2005/2006

THE
WORLD
GUIDE

A VIEW FROM THE SOUTH

The World Guide 2005/2006

New Internationalist Publications Ltd has an exclusive license to publish and distribute the English language print and CR-ROM editions of The World Guide throughout the world. While every care has been taken in preparing this edition, the publisher and distributors make no representation, express or implied, with regard to the accuracy of the information contained in this book and cannot accept any legal responsibility or liability for any errors or omissions, or for any action taken or not taken as result of its content.

Third World Guide (English language edition) 1986, 1988, 1990, 1992.

The World Guide (English language edition) 1995, 1997, 1999, 2001, 2003, 2005.

Copyright © 2005 by Instituto del Tercer Mundo

ISBN 1 904456 11 1

New Internationalist™ Publications Ltd,

Registered Office: 55 Rectory Road,

Oxford OX4 1BW, United Kingdom.

Fax: +44 1865 793152

www.newint.org

Printed on recycled paper by C&C Offset Printing Co. Ltd., Hong Kong, China.

General index

World Guide 2005/2006

The world guide section by section

SECTION I:

Global issues

Theme Article Summary

Article Text

Table Statistics Figures

I. DEMOCRACY, DEVELOPMENT AND ETHICS

19.

Latin America: an eroded democracy

A paradoxical combination: Latin America, the most unequal region in the world, is also the most democratic of developing regions, at least statistically. This combination is inherently unstable and potentially explosive. Democratic political systems survive only if they manage to offer their citizens a clear perception of their usefulness and not just a supposed guarantee of freedom, especially in a region that has known little democracy and even less democratic stability.

21.

Democracy in sub-Saharan Africa: show but no substance

In the 1990s, a current of 'Afro-optimism' swept through the world. A wave of democracy was to be followed by reforms. But the trends since then have been contradictory and have not necessarily led in the direction of more political democracy.

NEPAD: hope for change?

22.

The ethics of disaster: humanitarian aid and political power

A globalized policy, with international efforts mainly focused on the war on terrorism, presents major ethical dilemmas around the legitimacy of humanitarian agencies. According to a recent world report by the International Federation of Red Cross and Red Crescent Societies, humanitarian intervention in certain disasters is no longer defensible unless the causes of those disasters are addressed.

Disasters: statistics and trends 1993-2002

II. FREEDOM FROM FEAR, FREEDOM FROM WANT

24.

Human security: protecting vital freedoms

Security has been the subject of a heated debate all over the world: debate about policies that would make the world and the societies in it more secure; debate about the factors causing uncertainty, fear and insecurity among people and within nations. In this global re-assessment of security, the concept of human security can help shift the focus of the debate away from the stipulations of a few countries and their specialized security bodies towards a focus on what humanity really wants.

25.

Privatizing basic services: a violation of human rights?

The deepening inequalities of income and opportunity between and within nations has led to an increasing number of people being without adequate and secure housing. The continuing deterioration of conditions faced by the majority of the poor around the world has caused tremendous concern that unfettered globalization cannot bring about the fulfilment of economic, social and cultural rights, including the right to adequate housing.

Private operators versus accountability

(Table) **Sexual Minorities and the Law: a World Survey**
Sources: *International Lesbian and Gay Association World Survey*; Commission for Lesbian and Gay Human Rights; *The Penguin Atlas of Human Sexual Behaviour*; *The No-Nonsense Guide to Sexual Diversity*.

III. GLOBALIZATION

32.

Global markets, global divide

A series of unprecedented economic, social and cultural metamorphoses took place during the latter decades of the 20th century. Walls and barriers between nations collapsed as information technology speeded up the process of liberalization. At the same time the development gap between North and South, rich and poor, continues to grow.

(Table) **Gross National Income as Indicator of Wealth**
- Indicators: Gross National Income (per capita), 2002.
Source: World Development Indicators 2003, World Bank.

34.

Cleaning up the dirt: money laundering

As those in power attempt to curb international money laundering, seeing it as a source of terrorist activity, Southern governments under pressure from globalizing forces feel it may be one of the few ways of attracting the capital that they desperately need.

International, regional and offshore financial centers

For a few million dollars more

(Table) **Index of bribe-payers**
Source: Transparency International 2003

(Table) **Corruption perception index**
Source: Transparency International 2003

37.

For good or ill: cultural globalization

Globalization as a cultural phenomenon occurs, like the economy, as a result of the expansion of capitalism. All civilizations and cultures are entering the new world of modernity and cannot fail to be affected by it, for good or for ill.

47.

The missing girls of China

When the Chinese Government, worried about increasing population and food and water scarcity, began limiting reproduction to one child per couple in 1979, many tried to ensure that child would be male. The program allowed for some exceptions: a second child was allowed in rural areas to help with the chores if the first-born was female, and if several years had passed since her birth; certain ethnic minorities were allowed up to three children. But the percentage of males has in fact risen steadily since that date.

World population growth

(Table) **Under 5 mortality**
- Indicators: Under 5 mortality rate (per 1,000 live births), 2002.
Source: *The State of the World's Children 2004*, UNICEF.

49.

Perishable merchandise: child slaves

Trafficking in human beings forces people to live in conditions of slavery. This practice affects all continents and most countries, but in Africa it is out of control. Extreme poverty turns anything into a commodity, even people's children.

(Table) **AIDS in figures**
- Indicators: HIV prevalence rate, aged 15-49, per cent; AIDS estimated deaths;
Children orphaned by AIDS (one or both parents), currently living.

Source: UNAIDS.

51.

The children of AIDS

Some 11 million of the 14 million children orphaned by AIDS live in Sub-Saharan Africa, one of the poorest regions on the planet. A World Bank report counts the costs of the epidemic.

Haiti: magic not microbes

51.

Children who work to death

Every year, child labor takes 22,000 lives. Millions of children - one third of them under ten - are part of the global labor force, many working to pay their family's debts.

52.

Deprived of a future: girls without education

While poverty forces increasingly young children to enter the labor market, girls suffer more than boys due to disparities in income distribution. The UN's Millennium Goals include ensuring elementary education to both girls and boys by 2015. But in practice this is going to be a difficult target to meet.

52.

Boys: the turning point

While there are fewer girls than boys in schools, there is a new trend in some countries - girls are doing better than boys in education. There are many reasons for this, but the reforms that make school safer and more relevant for girls also make schools into places where boys can flourish.

(Table) **Education imbalances**
- Indicators: Primary pupil to teacher ratio, 2000.
Source: *World Development Indicators 2003*, World Bank.

53.

Tackling child pornography on the net

There are more than 2,000 child pornography websites which depend on presumed consumer anonymity for their success. Their eradication is difficult and they generate parallel crimes, such as financial fraud.

54.

Millennium Development Goals: a new challenge

The year 2015 will bring an end to the timeframe set to achieve the eight Millennium Development Goals (MDGs). The first seven aim at reducing poverty, promoting human dignity and equality and achieving peace, democracy and a sustainable environment. In order to achieve these, the final goal of the Declaration includes several commitments by rich countries in the North to increase aid to poor countries in the South.

(Table) **Workers in figures**
- Indicators: Labor force (percentage of total population), 2002. Male and female employment percentage in: agriculture, industry, services, 1995/2001.
Sources: *World Development Indicators 2003*, World Bank; *Human Development Report 2003*, UNDP; LABORSTA database, ILO Web Site.

(Table) **AID in figures**
- Indicators: Total net official development assistance (ODA) disbursed, 2001.
Source: *Human Development Report 2003*, UNDP.

(Table) **Debt in figures**
- Indicators: Total external debt (millions $), 2001; debt service as percentage of exports, 2001; External debt $ per capita, 2001.
Source: *World Development Indicators 2003*, World Bank.

(Table) **Literacy**
- Indicators: Adult literacy rate (percentage), 2000.
Source: *The State of the World's Children 2004*, UNICEF.

(Table) **Women in political and economic life**
- Indicators: Percentage of women in labor force, 2002; percentage of professional and technical workers; female legislators, senior officials and managers (as per cent of total); women's earned income share (percentage); percentage of ministerial posts occupied by women, 2000; percentage of parliamentary seats occupied by women, 2003.
Sources: *World Development Indicators 2003*, World Bank; *Human Development Report 2003*, UNDP.

61.

The MDGs are not 'mission impossible'

The purpose of the Millennium Development Goals (MDGs) is to keep the eyes of the world focused on human development and on fundamental social and economic rights. Although all member states of the UN have pledged to: 'spare no effort to free our fellow men, women and children from the abject and dehumanizing conditions of extreme poverty', global progress towards the MDGs has been slow and very uneven.

62.

David and Goliath: the emergence of the Group of 20

The emergence of the Group of 20 (G-20 or G-20 plus), within the context of the fifth World Trade Organization (WTO) Ministerial Conference in 2003 has turned into an historical event since it opened the doors to a new kind of multilateral trade regime and to economic cooperation between countries from the South.

(Table) **International Trade**
- Indicators: Exports (millions $), 2002; imports (millions $), 2002.
Source: *World Development Indicators 2003*, World Bank.

VII. LATIN AMERICA: A LABORATORY FOR CHANGE

65.

Populism: a new suit for an old habit?

Ever since the 19th century processes of independence, Latin America has struggled to survive without getting swept into the whirlwind created by its huge neighbor to the North. Since the end of the World War I, there has been considerable resistance from all social sectors to US economic, social, political and military influence.

Zero Hunger Brazil: no grassroots mobilization

Billion dollar bonus: money from migrant workers

Remittances - the money that emigrant workers send to their relatives in their home countries - have become a growing source of financial income for Latin America and the Caribbean. The amount sent increased from $10 billion in 1996 to $40 billion in 2003 and continues to grow. The United Nations has said that remittances are one of the most efficient weapons in the fight against poverty in the region. But many of the 20 million Latin Americans abroad are working illegally.

Extreme poverty in the world's most unequal region

Remittances in Latin America

Maquilas: the crumbs from the giant's lunch

Maquilas have been present in Latin America for centuries. Today, they are the profitable outposts of transnational corporations, which have been encouraged by laws favoring companies and foreign capital and by the creation of Free Trade Zones (FTZs). But there are big questions about how much workers and host governments benefit. And now the boom in the Caribbean is threatened by the export of the maquila idea to China.

Host countries lose out

VIII. IN GOD THEY TRUST

A beacon of freedom?: the Christian right and Washington's foreign policy

The US Government of George W Bush seems to be increasingly dominated by a fundamentalist Christian agenda that believes America to be doing God's will.

Darwin on trial

US religious groups are challenging the way evolution theory is taught, in a debate which has sparked renewed controversy over the origin of life.

Intelligence: from the Inquisition to Iraq

Information is essential to policymaking. Managing accurate information does not guarantee the best decisions, but as history has repeatedly shown, inadequate information leads to disaster. The task of the intelligence agencies is to gather information efficiently, to interpret it using the necessary levels of sophistication, and to communicate it swiftly wherever it is needed. To do this they use whatever means they have at their disposal - and have always done so.

A torturer's truth

The world according to...

The World Bank, UN Development Program and UNICEF

IX. NON GOVERNMENTAL ORGANIZATIONS /CAMPAIGNS DIRECTORY

SECTION II:
Countries

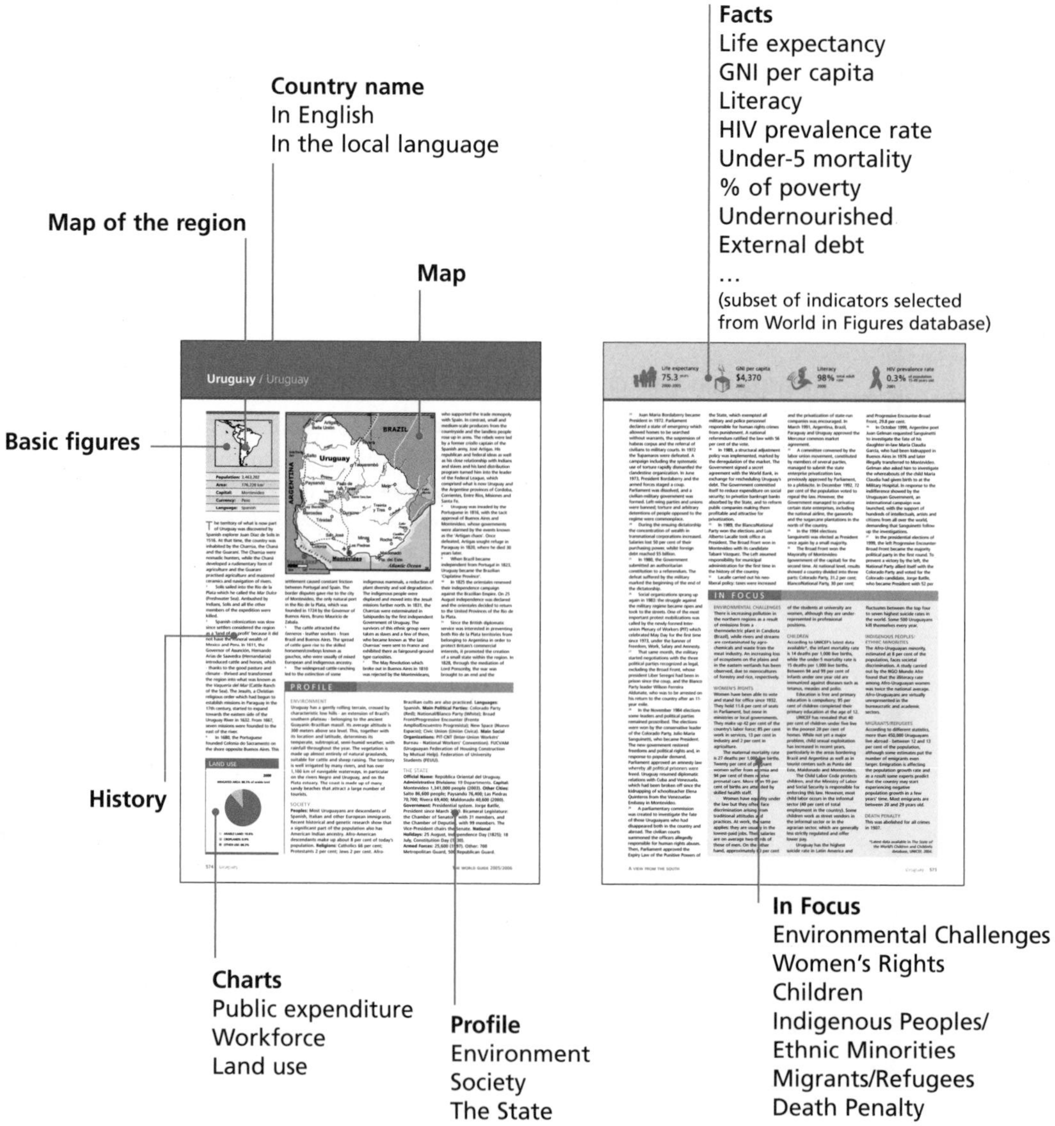

Country name
In English
In the local language

Map of the region

Map

Facts
Life expectancy
GNI per capita
Literacy
HIV prevalence rate
Under-5 mortality
% of poverty
Undernourished
External debt
…
(subset of indicators selected
from World in Figures database)

Basic figures

History

Charts
Public expenditure
Workforce
Land use

Profile
Environment
Society
The State

In Focus
Environmental Challenges
Women's Rights
Children
Indigenous Peoples/
Ethnic Minorities
Migrants/Refugees
Death Penalty

228	El Salvador	356	Luxemburgo	479	Samoa, American
231	Equatorial Guinea	357	Macedonia, TFYR	480	San Marino
233	Eritrea	359	Madagascar	481	São Tomé and Príncipe
234	Estonia	361	Malawi	483	Saudi Arabia
236	Ethiopia	363	Malaysia	486	Senegal
214	Faeroe Islands	366	Maldives	489	Serbia and Montenegro
239	Fiji	368	Mali	492	Seychelles
241	Finland	370	Malta	494	Sierra Leone
243	France	101	Malvinas/Falklands	496	Singapore
246	France's Overseas Departments and Territories	371	Marshall Islands	498	Slovakia
		372	Martinique	500	Slovenia
		373	Mauritania	502	Solomon Islands
101	Falklands/Malvinas	376	Mauritius	503	Somalia
247	French Guiana	190	Mayotte	504	Somaliland
248	French Polynesia	512	Melilla	506	South Africa
249	Gabon	379	Mexico	511	Spain
251	Gambia	383	Micronesia	515	Sri Lanka
253	Georgia	384	Moldova	518	Sudan
255	Germany	386	Monaco	521	Suriname
259	Ghana	387	Mongolia	523	Swaziland
514	Gibraltar	390	Montserrat	525	Sweden
262	Greece	391	Morocco	528	Switzerland
214	Greenland	394	Mozambique	531	Syria
265	Grenada	397	Myanmar/Burma	184	Taiwan
267	Guadeloupe	399	Namibia	534	Tajikistan
268	Guam	402	Nauru	536	Tanzania
269	Guatemala	403	Nepal	539	Thailand
273	Guinea	405	Netherlands	182	Tibet
275	Guinea-Bissau	408	Netherlands Antilles	542	Timor-Leste
277	Guyana	410	New Zealand/Aotearoa	544	Togo
279	Haiti	412	Niue	413	Tokelau
282	Honduras	414	Nicaragua	546	Tonga
183	Hong Kong	417	Niger	547	Trinidad and Tobago
284	Hungary	420	Nigeria	474	Tristan da Cunha
287	Iceland	109	Norfolk Island	549	Tunisia
289	India	423	Northern Marianas	551	Turkey
293	Indonesia	424	Norway	555	Turkmenistan
296	Iran	427	Oman	557	Turks and Caicos
299	Iraq	429	Pakistan	558	Tuvalu
302	Ireland	432	Palau	559	Uganda
305	Israel	433	Palestine	562	Ukraine
309	Italy	437	Panama	564	United Arab Emirates
312	Jamaica	440	Papua New Guinea	566	United Kingdom
314	Japan	442	Paraguay	570	United States
319	Jordan	445	Peru	573	US Dependencies
321	Kanaky/New Caledonia	448	Philippines	574	Uruguay
323	Kazakhstan	451	Pitcairn	577	Uzbekistan
325	Kenya	452	Poland	579	Vanuatu
328	Kiribati	455	Portugal	580	Vatican City
329	Korea	458	Puerto Rico	581	Venezuela
331	Korea, North	505	Puntland	584	Vietnam
333	Korea, South	460	Qatar	587	Virgin Islands (US)
335	Kuwait	462	Réunion	588	Virgin Islands (British)
338	Kyrgyzstan	463	Romania	246	Wallis & Futuna
340	Laos	466	Russia	589	Western Sahara
342	Latvia	471	Rwanda	592	West Papua
344	Lebanon	474	St Helena	593	Yemen
347	Lesotho	475	St Kitts-Nevis	596	Zambia
349	Liberia	476	St Lucia	598	Zimbabwe
351	Libya	246	St Pierre et Miquelon		
353	Liechtenstein	477	St Vincent and Grenadines		
354	Lithuania	478	Samoa		

History

1 A range of sources has been used to update the texts on each country. In many cases this meant checking with local sources and contributors, documentation centers linked to electronic mail networks and grassroots organizations throughout the world. This input went into our database in Montevideo, where the final editing was done.

2 Efforts were made to avoid the most frequent bias of Western reference books, such as appearing to make history start with the arrival of the Europeans (particularly in the case of African and Latin American countries) or ignoring the role of women.

3 The last overall updating of the database before printing was done in June 2004, but in several cases events as late as August were included. ∎

Statistics database

DEMOGRAPHY

Area
Surface area is a country's total area (in square kilometers), including areas under inland bodies of water and some coastal waterways (2002). SOURCE: 1

Total population
Total population, according to 2002 United Nations Population Division. In some cases, figures have been corrected through consultation with other sources (2005). SOURCE: 2

Demographic growth
Average annual rate (%) of population growth during the period 1985/2000 and projections of population growth (%) during the period 2000/2015 (1985-2000). SOURCE: 2

Total population estimate for year 2015
The population projections (thousands) for the year 2015 are calculations based on current data on population, rates of growth, and trends of these rates to increase or decrease (2002). SOURCE: 2

Population density
Midyear population divided by land area in square kilometers. Land area is a country's total area, excluding area under inland water bodies, national claims to continental shelf, and exclusive economic zones (2005). SOURCE: 2

Urban population
Percentage of total population living in urban areas. Figures are to be treated with care since definitions of 'urban zones' differ from country to country (2005). SOURCE: 2

Urban population, annual growth
Annual growth rate (%) of the urban population (2000-2005). SOURCE: 2

2015 urban population (%)
Projections of the percentage of total population living in urban areas for the year 2015 (2002). SOURCE: 2

HEALTH

Life expectancy at birth
Indicates the number of years a newborn infant, male or female, would live if prevailing patterns of mortality at the time of birth were to stay the same throughout the child's life (2000-2005). SOURCE: 2

Total fertility rate (children per woman)
Represents the number of children that would be born per woman were she to live to the end of her child-bearing years and bear children at each age in accordance with prevailing age-specific fertility rates (2002). SOURCE: 3

Crude birth rate
Indicates the number of live births occurring during the year, per 1,000 population estimated at midyear (2000-2005). SOURCE: 2

Crude death rate
Indicates the number of deaths occurring during the year, per 1,000 population estimated at midyear (2000-2005). SOURCE: 2

Contraceptive use
Contraceptive prevalence rate is the percentage of women who are practising, or whose sexual partners are practising, any form of contraception. It is usually measured for married women ages 15-49 only

(1995-2002). SOURCE: 3

Maternal mortality (per 100,000 live births)
Maternal mortality ratio refers to the number of female deaths that occur during pregnancy and childbirth per 100,000 live births. Due to changes in the model of estimation, 1995 and 2000 data are not comparable. The data are official estimates from administrative records, survey-based indirect estimates, or estimates derived from a demographic model developed by the World Health Organization (WHO) and the United Nations Children's Fund (UNICEF) (2000). SOURCE: 3

Births attended by trained health personnel
Percentage of deliveries attended by personnel trained to give the necessary supervision, care, and advice to women during pregnancy, labor and the postpartum period, to conduct deliveries on their own, and to care for the newborns (1995-2002). SOURCE: 3

Infant mortality rate
Number of infants dying before reaching one year of age, per 1,000 live births in a given year (2002). SOURCE: 3

Under-5 mortality rate
Number of infants dying before reaching five years of age, per 1,000 live births in a given year (2002). SOURCE: 3

Low weight at birth
Newborns weighing less than 2,500 grams, with measurement taken within the first hours of life, before significant postnatal weight loss has occurred (1998-2002). SOURCE: 3

Child malnutrition
Prevalence of child malnutrition (weight for age) is the % of children under five whose weight for age is less than minus two standard deviations from the median for the international reference population ages 0 to 59 months (1995-2002). SOURCE: 3

Undernourished people
Undernourishment is the result of food intake that is insufficient to meet dietary energy requirements continuously. The World Health Organization recommends that the average person needs to take a minimum of 2,300 Kcal per day to maintain body functions, health and normal activity. This global minimum requirement of calories is broken down into country-specific differentials that are a function of the age-specific structure and body mass of the population (1998-2000). SOURCE: 5

Breastfeeding
Exclusive Breastfeeding Rate (% of under-6-months children) (1995-2002). SOURCE: 3

Calorie consumption
Daily per capita calorie supply. Shown as a national average, though a country's income distribution may create a wide gap between the average, the highest and the lowest strata. Minimum calorie requirements vary in different countries, depending on climate and nature of the main activities (2001). SOURCE: 7

Doctors per 100,000 people
Traditional medicine and community health care practised by health personnel who are not officially recognized are not included in these statistics, although they may be the only health service available for the majority of the population in many countries (1990-2002). SOURCE: 4

Nurses per 100,000 people
All persons who have completed a programme of basic nursing education and are qualified an registered or authorized by the country's authorities to provide responsible and competent service for the promotion of health, prevention of illness, care of the sick and rehabilitation (1997). SOURCE: 5

Access to improved water sources
The United Nations includes the percentage of population with 'reasonable' access to safe water sources. They include treated surface waters and untreated but uncontaminated water from springs, wells and protected boreholes in the 'reasonably safe water' category (2000). SOURCE: 3

Access to sanitation services
Percentage of the population with at least adequate excreta disposal facilities (private or shared, but not public) (2000). SOURCE: 3

EDUCATION

Literacy
Indicates the estimated percentage of people, male or female, over the age of 15 who can read and write (2000). SOURCE: 3

School net enrolment ratio
Primary/secondary net school enrolment ratio. Number of people, male or female, (of the age group officially corresponding to primary/secondary school level) enrolled in primary/secondary school level, divided by the population of the age group officially corresponding to that level (2000). SOURCE: 1

Tertiary gross enrolment ratio
Ratio of total enrolment, regardless of age, to the population of the age group that officially corresponds to the level of education shown. Tertiary education, whether or not to an advanced research qualification, normally requires, as a minimum condition of admission, successful completion of education at secondary level (1997). SOURCE: 1

Primary pupil to teacher ratio
Primary school teachers/students ratio (students per teacher) (2000). SOURCE: 1

COMMUNICATIONS

Mass media
Estimation of the print run of daily newspapers (1997/2001), the number of working radio receivers (1997/2001) and TV sets (2001) per 1,000 people. The latter figure may rely on the number of licences granted or the number of declared receivers. SOURCE: 1

Telephones
Telephone mainlines per 1,000 people (2001). SOURCE: 1

Computers

Personal computers per 1,000 people (2001). SOURCE: 1

ECONOMY

International Poverty Line

Percentage of the population living on less than $1.08 a day at 1993 international prices (equivalent to $1 in 1985 prices, adjusted for purchasing power parity)

GNI per capita

Gross national income, converted to US dollars using the World Bank Atlas method, divided by the midyear population. GNI is the sum of value added by all resident producers plus any product taxes (less subsidies) not included in the valuation of output plus net receipts of primary income (compensation of employees and property income) from abroad (2002). SOURCE: 1

GDP per capita

GDP (PPP, current $) is the value of the total production of goods and services of a country's economy within the national territory. GNP is GDP plus the income received from abroad by residents in the country (such as remittances from migrant workers and income from investments abroad), minus income obtained in the domestic economy which go into the hands of persons abroad (such as profit remittances of foreign companies) (2002). SOURCE: 1

GDP annual growth

Annual growth rate (%) of GDP per capita based on constant local currency (2002). SOURCE: 1

Annual inflation rate

Annual inflation rate as GDP implicit deflator (average annual $ growth), measures the average annual rate of price change in the economy (2002). SOURCE: 1

Consumer price index

Reflects changes in the cost to the average consumer of acquiring a fixed basket of goods and services (1995 = 100) (2002). SOURCE: 1

External debt

Public state guaranteed and private foreign debt (million $) accumulated by 2001. Per capita debt ($) was calculated from total external debt and total population (2001). SOURCE: 1

Debt service

Debt service as % of exports of goods and services.
The service of a foreign debt is the sum of interest payments and repayment of principal (capital loaned, regardless of yield). The relation between debt service and exports of goods and services is a practical measurement commonly used to evaluate capacity to pay the debt or obtain new credits.

These coefficients do not include private foreign debts without state guarantees - a considerable amount in some countries (2001). SOURCE: 1

Official development assistance

ODA consists of money flows from official governmental or international institutions for the purpose of promoting economic development or social welfare in developing countries. These funds are supplied in the form of grants or 'soft' loans, i.e. long-maturity loans at interest rates lower than those prevailing on the international market. We included the total and per capita net ODA received in dollars and as % of receptor country GDP; and total net ODA disbursed by the countries in dollars and as % of donors GDP (2001). SOURCE: 4

Energy use consumption (oil equivalent) per capita (kg)

These statistics refer only to commercial energy, and do not include, for example, that which rural people in poor countries produce by their own means (mainly firewood). Energy consumption of the country is measured in kilograms of 'oil-equivalent' per capita (1.000 kWh electrics = 0.222 million tep -centrales thermiques classiques) Energy imports are given as a percentage of energy consumption. Figures are negative in those countries that are net exporters of energy products (2000). SOURCE: 1

Public expenditure

Defense expenditure (2001), health services (2000) and education services (2001) as % of GDP (2001). SOURCE: 1

TRADE

Imports and exports

Annual value in US dollars f.o.b. (free on board) for *exports* and c.i.f. (costs, insurance and freight) for *imports* (2002). SOURCE: 1

Cereal imports

The cereals are wheat, flour, rice, unprocessed grains and the cereal components of combined foods. This figure includes cereals donated by other countries, and those distributed by international agencies (2002). SOURCE: 7

Food production and imports

Food production per cápita index (1981-91=100).
Imported food in relation to the food available for internal distribution. This means the total of food production, plus food imports, minus food exports (2001). SOURCE: 1

Weapons imports and exports

Imports and exports of conventional weapons ($ million, 1990 prices) (2002). SOURCE: 4

LABOR FORCE

Labor force as % of total population

Total labor force comprises people who meet the International Labour Organization definition of the economically active population: all people who supply labor for the production of goods and services during a specified period. It includes both the employed and the unemployed. While national practices vary in the treatment of such groups as the armed forces and seasonal or part-time workers, in general the labor force includes the armed forces, the unemployed, and first-time job-seekers, but excludes homemakers and other unpaid caregivers and workers in the informal sector (2002). SOURCE: 1

Unemployment rate

Unemployment refers to the share of the labor force that is without work but available for and seeking employment. Definitions of labor force and unemployment differ by country (2002). SOURCE: 6

Employment and unemployment

The male and female labour force percentage (2002), excluding housewives and other unpaid workers; Employment rate by sex and activity sector (agriculture, industry and services, years). Unemployment rate (1995/2002). SOURCE: 1, 4

LAND USE

Land use

Forest and woodland as percentage of land area (2000). Arable land as percentage of land area (2000). Irrigated area as percentage of arable land area (2000). Fertilizer use (kgs per ha) (2000). SOURCE: 1

Fertilizer use

Refers to purchases of nitrate, potassium and phosphate based fertilizers used on arable land (1999). (kgs per ha) (2000). SOURCE: 1

WOMEN'S SITUATION

% of women in professional and technician workers; % of women legislators, senior officials and managers; Earned income shared (% to women), % of ministerial posts occupied by women, % of parliamentary seats occupied by women. SOURCE: 4

Sources

1   World Development Indicators 2003, World Bank

2   World Population Prospects -The 2002 Revision. United Nations

3   The State of the World's Children 2004, UNICEF

4   Human Development Report 2003, UNDP

5   WHOSIS - WHO Statistical Information System, Web Site WHO 2003

6   LABORSTA database, ILO Web Site

7   FAOSTAT - Statistical Database - FAO Web site 2004

Index to Special Boxes

ENVIRONMENT

Estimates of area are based on UN official estimates according to internationally recognized borders; these include inland waters but not territorial ocean waters. Except where otherwise specified, territories claimed by certain countries but not under their effective jurisdiction are not taken into account, though this implies no judgment as to the validity of the claims.

SOCIETY

Peoples, Languages and Religions: Very few countries keep official ethnic and religious data, and UN-related institutions definitely do not do so. The ethnic and religious make-up of a society is a historical-cultural factor which is in constant change. Certain forces promote tribal or ethnic divisions to favor their own plans of domination, while others favor whatever makes for integration and national unity. In many countries the political and social problems cannot be grasped without reference to these factors.

Main Political Parties and Social Organizations: It is practically impossible to make a complete listing of all parties and other movements of any country, since they are permanently changing and in most cases would add up to several hundred names. Thus only major organizations are mentioned, even though 'major' is subjective when votes, parliamentary representation or number of members cannot be verified, where parties are outlawed or the right to associate is restricted.

THE STATE

Official Name: Complete name of the state in the official language Administrative divisions, the capital and other cities: Population figures are for the most recent available year. The legal limits of a city frequently do not match its real borders. Thus the information may refer only to the core area, which is a minor part of the whole city.

Government: Names of the major authorities and institutional bodies as of June 1998.

National Holiday: When more than one holiday is commemorated, Independence Day (if it is a holiday) is indicated.

Armed Forces and Others: The total number of personnel for the year indicated. 'Other' forces are those trained and equipped beyond the level of a Police Force (though some fulfill this role) and whose constitution and control means they can be used as regular troops.

ENVIRONMENTAL CHALLENGES

The main issues compromising sustainable development of the country's land resources.

WOMEN'S RIGHTS

Respect for women's rights; gender discrimination; political and economic involvement; access to the labor market; education and health services.

CHILDREN

Their health and education. Statistics and data on infant mortality, domestic violence, HIV/AIDS, child labor, exploitation and trafficking.

INDIGENOUS PEOPLES/ ETHNIC MINORITIES

The current situation of indigenous peoples and/or of minorities who are displaced, discriminated against or at risk.

MIGRANTS/REFUGEES

Recent emigration from and immigration to the country. The situation of refugees and asylum seekers in the country - and of local citizens who have sought refuge in other nations.

DEATH PENALTY

Information on whether or not capital punishment applies and under what circumstances. The date of the last execution.

SECTION III:

The world in figures

Indicators
Demography
Health
Education
Communications
Economy
Labor force
Land use
Trade
Women's situation

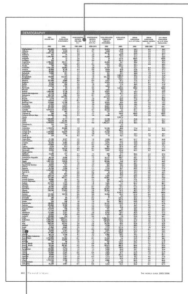

Countries

Preface

The other shore

Nasreddin Hodja sat on a river bank when a foreigner shouted to him from the opposite side:

 — 'Hey! how do I get across?'

 — 'You are across!' Nasreddin shouted back.

Hodja, a famous scholar (and humorist) is said to have lived in present-day Turkey a thousand years ago. His words still carry a powerful message, relevant to the deeply divided world we now live in.

Hodja's reply is telling the foreigner that both points of view are equally valid, and he shouldn't take his own stand as the standard for his interlocutor. Hodja does not hinder the traveler from reaching the other side, but definitely helps him to do so with due respect for the local views when he eventually crosses.

War and violence are always against the 'other', the 'different', the foreigner, those who do not accept our obvious righteousness.

The Third World Institute gathers researchers and collaborators from around the world to edit this World Guide. All care is taken to check for the accuracy and relevancy of the information. And still we the authors announce on the cover that this is 'a view from the South'. Why? Because, like Hodja, we want the reader to ask herself who is 'across'.

Roberto Bissio
Montevideo, September 2004

THE WORLD GUIDE

INSTITUTO DEL TERCER MUNDO

Executive Board

President:
Clara Píriz

Secretary:
Luis Álvarez

Director:
Roberto Bissio

THE WORLD GUIDE

Editor:
Amir Hamed

Editorial Co-ordinator:
Inés Bortagaray

Research and Editing:
Joaquín Olivera
Carmen Ridao
Dina Yael Kaganovicius

Collaborators:
Paula Cladera
Sandra López Desivo
Gustavo Alzugaray
Paulina López Rivero
María José Santacreu
Andrea Tutté
Gustavo Espinosa
Virginia Martínez
Fabián Muro
Sofi Richero
Leo García
María Eugenia Méndez
Lucila Bortagaray
María Fernanda Cortinas
Paola Pintos

Statistics:
Daniel Macadar

Translators:
Álvaro Queiruga
Patricia Draper
Elizabeth Ardans
Ana Ridao
Fernanda Trías
Susana Medina
Susan Day
Anthony Shaw
Victoria Swarbrick
Elena Vasilisky

English version:
Niki Johnson
Stephanie Wildes
Valerie Dee

Graphic Design:
Monocromo

Administration:
María Lucía Rivero
Maika Flores

NEW INTERNATIONALIST PUBLICATIONS LTD
(English language edition)

Editors:
Troth Wells, Chris Brazier
and Nikki van der Gaag

Production:
Fran Harvey and Dean Ryan

Marketing and Distribution:
Bev Laing and Jo Lateu

This book is the result of documentation, research, writing, editing and design work done by the Instituto del Tercer Mundo (Third World Institute), a nonprofit institution devoted to information, communication and education, based in Montevideo, Uruguay.

The World Guide 2005/2006 is a fully updated, corrected and expanded edition of The World Guide 2003/2004, with a heavier emphasis on civil society issues. This reference book was published for the first time in Mexico in 1979, on the initiative of Neiva Moreira, to complement the dissemination work of The Third World magazine he had begun publishing. In 1980 the first Portuguese version of the Guide was published. The first English version was published in 1984. New Internationalist Publications Ltd, in Oxford, England, has been in charge of the English version and its distribution in English-speaking countries since 1996. In 1999, SERMIS-EMI (Editrice Missionaria Italiana), from Bologna, launched the Italian version of The World Guide. Since 1992, The World Guide has been published on CD-ROM. Since 1997, through the Internet and together with the updating service, the Spanish version of The World Guide has been available in Web Pages.

The World Guide is a cumulative work, building on the efforts of former staff members. We would like to mention the contributions of: Carlos Abín, Mohiuddin Ahmad, Carlos Afonso, Andrés Alsina, Claude Alvares, Iván Alves, Juan José Argeriz, Maria Teresa Armas, Marcos Arruda, Iqbal Asaria, Gonzalo Abella, Susana de Avila, Víctor Bacchetta, Edouard Balby, Artur Baptista, Roberto Bardini, Luis Barrios, Cedric Belfrage, Max van den Berg, Alicia Bidegaray, Beatriz Bissio, Ricardo de Bittencourt, Samuel Blixen, Gerardo Bocco, José Bottaro, Dirk-Jan Broertjes, Alberto Brusa, José Cabral, Luis Caldera, Juan Cammá, Altair Campos, Paulo Cannabrava Filho, Carmen Canoura, Cristina Canoura, Gerónimo Cardozo, Diana Cariboni, Gustavo Carrier, Virgilio Caturra, Macário Costa, Anne-Pieter van Dijk, Carlos María Domínguez, Rodrigo Egaña, Roberto Elissalde, Wáshington Estellano, Marta Etcheverrigaray, Carlos Fabião, Marcelo Falca, Helena Falcão, Wilson Fernández, Cecilia Ferraría, Alejandro Flores, Lidia Freitas, Sonia Freitas, Marc Fried, Héctor García, José Carlos Gondim, Leo van Grunsven, Goran Hammer, Mario Handler, David Hathaway, Ann Heidenreich, Bill Hinchberger, Etevaldo Hipólito, Mohammed Idris, Sytse Kujik, Heraclio Labandera, Peter Lenny, Arne Lindquist, Cecilia Lombardo, Linda Llosa, Geoffrey Lloyd Gilbert, Fernando López, Hakan Lundgren, Carlos Mañosa, Pablo Mazzini, Daniel Mazzone, Carol Milk, Fernando Molina, João Murteira, Abdul Naffey, Claudia Neiva, Ruben Olivera, Hattie Ortega, Pablo Piacentini, Ana Pérez, Christopher Peterson, Virginia Piera, Carlos Pinto Santos, Sieni C. Platino, Hans Poelgrom, Artur José Poerner, Graciela Pujol, Roberto Raposo, Felisberto Reigado, Malva Rodríguez, Maria da Gloria Rodrigues, Julio Rosiello, Ash Narain Roy, Ana Sadetzky, Alexandru Savulescu, John Sayer, John Schlanger, Dieter Schonebohm, Gregorio Selser, Irene Selser, Eunice H. Senna, Baptista da Silva, Herbet de Souza, Yesse Jane V. de Souza, José Steinleger, Firiel Suijker, Sjef Theunis, Carolina Trujillo, Pedro Velozo, Horacio Verbitsky, Amelia Villaverde, Anatoli Voronov, Germán Wettstein and Asa Zatz.

The editorial staff acknowledges the valuable contributions made by the libraries of the following institutions: UNDE, UNESCO, CLASH, FE, the UN Information Center in Montevideo, Iepala in Madrid and the UNCLAD in Geneva.

The Third World Network, Penang, Malaysia provided ideas, documents and links with many contributors. Novib in the Netherlands offered vital early support.

To all of them we offer our thanks. This fully expanded World Guide 2005-2006 has benefited from the contributions of Jens Martens and Jonna Schürkes, from the World Economy, Ecology & Development Association (WEED), Germany, and of Fernanda Carvalho and Mauricio Santoro, from the Instituto Brasilero de Análises Sociais e Econômicas (IBASE).

Thanks also to the hundreds of readers who keep volunteering their comments, suggestions and detailed information. The judgements and values contained in this book are the exclusive responsibility of the editors and do not represent the opinion of any of the people or institutions listed, except for the Third World Institute.

INSTITUTO DEL TERCER MUNDO
Juan D. Jackson 1136, Montevideo 11200, Uruguay.
Phone: 598 2 419 6192; Fax: 598 2 411 9222.
E-mail: item@item.org.uy/
Website: http://www.item.org.uy

NEW INTERNATIONALIST PUBLICATIONS LTD
55 Rectory Road, Oxford OX4 1BW, United Kingdom
Phone: (44) 1865 728181; Fax: (44) 1865 793152
E-mail: ni@newint.org
Website: http://www.newint.org/

Global issues

Key challenges for our times

Latin America: an eroded democracy

A PARADOXICAL COMBINATION: LATIN AMERICA, THE MOST UNEQUAL REGION IN THE WORLD, IS ALSO THE MOST DEMOCRATIC OF DEVELOPING REGIONS, AT LEAST STATISTICALLY. THIS COMBINATION IS INHERENTLY UNSTABLE AND POTENTIALLY EXPLOSIVE. DEMOCRATIC POLITICAL SYSTEMS SURVIVE ONLY IF THEY MANAGE TO OFFER THEIR CITIZENS A CLEAR PERCEPTION OF THEIR USEFULNESS AND NOT JUST A SUPPOSED GUARANTEE OF FREEDOM, ESPECIALLY IN A REGION THAT HAS KNOWN LITTLE REAL DEMOCRACY AND EVEN LESS DEMOCRATIC STABILITY.

When the 20th century was drawing to an end, almost all the Latin American countries had political regimes which, in principle, would undoubtedly be considered democratic. However, no politician, citizen or analyst would be willing to accept the claim that these democracies are 'consolidated'. There is a suspicion that, although substantial political progress has been made in the region, something is not quite right. Electoral democracies have persisted, and regimes are not openly authoritarian, but it is also possible to observe processes which erode confidence in the stability, quality, and substance of these 'democratic' governments.

Most Latin American countries show inequality and poverty levels that a decade of democracy has not been able to tackle. Between 1950 and 1970 there was some kind of relationship between wealth and democracy, but this has disappeared since 1970. In many cases poverty has increased since then, or has remained at unacceptably high levels. Inequality has grown almost everywhere.

This presents a double challenge to the region's democratic future: to strengthen, or rather, build the social base of democracy, and to be able to show its social functions to its citizens. The latter does not mean the achievement of economic equity, but rather the demonstration that, in the long term, democracy seeks to protect the majority in critical times and tries to benefit it during periods of expansion.

If this does not happen, there is a real risk that democracy will become an increasingly hollow word. That the region's political regimes do not turn authoritarian does not mean they are, or will be, democratic. If Latin America is not able to match democracy with growth and equality, in the near future its fate will be far from democratic, at least in any way that approximates to the basic concept of what democracy means.

A botched experiment

Many Latin American countries faced major political crises during the 1990s, some of which found their way out through democratic paths without many obstacles. Others took the dangerous route of plebiscitary democracy or 'constitutional' authoritarianisms. A considerable number of countries witnessed growing citizen apathy and a lack of interest and distrust in the democratic process. In some cases, these citizens chose to express themselves in non-electoral and non-partisan ways.

Such expressions have often followed organized and essentially positive parameters, but sometimes they have taken violent shapes, affecting the stability of elected governments and sometimes whole regimes. This challenge is synthesized in the concept of a 'representation/participation deficit' and the problem of the social and political *anomie* of the masses. This representation deficit is also clearly rooted in the pronounced ideological deflation process that prevailed in the late 1980s and throughout most of the 1990s, generating a loss of real meaning in the political-electoral continuum.

For a long time, Latin America has been a unique laboratory for the study of social and political development. No region in the world has embraced and failed so many times in its attempt to emulate the wealthy West. Although the colonies settled by Anglo-Saxon whites are successful examples in this respect, most of Asia and Africa are examples of alternatives to the Western model.

In Latin America, republican attempts turned into oligarchies, democratic efforts were reduced to dictatorships, searches for order fell into chronic instability and anarchy. The region also sought social modernity through the urban and industrial development of its societies, only to beget megacities characterized by the social exclusion of their citizens. It also came up with the utopia of a solid middle class, seldom achieved. It embraced the mirage of education, which vanished after the 1950s when it became a powerless witness to the superior educational achievements of Western Europe, then of Asia, and now of recently transformed Eastern Europe. Latin America began to distance itself more and more from the increasingly educated populations of the West.

The current democratic wave that began in the 1980s, and the hegemony of the market ideology of the last 25 years represented, in the eyes of many, a new promise of growth, well-being and political and democratic stability. This illusion was crushed, once again, with the advent of the 21st century. Only Chile seems to be on its way to a relatively stable and modern sociopolitical model, based on an economy that has apparently overcome the classic cycles of the stop-and-go syndrome. And Chile is arguably a current example of neo-liberal and neo-developmental policies.

The rest of the region has huge social, political and economic problems. Argentina faces the worst economic and social crisis in its history, while the political system tries to overcome its own shortcomings, as well as the wrath and disaffection of its citizens. Venezuela wavers between 'constitutional' authoritarianism and the opposition's active hesitation. Most of the remaining countries show confusing scenarios, where even though democracy as a whole does not seem to be in question, its quality and governance are, as well as the honesty and competence of its ruling élites. Even Chile and Mexico face the challenges of decreasing their poverty levels and cutting down inequality.

The Washington Consensus, poverty, inequity

Although it can be said that democracies in the region made a significant effort when it came to social policies, this has not been reflected in the overall social structures. On many occasions, increased spending did not have an impact on social indicators because of how and where it was allocated. Cronyism, a lack of technically trained state agents, the collusion of private service-providers and other issues have negatively affected education reforms in Chile, the decentralization of social services in Brazil, Honduras and Bolivia, targeted programs in Mexico and Argentina, and many other initiatives.

Likewise, throughout the region a significant part of the growth in state social expenditure was focused on financing the transition from a social-security distributive model to an individual or mixed capitalization one when it came to pensions. Even though it is expected that in the long run this will mean a decreased fiscal burden for the state, during the transitional period it undoubtedly implies a greater burden. This is because the treasury has to honor present pensions although they may be lacking a part or the whole of workers' contributions, since these contributions end up, in part or in total, in each worker's individual equity fund.

Beyond these factors, what accounts in greater measure for the poor social performance of the 1990s is the development of markets and national economies and their ensuing redistributional effect. The new economic model has in fact caused levels of inequity which no social policy can address, least of all one with severe technical and fiscal restrictions.

The traits of this model have come together under what is called the 'Washington Consensus', and have encompassed the following transformations: falling import quotas and tariffs, financial/labor market liberalization, privatizations, fiscal austerity measures and income tax reform with an emphasis on indirect taxation (VAT). All these measures cause greater inequity and/or poverty in the short term.

Trade liberalization destroys more labor demand than it creates. Labor market deregulation decreases employer costs by facilitating the total transfer of this adjustment in labor demand to the working population through layoffs and the lowering or suppressing of minimum wages. Fiscal reforms focused on indirect taxation seek to have a neutral effect, at best. However, when tax collection increases the tax base but the population benefiting from public spending is still a privileged segment, the overall effect is regressive. This is the case with social security, corporate subsidies, free university education, spending in secondary education, and with generic subsidies to the private delivery of goods and services.

Privatizations and financial liberalization may contribute to equity if they lower the cost of money (interest rates) as well as the cost of service delivery (tariffs). This happens when and if there is an adequate credit market; when privatized services are not or do not become monopolies or oligopolies, or incur two-tier service delivery or cutbacks to basic public services for those unable to pay rates that used to be subsidized by charging higher rates to those with higher incomes. This is not always the case, as has been bitterly proven by the greater part of Latin America.

When the possibility of translating citizens' preferences into public policy does not exist, the very core of the notion of democracy is eroded in the eyes of the population. The Thatcherite neo-conservative principle of 'there is no

alternative' takes its place. Although sometimes this process can be reasonable or inevitable, its effect on the muscle tone of these besieged and tired democracies is deeply destructive. The words of José Dirceu, Brazilian president Lula da Silva's right-hand man, when replying to criticism from his own PT party are eloquent: 'The PT is a left-wing party, but the PT government is not left-wing'. Even so, and perhaps because of this ambiguous sincerity shown recently by the PT leadership, Latin America still hopes for significant change from a party that has been a product of the construction of a successful national political democratic system.

The limits to national democracies

Financier George Soros observed recently that the main reason why the new international financial system is an inescapable trap for developing countries is that international financial capital discounts its own future behavior in the interest rates that it charges poor countries in need of credit. This behavior is - in the opinion of several analysts who critically observe these new global players - unstable, speculative and, eventually, predatory. It capitalizes on, and contributes to, speculative bubbles while at the same time manufacturing destruction. It then opts for greener pastures where the cycle is often repeated.

Meanwhile, the International Monetary Fund (IMF), as a central player in this game, plays a notoriously pro-cyclic role, very different from the anti-cyclic role it was mandated with upon its creation. The IMF favors and grants loans in expansive economic and fiscal contexts, while demanding austerity cutbacks in contracting or recessive contexts. According to economics Nobel Prize winner Joseph Stiglitz, author of *Globalization and its Discontents*, the IMF adds technical incompetence and a conflict of interests with international financial capital to this mutation of its original commitments and mandate. Other authors have written stinging analyses focusing on the mistakes made by international financial institutions and the effect that unbridled financial liberalization can have on countries thirsty for fresh credit and capital.

The problem with the cycles generated by capital, and the IMF's role as arbiter and moneylender of 'last resort', is not just economic but also political. The indebted countries, especially those that face problems of sustainability or an inability to repay, have to renounce their sovereignty in a way that threatens the democratic process.

Democracies under siege

American political writer Samuel Huntington (author of *The Clash of Civilizations*) observed that praetorian democracies were characterized by a vicious cycle that went from populism, to fiscal and economic anarchy, to the eruption of the military and economic élites who closed the channels of participation, to a technocratic

political model which led to a governmental loss of legitimacy and accountability. This gave way to a new eruption, this time from the popular masses, led by populist rhetoric, and so on. The pendulum swung between an excluding authoritarianism and a plebiscitary and often authoritarian populism. The central players were the isolated popular sectors, the populist leaders, and the technocratic coup-prone sectors.

The key to this Sisyphus-like fate lay in the impossible task of building institutional systems which by mediating, channeling, arranging and postponing demands, retained an inkling of legitimacy and accountability.

From a similar perspective, Robert A Dahl, Professor Emeritus of Political Science at Yale University, observed that when the costs of incorporation exceed the costs of suppression the tendency is towards a system of exclusion. This vicious cycle was violent and bloody at times, swaying between societal and state violence. Like every cycle, one can argue that the problematic starting point is not institutional but societal. Deep inequalities help to create élites disinclined to democratic tolerance and peoples skeptical of democracy's channels of representation.

The century has changed and, for many, the cycle was broken. There is some undeniable truth to this perception. For more than a decade, electoral democracies have persisted, and violence, at least in its massive and acute manifestations, has moderated and even disappeared. But what seems to be incorrect is that the vicious cycle has disappeared: what has disappeared is its political violence.

The pendulum swing between excluding technocratic models and plebiscitary populisms is still present in most of Latin America. What has changed are the actors at the base. It is no longer the domestic economic and military coup-prone élites who close the participatory channels. International finance and multilateral credit agencies have replaced them in a politically (albeit not socially) innocuous manner. The same parties administer the populist opening as well as the technocratic closing of democracy. When they fail, the party system is left in shambles, with a trail of partisan corpses in its wake. Once again the popular masses erupt, but in an even more isolated way than before. They lack guilds and unions. Their axis pivots around consumption, not work. Only state corporations that have been leveled by the state's own vices seem to resist, in a never-ending retreat from the old development model. ■

Source: Fernando Filgueira and Cecilia Rossel, *Desigualdad, pobreza y exclusión: impotencia, fatiga y asedio en las democracias latinoamericanas*, in H enciclopedia, http://www.henciclopedia.org.uy

Democracy in sub-Saharan Africa: show but no substance

IN THE 1990s, A CURRENT OF 'AFRO-OPTIMISM' SWEPT THROUGH THE WORLD. A WAVE OF DEMOCRACY WAS TO BE FOLLOWED BY REFORMS. BUT THE TRENDS SINCE THEN HAVE BEEN CONTRADICTORY AND HAVE NOT NECESSARILY LED IN THE DIRECTION OF MORE POLITICAL DEMOCRACY.

In the early 1990s, Africa seemed to be going through a second liberation process. This was marked by the end of brutal post-colonial dictatorships and the consolidation of citizens' participation in political and public affairs.

During the previous decade, the legitimacy of the development model of pro-independence nationalisms had been wiped out and a series of institutional reforms implemented throughout the continent. But Africa is now being pulled in a number of different directions at the same time, according to Achille Mbembe, professor at the Institute for Social and Economic Research at the University of Witwatersrand, South Africa. On the one hand, elections are being held, on the other, states are disintegrating.

The authoritarian African state, based on repressive mechanisms and unable to fulfil its pledges of modernization, is currently engulfed in a deep financial crisis that also threatens its legitimacy. Post-colonial rulers face a reduction in their resources, brought about by the deterioration of the terms of trade for the continent's commodities; the implementation of structural adjustment plans (SAPs), and the self-destructive and extenuating dynamics of the electoral gift-giving system that prevailed in African countries. As a result, they do not have the funds to meet the demands of the electorate.

Democracy and the legacy of SAPs

With the end of the Cold War, the superpowers (the US and the countries of the former USSR) ended their unconditional support for tyrannical regimes. At the same time, the form of liberal democracy that prevailed in Western states now became the only model of political legitimacy. The end of Soviet regimes in Eastern Europe sent ripples of excitement through African opposition members. They now openly questioned the official doctrine - based on cultural or economic arguments - that rejected democracy as an appropriate system for Africa.

The Structural Adjustment Programs (SAPs) promoted by the International Financial Institutions (IFIs) in the 1980s as a means of resolving the debt crisis also had political implications. In the long term, the SAPs - although apparently apolitical - sought the formation of a middle class who would be independent from the state and supported by commercial activities. They would be the foundation of an empowered civil society capable of counterbalancing the power of the state.

In practice, the SAPs had the opposite effect. They toughened the state's authoritarian and repressive practices, because governments had to quell

NEPAD: hope for change?

THE HISTORIC FOUNDATION of the Organization of African Unity (OAU) on 25 May 1963, in Addis Ababa, Ethiopia, was one of the most significant events of Africa's post-independence years. The OAU agreements sought to eradicate all forms of colonialism in Africa and promote progress in general throughout the continent. They aimed to enhance unity and solidarity among African states; to coordinate and intensify their cooperation and efforts to achieve a better life for their peoples and defend their sovereignty, territorial integrity and independence. They also maintained a principle of non-interference in domestic affairs and a policy of non-alignment.

For almost 40 years, the OAU had its ups and downs, but it left a positive legacy to its heir, the African Union (AU), which took on its predecessor's principles with new and wider goals. In March 2000, the heads of state and government of the 53 member countries approved the Union's act of constitution.

During the OAU's last Extraordinary Summit held in Sirte, Libya, on September 1999, Presidents Thabo Mbeki, of South Africa, and Abdelaziz Bouteflika, of Algeria, were commissioned to negotiate with Africa's creditors on the cancelling of the continent's foreign debt. In January 2001, Mbeki attended the World Economic Forum in Davos, Switzerland, to introduce a development proposal for Africa called the 'Millennium African Renaissance Program'. In July 2001, Mbeki took the proposal to the summit of the Group of Eight (G-8, the world's seven wealthiest countries in the world plus Russia) in Genoa, Italy. After revising the proposal, the G-8 leaders requested the inclusion of items that would ensure transparency and accountability. Based on the G-8 requests, and after consulting with the International Financial Institutions (IFIs) and the leaders of Nigeria and Algeria, Mbeki launched the 'New Partnership for Africa's Development' (NEPAD) in 2002.

NEPAD's main goal was to attract foreign direct investment to its agriculture, power, communications and human-resources sectors. NEPAD advocates hoped that with $64 billion in annual public and private investment the member states would reach a seven per cent growth rate.

Under NEPAD, African countries offered transparency and accountability in exchange for financial aid. To ensure governance and monitor the use of funds, a system of peer evaluation was proposed. In any case, any money granted to NEPAD would be strongly conditioned and restricted to those countries that met the political and economic criteria imposed by the G-8.

African governments were once again invited to the G-8 summit in Kananaskis, Canada, in June 2002. Here, the G-8 presented its own 'Africa Action Plan', committed to the process initiated by the NEPAD. But no concrete and significant actions were undertaken by the G-8 in the following year. The enthusiasm originated in Canada gave way to skepticism and disappointment with the process.

In June 2003, African leaders were again invited to the G-8 summit in Evian, France, where Africa was promised development aid. But key issues for the African population, such as access to affordable drugs, were not addressed.

It remains to be seen whether the promise of NEPAD can fulfil the original principles set out by the OAU more than 40 years ago. ∎

protests and uprisings against the new economic policies that reduced state spending and already dwindling social services. But they also contributed to articulate pro-democracy demands. This was more because of their adverse effects on Africans' quality of life than because of their contribution to the emergence of new middle classes.

When it became evident that the SAPs were not generating the expected economic recovery, Western donors - and to a lesser degree the IFIs - introduced a concern for 'governance', government systems, law enforcement and human rights. Economic conditioning, pegged to aid, started to include a vague political conditioning as well.

Meanwhile, because of the authoritarian and militaristic way in which African governments were fashioned during the first years of independence, the new educated élites were left without a space of their own in the circles of power. These alternative élites see multiparty democracy as a new way of reaching power and the resources it brings.

New formulas, old methods
Institutional transformations have not always led to more democratic governments, especially in Sub-Saharan Africa. Formulas from previous governments have often been copied to pursue, jail or torture the opposition, now legalized in the new political era. Observers such as Mbembe believe that the so-called African transitions to democracy come down to a reshuffling of power. They are one of the multiple transformations going on throughout the continent, which seems to be headed in different directions at the same time.

Electoral processes have been used by many of the old autocrats in power or by the winners of civil conflicts as a way to legitimize their government, or their victory, and to keep receiving international aid. Elections have become a matter of maintaining the international image of old dictators such as Arap Moi, from Kenya, or Obiang Nguema, from Equatorial Guinea. Authoritarian mechanisms of domination have been adopted even when there has been a change of government, as in Zambia with Frederick Chiluba.

Some of the contradictions are caused by the fact that those in power are trying to respond to external, rather than to domestic, pressures. The adoption of foreign-imposed political measures not only undermines democracy itself, but also reveals deep inconsistencies. First, because the political players - more concerned about the international than the national or local effects of their decisions - tend to convert democracy into a show with no substance. Second, because the international agenda is never aimed solely at increasing the participation of Africans: there is always a diversity of goals driving donors' foreign policies.

Politics in Africa continues to be a struggle for scarce resources. There is too much at stake for a peaceful change of power to take place. The state (often in the hands of corrupt governments) is currently the main instrument of accumulation. At the same time, it faces ever-decreasing resources; the struggle sometimes develops into civil war. In this context, the electoral mechanism as it stands does not offer a way of reaching political and social consensus.

Perhaps NEPAD's negotiations (see box) will manage to force African Governments to take on more responsibility and ensure more transparency in exchange for debt reduction or cancellation. And maybe this will put an end to the cycle of corruption and endemic poverty. ∎

Sources: *Rebelión* and Information and Documentation Centre on Africa

The ethics of disaster: humanitarian aid and political power

A GLOBALIZED POLICY, WITH INTERNATIONAL EFFORTS MAINLY FOCUSED ON THE WAR ON TERRORISM, PRESENTS MAJOR ETHICAL DILEMMAS AROUND THE LEGITIMACY OF HUMANITARIAN AGENCIES. ACCORDING TO A RECENT WORLD REPORT BY THE INTERNATIONAL FEDERATION OF RED CROSS AND RED CRESCENT SOCIETIES, HUMANITARIAN INTERVENTION IN CERTAIN DISASTERS IS NO LONGER DEFENSIBLE UNLESS THE CAUSES OF THOSE DISASTERS ARE ADDRESSED.

Humanitarian aid aims to save the lives of those most in need, while respecting the dignity of each person affected by armed conflict, hunger, diseases or natural disasters. In its 2003 *World Disasters Report* (www.ifrc.org/publicat/wdr2003) the International Federation of Red Cross and Red Crescent Societies (IFRC/RCS) focuses on ethics in aid. It analyzes specific issues, such as the famine that affected 15 million people in Southern Africa in early 2003. It denounces a lack of prevention and points out inefficiencies and delays in the implementation of aid measures. The combination of the famine with the AIDS epidemic and poverty dramatically complicated the situation and generates questions about the relevance of intervening in certain conflicts without attacking their structural causes. Afghanistan is another case where international aid has failed to tackle the root of the problem - many security and human-rights issues have been aggravated since the US-led invasion.

Emma Bonino, former European Commissioner for Humanitarian Affairs, warned that we must avoid situations where humanitarian aid is used as a substitute for foreign policy or as a scapegoat for the fact that there is no such policy. Humanitarian aid, no matter how justifiable, is no more than a stop-gap, a drop in the ocean, unless it has political backing from the European Union, the United States or the United Nations during a crisis situation. At the same time, the goal should not be to politicize aid, but rather to make foreign policy more humanitarian. Pragmatic solutions rather than principles (no matter how respectable) are the best way to resolve crises. A foreign policy based solely on national or regional interests has no future. That is why Bonino insists that Europe needs a foreign policy based on sound ethical foundations, principles and values which are universally accepted. These are the only principles, she says, that can be explained and defended to citizens and national parliaments.

Neutrality and independence

Humanitarian ethics should be ruled by two principles: neutrality and independence. The *World Disasters Report* notes five 'moral hazards' that it says should be considered with regard to humanitarian aid: 'complicity in abuses (feeding refugees may help armed factions regroup); legitimizing violations (prioritizing aid over investigating rights violations may encourage a climate of impunity); aid's negative effect (too much aid may undermine local markets or depopulate areas); targeting and triage (the most needy may be left to die if others can be more effectively helped); advocacy or access (condemning abuses can mean agencies are expelled).'

The International Red Cross and Red Crescent Movement, supported by more than 200 non-governmental organizations, has set up a 'behavior code' for humanitarian relief. This characterizes the immediate relief of suffering as the priority, while the principles of impartiality, non-political action and independence help ensure this can be achieved. The Code also commits its signatories to 'respect culture, build local capacities, encourage participation, reduce vulnerabilities and be fully accountable'.

The IFRC/RCS notes that these principles are not equally honored everywhere. Humanitarian aid tends to favor the major disasters that attract public attention. Jonathan Walter, the Report's editor, observes that: 'this trend is growing in the war on terrorism'. The greatest flows of aid are directed to those countries that are 'targets of the war on terror', but humanitarian aid does not lend the same hand to all those that suffer consequences from armed conflicts, diseases or disasters.

In 2002, $5.9 billion was given in aid. But this unprecedented amount was not grounded in ethical criteria. For example, that year, the northern Caucasus received 89 per cent of its UN appeal, while Somalia only received 22 per cent. Per capita assistance ranged from $10 in Uganda to $185 in Southeast Europe. A few weeks after toppling Saddam Hussein, $1.7 billion was raised to aid Iraq, but only half the humanitarian aid promised to millions of starving Africans was received.

Disaster evaluation: challenges, possibilities and ethics

In the hours and days that make up the aftermath of a disaster, before the arrival of international aid, local communities undertake the tasks of search and rescue, damage evaluation, collection of bodies and distribution of aid supplies. In slowly developing disasters such as famine, which do not immediately capture the attention of donors or the media, local organizations are usually the first to heed the call. They continue to reduce future

risks once international organizations have left. The aid agencies should improve the capacity of local institutions to assume control of decisions that affect their own communities. It is not just about transferring knowledge, but about making available to local organizations the necessary resources and the means to evaluate the impact of international aid.

The impact of humanitarian aid is defined in terms of the 'significant or permanent change' that a particular operation has on people's lives. This change can be positive or negative, foreseeable or unforeseeable, direct or indirect.

Certain specific recommendations have been suggested in order to give an ethical foundation to evaluation methods:

- Avoid generating expectations that cannot be fulfilled

- Foster evaluations that are meaningful to those involved

- Respect the personal and time restrictions of those who are reporting

- Realize that evaluations may heighten tensions and place people at risk

- Guarantee a voice to those excluded

- Fight to make sure evaluations and their conclusions are made public

- Change aid agencies' culture by making them more tolerant of, and receptive to, criticisms.

Insufficient or inaccurate information could lead to mistaken decisions which could cost lives or contribute to the

mismanagement of precious resources. The gathering and use of information, aside from facing practical difficulties (ie access to conflict or disaster zones), poses significant ethical challenges. When the need for humanitarian aid is urgent, immediately after a disaster, should precious time and valuable resources be spent in data collection, or in saving lives? Some claim that it is immoral to postpone life-saving interventions until data is collected. Others say that aid should be based on objective evaluations of need.

It is also of the utmost importance to avoid the manipulation of information for political, military or commercial purposes. This could be achieved by establishing an international code of ethics on the collection and use of data, for example, based on Project Sphere (www.sphereproject.org), which was launched in July 1997 by a group of humanitarian NGOs and the IFRC/RCS. Sphere is based on two core beliefs: 'first, that all possible steps should be taken to alleviate human suffering arising out of calamity and conflict, and second, that those affected by disaster have a right to life with dignity and therefore a right to assistance.'

Sphere is three things: a handbook, a broad process of collaboration and an expression of commitment to quality and accountability. It has developed a 'Humanitarian Chart' and a series of basic universal standards in key areas of humanitarian aid: water supply and sanitation, nutrition, food aid, shelter, settlements and health services. ∎

Disasters: statistics and trends 1993-2002

DURING THE 1993-2002 decade the death toll for both natural and human-made disasters decreased by 38 per cent in comparison to the previous decade, but the total number of people affected during the same period rose by 54 per cent. Weather-related disasters kept climbing: the annual average went from 200 during 1993-1997 to 331 during 1998-2003. Famine was the deadliest disaster throughout the decade, when at least 275,000 people starved to death. Some 140 million people were affected by floods.

In 2002:

- There were more disasters in than any other year in the decade.

- Although fewer lives were lost (24,500 lives lost against the decade's annual average of 62,000), the number of victims (608 million) was three times the 1992-2001 annual average (excluding those affected by armed conflict).

- Countries with high human development (HHD) only had six per cent of the total death toll; 18 casualties for each disaster.

- Countries with low human development (LHD) had a lower number of disasters, but a much higher death toll - 555 for each disaster.

- The global cost of disaster damage climbed to $27 billion, more than two-thirds of which belonged to HHD countries, while LHD countries represent only 0.15 per cent of that amount. The main reason behind this difference is the high value of financial infrastructure in developed countries. ∎

Source: Jonathan Walter, *World Disasters Report 2003*.

Human security: protecting vital freedoms

SECURITY HAS BEEN THE SUBJECT OF HEATED DEBATE ALL OVER THE WORLD: DEBATE ABOUT POLICIES THAT WOULD MAKE THE WORLD AND THE SOCIETIES IN IT MORE SECURE; DEBATE ABOUT THE FACTORS CAUSING UNCERTAINTY, FEAR AND INSECURITY AMONG PEOPLE AND WITHIN NATIONS. IN THIS GLOBAL RE-ASSESSMENT OF SECURITY, THE CONCEPT OF HUMAN SECURITY CAN HELP SHIFT THE FOCUS OF THE DEBATE AWAY FROM THE STIPULATIONS OF A FEW COUNTRIES AND THEIR SPECIALIZED SECURITY BODIES TOWARDS WHAT HUMANITY REALLY WANTS.

The concept of 'human security' appeared in the context of research for peace in the 1980s as a counterpoint to the concept of 'national security' predominant during the Cold War. It came into widespread use internationally in 1994 when it became the premise on which the United Nations Development Programme (UNDP) built its annual *Human Development Reports*. UNDP maintains that vulnerability is at the core of human insecurity and that we must ask ourselves how people can be protected, insisting on their direct involvement and on a close link between development and security. As a starting point, UNDP identified eight dimensions of human security (and therefore, human insecurity): economic, financial, food, sanitary, environmental, personal, gender, community and political.

A few years later, governments in countries such as Japan, Norway and Canada integrated the ideas underlying this concept into the design of their foreign policies. They also aimed to pursue particular security-related goals, including the prohibition of anti-personnel mines, the control of light arms, the prevention of recruitment of child soldiers, the promotion of International Humanitarian Law, support for new human-rights bodies set up by the United Nations, assistance for refugees and participation in peacekeeping operations.

The concept of human security, then, is evolving, and the discussion that it generates is an excellent opportunity to redefine the old security schemes based on military force, and to identify the needs of the planet as a whole, in all its diversity. These aspects have rarely been considered in general public policies.

According to the Commission on Human Security, human security 'means protecting vital freedoms. It means protecting people from critical and pervasive threats and situations, building on their strengths and aspirations. It means creating [political, social, environmental, economic, military and cultural] systems that give people the building blocks of survival, dignity and livelihood'.

The emphasis on people

Human security is complementary to the notion of territorial security of the State in that it is more concerned with the individual and the community than with the State itself. It is therefore possible to differentiate clearly between 'national security' policies which focus on the State's territorial integrity and the freedom to determine its form of government, and 'human security' which emphasizes people and communities, and in particular civilians who are in situations of extreme vulnerability, whether owing to war or social and economic marginalization. Dangers to people's security include threats and situations which, from the point of view of state security, are not always classified as threatening. Moreover, the human security focus widens the range of actors involved in such a way that the State is not the exclusive actor. The aim of human security is not only to protect people but to empower them so that they can fend for themselves.

Leading academics like Economics Nobel Prize winner Amartya Sen have been calling for years for the adoption of this new human-security perspective as an instrument for rethinking the future and for reassessing the concept of development itself, which is not only related to the growth in per capita income but also to the expansion of people's freedom and dignity. Sen advocates redefining the old international institutions that were set up in the 1940s and drawing up an agenda of the changes most needed. Among others, he includes trade agreements, patent laws, global health initiatives, universal education, dissemination of technology, environmental policies, foreign debt, conflict management and disarmament. An agenda, in short, that will make human security viable.

The objectives of human security are also part and parcel of the 1999 Programme of Action on a Culture of Peace, and the Millennium Declaration adopted by the UN General Assembly. Although the idea of human security and the early work in this sphere originated in predominantly Western circles and governments, from the very start the debate acquired an international dimension and has included all the different shades of opinion and divergent positions which characterize the political and cultural diversity of the world. The academic and political debate is centred on whether human security should focus on first-generation political rights or whether it should also include second- and third-generation rights, including the rights to development and to food.

Human security is inclusive and people-centred. It emerges from civil society in an attempt to protect individuals and their communities. It goes beyond issues of territorial defense and military power. And it is based on the notion of personal security, on the understanding that not only the State but also non-State actors and human beings are responsible for development and must become involved in promoting policies and actions that will strengthen people's security and development.

A multi-dimensional concept

Human security is multi-dimensional. It seeks to define the political, economic, social, cultural and environmental dimensions which affect people's security, and identify traditional and non-traditional threats to security based on the fact that security is not one-dimensional but encompasses many spheres.

Human security emphasizes association and joint effort, that is to say, multilateralism and co-operation. The current international context and the results of globalization have changed the scale of the problems, which were formerly seen from an exclusively national perspective. We are now faced with a new international order in which the capacity to interact is essential if States are to recover their ability to work with other actors and generate a system able to meet people's demands at national, regional and international levels.

Freedom from fear, freedom from want

As UN Secretary General Kofi Annan has said, human security, 'in its broadest sense, embraces far more than the absence of violent conflict. It encompasses human rights, good governance, access to education and healthcare and ensuring that each individual has opportunities and choices to fulfil his or her potential. Every step in this direction is also a step towards reducing poverty, achieving economic growth and preventing conflict. Freedom from want, freedom from fear, and the freedom of future generations to inherit a healthy natural environment, these are the interrelated building blocks of human - and therefore national - security.'

The paradigm of human development links human security to equity, sustainability, growth and participation, since it allows an assessment of the degree of life security attained by people in society, as well as interpreting the possibilities and challenges that society may encounter in its progress toward full and sustainable human development.

From the perspective of human security, what matters is not so much that States and societies should be concerned with guaranteeing peace from external threat, but rather that they should guarantee the minimum conditions for people to be secure and to feel secure within their societies.

The two basic dimensions

There are two basic dimensions to human security. The first is to protect people against chronic threats like hunger, disease and repression; the second is to protect them against sudden and damaging changes in their daily lives, whether it is in the home, in employment or in the community. These threats can have a negative impact on people at all income levels and stages of development in a country.

Human security complements state security, enhances human rights and promotes human development, extending its scope beyond the notion of 'growth with equity'. Respect for human rights lies at the core of protecting human security. The promotion of democratic principles is a step toward achieving human security and development in that it permits people to participate in governance structures,

thus allowing their voices to be heard. In order to achieve this it is necessary to set up stable institutions which establish the rule of law and empower people.

Human security is only possible when it is based on sustained development. This presupposes security at different levels for all members of society - from physical danger and threats, of income, in education, housing, health and the environment.

To sum up, the three most serious obstacles to human security are: first, threats to the security of individuals and their communities, in particular to the most vulnerable sectors of society; second, conflicts, threats and different kinds of violence (inter-state conflicts, breakdown of states, human-rights violations, terrorism, organised crime, etc); and third, poverty and economic exclusion. At a world level, human security will be achieved when all human beings live in conditions of justice, equity, freedom, tolerance, good health, and have access to adequate food, education and a healthy environment. In other words, the conditions that allow us all to live in dignity. ▪

Source: Karina Bathyany, 'Obstacles to Human Security', *Social Watch 2004*

Privatizing basic services: a violation of human rights?

THE DEEPENING INEQUALITIES OF INCOME AND OPPORTUNITY BETWEEN AND WITHIN NATIONS HAS LED TO AN INCREASING NUMBER OF PEOPLE BEING WITHOUT ADEQUATE AND SECURE HOUSING. THE CONTINUING DETERIORATION OF CONDITIONS FACED BY THE MAJORITY OF THE POOR AROUND THE WORLD HAS CAUSED TREMENDOUS CONCERN THAT UNFETTERED GLOBALIZATION CANNOT BRING ABOUT THE FULFILMENT OF ECONOMIC, SOCIAL AND CULTURAL RIGHTS, INCLUDING THE RIGHT TO ADEQUATE HOUSING.

It is estimated that 600 million urban dwellers and over a billion rural people now live in overcrowded and poor-quality housing without adequate water, sanitation, drainage or garbage collection. More than 1.2 billion people still have no access to safe drinking water and 2.4 billion do not have adequate sanitation services. This grave situation puts lives and health continually at risk. It also threatens a range of human rights, including the right to adequate housing.

The right to an adequate and secure home

Every woman, man, youth and child has the human right to a secure home and a community in which to live in peace and dignity. This human right has received global recognition and is firmly established

in a number of international human rights instruments, most notably the International Covenant on Economic, Social and Cultural Rights (CESCR). By ratifying these treaties and instruments, States have accepted the obligations to progressively realize the right to food, health, adequate housing and a range of other rights and services, including water and sanitation, which are essential for the wellbeing of their citizens. But globalization and increasing economic integration have limited the capacity of States to provide adequate resources to fulfill the economic, social and cultural rights of their citizens. Several macroeconomic factors influence the availability of resources for social spending, including:

- Small or even negative returns from trade liberalization by developing

countries, particularly Least Developed Countries (LDCs).

- Financial volatility following the deregulation of capital flows, coupled with interest-rate hikes which affect access to credit and mortgages.

- Increased land speculation as a result of more competition for prime locations in rapidly globalizing cities. This often forces out low-income residents to less desirable locations with poor service availability.

- Heavy burdens of debt servicing.

- Fiscal constraints and austerity measures imposed by the IMF and the World Bank which are primarily designed to reduce public spending, and invariably lead to reductions in financial allocations to social sectors

- The process of public-sector reform, particularly through decentralization and privatization.

Increased competition among cities to attract capital and businesses for generating employment and sources of tax revenues has led to widening inequalities between these cities, with consequent discrepancies in the levels of essential services provided to their citizens. In the urban housing sector, reliance on market mechanisms has tended to result in neglect of the poor.

Despite the constraints and difficulties placed upon them, central governments have the responsibility to make targeted interventions in order to ensure universal access to public services, including water and sanitation, on a fair and equitable basis; this is fundamental for the fulfilment of the right to adequate housing.

Privatization and vulnerable groups

Privatization often results in reduced access by the poor to basic social services. In developing countries, finding safe and affordable water is a daily struggle for the majority poor population. In many cities and towns, between 50 and 70 per cent of the population live in slums and squatter settlements without adequate housing or basic services. Many of the poor end up paying up to 20 times more than the rich for water. And higher prices for water mean the poor have to use less or go without.

In addition, privatization can cause interruptions in service, or deterioration in the quality of water, which pose serious health hazards. These can occur when projects fail (Tucuman, Argentina), contracts become unworkable (Dolphin Coast, South Africa), the company fails (Azurix, Buenos Aires province, Argentina), there are socially unsustainable price increases (Cochabamba, Bolivia), or when there is corruption and distorted accounting (Grenoble, France).

Women and inadequate housing, water and sanitation

The consequences of having inadequate or no access to water are devastating, especially for women and children. When water is not readily available, it is the women and children in particular who have to spend a large amount of time fetching water. This has a detrimental impact on their health, security and education.

It has been found that where there are no latrines, girls commonly do not go to school. Women and girls carry the bulk of the burden in providing water for households in rural areas and often have to walk great distances in search of water to meet minimal household needs. In poorer countries, one in five children dies before the age of five, mainly from infectious diseases related to inadequate or impure water.[1]

Water stress contributes to many other hardships for women. For example, in parts of India, because of the low availability of water, there is little vegetation growth. This means there is less green fodder, decreasing the production of milk and of cow dung, which is used for fuel and manure. Lower production of cow dung leads to a reduction in agricultural yields, which affects food quality and the nutrition of women. There is thus a vicious cycle of water and ecological destruction which impacts on the health of women and causes 'eco-stress'.

As women increasingly take up paid employment, their time also begins to carry monetary value. In many instances in rural areas, if this cost is included in the decision-making about the choice of technology and strategies for household water security, women and girls end up paying far more for water than they do in urban areas.

Lack of sanitation facilities affects both men and women, but sanitation needs and demands differ. Women have particular needs and concerns about privacy, dignity and personal safety. A lack of sanitation facilities in the home can force women and girls to use secluded places, often away from home, exposing them to the risk of sexual abuse; in other circumstances, girls are forced to defecate only at home and help their mothers to dispose of human and solid waste. Because of this extra work girls might have to stop attending school.

The lack of access to clean and sufficient water and sanitation facilities contributes to diseases, which results in more cost for the family, and means that someone (usually a girl or a woman) has to be kept at home to look after ailing family members. This leads to reduced school attendance and poorer educational performance.

Studies have also found that the access to sewage disposal often depends on the sex of the head of household; for example in Nairobi, Kenya, about 9.2 per cent of female-headed households used the bush for fecal disposal, whereas in the male-headed households the rate dropped to 2.2 per cent.

In many countries women and men do not enjoy equal access to basic resources and services. Female-headed households have less access than males, and if the services are privatized then the problem increases. Greater attention needs to be paid to the discrimination women face and to policies

---

1 *Human Rights, Poverty Reduction and Sustainable Development: Health, Food and Water*, OHCHR Background Paper, WSSD Johannesburg, 26 August-4 September 2002.

and measures adopted to alleviate it. There is also a need for laws and policies that regulate or define the habitability of housing to take into consideration the special needs of women.

International cooperation

The Millennium Declaration adopted by the General Assembly recognized 'solidarity' and 'shared responsibilities' as fundamental values essential to international relations in the 21st century. Such recognition is necessary for evolving strategies for distributive justice, including land reform and increases in social spending on areas critical to the realization of the right to adequate housing, such as access to potable water and sanitation. Such a reallocation or redistribution needs to be balanced with targeted support from international cooperation, including 'joint' and 'separate' action by States, as called for by the general obligations to international human-rights instruments.

In achieving these objectives, it is critical to recognize the obligations on States implicit in the legal provisions on international cooperation, given the current global reality of growing income disparities and attendant increases in poverty and marginalization. Serious attention must be paid to the need to assist developing countries in their efforts to improve the housing and living conditions of the poor and inadequately housed, through 'joint and separate action' as provided in Article 2.1 of the Covenant on Economic, Social and Cultural Rights (CESCR). This also means ensuring that States' international policies, or policies evolved at multilateral fora and institutions, respect the full realization of economic, social and cultural rights for all.

The solidarity and fraternity dimensions of international co-operation under international human-rights instruments mean that no action may be taken, or global social policies adopted, which could inhibit States' abilities to implement the commitments stemming from their obligations under these instruments. Most recently, in General Comment No 15 on the right to water, the CESCR stated: 'To comply with their international obligations in relation to the right to water, States parties have to respect the enjoyment of the right in other countries. International co-operation requires States... to refrain from actions that interfere, directly or indirectly, with the enjoyment of the right to water in other countries.' The Comment continues, 'steps should be taken by States... to prevent their own citizens and companies from violating the right to water of individuals and communities of other countries.'

States also need to examine policies - their own and others' - on international institutions and international agreements, to ensure they are consistent with covenanted obligations on the right to adequate housing, including access to basic social services. Such reviews should include the human-rights implications of World Trade Organization trade agreements, particularly the General Agreement on Trade in Services (GATS) and the Agreement on Trade-Related Aspects of Intellectual Property Rights (TRIPS); country assistance agreements and agreements with the World Bank and IMF; as well as poverty reduction strategies such as the Poverty Reduction Strategy Papers (PRSPs).

Numerous UN human-rights bodies have urged caution in the face of the existing international thrust on trade in services. The human-rights obligations, both at national and international levels, give a clear warning to the negotiators of trade agreements to step back from the expansion of any agreements such as GATS, that lead to the privatization of social services and the entry of corporations into the arena of providing social goods such as water. Such a step would, given the experience thus far, impact negatively on the realization of human rights. Human-rights obligations, in fact, provide legal instruments for conscientious states to argue against the expansion of global trade and investment agreements into the sphere of recognized human rights.

The way forward
It is essential that policies and programmes for international cooperation be aimed at assisting States to develop strategies for social justice and equitable distribution of resources and opportunities, including through land reform and well-targeted spending on essential social services such as credit, potable water, electricity, heating and sanitation.

It is important to employ a human-rights approach in assessing whether privatization is the correct option, and in monitoring the privatization of essential social services. Such an approach would aim to achieve sustainable development and poverty reduction; it would take gender perspectives into account, and empower people by ensuring their

participation; it would ensure that subsidies are guaranteed for those who cannot afford to pay.

Such an approach would also sharpen the focus on key 'gaps' - the divide between the 'haves' and the 'have-nots' - in different sectors, and highlight the accountability of institutions of governance. The areas where some of the most problematic gaps appear are: water supply and sanitation, gender equity and empowerment, and institutional and financial restructuring. Sanitation, for example, is deemed to be a key determinant of vulnerability to water-related diseases, and the 'sanitation gap' may indicate where investment in water

supply should be redirected towards sanitation and hygiene improvements.

Local authorities and civil society organizations in many cities around the world are seeking to provide alternative approaches to urban development and management. Among these is the 'Human Rights Cities' initiative, in which towns and cities have made commitments to implementing participatory budgets, preparing local development plans, or attempting to guide municipal decision-making by adopting a human-rights framework, implementing thoroughgoing administrative decentralization and decision-making through democratic processes. ■

Private operators versus accountability

PRIVATIZATION can reduce accountability and local control. In many cases, governments make long-term deals with water companies, granting them exclusive distribution rights, thus sanctioning monopolies. Transnational corporations are accountable to their shareholders, not to the citizens in the countries where they operate. There have been cases of corruption in the privatization process, where the system of checks and balances is weak. Contract workings and details are usually done behind closed doors and this encourages bribery, while ordinary citizens, who are directly affected, are kept in the dark.

Privatization also undermines water quality and ecological sustainability. Water companies work to weaken water-quality regulations and environmental standards when they are perceived as increasing the costs of doing business. Any private corporation driven by the profit motive is also likely to want to encourage consumption. In 1996, a World Bank

team criticized leakage levels of between one and five per cent in Germany's public sector system for being too low. According to the report, water should be allowed to leak away if the cost of stopping the leak is greater than the price for which the water could be sold at a profit. The team not only thought that the private water companies would waste more water - they encouraged it.

Aware of the bleak water predictions, corporations are in a rush to obtain access to water, which they can sell at huge profits. Mass extraction of water from its natural sources can result in ecological imbalances such as aquifer depletion and groundwater contamination. Once aquifers are depleted or contaminated, they are almost impossible to restore. ■

Source: Miloon Kothari, 'Privatizing human rights - the impact of globalization on adequate housing, water and sanitation' in *Social Watch 2003*.

SEXUAL MINORITIES AND THE LAW: A WORLD SURVEY

Today the issues of homosexuality and transgender are being hotly debated in parts of the world where they had been just a hushed whisper. It has become harder for political and religious leaders to maintain that 'homosexuality is not part of our culture' as home-grown lesbian, gay, bisexual or transgender groups have sprung up in Africa, Asia and Latin America, to fight unjust laws and demand freedom from discrimination and persecution. This 'internationalization' of sexual minority rights has coincided with the rise in internet activism and support from international human rights organizations. However, the situation for many lesbian, gay, bisexual or transgender (LGBT) people in the world remains dire. In nine countries homosexuality incurs the death penalty, while in some 80 states it is illegal, sometimes incurring long prison sentences. Currently, many governments are making constitutional and legal changes to combat centuries of discrimination. Pioneers in this area have included countries like The Netherlands or Denmark, with established liberal traditions, but also South Africa, Brazil and, more recently, the Philippines.

AFGHANISTAN
Homosexuality: Illegal. Death penalty applies under Sharia law.
Transgender: No data or legal situation unclear.

ALBANIA
Homosexuality: Legal. Age of consent higher for lesbians and gay men (18).
Immigration: LGBT citizens have been granted asylum by other countries.
Transgender: Gender reassignment (sex change) is illegal.

ALGERIA
Homosexuality: Illegal. Imprisonable for up to 3 years.
Immigration/Asylum: LGBT citizens have been granted asylum by other countries.
Transgender: No data or legal situation unclear.

ANDORRA
Homosexuality: Legal.
Transgender: Gender reassignment illegal.

ANGOLA
Homosexuality: Illegal.
Transgender: No data or legal situation unclear.

ANTIGUA AND BARBUDA
Homosexuality: Legal.
Transgender: No data or legal situation unclear.

ARGENTINA
Homosexuality: Legal.
Immigration/Asylum: LGBT citizens have been granted asylum by other countries
Employment: Lesbians and gay men are banned from the armed forces.
Transgender: Gender reassignment ('sex change') legal or openly performed without prosecution.

ARMENIA
Homosexuality: Legal.
Immigration/Asylum: LGBT citizens have been granted asylum by other countries, but now some support for LGBT refugees from elsewhere. Some residence rights for bi-national gay couples.
Transgender: No data or legal situation unclear.

ARUBA
Homosexuality: Legal. Some legal protection for sexual orientation.
Transgender: No data or legal situation unclear.

AUSTRALIA
Homosexuality: Legal. Age of consent higher for gay men in CT (18), NT (18), Q'land (18), WA (21). Some sexual orientation protection in some states.
Immigration/Asylum: Prepared to grant asylum to LGBT refugees.
Parenting: Lesbians and single women entitled to use state donor insemination services in the state of Tasmania but denied in other states. Some same-sex couple adoption.
Transgender: Gender reassignment legal in some states. Specific protection from discrimination exists for transgendered people.

AUSTRIA
Homosexuality: Legal.
Immigration/Asylum: Prepared to grant asylum to LGBT refugees.
Transgender: Gender reassignment legal or openly performed without prosecution. All personal documents may be reissued following change.

AZERBAIJAN
Homosexuality: Legal. Age of consent equal.
Transgender: No data or legal situation unclear.

BAHAMAS
Homosexuality: Legal. Age of consent higher for lesbians and gay men (18)
Transgender: No data or legal situation unclear.

BAHRAIN
Homosexuality: Illegal. Imprisonable for 10 years (Article 377 Penal Code)
Transgender: Gender reassignment illegal.

BANGLADESH
Homosexuality: Illegal. Imprisonable for up to 10 years.
Immigration/Asylum: LGBT citizens have been granted asylum by other countries
Transgender: No data or legal situation unclear.

BARBADOS
Homosexuality: Illegal.
Transgender: No data or legal situation unclear.

BELARUS
Homosexuality: Legal. Age of consent higher for gay men (18).
Employment: Lesbians and gay men are banned from the armed forces.
Transgender: Gender reassignment legal or openly performed without prosecution. No data on reissue of documents.

BELGIUM
Homosexuality: Legal. Age of consent equal. Legal recognition of same-sex partnerships.
Parenting: Legal recognition of non-biological parents. Same-sex couples have been allowed to adopt.
Immigration/Asylum: Prepared to grant asylum to LGBT refugees.
Transgender: Gender reassignment legal or openly performed without prosecution. All personal documents may be reissued following change.

BELIZE
Homosexuality: Legal.
Transgender: No data or legal situation unclear.

BENIN
Homosexuality: Illegal.
Transgender: No data or legal situation unclear.

BERMUDA
Homosexuality: Legal.
Transgender: No data or legal situation unclear.

BHUTAN
Homosexuality: Illegal (for men, women not mentioned in law). Imprisonable for life (Section 377 Indian Penal Code)
Transgender: No data or legal situation unclear.

BOLIVIA
Homosexuality: Legal.
Transgender: No data or legal situation unclear.

BOSNIA & HERZEGOVINA
Homosexuality: Legal.
Transgender: No data or legal situation unclear.

BOTSWANA
Homosexuality: Illegal (for men, women not mentioned in law). Imprisonable for 7 years (Section 164 Penal Code).
Transgender: No data or legal situation unclear.

BRAZIL
Homosexuality: Legal. Age of consent equal. Anti-discrimination and anti-vilification laws exist in several states.
Immigration/Asylum: LGBT citizens have been granted asylum by other countries
Transgender: Gender reassignment ('sex change') legal or openly performed without prosecution.

BRUNEI
Homosexuality: Illegal. Imprisonable for 10 years (Sections 292,294,377 Penal Code).
Transgender: No data or legal situation unclear.

BULGARIA
Homosexuality: Severe discrimination in criminal law but not technically illegal. Age of consent higher for lesbians and gay men.
Transgender: No data or legal situation unclear.

BURKINA FASO
Homosexuality: Legal. Age of consent higher for lesbians and gay men (21).
Transgender: No data or legal situation unclear.

BURMA
Homosexuality: Illegal (for men, women not mentioned in law). Imprisonable for 10 years (Sections 1882-88 Penal Code)
Transgender: No data or legal situation unclear. Traditionally transgendered people have accepted place in society.

BURUNDI
Homosexuality: Illegal.
Transgender: No data or legal situation unclear.

CAMBODIA
Homosexuality: Legal. Age of consent equal.
Transgender: No data or legal situation unclear.

CAMEROON
Homosexuality: Illegal.
Transgender: No data or legal situation unclear.

CANADA
Homosexuality: Legal. Age of consent higher for anal sex (18). Legal recognition of same sex partnerships in Quebec, followed by other states. Protection from discrimination in human-rights codes of 11 provinces.
Immigration/Asylum: Prepared to grant asylum to LGBT refugees.
Parenting: Same sex couples have been allowed to adopt.
Employment: equal workplace benefits in 8 provinces.
Transgender: Gender reassignment legal in some states and provinces.

CAPE VERDE
Homosexuality: Illegal.
Transgender: No data or legal situation unclear.

CAYMAN ISLANDS
Homosexuality: Legal.
Transgender: No data or legal situation unclear.

CENTRAL AFRICAN REPUBLIC
Homosexuality: Legal. Age of consent equal.
Transgender: No data or legal situation unclear.

CHAD
Homosexuality: Legal. Age of consent equal.
Transgender: No data or legal situation unclear.

CHILE
Homosexuality: Legal. Age of consent higher for lesbians and gay men (18).
Immigration/Asylum: LGBT citizens have been granted asylum by other countries
Transgender: No data or legal situation unclear.

CHINA
Homosexuality: Legal position unclear. May be prosecuted under 'hooliganism' laws.
Immigration/Asylum: LGBT citizens have been granted asylum by other countries.
Transgender: Gender reassignment ('sex change') legal or openly performed without prosecution.

COLOMBIA
Homosexuality: Legal. Age of consent equal.
Immigration/Asylum: LGBT citizens have been granted asylum by other countries
Transgender: First country to restrict genital mutilation of intersex children from without their, or before age of, consent.

CORMOROS
Homosexuality: Legal.
Transgender: No data or legal situation unclear.

CONGO
Homosexuality: Legal. Age of consent equal.
Transgender: No data or legal situation unclear.

CONGO DEM REP
Homosexuality: Illegal. Imprisonable for to 5 years under 'crimes against the family' laws.
Transgender: No data or legal situation unclear.

COOK ISLANDS
Homosexuality: Illegal (for men, women not mentioned in law). Imprisonable for 7 years (Section 155 penal Code).
Transgender: No data or legal situation unclear.

COSTA RICA
Homosexuality: Legal. Age of consent equal.
Transgender: No data or legal situation unclear.

CÔTE D'IVOIRE
Homosexuality: Legal.
Transgender: No data or legal situation unclear.

CROATIA
Homosexuality: Legal. Age of consent higher for lesbians and gay men (18).
Immigration/Asylum: LGBT citizens have been granted asylum by other countries.
Transgender: No data or legal situation unclear.

CUBA
Homosexuality: Severe discrimination in criminal law but not technically illegal.
Immigration/Asylum: LGBT citizens have been granted asylum by other countries.
Transgender: No data or legal situation unclear.

SEXUAL MINORITIES AND THE LAW: A WORLD SURVEY

CYPRUS
Homosexuality: Legal. Age of consent equal.
Transgender: Gender reassignment illegal.

CZECH REPUBLIC
Homosexuality: Legal. Age of consent equal.
Transgender: Gender reassignment ('sex change') legal or openly performed without prosecution. Some personal documents may be reissued.

DENMARK
Homosexuality: Legal. Age of consent equal. Legal recognition of same sex partnerships (also applies in Greenland).
Immigration/Asylum: Prepared to grant asylum to LGBT refugees.
Parenting: Legal recognition of non-biological parents.
Employment: Laws provide protection from discrimination on the grounds of sexual orientation.
Transgender: Gender reassignment ('sex change') legal or openly performed without prosecution. All personal documents may be reissued following change.

DJIBOUTI
Homosexuality: Illegal.
Transgender: No data or legal situation unclear.

DOMINICAN REP.
Homosexuality: Legal. Age of consent equal.
Transgender: No data or legal situation unclear. Cultural acceptance of transgendered guevedoche or 'pseudo-hermaphrodites'.

ECUADOR
Homosexuality: Legal. Second country in the world to have equality written into the Constitution; discrimination based on sexual orientation is illegal.
Parenting: Custody rights for lesbians.
Transgender: No data or legal situation unclear.

EGYPT
Homosexuality: Technically legal but effectively illegal. A variety of laws are applied.
Transgender: Gender reassignment ('sex change') legal or openly performed without prosecution.

EL SALVADOR
Homosexuality: Legal.
Immigration/Asylum: LGBT citizens have been granted asylum by other countries.
Transgender: No data or legal situation unclear.

EQUATORIAL GUINEA
Homosexuality: Information on sexual offences law unclear or unavailable.
Transgender: No data or legal situation unclear.

ERITREA
Homosexuality: Legal.
Transgender: No data or legal situation unclear.

ESTONIA
Homosexuality: Legal. Age of consent higher for homosexual anal intercourse (16).
Transgender: Gender reassignment ('sex change') legal or openly performed without prosecution. All personal documents may be reissued following change.

ETHIOPIA
Homosexuality: Illegal
Transgender: No data or legal situation unclear.

FIJI
Homosexuality: Illegal (for men, women not mentioned in law). Imprisonable for 14 years or more (Section 175 Penal Code, with or without corporal punishment). A 1998 clause prohibiting discrimination based on sexual orientation has since been removed from the Constitution.
Transgender: No data or legal situation unclear.

FINLAND
Homosexuality: Legal. Age of consent equal. Some legal protection for sexual orientation.
Immigration/Asylum: Prepared to grant asylum to LGBT refugees.
Parenting: Legal recognition of non-biological parents. Lesbians and single women have right to use state donor insemination services.
Employment: Laws provide protection from discrimination on the grounds of sexual orientation.
Transgender: Gender reassignment ('sex change') legal or openly performed without prosecution. All personal documents may be reissued following change.

FRANCE
Homosexuality: Legal. Age of consent equal. Legal recognition of same sex partnerships. Some legal protection for sexual orientation.
Immigration/Asylum: Prepared to grant asylum to LGBT refugees.
Employment: Laws provide protection from discrimination.
Transgender: Gender reassignment ('sex change') legal or openly performed without prosecution. Some personal documents may be reissued after change.

FRENCH GUYANA
Homosexuality: Legal.
Transgender: No data or legal situation unclear.

GABON
Homosexuality: Legal. Age of consent equal.
Transgender: No data or legal situation unclear.

GAMBIA
Homosexuality: Illegal. Imprisonable for 14 years or more. (Article 144 Criminal Code).
Transgender: No data or legal situation unclear.

GEORGIA
Homosexuality: Legal. Age of consent equal.
Transgender: Gender reassignment ('sex change') legal or openly performed without prosecution.

GERMANY
Homosexuality: Legal. Age of consent equal. Legal recognition of same-sex relationships in some regions. Some legal protection in some states.
Immigration/Asylum: Prepared to grant asylum to LGBT refugees
Transgender: Gender reassignment ('sex change') legal or openly performed without prosecution. All personal documents may be reissued after change.

GHANA
Homosexuality: Illegal for men.
Immigration/Asylum: LGBT citizens have been granted asylum by other countries.
Trangender: Gender reassignment (sex change) is illegal.

GREECE
Homosexuality: Legal.
Immigration/Asylum: Prepared to grant asylum to LGBT refugees.
Parenting: Lesbians and single women have right to use state donor insemination services.
Employment: Lesbians and gay men are banned from the armed forces.
Transgender: Gender reassignment ('sex change') legal or openly performed without prosecution. All personal documents may be reissued after change.

GRENADA
Homosexuality: Illegal (for men, women not mentioned in law).
Transgender: No data or legal situation unclear.

GUAM
Homosexuality: Information on sexual offences law unclear or unavailable.
Transgender: No data or legal situation unclear.

GUATEMALA
Homosexuality: Legal.
Transgender: No data or legal situation unclear.

GUINEA
Homosexuality: Illegal. Imprisonable for up to 3 years.
Transgender: No data or legal situation unclear.

GUINEA-BISSAU
Homosexuality: Legal.
Transgender: No data or legal situation unclear.

GUYANA
Homosexuality: Illegal (for men, women not mentioned in law). Imprisonable for life (Section 353 Penal Code).
Transgender: No data or legal situation unclear.

HAITI
Homosexuality: Legal.
Transgender: No data or legal situation unclear.

HONDURAS
Homosexuality: Legal.
Immigration/Asylum: LGBT citizens have been granted asylum by other countries.
Transgender: No data or legal situation unclear.

HUNGARY
Homosexuality: Legal. Age of consent higher for lesbians and gay men (18). Legal recognition of same sex partnerships.
Employment: Lesbians and gay men are 'recommended' not to enter the armed forces.
Transgender: Gender reassignment ('sex change') legal or openly performed without prosecution. Legal situation unclear on document issue.

ICELAND
Homosexuality: Legal. Age of consent equal. Some legal protection for sexual orientation. Legal recognition of same-sex partnerships.
Parenting: Legal recognition of non-biological parents.
Transgender: Gender reassignment ('sex change') legal or openly performed without prosecution. Legal situation unclear on document issue.

INDIA
Homosexuality: Illegal (for men, but law has been used against women and transsexuals too). Imprisonable for life (Section 377 Indian Penal Code).
Transgender: No data or legal situation unclear. Traditionally eunuchs have an accepted place in society.

INDONESIA
Homosexuality: Legal.
Transgender: Gender reassignment ('sex change') legal or openly performed without prosecution. Transgender people have an accepted place in society.

IRAN
Homosexuality: Illegal. Death penalty applies. Executions have taken place during past 10 years.
Transgender: Gender reassignment (sex change) is illegal.

IRAQ
Homosexuality: Legal.
Transgender: No data or legal situation unclear.

IRELAND
Homosexuality: Legal. Age of consent higher for gay men and for anal sex (17). Some legal protection for sexual orientation.
Immigration/Asylum: Prepared to grant asylum to LGBT refugees.
Employment: Laws provide protection from discrimination on the grounds of sexual orientation.
Transgender: Gender reassignment ('sex change') legal or openly performed without prosecution. It is illegal to change birth certificate or marry after gender reassignment.

ISRAEL
Homosexuality: Legal. Age of consent equal.
Employment: Some legal protection for sexual orientation.
Transgender: Gender reassignment ('sex change') legal or openly performed without prosecution.

ITALY
Homosexuality: Legal. Age of consent equal.
Transgender: Gender reassignment ('sex change') legal or openly performed without prosecution. Some personal documents may be reissued after change.

JAMAICA
Homosexuality: Illegal (for men, women not mentioned in law). Imprisonable for 10 years (Sections 76-79 Penal Code, can be accompanied by hard labour)
Transgender: No data or legal situation unclear.

JAPAN
Homosexuality: Legal. Employment: Homosexuals are banned from the armed forces.
Transgender: Gender reassignment ('sex change') legal or openly performed without prosecution.

JORDAN
Homosexuality: Legal.
Immigration/Asylum: LGBT citizens have been granted asylum by other countries.
Transgender: No data or legal situation unclear.

KAZAKHSTAN
Homosexuality: Legal.
Transgender: No data or legal situation unclear.

KENYA
Homosexuality: Illegal (for men, women not mentioned in law). Imprisonable for 14+ years ((Section 162-165 Penal Code).
Transgender: No data or legal situation unclear. Traditionally transgendered people have an accepted place in society.

KIRIBATI
Homosexuality: Illegal (for men, women not mentioned in law). Imprisonable for 14 years (Section 153 Penal Code).
Transgender: No data or legal situation unclear.

KOREA, N
Homosexuality: Anal intercourse between men illegal. Punishable by up to 10 years' imprisonment. Women not mentioned in law.
Transgender: No data or legal situation unclear.

KOREA, S
Homosexuality: Legal.
Transgender: No data or legal situation unclear.

KUWAIT
Homosexuality: Illegal (for men, women not mentioned in law). Imprisonable for 7 years (Section 193 penal Code). Laws denying freedom of expression and/or association also apply.
Transgender: No data or legal situation unclear.

KYRGYZSTAN
Homosexuality: Legal.
Transgender: No data or legal situation unclear.

LAOS
Homosexuality: Severe discrimination in criminal law but falling short of total illegality.
Transgender: No data or legal situation unclear.

LATVIA
Homosexuality: Legal.
Immigration/Asylum: Prepared to grant asylum to LGBT refugees
Transgender: Gender reassignment ('sex change') legal or openly performed without prosecution. Some personal documents may be reissued after change.

LEBANON
Homosexuality: Illegal. Laws denying freedom of expression and/or association apply.
Immigration/Asylum: LGBT citizens have been granted asylum by other countries
Transgender: No data or the situation unclear.

LESOTHO
Homosexuality: Legal.
Transgender: No data or legal situation unclear.

LIBERIA
Homosexuality: Illegal.
Transgender: No data or legal situation unclear.

LIBYA
Homosexuality: Illegal.
Transgender: No data or legal situation unclear.

LIECHTENSTEIN
Homosexuality: Severe discrimination in criminal law but not technically illegal. Age of consent higher for gay men (18).
Transgender: No data or legal situation unclear.

LITHUANIA
Homosexuality: Legal. Age of consent higher for gay men (18).
Transgender: Gender reassignment illegal.

LUXEMBOURG
Homosexuality: Legal. Age of consent equal.
Employment: Lesbians and gay men are banned from the armed forces.
Transgender: Gender reassignment ('sex change') legal or openly performed without prosecution. Some personal documents may be reissued after change.

MACEDONIA, TFYR
Homosexuality: Legal. Employment: Gays barred from joining the legal profession.
Transgender: Gender reassignment (sex change) is illegal.

MADAGASCAR
Homosexuality: Legal.
Transgender: No data or legal situation unclear. Transgendered people have an accepted place in society.

MALAWI
Homosexuality: Illegal.
Transgender: No data or legal situation unclear.

MALAYSIA
Homosexuality: Illegal (for men, women not mentioned in law). Imprisonable for 20 years (Articles 377A and 377B Penal Code).
Immigration/Asylum: LGBT citizens have been granted asylum by other countries.
Transgender: No data or legal situation unclear.

MALDIVES
Homosexuality: Illegal (for men, women not mentioned in law). Imprisonable for life. (Section 377 Penal Code).
Trangender: No data or legal situation unclear.

MALI
Homosexuality: Information on sexual offences law is unclear or unavailable.
Transgender: No data or legal situation unclear.

MALTA
Homosexuality: Legal. Age of consent equal.
Transgender: Gender reassignment illegal.

MARSHALL ISLANDS
Homosexuality: Illegal (for men, women not mentioned in law). Imprisonable for 10 years (Section 53 Penal Code).
Transgender: No data or legal situation unclear.

MAURITANIA
Homosexuality: Illegal. Death penalty applies.
Immigration/Asylum: LGBT citizens have been granted asylum by other countries
Transgender: No data or legal situation unclear.

MAURITIUS
Homosexuality: Illegal. Imprisonable for up to 3 years.
Transgender: No data or legal situation unclear.

MEXICO
Homosexuality: Legal.
Immigration/Asylum: LGBT citizens have been granted asylum by other countries.
Transgender: No data or legal situation unclear.

MICRONESIA
Homosexuality: Not mentioned in law.
Transgender: No data or legal situation unclear.

MOLDOVA
Homosexuality: Legal. Age of consent higher for homosexual anal sex (18).
Transgender: Gender reassignment ('sex change') legal or openly performed without prosecution. All personal documents may be reissued following change.

MONACO
Homosexuality: Legal. Age of consent equal.
Transgender: Gender reassignment ('sex change') legal or openly performed without prosecution. All personal documents may be reissued following change.

MONGOLIA
Homosexuality: Not mentioned in law but penal code prohibiting 'immoral gratification of sexual desires' is used against gay people.
Transgender: No data or legal situation unclear.

MOROCCO
Homosexuality: Illegal.
Immigration/Asylum: LGBT citizens have been granted asylum by other countries.
Transgender: Legal situation unclear.

MOZAMBIQUE
Homosexuality: Illegal (for men, women not mentioned in law).
Transgender: No data or legal situation unclear.

NAMIBIA
Homosexuality: Illegal (for men, women not mentioned in law).
Partnership/Immigration: Legal precedent giving immigration rights to same-sex lesbian partnership.
Employment: Some anti-discrimination provision applies, paradoxically, in spite of illegality.
Transgender: No data or legal situation unclear.

NAURA
Homosexuality: Illegal (for men, women not mentioned in law).
Transgender: No data or legal situation unclear.

NEPAL
Homosexuality: Illegal (for men, women not mentioned in law). Imprisonable for life. (Section 377 Penal Code).
Transgender: No data or legal situation unclear.

NETHERLANDS
Homosexuality: Legal. Age of consent equal. Some legal protection for sexual orientation. Legal recognition of same sex partnerships.
Parenting: Legal recognition of non-biological parents. Same-sex couples have been allowed to adopt. Lesbians and single women have right to use state donor insemination services.
Immigration/Asylum: Prepared to grant asylum to LGBT refugees.
Transgender: Gender reassignment ('sex change') legal or openly performed without prosecution. Some personal documents may be reissued after change.

NEW ZEALAND/AOTEAROA
Homosexuality: Legal. Age of consent equal. Legal protection for sexual orientation under the Human Rights Act. Same-sex partnerships recognized in a number of areas.
Immigration/Asylum: Prepared to grant asylum to LGBT refugees.
Transgender: Gender reassignment ('sex change') legal or openly performed without prosecution. Transgendered people can have all official documents reflecting their gender choice.

NICARAGUA
Homosexuality: Illegal.
Immigration/Asylum: LGBT citizens have been granted asylum by other countries.
Transgender: No data or legal situation unclear.

NIGER
Homosexuality: Legal.
Transgender: No data or legal situation unclear.

NIGERIA
Homosexuality: Illegal (for men, women not mentioned in law). Imprisonable for up to 14 years. In Northern provinces death penalty under sharia law applies.
Transgender: No data or legal situation unclear.

NIUE
Homosexuality: Illegal (for men, women not mentioned in law). Imprisonable for 10 years (Section 170 Penal Code).
Transgender: No data or legal situation unclear.

NORWAY
Homosexuality: Legal. Age of consent equal. Legal recognition of same-sex partnerships.
Immigration/Asylum: Prepared to grant asylum to LGBT refugees.
Parenting: Legal recognition of non-biological parents.
Transgender: Gender reassignment ('sex change') legal or openly performed without prosecution. Some personal documents may be reissued to reflect change.

OMAN
Homosexuality: Illegal.
Transgender: No data or legal situation unclear. Transgendered people have an accepted place.

PALESTINE
Homosexuality: Illegal. Imprisonable for 10 years.
Transgender: No data or legal situation unclear.

PAKISTAN
Homosexuality: Illegal. Death penalty applies under sharia law.
Immigration/Asylum: LGBT citizens have been granted asylum by other countries.
Transgender: No data or legal situation unclear.

PANAMA
Homosexuality: Legal.
Transgender: No data or legal situation unclear.

PAPUA NEW GUINEA
Homosexuality: Illegal (for men, women not mentioned in law). Imprisonable for 14+ years (Section 210 Penal Code).
Transgender: No data or legal situation unclear.

PARAGUAY
Homosexuality: Legal. Age of consent equal.
Transgender: No data or legal situation unclear.

PERU
Homosexuality: Legal.
Immigration/Asylum: LGBT citizens have been granted asylum by other countries.
Employment: Lesbians and gay men are banned from the armed forces.
Transgender: No data or legal situation unclear.

PHILIPPINES
Homosexuality: Legal. Age of consent equal. Bill criminalizing discrimination on the basis of sexual orientation and gender identity was being discussed in 2004.
Transgender: Gender reassignment ('sex change') legal or openly performed without prosecution.

POLAND
Homosexuality: Legal. Age of consent equal.
Immigration/Asylum: LGBT citizens have been granted asylum by other countries.
Employment: Lesbians and gay men are banned from the armed forces.
Transgender: Gender reassignment ('sex change') legal or openly performed without prosecution. Some personal documents may be reissued to reflect change.

PORTUGAL
Homosexuality: Legal. Age of consent higher for lesbians and gay men (16).
Employment: Lesbians and gay men are banned from the armed forces.
Transgender: Gender reassignment ('sex change') illegal.

QATAR
Homosexuality: Illegal. Imprisonable for up to 5 years.
Transgender: No data or legal situation unclear.

ROMANIA
Homosexuality: Legal.
Transgender: Gender reassignment ('sex change') legal or openly performed without prosecution. Legal situation unclear on document issue.

RUSSIAN FEDERATION
Homosexuality: Legal. Age of consent equal.
Immigration/Asylum: LGBT citizens have been granted asylum by other countries
Transgender: Gender reassignment ('sex change') legal or openly performed without prosecution. All personal documents may be reissued to reflect change. Traditionally, transgender people have an accepted place in Siberian society.

RWANDA
Homosexuality: Legal.
Transgender: No data or legal situation unclear.

ST KITTS & NEVIS
Homosexuality: Information on sexual offences unclear or unavailable.
Transgender: No data or legal situation unclear.

ST LUCIA
Homosexuality: Illegal. Imprisonable for 25 years.
Transgender: No data or legal situation unclear.

ST VINCENT & THE GRENADINES
Homosexuality: Legal situation unclear.
Transgender: No data or legal situation unclear.

SAN MARINO
Homosexuality: Legal. Age of consent equal.
Transgender: Gender reassignment illegal.

SAO TOME AND PRINCIPE
Homosexuality: Legal.
Transgender: No data or legal situation unclear.

SAUDI ARABIA
Homosexuality: Illegal. Death penalty applies under sharia law. Executions have taken place during past 10 years.
Transgender: No data or legal situation unclear.

SENEGAL
Homosexuality: Illegal.
Transgender: No data or legal situation unclear.

SERBIA & MONTENEGRO
Homosexuality: Legal. Age of consent is higher for male homosexual anal sex (18).
Transgender: No data or legal situation unclear.

SEYCHELLES
Homosexuality: Illegal (for men, women not mentioned in law).
Transgender: No data or legal situation unclear.

SIERRA LEONE
Homosexuality: Illegal (for men, women not mentioned in law).
Transgender: No data or legal situation unclear.

SINGAPORE
Homosexuality: Illegal (for men, women not mentioned in law). Imprisonable for life (section 377 Penal Code)
Immigration/Asylum: LGBT citizens have been granted asylum by other countries.
Transgender: Gender reassignment ('sex change') legal or openly performed without prosecution.

SLOVAKIA
Homosexuality: Legal.
Transgender: Gender reassignment ('sex change') legal or openly performed without prosecution. Some personal documents may be reissued to reflect change.

SLOVENIA
Homosexuality: Legal.
Employment: Laws provide protection from discrimination on the grounds of sexual orientation.
Trangender: Gender reassignment (sex change) is illegal.

SOLOMON ISLANDS
Homosexuality: Illegal. Imprisonable for up to 14 years (Section 153, Penal Code).
Transgender: No data or legal situation unclear.

SOMALIA
Homosexuality: Illegal (for men, unclear whether law applies to women). Imprisonable for up to 3 years.
Transgender: No data or legal situation unclear.

SOUTH AFRICA
Homosexuality: Legal. First country in the world to include equality and sexual orientation protection in its Constitution. Age of consent higher for lesbians and gay men (19), however.
Immigration/Asylum: Prepared to grant asylum to LGBT refugees.
Parenting: Same-sex couples have been allowed to adopt children.
Employment: Labour Relations Act of 1995 provides protection from discrimination on the grounds of sexual orientation.
Transgender: Gender reassignment ('sex change') legal or openly performed without prosecution.

SPAIN
Homosexuality: Legal. Age of consent equal. Some legal protection for sexual orientation. Recently legalized same-sex marriage.
Parenting: Lesbians and single women have right to use state donor insemination services.
Transgender: Gender reassignment ('sex change') legal or openly performed without prosecution. All personal documents may be reissued to reflect change.

SRI LANKA
Homosexuality: Illegal (for men, women not mentioned in law). Imprisonable for 10 years (Section 365A Penal Code).
Transgender: No data or legal situation unclear.

SUDAN
Homosexuality: Illegal. Death penalty applies under sharia law.
Transgender: No data or legal situation unclear.

SURINAME
Homosexuality: Legal but severe discrimination in criminal law. Age of consent higher for lesbians and gay men (18).
Transgender: No data or legal situation unclear.

SWAZILAND
Homosexuality: Illegal
Transgender: No data or legal situation unclear.

SWEDEN
Homosexuality: Legal. Age of consent equal. Some legal protection for sexual orientation. Legal recognition of same-sex partnerships.
Immigration/Asylum: Prepared to grant asylum to LGBT refugees.
Transgender: Gender reassignment ('sex change') legal or openly performed without prosecution. All personal documents may be reissued to reflect change.

SWITZERLAND
Homosexuality: Legal. Age of consent equal. Anti-discrimination on the basis of 'lifestyle' clause in the Constitution.
Transgender: Gender reassignment ('sex change') legal or openly performed without prosecution. All personal documents may be reissued to reflect change.

SYRIA
Homosexuality: Illegal. Imprisonable for up to 3 years.
Immigration/Asylum: LGBT citizens have been granted asylum by other countries.
Transgender: No data or legal situation unclear.

TAIWAN
Homosexuality: Legal. Age of consent equal.
Transgender: Gender reassignment ('sex change') legal or openly performed without prosecution.

TAJIKISTAN
Homosexuality: Illegal (for men, women not mentioned in law).
Transgender: No data or legal situation unclear.

TANZANIA
Homosexuality: Illegal (for men, women not mentioned in law). Imprisonable for 14 years (Sections 154-157 Penal Code).
Immigration/asylum: LGBT citizens have applied for asylum in other countries.
Transgender: No data or legal situation unclear.

THAILAND
Homosexuality: Legal. Age of consent equal.
Transgender: Gender reassignment ('sex change') legal or openly performed without prosecution.

TOGO
Homosexuality: Illegal. Imprisonable for up to 3 years.
Transgender: No data or legal situation unclear.

TONGA
Homosexuality: Illegal (for men, women not mentioned in law). Imprisonable for up to 10 years.
Transgender: No data or legal situation unclear.

TOKELAU
Homosexuality: Illegal (for men, women not mentioned in law). Imprisonable for 10 years (Section 170 Penal Code).
Transgender: No data or legal situation unclear.

TRINIDAD AND TOBAGO
Homosexuality: Illegal. Imprisonable for 10 years (Sections 13 and 16 Sexual Offences Act 1986).
Transgender: No data or legal situation unclear.

TUNISIA
Homosexuality: Illegal. Imprisonable for up to three years.
Immigration/Asylum: LGBT citizens have been granted asylum by other countries.
Transgender: Rights only for born hermaphrodites.

TURKEY
Homosexuality: Legal. Age of consent equal.
Immigration /Asylum: LGBT citizens have been granted asylum by other countries.
Employment: Lesbians and gay men are banned from the armed forces.
Transgender: Gender reassignment ('sex change') legal or openly performed without prosecution. All personal documents may be reissued to reflect change.

TURKMENISTAN
Homosexuality: Information on sexual offences law unclear or unavailable.
Transgender: No data or legal situation unclear.

TURKS AND CAICOS
Homosexuality: Legal.
Transgender: No data or legal situation unclear.

TUVALU
Homosexuality: Illegal (for men, women not mentioned in law). Imprisonable for 14 years (Section 153 Penal Code).
Transgender: No data or legal situation unclear.

UGANDA
Homosexuality: Illegal (for men, women not mentioned in law). Imprisonable for life (Section 140 Penal Code).**Immigration/Asylum:** LGBT citizens have been granted asylum in other countries.
Transgender: No data or legal situation unclear.

UKRAINE
Homosexuality: Legal. Age of consent equal.
Transgender: Gender reassignment ('sex change') legal or openly performed without prosecution. All personal documents may be reissued to reflect change.

UNITED ARAB EMIRATES
Homosexuality: Death sentence applies (354 Federal Penal Code).
Transgender: No data or legal situation unclear.

UNITED KINGDOM
Homosexuality: Legal. Age of consent equal.
Immigration/Asylum: Prepared to grant asylum to LGBT refugees. Immigration requires proof of 2-years cohabitation.
Parenting: Same sex couples allowed to adopt in some areas.
Employment: no legal protection against discrimination.
Transgender: Gender reassignment ('sex change') legal or openly performed without prosecution. Some personal documents may be reissued.

UNITED STATES
Homosexuality: Legal. In 2003 a US Supreme Court ruling overturned anti-sodomy laws which applied in 20 states. Progressive anti-discrimination laws and legal recognition of same-sex partnerships apply in some states and municipalities.
Immigration/Asylum: Prepared to grant asylum to LGBT refugees.
Parenting: Same-sex couples allowed to adopt in some states.
Employment: Legal protection against discrimination in some states.
Transgender: Gender reassignment ('sex change') legal or openly performed without prosecution in some states. Traditional Native American acceptance of transgender.

URUGUAY
Homosexuality: Legal.
Transgender: No data or legal situation unclear

UZBEKISTAN
Homosexuality: Illegal (for men, women not mentioned in law). Imprisonable for up to three years.
Immigration/Asylum: LGBT citizens have been granted asylum by other countries.
Transgender: No data or legal situation unclear.

VANUATU
Homosexuality: Legal.
Transgender: No data or legal situation unclear.

VATICAN/HOLY SEE
Homosexuality: Not mentioned but de facto forbidden.
Transgender: Condemned as 'repugnant'.

VENEZUELA
Homosexuality: Legal. Some legal protection for sexual orientation.
Immigration/Asylum: LGBT citizens have been granted asylum by other countries.
Parenting Employment: Lesbians and gay men not permitted to serve in the armed forces.
Transgender: No data or legal situation unclear.

VIETNAM
Homosexuality: Legal. Age of consent equal.
Transgender: No data or legal situation unclear.

WESTERN SAMOA
Homosexuality: Illegal. Imprisonable for 7 years (Sections 58b-58j Penal Code).
Transgender: No data or legal situation unclear. Some traditional acceptance of transgender people.

WESTERN SAHARA
Homosexuality: Illegal in territory occupied by Morocco.
Transgender: Legal situation unclear.

YEMEN
Homosexuality: Illegal. Death penalty applies.
Transgender: No data or legal situation unclear.

ZAMBIA
Homosexuality: Illegal (for men, women not mentioned in law). Imprisonable for 14 years (Section 155 Penal Code).
Transgender: No data or legal situation unclear.

ZIMBABWE
Homosexuality: Illegal (for men, women not mentioned in law).
Immigration/Asylum: LGBT citizens have been granted asylum by other countries.
Transgender: No data or legal situation unclear.

Note: In the countries of the European Union cases of discrimination against sexual minorities can be challenged by referring to the Human Rights Act of 2000 providing another right (to 'privacy', for example) has also been breached.

Sources: International Lesbian and Gay Association World Survey www.ilga.org; International Commission for Lesbian and Gay Human Rights www. iglhrc.org; *The Penguin Atlas of Human Sexual Behavior*, Judith Mackay, Penguin, 2000; New Internationalist, October 2000; *The No-Nonsense Guide to Sexual Diversity*, Vanessa Baird, New Internationalist/Verso, 2001.

Research by Rob Wintermute, Kings College Law School, London. Amnesty International, AI-LGBT website www.ai-lgbt.org/status_worldwide.htm
Research by Ian Sumner, Molengraft Institute, Utrecht, Netherlands, May 2003.
IGLHRC Survey of Laws Around the World, www.sodomy laws.org February 2004.

The World Guide welcomes corrections and updates to information. Please send these to: vanessab@newint.org
Updated August 2004

Global markets, global divide

A SERIES OF UNPRECEDENTED ECONOMIC, SOCIAL AND CULTURAL METAMORPHOSES TOOK PLACE DURING THE LATTER DECADES OF THE 20TH CENTURY. WALLS AND BARRIERS BETWEEN NATIONS COLLAPSED AS INFORMATION TECHNOLOGY SPEEDED UP THE PROCESS OF LIBERALIZATION. AT THE SAME TIME THE DEVELOPMENT GAP BETWEEN NORTH AND SOUTH, RICH AND POOR, CONTINUES TO GROW.

Globalization and integration are intertwined; the process is happening worldwide in countries, regions, markets, economies, traditions, cultures, etc. But there is a problem: no-one can really agree what 'globalization' actually means.

The system we see today has been slowly established through a succession of historical movements that led to the expansion of market capitalism. The scene was set in the Industrial Revolution between the 16th and 19th centuries, and it was nurtured by colonialism and imperialism. This in turn fostered and intensified a particular way of life - social, cultural, political and economic - throughout the globe; a way of life that is based on global consumer demand.

Today, this process is also accompanied by political and cultural arrangements which establish, at a global level, a new definition of the roles played by governments, states, corporations, non-governmental organizations (NGOs) and others in strategic power alignments. The ultimate goal of these is the capture of global markets which transcend national economies. This must be done by means of competition, where the only thing that matters is enhancing production quality in order to reach more markets - even though this may be detrimental to human beings.

Increased integration of market economies is achieved through a number of factors, including a growth in direct foreign investment and corporate joint ventures, and the integration of international financial markets. National and local markets are 'liberalized'; that is, opened up by governments by means of fiscal policies, budgets, exchange rates and taxes. Thanks to an increase in information flows (electronic commerce), capital markets enjoy the freedom to operate beyond the reach of national regulations. But the growth of short-term investment capital within the global flow of international capital leads to greater possibilities of economic and social instability.

For the countries of the North, liberalization is a way of accessing new riches. For Southern countries, it is a fiscal necessity in order to activate the economic cycle and ensure growth. The main instrument used to force poor countries into liberalization, privatization, deregulation and the detachment of the state from socio-economic activities has been the mechanism of tying loans to the adoption of tough fiscal policies. But if these 'structural adjustments' are not supplemented with appropriate social policies (poverty reduction, health care, education, etc), they then exclude the poor from the benefits of economic growth and contribute to their further impoverishment.

The national policies of the industrialized countries themselves are riddled with contradictions. Immigration is a case in point; many countries restrict population flow across their borders, going against the growing liberalization of the finance, goods and services markets.

Globalization and the growth of inequity

According to Martin Khor, director of the Third World Network, globalization is possible thanks to national and international political choices which enable a rapid liberalization of finance, trade and investment. Although it is true that Southern countries took part in the process of integration, the political decisions are taken by international institutions and governments from the developed world.

Khor also emphasizes in his book *Globalization and the South* that this is a very unequal process in which profits and losses are not evenly distributed. He argues that this imbalance widens the gap between the few countries and corporations that profit from globalization and the many nations and social sectors that lose out or are marginalized in some way. This includes most developing countries.

Thus globalization affects countries differently, whether they are technologically developed or not. This phenomenon can be explained as follows:

- growth and expansion in countries that lead or participate fully in the process.

- moderate or fluctuating growth in economies that try to incorporate the process of liberalization and globalization.

- marginalization and deterioration in the many countries that cannot overcome pressing problems like the low price of commodities, foreign debt, conflicts brought on by liberalization, and exclusion from export opportunities.

Consecutive United Nations Development Programmes human development reports show how the economic status of poor and rich countries drifts further apart every year. Over the past two decades, income inequality worsened in 33 out of 66 developing countries with data. Poverty has increased even in some countries which have achieved economic growth (*Human Development Report 2003*). The income received by the richest 20 per cent has increased almost everywhere since the early 1980s, while the poorest have not improved their condition at all. Middle-class income in developing countries has also collapsed. Increasing numbers of developing countries in every region are affected.

Some aspects of this growing inequality are of particular concern. First, the progressive concentration of national income in the hands of a few has not translated into more investments or faster growth. Second, those same factors that cause disparities in a globalized world are the ones that prevent investments and hamper growth worldwide.

The Secretary General of the United Nations, Kofi Annan has noted the 'negative transfer' of resources to developing countries (an accounting euphemism to describe the exodus of money from the poor countries to the developed ones) defining it as 'constant' since 1997. The causes include the fall in the prices of raw materials, the non-reinvestment of earnings, the exodus of capital, corruption and foreign debt. The political conditions tied to loan renegotiation packages were an obstacle to the recovery of several countries and led to a deterioration in social services. Technological development, particularly in the information and communications sectors, only widens the gap formed by the different capabilities of developed and underdeveloped economies. The speed of liberalization causes more harm than good, due to the lack of capacity and preparation.

The weaknesses of developing countries arise partially from their lack of strength in international negotiations. Their foreign debt and dependency on donor countries and on loans granted by multilateral agencies leads to a loss of bargaining power, not least in relation to the loan conditions themselves.

Industrialized countries are well positioned to decide the agenda of globalization; they have good domestic organization, departments well-staffed to deal with trade and foreign finance, academics who participate in, and debate, the issues, and experts who help to gather information and implement policies and strategies. Developing countries, on the other hand, lack good domestic organization or specialized staff who can keep up to speed with globalization in all its manifestations. ∎

GROSS NATIONAL INCOME AS INDICATOR OF WEALTH

Gross National Income per capita (in dollars), 2002. **Source:** *World Development Indicators 2003*, World Bank.

The gap between the richest countries and the poorest continues to widen. While income per capita continues to soar in the wealthiest nations - there are now six over $30,000 per year - the poorest countries, almost all from sub-Saharan Africa, are standing still.

Country	GNI	Year	Country	GNI	Year	Country	GNI	Year
Luxembourg	38,830	2002	St Lucia	3,840	2002	Azerbaijan	710	2002
Switzerland	37,930	2002	Lithuania	3,660	2002	Indonesia	710	2002
Norway	37,850	2002	Malaysia	3,540	2002	Congo R.	700	2002
United States	35,060	2002	Grenada	3,500	2002	Equatorial Guinea	700	2001
Japan	33,550	2002	Latvia	3,480	2002	Angola	660	2002
Denmark	30,290	2002	Dominica	3,180	2002	Georgia	650	2002
Iceland	27,970	2002	Gabon	3,120	2002	Côte d'Ivoire	610	2002
United Kingdom	25,250	2002	Botswana	2,980	2002	Bhutan	590	2002
Sweden	24,820	2002	Belize	2,960	2002	Solomon Is.	570	2002
Hong Kong SAR, China	24,750	2002	Brazil	2,850	2002	Cameroon	560	2002
Brunei	24,100	1998	Jamaica	2,820	2002	Papua New Guinea	530	2002
Netherlands	23,960	2002	St Vincent	2,820	2002	East Timor	520	2001
Ireland	23,870	2002	South Africa	2,600	2002	Yemen	490	2002
Finland	23,510	2002	Turkey	2,500	2002	India	480	2002
Austria	23,390	2002	Marshall Is.	2,350	2002	Lesotho	470	2002
Belgium	23,250	2002	Dominican Republic	2,320	2002	Senegal	470	2002
Germany	22,670	2002	Fiji	2,160	2002	Zimbabwe	470	1999
Canada	22,300	2002	Russia	2,140	2002	Moldova	460	2002
France	22,010	2002	Maldives	2,090	2002	Uzbekistan	450	2002
Singapore	20,690	2002	El Salvador	2,080	2002	Haiti	440	2002
Australia	19,740	2002	Peru	2,050	2002	Mongolia	440	2002
Italy	18,960	2002	Tunisia	2,000	2002	Vietnam	430	2002
Kuwait	18,270	2001	Micronesia	1,980	2002	Guinea	410	2002
Israel	16,710	2000	Thailand	1,980	2002	Mauritania	410	2002
French Polynesia	16,150	2000	Suriname	1,960	2002	Pakistan	410	2002
Bahamas	14,860	2000	Romania	1,850	2002	Comoros	390	2002
Spain	14,430	2002	Colombia	1,830	2002	Benin	380	2002
Macau SAR, China	14,380	2001	Bulgaria	1,790	2002	Nicaragua	370	1998
Kanaky-New Caledonia	14,050	2000	Namibia	1,780	2002	Bangladesh	360	2002
New Zealand-Aotearoa	13,710	2002	Jordan	1,760	2002	Kenya	360	2002
Cyprus	12,320	2001	Guatemala	1,750	2002	Sudan	350	2002
Greece	11,660	2002	Algeria	1,720	2002	Zambia	330	2002
Bahrain	11,130	2001	Iran	1,710	2002	Laos	310	2002
Puerto Rico	10,950	2001	Macedonia, TFYR	1,700	2002	Kyrgyzstan	290	2002
Portugal	10,840	2002	Kazakhstan	1,510	2002	Nigeria	290	2002
Korea, South	9,930	2002	Egypt	1,470	2002	São Tomé and Príncipe	290	2002
Slovenia	9,810	2002	Ecuador	1,450	2002	Cambodia	280	2002
Barbados	9,750	2001	Samoa	1,420	2002	Gambia	280	2002
Antigua	9,390	2002	Tonga	1,410	2002	Tanzania	280	2002
Malta	9,200	2001	Serbia and Montenegro	1,400	2002	Ghana	270	2002
Saudi Arabia	8,460	2001	Albania	1,380	2002	Togo	270	2002
Oman	7,720	2001	Belarus	1,360	2002	Central African Rep.	260	2002
Palau	7,140	2002	Cape Verde	1,290	2002	Uganda	250	2002
Seychelles	6,530	2001	Bosnia-Herzegovina	1,270	2002	Madagascar	240	2002
Trinidad and Tobago	6,490	2001	Turkmenistan	1,200	2002	Mali	240	2002
St Kitts-Nevis	6,370	2002	Morocco	1,190	2002	Nepal	230	2002
Mexico	5,910	2002	Swaziland	1,180	2002	Rwanda	230	2002
Czech Republic	5,560	2002	Paraguay	1,170	2002	Burkina Faso	220	2002
Hungary	5,280	2002	Syria	1,130	2002	Chad	220	2002
Croatia	4,640	2002	Vanuatu	1,080	2002	Mozambique	210	2002
Poland	4,570	2002	Philippines	1,020	2002	Tajikistan	180	2002
Uruguay	4,370	2002	China	940	2002	Niger	170	2002
Chile	4,260	2002	Palestine	930	2002	Eritrea	160	2002
Estonia	4,130	2002	Honduras	920	2002	Malawi	160	2002
Costa Rica	4,100	2002	Bolivia	900	2002	Guinea-Bissau	150	2002
Venezuela	4,090	2002	Djibouti	900	2002	Liberia	150	2002
Argentina	4,060	2002	Guyana	840	2002	Sierra Leone	140	2002
Panama	4,020	2002	Sri Lanka	840	2002	Burundi	100	2002
Lebanon	3,990	2002	Kiribati	810	2002	Ethiopia	100	2002
Slovakia	3,950	2002	Armenia	790	2002	Congo D.R.	90	2002
Mauritius	3,850	2002	Ukraine	770	2002			

Cleaning up the dirt: money laundering

AS THOSE IN POWER ATTEMPT TO CURB INTERNATIONAL MONEY LAUNDERING, SEEING IT AS A SOURCE OF TERRORIST ACTIVITY, SOUTHERN GOVERNMENTS UNDER PRESSURE FROM GLOBALIZING FORCES FEEL IT MAY BE ONE OF THE FEW WAYS OF ATTRACTING THE CAPITAL THEY DESPERATELY NEED.

Money laundering is one of the forms of corruption which has extended its influence in today's world. Many developing countries see it as an alternative means of income when faced with the inefficient financial policies imposed by the multilateral financial institutions. They feel they have to welcome this 'fly-by-night' capital in order to curb economic recession and depression.

Now those who indirectly created that necessity are demanding greater controls (but within the model of ever-increasing liberalization and privatization). The US, insisting that money laundering provides the economic basis for terrorism - apparently the only issue that really worries the US Government - is taking advantage of the situation to drum up international support and establish criteria for fighting the phenomenon.

Money laundering can be defined as a process by which earnings or profits from illegal activities, or 'dirty money', are channeled into the legal economy to turn it into 'clean money'. The launderer (any person or organization) must create a convincing explanation to justify the large amounts of capital being handled, in order to avoid detection of the real origin of the money. This erasing of the tracks left by the funds can be achieved by converting the cash into material goods, or transferring it to a safer place.

The operation is performed through financial companies (stockbrokers, banks, exchange bureaux, brokers of products) or commercial companies (casinos, insurance companies, travel agencies, car sales companies, real estate). In the US and Latin America, exchange bureaux are almost a parallel banking system.

Successful money laundering
A successful money-laundering process generally consists of three steps:

In the first, known as 'Placement', the cash is introduced into the legal economic system, normally through deposits in bank accounts. Eighty per cent of the funds which come from drug trafficking in the US enter the financial system through bank deposits, according to Mateo Bermejo from the Organization of Economic Co-operation and Development (OECD).

In the second step, 'Stratification' or 'Shadowing', the illegal origin of the cash is covered up by means of a great number of financial transactions. This way, the connection between the capital and the criminals is rendered very hard, or even impossible, to track.

The last step, 'Integration', entails providing a legal justification for such large returns.

Some of the many techniques used in money laundering are:

a) Dividing the total sum into smaller amounts, to be managed by different people or independent companies, in order to avoid drawing attention to a large sum.

b) Depositing amounts in banks where the employees tend to 'forget' or 'make mistakes' when registering the data required for a transaction.

c) Taking the cash across borders (currency contraband).

d) Pouring funds into a pre-existing business which serves as a 'front company' under which to operate.

e) Creating portfolio or nominal companies. These can be legally established companies which do not operate in the market until they are needed (a 'shell company'), or held by a state-authorized proxy or agent until the client appears ('shelf company').

These activities have several damaging effects on the economy. The US State Department's 2001 report cites the following: unfair competition, with prices below costs; loss of taxes due to the illegal entry of the money; bankruptcies in banks due to sudden capital flight, and the monopoly exercised over certain aspects of the market which end up distorting it.

Offshore Financial Centers
In the last 30 years, Offshore Financial Centers (OFCs) have come to represent the main component of financial systems in developing countries, and have made the money launderer's task easier by offering ideal services for their activities. 'Offshore' means any financial center that has out-of-country activity, taking (in the form of deposits, collective savings funds, etc) money from non-residents and lending it to other non-residents. The basic function is to make large amounts from a variety of deposits available to investors abroad, maintaining (in the case of the OFCs) strict discretion regarding information at both ends of the chain. The OFCs, located in markets with minimal or non-existent state controls and low taxes, and where employees are easily corruptible, are an invaluable instrument for laundering shady funds.

According to Suisse Capital, a company which provides a complete service in such matters, the centers exist as a consequence of the difference in taxes and rates that taxpayers are charged in different parts of the world. The explosive growth in this form of managing capital has sounded the alarm in countries which, having strict legislation and regulations in place, have seen their funds take off to warmer climes. For that reason, global institutions and

International, regional and offshore financial centers

ACCORDING TO some analysts, there are three types of Financial Centers, although their classification may not always be cut-and-dried.

a) International Financial Centers (IFC): large centers like New York, Tokyo and London, with strict financial control systems, high taxes, large domestic economies, deep, liquid markets and strict regulatory frameworks. They generally request short-term loans from non-residents and lend non-residents long-term loans.

b) Regional Financial Centers (RFC): similar to the IFCs, with well-developed financial markets and infrastructure, but located in places with relatively small internal economies, like Singapore, Hong Kong, and Luxembourg.

c) Offshore Financial Centers (OFC): the volume of the financial activity comes exclusively from out-of-country, the capital belongs to foreigners, the transactions are initiated elsewhere and the majority of the institutions are controlled by non-residents. Based in emerging countries with very small economies, they offer limited services. Their interest is focused on business with foreigners. Deposits enjoy tax incentives and are free of interest and controls. ■

international organizations, the OECD in particular, together with the most heavily affected countries, have joined forces to try to exert some kind of control over the offshore centers.

The charm of capital

While the struggle for the deregulation of small economies continues, driven by the world's large decision-making centers, the new model is starting to show some cracks.

Balanced accounts used to be, until a short while ago, the first requirement for obtaining fresh money. Nevertheless, the 'rotating door' effect (which allows the entrance of money into a country and its immediate return to the lender in the form of debt servicing) is one of the reasons why this equilibrium is impossible. Joseph Stiglitz, former Chief Economist at the World Bank (WB), says the benefits of privatization policies have been overstated and the costs underestimated. Other analysts have stated even more frankly that privatizations have spread corruption, and acted as a suction pump channeling riches from the South to the North.

In 1999, the WB admitted that the liberalization of the economy could open up new routes of corruption due, among other reasons, to the reduction of controls and regulation by local governments. The 'history of horror in East Asia' (a quote from WB president Jean Michel Severino) arising from corruption, or the weakening of democracy and coup d'etats instigated by foreign countries (like the one in Venezuela), are the result of prescriptions handed down to others but not applied by those who write them out.

It is in this context that some countries, in search of quick capital, opt for the less prestigious but easier route of becoming 'attractive financial markets'. In order to achieve this, they ease controls, lower interest rates and attempt to improve performance by privatizing or outsourcing services. This creates ideal conditions for money launderers, who rapidly respond to the call. The result, in many cases, is a total loss of control over their economies, widespread corruption, financial scandals and the flight of the country's scant wealth.

The capital, which is just 'passing through', is often abruptly withdrawn from these small markets, triggering bankruptcies, the

---

For a few million dollars more

THE OFCs may be used for legitimate reasons (like taking advantage of the benefits mentioned previously) or 'shady' ones like tax evasion and money laundering. The former can act as a cover-up for the latter. They are almost impossible to separate. Merrill Lynch International and Gemini Consulting, in their *Wealth Report*, estimate that one-third of the fortune of the wealthiest individuals in the world (around $6 trillion of a total $17.5 trillion) is managed today in offshore accounts.

Some famous names of account-holders appear in an article by Sue Hawley from The Corner House, June 2000:

- Omar Bongo, president of Gabon, transferred $100 million to branches of Citibank in New York.
- Asif Ali Zardari, husband of former Pakistani prime minister Benazir

Bhutto, deposited $40 million in accounts at the same bank.

- The three sons of Nigerian General Sani Abacha hold $110 million in accounts (several of which are in the name of shell companies).
- Raul Salinas, brother of former Mexican president Carlos Salinas, deposited between $80 and $100 million in Citibank between 1992 and 1994.

In her work, Hawley quotes US Senator Carl Levin, who stated that 'America cannot have it both ways. We cannot condemn corruption abroad, be it officials taking bribes or looting their treasuries, and then tolerate American banks making fortunes off that corruption.' ∎

---

closure of companies and failures in the chain of payments. Efforts to return to the previous financial system are usually futile. It is no longer enough to be able to promise fiscal balance and stability. Now, with this new 'record', the requirements of lenders are different. So are the necessities of those who apply for loans.

The anti-money-laundering system

The Financial Action Task Force (FATF), an independent international body whose secretariat is based at the OECD, is made up of 31 members (29 countries plus the European Commission and the Gulf Co-operation Council). It was created in 1989 with the aim of protecting the financial system, to prevent it from being used to launder profits coming from illegal activities like arms and drug trafficking, child sex exploitation, tax evasion, fraud, etc. Since President George W Bush took office in the US, another task has been added to its functions: a heavy focus on uncovering possible sources of terrorist financing.

With the addition of eight special recommendations to the 40 concerning money laundering, the FATF aims to build a shield to keep international terrorism at

bay, cutting off its main sources of financing. The second of these special recommendations states that: 'Each country should criminalize the financing of terrorism… Countries should ensure that such offences are designated as money laundering predicate offences.'

The FATF encourages all countries and jurisdictions to follow their example and specifically comply with these recommendations. To this end, agreement was reached with the United Nations, the International Monetary Fund, the World Bank, the recently created Group of Action against Terrorism and other 'donors' to give priority in financial assistance to countries in accordance with their progress in implementing and complying with these 'norms'.

Since October 2002, joint evaluations have been performed, dividing the countries into three categories:

a) Co-operative: They meet international standards of control and fiscalization (eg, Switzerland, Luxemburg, Singapore, etc).

b) Somewhat co-operative: They make an effort but have not yet met the

---

INDEX OF BRIBE-PAYERS

The Corruption Perception Index (see page 36) gives an indication of those countries whose officials may accept bribes or other inducements - but who offers these? Transparency International's Gallup Poll ranks the top exporting countries of the world according to the degree their companies were perceived to be paying bribes abroad. The countries at the bottom are those with the higher propensity to bribe overseas.

RANK	COUNTRY	SCORE	RANK	COUNTRY	SCORE	RANK	COUNTRY	SCORE
1	Australia	8.5	8	United Kingdom	6.9	15	Malaysia	4.3
2	Sweden	8.4	9	Singapore	6.3	16	Hong Kong	4.3
3	Switzerland	8.4	10	Germany	6.3	17	Italy	4.1
4	Austria	8.2	11	Spain	5.8	18	South Korea	3.9
5	Canada	8.1	12	France	5.5	19	Taiwan	3.8
6	Netherlands	7.8	13	United States	5.3	20	People's Republic of China	3.5
7	Belgium	7.8	14	Japan	5.3	21	Russia	3.2

Notes: The survey asked: 'In the business sectors with which you are familiar, please indicate whether companies from the following countries are very likely, quite likely, or unlikely to pay bribes to win or retain business in this country.' The standard error in the results was 0.2 or less.

standards (eg, Barbados, Bermuda, Monaco).

c) Non-co-operative: Fifteen countries that have failed to meet international standards, including the Cayman Islands and the Bahamas.

The countries in Category c are the focus of the new 'international financial police'. The FATF works full-time attempting to raise the countries' awareness of the dangers posed by money laundering, while tightening controls and expanding the number of countries targeted.

The US, through State Department reports like *The Consequences of Money-Laundering and Financial Crime* by John McDowell and Gary Novis, or reports from US embassies, such as those that appear on the Colombian Embassy website, continues to exert pressure to make the fight against money laundering a concern of the entire international community. ■

CORRUPTION PERCEPTION INDEX (CPI)

Based on surveys by independent institutions, commissioned by Transparency International (TI), this charts the degree of corruption (for example in receiving bribes) perceived to exist among officials and politicians. TI requires at least three sources of information for a country to be included in the CPI; however there are many countries for which this information is not yet available.

Corruption is perceived to be pervasive in Bangladesh, Nigeria, Haiti, Paraguay, Myanmar, Tajikistan, Georgia, Cameroon, Azerbaijan, Angola, Kenya, and Indonesia, countries with a score of less than 2. Countries with a score of higher than 9, with very low levels of perceived corruption, are rich countries, namely Finland, Iceland, Denmark, New Zealand, Singapore and Sweden

RANK SCORE	COUNTRY	CPI 2003	SURVEYS USED	STANDARD DEVIATION	HIGH-LOW RANGE	RANK SCORE	COUNTRY	CPI 2003	SURVEYS USED	STANDARD DEVIATION	HIGH-LOW RANGE
1	Finland	9.7	8	0.3	9.2 - 10.0		Sri Lanka	3.4	7	0.7	2.4 - 4.4
2	Iceland	9.6	7	0.3	9.2 - 10.0		Syria	3.4	4	1.3	2.0 - 5.0
3	Denmark	9.5	9	0.4	8.8 - 9.9	70	Bosnia & Herzegovina	3.3	6	0.7	2.2 - 3.9
	New Zealand	9.5	8	0.2	9.2 - 9.6		Dominican Republic	3.3	6	0.4	2.7 - 3.8
5	Singapore	9.4	12	0.1	9.2 - 9.5		Egypt	3.3	9	1.3	1.8 - 5.3
6	Sweden	9.3	11	0.2	8.8 - 9.6		Ghana	3.3	6	0.9	2.7 - 5.0
7	Netherlands	8.9	9	0.3	8.5 - 9.3		Morocco	3.3	5	1.3	2.4 - 5.5
8	Australia	8.8	12	0.9	6.7 - 9.5		Thailand	3.3	13	0.9	1.4 - 4.4
	Norway	8.8	8	0.5	8.0 - 9.3	76	Senegal	3.2	6	1.2	2.2 - 5.5
	Switzerland	8.8	9	0.8	6.9 - 9.4	77	Turkey	3.1	14	0.9	1.8 - 5.4
11	Canada	8.7	12	0.9	6.5 - 9.4	78	Armenia	3	5	0.8	2.2 - 4.1
	Luxembourg	8.7	6	0.4	8.0 - 9.2		Iran	3	4	1	1.5 - 3.6
	United Kingdom	8.7	13	0.5	7.8 - 9.2		Lebanon	3	4	0.8	2.1 - 3.6
14	Austria	8	9	0.7	7.3 - 9.3		Mali	3	3	1.8	1.4 - 5.0
	Hong Kong	8	11	1.1	5.6 - 9.3		Palestine	3	3	1.2	2.0 - 4.3
16	Germany	7.7	11	1.2	4.9 - 9.2	83	India	2.8	14	0.4	2.1 - 3.6
17	Belgium	7.6	9	0.9	6.6 - 9.2		Malawi	2.8	4	1.2	2.0 - 4.4
18	Ireland	7.5	9	0.7	6.5 - 8.8		Romania	2.8	12	1	1.6 - 5.0
	USA	7.5	13	1.2	4.9 - 9.2	86	Mozambique	2.7	5	0.7	2.0 - 3.6
20	Chile	7.4	12	0.9	5.6 - 8.8		Russia	2.7	16	0.8	1.4 - 4.9
21	Israel	7	10	1.2	4.7 - 8.1	88	Algeria	2.6	4	0.5	2.0 - 3.0
	Japan	7	13	1.1	5.5 - 8.8		Madagascar	2.6	3	1.8	1.2 - 4.7
23	France	6.9	12	1.1	4.8 - 9.0		Nicaragua	2.6	7	0.5	2.0 - 3.3
	Spain	6.9	11	0.8	5.2 - 7.8		Yemen	2.6	4	0.7	2.0 - 3.4
25	Portugal	6.6	9	1.2	4.9 - 8.1	92	Albania	2.5	5	0.6	1.9 - 3.2
26	Oman	6.3	4	0.9	5.5 - 7.3		Argentina	2.5	12	0.5	1.6 - 3.2
27	Bahrain	6.1	3	1.1	5.5 - 7.4		Ethiopia	2.5	5	0.8	1.5 - 3.6
	Cyprus	6.1	3	1.6	4.7 - 7.8		Gambia	2.5	4	0.9	1.5 - 3.6
29	Slovenia	5.9	12	1.2	4.7 - 8.8		Pakistan	2.5	7	0.9	1.5 - 3.9
30	Botswana	5.7	6	0.9	4.7 - 7.3		Philippines	2.5	12	0.5	1.6 - 3.6
	Taiwan	5.7	13	1	3.6 - 7.8		Tanzania	2.5	6	0.6	2.0 - 3.3
32	Qatar	5.6	3	0.1	5.5 - 5.7		Zambia	2.5	5	0.6	2.0 - 3.3
33	Estonia	5.5	12	0.6	4.7 - 6.6	100	Guatemala	2.4	8	0.6	1.5 - 3.4
	Uruguay	5.5	7	1.1	4.1 - 7.4		Kazakhstan	2.4	7	0.9	1.6 - 3.8
35	Italy	5.3	11	1.1	3.3 - 7.3		Moldova	2.4	5	0.8	1.6 - 3.6
	Kuwait	5.3	4	1.7	3.3 - 7.4		Uzbekistan	2.4	6	0.5	2.0 - 3.3
37	Malaysia	5.2	13	1.1	3.6 - 8.0		Venezuela	2.4	12	0.5	1.4 - 3.1
	United Arab Emirates	5.2	3	0.5	4.6 - 5.6		Vietnam	2.4	8	0.8	1.4 - 3.6
39	Tunisia	4.9	6	0.7	3.6 - 5.6	106	Bolivia	2.3	6	0.4	1.9 - 2.9
40	Hungary	4.8	13	0.6	4.0 - 5.6		Honduras	2.3	7	0.6	1.4 - 3.3
41	Lithuania	4.7	10	1.6	3.0 - 7.7		Macedonia	2.3	5	0.3	2.0 - 2.7
	Namibia	4.7	6	1.3	3.6 - 6.6		Serbia & Montenegro	2.3	5	0.5	2.0 - 3.2
43	Cuba	4.6	3	1	3.6 - 5.5		Sudan	2.3	4	0.3	2.0 - 2.7
	Jordan	4.6	7	1.1	3.6 - 6.5		Ukraine	2.3	10	0.6	1.6 - 3.8
	Trinidad and Tobago	4.6	6	1.3	3.4 - 6.9		Zimbabwe	2.3	7	0.3	2.0 - 2.7
46	Belize	4.5	3	0.9	3.6 - 5.5	113	Congo, Republic of the	2.2	3	0.5	2.0 - 2.8
	Saudi Arabia	4.5	4	2	2.8 - 7.4		Ecuador	2.2	8	0.3	1.8 - 2.6
48	Mauritius	4.4	5	0.7	3.6 - 5.5		Iraq	2.2	3	1.1	1.2 - 3.4
	South Africa	4.4	12	0.6	3.6 - 5.5		Sierra Leone	2.2	3	0.5	2.0 - 2.8
50	Costa Rica	4.3	8	0.7	3.5 - 5.5		Uganda	2.2	6	0.7	1.8 - 3.5
	Greece	4.3	9	0.8	3.7 - 5.6	118	Cote d'Ivoire	2.1	5	0.5	1.5 - 2.7
	South Korea	4.3	12	1	2.0 - 5.6		Kyrgyzstan	2.1	5	0.4	1.6 - 2.7
53	Belarus	4.2	5	1.8	2.0 - 5.8		Libya	2.1	3	0.5	1.7 - 2.7
54	Brazil	3.9	12	0.5	3.3 - 4.7		Papua New Guinea	2.1	3	0.6	1.5 - 2.7
	Bulgaria	3.9	10	0.9	2.8 - 5.7	122	Indonesia	1.9	13	0.5	0.7 - 2.9
	Czech Republic	3.9	12	0.9	2.6 - 5.6		Kenya	1.9	7	0.3	1.5 - 2.4
57	Jamaica	3.8	5	0.4	3.3 - 4.3	124	Angola	1.8	3	0.3	1.4 - 2.0
	Latvia	3.8	7	0.4	3.4 - 4.7		Azerbaijan	1.8	7	0.3	1.4 - 2.3
59	Colombia	3.7	11	0.5	2.7 - 4.4		Cameroon	1.8	5	0.2	1.4 - 2.0
	Croatia	3.7	8	0.6	2.6 - 4.7		Georgia	1.8	6	0.7	0.9 - 2.8
	El Salvador	3.7	7	1.5	2.0 - 6.3		Tajikistan	1.8	3	0.3	1.5 - 2.0
	Peru	3.7	9	0.6	2.7 - 4.9	129	Myanmar	1.6	3	0.3	1.4 - 2.0
	Slovakia	3.7	11	0.7	2.9 - 4.7		Paraguay	1.6	6	0.3	1.2 - 2.0
64	Mexico	3.6	12	0.6	2.4 - 4.9	131	Haiti	1.5	5	0.6	0.7 - 2.3
	Poland	3.6	14	1.1	2.4 - 5.6	132	Nigeria	1.4	9	0.4	0.9 - 2.0
66	China	3.4	13	1	2.0 - 5.5	133	Bangladesh	1.3	8	0.7	0.3 - 2.2
	Panama	3.4	7	0.8	2.7 - 5.0						

For good or ill: cultural globalization

GLOBALIZATION AS A CULTURAL PHENOMENON OCCURS, LIKE THE ECONOMY, AS A RESULT OF THE EXPANSION OF CAPITALISM. ALL CIVILIZATIONS AND CULTURES ARE ENTERING THE NEW WORLD OF MODERNITY AND CANNOT FAIL TO BE AFFECTED BY IT, FOR GOOD OR FOR ILL.

Globalization is not just economic but also cultural and ideological. The cultural aspects have accompanied the commercial, political and consumption processes. This has tied the social and cultural dimension of globalization to a more technical and organic vision of capital. Jointly, these aspects have put the most diverse traditions into mutual contact.

One can be certain that although the social and cultural content - as a process which goes back to the dynamics of globalization - has been present since the dawn of civilization; its omnipresence is related to capitalist relations of production.

The cultural dimension of globalization can be seen as an objective process resulting from the increasingly intensified worldwide social relations of production, connecting places far and wide, in an economically, socially, culturally, demographically, politically and historically diverse world. From another angle, there are those who define globalization as the current phase of modernity, understood as an attempt to unify the world's collective cultural imaginations. This idea proposes modernity is at the core of cultural globalization. Modernity can be understood as a progressive notion, but also as an all-encompassing vision of reality; as a phenomenon lacking values or interests of its own that takes the shape of the class and power structures in which it is cast.

At a more general level, globalization is understood by some analysts as the call to bring everything to the same economic, political and cultural level, in a global context completely under the control of transnational players which dominate and design the axis on which global society pivots.

How far is it possible?

According to Cuban psychologist Miguel Jusidman, globalization is a phenomenon which cannot be stopped. On the other hand, no matter how brilliant the arguments in favor of globalization may be, they all fail, because they assume there are common principles and values which are permanent, universal and even generally accepted.

Globalization is, essentially, a model created by Northern cultures. The cultures that are supposed to be globalized come from regions with specific traits. These cultures originally arose in specific geographical conditions, with their own mineral and water resources, climates and soils, flora and fauna. Jusidman points out

that these conditions created behaviors in the human groups which inhabited these regions, generating cultures that expressed themselves through language, religion, art, architecture, food, dress, education, folklore, work habits, etc. Inherent in globalization may be a confrontation between its own characteristics and each people's particular traits, such as power management, trade skills, quality of life, and styles of work.

The imposition of a behavior model alien to the group may lead to a loss of identity which creates mistrust and resistance to change. Jusidman also argues that lack of a full understanding as to how change affects the life of society and its individuals causes mistrust and resistance to change. People adopt change when they perceive in it real benefits for themselves and their families, he adds. Trying to impose strange behavior models, which are sometimes alien to the 'natural' culture of a society and its individuals, generally leads to their being openly rejected or simply practised without conviction, and therefore with little real effect. Jusidman says it is not likely that: 'Latin American indigenous peoples will behave like big capitalists or change their world view for a more practical and productive one in a short time'.

Culture and mass media

According to Florence Toussaint, professor at the National Autonomous University of Mexico (UNAM), the mad swirl of globalization takes everything in its path, both good and bad. People are caught in a whirlwind, not knowing when they will get out - or even if they want to. In many instances they are not aware of where they are headed, but are nonetheless compelled to continue down the path of globalization. Development and modernization are powerful currents engulfing whoever opposes them. Toussaint points out that in such a society it is inevitable that 'all that is solid vanishes into thin air'.

British writer Anthony Giddens has written extensively about globalization and modernity from a sociological perspective, dealing mostly with its cultural aspects. Giddens regards globalization as the result of an intensive process of communication between different regions linked through exchange networks around the globe.

The so-called mass media, with its accelerated eruption onto the modern stage, has undoubtedly transformed both

the notion of culture and of communication. The symbolic universe is not the same since the atmosphere was flooded by hertz waves, antennae grew on roof tops, cinemas lined the streets, and power wires and spectacular advertisements sprouted everywhere, while homes were filled with radios and television sets, video players, phones and fax machines.

Never before had communication had so many tools to develop in so many ways, among so many people, with such intensity, and in places so far away from each other. Voices have been amplified, recorded, and reproduced by the millions. The images grasped by our brain during one week of television viewing bear no relationship with those a 19th-century citizen could have seen in a lifetime.

Pop culture has been absorbed by audiovisual media which, using industrial production methods, have redefined the meaning of history, traditions, holidays and characters, and reinvented many more, using elements originally born within the social groups. This makes people identify with mass production and allows it to take root in the collective imagination.

Thus, in this gradual way, culture has a major source of creativity and transformation in the audiovisual media. To the extent that the media become increasingly omnipresent in people's everyday lives, culture soaks through and prevails and the exposure to its products grows and consolidates. This is mass culture, the industrial culture of modernity.

Social movements

These changes may or may not be beneficial for the cultures where they are being introduced, but they always cause conflict. This is because society is not indifferent in the face of these outbursts of change. A social movement has formed in reaction to the inequalities caused by globalization and the destabilization of cultural values. This movement - of farmers and environmentalists, students and workers - aims to mitigate the negative impact of globalization and to bring about social change and greater social representation. Their political platform is generally defensive and grassroots. Globalization has achieved at least one thing: for the first time the most diverse population in the world is united in the face of the same phenomenon. ∎

Technology: shaking the structures of society

SOME PEOPLE BELIEVE THAT GLOBALIZATION STEMS FROM A TECHNOLOGICAL REVOLUTION. OTHERS MAINTAIN THAT IT IS THE RESULT OF ANOTHER REVOLUTION, NOT JUST TECHNOLOGICAL BUT INSTITUTIONAL, ORGANIZATIONAL AND IDEOLOGICAL. TECHNOLOGICAL GLOBALIZATION IS ALSO KNOWN AS THE 'THIRD INDUSTRIAL REVOLUTION'.

For many people, globalization is the fruit of the technological revolution. There are others who hold that it is the result of other institutional, ideological and organizational revolutions, all based on what they have come to call the 'holy trinity' of the modern world: liberalization, deregulation and privatization. It is clear that without these three elements the technological revolution would never have happened. In the same way without the revolution in the Information and Communication Technologies (ICTs), liberalization, deregulation and privatization would not have occurred.

Technology is defined as 'the use of scientific knowledge to specify ways of doing things that can be reproduced'. The term includes all the information technologies: microelectronics, computer science, telecommunications, optoelectronics (fiber optics and laser transmissions), and genetic engineering. These technologies have undergone a massive revolution in a matter of two decades (1970-1990). All these technical advances were made possible thanks to an industrial, institutional and epistemological maturity; a new economic mentality and, above all, the presence of agents willing to learn how to use these new breakthroughs. These circumstances have enabled the creation of new materials, the discovery of new sources of energy, and an improvement in manufacturing techniques.

The process of liberalization, deregulation and privatization accelerated when the US started to use the technological revolution to increase capital earnings, whose profit margins had decreased during the 1960s. During the early 1970s, Japan and Western Europe followed this logic of technological innovation in order to improve capital profit rates. Since then, these countries have used these tools to establish a predominance of well-defined economic forces. This is why some authors, such as US political scientist Benjamin Barber, believe that globalization is the result of an affirmation of US imperialist power.

According to Peter Marcuse, urban planning professor at Columbia University, the link between technological progress and the concentration of economic power is no accident. Computerization, faster communications thanks to the progress of information technology, the ability to enforce and radiate control from a center

to the five continents, the growing speed and efficiency of transportation (both of goods and people), the benefits of flexible production, automation of routine tasks: all of these are essential to the substantial expansion of the economic power concentration we witness today.

Technological breakthroughs could translate into the same quantity of goods and services being produced with less effort, or producing more with the same effort. In any case, the theory goes, we all benefit since we either work less or have more. In fact, technology is in the hands of those in power who use it to have more power. According to Marcuse, technology should be used instead to upset the balance of power between the classes.

Many of today's discoveries are not destined to improve production conditions but to appropriate technological progress. Companies prefer technological change coming from the laboratory to that which comes from the experience and learning of workers. Technological confrontation leaves Adam Smith's 'invisible hand' principle without effect; monopoly power arises when smaller rivals are displaced. Whoever gains advantage is in a privileged position to take out their competitors and monopolize the market. The priority is not to produce more cheaply, but to keep the technology in the parent companies.

Breakthroughs in aviation, the internet and pharmaceuticals have generated consumption that previously did not exist, aimed at higher-income groups. Since companies prefer highly skilled professionals, individuals strive harder to obtain degrees and thus demand higher salaries. Progress in computer science has given place to complex processes that do not lead to better results; science has ceased to be neutral.

Significant progress in technology has brought about greater innovation and the creation of new entities, but it has also meant the destruction of businesses and diminished employment opportunities. This is reflected in an alarming increase in inequality, fuelled by knowledge that is induced by profit. As with the steam engine and electricity revolutions of the past, many have fallen victim to greater-than-life expectations. It was assumed that production rates would grow at an annual four per cent, double the historical average. The truth is that the fictions of the new industrial revolution or

technological globalization were perceived only when the bubble burst in 2000, forcing the collapse of the US economy.

Consequences

A new society is developing globally. This new society depends on the uncontrollable structures of information capitalism. It is in constant change and flux. Globalization can be envisaged as a process in which all cultural realms are influenced by, and in turn, influence, this society. Each technological innovation produces imbalances, causing a chain reaction which affects every aspect of traditional cultural systems. In other words, capitalism, in the form of national markets mixed with the birth of digitalization has caused a social and economic change which shakes the very structures of society. ■

Net stats

Number of internet users (in millions), February 2002:

World Total: 544.2

Africa: 4.15

Middle East: 4.65

Latin America: 25.33

Asia/Pacific: 157.49

Europe: 171.35

Canada and US: 181.23

Source: *Internet Users Association*

Internet language distribution (%), March 2003:

English: 40.2

Chinese 9.8

Japanese: 9.2

Spanish: 7.2

German: 6.8

Korean: 4.4

French: 3.9

Italian: 3.6

Portuguese: 2.6

Dutch: 2.1

Russian: 2.0

Other: 8.2

Source: *Global Reach*

Inequity.com: the digital divide

THE TERM 'DIGITAL DIVIDE' REFERS TO THE GROWING GAP BETWEEN THOSE WHO HAVE ACCESS TO NEW INFORMATION AND COMMUNICATION TOOLS, SUCH AS THE INTERNET, AND THOSE WHO DO NOT. THE GAP IS NOT JUST BETWEEN NORTH AND SOUTH, BUT ALSO WITHIN COUNTRIES AND COMMUNITIES. IT IS SEEN BY SOME AS ONE OF THE MOST COMPLEX CIVIL-RIGHTS CHALLENGES OF THE MILLENNIUM.

The growing global divide following the revolutionary advent of the internet is caused by a lack of equal opportunities in accessing information, knowledge and education. In July 2000, ABC News noted that one in 20 people on the planet were connected to the internet. The US is home to more than 60 per cent of web users, despite representing only five per cent of the world's population. Meanwhile, Africa has barely 14 million telephone lines, less than Manhattan or Tokyo.

The overwhelming growth of the internet during the last few years was shown in a July 2000 study made by BH Murray and A Moor from Cyveillance, a company that supplies electronic business information. At that time there were 2.1 billion websites, with a daily growth rate of 7.3 million sites. More recently, the search engine *Google* recorded the existence of more than 4.2 billion sites.

Inequity in internet access is not confined to countries with uneven economic characteristics, but is also within areas of similar economic development, like Europe and the US, and even between residents of the same country, due to differences arising from income, ethnic origin, education or age.

Unfair costs

The growth of the digital divide has caused great concern among international organizations, non-governmental organizations and also corporations, since Southern countries - with few resources to benefit economically from the new ICTs - may fall even further behind in the information revolution.

A study by the World Intellectual Property Organization (WIPO), an intergovernmental agency which administers treaties protecting human creations, published in January 2003 by *Revista del Sur* magazine (www.redtercermundo.org.uy/revista_del _sur/) concluded that the global intellectual property system could be used to reduce the digital divide between industrialized and technologically developing countries. Data cited in the study illustrated the size of the divide: the cost of accessing telecommunications infrastructures varies between countries and regions, although the usually higher prices in developing countries put them at a

disadvantage regarding the speed and growth of electronic commerce. For example, the monthly connection charge to the internet in Nepal amounts to 278 per cent of the population's average monthly income; in Sri Lanka it equals 60 per cent; in the US it hardly reaches 1.2 per cent.

The Geneva Summit

On 18 June 2003, at the conference 'The Net World Order: Bridging the Global Digital Divide', United Nations Secretary-General Kofi Annan addressed business leaders on the role of industry in bridging the divide. This paved the way for the World Summit on the Information Society (WSIS), held in Geneva in December 2003. The 'Declaration of Principles' of the WSIS, 'Building the Information Society: A Global Challenge in the New Millennium', had three parts:

1) Our common vision of the information society

2) An information society for all: key principles

3) Towards an information society for all based on shared knowledge.

After a series of considerations, which include references to articles 19 and 29 of the Universal Declaration of Human Rights (on freedom of speech and the rights of individuals towards the community), paragraph ten under the first heading states:

'We are... fully aware that the benefits of the information technology revolution are today unevenly distributed between the developed and developing countries and within societies. We are fully committed to turning this digital divide into a digital opportunity for all, particularly for those who risk being left behind and being further marginalized.' Paragraph 17 says: 'We recognize that building an inclusive Information Society requires new forms of solidarity, partnership and cooperation among governments and other stakeholders, ie the private sector, civil society and international organizations. Realizing that the ambitious goal of this Declaration - bridging the digital divide and ensuring harmonious, fair and equitable development for all - will require strong commitment by all stakeholders, we call for digital solidarity, both at national and international levels.'

The second meeting of the WSIS will take place in Tunis in December 2005.

Big fish on the net

Appealing to corporate leaders seems to be the main way of addressing the issue at present. Leaders from the Group of Eight most industrialized countries in the world (G-8) set up a Digital Opportunity Task Force (DOT Force) in 2000 to find ways of bridging the divide between technologically developed and underdeveloped countries (www.dotforce.org). One of the DOT Force's goals is to foster the development of a communications infrastructure in Southern countries, incorporating them into the economic revolution caused by the internet. The Task Force brought together governments from around the world with the leading lights in information technology, media, communications and entertainment from many different parts of the world.

But there are also many critics who hold that globalization - understood within the context of the cultural effects of communications technology - simply reinforces and expands the colonization of the Southern countries by the North, while increasing the divide between rich and poor. They also feel that, although information technology is conducive to economic prosperity, it fails to foster social equity. There are a number of interest groups which maintain that the efforts to bridge the digital divide respond to commercial and marketing interests rather than the purported equal distribution of the benefits of technology, thus conditioning internet content.

The subordination of cultural and social interests by corporate interests is evident in the March 2004 conflict between Microsoft and the European Commission (EC). According to the Commission, Microsoft has not given enough information to its competitors about its Windows operating system and has hindered the incorporation of competing audiovisual software into its system. Both Microsoft and the EC have tried unsuccessfully to reach an agreement and, according to various sources, negotiations continue. Press reports noted that the Commission's draft decision demands that Microsoft shares information with its rivals and offers computer manufacturers a more user-friendly version of Windows.

Digital opportunity vs Pokemon

According to a magazine article written by Andy Carvin (www.infotoday.com/MMSchools/Jan00/carvin.htm) the digital divide is one of the most serious civil-rights challenges of the new millennium. Carvin belongs to the Benton Foundation (a Washington DC-based organization which promotes awareness of the digital divide). He is also co-editor of the Digital Opportunity Channel (wwwdigitalopportunity.org), an internet gateway focused on the use of information technologies for sustainable development. One of the main objectives is to see that the internet's power to mobilize and distribute alternative ideas does not vanish due to a lack of resources or massive marketing by corporate campaigns. According to Carvin, the digital divide is a five-piece puzzle: access, contents, literacy, education and community.

1. *Access:* The internet has sufficient potential to bring its users new capacities and perspectives. Not having this technology means being relegated to the fringes of public life.

2. *Content:* Until the internet has content with real value for all its potential users, it will remain a place for an élite. If most of what we find on the Net is online shopping, pornography or Pokemon trade clubs, one could assume that having access or no access to the internet is not so important. Although the World Wide Web is a place with great variety, it pales in comparison when confronted with the rich cultural diversity of real-world humanity.

3. *Literacy*: The digital divide is related to illiteracy levels in underdeveloped countries, but literacy is also one of the US's 'dirty little secrets'. Carvin reminds us that a functional illiteracy exists in his country. Millions of youth and adults - 44 million, one out of four in 1993 - have serious difficulties in filling out forms, following written instructions or even reading a newspaper. Another important parameter to consider when it comes to internet use is computer literacy and its significance.

4. *Education*: Internet school access lacks meaning if teachers are not trained to benefit from the technology. Carvin argues that teachers who use interaction as a teaching tool are more inclined to use the internet. However, obsolete teaching practices are not interested in interaction in the classrooms, excluding the Net from schools.

5. *Community:* The digital divide is related to whether or not we foster internet use in the community. Public spaces/forums are needed in the internet in order for people to get together without being overwhelmed by advertisers. If individuals are not able to build meaningful ties online, it is difficult for them to be attracted to the Net. ∎

COMMUNICATIONS IN FIGURES

A = Main telephone lines per 1,000 people, 2001. **Source:** *World Development Indicators 2003*, World Bank.

B = Personal computers per 1,000 people, 2001. **Source:** *World Development Indicators 2003*, World Bank.

The poorest countries in Africa are starting to take advantage of mobile/cell phones rather than installing expensive landlines. In this table in the last World Guide only the US had more than 500 computers per 1,000 people; now there are 8 countries in this position.

	A	B		A	B		A	B		A	B
Afghanistan	1.5		Dominica	290.6	75.0	Lebanon	194.9	56.2	Samoa, American	211.3	
Albania	49.7	7.6	Dominican Republic	110.2		Lesotho	10.3		São Tomé and Príncipe	36.3	
Algeria	61.0	7.1	Ecuador	103.7	23.3	Liberia	2.2		Saudi Arabia	144.8	62.7
Andorra	438.3		Egypt	103.6	15.5	Libya	109.3		Senegal	24.5	18.6
Angola	5.9	1.3	El Salvador	93.4	21.9	Liechtenstein	608.2		Serbia and Montenegro	228.8	23.4
Antigua	481.3		Equatorial Guinea	14.7	5.3	Lithuania	312.9	70.6	Seychelles	261.1	146.5
Argentina	223.8	91.1	Eritrea	8.2	1.8	Luxembourg	779.9	517.3	Sierra Leone	4.7	
Armenia	140.3	7.9	Estonia	352.1	174.8	Macedonia, TFYR	263.5		Singapore	471.4	508.3
Aruba	350.3		Ethiopia	4.3	1.1	Madagascar	3.6	2.4	Slovakia	288.0	148.1
Australia	518.9	515.8	Faeroe Is.	554.5	67.1	Malawi	5.2	1.3	Slovenia	400.9	275.7
Austria	468.1	335.4	Fiji	112.3	60.9	Malaysia	195.8	126.1	Solomon Is.	17.1	50.9
Azerbaijan	111.3		Finland	547.6	423.5	Maldives	99.4	21.9	Somalia	3.5	
Bahamas	400.3		France	573.5	337.0	Mali	4.3	1.2	South Africa	112.5	68.5
Bahrain	246.6	141.8	French Polynesia	222.6	280.0	Malta	530.0	229.6	Spain	431.1	168.2
Bangladesh	4.3	1.9	Gabon	29.5	11.9	Marshall Is.	59.8	50.0	Sri Lanka	44.3	9.3
Barbados	476.3	92.3	Gambia	26.2	12.7	Mauritania	7.2	10.3	St Kitts-Nevis	568.8	174.5
Belarus	278.8		Georgia	158.6		Mauritius	257.4	109.1	St Lucia	313.5	146.8
Belgium	497.9	232.8	Germany	634.2	382.2	Mayotte Is.	69.8		St Vincent	219.6	116.1
Belize	144.4	135.2	Ghana	11.6	3.3	Mexico	137.2	68.7	Sudan	14.2	3.6
Benin	9.2	1.7	Greece	529.2	81.2	Micronesia	84.0		Suriname	175.8	45.5
Bermuda	869.2	495.4	Greenland	467.4	107.4	Moldova	154.0	15.9	Swaziland	31.4	
Bhutan	25.4	5.8	Grenada	327.5	130.0	Mongolia	51.8	14.6	Sweden	739.1	561.2
Bolivia	62.2	20.5	Guam	508.9		Morocco	40.8	13.7	Switzerland	745.6	540.2
Bosnia-Herzegovina	110.7		Guatemala	64.7	12.8	Mozambique	4.4	3.5	Syria	103.0	16.3
Botswana	91.5	38.7	Guinea	3.2	4.0	Myanmar-Burma	6.1	1.1	Tajikistan	35.9	
Brazil	217.8	62.9	Guinea-Bissau	9.8		Namibia	65.7	36.4	Tanzania	4.1	3.3
Brunei	264.0	74.6	Guyana	91.9	26.4	Nepal	13.1	3.5	Thailand	98.7	27.8
Bulgaria	359.4	44.3	Haiti	9.7		Netherlands	621.1	428.4	Togo	10.3	21.5
Burkina Faso	4.9	1.5	Honduras	47.1	12.2	Netherlands Antilles	372.3		Tonga	109.2	
Burundi	2.9		Hungary	374.0	100.3	New Zealand-Aotearoa	477.1	392.6	Trinidad and Tobago	239.9	69.2
Cambodia	2.5	1.5	Iceland	663.9	418.1	Nicaragua	31.2	9.6	Tunisia	108.9	23.7
Cameroon	6.7	3.9	India	37.5	5.8	Niger	1.9	0.5	Turkey	285.2	40.7
Canada	675.8	459.9	Indonesia	34.5	11.0	Nigeria	4.6	6.8	Turkmenistan	80.2	
Cape Verde	142.7	68.6	Iran	168.7	69.7	Northern Marianas	395.9		Uganda	2.8	3.1
Cayman Is.	821.2		Iraq	28.6		Norway	720.4	508.0	Ukraine	212.1	18.3
Central African Rep.	2.4	1.9	Ireland	484.5	390.7	Oman	89.7	32.4	United Arab Emirates	339.7	135.5
Chad	1.4	1.6	Israel	476.3	245.9	Pakistan	23.3	4.1	United Kingdom	588.0	366.2
Chile	232.5	106.5	Italy	471.5	194.8	Palestine	77.6		United States	667.1	625.0
China	137.4	19.0	Jamaica	197.3	50.0	Panama	148.3	37.9	Uruguay	282.9	110.1
Colombia	170.5	42.1	Japan	597.1	348.8	Papua New Guinea	11.7	56.7	Uzbekistan	65.8	
Comoros	12.2	5.5	Jordan	127.4	32.8	Paraguay	51.2	14.2	Vanuatu	33.6	
Congo D.R.	0.4		Kanaky-New Caledonia	231.2		Peru	77.5	47.9	Venezuela	109.3	52.8
Congo R.	7.1	3.9	Kazakhstan	113.1		Philippines	42.4	21.7	Vietnam	37.6	11.7
Costa Rica	229.7	170.2	Kenya	10.4	5.6	Poland	295.1	85.4	Virgin Is. (Am.)	563.7	
Côte d'Ivoire	18.0	7.2	Kiribati	42.1	23.2	Portugal	426.8	117.4	Yemen	22.1	1.9
Croatia	365.2	85.9	Korea, North	22.5		Puerto Rico	336.4		Zambia	8.0	7.0
Cuba	51.0	19.0	Korea, South	485.7	256.5	Qatar	274.5	163.9	Zimbabwe	18.6	12.1
Cyprus	630.9	246.6	Kuwait	239.7	131.9	Romania	183.8	35.7			
Czech Republic	375.1	145.7	Kyrgyzstan	77.9		Russia	243.3	49.7			
Denmark	719.2	540.3	Laos	9.8	3.0	Rwanda	2.7				
Djibouti	15.4	10.9	Latvia	308.3	153.1	Samoa	64.1	6.7			

Too hot to handle: climate change

THE PLANET IS GETTING HOTTER. THE DECADE OF 1994-2004 WAS THE WARMEST SINCE RECORDS BEGAN AND SCIENTISTS BELIEVE THAT FUTURE YEARS WILL BE EVEN WARMER. MOST EXPERTS AGREE THAT HUMANS IMPACT DIRECTLY ON THIS HEATING PROCESS, GENERALLY KNOWN AS THE 'GREENHOUSE EFFECT'. ACCORDING TO A LARGE MAJORITY OF THE INTERNATIONAL SCIENTIFIC COMMUNITY, RISING TEMPERATURES WILL LEAD TO GREAT CHANGES IN GLOBAL ECOSYSTEMS.

Weather is the result of the global circulation of the air mass that surrounds the earth. This is affected by solar radiation and its exchange with oceans and land, thus maintaining a dynamic and very complex balance. Global climate has evolved along with the earth, undergoing more or less cyclical variations.

Global climatic changes have been great and diverse during the earth's approximate 4.6-billion-year history. The global climate has undergone more or less cyclical variations. Some epochs have seen a warm climate, some cold, and, in many instances, there was an abrupt change from one to the other. The current scientific community strongly agrees that global climate will be significantly altered during this century, as a result of the growing concentration of greenhouse emissions such as carbon dioxide, methane, nitrous oxides and chlorofluorocarbons.

It seems logical then that a larger concentration of greenhouse gases will result in a greater increase in global temperatures. Scientists have been saying since the late 1970s that a growing concentration of greenhouse gases in the atmosphere would result in a 1.5-4.5°C increase of the earth's surface temperature. More recent studies suggest that warming will occur faster on solid ground than in the sea.

It is difficult to forecast how this situation will affect us since global climate is a very complex system. If a key aspect is altered, such as average global temperature, ramifications from this change will have far-reaching consequences. Wind and rain patterns prevalent during hundreds or even thousands of years (and on which the lives of millions of people depend) could change; sea levels could rise and threaten islands and low-lying coastal regions. This might result in massive migrations, famines and natural catastrophes unprecedented in their severity.

Climate and development
Climate change is no longer an environmental problem but is now also a development issue, since it threatens to increase poverty, hunger and disease and affects national, regional and international security. It is well known that industrialized countries are the main culprits when it comes to greenhouse emissions, while developing countries are the least protected.

For example, there are 1.3 billion people worldwide without access to clean water, two billion without sanitation and as many without electricity, and 800 million are malnourished. Climate change could compound these problems, since it would diminish the quality and quantity of water, worsen droughts, floods and insect-transmitted diseases, reduce agricultural yields and increase human displacement.

Social problems derived from an increase in global temperature will also lead to more conflicts, since poor countries have fewer means of adapting to climate change. Developed countries can modify their infrastructures in order to resist, but the poorest countries cannot undertake these changes, nor buy solutions.

The greenhouse effect
The energy the earth receives from the sun has to be balanced by the radiation emitted from the earth's surface. This is known as the 'earth's effective radiating temperature'. For example, without an atmosphere, surface temperature would be approximately -18°C. In fact, the earth's surface temperature is approximately 15°C.

The reason behind this difference in temperature is that the atmosphere is almost transparent to short-wave radiation, but it absorbs most of the long-wave radiation issued by the earth's surface. Several atmospheric elements such as water vapor and carbon dioxide have vibrating molecular frequencies within the spectral range of the earth's radiation. These greenhouse gases absorb and re-emit long-wave radiations, bringing them back to the earth's surface, thus causing an increase in temperature which is called the 'greenhouse effect'.

The glass in a greenhouse is similar to the atmosphere: transparent to sunlight and opaque to earth radiation, but trapping the air inside and preventing hot air from escaping. But the greenhouse effect is different; the inside of a greenhouse keeps warm since the glass does not allow the heat to escape through convection to the surrounding air: it gets hotter and hotter. That is why the atmospheric phenomenon is based on a different process to that of a greenhouse, but the term has become so popular that there is no chance of establishing a more precise one.

One of the many threats to life-sustaining systems comes directly from an increase in the use of resources. Carbon dioxide is released with the burning of fossil fuels and the clearing and burning of forests. The accumulation of this gas, along with others, traps solar radiation close to the earth's surface, causing global warming. One of the results of the greenhouse effect is maintaining a concentration of water vapor in the lower troposphere (the innermost part of the atmosphere, approximately ten kilometers in height, composed of air), much higher than would be possible in the low temperatures that would prevail if the phenomenon did not exist.

The Kyoto Protocol
The Kyoto Protocol, which was agreed in Japan in 1997, is the only international instrument which includes obligations for industrialized countries: a 5.2 per cent reduction in greenhouse emissions by industrialized countries during 2008-2012, based on 1990 figures. To be enforced, the treaty needs to be ratified by 55 industrialized member nations, amounting to at least 55 per cent of global greenhouse emissions. In late 2003 the ratifying countries were responsible for 44.3 per cent of these emissions.

If the US were to take part in this agreement - having withdrawn from it in 2001 after a decision by President George W Bush - that proportion would rise to 80 per cent. If Russia ratifies it, as recommended by the Putin Cabinet in September 2004, the proportion of committed emissions would rise to 61 per cent. If both countries took part, the proportion would rise to 97 per cent. However, due to its modest goals, the implementation of the Kyoto Protocol is in fact only a small step. Rather than 5.2 per cent, a 60 to 80 per cent reduction in greenhouse emissions would be needed to stabilize carbon dioxide concentration in the atmosphere to normal levels (between 0.03 and 0.04).

It seems ironic that while the US leads a war to defend the world from terrorism, at the same time it punishes that same world with carbon dioxide emissions, causing 36 per cent of the damage related to global warming. This can only be classified as terrorist attack on a global scale.

Also, among industrialized countries, the Netherlands, Finland, France, Greece, Spain, Austria, Denmark, Belgium and Ireland are well below the level of controls they should apply in order to reduce greenhouse emissions. This is due mainly to the indiscriminate use of transportation by land and their huge industries. Only the UK and Sweden will meet the objectives of the accord within the established targeted timeframes.

Contradictory opinions

Although there is a strong scientific consensus about the causes and consequences of climate change, a group of scientists from the US believes that such theories are only hypotheses that have not been proven. These researchers suggest that emissions which 'produce' the greenhouse effect may not be the main cause of global warming.

Among the most salient criticisms these researchers make are that predictions on climate change are based on models and presumptions that are: 'not only unknown but impossible to ascertain within the relevant limits for the implementation of rules'; the models used do not adequately describe clouds, water vapors, aerosols, ocean currents and solar effects.

At the same time, these scientists also state that temperature simulations made by the UN Panel on Global Climate Change look more like an arbitrary model of curves than a genuine demonstration of humanity's influence on the global climate.

Facts and predictions

Nevertheless, some of the effects of climate change are already being felt. The Arctic polar cap has lost 42 per cent of its thickness and 27 per cent of coral reefs in the world have disappeared.

According to forecasts by some experts, there would be greater snow- and rain-falls in the higher latitudes during winter due to the possible interruption or decrease of the Gulf Stream which is responsible for maintaining high median temperatures in the north of Europe.

The countries of the South would experience an intensification of droughts and an expansion in areas today affected by desertification such as the Sahel, North Africa, Southeast Asia, India, Central America and the Mediterranean Basin. This includes Spain, where it is predicted the problem will achieve significant proportions.

Furthermore, if there is increased precipitation, it will not be in the form of more rainy days, but rather a decrease in the number of days and an increase in the intensity of rain. This will cause floods, mudslides and increased soil erosion. There will also be more natural catastrophes such as hurricanes, cyclones and tornadoes, extending to areas which were previously unaffected. Median sea level will rise due to the thermal expansion of water and the melting of mountain glaciers. The increase is calculated to be between 10 and 30 centimeters by 2030 and up to a meter by 2050. This rise would mean the contamination of water reservoirs with marine waters, receding coastlines and wetlands on a scale which is thought could do away with 15 per cent of Egypt's and 14 per cent of Bangladesh's fertile lands.

At the same time, forests will recede to the interior of continents, leaving behind deteriorated ecosystems. The lack of water and food in some places will cause serious problems which in turn could result in an increase in the number of wars. Diseases endemic to tropical areas such as malaria, dengue or Nile fever will spread according to the variations in climate. ■

Climatic Armageddon

ALTHOUGH these warnings on the phenomenon of global climate change have been around for more than four decades, they had never been accepted by institutions such as the Pentagon and the World Bank. But in 2003, both institutions warned of the terrible geopolitical consequences climate change could have on humanity.

A secret report by the Pentagon published by UK's *The Observer* in late 2003 warns that major European cities would be submerged by rising seas, while by 2020 Great Britain's climate would be similar to that of Siberia. Major famines, generalized uprisings and nuclear conflicts over the control of resources could take place worldwide.

The document warns that abrupt climate change caused by polluting industrial gas emissions could take the planet to the brink of anarchy while countries develop their nuclear capacity to defend and secure the provision of food, water and energy. According to the Pentagon report, the threat to global stability is greater than that of terrorism. The Pentagon goes on to say that 'disturbances and conflicts will be endemic features of life'.

The report adds that, as soon as 2007, climate change will generate violent coastal storms, causing some areas in the Netherlands, for instance, to become uninhabitable. On the other hand, the report flatly dismisses the idea that the planet's resources could sustain all of humanity as long as there was a fair distribution of wealth. In other words, the relationship of sustainability between the planet and human beings will become seriously unbalanced.

Another report, this time by the World Bank, admits that the planet is in grave danger and that the main challenge for the future is not terrorism but rather human dependency on fossil fuels. Ninety-four per cent of World Bank energy investments are in fossil fuels and six per cent in renewable sources of energy. The report suggests that investments in renewable energy should increase by a minimum of 20 per cent. If current levels of fossil fuel consumption continue, global warming and polar ice cap meltdown could multiply the rise in sea levels by four in ten years in relation to 2003 levels.

The report recommends immediate action in order to counteract the effects of global warming. ■

Water in King Midas' hands

THERE IS THEORETICAL AGREEMENT AMONG THE COUNTRIES OF THE UNITED NATIONS THAT WATER SHOULD BE CONSIDERED A SOCIAL, RATHER THAN AN ECONOMIC, BENEFIT. BUT WATER IS WORTH ITS WEIGHT IN GOLD, AND IS NOW BECOMING JUST ANOTHER COMMODITY. MANY OF THESE SAME COUNTRIES ARE PROMOTING WATER PRIVATIZATION, WHICH LEADS TO A RISE IN WATER PRICES FOR THOSE WHO CAN LEAST AFFORD IT.

Without water, people cannot live with dignity. Lack of water also violates other human rights. It should be treated as a social and cultural benefit, and not exclusively an economic one, says the Committee on Economic, Social and Cultural Rights (CESCR).

One of the goals set forth at the Millennium Summit by the member countries of the UN was to halve the number of people with no access to drinking water by 2015. This was put on a par with the reduction of maternal and under-five mortality. So how has it come about that water has become such a problem, not only in regions where access is naturally difficult, but also in those where historically there have not been any water shortages? One of the problems is that water is increasingly being viewed as a privatizable commodity as countries liberalize under trade agreements such as GATS.

Water and the Washington Consensus

The World Bank uses the model of the 'Washington Consensus' to promote the interests of a handful of transnational water providers, pressuring countries to privatize their resources through conditions attached to their economic 'aid' packages. The 'Washington Consensus' is a political/economic/intellectual complex created in 1990 against the new global backdrop caused by the fall of socialism. It is composed of international agencies (IMF, World Bank), the US Congress, the US Federal Reserve, high-ranking government officials and think-tanks. Hailed as the economic paradigm of the post-socialist era and the sole model for emerging countries, it recommends a range of measures beneficial to corporations from Northern countries, such as opening up to direct foreign investment, privatizing and deregulating.

According to an article by Maude Barlow and Tony Clarke (*Economic Justice News*, Vol 7, January 2004), there are currently ten large corporations which provide water services for a profit. The three largest - the French Suez and Vivendi (now Veolia Environment), and the German RWE-AG - supply water to almost 300 million customers in over 100 countries, and compete with others like Bouygues SAUR, Thames Water (owned by RWE) and Bechtel-United Utilities for world market

coverage. Ten years ago they served 51 million people in 12 countries. At the present rate, in the next ten years they will come to control more than 70 per cent of European and North American water systems. The same article states that the growth in company earnings was just as explosive. Vivendi went from $5 billion in the early 1990s to $12 billion in 2002. RWE grew 9,786 per cent in ten years. These growth rates surpass those of many host countries.

According to the authors, the World Bank lent around $20 billion for water service-related projects, thus becoming the main financing institution for such privatizations. The World Bank has just announced an increase in funds for these loans from $1.3 billion in 2003 to $4 billion for 2004.

Water into gold

Water is one of the essential social services, directly and indirectly satisfying human needs. Paradoxically, this also makes it viable as an economic commodity, being both 'scarce' and 'transferable'. The worldwide market value of water (according to the World Bank) is $800 billion, comparable to petroleum. This is where the Midas effect comes in. Whatever King Midas touched turned to gold.

In many cases governments have reached agreements with water companies, conceding real monopolies. These transnational companies are responsible to their shareholders, not to the citizens of the countries where they work. Cases of corruption, bribes or excessive costs for

services have been reported in many places (in, for example, South Africa and France).

Privatization seems to lead to a rise in water prices, as indebted governments are pushed by international organizations to raise the rates to attract private investment. The benefits are guaranteed by parcelling out the service. The more profitable areas are sold, and the rest are kept in the public sphere, which continues to have scarce resources. This contributes to growing social polarization.

To increase returns, companies often do not comply with promises made at the time they invested, instead minimizing maintenance and quality. The host countries have few tools of control. In Cochabamba, Bolivia, there was an increase in water rates of 200 per cent before any of the promised investment in infrastructure appeared, and this led to popular uprisings and violent confrontations. Negotiations broke down (*Social Watch 2003*). The case showed just how incompatible private and public interests can be. The over-exploitation of the water reserves in northern Chile, which led to desertification of vast areas, is another example of this.

GATS and the water in the Green Room

The General Agreement on Trade in Services (GATS) is also likely to have an effect on the availability of water to the poor. The GATS is an international trade agreement that came into effect in 1995

One Californian equals 27 Sudanese

US EX-PRESIDENT Bill Clinton said that a quarter of the world's population has never held a glass of drinking water in their hands (*Los Angeles Times* 2002). This implies that there is not enough water for everyone. The numbers would seem to back this up: 97 per cent of the water on earth is in the oceans and salty seas. Only the other three per cent is suitable for human consumption. And even this precious three per cent is not easily accessible or usable. Seventy-nine per cent is polar ice and glaciers and 20 per cent is made up of water reserves and underground currents. Only 0.03 per cent

of the total (one per cent of the three per cent) is on the surface to be used. The desalinating of the other 97 per cent would be slow and extremely costly.

However, even this percentage would be more than enough to sustain life for everyone on the planet. But water is wasted, and it is not evenly distributed. In California, for example, the average amount of water used by one person is 191,000 liters per year, while in Sudan it is 7,000 liters (OECD1989). In terms of water consumption, one Californian is equal to 27 Sudanese. ∎

and operates under the umbrella of the World Trade Organization (WTO). The aim of the GATS is gradually to remove all barriers to trade in services and to open them up to international competition between transnational firms. In 1999, the European Commission said: 'The GATS is... first and foremost an instrument for the benefit of business.'

The GATS negotiations are not in the public arena. They are managed through confidential requests which do not allow for debate. It is hard not to also assume that the so-called 'Green Room effect' (which in the language of the WTO describes the form of some of the most important decisions taken by the organization), is the norm. The four or five most influential countries meet in the (green) office of the Director General, agree among themselves, and then exert pressure on the rest of the representatives (they call it 'search for consensus') until final approval is achieved.

Since February 2000, negotiations have been under way in the WTO to expand and 'fine-tune' the GATS. These negotiations have aroused worldwide concern. One of the criticisms is that the GATS will have a negative impact on universal access to basic services such as healthcare, education, transport - and water (www.gatswatch.org).

Although the trading of drinking water is not included in the GATS, the European Union (EU) proposes to liberalize it. Companies would compete in gaining access to water, which they could then sell later, maximizing their gains. But uncontrolled and massive extraction could cause water reserves to run dry, or underground contamination. This might result in extensive and irreversible environmental imbalances which in turn may cause 'ecological stress'; a vicious cycle of water scarcity, a reduction in resources and human under-nourishment.

Much depends on whether and how governments conform to the GATS. Either the plunder of the globe continues to pare poor consumers to the bone, or an appeal for a less fragmented and more integrated world prospers, as those same governments proposed in the Millennium Development Goals. For the latter to be possible, representatives of the international organizations must avoid manifesting a sort of schizophrenia when addressing economic and social topics, where voting seems to depend on the tapestry of the chair they are sitting in.

The nations of the South will no longer be content with listening to the good news of how they should be thankful for the arrival of investment capital (presented as the only way out of their crisis) and how they should forget their inefficient public services (which will be replaced by efficient private management). Water is too precious to be privatized. The peoples of the South know that you cannot drink gold. ∎

Gene dreams, gene schemes

GENETIC ENGINEERING IN FOODSTUFFS IS THE OBJECT OF DEEP CONTROVERSY. SEVERAL ORGANIZATIONS (FROM NON-GOVERNMENTAL ORGANIZATIONS TO BIOTECHNOLOGICAL COMPANIES) ESPOUSE CONFLICTING VIEWPOINTS. ALL SHIELD THEIR INTERESTS BEHIND A PRESUMED SCIENTIFIC CLAIM TO OBJECTIVITY.

Companies using genetic engineering (GE) in food production to promote the consumption of their products face resistance from organized consumer groups and other civil-society institutions. This confrontation has generated a battery of arguments on either side. Those who press for genetic manipulation say:

- Thanks to new genetic engineering technology it is possible to develop large quantities of more nutritious foods. Therefore, genetic modification should be put in practice for humanitarian reasons.

- GE is a natural extension of the traditional process which leads to more valuable and productive harvests and cattle.

- While natural rearing is an imperfect and uncontrolled combination of thousands of genes, GE is precise, since it allows for the selection of specific genes and the use of other techniques to incorporate them into the desired organism.

- All genetically modified foods have been scientifically tested before reaching the markets. These foods have been sold in the US for several

years and there is no evidence proving that they are detrimental to health.

- Certain types of transgenic potatoes and corn produce their own Bt, a pesticide that protects crops against insects, thus lowering costs and increasing yields without adverse impacts to health.

- Increasing harvest productivity through GE reduces the demand for land and the use of herbicides and pesticides, therefore reducing environmental harm.

- GE produces specific and identifiable changes in the live organism genome which can be patented, thus accelerating the development of newer and better food sources.

- Since transgenic foods that are introduced into the market have no significant differences in flavor or nutritional value from other foods, there is no need to label them as such.

On the other hand, those that question the use of biotechnology in food production maintain that:

- Each new scientific technology has side effects. Long-term tests are needed on

the effects of GE on health and the environment.

- GE techniques are contrary to natural reproductive barriers and combine genes from different species in a way that would never occur naturally, altering genetic models that have taken a long time to develop and increasing the probability of uncontrollable and unpredictable events.

- The unpredictable interruptions in normal DNA functioning caused by GE could produce unwanted and unknown side effects, including toxins and allergens. Only human testing can evaluate these possibilities.

- Even if it were carried out to acceptable standards, the merely scientific evaluation of GE does not take into account that, for many people, food has cultural, ethical and religious dimensions that should also be considered.

- Throughout the years, farmers have created a variety of global harvests with natural growing techniques. The control by a few companies of seeds used around the world threatens the autonomy of many countries.

- Transgenic food should be labeled as such. Most people in countries where surveys were carried out want transgenic foods labeled in order to be better informed at the time of choosing.
- Genetically modified foods containing pesticides should be considered and labeled as such.

Bioethics

The appropriation of scientific knowledge is one way in which power can be concentrated. One of the tools through which this is carried out is legislation which protects intellectual property. More than 90 per cent of patents are issued in the dominant economic blocs - the US, Europe and Japan. But companies can do research with lower costs and lower standards in the poorer regions than in their countries of origin.

The companies which hold the intellectual property rights can exert complete control over their 'products'. For example, the Technology Protection System (TPS), known as 'Terminator' technology, incorporates a feature that kills developing plant embryos in such a way that they may not be stored and replanted in subsequent years. 'Traitor', officially known as Trait Specific Genetic Use Restriction Technology (or T-Gurt), is a control mechanism which requires annual applications of a patented chemical substance in order to activate the desired characteristics in the crop. The farmer can store and replant the seeds, but may not reap the benefits of the controlled traits unless he or she pays each year for the activating chemical substance.

Those who promote the use of TPS maintain that transgenic crops will not pass their genes onto neighboring plants. TPS genes are transferred through pollen and, therefore, any plant pollinated by a TPS will produce dead seeds. This will avoid the accidental transfer of genes from transgenic crops to the wild flora. Although this may be considered beneficial, preventing the transfer of transgenic traits to populations of wild plants could have a negative impact on their ability to maintain themselves. Depending on the crop's likelihood to crossbreed with wild plants, some species of rare or endangered plants could be threatened by TPS crops.

On the other hand, farmers that depended on their ability to sow seeds year after year will have to buy new seeds every year. Many organizations, including the Union of Concerned Scientists (UCS), are worried about the implications of this technology, particularly in the developing world, where seed storage is a regular practice. According to an article published by the UCS (www.ucsusa.org), 'poor farmers are particularly alarmed with the possibility that seed markets fall under control of multinational corporations selling sterile seeds.. they [the poor farmers] fear that seed costs increase and that they will lose control over their own food supply'. Hope Shand, of ETC group (Action Group on Erosion, Technology and Concentration), stated that 'the final goal of seed sterilization is neither biosecurity nor agricultural benefit but rather biological slavery' (www.etcgroup.org).

Hunger as an excuse

These issues involve diverse economic and political interests. One of the sectors affected is the US food industry, which faces what an *International Herald Tribune* report (29 May 2003) defined as 'the biotechnological war reformulated as a matter of hunger'. Here are some episodes in that war:

- Washington threatens to initiate legal actions through the World Trade Organization (WTO) against the European Union (EU) on the issue of genetically modified foods.

- Robert Zoellick, US Trade Representative, travels to Brazil to lobby against that country's policies, which ban genetically modified crops.

- During the Earth Summit (Johannesburg, September 2002), Secretary of State Colin Powell tries to pressure South African countries to accept transgenic foods. Zambia refuses to yield to US pressure.

- The US embassy pressures India's Ministry of the Environment to approve the imports of transgenic wheat, facing a grassroots mobilization that manages to turn back two ships carrying 10,000 tons of such wheat. The president of the Genetic Engineering Approval Committee which rejected the cultivation and importation of genetically modified foods is later dismissed, along with the Minister of Agriculture.

According to the *Herald Tribune* report, hunger is an excuse to promote and impose genetic engineering. Transgenic foods have more to do with the ambition of corporations than with the hunger of the poor. Genetic engineering technology does not seek to eradicate food scarcity, but to create a food and seed monopoly. Even US food aid has been questioned by some critics - is it being used to get rid of the transgenic food surpluses and thus avoid the collapse of the biotechnological industry?

The adventures of bio-imperialism

Monsanto is one of the largest biotechnology corporations in the world, owning most of the transgenic seed patents. The US has pressured India to change its patent laws under the TRIPs (Trade-Related Aspects of Intellectual Property Rights) Agreement. The main beneficiaries of India's second amendment of its Patents Act are corporations such as Monsanto that seek to patent genetically modified crops.

Monsanto also pressured the Government of Brazil to temporarily lift the ban on transgenics.

Genetic engineering is not only causing the genetic pollution of our biodiversity and creating bio-imperialism, it is also generating contaminated knowledge and undermining scientific independence by creating monopolies on knowledge and information.

Monsanto's promises about the benefits of Bt cotton in India are one example of

Food aid or agricultural subsidies?

SOME non-governmental organizations see US food donations as a hidden subsidy by the US Government and the Department of Agriculture in order to protect its important biotechnology industry (which ranges from seeds, agrochemicals and machinery manufacturers to marketing companies) from restrictions and embargoes imposed upon transgenic food in other parts of the world.

Apart from allowing the production of transgenic crops, humanitarian aid is allocating highly lucrative contracts to US companies which trade in grains, such as Archer Daniels Midland (ADM) and Cargill. In 2001 alone, these two companies were awarded a third of all food-aid contracts given by the World Food Programme (WFP), amounting to more than $140 million.

It is no wonder, therefore, that the US is currently the WFP's main aid donor and is the first country which the UN-affiliated WFP appeals to when a food crisis arises in the world. For example, in September 2002 development and humanitarian aid agencies based in Africa asked for immediate food relief to Zimbabwe, Zambia, Malawi, Mozambique, Lesotho and Swaziland, where more than 13 million people faced starvation due to the loss of crops caused by the prolonged drought affecting Southern Africa. The US announced an urgent shipment to the area, through the WFP, of 87,000 tons of transgenic corn and another 160,000 tons to be delivered in successive shipments until the first months of 2005.

It should also be noted that the WFP's executive director at that time was Catherine Bertini, a former US Department of Agriculture employee from Illinois, home to the largest genetically modified corn plantations. ∎

the promotion of an unnecessary and dangerous technology through the use of pseudo-science. While transgenic cotton production decreased by 80 per cent and its quality declined, farmers' losses amounted to nearly 6,000 rupees per acre, and the cost of seeds increased by 300 per cent,

Monsanto used Martin Qaim (Bonn University) and David Zilberman (University of California at Berkeley) to publish an article which affirmed that Bt cotton production increased by 80 per cent. Qaim and Zilberman published their work based on data submitted by Monsanto and not on

the work of farmers during the first year of commercial production.

On 25 April 2003, the Indian Government's Genetic Engineering Approval Committee (GEAC) decided to bar Monsanto from selling Bt cotton seeds in north India. ∎

FOOD IN FIGURES

A = Food production per capita index (1989/91=100), 2001. **Source:** *World Development Indicators 2003*, World Bank.
B = Food imports (as % of merchandise imports), 2001. **Source:** *World Development Indicators 2003*, World Bank.
C = Cereal imports (metric tons), 2002. **Source:** FAOSTAT - Statistical Database - FAO Web site 2004. http://apps.fao.org

Japan is by far the biggest food importer in the world, with almost twice the amount imported by the next biggest, Mexico.

	A	B	C		A	B	C		A	B	C
Albania		19	470,073	Ghana	174	18	740,786	Oman	159	22	521,981
Algeria	139	28	8,610,899	Greece	102	12	2,246,199	Pakistan	144	13	285,380
Andorra		20		Greenland	106	18	2,662	Palestine			832,765
Angola	149		581,013	Grenada	94	20	11,615	Panama	104	12	400,414
Antigua	99	22	6,758	Guadeloupe			0	Papua New Guinea	124	18	578,525
Argentina	146	6	14,626	Guam	129		11,989	Paraguay	144	14	16,221
Armenia	71	25	420,090	Guatemala	138	14	1,135,767	Peru	176	13	2,491,230
Aruba		19	6,623	Guinea	159	24	429,590	Philippines	136	9	4,620,238
Australia	145	5	64,745	Guinea-Bissau	145	44	33,251	Poland	86	6	648,162
Austria	104	6	767,312	Guyana	194	7	37,940	Portugal	100	11	3,325,124
Azerbaijan	86	16	728,234	Haiti	100		735,809	Puerto Rico	84		
Bahamas	140	16	15,743	Honduras	113	18	452,109	Qatar	178	11	143,833
Bahrain	139	12	138,683	Hungary	84	3	57,293	Réunion			0
Bangladesh	141	15	2,574,625	Iceland	110	10	63,724	Romania	100	8	371,867
Barbados	100	17	56,765	India	129	5	2,805	Russia	66	21	1,424,420
Belarus	61	12	859,079	Indonesia	117	10	7,927,166	Rwanda	110		30,460
Belgium	112	9	0	Iran	130	16	6,550,800	Samoa	99		10,592
Belize	176	14	27,251	Iraq	68			Samoa, American	96		105
Benin	159	20	184,377	Ireland	114	7	762,477	São Tomé and Príncipe	166		13,352
Bermuda	78	20	2,004	Israel	115	5	3,072,451	Saudi Arabia	83	16	5,673,790
Bhutan	118	18	34,434	Italy	103	9	9,803,141	Senegal	137	27	1,176,309
Bolivia	147	15	489,503	Jamaica	119	16	478,640	Serbia and Montenegro	104	9	20,631
Bosnia-Herzegovina			518,932	Japan	92	13	26,605,400	Seychelles	138	20	13,781
Botswana	96		2,956	Jordan	139	18	1,227,522	Sierra Leone	80		96,427
Brazil	151	6	7,809,248	Kanaky-New Caledonia	129	15	39,642	Singapore	40	4	836,135
Brunei	205	17	29,120	Kazakhstan	74	9	60,917	Slovakia	73	6	80,889
Bulgaria	65	5	177,225	Kenya	106	14	707,824	Slovenia	114	6	373,729
Burkina Faso	137	22	110,816	Kiribati	134	37	60,429	Solomon Is.	147	16	9,443
Burundi	96	23	22,269	Korea, North			1,825,472	South Africa	105	5	2,771,719
Cambodia	157		100,824	Korea, South	130	6	13,388,837	Spain	115	10	12,299,681
Cameroon	132	16	364,556	Kuwait	229	17	593,159	Sri Lanka	123	14	1,292,523
Canada	119	6	4,564,376	Kyrgyzstan	121	14	254,611	St Helena			76
Cape Verde	136	34	62,682	Laos	170		43,102	St Kitts-Nevis	94	17	4,494
Cayman Is.	85		687	Latvia	42	12	31,199	St Lucia	74	27	35,178
Central African Rep.	143	12	52,951	Lebanon	148	18	765,267	St Pierre and Miquelon			14
Chad	135	24	70,997	Lesotho	129		57,675	St Vincent	77	27	28,694
Chile	145	7	1,694,649	Liberia			221,716	Sudan	168	15	1,326,454
China	179	4	9,430,873	Libya	163	28	2,257,322	Suriname	77	18	39,886
Colombia	122	12	3,644,651	Liechtenstein	91			Swaziland	87		162,389
Comoros	122	22	69,906	Lithuania	56	9	182,278	Sweden	97	7	304,753
Congo D.R.	83		331,099	Luxembourg			44,763	Switzerland	93	6	552,076
Congo R.	130	21	249,408	Macedonia, TFYR	87	14	94,914	Syria	153	19	1,189,177
Cook Is.			814	Madagascar	107	14	126,487	Tajikistan	55		454,448
Costa Rica	149	8	812,406	Malawi	163	20	305,133	Tanzania	104	16	537,954
Côte d'Ivoire	134	17	1,081,550	Malaysia	148	5	5,123,885	Thailand	120	5	991,623
Croatia	68	9	88,959	Maldives	130	23	37,513	Togo	132	23	223,283
Cuba	61		1,684,818	Mali	125	19	127,735	Tokelau			0
Cyprus	129	17	583,641	Malta	118	11	169,249	Tonga	98	33	8,587
Czech Republic	79	5	155,380	Martinique			0	Trinidad and Tobago	115	9	216,462
Denmark	105	12	1,140,837	Mauritania	112	26	428,795	Tunisia	127	8	3,544,323
Djibouti	90	27	274,768	Mauritius	112	16	307,239	Turkey	110	4	2,645,500
Dominica	85	23	7,381	Mexico	138	5	14,092,111	Turkmenistan	137	12	10,468
Dominican Republic	118		1,398,788	Micronesia	18,866		9,415	Tuvalu			1,707
East Timor			12	Moldova	46	14	80,331	Uganda	137	12	205,588
Ecuador	162	8	885,072	Mongolia	103	17	315,987	Ukraine	53		387,787
Egypt	158	26	10,322,252	Montserrat			349	United Arab Emirates	291	10	2,096,378
El Salvador	114	17	716,033	Morocco	106	14	5,032,115	United Kingdom	89	8	3,489,282
Equatorial Guinea	115		10,255	Mozambique	124	14	694,970	United States	122	4	5,014,779
Eritrea	127		228,211	Myanmar-Burma	171	15	113,709	Uruguay	134	11	399,514
Estonia	43	11	213,339	Namibia	115		138,566	Uzbekistan	124		238,200
Ethiopia	142	7	697,017	Nauru			465	Vanuatu	111	22	21,031
Faeroe Is.	97	20	8,679	Nepal	133	13	27,371	Venezuela	123	12	1,527,792
Fiji	99	16	138,130	Netherlands	101	11	7,759,754	Vietnam	155		1,423,167
Finland	90	6	334,481	Netherlands Antilles	164	9	202,684	Virgin Is. (Am.)	103		0
France	102	8	1,563,953	New Zealand-Aotearoa	133	9	446,208	Virgin Is. (Br.)			278
French Guiana			0	Nicaragua	155	16	277,323	Wallis and Futuna Is.			1,181
French Polynesia	93	20	38,896	Niger	146	44	129,577	Yemen	136	35	2,298,947
Gabon	117	19	169,296	Nigeria	157	20	3,711,664	Zambia	108	8	367,321
Gambia	153	35	121,891	Niue			65	Zimbabwe	110	9	685,847
Georgia	79		242,744	Norfolk Is.			167				
Germany	99	7	3,631,290	Norway	89	7	450,847				

The missing girls of China

WHEN THE CHINESE GOVERNMENT, WORRIED ABOUT INCREASING POPULATION AND FOOD AND WATER
SCARCITY, BEGAN LIMITING REPRODUCTION TO ONE CHILD PER COUPLE IN 1979, MANY TRIED TO ENSURE
THAT CHILD WOULD BE MALE. THE PROGRAM ALLOWED FOR SOME EXCEPTIONS: A SECOND CHILD
WAS ALLOWED IN RURAL AREAS TO HELP WITH THE CHORES IF THE FIRST-BORN WAS FEMALE, AND
IF SEVERAL YEARS HAD PASSED SINCE HER BIRTH; CERTAIN ETHNIC MINORITIES WERE ALLOWED UP
TO THREE CHILDREN. BUT THE PERCENTAGE OF MALES HAS IN FACT RISEN STEADILY SINCE THAT DATE.

The first family-planning campaign was launched in 1972, when Chinese women had an average of six children. The campaign, conducted under the motto 'no juvenile weddings, more time between pregnancies, and fewer children' suggested people should wait longer to get married and have children, prolong the time between pregnancies and have smaller families. This first attempt at family planning was considered positive. The birth control message had reached the masses and birth rates dropped from 5.8 children per woman in 1970 to 2.7 in 1979.

Faced with extraordinary demographic growth in 1979 - at one billion people, then almost a quarter of the world's population - the Government of the People's Republic of China implemented a severe family-planning policy which consisted of limiting couples to one child. The policy was called 'One family, one child'. In order to reduce birth rates, the Government imposed fines on parents with more than one child, raised the legal marrying age and demanded the use of family planning methods such as IUDs, abortion and permanent sterilization.

In 1984, the program demanded that the legal marrying age be raised from 18 to 20. The officially recommended age has been higher: 23 for rural women and 25 for urban women. Since 1982, the average marrying age has been more than 20 in every Chinese province.

The program was effective in reducing overall birth rates. Although the goal was not to exceed 1.2 billion people by 2000, that year's census revealed a population close to 1.3 billion. This could be seen as a failure, but had the policy not been implemented it is estimated the country would now have 1.6 billion people (currently the Chinese demographic projection for 2050). However, for 24 years the program led to the hidden and massive extermination of millions of girls - the unwanted sex in Chinese society - either before or after their birth, with the resulting eradication of their reproductive potential.

The preference for sons is traditional in China. Some studies suggest that the cutback in the number of females was already mentioned in the chronicles of Imperial China and during the republican era. Lineage is handed down through males, who take care of their aging parents. Women marry and take care of their husband's family. Through different times and situations, Chinese families used infanticide to regulate family size and the sex of their children. Due to the current one-child limit, many couples have only one legal chance to have a child, so they trust ultrasound techniques to identify fetuses and abort females. The program allows for a second child in rural areas - where some two thirds of China's population lives - but if the first child is a girl, a second girl is often aborted or abandoned until a boy is born.

More than 90 per cent of children in orphanages are abandoned girls between one and four years old, many of them the second female born to rural families. Many peasants consider it a great dishonor to their ancestry not to have a male heir. Couples whose first child is male often sign the one-child-per-family certificate, while those whose first born is female keep

trying to have a son at the risk of paying preposterous fines, or, as has happened in remote rural areas, the destruction of their home by Family Planning officials. In Rongshui county, a very poor area peopled mostly by Miao and Dong ethnic groups, parents with more than two children have to pay a $6,000 fine, although the average annual income among peasants barely amounts to $60.

Fewer women

According to the China Internet Information Center, 'thanks to family planning policies people have changed their ideas about marriage, reproduction and family, and accept the late marriage and low procreation policy, as well as eugenics'. These policies also, 'free women from frequent pregnancies, heavy family loads and improve maternal and children's health'. According to Zhang Weiqing, minister of the State Family Planning Commission, the one-child policy prevented 330 million births in the last three decades.

The program has reduced birth rates. Urban areas such as Beijing and Shanghai, for instance, have enforced the policy. Meanwhile, rural areas have reached an

World population growth

ACCORDING TO THE UN annual report the *State of World Population 2003*, global population growth has slowed down, in part due to 'efforts made in the last 30 years to raise awareness on the dangers of overpopulation'. Although the report states that the growth rate will continue to drop during the next decades, high birth rates in the past determine a demographic inertia which generates approximately 80 million births per year.

The report states that although in several European countries people over 60 currently make up 20 per cent of the population, in 2050 this will amount to

35 per cent, and by 2100 to 45 per cent. While more than half of the Japanese population will be over 65 in the year 2100, in China the proportion will triple from the current 10 per cent to 30 per cent in 2050. This would mean that by then there will be only three active workers for every retired person, while today there are ten.

The world had three billion people in 1960, five billion in 1987, and six billion in 1999. It is estimated that by 2070 the world population will reach a peak of nine billion, after which it will start to decline, reaching approximately 8.4 billion in 2100. ■

average of two children per family. However, the policy is already leading to an imbalance in the male-female population. The female population has decreased significantly since 1979 and there are 116.9 boys for every 100 girls born today in China, compared to an average of 105-106 boys per 100 girls in other countries.

The gender ratio imbalance began in late 1980, when portable ultrasound equipment arrived in villages and remote areas. In Hubei province, the number of males born for every 100 females increased from 107 in 1982 to 109.5 in 1989. By 1995, it was 130.3 boys for every 100 girls. By 1998, the ratio was 120 boys to 100 girls.

Various means are used to curtail the female birth ratio: deliberate omission of female registration in census and statistical surveys, infanticide, abandonment, criminal negligence and selective abortion.

Simple procedure

China has more than 200,000 clinics and local doctors' offices with modern ultrasound equipment. Women interviewed in Ping Yu say 'the procedure is simple', since they do not even have to travel the 160 kilometers to get to Beijing. They can simply travel to Shi Du city where, less than 30 minutes away by bus, doctors carry out tests that will allow the mother to know the sex of her future child. Although gender-selective abortion is prohibited, the ultrasound test which determines the baby's sex is usually provided through bribes.

In Shandong province, where gender ratios had reached 125 males to 100 females, a new law was enforced in January 1999 banning doctors from having ultrasound equipment and even from performing abortions. Two-dimensional ultrasound equipment can only establish the sex of the unborn baby during the fourth or fifth month into a pregnancy. This leads to late-term abortions with permanent health complications for women. According to official statistics, 97.5 per cent of aborted babies are female.

Absent girls

The 2000 census counted approximately 12.8 million fewer girls born between 1980 and 2000 than would have been born if China had had normal birth and mortality rates. Among these 12.8 million girls there are those definitely and actually lost (victims of selective abortions, negligence and abandonment after birth;

UNDER FIVE MORTALITY

Under 5 mortality rate (per 1,000 live births), 2002. **Source:** *The State of the World's Children 2004*, UNICEF.

Sweden's under-five mortality rate is now only 3, the lowest rate in history. But while most countries continue to improve their child-mortality rates, many African nations are now going backwards thanks to the devastating impact of HIV/AIDS. Since 1990, for example, Zambia's child-death rate has soared from 122 to 192, and Zimbabwe's from 87 to 123.

Sweden	3	Barbados	14	Jordan	33	Azerbaijan	105
Denmark	4	Dominica	15	Armenia	35	Pakistan	107
Iceland	4	Uruguay	15	Brazil	36	Yemen	107
Norway	4	Bahamas	16	Cape Verde	38	Congo R.	108
Singapore	4	Bahrain	16	Dominican Republic	38	Myanmar-Burma	109
Austria	5	Bulgaria	16	Philippines	38	Botswana	110
Czech Republic	5	Qatar	16	China	39	São Tomé and Príncipe	118
Finland	5	Seychelles	16	El Salvador	39	Kenya	122
Germany	5	Bosnia-Herzegovina	18	Peru	39	Haiti	123
Greece	5	Argentina	19	Vietnam	39	Zimbabwe	123
Japan	5	Libya	19	Belize	40	Iraq	125
Korea, South	5	Mauritius	19	Suriname	40	East Timor	126
Luxembourg	5	Serbia and Montenegro	19	Egypt	41	Gambia	126
Malta	5	Sri Lanka	19	Nicaragua	41	Madagascar	136
Monaco	5	St Lucia	19	Honduras	42	Cambodia	138
Netherlands	5	Belarus	20	Iran	42	Senegal	138
Slovenia	5	Jamaica	20	Turkey	42	Togo	141
Australia	6	Tonga	20	Vanuatu	42	Uganda	141
Belgium	6	Trinidad and Tobago	20	Morocco	43	Djibouti	143
Brunei	6	Ukraine	20	Indonesia	45	Swaziland	149
Cyprus	6	Fiji	21	Algeria	49	Equatorial Guinea	152
France	6	Latvia	21	Guatemala	49	Benin	156
Ireland	6	Romania	21	Tuvalu	52	Tanzania	165
Israel	6	Russia	21	Korea, North	55	Cameroon	166
Italy	6	Venezuela	22	Kyrgyzstan	61	Guinea	169
New Zealand-Aotearoa	6	Colombia	23	South Africa	65	Ethiopia	171
Portugal	6	Cook Is.	23	Marshall Is.	66	Côte d'Ivoire	176
San Marino	6	Micronesia	24	Namibia	67	Central African Rep.	180
Spain	6	Solomon Is.	24	Uzbekistan	68	Malawi	183
Switzerland	6	St Kitts-Nevis	24	Kiribati	69	Mauritania	183
Andorra	7	Grenada	25	Bolivia	71	Nigeria	183
Canada	7	Palestine	25	Mongolia	71	Rwanda	183
United Kingdom	7	Panama	25	Guyana	72	Burundi	190
Croatia	8	Samoa	25	Tajikistan	72	Zambia	192
Malaysia	8	St Vincent	25	Kazakhstan	76	Mozambique	197
United States	8	Macedonia, TFYR	26	Bangladesh	77	Chad	200
Cuba	9	Tunisia	26	Maldives	77	Congo D.R.	205
Hungary	9	Saudi Arabia	28	Comoros	79	Burkina Faso	207
Lithuania	9	Syria	28	Lesotho	87	Guinea-Bissau	211
Poland	9	Thailand	28	Eritrea	89	Mali	222
Slovakia	9	Ecuador	29	Gabon	91	Somalia	225
United Arab Emirates	9	Georgia	29	Nepal	91	Liberia	235
Kuwait	10	Mexico	29	India	93	Afghanistan	257
Costa Rica	11	Palau	29	Bhutan	94	Angola	260
Liechtenstein	11	Albania	30	Papua New Guinea	94	Niger	265
Chile	12	Nauru	30	Sudan	94	Sierra Leone	284
Estonia	12	Paraguay	30	Turkmenistan	98		
Oman	13	Lebanon	32	Ghana	100		
Antigua	14	Moldova	32	Laos	100		

or adopted by foreign couples and taken abroad) and those that are nominally lost (not counted in the census or excluded from statistics), who are alive but hidden from official population counts. One-third of those nominally absent are 'hidden' and two-thirds are in fact missing, meaning that the real number of girls born between 1980 and 2000 and lost is approximately 8.5 million.

Even leaving aside the human-rights dimension, the long-term demographic impact of these missing girls is considerable, since their reproductive potential is also lost. The 'actually missing' girls are likely to reduce China's future population by 3.2 per cent in 100 years. This would imply that in 100 years the population will be 5.4 per cent less than it would have been if those girls had existed. And if the number of the absent girls in 2000 were projected for 100 years, China's population would decrease by 13.6 per cent.

No more than a third of those 'nominally lost' between zero and four years of age would be hidden. The Latin American organization Analisis Internacional

(www.analisisinternacional.com) estimates that, since the family-planning policies began, between 10 and 20 million girls have 'ceased to be born'. Unlike the hidden girls, the actually absent girls never go to school, enter the work force, marry or have children. By virtue of their absence they have a real demographic impact.

The influence on population growth does not show so much in the direct elimination of girls, but rather in the elimination of their reproductive potential. Not only does a missing girl not contribute to the population, but neither does her child, or her child's child. The reproductive potential of 'actually lost' girls is lost for all future generations.

In 2002, China had 1,294,377,000 people. The population is unevenly distributed throughout the country. Approximately 95 per cent of people live in the south-eastern half of the country. The central government has tried to encourage migration to the northwest by offering economic incentives for those who move to Tibet, Qinghai and Gansu. This has created ethnic strife between the non-Han

population from the northwest and Han immigrants, who receive better pay and benefits. Between 1982 and 1990 the Chinese urban population increased from 21 to 26 per cent. The trend since then has become even more marked. Today, 36 per cent of Chinese people live in towns and cities. It is estimated that anywhere from 700 to 800 million people live in rural areas.

The population growth rate has decreased by a yearly average of 1.07 per cent between 1990 and 2000. In 2001 it stood at 0.88 per cent. Although China has made the transition from high to low birth and death rates, each year the number of births still exceeds the number of deaths by close to nine million. ∎

Perishable merchandise: child slaves

TRAFFICKING IN HUMAN BEINGS FORCES PEOPLE TO LIVE IN CONDITIONS OF SLAVERY. THIS PRACTICE AFFECTS ALL CONTINENTS AND MOST COUNTRIES, BUT IN AFRICA IT IS OUT OF CONTROL. EXTREME POVERTY TURNS ANYTHING INTO A COMMODITY, EVEN PEOPLE'S CHILDREN.

According to UNICEF, each year 1.2 million children are traded worldwide. Most of the trafficking comes from West African countries, such as Sierra Leone, impoverished by the civil war. There is also trafficking from the south of Sudan, mostly of black people, to Arab countries in the northern part of the continent.

Child slavery generally implies an economic agreement with the child's family. Parents that cannot feed, dress or heal their children will seek somebody to take responsibility for them. In poor areas with weak social security institutions this can mean the sale of the children, who end up in plantations or as domestic workers in other African countries, at great profit to traffickers.

US government statistics published in 2002 indicate that 700,000 people are victims of the slave trade, mostly women and children. The International Organization for Migration (IOM) raises the number of people subject to internal and

international trafficking to four million. The International Labor Organization (ILO) states that difficulties in measuring this phenomenon are similar to those that do not allow accurate child labor statistics to be kept: one of the main problems is that incidences are not reported.

Global crime, continental reality
Yet no country in the world allows trafficking in children. In fact, slavery was abolished by law in every country during the 19th and 20th centuries. It is banned in international treaties and particularly in the UN Convention on the Rights of the Child.

But the next African generations will continue to suffer this scourge as long as poverty is not alleviated. According to the World Bank, more than 350 million Africans - more than half of the population - survive on less than a dollar a day.

Poverty is the driving force behind child slavery since it supplies traffickers with exploitable children and desperate

families. The AIDS epidemic has brought a new dimension to this which has left millions of orphans struggling for survival.

'The human vultures will swoop down to grab those orphans', the South African Protestant cleric Jabulani Dlamini was quoted as saying: 'Unless we take responsibility for each child and establish institutions and programs to see to their needs, they will be stolen by traffickers and we will never see them again.'

As in other instances, speculators and desperate families together transform children into merchandise. In this state of things, the trade in slave children (which is also selling the hope of better options to the victims) is no different from the kinds of trade that have exhausted other natural resources in the continent for centuries. Demand and supply are intimately connected. Extreme poverty is the fertilizer that allows the production of slave children; they become simply perishable merchandise. ∎

AIDS IN FIGURES

A = HIV prevalence rate, aged 15-49, per cent. **Source:** UNAIDS estimates, 2001.

B = AIDS estimated deaths. **Source:** UNAIDS estimates, 2001.

C = Children orphaned by AIDS (one or both parents), currently living. **Source:** UNAIDS, 2001.

The HIV prevalence rates in parts of Southern Africa have reached truly terrifying levels: in Botswana 4 in every 10 people aged 15 to 49 now carries the virus.

Country	A	B	C
Algeria	0.1		
Angola	5.5	24,000	100,000
Argentina	0.7	1,800	25,000
Armenia	0.1	1,000[1]	
Australia	0.1	1,000[1]	
Austria	0.2	1,000[1]	
Azerbaijan	0.1[1]	1,000[1]	
Bahamas	3.5	610	2,900
Bahrain	0.3		
Bangladesh	0.1[1]	650	2,100
Barbados	1.2		
Belarus	0.3	1,000	
Belgium	0.2	1,000[1]	
Belize	2	300	950
Benin	3.6	8,100	34,000
Bhutan	0.1[1]		
Bolivia	0.1	290	1,000
Bosnia-Herzegovina	0.1[1]		
Botswana	38.8	26,000	69,000
Brazil	0.7	8,400	130,000
Bulgaria	0.1[1]		
Burkina Faso	6.5	44,000	270,000
Burundi	8.3	40,000	240,000
Cambodia	2.7	12,000	55,000
Cameroon	11.8	53,000	210,000
Canada	0.3	500[2]	
Central African Rep.	12.9	22,000	110,000
Chad	3.6	14,000	72,000
Chile	0.3	220	4,100
China	0.1	30,000	76,000
Colombia	0.4	5,600	21,000
Congo D.R.	4.9	120,000	930,000
Congo R.	7.2	11,000	78,000
Costa Rica	0.6	890	3,000
Côte d'Ivoire	9.7	75,000	420,000
Croatia	0.1[1]	10[3]	1,000
Cuba	0.1[1]	120	
Cyprus	0.3		
Czech Republic	0.1[1]	10[3]	
Denmark	0.1[1]	1,000[1]	
Dominican Republic	2.5	7,800	33,000
Ecuador	0.3	1,700	7,200
Egypt	0.1[1]		
El Salvador	0.6	2,100	13,000
Equatorial Guinea	3.4	370	
Eritrea	2.8	350	24,000
Estonia	1	1,000[1]	
Ethiopia	6.4	160,000	990,000
Fiji	0.1		
Finland	0.1[1]	1,000[1]	
France	0.3	800	
Gambia	1.6	400	5,300
Georgia	0.1[1]	1,000[1]	
Germany	0.1	660	
Ghana	3	28,000	200,000
Greece	0.2	1,000[1]	
Guatemala	1	5,200	32,000
Guinea-Bissau	2.8	1,200	4,300
Guyana	2.7	1,300	4,200
Haiti	6.1	30,000	200,000
Honduras	1.6	3,300	14,000
Hungary	0.1[1]	1,000[1]	
Iceland	0.1	1,000[1]	
India	0.8		
Indonesia	0.1	4,600	18,000
Iran	0.1[1]	290	
Iraq	0.1[1]		
Ireland	0.1	1,000[1]	
Israel	0.1		
Italy	0.4	1,100	
Jamaica	1.2	980	5,100
Japan	0.1[1]	430	2,000
Jordan	0.1[1]		
Kazakhstan	0.1	300	
Kenya	15	190,000	890,000
Korea, South	0.1[1]	220	1,000
Kyrgyzstan	0.1[1]	1,000[1]	
Laos	0.1[1]	150[4]	
Latvia	0.4	1,000[1]	
Lesotho	31	25,000	73,000
Libya	0.2		
Lithuania	0.1[1]	1,000[1]	
Luxembourg	0.2	1,000[1]	
Madagascar	0.3		6,300
Malawi	15	80,000	470,000
Malaysia	0.3	2,500	14,000
Maldives	0.1		
Mali	1.6	11,000	70,000
Malta	0.1[1]	1,000[1]	
Mauritius	0.1	1,000[1]	
Mexico	0.3	4,200	27,000
Moldova	0.2	300	
Mongolia	0.1[1]		
Morocco	0.1		
Mozambique	13	60,000	420,000
Namibia	22.5	13,000	47,000
Nepal	0.5	2,400	13,000
Netherlands	0.2	110	
New Zealand-Aotearoa	0.1[1]	1,000[1]	
Nicaragua	0.2	400	2,000
Nigeria	5.8	170,000	1,000,000
Norway	0.1	1,000[1]	
Oman	0.1	4,500	25,000
Pakistan	0.1	1,900	8,100
Panama	1.5	880	4,200
Papua New Guinea	0.7	3,900	17,000
Peru	0.3		
Philippines	0.1[1]	720	4,100
Poland	0.1		
Portugal	0.5	1,000	
Romania	0.1[1]	350	
Russia	0.9	9,000	
Rwanda	8.9	49,000	260,000
Senegal	0.5	2,500	15,000
Serbia and Montenegro	0.2	1,000[1]	
Sierra Leone	7	11,000	42,000
Singapore	0.2	140	
Slovakia	0.1[1]	1,000[1]	
Slovenia	0.1[1]	1,000[1]	
Somalia	1		
South Africa	20.1	360,000	660,000
Spain	0.5	2,300	
Sri Lanka	0.1[1]	250	2,000
Sudan	2.6	23,000	62,000
Suriname	1.2	330	1,700
Swaziland	33.4	12,000	35,000
Sweden	0.1	1,000[1]	
Switzerland	0.5	1,000[1]	
Tajikistan	0.1[1]	1,000[1]	
Tanzania	7.8	140,000	810,000
Thailand	1.8	55,000	290,000
Togo	6	12,000	63,000
Trinidad and Tobago	2.5	1,200	3,600
Turkey	0.1[1]		
Turkmenistan	0.1[1]	1,000[1]	
Uganda	5	84,000	880,000
Ukraine	1	11,000	
United Kingdom	0.1	460	
United States	0.6	15,000	
Uruguay	0.3	500[2]	3,100
Uzbekistan	0.1	1,000[1]	
Venezuela	0.5		
Vietnam	0.3	6,600	22,000
Yemen	0.1		
Zambia	21.5	120,000	570,000
Zimbabwe	33.7	200,000	780,000

[1] Less than 0.10%

The children of AIDS

SOME 11 MILLION OF THE 14 MILLION CHILDREN ORPHANED BY AIDS LIVE IN SUB-SAHARAN AFRICA, ONE OF THE POOREST REGIONS ON THE PLANET. A WORLD BANK REPORT COUNTS THE COSTS OF THE EPIDEMIC.

There are more than 11 million children who have been orphaned by AIDS in sub-Saharan Africa. South Asia (mainly India, where there are 1.5 million orphans) is the second most affected region. At the end of 2003, 25 million people in sub-Saharan Africa were living with HIV, including three million children under 15 years of age.

According to Peter Piot, head of UNAIDS, by 2010, the number of children orphaned by AIDS could reach 25 million. Piot says the challenge for affected countries is to keep parents alive, protect children from violence and exploitation, and guarantee them health and education. To do this, studies estimate that affected countries would need $1 billion. Two out of three countries hit by HIV/AIDS lack strategies to guarantee minimum protection and care for their children.

In several African countries, the pandemic also leads to incalculable long-term economic damage. The World Bank has warned that HIV/AIDS could reduce African Gross Domestic Product (GDP) by more than 1.5 per cent.

The WB points out three fundamental contributory factors:

1. Human capital destruction, since it is adults with job-market experience and knowledge who have the highest death rates.

2. The weakening of mechanisms to regenerate that human capital. Once parents die, their children lack resources for education and development.

3. The fact that children themselves fall ill makes investing in their education less attractive.

The report also indicates that governments ought to consider a macroeconomic perspective on the loss of human capital and decreased productivity in relation to societies crippled by HIV/AIDS. ∎

Haiti: magic not microbes

IN HAITI, approximately 5,000 children are born carrying the HIV virus every year. UNICEF estimates that one child dies of AIDS every two hours, while 200,000 are orphaned.

Miriam Silva, a physician from the international organization Doctors without Borders, explained that: 'many infected people do not know they have AIDS; they think someone has cursed them.' Many Haitians, particularly among the five million in the countryside, believe that multiple diseases - AIDS among them - are caused by magic and not by microbes. ∎

Children who work to death

EVERY YEAR, CHILD LABOR TAKES 22,000 LIVES. MILLIONS OF CHILDREN - ONE THIRD OF THEM UNDER TEN - ARE PART OF THE GLOBAL LABOR FORCE, MANY WORKING TO PAY THEIR FAMILY'S DEBTS.

The International Labour Organization (ILO), reported in February 2004 that approximately 22,000 girls and boys die each year as a result of child labor. More than 211 million children work, of whom 186 million do so in unhealthy conditions and 73 million are under ten. Minors are employed in mines, brickworks, farms, domestic services and factories; some are sold and others are sexually exploited.

There is a very close relationship between child labor and poverty. Children that work are almost exclusively poor. Countries with compulsory and accessible education have lower rates of child labor than those without.

According to the ILO, school registration and the eradication of child labor would create, in the long term, a profit seven times greater than the amount invested in eradicating poverty. Initially this would have an adverse effect on poor families who depend on their children's wages. But in the long run most of them would benefit, since a person with a sound education has more chance of earning a living than someone who is illiterate.

Latin America: semi-slavery
In 1990 there were 7,300,000 children between 10 and 14 years old working in Latin America. UNICEF reported in 2004 that in Haiti there are between 250,000 and 300,000 minors (more than 75 per cent of them girls) working as domestic employees in conditions amounting to semi-slavery. Three-quarters are illiterate, many of them orphans. They work all day, feed on waste, sleep on the floor and, in the case of the girls, are often subjected to sexual abuse.

Rural families send their children to acquaintances in the city, who promise to grant them education, shelter and food in exchange for their domestic labor.

India: first place in child labor stakes
India has the highest number of workers between 4 and 14 years old, despite a 1986 law that bans child labor. The Government puts the figure at 17 million child workers, but the ILO estimates it at 45 million. Swami Agnivesh, from the Forced Labour Liberation Front, claims that in 1994 there were more than 60 million.

The *Asia Labour Monitor* (ALM) estimates that the children of rural landless families produce about 20 per cent of Gross Domestic Product (GDP), in sectors such as agriculture, mining, furnaces, factories (textiles, matches, fireworks, silk manufacturers) and in the giant urban sector (transporting loads, working in small shops, etc).

India's Supreme Court considers all child labor to be slavery, not only because child laborers have no option, but because they do not receive the minimum legal wage. Corporations and countries from the industrialized North accuse India and other countries from the South of unfair competition and say that their exports are based on child labor and exploitation.

At least five million Indian children are slaves who receive no wages at all. They are forced to work to pay off family debts or because their parents have obtained an advance payment on their work. Under these conditions, the minors are doubly enslaved: by the employers who use their work and by the parents who use their money. ∎

Deprived of a future: girls without education

WHILE POVERTY FORCES INCREASINGLY YOUNG CHILDREN TO ENTER THE LABOR MARKET, GIRLS SUFFER MORE THAN BOYS DUE TO DISPARITIES IN INCOME DISTRIBUTION. THE UN'S MILLENNIUM GOALS INCLUDE ENSURING ELEMENTARY EDUCATION FOR BOTH GIRLS AND BOYS BY 2015. BUT IN PRACTICE THIS IS GOING TO BE A DIFFICULT TARGET TO MEET.

According to UN Secretary General Kofi Annan: 'There is no more efficient development tool than the education of girls'. But a recent UNICEF report shows that in most countries, girls living in poverty have no access to education or basic health services. Of the 121 million children without schooling in the world, 65 million are girls. The 2004 report *Girls, Education and Development* emphasizes their disadvantaged position when it comes to schooling.

There are immediate and long-term consequences when a girl lacks the practical knowledge acquired through school. The report stresses that 'when a girl is without the knowledge and life skills that school can provide... she is exposed to many more risks than her educated counterparts and the consequences are bequeathed to the next generation'.

UNICEF's Executive Director Carol Bellamy notes that, when 'a girl gets an education ... she is more likely to be healthy. Her children are less likely to die before the age of five. She is more likely to make choices about her life... she becomes more of a functioning person in society.' In addition, the study shows that every extra year of education reduces the number of women who die in childbirth by two per thousand. UNICEF states that campaigns to educate girls also benefit boys due to the fact that it is rare for education to be offered to girls alone.

One of the main goals of the UN's Millennium Development Summit was to 'guarantee elementary education to every girl and boy' by 2015. But while some countries are making efforts to secure female access to education, in practice the projected goals are far from being accomplished, particularly in Sub-Saharan Africa, South Asia and the Middle East. ∎

Boys: the turning point

WHILE THERE ARE FEWER GIRLS THAN BOYS IN SCHOOLS, THERE IS A NEW TREND IN SOME COUNTRIES - GIRLS ARE DOING BETTER THAN BOYS IN EDUCATION. THERE ARE MANY REASONS FOR THIS, BUT THE REFORMS THAT MAKE SCHOOL SAFER AND MORE RELEVANT FOR GIRLS ALSO MAKE SCHOOLS INTO PLACES WHERE BOYS CAN FLOURISH.

In the majority of Southern countries, far fewer girls than boys attend school. But in Colombia, Haiti, Lesotho, Madagascar, Malawi, Mongolia, Suriname and Tanzania, according to a UNICEF report, it is boys who are disproportionately absent from school. In addition, in Latin America and the Caribbean, boys generally have higher repetition rates and lower academic achievement levels than girls, and in some countries, a higher rate of absenteeism. In the industrialized world, girls are also beginning to outperform boys.

From an educational point of view, the turning point for boys often comes in early adolescence, when their bodies and sense of themselves are changing, and they are forced to engage with the adult world and its expectations of them as men. This is becoming increasingly true in industrialized countries too, where for many years, there was an acceptance that girls did better than boys in language and humanities, and boys did better in mathematics and science, fields that had been traditionally closed to girls. However, more recently, after school-based initiatives and changes in social expectations of women, girls' participation and performance in science and math improved. The result is that in many countries girls are outperforming boys across the board.

The problem of boys' educational underachievement is complex. Socialization is one factor - girls may have to stay home and help with housework and childcare while boys are allowed more freedom. But this encourages them to concentrate and stay on task, thus enabling them to fit school behavioral requirements better than boys.

Another factor is that it is often difficult to disentangle boys' educational problems from their social class. In the Caribbean and Brazil, for example, boys' alienation from school and poor socio-economic circumstances go hand in hand. Poverty, as well as gender roles, influence boys' academic underachievement.

But boys can also be empowered and their social and educational development enhanced by helping to protect and promote girls' rights. Boys have become valuable allies in addressing girls' security and safety during the commute to and from school. This not only helps protect girls, but also strengthens boys' social development and helps them to confront violence and understand why it is unacceptable.

All this suggests that boys' disaffection from education may be connected to their traditional socialization as males. This factor underscores the necessity of fathers' involvement with their children from birth, participating in their care and development during early childhood and supporting their education.

Like many of the other strategies to help boys, this benefits both sexes. All children can also benefit from early childhood learning programmes, scheduling lessons to fit work at home or in the fields, and locating schools nearer to children's homes. Perhaps the most fundamental however is the development of the kind of gender-specific education that benefits each individual child - whether they are a boy or a girl. ∎

Source: 'What about boys?' *State of the World's Children 2005, UNICEF*

EDUCATION IMBALANCES

Primary pupil to teacher ratio, 2000. **Source:** *World Development Indicators 2003*, World Bank.

While there are 73 children to every teacher in the Central African Republic and 71 in Chad, there are just 5 in San Marino, 8 in Libya and 10 in the Netherlands.

Country	Value	Year	Country	Value	Year	Country	Value	Year	Country	Value	Year
Afghanistan	42.7	2000	Czech Republic	17.7	2000	Laos	29.9	2000	Samoa	24.0	2000
Albania	21.8	2000	Denmark	9.9	2000	Latvia	15.0	2000	Samoa, American	15.0	1991
Algeria	27.8	2000	Djibouti	35.6	2000	Lebanon	17.0	2000	San Marino	5.4	1999
Angola	35.2	2000	Dominica	20.7	2000	Lesotho	47.9	2000	São Tomé and Príncipe	34.3	2000
Antigua	18.7	2000	Dominican Republic	40.5	2000	Liberia	35.9	1999	Saudi Arabia	11.8	2000
Argentina	21.8	1999	Ecuador	23.1	2000	Libya	8.4	1998	Senegal	50.8	2000
Armenia	18.8	1996	Egypt	22.3	2000	Lithuania	16.0	2000	Serbia and Montenegro	19.9	2000
Aruba	18.9	2000	El Salvador	25.6	2000	Luxembourg	11.7	2000	Seychelles	14.7	2000
Australia	18.1	1996	Equatorial Guinea	41.5	2000	Macedonia, TFYR	21.6	2000	Sierra Leone	43.7	2000
Austria	13.5	1999	Eritrea	44.8	2000	Madagascar	49.6	2000	Singapore	25.4	1996
Azerbaijan	18.6	1999	Estonia	14.1	2000	Malawi	56.3	2000	Slovakia	19.5	2000
Bahamas	14.0	1998	Ethiopia	54.9	2000	Malaysia	18.2	2000	Slovenia	14.1	1998
Bahrain	17.2	2000	Fiji	23.0	1998	Maldives	22.7	2000	Solomon Is.	24.1	1994
Bangladesh	57.1	2000	Finland	15.5	2000	Mali	63.4	2000	South Africa	33.5	2000
Barbados	16.9	2000	France	18.7	2000	Malta	19.1	1999	Spain	14.3	2000
Belarus	17.1	2000	French Polynesia	14.3	1995	Marshall Is.	14.9	1998	Sri Lanka	27.8	1996
Belgium	12.1	2000	Gabon	49.2	2000	Mauritania	41.8	2000	St Kitts-Nevis	19.2	2000
Belize	22.8	2000	Gambia	37.5	2000	Mauritius	26.1	2000	St Lucia	22.3	2000
Benin	53.5	2000	Georgia	15.6	2000	Mexico	27.3	2000	St Vincent	25.0	2000
Bermuda	9.3	2000	Germany	14.8	2000	Micronesia	23.4	2000	Sudan	26.7	1999
Bhutan	41.1	2000	Ghana	33.0	2000	Moldova	20.3	2000	Suriname	17.1	2000
Bolivia	24.2	2000	Greece	12.7	2000	Monaco	15.6	1998	Swaziland	33.2	2000
Botswana	26.7	2000	Grenada	20.9	2000	Mongolia	32.3	2000	Sweden	11.4	2000
Brazil	26.0	2000	Guatemala	32.6	2000	Morocco	28.1	2000	Switzerland	13.6	2000
Brunei	14.6	1995	Guinea	44.4	2000	Mozambique	64.0	2000	Syria	24.1	2000
Bulgaria	17.7	2000	Guinea-Bissau	44.1	1999	Myanmar-Burma	32.3	2000	Tajikistan	21.8	2000
Burkina Faso	47.4	2000	Guyana	26.2	1999	Namibia	31.6	2000	Tanzania	40.4	2000
Burundi	50.2	2000	Haiti	34.7	1996	Nepal	37.0	2000	Thailand	20.8	2000
Cambodia	52.9	2000	Honduras	34.1	2000	Netherlands	9.8	2000	Togo	34.3	2000
Cameroon	62.7	2000	Hungary	10.5	2000	Netherlands Antilles	17.7	2000	Tonga	20.9	2000
Canada	15.0	1999	Iceland	10.9	1999	New Zealand-Aotearoa	15.6	2000	Trinidad and Tobago	19.8	2000
Cape Verde	28.4	2000	India	40.0	1999	Nicaragua	35.7	2000	Tunisia	22.7	2000
Cayman Is.	15.2	2000	Indonesia	22.2	2000	Niger	41.9	2000	Turkey	27.7	1994
Central African Rep.	73.5	2000	Iran	24.8	2000	Nigeria	33.8	1996	Uganda	59.1	2000
Chad	71.2	2000	Iraq	21.4	1999	Oman	23.7	2000	Ukraine	20.5	1998
Chile	25.2	2000	Ireland	21.6	1999	Pakistan	40.4	1996	United Arab Emirates	15.9	2000
China	19.8	1999	Israel	12.2	2000	Palau	15.3	1998	United Kingdom	18.2	2000
China, Hong Kong SAR	23.7	1995	Italy	10.7	2000	Panama	24.7	2000	United States	15.4	2000
China, Macau SAR	28.4	2000	Jamaica	35.5	2000	Papua New Guinea	36.0	1999	Uruguay	20.8	2000
Colombia	26.5	2000	Japan	20.4	2000	Paraguay	19.6	1998	Uzbekistan	20.6	1994
Comoros	35.9	2000	Jordan	21.1	1996	Peru	25.3	1998	Vanuatu	23.5	2000
Congo D.R.	26.0	1998	Kanaky-New Caledonia	20.4	1991	Philippines	35.2	2000	Venezuela	21.1	1996
Congo R.	50.7	2000	Kazakhstan	18.7	2000	Poland	11.1	2000	Vietnam	28.0	2000
Costa Rica	24.9	2000	Kenya	29.8	2000	Portugal	12.9	2000	Virgin Is. (Am.)	18.4	1992
Côte d'Ivoire	47.5	2000	Kiribati	24.4	1999	Qatar	12.6	2000	Yemen	29.8	1998
Croatia	18.3	2000	Korea, South	32.1	2000	Romania	19.6	1999	Zambia	45.0	2000
Cuba	10.7	2000	Kuwait	13.8	1999	Russia	17.3	2000	Zimbabwe	37.0	1992
Cyprus	17.2	2000	Kyrgyzstan	24.5	2000	Rwanda	51.4	2000			

Tackling child pornography on the net

THERE ARE MORE THAN 2,000 CHILD PORNOGRAPHY WEBSITES WHICH DEPEND ON PRESUMED CONSUMER ANONYMITY FOR THEIR SUCCESS. THEIR ERADICATION IS DIFFICULT AND THEY GENERATE PARALLEL CRIMES, SUCH AS FINANCIAL FRAUD.

According to UNESCO, up to half a million erotic images of children were found on the internet in 2001. Among other tools, pornographic rings use chat rooms where communication is carried out in private and 'conversations' cannot be seen by others.

The UK's National Hi-Tech Crime Unit (NHTCU) says that extortion, child pornography and financial fraud are the most common crimes on the internet. An NHTCU report revealed that pornographic rings have taken advantage of the fact that business transactions are increasingly carried out through the internet.

Through child pornography sites, expert programmers create fraud techniques against banks and corporations, but those most affected have been ordinary people. Offering low-price products (including child pornography codes) the pornography rings obtain credit card or bank account numbers in order to empty them later.

As in most fraud cases, these fraud artists prey on their victims' ambition and often on a certain willingness to commit fraud on their part, for example in cases of defrauded pedophiles. However, there is an underlying question for such 'victims':

does someone who buys a counterfeiting machine that does not work have a right to feel defrauded?

Policies: past and future
As with other rights of children that are violated on a daily basis, policies regarding child pornography should target both the past and the future. On the one hand, they need to address past crimes which have consequences for children, who may by now be adults, but who continue to react to their previous victimization. On the other, policies need to target child pornography as an industry still waiting to attract its child victims. ∎

Millennium Development Goals: a new challenge

THE YEAR 2015 WILL BRING AN END TO THE TIMEFRAME SET TO ACHIEVE THE EIGHT MILLENNIUM DEVELOPMENT GOALS (MDGS). THE FIRST SEVEN AIM AT REDUCING POVERTY, PROMOTING HUMAN DIGNITY AND EQUALITY AND ACHIEVING PEACE, DEMOCRACY AND A SUSTAINABLE ENVIRONMENT. IN ORDER TO ACHIEVE THESE, THE FINAL GOAL OF THE DECLARATION INCLUDES SEVERAL COMMITMENTS BY RICH COUNTRIES IN THE NORTH TO INCREASE AID TO POOR COUNTRIES IN THE SOUTH.

The Millennium Development Goals (MDGs) are eight sustainable development goals endorsed by 189 Heads of State during the 2000 UN Millennium Summit. They are:

1. To eradicate extreme poverty and hunger

2. To guarantee elementary education to every girl and boy

3. To promote gender equity and the empowerment of women

4. To reduce mortality rates of children under five by two-thirds

5. To reduce maternal mortality rates during birth by three-quarters

6. To stop and turn back the spread of AIDS and the incidence of malaria and other epidemic diseases

7. To guarantee environmental sustainability

8. To develop a global partnership for development.

1. Eradicate extreme poverty and hunger

a) Halve the percentage of people living in extreme poverty
According to the 2003 UNDP Human Development report, more than 1.2 billion people - one in five worldwide - survive on less than $1 a day. The number of people suffering extreme poverty decreased from 30 per cent to 23 per cent during the 1990s. But given global population growth, this number was reduced by only 123 million, a small fraction of the progress needed to reduce poverty. Most of the progress was, besides, in China, which lifted 150 million people out of poverty during the 1990s. In the rest of the world the number of people living on less than $1 a day actually increased by 28 million.

b) Halve the percentage of people suffering from hunger
The number of people suffering from hunger decreased by some 20 million during the 1990s. But, again, if China is excluded from the statistics, the number actually increased. South Asia and sub-Saharan Africa have the largest numbers of people suffering from hunger in the world.

2. Achieve universal primary education
Although more than 80 per cent of children in developing regions are enrolled in primary school, around 115 million children have no schooling at all. One in every six adults worldwide is illiterate. The gender gap persists: three fifths of the 115 million children without schooling are girls, and two thirds of the 876 million illiterate adults are women.

There is unequal access to basic education in most countries; the poorest 20 per cent of people receive much less than 20 per cent of state expenditures, while the richest 20 per cent receive much more. Primary education receives less funding than secondary and higher education. This situation discriminates against the poor, who most stand to benefit from elementary education.

3. Promote gender equity and empower women
The promotion of gender equity and the empowerment of women is a key objective of the Millennium Declaration, since women are agents for development and multipliers of productivity. They are the main caregivers in almost every society. Their education contributes in a greater measure than that of men to the health and education of the next generation; and even greater if they play a significant role in the family's decision making. Women who receive a better education and who are healthier also contribute to greater productivity and hence to higher household incomes. Women with schooling have fewer and healthier children, speeding up the transition towards lower birth rates.

4, 5 and 6. Reducing under-five child mortality by two thirds, reducing maternal mortality by three quarters, stopping and reversing the spread of AIDS, malaria and other epidemic illnesses.
Some 30,000 children a day - more than 10 million a year - die from preventable diseases. More than 500,000 women die each year during pregnancy or while giving birth. There are 42 million people worldwide living with HIV/AIDS, of which 39 million are in developing countries. Tuberculosis (along with AIDS) still has the highest mortality rates of all transmissible diseases among adults, causing up to two million deaths a year. Malaria causes a million deaths a year, but could kill double that number annually in the next 20 years. Many of these deaths are easily preventable through the use of mosquito nets, antibiotics, basic hygiene practices, midwives, and access to the Directly Observed Treatment Short-Course (DOTS) for tuberculosis, none of which need high technology.

Health systems lack resources (particularly in primary health treatment), are not universally accessible, and are inefficient. More than a billion people in developing countries (one in five) do not have access to safe drinking water, and 2.4 billion lack improved sanitation systems. Both are crucial to life. Those living in poor rural areas and in the poorest urban neighborhoods are the most affected.

7. Ensure environmental sustainability
There is an irregular geographical pattern when it comes to consumption, environmental damage and human impact. Rich countries cause most of the world's environmental contamination and deplete most of its resources. The poor are most vulnerable to environmental degradation and turmoil, like the anticipated effects of global climate change.

Soil degradation affects almost two billion hectares, threatening the livelihood of a billion people who live on arid land. Around 70 per cent of fisheries are depleted and 1.7 billion people - one third of the population in developing countries - live in areas that lack water. About 900 million of the rural poor depend on natural products as an important part of their livelihood. Up to a fifth of diseases in poor countries may be caused by environmental risk factors. Climatic changes could damage agricultural production in poor countries and increase risks by exposing them to floods and catastrophes.

8. Promote a global partnership for development
In order for developing countries to achieve the MDG goals one to seven by the year 2015, rich countries have to

change their approach. Poor countries cannot overcome the structural limitations which keep them poor by themselves. These limitations include rich countries' trade tariffs, and subsidies which restrict access to poor countries' exports, patents limiting access to life-saving technologies, and unsustainable debt owed to government and multilateral institutions from rich countries.

The goals must be seen as an indivisible whole if they are to become an instrument to manage globalization in favor of the poor. Although the objectives focus mainly on the first seven goals and on their impact on developing countries, their success or failure will eventually depend on achieving the eighth: the commitments by rich countries to increase financial assistance to the poor and to improve the rules of the international system.

New goals for a new era?
The MDGs tackle many of the most recurring setbacks of human development. The new goals are different from the objectives laid out during the first three UN 'Development Decades' in the 1960s, 1970s and 1980s, which were focused on economic growth. These goals give priority to human wellbeing and the reduction of poverty.

The MDGs reflect the main objectives established by different UN development conferences during the 1990s. These were the result of many consultations at national, regional and international levels in which millions of people took part. They represented a great variety of interests, including governments, grassroots organizations and the private sector.

Since the first Decade for Development during the 1960s, the international community, often led by the UN, has set development objectives. It has also experienced multiple setbacks. For instance, in the 1977 'Alma Ata Declaration', the world made the commitment to healthcare for all by the end of the century. However, in 2000, millions of poor people died from pandemic diseases, many of them easily preventable and treatable. During the 1990 World Summit for Children, the commitment was to provide universal primary education by the year 2000, but this goal was also not achieved.

Nevertheless, some UN goals have been successfully met. Thanks to the goal of universal immunization, coverage in more than 70 countries grew from 10 or 20 per cent in 1980 to more than 70 per cent in 1990. And even if the quantitative goals were not met within the terms set, progress has been speeded up.

Economic growth is not enough
During the 1980s and most of the 1990s, efforts by financial institutions and the main donor countries to promote development were carried out in the belief that market forces would lead poor countries toward self-sustaining economic development. Globalization seemed to be the great new engine behind global economic progress.

The development debate focused on three main themes. The first was the need for economic reforms in order to achieve macroeconomic stability. The second was the need for sound governance and institutions which would manage to stem corruption and uphold the law. The third was the need for social justice and citizen participation in the decision making process.

These are crucial issues for sustainable human development and continue to merit priority attention from policymakers. Nevertheless, there is a fourth factor that has not been taken into account: the structural limitations that impede economic growth and human development. Poor countries were supposed to achieve economic growth as long as they followed sound economic principles based on macroeconomic stability, market liberalization and the privatization of economic activity. Economic growth was supposed to bring general improvements in health, education, nutrition, housing and access to basic infrastructure such as safe drinking water and sanitation systems, allowing countries to climb out of poverty. But despite the improved living standards that globalization has brought to some parts of the world, hundreds of millions of people have experienced economic setbacks instead of progress and more than a billion still struggle daily against the scourge of hunger and poor health.

Economic growth is not enough because it sidesteps the poorest peoples and areas of the world. Economic growth is useless if human development is not a part of public policy.

The uniqueness of the MDGs lies in the clear recognition that poverty eradication can only be achieved through a closer co-operation between all development players, and with more action from rich countries, such as the opening up of trade, debt relief, the transfer of technology and increased aid.

Following up the MDGs
The last 30 years have produced great improvements in developing countries. However, progress in human development continues to be too slow.

For many countries, the last 15 years were desperate. Around 54 are poorer today than they were in 1990. In 21 countries, the percentage of people who go hungry has increased. In another 14, more children under five are dying. In 12, primary school enrolment is decreasing. In 34, life expectancy has also decreased. Rarely have there been such setbacks in survival rates.

Another sign of the development crisis is the fact that 21 countries lost points in the Human Development Index (the HDI measures the three components of human development: enjoying a long and healthy life, receiving education and having an adequate standard of living). This was rare until the late 1980s, since the abilities measured by the HDI are not easily lost.

If global progress continues at the same rate as the 1990s, the only Millennium Development Goals (MDGs) with a chance of being met are those seeking to reduce by half both income poverty and the number of people without access to safe drinking water. Mostly, this will be the effect of the statistical influence of China's and India's economic growth.

At this rate, and from a regional perspective, sub-Saharan African countries will not meet the poverty goals until 2147. With respect to HIV/AIDS and hunger, the trend in that region is still increasing rather than decreasing.

The fact that so many countries in the world are so far from achieving the MDGs before 2015 points to the need for an urgent change in strategy. However, development progress made so far shows what even very poor countries are capable of accomplishing.

The Millennium Project review
The international community needs to establish an order of priorities to achieve the MDGs. These must be based on an objective analysis of the major challenges and obstacles ahead, on information about what has and has not worked, and on ideas about new initiatives that can speed up progress.

To carry out this analysis, the UN Secretary General has created the Millennium Project. This initiative includes almost 300 international experts from the academic world, civil society, international organizations, state and private sectors, who will be issuing a final report in 2005 (www.unmillenniumproject.org/html/about .shtm).

Criticism from civil society
The contents of the MDGs spring from an exhaustive process of cumulative work where civil-society organizations played a fundamental role. But the fact that they participated indirectly rather than by right has led civil-society groups to see the summit goals as alien. They believe the MDGs reflect the dominant official position about development and the consensus achieved between rich and poor countries at a governmental level, which is still foreign to civil-society organizations, where mixed positions have emerged.

Civil-society organizations (CSOs) had no direct participation in the Millennium Summit, the Millennium Declaration, or the drafting of the goals. As a result, reactions have been mixed: although government support for the initiative was seen as an important sign of commitment, there is a well-founded concern about the apolitical, minimalist and quantitative nature of the objectives. Some civil-society groups believe the Millennium Declaration entails a significant international political consensus, but that it does not represent a development strategy as such. They do not believe the goals address the systemic causes of continuing poverty or increasing inequality and global polarization. They feel they are significantly lacking in ambition compared with the resources that exist, and as objectives they are on the fringe of what is morally acceptable

A third of the groups polled for a 2002 report (WFUNA-North-South Institute) said they were not fully aware of the contents of the goals, while 53 per cent of those that were informed found them insufficient. If this data is broken down by region, the goals were better received among rich and less developed countries and fared worse among developing or unevenly developed countries.

Representatives from civil-society organizations present five basic arguments about the MDGs:

1. Are the MDGs viable? Why should the population mobilize for the UN's latest goals when so many previous objectives remain incomplete?

2. The new goals are minimal in comparison with previous ones, for example, the goal of reducing poverty by half is considered to exclude 50 per cent of the poorest of the poor because of the way it was drafted.

3. The goals are blamed for reducing development policies so that they become aid measures. These do not address the growing inequality that affects the overall population.

4. The fourth demands a just balance between getting rich countries to commit to alleviating the situation of the poorest, and abandoning or diluting the discussion about systemic problems related to the global financial architecture, which have a negative impact on the world population.

5. There is an objection to the undefined and vague way in which the goals are worded when referring to commitments by rich countries. Debt relief, market access and increases in aid were not tied to any timetable or specific indicator, while the commitments of poor countries regarding basic services and the environment may undermine their sovereignty over natural resources and leave these countries even more exposed to the dictates of international financial institutions. ∎

WORKERS IN FIGURES

A = Labor force (% of total population), 2002. **Source:** World Development Indicators 2003, World Bank.

B = Female employment (% in agriculture), 1995/2001. **Source:** Human Development Report 2003, UNDP.

C = Female employment (% in industry), 1995/2001. **Source:** Human Development Report 2003, UNDP.

D = Female employment (% in services), 1995/2001. **Source:** Human Development Report 2003, UNDP.

E = Male employment (% in agriculture), 1995/2001. **Source:** Human Development Report 2003, UNDP.

F = Male employment (% in industry), 1995/2001. **Source:** Human Development Report 2003, UNDP.

G = Male employment (% in services), 1995/2001. **Source:** Human Development Report 2003, UNDP.

H = Unemployment (%). **Source:** LABORSTA database, ILO Web Site.

	A	B	C	D	E	F	G	H UNEMPLOYMENT	DATE
Afghanistan	41.8								
Albania	50.4							15.8	2002
Algeria	35.0							27.3	2001
Angola	46.1								
Argentina	41.4		10	89	1	34	65	19.6	2002
Armenia	63.7							9.4	2002
Australia	51.0	3	10	86	6	31	63	6.3	2002
Austria	46.8	7	14	79	6	43	52	4.0	2002
Azerbaijan	45.7							1.3	2002
Bahamas	55.0	1	5	93	6	24	69	7.7	1998
Bangladesh	53.4	78	8	11	54	11	34	3.3 3	2000
Barbados	53.5	3	11	85	5	31	64	10.3	2002
Belarus	53.2							3.0	2002
Belgium	41.4	2	13	86	3	37	60	7.5	2002
Belize	35.2	6	12	81	37	19	44	12.8	1999
Benin	45.4								
Bhutan	48.0								
Bolivia	41.2	2	16	82	2	40	58	7.4	2000
Bosnia-Herzegovina	46.9								
Botswana	44.7							15.8	2000
Brazil	46.8	19	10	71	26	27	47	9.4	2001
Brunei	45.8								
Bulgaria	51.5							17.6	2002
Burkina Faso	49.0								
Burundi	55.0							14.0	1999
Cambodia	53.2							1.8	2001
Cameroon	40.9								
Canada	53.6	2	11	87	5	32	63	7.7	2002
Cape Verde	42.0								
Central African Rep.	48.3								
Chad	48.5								
Chile	41.6	5	14	82	19	31	49	7.8	2002
China	60.1							4.0	2002
Colombia	44.4		20	80	2	30	68	15.7	2002
Comoros	46.0								
Congo D.R.	41.5								
Congo R.	41.5								
Costa Rica	40.5	4	17	79	22	27	51	6.1	2001
Côte d'Ivoire	40.4								
Croatia	47.3	17	22	61	16	38	46	14.8	2002
Cuba	49.9								
Cyprus	48.7	10	18	71	11	30	58	3.3	2002
Czech Republic	55.9	4	28	69	6	49	48	7.3	2002
Denmark	54.4	2	15	83	5	37	58	4.7	2002
Dominica		14	10	72	31	24	40		
Dominican Republic	44.8	3	20	77	24	27	49	15.9	1997
Ecuador	40.0	2	14	84	11	26	63	9.3	2002
Egypt	39.0	35	9	56	29	25	46	9.2	2001
El Salvador	44.3	6	25	69	37	24	38	6.2	2002
Equatorial Guinea	41.9								
Eritrea	50.4								
Estonia	56.1	7	23	70	11	40	49	10.3	2002
Ethiopia	43.0	88	2	11	89	2	9		
Fiji	41.6							5.4	1995

WORKERS IN FIGURES

	A	B	C	D	E	F	G	H	UNEMPLOYMENT DATE
Finland	49.7	4	14	82	8	40	52	9.1	2002
France	45.4		13	86	2	35	63	8.9	2002
Gabon	45.3							18.0	1993
Gambia	50.7								
Germany	49.8	2	19	79	3	46	50	8.7	2002
Ghana	47.9								
Greece	43.4	20	12	67	16	29	54	9.6	2002
Grenada		10	12	77	17	32	46		
Guatemala	37.7	14	19	68	37	26	38	1.8	2002
Guinea	47.4								
Guinea-Bissau	46.9								
Guyana	44.5								
Haiti	43.9								
Honduras	38.6	9	25	67	50	21	30	4.2 4	2001
Hungary	47.8	4	25	71	9	42	48	5.8 2	2002
Iceland	56.5	5	15	80	12	34	53	3.3	2002
India	44.8								
Indonesia	49.2	42	16	42	41	21	39	9.1	2002
Iran	32.2							12.3	2002
Iraq	28.2								
Ireland	42.9	2	15	83	12	38	50	4.6	2002
Israel	44.0	1	13	86	3	35	61	10.3	2002
Italy	44.5	5	21	74	6	39	55	9.0	2002
Jamaica	53.1	10	9	81	30	26	45	16.0	1996
Japan	53.5	6	22	73	5	38	57	5.4	2002
Jordan	30.4								
Kazakhstan	49.4							9.3	2002
Kenya	52.0	16	10	75	20	23	57		
Korea, North	52.4								
Korea, South	51.6	13	19	68	10	34	56	3.1	2002
Kuwait	41.9							1.1	2002
Kyrgyzstan	44.1	53	8	38	52	14	34		
Laos	47.9								
Latvia	55.1	14	18	69	17	35	49	12.0	2002
Lebanon	36.1								
Lesotho	41.4								
Liberia	40.0								
Libya	28.8								
Lithuania	52.3	16	40	63	24	33	43	13.8	2002
Luxembourg	42.4							3.0	2002
Macedonia, TFYR	47.3							31.9	2002
Madagascar	47.4								
Malawi	48.1								
Malaysia	42.3	13	29	58	21	33	46	3.8	2002
Maldives	40.8								
Mali	48.9								
Malta	37.9							6.8	2002
Mauritania	46.3								
Mauritius	43.3	13	43	45	15	39	46	9.7	2002
Mexico	41.9	7	22	71	23	29	47	1.9	2002
Moldova	50.7							6.8	2002
Mongolia	50.9							3.4	2002
Morocco	40.8	6	40	54	6	32	63	18.3	2002
Mozambique	52.0								
Myanmar-Burma	53.5								
Namibia	41.3	39	8	52	38	19	43	33.8	2000
Nepal	46.7								
Netherlands	46.2	2	9	84	4	31	63	2.7	2001
New Zealand-Aotearoa	50.1	6	12	81	11	32	56	5.2	2002
Nicaragua	41.5							12.2	2002
Niger	47.1								
Nigeria	39.9	2	11	87	4	30	67		
Norway	51.8	2	9	88	6	33	61	3.9	2002
Oman	26.7								
Pakistan	38.1	66	11	23	41	20	39	7.8	2000
Panama	42.8	2	10	88	25	22	52	14.1	2002
Papua New Guinea	49.3								
Paraguay	40.1	3	10	87	7	31	62	14.7	2002
Peru	38.8	3	11	86	8	25	67	7.9	2001
Philippines	42.8	27	13	61	47	18	36	9.8	2001
Poland	51.6	19	21	60	19	41	39	19.9	2002
Portugal	50.7	14	24	62	11	44	45	5.1	2002
Puerto Rico	38.2							12.3	2002
Qatar	53.1								
Romania	48.1	45	22	33	39	33	29	8.4	2002
Russia	53.8	8	23	69	15	36	49	8.9	2001
Rwanda	59.1							0.6	1996
Saudi Arabia	33.1							4.6	2001
Senegal	44.9								
Serbia and Montenegro	48.1							13.8	2002
Sierra Leone	37.5								
Singapore	49.2		23	77		33	67	5.2	2002
Slovakia	54.9	5	26	69	10	49	42	18.5	2002
Slovenia	50.5	11	28	61	11	46	42	5.9	2002
Solomon Is.	51.3								
Somalia	42.8								
South Africa	39.9							30.0	2002
Spain	44.3	5	14	81	8	41	51	11.4	2002
Sri Lanka	44.3	49	22	27	38	23	37	8.7	2002
St Lucia		16	14	71	27	24	49		
Sudan	40.3								
Suriname	39.1	3	10	86	7	32	56	14.0 2	1999
Swaziland	37.1								
Sweden	53.8	1	12	87	4	38	59	4.0	2002
Switzerland	53.9	4	13	83	5	36	59	2.9	2002
Syria	32.9							11.7	2002
Tajikistan	40.6							2.7	1997
Tanzania	51.5							5.1	2001
Thailand	60.8	47	17	36	50	20	31	2.6	2001
Togo	41.6								
Trinidad and Tobago	45.6	3	13	83	11	37	52	10.8	2001
Tunisia	40.5							14.9	2002
Turkey	46.7	72	10	18	34	25	41	10.6	2002
Turkmenistan	44.3								
Uganda	49.1								
Ukraine	51.1							10.1	2002
United Arab Emirates	49.2							2.3	2000
United Kingdom	50.0	1	12	87	2	36	61	5.1	2002
United States	51.4	1	12	86	4	32	64	5.8	2002
Uruguay	46.2	1	14	85	6	34	61	17.0	2002
Uzbekistan	43.4							0.4	1995
Venezuela	41.7	2	13	85	16	29	55	15.8	2002
Vietnam	52.0								
Yemen	31.8							11.5	1999
Zambia	42.9								
Zimbabwe	46.6							6.0	1999

AID IN FIGURES

Total net official development assistance (ODA) disbursed, 2001. **Source:** Human Development Report 2003, UNDP.

A = As % of GNI

B = Millions $

The long-established UN target for aid donors is 0.7 per cent of GNI but this is only matched by five countries, with Denmark by far the most generous. The US gives a lower proportion of its national income in aid than any other donor country - though it still has the largest aid budget, simply because its economy is so huge.

	A	B		A	B		A	B
Australia	0.25	873	Greece	0.17	202	Portugal	0.25	268
Austria	0.29	533	Ireland	0.33	287	Spain	0.30	1,737
Belgium	0.37	867	Italy	0.15	1,627	Sweden	0.81	1,666
Canada	0.22	1,533	Japan	0.23	9,847	Switzerland	0.34	908
Denmark	1.03	1,634	Luxembourg	0.82	141	United Kingdom	0.32	4,579
Finland	0.32	389	Netherlands	0.82	3,172	United States	0.11	11,429
France	0.32	4,198	New Zealand-Aotearoa	0.25	112			
Germany	0.27	4,990	Norway	0.83	1,346			

DEBT IN FIGURES

A = Total external debt (million $), 2001. **Source:** World Development Indicators 2003, World Bank.

B = Debt service as % of exports, 2001. **Source:** World Development Indicators 2003, World Bank.

C = External debt $ per capita, 2001. Calculated from total external debt and total population. **Source:** World Development Indicators 2003, World Bank.

The country with the highest foreign debt per capita is the Caribbean island state of St Kitts-Nevis, closely followed by Malta, Argentina and Lebanon.

	A	B	C		A	B	C		A	B	C
Albania	1,094	2.2	350	Gambia	489	3.8	362	Pakistan	32,019	25.8	219
Algeria	22,503	21.2	732	Georgia	1,714	7.8	328	Panama	8,245	12.9	2,742
Angola	9,600	27.6	752	Ghana	6,759	13.0	338	Papua New Guinea	2,521	12.7	462
Argentina	136,709	66.3	3,643	Grenada	215	8.2	2,664	Paraguay	2,817	12.5	503
Armenia	1,001	8.3	324	Guatemala	4,526	9.0	386	Peru	27,512	22.0	1,044
Azerbaijan	1,219	5.3	148	Guinea	3,254	12.3	395	Philippines	52,356	18.7	679
Bangladesh	15,216	7.3	108	Guinea-Bissau	668	41.1	475	Poland	62,393	28.0	1,614
Barbados	701	4.5	2,610	Guyana	1,406	6.6	1,846	Romania	11,653	18.8	519
Belarus	869	2.8	87	Haiti	1,250	5.2	154	Russia	152,649	14.5	1,054
Belize	708	25.1	2,886	Honduras	5,051	11.2	763	Rwanda	1,283	11.4	159
Benin	1,665	7.9	261	Hungary	30,289	37.2	3,039	Samoa	204	10.8	1,170
Bhutan	265	4.2	125	India	97,320	11.8	94	São Tomé and Príncipe	313	22.9	2,045
Bolivia	4,682	31.1	552	Indonesia	135,704	23.6	633	Senegal	3,461	13.3	360
Bosnia-Herzegovina	2,226	19.1	547	Iran	7,483	4.9	111	Serbia and Montenegro	11,740	2.4	
Botswana	370	1.7	211	Jamaica	4,956	14.3	1,904	Seychelles	215	2.6	2,700
Brazil	226,362	75.4	1,301	Jordan	7,479	10.7	1,443	Sierra Leone	1,188	102.0	260
Bulgaria	9,615	17.3	1,197	Kazakhstan	14,372	31.6	925	Slovakia	11,121	17.0	2,062
Burkina Faso	1,490	11.8	122	Kenya	5,833	15.4	188	Solomon Is.	163	6.9	361
Burundi	1,065	39.8	166	Korea, South	110,109	13.9	2,336	Somalia	2,532		279
Cambodia	2,704	1.3	201	Kyrgyzstan	1,717	29.8	344	South Africa	24,050	11.6	541
Cameroon	8,338	12.6	540	Laos	2,495	9.0	462	Sri Lanka	8,529	9.7	455
Cape Verde	360	5.5	808	Latvia	5,710	13.6	2,429	St Kitts-Nevis	189	12.6	4,505
Central African Rep.	822	11.9	218	Lebanon	12,450	43.7	3,520	St Lucia	238	6.5	1,620
Chad	1,104	7.9	136	Lesotho	592	12.4	330	St Vincent	194	7.8	1,641
Chile	38,360	28.1	2,488	Liberia	1,987	0.5	641	Sudan	15,348	2.3	477
China	170,110	7.8	132	Lithuania	5,248	31.0	1,506	Swaziland	308	2.7	291
Colombia	36,699	35.3	857	Macedonia, TFYR	1,423	12.9	699	Syria	21,305	3.4	1,256
Comoros	246	3.6	339	Madagascar	4,160	43.3	253	Tajikistan	1,086	11.2	177
Congo D.R.	11,392	1.7		Malawi	2,602	7.8	224	Tanzania	6,676	10.3	188
Congo R.	4,496	4.2	1,269	Malaysia	43,351	6.0	1,845	Thailand	67,384	25.1	1,095
Costa Rica	4,586	9.0	1,143	Maldives	235	4.6	783	Togo	1,406	6.6	300
Côte d'Ivoire	11,582	13.5	719	Mali	2,890	8.8	236	Tonga	63	2.8	624
Croatia	10,742	27.9	2,417	Malta	1,531	3.5	3,916	Trinidad and Tobago	2,422	4.7	1,872
Czech Republic	21,691	11.2	2,115	Mauritania	2,164	22.7	795	Tunisia	10,884	12.9	1,131
Djibouti	262	5.5	385	Mauritius	1,724	6.9	1,440	Turkey	115,118	40.0	1,661
Dominica	207	11.5	2,642	Mexico	158,290	26.1	1,576	Turkmenistan	2,259	31.8	
Dominican Republic	5,093	6.0	600	Moldova	1,214	19.3	284	Uganda	3,733	7.0	154
Ecuador	13,910	21.4	1,103	Mongolia	885	7.7	350	Ukraine	12,811	10.6	260
Egypt	29,234	8.9	423	Morocco	16,962	17.8	573	Uruguay	9,706	36.3	2,883
El Salvador	4,683	6.3	742	Mozambique	4,466	3.4	245	Uzbekistan	4,627	25.9	183
Equatorial Guinea	239	0.1	510	Myanmar-Burma	5,670	3.1	118	Vanuatu	66	1.0	326
Eritrea	410	1.7	106	Nepal	2,700	4.9	112	Venezuela	34,660	24.6	1,400
Estonia	2,852	7.4	2,108	Nicaragua	6,391	26.2	1,228	Vietnam	12,578	6.7	159
Ethiopia	5,697	18.5	85	Niger	1,555	6.8	140	Yemen	4,954	4.9	266
Fiji	188	2.0	229	Nigeria	31,119	12.4	264	Zambia	5,671	11.7	536
Gabon	3,409	13.9	2,658	Oman	6,025	14.2	2,242	Zimbabwe	3,780	6.8	296

LITERACY

Adult literacy rate (%), 2000. Source: The State of the World's Children 2004, UNICEF.

A = Total

B = male

C = female

The countries with the lowest literacy rates in the world are the West African states of Niger (just 16%) and Burkina Faso (24%). The biggest gap between male and female literacy rates is to be found in Yemen, the poorest of the Arab states - a massive 43% - though there is also a 35% male-female divide in the Himalayan kingdom of Nepal.

	A	B	C		A	B	C		A	B	C
Afghanistan	36	51	21	Gambia	37	44	30	Nicaragua	64	64	64
Algeria	63	75	51	Georgia	100	100	99	Niger	16	24	9
Antigua	82	80	83	Ghana	72	80	63	Nigeria	64	72	56
Argentina	97	97	97	Greece	97	99	96	Niue	81	80	83
Armenia	98	99	98	Guatemala	69	76	61	Oman	72	80	62
Azerbaijan	97	99	96	Guinea	41	55	27	Pakistan	43	57	28
Bahamas	95	95	96	Guinea-Bissau	38	54	24	Panama	92	93	91
Bahrain	88	91	83	Guyana	99	99	98	Papua New Guinea	64	71	57
Bangladesh	40	49	30	Haiti	50	52	48	Paraguay	93	94	92
Barbados	100	100	100	Honduras	75	75	75	Peru	90	95	85
Belarus	100	100	100	Hungary	99	100	99	Philippines	95	95	95
Belize	93	93	93	India	57	68	45	Poland	100	100	100
Benin	37	52	24	Indonesia	87	92	82	Portugal	92	95	90
Bhutan	47	61	34	Iran	76	83	69	Qatar	94	94	94
Bolivia	85	92	79	Iraq	39	55	23	Romania	98	99	97
Bosnia-Herzegovina	93	98	89	Israel	95	97	93	Russia	100	100	99
Botswana	77	75	80	Italy	98	99	98	Rwanda	67	74	60
Brazil	87	87	87	Jamaica	87	83	91	Samoa	99	99	98
Brunei	92	95	88	Jordan	90	95	84	Saudi Arabia	76	83	67
Bulgaria	98	99	98	Kazakhstan	99	100	99	Senegal	37	47	28
Burkina Faso	24	34	14	Kenya	82	89	76	Serbia and Montenegro	98	99	97
Burundi	48	56	40	Korea, North	98	99	96	Sierra Leone	36	51	23
Cambodia	68	80	57	Korea, South	98	99	96	Singapore	92	96	88
Cameroon	71	79	64	Kuwait	82	84	80	Slovakia	100	100	100
Cape Verde	74	85	66	Laos	65	76	53	Slovenia	100	100	100
Central African Rep.	47	60	35	Latvia	100	100	100	South Africa	85	86	85
Chad	43	52	34	Lebanon	86	92	80	Spain	98	99	97
Chile	96	96	96	Lesotho	83	73	94	Sri Lanka	92	94	89
China	85	92	78	Liberia	54	70	37	Sudan	58	69	46
Colombia	92	92	92	Libya	80	91	68	Suriname	94	96	93
Comoros	56	63	49	Lithuania	100	100	100	Swaziland	80	81	79
Congo D.R.	61	73	50	Macedonia, TFYR	96	97	94	Syria	74	88	60
Congo R.	81	88	74	Madagascar	67	74	60	Tajikistan	99	100	99
Costa Rica	96	96	96	Malawi	60	75	47	Tanzania	75	84	67
Côte d'Ivoire	49	60	37	Malaysia	87	91	83	Thailand	96	97	94
Croatia	98	99	97	Maldives	97	97	97	Togo	57	72	43
Cuba	97	97	97	Mali	26	36	16	Trinidad and Tobago	98	99	98
Cyprus	97	99	95	Malta	92	91	93	Tunisia	71	81	61
Djibouti	65	76	54	Mauritania	40	51	30	Turkey	85	93	77
Dominican Republic	84	84	84	Mauritius	85	88	81	Uganda	67	78	57
Ecuador	92	93	90	Mexico	91	93	89	Ukraine	100	100	100
Egypt	55	67	44	Micronesia	67	66	67	United Arab Emirates	76	75	79
El Salvador	79	82	76	Moldova	99	100	98	Uruguay	98	97	98
Equatorial Guinea	83	93	74	Mongolia	98	99	98	Uzbekistan	99	100	99
Eritrea	56	67	45	Morocco	49	62	36	Venezuela	93	93	92
Estonia	100	100	100	Mozambique	44	60	29	Vietnam	93	95	91
Ethiopia	39	47	31	Myanmar-Burma	85	89	81	Yemen	46	68	25
Fiji	93	95	91	Namibia	82	83	81	Zambia	78	85	72
Gabon	71	80	62	Nepal	42	59	24	Zimbabwe	89	93	85

WOMEN IN POLITICAL AND ECONOMIC LIFE

A = % of women in labor force, 2002. **Source:** World Development Indicators 2003, World Bank.

B = % of professional and technical workers, UNDP 2003. **Source:** Human Development Report 2003, UNDP.

C = Female legislators, senior officials and managers (as % of total) UNDP 2003. **Source:** Human Development Report 2003, UNDP.

D = Women's earned income share (%), UNDP 2003. **Source:** Human Development Report 2003, UNDP.

E = % of ministerial posts occupied by women, 2000. **Source:** Human Development Report 2003, UNDP.

F = % of parliamentary seats occupied by women, 2003. **Source:** Human Development Report 2003, UNDP.

The only country in the world where women make up a bigger percentage of legislators, senior officials and managers than men is the Philippines, with 58%.

Country	A	B	C	D	E	F
Afghanistan	35.8					
Albania	41.5				15.0	5.7
Algeria	29.0				0.0	6.0
Angola	46.2				14.7	15.5
Antigua					0.0	8.3
Argentina	34.4				7.3	31.3
Armenia	48.6					3.1
Australia	44.0	45	25	0.70	19.5	26.5
Austria	40.4	48	29	0.50	31.3	30.6
Azerbaijan	44.7				2.6	10.5
Bahamas	47.4	56	31	0.64	16.7	23.2
Bahrain	21.6					6.3
Bangladesh	42.5	25	8	0.56	9.5	2.0
Barbados	45.9	55	40	0.61	14.3	20.4
Belarus	48.9				25.7	18.4
Belgium	41.1	50	19	0.44	18.5	24.9
Belize	24.3	53	33	0.24	11.1	13.5
Benin	48.3				10.5	6.0
Bhutan	40.0					9.3
Bolivia	38.0	40	36	0.45		17.8
Bosnia-Herzegovina	38.2					12.3
Botswana	45.1	52	35	0.60	26.7	17.0
Brazil	35.5	62			0.0	9.1
Brunei	36.3				0.0	
Bulgaria	48.0				18.8	26.3
Burkina Faso	46.5				8.6	11.7
Burundi	48.6				4.5	18.5
Cambodia	51.5	33	14	0.77	7.1	9.3
Cameroon	38.2				5.8	8.9
Canada	46.0	53	35	0.63	24.3	23.6
Cape Verde	38.8				35.0	11.1
Central African Rep.						7.3
Chad	44.8					5.8
Chile	34.5	50	24	0.38	25.6	10.1
China	45.2	.			5.1	21.8
Colombia	39.1	49	38	0.47	47.4	10.8
Comoros	42.2					
Congo D.R.	43.3					
Congo R.	43.5					11.1
Costa Rica	31.6	28	53	0.38	28.6	35.1
Côte d'Ivoire	33.6				9.1	8.5
Croatia	44.4	50	25	0.55	16.2	16.2
Cuba	39.9				10.7	36.0
Cyprus	38.9	43	18	0.47		10.7
Czech Republic	47.2	53	26	0.55		15.7
Denmark	46.5	51	21	0.71	45.0	38.0
Djibouti					5.0	10.8
Dominica					0.0	18.8
Dominican Republic	31.4	49	31	0.36		15.4
East Timor	44.7					
Ecuador	28.7	44	25	0.30	20.0	16.0
Egypt	31.0	29	10	0.39	6.1	2.4
El Salvador	37.3	47	33	0.35	15.4	9.5
Equatorial Guinea	35.7					5.0
Eritrea	47.4				11.8	22.0
Estonia	48.9	70	35	0.63	14.3	17.8
Ethiopia	41.0				22.2	7.8
Fiji	31.8				20.7	5.7
Finland	48.2	57	28	0.70	44.4	36.5
France	45.3				37.9	11.7
Gabon	44.8				12.1	11.0
Gambia	45.2				30.8	13.2
Georgia	46.8	60	23	0.41	9.7	7.2
Germany	42.4	50	27	0.57	35.7	31.4
Ghana	50.4				8.6	9.0
Greece	38.2	47	25	0.45	7.1	8.7
Grenada					25.0	17.9
Guatemala	30.1				7.1	8.8
Guinea	47.2				11.1	19.3
Guinea-Bissau	40.5				8.3	7.8
Guyana	34.4					20.0
Haiti	42.8				18.2	9.1
Honduras	32.6	51	36	0.37	33.3	5.5
Hungary	44.8	61	34	0.58	35.9	9.8
Iceland	45.4	55	31	0.63	33.3	34.9
India	32.5				10.1	9.3
Indonesia	41.2				5.9	8.0
Iran	28.4				9.4	4.1
Iraq	20.4					
Ireland	35.0	49	28	0.40	18.8	14.2
Israel	41.7	54	27	0.53	6.1	15.0
Italy	38.7	44	19	0.45	17.6	10.3
Jamaica	46.2				12.5	13.6
Japan	41.7	45	9	0.45	5.7	10.0
Jordan	25.6				0.0	3.3
Kazakhstan	47.1				17.5	8.6
Kenya	46.1				1.4	7.1
Korea, North	43.3					
Korea, South	41.8	34	5	0.46	6.5	5.9
Kuwait	32.1				0.0	0.0
Kyrgyzstan	47.2					6.7
Laos					10.2	22.9
Latvia	50.5	68	38	0.70	6.7	21.0
Lebanon	30.1				0.0	2.3
Lesotho	37.0					17.0
Liberia	39.6					
Libya	24.0					12.5
Lithuania	48.0	69	47	0.66	18.9	10.6
Luxembourg	36.8				28.6	16.7
Macedonia, TFYR	42.0				10.9	18.3
Madagascar	44.7				12.5	6.4
Malawi	48.4				11.8	9.3
Malaysia	38.3	45	20	0.47		14.5
Maldives	43.5	40	15			6.0
Mali	46.1				33.3	10.2
Malta	28.3				5.3	9.2
Mauritania	43.5				13.6	3.0
Mauritius	33.0				9.1	5.7
Mexico	33.8	40	25	0.38	11.1	15.9
Moldova	48.4	66	37	0.65		12.9
Mongolia	47.1				10.0	10.5
Morocco	34.9				4.9	6.1
Mozambique	48.4					30.0
Myanmar-Burma	43.4					
Namibia	41.0	55	30	0.51	16.3	21.4
Nepal	40.5				14.8	7.9
Netherlands	40.9	48	26	0.53	31.0	33.3
Netherlands Antilles	42.8					
New Zealand-Aotearoa	45.2	53	38	0.68	44.0	29.2
Nicaragua	36.6				23.1	20.7
Niger	44.3				10.0	1.2
Nigeria	36.7				22.6	3.3
Norway	46.5	48	26	0.65	42.1	36.4
Oman	18.9					
Pakistan	29.5	26	9	0.32		20.6
Palestine		32	11			..
Panama	35.7	46	33	0.42	20.0	9.9
Papua New Guinea	42.4				0.0	0.9
Paraguay	30.4	54	23	0.33		8.0
Peru	31.9	44	27	0.26	16.2	18.3
Philippines	38.0	62	58	0.59		17.2
Poland	46.5	60	32	0.62	18.7	20.7
Portugal	44.1	50	32	0.53	9.7	19.1
Puerto Rico	37.8					
Qatar	16.4				0.0	
Romania	44.5	57	29	0.58	20.0	9.9
Russia	49.2	64	37	0.64		6.4
Rwanda	48.7				13.0	25.7
Samoa					7.7	6.1
São Tomé and Príncipe						9.1
Saudi Arabia	17.7					
Senegal	42.6				15.6	19.2
Serbia and Montenegro	43.1					
Seychelles					23.1	29.4
Sierra Leone	37.1				8.1	14.5
Singapore	39.2	43	24	0.50	5.7	11.8
Slovakia	47.7	61	31	0.65	19.0	19.3
Slovenia	46.6	54	31	0.62	15.0	12.2
Solomon Is.	46.4					0.0
Somalia	43.4					
South Africa	37.9				38.1	30.0
Spain	37.5	45	32	0.44	17.6	26.6
Sri Lanka	36.9	49	4	0.50		4.4
St Kitts-Nevis					0.0	13.3
St Lucia					18.2	20.7
St Vincent					0.0	22.7
Sudan	30.0				5.1	9.7
Suriname	34.2	51	28			17.6
Swaziland	37.8				12.5	6.3
Sweden	48.1	49	30	0.68	55.0	45.3
Switzerland	40.8	43	24	0.50	28.6	22.4
Syria	27.6				11.1	10.4
Tajikistan	45.2					12.4
Tanzania	49.0					22.3
Thailand	46.2	55	27	0.61	5.7	9.6
Togo	40.0				7.4	7.4
Trinidad and Tobago	34.9	51	40	0.45	8.7	25.4
Tunisia	32.1				10.0	11.5
Turkey	38.1	31	8	0.46	0.0	4.4
Turkmenistan	45.9					26.0
Uganda	47.6				27.1	24.7
Ukraine	48.8	63	37	0.53		5.3
United Arab Emirates	15.9	25	8	0.21		0.0
United Kingdom	44.3	43	30	0.60	33.3	17.1
United States	46.2	54	46	0.62	31.8	14.0
Uruguay	42.2	52	37	0.52		11.5
Uzbekistan	46.9				4.4	7.2
Vanuatu						1.9
Venezuela	35.4	58	24	0.41	0.0	9.7
Vietnam	48.7					27.3
Yemen	28.3	15	4	0.30		0.7
Zambia	44.6				6.2	12.0
Zimbabwe	44.5				36.0	10.0

The MDGs are not 'mission impossible'

THE PURPOSE OF THE MILLENNIUM DEVELOPMENT GOALS (MDGs) IS TO KEEP THE EYES OF THE WORLD FOCUSED ON HUMAN DEVELOPMENT AND ON FUNDAMENTAL SOCIAL AND ECONOMIC RIGHTS. ALTHOUGH ALL MEMBER STATES OF THE UN HAVE PLEDGED TO: 'SPARE NO EFFORT TO FREE OUR FELLOW MEN, WOMEN AND CHILDREN FROM THE ABJECT AND DEHUMANIZING CONDITIONS OF EXTREME POVERTY', GLOBAL PROGRESS TOWARDS THE MDGS HAS BEEN SLOW AND VERY UNEVEN.

The Millennium Declaration was in part prompted by the slow progress observed in the 1990s, as well as by the growing realization that most of the progress had by-passed the most vulnerable and disadvantaged segments in society. Indeed, the countries and people who most needed progress usually saw the least of it. The number of countries that saw a decline in their human development index (HDI) in the 1990s rose to 21; up from only four during the 1980s. Most of these reversals stemmed from the HIV/AIDS pandemic and economic crises, particularly in sub-Saharan Africa and in the transition economies.

In short, it is hard to argue that the glass is more than half full. At the current pace, most countries will fail to achieve most MDG targets. Yet, there have been several success stories in recent years, including in Africa. They confirm that the MDGs are not 'mission impossible', provided there is determined political leadership and awakened public interest.

On the education front, an estimated 115 million children are 'out of school' and perhaps three times as many are 'out of education' in the sense that they have not acquired basic literacy and numeracy. Failure to meet the education target will reduce the chances of reaching other MDGs because of its instrumental value for enhancing productivity and gender equality. On the positive side, the gender gap in primary enrolment has narrowed, although an estimated 60 per cent of the out-of-school children are girls. Africa, South Asia and the Middle East are the regions that fall short of the target.

In 2000, more than ten million children under the age of five died, mostly due to preventable causes such as pneumonia, measles, malaria and malnutrition. In sub-Saharan Africa, where almost half of the under-five deaths occur, there has been no significant progress since 1990. Actually, the HIV pandemic is pushing the child mortality rate upwards - an unprecedented trend after decades of steady decline.

HIV/AIDS has turned into the leading cause of death in sub-Saharan Africa. Worldwide, it numbers four in the league of major fatal diseases. Other regions are also experiencing rapid increases in the incidence of HIV, including South Asia, the CIS and the Caribbean. The pandemic may prove to be the greatest impediment to achieving the MDGs by 2015. In addition, the global MDG targets may not have been set in a way that is conducive to success. By and large, global MDG targets were set on the premise that the global trends observed in the 1970s and 1980s would continue till 2015 - ie during the lifetime of one generation. While a separate target for halting and reversing HIV was inserted in the Millennium Declaration, the quantitative targets for health, water, education, income poverty, and hunger were set as if no HIV pandemic existed, thereby ignoring the undeniable fact that HIV was already slowing down global progress in health and beyond.

Globally, every minute one woman dies of a pregnancy- or childbirth-related cause. It is not possible with available data to reliably assess progress, but there is little indication of measurable progress anywhere in the developing world sufficient to meet the target except in a few countries.

The goal of enhancing environmental sustainability has not seen much progress either. Around 2.4 billion people do not have access to improved sanitation and an estimated 1.2 billion people do not have access to an improved source of water. The picture is clouded by measurement problems and by the fact that much of the progress of the 1990s may not be sustainable as many parts in the world face growing shortages.

If the MDGs are to be achieved, all partners must keep their end of the bargain. Developed countries need to fulfil their commitment to increase development assistance while relieving the debt burden of poor nations. They must also keep the promises of the Doha round of international trade negotiations, including reducing agricultural subsidies, which have been undercutting livelihoods in developing countries. Overall, progress towards the global partnership for development has been disheartening in terms of more aid, fairer trade and steeper debt relief. Ultimately, the financial cost of reaching the MDGs is modest, whereas the benefits that beckon are enormous.

Despite slow progress so far, the MDGs remain technically do-able and financially affordable. Experience shows that determined leadership and awakened public interest can put the world back on the MDG track. This will require pro-poor policies and development strategies that are truly home-grown. Hence, there is an urgent need to scale up action on behalf of all parties involved. Small is beautiful, but big has become necessary. The challenges for the global community are to generate stronger political commitment and to mobilize more financial support around priorities that are set by national stakeholders, including civil-society organizations and the private sector.

To achieve the MDGs, pro-poor policies need to be placed at the centre of any national and international development framework. In addition, stronger support is required from developed countries and international agencies. Hence, more and better aid and steeper debt relief will be indispensable, especially - but not exclusively - for the least developed countries.

In order to advance the MDG agenda, civil society must be nurtured, public interest awakened, ambition stirred and expectations raised. The MDGs encourage all stakeholders to think global but to act local. Thus, the targets need to be tailored to the national context and local priorities. Targets must be customized through an inclusive dialogue because only genuine participation will result in a consensus centered on a pro-poor development agenda. Furthermore, monitoring and good statistics must be used to inform political leaders, parliamentarians, journalists, NGO activists and the general public. Monitoring must go beyond averages and aggregates. Data must be broken down according to gender, age, geographical location and socio-economic groups. Comparing the performance of neighboring localities and communities can be a catalyst for change.The task in hand is to raise everyone's interest in the MDGs so that people can hold their government accountable vis-à-vis the promises made. It is not too late to realize the dream by 2015. ∎

Jan Vandemoortele and Elham Seyedsayamdost, from the Poverty Group, UNDP, for *The World Guide 2005-2006.*

David and Goliath:
the emergence of the Group of 20

THE EMERGENCE OF THE GROUP OF 20 (G-20 OR G-20 PLUS), WITHIN THE CONTEXT OF THE FIFTH
WORLD TRADE ORGANIZATION (WTO) MINISTERIAL CONFERENCE IN 2003 HAS TURNED INTO
AN HISTORICAL EVENT SINCE IT OPENED THE DOORS TO A NEW KIND OF MULTILATERAL TRADE
REGIME AND TO ECONOMIC COOPERATION BETWEEN COUNTRIES FROM THE SOUTH.

Southern governments have decided to join forces to advance towards more equitable world trade conditions. The so-called Group of 20 (G-20) was born in August 2003 and appeared on the scene during the fifth World Trade Organization (WTO) Ministerial Conference, in September 2003 in Cancun, Mexico. It was exclusively focused on agricultural issues, particularly lobbying to eliminate agricultural subsidies. Even though it was initially centered on positions held by Brazil, India, China and South Africa, it has involved countries from all continents, amounting to more than half of the world's population.

The Cancun conference failed to reach agreement. One of the main effects of this failure was that a negative agreement was avoided, thus illustrating the unfair relations in international trade, in general, and in the agricultural sector, in particular.

Many Southern countries were empowered by the experience, especially the coalitions of African, Asia-Caribbean-Pacific and G-20 nations. At the same time, the opposition of several Northern countries to the South's development became evident. For many African and Asian nations, whose participation in global trade is minimal, there is no sense in taking part in a multilateral trade system which only serves to legitimate the rules which exclude them.

The Cancun collapse was followed by a deterioration of the WTO's image, which confirms the growing delegitimization of multilateral regulatory bodies such as the International Monetary Fund (IMF) and the World Bank (WB). Rich nations tried to force the pace by threatening retaliation along with trade accords and aid offers. The poor nations said no.

As a result, the whole multilateral trade system was damaged and we have yet to gauge the real impact. For many, this may strengthen the trend of regional and multilateral accords, but it is also possible that world trade may become fragmented into asymmetrical bilateral relations, where the strongest dominate.

The conference in September 2003 left the WTO's weaknesses out in the open and delegitimized the power of the strongest, but left behind the hope that if governments commit themselves to productive and inclusive development initiatives, changes are possible. If the WTO does not recover from the setback in Cancun, there is a risk of a new wave of protectionism and global trade fragmentation. Then there would need to be an urgent search for alternative forums of multilateral cooperation.

A creative strategy
It is very likely that the unity of the G-20 could become increasingly compromised as agricultural issues are discussed. Here, there are three divergent and distinct tendencies within the G-20. First, there are the export-oriented countries (part of the Cairns Group of 18 agricultural-exporting countries that oppose agricultural subsidies and other trade barriers, formed in 1986), whose main concern is internal support and subsidy policies for developed nations' exports. Second, there are countries such as China and India, and some smaller ones (related to those two giants) whose main concern is to protect their farmers, the great masses of small and marginal producers, from the whims of international agricultural market forces. And third, there are countries like Egypt, whose main concern is the eventual disappearance of cheap subsidized food imports from the powerful North.

If trade powers apply intelligent measures to satisfy the first and third tendencies, the second group could be isolated. Even China, with its thriving trade surplus with the US, could be forced to act with caution, taking care not to upset the momentum of the negotiations by insisting on strong positions in any sector under negotiation. The possibility that the second tendency might lose its cohesion could lead to adverse consequences for countries such as India, setting them back to pre-G-20 times.

It is therefore in the best interests of India and other G-20-founding nations to attempt to persuade the coalition to formulate a creative strategy that reconciles these opposing tendencies. It is clear that even if the first tendency leaves the agricultural model uncontested, the objective roles of the other two are not compatible with this model.

A change of paradigm?
After Cancun, the WTO entered a kind of slumber due to the confrontation between the Northern countries - which have been imposing their rules for years - and the countries of the South, which for the first time managed to hold firm to their positions. According to some analysts, the G-20 is the only hope the WTO has of remaining in place. Mario Marconini, director of the Brazilian Center for International Relations, believes the WTO negotiations have lacked leadership for years and especially now that the US abandoned its traditional position and has become protectionist in the textile, agricultural, and steel sectors.

Washington always led negotiations such as the Uruguay Round, which was finalized in 1994 and gave way to the WTO, and the current Development Round initiated in Doha, 2001. But the US is no longer interested in multilateralism, because its private sector no longer wants markets to be open.

Marconini underscores that since the European Union (EU) never leads but only reacts to these rounds, and is currently more concerned with its own integration and the incorporation of more countries, the multilateral trade system depends on the strength of developing countries to thrust negotiations forward. And, according to many critics, the Uruguay Round was wrongly implemented, harming developing countries, especially in the agricultural realm, but also in the textile sector. After the Cancun conference, the WTO Director General, Supachai Panitchpakdi recognized the importance of the G-20 in lifting the negotiations out of their quandary.

Marconini adds that the G-20 may be regarded as a laboratory in which tests are made to achieve major reductions in agricultural subsidies, with the advantage that all its members paid the price for opening up their markets - as China did to join the WTO - and now want something in exchange.

The G-20 started off with 20 members, then three more joined, but by the time of the WTO Ministerial Conference, Panama was no longer a member. It then became known as the Group of 22 (G-22). Its membership has varied, but the largest economies have always been present. The G-20 plus included some members that do not belong to the Cairns Group, but which showed no cohesion or flexibility in Cancun when replying to the reduction of subsidies proposed by the US and the EU. Brazil made concessions to China and India, demanding more access to their markets. A major obstacle that prevents developing countries from importing more is not tariffs, but the low buying power of their populations. That is why lowering tariffs, as the US does, does not make sense.

The Cancun failure, together with the appearance of the G-20, points to a change of paradigm, a role reversal, with developing countries leading the struggle for trade liberalization, opposed by the rich countries who once disciplined 19th-century industry but want to protect the industry of the 21st century. ∎

INTERNATIONAL TRADE

A = Exports (millions $), 2002. **Source:** World Development Indicators 2003, World Bank.
B = Imports (millions $), 2002. **Source:** World Development Indicators 2003, World Bank.

The US trade deficit of $364 billion dwarfs any other. But the deficits of small Pacific island states such as Kiribati and the Marshall Islands are much higher in percentage terms.

	A	B	Date		A	B	Date
Albania	923,466,368	2,057,503,488	2002	Cyprus	4,112,425,728	4,464,793,088	1999
Algeria	18,629,492,736	13,044,016,128	2002	Czech Republic	40,344,735,744	41,902,632,960	2001
Angola	7,057,233,408	5,887,914,496	2001	Denmark	73,654,378,496	63,294,304,256	2001
Antigua	469,814,816	541,296,320	2001	Djibouti	246,514,080	347,224,736	2000
Argentina	30,694,342,656	27,315,230,720	2001	Dominica	134,651,856	167,918,512	2001
Armenia	691,862,400	1,084,603,520	2002	Dominican Republic	5,071,758,848	6,800,975,872	2001
Australia	88,780,496,896	88,370,601,984	2000	Ecuador	5,613,000,192	6,608,000,000	2001
Austria	98,444,402,688	99,140,501,504	2001	Egypt	16,396,546,048	21,014,104,064	2002
Azerbaijan	2,306,297,344	3,198,275,840	2002	El Salvador	3,976,699,904	5,891,599,872	2001
Bahrain	6,403,893,760	4,694,539,776	2001	Equatorial Guinea	463,766,848	790,742,848	1998
Bangladesh	6,849,999,872	9,061,000,192	2002	Eritrea	118,198,544	530,638,560	2002
Barbados	1,311,092,224	1,447,322,624	2001	Estonia	5,684,724,736	5,943,610,880	2002
Belarus	8,290,245,120	8,722,540,544	2001	Ethiopia	909,425,088	2,004,940,544	2002
Belgium	193,830,928,384	186,181,795,840	2001	Fiji	1,131,571,712	1,034,910,912	2000
Belize	443,649,984	596,600,000	2001	Finland	48,804,040,704	38,162,522,112	2001
Benin	385,023,744	719,402,432	2002	France	365,625,344,000	345,071,648,768	2001
Bhutan	122,238,576	228,773,504	2001	French Polynesia	168,811,808	835,298,176	2000
Bolivia	1,461,856,256	1,951,777,408	2001	Gabon	2,956,725,504	1,961,710,720	2002
Bosnia-Herzegovina	1,410,342,784	2,658,416,640	2002	Gambia	208,986,000	267,979,760	2002
Botswana	3,295,568,640	3,222,602,496	2002	Georgia	900,958,016	1,301,694,976	2002
Brazil	67,141,423,104	72,338,833,408	2001	Germany	645,542,313,984	610,571,714,560	2001
Bulgaria	7,995,599,872	9,297,021,952	2002	Ghana	3,068,816,384	4,042,381,568	2002
Burkina Faso	288,240,160	720,241,728	2002	Greece	27,966,531,584	36,862,779,392	2000
Burundi	47,220,560	136,019,456	2002	Grenada	233,940,736	279,107,392	2001
Cambodia	1,813,941,632	2,091,241,728	2001	Guatemala	3,817,200,896	5,746,100,736	2001
Cameroon	2,464,675,328	2,533,831,936	2002	Guinea	868,281,856	1,004,446,080	2002
Canada	304,276,111,360	268,354,502,656	2001	Guinea-Bissau	81,032,416	146,565,776	2001
Cape Verde	145,625,520	322,043,168	2001	Guyana	662,986,112	777,155,904	2001
Central African Rep.	128,555,984	176,942,736	2002	Haiti	468,847,552	1,246,721,024	2001
Chad	234,867,680	1,217,667,712	2002	Honduras	2,447,399,936	3,511,500,032	2001
Chile	23,042,508,800	21,700,268,032	2001	Hungary	31,400,114,176	32,511,571,968	2001
China	332,366,807,040	313,802,293,248	2002	Iceland	3,117,863,680	3,154,049,280	2001
Colombia	15,983,960,064	15,693,706,240	2001	India	78,155,825,152	82,908,504,064	2002
Comoros	37,724,196	78,557,008	2002	Indonesia	61,210,357,760	49,363,251,200	2002
Congo D.R.	1,047,449,472	1,223,523,072	2002	Iran	28,847,622,144	19,065,970,688	2002
Congo R.	2,309,221,376	1,512,220,672	2002	Ireland	98,540,503,040	83,144,671,232	2001
Costa Rica	6,899,774,976	7,258,940,416	2001	Israel	44,146,860,032	51,812,720,640	2000
Côte d'Ivoire	4,448,260,096	3,701,395,200	2002	Italy	307,804,667,904	290,358,034,432	2001
Croatia	9,465,854,976	10,690,798,592	2001	Jamaica	3,228,048,128	4,344,316,928	2001

	A	B	Date		A	B	Date
Japan	432,547,299,328	406,428,418,048	2001	Portugal	34,733,293,568	45,286,305,792	2001
Jordan	4,192,499,968	6,664,900,096	2002	Puerto Rico	54,836,199,424	68,198,600,704	2001
Kanaky-New Caledonia	399,928,544	1,008,558,912	1999	Qatar	4,079,670,272	4,052,197,888	1997
Kazakhstan	11,128,787,968	11,937,626,112	2002	Romania	15,518,815,232	18,803,372,032	2002
Kenya	3,097,598,464	3,835,494,144	2002	Russia	108,762,718,208	78,024,540,160	2002
Kiribati	4,263,235	38,694,852	1992	Rwanda	140,397,312	434,691,040	2002
Korea, South	190,740,938,752	183,884,988,416	2002	Samoa	77,149,512	193,254,368	2000
Kuwait	17,952,397,312	12,266,057,728	2001	São Tomé and Príncipe	18,851,284	41,655,508	2002
Kyrgyzstan	629,699,968	690,700,032	2002	Saudi Arabia	78,213,619,712	45,588,783,104	2001
Laos	466,700,000	612,099,968	1998	Senegal	1,448,400,000	1,833,299,968	2002
Latvia	3,843,054,848	4,525,592,064	2002	Serbia and Montenegro	2,854,000,128	5,724,000,256	2002
Lebanon	2,399,460,352	7,064,828,416	2002	Seychelles	535,317,728	608,225,024	2002
Lesotho	397,878,656	704,174,720	2002	Sierra Leone	126,600,000	333,500,000	2002
Libya	12,139,646,976	5,278,960,640	2000	Slovakia	17,241,765,888	19,111,636,992	2002
Lithuania	6,211,739,648	7,037,521,408	2002	Slovenia	11,299,746,816	11,373,897,728	2001
Luxembourg	29,383,610,368	25,423,689,728	2000	South Africa	29,384,044,544	27,760,775,168	2002
Macedonia, TFYR	1,430,988,544	2,159,687,424	2002	Spain	174,076,297,216	182,681,141,248	2001
Madagascar	764,454,400	1,027,975,488	2002	Sri Lanka	5,824,500,224	6,964,251,648	2002
Malawi	441,564,352	910,623,616	2002	St Kitts-Nevis	151,185,184	250,037,040	2001
Malaysia	108,260,786,176	91,695,529,984	2002	St Lucia	317,711,488	404,967,552	2001
Maldives	545,274,816	442,253,152	2001	St Vincent	162,592,592	220,000,000	2001
Mali	833,600,256	1,119,474,304	2001	Sudan	1,648,999,936	2,023,000,064	2001
Malta	3,172,184,064	3,335,258,880	2001	Suriname	518,365,856	644,498,496	2001
Marshall Is.	7,700,000	68,900,000	1999	Swaziland	712,530,944	840,266,368	2002
Mauritania	362,000,000	516,700,000	2002	Sweden	97,462,419,456	85,108,244,480	2001
Mauritius	2,876,852,224	2,866,700,800	2002	Switzerland	112,355,008,512	101,620,326,400	2001
Mexico	170,587,734,016	185,154,306,048	2001	Syria	7,784,999,936	6,467,459,072	2002
Micronesia	62,100,000	114,900,000	1998	Tajikistan	745,000,000	855,000,000	2002
Moldova	799,373,312	1,206,182,784	2002	Tanzania	1,533,299,968	2,289,700,096	2002
Mongolia	672,460,480	838,865,216	2001	Thailand	81,865,154,560	72,709,079,040	2002
Morocco	11,152,277,504	13,362,131,968	2002	Togo	457,683,488	692,694,656	2002
Mozambique	1,070,434,688	2,011,933,184	2002	Tonga	29,071,038	71,346,384	1992
Namibia	1,332,458,240	1,691,579,264	2002	Trinidad and Tobago	4,841,299,968	3,798,899,968	2001
Nepal	1,016,857,024	1,609,579,136	2002	Tunisia	9,633,609,728	10,666,307,584	2002
Netherlands	247,327,539,200	227,046,735,872	2001	Turkey	52,662,620,160	46,424,911,872	2002
New Zealand-Aotearoa	18,656,620,544	17,812,969,472	2000	Turkmenistan	2,776,600,064	2,807,300,096	2001
Nicaragua	761,366,080	1,664,701,056	1998	Uganda	699,474,944	1,636,409,344	2002
Niger	349,647,232	548,359,360	2002	Ukraine	23,177,859,072	22,442,438,656	2002
Nigeria	16,405,668,864	18,977,136,640	2002	United Arab Emirates	31,313,819,648	31,313,819,648	1998
Norway	75,393,540,096	49,253,101,568	2000	United Kingdom	386,216,165,376	416,943,636,480	2001
Oman	5,594,278,400	4,494,148,096	1994	United States	1,103,099,985,920	1,466,900,021,248	2000
Pakistan	10,735,265,792	10,900,202,496	2002	Uruguay	3,478,018,816	3,712,440,576	2001
Palau	18,300,000	99,100,000	2001	Uzbekistan	3,829,155,072	3,785,710,848	2002
Palestine	603,791,680	3,085,316,352	2000	Vanuatu	100,683,672	122,106,440	1995
Panama	3,570,395,904	3,658,795,776	2002	Venezuela	28,316,385,280	21,942,460,416	2001
Papua New Guinea	1,610,853,760	1,502,973,824	1999	Vietnam	18,008,315,904	18,676,899,840	2001
Paraguay	1,676,245,888	2,754,469,888	2001	Yemen	2,681,899,008	2,936,684,032	2002
Peru	8,547,678,720	9,341,280,256	2001	Zambia	1,087,358,208	1,662,272,000	2002
Philippines	37,714,059,264	36,873,691,136	2002	Zimbabwe	1,999,000,064	1,807,000,064	2002
Poland	36,386,336,768	48,028,770,304	2002				

Populism: a new suit for an old habit?

EVER SINCE THE 19TH CENTURY BROUGHT INDEPENDENCE, LATIN AMERICA HAS STRUGGLED TO SURVIVE WITHOUT GETTING SWEPT INTO THE WHIRLWIND CREATED BY ITS HUGE NEIGHBOR TO THE NORTH. SINCE THE END OF THE FIRST WORLD WAR, THERE HAS BEEN CONSIDERABLE RESISTANCE FROM ALL SOCIAL SECTORS TO WASHINGTON'S ECONOMIC, SOCIAL, POLITICAL AND MILITARY INFLUENCE.

The 20th century's populist governments were one of the ways Latin America dealt with this ambiguous, love-hate relationship. At the dawn of the 21st century, economic and political fads have changed a lot. But judging by new political developments which to some resemble those 19th-century movements, Latin America threatens to come onto the world stage in the same costume. Perhaps because the oldest of suits is also the newest if it is the only one you have.

Historical populism
According to the 18th-century French Jacobins, consensus is the normal situation in a society whose legitimate interests are those of the group. Dissent and difference were to them symptoms of an anomaly in the social system. Jean Jacques Rousseau's Jacobinism rejects representative democracy since elected officials always have the chance of altering the people's will. Representative democracy must be replaced by direct democracy. But even for Rousseau, representation was inevitable in a complex society, although he added that it had to be minimal, permanent and transparent.

Two developments combine to generate a characteristic Latin American political model: the radio, which became the mass medium for political propaganda during the Second World War, and the concept of the 'popular masses' or 'the people', emerging from the French Revolution.

Populism is a non-proletarian regime searching for support from the dispossessed, the 'shirtless', in order to defend the interests of those classes in power that support the leader. Massive and popular propaganda and a leader with 'the people's' direct support are at the center of a political model which also has a peculiar coincidence with fascism. In *Mein Kampf*, Adolf Hitler says that the majority of humans are negligent and cowardly, resigning themselves to passive knowledge. Hitler believed that this is where propaganda should act, sending the message in a 'colloquial' language, accessible to the understanding of the most ignorant of those it is aimed at.

But populism is as ambiguous as it is interesting. It is not a closed concept, but an open political category with some general common traits and enormous differences in its local applications. It appeared in Latin America towards 1930 and quickly became the prevailing political model, only to decline towards 1955. Among the many and varied forms of populism, three stand out for the significance they had in their time and for their current impact: Mexico under the rule of the Revolutionary Party (after the death of Lázaro Cárdenas), the Brazil of Getulio Vargas and Peronism in Argentina.

Ambiguity is the essential feature of populism, appealing to 'the people' to effect change, but not allowing them to organize or decide freely. It exercises strong state control, particularly among trade unions. Populism focuses collective fervor around a simple goal: redistributive justice, but without proposing concrete ways of implementation. The tool is to rebel against the system, without the need to define the pillars for a new system. It calls forth a demagogic nationalism: mobilization against everything foreign (bordering on xenophobia) and the return of pillaged possessions to 'the people'. Mobilization consists simply in the adoration of a quasi-mythical leader who will save the motherland.

The 'people' are conceived as a shapeless mass guided by irrational arguments. The concept is similar in a way to the Nazi and Fascist models, and very different from Marxism, which attributes 'class consciousness' to the masses. Argentine professor Ernesto Laclau argues in his book *The Populist Reason* that the 'people' notion in populist speeches is never a fact but is essentially a political construct. It is a process which historians call 'equivalence', which equalizes different demands from different groups. Laclau believes 'those from below' are an historical agent, created by the representatives to question the institutional order. They constitute an ambiguous, insufficiently defined concept opposed to the rest of the community. Populisms arise when this 'us', built by increasingly general (all-encompassing) demands, prevails.

Populist resurgence
In today's new global reality, so different to that of the mid-20th century, it would not be appropriate to expect the resurgence of a model so tightly bound to the concrete and unique conditions of that particular historical period. However, the election of several South American leaders raises some concerns about such a possibility. Hugo Chávez in Venezuela, Inácio (Lula) da Silva in Brazil, Néstor Kirchner in Argentina and the eventual triumph of Tabaré Vázquez in Uruguay are being analyzed from a variety of perspectives. Liberal and far-left sectors try to group them into a supposed emerging 'neo-populism', while in the US they are called 'radical populisms'.

Uruguayan writer Carlos Maggi has said that the current forms of direct democracy - such as plebiscites - are of clannish origin: 'every demagogue wants to solve problems with the people he sways'. Maggi contends that people vote *en masse*, swept away like sheep and without a deep understanding of the issues. He believes that is why direct democracy is so dangerous, so suitable to Hitler, his followers and to all populists nowadays.

General James T Hill, commander of the US Southern Command, speaking before the US House of Representatives Armed Services Committee on 24 March 2004, said that: 'In Latin America... these traditional threats (terrorism and others) are now complemented by an emerging threat best described as radical populism, in which the democratic process is undermined to decrease rather than protect individual rights.' He warned that: 'some leaders in the region are tapping into deep-seated frustrations of the failure of democratic reforms to deliver expected goods and services... [frustrations caused by] social and economic inequality... [these leaders are] able to reinforce their radical positions by inflaming anti-US sentiment.

Additionally, other actors are seeking to undermine US interests in the region by supporting these movements.'

Hill admitted that: 'populism in and of itself is not a threat. The threat emerges when it becomes radicalized by a leader who increasingly uses his [sic] position and support from a segment of the population to infringe gradually upon the rights of all citizens'.

Hill mentioned Haiti, Venezuela and Bolivia as examples. He added that: 'The Argentine economic crisis has caused many to question the validity of neo-liberal reforms, manifested in the Buenos Aires Consensus signed last October [2003] by Presidents Kirchner and Lula and stressing "respect for poor countries"'.

A region under surveillance

Hill considers that these regional tendencies 'paint a negative picture in many regards' and have to be monitored carefully. 'We will maintain vigilance' and 'we continue to work to improve both the capabilities and professionalism of our partner nations' militaries, so they can maintain their own security and can assist in combating common transnational threats,' said the General.

He concluded that, in spite of some successes in the region, not enough has been done to stem the 'growth of radical populism and popular dissatisfaction in some countries where reforms have failed to solve underlying social and economic woes'.

Those who form part of the Washington Consensus believe that Latin America first has to solve the fiscal crisis which they consider to be closely tied to statism and populism. The solution to both lies in applying a set of uniform and universal recipes. This is how populism has become a new enemy of the 'international community', spread through a whole new language and a 'consensual' way of thinking repeated *ad infinitum* by the mass media.

Populism, according to historian Agustín Cueva is: 'A kind of substitute for the democratic-bourgeois and anti-imperialist revolution' which in Latin America did not occur at the same time as it did in Europe. Antonio Gramsci described it as: 'one of the means of political realization of the passive bourgeois revolution, through which some essential tasks are realized for the transition from an oligarchic society to the modern bourgeois society'.

Meanwhile, Laclau thinks that asking whether a movement is populist or not is the wrong question to begin with. The question is: 'How much populism does a movement have?' Or, similarly, in what measure is its ideology dominated by a logic of equivalence?

Three cases of populism today: Brazil, Venezuela and Argentina

1. Lula, an uphill ride

Metal worker and union leader, child of illiterate parents, Luiz Inácio Lula Da Silva was born in 1945 in Pernambuco (one of the poor North-eastern Brazilian states). He was sworn in as Brazilian president on 1 January 2003. After three electoral defeats and long years of learning how to succeed, Lula had a change of image, toning down his body language, and focusing on a more reconciliatory discourse which appealed more to his voters' sensibility than their rebelliousness.

Lula supports those who are against intolerable inequalities between rich and poor, whether among countries or among social classes within a country. However, in a more moderate tone, he favors the free market and the system of variable exchange rates for the *real* applied by his predecessor, Fernando Henrique Cardoso, in compliance with the Washington Consensus.

Lula proposes land reform requested by the Landless Peasant Movement, but asks for their patience and calms the international consensus by insisting that private property will be respected. He promises to eradicate child hunger through his 'Zero Hunger' campaign, while facing increasing unemployment.

The class-conscious President is caught up in a reality which adds another problem to that of his opponents (transnationals, financial capital, and conservative sectors with whom he is ready to debate): the demands of the immense masses of unorganized, unemployed and underemployed. They do not demand wages, job security or even work. They ask for food and shelter, and they cannot wait.

There are too many Brazilians who feel they have given power to 'their man', who will pull them out of misery. Now they expect quick answers. These people do not fit into any of the old molds, not even the Marxist one. For the state to implement aid programs initially designed to function spontaneously (Betinho's hunger campaign, see next page) is much more complex than it seems and an uphill ride, as Lula's government has discovered.

2. Chávez, doing it the old way

In 1992, then Lieutenant Colonel Hugo Chávez, commanding a parachute regiment, jumped into Venezuelan politics heading 'Operation Ezequiel Zamora' in an attempt to overthrow President Carlos Andrés Pérez. After the failed coup he was incarcerated and, following a bloody attempt to free him by loyal military forces in 1994, he

was freed and discharged from the Venezuelan army.

Chávez began his political career by showing up in public dressed in a camouflage uniform, announcing that his words would be: 'Munitions aimed at those opponents acting on behalf of discredited political parties', and that it was necessary to 'remove politicians from power so wealth may be redistributed with justice and equity.' At the same time Chávez stressed that his political project is 'the search for the human side of capitalism, distancing ourselves from what the Pope calls 'savage neoliberalism'. We propose an economic model which is humanist, diversified, aimed at production and job creation.'

Chávez won the 1998 elections by a landslide with a vaguely left-wing ideology, often citing Simón Bolívar and not forgetting the Bible as a constant source of inspiration. Shortly after taking power, he announced that there would be 'as much state as necessary and as much market as possible'.

By late 2001, the President had decreed 49 laws, including the Lands and Agricultural Development Act (a Napoleon Bonaparte-style land reform which leaves private property untouched but fights large landowners), the Hydrocarbons Act (which sets a minimum of 51 per cent of state participation in oil extraction) and the Fisheries Act (which protects small fisherpeople against industrial fishing and which, according to employers, has meant the loss of 15,000 jobs). These measures, which initially alarmed the international lending institutions, were followed in February 2002 by a floating currency. This ensured the International Monetary Fund's blessing for the Government.

After the failed 2002 coup by the army, Chávez's return to power brought some changes. Negotiations with the military determined that the army would be left out of the President's new political discourse. He abandoned the military uniform and softened his 'revolutionary' tone.

3. 'Consistency with his time': Kirchner

Of the three cases, Argentina's (whose frequent popular chant 'all of you leave', usually leads to the return of the military) is the most peculiar, given the way Néstor Kirchner achieved power, with less than 22 per cent of the vote, almost by default. When Carlos Menem decided not to run in a second ballot, he sought to repeat the historical behavior of kicking the chess board when the game is going against you. The absence of a second round meant the new president did not get greater support.

In spite of this, the incoming president was not intimidated and from the beginning forged ahead with pronouncements long awaited by the neediest sectors of society. Kirchner sees the state as the remedy for inequalities, generating social justice through income distribution, particularly addressing the middle classes and trying to pull those who suffer from it out of extreme poverty. A transparent state with strong institutions for whom a vigorous 'cleansing' of some of its most corrupt bodies, like the police and the judiciary, is carried out.

Kirchner assures his populace that he will not pay foreign debt with the hunger of the Argentine people, and he tries to negotiate a partial write-off. He was firm on this during his visit to the US in early 2004. Today, the leader who became president with the least experience and popular support of the three seems to be the strongest when it comes to facing the powerful resistance of the status quo. Without public assemblies or official demonstrations, the Argentine President shows signs of consistency with his time.

A new ceremony?

Do populist models apply in the midst of growing globalization, a unipolar world, societies' scarce ideological commitment, and the absence or (in the best of cases) unprecedented historical weakness of the union movement (caused by the near demise of big industry, among other things)? Or are we witnessing a new development? The first Chávez had,

without a doubt, points in common with Peronism; the second does not.

There is a tendency towards a 'state capitalism' (according to some experts) or 'national capitalism' (according to Kirchner) which refers to the regulatory position that the state would need to solve the serious problems of the large sectors of the population living below all indicators. It would need to do this without giving up the idea of opening up to the world, while at the same time taking care of what the market disregards. This idea can be confused with British philosopher Anthony Giddens' 'Third Way' as it foresees forums of direct democratic participation for issues such as the environment and the rights of women, children, and animals, among others.

It resembles the 'non-threatening populism' referred to by General Hill. It also seems another step in capitalist evolution, and a reminder of Peron's advice to let the people decide on 80 per cent of the country's issues, as long as the remaining 20 per cent are the most important. The other populism, (the 'radical populism' feared by Hill that will be closely monitored by the US Army) is the alternative to the failure of these processes, which could lead to a spontaneous, non-ideological uprising by the people with nothing to lose.

It may be that the articulateness of content which Laclau observes in the populist models is, once again in Latin America, the inevitable way of reconciling the imminent urgencies of some nations with the limited possibilities of their government. It may also be that all alternative channels, extremely weakened, are completely overwhelmed and, instead of the logic of equivalency, the logic of mere chaos prevails. ∎

Zero Hunger Brazil: no grassroots mobilization

THE HUNGER CAMPAIGN, or 'Citizens' Action Against Hunger and For Life' launched by Herbert 'Betinho' de Souza in June 1993, organized tens of thousands of committees throughout the country to collect and distribute food and obtain more jobs. Two million people joined the movement. By August 1994, over four million families had received food aid. The program achieved up to 90 per cent support levels in Brazil. The absolute commitment shown by de Souza - rejected as a factory worker because nobody wanted to hire a puny man who weighed less than 50 kg - was based on the simple and devastating logic that a hungry person 'has a face and is always known by someone.'

The idea had many points in common with educator Paulo Freire's *Pedagogy of the Oppressed*, which underlines the potential of each individual's environment as a tool to interpret

reality with the goal of changing it, and not merely adapting it or blaming those responsible.

The Hunger Campaign became a major electoral campaign issue and was transformed into Government policy by President Lula, through his Zero Hunger programme. The role of government in this respect is to provide a regulating framework for citizen initiatives and to generate opportunities so that 'all families and persons in Brazil may ensure their food and nutrition security through their work'. As Betinho had done, Lula called on each Brazilian to do their part in taking care of 11.4 million families, thus avoiding welfare, by the end of his mandate in 2007.

The program had taken care of 3.6 million families by early 2004. Some critics argue that all it did was to give through the Family Fund 70 *reals* ($23) a day for the purchase of food; according

to the Government, this was complemented with advisors in hygiene, education, training in family agriculture and small production cooperatives.

According to Betinho, the root of poverty in Brazil is the land issue. Land occupations by the Landless Rural Workers' Movement (MST) are starting to cause trouble for Lula, who reaffirmed his dream of 'land reform in this country' at the third World Social Forum. During the First National Workshop (*Talheres*) Meeting held in October 2003, Ivo Poletto, one of the programme's coordinators, said implementation is hindered by confrontations with local powers, the current system of social class domination and exploitation, and resource scarcity. Clearly, an adequate implementation of the program (as conceived) will be seriously challenged if it lacks its original source of strength, grassroots mobilization. ∎

Billion dollar bonus: money from migrant workers

REMITTANCES - THE MONEY THAT EMIGRANT WORKERS SEND TO THEIR RELATIVES IN THEIR HOME COUNTRIES - HAVE BECOME A GROWING SOURCE OF FINANCIAL INCOME FOR LATIN AMERICA AND THE CARIBBEAN. THE AMOUNT SENT INCREASED FROM $10 BILLION IN 1996 TO $40 BILLION IN 2003 AND CONTINUES TO GROW. THE UNITED NATIONS HAS SAID THAT REMITTANCES ARE ONE OF THE MOST EFFICIENT WEAPONS IN THE FIGHT AGAINST POVERTY IN THE REGION. BUT MANY OF THE 20 MILLION LATIN AMERICANS ABROAD ARE WORKING ILLEGALLY.

The money sent by Latin American emigrants to their families in their home countries (known as remittances) is one of the major sources of financial income in the region. According to a study by the Economic Commission for Latin America and the Caribbean (ECLAC), remittances in 2003 amounted to approximately $40 billion, a figure similar to the total GDP of Ecuador and equal to one per cent of the GDP of all Latin American countries.

Other ECLAC reports show there are about 20 million Latin Americans living and working abroad who send money home to their families. In 2001, this sum amounted to 33 per cent of foreign direct investment attracted by the region.

Worldwide, the main destination of remittances is India, which in 2001 received $10 billion.

Remittances play a significant role in Latin American economies, increasing savings levels and financing consumption. Almost 60 per cent of all remittances is spent on food, medicine and home rentals. The United Nations has stated on several occasions that remittances are one of 'the most efficient weapons to fight poverty in Latin America.'.

In Central America, according to Inter-American Dialogue, remittances are responsible for economic stability, and they are the key factor in sustaining dollarization in El Salvador and exchange stability in Guatemala and Honduras. In 2003, the $3.5 billion in remittances sent to the region exceeded by far the $2.1 billion averaged by development aid and direct investment.

Remittances are also very important for the Caribbean. In 2003, they had virtually doubled since 1996, to $4.5 billion, compared with $500 million in official development aid and $2.7 billion in direct foreign investment.

In both Latin America and Mexico, remittances are less significant macroeconomically but still play an important role in their economies. The $10 billion received in remittances by Mexico in 2003 amounted to half the average of direct investment and development aid. Meanwhile, in Latin America that year, remittances equaled 66 per cent of direct foreign investment and exceeded the $3.7 billion the region received in official development aid.

According to ECLAC, remittances tend to be more stable than capital flows, known for their volatility. This is why remittances benefit local economies, since they do not follow economic cycles in times of crisis or recession.

Since the early 1980s, the money sent by emigrants has grown at an average annual rate of 12.4 per cent. It is estimated that almost 20 million Latin Americans and Caribbeans live outside their countries and that they send, on average, $2,000 per year to their families.

Most Latino emigrants are found in the US, Spain and Italy, most of them without the required legal documentation. According to estimates, their average income amounts to $26,000 a year.

Each emigrant in the US sends home an average of between $200 and $300 a month, and each time they send money they have to pay between $15 and $30 for transference costs. The Inter-American Development Bank (IDB) has pointed out that reducing the costs of remittance transactions would be equal to increasing net capital flows. Economies in the region would receive an additional three billion dollars per year, according to the IDB and the UN. ∎

REMITTANCES IN LATIN AMERICA, 2001 (BILLION $)	
Mexico	9.3
Dominican Republic	2.0
El Salvador	1.9
Colombia	1.8
Brazil	1.5
Ecuador	1.4

Extreme poverty in the world's most unequal region

THERE IS NO END to hunger and poverty in Latin America and the Caribbean. In several cases, regional averages mask humanitarian catastrophes. Without working women's contribution, extreme poverty would further increase by ten per cent. The region mutilates its own future in every one of its malnourished children.

- 220 million Latin Americans are poor; 95 million are extremely poor.

- While the richest 10 per cent have more than 30 per cent of the wealth, the poorest 40 per cent have less than 20 per cent of total income.

- Poverty has not declined in the region since 1997 due to the deep and growing inequities in these countries.

- 55 million Latin Americans and Caribbeans are undernourished. One in ten children under 5 suffers from acute malnutrition; 1 in 5 from chronic malnutrition.

- The 8 per cent regional average for malnourished populations hides dramatic national realities: 10 per cent in Brazil; 12 per cent in El Salvador, Nicaragua and Guyana; 15 per cent in Ecuador; 24 per cent in Guatemala; 25 per cent in Honduras; 28 per cent in Haiti.

- Hunger is not the result of lack of food, but of poverty and the unequal distribution of income and consumption. Inequity has also been a barrier to economic growth.

- Most extremely poor homes are headed by women.

- Although the number of working women grows continuously, they earn on average 75 per cent of a man's wage, despite having more years of schooling. ∎

Sources: CEPAL and World Bank

Maquilas: the crumbs from the giant's lunch

MAQUILAS HAVE BEEN PRESENT IN LATIN AMERICA FOR CENTURIES. TODAY, THEY ARE THE PROFITABLE OUTPOSTS OF TRANSNATIONAL CORPORATIONS, WHICH HAVE BEEN ENCOURAGED BY LAWS FAVORING COMPANIES AND FOREIGN CAPITAL AND BY THE CREATION OF FREE TRADE ZONES (FTZs). BUT THERE ARE BIG QUESTIONS ABOUT HOW MUCH WORKERS AND HOST GOVERNMENTS BENEFIT. AND NOW THE BOOM IN THE CARIBBEAN IS THREATENED BY THE EXPORT OF THE MAQUILA IDEA TO CHINA.

The term 'maquila' originated in medieval Spain to describe a system whereby wheat was ground in someone else's mill, and the mill-owner was paid with part of the ground flour. In Latin America this same system operated in the sugar mills of the Antilles in the 19th century, where the sugar planters paid the mills partly in sugar.

Today, the maquila still maintains its principal characteristics, although the 'owner' now tends to be a transnational company which uses someone else's land, labor and services to produce goods that are usually designed for export. This often involves installing an offshore company in another country (see Money Laundering: in search of the criminally correct) which plays a limited role in the production process. The transnational company (under the form of different companies) manages to buy and sell itself raw material and produce. Protected by Free Trade Zone (FTZ) regimes or situated in export-processing zones (EPZs), the transnationals take advantage of the facilities the host country offers them. The maquiladoras are part of an international 'production line' which fixes the different steps of the production process in the most convenient places.

For the large industrial corporations, the poorer the country, the more 'competitive' it is. There is stiff competition among maquilas, even from regions in the same country, to attract business. Governments implement changes in labor laws, foreign trade, treatment of foreign capital, environmental issues, natural resources and biological diversity (biodiversity) in a desperate and futile attempt to solve structural problems by modifying the legal system.

Investing in the miracle
The foreign debt crisis in Latin America in 1982 did not stop the application of the neo-liberal model, as might have been expected, nor did it make banks or the creditors less inflexible. In fact, it actually intensified these policies, particularly concerning favorable treatment of foreign capital in the region and the elimination of restrictions to direct foreign investments. For the countries in question, the aim of these measures was to increase entry of capital in the short term. In many

Caribbean countries, the maquilas were considered a quick way to achieve this.

In Central America, there are a large number of companies, attracted by cheap and abundant labor, fiscal benefits, a privileged geographic emplacement and commercial preferences granted by the Caribbean Basin Initiative (CBI). Countries like Mexico, Guatemala, Honduras, Haiti, El Salvador and the Dominican Republic are the favorites. Costa Rica is trying to offer better qualified labor in exchange for better wages.

The maquilas are not situated in unhealthy, remote, isolated areas. They need a minimum infrastructure, which often means prior investment by governments (in telecommunications, ports, electric power, roads, etc) in order to attract them. The sum total of these investments, plus labor legislation which disciplines workers and obstructs the formation of trade unions, generates facilities which in fact constitute indirect subsidies to foreign capital.

To increase competitiveness, the companies try to reduce production costs as much as possible. Abundant labor allows for low wages, generating competition for jobs which are increasingly scarce.

In the Dominican Republic, according to Professor Raul Fernandez, from the University of California, wages went from $1.33 in 1984 to $0.56 in 1997. While in 1998 the best-paid workers in Latin America earned an average of $1.51 per hour, in the US, doing the same job, workers earned $17.2 (11 times more). This difference is even greater if we consider wages in Germany or Japan.

Young women between the ages of 15 and 25, without children, with no work experience and not pregnant (in Mexico and El Salvador, for instance, certificates are required and pregnancy is a cause for immediate firing), are generally preferred for the jobs. They are seen as more docile than men, with lower wage expectations.

Some of the complaints registered by certain Honduran NGOs refer to sexual harassment, corporal punishment, long workdays on their feet and bad ventilation in work areas. In the Guatemalan maquilas the working day was increased to 12 hours and stimulants have been used to raise performance at

work. According to a report filed at the Guatemalan Workers Trade Union (UNSINTRAGUA), the drugs administered to pregnant women caused malformations in newborns.

In many cases, the companies have also been accused of discriminating against their workers (for example, Mayan women in Guatemala must abandon their traditional dress), contaminating the environment by not respecting the law, and refusing to support the communities where they have settled.

In addition, most of the workers in the maquilas do not work in the communities they live in. As most are women, this distorts traditional family organization due to very long work days. If they bring their children with them, they stay (in the best of cases) in care centers, some of them belonging to the company the mother works for. It is as if the workers were emigrants in this enclave of the industrialized world in their own country. The difference in favor of the real emigrants (even those who are illegal) is that they send remittances home, following a very established custom in Caribbean countries (see Billion dollar bonus: money from migrant workers).

Flexible production in a non-flexible structure
The transfer of factories to peripheral countries also causes social and economic conflicts in the industrialized world, since thousands of jobs are lost due to closures of factories which are relocating overseas. According to extra-official data, during the 1990s, in the US, more than 900,000 jobs were lost in the textile industry and 200,000 in the electronics industry.

In Mexico, this phenomenon peaked after 1984 when the 'Law to Promote Mexican Investment and Regulate Foreign Investment' was modified to incorporate new guidelines and rules. Projects oriented towards export were given priority. Foreign capital, which had previously been limited to 49 per cent, was allowed to reach 100 per cent. According to data from the Mexican National Institute of Statistics, Geography and Data Processing, between 1980 and 1990, the number of maquilas grew by 200 per cent.

Raul Fernandez points out that, in today's worldwide economic model, the maquila stands out as a banner of flexible production, playing a decisive role in the increase of inequalities between and within the countries of the world. He maintains that the *maquila* uses modern technology with a flexible 19th-century-style labor force.

If a Mexican earns in one day the same as a North American earns in one hour, Central America has a serious problem which is solved cleanly and quickly by the inexorable laws of monopolistic capitalism.

More for less: the reverse of profitability.

China has an even more serious problem; its workers earn in a week what a Mexican earns in a day. For China, the main obstacle is the distance from the economic centers. Because of this, it has started to draw up new strategies. Instead of offering a partial service, like that of the *maquilas*, it offers a complete package, from raw materials to design and even the shipping of the finished products to the centers of distribution, at a very competitive final price.

The growth of manufacturing industry in China and its entry in the World Trade Organization (WTO) are of concern to the *maquila* businesspeople in Latin America.

The US has made a commitment to the WTO to increase its import quota from Asia as of 31 December, 2004. This may well impact on the *maquilas* in Latin America.

Already, many hundreds of *maquila* plants on the Mexican border with the US have closed their doors due to the implementation of the North America Free Trade Agreement (NAFTA). One chapter of the agreement specifies that, as of 2002, only 'national' products (those originating in Canada, the US and Mexico are considered as such) can be put together in the *maquilas* in Mexico. In order to use others (European or Japanese), high import taxes must be paid. The aim is to exclude Japan and Europe from the area, reserving local labor for US companies.

This situation caused a hasty withdrawal of numerous non-US factories - and they are relocating to China. ∎

Host countries lose out

IN 1996, *Maquilas* in El Salvador exported $ 709.7 million and imported $541.5 million. The difference left to the host country, was barely $168.2 million (this includes the costs of electric power, drinking water, salaries, machinery maintenance, rentals, etc). No national or municipal taxes or custom rights were paid on exports or imports. No national raw materials were used (these were completely imported), nor was any knowledge or technology acquired (Oxfam International, 2002 report).

With similar numbers, all the countries in the region that have invested in *maquilas*, see capitals flow in and then out again. Of course the governments validate the large amounts. When the time comes to enumerate achievements: they can say: 'This year we exported...', or 'So many jobs were created...'. But the companies only pay for what they use and they do not generate riches or earnings for the governments. It's a story which repeats itself throughout the continent. ∎

A beacon of freedom?: the Christian right and Washington's foreign policy

THE US GOVERNMENT OF GEORGE W BUSH SEEMS TO BE INCREASINGLY DOMINATED BY A FUNDAMENTALIST CHRISTIAN AGENDA THAT BELIEVES AMERICA TO BE DOING GOD'S WILL.

'We have been working for freedom for centuries. Tonight we lead the world as we face a threat to our human dignity and sense of decency. What's at stake is something more than the fate of a small country; it's a great idea, a New World Order where several nations unite with the common universal aspirations of humanity: peace and security, freedom and the rule of law…Yes, the United States carries a good share of the leadership in this effort. Of all of the world's nations only the United States of America has had the resources as well as the moral strength to support it. We are the only nation on earth capable of summoning the forces of peace. This is the responsibility of leadership and strength that has made America a beacon of freedom… May God bless the United States of America.'

This was how President George Bush Sr justified the 1991 attack on Iraq while at the same time announcing a 'New World Order'. A decade later, President George W Bush (whose rehabilitation from alcohol when he was 40 years old through 'divine intervention' is ironically portrayed by the media with the phrase: 'Goodbye Jack Daniels, hello Jesus') made himself heard with the same sense of transcendence, announcing the beginning of the 'crusade' of good versus evil and stigmatizing those who would not support his country in the struggle against terrorism.

As can be seen, the belligerent behavior by the US during the last Republican administrations has been supported by a Messianic rhetoric which portrays its interventions as chapters in sacred history: a 'New Order' that encompasses the struggle against the 'Axis of Evil' (North Korea, Iran, Iraq-Libya, Syria, Cuba); that justified the 'Enduring Freedom' operation against Afghanistan and the latest 'Preventive War' which determined the recent invasion and occupation of Iraq. These actions have been analyzed from different angles; there are those who suspect the slogans on which they are based are euphemisms behind which lies an attempt to camouflage the desire to control the oil fields and other riches. The argument that these operations arise from a need to maintain and potentially

develop the arms industry also runs along economic lines.[1]

In spite of this apocalyptic tone, some analysts have pointed out (without dismissing geopolitical and/or economic aspects) the religious motivations that inspire these war expeditions. We are thus faced with a paradoxical situation: there is a war or series of wars whose agents (a nation born in the midst of the Enlightenment, which has been seen as a symbol of Modernism, both inside and out) present themselves as defenders of Freedom, Civilization and Tolerance against religious fundamentalisms. But that war is a holy war.

Baghdad-bound - on the Mayflower

In 1620 a group of English Puritans, funded by a London company, crossed the Atlantic on board the *Mayflower*. They settled first in Plymouth, Massachusetts, then in Connecticut, where they established a colony whose government would have to abide strictly by the fundamental values of Christian morality. According to the pioneers, these values had been ignored by the negligence and corruption of the English political and religious authorities. The term 'Puritans' used to describe this religious group had originally been used in a derogatory manner in order to single out those that pretended to purify the Anglican Church of certain practices which distanced it from Christian values and brought it closer to Catholicism. The Anglican Church had separated from the Catholic Church in the 16th century, during the reign of

---

1 'Once the Iraq war is over, to the benefit of its military industry, the US will have to replace all the weapons used against that country already devastated by a 13 year-old embargo. The replacement of those weapons and others that will be used or destroyed by the end of the war will give a tremendous boost to the US weapons industry, which since the first Gulf War in 1991 had not known such a promising business opportunity. In the latest 'Congressional Budget Justification for Foreign Operations', the US State Department predicts that US arms sales are expected to reach over 14 billion dollars this year, the largest total in almost two decades, compared to 12.5 billion dollars in 2002. 'A tragic indicator of the values of our civilization is that there's no business like war business, 'says Douglas Mattern of the New York-based War and Peace Foundation.'
Thalif Deen, 'IRAQ-US: The great war business' *El Puente, encuentro de las culturas*, 15 April 2003.

Henry VIII, and as it became increasingly assimilated to Calvinism, confrontation with the Catholic Church increased.

The reasons behind the emigration of the *Mayflower* pilgrims are still an object of controversy among historians. Some say they were persecuted by the official religion during the reign of James I (1603-1625); others state there was no such persecution since even though Puritan beliefs were not part of the state religion, they were free to practise them in public. In any case, the goal of the Puritans in the new world had been just that: to establish a New World, far from the alleged Anglican and Papal corruption, a kind of Utopia whose government closely adhered to Calvinist biblical precepts. Only church members had the right to vote in the Protestant colonies established in New England, while their salaries were paid by taxing the people. Evangelical law thus imposed itself over the law of the Church and the State. Although this institution did not govern directly, it proposed the means to do so and to choose its representatives. A strict moral code began to develop which expressed itself in the rigorous persecution of adulterers, drunkards, witches and heretics. Some writers maintain even today that this tradition is the foundation of certain domestic and foreign policy decisions in the US.

Predestination - from grace to war

One of reformer John Calvin's (1509-1564) most peculiar concepts, eagerly incorporated by the Puritans, is that of predestination. From eternity immemorial, an omnipotent God determines who is saved and who is damned. According to this idea, which is closely tied to the idea of grace and providence, humans - ever since original sin - suffer from a 'moral incapacity' to do good deeds; only those chosen by the grace of God (impossible to resist) are capable of good actions. Thus, good deeds will not lead people to salvation under Calvinist-rooted Puritanism. There is a reversal of cause-effect relations with respect to other versions of Christianity: edifying deeds and graceful actions are symptoms, consequences or a way of proving that one is among God's chosen creatures. It is

precisely this will to exhibit the influence of grace, the desire to show one's ability to control perverse inclinations, which make the members of this community particularly active and entrepreneurial, constantly interested in designing government and society according to the will of God as revealed in the Bible. If we project these attitudes and beliefs onto a wider canvas, through a more historically informed reading, we will see how today's descendants of those Puritans perceive themselves: they are creatures chosen by God to overthrow History's cosmic drama and institute a New World Order. George W Bush has mentioned predestination as a source of his belligerent political decisions: 'President Bush's war plans are risky, but Mr Bush is no gambler. In fact, he denies the very existence of chance: 'Events aren't moved by blind chance but by the hand of a just and faithful God'. From the outset he has been convinced that his presidency is part of a divine plan, even telling a friend while he was Governor of Texas:
'I believe God wants me to run for president'. This conviction that he is doing God's will has surfaced more openly since 11 September 2001.'[2] There is a need to manifest and constantly update God's irresistible preordained destiny.

Manifest destiny
The US went through a great period of expansion during the 19th century. While in 1800 the population was estimated at less than five million, by 1850 it had grown to 23 million. The territory grew in size until it reached the Pacific Ocean. The doctrine of predestination and a Messianic discourse also informed the determining economic, demographic and technological factors of that expansionist policy which caused domestic controversies at the time. Alexis de Tocqueville (1805-1859), French historian and author of *La Democracie en*

Amérique, observed: 'In the United States religion is at the heart of all and every one of the national customs and in all of the national sentiments that the word motherland evokes.'

Around that time the concept of 'manifest destiny' was used for the first time in an article about the annexation of the Texas territory by reporter John L O'Sullivan. He argued that political and economic superiority granted the US the right to expand over the rest of the American landscape and, furthermore, that superiority was evidence they were destined to do so by divine grace. The words of a Senator Taylor are clear evidence of the typical arrogance the self-proclaimed 'enlightened' of those times exhibited: 'We are standing on earth's pedestal, where we reign supreme, and nothing stands over us except God'. The concept of a manifest destiny, according to which only the US has the 'moral strength' to achieve 'universal aspirations' lives on in the current discourse which evokes God's blessing when carrying out American campaigns.

Playing God
'Steven Spielberg's latest film depicts a future government incarcerating potential criminals before they commit to or even think of engaging in terrorism. This could be more than just fiction.'

Nat Hentoff, *Village Voice*,
10 September 2002

The concept of 'preventive war' is another ingenious strategy which has been presented in order to legitimize US foreign policy. It entails striking those countries which could, supposedly, carry out future actions against America. This strategy has been likened by some analysts to the plot of the science-fiction film *Minority Report*. In that film we see a

kind of anti-utopia where an implacable law and order establishment is in charge of prosecuting future criminals on a preventive basis. The Preventive War concept is currently also being applied in the US, where some citizens are being detained as potential terrorists without right to legal counsel or due process of law. A *New York Times* editorial published on 8 August 2002 stated: 'The Bush Administration seems to believe, without much legal authority, that by calling its citizens "illegal combatants" in the war on terrorism, it can jail them indefinitely while denying them defense lawyers. This challenge to the courts flies in the face of two centuries of constitutional law and threatens the very liberties President Bush claims to defend in the fight against terrorism.' In the words of historian Arthur J Schlesinger, two-time Pulitzer-Prize winner and former advisor to President Kennedy: 'It is obvious that Vice President Cheney and Defense Secretary Donald Rumsfeld see themselves as Steven Spielberg's pre-cops, two telepathists physically equipped to detect crimes that are about to happen.'

According to the concept of predestination as presented here, world history is akin to a script written by God in his infinite wisdom. In this script, not just every person, but 'all parts and each particle in the world' - to use Calvin's words - have a pre-established role following an 'incomprehensible wisdom'. Perhaps these divine designs are revealed only to those that regard themselves as touched by an irresistible grace, in other words, those who are predestined. In this regard, Herbert Butterfield, an English historian quoted by Schlesinger, said: 'History shows us that the heaviest blows from heaven fall upon those that imagine they can sovereignly control things by playing God, not only to themselves, but also to the distant future.' ∎

2 www.bushwatch.com

Darwin on trial

US RELIGIOUS GROUPS ARE CHALLENGING THE WAY EVOLUTION THEORY IS TAUGHT, IN A DEBATE WHICH HAS SPARKED RENEWED CONTROVERSY OVER THE ORIGIN OF LIFE.

There is a deeply held belief among many fundamentalist Christians in the US that unquestioning adherence to the theory of evolution has often been used as an argument against the existence of God. This is true at the highest levels of government: during his 2000 election campaign, President George W Bush himself cast doubt on the theory of evolution: 'On the issue of evolution, the verdict is still out on how God created the Earth'.

In the early 20th century, Christian groups tried to get the Biblical explanation of creation taught as scientific fact. Today, supporters of the 'Intelligent Design' theory want the concept to be added to science curricula in Ohio state schools, alongside Darwin's theory of evolution. But what is being discussed in Ohio in the first years of the 21st century represents more than just a simple return to 'Creationism', as a literal belief in the Bible story is called.

A history of evolutionism versus creationism

The controversy over the value of the theory of evolution is nothing new. The best-known exponent of the Intelligent Design theory was English theologian William Paley, who in 1802 created a watchmaker analogy. Paley wrote that if we find a pocket watch in a field, we immediately infer that it was produced not by natural processes acting blindly but by a designing human intellect. He reasoned that, in the same fashion, the natural world contains abundant evidence of a supernatural creator. This argument of design prevailed as an explanation of the natural world until the publication of Darwin's *On the Origin of Species* in 1859.

At this point, Christian fundamentalists' opposition to science intensified. They believed this was just another step towards a materialist vision of the world, opposed to the moral and religious values of Christianity. In the 1920s, a popular crusade erupted against instruction on the theory of evolution in public high schools. In 1925, Tennessee became the first state to outlaw evolutionary teaching.

The US Constitution says the state cannot advocate or ban the instruction of any religious creed. However, fundamentalists have sought many ways to promote the teaching of the Bible and to exclude evolution from school curricula. During the first decades of the 20th century, several US states passed laws banning the instruction of evolution in state schools and colleges. In 1968, the Supreme Court decided that those laws were unconstitutional.

So the fundamentalists then adopted a strategy of passing laws that made the instruction of creationist theory compulsory alongside that of evolution, arguing that the former was also a scientific hypothesis. The first of such laws was passed in Arkansas in 1981 and was declared unconstitutional by a federal court the following year. The state of Louisiana passed a similar law which was appealed all the way to the Supreme Court. It was also finally declared unconstitutional.

It seems to be of little use that theologians and bishops, both Catholic and Protestant, preach that there is no radical conflict between science and the Christian faith. In October 1996, Pope John Paul II confirmed the scientific validity of the theory of evolution in a speech delivered at the Pontifical Academy of Sciences. The Pope had already said in 1981 that the Bible's purpose was not to instruct us on astronomy and the origin of the universe, but on how to get to Heaven.

In 1991, the adherents of the Intelligent Design movement launched a new assault with Phillip E Johnson's book *Darwin on Trial*. This accepts that the universe is much more than 6,000 years old (the original belief of the creationists which they said was based on the Bible) and that some species do change; it rejects the idea that evolution accounts for the wide range of species that exist.

In its late 20th century revamp in the US, the Intelligent Design movement crystallized 1996 as the Center for the Renewal of Science and Culture (CRSC). This was sponsored by the Discovery Institute, a conservative Seattle think tank. Johnson assembled a group of supporters who promote design theory through their writings, financed by CRSC fellowships. According to an early mission statement, the CRSC seeks: 'nothing less than the overthrow of materialism and its damning cultural legacies'.

Darwin is no 'divine' creation

The creationist argument is that evolution is a theory, not a fact. Science is based on observation, they say, but nobody has observed the origin or the evolution of the universe or of the species. The theory of evolution states that human beings and chimpanzees descend from a common ancestor. This is based on the assumption that both species are genetically quite similar - for example, humans share 98 per cent of their DNA with chimpanzees.

Creationists still blame Darwin's *On the Origin of Species* for modern society's decadence, marked by promiscuousness, birth control, abortions, pornography, violent crime, etc. Recently, they have introduced a new offensive strategy: to criticize the theory of evolution with scientific arguments. They argue that the methods used by scientists to determine the age of facts are not trustworthy and that there is no reason to doubt the date of Biblical creation. Likewise, they attack the validity of fossil data, maintaining that there are no fossils that show the transitory forms between the different types of life. However, for a long time now there have been methods and equipment, such as the use of radioactive isotopes, that enable us to determine the age of fossils with reasonable precision. But Johnson, and the Inteligent Design Movement do not question the age of the world, but some aspects of Darwin's theory. They accept evolution 'up to a point', but leave the bulk of the creation of life to a Great Designer.

Intelligent Design: a back door into schools?

Critics argue that what the movement is really about is finding a back door to get creationism into schools. Some people still believe that it would be reasonable for schools to teach both creationism and evolutionism. But most scientific facts cannot be contested. When we get on a plane or cross a bridge, we assume they have been made according to scientific principles and that they will work. We know that the sun is not the center of the universe, that the earth is not flat, that gravity exists. But we also know that science is constantly evolving and new ideas and new discoveries emerge all the time; if children in schools are not taught to learn and to question, their education - and their whole approach in their future lives - will be narrow indeed. ∎

Intelligence: from the Inquisition to Iraq

INFORMATION IS ESSENTIAL TO POLICYMAKING. MANAGING ACCURATE INFORMATION DOES NOT GUARANTEE THE BEST DECISIONS BUT, AS HISTORY HAS REPEATEDLY SHOWN, INADEQUATE INFORMATION LEADS TO DISASTER. THE TASK OF THE INTELLIGENCE AGENCIES IS TO GATHER INFORMATION EFFICIENTLY, TO INTERPRET IT USING THE NECESSARY LEVELS OF SOPHISTICATION, AND TO COMMUNICATE IT SWIFTLY WHEREVER IT IS NEEDED. TO DO THIS THEY USE WHATEVER MEANS THEY HAVE AT THEIR DISPOSAL - AND HAVE ALWAYS DONE SO.

The nature and functions of intelligence agencies are illustrated by a US presidential order, Executive Order 12333, December 1981, where the national intelligence services are mandated to provide: 'information on which to base decisions concerning the conduct and development of foreign, defense and economic policy, and the protection of United States national interests from foreign security threats'. The document also emphasizes the role of detecting espionage operations and other threats coming from foreign intelligence services.

But these official definitions omit an essential function of the intelligence apparatus: the secret intervention in the political or economic affairs of other nations, ie, its covert activities.

These intelligence, counterintelligence and undercover tasks include a wide gamut of government activities and have determined the development of a vast international industry which generally progresses more or less secretly. It is impossible to accurately determine the costs of this industry; it is estimated that towards the end of the Cold War the US and the USSR were each spending at least $12 billion.

From the Bible to James Bond

According to the Encyclopedia Britannica, the most remote descendants of modern intelligence agencies were the old fortune-tellers - such as those of the Delphi oracle in Greece - which claimed the ability to examine the will of the gods and predict the future, for which they were consulted by politicians. As is often the case now with the intelligence apparatus, their reports used to be ambiguous - or simply ignored by those they were intended for.

Spies also existed in the Old Testament. In Numbers, 13, God commands Moses to send agents to the land of Canaan. Forty days later, the 12 returned, saying that the inhabitants of that territory were stronger than the Israelites. For saying this they were punished by God.

Another prestigious document about intelligence activities in antiquity is *The Art of War*, written around 400 BC, by Sun-Tzu, who was of Chinese origin. This classic treatise, apparently consulted by strategists from the People's Republic of China, establishes categories which correspond with modern intelligence concepts (secret agents, double agents, etc) and stresses the importance of counterintelligence and psychological warfare.

Intelligence started to be used systematically during the Middle Ages but it came across practically insurmountable technical difficulties, like the impossible task of maintaining troop- or ship-movements in secret, and slow communications. Already by the 15th century Italian city-states had established permanent embassies in European capitals, often using them as intelligence sources and developing codes and systems of encrypted writing.

In England during the 16th century, Francis Walsingham, Secretary of State to Elizabeth I, hired a team of Oxford and Cambridge graduates to create an espionage ring and develop systems to develop and break codes. Later, John Truloe, Oliver Cromwell's intelligence chief, developed a rather sophisticated intelligence system.

In the 18th century, the main breakthroughs in organization and doctrine are attributed to the German monarch Frederick the Great. A century later, the Prussians, under Bismarck and his assistant Wilhelm Steiber, organized intelligence activities as part of state functions, creating an agency dedicated solely to military intelligence and what could be considered the first large-scale espionage ring.

In spite of this historical development and the perfection of military and communications technology, the major Western powers entered the 20th century with an inadequate intelligence apparatus. It is often said that the First World War was not what the warring powers wanted it to be. Among other factors, this suggests the failure of their respective intelligence systems. French services were bogged down in internal intrigue and had been undermined by the Dreyfus affair, which led them, among other errors, to underestimate German military power. Nor was the German intelligence system efficient, while the Russians were initially successful because of the desertion of an Austrian official, but during the War itself they were no more efficient than the rest. The British on the other hand, achieved a measure of success, cracking German naval codes. Upon joining the War, the US Army's intelligence department was composed of two officers and two civil servants. By the time the War ended, this service had grown to almost 1,200 personnel, most of them amateurs.

Improvement and specialization continued during the following decades, particularly in expansionist regimes, but the qualitative jump was made in the Second World War, when the US created the Office of Strategic Services (OSS) in order to deal with unprecedented challenges related to new technological developments such as the development of radio technology and its penetrating effects in psychological warfare. Some events, like the Japanese surprise attack on Pearl Harbor in December 1941, or the unexpected German resistance to Allied bombing, can be read as the failure of policymakers or their strategists to interpret the reports of their respective services or to take the appropriate decisions.

One of the most famous feats in the field of intelligence also took place around this time: Operation Ultra, which enabled English intelligence services to break German military codes after acquiring a German Enigma coding machine with Polish and French aid. The Allies were thus able to read the German strategists' minds during most of the War.

The Cold War generated the spectacular, sometimes chaotic, and not always efficient growth of the intelligence apparatus and a complicated and powerful bureaucracy. The media made these intelligence systems familiar to the public; agencies such as the US Central Intelligence Agency (CIA), the Soviet KGB or Israel's Mossad. The entertainment industry also created the espionage epic, decorating the intelligence services with novelesque excitement. This was far from the truth according to the Encyclopaedia Britannica, which describes them as: 'tedious, insipid and immoral'.

Types and sources of intelligence

- Among the various intelligence categories, the most highly valued and the least trustworthy is *political intelligence*. It is responsible for anticipating the behavior of foreign political forces, using reports from open sources provided by diplomatic personnel - particularly military attachés - complemented by investigations done through the professional intelligence apparatus. The most valued information in this field is related to military organization, ironically more accessible and less efficiently protected in war than in peacetime.

- The collection of information on trade, finances, natural resources, industrial capacity, etc, belongs to the realm of *economic intelligence*, as well as the analysis of this relevant information for guiding purposes of foreign policy.

- Technological progress has generated an endless race between military capacities and defense measures, as well as between new access to information methods and new techniques to protect secret information. *Technological intelligence* plays a crucial role in these processes.

- If intelligence systems need to make predictions about the behavior of foreign states, the need for *personal intelligence* is obvious, ie, tools for the detection and systematization of policymakers' personal and biographical characteristics.

- The significance of cultural, environmental and other factors has grown lately. They could determine the appearance of *new specializations* in intelligence systems.

According to other criteria, intelligence services can be categorized as: strategic intelligence, tactical intelligence and counterintelligence. The first obtains information about capabilities and other countries' intentions. Tactical intelligence is also called 'operational' or 'combat' intelligence, and has military objectives. Counterintelligence is dedicated to the protection of its own intelligence systems with respect to foreign colleagues, and to preserve a state's advanced technology. This is the world of double agents and spies.

As far as sources are concerned, the bulk of the work is done through the meticulous searching of public sources: monitoring of radio and television broadcasts, analysis of all kinds of publications, compilation of reports by diplomats, businesspeople (some can be women) and other observers. All this is done by bureaucrats or university professionals. The non-public sources - in descending order of significance - are: air and satellite reconnaissance, electronic surveillance and the decoding of codes and passwords, and - finally - secret agent espionage.

The US and the CIA: a paradigm

The US intelligence system has served as organizational model for many Western nations. It is very powerful, vast and complex. Among its information-gathering agencies we find: the Central Intelligence Agency (CIA) with its Operations and Science and Technologies Directorates; organizations attached to the Defense Department such as the National Security Agency (NSA), Defense Intelligence Agency (DIA), National Reconnaissance Office (NRO), Defense Airborne Reconnaissance Office (DARO), Central Imagery Office (CIO); plus the Army, Navy and Air Force intelligence departments. During the stage when gathered information is interpreted, other agencies come into play: the National Intelligence Council (NIC), the CIA's Directorate of Intelligence (DI) and the Department of State's Bureau of Intelligence and Research (INR). The main counterintelligence organism is the FBI's National Security Division. There are other more specialized or focal agencies such as the Department of Energy's Office of Intelligence and the Department of Treasury's Office of Intelligence Support.

This intricate network also has administration and coordination organisms: the Director of Central Intelligence (DCI), who is the President's top advisor in matters of security as well as the head of the Intelligence Community and the head of the CIA; the National Foreign Intelligence Board, which is responsible for international coordination and the development of policies to protect source and intelligence methods; and finally, the Intelligence Community Executive Committee (IC/EXCOM), the main advisory group to the DCI.

The most representative model of this gigantic apparatus is the CIA. It was founded in September 1947, when the end of the Second World War brought about the need to centralize intelligence activities (after intense debates about the necessary degree of centralization). The CIA is under the jurisdiction of the National Security Council (NSC) and its mandate is to advise the NSC in intelligence matters related to national security, recommend measures to the NSC for the efficient coordination of intelligence activities for other departments and agencies, evaluate intelligence activities and the Government's internal communication, centralize additional services determined by the NSC, and carry out any other task related to national security according to NSC directives.

The agency has grown beyond these basic commitments and has widened its objectives. It is believed that in the late 1980s it employed 18,000 people in the US alone, and several thousands more abroad. CIA-controlled military and paramilitary unit activities do not figure in the agency's annual budgets. The guidelines and policies that bind it are contained in presidential executive orders and directives from the National Security Intelligence Council (which are classified).

Since 1947 the CIA has carried out the following activities: gathering, evaluation and communication of foreign intelligence activities; counterintelligence abroad; psychological warfare and foreign paramilitary operations. The first two objectives are clearly established in its statutes; the other is the result of a very loose interpretation of these statutes. The already mentioned Directorate of Operations is also known as the 'Dirty Tricks Department', often dealing with undercover operations such as espionage missions, political interventions, recruitment of defectors and other undercover activities. ∎

Sources: 'intelligence' Encyclopaedia Britannica Premium Service. www.britannica.com/eb/article?eu 109 301

For an overview on the Intelligence Community see www.access.gpo.gov/int/int023.html

A torturer's truth

THE SOURCES that helped to produce this article do not mention torture as one of the proceedings employed to obtain information. According to the Encyclopaedia Britannica, torture (from the Latin *tortura*) is the infliction of excruciating physical or psychological pain for such reasons as punishment, intimidation, coercion, the extraction of a confession, or the obtainment of information. This methodology goes back a long way, and some of its historic episodes, such as the Holy Office of the Inquisition, implemented from the 13th century onwards, are preserved in museums.

Experts say torture is far from being an ideal tool to obtain information, since most of the victims reveal not the truth, but the truth they believe their torturers want to hear. As Michel de Certeau pointed out in his study *The Institution of Rot*, on the methods employed by the Inquisition to eradicate heresy, the torturer's ultimate goal is to make the persons under torture renounce their truth.

Such proceedings also seem to be in force in the 21st century, in the so-called 'War on Terror' led by the United States. As has become notorious, military jail guards in Iraq and Afghanistan have forced tortured inmates to renounce the Qur'an, eat pork, take their clothes off, etc. These are all elements that, above all, are meant to annihilate the tortured person's identity. Under strict 'intelligence' terms, it may be said that the information sought by the torturer is mainly to confirm that the 'enemy' is no longer the

The world according to...

...The World Bank Ranked by income (Gross National Income, GNI, per capita). See page 497.

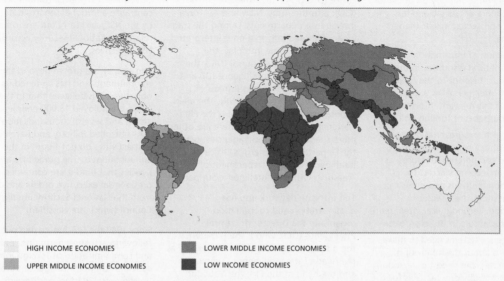

HIGH INCOME ECONOMIES

UPPER MIDDLE INCOME ECONOMIES

LOWER MIDDLE INCOME ECONOMIES

LOW INCOME ECONOMIES

...UNDP (UN Development Program) Ranked by Human Development Index. See page 497.

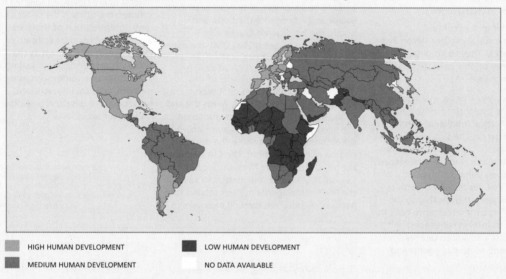

HIGH HUMAN DEVELOPMENT

MEDIUM HUMAN DEVELOPMENT

LOW HUMAN DEVELOPMENT

NO DATA AVAILABLE

...UNICEF (UN children's agency) Ranked by under-5 mortality rate. See page 497.

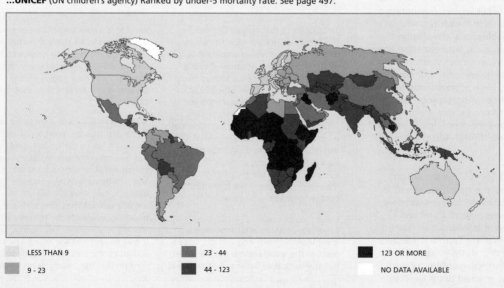

LESS THAN 9

9 - 23

23 - 44

44 - 123

123 OR MORE

NO DATA AVAILABLE

ACORD (Agency for Co-operation and Research in Development)
Dean Bradley House
52 Horseferry Road
London SW1P 2AF
UK
www.acord.org
An international consortium of NGOs working under the trusteeship of its member agencies. There are 11 member agencies, each in a different country. Its main role is to help establish or strengthen local non-governmental structures with a view to promoting self-reliant, participatory development. It also acts in emergency situations which seem likely to give rise to new development needs.

Amazon Basin Indigenous Organizations Co-ordinating Committee
www.coica.org
Founded in 1984, its aim is to strengthen local organizations and ties among indigenous peoples in their struggle to defend their rights and their native lands.

Amnesty International (AI)
1 Easton Street
London WC1X 8DJ
UK
www.amnesty.org
Founded in 1961, AI is a worldwide campaigning movement (active in over 140 countries) that works to promote all the human rights enshrined in the Universal Declaration of Human Rights and other internationally recognized human-rights agreements. In particular, AI campaigns to free all prisoners of conscience; ensure fair and prompt trials for political prisoners; abolish the death penalty, torture and other cruel treatment of prisoners; and end political killings and 'disappearances'.

AMREF (African Medical Research Foundation)
www.amref.org
AMREF is Africa's largest indigenous health charity. It was founded in 1957 in Kenya and works with local communities and governments in sub-Saharan Africa to research and alleviate the region's health problems, with a special emphasis on primary healthcare. It also incorporates the Flying Doctor Service. It is supported by funds raised by 11 offices in Europe and North America.

Anti-Slavery International
Thomas Clarkson House,
The Stableyard
Broomgrove Road
London SW9 9TL
www.antislavery.org
Founded in 1839, Anti-Slavery International is the world's oldest human-rights organization and has consultative status with the UN Economic and Social Council. It exposes current cases of slavery and campaigns for their eradication, pressing for more effective implementation of international laws against slavery. It focuses on all forms of slavery, including exploitative child labor, bonded labor, forced labor, trafficking of women and children, forced marriage and 'chattel' slavery.

ATTAC (Association for the Taxation of Financial Transactions for the Aid of Citizens)
www.attac.org
The international ATTAC movement was created at a meeting in Paris in December 1998. It describes itself as 'the international movement for democratic control of financial markets and their institutions'. It is a network with neither hierarchical structures nor a geographical center. The network now covers 33 countries and 15 languages.

Care International
www.care.org
An international network of 12 national organizations aiming to serve individuals and families in the poorest communities in the world. It works in the following fields: water; agriculture; emergency relief; health; urban priorities; micro-finance; and education.

Caritas Internationalis
www.caritas.org
A worldwide confederation of 162 Catholic relief and development organizations.
Palazzo San Calisto
00120 Vatican City

CEE Bankwatch Network
An international network with member organizations in 12 countries of the CEE/CIS region. The basic aim of the network is to monitor activities of International Financial Institutions (IFIs) in the region, and to propose constructive alternatives to their policies and projects, with particular attention to the environment, energy and transport.
www.bankwatch.org

EarthAction
www.earthaction.org
Created in 1992, its goal is to mobilize growing numbers of people around the world to press their governments (or sometimes corporations) for stronger action to solve global problems: environmental degradation, poverty, war and the abuse of human rights. Has international offices in Chile, the UK and the US and partner organizations in 162 countries.

Earth Rights International (ERI)
1612 K St. NW, Suite 401
Washington, DC 20006
US
www.earthrights.org
ERI is a nonprofit group of activists, organizers and lawyers with expertise in human rights, the environment, and corporate and government accountability. It also has an office in Southeast Asia.

Focus on the Global South
c/o CUSRI, Chulalongkorn University,
Wisit Prachuabmoh Building,
Bangkok-10330
Thailand
www.focusweb.org
Focus on the Global South is a program of development policy research, analysis and action. It was founded in 1995, the same year the World Trade Organization came into existence, and reflects the priorities of a people's movement grappling with the impact of corporate-driven globalization on the daily lives and struggles of the poor and marginalized people in the South.

Friends of the Earth International
PO Box 19199
1000 GD Amsterdam
The Netherlands
Tel: +31 20 622 1369
Fax: +31 20 639 2181
info@foei.org
www.foei.org
Friends of the Earth International is a federation of autonomous environmental organizations from all over the world. Its members, in 68 countries, campaign on the most urgent environmental and social issues of the day, while simultaneously catalyzing a shift toward sustainable societies.

Greenpeace International
Ottho Heldringstraat 5
1066 AZ Amsterdam
The Netherlands
www.greenpeace.org
Greenpeace focuses on the most crucial threats to our planet's biodiversity and environment. It campaigns to: stop climate change, protect ancient forests, save the oceans, stop whaling, say no to genetic engineering, stop the nuclear threat, eliminate toxic chemicals and encourage sustainable trade. Formed in 1971, it now has a presence in 40 countries across Europe, the Americas, Asia and the Pacific. It uses research, lobbying and quiet diplomacy to pursue its goals, as well as high-profile, non-violent conflict to raise the level and quality of public debate.

HelpAge International
www.helpage.org
Founded in 1983, this is a global network of not-for-profit organizations with a mission to work with and for disadvantaged older people worldwide to achieve a lasting improvement in the quality of their lives.

Human Rights Watch
www.hrw.org
Originally a US organization, it now also has offices in London, Brussels, Sarajevo, Moscow, Tbilisi, Tashkent, Dushanbe and Rio de Janeiro. It is dedicated to protecting the human rights of people around the world, investigating and exposing human-rights violations and holding abusers accountable. It also challenges governments to end abusive practices and respect international human-rights law.

Institute for War and Peace Reporting
Lancaster House, 33 Islington High Street,
London N1 9LH
UK
www.iwpr.net
Also has offices in Armenia, Azerbaijan, Georgia, Kazakhstan, Kosovo, Kyrgyzstan and Serbia. Works to inform the international debate on conflict and support the independent media in regions in transition. Publishes the magazine *WarReport*.

International Alert
1 Glyn Street
London SE11 5HT
UK
www.international-alert.org
A charity committed to the just
and peaceful transformation of
violent conflicts. International
Alert seeks to advance individual
and collective human rights by
helping to identify and address
the root causes of violence.

**International Baby Food Action
Network (IBFAN)**
www.ibfan.org
IBFAN consists of public interest
groups working around the world
to reduce infant and young child
morbidity and mortality. It co-
ordinates international
campaigning against and boycotts
of companies breaching the
International Code of Marketing
of Breastmilk Substitutes, which
continue to cause the deaths of
babies and young children in the
developing world.

**International Campaign to Ban
Landmines**
110 Maryland Ave NE
Box 6, Suite 509
Washington DC 20002
US
www.icbl.org
An international network of more
than 1,400 NGOs in 90 countries
working for a global ban on
landmines. The organization won
the 1997 Nobel Peace Prize.

**International Community of
Women Living with HIV/AIDS**
2C Leroy House, 436 Essex Road
London N1 3QP
UK
www.icw.org
Formed at the International AIDS
Conference in Amsterdam in 1992
in response to the desperate lack of
support and information available
to HIV-positive women worldwide.

International HIV/AIDS Alliance
Queensberry House, 104–106
Queens Road
Brighton BN1 3XF
UK
www.aidsalliance.org
Established in 1993 as an
international NGO supporting
community action on HIV and
AIDS in developing countries.

**International Planned
Parenthood Federation (IPPF)**
Regent's College, Inner Circle,
Regent's Park
London NW1 4NS, UK
www.ippf.org
Founded in Mumbai, India, in
1952, IPPF is the world's leading
voluntary organization in this
field. It exists to support sexual
and reproductive health
programmes – including family
planning – through more than 150
national family planning
associations in over 100 countries.

**International Red Cross and
Red Crescent Movement
International Committee of the
Red Cross**
www.icrc.org
**International Federation of
Red Cross and Red Crescent
Societies**
www.ifrc.org
The International Red Cross and
Red Crescent Movement is the
largest independent humanitarian
organization in the world. It was
inspired by a Swiss entrepreneur
who, appalled by the suffering of
thousands left to die after the
Battle of Solferino in 1859,
proposed setting up national relief
societies of volunteers that would
provide neutral and impartial help
in times of war. The movement's
key principles are: humanity;
impartiality; neutrality;
independence; voluntary service;
unity; and universality.
The Federation is the focal point
for the national societies and is
primarily concerned with the
victims of natural disasters; the
ICRC is concerned with the victims
of war. The Movement enforces
the Geneva Conventions.

Médecins Sans Frontières (MSF)
www.msf.org
Formed in 1971, MSF provides
emergency medical assistance to
populations in danger in more than
80 countries. MSF works in
rehabilitation of hospitals and
dispensaries, vaccination
programmes and water and
sanitation projects. MSF also works
in remote healthcare centres, slum
areas and provides training of local
personnel. All this is done with the
objective of rebuilding health
structures to acceptable levels.

Minority Rights Group (MRG)
International Secretariat
379 Brixton Road
London SW9 7DE
UK
www.minorityrights.org
MRG works to secure rights for
ethnic, religious and linguistic
minorities worldwide, and to
promote co-operation and
understanding between
communities. To this end it engages
in advocacy, training, publishing,
facilitating and outreach.

One World International
9 White Lion Street
London NW1 9DB
www.oneworld.org
Originally launched as One World
Online in 1995, it became a global
organization in 1999 and now has
centres in Austria, Costa Rica,
Finland, India, Italy, the
Netherlands, the UK, the US and
Zambia. Partner organizations
form a global network sharing a
common aim of using the internet
to promote human rights and
sustainable development.

Oxfam International
www.oxfam.org
Originally a British aid organization
formed in 1942, Oxfam
International is now a
confederation of 12 organizations
working together with over 3,000
partners in more than 100 countries
to find lasting solutions to poverty,
suffering and injustice. It seeks
increased worldwide public
understanding that economic and
social justice are crucial to
sustainable development.

**Peoples' Global Action (PGA)
c/o Canadian Union of Postal
Workers (CUPW),**
377 Bank Street,
Ottawa, Ontario, Canada
www.agp.org
Formed in 1998 to co-ordinate
worldwide resistance to the global
market, the alliance's full title is
Peoples' Global Action against
'Free' Trade and the World Trade
Organization. Its major activity has
been coordinating decentralized
Global Action Days around the
world to highlight the global
resistance of popular movements
to capitalist globalization.

Pesticide Action Network (PAN)
www.pan-international.org
Pesticide Action Network (PAN) is a
network of over 600 participating
NGOs, institutions and individuals
in over 90 countries working to
replace the use of hazardous
pesticides with ecologically sound
alternatives. Its projects and
campaigns are co-ordinated by five
autonomous regional centers in
North America, Latin America,
Europe, Africa and Asia-Pacific.

**Save the Children
International Save the Children
Alliance**
Second Floor, Cambridge House
100 Cambridge Grove
London W6 0LE
UK
www.savethechildren.net
27 Save the Children organizations
make up the International Save
the Children Alliance, which works
in over 115 countries. The
organization fights for children's
rights while aiming to deliver
immediate and lasting
improvements to children's lives
worldwide.

Third World Network
121-S, Jalan Utama, 10450
Penang
Malaysia
www.twnside.org.sg
Third World Network is an
independent non-profit
international network of
organizations and individuals
involved in issues relating to
development, the Third World and
North-South issues. Its objectives
are to conduct research on
economic, social and

environmental issues pertaining to
the South; to publish books and
magazines; to organize and
participate in seminars; and to
provide a platform representing
broadly Southern interests and
perspectives at international
forums such as the UN conferences
and processes. It also has offices in
Delhi, India; Montevideo, Uruguay;
Geneva; and Accra, Ghana.

Transparency International (TI)
International Secretariat, Otto-
Suhr-Allee 97/99, 10585 Berlin,
Germany
www.transparency.org
Founded in 1993 as a global
coalition against corruption, TI has
more than 85 independent national
chapters and annually publishes the
Global Corruption Report.

**World Rainforest Movement
(WRM)**
International Secretariat
Maldonado 1858
11200 Montevideo
Uruguay
www.wrm.org.uy
Established in 1986, the WRM is an
international network of citizens'
groups of North and South
involved in efforts to defend the
world's rainforests. It works to
secure the lands and livelihoods of
forest peoples and supports their
efforts to defend the forests from
commercial logging, dams, mining,
plantations, shrimp farms,
colonization, settlement and other
projects that threaten them.

**Worldwide Fund for Nature
(WWF)**
www.panda.org
World Wildlife Fund was founded
in 1961 to preserve wildlife and
natural habitats. In 1989 it
changed its name to the
Worldwide Fund for Nature and its
key aims are now expanded to:
conserving the world's biological
diversity, ensuring that the use of
renewable natural resources is
sustainable and promoting the
reduction of pollution and
wasteful consumption.

World Social Forum
www.worldsocialforum.org
The World Social Forum, which
takes place annually in January, is
an open meeting place where
groups and movements of civil
society opposed to neo-liberalism
and a world dominated by capital
or by any form of imperialism, but
engaged in building a planetary
society centred on the human
person, come together to debate
ideas, to formulate proposals, to
share experiences freely and
network for effective action.
Regional and local social forums
are also increasingly active and
important.

Countries of the world

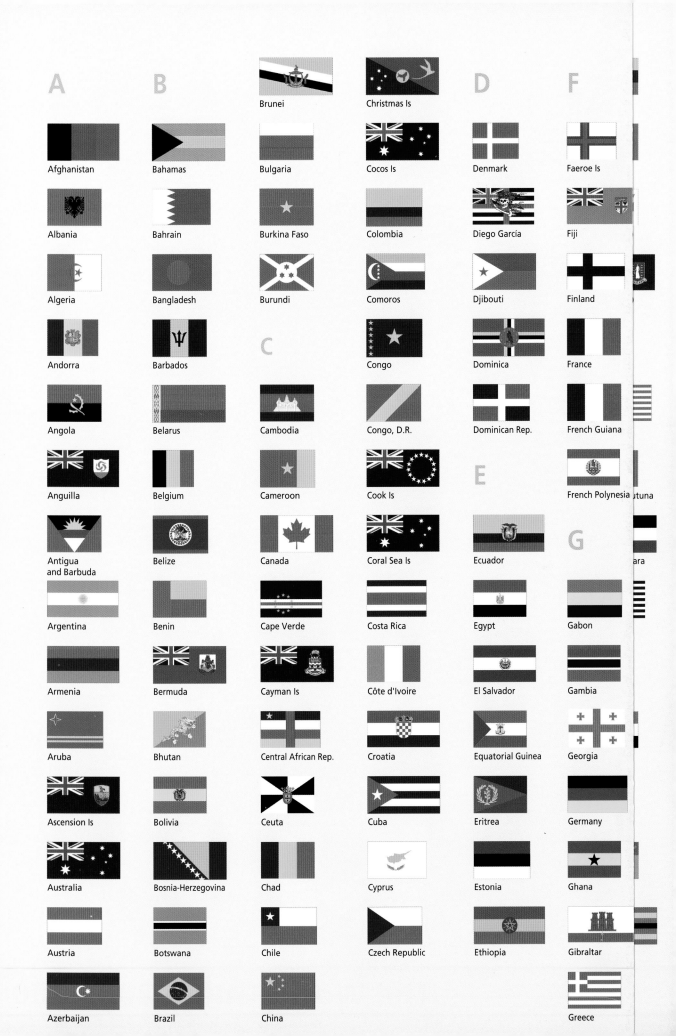

A

Afghanistan

Albania

Algeria

Andorra

Angola

Anguilla

Antigua and Barbuda

Argentina

Armenia

Aruba

Ascension Is

Australia

Austria

Azerbaijan

B

Bahamas

Bahrain

Bangladesh

Barbados

Belarus

Belgium

Belize

Benin

Bermuda

Bhutan

Bolivia

Bosnia-Herzegovina

Botswana

Brazil

Brunei

Bulgaria

Burkina Faso

Burundi

C

Cambodia

Cameroon

Canada

Cape Verde

Central African Rep.

Ceuta

Chad

Chile

China

Christmas Is

Cocos Is

Colombia

Comoros

Congo

Congo, D.R.

Cook Is

Coral Sea Is

Costa Rica

Côte d'Ivoire

Croatia

Cuba

Cyprus

Czech Republic

D

Denmark

Diego García

Djibouti

Dominica

Dominican Rep.

E

Ecuador

Egypt

El Salvador

Equatorial Guinea

Eritrea

Estonia

Ethiopia

F

Faeroe Is

Fiji

Finland

France

French Guiana

French Polynesia

G

Gabon

Gambia

Georgia

Germany

Ghana

Gibraltar

Greece

THE POLITICAL WORLD

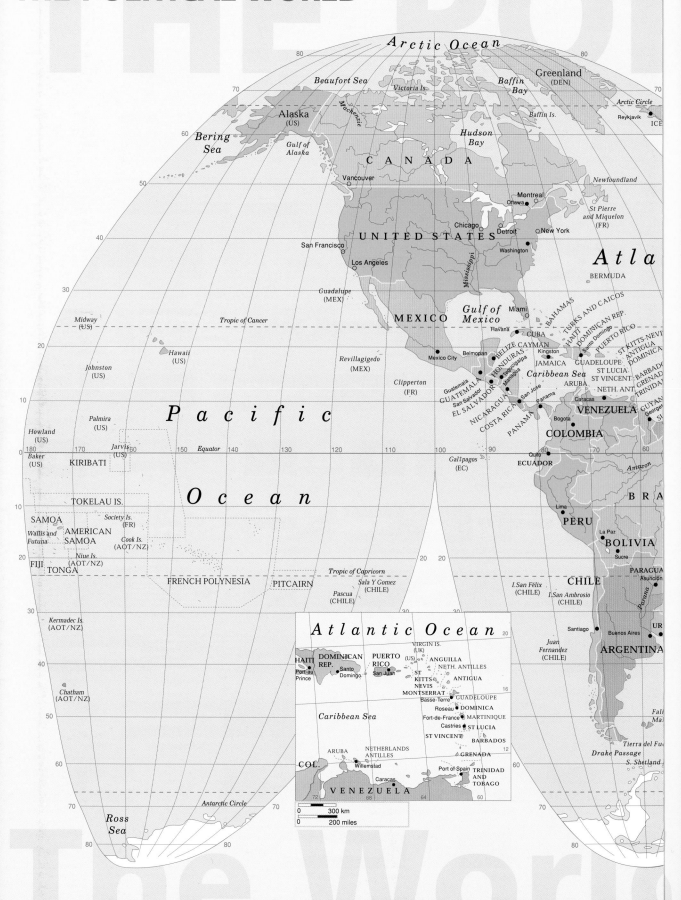

Arctic Ocean

Greenland
(DEN)

Beaufort Sea

Baffin Bay

Victoria Is.

Baffin Is.

Arctic Circle

Alaska
(US)

Mackenzie

Reykjavik

ICE

Bering Sea

Gulf of Alaska

Hudson Bay

C A N A D A

Newfoundland

Vancouver

Montreal

St Pierre and Miquelon
(FR)

Ottawa

Chicago

Detroit

New York

San Francisco

U N I T E D   S T A T E S

A t l a

Washington

BERMUDA

Los Angeles

Mississippi

Guadalupe
(MEX)

MEXICO

Gulf of Mexico

Miami

Havana

CUBA

BAHAMAS

TURKS AND CAICOS

DOMINICAN REP.

Tropic of Cancer

ST KITTS-NEVIS

ANTIGUA

Midway
(US)

Hawaii
(US)

Revillagigedo
(MEX)

Mexico City

Belmopan

BELIZE CAYMAN

Kingston

Santo Domingo

PUERTO RICO

GUADELOUPE

DOMINICA

Johnston
(US)

Clipperton
(FR)

Guatemala

HONDURAS

Tegucigalpa

Managua

Caribbean Sea

ST LUCIA

ST VINCENT

BARBADO

San Salvador

GUATEMALA

JAMAICA

ARUBA

NETH. ANT.

GRENAD

TRINIDA

P a c i f i c

EL SALVADOR

NICARAGUA

San José

Panama

Caracas

VENEZUELA

GUYAN

Palmira
(US)

COSTA RICA

PANAMA

Bogotá

Georget

SI

Howland
(US)

Baker
(US)

Jarvis
(US)

Equator

Gal‡pagos
(EC)

Quito

ECUADOR

COLOMBIA

KIRIBATI

O c e a n

Amazon

B R A

TOKELAU IS.

SAMOA

Society Is.
(FR)

Lima

PERU

Wallis and Futuna

AMERICAN SAMOA

Cook Is.
(AOT/NZ)

La Paz

BOLIVIA

FIJI

Niue Is.
(AOT/NZ)

Sucre

TONGA

Tropic of Capricorn

PARAGUA

FRENCH POLYNESIA

PITCAIRN

Sala Y Gomez
(CHILE)

CHILE

Asunción

Parana

Kermadec Is.
(AOT/NZ)

Pascua
(CHILE)

I.San Félix
(CHILE)

I.San Ambrosio
(CHILE)

UR

Juan Fernandez
(CHILE)

Santiago

Buenos Aires

UR

Chatham
(AOT/NZ)

ARGENTINA

Fal

Ma

Tierra del Fue

Drake Passage

S. Shetland

Ross Sea

Antarctic Circle

Atlantic Ocean

VIRGIN IS.
(UK)

ANGUILLA

NETH. ANTILLES

HAITI

DOMINICAN REP.

PUERTO RICO

Port-au-Prince

Santo Domingo

San Juan

ST KITTS & NEVIS

ANTIGUA

MONTSERRAT

GUADELOUPE

Basse-Terre

Roseau

DOMINICA

Caribbean Sea

Fort-de-France

MARTINIQUE

Castries

ST LUCIA

ST VINCENT

BARBADOS

ARUBA

NETHERLANDS ANTILLES

GRENADA

COL.

Willemstad

Port of Spain

TRINIDAD AND TOBAGO

VENEZUELA

Caracas

0	300 km
0	200 miles

6

Afghanistan / Afghanestan

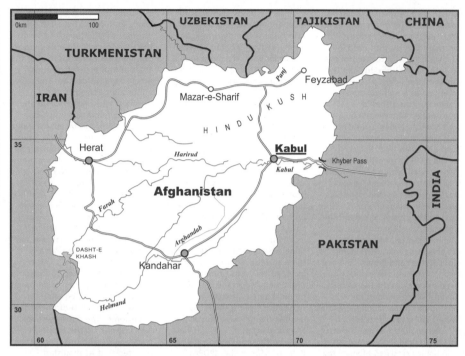

Population:	25,971,254
Area:	652,090 km²
Capital:	Kabul
Currency:	Afghani
Language:	Pashtu

T he territory now known as Afghanistan is believed to have been inhabited in the Neolithic era, 100,000 years BC. In a cave at Darra-i-Kur, in Badakhshan, fragments were found of a Neanderthal skull. During the Bronze Age, in the third and second millennia BC, with the rise in commerce with Mesopotamia and Egypt, and the export of lapis lazuli extracted from the Badakhshan mines, the first urban centers were founded: Mundigak and Deh Murasi Ghundai. While the mesa region of Persia, the Central Asian steppes and the Indo valley saw important population growth, the region became a migration route, and the Khyber Pass turned into a gateway to northern India.

2   Throughout its history, the territory has been known primarily by three names: Ariana, when the Arian tribes settled there around 2000 BC, Khurasan in the medieval period, and Afghanistan in the modern era. It is thought that Kabul was founded during the Arian settlement and that the *Rig-Veda*, one of the founding texts of Hinduism, was written in Ariana.

3   The region was incorporated into the Persian Empire of Cyrus the Great in the 6th century BC, and there is speculation that around this time the Zoroastrian

LAND USE

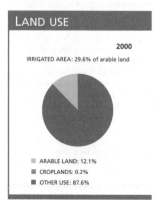

2000

IRRIGATED AREA: 29.6% of arable land

- ■ ARABLE LAND: 12.1%
- ■ CROPLANDS: 0.2%
- ■ OTHER USE: 87.6%

WORKERS

LABOR FORCE   2002

■ FEMALE: 35.8%   ■ MALE: 64.2%

religion was introduced in what is known as Bactria. Three centuries later, Alexander of Macedonia (who founded Alexandropolis, present-day Kandahar) pushed out the Persians and incorporated the territory into the Alexandrian empire. Upon his death, in 323 BC, the eastern Satraps came under the dominance of the Seleucid dynasty, which governed from Babylon. In 250 BC, Diodoth, a local Greco-Bactrian governor, declared the Amu River plains independent. The Greco-Bactrians expanded southwards and, in 180 BC, established their dominion in Kabul and Punjab. The Parthians of eastern Iran broke off from the Seleucids, taking over Seistan and Kandahar.

4   A confederation of five Central Asian nomad tribes, known as the Yüeh-chih, deposed the Greco-Bactrian kingdom and, united under the Kusana tribe, conquered the rest of the territory, establishing a kingdom of the same name, which turned into a trade center between Rome, India and China, opening the way for the 'silk route'. In the 2nd century AD, the empire of

King Kaniska stretched from Mathura, in north and central India, to the Chinese borders in Central Asia.

5   The Sassanian Persian Empire annexed part of the Kusana empire in the 3rd century and in the following century a new wave of Central Asian nomads, known as Heftali, took control of the territory. In 550 AD, the Persians re-conquered what is Afghanistan today, though they faced repeated uprisings by the Afghan tribes.

6   Islam was introduced when Muslim forces defeated the Sassanians in 642 in Nahavand (near present-day Hamadan, in Iran) and spread to Afghan territory. The 9th and 10th centuries saw the rise of various local Islamic dynasties, one of the first being that of the Tahirids, established in Khorasan, and whose dominion included Balkh and Herat. That dynasty was succeeded by the Saffarids, natives of Seistan. The northern areas soon became feudatories of the powerful Samanids, who ruled from Bujara, making their grandeur known in Samarcanda, Balkh and Herat.

7   The Mongols, under the command of Genghis Khan, invaded the eastern portion of Sultan Ala ad-Din's empire in 1219, and conquered the territory in 1221, making it part of their own vast empire. With the breakup of the empire following Genghis' death in 1227, some local leaders were able to maintain autonomous fiefdoms, while others swore servitude to

the Mongol princes. In 1360, they fell under the reign of Timur Lenk (Tamerlane), the Turkish conqueror of Islamic faith, whose descendants governed Khorasan until the beginning of the 16th century.

8   With the rise of the third Persian Shi'a empire (1502) and the empire of the Great Mogul in India (1526), the region became the scene of constant battles between the Mongols who dominated Kabul, the Saffavid Persians who controlled the southern region, and the Uzbek descendants of Tamerlane who ruled the northwest. The battles and political upheaval gave way to unification in 1747 when an assembly of local chieftains elected Shah Ahmad Durrani, a military commander who had previously served Persian sovereigns. Ruling by military might, the new shah consolidated the national borders, which would be threatened by the expansionism of Czarist Russia and the interests of Britain, which controlled India.

9   The first British-Afghan War (1839-1842), which the British Empire lost, reinforced Dost Muhammad Shah's slightly pro-Russian sympathies. He sought to increase his influence in northern India by encouraging anti-British movements. His son Sher Ali Shah continued this policy, which led British forces to invade the country once again.

10   As a result of the second British-Afghan War (1878-1880), the Durrani dynasty was

Life expectancy
43.1 years
2000-2005

Literacy
36% total adult rate
2000

overthrown. Afghanistan lost its territories south of the Khyber and became a buffer state between Czarist Russia and India. The country thus lost control over its foreign relations. In 1893, the Durand Line, which was not intended as a political border, delineated the zones of responsibility for maintaining law and order between British India and Emir Abdor Rahaman Khan, who governed from Kabul.

[11] In 1919, after a third British-Afghan war, lasting four months, the country was freed from British protection. Independence leader Emir Amanullah Khan (the heir and grandson of the British-imposed ruler) came to power and modernized the country. He enacted a relatively liberal Constitution and became the first head of state in the world to establish diplomatic ties with the Soviet Union, marking the beginning of special relations that would last seven decades.

[12] Amanullah was overthrown in 1929 by the Mohammadzai clan, which crowned Muhammad Nadir Shah. A new Constitution in 1931 recognized the autonomy of local leaders. The new Shah was assassinated in 1933 and the crown went to his son Zahir, who for the first 20 years of his reign attempted to consolidate the country, expanding foreign relations and promoting internal development. Once Pakistan became independent in 1947, the old Durand Line left the country with the problem of determining the political status of the Pashtuns who lived on the Pakistani side.

[13] Lt-Gen. Muhammad Daud Khan, the Shah's cousin and brother-in-law, became Prime Minister in 1953 and launched a new modernization process: he nationalized utilities, built roads, irrigation systems, schools and hydroelectric facilities (with US funding); he reorganized the armed forces (with Soviet assistance); and maintained neutrality throughout the Cold War. Furthermore, he abolished the obligatory use of the *chador* (veil) by women, and *purdah*, or the prohibition of women in the public sphere.

[14] Finding itself in the middle of the zone of conflict, Afghanistan attempted early in the Cold War to remain equidistant between the US and the USSR. But it grew increasingly dependent upon the USSR due to the ongoing US support of Pakistan. As of 1955, thousands of Afghans were regularly being sent to study in the Soviet Union, and particularly to receive military training.

[15] The Pashtuns' demands for independence prompted Daud to take repressive measures against them, leading Pakistan to close its border with Afghanistan in 1961. Soviet influence became evident in some Marxist leanings in the press and the government, which displeased those allied with the king. In March 1963, King Zahir 'accepted Daud's resignation' and, two months later, Pakistan reopened the border.

[16] Muhammad Yusuf was appointed prime minister. He proposed a Cabinet of technocrats and intellectuals, and pushed for a new Constitution based on the principle of individual freedom that at the same time upheld the values of Islam and the monarchy. Enacted in 1964, the Constitution for the first time allowed the creation of political parties and the holding of elections, but it indirectly banned the participation of Marxist parties.

[17] The People's Democratic Party of Afghanistan (PDPA), founded as an underground organization, staged its first anti-monarchy demonstrations in 1965. Shortly thereafter, the PDPA was split between the Khalk (consisting of the ethnic Takjik or Afghan-Persians), which advocated revolution through a worker-peasant alliance, and the *Parcham*, or Banner (of the Pashtun), which sought to establish a broad-based front involving intellectuals, the national bourgeoisie, urban middle class and military.

[18] Workers and students began to organize actively in the country's industrial regions. Demonstrations and criticisms of the king grew more frequent. Moscow, which had not fully accepted Daud's replacement, supported the naming of Daud as president in 1973 while King Zahir was abroad. With the support of the PDPA, he proclaimed Afghanistan a republic and annulled the 1964 Constitution.

[19] Daud designed a platform based on democracy and socialism, nearly identical to the one published four years earlier in the first edition of Parcham newspaper, particularly in the areas of agrarian reform, bank nationalization, industrial development and social justice. The new single-party Constitution, based on the models of Algeria and Nasser's Egypt, was approved in April 1977. Daud, who had thrown out the communist ministers and lost Moscow's backing, was elected President for a 10-year term.

[20] Daud travelled to Kuwait, Saudi Arabia and Egypt, in an attempt to re-establish ties with the Islamic world. In a desperate bid, he tried to reconcile with the Shah of Iran in 1978, which only accelerated his demise. The military organized by the Parcham assassinated Daud and his entire family, and replaced him with Nur Muhammad Taraki, who was also named Secretary-General of the PDPA. Hafizulah Amin, leader of a rival communist faction, and Babrak Karmal, leader of the Parcham, were appointed vice-premiers. Conflicts between the two were resolved in April 1979, when Amin was appointed Prime Minister. In September, Amin overthrew and assassinated his one-time ally Taraki.

[21] Amin introduced changes such as a literacy campaign based on secular values, equality for women, agrarian reform and the abolition of the dowry system, which shook up the country's traditional standards. Though he asserted that Afghanistan considered itself a non-aligned nation, the peasants, familiar with the radio broadcasts from Moscow, assumed that the new government was Marxist, pro-Soviet and, therefore, atheist. In February 1979, the US ambassador to Kabul was kidnapped and murdered. The US withdrew economic assistance and increased its hostilities towards what it considered a pro-Soviet government.

[22] Amin was assassinated in a coup, which was backed by the Soviet troops that had entered the country in December 1979 for strategic reasons. Babrak Karmal was installed as Prime Minister, president of the Revolutionary Council and PDPA Secretary-General. In several areas of the country, resistance against the Soviet invaders began to grow and *mujahedin*, or Islamic guerrillas, were organized. Islamic fundamentalists traveled to Afghan territory in volunteer expeditions financed by Saudi Arabia. Meanwhile, millions of Afghan peasants sought refuge in neighboring Pakistan and Iran.

[23] The mujahedin guerrillas, divided among various factions backed by different countries (Iran, Pakistan, Saudi Arabia and the US), coincided with the deepening divisions in Kabul. In May 1986, Mohammed Najibullah, a young doctor of Pashtun origin, replaced Karmal as PDPA Secretary-General. He announced a unilateral ceasefire in January 1987, with guarantees for guerrilla leaders willing to negotiate with the Government,

an amnesty for rebel prisoners, and the promise of a prompt withdrawal of Soviet troops. The mujahedin, however, continued their armed struggle.

[24] After six years of negotiations, an Afghan-Pakistani accord was signed in Geneva, guaranteed by both the US and USSR. The agreement ensured the voluntary return of refugees, who by then numbered more than 4 million. Another document, signed by Afghanistan and the USSR, provided for the withdrawal of Soviet troops. The PDPA was renamed Watan Party, or Party of the Homeland.

[25] In September 1991, the US and USSR agreed to stop sending arms to the Afghan Government and guerrillas, sparking confrontation between Saudi Arabia and Iran, and the Afghan mujahedin groups they each financed. The Kabul regime was left without foreign support following the break-up of the USSR. After Najibullah sought refuge at the UN headquarters in Kabul, in April 1992 (marking the collapse of the communist regime), the Government was left in the hands of the four vice-presidents.

[26] The Government announced its willingness to negotiate with the rebel groups, but its meeting with commander Ahmed Shah Massud, of the Jamiat-i-Islami, triggered demonstrations among the mujahedin belonging to the Pashtun majority in the country's south and east. From Pakistan, Gulbuddin Hekhmatyar, the head of fundamentalist group Hezb-i-Islami, threatened to start bombing the capital if the Government refused to step down. In the days that followed, the forces of Massud and Hekhmatyar clashed in Kabul itself.

[27] The alliance of 'moderate' Muslim groups, headed by Massud (the new defense minister), gained control of the capital, expelling the Islamic fundamentalists led by Gulbuddin Hekhmatyar. In May, the Interim Council formally dissolved the Watan Party (former PDPA). The KHAD, or secret police, and the National Assembly were also dismantled.

[28] Some of the Government's measures reimposed Islamic law: the sale of alcohol was outlawed, and new rules required women to cover their heads and wear traditional Islamic dress. Hekhmatyar continued fighting Kabul, demanding the withdrawal of Massud and of the militia loyal to Abdul Rashid Dostam, who had been a member of the communist government,

Under-5 mortality

257 per 1,000 live births

2002

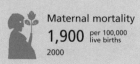

Maternal mortality

1,900 per 100,000 live births

2000

but had defected to join the Muslim guerrillas that took power.

29 By this time, the economy had come to a standstill and 60 per cent of its productive structure had been destroyed. Afghanistan had become the world's largest producer of opium. The Pakistani Government decided to put a stop to the arms and food contraband across its border with Afghanistan in order to weaken Hekhmatyar, whom it held responsible for the deterioration in relations between the two countries.

30 Beginning in 1993, the president in Kabul and head of the Jamiat-i-Islami, Buranuddin Rabbani, Hekhmatyar and Dostam were the main leaders of the conflict, marked by pacts and betrayals. The emergence in the south in 1995 of the armed Taliban (Persian, for 'students of the Qur'an'), changed the course of the war. These guerrillas, trained in Pakistan, aimed to create a united Islamic government in Afghanistan. The Taliban proclaimed that the three aforementioned leaders were a fundamentalist-communist alliance that offended Islam.

31 Pakistan, Saudi Arabia and the US supported the Taliban army, which took control of Kabul in September 1996, while the Government fled to the north. Mohammed Omar Akhunzada (Mullah Omar) was elected in April 1996 as 'Commander of the believers' (*amir ol momumin*) in the Taliban territories. In June 1977 the United National Islamic Front for the Salvation of Afghanistan, better known as Northern Alliance (NA) or United Front, was formed, made up mainly by Tajik, Uzbek and Hazara factions.

32 Once in control of Kabul, and following its principle to rule according to its own interpretation of the *Qur'an*, the Taliban banished women from the public sphere, excluding them from education and reviving purdah. At the same time, it outlawed music and singing (except religious hymns), cinema, theater and alcohol, declaring them 'non Islamic'. By late 2000, the Taliban army controlled more than 95 per cent of Afghan territory.

33 On September 3 2001, the NA leader Massud was assassinated - supposedly under orders from Mullah Omar - which would have been a mortal blow for the opposition's aspirations had it not been for the terrorist attacks of September 11 against New York and Washington. These unleashed US wrath in the 'war on terrorism' against terrorist

organization al-Qaeda, led by Saudi Osama bin Laden, a former mujahed who lived in Afghanistan along with thousands of his men, sheltered by the Taliban.

34 In September 2001, the Council of Elders, meeting in Kabul, asked the Taliban regime to persuade Bin Laden to leave the country of his own free will. The council also resolved to call for a *jihad* (holy war) in case the US attacked Afghanistan.

35 The US began its air raids on Afghanistan on October 7, in the context of a campaign initially called Infinite Justice and later Enduring Freedom by President George W Bush. The coalition against Afghanistan had direct participation from the US, UK, Australia and Canada and the support of the EU and NATO (including Turkey), China, Russia, Israel, India, Saudi Arabia and former Taliban ally Pakistan. Iran and Iraq condemned the attacks. Rabbani not only welcomed Western military intervention, but linked the future of Afghanistan to the 'destruction' of the Taliban.

36 As the war evolved, Rabbani's leadership weakened hugely and

a triumvirate - formed by Abdullah Abdullah, Foreign Minister and main spokesperson of the Front, Yunus Qanuni, Home Minister, and Mohammad Qasem Fahim, Defense Minister - took his place. The first two represented the new generation of leaders formed abroad and with a strong secular orientation, while Massud's right-hand man, Fahim, was more like Rabbani in orientation.

37 After air raids that lasted several weeks, the NA recovered two-thirds of the country. Finally, on November 13, and breaking its

IN FOCUS

ENVIRONMENTAL CHALLENGES
The increasing rate of deforestation is a key environmental issue. Safe water resources are very scarce. Huge areas of land and buildings were devastated by the war.

WOMEN'S RIGHTS
Women have voted and run for office since 1963. Most of their rights were severely curtailed between 1992 and 2001. The female suicide rate rose considerably in that period. Since 2001 the transitional Government has been under pressure from the international community and international human rights NGOs to improve the oppressive situation of Afghan women. Among other restrictions they still face inadequate access to healthcare and nutrition services. Making blood transfusions safe is specially important for maternal health care and to prevent the spread of HIV in the region.

Unfortunately, there is no accurate data on the disease in the country. Afghanistan has one of the highest maternal mortality ratios, together with low life expectancy and severe malnutrition. Girls make up 30 per cent of all school students, a massive increase compared with previous years*. However, in southern and eastern Afghanistan, female enrolment remained extremely low.

CHILDREN
Under-5 mortality maches at 257 per 1,000 live births, the second-highest rate in the world*. A lack of immunization against common childhood diseases has resulted in measles killing 35,000 children every year. Although 80 per cent of

children were immunized in 2002 against measles and polio, this coverage must continue because of the risk of cross-border transmission of polio. Goitre and stunting are common, due to a lack of minerals (iodine, iron) among mothers and children.

The shortage of drinking water causes frequent child diarrhea in the summertime. Almost 65 per cent of the urban population and 81 per cent of the rural population have no access to drinking water. Three million children received some type of education in 2002, mostly primary. The school system is overwhelmed by the demand, and classrooms, materials and teachers are needed. Landmines threaten the lives of the population. It was estimated that between 150 and 300 Afghans were killed or injured by mines every month in 2002.

INDIGENOUS PEOPLES/ETHNIC MINORITIES
The Hazara speak Farsi, are Shi'a Muslims and live in the central hills (Hazarajata) of Afghanistan. The Hazara lived in other parts of the country in the past, but were displaced by the Sunni and Pashtun in the 18th and 19th centuries. Their political, economic and cultural status is vulnerable since they are both an ethnic and religious minority. The Hazara territory was used as a battlefield during the Afghan civil war. Several massacres of Hazara civilians took place between 1998 and 2000.

The Uzbek, Sunni Muslims, are Turkic from an ethnic and linguistic point of view, and live and work in the northern agricultural region of the country, bordering their relatives in Uzbekistan. Uzbek women are renowned as carpet weavers, and this has historically supplied their community with extra income. This

economic advantage has given way to political ones, and Uzbeks have held political office in several Afghan governments.

MIGRANTS/REFUGEES
In 2002, more than 3.5 million Afghans were refugees, especially in Iran and Pakistan. Some 30,000 lived in other countries of the region, such as India and Tajikistan. Millions of refugees and internally displaced people returned to their country or community that year. Hundreds of famillies returned unattended, and many resettled in Kabul and not in their original places of residence, where rebuilding their old homes or livelihoods was impossible. In 2002 there were some 700,000 displaced people.

Some 30,000 Afghans requested asylum in Europe, North America and Oceania in 2002, above all in the United Kingdom, Germany, Hungary and Slovakia.

Human rights groups reported that Iran and Pakistan may have forced the repatriation of Afghan refugees in 2002, based on reports of police abuse against refugees and restrictions to jobs, healthcare and education.

In addition, refugees and internal displaced people are particularly vulnerable to HIV for various reasons, including exposure to sexual abuse, violence and lack of access to information and education.

DEATH PENALTY
It is currently applied as a punishment, even for common crimes.

*Latest data available in *The State of the World's Children* and *Childinfo* database, UNICEF, 2004.

Malnutrition
48% under-5s
1995-2002

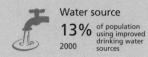

Water source
13% of population
using improved
2000   drinking water
sources

promise not to take over Kabul until a transition government had been formed, NA forces took the city. Most of the population welcomed the NA's arrival, which put an end to the Taliban regime and US bombings.

[38] The Taliban's collapse was apparent when the inter-Afghan Conference was held in Bonn. For the first time, two women took part in such a debate. An agreement was reached to create an Interim Administration of 30 members, with monarchist Pashtun Hamid Karzai as chairman. A two-and-a-half-year schedule was agreed to prepare for general elections, and prior to that there would be an emergency Loya Jirga (assembly), a Transitional Authority and a Constitutional *Loya Jirga*, assisted by an International Security Force from the UN. The NA obtained 18 out of the 29 Ministries. Abdullah, Qanuni and Fahim were confirmed in the roles they held in the Alliance Government, while former king Mohamed Zahir Shah was to open the Loya Jirga. Rabbani accepted the decisions taken on December 12, even when - according to him - Karzai was a President 'imposed from abroad'. Karzai took office on December 22.

[39] In February 2002 Bush gave the order to resume trade relations with Afghanistan, suspended in January 1986 after the Soviet invasion. Fighting continued between different factions, while Osama bin Laden and Mullah Omar, targets of the global anti-terrorist hunt headed by the US, had not been found.

[40] In spite of the so-called end of the war, Afghanistan was still subject to attacks. In July 2002 almost 50 Afghan civilians were killed and more than 100 injured by a US military aircraft in the southern village of Deh Rawud. Some days later Deputy President Haji Abdul Qadir and his driver died in a hail of bullets in Kabul as the car drove through the entrance of the Public Works Ministry. Qadir, a Pashtun, had helped fight the Taliban as a former NA commander in eastern Afghanistan.

[41] In September Karzai survived an assassination attempt in Kandahar, by a suspected member of al-Qaeda. The gunman - later identified as Abdul Rahman - fired four rounds into his car, wounding the Kandahar governor Gul Agha Sherzai and a bodyguard. As US soldiers guarding the President fired back, the attacker and an Afghan bodyguard were killed. This attack happened only hours after a car bomb exploded and killed at least 10 people in Kabul.

[42] The Afghan territory was one of the most heavily mined in the world in late 2002, after more than two decades of armed conflict.

[43] Most of the country was under control of powerful warlords who carried on without interference from the central government and with the support of the US. President Karzai's authority was mostly limited to the capital.

[44] In the context of a virtual opening-up to the world, in March 2003 Afghanistan launched its own domain in cyberspace: .af. Under the Taliban regime the use of the web by persons not belonging to the Government was punished by death.

[45] Despite the disappearance of the Taliban regime, the plight of women remained dire. Women outside of Kabul who wished to study or work were persecuted, girls were still forced to marry, and a large number of Afghan children - some as young as 4 - were kidnapped to be sold abroad as sex or work slaves.

[46] NATO launched a peace mission in the country in August 2003, the first outside Europe in the 54-year history of the organization. NATO was to be in charge of planning, supervising, commanding and controlling the International Assistance Security Force in Afghanistan, under the auspices of the UN.

[47] As a first step toward the June 2004 elections, the UN and the Afghan Government signed in August an agreement to adopt an electoral registration programme, in preparation for the first national elections in 30 years. The groups that travelled throughout the country included female teams, in order to facilitate the registration of women voters.

[48] In November, a draft for a Constitution was sent by the Constitutional Revision Commission to President Karzai and the UN special envoy, Lakhdar Brahimi. The draft provides for the creation of an Islamic republic with equal rights for all its citizens. There is no reference made to the *sharia* or Islamic law, but it is assumed no laws shall contradict Islam. If the text is approved, women would have a representation quota in the two-chamber Parliament, and would receive special attention in education and health. However, Amnesty International warned the draft does not protect women's rights since it does not specifically ban gender-based discrimination and does not fully recognize equality between men and women.

[49] In the midst of growing instability, the UN suspended in November all its activities in the province of Ghazni, in eastern Afghanistan, after the murder of a female worker belonging to its refugee agency.

[50] Nine Afghan children and one adult were killed in December after a US plane bombed a town in the province of Ghazni. The UN condemned the attack and demanded an immediate investigation of the incident.

[51] The non-governmental organization Human Rights Watch (HRW) denounced in May 2004 the 'systemic mistreatment' of Afghan prisoners by US troops and called for the immediate release of details on the deaths of three of them. The NGO documented 'numerous cases of mistreatment of detainees', similar to those reported in Iraq, also by US troops, that violated international law. The detainees were deprived of sleep, exposed to freezing temperatures, severely beaten, stripped and photographed naked. Also, Manoel de Almeida e Silva, the UN spokesperson, stated that he had been receiving reports of violations for the past two years. At least 300 Afghans were believed to be held at the main US base at Bagram, north of Kabul, while an unknown number was being held at other (secret) sites.

[52] In October 2004 Hamid Karzai won the country's first-ever democratic presidential election, which was supervised by the UN against a backdrop of fraud, intimidation and violence. ∎

PROFILE

ENVIRONMENT

The country consists of a system of highland plains and plateaus, separated by east-west mountain ranges (principally the Hindu Kush) which converge on the Himalayan Pamir. The main cities are located in the eastern valleys. The country is dry and rocky though there are many fertile lowlands and valleys where cotton, fruit and grain are grown. Coal, natural gas and iron ore are the main mineral resources.

SOCIETY

Peoples: Pashtun 44 per cent, Tajik 25 per cent, Hazara 10 per cent and Uzbek 8 per cent. The rest is composed of peoples of Turkic origin and nomads of Mongolian origin.
Religions: 99 per cent of the population is Muslim (74 per cent Sunni, 15 per cent Shi'a, and 10 per cent others).
Languages: Pashtu and Persian (Dari) are the official languages. There is also a great variety of languages, mainly of Persian or Turkic root: Hazaragi, Turkmen, Uzbek, Aimaq, among others.
Main political parties: Among those parties that made up the United National and Islamic Front for the Salvation of Afghanistan - usually known as Northern Alliance or United Front, - and supported the new government are: Islamic Society, Islamic Unity Party, Islamic Movement, National Islamic Movement. The Taliban Party was militarily defeated and was left out of the government.
Main Social Organizations: Trade unions are very weak because industrial activity is not significant. Other social organizations operate especially among Afghans living abroad, such as: Revolutionary Afghan Women's Association (RAWA); Humanitarian Assistance for the Women and Children of Afghanistan (HAWCA), Co-ordinating Council for National Unity and Conciliation in Afghanistan.

THE STATE

Official name: Doulat i Islami-ye Afghánistan (Islamic State of Afghanistan). Emirat i Islami ye Afghánistan (name under Taliban rule).
Administrative Divisions: 31 provinces.
Capital: Kabul 2,956,000 people (2003).
Other Cities: Kandahar 329,300 people; Herat 161,700; Mazar-e-Sharif 232,800 (2000).
Government: The Pashtun and monarchist Hamid Karzai was interim president since 22 December 2001; elected president in June 2002 (term runs until the elections of 2004) by the *Loya Jirga*, grand assembly of 2,000 delegates (1,051 elected members, 160 for women, 53 for current government, 106 seats for refugees and internally displaced Afghans, 25 for nomads).
National Holiday: 19 August, Independence Day (1919).

Albania / Shqipëria

Population:	3,220,164
Area:	28,750 km²
Capital:	Tirana (Tiranë)
Currency:	New lek
Language:	Albanian

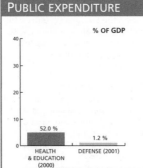

The Albanians descend from the ancient Illyrians, an Indo-European people who had migrated southward from Central Europe to the north of Greece by the beginning of the Iron Age. The southern Illyrians were much in contact with Greek colonies, while the northern Albanian tribes were mostly united under local kings. The most important of them was Argon, whose kingdom (latter half of the 3rd century BC) expanded from Dalmatia in the north to the Vijose river in the south. In the year 168 BC, the Romans conquered all of Illyria and then the Albanians became part of the prosperous Roman province of Illyricum. After 395 AD, with the decline of the Roman Empire, the area remained connected with Constantinople (now Istanbul) for administration purposes. From 491 to 565 AD three Byzantine emperors were of Illyrian origin: Anastasius I, Justin I and the most acclaimed emperor of all, Justinian I.

2   Despite the Hun incursions during the 3rd to 5th centuries, and the Slavic invasions during the 6th and 7th centuries, the Illyrians kept their own language and customs. With the passing of centuries and under the impact of the Roman, Byzantine and Slavic cultures, the old Illyrian population turned into the Albanian one. Between the 8th and 11th centuries AD, the name of Illyria started to make way for that of Albania. When the Christian Church split in 1054, southern Albania maintained links with Constantinople, while the north fell under Roman jurisdiction, marking the first significant religious fragmentation of the country.

3   When the Turks invaded in 1431, the Albanians put up stiff resistance, but succumbed 47 years later. In the late 16th century, the Ottoman Turks imposed Islam upon the country, and they kept up the Islamic pressure over the following century. By the early 18th century, two-thirds of the Albanian population had converted to Islam. More than 25 of the great Viziers of Turkey were of Albanian origin.

4   The ideologists of the nationalist movement of the 19th century, in order to overcome the religious divisions and encourage national unity, adopted the slogan 'The religion of the Albanians is Albania'. The Albanian League - which had both political and cultural aims - was founded in 1878 in the Kosovan town of Pritzen. The League tried without success to bring the Albanian territories of Kosovo, Monastir, Shkodër and Jänina (which were then divided into four provinces) together as a single state within the Ottoman Empire. On the cultural front, language, literature and an educational system which would foster nationalism were promoted.

5   The Empire suppressed the League in 1881. In 1908, Albanian leaders met in Monastir (part of present-day Macedonia) and adopted a national alphabet mainly based on Latin, which

LAND USE

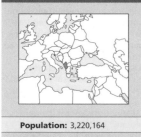

2000

IRRIGATED AREA: 48 6% of arable land

- ARABLE LAND: 21.1%
- CROPLANDS: 4.4%
- OTHER USE: 74.5%

PUBLIC EXPENDITURE

% OF GDP

HEALTH & EDUCATION (2000)	DEFENSE (2001)
52.0 %	1.2 %

WORKERS

UNEMPLOYMENT: 15.8% (2002)

LABOR FORCE   **2002**

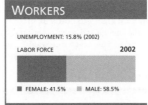

- FEMALE: 41.5%
- MALE: 58.5%

Life expectancy
73.7 years
2000-2005

GNI per capita
$1,380
2002

supplanted the previous Arabic and Greek versions. Also that year, the Young Turks took power in Istanbul and ignored their promises of bringing in democratic reforms and guaranteeing Albanian autonomy, which led to three years of armed conflict. Turkey finally accepted the Albanian demands in 1912, and independence was declared.

[6] Due to pressure from Albania's neighbors, the European powers assigned Kosovo to Serbia when drawing up the borders of the new country, allowing Greece the bulk of Sameria and a portion of Epirus. Half the Albanian population and territory was left beyond the Albanian borders.

[7] In 1914, the international powers appointed German prince Wilhelm zu Wield as King of Albania, who quickly abandoned the country due to his lack of familiarity with the Albanians. During World War I, Albania was occupied by the Austro-Hungarian, French, Italian, Greek, Montenegran and Serbian armies. US President Woodrow Wilson vetoed a plan by the French, British and Italians that aimed to divide the territory amongst its neighbors.

[8] A national congress, established in January 1920, set the basis for a new government and that same year Albania was admitted to the League of Nations. In 1927, Ahmed Zogu, president since 1925,signed a treaty with Mussolini, turning the country into a virtual Italian protectorate. In 1928 Zogu proclaimed the country a monarchy.

[9] In April 1939, Italy occupied and formally annexed Albania to the kingdom of Victor Emmanuel III. The Communists, led by Enver Hoxha, organized guerrilla resistance. The anti-Fascist front forced the withdrawal of the occupying forces on 29 November 1944, and the People's Republic was declared on 11 January 1945.

[10] Despite its desire for independence, Albania matched its internal options to external events. Upon the split between Tito and Stalin in 1948 (see former Yugoslavia), the Albanian Workers' Party sided with the KOMINFORM (communist parties allied with the Soviet Union). Albania broke with Moscow after the de-Stalinization of the early 1960 sand established close ties with the People's Republic of China, with which it eventually broke in 1981, when the Maoists

of the Cultural Revolution fell from power.

[11] The break with China became official at the Eighth Workers Party Congress, where a party line was put forth against US imperialism, Soviet socialist-imperialism, Chinese and Yugoslavian revisionism, Euro-Communism and social democracy, while condemning the policies of non-alignment and European detente, as set out in the Helsinki accords.

[12] Until Albania's liberation from Italian Fascist occupation in 1944, 85 per cent of the population lived in the countryside, and 53 per cent lacked even a patch to grow their own vegetables. In 1967 the Government established collective farming which, according to official statistics, in 1977 made the country self-sufficient in wheat. According to official figures, between 1939 and 1992 industrial output increased over 120-fold, materials 262 times over, and electricity more than 300-fold.

[13] In 1989, Ramiz Alia, - head of state since Hoxha's death in 1985 - initiated a process of restructuring. Border immigration procedures were simplified to encourage tourism; religious

worship was authorized; home ownership was permitted; capital punishment was abolished for women and the number of crimes punishable by death was reduced from 34 to 11. One year later, Alia authorized the activity of independent political parties and called for general elections after 46 years of communist rule. Diplomatic relationships were resumed with the USSR in July 1990 and with the US in February 1991.

[14] In March 1991, one thousand candidates from 11 political parties stood for election. Amidst accusations of fraud the Communists won 156 of the 250 parliamentary seats. In May, more than 300,000 workers went on strike demanding the resignation of the Government, and a 50 per cent salary increase. Prime Minister Fatos Nano dissolved his cabinet, seeking an alliance with the opposition.

[15] At the height of the economic collapse, with an 80 per cent abstention rate, the parliamentary elections of March 1992 gave the Democratic Party (DP), a spectacular triumph over the Socialist Party (SP). Sali Berisha, leader of the DP, replaced Ramiz Alia as president,thus becoming the first

IN FOCUS

ENVIRONMENTAL CHALLENGES
Most forests are degraded, wild fauna is threatened and crops are being cultivated in wooded areas. Deforestation and floods have caused significant erosion. Oil and mineral extraction have polluted air, soil and underground water, especially in the central region, while water resources are affected by non-treated domestic and industrial waste. Air pollution brought about by metallurgic, chemical and oil plants is particularly serious.

WOMEN'S RIGHTS
Albanian women have been able to vote and run for office since 1920. Between 1995 and 2000, the percentage of seats held by women in parliament fell from 11 to 5 per cent, while the percentage of ministerial and equivalent positions grew from 0 to 11 per cent.

In 2000*, illiteracy among women was 3.6 per cent, while among men it was 0.9 per cent*.

After the Kosovo War, the number of cases of neonatal tetanus increased as more mothers transmitted the

disease. The women refused to be vaccinated because of the rumor that Serbian doctors use the vaccination to sterilize Albanian women and thus limit the population.

Women make up 41 per cent of the workforce. Between 1990 and 2000, 27 per cent worked in agriculture, 45 per cent in the industrial sector and 28 per cent in services. The female unemployment rate increased between 1995 and 2000 from 13.7 to 20.9 per cent while the male rose from 11.5 to 15.8 per cent.

CHILDREN
Basic health and education services, freely available during the Communist era, are severely diminished. Child and maternal mortality rates are very high by European standards, due to malnutrition (14 per cent of children under 5*) and poor access to basic health services, especially in rural areas. An outbreak of polio in 1996 led to international co-operation which increased vaccination coverage for common childhood diseases. But Albania still lacks vaccines for diseases which have been eradicated in

industrialized countries, such as German measles and neonatal tetanus.

Sixty per cent of children experience violence in their family. In 2002 it was estimated 15,000 children were trafficked out of the country via Italy or Greece. Hundreds of children are locked up by their parents, deprived of schooling and social life, for fear they could be killed by members of feudal families that still apply the *Kanun* (a medieval code of honor, lately re-established in the poorest areas of the country).

INDIGENOUS PEOPLES/ ETHNIC MINORITIES
This is the European country with the greatest ethnic homogeneity, with Albanians making up more than 95 per cent of the population.

MIGRANTS/REFUGEES
It is estimated that there are about seven million Albanians scattered throughout the world, most of them in bordering countries. Kosovo has an Albanian majority but there are also communities in Italy, Greece, Bulgaria and

Rumania, and since 1970, the Diaspora has been extended to the rest of Europe and the US.

In 2002, almost 9,900 Albanians sought asylum in other countries: more than 5,000 in the US and the rest in the UK. Surveys carried out in 2003, show that 44 per cent of young people intend to emigrate when they come of age. Notwithstanding, most of those who emigrated during the 2001 conflict with Macedonia, returned voluntarily towards the end of that year.

Unlike 1998 and 1999, a period of massive migratory inflow, refugee situations were scarce in the country during 2002, when the National Commission for Refugees revoked a temporary protected status that had been agreed with Kosovars.

DEATH PENALTY
This still applies, though there have been no executions since 1995.

*Latest data available in *The State of the World's Children* and *Childinfo* database, UNICEF, 2004.

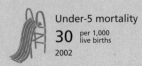
Under-5 mortality
30 per 1,000 live births
2002

Debt service
2.2% exports of goods and services
2001

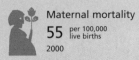
Maternal mortality
55 per 100,000 live births
2000

non-Marxist president since the end of World War II.

[16] In 1993, the Government put the main political figures of the previous regime on trial. Naxhmija Hoxha, widow of Enver, ex-President Alia and ex-Premier Nano, among others, were sent to prison convicted of misuse of public funds.

[17] The parliamentary elections of 1996, with the main opposition leaders proscribed, gave an overwhelming victory to the DP, which was accused of fraud by the US and several European countries interested in investing in Albania.

[18] In 1997, the collapse of a series of pyramid investment funds, led to a bloody social and political uprising. One in six Albanians was left penniless and the biggest cities, including the capital, Tiranë, rose in arms. Eighty per cent of weapons fell into civilian hands, after people sacked forts and barracks abandoned by the army and the police, who had joined the rebels. Armed confrontations caused 1,500 deaths. President Berisha was forced to bring forward parliamentary elections to June 1997. The SP, led by Nano (now out of jail) won the elections.

[19] Nano, back as Prime Minister had regained control of the country by the end of the year and was able to reduce inflation. The socialist government pledged to carry out reforms that included the revitalization of the economy through an extensive privatization plan.

[20] In March 1998, the IMF praised Nano's management and promised funding for three years to support Albania's economic reform. But in September that year an internal quarrel within the SP led the Prime Minister to stand down. The administration was left in charge of Pandeli Majko, who in turn had to hand over to Ilir Meta, also from the Socialist Party, in 1999.

[21] As civil war was well advanced in the former Yugoslavia (now Serbia and Montenegro), Albania called for NATO intervention to protect Kosovan Albanians and both countries broke off diplomatic relationships. Local mafias supplied weapons to the Kosovo Liberation Army (KLA), while Albania accepted tens of thousands of refugees and served as a base for the Alliance troops. Diplomatic relationships were re-established in 2001.

[22] Although the SP won a second term in the 2001 elections, new internal disputes paralyzed the Government, which was denounced by Nano as corrupt

and incompetent, leading his followers to block the appointment of new ministers. With both the Government and the economy crippled, a power shortage was compounded by a particularly harsh winter. Without funds for imports, Meta declared a state of emergency. Some areas spent up to 20 hours a day without electricity.

[23] In August 2002, after new political disputes and a series of resignations, Nano became head of government for the third time and also chair of the SP. By now the pretender to the Albanian throne, Leka Zogu, son of former King Ahmed Zogu, returned to Albania with his family after 63 years of exile.

[24] A gun culture prevails in Albania. Hundreds of thousands of weapons stolen from the police in 1997 are still circulating - many of them are trafficked in different countries around the world - and any Albanian can get hold of Russian guns, Chinese machine-guns or anti-aircraft weapons.

[25] In March 2003, during the Chemical Weapons Convention (CWC), Albania declared that it possessed chemical weapons. One month later, 110 out of the 151 members of the CWC agreed to improve the implementation of the non-proliferation treaty and the destruction of such weapons was begun right away.

[26] From 1990 the number of motor vehicles in the country grew 12 times. Although the World Health Organization (WHO) sets a limit of 50 micrograms of particles per cubic meter of air, in the streets of downtown Tirana the average daily exposure amounts to 483 micrograms. Respiratory illnesses and malignant tumors linked to pollution are a frequent cause of death.

[27] The reduction of pollution caused by cement, steel and chrome factories grouped in the industrial centre of Elbasan is possible, according to Minister of the Environment Et'hem Ruka, thanks to the development of new less contaminating techniques. However, their implementation would lead to more unemployment. In 2004 it was estimated that 37 per cent of the population lacked a stable job. The industrial sector is the most affected: seven out of 10 workers lost their jobs in the 1990s.

[28] On 10 January 2004, 21 Albanians froze to death when they attempted to cross over to Italy.

[29] In February 2004 thousands of Albanians filled the streets under the slogan 'Nano out' to accuse Prime Minister Fatos Nano

PROFILE

ENVIRONMENT

A Balkan state on the Adriatic Sea. Albania's seacoast comprises two distinct regions: from the border with Serbia and Montenegro to the Bay of Vlöre it has alluvial plains, which become partially swampy in the winter; further to the south, the coast is surrounded by mountains and has a Mediterranean climate. The soil of the mountainous inner region is very poor and cattle-raising predominates there. Cotton, tobacco and corn are grown on the plains; rice, olives, grapes and wheat are produced on the valleys. The country has large areas of forest and is rich in mineral resources, including oil deposits.

SOCIETY

Peoples: Albanians (96 per cent) are a homogeneous ethnic group, although there is an important division between the Gegs - from the north - and the Tosks - from the south. There are Greek, Bulgarian and other minorities.
Religions: Freedom of worship was authorized in 1989, having been banned since 1967. Islam (70 per cent): Sunni majority and a Shi' a-bektashi minority; Christians: Orthodox (20 per cent) and Catholic (10 per cent).
Languages: Albanian-Tosk (official) and other dialects; Greek; Macedonian, Romanian and Romani.
Main political parties: A multiparty system was established by the constitution that has been in effect since April 30 1991. Socialist Party (SP), formerly communist, now advocates democratic socialism within a free market economy; Union for Victory (made up of: Albanian Democratic Party, a liberal democratic party that supports a free market economy; National Front Party, nationalist; Republican Party-PRA, conservative; Movement of Legality, monarchic; Liberal Union Party). Other parties: Democratic Party; Social Democratic Party (PSD), supports gradual economic reforms; Unity for Human Rights; Democratic Alliance Party.
Social Organizations: The Union of Independent Trade Unions of Albania (BSPSH) and the Confederation of the Trade Unions of Albania (KSSH) are the main union federations.

THE STATE

Official Name: Republíka e Shqipërísë.
Administrative Divisions: 36 districts.
Capital: Tirana (Tiranë) 367,000 people (2003).
Other Cities: Elbasan 101,300 people; Durrës 98,400; Shkoder 84,300; Vlöre 81,000 (2000).
Government: Parliamentary republic. Alfred Moisiu, President of the Popular Assembly since July 2002. Fatos Nano, Prime Minister and Head of Government, since July 2002. Single-chamber legislature: People's Assembly, made up of 140 deputies elected by universal suffrage every four years.
National holiday: 28 November, Independence from the Turks (1912).
Armed forces: 27,000 (2001).

of leading the country into corruption and organized crime. Nano was also accused with electoral fraud. More than 2,000 police agents controlled the march held 13 years after 100,000 demonstrators toppled communist leader Hoxha's statue, on an occasion that marked the beginning of the current transition.

[30] The Prime Minister is under pressure due to rises in public utilities fees and in unemployment, among other things.

[31] It is estimated there are 4,000 Albanian children in Greece who

crossed the border on their own seeking a better future, and who are sexually or commercially exploited. Many of them are considered missing.

[32] In April a report by UNEP, the United Nations Environment Programme, revealed that thousands of Albanians were being poisoned each day by deadly toxins in their environment. The toxic levels found on land where children played and crops were grown were thousands of times higher than those permitted in EU states. ∎

Algeria / Al Jaza'ir

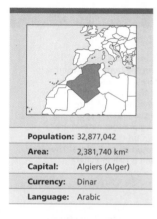

Population:	32,877,042
Area:	2,381,740 km²
Capital:	Algiers (Alger)
Currency:	Dinar
Language:	Arabic

The kingdoms that arose in Algeria dating back to antiquity were linked to the region's two power centers: Tunisia, from the Carthage era (10th century BC), and Morocco, following the Arab conquest of the Iberian Peninsula (711 AD). That intermediate position facilitated the concentration there of dissent against discrimination practised between born Muslims and recent converts. This dissent later led people to the Jariyite sect that promoted egalitarian principles and the belief that caliphs did not have to be descendants of Muhammad or his family: thus, any Muslim could ascend to the caliphate regardless of race, color or social status. This sect appealed especially to the Berbers (the name comes from the Romans' name for them: 'barbarians'). They had resisted the Arab invasion in the 7th century AD but eventually converted to Islam and played a role in the Arab conquest of the Iberian Peninsula. Berbers remained subordinate to the Arabs who were politically dominant, though fewer in number. In the 12th century, invading Bedouin Arabs destroyed the Berbers' peasant economy in coastal North Africa; as a result, many became nomadic.

² With the downfall of the Almohad Empire in 1212, Yaglimorossen ibn Ziane founded a new state on the Algerian coast. Its borders were consolidated as economic prosperity and cultural development led nomadic peoples to settle. Ziane and his successors governed the country between 1235 and 1518. After the Christians had put an end to seven centuries of Muslim domination, in 1492 the Zianids were confronted with a series of Spanish military incursions in which various strategic sites, like Oran, were taken.

³ Algeria and Tunisia both became part of the Ottoman (Turkish) Empire in the 16th century. The Arroudj and Kheireddine brothers drove the Spanish from the Algerian coast and expanded the state's authority over a sizeable territory. The Empire's mighty fleet won respect for the nation, and its sovereignty was acknowledged in a series of treaties (with the Low Countries in 1663, France in 1670, Britain in 1681 and the US in 1815).

⁴ Wheat production gradually increased until it became an export crop once again, for the first time since the Hilalian invasion (see Mauritania). Wheat exports became the indirect cause of European intervention. At the end of the 18th century, the French revolutionary government bought large amounts of wheat from Algeria but failed to pay. Napoleon, and later the Restoration monarchy, delayed payment until the Dey of Algiers demanded that the debt be paid. Reacting to further excuses and delays, he slapped a perplexed French official in the face - a show of temper that would cost the Turkish Pasha dearly. 36,000 French soldiers disembarked to 'avenge the offense', a pretext used by the French to carry out a long-standing project: to re-establish a colony on the African coast opposite their own shores. However, the French encountered heavy resistance, and were defeated.

⁵ In 1840, disembarking with 115,000 troops, the French set out once again to conquer Algeria. Successive rebellions were launched against the invaders. In the South the nomadic groups remained virtually independent and fought the French until well into the 20th century (see Western Sahara). In 1873, France decided to expropriate land for French settlers, or *pieds-noirs* as they were known, who wished to remain in the colonies (they numbered 500,000 by 1900, and over a million after World War II). As a result, the French pieds-noirs came to monopolize the fertile land, and the country's economy was restructured to meet French interests.

⁶ Nationalist resistance grew stronger from the 1920s until in 1945 it exploded when the celebration of the victory over Nazi-Fascism turned into a popular rebellion. The French forces tried to put down the rebellion and according to official French reports, 45,000 Algerians and 108 Europeans were killed in the ensuing massacre.

⁷ Shortly thereafter, the Algerian People's Party, founded in 1937, was restructured as the Movement for the Triumph of Democratic Liberties (MTLD) which participated in the 1948 and 1951 elections called by the colonialists.

⁸ Convinced of the futility of elections under colonial control, nine leaders of the OS (Special Organization, the military wing of the MTLD) founded the Revolutionary Committee for Unity and Action (CRUA). In November 1954, this committee became the National Liberation Front (FLN) that led the armed rebellion. Frantz Fanon, a doctor from Martinique, who had fought in the liberation of France during World War II, joined the FLN and came to exert great intellectual influence not only in Algeria but also throughout the sub-Saharan region.

⁹ In order to maintain 'French Algeria' and the pieds-noirs, the French colonial regime destroyed 8,000 villages, killing more than a million civilians, made systematic use of torture and deployed more than 500,000 troops. Right-wing French residents of Algeria formed the Secret Army Organization (OAS), a terrorist group which blended Neo-Fascism with the demands of the French colonials, who resented the growing power of the Algerians. Finally, on 18 March 1962, French President De Gaulle signed the Evian Agreement, agreeing to a cease-fire and a plebiscite on the proposal for self-determination.

¹⁰ Independence was declared on 5 July 1962, and a Constituent Assembly was elected later that year. Ahmed Ben Bella was named Prime Minister. Almost all foreign companies were nationalized; 600,000 French nationals

LAND USE

2000

IRRIGATED AREA: 6.8% of arable land

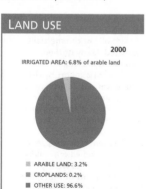

- ■ ARABLE LAND: 3.2%
- ■ CROPLANDS: 0.2%
- ■ OTHER USE: 96.6%

PUBLIC EXPENDITURE

% OF GDP

- 7.8 % — HEALTH & EDUCATION (2000)
- 3.5 % — DEFENSE (2001)

WORKERS

UNEMPLOYMENT: 27.3% (2002)

LABOR FORCE — **2002**

- ■ FEMALE: 29.0% ■ MALE: 71.0%

Life expectancy
69.7 years
2000-2005

GNI per capita
$1,720
2002

Literacy
63% total adult rate
2000

HIV prevalence rate
0.1% of population 15-49 years old
2001

abandoned the country taking everything they could with them, and 500,000 Algerians returned, to share the lot of 150,000 landless and hungry peasants. A system of local agricultural and industrial operations was introduced by the new government.

11 However, Ben Bella's self-management program came up against the reality of a government with little administrative expertise. In June 1965 a revolutionary council headed by Houari Boumedienne took power and jailed Ben Bella. A new emphasis on centralization and state power began to prevail over Ben Bella's self-management notions. Under Boumedienne, there was further nationalization and a program of industrialization based on oil and liquid natural gas exports. The country entered a period of economic expansion, which was not reflected in the countryside. Population grew more rapidly than agricultural production, and Algeria went from exporting to importing food. Strikes broke out in several cities.

12 Houari Boumedienne died in December 1978, after a long illness, just as the country's political institutions were beginning to consolidate. In 1976, a new National Charter was approved and, in 1977, the new members of the National People's Assembly were elected, with Colonel Chadli Ben Jedid appointed president.

13 The new President initiated a policy of reconciliation by releasing Ben Bella, who had been imprisoned for 14 years. Restrictions on travel abroad were lifted, taxes reduced and prohibitions removed on private housing. The restructuring of inefficient public enterprises gave an impetus to private companies.

14 Ben Jedid was re-elected in January 1984. In October 1988, a wave of protests broke out in several cities due to the lack of water and basic consumer goods; the legitimacy of the FLN and the military was called into question. Among the main groups participating in these mass protests were militant Islamists. Some mosques - especially in poorer neighborhoods - became sites of political demonstrations.

15 Some sectors of the most radical forms of Islam, influenced by Iran, began sending volunteers to fight in Afghanistan, to carry out the *jihad* or 'holy war' against the Soviet-backed Kabul regime. In mid-1989, against a background of protest and upheaval, Ben Jedid presented a new constitution which

IN FOCUS

ENVIRONMENTAL CHALLENGES
Several species of mammals, reptiles and birds run a serious risk of extinction. Desertification affects regions bordering the Sahara desert. Severe erosion, affecting 45 per cent of agricultural lands (12 million hectares), together with oil industry waste and dumping of untreated domestic and industrial residual waters, have caused a significant pollution of waterways and the Mediterranean coast.

WOMEN'S RIGHTS
Algerian women have voted and run for office since 1962. The number of Parliamentary seats held by women fell from 7 to 3 per cent between 1995 and 2000, while ministerial or similar positions fell from 4 to 0 per cent. Women made up 28 per cent of the workforce in 2000. More than 49 per cent lived in rural areas and took part in agriculture, though not always on a paid basis*. In 2000*, access to primary education was 98 per cent for men and 97 per cent for women. Illiteracy among women between 15 and 24 amounted to 16.4 per cent*. Eight per cent of childbirths are unattended by qualified staff*. In major cities, 96 per cent of pregnant women received prenatal care; 75 per cent in smaller towns and only 46 per cent in rural areas*.

CHILDREN
The percentage of underweight children under five years of age fell 13 to 6 per cent, but in 2000* some 18 per cent still had

growth problems. Only 13 per cent of children under six months were fed solely with maternal milk. Infant mortality has fallen 33 per cent since 1990*. In 2003 the Government prioritized immunization against polio and other preventable childhood diseases, and implemented programs against child malnutrition, diarrhea and respiratory infections. A large number of HIV cases are transmitted from mother to child at birth. The Government launched in 2002 an Economic Development Plan aimed at improving the situation of women and children, especially in rural provinces, where women's access to education and healthcare has been falling.

INDIGENOUS PEOPLES/ ETHNIC MINORITIES
In ethnic terms, the Berbers represent almost 80 per cent of the population, but arabization has threatened their identity and their language, Tamazight. Thus, only 25 per cent of Algerians identify themselves as Berbers. Algeria has the largest Berber community in North Africa. The Berber Cultural Movement, closely linked to the two Berber political parties, succeeded in making Tamazight an official language in 2002. The Tuaregs speak Tamazight dialects - Tamahak or Tamashek - and preserve a distinct alphabet, the Tifinagh. Between 100,000 and 300,000 Tuaregs live in Algeria, Libya, Mali, Nigeria and Burkina Faso. Before they were colonized, their system of nomad confederations enabled a rational administration of their huge territory. After 30 years of Tuareg

resistence, the conquerors split up the confederation into a myriad of smaller tribes.

MIGRANTS/REFUGEES
In late 2002 there were between 100,000 and 200,000 internally displaced people. In 10 years, thousands of families have fled from violence to rural areas, where they live with relatives or friends in irregular settlements, state buildings or improvised shelters. The authorities withhold information and limit the investigations of international humanitarian agencies. International organizations state that almost 30,000 people have sought shelter in the town of Tiaret, southwest of Algiers. Some 30,000 more live on the outskirts of Saida, 330 kilometers from the capital. Some 10,000 Algerians sought asylum in industrialized countries during 2002, a trend sustained since 1992. That year, Algeria received almost 85,000 refugees, some 80,000 from Western Sahara and the rest Palestinians. Since the Moroccan invasion of Western Sahara in 1975, Algeria has housed most of the occupied country's people in refugee camps around the desert town of Tindouf.

DEATH PENALTY
Currently there are more than 600 people under sentence of death. There have, however, been no executions since 1993.

*Latest data available in *The State of the World's Children* and *Childinfo* database, UNICEF, 2004.

introduced a modified multiparty system, breaking the monopoly which the FLN had held.

16 More than 20 opposition groups - including Muslims - openly expressed their views. The most significant were the Islamic Salvation Front (FIS), the Dawa Islamic League, the communist-socialit Avant Garde Party (PAGS) and the strongly Kabbyle (an ethnic minority of Berber origin) Rally for Culture and Democracy (RCD). Mouloud Hamrouche, a leading reformer, was appointed Prime Minister. In the first multiparty elections since Algeria's independence from France in 1962, the FIS defeated the FLN in the June elections.

17 Hamrouche and his cabinet resigned in June 1991, against a background of social agitation from the mosques. In early June,

a state of siege was declared throughout the country in the face of massive protests by FIS agitators who demanded that presidential elections be held ahead of schedule and that an Islamic state be proclaimed. Sid Ahmed Ghozali, an oil technician who had been Foreign Minister during the previous administration, was appointed Prime Minister. Legislative and presidential elections were scheduled for later in the year, and the FIS suspended its campaign of social and political agitation.

18 The country requested loans from the IMF in order to alleviate fluctuations in the price of oil. Ghozali proposed parliamentary reforms in order to ensure the transparency of the electoral system, but the proposals, which

included the possibility of withdrawing a man's right to vote for his wife, were boycotted by the FLN's parliamentary majority.

19 In the December 1991 elections, 40 per cent of the 13 million registered voters abstained. The first round, for 430 seats in Parliament, gave the victory to the FIS. The anti-fundamentalists - alarmed by the FIS victory in the first round and headed by the Workers' Center, UGTA and the FFS - raised a demonstration of 100,000 in central Algiers. Women's, professional and intellectual movements also participated.

20 President Chadli Ben Jedid resigned under strong pressure from the military and politicians fearful of a FIS victory. A Security Council made up of three military leaders and the Prime Minister

Under-5 mortality
49 per 1,000 live births
2002

Poverty
<2% of population living on less than $1 per day
1995

Debt service
21.2% exports of goods and services
2001

Maternal mortality
1,900 per 100,000 live births
2000

was put in power. Shortly after, a High Council of State was appointed, headed by Mohamed Boudiaf, a dissident FLN leader. The arrest of FIS leaders followed immediately and the election was annulled. In February, the High Council of State proclaimed a nationwide state of emergency for a year.

[21] In March 1992, the FIS was outlawed. The Government dissolved nearly 400 local councils controlled by FIS members, and the Supreme Court ratified the illegality of the FIS. In June, Boudiaf was assassinated by one of his bodyguards whilst making a public speech. The Government of Prime Minister Belaid Abdelsalam decreed a series of 'anti-terrorist' measures, including extending the death penalty for various crimes.

[22] In February 1993, the High Council of State extended the state of emergency indefinitely, imposed a curfew on Algiers and in five provinces, and dissolved all associations linked to the FIS. Following a long series of failed negotiations, the Government named Defense Minister Lamine Zeroual president of the country for three years.

[23] In a climate of increasing factionalism among all political groupings, the Islamic guerrillas split into the Armed Islamic Group (GIA) and the Armed Islamic Movement. In one of their most spectacular acts, the fundamentalists allowed 1,000 prisoners to escape from the Tazoult high security prison.

[24] In early 1995, following a meeting in Rome, the FIS, FLN, FFS and some moderates from the Islamic group Hamas proposed an end to the violence, the release of the political prisoners and the formation of a national unity government to organize elections. Despite international support, the proposal was not accepted by Zeroual, who responded by setting elections for November.

[25] The FIS, FLN and FFS boycotted the elections, which Zeroual won with 61 per cent of the votes against the moderate Islamic Mahfoud Nahnah's 25 per cent. Despite the presence of international observers, there were still strong doubts over whether the elections had truly been free and fair.

[26] In early 1996, Zeroual's government, apparently supported by the new leaders of the FLN, gained important military victories and followed an IMF-recommended structural adjustment plan which increased poverty across a large section of the middle class and the most

PROFILE

ENVIRONMENT

South of the fertile lands on the Mediterranean coast lie the Tellian and Saharan Atlas mountain ranges, with a plateau extending between them. Further south is the Sahara desert, rich in oil, natural gas and iron deposits. Different altitudes and climates in the north make for agricultural diversity, with Mediterranean-type crops (vines, citrus fruits, olives and so on) predominating.

SOCIETY

Peoples: Algerians are mostly Arab (80 per cent) and Berber (17 per cent). Nomadic groups linked to the Tuareg of Nigeria and Mali live in the south. Nearly a million Algerians live in France.
Religion: Islam.
Languages: Arabic and Tamazight (Berber) are the official languages. Many people speak French, but Arabic has gradually been replacing it in education and public administration.
Main Political Parties: National Rally for Democracy (RND), headed by Lamine Zeroual; Front for National Liberation (FLN), led by former Premier Alí Benflis. Movement of the Society for Peace (MSP) and Islamic Renaissance Movement (MRI), both Islamist; Socialist Forces Front (FFS); the Islamic Salvation Front (FIS) has a large following. The 1989 reforms brought forth a multiparty system.
Social Organizations: General Union of Algerian Workers (UGTA), National Union of Algerian Peasants, National Union of Algerian Women, National Youth Union.

THE STATE

Official Name: Al-Jumjuriya al-Jazairia ash-Shaabiya.
Capital: Algiers (Alger) 3,060,000 people (2003).
Other Cities: Oran 712,300 people; Constantine 501,900; Annaba 233,600 (2000).
Government: Abdel-Aziz Bouteflika, President since 1999, re-elected in April 2004. Ahmed Ouyahia, Prime Minister since 2003.
National Holiday: 1 November, Anniversary of the Revolution (1954).
Armed Forces: 121,700 (65,000 conscripts). Other: 180,000 (Gendarmerie, National Security Forces, Republican Guard).

deprived sections of the population.
[27] As the June 1997 elections approached, the violence increased. The elections gave a relative majority to the ruling party, which took 155 of the 380 seats. The FIS, which had called for a boycott on the elections, declared itself satisfied with an abstention rate of 34 per cent.
[28] In August 1997, the recently freed FIS leader Abasi Mandana confirmed his movement's desire to end the violence through dialogue with the Government. However, the massacre of some 300 people in a village south of Algiers once again reduced the possibility of bringing an end to the conflict. Witnesses said members of the Algerian army could have prevented the event, but had preferred not to intervene.
[29] The President stood down and called new elections. In April 1999 Abdelaziz Bouteflika took over, immediately calling a referendum on a law of reconciliation. The response was hugely in favor (98.6 per cent), with overwhelming FIS

participation and support. The President announced a general amnesty for those giving up their weapons and joining the legal political battle, which was rejected by the GIA and the Salafist Group for Preaching and Combat (GSPC).
[30] Abdelkader Hachani, the number three in FIS, was murdered in a fundamentalist neighborhood of Algiers in November 1999. The murder was seen as an attack on the peace process by radical Muslims opposed to Hachani's line of dialogue with the Government.
[31] The army's behavior in the conflict was condemned by public opinion and part of the international community after it was exposed in the book *The Dirty War*, by retired colonel Habib Souaidia, which stated that Algerian troops disguised as rebels took part in civilian massacres in the 1990s, and that the Army tortured Islamic militants to death. The Bouteflika Government refused to carry out a thorough and public investigation, as human rights activists demanded.

[32] In February 2001, Bouteflika, who a month earlier had promised to 'fight with an iron fist' against active rebels, was seriously criticized for being unable to put a stop to massacres caused by the GIA's boldest and bloodiest attacks yet.
[33] A series of large demonstrations in April, organized by Berber leaders seeking cultural and social recognition, led to clashes with security forces that left 60 civilians dead, prompting the Rally for Culture and Democracy (RCD) to abandon the Government.
[34] Since the Berbers' important role in the independence war has been downplayed by the Arab majority, tens of thousands of Berbers carried out an 'official' ceremony in August in the Soummam valley, in the heart of the Kabbyle region, to mark a key date in the history of independence. The Berber blocked roads, forcing government delegations to keep their distance.
[35] Bouteflika announced in March 2002 that the Berber language, Tamazight, would be recognized as a national language.
[36] The Berbers, who make up 17 per cent of the population, boycotted the May parliamentary elections demanding recognition for their cultural identity, better social conditions and job opportunities.
[37] An attack on a market near the capital killed 30 people during celebrations of the 40th anniversary of Algerian independence from France. The authorities blamed radical Islamic groups.
[38] Three days of national mourning were declared in May 2003 after an earthquake killed 1,100 people and injured 7,000.
[39] The Bouteflika Government announced the Civil Reconciliation Law, which in July freed the main two leaders of the FIS, Abassi Madani and Ali Belhadj, who had been in prison for the last 12 years. Ahmed Ouyahia, from the National Rally for Democracy (RND), was appointed Prime Minister in May.
[40] Thousands of soldiers and agents from government-backed militias attacked the GSPC in September in the Babor mountains, in the province of Setif. In November, the Algerian army arrested GIA leader Rachid Abou Tourab, in Saoula.
[41] Bouteflika was re-elected in April 2004. At the swearing-in ceremony he promised to devote his government to national reconciliation. ∎

Andorra / Andorra

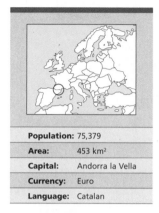

Population:	75,379
Area:	453 km²
Capital:	Andorra la Vella
Currency:	Euro
Language:	Catalan

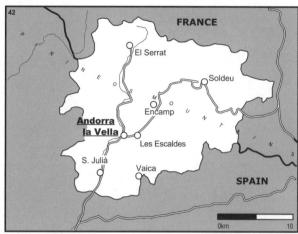

Evidence from cave paintings and funerary offerings shows that the territory of present day Andorra was inhabited in Neolithic times. Some historians believe that the original settlers of the Andorra valley are related to the Basque peoples of northern Spain, and that the name is therefore derived from the Basque language (Euskera). Other pre-Roman settlers, mentioned by Greek historian Polybius in his first century BC description of the Punic Wars, included some migratory Celtic (see box 'The Celts') and Southern Iberian peoples, along with a small group called Andosinos (the ancestors, some believe, of Andorrans).

[2] After the fall of the Roman Empire, Andorra once again became a thoroughfare for barbarians from the northern Gaulish Roman provinces to the Iberian peninsula. Several of these left their mark, including the Alans, Visigoths and Vandals.

[3] When the Muslims arrived, having made their way to northern Spain from Africa, the people in Andorra were predominantly Christian with some pagan settlements in more remote areas.

[4] The Holy Roman Emperor Charlemagne is said to have liberated the territory from Muslim occupation in 803 AD, but the first document citing the name Andorra is an order from Charles the Bald, Charlemagne's grandson. This document, dated 843 AD, cedes the valleys of Andorra to Sunifred, Count of Urgell, from the nearby Spanish city of La Seu d'Urgell. The Act of the Consecration of La Seu cathedral, dated 860, mentions this Pyrenean parish as a dominion of the Counts of the nearby Segre valley.

[5] During the Middle Ages, in-fighting between the small kingdoms and constant Arab invasions forced the Counts of Urgell to seek help and form an alliance with the Counts of Caboet (a very powerful family within the area) to protect Andorran settlements. In 1159, an agreement was signed, in which the Bishop of Urgell was granted sovereignty over Andorra and the territory was donated as a feud to the House of Caboet with shared rule of the Principality. Since then, the territory has been ruled by a system of co-principality between the Spanish Bishop of Urgell and the French Head of State.

[6] In 1610 the heir to the House of Caboet, Count Henry de Foix, was made King Henry IV of France and the rights of the Principality went to the French throne. Years later his son Louis XIII confirmed that sovereignty was to be shared by the two feudal lords: the Bishop of Urgell (Spanish) and the King of France.

[7] The French Revolution (1789) exterminated the monarchy in France and left the Principality orphaned from secular rule, and at the mercy of the Spanish, until the arrival of Napoleon in 1806. He re-established the co-principality at the request of the Andorrans. Since that day, the Head of State has been the 'co-prince,' a post held by all presidents of the French Republic.

[8] As time passed, Andorra modified its structures, but maintained its sovereignty. In 1866 the New Reform was announced, bringing in the General Council of the Valleys - a Parliament. In 1933 all Andorran men aged over 25 were given the right to vote; previously only the head of the family had had the vote. In 1970 women were granted suffrage.

[9] In 1982 the first Government of the Principality was created, separating the Legislative Power from the Executive Power. In 1988 the Universal Declaration of Human Rights (adopted by the United Nations in 1948) became law.

[10] In December 1989 the first elections were held under the new constitution. A majority of moderate reformers, led by Oscar Ribas Reig, took over the General Council of the Valleys. Reig had already run the country from 1982 to 1984, until he was ousted for being too slow with reforms.

[11] In 1993, the General Council approved a new constitution. The first article defines Andorra as an independent state in law, democracy and society, with a political regime described as 'institutionalized parliamentary co-principality,' as befitting tradition, with the co-princes - the Bishop of Urgell and the President of the French Republic - as Heads of State, in a joint and indivisible manner.

[12] The principality joined the UN in 1993 and in 1994 it became the 33rd member of the Council of Europe.

[13] In the first legislative elections, held in 1993, Oscar Ribas Reig was re-elected, but he left the post that same year after losing the support of his allies over disagreements about budgets.

[14] In 1997 the Andorran Government approved the Law of Linguistic Ordering, aiming to guarantee the use of the official language, Catalan, in all areas of public life, the media, cultural activity and sport.

[15] Legislative elections were held in 2001. Marc Forné Molné, President of the current government and of the Liberal Party of Andorra, gained an absolute majority in the General Council.

[16] In 2002, the Organization for Economic Cooperation and Development (OECD) included Andorra in a list of seven tax havens that had failed to meet its standards on financial transparency. This could result in the country facing sanctions and the resulting reduction of investment.

[17] Only 2 per cent of Andorran land is arable. The agricultural activity is focused on sheep raising and on growing small quantities of tobacco, rye, wheat, olives, grapes and potatoes. Industry is limited to the processing of those products and, owing to the scarcity of arable land, most food has to be imported. Tourism accounts for 80 per cent of the gross domestic product. It is estimated that every year 9 million people visit Andorra, attracted by the country's duty-free status and by winter and summer resorts. The banking sector, with its 'tax haven' status, also contributes substantially to the economy. Numerous immigrants, both legal and illegal, are attracted by the thriving economy of the country. ■

PROFILE

ENVIRONMENT

Located in the eastern Pyrenées, the Principality of Andorra is made up of deep ravines and narrow valleys surrounded by mountains between 1,800 and 3,000 meters high. The Valira de Ordino and Valira de Carrillo rivers join in Andorran territory under the name of the Valira river. Wheat is grown in the valleys, but livestock (especially sheep) has given way to tourism as the primary economic activity.

SOCIETY

Peoples: Spanish 44.4 per cent; Andorran 20.2 per cent; Portuguese 10.7 per cent; French 6.8 per cent; other 6.6 per cent.
Religions: Catholic 92 per cent; Protestant 0.5 per cent; Jewish 0.4 per cent; other 7.1 per cent. **Languages:** Catalan (official), French and Spanish. **Main political parties:** Liberal Party of Andorra (ruling party); Social Democratic Party (main opposition).
Social organizations: There are no organized trade unions. Many workers have joined French trade unions.

THE STATE

Official Name: Principat d'Andorra. **Administrative divisions:** 18 provinces. **Capital:** Andorra la Vella 21,000 people (2003).
Other Cities: Les Escaldes 16,000 people; Encamp 10,800 (2000).
Government: Parliamentary republic. The Bishop of Urgell (Spanish jurisdiction) and the President of France, respectively represented by Francesc Badia-Batalla and Louis Deblé, are 'co-princes' of the territory. Marc Forné Molné is President of the Executive Council and Head of Government since December 1994. Single-chamber Legislature (General Council), with 28 members, elected by direct vote every four years. At some point in the future, total independence from France and the Spanish bishopric is foreseen.
National holiday: 8 September, Our Lady of Meritxell Day (1278).

Angola / Angola

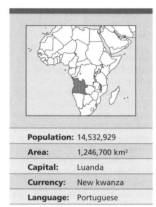

Population:	14,532,929
Area:	1,246,700 km²
Capital:	Luanda
Currency:	New kwanza
Language:	Portuguese

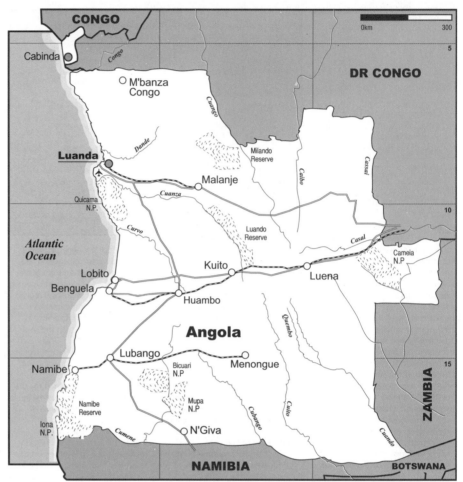

The original inhabitants of the current territory of Angola were Khoisan-speaking hunter-gatherers. The large-scale migrations of Bantu-speaking peoples in the first millennium AD made them dominant in the Khoisan area. The Khoisan - named Bushmen by the Europeans - still live in small groups in some zones of southern Angola.

[2] The Bantu-speakers were farming, hunting and gathering people who probably began their migration from the rainforest in what is the present-day border of Nigeria and Cameroon. Their expansion took place as small groups relocated in response to political and economic circumstances. Between the 14th and 17th centuries, the Bantu set up a series of kingdoms. In Angola the most important one was the Congo, covering the strip that today forms the frontier between Angola and Zaire, and reaching its apogee from the mid-13th to 14th centuries.

[3] In 1482, a Portuguese fleet commanded by Diogo Cao entered the Congo river mouth. He made the first contact with the Angolans of the old kingdom of Congo and began the colonization process. This process was started by missionaries and traders, later giving way to military expeditions against the peoples of the Angolan interior.

[4] Various kingdoms within the country opposed foreign occupation until the mid-18th century. Wars and slavery reduced the Angolan population from 18 million in 1450, to barely eight million in 1850. Even so, the Angolan people never gave up their opposition to Portuguese colonization, with figures like Ngola Kiluange, Nzinga Mbandi, Ngola Kanini and Mandume leading the resistance.

[5] Portugal intensified its military incursions following the 1884 Berlin Conference that divided Africa among the European colonial powers. Nonetheless, it took 30 years of military campaigns (1890-1921) to 'pacify' the colony.

[6] From then on, Portuguese settlers arrived in ever-increasing numbers. In 1900, there were an estimated 10,000, in 1950, 80,000 and in 1974, less than a year before independence, 350,000. Only one per cent lived on farms inland. The colonial economy was parasitic, built upon the exploitation of mineral and agricultural wealth (diamonds and coffee), with the bulk of profits going to Portuguese merchants.

[7] In 1956, several small nationalist groups joined together to form the Popular Movement for the Liberation of Angola (MPLA). Their aim was to pressure the Portuguese Government into recognizing the Angolan people's right to self-determination and independence. When Britain and France began to withdraw from their overseas colonies in the 1960s, Portugal did not follow suit and frustrated all Angolan attempts to win independence by peaceful means.

[8] In 1961, a group of MPLA militants from the most underprivileged classes stormed Luanda's prisons and other strategic points in the capital. This spurred resistance in other Portuguese colonies. Their agenda was clear: they were fighting not just colonialism but also the international power system that sustained it. In addition, they were fighting racism and ethnic chauvinism.

[9] In the years that followed, other independence movements with different regional origins sprang up: the National Front for the Liberation of Angola (FNLA) led by Holden Roberto; the Cabinda Liberation Front (FLEC); and the Union for the Total Independence of Angola (UNITA) led by Jonas Savimbi. Under the direction of Agostinho Neto, the MPLA militants held a conference in January 1964 to discuss and define their strategy of a prolonged people's war.

[10] Portugal's domestic problems, coupled with military setbacks in Angola, Mozambique and Guinea-Bissau and repeated shows of international solidarity with the independence fighters, dashed

LAND USE

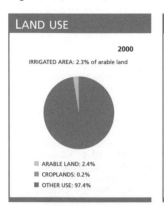

2000

IRRIGATED AREA: 2.3% of arable land

- ARABLE LAND: 2.4%
- CROPLANDS: 0.2%
- OTHER USE: 97.4%

PUBLIC EXPENDITURE

% OF GDP

4.7 % — HEALTH & EDUCATION (2000)

3.1 % — DEFENSE (2001)

Life expectancy
40.1 years
2000-2005

GNI per capita
$660
2002

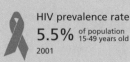
HIV prevalence rate
5.5% of population 15-49 years old
2001

Portuguese army hopes of a military solution. An uprising led by the Armed Forces Movement (MFA) overthrew the Portuguese regime of Oliveira Salazar and Marcelo Caetano in1974. The MFA expressly recognized the African colonies' right to self-determination and independence.

[11] The MFA immediately invited the MPLA, FNLA and UNITA to participate with Portugal in a transitional government for Angola in the interim period, the mechanisms of which were established in the Alvor Accords, signed in January 1975. By this time, political and ideological divergences among the three groups had become irreconcilable; the FNLA was directly assisted by US intelligence services and received military aid from Zaire (now DR Congo). UNITA received overt backing from South Africa and Portuguese settlers while the MPLA was aligned ideologically with the socialist countries. The accords were never implemented.

[12] The FNLA and UNITA unleashed a series of attacks on MPLA strongholds in Luanda, and a bloody battle for control of the capital ensued. Between September and October 1975, Angola was attacked on all sides: Zaire invaded from the north while South Africa, with the complicity of UNITA, attacked from the south to prevent a Marxist Government.

[13] On 11 November 1975, the date agreed for the end of colonial rule, the MPLA unilaterally declared independence in Luanda, pre-empting the formal transfer of sovereignty. Some 15,000 Cuban troops aided the new government in fighting off the South African invasion. In 1976, the United Nations recognized the MPLA Government as the legitimate representative of Angola. However, the South African attacks supporting UNITA continued from Namibia.

[14] The Angolan economy was severely debilitated. The war had paralyzed production in the far north and south of the country. The Europeans had emigrated en masse, taking all that they could with them and effectively destroying the productive capacity.

[15] Under these circumstances, the Angolan Government began to restore the chief production centers, and to train the largely unskilled and illiterate workforce. In this way, a large public sector emerged which was to become the economy's driving force, and banking and strategic activities were nationalized.

[16] In 1977, Nito Alves led a faction of the MPLA committed to 'active revolt', in a coup attempt.

Six leading MPLA members were killed but the conspiracy was successfully put down within hours. Seven months later, at its first congress, the MPLA declared itself Marxist-Leninist and adopted the name of MPLA-Workers' Party. In 1978, closer political and economic links were established with the countries of the socialist Council for Mutual Economic Assistance.

[17] The country's first president, Agostinho Neto, died of cancer in Moscow in 1979 and was succeeded by Planning Minister José Eduardo dos Santos.

[18] In August 1981, South Africa launched 'Operation Smokeshell', in which 15,000 soldiers with tanks and air support advanced 200 kilometers into Cunene province. Pretoria justified this aggression as an operation against guerrilla bases belonging to the Namibian liberation movement, the South West African People's Organization (SWAPO). But their

real aim seemed to be to establish a 'liberated zone' where UNITA could install a parallel government inside Angolan territory capable of obtaining some degree of international recognition.

[19] This incursion and successive attacks in the years that followed were contained by effective Angolan and Cuban military resistance. The cost of the war, plus international pressure and the mounting anti-apartheid campaign at home, obliged South Africans to resume diplomatic discussions with the MPLA. In December 1988, Angola, South Africa and Cuba signed a Tripartite Accord in New York, which put an end to the war between Luanda and Pretoria, and provided for the independence of Namibia and withdrawal of South African and Cuban troops from Angola.

[20] In Lisbon, 1990, the Angolan authorities announced they would resume conversations with the UNITA, with the intention of

achieving a final ceasefire. That year Jonas Savimbi officially acknowledged José Eduardo dos Santos as Chief of State. The MPLA introduced some reforms, and in May 1991, a law on political parties was published, which brought one-party rule to an end. That same month, the law banned political participation by active members of the armed forces, the police or the judiciary. Political amnesty was granted, and the last Cubans left Angola.

[21] After 16 years of civil war, a peace settlement was signed on 31 May by the Angolan Government and UNITA, in Estoril, Portugal. This agreement included an immediate cease-fire, as well as a promise to hold democratic elections in 1992 and the creation of a Joint Politico-Military Commission (CCPM), charged with establishing a national army made up of soldiers from both opposition groups. Portugal, the US and the Soviet Union were

IN FOCUS

ENVIRONMENTAL CHALLENGES
In recent years there has been an extensive use of pasture land and further erosion of the soil, due to the overpopulation of certain areas and the deforestation of the tropical rainforests for the export of wood and fuel. Though Angola is the second-biggest oil exporter in Africa, only in the capital Luanda is it used as an alternative to firewood. Deforestation is particularly serious in the central hill region, where there is not only loss of biodiversity but also water pollution and sedimentation in rivers and dikes. More topsoil is washed away every year during the rainy season.

WOMEN'S RIGHTS
Women have been able to vote and be elected since 1975. In the period 1995-2000 their parliamentary representation increased from 10 per cent to 16 per cent; their places in the Cabinet or equivalents increased from 7 per cent to 14 per cent. Of the six million people that constituted the labor force of the country in the year 2000, 46 per cent were women. Only 25 per cent of Angolan women receive prenatal care, 30 per cent of pregnant women suffer from anemia and more than 77 per cent of deliveries are not attended by qualified staff; 1,700 mothers die for every 100,000 live births*.

CHILDREN
Sixty per cent of Angolans are children. After almost 40 years of war there are as many mines as there are children, and healthcare and education services are devastated. Two generations of children - many of them soldiers - went missing during a decade of civil war, 100,000 minors were separated from their families and 4.5 million children were not registered at birth.

Almost 50 per cent of children do not attend school, 45 per cent suffer from chronic malnutrition and one in four dies before the age of five*. Angola has the fourth highest child mortality rate in the world. Following peace in 2002, the State and organizations such as UNICEF began the immunization of 7.1 million children and launched the 'Back to school' campaign that benefited around 500,000 children in 2003.

INDIGENOUS PEOPLES/ ETHNIC MINORITIES
The ethnic groups at risk during the war were the Bakongo (13 per cent), the Kimbundu (25 per cent), the Cabinda and the Himba. In 2002 the sacred places of the Himba community were affected by international tourism promoted by the Government after the end of the war.

Likewise, in their search for oil, transnationals like Chevron and Texaco have altered the way fisher people and other tribal groups that inhabit the coastal

areas of the south of the country earn their living.

MIGRANTS /REFUGEES
In 2002 there were between 2 and 3.5 million displaced people within the territory and around 410,000 refugees were seeking asylum outside the country. Almost 190,000 Angolans took refuge in Zambia, around 150,000 in DR Congo, 30,000 in Congo, 25,000 in Namibia, 5,000 in South Africa and 2,000 in Botswana. By the end of 2002 there were around 7,000 new people seeking asylum in industrialized countries.

When the war ended, around 800,000 Angolans (displaced people and refugees) returned to their homes. Many of them returned against their will, forced by government officers, and at least 80,000 refugees were repatriated from neighboring countries where they had not enough assistance. Most repatriated people were relocated in the borderline provinces near Zambia and DR Congo. Around 12,000 refugees, who arrived from DR Congo more than ten years ago, were still living in the environs of Luanda at the end of 2002, half of which depended on food aid.

DEATH PENALTY
Abolished in 1992.

*Latest data available in *The State of the World's Children* and *Childinfo* database, UNICEF, 2004.

Under-5 mortality
260 per 1,000 live births
2002

Malnutrition
31% under-5s
1995-2002

Debt service
27.6% exports of goods and services
2001

Maternal mortality
1,700 per 100,000 live births
2000

involved in the discussion and drawing up of the agreement, as was the United Nations, which was put in charge of supervising compliance with the terms of the peace agreement.

22   Holden Roberto, leader of the FNLA, and Jonas Savimbi, president of UNITA, returned to Luanda in August and September 1991 respectively - after 15 years of exile - to launch their election campaigns. The US continued to support UNITA, and as a result tensions increased as the 1992 elections drew near.

23   Plagued by a foreign debt of more than $6 billion, the Government appealed to the international community for economic aid. The US refused to suspend the economic and diplomatic blockade, alleging that Angola was a Marxist nation and announcing it would not grant diplomatic recognition until after the 1992 elections. Consequently, the US companies in Angola were unable to get loans from banks in their own country.

24   Following intense negotiations between the Government and UNITA, elections were set for September 1992. The ruling MPLA obtained nearly 10 per cent more votes than UNITA. Savimbi refused to recognize defeat and hostilities resumed. In their advance, the UNITA troops occupied the diamond mines of the interior, leaving the Government with oil as the only stable source of income (between $1.6 and $1.7 billion per year).

25   In November 1993, peace talks were re-started in Lusaka, the capital of Zambia. A year later in November 1993 a peace agreement was signed. The main points (a ceasefire and constitutional changes so that Savimbi could become Vice-President) were not put into practice until late 1995 and the fighting continued.

26   Some progress was seen during 1996. In May, an amnesty law was approved and UNITA soldiers began to be absorbed by the armed forces. Savimbi withdrew most of his troops to barracks and handed over some of the weapons. The civil war caused the most serious social and economic crisis in Angolan history. The adoption of IMF and World Bank economic liberalization measures did not improve matters for ordinary people.

27   In 1997, hard negotiating ended with UNITA accepting to join the Government at executive, legislative and military levels. Even though its position in the capital was weak, UNITA's troops still controlled 40 per cent of the territory. The fall of Mobutu Sese Seko in Zaire (now DR Congo) in May weakened UNITA even further, and they were forced to abandon areas of the northern frontier. The Angolans wanted to avoid the infiltration of Mobutu's troops - formerly allied to Savimbi - into their territory. Mobutu's soldiers were fleeing from the government of the new DR Congo leader Laurent Kabila, a former ally of dos Santos.

28   In 1998, thousands of demobilized soldiers mostly with little or no education encountered serious difficulties in returning to their home villages, given the scarce employment possibilities there and the slow arrival of economic aid. Since 1994, only 300,000 of the 4.5 million people uprooted by the civil war had been able to resettle according to the United Nations figures. The presence of large numbers of land mines across the country increased the insecurity of the population.

29   In April 1999, the Government announced the formation of a self-defense front with Zimbabwe, Namibia and DR Congo. This reflected the interconnected nature of regional conflicts, which transcended frontiers established by former colonial powers. In late 1999, after winning back Andulo and Bailundo - the main cities under opposition control - and following a run of military victories the Government felt confident in announcing that the end of the war was in sight.

30   However, after a period of relative peace, fighting between the Government and UNITA resumed in 2000. The UN Security Council decided to withdraw its peace mission from Angola, present since 1995 to mediate between the Government and UNITA.

31   Jonas Savimbi, leader of UNITA since 1975, was killed in combat on 22 February 2002, in the central province of Moxico. Vice-President Antonio Dembo took over the organization's leadership. After the rebel chief's death, the Government called for the end of the civil war. President dos Santos said the death of Savimbi had opened the way for general elections, but added that security had to be ensured first. In order to achieve it, he began to make contacts with Dembo. The ceasefire remained precarious.

32   In April the Government and UNITA signed a formal ceasefire and four months later UNITA finally disbanded its armed wing, which led the Defense Minister to announce that the war was over. Angola's civil war, the longest African conflict of this kind, had lasted 27 years.

33   The successive understandings with UNITA allowed expanding the exploration for minerals, damaged by the international traffic of diamonds in exchange for weapons, which benefited rich countries such as Belgium, France and Italy. A report issued by the UN on October 2002 stated that six months after the ceasefire, UNITA still kept illegal diamonds hidden. The requirement of a certificate of origin for the diamonds extracted from Angola, in force since the year 2000, proved to be useful in restraining the traffic. Before its independence, Angola was the world's fourth-largest diamond exporter.

34   In February 2003, the UN began an operation designed to observe the peace process. Transformed into a political party, UNITA elected Isaias Samakuva as their new leader in June.

35   The country has great challenges ahead, which include the reconstruction of roads and the railway system. The complete road network amounted to 17,000 kilometers in 1973. During the civil war, it became impossible to travel on the roads, except in armed convoys; besides, several bridges were destroyed and the town-to-town bus services stopped working. The agricultural sector, which was flourishing before independence, decayed later, due to the deterioration of transport, lack of security and the increase in export taxes, among other causes. Less than ten per cent of Angolan soil is fertile, and given the combination of poor compost and scarce rain, farmers face many obstacles. ■

PROFILE

ENVIRONMENT

The 150 kilometer-wide strip of coastal plain is fertile and dry. The extensive inland plateaus, higher to the west, are covered by tropical rainforests in the north, grasslands at the center and dry plains in the south. In the more densely populated areas (the north and central west) diversified subsistence farming is practiced. Coffee, the main export crop, is grown in the north; sisal is cultivated on the Benguela and Huambo plateaus; sugarcane and oil palm along the coast. The country has abundant mineral reserves: diamonds in Luanda, petroleum in Cabinda and Luanda, iron ore in Cassinga and Cassala. The port of Lobito is linked by railway to the mining centers of Zaire and Zambia.

SOCIETY

Peoples: As a consequence of centuries of slave trade the population density is still very low. To maintain control over the country, the Portuguese colonizers fostered local divisions between the various ethnic groups: Bakongo (13 per cent), Kimbundu (25 per cent), Ovimbundu (37 per cent), others (22 per cent). There are also small minorities of Europeans (1 per cent) and Afro-Europeans (2 per cent).
Religions: The majority practise traditional African religions; 38 per cent are Catholic, and 15 per cent Protestant. However, there are forms of syncretism which make it impossible to establish clear boundaries between one religion and another.
Languages: Portuguese (official) and 41 African languages including Ovidumbo, Kimbundu and Kikongo.
Main Political Parties: The People's Movement for the Liberation of Angola (MPLA), founded by Agostinho Neto on December 10 1956 dominates the Government of Unity and National Reconciliation. The main opposition party is the National Union for the Total Independence of Angola (UNITA).
Social Organizations: National Union of Angolan Workers (UNTA); Organization of Angolan Women (OMA).

THE STATE

Official name: República Popular de Angola.
Administrative Divisions: 18 provinces.
Capital: Luanda 2,623,000 people (2003).
Other Cities: Huambo (Nova Lisboa) 165,700 people; Lobito 133,100; Benguela 129,800 (2000).
Government: José Eduardo dos Santos, President since September 1979, re-elected in 1992; Fernando da Piedade Dias dos Santos, Prime Minister since December 2002. Unicameral legislature. 223 -member National Assembly, elected by direct popular vote.
National Holiday: 11 November, Independence Day (1975).
Armed Forces: 120,000 (2001) Other: 20,000 Internal Security Police.

Anguilla / Anguilla

Population:	12,246
Area:	96 km²
Capital:	The Valley
Currency:	EC dollar
Language:	English

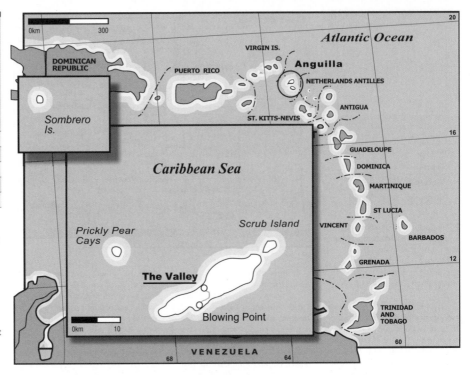

Anguilla is the most northerly of the Leeward Islands. Called Malliouhana by the Arawaks, who inhabited it until their extermination by the Caribs, its present name was first mentioned by explorer Pierre Laudonnaire, after it was sighted by a French expedition in 1556. In 1650 it was colonized by the British Empire but in 1656 the Caribs attacked the island, to be followed by several failed attempts of domination from Ireland (1698) and France (1745 and 1756). Its small size and its agriculturally unfit land made the island unattractive to the British Empire, factors that determined the failure of slavery on the island, although abolition was formalized as late as 1838.

² From 1816 to 1871 Anguilla, St Kitts-Nevis and the Virgin Islands were administered together as one colony. The Virgin Islands were split off in 1871, leaving the others as a colonial unit ruled from St Kitts.

³ Colonialism lasted until the St. Kitts-Nevis-Anguilla colony became one of the five Caribbean 'States in Association with the United Kingdom'. Anguillans opposed the agreement and in 1967 rebelled against the St Kitts Government, deposing the authorities. Under the leadership of local entrepreneur Ronald Webster, Anguilla demanded a separate constitution through a referendum and headed its own administration until 1969, when British troops regained control of the island.

⁴ In 1976 a new constitution was approved by Britain, establishing a parliamentary system of government under the patronage of the British Commissioner. But it was not until 1980 that Anguilla was able formally to withdraw from the Associated State arrangement with St Kitts-Nevis, gaining the status of 'British Dependent Territory'.

⁵ The 1976 constitution provided for a governor appointed by the British Crown, responsible for defense, foreign relations, internal security (including the police),

utilities, justice and the public audit. The Governor presides over the Executive Council.

⁶ The first general elections, held in March 1976, voted in the People's Progressive Party (PPP) leader, Ronald Webster, as Chief Minister. In the following changes of government, Webster's party (which dissolved the PPP in 1981 and created the Anguilla People's Party) and the opposition Anguilla National Alliance (ANA), headed by Emile Gumbs, alternated in

government until 1994, when alliances among the parties were necessary in order to rule.

⁷ The Constitution was changed in 1982 to modify the number of ministers. This led to a series of constitutional discussions and eventually to the creation, in 1990, of the Constitutional and Electoral Reform Consultative Forum of Anguilla.

⁸ Through the 1980s construction for the tourism industry reduced unemployment

from 26 per cent to 1 per cent, and income generated from livestock, salt production, lobster fishing, and remittances from émigrés were gradually overtaken by the construction, tourism and international financial service sectors.

⁹ In the 1994 elections, Hubert Hughes was elected Chief Minister after an alliance between the Anguilla United Party and the Anguilla Democratic Party (ADP). Development in the tourism industry led to an average annual growth of 7 per cent in 1997 and part of 1998. In 1999 Anguilla joined the Caribbean Community Common Market as an associate member.

¹⁰ The 2000 parliamentary elections were won by a coalition formed between the ANA and the ADP, known as the United Front. Osbourne Fleming became Chief Minister.

¹¹ The Organization for Economic Co-operation and Development (OECD) listed Anguilla as a tax haven in November. According to OECD, the countries on this list were supposed to have adopted a program to eliminate practices allowing tax evasion by 31 December 2001.

¹² On 9 May 2001 a new General Population and Housing Census was held, which concluded there was a 22 per cent growth in population, slightly less than expected, although the number of children grew 30 per cent, 2 per cent more than expected. ■

Antigua and Barbuda / Antigua and Barbuda

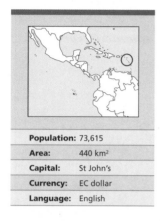

Population:	73,615
Area:	440 km²
Capital:	St John's
Currency:	EC dollar
Language:	English

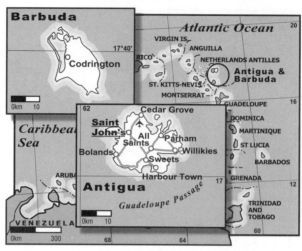

The Caribs (see chart) inhabited most of the islands in the sea which took their name, but abandoned many of them, including Antigua, in the 16th century due to the lack of fresh water.

[2] In 1493 the name Antigua was given to one of the Antilles by Christopher Columbus in honor of a church in Seville. Other Europeans settled later (the Spanish in 1520, the French in 1629) but again left because of the scarcity of water. However, a few English were able to settle by using appropriate techniques to store rainwater. The nearby island of Barbuda was colonized in 1678 and granted by the crown to the Codrington family in 1685. Although it was planned as a slave-breeding colony, the slaves who were imported came to live self-reliantly in their own community.

[3] By 1640, the number of English families on Antigua had increased to 30. The few Indians who had dared to stay were eventually murdered by the settlers, who imported African slaves to work the tobacco plantations and later sugar plantations. In 1666, the French governor of Martinique invaded the island, kidnapping all the African slaves. When England regained control in 1676, a rich colonist from Barbuda, Colonel Codrington, acquired large quantities of land and brought new African slaves.

PUBLIC EXPENDITURE

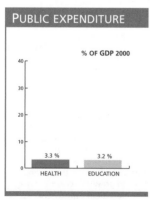

% OF GDP 2000

HEALTH 3.3 % EDUCATION 3.2 %

Thus sugar production was reinstated on the island.

[4] Slavery was abolished in the British colonies in 1838. The workers' situation did not noticeably change and quasi-slavery continued for many decades, until the early 20th century when trade unions began to appear. The first trade union, led by Vere Bird, was formed on January 16 1939. The Antigua Labor Party (ALP), the first political party, was originated within a trade union. It was also led by Vere Bird.

[5] In the elections of April 1960, Bird's party won and he became Prime Minister. In 1966, a new constitution introduced self-government with a Parliament elected by Antiguans and Barbudans. Britain remained responsible for defense and foreign relations. Bird was again successful in the 1967 elections.

[6] On 1 November 1981, Antigua and Barbuda became independent as a sovereign, democratic and united state and were admitted into the United Nations and the Caribbean Community (Caricom). Independence also gave the islands the right to become indebted to the IMF and the World Bank. The foreign debt grew dramatically and reached almost half of the GDP by the end of that year.

[7] The Prime Minister maintained close relations with the US, who rented part of the island's territory for military purposes. The alliance with the US was further consolidated in 1983, when Antigua participated in the US invasion of Grenada. Parliamentary elections were held in April 1984, and despite accusations during the electoral campaign, Bird was re-elected. His victory was attributed to approval of his stance on the Grenada issue.

[8] Lester Bird, Vere's son, replaced him at the head of ALP and won the elections in 1994 and

1999. His government was affected by a series of scandals, including money laundering, arms trafficking and a case brought against his brother Ivor, for cocaine smuggling. In June 1999 Vere Bird died.

[9] In 2002 Antigua and Barbuda joined other states of the Caribbean under the protection of a program of the Organization for Economic Co-operation and Development (OECD), which was in charge of safeguarding governmental transparency and the prevention of tax frauds in those states. This concession prevented the country from being included in the OECD blacklist, which would have imposed severe sanctions on them.

[10] In 2003, the Caribbean Financial Action Task Force (CFATF), an organization formed by the 29 States of the Caribbean Basin, that had agreed to take countermeasures against offenses such as money laundering and terrorism financing, appointed as their President Ronald Sanders, then foreign minister of Antigua and Barbuda. That same year, Antigua joined as a member of the Latin America and the Caribbean Organization for the Prohibition of Nuclear Weapons (OPANAL), an intergovernmental organization created by the Treaty for the Proscription of Nuclear Weapons in Latin America and the Caribbean (Tlatelolco Treaty). ■

PROFILE

ENVIRONMENT

The islands - Antigua with 280 sq km, and its dependencies Barbuda with 160 sq km and Redonda with 2 sq km - belong to the Leeward group of the Lesser Antilles. Antigua is endowed with beautiful coral reefs and large dunes. Its wide bays distinguish it from the rest of the Caribbean because they provide safe havens. Barbuda is a coral island with a large lagoon on the west side. It consists of a small volcano joined to a calcareous plain. Redonda is a small uninhabited rocky island, and is now a flora and fauna reserve. Sugar cane and cotton are grown along with tropical fruits; seafood is exported. The reduction of habitats due to the reforestation of native forests with imported species is the main environmental problem of most of the Caribbean islands.

SOCIETY

Peoples: The majority of Antiguans and Barbudans are of African origin (91.3 per cent); Europeans; Mestizo; Syrian-Lebanese; Indo-Pakistanis.
Religions: Protestants 73.7 per cent (Anglicans 32.1 per cent, Moravians 12 per cent; Methodists 9.1 per cent; Seventh Day Adventists 8.8 per cent; and others); Catholics 10.8 per cent; Jehovah Witnesses 1.2 per cent; Rastafarians 0.8 per cent.
Languages: English is the official language, but in daily life a local Patois dialect is spoken.
Main Political Parties: The Antigua Labor Party (ALP); The Antigua Caribbean Liberation Movement (ACLM); The United National Democratic Party (UNDP); The United Progressive Party (UPP).
Main Social Organizations: Antigua Workers' Union, linked to the UNDP; Antigua Trades and Labor Union, with ALP leadership; People's Democratic Movement.

THE STATE

Official Name: Associated State of Antigua and Barbuda.
Capital: St John's 28,000 people (2003).
Other Cities: Parham 1,400 people; Liberta 1,400 (2000).
Government: James Carlisle, Governor-General since June 1993, representative of Queen Elizabeth II (Head of State). Baldwin Spencer, Prime Minister since March 2004. Bicameral Legislature: House of Representatives, with 19 members, and the Senate, with 17 appointed members.
National Holiday: 1 November, Independence Day (1981).
Armed Forces: 90 troops (1994).

Argentina / Argentina

Population:	39,310,826
Area:	2,780,400 km²
Capital:	Buenos Aires
Currency:	Peso
Language:	Spanish

Around 300,000 indigenous people inhabited the territory currently occupied by Argentina when the first expeditionaries of the Spanish Crown arrived in these lands searching for gold towards the beginning of the 16th Century. The Pampean Patagonian peoples in the south, such as the Tehuelch and the Pehuelch, were nomadic hunters and gatherers, while the tribes of the Chaco in the north-east the Mataco, the Guaycurúe and the Guaraníes had begun to settle down. The Andean peoples, such as the Diaguita and the Huarpes, through contact with the Incas, perfected their agricultural system, introducing terracing and artificial irrigation. This gave rise to commercial trade with the northeastern and western regions. They also made handicrafts and raised llamas. Little is known about the Omahuacas, the Patamas, the Capayanes, the Comechingones and the Algarrobero peoples.

[2] In 1526, Sebastian Cabot founded a fort on the banks of the Carcarañá river which was the first European settlement of present-day Argentina.

[3] To check the Portuguese advance, Spain sent Pedro de Mendoza to the region on a contract granting the conquistador established political and economic privileges. In 1536, de Mendoza founded Santa Maria del Buen Ayre (Buenos Aires), a small town which was abandoned in 1541 after being besieged by the indigenous peoples.

[4] Using Asunción (in today's Paraguay) as a focus for colonization, the Spanish founded several cities in what is now Argentine territory (Santiago del Estero, Córdoba, Santa Fe), until they came to the second founding of Buenos Aires in 1580. Under colonial administration, the region was in principle subject to the Vice-Royalty of Peru. Three cities succeeded each other in predominance. Tucumán, linked with gold exploitation in Upper Peru, was the center during the

16th century. Córdoba, where the first university of the region was established in 1613, was the intellectual center during the 17th and 18th centuries. And after the new administrative divisions in 1776, the port city of Buenos Aires became capital of the new Viceroyalty of the River Plate, which covered what are now Bolivia, Paraguay, Argentina and Uruguay.

[5] In the 17th and 18th centuries, the Spanish conquest pushed the Mapuche - Araucans by the Europeans - from Chile into the center and south-east of present-day Argentina resulting in the 'Araucanization' of the local inhabitants. The abundance of cattle, the main product the viceroyalty sent to Spain, caused great ethnic and cultural changes. Outside the cities, vast plains of good pasture were ranged by horsemen, some of whom were indigenous people (who modified their diet to feed on beef). The rest were gauchos - mixed-race cowboys who lived by working the cattle.

[6] The strong bourgeoisie of the port area who favored free trade initiated the revolutionary movement of 1810, which created the United Provinces of the River

Plate and overthrew the Viceroy, accusing him of a lack of loyalty to Spain, which was at that time occupied by Napoleon's troops. Gauchos and Indians swelled the ranks of armies organized in Buenos Aires to fight the Spanish crown beyond the frontiers of the Viceroyalty. General José de San Martín led the armies which defeated the royalists and contributed decisively to the independence of Chile and Peru.

[7] Even though the Spanish were quickly expelled, discrepancies between Buenos Aires and the rest of the United Provinces of the River Plate (including the present-day Republic of Uruguay) kept the region in a permanent state of war. The Unionists defended the centralism of Buenos Aires, which threatened the economy of the interior, while the Federalists pursued a more equitable agreement for all the provinces.

[8] In 1829 Juan Manuel de Rosas, a land-owner with federal roots (opposed to Buenos Aires' centralism), took over as governor of Buenos Aires. Rosas, who had himself proclaimed Restorer of the Laws, gained fame in the 'Desert Campaign' where Buenos Aires

expelled the indigenous peoples from its surroundings. He used political means and force to pacify the interior, bringing most of the governors together and deploying troops from Buenos Aires as far as the frontiers with Bolivia and Chile.

[9] Since Buenos Aires was the gateway to the Paraná and Uruguay rivers - main arteries for French and British trade with the provinces of the interior and Paraguay - Rosas brought in a customs law which restricted access to foreign vessels and products. The Rosas Government was attacked by armies from both powers, which blockaded the port of Buenos Aires intending to crush the Government and support Rosas' more liberal rivals. During the campaign to put pressure on Rosas in 1833 Britain occupied the Malvinas (Falkland Islands).

[10] The 'Great War' (waged in Argentina and Uruguay between 1839 and 1852) involved Argentina, Uruguay, Paraguay and Brazil, and saw direct intervention from Britain and France, bringing an end to Rosas' 20 years in power.

[11] Justo José de Urquiza, Governor of Entre Rios, then presided over the Argentine Confederation with its capital in Paraná in accordance with the federal constitution of 1853. However, there was resistance from Buenos Aires, which proclaimed independence and declared itself a separate state, even having diplomatic representation abroad. After 10 years of fighting, in 1861 Buenos Aires got its own way.

[12] Bartolomé Mitre (President from 1862 to 1868) made an alliance with Pedro II, Emperor of Brazil, and Venancio Flores, President of Uruguay, to wage the 'War of the Triple Alliance' on Paraguay. The fighting started in 1865 and ended in 1870 with the death of Paraguayan President Francisco Solano López and most of the Paraguayan population. By the time 'victory' came, Domingo Faustino Sarmiento had taken over from Mitre.

[13] Once the war was over, the rest of what is now Argentina was occupied through successive incursions against the indigenous peoples of Patagonia, the Chaco and the Andean regions of Río Negro. In 1879, General Julio Roca (President from 1880-86 and 1898-1904) ended Argentina's 60-year military campaign to exterminate the indigenous peoples. The railway, symbol of modernization, ensured the Buenos Aires Government's control over the territory. The mass immigration of European workers, above all Spaniards and Italians, changed the face of the nation which underwent unprecedented

Life expectancy
74.2 years
2000-2005

GNI per capita
$4,060
2002

Literacy
97% total adult rate
2000

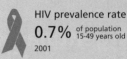
HIV prevalence rate
0.7% of population 15-49 years old
2001

industrial, agricultural and commercial growth. The population grew from less than a million people in 1869 to almost eight million in 1914.

[14] Up until the electoral law of President Roque Sáenz Peña in 1912, which guaranteed universal, secret and obligatory suffrage for adult men, political power had never been a matter of democratic elections, rather the product of permanent fraud. This was the cause of the 1874, 1890, 1893 and 1905 rebellions led by Mitre, Leandro Alem, Aristóbulo del Valle and Hipólito Irigoyen, respectively.

[15] The Sáenz Peña Law helped the Radical Party, led by Irigoyen, into power in 1916. During World War I, in which Argentina was neutral, the country sold food to Europe and experienced industrial growth. One result of this was that the unions became far stronger.

[16] Despite being re-elected by a margin of two to one in 1928,

Irigoyen was unable to ride the consequences of the world economic crisis of 1929, which drastically undermined the agro-exporter model. Irigoyen was ousted a year later in a military coup led by General José Félix Uriburu. The coup marked the end of a period of constitutional continuity which had lasted 68 years, as well as a long period of economic expansion based on the export of raw materials which had doubled between 1913 and 1928.

[17] During World War II, President Ramón S Castillo maintained Argentina's neutrality, provoking opposition. Another military coup ousted Castillo in 1943. The ensuing dissent within the army - which wanted neither to restore democracy nor to prolong an indefinite dictatorship - together with pressure from political groups and the United States (which wanted Argentina to support the Allies) brought Colonel Juan

Domingo Perón to the presidency from his post in the Employment Ministry.

[18] With the support of the unions, Perón won the 1946 elections by a narrow margin. Backed by the General Labor Confederation (CGT), he declared a state of civil war, which allowed him to get round the opposition and extend his authoritarian power. He nationalized foreign trade, the banks, the railway, gas and telephones; extended the fleet and created the air force; increased the workers' share of the national income to 50 per cent and framed advanced social legislation. Furthermore, he organized workers and bosses into national confederations with whom he negotiated economic and social policy. His wife Eva ('Evita') formed an exceptionally charismatic nexus between Perón and the workers, whom she dubbed 'the Shirtless Ones'. It was Eva Perón who was

largely responsible for Argentina giving women the vote in 1947. In foreign affairs Perón took the 'Third Position' between the two superpowers of the Cold War, which brought him into conflict with the US.

[19] Re-elected in 1951, Perón lost army support by confronting the Church. He was ousted in a coup in 1955 and forced into exile. A dictatorship headed by Pedro Aramburu replaced him, embracing the National Security Doctrine which passed responsibility for defending the region against 'the enemies of democracy' to the US. The dictatorship imposed a regressive wealth distribution system and opponents from both army and civilian ranks were executed in the 1956 'Operation Massacre', a precursor of decades of political violence.

[20] 'Peronism' was outlawed, but it was the Peronist vote which brought the pro-development government of Arturo Frondizi to power in 1958, opening the country to oil and automobile transnationals, and implanting a model of growth and wealth concentration which fed serious social confrontations. Frondizi legalized 'Peronism', and in the 1962 parliamentary elections the Peronists won in 10 provinces. This provoked another coup from the army which toppled Frondizi. Following two serious confrontations between separate factions of the army, General Juan Carlos Onganía emerged as the new strongman.

[21] With Peronism banned once again, the Radical Party's Arturo Illia was elected in 1963 in the first administration for 40 years not to apply a State of Emergency nor other special measures for repression or cultural censorship. His term in office was marked by friction with the Peronist unions who organized strikes, demonstrations and occupations of factories.

[22] In June 1966, Illia was overthrown by the 'Argentinean Revolution' of General Juan Carlos Onganía, who brought in a new authoritarian model, politically clerical and corporatist, economically liberal and defender of the 'ideological borders' in foreign policy. Onganía consecrated the country to the Sacred Heart, banned political parties, intervened in the universities and the CGT and denationalized the economy: bankrupted companies were bought up extremely cheaply by US, British and German consortia.

[23] A succession of social uprisings, like the 1969 'Cordobazo', and the emergence of a guerrilla force, threatened to split the army. General Agustín Lanusse took over

IN FOCUS

ENVIRONMENTAL CHALLENGES
Deforestation, soil degradation, desertification and pollution of the air and the water are all significant problems. Untreated sewage has polluted several rivers, particularly the Matanza-Riachuelo river in Buenos Aires. Soil erosion is growing, mainly in the north of the humid Pampa. In the 1999 Convention on Climate Change Argentina announced that it would reduce its predicted CO_2 emissions for the period 2008-2012 by between 2 and 19 per cent.

WOMEN'S RIGHTS
Argentinean women have been allowed to vote and to run for office since 1947. The 'quota' system of 1991 ensured that the proposed candidate ballots allocate at least 30 per cent of the positions to women. A ballot that does not comply with these requirements is not valid. In 2003, 25 out of 69 senators and 79 out of 257 representatives were women. Argentinean doctor Mirta Roses has been the Director of 'The Pan American Health Organization' (PAHO) since 2002.

In 1995, unemployment among women was higher than that among men by 5.8 per cent. In 2000, 10 per cent of women workers were in the industrial sector and 90 per cent in the services sector.

Out of every 1,000 pregnant women, 60 are teenagers aged between 14 and 19. 26 per cent of pregnant women are anemic, and 98 per cent of the deliveries are attended by qualified staff*.

There is universal enrolment in primary education but more girls than boys stay within the education system. Two thirds of students in tertiary education are female.

CHILDREN
In 2001, 12.3 million Argentineans were under 18 and 3.5 million under 5; over 85 per cent of these children lived in urban areas. In 2000* 95 per cent of children reached the fifth grade of primary school and over 90 per cent enrolled in secondary school. Between 5 and 19 per cent of the child population suffer from hunger, depending on the province. The economic and financial crisis that took shape towards the end of 2001 led to sharp increases in child mortality and hunger, especially in the northern provinces, and affected children's access to education, nutrition and health services.

Soup kitchens set up for school children were the means of keeping many of the poorest children at school. In 2003 it was decided that more than 1,500 schools should remain open during the holidays in three provinces, providing 330,000 children with one meal a day and basic care.

INDIGENOUS PEOPLES/ ETHNIC MINORITIES
Indigenous organizations estimate that there are between 800,000 and 2,000,000 native inhabitants in the country. Some provinces' populations are 17-25-per-cent indigenous. While other citizens have several state offices where they can file their complaints, indigenous people are able to do so

only before the National Office for Native Affairs. Indigenous people were supposed to have representatives designated by their communities, but this was never implemented.

MIGRANTS/REFUGEES
Towards the end of 2002, there were 2,700 refugees in Argentina, including Peruvians, Cubans and Armenians. According to UNHCR 1,100 of these refugees had requested residence a year before. That same year, the country witnessed 300 more Peruvians, Cubans and Senegalese seeking asylum. The Government approved 78 of those requests and rejected 520 (including previous ones). 'Temporary residence' is granted to these refugees, which authorizes them to work, study and live in Argentina.

The emigration of Argentineans owing to the economic crisis peaked in 2001-2 most of them bound for Spain, the US and Italy. Almost 155,000 people left the country in those years, many never to return. In 2003 there was a short break in this population drain, based maybe on hopes aroused by the new government's proposed changes.

DEATH PENALTY
In 1984 it was abolished for ordinary crimes.

*Latest data available in *The State of the World's Children* and *Childinfo* database, UNICEF, 2004.

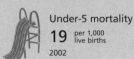

Under-5 mortality
19 per 1,000 live births
2002

Debt service
66.3% exports of goods and services
2001

Maternal mortality
82 per 100,000 live births
2000

the presidency in 1971 and in order to preserve the military institution he announced elections, although he banned Perón, exiled in Madrid, from taking part.

[24] Héctor Cámpora, the 'Justicialista' Liberation Front candidate - a Peronist electoral coalition - received 49 per cent of the vote in the March 1973 elections, taking office in May 1973, and resigning two months later to allow new elections after Perón's return to the country. On 23 September, Perón was re-elected in a new contest with 62 per cent of the vote, and the vice-presidency went to María Estela 'Isabelita' Martínez de Perón, his third wife.

[25] The Peronists resumed diplomatic relations with Cuba, proposed a reorganization of the Organization of American States (OAS) to serve Latin America's interests, promoted Argentina's participation in the Non-Aligned Movement and increased trade with socialist countries. After the Ezeiza massacre on 20 June, the day Perón returned to Argentina, friction grew among various Peronist factions and open warfare broke out between the old-time labor leaders and the 'special squads', as Perón used to call the guerrillas.

[26] When Perón died in 1974, his widow Isabelita took office. Her Social Welfare Minister (Perón's former secretary), José López Rega, set up the 'Triple A' (Argentine Anticommunist Alliance), a paramilitary hit squad that murdered Marxist opponents and left-wing Peronists.

[27] On 24 March 1976, a military coup put an end to Isabelita's inefficient and corrupt administration. A military junta led by General Jorge Videla suspended all civil liberties and set in motion a cycle of kidnapping, torture, betrayal and murder. The term 'missing person' became ominously commonplace, and government priorities were dictated by the newly adopted 'National Security' doctrine. Human rights organizations drew up a list of over 25,000 missing people, who had been arrested by the police in front of witnesses. Their fate has never been determined with certainty.

[28] The Junta encouraged imports to the point of liquidating a third of the country's productive capacity. Fifty years of labor gains were wiped out, real wages lost half their purchasing power, and regional economies were choked by high interest rates. The country's cattle herds decreased by 10 million head and foreign debt climbed to $60 billion, a quarter of which had been spent on arms. It was the era of what Argentines called the *patria financiera* (financial

fatherland), when government economic policies encouraged most of the country's productive sector to turn to speculation. In 1980, a wave of bankruptcies hit banks and financial institutions.

[29] In 1981, Videla was replaced by Roberto Viola who was in turn replaced by General Leopoldo Galtieri. Galtieri thought he had US President Reagan's unconditional support and decided to ward off the domestic crisis by recovering the Malvinas Islands, in British hands since 1833. His troops landed there on 2 April 1982. Galtieri's error soon became evident. Britain deployed a powerful fleet that included nuclear submarines, and the United States backed its North Atlantic ally. After 45 days of fighting Argentina surrendered on 15 June; 700 Argentineans and 250 British soldiers had been killed during the conflict. Two days later Galtieri was forced to resign from both his military and presidential posts.

[30] The junta set elections for 30 October 1983. The Radical Civic Union's new leader, Raul Alfonsín, won the election with 52 per cent of the vote.

[31] The new government started well but ended with the complete discrediting of Alfonsín. On the political front, the Government wanted to try the military leaders who had taken part in the 'Dirty War', responsible for the disappearance of more than 30,000 people. On the economic front, it aimed to tackle inflation head on, as this had reached astronomical proportions - 688 per cent by the end of 1984 - by reducing public spending and launching the Austral Plan, which froze prices, fees for services and established a new currency, the Austral, initially worth more than the dollar.

[32] On the basis of revelations made in studies by the National Commission of Missing Persons, nine Commanders in Chief of the dictatorship were put on public trial accused of having ordered the crimes of that period. The sentences meted out to several high-ranking army leaders - including former President Videla - and the later extension of the trials to lower ranking officers prompted a strong reaction from the military and between 1987 and 1989, Alfonsín had to put down four military uprisings. In 1987, the President sent Congress the 'Due Obedience' bill, which was approved, exempting most military personnel accused of human rights violations, claiming they were simply obeying orders from above.

[33] The failure of the Austral Plan led to thousands of jobs being lost between December 1983 and April 1989, salaries were drastically

reduced and some 10 million inhabitants - almost 30 per cent of the population - were virtually pushed out of the consumer market. In this period, the CGT organized 14 general strikes and shops were raided in various areas of the capital and some cities of the interior.

[34] The May 1989 presidential elections brought the Peronist Carlos Saúl Menem to power. The magnitude of the economic troubles resulted in the new

president being asked to take office a couple of months early. Menem, who had been governor of La Rioja, established a program of privatizations based on the August 1989 State Reform Act. In his first year in power, the privatization of the state oil company was promoted, as well as that of several mass media and communications companies and the state airline. The economic liberalization policy caused a schism in the CGT between the sectors supporting the

PROFILE

ENVIRONMENT

There are four major geographical regions. The Andes mountain range marks the country's western limits. The sub-Andean region consists of a series of irrigated enclaves where sugarcane, citrus fruits (in the north) and grapes (central) are grown. A system of plains extends east of the Andes: in the north, the Chaco plain with sub-tropical vegetation and cotton farms; in the center, the Pampa with deep, fertile soil and a mild climate where cattle and sheep are raised, and wheat, corn, forage and soybeans are grown, and to the south stretches Patagonia, a low, arid, cold plateau with steppe vegetation where sheep are extensively raised and oil is extracted. Argentina claims sovereignty over the Malvinas (Falkland) Islands and a 1,250,000 sq km portion of Antarctica.

SOCIETY

Peoples: Most Argentinians are descendants of European immigrants (mostly Spaniards and Italians) who arrived in large migrations between 1870 and 1950. Among them is the largest Jewish community in Latin America. According to unofficial figures, the indigenous population of 447,300 is made up of 15 indigenous and 3 mestizo peoples mainly in the north and southeast of the country, and in the marginal settlements around the major cities. The Mapuche, Kolla and Toba constitute the largest ethnic groups. The indigenous peoples in the east, center and southernmost tip are in decline.
Religions: Catholic (92 per cent, official); Protestant, Evangelical, Jewish and Islamic minorities. Languages: Spanish. Minor groups maintain their languages: Quechua, Guarani and others.
Main Political Parties: 'Justicialist' or 'Peronist' Party (PJ), currently in power; the Radical Civic Union (UCR), and the Frepaso (a coalition made up of former communists, socialists, independents, members of the Intransigent Party, former Peronists and the People's Socialist Party); Alternative for a Republic of Equals (ARI), center-left; RECREAR, center-right; Front for Change/Social Area (FC); Union of the Democratic Center (UceDé).
Main Social Organizations: The General Labor Confederation (CGT), 'Peronist' in orientation, founded in 1930. In reaction to the Government's economic and labor policies in the 1990s, the confederation has split into three factions. Argentine Workers' Central; Mothers of Plaza de Mayo (different groupings); Argentine Agrarian Federation; Argentine University Federation; Ecumenical Movement for Human Rights; Indigenous Peoples.

THE STATE

Official Name: República Argentina.
Administrative Divisions: 4 Regions with 23 Provinces and the Federal Capital of Buenos Aires.
Capital: Buenos Aires 3,047,000 people; Greater Buenos Aires 13,047,000 people (2003).
Other Cities: Cordoba 1,521,700 people; Rosario 1,339,100; Mendoza 957,400; La Plata 813,800 (2000).
Government: Presidential system. Néstor Kirschner has been president since 2003. The National Congress (Legislature) has two chambers: Chamber of Deputies of the Nation, with 257 members, and the Senate of the Nation, with 72 members. Each province and the Federal District have three seats in the Senate.
National Holidays: 25 May, Revolution (1810); 9 July, Independence Day (1816).
Armed Forces: 67,300: army 60 per cent, navy 26.8 per cent, air force 13.2 per cent.

Malnutrition
5% under-5s
1995-2002

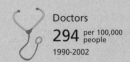
Doctors
294 per 100,000 people
1990-2002

Primary school
100% net enrolment rate
2000

Government and those opposing them.

[35] Menem re-established relations with the United Kingdom (leaving the key issue of sovereignty over the Malvinas under an ambiguous 'protective umbrella') and in two stages pardoned all the army officers responsible for the 'Dirty War'.

[36] Despite constant scandal and accusations of corruption, Menem maintained his image thanks to the economic stability achieved by the Convertibility Plan, which drastically reduced public spending and established parity between the new monetary unit - the peso - and the US dollar. Inflation fell and reached a historical low: in 1993 it was 7.4 per cent.

[37] There was strong economic growth but the unequal wealth distribution across the various regions worsened.

[38] The big surprise of the 1994 constituent elections was the performance of the leftist Frente Grande (Broad Front), which became the third strongest political force in the nation and triumphed in the Federal Capital with 37.6 per cent of the vote. It also won in the southern province of Neuquén. In Buenos Aires it became the second political force with 16.4 per cent of the vote. However, Peronists and Radicals obtained the majority necessary to ensure the constitutional reform which allowed Menem to stand for re-election.

[39] Shortly before Menem won the elections with 50 per cent of the vote in May 1995, scandal struck at the heart of his family, when his son, Carlos Menem Junior, was killed in a dubious helicopter crash.

[40] In the first quarter of 1996, Menem sacked Economy Minister Domingo Cavallo for having reported facts which linked the President with the murder of José Luis Cabezas, a photographer for a magazine critical of the government. The new Economy Minister, Roque Fernández, kept the economy going along the same lines as his predecessor had.

[41] In the 1999 presidential elections, the candidate for the Alliance (a coalition formed by the UCR and the Frepaso, derived from the Frente Grande), the radical Fernando de la Rúa, was victorious with almost 50 per cent of the vote in the first round.

[42] Economic recession deepened in 2000 and the new administration, which had promised to fight corruption, was involved in a scandal. In September, Vice President Carlos 'Chacho' Álvarez revealed that the Government had bribed several legislators in April, with money from expenses reserved for Intelligence services, so they would pass a new labor law. That

month, Senator Silvia Sapag, from Neuquen province, revealed that a Justicialist senator, chair of the Energy Commission, had offered her money, supplied by oil companies, for her to vote for the new hydrocarbons bill. Álvarez requested the suspension of those involved, but De la Rúa confirmed them in office, resulting in the Vice President's resignation in October.

[43] In late 2000, the IMF granted Argentina 40 billion dollars in aid to cover social needs, but the country continued to have difficulty obtaining funds from foreign private investors. Debt grew and Argentina found itself paying 2.7 billion dollars per year to the IMF, only one of its many creditors.

[44] After failing to reactivate the economy and once the country risk index reached 800 points, Economy Minister José Luis Machinea resigned in March 2001. The following day, De la Rúa requested his Cabinet's resignation. Liberal Ricardo López Murphy became the new Economy Minister and confirmed he would reach the goals agreed with the IMF. But when the new minister presented his plan, which implied a cut in government expenses to reduce the fiscal deficit, three ministers and six high officials resigned in protest. To replace López Murphy, De la Rúa appointed Cavallo, who announced he would reduce the state deficit to zero, through spending cuts. The Senate passed a law binding the State to spend only what it had collected, and included a 13 per cent cut in state wages and pensions.

[45] In early December, the IMF denied Argentina a new loan, arguing that an economic policy that combined fiscal deficit, high debt and a fixed exchange-rate system (the convertibility that pegged the peso to the dollar) was unsustainable, and demanded more budget cuts. By then, Argentina owed international organizations more than $140 billion (54 per cent of its GDP) and, as a result of the crisis, had lost approximately $19 billion in investments.

[46] The massive withdrawal of deposits forced the Government to apply a series of temporary restrictions on accounts. The measure, announced on 1 December for an initial period of 90 days, came to be known as the 'corralito' - little corral. Unemployment, which had reached 18.3 per cent, and social discontent were translated into a nationwide strike which paralyzed the country and ended with Cavallo's resignation.

[47] After failing to form a national unity government, De la Rúa resigned on 20 December, amidst massive street protests. The demonstrations, which included

looting in supermarkets and other businesses in downtown Buenos Aires, were severely repressed by security forces, which opened fire on the demonstrators, killing six and injuring dozens. Hundreds of people were detained.

[48] After De la Rúa resigned, Senate chairman Ramón Puerta, a Justicialist, first in the succession line due to the absence of a Vice-President, took office as President. Shortly after, the Legislative Assembly named another Justicialist, Adolfo Rodríguez Saá, who during the five days of his Presidency, announced the suspension of foreign debt payments and promised to create one million jobs. Rodríguez Saá resigned on 30 December, pressured by his own party. Eduardo Camaño, Chamber of Deputies chairman and also from the PJ, was sworn in as interim President and called the Legislative Assembly. Finally, Eduardo Duhalde - the main Justicialist opposed to Menem - was chosen at a special session held on 1 January 2002. Duhalde was allowed to preside over the Argentine Government until September 2003 and elections scheduled for 3 March were cancelled.

[49] The Government announced in January 2002 that the corralito would be enforced until 2003 and people would only recover their money in installments. The Central Bank was forced to intervene in the exchange-rate market to prevent the peso from crashing. Protests continued throughout the country, causing destruction in banks and automatic telling machines. Duhalde, who had undertaken in early January that those with deposits in dollars would get dollars in return, broke his promise and announced the blocked deposits would be returned only in devalued pesos. The total amount of savings in US currency, according to the Argentine Central Bank, reached $44.8 billion.

[50] A massive nationwide 'cacerolazo' (pot-banging protest carried out mostly by the middle class) took place on 26 January against corruption, the corralito and the Supreme Court of Justice. The population's discontent with the Court increased, among other things, after the judges freed former President Menem, who had been detained for arms smuggling to Croatia and Ecuador.

[51] The Impeachment Commission of the Chamber of Deputies initiated in February impeachment proceedings against Supreme Court judges, who were charged with corruption. Duhalde denounced the judges for blackmail. After several months, the judges declared the corralito unconstitutional, to avoid going to trial.

[52] In February the Government 'peso-ed' the economy and freed the dollar to float, while the Argentinian peso exceeded the 3 per dollar barrier. Without political backing from Congress to approve the Bonex plan - which aimed to turn dollar deposits, tied at 1.4 pesos in January, into a bond in pesos with a 5-year expiry date - Economy Minister Jorge Remes Lenicov resigned in April. Duhalde replaced him with Roberto Lavagna, who started to devise a plan to avoid the dollar's uncontrollable rise and started a long period of hard negotiation with the IMF to reach an agreement in January 2003. By this time, the IMF agreed temporarily to postpone Argentina's repayments to it and to other multilateral credit agencies. Reports indicated that 14 million Argentinians, almost half the total population, were living in poverty.

[53] Duhalde brought the elections forward to May and backed Néstor Kirchner, a lawyer who was at the time governor of the province of Santa Cruz and who, until then, had had a secondary role in the political sphere. In the first round, Kirchner obtained second place, with 22 per cent of the votes, behind Menem (24 per cent). Menem decided to withdraw from the elections because of the ample margin by which the polls stated that Kirchner would be the winner. In accordance with the Constitution, this made Kirchner president.

[54] In a few months, 54-year-old Kirchner reached a popularity of almost 80 per cent, having most of the non-Peronist population on his side. Coming from the left of Peronism, in his opening speech, Kirchner declared himself 'son of the Mothers and Grandmothers of May' (who have struggle on behalf of their 'missing' relatives since the beginning of the military regime) and promised to boost a 'united, serious and fair Argentina', which should become 'a normal country' again, making reference to the political, institutional, economic and social frailty of the country at the time.

[55] Kirchner appointed ministers who were mainly of his own generation and inaugurated an expeditious and bold leading style. He immediately made clear his authority before the Armed Forces, when he made dozens of military men involved in the repression apply for retirement in June, challenged the exculpatory laws and pursued research on the 'missing' people issue. Two months later he carried out a 'screening' process within the Federal Police, in which he removed from their posts those officers who were involved in cases of corruption.

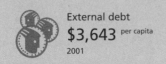

56 Through the Anti-Corruption Office, prosecution started for magistrates of the Supreme Court involved in the buying of laws, who in December, had been banned from leaving the country, together with former President Fernando De la Rúa.

57 On the economic front, Kirchner recovered the leading role of the state. He established during 2003 raises in private-sector wages and salaries and revoked the law on work flexibilization passed during the Menem era. He also improved state salaries and started a series of inspections to beat undeclared work and to increase tax revenue, which rose 45 per cent in that year. What is more, he froze gas and electricity rates and extended the plan 'Jefas y Jefes de ayuda a desocupados' (a subsidy for unemployed heads of family) initiated by Duhalde and returned the money frozen in the corralito to those small creditors who were private citizens. 'Our aim is to boost reactivation through demand,' reaffirmed Lavagna.

58 When Kirchner took office, external debt was reaching 178 billion dollars. Before the General Assembly of the UN held in New York in September, Kirchner demanded a reform of the payment plan to the IMF and stated that 'the multilateral organisms that encouraged indebtedness will now have to take on the responsibility.' In October, Lavagna stated before the IMF that Argentina would only pay on condition that the face value of the indebted bonds be reduced by 75 per cent and he did not pay the interests set for that month. In November, Kirchner stressed the fact that the money of the 2004 budget was not going to be used to pay the external debt, but that it would be allocated to social plans.

59 Felipe Solá (PJ), a Kirchner ally, became governor of the province of Buenos Aires in the August elections. Aníbal Ibarra (Frente Grande) became mayor of the capital in September, thanks to the support of several groups called by Kirchner to unite against Mauricio Macri, who represented a powerful economic group consolidated under the Menem administration. Duhalde supported Macri, which signaled a new crack in the PJ.

60 The unemployed 'pickets' movement held constant protests in these years. This consisted in blocking the traffic in the streets. This disorderly conduct along with a wave of kidnappings made the middle class worry mainly about law and order. This was the main challenge for the Kirchner team, whose term of office is to finish in 2007, together with the need to create real jobs to fight the

Falkland Islands / Islas Malvinas

Population: 3,063
Area: 11,410 km²
Capital: Port Stanley (Puerto Argentino)
Currency: Pound sterling
Language: English

When the islands were sighted for the first time in 1520 by a Spanish ship they were uninhabited. In the 18th century, they were baptized the 'Malouines' in honor of Saint Malo, port of origin of the French fisherpeople and seal hunters who settled there. In 1764, Louis Antoine Bougainville founded Port Louis on Soledad Island. This move brought Spanish protests, and France recognized Spain's prior claim. That same year the British, who since 1690 had called the islands 'Falkland', founded Port Egmont, renamed Puerto Soledad when the islands were returned to Spain in exchange for £24,000.

2 In 1820, shortly after independence, Argentina appointed Daniel Jewit as first Governor of the Malvinas. In 1831, Governor Vernet impounded two US ships on charges of illegal fishing. A US fleet that was visiting South America avenged this act of 'piracy' by destroying houses and military facilities at Port Soledad. On 3 January 1833, the English corvette Clio landed a contingent of settlers, which the small local force was unable to repel.

3 After World War II, the United Nations Decolonization Committee included the Malvinas and their dependencies on the list of 'non-autonomous' territories and established that, as the inhabitants were British, the principle of self-determination was not applicable. The only legally valid solution to the problem was to recognize Argentinian sovereignty.

4 On 2 April 1982, Argentinian forces occupied the Malvinas. British Prime Minister Margaret Thatcher, whose popularity rating had been rock bottom before the conflict, responded by going to war. Two months later, at the cost of more than 1,000 lives, the Union Jack was once again hoisted over the islands.

5 At the beginning of his administration, Menem renewed relations with London, but the intractable issue of the Malvinas' sovereignty was left unresolved. During his first official visit to the Malvinas, British Foreign Minister Douglas Hurd emphasized London's determination to maintain the islands under British sovereignty. In November 1991 Britain authorized the Governor of the Malvinas to award contacts for exploration and exploitation of possible underwater oil deposits around the islands.

6 In March 1994, the Argentinian Minister of Defense reported that Argentinian soldiers had died at the hands of British forces, in circumstances that violated the Geneva Convention on the treatment of prisoners of war. There were still some 15,000 live mines on the islands.

7 An understanding reached between President Carlos Menem and Prime Minister John Major at the United Nations, in September 1995, established that Argentina and the United Kingdom would jointly exploit the west of the islands, along the border with Argentina.

8 The giant US oil company Amerada Hess announced in May 1998 the presence of 'minor hydrocarbons' while drilling a pilot well 120 miles off the north of the islands.

9 In October 1999, as a result of an agreement between the Argentinian and British Governments, a group of Argentinians flew to the island, the first such visit since 1982. The ex-combatants and journalists who made up the party paid tribute to those who died in the war.

10 In April 2003, on the 21st anniversary of the war, Senator Eduardo Duhalde, interim president of Argentina from January 2002, declared that 'the Malvinas have been, are and will continue to be Argentinian'. ∎

PROFILE

ENVIRONMENT
An archipelago with nearly 100 islands located in the South Atlantic. It includes South Georgia, South Sandwich and South Shetland Islands. There are two main islands - Soledad (East Malvina) and Gran Malvina (West Malvina) - separated by the San Carlos Channel. The coast is rough and mountainous. More than half of the population lives in the capital on Soledad. The main economic activity is sheep rearing. The islands' territorial waters are believed to contain oil reserves. There is also hope that krill (a microscopic crustacean rich in protein) can be marketed. Its proximity to Antarctica also gives the archipelago strategic importance.

SOCIETY
Peoples: 3,000 descendants of English colonists (est. 2005). **Language:** English.
Religion: Mostly Anglican; Catholics, other Protestant churches.

THE STATE
Capital: Port Stanley (Puerto Argentino) 2,000 people (2003).
Government: Howard Pearce, Governor since 2002, appointed by Britain. The Legislative Assembly has 10 members, 8 members elected for a four year term and 2 members ex officio. In November 2001 elections, only non-partisans have been elected, with a turnout of 68.7 per cent.
Armed Forces: 4,000 UK soldiers since June 1982.

poverty of 54 per cent of the population and the indigence of 26 per cent. The economy, though, grew 6 per cent in 2003 and the dollar remained stable at around 3 pesos.

61 Kirchner and Brazilian president Luiz Ignacio 'Lula' da Silva, also left-wing, started in July a plan to enlarge and strengthen the MERCOSUR so as to create a solid Latin American platform. They hoped to improve negotiating conditions with Europe and the US and to prevent the advance of the Free Trade Area of the Americas, which they both agreed was a priority. ∎

Armenia / Hayastan

Population:	3,042,663
Area:	29,800 km²
Capital:	Yerevan
Currency:	Dram
Language:	Armenian

The first historical reference to the country 'Armina' (Armenia) was made in the cuneiform writings from the era of King Darius I of Persia (6th-5th centuries BC). But the name Hayk, as the Armenians are called, comes from the name of the country, Hayasa, mentioned in the Hittite writings from the 12th century BC. The Urartians, direct ancestors of the Armenians, founded a powerful state in the 9th to 6th centuries BC; its capital was the city of Tushpa (today Van, in Turkey). In the year 782 BC, they founded the fortress of Erebuni, in the north of the country (today Yerevan, capital of Armenia).

[2] With the collapse of Ur state, the ancient Kingdom of Armenia emerged in its territory. The first rulers were the *satraps* (viceroys) of the shahs of Persia. This period was recorded in the works of Xenophon and Herodotus. In *Anabasis*, Xenophon described how the Armenians turned back 10,000 Greek mercenaries between 401- 400 BC. His writings also describe Armenia's prosperous production, and its wealth in wheat, fruit and delicious wines.

[3] After the expeditions of Alexander the Great and the rise of the Seleucid Empire, Armenia came under extensive Greek influence, which gave a boost to the country's cultural life. The Seleucid State fell into the hands of the Romans in 190 BC, and Armenia became independent. The local government named Artashes (Artaxias) King of Greater Armenia.

[4] Armenia reached the pinnacle of its prosperity during the reign of Tigranes the Great (95-55 BC), an age known as the Golden Age. King Tigranes united all Armenian-speaking regions and annexed several neighboring areas. Its borders extended as far as the Mediterranean to the south, the Black Sea to the north and the Caspian Sea to the east. Tigranes' empire soon fell into the hands of the Romans and the Parthians, and Armenia was proclaimed 'friend and ally of the Roman people', a euphemism for the vassals of Rome.

[5] In 301 AD, Armenia became the first country in the world officially to adopt Christianity as a state religion. At that time, St Gregory the Illuminator, the first pontiff, founded the monastery at Echmiadzin, still extant as the headquarters for the patriarchs of the Armenian Church. The country lost its state integrity and disappeared in the year 428, when it was divided between the Roman Empire and the new Persian kingdom. Garni, a Greek temple dating from the 1st Century near Yerevan, is one of the monuments that reflect this period. The Church, identified with Armenian national feeling, allowed people to remain united even after they lost their organization as a state.

[6] In 405, the monk Mesrop Mashtots devised an alphabet that formed the basis of the Armenian writing system. The characters of this alphabet have remained unchanged, achieving a continuity which spans the centuries and links ancient, medieval and modern cultures. The 5th century was the golden age of religious and secular literature and of Armenian historiography; the natural sciences also developed during a later period. In the 7th century,

Ananias Shirakatsi wrote that the world was round and formulated the hypothesis that there were several worlds inhabited by beings endowed with some form of intelligence.

[7] In the 5th and 6th centuries, Armenia was divided between Byzantium and Persia. The Persians tried to stamp out all traces of Christianity in the eastern Armenian regions triggering a massive rebellion. Prince Vartan Mamikonian, commander of the Armenian army, assumed the leadership of the rebellion. In the year 452, he led an army of 60,000 troops into battle against a vastly superior Persian force, in the Avaraev valley. The Armenians were defeated and Prince Vartan was killed, but the Persians also suffered heavy losses, and subsequently gave up their attempts to convert the Armenians to Islam. All those who lost their lives in this battle were later canonized by the Armenian Church.

[8] In the 7th century, Arab forces invaded Persia, bringing about the collapse of the Persian Empire. The new Muslim leaders also established control over the Armenian regions. The people resisted, fighting for their independence until the late 9th century, when Prince Ashot Bagratuni was named King of Armenia, and established an independent government.

[9] The prosperity of the Bagratids' reign was short-lived, for in the 11th century the

LAND USE

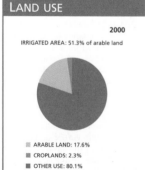

2000

IRRIGATED AREA: 51.3% of arable land

- ARABLE LAND: 17.6%
- CROPLANDS: 2.3%
- OTHER USE: 80.1%

PUBLIC EXPENDITURE

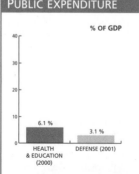

% OF GDP

6.1 % — HEALTH & EDUCATION (2000)
3.1 % — DEFENSE (2001)

WORKERS

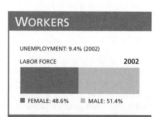

UNEMPLOYMENT: 9.4% (2002)

LABOR FORCE — **2002**

- FEMALE: 48.6%
- MALE: 51.4%

Life expectancy
72.4 years
2000-2005

GNI per capita
$790
2002

Literacy
98% total adult rate
2000

HIV prevalence rate
0.1% of population 15-49 years old
2001

Byzantines and Seleucids began bearing down on the Transcaucasian region from Central Asia. Many Armenian princes ceded their lands to the Byzantine Emperor, in exchange for lands in Cilicia (in modern-day Turkey). The inhabitants of other Armenian regions began flocking to Cilicia, fleeing the Turkish raids.
[10] In the 11th century, the Rubenid dynasty founded a new Armenian state in Cilicia, which lasted 300 years. Cilicia had close ties to the western European states; Armenian troops took part in the Crusades, and intermarriage with other ruling dynasties introduced the Rubenids to the circle of European rulers. In 1375, Armenian Cilicia fell to the Mamelukes of Egypt, who retained Cilician science, culture and literature. In the meantime, the region that had originally been Armenia was devastated by invasions and wars.
[11] In the 13th century the Ottoman Turks replaced the Seleucids and began their conquest of Asia Minor. In 1453, they took Constantinople and marched eastwards, invading Persia. Armenia was the scene of numerous wars between Turkey and Persia, until the 17th century, when the country was divided between the two Islamic empires.
[12] In 1722, Russian troops sent an expedition to Transcaucasia, occupying the city of Baku and other territories belonging to Persia. Armenian princes in Nagorno-Karabakh and other neighboring areas seized the opportunity to join forces with the Russians, and organized a revolution against the Persians. The uprising was led by the Armenian national hero David-bek. However, Armenian hopes were dashed when the Russian Czar, Peter the Great, died. He had promised to support the Armenians, but on his death Russia signed a peace treaty with Persia. Another war between Russia and Persia, one hundred years later, ended in 1813 with the Treaty of Gulistan. According to the terms of this, Karabakh and other territories that had historically belonged to Armenia became part of the Russian Empire.
[13] Russia was at war with either Turkey or Persia during most of the 19th century; with each war, Russia annexed more and more Armenian territory. Finally, almost the entire eastern part - home to more than 2 million Armenians - was swallowed up. However, the major part of Armenia's historic lands - with a population of more than 4 million - belonged to Turkey. Protected by Russia

against wars and invasions, Eastern Armenia prospered, while within the Ottoman Empire the Armenians were the objects of abuse and persecution. There were frequent disturbances and riots, which were cruelly suppressed by the Turks in 1915. During World War I, citing the Armenians' pro-Russian sympathies, the 'Young Turk' Government perpetrated the genocide that killed almost two million Armenians. While the men were executed in the villages, the women and children were sent to the Syrian deserts, where they starved to death. Survivors of these atrocities sought refuge in Armenian expatriate communities.

[14] At the fall of the Russian Empire, Armenia's independence was proclaimed in Yerevan. Turkey attacked Armenia in 1918 and again in 1920. In spite of some resounding victories on the part of the Armenian troops, the young republic's economy suffered and it also lost a significant part of its territory. In late 1920, a coalition of communists and nationalists proclaimed the Soviet Republic of Armenia. The nationalists were eased out of power and in February 1921 the Communist Government was brought down. However, with the help of the Red Army - which came into Armenia from Azerbaijan - the Communists were back in power after three months of fighting.

[15] In 1922, Armenia, Georgia and Azerbaijan formed the Transcaucasian Soviet Federated Socialist Republic, which became a part of the USSR. In order to avoid friction between Christian Armenians and Muslim Azeris, the Soviet regime adopted the policy of separating nationalities into different political/administrative entities, which involved relocating large segments of the population. In 1923, the Nakhichevan (Nachicevan) Autonomous Soviet Socialist Republic was created as a dependency of Azerbaijan, from which the entire Armenian population had been removed. Azerbaijan was also given Upper Nagorno-Karabakh, a region which had historically been

IN FOCUS

ENVIRONMENTAL CHALLENGES
The energy crisis in 1990 caused massive deforestation, since firewood became an alternative source of energy. The pollution of the Hrazdan and Aras rivers, and the desiccation of Lake Sevan, which were also a consequence of the extensive use of water as a source of energy, compromised water supplies. Another serious challenge Armenia faces is the reopening of the Metsamor nuclear power plant, which is located in an area of seismic activity. Part of the soil is contaminated with highly toxic chemicals, such as DDT.

WOMEN'S RIGHTS
Armenian women have been able to vote and be elected since 1921.
During the period 1995-2000, the proportion of women occupying legislative seats declined from 6 per cent to 3 per cent; in 2000 women occupied no ministerial offices or equivalents (in 1995 they occupied 3 per cent). In 2002 women represented 48 per cent of the labor force but women's unemployment rate was three times that of men. Almost 8 per cent of women receive no prenatal care whatsoever, and 97 per cent of births are delivered without skilled attendants*.
In 2000*, 2 per cent of women older than 15 were illiterate. Enrollment in higher education is 22 per cent for women and 18 per cent for men.

CHILDREN
In 2002, more than 55 per cent of the population lived below the poverty line and 8.5 per

cent lived in extreme poverty. Families with children under five years old comprised 60 per cent of poor people. Low income and high unemployment make it extremely difficult for parents to support the chronic malnutrition among children under five years old which increased from 12 to 14* per cent and affect a fifth of Armenian refugees.
In 2000, UNICEF reported Armenia as one of the seven countries with highest level of child sexual exploitation and child trade. Spending that year on education was a quarter what it had been in 1990. Malaria reappeared after 30 years, and 2,000 cases were reported in 1999.

INDIGENOUS PEOPLES/ ETHNIC MINORITIES
In Armenia ethnic minorities only represent around 3 per cent of the population. In 2003, there were 20 ethnic, among them 45,000 Yezidis, 8,000 Assyrians, 6,000 Greeks, 4,000 Ukrainians, more than 1,000 Kurds, some Georgians, Germans and Polish, besides the Armenian gypsies and Armenian 'Tats'. The Armenian subgroups are distinguished by their religious beliefs, their customs, and especially by their language, in the case of the gypsies a sort of Armenian slang that is on its way to extinction and has been corrupted and, in the case of the Tats, Farsi, which nowadays is only spoken by people over 50 years old.

MIGRANTS/REFUGEES
Between 800,000 and 1.2 million Armenians have abandoned the country since 1988. The first wave was caused by the earthquake of 1988, the second by the conflict

with Azerbaijan over Nagorno-Karabakh and the third by a combination of poverty and particularly bitter winters in which energy was short. At the end of 2002, around 256,000 ethnic Armenians from Azerbaijan lived 'as refugees', though UNHCR (United Nations High Commissioner for Refugees) did not consider them refugees and therefore refused to give them any assistance. That year UNHCR did shelter 11,000 ethnical Armenians who had escaped from the conflicts in Chechnya and Georgia, and had not yet received government support.
In the early 1990s there were around 50,000 internally displaced Armenians, especially farmers uprooted from near the Azerbaijan border. The internally displaced people received less governmental and international attention than those 'given refuge', or than the 100,000 people displaced by the 1988 earthquake. The Government eventually helped almost 40,000 of them go back to the border regions and gave assistance to those who returned by themselves.
In 2002, around 12,000 Armenians requested asylum in Northern countries, particularly Austria, France, Germany and the US.

DEATH PENALTY
Parliament abolished the death penalty in September 2003 and ratified Protocol 6 of the European Convention of Human Rights.

*Latest data available in *The State of the World's Children* and *Childinfo* database, UNICEF, 2004.

Under-5 mortality
35 per 1,000 live births
2002

Poverty
12.8% of population living on less than $1 per day
1998

Debt service
8.3% exports of goods and services
2001

Maternal mortality
55 per 100,000 live births
2000

Armenian and which Azerbaijan had previously relinquished in 1920.

16 In 1936, the Transcaucasian Federation was dissolved, and the republics joined the Soviet Union as separate constituent republics.

17 In 1965, Armenians around the world commemorated the 1915 genocide for the first time. In the Armenian capital, demonstrators clamored for the return of their lands, referring to the region of Upper Karabakh. The first petition for the reunification of Nagorno-Karabakh and Armenia - signed by 2,500 inhabitants of the former - was submitted to Nikita Krushchev, president of the USSR, in May 1963. Since that time, there have been two diametrically opposed positions: Armenia, in favor of reunification, and Azerbaijan, against. In 1968, fighting broke out between Armenians and Azeris in Stepanakert, the capital of Nagorno-Karabakh (see Azerbaijan).

18 In 1988, encouraged by the political opening of the USSR (known as *glasnost*), Nagorno-Karabakh Armenians (80 per cent of the local population) began a campaign t o join Armenia. Karabakh's Regional *Soviet* (Parliament) approved the resolution and in Armenia, the Karabakh petition for reunification was received enthusiastically. Moscow reacted violently and sent in troops to crush the demonstrations in Yerevan and Stepanakert.

19 In the 1991 referendum, 99.3 per cent of the electorate voted in favor of secession from the USSR. The Armenian Soviet proclaimed independence and in October Levon Ter-Petrosian was elected President with 83 per cent of the vote. In October 1991, Nagorno-Karabakh also declared independence after 99 per cent of the electorate approved separation. Azerbaijan responded with an economic and military blockade, sparking a war between the two republics. In December 1991 Armenia joined the Commonwealth of Independent States (CIS) and in 1992 was admitted to the UN.

20 In 1993, pro-Armenian forces achieved important victories in Nagorno-Karabakh, but Yerevan withdrew its unconditional support -at least officially. In 1994 - when, according to Azerbaijan, the Armenian forces had taken over 12,000 square km of disputed territory - Russian pressure made a ceasefire possible. Some 20,000 people had been killed in the war and one million displaced from their homes.

PROFILE

ENVIRONMENT

Armenia is a mountainous country, bounded to the north by Georgia, in the east by Azerbaijan and in the south, by Turkey and Iran. With an average altitude of 1,800 meters, high Caucasian peaks - like Mount Aragats (4,095 meters) - alternate with volcanic plateaus and deep river valleys. The most important river is the Aras, a tributary of the Kura, which forms a natural boundary with Turkey and Iran. The climate is dry and continental; the summers are long and hot and the winters extremely cold. On the plains, wheat, cotton, tobacco and sugar beet are grown. There are also vineyards, from which good quality wine is made. Cattle-raising is generally limited to the mountains. There are important copper, aluminum and molybdenum deposits.

SOCIETY

Peoples: 93.3 per cent Armenian; 2.6 per cent Azeri; 2.3 per cent Russian; 1.7 per cent Kurd.
Religions: Most belong to the Armenian Church (a branch of the Christian Orthodox Church).
Languages: Armenian (official), Russian, Azerbaijani and Kurdish.
Main Political Parties: Republican Party of Armenia, People's Party of Armenia. Communist Party of Armenia, Law and Unity Party (IM) (coalition); Armenian Revolutionary Federation (Dashnaktsutyun Party), social-democratic.

THE STATE

Official Name: Hayastani Hanrapetut'yun (Republic of Armenia).
Administrative divisions: 10 provinces.
Capital: Yerevan (Erevan) 1,079,000 people (2003).
Other Cities: Gyumri 130,400 people; Alaverdi 30,800; Dilijan 27,800; Goris 27,900 (2000).
Government: Robert Kocharian, President since February 1998; Andranik Markaryan, Prime Minister since May 2000. Single chamber National Assembly with 131 members.
National Holiday: 28 May, Independence (1918).
Armed Forces: 57,400 (1996).

21 In 1995, the President was granted more powers and the Government declared the liberalization of prices and a series of privatizations. Ter-Petrosian started a second term as President after winning the September 1996 elections, although fraud was suspected. The social situation - 20 per cent unemployment and public protests against the policies on Nagorno-Karabakh - forced him to resign in 1998. In the elections for the remaining term, Robert Kocharian, a native of Nagorno-Karabakh, defeated Karen Demirchian, leader of the Communist Party during the Soviet era.

22 Demirchian, now in the Miasnutiun (Unity) Alliance, was avenged in the June 1999 parliamentary elections, when he was elected president of the legislature. But in October an armed group with no ties to political organizations entered Parliament and killed Prime Minister Vazgen Sarkisian, Demirchian and other lawmakers, including two ministers. As a result of negotiations with Kocharian, the attackers stepped down in exchange for guarantees of their personal safety and Aram

Sarkisian (brother of their dead leader) was appointed Prime Minister. In 2000, the opposition accused the President of obstructing the investigations into the attack on Parliament. To control the crisis, Kocharian removed Aram from office and appointed Andranik Markarian in his place.

23 In 2001, Armenia joined the Council of Europe as a full member. The European Parliament unanimously upheld a 1987 resolution establishing that Turkey could only enter the EU as a full member once it publicly recognized the 1915 Armenian genocide.

24 Pope John Paul II visited the country for the first time in 2001 and resumed contact with the Armenian Apostolic Church, which had broken off relations with the Vatican in the 6th Century.

25 That same year, Russian President Vladimir Putin made the first visit by a Russian leader to independent Armenia. Moscow and Yerevan signed a treaty on economic co-operation, which also authorized the Russian army to defend Armenia's Turkish and Iranian borders. This treaty was the basis for the creation of the

Collective Security Committee, consisting of Armenia, Russia, Belarus, Kazakhstan, Kyrgyzstan and Tajikistan, which was strengthened a year later in Yerevan to include military cooperation against Islamic extremism.

26 Robert Kocharian won the 2003 elections with almost 50 per cent of the vote. His main opponent, Stepan Demirchian (son of Karen Demirchian, who had been murdered), member of the Popular Party and born in Yerevan, obtained almost 30 per cent of the vote. The elections were held even though fraud was suspected, and while some partisans of Demirchian were being placed under arrest, both in the capital city and in the provinces. The Armenian Constitutional Court determined that the arrests violated the European Convention on Human Rights, while the European Council reaffirmed their request to reform the country's Code of Administrative Offences, which dated from the Soviet era.

27 Until independence, the country's economy was based on the chemical industry, machinery, electronic products, processed food, synthetic rubber and was highly dependent on foreign resources. After the disintegration of the USSR, Soviet investment in and support for industry disappeared. The closure of the border with Azerbaijan and Turkey devastated the economy, which was dependent on oil and raw materials from abroad.

28 Since 1995, the economy has become more oriented to the processing of precious stones, jewelry making, communication technology and tourism, which has led to significant growth. This economic progress has made it possible to access loans from the IMF, the World Bank as well as from some foreign countries. To continue growing in the 21st century, Armenia will have to reduce its budgetary deficit, stabilize its currency, and stimulate the development of agriculture, food processing and transport as well as strengthen its health and education systems.

29 Parliament abolished the death penalty in September 2003 by 92 votes to 1, ratifying Protocol No 6 of the European Convention of Human Rights. Parliament was concerned to be in accord with the European Council, which considers the abolition of the death penalty a priority (41 out of its 45 members have ratified the Protocol). President Kocharian commuted the death sentences of 42 prisoners to life imprisonment. ∎

Aruba / Aruba

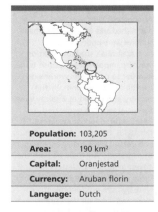

Population:	103,205
Area:	190 km²
Capital:	Oranjestad
Currency:	Aruban florin
Language:	Dutch

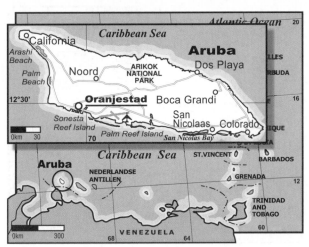

The Caiquetios, an Arawak nation originating in the Orinoco River basin, settled on the island now known as Aruba some 2,000 years ago (see box 'Arawaks and Caribs: Genocide in paradise'). Their culture and livelihood, based on intensive cultivation of manioc/cassava, sweet potato and maize, as well as hunting and gathering, underwent a dramatic change in 1499 when the island caught the attention of Spaniard Alonso de Ojeda. Within two decades, most of the population had been decimated by the diseases and slavery introduced by the Europeans.

2 In the 16th century, some convicts sent to South America by the Spanish Crown inhabited the island, called then 'La Española', as Spain was not interested in the territory.

3 In 1633, the Dutch, who were engaged in the 80 Years War with Spain, took the island. By the Treaty of Westphalia (1648), the Netherlands ruled over Aruba, Curaçao and Bonaire.

4 Throughout the 18th century, the colonial authorities used Aruba as a feed-lot for their horses. At the beginning of the 19th century, land began to be sold to the colonists.

5 In 1800, with the burial of the last of the Caiquetios the culture and language of the first islanders disappeared.

6 The Netherlands retained control over the island except for a period of UK domination (1805-1815). Aruba required little labor to support its horse and cattle-raising industry. For this reason there was little need for slaves, and only 12 per cent of the population was of African origin by the time slavery was abolished (mid-19th century).

7 Gold was found in 1825, leading to a transformation of the economy. However, in 1913 the gold mines were so depleted that mining was phased out.

8 The discovery of petroleum and the installation of large oil refineries on Aruba at the beginning of the 20th century generated a wave of migrant skilled workers, particularly from the US. Aruba's economic growth created problems with Curaçao, which was by then the colonial capital city.

9 In 1954, the Dutch Government gave Aruba and the other five islands of the colony (Bonaire, Curaçao, St Maarten, St Eustacio and Saba) their autonomy. This gave rise to the Netherlands Antilles Confederation. The political parties in power were the Aruba People's Party (AVP) and the Aruban Nationalist Union (UNA).

10 Juancho Irausquin, a former AVP member, founded the Aruban Patriotic Party (PPA) in 1971 and was its leader through the following decades. Gilberto 'Betico' Cores was the opposition leader and founder of the People's Electoral Movement (MEP). This supported each island's right to its own Constitution and autonomy within the Dutch commonwealth.

11 In 1979 the Antiyas Nobo Movement (MAN), won a significant electoral victory in Curaçao. With the MEP and the Bonaire Patriotic Union (UPB), it established the first left-of-center coalition Government. But while MAN favored a federation with broad autonomy for each island, the MEP insisted on the secession of Aruba. These differences led to the disintegration of the governmental alliance in 1981.

12 The MEP demanded separation from the Curaçao administration. In 1985, the Dutch Government granted Aruba separate status, and on 1 January 1986, Aruba became a separate entity within the Dutch commonwealth, then made up of The Netherlands, Aruba and the Netherlands Antilles.

13 Aruba's economy continued to be underwritten by Holland. The bulk (98.9 per cent) of its economic resources came from refining Venezuelan oil. But in 1985 Exxon, who owned the refinery, withdrew from the country and the island's unemployment rose to 20 per cent. Since then, the Government has turned to the tourism industry, which now provides most of the country's GDP.

14 Henry Eman, of the AVP, was elected Prime Minister in 1994 and re-elected in 1997. That year, the Government of Aruba, along with those of the Netherlands and Netherlands Antilles, decided to postpone indefinitely transition to complete independence.

15 The MEP won the 28 September 2001 elections, and for the first time since 1980 a single party had overall control of Parliament. The MEP obtained 12 of the 21 seats and its leader Nelson Oduber was named Prime Minister.

16 At the beginning of 2002, the OECD announced that Aruba, among other countries, was no longer on their 'black list' of tax havens - ie places where 'harmful tax practices' such as tax evasion are permitted.

17 According to UN figures, in March 2002 women held 30 per cent of seats in Parliament, one of the highest percentages of Latin America and the Caribbean.

18 In 2003, the Government of Aruba decided that it would accept euros, the main European currency, as a means of encouraging more visitors from that region. ∎

PROFILE

ENVIRONMENT

Located off the coast of Venezuela, the island of Aruba was until January 1986 one of the 'ABC Islands', otherwise known as the Netherlands Antilles, together with Curaçao and Bonaire. The climate is tropical, moderated by ocean currents. Tourism is the main economic activity.

SOCIETY

Peoples: Predominantly of European and Carib origin, its inhabitants intermingled with Latin American and North American immigrants.
Religions: Mainly Catholic (82 per cent). There is also a Protestant (8 per cent) minority and small Jewish, Muslim and Hindu communities.
Languages: Dutch (official). The most widely spoken language, as on Curaçao and Bonaire, is Papiamento, a local dialect based on Spanish with elements of Dutch, Portuguese (spoken by the Jewish community), English and some African languages.
Main Political Parties: Aruba People's Party (AVP); People's Electoral Movement (MEP); Aruban Liberal Organization (OLA); National Democratic Action (ADN); Aruban Patriotic Party (PPA); Aruba Solidarity Movement (MAS).
Main Social Organizations: The Aruba Workers' Federation.

THE STATE

Official name: Aruba.
Capital: Oranjestad 29,000 people (2003).
Other Cities: St Nicolaas 17,400 people (2000).
Government: Fredis Refunjol, Governor appointed by Holland, since May 2004. Nelson Oduber, Prime Minister and Minister of General Affairs since 2001. Holland continues to be in charge of defense and foreign relations. Single-chamber legislature; Parliament made up of 21 members elected for a 4-year term.
National holiday: 18 March, Flag Day (1976).

Australia / Australia

Population:	20,092,317
Area:	7,741,220 km²
Capital:	Canberra
Currency:	Australian dollar
Language:	English

The first inhabitants of Australia are thought to have come from Southeast Asia between 60,000 and 120,000 years ago, but whether or not they constituted one homogeneous ethnic group at the time of their arrival is not known.

[2] These peoples, named 'Aborigines' by the Europeans, spoke over 260 different languages that embodied distinctive cultures. However, they had common traits: they were all semi-nomadic hunters and gatherers. The clan, the basic economic and social unit, administered the use of the land and resolved ecological and social differences. Their principal social unit was the family, which was self-sufficient for food and supplies within the clan.

[3] In the 12th century AD Portuguese cartographers and navigators debated the existence of an unknown *terra australis*. In the 17th century, Dutch navigators sighted the northwest and southeast parts of the Australian coastline but took no territorial interest. It was not until the 18th century that the voyages of the British navigator James Cook began the colonization of Australia.

[4] In 1788, Britain established a penal settlement on the east coast of Australia at Botany Bay, to which it first sent 736 convicted criminals: it had recently lost its American colonies, which had previously absorbed some of its convict population. The new arrivals divested the natives of their richest cultivating and grazing lands, even though international and British legislation recognized the Aborigines' right to their territory until such a time as it was abolished by mutual agreement. British officers, then free settlers, farmed the land and from 1797 built successful industries (such as sheep farming and textile trades) that were to become the backbone of the Australian economy for more than a century. To do this, they utilized slave-like labor, since they used the convicts to build bridges and roads; clear and farm the land;

and act as servants to an emerging landed gentry.

[5] From 1787 to 1857, Britain transported 160,000 of its convicts (petty thieves, deserters from the Royal Navy and members of Irish opposition groups) to Australia. In the various colonies across the country, penal administration and local government remained in the hands of high-ranking military officers, appointed by the Crown until well into the 19th century. Their functions were to oversee the prison population and take charge of defense against possible attacks by other European powers.

[6] The battle to gain control of the land claimed the lives of 80 per cent of the Aborigines. As resistance was

broken, Aborigines were progressively relegated to Australia's more inhospitable areas. If genocide was not intended, in some parts of the country this was the effect. By 1871, records reveal only 879 Aborigines in Victoria, while in Tasmania less than 10 were on record as having survived. Exposure to European diseases claimed many. Entire families were poisoned, forcibly removed from their lands or confined to British reservations. Many of those that survived, completely defeated, were forced to sign with a mark 'work contracts' written in English - a language they did not understand - committing them to work in slave-like conditions as household servants or farmhands subject to severe

disciplinary measures. In the process, Aborigines' rights over land diminished and, little by little, their cultures were undermined.

[7] Australia's strategic location was also important for British trade, in order to control its worldwide maritime network. Initially the country also served as a safety valve for social tensions generated by Britain's rapid industrialization. By the 1830s, the poor classes in Britain and Ireland were being encouraged to migrate to Australia by both their government and by letters from those who had already settled and were by then enjoying plentiful work and meat on their tables.

[8] The development of the livestock industry and the subsequent discovery of gold and other precious metals boosted the economy between 1830 and 1860. Prospectors in search of gold from Britain, America, Poland, Germany, Italy and China rushed into the colonies of New South Wales and Victoria during the early 1850s. In November and December 1854, gold miners at Ballarat, Victoria, revolted against exorbitant license fees and those that imposed them. Under the Southern Cross flag, 10,000 of them met at Bakery Hill and demanded the right to vote in elections. Thirty of them later died defending the Eureka Stockade, which the miners had built to resist the aggression of the colony's soldiers. The Southern Cross flag remains a popular symbol of resistance to authoritarian rule to this day.

PROFILE

ENVIRONMENT

Australia occupies the continental part of Oceania and the island of Tasmania, and has a predominantly flat terrain. The Great Dividing Range runs along the eastern coast. Inland lies the Central Basin, a desert plateau surrounded by plains and savannas. The desert region runs west to the huge Western Plateau. Rainfall is greatest in the north where the climate is temperate, with dense rainforests. Some 75 per cent of the population is concentrated around the southeastern coastline, which has a temperate climate and year-round rainfall. Oats, rye, sugar cane and wheat are grown there; Australia is one of the world's largest producers of the latter. Australia has the largest number of sheep of any country in the world, located in the inland steppes and savannas, and is also the world's largest exporter of wool. It also exports meat and dairy products and is one of the world's largest producers of minerals: iron ore, bauxite, coal, lead, zinc, copper, nickel and uranium. It is self-sufficient in oil and has a large industrial zone concentrated in the southeast.

SOCIETY

Peoples: When the British 'discovered' Australia in 1788, there were 250,000 Aborigines in approximately 500 different tribes. In 1901, only 66,000 of their descendants were still alive. Today, there are 460,000, representing just 2.4 per cent of the national population. Descendants of British immigrants make up two-thirds of the population.

The rest are immigrants from Asia, Europe and Latin America. **Religions:** Christians 74 per cent (Catholic 27 per cent, Anglican 24 per cent, Methodist 8 per cent). Buddhist, Muslim, Confucian and other, 13 per cent. **Languages:** English.
Main Political Parties: Australian Labor Party (ALP) founded in 1901; Liberal Party, a right-of-center party; National Party (NP), which represents the interests of farmers; Australian Democrats (moderate).
Main Social Organizations: The Australian Council of Trade Unions (ACTU) is the largest labor confederation, with 133 union affiliates.

THE STATE

Official Name: Commonwealth of Australia.
Administrative Divisions: 6 states and 2 territories.
Capital: Canberra 373,000 people (2003).
Other Cities: Sydney 3,985,800 people; Melbourne 3,317,300; Brisbane 1,535,300; Perth 1,365,600; Adelaide 1,115,900 (2000).
Government: Parliamentary monarchy. Michael Jeffery, Governor General, appointed by the British Queen in August 2003. John Howard, Prime Minister since March 1996, re-elected in 1998 and 2001. Bicameral Legislature: the House of Representatives, with 150 members, and the Senate, with 76 members. **National Holiday:** 26 January, Australia Day. **Armed Forces:** 59,000 (7,500 women included).
Dependencies: Cocos Islands, Coral Sea Islands, Christmas Island, Norfolk Island.

Life expectancy
79.2 years
2000-2005

GNI per capita
$19,740
2002

HIV prevalence rate
0.1% of population
15-49 years old
2001

[9] Large tracts of land leased by British administrators meant that by the end of the Gold Rush all the good land in the colonies was held by wealthy farmers ('squatters'). Following broad support for 'unlocking the land', the colonies passed laws to enable the squatters' land to be subdivided and made available to 'selectors' - small farmers who would settle in the land. Although the success of these laws was limited, the stranglehold of the squatters was broken in parts of South Australia, Queensland and Victoria.

[10] In the meantime, a labor movement began to appear in the cities, and it soon had a significant following. In the 19th century, the Australian unions gained important victories and concessions which Europe's working classes were still a long way from obtaining (such as the eight-hour day obtained by stonemasons in New South Wales and Victoria in 1856). Urbanization went hand-in-hand with industrial development. Sydney and Melbourne turned into large urban centers. A demand for Australia's products on the world market and the low cost of land encouraged massive waves of immigrants, mainly British. A middle class developed alongside a wealthy industrial bourgeoisie, utterly transforming Australian life. Liberal governments dominated the country's political scene between 1860 and 1890.

[11] With major strikes by miners, wharfies and shearers during the 1890s, a political power base emerged to unify and represent the working classes. In 1891 labour candidates contested 45 seats in the New South Wales Legislative Assembly election and won 36 to hold the balance of power. By 1908 an Australian Labor Party (ALP) politician had become prime minister.

[12] Confederation of the separate Australian colonies arrived after a constitution, drafted in 1897-1898, was approved by the British parliament. In 1901 the six colonies (New South Wales, Victoria, South Australia, Western Australia, Queensland and Tasmania) were federated in the 'Commonwealth of Australia', governed by a federal parliament. The Commonwealth took over the administration of the Northern Territory and the federal capital in 1911. One of the first laws to pass the new nation's parliament authorized a dictation test to screen out 'undesirable' immigrants of particular nationalities from entering Australia, effectively implementing the 'White Australia' policy. This legislation was not repealed until 1958.

[13] A prolonged period of economic prosperity financed a series of social reforms, impelling

IN FOCUS

ENVIRONMENTAL CHALLENGES
Unique species, animal and vegetable, are in danger of extinction due to the destruction of their habitat. The erosion of the land due to extensive grazing, industrial development, unplanned urbanization and inadequate farming are of great concern; there is also an increase in salinity. The largest coral reef in the world, near the northeast coast, is threatened by shipping and by its increasing popularity as a tourist site. As the country contains some of the driest places on Earth, natural water resources for human use are limited.

WOMEN'S RIGHTS
White Australian women have been able to vote and run for office since 1902. The right to political participation was, however, not extended to indigenous women until 1967, although their registration on the electoral roll was not compulsory. Between 1995 and 2000 female representation in Parliament increased from 16 to 20 per cent; in ministerial or equivalent posts, the number of women increased from 13 to 14 per cent.

In 2000 women comprised 44 per cent of the labor force. Of these, 3 per cent worked in agriculture, 10 per cent in industry and 86 per cent in services. Those women belonging to ethnic minorities face discrimination due to gender and to race. In 2003 there was a flourish of media coverage on the trafficking of women for prostitution, as well as of arrests made in accordance with the 1999 sexual slavery legislation.

CHILDREN
Australian children enjoy maximum access to all basic elements which will ensure their well being (education, nutrition, health, clothing, shelter, social participation) - as long as they do not belong to the indigenous minority. The life expectancy of Australian Aborigines is 20 years lower than that of Australians of European origin (see Indigenous people).

INDIGENOUS PEOPLES/ ETHNIC MINORITIES
In 2002, around 458,500 Aborigines lived in Australia (nearly 2.4 per cent of its total population). Even though discrimination is considered illegal in Australia since the 1975 Law was passed, and despite the government's investments in programmes to improve Aborigines' economic and social status, they are still victims of discrimination throughout the country. Indigenous families are socially considered a 'problem' and Aboriginal children are 6 times more likely to be removed from their homes for 'welfare' reasons than non-Aboriginal children. Aborigines comprise over 20 per cent of the population in adult prisons and over 40 per cent of the youths arrested since 1997: Aboriginal youths are 21 times more likely to be arrested than white youths. The suicide rate among Aborigines is 6 times higher than the average for the whole population. Since

Federation, only two Aboriginal people (both men) have sat as members of the Federal Parliament.

MIGRANTS/REFUGEES
Towards the end of 2002, Australia was hosting around 25,000 refugees and people of diverse nationalities seeking asylum, among them 4,000 Kosovo-Albanians and 1,800 Timorese. The majority of Kosovars had returned home by 1999, and some of the Timorese temporary refugees were repatriated in 1999 and 2000 - in some cases under pressure from government action, such as the interruption of basic services.

Since September 2001, the country has been in the international spotlight for its zero-tolerance policy on the unauthorized arrival of boats with people seeking asylum. Through the so-called 'Pacific Solution', which remained in effect during 2002, the Government has denied the boats access and, in most cases, sent the refugees to other countries in the Pacific, such as Nauru and Papua New Guinea. Towards the end of 2002, over 500 Afghans and Iraqis remained in those two places outside Australian territory. Some 300 Afghans obtained economic assistance to return to their own country.

DEATH PENALTY
The death penalty was abolished in 1985, the last execution having taken place in 1967.

the country towards an open society. South Australia granted women the right to vote in 1893; in 1902, the Commonwealth of Australia became one of the first countries in the world to grant women the right to vote when it gave the vote to all British subjects of six months' residence and over 21 years of age - except for Aborigines, Asians and Africans.

[14] World War II, in which 30,000 Australians died and 65,000 were wounded, loosened the ties between Britain and Australia, and the US guaranteed security in the region.

[15] The Korean War (1950-1953) triggered a sharp increase in the price of wool, and consolidated Australia's economy, helping to diminish the gap between well-being in urban and in rural areas.

[16] During the Cold War, the ANZUS military assistance treaty was signed in 1951 by Australia, New Zealand/Aotearoa and the US. The aim of the treaty was to guarantee

the security of US and allied interests in the region. This military alliance also committed the Australians to fight in the Vietnam War (as well as in other conflicts), which damaged the treaty's image internationally, and triggered an important anti-war movement.

[17] A referendum held in 1967 granted Australian Aborigines full citizenship rights (including the right to vote) and placed the Aboriginal issue under the jurisdiction of the Federal Government.

[18] In 1972, a group of Aborigines set up a tent embassy outside the Federal Parliament, swearing to stay until land rights were achieved. In the following five years both Liberal and Labor governments began to put in place policies and laws for the return of some indigenous lands. But in 1983, the commitment to pass a law in defense of the Aborigines' territorial claims was shelved, when the enterprises developing mineral resources (gold, uranium, bauxite and iron) argued, against public

opinion, that the Aborigines' defense of their territorial claims could compromise the country's economic growth.

[19] Aborigines in Australia by now represented 2.4 per cent of the country's total population, many retaining their original languages. Two thirds of them no longer live in tribal groups. A substantial minority continues to live in areas which Europeans consider to be inhospitable, like the central desert, where they have managed to keep their own religious and social traditions alive.

[20] After slowly dismantling the White Australia policy, leaders on both sides of politics in the 1970s proclaimed Australia to be multicultural. Closer economic and political ties with Asia were formed. In 1989 the Asian Pacific Economic Co-operation Organization (APEC) was formed in 1989, led by Australia. The project promoted the formation of a common market in the region, and hoped to become

Under-5 mortality
6 per 1,000 live births
2002

Aid
0.26% Official development assistance as % of donors' GNI
2001

Maternal mortality
8 per 100,000 live births
2000

Cocos Islands

Population: 630
Area: 14 km²
Capital: West Island
Currency: Australian dollar
Language: English

The Cocos were discovered in 1609 by captain William Keeling of the East Indies Company, but it was not until 1826 that a settlement was established by Alexander Hare from Britain.

[2] The Clunies-Ross Company, founded by Scotland's John Clunies-Ross in the early 1800s, established a second settlement as the real owner of the islands, in spite of their formal British status (since 1857). Queen Victoria ceded the islands to the Clunies-Ross family in 1886 in exchange for the right to use the land for public ends. Clunies-Ross brought in Malayan workers - in conditions that were close to slavery - to work the coconut groves.

[3] In 1978, after many years of negotiation, Australia bought the islands from the Company. However, the Company kept a monopoly on the production and commercialization of copra. The transfer was designed to give Home Island residents formal ownership of their plots of land in order to alleviate social tensions. On West Island, Australia also had a military base, purchased in 1951.

[4] In a 1984 referendum, the population voted in favor of Australian nationality for the islanders and full annexation of the territory to Australia. The UN General Assembly validated the results of the plebiscite and Australia was freed from the obligation of reporting to the Decolonization Committee.

[5] Australia purchased the remaining Clunies-Ross properties in 1993.

[6] In June 2000 an earthquake measuring 7.5 on the Richter scale hit the Indian Ocean, near the Cocos Islands. Significant shaking was felt in the islands but there was no structural damage.

[7] In December 2001, the population of West Island doubled as a result of illegal immigrants - mostly from Sri Lanka - arriving by sea. Tourism operators complained that this could affect tourism in the islands. ■

ENVIRONMENT
A group of coral atolls in the Indian Ocean, southwest of Java, Indonesia. Of the 27 islets, only two are inhabited, West and Home. The climate is tropical and rainy, and the land is flat and covered with the coconut groves that give the islands their name. Direction Island has a military base.

SOCIETY
Peoples: The inhabitants of Home Island are descended from Malayan workers. Australians and Sri Lankans predominate on West Island. **Religions:** Sunni Muslims (57 per cent). Christians (22 per cent). Other: 21 per cent. **Languages:** English and Malay.

THE STATE
Capital: West Island 250 people (1999). **Government:** Bill Taylor, administrator appointed by the Australian Government, since February 1999. The territory does have a five-person police force.

Christmas Island

Population: 433
Area: 135 km²
Capital: The Settlement
Currency: Australian dollar
Language: English

The island, formerly a dependency of the British colony of Singapore, was transferred to Australia on 1 October 1958 and its residents were accepted as Australians as of 1981. In 1984, social benefits and political rights were granted, and in 1985 income tax was imposed.

[2] Phosphate mining, the core economic activity and sole source of employment, was shut down in 1987 and reopened by private companies in 1990 under strict environmental conservation measures. Two-thirds of the island were declared a national park, and since 1991 the Government has attempted to promote tourism as an economic alternative. In 1993 a private casino was opened with state support and an investment of $34 million. Also under consideration is the possibility of building a space rocket launch site.

[3] In August 2001, some 460 illegal migrants, mostly Afghans, though also Sinhalese and Thais, were rescued by a Norwegian freighter when their boat foundered. The ship tried to place the migrants on Christmas Island, but Australia refused them entry. A new Australian law excluded Christmas Island and other Australian dependencies from its migration zone. At the same time Canberra asked other Pacific islands - like Nauru, Palau, Fiji and Tuvalu - to install temporary camps for migrants seeking asylum, who were rejected by Australia.

[4] In January 2003, a young woman from Iraq, who was detained in the Island, was flown to a West Australian hospital, where she died. The extremely high levels of cadmium, where no plants can grow, mades the island a inadequate place to hold the asylum seekers. A refugee group, Project SafeCom, started a prosecution against the Howard Government for its human rights abuses.

ENVIRONMENT
An island in the Indian Ocean, 2,500 km northeast of Perth, Australia, and 380 km south of Java, Indonesia. Mountainous and arid, it has a dry climate. ■

SOCIETY
Peoples: Nearly two-thirds of the population are of Chinese origin. There are some Malays and a minority of Australians. There are no native inhabitants. **Religions:** Christianity (Protestants), Confucianism and Taoism. **Languages:** English, Malay, Mandarin and Cantonese. **Capital:** Flying Fish Cove. **Government:** Bill Taylor, Administrator appointed by the Australian Government, since February 1999. The assembly of 9 members is renewed every two years. There are no political parties.

the spokesperson for food-exporting countries, promoting the 'Cairns Group' in the Uruguay Round of the GATT.

[21] In 1991, unemployment figures reached more than a million, putting constant pressure on Bob Hawke's Labor Government. The economic liberalization driven by Hawke in the 1980s continued under the government of his successor, Paul Keating. The following year, unemployment reached 11.1 per cent. The Government approved legislation aimed at increasing employment and reducing immigration by 29 per cent.

[22] In the 1992 Mabo judgment, the Australian High Court recognized for the first time that those indigenous people who could demonstrate that they and their ancestors had occupied and worked Crown land, possessed native title and could claim the land. In the 1993 general elections, Keating won by a narrow margin. One of Keating's campaign promises was to give the Aboriginal issue a high priority. However, his government presented a package of measures that limited the effect of the Mabo judgment by protecting mineral exploitation and livestock herding on land that could be claimed by the Aborigines. Keating's package divided Aboriginal leaders, with many opposing the measures and accusing Keating of going back on his electoral promises.

[23] The resumption of French nuclear testing on Mururoa atoll provoked massive public protests throughout Australia, causing the Keating Government to remonstrate with France. The British Government's refusal to confront France strengthened the argument for Australia to sever its ties with Britain and become a republic.

[24] The Liberal Party under John Howard won the general elections held in 1996. In a further ground-breaking judgment for Aboriginal people that year, the High Court upheld a claim by indigenous Australians to land leased by governments to pastoralists. The Howard Government responded immediately, limiting the effect of the decision. In 1997, the start of new uranium mining activities in the north caused strong resentment among Aboriginal groups. Their leaders claimed the land would be contaminated. Since then,

Water source
100% of population using improved drinking water sources
2000

Doctors
260 per 100,000 people
1990-2002

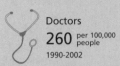

Primary school
96% net enrolment rate
2000

Aboriginal groups have filed suits for the recognition of their property over vast coast and sea areas, though few of these have been successful.

²⁵ The coalition formed between the Liberal Party and the National Party won the 1998 elections by a narrow margin and Howard was re-elected. The November 1999 referendum on Australia becoming a republic was won by the monarchists, with 54 per cent of voters deciding in favor of Britain's Queen Elizabeth II remaining head of State. The opposition blamed this defeat on Prime Minister Howard, as the referendum question favoring a republic envisaged that the future head of state would be elected by the Prime Minister himself, with the agreement of the leader of the opposition and parliamentary approval. Many voters supportive of a republic voted against the option because they wished to elect the head of state by direct ballot.

²⁶ The 2001 World Economic Forum meeting in Melbourne, was disrupted when some 10,000 demonstrators prevented several delegates from entering the meeting in the Crown Casino. The police - under pressure from event organizers - used violence to put down the protest. In November Howard obtained his third mandate in the general elections - snatching victory when large sections of the Australian public supported his government's decision to turn back boats containing Afghan and Iraqi refugees.

²⁷ In 2002, over 200 refugees, mainly Afghans, detained in a camp in Woomera, went on hunger strike in protest against the detention conditions and the difficulties in getting their asylum requests granted. The UN High Commissioner for Refugees (UNHCR), Sergio Vieira de Mello, classed the policy of detaining undocumented asylum seekers as 'unnecessary' and 'unacceptable'. Meanwhile, Howard defended obligatory detention and expressed that 'neither the condemnation of international bodies, nor strikes nor suicide attempts' would lead to any change in his government's immigration policies.

²⁸ The UN requested that all member countries refrain from blocking asylum requests from Afghans. Canberra argued that the Afghans' situation changed with the fall of the Taliban regime in Afghanistan and offered to help them financially to return to their country. Several asylum seekers escaped from Woomera, assisted by hundreds of demonstrators who broke down the camp walls in protest at the treatment of the immigrants. Hassan Varasi, spokesperson for the Afghans in Woomera, declared in 2003 that the refugee contingent turned down the Australian Government offer. Varasi affirmed that Afghanistan was 'too dangerous' a country to encourage people to return.

²⁹ In 2002, Australian public opinion was shaken by the terrorist attacks in Bali (Indonesia). In 1995 the Keating Government had signed a 'Security Maintenance Treaty' with Indonesia. The Bali attacks left 190 victims, of which 94 were Australian tourists. Promising justice for the victims, Howard re-affirmed his support for the US in the war against terrorism, in spite of the concern of some religious leaders about the danger that this could entail for Australians.

³⁰ In January 2003, Australia sent troops to the Persian Gulf in support of the imminent war headed by the US, which caused strong public protests. In February, for the first time in its history, the Senate passed a vote of no confidence against a sitting prime minister, condemning Howard's assistance to Washington during the Iraq crisis.

³¹ In March, Howard agreed to send 2,000 soldiers in support of any future US operations to disarm Iraq, and he authorized the Australian Defence Force (ADF) to participate in allied operations. Polls indicated opposition to this measure among 71 per cent of the Australian population.

³² Although military service is not compulsory, the country has a strong military tradition. Even though there have been no wars on Australian territory (except for the Japanese attack during the Second World War), the growing importance of the Asian Pacific area on the world scene and the influence that could be posed by China's ambitions, could presage a change in the role played by the ADF.

³³ The National Party and the Labor Party both take a 'hard' stand on security. This vision is not approved by all the Australian defense community, nor is it in accord with the less negative position held by the Association of South-East Asian Nations (ASEAN) on the region's underlying security position. The Howard Administration initiated two revisions of the country's military strategy, proposing major changes in the administration, structure and deployment of the ADF, as well as a more expansive and active role in the 21st century.

³⁴ Howard also tried to reinvigorate bilateral defense ties with the US and successive Australian governments have become ever more sensitive to Washington's strategic policies in the region.

³⁴ In October 2004 Howard's Liberal Party, in alliance with the National Party, won a fourth consecutive term of office. ■

Norfolk Islands

Population:	1,853
Area:	36 km²
Capital:	Kingston
Currency:	Australian dollar
Language:	English

There are no records of the existence of an indigenous population before the arrival of the Europeans. British sailor Captain Cook arrived in 1774, and the island was used as a prison site between 1825 and 1855. It was transferred to Australia as an overseas territory in 1913. In November 1976, two thirds of the Norfolk Island electorate opposed annexation to Australia. Since 1979, the island has had autonomy. In December 1991, the local population rejected a proposal to become part of Australia's federal electorate. In August 2002, the murder of a woman resident - the first one in 150 years - forced the Australian federal police to fingerprint the whole population and tourists (680) who were visiting the island. ■

ENVIRONMENT
The island is located in southern Melanesia, northwest of the North Island of New Zealand. The subtropical climate is tempered by sea winds.

SOCIETY
Peoples: 1,853 inhabitants in 2003. A large part of the population descends from the mutineers of the British vessel HMS Bounty, who came from Pitcairn Island in 1856. **Religions:** Protestant. **Languages:** English (official). **Main Political Parties:** There are no political parties.

THE STATE
Official Name: Norfolk Island. **Capital:** Kingston 1,000 (1999). **Government:** Anthony J Messner, Administrator appointed by the Governor-General of Australia in August 1997. Geoffrey Robert Gardner, Chief Minister since December 2001. Legislative Assembly with 9 members.

Coral Sea Islands

Created in 1969 as a separate administrative entity, the territory consists of several islets located east of Queensland (eastern Australia). The major ones are Cato and Chilcott in the Coringa group, and the Willis archipelago. With the exception of a weather station on one of the Willis islands and lighthouses in several islands, the rest of the islands are uninhabited.

² The Constitutional Act by which the territory was created did not provide for Australian administration of the islands, but only for control over foreign visitors by the Canberra Government. However the discovery of oil fields and the expanding fishing industry may change this situation.

³ In 1997, the charter was amended in order to extend its boundaries and include the reefs of Elizabeth and Middletown, 160 km North of the Lord Howe island. At present, these reefs are considered part of the Australian continental shelf.

⁴ In 2004, Australia maintains automatic weather stations on the island, and claims a 200-km exclusive fishing zone. There is no permanent population, only a staff of four people to run the meteorological stations. No economic activity is registered. ■

Austria / Österreich

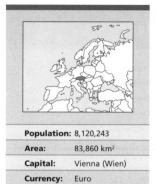

Population:	8,120,243
Area:	83,860 km²
Capital:	Vienna (Wien)
Currency:	Euro
Language:	German

The first traces of human settlement in the land that is now Austria date back to the Early Paleolithic age. From then on, the territory was occupied by various ethnic groups. The northern region of Hallstatt gave its name to the main culture in the Iron Age, from 800 to 450 BC. The origin of the Hallstatt culture cannot be ascribed to only one group; it was developed by the Illyrians and Venetians (among other peoples), but the main growth was achieved by the Celts (see Table), owing to their great knowledge of iron production techniques. This metal allowed the construction of vehicles which facilitated the crossing of the Alps, thus increasing commercial exchange. Archaeologists found 2,000 tombs within the region,.containing the corpses of salt miners. Cattle breeding, suitable for mountain areas, replaced agriculture; salt was used to preserve meat and meat consumption increased.

2 Celtic tribes moved into the Eastern Alps in the year 400 BC, and founded the kingdom of Noricum; in the west, the ancient race of Raetians was able to maintain its lands. Later, the Romans also settled here, attracted by the iron ore in the area and by its strategic military importance: Roman troops conquered the whole of the country around the year 15 BC. Raetia, Noricum and Pannonia became Roman provinces which were subdivided into municipalities. The Empire's dominions were extended as far as the Danube through a vast network of roads. The Pax Romana (see Table) ended with the arrival of Germanic tribes between 166 and 180 AD. Although Marcus Aurelius repulsed this invasion, the region did not recover its prosperity. Between the 4th and 6th centuries, the Huns and the Germans raided the area, putting an end to the Empire on the Danube.

3 In the 5th century, according to written records from the era, the Germanic tribes of the Rugii, Goths, Heruli and the *Langobardi* (Lombards), successively invaded the territory. In 488 a part of the population of the devastated province of Noricum was forced to emigrate to Italy. Following the departure of the Lombards in 568, after successive battles with Slavic tribes, the sway of the Bavarians - under the political influence of the Franks - reached as far as the Avar frontiers in the 6th century. When the Frankish king Dagobert I died, the Bavarian dukes were left virtually independent. Christianity survived through the Roman missionaires who remained in the west region and thanks to the support of the dukes. Under the protection of the Christian churches of Salzburg and Passau, led by the Slav apostles Cyril and Methodius, the Bavarians expanded both militarily and economically during the 8th century.

4 Charlemagne, king of the Franks, deposed Duke Tassilo III of Bavaria, and between the years 791 and 79 annexed the Avar lands in the south. The surviving Avars (mounted nomads possibly from Central Asia, who built an empire in Eastern Europe between the 6th and 9th centuries) were forced to settle in the western part of Low Austria, between the Fischa and Leitha rivers, and soon disappeared from the historical record, probably mixing in with the native population. Charlemagne took over as Holy Roman Emperor in the year 800, becoming the model of a Christian king and emperor. Even though the Empire disintegrated after his death, the German medieval monarchies - just like the French - derived their constitutional traditions from the Carolingian Empire.

5 At the end of the 9th century, the Magyar invaders took control of the low lands to the Rivers Enns and Styria to Koralpe. However, the Germans and Slavs continued to settle and after the German king Otto started expelling the Magyars in 955, the territory was predominantly German again.

6 Between the 10th and 13th centuries, during the period of Babenberg control, Austria was contested by the Pope and the Holy Roman Empire on several occasions in the battle for control of the German church. Meanwhile, the reformists gained ground, founding the monasteries of Gottweig, Lambach, and Admont in Styria. The Babenbergs maintained the duchies of Austria and Styria, expanding them north and south. New settlements were made by clearing the forests and moving into mountain areas. The colonization process changed the distribution of the German-speaking population and apart from in some Alpine regions, the Slavs were gradually assimilated, as were the Roman populations in Salzburg and the northern Tyrol.

7 The expansion of the German language was also encouraged by the attraction the Babenburg court held for the leading German poets. Decorated texts proliferated in monasteries, and in the early 13th century, the saga of the Niebelungs was composed by an unknown Austrian poet. In this era Austria also saw the flowering of the best romanesque and early gothic architecture.

8 Following the death of Frederick II, the Babenbergs' dominions were coveted by their neighbors. Premysl Otakar II of Bohemia became king in 1253, facing the opposition of the Austrian nobility after appointing foreigners in official positions, destroying fortresses built without his consent and dissolving his marriage. Rodolfo IV of Hapsburg came to the German throne in 1273 and pushed Otakar out with the help of the Hungarians.

9 Even though they were initially rejected by the local nobility and their neighbors, the Hapsburgs managed to maintain control over their dominions. In 1322, several defeats by the Swiss, and in particular that of Frederick I at the hands of Louis IV of Bavaria, threatened their dominion over the area of southern Rhine and Lake Constance. By passing the last years of his life on Austrian territory, and being buried in the Carthusian monastery of Mauerbach in 1330, Frederick was the first of his dynasty to consecrate Austria as a home for the Hapsburgs. The Hapsburg government and territories were known as *dominium austriae*, a term which would later be replaced by the concept of the House of Austria. Its consolidation was achieved through inheritance and marriage alliances. On the death of

Life expectancy
78.5 years
2000-2005

GNI per capita
$23,390
2002

HIV prevalence rate
0.2% of population
15-49 years old
2001

Frederick III, Maximilian I inherited the House of Austria and the German Empire. His son Philip I, married in 1496 to the Infanta Juana, gained the throne of Spain. A famous saying of the time ran: 'Let others make wars: you, fortunate Austria, get married'.

[10] The desire to expand Lutheranism, supported by the noble families, involved the Holy Empire in armed conflicts. In 1521, Protestant pamphlets were printed in Vienna, and bans on their dissemination had no practical effect in 1523. There were peasant revolts in Tyrol, Salzburg and Innerösterreich. Although the Anabaptists (opposed to the christening of children and rebaptized as adults) were joined by many peasants, they had no support from the powerful, which meant they suffered greater persecution. In 1528, in Vienna, Balthasar Hubmaier, reformist leader in the Danube and southern Moravia, was burned at the stake. In 1536, in Innsbruck, Jakob Hutter, a Tyrolian, was sentenced to the same fate after he had led his followers into Moravia.

[11] With the death of King Jagiellon of Bohemia and Hungary, Vienna took the chance to extend the power of the Hapsburgs, who held the union of Austria, Bohemia and Hungary as their driving policy. Ferdinand I was proclaimed King of Bohemia in 1526 but his troops were repelled with the help of the Turks when he tried to impose himself on the Hungarians. The 1562 Constantinople Peace Treaty divided Hungary into three possessions: the north and west which went to the Hapsburgs; the center held by the Turks; and Transylvania, with its neighboring territories, to Hungary's Janos Zapolya and his successors.

[12] In Austria, the Counter-Reformation started with the Jesuits, strong in Vienna, Graz and Innsbruck, and with the impetus of Melchior Klesl, apostolic administrator in Vienna, then Bishop and Cardinal as well as a key figure in Austrian politics. Maximilian II - successor of Ferdinand I as Emperor of Bohemia, a part of Hungary and the Austrian Danube - who had Protestant inclinations, promised his father he would keep the Catholic faith. His successor, Rudolf II, educated in Spain as a strict Catholic, expelled the Protestants from the court and put Klesl in charge of the conversion of the cities and markets. The Counter-Reformation caused mass emigration, including members of the nobility, to Protestant states and the imperial cities in southern Germany.

[13] The Catholic-Protestant controversy suffered ups and downs which made war inevitable. Upon the death of Emperor Matthias in 1619, Ferdinand II, who had been recognized a year earlier as king of Bohemia and Hungary, succeeded him as Head of the House of

IN FOCUS

ENVIRONMENTAL CHALLENGES
The gas emissions in large cities (from industrial plants, as well as from cars and trucks using the country in transit between northern and southern Europe), and the use of agrochemicals are the main causes of environmental degradation.

WOMEN'S RIGHTS
Women have been able to vote and stand for election since 1918. This is one of the 17 countries in which women's political representation has increased between 1987 and 2000, due to the Government's interest in the subject. In 2000, 27 per cent of parliamentary seats and 20 per cent of ministerial or equivalent positions were held by women. Women made up 40 per cent of the country's workforce. Of these, 79 per cent worked in services, 14 per cent in industry and 7 per cent in agriculture.

Since 1990, more than 17 organizations have been created, focusing on reproductive health, HIV/AIDS, sexual initiation, counselling for teenagers about contraception and support and information for sexual workers. A further 13 organizations provide assistance to the victims of domestic violence.

Since 1998, measures have been taken against human trafficking: the 'humanitarian visa' has been introduced and an intervention center has been set up for victims of trafficking and exploitation.

CHILDREN
Austria is the cradle of the SOS Children's Villages, an organization which was founded in response to the misery of thousands of children in need of care after World War II. The organization was founded in 1949 and managed, during its first 10 years of existence and at first by means of works of charity, to establish more than 20 villages in Austria, Germany, France and Italy. Today, more than 850 orphans live in 9 Austrian SOS Children's Villages.

INDIGENOUS PEOPLES/ ETHNIC MINORITIES
In 1999, there were between 40,000 and 60,000 Slovenes in the country. Under the post-World War II Treaty, which founded the Second Republic of Austria, the Slovenes are provided with minority rights in the areas of organization, education and administration, and all activities hostile to minorities are prohibited. However, pressure from nationalists has prevented full compliance with the Treaty. Within the Styria region, the existence of the Slovene minority is not recognized. In contrast, the ethnic minority in Carinthia, supported by Slovenia, operates with two central organizations and has developed autonomous financial, scientific and cultural activities.

The Roma (Gypsy) population includes the descendants of those who have lived in Austria for generations (many of Turkic or Indian origin), the immigrants or descendants of immigrants who came to the country in recent decades, and refugees and asylum-seekers from Central and Eastern Europe. Only people from the first group are part of the Roma-Gypsy Volksgruppe, which entitles them to special rights (state financial support for cultural projects, bilingual schooling). In general, the other gypsy groups face serious social disadvantages and prejudices in the areas of employment, housing and public spaces. Despite the small size of the Jewish community in Austria (there were about 7,000 in 2000), antisemitism is a serious problem, manifests itself in harassment, in the circulation of antisemitic material and graffiti, and in the desecration of cemeteries.

MIGRANTS/REFUGEES
At the end of 2002, Austria hosted some 30,900 refugees and asylum-seekers; 29,000 cases whose resolution is pending and 1,000 people who were granted official asylum. Asylum requests were 20 per cent up on the previous year, most of them from Yugoslavs, Iraqis, Afghans, Turks and Indians. Of the 5,100 pending cases, only 1,000 were approved (3 per cent less than in 2001).

DEATH PENALTY
The death penalty was abolished in 1968; the last execution was in 1950.

Hapsburg, and tried to impose Catholicism on his subjects. Lower Austria claimed the resignation of Ferdinand to Bohemia by means of a peace treaty and proposed religious concessions. The Bohemians were forced to withdraw and the territory was occupied by imperial troops.

[14] During the same year, the Diet (Legislature) - predominantly Protestant - unilaterally deposed Ferdinand, choosing to replace him with Frederick V on the Bohemian throne. Two days later, Ferdinand II was named Holy German Roman Emperor; who as a secular branch of the church, committed himself to continue imposing Catholicism. The conflict over the crown ran beyond the borders of the Empire and led to a series of conflicts known as the Thirty Years War.

[15] Bavaria and Saxony joined Ferdinand II, as did Spain - then at war with the Low Countries - to sustain Catholicism. After five years, the Bohemian army was defeated, and an imperial edict put down the Diet. Catholicism was imposed by force. Protestants emigrated en masse to Germany, which was invaded in 1630 by imperial troops of Adolf II, who won over many German princes to his anti-Catholic and anti-Roman cause. Although Germany was from then on the Gordian knot of the war, no throne in Europe was free of the conflict which drew in France, Poland and Denmark.

[16] In 1648, the Peace of Westfalia brought an end to the Thirty Years War and marked a new order in Europe. Holland became an independent republic, and the member states of the Holy Roman Empire were granted complete sovereignty. The old notion of a Catholic empire of Europe, led spiritually by the Pope and secularly by the Emperor, was abandoned for good. The modern structure of a community of sovereign states was established.

[17] Ferdinand II's heir Leopold was threatened by Hungarian rebels and by the Ottoman Turk Empire (over frontier disputes), which led him to form an alliance with Poland. In 1683, Vienna was besieged by the Turks, but the Austrians were rescued by Bavarian, Saxon, Frank and Polish forces, under the leadership of Polish king John III. In 1685, the Emperor signed a pact with Poland and the Republic of Venice, establishing the Holy League.

[18] Between the 17th and 19th centuries, the Hapsburgs were involved in all the European conflicts, several of them due to dynastic disputes, but the nature of these disputes was changed by the French Revolution. The Napoleonic Wars virtually dismantled the Austrian Empire, and it was only after Napoleon's abdication in 1814 that the House of Austria recovered most of its territory. In order to prevent a revolutionary uprising, the Austrian Chancellor Clemens Metternich created the Holy Alliance of the European powers at the Congress of Vienna in 1815. This upheld the principles of Christian authoritarianism and foreign intervention against liberal movements.

[19] In 1848, the repercussions of the Paris Commune reached Austria and a revolt broke out in Vienna, led by

Under-5 mortality
5 per 1,000 live births
2002

Aid
0.26% Official development assistance as % of donors' GNI
2001

Maternal mortality
4 per 100,000 live births
2000

crowds demanding the liberalization of the regime. Metternich's resignation, rather than bringing peace, unleashed a revolution throughout the Empire. At the same time, in Hungary, the liberal government demanded independence. In Germany the revolution installed a National Assembly in Frankfurt, which incorporated Austro-German liberals and conservatives interested in separation from the Hapsburg Empire. The Emperor accepted the Budapest petitions, except on two key points: budget and military autonomy. The Hungarian Parliament declared the power of the Hapsburgs null and void, and proclaimed a republic in 1849 but, soon after, the revolution was crushed.

20   From the 18th century, known as the Age of Enlightenment, until the 20th century, Austria was cradle and shelter of some of the most important personalities of European art and intellectual thought: including musicians like Joseph Haydn, Wolfgang Amadeus Mozart and Franz Schubert; thinkers like Sigmund Freud (founder of psychoanalysis); and the philosopher Ludwig Wittgenstein.

21   Counter-revolution annulled the Frankfurt Assembly, but the Austro-Prussian dispute persisted. The Hapsburg Empire weakened; it lost, ceded and decentralized its dominions until it disappeared in 1918, following its defeat in World War I. In that same year, a national assembly declared German Austria an independent state and, following the abdication of the Emperor, the Austro-German republic was proclaimed a component of the Republic of Germany. The Socialist Karl Renner headed the first republican government, a coalition in which his deputy was the Social Democrat Otto Bauer.

22   The economic chaos and hunger inherited from the war, forced the new government to confront - without consulting the old regime - the social unease and communist activism, that had been inspired by the Russian revolution in 1917 and by the Hungarian revolution of 1919. The personal prestige of Renner and Bauer helped them survive two attempted coups led by the Communists. The Social Democrats, who had support among the peasants and the Conservatives, had a majority in Vienna, where one-third of the population lived, while German nationalism fed on the urban middle classes.

23   The League of Nations supported Austrian postwar economic recovery, on condition that the country remained independent and did not join Germany. In 1922, the Government stabilized the country's finances by means of a loan until the great depression of 1929

which brought the Austrian economy to the verge of collapse. A customs agreement with Germany was fiercely opposed by the rest of Europe. Together with the rise of Nazism, German nationalism in Austria was showing signs of strengthening. In 1932, the Social Christian government of Engelbert Dollfuss attempted to take an authoritarian stance against the Social Democrats and the Nazis simultaneously. The Social Democrats rebelled and were declared illegal and in 1934 the Nazis murdered Dollfuss in a failed coup.

24   Taking advantage of the internal crisis and the Government's weakness, German troops invaded Austria in 1938, unchallenged by the European powers. A plebiscite carried out that same year in greater Germany recorded a vote of more than 99 per cent in favor of Hitler. In 1945 after his defeat in World War II, Austria was divided into 4 zones, occupied by US, French, British and Soviet troops.

25   In the first post-War election, the Conservatives obtained 85 seats in the National Council and the Social Democrats 76. Between 1945 and 1952, Austria fought for survival, since after being liberated from the Nazis, it suffered a severe economic collapse which was only overcome with the aid of the United Nations and the US, under the Marshall Plan. Heavy industry and banking were nationalized in 1946, and inflation was controlled by price and salary agreements. The interference of military groups with political and economic matters, within the Soviet zone of occupation, caused a considerable migration of capital and industry from Vienna and Lower Austria, to the agricultural areas of the western states. In the long run, this migration brought about a very important change in the social and economic structure of the country.

26   Conservatives and Socialists shared the government of the Second Austrian Republic, which only recovered full independence in 1955, with the Treaty of State and the withdrawal of the allied troops The country became a member of the UN in 1955 and of the Council of Europe in 1956. Since then, the key issues in foreign policy have been the dispute with Italy over Sudtirol (Bolzano), resolved in 1969, and its association with the European Economic Community (EEC).

27   The coalition ended in 1966, when the People's Party was elected. In the postwar period, Austria did not take part in any millitary alliance and during the Cold War, the country was liberal in its acceptance of political refugees from Poland; it was also a transit station for Soviet Jewish émigrés. The Socialist Party (SPÖ) won a narrow victory in 1970

forming a minority government led by Bruno Kreisky, an agnostic Jew, born in Vienna. Between 1971 and 1975, the SPÖ monopolized government, supported by great economic stability and a policy of moderate social reforms. Kreisky resigned when the SPÖ lost its majority in 1983. In coalition with the Liberal Party (FPÖ), the SPÖ maintained its social welfare policy and active neutrality in the international sphere.

28   In the last decade of the 20th century, the ultra-nationalist FPÖ led by Joerg Haider became the second strongest political force in Vienna. Haider was removed from his post as governor of Carinthia in 1991 for praising the full employment policy of the Hitler's Third Reich. He also accused foreigners resident in Austria of 'stealing' jobs from Austrians. In a widely circulated book, Hans Henning Scharsach highlighted the similarities between Haider and Hitler. The rise of Haider coincided with a debate on Austria's role in World War II. In 1992, after repeated attacks on foreign residents, the Government passed a law which punished neo-Nazi activities. In the same year, Thomas Klestil of the ÖVP was elected President.

29   A referendum in 1994 decided that Austria would join the European Union (EU). In theory this integration did not affect the country's neutrality. Almost 1,600 companies went bust in 1996, which was associated with an increase in economic competitiveness due to joining the EU. The Freedom Alliance (headed by the FPÖ) gained the same number of seats as the SPÖ in the European Parliament, overcoming the ÖVP. The Chancellor (head of government) Franz Vranitsky resigned in 1997 and was replaced by Viktor Klima, who masterminded an austerity economic plan. In 1998, Klestil was re-elected President.

30   In 1999 the decline of the Social Democrats was confirmed. Haider was re-elected in Carinthia and managed to transform the FPÖ into the second political force, beating the ÖVP. The Greens obtained 13 MPs, which proved to be inadequate for an alliance with the SPÖ. Klima, in spite of being a sharp negotiator, failed to form a government and accepted a conservative-liberal alliance. Before the new government was constituted, the EU warned that giving power to Haider and his Party would cool relations with the whole bloc. Even though Haider was not in the cabinet, the 14 remaining EU members decided in 2000 to restrict diplomatic contact and abstain from supporting Austrian candidates in the Union or other international bodies. Israel and other countries recalled their ambassadors from Vienna, accentuating the isolation of a government headed by the

conservative Wolfgang Schüssel. This isolation lasted for seven months.

31   In 2000, Austrian environmentalists protested on the border with the Czech Republic against a new nuclear power station at Temelin, 37 miles from the Austrian border. In 2001, after long disputes between both countries, Chancellor Schüssel and the Czech Government reached an agreement on legal measures to monitor the nuclear station and reduce its environmental impact. Austria does not have any nuclear power stations.

32   Chancellor Schüssel defended Austrian entry to NATO. The Russian President, Vladimir Putin, called on Austria to maintain neutrality on a visit in February 2001, stating this was good for Austria and Europe. The Russian ambassador in Vienna had previously declared that the end of neutrality would be seen, in Moscow's opinion, as a violation of international law.

33   In 2001, Austria agreed to compensate those Jews who had fallen victim to the Nazis during World War II, setting aside $360 million for the purpose. A fund was also set up for those suvivors who live outside Austria.

34   Czech premier, Milos Zeman fingered Haider as a pro-fascist populist charlatan, after Haider called for a veto on Czech entry to the EU and claimed there were security problems in the Temelin nuclear power station. This incident took relations between the two nations to their lowest point since the end of the Cold War, and the fragile Austrian governing coalition was rocked again. In the same year, 15 per cent of the Austrian electorate signed an FPÖ petition, demanding that the Czechs be refused entry to the EU and that the the Temelin nuclear power station be closed down.

35   In 2002, the government coalition collapsed: Schüssel called for early elections after the Vice-Chancellor (and FPÖ leader), Suzanne Riess-Passer, the finance minister, Karl-Heinz Grasser and other two members abandoned the coalition due to a political dispute with Haider, who wanted tax cuts implemented immediately rather than postponed to pay for reconstruction efforts following damage caused by floods along the Danube.

36   In 2003, the new coalition of Conservatives with the FPÖ was consolidated, promoted by Schüssel's previous conversations with the Social Democrats and the Green Party. During that year, the Government passed a law on political asylum which was considered one of Europe's most restrictive.

37   Heinz Fischer (SPÖ) was elected president in April 2004 with 52.4 per cent of votes; Foreign Minister Benita Ferrero-Waldner (Austrian People's Party) received 47.6 per cent. ■

Azerbaijan / Azärbaycan

Population:	8,527,280
Area:	86,600 km²
Capital:	Baku
Currency:	Manat
Language:	Azeri

Nakhichevan (Under Azerbaijan control)

Nagorno-Karabakh (Under Armenian control)

The Azeris came from the mix of ancient peoples of eastern Caucasus. Archaeological expeditions confirm that the territory has been inhabited by human beings since the Stone Age. A considerable number of primitive settlements - belonging to different periods of the Stone Age - refer in cave paintings to the existence of ancestors of Azeri people. The most famous cave is Azykh, located in the southern part of the Karabakh region. Items like utensils, stone tools and fireplaces were found there. Fire characterized the ancestors of Azeri people to the point that Azerbaijan was identified as 'The land of fire' by the Persians. Drawings on rocks at Gobustan (a city located near Baku), date back to the 8th century BC.

2   In the 9th century BC, the states of Mana, Media, Caucasian Albania and Atropatene emerged in the area of present-day Azerbaijan. General Atropates proclaimed the independence of this province in the year 328 BC, when Persia was conquered by Alexander the Great. The above-mentioned states were incorporated to the Persian Arsacid and Sassanid kingdoms. In the year 642, the Arab caliphate conquered Azerbaijan, which was still inhabited by several ethnic groups. The Arabs united the country under Shi'a Islam, despite some resistance. Between 816 and 837, an anti-Arab revolt was led by Babek.

3   Between the 7th and 10th centuries, the territory provided an important trade route which united the Near East with Eastern Europe. From the 11th to the 14th centuries the Seleucid Turks occupied Transcaucasia and the north of Persia. The peoples in the region adopted the Turkish language, and the Azeris' ethnic identity was consolidated. In the 15th and 16th centuries, the region of Sirvan (north of Azerbaijan), became an independent State.

4   Between the 15th and 16th centuries, the Setevid State emerged. Shah Ishmael I, founder of the dynasty, was supported by the nomadic Azeris who became the main power behind the State. The

Azeri nobility transferred its support to the Iranians and between the 16th and 17th centuries, East Transcaucasia was the scene of Iranian-Turkish rivalry. In the 18th century, Azerbaijan was disputed by the Russian Empire, which resulted in the emergence of more than 15 Azerbaijani Khanates dependent upon Iran. After several Russian wars against Turkey and Persia, the peace treaties of Gulistan (1813) and Turkmenchai (1828) were signed, granting Russia northern Azerbaijan (Baku and Yelisavetpol, corresponding to modern Gyanja).

5   The peasant reform of 1870 in Russia accelerated the development of Azerbaijan, which was supported by the abundance of oil in the region. With the Russian Revolution of 1905, the bourgeois nationalist Musavit (Equality) Party, which had a pan-Turkish, and pan-Islamic platform, was founded in Baku in 1911. After the triumph of the Bolsheviks in October 1917, the Commune of Baku established Soviet power in Azerbaijan. In 1918, Turkish-British intervention ousted the Commune and brought the Musavatists to power. Azerbaijan was

declared an independent state but Baku remained under the Communist Government, aided by the local Armenian army. In 1920, the Red Army re-established Soviet power throughout the country, proclaiming the Soviet Socialist Republic (SSR) of Azerbaijan.

6   In 1920, within the framework of Soviet policy on inter-ethnic problems, Moscow incorporated the regions of Upper Nagorno-Karabakh and Nakhichevan into Azerbaijan. These had previously belonged to Armenia as the ancient khanates of Karabakh and Nakhichevan. In 1922 Azerbaijan became part of the Transcaucasian Federation of Soviet Socialist Republics, along with Armenia and Georgia, which experienced considerable economic, urban and industrial development. Although Azeris held powerful positions in education, the republic was controlled by Moscow, especially during Stalin's period. The country was divided between traditional rural areas and the cosmopolitan city of Baku.

7   In 1923, the Autonomous Region of Nagorno-Karabakh was founded, and in 1924, the Autonomous Region of Nakhichevan; both had formerly belonged to the SSR of Azerbaijan. In 1929 an attempt was made to substitute Azeri script (in Arabic characters) for the Latin alphabet. In 1936, the Transcaucasian Federation was dissolved, and the SSR of Azerbaijan joined the USSR on its own. In 1940, the Cyrillic alphabet was introduced.

8   During 1980, socio-economic, political and ethnic problems exacerbated the feeling of discontent among Azeris. Between 1969 and 1982, the main leadership of the Communist Party of Azerbaijan was in the hands of Heydar Aliyev, who was known and trusted by the Secretary of the Soviet Communist Party, Leonid Brezhnev. In 1986, the new Soviet leader Mikhail Gorbachev initiated economic reforms (perestroika) and openness (glasnost) in the administration of the country, which encouraged popular discontent within the Union.

9   There was a wave of strikes, political rallies and demonstrations. New political movements came into being, like the leading People's Front of Azerbaijan (PFA) with a platform stressing civil rights, free elections and political and economic independence for the country, but opposing the long-standing aspiration of the Armenians of Nagorno-Karabakh to rejoin the Armenian republic. In 1989, Azerbaijan was proclaimed a sovereign state within the USSR. The ethnic conflicts between Azeris and Armenians led to the formation of extremist groups and Armenians were massacred in Sumgait and Baku. After the events in Baku, the

PROFILE

ENVIRONMENT
Located in the eastern part of Transcaucasia, Azerbaijan is bordered by Iran to the south, Armenia to the west, Georgia to the northwest, Dagestan (an autonomous region of the Russian Federation) to the north, and the Caspian Sea to the east. The mountains of the Caucasus Range occupy half of its territory; the Kura-Araks river valley lies in the center of the country; and the Lenkoran Valley in the southeast. The climate is moderate and subtropical, dry in the mountains and humid on the plains. The vegetation ranges from arid steppes and semi-deserts to Alpine-like meadows. The mountains are covered with forests. The country has important deposits of oil, gas, copper and iron and foreign corporations moved in to exploit the oil reserves during the 1990s.

SOCIETY
Peoples: Azeris, 90 per cent; Dagestanis, 3.2 per cent; Russians, 2.5 per cent; Lezghi, 2.2 per cent; Armenians, 2.0 per cent. There are also Ukranians, Tatars, Kurds and Talysh Georgian. **Religions:** Muslim (majority Shi'ite, 93.4 per cent), orthodox Russian (2.5 per cent), orthodox Armenian (2.3 per cent). **Languages:** Azeri (official) and Russian. Armenian, Kurmanji, Talysh, etc. **Main Political Parties:** New Azerbaijan Party; Popular Front of Azerbaijan; Musavat Pärty; Azerbaijan National Independence Party; Citizens' Solidarity Party; Communist Party. **Main Social Organizations:** Sadval, movement of the Lezgian people; movement of the Talysh people. There is also the self-proclaimed Nagorno-Karabakh Republic of Armenian People. There are some independent trade unions, such as the journalists' union.

THE STATE
Official Name: Azerbaycan Respublikasi. **Capital:** Baku 1,816,000 people (2003). **Other Cities:** Gyanja (formerly Kirovabad) 299,300 people; Sumgait 277,300; Mingechaur 98,900; Nakhichevan 67,100 (2000). **Government:** Ilham Aliev, President since October 2003 and Prime Minister since August 2003 Artur Rasizade acts as Aliev's deputy. The legislative body has 125 members. **National Holiday:** 28 May, Independence (1918). **Armed Forces:** 70,700 (1996). Other: Militia (Ministry of Internal Affairs) 20,000; Popular Front (Karabakh People's Defense) 12,000 (est).

Life expectancy
72.2 years
2000-2005

GNI per capita
$710
2002

Literacy
97% total adult rate
2000

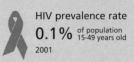
HIV prevalence rate
0.1% of population 15-49 years old
2001

Communist Government decreed a state of emergency and called in troops from the USSR to re-establish order; which led to the killing of more than 100 people.

[10] The Nagorno-Karabakh issue increased friction with Armenia and the Soviet (Council) of the Autonomous Region of Karabakh proclaimed its independence from Azerbaijan. In 1989, Armenia's Soviet approved the reunification, which Azerbaijan denounced as interference in its internal affairs. Karabakh, besieged and bombed by Azerbaijan forces, voted 99.3 per cent in favor of its independence in a plebiscite; the Azeri minority population refrained from voting. In 1991, the Republic of Nagorno-Karabakh declared independence from both Azerbaijan and Armenia. The status of Autonomous Region was annulled and the troops of the Commonwealth of Independent States (CIS) were withdrawn, though later on fighting between Azeri and Armenian guerrillas intensified. The People's Front of Azerbaijan (PFA) demanded the creation of an Azeri national army. Baku accused CIS troops of facilitating the union of Armenia and Nagorno-Karabakh.

[11] In 1991 Moscow approved Azerbaijan's independence. The state of emergency was lifted in Baku and the first presidential elections were held, the Communist Party of Azerbaijan been dissolved. Former Azeri Communist leader, Ayaz Mutalibov, who had supported the aborted coup against Gorbachev, was elected. The PFA called the elections 'undemocratic', and withdrew their candidate. Azerbaijan joined the CIS in 1991 and in 1992 it was admitted to the UN.

[12] In 1992, Mutalibov resigned, accused of being responsible for a massacre in Khojala (a territory of Karabakh), and Yuri Mamedov, assumed presidential powers. The fighting between Armenians and Azeris extended to Nakhichevan. Azerbaijan's Parliament, controlled by former communists, reinstated the deposed Mutalibov, who suspended planned elections and imposed a curfew. The PFA leaders, with the support of the national militia, responded by seizing the Parliament building in Baku, declaring the reinstatement of Mutalibov illegal. Despite fierce clashes in the capital, Mutalibov was ratified as president. The PFA assumed the directorship of the security services and of the official media.

[13] Later that year, due to the defeat of Azeri troops and the siege of Parliament by PFA forces, Mutalibov was forced yet again to resign and Abulfaz Elchibey of the PFA was elected. This prompted the return of Aliyev (former Soviet Communist Party and KGB) to a senior post. Over the following weeks, the Armenians launched a strong offensive and as a result there was a coup. Rebels led by Colonel Guseinov, took control of five regions of the country. Elchibey fled when the offensive against Baku started, leaving Aliyev as interim President. Armenian attacks intensified, and in May 1993 an offensive was launched on Stepanakert, the administrative center of Nagorno-Karabakh. During that year, Aliyev won the elections and successfully attacked Karabakh.

[14] In 1994, under Moscow's pressure, a ceasefire was declared and negotiations between the warring factions began. A coup by followers of Prime Minister Surat Husseynov failed. Parliamentary elections were held, without the participation of the powerful Musavit party, nor of communist or Islamic groups. Aliyev's party, New Azerbaijan (NA), won the elections.

[15] In 1995, the NA won the majority of parliamentary seats, in the country's first Presidential multi-party elections and a new Constitution was approved by referendum. In 1998, opposition leaders, among them Abulfez Elchibey, boycotted the Presidential elections in which Aliyev obtained 76 per cent of the vote. Observers denounced abnormalities and the opposition took to the streets claiming the elections were rigged, while editors of 20 daily newspapers began a hunger strike to press for the annulment of the elections.

[16] In 1997 Azerbaijan opened its oil fields in the Caspian Sea, made possible by a contract between the Government and a 12-company (40 per cent US) consortium. Azerbaijan, Kazakhstan and Turkmenistan possess the third largest oil reserves in the world.

[17] In 2000, elections gave another overwhelming majority to the NA of President Aliyev, and observers denounced once again the lack of integrity of the electoral system. Azerbaijan's democracy was condemned in 2001 by European Council officials, who criticized the lack of freedom of speech and the existence of political prisoners. Aliyev judged criticism to be rough interference in the internal affairs of the country. Despite this, Azerbaijan became a full member of the European Council that year.

[18] After the terrorist attacks of 11 September 2001 in Washington and New York, Aliyev allowed the US to use Azeri air space to mobilize troops and supplies for its bases in Central Asia and supported Washington's anti-terrorist campaign; in exchange the US lifted the sanctions imposed on Azerbaijan in 1992 because Baku had blocked a railroad to Armenia.

[19] A multi-million-dollar pipeline that will transport oil from the Caspian Sea in Azerbaijan to Turkey through Georgia was under construction in 2002. Hundreds of people demonstrated that year in Baku, demanding the end of poverty and denouncing the appalling conditions of their lives. In that year, Aliyev suffered a collapse during a ceremony on television and was hospitalized in Turkey; he appointed his son Ilham as Prime Minister.

[20] In October 2003, Ilham Aliyev won the Presidential elections, described by observers as being quite far from international standards. Opposition parties took to the streets and the protests were suppressed by police, which arrested hundreds of people. ∎

IN FOCUS

ENVIRONMENTAL CHALLENGES
There are problems with soil pollution from the use of pesticides such as DDT. Highly toxic defoliants have been used extensively on cotton crops. Water pollution is a serious problem; approximately half the population lacks sewage facilities and only a quarter of all water is treated. The situation of the Caspian Sea is alarming, especially near the Abseron Peninsula, considered as one of the world's most ecologically degraded areas with high levels of drying.

WOMEN'S RIGHTS
Women have been able to vote and stand for election since 1921. From 1995-2000 women held 12 per cent of Parliamentary seats and their representation in ministerial or equivalent positions increased from 5 to 10 per cent. In 2000, women made up 36 per cent of the workforce. Prenatal health care covered 68.7 per cent of pregnancies, while 84 per cent of births are attended by skilled health staff*.

Since then, risks to maternal health have increased due to the declining quality and rising cost of the public health care services, which have led many women to make their own diagnosis and to give birth at home. There are no family planning advice services, so abortion remains the main method of birth control. The UN estimates the maternal mortality ratio at 94 per 10,000 live births, much higher than the figure officially reported*.

CHILDREN
The principal causes of under-five mortality are respiratory conditions and parasitic infections. Vaccination has improved, reaching levels higher than 90 per cent. However, a survey for the Extended Programme on Immunization in 2002, indicated lower coverage among groups of Armenian refugees or internally displaced people. The incidence of iron deficiency is high, and iodized salt consumption reaches only 41 per cent of the population. In 2003, malaria became a new problem affecting the children in particular.

INDIGENOUS PEOPLES/ETHNIC MINORITIES
In 2000, the Lezgins represented 2.5 per cent of the total population of Azerbaijan. The Lezgins are a Sunni Muslim people whose lands are divided by the border between Russia and Azerbaijan. Today, most Lezgins speak Azeri as a second language, and are fairly well-integrated into the society of Azerbaijan.

The most frequent complaints by Lezgins include the lack of Lezgin language education and media in Baku but all Lezgin groups are increasingly willing to negotiate their grievances.

In 2001, the Armenian minority in Azerbaijan was still at a high risk of conflict as long as the Nagorno-Karabakh situation remained unsettled.

MIGRANTS/REFUGEES
By the end of 2002, more than 576,000 people remained internally displaced from the western regions of Azerbaijan - especially Nagorno-Karabakh - which have been under Armenian occupation since 1993. According to Government information, some 11,400 refugees and asylum-seekers - including some 10,000 from the Republic of Chechnya and 1,200 from Afghanistan - were living in the country by the end of 2002.

During that year, the UNHCR registered almost 1,800 asylum-seekers in Azerbaijan, most of them Chechens. There were also some 270,000 people living as refugees in Azerbaijan in 2002, most of them Azeris who came from Armenia in 1988 but also including 50,000 ethnic Turks who fled Uzbekistan in 1989. During 2002, nearly 4,900 people from Azerbaijan requested asylum in other European countries, less than a third the number the previous year.

DEATH PENALTY
Was abolished in 1998.

*Latest data available in *The State of the World's Children* and *Childinfo* database, UNICEF, 2004.

Population:	320,650
Area:	13,880 km²
Capital:	Nassau
Currency:	Bahamian dollar
Language:	English

The Bahamian archipelago was one of the few areas of the Caribbean from which the Arawak Indians, who mainly lived on fishing and the harvesting of seafood and molluscs, were not displaced by the Caribs (see chart 'Genocide in paradise'). The few remaining traces of their culture are pots, potsherds and petroglyphs.

2   Columbus probably first trod American soil on the Bahamian island of Guanahani (or San Salvador or Watling).

3   The Spanish historian Francisco de Gomara pointed out, 'over a period of 25 years, the Spaniards enslaved 40,000 Indians who were sent to work in mines on the other islands', such as Santo Domingo.

4   The Spaniards did not colonize the islands that lacked mineral resources. Instead, British privateers and pirates sought refuge in these islands after seizing the gold extracted by the Spaniards in other American territories.

5   From 1640 the British began to settle the Bahamas. Sugarcane and other tropical crops were grown in plantations worked by African enslaved laborers whose descendants today make up most of the local population. In 1873, the Treaty of Madrid settled the dispute over control of the Bahamas in favor of the British.

6   The British refused to accept the independence of this strategic archipelago, and it was not until 1973 that the Bahamas proclaimed their independence within the British Commonwealth. This change actually meant little to the islanders because in the meantime the country had become increasingly dependent on the United States.

7   In fact, most of the three million tourists who now visit the Bahamas come from the US, drawn to the beaches and casinos. The transnationals which use the Bahamas as their formal headquarters are also North American, taking advantage of the exemptions that make the country a 'tax-haven'. Also, US citizens are the chief buyers of lottery tickets, a source of fiscal revenues that contributes heavily to the state budget. The country's second economic activity is banking. By the end of 1986 there were more than 300 banks. In 1942, the US installed a naval base at Freeport, which helped control traffic from the Gulf of Mexico to the Atlantic, via the Florida Strait.

8   While other Caribbean nations sought ways to bring about regional integration, the Bahamas never joined any regional organization.

9   In 1956 the Assembly passed an anti-discriminatory resolution aimed at promoting ethnic equality. Thus, the Afro-Caribbean population was given access to places where they had never before been admitted.

10   In 1964 the new Constitution was passed and a ministerial form of government was established. The number of representatives to the Assembly was increased from 29 to 40.

IN FOCUS

ENVIRONMENTAL CHALLENGES
The warming of the seas, as well as the increasing frequency and intensity of tropical hurricanes, are growing threats to the islands' environment. The main difficulties are the pollution and deterioration of the coral reefs and the erosion of the coastal areas.

WOMEN'S RIGHTS
Women have been able to vote and be elected without restrictions since 1964. From 1995 to 2000 the parliamentary seats occupied by women increased from 8 to 15 per cent, while their representation in ministerial offices or equivalents reduced from 23 to 17 per cent.

In 2000, women constituted 47 per cent of the labour force (1 per cent in the agricultural sector, 5 per cent in the industrial sector and 94 per cent in the services sector), a number that had been increasing at a pace of 1 per cent a decade. 88 per cent of working women were employees. Female unemployment (9.7 per cent) was 3.7 per cent higher than male unemployment. The illiteracy rate among women between 15 and 24 years old is 1.7 per cent, 2.1 per cent lower than the rate registered in men within the same age range.

CHILDREN
Under-five mortality decreased from 29 per cent to 16 between 1990 and 2002*.

In 2001 there were 2,900 children who had been orphaned by HIV/AIDS.

INDIGENOUS PEOPLES/ ETHNIC MINORITIES
Unofficial estimates indicate that between 20 and 25 per cent of the population are Haitian or their descendants, which turns them into the country's largest and most visible ethnic minority. Around 40,000 Haitians are legally settled in Bahamas, while a similar number of them remain in the country with no official permit. In general, they are socially well-integrated, although they are mildly discriminated against in the labour market and there is a certain apprehension regarding the possibility of a massive Haitian immigration.

MIGRANTS/REFUGEES
Bahamas has not enacted legislation implementing the UN Convention relating to the status of Refugees and its Protocol, which it ratified in 1993. The Government determines asylum claims on an ad hoc basis, advised and assisted by the UNHCR.

Most asylum-seekers come from Haiti or Cuba. In 2002, only 4 of the 54 asylum applicants were recommended for refugee status. Many Haitians were deported, since Nassau determined that all illegal immigrants should be automatically deported.

DEATH PENALTY
The last execution took place March 1998. The death penalty may be applied to every kind of crime.

*Latest data available in *The State of the World's Children* and *Childinfo* database, UNICEF, 2004.

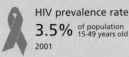

Life expectancy	GNI per capita	Literacy	HIV prevalence rate
67.1 years 2000-2005	**$14,860** 2002	**95%** total adult rate 2000	**3.5%** of population 15-49 years old 2001

[11] The Progressive Liberal Party (PLP), whose leaders were black, won the 1967 election, putting an end to white supremacy. Lynden Pindling became Prime Minister.

[12] In 1977, when the economic and social crisis started to bite, the Government decided to give even greater incentives to foreign capital. In an attempt to diminish the massive unemployment which threatened to create social tensions and changes in the archipelago, the Government opened an industrial estate of 1,200 hectares near a deep water port in Grand Bahama. It was meant to be used as a storage point for merchandise which was later to be re-exported after minimal local processing.

[13] During the 1977 electoral campaign the opposition parties - the Free National Movement, the Democratic Party of Bahamas, and the Vanguard Party - accused the Government of corruption and squandering public funds. Both left and right criticized the Government's policy towards transnationals. However, Pindling again won by a landslide and promised to lower unemployment. He opened the country's coasts to the transnationals, which resumed oil prospecting in 1979.

[14] In 1984, the political scene was further upset when the US NBC Network News directly charged Prime Minister Pindling with receiving large sums of money for authorizing drug traffic through Bahamian territory. An investigation immediately confirmed that Government officials were involved in smuggling but cleared Pindling of any responsibility in the affair.

[15] In 1987, the unemployment rate was estimated to be above 18 per cent, with that of young people under 25 as high as 35 per cent. Although they had strongly supported the Government in the past, labor unions now criticized the authorities for the lack of constructive, long-term programs aimed at solving the grave unemployment problem.

[16] Lynden Pindling won his sixth consecutive election on 19 June 1987. The PLP obtained 31 out of 49 seats. The opposition Free National Movement (FNM), led by Cecil Wallace Whitfield repeatedly asked Pindling to step down, charging him with fraud, corruption, and being 'soft' towards drug dealers.

[17] In 1991, there was a sharp decrease in the number of tourists, estimated at three million per annum. This was attributed to the fact that there had been a rise in crime, compounded by the Bahamas' extremely high cocaine consumption rate. Although there had been a slowdown in inflation and a slight fiscal surplus, this did not prevent people from taking to the streets.

[18] Tourism had generated over 65 per cent of the country's GDP, but in 1992 this fell by 10 per cent in relation to 1990 figures. Meanwhile the banking system lost customers to its competitors in the Cayman Islands. In addition, the Government was unable to increase agricultural production, making it necessary for the country to import 80 per cent of its food.

[19] Pindling's 25 years in office ended in 1992 when Hubert Ingraham, a former protégé of Pindling's and leader of the National Free Movement, won the parliamentary elections with 55 per cent of the vote. The new Government aimed to reduce unemployment through the liberalization of foreign investment laws and the re-establishment of the Bahamas as a major tourist destination.

[20] In February 1994, one of the prominent figures from Pindling's time, lawyer Nigel Bowe, was incarcerated in Miami for drug trafficking. That year, the Government appointed a commission to investigate Pindling, who was accused of having used the Hotel Corporation's funds to increase his wealth. Pindling denied the charges and sought protection in bank secrecy, which limited the Commission's progress.

[21] In 1995, foreign investors carried out the privatization of several hotels belonging to the Hotel Corporation. The most significant problems for the Government were unemployment and the presence of several thousands of Haitian and Cuban refugees. A repatriation agreement with Haiti was achieved, but the Cuban refugees refused to be sent back, and demanded to be transferred to the United States.

[22] In January the following year the conflict was resolved when the Bahamas signed an agreement with Cuba whereby Cubans living in Bahamian detention camps were returned to their home country. During 1996, 250 Cubans from the camps, and a further 70 living illegally were returned to Cuba. The Cuban Government agreed not to take retaliatory measures against the deportees.

[23] The death penalty was applied in March 1997 for the first time in 12 years when two prisoners were hanged. The National Free Movement won the Parliamentary elections held that month with 35 seats. The Progressive Liberal Party won five seats. Hubert Ingraham was reelected as Prime Minister.

[24] In February 1998, religious leaders in the country publicly demonstrated against visits from homosexual tourists, prompting a British Government representative to say the United Kingdom would oppose any type of discriminatory practices in the Bahamas.

[25] The Bahamas were ravaged in September 1999 by Hurricane Floyd, the worst storm in decades. Tens of thousands of people were evacuated, amid winds reaching speeds of 240 km per hour. They swept through whole villages, destroying boats and severing communications in Nassau.

[26] In spite of pleas for pardon from different human rights groups, a man was hanged in January 2000 for the murder of two German tourists. Amnesty International asked Bahamas Governor Orville Alton Turnquest to abide by international treaties, stop the execution and consider abolishing the death penalty.

[27] Late that year the Government enacted a series of laws to restructure the financial services sector and comply with certain demands of the Financial Action Task Force (FATF), the OECD and others that had included Bahamas on their 'blacklists'. A package of nine laws came into effect which covered, among other things, a complete revision of the Central Bank and the Private Banks and Trust Funds Acts, revenues from illegal acts, reports of financial transactions and the creation of a Financial Intelligence Unit.

[28] In November 2001, for the first time in the country's history, a woman, Ivy Dumont, took office as Governor General of Bahamas.

[29] The Bahamian oil tanker 'Prestige' was wrecked near the Galician coast of Spain in November 2002, spilling 60,000 tons of oil.

[30] In November 2003, Amnesty International complained that the Bahamian authorities were not complying with international treaties governing the treatment of immigrants. Cuban immigrants in particular have no access to a proper asylum procedure, and are kept in detention centers where they are treated as common criminals, enduring extremely poor sanitary conditions with almost no medical attention. ∎

PROFILE

ENVIRONMENT

The territory comprises over 750 islands, only 30 of them inhabited. The most important are: New Providence (where the capital is located), Grand Bahama and Andros. These islands, made of limestone and coral reefs, built up over a long period of time from the ocean floor. Despite the subtropical climate, the lack of rivers has prevented the favorable climatic conditions being fully exploited for agriculture. Farming is limited to small crops of cotton and sisal. The main economic activity is tourism, centered on New Providence.

SOCIETY

Peoples: Descendants of African slaves, 86 per cent, plus North Americans, Canadians and British (12 per cent); Asian and Hispanic people (2 per cent).
Religions: Predominantly Christian. Baptists 32 per cent; Anglicans 20 per cent; Roman Catholics 19 per cent and Methodists 6 per cent.
Languages: English (official) and Creole.
Main Political Parties: Free National Movement (FNM); Progressive Liberal Party (PLP) founded in 1953. The socialist Vanguard Party has no parliamentary representation.
Main Social Organizations: Trade Union Congress; trade unions of the different sectors: hotel caterers and related activities, teachers-professors, civil servants, airport employees, cab drivers, musicians and theatre.

THE STATE

Official Name: Commonwealth of the Bahamas.
Capital: Nassau 222,000 people (2003), on New Providence Island.
Other Islands: Freeport/Great Bahama 42,400 people; Eleuthera 3,300; Andros 2,800; Long Island 1,800 (2000).
Government: Queen Elizabeth II is Head of State, represented by Dame Ivy Dumont since 2001. Prime Minister Perry Christie, member of the PLP, elected in May 2002. There is a bicameral Legislature, with a 16-member Senate and a 40-member Assembly.
National Holiday: 10 July, Independence (1973).
Armed Forces: 2,550: Police (1,700); Defense Force (850).

Bahrain / Al Bahrayn

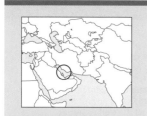

Population:	754,331
Area:	710 km²
Capital:	Manama
Currency:	Dinar
Language:	Arabic

From the time of the Sumerians, the area now called Bahrain was central to the intense maritime trade between Mesopotamia and India. This trade became particularly prosperous between the 11th and 15th centuries, as Islamic civilization expanded over all the territory from the Atlantic Ocean to the South Pacific.

2 Portuguese sailors occupied the island in 1507 and stayed there for a century until the Persians expelled them. Iran's claim to sovereignty over this part of the Persian or Arab Gulf dates from this period. Sheikh al-Khalifah took power in 1782, displacing the Persians the following year; his descendants are still in power. Independence lasted until 1861, when another Khalifah, afraid of Persian annexation, agreed to declare a 'protectorate' under the British.

3 During the two World Wars Bahrain was an important British military base. In 1932 the first oil wells in the Gulf were opened on the island. Nationalist movements demanding labor rights, democracy and independence grew during the 1950s, as they did in other parts of the Arab world. In December 1954, a strike broke out in the oil fields. British troops quashed the rebellion and, slowly, some reforms were carried out and local participation in public administration increased.

4 Finally, beginning in the early 1970s, the British decided to withdraw from their last colonies 'east of Suez', though they maintained their economic and strategic interests in Bahrain. Bahrain and Qatar refused to join the United Arab Emirates, so in 14 August, 1971 the country became independent under Sheikh Isa ibn-Sulman al-Khalifah.

5 The new nation authorized the US to set up naval bases in its ports. These were dismantled in 1973 following the Arab-Israeli conflict. Local elections were held the same year and the National Assembly came under the control of progressive candidates calling for freedom to organize political parties and greater electoral representation. The British felt their interests were being threatened, and, in August 1975, they backed al-Khalifah's decision to dissolve Parliament.

6 In the 1970s, Iran managed to eclipse Saudi control of the Emirates, forcing a virtual protectorate over them. Meanwhile, heavy migration into Bahrain threatened to create a large and active Iranian minority. The Emir responded by cracking down even harder on both Iranian or Shi'a immigrants and on all progressive movements. At the same time he drew closer to the other Arab governments, rejecting the Camp David agreement and signing mutual defense treaties with Kuwait and Saudi Arabia.

7 In 1981, the country joined the Gulf Cooperation Council (GCC). This was set up with US help to guarantee military and political control over the area, to stop the influence of the Iranian Islamic revolution, and to keep an eye on opposition groups in the member states.

8 One of the most closely watched movements was the

IN FOCUS

ENVIRONMENTAL CHALLENGES
The refineries, large storage tanks and transport pipelines for the treatment of petroleum have a major impact on the environment. Oil extraction in the region produces 4.7 per cent of the oil industry's contribution to world pollution.

WOMEN'S RIGHTS
Women have been able to vote and run for office since 1973, but interruptions in the country's democracy have led them have enjoyed full citizen rights only as of since 2002. From 1995 to 2000, parliamentary seats held by women fell from 12 to 5 per cent; in ministerial or similar posts, however, female representation grew from 0 to 11 per cent.

In 2000, women made up 21 per cent of the work force (0.5 per cent in agriculture, 32 per cent in industries and 67.5 per cent in the service sector). That year, illiteracy among women between 15 and 24 amounted to 1.4 per cent, compared with 1.8 per cent of men in the same age bracket.

CHILDREN
The economic boom of the 1970s and early 1980s established the basic infrastructure of socio-economic development, such as education, health, drinking water, environmental health and electricity. Apart from improving overall living standards, the Gulf countries have implemented extensive networks of free or subsidized services for their citizens, which have contributed to huge improvements in the survival, development and protection of women and children. Improvements are still needed in educational contents, school infrastructure and legislation.

The female association Be Free launched in 2003 a telephone hotline to support children victims of sexual abuse and neglect, and to counsel their parents. It is the first initiative of its kind in the Arab world and intends to raise social awareness of child abuse.

INDIGENOUS PEOPLES/ETHNIC MINORITIES
The Shi'a face political and economic discrimination, despite not being a minority. This is because they have historically opposed the Sunni minority, to which the monarchy belongs. Most Shi'a belong to the middle and lower economic and social classes. The Government often resorts to random arrests, lengthy detentions without trial and forced exile. The reforms of the year 2000 have, however, created a space for negotiations. Most of the opposition is moderate, while violence has diminished in the last years. After the death of Sheik Isa bin Sulman al-Khalifa in 1999 and the sporadic riots caused by Shi'a activists between 1994 and 1999 demanding the return to the representative system of the National Assembly and labor rights, the opposition has shown it is willing to end its protests. This conciliatory approach has reduced tensions. Although small activist groups continued to demonstrate in 1999 and 2000, their new leader, Sheik Hamad, accepted the 2000 Constitution, which paved the way for democracy.

MIGRANTS/REFUGEES
The kingdom hosts a significant number of immigrants. Human Rights' Watch estimated the immigrant population at 720,000, of whom 290,000 were non-Bahrainis (40 per cent in all). In 1991 foreigners made up 36 per cent of the population. The total number of workers in 2001 was 332,521, of whom 213,007 (or 64 per cent) were foreigners.

DEATH PENALTY
The death penalty still applies, even for minor crimes.

Life expectancy
74.0 years
2000-2005

GNI per capita
$11,130
2002

Literacy
88% total adult rate
2000

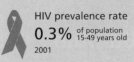
HIV prevalence rate
0.3% of population 15-49 years old
2001

Bahrain National Liberation Front, based in the UK and supported mainly by oil workers, students and professionals. This group was a member of the Gulf Liberation Front until 1981, along with other regional movements.

9 In November 1986, a super-highway was opened between Saudi Arabia and Bahrain, making Bahrain no longer truly an island. During the first year alone, the highway was used by more than a million vehicles.

10 In March 1991, after the Iraqi defeat in the Gulf War, the foreign ministers of Egypt, Syria and the six Arab member States of the GCC signed an agreement with the US in Riyadh in order to 'preserve regional security'. After Kuwait, Bahrain was the emirate most affected by the conflict.

11 In December 1994, Shi'a leader Sheikh al-Jamri was arrested, after signing a claim for the restoration of the Constitution and Parliament, dissolved in 1975. His arrest provoked anti-government demonstrations, in which two students and a police officer died. In April 1995, Emir Isa ibn-Sulman al-Khalifah met with 20 opposition leaders in an attempt to put an end to growing violence. In August, both parties reached an agreement that concluded with the release of 1,000 political prisoners.

12 In 1996, the demonstrations spread across the country, and some ended in violent confrontations with the police. The Government decided to use the death penalty to punish those 'responsible', a measure endorsed by the Courts. The UN Working Group on Arbitrary Detentions issued three declarations on the situation of the inmates of Bahrain's prisons.

13 On 6 March, 1999, after ruling Bahrain for 37 years, Emir Isa Ibn-Salman Al-Khalifah died. He was succeeded by his son, Hamad Ibn Isa Al-Khalifah, who pursued conciliatory policies with the Shi'a - who represent almost 70 per cent of the population but have traditionally been ruled by the Sunni minority - to which the royal family belongs. During May and June he freed more than 300 Shi'a political prisoners, but another 1,000 remained in jail awaiting trial.

14 In December 1999, in his Independence Day address, the new Emir spoke about democratic openness and promised to reinstate municipal councils. The following year, in addition to publicly promising to reinstate Parliament, the Emir for the first time named as members of the Consultative Council - a body created in 1992, made up of 40 people who monitor most of the government's policies - non-Muslim men and women, including a Jewish entrepreneur and four women, one a Christian.

15 In a February 2001 referendum, the Bahrainis overwhelmingly supported the political reforms proposed by the royal family. The reforms, entail converting the State into a constitutional monarchy, with the Emir becoming King, and separating the branches of government.

16 In December, the Ministry of Information tried journalist Hafez al-Shaikh for publishing articles critical of the Shi'a community. Al-Shaikh was accused of violating the country's press laws. He argued that the persecution was really due to his negative comments, published in a Lebanese daily, about Bahrain's collaboration with US incursions in Afghanistan.

17 In March, after lengthy conflicts between Bahrain and Qatar over the Hawar islands - which contain important reserves of natural gas - the International Court of Justice at The Hague delivered its verdict, in favor of Bahrain.

18 Throughout 2001 several political associations and non governmental organizations were officially recognized. In June, the General Committee of Workers was officially registered as the General Union of Bahrain Workers, and in September a trade union law was enacted. In July the Bahrain Human Rights Centre, the first institution of its kind in the Gulf region, was also registered. The Bahrain's Women Union, an advocate of women's rights, was recognized in November.

19 In May 2002 local elections were held in Bahrain and for the first time women were allowed to vote and stand as candidates. This was also the case for October's parliamentary elections. Despite the calls for a boycott from the Islamic National Accord Association (INAA), the main political party representing the majority Shi'a, there was a 50 per cent voter turnout. The Shi'a INAA opposition - which was the party of choice in the elections - had considered the electoral process undemocratic, since the legislative power would be divided between the elected chamber and an advisory council appointed by the King, who is Sunni.

20 In March the authorities blocked access to several websites, including that of the Bahrain Freedom Movement, which had strongly criticized the constitutional reforms approved by the King. The Al-Jazeera television network, based in Qatar, was banned in May. A royal decree enacted in October a new Press and Publications Act, whose article 68 punished with up to 5 years in prison the publication of articles offensive to the State religion, critical of the king or inciting people to depose or change the government.

21 Also in May, a colonel from the Security and Intelligence Service, Adel Jassem Fleifel, fled to Australia when the authorities began to investigate him on corruption charges. Opposition groups had long been accusing him of torturing and ordering the torture of detainees and political prisoners. That month, Amnesty International urged the Government to investigate all torture and other human rights violations supposedly committed by Fleifel and the Security and Intelligence Service. The fugitive returned to Bahrain in November and was arrested. In October, the King issued Decree 56, which clarified the contents of the general amnesty of February 2001 (Decree 10), effectively banning any judicial action against civilians or military officers who had committed or been implied in human rights violations before February 2001. Amnesty International wrote to the King in November urging him to revoke the decree.

22 The UN High Commissioner for Human Rights visited Bahrain in March and stated the need to investigate human rights violations committed in the past and to take those responsible to court. Shortly after, Bahrain ratified the UN Convention on the Elimination of All Forms of Discrimination against Women, with reserves on articles 2, 9, 15, 16 and 29. ∎

Bangladesh / Bangladesh

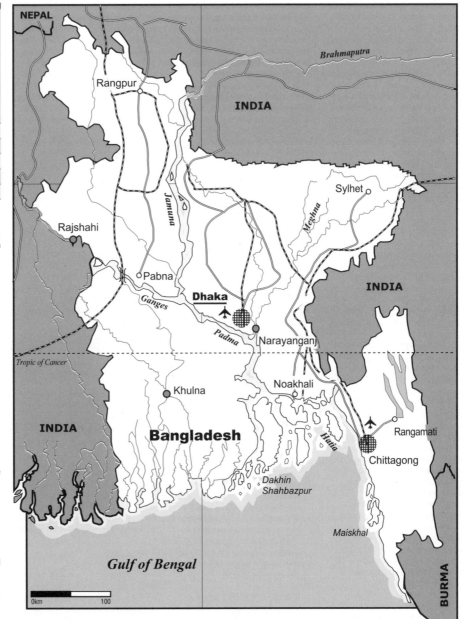

Population:	152,592,662
Area:	144,000 km²
Capital:	Dhaka (Dacca)
Currency:	Taka
Language:	Bangla/Bengali

The area comprising present-day Bangladesh and the Indian state of West Bengal was settled in about 1000 BC by Dravidian peoples who were later known as the Bang. The first Dravidian empire to spread over most of present-day India, Pakistan, and Bangladesh was the Mauryan Empire between the 3rd and 1st century BC. During the Mauryan Empire, a Buddhist chief named Gopala came to Bengal and took power becoming the first ruler of the Pala Dynasty (AD 750-1150). He and his successors provided stable government, security, and prosperity while spreading Buddhism throughout the state and into neighboring territories.

2 The Senas, militant Hindus, replaced the Buddhist Palas as rulers of a united Bengal until the Turkish conquest in 1202. Opposed to the Brahmanic Hinduism of the Senas with its rigid caste system, vast numbers of Bengalis, especially those from the lower castes, would later convert to Islam.

3 Turks ruled Bengal for several decades before the conquest of Dhaka by forces of the Mughal emperor Akbar the Great in 1576. The British East India Company, a private company formed in 1600 during the reign of Akbar and operating under a charter granted by Queen Elizabeth I, established a factory on the Hooghly River in Bengal in 1650 and founded the city of Calcutta in 1690.

4 Although the initial aim of the East India Company (EIC) was to seek trade under concessions obtained from local governors, the steady collapse of the Mughal Empire (1526-1858) enticed the Company to take a more direct involvement in the politics and military activities of the subcontinent. Siraj ud Daulah, governor of Bengal, provoked a military confrontation with the British at Plassey in 1757. He was defeated by Robert Clive, a young official of the Company. By 1815 the supremacy of the EIC was unchallengeable, and by the 1850s British control and influence had extended into territories that became the independent states of India and Pakistan in 1947.

5 In 1905 the British governor general, Lord George Curzon,

WORKERS

UNEMPLOYMENT: 3.3% (2002)

LABOR FORCE **2002**

■ FEMALE: 42.5%   ■ MALE: 57.5%

EMPLOYMENT DISTRIBUTION **1995/2001**

F
M

	F	M
■ AGRICULTURE	54.0%	78.0%
■ INDUSTRY	11.0%	8.0%
■ SERVICES	34.0%	11.0%

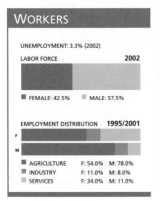

LAND USE

2000

IRRIGATED AREA: 49.4% of arable land

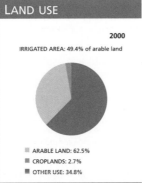

■ ARABLE LAND: 62.5%
■ CROPLANDS: 2.7%
■ OTHER USE: 34.8%

PUBLIC EXPENDITURE

% OF GDP

3.9 % HEALTH & EDUCATION (2000)

1.3 % DEFENSE (2001)

Life expectancy
61.4 years
2000-2005

GNI per capita
$360
2002

Literacy
40% total adult rate
2000

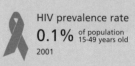
HIV prevalence rate
0.1% of population 15-49 years old
2001

divided Bengal into eastern and western sectors in order to improve administrative control of the huge and populous province. Thus, two new provinces were established: East Bengal, which had its capital at Dhaka, and West Bengal (the present-day state of West Bengal in India), with its capital at Calcutta, which also was the capital of British India. Many Bengali Muslims viewed the partition as recognition of their cultural and political differences from the majority Hindu population - the All-India Muslim League (ML) supported the partition -, but Curzon's decision was ardently challenged by the Indian National Congress (INC), a political organization dominated by Hindus, founded in 1885 and supported by Calcutta's elite. In 1912 the British voided the partition of Bengal, reconstituting the reunited province as a presidency, while moving the capital of India from Calcutta to the less conflictive area of New Delhi.

6   During World War I, the INC supported Great Britain in the hope that the British Crown would reward Indian loyalty with political concessions after the war. The ML was more ambivalent, perhaps because the dismemberment of the Ottoman Empire presaged the destruction of the last great Islamic power. In 1920 the Khilafat Movement (KM) was launched, combining Indian nationalism and pan-Islamic sentiment with strong anti-British overtones. KM leaders and Mahatma Gandhi, the leading figure in the INC, came to an agreement resulting in the joint advocacy of self-rule for India, agitation for the protection of Islamic holy places and the restoration of the caliph of Istanbul. In 1922 the Hindu-Muslim accord suffered a double blow when their noncooperation movement miscarried and the KM lost its purpose when the postwar Turkish nationalists abolished the sultanate, proclaimed Turkey a secular republic, abolished the religious office of the caliph, and sent the last of the Ottoman ruling family into exile. After the eclipse of the Hindu-Muslim accord, the spirit of communal unity was never reestablished in the subcontinent.

7   In August 1947, the British divided India, transforming part of the territory into Pakistan. Bengal was also divided. The mostly Muslim regions, known as East Bengal, became part of Pakistan, and the mostly Hindu regions, became part of India. In 1956, the new Constitution of Pakistan changed the name of

East Bengal to East Pakistan. The Bangladeshi people - discontented with the vast transfer of resources from the region to the rest of the country and with the military-bureaucratic oligarchy installed in West Pakistan - demanded regional autonomy, with the goal of establishing an autonomous government. Reacting to these attempts, the Pakistani military took strong measures against civilians. The people of East Pakistan - which adopted the name of Bangladesh - declared their independence, began a movement of armed resistence and formed a government in exile, in India, with Sheik Mujibur Rahman as president. In December 1971 the occupation forces were expelled, and a Constitution adopting parliamentary democracy was adopted in November 1972. Democracy, secularism, socialism, and nationalism were declared basic pillars of the State, and industries, banks and insurance companies were nationalized.

8   However, the challenge to improve an economy ravaged by war and other problems turned out insurmountable for the governing party - the Awami League - and its inexperienced leaders. Nationalist fervour was brief, giving way to generalized discontent and the appearance of armed political movements. In December 1974 the Government declared a state of national emergency, suspended fundamental civil rights, banned political parties and trade union activity. The only party remaining was Bakshal, formed mostly by Awami League members and pro-Soviet communists. Newspapers were closed and a new press act banned all opposition opinion.

9   In this context, an army rebellion of active and retired officers murdered the president, Sheik Mujibur Rahman, and his family, proclaiming martial law.

After several coups, General Ziaur Rahman, who had founded the Bangladesh Nationalist Party (BNP), was assassinated in a failed *coup d'etat*. In March 1982 the army overthrew the Government and placed General Hossein Mohammed Ershad as President. Ershad dissolved Parliament after the Jatiya Party (JP) won the 1986 national elections, amidst electoral fraud claims that led to massive popular uprisings. Confidence in political integrity had dwindled so that the 1988 elections were boycotted by the main parties, followed by a large percentage of voters.

10   The gradual islamization of politics led in 1989, through a constitutional amendment, to the declaration of Islam as official religion. According to the Constitution, a woman shall inherit only half of what her brother may inherit. In practice, this fraction ends up in the hands of her husband or kept for her

IN FOCUS

ENVIRONMENTAL CHALLENGES
A large part of the population is landless and lives and farms on sites prone to flooding. The tainting of groundwater by arsenic is a major health problem: people dependent on this water drawn up by tubewells are at severe long-term risk of cancer. This has reduced access to safe drinking water, as have droughts in the north and central regions. Although access to sanitation increased from 21 per cent in 1990 to 43.4 per cent in 2000, it is still a long way off the 80 per cent sought by the Milennium Development Goals.

WOMEN'S RIGHTS
Women held 9 per cent of parliamentary seats in the 1995-2000 period, while their representation at ministerial or equivalent positions drop from 8 to 5 per cent. Women made up 42 per cent of the workforce in the year 2000. In recent years there has been a major change in women's working patterns: in 1995 78 per cent of women worked in agriculture but by 2000 this had shrunk to 48 per cent, while over the same period the proportion in industry went up from 8 to 20 per cent and that in services from 11 to 32 per cent.

Three women die each hour due to pregnancy-related complications (26,000 each year). More than 90 per cent of births took place in the mother's home

and were not supervised by trained staff*.

Some 3,189 cases of rape and death by torture of women and children - 49 more than the previous year - were reported in 2002 (see history).

CHILDREN
Although the death rate among children under five has diminished 48 per cent between 1990 and 2001*, some 330,000 children die each year due to various diseases, accidents and malnutrition, leading to anemia, weakness and rickets. Among those born alive, 30 were underweight at birth*.

Child prostitution and child trafficking represent a growing problem. Many children are subject to hazardous or exploitative labour, whether in the workplace or the home.

Access to primary education is improving, both in the government sector and in schools run by the Bangladesh Rural Advancement Committee, an influential NGO, and increasing attention is also being paid to the quality of schooling.

INDIGENOUS PEOPLES/ ETHNIC MINORITIES
Some 11 different groups of indigenous peoples live in the Chittagong Hill Tracts: these increasingly refer to themselves by the collective name Jumma, drawn from the 'jhum' method of traditional cultivation. The hill peoples are increasingly being displaced by Bangladeshi settlers,

backed up by militarization. After two decades of armed resistance a peace accord was signed in 1997 but this seems to have consolidated the economic dominance of the settlers.

Transnational oil companies, such as Shell and Halliburton, and institutions such as the World Bank, are pressuring the Government to export oil and natural gas, threatening lands belonging to the Jumma with indiscriminate digging and deforestation. The destruction of mangrove swamps has displaced some 60,000 people from these ethnic groups.

MIGRANTS/REFUGEES
Of the 120,000 Rohingya people that have arrived in the country from Myanmar/Burma since 1993, barely 21,900 have been aided by UNHCR and acknowledged by Dhaka; the rest are considered illegal immigrants. Some 300,000 Biharis that arrived in 1947 from the Indian state of Bihar to what was then East Pakistan, still live as refugees.

Approximately 7,000 Bangladeshis sought asylum abroad in 2002 (mostly in Austria, Slovenia, and the US).

DEATH PENALTY
The death penalty still applies, even for minor crimes.

*Latest data available in *The State of the World's Children* and *Childinfo* database, UNICEF, 2004.

Under-5 mortality
77 per 1,000 live births
2002

Poverty
36.0% of population living on less than $1 per day
2000

Debt service
7.3% exports of goods and services
2001

Maternal mortality
380 per 100,000 live births
2000

dowry. Bangladeshi feminists state that women are treated as objects and not as individuals, since they belong to their parents in childhood, to their husbands in marriage (most marry at 13 years of age) and to their children when they grow old. Their work at home and as harvesters is not included in official production statistics, and divorce (a prerogative of men, under Islamic law) can be easily obtained if women's productivity falls. However, after Ershad was overthrown in 1991 and elections were called, both the Awami League (AL) and the Bangladesh Nationalist Party (BNP) slated women as their main candidates, both widows of former political leaders. Begum Khaleda Zia, from the BNP, was elected in March and declared her support for the establishment of a parliamentary regime. Five months after her victory at the polls, and with the unanimous approval of legislators of both parties, the Congress of Bangladesh replaced the presidential system with a parliamentary one.

11   The identity of Bangladesh as a Muslim country was reaffirmed with the Gulf War (1990-1991). This sentiment was intensified in 1992 with the repatriation of Muslim refugees. Early that year, Bangladesh received some 250,000 Bihari Muslims that had supported Pakistan in 1971. In June, some 270,000 Rohingya Muslims arrived, escaping from persecution in Myanmar, a mostly Buddhist country. Repatriation agreements signed by both countries in 1992 did not stem the flow of refugees.

12   Bangladesh has always been a predominantly rural society. About 4/5 of the work force is employed in agriculture or related activities. Agriculture makes up approximately half the GDP, while only 10 per cent is generated by industry. Before the 'Green Revolution' of the 1970s and 1980s, more than 7,000 varieties of rice were planted in Bangladesh. In recent times only one is extensively cropped.

13   Bangladesh has suffered human-made disasters. Oil tank leaks and industrial waste spread throughout the coast are destroying the coastal ecosystem. Sealife has been decimated - a catastrophe in a country where fishing makes up 6 per cent of the GDP. Some 15 million people remain at risk from the pollution by arsenic of wells (the population's main source of access to water).

14   By 1992, Bangladesh was strongly dependent on international aid. Almost 95 per

cent of development programs were financed by the United States, Japan, the Asian Development Bank and the World Bank.

15   Although the 1996 elections - carried out under army control - were considered fraudulent, Khaleda Zia remained in power. The Awami League called for national strikes which paralyzed the country, followed by clashes between police and opposition activists. Violence did not stop with Zia's fall, and the government was transferred by former Supreme Court of Justice chief, Mohammed Habibur Rahman, to Sheik Hasina Wajed, chosen prime minister in the second elections within four months. Social conflict continued throughout 1997, increasing in December with several strikes called by opposition parties protesting against the agreement signed by the Government to put an end to armed resistance in the southeast. For several days, both supporters and opposers of these strikes marched in various cities - Dhaka, Chittagong, Barisal, Syleht and Rajsani, among others - and in many small towns, leaving the country in a state of semi-paralysis.

16   In the context of the US war on terrorism, in September 2001 Dhaka granted Washington's request to use its air space, ports and airports in case of an invasion of Afghanistan. In November, head of state Badruddoza Chowdhury travelled to Washington to meet with Secretary of State Colin Powell. While the US sought to confirm the support of Bangladesh - one of the largest Muslim countries - in its campaign against Afghanistan, Chowdhury sought economic benefits for his country in exchange for its support.

17   After three days of talks, high officials from Bangladesh and India announced, in March 2002, new measures to reduce the tension throughout the 4,000 kilometers of their common border. Among other things, they decided joint patrols of the area, and regular meetings between their commanders in charge. In June 2002, Chowdhury resigned the presidency and in September 2002, Iajuddin Ahmed was sworn in as president.

18   A dramatic rise in violence against women led, in March 2002, to the adoption of laws punishing attacks with sulphuric acid with the death sentence. While the use of acid rose 50 per cent between 2000 and 2002, according to police records, in 2001 there were 13,339 cases of domestic violence, six times more

PROFILE

ENVIRONMENT

Located on the Padma River Delta, formed by the confluence of the Meghna with the Ganges and the Brahmaputra, Bangladesh is a fertile, alluvial plain where rice, tea and jute are grown. There are vast rainforests and swamps. A tropical monsoon climate predominates, with heavy summer rains from June to September generally accompanied by hurricanes and floods of catastrophic consequences. Low-quality coal and natural gas are the only mineral resources.

SOCIETY

Peoples: The people of Bangladesh are ethnically and culturally homogeneous, as a result of 25 centuries of integration between the local Bengali population and immigrants from Central Asia. There are small Urdu and Indian minorities. The Chittagong hill tracts are home to 11 ethnic groups known as a whole as Jumma.
Religions: Mostly Islamic (83 per cent) and Hindu (16 per cent), with Buddhist and Christian minorities.
Languages: Bangla/Bengali (98 per cent); others: dialects related to the Tibeto-Burman group of languages.
Main Political Parties: Bangladesh Nationalist Party, right of center (Bangladesh Jatiyatabadi Dal, BNP); Bangladesh Awami League (AL), in favor of a mixed economy; National Party (coalition), an Islamic-inspired alliance of five nationalist parties; Islamic Conference Bangladesh; Islamic Unity Front; National Socialist Party-Rob and other minor parties.
Main Social Organizations: Jana Sanghati Samiti, fighting for the rights of the tribal people; Women for Women.

THE STATE

Official Name: Gana Prajatantri Bangladesh.
Administrative Divisions: 4 districts.
Capital: Dhaka (Dacca) 11,560,000 people (2003).
Other Cities: Chittagong 2,500,900 people; Khulna 1,168,800; Rajshahi 687,300 (2000).
Government: Parliamentary republic. Iajuddin Ahmed, President and Head of State since September 2002. Khaleda Zia, Prime Minister and Head of Government since October 2001. Single-chamber legislature: Parliament made up of 330 members (300 elected by direct vote and 30 reserved for women, nominated by Parliament, for 5-year term).
National Holidays: 26 March, Independence Day (1971); 16 December, Victory Day (1971).
Armed Forces: 115,500 (1995). Other: Bangladesh Rifles: 30,000 (border guard); Ansars (Security Guards): 20,000.

than those registered in 1995 (2,048). In Bangladesh - and Myanmar, Cambodia, Pakistan, among others - sulphuric acid, cheap and easily obtained, is used by men to disfigure and sometimes kill, women and girls; the reasons for these attacks are refusal to accept marriage proposals, domestic fights and conflicts about the property of goods. Khaleda Zia, who was reelected prime minister in 2001, introduced two additional laws to stem the tide. Throughout the year, 2,343 people were arrested for domestic violence. One year later, not one had been punished for their actions.

19   A rise in the slave trade also took place. It is estimated that, every year, between 5,000 and 6,000 women and children are victims of this trade, mainly from rural areas toward the cities and to India and Pakistan.

Representatives of the organization Caritas Bangladesh stated in April 2003 that the slave trade, linked to drug and arms traffic, is closely connected to Bangladeshi political leaders. The main victims of this traffic are children and poor women who have been stigmatized due to marriage failure or pregnancy out of wedlock.

20   In May 2004 the AL, then in opposition, accused the ruling Bangladesh National Party of seeking to increase its majority. Parliament amended its constitution to reserve 45 seats for women. Female MPs would be selected in proportion to each party's support at the last election and the total number of MPs was raised to 345. The opposition AL called two general strikes, accusing the Government of corruption and also demanding early elections. ∎

Barbados / Barbados

Population:	272,214
Area:	430 km²
Capital:	Bridgetown
Currency:	Barbadian dollar
Language:	English

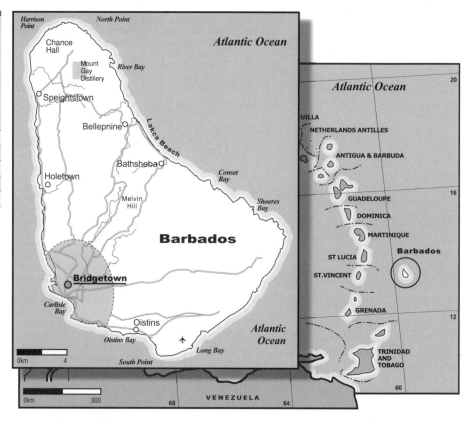

The peaceful and nomadic Arawak people expanded throughout the Caribbean region, and although they were dislodged from many islands by the Caribs (see box), they remained on others - as in the case of Barbados.

2   The Spanish landed on the island early in the 16th century and christened it the 'island of the bearded fig tree'. Satisfied that there was no natural wealth they withdrew, but not before massacring the native population, taking a few survivors with them to amuse the Spanish court. In 1625 the British arrived and found a fertile, uninhabited territory.

3   Around 1640 the island had close to 30,000 inhabitants. The majority were farmers and their families, and some were political and religious dissidents from Britain. The settlers grew tobacco, cotton, pepper and fruit on small plots, raising cattle, pigs and poultry.

4   Sugarcane was introduced, with the support of the British, and caused extensive social change. Plantation owners purchased large plots to improve profitability, and small landowners - most of them in debt - sold off their land to the plantation owners. The importation of slaves from Africa to work the sugar plantations began during this period.

5   In 1667, 12,000 farmers emigrated to other Caribbean islands or to the 13 colonies of North America. Nonetheless, the island had a commercial fleet of 600 vessels and, as recorded by a French traveler in 1696, was 'the most powerful island colony in America'.

6   Towards the end of the 18th century, the island was one huge sugar-producing complex which included 745 plantations and over 80,000 African slaves. By that time there was no woodland left on an island described in a 16th century account as 'entirely

covered with trees'. Its ecological balance seriously impaired, the island fell victim to drought in the early 19th century and parts of it suffered soil exhaustion.

7   The pursuit of increased profitability and an economy oriented toward foreign trade resulted in underdevelopment. A different approach might have led to development along the lines of the other North American colonies.

8   Slavery was abolished in 1834 but the plantation economy

still dominated the island's fiscal system. European landowners controlled local politics until well into the 20th century.

9   In 1938, following the gradual extension of political rights, the Barbados Labor Party (BLP) led by Grantley Adams developed from within the existing labor unions. Universal suffrage was declared in 1951, and Adams became leader of the local government.

10   Internal autonomy was granted 1961, and in 1966

independence was proclaimed within the British Commonwealth. Errol Barrow was elected Prime Minister. Unlike the rest of the West Indies, Barbados never severed its links with the colonial capital in spite of its political independence.

11   After 1966, Errol Barrow's Democratic Labor Party (DLP) contributed to the creation of the Caribbean Free Trade Association (CARIFTA) which became CARICOM in 1973,

PROFILE

ENVIRONMENT
Of volcanic origin, Barbados is the easternmost island of the Lesser Antilles. The fertile soil and rainy tropical climate favor intensive farming of sugarcane, rotated with cotton and corn.

SOCIETY
Peoples: Most are of African origin (92.5 per cent), with a minority of Europeans (3.2 per cent) and 2.8 per cent of mixed descent. It is one of the most densely populated countries in the world, with an average of 616 people per sq km.
Religions: 33 per cent Anglican, 29.8 per cent belong to other Protestant faiths; 4.4 per cent are Catholic.
Languages: English (official), Creole (Bajan).
Main Political Parties: Barbados Labor Party (BLP); Democratic Labor Party (DLP); National Democratic Party (NDP); Workers' Party of Barbados, People's Progressive Movement.

Main Social Organizations: Barbados Workers Union; National Organization of Women; Barbados Gays and Lesbians against Discrimination; Mothers' Union of Barbados.

THE STATE
Official Name: Barbados.
Administrative Divisions: 11 parishes.
Capital: Bridgetown 140,000 people (2003).
Other Cities: Speightstown 820 people; Holetown 720; Bathsheba 720 (2000).
Government: Owen Arthur, Prime Minister since September 1994, re-elected in 1999 and ratified in 2003; Sir Clifford Husbands, Governor-General, appointed by Queen Elizabeth II in 1996. Parliament is bicameral: the Senate, with 21 members, and the Legislative Assembly, with 30 members.
National Holiday: 30 November, Independence Day (1966).
Armed Forces: 610 army (1995).

Life expectancy
77.2 years
2000-2005

GNI per capita
$9,750
2002

Literacy
100% total adult rate
2000

HIV prevalence rate
1.2% of population 15-49 years old
2001

involving 12 islands of the region. Barrow showed great interest in the Non-Aligned Movement. In 1996 Barbados became a UN member-country, and in 1997 it joined the Organization of American States (OAS).

[12] Free education and new electoral laws were not followed by any significant change in DLP policies towards the owners of sugar refining plants. The rise in unemployment diminished DLP support and resulted in the Party's electoral defeat.

[13] In 1970, the country became a member of the International Monetary Fund (IMF).

[14] The BLP won 17 of the 24 available seats in 1976. Tom Adams, Grantley Adams' son, was elected Prime Minister. He promised to fight corruption and described himself as a social democrat (the BLP became a member of the Socialist International in 1978). However, the Government protected the interest of investors in sugar and tourism transnationals, while encouraging foreign investment.

[15] Adams pressured Washington to withdraw from its naval base on nearby St Lucia, which it did in 1979. In 1981, Adams was re-elected and consolidated relations with Washington. Barbados supported the US invasion of Grenada.

[16] In order to attract foreign capital, the Government passed new tax exemption laws and liberalized ship registration. In 1986, an agreement between the US and Barbados led to 650 new companies registering in the off-shore sector. Unemployment and inflation within Barbados continued to grow.

[17] The 1986 election was won by the DLP. Prime Minister Errol Barrow committed the Government to changing the policy toward the US that had been followed by the BLP Government in the preceding 10 years. In 1987, Barrow died of a heart attack and was succeeded as Prime Minister by Erskine Sandiford. Two years later, as a result of a split within the DLP, a new opposition group was founded, the right-wing National Democratic Party (NDP), under the leadership of Richard Heynes.

[18] In 1991, the DLP was re-elected with 49 per cent of the vote although it lost 2 of its 20 seats. In November, riots and protests due to an 8 per cent cutback on civil servants' wages led to a general strike. Despite this challenge, Sandiford remained in office.

[19] In 1992 the Government obtained an IMF loan amounting to $64.9 million and the Prime Minister announced further wage reductions in the public sector, a rise in interest rates and cutbacks in the social system, as well as the privatization of oil and cement production and the tourism industry.

[20] After two successive finance ministers resigned, Sandiford himself assumed the post in late 1992, attempting to transform the country into a financial center.

[21] In June 1994, the BLP withdrew its support for the Prime Minister and won the elections held in September. Owen Arthur, the new Prime Minister, canceled planned wage reductions, and this became law in February 1995.

[22] The island's Governor-General, Dame Nita Barrow, sister of former Prime Minister Errol Barrow, died on 19 December 1995. After a brief interregnum by Denys Williams, Clifford Husbands became premier on 1 June 1996.

[23] The legislative assembly voted in February 1996 for civil servants' salaries to be brought back up over a two-year period. The measure, promoted by the BLP, was a response to the salary reduction policy applied in 1994 by the Democratic Labor Party.

[24] In April 1998, during the summit of American Presidents in Santiago, Chile, the Prime Minister of Barbados, Owen Arthur, said he was in favor of Cuba's inclusion at the next meeting.

[25] The January 1999 elections saw a broad victory for the BLP, which took 26 out of the 28 disputed seats, while the other two remained in DLP hands. Owen Arthur was returned to his post.

[26] A Financial Intelligence Unit (FIU) was set up to fight money laundering. The new body was advised by members of the UN's International Drug Control Program (UNIDCP).

[27] In late 2000, the 20-year - long fishing rights dispute between Barbados and Trinidad and Tobago peaked when two Barbadian fishermen were arrested by maritime patrols from Port of Spain. Premier Arthur threatened Trinidad and Tobago with economic sanctions and warned he would apply the Immigration Act to expel illegal Trinidadian immigrants.

[28] Barbados enacted a law on international companies in 2001 in order to attract foreign investment. The law created a 2.5 per cent maximum income tax, exemptions on every other tax and on tariffs on the imports

IN FOCUS

ENVIRONMENTAL CHALLENGES
Serious environmental problems include: untreated domestic waste waters, the final disposal of solid waste, erosion of the soil and of coastal areas. Pollution of the sea is growing, as well as the excessive use of its resources.

WOMEN'S RIGHTS
Women have been able to vote and run for office since 1950. From 1995 to 2000 women held 11 per cent of seats in Parliament, and their presence in ministerial or equivalent posts increased from 0 to 27 per cent. In 2000 women made up 46 per cent of the work force (3 per cent in agriculture, 12 per cent in industries and 85 per cent in services). That year, 11.5 per cent of the female workforce was unemployed, compared to 7.4 per cent of the male workforce.

Only 9 per cent of births are unattended by trained staff*. Out of every 1,000 births, 51 are from teenage mothers*.

CHILDREN
Immunization rates are in excess of 90 per cent. HIV/AIDS is a big challenge in 2002. It is transmitted generally through heterosexual intercourse, and it is growing rapidly. Teenagers between 15 and 19 are particularly vulnerable, because they engage in sex at an early age and lack education on the matter. It is estimated that in the Caribbean Community (CARICOM) area, some 3,000 children were born in 2001 from mothers living with HIV.

There were 264 cases of sexual child abuse reported in 2000.

MIGRANTS/REFUGEES
In February 2003, UNHCR announced that, although states have the right to adopt their own policies on migration, they should also take into consideration the jurisprudence of international organisms that supervise human rights. It encouraged Barbados to strengthen its legal framework for the protection of asylum-seekers, potential refugees and stateless people, since the country did not adopt the 1951 Convention relating to the Status of Refugees, or later instruments.

Less than 20,000 people emigrated between 1995 and 2000.

DEATH PENALTY
Barbados applies the death penalty for ordinary crimes.

*Latest data available in *The State of the World's Children* and *Childinfo* database, UNICEF, 2004.

of materials for production, the exemption of foreign exchange controls, and a deduction of 150 per cent on the cost of research and development activities on exports.

[29] In June 2001, Barbados hosted the preparatory Regional Round Table for the World Summit on Sustainable Development, held in Johannesburg, South Africa, in September 2002. The General Assembly of the OAS was held in June 2002 in Bridgetown, the capital of Barbados.

[30] In the May 2003 elections, the BLP won for the third time in a row, and Owen Arthur was ratified as Premier. The BLP won 21 seats and the DLP only 7 out of the 30 at stake. Both parties focused their electoral campaign on reducing taxes - Barbados has one of the highest tax rates in the Caribbean - and job creation. In 2002 the Government presented a plan to reduce income tax from 25 per cent to 22.5 per cent, announcing it would fall to 20 per cent in 2004. The two rival parties were also concerned about unemployment, which rose from 9.9 per cent in 2001 to 10.3 per cent in 2002. The Opposition emphasized the Government's mismanagement of public funds and, especially, the millions of dollars spent on paying off hotel industry debts.

[31] An alarming proportion of the Barbados population lives with HIV/AIDS in relation to other Caribbean states, according to UN reports issued in 2003. In June 2000 some 2,415 people were HIV-positive, of whom only 1,252 had been diagnosed. It is estimated that reported cases amount to only one fifth of the total population living with HIV in Barbados. From 1985 until April 2001 the Ministry of Health managed the National AIDS Program of Barbados, when, as the National HIV/AIDS Commission, it agreed common policies with other CARICOM (Caribbean Community) countries, with the Joint United Nations Programme on HIV/AIDS (UNAIDS) and the Caribbean Epidemiology Centre. ∎

Population:	9,808,724
Area:	207,600 km²
Capital:	Minsk (Mensk)
Currency:	Rouble
Language:	Belarusian

According to archeological evidence, the territory of present-day Belarus has hosted Upper Paleolithic and Neolithic cultures. Between the 6th and 8th centuries, the territory was inhabited by the Slav tribes: Krivichi, Dregovichi, and Radimichi In the 9th century, the eastern Slav peoples formed the Kiev Rus, the ancient Russian State (see history of Russia) which gave rise to modern Russia, Ukraine and Belarus.

[2] In the 14th century, Lithuanian principalities annexed themselves to the Western Rus. Between the 14th and 16th centuries, the Belarusian culture began to differentiate itself from that of the Russians and the Ukrainians, and to develop its own language, different from the old Russian language. Gueorgui Skorina became the first Belarusian printer.

[3] With the first partition of Poland in 1772, Russia kept the eastern part of Belarus. Between 1793 and 1795, the rest of Belarus became part of the Russian Empire.

[4] In 1861, the Russian Czar put an end to the serf system and the peasants' feudal bondage to the landed nobility, but this failed to solve the land problem. Only 35 per cent of the land was handed over to Belarusians, which triggered a number of uprisings, the most important in 1863 led by K. Kalinovski.

[5] In March 1899, the 1st Congress of the Social Democratic Workers' Party of Russia (SDWPR) was held secretly in Minsk. This group was inspired by Marxist socialism and was determined to bring down the Czar. Other sectors of the intelligentsia took their cue from the peasants' discontent, and founded an autonomous Belarusian movement in 1902, which sought to revive the nation's culture. During this period, the czarist regime deported Jews to Belarus, where they came to account for a fifth of the local population: the majority of these died under the Nazis.

[6] During World War I (1914-1917) part of Belarus was occupied by German troops. After the Russian Revolution of February 1917, councils (soviets) made up of workers' representatives were formed in Minsk, Gomel, Vitebsk, Bobruisk and Orsha.

[7] Soviet power began to be established at the end of 1917. In February 1918 the large landholdings were nationalized. A few months later, land began to be distributed to the peasants. At the insistence of the Bolsheviks (socialist revolutionaries of the SDWPR), the first collective farms (koljoses) were set up, while the land gradually went into State control.

[8] The 6th Party Conference of the Russian Communists (Bolsheviks) - formerly the SDWPR - held in Smolensk, approved the decision to found the Soviet Socialist Republic of Belarus (SSRB). In January 1918, the 1st Congress of the SSRB soviets decided to join Lithuania. Lithuania approved this motion. On 28 February 1919, in the city of Vilno (today's Vilnius, the capital of Lithuania) the Government of the Soviet Socialist Republic of Lithuania and Belarus was elected, with Mickevicius-Kapsukas as head of state.

[9] After the occupation of a considerable part of Belarus in February 1919, and according to the Treaty of Riga, signed between Soviet Russia and Poland (1921), Western Belarus became part of Poland. On 1 August 1920 the Assembly of representatives of the Lithuanian and Belarusian Communist Parties and of labor organizations in Minsk and its surrounding areas approved the foundation of the independent Belarusian republic.

[10] On 30 December 1922, Belarus joined the Union of Soviet Socialist Republics (USSR) as one of its founders, along with the Russian Federation, Ukraine and the Transcaucasian Federation (Armenia, Georgia and Azerbaijan).

[11] The industrialization and collectivization of agriculture began in the second half of the 1920s. On 19 February 1937 the 12th Congress of the Soviets of Belarus approved the new constitution. In November 1939, as a result of the Molotov-Ribbentrop Pact - signed between the USSR and Germany - Western Belarus was reincorporated into the Soviet Union.

[12] In June 1941 the state became the first of the Soviet republics to suffer Hitler's aggression. The fortress at Brest offered fierce resistance. Guerrilla warfare extended throughout the country. At the end of World War II, more than 2 million Belarusians had lost their lives.

[13] After Germany's defeat in 1945, Belarus' current borders were established. It became a charter member of the United Nations that same year, with a delegation independent of the USSR (the same as Ukraine).

[14] Between the 1920s and the 1980s, Belarus ceased to be a rural country in which 90 per cent of the population lived from traditional farming and livestock raising, becoming a urban, industrialized country. Belarus became an important producer of heavy trucks, electrical appliances, radios and television sets.

[15] Belarus was, among the Soviet republics, one of the few that maintained a majority of its local population - more than 80 per cent - with minimal influence from Russian or other immigration.

PROFILE

ENVIRONMENT
Belarus is located between the Dnepr (Dnieper), Western Dvina, Niemen and Western Bug rivers. It is bounded in the west by Poland, in the northwest by Latvia and Lithuania, in the northeast by Russia and in the south by Ukraine. It is a flat country, with many swamps and lakes, and forests covering a third of its territory. Its climate is continental and cool, with an average summer temperature of 17-19°, and 4-7° below zero in winter.

SOCIETY
Peoples: Belarusians, 81.2 per cent; Russians, 11.4 per cent; Poles, Ukrainians and others 7.4%. **Religions:** Christian Orthodox in the east and Catholic in the west. **Languages:** Belarusian (official); Russian (second language for most of the population); Polish; Ukrainian; Yiddish and Tatar. **Main Political Parties:** Communist Party; Women's Political Party 'Nadzeya' (Hope). Belarusian People's Front-Revival; United Civic Party; Stop Luka. **Main Social Organizations:** Labor Union Federation of Belarus; Free Union, formed by the new strike committees; Belarusian Assembly of Democratic NGO's; Charter '97, democractic movement for civil rights and civil freedom; Women's Christian Association; Zubr, young people's movement in favour of democracy.

THE STATE
Official Name: Respublika Belarus. **Administrative Divisions:** Six regions (Brest, Gomel, Grodno, Mensk, Moguiliov and Vitebsk). **Capital:** Minsk (Mensk) 1,705,000 people (2003). **Other Cities:** Gomel 503,400 people; Mogiliov 372,700; Vitebsk 356,000; Grodno 311,500; Brest 304,200 (2000). **Government:** Aleksander Lukashenka, President since July 1994, re-elected in September 2001; Sergei Sidorsky, Prime Minister since July 2003. The National Assembly has two chambers: Representatives with 110 members and the Soviet with 64 seats. **National Holiday:** 25 August, Independence (1991). **Armed Forces:** 86,654 (2003). Other: Border Guards (Ministry of Interior): 8,000.

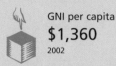
[16] Until 1985, the Communist Party and the Belarusian Government followed the course established by the Communist Party of the Soviet Union. Among the outstanding communist leaders of this period was Piotr Masherov, who died in a car accident.

[17] Because of the policies of *glasnost* (openness) and *perestroika* (economic reform) initiated by President Mikhail Gorbachev, there was no strong pressure within Belarus to secede immediately from the USSR, although there were movements favoring a multiparty political system, as well as protest demonstrations against high food prices.

[18] The catastrophe at the Chernobyl nuclear plant, Ukraine, in 1986, brought about serious consequences in Belarus, the most affected neighboring country. According to foreign researchers, in the following years there was a rapid increase in cases of cancer, leukemia and birth defects.

[19] In June 1991, Belarus declared independence and in October signed an economic integration agreement with Kazakhstan and Uzbekistan. On 8 December that same year, the presidents of the Russian Federation and Ukraine, Boris Yeltsin and Leonid Kravchuk, and of the Belarus Parliament, Stanislav Sushkevich, signed an agreement that put an end to the USSR and founded an association of sovereign states. On 21 June, in Alma-Ata (now Almaty, in Kazakhstan), 11 republics signed an agreement creating the Commonwealth of Independent States (CIS), whose members requested admission to the UN as separate countries. Belarus and seven of the republics pledged to implement structural reforms which would convert them into market economies.

[20] In March 1994, Parliament approved the new constitution and the country became a presidential republic with a 260-seat Parliament. Alexander Lukashenka became President after having obtained 80 per cent of the vote.

[21] In spite of having criticized in his electoral campaign his predecessors' policy of rapprochement with Moscow, in April 1996 Lukashenka signed a political and economic integration agreement with Russia. By the end of the year, a constitutional reform had granted more powers to Lukashenka. The opposition denounced the establishment of a dictatorship.

[22] In April 1999 Senate approval was given for integration with Russia, which caused some protest

IN FOCUS

ENVIRONMENTAL CHALLENGES
Due to its proximity to Ukraine, Belarus received heavy radioactive fall-out following the disaster at the Chernobyl nuclear plant in 1986. A quarter of the country's arable land shows signs of chemical pollution from the overuse of pesticides.

WOMEN'S RIGHTS
Belarusian women have been able to vote and stand for election since 1919. In 2000 women had 5 per cent of the seats in Parliament, compared with none in 1995; 3 per cent of ministerial or equivalent positions were held by women.

In 2000, women represented 49 per cent of the workforce.

Women, children and young people of Belarus continue to bear the costs of the lengthy economic and social transition from communism to capitalism. Despite modest economic growth poverty remains widespread.

In 2000, the unemployment rate for both sexes represented 8 per cent of people with primary education, 18 per cent of women and 10 per cent of men with secondary education, 74 per cent of women and 82 per cent of men with tertiary education.

Out of the 15,000 AIDS cases that were confirmed in the country in 2001, 3,700 were women.

CHILDREN
Poverty affects 30 per cent of the population. The increasing number of orphans is one of the most worrying manifestations of the social and economic crisis. The alcoholism of parents, which has reached unprecedented levels, is the leading cause of child abandonment, neglect and abuse. In 1999, alcohol sales, expressed in litres of pure alcohol per capita, were 1.7 times higher than they had been in 1990. The health of children has been seriously affected by the Chernobyl disaster. Besides, there has been a decline in public health services. From 1991 to 1999, the morbidity rate increased by 40.5 per cent. A high percentage of children suffer from psychological disorders.

INDIGENOUS PEOPLES/ ETHNIC MINORITIES
The Polish minority lives near the border with Poland. Poles have only recently experienced significant discrimination or disadvantage. Their situation started to change after the election of Aleksandr Lukashenka as President in 1994. In 1995, the State Committee for Religious and Ethnic Affairs suggested that changes should be made to the Law on Public Associations, in order to debar national and cultural associations from political activity. This was directly addressed to the Association of Belarusian Poles (ABP), blamed for 'straining relationships with state agencies and taking part in opposition activities'. The proposal violated the Polish-Belarusian treaty which guaranteed the right of setting up organizations that would represent national minorities. There are also signs of religious discrimination against Poles, manifested in the strong official support to the Belarusian branch of the Russian Orthodox Church, and by the restriction of activities of other religious groups.

MIGRANTS/REFUGEES
At the end of 2002, about 3,600 asylum seekers and refugees were living in Belarus. Among these, 656 were recognized as refugees by the Government and 2,010 (from Russia and Afghanistan) had been rejected by Minsk but remained under the protection of the UNHCR. Belarus lacks a formal policy on providing humanitarian protection to refugees fleeing generalized violence that do not meet the criteria for asylum under the UN Refugee Convention.

Since 1997 about 600 people have been granted refugee status, mostly Afghans. In 2002 refugee status was granted to half of 106 cases (Afghans and Georgians).

During 2002, more than 4,400 persons from Belarus sought asylum abroad, most of them in Western Europe. Another 16,900 stateless persons of former Soviet origin were living in Belarus in refugee circumstances. In 2001, 10,500 stateless persons were granted citizenship.

DEATH PENALTY
The death penalty still applies.

in the south of the country but was broadly supported in the north, where Russian influence is stronger. Among other things, it was agreed that citizens of both countries would enjoy identical rights on either side of the border.

[23] Belarus entered the 21st century with over 70 per cent of the population living below the poverty line. The value of the national currency, the rouble, fell against the dollar and inflation grew. In 2003, unemployment reached 250,000.

[24] In the October 2000 Parliamentary elections, several candidates were banned because they called for a boycott of the elections. The electoral commission said that more than 60 per cent voted, which was considered sufficient to validate the victory of the governing party. According to European observers, however, the counting of the votes did not meet democratic international standards. The same happened in 2001: the opposition, several of whose candidates had been banned, called for a boycott of the parliamentary elections. However, Lukashenka was re-elected.

[25] In March 2001, in view of the pressure exerted by the opposition and observers, Lukashenka supported the re-run of parliamentary elections in 13 districts which had had a very low turnout. The result was declared valid, and in Minsk police cracked down on a demonstration against the President by thousands of people.

[26] In 2002, Russian President Vladimir Putin condemned the federal council (soviet) model, a cornerstone of Lukashenka's policy, stating that since the Belarusian economy amounts to 3 per cent of the Russian economy, equity makes no sense. Putin suggested a model for state unification or union according to the principles of the European Union. Lukashenka, however, mentioned the 1999 treaty signed with Boris Yeltsin, in which the sovereignty of both states was preserved.

[27] Freedom of expression is severely limited by the Government: more than 20 newspapers have been closed down; journalists and politicians have denounced tortures and others have disappeared. The Government does not co-operate with the investigation of such cases and Parliament's participation, in the majority of cases, is very limited. In September 2002, the Parliamentary Assembly of the Council of Europe expressed concern about the violation of human rights and fundamental freedoms. ▪

Belgium / België - Belgique

Population:	10,359,127
Area:	33,100 km²
Capital:	Brussels (Brussel - Bruxelles)
Currency:	Euro
Language:	Dutch, French and German

B elgium, Holland, Luxembourg and a part of northern France make up the Low Countries, which had a common history until 1579 (see Netherlands). The linguistic separation which took place between the Roman and Germanic languages coincided with the borders of the Holy Roman Empire, which divided the Low Countries in two.

2   Between 1519 and 1814, the southern provinces were successively ruled by Spain (1519), Austria (1713) and France (1794). After the fall of Napoleon in 1814, the European powers enforced reunification with the north. The southern provinces had already forged an identity of their own, and were unwilling to accept Dutch authority.

3   The region's economy was based on the production of linen and textiles. Industrialization was facilitated by the fact that manufacturers and landowners were often one and the same, and that textile mills were concentrated in the hands of a few owners.

4   In 1830, the Brussels' bourgeoisie took up arms against the Dutch authorities. When the conflict spread and proved substantial, European powers recognized the independence of the southern provinces, which were henceforth known as Belgium. Congress adopted a parliamentary monarchy, with an electoral roll made up of property owners. Parliamentary monarchy, institutionalized in 1830, has survived until today.

5   By the end of the 19th century, workers forced the government to pass laws aimed at providing housing for working-class people, and improving conditions in the workplace, especially for women and children. At the same time, Parliament changed the constitution and in 1893, established limited male suffrage. General male suffrage was introduced in 1919.

6   Between 1880 and 1885, Leopold II financed international expeditions to the Congo, making it effectively his 'private' colony. Substantial deficits and protests from several European nations against the severe repression and exploitation occurring in the Congo, forced the Belgian Government to take it as a colony in 1908. With this, the worst excesses ended, but the Belgian Government, businesses and the Church increased their influence over the following years.

7   In the 20th century, the Belgian democratic system was threatened twice by a major world war, but each time democracy prevailed. In 1914, Belgium refused to give way to the Germans and was drawn into war. The Treaty of Versailles granted the territories of Eupen and Malmedy to Belgium. In Africa, Belgium colonized the former German colonies of Rwanda and Burundi after the League of Nations granted them a mandate. In 1920 Belgium signed a military assistance treaty with France, and the following year, it formed an economic alliance with Luxembourg.

8   During World War II Belgium was occupied by Germany between 1940 and 1944. The return of the king from imprisonment by the Germans unleashed a major controversy. In a plebiscite, 57 per cent of the population voted in favor of his return to the throne, but continuing tension in Wallonia forced Leopold III to abdicate in favor of his son Baudouin (1950).

9   In 1947, Belgium, the Netherlands and Luxembourg formed an economic association known as the Benelux. This association can be considered as the cradle of the present European Union. Belgium also became a member of NATO in 1949. In 1960 the Belgian Congo became independent, but Belgium and the Western powers continued to intervene in the former colony (which became Zaire, and is now the Democratic Republic of Congo). In 1962 Rwanda and Burundi became independent.

10   Female suffrage was granted without restrictions in 1948. In 1975, Belgian women gained the right to equal pay.

11   In 1970, linguistic communities were granted autonomy in cultural matters. In 1980, a new federal structure was approved by Parliament, made up of Flanders, Wallonia, and Brussels as the bilingual capital district. This marked the beginning of a process of decentralization that would continue for the next 30 years and is still ongoing.

IN FOCUS

ENVIRONMENTAL CHALLENGES
Water protection laws, passed in 1971, did not prevent the River Mosa's pollution by steelworks. This river provides water resources to 5 million people. The increase in the concentration of nitrates and the proliferation of algae in many rivers are due to contamination by manure and the intensive use of fertilizers in agriculture.

WOMEN'S RIGHTS
The first women (war widows) were able to stand for election in 1921. Since 1948 there have been no restrictions on women's political participation. In the period 1995-2000 their parliamentary representation increased from 12 to 23 per cent; in ministerial or equivalent positions it was 18.5 per cent in 2000. In that year, women made up 41 per cent of the workforce (2 per cent in agriculture, 13 per cent in industries and 85 per cent in services).

In 2002 the country was one of the three main destinations for trafficked African women, particularly from Ghana and Nigeria.

CHILDREN
School is compulsory up to 18 years old. Those between 15 and 18 years old are able to work part time or full time during school holidays.

Those between 15 and 18 years old are able to combine work and school.

INDIGENOUS PEOPLES/ ETHNIC MINORITIES
The country has a multicultural and multi-linguistic population. In addition, ethnic minorities have been integrating into Belgian society as immigrants, refugees or people in need of assistance from non-industrialized countries. Some initiatives were launched to fight racism and to promote intercultural dialogue. Belgium has an anti-racism law since 1981. In 1993, a Centre for equal

Opportunities and against Racism has been established. Its main task is to act against racism, and to follow up Belgian integration policy.

MIGRANTS/REFUGEES
At the end of 2002, Belgium sheltered around 30,300 refugees and asylum-seekers. About 1,700 obtained asylum during that year, while 24,400 new petitions were placed. To estimate the real number of people in need of protection, as the Belgian Government only registers adults, some international refugee committees use a 1.3 multiplication factor. The native countries of most of these people were Congo Democratic Republic, former Yugoslavia, the Russian Federation, Turkey and Angola.

DEATH PENALTY
Abolished in 1996. The last execution took place in 1950.

Life expectancy
78.8 years
2000-2005

GNI per capita
$23,250
2002

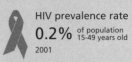

HIV prevalence rate
0.2% of population
15-49 years old
2001

[12] In 1983, the installation of NATO nuclear missiles on Belgian soil unleashed a nationwide controversy. The missiles were withdrawn in 1988, after an arms reduction agreement was signed between the US and the USSR. The mass peace movement disappeared along with the missiles.

[13] The Government closed its 1997 budget with a national deficit of 2.7 per cent of GDP. In spite of this enormous public debt, which clearly exceeded the criteria of the Maastricht Treaty, Belgium was allowed to join the European Monetary Union.

[14] On 31 July 1993, King Baudouin died after a reign of 42 years and was succeeded by his brother Albert.

[15] The 1994 European elections reflected the population's lack of confidence in the governing coalition. Thus, in the European elections held in June and in the municipal elections of October the French-speaking Socialists lost votes. In the municipal elections, the Vlaams Blok became the second party in Antwerpen, by winning 18 out of the 55 seats at stake on the city council.

[16] Meanwhile, Parliament had agreed on major constitutional changes that turned the country into a federal state. On 21 May 1995, voters not only elected their members of parliament, but also the three new regional assemblies of Brussels, Flanders and Wallonia. The government alliance led by premier Jean-Luc Dehaene had a clear victory in the national elections, allowing him to continue as head of government.

[17] In 2001, the Lambermont agreements continued the reform of the state through decentralization. Federal powers concerning agriculture and foreign trade were transferred to Flanders and Wallonia. A principle decision was taken to transfer competence for development cooperation as well, but the execution of this decision is still pending. Food security however remained a federal issue due to the different food scandals that had threatened the country for years, including swine fever, mad cow disease, foot-and-mouth disease and the dioxin scandal. This situation brought Dehaene down and allowed into the political arena a coalition headed by Guy Verhofstadt, leader of the Flemish Liberal Party (VLD). Verhofstadt formed a coalition with Socialists and Greens from both communities, leaving the Christian Democrats out of office for the first time in 41 years.

[18] On the basis of the genocide law of 1993, crimes against humanity, committed anywhere in the world, can be prosecuted in Belgium. This happened in 2001, when four Rwandan citizens were sentenced in Brussels for taking part in the 1994 genocide. In the same year, the existence of the genocide law prompted the Israeli premier Ariel Sharon to cancel his visit to Belgium as result of denunciations made by several Palestinians, survivors of the 1982 Sabra and Shatila massacre. Following diplomatic pressure, Louis Michel considerably weakened the Genocide law in 2003.

[19] In 1996 Marc Dutroux was arrested for the abduction, rape and murder of several children. Public opinion was shocked that this could occur and lost confidence in the police and justice apparatus. The demission of an highly appreciated inquiry judge during the inquiry procedure, unleashed a mass protest against the judicial changes (White March). As a result of the protest, police apparatus has been reformed and measures concerning the judiciary have been taken.

[20] In 2001 Belgium resumed diplomatic links with DR Congo. Premier Verhofstadt and Minister of Foreign Affairs Michel visited the former colony to further the peace negotiations that should end the civil war in the eastern part of the country.

[21] The flow of refugees from Third World and former communist states became a political issue in Europe. Belgium followed the European trend, abolishing all financial support to refugees and by introducing a fast deportation procedure. The Belgian asylum policy was criticized by Amnesty International.

[22] In July 2001, Belgium took over the chair of the European Union. It put the Tobin Tax, the taxation of international financial transactions, on the European agenda. Since 1 July, 2004 a law on the Tobin Tax has been voted in the Belgian Parliament. The law will only come into force when all other EU member states also vote a Tobin Tax law. On 1 January 2002, the Euro replaced the Belgian franc as the national currency.

[23] The Belgian section of the anti-globalization movement, consisting of trade unions, peace groups, ecological and Third World movements and several non-governmental organizations, occupied the streets of Gent and Brussels in the autumn of 2001, protesting against EU policy and other international organizations.

[24] The study by a committee of distinguished historians of the deaths of 10 million Congolese people at the hands of Leopold II's private army was completed. In 2001 the Government apologized for Congolese Prime Minister Patrice Lumumba's death, which occurred after the coup led by Mobutu Sese Seko.

[25] In September 2002 Belgium became the second country in the world, after the Netherlands, to legalize euthanasia.

[26] In August 2002 the Government agreed to sell military equipment to Nepal. According to the opposition, this transaction was against the law prohibiting weapons trading with countries in a state of civil war. After the federal elections in June 2003, the weapon trade law was decentralized: decisions on weapon trades are now a competence of the regions.

[27] The governing coalition survived until the federal elections held in June 2003, where two of the coalition parties got most of the votes. The Green Party, however, was voted out of office and federal parliament. ∎

PROFILE

ENVIRONMENT

Northwestern Belgium is a lowland, the Plains of Flanders, composed of sand and clay deposited by its rivers. In southern Belgium the southern highlands rise to 700 m on the Ardennes Plateau. One of the most densely populated European countries, its prosperity rests on trade, helped by its geography and by the transport network covering the northern plains, converging at the port of Antwerpen. Belgium has highly intensive agriculture, and a major industrial center. Heavy industry was located near the coal fields of the Sambre-Meuse valley, and textiles were traditionally concentrated in Flanders.

SOCIETY

Peoples: The country's two major language-based groups are the Flemish (55 per cent) and the Walloons (44 per cent). There is also a German minority (0.7 per cent). Over 7 per cent of the economically active population (about 250,000 people) are immigrants (Italian, Moroccan and, in lesser numbers, Turkish and African).
Religions: Mainly Catholic. There are Protestant, Muslim and Jewish minorities.
Languages: Flemish (58 per cent) and French (32 per cent) are the official languages. French is the main language spoken in the south and east, and Flemish in the north and west. German is spoken by about 0.6 per cent of the population.
Main Political Parties: Social Democrats (SP-A/PS), Christian Democrats (CD&V/CDH), Liberals (VLD/MR), Flemish Nationalist Parties (SPIRIT, NVA), Greens (GROEN!, ECOLO), Extreme right parties (Vlaams Blok/Front National).
Main Social Organizations: Confederation of Christian Labor Unions of Belgium (ACV/CSC) 1,300,000 members; the General Labor Federation of Belgium (ABVV/FGTB) 1,100,000 members.

THE STATE

Official Name: Koninkrijk België/Royaume de Belgique.
Administrative Divisions: 10 provinces.
Capital: Brussels (Brussel/Bruxelles) 998,000 people (2000). Brussels is also the capital of the European Union.
Other Cities: Antwerpen 945,800 people; Liège 620,900; Gent 223,000 (2000); Charleroi 201,700.
Government: Federal parliamentary state since 1993, under a constitutional monarch. Belgium has in total 6 regions and communities, each of them having a parliament, a government and an administration: Flemish region and community, Walloon Region, French speaking community, German speaking community and Brussels Capital. There are three official language communities: Flemish, French and German. King Albert II, Head of State since August 1993. Guy Verhofstadt, Prime Minister since July 1999, re-elected in 2003. Bicameral Legislature: Chamber of People's Representatives, with 150 members; Senate, with 71 members.
National and Regional Holiday: 21 July, National Day (the day King Leopold I came to the throne in 1831). 11 July (Flemish official holiday). 27 September (Waloon official holiday).
Armed Forces: 53,000 (including women). Conscription was abolished in 1994. Belgium now has only a professional army.

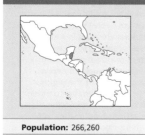

Population:	266,260
Area:	22,960 km²
Capital:	Belmopan
Currency:	Belize dollar
Language:	English

N ative American people known as the Itzae were the original occupants of what is now Belize (formerly British Honduras). Belize, together with Guatemala and southern Mexico, formed part of the Mayan Empire. In Belize, the Mayas built the cities of Lubaatún, Pusilhá, and a third which archaeologists call San José.

[2] In 1504 Columbus sailed into the bay naming it the Gulf of Honduras. Spain was nominally the colonial power in the region, but never pushed further into Belize, because of tough resistance from the local people. According to the terms of the Treaty of Paris (1763) Spain allowed the British to start exploiting timber in the area. This authorization was later confirmed in the Treaty of Versailles (1783). In 1798 the British gained control of the colony, although Spain retained sovereignty until it became a British colony in the 1840s, and its name changed to British Honduras.

[3] The first settlers in Belize were British Puritans, attracted by the cedar, campeche wood and timber. They began to establish themselves in the coastal areas, importing African slaves to work their estates. Shortly afterwards, slaves outnumbered Europeans, and in 1784 only 10 per cent of the population was of European extraction.

[4] The ethnic base became more heterogeneous in the early 19th century. By that time, Garifuna migrants had settled on the Southern coast of Belize. The War of Castes in Yucatan between 1847 and 1901 displaced thousands of Spanish-speaking inhabitants to the northern coast of Belize, while several Maya communities re-settled in the northern and western areas of the country. These immigrants introduced changes in agricultural techniques that set the pattern for subsistence farming and for sugar, banana and citrus production. During the 1860s and 1870s, sugarcane plantation owners sponsored the migration of several thousand workers from China and India. By the end of that century, Maya and Kekchi indigenous peoples, who had escaped oppression in Guatemala, established self-sufficient communities in the south and west of Belize.

[5] By the early 20th century, the economy was stagnant and the British colonial administration prevented any democratic participation. In 1931, a hurricane destroyed a large part of Belize City. That same year, a series of strikes and demonstrations by workers and the unemployed gave rise to unions and increasing demands for democracy. Eligibility for voting was legally introduced in 1936, but it was heavily restricted by level of literacy, land title and gender.

[6] In 1949 when the Governor devalued the national currency, union leaders and the local middle class joined in a People's Committee that demanded constitutional changes. As a result, in 1950 the People's United Party (PUP) was founded, led by George Price. First organized as a 'people's committee' to fight against arbitrary treatment by the colonial administration, the PUP won its first elections by a landslide majority. In 1954 the direct election of the legislative representatives was approved. In 1961 a ministerial system of government was established, and in 1964 the country was granted internal autonomy, with Price becoming Prime Minister. On 1

IN FOCUS

ENVIRONMENTAL CHALLENGES
Sea pollution, soil erosion and deforestation are problems shared with other Caribbean countries. Close to the cities, the surface of the water is covered with residual wastes and by-products of sugarcane production. Industrial waste, dumped in the water, has generated public health problems and killed fish stocks. Final disposal of household wastes and sewage water treatment are unsatisfactorily resolved issues.

WOMEN'S RIGHTS
Women have been able to vote and run for office since 1954. From 1995 to 2000, female legislative seats rose from 3 per cent to 7 per cent; while their representation in ministerial or equivalent positions went from 6 per cent to nil.

CHILDREN
Over 48 per cent of the population is under 18 years old. High rates of crime and violence persist among youngsters. Between 1990 and 2000, there has been an increase in the number of institutions devoted to childhood and adolescence. In 2001 and 2002 there was a 150 per cent increase in AIDS infection rate amongst infants under one year old. Most mother-to-child-transmissions during delivery were in HIV -positive single mothers. The percentage of pre-school national health coverage is low: a total of 27.5 per cent, with higher figures in Belize City (60.4 per cent) than in other districts, particularly Toledo (2.7 per cent). Male and female participation in school courses was almost equal in 2001*. The course repeat rate was 8.3 per cent, 2 per cent less than in 1996-1997. Under-five mortality decreased from 52 in 1992 to 40 in 2002*. However, not all deaths are reported.

INDIGENOUS PEOPLES/ ETHNIC MINORITIES
Garifuna (African-Carib Indian) which are 7 per cent of the population, were recognized by the Government as a people in 2001. The Government announced its intention to work with UNESCO in protecting their culture. However their land ownership claims are still questioned.

Maya culture (11 per cent of the population) is threatened by the plans to build a dam by Belize's electricity company and Fortis (a Canadian transnational), which could flood their community's main location, destroying ancient Maya sites.

MIGRANTS/REFUGEES
In 2000, Belize sheltered around 1,700 refugees and asylum-seekers, mainly from El Salvador. During that year some Nigerians requested asylum and by the end of the year all the cases were still under review. Even though Belize is part of the UN Convention and Protocol on refugees, and has had national laws on this since 1991, no refugee status was granted between 1995 and 1999. UNHCR's office in Belize was closed in 1998 and since then UNHCR-Mexico has covered the country's refugees. In 1999 there was a change in government decisions on giving legal residence to refugees and illegal immigrants. In that year, out of 4,800 families of illegal refugees, 1,700 got permanent residence; 1,150 refugees from El Salvador, Guatemala and Nicaragua were given citizenship, with support from UNHCR, which considered them 'cases of concern'.

DEATH PENALTY
It is currently applied.

*Latest data available in *The State of the World's Children* and *Childinfo* database, UNICEF, 2004.

Life expectancy
71.4 years
2000-2005

GNI per capita
$2,960
2002

Literacy
93% total adult rate
2000

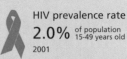

HIV prevalence rate
2.0% of population 15-49 years old
2001

June 1973 the country changed its name to Belize.

[7] Guatemala claimed to have inherited sovereignty over Belize from Spain, and did not recognize the Guatemala-Belize border. In March 1981, Guatemala and Britain signed a 16-point agreement. Britain assured the future independence of Belize in exchange for some concessions to the Guatemalan regime, such as free and permanent access to the Atlantic, joint exploitation of the marine resources, the building of a pipeline, and an 'anti-terrorist' agreement.

[8] Price and the PUP were accused of partiality towards the 'revolutionary' Cuba and Nicaragua, an issue exploited by the right-wing opposition, the United Democratic Party (UDP), which won the December 1984 elections.

[9] The new Prime Minister, Manuel Esquivel, a US-educated physics professor, adopted a liberal economic policy and supported the private import-export sector, which was in the hands of inexperienced family business ventures. He also developed favorable policies to encourage foreign investment and attracted US, Jamaican and Mexican investments in tourism, energy, and agriculture.

[10] Sugarcane generated 50 per cent of the country's revenue, but a fall in international prices badly affected the economy. The industry only survived because of import quotas guaranteed by the US and EEC markets, which took 60 per cent of the sugar output, with the remainder being sold at a loss.

[11] In March 1986, Prime Minister Esquivel proposed a plan for the sale of Belizean citizenship, aimed primarily at Hong Kong business people. Anyone investing $25,000 in government bonds - really worth only $12,500 - would be granted instant citizenship of Belize.

[12] During the 1980s, the country received approximately 40,000 Salvadoran, Guatemalan, Honduran and Nicaraguan refugees. In spite of official tolerance, some officials blamed immigrants for the rise in marijuana trafficking and crime.

[13] When Vinicio Cerezo became President of Guatemala in 1986, relations between the countries changed substantially. In December 1986, Cerezo's government re-established diplomatic relations with Britain, broken off two decades earlier over Guatemalan claims to Belizean territory. A Permanent Joint Commission was formed with Belizean, Guatemalan and

PROFILE

ENVIRONMENT

Belize covers the southeastern tip of the Yucatan Peninsula. The land is low, and the climate warm and rainy in the north. In southern Belize, the hillsides sustain a variety of crops. The northern coastline is marshy and flanked by low islands. In the south there are excellent natural harbors between reefs. Significant oil and gas deposits are believed to exist off the coast.

SOCIETY

Peoples: Spanish-Indian descendants 43.6 per cent; Creole (predominantly black) 29.8 per cent; Mayan Indian 11.0 per cent; Garifuna (African-Carib Indian) 6.7 per cent; white 3.9 per cent; East Indian 3.5 per cent; other or not stated 1.5 per cent.
Religions: 60 per cent are Catholic, most of the rest are Protestant (Anglican, Methodist, Seventh-Day Adventist, Pentecostal, Jehovah's Witness). **Languages:** English (official); common language is Creole. Spanish, Quiché, Yucatan Mayan and Garifuna are also spoken. **Main Political Parties:** The People's United Party (PUP), founded in 1950; The United Democratic Party (UDP); the National Alliance for the Rights of Belize, founded in 1992 by members of the UDP opposed to compromise with Guatemala.
Main Social Organizations: The General Workers' Union, the Christian Workers' Union (CWU), the United General Federation, the General Federation of Workers and the Public Service Union of Belize.

THE STATE

Official Name: Belize. **Administrative Divisions:** 6 districts.
Capital: Belmopan 9,000 people (2003). **Other Cities:** Belize City 50,200 people; Orange Walk 13,800; San Ignacio 13,600; Dangriga (formerly known as Stann Creek) 9,000; Corozal 8,100 (2000).
Government: Parliamentary monarchy, Queen Elizabeth II of England is Head of State. Colville Young, Governor-General since November 1993. Said Wilbert Musa, Prime Minister since August 1998, re-elected in 2003. Legislative power lies with the House of Representatives, which has 29 members and is elected by universal suffrage, and a 9-member Senate appointed by the Governor-General. **National Holidays:** 10 September, National Day; 21 September, Independence Day (1981).
Armed Forces: 1,065 (1995).

British representatives to find a peaceful solution to the issue. However, Belize feared a Guatemalan invasion and kept a standing army of 1,800 British troops. Esquivel declared in Mexico that he 'would not allow the installation of US military bases', stressing that he did not wish to become involved in the Central American crisis.

[14] However, the number of US embassy personnel grew sixfold after independence and the number of Peace Corps volunteers was ten times higher. Dean Barrow, Minister of Foreign Affairs and Economic Development, admitted that he was aware of the country's dependence upon the US. But he also stated that Belize could defend its territorial integrity through the Non-Aligned Movement.

[15] Drug-trafficking - or the sale of 'Belize breeze' as marijuana is known - showed spectacular growth. According to some foreign economists, it became the country's main export, and it was estimated that some 700 tons - worth at least $100 million - had been taken into the US, being its

market price 10 times this sum. The area under cultivation increased by at least 20 per cent in spite of a US-sponsored herbicide-spraying campaign.

[16] George Price was returned to power when the PUP won the September 1989 elections. In September 1991, Guatemalan President Jorge Serrano Elias finally recognized Belize's sovereignty and right to self-determination. The Government of Belize in turn gave Guatemala free access to the gulf of Honduras.

[17] At the end of the 1980s and early 1990s a large number of Haitians went to Belize as agricultural laborers, attracted by higher wages than at home. Lower inflation rates and more equal income distribution were incentives for immigration, and they also had access to health and education services. The social services consequently became overloaded, triggering a backlash from Belizeans who demanded that the immigrants be deported.

[18] Banana, sugar and citrus production increased, representing 40 per cent of the

country's total production and four-fifths of its exports. Fishing was the fourth biggest economic activity. Tourism became the sector with the greatest potential. Mayan archeological discoveries attracted many visitors.

[19] Hours after Guatemala's President Serrano was ousted on 1 June 1993, Price brought the election date forward 15 months, counting on a new PUP victory to ratify agreements made with this neighbor. His opponent Manuel Esquivel questioned the validity of Price's concessions to Guatemala, and proposed that these be legitimized by a referendum.

[20] In the June 1993 elections the PUP was defeated by the UDP, led by Esquivel and dominated by Spanish-Indian descendants. The Government formed a group of economic advisors to look into establishing facilities for the capital and tourist markets, and the development of more free zones. The fear of new territorial demands from Guatemala and the withdrawal of British troops led to an increase in defense spending and new recruitment for the armed forces.

[21] Victory in the August 1998 general elections went to the PUP and Said Wilbert Musa became the new Prime Minister. The UDP was reduced to just three seats.

[22] On 24 February 2000 four members of the Belize security force where apprehended in Guatemala for allegedly entering that country's territory illegally. The incident intensified the dispute between Belize and its neighbor. Almost immediately the Caribbean Community (CARICOM) accused the Guatemalan Government of invading territory and kidnapping Belizeans.

[23] In October, Hurricane Keith caused widespread destruction. The storm left many dead, and the subsequent floods severely damaged the country's infrastructure.

[24] Another tragedy struck Belize in 2001 when Hurricane Iris buried entire towns and left more than 13,000 homeless. The hurricane, the most destructive in Central America in three years, flattened whole forests, destroyed the banana plantations and claimed around 20 lives.

[25] On 7 February 2003 Belize, Guatemala and Honduras, under the supervision of the OAS, signed an agreement to give Guatemala access to the Caribbean Sea. At the same time, a tripartite commission was set up to oversee fishing in the Gulf of Honduras. ∎

Benin / Benin

Population:	7,103,140
Area:	112,620 km²
Capital:	Porto Novo
Currency:	CFA franc
Language:	French

Benin (known as Dahomey until 1975) is among the poorest countries in the world. It lies in the region of the Yoruba culture, which developed at the ancient city of Ife. It was here that the Ewe peoples, who came from the same linguistic family, developed into two distinct kingdoms during the 17th century: Hogbonu (today known as Porto Novo) and Abomey, further inland. These states developed around the booming slave trade, serving as intermediaries.

2   The traditional rulers of Abomey, the Fon, built a centralized state that extended east and west beyond Benin's present-day frontiers. A well-disciplined army, with European rifles and a large contingent of female soldiers enabled them to end the patronage of the Alafin of Oyo (Nigeria) and capture various Yoruba cities. After the 17th century, Ouidah became the main port for British, French and Portuguese slave traders receiving their human cargo.

3   The ruling group of Abomey suffered a setback in 1818 when Britain banned the slave trade, although Ghezo who ruled between 1818 and 1856 maintained a thriving clandestine traffic to Brazil and Cuba. He also promoted the development of agriculture and established a strict state monopoly on foreign trade.

4   In 1889, Ghezo's grandson Benhanzin inherited a prosperous state, but one already threatened by colonialism. In 1891, Fon troops resisted the French invasion only to be defeated a year later. The King and his army retreated to the forests, where they held out until 1894. Benhanzin, who became a symbol of anti-colonial resistance, died in exile in Martinique in 1906.

5   The colonists destroyed the centralized political structure of the ancient Fon state. Traditional

Fon society was dismantled and replaced with a system based on the exploitation of farm labor. The French also declared a monopoly on the palm-oil trade and ruined families that had resisted foreign penetration for nearly a century.

6   By the beginning of the 20th century, the colony of Dahomey (as the French called it), was no longer self-sufficient. When it gained independence in August 1960, oil-seed exports stood at 1850 levels, while the population had tripled.

7   Independence came as a direct consequence both of France's weakness at the end of World War II and the activities of European-educated nationalists, led by Louis Hunkanrin, who waged a stubborn 20-year struggle against the compulsory labor imposed by the French. All forms of political organization were banned and in retaliation, Hunkanrin created the Human Rights League. A period of ruthless repression followed: hundreds of villages were burned down, nearly 5,000 people were

killed, and Hunkanrin took refuge in Mauritania.

8   By 1960, Dahomey had become an unbearable economic burden and France agreed to

independence. The new Government inherited a bankrupt economy and a corrupt infrastructure. A series of 12 military and civilian governments marked a 16-year period of instability.

9   The neocolonial élite collapsed in 1972 when then-Major Mathieu Kérékou headed a coup by a group of young officers opposed to political corruption and official despotism. Two years later, a Marxist-Leninist state was proclaimed and its name changed to Benin, with a communitarian political and economic system. All foreign property was nationalized, and a single-party system was introduced with the creation of the People's Revolutionary Party.

10   The revolutionary government became the target of several conspiracies plotted abroad. There was an unsuccessful invasion in January 1977 with the participation of French mercenaries and the support of Gabon and Morocco.

11   In 1980, a new Revolutionary Assembly was elected through direct vote. The Government switched to a more pragmatic foreign policy and diplomatic relations with France were resumed. Although palm-oil production continued to fall as the trees grew older and were not replaced, cotton and sugar sales rose. High unemployment continued, but in 1982 offshore oil was discovered thus guaranteeing energy self-sufficiency. In addition large phosphate deposits were discovered in the northern Mekrou region.

12   Hopes of recovery dimmed as drought reached the northern provinces. Desertification was exacerbated, and the region was unable to supply its own food even in traditional subsistence crops such as cassava/manioc, yams, corn and sorghum.

13   The economic crisis forced the Government to accept the terms of the International Monetary Fund (IMF), including a 10 per cent income tax and a 50 per cent reduction in non-wage social benefits.

14   On 8 December 1989, disappointed with results and besieged by street demonstrations, President Kérékou announced that he was abandoning his Marxist-Leninism. A new constitution was drawn up, providing for a series of political and economic reforms, especially the promotion of free enterprise.

15   On 24 March 1991 Prime Minister Nicéphore Soglo defeated President Kérékou with 68 per cent of the votes in the

PROFILE

ENVIRONMENT
Benin is a narrow strip of land that extends north from the Gulf of Guinea. Its 120-km sandy coast lacks natural ports. Several physical regions cut across the country from south to north: the coastal belt where oil palms are cultivated; the tropical wooded lowlands; and the plateau which rises gradually towards the headwaters of the Queme, Mekrou, Alibori and Pendjari rivers, in a region of tropical hills.

SOCIETY
Peoples: Benin's people stem from 60 ethnic groups. The Fon (47 per cent), Adja, Yoruba and Bariba groups are the most numerous and before French colonization they had already developed stable political institutions. There is a European minority.
Religion: Around 70 per cent practice traditional African religions, 15 per cent are Muslim and 15 per cent Catholic.
Languages: French (official). Other widely-spoken languages are Fon, Fulani, Mine, Yoruba and Massi.
Main Political Parties: Action Front for Renewal and Development (FARD); Renaissance Party of Benin (PRB), Democratic Renewal Party (PRD); Social Democratic Party (SDP); African Movement for Democracy and Progress (MADEP). Extra-parliamentary parties: Benin Communist Party (PBC); Marxist-Leninist Party of Benin (a 1999 split from the PBC).
Main Social Organizations: The Benin Workers' National Trade Union (UNSTB) is the only union.

THE STATE
Official name: République Populaire du Bénin.
Administrative Divisions: 6 provinces.
Capital: Porto Novo 238,000 people (2003).
Other Cities: Cotonou 704,900 people; Djougou 177,300; Parakou 141,100; Abomey-Calavi 86,900 (2000).
Government: Presidential republic with a strong Head of State. Mathieu Kérékou, President, Head of State and Government since 1996 (second term); re-elected in 2003. Since 1998 he has also taken the role of Prime Minister. Single chamber parliament of 83 members. **National Holidays:** 1 July, Independence (1960); 30 November, Revolution Day (1974).
Armed Forces: 4,800. Other: Gendarmerie and Peoples' Militia: 4,000.

Life expectancy	GNI per capita	Literacy	HIV prevalence rate
50.6 years	**$380**	**37%** total adult rate	**3.6%** of population 15-49 years old
2000-2005	2002	2000	2001

IN FOCUS

ENVIRONMENTAL CHALLENGES

The process of deforestation and desertification is among the major environmental problems, which has been made worse in recent years by a significant decrease in rainfall. The absence or precariousness of sanitary facilities does not ensure safe access to drinking water and 65 per cent of the population runs the risk of being contaminated, especially in rural areas.

WOMEN'S RIGHTS

Women can vote and stand for election since 1956. From 1995 to 2000, women seats in Parliament fell from 7 per cent to 6 per cent; representation in ministerial or equivalent positions increased from 10 to 13 per cent.

In 2000, women represented 48 per cent of the total workforce (65 per cent of them in agriculture, 4 per cent in industry and 30 per cent in services). 41 per cent of pregnant women are anemic*. The fertility rate stands at 5.7 children per woman*. Meanwhile 44 per cent of women receive no perinatal assistance; for every 100,000 live births, 850 women die*. In 2000*, the rate of adult female illiteracy was enormous (76 per cent), far worse than that of men (48 per cent)*. The illiteracy rates for young people aged 15-24 are marginally better (64.0 per cent for women and 29.5 per cent for men in 2000) but the gender gap is still vast. The frequency of HIV/AIDS in women aged 15 to 20 was 2.2 per cent (compared with 0.9 per cent for men of the same age); for women aged 20 to 24 the prevalence rate increased to 4.8 per cent.

CHILDREN

Poverty, illiteracy and illnesses are some of the factors hindering progress towards the achievement of child rights in the country. In 2003, only 38 per cent of children under 6 months old were exclusively fed on breast milk. In 2001, 27 per cent of children under 3 years old suffered from chronic malnutrition – a slight increase since the 25 per cent incidence in 1996. Also in 2001, 8 per cent of children suffered from acute malnutrition – an improvement on the 1996 figure of 14 per cent. Chronic malnutrition is almost equally distributed among girls and boys, while acute malnutrition is more prevalent among boys.

In 2001, there were 34,000 children orphaned by HIV/AIDS. By the end of that same year, 12,000 children between 0 and 12 years old were carrying the virus. Forty per cent of children under 5 years old who had flu as a symptom of malaria were not receiving medication against the disease.

INDIGENOUS PEOPLES/ETHNIC MINORITIES

Benin is part of French-speaking Africa but there are still 51 separate ancestral languages alive in the country, among them Yoruba, Bariba and Awuna. Some of these are also still spoken in parts of Latin America, having been carried there by slaves transported from the region of present-day Benin. In addition, Benin and Nigeria are the cradles of Vodou, a form of ancestral cult which was also carried to Latin America and the Caribbean by slaves and was syncretized with other religious practices to create voodoo. One of the current dangers faced by indigenous peoples such as the Ogoni and the Ijaw in Benin and neighboring countries is the threat to their environment by transnational oil companies. This is part of an agreement with the Government of Nigeria for the construction of a gas pipeline designed to traverse 600 miles (1,000 km) from Benin up to Togo and Ghana.

MIGRANTS/REFUGEES

At the end of 2001, Benin hosted some 5,000 refugees from Togo, Congo DR and other countries. During that year, the UNHCR offered partial humanitarian assistance to 2,500 of the total number of refugees within the country. One thousand registered Togolese lived in Benin, but according to estimates, there were 1,000 additional unregistered Togolese who remained in the country. Some refugees lived in a camp near Cotonou, the largest city, while others lived on their own in Cotonou. Some Togolese remained concerned for their safety, fearing infiltration into Benin by Togolese government agents. Benin's largest refugee camp, Kpomasse, located 30 miles (50 km) from the capital, housed about 1,000 refugees of various nationalities. Refugees from Nigeria complained that UNHCR failed to give them adequate protection from alleged mistreatment by Nigerian government agents and Benin's police.

The Benin Government continued to offer a permanent home to a modest number of refugees who were unable to repatriate safely or resettle in other countries. In 2000 and 2001, permanent resettlement in Benin was only granted to 140 refugees.

DEATH PENALTY

It is still applied. There have been no executions since 1986.

*Latest data available in *The State of the World's Children* and *Childinfo* database, UNICEF, 2004.

---

country's first presidential election in 30 years. In 1992, former president Kérékou, who had been prosecuted for his activities following the 1972 coup, was granted an amnesty, and political prisoners were released.
[16] Soglo continued the economic liberalization and privatization policy initiated by Kérékou in 1986. Debt servicing still represented a high percentage of the resources annually obtained (in 1992 debt service was equivalent to 27 per cent of the country's income).
[17] The 100 per cent devaluation of the CFA franc decreed by France in January 1994 provoked contradictory effects in Benin's economy. GDP continued to grow at a 4 per cent annual rate and cotton exports increased. However, public expenditure cuts - aimed among other things at curbing inflation after the devaluation - brought about drastic reductions in social spending schemes.
[18] In July 1994, Soglo assumed the leadership of the Renaissance Party of Benin (PRB), founded by his wife Rosine in 1992. The PRB was defeated in the legislative and municipal elections of March 1995 by the opposition Democratic Renewal Party (PRD).
[19] Soglo's clannish style and his tendency to rule together with his family angered the political class in Benin. In the general elections held in March 1996, Soglo suffered a narrow defeat by Kérékou, the former leader of the Marxist regime.
[20] Between August and October 1997, disease killed around 60,000 pigs - 10 per cent of the country's stock of swine. The spread of HIV/AIDS was a factor in causing life expectancy in the country to drop by ten years.
[21] The country's five unions called for a strike in February 1998 against 'the antisocial budget for 1998, the dictates of the IMF, the World Bank and the European Union, as well as widespread corruption encouraged by Kérékou's government'. The Government answered with a $10 million increase in public spending, a move deemed insufficient by the unions, which now called for a general strike.
[22] The March 1998 parliamentary elections saw the presidential faction win over the other 55 parties. Prime Minister Adrien Houngdedji stood down and his role was taken on by Kérékou.
[23] In January 2000, the President denounced a conspiracy against his government by some of the military, particularly former members of regional peacekeeping forces. A group such as this had led a coup in Côte d'Ivoire in December 1999 and similar action in Mali had been narrowly avoided when another group attempted to claim outstanding pay.
[24] In July 2000, Benin qualified for the Broad Initiative for Heavily Indebted Poor Countries with a $460 million reduction in its foreign debt.
[25] A boat carrying dozens of children made Benin the center of an international search in April 2001, highlighting slave trafficking in that country and the region. In many cases the children are sold to work in cocoa and coffee plantations in neighboring countries. In October 2003, the Presidents of Nigeria and Benin decided to undertake a joint mission for the repatriation of slave children, with the support of UNICEF and the NGO Terre des Hommes. According to estimates by the Brigade for the Protection of Minors, 6,000 Beninese children are exploited as slave labor in Nigeria.
[26] In January of the same year, a law was passed banning all female genital mutilation, setting fines and penalties ranging from six months to three years in prison for practitioners. The penalties increase up to five years if the woman is a minor, and could be 10 years if she dies as a result of mutilation.
[27] In the parliamentary elections of March 2003, the Kérékou faction again won a parliamentary majority with 55.8 per cent of votes. ∎

Bermuda / Bermuda

Population:	82,729
Area:	50 km²
Capital:	Hamilton
Currency:	Bermuda dollar
Language:	English

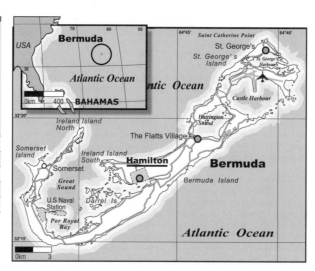

The Bermuda archipelago was the first colony of the British Empire. Sighted by the Spanish navigator Juan Bermúdez in 1503 (the place was named after him), it was settled in 1609 when British emigrants on their way to America were shipwrecked nearby.

2   From 1612, the colony welcomed religious and political dissidents. In 1684, it began to be administrated by the British Crown, and the first parliament was installed. Even though African slaves formed the majority, only plantation owners could elect representatives.

3   Agriculture almost disappeared in the 20th century, being replaced by tourism, gambling and transnational corporations lured by numerous tax exemptions. Today, Bermuda is one of the most densely populated places in the world (more than 1,000 people per km²). The residents of this tourist and tax haven do not receive much of the huge wealth that circulates there. In the last century, during the Prohibition (1919-1933) traffickers living in Bermuda smuggled rum into the United States. From 1941, Washington set up air and naval bases on the islands.

4   After the creation of the Bermuda Industrial Union (BIU), in 1963, workers founded the Progressive Labor Party (PLP), which favored the country's total independence and the introduction of an income tax. The following year, the Right organized the United Bermuda Party (UBP).

5   Britain granted the island greater administrative autonomy in 1968, and the majority party was given the right to name the prime minister. The period leading up to the elections was marked by racial and political violence. The assassination of the governor led to intervention by British troops. When the election was held, the UBP won by a large margin. The PLP increased its number of seats in the 1976 election. From its

position in opposition, the PLP continued to demand greater autonomy for the island.

6   In 1977, two members of the 'Black Cadre' were sentenced to death, for participating in armed anti-colonial activities. Their execution unleashed a wave of protests, with British troops intervening once again. The Minister of Communal (Race) Relations was sacked, and his duties delegated to the Bermuda Regiment, responsible for putting down protest and discontent. The 1979 Bermuda Constitutional Convention failed to reach a consensus on representation and the minimum voting age. However, a reduction in the number of non-Bermudan voters went into effect that December.

7   The UBP won both the 1980 and 1983 elections, although the opposition increased its representation. With the UBP in power, the country continued without self-determination as the

Government claimed that the majority was against this. The island's strategic location along North Atlantic routes explained the continued presence of British, Canadian and US troops.

8   During 1989 and 1990, unemployment rose by 0.5 per cent and 2 per cent, respectively. The US recession continued to affect tourism in the first few months of 1992. London rejected plans for independence.

9   In 1992, the economic crisis caused the French naval base to close and cutbacks in personnel at the US air base. The Bermuda Human Rights Alliance, an organization for the protection of gay rights set up in 1992, launched a campaign to reform the Criminal Code that penalized sex between men with up to 10 years in prison. In May 1994 sex between men over 18 years old was legalized.

10   In August 1995 the question of independence was put to a referendum. The result was against independence, so the status of British colony was maintained.

11   The PLP won the 1998 elections and Jennifer Smith became Prime Minister, putting an end to the 30-year-PUB government. However, despite this fact, Smith's leadership validity was questioned by vast factions of the PLP and she was forced to resign. Alex Scott took her place.

12   Although there had been no executions in Bermuda since 1977, capital punishment had remained on the statute book. However, death penalty and corporal punishment were finally abolished in December 1999.

13   In June 2002 Bermuda was excluded from the Organization for Economic Co-operation and Development (OECD) report on tax havens, as a result of the Government's commitment to reform their tax system before 31 December 2005. In March 2003, a constitutional reform reduced the members of the Assembly from 40 to 36 and in December, the Education Law was reformed, establishing that parents are responsible for their children's behavior at school, and imposing a fine on those who break the law. The Black Alliance, an organization for the protection of African descendants' rights, claimed that the Law was discriminatory, and that it tended to criminalize the poor, since it was only applied to public education, which is mostly used by the working class and black people. ■

PROFILE

ENVIRONMENT
This Atlantic archipelago is made up of 360 small coral islands, characterized by chalky, permeable soil. Bermuda includes 150 of these islands, of which 20 are uninhabited. The warm Gulf Stream current produces a mild climate which attracts tourists, mainly from the US. Pollution, especially from the US, caused by former military bases, is one of the country's main environmental problems.

SOCIETY
Peoples: Approximately 60 per cent are of African descent; there are also descendants of Portuguese from Madeira and the Azores; mixed European and Indian descendants and a minority of European origin. **Religions:** Anglican majority (28 per cent), in addition to Methodists (12 per cent), Adventists (6 per cent), Catholics (15 per cent) and members of other religions. **Languages:** English (official): Portuguese.
Main Political Parties: Progressive Labor Party (PLP); The United Bermuda Party (UBP); National Liberal Party of Bermuda; Environmental Party.
Main Social Organizations: Bermuda Industrial Union, Bermuda Public Service Association, Audubon Society of Bermuda, The Bermuda Human Rights Alliance and the Black Alliance.

THE STATE
Official Name: Bermuda. **Administrative Division:** 9 counties.
Capital: Hamilton 1,000 people (2003).
Other Cities: St George's 1,800 people (2000).
Government: British dependency. John Vereker, Governor since April 2002; nominated by Queen Elizabeth II. Prime Minister Alex Scott since 2003. The Prime Minister appoints the cabinet on approval by the Governor. Bicameral parliament: Senate has 11 members, 5 elected by the Prime Minister, 3 by the opposition leader and 3 by the Governor. Assembly has 36 members elected by direct voting for a 5-year term.
National Holiday: 24 May, Bermuda Day.

Bhutan / Druk Yul

Population:	2,391,782
Area:	47,000 km²
Capital:	Thimbu
Currency:	Ngultrum
Language:	Dzongkha

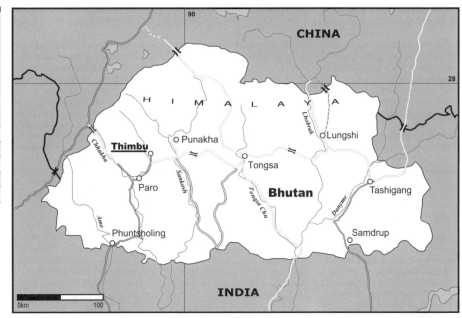

B hutan lies in the heart of the vast Himalayan mountains. Early explorers and envoys of the British colonial Government called it Bootan, land of the Booteas, or sometimes Bhotan. Wedged between giant neighbors China and India and cut off by some of the world's highest peaks, it was little known to the rest of the world. Even today, the origin of its name remains unknown. Perhaps it came from the Sanskrit. To the people of Bhutan it is Druk or Druk Yul, land of the Thunder Dragon.

[2] From the 12th century, the Drukpa Kargyud tradition became dominant. After a long period of rivalry among various groups, the country was united in the 17th century by a Drukpa Kargyud Lama named Ngawang Namgyal. Druk, the country's endogenous name, derives from the Kargyud sect of the Mahayana Buddhism (*drukpa*), which is currently the official religion. Namgyal, popularly known as Shabdrung ('at whose feet one submits'), was both the country's spiritual and secular ruler. Factionalism gradually eroded the power of the subsequent Shabdrungs. On 17 December 1907 Ugen Wangchuk reunified the country and established Bhutan's first hereditary monarchy.

[3] The British colonial administration in India signed important treaties with Bhutan in 1774 and 1865. The 1910 Treaty of Punakha stipulated that the British would not interfere in Bhutan's internal affairs, but made the country a British protectorate in terms of external relations. Similar provisions were included in the 1949 treaty signed between Bhutan and independent India.

[4] Bhutan emerged from its isolation in the 1960s and joined the Colombo Plan for Co-operative, Economic, and Social Development in Asia and the Pacific and the UN in 1962. Bhutan also joined the Non-Aligned Movement.

[5] Bhutan is still one of the poorest countries in Asia, although the emergent industrialization and recent development make exploitation of its natural resources feasible. For example, the forests that cover 65 per cent of the territory could be used if Bhutan were to sell its 'pollution rights.' The

LAND USE

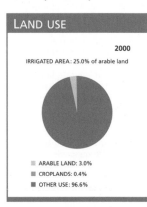

2000

IRRIGATED AREA: 25.0% of arable land

- ARABLE LAND: 3.0%
- CROPLANDS: 0.4%
- OTHER USE: 96.6%

PROFILE

ENVIRONMENT
This Himalayan country is made up of three distinct climatic and geographical regions. The Duar plain in the south, humid and tropical, is densely wooded and ranges in height from 300 to 2,000 meters. At the center lies a temperate region with mountains of up to 3,000 meters. Finally, there are the great northern heights, with year-round snow and peaks up to 8,000 meters. Forests are the country's mainstay. Rivers and waterfalls have been exploited and they supply energy to the country and neighboring areas. There are graphite, marble, granite and limestone deposits. Approximately half of the arable land lies on steep slopes; of this nearly 15 per cent is merely topsoil.

SOCIETY
Peoples: The main ethnic groups are the Bhutias, Drukpas and the Tibetans (50 per cent). The ethnic minorities are geographically divided: the Ngalong live in the west area, the Scharchops live in the east and the Nepalis (35 per cent of the population; known as Lhotsampas) live in the south. There are also Lepchas, indigenous people, and Santal, descended from Indian immigrants. 95 per cent of the teachers and 55 per cent of public servants are of Indian origin.
Religions: Buddhist 69.6 per cent; Hindu 24.6 per cent; Muslim 5.0 per cent; other 0.8 per cent (1980).
Languages: Dzongkha (official). Nepalese and other dialects are also spoken.
Main Political Parties: there are no legal parties. Political groups from the Nepali minority operate from exile: the Bhutan People's Party (BPP), founded in Nepal in 1990 represents the Nepali minority; the National Bhutanese Congress (DNC) founded in 1992, in Nepal and India; the United People's Liberation Front (UPLF), also founded in 1990. Social Organizations: the People's Forum of Human Rights (PFHR), covering five refugee camps in Nepal; the National Women's Association

THE STATE
Official Name: Druk Yul.
Administrative Divisions: 18 Districts.
Capital: Thimbu 35,000 people (2003).
Other Cities: Phuntsholing 54,300 people; Punakha 20,700; Samdrup Jongkhar 13,200 (2000).
Government: Jigme Singye Wangchuk, King since 21 July 1972; hereditary absolute monarchy. The monarch is assisted by a council of 9 members, of whom 5 are elected by the people, 2 are appointed by the monarch and 2 by the Buddhist religious dignitaries whose 6,000 lamas (monks) are headed by the Je Khempo. Lyonpo Yeshey Zimba, Prime Minister since August 2004. There is also a consultative assembly (Tsogdu) of 150 members 101 of whom are elected and 49 appointed, most being Buddhist monks. The ruler also dispenses justice.
National Holidays: 8 August, Independence Day (1949, from India); 17 December, National Day (1907); 2 August, Buddhist Lent; 30 October, end of Buddhist Lent.
Armed Forces: 7,000 royal troops (1993)

Life expectancy
63.2 years
2000-2005

GNI per capita
$590
2002

Literacy
47% total adult rate
2000

HIV prevalence rate
0.1% of population 15-49 years old
2001

IN FOCUS

ENVIRONMENTAL CHALLENGES
Most arable soil is thin and is located in steep areas, which makes the territory very susceptible to erosion. Access to drinking water is becoming increasingly difficult.

WOMEN'S RIGHTS
Women, who have had the vote and been eligible for office since 1953, have been excluded, discriminated against and exploited. They have never been appointed to ministerial posts or equivalents. In 2000, women occupied only 2 per cent of the parliamentary seats and 2 per cent had low-skilled jobs, while the rest mainly worked in agriculture. They have no economic autonomy, and more than 90 per cent of them are illiterate. Their health situation is poor, with high maternal mortality and anemia during pregnancies.

Sexual exploitation of women is common. A discriminatory law has been in force since 1988, which regulates mixed marriages between men from dominant ethnic groups (Drukpa or Ngalong) and Lhotsampa women (Lhotsampas are Bhutanese Hindus of Nepali origin), or between Lhotsampa men and non-Bhutanese women. The Bhutanese men who marry Lhotsampa women - and their children - automatically lose their civil, economic and social rights. In addition, foreign wives of Lhotsampa men are discriminated against - particularly Nepalese or Indian women - and the couple is deprived of civic rights: this does not happen when the Drukpas marry foreigners. This legislation is retroactive, which means that it applies to such marriages solemnized before 1988. More than 10,000

Lhotsampas' wives are deprived of their nationality.

CHILDREN
In 1990, 65 per cent of the population was under 30 years old, and 40 per cent was under 15. In 1999, the percentage of working minors aged 10 to 14 years old was the highest in Asia (55 per cent), despite the fact that in 1990 Bhutan had signed the Convention on Children's Rights. This is the main reason for the low school enrolment rate - despite the Kingdom's claim to have universal primary education: only 47 per cent of girls, 11 per cent below the rate registered for boys. The Government closely monitors secondary and further education, using exams as barriers. Children mainly work in agriculture, housework or in the building sector. Malnutrition and anemia are particularly high. In 2003, 40 per cent of children suffered from arrested development. By the end of the decade of 1990, 5 per cent of the armed forces were under 18 years old.

INDIGENOUS PEOPLES/ ETHNIC MINORITIES
The Lhotsampas - Bhutanese Hindus of mainly Nepali origin, whose language derives from Sanskrit - have very different traditions from those of the Drukpas or the Ngalongs. They have mainly settled in the warmer southern areas of the country, while the Ngalong - Buddhists who speak the Tibetan language - live in the colder north of the country.

The 1985 Citizenship Act deprived the Lhotsampas of citizenship; claiming they were illegal immigrants, the Bhutanese authorities arrested, tortured and murdered many of them, confiscated their properties and documents and forced them into exile. In 1997, the Bhutanese National Assembly decreed that

the 'Nepalese nationals' - the Lhotsampas - could not work in Bhutan, and allowed the Drukpas or the Ngalongs to settle on the land of those Lhotsampas who had fled to neighboring countries. In 2001, Bhutan and Nepal began jointly to 'verify' the potential candidates for repatriation, but by the end of 2002, disagreements about the verification process - together with the continuing occupation of Lhotsampas' ancestral land by Bhutanese people - prevented the repatriation process from succeeding. In October 2003, after the verification process in one of the 7 refugee camps was completed, only 3 per cent of the refugees were allowed to return to Bhutan.

The six NGOs that visited the Khundunabari refugee camp, rejected this 'solution' to the refugee issue because of the low repatriation rate and the irregularities found in the verification process: the UN High Commissioner for Refugees was not allowed to monitor it and was denied access to the places of return.

MIGRANTS/REFUGEES
In 2002, around 127,000 Bhutanese people lived as refugees in neighboring countries; 49 per cent of them were women and 40 per cent children. Almost all were Lhotsampas or Bhutanese of Nepalese or Indian origin, who lived in the southern plains of Bhutan. Most of them fled to Nepal and India during the first years of 1990 to escape the hostility, the harassment and expulsion by the Bhutanese authorities.

DEATH PENALTY
It is still in force. The last execution was in 1964.

[8] In 1998, the King, who was also head of state, government and head of the Court of Appeals, appointed a prime minister and a cabinet, whilst also granting the Consultive Assembly the right to initiate ideas or veto his decisions, and even call for his abdication. The opposition accused him of planting his followers in key positions in the Assembly. Bhutan still does not have a constitution and a bill of civil rights.

[9] Singye Wangchuk set out his own philosophy of development, which states that economic growth and material progress are not the only way to achieve personal success, as equal emphasis must be placed on emotional and spiritual security. As State ideology, this implies the aim to be achieved is Gross National Happiness (GNH) above Gross Domestic Product. GNH formed the framework for an agreement signed in 2001 by Bhutan and the Asian Development Bank. The agreement prioritizes poverty reduction in the country, and the Bank is supposed also to take into account the non-material elements of well-being.

[10] In December 2002, the Government announced it had finished drawing up the first draft of the Constitution and that the first round of consultational talks would begin, which would allow Bhutan to evolve into a parliamentary monarchy. The main issue was whether a multiparty system would be adopted or not.

[11] In September 2003, the Bhutan and Indian authorities agreed to find a solution that would allow the armed groups who fought for the independence of the Indian state of Assam to leave Bhutan. The Indian Government estimates that 3,000 members of these forces run 20 training camps in Bhutanese territory.

[12] In October 2003, as a result of international pressure, the Bhutan and Nepali governments agreed to find a solution to repatriate the Bhutanese refugees and decided to grant the rest of them Nepali citizenship. However the six NGOs that watched over the process rejected that solution because of the low repatriation rate and lack of UNHCR involvement, among other reasons.

[13] Bhutan is one of the countries that signed the bilateral agreements that grant US citizens charged with genocide, crimes against the humanity and war crimes, immunity from prosecution by the International Criminal Court. ■

country has one of the 10 most important protected areas of biodiversity on the planet.

[6] President-monarch, Jigme Singye Wangchuck, was crowned in 1972 and since ascending the throne the kingdom has begun a slow process of opening up to the world. Alongside this, a policy was initiated for the Bhutanization of the country. Since the Decree of Citizenship in 1985, many southerners were declared illegal immigrants. After the 1988 census, the monarch imposed the use of

national dress and the Dzongkha language in public places. Education in Nepalese was banned and work permits for foreigners were stopped. The political crisis arising from these measures led to the displacement of 100,000 Nepali Bhutanese to Nepal, where they lived in refugee camps. This event constitutes one of the largest ethnic expulsions in human history. Since 1990, Bhutan has considered the refugees, known as Lhotsampas, as people of no nationality.

[7] The seventh five-year plan started in 1992, with the objective of increasing exports, environmental conservation, regional balance and the institutional promotion of women. The Government encouraged foreign investment and began a cautious privatization program. In the 1990s, Bhutan signed bilateral agreements with Holland, Norway, Japan and Switzerland (among others), which provided funding for development programs.

Bolivia / Bolivia

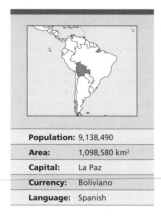

Population:	9,138,490
Area:	1,098,580 km²
Capital:	La Paz
Currency:	Boliviano
Language:	Spanish

I n 2000 BC the region of modern-day Bolivia was inhabited by farmers in the Andes, and forest hunter-gatherers in the east. Their terrain ranged from high mountain areas, *puna*, to hot valleys and forests. They raised livestock and grew potatoes, cotton, maize, and coca; they also fished and mined. This region, rich in natural resources, sustained several kingdoms and fiefdoms around Lake Titicaca, with the Tiahuanaco-Huari (600 BC-1000 AC) civilization at their center.

2   The basic social unit was the *ayllu* kinship group, in which there was no private land ownership. The society was stratified into farmers, artisans and the ruling ayllu, of priests and warriors, who appointed the *malku* (chief).

3   By 800 AD, Tiahuanaco formed the first Pan-Andean empire. By 1100, the Incas, from the Cusco Valley in Peru, had colonized the other Andean peoples and formed a confederation of states called the Tahuantinsuyo. Also known as the Inca Empire, it adopted elements of Tiahuanaco culture, technology, religion and economics, particularly the *ayllu* social unit.

4   Through the *mita*, each worker would render service to the centralized state. This system was later cruelly exploited by the Spaniards. Social organization was

WORKERS

UNEMPLOYMENT: 7.4% (2002)

LABOR FORCE   **2002**

■ FEMALE: 38.0%   ■ MALE: 62.0%

EMPLOYMENT DISTRIBUTION   **1995/2001**

F

M

■ AGRICULTURE	F: 2.0%	M: 2.0%
■ INDUSTRY	F: 40.0%	M: 16.0%
■ SERVICES	F: 58.0%	M: 82.0%

based on self-sufficient, communal production.

5   When the Spanish arrived at the beginning of the 16th century, the Tahuantinsuyo extended from southern Colombia, through Ecuador and Peru, to northern Chile, and from Lake Titicaca and the *altiplano* highlands to northern Argentina, embracing the mountain valleys and the eastern plains. One million people were estimated to have been living within the area of the present Bolivia, and from 12 to 13 million in the Tahuantinsuyo as a whole, making it the most densely populated area of South America. This society included a number of ethnic groups, predominantly Aymara (around Lake Titicaca) and Quechua. The eastern plains were inhabited by dispersed groups of Tupi and Guaraní, with no central nucleus. To this day, Aymara and Quechua are the most widespread languages in Bolivia.

6   In 1545 the Spanish discovered silver at Potosi. They extracted immense quantities of the metal, which contributed to the capital accumulation of several European powers. Millions of Native Americans died there, cruelly exploited to the point of exhaustion. Potosi was one of the three largest cities of the 17th century, growing up at the foot of the hill. It became the economic nerve center for vast regions of Chile and Argentina, and nurtured a rich mining bourgeoisie, guilty of corruption, ostentation and wastefulness.

7   Decades of popular struggle against the Spanish reached their peak with the successive rebellions of Tupac Katari (1780-82) and in the Protective Board of La Paz

(1809). The pro-independence movement was subsequently taken up by the *criollos* (Spaniards born in America), who distorted it by advocating social, economic and political systems based on the models of emerging European capitalist powers. A British blockade interrupted the supply of mercury, essential for treating the silver, and the Bolivian mining industry went into decline. The Buenos Aires based trading bourgeoisie soon lost interest in Upper Peru (Bolivia) and offered little resistance when it fell under the influence of the independence leader Simon Bolivar. The country was renamed after him when the Assembly of Representatives proclaimed independence in 1825.

8   Peru exerted great influence over the independent Bolivia until 1841. Bolivian president Marshall Andrés de Santa Cruz tried to modernize Bolivia, founding universities and the Supreme Court of Justice, and compiling law codes.

9   A mine-owning oligarchy including Patiño, Aramayo and Hochschild worked with the politicians and generals, who were their associates, treating the Bolivian republic as if it were part of the tin business. British imperialist interests, initially in the saltpeter at Antofagasta and later in Bolivia's southern oil reserves, triggered two wars in South America: the Pacific War (Chile against Bolivia and Peru from 1879-83), and the Chaco War (Paraguay and Bolivia, from 1932-35). As a result of these conflicts, Bolivia lost its coast and three-quarters of its territory in the Chaco region. The ceding of Amazonian Acre to Brazil, in 1904, completed the country's dismemberment.

10   On 21 July 1946 Bolivian president Gualberto Villarroel - accused by left and right parties as 'fascist' - was overthrown, assassinated, and his body hung from a lamp-post in downtown La Paz. Villarroel who had overthrown elected-president General Enrique Peñaranda, confronted the owners of the mines imposing taxes and organizing the miners' trade unions. He also mobilized peasants for the first time, gathered in the Indigenous Congress.

11   Nationwide frustration at these humiliations gave way to a powerful current of reformism and anti-imperialism. The MNR grew up alongside progressive labor and peasant movements. After several uprisings, and a 1951 electoral victory that was not honored, the MNR led a popular insurrection in 1952. Civilians defeated the oligarchy army in the streets, and they carried first Victor Paz Estenssoro, and then Hernan Siles Zuazo, to the presidency. The Bolivian revolution nationalized the tin mines, carried out agrarian reform and proclaimed universal suffrage. Workers' and peasants' militias were organized and together with the Bolivian Workers' Confederation (COB) formed a coalition with the MNR.

12   Troubled by internal divisions, the MNR gradually lost its drive and was defeated in November 1964 by a military junta led by René Barrientos. Ernesto 'Che' Guevara tried to establish a guerrilla nucleus in the Andes to spread revolutionary war throughout South America, but he was caught by US-trained counter-insurgency troops, and assassinated on 8 October 1967.

13   Division within the army coupled with pressure from the grassroots level led to an anti-imperialist faction taking over government in 1969, with General Juan José Torres as the leader. During his short time in office, there was a significant increase in the number of grassroots organizations. The People's Assembly was formed, with links to the COB and the parties of the Left. In August 1971 he was ousted by Colonel Hugo Bánzer Suárez, who formed a government with MNR support. The civilian-military coalition government remained in power until July 1978, with an authoritarian but development-oriented administration encouraging agribusiness and stressing infrastructure projects, bolstered by the high price of oil and other minerals.

14   Military uprisings and disregard for election results occurred repeatedly between 1978 and 1980. On 29 June 1980, the elections were won by the

Life expectancy
63.9 years
2000-2005

GNI per capita
$900
2002

Literacy
85% total adult rate
2000

HIV prevalence rate
0.1% of population 15-49 years old
2001

IN FOCUS

ENVIRONMENTAL CHALLENGES

The intensive agricultural production using poor crop methods and free timber exploitation increase soil erosion, desertification and biodiversity loss, thus threatening forest and fauna diversity and water resources. Air contamination increased in La Paz, as a consequence of industrial emissions and the increasing number of vehicles. Drinking and irrigation water resources are polluted by untreated industrial waste waters.

WOMEN'S RIGHTS

All Bolivian women have had the vote and have been able to stand as candidates since 1952 (between 1938 and 1952 a limited number of women were allowed to participate in politics). From 1995 to 2000 parliamentary seats held by women increased from 7 to 12 per cent; in ministerial or similar positions female representation grew from nil to 6 per cent and in local government it reached 4 per cent.

In the year 2000, women comprised 38 per cent of the workforce. Of those between 15 and 24 years old, 6.4 per cent were illiterate. Amongst those older than 15 that percentage was 20.8 per cent, while male illiteracy was 8.1 per cent for the same age range*.

The percentage of anemic pregnant women is 54 per cent (69 per cent of pregnant women receive antenatal health care and 69 per cent of the deliveries are assisted by qualified personnel)*. 1,200 women between 15 and 49 years old lived with HIV/AIDS in 2001.

CHILDREN

Anemia and chronic infant undernourishment persist among children under 5 years old. Between 1990 and 2000 mortality rates decreased due to the implementation of a Basic Health Insurance which covered pregnant women and children under 5 years old. Ten per cent of the children of this age were underweight in 1998*.

Immunization against common illnesses has improved, as has school enrolment, but these are both worse in the rural areas. In 2001 more than 800,000 people under 18 years old worked in mines, sugarcane harvest and prostitution. Around 12,000 children lived in institutions where their basic rights were not respected and more than 2,500 lived on the streets of the main cities. In the same year, 13 per cent of the teenage girls were pregnant or had already been mothers. The spread of sexually transmitted diseases, including HIV/AIDS, among children and teenagers is increasing.

INDIGENOUS PEOPLES/ ETHNIC MINORITIES

There are several indigenous peoples' associations to defend their rights and work against the discrimination they have suffered for 5 centuries. One of them is the Confederation of Indigenous Peoples of the Eastern Region, which groups 34 peoples from the east, Chaco, Amazonia and some areas of the Bolivian *altiplano* highlands, and was founded in Santa Cruz de la Sierra in 1982 with representatives of four indigenous peoples: Guaraní-izoceños, Chiquitanos, Ayoreos and Guarayos.

The unification process of the Eastern indigenous peoples began in 1979, when the first contacts between representatives of the aforementioned peoples took place. This was the initiative of Guraní Mburuvichaguasu Bonifacio Barrientos Iyambae, a Guaraní activist.

MIGRANTS/REFUGEES

Those recognized as refugees can get a permit to live in Bolivia indefinitely or temporarily, with travel and identity documents. There are yet many difficulties for recognized refugees to get such documents. In 1999 according to UNHCR's definition only 350 refugees were registered and 10 Bolivians requested asylum in other countries.

Between 1999 and 2000, over 200,000 Bolivian emigrants chose South American countries, especially Brazil and Argentina, as their destination, seeking informal sector jobs; they stayed as illegal immigrants for long periods of time. Many of them returned to Bolivia during the Argentinian economic crisis of 2001. Since 2003 Bolivians are included among those Americans to whom mobility, residence and work will not be restricted within the MERCOSUR countries. This will benefit many Bolivians who have been living in these countries for decades, as well as possible new emigrants.

DEATH PENALTY

The death penalty was abolished in 1997. The last execution took place in 1974.

*Latest data available in *The State of the World's Children* and *Childinfo* database, UNICEF, 2004.

Democratic Popular Union (UDP), a center-left coalition whose candidate, Hernan Siles Zuazo, was prevented from taking office by another bloody coup engineered by General Luis Garcia Meza. According to reports received by Amnesty International, thousands of people were killed or tortured.

[15] By 1982 internal dissent and the erosion of the regime's international standing because of its connections with drug trafficking, plus the dogged popular resistance led by the Bolivian Workers' Confederation (COB), resulted in the fall of the military regime. Hernan Siles Zuazo took office in a legal constitutional model that has continued ever since.

[16] Siles Zuazo, with a populist/nationalistic outlook, handed administration of the state-owned mines to the labor unions. He also announced the non-payment of Bolivia's foreign debt. The labor movement and the peasants exerted pressure on the government through demonstrations, and several laws passed by his administration allowed these groups to participate in the economic policy decisions of large businesses, and in local committees dealing with food, health and education issues. In response to these measures, creditor banks, the IMF and the World Bank blocked credits to Bolivia placing an embargo on its international trade, provoking a fiscal crisis and uncontrolled hyperinflation.

[17] Under heavy pressure from all social sectors, the Government cut short its term and called elections for July 1985. As neither candidate secured over 50 per cent of the vote, the decision was put to Congress, who elected Victor Paz Estenssoro (MNR) as constitutional president, though Hugo Banzer (ADN) had marginally more votes.

[18] The Estenssoro Government decreed a program of neo-liberal measures to end subsidies and close down state enterprises. It eliminated price controls and the official listing of the dollar against the local currency. Mines were closed down, and others rented out, leaving thousands of miners jobless, while investment ground to a standstill.

[19] In the 1989 national elections, Jaime Paz Zamora's Revolutionary Movement of the Left (MIR) proved itself a potent new political force, coming third with 19 per cent of the votes (double that of previous elections). The MNR candidate, Gonzalo Sánchez de Losada, obtained 23 per cent and Banzer's Nationalist Democratic Action (ADN), 22.6 per cent. As no party had achieved a majority, an agreement known as the Patriotic Accord (AP) between the MIR and the ADN made it possible for Paz Zamora to be nominated president by the National Congress. The Patriotic Accord continued Paz Estenssoro's neo-liberal economic policy.

[20] The Government embarked upon privatization of state enterprises, except those considered strategic. Congress passed a law permitting the state to sell off 22 of the existing 64 public enterprises, though the Supreme Court ruled it unconstitutional. The Government promoted joint ventures between the state-owned Mining Corporation (COMIBOL) and private companies. The Federation of Mining Workers (FSTMB) launched a series of hunger strikes and threatened to occupy the mines, defending the principle of continued state ownership.

[21] In April 1991, Bolivia's Congress authorized US military officers to come and train local personnel in the war against drugs. Despite military action and the policy of crop substitution - a program called 'development in place of coca' - the area under coca cultivation increased. It was estimated that in 1992 there were some 200,000 people involved in coca-cocaine production, and that the national net earnings from this crop reached $950 million per year.

[22] The loss of power in the workers' movement was compensated for by new organizations of indigenous peoples and communities. Several congresses of the Confederation of Indigenous Peoples of the Eastern Region, the Chaco and the Bolivian Amazon Region (CIDOB) and of the Guaraní People's Association, among other organizations, were held. Their demands include assignation of lands, habitat's preservation and the use of their native languages in the educational system.

At this time, the population of Bolivia's eastern region included 250,000 people of 10 linguistic groups and 35 ethnic groups.

[23] In September 1990, a group of peoples from this region carried out a 750 km march from the east

Under-5 mortality		Poverty		Debt service		Maternal mortality	
71	per 1,000 live births 2002	**14.4%**	of population living on less than $1 per day 1999	**31.1%**	exports of goods and services 2001	**420**	per 100,000 live births 2000

to the capital with the slogan 'Land and Dignity'. Paz Zamora's government approved a National Plan for the Defense and Development of the Indigenous Peoples, and in August 1991, recognized the Santa Ana de Horachi Mosetana Community's right to 8,000 hectares of land, which they consider collective property. These resolutions were opposed by companies that were exploiting the region's vast forestry resources.

24   In January 1992, Presidents Paz Zamora and Alberto Fujimori (of Peru) signed an agreement whereby Peru ceded an area of 327 hectares to Bolivia for it to develop a free zone at the port of Ilo, so Bolivia gained a free port for its international trade.

25   The MNR won the national elections of June 1993, with 36 per cent of the vote. Its presidential candidate was Gonzalo Sánchez Losada, and the vice-presidential candidate was Victor Hugo Cardenas, an Aymara sociologist and leader of the Tupac Katari Movement.

26   In its first year the Government established the right to education in the Indian languages (Aymara, Quechua, Guaraní). The Capitalization Bill aimed to privatize 50 per cent of the main public industries (telecommunications, electricity, oil, gas, railways, airlines) on the basis of transferring half the shares to the Bolivian citizens as pension funds. The aim was to attract foreign investment, reduce unemployment and increase GDP.

27   The burning of coca plantations by the US led to continuous confrontations between the rural workers and the military. Meanwhile, the World Bank reported that 97 per cent of the rural population were living in poverty.

28   The Capitalization Bill, unpopular amongst workers, led to a series of strikes in 1995. The Government declared a state of emergency on two occasions, granting the police special powers and imposing a curfew.

29   As part of its regional campaign to control the northward flow of cocaine, the US demanded that the Bolivian parliament approve a law against the drug-money laundering in February 1997.

30   In the national elections in June, the ADN won with 22 per cent of the vote, followed by the MNR, MIR, UCS and CONDEPA. Hugo Banzer became president once again after complicated negotiation in Parliament between the parties, themselves divided.

31   In August, the 100 coca syndicates agreed voluntarily to

reduce the production to comply with US requirements, as the US had promised to give $40 million to Bolivia to help in the war on drugs. In January 1999 Washington stated the plan had been a success and that Bolivian coca production had been reduced by 50 per cent.

32   According to Human Rights Watch (HRW), cocaine traffickers are very influential within the executive, Congress, armed forces, police, political parties and other public institutions. Drug trafficking and corruption prevent Bolivia from developing public institutions rooted within the law.

33   Quiroga replaced Banzer as president in August 2001, the latter was suffering from cancer.

34   The coca eradication plan hit another obstacle in December when poor farmers rejected a government offer of $900 per head per year to stop planting. The same month, farmers' leader Casimiro Huanca was shot dead by police.

35   In Cochabamba, the country's third-largest city, local citizens rebelled in 2000 against a World Bank-imposed privatization of the local public water system, leased off to the US engineering transnational, Bechtel. Angry over steep increases in water prices, Cochabambinos shut down their city for a week and forced Bechtel out of the country.

36   Two candidates topped the poll in the June 2002 national election: Sánchez de Lozada, with 22.46 per cent of the vote and Evo Morales, the Indian leader of the coca growers and candidate for Movement towards Socialism (MAS), who received 20.94 per cent. Since neither won an outright majority, Congress had to vote and Sánchez de Lozada was elected president in August.

37   In January 2003 10 peasants and 2 soldiers were killed in a crude act of aggression that occurred after the blockade of the country's main road by coca planters. After two weeks of intransigence, Sanchez de Lozada started a dialogue with peasants, who wanted an increase in the authorized coca plantation quota and a radical change in the Government's policies.

38   On 1 September 2003, a group of peasants and workers marched from Caracollo town to La Paz, opposing the export of gas, through Chile to the US, and demanding the resource be reserved in the first instance for domestic use and internal development. The protest grew for a month, with pickets, marches and road blockades. On the 29th day, COB called an indefinite general strike. Thousands of mineworkers marched to the capital and a few kilometers outside the city they

were stopped by the police. This confrontation killed two and injured many more. President Sánchez de Lozada accused the workers' and peasants' leaders of being 'anarchists and drug dealers'.

39   On 10 October, demonstrators virtually laid siege to La Paz. The Government called the riot 'a coup d'etát led by the MAS'. The unrest spread throughout the country after the army opened fire on the crowd, leaving 26 dead and many injured in El Alto on 12 October.

40   The biggest march in Bolivia's history took place on 16 October 2003. Human rights activists, intellectuals and middle-class people on hunger strike demanded that the President step down in

favor of Vice-President Carlos Mesa. On the 17th, Sanchez de Losada resigned, fleeing to Miami with his family and some of his ministers. That night Mesa was declared President in a special session of the Congress.

41   Mesa promised to review the hydrocarbon law and demand 50 per cent of oil transnationals' profits, instead of 18 per cent. He also promised to call a Constituent Assembly to 're-found Bolivia' and to organize a referendum to decide on gas policy. Thus the President took up the main claims of the people and opposition parties.

42   The so-called 'gas war' had left 74 dead and hundreds injured, mostly indigenous people. ■

PROFILE

ENVIRONMENT

A landlocked country with three geographic regions. 70 per cent of the population live in the cold, dry climate of the altiplano, an Andean highland plateau with an average altitude of 4,000 meters. This region holds the country's mineral resources: tin (second largest producer in the world), silver, zinc, lead and copper. The subtropical valleys *(yungas)* of the eastern slopes of the Andes form the country's main farming area, where coffee, citrics, cocoa, sugarcane, coca and bananas are grown. The tropical plains of the East and North, a region of jungles and grasslands, produce cattle, rice, corn, and sugarcane. The area is also rich in oil. Bolivia is made up of three drainage basins: Lake Titicaca (closed basin), the Amazon in the north and the Río de la Plata in the south.

SOCIETY

Peoples: 57 per cent of Bolivians are Quechua and Aymara. *Mestizos* and *Cholos* account for 25 per cent of the population. A minority of European descent has ruled the country since the Spanish conquest. The Tupí and Guaraní peoples live in the eastern forests. **Religions:** Mainly Catholic (95 per cent). Syncretism in indigenous communities. Protestant and Jewish minorities. Freedom of religion. **Languages:** Spanish, Quechua and Aymara (all official). More than half the population speaks native languages (including Guaraní); there are 39 ethnic-linguistic groups. **Main Political Parties:** the Free Bolivia Movement (MBL)/Nationalist Revolutionary Movement (MNR) of former President Gonzalo Sánchez de Lozada; the Movement towards Socialism (MAS) of the indigenous leader of the coca planters, Evo Morales; the New Republican Force (NRF) led by Manfred Reyes Villa; the Movement of Revolutionary Left (MIR) of former President Jaime Paz Zamora; The Nationalist Democratic Alliance (ADN), led by former dictator and President Hugo Banzer. **Main Social Organizations:** The Bolivian Workers' Confederation (COB) and the Sole Labor Union Confederation of Farm Workers of Bolivia (CSUTCB), mainly indigenous. Indigenous Confederation of the Eastern region, Chaco and Bolivian Amazon Area (CIDOB); the Guaraní People's Assembly (APG); the Aymara People Parliament (PPA); the Federation of Campesino Women; the Federation of Neighborhood Commissions; and the Bolivian Forum on Environment and Development (FOBOMADE).

THE STATE

Official Name: República de Bolivia. **Administrative Divisions:** 9 Departments. **Capital:** Sucre (212,000 people) is the constitutional capital, and seat of the judiciary. La Paz 1,477,000 people (2003) - including El Alto (766,100 people) which became a separate city in 1988 - functions as the seat of the Government. **Other Cities:** Santa Cruz de la Sierra 1,089,400 people; Cochabamba 558,500; Sucre 172,000 (2000). **Government:** Carlos Mesa Gisbert, President and Head of the Government since 17 October 2003. Bicameral legislature: Chamber of Deputies, made up of 130 members; Senate with 27 members. **National Holiday:** 6 August, Independence Day (1825). **Armed Forces:** 25,000 (1993). Other: 23,000 Police.

Bosnia-Herzegovina / Bosna i Hercegovina

Population:	4,208,630
Area:	51,130 km²
Capital:	Sarajevo
Currency:	Konvertibilna marka (KM)
Language:	Serb, Croat and Bosnian

The earliest inhabitants of what is now Bosnia-Herzegovina were Illyrians and Celts (see Table). The Roman Empire crossed the Adriatic Sea in the mid-2nd century BC, and created the province of Illyria, where the border between East and West was drawn according to the division of the Roman Empire. Slavs settled in the area in the 7th century AD, coming from present-day Polland and Ukraine, gradually absorbing Illyrians and Celts.

2   In the mid-12th century, the region came under the jurisdiction of the Hungarian archbishop of Kalocsa. The combined efforts of the papacy and of the Hungarians to impose their religious authority, gave rise to strong national resistance. Bosnia was a bastion of the Bogomils (or Cathari), one of southern Europe's main heretical movements. Neighboring Christians - both Orthodox Serbs and Catholic Croats - organized several crusades against this heresy.

3   Ban Prijezda founded the Kotromanic dynasty (1254-1395) under which Bosnia conquered the province of Hum (Herzegovina, took its name from the Duke (Herceg) Stejpan Vukcic, who ruled the southern area of the present republic until the arrival of the Turks). In 1377, Tvrtko crowned himself King of Serbia, Bosnia and the coastlands. The Turkish invasion of 1386 defeated the Serbs in Kosovo (1389), but Tvrtko carried out further conquests in the west, and in 1390 was crowned King of Rashka, Bosnia, Dalmatia, Croatia and the coastlands.

4   The Ottoman Empire conquered Constantinople in 1453 and occupied Serbia in 1459. The Pope called for a war against the Turks but this was not supported. Bosnia became a province of the Ottoman Empire in 1463. Hum resisted, but in 1482 the port of Novi (now Herzegnovi) fell, and Herzegovina too became an Ottoman province. Bosnian Bogomils converted to Islam. In addition to Catholic Slavs and Christian Orthodox Slavs, there were now Muslim Slavs. Muslims were the élite and Christians the *raia* (poor); relations between the three communities were strained, and religion became the decisive social factor.

5   The Turkish governor (Pasha) had his headquarters in Banja Luka, but later transferred them to Sarajevo. In 1580, Bosnia was divided into 8 *sanjaks* (sub-regions), under the jurisdiction of 48 hereditary Kapetans, who exercised a feudal power over their territories where the manufacture of wrought metals and weapons was developed. In the 16th and 17th centuries, Bosnia played an important role in the Turkish wars against Austria and Venice. In 1697, Prince Eugene of Savoy captured Sarajevo. By the Treaty of Karlowitz (1699) the Sava river (Bosnia's northern border), also became the northern boundary of the Ottoman Empire. Herzegovina and the part of Bosnia east of the Una river were ceded to Austria in 1718, and returned to Turkey in 1739.

6   In the 19th century, Bosnia's nobility resisted Turkish interference. In 1837, Herzegovina's regent declared independence. Uprisings became chronic, bringing Christians and Muslims together, despite their differences, against the bureaucracy and corruption of the Empire. In 1875, a local Herzegovinian conflict unleashed a rebellion, which spilled over into Bosnia. Austria, Russia and Germany tried unsuccessfully to mediate between Turkey and the rebels. The Sultan's promise to reduce taxes, grant religious freedom and install a provincial assembly was rejected.

7   By a secret agreement in 1877, Russia authorized Austria-Hungary to occupy Bosnia-Herzegovina, in exchange for its neutrality in Russia's upcoming war against Turkey. After the Russo-Turkish War (1877-1878), the Congress of Berlin disregarded Serbian wishes, and assigned Bosnia and Herzegovina to the Austro-Hungarian Empire (although nominally they continued to be under Turkish control). In 1878, Vienna put down armed resistance from Bosnia-Herzegovina with an army of 200,000 soldiers.

8   The revolution launched by the Young Turks in 1908 brought on a crisis within the Ottoman Empire. The Turkish Government asked Bosnia-Herzegovina to participate in the new parliament at Istanbul, which strengthened the nationalist feeling. Austria-Hungary ended that process by annexing the two provinces in 1908, with Russian consent. Vienna established a provincial assembly (Sabor), without representation in Vienna or Budapest. The 1910 Constitution was promoted by the Empire to consolidate social and religious differences by establishing three electoral colleges - Orthodox, Catholic and Muslim - each with a fixed number of seats in the Sabor.

9   The influence of the Mlada Bosna (Young Bosnia) movement and other revolutionary groups led the Empire's authorities to close Bosnia's Sabor, and dissolve several Serbian political groups. In 1914, the Archduke Franz Ferdinand (heir to Austria's crown) and his wife the Duchess of Hohenberg were assassinated in Sarajevo by a Bosnian Serb student. Austria declared war on Serbia and thus triggered World War I.

10   In 1915, emigrants in Peru founded the Yugoslav Committee (Yugoslav means 'southern Slavs'), which began an intense campaign in favor of independence and the unification of the 'Yugoslavs'. The kingdom of the Serbs, Croats and Slovenians was proclaimed on 1 December that year, and included Bosnia-Herzegovina. In 1919 the Yugoslav Communist Party was founded, and won 14 per cent of the parliamentary seats. It was banned in 1920. The country was renamed the Kingdom of Yugoslavia in 1929, following an authoritarian coup that persecuted communists, trade unionists, and opponents of Serb dominance.

11   The Nazis occupied Yugoslavia in 1941. Bosnia-Herzegovina was subjected to the puppet administration of Croatia. In the two provinces, Croat Ustashes (Fascists) massacred the Serbs. The continuing rivalry between Muslim, Serb and Croat degenerated into deep hostility. The Communists, led by Tito, organized a guerrilla resistance movement with the support of the allies. At the end of World War II the country remained a federation of republics, one of which was Bosnia-Herzegovina. The slogan of the Yugoslav federated socialists was 'Brotherhood and Unity', but ethnic confrontation was visible in the arts, and literature.

12   The federal system and Tito's leadership achieved a half-century of domestic peace. Development plans favored the poorer regions and diverse communities were successfully integrated. Following Tito's death in 1980, a collegial executive was established with representation from all the republics and a yearly rotation of the presidency among them. But instead of pacifying the rivalries between the federated entities, this mechanism seemed to exacerbate them.

13   After the fall of the Berlin Wall in 1990, the Yugoslav Communist League withdrew its monopoly over the political system. Political demagogues incited discontent, stirring up local and ethnic demands. That year, in the post-war period's first multi-party legislative elections, the Bosnian electorate chose candidates who were ethnic standard-bearers. The nationalist parties elected 73 Serbs and 44 Croats, while the candidates of the Democratic Reform Party (ex-Communist) and the liberal technocrats lost political ground.

14   The Muslims were represented by the Democratic Action Party (DAP). Their leader, Alija Izetbegovic, who held a doctorate in theology, was elected president of the republic. The Bosnian Croat and Muslim leadership sought to follow the example of Slovenia and Croatia in seceding from Yugoslavia, encouraged by Western Europe and fearful of the advance of Serbian nationalism. The Bosnian Serbs favored remaining within the Yugoslav federation. In 1991, Bosnia-Herzegovina's Sabor approved a declaration of independence and in 1992 called for a plebiscite on the issue of separation. Izetbegovic, in order to

Life expectancy	GNI per capita	Literacy	HIV prevalence rate

 Life expectancy
74.0 years
2000-2005

 GNI per capita
$1,270
2002

 Literacy
93% total adult rate
2000

HIV prevalence rate
0.1% of population 15-49 years old
2001

IN FOCUS

ENVIRONMENTAL CHALLENGES

Only half of the region's water supplies are considered safe; the Sava River being the most polluted of all. In addition, air pollution caused by metals plants in urban areas and other environmental problems are evident as a result of the widespread destruction of infrastructures during the 1992-1996 war. There are insufficient facilities for the final disposal of solid waste.

WOMEN'S RIGHTS

Women have been able to vote and be elected since 1949. In 2000, women held 29 per cent of the total seats in parliament; this fell to 12.3 per cent in 2003. In 2000, their representation in ministerial or equivalent positions was 6 per cent of the total.

In that year, women were 38 per cent of the labor force. In the period 1990-2000, interrupted by the civil war, the female labor force was divided approximately into 16 per cent in agriculture, 37 per cent in industry and 48 per cent in services.

Almost all pregnant women are given perinatal care*. The socialist system's institutions for maternal and child welfare are being steadily eroded, and while war and post-war international humanitarian aid decreases, assistance to women and children tends to diminish.

Lured by the promise of lucrative jobs in Western Europe, women and girls from Moldova, Ukraine and Romania instead found themselves trapped and sold as servants or forced into prostitution in Bosnia. Human Rights Watch denounced the corruption of government officers and the UN, after the 2000-2003 investigation which concluded that in 2003 there were still 2,000 victims of this trafficking, many of them sold for prices ranging from $700 to $2,300.

CHILDREN

In 2000*, 3.5 per cent of children suffered from low birth weight. That year, 4.1 per cent of children under 5 were moderately or severely underweight; 1 per cent were severely underweight, 6.3 per cent suffered severe and moderate weakness and 9.7 per cent were moderately or severely stunted.

Immunization rates for children have risen though they are not yet back at pre-war levels*.

There is some difference between official statistics and household surveys as to school enrolment/attendance levels. Marginalized groups of children, including Roma, returnees or children with disabilities, face difficulties of access to schooling. All children and young people cope with some traumatic experience relating to the war and post-war period. The 1 million landmines still scattered throughout the country in 2001 posed a serious danger for both children and adults, and especially for displaced people wanting to return to their homes. UNICEF assumes that the HIV/AIDS cases will increase among young people in the near future, given the trends of high-risk behavior (injecting drug use, sex trade and some sexual practices), since many people still do not perceive the virus as a threat.

MIGRANTS/REFUGEES

At the end of 2002, more than 530,000 Bosnians were still displaced as a result of the war. Some 368,000 were internally displaced, although this figure is hard to confirm, and the rest were refugees and asylum-seekers abroad. That year, more than 160,000 Bosnian refugees remained in Yugoslavia, Germany and Croatia and 37,000 refugees returned to the country during the year. The number of residents in foreign government-funded housing fell from 43 per cent from 2001, reaching 3,200 people. Some of those who returned were deported from Germany, Croatia and Switzerland.

In 2002, around 8,000 Bosnians filed asylum applications in 29 industrialized countries, down from 11,000 in 2001.

In 2002, Bosnia hosted 34,000 refugees, among them people from Yugoslavia and Croatia. Some 6,000 persons with temporary admission status in Bosnia asked for the extension of their permit. Less than 300 were resettled to other countries such as the US.

DEATH PENALTY

Still applies for exceptional crimes; it was abolished for common offenses in 1997.

*Latest data available in *The State of the World's Children* and *Childinfo* database, UNICEF, 2004.

maintain the unity and integrity of the republic, promised that Bosnia-Herzegovina would not become a Muslim state, and guaranteed the rights of all nationalities. During that year, conflict broke out when independence was ratified in the referendum by 99.4 per cent of the Muslims and Croats.

[15] In 1992, the EU and the US recognized the independence of Bosnia-Herzegovina. The Bosnian Republic was accepted as a member state in the Conference of Security and Co-operation in Europe, and joined the UN. At the same time, the Serb community proclaimed the independence of the 'Serb Republic of Bosnia-Herzegovina' in the areas under Serb control (Bosnian Krajina, with its center at Banja Luka). The conflict quickly extended throughout the entire region. Local Croat forces also controlled certain areas of the Republic; there were sporadic confrontations with Bosnian government troops. Finally, that year, Croatia and Bosnia signed a mutual recognition pact.

[16] In 1993, Serb troops killed Bosnian deputy prime minister, Hakija Turajlic, in Sarajevo. The UN decreed a cease-fire in that city: at that point, there were numerous reports on the existence of Serb concentration camps, as well as an 'ethnic cleansing' campaign (forced and violent expulsion and sometimes murder of members of rival ethnic groups). According to Amnesty International, thousands of civilians, as well as soldiers that had been captured or wounded, were deliberately executed and prisoners were submitted to torture. According to UN figures, a total of 40,000 women had been raped. Although atrocities were committed by all sides, the Serbs bore the major responsibility, while the Muslims were the main victims. The UN Protection Forces (UNPROFOR) sent in some 20,000 peacekeeping troops. The US refused to send troops to Bosnia, despite pressure from the UN and European countries. Several security zones were decreed in Tuzla, Zepa, Gorazde, Bihac and Sarajevo, which were not always observed, just as successive ceasefires were consistently violated.

[17] In 1993, Serb occupation of Bosanki Brod opened up a corridor between Serbia and Bosnian Krajina. Serbs controlled 70 per cent of the territory, due to their superior artillery and armored vehicles, as well as their control of the bridges over the Drina river - border between Serbia and Bosnia - which allowed them illegally to receive arms and other supplies from the Yugoslav Federation. On account of this support, the UN called for an economic blockade on the Federation, and an arms embargo aimed at Bosnians and Croats. The Muslims found themselves cornered in Sarajevo and a few other minor sites, receiving what little financial and moral support they could from a few Islamic countries and sporadic UN humanitarian aid flights, subject to the authorization of Serbian - Bosnians besiegers.

[18] During the same year, Serb President Slobodan Milosevic and his Croatian counterpart, Franjo Tudjman, announced the partition of Bosnia into three ethnic entities (Serb, Croatian and Muslim), within the framework of a federal state, coinciding with a peace proposal by the UN and the EU that the territory should be divided into three semi-autonomous provinces, controlled by each ethnic group. The Croats, faced with the partition of Bosnia, sought to gain the upper hand to negotiate from a position of strength and launched an offensive against Mostar, capital of Herzegovina. The UN Human Rights Commission reported that 10,000 Muslims had been held in Croatian concentration camps, suffering torture and summary executions.

[19] In the meantime, conditions in Sarajevo grew worse: there were epidemics, and no electricity, water or food. The 300,000 inhabitants managed to survive on minimal rations, while international aid agencies faced difficulties getting the supplies in. In 1994, the mediators (UN and EU) put forward a proposal which included the partition of Bosnia into three ethnically homogeneous republics: Serbs would receive 52 per cent, Muslims 30 per cent and Croatians 18 per cent. The Bosnian Government rejected the proposal since it called for the transfer of people from one sector to another and implied the legitimacy of 'ethnic cleansing'. The UN's Human Rights Commission for the former Yugoslavia criticized the creation of ethnic boundaries and defended a reform of the democratic system.

[20] In 1994, the US and Russia exerted growing pressure upon the Serbs to accept the proposal. Croatians and Muslims approved a federal agreement between the two communities: 51 per cent of the territory would remain among Bosnians and Croatians while Serbs would be in control of 49 per cent, without the need to divide Bosnia into three ethnically distinct states. With support from the EU, Washington and Moscow, the federal agreement was signed by presidents Franjo Tudjman of Croatia and Alija Izetbegovic of Bosnia, but the Serbs rejected it. Negotiations were hampered because Serb president Milosevic (who represented the Serbs diplomatically) stated he had no authority over the self-proclaimed Republic of Srpska.

[21] In 1995, the Bosnian-Serbs held several UN troops hostage and took

Under-5 mortality
18 per 1,000 live births
2002

 Malnutrition
4% under-5s
1995-2002

Debt service
19.1% exports of goods and services
2001

Maternal mortality
31 per 100,000 live births
2000

Bihac. The situation was radically changed by NATO's bombing of Bosnian-Serb positions in the siege of Sarajevo. Almost at the same time, Croatia expelled Serb-Croat forces from the eastern side of the country forcing their delegates to negotiate. Under US military pressure, the peace process launched in Dayton (Ohio, US) stipulated elections to be held in 1996, with the aim of promoting more tolerant leaders among each of the nationalities in conflict. The presence of American troops forced a peaceful settlement that was signed in Paris (1995) and froze the political situation.

[22] The Dayton Accords acknowledged two ethnically based mini-states (the Bosnian-Serb Republic - Srpska - and the Croatian-Muslim Federation) that resulted from the physical elimination or expulsion of ethnic minorities. The International Criminal Tribunal at the Hague convicted Radovan Karadzic, leader of the Srpska Republic and his military commander Ratko Mladic, for genocide. The Dayton peace accords banned the electoral participation of people accused of war crimes. In spite of being convicted and banned, neither was incarcerated, and they retained considerable influence in the republic's political life.

[23] Seventy-three per cent of voters took part in the general elections of 1996. Izetbegovic's DAP-Muslim Party won the majority of votes with 19 of the 42 parliamentary seats. Momcilo Krajisnik's Democratic Serbian Party (DSP) obtained nine seats with 24 per cent of votes, and Kresimir Zubak's Croat Democratic Union (CDU), gained 14 per cent of votes and eight seats. In 1997, the Croatian and Bosnian presidents met in Split to relaunch the Muslim-Croatian federation, pledging once again to facilitate the return of the refugees. Radovan Karadzic (Serb war leader involved in genocide and crimes against humanity) questioned the legislative elections, accusing Western representatives of having fixed the results in favor of the Muslim and Croatian parties.

[24] High Commissioner for the republic, Carlos Westendorp, imposed unification measures, like the creation of a common flag and national symbols for Bosnia-Herzegovina, which brought new confrontation. Each group maintained their own armed forces and the federation between Croats and Muslims was shaped as a combination of both groups and not a unified identity.

[25] The new currency, the mark, introduced in 1998, was widely accepted in the domestic market. It was not until 2001 that the privatization of companies and banks was accelerated, having been initiated two years earlier with a loan from the World Bank. In 1991, all the communist era payment offices had been closed. The country had depended on humanitarian aid from the international community for its reconstruction.

[26] The 2000 parliamentary elections gave the non-nationalists a slight majority, but the process of forming a new government was paralyzed by the power struggle amongst the nationalist parties. The international High Commissioner, Wolfgang Petritsch, sacked the Croat president in the rotating presidency, Ante Jelavic, accusing him of diminishing the Dayton accords by supporting the creation of a Croat mini state. In 2001, the World Bank and the IMF warned that they would grant no more loans until the crisis was resolved. Finally, that year a new, non-nationalist government took power.

[27] At the end of the war there had been 60,000 international peace-keepers, but by 2001 barely 18,000 were left. The US proposed the withdrawal of its 3,000 blue helmets, causing Petritsch to state in 2002 that Bosnia-Herzegovina was still far from being 'a viable state that can maintain itself alone'. According to Petritsch, a further three to four years were needed before the country could function independently, without an international administrator.

[28] The 2002 elections meant the return to power of the nationalist parties, which came to occupy the tripartite presidency. This return of the nationalists to key positions was mainly due to the poor performance of the pro-reform parties. European analysts suggested that being out of power for a decade had softened the line that had led them to the civil war.

[29] In 2003, Mirko Sarovic, Serb member of the presidency, resigned after being accused by a Western intelligence service of participating in the illegal sale of weapons to Iraq. There were also accusations of espionage against international officers. Borislav Paravac, of the DSP, became president in his place. During that year, the international High Representative, Paddy Ashdown (in office since 2002) abolished the Republika Srpska's Supreme Defense Council and removed some provisions of both the Federation of Bosnia-Herzegovina and Srpska that made any references to the entities having state power.

[30] In April 2003, Commander Naser Oric was arrested and charged at the Tribunal at The Hague with 'violations of the laws and customs of war', including murder, persecution, wanton destruction, and plunder against Serbs in Srebrenica between 1992-1995. The Tribunal decided not to make his indictment public.

[31] In August, a ceremony was held at the Mostar Bridge, known as the bridge of hope and reconciliation, and the keystone was laid to establish the country's post-war reconstruction. The bridge (a Unesco world heritage site), one of the oldest and most beautiful monuments destroyed in Bosnia by Croat forces in 1993, had survived numerous conflicts within the region, including both World Wars. The Old Bridge, which is of no strategic or military importance, has turned with the passing of centuries into a symbol of tolerance and diversity among the communities of Mostar and Bosnia. ∎

PROFILE

ENVIRONMENT

Bosnia-Herzegovina has a 20-kilometer coastline on the Adriatic Sea. In the north and west it is bordered by Croatia; in the southeast by Montenegro and in the east by Serbia. The major part of the country lies in the Dinaric Alps, with elevations of around 4,265 meters, making overland communication difficult. The country is drained by the Sava and Neretva rivers and their tributaries. The territory takes its name from the Bosna River, a tributary of the Sava. Half of the country's area is covered by forests (on account of which there is an important wood industry), and another part consists of arable lands, mainly in the Sava and Drina river valleys. The main crops are grains, vegetables and grapes; there is also livestock rearing. There is a wealth of mineral resources, including coal, iron, copper and manganese. Because of air pollution, respiratory ailments are very common in urban areas. Barely half of the region's water supplies are considered safe, the Sava River being the most polluted of all. There are multiple environmental problems due to the conflict of 1992-1996.

SOCIETY

Peoples: From a common Slav origin, ethnic differences are historo-religious: for example Muslim Slavs (Bosnian), 49.2 per cent; Orthodox Serbs, 31.3; Catholic Croats, 17.3. Serbs are a majority in north-east Bosnia, with the center in Banja Luka; and the Croats in Herzegovina in the west, centered on Mostar. Ethnic distinctions are less clear in other regions. In the capital, Sarajevo, there are Muslims (majority), Croats and Serbs. Until 1992 there was a 1,200 strong Jewish community. There is also a large Roma (gypsy) minority.
Religions: The majority is Muslim. Other: Christian Orthodox and Roman Catholic.
Languages: Serb, Croat and Bosnian (all official) (very similar and previously known as Serbo-Croat).
Main Political Parties: in the Government: Democratic Action Party (DAP - Muslim); Social Democratic Party (SDP - multiethnic); Democratic Serbian Party; Croat Democratic Community (CDC); Party for Bosnia Herzegovina (moderate Bosnian - Muslim).
Main Social Organizations: Unions are currently in the process of being reorganized as are other organizations; some environmental groups operated even during the conflict.

THE STATE

Official Name: Republika Bosna I Hercegovina.
Administrative Divisions: 50 Districts. **Capital:** Sarajevo 579,000 people (2003), reduced to less than 50,000 in September 1995.
Other Cities: Banja Luka 175,700 people; Tuzla 111,900; Mostar 72,000 (2000).
Government: There are two entities, each with their own government and national assembly: the Bosnia-Herzegovina Federation (the Croat and Muslim zones) and the Srpska Republic (mostly Serbians) although the city of Brcko is autonomous. At state level, BiH has a 2 chamber parliament. The current BiH President is Borislav Paravac (since April 2003), sharing this role on a rotating basis with Sulejman Tihic and Dragan Covic (all three from different ethnic groups). Prime Minister: Adnan Terzic, since December 2002.
National Holiday: 1 March, Independence Day (1992).
Armed Forces: approximately 60,000. 120,000 reserves (1993). Due to the conflict the United Nations Protection Force (UNPROFOR) deployed several thousand troops. As part of the peace agreements two separate armies are kept in the nation, one for the Federation and one of the Serb Republic. There are more than 150,000 troops from the Federal Yugoslav Army and Serb nationalist militias operating in the country.

Botswana / Botswana

Population:	1,800,577
Area:	581,730 km²
Capital:	Gaborone
Currency:	Pula
Language:	Setswana

The first inhabitants of what is now Botswana were probably the ancestors of the San (also known as Bushmen), hunters and gatherers who today inhabit the semi-arid plains of southwestern Botswana, and the Khoikhoi from the north. Bantu-speaking populations reached the region in the first century BC. The ancestors of the Tswana, currently the country's majority group, settled between the 11th and 12th centuries in the plains of the Vaal River (in what is now South Africa). The Tswanas were divided among eight powerful clans. Clan rivalry stood in the way of establishing a kingdom like those of other nations in southern Africa.

2   The history of Botswana - the 'fatal crossroads' located in the heart of southern Africa - is the history of the Kalahari Desert, a passage between the northeastern inhabited savanna and the southeastern plains. The pre-colonial movement facilitated settlement for British, Dutch and Portuguese colonists since the 18th century. The British tried to unite the continent from south to noth (from South Africa to Egypt), taking the 'missionaries' road'. The Portuguese wanted to unite the colonies of Angola and Mozambique. The region became a real focal point for the different colonial strategic interests, and for the clash between these interests and the Tswana who had inhabited those areas since the 17th century.

3   In 1840, Boer colonists of Dutch origin (also known as Afrikaners), fleeing from Cape Town to escape the British, were settled in eastern Botswana. The Boers (farmers) fought with the Tswanas for the scant fertile lands, thus provoking clashes between Tswanas and the Zulus who had been driven out from southern Africa by settlers. In 1895, three Tswana kings traveled to London, seeking support against the Boers and against the German expansion in Southwest Africa (that became Namibia). Later, Botswana became a British protectorate, known as Bechuanaland. The kings had to allow, in exchange for protection, the construction of a railway between their lands and Zimbabwe (Southern Rhodesia) by the British South Africa Company. British trusteeship prevented political absorption by South Africa but paved the way for the Afrikaners' economic supremacy.

4   In spite of its large semi-arid area, Botswana became one of southern Africa's major cattle and meat exporters. At the beginning of the 20th century, 97 per cent of the population lived in rural areas, every family owned at least a couple of cows, and the richest had oxen to plough their fields. In 1966, when Botswana gained independence, the urban population reached 15 per cent and almost 40 per cent of the

IN FOCUS

ENVIRONMENTAL CHALLENGES
The spread of cattle-raising has meant a reduction in the areas originally occupied by wild species. Intensive cattle-raising rapidly depletes the soil, bringing about desertification and erosion. Limited water resources are available for human consumption.

WOMEN'S RIGHTS
Women have been able to vote and stand for office since 1966. Between 1995 and 2000, women held 9 per cent of seats in Parliament and their representation in ministerial or equivalent positions increased from 6 to 14 per cent.

The national illiteracy rate for women over 15 is 20.2 per cent; the illiteracy rate for young women aged 15 to 24 is much lower at 7.9 per cent*.

In 2000, 40 per cent of pregnant women receiving prenatal care were HIV positive.

CHILDREN
Since independence, there has been better access to basic services (water, primary education, health) and wider vaccination coverage against common infant

diseases. However, Botswana has the highest HIV/AIDS infection rate in the world (39 per cent of adults are HIV positive). Among children, the greatest impact is seen in girls, who are at least 4 times more susceptible to early infection than boys. The pandemic has left some 80,000 orphans under 15 years old, most of them orphaned in 2001. More than 25,000 receive food aid or other kind of support from the Government. If the present trend of the epidemic continues, the traditional caring mechanism for orphan minors will soon be unable to cope, since 9,500 babies will become infected from their mothers each year if preventive measures are not taken and anti-retroviral medication not made available.

In 2001, 35 per cent of pediatric cases admitted in urban hospitals were HIV/AIDS-related, as were almost 70 per cent of infant deaths in hospitals. In 1999, over 37,000 children under 5 were HIV-positive, mainly through mother-to-child transmission. Other causes of under 5 mortality are intestinal, respiratory and neonatal infections.

Although access to primary education has been improved, only 9 per cent of preschool children have

access to educational services, since such facilities are few in number, mainly in urban areas and fee-paying.

INDIGENOUS PEOPLES/ ETHNIC MINORITIES
Some of the San - Bushmen - are among the world's last nomadic hunter-gatherers. They speak a variety of Khoisan languages and are not related to the majority Tswanas. San people are concentrated in the central region of Kalahari Desert. Since 1997, the Government has been resettling them in reserves - where there are few basic sanitation, water and health services - and does not fulfil its promises of improving their living conditions. San people are the poorest group with the highest unemployment rates. More than half live below the poverty line. They face restrictions in social services, as well as social exclusion. As a result, alcoholism is widespread and there is a high rate of arrests; sentences are harsher than for other ethnic groups. Their traditional chiefs are denied recognition. Since 1989, they have begun to organize and publicize their main grievances: lack of access to traditional lands, recognition for their groups and leaders, more say in government,

protection and promotion of their culture and language.

MIGRANTS/REFUGEES
By the end of 2002, the country had hosted some 4,000 refugees and asylum-seekers, most of them from Angola and Namibia, from where they had fled during the 1998 insurrection in the Caprivi Strip. Some Barakwena refugees had difficulty in adapting to sedentary life in camps, since they were nomadic. With help from UNHCR, some of them returned to Namibia in 2002 when violence diminished.

However, the bulk of immigrants are from Zimbabwe: in 2004 the figure was put at 130,000 by Botswana's Department of Immigration.

UNHCR took steps to try and prevent the spread of HIV since at least one-fourth of all pregnant refugee women were HIV-positive in 2002.

DEATH PENALTY
It is currently applied, even for common crimes.

*Latest data available in *The State of the World's Children* and *Childinfo* database, UNICEF, 2004.

| | Life expectancy
39.7 years
2000-2005 | | GNI per capita
$2,980
2002 | | Literacy
77% total adult rate
2000 | 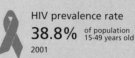HIV prevalence rate
38.8% of population 15-49 years old
2001 |

rural population had no cattle. Due to the economic concentration, the Afrikaners dominated agriculture and controlled 60 per cent of meat exports.

[5] The struggle for independence had become entangled with the wedding of Seretse Khama, a leader of the major Bamagwato chiefdom who went to England to study law. He married Ruth Williams, a British woman. This upset both the British and the Afrikaners who prevented Seretse from returning home. He withstood every pressure including offers of money from the British and, firmly supported by his people, he retained leadership of the country's main ethnic group. He did not come back until 1956. Nine years later, his Botswana Democratic Party (BDP) polled 80 per cent of the vote in general elections.

[6] At independence, Seretse was elected as first president of the country. In 1967, he was knighted by the British. The BDP carried out a conciliatory policy towards Europeans, who controlled 80 per cent of the economy. Besides, Botswana was highly dependent upon South Africa; almost all its imports came through there, and 60 per cent of its exports were purchased by South Africans. Nevertheless, in the political arena, Seretse maintained his distance from apartheid South Africa, and supported the region's anti-racist movements. Botswana was one of the 'frontline nations' fighting apartheid (see South Africa), and a member of the SADCC (see International Organizations), a grouping of the nine southern African countries seeking to end the economic dependence on South Africa.

[7] Seretse Khama died of cancer in 1980 and was succeeded by the Vice-President, Quett Masire, who studied economics at Oxford. Strong pressures were exerted on Masire by revolutionary socialist groups to limit the concentration of arable land in European hands and to increase the area allotted to cooperatives. The rural poor accused large landowners of overgrazing, causing a rapid deterioration in the quality of the land. A movement also arose demanding the nationalization of rich diamond, iron, copper and nickel deposits exploited by South African companies.

[8] Between 1978 and 1988, Botswana became the third largest diamond producer in the world, behind Australia and the DR Congo (then Zaire). The national economy grew at a record rate of 12 per cent a year. Despite this, three-fifths of the population lived on subsistence crops or 'non-institutionalized' activities, that is, off the statistical record, beyond fiscal control and the commercial circuit.

[9] In 1985 there were repeated flare-ups along the frontier with South Africa due to the Botswana Government's support for the African National Congress (ANC) anti-apartheid campaign. In 1987, South Africa applied pressure blocking the roads to Botswana's capital, Gaborone.

[10] In 1989, Masire was re-elected President, and the Government had to confront successive economic and political problems, fundamentally due to a fall in the international demand for diamonds. Increased unemployment and opposition criticism brought government corruption into the open, forcing several ministers to resign. In 1991, three of the seven opposition parties created the People's Progressive Front (PPF) in opposition to the ruling BDP. That same year, the country suffered the biggest strikes since independence. Public sector workers demanded a 154 per cent pay increase and the Government sacked 18,000 state employees. Despite having maintained economic growth for decades, according to some studies, Botswana has some of the most severe social inequalities in the world.

[11] In 1992, unemployment reached 25 per cent. In an attempt to increase employment and lift the flagging fortunes of the BDP, the Government initiated an incentive policy for non-mining industries. Severe drought forced the authorities to declare a state of emergency. Public spending was drastically reduced, and more than a third of the workers employed directly or indirectly by the State were laid off. Despite the economic and social problems, the BDP kept its majority in the 1994 parliamentary elections, while losing nine seats.

[12] The country - today the second most important diamond exporter after Russia - has always depended on its mineral exports. Partly as a result of its diamond wealth, the economy flourished and, according to the World Bank (WB), it had the fastest-growing economy in the world during the period 1965-1996, when per capita income grew at 9.2 per cent. During those years, tourism became the second largest income earner. The rapid growth led to increasing disparities between rich and poor people.

[13] The Government, while still keeping the budget in the black, failed to solve the most pressing problems of a population lacking, amongst other things, decent healthcare. In 1998, 30 per cent of Botswana's adults were HIV-positive (the most recent figure is now 39 per cent - one in 3 people). The disease has orphaned more than 80,000 children and has dramatically reduced life expectancy. Following action taken by South Africa and Kenya to import generic - cheaper - versions of HIV/AIDS drugs, corporations agreed to reduce prices on medicines.

[14] In 1998, Botswana attempted for the second time buy Belgian weapons. This prompted German intervention to prevent the purchase. In 1996, Germany blocked Botswana's attempts to buy arms from the Netherlands. Despite these setbacks, the BDP Government appears determined to acquire such weapons.

[15] The civil war in Namibia in the Caprivi Strip, a corridor 460 kilometers by 30 kilometers, affected Botswana's relations with its neighbor. In 1999, almost 2,000 residents of this area - many of them separatists - fled to Botswana. The decision to grant them asylum worsened relations with Windhoek. Both countries were also involved in a border dispute over an island in the Chobe river. During that same year, the BDP was again the winner in the elections, taking 33 of the 40 seats open to direct vote. Its candidate, Festus Gontebanye Mogae, was reconfirmed in the presidency he had held since Masire stood down in 1998.

[16] In 2002, the Government relocated the last 2,200 San people into settlements, having first deprived them of water and food, removing them from lands they had occupied for 30,000 years. From 1985 until now, 50,000 San have been confined in 23 camps to force them to give up their nomadic lifestyle. In 2003, there was conflict between Gaborone and the organization Survival International (SI), which was opposed to the mistreatment and relocation of the San and Basarwa people. The Kalahari zone, the San ancestral lands, is rich in diamonds. Under Botswana's legislation indigenous communities may not engage in mining activities nor possess minerals, despite the fact that they reside in mining areas.

[17] In 2003, after many years of conflict among different ethnic minorities, the Government promised to remove three discriminatory clauses from the constitution by the end of the year. According to President Mogae, the aim is to promote unity and cultural diversity, thereby building a better country.

[18] In 2004 the Department of Immigration estimated there were around 130,000 illegal Zimbabwean immigrants in Botswana who fled Robert Mugabe's terror tactics. ∎

PROFILE

ENVIRONMENT

An extensive and sparsely populated country, Botswana is divided into three large regions. In the center and southwest, the Kalahari basin is a desert steppe where grazing is only possible in certain seasons. The Okavango River basin in the northeast has a tropical climate suitable for agriculture. Eighty per cent of the population lives within a strip in the east, stretching along the railroad. Traditionally pastoral, the country is beginning to exploit its mineral resources (manganese, copper, nickel and diamonds).

SOCIETY

Peoples: Tswana make up 90 per cent of the population; Minorities include: Kalanga and Basarwa. **Religions:** Some are Catholic and Protestant, some follow African religions; sometimes the distinction between these and Christian practices is blurred. There are also Muslim and Hindu minorities. **Languages:** Setswana (national) and English (official). There are diverse local languages, among them Kalanga, Mbukushu and Herero. **Main Political Parties:** The Botswana Democratic Party (BDP), founded by Seretse Khama in 1961; the Botswana National Front (BNF) was founded in 1978 as a coalition of leftist and center-left parties; Botswana Congress Party (BCP). The latest attempts towards opposition unity were: PPF (People Progressive Front) in 1990; UDF (United Democratic Front) in 1994 and lately BAM (Botswana Alliance Movement) in 1999. **Main Social Organizations:** 5 of the 13 local trade unions form the Botswana Federation of Trade Unions, founded in 1976. BOCONGO, Botswana's NGO Council, includes diverse groups as the Forum on Sustainable Agriculture, First People in the Kalahari; Task Force on Indigenous Minorities in the South of Africa.

THE STATE

Official Name: Republic of Botswana.
Administrative Divisions: 4 Districts. **Capital:** Gaborone 199,000 people (2003). **Other Cities:** Francistown 101,700 people; Selebi-Phikwe 47,200 (2000). **Government:** Festus Gontebanye Mogae, President since 1998, confirmed in October 1999 elections. The single chamber National Assembly has 47 members. **National Holiday:** 30 September, Independence Day (1966). **Armed Forces:** 7,500 (1997). **Other:** 1,000 Transport Police.

Brazil / Brasil

Population:	182,797,708
Area:	8,547,400 km²
Capital:	Brasilia
Currency:	Real
Language:	Portuguese

The huge territories which were to become today's Brazil were initially inhabited by small bands belonging mainly to the Tupi Guarani, Carib and Arawak linguistic groups. The indigenous peoples from the Amazon basin fished and farmed while the inhabitants of the dry savanna lived by hunting and gathering. When the first Portuguese ships arrived at the coast of what today is Bahia de Todos os Santos in 1500, more than two million people inhabited those lands.

2   Under the Tordesillas Treaty (1494) which divided the non-European world between Spain and Portugal, the latter was assured its rights over these lands. Sailing towards India, Pedro Alvarez Cabral landed at Bahia de todos os Santos in 1500 and christened the area the Island of Vera Cruz. Between 1501 and 1502 a naval expedition headed by Gaspar de Lemos charted the region between Rio Grande and the Río de la Plata; Cabral's error (he thought he had reached an island) was thus corrected and the region came to be known by the Europeans as Santa Cruz Land.

3   For the Portuguese, these lands were far less lucrative than Africa and India. The strip of coast did not reveal major deposits of precious metals and was inhabited by semi-settled indigenous peoples, the Tupi, related to the Guaraní, whom the Spanish would later find in Paraguay. At first the Portuguese crown only valued those lands as places to trade slaves or barter metals and trifles with the Indians in exchange for brazilwood. The pulp from this tree, used to make a fire-colored dye, would give the country its final name - 'brasa' in Portuguese means embers.

4   Wood industry did not lead to the creation of major cities or other signs of European development in the region, in spite of being quite significant. Although the Indians were used to felling trees in order to clear the forests, they lacked a commercial tradition in wood and could not cut trees on a large scale. The Portuguese supplied axes and saws and trading agents had the timber ready for shipment. Trading posts were often established on islands on the Atlantic ocean and, shortly after, the first Portuguese settlements were also established on these islands. Only a few Portuguese exiles inhabited the continent by that time, together with the indigenous communities. On several occasions, these exiles helped other mainland Portuguese make fruitful alliances with the natives.

5   Around 1530, the Portuguese were forced to increase their involvement with Brazil. Other European traders, particularly the French, started to arrive. Commerce with India had slumped and the achievements of Spanish conquistadors in other parts of the continent represented both an incentive and a threat. In order to expel the French and establish its authority, the Portuguese crown sent an expedition along with some settlers. In 1532, the first official Portuguese settlement, São Vicente, was established on an island close to São Paulo.

6   The Spanish expanded their empire through the conquest of lands under the strict control of the Crown. The Portuguese however, due to their maritime commercial tradition, divided the Brazilian coast into captaincies which were awarded to donatarios, prominent individuals who supposedly had the wealth required to occupy and exploit the lands. The captaincies were hereditary, with extensive judicial and administrative powers, although several were never occupied and others survived for a brief time. Four of them became permanent settlements and two (Pernambuco to the north and São Vicente to the south) would turn out to be viable and lucrative.

7   Just like in the Spanish colonial outposts, the first Portuguese settlements had to be fortified to defend them from Indian attacks. Procurement of supplies was difficult and for a while the Portuguese obtained most of their food by trading with the indigenous peoples and became used to eat cassava instead of wheat, which was hard to grow in most of the region. Two agricultural systems developed, the *rozas* or farms and the large *fazendas*, given over to exports, mainly of sugarcane. In spite of favorable conditions, the fazendas took a long time to prosper, due to the lack of capital and labor. Besides, agriculture and the discipline imposed on the plantations were foreign to the local peoples, whom the Portuguese forced to toil in exchange for European products. The settlers decided to obtain slave workers either through expeditions which directly hunted for Indians or through other Indians acting as intermediaries.

8   During the second half of the 16th century, Indians have already been decimated by European illnesses (influenza, smallpox, measles) or had fled to other areas. African slaves were then imported to grow sugar and the trade grew to the point that, between the 16th and 19th century, it is estimated that from three to four million Africans arrived in Brazil In 1548, as a result of pressures similar to those of 1530, the Crown opted for a direct representation in Brazil and appointed a general governor, who with 1,000 men established the capital of the country in Bahia (northeastern coast). A bishopric was created in 1551. Only 50 years after the first contact, Brazil had reached the same degree of European institutionalization which characterized the Spanish territories.

9   The Jesuits started to arrive by that time, and soon became the strongest branch of the Catholic Church, unlike in Spanish America, where they arrived much later than other orders. The Jesuits learnt the Guaraní language to convert Indians to Catholicism and established villages very similar to the missions in the Spanish areas. The main contacts between Indians and Europeans (war, trade, slavery and missions) were the same as in the Spanish areas. Due to these contacts, Guaraní became the language used in the 16th century for all kinds of exchanges.

10   Brazil carried out major expansions towards the west of the Tordesillas line, whose meridian was drawn up 370 leagues to the west of Cape Verde. The expansion reached the slopes of the Andes mountain range and, from north to south, from the Amazon to the Río de la Plata. In the north, the movement led by the Jesuits established several missions along the Amazon. In the northeast, cattle farmers from the sugar areas of Pernambuco and Bahia ventured to the heart of the continent, looking for new grazing lands and reached today's Piauí, Goiás and Maranhao regions.

11   The westward march was led by the paulistas (São Paulo settlers) who in the search for Indian slaves, gold and precious stones, set up major expeditions to the interior, known as bandeiras. The incorporation of Portugal into the Spanish kingdom in 1580 facilitated the paulistas' incursions, since internal borders were broken and the Tordesillas division became ineffective. The bandeiras took the paulistas to Peru's mining regions and even to Bogotá (Colombia), also exploring the region of Mato Grosso. To the south, they attacked local *reducciones* (missions), particularly those of Guaira, where the Guaraní people lived already relatively immune to disease and were accustomed to collective agricultural work. The Indians and Jesuits who were protecting them, offered resistance but human hunts were so devastating that the missions were forced to move further and further south until they finally were located in the 'Seven Towns' (today's Rio Grande state).

Life expectancy
68.1 years
2000-2005

GNI per capita
$2,850
2002

Literacy
87% total adult rate
2000

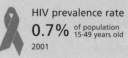
HIV prevalence rate
0.7% of population 15-49 years old
2001

[12] Apart from the paulistas who penetrated the dense forests, thousands of Africans sought refuge there, fleeing from the coastal plantations. Africans, indigenous Americans and their mixed descendants joined forces in constant war against the colonial military expeditions, founding villages known by the African terms *quilombo* or *mokambo*, the most famous of which were at Palmares (1630-1695), in northeastern Brazil, where the legendary Zumbi led the struggle. The Brazilian anti-racist movement still commemorates the date of Zumbi's death in battle, 20 November, as Black Consciousness Day.

[13] Brazil found itself involved in a war of independence between the Netherlands and Spain.

Flanders and the Netherlands had been 'inherited' by the Spanish Crown. Between 1630 and 1654, the Dutch reasserted their control over Pernambuco after a failed attempt to conquer Bahia, which was repulsed by the joint efforts of native Americans, Africans and Portuguese. The separation of Spain and Portugal that followed could not reinstate the Tordesillas Treaty since events had surpassed the shifting of colonial borders. In 1696, a bandeirantes expedition struck the first gold in what is now Minas Gerais. Gold mining peaked in the 18th century. The viceregal capital was transferred from Salvador to Rio de Janeiro in 1763 mostly due to the impact of these mines on the Brazilian economy.

[14] The local ruling class began to benefit from an expanding export economy and soon expressed a growing desire to dispense with the Portuguese role as intermediaries in their trade with Europe. The first moves towards independence came in the late 18th century and were rapidly crushed by the colonial power. Brazil's main freedom figure, Ensign Tiradentes, was executed in 1792 for his leading role in the Minas Conspiracy of 1792.

[15] When Napoleon invaded the Iberian peninsula in 1808, Portuguese King Dom João VI had to transfer his court to Brazil, making the country semi-independent. Portugal ceased to be an intermediary and Brazil then dealt directly with its main

customer, Britain. The Brazilian merchants prospered at the expense of other sectors linked to the Portuguese monopoly. The 1821 Oporto revolution in Portugal was an attempt to reinstate the old colonial system based on monopoly. When the King returned to Lisbon, the Brazilian merchants - determined to secure their gains - declared independence with British blessing. Brazil became an empire and Pedro I, the prince-regent, became its emperor.

[16] The following decade was one of the most turbulent in Brazilian history. From 1831 to 1835, a regency unsuccessfully tried to put an end to the civil war in the provinces and to the army's insubordination. In 1834, the Constitution was amended to decentralize the government, with the creation of provincial assemblies with considerable local powers, and to choose a regent for a period of four years. In 1835, Diego Antonio Feijóo, a priest, was elected as regent and fought for two year against the break-up in the revolts in Rio Grande do Sul, known as *Guerra dos Farrapos*, 1835-1845 (War of the Ragged Ones). Feijóo was forced to resign in 1837, being replaced by Pedro Araújo Lima. Impatient with the regency, Brazilians hoped to find in an Emperor the figurehead that would unite them. In 1840, Pedro de Alcántara was declared of age and enthroned with the name of Pedro II.

[17] During the Empire that lasted from 1822 to 1889, Brazil consolidated its national unity and extended its borders over the areas settled by bandeirantes (17th and 18th centuries). The territorial expansion included the annexation of the Cisplatine Province (now Uruguay), the war of the Triple Alliance against Paraguay, in which Brazil annexed 90,000 square kilometers of Paraguayan territory; and, towards the end of the century, the annexation of Bolivia's Acre territory.

[18] Under the rule of Pedro II, the population grew from 4 to 14 million, but the economy continued to depend on large estates and the export of tropical agricultural products, mainly coffee. Slavery was not abolished until 1888, which accelerated the fall of the monarchy, but brought little change in the social and political conditions of blacks, who as illiterate people, were denied the right to vote and therefore political freedom.

[19] By the end of the 19th century, the gap between urban and rural areas was widening. The urban middle class, the military

IN FOCUS

ENVIRONMENTAL CHALLENGES
The Amazon region is being devastated by the unrestrained felling of trees, which has destroyed the habitat of many plant and animal species, as well as that of indigenous peoples. There are serious pollution problems in cities like Rio de Janeiro and São Paulo. The main causes for the pollution of important aquiferous sources are mining activities, degradation of wetlands and oil leakages.

WOMEN'S RIGHTS
In 2003, when the present government came into power, women held 8.2 per cent of seats in the Chamber of Deputies and 5.9 per cent in the Federal Senate (more than a 40 per cent increase over the previous administration). In addition, 4 ministers were women (one of them being Afro-Brazilian).

In 2000*, 80 per cent of women over 15 were literate (5 per cent less than adult men).

Maternal mortality continues to be a problem, although 88 per cent of deliveries take place in hospital*. Pre-natal care is often of low quality and there is unequal access for different segments of society and regions of the country.

CHILDREN
In 2001, 54 million Brazilians were living below the poverty line. The infant mortality rate has fallen to 30 per 1,000 live births within the last decade*, but remains disproportionate to national production capacity and available technology. Brazil

is, together with Mexico, the country of the Americas with the most street children. There are many young women - especially from the poor Northeast - who migrate to the big southern cities looking for domestic work, but in countless cases they end up in prostitution or pornograhy.

According to the National Secretary for Human Rights, between May and October 2003 more than 3,300 calls were registered on their helpline reporting cases of abuse, sexual exploitation and ill-treatment of children. Those reports mainly came from the state of Rio Grande do Sul, Rio de Janeiro and São Paulo.

INDIGENOUS PEOPLES/ ETHNIC MINORITIES
The 200+ indigenous groups comprise about 350,000-500,000 people (from 0.2 per cent to 0.3 per cent of the country's population). They are mostly located in the Amazon and central regions (small communities, missions, national parks - there are four - and reserves appointed by the Government). There are groups of farmers, hunter-gatherers and others which are semi-nomadic. The Amazon indigenous groups are highly dependent on the land and river to develop their way of life, but they are threatened by the gold mining, agriculture and timber and oil industries. The exploitation of these natural riches has caused the decline of the indigenous population, partly as a result of confrontations with non-indigenous people, some of whom consider them 'less than complete people', and also because of the introduction of new diseases in their habitat. During Fernando Henrique Cardoso's administration,

the privatization of part of their lands was encouraged, threatening their way of life. The organization of the different groups is mainly local, because of the remoteness and distances between them. The National Indian Foundation, FUNAI, is the only state-based organization devoted to the study of indigenous peoples; it estimates that the Guarani, Yanomami, Kaingang, Terena and Kaiwa groups are the largest within the country.

MIGRANTS/REFUGEES
At the end of 2000, 1,887,893 Brazilians were living in foreign countries, including Germany, Switzerland and Italy. Although Brazil is one of the world's largest economies, the income distribution is far from equitable which makes many people seek better opportunities in other countries.

The policy on refugees in Brazil has changed frequently but since the early 1990s, the country has specific legislation. In 2002, practical programs arising from the Refugee Act began to be implemented, giving priority initially to Afghan asylum-seekers by settling them in Brazilian cities, organized in cooperation between the National Commission for Refugees and the UNHCR.

DEATH PENALTY
The last execution was in 1855; in 1979 it was abolished for common crimes.

*Latest data available in *The State of the World's Children* and *Childinfo* database, UNICEF, 2004.

Under-5 mortality	Poverty	Debt service	Maternal mortality
36 per 1,000 live births 2002	**9.9%** of population living on less than $1 per day 1998	**75.4%** exports of goods and services 2001	**260** per 100,000 live births 2000

and coffee growers pressed for the country's modernization. For them, the monarchy was too closely linked to the old systems of production and to cattle-raising landowners. A republic was the preferred modernization model for these three groups. In 1889, the army backed a conspiracy of modernists. Pedro II abdicated and was exiled in Europe. The abolition of slavery, together with the fall of the Empire, brought about social, political and economic changes which accelerated modernization, though not without causing political, social and religious disorders.

20   The establishment of republican institutions was difficult. Prudente de Morais was elected first civilian President in 1894. The Federal Republican Party was founded in 1893, but the Navy rebelled both that year and the following. From 1893 to 1895, Brazil suffered a federalist rebellion in Rio Grande do Sul. From 1896 to 1897, the Canudos war, in which a religious community was wiped out by the republic's troops, took place in the northeastern provinces. This war was due to a clash between the interior - poor, illiterate and desperate - and the coast - literate, with a developed economy and seeking modernization.

21   Until 1920, uprisings, outbreaks of authoritarianism and fights among the regional oligarchies were frequent. Neither electoral justice nor the secret ballot was yet instituted and dissatisfaction with election results was widespread. Elections were rigged since the electoral rolls often included deceased voters. The period since the declaration of the Republic up to 1930 was known as the Old Republic.

22   Coffee was consolidated as the major export. Between 1914 and 1918, World War I brought an economic boom to Brazil, since the country was one of the main suppliers of commodities to the powers at war. However. between 1920 and 1930, coffee prices tumbled as international competition reduced sales and, in 1929, due to that year's world slump, 29 million bags of coffee were left unsold. In 1930 a coup resulted in the appointment of Getulio Vargas as president. The Revolution of 1930 marked the end of the landowners' predominance, already weakened by the crisis that had destroyed the coffee industry. Vargas introduced the 'import substitution' model and gave priority to national industrial development, especially in iron

and steel during World War II. Vargas held power from 1937 to 1945 as dictator of the New State.

23   Fearing Vargas would attempt to retain power, the military forced him to resign in 1945. General Eurico Gaspar Dutra won the presidential election in that year and Vargas was elected to a seat in the Senate. In reaction against Vargas, the constitution promulgated in 1946 sought to prevent the rise of another all-powerful president. The three branches of government were separated, ensuring Congress of its independence and freedom in the election of its members. The Constitution set restrictions to prevent abusive federal intervention in the internal affairs of the states.

24   In 1950 Vargas was elected again as constitutional president. Nationalism and reformist defense of workers' rights, *trabalhismo* (laborism), the name of his movement, were the two outstanding features of his government. In 1953 the state oil monopoly was established with the creation of Petrobras and social security laws were passed. Vargas committed suicide in 1954 leaving a letter accusing 'dark forces' (referring to imperialism and its local accomplices) of blocking his efforts to govern according to popular and national aspirations.

25   By means of a development policy, Juscelino Kubitschek's administration (1956-61) admitted transnationals to the Brazilian market, granting them exceptional privileges. Brasilia city was built during his term in office, to mark a new era in the country's economic development. In 1960, the federal capital, previously at Rio de Janeiro, was transferred there. Kubitschek's successor, Janio Quadros, initiated some changes in foreign policy but resigned in unclear circumstances, seven months after taking office.

26   In 1961, Vice-President João Goulart, the Labor Party leader and Getulio Vargas' political heir, assumed the presidency. High-ranking military officers opposed his appointment but he was backed by a civilian/military movement which wanted a legal government, led by Leonel Brizola, governor of Rio Grande do Sul. A compromise parliamentary solution was adopted, with Tancredo Neves becoming Prime Minister. In 1963 a national referendum reinstated the presidential system. Goulart attempted to introduce measures like the agrarian reform and legislation to regulate profit transfers abroad by foreign companies. A US-backed military coup deposed him in 1964.

27   The new government passed Institutional Act No. 1, which repealed the 1946 liberal constitution, allowing the revocation of parliamentary mandates and the suspension of political rights. A string of arrests all over the country forced major political leaders such as João Goulart, Leonel Brizola, Miguel Arraes and later even Juscelino Kubitschek into exile or to fight underground. The military junta appointed General Humberto de Alencar Castello Branco head of government for the remainder of the constitutional period, but his mandate was later extended until 1967. In some of the 1965 state elections, opposition candidates won in Rio de Janeiro and Minas Gerais. The military retaliated with Institutional Act No. 2, stating that the President would henceforth be appointed by an electoral college and banning existing political parties. A two-party system was created formed by the majority and pro-government National Renewal Alliance (ARENA), and the Party of the Brazilian Democratic Movement (PMDB), from the opposition but without possibilities of reaching power.

28   During 1967, a new Constitution came into effect and General Arthur da Costa e Silva became President. In 1968, to confront growing electoral support for the popular opposition, Institutional Act No. 5 was passed, granting full autocratic powers to the military regime. In 1969, Costa e Silva was replaced by a Military Junta that remained in power for a month, when another army general, Emilio Garrastazú Médici, former head of the National Information Services (SNI), became President. His administration was marked by extreme repression of both the legal and illegal opposition, and by an economic policy which fed middle class consumerism.

29   In 1974, General Ernesto Geisel was appointed President, putting an end to the state oil monopoly, signing a controversial nuclear agreement with West Germany and granting further prerogatives to foreign investors. Its arms industry placed Brazil fifth among the world's main arms exporters. Under the Geisel administration there was a gradual relaxation of political controls, which allowed the democratic process to evolve. Between 1974 and 1978, despite media censorship, the PMDB achieved significant victories at the polls. At the end of his mandate, Geisel delivered the reins of government to General João Baptista Figueiredo (former SNI head). Figueiredo came to power

in 1979, announcing that he intended to complete the softening of political restrictions. A month later, a strike by 180,000 metalworkers in Sao Paulo led by Luis Inácio 'Lula' da Silva was settled without violence, as a result of negotiations between the Labor Ministry and the Union. By the end of that year, the Congress passed a bill granting a far broader amnesty to political opponents than the Executive had originally intended; political prisoners were released and exiles began to return.

30   In the economic-financial arena, the after-effects of the monetary policies applied by successive military governments were felt during the Figueiredo administration. Foreign debt spiraled and in the early 1980s, Brazil became an early exporter rather than importer of capital in its efforts to find funds to pay off the interest on its $100 billion debt. In 1985, according to official data there were 6 million unemployed·and 13 million under-employed, out of a population of more than 130 million, of which over 50 per cent lived below the poverty line and outside the formal economy, in cities alone. Ministry of Labor officials stated that 'not even 7 per cent growth per year for 20 years, would be enough to improve these peoples' living conditions'.

31   The opposition's electoral victory in 1983 reflected enormous popular discontent. The central government held only 12 states while the opposition won 10, including the economically decisive states of São Paulo, Rio de Janeiro and Minas Gerais which accounted for 59 per cent of the population and 75 per cent of the country's GDP. Tancredo Neves, governor of Minas Gerais, was the chief co-ordinator of the opposition front. A popular campaign for direct elections in 1984 failed, but the opposition won the Electoral College due to divisions within the ruling party. Neves was elected President and José Sarney, who had been formerly president of the Government party, became Vice President. Neves announced plans for a new social order: the New Republic.

32   The day before his inauguration, Neves was hospitalized and rushed into surgery. Sarney was sworn in as interim president and came to power after Neves died in 1985, legalizing the Communist Party and left-wing organizations, which had been banned for 20-40 years. Democratization was strengthened: direct election for President of the Republic and mayors of state capitals were

 Malnutrition
6% under-5s
1995-2002

 Water source
87% of population using improved drinking water sources
2000

Doctors
158 per 100,000 people
1990-2002

 Primary school
97% net enrolment rate
2000

approved, a national assembly was convened for 1987 to draft a new constitution and illiterate people were granted the right to vote.

[33] In 1986 Sarney declared a moratorium on the foreign debt and launched the Cruzado Plan that aimed at fighting inflation. The plan produced impressive short-term results: a boom in consumption and economic growth. This startling prosperity coincided with the 1987 parliamentary elections which the PMDB won by a landslide. The new Congress drafted a new constitution that would inaugurate the return to democracy. It set Sarney's term at five years, after considerable pressure from the Executive to ignore the groups who followed Neves and wanted to reduce the term to four years.

[34] The Cruzado Plan could not be maintained without fighting the excessive speculation and halting pressure from the financial sector. After the Parliamentary election, the price freeze came to an end and inflation leapt to a monthly rate in double figures. The planned agrarian reform was gradually reduced.

[35] In 1988, landowners from the Acre region murdered Chico Mendes, leader of the *seringueiro* (rubber tappers) movement and the Amazonian indigenous peoples. Mendes had organized an original *empates* struggle (linking arms to stop trees being felled) to prevent the clearing of the forests, and proposed the creation of reserves, to guarantee their right to live and work in the forest without destroying it.

[36] The first direct presidential elections in 29 years were held in 1989. Nearly 80 million people voted and the final round was fought between conservative candidate Fernando Collor de Mello and Workers' Party (PT) leader, Luiz Inacio 'Lula' da Silva. Collor de Mello, a young politician who had begun his career under the military regime, won the second round with 42.75 per cent to his opponent's 37.86 per cent of the vote. Collor adopted the neo-liberal model in economics, with the privatization of state enterprises and the reduction of tariff barriers for foreign products, but he failed to control inflation, and neither held off recession nor unemployment.

[37] Besides this complex economic setting, the Government faced a critical social situation and the escalation of violence. In 1991, more than 350 street children were murdered in Rio de Janeiro. The parliamentary commission that investigated these murders estimated that over 5,000 children

had been killed in this way within three years. The same commission reported that the persecution of homeless children - 7 million according to estimates of the Brazilian Center for Childhood and Adolescence - was carried out by paramilitary groups financed by shop owners.

[38] The accelerated destruction of the tropical forest in order to exploit its mining and timber potential and to turn it into grassland or mining areas, kept devastating indigenous peoples: apart from suffering epidemics, the degradation or loss of natural resources, pollution and a systematic fall in their standard of living, they are being murdered and subject to violence by miners and by the police.

[39] In 1991, thousands of people from the Landless Movement of Brazil (MST) staged a march in the state of Rio Grande do Sul, where there were 150,000 families of landless farmers alongside nine million hectares of land not in production. The protesters demanded settlements to work and that the 4,700 million cruzeiros earmarked for agrarian reform should be spent, of which only 800 million had actually been used. Figures provided by the Pastoral Commission of the Earth, in 1992 showed that there were 15,042 rural slaves - triple the number recorded the previous year. According to data gathered by the Federal Bureau of Statistics, nearly four million people living in rural areas worked under conditions of virtual slavery. Collor's administration had zoned 20 million hectares as new land for indigenous peoples, which alleviated but did not solve their situation.

[40] In 1992, a Parliamentary Investigating Commission studied government corruption, which took the form of influence-peddling in exchange for deposits made to the President's personal accounts. Demonstrations against corruption and the discovery of evidence implicating other government figures in these schemes led all the political parties to vote for the President's impeachment. Congress voted to relieve Collor of his duties, so that he could be put on trial. Vice-President Itamar Franco became President. In 1992, Collor was found guilty by the Senate of 'criminal responsibility' and his presidential mandate was removed and his political rights suspended until the year 2000. Franco officially assumed the presidency.

[41] The Citizens' Action Against Hunger and for Life group, founded in 1993 by Herbert de Souza, organized tens of

thousands of committees throughout the country to collect and distribute food and obtain more jobs. Two million people, mostly women, priests and trade unions joined this grassroots movement. In 1994, over four million families had received food aid.

[42] In 1993, Economy Minister Cardoso presented the Plan Real, an economic stabilization project which ended index-linking and created a new currency, the Real, in 1994. The success of this anti-inflationary policy rapidly made Cardoso the most popular candidate for the October elections. In the first round he beat the previous favorite Luis Ignacio 'Lula' da Silva, of the PT. Cardoso began the privatization of state companies, including part of Petrobras and the telecommunications sector, but economic recession led to the rise of unemployment, urban labor conflicts, crime and land seizures by poor peasants.

[43] In 1995, the President announced a government Multi-Year Plan with investments amounting to $153.39 billion, mainly focused on economic infrastructure. According to statistics revealed during that year, 10 per cent of the population received 48 per cent of the income - four times the amount earned by the poor half of the country. World Bank figures showed that 43 per cent of fertile land belonged to 0.83 per cent of landowners in 1997. These figures placed Brazil among countries with extreme social inequality.

[44] During that year, Parliament passed a constitutional reform that permitted presidential re-election, and the Government issued a decree which guaranteed indigenous peoples the exclusive use of 23 plots of land covering 8.4 million hectares, some 10 per cent of Brazilian territory. The marches and seizures by the MST were supported by the Vatican's Pontifical Council of Justice and Peace in 1998, in the document 'For better land distribution: the land reform challenge'.

[45] In 1998, Cardoso was re-elected President, with 53.1 per cent of the vote in the first round, 20 percentage points above Lula da Silva. In 1999, former president Itamar Franco, Governor of Minas Gerais, declared a moratorium on debt with the Federal Government. The Government freed the real against the dollar (a measure that was denied until the day before its implementation) resulting in a 10 per cent devaluation of the real. The president of the Central Bank resigned 'so that investors can

regain confidence' but the real continued its slide with devaluation reaching 50 per cent in a month. The real crisis hit consumption, industry (in need of imported resources) and Brazil's relations with its Mercosur partners, but benefited the country's export sector.

[46] In 2000, to 'counter-commemorate' the fifth centennial of the Europeans' arrival in Brazil, 2,000 Indians met at a beach in northeast Bahia, carrying protest banners. Of the five million inhabitants there when the Portuguese arrived, only 350,000 remained. The 1,000 groups that existed at the time of colonial contact were reduced to 210 (of which 50 have stayed beyond contact). The average life expectancy among Brazilian Indians is 42.6 years (the country average is 67).

[47] In order to reduce the inequality in land ownership, the Government suspended the property titles of some 1,900 landowners, since they were not able to justify the origin or legality of their property titles. Some 62 million hectares of land (roughly the size of Central America) was unlawfully held. The accumulation of lands with fake documents is a widespread and centuries-old practice in Brazil. It is estimated that a third of all landowners have built their estates with false papers. Nowadays, 90 per cent of all arable lands are in the hands of 20 per cent of the population, while 40 per cent of the poor population holds barely 1 per cent of land fit for agriculture.

[48] In 2001 Cardoso closed two government development agencies, which were accused of corruption involving more than $1 billion. Federal police discovered that projects promoted by these agencies, to develop the Amazon and poor areas in the northeast, were no more than façades to embezzle money. Both the Senate chairman Jader Barbalho and his wife were investigated.

[49] In 2001, José Nilson Pereira da Silva and Juliano Filipini Sabino were sentenced to 21 years in prison for the death of Edison Neris da Silva, a gay man who was beaten to death in early 2000 by a group of skinheads in São Paulo. The trial and sentence were considered landmark rulings by human rights and gay groups, since it was the first time a sexual discrimination crime was sentenced in Brazil. According to Bahia's Grupo Gay, 299 homosexuals were murdered in Brazil between 1999 and 2000; 30 per cent of the victims were transvestites and 3 per cent were lesbians. Two thirds of the murders

External debt	Imports (millions)	Exports (millions)	Received Aid
$350 per capita 2001	$27,315 good and services 2002	$30,694 good and services 2002	$2 per capita 2002

were committed in northeastern Brazil.

50   During that same year, the Government, as part of its AIDS prevention program, hired a producer of pornographic films, Sexy Videos, to show movies in which the actors wore condoms. The films had a special message about AIDS prevention which was shown at the beginning; this then became compulsory for all adult films produced within the country. The AIDS program includes lessons in school where teenagers are taught how to put on a condom using a clay model. According to the organization Médecins sans Frontières (MSF), AIDS-related deaths in Brazil fell more than 60 per cent. The HIV and AIDS program in Brazil is renowned worldwide for its success: the State delivers free treatment to 90,000 patients at a cost of $5,000 dollars per year (less than half of what it would cost to assist one patient in the US).

51   Free access to the AIDS drugs-cocktail treatment is the main basis of the program. A 1996 law states that, if foreign firms do not make their drugs locally, they will lose their patent in Brazil after a three-year period. The law states that in situations of 'public interest', the local industry can break the patents. Currently, Brazil manufactures 8 out of the 12 drugs that are part of the drug-cocktail received freely by patients at state clinics. Those opposing the program argued that poorer patients might not be able to follow the cocktail's complicated instructions. The Government solved the problem by putting labels with suns, moons and drawings of food on each medication.

52   In Brazil, the distribution of of wealth is highly uneven. In 2001, the average income per person among whites was 2.5 times that of black people, while 69 per cent of Brazil's poor people are black. The African descendants are 45.3 per cent of the total population. Unemployment amounted to 11 per cent among blacks and 7.5 per cent among whites. Only 2 per cent of blacks are university educated, compared to 11 per cent of whites.

53   In 2002, with the title 'Towards a Globalization of the World Social Forum (WSF)', the second meeting of the WSF was held in Porto Alegre, thus institutionalizing this global assembly which had been launched a year earlier in that same city. The WSF, which is held around the same time as the World Economic Forum, was attended by 5,000 organizations to analyze, share ideas, debate and define parameters and

alternatives in the anti-globalization struggle.

54   In 2002, some 500 activists from the Landless Movement (MST) invaded the estate of President Cardoso's children some 700 kilometers southeast of Brasilia, in order to force the Government to free lands for redistribution in the region. The general coordinator of the MST, João Pedro Stédile, stressed the invasion was an 'extreme measure taken by landless workers due to a lack of solution to their demands'. The main demand, presented to the Government before, was the delivery of lands to some 200 farmer families together with their property titles and credit for production in the state of Minas Gerais.

55   Given the predicted triumph of the left in the 2002 elections and the financial instability of the region, the dollar began to rise in response to pressure from the financial sectors of the market. To keep the financial market stable, Cardoso asked the International Monetary Fund for a loan of $30,000 million.

56   During that year, at his fourth attempt to win the presidency, Lula da Silva triumphed over José Serra, the candidate of the party in power, and led Brazil's left to government. That victory, with an overwhelming majority in the second round of elections, was helped by the alliance of the Workers Party with conservative elements from center and right, in an attempt to allay the market's fears.

57   The Workers' Party committed its administration to complying with the repayment schedules agreed with multilateral credit organizations. In spite of the many economic and political conditions, Lula came into government backed by 52 million votes and promised to strengthen Brazil's economic independence, supporting the common strategies of the Southern Cone Common Market and applying a gradual economic redistribution policy that would reduce the extreme inequality that has prevailed for decades.

58   In March 2003, the Landless Movement (MST) began a new series of occupation of estates, in order to accelerate agrarian reform. That same year, the launching of a rocket in Alcantara caused an explosion which killed 21 people. That same year, the International Monetary Fund and President 'Lula' agreed on a new loan for Brazil for the following year, which according to the Government, was requested as a precaution in the event of future economic turbulence. The IMF also

PROFILE

ENVIRONMENT

There are five major regions in Brazil. The Amazon Basin, in the North, is the largest tropical rainforest in the world. It consists of lowlands covered with rainforest and rivers. The Carajás mountain range contains one of the world's largest mineral reserves, rich in iron, manganese, copper, nickel and bauxite. The economy is mainly extractive. The northeastern sertao consists of rocky plateaus with a semi-arid climate and scrub vegetation. Raising cattle is the main economic activity. The more humid coastal strip, situated on the 'Serra do mar' (Coastal Sierra), has numerous sugarcane and cocoa plantations. In the southeast, the terrain consists of huge plateaus bordered in the east by the Serra do Mar mountain range. The main crops are coffee, cotton, corn and sugarcane. The southern plateau, with sub-tropical climate, is the country's main agricultural region, where coffee, soybeans, corn and wheat are grown. In the far south, on the Rio Grande do Sul plains, cattle raising is the main economic activity. Finally, the mid-west region is made up of vast plains where cattle-raising predominates.

SOCIETY

Peoples: Brazilians come from the ethnic and cultural integration of indigenous people (mainly Guaraní), African slaves and European (mostly Portuguese) immigrants. Arab and Japanese minorities have also settled in the Rio-São Paulo area. There are also many Indian peoples. Contrary to what is commonly admitted, racial discrimination does exist although the 1988 Constitution includes racism as a crime.
Religion: Most are baptized Catholic; but there is considerable merging into syncretic Afro-Brazilian cults (macumba, candomblé and umbanda). **Language:** Portuguese is the official and predominant language. Many Indian languages are spoken (ie Bariwa and Guajajára). **Main Political Parties:** Party of the Liberal Front, led by Jorge Bornhausen; Party of the Brazil Social-Democracy (PSDB), of Fernando Henrique Cardoso; Party of the Brazilian Democratic Movement (PMDB), led by Luis Henrique da Silveira; Workers' Party (PT), headed by Rui Falcao; Brazilian Labor Party (PTB); Communist Party of Brazil.
Main Social Organizations: Workers are grouped together primarily in the Consolidated Union of Workers (CUT), the General Confederation of Workers (CGT) and the Labor Union Force. Many labor unions do not belong to any of these, preferring to remain independent. Landless Movement of Brazil (MST), an association of workers without land whose agenda is agrarian reform in rural areas, and land for the construction of housing in urban areas. National Union of Indigenous Peoples (UNI), an association of Brazil's different indigenous groups. Pastoral Commission of the Earth (CPT) and Indigenous Missionary Council (CIMI), pastoral groups of the Catholic Church involved in social action in these areas. Defense Network of the Human Race (REDEH), an eco-feminist organization. 'Torture No More', state groups committed to the defense of human rights.

THE STATE

Official Name: República Federativa do Brasil.
Administrative Divisions: 26 States, 1 Federal District.
Capital: Brasilia 3,099,000 people (2003). Other Cities: São Paulo 17,800,000 people; Rio de Janeiro 10,600,000; Belo Horizonte 4,310,000; Porto Alegre 3,576,500; Recife 3,377,600.
Government: Luis Inacio (Lula) da Silva, President since 2003. Bicameral legislature: The National Congress has two chambers: the Chamber of Deputies has 513 members, and the Federal Senate has 81 members. **National Holiday:** 7 September, Independence Day (1822). **Armed Forces:** 295,000 troops (1996). Other: 243,000 Public Security Forces.

extended Brazil's debt repayment deadlines to 2005 and 2006.

59   In 2003, the Brazilian Senate discussed a bill to outlaw the carrying of guns in public by civilians; the same bill would tighten rules on gun permits and create a national firearms register, with strict penalties for owning an unregistered gun. A referendum will be held in 2005 on whether to ban gun sales outright. About 40,000 people are shot each year in Brazil, mainly in urban areas, giving the country one of the worst murder rates in the world. ∎

Brunei / Brunei

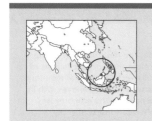

Population:	374,242
Area:	5,770 km²
Capital:	Bandar Seri Begawan
Currency:	Brunei dollar
Language:	Malay

The ancient history of Brunei is not well documented, although there is information that its inhabitants were trading with and paying tribute to China in the 6th century AD. Later, it came under Hindu influence through allegiance to the Majapahit kingdom in Java. From the 13th century, Brunei was under the Islamic empire that covered most of the island of Borneo, from which it derives its name. Although the European presence - Portuguese, Spanish and Dutch - became constant in the region from the 16th century onwards, it was only in the early 19th century that the colonial powers decided to occupy the large island. The Dutch advanced from the south, while Sultan Bolkiah (1473-1521), turned to the British in an attempt to preserve independence.

[2] In 1841, as payment for help in quelling the 1839-1840 rebellion, the Sultan had to turn the province of Sarawak over to James Brooke, who became a European Rajah over a Malayan state. In 1846 the British annexed the strategic island of Labuan, and in following years paved the way for the secession of the province of Sabah. In 1888, the British consolidated their position and established separate protectorates over Brunei, Sarawak and Sabah.

[3] Following World War II, despite Britain's efforts, the island began the decolonization process. An agreement signed with the incumbent Rajah Brooke in 1946 made Sarawak and Sabah into British colonies while Kalimantan (former Dutch Borneo) gained independence in 1954 as part of Indonesia.

[4] All that was left of the British protectorate was the Sultanate of Brunei, reduced to a tiny enclave between two Malaysian provinces, scarcely 40 km from the border with

IN FOCUS

ENVIRONMENTAL CHALLENGES
Brunei is one of the world's main exporters of liquid gas, production of which threatens the environment in various ways. In drought periods, fires in the Indonesian forests result in heavy smoke or haze cover.

WOMEN'S RIGHTS
The participation of women (and men) in politics is restricted by the Sultan's or his counsellor's decisions. Whatever participation there is takes place within the framework of an interim regime which is renewed monthly. Women made up 47 per cent of the total population in 1999.

In 2000, they were 36 per cent of the workforce. Since then, there has been an increase in employment for women, with more variety in their jobs (traditionally, they only did domestic work). During that year, illiteracy for women over 15 reached 12 per cent. There were 93 literate women for every 100 men. Since 1999, there was also an increase in the number of women attending university; women now make up almost two-thirds of university registration. In July 1999, a Married Women's Law came into effect, improving the rights of non-Muslim women over maintenance, property and domestic violence. In the same year, the Islamic Family Law was also amended to improve Muslim women's rights in marriage and divorce.

CHILDREN
In 2001, there were 34,000 children under 5 years old and 124,000 under 18. During the three previous decades, all indicators relating to child welfare (including under-5 mortality, education, health and maternal care) had improved, mirroring the country's growth in prosperity from its energy indsutry.

Women married to foreigners or bearing children by foreign fathers cannot pass citizenship to their children, even when such children are born in Brunei. This has resulted in a population of 5,000 or so stateless children who can live in Brunei and have travel documents, but who may not enjoy the full privileges of citizenship, including the right to own land.

INDIGENOUS PEOPLES/ ETHNIC MINORITIES
Most of the population is Malay and includes Kedayan, Tutong, Belait, Bisaya, Dusun and Murut - groups that in 2000 made up 67 per cent of the population. Other indigenous groups like Iban, Dayak and Kelabit are 5.9 per cent (19,600 people); 11.6 per cent of the population belongs to other non-specified racial groups.

MIGRANTS/REFUGEES
The economy is dependent on the oil industry and historically has used migrant labor from Southeast Asia. In 1986, immigrants were already 32 per cent of the total workforce. Two years later, in the private sector alone, the figure was 71 per cent. In 2000, it was estimated that migrant labor would constitute more than 35 per cent of the total workforce.

DEATH PENALTY
The death penalty is in force for ordinary crimes but the last execution was in 1957.

Life expectancy
76.3 years
2000-2005

GNI per capita
$24,100
2002

Literacy
92% total adult rate
2000

Indonesia. In 1929, the transnational Shell discovered oil deposits in the area. In the following decades, drilling for oil and natural gas began, reaching production rates of 175,000 barrels a day.

⁵ In 1962, Sultan Omar Ali Saiffudin accepted a proposal from Malaysian Premier Abdul Rahman to join the Federation of Malaysia, which at the time joined Sabah and Sarawak to Singapore and the provinces of the Malayan peninsula. The Brunei People's Party, (Rakyat) which held 16 seats in the 33-member Legislative Council, opposed the move and pressed for the creation of a unified state comprising Northern Borneo, Sarawak and Sabah, but excluding peninsular Malaya.

⁶ During that year, a mass uprising broke out, staged by the Rakyat, backed by the Barisan Sosialis (Socialist Party) of Singapore, with support from the anticolonialist Sukarno regime in Indonesia. The rebels opposed integration to the Federation of Malaysia, demanding participation in administration and the end of the autocratic regime. The rebellion was rapidly stifled, the People's Party outlawed and the leaders arrested or forced into exile. Finally, in spite of ethnic, historical, and cultural ties with Malaya, Sultan Omar decided to keep out of the Federation. He was not satisfied with arrangements for power-sharing with the other Malayan rulers and least of all with Federation hopes of a share in his territory's oil resources.

⁷ In 1976, with Malaysian prompting and UN support, the renegotiation of the anachronistic colonial statute was taken into consideration, when the newly-elected Malaysian Prime Minister Datuk Hussain Onn promised to respect Brunei's independence. Full independence from the UK became effective on 1 January 1984. Power was formally transferred on that date, but celebrations were postponed until 23 February 1985, so that foreign guests could attend.

⁸ One month after independence, Hassanal Bokiah, son of Sultan Omar, who had abdicated in his favor in 1967, dissolved the Legislative Council and went on to govern by decree. From that time, the main sources of tension were the power struggle within the ruling family and the presence of foreigners in all the key positions of public office, the economy and the army. Problems on the domestic front included poor basic education and the issue of minority groups, especially the Chinese. In spite of progressive legislation, including a student transport allowance and free accommodation, the illiteracy rate kept climbing (in 1982, 45 per cent of the population was illiterate), posing a serious obstacle to filling civil service posts with Brunei nationals.

⁹ Brunei obtained its independence in particularly favorable conditions for a Third World country. It had: a relatively small population, an annual per capita income of $20,000, low unemployment, a generous social security system and considerable foreign exchange reserves ($14 billion in 1984). However, 20 per cent of the population was living below the poverty line and, 90 per cent of consumer goods, including food, were imported, which made the cost of living extremely high.

¹⁰ The Sultan however was aware that the country depended on a non-renewable resource, and food imports. Consequently, with a view to achieving self-sufficiency in food production, he attempted to diversify the economy and promote a new land-owning class. Only 10 per cent of the arable land was cultivated, and small farmers, especially rubber-tree growers, tended to emigrate to the city.

¹¹ Economically, Brunei depended upon the complex interplay of transnational interests. The Government's partnership in exploiting natural gas reserves with Brunei Shell Petroleum Co. and Mitsubishi, a shipping contract with Royal Dutch Shell and oil field concessions to Woods Petroleum and Sunray Borneo, introduced powerful new parties into the process of national decision-making. In 1985, the Government created an Energy Control Board to supervise the activities of the Brunei Shell Petroleum Company, a company funded equally by the Government and Shell.

¹² In 1987, it was reported that a request from Colonel Oliver North, of President Reagan's administration in the US, for 'non-lethal' aid to the Nicaraguan contras resulted in the Sultan of Brunei depositing a $10 million donation in a Swiss bank account.

¹³ In 1991, Sultan Hassanal Bolkiah freed six political prisoners who had been detained after the failed 1962 revolt. The release was ascribed to political pressure by the British Government. This same year Brunei signed a contract for almost $150 million with the United Kingdom in order to modernize its army.

¹⁴ In 1992, Brunei joined the Non-Aligned Movement, together with Vietnam and India. Together with other members of ASEAN - Indonesia, Singapore, Thailand, Malaysia and the Philippines - it signed an agreement to create the first integrated market in Asia in 2007. This project stipulates the creation of 'growth triangles' - association between some ASEAN members to deregulate trade in certain economic sectors, allowing the overall liberalization planned for 2007.

¹⁵ In 1994, Brunei created - with the Philippines, Malaysia and Indonesia - a sub-regional market to intensify trade in tourism, fishing, and transport by sea and air. In 1995, the country joined the World Bank (WB) and the IMF. Negotiations with southeast Asian leaders were intensified following the regional stock market crisis in 1997, in order to co-ordinate policies to stabilize the regional economy and establish a recovery strategy. In the negotiations, the possibility was discussed of using local currencies instead of the US dollar for trade transactions within the area.

¹⁶ In 1998, uncontrollable fires in the Indonesian part of the island of Borneo caused dense smoke clouds over Brunei, affecting daily life in the Sultanate. The smoke clouds spread to several other nations of the region, affecting tourism.

¹⁷ That same year, the Sultan named his eldest son, Al-Muhtadee Billah, as successor to the oldest Islamic dynasty in the region - in existence for over six centuries. The announcement was made in the midst of the worst economic crisis since independence. Construction and the export sectors began a slow recovery during 1999. The Government announced plans to train a large part of the workforce in a period of five years, with the aim of diversifying the economy and developing other sectors, apart from tourism.

¹⁸ In 2000, the authorities indicted the Sultan's younger brother, Prince Jefri, for embezzling public funds during his terms as minister of Finance and president of the State Investment Agency, where he served until 1998. Jefri had been removed and forced to declare bankruptcy of his private company, to which he had transferred large sums of government funds during his ten years in office. A year after the trial, an auction was held in which some 10,000 of the prince's belongings were sold.

¹⁹ During the ASEAN summit in Brunei in 2001, the leaders agreed to cooperate in the US-led war against terrorism. They also postponed the launch date for the Asian Free Trade Area (AFTA), to be set for some time between 2006 and 2010.

²⁰ In February 2003, Brunei and Zambia established diplomatic relations. In March, the National Petroleum Company signed and agreement with a consortium of three foreign companies, TotalFinaElf Deep Offshore Borneo BV, BHP Billiton, and Amerada Hess.

²¹ Brunei boasts fine jewelry, ornaments and objects made of silver and brass. Brass is used to make household gongs, ceremonial cannons and ornaments. The jewelry and ornaments, found in most homes, depict verses from the Qu'ran, animals and other cultural references. ∎

PROFILE

ENVIRONMENT
Brunei comprises two tracts of land located on the northwestern coast of Borneo, in the Indonesian Archipelago. It has a tropical, rainy climate slightly tempered by the sea. Rubber is tapped in the dense forests. There are major petroleum deposits along the coast. The country is one of the world's main exporters of liquid gas.

SOCIETY
Peoples: Malay 67 per cent; Chinese 15 per cent; indigenous 6.0 per cent; Indian, European and other. **Religions:** Islam is the official religion. Muslims, 67 per cent; Buddhists 12.8 per cent; and Christians 10 per cent. **Languages:** Bahasa Malay (official), Chinese, English, local languages. **Main Political Parties:** were banned in 1988. There had been five political organizations: Brunei National Democratic Party (BNDP), founded in 1985 - first political party in Brunei; Brunei National United Party (BNUP), formed in 1986 by dissidents of the BNDP; Brunei People's Party (BPP), whose leaders are in exile; The Popular Independence Front, (inactive); People's National United Party, (inactive). The only authorized party is Brunei Solidarity National Party.

THE STATE
Official Name: Negara Brunei Darussalam.
Administrative Divisions: 4 districts. **Capital:** Bandar Seri Begawan 61,000 people (2003). **Other Cities:** Kuala Belait 26,600 people; Seria 23,000; Tutong 16,300 (2000). **Government:** Hassanal Bolkiah Muizzaddin Waddaulah, Sultan since 1967. He is also Prime Minister, Minister of Finance and the Interior, assisted by five Councils: religious, private, ministerial, legislative and of succession. The Legislative Council is made up of 20 members and has only an advisory role. **National Holiday:** 1 January, Independence Day (1984); 15 July, the Sultan's birthday.
Armed Forces: 4,900 (1995). Others: Gurkha Reserve Unit: 2,300; Royal Brunei Police: 1,750.

Bulgaria / Balgarija

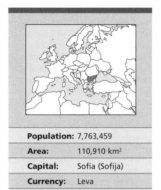

Population:	7,763,459
Area:	110,910 km²
Capital:	Sofia (Sofija)
Currency:	Leva
Language:	Bulgarian

Evidence of human habitation in the Bulgarian area dates from the Middle Paleolithic period (100,000 to 40,000 BC). The first agricultural communities appeared in the Neolithic Period (7,000 to 3,000 BC). Thracian peoples - ethnically Turks - arrived from Central Asia around 3,500 BC, settled there and developed their culture, the traces of which remain in their monuments devoted to horse-worship and acting. Thanks to their aptitude for combat, the Thracians resisted several Macedonian and Persian attacks as well as the Roman Empire for 150 years, which finally managed to subdue them in the first years of our era. In Roman times Bulgaria was divided between the provinces of Moesia and Thrace and was crossed by the main land route from the west to the Middle East.

[2] The Bulgarians came to the region towards the end of the 5th century, among the peoples that followed the devastating Mongolian invasion, led by Attila. They were fierce warriors who lived by warfare and plunder. They first settled temporarily on the steppes north of the Black Sea and northeast of the Danube.

[3] Towards the end of the 6th century, the region was occupied by Slav immigrants coming from the east, who spread across the area between the Danube and the Aegean Sea. That land was deserted after the Goths (Germanic), the Huns (barbaric people who came from Upper Asia during the 5th century; they built a powerful state in the Danube area, survived the Roman Empire and disappeared after it fell) and the Avars (nomadic warriors from Central Asia) passed by. During the 7th century, the Avars forced the Bulgarians across the Danube and subdued the Slavs.

[4] In the year 681, after the Bulgarians won several battles for territory - Moesia was under the control of the Byzantine Empire - Emperor Constantine IV formally recognized the State of Bulgaria.

[5] When the Patriarch of Byzantium recognized the independence of the Bulgarian Church in the year 864, Bulgaria's political autonomy was finally consolidated. This achievement favored the cultural assimilation of Slavs and Bulgarians, who developed an original identity, as seen in the creation of the Slav alphabet and the establishment of the official language in 863. Literature and arts flourished during that period and several schools and universities were opened.

[6] Under Simeon (893-927), the Bulgarian State extended its domain as far as the Adriatic, subduing the Serbs, and becoming the most powerful kingdom of Eastern Europe.

[7] Bulgaria's power declined after Simeon's death. Internal disputes among the nobility, the opposition of the peasants and renewed attacks from abroad led to its downfall. In 1014, Bulgaria lost all its territory to the Byzantine Empire, which kept control for more than 150 years. After a large uprising in 1185, the northern part of Bulgaria recovered its independence.

[8] During the reign of Ivan Asen II (1218-41) Bulgaria regained power. However, none of Ivan's successors managed to impose a central authority over these diverse areas where feudalism was the norm. By 1393 the whole of Bulgaria had fallen under Turkish rule.

[9] In the 17th and 18th centuries, after the wars with Austria and the unsuccessful siege of Vienna, the Ottoman Empire began to decline, though it still retained much of its territory. The former Bulgarian State was twice invaded by Russia, in 1810 and 1828.

[10] Throughout the invasion period the Bulgarians maintained their cultural identity; keeping their language, music and folklore alive. Under Turkish domination, the Greek Orthodox Church assumed religious leadership, suppressing the independent patriarch. In this way Bulgarian monks were among the precursors of the national liberation movement.

[11] The Bulgarian Church fought for 40 years to recover its independence. In 1870, the Sultan gave permission for the Church to create an exarchate (sub-Patriarchy). The first exarch (deputy patriarch) and his successors were declared schismatic and were excommunicated by the Greek patriarch; this further strengthened Bulgarian nationalism.

[12] From 1876 onwards, a series of revolts was cruelly put down. Some Bulgarian volunteers joined the ranks of the Serbian and Russian armies, who went to war against the Empire. One of Moscow's conditions for the Treaty of St Stephen (1878) was the creation of a Bulgarian state. The European powers feared the creation of a Russian satellite in the Balkans so they blocked the motion.

[13] In the 1878 Berlin Congress, the 'autonomous province' of Rumelia was created in the south, and the State of Bulgaria in the north. Rumelia was nominally under the Sultan's control, and Macedonia was to continue as part of the Ottoman Empire. An Assembly of Notables was in charge of drawing up a law and appointing the ruler of the new state.

[14] The assembly approved a liberal Constitution, establishing a constitutional monarchy. Prince Alexander of Battenberg, grandson of Alexander II of Russia, was elected and assumed the Bulgarian throne in July 1878, swearing to uphold the Constitution. He suspended it two years later.

[15] The Prince set up a dictatorship, headed by Russian general Leonid Sobolev and other conservatives. The Russian Emperor's death modified Alexander's behavior, making him more attuned to Bulgarian issues. In 1885, he supported the liberal rebellion in Rumelia, the governor there was replaced and union with Bulgaria was proclaimed.

[16] In 1886, several treaties were signed that recognized Prince Alexander as the ruler of Rumelia and Bulgaria. However, he was subsequently taken to Russia against his will and forced to abdicate. Looking for someone who would be acceptable to Russia, as well as the rest of Europe, the Bulgarians finally appointed Ferdinand of Saxe-Coburg-Gotha as his replacement.

[17] Although initially distrusted, Ferdinand was able to gain the support of Vienna, London, Rome and Russia. He then concentrated on the reunification of the Bulgarians. Prince Ferdinand proclaimed Bulgaria's independence in 1908.

[18] In 1912, Bulgaria encouraged the formation of the Balkan League, together with Greece, Serbia and Montenegro to fight Turkey in the first Balkan War that began in October. In May, Turkey ceded its European dominions on the Black Sea.

[19] The allies did not agree with the distribution; Bulgaria confronted Greece, Serbia and Romania. The Second Balkan War quickly ended in Bulgarian defeat. In Bucharest, in August 1913, Macedonia was divided between Greece and Serbia, and Romania gained an area of northern Bulgaria, rich in natural resources.

[20] In 1913, the Bulgarian Government abandoned its traditionally pro-Russian stance, seeking closer ties with Germany. When World War I broke out the Bulgarian people and the army disapproved of the official policy, even though Serbia was beaten. Ferdinand surrendered to the Allies in 1918 and abdicated in favor of his son Boris.

[21] Having lost much territory, Bulgaria was disarmed and forced to pay extensive war damages. With the restoration of the 1878 Constitution, elections were held in 1920. The anti-war reaction gave the Agrarian Party a wide margin. Working on a Soviet model, the Government started radical agrarian reforms. The Government was not pro-Soviet, however, and local Communists were persecuted.

[22] Bulgaria joined the League of Nations and followed a conciliatory line of diplomacy for some time. However, its territorial losses and the pressure exerted by expatriots abroad soon led to new tensions with its neighbors. Aleksandur Stamboliyski, the leader of the Agrarian Party and head of the Government, was ousted and assassinated by a conspiracy of Macedonians and opposition figures in 1923.

[23] Aleksandur Tsankov assumed control of the Government, heading a multiparty alliance which excluded the Liberal, Communist and Agrarian parties. Uprisings and armed activity by the opposition led to hundreds of executions and assassinations. The Government declared martial law and reinforced the army in order to avoid outright rebellion.

[24] In 1926, Tsankov resigned in favor of Andrei Liapchev, leader of the Democratic Party, to make way for more liberal policies.

[25] In 1934, fearing the effects of the worldwide economic depression and taking a cue from his neighbors, King Boris III set up a dictatorship. All political parties were proscribed,

Life expectancy
70.9 years
2000-2005

GNI per capita
$1,790
2002

Literacy
98% total adult rate
2000

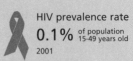

HIV prevalence rate
0.1% of population 15-49 years old
2001

there was censorship of the press, the universities were closed and an ultra-right youth movement was established.

26 Tension with Turkey eased and in 1937, a peace and friendship treaty was signed with Yugoslavia. The following year, Bulgaria signed a non-aggression pact with the Balkan alliance, in exchange for the rearmament of the Bulgarian army. While the King was once again seeking rapprochement with Germany, the Bulgarian dream of re-establishing its former borders was gathering strength.

27 In 1940, Germany made Romania return the parts of Bulgaria which it had won in the second Balkan War. Bulgaria signed the Anti-Komintern pact and German troops set up bases aimed at Greece and Yugoslavia on Bulgarian soil. In exchange, Bulgarian troops were allowed to occupy the part of Thrace belonging to Greece, the part of Macedonia belonging to Yugoslavia, and part of Serbia.

28 When Bulgaria refused to declare war on the Soviet Union, King Boris was assassinated, and a new pro-German Government was formed. Growing anti-Nazi resistance, led by the Communists, contributed to the formation of the Patriotic Front in 1942. The Republicans, left-wing Agrarians, Democrats and independents all subsequently joined.

29 In May 1944, paralyzed by the civil war, the pro-German Boshilov resigned, and was replaced by Bagrianov. While Soviet troops advanced toward the Danube, Bagrianov sought an agreement with the Allies. In August, Bulgaria proclaimed its neutrality, and ordered the disarmament of the German troops on its soil.

30 The USSR and the Red Army entered Bulgarian territory on 5 September. The resistance fanned local insurrection. On 8 September, the Red Army took the capital, and the Patriotic Front formed a Government headed by the Republican Kimon Georgiev.

31 Sofia signed a treaty with the allies in October 1944. Bulgarian troops, under Soviet command, collaborated in the defeat of the German forces in Hungary, Yugoslavia and Austria. During 1945, war trials led to the imprisonment and execution of thousands of people.

32 In March 1945, Communist leader Giorgi Dimitrov returned to Bulgaria after several years at the Komintern headquarters, in Moscow. A crisis erupted a few months after and the elections were postponed.

33 In a referendum held in September 1946, 92 per cent of the electorate approved of the creation of the Republic of Bulgaria. The Patriotic Front won the elections, as the Communist Party (BCP) obtained an absolute majority of votes. Dimitrov became Prime Minister.

34 In 1947, Britain and the US recognized the government. The National Assembly ratified the peace treaty with the Allies, the new Constitution went into effect and, at the end of the year, the Soviet troops withdrew from the country. After joining the BCP opposition, some of the Patriotic Fronts former leaders were arrested and sentenced to death for conspiracy.

35 Under the leadership of the BCP, the Bulgarian State adopted the Soviet socio-economic model. A process of accelerated industrialization was set in motion, without taking into account the lack of raw materials or the technical preparation of the labor force. This industrialization led to urbanization that determined the demographic expansion of Sofia, whose population increased fourfold in two generations. In the countryside, collective farming was enforced.

36 Dimitrov resigned from the administration in 1949. Vulko Chervenkov succeeded him. In 1954, Todor Zhivkov was named First Secretary of the BCP, becoming Prime Minister in 1962. Bulgaria was the USSR's closest ally among the Warsaw Pact countries, and in 1968 Bulgarian troops accompanied Soviet troops in the invasion of Czechoslovakia.

37 In the 1980s Bulgaria was accused of imposing a policy of forced assimilation on the country's Turkish minority. In 1986, Sofia refuted Amnesty International's accusation that more than 250 Turks had been detained or imprisoned for refusing to accept new identity cards.

38 In 1988, Bulgaria and Turkey signed a protocol governing bilateral economic relations. The dialogue was interrupted in the following year, when it was revealed that the Bulgarian militia had used violence to put down a protest by 30,000 Turks, who had been demonstrating against the Government's policy of assimilation.

39 In June 1989, more than 80,000 Turks were expelled from Bulgaria. Turkey promised to accommodate them all, but towards the end of August, after receiving 310,000 Bulgarian Turks, it closed its borders. 30,000 of these refugees subsequently returned to Bulgaria.

40 The largest protest meeting since the War was held in November in front of the National Assembly. A group known as 'Eco-glasnost' demonstrated against a proposed nuclear power plant on an island in the Danube and against the construction of a reservoir in one of the country's largest nature reserves.

41 In December members of a Muslim minority group -with an estimated 300,000 members- demanded religious and cultural freedom.

IN FOCUS

ENVIRONMENTAL CHALLENGES
Heavy metals, nitrates, petroleum derivatives and cleansing agents damage the medium and lower courses of the most important rivers that flow into the Black Sea, which is highly contaminated. One fourth of the forests suffer the effects of air pollution, such as acid rain, which is a consequence of metallurgical and industrial plants' emissions.

WOMEN'S RIGHTS
Bulgarian women have been able to vote since 1937 and to be elected since 1944. From 1995 to 2000, the parliamentary seats occupied by women went down from 13 per cent to 11 per cent. In 2000 women represented 48 per cent of the labor force. In 2000, 10,000 Bulgarian women were forced to work as prostitutes in industrialized countries and in 2003, 13 Bulgarian citizens were arrested in Italy for being part of the chain 'distributing' women, for fees ranging from $3,000 to $8,000, depending on the woman's 'quality'.

CHILDREN
The indicators of progress regarding commitment to child welfare have improved between 1970 and 2000 (mortality rate of children under five and mothers decreased, while the percentages of vaccination and access to health care and education of children increased). However although vaccination has been widespread, cases of polio were detected in 2001. On the other hand, that year only 32 per cent of the babies were exclusively breastfed until 4 months old. Education is compulsory up to the age of 14. The enrolment rate of school-age children increased to 94 per cent in 2000; according to the figures available*, 45,000 children drop out of school every year. The highest dropout rates (32 per cent) are among children from families of Roma origin, followed by Bulgarian girls (8 per cent) and Turkish girls (6 per cent). Some children from the Roma community go to the so called 'gipsy schools', where the study conditions are not good. There is a high proportion of Roma children in schools for children with learning difficulties.

INDIGENOUS PEOPLES/ ETHNIC MINORITIES
In 2000, most Turks lived in two main areas where they were the majority of the inhabitants; one in the northeast (Silistra-Varna) and another in the southeastern corner (Haskovo-Kurdzali). The forced 'Bulgarization' of the Turk minority in the1980s is daily becoming less common. In 2000 a law that allowed broadcasting in Turkish was approved, as well as a new law on minorities by which everybody could communicate in his/her mother tongue. In political terms, the Turks have representatives in the legislature and the executive as well as at the local level in areas where they form the majority. Their main grievances have to do with the economic situation and with needing more governmental support for their language and cultural traditions.

In 2002, the Roma were discriminated against in terms of access to housing, public services, education and health care. They remained a focus of police violence. The Government took some measures towards the implementation of a 'Framework Program for Equal Integration of Roma in Bulgarian Society', signed in April 1999. Among other things, this promised to improve Roma settlements and to grant them funds for the diffusion of their culture - but neither had been implemented by the end of 2002.

MIGRANTS/REFUGEES
By the end of 2002, the country sheltered around 1,200 refugees and people seeking asylum or protection. During that year, there were 2,900 asylum requests, almost 20 per cent more than in 2001. Most came from Iraq, Afghanistan, Armenia and Nigeria. Some of the people who were denied asylum were granted residence permits for humanitarian reasons for different periods of time; an exception that was in most cases granted to Iraqi and Afghan citizens. Almost 5,000 Bulgarians, apparently from Roma stock, requested asylum in other European countries during that year, joining the almost 3,000 people that had done so in 2001.

DEATH PENALTY
It was abolished in 1998.

*Latest data available in *The State of the World's Children* and *Childinfo* database, UNICEF, 2004.

⁴² The Central Committee of the BCP replaced Zhivkov as Secretary General, a post he had held for 35 years and as president of the State Council. He was succeeded by Petur Mladenov, who was considered to be a proponent of liberalization of the regime.

⁴³ The National Assembly lifted the ban on anti-government demonstrations, and granted amnesty to political prisoners. There was an immediate increase in the number of political demonstrations demanding reforms and elections. Social pressure forced the Government to amend the Constitution to introduce an electoral law that allowed elections to take place.

⁴⁴ In March 1990, the Union of Democratic Forces (UDF), made up of 16 opposition parties, and the BCP agreed to the election of a Constitutional Assembly. The July election was won by the Bulgarian Socialist Party, BSP (formerly BCP). In October, the BSP was forced to enter a new coalition, led by Yelio Yelev, a dissident during the 1970s and leader of the Social Democratic wing of the UDF.

⁴⁵ The new coalition government adopted a program of economic reforms in consultation with the IMF and the World Bank. They reached an agreement with the labor unions for a 200-day 'social peace' until the reforms could go into effect.

⁴⁶ In July 1991, the new Constitution was approved, establishing a parliamentary system, allowing personal property, and freedom of expression. After the October election, Parliament named Filip Dimitrov as Prime Minister. Virtually alienated from the Social Democrats and the 'Greens' - co-founders of the UDF - Dimitrov was chosen because of the support he had from the right-wing of the opposition coalition and the Movement for Freedom and Human Rights (of the Turkish minority).

⁴⁷ In the January 1992 election, Yelev - leader during the political transition and author of the rapprochement toward the West - was elected President of the Republic.

⁴⁸ In June Bulgaria joined the Council of Europe. During that year, former Communist leader Todor Zhivkov, three former Prime Ministers and another former member of government prior to 1991, were arrested and charged with corruption in the exercise of their duties. The economic situation led the Movement for Rights and Freedoms (MRF) to withdraw its support of Dimitrov, which caused the downfall of his cabinet.

⁴⁹ The new Prime Minister Liuben Berov stated he was willing to restore the lands confiscated by the Communists to the Turkish minority.

PROFILE

ENVIRONMENT

Located in the Balkans, Bulgaria comprises four different natural regions. The fertile Danubian plains in the north are wheat and corn-producing areas. South of these lie the wooded Balkan Mountains, where cereals and potatoes are cultivated, cattle and sheep are raised, and the country's major mineral resources - iron ore, zinc and copper, are found. Cattle are also raised on the Rhodope Mountains in southern Bulgaria. South of the Balkan mountains there is a region of grassland, crossed by the Maritza River, where tobacco, cotton, rice, flowers and grapes are cultivated.

SOCIETY

People: The majority are Bulgars of Slav origin (85 per cent). There are also Turks (9.4) and Roma (gypsies, 3.6), plus immigrant communities of Macedonians, Armenians, Tatar, Gagauz, Circassians, Russians.
Religions: Orthodox Christian Church of Bulgaria, 83 per cent, Muslim 13, Catholic 1.5, Jewish 0.8 and Protestants, Gregorian Armenians.
Languages: Bulgarian (official and predominant); also spoken: Romani, Turkish, Macedonian, Gagauz and Armenian.
Main Political Parties: There are many small parties, hence the formation of coalitions like the Union of Democratic Forces (UDF) (7 parties); Democratic Left, including the Bulgarian Socialist Party, the Ecologist Party, and the Rural Farmers' Union; National Movement Simeon the Second; National Salvation Union; Movement for Liberty and Human Rights (of the Turkish minority); the Euro-Left Coalition; the Bulgarian Businesses Bloc; the Communist Party; and the Union of the Monarchy. Ethnic parties are banned.
Main Social Organizations: The Confederation of Independent Unions of Bulgaria was founded in 1990 and is the biggest (1.6 million members). Since January 1990 the Confederation of Labor Podkrepa has been legal, becoming a new union axis, headed by Constantin Trenchev. Importance of the agrarian movement led by the National Agrarian Union of Bulgaria and the national 'Nikola Petkov' union. There are many regional, ethnic and national groups with varied agendas, one of the most active is the Internal Macedonian Revolutionary Organization.

THE STATE

Official Name: Narodna Republika Balgarija. **Capital:** Sofia (Sofija) 1,076,000 people (2003). **Other Cities:** Plovdiv 344,500 people; Varna 293,600; Burgas 192,900 (2000). **Government:** Georgi Parvanov, President since January 2002; Simeon Saxe-Cobourg, Prime Minister since July 2001. National Assembly has 240 members.
National Holiday: 3 March, National Liberation Day - Independence (1878). **Armed Forces:** 102,000. Other: Border Guards (Ministry of Interior): 12,000; Security Police: 4,000; Railway and Construction Troops: 18,000.

⁵⁰ Transition from a centralized planned economy to a free market economy continued to be difficult and caused paradoxical situations. When the former Soviet Union stopped buying two-thirds of Bulgaria's exports, foreign trade was significantly reduced. UN sanctions imposed on neighboring former Yugoslavia caused losses of $1.5 million to Bulgaria. In 1993, Berov went on with the transition to a market economy at a rate considered excessively slow by the IMF, which caused a certain amount of tension between Sofia and the international organization.

⁵¹ In June 1994, Berov was able to pass the privatization law. His economic policies and the rights of Bulgarians of Turkish origin were being sharply questioned and so three months later he resigned. President Yelev dissolved Parliament and called new elections. The BSP won an absolute majority in the National Assembly.

⁵² In January 1995, socialist leader Zhan Videnov formed a new Government which included members from the BSP, the Bulgarian Agrarian National Union and the Eco-glasnost Political Club. His cabinet was the first in the history of post-Communist Bulgaria with an absolute majority at the National Assembly. Differences between the new Government and Yelev were frequent. In July, the President criticized the Government because he thought market reforms were not being implemented swiftly enough, suggesting the BSP was 'genetically connected' to organized crime.

⁵³ Petar Stoyanov's Union of Democratic Forces won the presidential elections in 1996. That year Bulgaria became a member of the World Trade Organization.

⁵⁴ Harrassed by his political enemies, Prime Minister Zhan Videnov resigned. The conservative groups that backed Stoyanov called for the dismissal of the Government

that was supported by the parliamentary majority of the socialists and their allies. A series of public demonstrations in the capital and other cities demanded new elections. In January 1997, Stoyanov became President.

⁵⁵ The legislative elections were won by the Union of Democratic Forces (UDF) in April 1997. The new government implemented a purely neo-liberal economic policy, following IMF guidelines, planning the privatization of state companies considered to be loss-making and the elimination of 60,000 jobs in the public sector. Services were liberalized with the aim of reducing inflation. In May 1998 agricultural subsidies were abolished and the State telecommunications company, several banks and the Bulgarian airline were privatized. The Government declared its objective would be fiscal balance. A few weeks later the IMF agreed an $800 million loan. The last loan, for $300 million, was granted by the end of 2001.

⁵⁶ To be accepted as a member of the European Union in 2007, Bulgaria was forced to shut down two of its oldest nuclear reactors and made a commitment to shut down two of the remaining four by 2006.

⁵⁷ Former king Simeon II - crowned at the age of six and reigning for three years from 1943 - launched the Simeon II National Movement in 2001. Simeon Saxe-Cobourg won the parliamentary elections and became Prime Minister in July, thus becoming the first former monarch of Eastern Europe to return to power. His campaign agenda did not include the restoration of the monarchy, but promised to end poverty, unemployment and other ills that plagued Bulgaria after the fall of Communism. Bulgaria is currently the major entry point into Western Europe for heroin and cocaine smugglers from Asia.

⁵⁸ However 100 days after the election, thousands thronged the streets of the capital protesting that promises had not been fulfilled. That same month the Socialist Party leader, Georgi Parvanov, was elected president. The electoral turnout was the lowest since the fall of communism (41 per cent).

⁵⁹ Bulgaria, like Romania, hoped to be invited to join NATO. The organization invited both countries to participate as guests in the Vienna summit held in 2002. In 2003 NATO expressed its intention to relocate its German military bases to Bulgaria and Romania during 2004.

⁶⁰ In October 2003 local elections were held. The BSP won with 33 per cent of the votes, followed by the UDF with 21 per cent, while Simeon's party got 10 per cent. Voter participation was below 40 per cent. The presidential elections are due to be held in 2005. ■

Burkina Faso / Burkina Faso

Population:	13,797,527
Area:	274,000 km²
Capital:	Ouagadougou
Currency:	CFA franc
Language:	French

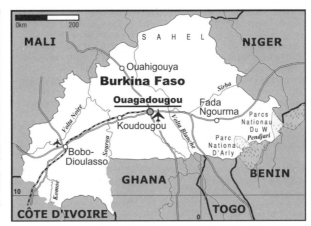

During the 11th century, indigenous peoples, ancestors of the Lobi and Bobo, settled in the western region of the Mouhoun River (or Volta Noire/Black Volta). Though they never developed a centralized political system, the populations that migrated from the Dagomba region (present-day Ghana) founded the Mossi dynasty in the north. The Mossi kings imposed their military aristocracy over the region of the Volta Rivers (Volta Noire, Volta Blanche and Volta Rouge - black, white and red).

[2] Several well organized kingdoms were created in the following two centuries. TheYatenga and Uagadugu were the most important kingdoms. The monarchs of the Uagadugu kingdom were chosen from the members of the royal family by four ministers who had to maintain the balance between the Mossi aristocracy and the Mande people.

[3] The Mossi and Mande resisted attempts at annexation by the Mali and Songhai empires (see Mali and Guinea) and remained independent throughout the Fulah invasions of the 18th and 19th centuries.

[4] In a series of military incursions between 1896 and 1904, the French laid waste the central plains, burning houses, and slaughtering people and animals. The ensuing reign of terror finally sparked off an insurrection in 1916, which met with such violent repression that millions were forced to emigrate, mostly to Ghana.

[5] Called Upper Volta by the French, the country was administered as part of the colony of Haute Sénégal-Niger, when it became an independent protectorate. In 1932 it was split between Côte d'Ivoire, Niger and Sudan, and reconstituted as a separate colony in 1947. Finally, in line with French neo-colonial strategy, the country was declared independent in 1960.

[6] 1960's elections were won by the Voltanese Democratic Union (UDV), a party backed by landowners and private enterprise. Maurice Yameogo was elected President and was re-elected in 1965 amidst intense trade-union agitation, which occurred in response to administrative chaos and austerity measures. Yameogo was overthrown a year later in a military coup led by army chief-of-staff, General Sangoulé Lamizana.

[7] The 1970s witnessed a succession of elections, military coups, and more or less fraudulent re-elections orchestrated by General Lamizana. Starvation was widespread, herds were dwindling and an estimated quarter of the population had emigrated to neighboring states.

[8] In 1980 Colonel Saye Zerbo led a coup d'état, but was in turn ousted in 1982 by Major Doctor Jean-Baptiste Ouedraogo. Ouedraogo was overthrown by a young officer, Thomas Sankara, who was popular among soldiers and the rural poor as he brought in an anti-corruption campaign and organized brigades to assist victims of the prolonged drought and deforestation.

[9] Under Sankara's government Upper Volta was renamed Burkina Faso - 'land of the incorruptible'; the national anthem was sung in African languages; land reform was carried out and popular courts were set up to dispense justice.

IN FOCUS

ENVIRONMENTAL CHALLENGES
Burkina Faso suffers from desertification, caused by serious droughts and the intensive production of export crops such as millet, peanuts and cotton. One of the harmful consequences of desertification is the lack of wood for domestic use. In the main cities, air pollution (due to usage of petroleum derivatives as vehicle fuel and also to industrial emissions) is the major environmental problem.

WOMEN'S RIGHTS
Since 1958 women have been able to vote and stand as candidates. From 1995 to 2000 the percentage of women in parliament rose from 4 to 8 per cent, and in ministerial or similar positions from 7 to 10 per cent. In the year 2000, women comprised 47 per cent of the country's work force. Moreover poverty in general disproportionately affects women. Most of the polygamous households (58 per cent), with three or more women per man, were poorer in 2001 than monogamous or single person households.

Only 61 per cent of pregnancies benefited from health care and only 31 per cent of the deliveries were assisted by qualified personnel*. 6.2 per cent of pregnant women between 15 and 19 years old were HIV-positive in 1998, and 8.8 per cent of those between 20 and 24 years old. Since 1996, female genital mutilation has been forbidden, but its practice has not been totally eradicated. In the year 2000, only 13 per cent of the women and 33 per cent of the men in the country were literate.

CHILDREN
In 2001 there were 270,000 orphans due to HIV/AIDS. By the end of that year it was estimated that 61,000 of the children between 0 and 14 years old were HIV positive or had HIV/AIDS. Before the year 2000, percentages of mortality among children were decreasing (6 per cent*), even among the under-fives. Now, however, malaria, respiratory and intestinal infections and undernourishment, due to generalized poverty, are worsening the health of women and children in particular. 34 per cent of children under five years old were classified as underweight; 12 per cent were critically so*. 13 per cent of the children in this age range were weakened by undernourishment, and 37 per cent suffered from moderate or severe growth delay. Only 25 per cent of the population have access to safe drinking water.

INDIGENOUS PEOPLES/ ETHNIC MINORITIES
There are more than 60 ethnic groups in the country, each one with its particular social and cultural characteristics, even though all of them are of Burkinabe origin. The major group is the Mossi, descendants of the Moro-Naba dynasty. Tuaregs face discrimination and, in some cases, danger (see Argelia).

MIGRANTS/REFUGEES
Almost a thousand refugees and people requesting asylum - from more than 20 African countries - lived in Burkina Faso, mostly in the capital, Ouagadougou, at the end of the year 2000. 400 of them received assistance from UNHCR, including for recent refugees a 120-dollar stipend for three months, subsidized health care, loans up to 400 dollars to start small businesses and more than 60 scholarships.

Since 1998 Burkina Faso has been one of the few countries which has agreed to give permanent residency to those refugees who could no longer stay in other African countries.

Thousands of Burkinabes, who had emigrated in the 1990s to Côte d'Ivoire searching for jobs, were obliged to return in the year 2000 due to anti-foreigner pressure in that country. Some of them, descendants of Burkinabes but born in Côte d'Ivoire, thus had little connection with Burkina Faso.

DEATH PENALTY
The country retains the death penalty for ordinary crimes such as murder, but can be considered abolitionist in practice in that they have not executed anyone during the past 10 years.

*Latest data available in *The State of the World's Children* and *Childinfo* database, UNICEF, 2004.

Life expectancy
45.7 years
2000-2005

GNI per capita
$220
2002

Literacy
24% total adult rate
2000

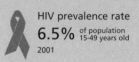
HIV prevalence rate
6.5% of population 15-49 years old
2001

[10] Sankara, leading a National Revolutionary Council, set a target of two meals and 10 liters of water per person per day. The implementation of such measures presented a considerable challenge in a country where 82 per cent of adults were illiterate and absolute poverty was the norm. But a series of radical initiatives were launched: the rural poll tax was abolished; Operation Vaccination Commando immunized 2.5 million children against meningitis, yellow fever and measles in 15 days in November 1984; 1985 saw a massive public housing construction programme and a campaign to plant 10 million trees to slow the Sahara's advance; Operation Alpha Commando from February to April 1986 involved 35,000 people in a literacy campaign in nine indigenous languages.

[11] On 15 October 1987, Sankara was overthrown, prosecuted and executed along with twelve of his supporters in a coup led by his second-in-command, Blaise Compaoré, who pledged to continue the Popular Front and 'rectify' the regime internally.

[12] Contrasting with the image of Sankara, a man of austere habits who shunned personal property and refused to use air conditioning because it was unavailable to ordinary Burkinabes, Compaoré built a government palace and purchased a presidential plane. His economic strategy included encouraging private enterprise and foreign capital, and consideration of denationalization, deregulation and agreements with international lending institutions.

[13] In the years following 1987, political groups opposed to the rectification process were organized, including the Popular and Democratic Union Thomas Sankara, which demanded trade union freedom, amnesty for political prisoners and free elections, and the Revolutionary Burkina's Workers Party (PRTB), which maintained that the cause of Sankara's overthrow was his anti-corruption campaign.

[14] In December 1992 and March 1993 there were two general strikes against the implementation of the structural-adjustment plan recommended by the IMF. Devaluation of the CFA franc in January 1994 led to further popular dissatisfaction. In July, in spite of protests from the opposition, Parliament passed a law that allowed the government to privatize 19 national companies.

[15] The Government continued its policy of economic liberalization and officially took Burkina Faso into the World Trade Organization in June 1995. A project to restructure the recently privatized railways, resulting in 500 lay-offs, caused a major general strike that led the country once again toward a tense situation.

[16] The economy grew 5 per cent in 1996. In June, the IMF approved a new $57 million loan to support the implementation of a structural-adjustment program in the subsequent three years. In 1997, a drought decimated food production and left the country in a critical situation. The deficit in food production, which added up to 32 per cent of the GDP and employed 90 per cent of the population, was estimated at 156,000 tonnes for the 1997-1998 period. In December 1997, Ouagadougou had to call on the international community for 67,000 tonnes of grain to tackle the crisis.

[17] Marijuana plantations grew swiftly in Burkina Faso, as well as in other countries of the region. It replaced some 'traditional' cash crops whose price had fallen. The devaluation of the CFA franc caused a reduction in the import of medicines, which further complicated the fight against the two major diseases that ravage the population: malaria and AIDS. In the country in 1998, there was only one doctor for every 25,000 people.

[18] The 1998 elections were boycotted by the opposition granting the president-candidate victory. A series of protests led to the resignation of the cabinet, but the President confirmed most of the ministers in their posts in January 1999.

[19] The murder of journalist Norbert Zongo, in December 1998, brought the Government under suspicion. Zongo had made important revelations about the supposed responsibility of François Compaoré, the President's brother, for the murder of his chauffeur, following torture inflicted by members of the presidential security staff. A year after Zongo's death, despite Compaoré's attempts to silence the protests, 30,000 people demonstrated in Ouagadougou, clamouring for justice. Four of the six guards accused of Zongo's murder were finally condemned, but the President's brother only ever made one statement.

[20] In February 2000, the Commission for National Reconciliation, formed by Compaoré as a way of easing the tension caused by the Zongo case, requested the rehabilitation of former president Thomas Sankara, assassinated in Compaoré's coup.

[21] A report by the UN stated in 2000 that Compaoré acted as middleman in arms smuggling from the Soviet bloc to rebel groups such as UNITA in Angola and the RUF in Sierra Leone in violation of an international embargo on arms to these groups. His services were paid for with diamonds, whose trade for this purpose is also forbidden (see box 'Diamonds of war'). In December, the Government finally accepted the presence of a United Nations' supervisory committee to monitor the import of weapons.

[22] In 2001, a meningitis epidemic killed more than 1,500 people; it was estimated that more than 10 per cent of the population was HIV-positive, making Burkina Faso one of the countries most affected by the pandemic.

[23] There were legislative elections in 2002. These had been initially scheduled for 28 April 2002, but were postponed to 5 May because of low voter registration. This time, the opposition also took part, having boycotted the Presidential elections in 1998 and the local elections in 2000.

[24] In October 2003 12 members of the presidential guard and the armed forces, accused of planning a coup against Compaoré, were imprisoned. One of them, Naon Babou, revealed details of Zongo's murder that implicated the President's brother. Burkina Faso held the neighbouring and more prosperous Côte d'Ivoire responsible for financially supporting the coup attempt. The relationship between these countries has become tense due to Côte d'Ivoire's civil war, which started in September 2002. President Laurent Gbagbo has accused Compaoré of supporting the rebels occupying the northern area of the country. As a consequence of this war, 350,000 Burkinabe migrants returned home. ■

PROFILE

ENVIRONMENT

A landlocked country, Burkina Faso is one of the most densely populated areas of the African Sahel (the semi-arid southern rim of the Sahara). The Mossi plateau slopes gently southwards and is traversed by the valleys of the three Volta Rivers (Black Volta, White Volta and Red Volta). Export crops such as millet, peanuts and cotton are produced, mainly in the southwest.

SOCIETY

Peoples: Over half of the population are Mossi. Peulh herders and the Tamajek clans with their vassals, the Bellah, amount to around 20 per cent. Djula peasants and traders are indigenous minorities. The language of these three population groups is the linguistic bridge between the various regions. Senufo and Bobo-Fing cultures inhabit the western plains where the savanna merges into the forest. In the south, the predominant Lebi, Bobo-Ule, Gurunsi and Bissa cultures extend into several states. The savanna to the east holds the great Gurmantehé civilization, while the Sampo, Rurumba and Marko cultures live in the desert regions to the north and northeast. **Religions:** 50 per cent are Muslims; traditional African religions, 40 per cent; Christian (mostly Catholic), 10 per cent. **Languages:** French (official); 71 languages from the Sudanic family, spoken by 90 per cent of the population (most common are Mossi, Bobo, Bissa and Gurma).
Main Political Parties: African Democratic Rally-Alliance for Democracy and Federation (RDA-ADF); Confederation for Federation and Democracy (CFD); Congress for Democracy and Progress (CDP-left-wing); Tolerance and Progress Movement (MTP); Party for African Independence (PIA); Party for Democracy and Progress (PDP-social democratic); and Burkina Green Party (PVB).
Main Social Organizations: Burkina General Work Confederation (CGTB); Burkina Human Rights Movement (MBDHP); February 14 Group; Burkina Workers National Confederation (CNTB); Free Syndicates National Organization (ONSL); surveillance groups on political action in different organizations and communities.

THE STATE

Official Name: République de Burkina Faso. **Administrative Division:** 45 provinces, 300 departments and 7,200 villages. **Capital:** Ouagadougou 821,000 people (2003). **Other Cities:** Bobo-Dioulasso 474,300 people; Koudougou 124,400; Ouahigouya 74,000 (2000).
Government: Republican parliamentary system, with a powerful head of state. Blaise Compaoré, President and Head of State, in power since October 1987 after a coup d'état; elected in 1991 and re-elected in 1998. Paramanga Ernest Yonli, Prime Minister and Head of Government since November 2000. Bicameral Parliament: the National Assembly, with 111 members, and the House of Representatives, with 178 members. **National Holiday:** 5 August, Independence (1960). **Armed Forces:** 8,700 (including Gendarmerie). Others: 1,750.

Burundi / Burundi

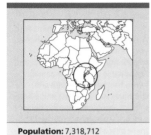

Population:	7,318,712
Area:	27,830 km²
Capital:	Bujumbura
Currency:	Burundi franc
Language:	Rundi, Kirundi and French

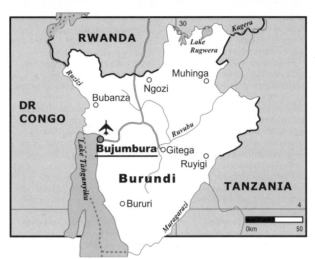

Pieces of metal found in what is now Burundi are thought to date from around the 7th century BC, according to the scarce archeological evidence. There is little detailed knowledge about what took place after that time and up to the 15th century, but in general it was a period of progressive land occupation and the development of agriculture using natural irrigation. There was also herding and some hunting and gathering.

2   The progressive organization of Burundian society, between the 15th and 16th centuries, led to the formation of a monarchy ruled by a Mwami (King). The State was structured as a feudal system (feudal and semi-autonomous organization and division of power held by *ganwas*, the equivalent of feudal lords in the Middle Ages) which assimilated political and religious functions and assured the pacific coexistence among ethnic groups. No ethnic conflict was registered until the second phase of the colonial period (20th century).

3   In the 19th century, anthropologists characterized the population of the area now known as Burundi as having three ethnic groups: the Twa (Pygmies indigenous to the area), Hutus (a Bantu group that came from Chad and Nigeria) and Tutsis (a Hamitic group from the Nile valley area).

4   The first Catholic mission was set up in Burundi in 1879. In 1885, the Congress of Berlin placed Burundi in the German sphere of influence and it became part of German East Africa. In 1897, Germany founded its general headquarters in Usumbura, within a district that included Rwanda and Burundi, which became known as Ruanda-Urundi. On 6 June 1903, King Mwezi Gizabo, after resisting the Germans, accepted the Treaty of Kiganda and acknowledged the protectorate. The Germans established an indirect administration policy and maintained local customs and authorities. Large quantities of ivory were exported, coffee-growing was started, a railway was built and the first

German civil settlements were set up in 1906.

5   After World War I, in 1919 Belgium was granted a mandate over Ruanda-Urundi by the Allied Supreme Council. In 1922 the League of Nations gave Belgium the mandate for the region, which Belgium took up in 1924.

6   After breaking up the traditional political-administrative ties, Belgium destroyed the political organization that kept the balance within Burundian society. The notion of 'chief' was radically changed from defender and regulator of social relationships to a bureaucratic official, who made excessive use of force. Privileges were accorded to the minority Tutsis, which caused

severe disruption and violence among the ethnic groups.

7   In 1925, a law was passed that established the administrative union of Ruanda-Urundi within the Belgian Congo (now DR Congo). This forced Burundi to provide cheap labor to mining centers in Katanga. The Belgians put a paternalistic policy into practice which among other things led to a system of barter, with little money in circulation. The construction of roads did not begin until after the famine of 1928-1929.

8   In 1946, after the end of World War II, Burundi became a UN trust territory under Belgium, with the condition that its economic development was assured and the country was led towards

independence. However, the Belgian control of local authorities was intensified: the Mwami was personally appointed by the Vice-Governor in charge of the region. This administrative change, which ended the traditional aristocracy, together with the extension of the Belgian Congo's control over Ruanda-Urundi, brought about the loss of national identity. The Belgian administration was supported by the Catholic Church which expanded rapidly in Burundi.

9   By means of a 1952 decree, Belgium revised its policy on the local population's political participation and created elected councils, promoting the creation of multiple parties (especially, the Democratic Christian Party), in order to prevent the formation of a single and totalitarian movement. Between 1958 and 1960, 25 political parties were founded.

10   On 18 September 1961, Burundi's first multiparty elections were held, although the franchise was limited. The Union for National Progress (UPRONA) won. Its founder, Tutsi Prince Louis Rwagasore, was appointed Prime Minister. His pressure for independence led to his assassination by the Belgians on 30 October. He was replaced by another member of the Tutsi élite, who changed the country's policy by giving support to the Hutus. In the midst of this political turmoil, Belgium granted Burundi's independence on 1 July 1962.

IN FOCUS

ENVIRONMENTAL CHALLENGES
Deforestation, due to the indiscriminate felling of trees for firewood, is one of the country's worst problems, aggravated by the growing incidence of farming on unsuitable lands. By 2000, 22 per cent of population had no access to drinking water.

WOMEN'S RIGHTS
Burundian women have been able to vote and stand for office since 1961. In 2000, women held 6 per cent of seats in Parliament and their representation in ministerial positions amounted to 8 per cent. The extended armed conflict has had a devastating impact on the country's economy and humanitarian conditions, particularly for children and women.
      Burundi has some of the worst health indicators in the world and continues to register worsening infant and maternal mortality rates*. The fertility rate has remained constant in 1960, 1990 and 2001 at 6.8 children per women*.

CHILDREN
In 2000, severe malnutrition, epidemic levels of malaria and smallpox and a rise in cholera and dysentery hit the country. That year, the decline in the rate of exclusive breastfeeding to 89 per cent of babies under four months old signalled deteriorating child-care practices. Under-five chronic malnutrition rates rose from 48 per cent in 1987 to 56.8 per cent in 2000*. The number of HIV/AIDS cases continues to rise dramatically, particularly in rural areas. In 2001, the total estimated number of HIV-positive children under 14 years old was 55,000. Infection rates in girls aged 15 to 19 were four times higher than boys of the same age.

MIGRANTS/REFUGEES
At the end of 2002, more than 400,000 Burundians were living as refugees in other countries, most of them in Tanzania, DR Congo, Malawi, Rwanda and South Africa. In addition, some 47,000 Burundians were living in western Tanzanian settlements without official refugee status.

Approximately 400,000 or more Burundians were internally displaced by the year's end; out of the 1 million or so people that had been uprooted during the year, only 300,000 were in refugee camps.
      Some 50,000 Burundians have returned to some provinces in the north and east of the country, primarily from Tanzania since 2002. Unable to return to their villages because of poor security, many Burundians have crowded into camps for internally displaced people.
      Nearly 40,000 people from DR Congo were living in Burundi at the end of 2002; about half of these had arrived in October that year. One-third lived in two UNHCR-administered transit centers and two refugee camps near the Burundi-DR Congo border.

DEATH PENALTY
It is in force for all types of crimes.

*Latest data available in *The State of the World's Children* and *Childinfo* database, UNICEF, 2004.

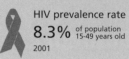
11   In November 1966, Prime Minister Captain Michael Micombero staged a coup and proclaimed the Republic of Burundi. The new President carried out a purge of Hutu government officials. In 1971, 350,000 Hutus were killed and an additional 70,000 went into exile.

12   From that point, the disputes over the control of political power fueled ethnic conflicts between Tutsis and Hutus. In 1972 a series of massacres between the groups became known as 'the 1972 crisis'. During the first four years of autonomous rule, there were five different Prime Ministers.

13   In 1976, Lt-Col Jean Baptiste Bagaza seized power in a coup and proclaimed the Second Republic. Bagaza broadened UPRONA, put a land reform program in operation, in defiance of the Tutsi élite and their foreign capitalist allies, and also rehabilitated labor unions. Until 1980, violent confrontations were prevented through a policy of silence on the topic of ethnicity which was considered a taboo subject, and religious freedom was restricted. In foreign policy, the new government drew closer to Tanzania, and China sent aid to develop Burundi's mineral resources.

14   A new Constitution became effective in 1981. It prevented the exploitation of the Hutu majority by the Tutsi minority, prompted the modernization of the political structure, adopted a socialist stance and gave men and women equal rights. The new constitutional reforms provoked strong feelings between the Government and the Catholic Church, leading to the confiscation of properties and deportation of 63 missionaries.

15   Elections held in 1982 (the first by universal suffrage), upheld Bagaza's policies. Despite Burundi's established political independence, the economy was in tatters. Being a landlocked country raised the price of both imports and exports (coffee was the leading export). The vast majority of Burundi's population lives in the north where overuse of the land has caused soil erosion, affecting its fertility. Wood is the main source of domestic fuel, although between 1960 and 1980 half of the country's forests were logged. Ninety per cent of agricultural products were consumed by the domestic market and rich nickel deposits were exploited. Belgian and US companies were developing the Musongati mines that also have large cobalt and uranium deposits.

16   In September 1987, Bagaza was overthrown by army major Pierre Buyoya (UPRONA) in another coup. In August 1989, strife between Hutu and Tutsis broke out in the north; several thousands of people, mostly Hutus, were massacred by the military, which was dominated by Tutsis. About 60,000 Hutus sought refuge in Rwanda. The Government responded by appointing a Hutu Prime Minister, Adrien Sibomana, and a new cabinet with equal representation of Hutus and Tutsis.

17   In 1989, there was reconciliation between the military government and the Catholic Church, which had regained its properties. A structural adjustment program was initiated which included the privatization of public enterprises and the creation of a 'watchdog' tribunal to combat corruption. In 1992, Buyoya enacted a multiparty constitution and called elections for October 1993, in which he was defeated by Melchior Ndadaye, from the opposition Front for Democracy in Burundi (FRODEBU) composed mainly of Hutus.

18   Three months after he was elected, Ndadaye was assassinated during an attempted coup. Prime Minister Sylvie Kinigi managed to keep the situation under control. The leaders of the rebellion were either arrested or fled to Zaire (now DR Congo). Cyprien Ntaryamira - a Hutu like Ndadaye - was appointed President by Parliament.

19   In spite of the failed coup, Ndadaye's assassination led to one of the worst massacres in Burundi's history. Supporters of the former president attacked UPRONA members - Tutsis or Hutus - causing the death of tens of thousands of people and the flight of some 700,000. The so-called 'extremist armed militias' - hostile to living alongside the other ethnic groups - were consolidated by this time, as were the 'Undefeated' Tutsis and the *Intagohekas* ('those who never sleep') Hutus. Violence spread.

20   On 6 April 1994, Ntaryamira died along with Rwandan president Juvenal Habyarimana when their plane was shot down. Another Hutu, Sylvestre Ntibantunganya, replaced the assassinated president. Violence intensified, especially between militias backing Hutu power and the Tutsi-controlled army. In February 1995, UPRONA left the Government in order to force Prime Minister Anatole Kanyenkiko to resign. His resignation paved the way for nomination of Tutsi Antoine Nduwayo and UPRONA's return to the coalition government alongside FRODEBU.

21   Fearing that the Burundian conflict would extend to neighboring countries, the UN and the Organization for African Unity decided to intervene. Pierre Buyoya, claiming the need to prevent an intervention by inter-African forces in the country, staged a new and successful coup in July 1996 and became the new president of Burundi. After this action, Ethiopia, Kenya, Rwanda, Tanzania, Uganda and Zaire (now DR Congo) imposed an embargo on the country. Amnesty International reported that it was was very difficult to distinguish between government and rebel responsibility for the massacres that took place after this coup.

22   In late 1997, the UN declared that international sanctions had had devastating effects, significantly degrading the living conditions of poor Burundians and questioned the embargo's usefulness. In September, Buyoya accused Tanzania of protecting more than 200,000 Hutu rebels and of intending to 'annex' Burundi. In October, Bujumbura reported the attacks of Tanzanian forces in the southern towns of Kubonga and Mugina. At the end of 1998, the number of victims of the civil war since 1993 was estimated at more than 250,000.

23   On 16 July 1998, the Transitional National Assembly was created, with the admission of 40 new representatives from the two political parties and the public. Until then, FRODEBU held 65 seats and UPRONA 16.

24   In January 2000, former South African President Nelson Mandela was chosen as mediator for negotiations between Burundi and Tanzania, in Arusha (Tanzania), which had begun in 1998 and continues still. Mandela was offered then US President Clinton's personal support. Agreements reached in these peace talks were violated several times by both countries and confrontations continued. As part of these agreements, in 2001 the appointment of a new transitional Government was set for 2003.

25   In December 2001, Buyoya received loans of $764 million for reconstruction from the international financial bodies.

26   Domitien Ndayizaye, the country's fourth Hutu President, took office in April 2003 as President of the transitional Government, which had been agreed in Arusha in 2001; however some feel that these negotiations are running into the sand. ■

PROFILE

ENVIRONMENT

Most of the land is made up of flat plateaus and relatively low hills covered with natural pastures. Located in the Great Lakes region (Lakes Tanganyika, Victoria), the Ruvubu River valley stretches through the country from north to south. Tropical forests are found in the low, western regions. Most inhabitants engage in subsistence agriculture (corn, cassava, sorghum, beans). Coffee is the main export. Internal communications are hampered by natural barriers and the nearest sea outlet is 1,400 km beyond the border, a fact which makes foreign trade difficult.

SOCIETY

Peoples: Most Burundians (86 per cent) belong to the Hutu ethnic group, an agricultural people of Bantu origin. They were traditionally dominated by the Tutsi or Watusi (13 per cent), pastoralists of Hamitic descent. There is a small minority (1 per cent) of Twa pygmies.
Religions: Christians, 67 per cent; 32 per cent follow traditional African religions and 1 per cent are Muslim. **Languages:** Rundi, Kirundi and French, official, with Swahili the business language.
Main Political Parties: Front for Democracy in Burundi (FRODEBU), of Ndadaye (assassinated in 1993); Union for National Progress (UPRONA). Also there are approximately 17 parties that do not take part in government but which signed the peace document in Arusha. Rebel groups that do not take part in the peace process include the National Council for Defense of Democracy (CNDD), with its armed branch (FDD); and the National Liberation Forces (PALIPEHUTU-FNL - Parti pour la libération du peuple hutu-Forces nationales de libération), another armed group.
Main Social Organizations: As a result of civil war, organizations are restructuring but there are many foreign non-governmental organizations (NGOs) and local NGOs like the Association for the Economic Promotion of Women.

THE STATE

Official Name: Republika y'u Burundi. **Administrative Divisions:** 15 Provinces. **Capital:** Bujumbura 378,600 people (2003).
Other Cities: Gitega 95,300 people (1986). **Government:** President Domitien Ndayizaye, a Hutu, elected in April 2003. Vice-President Alphonse Kadege, a Tutsi, elected in 2003. The National Assembly has 81 members, elected for a five-year period, which proportionally represents the two parties. FRODEBU has 65 seats and UPRONA 16. On 16 July, 1998, the Assembly was reformed into a Transitional National Assembly with the admission of 40 new legislators, representing the political parties and the public. **National Holiday:** 1 July, Independence (1962). **Armed Forces:** 12,600. Others: 1,500 Gendarmerie (1993).

Cambodia / Kâmpuchéa

Population:	14,825,135
Area:	181,040 km²
Capital:	Phnom Penh
Currency:	Riel
Language:	Khmer

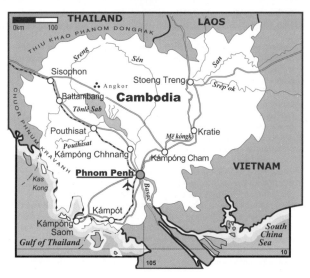

There is still debate and various theories about how long people have lived in what is now Cambodia, where they came from, or what languages they spoke before the introduction of writing in 300 BC. Carbon-dating evidence shows that there was pottery-making in the region and therefore human habitation from as early as 4000 BC. Ongoing studies indicate that those early inhabitants built their houses on piles of wood and lived on fish, pork and buffalo.

2   The land of Cambodia takes its name from a *rishi* (sage), for the first Cambodian kings proclaimed themselves descendants from the great sage Cambu Svayambhuva. The first kingdom of Cambodia was known in Chinese texts under the name of Funan and was founded by the Mon and Khmer peoples who migrated from the north in the first century AD. During these first centuries, a strong Indian influence was registered since Indian and Chinese pilgrims used to visit these coasts and exchanged silk and metals for spices, aromatic wood and gold.

3   For centuries Khmer people have practised the cult of Devaraja or god-king, who demanded absolute obedience in exchange for prosperity. Among the legends of this community is the 'Churning of the Ocean Milk', according to which the God Vishnu becomes a turtle and offers its shell to support a mountain. Gods and demons coil a rope around it and start to swivel it back and forth, beating the surrounding ocean of milk in order to create the ambrosia that will bring happiness and wealth. The most beautiful and impressive architectural works in the country date from the Angkor Empire period (the Khmers dominated the region from the ninth to the fifteenth century AD). The most outstanding are Angkor Wat, the 'capital that is a temple', and Angkor Thom, the 'great capital' (Wat, meaning 'temple').

4   Chinese sources reveal the scope of Indian influence by the example of the sage Kaundimnya, who married princess Soma, of Nagi origin (that is, semi-divine) and transformed the Khmer institutions along Indian lines. One of the modifications was probably the introduction of large-scale irrigation, which allowed the production of up to three rice harvests a year. Another was the worship of the Indian god Shiva, who became seen as a guardian ancestor and the spirit of land by the Khmer. A third modification ascribed to Kaundimnya was the coexistence of Buddhism and Hinduism, which characterized Cambodia for more than 1,000 years.

5   According to Chinese writings, the Funan created a centralized state machinery, headed by an absolute ruler, who ran agricultural labor and used farming surpluses to maintain his lifestyle and that of a caste of priests, and also to build fortresses, palaces and temples.

6   The first Sanskrit writings date from the 6th century and the first ones found in the Khmer language are from the 7th century. The developments between the decline of Funan and the foundation, three centuries later, of a new centralized state in the Cambodian north-eastern region (called Chenla in Chinese texts of that period) have not been clarified as yet. Chinese sources cite the existence of at least two Cambodian kingdoms, which - under the sovereignty of the Java Kingdom - requested recognition from China. Sanskrit and Khmer sources reveal that, during the 7th, 8th and 9th century, multiple kingdoms paid homage and fealty to the Java Kingdom.

7   In 790 AD, a Cambodian prince, born and raised in the Javanese court of the Sailendra dynasty, proclaimed himself descendant of the Funan rulers. He declared the Khmer territory independent from Java and was crowned Prince Jayavarman II. Ten years later, Jayavarman extended his power north, controlling vassal states and reached the river valley. In 802, he was named again in northeastern Cambodia, this time Chakravartin (old Sanskrit term meaning 'world ruler'). Jayavarman was the first 'national' king of Cambodia.

8   In 887, Indravarman I usurped the throne that belonged to his cousin Jayavarman III. During his reign, a large dam surrounding the capital city Roluos was built, which was the first of a vast system of dams, channels and irrigation canals that made these lands productive and allowed the Khmer to maintain a densely populated and centralized State in the area, which otherwise would have remained infertile. In 889, Yasovarman I became king of Khmer and built Angkor city (then called Yasodharapura) on the same site, which became capital of the Khmer Empire. In 1002, Suryavarman I usurped the throne and extended the Kingdom of Angkor to parts of today's territories of Thailand and Laos. In 1080, Angkor being conquered by the Kingdom of Champa, a Khmer ruler of a northern province proclaimed himself king under the name of Javayarman VI, ruling from his home province rather than from Angkor.

9   In 1177 Angkor was conquered again by Champa forces. Jayavarman VII became king in 1181 and conquered Vijaya, capital of Champa (in present-day Vietnam). Under his rule, the Khmer Kingdom reached its height, including virtually the whole of today's Thailand and Laos and even reaching Myanmar/Burma, Malaysia and Vietnam. Jayavarman VII converted from Hinduism to Buddhism, which became the national religion.

10   In 1200, work began on building the new capital city of Angkor Thom. This undertaking depleted the royal coffers and the Kingdom experienced economic problems in the following decades. The decline of Angkor coincided with the rise of the Thai Kingdom to the west and the Vietnamese one to the east. Turned into a small buffer state between both, the Khmer Kingdom alternately depended on the power of the Thais or the Vietnamese, since in order to be free from one conqueror, it needed the aid of the other. In 1432, when the Thais conquered Angkor once again, the Khmer people abandoned the city to the jungle.

11   During more than 400 years, the Kingdom was alternately conquered by the Thai and Vietnamese forces, until 1864, when Cambodian King Norodom accepted the status of French 'protectorate' for his country, in the hope that the French would protect them from Siam (Thailand) and Vietnam. The French were not able to prevent the Siamese (Thais) from temporarily annexing some west Cambodian areas, including the city of Battambang. However, by recognizing the French authority, King Norodom managed to prevent the country from being divided and distributed between Vietnam and Siam (Thailand). During the previous centuries, Vietnam had taken control of large tracts of Cambodia. The Mekong Delta area was inhabited by Cambodians until the 18th century.

12   In 1884, with the consent of King Norodom, Cambodia became a French colony. France's political influence increased and, together with Vietnam and Laos, Cambodia became a part of the Indo-Chinese Union. Later on, the colonial empire installed a European administrative system in Cambodia and developed the country's infrastructure. The economic development of the French Indo-Chinese Union did not reach the levels attained by Burma or India under British rule.

13   After France was invaded by Germany, Japanese forces occupied Indochina in 1940, with virtually no resistance. This enabled the Japanese to use the military facilities in exchange for allowing France to maintain administrative control. As a result Cambodia suffered less damage during World War II than the South Pacific islands, which were fiercely disputed by opposing forces.

14   In 1941, French authorities appointed the 18-year-old Prince Norodom Sihanouk as King of Cambodia, in the hope of

Life expectancy
57.4 years
2000-2005

GNI per capita
$280
2002

Literacy
68% total adult rate
2000

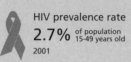

HIV prevalence rate
2.7% of population 15-49 years old
2001

controlling the politics of an inexperienced youngster. However, when the Japanese invaders withdrew, in 1945, Norodom Sihanouk declared independence. But the French occupied Indochina again. While Vietnam began an anti-colonial war, in Cambodia the King managed to gain greater autonomy from France.

[15] In 1947, a new constitution kept King Sihanouk on the throne, his power being limited by parliament. In 1949, Cambodia's legal system was re-negotiated, with Paris retaining control over military and foreign affairs and the remaining functions carried out by the 'protected' local Government. In 1953, the Vietnamese offensive forced French troops to withdraw from Cambodia, leaving the country fully independent. In 1955, Sihanouk abdicated in favor of his father, in order to participate in political life (consitutionally barred to the King). In 1960, the former King, now Prince Sihanouk, became head of state.

[16] During the first years of US aggression against Vietnam, Cambodia sought to maintain political and territorial neutrality. In 1965, however, Cambodia was bombed by South Vietnamese forces, under US orders, and Sihanouk's government moved closer towards the Chinese/Russian camp. In 1968 the US began air strikes on the so-called Ho Chi Minh Trail which came through Cambodian territory and was the supply-line from North Vietnam for the Viet Cong resistance in the South.

[17] While taking diplomatic action abroad to protect his country's sovereignty, Sihanouk was ousted in a CIA-backed coup in 1970. He was replaced by Lon Nol who, during his 5-year rule, received $1.6 billion in aid from Washington. During that period, the US invaded Cambodia to bomb the Communist Khmer Rouge guerrillas. As a result of this bombing, 100,000 Cambodians were killed. Sihanouk went into exile in Peking (now Beijing), and from there, supported by the Khmer Rouge, he organized the National United Front of Kâmpuchéa (NUFK) using the name of the country in Khmer language.

[18] In 1975, before the Viet Cong took Saigon, the Khmer Rouge entered Phnom Penh and proclaimed the Democratic Republic of Kâmpuchéa. In 1976, together with a new Constitution, the People's Congress confirmed Sihanouk and Khieu Samphan as head of state and Government, respectively. However, on his return from exile, Sihanouk was forced to resign and kept under house arrest, while Pol Pot rose to the fore as the regime's new leading force. Cambodia closed its borders even

IN FOCUS

ENVIRONMENTAL CHALLENGES
Deforestation has been caused by defoliants and mine and bomb damage during the war (1965-1975), in which the country lost approximately three-quarters of its fauna. The Taiwanese toxic wastes dumped in 1998 led to the increase in pollution for the population in the central areas. The illegal exploitation of forest products throughout the country and the plundering of precious stones from mines in the western region - bordering Thailand - have devastatated the environment and weakened biodiversity. In particular the destruction of the mangrove swamps threatens fishing.

WOMEN'S RIGHTS
Cambodian women have had the right to vote since 1995. During the period 1995-2000 the number of parliamentary seats held by women increased from 6 per cent to 8 per cent. However, they occupied no ministerial offices or equivalents.

The illiteracy rate for women over 15 decreased significantly in the period 1980-2000. In 1980 there were 60.9 per cent illiterate women (compared with 25.6 per cent men), while in 2000* those percentages were reduced to 43 per cent and 20 per cent respectively.

Among the 15-24 year old population, HIV/AIDS is more frequent in women (2.2 per cent) than in men (1.2 per cent).

In 2000, Cambodian women constituted 38 per cent of the total labor force, which was 1,113,000

people. In 1995, 79 per cent worked in the agricultural sector, 3 per cent in industry and 18 per cent in services.

CHILDREN
As a consequence of the increase in HIV/AIDS infection, there is a growing number of children born to HIV-postiive mothers. UNICEF's recent campaigns have tried to reduce micronutrient deficiencies and to promote appropriate nutritional practices and care.

School enrolment rates are similar in girls and boys between 6 and 11 years old, but the drop-out rate in girls over 11 years old has increased.

Sexual exploitation and trafficking are serious problems. There is a significant number of children living or working on the streets or experiencing working conditions that adversely affect their normal development.

Forty five per cent of children under five were moderately or severely underweight, while approximately the same percentage suffered from moderate or severe arrested development.

INDIGENOUS PEOPLES/ ETHNIC MINORITIES
Vietnamese people are widely dispersed across the territory. Most of them moved there in the post-1945 era. Another group migrated to Cambodia in 1979, after the Vietnamese invasion. They have assimilated the Khmer language, and most of them practice Buddhism. The status of the Vietnamese living in Cambodia has been affected by the relations between Hanoi and Phnom Penh, and by domestic disputes between the different ideological factions

battling for control of the Government.

MIGRANTS/REFUGEES
By the end of 2002, there were around 16,000 Cambodian refugees in Vietnam. The majority of them were Vietnamese ethnic groups that had left Cambodia between 1990 and 1995.

Cambodia sheltered at least 280 refugees throughout 2002, 144 of whom were of the Vietnamese Montagnard minority that had entered the country between 2001 and 2002 and were waiting for the US to grant them asylum. In the meantime, UNHCR granted refugee status to 54 other people of different nationalities, with 81 others waiting for refugee status. In 2001, more than 1,000 Montagnards had settled in the Northern provinces of Mondolkiri and Ratanakiri, escaping the ethnic conflicts in Vietnam. Around 250 Montagnards returned to Vietnam in 2001. Although the Vietnamese Government's first reaction was to arrest and deport the members of this group, the Cambodian Government demanded their repatriation, stating that they had illegally abandoned the country. Phnom Penh allowed UNHCR to intercede - as a result of international pressure - and to relocate them in areas under their control within Cambodia. The US accepted 791 as refugees.

DEATH PENALTY
It was abolished in 1989.

*Latest data available in *The State of the World's Children* and *Childinfo* database, UNICEF, 2004.

to diplomats of friendly countries. Under Pol Pot's regime, money was eliminated and large numbers of the urban population were transferred to the countryside, enforcing the return to an agricultural lifestyle. Mass purges and executions, hunger and illness, left at least a million people dead.

[19] The Pol Pot regime strengthened ties with China and broke off relations with Vietnam. By refusing to recognize borders 'established by colonialism' which had been established by Hanoi and Sihanouk's government in 1973 in the absence of accurate historical boundary documentation - Khmer Rouge troops were sent to invade Vietnamese territory in late 1977. In 1978, a pro-Vietnamese faction of the Khmer Rouge created the United Front for the Salvation of Kâmpuchéa (KNUFNS), under the

presidency of General Heng Samrin. In 1979, the Vietnamese forces and those of the United Front entered Phnom Penh and proclaimed the People's Republic of Kâmpuchéa (PRK), establishing a People's Revolutionary Council to rebuild the country.

[20] While Pol Pot was tried in absentia for war crimes, his forces turned to guerrilla warfare. With the support of China and the US, the Khmer Rouge maintained UN recognition as the country's legitimate Government. In 1982, Sihanouk and the Khmer Serei, led by Son Sann, joined the Government of Democratic Kâmpuchéa in exile, together with the Khmer Rouge. The Government of Phnom Penh aimed at reactivating the industrial, agricultural and transportation sectors. The Soviet Union and other

socialist countries gave aid which was focused on the reconstruction of power sources and the formation of a very basic industrial infrastructure.

[21] Municipal and legislative elections were held in 1981, with many candidates for each post. The Non-Aligned Movement summit meeting in New Delhi, decided to leave Cambodia's seat vacant, as they could not decide which of the two civil war protagonists was the legitimate representative. In 1985, the Vietnamese announced the withdrawal of 150,000 troops over a period of five years. In spite of the dissolution of the Communist Party in 1981, the Khmer Rouge's entry into the political arena posed the main obstacle to a negotiated settlement.

[22] Difficulties stemming from the war affected the Cambodian

Government, especially the international isolation since it was only officially recognized by some 30 countries. Still, it managed to bring about a steady increase in the production of rice, cattle, pigs and poultry.

23   In 1986 the Phnom Penh Government made overtures to Sihanouk within the context of a general agreement, offering him the position of head of state in a Government from which the Khmer Rouge would be excluded. Between 1987 and 1989, Prime Minister Hun Sen met with Sihanouk on six occasions. The main disagreement each time was whether the Khmer Rouge would be admitted to a new provisional government or not. In 1989, a curfew in effect since 1979 was lifted and private ownership of some 'non-strategic' enterprises was permitted. Land and transportation services were privatized. During that year, to complete the transformation and diminish international isolation, the country changed its name to the State of Cambodia.

24   In Paris, that same year, the International Conference for Peace in Cambodia ended in failure as the factions of the armed opposition could not come to any agreement. The two main points of disagreement were UN monitoring of the Vietnamese withdrawal and Khmer Rouge participation in government. Vietnamese troops withdrew completely that year. In 1990, a Phnom Penh military offensive eliminated rebel bases and opposition forces retreated to the Thai border. Bangkok sponsored a new Sihanouk-Hun Sen meeting and both leaders agreed to the installation of a supernational agency which would symbolize the sovereignty and national unity of Cambodia, under an 'adequate' UN supervision. In 1990, the US announced they would withdraw recognition to Democratic Kâmpuchéa and would initiate negotiations with Vietnam over a peace settlement.

25   In 1991, a peace treaty was signed. The Supreme National Council was created, with representatives of the Phnom Penh Government and part of the opposition, chaired by Sihanouk who was to govern the country until elections in 1993. In 1992, the UN sent a peacekeeping force to enforce the cease-fire and organize the elections.

26   In the constituent elections of 1993, boycotted by the Khmer Rouge, the supporters of FUNCINPEC, led by Sihanouk's son Norodom Ranariddh, won the majority of seats. In the new Government, Ranariddh and Hun Sen shared the post of Prime Minister. That year, a new Constitution was enacted which turned the National Assembly into a Parliament and established a parliamentary monarchy. Sihanouk was appointed King, 'independent' of all political parties. The King, who spent most of 1994 in China undergoing medical treatment for cancer, continued to advocate a 'national reconciliation' Government, with the inclusion of the Khmer Rouge.

27   In 1996, the Khmer Rouge began to show signs of weakness. Many defections suggested that the Government policy aim of splitting the Khmer Rouge was proving successful. Accused of treason and of planning a civil war alongside the Khmer Rouge, Prince Ranariddh was ousted in 1997 by Cambodian army officials loyal to the second Prime Minister Hun Sen. From China, King Sihanouk approved Hun Sen's proposal to appoint foreign minister Ung Huot (FUNCINPEC), as first Prime Minister. In 1998 the monarch pardoned his son - sentenced to a 30-year prison term - in an attempt to delay the political chaos which followed Ranariddh's expulsion and as a means to secure international financial aid which had been interrupted since the coup.

28   After the death of Pol Pot in Thailand in 1998, Ranariddh returned to Cambodia to compete in the election held that year, which Hun Sen won by a narrow margin. Ranariddh's FUNCINPEC and the opposition party's leader, Sam Rainsy (SRP), denounced irregularities in the elections, including the disappearance of ballot papers, pressure on voters, errors in the count and an insufficient number of international observers. According to the 600 observers, there were no defects in the count.

29   In 1999, under the effects of the South East Asian economic crisis that started in 1997, Cambodia joined ASEAN as its tenth member. Opposition leader Sam Rainsy was fearful that that ASEAN would destroy Cambodia's industry, which found it hard to compete, leaving the country reduced to exporting raw materials.

30   Spien Kizuna, the first bridge over the Cambodian stretch of the Mekong river, was opened. The 1.5 km bridge, built with Japanese money, lies 75 km northeast of the capital. The Government hoped it would stimulate domestic trade, since it connects the country by land from east to west and would strengthen links with Laos and Vietnam, countries which border the river with Cambodia.

31   In 2002, the first local elections in many years were held. Hun Sen's Cambodian Pracheachon Party won 1,597 of the 1,620 communes in the whole country and the opposition only won 23 (10 for FUNCINPEC and 13 for Sam Rainsy's SRP). Although not totally free and held in a very violent atmosphere - at least 20 FUNCINPEC and SRP candidates were murdered during the campaign - it was estimated that their long-term effect would be positive.

32   That year, the Government imposed a three month deadline on UN attempts to restart negotiations on the trial of Khmer Rouge leaders. (In 1999, Cambodia had agreed with the UN for a tribunal to try former Khmer Rouge leaders for crimes against humanity committed under the Pol Pot regime). According to the Cambodian Government, low-ranking officials will not be judged and the trial will be focused on leaders with direct responsibiliy in genocide. The UN withdrew its support for the process in 2002, stating that the independence and impartiality of the court could not be guaranteed, since the national law would take precedence over the agreement with the UN.

33   The Government accepted the repatriation of some 900 Montagnards - people from the mountains of Vietnam - who fled to Cambodia in 2001 after suffering persecution at the hands of the Vietnamese Government (see Vietnam). Human rights groups have condemned a repatriation agreement between Phnom Penh and Hanoi, as they consider it opens the way for forced expulsions of the Montagnards to Vietnam. In 2002, for the first time, a Vietnamese newspaper accused the Cambodian Government of forcibly repatriating the mountain people.

34   After intense negotiations during the Cancun Ministerial Conference in September 2003, the World Trade Organization (WTO) approved Cambodia's membership. This would allow Cambodia to achieve greater regional and global economic integration. Australia and Cambodia signed a bilateral agreement which covered current and prospective exports interests in goods and services of both countries.

35   In October 2004 King Sihanouk announced that he was abdicating the throne at the age of 81. ∎

PROFILE

ENVIRONMENT

The territory is mainly a plain surrounded by mountains, like the Cardamour Mountains in the southwest. In the north, the Dangrek range rises abruptly from the plain. The central basin of the country, occupied by the Tonle Sap (Great Lake) depression, is the point of confluence into the Mekong, one of the largest rivers in Asia. The country has a sub-tropical climate with monsoon rains. The population is concentrated in the central basin where rice, the mainstay of the diet and principal export crop, is grown. The country also exports rubber. The mineral reserves of phosphate, iron ore and limestone are as yet mainly unexploited.

SOCIETY

Peoples: the Cambodians represent a culturally homogeneous ethnic group that extends beyond the present boundaries of Cambodia. There are Vietnamese (5 per cent), Chinese (1 per cent) and Laotian minorities.

Religions: In 1986 Buddhism - the religion of the majority - became the country's official religion. There is an Islamic minority (Cham).

Languages: Khmer, official and predominant, together with other minority languages. **Main Political Parties:** Cambodian People's Party (Pracheachon), led by Chen Sim; Cambodian People's Party United National Front for an Independent, Neutral, Peaceful and Cooperative Cambodia (Funcinpec); Sam Rainsy Party. As extra-parliamentary parties: Liberal Democratic Buddhist Party, of Son Sann; and the Khmer Rouge that keeps the name 'Democratic Kâmpuchéa'.

THE STATE

Official Name: Kâmpuchéa. **Administrative Divisions:** 22 provinces. **Capital:** Phnom Penh (Phnum Pénh) 1,157,000 people (2003). **Other Cities:** Battambang 183,600; Kompong Cham 53,800 (2000). **Government:** Parliamentary monarchy. King Norodom Sihanouk since September 1993. Executive Power held by Prime Minister, Samdech Hun Sen since November 1998. Bicameral Legislature: 122-member National Assembly; 61-member Senate. **National Holiday:** 9 November, Independence Day (1953). **Armed Forces:** The Royal Cambodian Armed Forces (87,700) were created in 1993 by the merger of the Cambodian People's Armed Forces and the two non-communist resistance armies. Other: the Khmer Rouge forces estimated in about less than 5,000 by the end of 1994. **Foreign Forces:** United Nations (UNTAC): 16,000 plus 3,540 civil police officers.

Cameroon / Cameroun

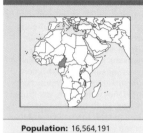

Population:	16,564,191
Area:	475,440 km²
Capital:	Yaoundé
Currency:	CFA franc
Language:	French and English

The indigenous inhabitants of Cameroon, the Bakas (pygmys), today live in the forests in the south and east of the region. Bantu-speaking people, originally from the highlands, were the first group to migrate, after 200 BC, east and south, spreading new crop varieties and methods for working iron. Archeological evidence shows that humans lived in the region 50,000 years ago, in large kingdoms and states, and also in recent times, for example the kingdom of Sao near Lake Chad, around the 5th century AD.

[2] The migration of Fulani herders from the western Sahel region - they were among the first Muslims to spread out across West Africa - helped transform the local economies into part of a regional nexus which later gave rise to the Emirate of Adamaua in the north central region, dominating and displacing non-Muslim inhabitants. The nomadic Fulanis lived in portable huts and rarely killed cattle for meat. The urban Fulanis were strong Muslims, whereas the herders were less inclined to religion.

[3] In 1472, Portuguese explorer Fernando Po named the river Wouri *Cameroes* (Portuguese for shrimp) because of the great number of crustaceans in it. The name eventually became Cameroon. The Portuguese arrived in 1500, working with sugarcane and the slave trade. Malaria and other diseases hindered the proliferation of European colonies and the conquest of the hinterland until 1800, when quinine (medicine for malaria) became available.

[4] German penetration began in 1884 when envoy Gustav Nachtigal agreed with the Doualas, a coastal people, to make the region a protectorate. In 1885 the Berlin Conference awarded Cameroon to Germany. In 1894 Adamaua, which the British wanted, was formally included. The Protectorate was conflictual: the Doualas dominated trade that the Germans wanted to control between the coast and Yaoundé, the trade center between

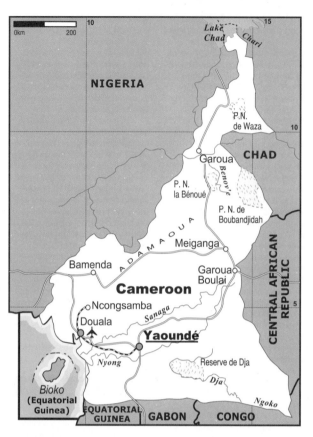

Adamaua and the south. In 1897, the Doualas began a bloody 4-year war against the Germans, who appropriated the most fertile lands, while the Africans died of hunger by the thousands.

[5] In 1918 France and Britain invaded Cameroon: the French took three-quarters of the territory, and the British took the rest. The cause of the independence organizations was facilitated by tensions between the colonial powers. In 1945, the People's Union of Cameroon (UPC) was founded, headed by Rubem Um Nyobé. With great popular support it launched a series of legal campaigns between 1948 and 1956, when it was outlawed. Nationalist leaders fled to the British-held western sector and organized a guerrilla movement. The UPC established liberated zones in the southern forests, setting up autonomous governments - a first for sub-Saharan Africa. The efficiency of the guerrillas made it possible for them to resist constant French attacks, until 1960 (Nyobé died in 1958, but the revolution continued).

[6] UPC resistance forced the French to adopt a new strategy, adding political maneuvering to their repressive tactics. Paris created the National Union of Cameroon (UNC), merging two conservative, predominantly Islamic, northern-based parties. In 1960 UNC leader Alhaji Ahmadou Ahidjo became president after the French Cameroon gained full independence as the Republic of Cameroon. In 1961 it became the Federal Republic of Cameroon, after unification with the southern part of British Cameroons. UPC nationalists were unable to help shape their long-held dream of an independent Cameroon as they were mostly underground or in exile. Ahidjo developed one of sub-Saharan Africa's most efficiently repressive systems. European human rights groups revealed the existence of thousands of political prisoners in the country.

[7] In 1982 Ahidjo suddenly resigned and was succeeded by his

PROFILE

ENVIRONMENT

The country is divided into three regions: the plains of the Lake Chad basin in the northern region (savanna where cattle are raised and corn and cotton are grown); the central part, made up of humid grasslands; and the southern part, an area with rich volcanic soil where the main cash crops (coffee, bananas, cocoa and palm oil) are grown. It is in the latter that most of the population lives. Drought and desertification are the main concerns in the southern region, which covers 25 per cent of the nation's land area, and houses over a quarter of the population.

SOCIETY

Peoples: There are some 200 ethnic groups, the main ones being the Doualas, Bamilekes, Tikars and Bamauns in the south; the Euondos and Fulbes in the west, and the Fulanis in the north. In the southeast live the Baka Pygmies, who live by hunting and fishing.

Religions: Half the population practice traditional African religions. Christians are a majority in the south while Muslims predominate in the north.

Languages: French and English are the official languages. There are nearly 200 African languages (Beti and Bulu being the most widely spoken). German is also spoken.

Main Political Parties: Democratic Alliance of the People of Cameroon (RDPC, formerly the only party),

Movement for the Defense of the Republic, Social Democratic Front (FSD), Social Democratic Movement, National Union for Democracy and Progress (UNDP), Democratic Union of Cameroon, Union of the Peoples of Cameroon.

Main Social Organizations: In 1971, the Government banned the Workers' Union of Cameroon, heir to the labor movement from the previous century. The Government-run National Workers' Union of Cameroon was created. Trade Union Confederation of Cameroon Workers. There is a strong separatist movement in the English-speaking area of Cameroon. People's Conference of 'Southern Cameroons' (SCPC) unites several parties and organizations.

THE STATE

Official Name: République du Cameroun.
Capital: Yaoundé 1,616,000 people (2003).
Other Cities: Douala 1,409,200 people; Garoua 180,900; Ncongsamba 106,800 (2000).
Government: Parliamentary republic. Paul Biya, President since 1982, re-elected in 1992 and 1997. Peter Mafani Musonge, Prime Minister since September 1996. Unicameral Legislature: National Assembly, with 180 members. **National Holidays:** 1 January, Independence Day (1960); 1 October, Reunification (1961); 20 May, proclamation of the Republic (1972). **Armed Forces:** 14,600.

| Life expectancy **46.2** years 2000-2005 | GNI per capita **$560** 2002 | Literacy **71%** total adult rate 2000 | HIV prevalence rate **11.8%** of population 15-49 years old 2001 |

former Prime Minister, Paul Biya, who maintained his predecessor's political and economic policies, though many of Adhidjo's followers supported an attempted coup by a group of military officers. Young people - especially students - resisted this by taking to the streets. Growing unemployment and food shortages undermined Cameroon's traditionally prosperous image. Biya attempted to reinforce his control by calling early elections in 1984. Political parties were banned, and he was re-elected. Nevertheless, overall instability led to a new coup attempt, followed by a series of bloody incidents in which 200 people were killed. In the 1980s, the UNC changed its name to 'Democratic Group of the People of Cameroon' (RDPC), but its political line remained the same.

8   The UPC later adopted a more flexible stance in order to broaden its social scope, and Biya created new northern provinces to reduce the economic and political power of the Muslim north. Disagreements over oil revenues aggravated inter-ethnic and inter-regional friction. Economic problems stemming from a drop in world prices for coffee, rubber and cotton were exacerbated by Cameroon's dependence on French companies which controlled almost 44 per cent of the export market. Faced with the fall in oil prices and foreign debt payments, the Government sought World Bank and IMF support to stabilize its finances. By reducing imports and state expenditure, privatizing public enterprises and reorganizing the banking system, the country's debts were renegotiated with the Paris Club.

9   In 1990 the Government authorized the creation of political parties: some 70 groups were granted legal recognition. The following year, the Government set legislative elections for 1992. The opposition wanted the constitution and electoral law to be modified prior to the elections. In 1992, in the country's first multiparty elections, Biya was re-elected, press censorship increased and the position of prime minister was eliminated. The RDPC won 88 of the 180 parliamentary seats. The National Union for Democracy and Progress (UNDP) came in second.

10   Seven parties fielded candidates: among them, the Social Democratic Front (FSD) led by John Fru Ndi, the main opposition party representing the English-speaking community; and the Democratic Union of Cameroon, led by Adamu Ndam Njoya. Amid widespread accusations of fraud, the Government's victory (39.98 per cent against the FSD's 35.97 per cent) provoked incidents in the English-speaking Northwestern Province, Fru Ndi's territory. International

ENVIRONMENTAL CHALLENGES
The region's forests are one of the 25 places in the world with endangered biodiversity. Cameroon's mountain range is isolated and so its inhabitants depend on it for their basic resources. Deforestation has caused many streams and much wildlife to disappear. Water-borne diseases, exhaustion of the land from extensive cattle rearing, desertification and indiscriminate hunting and fishing are some of the country's major problems.

WOMEN'S RIGHTS
Between 1995 and 2000 the number of women in parliament fell from 12 per cent to 6 per cent, while their presence in ministerial offices or equivalents increased from 3 per cent to 6 per cent.

In 2000, 8 per cent of men and only 1 per cent of women were enrolled in higher education. Although adult illiteracy has diminished, it was still higher among women*: rates fell to 36.3 per cent for women and 20.9 per cent for men.

In 2000*, 44 per cent of pregnant women suffered from anemia, and 7.8 per cent of women aged 15-24 were living with HIV/AIDS.

CHILDREN
In 2002, the mortality rate for children under five was 166 for every 1,000 live births. Fifty-one per cent of the population lives below the poverty line; among these, most are women. 56 per cent of the people are 20 years old or under. Eleven per cent of the children are born underweight*.

Six out of ten children may become victims of human trafficking; the main reasons for this high rate are: poverty, lack of opportunities in rural areas, lack of access to education and high demand for cheap labor in the informal sectors of the economy.

In 2001, 210,000 children between 0 and 14 years old were orphaned by HIV/AIDS.

INDIGENOUS PEOPLES/ ETHNIC MINORITIES
The Baka, the Gyeli and the Tikar, nomadic peoples also called Pygmies, live in the southeast and southwest forests. The Government and the Catholic Church have tried to make them settle in 'pilot' villages. Farmers, timber merchants and plantations pay them less than the minimum wage and build roads across their forests. Children of forest nomads may often be denied access to local schools; educational curricula are not always relevant for their culture and their real economic prospects. The Chad-Cameroon oil pipeline poses a threat to the Gyeli.

During the 17th century the Fulani - an Islamic nomadic group - entered the territory, and 100 years later they built the Adamaua Emirate in the north-central region. The Bamileke (27 per cent) and a group of Bantu peoples dominate the economic and cultural life of West Cameroon; the westerners (around 20 per cent) are Christian English-speaking minorities; the Fulani (8 per cent), whose power base is in the north, are made up of 21 chieftaincies.

After World War I, the British controlled the western part (10 per cent of the territory), while the rest of the territory was under French

control. The French-speakers dictated the terms of the 1961 reunification. In the 1990s, the growing hostility and repression by the central government, which had favored French-speakers - for example by granting them royalties from the oil extracted in the west of the country - led the English-speaking lobbies to demand autonomy for their region and a return to the 1972 federal structure.

MIGRANTS/REFUGEES
During the 1970s and 1980s, large groups of Chadians arrived in Cameroon, fleeing from Chad's civil war and the insurrection. Although 7,000 people have returned, helped by the voluntary repatriation operation launched in 1999 by UNHCR, by the end of 2002 there were still around 30,000 refugees in Cameroon. More than 20,000 Nigerians - mostly Fulani who had entered the country with hundreds of thousands of livestock after escaping ethnic persecution - found refuge during 2002, joining others who had already settled there. Around 8,000 Nigerians returned home that year, but some 15,000 remained in Cameroon. There were also about 2,000 refugees from other African countries, most of them in Yaounde.

Around 5,000 Cameroonians were seeking asylum in Europe.

DEATH PENALTY
The death penalty is in force, even for ordinary crimes.

*Latest data available in *The State of the World's Children* and *Childinfo* database, UNICEF, 2004.

observers confirmed the fraud, but the Supreme Court refused to annul the election. Fru Ndi proclaimed himself President, and the Government decreed a state of emergency in the Northwest. Fru Ndi and his supporters were immediately placed under house arrest.

11   In late 1992 government repression intensified, bringing international condemnation, particularly when four members of the Bar Association were arrested in December for leading protests and one died as a result of torture. The United States suspended aid to the country; Biya ended the state of emergency and released Fru Ndi.

12   Biya was re-elected in 1997 in a poll challenged by the opposition parties, some of which had called for a boycott of the elections. Just three million of the six million registered voters were called on to cast ballots.

The rest were excluded by the Government, which insisted they were 'foreigners'.

13   In the wake of the 1999 publication of a Transparency International report that ranked Cameroon as the second most corrupt country in the world, Biya announced in January 2000 a campaign to fight corruption in his government as well as continued economic reforms. He promised to implement the constitutional changes that had been approved by Parliament in 1996, which included the creation of a Senate, of regional councils and of a constitutional council.

14   A trial of English-speaking secessionists in 2000 ended with prison sentences for 33 of the defendants. Two of them, members of the RDPC, were also sentenced on embezzlement charges. The FSD

continued to support the separatist cause of the National Council of South Cameroon. The UN reported that torture and mistreatment were 'systematic and widespread' at Cameroon's police stations.

15   In 2002 the International Court at The Hague ruled in favor of Cameroon over its border dispute with Nigeria, a case put before the Court in 1998. The case, which began in 1994 with a claim by Cameroon over sovereignty of the Bakassi peninsula - which is rich in fishing and has potential oil wealth - turned into a question of defining the border between the two countries, and also affected Equatorial Guinea. Nigeria rejected the ruling, keeping its occupation forces in the area. In 2003, after talks in Cameroon, Nigeria decided not to leave the peninsula, at least for a further three years. ■

Canada / Canada

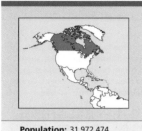

Population:	31,972,474
Area:	9,970,610 km²
Capital:	Ottawa
Currency:	Canadian dollar
Language:	English and French

Sometime between 20,000 and 35,000 years ago, during the last Ice Age, the first humans to make their homes in North America migrated from Asia. Unknown numbers of people moved southward along the western edge of the North American ice cap. Archaeological evidence and oral traditions help rebuild the period that preceded contact with Europeans. There were 12 major language groups among the peoples living in what is now Canada: Algonquin, Iroquois, Siouan, Athabascan, Kootenaian, Salishan, Wakashan, Tsimshian, Haidan, Tlinglit, Inuktitut, and Beothukan. Within each language group there were usually political and cultural divisions. These subgroups were also divided; at the time of contact the Iroquois had organized themselves into a confederacy, the Iroquois League, consisting of the Mohawk, Oneida, Onondaga, Cayuga, and Seneca. A sixth group, the Tuscarora, joined later. The Inuit (Eskimo) who live in Canada's Arctic regions today were the last of the aboriginal peoples to reach Canada. The European colonists who came to North America in the 16th century estimated the indigenous population of the continent to be between 10 and 12 million.

² The peoples of the Eastern Woodlands (Huron, Iroquois, Petun, Neutral, Ottawa, and Algonquin), created a mixed subsistence economy of hunting and agriculture supplemented by trade. The Huron and the Iroquois formed political and religious confederacies and both created extensive trade systems and political alliances with other groups. Peoples living in the far north did not appear to have formed larger political communities, while those of the West Coast and the Eastern Woodlands formed sophisticated political, social, and cultural institutions. All the groups were self-governing and politically independent.

³ In AD 985 Norse (Viking) sailors sailing from Iceland to Greenland were blown far westward off their course and sighted the coast of Labrador. In 1000 AD Leif Ericson became the first European to land in North America. A colony was established in what the Vikings described as Vinland, which died out during the 14th and 15th centuries.

⁴ Italian navigator Giovanni Caboto (Cabot) sailed from Bristol in 1497 under a commission from the English king to search for a short route to Asia (what became known as the Northwest Passage). As Cabot and his sons explored the coasts of Labrador, Newfoundland, and possibly Nova Scotia they discovered that the cold northwest Atlantic waters were teeming with fish. Soon Portuguese, Spanish, and French fishing crews braved the Atlantic crossing to fish in the waters of the Grand Banks. Some landed on the coast of Newfoundland to dry their catch before returning to Europe. The English paid little heed to the Atlantic fishery until 1583, when Sir Humphrey Gilbert laid claim to the lands around present-day St John's in Newfoundland. The French also claimed parts of Newfoundland, primarily on the north and west coasts of the island. The initial period of contact between the Indians and the Europeans was based on the fishery. Although each was deeply suspicious of the other, the fishing crews and the Indians carried on a sporadic trade. Chiefly as a sideline of the fishing industry, there continued an unorganized traffic in furs.

⁵ Between the 17th and 19th centuries, these territories were colonized by Britain and France. Some areas changed hands several times until the Parliament and the King granted Canada to Britain. Colonization increased thanks to the profitable fur trade, with the local population growing to almost half a million by the end of the 19th century. The British North America Act of 1867 determined that the Canadian constitution would be similar to Britain's, with executive power vested in the King and delegated to a Governor General and Council. The legislative function would be carried out by a Parliament composed of a Senate and a House of Commons.

⁶ In 1931, the Statute of Westminster released Britain's dominions from the colonial laws under which they had been governed, giving Canada legislative autonomy. That same year, Norway recognized Canadian sovereignty over the Arctic regions to the north of the main part of its territory. In 1981, the Canadian Government reached an agreement with the British Parliament over constitutional transition. The following year, the 1867 Constitution was replaced by the Act of Canada, which granted Canada the autonomy to reform its own constitution. The Constitution Act of 1982 included a Charter of Rights and Freedoms, which recognized the country's pluralistic heritage and the rights of its indigenous peoples. It set forth the principle of equal benefits among the country's ten provinces, and the sovereignty of each province over its own natural resources. The largely French-speaking province of Quebec did not sign the agreement.

⁷ The religious sentiment and political nationalism evoked in Quebec's French population when the territory was occupied by English Protestants in 1760 led Quebec to take on a special role as guardian of the Catholic faith, the French language and the French heritage in North America. It was a role that it performed well. From a French population of 6,000 in 1769, the number of Québecois had increased to 6 million by 1960. In Quebec, four-fifths of the population speak French as a first language and preserve their cultural identity. Provincial autonomy was, and remains, a delicate issue. In 1977, the ruling separatist Parti Québecois (PQ), led by René Lévèsque, adopted French as the official language of education, business and local public administration. Lévèsque discarded unilateral separation, proposing instead a concept of 'sovereignty-association' with a monetary and customs union, but voters rejected this proposal by 59.5 to 40.5 per cent in a plebiscite held in 1980. In 1990, a poll revealed that 62 per cent of Québecois were in favor of their province's secession.

⁸ Antiquated British law governed gender issues in North America for a long time, and it was only in 1929 that Canadian women obtained full legal rights. True sexual equality was finally established with the 1982 Constitution. Each province has an equal rights law, guaranteeing access to housing, jobs, services and other facilities, without discrimination on the basis of race, religion, age, nationality or gender. The marriage of gay and lesbian people is now legal in Canada - one of the few places where this is the case.

⁹ Liberal governments, led by Pierre Trudeau, were elected in 1968, 1972, 1974 and again in 1980, after a brief Conservative interlude. Trudeau loosened Canada's traditional ties with Western Europe and the US, and strengthened those with the Far East, Africa and Latin America. In addition, he refused to participate in the economic blockade against Cuba. Economic difficulties stemming from the worldwide recession triggered a sharp drop in the Liberal Party's (LP) popularity, in favor of the Conservative Party (CP). In 1983, Conservative leader Brian Mulroney, a labor relations lawyer and businessman from Quebec, became Prime Minister, replacing John Turner, who had succeeded Trudeau as head of the LP. Mulroney re-established a 'special relationship' between Canada and the US, starting negotiations for a free trade agreement in 1985. This agreement, which went into effect in January 1989, provoked criticism from the Liberals and other members of the opposition, who claimed that the terms of the agreement were overly favorable to the US. Nevertheless, it received majority support from the voters in the 1988 election.

¹⁰ The Conservative victory was made possible by the Québecois votes (reflecting the growing economic importance of French-speaking voters) and by the impact

Life expectancy
79.3 years
2000-2005

GNI per capita
$22,300
2002

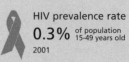

HIV prevalence rate
0.3% of population,
15-49 years old
2001

of the Meech Lake Accord initiated by Mulroney and signed in 1987. In it the Federal Government ceded important powers to the provinces, granting Quebec for the first time recognition of its unique cultural status. To be implemented, the Meech Lake Accord had to be ratified by the unanimous consent of each of the provinces but Newfoundland and Manitoba blocked it. In Manitoba the one vote against came from a Native Canadian who did not accept the 'distinct society' clause for Quebec.

[11] Canada's first trading partner is the US, and vice versa, but while the volume of Canada's sales to the US accounts for one-fifth of its total production, American exports to Canada represent less than 3 per cent. No other major Western economy maintains a trade imbalance of such magnitude. It is comparable only to the dependence of Southern countries in relation to the industrialized countries. With the 1989 free trade agreement Canada's integration with the American economy was accentuated. Through trade, the extension of credit, and investments in Canada, the US secured ever greater control over Canadian natural resources and majority control over shares in some Canadian industries. This degree of dependence has been labeled 'colonial', even though Canada is the world's eighth largest industrial power, with a standard of living ranked tenth in the world (according to OECD statistics).

[12] The Canadian Armed Forces (CF) are charged with protecting national interests both inside and outside the country, with defending North America in cooperation with the US, and complying with its NATO commitments; in addition, it participates in UN Peacekeeping. Relations between Canada and the US became tense in 1985, when a US Coast Guard vessel passed through the Northwest Passage without Canadian authorization. The US recognizes Canadian sovereignty over the Arctic islands but not over its waters. A similar dispute exists with relation to the waters surrounding the French islands of St Pierre and Miquelon. Canada made little headway in getting the US to control industrial pollutants, which drift over Canadian territory, bringing with them acid rain. The Canadian Government made a commitment to reduce its industrial emissions by half, anticipating a reduction of 20 per cent by the year 2005.

[13] In 1991, Quebec's Prime Minister Robert Bourassa started the second phase of the James Bay hydroelectric project, damming and diverting 9 rivers which run into James and Hudson Bays, covering 350,000 sq km in the northwest of the province. The first phase, called 'La Grande' (the big one) generates more than 10,000 megawatts. James Bay produces a total power of 27,000 megawatts (more than in Itaipú, Brazil or China's Three Gorges). Almost 11,000 Cree and 7,000 Inuit have been hunting and fishing in this area for 5,000 years. In addition, the greatest population of beluga whales, the biggest herds of caribou and many of the world's seals live in this region. More than 13,000 sq km were flooded in order to complete the project. When a floodgate was opened at 'La Grande' dam in 1984, about 10,000 caribou drowned.

[14] The project's second phase will complete the damming of the rivers and flood a further 10,000 sq km. The James Bay project will enable Canada to sell electricity to the US, as well as boost internal energy consumption such as for the energy-intensive aluminum industry. The consequences of this project on the region's environment are unforeseeable: in 1973 hunting and fishing provided two-thirds of the local population's food. By 1993 these provided just one quarter. An agreement allowed local people to keep part of their territory while receiving compensation for the lost lands. But the traditional way of life has suffered, provoking a health crisis among indigenous youth alienated from the land.

[15] The Inuit, who inhabit the Belcher Islands in the Hudson Bay and navigate the frozen waters in search of fish and game, were not taken into account in these agreements. Today, 326,000 First Nation Peoples live in Canada, comprising 577 groups. Inuit people number 25,000. At least 100,000 Métis and First Nation People are assimilated into the dominant culture (4 per cent of the total population). Canada's original

IN FOCUS

ENVIRONMENTAL CHALLENGES
Industrial emissions from Canadian and American plants, together with the high level of vehicle emissions, contribute to the acid rain problem that has already damaged thousands of lakes and forests. The building of hydroelectric plants in Quebec threatens to destroy the land and economy of indigenous populations. Toxic waste from industrial, mining and agricultural activities pollute the sea.

WOMEN'S RIGHTS
During World War I, nurses serving in Europe were allowed a postal vote, and became in 1917 the first Canadian women to vote. However, it was not until 1920 that they were allowed to stand for office. In 2000, women held 21 per cent of parliamentary seats and in 1995 they held 14 per cent of ministerial positions.

Women make up 46 per cent of the labor force. Sixty-three per cent are employed in services, 32 per cent in industry and 5 per cent in agriculture. There is low population growth: 1.5 children per woman* (below the population replacement level of 2.1). Population has grown by 4 per cent since 1996, lower than the US growth rate, for the first time in 100 years.

During 2002, a total of 27,100 rapes were reported. Canada is a destination country and transit point to the US for traffic in women and children for the sex trade, forced labor and drug-trafficking. Thousands of Asian women are persuaded to emigrate on the promise of being better off economically; once in Canada, they are forced to engage in prostitution.

CHILDREN
The infant mortality rate is 5 deaths for every 1,000 live births, while the under-5 mortality rate is 7 deaths for every 1,000 live births*. Six per cent of babies have low birth weight, and between 89 and 96 per cent of children under one were immunized against diseases like polio, measles and tetanus.

Education is free and compulsory until the age of 16 in the whole country. Legislation protects children against sexual abuse, child labor and discrimination, imposing severe penalties on those who infringe these laws. In spite of existing controls, trafficking in children mainly from Asia and Latin America to work in the sex industry still poses a problem for which no lasting solution has been found.

INDIGENOUS PEOPLES/ ETHNIC MINORITIES
There are about 800,000 First Nations people, some living a traditional lifestyle in isolated areas, particularly in the far north, some living on protected reserves, and some living in cities. These aboriginal groups have inhabited the continent for millennia and had autonomous societies before the Europeans' arrival. The majority of the ancient Canadian residents speak their native languages - the most common are Inuit, Cree, Ojibwa, Inukitut - and one of the official languages, French or English.

Life expectancy for aboriginal peoples - 3.1 per cent of the population - is lower than for the rest of Canadians. There are numerous cases of alcoholism, suicide and drug abuse. They also have higher birth and unemployment rates. Housing conditions are poor and residual waters are common in reserves. Only 25 per cent of aboriginal students complete secondary education. Almost 70 per cent of those who are 'registered' have been in jail before they reach the age of 25. Although there is no discriminatory legislation against these peoples, former restrictions have contributed to a lower standard of living among some.

MIGRANTS/REFUGEES
By the end of 2002 Canada had taken in around 78,500 refugees and people seeking asylum or protection. There were 52,800 outstanding cases; 15,200 applications accepted by the Office for Immigration and Refugees (which turned down 58 per cent of requests, 47 per cent more than in 2001) and 10,400 refugees coming from abroad, mainly Pakistan, Colombia, Mexico, China and Sri Lanka.

In 2002, in response to the imminent enforcement of the 'third safe country' agreement signed that year by Washington and Ottawa (which allowed Canadian immigration authorities to send back would-be migrants entering from the US), several asylum-seekers entered from the Middle East, South Asian and North African countries. Many of them were undocumented citizens living in the US who feared deportation. Although the agreement gave the US reciprocal rights, it received only 200 asylum applications compared with Canada's 15,000.

DEATH PENALTY
The death penalty was abolished in 1998; the last execution was performed in 1962.

*Latest data available in *The State of the World's Children* and *Childinfo* database, UNICEF, 2004.

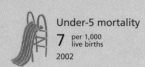
Under-5 mortality
7 per 1,000 live births
2002

Aid
0.28% Official development assistance as % of donors' GNI
2002

Maternal mortality
6 per 100,000 live births
2000

inhabitants have now become better organized and between the 1960s and 1970s this resulted in the creation of the National Indian Brotherhood (NIB) to represent them and their interests. The NIB was subsequently replaced by the Assembly of First Nations (AFN). Indigenous peoples are fighting for government respect of the treaties that affirm their rights to their land and resources. Those who still live from hunting and fishing are committed to the self-government of indigenous communities.

16 The Northwest Territories - one third of the country's area with a population of just 52,000 people - is split into two regions with autonomous governments, Nunavut and Denendeh. This plan was passed by the local parliament in 1987, and was ratified by referendum. In 1992 the Tungavik Federation of Nunavut (TFN), the federal Government and the Government of the Northwest Territories (NT) signed an agreement confirming the splitting of these lands and the creation of the Government of the Nunavut territory.

17 In 1990, the Canadian Parliament passed laws on refugees, which came into force in 1991, stating that people who entered the country without residence rights would be sent back. The Parliamentary opposition and humanitarian organizations accused the Government of inconsistency in its approach to this

issue. The authorities replied that it was not closing the frontiers - 13,000 asylum-seekers and 10,000 residents' relatives were admitted. In 1991, the International Work Group for Indigenous Affairs (IWGIA) stated that the Canadian Government was not respecting the religious rights of the Mohawk population and reported several acts of aggression towards them, including allowing the building of golf courses on their sacred sites. In the same year, delegates from 22 American countries came to a conference organized by the Canadian '500 Indigenous Women Committee'. They rejected the male domination and discrimination and decided to regain some of the leadership women held in indigenous society before the arrival of the Europeans.

18 In 1991 US and EU farm subsidies left Canadian farmers at a disadvantage. The country recorded its first trade deficit in 15 years (in September, the trade deficit was $275 million). Economic recession, higher taxes, corruption scandals, increasing separatist feelings and a decline in Mulroney's popularity characterized the year. That same year, Canadian forces took part in the Gulf War, after the Iraqi invasion of Kuwait.

19 In 1992, there was intense debate over Quebec's growing demands for autonomy. The Province rejected the Federal Government's scheme to grant it 'special' status. This was considered

'insufficient'. That year after 18 months of negotiations, Canada, the US and Mexico signed an agreement creating a free trade zone (North American Free Trade Agreement, NAFTA). In 1993, Mulroney resigned as Prime Minister. Kim Campbell, former Defense Minister, became Canada's first woman Prime Minister. She reduced the Cabinet from 35 to 25 members. In the same year, Parliament ratified the NAFTA treaty. Campbell traveled the country promoting the adoption of austerity measures to combat the budget deficit, while her rival, Liberal Jean Chrétien, gave high priority to the creation of new jobs.

20 In the 1993 general elections, the LP regained power after 9 years, with a major victory over the CP, whose representation in the House of Commons dropped from 155 seats to 2. The Liberals won 178 seats, up from 79 in the previous legislature. The separatist Bloc Québecois (BQ) (54 seats) and the right-of-center Reform Party (RP) (52 seats) both made significant gains. This was the worst defeat for a governing party in Canada's 126-year history. Prime Minister Chrétien took office in November and the following month Kim Campbell resigned from her post as leader of the CP.

21 The reduction in the public deficit and Federal Government spending, an increase in unemployment to more than 10 per

cent and separatist tendencies in Quebec were the main Government concerns during 1994 (when inflation dropped for the first time in 40 years) and 1995. The Parti Québecois (PQ) again brought up the possible secession of Quebec from Canada in 1994. Chrétien's popularity had increased 13 per cent since the elections, but the PQ triumphed in Quebec. The provincial Premier, Jacques Parizeau, promised to do everything possible to make Quebec a sovereign state.

22 The geopolitical context of NAFTA meant that the Quebec issue was followed with great attention in Mexico and the US, even though the PQ had promised that the province would meet the obligations assumed by Canada. However, on 30 October 1995, separation was rejected by 50.6 per cent of the electorate. The Quebec secession threat faded in 1996, despite the high number of votes received by the separatist option (49 per cent). The Federal Government transferred some powers to the provinces attempting to calm the nationalist movement. Lucien Bouchard, a separatist leader, replaced Parizeau as Premier of Quebec when the latter resigned following the referendum defeat. Unemployment continued to rise in 1996, despite the economic growth. Disagreements continued throughout the year with the US over Canadian companies dealing with Cuba.

Water: plentiful and badly managed

CANADA HAS 9 PER CENT of the world's renewable fresh water. Most of this is underground water and its volume is estimated to be 37 times greater than that of the surface water in the country's lakes and rivers. Underground water is known to supply 22 per cent of Lake Erie and 42 per cent of Lakes Huron and Ontario. More than one quarter of Canadians are supplied by underground water for domestic use. In spite of having so much drinking water available, the population only has access to 40 per cent of it. This is due to the fact that in many regions, subterranean water is not replenished in proportion to its use. Canada is suffering from pollution in some areas from petrochemical industries, pesticides, sewage, nitrates, chemical waste and bacteria. Contaminated aquifers can kill people,

especially children and vulnerable older people.

In Canada, the daily consumption of water for household and gardening uses is on average 343 liters per capita. The Governor of the US state of Montana announced the intention to renegotiate an international agreement with Canada, dating from 1921, since according to the results of a recent study, Canadian irrigators have been allowed to take more water than the agreed share from the St Mary and Milk rivers. Montana farmers in the Milk river basin allege that they have received nearly 90,000 acre-feet less water during the last 50 years, according to the above study. An acre-foot of water is around 325,851 gallons.

Some 20,000 Canadian lakes have fallen victim to acid rain. It is estimated that in the 21st century, water supply will be a greater problem than that of food and energy resources. According to Terence Corcoran, editor of the Toronto-based Financial Post, water will be 'the oil of the 21st century'. Canadians, including the prestigious Council of Canadians, are concerned that a water-hungry and profligate US will look north as a way of solving its water needs. However, there is not universal agreement about predictions of shortage. Anil Agarwal, when director of the Center of Science and Environment (CSE) in New Delhi, declared that 'there is no lack of water', and that the solution to the crisis is to end the bad management of water. ∎

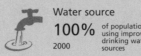

Water source
100% of population using improved drinking water sources
2000

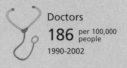

Doctors
186 per 100,000 people
1990-2002

Primary school
99% net enrolment rate
2000

23 In 1997, Chrétien's party again won the parliamentary elections, gaining 155 of the 301 seats, followed by the RP and the PQ, and then the New Democratic Party with 21 and the CP. In 1998, after pressure from the separatists, the Government prohibited the display of the Canadian flag inside the House of the Commons. That year, the Supreme Court ruled that Quebec could not separate without the consent of Federal Government, which in turn promised to negotiate the secession, if the Quebecois majority agreed. The Prime Minister, a native of Quebec and ardent opponent of secession, said the ruling supported the principal arguments of Federal Government, by establishing that Quebec lacked authority, within Canadian law, to execute unilateral independence.

24 In 1999, a study by the David Suzuki Foundation stated Canada had the highest per capita oil and gas consumption and that 16,000 people there die each year from air pollution. The study named Canada as the leading per capita producer of greenhouse gases. That year, Julie Payette - from Quebec - became the first Canadian woman in space.

25 After 50 years of federal rule, in 1999 the Inuit finally achieved the devolution of one-fifth of Canadian territory, in Nunavut. Given the lack of infrastructure to tap Nunavut's mineral resources, the 25,000 Inuit that live there are still dependent on Canadian Government subsidies and welfare.

26 The Jantzi Social Index (JSI) came in effect in the year 2000 in Canada, formed by 60 companies selected for their respect of environmental and social matters. It gave investors who do not wish their funds to contribute to the arms industry or companies that hire child labor at poverty wages the chance to select whom they support. The JSI also excludes those companies linked to nuclear power, military production and tobacco. Nevertheless companies linked with alcohol and gambling were included.

27 In response to a wave of criticism of his Government, Chrétien - against the opinion of members of his party - brought forward the elections to 2000. He won an overall majority in the House of Commons, and received 17 more seats than in 1997. Also, his LP won seats in Quebec, which weakened the separatists. The performance of the Canadian economy encouraged voters to support the Prime Minister and his team. The country was also ranked top of the UN's Human Development Index.

28 In 2001, 34 heads of state met, behind police barriers, at the Summit of the Americas held in Quebec City. The Summit reaffirmed the commitment to create the largest free trade area in the world by 2005. Tens of thousands of anti-globalization protesters rallied against the summit.

29 The Government passed new legislation in March 2001 against child pornography, making it a crime to produce or publish 'indecent' images of children or to access them on a website. Individuals who commit crimes described in this new law, regardless of where in the world they commit them, may be taken before Canadian courts. Internet providers warned it would be very difficult to control everything that is published and seen on the worldwide web. In July Canada became the first country in the world to legalize the therapeutic use of marijuana and began to grow the drug for medicinal purposes. Commercial production and its sale for non-medicinal purposes remain illegal, but possession of small quantities is punishable only by a fine.

30 Following secret negotiations between the Quebecois Government and leaders of the Cree community, it was agreed the Cree would receive Can $2.2 billion in exchange for an environmental survey that would enable the construction of a hydroelectric dam. For many of the 12,000 Cree, who had struggled for decades against the project, the agreement amounted to a sell-out by their leaders and goes against their conviction that land is sacred and should not be harmed.

31 After the September 11 attacks on the US, Canadian troops took part in US President Bush's war on terrorism. In 2002, US bombs killed four Canadian soldiers serving in Afghanistan. That fall, Chrétien stated in a TV interview that the West should learn from the 9/11 attacks on New York and Washington that 'you cannot exert your powers to the point of humiliating others', and that 'the West is becoming excessively rich in relation to poor countries'. At the same time, Canada refused to support any kind of military action against Iraq without UN backing. This earned Chrétien much fierce criticism from conservative opponents, who demanded he apologize to the US Government.

32 In 2003 the greatest worker stayaway in Toronto's history was caused by an outbreak of SARS, an acute respiratory syndrome, which not only paralyzed the city but also made the WHO warn travelers against visiting Toronto unless absolutely necessary. This advice angered Canadian authorities. Later that year, Toronto experienced the largest blackout in its history, which also affected Ottawa and cities of northeastern US.

33 In the same year, the LP won Quebec's local elections, ending the PQ's 9-year rule. Jean Charest became the Province's Premier, succeeding Bernard Landry (Bouchard's successor). The LP won 75 of Quebec's 125 National Assembly seats. Paul Martin (Finance Minister) won the Liberal leadership and became federal Prime Minister when Chrètien retired after 10 years in office. ■

PROFILE

ENVIRONMENT

Canada is the second largest country in the world in land area, divided into five natural regions. The Maritime Provinces along the Atlantic coast are a mixture of rich agricultural land and forests. The Canadian Shield is a rocky region covered with woods and is rich in minerals. To the south, along the shores of the Great Lakes and the St Lawrence River, there is a large plain with fertile farmlands, where over 60 per cent of the population is concentrated, and the major urban centers are located. Farming (wheat, oats and rye), is the mainstay of the central prairie provinces. The Pacific Coast is a mountainous region with vast forests. The north is almost uninhabited, with very cold climate and tundra. There are ten provinces, and three territories; the Yukon, Northwest and Nunavut (the latter created in 1999 as land for Inuit people). Canada has immense mineral resources; it is the world's largest producer of asbestos, nickel, zinc and silver and the second largest of uranium. There are also major lead, copper, gold, iron ore, gas and oil deposits.

SOCIETY

Peoples: There are about 800,000 First Nations People or Native Americans, Métis (mixed race) and Inuit (Eskimos) ranging from highly acculturated city-dwellers to traditional hunters and trappers living in isolated northern communities. There are six distinct culture areas and ten language families; many native languages such as Cree and Ojibwa are still widely spoken. About 326,000 native people are classified as such: that is, they belong to one of 577 registered groups and can live on a federally protected reserve (though only about 70 per cent actually do so). Métis and those who do not have official status as 'native people' have historically enjoyed no separate legal recognition, but attempts are now being made to secure them special rights under the law. About 45 per cent of the Canadian inhabitants descend from British settlers, while 29 per cent are French. Today Canada is multicultural with many people from Asia, the Caribbean and Europe (Germans 3.4 per cent; Italians 2.8 per cent; Chinese 2.2 per cent; Ukrainian 1.5 per cent, Dutch 1.3 per cent; also Portuguese, Polish, Pakistani, Filipino).
Religions: Roman Catholic 45.7 per cent; Protestant 36.3 per cent. There are also Jews, Muslims, Buddhists, Hindus; 12.4 per cent of the population considers itself non-religious.
Languages: English and French, both official. 13 per cent of the population is bilingual, 67 per cent speak only English, 18 per cent only French, and 2 per cent speak other languages (Italian, German and Ukrainian and indigenous languages).
Main Federal Political Parties: The Liberal Party; the Conservative Party; Bloc Québécois; New Democratic Party; Green Party.
Main Social Organizations: Canadian Labour Congress, with more than 2.3 million members; Confédération des syndicats nationaux; Fédération de travailleurs et travailleuses du Québec; Canadian Federation of Students. Non-union: Assembly of First Nations; Council of Canadians.

THE STATE

Official Name: Canada.
Administrative Divisions: 10 Provinces and 3 Territories.
Capital: Ottawa 1,093,000 people (2003).
Other Cities: Toronto 5,411,300 people; Montreal 3,490,600; Vancouver 1,922,000 (2000).
Government: Paul Martin, Prime Minister and Head of Government since December 2003. Canada is a federation of ten provinces and a member of the British Commonwealth, with a parliamentary system of government. Senate has 104 members and the House of Commons 301. Governor-General Adrienne Bing Chee Clarkson (1999) represents Queen Elizabeth II.
National Holiday: 1 July, Canada Day (1867).
Armed Forces: 70,500 (1996). Others: 6,400 (Coast Guard).

Cape Verde / Cabo Verde

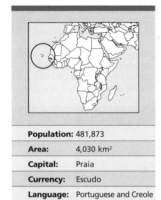

Population:	481,873
Area:	4,030 km²
Capital:	Praia
Currency:	Escudo
Language:	Portuguese and Creole

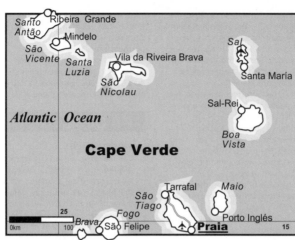

When the Portuguese settled on the Cape Verde archipelago in the 15th century, the islands were deserving of their name (Green Cape). They were covered by lush tropical vegetation that stood out against the black volcanic rock and the blue sea. There is no evidence of the islands having been inhabited prior to the arrival of settlers, although it is believed that the Moors had visited the Island of Sal to collect salt supplies in previous centuries. In 1462, the first settlers landed on what today is known as São Tiago and founded the oldest European city in the tropics (now called Cidade Velha). The Portuguese introduced the cultivation of sugarcane which was not successful because of the dry climate. Cape Verde's prosperity came as a result of the slave trade (mainly from the West African coast). After 400 years of Portuguese colonization the islands were transformed into a 'floating desert', with most of the population emigrating to escape starvation.

[2] For Portugal, the islands' position between Africa, South America and Europe, represented an important strategic interest. In the 16th century, Cape Verde was port of call for ships carrying slaves to America (slavery was abolished in 1876). The frequent incursions by French, British and Dutch pirates made Portugal bring farmers from its Alentejo region (in southeastern Portugal and known as the 'barn' of that country) to the islands. Their style of agriculture eroded the fertile soil and periodic droughts have struck the country ever since. Between the 17th and 19th centuries, cotton was the prized export, but later falling farm production caused huge out-migration of Cape Verdeans. Most went to Guinea-Bissau, another former Portuguese colony with close ties to the archipelago. There was further migration to Angola, Mozambique, Senegal, Brazil and in particular the US. In 1800, the prosperity of the islands was slowly

disappearing due to poverty, hunger, bad administration and the colonial government's corruption.

[3] In 1951, Cape Verde's status changed to overseas province. During the independence struggle, the islands developed closer ties to Guinea-Bissau (see Guinea-Bissau). In 1956, the African Party for the Independence of Guinea and Cape Verde (PAIGC) was created, with supporters in both colonies. Amilcar Cabral, founder and ideologist, thought that they could fight together for freedom and development, on the basis that they were two economically similar countries. In 1961, guerrilla war broke out on the mainland, and hundreds of Cape Verdeans joined the fight. Cabral was assassinated in 1973. The following year, the colonial regime was overthrown and after a transition government in 1975, independence was proclaimed. For the first time ever one political party, the PAIGC, took office in two different countries at the same time. Aristides Pereira became President of the Republic of Cape Verde and commander Pedro Pires its Prime Minister. The

PAIGC took the first steps towards a federation between Cape Verde and Guinea-Bissau: the national assemblies of the two countries sat together as the Council of the Union.

[4] From 1975 onwards, the forested areas of Cape Verde increased from 3,000 to 45,000 hectares. The Government predicted that in the next 10 years a further 75,000 hectares would be planted making the islands self-sufficient in firewood. In rainy seasons, men and women left their homes and offices to spend a week planting trees. The land reform program was implemented, giving priority to food production to meet the needs of the population (local production amounted barely to 5 per cent) instead of favoring the export crops of the colonial period. In spite of these actions, agricultural production declined due to severe droughts which led the Government to invest in fisheries.

[5] Cape Verde supported Angola during its 'second liberation war' (see Angola) by allowing Cuban planes to land on the archipelago,

helping to defeat the invasion of Angola by former Zaire and South Africa and adopted a policy of non-alignment, declaring that no foreign military bases would be allowed in their territory.

[6] In 1981, while the PAIGC was discussing a new constitution for Guinea-Bissau and Cape Verde, Guinea-Bissau's President Luiz Cabral was overthrown. João Bernardo Vieira took office in his place, and was hostile to integration with Cape Verde. That same year, the PAIGC held an emergency meeting in Cape Verde to discuss political developments in Guinea-Bissau. After the ratification of the principles of Cabral, the party changed its name to 'the African Party for the Independence of Cape Verde' (PAICV) stressing its independence from the party of Guinea. Relations between the two governments became tense, until mediation efforts by Angola and Mozambique in 1982 paid off and Mozambique's President Machel brought Pereira (re-elected in 1981) and Vieira together in Maputo. At the Conference of Former Portuguese Colonies in Africa (1982), held in Praia, Cape Verde, Vieira met with colleagues from Angola, Mozambique, Cape Verde and São Tomé. Diplomatic relations returned to normal, although the party was not reunited and plans for reunification were abandoned.

[7] In 1984, after severe drought crop yields fell by 25 per cent below those of the previous 5 years, trade deficit stood at $70 million and foreign debt reached $98 million. The food distribution system and efficient state management prevented famine. Being poor in natural resources, with just 10 per cent of arable land, Cape Verde is highly dependent on imported food, mainly from aid agencies. Dependency on foreign aid also

PROFILE

ENVIRONMENT
An archipelago of volcanic origin, composed of Windward Islands Santo Antao, São Vicente, São Nicolau, Santa Luzia, Sal, Boa Vista, Branco and Raso; and Leeward Islands Fogo, Santiago, Maio, Rombo and Brava. The islands are mountainous (heights of up to 2,800 meters) without permanent rivers. The climate is arid, influenced by the cold Canary Islands current. Agriculture is poor; nonetheless it employs most of the population.

SOCIETY
Peoples: Cape Verdeans are descended from Africans, mainly from Bantu-speaking peoples, and from Europeans. Today the population is 71 per cent of mixed descent; 28 per cent African and 1 per cent European. **Religions:** Mainly Roman Catholic 93.2 per cent (with influence of local practices); Protestant 6.8 per cent (mainly from the Nazareth Church). **Languages:** Portuguese is the official language, but the national language is

Creole, based on old Portuguese with West African vocabulary and structures.
Main Political Parties: African Party for the Independence of Cape Verde (PAICV); Movement for the Democracy (MPD); Democratic Alliance for Change (ADC); Party of Work and Solidarity (PTS).
Main Social Organizations: National Cape Verde Workers' Union-Central Trade Union Committee (UNTC-CS); Cape Verde Confederation of Free Trade Unions.

THE STATE
Official Name: República do Cabo Verde.
Administrative Divisions: 9 islands and 14 counties.
Capital: Praia 107,000 people (2003).
Other Cities: Mindelo 64,000; Santa Maria 13,400 (2000). **Government:** Parliamentary republic. Pedro Pires, President since March 2001. José Maria Neves, Prime Minister, since February 2001. National Assembly with 72 members. **National Holiday:** 5 July, Independence Day (1975). **Armed Forces:** 1,100.

Life expectancy
70.2 years
2000-2005

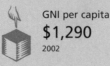
GNI per capita
$1,290
2002

Literacy
74% total adult rate
2000

limited the scope of the First Development Plan. In 1986, the Second Development Plan prioritized private enterprise especially in the informal sector, and the fight against desertification. Up to 1990, the plan was to recover more than 500 sq km, and establish a centralized system of administering water reserves for the whole country. During the first phase, more than 15,000 dams were built to store rainwater, and 231 sq km were forested. Despite droughts, farm production gradually increased to make the country practically self-sufficient in meat and vegetables, without resorting to imports.

[8]   In 1991, Antonio Mascarenhas Monteiro (President of the Supreme Court during the previous decade) was elected President in the first free and multiparty elections. The transition to a free-market economy with the privatization of insurance companies, fishing and banking began, in line with the requirements of international agencies. Foreign aid accounted for 46 per cent of the GDP, while remittances from the 700,000 Cape Verdeans residing abroad, constituted another 15 per cent of it. The MPD government (center-right), faced with a 25 per cent unemployment rate, announced the restructuring of the state. In 1993, a 50 per cent reduction of the 12,000 civil servants began, together with a gradual deregulation of prices. The 1994 budget, despite making cuts in public expenditure, increased public investment (in transport, telecommunications and rural development) from $80 million in 1993 to $138 million in 1994.

[9]   In 1995, Prime Minister Carlos Veiga introduced changes to 'facilitate the country's transition to a free-market economy' and merged the Ministries of Finance, Economic Coordination and Tourism, and Industry and Commerce into one Ministry of Economic Coordination. In 1997, unemployment remained at 25 per cent and more Italian investments in the tourism sector were announced. The African Development Bank granted a $4.9 million loan for road building. Cape Verde also received economic support from China and created an association with Angola to invest in health and social welfare.

[10]   Reports of police brutality to prisoners recurred throughout 1998 and 1999. The number of prisoners exceeded the capacity of prisons which offered way below minimum reasonable conditions. Opposition politicians criticized the pro-government media for not carrying out their critical function - self-

censorship is frequent in Government-controlled media. The authorities, using the law to suit themselves, have tried, fined and often imprisoned editors and journalists.

[11]   In 2001, presidential elections - deemed fraudulent by the main opposition leader and former Prime Minister Carlos Veiga (MDP) - gave too slight a margin (50.05 per cent against 49.95 per cent), and new elections were held. In the second round, the Electoral Commission halted the public recount and carried out another. The final result was decided by the Supreme Court

after complaints of irregularities in the election. Pedro Pires won by 17 votes and succeeded Monteiro as the third President since independence. Jose Maria Pereira Neves was elected Prime Minister. Veiga declared he would abide by the Court's decision and its consequences. In 2002 Pires' Government began to step up efforts to decentralize and privatize its public sector and signed a cooperation agreement with France for 610 million euros, which would facilitate this.

[12]   In June 2003, during the celebration of the African

Children's Day, Neves declared that the main goal of his Government was to succeed in providing access to water and electricity to all Cape Verdeans before 2013. Following privatizations, the cost of basic services increased and access to clean water, especially outside the capital, was low. Neves added that the Government planned for all schools to have access to at least one computer within five years. He announced the start of a development plan 'Operation Hope' and emphasized that his investiture 'is a guarantee to the future of Cape Verdean children'. ∎

IN FOCUS

ENVIRONMENTAL CHALLENGES
Although an island, Cape Verde lies within the Sahel belt, which is undergoing increased desertification, with periodic droughts and a high demand for wood - used as fuel - that generates serious deforestation. These phenomena are made worse by factors such as the topography of rolling hills, high winds and the islands' small size. The environmental damage threatens different species of birds and reptiles. Illegal beach-sand extraction and indiscriminate fishing have been recorded

WOMEN'S RIGHTS
Cape Verdean women have been able to vote and stand for election since 1975.
     Although illiteracy in women over 15 years old was reduced during the period 1980-2000 (from 60.2 to 34 per cent), the difference between men and women was maintained in the year 2000*, with only 15 per cent of men illiterate.
     Poverty affects a significant portion of the population, especially women. Food production is insufficient and only provides 10 per cent of the country's needs, the rest coming from multilateral aid agencies. The economy depends on development assistance programs (around 20 per cent of the country's income) and on remittances sent by emigrants (by the end of 1990 these represented between 25 and 30 per cent of the country's income).

CHILDREN
A high percentage of children show signs of chronic malnutrition. In 1998* 13 per cent of children suffered from low birth weight.
     Frequently, girls drop out of school as a result of sexual abuse

and teenage pregnancy, which becomes intertwined with sexually transmitted infections and the potential spread of HIV/AIDS (for the period 2002-2006, the Government has implemented a national plan to control this disease).
     Adolescents face numerous risks: sexual exploitation, alcohol, tobacco and drug abuse and delinquency. The child protection program implemented by UNICEF is concerned at cases of sexual violence and exploitation of children. Child prostitution primarily affects girls, but also boys, such as on the island of Sal. The increasing tourism may possibly increase sexual exploitation and trafficking in children. The present criminal code forbids the promotion of the practice of prostitution with minors under the age of 14. The punishment is imprisonment for 9 to 19 years, but if the victim is between 14 and 16 years of age, the punishment is reduced to 2 to 8 years of imprisonment.

INDIGENOUS PEOPLES/ ETHNIC MINORITIES
According to Marian Aguiar, from the Boston University, bi-racial origins of the Cape Verdeans are a legacy of Portuguese settlement and the African slave trade. The small and elitist white population, former slaveholders, determined social position according to origins as well as race. In addition, as the islands' *mestizo* (or mixed, of indigenous and European descent) population grew, racial lines became increasingly difficult to draw. From almost the moment of settlement, the Portuguese brought slaves to or through the islands. The Africans who left their mark on Cape Verde were called *pretos* (blacks). More than 50 per cent of the resident slaves were female. Often 'whiteness' or 'blackness' was as much a signifier of class position as it was of 'blood'. Today the

connotation of other markers, such as class or education, makes it possible for an individual to become 'more white' by moving up in society.

MIGRANTS/REFUGEES
Emigration is among the highest in the world; the diaspora outnumbers the resident population and every family has at least one emigrant among its members. According to the 2000 census, half of all emigrants during the period 1995-2000 chose Portugal as their destination, followed by the US, France and the Netherlands. During the same period, there was significant emigration to Italy, Spain and Luxembourg. In proportion to the total financial flow, remittances to Cape Verde have increased by 35 per cent within the last 20 years.
     Cape Verde shows the results of the tightening of immigration policy by the EU and US: between 1970 and 1990, migration flows have fallen substantially. Meanwhile, in recent decades, policies to promote migration to Cape Verde have been implemented, with the result of an increase in population growth. Over the last 20 years, it has tripled, almost reaching an annual 2.5 per cent growth rate. Currently, women are the main emigrants. This is largely because when men who migrated to Europe in the 1960s and 1970s brought their families over in the 1980s. In addition, women are now migrating in their own right to get jobs as domestic workers in Italian, Portuguese and Spanish homes.

DEATH PENALTY
It was abolished in 1981.

*Latest data available in *The State of the World's Children* and *Childinfo* database, UNICEF, 2004.

Cayman Islands / Cayman Islands

Population:	42,785
Area:	260 km²
Capital:	Georgetown
Currency:	Cayman dollar
Language:	English

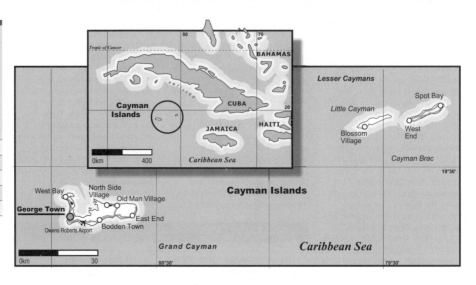

In his last voyage to the West Indies in 1503 Christopher Columbus sighted the Cayman Islands (Grand Cayman, Cayman Brac and Little Cayman) and named them the 'Turtles' because of the vast numbers of turtles there (in the late 18th century; over-fishing virtually killed off this resource). Shortly afterwards, buccaneers and privateers took over the islands which were loosely under French control. For a good part of the 17th century, the Caymans were the pirate headquarters of the Antilles.

[2] Conflicts among European powers affected the Antilles and particularly the Cayman islands. When Jamaica was ceded to Britain under the Treaty of Madrid (1670), the Cayman Islands became a Jamaican dependency. The first permanent colonial settlement was established on Grand Cayman and most of the settlers were British sailors, castaways from buccaneer ships, African slaves and Jamaican landowners. When slaves were freed (1835), the islands' society became homogeneous. In 1959, with Jamaican independence, they were given the status of British dependent territory.

[3] In 1972, a new constitution granted some local autonomy on domestic matters. The Governor, appointed by the Crown, became responsible for defense, foreign affairs, internal security, and some social services. There was also an Executive Council and a Legislative Assembly.

[4] Their tax-exempt status has encouraged the establishment of a strong financial center: in 1987 there were 515 banks in the Cayman Islands. By the end of the decade, a quarter of the economically active population worked in tourism (the islands were visited that year by more than 600,000 tourists). There are many hotels and the influx of visitors has produced considerable immigration, which in 1988 accounted for 35 per cent of the population.

[5] With the exception of turtle farming (which replaced fishing), local industry and agriculture only meet domestic needs. The Caymanese are renowned boat-builders and sailors. One of the country's main sources of revenue is the money sent home by sailors. Fishing declined seriously in the 1980s and has not recovered.

[6] In 1991, McKeeva Bush, a member of the Assembly, founded the first political party in the Caymans. The DPP (Democratic Progressive Party) aimed to change the legal status of the islands from being British dependencies. The DPP campaigned for constitutional reform, seeking the creation of a party system, more members of the Executive Council, the creation of the post of Prime Minister, and an increase in the Legislative Assembly to 15 members. The Governor would become the President of the extended Executive Council.

[7] In 1996, the capture of a drug trafficker from Mexico - the third main country supplying cocaine to the US - revealed the role of the Caymans' banking system in a money-laundering circuit running from Texas to Switzerland. In 1998 the Government denied entry to 910 gay tourists, mostly US citizens, alleging that they did not fulfill the 'appropriate behavior requirements'. The British Government distanced itself from this 'discriminatory' policy.

[8] In 2000 concern about illegal financial practices led international monitors to categorize the Cayman Islands as 'reluctant' to collaborate in fighting money-laundering. The country was removed from the blacklist in June 2001 after enacting regulations that banking authorities said were already being followed. Even so, anyone engaged in the finance industry, from banks to lawyers, must now verify the identity and source of income of each client. In 2002 it was discovered that US company Enron used some 700 partnerships registered in the archipelago to evade federal taxes. The islands signed an agreement with the US Government to share tax information to uncover offenders.

[9] In 2003 the Caymans were implicated in the Italian company Parmalat's fraudulent accounting - almost 4 billion euros were missing - leading to the largest corporate scandal of the year. The Bank of America (third largest US bank) stated that a Parmalat certificate for $3,950 million in cash and bonds was false. It was held by Caymans-registered Bonlat Financing Corporation. ∎

PROFILE

ENVIRONMENT

Located west of Jamaica and south of Cuba, this small archipelago is part of the Greater Antilles. It comprises the Grand Cayman islands, where most of the population live, Little Cayman, and Cayman Brac. The archipelago is of volcanic origin, and has rocky hills and considerable coral formations. The climate is tropical and rainy, tempered by oceanic influences. The shortage of freshwater is a major problem for the inhabitants.

SOCIETY

Peoples: 50 per cent of the population are of mixed European and Indian descent; 25 per cent are of European descent; 25 per cent are of African origin.
Religions: Protestant.
Languages: English.
Main Political Parties: Democratic Progressive Party (DPP). Groups of independent citizens are formed to elect the local government. In the last elections, only independent candidates were elected.

THE STATE

Official Name: Cayman Islands.
Administrative Divisions: There are eight districts (Creek, Eastern, Midland, South Rown, Spot Bay, Stake Bay, West End, Western).
Capital: George Town 24,000 people (2003).
Other Cities: West Bay 9,800 people; Bodden Town 5,900 (2000).
Government: Bruce Dinwiddy, Governor since May 2002. There is an 18-member Legislative Assembly (15 elected by direct popular vote and 3 named by the Governor).
National Holiday: Constitution Day, first Monday in July.
Armed Forces: The UK is responsible for the defense of the Islands. There is a civil guard for internal security.

Central African Republic / République Centrafricaine

Population:	3,961,846
Area:	622,980 km²
Capital:	Bangui
Currency:	CFA franc
Language:	French

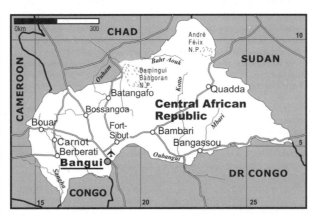

Diamonds and carved quartz that are at least 8,000 years old and a megalith set up about 500 BC attest to the existence of humans here before 800 BC. The first inhabitants of the present-day Central African Republic (CAR) were Pygmies - hunters and gatherers whose descendants still live in the forest (to the southwest).

[2] The first state structure was the Kanem Kingdom, founded in the 9th century; it became Muslim in the 11th century, spreading from Chad. It is presumed that peoples related to the Nubians (that came from Egypt and Sudan) settled two Kingdoms during the 15th and 16th centuries in other Central African regions.

[3] In the 1750s, the Sudan sultanates deported many people who lived by the Oubangui river (Sango-speaking traders). From 1780, the Portuguese removed many in the slave trade. These were mainly Gbaya-Mandja and peoples that lived in the central and northern savanna who, at that time, numbered half the country's current population.

[4] Most of today's Central African people are descended from different ethnic groups that were settling by the end of the 18th century and the formal abolition of slavery. Images made with butterfly wings and some ebony and ivory sculptures that have been found attest to the art that was disrupted by European colonization. Today several of these small diverse groups (ranging from hunters to farmers), still practise some of the same animist rituals, singing and drumming.

[5] During the last decades of the 19th century, the Belgians, British and Germans competed for control over the territory in search of raw materials. In 1887, France and Belgium divided their domain along both sides of the Oubangui river. In 1888 in this region, the French founded an administrative entity known as French Congo, with an outpost at Bangui, capital of today's CAR. In 1891, the French-occupied territory was called Oubangui-Chari; colonial status was conferred in 1903

so that it could be annexed to French Equatorial Africa in 1910.

[6] During World War I, hundreds of people from the region were sent to fight for the French against German forces in Africa in a bid to conquer Germany's territories. From the outset, the French military occupation of today's CAR, was brutal, with the system of *corvée*, or forced labor, and constant

expeditions against Sultan Rabah (in Sudan). About 40 Europeans controlled the exploitation of rubber, ivory and diamonds as well as the cotton and coffee plantations. Railways were built to make transport possible.

[7] There were further rebellions in the 1930s, provoked by the forced labor system. During WWII, cotton and diamond exports reached record

levels and France was reluctant to relinquish this source of wealth. In the end, in 1946, France granted the status of 'overseas territories' to Oubangui-Chari and other colonies. This new statute gave the right of representation in the French Legislative Assembly. The first Deputy from the region was the Catholic priest Barthélemy Boganda (1910-1959). In spite of these reforms, France retained control of foreign trade, defense and tax collection.

[8] From 1949, after founding the Movement for the Social Evolution of Black Africa (MESAN), Boganda led the fight for independence. The French carried out campaigns to discredit him, and in 1956 they managed to bribe his main advisers. His nephew and associate David Dacko took over but MESAN degenerated into a French controlled agency. Abel Goumba broke away to form The Movement for the Democratic Evolution of Central Africa (MEDAC) which was banned by the French in 1960 and its leaders arrested.

IN FOCUS

ENVIRONMENTAL CHALLENGES
Bad land management has increased soil erosion and reduced fertility. The scarcity of water and pollution of rivers pose serious problems. Indiscriminate hunting and fishing have damaged the country's natural reserve, and desertification and deforestation are worsening.

WOMEN'S RIGHTS
Women have had the right to vote and to stand for election since 1986.

Although between 1980 and 2000* the percentage of female illiteracy fell from 88.8 to 65 per cent, the differential with men remains; male illiteracy fell from 64.2 to 40 per cent over the same period.

In the year 2000*, the net rate of school registration was 45 per cent for girls and 64 per cent for boys.

Among the 15 to 24-year-old population, 14.1 per cent of women were HIV-positive in the year 2000; for men in this group the figure was less than half at 6.9 per cent.

Life expectancy for women in the CAR fell from 49 in 1980 to 40.6 in 2000*.

CHILDREN
In 2001, 144,000 births and 26,000 deaths of under fives were recorded. By the end of 2001, it was estimated that 25,000 children under 14 were

HIV-positive and that 110,000 of these were HIV/AIDS orphans.

CAR is one of the 10 countries worst affected by the pandemic of HIV/AIDS. In 2002*, out of the 144,000 children that are born every year, more than 16,500 will die before their first birthday and another 26,000 before reaching their fifth birthday. The leading causes of infant morbidity and mortality are HIV/AIDS and malnutrition.

INDIGENOUS PEOPLES/ ETHNIC MINORITIES
Mbum, Mbororo, Ba'aka and Hausa people are the main minorities. In the 20th century, the Mbum (4 per cent of the population) fled from the mountainous region of the country to avoid the Mbororo roundups. Today they are marginalized, living in extreme poverty. The Mbororos - of the Fulani ethnic group - are descended from the semi-nomadic herders of the western grasslands. Because of their relative cattle wealth, they have been the subject of attacks and extortion.

The Muslim Hausa are less than 1 per cent of the total population, yet constitute three-quarters of the small traders.

The Ba'aka people - also known as pygmies, a group of some 20,000 members - are mainly hunters, gatherers and inhabit the southern tropical forest of the country. They are particularly threatened by the political instability of the region (especially in DR Congo).

MIGRANTS/REFUGEES
Almost 15,000 people from CAR were refugees or were seeking asylum by the end of 2002, including some 10,000 in DR Congo, almost 3,000 in Congo and another 1,000 in Chad. Some 10,000 were internally displaced.

Some 50,000 refugees from other countries were in the CAR at the end of 2002: at least 35,000 Sudanese; 11,000 from DR Congo; almost 2,000 from Chad and 2,000 from elsewhere.

The sporadic political violence and instability that has prevailed since the mid-1990s has caused tens of thousands of people to flee Bangui.

Out of the more than 35,000 Sudanese refugees, who arrived in the early 1990s fleeing civil war in their own country, only a few have been repatriated.

Several Rwandan asylum-seekers have attracted controversy because they are accused of taking part in the Rwanda's 1994 genocide and in the 1991 coup attempt in the Central African Republic. The Government classifies the Rwandan population as 'asylum-seekers in transit' and refuses to provide aid or identity documents to most of them.

DEATH PENALTY
Although it still applies, there have been no executions since 1981.

*Latest data available in *The State of the World's Children* and *Childinfo* database, UNICEF, 2004.

Life expectancy
39.5 years
2000-2005

GNI per capita
$260
2002

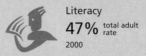
Literacy
47% total adult rate
2000

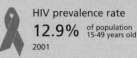
HIV prevalence rate
12.9% of population 15-49 years old
2001

9   In 1958, the country became the Central African Republic as part of the Franco-African Community (CFA). Boganda became Prime Minister and clearly had vision for his country and the region. However, in 1959, he died in a mysterious plane crash.

10   On 13 August 1960, independence was declared. Dacko became the President and in 1964 promoted a constitutional reform which granted him full powers. He purged the more progressive elements within the MESAN and drew increasingly closer to the French. He made French the official language and Sango the national language and granted US companies concessions for mining the uranium and cobalt reserves.

11   Dacko rapidly lost the support he had inherited from Boganda, as a result of his corrupt administration. The country plunged into a deep economic and political crisis. In 1965, Dacko was ousted in a coup led by one of his cousins, General Jean-Bedel Bokassa (1921-1996). Bokassa was pro-France, having served in the French Army for 22 years. In 1972, he proclaimed himself President-for-life.

12   In 1977, Bokassa decided to crown himself Emperor of the country (renaming it as Central African Empire). The coronation ceremony cost $28 million and was financed by France, Israel and South Africa. The Emperor gave away diamond-rich lands to foreigners and hired notorious international arms dealers as his military advisers.

13   The Emperor and the then President of Zaire (now DR Congo), Mobutu Sese Seko, established close military collaboration to repress the continuing popular rebellions in both countries. In 1979, a massacre of students shook the world's public opinion.

14   France decided to depose the Emperor, attempting to erase the negative image it had created by supporting his coronation. On 20 September 1979, he was overthrown and former President David Dacko came back to power, protected by 1,000 French troops.

15   Dacko dissolved the Empire and reinstated a republic, granting France a 10-year lease on the big Bouar (west) air base. Dacko's return amounted to no more than a change of name as corruption and repression continued. Political opposition was ruthlessly repressed and almost all opposition leaders were sent to prison or exiled.

16   Amidst countless conspiracies, Dacko was overthrown by another military coup in September 1981, which brought General Kolingba to power. Kolingba asked the French to pay the salaries of 24,000 civil servants for the period of one year. In an attempt to draw closer to the US, he granted them new economic concessions, allowing the exploitation of uranium resources.

17   The planned return to democracy, initially set for 1982, became rather an election barred to the opposition on 21 November 1986. Kolingba was elected President with his CAR Party of Democratic Recovery (PCRD). A constitution was passed establishing a one-party system, and in July 1987, the members of the General Assembly were chosen from PCRD members.

18   During that period, an IMF structural adjustment plan was launched, which did not improve the catastrophic situation shown by socio-economic indicators. The intensification of malnutrition, infant mortality and the spread of diseases like HIV/AIDS (which reached 12 per cent of the population in 2003), among others, are clear signs of the suffering of Central Africans after the adoption of successive economic policies.

19   In 1986 Bokassa returned from exile in France. Being accused of murder, cannibalism and misappropriation of public funds, he had been sentenced to death in absentia. Upon his return, he was arrested, tried again and sentenced to life imprisonment.

20   Municipal elections were held in May 1988, with universal suffrage. In 1991 a plan was approved for constitutional reform and for the adoption of a multiparty system. Elections were scheduled for October 1992, but shortly after the voting started Kolingba annulled the process claiming there had been irregularities. A Provisional National Council of the Republic was formed, made up of the five presidential candidates.

21   The first round of the presidential elections took place in August 1993. Kolingba, who came fourth, annulled the result by decree once again. However France threatened to suspend its military and financial aid, forcing him to allow the second round to go ahead and to free political prisoners, including former emperor Bokassa.

22   On 19 September, Ange-Felix Patassé, Bokassa's former Prime Minister, was returned as President with 52.47 per cent of the vote. In 1996, Patassé requested French military intervention to crush rebel soldiers. After the intervention, Bangui saw some violent expression of hostility towards the presence of French soldiers.

23   In June, the President announced a new Government of national unity and named former ambassador in France, Jean-Paul Ngoupande, Prime Minister. In spite of a truce, in early 1997 France launched an offensive against rebel troops in Bangui in retaliation for the death of two French soldiers. This led Patassé and the rebel leader Anicet Saulet to agree the replacement of French troops by a guard from African countries, although funded by Paris.

24   In February, Patassé formed a new Government, including some opposition members, and most of the rebels returned to the barracks. Some months later, the President demanded French withdrawal from the military bases. At the same time, he tried to strengthen links with the US, whose influence over the region had increased.

25   In March 1998, the UN Security Council authorized the deployment of the UN Mission in the Central African Republic (MINURCA), made up of some 1,400 troops. In May, the Government announced the elimination of customs subsidies, as a way to fulfil IMF-imposed conditions.

26   In the elections that year, the ruling National Liberation Movement (NLM), led by Patassé, and his allies took 49 of the 109 seats. However, the nomination of the new cabinet sparked violent street demonstrations in Bangui, in early 1999. In the presidential elections Patassé took 51 per cent of the vote, but the opposition called for the elections to be annulled, accusing the Government of fraud.

27   Shots between the presidential guard and a military squadron which had been loyal to President Patassé through the two previous coup attempts caused panic in the capital in January 2000. In December, civil servants went on strike demanding back wages; some were owed for 30 months. The leaders of Economic Community of Central African States (ECCAS), meeting in Cameroon in 2001, called for dialogue and respect of all parties for the constitution of the Central African Republic. A presidential spokesperson declared there was no conciliation possible with the leader of the uprising, François Bozize, former Chief of Staff of the Army.

28   In February 2002, the population of Bangui demonstrated against the arrival of Libyan troops, ostensibly there to protect the President. These troops controlled radio and TV stations and the airport. Opposition leader Bozize, who had taken refuge in Chad and France, returned in October. At the same time, rebels loyal to him crossed the border from Chad attacking many towns and taking over a third of Bangui, demanding that Patassé should resume the dialogue or else resign.

29   Four years after having 'definitively' withdrawn their military bases from the Central African Republic, France sent troops, along with Chad and the Republic of Congo, to secure the coup, which took place on 14 March 2003 and allowed General Bozize to become President. The different intervention forces agreed with the new President that democratic elections would be held in 2004. From exile in Togo, Patassé had declared in May that he was prepared to negotiate to achieve a 'consensual transition'. ∎

PROFILE

ENVIRONMENT

This is a landlocked country in the heart of Africa. It is located on a plateau irrigated by tributaries of the Congo River, like the Oubangui, the main export route, and of Lake Chad. The southwestern part of the country is covered by a dense tropical forest. Cotton, coffee and tobacco are the basic cash crops. Diamond mining is a major source of revenue.

SOCIETY

Peoples: Most Central Africans belong to the ethnic group Baya (Gbaya), 33 per cent; followed by Banda, 27 per cent; Mandjia, 13 per cent; Sara, 10 per cent; Mboum, 7 per cent; M'baka, 4 per cent; Yakoma, 4 per cent; Ba'aka, 1.3 per cent and other 2 per cent.
Religions: There is no official religion. 24 per cent practise traditional African religions; 25 per cent are Protestant; 25 per cent Roman Catholic; and 15 per cent Muslim. **Languages:** French (official); Sango is the national language, used for communication between the various ethnic groups. **Main Political Parties:** National Liberation Movement; Central African Democratic Rally; Central African Democratic Union; Movement for Democracy and Development.

THE STATE

Official Name: République Centrafricaine / Ködrö tî Bê-Afrika.
Administrative Divisions: 16 Prefectures, 52 Sub-prefectures.
Capital: Bangui 698,000 people (2003). **Other Cities:** Berberati 61,400 people; Bouar 53,800; Carnot 51,900; Bambari 49,900 (2000).
Government: General François Bozize, President and Head of State since 15 March 2003 by a coup. Prime Minister and Head of Government: Abel Goumba, since 15 March 2003, appointed by the President. Parliament: National Assembly with 109 members, elected for a five-year term. **National Holiday:** 1 December, Independence Day (1960). **Armed Forces:** 2,650 (1996). Other: 2,700 Gendarmes.

Chad / Tashad - Tchad

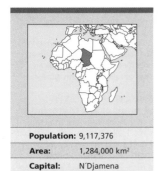

Population:	9,117,376
Area:	1,284,000 km²
Capital:	N'Djamena
Currency:	CFA franc
Language:	Arabic and French

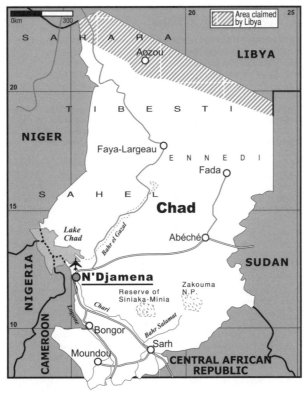

The Sahel region, of which the Republic of Chad is part, has been inhabited from time immemorial and could be the place where the first hominids lived, according to the July 2002 discovery of a 7-million-year-old fossil skull of a specimen named Sahelanthropus tchadensis.

2　By the end of the 18th century, European missionaries converted some of the southern peoples to Christianity and gave them a European-style education. These converts sided with the Europeans against the native peoples of the north.

3　France 'acquired' Chad in 1885 after the Berlin Conference, but did not establish in the territory until a 1920 invasion by the notorious French Foreign Legion which defeated the northern Muslim groups.

4　The colonizers introduced cotton farming in 1930, and small parcels of land were distributed to peasants to grow this crop, while the French monopolized its trade. The result was a cotton surplus and a food shortage, accompanied by famine.

5　In August 1960 when France granted Chad its independence, southern leaders who had been negotiating with the colonizers since 1956 assumed power. However Chad's first president, François Tombalbaye, leader of the Chad Progressive Party, was unable to unite a country where frontiers still reflect the arbitrary colonial divisions.

6　The Chad Liberation Front (FROLINAT), founded in 1966, was crushed by the French troops. The Front had become fully active about the time that southern peasants rebelled against the French company Cotonfran which controlled the cotton industry.

7　In 1970, the Front controlled two-thirds of the national territory, and by 1972 FROLINAT guerrillas were within range of N'Djamena, the capital. In 1975 Tombalbaye was ousted and killed in a French-staged coup that put General Felix Malloum in power.

8　Paris supported Hissene Habré's faction - the Armed Forces of the North (AFN) - because he opposed Goukouni Oueddei, FROLINAT's president and leader of the People's Armed Forces (PAF), who was receiving support from Muammar Qadhafi's Government in Libya.

9　In 1979 Chad's 11 major political groups formed a Provisional Government of National Unity (PGNU). Habré was named Minister of Defense in Malloum's Government. However, the French were displeased with the make-up of the Cabinet because of their strategic interest in Chad - linked to the Maghreb and to the uranium and oil discoveries in the 1960s. In March 1980 Habré resigned, broke the alliance, and unleashed civil war.

10　The PGNU split into three factions. In May 1980, Oueddei requested military aid from Libya, and Qadhafi sent 2,000 troops.

11　That same year, over 100,000 refugees fled the country, after the bombing of N'Djamena by Habré's forces. In October, Libyan troops reached the capital, mediation efforts by the Organization for African Unity (OAU) failed, and the defeated Habré fled to Cameroon in December 1980.

12　France led an international campaign against Libyan expansionism in Africa, with support from the United States, Egypt, Sudan, and other African countries, fearful that Qadhafi's revolutionary drive would eventually 'infect' poor Islamic populations of the Sahel region, south of the Sahara.

13　Habré was accused of being opportunistic and corrupt; however, Libyan support made it possible for France to divide Oueddei's allies. In April 1981, backed by France, Habré reorganized his followers in Sudan. In July, in Nairobi, the OAU decided to send a peacekeeping force to Chad, with the help of the French and troops from six African countries. Oueddei, yielding to foreign pressure and tensions within the PGNU, requested the withdrawal of Qadhafi's troops in November.

PROFILE

ENVIRONMENT

40 per cent of the territory is part of the Sahara Desert, with the great Tibesti volcanic highlands. The central region, the Sahel, which stretches to the banks of Lake Chad, is a transition plain where nomadic pastoralism is common. The lake, only half of which lies within Chad's borders, is shallow and mostly covered with swamps. Thought to be the remnant of an ancient inland sea, its waters are fed by the rivers Logane and Chari. The banks of these rivers, fertilized by flooding, contain the country's richest agricultural lands and are the most densely populated areas. In colonial times, economic activity was concentrated there. Cotton is the main export product but subsistence agriculture, though hampered by droughts, still predominates. In recent years, mineral reserves of uranium, tungsten and oil have attracted the attention of the transnationals.

SOCIETY

Peoples: Northern Chadians, mostly nomadic shepherds of Berber and Tuareg (Toubou, Ouaddai, Kotoko, Maba) origins, have traditionally opposed the majority population of the south, where the farming Sara, Massa, Mundani and Hakka peoples predominate. Due to droughts in the Sahel region, there is a constant process of internal migration, from the north to the fertile regions of the south, which heightens conflicts. **Religions:** An estimated 50 per cent of the population is Muslim, 27 per cent practice traditional African religions, 23 per cent Catholic. Muslims are mostly concentrated in the north, non-Muslims in the south. **Languages:** Arabic and French are the official languages. There are more than 100 local languages, the most widely spoken being Sara (in the southern region).

Main Political Parties: Patriotic Salvation Movement (MPS) led by President Idriss Déby. Union for Renewal and Democracy (URD), National Union for Democracy and Renewal (UNRD); Liberty and Freedom Party, Federation and Action for the Republic Party.

Main Social Organizations: Chad Federation of Labor Unions, Chadian Human Rights League, Chad Non-violence, Chadian Association for the Promotion and Defense of Human Rights.

THE STATE

Official Name: République du Tchad.
Administrative Divisions: 14 Prefectures.
Capital: N'Djamena 797,000 people (2003).
Other Cities: Moundou 111,200; Sarh 84,400 people; Abéché 61,100 (2000). **Government:** Idriss Déby, President since December 1990, re-elected in 2001. Moussa Faki Mahamat, Prime Minister since December 2003. Council of the Republic with 31 members, appointed by the President. National Assembly with 155 members elected every four years. **National Holiday:** 11 August, Independence Day (1960). **Armed Forces:** 25,200. Other: 4,500 Gendarmes.

Life expectancy	GNI per capita	Literacy	HIV prevalence rate
44.7 years 2000-2005	**$220** 2002	**43%** total adult rate 2000	**3.6%** of population 15-49 years old 2001 ∎

14 After his defeat by Habré's forces in June 1982, the exiled Oueddei set up a Provisional National Salvation Government in October. The new civil war split the country in two: northern Chad, under the control of a recently formed National Liberation Council with Libyan support; and southern Chad, with the Habré Government dependent on French troops.

15 When Habré seized power, bringing this phase of the civil war to an end, the country was in ruins. The population of N'Djamena had dropped to 40,000, and half of its businesses and small enterprises had closed. Outside the cities, 2,000 wells and all the water towers had been destroyed, and the health and educational infrastructures were practically non-existent.

16 In 1987, the southern forces supported by France took Fada, Faya Largeau and the frontier strip of Aozou, claimed by Libya. In 1989, Chad and Libya signed an agreement on this 114,000 sq km territory, which included the return of prisoners and the presentation of a territorial lawsuit before the International Court in The Hague.

17 In 1990, Idriss Déby (leader of the Patriotic Salvation Movement, supported by France) ousted Habré, who fled to Senegal. During the deposed president's term in office in the 1980s, some 40,000 people were executed or 'disappeared'.

18 Déby inaugurated a national conference in 1993 to 'democratize' Chad, with the participation of some 40 opposition parties, another 20 organizations and six armed rebel groups. Fidele Moungar was appointed interim Premier during the transition period.

19 In February 1994, the International Court in The Hague ruled that the Aozou strip belonged to Chad. In April the Transition High Council postponed the elections for one more year. In May, Libya officially returned the Aozou strip to N'Djamena.

20 In March 1995, the Transition High Council once again postponed the elections for 12 months. In the Presidential elections, finally held in June and July 1996, Déby was elected constitutional President with 69 per cent of the vote.

21 That was a year of 'reconciliation', as several rebel groups signed peace agreements with the Government and in August, Déby signed an agreement with the armed forces of the south to establish a federal republic, bringing the fighting to a close.

22 Southern Chad was at the heart of an international controversy in December 1997 when the Campaign for the Reform of the World Bank, supported by dozens of NGOs, opposed a megaproject planned by the Bank

IN FOCUS

ENVIRONMENTAL CHALLENGES
Desertification and drought are endemic to the region and affect all aspects of daily life. Supplies of drinking water are inadequate. Ineffective waste disposal contributes to soil and water pollution.

WOMEN'S RIGHTS
Women have had the vote and been able to stand for office since 1958. From 1995 to 2000 the percentage of parliamentary seats held by women decreased from 17 to 2 per cent. In 1995 women comprised 5 per cent of the ministers, while in 2000 there were no women in these positions.

Women make up 45 per cent of the country's workforce.

Life expectancy for women has only increased from 44 to 45,7 years*. Only 5 per cent of women aged 15-24 have information on HIV/AIDS protection and prevention*.

In 2000*, the estimated time at school was just 4 years. Adult female illiteracy was 66 per cent (down from 90.7 per cent 20 years ago) and for men it was 48.4 per cent.

CHILDREN
In 2001 396,000 children were born and 79,000 under five died. Between 1995 and 2000, 24 per cent of the children were born underweight, while between 1995 and 2001 28 per cent of under-5s suffered from severe and moderate low weight.

By the end of 2001, 18,000 children under 14 were HIV-positive and 72,000 were HIV/AIDS orphans.

The political instability of recent decades has slowed economic and social development; women and children have been the worst affected.

INDIGENOUS PEOPLES/ ETHNIC MINORITIES
As a result of contacts with Sudan and Egypt, the southern and eastern regions are largely populated by Arabs, while southerners integrated into European culture under French colonial rule. Southerners - Sara, Massa, Moundang and Hakka - comprise 46 per cent of the country's total population. They are mainly Christians or Animists, living by agriculture in up to 10 per cent of the country's total area.

Other ethnic groups include Toubou, Teda and Daza in the northern prefectures of Bourkou, Ennedi and Tibesti (known as the BET region - one third of the country, with 6 per cent of the population). Hadjerai people live in the mountainous central region; Zagawa or Bidaye (one of the Ouaddian groups) live in the north and east straddling the Sudan-Chad border; and the Buduma, fishing people, around Lake Chad. The Arabs comprise 25 to 30 per cent of the total population; most of them are nomads or semi-nomads living in the Salamat area in the southeast or settled in the central regions. They are predominantly Muslim.

MIGRANTS/REFUGEES
By the end of 2002 Chad hosted nearly 20,000 refugees, including some 15,000 from Sudan, and 1,000 from Central African Republic (CAR). Most of the Sudanese refugees arrived in the eastern part of the country - near Abéché - in the late 1990s fleeing the civil war. In 2001 UNHCR stopped food distribution to them, judging them economically self-sufficient. In late 2002, refugees from CAR fled into Chad's southern border areas - where they were helped by local residents - after escaping clashes between CAR rebels and Government troops.

About 7,000 Chadians were refugees at year's end, including some 3,000 in Nigeria, 2,000 in Gabon, and 2,000 in CAR (but almost 10,000 returned to Chad recently because of violence in CAR). About 30,000 Chadians live in refugee-like circumstances in Cameroon, but are unlikely to return.

DEATH PENALTY
The death penalty still applies for ordinary crimes.

*Latest data available in *The State of the World's Children* and *Childinfo* database, UNICEF, 2004.

in this zone. The project included digging 300 oil wells and transporting oil to the Atlantic Ocean through Cameroon. The NGOs considered that funds for fighting poverty should not be used for this type of project. Despite the opposition the project went on.

23 From 1998, the most active guerrilla group, located in the country's desert north, was the Movement for Democracy and Justice in Chad (MDJT), led by Youssouf Togoimi, former Minister of Defense in Déby's Government.

24 In the presidential elections of 20 May 2001, Déby was re-elected with 67.4 per cent of the vote. The six defeated candidates claimed there was electoral fraud and called for the vote to be annulled, but international monitors stated they were mostly satisfied with the electoral process.

25 In February 2002, the Government and the rebels of the MDJT signed a peace treaty, ending three years of civil war. The accord proclaimed an immediate ceasefire, the release of prisoners, and the incorporation of the rebels into the armed forces and the Government.

26 In the parliamentary elections, President Déby's Patriotic Salvation Movement won 110 of 155 seats. However, the peace achieved in February soon showed its fragility and in May new clashes between the MDJT and Government forces left 64 people dead.

27 The Chad-Cameroon Oil Development and Pipeline Project was officially inaugurated in October 2003. The 1,070 km-long pipeline was financed by Exxon Mobil, Chevron Texaco, Petronas and the World Bank, despite strong opposition from several NGOs and environmental groups.

28 The Government promised to devote 80 per cent of the oil revenues to education, health and the environment, and to provide access to drinking water. This promise came after officials admitted that $4 million had been diverted to buy arms 2000. In 2002, according to Transparency International Chad was one of the African countries with the highest corruption index. Chad was forced to reimburse the IMF a $7.5 million loan in June 2003 since the Government had given false information on pending external payment accumulation.

29 Since Hissène Habré's fall, victims of regime, supported by several human rights organizations have tried to put him on trial for his crimes against humanity. The Senegalese President agreed to hold Habré until an international court sought his extradition, even though the Government of Senegal had declared in 2001 that its courts had no jurisdiction over crimes committed outside the country. The case was presented to the Belgian judge who has been investigating the numerous accusations against the former dictator.

30 The Government and the rebel groups signed two new peace agreements in 2003. On 10 January a ceasefire with the National Resistance Army (operating in the southeast) was signed in Gabon and on 22 December an agreement was reached with the MDJT rebels in Burkina Faso.

31 In January 2004 the UN started resettling more than 95,000 Sudanese refugees who fled to Chad because of the armed conflict between the Sudanese Government and Sudan's Liberation Army. ∎

Chile / Chile

Population:	16,185,450
Area:	756,630 km²
Capital:	Santiago
Currency:	Peso
Language:	Spanish

At the beginning of the 16th century, the north of Chile formed the southernmost part of the Inca empire (see: Peru, Bolivia and Ecuador). The area between Copiapo to the north and Puerto Montt to the south was populated by the Mapuche, later called Araucanians by the Europeans. Further south lived the fishing peoples: the Yamana and the Alacalufe.

2 Diego de Almagro set off from Peru in 1536 to begin the conquest of Chile. With an expeditionary force of Spanish soldiers and enslaved native Americans he covered nearly 2,500 km, when a mutiny by Spanish soldiers in Lima forced him to turn back.

3 Between 1540 and 1558, Pedro de Valdivia settled in what is now the port of Valparaiso and founded several cities including Santiago. The Mapuche, led by chief Lautaro, a capable military strategist, beat the invaders on several occasions, adapting their military tactics to changing conditions in the region. Valdivia died in one of these battles. His successor, Francisco de Villagra, defeated and killed Lautaro in 1557. And in a case unique in colonial America, the Mapuche maintained an independent territory on the Bio-bio river for more than 300 years, officially recognized by Spain as Araucaria. Creole -Spanish dominion only spread to all the territory in the second half of the 19th century.

4 In 1810 Santiago's town council became an autonomous ruling Junta. In 1811, led by José Miguel Carrera the Junta instigated the independence process. General Bernardo O'Higgins, the son of a former viceroy in Peru, joined this movement. War broke out between the independence army and the royalist forces, with their strongholds in Valdivia and Concepción. Helped by the army of José de San Martín, which crossed the Andes to fight the royalists, the independence army finally defeated the Europeans on 5 April 1818 in the Battle of Maipú.

5 In 1817, O'Higgins was designated Supreme Head of State,

while the royalist troops still maintained pockets of resistance. He laid the political foundations of the country, which were reinforced in the 1833 Constitution, during the Presidential term of Diego Portales. This 'aristocratic republic' denied all forms of political expression to the new urban sectors, the middle class and the rising proletariat. English companies, in alliance with the creole oligarchy, organized an export economy based on the rich saltpeter deposits of the north along the maritime coast of then non-landlocked Bolivia to Peru. Soon the English controlled 49 per cent of Chile's foreign trade. Chilean and British capital also owned 33 per cent of Peru's saltpeter, but they wanted total control.

6 The 'Nitrate War' or Pacific War of 1879-1884 was caused by this Chilean-British alliance. Chilean territory increased by a third and left Bolivia in its present landlocked state. The victory brought about the rapid growth of the saltpeter industry and its labor force.

7 Jose Manuel Balmaceda was elected President in 1886 and tried to break the oligarchic order. The nationalism fostered by war, economic growth, social diversification and the education of the wealthy helped to gain him support. He encouraged protectionism to develop national industry. The oligarchy reacted violently, supported by the English. The army defeated the President's partisans, and Balmaceda committed suicide in the Argentine embassy in 1891.

8 In 1900, the first union was founded in Iquique. In 1904, 15 unions with 20,000 members joined to form a federation called the National Convention. That year the unions clashed with the military in Valparaíso and three years later automatic weapons supplied by the US were used to massacre 2,500 workers and their families in a school in Iquique.

9 Housing, railroads and new mines continued to expand, stimulating trade, new services and public administration. In 1920, populist politician Arturo Alessandri became the leader of the new social factions that sought to subvert the oligarchic order and achieve representation in politics. Alessandri's Government promoted constitutional reform and welfare legislation with electoral rights for literate men over 21, direct presidential elections, an 8-hour working day, social security, and labor regulations.

10 Chile's economy, based on farm and mineral exports, was severely affected by the 1929-30 depression. Recovery did not come until the bourgeoisie was able to

impose an industrialization program to produce previously imported goods. Their proposal served as a base for the 1936 Popular Front, which marshaled support from Communists and Socialists. The front was led by Pedro Aguirre Cerda. The armed forces were purged and withdrew from the political scene for almost 40 years. Although the oligarchy was weakened, it made a pact with the Government on agrarian policies and Aguirre Cerda never allowed land reform or the formation of rural workers' unions.

11 The alliance worked out in the 1930s broke down during González Videla's term of office, 1946-1952. The climate created by the Cold War was used to legitimize the Law for the Permanent Defense of Democracy, which banned the Communist Party and deprived its members of the vote. On 9 January 1949, to compensate for these measures, the Government brought in female suffrage. The Radical Party's repressive and de-nationalizing policies, and the disabling of the Left enabled the populist Carlos Ibáñez to win the 1952 election.

12 Economic deterioration rapidly eroded the strength of the populist Government. In 1957, offshoots

from the National Falange (populist) and from the old Conservative Party (oligarchic), founded the Christian Democratic Party (PDC). The Communist Party was legalized and the Left rebuilt its alliances, forming the Popular Action Front. The people wanted change, but, sensitive to an aggressive anti-communist campaign, voted for Eduardo Frei's 'revolution in freedom', which initiated agrarian reform in 1964.

13 The UP (Popular Unity) coalition led by Salvador Allende won the 1970 election, obtaining 35 per cent of the vote, while the rest of the electorate was split between the Christian Democrats and the conservative parties. The UP coalition included the Socialist Party, the Communist Party, the United Popular Action Movement (MAPU) and the Christian Left. The following year the UP won almost 50 per cent of the vote in the local elections, leading the Right to fear a definitive loss of its majority.

14 Allende nationalized copper and other strategic sectors, together with private banks and foreign trade. He increased land reform, promoted collective production and created a 'social sector' in the economy, managed by workers.

15 The traditional élite, now out of power, conspired with the Pentagon, the CIA and transnational corporations, particularly ITT, to topple the Government. The Christian Democrats were indecisive, but finally supported the coup. Inflation, a shortage of goods and internal differences within Popular Unity contributed to the climate of instability.

16 On 11 September 1973 General Augusto Pinochet led a coup. The Presidential Palace at La Moneda was bombed by the air force, and President Allende died, possibly committing suicide, during the fighting. Violent repression ensued: people were shot without trial, sent to concentration camps, tortured, or simply 'disappeared'.

17 The Chilean military dictatorship was one of many that ravaged South America during the 1970s, inspired by the National Security Doctrine. This was supported by the Chilean oligarchy and the middle classes, as well as by transnational corporations who recovered the companies that had escaped their control.

18 After the coup, Chile's economic policy started to be based on neo-liberal doctrines. Inflation dropped below 10 per cent per year, unemployment practically disappeared and imported manufactured goods flooded the market. Alongside this ran a loss of earning power in workers' salaries

Life expectancy
76.1 years
2000-2005

GNI per capita
$4,260
2002

Literacy
96% total adult rate
2000

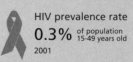

HIV prevalence rate
0.3% of population 15-49 years old
2001

and an overall impoverishment of the poorer classes.

[19]   The detrimental influence of these neo-liberal economic policies became evident in 1983, two years after a constitution containing a mandate for 'continuity' was approved in a referendum by 60 per cent of the voters. Unemployment reached 30 per cent, real salaries had been reduced by 22 per cent in just two years and 55 per cent of all families were living below the poverty line. This situation provided the background for the violent popular uprising which took place in November 1983, led by the National Labor Co-ordination Board and the National Workers' Command.

[20]   In 1984 the Church started talks. To participate in these, the opposition formed the Democratic Alliance, led by the PDC. The talks with Home Minister Sergio Onofre Jarpa failed and the break with the Church became evident. After this,

the Vicarate for Solidarity of the Archbishopric of Santiago played a key role in defending human rights.

[21]   The political left joined together under the Popular Democratic Movement (MDP), vindicating all forms of struggle against the dictatorship. The MDP and the PDC attempted to join in 1985, but the controversy on armed struggle kept them apart. One faction formed the Manuel Rodriguez Patriotic Movement (FPMR), an armed group which carried out numerous attacks, the most important being an attempted assassination of Pinochet on 7 September 1986.

[22]   The international isolation of the Chilean Government during the US Carter administration eased a little with the election of Ronald Reagan, and Margaret Thatcher in the UK. In August 1985 Chile authorized US space shuttle landings on Easter Island. At the beginning of 1986 a US delegation

proposed that Chile be condemned before the UN Human Rights Commission, thereby avoiding having to take more drastic action against the country.

[23]   On 5 October 1988, an 8-year extension of Pinochet's rule was submitted to a referendum. Widespread opposition ended his Government, bringing elections the following year.

[24]   Facing up to the defeat, Pinochet negotiated constitutional reform. Proposed changes included further restrictions of the power of future governments, an increase in the number of senators, shortening the Presidential term from 8 years to 4 and a liberalization of the proscription of left-wing parties. The reform was approved by referendum on 30 July 1989.

[25]   Elections were held on 14 December 1989. Patricio Aylwin, leader of the Christian Democrats, gained 55.2 per cent of the vote, taking office on 11 March, 1990.

[26]   In April, Aylwin appointed a Truth and Reconciliation Commission to investigate the issue of missing people. The Commission confirmed that there were at least 2,229 missing people, who were assumed dead. It also made a detailed study of repression during the dictatorship. When the facts were made public in March 1991 the President asked the nation for forgiveness in the name of the State. He announced that judicial procedures would follow and he requested the co-operation of the armed forces in these proceedings

[27]   The armed forces and the Supreme Court justified their conduct during the Pinochet dictatorship, and denied the validity of the Government report - thus discrediting the President.

[28]   On 2 April 1991, Senator Jaime Guzmán, former adviser and ideologue of the military regime, was murdered and the assassination attributed to radical left wing

IN FOCUS

ENVIRONMENTAL CHALLENGES
The southern part of the country is colder and heavily wooded; nevertheless, during the military dictatorship, 40,000 hectares of native forest were cut per year, causing death of wild fauna. Air contamination in Santiago reaches harmful levels several times a year.

WOMEN'S RIGHTS
In 1931 women over 25 were allowed to vote in municipal elections, but they were not given the franchise to vote in national elections until 1949. In 2000, women held 8 per cent of the Parliament seats and 13 per cent of the ministerial positions.
    Women comprised 34 per cent of the country's workforce in 2000: 5 per cent in agriculture; 14 per cent in industry and 82 per cent in services. In addition, 10.5 per cent were unemployed (unemployment rate was 10 per cent).
    In 2000 the average length of time in school for girls was 13 years; it was one year more for boys*. The illiteracy rate for women over 15 was 4.4 per cent.

CHILDREN
According to UNICEF, Chile's indicators compare favorably with other countries in the region. Although poverty has decreased in 10 years, other indicators, such as wealth distribution show a worsening situation.

In 2002 the Government launched a program, 'Chile Solidario', to focus on assistance to the poorest households (56,055 in 2002 and 60,318 in 2003). The program aims to boost the time children spend in school through measures such as expanding pre-school education; lengthening the school day and increasing the years of compulsory education from 9 to 12. By December 2005, it is hoped that 225,000 of the poorest families will be in the program and also that the 15,675 or so people over 65 will be helped out of their poverty.
    It is estimated that 64,954 children between 12 and 17 work (many of them as farm workers) or are seeking work. UNICEF, together with the Ministries of Education and Labor, decided to carry out a communication campaign aimed at preventing child labor, in order to dissuade children and adolescents living in rural areas from leaving school to work in the harvest season.

INDIGENOUS PEOPLES/ ETHNIC MINORITIES
Indigenous groups comprise 4.2 per cent of the Chilean population. The Mapuche community, which includes the Pehuenche and the Huilliche, makes up 90 per cent of the indigenous population and is the most organized. About a third of them are scattered in urban areas and in reservations first established by the Government in the 17th century. However their claims for ethnic and cultural recognition have often set them

on a collision course with government policies.
    For 350 years the Mapuche resisted first Spanish settlers and then successive governments and the army. In 1553, indigenous people led by Lautaro were very close to invading Santiago while Spanish expeditionary forces and Governor Pedro de Valdivia were founding the southern city of Concepción. When Chile became independent at the beginning of the 19th century, the Government and the wealthy thought that the 'Mapuche problem' had to be solved. In 1881 after the genocide of these people by the army, the 'Araucanian territory' was recovered. In 1883, after a series of pacts, Mapuche people were confined to 300,000 hectares (they had owned 5,000,000 hectares) and during the Pinochet era lost a further 200,000 hectares, which have since been exploited by private companies such as Forestal Mininco and Endesa.
    The Mapuche communities on the south bank of Bío Bío river have for many years been reporting the predation of their lands, destruction of their crops and the impunity granted to timber and electric energy corporations in the 200,000 hectares taken away during the military dictatorship (1973-1989).
    Since the 1980s Mapuche communities have lost 60 per cent of their territory. In 1997 the Mapuche Community Union was created - in 1999 they marched on Santiago - to demand that the State give back their lands and

prevent the companies' expansion on their territory.

MIGRANTS/REFUGEES
Before 1973, the year of the coup that deposed Allende, Chile sheltered thousands of refugees and political prisoners fleeing right-wing governments or to give support to what they considered a unique socialist experience. In the three years following the coup, UNHCR resettled in other countries foreign refugees who were unable to stay in Chile for political reasons. In September 1973 UNHCR opened an office in Santiago and a National Committee for Refugee Aid (CONAR) was created. Refugees from Chile's dictatorship dispersed and were granted asylum in about 110 countries.
    There are no accurate figures about the number of exiled people during the military dictatorship; the Inter-Intergovernmental Committee for European Migrations allowed 20,000 people to leave for Europe in 1980. Other estimates put the total of people exiled by the regime, either voluntarily or expelled, at no less 200,000 people.

DEATH PENALTY
It was abolished for common crimes in 2001, but still applies in exceptional cases.

*Latest data available in *The State of the World's Children* and *Childinfo* database, UNICEF, 2004.

Under-5 mortality
12 per 1,000 live births
2002

Poverty
<2% of population living on less than $1 per day
1998

Debt service
28.1% exports of goods and services
2001

Maternal mortality
31 per 100,000 live births
2000

groups. This enabled the Right to raise the issue of terrorism once more. Political life was slowly brought back to normal. On 23 April , the FPMR announced its decision to abandon armed struggle.

29 The Chilean economy maintained a 10-year expansion, with annual growth rates of over 6 per cent, mainly due to high levels of investment (especially fixed capital) and the expansion of the external sector.

30 During Aylwin's presidency, social indicators improved. In 1993, real salaries increased by 5 per cent, the unemployment rate fell to 4.5 per cent, social spending increased 14 per cent in two years and inflation stabilized around 12 per cent.

31 In August 1993, the Special Commission on Indigenous Peoples (a government agency) proposed introducing indigenous language instruction in Mapuche, Aymara and Rapa Nui at primary schools in communities where Spanish is not their mother tongue. This was considered vital to reduce the loss of cultural identity among indigenous children.

32 In 1993, Eduardo Frei, candidate for the Christian Democratic Party and the Concertación (agreement) coalition, won the presidency with 58 per cent of the vote. However, he did not achieve the parliamentary majority required to do away completely with the old authoritarianism because of eight 'designated' seats in the Senate which were a legacy from the Pinochet regime.

33 Before handing over the presidency, President Aylwin pardoned four FPMR activists, sentenced to death for the assassination attempt against Pinochet in 1986.

34 The Frei Government announced a plan to reduce the poverty which affected nearly a quarter of the population. In May 1995, the minimum salary was increased by 13 per cent. Taxes were introduced on the sale of cigarettes and motor vehicles to fund a 10 per cent increase in the lowest pensions and a 5 per cent increase in the education budget. In June, Chile requested associate membership of the Mercosur market and negotiated entry into the North American Free Trade Association (NAFTA).

35 Brigadier Pedro Espinoza and retired General Manuel Contreras were sentenced to imprisonment for their parts in the murder of former foreign minister Orlando Letelier in Washington in 1976. Pinochet reiterated his support for the sentenced officers, but then called for respect for the civil authorities. Then, the Government suspended investigations into corruption charges against the former dictator's son. In a later hearing, during February 1998, Contreras stated that the true leader of the DINA (the political police during the dictatorship) was Pinochet himself.

36 The Chamber of Deputies approved the trade agreement with Mercosur member nations by 76 votes to 26. Two right-wing parties the UDI and RN, came out against the agreement. The signing of the free trade agreement took place on 25 June 1996, establishing the 'four plus one' association between Argentina, Brazil, Paraguay, Uruguay and Chile. This formula was to remain in place until Chile became a full member of the agreement. The treaty with Mercosur came into operation on 1 October 1996.

37 A report from the National Society of Farmers (SNA) said the agreement would mean annual losses of $460 million for the Chilean agricultural sector, but, balancing this, the country would become integrated into a market of more than 200 million people.

38 Various studies in 1996 suggested the average economic growth of 6 per cent in the last 11 years had led to a reduction in 'extreme poverty' - but not in social inequality. Thus 20 per cent of the population still controlled 57 per cent of the national wealth, while the poorest 20 per cent handled only 3.9 per cent. During the first half of 1996, military and civil tribunals closed 21 cases of disappearances and extra-judicial killings involving 56 victims, without finding anyone responsible

39 Concertación retained the majority in the 11 December 1997 legislative elections, but lost ground to the right. The Government coalition took 50.6 per cent of the vote (compared with 56.1 per cent in the 1996 municipal elections), while the Right took 39 per cent (35 per cent in 1996).

40 After passing on the post of Commander-in-Chief of the armed forces to General Ricardo Izurieta, Pinochet entered the Senate on 11 March 1998, amidst general indignation. After the Senate vetoed President Frei's proposal for a referendum on whether or not to eliminate the post of 'senator for life', (Pinochet's position), Frei called for a new popular consultation. At the same time 21 parliamentarians stated that the constitutional clause which gave former presidents a Senate seat for life should not apply to Pinochet, since he had not been elected.

41 Pinochet's arrest in Britain in October 1998, following an extradition bid by Spanish judge Baltasar Garzón, deeply shook the Chilean political process. The Government and opposition united in calls for the General to be returned to Chile. But while the Right accused the Government of only making luke-warm efforts, Concertación suffered internally from having to defend the former dictator under the guise of defending national sovereignty. The legal comings and goings in London were accompanied by often violent demonstrations in Santiago both for and against the arrest

42 In November 1998, in a country where women only make up 32 per cent of the economically-active population, Mirella Pérez was appointed the first female general in Chile.

43 Confrontations between Mapuche and forestry planters in southern Chile in October 1999 led to the mobilization of a special armed group of 200 police officers with helicopter backing who surrounded the village of Temucuicui. The Government announced a plan whereby Mapuche would receive $275 million for roads, technical agricultural aid, student grants, paying off the state agricultural agency debt and the establishment of bilingual schools. However, Mapuche leaders saw this as a collection of old unfulfilled promises dressed up as a new offer. The Chilean Constitution offers no special treatment to indigenous communities, unlike many other regional nations.

44 Ricardo Lagos, the socialist Concertación candidate, won a slim victory in the January 2000 presidential elections leaving the new Government with very little room for maneuver. The Right, which took a moral victory with 49 per cent of the vote, promised an attitude of 'vigilant collaboration' with the president-elect.

45 In an unprecedented ruling, the Supreme Court of Justice recognized the ancestral rights of

PROFILE

ENVIRONMENT

Flanked by the Andes in the east and the Pacific in the west, the country is a thin strip of land 4,200 km long and never wider than 360 km. Its length explains its variety of climates and regions. Due to the cold ocean currents, the northern territory is a desert. The central region has a mild climate which makes it good for agriculture. The southern part of the country is colder and heavily wooded. The major salt and copper mines are located in northern Chile. 65 per cent of the population live in the central valleys. Chile exercises sovereignty over Easter Island/Isla de Pascua (Rapa Nui).

SOCIETY

Peoples: Chileans are descended from the native American population and European immigrants. 300,000 Mapuche Indians live mainly in southern Chile.
Religions: Mainly Catholic (77 per cent), Protestant 13 per cent.
Languages: Spanish, Mapudungun (Mapuche language), Rapa nui and other minority languages.
Main Political Parties: Concertation of Parties for Democracy (CPD), a coalition of the Christian Democratic Party (PDC), the Socialist Party (PS), the Democratic Party (PPD) and the Radical Party (RP). The National Renovation Party (RN); the Independent Democratic Union (UDI); the Liberal Party (PL), Communist Party of Chile (PCCh); Humanist-Green Alliance.
Main Social Organizations: The Central Workers' Union (CUT), was the main labor organization until 1973, when it was forbidden. Legalized in 1990, it became the most important union again in the early 90s; the Copper Workers' Confederation (CTC); the United Workers' Front (FUT); the National Labor Co-ordination Board (CNS). The indigenous movement has independent organizations as the Action Group for the Bío Bío (GABB), the Mapuche Inter-regional Council (CIM) and the Mapuche Ad-Mapu Organization.

THE STATE

Official Name: República de Chile.
Administrative Divisions: 12 numbered Regions and the unnumbered Metropolitan Region of Santiago.
Capital: Santiago 5,478,000 people (2003).
Other Cities: Viña del Mar 356,800 people; Concepción 963,800; Valparaíso 888,300; Temuco 280,200 (2000).
Government: Ricardo Lagos, President since March 2000. Bicameral Legislature: the National Congress is formed by the Chamber of Deputies, with 117 members, and the Senate, with 48 members.
National Holiday: 18 September, Independence Day (1810).
Armed Forces: 89,700 troops; 31,000 carabineros; 50,000 reservists (1996).

Malnutrition
1% under-5s
1995-2002

Water source
93% of population using improved drinking water sources
2000

Doctors
115 per 100,000 people
1990-2002

Primary school
89% net enrolment rate
2000

an indigenous community, against the interests of a powerful southern landowner who was occupying plots for commercial plantations. In its ruling, the Court recognized these were fiscal lands ancestrally held by the Huilliche.

⁴⁶ Pinochet returned to Chile in March, after the British justice system considered his 'bad physical and mental health' exempted him from being tried in Spain. A week later, Chilean Congress approved a constitutional amendment guaranteeing immunity to former presidents. In May, representatives from the Government (including the army) and civil society formed a Human Rights Committee to find the remains of the 'disappeared'. In August, the Supreme Court ruled that Pinochet had lost his immunity. In early 2001, Judge Juan Guzmán confirmed the charges of homicide and kidnapping against the former dictator and confined him to house arrest for his involvement with the 'Death Caravan', a military squad that traveled through Chile by helicopter, executing 75 political prisoners during the first weeks of the dictatorship.

⁴⁷ In July 2001, a Chilean court suspended the charges against Pinochet, claiming he was not able to stand trial since he was not 'in a state of mental capacity' enabling him to exercise 'efficiently the rights of due process'.

⁴⁸ Likewise, on September 11 of that year, a Washington DC (US) court began a trial against former Secretary of State Henry Kissinger for his involvement in the plan leading to the murder of Chilean general René Schneider in 1970. The trial was started by Schneider's relatives, based on the contradictions between CIA reports and Kissinger's statements on the case. The Supreme Court of Chile approved a request from judge Guzmán to interrogate Kissinger about the death of American journalist Charles Horman.

⁴⁹ Although passing a divorce law was one of President Lagos' campaign priorities, the Government had not acted to bring in the law by March 2002 as promised, due to the Catholic Church's opposition and pressure.

⁵⁰ On 21 February 2002, 25 members of the US Congress requested Attorney Roscoe Howard to present formal charges against Pinochet for terrorism and for his alleged responsibility in the 1976 murder of former Chilean Foreign Minister Orlando Letelier.

⁵¹ In the same month, a judge ordered the arrest of former Minister of Public Works Carlos Cruz - an old associate of President Lagos - and two other high-ranking officers, on bribery charges. This scandal resulted in the removal of five members of Parliament on corruption charges. Up to this time Chile had prided itself on being the least corrupt country in Latin America.

⁵² Between August and October 2003 the US and Chilean Senates passed a Free Trade Agreement (FTA) that came into force on 1 January 2004. The US admitted that this treaty was part of the Bush administration's strategy to force Brazil to join the Free Trade Area of the Americas (FTAA). Some weeks before, at the WTO meeting in Cancún, those developing countries including Chile which formed the G-22 group blocked the rich world's economic agenda. The rich world attempted to get greater liberalization and guarantees for access by transnational capital, while holding onto their protectionist measures in agriculture.

⁵³ On signing the agreement the FTA removed tariffs from 85 per cent of Chilean export goods to the US; and the rest of the tariffs will be phased out by 2014. Small and medium size enterprises and farmers, indigenous communities and culture creators and promoters are damaged by the agreement. Public health and education services are likely to be forced into a further privatization, since state subsidies resulting from tariffs will disappear.

⁵⁴ In December 2003 retired General Manuel Contreras and another two chiefs from the DINA were convicted by judge Guzmán for their involvement in the disappearance of nine people during Operation Condor, the program of repression by South American military regimes in the 1970s.

⁵⁵ In this climate, a new appeal to remove Pinochet's privileges was put to the Appeal Court. The case arose after an interview by Pinochet showed him to be both lucid and having good recall. ■

Operation Condor versus the truth

IN THE 1970s AND 1980s, the military dictatorships that ruled the Southern Cone countries (Argentina, Bolivia, Brazil, Chile, Paraguay and Uruguay) implemented and applied a US-backed cross-border intelligence and repression plan called Operation Condor or the Condor Plan. This scheme aimed to destabilize the internal opposition movements who were fighting the regimes.

Demands for justice and for clarification as to the fate of the disappeared have intensified in recent years, partly due to the shift to the left in those countries.

In 2003, the Argentinian Government declared null and void the Due Obedience and Full Stop laws enacted in the 1980s and repealed a 2001 decree which prevented the extradition of human rights violators. Argentina heads the list of countries that committed crimes against humanity in the region, with 30,000 disappeared people according to human rights organizations. On the other hand, it is also the country which has made the most progress towards bringing former repressors to justice. Of the six countries that took part in Operation Condor, Brazil and Uruguay are the only ones that have not brought to trial any former head of a repressive dictatorship.

In Brazil, the amnesty protected both opposition insurgents as well as the dictatorship's repressors who committed abuses, murders and tortures; most of the perpetrators having been identified. The Brazilian justice system attempted to investigate the deaths of members of the Communist Party, who were killed near the Araguaia river in northern Brazil between 1972 and 1974. However, the Government refused to declassify the relevant military documents.

In Uruguay, a 1986 law, ratified by referendum in 1989, put an end to prosecutions of soldiers and police accused of human rights abuses during the 1973-1985 dictatorship. After Jorge Batlle took office in 2000, a change was seen with the creation of a Peace Commission which investigated some 30 disappearances.

The Chilean Government also failed to repeal the amnesty law decreed by the Pinochet dictatorship covering the crimes committed from March 1973 until 1978. It was precisely during that period that most of the 3,000 disappearances and political murders were committed. However, when democracy was reinstated judges ruled that the amnesty law did not apply to cases of disappearances, since these were ongoing crimes. Based on that judgment, the Chilean Judge Juan Guzmán prosecuted Pinochet in March 2000 and managed to strip him of the immunity he enjoyed as senator-for-life. However, the legal process was cut short by Chile's Supreme Court which declared Pinochet mentally unfit to stand trial in July 2002. In May 2004, the Santiago Court of Appeals voted 14-9 to lift his immunity as former President.

Despite moves in some countries, however, Operation Condor is still alive, as seen in US-backed counter-insurgency efforts in Venezuela and Colombia. Washington's plan is to 'economically and militarily wipe out the social and indigenous movements in order to obtain their resources and territories', says Bolivian Congressman Evo Morales, echoing a view popular in the region. The driving force behind these plans is the same as over last 500 years - 'the eradication of indigenous cultures'. ■

China / Zhon Ghuo

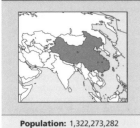

Population:	1,322,273,282
Area:	9,598,050 km²
Capital:	Beijing
Currency:	Renminbi (Yuan)
Language:	Chinese

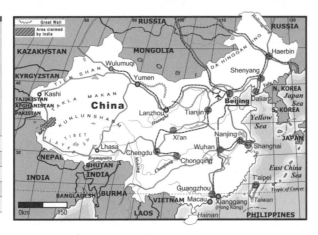

Chinese civilization is one of the oldest in the world, having reached unparalleled refinement long before Western cultures appeared. Its birth can be traced back to the 29th century BC, to the times of the mythical emperor Fu Hsi, in the Huanghe river basin, at the centre of present-day China.

2   The transition from tribal to feudal way of life took place between the 18th and 12th centuries BC, during the Shang dynasty. In that period iron replaced bronze, and new irrigation techniques were invented for agriculture.

3   By then, a cosmology that integrated opposites (life and death, micro and macro, material and immaterial, known and unknown, chaos and order, feminine and masculine, etc) as basic forces of vital cycles was deeply ingrained in Chinese culture. These notions were included in the *I Ching* (Book of Changes, 4th century BC) through the Yin ('the dark side', related to Earth) and Yang ('the light side', related to heaven) concepts.

4   The belief in the meaning of human existence as not being above that of any other living being, and as a product of an incomprehensible cosmic order, enabled the flourishing of a celestial mythology up to the beginning of the warring states period, between the 6th and 3rd centuries BC.

5   The *Tao Te Ching*, written by Lao Tzu in the 6th century BC, paid attention to human beings and their role as custodians of the laws of nature on Earth. Thus, it defined the precepts of an ethics of 'virtue'. A detailed analysis of human anatomy lay at the heart of its approach: the body's flow of blood would correspond to that of rivers, its 369 bone joints to the days of the ritual calendar, its five openings and senses to the basic elements of nature (water, fire, earth, wood and metal; air would be the essential source of energy). Its studies on the human body, biology, chemistry and

physics laid the foundations for the development of a medicine frequently, even today, more efficient and economic than that of the West.

6   Concepts within the *Tao Te Ching* ('The Way to Virtue') were interpreted and adapted several times throughout Chinese history. Power struggles between the kingdoms, typical of the warring states period, led learned man Kung Fu-Tzu (Confucius, 551-479 BC) to grant a social and political dimension to the ethics of individual submission. The stress Confucius put on respecting hierarchy and the preservation of order in every realm of social life (from the family to the highest political spheres), provided the ideological basis for the establishment, in the 3rd century, of a centralized and bureaucratic administration. The positive essence of Confucianism is present nowadays in popular beliefs, although relatively emptied of their sacred nature. In spite of several uprisings and foreign invasions, society was disciplined and means of domination were increasingly rationalized starting with the Ch'in dynasty (221-206 BC).

7   What would later become China was mostly unified for the first time in 221 BC, when the king of Qin (or Ch'in) state adopted the title of Shi Huangdi (First Emperor), a formulation previously reserved to deities or mythological emperors from sagas. The submission of the other six main states was mostly carried out through academic and legal advisors; centralization focused on the uniformity of legal codes, bureaucratic procedures, writing and coining systems, patterns of thought and study. A single system of writing through ideograms was created, and construction of the 5,000-km Great Wall was started to repel 'barbarians' from the north (it was reconstructed in the Sui, Jing and Ming periods). Many dissident Confucian scholars were banned or

executed, their books confiscated and burned.

8   Taocracy (defined as neo-Taoism because of Confucius' doctrinary reforms and because of Buddhist influence) expanded to all of modern China throughout the 2nd and 3d centuries, when light paper was invented under the Han dynasty (206 BC-220 AD). The first reference to Buddhism in China is found in writings from 65 AD, which revealed the interest shown by the imperial family in meditation techniques from India. Cloth and porcelain were painted to represent the coexistence of the 'three branches of the Chinese tree': Confucius (the scholar of society), Buddha (the monk) and Lao Tzu (the ascetic).

9   Far from living in harmony, these three doctrinary branches and their extensions became the excuse for various separatisms and territorial claims. Buddhist monasteries did not pay taxes and became autonomous centres of economic and military power, mainly in Tibet. These privileges caused protests in dominated regions burdened by taxes.

10   Between the 3rd and 13th centuries, territorial break-up and penetration by Mongols and Turks was avoided (partially in the case of the latter) through successive divisions of the territory among the aristocrats. With sporadic reunifications, six dynasties came to coexist, with conspiracies that led the eunuchs (castrated servants and counsellors) to attempt a coup d'état in 835. Foreign empires were the subject of satire and called barbarian by several literary works of the period in which Chinese culture had its first golden age (between the 8th and 10th centuries - T'ang dynasty), with the expansion of paper currency.

11   The Turks dominated Central Asia between the 6th and 13th centuries and by paying taxes occupied lands in China's far west. They traded some Chinese goods (such as silk and tea) abroad and introduced Islam to the region.

12   During the Song dynasty (1127-1279), in the south, took place the 'second golden age' of Chinese culture, when the printing press, the compass and gunpowder were invented. In 1206, Genghis Khan, advised by Tangut scholar Yeh-lu, invaded China and gradually imposed Mongolian domination until 1368. He created the Yuan dynasty and a system of dual government (Mongolian military administration allied with traditional Chinese bureaucracy and cultured aristocracy). China was finally conquered by his grandson, Kublai Khan.

13   Instead of fighting Chinese culture, Mongolians were overwhelmed by it and absorbed its doctrines (giving way to neo-Confucianism) and knowledge. In this period the Chinese made discoveries in astronomy, mathematics, navigation and weaponry, and had a first look at Christianity.

14   Tibetans maintained their autonomy under Mongolian power.

15   In 1368, amidst popular uprisings and a partially reassembled army, the Chinese overcame the Mongolians within their land and the Ming dynasty came to power until 1644. In order to control the economy the free movement of goods and individuals was banned, while Mongolians, Turks, Japanese and European sea expeditionaries, accused of piracy, were held back. However, in 1557 the Chinese granted the port of Macao to the Portuguese and allowed Europeans the use of some ports, although under strict conditions.

16   The northern Manchu took Beijing in 1644, taking advantage of the Ming dynasty's weakness, after several uprisings against large landowners, internal purges and its military defeat against Japan in Korea (1612). They founded the last Chinese dynasty, which fell in 1911.

17   The Manchu dynasty sought to consolidate its dominion in the continent's hinterland. In 1696 it recovered the protectorates of Tibet and Mongolia. This facilitated European penetration, interested in obtaining goods sought by metropolitan markets. In 1682, the Portuguese occupied Taiwan (Formosa), while the English and French attempted, at first, a peaceful approach.

18   French Jesuits reached the highest spheres of the Manchu dynasty and had an important role in the so-called 'third golden age' (1736-1796). Traditional academies were closed and the study of European Enlightenment ideas was imposed, especially with mathematics and astronomy that contradicted orthodox neo-Confucianism. In its effort to

Life expectancy
71.0 years
2000-2005

GNI per capita
$940
2002

Literacy
85% total adult rate
2000

HIV prevalence rate
0.1% of population 15-49 years old
2001

secularize culture, the Government promoted the proliferation of bookshops in the cities. But Chinese authorities continued to refuse trade with Europe.

19 In the latter half of the 18th century, British traders started to import opium from India, and were paid with silver, which was sent to London through the port of Canton. This enabled entrepreneurs to buy silk, tea and porcelain to be sold mostly in India, which allowed for the appearance of mafia groups in Canton. The widespread use of opium brought down the economy.

20 When China outlawed the opium trade in 1839, the British Crown declared war, sending 16 ships to attack Canton in 1840. London obtained the island of Hong Kong and five ports on the China Sea through the Nanking treaty (1841 - end of the First Opium War). An anti-European and anti-Japanese movement was formed in Canton, which led to a Second Opium War (1854-1860) that ended with Beijing (1860) falling to the English and French.

21 The Ch'ing Dynasty also suffered the Taiping political and religious rebellion (1851-1864), which was the largest civil war in Chinese history, devastating 17 provinces and killing 20 million people. Under the spiritual leadership of Hung Hsiu-ch'uan (God of Heavens), the Taiping practised a synchretic monotheism with influences from Protestant Christianity (individual relationship with God), neo-Confucianism (intolerance), and Taoism (extreme egalitarianism). They attacked the Manchu foreigners that ruled the country, formed an army of 1 million men with hungry peasants, workers and miners. Under the slogan a 'general treasure' (common property of land) they controlled part of southern China to carry out land reform and practised a type of primitive Communism of Taoistic inspiration. They were crushed with the help of Western troops.

22 The Chinese army was rapidly defeated in 1895 when the Japanese invaded Taiwan and part of the Korean peninsula.

23 An anti-Western rebellion broke out in 1898, headed by a secret society of Harmonious Fists or Boxers (with the unofficial support of Chinese authorities), but was crushed by a joint British, Russian, German, French, Japanese and US expedition. The victorious armies divided the country into regions of influence and demanded that China pay huge war reparations, as well as 'concessions' (of land) to put up factories near the Shanghai port.

24 Japanese victory over Russia in the 1904-1905 war awoke in China

a call for constitutionalism, which the Imperial Court eventually supported. Sun Yat-sen, a non-aristocrat ignorant of Chinese culture, obtained a pragmatic education in Japan and the US. He used army differences to get economic support and proclaim the republic in 1912, heading a disorganized revolutionary movement headquartered in Tokyo.

25 The first Parliamentary elections (1913) were won by the Kuomintang (KTM; anti-Manchu) nationalist movement, which hindered negotiations between Yuan, the chief of Government (committed to the Manchu) and foreign banks to get loans for China's modernization. Chinese society, shaken by the civil wars, awaited the elaboration of a final Constitution. Yuan closed the Parliament in 1914 and established a dictatorship.

26 During World War One (1914-1918), Japan supported the Allied forces. In 1915, the Japanese secretly presented Yuan with the so-called 21 Demands that aimed to turn China into a Japanese dependency. Yuan could not uphold his initial refusal, due to a lack of external support. Japan obtained privileges and concessions in Manchuria, and demanded exclusive trade. Yuan died in June 1916.

27 Vice President Li Yang-hung became President and continued the pro-Japanese dictatorship until 1927.

28 In 1915, Chen Duxiu, a young man who had studied in Japan and France, founded 'New Youth' magazine. This was the main propaganda source against Yuan. After his death it spread the iconoclastic ideas of Beijing University's avant-garde. In May 1919, students marched against the Chinese Government's acquiescence to the decision of the Versailles Peace Conference, that year, to transfer the former German concessions; they organized strikes and boycotts against Japanese assets.

29 Many of these university students, inspired by Karl Marx (1818-1883) and the Russian Revolution (1917), belonged to the Socialist Youth League (with 3,000 members). In 1921, some of them founded the Chinese Communist Party (CCP), in a congress with the presence of a Kremlin representative. In the two ensuing years, the Communists carried out a propaganda campaign favoring a nationalist revolution among train and factory workers, and sent members to Moscow to study the Soviet revolutionary process.

30 The CCP had 300 members in 1923, while the KMT, reorganized under the leadership of Sung, its

founder, was in process of consolidation and writing a constitution based on the Soviet model. That year, during the third congress, the CCP made an alliance with the KMT to join forces against the Government, which had the joint military support of the United States, Britain, France and Japan.

31 Moscow chose Chang Kai Shek (1887-1975), a KMT member, to organize an armed section of the Chinese revolutionary movement. Trained in the Soviet army, he was named commander of the Chinese revolutionary army in 1926. In 1927 his troops took the main cities. In Shanghai, conservative nationalist leaders and Chinese entrepreneurs convinced Chang Kai Shek to crush the General Workers' Union (controlled by the CCP, jointly with 700 other unions) and to expel the CCP from the Central Committee.

32 Between 1927 and 1937, the Chang Kai Shek Government had not been able to control the country nor organize its economy. Communists formed 15 agrarian bases in central China, defending them with their armed section (the Red Army, made up of peasants). In 1934 they advanced westward, taking land along the way (the Long March). In 1931 the Japanese occupied Manchuria; uprisings took place in several regions.

33 In 1935 the CCP Central Committee chose Mao Zedong (1893-1976), one of the party's founders, as Secretary General, while promoting the struggle against the Japanese as a first step to power. Thus, it concluded secret agreements with the KMT.

34 In 1937 both parties formed a United Front against the Japanese invasion in July. Never before had the Chinese army been so large (1,700,000). Agreements between the KMT and the CCP were broken several times until the Japanese withdrew in 1945, defeated in World War II (1939-1945).

35 The fight against the Japanese Empire enabled growth in the CCP, which was excluded from the Government, while Chang Kai Shek received financial aid from the US in 1946 to counter high inflation. By then, the KMT armed forces were larger than the Red Army's, but two years later, Mao Zedong had recruited more than 500,000 peasants willing to defend the land reform initiated by the CCP in several regions.

36 On 1 October 1949, after defeating the KMT, the communist leadership proclaimed the People's Republic of China and established a one-party system, similar to the Soviet Union's. The remnants of the KMT Government and army moved to the island of Taiwan. There, Chang Kai Shek claimed to be the sole legitimate authority of China

and, with US support, laid plans to reconquer the mainland.

37 As leader of China Mao faced the triple challenge of ensuring a transition from stagnation to economic growth, from social disintegration to discipline and from military to civilian rule. In December 1949 Mao made an official visit to Moscow and signed a treaty of friendship, alliance and bilateral assistance with Joseph Stalin (1879-1953)

38 The Government started by instituting land reform to the rest of China and nationalizing foreign property. Massive health and education plans were implemented. Most of the population was illiterate, partly because of the complex ideograms, so writing was simplified. Female prostitution was banned.

39 In 1950, the year after the CCP came to power, the Red Army faced the US in Korea. Although this gave Mao the support of the Chinese population, it forced him to pay less attention to domestic needs.

40 The first 5-year plan adopted by the CCP Central Committee, with technical and financial support from the Soviet Union, was launched in 1953. The process of land collectivization and the socialization of industry was begun, while business activity was regulated. The State gave peasants, which made up 80 per cent of the population, small lots of land and their means of production. This allowed them to trade their surpluses, while industrial production was left to the State.

41 Although China kept receiving financial aid from the USSR (allowing it, among other things, to build the atomic bomb in 1958), after Stalin's death relations between the countries deteriorated. Mao deemed it convenient for China to adopt a more neutral role in the Cold War (1950-1991) and to create a third pole of hegemonic power in world geopolitics.

42 In the 1950s, Nikita Khruschev (1894-1971) started the USSR's 'destalinization'. In 1958 Mao implemented an opposite domestic policy, implementing terror to restructure the economy and increase production, whose growth rate was below that of the population. These procedures caused 20 million deaths and were carried out until 1961 in what Mao called the Great Leap Forward.

43 Demonstrations for civil rights in Tibet in 1959 were met with severe repression by Chinese authorities and forced the Dalai Lama (the Tibetan Buddhist leader) to flee to India. This caused a row between both countries over Tibet's sovereignty.

44 In 1962 Mao delivered a public self-criticism of his economic policy

Under-5 mortality
39 per 1,000 live births
2002

Poverty
16.1% of population living on less than $1 per day
2000

Debt service
7.8% exports of goods and services
2001

Maternal mortality
56 per 100,000 live births
2000

IN FOCUS

ENVIRONMENTAL CHALLENGES

Coal is the main source of power, producing acid rain, pollution and large CO_2 emissions. Less than 13 per cent of the land is still forested. It has great potential for hydroelectric power, which is meant to be harnessed through the construction of the Three Gorges dam on the Yangtse river, one of the world's largest, whose human and environmental consequences are considered potentially catastrophic.

WOMEN'S RIGHTS

Women made up 48 per cent of China's population between 1980 and 2000. They have been able to vote and run for office since 1949. In 2000 22 per cent of members of parliament were women.

Women made up 45 per cent of the workforce, which totalled 757 million people.

An estimated 27.26 million young and middle-aged women learned to read between 1990 and 1999, thereby reducing the adult female illiteracy rate from 31 per cent in 1990 to 22 per cent in 2000*.

In 1979, due to its extraordinary population growth, the Government established a draconian family planning policy, called 'one family, one child'. It limited couples to one child. To reduce fertility, the Government fined parents with more than one child, increased the legal age for marriage and demanded the use of IUDs, abortion and sterilization. The policy was extremely harsh but was effective in reducing fertility rates: the fertility rate between 1995 and 2000* stood at 1.8 children per woman.

Although the goal was a population of 1,200 million for the year 2000 and the census of that year revealed it had reached 1,300 million, it is estimated that without such a policy, the country would have 1,600 million people (the present projection of China's population for the year 2050). However, the program has for the last two-and-a-half decades resulted in the abandonment or infanticide of millions of girls - not to mention the effect on the reproductive potential of hundreds of millions of women.

Preference for the boy child is traditional in China. Some studies suggest that a reduction in the number of women was reported in the chronicles of Imperial China and the republican era. Due to the present limitation of one child, many couples only have one legal chance to have a son and resort to ultrasound machines to identify the unborn and abort the girls. In rural areas - where approximately two thirds of the people live - the program allows for a second child, but if the firstborn is a girl, frequently the second girl is aborted or abandoned once born in order to have a boy.

CHILDREN

Opening up to global market forces could increase inequalities and put pressure on the poor. Meanwhile, it is difficult to measure the impact of recent disasters such as the SARS epidemic and natural catastrophes - floods, blizzards, earthquakes - to which children are always most vulnerable.

The main causes of death for children under 5 are pneumonia, diarrhea and injuries. Child malnutrition occurs mostly in rural areas: severe malnutrition is three times worse in rural than urban areas; in the cities, obesity is a problem.

There are major regional differences in economic development. The country has 30 million poor, mostly in western China. Child and maternal death rates are notoriously higher in the west than on the coast.

It is estimated that currently there are one million people living with HIV/AIDS in the country. The Academy of Preventive Medicine of China estimates there will be 7 million people with HIV in 2005, and between 10 and 15 million in 2010. The epidemic is transmitted mostly through heterosexual contact and blood transfusions.

It is estimated that 150,000 children live and work on the streets.

INDIGENOUS PEOPLES/ETHNIC MINORITIES

Hui Muslims make up 0.7 per cent of the population (8.7 million people) and live mostly in Ningxia and the provinces of Gansu, Qinghai, Henan, Hebei, Shandong, Yunnan and Xinjiang. They are a religious sect that have not carried out any protests in the last decades and have low levels of concentration, organization and cohesion. The Government has adopted some cultural interests of this group - of mixed Arab, Persian and Chinese blood, traced back to the 17th century, when Arab and Persian traders came to China - and it is not subject to any significant repression. Government interest in the development of western provinces could contribute to improving the group's status. They lack any political representation. In the past there have been conflicts between different Sufi sects among the Hui, between the group and the Chinese State and between Hui and Han groups.

The Hui do not seek autonomy: their major concern lies in the restriction of religious practices, economic backwardness and environmental deterioration in Ningxia.

More than 5,000 Chinese make an annual pilgrimage to Mecca; the first Islamic university started to operate in the country, and Xian has a system of Islamic education for children over 4 years old.

Tibetans - who have lived in the region since 127 B.C. and whose empire peaked between the 7th and 10th centuries and collapsed between the years 824 and 1247 - make up 0.44 per cent of the population (6 million people). Half live in the Autonomous Region of Tibet and the rest in the neighboring provinces of Qinghai, Gansu, Sicuani and Yunnan. They are highly organized and integrated as a group, with strong transnational support. In spite of Tibet's economic development the potential for rebellion persists, while China keeps limiting their cultural and religious activity, refuses any direct talks with their leader, the Dalai Lama, and insists on ignoring the Dalai Lama's request for regional autonomy.

Turkmen (Uigurs and Kazakhs; Turkic minorities that arrived in China in the 8th century) make up 0.7 per cent of the population (8.658 million people). Uigurs (who are Muslim) live mostly in the Xinjiang region, which they call East Turkestan and suffer religious and economic discrimination, in addition to receiving in their territory a constant inflow of Han groups. In the 1930s and 1940s, the Uigur moved to neighboring countries, but when the Soviet Union collapsed, they returned to Xinjiang (there are exiled communities in Afghanistan, Kyrgyzstan and Turkey, from which they receive help).

Throughout 2002, China kept repressing the Uigurs. An unknown number of Uigurs moved to Kyrgyzstan, Kazakhstan and other Central Asian countries, although most failed to find security. The United Nations Security Council added the Islamic Movement of East Turkestan - one of numerous separatist groups - to a list of terrorist groups, responding to a request from Beijing, with US support. However, Amnesty International has stated that China uses anti-terrorism as an excuse to suppress the Uigurs.

MIGRANTS/REFUGEES

Between 1999 and 2001 China was among the top 10 countries of destination for refugees. In 2002 it held more than 396,000 refugees and asylum seekers; most (296,000) came from Vietnam (mostly ethnic Chinese), having left that country in 1979 during the China-Vietnam war and settled in the southern provinces, while some 100,000 were from North Korea (although some NGOs estimate this figure to be as high as 300,000). Tens of thousands of North Koreans were repatriated during 2002, but thousands more kept coming to China. An unknown number of Kachin refugees from Myanmar were in the province of Yunnan.

Beijing kept committing human rights violations in Tibet during 2002 - repressing political dissidents and religious activity - while 2,000 Tibetans entered Nepal, where the UNHCR helped move them to India. An unknown number of Chinese asylum seekers, mostly from the province of Fujian, fled by ship to Canada, Australia, Japan and the United States. Several asylum seekers paid organized smugglers to take them, frequently in unsafe ships. To get to Europe they paid between 10,000 and 15,000 dollars per person; to get to the US they paid some 30,000 dollars. Although some receiving countries regard them as economic migrants, most asylum seekers say they were persecuted, because of the one-child policy or for being members of the Falun Gong spiritual group.

In the last decade there has been intense Chinese emigration that has added to the Chinese Diaspora, amounting to between 30 and 50 million people.

DEATH PENALTY

Applied to all kinds of offenses; in 2001 alone more than 2,500 people were executed.

*Latest data available in *The State of the World's Children* and *Childinfo* database, UNICEF, 2004.

mistakes and was replaced by Lao Shaoqi as chief of State, but kept on as head of the Party and had the support of the People's Liberation Army. In spite of this self-criticism, Mao became increasingly radical and accused Lao and his minister Deng Xiaoping (1904-1977) of 'revisionism' (reformism), for favoring a fledgling free trade in the cities.

45 In 1963 Beijing accused the Soviet Union, jointly with the United States and Britain, of conspiring against it, and broke off relations with Moscow. In 1965, the Red Army installed troops in Cambodia.

46 Throughout 1965 orthodox Maoists became radicalized in opposition to 'revisionist' sectors. In 1966, the army and young students of the Red Guards followed Mao in what they called the Great Proletarian Cultural Revolution (1966-1969). Radicalized by Mao and his *Little Red Book*, they launched ideological persecution in all levels of society. Lao Shaoqi was murdered and a civil war was unleashed, with millions of people killed or confined to 'rehabilitation' camps.

47 Mao feared that a Soviet invasion would interrupt the Cultural Revolution. His foreign policy focused on stopping the USSR from extending its area of influence to countries that were starting revolutionary processes. This led him to finance and oversee pro-Chinese parties and governments in Asia, Africa and Latin America. The covert control he had over Albania and the founding of the Non-Aligned Movement (1961) were the pillars of his 'third way' policy.

48 In 1968, the Red Guard, used by Mao in his increasingly intense confrontations with the CCP's reformist sectors, withdrew its support. In 1969, Chou Enlai was named prime minister.

49 In 1971, the UN admitted the Communist Government to replace Taiwan as representative of China. This was possible due to US abstention in the vote. Chou Enlai started talks with Washington, stating his intention of beginning a gradual process of industrial modernization using foreign capital. In 1971 Deng Xiaoping (restored to the Central Comittee) planned the future opening of the so-called Special Economic Regions near Macao and the world financial hub of Hong Kong.

50 US President Richard Nixon travelled to Beijing in 1972 to attend a ceremony marking the establishment of diplomatic relations with China.

51 In 1975, after Mao's death, reformist bureaucrats took control of the CCP, and the so-called Gang of Four (which included Mao's widow), were arrested and charged with conspiracy. They became scapegoats for the failures and excesses of the Cultural Revolution. In 1981 they were put on public trial, televised and broadcast throughout the world.

52 The first Special Economic Regions opened in 1978. Their lands were rented at low cost and their activities were tax-free.

53 Between 1978 and 1979 the Government implemented a contract system of employment replacing the lifetime assignment to a production unit. The State appropriated lands given by Mao to peasants, who became tenants. Production quotas were replaced by taxes, and peasants were permitted to sell their surpluses for cash.

54 Small businesses were allowed and price subsidies of consumer goods were gradually removed. Likewise, more decision-making power was passed to plant managers, in matters such as hiring or dismissing workers. The social security system was gradually phased out and control on labor activity was regulated, breaking international agreements.

55 The Deng Xiaoping Government rehabilitated victims of the Cultural Revolution, greater expression was tolerated, and censorship on music, dress and other cultural goods was lifted. The education system was redirected toward technical and scientific specialization, according to world standards. A Constitution was passed in 1982 that entails, in the long term, the institution of the right to property.

56 Between 1982 and 1985, the policy called by Deng Xiaoping 'one country, two systems' caused inflation and encouraged corruption within the CCP. In 1984 the Government authorized 14 more Special Economic Regions. In 1985 it implemented a 'rectification' campaign within the CCP, excluding corrupt officials, others who opposed economic reforms and still others who wanted more civil and political rights.

57 In that period the Government launched a birth-control plan called 'one family, one child', which included the widespread practice of abortion and sterilization. Spouses had to have a minimum age and request their bosses' permission to get married.

58 The reduction of purchasing power, linked to price hikes, caused popular discontent. The people could not protest through organized labor, therefore expressed themselves through numerous student marches between 1986 and 1989. Hu Yaobang, Secretary General of the CCP and in favor of political reforms, became a symbol of the struggle for democracy, after his expulsion from the Party in 1986 during the 'rectification' campaign.

59 The death of Hu Yaobang in April 1989 served as a pretext for massive protests of students and workers in a dozen cities, which did not stop until June, when army tanks were sent into Tiananmen Square (Gate of Heavenly Peace square) in Beijing. The image of tanks crushing demonstrators outraged Western public opinion. In the three days that ensued repression was unbridled, leaving hundreds dead, injured or jailed and subject to torture.

60 That year, police in Tibet opened fire on demonstrators protesting against cultural and religious persecution and demanding greater political rights. Widespread rioting resulted in martial law, lifted only in April 1990. Tibetan exiles reported detentions and several executions. Tibet had been invaded and annexed to China in 1950 and converted into an autonomous region in 1965.

61 The Tiananmen events caused political changes. Li Peng became Prime Minister and Beijing was briefly estranged from the West. In September 1991 Britain was the first to send representatives to the capital to sign an agreement on the construction of a new airport in Hong Kong, as part of the negotiations to return the British enclave to Chinese sovereignty in 1997.

62 That year, after the breakup of the USSR, China re-established diplomatic relations with Moscow and Hanoi.

63 In late November, the Government freed student leaders from the Tiananmen demonstrations. The following year, Amnesty International reported there were 20,000 political prisoners.

64 At the same time, Deng Xiaoping, aged 87, was called to lead international financial negotiations in an attempt to counter the deficit left by the estrangement of foreign investors following the Tiananmen episode.

65 In 1992 the People's National Congress decided to maintain Jiang Zemin as Secretary General of the CCP and appoint him both President of the Republic and commander of the Armed Forces, becoming the first person since Mao to combine those functions. Prime Minister Li Peng was confirmed in his post.

66 That year it was announced that the giant Three Gorges dam would be constructed with foreign funds. The construction would be finished in 2009 and would flood 10 cities and more than 800 towns. Hydrologists, seismologists, economists, human rights defenders and activists against economic globalization opposed the project, saying it would destroy the habitats of endangered species and leave millions of people exposed to earthquakes, landslides and floods.

67 In September, the Government said pro-independence action in Tibet would be 'implacably repressed'. An austerity plan was launched and taxes were increased on the rural population. A series of protests and demonstrations forced the Government to lift the measures a few months later.

68 In 1995 the Government maintained subsidies for state enterprises to stem unemployment which had affected 30 million workers in the sector without unemployment benefits.

69 That year, the CCP first secretary in Beijing, Cheng Xitong, was forced to leave his post for misappropriation of funds, along with important local leaders. In April, the deputy-mayor of Beijing, Wang Baosen, committed suicide, accused of having embezzled $37 million of Government funds.

70 In 1996 Amnesty International condemned the Chinese repression of Buddhist monks in Tibet. According to AI, 80 monks were injured for refusing to respect a ban on the public exhibition of pictures of the Dalai Lama. That year, two student leaders of the 1989 uprising were sent to prison for 11 and 3 years, accused of promoting the overthrow of the Government.

71 In 1997 China recovered its sovereignty over Hong Kong and named it a Special Administrative Region. Several foreign companies were authorized to convert local money into dollars or yen. A few months earlier, Jiang had made the first-ever visit of a Chinese President to South Korea.

72 Following the death of Deng Xiaoping in February 1997, the 15th CCP Congress confirmed Jiang Zemin as leader, reaffirming the political system. In March 1998 the People's National Congress ratified the changes decided by the CCP, by re-electing Jiang Zemin as Head of State and commander of the armed forces, with 98 per cent of the vote.

73 Hu Jintao, mentioned as a possible successor to Zemin, was elected Vice-President, while outgoing Prime Minister, Li Peng, became Head of Parliament. The Constitution prevented him from serving a third term as Head of Government. Zhu Rongji, former deputy Prime Minister in charge of the economy, was elected Prime Minister. The new cabinet, made up mostly of economic experts, faced

the preparation of the 370,000 State companies for free market rules.

[74] In June 1999, the Government issued an arrest warrant on militants of the 'exercise and meditation movement' Falun Gong and asked Interpol to arrest Li Hongzhi, the man who founded the sect in 1992 before emigrating to the United States. At the same time, the authorities destroyed more than one and a half million books on the group's beliefs. This confrontation with Falun Gong - seen by the Chinese leadership as the greatest threat to the Government since the demonstrations in 1989 - started after the group staged a silent protest against Government hostility in April when 25,000 of its supporters demonstrated opposite Jiang Zemin's residence.

[75] China, which had signed in 1992 the Non-Proliferation Nuclear Treaty, added in November 1999 100 missiles to its southeastern coast facing Taiwan. In 2003 China had 300 nuclear warheads, half the number held that year by the European Union.

[76] In December 1999, Macao was reunified with China, and became a Special Administrative Region, at least for the next 50 years.

[77] Between 1980 and 2000, China received almost half a trillion dollars in foreign investment. Although a factory worker's salary was around 2 dollars per day in 2003, in that period 25 per cent of all peasants moved to the cities. Also, 65 million Chinese had the buying power of the lower middle class in European countries.

[78] In late 2000, the Government announced that 11 people had been sentenced to death, among them Government officials and police, in the trial resulting from the country's worst corruption scandal. In total, 84 people were convicted for their involvement in a smuggling network that, through sexual favors and payoffs in billions of dollars, had bribed high officials. All were connected in some way with the Yuanhua Group, a mafia based in the port city of Xiamen, in the southeast.

[79] In March 2001 the Government amended the National Minorities act to minimize national autonomy and increase the central Government's power.

[80] From 1996 to 2001, the Communist Party (CP) added 7.5 million members under 45 years of age to its ranks. Although Chinese leaders asserted that these figures indicate that 'Marxism and revolutionary ideas continue to play an important role among Chinese youth', for some experts these new members were motivated by the connections the Party offers those who seek an entry into the business world.

[81] In June 2001, leaders from China, Russia, Kazakhstan, Uzbekistan, Tajikistan and Kyrgyzstan signed a treaty to fight ethnic and religious militancy, and promote trade accords.

[82] A month later, Jiang Zemin signed a 20-year friendship treaty with Russian President Vladimir Putin. The treaty stated that neither of the countries has territorial claims on the other. Voices of concern were raised in Russia about the potential for Chinese immigrant incursions in Russia's far east and in the Siberian regions, which China claimed from Moscow during the Cold War.

[83] China was admitted in November to the World Trade Organization (WTO).

[84] In December 2002 the first case of atypical pneumonia or SARS was reported in a southern Chinese town, an infectious disease that killed 700 people throughout the world in one year. Hong Kong quarantined several buildings in 2003 and demanded hundreds of people use mouth covers for a period of months.

[85] Beijing, which adopted anti-terrorist measures demanded by Washington after September 2001, abstained, along with other permanent members of the UN Security Council, from declaring itself in favor of the US-led invasion of Iraq in March 2003.

[86] In June, a peasant was executed in public after being tried and found guilty of infecting 40 people with the SARS virus. China executed 1,060 people in 2003, which made it the country with the highest number of executions that year.

[87] In 2003 China held many people under arrest for an indeterminate time before charging them and assigning them a lawyer. Apart from censoring all information sources, the Government forced internet servers to use filters which would stop access to sites with the words 'human rights' and 'Tiananmen Square'.

[88] In February 2003, the Government for the first time allowed Hollywood film distributors to sell their movies in China. In June the floodgates of the Three Gorges dam were closed to fill its reservoir. The Government announced that the two largest state banks (Bank of China and Construction Bank of China) would be turned into corporations in 2004, and that insurance companies would be allowed to operate.

[89] In March 2003 the Central Committee of the CCP chose Hu Yintao as President and Wen Jiabao as Vice President. India and the new authorities of China agreed in June on a new status for Tibet, which the press of both countries hailed as a 'triumph', although it was actually a meeting to increase trade and build a highway between the two large countries. According to Indian authorities, China recognized Indian sovereignty over Sikkim; according to the Chinese, India recognized Chinese sovereignty over Tibet.

[90] China became the third country to send a spaceship carrying humans into orbit in October 2003. Beijing announced it would start preparing for the 2008 Olympic Games that year.

[91] Exports in 2003 doubled those of 2002. In that year, Chinese GDP grew twice as much as that of the United States. Based on these figures, US investment bank Goldman Sachs estimated that, if it maintained its current growth rate, China would become the world's strongest economy in 2040. ■

PROFILE

ENVIRONMENT

The terrain of the country is divided into three main areas. Central Asian China, comprising Lower Mongolia, Sinkiang and Tibet, is made up of high plateaus, snow-covered in winter but with steppe and prairie vegetation in summer. North China holds the vast plains of Manchuria and Hoang-Ho, with extensive plantations of wheat, barley, sorghum, soybean and cotton (though China no longer has a surplus in farm products and has become a net importer). The North also has coal and iron ore deposits (Manchuria is the country's leading mining region). South China is a hilly region crossed by the Yangtse Kian and Si-kiang Rivers and has a warm, humid, monsoon climate. The country holds great mineral wealth: coal, petroleum, iron and non-ferrous metals.

SOCIETY

Peoples: There are 56 official recognized nationalities. Han (91.96 per cent), Chuang (1.37 per cent), Manchu (0.87 per cent), Hui (0.76 per cent), Miao (0.65 per cent), Uighur (0.64 per cent), Yi (0.58 per cent), Tuchia (0.50 per cent), Mongol (0.42 per cent), Tibetan (0.41 per cent), Puyi (0.23 per cent), Tung (0.22 per cent), Yao (0.18 per cent), Korean (0.17 per cent), Pai (0.14 per cent), Hani (0.11 per cent), Kazak (0.1 per cent), Tai (0.09 per cent), Li (0.09 per cent), other (0.51 per cent). Religions: No religion 59.2 per cent. Confucianism (a moral code, not a religion) combined with mystical elements from Taoism and Buddhism are what could be called the predominant 'beliefs'. Buddhist 6.0 per cent; Muslim 2.4 per cent; Christian 0.2 per cent; other 0.1 per cent.

Languages: Chinese (official) is a modernized version of northern Mandarin. Variants of this (many of which are mutually unintelligible) can be found in the rest of the country, the most widespread being Cantonese, in the south. Ethno-cultural diversity is reflected by the 205 registered languages.

Main Political Parties: The Chinese Constitution states that the Communist Party is the 'leading nucleus of all the Chinese people'. There are eight minor parties that participate in political life, including the Democratic Party of Workers and Peasants, the Revolutionary Committee of the Kuomintang and the League for the self-governance of democratic Taiwan. Hong Kong and Macau also have their own parties.

Main Social Organizations: Chinese Federation of Unions is the largest. Opposition groups of unknown size, based on ethnicity and religion, extending to the diaspora: movements in Tibet, Inner Mongolia, Xinjiang, as well as the Falun Gong group

THE STATE

Official Name: Zhonghua Renmin Gongheguo.
Administrative Divisions: 23 provinces (including Taiwan), 5 autonomous regions, 4 municipalities and 2 special administrative regions (Macau and Hong Kong). Capital: Beijing 10,848,000 (2003).
Other Cities: Shanghai 12,900,000 people; Tianjin 9,200,000; Xianggang (Hong Kong) 8,087,700; Shenyang 6,326,000 (2000).
Government: Socialist Republic. Hu Jintao, General Secretary of the Communist Party, President since March 2003. Wen Jiabao, Prime Minister since March 2003. The 2,979-member National People's Congress (NPC) sits for about two weeks a year to ratify laws. NPC delegates are drawn from various geographical areas and social sectors (army, minorities, women, religious groups).
National Holiday: 1 and 2 October, proclamation of the People's Republic of China.
Armed Forces: 2,930,000 (1995). Other: 1,200,000 Armed Peoples' Police, Defense Department.

Tibet

Little is known about the origin of the Tibetan people, the descendants of warring nomadic tribes known as Qiang (Chiang). The first known religion in the region was Bon, which combined a belief in gods, demons and ancestral spirits who were responsive to priests or shamans. Chinese Buddhism was introduced in ancient times -the first scriptures date back to the 3rd century AD - but mainstream Buddhist teachings came to Tibet from India in the 7th century. The blend of both produced the particular Lamaist Buddhism of the region and its many different sects.

2   When the Yarlung Empire spread throughout Central Asia, during the 8th century, Tibet controlled the Silk Road and received taxes from the Tang empire in China. In the 13th and 14th centuries, the Mongol empire conquered China and accepted Tibet's submission, without invading it, before conquering the majority of Eurasia. The Tibetans developed a phonetic alphabet about AD 600 and, after centuries of rivalry, a theocratic kind of feudal state was established in the early 10th century. Both political and religious powers were conferred on the lamas - Tibetan priests divided into sects with a complex hierarchy - who, as the ruling class, controlled the peasants and the produce of the land.

3   In 1247, Köden, the younger brother of Güyük Khan, symbolically invested the Sa-skya lama with temporal authority over Tibet. Kublai Khan, grandson of Genghis Khan, appointed the lama Phags-pa as his 'Imperial preceptor'. The politico-religious relationship between Tibet and the Mongol Empire was characterized as a personal bond between the Emperor as patron and the lama as priest. For one century, many Sa-skya lamas, living at the Mongol court, became viceroys of Tibet on behalf of the Mongol emperors.

4   During the Chinese Ming dynasty (1368-1644), Tibet was ruled independently by the Tibetan Pagmodru, Rinpung and Tsangpa dynasties. In the 17th century, China was reconquered by the Manchu, while Tibet was ruled between 1642 and 1682 by the fifth Dalai Lama. The country was gradually demilitarized and, to avoid having to keep an army, a protective alliance was negotiated with the Manchu Emperor around 1650.

5   The assassination of two Chinese high commissioners in 1751 brought an immediate and bloody response from the Manchu dynasty: the Emperor sent a military expedition to Lhasa. From that time onward, the Dalai Lama's relationship with China became more difficult than that of the Panchens - the other leaders of the religious hierarchy. Worldly competition between the two heads of the Lamaist Buddhism often fostered division and sectarianism.

6   In 1910 Chinese troops entered Lhasa. The Dalai Lama appealed to the British to help expel them - and was refused assistance. But the Chinese empire was in its death throes and fell to the Nationalists in 1911. Tibetans seized the chance to expel the invaders and in June 1912 the Dalai Lama proclaimed Tibetan independence. About ten years later, disagreements between the Dalai Lama and the Panchen Lama ended in the flight of the latter to Beijing. A boy born of Tibetan parents about 1938 in Tsinghai province, China, Bskal-bzang Tshe-brtan, was recognized as his successor by the Chinese Government and brought to Tibet in 1952. Eventually, he entered Lhasa under Communist military escort and was enthroned as head monk of the Tashilhunpo Monastery.

7   China invaded Tibet in 1950, the year after the Communist revolution led by Mao Zedong. Most of the Tibetan artistic, literary and architectural treasures were destroyed by the occupiers. Before the invasion there were some 6,250 Buddhist monasteries in Tibet; in 1979 only 13 remained. Monks and nuns were detained in concentration camps, murdered or simply forced to leave the monastic life.

8   The Dge-lugs-pa (Yellow hat sect) ruled political and religious life from the 17th century until 1959, when they launched a failed uprising against the Chinese Communists, who had abolished the feudal system, created the first 'Communist' communes and fought against the Tibetan religious system.

9   When the 1959 uprising failed, the Panchen Lama remained in Tibet while the Dalai Lama went into exile in India. From there he lobbied against the occupation and advocated a return to traditional society. Since the Panchen Lama refused to denounce the Dalai Lama as a traitor, the Chinese Government jailed him in 1964. He was freed in the 1970s and died in 1989.

10   In 1994 Chinese and Tibetan religious authorities declared a five-year-old Tibetan child Panchen Lama, but the Dalai Lama did not recognize the nomination. In late 1999, the 14-year-old Buddhist leader Karmapa Lama managed to flee Tibet to India, meeting with the Dalai Lama. This heightened hopes abroad for independence in Tibet, and India was concerned over possible confrontation with Beijing.

11   Tibet - presently one of the five Chinese autonomous regions - had a mostly Tibetan population until a large Han migration was encouraged by Beijing. The Han form the Chinese majority. Tibetans are no longer in a majority in the capital Lhasa. Furthermore, the region is settled by the Hui (Muslim Chinese), the Hu and the Monba, amongst others.

12   It is estimated that 1.2 million Tibetans have fled the region since Chinese occupation.

13   In November 2000, a delegation from the European Union approached the Chinese leader Li Peng with the proposal that the Dalai Lama be appointed governor of Tibet. This idea was rejected on the grounds that he would have to renounce his Tibetan citizenship and become Chinese before this could happen.

14   In 2001, the Chinese Government discovered the existence of an oil field estimated to hold 100 million tons of crude oil.

15   In October 2003, the Dalai Lama announced that 'a certain kind of cultural genocide' was taking place in his homeland.

16   The UN General Assembly has not implemented the resolutions adopted on Tibet in 1959, 1961 and 1965. The Tibetan Youth Congress, one of the most radical groups fighting for freedom in Tibet, started a hunger strike in front of the UN headquarters in New York, on 2 April 2004, demanding that the UN stop the execution by the Chinese authorities of a Tibetan religious leader and investigate the situation of the Panchen Lama, the second most important figure in Tibetan Buddhism. He is detained by the Chinese authorities in an undisclosed location.

17   China has implemented a surveillance system in Tibet's internet to control the activity of the occupied territory's activists on the web, according to the International Campaign for Tibet (ICT). The system, launched in Lhasa in 2003, requires Government permission to receive a log-in and password to be used in cybercafés. In this way the authorities can identify in real-time what the user is doing and where he or she is. More than 60 cyber-dissidents have been arrested since 1999. Several transnationals have been accused of supplying the Chinese Government with systems for Internet surveillance. ■

Hong Kong

H ong Kong (Xianggang) island was ceded to Britain 'in perpetuity' in 1842, when the British attacked China in the first Opium War. Eighteen years later, the British gained the rights over Kowloon, the mainland peninsula facing the island. In 1898, the British forced the Chinese to give them a 99-year lease on the rural zone north of Kowloon, known as the 'New Territories'.

2   Hong Kong was initially used as a trade center, constituting a point of entry to China. But in the 1950s, following the Communist victory in China, the United States and Britain imposed a trade embargo. Deprived of its supplies, Hong Kong was forced to import all its basic goods from overseas, therefore having to develop exports, rapidly transforming itself into a light industry center, exporting textiles, clothing, plastic and electronic goods. Just as in Taiwan and South Korea, this development was generously supported by Western powers interested in these 'bastions' of the Cold War.

3   Growth of trade and the export industry converted Hong Kong into a financial, communications and transport center. Government policy also contributed, setting low taxes and minimal customs tariffs, offering trustworthiness and freedom in the movement of capital.

4   In the late 1970s, China announced a stage of liberalization toward foreign trade and investment, and Hong Kong - armed with one of the best natural ports in the world, sophisticated investment and trade systems, as well as large terminals for containers - was in a position to take advantage of the situation. Almost the entire population of Hong Kong is of Chinese origin.

5   London and Beijing began negotiations on the future of the colony in the early 1980s, as the 99-year lease was due to end in 1997. The people of Hong Kong were not represented in these discussions.

6   Agreement was reached in 1984, giving China sovereignty over the entire territory, but allowing Hong Kong 'a high degree of independence' as a Special Administrative Area.

7   In September 1991, the people of Hong Kong elected the members of the Legislative Council for the first time in 150 years. The United Democrats of Hong Kong (UDHK) candidates - critical of the colonial government of Hong Kong and of China and calling for a strengthening of democracy - won most of the seats.

8   The last British Governor, Chris Patten, reformed the electoral system, totally separating the economic and legislative powers. China said this reform contradicted the principles of the Basic Law. In 1998, China appointed a Preparatory Committee for the Administrative Region of Hong Kong, made up of leading figures from Hong Kong, and consultants from the colonial government.

9   In 1994, Patten proposed a plan to increase the number of voters in the 1995 elections, causing further confrontations with Beijing. In September 1995 the Democrat Party, opposed to the official Chinese interpretation of the Basic Law, triumphed in the Legislative Council elections.

10   At 00:00 hours, on Tuesday 1 July 1997, China recovered control over Hong Kong after 155 years of British colonial dominion. Entrepreneur Tung Chi Hua was appointed head of the new Executive branch with the support of a Legislative Council.

11   According to the new law, Hong Kong would retain its rights and liberties, its legal independence and nature as an international financial and trade center, along with its way of life, for 50 years. The zone mints its own currency and is ruled by its own immigration and customs laws. Beijing would handle defense and foreign relations during this period.

12   Reunification put China in a 'one country, two systems' situation, combining the free market economy of Hong Kong with rigid political control over the rest of the country, a totally unprecedented situation.

13   The transfer took place against a backdrop of spectacular growth in the Chinese economy, which showed no signs of slowing down. The Hong Kong economy, meanwhile, was considered the third most powerful in the world, and the former enclave was also the third most important international financial center behind New York and London.

14   Hong Kong was much more severely hit by the Asian financial crisis than the rest of China. Exports declined, and the economy shrank 7 per cent in the third quarter of 1997. In the meantime, unemployment rose to its highest level since 1982.

15   In June 1999, Beijing was forced to intervene in Hong Kong's judicial system to avoid an immigration 'influx' which was seen as threatening to the city's stability. The local Supreme Court had extended the right of citizenship to all Chinese children born to Hong Kong citizens. The Court decision put Hong Kong at risk of being 'invaded' by almost two million people (equivalent to one third of its population).

16   In the May 1998 elections, the Democratic Party of Hong Kong won the majority of votes, but due to the inclusion of special constituencies (based on occupational groupings or corporations), the pro-China sectors gained control of the Legislative Council. In spite of having obtained 60 per cent of the votes, the so-called 'democratic' parties (pro-West), only won 33 per cent of the seats.

17   Between 2001 and 2002, the economy was affected by a deep recession. Unemployment peaked at 6.7 per cent in 2002, the highest level for 20 years.

18   In July 2003, the Chief Executive Tung Chee Hwa announced that voting on an anti-subversion bill would be postponed. This followed public protests against the bill on National Security, which would have provided for life imprisonment for any person convicted of subversive acts, sedition, or treason against China, while granting greater powers to the police. According to the Chinese Government, the only intention was to prevent foreign forces from attacking China through Hong Kong. ∎

Taiwan / T'aiwan

Population:	22,370,000
Area:	36,960 km²
Capital:	Taipei
Currency:	New dollar
Language:	Chinese (Mandarin)

The island of Taiwan was originally inhabited by Austronesian peoples, who also spread to the Polynesian archipelago and New Zealand/Aotearoa, and are still found among a dozen ethnic groups that have not assimilated into the Chinese culture.

[2] In 1590, the Portuguese landed on the island, renaming it Ilha Formosa. After a brief occupation by the Dutch in the early 17th century, the island was incorporated into the Chinese Empire during the Qing (Manchu) dynasty in 1683 and proclaimed a province of China in 1887. During this time, the political and administrative systems of mainland China were extended to Taiwan, and many people migrated there from the continent.

[3] After China's defeat in the 1895 Sino-Japanese war, Taiwan became a Japanese colony, but was returned to China after the defeat of Japan at the end of World War II.

[4] At first, the people of Taiwan rejoiced at the end of Japanese colonialism, but they soon discovered that life under the authoritarian Kuomintang (KMT) party led by Chiang Kai-Shek resembled colonialism.

[5] On 28 February 1947, there was a major demonstration against the KMT authorities. The KMT reacted at first by lifting martial law and inviting the opposition to form a Settlement Committee of politicians, trade unionists and student groups to discuss possible political reforms. Meanwhile, they drafted in 13,000 additional troops and when the opposition came forward, the KMT massacred large numbers of them, imprisoning others.

[6] In 1949, the entire KMT government, the remnants of its armies, and their relatives and supporters, fled to Taiwan after losing the mainland civil war to the Communist armies. From its refuge, backed by the United States, the KMT declared Taiwan to be the temporary base of the Republic of China pending recovery of the mainland.

[7] When the Korean War erupted, with China supporting the North Koreans, the US redoubled its military and economic commitment to Taiwan, protecting it as a front-line state in the battle to defend the 'free world'. During the Cold War Taiwan became a champion of anti-communism, and forged close relations with right-wing dictatorships, including Chile, Paraguay, Uruguay and South Africa.

[8] Democracy disappeared. Human rights were violated, demonstrations, strikes and political parties banned, and martial law imposed - all in the name of the battle to reconquer the mainland. The KMT set up a governmental system which claimed to represent the whole of China, with legislators representing each mainland province.

[9] Taiwan's remarkable industrialization began in the 1970s, when World Bank and US technocrats helped the Government apply an export-oriented development strategy. The US granted financial, trade and aid advantages to bolster an authoritarian political regime which, in turn, hectored Taiwan's disenfranchised and politically disorganized workforce.

[10] Output grew at an annual average of 8.6 per cent between 1953 and 1985, and Taiwan became one of the four newly-industrialized 'tigers' of East Asia, based on highly developed plastics, chemical, ship-building, clothing and electronics. Growth was entirely export-oriented, and the island developed the world's

second-largest trade surplus, along with the US, after Japan.

[11] In 1971, the US decided to seek closer ties with China, no longer vetoing the latter's admission to the UN. Taiwan therefore lost its representation in that world body. A few years later in 1979 the US officially broke off diplomatic relations with Taiwan.

[12] The country found itself at an economic crossroads. It was over-dependent on a few export markets and labor-intensive industries, importing nations were pressuring for more balanced trade and Taiwan's labor was no longer as cheap as that of many of its Asian neighbors.

[13] Technocrats insisted that Taiwan needed a more open political system in order to compete. The KMT also faced an internal succession crisis as aging politicians clung precariously to power.

[14] A significant portion of the opposition began to reject both the authoritarian policies of the KMT and Deng Xiaoping's unification proposal of 'one nation, two systems' with Taiwan becoming a Chinese dependency but maintaining its socioeconomic model, in similar fashion to Hong Kong.

[15] In September 1986 the Democratic Progress Party (DPP) was formed as the first opposition party to challenge the KMT's political stranglehold. Although technically illegal, the party was allowed to survive.

[16] Martial law was formally lifted on 15 July 1987. A huge upsurge in union activity took place and strong independent sections were formed in the trade union system. Its leaders founded parallel political structures in the Labor Party and Worker's Party.

[17] While the KMT was resolutely opposed to independence, some DPP members formed the New Wave group proposing self-rule. Other groups advocated a referendum for self-determination.

PROFILE

ENVIRONMENT
Located 160 km southeast of continental China, Taiwan is part of a chain of volcanic islands in the West Pacific which also includes Japan. A mountain range stretches from north to south along the center of the country. A narrow plain along the island's western coast constitutes its main agricultural area where rice, sugar cane, bananas and tobacco are cultivated. More than two-thirds of the island's area is densely wooded. Taiwan has considerable mineral resources: coal, natural gas, marble, limestone and minor deposits of copper, gold, and oil.

SOCIETY
Peoples: Most are Chinese who have migrated from the mainland since the 17th century and are known as 'Taiwanese'. Hundreds of thousands of Kuomintang Chinese fled to Taiwan during 1949-50. The island's indigenous inhabitants are of Malayo-Polynesian origin (recognized as a sub-group of the Austronesian-speaking family) and make up about 1.7 per cent of the population. **Religions:** More than half are Chinese Buddhist. There are also Muslim and Christian minorities. Indigenous religions in some areas. **Languages:** Chinese (Mandarin), official. Taiwanese, a derivative of the Chinese dialect from Fujian province, is the language of the majority. Hakka is the second Chinese dialect in Taiwan. There are several indigenous languages, such as Amis. **Main Political Parties:** Democratic Progressive Party (DPP), formed in 1986 with a very broad platform to restore political democracy in Taiwan; Kuomintang (Chinese Nationalist Party/KMT) founded in China in 1919, took political monopoly control of Taiwan when it fled from the continent in 1949 and ruled under martial law up to 1987; People's First Party (PFP); and Taiwan Solidary Union (TSU). **Main Social Organizations:** Every trade union has to be a member of the Chinese Federation of Labor, controlled by the Kuomintang, but in 1987 a few independent trade unions appeared (National Federation of Independent Unions and Tao-Chu-Miao Brotherhood).

THE STATE
Official Name: Republic of China. **Administrative Divisions:** 7 municipalities and 16 counties. **Capital:** Taipei (T'aipei) 7,423,000 people (2003). **Other Cities:** Kaohsiung 2,478,600 people; Taichung 2,070,300; Tainan 770,100 (2000). **Government:** Chen Shui-bian, President since May 2000, re-elected in 2004. Yu Shyi-kun, Prime Minister since February 2002. The National Assembly has 720 members; it is in charge of appointing the President for a six-year-period and is empowered to amend the Constitution. The President heads the legislative 'Yuan', with 225 members (including eight seats for indigenous representatives and eight for the Chinese diaspora), and appoints the Prime Minister who heads the executive 'Yuan'. Internal affairs are under the control of a Provincial Assembly of 77 members, which deals with administrative matters. **National Holiday:** 1 January, Day of the Republic; 25 February, Constitution Day. **Armed Forces:** 376,000 troops. Other: Military police 25,000.

18   The National Assembly elections in December 1991 were regarded as a plebiscite on the independence issue. The DPP's electoral platform, favoring a definitive separation from China, was supported by just 21 per cent of the electorate, against the KMT's 71 per cent.

19   From 1994, voices rose demanding an independent way for Taiwan, leaving behind the assumption of being a government representative of all Chinese. However, due to Beijing's opposition to any measure which could further lead the island toward independence, Taipei's efforts to be accepted into the UN were in vain.

20   The first multiparty municipal elections were held in December. Most of the vote went to the ruling Kuomintang and the DPP. In spite of opposition from environmentalists and anti-nuclear activists and DPP objections, the KMT supported the construction of a fourth nuclear plant on the island.

21   In 1995, economic relations with Beijing intensified. Taiwan became the second 'foreign' investor in the People's Republic after Hong Kong. However, political relations between the two countries deteriorated after a private visit from Taiwanese president Lee Teng to the US in June. Heedless of US warnings, Beijing carried out a series of missile launchings in July and August on waters just 140 kilometers from Taiwan.

22   In spite of losing ground in previous elections, the KMT won the December legislative elections. In the campaign prior to the March 1996 presidential elections, new Chinese military maneuvers near the coast of Taiwan led Washington to send warships in defense of Taiwan's allegedly threatened territorial integrity.

23   Lee Teng, of the KMT, triumphed on March 20 in the first presidential elections with direct suffrage in the history of the island.

24   In July, China made a show of military force off the coast of Taiwan, timed to coincide with the return of Hong Kong to Chinese control.

25   In August the Government announced the closure of its embassy on the island of St Lucia, following the Caribbean island's decision to strengthen links with China. The severing of diplomatic relations reduced the number of countries recognizing the Taipei Government to 30. Also that month, Prime Minister Lien Chan resigned and was replaced by Vincent Siew.

26   In April 1998, China and Taiwan decided to reopen direct negotiations, having broken off relations in June 1995.

27   In the weeks running up to the presidential elections of 2000, Beijing repeatedly announced it could resort to force if Taipei refused unification.

The announcement was made as a response to the DPP election campaign in which candidate Chen Shui-bian had stated he would hold a referendum to decide the future status of the island were he to win.

28   This external pressure did the KMT no good, and on 18 March it lost power on the island for the first time in its history. The DPP won, followed by an independent candidate, James Soong, a former KMT leader who led a new faction. The KMT immediately expelled more than 50 of its members, accusing them of supporting Soong instead of the ruling party candidate Lien Chan.

29   In response to the new Taiwanese President's actions (Chen sought rapprochement with Beijing since almost his first day in office) the Chinese Government ceased its threats and accepted Chen's victory. KMT supporters did not react so patiently: they blamed their leaders for their defeat and for allowing the division of nationalist voters.

30   In early 2001, after more than 50 years of isolation, Taiwan and China inaugurated the first direct links between their territories.

31   In 2001 Taiwanese exports and imports fell due to world recession, and unemployment reached an all time high of five per cent, while the crisis of the new technology (dot.com) companies and the slowdown of the US economy also harmed the local economy. That year Taiwan became the 144th member of the World Trade Organization, after China lifted its boycott.

32   The KMT lost its parliamentary majority in the December 2001 elections, putting an end to the political hegemony responsible for the 'Taiwanese miracle', which had ruled with an iron fist since 1949.

33   The Dalai Lama's visit to Taiwan in March 2002 irritated China, which claimed the trip of Tibet's spiritual leader had pro-independence political motives (China has occupied Tibet since the early 1950s). Taiwanese Government spokesperson, Su Cheng Ping, stated that the visit, the second of its type, would only foster the religious spirit of its citizens and promote traditional Tibetan culture.

34   In January 2002, President Chen reshuffled his economic team and for the first time, a woman, Christine Tsung, was appointed Economy Minister.

35   In late 2003 President Chen proposed holding a 'defensive referendum' to maintain the status quo and 'help to consolidate our people's psychological defense', aside from 'calling global attention to the military threat mainland China posed for Taiwan'. A law passed by the *Yuan* (Legislative Chamber) enables holding a referendum in case a foreign military threat seeks to change the status of Taiwan. The so-called 'defensive referendum' would be held in response to a threat from mainland China.

36   In March 2004 President Chen survived an assassination attempt, and was re-elected for a second term. In his campaign he advocated for 'one country in each extreme'. A new passport design added the word 'Taiwan' on the cover. China assured it would 'pay any price' to prevent Taiwan's independence.

37   Meanwhile, pro-independence groups guided by former president Lee Teng Hui launched a campaign for a new Constitution. ■

Colombia / Colombia

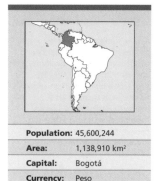

Population:	45,600,244
Area:	1,138,910 km²
Capital:	Bogotá
Currency:	Peso
Language:	Spanish

The best known of Colombia's indigenous cultures is that of the Chibcha or 'Muisca' peoples. Living in the north of Colombia, in present-day Panama, they were farmers and miners and developed a stratified society of feudal lords and vassals, with a matrilineal succession of power and patrilineal inheritance of property. The legend of *El Dorado* is attributed to a Chibcha ceremony in which a newly appointed chief was covered with gold dust and then bathed in a holy lake. The Chibcha culture and language remained isolated and, in spite of Spanish dominance, survive today in some areas of northern Colombia.

2   Spain conquered Colombia between 1536 and 1539. Gonzalo Giménez de Quesada's forces decimated the Chibchas and founded the city of Santa Fé de Bogotá which became the center of the Viceroyalty of New Granada in 1718. The population was subjected to thinly disguised forms of slavery, and by the 19th century, a large part of the indigenous population had been killed.

3   Extensive, export-oriented agriculture (coffee, bananas, cotton and tobacco) replaced traditional crops (potatoes, cassava, corn, wood and medicinal plants). African slaves were imported to work in the plantations.

4   The Revolt of the Comuneros (1781) started the process leading to the declaration of independence in Cundinamarca, in 1813. The road to independence was marked by constant struggles between the advocates of centralized Government and the federalists, headed by Camilo Torres. Antonio Nariño (who had drafted the declaration of independence) represented the urban bourgeoisie, linked to European interests, while Torres presided over the Congress of the United Provinces, representing the less privileged.

5   In 1816, Pablo Morillo reconquered this territory, executing Torres. Three years later, Simon Bolívar counter-attacked from Venezuela, liberated Colombia and founded the Republic of Greater Colombia, including Venezuela, Ecuador and the province of Panama. After the secession of Venezuela and Ecuador in 1829-30 the Republic of New Granada was proclaimed, and in 1886 adopted the name of Colombia.

6   From 1830 to the early 20th century, the country went through 9 civil wars, 14 local wars and two with Ecuador, three military uprisings and 11 constitutions. The Liberal and Conservative parties were created in 1849.

7   Between 1861 and 1885, a Liberal Party administration separated the Church from the State and created nine state companies.

8   Between 1921 and 1957 US firms made a profit of $1,137 million tapping Colombia's oil reserves, which led to their disappearance. These companies controlled the mining industry, 80-90 per cent of the banana trade and 98 per cent of electricity and gas.

9   In 1948, the 'Bogotazo' popular uprising killed leader Jorge Eliécer Gaitán. From that year - when a Liberal mayor organized the first guerrilla group - until 1957, the civil wars caused between 250 and 300 thousand deaths.

10   The Revolutionary Armed Forces of Colombia (FARC), led by Manuel 'Tiro Fijo' (Sure Shot) Marulanda and Jacobo Arenas, appeared on the scene in 1964. Guerrilla strategists included Camilo Torres Restrepo, a priest and co-founder of the National Liberation Army (ELN), who was killed in combat in 1965.

11   Large landowners organized, armed and paid 'self-defense' groups to fight these rural-based guerrilla movements. These were supported by members of the army and, in some cases, by foreign mercenaries. Closed out of official circles, the army also created paramilitary groups, later condemned by Amnesty International.

12   In 1974, President Alfonso López Michelsen, a Liberal, tried to give greater attention to popular demands, but vested economic interests led to the failure of this policy. Figures for 1978 reveal that only 30 per cent of industrial workers and 11 per cent of the rural workforce had social security benefits. Colombia was dependent on international coffee prices on the US and German markets for its foreign exchange, as these countries consumed 56 per cent of the Colombian product at that time.

13   Guerrilla movements, particularly FARC and the April 19 Revolutionary Movement (M-19), continued their activities into the late 1970s. Military repression grew during the Government of President Julio C Turbay Ayala (1978-82).

14   In 1980, M-19 guerrilla leader Jaime Bateman proposed a high-level meeting in Panama. Bateman subsequently died in an airline 'accident' and talks were suspended. The FARC and the Government reached an agreement which led to a ceasefire between them and to the adoption of political, social and economic reforms.

15   In 1982, a divided Liberal Party nominated two candidates, thus handing the victory to the Conservative Party's Belisario Betancur, a journalist, poet and humanist, who had actively participated in the peace process in Central America. Betancur proposed that Colombia join the Non-Aligned Movement and reaffirmed the right of debtor nations to negotiate collectively with creditor banks. Also, in 1983 he entered peace talks with leaders of the M-19.

16   Large landowners fiercely opposed talks between the Government and the guerrillas. The rural oligarchy, holding 67 per cent of the country's productive land, denounced the peace process as 'a concession to subversion' and proposed the creation of private armies. Paramilitary action started up again; subsequent investigations revealed the hand of the Muerte a los Secuestradores (MAS - 'death to the kidnappers'), which had opposed the withdrawal of the army from guerrilla-controlled areas. A one-year truce came into effect but M-19 withdrew five months later, claiming that the army had violated the ceasefire.

17   In January 1985, the Government passed a series of unpopular economic measures which worsened the recession: price hikes, lower real purchasing power, and a currency devaluation. The aim was to increase exports and reduce the $2 billion fiscal deficit by 30 per cent. A commission of 14 banks, presided over by the Chemical Bank, stated that the Government would have to reach a formal agreement with the IMF.

18   According to the Human Rights Commission, 80 detainees had disappeared in one year, political prisoners had been tortured and 300 clandestine executions were confirmed. The number of political activists who had disappeared rose to 325.

19   On 6 November 1985, 35 guerrillas from M-19 took over the Palace of Justice in Bogotá. The army attacked, causing a massacre. All the guerrillas were killed, along with 53 civilians.

20   Over 2,000 left-wing activists were killed by terrorists, and two presidential candidates were assassinated: Jaime Pardo Leal, a member of the Patriotic Union, in 1987, and Liberal senator Luis Carlos Galán, in 1989. They had promised to dismantle the paramilitary groups and fight drugs. War broke out between the Government and the drug mafia. In March 1990, Bernardo Jaramillo, the Patriotic Union's presidential candidate, was assassinated, with Carlos Pizarro (replacing Jaramillo) also killed 20 days later.

21   More than 140 paramilitary groups were present in the country, some of them financed by the drug

Life expectancy
72.2 years
2000-2005

GNI per capita
$1,830
2002

Literacy
92% total adult rate
2000

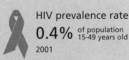

HIV prevalence rate
0.4% of population 15-49 years old
2001

mafia. Meanwhile, the US Drug Enforcement Agency allegedly bombarded coca plantations with chemical herbicides.

[22] The presidential elections of 27 May 1990 were won by Liberal Party candidate Cesar Gaviria, who received 48 per cent of the vote in an election where the abstention rate was 58 per cent. The following year, in elections for the constituent assembly, abstentions were at 65 per cent, and the ADM-19 (Alianza Democrática M-19/Democratic Alliance M-19) won 19 seats.

[23] In June 1991, members of Gaviria's Government met in Caracas with representatives of the Revolutionary Armed Forces of Colombia (FARC), the National Liberation Army (ELN) and the People's Liberation Army (EPL) - members of the Simón Bolívar Guerrilla Coordinating Committee, which controlled 35 per cent of the country. Talks dealt with the demobilization of guerrillas, the subordination of the armed forces to civilian authority, the dismantling of paramilitary groups and the reintegration of guerrilla fighters into areas where they could exert political influence.

[24] The new 1991 constitution created the office of vice-president; abolished presidential re-election; legalized civil divorce for Catholic marriages; promulgated direct election of local authorities; guaranteed democratic rights for indigenous peoples; added the democratic tools of referendum and grassroots legislative initiatives; guaranteed equal opportunities for women, and banned the extradition of Colombians for trial overseas. The Constitution met criticism from the Left for failing to give civilian courts jurisdiction over members of the military accused of committing crimes against civilians and for granting judicial powers to State security agencies.

[25] In October an agreement between the President and the three major political forces participating in the constituent assembly reduced the number of representatives. After the dissolution of Congress, parliamentary elections were held. The Liberal Party, split into several groups, obtained 60 per cent of the vote and support for the ADM-19 dropped to 10 per cent. In the March 1992 municipal elections, marked by a 70 per cent abstention rate, this trend was continued.

[26] The peace process reached a low point in 1992. After talks had been discontinued, the Government promoted its so-called 'Integral War', which authorized intervention in civilian organizations with suspected links to rebel groups.

[27] The Simón Bolívar Coordinating Committee resisted the army

IN FOCUS

ENVIRONMENTAL CHALLENGES
Pesticide abuse, intensive crops, and mining have degraded water and soil quality. Deforestation is significant. Two-thirds of bird species are at risk. Air pollution, especially in Bogotá, is caused by vehicle carbon emmission.

WOMEN'S RIGHTS
Colombian women have been able to vote and run for office since 1954.

Illiteracy among women over 15 was halved between 1980 and 2000, from 16.8 to 8.4 per cent. In 2000*, women made up 39 per cent of the workforce: 20 per cent worked in the industrial sector, 80 per cent in services. Women made up 24.5 per cent of the 20.5 per cent of unemployed in the country.

In 2000, 19 per cent of adult women were victims of physical violence. The rate of maternal deaths remains high (71.4 per 100,000 live births), due to poor access to prenatal and childbirth care.

CHILDREN
More than one million children between 5 and 17 are working. Sexual exploitation and international trafficking have increased. More than one million children have been displaced in the last 15 years. Some 7,000 fighters between 10 and 18, recruited by guerrillas and paramilitary groups, make up 20 per cent of these forces.

In 2002, some 300 children were kidnapped.

The average of school years completed increased from 3 to 3.7 among girls and from 3.1 to 3.8 among boys*. Indigenous and Afro-Colombian children from rural areas have poor access to education.

Sexual activity happens increasingly earlier, and marriage increasingly later. The number of births to 15-19-year-olds girls, increased from 70 per 1,000 in 1990 to 89 in 1995.

INDIGENOUS PEOPLES/ ETHNIC MINORITIES
Indigenous peoples make up one per cent of the population and live in 27 of the 32 departments, with large concentrations in the Amazon, Orinoquia, Pacific coast, Sierra Nevada de Santa Marta, Perija mountains, Guajira Peninsula and the *cordillera* or mountain range. There are between 80 and 90 groups, identified by the *cabildo* or department they live in, their languages (more than 64) and dialects (300), and by the collective claims established by their local organizations.

The efforts of indigenous organizations to implement land reform or claim ancestral lands lost during colonial and post-colonial periods have historically encountered legislative resistance and violence from military and paramilitary groups. Their main claims are: regional autonomy with limited power, greater political rights over their regions, equality of civil rights, equal distribution of funds and public services, protection of lands and resources from foreign oil companies,

protection from attack and occupation from military groups.

Blacks, descendants of slaves brought from Africa in the 18th century, make up four per cent of the population. The abolition of slavery after 1850 coincides with the movement of black workers to cities such as Medellin and Bogota and the inflow of whites in search of jobs in the mining, business, and wood industry sectors. In the cities, even today blacks work mostly as domestic employees and in non-qualified areas. They make up the majority of the workforce in the Antioquia coffee plantations and in the Choco mines.

MIGRANTS/REFUGEES
Between 1998 and 2003,1.5 million Colombians emigrated, fleeing from violence and persecution, or for economic reasons. Internally displaced, refugees and those waiting for asylum make up a population of almost three million. More than 325,000 Colombians lived as refugees abroad (at least 150,000 in the US; the rest in Ecuador, Venezuela, Costa Rica, and Panama).

Many people have been uprooted, and children may be vulnerable to recruitment by guerrillas as a result of this dispersal.

DEATH PENALTY
Abolished in 1910.

*Latest data available in *The State of the World's Children* and *Childinfo* database, UNICEF, 2004.

offensive, continuing its campaign. In response, paramilitary groups resumed their activities. Violence caused major population displacement from conflict areas to the interior, for fear of children being recruited into the conflict.

[28] In November 1992, the Government decreed a state of emergency after Pablo Escobar Gaviria (head of the Medellín Cartel, a powerful drug-trafficking ring) had escaped from prison earlier in the year, stepping up the Cartel's violence. In January 1993 a group appeared known as 'PEPES' - People Persecuted by Pablo Escobar. Within a two-month period, they killed 30 cartel members, destroyed several of Escobar's properties and harassed members of his family. The confrontation reached serious proportions, with car-bombs causing dozens of deaths. On 2 December, Escobar was killed in a shoot-out with police forces in Medellín. His death was a serious blow to the

political and social power of the Medellín Cartel.

[29] The Supreme Court of Justice decriminalized the use of cocaine, marijuana and other drugs, with the opposition of several political and religious circles, headed by President Gaviria.

[30] The coffee market crisis and the 1993 drought, as well as the reduction of banana quotas to the European Union, affected exports. However, with $2 billion per year from drug-trafficking and the discovery of oil in Casanare province, the country achieved a sustained growth of 2.8 per cent per capita. However, 45 per cent of the population were still living in deep poverty.

[31] President Gaviria was elected secretary-general of the Organization of American States (OAS), with the support of the United States, which welcomed the victory of Ernesto Samper, his party's candidate in the 1994 elections;

defeating Conservative Andrés Pastrana by 50 per cent to 48.6 per cent of the vote. Support for the ADM-19 dropped to 4 per cent of the vote, with abstentions slightly decreased to 65 per cent.

[32] The Samper Government began with a series of successful blows to drug-trafficking, but in September 1995 political scandal broke out when the Cali Cartel revealed details of that organization's contributions to both the Samper and Pastrana campaigns. Defense Minister Fernando Botero, Samper's former campaign director, was sent to prison for embezzling.

[33] In August 1996, Samper decreed a state of emergency to curb a wave of violence and kidnappings, a move considered an attempt to protect himself from drug-linked scandals. However, the murders of several opposition leaders and actions by FARC and the ELN, which attacked high-tension power lines, oil pipes, police and

Under-5 mortality
23 per 1,000 live births
2002

Poverty
14.4% of population living on less than $1 per day
1998

Debt service
35.3% exports of goods and services
2001

Maternal mortality
130 per 100,000 live births
2000

military facilities, continued. With fighting in almost 100 places, these two groups controlled growing areas in the economically powerful coffee region, the Caribbean and even in the vicinity of Bogotá and Medellín.

34 Efforts to eradicate coca and opium poppy plantations continued, as well as armed operations against the Cartel's bases. Some of the Cali Cartel's main leaders, responsible for 70 per cent of cocaine traffic worldwide, gave themselves up. In March 1996 the US took Colombia off its list of countries which co-operate in the war on drugs. This measure ended bilateral aid to Colombia and blocked its access to foreign financial sources. Washington denied an entry visa to Samper, in an attempt to corner him diplomatically.

35 Some 1,900 candidates decided not to run for the 26 October local elections because 49 mayors and city councilors had been killed and more than 180 kidnapped since the beginning of the year. In spite of the traditionally low turnout, over 5 million people enclosed symbolic 'vote for peace' slogans in their ballot papers.

36 In November the Human Rights prosecutor revealed that since August 1995 his office had ordered disciplinary measures, including 50 dismissals, against 126 military and police officers for human rights abuses. In the same period, more than 600 cases were investigated against security forces members, related with 1,338 victims of murder, torture or disappearance. Some 500 kidnappings mainly by FARC and ELN were reported in the period.

37 Several organizations estimated that since early 1997 one million Colombians had been displaced from their homes in conflict areas, mainly due to the activity of paramilitary groups. According to the Government, guerrilla groups obtained an annual net income of $750 million, substantially more than that earned by coffee. The only sectors with higher earnings were the drug cartels of Medellín and Cali.

38 In February 1998, US President Clinton acted, for 'national interest' reasons, to include Bogotá as a cooperating state in the war on drugs. According to the World Bank, high murder rates reduced GDP growth by 2 per cent each year.

39 In June 1998, former Bogotá Mayor Andrés Pastrana was elected President. The winner, from the conservative New Democratic Force party, obtained 50.4 per cent of the vote, ending the Liberal Party's 12-year hold on the presidency.

40 In August 2000, Pastrana announced the Plan Colombia,

inspired by the US, which sought to eradicate, from the air, 60,000 hectares of coca crops. The Plan encompassed the formation of three anti-narcotics battalions, trained and equipped by US special forces, backed by 60 helicopters. Colombia is currently the world's third-largest recipient of foreign military aid. The US also promised to contribute with $1.3 billion, mostly in military aid. The objective was to weaken the guerrillas' and drug barons' finances, rather than facing them in the battlefield. After the September 11 2001 attacks in the US, Colombia was included by Washington among the targets in its 'war on terror', although the US Government did not spell out any details. This enabled the US to overcome obstacles of its domestic legislation and cooperate actively.

41 Peace talks between the Government and FARC broke down on 20 February 2002, after the guerrillas kidnapped politicians in order to influence electoral results and force a swap with jailed guerrillas. On 10 March, when partial elections were being held, 12 politicians were held, including presidential candidate Ingrid Betancour. The Government lost the elections and forces allied to right-wing candidate Álvaro Uribe Vélez took power. Uribe had been linked to paramilitary forces under the United Self-Defense Groups of Colombia (AUC). The candidate's father had died under torture by the FARC, and Uribe opposed any peace agreement with the guerrillas.

42 After negotiations were broken off, several people died from FARC attacks. On 4 May 2002, violence against civilians reached an all-time high when FARC mortar-bombed a church where the population of Bojaya was taking refuge, killing 117 people, at least 40 of them children.

43 Washington approved $2.6 billion, twice the amount of Plan Colombia, in May 2002. Thus the US began a significant military intervention in the continent. At the same time, Pastrana held peace talks, in Cuba, with the ELN.

44 The Government put the Democracy Plan into action in April, a strategy through which 212,000 members of the army, police, air force and secret services aimed to guarantee the presidential elections on 26 May across Colombia. The few voters who turned out did so in an atmosphere intensified by guerrilla sabotage attempts, which left at least 11 paramilitaries and guerrillas dead. Abstention ran at 55 per cent. Independent candidate Uribe Vélez took the lead with 52.96 per cent of the vote to his rival Horacio Serpa's 31.77 per cent, breaking the traditional cycle of

liberals and conservatives. Uribe's campaign promise had been 'security for all Colombians' even if this implied hardline policies against all those involved in violent and illegal activity, including guerrillas, paramilitaries and drug traffickers. However, Uribe's close links with paramilitaries and drug traffickers meant his policies would concentrate on FARC without touching other violent sectors.

45 It is estimated there are more than 25,000,000 Colombians living below the poverty line; 11,000,000 of them are abjectly poor. The unequal distribution of wealth is reflected especially in the fact that 1.5 per cent of the population owns 80 per cent of the land suitable for agriculture.

46 In January 2003 Uribe requested Washington's direct intervention in the fight against the guerrilla and paramilitary groups, calling them terrorists. That month,

US special forces were deployed in the province of Arauca, becoming that country's first military troops to become directly involved in Colombia's civil war.

47 A referendum sought political reform in October 2003. The victory of Luis Eduardo Garzón, a candidate from the center-left Independent Democratic Pole (IDP), as mayor of Bogota (the most important office in the country after the presidency) was an historic shift in Colombian politics and a surprise for the two traditional parties. A left-wing movement had been consolidated nationwide.

48 According to a Human Rights Watch (HRW) report, more than 11,000 children and youngsters were recruited to fight for the guerrilla or the paramilitary. These children often commit atrocities and are forced to execute other child fighters who try to run away. ■

PROFILE

ENVIRONMENT

The Andes cross the country from north to south, in three ranges: the western range on the Pacific coast, and further inland, the central and eastern ranges, separated by the large valleys of the Cauca and Magdalena Rivers. North of the Andes, the swampy delta of the Magdalena River opens up, leaving flat coastal lowlands to the west - along the Pacific coast - and to the east, plains covered by jungle and savannas extend downward to the Orinoco and Amazon Rivers. This diversity results in great climatic variety, from perpetual snows on Andean peaks to tropical Amazon rain forests. The country's Andean region houses most of the population. Coffee is the main export item, followed by bananas. Abundant mineral resources include petroleum, coal, gold, platinum, silver and emeralds. Coca plantations in Colombia increased by almost 25 per cent in 2001, some 33,600 hectares out of a total of 169,800.

SOCIETY

Peoples: Colombians are descended from native Americans, Africans and Europeans. **Religions:** 93 per cent are Catholic. Although this is the country's official religion, there is religious freedom. **Language:** Spanish (official); there are dozens of Indian languages including wayuu, camsá and cuaiquer. **Main Political Parties:** The New Democratic Force (NFD), conservative. The Liberal Party (LP); the Social Conservative Party (SCP); M-19 Democratic Alliance (ADM-19); Independent Democratic Pole (IDP), representing the Colombian left wing, specifically center-left. **Main Social Organizations:** There are four major labor organizations: the Confederation of Colombian Workers; the Confederation of Workers' Unions, Workers' Union and the General Labor Confederation. Eighty per cent of all salaried workers affiliated to trade unions are members of the Unitary Workers Federation (CUT), founded in 1986. Regional Indigenous Council of Tolima (CRIT). Colombian Association of Peasant and Indigenous Women.

THE STATE

Official Name: República de Colombia.
Administrative Divisions: 32 departments and the capital district.
Capital: Bogotá 7,290,000 people (2003). **Other Cities:** Cali 1,718,900 people; Medellín 1,621,400; Barranquilla 1,064,300; Cartagena 745,700 (1995). **Government:** Álvaro Uribe Vélez, President since August 2002. The Congress (Legislature) has two chambers: the Chamber of Representatives, with 161 members, and the Senate of the Republic, with 102 members.
National Holiday: 20 July, Independence Day (1810).
Armed Forces: 146,300 troops; 40,400 conscripts (1996). Other: National Police Force, with 85,000 members.

Comoros / Komori - Comores

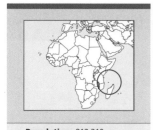

Population:	812,310
Area:	2,230 km²
Capital:	Moroni
Currency:	Comorian franc
Language:	Arabic and French

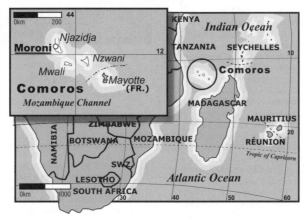

Comoros was inhabited around the 5th century by one of the last Indonesian migrations (see Madagascar). The Comoros Islands remained isolated from the continent until the 12th century when Muslim traders from Kilwa settled on the archipielago, founded ports and reproduced the civilization of the eastern African coast. In the 16th century Comoros had a prosperous economy but the Portuguese seized the islands and destroyed their active trade. When the Sultan of Oman finally drove the Portuguese from the region, Comoros came under the influence of Zanzibar and as a result of the slave trade the Bantu-speaking population increased considerably.

[2] In the 19th century, after Zanzibar split from the sultanate of Oman, European pressure became stronger and finally France occupied Mayotte in 1843. Colonial domination eventually spread to the entire archipelago, motivated by spice production and the islands' strategic position on the Cape route.

[3] The Comoros National Liberation Movement (MOLINACO) joined forces with the local Socialist Party (PASOCO) to form the United National Front (FNU) which pressured the French Government into holding a referendum in 1974. A large majority, 154,182 people, voted in favor of the islands' independence, and only 8,854 voted against.

[4] Most of those who wished to remain under French rule were Mayotte residents (63 per cent of its voters). France had air and naval bases on Mayotte and the economy was controlled by a few dozen Catholic families, sympathetic to France and politically represented by the Mahorés People's Movement (MPM), led by Marcel Henry.

[5] Ahmed Abdallah, the archipelago's leading rice exporter and Prime Minister of the semi-autonomous local Government, proclaimed the independence of Comoros in July 1975, before the French announced the result of the referendum. Abdallah was afraid that his Udzima (Unity) Party would

lose out to the FNU in a future assembly to draft a new constitution. The MPM took advantage of the situation to declare that Mayotte would continue under French rule. Paris supported the secession in order to maintain its military presence in the Indian Ocean, violating its previous commitment to respect the result of the referendum. France did not oppose the islands' membership in the UN but vetoed specific Security Council resolutions to reincorporate Mayotte into the archipelago.

[6] Less than a month after the declaration of independence, a

small group of FNU youths seized the national palace in Moroni and appointed their leader, the socialist Ali Soilih, as president, in place of Abdallah. France reacted by sending a task force of three warships and 10,000 soldiers to Mayotte; one soldier for every three inhabitants.

[7] In May 1978, a mercenary force, under the command of Ahmed Abdallah, in exile in Paris, landed on Grand Comoro (now Njazidja) overthrowing and assassinating Ali Soilih. At the head of the operation was the notorious French mercenary Bob Denard, who had been tried in 1977 for mercenary acts of war

against the Government of Benin. His presence in Comoros triggered international protests, to the point of the Comoros Islands' delegation being expelled from the Organization of African Unity. Madagascar tightened its diplomatic relationships with the islands and the UN threatened to apply economic sanctions to the regime.

[8] From then on, Denard became a key figure in the archipelago's politics, and Abdallah's control of the Government came to depend on support from Denard and his 650 troops. On 26 November 1989, a coup led by Denard ousted Abdallah, who was killed in the fighting.

[9] The French Government suspended all economic aid to the islands and initiated negotiations designed to oust Denard and his mercenaries. They surrendered to the French troops on 15 December and left for South Africa, where they were imprisoned.

[10] Restrictions on the formation of political parties ceased after Abdallah's death. A number of opposition groups returned from exile.

[11] In August 1991, the Supreme Court of the Islamic Federal Republic of the Comoros found President Said Mohammed Djohar unfit to govern and guilty of serious negligence. After a failed attempt to oust the President, the political parties and Djohar signed a national reconciliation pact. A new Government was formed, headed by Mohammed Taki, leader of the National Union for Democracy in Comoros (UNDC), who was dismissed in July by President Djohar, accusing him of appointing a former French mercenary to his cabinet.

[12] In October 1993, when Djohar, aged about 80, was outside the country, Prime Minister Caabi el Yachourtu Mohamed proclaimed himself 'interim President', refusing to give up power on Djohar's return.

[13] Djohar recovered a 'symbolic' Presidency in January 1996, while Taki, leader of the UNDC, won the elections held in March.

[14] The October 1996 Constitution replaced the 1992 one and included, among other innovations, the formation of a Council of Ulemas (Islamic teachers) to monitor the compliance of the laws with their interpretation of Islamic law. The death penalty, suspended in 1975, was reinstated.

[15] In August 1997, a separatist movement headed by Abdallah Ibrahim demanded the independence of Anjouan Island, where half the Comoran population lives. In March 1998, more than 99 per cent of Anjouan citizens voted for secession in a referendum, while

IN FOCUS

ENVIRONMENTAL CHALLENGES
Soil degradation and erosion result from crop cultivation on slopes without proper terracing. Furthermore, there is deforestation and cyclones occur during the rainy season.

WOMEN'S RIGHTS
Women have been able to vote and run for office since 1956. In 2000*, while illiteracy in women over 15 had decreased since 1980 (from 56 to 51.3 per cent), the differential with male illiteracy was the same (male illiteracy went from 40.4 to 36.8 per cent).
In 2000, women held 7 per cent of ministerial positions and made up 42 per cent of the workforce.

CHILDREN
Primary school enrolment rate is 60 per cent for boys and 52 per cent for girls. Girls' enrolment is therefore improving fast but the gap between girls and boys remains large.
Eighteen per cent of the children were born underweight, 25 per cent suffered from moderate or severe low weight conditions, and 42 per cent were stunted. In 2001* 28,000 births were registered and 2,000 children under five died.

INDIGENOUS PEOPLES/ ETHNIC MINORITIES
There are Arabs, descendants of Shirazi settlers, who arrived in the 15th century; the Cafres, an African group that settled on the islands before the Shirazi; a second African group, the Makoa, descendants of slaves brought by Arabs from the East African coast; and three groups of Malayo-Indonesian peoples - the Oimatsaha, the Antalotes, and the Sakalava, the latter having settled mainly in Mahoré.
Creoles, descendants of French settlers who married indigenous people, form a tiny (less than 100 people) but influential group in Mahoré. They are Roman Catholic and own small plantations. A small group of people descended mainly from the Portuguese sailors who landed on the Islands at the beginning of the 16th century live around the town of Tsangadjou on the east coast of Njazidja.

DEATH PENALTY
The death penalty applies for ordinary crimes.

*Latest data available in *The State of the World's Children* and *Childinfo* database, UNICEF, 2004.

Life expectancy
60.8 years
2000-2005

GNI per capita
$390
2002

Literacy
56% total adult rate
2000

Mohéli island also called for its independence. On 23 April 1999, in Madagascar, an agreement was proposed to grant more autonomy to Anjouan and Mohéli and to establish an interim Government and a rotating Presidency among the three islands. Anjouan delegates refused to sign it, alleging they had to consult their people first; this led to violent clashes both in Njazidja and Anjouan, which led to a bloody military coup on April 30. Colonel Azzali Assoumani became President, and promised to hold elections within 10 months.

[16] While Anjouan's political leaders were in Mohéli scrutinizing a constitutional draft on redefining the islands' relationships in August 2001, a military committee led by Major Mohamed Bacar took over Anjouan and granted the island 'regional autonomy from Comoros, but not total separation'.

[17] Two separatist coups within the military élite failed in Anjouan, and control was left in the hands of Bacar. Finally, a referendum in Njazidja supported the new constitution (already approved in the other two islands) that held the Federation, but granted more autonomy to each part. The Presidency would rotate among the three islands. The first four-year term went to Njazidja.

[18] After an election rife with protests of fraud, Assoumani was confirmed as federal President of Comoros by a new ad hoc electoral body, the Commission of Ratification, in May. The Commission declared Mohamed Fazul had won the elections in Mohéli, which had also been denounced as fraudulent. Bacar had won Anjouan's presidential elections and Abdou Soule Elbak was elected President of Njazidja (Grand Comoro).

[19] Continuing power struggles between Assoumani and Elbak about taxes, security and budget delayed the parliamentary elections slated for 2003. Neighboring countries, international organizations and social groups came up with a peaceful solution in December 2003 paving the way for elections in April 2004.

[20] In elections to the federal parliament held in April 2004, the national parties of the three autonomous islands won the majority of seats. The parties are united by nothing but their opposition to President Assoumani, who will now have to govern with an opposition-dominated federal parliament. ∎

PROFILE

ENVIRONMENT
The Comoros Islands are located at the entrance of the strategic Mozambique Channel, on the oil tanker route between the Arab Gulf and western consumer nations. The four major islands of this volcanic archipelago are: Njazidja, formerly Grand Comoro; Nzwani, formerly Anjouan; Mwali, formerly Moheli; and Mahore, also known by its former name of Mayotte. Njazidja has an active volcano, Karthala, 2,500 meters in altitude. The mountainous island is covered by tropical forests. Only 37 per cent of the cultivated land (100,000 hectares) is used to grow cash crops - vanilla and other spices; the rest is devoted to subsistence farming which is carried out without permanent rivers. The rainwater, which is stored in reservoirs, is easily polluted.

SOCIETY
Peoples: The original Malay-Polynesian inhabitants were absorbed by waves of Bantu and Arab migrations. Today, the latter groups predominate, co-existing with minority Indian and Malagasy communities. **Religions:** Islam (official 98 per cent), Catholic (2 per cent). **Languages:** Arabic and French are official. Most people speak Comoran, a Swahili dialect, and some groups speak Malagasy. **Main Political Parties:** Forces for Republican Action (FAR); Forum for National Renewal (FNR, an alliance of 12 parties); National Front for Justice (Islamic); National Union for Development (conservative alliance). **Main Social Organizations:** The failure of the political parties has led to the foundation of several social organizations, the main one being the Comoran Workers' Union. Citizen's Initiative has played a key role in the peace negotiations.

THE STATE
Official Name: Union des Comores. **Capital:** Moroni 53,000 people (2003). **Other Cities:** Mutsamudu 25,400 people; Domoni 14,000; Fomboni 12,200 (2000). **Government:** Parliamentary federal Islamic republic. Colonel Azzali Assoumani seized power in April 1999 in a coup; in May 2002 he was elected President. Legislature: General Assembly of 30 members (15 elected by local assemblies and 15 by universal suffrage).
National Holiday: 6 July, Independence Day (1975).

Mayotte

Population:	163,366,000
Area:	400 km²
Capital:	Mamoutzou
Currency:	Euro
Language:	French, Arabic, Swahili and Comoran

Known as the Island of Perfumes, Mayotte lies in the Indian Ocean, about halfway between Madagascar and the coast of Mozambique, 1,500 kilometers away from Réunion. Mahoré (Mayotte in Creole) comprises two main islands, Petite Terre and Grand Terre separated by two kilometers of sea and surrounded by a coral reef of 1,000 square kilometers.

[2] As a consequence of successive invasions since the 10th century, Mayotte is a combination of Arabic, Madagascan and French influence. After the treaty of 25 April 1841, Mayotte became a French colony. In 1974, after pressure from independence movements, France agreed to a referendum in the Comoros islands, of which Mayotte was part. Nationalist forces won and in 1975 the independence of the Comoros was proclaimed. However, those who wished to remain under French rule gathered in Mayotte and, supported by Paris, encouraged secession from the Comoros. Taking advantage of a movement that overthrew Ahmed Abdallah - prime minister of the semi-autonomous local government - 10,000 French troops occupied Mayotte.

[3] The policy statement of the Eighth Conference of Non-Aligned Countries (1986), declared that 'the Comoran island of Mayotte, still under French occupation, is an integral part of the sovereign territory of the Federal Islamic Republic of the Comoros'. In 1991, the UN General Assembly reaffirmed the sovereignty of the Comoros over Mayotte by an overwhelming majority.

[4] France maintains an important air-naval base on the island which is still under a French protectorate. In 1997, the islands of Nzwani and Mwali declared their independence from the Comoros, stating their desire to return to French rule. In 1999 a peace agreement was signed and the islands remained within the federation, but enjoying greater automomy. Voters on Nzwani rejected the peace agreement and endorsed independence in January 2000. The Organization of African Unity imposed economic sanctions on the island.

[5] In July 2000, the people of Mayotte accepted in a referendum an offer by Paris to increase the island's autonomy. The agreement granted Mayotte a status similar to that of a department, instead of an overseas territory.

[6] According to research published in September 2003 in Nature magazine, by 2020 a massive number of coral reefs in Mayotte - as well as in Comoros, Kenya, Tanzania, Mozambique and Madagascar - will have perished as a result of global warming. ∎

ENVIRONMENT
A mountainous island with tropical climate and heavy rainfall throughout the year. The island is of volcanic origin, has dense vegetation and is located at the entrance to the Mozambique Channel. Cyclones (hurricanes) are quite frequent.

SOCIETY
Peoples: Mayotte inhabitants are of the same origin as Comorans. There is an influential community of French origin that controls the island's commerce. **Religions:** 98 per cent Muslim. **Languages:** Arabic, Swahili, Comoran, and French (official). **Main Political Parties:** The Mayotte Federation for the Organization of the Republic (RPR); the Mahoré People's Movement (MPM).

THE STATE
In October 1991, the UN General Assembly reaffirmed the sovereignty of the Comoros over Mayotte by an overwhelming majority.
Official Name: Collectivité Territoriale de Mayotte. **Capital:** Dzaoudzi 13,500 people (1999). **Other Cities:** Mamoudzou 40,900 people (2000). **Government:** Jean-Jacques Brot, Prefect since July 2002, appointed by the French Government. Unicameral. **Legislature:** General Council, with 19 members. **National Holiday:** All French holidays. **Armed Forces:** Defense is the responsibility of France; a small contingent of French forces is stationed on the island.

Congo Democratic Republic
République Démocratique du Congo

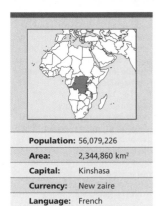

Population:	56,079,226
Area:	2,344,860 km²
Capital:	Kinshasa
Currency:	New zaire
Language:	French

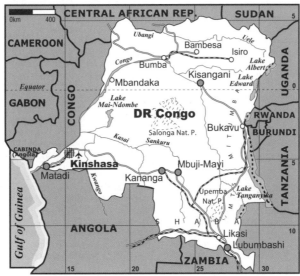

The first known state to emerge in what is now DR Congo was the Luba kingdom - Katanga (Shaba) region - created when a warrior named Kongolo subdued the small chiefdoms in the area and established a highly centralized state. To the northwest was the Kuba, a federation of numerous chiefdoms that reached its peak in the 18th century. Dr David Livingstone brought the region to the notice of the Western world through his explorations between 1840 and 1870. He met up with Henry Stanley, a journalist and adventurer, in Ujiji in 1871. In 1876, King Leopold II of Belgium founded the International Association for the Exploration and Civilization of Congo, a private organization that financed Stanley's expeditions. Stanley succeeded in signing more than 400 trade and/or protectorate agreements with local leaders along the Congo River. These treaties, and the Belgian trading posts established at the mouth of the river, devised a system for the economic exploitation of the Congo. The Berlin Conference (1884-1885) decided that the 'Free State of Congo' was the Belgian King's personal property. Consequently, Leopold II stopped British colonialist expansion, and made a fortune using slave labor to exploit rubber and ivory. It is estimated that 10,000,000 Congolese died from forced labor, starvation and systematic extermination during the period of Leopold II's kingdom.

2   The harsh working conditions did not change when the region formally became a Belgian colony in 1908. Military force was systematically employed to suppress anticolonial opposition and to protect the flourishing copper mining industry in Katanga (now Shaba).

3   In 1957, liberalizing measures permitted the formation of African political parties. This led countless tribal-based movements to enter the political arena, all trying to benefit from the general discontent. Only the National Congolese Movement led by Patrice Lumumba had a national outlook, opposing secessionist tendencies and supporting independence claims.

4   In 1959, the police suppressed a peaceful political rally triggering a series of bloody confrontations. King Baudouin of Belgium tried to appease the demonstrators by promising independence in the near future, but European residents of the Congo reacted with more oppressive measures. Independence was finally achieved in 1960, with Joseph Kasavubu as President and Lumumba as Prime Minister. A few days later, Moise Tshombe, then Premier of the Province of Katanga, initiated a secessionist movement.

5   Belgium sent in paratroopers and the United Nations, acting under US influence, intervened with a 'peacekeeping force'. Kasavubu staged a coup and arrested Lumumba, delivering him to Belgian mercenaries in Katanga who killed him. The civil war continued until 1963. Secessionist activity ceased when Tshombe, who represented the neo-colonial interests, was appointed Prime Minister. With the help of mercenaries, Belgian troops and US logistical support, he defeated the revolutionary forces. In 1965, he was forced to resign by Kasavubu who was in turn overthrown by army commander Joseph Desiré Mobutu. For the transnationals, Mobutu was the only person who could restore the conditions required for them to continue operating there.

6   Under the doctrine of 'African authenticity', Mobutu changed the name of the country to Zaire and his own to Mobutu Sese Seko. However, his nationalism went little further than this, and the 'Zairization' of copper, which he declared in 1975, only benefited an already wealthy economic elite and the state bureaucracy.

7   Although these measures caused some discomfort among US diplomats, Mobutu offered Washington his services in the region.

8   Zaire sheltered and actively supported the so-called National Front for the Liberation of Angola (FNLA). Mobutu encouraged secessionist groups in the oil-rich Angolan province of Cabinda, and Zaire's troops effectively cooperated with the South African racist forces in their war against the Angolan nationalists.

9   Meanwhile, in Zaire guerrillas continued the struggle in the interior. In 1978 and 1979, the major offensive launched by the Congolese Liberation Front was checked with the aid of French and Belgian paratroopers and Moroccan and Egyptian troops, again with US logistical support.

10   At the end of 1977, international pressure led to parliamentary elections being held for an institution which had been given limited legislative functions. This helped to divert international attention from human rights violations against students and intellectuals in the cities, the establishment of concentration camps for Mobutu's opponents and the brutal reception given to refugees who returned under an 'amnesty' decreed in 1979.

11   At this time Zaire was the world's largest cobalt exporter, the fourth biggest diamond exporter and among the top ten world producers of uranium, copper, manganese and tin. But corruption

was rampant throughout the country's administration, worsening the already unstable economic situation.

12   During 1980 and 1981, the major Western powers decided to seize direct control of the strategic mineral reserves in the country. The International Monetary Fund (IMF) took special interest in Zaire's economy, facilitating the renegotiation of its foreign debt, and imposing drastic measures against corruption. Zaire's economy was under direct IMF control, and the Fund's representatives in Kinshasa began to supervise the country's accounts personally.

13   In April 1981, Prime Minister Nguza Karl I-Bond sought political asylum in Belgium; he presented himself to the western powers as a 'decent alternative' to the official corruption in Zaire.

14   The elections of June 1984 officially gave Mobutu 99.16 per cent of the vote. In February 1985 Zaire signed a security pact with Angola to improve their relations.

15   The Angolan Government denounced the fact that $ 15,000,000 of covert aid for the FNLA was channeled by the Reagan administration through Zaire, and that Zaire effectively acted as an arsenal for the Front.

16   In April 1990, anticipating the process of democratization which he considered imminent, Mobutu decreed the end of the one-party system, opened up the labor movement and promised to hold free elections within a year. A rapid process of political organization began. Hundreds of associations and political groups demanded legal recognition from the Government. The extent of the popular reaction frightened the authorities and in May, Mobutu issued a statement saying that no party had yet been legalized and that it would be necessary to modify the constitution before holding elections, because the head of state wished to 'preserve his authority without exposing himself to criticism'.

17   The students at the University of Lubumbashi, in Shaba province, began calling for Mobutu's resignation; he reacted by sending in his presidential guard to silence the protests.

18   The troops stormed the university campus at dawn on 11 May. More than 100 students were killed and the terrified survivors fled to other provinces and Zambia, from where they condemned the massacre.

19   President Mobutu partially stifled the massacre's outcome, but the European Community called for an international investigation, while Belgium stopped its

Life expectancy
41.8 years
2000-2005

GNI per capita
$90
2002

Literacy
61% total adult rate
2000

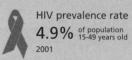
HIV prevalence rate
4.9% of population 15-49 years old
2001

economic aid. The political reform plan lost momentum, at least temporarily.

[20] The massacre at Lubumbashi University generated an anti-Mobutu wave which led to a series of strikes, like that at state-owned Gecamina, the country's most important mining company.

[21] In October 1990, under growing internal and external pressure, Mobutu decided to carry out a new political 'democratization' process and he authorized the unrestricted creation of new political parties. In December, the opposition - grouped together under the Holy Union, a front made up of the largest parties - demanded Mobutu's resignation and called for a National Conference to decide on the political future of Zaire without presidential intervention.

[22] Mobutu faced another national uprising in September 1991, provoked by a general price hike and the failure of a conference called in August to introduce democratic reforms. The uprising led to dozens of deaths and the intervention of France and Belgium, which sent hundreds of troops to evacuate their citizens.

[23] In November 1991, the Holy Union formed a 'shadow government', and appealed to the armed forces to depose Mobutu. The same month, the President appointed Nguza Karl I-Bond as his new Prime Minister - his fifth in that year. Nguza, a former opposition leader who had been Mobutu's head of government 10 years earlier, took office amidst a worsening economic crisis and growing international pressures, especially from the US.

[24] Early in 1992, the National Conference was set up. The opposition had long awaited this opportunity to press for constitutional reform and transition to democracy.

[25] In February of the same year, Prime Minister Nguza Karl-I Bond suspended the Conference, causing a faction of the army to rebel, taking over a state-run radio station and demanding President Mobutu's resignation. Some hours later the rebels were defeated and the army clashed with thousands of demonstrators, leaving many dead and injured. The European Community suspended financial aid to Zaire immediately, until the National Conference was reinstated.

[26] In March 1992, after meetings with Conference president Archbishop Monsegwo Pasinya, Mobutu announced the reopening of the National Conference. Etienne Tshisekedi, leader of the Holy Union, was made Prime Minister, to replace Nguza Karl-I Bond.

[27] Inter-ethnic strife erupted again in 1992. In Shaba there were outbreaks of violence after Karl-I Bond's dismissal. Lunda people, Karl-I Bond's group, attacked members of the Luba community, Tshisekedi's people. Some 2,000 people were killed, and thousands of Luba left Shaba as their homes had been destroyed.

[28] The 12 commercial banks operating in Zaire closed indefinitely in 1992, due to a lack of funds. Inflation reached 16,500 per cent. According to a report by the Washington-based Population Crisis Committee, in 1992 Zaire was among the 10 poorest countries in the world.

[29] In December, galloping inflation prompted the Prime Minister to put a new currency in circulation. Mobutu nonetheless ordered that troops receive their back pay in the old currency. In early 1993, battles broke out between the soldiers - furious at having been paid in worthless bills - and Mobutu's personal guard. This confrontation resulted in over 1,000 deaths in Kinshasa.

[30] On 24 February, Mobutu's soldiers surrounded the building housing the High Council of the Republic, a transitional body formed by the National Conference. They demanded that the legislators approve the old currency which Mobutu had put back into circulation.

[31] With the worsening situation, the US, Belgium and France sent a letter to Mobutu demanding that he share power with a provisional government headed by Tshisekedi. Mobutu responded by dismissing Prime Minister Tshisekedi.

[32] The US Department of State suggested Belgium and France should block Mobutu's wealth - calculated in more than $4 billion - as a punitive measure that would not harm the country's economy nor European and US business interests.

[33] The genocide in Rwanda and the arrival of large numbers of Rwandan refugees - amongst whom were thousands of soldiers responsible for the massacre - created great tension in eastern Zaire.

[34] When the Rwandan Patriotic Front (FPR) guerrillas came to power in Rwanda, several Western nations reduced the pressure on Mobutu - newly considered as a potential ally following the victory of 'the English-speaking Tutsis' in the neighboring country. This reinforced the President's power, facilitating the nomination of Léon Kengo Wa Dondo as Prime Minister.

[35] The tension between Zaire and Rwanda increased in 1996, after Rwandan and Zaire militias began ethnic cleansing in the Masisi region, ousting and killing the *Banyamulenge*, Tutsis who had

IN FOCUS

ENVIRONMENTAL CHALLENGES
Water pollution - especially untreated waste that flows into rivers - is the greatest source of disease. Some species of fauna run the risk of becoming extinct, due to poaching: among them, elephants and rhinoceros whose horns are sold as aphrodisiacs. Wooded areas have deforestation problems.

WOMEN'S RIGHTS
Women have been able to vote since 1967.

Women life expectancy is 42.8, almost nine years less than in 1980*.

Illiteracy among women over 15 decreased between 1980 and 2000*, from 79.2 to 50 (for men it was 27 per cent in 2000*). In 2000, women made up 43 per cent of the workforce.

CHILDREN
In less than five years of civil war - one of the bloodiest conflicts since World War II - some 3.3 million people were killed, mostly civilians. Children were the most vulnerable: hundreds died from malnutrition and other preventable diseases.

Thousands of children are recruited, one third of them by force; many are barely 10 years old. In the province of Itubi hundreds of women and children were raped, mutilated and murdered in 2002 and 2003.

Twelve per cent of children are born underweight and 31 per cent with moderate low weight*. Some 514 children under 5 died in 2001.

In late 2001 it was estimated that some 170,000 children between 0 and 14 were HIV-positive and some 930,000 had been orphaned by HIV/AIDS.

INDIGENOUS PEOPLES/ ETHNIC MINORITIES
There are more than 200 ethnic groups, mostly Bantu-speakers; the four largest groups - Mongo, Luba, Kongo and Mangbetu-Azande - make up 45 per cent of the population.

From the 18th onwards Hutus were treated as slaves or serfs in kingdoms ruled by Tutsis, who formed militias loyal to the royal authority.

The Twa, a hunting and gathering people of the tropical forests, face a dismal future. Deprived of rights, compensation or justice, and exposed to discrimination from other sectors of society, the Twa are suffering an alarming rise in malnutrition and disease. Together with the Twa, the Hutus and Tutis were one nationality, called *banyarwanda*. This collapsed with the genocide in Rwanda in 1994, when Hutu extremists murdered more than one million Tutsis and moderate Hutu. After the genocide, over a million Hutu refugees fled to DR Congo, fearing reprisals from the Tutsi, who formed the Rwandan Government and had recently carried out sporadic attacks against them.

The Tutsi minority (2 per cent of the population) are dominant politically and militarily, with sporadic outbreaks of violence against Hutus (3 per cent). These live in the eastern province of Kivu, densely populated and of difficult access due to its mountainous terrain. Although the Hutus are adversely affected by some economic decisions, they have political freedom.

MIGRANTS/REFUGEES
The civil war, the intervention of foreign armies, ethnic violence, political anarchy and economic meltdown have ravaged the country and its people. It is estimated 3,000,000 have died since 1998 of causes directly or indirectly related with the conflict.

More than 2.4 million people were displaced in 2002, including 2,000,000 internally displaced and almost 410,000 refugees and asylum-seekers. Around 140,000 people from DRC took refuge in Tanzania, 80,000 in the Republic of Congo, and tens of thousands in other African countries. Almost 15,000 applied for asylum in industrialized countries.

Meanwhile, 270,000 refugees from neighboring countries remained in DR Congo in late 2002, coming from Angola, Sudan, Uganda, Burundi, Central African Republic, Republic of Congo and Rwanda.

DEATH PENALTY
It still applies.

*Latest data available in *The State of the World's Children* and *Childinfo* database, UNICEF, 2004.

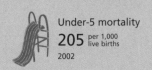
Under-5 mortality
205 per 1,000 live births
2002

Malnutrition
31% under-5s
1995-2002

Debt service
1.7% exports of goods and services
2001

Maternal mortality
990 per 100,000 live births
2000

lived in this part of eastern Zaire for generations.

[36] At the end of 1996, the conflict between armed Tutsi groups and the remnants of the Rwandan army (mostly Hutu), assumed civil war proportions. The confrontation spread with government forces participating to put a stop to the advance of the Tutsi rebels, who took several cities in the east of the country. The Mobutu regime became seriously threatened when various opposition forces formed an alliance led by the veteran guerrilla leader Laurent Kabila.

[37] In the first few months of 1997, opposition forces easily took over practically the whole country, and a group of states - South Africa, the US, France and Belgium included - attempted to mediate and seek a solution. Nelson Mandela arranged a meeting between Mobutu and Kabila which failed when Kabila demanded that Mobutu stand down.

[38] In March, Parliament sacked Prime Minister Kengo Wa Dondo; Tshisekedi was appointed for his third term in office, with Mobutu's approval. Tshisekedi offered Kabila six ministries, including Defense and Foreign Affairs, but Kabila rejected this and Tshisekedi was dismissed. Foreseeing the final outcome, the powerful mining companies began to negotiate with Kabila to protect their interests in Zaire.

[39] On 16 May, Mobutu fled to Morocco and opposition troops entered Kinshasa the following day. Kabila declared himself President. Mobutu died in Rabat on 13 September and the new strongman took over as president that month with full military, legislative and administrative powers. The new government changed the name of Zaire to the Democratic Republic of Congo (DR Congo/DRC) and announced a series of economic recovery measures.

[40] A study by Médecins Sans Frontières (MSF) in late 1997 exposed the massacres committed by Kabila's forces and the Rwandan troops that supported him in ousting Mobutu. Members of the Union for the Republic and Democracy (URD, former members of the AFDL founded by Kabila himself) accused Kabila of returning to tribalism, and under the leadership of Ernest Wamba dia Wamba - an intellectual - armed groups of Tutsi refugees and demobilized Congolese soldiers took half the country using weaponry and officers provided by the Rwandan and Ugandan governments. Kabila launched resistance under the slogan of a 'threat to the African civilization'.

[41] The conflict rapidly raised international concern and, in April 1999, in response to the attack, Kabila and the Angolan, Zimbabwean and Namibian leaders announced an alliance to provide a joint response if any of the members were attacked. Hence Angola, Zimbabwe and Namibia supplied Kabila with troops and weapons, while Uganda and Rwanda stepped up support of the rebels.

[42] Two years into the civil war which brought Kabila to power, whole provinces were under Ugandan and Rwandan control. The Congolese Parliament was dissolved in 2000, and the President replaced it with a 300 member government assembly.

[43] Kabila was assassinated by one of his bodyguards in January 2001 while the Franco-African summit was meeting in the presidential palace. His son Joseph immediately replaced him as President, with support from the former president's allies.

[44] There was a first withdrawal of troops monitored by the UN in May 2001. As troops were removed from combat, aid agencies discovered the full impact of the conflict which had pushed most of the population into remote areas where they lacked food, medicine or shelter. According to figures from the International Rescue Committee (IRC), five per cent of the Congolese population died during the war. In the eastern region of the country alone, two and a half million people had died, mostly due to malaria, diarrhea and violence.

[45] In July 2002, Kabila and Paul Kagame, President of Rwanda, signed a peace treaty ending 4 years of civil war in the DRC. The conflict, called the 'World War of Africa', involved the armies of 6 nations, divided the DRC into regions controlled by rebel forces and by the Government and caused the death of almost 3,000,000 people, mostly from illness and starvation. With the agreement signed in Pretoria, South Africa, Kabila promised to disarm, arrest and repatriate almost 12,000 fighters from the Rwandan Hutu militias, while Rwanda would withdraw its 30,000 soldiers from DRC's eastern region.

[46] In December, the Kabila Government, guerrilla groups and opposition political parties signed an agreement ending the war. The agreement included the formation of a bicameral Parliament and the distribution of ministries between the Government, the guerrillas and opposition parties.

[47] In July 2003 a transition Government was installed. This was a military junta presided over by Kabila and four vice-presidents: two leaders from the largest rebel groups, one from the opposition and one from the Government. It undertook to lead the country toward its first elections in 40 years.

[48] However, violence continued in Ituri, in the east, where fighting between the Hema and Lendu peoples cost 50,000 lives in the 4-year war. The UN transferred, in December 2003, 80 per cent of its 10,000 blue helmets to Bunia, capital of Ituri, in an attempt to disarm the local militias and protect civilians.

[49] As an outcome of the war, HIV/AIDS became a major threat to security. The mobility of soldiers in the battlefield, and in particular the widespread rape of women, from girls as young as 5 to elderly women, drastically increased the number of those living with HIV/AIDS.

[50] In December 2003 it was estimated that for each woman out of the 150 that sought humanitarian aid each month, 30 more had been raped. ■

PROFILE

ENVIRONMENT

Located in the heart of the African continent, DR Congo's territory covers most of the Congo River basin and has a narrow outlet into the Atlantic. The center and northern regions are covered with rainforests and are sparsely populated. Small plots of subsistence farming are found here. In the southeast, a plateau climbs to 1,000 meters in the Shaba region (former Katanga). Most of the nation's resources and population are located in the southern grasslands, where cotton, peanuts, coffee and sugarcane are grown. There are also large palm-oil and rubber plantations. The country's mineral wealth is concentrated in Shaba: copper, zinc, tin, gold, cobalt and uranium. Local industry is found in the mining areas too. The small eastern region, Ituri, is home to the world's richest goldfield, the Kilo Motu, and is already the locus of significance for oil exploration. Eastern Congo has also more than half the world's supply of Coltan, used in chips in cell phones and computers, and which has at times rivaled gold in price per ounce.

SOCIETY

Peoples: The people of Congo are made up of several major African ethnic groups. West African people live in the northwest, while Nilo-Hamitic descendants live in the northeast and a large pygmy minority lives in the eastern center. There are more than 200 ethnic groups, mainly: Luba (18 per cent), Mongo (13.5 per cent), Azande (6.1 per cent), Bangi and Ngale (5.8 per cent), Rundi (3.8 per cent), Teke (2.7 per cent), Boa (2.3 per cent), Chokwe (1.8 per cent), Lugbara (1.6 per cent), Banda (1.4 per cent), other (16.6 per cent).
Religions: It is difficult to pinpoint the religion of peoples in the DRC due to high levels of religious syncretism. There is a large Christian population, above all Catholic (41 to 50 per cent), a Muslim minority (1.2 to 10 per cent) and many traditional religions. Protestant 32 per cent.
Languages: French (official). The most widely-spoken local languages are Swahili, Shiluba, Kikongo and Lingala (the army's official language).
Main Political Parties: Parliament is currently dissolved, so these are non-parliamentary parties. Union for Democracy and Social Progress (UDPS, liberal); Union for the Republic and Democracy; Congolese Rally for Democracy; Congolese-Liberation Movement (RCD-ML); Rally for a New Society (RNS); Convention of Democratic and Social Institutions (CIDES).

THE STATE

Official Name: République Démocratique du Congo.
Administrative Divisions: 10 provinces and a capital.
Capital: Kinshasa 5,277,000 people (2003).
Other Cities: Lubumbashi 1,044,200 people; Mbuyi-Mayi 1,018,100; Kisangani 792,400; Kananga 521,900 (2000).
Government: Joseph Kabila, acting President since January 2001. There is a provisional 300-member government assembly appointed by former President Laurent Kabila in 2000.
National Holiday: 30 June, Independence Day (1960).
Armed Forces: Between 20,000 and 40,000 of Kabila's troops constitute the new Armed Forces of the country.
Other: Gendarmerie: 21,000; Civil Guard: 19,000.

Congo / République du Congo

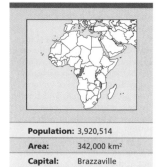

Population:	3,920,514
Area:	342,000 km²
Capital:	Brazzaville
Currency:	CFA franc
Language:	French

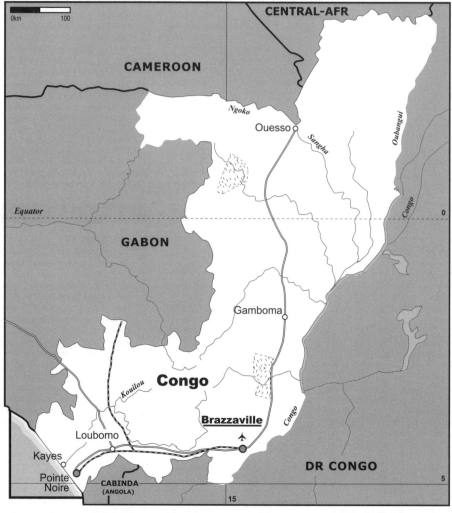

Today's Congo was originally populated by Pygmies and Bushmen (San). By the 16th century it comprised the Bantu states of Luango and Kacongo, for many years ruled by the Manicongo. These nations managed to stave off early Portuguese attempts at colonization. Instead, for three centuries, under the Batekes of Anzico, they acted as suppliers and intermediaries of British and French slave dealers.

2   Towards the end of the 19th century, trade in rubber and palm oil replaced slave traffic and brought with it French colonization.

3   In 1880 French troops led by Savorgnan de Brazza began to colonize the Congo by force, and by the 1920s, two-thirds of the local population had been killed, which resulted in the emergence of independence movements with strong religious beliefs, under the leadership of Matswa.

4   At the start of the decolonization process, the French sponsored Friar Fulbert Youlou who led the Democratic Union for the Defense of African Interests and was the first president of independent Congo in 1960. The growing mass participation never accepted Youlu's neo-colonialist policies and a wave of demonstrations against corruption and the banning of trade unions

LAND USE

2000

IRRIGATED AREA: 0.5% of arable land

- ARABLE LAND: 0.5%
- CROPLANDS: 0.1%
- OTHER USE: 99.4%

ended in a popular uprising during the 'three glorious days' (13-15 August) of 1963.

5   Youlou resigned and the self-proclaimed socialist Alphonse Massemba-Debat, took office and forced the French troops stationed in the country to withdraw. He then founded the National Movement of the Revolution (MNR) as the country's sole party.

6   This force could not coexist with the neo-colonial army, equipped and trained by the French, and the consequent crisis led Massemba-Debat to resign on 1 January 1969. He was replaced by Major Marien N'Gouabi, backed by left-wing army officers.

7   Political life was re-organized and a Marxist-Leninist party called the Congolese Workers' Party (PCT) was created. In 1973, a new constitution was approved, proclaiming the Congo a People's Republic.

8   In December 1975, N'Gouabi made a public self-appraisal, issued a call to 'extend the revolution', and launched a general review of party structures,

the state apparatus and mass organizations. N'Gouabi began educational reforms and modified the structure of Government.

9   On 18 March 1977, N'Gouabi was assassinated by followers of ex-president Massemba-Debat. The conspirators failed in their efforts to seize power, however, and Massemba-Debat was executed.

10   The new president, Colonel Joachim Yombi Opango, did not maintain the previous austere style and was forced to resign on 6 February 1979, charged with corruption and abuse of power. Denis Sassou N'Guesso replaced him.

11   N'Guesso launched a anti-corruption campaign within the public sector, and administrative and ministerial reforms. By the end of 1981, the Congo faced foreign trade difficulties arising from inefficiency in state enterprises.

12   In 1982, the Congo's finances improved. Part of the recovery was attributed to oil exports, which financed 49.44 per cent of the

budget. Oil was exploited in partnership with French, US and Italian firms, which as a whole, reached annual exports of approximately 8 million tons of crude (1988).

13   President N'Guesso's foreign policy was pragmatic; he maintained economic relations with Eastern Europe, US and France. He played a leading role in negotiations between Angola, South Africa and Cuba. This culminated in the signing of a peace settlement for the region on 13 December 1988, in Brazzaville, paving the way for Namibia's independence.

14   The fall of the Berlin Wall and the demise of the Soviet Union precipitated political and economic changes. In December 1990, the country adopted a multiparty system. In July 1991, André Milongo took the post of Prime Minister until presidential elections could be held.

15   This decision caused confrontation in the streets and the formation of a transition Government with army

Life expectancy
48.2 years
2000-2005

GNI per capita
$700
2002

Literacy
81% total adult rate
2000

HIV prevalence rate
7.2% of population 15-49 years old
2001

ENVIRONMENTAL CHALLENGES
Problems arise from haphazard urban development, waste and lack of sewage facilities, contagious diseases, pollution, deforestation and disappearance of fauna.

WOMEN'S RIGHTS
Women have been able to vote and be elected since 1963. In 2000 they held 12 per cent of Parliamentary seats and 6 per cent of ministerial positions.

In 2000*, illiteracy among women over 15 was 25.6 per cent; women make up 44 per cent of the workforce. Life expectancy is 49.7 years old for women*; 6.5 per cent of women between 15 and 24 were HIV-positive (double the percentage of men: 3.2 per cent).

The fertility rate (children per woman) is 6.3*.

CHILDREN
In 2001, approximately 139,000 children were born; 780,000 children under 14 became orphans.

Armed conflicts and economic crisis have worsened the human rights situation of women and children - the most vulnerable to insanitary conditions, diseases and death. The main cause of death among children is malaria and diarrhea. UNICEF has set up programs to combat malnutrition and cholera, and the registration of the newborn (more than one third of children under 5 are undocumented). Nutrition programs promote breastfeeding and the provision of iron supplements to pregnant women.

INDIGENOUS PEOPLES/ ETHNIC MINORITIES
There are several ethnic groups in different regions. The Lari live in the south, along with Bakongo, Vili, Yombe and Bembe peoples. Historically, the Lari - who make up 20 per cent of the population - have been political rivals of the M'boshi, from the north, along with the Teke (17 per cent of the population). The Lari are politically discriminated against. The M'boshi, President N'Guesso's people, are favored by the Government.

MIGRANTS/REFUGEES
Almost 25,000 Congolese were refugees or awaiting asylum in late 2002: 15,000 in Gabon, 3,000 in Democratic Republic of Congo and almost 5,000 in the West.

Almost 100,000 were internally displaced. Tens of thousands had been uprooted by the recent conflict after a brief period of peace between 2000 and 2001.

In late 2002 almost 120,000 refugees from other countries were living in Congo: approximately 80,000 were from DR Congo, 30,000 from Angola, some 5,000 from Rwanda, and 3,000 from Central African Republic.

DEATH PENALTY
Although it is still in force, there have been no executions since 1982.

*Latest data available in The State of the World's Children and Childinfo database, UNICEF, 2004.

participation. In the following elections of August 1992, Pascal Lissouba succeeded Sassou N'Guesso.
[16] In the early legislative elections of May 1993, the ruling party won 62 seats against the opposition coalition's 49. The opposition accused the Government of fraud and further clashes between demonstrators and the military left six people dead.
[17] President Lissouba named Jacques Yhombi-Opango as Prime Minister, which led the opposition to form a parallel Government led by Bernard Kolelas. Between July 1993 and January 1994, fresh disturbances caused the death of 180 people.
[18] An agreement between the opposition and the Government, in mid-March, marked the beginning of a cease-fire. The election of Kolelas as mayor of Brazzaville further calmed the situation, allowing for public reconciliation.
[19] In 1994, Lissouba accepted the IMF structural adjustment program, including the reduction of the number of civil servants. Competition between various oil multinationals threatened the dominance of the French Elf in Congo, leading the company to increase the amount of profit reinvested in the country from 17 to 31 per cent.
[20] Civil war began when the Government sought to disarm and arrest Denis Sassou N'Guesso and his followers in June 1997. In November, opposition forces defeated Lissouba, with the aid of Angolan troops. N'Guesso formed a new Government in Brazzaville and decided to wipe out 'ninja'

militias, self-proclaimed resistance forces led by Kolelas.
[21] A cease-fire agreement was signed in November 1999. In compliance with the agreement, N'Guesso freed prisoners and during January 2000 thousands of rebels gave up their weapons. In February, Kolelas ratified his recognition of N'Guesso as President.
[22] In December 2001, 11 cases of ebola were identified in December 2001, in spite of health controls in the borders.
[23] The first Presidential elections after the end of the civil war were held in February 2002, with an 80 per cent turnout. Incumbent

President Denis Sassou-N'Guesso won with 74.7 per cent of the vote. Although the elections were peaceful, the main opposition candidates were either in exile or withdrew their candidacy at he last minute, saying the the electoral process was a 'charade'.
[24] However, soon after the elections, the Government denounced attacks by 'ninja' rebels on military positions in Pool region. By April, the conflict had spread and in June attacks were launched on Brazzaville.
[25] In March 2003, the Government reached a new peace agreement and 2,300 rebels voluntarily surrendered their

weapons. On 30 August, the National Assembly unanimously approved the amnesty for rebels. However, the NGO Congolese Human Rights Observatory called the amnesty 'selective', since it did not include all protagonists of conflict, especially Lissouba, Opango and Kolelas, who remain in exile.
[26] In 2003-2004, the UN continued to develop extensive aid programs, focused on the emergency needs of people displaced by the conflict, medical assistance and control of HIV/AIDS epidemic and reduction of poverty.
[27] New cases of ebola caused the death of 136 people in 2003. ∎

ENVIRONMENT
The country comprises four distinct regions: coastal plains; a central plateau (separated from the coast by a range of mountains rising to 800 meters); the Congo River basin in the northeast; and a large area of marshland. The central region is covered with dense rain forests and is sparsely populated. Two-thirds of the population live in the south, along the Brazzaville-Pointe Noire railroad. Lumber and agriculture employ more than one third of the population. The country has considerable mineral resources including oil, lead, gold, zinc, copper and diamonds.

SOCIETY
Peoples: The Congolese are of Bantu origin; the Bakongo prevail in the South, the Teke (or Bateke) at the center; the Sanga and Vilil in the North. There is also a Pygmy minority.
Religions: Approximately half of the population are Christians and the others practise traditional African religions, with some fusion of the two. There is a Muslim minority (2 per cent).
Languages: French (official), Kongo, Lingala, Téké.
Main Political Parties: Congolese Workers' Party (PCT), founded in 1969, the only party until 1990.

Since then, more than 30 parties and movements have been formed. Pan-African Union for Social Democracy. Party of the Poor. Convention for Democracy and the Republic. Congolese Union of Republicans. Liberal Republican Party.
Main Social Organizations: The four existing labor organizations merged in 1964 to form the Congolese Labor Confederation (CSC), Revolutionary Union of Congolese Women.

THE STATE
Official Name: République du Congo.
Administrative Divisions: 9 regions and 6 communes.
Capital: Brazzaville 1,080,000 people (2003).
Other Cities: Pointe Noire 765,300 people; Loubomo 84,500 people (2000).
Government: Parliamentary republic. Denis Sassou N'Guesso, President since October 1997, re-elected in March 2002. Two-chamber Parliament: the National Assembly made up of 153 members and the Senate made up of 66 members.
National Holiday: 15 August, Independence Day (1960).
Armed Forces: 10,800 (1996). Other: 6,100: Gendarmerie (1,400); People's Militia (4,700).

DR Congo and the Great Lakes region

BEHIND THE PAIN and bloodshed of the recent war in the Democratic Republic of Congo (DRC) lies a revealing history. The countries involved have all been hungry for its wealth and territory.

The war broke out in 1997 when veteran guerrilla Laurent Kabila fought his way to the capital Kinshasa and proclaimed himself president. On taking power, Kabila and his Congolese Liberation Front (CLF) brought an end to 30 years of another civil war, ousting former dictator Mobutu Sese Seko, who died days later in exile in Morocco. But the peace was too fragile to last.

The conflict in the DRC operated on various fronts, with a wide range of causes and elements behind it. Apart from Zambia, all the Great Lakes countries have been involved in the DRC conflict: Uganda, Rwanda, Burundi, Kenya and Tanzania. Rebel groups with Ugandan and Rwandan military and economic backing tried to depose Kabila. Government troops meanwhile welcomed the support offered them by Angola, Namibia and Zimbabwe.

The forces settled in the DRC. They were joined by UN peace-keeping forces (MONUC), at that time consisting of 5,500 troops drawn from 20 or so African, Asian, European and South American countries. The African troops included some from Tanzania and Kenya - countries implicitly involved in the DRC's civil war in the 1960s when they had supported Laurent Kabila's resistance to Mobutu.

TEARING OUT THE HEART OF AFRICA
The DRC lies at the heart of Africa. The vast country is rich in gold, iron, copper, manganese, cobalt, diamonds, uranium and also oil, a seam of mineral wealth that reaches from Nigeria in the north to Angola in the south. The multiplicity of interests in play reflect the number of countries and foreign companies fighting for what they consider their share.

The various conflicts of the Great Lakes region have been exacerbated by famine, malaria and cholera, as well as tuberculosis and HIV-AIDS. As a result there are hundreds of thousands of refugees who represent a different kind of battle front maintained by human rights organizations such as Médecins Sans Frontières and some UN agencies. In an attempt to mitigate these diseases, the aid agencies - some funded by the World Bank - involuntarily provided another source of conflict as the refugee camps were frequently moved by the Congolese

authorities to serve as a human shield against attacks from rebel groups or the enemy of the moment.

In addition, the region has the legacy of the thousands of people killed and maimed by so many years of civil war, for example in the Rwandan genocide of 1994. Some battlegrounds are littered with by myriad tiny antipersonnel mines, that only detonate when trodden on.

WAR IN THE BELGIAN CONGO
The civil war in the Belgian Congo (as the DRC then was) began in1960, when this country gained independence. But the origins of this conflict - like the others in the region - hark back to the colonial legacy.

In 1884 at the Berlin Conference, the European powers partitioned Africa, mapping out 48 new states. Their officials rode roughshod over the empires, kingdoms and ancient civilizations which messily straddled or stood in the way of the new national borders. Ethnic differences and conflicts were often exploited by the colonizers to suit their ends - such as the control of resources. Once the decolonization processes began in earnest in the mid-20th century, the African nations were forced to adopt systems of government alien to their historical traditions. Countries were pressed by the West to modernize along the lines of Western-style democracy.

After independence, aid to the poverty-stricken region came initially from the International Monetary Fund (IMF) and the World Bank, as well as from US interests at the height of the Cold War. Then came the structural adjustment plans which ensured the countries would continue to hand over their their minerals and commodities and open up their markets.

MOBUTU AND THE ALLIANCES
When army commander Mobutu came to power in a coup in 1965, he renamed the country Zaire and began to form alliances in order to shore up his position. For France, Belgium and the US (and its Central Intelligence Agency, the CIA), the dictator Mobutu was their best defense against the advance of 'communist' forces such as Laurent Kabila's CLF.

With military aid for arms and training, Mobuto was able to repel rebel advances for years and also cultivate friends and enemies. However, when the rebel advance could no longer be contained,

international aid began to fall off or to change. Mobutu played the leading role in this complex tapestry of alliances. He requested help from Uganda and Rwanda, both fighting in Zairean territory against Burundian and Rwandan Hutu and Tutsi refugees. With the support of these countries, Mobutu created a new dimension by allowing their soldiers and refugees to exploit and sell gold from the mining areas close to their borders. Slowly, the foreign armies occupied more territory and became entrenched. The conflict in Zaire became more international, and the country was disempowered.

ZAIRE AND THE END OF APARTHEID
The CLF meanwhile also created alliances. During the 1960s and 1970s Laurent Kabila was in exile in Dar es Salaam, capital of Tanzania, shaping his plans and directing his troops from there. His forces were armed and trained by Cuba, which in 1965 had sent the famous guerrilla fighter Ernesto Che Guevara to lend his support. From exile, Kabila cemented a friendship with Agostinho Neto of Angola. Neto appeared to be the leader of Angolan independence, and his People's Movement for the Liberation of Angola (MPLA) later formed the first post-independece government. By contrast, Mobutu supported Jonas Savimbi's National Union for the Total Independence of Angola (UNITA), and Uganda did the same. The civil wars in both countries were closely related.

Kabila's troops - with backing from Cuba and the MPLA - helped expel the South African army from Angola. The turning point for the South Africans, and therefore also for Angola and its allies, was the battle of Cuito Cuanavale. Until that moment, whites had not died in this combat. In December 1988 South Africa signed an agreement to withdraw its forces from Angola, and also from Namibia. In this way, the victory for the MPLA, supported by Laurent Kabila and Cuba, was also significant in the struggles to end apartheid in South Africa, and to achieve Namibian independence.

FRAGILE PEACE
Joseph Kabila succeeded his murdered father in 2001. A peace deal and the setting up of a transitional government in 2003 appeared to signal the end of the five-year conflict. An estimated 3 million people have died from the fighting and associated privations. With so much at stake, and renewed fighting round Ituri in the northeast, hopes for a lasting peace are slim. ∎

Costa Rica / Costa Rica

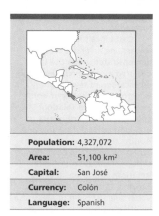

Population:	4,327,072
Area:	51,100 km²
Capital:	San José
Currency:	Colón
Language:	Spanish

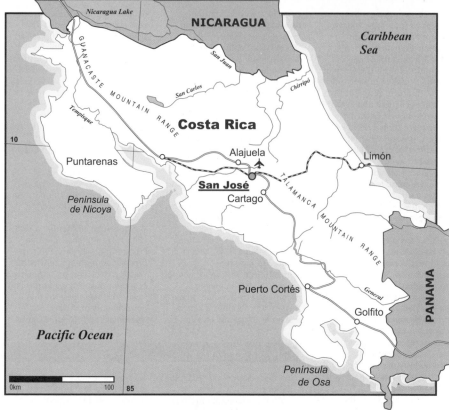

W hen Christopher Columbus reached the coast of Costa Rica - 'the rich coast' - on his last voyage in 1502, the territory of present-day Costa Rica was populated by small groups of the Chorotega, Cobici, Carib and Boruca nations. Although the first contact was friendly, Europeans did not easily dominate the local people, and it took nearly 60 years for a permanent settlement to be established in the region.

2   Gaspar de Espinosa, Hernán Ponce de León and Juan de Castañeda traveled along the coast of the territory between 1514 and 1516. Between 1560 and 1564, they were followed by Juan de Cavallón, Juan de Estrada Rabago and Juan Vásquez de Coronado. The conquest of the territory was consolidated in the second half of the 16th century.

3   The Spanish established the first permanent settlement, the town of Cartago, on the central plain in 1564. This was assigned to the political jurisdiction of the Captaincy-General of Guatemala, while remaining under the spiritual guidance of the bishop of Nicaragua.

4   The indians' resistance kept the colonizers isolated. They were unable to establish a system of *encomiendas* - the virtual enslavement of the Indian work

force. Thus, a patriarchal society of small landowners was formed, with no powerful land-owning oligarchy as in the neighboring countries. This might explain how, instead of becoming a nation scourged by civil wars and military dictatorships, modern Costa Rica maintained greater democratic stability and has not established a regular army like the other countries in the region.

5   When Mexico declared independence from Spain in 1821, Costa Rica, along with other former Spanish colonies in Central America, formed part of the Mexican empire. In 1823, Costa Rica helped create the United Provinces of Central America and remained a part of this federation until its dissolution in 1840. A persistent

opponent to the 'Balkanization' brought about by British imperialism, Costa Rica's territory was used as a base for operations by Francisco Morazán - an advocate of Central American unity - until its independence in1848.

6   In the mid-19th century, William Walker - a US national who had taken control of Nicaragua - tried to extend his dominion over the Central American isthmus. Forces commanded by the Costa Rican President Juan Rafael Mora defeated him. Material progress reached Costa Rica during the regime of General Tomás Guardia, who ruled the nation from 1870 to 1882. While his administration took away some liberties and increased foreign

debt, coffee and sugar production rose and more schools were built. The Constitution adopted in 1871 remained in place until 1949.

7   The last decades of the 19th century were marked by a gradual reduction of Church influence in secular affairs. Cemeteries were secularized and the Jesuits expelled from the country for a few years. In 1886, primary education became obligatory and free; schools were founded, along with a museum and a national library. In 1890, José Joaquín Rodríguez was elected President in what were considered the first free and fair elections in Central America.

8   In 1916, Nicaragua gave the US permission to use the San Juan river, which forms the frontier with Costa Rica. The San José Government protested that its rights had been overlooked and the complaint was taken to the Central American Court of Justice, which ruled in favor of Costa Rica. Nicaragua rejected the verdict and withdrew from the Court. This was one of the main reasons for the dissolution of the Court a year later.

9   Costa Ricans had their first elections with direct voting in 1913. There was no outright winner and the Legislative Assembly designated Alfredo González Flores as President. General Federico Tinoco

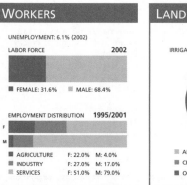

WORKERS

UNEMPLOYMENT: 6.1% (2002)

LABOR FORCE   **2002**

■ FEMALE: 31.6%   ■ MALE: 68.4%

EMPLOYMENT DISTRIBUTION   **1995/2001**

F

M

■ AGRICULTURE   F: 22.0%   M: 4.0%
■ INDUSTRY   F: 27.0%   M: 17.0%
■ SERVICES   F: 51.0%   M: 79.0%

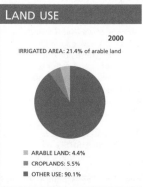

LAND USE

2000

IRRIGATED AREA: 21.4% of arable land

■ ARABLE LAND: 4.4%
■ CROPLANDS: 5.5%
■ OTHER USE: 90.1%

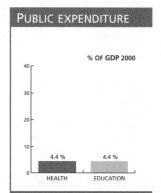

PUBLIC EXPENDITURE

% OF GDP 2000

4.4 %   4.4 %

HEALTH   EDUCATION

Life expectancy
78.1 years
2000-2005

GNI per capita
$4,100
2002

Literacy
96% total adult rate
2000

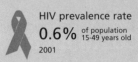
HIV prevalence rate
0.6% of population 15-49 years old
2001

Granados, unhappy with the reforms proposed by González, led one of the few coups experienced by the nation, in 1917. But the lack of US recognition for his Government and the threat of intervention forced Tinoco to resign in 1919.

[10] Between 1940 and 1948 the Government was backed by coffee plantation owners and bankers. However in 1948 opposition leader Otilio Ulate, nominated by the National Unity Party, won a presidential election which was annulled by Congress. This unleashed civil war which ended with a junta seizing power, presided over by José Figueres Ferrer. The junta issued a call for the election of new representatives, who in turn confirmed Ulate's victory. A year later, the new Constitution was promulgated.

[11] The new Constitution of 1949 not only gave women and African descendants the right to vote but it also abolished the army (replaced with a civil guard). This decision subsequently marked the country internationally as being pacifist and a promoter of demilitarization. Costa Rica stood apart from the other Central American countries because it did not suffer military coups and because it earmarked greater resources to areas key to the country's development, such as education and health.

[12] This heralded the so-called 'Welfare State Capitalism'. Figueres was elected President in 1954 and during his administration Costa Rica became a strongly anti-communist welfare state. In 1958, the conservatives defeated Figueres and imposed a US-backed import-substitution development model.

[13] The traditional antagonism between liberals and conservatives gave way to new tensions between the National Liberation Party (PLN), led by Figueres, and a heterogeneous group consisting of various small parties. In 1966 the United National Opposition elected José Joaquín Trejos to the presidency.

[14] After the 1970 election, the PLN returned to power with Figueres, who remained in office until 1974, when Daniel Odúber Quirós, co-founder of the Party in 1950, was elected President.

[15] Odúber tried to restore unity to the Central American Common Market, left in a critical situation after the 1969 war between El Salvador and Honduras. However, his obvious pro-democracy stance did not meet with the approval of Somoza's regime in Nicaragua.

Costa Rica was constantly harassed by its neighbor and became a safe haven for thousands of political refugees.

[16] 1975 saw a rise in wages due to favorable conditions resulting from the nationalization of transnational oil companies and the rise in coffee prices on the world market.

[17] In 1978 presidential elections were won by a conservative coalition which had been critical of Figueres's administration. The leftist bloc, grouped in the United People's Coalition, made considerable gains.

[18] The new President, Rodrigo Carazo Odio, imposed an unpopular economic policy prescribed by the International Monetary Fund (IMF), which resulted in growing confrontation with labor and left groups. In 1979 however, encouraged by popular sympathy towards the Sandinista rebels, and under threat of invasion by

neighboring dictator Anastasio Somoza, the Costa Rican Government actively supported the Nicaraguan Sandinistas.

[19] A radically different attitude was taken in 1980 with regard to El Salvador's insurgency. In spite of human rights violations in that country, the San José Government supported the Salvadoran military junta. In 1981 President Carazo broke off diplomatic relations with Cuba.

[20] In January 1982, the US-backed Central American Democratic Community was set up in San José with the purpose of isolating revolutionary Nicaragua.

[21] Luis Alberto Monge, a right-wing PLN candidate, became President in February 1982. He proclaimed his alignment with Western democracies, announced economic austerity measures and fostered closer ties with the governments of El Salvador, Guatemala and Honduras, thus

aggravating relations with Nicaragua.

[22] Costa Rica's hostile attitude towards its neighbor was clearly demonstrated when the US declared a commercial embargo on Nicaragua's revolutionary Government. A series of border incidents brought relations between the two countries to breaking point during July and August 1985. However, prompt action taken by the Contadora Group (organization of Latin American countries - Mexico, Panama, Colombia and Venezuela - formed in 1983, at a meeting on Panama's Contadora island, to achieve a peace agreement for Central America) prevented mounting tension in the area. Both governments agreed to place neutral observers along the common frontier to arbitrate any further border clashes.

[23] The winner of the February 1986 presidential election was

IN FOCUS

ENVIRONMENTAL CHALLENGES
Deforestation has been partially responsible for soil erosion. Coastal marine pollution and air contamination are observed. Reduced soil fertility, particularly in the Huetar Norte Region, is caused by the expansion of timber plantations. The rich biodiversity of the forests (there are about 150 different tree species in the country) actively needs safeguarding.

WOMEN'S RIGHTS
Women have been able to vote and run for office since 1949. In 2000, they held 19 per cent of Parliamentary seats, 15 per cent of the ministerial positions and 5 per cent of local government posts.

They made up 31 per cent of the country's workforce in 2000. Unemployed women were 6.9 per cent of the total jobless (5.2 per cent of the total workforce).

There are as many illiterate women as men*.

CHILDREN
Even though Costa Rica has met the majority of the goals of the World Summit for Children - particularly in health - as well as most of its commitments under the UN Millennium Goals, social and territorial inequalities are increasing. Commercial sexual exploitation of minors, sexual abuse, as well as child labor

have become more prevalent. 30 per cent of poor Costa Ricans are children and adolescents.

Although the country had a net rate of 91 per cent for primary education enrolment, in 2000* the serious problems of grade repetition and drop-outs still exist. Three out of every 10 children drop out of school before completing basic general education; eight out of 10 do not complete secondary studies within the allotted time frame and 40 per cent of adolescents have left the education system.

According to the Responsible Paternity Law, adopted in 2001, when a mother registers the birth of an illegitimate child she must declare both paternity and maternity. If the father is absent, the mother is authorized to declare and register paternity (assuming she knows who the father is). The man may attempt to prove he is not the father, using DNA evidence. If the alleged paternity is proven the father is obliged to pay child support. 30 per cent of the children lack official acknowledgement of paternity. There are still institutional and cultural difficulties in applying this law, but it is nonetheless an international milestone in this field.

INDIGENOUS PEOPLES/ ETHNIC MINORITIES
The black community, mainly the descendents of immigrants who came from Jamaica since 1870, is

split into a wealthy élite at one end and the poor at the other.

MIGRANTS/REFUGEES
By the end of 2002, there were 12,750 refugees living in Costa Rica: 7,600 Colombians, 2,700 Nicaraguans, 1,100 Cubans and 1,350 people from another 28 countries. Another 20,000 to 50,000 Colombians were living in Costa Rica in refugee-like circumstances. 58 per cent of their asylum applications had been approved.

Costa Rica grants equal rights to its citizens and refugees, who can apply for permanent residence after living in the country for two years. The UNHCR provides legal, economic, social and psychological assistance to refugees through a non-government local agency.

Refugees in Costa Rica are largely urban, middle-class and live in the biggest cities of the country. Though they are allowed to work, their relative unemployment rate is high, since many employers are not aware that it is legal to employ refugees.

300,000 Nicaraguans have migrated to Costa Rica over the last 20 years.

DEATH PENALTY
The death penalty was abolished in 1877.

*Latest data available in The State of the World's Children and Childinfo database, UNICEF, 2004.

	Under-5 mortality		Poverty		Debt service		Maternal mortality
	11 per 1,000 live births 2002	$	**6.9%** of population living on less than $1 per day 1998		**9.0%** exports of goods and services 2001		**43** per 100,000 live births 2000

Social Democrat Oscar Arias, who won a tight victory with 52 per cent of the vote. Arias devoted himself to the task of designing a policy that would break both the logic of war and the escalating tension within the region.

24 In August 1987 he presented a peace plan at a summit meeting held in Esquipulas, Guatemala. This was accepted and signed by the Presidents of El Salvador, Nicaragua, Guatemala and Honduras. The focal points of the plan were: a simultaneous cease-fire in Nicaragua and El Salvador, an immediate end to American aid to the Nicaraguan contras, a democratization time-table for Nicaragua which included holding free elections and putting an end to the use of foreign territory as supply or attack bases.

25 The signing of this peace plan, known as 'Esquipulas II', earned Costa Rica a special place in international relations, and constituted a personal triumph for President Arias, who received the Nobel Peace Prize in October 1987.

26 During his term, Arias instituted two structural adjustment programs (PAE I and PAE II), with World Bank support. Their objective was the transformation of industry through technological modernization, increased efficiency and greater productivity. Neo-liberal formulas were applied, following the dictates of international financial organizations. However, according to the labor unions, these 'prescriptions' were formulated without looking at their social effects.

27 In July 1989, a parliamentary commission on drug trafficking produced a report. It stated that both the main political parties (the PLN and the PUSC) were guilty of receiving drug money during the 1986 electoral campaign. At the same time, another scandal broke out over the financing of electoral campaigns, with accusations that both parties - and Oscar Arias individually - had received money from Panamanian General Noriega in 1986.

28 In 1990, women officially made up 29.9 per cent of the economically active population, but their number in the informal sector was reckoned to be around 41 per cent. Teenage prostitution increased through organized crime rings, which have become multi-million-dollar businesses for their owners.

29 Under the slogan of 'change' and focusing specifically on low-income groups with lower educational levels, the Social Christian candidate Rafael Angel Calderón won the election held in February 1990 and obtained an absolute majority in the legislature.

30 The application of a severe economic adjustment program led to a reduction in the State apparatus as well as in the fiscal deficit, which had reached 3.3 per cent of GDP. As a result of these cuts, unemployment rose and popular discontent increased.

31 In the 1994 elections, social democrat candidate José María Figueres Olsen (José Figueres' son) defeated Government candidate Miguel Rodriguez by a narrow margin, after a campaign with few differences in their political positions but with notably harsh speeches from the rival parties.

32 A free trade agreement was signed with Mexico in January 1995. However, the deterioration of the economy, with rising inflation and a fiscal deficit led the Government to increase taxes in order to balance the budget. The World Bank rejected the economic plan and refused to finance the structural adjustment schedule. In April, the PLN accepted the liberalization of the banking system and the privatization of the insurance, petroleum and telecommunications state enterprises proposed by the Christian opposition in exchange for the tax package approval. Unions organized strikes against these measures, particularly the dismissal of several civil servants.

33 In 1996, the governing PLN agreed a budget plan with the opposition which limited the Government deficit to 1 per cent of the GDP. In late July, Hurricane Caesar struck Costa Rica, especially the south, causing some 30 deaths. The damage was estimated at around $100 million.

34 In February 1998, Miguel Angel Rodriguez, the Social Christian Unity Party (PUSC) candidate was elected president, with the PUSC also gaining the majority of seats in the parliamentary elections.

35 In March, the US ambassador, Thomas Dodd, was accused by the Commission for the Defense of Human Rights in Central America (Codehuca) of interfering in the internal affairs of the country. Dodd had declared that his Government might impose economic sanctions following the death of a US citizen in a private dispute.

36 A nutrition survey in March 1999 revealed that 75 per cent of infants aged 1-2 years, 26 per cent of pre-school children, 33 per cent of people living in rural areas and 16 per cent of urban dwellers had some degree of anemia.

37 In order to address the growing violence, and to avoid the country becoming a refuge for criminals operating in neighboring countries, in December the Government brought in the obligatory registration of weapons and offered a 12-month amnesty to those who gave up their arms.

38 For the first time in the country's electoral history, a run-off vote was necessary in the presidential elections because no candidate achieved the required 40 per cent of the vote. In April 2002 the PUSC candidate, Abel Pacheco, won 58.2 per cent, defeating his PLN rival, Rolando Araya, and became the new President. Another new factor in the elections was the rise of the Citizen Action Party (PAC), an independent movement that won 26 per cent of the vote, weakening the country's long-dominant two-party system.

39 In May 2003 electricity and telecommunication workers, opposed to the Government's privatization plans, together with teachers demanding a wage rise, organized a strike which led to the resignation of three ministers.

40 In December 2003 Costa Rica's representatives walked out of negotiations with the US on a Central America Free Trade Agreement (CAFTA). Separate negotiations set for 2004 were motivated by the threat to state insurance and telecommunications monopolies. ∎

PROFILE

ENVIRONMENT

A mountain range with major volcanic peaks stretches across the country from northwest to southeast. Costa Rica has the highest rural population density in Latin America, with small and medium sized farmers who use modern agricultural techniques. Coffee is the main export crop. The lowlands along the Pacific and the Caribbean have different climate and vegetation. Along the Caribbean coast there is dense, tropical rainforest vegetation. Cocoa is grown in that region. The Pacific side is drier; extensive cattle raising is practiced along with artificially irrigated sugarcane and rice plantations.

SOCIETY

Peoples: Costa Ricans, usually called *ticos* in Central America, are descended from the integration between native Americans and European migrants, mainly Spanish. African descendants, who were brought in from Jamaica, make up 3 per cent of the population and are concentrated along the eastern coast. Indigenous peoples, 1 per cent.
Religions: 76.3 per cent of the population are Catholic; Evangelical Protestant 13.7 per cent, Jehovah witnesses 1.3 per cent.
Languages: Spanish is the official language, spoken by the majority. Mekaiteliu, a language derived from English, is spoken in the province of Limón (east coast). Several indigenous languages.
Main Political Parties: Social Christian Unity Party (PUSC); National Liberation Party, social democrat (NLP); Citizens' Action Party (CAP); Libertarian Movement (LM); Costa Rica Renewal Party (CRRP); Democratic Force (DF).
Main Social Organizations: The Unitary Workers' Union (CUT); the 50,000-member CUT groups both workers and peasants from the National Federation of Civil Servants, the National Peasant Federation; the Federation of Industrial Workers, regional federations and smaller unions. 375 cooperatives.

THE STATE

Official Name: República de Costa Rica.
Administrative Divisions: 7 Provinces: Alajuela, Cartago, Guanacaste, Heredia, Limon, Puntarenas, San José.
Capital: San José 1,085,000 people (2003).
Other Cities: Alajuela 716,286 people; Cartago 432,395; Limón 339,295 (2000).
Government: Abel Pacheco, President since May 2002. Unicameral Legislature: the Legislative Assembly, made up of 57 members, elected by proportional representation in each province for a four-year term.
National Holiday: 15 September, Independence Day (1821).
Armed Forces: Abolished in 1949.
Other: 7,500: Civil Guard (4,300), Rural Guard (3,200), (1995).

Côte d'Ivoire / Côte d'Ivoire

Population:	17,164,505
Area:	322,460 km²
Capital:	Abidjan, Yamoussoukro
Currency:	CFA franc
Language:	French

According to Baulé tradition, in 1730 Queen Aura Poka emigrated westwards with her people and founded a new state in the center of a territory known since the 15th century as the Côte d'Ivoire (or Ivory Coast) because of the active trade in elephant tusks.

[2] This Ashanti state soon grew and became a threat to the small states of Aigini, on the coast, and Atokpora, inland. In 1843, these states requested French protection, thus enabling France to obtain exclusive rights over the coastal trade and, later, the opportunity to annex Côte d'Ivoire to its other territories, now called Guinea, Mali and Senegal.

[3] However, the French met with stiff resistance from Samori Touré. He had set up a state in the heart of the region that the Europeans were planning to unify (See Guinea).

[4] In 1898 Touré was defeated and the leaders of the dominant groups signed colonial agreements with the French.

[5] The area became known as French West Africa, comprising Senegal, French Sudan (now Mali), Guinea and Côte d'Ivoire. Later, what are now Chad, Burkina Faso and Mauritania were also annexed. The French hoped to balance the poorer regions of Chad and Burkina Faso with the better off Senegal and Côte d'Ivoire.

[6] Modern political activities began in 1946 with the creation of the African Democratic Union (ADU), a political party with branches in Senegal, Mali and Guinea. The ADU promoted independence and unity for French colonies in the area.

[7] Felix Houphouët- Boigny, physician and well-to-do farmer, was appointed party president, based on his experience leading a farmers' association which had fought against colonial policies.

[8] Tactically allied to the French Communist Party, the ADU staged strikes, demonstrations and boycotts of European businesses. The nationalist cause was savagely suppressed, leaving dozens of activists dead and thousands imprisoned, giving Houphouët-Boigny grounds for ending his alliance with the French communists in 1950. He soon reached a new agreement with François Mitterrand, then Minister for Overseas Territories. This move undermined the ADU's standing, and Houphouët-Boigny was only just able to maintain his prestige in his own land.

[9] Between 1958 and 1960 all of French West Africa became independent and the new states joined the UN. Aware of their meager economic prospects, the political leaders proposed to form a federation. However Houphouët- Boigny, confident in the relative prosperity of his country and his privileged neo-colonial relations with France, opposed the idea.

[10] As a major producer of cocoa, coffee, rubber and diamonds, Côte d'Ivoire was able to attract transnational investors, offering them political stability produced by Houphouët-Boigny's paternalistic, authoritarian rule and cheap labor, mostly supplied by neighboring countries.

[11] The economic growth rate, which remained between 8 and 10 per cent a year from 1966 to 1976, declined as the West went into a recession after 1979. Agricultural exports fell from $4 billion to barely $1 billion between 1980 and 1983. Half the industries set up between 1966 and 1976 closed down, pushing unemployment figures up to 45 per cent. The foreign debt in 1985 was five times greater than in 1981.

[12] In 1985 the 8th congress of the Côte d'Ivoire Democratic Party (PDCI) proposed Houphouët-Boigny for a sixth presidential term. The appointment was confirmed by apparently 99 per cent of the vote in that year's election.

[13] The Government built the largest basilica in Africa in a country where only 12 per cent of the population is Christian.

[14] Côte d'Ivoire suffered a blow to its main export, cocoa. Between July and October 1987, cocoa prices plummeted 50 per cent on the international market.

[15] After the death of the President in December 1993, Henri Konan-Bédié, leader of the National Assembly, assumed the post. He consolidated his power within the ruling Democratic Party in spite of opposition from former prime minister Alassane Ouattara.

[16] In 1994 the Government faced a strong labor movement demanding compensation after the 100 per cent devaluation of the CFA franc in January. In what was seen as a reward for having accepted the devaluation - imposed by France and the IMF - half of Côte d'Ivoire's debt to the Paris Club was cancelled. However,

PROFILE

ENVIRONMENT
Located on the Gulf of Guinea, the country is divided into two major natural regions: the South, with heavy rainfall and lush rainforests, where foreign investors have large plantations of cash crops like coffee, cocoa and bananas; and the North, a granite plain characterized by its savannas, where small landowners raise sorghum, corn and peanuts.

SOCIETY
Peoples: The population includes five major ethnic groups, the Kru, Akan, Voltaic speakers, Mande and Malinke, some from the savannas and others from the rainforests, sub-divided into approximately 80 smaller groups. There are many 'non-Ivorian' living in the country, mostly from the neighboring countries.
Religions: It is difficult to quantify the religions and mixture of beliefs of 'non-Ivorians'. They are divided more or less equally among traditional beliefs, Islam and Christianity.
Languages: French (official). There are as many languages as ethnic groups; the most widely spoken are Diula, in the North; Baule, in center and West; and Bete in the Southeast.
Main Political Parties: Ivorian People's Alliance (FPI); Côte d'Ivoire Democratic Party (PDCI); Rally of the Republicans (RDR); Côte d'Ivoire Workers' Party.
Main Social Organizations: The General Workers' Union (UGT) is the only recognized union. Several opposition unions work underground.

THE STATE
Official Name: République de Côte d'Ivoire.
Administrative Divisions: 49 departments.
Capital: Abidjan (economic center) 3,337,000 people; Yamoussoukro (political center since 1983) 416,000 (2003).
Other Cities: Bouaké 741,100 people; Daloa 184,300; Korhogo 164,400 (2000).
Government: Parliamentary Republic. Laurent Gbagbo, President since October 2000. Affi N'Guessan, Prime Minister since October 2000. Unicameral Legislature: National Assembly, with 225 members.
National Holiday: 7 August, Independence (1960).
Armed Forces: 8,400. Other: 7,800.

Life expectancy
41.0 years
2000-2005

GNI per capita
$610
2002

Literacy
49% total adult rate
2000

HIV prevalence rate
9.7% of population 15-49 years old
2001

the country continued to have the world's highest per capita foreign debt.

[17] In 1995, Bédié won a presidential election that the opposition boycotted. For the first time since the country's independence, residing foreigners were not allowed to vote, nor were Côte d'Ivoire citizens who had foreign parents. This permitted Bédié to dispose of Ouattara, whose father was from Burkina Faso.

[18] A military coup led by General Robert Guéi overthrew Bédié, who fled the country. The US and the European Union urged the military junta to return to democracy. In January 2000, after declaring that the state coffers were empty, Guéi took over as interim president and announced a referendum that modified the Constitution and set elections for October.

[19] The constitutional changes gave the right to vote to those age 18 and over (which Bédié had originally opposed, fearing that the younger segment of the population - affected by his social policies - would tend to vote against him). Last minute amendments stipulated that both parents of presidential candidates must be 'of Ivorian origin', a change that once again excluded Ouattara.

[20] The abstention rate was over 60 per cent in the October 22 2000 elections. Two days later, when the re-count gave the victory to the socialist candidate of the Ivorian People's Front (FPI), Laurent Gbagbo, with 51 per cent of the vote, Guéi declared himself President. The presidential guard took over the Electoral Commission and the director said errors had been made in the re-count and denounced fraud committed by Gbagbo's party. The streets filled with protesters, but neither the army nor the police intervened. The Electoral Commission reappeared, but this time with the true results: Gbagbo 60 per cent; Guéi 32 per cent. Gbagbo took office while Guéi was in Benin.

[21] Initially the three majority parties were united against Guéi, but after the official announcement of Gbagbo's victory, Ouattara's supporters demanded new elections. The dispute triggered an anti-North uprising. In the South, mosques were burned and and FPI militants supported by the army and the police massacred some 500 Muslim northerners.

[22] Ouattara and Gbagbo met to seek a way out of the crisis and urged peace, but the new President refused to repeat the elections. The first actions of the Gbagbo administration included investigating the killings of the

IN FOCUS

ENVIRONMENTAL CHALLENGES
Côte d'Ivoire currently has one of the fastest rates of deforestation in the world. Its forests, once the largest in West Africa, have been almost completely cleared. Industrial and agricultural wastes contaminate water sources.

WOMEN'S RIGHTS
Women have been able to vote and be elected since 1952.

Women made up 33 per cent of the total workforce (6,000,000 people) in 2002.

Women's life expectancy is 41.2 years and the fertility rate is 4.8 births per woman*. 9.5 per cent of the women aged 15-24 are HIV-positive. In the population as a whole the prevalence rate is 3.8 per cent.

CHILDREN
Côte d'Ivoire is one of Africa's richest countries, but instability and internal fighting have displaced the population and disrupted access to essential services. Hundreds of thousands of primary school children had no regular lessons as schools closed in the conflict-affected areas (north and west). Many health centers have been forced to cut services as staff fled and

provisions of essential medical supplies dwindled. UNICEF is providing humanitarian assistance.

In 2001, 581,000 children were born; 102,000 under five died. Seventeen per cent of the children are considered low birthweight and 21 per cent of those under five years old suffer from moderate and severe underweight*.

By the end of 2001, an estimated 84,000 children under 14 were HIV-positive, while 420,000 became AIDS orphans.

INDIGENOUS PEOPLES/ ETHNIC MINORITIES
The population of Côte d'Ivoire is diverse, with over 60 ethnic groups. The main ones include the Akan-speaking peoples of the south-east, Mande peoples in the north, the Voltaic groups of the north-east, and the Kru of the south-west. About 12 per cent of the Ivorian inhabitants are Baoulé, an Akan-speaking people and the largest group in the country. Meanwhile, immigrants from Burkina-Faso, Mali and Ghana form 30 per cent of the country's population.

About one quarter of the population is Muslim, while one in eight people is Christian; the remainder follow traditional beliefs.

MIGRANTS/REFUGEES
Hundreds of thousands people from Mali and Burkina Faso have emigrated to Côte d'Ivoire in the last 20 years.

In 1990 167,000 Ivorians lived in France; in 1999 305,000 were in the US. In 2000 around 2,500 Ivorians lived in German, 83 in Portugal and 696 in the UK, the Netherlands and Switzerland.

By the end of 2002 - the year of the civil war - there were over half a million uprooted Ivorians: 500,000 internally displaced and about 25,000 refugees or asylum-seekers. There were 20,000 refugees in Liberia and at least 2,000 in Guinea, plus 1,000 in Mali and almost 2,000 asylum-seekers in industrialized countries. In that year an estimated 80,000 people left the country.

About 50,000 refugees, mostly from Liberia lived in Côte d'Ivoire. 20,000 new refugees came from Liberia in 2002, while another 20,000 returned, fleeing the violence in Côte d'Ivoire.

DEATH PENALTY
It was abolished in 2000.

*Latest data available in *The State of the World's Children* and *Childinfo* database, UNICEF, 2004.

young Muslims linked to the Rally of the Republicans (RDR) and punishing the perpetrators, and also creating a national reconciliation committee consisting of 29 representatives of the various sectors of civil society.

[23] The return to democracy improved international relations, and with them the expectation of economic growth. In April 2002, the European Union and the Paris Club cancelled $911 million of Côte d'Ivoire's debt. In exchange, the Government promised to implement broad structural reforms, which would include privatizing state companies, reducing subsidies and liberalizing trade.

[24] In September, armed violence broke out in Abidjan and other cities in the north. The rebellion - led by the so-called Côte d'Ivoire Patriotic Movement and backed by the majority of the northern population, mostly Muslims - initially sought the re-instatement of around 800 soldiers that had been discharged. Afterwards, the rebels demanded the removal of Gbagbo and also new elections. During the military uprising, France evacuated foreigners from the city of Bouaké, which was the rebel headquarters during the fighting. Thousands of residents had to abandon their

homes, escaping from the guerrillas. The Minister of the Interior, Emile Boga Doudou, and the former president Guéi were murdered in Abidjan during the uprising.

[25] In October 2002, on the arrival of a group of Ministers from ECOWAS (Economic Community of West African States), the rebels agreed to a ceasefire in the besieged city. However a new offensive by Government forces broke this truce. The rebels captured the city of Daloa, and after the Government troops expelled them, a new ceasefire was signed in the northern bastion of Bouaké. Gbagbo accepted the new peace accord which was signed by the rebels and seconded by several neighboring countries. It supported the formation of an intermediary regional force to monitor the truce between rebel and Government forces, thus avoiding hostilities during the negotiations.

[26] The civil war had caused the displacement of almost 600,000 people, according to UNI-Africa in February 2003. Half the country was under different rebel groups' control and riots took place in Abidjan against the peace plan.

[27] In November 2003 the UN Security Council extended its mission in Côte d'Ivoire, after a new

peace agreement was signed in France between the Ivorian army and the rebel *Forces Nouvelles* to put an end to the bloodshed that occurred by the end of the year 2002. The Security Council also authorized more soldiers to protect civil rights in the run-up to the 2005 elections.

[28] In November 2004, President Gbagbo ended the 18-month ceasefire with air strikes on rebel-held towns in the north. On 6 November nine French soldiers were killed and 22 wounded when Ivorian jets bombed a French base in Bouake. French President Chirac retaliated by ordering the destruction of most of the planes and helicopters in the Ivorian air force. Riots broke out in protest in Abidjan and Yamoussoukro and angry mobs hunted Europeans through the streets. French helicopters plucked people to safety as mobs burst into residential blocks in Abidjan and French troops killed some rioters. Ivorian government figures fanned the flames by urging people to rise up against the former colonial power.

[29] The UN Security Council held an emergency session and discussed imposing an arms embargo and banning Ivorian officials from traveling. ∎

Croatia / Hrvatska

Population:	4,405,173
Area:	56,540 km²
Capital:	Zagreb
Currency:	Kuna
Language:	Croatian

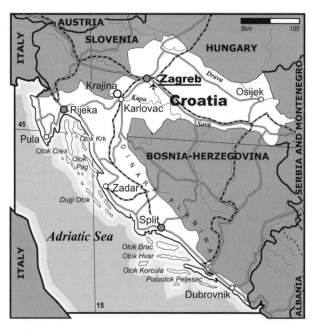

The Croats, a Slav people, emigrated in the 6th century AD from White Croatia, a region today in the Ukraine. They moved on toward the Adriatic Sea, where they conquered the Roman stronghold of Salona, in 614. Once established in Pannonia and Dalmatia, the Croats freed themselves from the Avars and began developing independently. Even though the territory was under the Byzantine empire, the Croats accepted the Roman Catholic Church, whilst preserving the Slav liturgy.

2   In the 8th century, Croats set up the dukedoms of Pannonia and Dalmatia. The first one was under the French Empire's rule and the second under Byzantium, as a result of the 812 peace treaty between the two empires. Both dukedoms broke free by mid-9th century and joined to develop the first independent Croatian kingdom.

3   In the 9th century, an independent Croat State developed in Dalmatia. During the reign of Tomislav (910-928) this achieved great military development. Tomislav and his heirs defended themselves from the Bulgar Empire in Pannonia and the Venetian expansion along the Dalmatian coast. The Byzantine Empire helped King Stjepan Drzislav (969-997) to defend himself from the Venetians, and re-established its influence in the Adriatic. King Peter Kresimir (1058-1074) broke with Byzantium and strengthened links with the papacy. In that period, Croatia reached the peak of its power and territorial expansion.

4   During Kresimir's rule, the country split in two, with one group favoring the king, and an opposition group backed by popular support. When Dimitrije Zvonimir tried to involve the Kingdom in a war against the Seljuk Turks, the opposition accused him of being the Pope's vassal and assassinated him in 1089. The civil war that was then unleashed marked the beginning of the decline of the Croatian Kingdom.

5   The Byzantines recovered Dalmatia. Lazlo I of Hungary conquered Pannonia in 1091, laying claim to the Croatian crown. He founded a bishopric at Zagreb in 1094, which became the center of the Church's power in the region. The Dalmatians crowned Petar Svacic - the last king of Croat blood - but the Pope considered him a rebel, and unseated Svacic in 1097.

6   After an extended war Kalman signed a treaty, the *Pacta Conventa*, with the Croat representatives. Only Bosnia, then a part of the Croatian kingdom, refused to submit to a and turned to King Kalman of Hungary who invaded the country foreign monarch. For the next eight centuries, Croatia was linked to Hungary. In the 14th century, Dalmatia became a part of Venice, which ruled over it for 400 years.

7   After the defeat of the Croatian and Hungarian forces in the battles of Krbavsko Polje (1493) and Mohacs (1526), most of Pannonia and Hungary fell into Turkish hands.

8   Turkish domination altered the ethnic composition of Pannonia, as many Croats migrated northwards, some even going into Austria. In the meantime, the Turks brought in German and Hungarian settlers, and gave incentives for Serbians fleeing the Balkans to settle in the Vojna Krajina.

9   When the Turks were driven back in the 17th century, Austria tried to limit Croatia and Hungary's state rights, to make them mere provinces of the Austrian Empire. The Croatian and Hungarian nobility conspired together to organize an independence movement, which failed. The Croatian leaders were executed and their lands were distributed among foreign nobles.

10   After the annexation of Rijeka (Fiume) in the 1770s, Hungary tried to impose its language, but this triggered a nationalist reaction among the Croatians. The French Revolution and the Napoleonic Wars which had incorporated Dalmatia,

IN FOCUS

ENVIRONMENTAL CHALLENGES
There is air pollution (from the metals industry) and the resulting acid rain is damaging the forests. There is coastal pollution from both industrial and domestic waste. After the 1992-95 civil war, a campaign started to remove landmines and to rebuild the country's infrastructure.

WOMEN'S RIGHTS
Croatian women have been able to vote and run for office since 1945. In 2000, 8 per cent of the parliamentary seats were held by women, while in ministerial positions their representation rose from 4 per cent (1995) to 12 per cent.

Women comprise 44 per cent of the country's 2 million workforce; 17 per cent work in agriculture, 22 per cent in industrial jobs and 61 per cent in services. While the total unemployment rate is 20.6 per cent, female unemployment is 14.5 per cent.

CHILDREN
In 2001 54,000 children were born and there were 264,000 under five. Six per cent of babies had low birthweight*.

The new government coalition has committed itself to ending Croatia's international isolation and to democratic reforms. Nonetheless, the country continues to deal with the impact of the war on the physical and psychological well-being of children.

A gun culture has developed since the war, with 21 per cent of housekeepers keeping weapons in their homes.

INDIGENOUS PEOPLES/ ETHNIC MINORITIES
The number of Roma (Gypsies) is estimated at between 200,000 and 300,000. Discrimination against the Roma in Croatia has been persistent over the last decade. Within the past couple of years, there have been reports of official discrimination including inadequate investigations of complaints by the police, public demonstrations against the presence of Roma in some cities. However, the prospects for an improvement in their situation are not completely bleak, according to the US Committee for Refugees, since Croatia's Government is expected to cooperate on initiatives to improve their status. In 1999 the Government committed itself to a policy of promoting Roma education and enhancing cultural awareness.

An estimated of 219,000 Serbs lived in Croatia in 2002. As the country wants to join the EU, it has to pay attention to treatment of its minorities; but the long history of animosity between Serbs and Croats does not make for favorable conditions for the Serb minority. Serbs are excluded from political and economical decisions and can not count on Serb military support.

MIGRANTS/REFUGEES
Croatia is one of the 10 countries in the world with the highest number of refugees living abroad. In 1995 351,000 asylum-seekers left the country. By the end of 2002 at least 251,000 refugees remained abroad, most of them in Serbia and Montenegro (228,000) and Bosnia (22,000). In 2002, about 1,000 Croats sought asylum in different countries.

DEATH PENALTY
It was abolished in 1990.

*Latest data available in *The State of the World's Children* and *Childinfo* database, UNICEF, 2004.

Life expectancy
74.2 years
2000-2005

 GNI per capita
$4,640
2002

Literacy
98% total adult rate
2000

 HIV prevalence rate
0.1% of population 15-49 years old
2001

Pannonia and the area south of the Sava river to the French Empire, further stimulated Croatian nationalism. Upon the fall of Napoleon, relations between Hungary and Croatia rapidly deteriorated.

[11] In April 1848, the Hungarian Parliament adopted a series of measures limiting Croatian autonomy. The Croatian Diet (Parliament), dissolved in 1865, declared its separation from Hungary, abolishing serfdom and approving equal rights for all its citizens. Hungary's troops were weakened by this conflict, making it easier for the Hapsburgs to put down the Hungarian Revolt and regain power later that year.

[12] With the division of the crown, Germany and Hungary became the major nations of the Austro-Hungarian Empire. In 1868, Hungary accepted the union of Croatia, Slavonia and Dalmatia as a separate political entity, though Austria refused to relinquish its claim to Dalmatia.

[13] In the early 20th century, Croatian nationalists intensified their activity. An alliance of Croatian and Serbian leaders adopted the 'Rijeka resolution', a plan of action which enabled them to win the 1906 elections. The Croatian Peasant Party began political activity among the peasants. The Crown responded by increasing repression.

[14] In 1915, Croatian, Serbian and Slovenian leaders organized the Yugoslav Committee in Paris to push for separation from the empire and union with an independent Serbia. Austria-Hungary's defeat in World War I accelerated the creation of the Yugoslav kingdom in 1918.

[15] The Serbian dynasty's policy of amalgamating the regions immediately came into conflict with Croatian desires for independence. Croatia demanded the creation of a Yugoslav federation. As of 1920, the Peasant Party, led by Stjepan Radic, headed the Croatian opposition. The assassination of Radic and other opposition members in 1928 led to a serious crisis.

[16] When World War II broke out, Yugoslavia was divided internally, so it was easily occupied by Hitler in 1941. The German army set up a puppet regime in Croatia, which launched a racist campaign. Serbs, Jews, Gypsies and Croats opposed to Fascism were massacred by 'Utashi' (Fascists) in their homes or in concentration camps or forced into exile.

[17] During the communist-led resistance to the Nazi occupation, local committees were created in the recently liberated regions. After the anti-Nazi guerrillas had occupied Zagreb in May 1945, the Anti-Fascist Council of National Liberation of Croatia assumed control of the Government. By the end of the year, Croatia was part of the new People's Federated Republic of Yugoslavia.

[18] Within the Yugoslav socialist system, Croatia maintained and strengthened its national independence, and in 1972, the Matica Hrvatska, the Croatian cultural organization, was suspended.

[19] At the end of 1980, Yugoslavia modified its political system. The Yugoslav League of Communists (YLC) renounced the monopoly and leading role assigned to it by the constitution, and in April 1990, the first multiparty elections since World War II were held in the different regions (see Serbia and Montenegro for information on Popular Federal Republic of Yugoslavia's history).

[20] Following the collapse of Communism in Eastern Europe, Croatia saw the first free elections in 50 years. The Communists were defeated by the Democratic Croat Union (DCU), led by Franjo Tudjman. In June 1991, Croatia declared independence but the European Community and the US withheld recognition. The eastern Serbo-Croats expelled the Croats with help from the Yugoslav army. In late 1991, nearly a third of Croat territory was under Serb control. The Serbs declared the republic of Krajina (in southern Croatia) as a new member of the Yugoslav federation. In 1992 a peace plan between Serbia and Croatia was mediated by the European Community.

[21] In May 1992 the UN accepted membership of former Yugoslavian republics Croatia, Slovenia and Bosnia-Herzegovina. In November that year, the Bosnian Serb leader Radovan Karadzic announced the formation of the Serb Republic of Bosnia-Herzegovina and the Serb Republic of Krajina (in Croatia), leading to renewed hostilities. Although less bloody than the conflict in Bosnia, there were nonetheless tens of thousands of civilian deaths in Croatia. In late 1993, Tudjman and President Izetbegovic of Bosnia-Herzegovina signed a ceasefire agreement.

[22] In June 1994 Croatia re-established the Kuna, the currency issued in World War II by the Nazi-imposed government. This replaced the Dinar, which had been adopted after independence. Tudjman, re-elected President in 1992, signed the Dayton peace accords in 1995, putting an end to the war in Bosnia-Herzegovina. In 1996, diplomatic relations were restored with Serbia. Even though the Croat re-occupation of Krajina was considered one of the biggest ethnic cleansing operations of the war in the former Yugoslavia, by May 1996 only eight Croats had been tried in *absentia* at the war crimes tribunal in The Hague.

[23] In April 1999 a court ruled there was not enough evidence to convict six former Croat soldiers of war crimes against Serbian rebels, despite the fact that one of the accused had admitted his guilt to the press. The court case was the first in which Croats were prepared to be judged for their own crimes.

[24] Tudjman died that year. In January 2000, his UDC party was defeated by a coalition led by the Social Democrats and the Social-Liberals. They promoted constitutional changes to avoid a concentration of power. In February, when Stjepan Mesic of the Croat Peoples Party became President, he announced Croatia's intention of joining NATO and the European Union. According to the new Constitution, approved in 2000, Parliament rather than the President had the power to appoint and dissolve government.

[25] In February 2001, hundreds of thousands of people, led by war veterans, protested against attempts to arrest General Mirko Norac to face accusations of war crimes. This change in policy from the Social Democratic Government led the Right to accuse them of treason with the intention of bringing down the Mesic Government and Prime Minister Ivica Racan.

[26] Racan was accused of treason in July 2001 because he decided to comply with the Hague Tribunal request for the extradition of generals Ademi and Gotovina. The parliamentary vote allowed the premier to continue in his post. Croatia returned to Serbia some Orthodox icons that had been pillaged by its army following the fall of Vukovar, 10 years previously.

[27] The Democratic Croat Union, a nationalistic political party, won the November 2003 elections from the center-left coalition led by former Prime Minister Racan. The UDC and its two allied parties regained power with 75 of the 140 Parliament seats. The Social Democratic Party coalition had 63 seats.

[28] Ivo Sanader, the new leader, undertook to keep Croatia's international commitments, including the co-operation with the UN War Crimes Tribunal - International Court. Other campaign pledges were to join NATO in 2006 and the EU in 2007. ∎

PROFILE

ENVIRONMENT
Croatia is bounded to the north by Slovenia and Hungary, and to the east by Serbia. The Dalmatian coast - a 1,778-kilometer coastline on the Adriatic, with numerous ports and seaside resorts, as well as a thousand islands - lies in southern and western Croatia. The territory is made up of three regions with different landscapes: rolling hills in the north, around Zagreb; rocky mountains along the Adriatic coast and the inland valleys of the Pannonian Basin. The coast mountains are the Dinaric Alps and the Valebit and Velika Kapela mountain systems, between 700 and 2,200 meters high. The inland valleys are washed by the mid and upper streams of River Sava, which runs through the country from the northwest to the southeast, and it is part of the borderline shared with Bosnia-Herzegovina. The River Drava forms part of the border between Serbia and Croatia. It runs from the north along the border with Hungary and flows into the Danube.

SOCIETY
Peoples: 78.1 per cent Croats; 12.1 Serbs; Slav-Muslims 1.0; Hungarians 0.5; Slovenians 0.5. Czechs, Italians, Roma.
Languages: Croatian (official) 96 per cent. Istrian, Romani, Czech, Slovac, Italian. **Religions:** Roman Catholic 76 per cent; Orthodox 11 per cent; Muslims 1 per cent. **Main Political Parties:** The Social Democratic Party (SDP); the Croatian Democratic Union (CDU); the Croat Socio-Liberal Party (CSLP); the Croat Peasant Party; Istrian Democratic Assembly (IDS); Croatian Party of Rights (HSP)
Main Social Organizations: Association of the Independent Trade Unions of Croatia, Union of Autonomous Trade Unions of Croatia, Railworkers' Union of Croatia, Metalworkers' Trade Union of Croatia, Croatian Journalists' Association.

THE STATE
Official Name: Republika Hrvatska. **Administrative Divisions:** 102 Districts. **Capital:** Zagreb 688,000 people (2003).
Other Cities: Split 200,800 people; Rijeka 180,000 (2000).
Government: Stjepan Mesic, President since February 2000. Ivo Sanader, Prime Minister since November 2003. The bicameral parliament (Sabor) is one of Europe´s oldest: the Chamber of Deputies has 127 members and the Chamber of Districts has 68 members, elected for a 4-year term. **National Holiday:** 25 June, Independence (1991). **Armed Forces:** 105,000 (1995). Other: 24,000 Police (1,000 deployed in Bosnia).

Cuba / Cuba

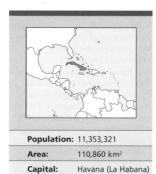

Population:	11,353,321
Area:	110,860 km²
Capital:	Havana (La Habana)
Currency:	Peso
Language:	Spanish

Until the 16th century the island of Cuba was inhabited by several ethnic groups, mainly the Taino or Arawak and Ciboney. Christopher Columbus arrived there on 27 October 1492 but it was not until 1509 that a voyage was made around the coast proving that Cuba was an island. The conquest which was begun in 1511 by Diego Velázquez de Cuéllar, ended in 1514 when the Spanish were defeated by the local forces led by chieftains Hatuey and Guama.

2 The Spanish expeditions which would subsequently conquer a large part of the Caribbean, Mexico and Central America, departed from Cuba. It was described in a mid-16th century document as 'high and mountainous' with small rivers 'rich in gold and fish'. In 1511, colonists from Santo Domingo started mining Cuban gold. It was a short-lived economic cycle, probably because the Indian population was rapidly exterminated. As the number of African enslaved workers on the island was insufficient, economic life soon declined and did not recover until the end of the 16th century, with the advent of sugar production.

3 As early as the 17th century, economic diversification was achieved through shipbuilding and the developing leather and copper industries. The economic center of the island gradually moved from Santiago, on the southern coast, to Havana, in the north, a port of great importance in the mid-17th century.

4 Towards 1840, the slave labor in the sugar plantations represented 77 per cent of the total Cuban workforce. There is evidence that there were *palenques*, settlements of escaped slaves, similar to the so-called *quilombos* in other parts of America (see Brazil) on the island, and there was an abortive slave revolt known as 'La Escalera' in 1843.

5 In addition to the British efforts to end slavery, actions taken by the slaves themselves during the Ten Years War contributed decisively to abolition of slavery in 1886.

6 As in the other Spanish colonies in the Americas, the struggle for independence began in the first few decades of the 19th century. Spain reinforced its military presence and, in 1818, a liberalizaton of trade policies took effect, allowing the export of sugar to the US. The second war of independence began in 1895, led by José Martí, Antonio Maceo and Máximo Gómez. In 1898, aware that the victory of the Cuban patriots was inevitable, the US declared war on Spain and landed at Guantánamo.

7 US occupation forces ruled the country from 1899 to 1902, imposing a constitution including the so-called 'Platt Amendment'. This secured the US rights to intervene in Cuba and to retain Guantánamo, where they set up a powerful military base, still in operation. The 'right' to intervene has been exercised on various occasions, with US Marines remaining on Cuban soil for extended periods of time.

8 In 1933, a popular uprising overthrew Machado from power. Grau San Martín tried to implement several popular and anti-imperialist measures but he was forced to resign by US pressure. Fulgencio Batista emerged as a key-figure during a turbulent period characterized by corruption and gangsterism under the auspices of the US. On 10 March 1952, Batista engineered yet another coup, establishing a dictatorial regime which was responsible for the death of 20,000 Cubans.

9 On 26 July 1953, Fidel Castro and a group of revolutionaries attacked the Moncada Army Base in Santiago de Cuba. Although the attack itself failed, it marked the beginning of the revolution. Castro's revolutionary program had been defined during his trial after the failed initial uprising, ending with his well-known words:

'History will absolve me'. After a period of imprisonment and subsequent exile in Mexico, he landed in Cuba with a small force in December 1956.

10 At the end of 1958, Batista fled from Cuba as guerrilla forces led by Ernesto 'Che' Guevara and Camilo Cienfuegos, vanguard of the Rebel Army, closed on Havana. In just over two years, the guerrillas of the '26th of July' Movement broke the morale of Batista's corrupt army.

11 In 1961, counter-revolutionaries backed by the US disembarked at Playa Giron (Giron Beach), in the Bay of Pigs, in an attempt to bring down the regime which had carried out agrarian reforms and expropriated various American enterprises. They had counted on a popular uprising against the revolutionary Government, but this did not materialize. After 72 hours of fierce fighting, the Bay of Pigs invasion ended in the defeat of the invading forces. Two days before the invasion, on 15 April, while the victims of the Havana Airport bombing were being buried, Castro proclaimed the socialist nature of the revolution and its political alignment with the Soviet bloc.

12 Also in that year, all the pro-government organizations joined together in a common structure. This was initially known as the Integrated Revolutionary Organizations (ORI), and later became the United Party of the Socialist Cuban Revolution (PURSC).

13 In 1962, the US had Cuba excluded from the Organization of American States (OAS). It also put pressure on other countries to sever diplomatic relations, engineering an economic blockade of the island under the pretext of Cuban support to revolutionary movements in Latin America. In October, the setting up of Soviet nuclear missile launching sites on the island made the possibility of a war between the US and the Soviet Union (USSR) into a near-probability. The end of the crisis was negotiated between

Washington and Moscow. Cuba was denuclearized and the US pledged not to invade it, but disregarded the Cuban Government's demands for an end to the blockade, the withdrawal of US troops from Guantánamo and an end to US-managed terrorist activities.

14 The literacy campaign during these years soon bore fruit, and by 1964, Cuba was free of illiteracy. Improvements in health were also one of the Government's priorities. In October 1965, the PURSC was turned into the Cuban Communist Party (PCC). In 1967 Che Guevara was killed in Bolivia.

15 The economic and political ties with the USSR were strengthened in the following years. Cuba began lending technical assistance to like-minded peoples and governments of the Third World. In 1975, troops were sent to countries like Ethiopia and Angola, who requested help to resist invading forces.

16 The revolution began to be institutionalized after the first PCC congress in 1975. A new constitution was approved in 1976 and there were subsequent elections of representatives for the governing bodies at municipal, provincial and national levels. In 1979, Castro and the leaders of the PCC launched a campaign of revolutionary requirements to correct weaknesses in the administrative and political management areas of the revolutionary process.

17 Tension between Cuba and the US increased when Ronald Reagan came to the White House in 1979. In the mid-1980s, some 120,000 people left Port Mariel bound for Florida. During this period, Washington's two-sided policy towards Cuban immigration was intensified. On the one hand, the illegal departure from the island was supported and propagandized by the US, but on the other hand entry applications were restricted.

18 Cuba's relations with many Latin American countries improved after the 1982 Malvinas/Falklands war. During 1985, several meetings were held in Havana on the debt issue, which also drew Cuba closer to the rest of the region.

19 After the Third PPC Congress in 1986, a 'process of the rectification of errors and negative tendencies' was initiated. This coincided with the changes which were taking place in the USSR, but the Cubans avoided adopting the eastern European model.

20 In June 1989, a high-ranking group of Army officers and officials of the Ministry of the Interior were brought to trial and four of them were executed for being involved in drug trafficking. Among them was Arnaldo Ochoa, the main

Life expectancy
76.7 years
2000-2005

Literacy
97% total adult rate
2000

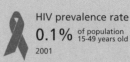
HIV prevalence rate
0.1% of population 15-49 years old
2001

military chief after Fidel's brother (and potential successor), Raúl.

[21] In early 1990, the George Bush (senior) administration increased US pressure on Cuba, with important military maneuvers at Guantánamo Base and in the Caribbean. The US also violated Cuban television airspace with transmissions by 'Televisión Martí', which was supported by 'The voice of America'. However, this broadcast was only picked up on the island for one day, after which it was jammed.

[22] At about this time, the last of Cuba's troops returned home from DR Congo, Ethiopia and Angola, ahead of Namibia's independence and the first steps towards the abolition of apartheid. More than 300,000 Cubans had served in Angola, with the loss of 2,016 lives.

[23] The 4th PCC Congress took place in October 1991. Together with changes in the top leadership it was decided to reform the Constitution so that members of the National Assembly could be elected directly, the single-party system was ratified, religious freedom was extended and the Government recognized the need for joint ventures, especially with Latin American investors.

[24] With the changes in Eastern Europe, and the disappearance of the Council for Mutual Economic Assistance allies, some of Cuba's basic supplies dropped to critical levels. To ease this crisis, the Government strengthened its ties with China, Vietnam and North Korea, and looked for ways to capitalize on its recent technological advances, particularly in biotechnology and medicine (like the meningitis vaccine).

[25] With the collapse of the Soviet Union - Cuba's main trade partner - the Cuban economy went into free fall. From 1989 to 1993, its gross domestic product (GDP) fell by half, from $19.3 to $10 billion. When Moscow scrapped its oil-for-sugar deal and cut oil shipments by 25 per cent between 1989 and 1991 the country lost most of its petroleum supplies. Imports fell by a huge 75 per cent - much of that was food, spare parts, agrochemicals and industrial equipment.

[26] The years since 1989 are known as the special period, a time when the Cuban people had to figure out a way of coping with this massive economic dislocation. The State moved dramatically to restructure the economy. In essence it adopted its own, self-imposed structural-adjustment program.

[27] The loss of Cuba's main trading partners and the re-enforcement of the US blockade led to the creation of a Special Plan, aimed at distributing scarce resources equitably. In 1990, bread was rationed at 100 grams per person per day, three newspapers ceased publication, and the official newspaper, *Granma*, was forced to cut its circulation by over half. The tourist industry was strengthened. A further initiative was joint ventures with tens of investors, specially from Spain.

[28] In early 1993, National Assembly (parliament) elections were held, and deputies were elected directly for the first time. Ricardo Alarcón, foreign minister, was designated president of the National Assembly, and Roberto Robaina, secretary-general of the Communist Youth organization, became foreign minister.

[29] On 26 July 1993, the 40th anniversary of the attack on Moncada barracks, Castro announced that it would henceforth be legal for Cubans to possess and use foreign currency, and to be self-employed. Later that year, the National Assembly organized a debate on the financial crises in workplaces. These 'Workers' Parliaments', held in 1994, provided opinions about the workplaces and their economic management. The sugar harvest (then Cuba s top foreign-exchange earner) had plummeted from 8.4 million tons in 1990 to 4.2 million tons in 1993. In the same year, at the height of the crisis, Cuba was spending 60 per cent of its import bill on food and oil.

[30] In April 1994, a meeting entitled 'The Nation and Emigration' was held in Havana on the initiative of Foreign Minister Robaina, and it was attended by some groups of Cubans living abroad. Shortly afterwards, there was a series of incidents in Havana involving people who wanted to leave the country illegally in frail boats. When Cuba announced it would not stop the 'boat people' from leaving, the US started official negotiations to regulate the illegal departure of the immigrants.

[31] In July, Cuba entered the Association of Caribbean States (ACS) as a full member. Its participation in the ACS, a group emerging as a new economic bloc, encouraged greater integration of the Cuban economy in the region, offering tariff benefits and trade facilities.

[32] In 1995, the fiscal deficit fell for the third year running, due to the reduction of public services and cutbacks in subsidies. A system of convertibility of the peso with the dollar was introduced and holding US currency was legalized. The Cuban parliament approved a new investment law, allowing for totally foreign-owned companies to be established, including by Cuban residents abroad. US Congress approved the Helms-Burton law which penalized companies dealing with Cuba through third-party countries. The international community, especially the EU, harshly criticized this measure for violating the WTO and GATT agreements on free trade.

[33] In February 1996, the Cuban air force shot down two light aircraft flown by a group of Cuban exiles in Miami known as 'Brothers to the Rescue'. According to

IN FOCUS

ENVIRONMENTAL CHALLENGES
There is evidence or air and water pollution (especially noticeable in Havana Bay). The environmental pollution caused by nickel plants at the location of Moa, Holguin Province, has damaged the health of residents, who have complained to the local authorities (but with no answer or solution so far). Biodiversity is weakened as a result of pollution, and overhunting threatens wild species.

WOMEN'S RIGHTS
Cuban women have been able to vote and stand for office since 1934. While in 1990 they held 34 per cent of seats in Parliament, in 2000 they had 28 per cent; 5 per cent of ministerial positions belong to women.

In 2000, women represented 40 per cent of the 6 million labor force.

Iron deficiency is the main cause of anemia, which affects 27 per cent of pregnant women, 25 to 35 per cent of women of child-bearing age and approximately 46 per cent of children under two.

The illiteracy rate for women between 15 and 24 years old is 0.2 per cent. Among those over 15 it reached 3 per cent*. There is no significant difference in illiteracy rates between men and women. All children have an average of 12 years' schooling.

In 2000*, 100 per cent of births were attended by trained medical personnel.

CHILDREN
In 2001, 134,000 children were born; meanwhile, 1,000 under-5s died.

In 2000*, the net school registration and attendance rate was 97 per cent.

Accidents are the leading cause of death in children under 19 and the third major cause of death in children under one year. Accidents account for three per cent of infant deaths (under one year of age).

HIV/AIDS is perceived by the Cuban authorities as an epidemic that can be contained, partly because for example blood transfusions are regulated. However the prevalence rate in the 15-34 age group went up from 9.5 per 100,000 inhabitants in 2000 to 12.1 in 2001. If the present trend continues, the number of people living with HIV/AIDS will at least triple within the next 10 years.

INDIGENOUS PEOPLES/ ETHNIC MINORITIES
Afro-Cubans make up between 34 and 62 per cent of the population; the variance is because statistics are based on people's self-perception. The Cuban mulatto community is highly integrated within itself: there is a process of ethnic mix. The Afro-Cubans live mainly in the eastern part of the island and Havana neighborhoods.

MIGRANTS/REFUGEES
In 2002, about 34,200 Cubans were seeking refuge in foreign countries, mainly in the US. Approximately 25,300 arrived there by boat or through the Mexican border. They were admitted with conditions, but were free to seek permanent residence, under the Cuban Adjustment Act. The US Commitee for Refugees defines them as people that require international protection. The US admitted 1,900 Cubans as refugees directly from Havana. There were about 1,200 Cuban refugees or asylum-seekers in Spain, 1,100 in Costa Rica, 900 in Peru and hundreds scattered worldwide. Throughout 2002, the US refused entry to 700 Cubans coming by boat and repatriated them.

Cuba hosted 1,000 refugees and asylum-seekers at the end of 2002. During 2002, 9 were granted asylum status and 33 applications were rejected.

DEATH PENALTY
It is still in force for all types of crimes.

*Latest data available in *The State of the World's Children* and *Childinfo* database, UNICEF, 2004.

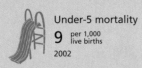

Under-5 mortality
9 per 1,000
live births
2002

Maternal mortality
33 per 100,000
live births
2000

PROFILE

ENVIRONMENT

The Cuban archipelago includes the island of Cuba, the Isle of Youth (formerly the Isle of Pines) and about 1,600 nearby keys and islets. Cuba, the largest island of the Antilles, has rainy, tropical climate. With the exception of the southeastern Sierra Maestra highlands, wide and fertile plains predominate in the country. Sugarcane farming takes up over 60 per cent of the cultivated land, particularly in the northern plains. Nickel is the main export mineral resource. Caribbean beaches are exploited as a resource for the tourism industry.

SOCIETY

Peoples: Cubans call themselves 'Afro-Latin Americans', because of the European and African influence in their heritage. Population of mixed descent (mulattos) 51 per cent; whites 37 per cent, blacks 11 per cent, Chinese and others 1 per cent.
Religions: Catholic 39.6 per cent; atheist 6.4 per cent; Protestant 3.3 per cent; and Afro-Cuban syncretists.
Languages: Spanish (official). Some Lucumi words are used in Santeria (voodoo) rituals.
Main Political Parties: The Cuban Communist Party (PCC) is defined by the constitution as the 'supreme leading force of society and the state'. It was founded in October 1965, stemming from the United Party of the Socialist Cuban Revolution which had been created in 1962 from the Integrated Revolutionary Organizations. This political front was formed in 1961 by the merger of the July 26th Revolutionary Movement, the People's Socialist Party, and the March 13th Revolutionary Directory. Illegal parties: Cuban Liberal Union; Christian Democrat Party; Democratic Solidarity Party, Social Democratic Coordinator.
Main Social Organizations: Cuban Workers' Union (CTC). The CTC has nearly 3,000,000 members, and represents 80 per cent of the Cuban active labor force. The National Association of Small Farmers, 200,000 members with more than 3,500 grassroots organizations (member of the farmers' international network Via Campesina). The Federation of Cuban Women (FMC), with more than 2,000,000 members. The University Student Federation (FEU) and the Federation of Secondary School Students (FEEM), 500,000 student members. The José Martí Pioneers' Union, 2,000,000 children and young people; the Revolution Defense Committees that are organized in neighbourhoods.

THE STATE

Official Name: República de Cuba.
Administrative Divisions: 14 Provinces, 169 Municipalities including the special municipality of Isla de Pinos.
Capital: Havana (La Habana) 2,189,000 people (2003).
Other Cities: Santiago de Cuba 534,600 people; Camaguey 342,900; Holguín 305,000; Guantánamo 264,100; Pinar del Río 172,300 (2000).
Government: Fidel Castro Ruiz, President of the Council of State and the Council of Ministers since December 1976, elected by the National Assembly of People's Power (with 601 members). The 1976 constitution states that the power is exercised through the Assemblies of People's Power. The local Assemblies delegate power to successively more encompassing representative bodies until a pyramid is formed which peaks in the National Assembly. Representatives are subject to recall by the voters.
National Holidays: 1 January, Liberation Day (1959); 26 July, Assault on the Moncada barracks (1953).
Armed Forces: 105,000 (1995). Other: 1,369,000 Civil Defense Force, Territorial Militia, State Security, Border Guard.

Havana, they had violated Cuban air space to drop anti-governmental leaflets on the island. Amnesty International denounced the imprisonment of several people linked to the Cuban Council. According to Amnesty, the Council included 140 groups of opponent journalists, professionals and union activists, while the Cuban Government linked it with US intervention.

[34] The Helms-Burton law barred Cuban access to loans from international institutions like the World Bank or the IMF. However the foreign companies continued to invest in Cuba by using various subterfuges such as pseudonyms, and the economic reforms continued to be implemented. In mid-1996, productivity was up 8 per cent on 1995 figures, while the GDP had increased 9.6 per cent.

[35] Cuban exiles in Miami suffered two setbacks in late 1997. The first was the death of its leader Más Canosa, and second came with Castro's political coup with Pope John Paul II's visit to the island. Following the PCC meeting in 1991 and constitutional amendments of 1992, relations between Cuba and the Vatican improved considerably. As a run-up to the visit, the Pope condemned the US embargo on the island and Castro declared Christmas 1997 a national holiday.

[36] In April 1998, Grenada and Cuba re-established diplomatic relations which had been suspended since the US invasion of the former in 1983. Grenada's prime minister Keith Mitchell made an official visit to Cuba where agreements on economic co-operation were signed.

[37] In February, the UN Historical Verification Commission blamed the US for backing the Guatemalan army in massacres of the population, whilst pointing out that Cuba's Government had supported the left-wing guerrillas here, even sending supplies of weapons.

[38] The tensions between Castro and successive US administrations were aggravated in November 1999 when a child, Elián González, was the only survivor of a Cuban boat that sank on its way to Miami. Cuba demanded the return of Elián while US political groups used the boy's situation as a banner for the 2000 elections. Ignoring the US justice system, which ruled that he should be returned to Cuba, they requested Congress to make the boy a US citizen. In Cuba, Elián also became a symbol of the struggle against the US and its 40-year blockade. Finally, in June 2000, the boy returned to the island.

[39] In November 2001, Hurricane Michelle hit the island, killing 20 people and destroying homes and plots. 481,300 people were evacuated. The US, for the first time in 40 years, exported food to the island to help overcome the disaster's effects.

[40] Hundreds of Afghan prisoners were confined in the US military base at Guantanamo Bay, in January 2002, awaiting interrogation as suspected members of terrorist Al-Qaeda network. The US, without granting them prisoner of war status, called them 'illegal warriors', a legal term unknown in international law.

[41] The Russian military base, Lourdes, located 20 km away from Havana, which had been set up in 1964 to monitor US movements and communications, was closed in January 2002. Although Moscow claimed the decision was taken due to its high costs, Cuban authorities accused Russian President Vladimir

Putin of closing it as a gesture to the US, part of a rapprochement policy adopted after the September 11 terrorist attacks in New York and Washington, and by US threats of suspending financial aid to Russia.

[42] On 20 April 2002, the UN High Commissioner for Human Rights (UNHCR) passed a resolution against Cuba, urging the Government to grant more individual liberties and political rights, and to allow the visit of a UN envoy to monitor progress in this area. The initiative was begun by Uruguay (see Uruguay). *Granma* reacted angrily against the resolution, denouncing that Washington planned more trickery for Cuba. The resolution was supported by 23 countries and rejected by 21, while 9 abstained. Of the Latin American countries, Brazil and Ecuador abstained and Venezuela and Cuba voted against.

[43] That month, Castro released the tape of a phone call with Mexican President Vicente Fox to confirm that the Mexican Government had asked him to cancel or cut short his stay at the March 2002 UN summit held in Monterrey (Mexico). He had also been told not to criticize the US in his speech. Castro also accused Mexican foreign minister Jorge Castaneda of being the main supporter of the change in Mexican policy toward Cuba, giving in to pressures from Washington. Mexico had been the only country in the region to maintain relations with Cuba after the blockade was imposed.

[44] In May 2002, former US President Jimmy Carter made a 6-day visit - the first US President (either in office or not) to do so since Castro came into power. After visiting a laboratory that Washington alleged was manufacturing biological weapons, Carter declared that this was not the case. Cuba was accused by US of being part of the 'axis of evil'.

[45] Between March and April 2003, according to Amnesty International, Cuban authorities 'carried out an unprecedented crackdown on the Cuban dissident movement'. 75 dissidents were detained, brought to trial without respecting the due process of law, and sentenced to up to 28 years in prison.

[46] On 11 April three men were executed for hijacking a Cuban ferry and attempting to sail to the US. The executions by firing squad, carried out less than a week after the trials began, ended a 3-year period without executions on the island. Amnesty International pointed out that the US economic embargo has contributed to the climate in which human rights violations occur. ■

Cyprus / Kipros

Population:	813,311
Area:	9,250 km²
Capital:	Nicosia (Levkosia)
Currency:	Pound
Language:	Greek and Turkish

TERRITORY UNDER TURKISH CONTROL

Mediterranean Sea

Morphou Bay — Kyrenia — Trikomo — *Famagusta Bay*

Levkosia (Nicosia) — (Salamis) — Ammókhostos (Famagusta)

Cyprus T R O D O S — Lárnax (Larnaca) — UK Sovereign Air-Base

Paphos — Limassol

UK Sovereign Air-Base

0km — 50

There is early evidence of human presence in Cyprus, tools and instruments dating back around 10,000 years. The first known settlement was in Khirokitia (near the south coast), where some 2,000 inhabitants built their houses of stone. The discovery of small quantities of obsidian - a type of volcanic rock not found on the island - is the only sign of contact with other cultures. Khirokitia and other smaller associated settlements disappeared after few centuries, leaving the island deserted for about 2,000 years. Hittites, Phoenicians, Greeks, Assyrians, Persians, Egyptians, Romans, Arabs and Turks trooped through its valleys and over its hills until 1878, when the British Empire - in need of

a base for eastward expansion - negotiated its occupation with Turkey. The Ottomans, after over 300 years of domination, ceded Cyprus to England, in exchange for British protection against Czarist Russia.

[2] In 1931, various movements appeared favoring *enosis* (annexation) of Cyprus by Greece (in view of the example of the incorporation of Crete to Greece in 1913). Enosis was promoted by the Greek Orthodox Church, the religion of the Greek Cypriots, who make up the majority of the island's population but Turkey - Greece's rival - feared being surrounded by a hostile neighbor on its Mediterranean coast. The British exiled various Greek Cypriot priests but, after World War II, the country's

most important political figure was Archbishop Vaneziz Makarios (original name was Mikhail Khristodolou Mouskos), who had been exiled in the Seychelles. Makarios headed the Cypriot pro-independence movement from exile.

[3] In 1959, representatives of the Greek and Turkish communities, of Makarios' Democratic Party and of British colonial interests, reached an agreement for the creation of the Republic of Cyprus, with constitutional guarantees for the Turkish minority, and British sovereignty over the island's military bases. Independence was proclaimed on 16 August, 1960, and Makarios (considered the 'Mediterranean Fidel Castro' by the US Government) took office as President. An active supporter of anti-colonialism, the

President played an important role in the Movement of Non-Aligned Countries (he was re-elected in 1968 and 1973). Tensions between Greece and Turkey persisted and had frequent repercussions in Cyprus where conflicts erupted between the Greek and Turkish communities.

[4] In 1963 there was an unsuccessful coup attempt by members of the radical right (who supported enosis). In 1974, the Cypriot National Guard, under the command of Greek army officers, ousted Makarios (who fled to Britain) and Nikos Sampson, who favored annexation by Greece, was appointed President. Turkey immediately invaded Northern Cyprus, bombed Nicosia, and drove 200,000 Greek Cypriots southward, under the pretext of protecting the Turkish minority. That same year, Sampson turned the presidency over to Glafcos Klerides (President of the House of Representatives) and facing the prospect of a war with Turkey - added to domestic opposition and world-wide repudiation - the Greek military junta (in power since 1967) also stepped down.

[5] Towards the end of 1974, Makarios returned to Cyprus and held the Presidential office until his death in 1977. Spyros Kyprianou succeeded Makarios and followed the same policy (refusing to recognize the division of Cyprus and retaining membership of the Non-

IN FOCUS

ENVIRONMENTAL CHALLENGES
Although the atmospheric pollution index has risen on account of traffic and industry, it is at an acceptable level. Soil deterioration is mainly due to the excessive use of agrochemicals. The coastal ecosystem has borne the adverse effects of tourism, particularly the construction of large hotels and high-rise apartment buildings.

WOMEN'S RIGHTS
Cypriot women have been able to vote and stand for office since 1960. In 2000, 5 per cent of the parliamentary seats were occupied by women; the percentage of women in ministerial positions was nil, compared with 7 per cent in 1995.

In the year 2000 they constituted 39 per cent of the labor force. Women's unemployment rate is 4.2 per cent compared with the island's total unemployment rate of 3.3 per cent. Ten per cent of women work in agriculture, 18 per cent

in industry and 71 per cent in services.

In the year 2000*, the illiteracy rate was 15 per cent among women over 15, while it was 1 per cent among men. That year, the average number of years' schooling for Cypriot women was 13.

CHILDREN
In 2001, 11,000 children were born and the gross birth rate was 13 per cent.

All of the elementary school students reached 5th grade*.

The net rate of elementary school enrollment and attendance is 95 per cent*.

The death rate for under-fives is 6 per cent.

INDIGENOUS PEOPLES/ ETHNIC MINORITIES
Even though historically Turkish and Greek settlers had lived together peacefully, their relations deteriorated after independence from British rule in 1960, and ended in the division of the island by the the Turkish army in 1974 with Greeks in the South, Turks in the North, and thousands of people

murdered and displaced. The main conflict was for control and administration of the territory: the violent confrontations between communities at independence revealed the lack of a Cypriot identity and the fact of two peoples closely linked to their mainlands.

In 1983, the Turkish minority (12 per cent of the island's population) established the Turkish Republic of North Cyprus. Although it has only been recognized by Ankara since its formation, poor relations between Turks and the Greek Cypriot majority (85 per cent) have ground to a halt. In the North, Turkish is spoken and Islam is the religion.

At present, there is tension on both sides which prevents reaching a settlement that would allow their entry to the EU. The history of tension suggests that violence could continue between the communities, but international attention would inhibit Turkish military activities - backed by Ankara - and reduce the polical isolation.

Other minorities also reside in Cyprus: since 1960, some 8,000 Maronites, Armenians and Italians have emigrated to the Greek sector.

MIGRANTS/REFUGEES
At the end of 2002, Cyprus accommodated over 1,800 refugees plus around 950 asylum-seekers - most of these from Iran (400) and the Gaza Strip (170). The total includes over 1,700 asylum-seekers awaiting decisions and 90 whose applications had been granted during the year (of these, 62 were Iranians).

Around 265,000 people were still internally displaced in 2002: 200,000 Greek Cypriots in the south and about 65,000 Turkish Cypriots in the north.

The Cypriot Government has been processing asylum applications since 1 January 2002. Prior to that, UNHCR processed them in Cyprus (it still does in the Turkish sector and had 5 applications in 2002).

DEATH PENALTY
It was abolished in 2002; the last execution was in 1962.

*Latest data available in *The State of the World's Children* and *Childinfo* database, UNICEF, 2004.

Life expectancy
78.3 years
2000-2005

GNI per capita
$12,320
2002

Literacy
97% total adult rate
2000

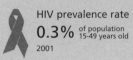

HIV prevalence rate
0.3% of population 15-49 years old
2001

Aligned Movement). The Turkish forces, who were occupying 40 per cent of the island, refused to return to the situation which had prevailed prior to the coup, and remained in the country: a Turkish Cypriot Federal State was proclaimed in the northern part of the island, under the presidency of Rauf Denktash (1975).

6   Denktash and Makarios had set four basic conditions for a negotiated peace settlement: a) the establishment of a binational, non-aligned and independent federal republic; b) an exact delimitation of the territories that each community would administrate; c) the discussion of - among other issues - internal restrictions on traveling, ownership rights and a federal system with equal rights for both communities; d) sufficient federal power to ensure Cyprus' unity. The Turkish refusal to withdraw the troops, an essential condition for the Greek Cypriots, meant that no substantial progress was made: in 1983, the Turkish Republic of North Cyprus (TRNC) was proclaimed, but only Turkey acknowledged the new state.

7   Since 1983, Cyprus has enjoyed a period of economic prosperity brought by tourism, foreign aid, and international business that made the island an international financial center, (replacing Beirut, whose money markets had been paralyzed by the Lebanese civil war). The main beneficiary of this was the Greek Cypriot bourgeoisie. In the northern part of the island there was a large influx of Turkish immigrants (more than 40,000 people) which, when added to almost 35,000 Turkish soldiers and the migration of some 20,000 Turkish Cypriots, created a change of profile in the population. In the 1990s there was one continental Turk for every Turkish Cypriot.

8   In 1985, a Constitution for the TRNC was submitted to referendum: 65 per cent voted in favor. However, 30 per cent of the registered voters abstained, and this was seen as a reflection of distrust in the State's legitimacy.

9   Giorgis Vassiliu was elected President of Cyprus in 1988. He re-established the negotiations with Denktash that had been stalled since 1985: leaders and representatives of the 350 thousand Cypriots in exile called for 'constructive flexibility' on the part of the two leaders. The Greek community - buoyed by their economic prosperity and the fact that they were numerically the majority - wanted independence to be guaranteed by the UN. They also sought freedom of movement and property rights across the island. The Turkish Cypriots - based on the superior strength of the Turkish army - demanded a binational federation under Turkey's

protection. Talks were again broken off in 1989.

10   In 1990, Denktash was re-elected President of the TRNC. With the support of US President George Bush in 1991 Turkey proposed a summit among representatives from Ankara, Athens and both Cypriot communities. Greece and the Greek Cypriot authorities considered Washington's support of the initiative as compensation for the aid given by Turkey during the Gulf War. In 1992, the UN declared Cyprus a bi-communal and bi-regional country, with equal political rights for both communities. In 1993, Glafkos Klerides defeated Vassiliu in the presidential elections.

11   In 1994 the European Court of Justice declared that direct trade between the TRNC and the EU was illegal. In 1996 violence and tension increased in the north of the island. Klerides and Denktash met throughout 1997, with UN mediation: their aim was reunification, ahead of admission to the EU. However, direct negotiations between the EU and Greek Cypriot authorities stalled dialogue within Cyprus and the drive for reunification broke down. The rivalry between Greece and Turkey on this issue also impeded the initiative. The EU stated that, if the island were not reunited, the Greek area could be admitted as if it were an independent state, leaving out the Turkish area. Denktash considered that the political legitimacy of the Turkish Cypriot Region (TRCN) should be acknowledged and the whole of Cyprus admitted to the Union.

12   In 1998, Klerides was re-elected President by a small margin. That year, the Foreign Ministers of all 15 EU countries agreed to initiate talks for the incorporation of the Greek sector into the EU. In 1999, Greece's withdrawal of its veto on Turkey's entry to the EU, plus the aid it provided the Turkish Government after a devastating earthquake (see Turkey), marked a change in the political climate with regard to Cyprus.

13   In the year 2000, negotiations were renewed between Klerides and Denktash within a UN framework. These were held as 'proximity talks', avoiding direct contact between the parties: the third round of negotiations that year, ended with no progress. Klerides boycotted the indirect talks in New York in protest against a statement by UN Secretary-General Kofi Annan, which granted equal authority to the TRCN and the internationally recognized Cypriot Government. Annan modified his stance, stating that any accord involving Cyprus would be based on the premise of single sovereignty. The positions of the two sides continued to be irreconcilable on

the future structure of Cyprus: the Cypriots advocated a reunified bi-communal federation; the Turkish Cypriots wanted one based on equal sovereignty. Once the Geneva rounds ended, Denktash threatened not to negotiate as long as the TRNC did not have international recognition.

14   In 2001, as an expression of its desire to overcome the differences with Greece, Turkey withdrew its veto, conditionally, on the agreement between the EU and NATO, which blocked the creation of a new European defense structure. Shortly after, the Cypriot Heads of State held an historic meeting: for the first time in the 27 years that the country had been divided, Klerides crossed the 'green line'; in Nicosia to meet Denktash. The imminent entry of Cyprus to the EU breathed new life into the dialogue between the Greek and Turkish Cypriot. However as Ankara had made the TRNC's entry conditional on its own admission, the TRNC refused to negotiate EU membership alongside the Republic of Cyprus (the Greek sector).

15   In 2002, Turkey's intransigence exasperated the EU, which then seemed set to accept only the Greek sector if no agreement was reached.

However, that year Klerides and Denktash re-started negotiations with UN mediation, focusing on their aim of EU membership. Toward the end of 2002, Kofi Annan presented a peace plan that proposed a federation of the two sectors, governed alternately. That year, the EU invited Cyprus to the 2004 Copenhagen summit, foreshadowed in the UN plan in the event of an agreement being reached in 2003: again, without reunification, only the Greek Cypriot sector would be admitted.

16   Tassos Papadopoulos was elected in the 2003 elections, a few weeks prior to the UN deadline for agreement on the island's future: the date passed with no reunification agreement. Annan admitted his plan had failed. That same year, for the first time in three decades, both the Turkish and Greek Cypriots crossed the 'green line': 17,000 people made the crossing, marking a milestone in the island's history.

17   In twin referendums in April 2004 the Greek Cypriots rejected a UN plan for reunification of the island while the Turkish Cypriots backed it. Because of the Greek rejection, only the Greek side entered the European Union as part of Cyprus on 1 May. ■

PROFILE

ENVIRONMENT
Once part of continental Europe, the island of Cyprus is located in the eastern Mediterranean, close to Turkey. Two mountain ranges - the Troodos in the southwestern region, and the Kyrenia in the north Cyprus - enclose a fertile central plain. The temperate Mediterranean climate, with hot, dry summers and mild, rainy winters, is good for agriculture.

SOCIETY
Peoples: Cypriots are divided into Greek (85 per cent) and Turkish (12 per cent) communities; they have separate political, cultural and religious organizations. **Religions:** Greek Orthodox and Islam. **Languages:** Greek and Turkish (official); English. **Main Political Parties:** Democratic Union - of the Greek Cypriot Community (right wing); Democratic Party (center-right); Progressive Party of the Working People (AKEL-Anorthotikon Komma Ergazemenou Laou, communist); Social Democrats Movement (KISOS-Kinima Sosialdimokraton); United Democrats (EDI-Enomeni Dimokrates, center-left); National Unit - of the Turkish Cypriot Community (right wing). **Main Social Organizations:** There are two major organizations representing approximately 30 unions, the Pancypriot Federation of Labor, and the Cyprus Worker's Confederation.

THE STATE
Official Name: Kypriaki Dimokratia-Kibris Cumhuriyeti. **Capital:** Levkosia (Nicosia) 205,000 people (2003). **Other Cities:** Larnaca 44,600 people; Limassol 26,700; Paphos 16,300 (2000). **Government:** Tassos Papadopoulos, Head of State and of the Government since February 2003. Single-chamber legislature with 71 members. Rauf Denktash - re-elected in April 2000 - has held the presidency of the Turkish Republic of North Cyprus since1983. This Government, based upon Turkish occupation and recognized only by Turkey, exercises an independent administration, including its own Judicial System and a 50-member Legislative Assembly, elected every five years. **National Holiday:** 1 October. Independence: 16 August 1960. The Turkish Republic of North Cyprus (declared in 1983) celebrates Independence on 16 November. **Armed Forces:** 10,000 (including 400 women). Other: Armed Police: 3,700.

Czech Republic / Ceska Republika

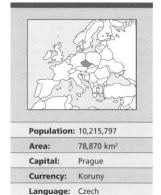

Population:	10,215,797
Area:	78,870 km²
Capital:	Prague
Currency:	Koruny
Language:	Czech

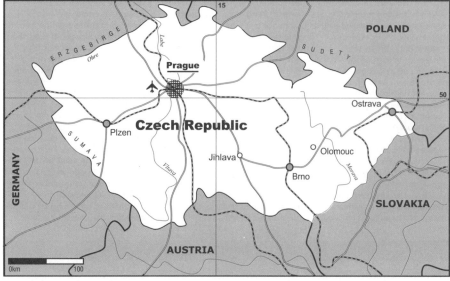

The exact origin of the first inhabitants of the Mid-Danube region remains uncertain, although there are signs left by the Boii, a Celtic people whose name gave rise to the Latin name 'Bohemia'. The Celts were displaced without major conflict by Germanic peoples and later, in the 6th century, by the Slavs, while the Germans continued their migration southward.

2 The inhabitants of mountain and forest areas had the natural protection of these areas. However, the lowlands were repeatedly invaded by the Avars. The Slavs were able to repel these invasions when they had leaders strong enough to unite the tribes, such as the Frankish merchant Samo. In the 8th century, peace was restored to Bohemia with the defeat of the Avars at the hands of Charlemagne.

3 In the early 9th century, three potential political centers emerged: the plains of Nitra, the Lower Morava Basin and Central Bohemia. The Slavs of Bohemia, called the Czechs, gained the upper hand in most of the region. The first Czech Prince was Mojmir I, who extended his realm as far as Nitra. His successor, Rostislav I, institutionalized the State and consolidated political relations with the Eastern Frankish Empire, as a way of maintaining his own sovereignty.

4 The Franks organized the first missions at Nitra and in Bohemia, but Rostislav would not allow Latin to be taught, and asked the Byzantine emperor to send preachers who spoke the Slavic language. Constantine (Cyril) and Methodius arrived in 863, leading a group of Greek missionaries; they developed the first Slavic alphabet and translated religious texts.

5 Methodius won recognition from Rome for his work in Moravia and in Panonia, which became an ecclesiastical province linked to the Archbishop of Sirmium. The Franks came to consider Methodius an enemy; he was captured and kept prisoner until 873, when he returned to Moravia.

6 Rostislav was the founder of Great Moravia, uniting the territories inhabited by the Slavs of the region and Slovakia, bordered by the northern ring of the Carpathian Mountains and by the Morava River.

7 After the death of Methodius in 885 the Frankish Bishop Wiching displaced Methodius's disciples and the new Pope outlawed Slavic liturgy.

8 King Arnulf sent a military expedition to Moravia in 892, allying himself later with the Magyars to defeat the principality. Between 905 and 908, Great Moravia went through several foreign occupations, until an agreement was reached between Mojmir II and Arnulf.

9 In the 10th century, between the strengthening of Germania and the restoration of the Holy Roman Empire, Bohemia lost the major part of its possessions. When Bfetislav I ascended the throne in 1034, the principality recovered part of Moravia and invaded Poland in 1039. However, King Henry III of Germania forced a retreat, and the Hungarian Crown kept Slovakia.

10 In order to maintain its independence, Bohemia found it necessary to be actively involved in the campaigns of the Holy Roman Empire. Thus, the situation arose whereby the Bohemian princes were being crowned king by both the rival powers.

11 In the early 13th century the Church separated from the State, and the feudal lords began demanding greater political participation. At the same time, Germanic immigration increased the population, building new urban centers and exploiting mineral resources, which gave rise to a new class of tradesmen and entrepreneurs.

12 Under the Przemysl dynasty, which lasted until 1306, Bohemia controlled part of Austria and the Alps; at one point a single king ruled over Bohemia and Poland. This dynasty was succeeded by the Luxembourgs in 1310. With the coronation of Emperor Charles I in 1455, Bohemia and the Holy Roman Empire were joined together. As the capital of the Kingdom and the Empire, this was Prague's greatest moment.

13 The religious reform movement strengthened in the 14th century and became even more radical under the influence of Father John Huss. Excommunicated by the Pope, Huss was later tried for heresy and sedition by the Council of Constance, and was burned alive in 1415 after refusing to recant.

14 The anger that followed Huss' execution marked the birth of the Hussite movement in Bohemia and Moravia. The Germanic peoples remained faithful to Rome, however, and in addition to these religious differences, the ethnic issue remained, triggering political conflict between them. The Holy Roman Empire, allied with the German princes, launched several military campaigns in Bohemia, but they were repulsed by the Hussites.

15 Religious differences prevented political union between Bohemia and its former possessions for many years. Vladislav II reigned over Bohemia from 1471 but Moravia, Silesia and Lusacia were ruled by Mathias, of Hungary. Only after his death in 1490, Vladislav II was elected king of Hungary and the territories were reunited.

16 The death of Louis II in 1526, paved the way for the rise of the Hapsburgs. Ferdinand I, Louis' brother-in-law, became king by currying favor with the nobility. Austria's victory over the Protestant Society of Schmalkaldica in 1547 permitted Ferdinand to impose the right of hereditary succession to the throne upon Bohemia and its states.

17 The Hapsburgs strengthened the Counter-reformation throughout the region. Slovakia

WORKERS

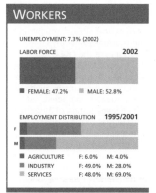

UNEMPLOYMENT: 7.3% (2002)

LABOR FORCE   2002

■ FEMALE: 47.2%   ■ MALE: 52.8%

EMPLOYMENT DISTRIBUTION   1995/2001

	F:	M:
■ AGRICULTURE	6.0%	4.0%
■ INDUSTRY	49.0%	28.0%
■ SERVICES	48.0%	69.0%

LAND USE

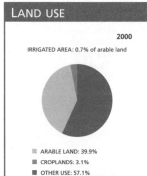

2000

IRRIGATED AREA: 0.7% of arable land

■ ARABLE LAND: 39.9%
■ CROPLANDS: 3.1%
■ OTHER USE: 57.1%

Life expectancy
75.4 years
2000-2005

GNI per capita
$5,560
2002

HIV prevalence rate
0.1% of population 15-49 years old
2001

remained within its realm because the Hapsburgs had retained it when Hungary was invaded by the Ottoman Empire, in 1526.

[18] Rudolf II (1576-1612) transferred the seat of the empire to Prague, making it once again one of the continent's most important political and cultural centers. Many key positions of the kingdom were filled by Catholics during Rudolf's reign, as he himself was Catholic. However, this triggered a rebellion by the non-Catholic (Reformed church) majority, and the king was deposed in 1611.

[19] After a stormy succession, Ferdinand II of Styria, with the support of Maximilian I of Bavaria, defeated the Protestants and ruled with a strong hand. The Germanic language was added to the traditional use of Czech, and only the Catholic religion was authorized.

[20] Unlike Bohemia, Moravia did not become involved in the fight against the Hapsburgs and therefore did not suffer the effects of civil and religious strife as severely. In Moravia there was religious tolerance allowing the growth of Protestantism in the state, which remained separate from the Austrian Crown until 1848.

[21] Despite the hegemony of the Germans, the Czechs conserved their ethnic identity, their language and their culture. Something similar had also occurred in the Hungarian counties inhabited by Slovaks. This set the scene for a resurgence of nationalism in the early 19th century, which strengthened the traditional ties between these two peoples.

[22] Czechs and Slovaks, together with the inhabitants of the German republics, helped put a stop to the absolutist doctrine, amidst a revolutionary wave which swept Europe in 1848. In 1867, the empire split in two: Austria, where ethnic Germans outnumbered the Czechs, Poles and other nationalities; and Hungary, where the Magyars subdued the Slovaks.

[23] With World War I the fall of the Austro-Hungarian Empire finally brought about the recognition of the Republic of Czechoslovakia. The new state's borders established in 1919 by the victorious powers included parts of Poland, Hungary and the Sudetenland, where there lived around three million Germans, source of potential conflict.

[24] Czech and Slovak leaders charged the National Assembly with drawing up a Constitution. The Assembly opted for a strict parliamentary system, in which the President and his cabinet would be responsible to two legislative chambers. Women's right to vote or to be elected was granted for the first time.

[25] The 1930s world-wide depression affected the Sudetenland intensely, as it was a highly industrialized region. It also accentuated nationalistic feeling among the German people there, who developed a separatist movement alongside Hitler's rise to power in 1933. Britain, France and Italy negotiated the ceding of the Sudetenland to Germany in 1938, thus paving the way for the German occupation of Czechoslovakia in 1939.

[26] After Hitler's defeat in World War II, and under the occupation of the Soviet army, Czechoslovakia recovered its 1919 borders, while the German population was almost entirely expelled from the country.

[27] The Communist Party (CKC) obtained 38 per cent of the vote in the 1946 election, increasing to 51 per cent in 1948. In June, a People's Republic was proclaimed, and the CKC applied the economic model in effect at the time in the USSR. Czechoslovakia joined the Council for Mutual Economic Assistance (CMEA) and the Warsaw Pact.

[28] In 1960, the People's Republic of Czechoslovakia added 'socialist' to its name. In political terms, this decade was a turning point. Slovak leaders, expelled from the party in the 1950s, were rehabilitated. The Slovak struggle for autonomy (which had been even further restricted by the new socialist constitution) together with the 1967 student strikes brought an end to Antony Novotny's leadership of the CKC.

[29] In early 1968, the election of Alexander Dubcek as Secretary of the CKC, and of Ludwik Svoboda as the country's president, led to the implementation of a program to decentralize the economy, and affirm national sovereignty, against a background of broad popular support.

[30] The USSR and other members of the Warsaw Pact viewed the possibility of Czechoslovakian

IN FOCUS

ENVIRONMENTAL CHALLENGES
Sulfur dioxide emissions - produced by electricity generation - are very high, causing acid rain. Air pollution has destroyed or damaged large areas of forest. Approximately three-quarters of all the country's trees show a high degree of defoliation. Water pollution levels are also very high, especially in rural areas. Waste from industry, mining and intensive farms threatens the purity of the water, both above and below ground.

WOMEN'S RIGHTS
Women have been able to vote and run for office since 1920. Fifteen per cent of seats in Parliament and 17 per cent of ministerial positions were held by women in 2000.

The estimated years of schooling were 14 in 2000, both for men and women.

Twenty-three per cent of pregnant women suffer anemia.

The female labor force was 47 per cent of the total in 2000. 10.6 per cent of the women were unemployed (in 2000, the unemployment rate was 8.8 per cent). Among female workers, 4 per cent worked in agriculture, 28 per cent in industry and 69 per cent in services.

CHILDREN
In 2001, 90,000 children were born.

The Czech Republic, along with Romania, Poland and Slovakia, is thought to be the base for criminal networks that exploit children between 9 and 13 years, using them to steal and act as drug couriers.

In addition, there is child trafficking from the Czech Republic into Germany, Netherlands, Belgium and the UK.

INDIGENOUS PEOPLES/ ETHNIC MINORITIES
In August 2003, the UN Committee on the Elimination of Racial Discrimination advised the Government to approve a law against the discrimination of national minorities. The Committee praised 'the numerous measures, programs and strategies adopted in order to improve the situation of Roma Gypsies and other marginalized groups, including refugees'. However, the Committee was concerned about the acts of racial violence, the persistence of racial hatred and intolerance and the de facto segregation particularly of Roma Gypsies.

Discrimination towards Roma in employment, housing and education was marked in 2002. This group, made up of 267,000 people - 2.6 per cent of the population, most of them very poor - was victim of hate crimes and violence. There were prosecutions of neo-Nazis who attacked and murdered Roma, but the crimes were punished lightly. The Government announced plans to stop Roma seeking asylum in EU countries and to limit public assistance for Roma who returned after unsuccessfully seeking asylum abroad. The authorities also proposed to create a special police force to fight money-lending in Roma communities. Fear of money-lenders' retribution when they default on debt is apparently a major reason why some Roma migrate.

The Slovak population represents another minority group (309,000 people), mainly in Prague, Brno, Karvina, Olomouc, Tabor and Kladno. Unlike the Roma, this minority group has improved living conditions over the last years. They do not face political or cultural restrictions (although there is lack of Slovak-language education) and there are several organizations representing their interests. They have no representation in Parliament, mainly because Czech Slovaks tend to vote for the broader political parties.

MIGRANTS/REFUGEES
At the end of 2002, the Czech Republic hosted more than 6,300 refugees, in addition to 6,200 asylum-seekers awaiting the Government's decision.

Approximately 8,500 asylum-seekers filed applications to stay in the country (in 2001 the number was 18,000); they came from Ukraine (1,700), Vietnam (900), Slovakia (800) and Moldova (700). The approval rate was 2 per cent. Applicants from Russia, Belarus, and Afghanistan were the most successful. About 5,100 applications were rejected (mostly from people from Ukraine, Slovakia, Moldova, Vietnam and China).

Although the Minister of the Interior rejected the applications of 27 Iraqis and Afghans, it was decided not to deport them. They were granted a 'tolerance visa' which would allow them to stay temporarily, while the conflicts in their own countries were continuing.

In 2002, about 3,000 Czech people, most of them Roma Gypsies, were seeking asylum in foreign countries (mainly in the UK).

DEATH PENALTY
It was abolished in 1990.

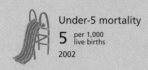
Under-5 mortality
5 per 1,000 live births
2002

Poverty
<2% of population living on less than $1 per day
1996

Debt service
11.2% exports of goods and services
2001

Maternal mortality
9 per 100,000 live births
2000

reforms as a threat to the integrity of the socialist camp; in August 1968, Soviet forces intervened in the country. The leaders of the 'Prague Spring' were expelled from the CKC and political alignment with the USSR was re-established.

[31] Soviet Communist Party Secretary Mikhail Gorbachev's reform process brought about changes in Czechoslovakia. In 1989, despite violent repression, anti-Government protests continued, precipitating a crisis within the regime.

[32] The Government was forced to negotiate with the Civic Forum, an alliance of several opposition groups. Among other reforms, Parliament approved the elimination of the CKC's leadership role. In late 1989, a provisional Government was formed, with a non-communist majority.

[33] In December 1989, the Civic Forum declared that the CKC had redistributed cabinet positions in such a way as to keep its own people in the key positions. 200,000 people gathered in Prague to demand a greater opposition representation in the cabinet. Gustav Husak resigned the presidency of the federation and was replaced by Vaclav Havel, who immediately granted amnesty to all political prisoners and called elections for June 1990. Havel was confirmed in the presidency and the Czech and Slovak Federal Republic was proclaimed.

[34] Following the elections, the Forum divided into the Civic Democratic Party, the self-proclaimed 'right with a conservative program', and the Civic Movement. The Slovakian Party 'Public against Violence' split into two oppositional groups. The Movement for a Democratic Slovakia - the most important one - summoned the people to fight against the right wing profile the country was acquiring

[35] In the June legislative elections, the Czech Civic Democratic Party and the Slovak group, Democratic Slovakia, won in their respective republics. When negotiations over the statutes of the new federation came to an impasse, Czech and Slovak leaders admitted that separation was inevitable. Czechoslovakia disappeared from the world map, replaced by the Czech Republic, with its capital Prague (Praha), and the Republic of Slovakia, with its capital Bratislava.

[36] Vaclav Havel, the former president of Czechoslovakia who had resigned on 17 July 1992 after the National Assembly declared the independence of Slovakia, was elected President of the Czech Republic in 1992. Vaclav Klaus

became the first Prime Minister of the new independent State.

[37] The national debt continued lower than that of other former communist countries of the region, while foreign investment was amongst the highest. Prime Minister Klaus planned an economic reform based on a rapid privatization. In 1995, the banking system saw a high number of deposits, many of which came from illegal economic activities. This same year, the Czech Republic became the first former Communist OECD member.

[38] In December 1996, the Czech Republic and Germany signed a reconciliation document, in which Germany asked forgiveness for the behavior of the Nazi regime during World War II, while the Czech Government apologized for the expulsion of three million Germans from the Sudetenland following the War.

[39] During 1997, the devaluation of the national currency, the koruny, brought political chaos. The Civic Democratic Party led by Klaus was accused of encouraging financial groups which bribed several of its members with 'hidden commissions' during the privatization process. Havel publicly called for Klaus' resignation, which was received in November. Josef Tosovsky became the new Prime Minister.

[40] The economic crisis coincided with increasing xenophobia. This violence appeared to be supported by a large and increasing percentage of the population.

[41] In April 1998, the Czech Republic was admitted to NATO. The Social Democratic Party (SDP) won the June elections with 32.3 per cent of the vote. Given the difficulty in obtaining a majority, the Civic Democratic Party (CDP) agreed to give the SDP control in return for their leader, Klaus, being appointed parliamentary speaker. The Government, the first of the Left in the post-communist era, aimed to wipe out corruption, raise the national minimum wage and halt the 'devolving' of property to the Catholic Church. But it was unable to improve the economic situation, which by the end of the year had reached record levels of unemployment and inflation surpassing 11.5 per cent.

[42] In March 1999 the country finally entered NATO, which marked the transition to the West. Other members criticized the fact that moves to join the EU were going slowly.

[43] In November, the Government gave in to international pressure and ordered that a controversial wall in the north of Usti nad Labem - built to separate Roma

houses from those of other residents - be pulled down.

[44] In late September 2000, the World Bank and the International Monetary Fund - meeting for the first time in Prague - intended to show off the Czech Republic as their first economic success in a former Iron Curtain country. Its poverty rate of 5 per cent was much lower than other former socialist countries. But massive acts of civil disobedience and protest organized by international anti-globalization groups forced the meeting to end a day earlier than planned.

[45] In October 2000 the first reactor at Temelin nuclear plant was activated, causing conflict with Austria, which tried to block the Czech Republic's entry to the EU.

[46] A journalists' strike and several large protests, the biggest since the end of communism, led to the resignation of Jiri Hodac, the Director-General of state TV. Hodac was seen as a Government stooge, which compromised editorial freedom.

[47] In November 2001, the Government settled the dispute with Austria over the nuclear plant by agreeing to safety measures

and to monitor its environmental impact.

[48] In 2002 Parliament unanimously rejected the neighboring countries' request to annul the 'Benes decrees' - the controversial post-war decrees under which 2.5 million ethnic Germans were expelled from Czechoslovakia and thousands of ethnic Hungarians dispossessed.

[49] After forming a coalition with the center alliance Christian Democratic Party and Free Union, the Social Democrat Party, led by Vladimir Spidla, won 70 of the 200 parliamentary seats.

[50] In August, the Vltava River flooded Prague, the worst flood in 200 years.

[51] In December, at the Copenhagen summit, the Republic was invited to join the EU. The integration, planned for 2004, was decided by a referendum in June 2003.

[52] The former Prime Minister Vaclav Klaus was appointed President in the February 2003 election, replacing Vaclav Havel.

[53] The Czech Republic formally joined the European Union on 1 May 2004 and was the first former Soviet bloc country to hold elections to the European Parliament in June. ■

PROFILE

ENVIRONMENT
The Bohemian massif occupies the western region, bordered by the Moravian plains to the southeast. Cereals and sugar beet are cultivated in the lowlands, where cattle and pigs are also raised. Rye and potatoes are grown in the Bohemian valleys. The region has rich mineral deposits: coal, lignite, graphite and uranium, while Moravia is rich in coal.

SOCIETY
Peoples: Czechs, 81.2 per cent; Moravians, 13.2 per cent; Slovaks, 3 per cent.
Religions: Catholic (39 per cent); Protestant (4.3 per cent); Orthodox (3 per cent). 40 per cent of the population are atheist.
Languages: Czech (official). Romani is spoken by the Roma (gypsy) community (200,000).
Political parties: Czech Social Democratic Party (SDP); Civic Democratic Party (CDP); Communist Party of Bohemia and Moravia, Christian Democratic Union-Czechoslovakian People's Party (continued to exist after country's separation), Republican Party (extreme right).
Social Organizations: Czech and Moravian Confederation of Trade Unions; Autonomous Democracy Movement of Moravia and Silesia; groups of activists against economic globalization (INPEG).

THE STATE
Official Name: Ceska Republika. **Administrative Divisions:** 8 regions, 73 districts and 4 municipalities.
Capital: Prague 1,170,000 people (2003).
Other Cities: Brno 382,800 people; Ostrava 320,900; Olomouc 102,800 (2000).
Government: Parliamentary republic. Vaclav Klaus, President since March 2003. Vladimir Spidla, Prime Minister since July 2002. The Parliament of the Czech Republic (Legislature) has two chambers: the Chamber of Representatives, with 200 members, and the Senate, with 81 members.
National Holiday: 28 October, Czech Founding Day (1928); 1 January, Independence (1993, from Czechoslovakia).
Armed Forces: 58,000 (2000).

Denmark / Danmark

Population:	5,385,540
Area:	43,090 km²
Capital:	Copenhagen
Currency:	Kroner
Language:	Danish

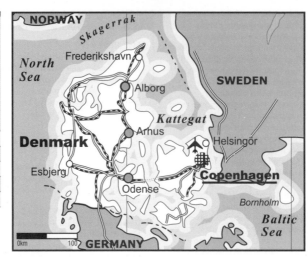

The first hunting peoples established themselves in Denmark in about 10,000 BC as the Neolithic period drew to a close. This was followed by a flourishing Bronze Age civilization, about 1000 BC. Around the year 500 AD, northern Germanic peoples began settling on the islands as fishers and navigators. Certain place names bear witness to the worship of Scandinavian gods, such as Odin, Thor and Frey.

[2] The first evidence of hierarchical society in Denmark comes from the Viking age, mostly from cemeteries and settlement sites. The Vikings were Scandinavian farmers, navigators, merchants and above all raiders who ruled the northern seas between the 8th and 10th centuries AD.

[3] Archeological remains indicate that Roskilde on the island of Sealand, Hedeby, south of Jutland, and Jelling in the north, were the most intensely populated areas. After the Danish victory over the Germans the Eider River became the final southern border. A huge wall was built to the south and west of Hedeby.

[4] In the 10th century, after continuous conflict with rival kingdoms, the center of the kingdom's power was transferred to Jelling, where Gorm became king of Jutland. His son Harald Bluetooth (Blatand) is credited with uniting Denmark and conquering parts of Norway.

[5] Subsequent Viking reigns extended Danish possessions as far as modern-day England and Sweden. In 1397 Queen Margrethe managed to unite Denmark, Norway, Iceland, Greenland, Sweden and Finland in the 'Union of Kalmar'.

[6] The introduction and spread of Christianity and strengthening of the Hanseatic League went hand-in-hand with the weakening of Denmark's military power.

[7] The Danish kings were involved in successive wars between themselves, campaigns which were interspersed with peasant rebellions and bourgeois revolts; a large and powerful middle class had developed as a result of growing mercantile activity. These conflicts ceased in the 17th century, when a weakened nobility gave the King power as absolute sovereign. He was then able to create laws to be imposed throughout the land.

[8] During the 18th century, Denmark colonized the Virgin Islands. The Danish colonists organized local production using African slave labor and in 1917 the islands and their population were sold to the United States. (See US Virgin Islands)

[9] Peace existed in Denmark and Norway from 1720 until the Napoleonic Wars. After Napoleon's defeat, Sweden attacked Denmark and, under the Kiel Peace Treaty, annexed Norway in 1814.

[10] The loss of Norway, combined with British trading impositions brought on an economic collapse which worsened as a result of low wheat prices. The ensuing agricultural crisis forced land reform to a standstill. The situation later improved when agricultural prices stabilized, trade increased and industrialization began. In 1814 an educational reform made schooling obligatory.

[11] After the European revolutions of 1848, King Frederick VII called an assembly which established parliamentary monarchy and abolished absolutism. The 1849 Constitution guaranteed freedom of the press, of religion and of association, as well as the right to hold public meetings. The main trends of the period were nationalism and liberalism.

[12] A territorial dispute with Germany over the Duchies of Schleswig and Holstein reinforced nationalistic sentiment. In 1864, when Denmark was defeated by Prussia and Austria, it lost its claim to these lands and the national-liberal government was brought down.

[13] The 1866 Constitution maintained the monarchy. In 1871, Louis Pio, a former military officer, attempted to form a socialist party. A series of strikes and demonstrations organized by the socialists was put down by the army, and Pio was deported to the US. The Social Democratic Party, mainly supported by intellectuals and workers, was formed in 1876.

[14] The peasants and emerging middle class weakened the monarchy on three fronts: the farm co-operative movement, a liberal bourgeois party (popularly referred to as 'leftist') and the social democrat party. In 1901 the United Left (Liberal) came to power establishing a new government. The emergence of the UL and the Social Democrats as a leading force at the turn of the century was the result of agrarian reform, industrialization and the development of railroads. The growth of urbanization and overseas trade (accelerating the formation of labor unions throughout the country and the rise of co-operatives in the countryside) was the main reason for these changes.

PROFILE

ENVIRONMENT

With an average altitude of only 35 meters above sea level, Denmark is one of the lowest countries in Europe. The land is divided into the mainland - the Jutland peninsula - and the islands (including the islands of Sjaeland and Jelling) which represent one third of the territory. The continental summers are relatively warm and rainy. The land is intensely cultivated, in spite of cold winters. Denmark is a supplier of livestock products and has important maritime activity.

SOCIETY

Peoples: 95.5 per cent of the population is of Danish origin. A German minority lives in Jutland. There are immigrant communities from Turkey (1.5 per cent), Asia (1.6 per cent), Africa (0.3 per cent), former Yugoslavia (0.5 per cent) and other Scandinavian countries (0.4 per cent). There are 250,000 immigrants from different countries.
Religions: 96 per cent of the population belong to the Lutheran Church; minorities of Catholics and Jews.
Languages: Danish (official). English is spoken as a second language.
Main Political Parties: Liberal (Venstre); Conservative People's Party; Social Democratic Party; Socialist People's Party; Danish Nationalist Party; Center-Democrats. Several parties out of Parliament are against joining the European Union.
Main Social Organizations: The Danish Confederation of Trade Unions (LO) has 1,500,000 members (49 per cent women) from 40 different unions; Confederation of Salaried Employees and Civil Servants in Denmark (FTF), 330,000 members; Danish Confederation of Professional Associations (AC), 100,000 members; and the Women Workers' Union in Denmark (KAD).

THE STATE

Official Name: Kongeriget Danmark.
Administrative Divisions: 14 departments (Amtskommuner), Frederiksberg, Copenhague.
Capital: Copenhagen 1,066,000 people (2003).
Other Cities: Århus 645,300 people; Odense 145,200; Ålborg 119,800; Frederiksberg 91,200 (2000).
Government: A constitutional parliamentary monarchy. Queen Margrethe II, since January 1972. Prime Minister, Anders Fogh Rasmussen, since November 2001. Unicameral Parliament: People's Diet, with 179 members, including 2 from Greenland and 2 from the Faeroe Islands.
National Holiday: 5 June, Constitution Day (1953); 16 April, Queen's birthday (1940).
Armed Forces: 33,100 (1995).

Life expectancy	GNI per capita	HIV prevalence rate
76.6 years	**$30,290**	**0.1%** of population 15-49 years old
2000-2005	2002	2001

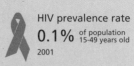

[15] In 1915, the Constitution was revised. The voting age of 35 was maintained, but the right to vote was extended to women, servants and farm hands. There were judicial reforms, bringing in trial by jury, and land distribution in the largest states. Also in 1915 women recovered the right (held since Viking times) to stand for election. The first woman was appointed to the cabinet in 1924.

[16] After the 1870-71 Franco-German War, Denmark adopted a neutral international stance. World War I gave Copenhagen trading opportunities with the warring nations, but also affected its supplies. During World War II Denmark was invaded by Germany, although it officially maintained its independence until 1943.

[17] When Hitler attacked the USSR, Denmark created a volunteer army and outlawed communist activity. The 1943 election was an anti-Nazi plebiscite, with the electorate throwing its support behind the democratic parties. Resistance to the Nazi regime, strikes, and the Government's refusal to enforce Nazi rule, led the German occupation forces to declare a state of emergency dissolving Denmark's police and armed forces.

[18] In September 1943, the Danish Freedom Council was created to co-ordinate the anti-Nazi opposition. When Germany finally surrendered, a transition government was formed, with representatives from the Council and the traditional parties. The 1945 election was won by the liberals.

[19] The Faeroe Islands, under Danish control since 1380, were occupied by Britain during the war and subsequently returned to Denmark. The 1948 Constitution gave the islands greater autonomy, though the Danish Parliament retained control of defense and foreign affairs.

[20] Denmark was responsible for foreign policy and justice of Greenland, a territory controlled by the Danes since 1380. In 1979, the island obtained the right to have its own legislative assembly (*Landsting*), which has power over internal affairs. Other areas are dealt with by the Danish Parliament which has two representatives from the island.

[21] Denmark joined NATO in 1949, increasing its military power with the help of the US. A US proposal for setting up air bases on Danish soil was turned down.

[22] The Constitution was amended in 1953, reducing the Legislature to a single chamber (*Folketing*). In 1954 the post of 'ombudsman' was created to ensure that municipal and national government complied with the law, and to protect

IN FOCUS

ENVIRONMENTAL CHALLENGES
The North Sea is polluted with nitrates and phosphates from vehicle and power plant emissions. Groundwater has been polluted by animal and factory wastes and agrochemicals. In 2003, Denmark imposed a ban on the spraying of glyphosate, the active ingredient in Monsanto's Roundup herbicide, following the release of data which found that it has been contaminating the drinking water resources. The chemical leached through the soil to pollute the groundwater at a rate of five times more than the permissible level for drinking water, according to tests done by the Denmark and Greenland Geological Research Institution (DGGRI).

WOMEN'S RIGHTS
Danish women have been able to vote and be elected in all elections since 1915. In 1924-1925 Nina Bang was the Minister of Education, the world's first female senior minister. In the 1980s women held 23 per cent of all parliamentary seats and in 1982 two women headed the ministries of Labour and Ecclesiastical Affairs.

In the 1990-2000 period, the number of women in Parliament rose from 31 to 37 per cent, and the percentage of ministerial or equivalent positions amounted to 41 per cent, as a result of a quota system that will gradually increase the percentage.

Women make up 46 per cent of the workforce: 2 per cent in agriculture, 83 per cent in services and 15 per cent in the industrial sector.

The trafficking of women from Eastern Europe for sexual exploitation, although widely unseen, is a problem.

CHILDREN
In 2001, children under 18 made up 21.37 per cent of the population, while those under 5 amounted to 6.02 per cent. Low birthweight affects 6 per cent of all newborns*. Approximately 96 per cent of children are immunized against polio, measles and tetanus*.

Save the Children Denmark has reported to the authorities cases of child trafficking and prostitution. In spite of this, the Government has not implemented any remedial policy and lacks official statistics on the topic.

INDIGENOUS PEOPLES/ ETHNIC MINORITIES
The Inuit live on the island of Greenland, with a current population of 44,000. The Danish government expelled them in 1950 from Thule and the US installed a military base there. A Danish court confirmed in December 2003 that the expulsion had been illegal. The Inuit demand the closing of the base and the return of their land; however they lost their case in the High Court in January 2004.

The Faeroese, from the Faeroe Islands, have lived in the area for the last 12,000 years.

There are small groups of Turks, and a larger number of Germans. The Germans' ancestors came to what is now Denmark 11,000 years ago. Today they are seeking greater recognition, access to public and political positions. They are Christian Protestants, and although their

official language is Danish, most of them speak German.

MIGRANTS/REFUGEES
In late 2002, Denmark received some 5,200 refugees and asylum-seekers, mostly from Afghanistan (1,200), Iraq (1,045) and former Yugoslavia (1,030). About 350 people sought asylum in Danish embassies, but it was only granted to 43, mainly Iraqis (23) and Afghans (15).

Overall, Iraqis (890), Afghans (880) and Somalis (650) have the highest acceptance rates for asylum applications.

Denmark, like other European countries, has experienced a growing rate of xenophobia in the last two decades. When the Government decided in August 2002 to repatriate the Somali refugees who insisted on staying, the populist extreme right proposed dropping the refugees by parachute over Somalia.

Immigration has exceeded emigration in the last decades. There are some 250,000 immigrants.

The proportion of foreigners amounted to 4.8 per cent of the population in 1999, compared to 2 per cent in 1984. More than half of all foreign citizens live in metropolitan Copenhagen, and more than one quarter of them come from Nordic or EU countries.

DEATH PENALTY
Abolished in 1978.

*Latest data available in *The State of the World's Children* and *Childinfo* database, UNICEF, 2004.

'ordinary' citizens from the misuse of power on the part of government officials or agencies.

[23] Denmark became the founding member of the European Free Trade Association (EFTA) in 1959. In 1972, 63.7 per cent of the electorate voted yes in a referendum to join the European Economic Community.

[24] In 1986, the Parliament passed a strict environmental protection law which entailed significant costs for industry and agriculture, in a country without nuclear plants.

[25] Marriage between people of the same sex was authorized in 1989. An amendment to the social security system in 1990 enabled parents to take up to 52 weeks' leave in the case of serious illness of a child under 14 years old.

[26] In 1993 the Danes finally approved the Maastricht Treaty, the formation of the European Union,

after rejecting it the previous year, on condition that the country would not join the Economic and Monetary Union.

[27] In 1994, Denmark implemented the UN recommendation to contribute at least 1 per cent of its GDP to development aid.

[28] Social Democratic Prime Minister Poul Nyrup Rasmussen was reelected in 1994, after having been chosen for office the previous year as a result of the fall of the liberal-conservative government which broke refugee laws. Former Justice minister Erik Ninn Hansen had been found guilty of having prevented the family reunion of Tamil refugees from Sri Lanka.

[29] Economic growth reached its peak in 1994, with 4.4 per cent GDP growth and a 2 per cent rise in inflation.

[30] Danish cinema, flourishing since 1910, became internationally

famous in 1995 with movies produced according to the 'Dogma manifesto'. Established by directors Lars Von Trier and Thomas Vinterberg, the Dogma stated that genre movies were not acceptable; that cameras should be hand-held; that sound is incidental and that the final work should not be credited to the director.

[31] Pia Kjaersgaard, leader of the Danish People's Party (DPP), received more than 6 per cent of the vote in the local Copenhagen elections in November 1997. She based her campaign on the 'danger' posed to her country by Third World immigrants. In early 2000, surveys showed the DPP had risen to third place in Danish politics. The party slogan stated: 'Muslims are just as good as us, but they are a problem for a Christian country'.

[32] After 7,000 years of geographic separation, a 16-

Under-5 mortality
4 per 1,000
live births
2002

Maternal mortality
5 per 100,000
live births
2000

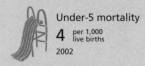

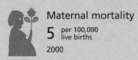

Faeroe Islands

Population: 47,457

Area: 1,400 km²

Capital: Torshvn

Currency: Danish kroner

Language: Faeroese, Danish

ENVIRONMENT

The climate is generally rainy and cloudy, with mild temperatures both in summer and winter. Only 6 per cent of the land is cultivated. Agricultural production mainly consists of vegetables as the land is not suitable for grain. Sheep are raised throughout the islands and there is mining in Suderoy. 20 per cent of the population are employed in handcraft production and 21 per cent in fisheries, which provide 90 per cent of the islands' exports. The Faeroe Islands are one of 10 largest salmon breeders in the world. To protect the fishing industry, a 200-mile zone was established in 1977. Modernization of the island's fishing fleet and methods was financed through a series of foreign loans, which totaled $839 million in 1990 - $18,000 per capita. Maritime oil prospecting was initiated. ■

SOCIETY

Peoples: The population is of Scandinavian origin.
Religions: Lutheran. There are a large number of Baptists and a small Catholic community. **Languages:** Faeroese; Danish.
Main Political Parties: Social Democratic and Union (liberal) parties, which favor ties with Denmark; the Republican 'Left', Popular and Progressive parties, favor independence.

THE STATE

Capital: Torshavn 18,000 people (2003). **Other Cities:** Klaksvik 4,800 people; Runavík 2,500 (2000). **Government:** The parliament (Løgtinget) has 32 members elected based on proportional representation. Parliament names a cabinet (Landstyret) of six ministers. The Prime Minister is Jóannes Eidesgaard (2003). Birgit Kleis (since 2001) is the High Commissioner (Rigsombudsman) who represents the Crown. The islands send two representatives to the Danish Parliament. **Diplomacy:** In January 1974 the Løgtinget resolved not to join the EEC and the aspiration for independence continues. **National Holiday:** 29 July, Olaifest (local holiday). **Armed Forces:** Defense is responsibility of Denmark; no organized native military forces; only a small Police Force and Coast Guard are maintained.

Greenland

Population: 56,963

Area: 341,700 km²

Capital: Nuuk (e-Godhaab)

Currency: Danish kroner

Language: Greenlandic, Danish and Inuit

ENVIRONMENT

Located in the Arctic Ocean, the island is the second largest tract of frozen land on the planet. Nearly four fifths of its surface is covered by an ice cap. In the month of June, soon after the rapid thaw, moss and lichen vegetation appear on certain parts of the coast. Most of the population is concentrated in the western region, where the climate is less severe. The country has lead, zinc, and tungsten deposits. Cryolite from the large reserves in Ivigtut is also exported. Fishing forms the basis of the economy, although fish stocks are approaching exhaustion in national waters, salted and frozen fish is exported, as well as whale oil. The island is encouraging tourism as an alternative source of income, with 35,000 visitors each year. There are highly protective policies on the nordic environment. Its ice covered coastlines are melting at a rate of more than a metre each year. ■

SOCIETY

Peoples: 80 per cent are Inuit. The remaining 20 per cent are Danish or other short-term European residents. **Religions:** Lutheran. The Greenlandic Church comes under the jurisdiction of the Bishop of Copenhagen and the minister of ecclesiastical affairs.
Languages: Greenlandic Inuktitut (Inuit/Aleut language) and Danish (official). There are three linguistic groups amongst the Inuit population; Kalaallit (west coast), Inughuit (north) and Lit (east coast). **Main Political Parties:** Siumut (Forward), social-democratic; Atássut (Feeling of Community), liberal; Inuit Atgatigiit (Eskimo Community), communist; Katusseqatigiit (Independents).

THE STATE

Official Name: Kalaallit Nunaat. **Administrative Division:** 3 districts: Avannaa, Tunu y Kitaa. **Capital:** Nuuk 14,000 people (2003). **Other Cities:** Sisimiut 5,200 people; Ilulissat 4,100 (2000). **Government:** Queen Margrethe II of Denmark, Head of State; Gunnar Martens, High Commissioner since 1995; Anders Fogh Rasmussen, Prime Minister since November 2001. Unicameral Legislature: The *Diet*, with 31 members elected by people for a four-year term. Greenland elects two representatives to the Danish *Folketing*, and has one representative on the Nordic Council. **Diplomacy:** Greenland is not part of the European Union. **National Holiday:** 21 June, Longest Day; 5 June, Danish Constitution (1953). **Armed Forces:** Defense is responsibility of Denmark.

---

kilometer-long bridge and tunnel now connects Copenhagen and Malmo, Sweden, in 15 minutes. The work was opened by King Carl Gustav of Sweden and Queen Margrethe of Denmark, in July 2000.

[33] In a referendum in September 2000, Denmark rejected replacing its kroner with the euro.

[34] In January 2001, Denmark reacted against the independence plan put forward by the Faeroe Islands, which included extending Danish subsidies until 2012. Oil prospects in the islands' sea platform had heightened calls for independence.

[35] In Jutland, the livestock region, Danish farmers complained that the arrival of the Dutch - wealthier than the Danes - had increased the price of land, making it difficult for many to compete. In 2001, ten per

cent of Danish milk was produced in Dutch farms and 60 per cent of the farms on sale were bought by Dutch farmers.

[36] The Liberal party won the general elections in November 2001, after 9 years of Social-Democrat Government. Although no more than 5 per cent of the population is made up of foreigners the Liberals had focused their campaign in the promise of passing tougher immigration laws.

[37] Social reform passed in January 2002 extended parental leave after the birth of a child from 32 to 52 weeks. That month, the Government introduced a bill in Parliament, aiming to reduce the number of asylum-seekers and immigrants. The bill stated that permanent residence would only be granted after seven years and in that period, the applicants would

receive half the value of social benefit entitlements given to Danish citizens. It also said that non-Europeans who wished to marry a Dane should be over 24 and that the Government would have the right to investigate whether or not the couple had relatives or other links in a foreign country. The bill was passed in May, although the UNHCR and the Swedish, Belgian and French governments warned that it contravened human rights laws and international agreements.

[38] The EU-Russia summit was moved from the Danish capital to Brussels in November, in midst of a diplomatic row between

Copenhagen and Moscow regarding Chechen exiles. Russian president Putin had threatened to boycott the summit in Copenhagen when Denmark did not extradite Akhmed Zakayev, a Chechen guerrilla leader.

[39] When US troops detained captured Iraqi president Saddam Hussein (see Iraq) in December 2003, and after President Bush stated that Saddam deserved the death penalty once he was brought to trial in Baghdad, Prime Minister Fogh Rasmussen - who had supported the US invasion of Iraq - stressed his opposition, shared widely among Danes, to the capital punishment. ■

Djibouti / Djibouti

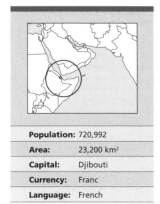

Population:	720,992
Area:	23,200 km²
Capital:	Djibouti
Currency:	Franc
Language:	French

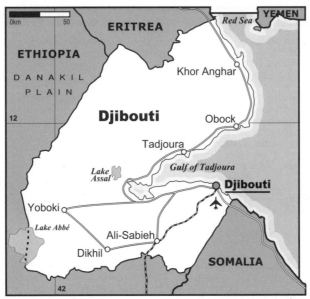

I n about the 3rd century BC Ablé immigrants came from Arabia and settled in the north and parts of the south. The Afars, or Danakil, are descendants of these peoples. Later the Somali Issas pushed the Afars out of the south and settled in the coastal regions. In AD 825 Islam was brought to the area by missionaries. Arabs controlled the trade in this region until the 16th century, when the Portuguese competed for it. In 1862, Tadjoura, one of the Sultanates on the Somalian coast (see Somalia), sold the port of Obock and adjoining lands to the French for 52,000 francs and in 1888 French Somaliland (Côte Français des Somalis) was established.

2   Djibouti became the official capital of this French territory in 1892. A treaty with Ethiopia in 1897 reduced the territory in size. A railway was built to connect Djibouti with the Ethiopian hinterland, reaching Dire Dawa in 1903 and Addis Ababa in 1917. The interior of the area was effectively opened up between 1924 and 1934 by the construction of roads and administrative posts. After World War II Djibouti port lost trade to the Ethiopian port of Asseb (now in Eritrea). In 1946 French Somaliland acquired the status of an overseas territory (from 1967 called the French Territory of the Afars and Issas),

and in 1958 it voted to become an overseas territorial member of the French Community under the Fifth Republic.

3   Independence and the reunification of neighboring Somalia stimulated the emergence of anti-colonialist movements such as the Somaliland Liberation Front and the African League for Independence, both of which used legal and armed branches.

4   During the 1970s, renewed resistance forced acting governor Ali Aref to resign. France called a plebiscite on 8 May 1977, and 85 per cent of the population voted for independence. Hassan Gouled Aptidon, main leader of the African League for Independence,

became President of the fledgling Republic.

5   In an attempt to overcome old ethnic divisions, Gouled granted governmental participation to various groups. He even appointed several Afar ministers. Though French remained the official language, Djibouti was admitted into the Arab League.

6   The new state, created for strategic reasons by colonialism, today transports much of Ethiopia's foreign trade through its port, earning revenue.

7   Ethiopia and Somalia, its two neighbors, both had territorial designs on Djibouti. Ethiopia's interest was geopolitical, because of Djibouti's strategic location as a

route to the Red Sea. When Eritrea gained independence, Ethiopia became a landlocked territory. If an agreement could not be reached for the use of Eritrean ports, Djibouti would be its only available port. Somalia's interest was in unifying the Somali nation.

8   In mid-1979, President Hassan Gouled resumed relations with Ethiopia and Somalia, signing trade and transportation agreements with them. The participation of Afars in the Government and in the newly-formed army was encouraged as a way of securing national unity. Foreign aid was basically used for irrigation works and to improve the situation of refugees from the Ogaden war.

9   After 8 years as an independent country, Djibouti was determined to follow its own path, contrary to earlier expectations that it would be annexed by Ethiopia or Somalia.

10   In spite of a successful performance in diplomatic relations, Gouled faced serious domestic problems, particularly ethnic rivalries between Afars and Issas. Afars, 35 per cent of the population, complained of political and economic discrimination. The Issas, 60 per cent of the population and holding key positions in the Government, refuted all accusations of favoritism, and supported Gouled's radical policies to neutralize the opposition. After the prohibition of the Popular Liberation Movement in 1979, the Afars tried to reorganize as

PUBLIC EXPENDITURE

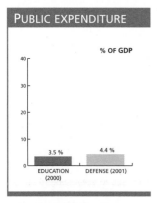

% OF GDP

EDUCATION (2000): 3.5 %
DEFENSE (2001): 4.4 %

PROFILE

ENVIRONMENT

Located in the Afar triangle, facing Yemen, Djibouti is one of the hottest countries in the world (average annual temperature 30° C). The land is mostly desert; its only green area is found in the basalt ranges of the northern region. Extensive cattle-raising is practised by nomads. Economic activity is concentrated around the port.

SOCIETY

Peoples: Djiboutians are divided into two major ethnic groups of equal size: the Afars, scattered throughout the country, and the Issas, of Somalian origin, who populate most of the southern territory and predominate in the capital. There are also French, Yemeni, Ethiopian, Italian, Greek and Pakistani minorities, among others. **Religions:** Sunni Muslims. There is a small Christian minority (5 per cent). **Languages:** Afar and Issa (Somali), French (official) and Arabic (religious). **Main Political Parties:** A constitutional reform in September 2002 established a multiparty system.

Democratic Renovation Party (PRD); Democratic National Party; Union for Presidential Majority. **Main Social Organizations:** Union of Djiboutian Workers (UDT), a national labor federation; Union of Construction and Public Works Workers (SB-BTP).

THE STATE

Official Name: République de Djibouti.
Administrative Divisions: 5 districts.
Capital: Djibouti 502,000 people (2003).
Other Cities: Ali-Sabieh 12,200 people; Tajurah 11,500; Dikhil 9,900 (2000).
Government: Ismail Omar Guelleh, President since May 1999. Dileita Muhammad Dileita, Prime Minister since March 2001. The Prime Minister is traditionally Afar to counterbalance the power of Gouled, who is Issa. The National Assembly has 65 members.
National Holiday: 27 June, Independence Day (1977).
Armed Forces: 9,000 (1997) Other: Gendarmerie (Ministry of Defense): 600; National Security Force (Ministry of Interior): 3,000.

Life expectancy
45.7 years
2000-2005

GNI per capita
$900
2002

Literacy
65% total adult rate
2000

IN FOCUS

ENVIRONMENTAL CHALLENGES
Most of the land is desertified and not suitable for farming. Agriculture, concentrated in oases and some coastal areas, produces only about a quarter of local needs. Drinking water is scarce. A great variety of animal and plant species are in danger due to the encroachment of the desert.

WOMEN'S RIGHTS
Women have had the vote since 1946 and been able to stand for office since 1986. However, only in 2003 was a woman voted into Parliament. In 2000, women were 43 per cent of the 1.1 million workforce; 88 per cent of women worked in services, 1 per cent in the industrial sector and the 11 per cent in other jobs.

Between 45 and 48 per cent of primary and secondary students are women, and only 9 per cent of tertiary students are women. Anemia affects 40 per cent of pregnant women. Some 76 per cent receive prenatal care, and the maternal mortality rate is 730 for every 100,000 births*. Genital mutilation is common.

CHILDREN
Djibouti's under five mortality rate, although it fell 18 per cent in the last decade*, is one of the highest in the world: 143 deaths per 1,000 live births. One of the main causes of infant mortality is polio. Poor access to medicines and lack of skilled birth attendants increase the number of deaths. Some 18 per cent of children under 5 suffer malnutrition or low weight*.

Child prostitution is increasing. According to UNICEF, 73 per cent of streetchildren aged 8-17 are prostitutes. Most are girls who do not speak French, trafficked from Ethiopia.

Since 1995, the Open Doors Association together with the French Government, the police and UNHCR are working to rescue, repatriate and rehabilitate the trafficked children. Some 400 children have been rescued of whom around 65 per cent have been able to rehabilitate into society.

INDIGENOUS PEOPLES/ ETHNIC MINORITIES
The Afar, present in Djibouti and Ethiopia, are a cohesive group. They did not support the 1977 division of their traditional lands between Ethiopia, Djibouti and Eritrea. Their situation has improved over the previous decade. However, in spite of some political reforms, the Somali Issas who belong to the ruling party are dominant. This has caused friction between the two groups.

MIGRANTS/REFUGEES
Currently there are 23,000 documented immigrants and/or refugees; 21,000 from Somalia and 2,000 from Ethiopia. Thousands of non-documented people from neighboring countries live on the outskirts of urban areas. Most Somali immigrants arrived between 1988 and 1990, fleeing from civil war. More than 40,000 Ethiopians arrived during Ethiopia's civil war. Once it ended, in 1996, more than 90 per cent returned, but a small number decided to remain in Djibouti.

DEATH PENALTY
Used for all kinds of offenses.

*Latest data available in *The State of the World's Children* and *Childinfo* database, UNICEF, 2004.

---

the Djibouti Popular Party in 1981, but this was also banned.
[11] In October 1981, President Gouled amended the Constitution to introduce a single-party system. The official Popular Association for Progress (RPP) became the sole legal party and the other groups were banned. It was argued that they had racial or religious aims and in consequence were potentially harmful to national unity.
[12] During 1983, the first steps were taken in a project to radically alter Djibouti's economy and transform it into the Middle East's Hong Kong. The plan included the creation of a financial hub and a free trade port. Six foreign banks opened offices in Djibouti, mainly attracted by a solid national currency backed by dollar deposits in the US.
[13] By the end of 1984, the first results were not encouraging: the number of passengers and goods in transit to Ethiopia and Somalia had dropped considerably and, therefore, customs revenues and bank activities had decreased. The continuing conflict in the area has been seen as the major cause for the withdrawal of European capital.
[14] With the support of the UN High Commissioner, Gouled's Government resumed the voluntary repatriation of more than a hundred thousand refugees, a process which had been interrupted in 1983. At the same time, bilateral agreements were signed with Ethiopia to combat contraband and promote peace in the border areas. These had been closed in 1977, at the outset of the conflict with Somalia over the Ogaden region.
[15] In August 1987, foreign military presence in Djibouti grew as French bases were also used by US and British forces participating in maneuvers in the Persian Gulf.
[16] France wrote off Djibouti's debt in 1990 by granting it $40,000,000 as public development aid. In 1991, confrontations between the Government and the Front for the Restoration of Unity and Democracy (FRUD) guerrillas were renewed. In November, Amnesty International accused the Government of the torture of 300 prisoners.
[17] In the May 1993 presidential elections, Gouled was again re-elected, with over 60 per cent of the vote. However, encouraged by the FRUD, half of the electorate abstained from voting and the opposition considered the elections a 'fraud'.
[18] Armed confrontations between government troops and guerrillas escalated in the weeks following the elections, which led thousands to seek refuge in Ethiopia. Acting as mediator, the French Government sought a cease-fire and negotiations began. Meanwhile, Gouled believed the rebellion was part of a plan orchestrated by Ethiopia.
[19] In June 1994, Gouled and the FRUD jointly decided to end the two-and-a-half year war. That month, a demonstration of mostly Afar residents from the Arhiba district, opposed to the demolition of their homes for 'security reasons', was quelled by the police. The intervention left four dead, 20 injured and 300 arrests, including that of Muhammad Ahmad Issa, United Opposition Front president.
[20] The movement's leaders in October banned Ahmad Dini Ahmad and Muhammad Adoyta Yussuf, another breakaway leader, from holding any 'activity or responsibility' in the FRUD. In 1995, after the Constitution was revised, a section of the FRUD formed an alliance with the ruling party. Dini Ahmad said this alliance amounted to 'treason'.
[21] In mid-1995 under pressure from the IMF, the Government reduced public spending and took measures to increase fiscal income. The following year, the IMF granted Djibouti a $6.7 million credit.
[22] In Addis Ababa, Ethiopia, 17 opponents of the Gouled regime were abducted on 26 September and made prisoners of the Djibouti Government.
[23] On 18 February 1998, despite Djibouti's having signed the African Human Rights Charter, guaranteeing freedom of speech and information, the editor of the bimonthly *Al Wahda*, Ahmed Abdi Farah, and journalist Kamil Hassan Ali were arrested for an article critical of the Government published a year earlier.
[24] April 1999 marked the first time since independence for citizens to vote for a president, with Ismail Omar Guelleh elected by a wide margin. As the second President in the history of the country Guelleh's campaign, centered on promises to alleviate poverty. His political rivals accused him of having assassinated members of the opposition during two decades when he was a key advisor to and director of special police corps.
[25] General Yacin Yabeh Galab, chief of police, led a failed coup attempt in December 2000. The Government and the most radical faction of the FRUD signed a peace treaty in May 2001 that ended the civil war. Ahmad Dini returned to Djibouti after 9 years in exile.
[26] As a first gesture toward the FRUD, Guelleh restructured the Government. However, in spite of previous speculation, no FRUD representative was named among the nine new Cabinet members.
[27] In January 2002, the US installed an anti-terrorist military base for the Horn of Africa in Djibouti, for which it promised to pay $31 million that year.
[28] The 1992 law allowing only three opposition parties to compete with the ruling party expired in September 2002, opening the way for multiparty politics. However, the Government has shown little tolerance for groups and individuals that question the political status quo.
[29] Also in September, Djibouti stressed it would not be used as a base for attacking other countries in the region. Nine hundred US troops were stationed there, supporting the war against terrorism.
[30] In January 2003 the coalition supporting President Omar Guelleh - the Union for Presidential Majority - won the first multiparty elections since independence in 1977.
[31] In May 2003, France agreed to increase its annual payment from $20 to $34 million for its military base of 2,700 troops. ∎

Dominica / Dominica

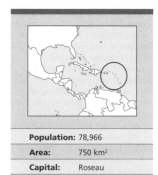

Population:	78,966
Area:	750 km²
Capital:	Roseau
Currency:	EC dollar
Language:	English

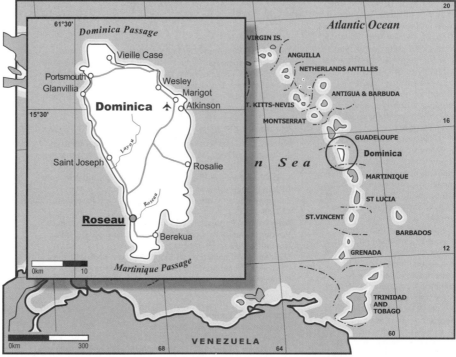

On Sunday, 3 November 1493, Genoese navigator Christopher Columbus reached an island, which he named Dominica. He planted a cross to claim Spanish sovereignty over the newly discovered territory in the name of Queen Isabella and King Ferdinand of Spain.

[2] The indigenous population was rapidly exterminated, as in other Caribbean islands. By 1632 there were only an estimated 1,000 Caribs on the island (see box *Arawaks and Caribs: Genocide in paradise*). Today, there are only 2,000 living in reservations.

[3] The forests were felled to clear the land for sugar plantations, worked by thousands of slaves transported from Africa.

[4] In the 17th century, the Spanish withdrew and the French took their place. They introduced cotton and coffee. In the following two centuries, frequent British attempts to seize the island from French hands culminated in Dominica becoming a British colony in 1805.

[5] French influence still persists. Catholic religion predominates despite strong competition from well-financed Protestant sects, and Creole, the language spoken by the people, is based on French mixed with African languages.

[6] After five centuries of colonization, the Dominicans inherited a rudimentary agrarian economy based on the mono-cultivation of bananas for export. These are the only significant export item, because most of the land went over to banana production when sugarcane became unprofitable at the end of the 19th century.

[7] The political system adopted on achieving internal autonomy in 1967 was a copy of the British model. The Constitution established the 'free association' of the Associated States of the West Indies with Britain. Britain retained responsibility for defense and foreign relations and each member island elected its own state government. The seat of the federal government was in Barbados. The Legislative Council was replaced by the Assembly Chamber; the administrator by the Governor, and the Chief Minister was renamed Prime Minister.

[8] From 1975, independence was negotiated separately by each State. In the case of Dominica the negotiations were conducted by Labor Party premier, Patrick John. In 1978, the British Parliament approved a new statute for the island and on 3 November 1978, exactly 485 years after the arrival of Columbus, Dominica became an independent country once more.

[9] The protest rallies that took place that day were an indication of the difficulties that lay ahead. Two trends became evident with a conservative group of veteran politicians opposed to independence on the one hand, and a progressive sector supported by young people unhappy with the Government on the other.

[10] Since the island lacked the natural resources to attract transnationals and tourism, Dominica could not compete with its neighbors. Many young people emigrated to neighboring Guadeloupe, while others found political inspiration in the US black power ideology.

[11] In May 1979, the police fired at demonstrators protesting against two decrees limiting union activities and press freedom. At the same time, secret agreements between John and the South African regime were revealed. The Dominican premier had helped to plan a mercenary attack on Barbados and intended to supply Pretoria with oil refined in Dominica. Patrick John was forced to resign. His successor, Oliver Seraphine, from the progressive wing of the Labor Party, called elections and strengthened Dominica's ties with progressive neighboring governments.

[12] In the July 1980 election, Mary Eugenia Charles won a landslide victory and became the first woman to head a Caribbean government. In the 1985 election, Charles' Dominica Freedom Party (DFP) obtained 15 of the 21 Parliamentary seats, although the opposition demanded an investigation into a $100,000 donation made by the CIA for alleged government collaboration in the US invasion of Grenada.

[13] The third election since independence was won by the ruling party, which held on to 11 of the 21 seats. The United Workers' Party (UWP), led by Edison James, won 6 seats, while Douglas' Labor Party took the 4 remaining seats.

[14] In 1990, Prime Minister Charles signed an agreement with

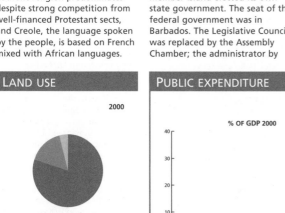

LAND USE

2000

- ARABLE LAND: 4.0%
- CROPLANDS: 16.0%
- OTHER USE: 80.0%

PUBLIC EXPENDITURE

% OF GDP 2000

	HEALTH	EDUCATION
	4.3 %	5.1 %

WORKERS

EMPLOYMENT DISTRIBUTION   **1995/2001**

F
M

AGRICULTURE	F: 31.0%	M: 14.0%
INDUSTRY	F: 24.0%	M: 10.0%
SERVICES	F: 40.0%	M: 72.0%

GNI per capita
$3,180
2002

her counterparts James Mitchell of St Vincent, John Compton of St Lucia and Nicholas Braithwaite of Grenada, for the four islands to form a new state. In the same year the Regional Constitutional Assembly of the Eastern Caribbean was set up. It comprised government officials, religious authorities and representatives from social organizations.

[15] This integration project was in line with the Chaguaramas Treaty, which aimed at the unification of the entire English-speaking Caribbean community, although the three islands of St Kitts, Montserrat and Antigua refused to commit themselves to the process. The opposition parties of Grenada and St Lucia also stated they were against it. The seven mini-States of the Eastern Caribbean have a common Central Bank, which coins their shared currency.

[16] In 1991, the Government decided on a series of measures to stimulate the national economy, centering its efforts on the development of agriculture and communications.

[17] The Prime Minister narrowly escaped censure in April through a motion presented by the United Workers' Party. At the end of 1991, Charles attempted to enact legislation making it illegal for civil servants to protest against the Government.

[18] In April 1994, the Government decision to increase the number of transport vehicle licenses caused protests and public disorder in Roseau. The Prime Minister accused the opposition of trying to bring forward the elections, and the crisis continued until an agreement was signed on May 6.

PROFILE

ENVIRONMENT

The largest Windward Island of the Lesser Antilles, located between Guadeloupe to the north and Martinique to the south, Dominica is a volcanic island. Its highest peak is Morne Diablotin, at 2,000 meters. The climate is tropical with heavy summer rains. The volcanic soil allows for some agricultural activity, especially banana and cocoa plantations.

SOCIETY

Peoples: Descendants of Africans 89 per cent; descendants of Europeans and Africans 7.2 per cent; Caribs living in reservations 2.4 per cent; Europeans 0.4 per cent; Other 0.7 per cent.
Languages: English (official). Creole, a local French patois, with African elements, is widely spoken.
Religions: Roman Catholic 77 per cent; six largest Protestant groups 17.2 per cent.
Main Political Parties: United Workers' Party (UWP); Dominica Freedom Party (DFP); Dominican Labor Party (DLP); Dominica Liberation Movement (leftist).
Main Social Organizations: National Workers' Union; Officials of Dominica Labor Union; Association for the Conservation of Dominica (environmentalist).

THE STATE

Official Name: Commonwealth of Dominica.
Administrative Divisions: 10 parishes.
Capital: Roseau 27,000 people (2003).
Other Cities: Portsmouth 3,600 people; Marigot 2,900; Atkinson 2,500 (2000).
Government: Parliamentary system. Dr. Nicholas Liverpool, President since October 2003; Roosevelt Skerrit, prime minister, replaced Pierre Charles, who passed away in January 2004.
National Holidays: 3 November, Independence Day (1978) and Discovery by Christopher Columbus (1493).
Armed Forces: Commonwealth of Dominica Police Force (includes Special Service Unit, Coast Guard).

[19] That month, Dominica voted against the creation of a whale sanctuary in the South Atlantic. The country was threatened with a tourism boycott from the International Wildlife Coalition. The measure would have seriously affected the island's economy - dependent on tourism - but was not implemented.

[20] In June 1995 the UWP won 11 of the 21 Parliament seats. The new Prime Minister, Edison James, supported the banana industry and privatized state companies to invest in social infrastructure.

[21] In August and September 1995, a succession of hurricanes and tropical storms destroyed the

plantations and crops for export. Houses, bridges, roads and hotels were also destroyed and had to be rebuilt, at great cost.

[22] In October 1998 the Assembly appointed Vernon Lorden Shaw, a retired civil servant, seventh president of Dominica. Shaw promised to boost Dominica's sources of income which had been badly hit by climatic disasters and the global economic crisis. That year, the Government announced plans to make the country into the main supplier of offshore financial services, 'not only in the Caribbean, but in the whole world'.

[23] In February 2000, Rosie Douglas became Prime Minister. That same month, Dominica and Cuba signed a bilateral co-ordination and consultation agreement, to strengthen cultural, social and political co-operation. Cuban-Dominican co-operation on education would extend to tourism.

[24] Douglas died unexpectedly on 1 October, aged 58, and was succeeded by Pierre Charles, leader of the Labor Party. Charles had drawn attention to himself after criticizing the US invasion of Grenada in 1983 and, more recently, the US embargo on Cuba and its intervention in Afghanistan.

[25] In February 2002, Parliament passed a law against money-laundering aimed at allowing foreign investigators to scrutinize offshore bank accounts. In May Charles announced a tight budget to help the economy battered by economic and financial crises, low exports and fewer tourists.

[26] In the October 2003 elections, Nicholas Liverpool was elected President.

[27] The country has no daily papers, and only two independent weeklies. There are no state TV channels, only a private network that broadcasts to part of the island.

[28] In January 2004, Pierre Charles died aged 49. The Labor Party chose former teacher Roosevelt Skerrit, 31, as his successor.

[29] In March, the Government discontinued diplomatic relations with Taiwan, favoring ties with China. Beijing agreed to give aid (worth more than US$100 million over five years) to the country.

[30] In April WRB Enterprises Ltd. bought 72 per cent of Dominica Electricity Services, Domlec. The World Bank tried to discourage the purchase, arguing that it threatened the Government's plans to downsize its budget and address the country's chronic fiscal deficits. ■

IN FOCUS

ENVIRONMENTAL CHALLENGES
Dominica is known as the 'Caribbean Paradise' due to its wonderful scenery and great animal and plant diversity. It has an extended system of protected natural parks, including Boiling Lake, one of the largest cauldrons of volcanic thermal waters in the world.

WOMEN'S RIGHTS
Women have been able to vote since 1951. Nine per cent of Parliamentary seats are held by women, 1 per cent less than in 1990. Local governments have 27 per cent female representation, while 20 per cent of ministerial positions are held by women. Women made up 43 per cent of

the workforce in 2000. Of these, 75 per cent work in services, 11 per cent in agriculture and 14 per cent in the industrial sector.

One hundred per cent of women receive medical care before and during birth*; on average they have 2.1 children*. Between 45 and 48 per cent of primary and secondary students are girls. Only 9 per cent of women reach tertiary level education.

CHILDREN
The mortality rate among children under 5 has fallen 35 per cent in the last decade*. Currently it is 15 per 1,000 live births*. The mortality rate for children under 1 totals 13 per 1,000 live births*. Malnutrition

affects 1.4 per cent of births*, one of the lowest rates in the Caribbean. Some 99 per cent of children are immunized against measles, polio and tetanus*.

INDIGENOUS PEOPLES/ ETHNIC MINORITIES
The indigenous population, the Caribs, were virtually exterminated during the Spanish colonization. Currently there are some 2,000 Carib descendants living in reservations.

DEATH PENALTY
Applied to all kinds of offenses.

*Latest data available in *The State of the World's Children* and *Childinfo* database, UNICEF, 2004.

Dominican Republic / República Dominicana

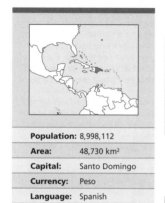

Population:	8,998,112
Area:	48,730 km²
Capital:	Santo Domingo
Currency:	Peso
Language:	Spanish

T he island of Quisqueya is now two countries: Haiti and the Dominican Republic. The first inhabitants belonged to several ethnic groups: the Lucayo, the Ciguayo, the Taino and the Carib. They were fishers and gatherers who practised basic agriculture. There was always a great deal of contact between the Caribbean islands and trade between the groups.

[2] In December 1492 Christopher Columbus reached the island of Quisqueya, which he renamed Hispaniola. With the wood from one of his vessels he built a fort, initiating the European colonization of America. Within a few years, the Europeans had appropriated the whole island, subduing the Carib population. The terrible living and working conditions imposed by the Spaniards nearly exterminated the indians. Faced with this shameful situation, Bishop Bartolomé de Las Casas proposed that they replace local slave labor with Africans, millions of whom were distributed in the centuries that followed throughout the American continent.

[3] Dominican historical records show that in 1523 a group of rebel African slave workers founded the first *quilombo* (former slave settlement) on the island. Subsequent rebel groups, in 1537 and 1548, set up their

own quilombos. The replacement of indigenous labor with African slaves accompanied a change from panning for gold to sugar plantations and extensive cattle raising. As historian Pierre Vilar pointed out, the gold cycle in Hispaniola was destructive, not of raw materials, but rather, of the labor force. During the colonial period the extraordinary economic potential of the Dominican Republic was comparable only with that of Brazil. The island was successively the greatest gold producer in the Antilles; one of the largest producers of sugar in the New World between 1570 and 1630; and finally, such an important cattle producer that there were 40 cattle per person on the island.

[4] 'Santo Domingo is like a microcosm of all American history', said one contemporary historian. 'Its history not only anticipates but also highlights evolutions that in other places occur less noticeably'.

[5] As a major sugar producer with a key position on the trade route from Mexico and Peru to Spain, Hispaniola was coveted by the other colonial powers. In 1586, the English buccaneer Francis Drake raided the capital and in 1697 the French occupied the island's western half. When they were given official ownership under the Treaty of Ryswick, they renamed it Haiti. Later, the whole island fell under French rule but was partially recovered by Spain in 1809, after the first Afro-American republic had been established (in Haiti).

[6] Haiti's government regained control over the whole island in 1822. The Spanish descendants' (*criollo*) resistance came to a head after an uprising in Santo Domingo. The independence of the Dominican Republic was proclaimed, but in 1861 the Government asked Spain to reinstate colonial status, in an attempt to gain support for the criollos, whose dominance was

threatened by the black and mulatto majorities.

[7] However, Spain did not defend its colony effectively and the Dominican Republic became independent again in 1865 after a mulatto uprising. The economic system remained unchanged.

[8] By that time the US, fully recovered from its civil war, began to gain influence in the West Indies. In 1907 the US imposed an economic and political treaty on the Dominican Republic, prefiguring dollar diplomacy, which laid the groundwork for its 1916 invasion. It imposed a protectorate that lasted until 1924.

[9] In 1930, when the country was autonomous again, Rafael Leónidas Trujillo seized power. He was Chief of Staff of the National Guard, elected and trained by the American occupation forces. He set up a dictatorial regime, with US backing, without nominally occupying the presidency. His crimes were so numerous and so apparent that he finally became too embarrassing even for the US, and the CIA planned his assassination which was carried out in May 1961. Trujillo owned 71 per cent of the country's arable land and 90 per cent of its industry.

[10] In 1963, following a popular rebellion, the first democratic elections were held and writer Juan Bosch was elected president. Seven months later, he was overthrown by military officers from the Trujillo regime. In April 1965, Colonel Francisco Caamaño Deñó led a constitutional armed rebellion. Accusing the

WORKERS

UNEMPLOYMENT: 15.9% (2002)

LABOR FORCE 2002

■ FEMALE: 31.4%   ■ MALE: 68.6%

EMPLOYMENT DISTRIBUTION 1995/2001

F

M

■ AGRICULTURE	F: 24.0%	M: 3.0%
■ INDUSTRY	F: 27.0%	M: 20.0%
■ SERVICES	F: 49.0%	M: 77.0%

LAND USE

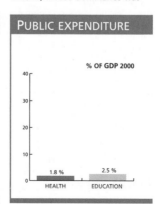

2000

IRRIGATED AREA: 17.2% of arable land

■ ARABLE LAND: 22.7%
■ CROPLANDS: 10.3%
■ OTHER USE: 67.0%

PUBLIC EXPENDITURE

% OF GDP 2000

1.8 %	2.5 %
HEALTH	EDUCATION

Life expectancy
66.7 years
2000-2005

GNI per capita
$2,320
2002

Literacy
84% total adult rate
2000

HIV prevalence rate
2.5% of population 15-49 years old
2001

nationalists of having Pro-Castro (communist) sympathies, the US intervened once again, sending in 35,000 Marines who suppressed the insurgency.

[11] Before leaving the country, the Marines paved the way for a Trujillo supporter, Joaquín Balaguer, to rise to power. In return, he opened the country to transnationals. The sugar industry fell under Gulf and Western control. The corporation also bought shares in local banking, agro-industry, hotels and the cattle industry, becoming very influential.

[12] The nationalist opposition kept up its resistance and in 1973 Francisco Caamaño was killed while leading a güerrilla group. The Dominican Revolutionary Party (PRD), originally led by Juan Bosch, split. The right wing (led by landowner Antonio Guzmán) eliminated the main reformist measures from its program. This action made it acceptable to the State Department and in 1978, when the PRD won the elections, the US used its influence - in the name of human rights - to ensure that the results would be respected.

[13] The PRD program re-established democratic freedoms and popular organizations took advantage of the new situation to reorganize their weakened structures after decades of harsh repression.

[14] New presidential elections were held on 16 May 1981, and Salvador Jorge Blanco became president in the PRD's second successive victory. José Francisco Peña Gómez, one of the Latin American leaders in the Socialist International, was elected mayor of Santo Domingo. On 4 July, departing president Antonio Guzmán killed himself, generating political tension which ended with the announcement of the electoral result.

[15] Blanco tried to tackle the situation by applying IMF-tailored austerity measures. But during 1983, the international price of sugar fell 50 per cent below the cost of production, and sugar accounted for 44 per cent of Dominican exports. In 1984, the Government withdrew the subsidies on several products, and imposed a 200 per cent price increase on staple and medical goods. These measures brought about protest rallies led by leftist organizations and labor unions. In return, the Union headquarters were occupied by soldiers leaving 100 dead, 400 injured and over 5,000 imprisoned.

[16] In 1985, the US reduced its Dominican Republic sugar quota again, causing another decrease in exports. Unemployment rose abruptly. The Government continued to toe the IMF line, harshly repressing all the strikes and protests against its policies. The Dominican Republic Association of Economists noted that since 1980, poverty - which had been limited to the low-income groups - had spread to the middle classes.

[17] For the poorer people, the situation was untenable. Committees for Popular Struggle began to appear and grass roots movements organized to resist price rises on basic goods and services. In April, dockworkers found 28 young Dominican Republic women asphyxiated in a ship's container. They could not find work and had expected to find a way of making a living on another island. It was disclosed that every two weeks a cargo of young women from the Dominican Republic left for the Franco-Dutch island of St Martin, where a brothel manager sold them to other Caribbean islands for between 800 and 1,000 German marks.

[18] Chaotic national elections were held on May 16 1986, with three presidential candidates: Jacobo Majluta for the Dominican Revolutionary Party (PRD), Joaquín Balaguer for the Social Christian Reformist Party (PRSC) and Juan Bosch for the Marxist-inspired Dominican Liberation Party (PLD). Balaguer was elected President by a slight margin, while the opposition claimed there had been fraud.

[19] Clearly a conservative, without a parliamentary majority and faced with highly organized social opposition, Balaguer did not even have the necessary power to impose a more restrictive economic program to get new loans from the IMF.

[20] Balaguer was re-elected in the 16 May 1990 elections. His rival, Juan Bosch, leader of the PLD, accused him of an electoral fraud. The third candidate, PRD's Peña Gómez, suggested a recount at the polling stations. This recount confirmed Balaguer's victory, with 35 per cent, to Bosch's 34 and Peña Gómez' 23. The opposition was not appeased.

[21] From 1990 to 1991 there were hundreds of thousands of Haitian immigrants working as cane-cutters in the Dominican Republic sugar industry. In June 1991, Balaguer expelled them as illegal immigrants.

[22] Negotiations by Balaguer made it possible to refinance the foreign debt. In 1993 tourism grew, making the country one of the most important tourist destinations in the Caribbean.

[23] As a result of the political crisis in neighboring Haiti, contraband goods were taken across the border from the Dominican Republic into Haiti. This practice foiled the international embargo against the Haitian regime. Oil was the main product smuggled into the country.

[24] Economic problems caused hundreds of Dominican Republicans to leave the country each year with forged visas and documents. Many sailed in unseaworthy vessels, bound for Puerto Rico, normally as a

IN FOCUS

ENVIRONMENTAL CHALLENGES
The country lost a significant amount of its forested areas between 1962 and 1980. Coral reefs suffer from pollution and degradation, which significantly reduce the fish population. Eighty per cent of water tables have less water as a result of deforestation and soil erosion; productivity of the land has severely declined.

The country has plenty of surface water, in excess of demand, but there is inadequate infrastructure to deliver enough drinking water; sanitation is also a problem.

WOMEN'S RIGHTS
Since 1942 women have had the vote and been eligible to stand for office. The number of women in ministerial or equivalent positions rose from 4 per cent in 1995 to 10 per cent in 2000; in that period the percentage of women MPs doubled from 8 to 16 per cent.

Of the more than two million people that make up the workforce, 31 per cent are women (75 per cent in services, 14 per cent in industries and 11 per cent in agriculture).

Some 98 per cent of pregnant women receive prenatal medical care, and 98 per cent of births are attended by medical staff*; there are 150 maternal deaths per 100,000 births*.

CHILDREN
38 children under 5 die for every 1,000 live births*. A certain amount of them are underweight. Only 33 per cent of teenagers are aware how HIV/AIDS is transmitted and how to prevent its spread. UNICEF reports that psychological and physical abuse among children, teenagers and women is a serious problem. The country has a large sex industry: Over 25,000 children and teenagers between 12 and 17 are involved in prostitution. Many youngsters are taken to Europe as prostitutes.

INDIGENOUS PEOPLES/ETHNIC MINORITIES
Approximately 11 per cent of the population are descended from Europeans; the rest are of Euro-African origin. There is racial discrimination against blacks.

Haitian immigrants are the poorest social group, earning 60 per cent less than the average. They are under-nourished, do not receive adequate medical care and do not participate in the country s political, social or cultural life. In most cases they work in sugar plantations, under slave-like conditions. They work for $1.5 per day, and in some cases receive no pay. Haitians born in the Dominican Republic are more accepted by society than other Haitians. In 1937, on the orders of dictator Rafael Leonidas Trujillo, the army murdered more than 25,000 Haitians.

MIGRANTS/REFUGEES
There are 700,000 people from the Dominican Republic in the US.

In 2002 the Dominican Republic received 250 asylum-seekers, most from Haiti. At the border refugees are generally allowed to enter the country and request asylum. However, the Government occasionally closes the borders for political reasons.

Dominican Republic authorities estimate that more than 1 million Haitians live in the country, but often some are deported. The few that are granted asylum have to overcome myriad official procedures. The Government regards most Haitians as 'in transit', therefore denying them citizenship. The children of Haitians born in the Dominican Republic are considered citizens.

DEATH PENALTY
Abolished in 1966.

*Latest data available in *The State of the World's Children* and *Childinfo* database, UNICEF, 2004.

Under-5 mortality	Poverty	Debt service	Maternal mortality
38 per 1,000 live births 2002	**<2%** of population living on less than $1 per day 1998	**6.0%** exports of goods and services 2001	**150** per 100,000 live births 2000

stopover on their way to New York.

25 More than a million expatriates live in the United States, and half are illegal. There are also an estimated 20,000 in Spain, half of them illegal. The majority are women who work as domestics, while another 25,000 women work as prostitutes throughout Europe, most of them lured by false promises of employment.

26 Although he had announced his retirement, Balaguer, 87, sought re-election in 1994. His perennial opponent Juan Bosch also ran. To avoid another case of electoral fraud, four of the five participating parties signed a civility pact, with the Catholic Church acting as guarantor. In spite of this, the electoral campaign turned violent, with hundreds of people injured and 12 people killed.

27 International observers were called in to supervise the voting. The PRD condemned the election stating that some 200,000 voters were unable to vote as a result of official party manipulation. According to official figures, Balaguer obtained 43 per cent of the vote, leading Peña Gómez by 1.5 per cent.

28 Peña Gómez and Balaguer agreed to hold national elections on 16 November 1995, and to amend the Constitution to ban presidential re-election. Meanwhile, Balaguer was sworn in as President.

29 On 30 June 1996, Leonel Fernández Reyna of the PLDP won the elections after forming an alliance with the conservative PRSC. On August 18 he succeeded Joaquín Balaguer, who had served seven terms as president.

30 After the election, the PRSC signed an agreement with the PRD giving them control of the Senate, and the PRD dominated the Chamber of Deputies. The PLD remained in a minority in both chambers, preventing the President from implementing several of the initiatives announced in his electoral campaign.

31 Increasing prices, unemployment of more than 30 per cent, and the poverty that affected 70 per cent of the population led to an increase in social tension. There were demonstrations in the streets, some violent. Despite this, the overall economy saw exceptional growth of 6.9 per cent in the first half of the year.

32 A law approved in June allowed private capital to invest in state companies, including the sugar and electricity sectors. The

PROFILE

ENVIRONMENT

The Dominican Republic comprises the eastern part of the island of Hispaniola, the second largest of the Antilles group. The Cordillera Central, the central mountain range, crosses the territory from northwest to southeast. Between the central and northern ranges, lies the fertile region of the Cibao. Sea winds and ocean currents contribute to the tropical, rainy climate. Between 1962 and 1990, the country lost a significant portion of its woodlands. Coral reefs are suffering the effects of pollution, which has harmed marine habitats and reduced fish populations. Hurricanes cause serious damage.

SOCIETY

Peoples: Most are of Spanish and African descent, with a small native American component.
Languages: Spanish.
Religions: Roman Catholic 91.3 per cent; other 8.7 per cent.
Main Political Parties: Dominican Revolutionary Party; Dominican Liberation Party; Social Christian Reformist Party. Minor parties: Strength of the Revolution; Quisqueyano Democrat Party.
Main Social Organizations: Most workers are represented by the General Workers' Union (CGT) and the Unity Workers' Union (CUT). In March 1991, 4 major labor groups, 57 federations and 366 labor unions merged within the CUT.

THE STATE

Official Name: República Dominicana.
Administrative Divisions: 26 Provinces, 1 National District.
Capital: Santo Domingo 1,865,000 people (2003).
Other Cities: Santiago de Los Caballeros 446,800 people; La Vega 416,300: San Pedro de Marcorís 257,700 (2000).
Government: Rafael Hipólito Mejía Domínguez, President since August 2000. Presidential system with a bicameral legislature. Congress of the Republic: a 30-member House of senators and a 149-member House of Representatives, all elected by popular vote.
National Holiday: February 27, Independence Day (1844).
Armed Forces: 24,500 (1995). Other: National Police, 15,000.

Government aimed to thus balance the state accounts.

33 Towards the end of 1997, the Presidents of the Dominican Republic and Haiti agreed to stop the large-scale repatriation of Haitians and to respect human rights. The Haitians often worked in the worst conditions, and so the state sugar company had announced a plan to employ 16,000 Haitian cane-cutters. This cheap workforce was transported from the frontier to the various sugar plantations to work and then taken directly back to Haiti. However, pressure against the arrival of more Haitians did not stop: anti-immigrant protests led to the expulsion of some 2,500 undocumented Haitians and strengthened frontier controls.

34 On 16 April 1998, the Dominican Republic and Cuba restored diplomatic relations. The Government sent a consular representative to Havana, later followed by a delegation of ministers that formally inaugurated the diplomatic headquarters. The US protested

against the measure, deeming it inappropriate.

35 The May 1998 legislative and municipal elections gave a clear advantage to the opposition DRP, which took 83 seats in Parliament and 24 in the Senate. The DLP retained just 49 seats in parliament and 4 in the Senate (120 and 30 members respectively).

36 Fresh disturbances shook Santo Domingo in January 1999 following the outcome of elections for the new president of the municipal league, a body which handled a $100 million budget to aid local governments.

37 The May 2000 elections gave the Presidency to Hipólito Mejía, candidate of the PRD, who received a big enough margin to avoid a second round. Balaguer ended up third.

38 The new President took office in August, promising to create jobs and fight corruption and poverty. In November, a march held by Fernández Reyna to denounce the imprisonment of four members of his government was suppressed by the police. The

former President, who was hospitalized as a result of police tear gas, claimed the prison sentences aimed to incriminate him in corruption cases.

39 In October 2000, the Government refused to extradite seven Haitian police accused of taking part of a plot to destabilize the Haitian Government. Hugo Tolentino Dipp, Dominican Republics Minister of Foreign Affairs, stated the seven would be held in his governments custody.

40 The following year, in May, the Court of Appeals annulled a trial against former President Salvador Jorge Blanco on corruption charges.

41 Since a wave of murders and kidnappings jeopardized the arrival of tourists - one of the country's main sources of income - Mejía sent the army to patrol the streets, seeking to contain crime.

42 In November 2001 an American Airlines plane from New York to Santo Domingo crashed in Queens, US, killing 225 people including many from the Dominican Republic. At first it was thought it might be linked to the 9/11 attacks by al-Qaeda on the US, but this was later dismissed.

43 In July 2002 Balaguer died at 95, having served more than 20 years as President.

44 After months of demonstrations, a general strike took place in November 2003. The police arrested hundreds of demonstrators, and six people were killed. Mejía declared there would be 'no mercy' in the response to public order disturbances.

45 In December 2003, tropical storm Odette forced the evacuation of 10,000 people. Civil defense forces warned the population to leave their homes, but without giving them alternative shelter. The storms are a constant danger, especially for those living near the sea

46 After the new government in Spain announced the pullout of its troops from Iraq, Mejía ordered the withrawal of Dominicans troops in April 2004. Dominican troops were part of the Plus Ultra Brigade, under Spanish command and comprising forces from Honduras, El Salvador and Nicaragua.

47 In May 2004, Mejía was re-elected, winning 72.8 per cent of the vote (52,400 Dominicans were registered to vote in various US cities, as well as in Puerto Rico, Canada, Spain and Venezuela). ∎

Ecuador / Ecuador

Population:	13,378,641
Area:	283,560 km²
Capital:	Quito
Currency:	US dollar
Language:	Spanish and Quechua

The territory now known as Ecuador has been inhabited at least since 2500 BC. The region was largely a border zone influenced by the Nazca, Tiahuanaco-Huari, Chibcha and also Mexica civilizations, among others. It has been suggested that there was contact with peoples of the Pacific, Japanese or Polynesians, though there is still much debate on that point. In the early 15th century AD, the Cara nation, led by the Shiri dynasty, expanded to the north and central Andean foothills. The Cara settled in the Quito kingdom, which was the largest unit of a confederation that left no historical records. In the same era, both the Chimu nation, originating in Peru's northern coastal zone, and the Inca empire began to exert pressure on the Cara and other peoples settled in the region.

[2] In 1478, Inca Topa Yupanqui united the Ecuadorean agricultural peoples. Within a few years the northern region of the Tahuantinsuyu, acquired great economic importance and Quito became its commercial center. But the rivalry for succession between Atahualpa (from Quito) and Huascar (from Cuzco) weakened the power of the Empire (see History of Peru).

[3] The Spanish conquistadors, under the command of Sebastián de Benalcázar, took advantage of the situation to usurp the kingdom of Quito in 1534. In the first era of the colonial period, the territory formed part of the Viceroyalty of Peru and was known as the Real Audiencia of Quito. Crude textiles were the only industry of the Royal District of Quito at the time.

[4] With the reorganization carried out by the Bourbons in 1717, Quito was transferred to the Viceroyalty of Nueva Granada, which comprised present-day territores of Ecuador, Colombia, Panama and Venezuela. In 1809 there was an uprising against the authority of the Crown. In 1822, the armies of Simón Bolívar and Antonio José de Sucre invaded from

Colombia, in support of the patriot rebels. On 24 May of that year, in Pichincha, near Quito, Sucre defeated the Spanish and won the emancipation of Ecuador, which was thus incorporated into Bolívar's Greater Colombia scheme.

[5] In 1830, the Real Audiencia of Quito seceded from Greater Colombia and adopted the name Republic of Ecuador.

[6] In 1895, the Liberal Revolution led by Eloy Alfaro raised the hopes of the majority of peasants for a solution to the agrarian issue. The Church property was nationalized, but the large landowners were not

affected. Alfaro was assassinated in 1912.

[7] In 1914 Ecuador ceded to Colombia the territory between river Caquetá and river Putumayo. In 1916, the elected president - the liberal Alfredo Baquerizo Moreno - promulgated the eight-hour working day.

[8] A military coup led by young officers paved the way for a new reformist period in 1925, but the regime did not survive the world economic crisis of 1929. A period of instability began and saw 23 different presidents from 1925 to 1948.

[9] In 1941, after a brief war with Peru, Ecuador was forced to renounce its claims to sovereignty over an extensive area of the Amazon, losing the province of El Oro. The Peace Protocol signed in 1942 in Rio de Janeiro, with Argentina, Brazil, Chile and the United States as guarantors, established the border between the two countries, but much of it was not demarcated within the territory.

[10] A popular uprising in 1944 ousted President Carlos Arroyo, ushering in a populist government led by José María Velazco Ibarra and consisting of conservatives, communists and socialists, under the name of Democratic Alliance. The Cold War made it impossible for this alliance to continue and soon the left became the target of persecution. In 1962, under pressure from the United States, the government of Carlos Arosemena broke off diplomatic relations with Cuba.

[11] In 1972, Ecuador began to export petroleum, which became the leading sector of the economy, replacing bananas, coffee and cocoa. That same year, the political situation changed, as veteran populist leader Velazco Ibarra was ousted for the fourth time by the armed forces. Under the government of General Guillermo Rodríguez Lara, the country joined OPEC, the state purchased 25 per cent of Texaco-Gulf shares and asserted its rights over the 200 miles of territorial waters when faced with US pressure for fishing interests, leading to what was dubbed the 'tuna war'.

[12] Jaime Roldós, nominated by the Convergence of People's Forces

PROFILE

ENVIRONMENT
The country is divided into three natural regions: the coast, the mountains and the rainforest. More than half of the population lives along the coast, where cash crops of bananas, cocoa, rice and coffee are grown. In the highlands, extending between two separate ranges of the Andes, subsistence crops dominate. In the eastern Amazon region, the exploitation of oil fields generates profits at the cost of environmental destruction. The Colón archipelago or Galapagos Islands belongs to Ecuador.

SOCIETY
Peoples: 65 per cent mestizos, 25 per cent indigenous, 3 per cent Afro-Americans, 7 per cent Indo-European. There are several indigenous nationalities: Huaorani, Shuar, Achar, Siona-Secoya, Cofan, Quechua, Tsachila and Chachi. There are over 1.5 million Quechua living in the inter-Andean valley. **Religions:** Mainly Catholic (95 per cent). **Languages:** Spanish (official), although 40 per cent of the population speaks Quechua and other indigenous languages. **Main Political Parties:** The Social Christian Party (PSC), of Jaime Nebot; the

United Republican Party (PUR), conservative; the Ecuadorean Roldosista Party; the Democratic Left, social democratic, affiliated to the Socialist International; the Conservative Party. **Main Social Organizations:** The Ecuadorean Central Organization of Class Unions (CEDOC), and the Central Organization of Ecuadorean Workers (CTE) are coordinated with the United Workers' Front (FUT); Confederation of Indigenous Nationalities of Ecuador (CONAIE); University Students Federation of Ecuador (FEUE).

THE STATE
Official Name: República del Ecuador. **Administrative Divisions:** 22 Provinces. **Capital:** Quito 1,451,000 people (2003). **Other Cities:** Guayaquil 2,627,900 people; Cuenca 271,400; Machala 211,300 (2000). **Government:** Lucio Gutiérrez, President since January 2003. One-chamber parliament: National Congress with 82 members. **National Holidays:** 24 May, Independence (1822); 10 August, First Shout of Independence of Quito (1809). **Armed Forces:** 57,100 troops (conscripts). 100,000 reserves (1996). Other: 200 Coast Guard and 6 coastal patrol units (1993).

Life expectancy
70.8 years
2000-2005

GNI per capita
$1,450
2002

Literacy
92% total adult rate
2000

HIV prevalence rate
0.3% of population 15-49 years old
2001

(CPF) and the People's Democratic Party, became president in August 1979. Ecuador renewed diplomatic relations with Cuba, China and Albania. The Government also initiated a program aimed at integrating marginalized rural and urban populations. However, it encountered a hostile Congress, as well as US opposition to its human rights policies and its antagonism to the dictatorships that were ruling South America.

[13] Toward the end of January 1981, the Five Day War broke out between Ecuador and Peru, with skirmishes along borders which had not been clearly delineated by the 1942 Protocol.

[14] Roldós died in a suspicious plane accident in 1981. The 1984 election was won by León Febres Cordero of the Social Christian Party, a conservative who promoted free-enterprise policies and supported US President Reagan's Central America policies. From 1988 the Social Democrat Rodrigo Borja held power before conservatives regained the presidency in the shape of Sixto Durán Ballén of the United Republican Party.

[15] In the following decade, the Durán Ballén government promoted privatization of state companies and rigid structural adjustment; however, the economy did not improve, a factor which aided the populist Abdala Bucaram into power. He was later deposed following massive price rises on essential services (and after being declared 'insane' by parliament) and Jamil Mahuad took office in his place.

[16] In 1990 the indigenous people's movement erupted onto the political stage for the first time. The Confederation of Indigenous Nationalities of Ecuador (CONAIE) campaigned for the 1997 Constitution to recognize the pluri-cultural and multi-ethnic nature of the State (and, therefore, the right of indigenous people and Afro-Ecuadorians to participate in equality), and there were seven large demonstrations.

[17] Amidst nation-wide demonstrations, Mahuad announced the economy would be pegged to the dollar, precipitating an indigenous uprising. Parliament and Government buildings were invaded, with the support of military groups. A government council formed by representatives of the army, judicial power, indigenous people and unions, was well received by the population. However, pressure from the US, led to the arrest of the insurrectionist soldiers - among which was the current president Lucio Gutierrez. Mahuad was replaced by Vice-President Gustavo Noboa, an Opus Dei (right-wing Catholic organization) militant, who implemented the dollarization of the economy.

[18] In 2000, the Government signed an agreement with UNICEF aiming at reducing the level of teenage pregnancy in the country - the highest in Latin America. For adolescents in rural areas, pregnancy was seen by some as a way of getting a monthly poverty allowance of $10, granted by the State to single mothers.

[19] On 20 February 2002 indigenous groups from Sucumbios and Orellana, two provinces from the Amazonian northeast, demanded that oil production in the country be stopped and began a strike. The trigger for the protests was the new pipeline for crude oil built by the consortium OCP Ecuador Inc. The provinces demanded that the Government pressure OCP company to give $10 million to be used in social programs in compensation for the damage caused by their works.

[20] The strike ended on 4 March, with three people dead and several injured and arrested. There were also losses of almost $3 million as a result of the break in oil production.

[21] Lucio Gutiérrez (a Colonel retired from the army after an amnesty for military and political crimes committed during the insurrection against Mahuad and confessed admirer of the Venezuelan President Hugo Chávez) and the Banana tycoon Alvaro Noboa - who claimed to be a central liberal and was considered the richest man in the country - were the two candidates that made it to the second round of the presidential elections that were held on 24 November. Gutiérrez, who had received more than half of the votes in the first round, finally became president after polling 54.3 per cent of the votes. Gutiérrez had pledged to fight corruption and to provide cheap housing and free health care during his campaign.

[22] In October 2003 the trial began of a Chevron-Texaco subsidiary. The company was accused of destroying large areas of rainforest and contaminating land and rivers in Sucumbios province.

[23] Angel Shingre, an activist campesino leader, was kidnapped and murdered in Orellana on 4 November. Since he had been active in the Chevron-Texaco trial, the transnational corporation's directors became the main suspects. However the crime was not resolved.

[24] During the same month, Lucio Gutierrez was accused of accepting money for his political campaign from people linked to drug-trafficking. This prompted the resignation of his entire Cabinet and the resignation of Napoleon Villa, head of the ruling Patriotic Society Party and Gutierrez's brother-in-law. ■

IN FOCUS

ENVIRONMENTAL CHALLENGES
In the coastal region, 95 per cent of the woodlands have been felled. Soil depletion and consequent desertification has increased by 30 per cent over the last years. Oil companies cause serious pollution, especially in fragile areas like the Galapagos Islands.

WOMEN'S RIGHTS
Although Ecuador was the first Latin American country to grant the vote to literate women (1929), it did not became universal until 1967.

In 2000, women held 17 per cent of parliamentary seats and 26 per cent of ministerial positions, an increase of 20 per cent in 5 years. They were 28 per cent of the labor force. Two per cent worked in agriculture, 14 per cent in industry and 84 per cent in services.

The illiteracy rate for women over15 was 10.1 per cent in 2000*, half the 1980 rate. Maternal mortality is higher in indigenous areas, where only 20 per cent of births take place in health centers.

CHILDREN
According to UNICEF, social public investment doubled between 1999 and 2003, which increased coverage of child immunization (by 25 per cent), school scholarships, school feeding and nutrition programs for children.

However, nearly 70 per cent of children live in poverty. Approximately 430,000 children work. Malnutrition affects 15 per cent of under-5s and childhood development programs reach only 8.4 per cent of children*.

Boys and girls have equal access to education, but indigenous and afro-Ecuadorean children do not: 90 per cent of these live in poverty and only 39 per cent complete primary school.

Seven out of 10 children under one year old are anemic. HIV/AIDS has not reached pandemic levels, but its incidence has increased seven-fold since 1990. By the end of 2001, it is estimated that 660 children between 0 and 14 years old were HIV-positive, and that 7,200 children were AIDS orphans.

INDIGENOUS PEOPLES/ ETHNIC MINORITIES
The Afro-Ecuadoreans (10 per cent of the population) live on the northern coast, mainly in the province of Esmeraldas. They first arrived in the country as slaves; in 1851 slavery was abolished and they started to control the political and economic life of the regions they inhabited. Nowadays, they are poor and suffer social discrimination.

Ecuadorean Coastal and Sierra Indians represent 28.5 per cent of the population, mostly mestizos (55 per cent). While Sierra Indians produce food for domestic markets, Coastal Indians mainly work in export agriculture.

Although there is still political and economic discrimination against indigenous peoples, the mobilization of Ecuador's indigenous groups is remarkable. These communities are supported by international organizations.

MIGRANTS/REFUGEES
In 2002, it was estimated that Ecuador hosted 9,100 refugees. All but 126 people were Colombians: most of those who arrived were fleeing civil war. In 2002, the number of asylum applications by Colombians in Ecuador increased significantly, to 500 per month.

The Ecuadorean Government and people have welcomed Colombians with fewer restrictions than Venezuela and Panama: they enjoy all rights accorded to any foreigner and they can even apply for citizenship. Undocumented Colombians usually live in towns like Ibarra, Santo Domingo de los Colorados, and Lago Agrio. According to an article published in 2002 by the *New York Times*, it is estimated that more than 200,000 Colombians have entered Ecuador in recent years and are still there.

Ecuador's population is, at the same time, traditionally emigrant. Ecuadoreans represent the second largest South American group in the US, after Colombians. Throughout the 1970s, emigration to US grew at an annual average 8.5 per cent, increasing even more during the 1980s and 1990s. It is estimated that 531,987 Ecuadoreans left the country between January 1992 and April 2001 and did not return. In 2002, Ecuador received $1,400 million by way of remittances.

DEATH PENALTY
It was abolished in 1906.

*Latest data available in *The State of the World's Children* and *Childinfo* database, UNICEF, 2004.

Discrimination in Latin America

LATIN AMERICA and the Caribbean are home to some 40 million indigenous peoples, amounting to almost nine per cent of the regional population of close to 500 million. They live in all the region's countries except Uruguay, where they were exterminated in the 19th century. Today, over 90 per cent of the region's indigenous population is concentrated in just six countries. The one with the largest indigenous population is Mexico (with 12 million), followed by Peru (9 million), Guatemala (5.3 million), Bolivia (4.5 million), Ecuador (4 million) and Chile (1 million). The Afro-descendant and indigenous population of Latin America endured centuries of exclusion and today the vast majority live in poverty. The black and mestizo people number 150 million, equivalent to 30 per cent of the regional population. The mestizo population is concentrated in Brazil (50 per cent), Colombia (20 per cent) and Venezuela (10 per cent).

Compared with the white population, the African descendants and indigenous peoples have very poor access to health, education, employment, justice and political participation. In many cases, they have lost their main basic means of survival, their land and natural resources. This is the reason why, for several decades, they have been moving to the cities in the hope of a better life. But sadly often all they find are precarious and badly paid jobs which are dangerous and even life-threatening.

According to the Economic Commission for Latin America and the Caribbean (ECLAC), the 'progressive loss of lands and the rupture of community economies' are two of the main factors that contribute to poverty in these countries.

The health of the minority groups is significantly worse than that of the general population, because of inadequate diets and lack of basic medical services. In many of the region's countries, big development projects often have negative effects on indigenous populations. The indiscriminate clearing of natural forests, oil extraction and the construction of dams and reservoirs have brought devastation to many communities.

Education is another area where minority people lose out. In Ecuador, for example, only 53 per cent of the indigenous population has access to primary education, 15 per cent to secondary education and barely one per cent to university.

'In Latin America there are no clear plans or government policies to address the poverty of 40 million indigenous peoples that survive in the region', said the statement issued by the First International Indigenous Summit of the Americas, held in Mexico in October 2000.

The indigenous communities allege that governments, politicians and candidates for public office only address indigenous issues when they talk about extreme poverty, and do not have plans or policies to respond to their demands and needs, such as respect for their territories, protection of biodiversity and full recognition of their rights.

BRAZIL'S CASE

The Afro-descendants and mestizos are not much better off than indigenous peoples in this region. In Brazil, for example, the Afro-descendant population suffers more intensely the problems of unemployment, low salaries and lack of access to key political positions. Discrimination is also reflected in the unequal distribution of income. The UN Committee on the Elimination of Racial Discrimination advised the country to end the inequalities that affect Afro-descendants, mestizo and indigenous peoples, and requested more studies to evaluate the situation.

In Brazil too, this group of people is more seriously affected by illiteracy. Commonly they are not aware of their rights, in particular of their democratic right to vote and be elected to public office. On the other hand, the State has neither granted indigenous people the 'effective possession' of their lands, nor verified their numbers or their needs for the provision and supervision of resources and development of their lands.

It is vital that all Latin American states amend their constitutions to incorporate the recognition of ethnic and racial diversity, as laid out in the ILO Convention 169. This has already been ratified by Bolivia, Colombia, Ecuador, Guatemala, Costa Rica, Honduras, Paraguay, Mexico and Peru.

THE AMAZON AND EXTINCTION

However, the bleak truth is that even if governments and laws were to guarantee the existence of the isolated indigenous groups still living in the Brazilian, Ecuadorian and Peruvian Amazon forest and in Paraguay's Chaco region, it may already be too late. Their path to extinction appears to be mapped out already, since these isolated communities are facing a cultural genocide.

According to the 1992 UN study, *Amazonia without myths*, when the Europeans arrived in the Americas, the Amazon region was home to some 2,000 indigenous groups that amounted to about 7 million people. More than five centuries later, after slavery and exploitation, persecution, and European diseases to which local people had no immunity, less than 400 groups and only about 2 million individuals remain. Of these, less than 5,000 still shun contact with 'civilization'. ∎

Egypt / Misr

Population:	74,878,313
Area:	1,001,450 km²
Capital:	Cairo (Al-Qahirah)
Currency:	Pound
Language:	Arabic

Six thousand years ago, a civilization began to form in the Nile valley (Nahr-an-Nil) and developed into a centralized state. Around 6000 BC, Pharaoh Menes, from Upper Egypt, united the two kingdoms - Upper (south) and Lower (north) Egypt - that coexisted for some time.

2 A powerful and centralized empire arose in the third millennium BC (the Ancient Empire); during those times Egypt carried out several successful military campaigns against the Nubians and the Libyans, beginning a prosperous sea trade. The Ancient Empire saw its demise with the collapse of the central authority during the Sixth Dynasty, due in large part to widespread famine.

3 The Third Dynasty developed the practice of constructing monumental tombs for the monarchs, the Pharaohs. These monuments or pyramids, also built for members of the elite, and the funeral ceremonies of the poor were closely linked to the belief in life after death. The pyramids and the decorated walls of the pharaonic tombs, the creation of a complex writing system and broad knowledge of medicine and agriculture are just a few examples of the level of civilization achieved by Egyptian society.

4 Egypt reached its height of power, wealth and territorial

LAND USE

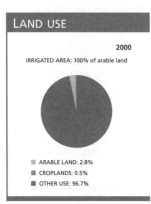

2000

IRRIGATED AREA: 100% of arable land

- ARABLE LAND: 2.8%
- CROPLANDS: 0.5%
- OTHER USE: 96.7%

dominance around 1500 BC. Reconverted into a military state, Egypt launched a series of campaigns to win control of Palestine, Syria and the north of the Euphrates. Territorial expansion led to the development of a complex diplomatic system of alliances and treaties.

5 In the last millennium BC, the decline of this remarkable civilization opened the way to foreign Pharaohs (Libyan and Sudanese dynasties). Toward the end of the 20th dynasty, the weakening of the Pharaohs led to renewed division between Upper and Lower Egypt and, after the Persian Cambises deposed the Pharaoh, the territory formed part of other empires (Persian, Greek and Roman).

6 During the period of Greco-Roman domination, Alexandria (Al-Iskandariyah) was one of the most influential cultural centers in the classical world, and its famous library was the largest until it was burned down in Julius Caesar's time. It brought together the most outstanding philosophers, scientists and scholars of the era. In 642 AD, when the Arabs conquered the country, little remained of its highly developed past and the Egyptians adopted Islam and the Arabian language.

7 Three centuries later, under the government of the Fatimid Caliphs, the new capital, Cairo (Al-Qahirah), became one of the major intellectual centers in the Islamic world and scholars, particularly African Muslims, were attracted by its university.

8 Between the 10th and 15th centuries, Egypt benefited from its geographic location, becoming the trade center between Asia and the Mediterranean. The Venetians and Genoese came to trade here, and even the constant warfare provoked by the European Crusades in Palestine, in the 11th to 13th centuries, did not stop active trade.

9 Once the Crusaders were driven out, it seemed that Egypt would naturally become the center of the ancient Arab empire. However the Sultanate of the Ottoman Turks was the rising power in the Islamic world at the beginning of the 16th century, and it soon conquered Egypt. The opening of the sea route between Europe and the Far East had already put an end to Egypt's previous trade monopoly, reliant on its dominion over the Red Sea, and Egypt had begun its economic decline.

10 Until the 19th century, Turkish domination was little more than nominal and the real power lay in the hands of Mameluke leaders. In 1805, Muhammad Ali, an Albanian military leader, took power. He forcibly eliminated local Mameluke leaders, established a centralized regime, reorganized the army, declared a state monopoly on foreign trade of sugarcane and cotton and achieved increasing autonomy from the Sultan of Istanbul, laying the foundations of a modern economy.

11 The economy was poorly managed by Muhammad Ali's successors, the crisis deepened and dependency on Europe increased. In 1874, Egypt was forced to sell all its shares in the Suez Canal, built as a joint Egyptian-French project between 1860 and 1870, to pay its debts to the British.

12 The situation continued to deteriorate, loans piled up and in 1879 the creditors imposed a Bureau of Public Debt formed by three ministers, one English, one French and one Egyptian. This bureau assumed the management of the country's finances.

13 This degree of interference awakened an intense nationalistic reaction, supported by the army. That year, the military overthrew Muhammad Ali's successor Khedive Ismail, forcing his son, Tawfiq, to expel the foreign ministers and appoint a nationalist cabinet. The colonial power reacted promptly: in 1882 English troops landed in Alexandria, seizing military control of the country.

14 The occupation was 'legalized' in 1914, when Egypt was formally declared a protectorate. The British installed King Fuad I on the throne in 1917. This situation continued until 1922, when an Egyptian committee in London negotiated their independence. But as before, despite the nominal independence, the British retained control.

15 In 1948 the state of Israel was created in Palestine and Egypt and other Arab nations launched an unsuccessful war against the new state, and the frustration of defeat brought about massive demonstrations against the royal government. Against a background of widespread government corruption, a nationalist group known as the 'Free Officials' was formed within the Egyptian Army, led by General Mohammed Naguib and Colonel Gamal Abdel Nasser.

16 On 23 July 1952 this group ousted King Faruk and, in June 1953, proclaimed a Republic. Three years later, Nasser became President.

17 The new regime declared itself nationalist and socialist, deciding to improve the living conditions of the *fellahin*, the country's impoverished peasants. Land reform was started, limiting the landowners' monopoly of the majority of the land.

18 The Government's reform program gave priority to the construction of the Aswan dam, one of the world's largest dam projects. The construction was carried out by the Soviet Union, after the Western powers had refused to take it on. The dam, which had been hailed as the key to the country's industrialization and 'development', in fact caused serious environmental disruption.

19 In 1955, Egypt was one of the leading organizers of the Bandung Conference, a forerunner neutralist Afro-Asian movement which preceded the Movement of Non-Aligned Countries. Twenty-

Life expectancy
68.8 years
2000-2005

GNI per capita
$1,470
2002

Literacy
55% total adult rate
2000

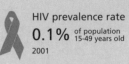
HIV prevalence rate
0.1% of population 15-49 years old
2001

nine Afro-Asian countries condemned colonialism, racial discrimination and nuclear armament.

[20] In October 1956, after the nationalization of the Suez Canal, French, British and Israeli troops invaded Egypt. The Government responded by distributing weapons to civilians. A diplomatic battle was also launched; as a result of UN intervention and joint US-Soviet disapproval, France, Britain and Israel were forced to withdraw and the Canal finally came under Egyptian control.

[21] After Nasser's re-election in 1965, Egypt gave high priority to the conflict with Israel. However, its attempt to economically paralyze Israel by blockading the Gulf of Aqaba failed during the Arab-Israeli conflict, the 'Six-Day War' of June 1967. This ended in another defeat of the Arab countries - Egypt, Syria and Jordan - when Israeli forces occupied the Sinai Peninsula, the Gaza strip, the West Bank, and the Syrian Golan Heights. The cost of the war aggravated Egypt's financial problems.

[22] Gamal Abdel Nasser died in 1970, and Vice-President Anwar Sadat, a member of the right wing of Nasser's Arab Socialist Party, took his place. Sadat put the *infitah* into practice. This was a government plan that meant an opening to Western influence, the de-nationalization of the Egyptian economy and the end of the one-party system. Furthermore, the new Government broke off relations with the Soviet Union and US economic and military aid flowed into Egypt.

[23] In 1973, Egyptian troops crossed the Suez Canal to bring to an end Israeli occupation of Sinai, beginning the fourth Arab-Israeli war. The brief war led OPEC to substantially increase oil prices. This move did not produce the desired effect, and Israel retained the rest of the occupied territories.

[24] Substantial price rises and unemployment worsened the living conditions of workers and resulted in massive anti-government demonstrations in 1976 and 1977. Peasants rebelled against the land redistribution of 1952, and the Islamic parties began to conspire openly against Sadat, accusing him of paving the road for a new period of foreign domination.

[25] Sadat's visit to Jerusalem in November 1977 raised a wave of protest in the Arab world. The process of rapprochement with Israel reached its apex in March 1979, with the signing of the Camp David Agreement, wherein the US negotiated the return of Sinai to Egypt. From then on, Egypt became the main beneficiary of US military aid, aimed at turning the country into the new US watchdog in the Arab World, as Shah Pahlevi of Iran had recently been deposed.

[26] In October 1981, Sadat was killed in a conspiracy organized by sectors of the military opposed to infitah and the repression of fundamentalist Islamic movements. Vice-President Hosni Mubarak became President on 14 October.

[27] Mubarak ordered an inquiry into the wealth accumulated by the Sadat family in an attempt to neutralize the general discontent. He also extended further concessions to foreign companies.

[28] There were some improvements in Egyptian foreign affairs during 1984. Egyptian diplomacy managed to overcome the most adverse reactions to the Camp David agreements. Their new position on the Palestinian question argued that any fair settlement of the Middle East crisis had to contemplate the rights of the Palestinian people and that Arab solidarity was 'the only way to recover the usurped rights'.

[29] Between 1980 and 1986 there was a dramatic increase in the role of foreign capital in the national economy and US aid continued to be a very important source of income. The Government received almost $3 billion per year, $1.3 billion of which was spent on defense. The IMF granted a further $1.5 billion loan in October 1986. Foreign debt increased from $2.4 billion in 1970 to $35 billion in 1986; the military debt increased sevenfold.

[30] In August 1990 Iraqi troops invaded Kuwait; Egypt was among the first Arab countries to condemn the action, sending troops to the Gulf immediately. When the land offensive started in January 1991, the US announced the cancellation of the Egyptian military debt, which amounted to $7 billion.

[31] In May 1991, the IMF approved a stand-by loan of $372 million to Egypt, conditional on an economic 'structural adjustment plan'. Cairo committed itself to privatizing State-run companies, to eliminating controls on production and investment and to reducing the current fiscal deficit from 21 per cent to 6.5 per cent of the

IN FOCUS

ENVIRONMENTAL CHALLENGES
Egypt suffers periodic droughts, earthquakes, floods and sandstorms. The main environmental problems are the unchecked growth of the cities which has swallowed up fertile lands, leading to soil erosion and water pollution.

WOMEN'S RIGHTS
Egypt women have been able to vote and be elected since 1956. In 2000, they held 2 per cent of seats in Parliament and 6 per cent of ministerial positions.

Women were 30 per cent of the labor force in 2000. That year, female unemployment reached 19.9 per cent. 35 per cent of women worked in agriculture, 9 per cent in the industrial sector and 56 per cent in services.

In 2000, 53 per cent of pregnant women received prenatal care. In 1995, 34 per cent of women were victims of physical violence.

It is estimated that 97 per cent of Egyptian women have been subjected to genital mutilation, which has been banned since 1996. According to an study conducted by AFROL (African News Agency) in 1997, 86 per cent of girls between 13 and 19 years old have been circumcised in this way. The local UNDP is supporting a campaign in 60 villages of Upper Egypt to stop the practice.

CHILDREN
In the last decade, there have been achievements in child rights. In 2002 the infant mortality rate and under-5 mortality rate were halved, reaching 35 and 41 for each 1,000 born alive, respectively.

Net primary school enrolment ratio has been increasing: from 86 per cent in 1990 to 96 per cent in 2001/2002. Child labor is yet a high impact problem, while the number of boys and girls who work and do not attend school in Upper Egypt is disproportionately higher than elsewhere in the country.

INDIGENOUS PEOPLES/ ETHNIC MINORITIES
Although not ethnically distinct from other Egyptians, the Copts - the Egyptian Christians (9 per cent of the population) - are politically weak and have suffered persecution. They live mainly in Alexandria, Cairo and urban areas in Upper Egypt. Most belong to the Coptic Orthodox Church. Although they are an economically advantaged group, they receive little public spending and feel discriminated against, for example in getting university places, and in marriage, divorce and inheritance laws (based on Islamic practice). During the 1990s they were victims of attacks by Muslims.

The Nubians inhabit the Upper Nile valley. They are considered descendants of the ancient Kush kingdom and the Kushite dynasty. In the 1960s, several Nubian homelands were flooded when the Aswan dam was built and about 100,000 Nubians had to leave. They emigrated to the north of Aswan, Sudan, Uganda and Kenya.

The Bedouin people (1,300,000 or so, who speak Badawi) migrated to the Sinai peninsula, while others now live along the northern edge of the Sahara Desert.

The 5,800 Berbers, whose language is Tamazight, are dispersed throughout the country.

MIGRANTS/REFUGEES
At the end of 2002, Egypt hosted 80,000 refugees and asylum-seekers (50,000 Palestinians, 20,000 Sudanese, nearly 7,000 Somalis, and more than 3,000 refugees from other countries). Most Palestinian refugees were displaced from the West Bank and Gaza by the 1967 Arab-Israeli war.

Egypt is not a signatory to the UN Refugee Convention and has no domestic asylum laws. In 2002, the Government allowed UNHCR to determine the refugee status of asylum-seekers. UNHCR granted refugee status to 5,000 people during that year, and 19,000 cases remained pending (most of them Sudanese applications).

More than 3,000,000 Sudanese lived in Egypt in 2002. Until the late 1980s, Egyptian law made migration from Sudan to Egypt easy, but as a result of the large registered migration throughout the following decade, the authorities limited their numbers.

Over 2,000 Egyptians were seeking asylum in Western countries like the US, Canada and Australia.

DEATH PENALTY
It is in force for all types of crimes. In 2002, of the 22 people that were sentenced to death, 17 were executed.

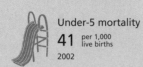
Under-5 mortality
41 per 1,000 live births
2002

Poverty
3.1% of population living on less than $1 per day
2000

Debt service
8.9% exports of goods and services
2001

Maternal mortality
84 per 100,000 live births ▪
2000

GNP. In order to achieve these goals the Government decided to cut back subsidies on basic products and to reduce the program of aid for the needy.

32 That year, foreign minister and deputy minister Esmat Abdel Meguid was named the new secretary-general of the Arab League. Coming upon the heels of the return of Arab League headquarters to Cairo (from Tunis) this appointment meant Egypt's recovery of its leadership role within the Arab world.

33 Islamic fundamentalists began to rebel, seeking the country's conversion into a Theocratic State. These groups had been fighting against Mubarak's government for ten years. The Government extended the state of emergency and executed 15 people in 1993.

34 In 1995, Mubarak still could not find a solution to the confrontation with the Islamic Fundamentalists. In January, Interior Minister al-Alfi met the Ministers of Internal Affairs of the Arab countries in an attempt to coordinate the fight against violent Islamic movements.

35 The ruling National Democratic Party won the 1995 parliamentary elections amidst violence and allegations of fraud.

36 In July 1996 the Health Minister banned female circumcision - the removal of the clitoris or part of it and/or the sewing together of the vaginal labia - a practice common in some regions of the country.

37 Attacks by armed Islamic groups continued throughout 1996 and 1997, along with government repression of all such groups, including those opposed to the use of violence, like the Muslim Brotherhood. By early 1998 an estimated 1,251 people had fallen victim to attacks and political killings, whilst the estimated number of political prisoners was between 10,000 and 30,000.

38 There was heated parliamentary debate in March 1999 over decrees on female circumcision. The rulings continued to provoke resistance in the traditionalist sectors.

39 The Parliamentary discussion over the status of women was resumed in January 2000. The Government had put forward an amendment to family law that authorized women to file for divorce and allowed them to leave the country without their husband's consent. The reform was expected to be finally approved, either by a vote or by presidential decrees, as previous reforms had been. Traditionalist sectors, however, considered the proposal 'non-Islamic', while the groups in favor of women's rights considered the measures were too 'restricted'.

40 The August 2000 Parliamentary elections were not free and fair, since opposition supporters were not allowed to vote.

41 In November that year, the Supreme Court ruled unconstitutional a decree from the Home Ministry that allowed men to prevent their wives from traveling abroad. In March that year, the Government had authorized women to file for divorce, with or without their husband's approval, for reasons of incompatibility. Until then, divorce could only be requested for serious causes, such as domestic violence. However a woman, on filing for divorce, has to return all money, property and gifts that she had received in the marriage and forgo alimony.

42 Due to domestic and regional pressure, Egypt was forced to resume relations with Iraq, disrupted since the 1991 war. Anti-American and anti-Israeli sentiment had grown among the population after Israel responded violently to the second *intifada* (Palestinian uprising). The existing offices were raised to embassy status, paving the way for the restoration of full diplomatic relations. Likewise, Egypt withdrew its ambassador in Israel in protest for the escalation of violence against Palestinians.

43 In December, Egypt, Lebanon and Syria signed an agreement to build a pipeline that would carry Egyptian natural gas under the Mediterranean to the Lebanese port of Tripoli, and also to Syria. Another pipeline would take gas to Turkey and the European markets. In March that year, Mubarak and the Presidents of Syria and Jordan had opened a line that connected the power grids of the three countries.

44 In 1997, the rebel organization al-Gamaa al-Islamiya claimed responsibility for several attacks that had taken place from 1981 to 1997. Among others, they admitted to the murder of 58 foreign tourists that year in Luxor.

45 Tourism - which was one of the country's main sources of income - suffered a strong fall after the terrorist attacks of September 2001 against the US. Egypt had to resort to loans from international organizations to cover its losses.

46 That same month, Mubarak visited Washington to inform President Bush of his own peace plan for Israel and Palestine. His goal was to promote a summit between the Israeli and Palestinian leaders in Egypt. Before starting his trip, Mubarak spoke by phone with

PROFILE

ENVIRONMENT

Ninety-nine per cent of the population live in the Nile valley and the delta although this constitutes only 30 per cent of the land. The remaining land is covered by desert except for a few isolated oases. The floods of the Nile set a pattern for the country's economic life thousands of years ago. Although controversial, and forcing wide-scale human displacement, the construction of dams, especially the Aswan in the south, has benefitted agriculture, particularly cash crops, and the economy. In addition to the traditional crops, wheat, rice and corn, cotton and sugarcane are also grown. The hydroelectric power supply, together with the northeastern oil wells, in the Sinai Peninsula, favored industrial development.

SOCIETY

Peoples: Egyptian society is ethnically diverse. While most people are Semitic-Hamitic in origin, there is a nomadic Bedouin minority in the desert east of the country. The other major group are the Nubians, African people settled for thousands of years in the Upper Nile region. The ethnic legacy of peoples that have passed through the territory are apparent, from the Romans and Greeks, to the Turks and Circasians, and more recently, to the English and French. **Religions:** Islamic, mostly Sunni. Orthodox Copts (under 10 per cent) and other Christian churches.
Languages: Arab (official); English and French are used by an educated élite; Nobiin/Nubian; Berber; Coptic (for religious matters). **Main Political Parties:** National Democratic Party; Progressive National Unionist Party; New Delegation Party; Liberal Party; National Progressive Unionist Party.
Main Social Organizations: The Egyptian Labor Federation is the only central labor organization; Union of Egyptian Students. Several NGOs work in defense of human rights. The Muslim Brotherhood.

THE STATE

Official Name: Jumhuriyah Misr al-'Arabiyah.
Administrative Divisions: 26 provinces.
Capital: Cairo (Al-Qahirah) 10,835,000 people (2003).
Other Cities: Alexandria (Al-Iskandariyah) 3,723,000 people; El-Giza 2,485,040; Subra al-Haymah 974,000 (2000).
Government: Presidentialist Republic. Hosni Mubarak, President since October 1981, re-elected in 1999. Ahmed Nazif, Prime Minister since July 2004. Single-chamber Legislature: the Majlis (People's Assembly) has 454 members, of which 10 are named by the President.
National Holiday: 23 July, Revolution Day (1952).
Armed Forces: 440,000 (incl. 270,000 conscripts). Other: Coast Guard, National Guard and Border Guards, 74,000.

Israeli Prime Minister Ariel Sharon, to inform him of the idea. 'We will not solve all issues in a minute, but this meeting can help change the political climate... by showing both of you sitting together', said Mubarak. Egypt's role as a close friend of Palestinian President Yasser Arafat made it the ideal peace mediator.

47 In April 2002 - a month that commemorates Israeli withdrawal from Egyptian territories in Sinai - Mubarak criticized Israel and accused it of resorting to state terrorism to crush Palestinians and abuse human rights. Likewise, it claimed Israel erased all traces of its crimes, for example in the Jenin refugee camp, and suggested that some international powers - referring to the US - did not honor their international responsibilities, losing all credibility. Cairo cut back its diplomatic relations with Israel to just those contacts that could help the Palestinians.

48 In September 2003, the Egyptian authorities set free the radical leader who had ordered Sadat's murder in October 1981. Karam Zohdy was one of the leaders of the Islamic group al-Gamaa al-Islamiya, the larger rebel army of the country.

49 Early in January 2004, Iranian Vice-President Mohammad Ali Abtahi confirmed that his country and Egypt would re-establish diplomatic relations.

50 In March Human Rights Watch reported the Egyptian police tortured and subjected arrested homosexuals to degrading examinations, in addition to wiretapping and using Internet chat rooms to get to them. The trial against 52 alleged homosexuals in 2001 was the most visible spot on discrimination and harassment against them. ▪

El Salvador / El Salvador

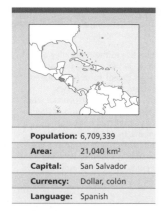

Population:	6,709,339
Area:	21,040 km²
Capital:	San Salvador
Currency:	Dollar, colón
Language:	Spanish

The region of El Salvador was inhabited from early times by Chibcha people (Muisca: see Colombia), most of whom were Pipile and Lenca. The Maya also lived within the region, but they were not very influential here.

[2] The Spaniards subdued the Aztecs in Mexico, and subsequently began the conquest of Central America under the leadership of Pedro de Alvarado. In 1525, Alvarado founded the city of El Salvador de Cuscatlan. The territory formed part of the Captaincy-General of Guatemala, a dependency of the Viceroyalty of Mexico. Central America became independent from Spain in 1821 and organized itself into a federation.

[3] In 1827, internal rivalries between 'imperialists' and 'republicans' led to civil war. In 1839, General Francisco Morazán, president of the Central American Republic, tried to prevent the break-up of the federation. From El Salvador, Morazán struggled to preserve the union with the support of some Nonulco natives, headed by Anastasio Aquino.

[4] When the federation was dissolved, Britain took advantage of the situation dominating the isthmus. In 1848, President Doroteo Vasconcelos refused to bow under British pressure, and the British blockaded Salvadoran ports.

[5] At the end of the century, the invention of artificial coloring destroyed the demand for indigo - El Salvador's principal export product - and its price fell to rock bottom. Indigo was replaced with coffee. Coffee required larger and more extensive farming areas, and the Liberal Revolution of 1880 drove thousands of peasants from their communal lands, forming a rural working class and a countryside full of anger and conflict. The coffee plantation owners became the dominant oligarchy and the ruling class of El Salvador.

[6] The 1929 financial crash caused the coffee market to collapse, crops were left unharvested, and thousands of sharecroppers and poor peasants starved. This led to a mass uprising on 22 January 1932, headed by the Communist Party of El Salvador and Farabundo Martí, a former secretary of Augusto Sandino in his campaign against the US invasion of Nicaragua.

[7] The rebellion was ruthlessly crushed by the troops of General Maximiliano Hernández Martínez, who had taken power in 1931. This started a series of military regimes that lasted half a century. Twelve thousand people died as a consequence of the repression.

[8] In 1960, the Alliance for Progress sponsored an industrialization program, within the Central American Common Market. High economic growth rates were attained without reducing the rampant unemployment that had caused 300,000 landless peasants to emigrate to neighboring Honduras. Population growth and competition between the local industrial interests, led to war between El Salvador and Honduras in June 1969. The regional common market collapsed after the 100-hour conflict, severely damaging Salvadoran industry.

[9] In the early 1970s unions and other civilian movements took on new life. Guerrilla fighters appeared in El Salvador and the legal opposition parties joined into a national front; the UNO, formed by the Christian Democrats (PDC), the Communists (UDN) and the Social Democrats (MNR). Colonel Arturo Molina, presidential candidate for the official National Conciliation Party, defeated the UNO's candidate Napoleón Duarte in a fixed election in 1972.

[10] In 1977, another fraudulent election made General Carlos Humberto Romero president. Mass riots broke out in protest but social unrest was suppressed leaving 7,000 dead.

[11] The lack of political alternatives helped the guerrilla organizations to prosper, focusing their actions as well as working with the democratic opposition forces.

[12] A civilian/military junta seized power on 15 October 1979. It included representatives of the social democrats and the Christian democrats. The Junta lacked real power and had no control over the ruthless repression campaigns carried out by police and military forces. Civilian members resigned and were replaced by right-wing Christian democrats from Duarte's party.

[13] On 24 March 1980, the Archbishop of San Salvador, Monsignor Oscar A Romero, was assassinated while performing mass in a clear reprisal for his constant defense of human rights.

[14] In October 1980, the five anti-regime political-military organizations agreed to form the Farabundo Martí Front for National Liberation (FMLN). On 10 January 1981 the FMLN launched a 'general offensive' and increased their actions throughout most of the country.

[15] In August 1981, the Mexican and French governments signed a joint agreement recognizing the FMLN and the Democratic Revolutionary Front (FDR) as 'a representative political force'.

[16] The US administration, led by President Ronald Reagan, saw the situation in El Salvador as a national security issue. The US became directly involved in the political and social conflict, and was the military and economic mainstay of the 'counter-insurgency' war, which the Salvadoran Army was unsuccessfully waging.

[17] On 28 March 1982, as instructed by Washington, the regime held an election for a Constituent Assembly. In response, the rebels launched an offensive ending in a one-week siege of Usulatán, a provincial capital.

[18] After continuous internal tussling for power, the presidency of the constitutional convention went to Roberto D'Aubuisson, the main leader of the ultra-right Nationalist Republican Alliance (ARENA) and the power behind the assassination of Archbishop Romero.

[19] Against a background of an upsurge in fighting, general elections were held in March 1984. These were boycotted by the FDR-FMLN; the abstention rate by voters was 51 per cent. Ostensibly supported by the US, the PDC - led by Napoleon Duarte - obtained 43 per cent of the vote, against the 30 per cent won by ultra-right candidate Major Roberto D'Aubuisson.

[20] The extreme right parties disputed the election, but quick responses from the Minister of Defense and the High Command, in support of Duarte, quashed any further reaction. It was the first time that the armed forces had publicly supported the reformists.

[21] In October 1986, a strong earthquake brought about a virtual cease-fire, which eventually led to the renewal of negotiations in October 1987. These talks took place within the new framework of regional peace making. The Central American governments had signed the Esquipulas agreements in August 1987, agreeing to strive for peace.

[22] Elections were held in October 1989; these were boycotted by some of the guerrillas, but civilian sectors of

WORKERS

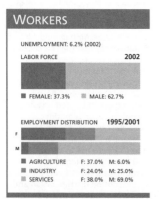

UNEMPLOYMENT: 6.2% (2002)

LABOR FORCE — 2002

■ FEMALE: 37.3%   ■ MALE: 62.7%

EMPLOYMENT DISTRIBUTION   1995/2001

■ AGRICULTURE   F: 37.0%   M: 6.0%
■ INDUSTRY   F: 24.0%   M: 25.0%
■ SERVICES   F: 38.0%   M: 69.0%

LAND USE

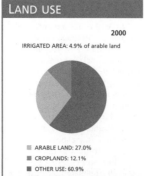

2000

IRRIGATED AREA: 4.9% of arable land

■ ARABLE LAND: 27.0%
■ CROPLANDS: 12.1%
■ OTHER USE: 60.9%

Life expectancy
70.7 years
2000-2005

GNI per capita
$2,080
2002

Literacy
79% total adult rate
2000

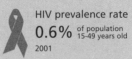
HIV prevalence rate
0.6% of population 15-49 years old
2001

the FDR (members of the social democratic and social Christian parties) participated, with Guillermo Ungo as their presidential candidate. Alfredo Cristiani, the ARENA party's candidate, won the election.

23   In November 1989, the FMLN launched an offensive occupying several areas of the capital and surrounding regions. The Government responded by bombing several densely populated areas of the capital. Six Jesuits, including the rector of the University of Central America, Ignacio Ellacuria, were tortured and killed by heavily armed soldiers. This provoked a world-wide outcry, especially from the Catholic Church, and American economic aid was threatened.

24   According to the El Salvador Human Rights Commission (non-governmental organization), women, students and members of labor unions were the people who suffered most from repression. During those twelve years of military repression, the human rights movement was led by mothers, wives, daughters and relatives of the thousands of victims of repression, and by the National Union of Salvadoran Workers (UNTS), challenging the military power and reporting the constant violation of human rights.

25   On 10 March 1991, the legislative and local elections reflected a new spirit of negotiation. For the first time in 10 years the FMLN did not call for the boycott of the elections, instead they decreed a 3-day unilateral truce. Abstention was still above 50 per cent, and there were acts of paramilitary violence immediately prior to the polls. On 12 March, the confrontations started over again.

26   In Mexico on 4 April 1991 delegates of the Cristiani Government and the FMLN started negotiations for a cease-fire agreement. On 19 April, two weeks before the Congress' mandate and the term granted by the FMLN for the peace-making came to an end, 10,000 demonstrators, from 70 social organizations, gathered in the Permanent Committee for National Debate (CPDN), demanded that the Constitution be reformed.

27   On 27 April, after several attempts, representatives of the Government and the Farabundo Martí Front signed the 'Mexico Agreements' restricting the function of the armed forces to the defense of national sovereignty and territorial integrity. The formation of paramilitary groups was banned, and it was agreed to reform article 83 of the Constitution to say that sovereignty 'resides in the people, and that it is from the people that public power emerges'. In New York another agreement was reached in June. The Salvadoran Government committed itself to dismantling the National Guard and the Rural Police (*Policía de Hacienda*), replacing it with Civilian Police including FMLN-members.

28   On 16 November, new talks began in the UN headquarters. This time, the FMLN declared an indefinite unilateral truce until a new, definite, cease-fire was signed. Meanwhile, a Spanish parliamentary delegation visited El Salvador and wrote a report on the murders of the six Spanish Jesuits from the Central American University (UCA). The report, submitted to the Spanish, European, Salvadoran, and US parliaments, accused the Salvadoran Government and the army of concealing evidence.

29   On 1 January 1992, after 21 weeks of negotiation and 12 years of civil war, both parties met in New York to sign agreements and covenants establishing peace in El Salvador. The war left 75,000 people dead, 8,000 missing, and nearly one million in exile. The period 1 February-3 October 1992 was designated as the time to cease all armed confrontation and to create an appropriate environment to apply the agreements and negotiations, which continued under the supervision of the UN and the OAS.

30   The final agreements were signed in the Mexican city of Chapultepec on 16 January 1992. They included substantial modifications to the Constitution and to the armed forces. They guaranteed to change rural land tenure and to alter the terms of employee participation in the privatization of State companies; they established the creation of human-rights organizations, and guaranteed the legal status of the FMLN.

31   According to the peace accords the Government was to reduce its troops by half by 1994, bringing the number down to 30,000; in addition, it was to disband its intelligence service. As of 3 March, a new civilian police was to be created, made up in part by former members of the FMLN. The FMLN, a legal political party since 30 April 1991, held its first public meeting on 1 February 1992 and called for the unification of all opposition forces for the 1994 election. After years of being underground, it was presided over by guerrilla commanders Shafick Handal, Joaquín Villalobos, Fernán Cienfuegos, Francisco Jovel and Leonel González.

32   In January 1992, the Law of National Reconciliation granted amnesty to all political prisoners. In addition, the Government pledged to turn over lands to the combatants and provide

IN FOCUS

ENVIRONMENTAL CHALLENGES
The country has some of the worst deforestation problems in Latin America, with erosion, water and soil pollution from toxic waste. A study in the 1990s stated that 90 per cent of all rivers were polluted, while two-thirds of all land suffered serious erosion. In January 2001 an earthquake reaching 7.6 on the Richter scale caused a landslide that killed more than 800 people. A month later another earthquake killed 255 people. Hurricanes are common.

WOMAN'S RIGHTS
In 1939 the Legislative Assembly extended the franchise to educated women over 21. Since the 1950 Constitution, all women have been able to vote and run for office. In 2000, 17 per cent of members of Parliament and 6 per cent of ministers were women. Eight per cent of local government positions were filled by women.
    In 2000 women made up 37 per cent of the workforce; 6 per cent worked in agriculture, 25 per cent in the industrial sector and 69 per cent in services. Fourteen per cent of pregnant women were anemic, and 76 per cent received prenatal care*. Some 0.3 per cent of females between 15 and 24 were living with HIV/AIDS.

CHILDREN
The Constitution bans all child labor, but out of the almost 2,000,000 Salvadorans under 18, more than 223,000 work. Most are boys and work in agriculture or fishing, while others work as street vendors, vulnerable to sexual exploitation. This is more acute in poor communities and when the parents have little schooling. Some 7,000 children aged under 5 died between 1995 and 2000. In 2001, 13 per cent of children were born underweight. In late 2001 there were 830 children under 14 living with HIV/AIDS, while 130,000 were orphaned by this disease.

INDIGENOUS PEOPLES/ ETHNIC MINORITIES
There are 288,000 indigenous people (5 per cent of all Salvadorans). They are poor and without access to education or health, living mostly in rural parts in southwestern region (Sonsonate, Ahuachapan, La Libertad and Santa Ana - a community better known as Panchimalco). Most speak Spanish as a first language, and few are familiar with Nahuatl, their own language. Although the Government implemented policies in 1992 to improve their situation and acknowledged past human rights abuses, they face economic discrimination. They are descended from the Pipils, a nomadic group of the Nahoa people in central Mexico. Since the beginning of the Spanish conquest, indigenous people and Europeans have coexisted in the same regions. In the 16th century intermarriage was common. In 1932, during an indigenous peoples' protest against government policies, 35 *ladinos* (non-indigenous inhabitants) were murdered.
In retaliation, between 35,000 and 50,000 native Americans were massacred, in an act called 'La Matanza' (The Massacre). During the 1980-992 civil war, thousands of indigenous people were victims of death squads. The present Constitution makes no specific provision for the rights of these peoples or their participation in decisions over the use of the land, their culture or the exploitation of natural resources.

MIGRANTS/REFUGEES
In late 2002 according to UNHCR there were 100 refugees, mostly Nicaraguans. The civil war in the 1980s caused wide-scale emigration, mostly to the US. In 1996 there were 40,000 Salvadorans living in Canada and 465,433 registered in the US. The US deported 3,743 people to El Salvador in 1997. In 2002 El Salvador was the 10th biggest recipient of remittances in the world, with $1,750 million per year.

DEATH PENALTY
Abolished for ordinary offenses in 1983. The last execution took place in 1976.

*Latest data available in *The State of the World's Children* and *Childinfo* database, UNICEF, 2004.

Under-5 mortality
39 per 1,000 live births
2002

Poverty
21.4% of population living on less than $1 per day
1997

Debt service
6.3% exports of goods and services
2001

Maternal mortality
150 per 100,000 live births
2000

assistance to *campesinos* belonging to both bands.

[33] On 15 February 1993, the last 1,700 armed rebels turned over their weapons in a ceremony which was attended by several Central American heads of state and by UN Secretary-General Boutros Boutros-Ghali. The National Civil Police was created, as well as a Human Rights Defense Commission and a Supreme Electoral Court.

[34] The result of the investigation of human-rights violations, carried out by the Truth Commission created by the UN, led to the resignation of Defense Minister General René Emilio Ponce, as being the one who ordered the assassination of six Jesuits in 1989. According to the Commission's final document, the military, the death squads linked to these and the State were responsible for 85 per cent of the civil rights violations committed during the war.

[35] The Truth Commission recommended the dismissal of 102 military leaders and that some former guerrilla leaders be deprived of their political rights. President Cristiani proposed a general amnesty for cases

where excesses had been committed; this proposal was approved on March 20 1993, only five days after the Truth Commission document had been made public. With this measure, the most serious crimes committed during the war met with total impunity.

[36] A year later on March 20 1994, the first elections since the civil war were held. The candidate of the left coalition, Democratic Convergence - made up of the FMLN and other groups - won 25.5 per cent in the first round, against 49.2 per cent for the right-wing candidate, Armando Calderón Sol, from the ARENA party. Although the Left considered the elections fraudulent, the UN observers confirmed that the elections were fair.

[37] According to UN the peace accords did not bring an end to the violence. In addition to the existence of intelligence activities within the armed forces, members of the military were linked to organized crime. And as there were few employment opportunities for discharged troops (from both sides), this led to an increase in petty crime.

[38] The long-promised award of land to demobilized fighters was slow and inefficient. By mid-1994, only one-third of the potential beneficiaries - 12,000 of a total 37,000 former members of the army or the guerrillas - had obtained plots. The rest remained inactive, living in substandard temporary housing and often drifting into organized crime.

[39] An agreement concluded on May 1995 between ARENA and the Democratic Party - split from the FMLN - enabled a 3 per cent rise of the valued added tax from 10 to 13 per cent. This raise was explained on the need to collect funds to finance land reform, infrastructure works and reconstruction of the country's electoral and judicial apparatus.

[40] In August 1996 demonstrators affected by the slowness of the process occupied streets and government buildings in downtown San Salvador. In May, the Democratic Party withdrew from its deal with ARENA, which left the Government without a parliamentary majority. In March 1997, the opposition's FMLN obtained an important victory in municipal elections, after winning in the capital and dozens of provincial cities, although ARENA still kept the majority of the votes. The turnout was 40 per cent.

[41] A study by the InterAmerican Development Bank, issued in March 1998, estimated that 25 per cent of El Salvador's potential economic growth was lost every year due to political and criminal violence.

[42] In May, the world crisis also affected the textile industry and 21 factories shut down in 1999, leaving some 9,000 people jobless. Francisco Escobar, chairman of the textile industry, asked the Government to realign the national currency against the dollar, in order to revitalize the sector. According to Escobar, another cause of the crisis were the 'high wages' received by workers, equivalent to $1.06 per hour of work, compared to 74 cents in Guatemala and 50 cents in Mexico. Likewise, the sugar sector requested the Legislative Assembly to lower interest rates from 12 to 6 per cent, and to be granted three years of grace. The request, according to the sugar workers, was rooted in the fact that the price of the sugar had fallen, in the last two harvests, from $14 to $4 per 100 kg, a price below production costs.

[43] The March 1999 elections ratified ARENA's dominance. At the age of 39 the elected candidate Francisco Flores became the youngest president in South

America, providing an image of rejuvenation. Flores' government program, 'The New Alliance', had four priorities: work, social investment, citizen security and sustainable development.

[44] The day after Flores was sworn in as President, he faced the first public demonstration by campesinos and environmental leaders in San Salvador demanding immediate action to deal with the chaos caused by Hurricane Mitch.

[45] Dollarization of the economy was enforced as of 1 January 2001, aiming to revitalize the economy and attract investors. Although the US currency was the new unit of the banking sector, citizens could carry out their transactions in colones.

[46] The earthquakes of 13 January and 13 February 2001 left 1,159 dead, 8,122 injured and 1.5 million homeless (25 per cent of the population). It is estimated the earthquakes aggravated environmental deterioration and caused 225,000 new poor.

[47] The World Food Program began giving out food in August 2001, as a result of one of the worst droughts in the last years. Approximately 2 tons of corn, beans and cooking oil were distributed among 20,000 families who had lost all of their yearly harvest.

[48] US President George W Bush visited San Salvador in March 2002, on the same day Archbishop Romero had been murdered 22 years before. Bush promised to support free trade policies, as the only solution to the region's problems. Even though US intervention during the civil war years had been widely proven, US officials claimed the purpose of the visit was to celebrate a story with a 'happy ending', which had involved George Bush Snr, George W's father, as one of the signatories of the peace in 1992.

[49] In July, a Court in Florida, US, found Carlos Eugenio Vides and José Guillermo García, Salvadoran retired generals, guilty of committing torture in their country during the 1980s

[50] El Salvador, Honduras, Nicaragua and Guatemala reached a free trade agreement with the US in December 2003. The Salvadoran business sector was uneasy, because the US offer was not as 'generous' as they had expected. The parliaments of the five countries still have to approve the agreement before it can come into force.

[51] After a virulent campaign ARENA's candidate, Antonio Tony, Saca, won the March 2004 presidential elections, defeating FMLN's Shafick Handal. ▪

PROFILE

ENVIRONMENT
It is the smallest and most densely populated country in Central America and the only one with no Caribbean coastline. A chain of volcanoes runs across the country from east to west and the altitude makes the climate mild. Coffee is the main cash crop in the highlands. Subsistence crops such as corn, beans and rice are also grown. Along the Pacific Coast, where the weather is warmer, there are sugarcane plantations.

SOCIETY
Peoples: 89 per cent of the Salvadoran population are mixed descendants of American natives and Spanish colonizers, 10 per cent are indigenous peoples, and 1 per cent are European.
Religions: Mainly Catholic. **Languages:** Spanish is the official and predominant language. Indigenous minority groups speak Nahuatl and Kekchi. **Main Political Parties:** The Nationalist Republican Alliance (ARENA) currently in power. The Farabundo Martí National Liberation Front (FMLN), founded in October 1980, comprises five political-military organizations. There is only two parties in the country, because in the March 2004 elections the other existing parties did not reach 3 per cent, least of the required suffrages for it's existence within the political map.
Main Social Organizations: National Union of Salvadoran Workers (UNTS); MUSYGES and the National Coordinator against Hunger and Repression (CNHR), formed in 1988. Coordinating Indigenous Salvadoran Council (CCNIS); Peasant Democratic Movement (ADC).

THE STATE
Official Name: República de El Salvador.
Administrative Divisions: 14 Departments. **Capital:** San Salvador 1,424,000 people (2003). **Other Cities:** Santa Ana 538,800 people; San Miguel 473,300; Soyapango 324,800; Mejicanos 152,900 (2000). **Government:** Antonio Elías 'Tony' Saca, President since June 2004. Parliament: Legislative Assembly with 84 members.
National Holiday: 15 September, Independence Day (1821).
Armed Forces: 30,500 troops (1995). Other: National Civilian Police, made up of former guerrillas, soldiers and police.

Equatorial Guinea / Guinea Ecuatorial

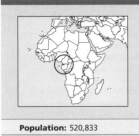

Population:	520,833
Area:	28,050 km²
Capital:	Malabo
Currency:	CFA franc
Language:	Spanish

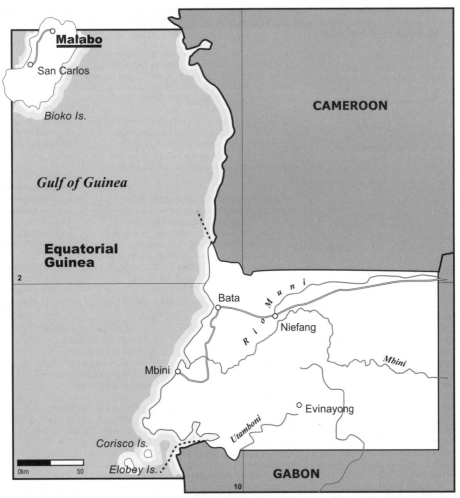

Malabo
San Carlos
Bioko Is.
CAMEROON
Gulf of Guinea
Equatorial
Guinea
2
Bata
Río Muni
Niefang
Mbini
Mbini
Corisco Is.
Evinayong
Utamboni
Elobey Is.
GABON
10
0km   50

F rom the 13th to the 15th century, Fang and Ndowe people settled in the River Muni area, north of Gabon, subduing the Bayele pygmy population, who now only exist in a few isolated groups. From the continental coast, these nations expanded onto the nearby islands that were described as 'densely populated' in the 15th century. In the colonial division of Africa, the Rio Muni area and the islands received the name of Equatorial Guinea.

2   The Ndowe became allies and intermediaries of Portuguese, Spanish, Dutch and English slave traders. Fang people, whose social organization did not include slavery, withdrew into the forests, convinced that the Europeans were cannibals.

3   The kings of Portugal, proclaiming themselves the lords of Guinea, ceded the entire 'District of Biafra' to Spain under the treaties of San Ildefonso and Pardo in 1777 and 1778, in exchange for Spanish territory in southern Brazil. In 1778, an expedition sailed out from Montevideo to occupy the islands. They lost their commanding officer, Argelejos, in a battle against the Annoboneuses, and the survivors, under their new leader, Lieutenant Primo de Rivera, turned back. The French and British gradually took over sections of the territory, with the British finally occupying it, founding the first settlements. They used it as a base for their conquest of Nigeria and turned the freed slaves, or 'Fernandinos', into their agents, creating a ruling group that, in many aspects, still exists today.

4   Between 1843 and 1858, the District was militarily re-conquered by Spain, re-establishing their 'rights' over the area. Bioko Spanish settlers supported Franco during the Spanish civil war in 1936 and then obtained control over the archipelago. At that time, economic activity centered on cacao, coffee and timber, but the territory was ineffectively controlled from a distance.

5   From 1963, the colony had a regime of internal autonomy which allowed for the legal existence of several political parties. Meanwhile, international pressure became so strong that Franco's Spain had to recognize the independence of Equatorial Guinea, officially proclaimed on 12 October 1968.

6   Francisco Macías Nguema took over the presidency a year later on the pretext of an alleged coup attempt. He instigated violent repression of the opposition, leaving a trail of thousands of political prisoners, killings, disappearances and 160,000 exiles.

7   In August 1979, a coup led by Lieutenant Colonel Teodoro Obiang Mba Nzago, the President's nephew, brought an end to Macías's power, and he was executed for 'crimes against humanity'. Obiang set up the Supreme Military Council.

8   The new regime continued the repression of its forerunner, and the groups which were benefited by the regime remained untouched, all now linked to the Democratic Party of Equatorial Guinea, the only legal party. In

elections held in 1984 and 1989 President Obiang was re-elected, unopposed. The National Alliance for the Recovery of Democracy formed in exile. Its attempts to negotiate with Obiang were fruitless. A coup attempt in 1986 sparked more arrests.

9   Initial rapprochement with the Soviet Bloc was undone when Obiang took the nation into the Customs and Economic Union of Central Africa, linking the national currency - the ekwele - to central banks of the region. This measure led to a drastic reduction in facilities offered by the Soviets and East Germans. The United States, France and Spain controlled iron and oil mining, and timber production.

10   Following his re-election in 1989, Obiang continued to apply IMF recipes in return for loans. The same year, he visited France and Equatorial Guinea later asked to join the French speaking African countries using the franc (CFA) as their currency.

11   Ten political parties were legalized in early 1993. In late March, the freeing of all political prisoners was agreed with the Joint Opposition Platform (a ten-party

coalition formed in November 1992 from legalized parties). In August the first multi-party elections were held but the Partido Democrático de Guinea Ecuatorial (PDGE) boycotted them and took 68 of the 80 seats.

12   Amidst accusations, arbitrary detentions and torture, the Government set presidential elections for early 1996. In February of that year, shortly before election day, the Government dissolved the Opposition Platform and detained several of its members. On February 25, Obiang romped home with 99 per cent of the vote in an election described as a farce by the oppositions. There was an 80 per cent abstention rate.

13   The nation's fortunes changed that year, when giant oil deposits were found. Oil exports brought about a extraordinary growth of the economy. Cocoa, coffee and timber were replaced by oil at the head of the list leading to marked economic growth. In 1997 GDP grew by 71.2 per cent, by 22 per cent in 1998 and 15 per cent in 1999, doubling the size of the economy in less than three years.

Life expectancy
49.1 years
2000-2005

GNI per capita
$700
2002

Literacy
83% total adult rate
2000

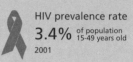
HIV prevalence rate
3.4% of population 15-49 years old
2001

14   In spite of the economic recovery, 80 per cent of the wealth was held by less than 5 per cent of the population, according to the UN. In 1999, the IMF complained because of the corrupt members of the Government who had kept $96 million of the $130 million from the oil income. Although the per capita income grew from $370 to $2,000 between 1995 and 2000, this disguised the continuing deeply unequal distribution of wealth. However, the economy's spectacular growth did allow for some positive improvements in health and education.

15   The discovery of natural gas deposits in 2001 caused a new leap in growth of over 50 per cent. Most local investment was poured into construction, and this dragged the other productive sectors in its wake, meaning some of the mineral wealth reached the worst-off sectors.

16   That was a relatively turbulent year politically. In February 2002, Cándido Muatetema Rivas was appointed Prime Minister, after Teodoro Obiang Nguema accused Ángel Serafín Seriche Dougan of causing a constitutional crisis and ousting him for 'not respecting the opinion of the people and the nation's interests'. The following month, eight opposition parties in exile formed a coalition in Spain to monitor the internal politics of the nation, stating that democracy under the Obiang government was only a headline.

17   In July, while Obiang was named PDGE party candidate for the 2003 election, the exiled

PROFILE

ENVIRONMENT
The country consists of mainland territory on the Gulf of Guinea (Río Muni, 26,017 sq km) and the islands of Bioko (formerly Fernando Po, and Macías Nguema) and Pigalu (formerly Annobon, Corisco, Greater Elobey and Lesser Elobey). The islands are of volcanic origin and extremely fertile; Río Muni is a coastal plain covered with tropical rainforests but without natural harbors. It is one of the most humid and rainy countries of the world, a characteristic that limits the variety of possible crops. The main exports are cocoa, wood and oil.

SOCIETY
Peoples: The population is mostly of Bantu-speaking origin. In the islands there are also Igbo and Efik peoples who migrated from Nigeria, subduing the local Bubi population. In Río Muni the inhabitants are mainly Fang and Ndowe. Nearly all of the Europeans and a third of the local population emigrated during the Macías regime.
Religions: Mainly Christian on the islands; traditional African beliefs in Rio Muni.
Languages: Spanish is official and predominant

language. French is also official. In Rio Muni, Fang is also spoken, and on the islands, Bubi, Ibo and English. **Main Political Parties:** Democratic Party of Equatorial Guinea (PDGE); People's Union; Convergence for Social Democracy.
Main Social Organizations: National Alliance for the Restoration of Democracy and other associations in exile (mainly in Spain) like the Platform for Peace and Human Rights in EG, Movement for the Self Determination of Bioko Island, Union of Workers of Equatorial Guinea.

THE STATE
Official Name: República de Guinea Ecuatorial.
Administrative Divisions: 4 continental and 3 island regions. **Capital:** Malabo 95,000 people (2003). **Other Cities:** Bata 43,000 people; Ela Nguema 14,700 (2000). **Government:** Teodoro Obiang Nguema Mbasogo, President since August 1979 (re-elected in December 2002). Miguel Abia Biteo Borico, Prime Minister since June, 2004. Parliament: Chamber of People's Representatives, with 80 members. **National Holiday:** 12 October, Independence Day (1968). **Armed Forces:** 1,300.

Florentino Ecomo Nsogo, leader of the Party for Reconstruction and Social Welfare, returned to the country. His party was the first to respond to the President's call for all opposition parties to register for the parliamentary elections in 2003.

18   In June 2002, 68 people - including the main opposition leader Plácido Micó Abogo - were arrested. They were accused of plotting to overthrow Obiang Nguema's regime. According to Amnesty International, many prisoners bore the marks of torture.

19   In the December 2002 elections the President was re-elected with 100 per cent of the vote, according to official figures. Opposition leaders said the election was rigged.

20   Although 60 per cent of the population live in poverty and HIV/AIDS affects 7 per cent of the people, over the last 10 years Equatorial Guinea was the country with the highest economic growth rate in the world (19 per cent annually) The country is nearing the Millennium Development Goals (MDGs) stated by UN for the year 2015.

21   In January 2004, Silvestre Siale Bileka, president of the Supreme Court, resigned. In his resignation letter to Obiang, Siale said that despite his best efforts in the Justice Department, there had been no major improvements. The opposition said that this resignation showed that Obiang's regime was incapable of controlling corruption.

22   Over the years of Obiang's rule, Amnesty International has repeatedly cited complaints of arrests, torture and murder. The Bubi minority have been regularly persecuted in their quest for self-determination for Bioko island. ∎

IN FOCUS

ENVIRONMENTAL CHALLENGES
A major environmental concern is the use of Pigalu island as a dump for industrial and toxic radioactive waste, resulting in pollution and diseases from contamination. Deforestation is in progress. Only 2 per cent of the population take advantage of 80 per cent of the country's natural resources.

WOMEN'S RIGHTS
Women have been able to vote and stand for election since 1963. In 2000, 5 per cent of the parliamentary seats and 4 per cent of the ministerial positions were held by women. Their life expectancy was 50.5 years. 2.8 per cent of 15-24 year-old women were HIV-positive or lived with AIDS (double the percentage for men).
        Eighty-six per cent of pregnant women receiv prenatal care and 65 per cent of all births are assisted by qualified staff*.

While the illiteracy rate for women over 15 was 25.6 per cent in 2000*, the equivalent figure for men was 7.5 per cent. The number of female secondary teachers went down from 11 per cent in 1995 to only 3 per cent in 2000. In 2000 the female labor force was 36 per cent of the total. From 1990 to 2000, 91 per cent worked in agriculture, 2 per cent in industry and 8 per cent in the service sector.

CHILDREN
In 2000*, the enrolment and attendance at secondary school was 38 per cent.
        Only half of the primary-school-aged children attend the 884 schools of Equatorial Guinea. At the end of 2001, 420 children under 14 were HIV-positive or lived with AIDS.

INDIGENOUS PEOPLES/ ETHNIC MINORITIES
The most important groups are formed by Bubis (15,000 people,

mainly Catholic), Fernandinos - people descended from intermarriage when the British administered Fernando Po in the 19th century; from Sierra Leone, or expelled from Cuba - Pagalos (Annoboneses), Ndowes, Combes, Bengas, Bujebas and Fangs or Pámues (including Okaks and Ntmus). According to oral tradition, Fangs originally came from what are now Gabon and Cameroon.
        The Fang people's main social institution, the 'house of word', is the place where neighbors get together to explain and solve their disputes openly in front of the whole community. There are around 35,000 Ibo and Hausa immigrants from Nigeria.

MIGRANTS/REFUGEES
Since 2000, this country with its rich mineral resources such as petroleum and minerals, has become a main destination for

skilled and non-skilled workers. From 1970 to 1980 many agricultural workers from Angola, Cameroon, the Central African Republic and Chad, started working on the cocoa, coffee and sugar plantations.
        During the Macías regime (1968-1979) 160,000 people left the country. Then, during the 20 years after the Obiang Nguema coup (1979), a few refugees returned; some were imprisoned and beaten. On release, they went into exile again.

DEATH PENALTY
It is applicable to all kind of crimes. In 2002, at least 18 people were executed.

*Latest data available in *The State of the World's Children* and *Childinfo* database, UNICEF, 2004.

Eritrea / Ertra

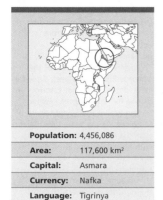

Population:	4,456,086
Area:	117,600 km²
Capital:	Asmara
Currency:	Nafka
Language:	Tigrinya

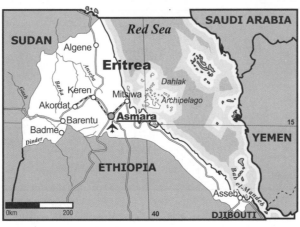

About 300 BC, Aksumite herders, who emigrated from Arabia to Mesopotamia, reached the shores of the Red Sea in the region now known as Eritrea. This area was linked to the beginnings of the Ethiopian kingdom, but it retained much of its independence until it fell under Ottoman rule in the 16th century. From the 17th to the 19th century control over the territory was disputed among Ethiopia, the Ottomans, the kingdom of Tigray, Egypt and Italy. In 1890, the Treaty of Wichale between Italy and Menilek II of Ethiopia recognized Italian possessions on the Red Sea, and the colony, created on 1 January 1890, was named by the Italians for the Mare Erythraeum ('Red Sea' in Latin) of the Romans.

[2] Eritrea was used as the main base for the Italian invasions of Ethiopia in 1896 and 1935-36. Italian rule continued until 1941 when the area came under British administration.

[3] On 2 December 1950, the United Nations declared that Eritrea should become a federated state within the Ethiopian Empire. The resolution rejected Ethiopian demands for outright incorporation, but also left the process of Eritrean self-determination undefined.

[4] In Eritrea, a national assembly was elected which enjoyed some autonomy until 1962, when Ethiopian leader Haile Selassie forced a group of Eritrean politicians to vote for its complete incorporation into Ethiopia. The decision was contested by nationalist groups, sparking a rebellion.

[5] The Eritrean Liberation Front (ELF) founded in 1958, in Cairo, by journalist and union leader Idris Mohamed Adem, began guerrilla activities in September 1961. In 1966, a split produced the Eritrean Popular Liberation Front (EPLF). In 1974, with Sudanese mediation, the two groups agreed to coordinate their actions and in the next few years, the EPLF imposed its leadership upon the rebel movement.

[6] During the pro-Soviet Mengistu government in Ethiopia, the Eritreans felt that the changes in Addis Ababa did not bring their self-determination closer, so they had no reason to stop fighting.

[7] In February 1990, the EPLF captured Asmara and the ports of Massawa and Asseb and almost all the Eritrean territory. The road between Asseb and Addis Ababa was the only way supplies could reach the Ethiopian capital by land.

[8] In 1991, Asmara and Addis Ababa started to relate as separate States. The Red Sea ports were opened again to enable the arrival of international aid.

[9] In the April 1993 referendum, 99.8 per cent of voters opted for independence. The EPLF formed a provisional government, led by Isaias Afwerki, which turned into a political party the following year, the People's Front for Democracy and Justice (PFDJ). After becoming a member of the UN in 1993, Eritrea joined the IMF in February 1994.

[10] In late 1997, Eritrea introduced the *nafka*, replacing the Ethiopian *birr*. As a countermeasure, Ethiopia announced that transactions between both countries would be carried out exclusively in US dollars.

[11] Fighting with Ethiopia resumed in February 1999. The war sucked in Nigeria, which supplied weapons to Eritreans, and Kenya, which mobilized forces along its border with Ethiopia.

[12] In June, Afwerki and his Prime Minister Meles Zenawi accepted the OAU's proposal for an immediate ceasefire and withdrawal of troops from the area in dispute. In September 1999, Eritrea accepted the peace plan proposed by the UN, while Ethiopia maintained minor differences.

[13] Eleven ruling party officials were arrested in September 2001, charged with 'defeatism' and 'treason' for criticizing the Government and demanding democratic reform. Likewise, the opposition press was closed and nine journalists were detained.

[14] In April 2002, the Permanent Court of Arbitration at The Hague decided on the border dispute between Eritrea and Ethiopia. The 1,000 km border was set by a court of five international specialists. The border cities of Zalembessa, Alitena and Bada were given over to Ethiopia, while Badme - the flashpoint of the war in 1997 - was given to Eritrea. According to experts, Ethiopia received a large part of its territorial demands.

[15] Eritrea produced less than 10 per cent of the cereals required for human consumption during 2002, due to the droughts. In 2003 the results of conflict with Ethiopia, the drought and increasing poverty triggered the worst food crisis since Eritrea's independence. The Government estimated that 80 per cent of the livestock could die from disease or starvation. In the first months of that year, 10 per cent of the animals were dead.

[16] According to UN surveys in 2003, 15-20 per cent of children under five were malnourished; 10,000 were severely malnourished, and urgently needed more food. Farmers, children, herders and peasants are particularly vulnerable to food shortages. These group together makes up about 1.4 million people. ∎

PROFILE

ENVIRONMENT
Eritrea is in the horn of Africa. The 1,000 km northeast coast is on the Red Sea; to the northeast lies Sudan; to the south, Ethiopia and to the southeast, Djibouti. The dry plains and extremely hot desert are inhabited by pastoralist herders.

SOCIETY
Peoples: The nine ethnic groups are the Tigrinya, Tigre, Bilen, Afar, Saho, Kunama, Nara, Hidareb and Rashaida. The majority are pastoralists or farmers; 20 per cent are urban workers. Half a million Eritrean refugees live in Sudan, 40,000 in Europe and 14,000 in the US.
Religions: Almost half of all Eritreans are Coptic Christians; most of the rest are Muslim, although there are Catholic and Protestant minorities.
Languages: Tigrinya; Afar, Beni-Amir, Tigré, Saho, Kunama, Arab and other local languages.
Main Political Parties: People's Front for Democracy and Justice (PFDJ) is the only party recognized by the Government. Formerly the Eritrean People's Liberation Front (EPLF), it adopted its new name in 1994.
Main Social Organizations: Eritrean Liberation Front, split into several fractions; Eritrean Islamic Jihad.

THE STATE
Official Name: Hagere Ertra.
Administrative Divisions: 8 provinces.
Capital: Asmara 556,000 people (2003).
Other Cities: Asseb 53,600 people; Keren 36,600; Mitsiwa 28,800 (2000).
Government: Parliamentary Republic. Isaias Afwerki, President since May 1993. Parliament: National Assembly with 104 members.
National Holiday: 24 May, Independence (1993).
Armed Forces: 35,000 (1997).

LAND USE

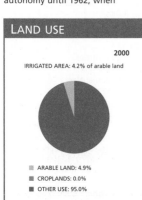

2000

IRRIGATED AREA: 4.2% of arable land

- ARABLE LAND: 4.9%
- CROPLANDS: 0.0%
- OTHER USE: 95.0%

Estonia / Eesti

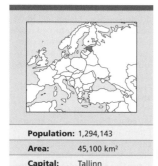

Population:	1,294,143
Area:	45,100 km²
Capital:	Tallinn
Currency:	Kroon
Language:	Estonian

The region was settled some 6,000 years ago. Estonians, a branch of the Finno-Ugric nations, have greater cultural and linguistic ties with the Finns to the north than with the Indo-European Balts to the south.

2 Around the year 400 AD, hunting and fishing activity began to be replaced by agriculture and cattle raising. At the same time, navigation and trade with neighboring countries along the Baltic Sea intensified. In the 11th and 12th centuries, combined Estonian forces successfully repelled Russia's attempts to invade the territory.

3 The Germans, Russians and Danes, invading Estonia in the 13th century, found a federation of states with a high level of social development and a strong sense of independence, keeping them united against foreign conquerors.

4 In the 13th century, the Knights of the Sword, a Germanic order which was created during the Crusades, conquered the southern part of Estonia and the north of Latvia, creating the kingdom of Livonia and converting the inhabitants to Christianity. German traders and landowners brought the Protestant Reformation to Estonia in the first half of the 16th century.

5 Between 1558 and 1583 Livonia was repeatedly attacked by Russia before being broken up in 1561. Poland conquered Livonia in 1569; a hundred years later, it ceded the major part of the kingdom to Sweden. In the Nordic Wars (1700-1721), Russia took Livonia from Sweden, and kept these lands under the Treaty of Nystad.

6 Russia received the Polish part of Livonia in 1772, with the first partition of Poland. The former kingdom of Livonia became a Russian province in 1783. Power was shared between the Czar of Russia and local German nobles, who owned most of the lands and the peasants lived in serfdom.

7 The abolition of serfdom in Russia and peasant land ownership rights (1804), strengthened Estonian nationalism.

8 In 1904, Estonian nationalists seized control of Tallinn, ousting the German-Baltic rulers. After the fall of the Czar in February 1917, a demonstration by 40,000 Estonians in Petrograd forced the Provisional Government to grant them autonomy.

9 In November 1917, with the election of a constituent assembly, the Estonian Bolsheviks obtained 35.5 per cent of the votes. On 24 February 1918, Estonia declared its independence from the Soviet Union and set up a provisional government. The following day, German troops occupied Tallinn and the Estonian Government was forced to go into exile.

10 After World War I, the Estonians successfully fought both the Red Army and the Germans. On 2 February 1920, with the Treaty of Tartu the Soviet Union recognized Estonia's independence. That year Estonia started the construction of what would become the world's first shale-oil distillery.

11 Estonia, Latvia and Lithuania, joined the League of Nations in 1921. The Government began the reconstruction of the country and initiated agrarian reform.

12 Estonia passed legislation guaranteeing the rights of minorities, and ensuring that all ethnic groups had access to schools in their own languages. The economic depression of the 1930s led Estonia to become a virtual dictatorship in 1933, before adopting a presidential-parliamentary system in 1937.

13 The secret protocols of the Molotov-Ribbentrop pact, signed in 1939, determined that Estonia - like its two Baltic neighbors - would remain within the Soviet sphere of influence. At the same time, Tallinn signed a mutual assistance treaty with Moscow giving the USSR the right to install naval bases on Estonian soil.

14 In June 1940, after demanding the right for his troops to enter Estonian territory under the pretext of searching for missing soldiers, Stalin deposed the Tallinn government and replaced it with members of the local Communist Party (CP). Elections were held during the Soviet occupation, after which the CP seized power.

15 Following the examples of Latvia and Lithuania, the new government adopted the name 'Soviet Socialist Republic of Estonia', joining the USSR voluntarily. More than 60,000 Estonians were deported to Siberia.

16 When the German offensive against the USSR began in 1941, Nazi troops invaded Estonia, establishing a reign of terror. The USSR recovered the Baltic States in 1944.

17 The Soviet regime imposed forced industrialization and collectivization of the countryside. Some 80,000 Estonians emigrated to the West, while Russian colonization gradually altered the traditional ethnic composition of the population.

18 Around 20,000 Estonians were deported between 1945 and 1946. The third wave of mass

PROFILE

ENVIRONMENT
Located on the northeastern coast of the Baltic Sea, Estonia is bounded by the Gulf of Finland in the north, Russia in the east and Latvia in the south. The Estonian landscape was formed by glaciers; there are numerous rivers and more than 1,500 lakes, the largest of which are Lake Peipsi (Europe's fourth-largest) and Lake Vorts. Forests make up 38 per cent of Estonia's territory; the highest elevation is Mount Suur Muna Magi (317 m). The climate is temperate, with average temperatures of 28° C in summer and around -5°C in winter. The Baltic coast is 1,240 km long and includes a number of fjords. Some 1,500 islands close to the coast make up around one-tenth of Estonia's territory. The Gulf of Finland has numerous ice-free bays, of which Tallinn is the largest. Estonia's most important mineral resources are shale-oil (which meets most of Estonia's energy needs), and phosphates.

SOCIETY
Peoples: Estonians 64.2 per cent; Russians 28.7 per cent; Ukranians 2.6 per cent; Belarusians 1.5 per cent Finnish and others 3.3 per cent (1998).

Religions: Lutheran (majority), Orthodox, Baptist.
Languages: Estonian (official); Russian and others.
Main Political Parties: Estonian Center Party; Fatherland Union, conservative; Estonian Reform Party; People's Party Moderates, social-democratic; Estonian Coalition Party, liberal.
Main Social Organizations: Confederation of Estonian Trade Unions (EAKL)

THE STATE
Official Name: Eesti Vabariik.
Administrative Division: 15 counties.
Capital: Tallinn 391,000 people (2003).
Other Cities: Tartu 98,400 people; Narva 72,100; Kohtla-Jarve 45,200; Pärnu 42,800 (2000).
Government: Parliamentary republic. Arnold Ruutel, President since October 2001. Juhan Parts, Prime Minister and Chief of State since August 2003. Unicameral Legislature: State Council (Riigikogu), with 101 members elected every 4 years.
National Holiday: 24 February, Independence (1918).
Armed Forces: 2,500 (1993). Other: 2,000 (Coast Guard).

LAND USE

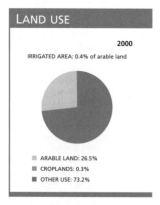

2000

IRRIGATED AREA: 0.4% of arable land

- ARABLE LAND: 26.5%
- CROPLANDS: 0.3%
- OTHER USE: 73.2%

deportations took place in 1949, when another 40,000 Estonians were sent to Siberia, most of them farmers who refused to accept collectivization of the land.

19 The reforms set in motion in 1985 by Soviet President Mikhail Gorbachev stimulated social and political activity within Estonia. In August 1987, a demonstration in Tallinn demanded the publication of the Molotov-Ribbentrop pact. Latvians and Lithuanians also asked that the contents of the protocols be revealed.

20 In January 1988, former Estonian political prisoners founded the Estonian Independence Party, defending the country's right to self-determination. In addition, this group called for the re-establishment of multiparty democracy, and the restoration of Estonian as the country's official language. Another group, the Estonian Heritage Society, began trying to locate and restore the country's historical monuments.

21 The Popular Front of Estonia (FPE), founded in April by nationalists and communists, organized a rally in June 1988 which was attended by 150,000 people. The outlawed Estonian flag was displayed on this occasion. In September, some 300,000 Estonians held another rally; a few days later, the ban on the flag was lifted.

22 In October, the first FPE congress reaffirmed Estonia's demand for autonomy, and asked Moscow for an admission of the fact that Estonia had been occupied against its will in 1940. The following month, Estonia's Parliament declared the country's sovereignty, and affirmed its right to veto laws imposed by Moscow without consent.

23 In August 1989, some two million Estonians, Latvians and Lithuanians formed a 560-km human chain from Tallinn to Vilnius to demand the independence of the Baltic States. In February 1990, a convention of Estonian representatives approved the Declaration of Independence, based on the 1920 Peace Treaty of Tartu.

24 In the May 1990 elections, the FPE and other nationalist groups won an ample majority within parliament. Moderate nationalist leader Edgar Savisaar was named as the leader of the first elected government since 1940. In August, parliament proclaimed the independence of Estonia, but Moscow did not consider it to be valid.

25 In late 1990 and early 1991, Moscow threatened to impede Estonia's separation from the USSR, by force, and skirmishes took place between Soviet troops and nationalist groups. In September, the USSR recognized the

IN FOCUS

ENVIRONMENTAL CHALLENGES
Estonia has an important fishing industry, although its fleet now has to fish further from its coastal waters because of pollution in the Baltic Sea, which contains toxic waste dumped by industries in several countries with Baltic coastlines. Neither Tallinn nor other cities have satisfactory sewerage systems. The northeast is polluted by power plant emissions of shale-oil. However, the level of polluting emissions has fallen drastically in the last two decades.

WOMEN'S RIGHTS
In 2000, 18 per cent of Parliament seats and 12 per cent of ministerial positions were held by women.

In 2000*, female school enrolment reached 97 per cent, and women teachers amounted to 82 per cent of all secondary-school teachers. The adult illiteracy rate remained at 0.2 per cent, both for women and men*.

Some 0.6 per cent of women between 15 and 24 were living with HIV/AIDS in 2000, while the percentage for men rose to 2.5 per cent.

Women made up 49 per cent of the labor force in the 1990-2000 period, with 7 per cent in agriculture, 23 per cent in industry and 70 per cent in services. Female unemployment reached 10.2 per cent in 2000.

CHILDREN
Four per cent of all children were underweight at birth. There was a 98 per cent net enrolment rate in primary school.

Some children and adolescents from the Tallin and Ida-Virumaa regions have drug problems. Young people hooked on injectable drugs may spend between 10,000 (approx $800) and 30,000 Estonian krooni per month on drugs. In 2002 the minimum wage was 1,600 Estonian krooni, then worth about $90; the average wage was 4,500 Estonian krooni, or $25). These adolescents have a hard time finding jobs, so they often end up in illegal activities such as drug-dealing, smuggling and prostitution.

A report by the ILO and the International Program on Elimination of Child Labor (IPECL) states that over the last years the number of 15 and 16 year-olds who have taken hard drugs has doubled. Fifty-three per cent of those seeking medical assistance started taking drugs before they were 18. The main first hard drug is heroin. Between 2000 and 2002 the number of HIV-positive users increased from 96 to 2,125. In 2000 there were 1,581 drug-related crimes.

INDIGENOUS PEOPLES/ ETHNIC MINORITIES
The Russian community is made up of 408,000 people living mainly in Tallinn and the border cities of Narva and Sillamae.This minority suffers political, economical and social discrimination and does not have any support for their demands from the Russian Government. The new citizenship act that promotes voting and political representation of Russians should lead to improvements. Nevertheless, Russians are better-off in Estonia than those living in other former Soviet countries.

Ukrainians are another minority group, making up 2.5 per cent of the total population.

MIGRANTS/REFUGEES
In 2001, 12 individuals requested asylum; 4 of them were from Syria. As in some other European countries, the Government puts asylum-seekers into reception centers, like the one in Illika, bordering Russia. Those who can financially support themselves are exempt.

In 2002 Estonia was seventh of 15 countries with the highest percentage of immigrants as a proportion of the total population (26.2 per cent). Most were Russian immigrants, who settled after independence.

DEATH PENALTY
Abolished in 1998.

*Latest data available in The State of the World's Children and Childinfo database, UNICEF, 2004.

independence of the three Baltic States, and that same month, they joined the United Nations.

26 In January, Savisaar and his government resigned in the face of growing criticism over its economic policy. Parliament named former transportation minister Tiit Vahi to head the new government. Estonia had to ration food and fuel when the Russian Federation began restricting and raising the price of its products.

27 On 20 June 1992, the new Constitution (based on the 1938 Constitution) was ratified by referendum. In September, the *Riigikogu* (Parliament) was elected. Lennart Meri, of the National Country Coalition Party (NCCP), was elected President on 5 October.

28 In June 1993, an overtly nationalistic law was approved, targetting foreigners - especially those of Russian origin who make up 30 per cent of the total population. The law obliges foreigners to apply for a discretionary residence permit.

29 The March 1995 elections led to the defeat of the coalition which had ruled Estonia since the former Soviet republic broke away from the USSR. The new Prime Minister, Tiit Vahi, caused a controversy when he named a 'disproportionate' number of former communist ministers in his government. In October his cabinet was forced to resign due to corruption charges against the Minister of the Interior. The new government was formed with the inclusion of Reform Party (RP) members.

30 In February 1998, Estonia, Latvia and Lithuania signed a Letter of Association with the US. In it, Washington committed itself to supporting the three states' integration into NATO. Russia announced it would normalize its relations with the Baltic states on condition that they normalize the situation of Russian-speaking minorities.

31 Mart Laar was appointed Prime Minister in March 1999. A new program was launched to help compensate for the social impact caused by the lay-offs of Russian-speakers who did not speak Estonian. One project, aimed at encouraging Estonian families in Narva to take in young people was set up in the Lake Peipus region. This area straddles the border with Russia and 95 per cent of the residents speak Russian.

32 In October 2001, Arnold Ruutel, former member of the Central Committee in the Soviet era, became President.

33 Laar resigned in January 2002, alleging the 'betrayal' of the Reform Party, which had 'given up' the city of Tallinn to the opposition. During his term, Estonia, as well as becoming the strongest economy of the former Soviet republics, had started talks on EU membership.

34 In 2003, a referendum was held in which 67 per cent of voters agreed to join the European Union.

35 In January 2004, the Presidents of Estonia and Cyprus signed two cooperation agreements, one on education and culture and the other to fight organized crime.

36 Estonia became a full member of the European Union on 1 May 2004. ∎

Ethiopia / Ityop'iya

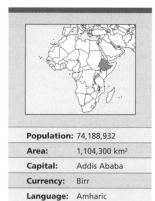

Population:	74,188,932
Area:	1,104,300 km²
Capital:	Addis Ababa
Currency:	Birr
Language:	Amharic

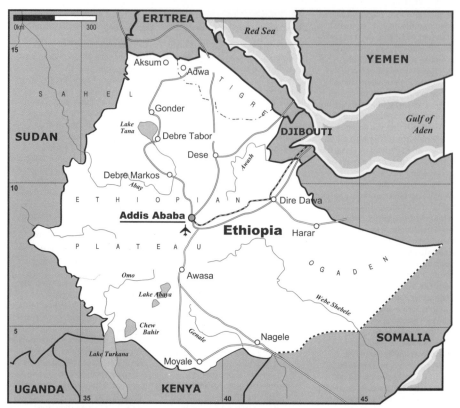

The first hominid, called Australopithecus or southern ape, appeared in the Ohma river valley in Ethiopia, two million years ago. The Australopithecus was characterized by walking upright; it made tools, fed on meat and lived in groups. The appearance of the Australopithecus marked the beginning of the cultural evolution of humankind.

[2] Axum, in the north of present-day Ethiopia, was the center of trade between the Upper Nile valley and the Red Sea ports which traded with Arabia and India; it reached its height in the first centuries AD. Ethiopia was a rich and prosperous state, which was able to subdue present-day Yemen, but which went through a crisis in the 7th century. Trade routes moved as Arab unification and expansion dominated the area, conquering Egypt.

[3] The Ethiopian ruling elite had converted to Christianity in the 4th century, further contributing to their isolation. Expansion towards the south, excessive growth of the clergy, and declining trade led to a process of social and economic stratification similar to that in feudal western Europe. By the 16th century, one third of the land belonged to the 'king of kings'; another third belonged to the monasteries and the rest was divided among the nobility and the rest of the population.

[4] The Muslim population that had developed a powerful trade economy on the coast of the Red Sea, instigated an insurrection, leading Ethiopia to resume its relations with Europe to request assistance. The aid took almost a century to arrive, but the Portuguese fleet, when it finally arrived in 1541, was decisive in destroying the Sultanate of Adal (See Somalia).

[5] For 150 years, Ethiopian emperors focused their efforts on the coast, giving Oromo (a people akin to the Hausa) a chance to gradually penetrate from the west until they became a majority. Their influence grew so great that an Oromo became emperor, between 1755 and 1769; though the Amhara ruling elite took great pains to oust him.

[6] This state of affairs continued until 1889 when Menelik II came to power. Designated heir to the throne in 1869, he spent the next 20 years training an army (with British and Italian assistance) and organizing the administration of his own territory, the state of Shoa. His efficiency was fortunate; in 1895 his former allies, the Italians, invaded the country claiming that previous commitments had not been honored. The final battle was fought in Adua in 1896 where 4,000 of the 10,000 Italian soldiers were killed. It was the most devastating defeat suffered by European troops on African soil until the Algerian War.

[7] In the diplomatic negotiations that followed their defeat, the Italians succeeded in obtaining two territories that Ethiopia did not really control: Eritrea and the southern Somalian coast. In 1906, the world powers recognized the independence and territorial integrity of what was then known as Abyssinia, in exchange for certain economic privileges.

[8] This arrangement saved Ethiopia from direct colonization until 1936, when Italian Fascist dictator Benito Mussolini invaded the country and overthrew Haile Selassie, Menelik's heir.

[9] During the five-year occupation, several industries as well as coffee plantations were started, and a system of racial discrimination was installed, similar to that of apartheid in South Africa.

[10] In 1948, Ethiopians won their autonomy back from Britain, which had taken over the country after Mussolini's defeat. When Selassie took the throne, his country was floundering in unprecedented crisis: foreign occupation had disrupted production; nationalist political movements had strengthened in the struggle for autonomy and rejected a return to feudalism; and poverty in the interior had grown considerably.

[11] Selassie denounced colonialism, favored non-alignment and supported the creation of the Organization for African Unity, which finally set up headquarters in Addis Ababa. He also maintained close links with Israel. Selassie's Government was dominated by a state bureaucracy, had a US-based educational system and the largest army in sub-Saharan Africa.

[12] The agrarian structure remained almost as it always had been: feudal landowners and the Orthodox Church held 80 per cent of the country's fertile lands. Plantations for export crops of cotton, and sugar began to expand in the 1950s, while the main crop, coffee, was mainly cultivated by small farmers. In 1974, after a series of strikes, student rallies and widespread protests against absolutism and food shortages, Haile Selassie was overthrown.

[13] An Armed Forces Coordination Committee, the Dergue

WORKERS

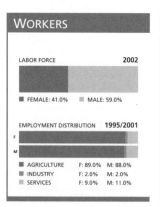

LABOR FORCE   **2002**

■ FEMALE: 41.0%   ■ MALE: 59.0%

EMPLOYMENT DISTRIBUTION   **1995/2001**

F

M

■ AGRICULTURE	F: 89.0%	M: 88.0%
■ INDUSTRY	F: 2.0%	M: 2.0%
■ SERVICES	F: 9.0%	M: 11.0%

LAND USE

2000

IRRIGATED AREA: 1.8% of arable land

■ ARABLE LAND: 10.0%	
■ CROPLANDS: 0.7%	
■ OTHER USE: 89.3%	

Life expectancy
45.5 years
2000-2005

GNI per capita
$100
2002

Literacy
39% total adult rate
2000

HIV prevalence rate
6.4% of population 15-49 years old
2001

('committee' in Amharic), headed by General Aman Andom abolished the monarchy and proclaimed a republic, suspending the Constitution and dissolving Parliament.

14   After subsequent internal crisis, Colonel Mengistu Haile Mariam rose to power in December 1977. He managed to hold the Dergue together and put an end to the military's internal struggles.

15   The military government nationalized foreign banks, insurance companies and heavy industry. US military bases were closed down. The key to the 'National Democratic Revolution' was the State's takeover of land, which put an end to the power of landowners. 'Scientific Socialism' was adopted as the official ideology in June 1976. The opposition was put down by the 'red terror' between 1977 and 1978. Thousands of people were executed during this period.

16   After settling this latest crisis, the Government was able to confront the two separatist movements which had been gaining strength since 1977, in Eritrea and the Ogaden desert. The Eritrean rebels considered that their independence struggle was valid, regardless of the existence of a progressive government in Addis Ababa, and the Somali population of the Ogaden desert (claimed by Somalia) took advantage of the domestic crisis in Addis Ababa to further their own separatist cause.

17   Faced with Somalia's attempt to annex the Ogaden, the USSR broke its military treaties with Somali President Siad Barre. In this modern armed war, Soviet and Cuban support was decisive in the defeat of Somali troops. The Eritrean separatists were forced to retreat after a major offensive in 1979. Meanwhile, a peasant-based guerrilla warfare had broken out in the Tigray region.

18   With the military situation temporarily resolved, Mengistu turned his attention back to domestic policy. In 1979, the Government set up the Ethiopian Workers' Party Organization Committee (COPWE). In that year, there was a 15 per cent increase in cultivated land, which raised the GNP by 6 per cent.

19   In 1984, the country was struggling under the effects of a drought which had begun in 1982, causing thousands of deaths from starvation. The drought affected twelve provinces, threatened five million lives and killed over half a million people.

20   That year, the Ethiopian Workers' Party (PWE) held their founding congress, approving a program to transform the country into a socialist state.

21   The newly-elected Assembly (the Shengo, or parliament) proclaimed the People's Democratic Republic of Ethiopia on 12 September, ratifying Mengistu Haile Mariam as head of state. Separatists extended operations in Eritrea and Tigray, as well as in Wollo, Gondar and Oromo in the south.

22   The new constitution provided for the creation of five autonomous regions and 25 administrative regions. Eritrea was able to legislate on all matters except defense, national security, foreign relations and its legal status in relation to central government. The separatists rejected the proposal, calling it 'colonial'.

23   The rebel military activity took a heavy toll on the Ethiopian army and in 1989 12 divisions (150,000 troops) stationed in the front line attempted a coup. Mengistu returned hastily from West Germany and put down the coup.

24   In September 1989, the last Cuban soldiers withdrew from Ethiopia. The Government had signed a peace agreement in April 1988, and no longer needed their services.

25   In 1990, within the framework of political changes in the Soviet bloc, the Central Committee of the Ethiopian Workers' Party decided to restructure the party and change its name to the Ethiopian Democratic Union Party (EDUP). While excluding the possibility of a multiparty system, the changes sought to lay the basis of 'a party of all Ethiopians', open to 'opposition groups'. The Marxist-Leninist tag was dropped. The Government established a mixed economy, including state enterprises, cooperatives and private businesses.

26   In May 1991, after overwhelming guerrilla victories in the north, Mengistu Mariam unexpectedly fled the country. The Government was left in the hands of Vice-President Tesfaye Gabre Kidane, considered a moderate, who initiated his transitional

IN FOCUS

ENVIRONMENTAL CHALLENGES
Many regions once rich in vegetation are now rocky, desert areas. Desertification and erosion have increased within the last years as a result of deforestation, intensive grazing and inappropriate use of water in agriculture. 4.2 million people suffer from lack of water.

WOMEN'S RIGHTS
Ethiopian women have been able to vote and be elected since 1955. In 2000, they held 2 per cent of seats in Parliament and 5 per cent of ministerial positions.

Women's life expectancy is 46.3 years old*. 42 per cent of pregnant women are anemic and 27 per cent receiv prenatal care*. Only 6 per cent of births are attended by trained health staff*.

In 2000, women made up 41 per cent of the total labor force. Between 1990 and 2000, 88 per cent worked in agriculture, 2 per cent in industry and 10 per cent in services.

In 1995, 45 per cent of Ethiopian women were victims of physical violence. It is estimated that 90 per cent of women have suffered genital mutilation.

In some regions, abduction is used to take a girl as wife. The girl is taken by a group of men and then raped by the prospective husband. The elders from the man's village apologize to the family of the victim and ask them to agree to the marriage. The family often consents because a girl who has lost her virginity will not be able to marry. Articles 558 and 599 of the 1957 Penal Code allow rapists to escape punishment by marrying the woman they rape.

CHILDREN
In 2001, 490,000 under-5s died. 47 per cent of children under 5 are moderately or severely under weight*.

Ethiopia is one of the countries worst affected by HIV/AIDS: 7.3 per cent of the adult population carries the virus. By 2001, there were 990,000 children orphaned by this disease. The drought may accelerate transmission of the virus, as people are forced to move and may become involved in sex work as a survival strategy.

INDIGENOUS PEOPLES/ ETHNIC MINORITIES
The Afar (2 per cent of the population) live in the east, practise both Islam and Christianity and are mostly nomadic pastoralists. They have inhabited these lands for over 2,800 years. They were among the first victims of colonialism in Africa, which decided the break-up of their territorial unit into the three states of Djibouti, Eritrea and Ethiopia.

Amhara people (27 per cent of the population) reside mainly in the north and in Addis Ababa. In 1,500 BC, together with the current Tigray peoples, they created the Axum Empire. In spite of being a minority within the population, their traditional leaders took part in the bureaucratic hierarchy of the empire.

The Oromo (30 per cent of the population) are the largest ethnic group in the country, mainly living in the south. They farm and raise cattle; practising Islam or Christianity, except for about 15 per cent of their rural population that follow traditional religions. Together with the Amhara and the Tigrayans they dominated the Government and

military classes of the Ethiopian Empire.

Somalis (39 per cent of the population) practise Islam and are pastoralists. On account of their opposition to the Ethiopian State, they did not take part in the Government until 1995. They inhabit two semi-autonomous regions: Dire Dawa and Ogaden, in eastern Ethiopia.

Tigrayans (5 per cent of the population) are Christians and mostly inhabit the northern Tigray province, where they work in agriculture. They are descendants of Semites who arrived in the region about 3,000 years ago. After a long exclusion from political power, the Tigrayan People's Liberation Front is part of the governing coalition and its leader Meles Zenawi is Prime Minister.

MIGRANTS/REFUGEES
At the end of 2002, Ethiopia hosted nearly 115,000 refugees, all from neighboring countries.

At that time, more than 20,000 Ethiopian refugees or asylum-seekers were registered in neighboring and European countries. Between 1991 and 2002, about 800,000 Ethiopian refugees came back after having fled their country during the 1974-1991 dictatorship. Some 90,000 Ethiopians were internally displaced at year's end, as a result of droughts and the 1998-2000 war with Eritrea.

DEATH PENALTY
In force for all crimes. After a period of time without executions, the practice was restored in 1998.

*Latest data available in *The State of the World's Children* and *Childinfo* database, UNICEF, 2004.

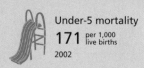

government by negotiating a cease-fire with the Eritrean rebels.

27 Kidane's government took part in peace talks, in London, presided over by the US, with the participation of the most important rebel groups. They aimed at reaching an agreement which would stave off civil war. Kidane resigned in late May, when the US advised the forces of the Ethiopian People's Revolutionary Democratic Front (EPRDF) to take control of Addis Ababa.

28 Ata Meles Zenawi, leader of the EPRDF, became interim president, until a multi-party conference could be held. He promised to bring the civil war to an end, re-establish democracy and put an end to hunger. Three months later, upon reopening Parliament and passing a new Constitution, Zenawi pledged to hold elections within a year.

29 In March 1992, the new regional Councils were elected. However the Oromo Liberation Front announced its withdrawal from the Council of Representatives, made up of 87 members, which legitimized the transitional government.

30 The transitional government promised to promote the market economy, stimulate agricultural production and reduce poverty, within a five year program coordinated by UN and the World Bank.

31 In 1994, the delivery of the $1.2 billion in five years planned in the economic program, slowed down considerably as the international organizations decided the Ethiopian government was privatizing too slowly. In a criticism of the structural adjustment plan proposed by the IMF and the World Bank, humanitarian organizations supporting Ethiopia said there should be greater investment in seeds, tools and livestock. Within the last 20 years, more than one million Ethiopians had died of starvation and another million had to seek refuge in neighboring countries.

32 In May 1994, the Council of Representatives, a temporary 87-member body, approved a draft Constitution which created the Federal Democratic Republic of Ethiopia. This draft was based on the 'ethnic federalism' doctrine, which put an end to the previous official unified vision of the nation. According to the approved document, the 'sovereignty resides in the nations, nationalities and peoples of Ethiopia' and not the people as a whole.

33 In June, elections were held for a Constituent Assembly, but were boycotted by main opposition parties, like the Oromo Liberation Front and the Ogaden National Liberation Front.

34 In May and June 1995, parliamentary elections were held, also boycotted by most of the opposition parties. The new federal republic was officially established in August, when Negasso Gidada, a Christian Oromo from the Welega region in the west of Ethiopia, took over the presidency. The outgoing president, Meles Zenawi, became Prime Minister and the 17 members of government were carefully selected to reflect 'the ethnic balance' of the country.

35 The Government went ahead with the privatization of state companies - 144 in 1995 - and the annual grain deficit stood at around a million tons. In 1996, there was an abortive assassination attempt against Mengistu. The World Bank announced a large reduction in the Ethiopian debt. In 1997, Amnesty repeated its plea for the liberation of members of the opposition and called for an end to arbitrary arrests, torture and disappearances.

36 In early 1998, food shortages threatened millions of Ethiopians. Due to the price increases set by the Government (13 per cent between August and December 1997) the satisfaction of basic needs become increasingly difficult for the poorer people. The Ethiopian Disaster Prevention and Preparedness Commission (DPPC) formally called on international organizations for help to avoid another famine.

37 Fighting against Eritrea began again in February 1999, following the short war that in May 1998 killed more than a thousand people. The UN Security Council called for an immediate cease-fire and a weapons and communications warfare embargo.

38 In March 1999, US President Bill Clinton proposed the cancellation of $70 billion of foreign aid paid to 46 African countries in a meeting of ministers in Addis. At this time, Clinton was under pressure from Congress to approve its 'Trade initiative with Africa'.

39 Heavily-armed troops from Ethiopia entered Eritrea in May 2000, capturing 300 prisoners. As in 1998, the UN Security Council issued a three-day ultimatum to stop fighting, and the US proposed an arms embargo on both countries which was rejected by Russia. Arms were allegedly being sold by the former Soviet republics of Eastern Europe. The ultimatum expired and the conflict continued.

40 Thousands of people celebrated the decision of the Permanent Court of Arbitration at The Hague, in April 2002, to mark the boundaries of Ethiopia's 1,000 kilometer border with Eritrea. The government in Addis considered it a victory for its demands, although

PROFILE

ENVIRONMENT

A mountainous country with altitudes of over 4,000 meters. Ethiopia is isolated from neighboring regions by its geography. In the mountains and plateaus, the vegetation varies with altitude. The Dega are cool, rainy highlands, above 2,500 meters, where grain is grown and cattle raised. The deep valleys which traverse the highlands are warm and rainy with tropical vegetation, known as the Kolla (up to 1,500 m). The drier, cooler, medium-range plateaus where coffee and cotton are grown (1,500 to 2,500 m) are the most densely populated parts of the country. To the East lies the Ogaden, a semi-desert plateau inhabited by nomadic shepherds of Somali origin.

SOCIETY

Peoples: There are more than 90 ethnic groups of which only seven have more than 1 million people. One-third of the population are Oromo, approximately a quarter are Amhara and a tenth are Tigrayan. There are also Gurage, Somali, Sidama and Wolaita. At present there are 22 recognized minorities.
Religions: The Amhara and Tigrayans are mostly Christians. The Somali, Afar and Aderi are mostly Muslims. African traditional religions are also practised. **Languages:** There are four major language families: Semitic (Amhara), Cushitic (Oromo, Somali, Afar), Omotic and Nilo-Saharan. Amharic is the official language, among other 80 registered languages. Tigrayans speak Tigrigna.
Main Political Parties: Ethiopian People's Revolutionary Democratic Front (EPRDF) is made up of several members: Tigray People's Liberation Front; Oromo People's Democratic Organization; Southern Ethiopian People's Democratic Union; Ethiopian People's Democratic Movement.

THE STATE

Official Name: Federal Democratic Republic of Ethiopia.
Administrative Divisions: There are nine ethnically-based states and 2 self-governing administrations (Addis Ababa and Dire Dawa). **Capital:** Addis Ababa (Adis Abeba) 2,723,000 people (2003). **Other Cities:** Dire Dawa 202,700 people; Harar 93,900 (2000). **Government:** Federal Republic. Girma Wolde-Giorgis, President since October 2001; Meles Zenawi, Prime Minister since August 1995, re-elected in 2000. Bicameral Legislature: the Federal Parliamentary Assembly is formed by the Council of People's Representatives, with 527 members, and Council of the Federation, with 117 members. **National Holiday:** 28 May, Overthrow of the Dergue (1991). **Armed Forces:** 120,000 (1995)

its claim over the port of Asseb was not taken into account by the commission.

41 In late April, Ethiopia decided to close its border with Eritrea to UN officials, accusing them of having taken journalists from Eritrea to the area without Ethiopian visas. The Eritrean Government accused Ethiopia of hampering the boundary setting process and of not complying with the recent border decision.

42 Also in April, UNICEF revealed that between 100,000 and 200,000 children lived on the streets and were exposed to danger from exploitation, sexual abuse, prostitution and HIV/AIDS.

43 In April and May 2002, demonstrations over the results of local elections spiraled into bloodshed between Ethiopian security forces and ethnic Sheko and Mezehenger populations in the southwestern Ethiopian town of Tepi. The violence killed more than 150 civilians, uprooted nearly 5,000

others, and destroyed some 1,000 homes.

44 In December 2002, the Swiss transnational Nestlé demanded $6 million in compensation from the nationalization carried out in 1975 by the Tafari Benti (1974-1977) Government. Nearly 40,000 people sent emails calling on Nestlé to withdraw its claim. In January, the transnational agreed to reduce its claim to $1.5 million which would be reinvested in national feeding programs.

45 In June 2003, more than 12.5 million Ethiopians were dependent on food aid.

46 In September 2003 Eritrea accused Ethiopia of violating international law by failing to accept a ruling on the boundary drawn up by an independent commission in 2002. Eritrea said Ethiopia was still claiming the village of Badme, the starting point of the war, despite the fact that it had been allotted to Eritrea by the commission. ■

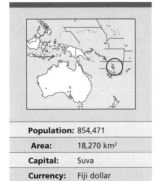

Population:	854,471
Area:	18,270 km²
Capital:	Suva
Currency:	Fiji dollar
Language:	English

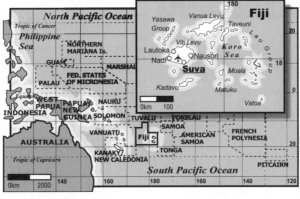

F our thousand years ago the Fijian archipelago was already populated. Melanesian migrations first reached the islands in the 6th century BC, and the Fijians had one of the leading Pacific cultures. In 1789, British Captain William Bligh (of Mutiny on the Bounty fame) visited the islands, writing the first detailed account of Fijian life.

2   Social life on the islands was organized in families and clans which gradually formed larger communities. One of these, ruled by traditional leader Na Ulivau, extended its influence from Ngau over the rest of the islands, achieving unification.

3   In 1830, the first Christian missionaries arrived from Tonga and 24 years later achieved a major victory by christening ruler Thakombau, son of Na Ulivau. This 'king' (formerly reported to be a 'cannibal') became such an enthusiastic admirer of the Western world that he offered to annex Fiji to the US. The White House, caught up in the turmoil of the Secession War, missed the opportunity to tack another star on the flag. The British, faced with a shortage of sugar, 'discovered' the archipelago's potential for growing cane and officially annexed the islands on 10 October 1874.

4   Fijian officials raised no objections to the purchase or expropriation of large tracts of land for the new crops, though the peasants were unwilling to leave their communal estates to work on the plantations. Consequently, a massive influx of bonded laborers were brought in, first from the Solomon islands, and then from India.

5   At the end of their contracts, Indian workers brought their families to Fiji and became small shop owners, craftspeople or bureaucrats in the colonial administration, and retained their language, religion and caste system.

6   Initial moves toward local autonomy resulted in a complicated electoral system securing political control by the 'natives' who were in the minority. Prime Minister Sir Kamisese Mara initiated an elaborate scheme of representation, which proved useful in preventing major disruptions during the transition to independence in 1970. His Alliance Party claimed to be multiracial, and marshaled support from some Indians and other minor groups, in addition to the Fijian electorate.

7   In 1976, the Government turned down a constitutional reform project which would have required multi-group cooperation in the country's administration.

8   The 1970s economic difficulties forced thousands of Fijians to emigrate to New Zealand (Aotearoa) in search of jobs. Individualism and private land ownership were encouraged, seeking to bolster the economic situation of 'natives' over that of the Indians. However, under these conditions, the rural workers gained few improvements; urban income increased by 3.5 per cent in 1978, but rural income increased only 0.3 per cent.

9   The difficult economic situation swelled the number of 'racist' groups such as the Nationalist Party, militant against the Indian majority, though Indians have been on the islands for five generations.

10   Former Prime Minister Kamisese Mara's conservative administration was deeply marked by racial and ideological trends. His government was the only one in the Commonwealth to maintain relations with the racist Rhodesian and South African regimes and to welcome Chilean dictator Augusto Pinochet on an official visit in early 1980.

11   In the 1982 election, the incumbent Alliance Party retained office with a small margin over the opposition National Federation Party (NFP), which had united its two rival factions despite growing conflict within the party.

12   In the 11 April 1987 election, the Indian majority won and Timoci Bavadra became premier, ending 16 years of government by Melanesians. A few days after the election, Bavadra was overthrown by a military coup led by Colonel Sitiveni Rabuka, who justified himself as 'attempting to solve the ethnic problem'. However, his real objective seemed to be the removal of the Indian Government, which believed in an independent foreign policy, and planned to join the treaty of Rarotonga. The treaty promoted regional denuclearization; endorsed by Australia and New

IN FOCUS

ENVIRONMENTAL CHALLENGES
Overfishing and pollution of the coastal waters threaten the marine environment. Deforestation and soil erosion on the islands are caused by intensive agriculture.

WOMEN'S RIGHTS
In the year 2000, women held 11 per cent of the parliamentary seats (showing a 7 per cent rise in just 5 years) and 10 per cent of the ministerial positions. They have had the vote and been eligible for office since 1963. Women comprise 31 per cent of the workforce. Total fertility rate is 2.9 children per woman*. Virtually all births are attended by trained health staff; however, 75 women die in childbirth or from pregnancy-related causes per 100,000 live births*.

CHILDREN
The under-5 mortality rate is 21 deaths per 1,000 live births*. Ten per cent of newborns are underweight; 95 per cent of the children are immunized against common childhood diseases such as polio, measles and tetanus*.

Fiji is a popular destination for sex tourists (tourism generates almost one third of the nation's income). Child abuse within the family is one of the main reasons children go into prostitution. The Committee on the Rights of the Child has expressed concern at the lack of information on child abuse, including prostitution, and also over the lack of both financial and human resources to prevent and combat child abuse.

INDIGENOUS PEOPLES/ ETHNIC MINORITIES
Ethnic Fijians constitute 50 per cent of Fiji's population while descendants of Indian immigrants brought to work on sugar plantations comprise 43 per cent. While 83 per cent of arable land belongs to indigenous people, 75 per cent of the Indian Fijians work on sugar plantations.
Ethnic Fijians are mainly settled in urban areas and in the southern islands. They speak Fijian and most of them are Methodist Christians. When the British colonized Fiji in 1874, Fijians cooperated with them in order to maintain their political and economical advantages over the other ethnic groups in the country.
Indians, who are dispersed all over the country, are the main population in the eastern areas where the sugar plantations are located. They speak Hindi and are primarily Hindus or Muslims. They were imported as laborers by the British but given few rights. They are still restricted in their political participation. Indians are seeking equal civil rights, a role in political decision-making and also freedom of religious and cultural expression.

MIGRANTS/REFUGEES
About 100 Fijians who had been internally displaced during the 2000-2001 coup returned in 2002. There is no data regarding refugees or asylum-seekers within Fiji.

DEATH PENALTY
The death penalty for ordinary crimes was abolished in 1979. There have been no executions since 1964.

*Latest data available in *The State of the World's Children* and *Childinfo* database, UNICEF, 2004.

Life expectancy	GNI per capita	Literacy	HIV prevalence rate
69.8 years 2000-2005	**$2,160** 2002	**93%** total adult rate 2000	**0.1%** of population 15-49 years old 2001

PROFILE

ENVIRONMENT

Fiji consists of nine large islands and 300 volcanic and coral islets and atolls, of which only 100 are inhabited. The group is located in Melanesia, in the Koro Sea, between Vanuatu (formerly New Hebrides) to the west and Tonga to the east, five degrees north of the Tropic of Capricorn. The largest islands are Viti Levu, where the capital is located, Vanua Levu, Taveuni, Lau, Kandavu, Asua, Karo, Ngau and Ovalau. The terrain is mainly mountainous. Fertile soils in flatland zones plus tropical rainy climate, mildly tempered by sea winds, make the islands suitable for plantation crops, sugarcane and copra.

SOCIETY

Peoples: Half of Fijians are of Melanesian origin with some Polynesian influence, the other are descendants of Indian workers who came to the archipelago early in the 20th century; plus those of European and Chinese origin. Banabans (see Kiribati) have bought the island of Rambi, between Vanua Levu and Taveuni, with the purpose of settling there since their own island was left uninhabitable by phosphate mining.
Religions: 53 per cent of Fijians are Christian (mainly Methodist and other Protestant sects) 38 per cent are Hindu and 8 per cent Muslim.
Languages: English (official), Urdu, Hindi, Fijian, Chinese. Rotuma and Kiribati (minority languages).
Main Political Parties: There are 26 registered political parties (2001). The main ones are: Soqosoqo Duavata Ni Lewenivanua/ United Fiji Party (UFP/SDL), led by Laisenia Qarase; Fiji Labor Party (FLP), led by Mahendra Chaudry; Conservative Alliance/Matanitu Vanua (MV), members include George Speight; New Labor Unity Party (NLUP); United General Party (UGP); National Federation Party (NFP).
Main Social Organizations: The Association of Fijian Young People and Students, Fijian Trade Unions Congress (FTUC).

THE STATE

Official Name: Republic of the Fiji Islands.
Administrative Divisions: 5 Regions divided into 15 Provinces.
Capital: Suva 210,000 people (2003).
Other Cities: Lautoka 45,000 people; Nadi 32,100; Nausori 22,500 (2000). **Government:** Ratu Josefa Iloilo, President since July 2000. Prime Minister, Laisenia Qarase, caretaker since March 2001; elected September 2001. Parliament: House of Representatives (Vale) has 71 members (23 Fijians, 19 Indians, 3 'others', 1 representative of Rotuma island, 25 open seats). The Senate (Seniti) has 34 members (24 appointed by the Great Council of Chiefs, 9 appointed by the Prime Minister, and 1 appointed by the council of Rotuma).
National Holiday: 10 October, Independence Day (1970).
Armed Forces: 3,900 (1995).

Zealand, but criticized by Britain and the US.

[13] The main Indian and Melanesian political parties reached an agreement, with added pressure from the Commonwealth, which appeared to appease the military. However, on 6 October 1987, Rabuka retaliated by proclaiming a Republic in a move intended to disavow the authority of the head of state, the British-appointed governor.

[14] In December, Rabuka resigned as head of state in an attempt to create an image of a joint civilian-military government, aimed at improving its foreign image. Penaia Ganilau was named President and Kamisese Mara, Prime Minister - a regime never subjected to the approval of the electorate.

[15] In July 1990 a new constitutional decree based on apartheid went into effect, assuring the indigenous people 37 of the Chamber of Representatives 70 seats and 24 of the Senate's 34 seats. A constitutional referendum announced for 1992 was finally cancelled. The following year, the UN's General Assembly, as well as Mauritius and India denounced the apartheid model.

[16] Rabuka founded the Fijian Political Party (FPP/SVT) and in 1992, amid growing political and social strains, a military officer was named Prime Minister.

[17] Fiji was not able to overcome its chronic balance of payments deficit: almost all of its fuel and manufactured products were imported and its main sources of income - sugar exports and tourism - were not enough to balance the budget.

[18] In November 1993 six FPP/SVT members voted together with the opposition against the budget, forcing general elections. Rabuka retained power with 31 of the 37 Fijian seats and support from independent and General Vote Party members. Dissidents formed a Fijian Association obtaining only five seats.

[19] In November 1994, the Government began a timid revision of the racist constitution. In 1995, Rabuka had to reorganize his Cabinet several times due to internal divisions in the coalition.

[20] In September 1996, a Commission completed a report on the new constitution, which created a 'multiracial council' and reserved a certain number of seats in Parliament for certain ethnic groups. The document was approved in July 1997, coming into operation a year later.

[21] In September 1997, Fiji was readmitted into the British Commonwealth, 10 years after the coup which took it out.

[22] In the first truly democratic elections since the coup, in May 1999, the victor was Mahendra Chaudhry, of the Fiji Labor Party (FLP). The Fijian Political Party (FPP/SVT) headed by Rabuka, won just six of the 71 parliamentary seats. Its ally, the General Voters Party, which had been the minority, did not win any seats.

[23] Although tens of thousands of Indians had fled Fiji since the 1987 coup, they represented nearly half the population. Ethnic tensions exploded on 19 May 2000, when an armed group led by Fijian entrepreneur George Speight entered Parliament and abducted Prime Minister Mahendra along with 30 others (including the daughter of President Kamisese Mara). Speight was seeking a reform of the Constitution to instate Fijian supremacy and thereby prevent an Indian minority from holding power.

[24] President Mara deposed the abducted Prime Minister, believing it would undermine Speight's importance and force a change of attitude. Commodore Frank Bainarama led a new coup on 29 May and overthrew the President, saying he had become weak and inoperative.

[25] The rebels were granted amnesty after releasing the hostages. In July, Ratu Josefa Iloilo was named interim President, while Laisenia Qarase was made Prime Minister, also interim. Because Speight had threatened to renew protests if the Cabinet did not include his supporters, the army arrested him and over 350 rebels.

[26] The coup left a deep wound in the country. Racial divisions intensified. In February 2001 the Fiji High Court ruled that the current military-backed government was illegal; the Government announced elections would be held in August that year.

[27] Ilikini Naitini (commonly known as George Speight) of the Conservative Alliance (MV) was elected Prime Minister while he was in prison awaiting trial for treason. The United Fiji Party/SDL won 46 per cent of the vote, capping the 38 per cent of Mahendra Chaudhry's Fiji Labor party (FLP); the MV came third with 8 per cent. Although the 1997 Constitution gave the parties the right to occupy a number of seats in the Cabinet proportional to their representation in Parliament, Qarase, still chief of the interim government, excluded Chaudry's party from the Cabinet. The Supreme Court reversed the decision and ordered Qarase to include Indians in the Cabinet.

[28] In December, Speight was removed from office and shortly after, he was sentenced to death, accused of treason. However, in February 2002, President Iloilo commuted his sentence to life imprisonment.

[29] The return to democracy meant a slow recovery of the country's economy, which depends mainly on the tourism and sugar industries. Political instability in 2000-2002 led to a 70 per cent decline in tourists, particularly those from Australia, New Zealand and the US, since their governments included Fiji in the list of countries they advised tourists to avoid.

[30] In November 2002 the sugar sector began a transformation, after the Government announced the privatization and restructuring of state industries. The sugar industry employs 200,000 workers and its revenues comprise 7 per cent of Fiji's GDP

[31] In November 2003, the US Government asked Fiji to send troops to 'maintain peace' in Iraq, offering to pay for the soldiers' uniforms, weapons and transport. The Fijian Government said it could not afford the costs of such a mission. About 100 Fijian soldiers took part in the invasion of Iraq as part of the British Armed Forces.

[32] The Asian Development Bank (ADB) granted Fiji $40,000 a year in loans for the period 2004-2006. The three-year program includes infrastructure projects to rebuild airports, upgrade roads and promote urban development. ■

Finland / Süomi

Population:	5,223,605
Area:	338,150 km²
Capital:	Helsinski
Currency:	Euro
Language:	Finnish

The ancestors of today's Sami people lived in nomadic groups, 7,500 years BC, in what is now Finland. According to archeological evidence, there were two Stone Ages, before the people were pushed to the north around 4,000 years BC, after the arrival of the Finno-Ugrics from the Urals area. It was then that Samis began practicing agriculture and domesticating animals.

² The Finno-Ugric immigration was made up of two groups: the ancestors of the *tavastlanders* who came from the Gulf of Finland, and the Carelians who arrived from the southeast. At that period, Scandinavian peoples (mostly Swedes) occupied the west coast, the archipelagos and Ahvenanmaa Island. The Scandinavians prevailed as an ethnic group in the subsequent evolution of the Finnish population.

³ In the 1st century AD, groups of Finns that had emigrated from the Volga regions of Russia, settled and fought against the *tavastlanders* and Carelians who, simultaneously, were fighting between themselves over land.

⁴ In the Viking Age (between the 8th and 9th centuries), the Finns did not take part in the expeditions. They mainly settled in the north, where they sold furs along the trade routes to Russia. Towards the end of this period, Finland's territory was a route for German and Russian goods.

⁵ Finland was claimed by both the Russian and Swedish empires from the 12th century until their respective demises. In 1172, the Pope advised the Swedes to control the Finns, to avoid their being proselytized by the Russian Orthodox Church. The Church of Sweden joined the Protestant Reformation in the 16th century. This unleashed a major peasant revolt. Peasants were dissatisfied with their poor living conditions and the foreign policy imposed by Sweden (Club War 1596-97). The translation of the New Testament in 1548 was the first book printed in Finnish.

⁶ Between 1634 and 1721, the territory of Finland was incorporated into the Kingdom of Sweden. This period of political stability and the spread of Protestantism helped unite the Finns.

⁷ The Kingdom of Sweden began to weaken after the Great Northern War (1721). Alexander I of Russia succeeded in occupying Finland in 1808 and in 1809 it became a grand duchy of Imperial Russia. He granted Finland certain autonomy, allowing the *Diet* (parliament) to operate, as well as the army and the local judicial system.

⁸ Once they became subjects of the Russian Empire, the Finns began to develop a national movement. They defended their religious identity by actively supporting the Lutheran Church. They also collected medieval pagan legends and myths about the early Finno-Ugric groups, as well as epic tales like the *Kalevala*, which was written in Finnish.

⁹ Until the mid-19th century, Swedish - which was only spoken by a minority - was the only language allowed in schools and universities and there were almost no publications in Finnish. In that period, the campaign for Finnish, the language of the majority, to be the main language became a key issue. The climax came in 1850 when the authorities banned the printing of all books in Finnish, except prayer books and bibles.

¹⁰ The Russian Empire allowed the opening of the first Finnish Grammar School in 1858 and promised to make Finnish the official language 25 years later. But, on the unification of Germany (1861-70), Czar Nicholas II strengthened the Russian military and civil presence in Finland and restricted the relative autonomy granted by his predecessors.

¹¹ The main opposition came from the Labor Party, founded in 1899, which four years later changed its name to Social Democratic Party (SDP), after joining the Second Socialist International (1889). The SDP formed a single front, together with the Constitutionalists who had been expelled from the Diet.

¹² After its defeat by Japan, Russia's weakness facilitated the complete reform of the parliamentary and voting systems in 1905. In 1906, a single-chamber Parliament was created, and universal and equal suffrage was established. Parliament was dissolved several times by the Russian Emperor until it was finally closed in 1910.

¹³ During World War I (1914-1918), Germany gave financial support and military training to the Finnish Liberation Movement.

¹⁴ After the triumph of the Bolshevik Revolution in Russia, Finland declared independence in December 1917. In January 1918, the SDP took Helsinki, with the support of Soviet troops, and the major industrial centers. The Government counterattacked, backed by Czarist and German troops under the command of General Mannerheim. In May, the civil war came to an end after causing the death of 30,000 people. The Socialist leaders that

PROFILE

ENVIRONMENT

Finland is a flat country (the average altitude is 150 meters above sea level) with vast marine clay plains, low plateaus, numerous hills and lakes formed by glaciers. The population is concentrated mainly on the coastal plains, the country's main farming area. The economy is based on forest (coniferous) products and mobile phones. Main export products are from the energy (high technology in electronics and communications), metallurgy, wood (paper paste and paper) and chemicals sectors.

SOCIETY

Peoples: 92.1 per cent of the population is Finnish and 7.5 per cent Swedish. There are Roma and Sami minorities. **Religions:** official churches: Evangelic Lutheran Church (more than 94 per cent of the population), Finnish Orthodox Church (2 per cent). **Languages:** Finnish (official and spoken by 93.2 per cent). Swedish (official and spoken by 6 per cent). Sami and Russian are spoken by minorities. **Main Political Parties:** The Social Democratic Party of Finland (SDP), center-left; Finnish Center, former Agrarian Party; the People's Democratic League; the National Rally, moderate conservative; the Swedish People's Party in Finland; the Green League. **Main Social Organizations:** Central Organization of Finnish Unions, about 1,000,000 members and 28 member unions. Finnish Confederation of Salaried Employees.

THE STATE

Official Name: Suomen Tasavalta. **Administrative Divisions:** 6 provinces. **Capital:** Helsinki 1,075,000 people (2003). **Other Cities:** Espoo 219,400 people; Tampere 197,200; Vantaa 182,700; Turku (Abo) 175,100 (2000). **Government:** Tarja Halonen, President since March 2000. Matti Vanhanen, Prime Minister since June 2003 (after the resignation of Anneli Jaatteenmaki, elected in March 2003). Unicameral Legislature: the Diet, with 200 members. Since 1996 there is a Parliament for the Sami minority (the samediggi) with limited autonomy on cultural matters. **National Holiday:** 6 December, Independence (1917, from Russia). **Armed Forces:** 31,200 (1994). Other: Border guards: 4,400.

Life expectancy
78.0 years
2000-2005

GNI per capita
$23,510
2002

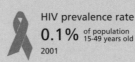
HIV prevalence rate
0.1% of population
15-49 years old
2001

could not escape to the USSR were sent to prison camps.

15 The country became a monarchy, and German Prince Frederick Charles of Hessen was elected king. After Germany's defeat in World War I, the monarchy collapsed and General Mannerheim was appointed regent, on condition that he would set up a republican system.

16 In the 1919 elections, in order to assure Mannerheim's defeat, the SDP supported Kaarlo Juho Stahlbergal, presidential candidate of the National Progress Party (center) who became elected.

17 The same year a Constitution was approved, establishing a parliamentary system with a strong presidential figure. In addition, it made the Prime Minister the head of the government, and the President head of state. Both Finnish and Swedish were recognized as official languages. Nationalist groups later demanded that Finnish be given priority which brought about a controversy that led to the creation of the Swedish People's Party.

18 The Constitution ratified the principle - established in 1868 and still in operation - of the relationship between the Lutheran Church and the Finnish State by which the latter promised to finance the Church, but at the same time it reserved its right to appoint bishops.

19 The country was ruled almost uninterruptedly after independence by alliances between the Social Democrats and the Centrists. From 1920 to 1930, these two political forces backed programs for the modernization of agricultural production and the timber industry, as well as a progressive legislation for the workers' rights. Agriculture employed 70 per cent of the active population until the 1960s. In the early 20th century, the Rural Party was founded, which later became the Center Party of Finland.

20 In 1926, the Marxist wing left the SDP and founded the Communist Party (FCP). The subsequent growth of the FCP gave rise to the ultra-right-wing Lapua (Lappo) Movement, which gained the support of conservative groups and some Rural Party sectors and banned the FCP in 1930. In 1931 the Lappo movement began to carry out attacks against the Social Democrats and the following year, it attempted a coup which was put down by the Government.

21 In 1939, after the German invasion of Poland, the USSR demanded part of the Karelian Province, a naval base on the Hanko peninsula and other islands of the Gulf of Finland. Given the refusal of the Finns to cede the lands, the USSR seized them by force and after a year of conflict, Finland had to give them up on signing the Treaty of Moscow.

IN FOCUS

ENVIRONMENTAL CHALLENGES
The atmospheric pollution caused by the sulfur dioxide emissions of factories and elecric power plants contributes to acid rain. The dumping of contaminated water with industrial waste and agrochemical products into the Baltic Sea poses a serious problem to the environment and has resulted in habitat loss and a threat to the survival of flora and fauna species.

WOMEN'S RIGHTS
In 2000, women held 37 per cent of seats in Parliament and their participation in ministerial or equivalent positions amounted to 34 per cent. They have been able to vote and stand for office since 1906. Finland was the first country in the world to grant women full political rights. Women make up 49 per cent of the labor force; 4 per cent work in agriculture, 14 per cent in industries and 82 per cent in services. There is discrimination at work; although women have access to important positions, they are paid lower wages than men holding the same positions and doing the same tasks.

One hundred per cent of pregnant women have access to prenatal, perinatal and postnatal care*. The maternal mortality rate is 6 per 100,000 live births, one of the lowest in the world*.

Fifty-two per cent of adult women have been victims of violence or physical or sexual threats since the age of 15. In the area of domestic life, 29 per cent suffer sexual violence at the hands of a member of their family. Immigrant women living in Finland, who belong to a minority group, face double discrimination based on ethnic origin and gender.

CHILDREN
The under-5 mortality rate is 5 per 1,000 live births; Finland is one of the countries with the lowest average rate*. Between 95 and 100 per cent of children are immunized against polio and measles.

The Government is concerned about the growing number of men that cross the border with Russia, seeking sexual services provided by minors in that country.

INDIGENOUS PEOPLES/ ETHNIC MINORITIES
The Sami are one among several other indigenous groups in Europe. Their total population is 75,000 and they inhabit lands in Norway, Sweden, Russia and Finland. More than half of their number speaks Sami or some related dialect. In Finland, there are 6,500 Sami, 4,000 of whom live in a 35,000 sq km reserve that includes a special region for the Skolt Sami who were located in this area after the end of World War II. In recent years, both the conditions of their lives and their participation in the social activities of the country have improved.

In 1994, the Government passed a new law that guaranteed Sami people the right to practise their language and culture.

MIGRANTS/REFUGEES
At the end of 2002, Finland hosted more than 1,000 refugees. In that same year, the number of asylum applications increased to 3,400, doubling the 2001 figures. Asylum was only granted to 14 persons, which represents a rate of 0.4 per cent, the lowest in the EU.

However, temporary asylum was granted to a significant number of foreigners who are unable to furnish conclusive proof that they are being persecuted but come from countries in conflict or show signs of torture. This type of asylum is granted for a three-year period and cannot be renewed. The holders of temporary asylum have the same rights as those who are granted 'normal' asylum. After residing in Finland for three months, asylum-seekers receive permission to work, although this is limited to specific job opportunities (those that citizens are unwilling to accept).

Finland annually resettles refugees selected by UNHCR. In 2003, the Government admitted 700 refugees.

DEATH PENALTY
This was abolished in 1972.

*Latest data available in *The State of the World's Children* and *Childinfo* database, UNICEF, 2004.

22 Finland had declared its neutrality at the beginning of World War II (1939-1945). However as a means to recover the territories ceded to Moscow, it agreed to cooperate with Germany. The 1944 Soviet counter-offensive and subsequent occupation of Karelia, caused the immediate resignation of President Ryti, architect of the alliance with Germany. He was succeeded by General Mannerheim, who signed an armistice with Moscow in 1944, recognizing the 1940 Treaty of Moscow. He organized the fight to expel German troops who were crushing resistance in the north, causing devastation.

23 During the war nearly 500,000 Finns had died. After it ended, Finland was forced to give goods to the USSR for six years by way of compensation. To achieve this, the country had to develop a metal and engineering industry. At the same time, it opened markets on both sides of the Berlin Wall, thus maintaining a neutral position on foreign policy. After joining the UN in 1955, during the Cold War (1950-1991), Finland was the only member of the Nordic Council that maintained relations with the EC and COMECON (Communist bloc).

24 With the disintegration of the USSR (1991), which had provided the market for over 25 per cent of Finland's exports, economic growth came to a standstill. Unemployment reached 20 per cent. Prime Minister Esko Aho, politically moderate, launched a drastic structural adjustment program which was resisted by workers. During the three previous decades, the State had allocated roughly half the GNP to social security programs.

25 Finland joined the European Union in 1995 and adopted the euro as its currency in 1999. It maintained its taxation and state health system. Unlike some other members of the EU, Finland frequently criticized NATO actions.

26 Social-Democrat Tarja Halonen won the January 1999 elections, becoming the first Finnish female head of state. The President, however, would carry out only representative functions, since the latest 2000 constitutional reform had installed a parliamentary system.

27 In March 2003, Anneli Jaatteenmaki of the Center Party was elected Prime Minister by just 6,600 votes. The election results forced the Center Party to form a coalition with the SDP and the Swedish Peoples' Party. Two months after taking office, the Prime Minister resigned, alleging that she had been threatened and feared for her personal security. Since Finland is considered both politically stable and virtually free of corruption, her comments startled many of her European counterparts.

28 In June, Matti Vanhanen (also of the Center Party) was appointed Prime Minister. Vanhanen, a journalist and academic, who was regarded as a specialist in EU affairs, expressed reservations about EU defense policy. He also was opposed to the construction of a fifth nuclear reactor and voiced concern about unemployment, which reached 10 per cent during 2003. Another concern is the increasing racial tension after the arrival of immigrants from Africa and southeast Europe. ■

France / France

Population:	60,711,094
Area:	551,500 km²
Capital:	Paris
Currency:	Euro
Language:	French

The two regions occupied by the Celts were known to the Romans as Gaul. The region between the Alps and Rome was Cisalpine Gaul, and beyond the Alps was Transalpine Gaul. With natural borders on all sides - the Alps, the Pyrénées, the Atlantic Ocean and the Rhine - Gaul covered not only what is now France, but also Belgium, Switzerland and the western banks of the Rhine.

2   Gaelic society was essentially agricultural, with almost no urban life. The few cities were used as fortresses, where the peasants sought refuge when under attack. Society was divided into the nobles (who were also warriors), the people and the Druids, keepers of Celtic wisdom and religious traditions.

3   The Romans came to Gaul in 125 BC. They conquered the area along the Mediterranean, the Rhone valley and Languedoc, calling the combined area 'Provincia'. Caesar divided Gaul into two regions; Provincia and Free Gaul. Free Gaul was subdivided into Belgian Gaul in the north, between the Rhine and the Seine; Celtic Gaul in the center, between the Seine, the Garonne and the lower Rhine; and Aquitaine, in the southwest.

4   In 27 BC, Augustus Caesar set up administrative centers in Gaul, to manage Rome's affairs

LAND USE

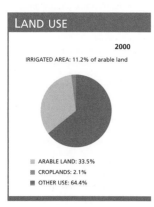

2000

IRRIGATED AREA: 11.2% of arable land

- ARABLE LAND: 33.5%
- CROPLANDS: 2.1%
- OTHER USE: 64.4%

encouraging urbanization. Bridges and an extensive road network were built throughout the region, facilitating an increase in trade. Wheat production was increased and vineyards were planted, with wine replacing beer as the traditional beverage. After a series of invasions by the Visigoths in the south and the Burgundians along the Saone and the Rhone, the northern Gauls conquered the rest of Gaul under the leadership of Clovis, adopting the name, 'Franks'.

5   Between the 5th and the 9th centuries France emerged as the Merovingian and Carolingian dynasties brought the entire region under the influence of Christianity. With the Islamic expansion and the fall of the Roman Empire, trade ceased, urban civilization was almost completely wiped out, population decreased and the culture became decadent.

6   By the 9th century, feudalism had become firmly established. Centralized authority practically disappeared, as local people were unable to repel the Scandinavians, Hungarians, Saracens, and other invaders of this era. By the end of the century, the previously united land was a conglomerate of more than 300 independent counties.

7   From the 10th century onward, the royal dynasties slowly recovered their power. They established hereditary succession to the throne, they shared power with the Church and became the main feudal landowners.

8   In the 13th century, an increase in commercial activity led to a remarkable rebirth of the cities, and agricultural techniques were improved, as the population

increased. The Crusades led to a greater circulation of people and goods, and the gradual disappearance of serfdom gave rise to greater social mobility. This was the 'Golden Age' of the French Middle Ages, when France had great power over, and influence upon Western civilization.

9   Paris was one of Europe's most important cities, and the prestige of its University was linked to its cultural pre-eminence. The University trained lawyers in Roman law, and their influence helped form a new concept of the State where the king was no longer a feudal lord, but rather the embodiment of the law. Over a period of time, nationalistic feelings began to develop.

10   Louis XIV, the 'Sun King', personified the concept of absolute monarchy. He came to the throne in 1661, and established the 'Divine Right of Kings'. He consolidated the unity of France, giving rise to the concept of the modern State. During his reign, French cultural influence reached its apogee.

11   The 1789 Revolution opened up a new era in the history of France. The National Assembly, convened in July of that year, replaced the absolute monarch with a constitutional monarchy. The fall of the Bastille on 14 July and the Declaration of the Rights of Man, on 27 August, brought the old regime to an end, thus paving the way for the rise of the bourgeoisie - the prevailing class of the towns - whose reforms came into direct conflict with the Church and the King. Finally, the Assembly overthrew the monarchy and proclaimed the First French Republic.

12   The rest of Europe joined forces against revolutionary France. Danton and Robespierre declared the nation 'to be in peril' and formed a citizen army. This Committee of Public Salvation was able to forestall foreign invasion but internal confrontations resulted in the 'Reign of Terror'. Robespierre and his companions were overthrown and executed in July 1794.

13   For the next five years, the revolutionaries tried to regain control of the country, which had fallen victim to corruption, internal strife and instability. Napoleon Bonaparte's coup (1799) brought an end to the dying regime. Seizing power, he had himself named Consul for Life in 1802 and then Emperor in 1804.

14   Although Napoleon's reign represented a return to absolutism, it preserved the main achievements of the Revolution. Legal, administrative, religious, financial and educational reorganization changed the country irrevocably. Napoleon strove hard to bring the rest of Europe under his control and his armies occupied the whole of the continent from Madrid to the outskirts of Moscow. Finally, exhausted by war, France was defeated at Waterloo, in 1815.

15   Rebellions in 1830, 1848 and 1871 rocked the country. In spite of this, the Industrial Revolution brought factories, railroads, large companies and credit institutions to France. The Third Republic, beginning in 1870, was to be France's longest-lasting regime in almost a century and a half.

16   With the establishment of universal male suffrage in 1848, the peasants and the urban middle class had the greatest electoral power. The Government managed to win their support by protectionism and the establishment of free, secular and mandatory primary education, which raised aspirations of greater social mobility.

17   Under the Republic, France started a period of colonial expansion with the conquest of Algeria in 1830, and continuing with other territories in Africa and the Far East. A large empire was built, with colonies in the Caribbean, Africa, the Middle East, the Indo-Chinese peninsula and the Pacific.

18   World War I enabled France to recover Alsace and Lorraine, territories annexed by Germany in 1870. The War left France devastated. More than 1.5 million people had been killed. Property damage coupled with the internal and foreign debt added up to more than 150 billion gold francs, and the nation's currency lost its traditional stability.

Life expectancy
79.0 years
2000-2005

GNI per capita
$22,010
2002

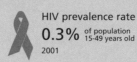

HIV prevalence rate
0.3% of population
15-49 years old
2001

19 The world-wide recession that started in the US in 1929, reached France in 1931. In 1936, the parties of the left, joined together to form the Popular Front, won the legislative elections and carried out important social reforms, such as paid vacations and the 40-hour working week, but they were unable to hold back unemployment or the looming economic crisis.

20 German's invasion in Poland led France and England to declare war on Germany in 1939. Germany went on to occupy almost one-third of France. In 1940, Marshal Pétain signed an armistice proclaiming the 'national revolution' transforming non-occupied France into a satellite of Berlin. The resistance fighters (or *maquis*) in the south did not militarily affect the occupation.

21 Once the German Army had been defeated on the Russian front, the Allied landing in Normandy led to France's liberation in 1944 and to its participation in the invasion of Germany. In October 1946, the Fourth Republic was proclaimed, led by General de Gaulle. In the 1946 elections the French Communist Party (PCF) obtained one of the highest votes in its history.

22 Funds from the US Marshall Plan led to the economic and social reconstruction of the country. Production reached a six per cent annual growth rate. Per capita income increased 47 per cent between 1949 and 1959; women were granted the right to vote; the banks were nationalized and a social security program came into effect.

23 After 1945, France was unable to re-establish its pre-war control over its colonies. This was partly a result of the growing sense of democracy and human rights. Having seen the anti-Fascist alliance and the birth of the League of Nations, many colonies (not just French ones) began to breathe the air of independence. French colonialism was based on the concepts of 'unity of the Republic' and 'cultural assimilation', which resulted in a centralized administration, with no autonomy for local governments. Thus, decolonization took place through fierce independence movements, with little room for negotiation.

24 In 1945, Syria and Libya were the first French colonies to become independent, followed by Morocco, Tunisia and Madagascar. Vietnam, Laos and Cambodia became independent only in 1954, after a long and bloody war. In May 1958, four years after the Algerian revolution began, the *pieds-noirs* - French people residing in the colony - dealt a mortal blow to the Fourth Republic, and the Government called in General de Gaulle to deal with the crisis.

25 The establishment of the Fifth Republic in 1958 and the 1962 decision to elect the President by direct universal suffrage laid the foundation for a regime with strong presidential powers. After the independence of Algeria in 1962 and the last remaining African colonies, France sought to achieve greater stability, based on strengthening the currency, growth of vanguard industries, scientific research, and development of a national independence strategy. France made use of 'deterrent' atomic power and in 1966 withdrew from the military structure of the North Atlantic Treaty Organization (NATO), but kept its membership in case of a 'surprise attack'.

26 France maintained enormous influence over its former African colonies, south of the Sahara. Diplomatic relations with Algeria, Vietnam, and other countries that had fought bloody wars for independence were not restored until 1982.

27 In May 1968, the greatest social and political crisis of the Fifth Republic took place. The regime's growing authoritarianism in the educational and social sectors gave rise to huge student protests and labor strikes throughout the country. For a whole month, the Government seemed to be seriously threatened, however, there were no political forces capable of toppling the Government, and the general strike was called off when a salary increase was promised.

28 The years which followed saw the birth of other groups based around social issues, such as the feminist, ecological and antinuclear movements. In 1972 the Socialist Party and the Communist Party created the Union of the Left. François Mitterand, the Socialist candidate, was elected President in 1981. His was the first left-wing cabinet since 1958.

29 The new government nationalized industrial and banking groups, granted new labor rights - the 35-hour working week, an increase in social benefits, retirement at the age of 60 - and decentralized power. However, unemployment, the economic crisis and an increase in imports led the Government to enforce a harsh economic policy and to carry out restructuring of the industrial sector, which made communist ministers resign. In 1981, a Ministry of Women's rights was created.

30 In March 1986, a right-wing coalition led by neo-Gaullist Jacques Chirac, the Mayor of Paris (1977-1995) defeated the Left in the legislative elections that saw the progress of Jean Marie Le Pen's ultra-right National Front. Chirac formed a new government and for two years the country experienced its first 'cohabitation' between a left-wing president (Mitterand) and a conservative council of ministers.

31 Chirac's government wiped out some of the 1981 and 1982 reforms with the privatization of several companies nationalized by the left but kept most of the social gains. In the field of individual liberties, the strong hand regarding legislation concerning foreigners living in France, was criticized by several humanitarian organizations.

32 In 1988, Mitterand defeated Chirac in presidential elections. Without 'cohabitation' this time, socialist Michel Rocard was appointed Prime Minister.

33 The Socialist economic policy did not differ substantially from that of the right and unemployment kept on the rise. In 1991 Edith Cresson became France's first female Prime Minister.

34 In 1993, the Left was defeated in legislative elections once again and Mitterrand named conservative

PROFILE

ENVIRONMENT

In the north is the Paris Basin, which spreads out into fields and plains. The Massif Central, in the center of France, is made up of vast plateaus. The Alps rise in the south-east. The southern region includes the Mediterranean coast, with mountain ranges, such as the Pyrénées, and plains. Grain farming is the main agricultural activity; wheat is grown all over the country, especially in the north. Grapes are grown in the Mediterranean region for wine exports. The main mineral resources are coal, iron ore and bauxite. France has the highest nuclear energy production per capita in the world. It runs second to the US in its nuclear power capacity; 77 per cent of the country's electricity comes from its 58 nuclear reactors.

SOCIETY

Peoples: Most of the population stem from the integration of three basic European groups: Nordic, Alpine and Mediterranean. Approximately 7 per cent of the population is of foreign descent, mainly from Northern Africa (Algeria, Morrocco, Tunisia), from the former French colonies in sub- Saharan Africa and from Europe (Spain, Italy and Portugal).

Religions: Mainly Catholic (81.4 per cent); Islam (6.8 per cent) practiced mostly by North African and West African immigrants; Protestants (2 per cent) and Jews (1 per cent).

Languages: French is the official and predominant language. There are also regional languages: Breton in Brittany, a German dialect in Alsace and Lorraine, Flemish in the northeast, Catalan and Basque in the Southwest, Provençal in the south-east, Occitan in the central south, Corsican on the island of Corsica. Immigrants speak their own languages, mainly Portuguese, Arab, Berber, Spanish, Italian and African languages.

Main Political Parties: Socialist Party (PSF); Union for a Popular Movement (UMP), led by President Chirac; National Front, an ultra-right-wing party; Union for the French Democracy (UDF); French Communist Party; the Greens; Revolutionary Communist League.

Main Social Organizations: General Labor Confederation (CGT), communnist; French Democratic Labor Confederation (CFDT), socialist; Workers' Force (FO); French Confederation of Christian Workers (CFTC). France has the lowest level of unionization in the European Community (about 10 per cent).

THE STATE

Official Name: République Française.

Administrative Divisions: 22 Regions with 96 Departments in France; 4 overseas departments (French Guiana, Guadeloupe, Martinique, Réunion); 4 overseas territories (French Polynesia, New Caledonia, Wallis and Futuna and the Southern and Antarctica French Lands) and the 2 overseas territorial collectivities (Mayotte, St Pierre and Miquelon).

Capital: Paris 9,794,000 people (2003).

Other Cities: Lyon 2,800,000 people; Marseille 2,800,000; Toulouse 800,000; Nice 933,080 (2000).

Government: Jacques Chirac, President since May 1995, re-elected in 2002. Jean-Pierre Raffarin, Prime Minister since May 2002. Bicameral Parliament: the National Assembly, with 577 members, and the Senate, with 321 members.

National Holiday: 14 July, Bastille Day (1789).

Armed Forces: 416,000 (2001). Other: 100,000 Gendarmes.

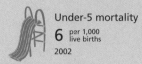

Under-5 mortality
6 per 1,000 live births
2002

Aid
0.38% Official development assistance as % of donors' GNI
2002

Maternal mortality
17 per 100,000 live births
2000

IN FOCUS

ENVIRONMENTAL CHALLENGES
Dependence on nuclear energy poses a serious problem. Nuclear reactors operating in the country generate three-quarters of the national consumption of electricity, making France the second largest producer of nuclear energy, after the US. There is also a nuclear-reprocessing plant (Cap de la Hague), which generates plutonium, with serious sanitary and environmental risks, such as acid rain which originates serious forest damage. Furthermore, industrial and vehicle emissions contribute to air pollution. River streams are polluted by urban and industrial wastes as well as by agricultural runoff.

WOMEN'S RIGHTS
Women have been able to vote and run for office since 1955. Eleven per cent of the Parliament seats and 12 per cent of the ministerial or equivalent positions in government were held by women in the year 2000. That same year women comprised 45 per cent of the country's workforce: 86 per cent of them worked in services, 1 per cent in agriculature and 13 per cent in industries. 99 per cent of births are assisted by trained personnel*. The maternal mortality rate is 17 per 100,000 live births*.

CHILDREN
France, like other Western European countries, is a major destination for child-traffickers. There are 12,000 to 15,000 street sex workers, of which 7,000 are based in Paris, but it is unclear how many of these are under 18. Some organizations place the total number of child victims of prostitution between 2,000 and 3,000, with hundreds in Paris. According to ECPAT, every year 2,000 to 3,000 new sex workers populate French streets and often their age is not clear because passports are confiscated or the victims don't have birth certificates from their home countries.

INDIGENOUS PEOPLES/ ETHNIC MINORITIES
Muslims: Most came from North Africa after World War II to meet the demand for low-paying labor. They mainly speak French and several Arabic dialects; most of them are Sunni Muslims. They suffer from social, economical, racial and cultural discrimination; they are often victims of attacks by ultra-right-wing groups.

Corsicans - from Corsica, a French dependency since 1768 when it was sold by Genoa - speak Corsican, a mixture of French and Italian. Many support autonomy for their island. The National Liberation Front of Corsica (FLNC) has been fighting for this since 1976. The Front has been behind several terrorist attacks in France.

The Roma-Gypsies (called *gitanes* in French) began to arrive in France in 1400. They spread out, searching for better economic opportunities, fleeing discrimination; they speak different languages and have varied religious beliefs. They are largely excluded form French society; many do not pay taxes and do not have access to health and education.

The Basques comprise a very small proportion of the country's population, and live in southwestern France; relatively few of them speak Basque/ Euskera. As they mostly live in poor regions, many suffer the effects of economic marginalization.

MIGRANTS/REFUGEES
France hosted over 27,600 refugees and asylum-seekers by the end of 2002. These included about 25,000 applications still awaiting decision at year's end and 2,600 individuals granted refugee status during the year. Accepted applicants are granted a one-year residence permit, which can be renewed twice. After three years, the holder is entitled to apply for permanent residence status. In 2002, the Refugee Appeals Commission (CRR) granted asylum to 2,600 individuals out of 21,700 applications, a 12 per cent approval rate.

Refugee advocates demand that French border police be trained to deal with asylum-seekers and respect their rights. Foreigners denied entry into France may be kept in detention for up to 20 days, pending deportation.

France signed a voluntary repatriation agreement with UNHCR and the Afghan Government in September 2002. Under the agreement, Afghans who voluntarily return receive a free flight and 2,000 euros cash.

France ranks fifth in the world for the largest number of immigrants. In 2003 6.3 million foreigners lived there.

DEATH PENALTY
The death penalty was abolished in 1981.

*Latest data available in *The State of the World's Children* and *Childinfo* database, UNICEF, 2004.

Edouard Balladur as Prime Minister. The corruption scandals, whose main targets had been socialist leaders, affected this time renowned right-wing politicians. Three of Balladur's ministers resigned in 1994.

[35] In the April 1995 presidential elections Chirac defeated socialist Lionel Jospin and appointed conservative Alain Juppé as Prime Minister.

[36] In December, the largest civil servants' strike since 1968 paralyzed the country for over three weeks. The social situation remained tense in 1996, which some observers linked with unfair income distribution - 20 per cent of the population received 44 per cent of total personal income - and property distribution, since 20 per cent of the French owned 69 per cent of national wealth.

[37] The Juppé administration continued its austerity policy that caused confrontation with labor unions in 1996. A new law was passed in 1997 to restrict the entrance and residence of immigrants in the country. Demonstrations against the measure mobilized over 150,000 people in one day.

[38] Unexpectedly, Chirac called for early legislative elections. In the second round, on 25 May 1997, the leftist opposition obtained an important victory. The Greens took seven seats. Lionel Jospin became the new Prime Minister.

[39] Several studies in 1998 published by *Le Monde*, showed that two out of every five French citizens openly admitted having racist sentiments. The country was top of the table for racism in the EU, closely followed by Belgium. These figures were surprising to the researchers since, second to Luxembourg, France is the most ethnically mixed country in the EU.

[40] In March 1999 the National Assembly approved a law giving legal status to unmarried couples, by 300 to 253 votes. Tens of thousands of citizens opposing the legislation demonstrated in the streets, fearing the law would allow gay couples to adopt children.

[41] The 35-hour week law came into effect on 1 February 2000. That day, truckers began a strike. While employers did not support a reduction of hours, workers did not support the cut in wages it implied.

[42] Scandal broke out in the political system when an illegal scheme of funding for political parties was revealed in August. Several of the President's collaborators were implicated. According to the public prosecutor, during Chirac's last years as Mayor of Paris in the 1990s, business people gave 'gifts' to the parties and were compensated with contracts - amounted to $3.7 billion - to build or remodel schools. A 1995 law banned companies from making donations to political parties, which are funded by public money.

[43] In April 2002, in a presidential election with the lowest turnout in the 44 years of the Fifth Republic, the first round unexpectedly put the National Front's Le Pen in second place (17.02 per cent), leaving Jospin out, who left politics altogether, leaving the Socialist Party without a leader. He called on his followers to vote in the second round for Chirac, who had won the first round with 19.67 per cent of the vote. Le Pen's electoral platform was based on immigration and the crime rate, factors considered by many among the French population to be firmly linked. Immigrants made up 5.4 per cent (3.2 million) of the French population. Large numbers of young people, who had previously been politically indifferent, held demonstrations against Le Pen.

[44] In the second round, on 5 May 2002, Chirac obtained 82 per cent of the vote. He greeted 'those French people committed to solidarity and freedom, open to Europe and the world'. World political leaders expressed their 'relief' at the results, but Le Pen's electoral advance was a clear triumph for the European right.

[45] Jean-Pierre Raffarin, Chirac's Prime Minister, started his term in office by reducing taxes by five per cent - in his campaign he had promised a 30-per-cent reduction in five years. He cut back the state infrastructure, and privatized gas and electricity in the face of strong opposition from unions.

[46] Together with Germany and Russia, France vigorously opposed a UN resolution authorizing the use of force to disarm Iraq, threatening to use its power of veto if the resolution was approved in the Security Council. The US and UK delegations abandoned the idea of a new resolution and attacked Iraq in March 2003.

[47] That month, amendments to the Constitution granting more autonomy on economic, tourism, cultural and educational issues and the power to call for local referenda were approved. However, a first referendum in Corsica was not able to calm separatist violence.

Doctors
303 per 100,000 people
1990-2002

Primary school
100% net enrolment rate
2000

48 A severe heatwave in Europe in August, led to the deaths of over 11,000 mostly elderly people in France. With temperatures over 40°C, heat caused also severe environmental damage - fires, deforestation, increasing pollution, problems with nuclear reactors.

49 Chirac promised to end chronic unemployment in France by 2004. In response to the demands of the employers' organization MEDEF, that supported Chirac's free market policies, he trimmed unemployment benefits - as well as pension contributions and support to young job-seekers - and also reduced taxes on higher incomes. Criticism came from social and workers' organizations, from the opposition and from Chirac's own supporters.

50 In December 2003 a Government commission recommended passing a law banning conspicuous religious symbols in school, for example the Islamic veil (*hijab*), the Jewish *kippa* and large Christian crosses. Most of the French supported this idea, on the basis that the state education's secular tradition should be defended from religious excess, particularly from Islamic radicalization.

51 Some Muslim, Christian and Jewish leaders felt that the law would only bring more religious discrimination. In January 2004 40,000 Muslims demonstrated against the measure in Paris, Marseilles, Lille and other cities. There were also protests in London, Berlin, Brussels, Cairo and Bethlehem. There are some five million Muslims in France. ■

Wallis and Futuna

Population: 14,888
Area: 274 km²
Capital: Mata-Utu
Currency: Cfp franc
Language: French

W allis was named after Samuel Wallis, a navigator who 'discovered' it in 1767. Marist missionaries arrived in the archipelago in 1837 and converted the inhabitants to Catholicism. It became a French protectorate in 1888, and in December 1959, after a referendum, the country adopted the status of French Overseas Territory.

2 Unlike other French dependencies in the Pacific, there are no independence movements on the islands. In 1983, the two kingdoms of Futuna achieved separation from Wallis, but maintained their relationship with France. The islands' economic prospects are poor: in addition to the devastating effect of cyclones that periodically hit the islands, the only bank on the islands was closed. Wallis and Futuna received FF55 million in aid from France in 1987 and still relies heavily on grants. Approximately 50 per cent of the economically active population has had to emigrate to other parts of Polynesia in search of work. Their remittances, together with public works projects, constitute the main source of income for the islands.

3 In the 1992 elections for the Territorial Assembly, the Left managed to defeat the neo-Gaullist Rassemblement pour la République (RPR), a party of the right, for the first time in 20 years. In 1997, the neo-Gaullist candidate Victor Brial gained the seat of deputy for Wallis in the French National Assembly.

4 In May 2004, Atolomako Puluiuvea, a Wallis islander who represents one of the Kings of Wallis - Lavelua Tomasi Kulimoetoke - announced for 2005 the inaugural flight of what was to be called ŒAir Wallis,. The only air service operating until that date between Wallis and New Caledonia, home to 20,000 Wallisians, was Air Calédonie International (AirCalin). ■

ENVIRONMENT
The territory consists of the Wallis archipelago (159 sq km), formed by Uvea Island - where the capital is located - and 22 islets, plus the Futuna (64 sq km) and Alofi Islands (51 sq km). This group is located in western Polynesia, surrounded by Tuvalu to the north, Fiji to the south and the Samoa archipelago to the east. With a rainy and tropical climate, the major commercial activities are copra and fishing.

SOCIETY
Peoples: Of Polynesian origin. Approximately two thirds of the population live on Wallis and the rest on Futuna. Nearly 12,000 inhabitants live in Kanaky and Vanuatu. **Religions:** Catholic.
Languages: French (official) and Polynesian languages.

THE STATE
Official Name: Territoire des îles de Wallis et Futuna.
Administrative Divisions: There are no defined administrative divisions, but there are three kingdoms: Wallis, Sigave and Alo.
Capital: Mata-Utu (located on Uvea) 1,500 people (1999).
Other Towns: Utuofa 820 people; Vailala 800 (2000).
Government: Overseas territory administered by a French-appointed Chief Administrator, Christian Job, since 2002, assisted by a 20-member Territorial Assembly elected for a 5-year term. The kingdoms of Wallis and Futuna (in Sigave and Alo) from which the country was formed, have very limited powers. They send one deputy to the French National Assembly, and another to the Senate.
Armed Forces: The defense is the responsibility of France.

St Pierre and Miquelon

Population: 6,357
Area: 242 km²
Capital: St Pierre
Currency: Euro
Language: French

ENVIRONMENT
Archipelago formed by two main islands: St Pierre (26 sq km) and Miquelon (which, with Langlade, amounts to 216 sq km) and some ten smaller islands off the Canadian coast in the North Atlantic. Economy almost exclusively depends on fishing.

SOCIETY
Peoples: the majority are descendants of French settlers.
Religion: Catholic.
Language: French.

THE STATE
Official Name: Departément de Saint Pierre et Miquelon (Territorial Collectivity of Saint Pierre and Miquelon - conventional).
Capital: St Pierre 6,000 people (1999).
Other Towns: Miquelon 1,100 people (2000).
Government: A French overseas department. The Head of State is Jaques Chirac (French President). Administered by a Prefect, Claude Valleix (since October 2002), who represents the French state. Unicameral Legislature: the General Council, with 19 members elected for a six-year term in single-seat constituencies. The territory has one deputy and one senator in the French Parliament and has representation in the European Parliament.

OVERSEAS DEPARTMENTS AND TERRITORIES

DEPARTMENTS:
Guadeloupe; Martinique; French Guiana; Réunion; St Pierre and Miquelon (see entries).

TERRITORIES:
Mayotte; New Caledonia (see Kanaky); Wallis and Futuna (see entries); French Polynesia (see entry).

SOUTHERN AND ANTARCTIC TERRITORIES:
Comprising two archipelagos: Kerguelen (7,000 sq.km, with 80 people in Port-Aux-Français) and Crozet (500 sq km, with 20 people); two islands: New Amsterdam (60 sq km, with 35 inhabitants.) and St Paul (7 sq km, uninhabited), located in the southern Indian Ocean; the Land of Adélie (500,000 sq km with 27 people at the Dumont Durville Base), in Antarctica. Administered from Paris by Administrateur Superieur Francois Garde (since 24 May 2000), assisted by Secretary General Jean-Yves Hermoso (since NA). Technical personnel at weather stations are the only inhabitants.

French Guiana / Guyane Française

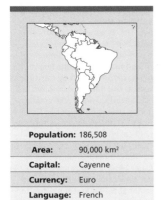

Population:	186,508
Area:	90,000 km²
Capital:	Cayenne
Currency:	Euro
Language:	French

The Arawaks were copper-skinned people with straight, black hair. They grew corn, cotton, yams and sweet potatoes. They built round huts with thatched, cone-shaped roofs, and slept in hammocks - an Arawak word which survived the culture which gave rise to it. They lived in balance with their surroundings. The Caribs displaced them from the area and later resisted the Spaniards who began to arrive toward the beginning of the 16th century.

2   In 1604 the French occupied Guiana, despite Carib resistance. The colony passed successively into Dutch, English and Portuguese hands, until the beginning of French domination in 1676. Towards the end of the 18th century, France sent more than 3,000 colonists to settle the interior. Few survived the tropical diseases, but those who did sought refuge in a group of islands off the coast, which they named Health Islands. The most famous among them is known as the Devil's Island, which was turned into an infamous prison in the 19th century. Hundreds of thousands of prisoners were sent there, among them Dreyfus and 'Papillon'.

3   In 1946, Guiana became a French 'Overseas Department'. Nine-tenths of the country is covered by forests, and although the country is fertile, most of the food is imported. The creole (African and mestizo) 80 per cent of the population are limited to minor positions in the local bureaucracy or police. The country is heavily reliant on French funding which provided 70 per cent of the GNP in 1989.

4   In 1967, the National Center for Space Studies was established. Over 1,300 foreign technicians work there, earning First World salaries, as well as 1,500 French Guyanan nationals. Thirty Ariane voyages have been launched from the base at Kourou, with all the satellites sent into space financed by European consortia.

5   During the 1970s, the autonomist Socialist Party of Guiana (PSG) became the majority party at the local level. Early in the 1980s, armed groups attacked 'colonialist' targets, but tensions were defused with the victory in France of the French Socialist Party in 1981.

6   At the 'First Conference of the Last French Colonies' held in Guadeloupe in 1985, there was severe criticism of the availability of French visas and citizenship for east Asians, while Haitians, Brazilians and Guianans, with closer cultural ties, underwent persecution and discrimination.

7   In 1986, Guiana's representation in the French National Assembly increased to two members. In the 1989 municipal elections, Cayenne and 12 other districts, out of the 19 at stake, were won by the Left. Georges Othily, a PSG dissident was elected for the French Senate.

8   In 1992, a week-long general strike was called by unions and business leaders. As a result, Paris agreed to finance a plan to improve infrastructure and education. In 1994, French Guiana joined the Association of Caribbean States as an associate member.

9   The French Government, after acknowledging the critical economic situation of its possession, announced a new 'development plan' for French Guiana in November 1997.

10   The March 2000 visit by Jean-Jacques Queyranne, under-secretary of Overseas Territories, triggered protests that ended in clashes between the police and the demonstrators who demanded independence. The crowds looted businesses and set cars on fire, and several people were injured. The pro-independence Workers' Union of Guiana led a general strike.

11   In 2001, French and Spanish authorities seized nearly seven tons of cocaine from two ships in territorial waters.

12   In December, many communities filed complaints with the French Government for its inaction in enforcing the environmental laws in the mining sector. Mercury, used in extracting gold from the ore, contaminates rivers and kills fish, the main source of food for the Wayana and Emerillon peoples.

13   Europe's largest and most expensive satellite was launched from the Kourou base in French Guiana in 2002, to monitor the health of the planet from outer space. Until that year, more than 125 commercial satellites had been launched from French Guiana.

14   During 2003, European scientists continued to launch more space probes. The 2004 European Agenda proposed strengthening the space research program, which would increase the flow of scientists and specialists from all over the world to Kourou, with benefits for the economy. ∎

PROFILE

ENVIRONMENT

French Guiana, the smallest and least populated country in South America, is located slightly north of the Equator. Due to its hot and rainy climate, only the coastal alluvial lowlands are suitable for agriculture (cocoa, bananas, sugar cane, rice and corn). The hinterland mountains are covered with rainforests. The country has large reserves of bauxite and gold. Mining activities have polluted the Moroni River, the principal source of food for the indigenous peoples of the area

SOCIETY

Peoples: Mostly of mixed European and African slave roots. There are 4,000 indigenous peoples, including the Wayana, Oyami and Emerillon in the interior jungles, and the Arawak, Galibi and Palikur along the coast. There are minority groups from China, India and France. Also in the jungles there are Cimarrones, descendants of rebel or fugitive African slaves. **Religions:** Mainly Roman Catholic, also Hindu and Islam.
Languages: French (official), local Creole. Some groups continue to speak their own languages.

Main Political Parties: Socialist Party of Guiana (PSG), Union for the Republic (RPR), Union for French Democracy (UDF), De-Colonization and Emancipation of Guiana Movement.
Main Social Organizations: Workers' Union of Guiana.

THE STATE

Official Name: Département d'Outre-Mer de la Guyane française.
Administrative Divisions: 2 Districts.
Capital: Cayenne 56,000 people (2003).
Other Cities: Kourou 21,000 people; St Laurent-du-Maroni 21,000 (2000).
Government: Jacques Chirac, Chief of State since May, 1995; re-elected May 2002. Ange Mancini, Prefect appointed by France (2002). Regional parliament (consultative body): General Council, made up of 19 members, and Regional Council, with 31 members. The department has 2 representatives in the National Assembly and 2 in the French Senate.
National Holiday: All French holidays.
Armed Forces: 8,400 French troops.

French Polynesia / Polynésie Française

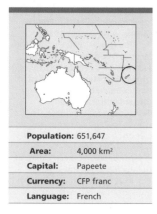

Population:	651,647
Area:	4,000 km²
Capital:	Papeete
Currency:	CFP franc
Language:	French

There are various theories on the origins of Polynesia's first inhabitants. Some say they came from Latin America, others say it was from Indonesia; but the evidence is inconclusive.

2   In 1840 France occupied the islands and in 1880, despite native resistance, they were officially made a colony under the name of 'the French Establishments of Oceania'. In 1958, they became an Overseas Territory.

3   Except for some concessions on the domestic front, France maintains its control over the islands, with a hard-line policy because of their strategic location and the atomic tests that have taken place on the Mururoa atoll since 1966. In 1975 France also carried out tests on the Fangataufa atoll, despite strong opposition from the population and countries such as New Zealand (Aotearoa).

4   The 'nuclearization' of the area rapidly resulted in the destruction of French Polynesia's traditional economic base, which depends upon the French military budget. In a few years, the economy went from self-sufficiency to dependence upon imported goods. By the end of 1980, 80 per cent of basic foodstuffs were imported.

5   Since 1984, French Polynesia is ruled by an autonomy statute (ratified in 1996), which stated power would be shared between France and the Territory.

6   Both the environment and the health of the islands' inhabitants has deteriorated over the last decades, with a high incidence of brain tumors, leukemia and thyroid cancer.

7   In 1985, the explosion of a bomb planted by two French secret agents killed an ecology activist and destroyed a Greenpeace ship that was heading for Mururoa in order to protest against nuclear testing. In 1992, French President François Mitterrand decreed a temporary suspension of nuclear tests and Paris began negotiations with Papeete for an economic plan to be carried out after the permanent closure of the experiment centers in Mururoa and Fangataufa.

8   The 'Progress Pact' between Paris and French Polynesia was based on assumptions similar to those in structural adjustment programs advocated by institutions such as the IMF, i.e. economic liberalization, privatization and 'major balancing' in public finance. However, the main pro-autonomy political party, Tavini Uiraatira (that means 'serving the people' in the Polynesian language) led by Oscar Temaru and representing 15 per cent of the voters, proposed nationalization and the extension of free services.

9   French President Chirac carried out further nuclear tests in 1995. After a controversial series of six explosions there were disturbances and fighting in French Polynesia. In January 1996, Chirac announced the permanent suspension of nuclear tests.

10   In 1998 it was revealed that tourism, above all from Japan and Italy, had increased 35 per cent during 1997. This was partly due to the suspension of nuclear tests.

11   Gaston Flosse, the President of Polynesia and a member of the French Senate, was prosecuted and found guilty of corruption by a French court of law. He received a prison sentence for having accepted tens of thousands of dollars in exchange for illegal gambling permits in Tahiti. Flosse refused to resign and stated he intended to appeal.

12   In May 2001, The President's party, the Tahoeraa Huiraatira/Rally for the Republic (RPR), won Parliamentary elections obtaining 28 seats, compared to 13 obtained by the Tavini Huiraatira (TH). Flosse was re-elected President on 18 May.

13   In early 2002, official statistics showed that, after the terrorist attacks of September 2001 in the US, tourism had fallen by 9.7 per cent in early 2002. French Polynesia is the second most popular tourist destination in the region, after Fiji.

14   In July 2003 President Chirac visited French Polynesia for the first time. While Flosse welcomed Chirac, pro-independence leader Oscar Temaru boycotted the reception. He organized a demonstration to remind the French President that France 'has the duty to lead the peoples under its responsibility toward independence and sovereignty'.

15   Chirac gave assurances that, according to International Atomic Energy Agency (IAEA), people's health would not be affected by the French nuclear tests in the area. However, the President announced that, as a precaution, France would monitor the atolls where the tests took place. ∎

LAND USE

2000

IRRIGATED AREA: 4.3% of arable land

- ARABLE LAND: 0.8%
- CROPLANDS: 5.5%
- OTHER USE: 93.7%

PROFILE

ENVIRONMENT

The territory is located in the southeast portion of Polynesia. Most of the French Polynesian islands are of volcanic origin but they also have major coral formations. The islands are largely mountainous, with a tropical climate and heavy rainfall. Relatively fertile soils favor agricultural development. The Windward and Leeward Islands form the Society Islands archipelago. Nuclear tests on atolls such as Mururoa and Fangataufa carried out by France over a 26-year period have caused damage to the environment and people that is difficult to evaluate.

SOCIETY

Peoples: Polynesian 78 per cent, Chinese 12 per cent, French descendants 6 per cent. **Religions:** Mostly Christian, 54 per cent Protestant, 30 per cent Catholic. **Languages:** French (official), Tahitian (national). **Main Political Parties:** Tahoeraa Huiraatira/People's Front-Rally for the Republic (RPR), conservative; Tavini Huiraatira/People's servant, an anti-nuclear and independence movement; Fetia Api/New Star.
Main Social Organizations: The Pacific Christian Workers' Central (CTCP), the Federation of French Polynesian Unions (FSPF) and the Territorial Union of the General Labor Confederation 'Workers' Force' (UTSCGT).

THE STATE

Official Name: Territoire d'Outre-Mer de la Polynésie française.
Administrative Divisions: Windward Islands, which include Tahiti, Murea, Maio; Papeete constitutes the center of the district. Leeward Islands, with the capital in Utoroa on Ralatea island. It also includes the islands of Huahine, Tahaa, Bora-Bora and Maupiti. Tuamotu and Gambier Archipelagos, the Austral Islands and the Marquesas Islands.
Capital: Papeete 126,000 people (2003).
Other Cities: Punaauia 22,700 people; Pirae 16,200 (2000).
Government: The French Government is represented by a High Commissioner, who controls defense, foreign relations and justice, Michel Mathieu since October 2001. President: Gaston Flosse since 2001. A local 49-member Territorial Assembly is elected by proportional representation for a 5-year term.
National Holiday: All French holidays.
Armed Forces: Defense is responsibility of the French Government. French Forces (includes Army, Navy, Air Force), Gendarmerie.

Gabon / Gabon

Population:	1,375,223
Area:	267,670 km²
Capital:	Libreville
Currency:	CFA franc
Language:	French

Tools found in the Gabon forests indicate that this region has been inhabited since the Palaeolithic age. In the 16th century, the same migrations that triggered the crisis in the ancient state of Congo brought the Myene and, in the 17th century, the Fang to Gabon. Thereafter, they monopolized the slave and ivory trade together with the Europeans.

² The Portuguese arrived in 1472. Around the middle of the 19th century, the French, Dutch and British established a permanent trade of ivory, precious woods and slaves. In 1849, Libreville was founded and established as a settlement for freed slaves from other French colonies. The territory was of little economic interest to the French, who used it as a base for expeditions into the heart of the continent.

³ The quest for independence was relatively uneventful because the two local parties (the Joint Mixed Gabonese Movement of Leon M'Ba and the Democratic and Social Union of Jean-Hillaire Aubame) were willing to accept neo-colonialism. In 1960, independence was declared and a military treaty was signed between Libreville and Paris.

⁴ Gabon has abundant resources: iron ore, uranium, manganese, timber and oil. Until

a few years after independence, timber was the only local industry of any size. The discovery of large oil reserves prompted the transnational companies Shell, Elf, Amoco and Braspetro to exploit them and to initiate a process of industrialization when they realized that Gabon could serve as a spearhead to penetrate the markets of Central Africa.

⁵ This 'development', relying on foreign capital has only exacerbated social conflicts and the promise of jobs in the cities

has encouraged urban migration. Gabon's social structure is changing as independent producers become suppliers of cheap labor for transnational industries.

⁶ When M'Ba died in 1967, he was succeeded by Omar Bongo, who faithfully followed his predecessor's style. Applying the US thesis of 'sub-imperialisms' to French interests, Bongo became its watchdog in central Africa, with Gabon a base for aggression against neighboring progressive

regimes. In January 1977, Gabon provided the planes and arms used by a mercenary group in an unsuccessful attack on Benin.

⁷ Bongo's foreign policy maintained good relations with several states in the region, including Angola, without altering the country's privileged relationship with France. Like Senegal, Ivory Coast, Chad, and the Central African Republic, Gabon also had French troops on its soil.

⁸ In 1979 and in 1986, Bongo was re-elected with 99 per cent of the vote, in presidential elections in which he was the only candidate.

⁹ His squandering of the country's income led to violent protests in the early 1980s. The revolt spread to the police who in 1982 organized a demonstration, demanding an increase in wages and the withdrawal of French advisors. The protests were brutally repressed by Gabon's secret police, officially known as the 'Documentation Center'.

¹⁰ The Government repressed the National Reorientation Movement (MORENA), formed by intellectuals, workers, students and nationalist politicians. The movement was accused of having expropriated 30 tons of weapons, in 1982, when the Bongo family and French military installations were the target of armed attacks. At least 28 MORENA leaders were sentenced to 15 years' imprisonment.

¹¹ Together with the advent of political changes in Eastern

LAND USE

2000

IRRIGATED AREA: 3.0% of arable land

- ARABLE LAND: 1.3%
- CROPLANDS: 0.7%
- OTHER USE: 98.1%

PROFILE

ENVIRONMENT
Irrigated by the Ogooué River basin, the country has an equatorial climate with year-round rainfall. The land is covered by dense rainforest. The timber industry - especially that of okoumé wood (used in plywood) - employs a large part of the population, together with the extractive industries (manganese, petroleum, uranium and iron), which make up 80 per cent of the country's exports.

SOCIETY
Peoples: Gabon was populated by Babinga (pygmies). In the 16th century it was invaded by Myene and other groups. Today over half of the population are Bantu-speaking peoples divided into more than 40 different groups including Galoa, Nkomi, and Irungu, among others. One third of the population are Fang and Kwele, in the northern part of Gabon, while there are Punu and Nzabi minorities in the south; plus Baka and Babongo pygmy people.
Religions: Mainly Christian. More than one third practice traditional African religions and there is a small Muslim minority.
Languages: French (official). There are as many languages as ethnic groups. Bantu languages are predominant, divided into 10 main linguistic groups; pygmy languages also spoken.

Main Political Parties: Gabonese Democratic Party (PDG), pro-government; National Woodcutters' Rally, in the opposition; Gabonese Party of Progress; Social Democratic Party; Union of the People of Gabon.
Main Social Organizations: Gabonese Confederation of Free Trade Unions (CGSL).

THE STATE
Official Name: République Gabonaise.
Administrative Divisions: 9 provinces and 37 prefectures.
Capital: Libreville 611,000 people (2003).
Other Cities: Port Gentil 99,300 people; Masuku 39,100; Oyem 28,100 (2000).
Government: Parliamentary republic with strong head of state. El Hadj Omar Bongo, President and head of State, since November 1967 and re-elected in 1998 for a seven-year term. Jean-François Ntoutoume-Emane, Prime Minister since January 1999 and re-elected in 2002. Bicameral Legislature: National Assembly, with 120 members elected every five years, and the Senate, with 91 members.
National Holiday: 17 August, Independence Day (1960).
Armed Forces: 4,750 (1995). Other: Coast Guard: 2,800; Gendarmerie: 2,000.

Life expectancy
56.6 years
2000-2005

GNI per capita
$3,120
2002

Literacy
91% total adult rate
2000

IN FOCUS

ENVIRONMENTAL CHALLENGES
Deforestation is one of the most serious environmental problems, together with the depletion of the country's wildlife.

WOMEN'S RIGHTS
Women have been able to vote and be elected since 1956. In 2000, women held 3 per cent of ministerial positions.

In 2000, women made up 45 per cent of the labor force, composed of 1 million people. Fifty-nine per cent worked in agriculture, 10 per cent in industry and 32 per cent in services.

In 2000*, the net school enrolment rate for girls was 87 per cent; 16 per cent of secondary school teachers were female. The illiteracy rate is around 48 per cent in women over 15; for men over 15 the rate is 20 per cent. There are 400,000 illiterate women*.

Some 86 per cent of births are attended by skilled health staff; meanwhile, 86 per cent of pregnant women receiv prenatal care*.

The UN Human Rights Committee demanded that Gabon ban polygamy.

CHILDREN
In 2001, 48,000 children were born and 4,000 children under 5 died.

In 2000*, the net primary school enrolment and attendance rate was 88 per cent.

Twelve per cent of children under 5 are of moderate or severely low weight*.

The Government has made a commitment to make vaccines available in all health centers; however, immunization coverage is still very poor. Within the last years, there have been epidemics of measles and the northern part had an outbreak of Ebola hemorragic fever, a contagious disease.

Child-trafficking is now an offense in the Penal Code. In addition, a decree was promulgated prohibiting child labor.

INDIGENOUS PEOPLES/ ETHNIC MINORITIES
Baka people are one of the Pygmy groups of Africa (the name derives from the Greek word *pyme* which means 'a cubit in height'). They were traditionally hunters and gatherers and were probably the first inhabitants of Equatorial Africa. Today, the different groups inhabit Rwanda, Burundi, Uganda, DR Congo, Gabon, Central African Republic and Cameroon, totaling 200,000 people.

There are also Bantu-speaking groups in the region, that have deeper historical roots in the territory: the Babongo or Obongo (in southern and central Gabon), the Barimba and Bagama (southwest). The Babongo group (formerly nomadic and hunter-gatherer communities) is made up of some 2,000 people settled in Gabon and Congo.

MIGRANTS/REFUGEES
At the end of 2002, Gabon hosted nearly 20,000 refugees and asylum-seekers (including about 15,000 from DR Congo (DRC) - who had arrived in 1999, fleeing civil war - 2,000 from Chad and 3,000 from other countries).

Although UNHCR estimated that within the year 6,000 repatriations for DR Congo would be registered, only 100 refugees were voluntarily repatriated in 2002. About 90 per cent of the DRC refugees live in the urban areas of three southern provinces along Gabon's border with DR Congo. Two-fifths of the refugees are under 18 years old.

A majority of refugees has received some assistance, including food, special rations for malnourished children, tools and seeds for farming, and education benefits.

The mining sector attracted many migrants from the Africa's central region, who arrived in Gabon during the 1990s. In 2000, 20.3 per cent of the population were immigrants.

In Europe, most part of the Gabonese diaspora has settled in France (3,000), Germany (238) and Italy (194).

DEATH PENALTY
It is applied to all types of crimes.

*Latest data available in *The State of the World's Children* and *Childinfo* database, UNICEF, 2004.

[17] Despite the fact Gabon had per capita income of $3,490 per year due to the oil income, in 1997 life expectancy was below 55 and the infant mortality rate stood at 87 per 1,000 live births.

[18] Early in 1998, Mayor Mba-Abessole requested the UN to supervise presidential elections that were to be held later that year in order to avoid the 'fraudulent reelection of Omar Bongo'. The elections were in fact won by the president, who defeated Mba Abessole and Pierre-Andre Kombila. Jean-François Ntoutoume-Emane became Prime Minister.

[19] The authorities sought the UN's humanitarian assistance due to the constant influx of refugees from the Republic of Congo. In October 1999, the country had approximately 10,000 refugees.

[20] In July 2000 two freighters, one Greek and one French, collided in Gabonese waters, causing a 400-ton oil spill.

[21] Like other Central and Western African countries, Gabon suffers from child smuggling, mostly coming from Nigeria. The children smuggled to Gabon work in plantations, as domestic employees, in the sexual trade, and in the streets. The ratification of an agreement against child smuggling, signed by Gabon and neighbors in the region, was expected for 2004. Once signed, the situation will be regulated and the children will be repatriated.

[22] The PDG again won the Parliamentary elections of 2001-2, with 84 out of the 120 seats of the National Assembly. In response to an invitation from Bongo to form a Government coalition, Abessole persuaded his followers to join the new administration in January 2002.

[23] In 2002, about 50 people died in the north after an outbreak of Ebola fever. The region of Mekambo and the border with the Republic of Congo were the most affected areas.

[24] In January 2003, after the PDG election victory Bongo pledged that his new administration would be an open one.

[25] On 6 May Faustin Boukoubi, Minister of Public Health, announced that the Ebola outbreak had ended.

[26] On 24 July, police forces destroyed four fishing villages near Libreville, leaving hundreds of people homeless. According to the Government, these villages were allegedly used as a base for drug-trafficking. They were razed as part of a war against crime. ∎

Europe, in late 1989 there were signs of democratic participation for Gabon's opposition forces. After violent confrontations in the streets the President had the constitution amended, introducing a multiparty system and lifting censorship of the press. In the meantime, he invited opposition leaders to join the cabinet.

[12] In May 1990, Joseph Redjambe, president of the Gabonese Progressive Party, was murdered. His death provoked strong reactions against the Government. The resulting incidents left six dead and a hundred wounded. A state of rebellion through the Port Gentil region lasted ten days and the French Government evacuated 5,000 French residents, charging the presidential guard with re-establishing order.

[13] In June, all political and social groups met in a National Conference and an agreement

was reached whereby free presidential elections would be held. Although this was a major victory for the opposition, who extracted promises of multiparty elections from the President, Bongo advanced the election date from 1992 to late 1990, contrary to what the opposition wanted. Bongo used the power base he had built up over the past 20 years in office to carry out his campaign, while the opposition - repressed for decades - had no time to organize itself adequately and faced the election with internal divisions. In September 1990, President Bongo's Gabonese Democratic Party (PDG), obtained a majority in the National Assembly. The new constitution, approved in March 1991, formally established a multiparty system.

[14] In 1991, the country was rocked by a new outbreak of political and social violence. At the same time, the economic crisis

continued to worsen. The IMF and World Bank stabilization program and structural adjustment plan failed to generate much hope among social and political groups.

[15] The 1993 presidential elections, which returned Bongo to power, were questioned by the opposition. In February 1994, the protests continued and were harshly repressed leaving 30 dead. Between September and November 1994, a coalition government was formed until new elections could be held.

[16] In July 1995, the President gained the support of 96 per cent of the voters in a referendum for constitutional reform in order for presidential and legislative elections to be held. The National Assembly elections in December 1996 gave the Democratic Party (PDG), led by Bongo, 47 of the 55 seats. Meanwhile, the opposition leader Paul Mba-Abessole became Mayor of the capital Libreville.

Gambia / Gambia

Population:	1,499,176
Area:	11,300 km²
Capital:	Banjul
Currency:	Dalasi
Language:	English

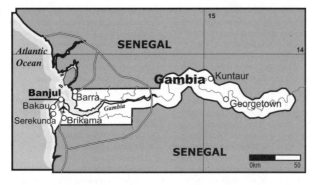

The earliest settlers of the Gambia river valley came from what is now Senegal. Attracted by Gambia's coast, which lent itself to trade and navigation, they settled along the river, carrying out subsistence farming.

[2] In the 15th century, the region was colonized by the Mandingo who, together with the Mali Empire, founded several kingdoms in the Gambia valley, which controlled coastal trade and enabled them to develop economically and culturally.

[3] With the arrival of the Portuguese in 1455, most of the region's domestic trade was displaced toward the Atlantic coast, bringing about the decline of the riverine people. For the Portuguese, Gambia became the point of departure for their precious metals and a prosperous enclave on their route to the Orient.

[4] However, in 1618 the Portuguese Crown sold its commercial and territorial rights to the British Empire, which at the height of its naval prowess was trying to assert its dominance as a colonial power by acquiring a foothold in Africa.

[5] At that time, a war began between Britain and France (controlling all of what is now Senegal) which was to last for over 200 years. As of 1644, the British used this coastal area as a source of slaves: British merchants set up alliances with princes inland to obtain slaves for Britain's colonies and for its slave trade with other colonial powers.

[6] The British therefore limited themselves to establishing a rudimentary trading post in the area, founded in 1660. Border disputes between the British and French increased during the 18th century.

[7] Throughout the 19th century a series of religious wars resulted in the complete Islamization of the country, with an increase in Muslim immigration from other parts of Africa.

[8] The region lost economic significance when the slave trade was abolished in Britain. It did however gain strategic importance by being a British enclave inserted into the heart of Senegal, a region instrumental in France's designs on sub-Saharan Africa. Slavery actually continued within the colony until the 20th century, not being abolished until 1906.

[9] In 1889, France and Britain reached an agreement as to the boundaries of their respective colonies, ensuring peace in the region and the formal recognition of British sovereignty over Gambia by other European powers.

[10] Gambia's status as a British colony remained unchanged throughout the first half of the 20th century. In 1963, it received partial administrative autonomy under the decolonization process begun after World War II.

[11] In 1965, Gambia obtained full independence and joined the British Commonwealth. At the time of its independence, some felt that Gambia did not constitute a nation as such because of its ethnic, cultural and economic complexity.

[12] Following independence, the territory's social and economic structures remained unchanged. Peanut exports continued to be vital to the economy. Traditional social structures remained so powerful that they were finally legitimized by the 1970 Constitution, which guaranteed legislature seats to five regional leaders.

[13] Dawda Jawara, a veterinary doctor and the founder of the People's Progressive Party (PPP), dominated Gambian politics as of the 1960s. He won the 1962 elections, but failed to assume office as the opposition forced a vote of no confidence. However, he again won in 1970 when the country was proclaimed a republic and embraced the presidential system.

[14] The success of Alex Haley's 1976 book *Roots* placed Gambia in the limelight. In the late 1970s it became a popular destination for tourists. Prostitution and drug-trafficking increased.

[15] The lack of border controls in Gambia led to it becoming a paradise for West African smuggling and a large part of Senegal's agricultural produce was illegally shipped through the port of Banjul. This close economic relationship between the countries led the government of Dawda Jawara to accept a project for union with Senegal in 1973.

[16] In July 1981, Muslim dissidents attempted to overthrow Jawara, aiming to end official corruption through the establishment of a revolutionary Islamic regime. The revolt was crushed by Senegalese troops who entered Gambia at the request of President Dawda, who was in London at the time.

[17] The proposed union with Senegal had been planned for 1982, but the coup attempt against Gambia's government accelerated plans for creating the Senegambian confederacy.

[18] Senegambia officially existed from February 1982 to the end of 1989 with Abdou Diouf of Senegal as its first president, assisted by a confederate council of ministers and a bi-national parliament. The treaty ensured that Dawda Jawara gained protection against internal rebellions and Senegal gained greater control over the leak of export tax revenues through

LAND USE

2000

IRRIGATED AREA: 0.9% of arable land

- ARABLE LAND: 23.0%
- CROPLANDS: 0.5%
- OTHER USE: 76.5%

PROFILE

ENVIRONMENT
One of the smallest African countries, Gambia stretches 320 km along the Gambia River, which is fully navigable and one of the main waterways in the area. The climate is tropical; there are rainforests along the river-banks and wooded savanna further inland. Only one sixth of the land is fit for cultivation, so peanuts are the only exportable agricultural resource. The economy is also based on tourism.

SOCIETY
Peoples: The majority of Gambians (40 per cent) are Mandingos; 14 per cent Futa, 13 per cent Wolof who belong to the same root, and 7 per cent are Diula. There are smaller groups inland (Serahuilis, Akus). Five thousand to ten thousand laborers migrate from Mali, Senegal and Guinea-Bissau every year, returning home after the harvest.
Religions: The majority of Gambians (approximately 95 per cent) are Muslims; a minority practice traditional religions and Christianity, mostly Protestant. **Languages:** English (official); the most widespread local languages are Mandingo, Fulani and Wolof. **Main Political Parties:** Alliance for Patriotic Reorientation and Construction (APRC), of President Yahya Jammeh; the United Democratic Party (UDP); the National Reconciliation Party (NRP); People's Democratic Organization for Independence and Socialism (PDOIS).
Main Social Organizations: There are three trade union federations: the Gambia Workers' Union (GWU), linked to the Government; the Gambia Labor Union; the Gambia Salesmen's and Merchants' Union. Gambia Students' Union (GAMSU).

THE STATE
Official Name: Republic of The Gambia.
Administrative Divisions: 5 provinces and the Capital. **Capital:** Banjul 372,000 inhabitants (2003). UPDATE. **Other Cities:** Serekunda 200,000 inhabitants; Brikama 56,100; Bakau 50,200 (2000).
Government: Lieutenant Yahya Jammeh (former dictator), President since October 1996, re-elected in 2001. Single-chamber Parliament: National Assembly, with 45 members elected directly by the people and 4 appointed by the President.
National Holiday: 18 February, Independence (1965). **Armed Forces:** 875 (1997).

Life expectancy
54.1 years
2000-2005

GNI per capita
$280
2002

Literacy
37% total adult rate
2000

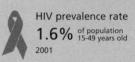

HIV prevalence rate
1.6% of population 15-49 years old
2001

smuggling. Both countries retained their individuality and internal organization.

[19] In the mid-1980s, Jawara became reluctant to consolidate his ties with Senegal and failed to comply with military aid agreements. In late 1989 Gambia signed a mutual defense pact with Nigeria which in practical terms meant the dissolution of Senegambia.

[20] Cordial relations were reinstated with a treaty of friendship and co-operation in 1991; however the confederacy was not restored.

[21] In 1993, agriculture and tourism were hit by the consequences of the European economic crisis. Gambia's trade with Senegal was damaged when the Central Bank of the Western Africa States decided to stop financing trade based upon the African franc (CFA) outside the area comprised by countries using this monetary system. That same year,

the Government took measures to initiate a national reconciliation process, including an amnesty granted to rebel movements fighting to oust the regime.

[22] In July 1994, a military coup overthrew President Dawda Jawara who sought asylum in Senegal after taking refuge in a US warship visiting the country. The presence of this ship in Banjul suggested complicity of the US with the military. The coup, headed by Yahya Jammeh, began with the protests of soldiers who demanded payment for their peace mission carried out in Liberia.

[23] Two members of the Provisional Armed Forces Council were arrested in January 1995 after trying to hand the Government over to civilians. In March, Jammeh also arrested the former Justice minister and general prosecutor for promoting the return of civilian rule. In November, the military junta expanded the powers of the security forces.

[24] In August 1996, following a referendum, a new Constitution was approved and Jammeh, until then chief of the Armed Forces Government Junta, became Gambia's second elected President. Arrests of Islamic leaders were frequent in 1998.

[25] In May 1999, Ousainou Darboe of the dissident United Democratic Party (UDP) accused the Government of 'arresting' their followers and maintaining a democracy with 'untruthful' laws. On 9 June, Jammeh berated Western 'donor' countries for making aid conditional on human rights and democracy. Days later, rebel leaders of Casamance, Senegal, met in Gambia to draw up a peace strategy.

[26] In September, Jammeh criticized the UN's 'lack of responsibility and inaction regarding the conflicts faced by Africa'. A month later, the Press Union denounced governmental measures against freedom of the press (raids on their

buildings and the power of the minister of information to confiscate their records). The security forces prevented an 'attempted coup d'état' in January 2000 and arrested the two officers allegedly responsible for the uprising.

[27] Gambia, with another 44 countries - mostly African - lost its right to vote in the UN General Assembly on 2 February 2000, for 'falling into arrears with its debt repayments'.

[28] The Community of Sahelian-Saharan States (COMESSA), accepted Gambia, Senegal and Djibouti as new members. The 11 members agreed not to interfere in members' domestic affairs and not to aid hostile forces of any of the countries.

[29] The President decided to lift the ban on political parties for the coming elections. In October 2001, Jammeh won the presidential elections, receiving the approval of international observers. However, the opposition argued strongly that the elections had been fraudulent.

[30] Gambia does not comply with international standards of respect for human rights. Journalists are arrested, there are extrajudicial executions and limitations of freedom of speech.

[31] In May 2002, Parliament passed a law on mass media that went against the 1997 Constitution. This law established an organization with powers to register journalists and to compel them to reveal their sources. It also could impose fines when 'unauthorized' articles were published, and ultimately shut down newspapers.

[32] In December 2003, a scandal known as 'Babagate' broke. Baba Jobe, a representative of the Government APRC party in the National Assembly and former associate of President Jammeh, was arrested on charges of money-laundering and fraud. Jobe was the President of the 'Youth Development Project', a job-creation program that managed imports. The company allegedly did not pay taxes to the Gambian Port Authority for its rice imports. The Authority demanded payment of its 65 million dalasis ($2 million) debt, but Jobe paid with counterfeit checks.

[33] On 23 January 2004, five high officials of the Central Bank were accused of multiple financial offenses against the State. During 2002 and 2003 the Bank had received nearly 9,000,000 Swiss francs in an effort to stabilize the dalasi's fluctuation. The stabilization, which should have only taken two days, was delayed for two years. During that time, the five accused officials drew up illegal contracts to finance four companies. Baba Jobe was the main shareholder of two of these companies. ∎

IN FOCUS

ENVIRONMENTAL CHALLENGES
Large areas of forest have disappeared as the land was taken over for growing export crops. Wood is also used as a major source of fuel. As a result, desertification has increased. The low-lying capital, Banjul - one meter above sea-level - risks being submerged in the next few decades by rising sea-levels, a consequence of global warming.

WOMEN'S RIGHTS
Women have been able to vote and be elected since 1960. In 2000, two per cent of the parliamentary seats and 29 per cent of the ministerial positions were held by women.

Female life expectancy increased from 42 to 55 years between 1980 and 2000*.

In 2000* the illiteracy rate for women over 15 was 70.3 per cent.

Women comprised 45 per cent of the labor force, in 2000; the total workforce was 1 million. Between 1990 and 2000, 92 per cent worked in agriculture, 6 per cent in services and 2 per cent in industry. That year, the unemployment rate among women was 12.2 per cent (up from 7.6 per cent in 1995).

55 per cent of the births are attended by qualified personnel, 10 per cent more than two decades earlier*. However, 80 per cent of expectant mothers are anemic*.

An estimated 60 to 90 per cent have been circumcized (female genital mutilation).

CHILDREN
In 2001, 51,000 children were born and 6,000 under-5s died. In 2000* the net rate of elementary school enrolment and attendance was 69 per cent.

Almost 49 per cent of the population is under 18; 19 per cent is aged between 15 and 24. Approximately 69 per cent live below the poverty line. In rural areas, 60 per cent of families are extremely poor. Fourteen per cent of the children were born underweight*. Twelve per cent of the under-5s were moderately or severely underweight*.

The involvement of young people in HIV/AIDS education helped break the culture of silence surrounding the disease. UNICEF's criticism of arranged or early marriages, adolescent pregnancy and violence against girls and women also contributed to the debate.

Community participation has been fostered by NGOs in order to increase girls' enrolment and attendance to school.

Breast-feeding for 6 months is encouraged. Towards the end of 2001, it was estimated that 460 children under 14 were living with HIV/AIDS, and there were 5,300 AIDS orphans.

INDIGENOUS PEOPLES/ ETHNIC MINORITIES
The Mandingo groups (42 per cent) along with other Mande-speaking groups, originally were part of the 13th-century Malian Empire. Wolof (16 per cent) mainly live south of the Gambia river, where they work in agriculture or trade. Jola people (10

per cent) are one of the oldest groups in the region. During the 18th century, they had to pay tribute to the Mandingo. The Serahuli (9 per cent), who live in what was the Wuli Kingdom, are a mix of Berbers, Mandingos and Fulanis. The Fulani (18 per cent) are pastoralists; they dominated during the Tekrur Kingdom until the 11th century. The Aku peoples (3.5 per cent) are mostly descendants of Yorubas who were freed there before they could be shipped as slaves to the Americas. They settled in the country during the 1820s and 1830s. By the late 19th century and during the 20th century, some had positions in government; they adopted Western customs and excelled as traders.

MIGRANTS/REFUGEES
At the end of 2002, the country accommodated around 10,000 refugees (5,000 from Senegal and 5,000 from Sierra Leone). A further 4,000 Senegalese refugees escaped from the conflict in the Casamance region that year, but many were repatriated a few weeks later, when Senegalese security was reinforced.

DEATH PENALTY
Even though it has not been abolished for ordinary crimes, the last recorded execution took place in 1981.

*Latest data available in The State of the World's Children and Childinfo database, UNICEF, 2004.

Georgia / Sak'art'velo

Population:	5,025,885
Area:	69,700 km²
Capital:	Tbilisi
Currency:	Kupon
Language:	Georgian

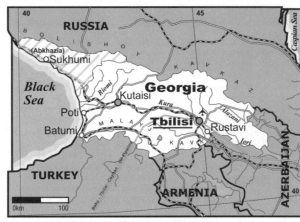

The cultivation of grain in what is now Georgia dates back to the last period of the Stone Age, some 12,000 years ago. The agricultural and cattle-raising activities during that period, are attested to by finds of hoes and other stone plowing instruments. The Caucasian peoples are thought to be the inventors of metallurgy, with their use of bronze, in the 3rd millennium BC.

[2] Vessels in gold and silver that are engraved with ritual scenes suggesting Asiatic cults have been found in majestic tombs of the 2nd millennium BC, giving the idea as to the origin and wealth of certain chieftains. Within the 1st millennium BC, Georgia was inhabited by groups of Assyrians (from Babylon), Armenians and Cimmerians (of Thracian origin, Turkey). The fusion of the latter with indigenous peoples would have formed the group called Kolkhida.

[3] The kingdom of Kolkhida in the 6th century BC, situated at the eastern end of the Black Sea, was conquered by Greece at the end of the 5th century BC, and then by Rome in the year 66 AD. Also invaded was the kingdom of Iberia, created in what is now southeastern Georgia during the 2nd century BC. As a result of Pompey's (106 BC - 48 BC) campaigns, Roman hegemony was established over the whole territory of present-day Georgia.

[4] Just like the other dependencies of the Roman Empire, Georgia was converted to Christianity by Constantin in 337. During the three following centuries, the country was drawn into the conflict between Constantinople and Persia. The ancient kingdom of Kolkhida fell under the control of Constantinople and the previous territory of Iberia came under Iranian control.

[5] Apart from the local authority exercised by the faithful magnates of each province, after 654, Arab caliphs established an emirate at Tbilisi (the capital of Georgia previously known as Tiflis). At the end of the 8th century, Bagratid Ashot I profited from the weakness of the Byzantine emperors and the Arab caliphs to set himself up as hereditary Prince in Iberia.

[6] King Bagrat III (975-1014) united eastern and western Georgia into one state. Tbilisi was not recovered from the Muslims until 1122. Georgia reached an apex under Queen Tamara, who formed a pan-Caucasian empire between 1184 and 1213 marked by the flourishing of architecture and religious arts.

[7] The Mongol invasions of 1220 brought Georgia's golden age to an end. The massacres of Turk conqueror, Tamerlane (1336-1405) displaced Mongols and destroyed Georgia's economy and culture. The introduction of Christianity brought about the emergence of the alphabet and literature, enhanced by contributions from Arabic culture.

[8] The last king of united Georgia was Alexander I, between 1412 and 1443, under whose sons the realm was divided and subsequently disintegrated.

[9] The fall of Constantinople to the Ottoman Turks, in 1453, left it isolated from the rest of the Christian world. Within the three following centuries, Georgia became the object of territorial disputes between Turkey and Iran.

[10] During that period of time, several revolts took place and hundreds of Christians were deported to Iran. During a respite registered between 1638 and 1723, Iran introduced printing to Georgia and appointed a commission of scholars to edit the Georgian annals.

[11] Ivan IV the Terrible (1530-1584) showed interest in Georgia as had his predecessors. The Russians managed to enter in 1789, and occupied the whole territory after defeating both Turks and Persians in 1878.

[12] The local language was eliminated from administrative documents and the use of Russian language imposed. The Georgian Church started to be ruled by Russian Orthodox bishops.

[13] Following the liberation of the Russian serfs (1861), the Georgian peasants also received freedom in 1864. The affluence of entrepreneurs from Western Europe (after the Napoleonic invasions) and the construction of connecting railroads, fostered the emergence of nationalist and freedom movements. In 1893, the Social Democratic Party was secretely founded and five years later, the Georgian Joseph Stalin became one of its members.

[14] After frequent rebellions, the Georgian population confronted the Cossacks during the 1905 Russian Revolution.

[15] When World War I broke out (1914-1918), the Caucasus saw fighting between Russia and Turkey. The Georgians formed a legion to fight alongside the Turks and in February 1917 they brought down the czarist regime.

[16] In November, after the Bolshevik triumph in Petrograd, power in Transcaucasia (Georgia and adjacent territories) fell into the hands of the Mensheviks. Stalin's group abandoned the Caucasus to join the Bolsheviks led by Lenin. In May 1918, in Tbilisi, the United Government of Transcaucasia announced its separation from Soviet Russia - requesting German protection.

[17] Between 1918 and 1920, German, Turkish and British troops entered Georgia. In early 1921, the Red Army occupied Georgia and the Soviet Socialist Republic of Georgia was proclaimed. In March 1922, Georgia, Azerbaijan and Armenia were reorganized as the Transcaucasian Federation. In 1936, the federation was dissolved and Georgia became one of the 15 republics of the Soviet Union (USSR).

[18] During Stalin's despotic rule (1928-1953), Georgia suffered from repression of all expressions of nationalism, the forced collectivization of agriculture and also witnessed many purges.

[19] In the Soviet period, Georgia was industrialized. The Kremlin promoted the creation of Georgian cultural and administrative élites destined to take part in the central government. After Stalin's death, a

PROFILE

ENVIRONMENT

Located in the central western part of Transcaucasia, Georgia is bordered in the north by Russia, in the east by Azerbaijan and in the south by Armenia and Turkey, with the Black Sea to the west. Most of its territory is occupied by mountains. Between the Little and the Great Caucasus lies the Kolkhida lowland and the Kartalinian Plain; the Alazan Valley lies to the east. Subtropical climate in the west, moderate in the east; there is heavy rainfall in the western area, along the shores of the Black Sea. Principal rivers are the Kura and Rioni. Forty per cent of the republic is covered by forests. Georgia has important carbon and manganese deposits and is famous for its wine.

SOCIETY

Peoples: Georgians, 70 per cent; Armenians, 8.1 per cent; Russians, 6.3 per cent; Azeris, 5.7 per cent; Ossetians, Abkhazians and Adzharians. **Religions:** Georgian Orthodox (65 per cent), Muslims (11 per cent), Russian Orthodox (10 per cent), and Armenian Orthodox (8 per cent). **Languages:** Georgian (official), Russian, Abkhazian, Armenian, Azeri, Greek, Kurmanji, Turkish and various Caucasian languages. Main Political Parties: National Movement Party, Citizens' Union of Georgia; All-Georgian Union for Revival; Communist Party of Georgia. Independent movements: Aidguilara (national movement of the Abkhazians), Admon Nyjas (national movement of the South Ossetians). **Main Social Organizations:** the traditional trade unions have 2.6 million members. Currently, the Georgian Trade Union Association is the leading organization.

THE STATE

Official Name: Sakartvelos Respublika. **Capital:** Tbilisi 1,064,000 people (2003). **Other Cities:** Batumi 143,800 people; Sukhumi 63,800; Kutaisi 264,600; Rustavi 178,900 (2000). **Government:** Mikhail Saakashvili, President since January 2004. Zurab Zhvania, Prime Minister since January 2004. Single-chamber parliament with 235 member. **National Holiday:** 26 May, Independence (1991). **Armed Forces:** 13,000.

Life expectancy
73.6 years
2000-2005

GNI per capita
$650
2002

Literacy
100% total adult rate
2000

HIV prevalence rate
0.1% of population 15-49 years old
2001

IN FOCUS

ENVIRONMENTAL CHALLENGES

Bacterial pollution of 70 per cent of the Black Sea constitutes a serious problem. Only 18 per cent of the residual waters in the main port of Batumi undergo adequate treatment. Air pollution is marked, particularly in Rust'avi. Overuse of pesticides has resulted in soil deterioration.

WOMEN'S RIGHTS

Although women's right to vote was declared in 1918, it was not until 1921 that Georgian women were able to vote and stand for office freely. In 2000, they held 7 per cent of seats in Parliament and 4 per cent of ministerial positions. They made up 47 per cent of the labor force.

Ninety six per cent of births are attended by skilled health staff and 95 per cent of pregnant women receiv prenatal care*.

CHILDREN

In 2001, 56,000 children were born and 2,000 under-5s died.

In 2000*, the net primary school enrolment and attendance rate was 95 per cent. Pre-school enrolment has declined by half in rural areas. Since the collapse of the Soviet Union and political transition in the late 20th century, there has been an increase in the number of street children.

The Government, supported by UNICEF, aims to increase access to basic health services for women and children. However, due to budgetary constraints, limited funds are available for the social sector. Immunization coverage is relatively high and under-5 mortality rates (mostly caused by respiratory and gastro-intestinal infections and diseases) have not risen since 1990, but still remain high. Since 1994, UNICEF has provided vaccines, syringes and needles to support the national immunization program, and in 2000, mobile immunization teams were set up, reaching 4,000 children in remote areas.

INDIGENOUS PEOPLES/ ETHNIC MINORITIES

See box for RUSSIA.

MIGRANTS/REFUGEES

At the end of 2002, there were more than 262,000 internally displaced people. About 249,000 were ethnic Georgians displaced from Abkhazia between 1991 and 1993, when the separatist movement took control of the province, declared independence and expelled nearly 30,000 Georgians. Although a 1994 ceasefire initially enabled up to 60,000 people to return to their homes, tens of thousands were uprooted again when fighting resumed in the Gali

district in 1998. Many of them depend on humanitarian assistance. Red Cross delegates, responsible for the distribution of food, reported in 2000 being 'shocked by the miserable condition of the people requesting their aid'. Georgians allege that the Abkhazis are carrying out an ethnic cleansing campaign.

Meanwhile, nearly 12,400 displaced people remained in the region of South Ossetia, where Georgians and Ossetians were in conflict in 1991-1992.

Georgia continues to oppose the return of some 280,000 Meskhetian Turks who were deported en masse from southern Georgia to Central Asia during the Stalin era. Thousands fled persecution or were expelled a second time from Central Asia at the time of the breakup of the Soviet Union and were living as stateless persons in Ukraine or Azerbaijan. In 1999, a 10-year repatriation process was decreed, to begin in 2002; however, no repatriations were registered that year.

DEATH PENALTY

It was abolished in 1997.

*Latest data available in *The State of the World's Children* and *Childinfo* database, UNICEF, 2004.

freewheeling 'second economy' was developed, which supplied goods and services.

[20] In 1953, Moscow made Eduard Shevardnadze, a Communist Youth leader until then, chief of police. When Shevardnadze was appointed First Secretary of the Communist Party in 1972, a new nationalist feeling began to emerge with declarations in defense of the Georgian language and violent acts of sabotage against the Soviet administration.

[21] In 1978, the new constitution of the USSR triggered a wave of protest, as it made Russian the official language. However, Shevardnadze managed to have the measure abolished and allowed an anti-Stalin movie, 'Repent', to be screened. This marked the development of glasnost (openness) and perestroika (restructuring) process in Georgia.

[22] In 1985, Shevardnadze was made Foreign Minister of the Soviet Union. After the political changes made by Mikhail Gorbachev in the late 1980s, several independent movements and parties emerged in Georgia - frequently repressed by the Red Army - among them, a Green Party that denounced industrial pollution in the Black Sea and deforestation problems.

[23] In the 1990 elections for the Soviet (parliament), the 'Free Georgia Round Table' coalition won, led by Zviad Gamsakhurdia, a well-known opponent to the Soviet regime. After the disintegration of the USSR, Georgia declared independence in April 1991 and Gamsakhurdia was elected President. But Gamsakhurdia's authoritarian behavior soon drove many of his supporters into opposition.

[24] Georgia's economy, dependent on the USSR for its energy supply, was the most affected of all former Soviet Republics after the rupture.

[25] A civil war broke out and in January 1992 the President was deposed by a Military Council, which was subsequently replaced in March by a State Council, headed by Shevardnadze. Tbilisi's authorities fought against Gamsakhurdia's supporters and Ossetian separatists. In June, a cease-fire was called in South Ossetia, supervised by a peacekeeping force of Russians, Georgians and Ossetians.

[26] The following month, the Abkhazian authorities (in the northeast) resolved to limit the jurisdiction of Georgia's central government within their autonomous region, and in August government troops occupied Sukhumi (Abkhazia's capital).

In June, a Russian-mediated armistice came into effect. Three months later, a strong Abkhazian offensive took the Georgians by surprise and occupied Sukhumi, from where Shevardnadze managed to escape uninjured.

[27] In November, supporters of former president Gamsakhurdia launched a broad offensive, but were defeated with the help of Russian troops. In early 1994, Gamsakhurdia committed suicide according to official reports. In February, Georgia signed a friendship treaty with Russia, and in April a peace treaty with the Abkhazian rebels.

[28] In August 1995, Parliament approved a new Constitution making Georgia a presidential republic. Shevardnadze won the first presidential elections in November and his party, the Union of Citizens of Georgia won an absolute majority in Parliament. In 1997, the country became the first former Soviet republic to abolish the death penalty.

[29] Between 1998 and 1999, Shevardnadze narrowly escaped two assassination attempts. In both cases there were rumors of Moscow's involvement. Russian President Vladimir Putin accused Georgia's Government of harboring Chechen rebels on their territory.

[30] The Abkhaz parliament declared independence in October 1999 but Tbilisi did not recognize the new state. In March 2001, Georgia and Abkhazia signed an accord renouncing the use of force between them, but in October, new confrontations broke out between Georgian paramilitary forces and Abkhaz troops.

[31] In October 2001, following the closing of the private Rustavi-2 TV station, which was critical of the failure to fight corruption, massive popular protests demanded the resignation of the Shevardnadze government. His administration was blamed for corruption, civil war and impoverishment. Shevardnadze answered by sacking the entire administration. In November 2001, Nino Burdzhanadze, then Foreign Minister, was elected head of Parliament in an extraordinary session.

[32] The arrival in Georgia of US military advisors, in February 2002, was criticized by Moscow. Washington's stated objective was to support the local army in fighting an Islamic terrorist group allegedly linked to the al-Qaeda network and based on the Chechen border. Some observers believed that US troops were there to protect a pipeline being built through Georgia to carry Azerbaijani oil to Western markets. Afterwards, during the Iraq invasion led by President Bush in April 2003, speculations about a permanent US military presence were confirmed.

[33] In November 2003, parliamentary elections were held. At first, official results confirmed the victory of Shevardnadze's party, but thousands of people questioned the veracity of results and demonstrated in the streets. International observers reported many irregularities and crowds of opposition demonstrators broke into Georgia's Parliament. These results were annulled by the Supreme Court.

[34] That month, several opposition parties agreed to support Mikhail Saakashvili as presidential candidate. Saakashvili (37 years old; National Movement party), is a US-educated lawyer, who started his career under the protection of Shevardnadze, and led the 'Rose Revolution', a popular revolt that ousted the former President. Even though he was among the Ministers expelled in 2001, Saakashvili gained popularity by exposing government corruption and promising to fight poverty. Meanwhile, Nino Burdzhanadze was appointed as interim President.

[35] In January 2004, Saakashvili won the presidential election with an overwhelming majority (more than 96 per cent of the votes). The new President announced that 'special measures' would be taken in order to 'eradicate organized crime and corruption'. ∎

Germany / Deutschland

Population:	82,559,636
Area:	357,030 km²
Capital:	Berlin
Currency:	Euro
Language:	German

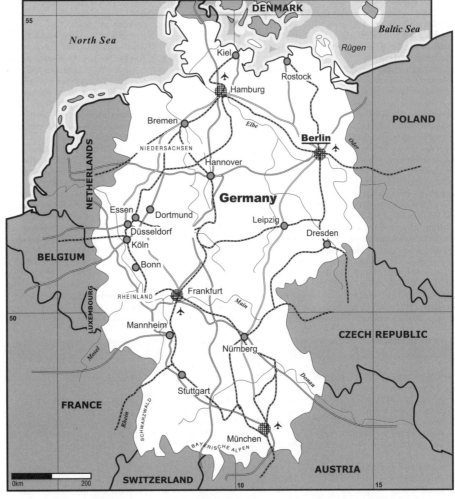

G ermanic peoples have lived in the area of what is now Germany since around 50 BC. The Gauls lived west of the Rhine. Greek and Roman writers such as Julius Caesar, who invaded part of Gaul around 50 BC, repeatedly mentioned the Germans. Between 260 and 276 AD, two German peoples, the Alemanni and the Franks, attacked Gaul.

2   When the Roman Empire fell in 476, the German tribes west of the Rhine were politically divided. Among the largest tribes were the Merovingians, Carolingians and Ottomans. Around 800 Charlemagne built a great empire that occupied the present Germany and France. After his death in 814 came a period of great social unrest. However, Otto I (936- 973) consolidated the empire once again.

3   During the 12th and 13th centuries Germany experienced a rapid growth in population, and continuous expansion.

4   The instability of royal dynasties strengthened secular and religious principalities. Princes were free to build fortresses, exploit natural resources and administer justice in their dominions.

5   In 1356, the authority of the king in relation to the papacy was consolidated in the Golden

Bull of Charles IV (1346-1378) establishing the right to appoint the King without the Pope's approval, and strengthened the hand of the principalities, on whose support the king depended.

6   During the 15th and 16th centuries internal instability persisted. In 1517 Martin Luther led the Protestant Reformation, which, coupled with political rivalries, frustrated reunification efforts.

7   The Reformation provided a forum for criticisms of secularization and corruption in the German Church, which had become an increasingly prosperous economic and financial institution. It owned a third of the land in some districts and profited from selling indulgences - one of the contributory factors to its downfall. After a succession of internal wars, including peasant uprisings, the Peace of Augsburg

was reached in 1555, giving equal rights to both Catholics and Lutherans.

8   Political and religious factions combined their strengths; in 1608 the Protestant Union was created, and the Catholic League a year later. The Bohemian rebellion triggered the Thirty Year War (1618-1648), which spread to the entire continent, reduced the population of central Europe by around 30 per cent, and ended in 1648 with the Peace of Westphalia.

9   In the 18th century, the Kingdom of Prussia emerged as an economic and political unit, responsible for creating tensions among the German states. Napoleon's victories over Prussia in 1806 and the formation of the Confederation of the Rhine put an end to the Holy Roman Empire.

10   In Central Europe during the 18th century, culture formed an outlet for intellectual energies, which could not be expressed through politics given that autocratic rulers dominated

WORKERS

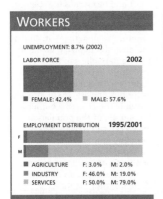

UNEMPLOYMENT: 8.7% (2002)

LABOR FORCE   2002

■ FEMALE: 42.4%   ■ MALE: 57.6%

EMPLOYMENT DISTRIBUTION   1995/2001

F

M

■ AGRICULTURE	F: 3.0%	M: 2.0%
■ INDUSTRY	F: 46.0%	M: 19.0%
■ SERVICES	F: 50.0%	M: 79.0%

LAND USE

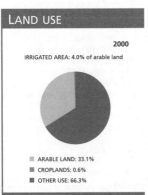

2000

IRRIGATED AREA: 4.0% of arable land

■ ARABLE LAND: 33.1%
■ CROPLANDS: 0.6%
■ OTHER USE: 66.3%

PUBLIC EXPENDITURE

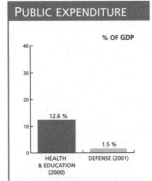

% OF GDP

40

30

20

10

0

12.6 %

1.5 %

HEALTH
& EDUCATION
(2000)

DEFENSE (2001)

Life expectancy
78.3 years
2000-2005

GNI per capita
$22,670
2002

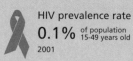
HIV prevalence rate
0.1% of population 15-49 years old
2001

political life. Philosophers like Kant and Herder, and writers like Goethe and Schiller, expressed the idealism and spiritualism that characterized the German art and literature of this time.

[11] When Napoleon fell, the German princes created a confederation of 39 states, which were independent except for foreign policy. Austrian and Prussian opposition to broader forms of representation increased popular unrest, leading to the 1830 revolts and increased repression.

[12] In 1834, Prussia threw its growing economic weight into the political realm, with the establishment of the German Customs Union, from which Austria was excluded. The main consequences of the Union were the duplication of trade among its members over the next ten years, as well as the formation of industrial centres and the emergence of a working class. Due to the rapid growth of the urban population, the supply of labor greatly exceeded the demand. The resulting impoverishment of industrial workers and artisans served as a breeding ground for the rebellions of subsequent years, culminating in the revolutionary wave of 1848-49.

[13] A National Assembly first met in Frankfurt on 18 May 1848; its representatives belonged mostly to liberal democratic sectors. They campaigned for German unity, and guarantees of political freedom. However, internal divisions facilitated the regrouping of the forces of the former regime, leading finally to the dissolution of Parliament in June 1849 and the repression of opposition organizations.

[14] With the revolutionary tendencies crushed, Austria and Prussia were free to dispute their respective roles in German unification. The issue was settled in 1866 with Prussia's victory in the Seven Weeks' War. The union was forged around the North German Confederation, a creation of the Prussian chancellor, Otto von Bismarck, which aimed to halt liberalism. The Parliament (*Reichstag*) was inaugurated in February 1867.

[15] Three years later, war broke out with France. Prussia's victory in 1871 was the last step in Bismarck's scheme to unite Germany under a single monarch, and Prussian domination.

[16] The Empire had to deal with opposing internal forces - the Church and social democracy. Bismarck passed the May Laws, secularizing education and some other activities. He later reversed this, securing the Church as an ally against socialism. Alarmed at the growth of social democracy, the regime used repression and social reform to neutralize the latter's potential.

[17] Bismarck's government introduced commercial protectionism to increase domestic income and foster national industry and the German economy grew substantially, especially in heavy industry, chemicals, the electro-technical area and production. The creation of the Triple Alliance with Austria and Italy, and the acquisition of colonies in Africa and Asia after 1884 made the German Empire a leading world power.

[18] German rivalry with France and Britain in the west, and Russia and Serbia in the east, triggered World War I. The capitulation of the Austro-Hungarian Empire and Turkey in November 1918 led to Germany's final defeat. The crisis was aggravated by an internal revolution that led to the abdication of the Emperor. Government was handed over to the socialist Friedrich Ebert, who was to call a National Constituent Assembly.

[19] German social democracy split into a moderate tendency favoring a gradual evolution to socialism, and a radical tendency promoting a revolutionary change. The radical group, the Spartacists, headed by Karl Liebknecht and Rosa Luxemburg, identified with the Russian revolution of October 1917 and wanted to set up a system similar to that of the Soviets. The Spartacist leaders were executed in January 1919 following a failed coup attempt. A few days later, the electorate returned a moderate socialist majority to power in the Constituent Assembly.

[20] Formally proclaimed in August of that year, the Weimar Constitution was welcomed as the most democratic of its time. The president elect had power to nominate the Chancellor, whose government needed approval of the lower chamber of parliament, or the Reichstag. It also provided for the constitution of an upper house or Länder, formed by delegates designate by the governments of the liberal states.

[21] The Weimar Republic had a short and hazardous life. Despite the virtues attributed to the Constitution, various factors came together to undermine it. One of the main destabilizing elements for the Republic was the conditions imposed on the country in Versailles by the victorious powers. These affected not only the economy but also the morale of the population, which refused to consider Germany 'guilty' of having caused the war in 1914 and was unable to accept the stipulations of the treaty that judged any German, from the Kaiser down, as a war criminal.

IN FOCUS

ENVIRONMENTAL CHALLENGES
There are hazardous waste dumps, though the Government has promised to stop using nuclear energy by 2015. The region of former East Germany was devastated by air pollution from chemical, electrochemical, metallurgic and iron and steel industries, as well as from coal-based energy sources. The emission of sulphur dioxide in the East is 15 times higher than in the West, adding to acid rain. Untreated waters from industrial waste mixed with heavy metals and toxic substances have affected eastern rivers, some of them tributaries of the polluted Baltic Sea.

WOMEN'S RIGHTS
Women have been able to vote and be elected since 1918. From 1995 to 2000, Parliament seats held by women rose from 26 to 31 per cent of the total. Female representation in ministerial or equivalent positions fell from 16 to 8 per cent.

In 2000 women made up 42 per cent of the workforce (2 per cent in agriculture, 19 per cent in industry and 79 per cent in services). Almost 92 per cent were waged workers, 6 per cent were independent and 2 per cent were underemployed. Female unemployment amounted to 8.6 per cent, 1 per cent higher than among males.

Parliament proposed in 2001 to legislate on the traffic of women in the country, focusing the punishment on those responsible for the business, rather than on the victims. Since 2000, between 150,000 and 500,000 women have entered the country illegally each year, mostly from Central or Eastern Europe.

CHILDREN
In 2001 children under 18 were 18.8 per cent of the population and those under 5 were 4.6 per cent. It is estimated there were 8,400 people under 50 and less than 500 children under 14 living with HIV/AIDS. There were 5,300 AIDS-related orphans in 2001.

Education and health indicators are good for children born in German families, but there are no clear figures for immigrants or refugees.

Germany was a pioneer of pre-school education in the Western world. It was begun by Fröbel in 1840 and focused on the pedagogical care and supervision of 3- to 6-year-old children.

INDIGENOUS PEOPLES/ ETHNIC MINORITIES
The Turks are an historical ethnic minority in Germany. The inflow of Turkish has been more or less constant since the 1950s. Now their birth rate is higher than the German population, which could change their present marginalization in the future. Turks are politically marginalized and still face barriers that prevent them from becoming citizens.

Barely 160,000 voted in the 1998 elections, and in Parliament there is only one Turk among 672 members.

All immigrant workers face legal problems. The State may restrict their freedom of association, movement or choice of occupation. Workers from other EU countries receive residence permits, automatically renewed. Non-EU workers, including Turks, become residents only after 8 years of constant work and residence. For those in the second and third generations, who no longer speak Turkish, integration to Turkish society would be as difficult as for any other German.

MIGRANTS/REFUGEES
There were 104,000 refugees and asylum-seekers in 2002, many of them Bosnian and Kosovar. That year, 91,500 people requested asylum, 20 per cent less than in 2001. Most came from Turkey, Yugoslavia, Russia and Iran. The Federal Refugees Office granted asylum to 3 per cent of all seekers (almost all of them Turks, Iraqis, Iranians and Syrians). Asylum was denied to 79,000 people, of whom 26,600 (34 per cent) were considered groundless requests.

DEATH PENALTY
Abolished in West Germany in 1949, and in East Germany in 1987.

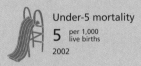

22 Even though the Republican Government managed to weather the serious economic crises, as in 1920-23 and events following the Wall Street Crash in 1929, the destabilizing influence of the Communists and the National Socialist Party, led by Adolf Hitler, were set to topple it. The National Socialist or Nazi Party had attempted a coup in 1923. Although this failed, the Party saw a sustained increase in its popularity throughout the decade, with rocketing support after the crisis in 1929. With barely 170,000 members in 1929, the number grew to 1,378,000 by 1932.

23 Field-Marshal Paul von Hindenburg, elected President in 1925, dissolved parliament in 1930. In the elections later that year, Communists and Nazis both saw a great increase in votes. The Nazis' promises to rebuild Greater Germany following the humiliation of the post-war treaties, and their campaign to blame the Jews and Communists for the economic crisis, gained ground when the Nazi Party doubled its share of the vote in the 1932 elections (37 per cent of the total).

24 The rise of Hitler and the National Socialist Party proved unstoppable. Despite the fact that Hitler's demands to become Chancellor had been refused, in January 1933 - as unemployment topped six million - Hindenburg was forced to hand him the reins of office. Hitler dissolved Parliament and called elections which the Nazis won.

25 In Potsdam in March 1933, the new parliament granted Hitler the power to issue decrees outside the Constitution without the approval of the legislative body or the President for four years. He had the power to set the budget, request loans and sign agreements with other countries, reorganize both his cabinet and the supreme ranks of the armed forces, and proclaim martial law. In July, Hitler abolished the German Federation and instituted absolute central power. He outlawed trade unions, strikes and all parties except his own. Germany also withdrew from the Disarmament Conference and the League of Nations. The Nazis dubbed their government the *Third Reich* (Third Empire).

26 After the death of President Hindenburg in August 1934, the cabinet was forced to swear personal allegiance to the Chancellor, Adolf Hitler. In 1935, in open violation of the Treaty of Versailles, he began to re-arm Germany. The European powers protested, but were unable to stop him. With the 1935 'Nuremberg Laws', the regime provided a legal framework for its racist ideology, laying the foundation for its subsequent policies of ethnic and religious persecution.

27 Germany and Italy signed a co-operation agreement in October 1936 which included support for General Franco in the Spanish Civil War. The following month Germany and Japan (the Axis powers) agreed to set up a military exchange, and in November 1937 Germany, Italy and Japan signed the Anti-communist Pact in Rome.

28 In March 1938, German troops invaded Austria, and Hitler annexed it. That same year, the pressure of Hitler and German nationalism on the Sudetenland forced the European powers to cede this Czechoslovakian region to Germany. On 'Kristallnacht', 9-10 November, the Government carried out a systematic destruction of Jewish commercial property and religious and cultural institutions.

29 In 1939, taking advantage of the disagreements between Czechs and Slovaks, German troops advanced into Prague; Bohemia, Moravia, and Slovakia became protectorates.

30 Britain assured Poland, Romania, Greece and Turkey that it would protect their independence, and Britain and France attempted to establish an alliance with the Soviet Union. In August 1939, however, the USSR signed a non-aggression treaty with Germany. On 1 September, German troops invaded Poland. Britain and France issued Germany an ultimatum which was disregarded. World War II broke out.

31 By 1940, Germany had invaded Norway, Denmark, Belgium, the Netherlands, Luxembourg and France. In 1941 Hitler started his offensive against the USSR, but German troops were halted a few miles outside Moscow. They were finally defeated after the siege of Stalingrad (Volgograd) in 1943.

32 From the outset, German aggression against its neighbours was accompanied by the systematic extermination of the Jewish population in concentration camps, primarily in Poland. Over six million Jews, and a million other people were killed.

33 The advance of the Red Army - culminating in the capture of Berlin - and the 1944 Allied landing in Normandy forced Germany to surrender in May 1945.

PROFILE

ENVIRONMENT

The northern part of the country is a vast plain. The Baltic coast is jagged, with deep, narrow gulfs. The center of the country is made up of very old mountain ranges, plateaus and sedimentary river basins. Of the ancient massifs, the most important are the Black Forest region and the Rhineland. The southern region begins in the Danube Valley, and is made up of plateaus (the Bavarian Plateau), bordered to the south by the Bavarian Alps. There are large deposits of coal and lignite along the banks of the Ruhr and Ens rivers, which provided the backbone of Germany's industrial development. Heavy industry is concentrated in the Ruhr Valley, mid-Rhineland and Lower Saxony. The south of the former German Democratic Republic is rich in coal, lignite, lead, tin, silver and uranium deposits. The chemical, electrochemical, metallurgical and steel industries are concentrated there.

SOCIETY

Peoples: German 91.1 per cent; Turkish and Kurdish 2.3 per cent; Yugoslav 0.7 per cent; Italian 0.7 per cent; Greek 0.4 per cent; Polish 0.4 per cent; Spanish 0.2 per cent; other 2.0 per cent.
Religions: Christian; Protestants (32 per cent) in the North and East; Catholics (33 per cent) were a majority in West Germany before reunification. Jewish and Muslim minorities (6 per cent).
Languages: German (official) and local dialects which, in spite of restrictions, are regaining popularity. Turkish, Kurdish.
Main Political Parties: Social Democratic Party of Germany (SPD); Christian-Democratic Union (CDU); Christian Social Union in Bavaria (CSU); Alliance-90/The Greens; Free Democratic Party (FDP).
Main Social Organizations: Workers' Federation (DGB); Social Watch; Heinrich Böll Foundation, linked to the Green Party; Association of German Development NGOs (Venro); Human Rights Forum.

THE STATE

Official Name: Bundesrepublik Deutschland.
Administrative Divisions: Federal parliamentary state made up of 15 Länder (federated states), as of 3 October 1990; 11 Länder made up what was formerly West Germany (Schleswig-Holstein, Hamburg, Bremen, Niedersachsen, Nordrhein-Westfalen, Hessen, Rheinland-Pfalz, Saarland, Baden-Württemberg, Bavaria and Berlin) while the former German Democratic Republic was divided into five Länder (Mecklenburg, Brandenburg, Sachsen-Anhalt, Sachsen and Thueringen).
Capital: Berlin (since 1990) 3,327,000 people (2003).
Other Cities: Hamburg 3,258,500 people; München (Munich) 2,342,500; Dresden 1,031,100; Köln (Cologne) 966,500; Frankfurt 645,500 (2002).
Government: Horst Köhler, President since July 2004; Gerhard Schröder, Chancellor since October 1998, re-elected in September 2002, appointed by the federal parliament. Parliament: The Bundestag (Federal Diet) has 598 members and the Bundesrat (Federal Council) has 69 members. Both have been in Berlin since 1999, while the Länder Chamber is still in Bonn.
National Holiday: 3 October, Unity Day (1990).
Armed Forces: 271,923 (2002). Other: Federal Border Guard 24,800; Coast Guard 535.

34 Four million Germans from neighbouring countries, and from the territories annexed by Poland and the USSR, were forced to move to the four zones that Germany was now divided into. The country remained occupied by the United States, France, Britain and the USSR. In 1949, discord between the former Allies over the future governance of Germany led to the creation of the Federal Republic of Germany (FRG), in the West, and the German Democratic Republic (GDR), in the East. The issue of the two Germanies became a bone of contention in post-war relations between the USSR and the US.

35 In 1955, the sovereignty of both Germanies was recognized by their occupying forces. During the Cold War, West Germany became a member of NATO while East Germany joined the Warsaw Pact. Foreign forces continued to be based in their territories and the two republics were still subject to limitations on their

Doctors

354 per 100,000 people

1990-2002

Primary school

87% net enrolment rate

2000

armed forces and a ban on nuclear weapons.

[36] The United Socialist Party (SED), formed from the union of Communists and Social Democrats in 1946, took over the government of East Germany. The USSR partly compensated them for war losses with money, equipment and cattle, and a social system similar to that of the USSR was set up. In 1953, the political and economic situation of East Germany led to a series of protests, which were put down by Soviet troops. In the meantime, emigration to the Federal Republic of Germany (FRG) increased.

[37] Between the state's formation and 1961, when the East German Government forbade all emigration to the West, some three million East Germans emigrated to West Germany. To enforce their resolution, the East closed its borders and built the Berlin Wall between the eastern and the western sections of the city. In 1971, Erich Honecker took over the leadership of the SED party, and later the GDR Government.

[38] Between 1949 and 1963, Chancellor Konrad Adenauer, a conservative Christian Democrat, oversaw the reconstruction of West Germany/FRG, under the slogan '(establishing) a social market economy'. With US support (the Marshall Plan) and huge amounts of foreign capital, the FRG became one of the most developed capitalist economies, playing a key role in the founding of the European Community (EC).

[39] With the victory of the Social Democratic Party (SPD) in the 1969 elections, the government of Chancellor Willy Brandt launched a policy of rapprochement toward Eastern Europe and the German Democratic Republic. In 1970 the first formal talks between the FRG and the GDR began, and in 1971 the occupying powers agreed to free access of FRG citizens to the GDR. A Basic Treaty of bilateral relations was signed by both Germanies in 1973; in September they were admitted to the United Nations.

[40] In the 1970s, the number of power stations producing nuclear energy increased. In response to this, a strong environmental movement was formed, with a network of hundreds of grassroots groups throughout the country.

[41] In 1974, after the discovery that his private secretary was an East German spy, Brandt resigned as Chancellor and was succeeded by Helmut Schmidt. The

modernization of Soviet medium-range missiles in East Germany, and the December 1979 NATO decision to do the same with its arsenal in West Germany, gave a strong impetus to the anti-nuclear movement in both states, with massive protests in the FRG.

[42] In 1982, the Social Democratic Party (SPD) had to leave power when the Liberal Party withdrew from the government alliance after 13 years. It was succeeded by the liberal-conservative alliance (CDU/CSU, FDP) led by Chancellor Helmut Kohl of the Christian Democratic Union (CDU).

[43] In mid-1989, Hungary liberalized regulations regarding transit across the border with Austria. Within a few weeks, some 350,000 Germans from the GDR had emigrated to the FRG. Street demonstrations demanding change brought on a crisis in the GDR. In August, Honecker resigned and was replaced by Egon Krenz. On 9 November the GDR opened up its borders and the Berlin Wall fell. Kohl immediately proposed the creation of a confederation of East and West Germany.

[44] In February 1990, the East German Government agreed to German unification and the withdrawal of all foreign troops from its territory. The fusion of the two states was officially recognized in August 1990, as the Federal Republic of Germany. Political union was made possible when the USSR accepted the East German entry into NATO. The only important difference between the two Germanies over the next two years was the East's preservation of a more liberal abortion law.

[45] In the first parliamentary elections of the new Federal Republic, in December 1990, the governing coalition of Christians Democrats and Liberals obtained 54 per cent of the vote and stayed in power. From 1991, the extreme right made important gains in places such as Bremen, where they increased their share of the vote by 7 per cent. During 1992, there were 2,280 attacks on foreigners and Jewish monuments, which left 17 people dead. After one incident which caused the death of a Turkish woman and two children, the Government outlawed three neo-Nazi organizations.

[46] Throughout the following year, the closure of most of the industry in the east of the country and economic recession - the worst since 1945 - caused a constant increase in unemployment. In May 1994, the conservative, Roman Herzog,

backed by Kohl, was designated president of Germany by a special electoral assembly, after defeating the Social Democrat Johannes Rau. Kohl triumphed again in the October general elections, although his majority fell to only 10 seats of the 672 in play.

[47] In 1995, the constant weakening of the Liberal Party (FDP) in various local elections prompted the resignation of Foreign Minister Klaus Kinkel. On the social front, Parliament adopted a new law which, despite again permitting abortion during the first 12 weeks of pregnancy, was more restrictive than the one annulled in 1993 for being unconstitutional.

[48] The discontent of many foreigners resident in Germany led to the formation of the Democratic Party of Germany, which stood for greater access to the electoral roll and citizenship - often restricted to people of German origin - for the children of immigrants.

[49] In 1996, five years after unification and three years after the frontiers fell for workers of the European Union, unemployment stood at around 10.6 per cent on a national level, and up to 16 per cent in the states of the former East Germany. Five million people were out of work.

[50] Racism and antisemitism continued to be issues for the Kohl administration. In October 1997, a television broadcast showed an army battalion giving Nazi salutes and shouting anti-Semitic and anti-US slogans. Amnesty International indicated that police abuse of foreigners could not be seen as isolated cases, due to the systematic repetition of the offences.

[51] In early 1998, the Deutsche Bank paid back Jewish organizations the money made from the sale of gold suspected to have been robbed from the Jews by the Nazis. At the same time, a Swiss foundation began to provide economic compensation - although with 'token' sums of money - to Roma (gypsy) residents in Germany who had survived the Nazi holocaust.

[52] The 1998 elections delivered an overwhelming victory for the Social Democrats and Gerhard Schröder was named Federal Chancellor. The SPD leader Oskar Lafontaine headed the Finance ministry. The former communists of former East Germany were well supported, winning 36 seats in the Federal Parliament.

[53] In March 1999, Lafontaine resigned from both posts

following discrepancies with the political line of the head of government, in what became a party crisis. A series of defeats in the 1999 local elections put the squeeze on the SPD and it seemed the public had returned to the Christian Democrats.

[54] But the CDU was hit by a corruption scandal in November 1999. Initially, former Chancellor Kohl was accused of authorizing the sale of armored vehicles to countries at war without parliament knowing, but later it was announced that he had accepted illegal contributions from private donors. Kohl refused to hand over the list of donors in order to protect them and had to stand down from honorary presidency of the CDU, found guilty of illegal handling of funds.

[55] Unemployment grew and, in November 2001, the number of unemployed reached 3,789,000, or 9.2 per cent of the working population.

[56] In March 2002 the lower chamber initiated the ratification process of the Kyoto Protocol, unanimously passing it into law. This commits the country to reduce its carbon dioxide emissions by one fifth by the year 2012.

[57] During the September 2002 electoral campaign, Chancellor Gerhard Schröder made public his deep opposition to a pre-emptive US attack on Iraq. This boosted his popularity with the voters, but worsened his relationship with George W Bush's government.

[58] In 2003 Germany maintained its opposition to the Iraq war. Massive demonstrations took place against the war. Before the attacks on Iraq started more than 80 per cent of Germans were against the war. However, the German Government supported the US when it allowed US Navy ships to sail the Germany's territorial waters to supply airplanes bombing Iraq.

[59] Structural changes took place in social security throughout 2003. The ruling SPD Party made cuts in public spending, including social security and public health. Unemployment and welfare benefits were reduced. Industrial workers were required to raise their working week from 35 to 40 hours and delay retirement by five years (until they were 65).

[60] Student demonstrations took place in November and December 2003 against the Government's budget cuts and the implementation of university fees. ∎

Ghana / Ghana

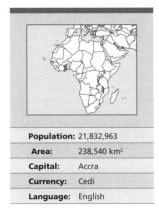

Population:	21,832,963
Area:	238,540 km²
Capital:	Accra
Currency:	Cedi
Language:	English

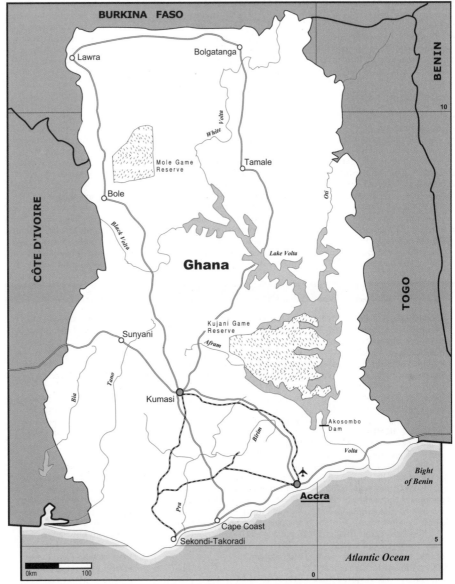

I n about 1300, the Akans or Ashantis moved into Ghana from the north. The Fanti State of Denkyira was already established on the coast so the Akans settled in the inland jungles where they founded a series of small states.

2   Around the 15th century the Ashantis began to trade in the markets of Sudan, on the border of present-day Côte d'Ivoire. They traded slaves and gold for fabrics and goods from other places (an ornate pitcher that had once belonged to Richard II, King of England between 1367 and 1400, was discovered in the treasure of a Kumasi ruler).

3   In the 17th century, the migration of peoples threatened the existence of the small states. The Akans united to confront and defeat the Doma invaders.

4   With the decline of the Songhai, the Moroccan incursions and the beginning of the Fulah expansion, the North African trade network collapsed with serious repercussions for the inland economy. The Ashanti were deprived of access to the coastal trading posts as these were in Denkyira Territory. So, they declared war on the Denkyira, defeated them and then organized a centralized state, ruled by the 'Ashantihene' (leader of the Ashanti nation) endowed with a powerful army. By 1700, the Ashanti had control of the slave trade and the flow of European goods to the interior.

5   The British stopped trading in slaves; meanwhile, the Ashanti were attempting to seize the shoreline from the Fanti, who had retained a significant share of the coastal trade. English backing of the Fanti led to the Anglo-Ashanti wars, 1806-1816, 1825-1828 and 1874. The British turned the Fanti territory into a colony, and in 1895 they proclaimed a protectorate over the northern territories.

6   While the coastal and northern regions were under British rule, the central region belonged to the autonomous Ashanti nation. In 1896, another Anglo-Ashanti war broke out. The capital, Kumasi, was razed by cannon fire, and the ruler was deposed and exiled. In 1900, an attempt to collect the debt owed by the Ashanti (50,000 ounces of gold in compensation for 'war damages') coupled with the British Governor's desire to sit on the gold throne, led to a general rebellion in which thousands of people were killed. In 1902 the Ashanti state was formally annexed to the Gold Coast Colony.

7   Early in the 20th century, a strong nationalist current developed in spite of the ethnic and religious differences within Ghana. There was an economic opposition between the north, where the traditional structures had remained intact, and the south, where a Westernized middle class and a relatively significant working class had developed.

8   Popular pressure on the colonial administration led to political concessions. In 1946, London admitted a few Africans into the colonial administration and in 1949 Kwame Nkrumah formed the Convention People's Party (CCP) to campaign for greater reform.

9   Nkrumah was one of the founding fathers of Pan-Africanism and African nationalism. He established a solid rural and urban party structure and, in 1952, he became Prime Minister of the colony. He proclaimed himself a 'socialist, Marxist and Christian', promising to fight against imperialism.

10   Nkrumah represented Ghana at the Bandung Conference in 1955 which marked the birth of the Movement of Non-Aligned Countries, together with Tito, Nasser, Nehru and Sukarno. In 1957 he achieved a major victory and Ghana became the first country in West Africa to gain independence. Known as *Osagyefo* (redeemer), Nkrumah enthusiastically embraced the African anti-colonialism. He initiated a series of internal changes based on industrialization, agrarian reform and socialist education.

11   Traditional and neo-colonial interests conspired against the Government and Nkrumah was overthrown. The pro-British coup leaders drew up a parliamentary constitution and held elections for a civilian government, where

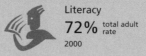
Nkrumah was not allowed to participate. He died in exile in Bucharest in 1972.

[12] That year, Colonel Ignatius Acheampong led a coup replacing the Government of Dr Kofi Busia. Acheampong dropped the ambitious industrialization and development plans, substituting an essentially agrarian policy which favored the owners of large cocoa plantations.

[13] Acheampong's Government survived eight coup attempts, but his economic policy was not as successful. Ghana had an inflation rate of 36 per cent, an oppressive foreign debt, a devalued currency and hundreds of imprisoned intellectuals and students, condemned for questioning government policy.

[14] In 1977, the so-called revolt of the middle class occurred. A period of social unrest began which ended with Acheampong's resignation in 1978. A new military regime was established, led by General William Frederick Akuffo. The opposition claimed this was simply a continuation of the previous government under a different figurehead. In June 1979, a coup led by Lt Jerry Rawlings overthrew Akuffo and called fresh elections. The Convention People's Party, which included Nkrumah's followers, won a large majority.

[15] In October 1979, with the acquiescence of the Revolutionary Council of the Armed Forces, Hilla Limann, a PNP leader, took over the presidency. Limann abandoned many of Nkrumah's nationalistic economic policies, replacing them with International Monetary Fund policies, in an attempt to reduce the fiscal deficit. To attract foreign investors and overcome the sharp fall in cocoa export revenues, the Government reduced all imports and, as a result, the purchasing power of workers fell drastically. This led to a series of strikes in 1980 and 1981.

[16] Inflation exceeded 140 per cent and the unemployment rate was more than 25 per cent. This created an unstable situation which culminated in a further coup, led by Rawlings on 31 December 1981. In spite of this, Rawlings still retained his popularity.

[17] A campaign against corruption in the public sector was launched, promising a social justice revolution in the country. Within a few months, more taxes had been paid, and cocoa-smuggling to neighboring countries was reduced. People's Courts were set up to pass judgement on irregularities committed by the authorities of the previous government.

[18] It became necessary to develop policy, and look for sources of foreign capital. Rawlings, who was willing to carry out an austerity program dictated by the IMF, strengthened relations with them in 1983. Ghana was granted generous loans by the IMF and the World Bank as a result.

[19] Taxes were increased, subsidies were removed, the Government salaries budget was reduced and financing for inefficient private enterprises was eliminated. These measures helped to reduce inflation from 200 to 25 per cent, the banking system improved and better prices were obtained for cocoa producers. However the costs soon became apparent.

[20] Ghana obtained loans on still more generous terms: $500 million payable in two installments, the first one due in 1994, at an annual interest rate of five per cent and the second with a ten-year grace period and 0.5 per cent interest rate. The major drawback of this scheme was that Ghana's finances were under rigid IMF control. The foreign debt approached $4 billion and the servicing of the debt used up two-thirds of the country's export earnings.

[21] The social cost of the structural adjustment program was high. Consumer prices rose by 30 per cent between 1983 and 1987; 45,000 public employees lost their jobs and there was a general loss of earning power leading to an increase in hunger, infant mortality and illiteracy.

[22] In the 1900s there had been just eight urban centers, but by 1984 the number had risen to 180. There was a strong migration towards the major cities, resulting in the creation of shantytowns with no drinking water or sanitation. At that time, in a poor quarter of Takoradi there were only 16 public toilets (seats or holes) per 3,250 people. In order to alleviate this situation, the Government launched a program to transfer 12,000 people a year to rural areas. In 1987, a Program of Action to Mitigate the Social Costs of Adjustment (PAMSCAD) was implemented, to analyze the impact of the economic recession on the poorest people, and to prioritize the action required.

[23] By the 1980s, the tropical forest - that used to cover 34 per cent of the land - was reduced to 7 per cent. Meanwhile, 42 per cent of the area which is officially considered 'forest', is in fact covered with timber plantations,

IN FOCUS

ENVIRONMENTAL CHALLENGES
Desertification, affecting the northwest, deforestation, soil deterioration caused by intensive grazing; hunting and habitat loss that threaten wild species; water pollution and a lack of drinking water are major environmental issues.

WOMEN'S RIGHTS
Women have been able to vote and stand for office since 1954. In 2000, 11 per cent of ministerial positions were held by women.

In 2000, they made up 51 per cent of the workforce (59 per cent were in agriculture and 32 per cent in services).

The illiteracy rate in women over 15 was reduced from 69.4 in 1980 to 36.8 per cent in 2000*. The rate for men in that age cohort in 2000* was 19.7 per cent.

Sixtyfour per cent of pregnant women are anemic*. It is estimated that between 15 and 30 per cent of Ghanaian women undergo genital mutilation.

CHILDREN
In 2001, 653,000 children were born and 65,000 children under five years old died.

Twenty-five per cent of under-5s suffer from moderate and severe low weight*.

The under-5 and maternal mortality rates have declined. Regional disparities are marked: in northern Ghana, the maternal mortality rate is twice as high and the under-5 mortality rate three times as high as in the south. Malaria, respiratory infections, diarrhea and measles are the leading killer diseases of children.

It is estimated that out of the 800,000 working children in Ghana, 20,000 live and work on the streets of Greater Accra.

Girls are also subject to female genital mutilation, early marriage and polygamy. Some are caught up in ritual servitude (*trokosi*). Trokosi means in the Ewe language 'slaves of the gods'. According to the tradition, families give virgin girls to priests to appease the gods for crimes committed by relatives.

There is a direct linkage between the spread of HIV/AIDS and polygamy. At the end of 2001, there were 34,000 HIV-positive children under14 and 200,000 AIDS orphans.

INDIGENOUS PEOPLES/ ETHNIC MINORITIES
Under Kwame Nkrumah (1947-1966), most people identified themselves as Ghanaians since his Convention Peoples Party (CPP) opened its membership to everyone, regardless of ethnic origin.

The Akan Ashanti people and Ewes have vied for power and influence. The Ewes (13 per cent) were favored while Jerry Rawlings ruled. They do not face political restriction or discrimination, but they are not as economically advanced as the Ashanti (28 per cent), which is the largest ethnic group, concentrated in the inland region of the country. In 2000, John Agyekum Kufour came into power with Ashanti support.

The Mossi-Dagomba (16 per cent) live in the northern part and form a cohesive group as a result of their relative isolation. In 1740, the Dagomba were dominated by the Ashanti, and by 1874, their kingdom had fallen apart. In comparison with the other main groups, they have less access to health and education. They inhabit an area with little mineral wealth, poor climate and soil conditions and they have to compete with the Ashanti for usable farm land.

MIGRANTS/REFUGEES
At the end of 2002, the country hosted more than 40,000 refugees (35,000 from Liberia, about 5,000 from Sierra Leone and nearly 1,000 from Togo). Most Liberians had fled to Ghana in 1990-1991 to escape civil war; likewise the refugees from Sierra Leone who also came in the 1990s. Approximately 3,000 new Liberian asylum-seekers arrived during 2002. The eruption of civil war in Côte d'Ivoire in 2002 led to the arrival of several hundred refugees.

Meanwhile, 10,000 Ghanaian refugees remained in Togo at year's end and another 2,000 were seeking asylum in Western countries. The ethnic and territorial conflict of 1994-1995 had uprooted about 100,000 people. The majority of them returned to their homes after the violence subsided.

DEATH PENALTY
Although the death penalty still applies, there have been no executions since 1993.

*Latest data available in The State of the World's Children and Childinfo database, UNICEF, 2004.

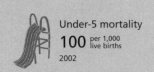
Under-5 mortality
100 per 1,000 live births
2002

Poverty
44.8% of population living on less than $1 per day
1999

Debt service
13.0% exports of goods and services
2001

Maternal mortality
540 per 100,000 live births
2000

secondary vegetation, or immature trees. For the people who live in the country, and for most of those who live in the cities, forest plants constitute the basis of their traditional medicine. Seventy-five per cent of the population rely on bush meat for their basic source of protein and forests also provide firewood, a basic household necessity.

24   These activities are ignored by official plans, which see the forest merely as a source of timber for export. Around 70,000 people are employed in the timber industry.

25   After the loss of millions of dollars because of the fall in export prices, Ghana was granted further loans of $900,000,000 in 1989. But, the hopes of growth collapsed, the current account deficit increased and earnings for exports were reduced. Between 1988 and 1989, around 120 industries closed down because their products could not compete with cheaper and higher-quality goods from China, South Korea, and Taiwan.

26   The crisis led Rawlings to initiate a democratization program and a devolution plan, favoring local administrations. In 1991, an advisory assembly of 260 members was elected to draft a new constitution. The National Council for Women and Development, a body with ministerial status, won ten seats.

27   In December 1991, Amnesty International denounced the Ghanaian policy of silencing or intimidating its opponents. In view of such serious and constant human rights violations, the Ghana Committee for Human and Popular Rights was created in 1992, the first such organization in the country.

28   In that year, a new constitution was approved and elections were held. Rawlings took 58.3 per cent of the vote in November and the three parties which supported him took 197 of the 200 seats in December. The opposition, which accused Rawlings of fraud and intimidation, boycotted the legislative elections which registered a voter turnout of only 29 per cent.

29   In 1993, representatives from 80 countries and international organizations attended Rawlings' investiture. This foreign support was attributed to the rigorous application of the IMF imposed structural adjustment plans and the prompt payment of debt service.

30   In 1994, confrontations over land ownership caused the death of more than a thousand people and the migration of 150,000. A state of emergency was declared

PROFILE

ENVIRONMENT

The southern region is covered with dense rainforest, partially cleared to plant cocoa, coffee, banana and oil palm trees. Wide savannas extend to the north. The rest of the territory is low-lying, with a few high points near the border with Togo. The Volta, Ghana's main river, has an artificial lake formed by the Akossombo dam. The climate is tropical, with summer rains. The subsoil is rich in gold, diamonds, manganese and bauxite.

SOCIETY

Peoples: Ghanaians come from seven main ethnic groups: the Akan (Ashanti and Fanti), 44 per cent, located in the mid southern part of the country; the Ewe, 13 per cent, and Ga-Adangbe, 8 per cent, on both sides of the Volta in southern and southeastern Ghana; the Mossi-Dagomba (16 per cent) in the northern savannas; the Guan, 4 per cent, and the Gurma, 3 per cent, in the valleys and plateaus of the northeastern territory.
Religions: 50 per cent Christian, 32 per cent traditional religions, 13 per cent Muslim.
Languages: English (official); Ga is the main local language, Fanti, Hausa, Fantéewe, Gaadanhe, Akan, Dagbandim and Mamprussi are also spoken.
Main Political Parties: New Patriotic Party (NPP); Convention People's Party (CPP); People's National Convention (PNC); National Democratic Congress (NDC).
Main Social Organizations: Ghana Trade Union Congress, of nearly 50 unions. The 31st December Women's Movement, headed by Nna Konadu Agyeman Rawlings, wife of the former president.

THE STATE

Official Name: Republic of Ghana.
Administrative Divisions: 10 regions, subdivided into 110 districts.
Capital: Accra 1,847,000 people (2003).
Other Cities: Kumasi 906,400 people; Tamale 259,200; Sekondi-Takoradi 164,400 (2000).
Government: John Agyekum Kufuor, President, Head of State and Government since January 2001. Alhaji Aliu Mahama, Vice-President since 2000. Unicameral Legislature, with 200 members elected for a four-year term.
National Holiday: 6 March, Independence Day (1957).
Armed Forces: 5,000. Other: People's Militia 5,000.

and in June an agreement was reached to bring an end to the violence.

31   Despite the New Patriotic Party and the People's Convention trying to settle their differences and form an alliance to present a common electoral platform, Rawlings won the December 1996 elections with 57.2 per cent of the vote. Amidst a severe energy crisis - produced by a fall in the water level of the Akosombo dam - Rawlings' Government sought for alternative sources which proved not to be feasible. In 1998, the Ministry of Science and Technology said Ghana could not pay the initial investment needed to develop a possible nuclear energy-based project. The crisis was partly resolved with help from Côte d'Ivoire, which increased the amount of electricity supplied to Ghana from 20 to 35 megawatts per day.

32   In August 1999, the police harshly put down a student demonstration against an increase in fees and costs passed by the Government. The authorities decided to close the University of

Ghana temporarily until the demonstrators could be pacified.

33   In December 2000 Rawlings stepped down. The next month John Kufuor from the NPP put an end to 20 years of NDC Government. He beat John Atta Mills (backed by Rawlings). The NPP also won the legislative elections, taking 97 of the 200 seats at stake, while the government party won only 86 seats. Kufuor assumed the Presidency, in the first occasion that a change of power took place through democratic means.

34   In late 2001, violent confrontations took place between Mamprusis and Kusasis, leaving 50 dead. New clashes took place in March 2002, causing the death of KngYa-Na Yakubu Andani II, an Andani, and of 27 other people. The Government declared a state of emergency and deployed its troops in order to calm both groups. Historically, Mamprusi people tended to favor the NPP, while the Kusasis tend to support the NDC.

35   Kufuor approved the creation of the National Reconciliation

Commission, with the aim of investigating cases of human rights abuses that took place during the 22 years of military dictatorships. This Commission would grant immunity to those who testify and would try to solve the 200 cases of disappeared persons, during Rawlings' military regime.

36   In May 2003, an arrangement under the Poverty Reduction and Growth Facility was approved by the IMF, granting Ghana $258 million for the Government's economic reform programs for the period 2003-2005. Despite tight public expenditure control, an annual growth of 4.9 per cent was expected together with a reduction in inflation.

37   In June of that year, the Government of Ghana and the African Development Fund signed a loan agreement to finance a health service rehabilitation project. The mission of the so-called Health Project III would be to control HIV/AIDS, malaria and blood transfusions. It also aimed at improving pre-natal care to reduce infant and maternal mortality, as well as reducing poverty.

38   In July, Parliament renewed the state of emergency in the north, in Dagbon, to keep the conflict there under control. However, this measure badly affected trade with neighboring Burkina Faso.

39   In September 2003, a group of 173 Ghanaian children, who had been sold by their parents to local fishermen for $180, were reunited with their families as part of an International Organization for Migration (OIM) program. The children were forced to do hard labor and some did not survive. In addition, they were poorly fed and ill-treated. The OIM offered the fishermen counseling and equipment, and also gave micro-credit to the children's parents so that they could set up small businesses to try and generate more income.

40   A thaumatin production facility was started in late 2003. Thaumatin is a low-calorie, natural sweetener, derived from the *katemfe* bush, which is 2,500 times sweeter than sugar. This enterprise could turn into a multi-billion industry, although the patents on the genes that contain the sweetening agent of the plant have been registered in the US, thus threatening the Ghanaian industry prospects.

41   In February 2004 former president Rawlings appeared before a human rights commission set up to investigate allegations of murder and torture during five military administrations, including his own. ∎

Greece / Ellás

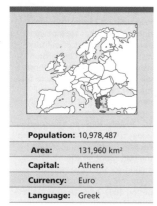

Population:	10,978,487
Area:	131,960 km²
Capital:	Athens
Currency:	Euro
Language:	Greek

Although the oldest records of Greece's official history date from 800 BC, agricultural tools were found that belonged to a period earlier than 6000 BC. The first Greeks, engaged in different cultivation activities and devoted to the cult of a Mediterranean goddess of fertility, would have lived more than 3,000 years, without fearing invasions, within a period evoked by the Greek legend as 'the golden age'.

[2] During the third millennium BC, the Minoic civilization emerged in Crete. Owing to its intense maritime trade, urban development and unique artistic talent, the Minoic was regarded as the first European civilization.

[3] In 1600 BC, the Achaeans (a fusion of Asia Minor and Indo-European peoples, in the third millennium BC) from Thessaly, in central Greece, invaded the Minoic, who originally came from the Middle East. The mixture of cultures, one peaceful and female-oriented (fertility), and the other one warlike, having Dyaus (Indo-European god of the sky, predecessor of Zeus) as main god, gave rise to the Mycenian civilization.

[4] Mycenae dominated Athens, Thebes, Pylos and Tiryns, among other cities. According to the Greek epic, Agamemnon, King of Mycenae, conquered the city of Troy (now Hisarlik in Asia Minor, where the Greek alphabet was created) in the 12th century BC, after a long war that would have led to the end of Mycenian civilization.

[5] The decline of Mycenae began during that century with the Dorian invasions. The Dorians, also of Indo-European origin, destroyed all that they came across in Crete and its dependencies (Thessaly, the Peloponnese and the Cyclade Islands) and subdued the population with iron weapons, which were unknown in Greece.

[6] The three centuries that followed the Dorian invasion were known as the Dark Age of Greek culture, characterized by the militarization of society. This period of terror resulted in the emergence of autonomous and fortified city-states in Athens, Sparta, Thebes, Corinth and Argos.

[7] Dorians and Mycenians developed a common religion and language. Homer's epic poems, written during the 9th century BC, incorporated deities from different locations into a coherent story (unified by Zeus) focused on the summit of Mount Olympus.

[8] Gods and heroes of the past (mortals gifted with god-like powers) took a leading part in those episodes that explained the cosmic laws that governed life on Earth. Likewise, the Greeks recognized obscure powers, hidden in an underworld, which were activated by guilt.

[9] The cult of each god - whose rituals included human sacrifice - took place both in private and in multitudinous festivals, where passages of the *Iliad,* the *Odyssey* and other Homeric poems were staged. The first event registered in the history of Greece were the Games organized at Olympia in 776 BC, to honor Zeus and the goddess Hera, which also marked the beginning of the Archaic Age.

[10] In the 8th century BC and the two following centuries, a demographic explosion spurred the Greeks to sail to the north of Africa, Spain, France, Italy and Asia Minor in search of land.

[11] Greek art, influenced by Asia Minor and Egypt, recovered the use of curves which had been replaced by the rectilinear geometrical forms imposed by Dorians since the Mycenian period. Athens, with its Attic style, displaced the Phoenicians (Semitic peoples) from the pottery and painting market and wealthy families started to order sculptures of gods and young aristocrats.

[12] By the end of the 7th century BC, commerce was radically changed by the use of coins which the Greeks had learnt from the Lydians. This accelerated the rise of merchants to political power. They joined the peasants to displace the nobility. Governmental structures underwent democratization in the different cities, except for Sparta, which remained an oligarchic state.

[13] In the 6th century BC, philosophers of Troy started to develop a rational critique of religious practices and beliefs. The Sophists continued this line of skeptical thought, as did dramatists like Euripides and Aristophanes. The lyric poetry of Lesbos (7th and 6th century BC) shocked the Greeks; some mathematics works by Pythagoras that date from the 6th century BC were never surpassed.

[14] The beginning of the Classical period (from 499 BC to 323 BC) was marked by the devastation of two Persian invasions as well as by the victory and consolidation of Athenian culture. The triumph of the confederated cities (in the Medic Wars, 499-479 BC) over a more powerful invader (the Persian Empire) gave Athenians - whose military intervention had been of the utmost importance - the glorious enthusiasm necessary to undertake the re-building of their city and the expansion of their own empire.

[15] After seizing the treasure of the Delos sanctuary, in 454 BC - a symbol of the union of the Greek city-states against the Persian enemy - Athens imposed the payment of tributes on all confederated cities of the League of Delos (476 BC).

[16] Pericles, governor of Athens between 443 BC and 429 BC, improved the governmental system - established in 594 BC - which would be later referred to as a 'slave holding democracy'. This was due to the exclusion of slaves and women from citizen status. The first definitions of citizenship and political pluralism involving rights and duties were set down in writing by Solon (640-558 BC).

[17] The works and ideas of scholars were exposed and debated in open spaces. Socrates (470-399 BC) developed the notion of dialectic thought and applied it to introspection; Plato (427-348 BC) went deep into the ethical and methodological principles of Socrates and founded his own school, the Academy; Herodotus (484-420 BC) used, for the first time, an objective method (examination of evidence) for historical research.

[18] Greek painters and sculptors engaged in the study of the human body, which turned into the main subject of their works. Sculpture was the most widely-known art and the practice of sports represented a sign of spiritual grandeur. Man, who was considered as 'the measure of all things', was examined in all his dimensions.

[19] The city of Sparta was a completely militarized state founded in the 9th century BC. It disputed with Athens the hegemony over Greece in continuous struggles between 431-404 BC (Peloponnesian War), which resulted in the fall of the Athenian empire (404 BC).

[20] The supremacy of Sparta (404-371 BC) was followed by that of Thebes (372-362 BC). These constant struggles weakened the Greeks and enabled Macedonians to conquer this domain under the rule of Philip II, in 338 BC, who aimed at annexing this territory to the Persian Empire, at a later stage.

[21] King Philip II had Demosthenes (384-322 BC), an Athenian master of rethoric, as his main advisor. Likewise, he chose Aristotle (384-322 BC), founder of formal logic and author of treatises on politics, metaphysics and physic, as tutor of his son Alexander.

[22] After the death of Philip II, in 340 BC, Alexander continued the plan set out by his father. He spread the area of influence of Greek culture by conquering territories in the east of the Mediterranean, the Arabian Peninsula, Mesopotamia and India. The exchange of knowledge and customs between the Greek culture and that of the conquered peoples, gave rise to what is known as 'Hellenism'.

[23] The political and cultural centers of the Hellenic world were Alexandria (Egypt) and Babylon (Mesopotamia). Upon the death of Alexander the Great in 323 BC, the

Life expectancy
78.3 years
2000-2005

GNI per capita
$11,660
2002

Literacy
97% total adult rate
2000

HIV prevalence rate
0.2% of population 15-49 years old
2001

empire was divided and Greece remained under the rule of the kings of Macedonia.

24   Rome formally established its rule over Greece in 146 BC, after defeating the Macedonian army and the Achaean League (of Greek confederated cities) in a war that lasted for 50 years. Although they subdued Greece from the economic and political point of view, in order to consolidate and spread their empire, the Romans (Italics, of Indo-European origin, who arrived in the 2nd millennium BC) had to assimilate the Greek culture. On account of this, Athens was granted special benefits and became the headquarters of the main university of the Roman Empire.

25   In Greco-Roman paganism, the field of ethics belonged to philosophers. Opposed doctrines, such as the Stoic (austere) or the Epicurean (sensual), oriented the life of learned citizens, without any conception of life after death. When Christianity became the official religion (3rd and 4th centuries), some of those doctrines that had emerged in Greece, acted as counter-cultures until the 6th century. At the same time, other doctrines like Neo-Platonicism contributed to strengthen what would turn into the new Western paradigm.

26   Christian sermons were well received among Greek slaves. Being mostly farmers, they hoped some authority would minimize the

difference between the extreme wealth of urban centers and the desolation of rural areas. From the 4th century, monasteries would partially fulfill this role.

27   Constantine I (280-337), crowned as Emperor in 313, transferred the capital of the Roman Empire to Byzantium (present-day Istanbul), which had been colonized by the Greeks in the 7th century BC. It was there that he founded Constantinople between 324 and 330, in order to avoid a Persian invasion and to control the Danube border, through which barbaric invaders entered.

28   Between the 3rd and 11th centuries, Greece witnessed devastating incursions of Germanic (Goths, Heruls and Vandals), Asiatic (Huns and Avars), and Norman (Scandinavians) peoples, as well as of Bulgars and Arabs.

29   During the 4th century, schools in Athens declined while paganism abandoned mythology. In 394, the prohibition of the Olympic Games was declared. Likewise, in the 6th century, the Emperor Justinian prevented pagan philosophers from teaching and limited access to texts by the great Greek thinkers to the elite groups in Constantinople.

30   Although some merchants prospered under the rule of Byzantium, the Greek economy was weakened. Byzantium was capital of the Eastern Roman Empire (394-1054), of the Greco-Oriental Empire (after the Schism of the Roman

Church in 1054 when Greek Christians pledged obedience to the Orthodox Church), and of the Latin Eastern Empire, under the Fourth Crusade occupation between 1204 and 1261.

31   The crusaders were displaced by Venetians, who gained control over wide land and maritime areas of the ancient Latin Empire, even after the taking of Constantinople by the Turkish-Ottoman Empire in 1454. It was not until 1718, when the Peace of Passarowitz was signed, that Venice promised to withdraw from Greece, and did not actually leave until 1797.

32   During the late Byzantine period (1204-1453), the Greek territories were occupied by Serbs, Catalans, Sicilians, French and mercenary companies, besides Venetians and Ottoman-Turks. Byzantium's political weakness brought about a revival of Hellenism in Greece, which was reinstated as a cultural center.

33   Within the first three centuries of Turkish-Ottoman occupation, Greece put up little resistance. The first sultans allowed Greeks to engage in trade activities and practice their own language and religion.

34   During the religious uprising of 1770, a partial victory over the Turks, together with the news about the US (1776) and French (1789) Revolutions, stirred a desire for freedom in Greeks which they were not able to define by common

criteria. Their lack of national unity and strength to fight the Turkish-Egyptian forces enabled the direct intervention of Russia, Britain and France, in the War of Greek Independence (1821-1832).

35   The anti-Turkish revolution comprised a first stage of local uprisings (from 1821 until 1825), which was followed, from 1826, by armed confrontations between the Turkish-Egyptians and the three European powers. The latter signed the Treaty of London in 1827, which declared Greece an independent state under their protection.

36   In 1832, the 17-year-old Otto of Bavaria was appointed king by the London Convention. Otto's permissive behaviour towards the outbursts of a Bavarian rebel group in Greece, called forth several insurrections between 1833 and 1843. That year, the rebel forces surrounded the royal palace, demanding Otto's resignation and forcing him to grant a constitution, which was promulgated in 1844.

37   In 1863, after being discredited by both the rivalries between the European powers and Turkish threats, Otto was replaced by William of Denmark. This was accomplished by a protocol signed in London - similar to the one signed in 1832 - which also stipulated the withdrawal of Britain from the Islands of Troy.

38   William named himself George I. He reigned in Greece between 1863 and 1913, set up an elective

IN FOCUS

ENVIRONMENTAL CHALLENGES
Increasing urbanization over the last five decades, has put pressure on coastal areas and caused sea pollution levels to rise. Solid and toxic waste is poorly managed. Arid areas suffer from a lack of drinking water and some desertification.

WOMEN'S RIGHTS
Greek women have been able to vote since 1952. In 2000, 6.2 per cent of parliamentary seats were held by women. Out of a total of 900 mayors in the country, only 14 are women. In 2000, women made up 38 per cent of the labor force, which was divided into services (67 per cent), agriculture (20 per cent) and industry (12 per cent). That year, 16.5 per cent of women were unemployed.

In 2000*, the illiteracy rate in Greek women over 15 was 4.1 per cent. The net primary school enrolment rate for girls reached 97 per cent*.

It is estimated that 83 per cent of Greek women have suffered from some form of domestic abuse.

CHILDREN
Eight per cent of children suffer from low birth weight*.

Between 1987 and 1998, Roma children were unable to attend local schools since the area inhabited by them was not within the enrolment boundaries of any school. Although a school for the Roma community was founded in 1998 and in 2002 some children even attended regular schools in the municipality, most of them dropped out soon and none of them graduated.

INDIGENOUS PEOPLES/ ETHNIC MINORITIES
Turkish Muslims (1.2 per cent) are concentrated in the area of Thrace and have a higher birth rate than Greeks. There are few teachers in Turkish schools and students are not allowed to learn Greek, which hurts them economically. Likewise, there are allegations of discrimination against non-Greek speakers seeking to enter university. The Government makes it easy to obtain land from Turks mainly through providing low interest loans. Meanwhile, there are

restrictions on the purchase and sale of property by Turks.

The Roma make up 1.7 per cent of the population. When confronted with social and cultural repression, they have traditionally preferred to move to a new location. Due to their nomadic lifestyle, the Roma as a group are not cohesive and organized. Also, their refusal to assimilate is not well received in Greece's nationalistic society. They have higher birth rates and poorer health conditions than the rest of the population.

MIGRANTS/REFUGEES
Greece has one of the lowest acceptance rates for asylum-seekers in Europe despite having some of the most liberal asylum laws. In 2002, only 4 per cent of applicants whose cases were decided were granted asylum.

In June 2002, a group of 47 human rights groups, including Amnesty International, Human Rights Watch, and the International Helsinki Federation, issued a joint statement criticizing human rights violations by Greek authorities against foreigners,

asylum seekers and undocumented migrants in Greece since they were denied competent translators, were not informed of their rights, were maintained in poor detention conditions and were even physically and verbally abused.

Every year, thousands of improperly documented migrants use the Greek coasts as a route into EU countries. In December 2002 alone, 24 deaths were recorded as a result of the harsh coastal conditions.

All Greek citizens are forced to identify their religion on their identity card, which makes Turkish people easy to identify and vulnerable to discrimination. Turkish employment in the police and military forces is restricted.

DEATH PENALTY
In 1993, it was abolished for ordinary crimes and the last execution took place in 1972.

*Latest data available in *The State of the World's Children* and *Childinfo* database, UNICEF, 2004.

Under-5 mortality
5 per 1,000
live births
2002

Aid
0.21% Official
development
assistance as
% of donors' GNI
2002

Maternal mortality
9 per 100,000
live births
2000

government and defined the king's role as a passive instrument of people's will within a system defined as 'monarchic democracy'. Eleutherios Venizelos gained popularity during the anti-Turkish struggles in Crete and managed to obtain its re-annexation to Greece in 1908. He also amended the Constitution in order to be elected Prime Minister in 1910, with 80 per cent of the vote.

39 Once a new Constitution was approved in 1911, Venizelos created the Balkan League. In November 1912, war was declared on Turkey, with Serbia and Bulgaria as allies, in order to recover the territory of Salonica, which had been lost after the Treaty of London of 1827. One month later, a second Balkan War broke out when Bulgars launched attacks on their two allies and Romania. Both wars, which ended in 1913, allowed Greece to spread its territory.

40 World War I (1914-1918) unleashed a confrontation between King Constantine and Venizelos. As a result, the Greek population was divided. The King proclaimed his neutrality but Venizelos denounced his alignment with Germany, on account of which he was expelled from government in 1915. In 1916, after establishing a rival republican government in Salonica, Venizelos helped the allied troops.

41 The interwar period was shaken by a warlike conflict with Turkey (1922-1923) - which caused over one million deaths - and another border conflict with Albania, which prompted Italy to launch an air raid (1923). Both conflicts prompted the intervention of the League of Nations. Venizelos was removed from the political arena in 1935.

42 Greece remained under Nazi occupation between 1941 and 1944. In 1949, the US launched its direct intervention to eliminate communist guerrillas, and from then on, it took control of the Greek economy. Greek soldiers were recruited to fight in the Korean War (1950-1953). Under US influence, Greece became a member of the Council of Europe (1949) and of NATO (1951).

43 In 1952, a new Constitution was approved. In the 1956 presidential elections women voted for the first time. Elections were won by Konstantinos Karamanlis, of the National Radical Union, who was forced to resign in 1963, after being accused of fraud by Socialist leader Andreas Papandreou.

44 In April 1967, upon the threat of a possible victory of the left in the upcoming elections, a group of colonels staged a coup. Martial Law was enforced, the Constitution was suspended and democratic movements were harshly repressed. Andreas Papandreou was condemned and sent to prison.

45 The Colonels' regime was supported by the US and by tycoons such as Onassis. Attempts were made to mask the dictatorship behind a unicameral Parliament in 1968, but in reality the military junta ruled by decree.

46 Between 1973 and 1974 the military government grew weaker. In July 1974, the junta promoted a coup in Cyprus by collaborating with the Cypriot National Guard. The coup succeeded in deposing president Archbishop Vaneziz Makarios and a minister in favor of Greek annexation was appointed. The Turkish army invaded Cyprus, allegedly defending the Turkish minority in the country. The Greek military government became even more discredited and internationally condemned, and they relinquished power immediately at the prospect of war with Turkey.

47 Karamanlis returned from exile and took over the government. In the 1974 elections his party won a parliamentary majority and a later referendum abolished the monarchy. In 1975, Parliament adopted a new constitution and Konstantinos Tsatsos, a Karamanlis partisan, was elected first President of the Republic.

48 In the 1981 parliamentary elections, PASOK (Pan-Hellenic Socialist Movement) led by Papandreou gained an absolute majority. That year, Greece joined the EEC. Papandreou's Government recognized the PLO and led a worldwide campaign in favour of handing back works of art that had been stolen during colonial domination to their countries of origin.

49 In the 1984 elections, PASOK won again. In 1986, successive austerity plans and salary freezes, applied since 1983, fuelled new protests and strikes. In June 1989, the Greek Left and the Communist Party formed the Left Alliance.

50 In the 1989 elections PASOK lost its majority, and the conservative New Democracy party received a large part of the vote. As there was no parliamentary majority and no agreement to form a government, the presidency went to the leader of the Left Alliance that formed a temporary government with New Democracy, aiming to investigate financial scandals. In November, a coalition government was formed.

51 Between 1983 and 1989, Greece and the US signed various agreements including the maintenance of four US military bases in the country, in return for economic and military assistance as well as US diplomatic support for

Greece in its disputes with Turkey. However, in 1990, Washington and Athens announced a new agreement to close two military bases.

52 In March 1990, a law was passed that established free negotiations between workers and bosses, putting an end to 50 years of State intervention, and including norms for the organization of the company and union committees.

53 Following Karamanlis' triumph in the 1990 presidential elections, a new government was formed headed by the conservative Constantinos Mitsotakis, who promoted public spending cuts, price liberalization and privatizations. The social cost of these measures contributed to the defeat of the conservative government in the 1993 legislative elections, in favour of Papandreou.

54 The public debt and pressures from the European Union regarding economic matters, complicated Papandreou's administration.

55 In 1995, at the end of Karamanlis' second term as President, Papandreou supported Kostis Stefanopulos, candidate of the small Political Spring party, who enjoyed a strong political reputation. He was elected in 1995 and re-elected in 2000, when he defeated the conservatives led by Karamanlis by a narrow margin.

56 Ill and increasingly criticized, Papandreou resigned in January 1996 and died five months later. His former Industry Minister, Konstantinos Simitis, replaced him. In September the Socialist Party, led by the new Prime Minister, won the legislative elections.

57 Backing its pro-regional integration position, in January 1998, Athens abolished a discriminatory constitutional article allowing 'non-ethnic Greeks' seeking to leave the country to be stripped of citizenship, which dated from the so-called 'dictatorship of colonels'. The article had been used against the Muslim minority of Turkish origin. Some 60,000 people had lost their Greek nationality since this measure was enacted.

58 In 2000, Simitis was appointed Prime Minister for the second time and stated that he would continue to adopt measures to reduce public spending, which still reached 50 per cent of the Greek GDP.

59 In 2002, Greece and Turkey signed an agreement to build a gas pipeline for Turkey to supply natural gas to Greece.

60 Simitis, who had committed himself to personally supervising the organization of the Olympic Games, to be held in Athens in September 2004, was accused by the International Olympic Committee of not complying with the agreed agenda. ∎

PROFILE

ENVIRONMENT
Located at the southeastern end of the Balkan peninsula, in the eastern Mediterranean, the country consists of a continental territory between the Aegean Sea and the Ionian Sea and numerous islands, including the island of Rhodes. Greece is a mountainous country, it has a Mediterranean climate with hot, dry summers. It is an essentially agricultural country (producing wine, olives, tobacco, wheat, barley); sheep and goats are raised in the mountains, where the soil is poor. Development of salt-water fish farming is under way. Greece produces lignite, bauxite and nickel. The traditional manufacturing industries include food, beverages, apparel, leather and paper. Other major industries are cement, chemicals, petrochemicals and mining.

SOCIETY
Peoples: Most people are of Greek origin and there is a small Turkish minority (1 per cent), plus Albanian, Macedonian and Roma.
Religions: Greek Orthodox. There is a Muslim minority.
Languages: Greek. **Main Political Parties:** Pan-Hellenic Socialist Movement (PASOK); New Democracy, conservative; Communist Party of Greece; Coalition of the Left and Progress, socialist; Democratic Socialist Movement. **Main Social Organizations:** The General Confederation of Greek Workers.

THE STATE
Official Name: Helleniké Demokratía. **Administrative Divisions:** 10 regions divided into 51 administrative units. **Capital:** Athens/Piraeus 3,215,000 people (2003). **Other Cities:** Patras 172,100; Thessaloniki 793,900; Peiraías 188,500 people (2000). **Government:** Head of State, Kostas Stephanopoulos, President since March 1995, re-elected in 2000. The President is elected by Parliament every five years. Kostantinos (Kostas) Karamanlis, Prime Minister since January 2004. The Prime Minister is appointed by the President. Unicameral Legislature: Greek Parliament (Vouli ton Ellinon), with 300 members (Parliamentary Republic). **National Holiday:** 25 March, Independence Day (1821). **Armed Forces:** 168,300 (1996). Other: Gendarmerie: 26,500; Coast Guard and customs: 4,000.

Grenada / Grenada

Population:	79,952
Area:	340 km²
Capital:	St George's
Currency:	EC dollar
Language:	English

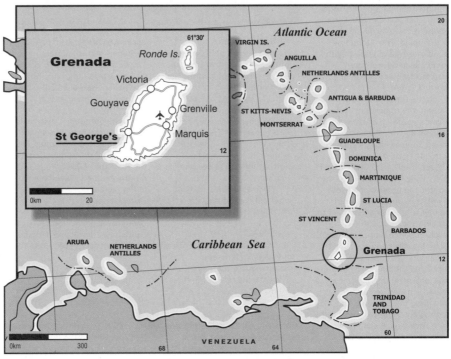

T he Carib Indians inhabited Grenada when Christopher Columbus arrived, around 1498, and named the island 'Concepción'. This European visit did not disrupt the island's peace but two centuries later in 1650 the governor of the French possession of Martinique, Du Parquet, decided to occupy the island. By 1674, France had established control over Grenada, despite fierce resistance from the Caribs.

2 In 1753, French settlers from Martinique had around 100 sugar mills and 12,000 slaves on Grenada. The indigenous population had been exterminated.

3 The British took control of the island towards the end of the 18th century and cultivated cocoa, cotton and nutmeg, using slave labor. In 1788 there were 24,000 slaves, a number which remained stable until the abolition of slavery in the following century.

4 The severe living conditions of workers resulted in the creation of the first union in the mid-20th century, the Grenada Manual and Metal Workers' Union. In 1951, a strike broke out and the labor struggle won considerable wage increases. Eric Matthew Gairy, a young adventurer who had lived away from the island most of his life, formed the first local political party, the Grenada United Labor Party (GULP) which favored

independence. In 1951, GULP won a legislative election and Gairy became leader of the assembly.

5 In 1958 Grenada joined the Federation of the British West Indies, which was dissolved in 1962. The country became part of the Associated State of the British Antilles in 1967. That year, Gairy was appointed Prime Minister, and his main objective was total independence from Britain.

6 GULP soon obtained semi-independence, which gradually

led to full independence. By that time, left-wing groups such as the New Jewel Movement (NJM, led by Maurice Bishop), had appeared on the island, opposing separation from Britain. Though apparently paradoxical, many Grenadians considered that Gairy was seeking independence for his personal benefit, manipulating a politically unprepared population.

7 In January 1974, an 'anti-independence' strike broke out to prevent Gairy from seizing power.

After some weeks of total paralysis of the country, the Mongoose Squad - similar to the Haitian *Tonton-Macoutes* - appeared. Its paramilitaries were on the Prime Minister's payroll and brutal repression was used to end the strike. Independence was proclaimed the following week.

8 As feared, Gairy exploited power for his own personal benefit. He distributed government jobs among the members of his party, and

LAND USE

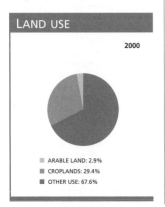

2000

- ◼ ARABLE LAND: 2.9%
- ◼ CROPLANDS: 29.4%
- ◼ OTHER USE: 67.6%

PROFILE

ENVIRONMENT
Grenada is the southernmost Windward island of the Lesser Antilles. The island is almost entirely volcanic. Lake Grand Etang and Lake Antoine are extinct volcanic craters. The rainy, tropical, climate, tempered by sea winds, is fit for agriculture, which constitutes the country's major source of income. It is famous for its spices, and is known as 'the Spice Island of the West'. The territory includes the islands of Carriacou (34 sq km) and Petite Martinique (2 sq km), which belong to the Grenadines.

SOCIETY
Peoples: Most are descended from African slaves (85 per cent); most of the others are of mixed descent (13 per cent) and European (0.7 per cent) and Indo-Pakistani (3 per cent) minorities.
Religions: Mainly Catholic (53.1 per cent); Protestant (38.1 per cent); other (7.4 per cent).
Languages: English (official and predominant). A patois dialect derived from French, and another from English are also spoken.
Main Political Parties: New National Party, conservative (NNP); National Democratic Congress, liberal (NDC); Grenada United Labor Party (GULP), People Labor Movement (PLM).

Main Social Organizations: Grenada Trades Union Council, which includes 8 organizations including those for public sector workers, teachers, seamen and dockers; Rural Farmers' Association; National Council of Students of Grenada.

THE STATE
Official Name: Grenada.
Administrative Divisions: 6 parishes and 1 dependency (Carricou and Petite Martinique).
Capital: St George's 33,000 people (2003).
Other Cities: Gouyave 3,200 people; Grenville 2,300 (2000).
Government: Queen Elizabeth II, Head of State; Daniel Williams has been the representative of the British Crown, (Governor-General) since August 1996. Keith Mitchell, Prime Minister since January 1995, re-elected in 1999 and 2003. Bicameral Legislature: a 15-member House of Representatives elected by direct popular vote and a 13-member Senate with 7 of them appointed by the Governor-General, 3 by the Prime Minister and 3 by the leader of the opposition.
National Holiday: 7 February, Independence (1974). **Armed Forces:** Royal Grenada Police Force (includes Special Service Unit), Coastguards.

promoted the paramilitary squad to the level of a 'Defense Force', making it the only military body on the island. The 'Mongoose Squad' received military training from Chilean advisers and recruited former inmates of St George's Prison.

[9] In the December 1976 election, the opposition People's Alliance, made up of the NJM, the National Party of Grenada and the United Popular Party, increased from one to six representatives out of a total of 15. On 12 March 1979, while Gairy was out of the country, the opposition seized power in a coup. Widespread popular support enabled them to establish the People's Revolutionary Government (PRG), led by Maurice Bishop.

[10] In four years, the PRG stimulated the formation of grass-roots organizations, and they created a mixed economy, expanding the public sector through agro-industries and state farms. However, Bishop allowed some private enterprise to continue.

[11] The PRG was constantly harassed by the US and some conservative neighboring countries because of its socialist policies. The US started a coordinated campaign to stifle Grenada economically, alleging that the modern Grenadian Point Saline airport could be used by Cuba to transport its troops to Africa.

[12] The Government based its foreign policy on the principles of anti-imperialism and non-alignment. Cuba agreed to collaborate in the construction of an international airport, conceived as a way to stimulate tourism, which employed 25 per cent of the country's workforce.

[13] Prime Minister Bishop faced constant pressure from the NJM's extreme left wing. Strife within the Party led to tragic consequences when Bishop was overthrown, possibly by his Minister of Finance backed by the military, in October 1983. Bishop was placed under house arrest, while General Hudson Austin, head of the army, seized power. Bishop was freed by a crowd of sympathizers, only to be shot dead by troops, as were his wife Jacqueline Creft - Minister of Education, the Foreign and Housing Ministers, two union leaders and 13 members of the crowd.

[14] The US used the upheaval as a pretext to invade - something that had been planned for over a year. On 25 October, 5,000 marines and Green Berets landed on the island. They were followed several hours later by a symbolic

IN FOCUS

contingent of 300 police from six Caribbean countries: Antigua, Barbados, Dominica, Jamaica, St Lucia and St Vincent, who joined the farce of a 'multinational intervention for humanitarian reasons'.

[15] Resistance from the Grenadian militia and some Cuban technicians and workers meant that the operation lasted much longer than expected. The US suffered combat casualties, and the press was barred from entering Grenada until all resistance had been eliminated. This made it impossible to verify how many civilians had been killed in attacks on a psychiatric hospital and other non-military targets.

[16] While strict US military control continued, Sir Paul Scoon, official British crown representative in Grenada, assumed the leadership of an interim government with the task of organizing an election. Voting was held in December 1984 to elect the members of a unicameral parliament. In turn, the representatives appointed Herbert Blaize Prime Minister. Blaize led a coalition of parties that was presented to public opinion as the New National Party (NNP) and received support from the US.

[17] Neither NATO nor the OAS dared to condone the aggression. Twenty days later, Barbados was rewarded for its 'co-operation' in the invasion with a $18.5-million US aid program.

[18] The new government reached a classic agreement with the IMF including a reduction of the civil service, a wage-freeze and incentives to private enterprise.

[19] The Regional Security System (RSS) permitting the Prime Minister to call on troops from neighboring Caribbean islands if Grenada was threatened was established by Blaize in December 1986, under the pretext that the trial of those involved in the 1983 coup was coming to an end. Bernard Coard, his wife Phyllis, and former army commander Hudson Austin were sentenced to death, along with 11 soldiers. Three others were tried, receiving prison sentences of 30 to 45 years.

[20] During his first years in government, Blaize achieved considerable economic growth, at between five and six per cent per year, basically from tourism. However, youth unemployment continued to increase, along with crime and drug addiction.

[21] In 1989, after Blaize's death, Ben Jones of the National Party took office, backed by big business and the landowners. On 12 March 1990 - the anniversary of the 1979 coup that overthrew Eric Gairy - the general elections were won by Nicholas Braithwaite, interim head of government after the invasion, and warmly regarded by the US.

[22] In 1994 unemployment reached 30 per cent and there was a clear pattern of emigration. The fall in international prices of bananas, coconuts, wood and nutmeg influenced this trend.

[23] In the June 1995 general elections, the governing NDC was pushed out by Keith Mitchell, former mathematics professor at the Howard University in Washington and leader of the New National Party (NNP). His victory was attributed to his promise to remove income tax, which had been revoked in 1986 and re-imposed by the NDC in 1994.

[24] In March 1997, the Government rejected a request from the Grenada Council of Churches to free the two men serving life sentences for the 1993 murder of former Prime Minister Maurice Bishop and a group of ministers and union leaders. In April, Grenada and Cuba re-established diplomatic relations, broken off during the US invasion.

[25] In the January 1999 elections, Mitchell's NNP won all the 15 seats in Parliament.

[26] In 2001 to 2002, Grenada was the Caribbean economy which showed the greatest growth, mainly due to a larger number of tourists, greater foreign investment and growth in farming. However, unemployment rates remain high, mainly affecting the youngest sector of the workforce.

[27] The increase in tourism investment generated controversy between the Government and defenders of the island ecology, as the construction of large hotel complexes threatened to damage tropical forests and erode the beaches.

[28] In October 2003, on the 20th anniversary of Bishop's murder and of the US invasion, Amnesty International published a report entitled 'The Grenada 17: the last of the Cold War prisoners'?, requesting the Grenadian authorities set up an independent review of the convictions of these prisoners who include Bernard Coard, Bishop's Minister of Finance, convicted of instigating the coup that toppled Bishop. The trial is thought to have been flawed, with irregularities in jury selection among other shortcomings.

[29] The international press has likened the 1983 US invasion of Grenada to events after the 2001 'war on terror' in Afghanistan. Guantanamo Bay, the US base in Cuba, which holds Afghan Taliban members and al-Qaeda suspects, is compared with Point Salines airport - US headquarters after the invasion - where prisoners were kept in wooden crates, having to crouch to get into them. George Bush senior was Reagan's vice-president when 'pre-emptive military intervention' - which his son turned into US national strategic doctrine in 2001 - was created: 'Get them before they are even remotely in a position to get you'.

[30] In November 2003 new members of the House of Representatives were elected. The NNP won 8 of the 15 seats and Keith Mitchell was sworn in for an unprecedented third term as Prime Minister. ∎

Guadeloupe / Guadeloupe

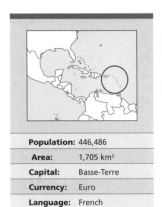

Population:	446,486
Area:	1,705 km²
Capital:	Basse-Terre
Currency:	Euro
Language:	French

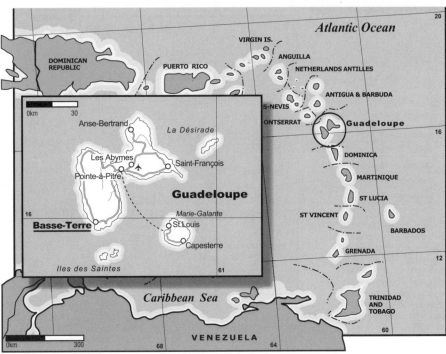

The entire archipelago of present-day Guadeloupe was inhabited by the Caribs. Originally from South America, they dispersed throughout the islands after overpowering the Arawak people. They resisted the Spanish invasion in 1493 but were defeated by the French two centuries later.

2   The French colonizers built the first sugar mill on the island in 1633 and began importing African slave laborers. By the end of the 17th century, Guadeloupe had become one of the world's main sugar producers. The colonists killed the last of the archipelago's surviving Caribs in the early 18th century.

3   With the abolition of the slave trade in 1815, France restructured its formal links with the Caribbean islands, giving them the status of colonies. In 1946, with the initiation of the new French constitution, Guadeloupe achieved greater political autonomy, as an Overseas Department.

4   French Government subsidies increased per capita income and the consumption of imported goods, but ruined the local economy.

5   The European Union's decision in 1992 to reduce the import quota of bananas from the 'French' Antilles to benefit imports from Africa and Latin America caused strong protests in Guadeloupe.

6   An important reduction in productive activities underlined the deficit in the trade balance. Exports, which amounted to barely 9.9 per cent of imports in 1995, were reduced to 5.2 per cent in 1996. The banana sector was also affected, since - due to the reduction in foreign demand and the competition from US-multinationals that managed plantations in Central America - it exported in 1996 less than half its exports of 1993.

7   Banana workers began a strike in late 1997. Union representatives accused the plantation owners of creating private militias and threatening to kill the workers to make them lift the strike. In February 1998, in a country with 40 per cent of the working population unemployed and with growing social inequity, the strike had extended to other sectors.

8   In 1999, Jean- François Carenco was appointed Prefect by the French Government. Jacques Chirac, President of France, visited the island in March 2000 to negotiate a special trade agreement between the EU and France's Overseas Departments in the Caribbean. Chirac's visit to the island coincided with a peak in independence protests in the regions's French dependencies.

9   In August 2001, Haitian immigrants complained to the public prosecutor about a TV show host for inciting hate and xenophobic racial violence against Haitian, Dominican and other residents. The accused, Ibo Simon, was also a Councillor on the Regional Council of Guadeloupe.

10   In 2002, shopkeepers refused to honor the 27 May holiday marking the abolition of slavery. The workers' union requested the closure of shops that day and responded violently against those who went to work. In June a union leader was arrested. This was met with violent protest in Pointe-a-Pitre, where seven policemen were injured. Also in 2002, Dominique Vian replaced Jean-François Carenco as Prefect.

11   In August 2003, several people were injured in a hold-up at a fast-food restaurant in Abymes. Sylvère Selbonne, a reporter-photographer for the daily *France-Antilles Guadeloupe*, was arrested while taking pictures in the restaurant. Police roughed him up, kicked him on the head and insulted him. Reporters Without Borders has written to Guadeloupe prefect, Dominique Vian, to complain about police mistreatment of the photographer. ∎

PROFILE

ENVIRONMENT

Includes the dependencies of Marie Galante, La Désirade, Les Saintes, Petite-Terre, St Barthélemy and the French section of St Martin forming part of the Windward Islands of the Lesser Antilles. The tropical, rainy climate is tempered by sea winds, and sugarcane is grown.

SOCIETY

Peoples: 90 per cent of African descent. There is a small European minority. There are immigrants from Lebanon, China and India (5 per cent).
Religions: mostly Catholic. There are also African, Hindu and several Protestant religions.
Languages: French (official).
Main Political Parties: Rally for the Republic (RPR), and Union for French Democracy (UDF), are the local branches of the French parties; the Communist Party of Guadeloupe (PCG); the Popular Union for the Liberation of Guadeloupe (UPLG), the Caribbean Revolutionary Alliance (ARC), the Christian Movement for the Liberation of Guadeloupe. **Main Social Organizations:** The Guadeloupe General Labor Confederation; the Department Organization of Trade Unions (CGT-FO), General Union of Guadeloupe Workers (UGTG).

THE STATE

Official Name: Département d'Outre-Mer de la Guadeloupe. **Administrative Divisions:** 3 Arondissements, 36 Cantons. **Capital:** Basse-Terre 12,700 people (1999). **Other Cities:** Pointe-à-Pitre 21,400 people; Les Abymes 64,400 (2000). **Government:** Jacques Chirac, Chief of State, represented by Paul Girot de Langlade, since August 2004. Legislative power: a 42-member General Council (chaired by Jacques Gillot since March 2001), and 41-member regional Council (chaired by Lucette Michaux Chevry since 1992). Guadeloupe has 4 deputies and 2 senators in the French parliament. **National Holiday:** 14 July. Bastille Day (1789).

Guam / Guam

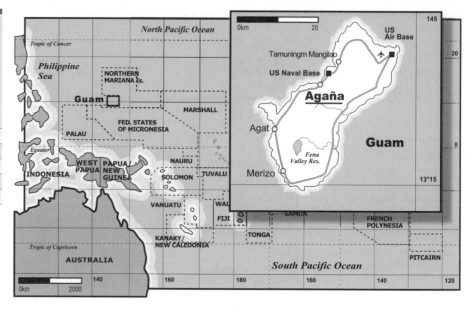

Population:	167,834
Area:	550 km²
Capital:	Agaña
Currency:	US dollar
Language:	English

G uam shares a common history with the rest of the Micronesian archipelago (see Micronesia). The population, which settled on the island thousands of years ago, became the victim of extermination campaigns at the hands of Spanish colonizers, between 1668 and 1695.

² As a result of armed aggression and epidemics (the people lacked immunity against European illnesses) the population declined from 100,000 at the beginning of the 17th century to fewer than 5,000 in 1741.

³ The few survivors intermarried with Spanish and Filipino immigrants, producing the Chamorro people who presently populate the island.

⁴ For three centuries, Guam was a port of call on the Spanish galleon route between the Philippines and Acapulco (Mexico), a major depot on the trade route to Spain.

⁵ Under the terms of the Treaty of Paris of 1898, Guam changed hands from Spain to the US, together with the Philippines. The island continued to serve as a stopover until it was invaded by the Japanese in 1941. Recovered in 1944, it became a US military base.

⁶ Since 1973, the United Nations has unsuccessfully urged Washington to permit the islanders to exercise their right to self-determination. In plebiscites held in 1982 and 1987 local people indicated their desire to redefine their relationship with the US, but the terms of the relationship have not been agreed.

⁷ The UN General Assembly held in December 1984 recommended that the US implement Guam's decolonization. The UN also reiterated its conviction that military bases are a major obstacle to self-determination.

⁸ In February 1987, former governor Ricardo Borballo, who had been elected in 1984, was found guilty of bribery, extortion and conspiracy.

⁹ Negotiations with the UN and US on the right to political self-determination and the creation of a Free Associated State were renewed in 1996. A landowners' organization demanded that the Government include the territory occupied by the US military bases in the talks. Washington considered Guam a key geo-strategic enclave.

¹⁰ In September 1996, the island served as a base of operations for US bombers carrying out a 'limited attack' on Iraq. The US Anderson air base is also used for Marine exercises, military maneuvers and war exercises.

¹¹ On 8 December 2002 typhoon Pongsona struck the island, destroying houses, trees and communication. Four people were killed and 400 were injured.

¹² In February 2004 a spokesperson for the US Air Force announced six B-52H bombers and 300 soldiers would be sent to reinforce troops installed there, mainly as a response to North Korea's nuclear program.

¹³ World War II hit Guam particularly hard. In 2003 the US Federal Advisory Committee Act established a Review Commission, which duly heard testimony from 70 survivors. The Commission is attempting to determine whether the US treated Guam similarly to other territories (such as the Philippines and Micronesia) when it paid compensation linked to Japanese occupation during World War II. ∎

LAND USE

2000

- ARABLE LAND: 10.9%
- CROPLANDS: 10.9%
- OTHER USE: 78.2%

PROFILE

ENVIRONMENT

Guam is the southernmost island of the Marianas archipelago, located east of the Philippines and south of Japan. Of volcanic origin, its contours are mountainous except for the coastal plain in the northern region. The climate is tropical, rainy from June to November (over 300 mm a month) and drier and colder from December to May. It has rainforest vegetation. One-third of the island is occupied by military installations.

SOCIETY

Peoples: Chamorro indigenous people account for approximately 47 per cent of the population; Filipino, 25 per cent. US troops and dependents, 10 per cent. Japanese, Chinese, Korean and other, 18 per cent.
Religions: 98 per cent of all Guamanians are Catholic.
Languages: English (official), Chamorro (a dialect derived from Indonesian), and Japanese.
Main Political Parties: Republican Party and Democratic Party, as in the US.

THE STATE

Official Name: Territory of Guam.
Capital: Agana 140,000 people (2003).
Other Cities: Tamuning 11,800 people; Mangilao 6,900 (2000).
Government: Felix P.P. Camacho, Governor since January 2003. His office reports to the US Interior Department and has less autonomy than the local military commander, as one-third of the island is under control of the US Navy and Air force. Although Guamanians formally possess US citizenship they have no representation in the US Congress nor do they participate in the presidential elections. Parliament: The Guam Legislature, with 15 members.
National Holiday: First Monday in March, Discovery Day (1521).
Armed Forces: Defense is responsibility of the US.

Guatemala / Guatemala

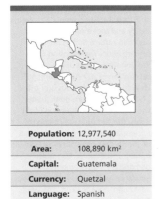

Population:	12,977,540
Area:	108,890 km²
Capital:	Guatemala
Currency:	Quetzal
Language:	Spanish

It is thought that the Maya culture appeared in 9,000 BC when hunters-gatherers lived on the *puuc* (hilltops) and along the Caribbean coast. An early complex social structure developed around farming. A new pre-classical era, from around 2,000 BC to 300 AC, has been determined after the discovery of pre-Maya figurines. The Maya civilization flourished during the first ten centuries AC in what is now Guatemala and parts of Mexico, Honduras, Belize and El Salvador (see box *Arawaks and Caribs: Genocide in Paradise*).

2   Historical research suggests that a religious caste ruled the Maya civilization, controlling government and religious affairs. Important events such as deaths, births, royal marriages, victories and defeats were carved on stone. Routes (*sacbes*), some longer than 100 km, linked important towns. These settlements were abandoned by the end of the classical period, probably because the resources could not support the population, but also perhaps because they were conquered by invaders from Mexico.

3   Spanish troops, under the command of Pedro de Alvarado, entered the country in 1524 and founded the city of Guatemala, gaining total control over the country two years later. This process was facilitated by the fact that the country was undergoing a gradual transition and readjustment among its various ethnic groups - the K'iche', Kaqchi', Mam, Q'eqchi', Poqomchi', Q'anjob'al, Tz'utujiil and others - all of which stemmed from a common Mayan ancestry. Though the situation favored the invaders, there were nevertheless frequent incidents in which they faced stiff resistance.

4   In the 18th century, the invention of synthetic dyes in Europe brought about a severe economic crisis in Guatemala since its most important export was vegetable dyes. After that, coffee became the prominent crop, grown on large plantations. On 15 September 1821, large landowners and local business interests joined forces with colonial officials, to peacefully proclaim the independence of the Vice-royalty of New Spain, including the five countries of Central America. In 1823, after independence from Mexico, Guatemala became the administrative and political center of the United Provinces of Central America (UPCA).

5   In 1831, under great debt pressure, the Government yielded large portions of territory to Britain for timber. This area later became British Honduras, now the independent nation of Belize. The UPCA collapsed in 1838 for two main reasons. One was the military coup by Rafael Carrera (in power until he died in 1865); the other was that British policy was to divide the American nations. In 1847 the State of Guatemala was formally created. In the 1871 Liberal Reform, indigenous people were deprived of their communal land, which was annexed to the coffee plantations. During the late 19th century, Guatemalan politics were dominated by the antagonism between liberals and conservatives.

6   Toward the end of the 19th century, Manuel Estrada Cabrera rose to power and governed Guatemala until 1920. He initiated an 'open door policy' (*cabrerismo*) for US transnationals, which eventually owned the railroads, ports, hydroelectric plants, shipping, international mailing services and the enormous banana plantations of the United Fruit Company (Unifruco).

7   General Jorge Ubico Castañeda, (the last of a generation of military leaders that went back to 1871), was elected President in 1931. He adopted a broadly paternalistic attitude towards indigenous people. However his was a harsh regime that banned unions and introduced a Vagrancy Law, forcing people into work whatever the conditions. Discontent grew with the economic crisis of World War II in 1941. Ubico was deposed in the 1944 Revolution.

8   The October Revolution resulted in new elections which were won by reformist Juan Jose Arévalo. He promoted democracy and social and economic reforms. In 1945, literate women were granted the right to vote. That same year the first campesino labor union was formed. The land reform program, under which extensive tracts of unused Unifruco land were expropriated, was considered a threat to US interests by Washington. An aggressive anti-communist campaign was launched, with the sole aim of harassing Arévalo and his successor, President Jacobo Arbenz Guzman (who was elected President in 1950 with the support of the communists and continued the reforms)

9   John Foster Dulles, US Secretary of State, but also a United Fruit Company shareholder and company lawyer, pressured the Organization of American States (OAS) to condemn Arbenz's reforms. Allen Dulles, director of the CIA and also a Unifruco shareholder, organized an invasion from Honduras in 1954. Arbenz was overthrown in this US-backed coup and was replaced by Colonel Carlos Castillo Armas. He gave the land back to Unifruco (renamed United Brands), reinstating foreign investments. Armas rooted out any communist influence, ended the land reform program and crushed labor unions. His ruthlessness was met with violence: he was assassinated in 1957.

10   Two decades of military regimes followed. Elections in 1970, 1974, 1978 and 1982, were fraudulent - with the top military candidates invariably elected. This kind of political atmosphere bred armed insurgency with groups such as the Rebel Armed Forces, the Guerrilla Army of the Poor and the Revolutionary Movement (MR-13). In 1982, the Guatemala National Revolutionary Unity (URNG), a guerrilla movement formed by various rebel groups and the Guatemala Labor Party (PGT), was founded. According to estimates from several humanitarian organizations, government repression had taken some 80,000 lives between 1954 and 1982.

11   In 1982, after elections that brought General Anibal Guevara to power, a group of discontented military seized control and installed General Efrain Ríos Montt. During his first year more than 15,000 people were murdered, 70,000 were forced into exile (mostly to Mexico) and about 500,000 fled to the mountains to escape the army. Hundreds of rural towns were razed. The number of 'model hamlets' increased systematically. Peasants were taken by force to these hamlets, where they were required to produce cash crops for export, rather than growing subsistence crops. Social and economic conditions grew worse due to the governmental inefficacy, and brutality, which led to a higher level of political violence.

12   In August 1983, another coup staged by the CIA deposed Ríos Montt and General Oscar Mejía Víctores came into power, promising a quick return to a democratic system. In 1984, a Constituent Assembly was set up to draft a new constitution (to replace the 1965 one), to include new constitutional guarantees, *habeas corpus* and electoral regulation. The Constituent Assembly approved the right to strike for civil servants, authorized the return from exile of leaders of the Socialist Democratic Party and called for elections in November 1985. These were won by Marco Vinicio Cerezo; some democratic progress followed.

WORKERS

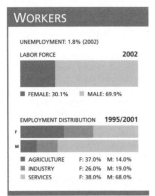

UNEMPLOYMENT: 1.8% (2002)

LABOR FORCE   **2002**

■ FEMALE: 30.1%   ■ MALE: 69.9%

EMPLOYMENT DISTRIBUTION   1995/2001

F
M

■ AGRICULTURE	F: 37.0%	M: 14.0%
■ INDUSTRY	F: 26.0%	M: 19.0%
■ SERVICES	F: 38.0%	M: 68.0%

IN FOCUS

ENVIRONMENTAL CHALLENGES

The area of forests, which covered 41.9 per cent of all the land in 1980, had been reduced to 33.8 per cent by 1990, putting at risk the diversity of the ecosystem. Logging is particularly heavy in the Petén tropical forest.

WOMEN'S RIGHTS

Women have been able to vote and stand for election since 1946. In 2000, 7 per cent of the parliamentary seats were held by women and they comprised 29 per cent of the labor force. Of these 68 per cent worked in the service sector, 19 per cent in industry and 14 per cent in agriculture.

45 per cent of the pregnant women are anemic; 41 per cent of births are attended by qualified staff*. The maternal mortality rate is 240 per 100,000 live births* for the country as a whole but in Maya indian areas such as Alta Veracruz and Huehuetenango it was even higher.

Nearly 60 per cent of female murders are the result of domestic violence. Estimates are that sexual abuse and incest affect 30 per cent of girls and 18 per cent of the boys.

In 2000, 0.9 per cent of women aged 15-24 were HIV-positive or lived with AIDS.

CHILDREN

In 2000, 409,000 children were born and 24,000 died before they were 5 years old. Due to drought, failed coffee harvests and resultant lack of income, nearly 75,000 children suffer malnutrition.

About 67 per cent of the indigenous children suffer chronic malnutrition.

Infant mortality is 36 per 1,000 live births; but for indigenous children it is 46 per 1,000*.

In primary schools there were 83.6 per cent girls and 81 per cent boys enroled in 2000*, but the quality of teaching was worse than before. The rate of absence and truancy is high. In urban areas, only 5 out of 10 children complete their primary education; in rural areas the figure is only 2 out of 10.

Although 60 per cent of the schoolage children live in rural areas, only 24.5 per cent of the schools are there.

From January to October 2002, 408 children and young people were murdered. At the end of 2001, there were 4,800 HIV-positive children under 14, and 32,000 AIDS orphans.

INDIGENOUS PEOPLES/ ETHNIC MINORITIES

Indigenous people number about 5,000,000 (42 per cent of the total population). The majority are Maya and are scattered mainly in the rural districts in the north and in the west of Guatemala City. The most common languages from the 26 spoken in the country are Quiché, Cakchiquel, Maya, Tzutujil, Achi and Pokomán.

They have only poor health services, and poor nutrition. They have been internally displaced and excluded both socially and politically. They have only restricted access to land and property. One of their main claims is protection and rights over the land which is used to benefit other groups, better jobs, pay and conditions. They are

campaigning to find and identify those who died or disappeared during the civil war; and for trials for war crimes and human rights' abuses. They claim the right to teach, publish and negotiate with the Government in their own language; the promotion of their culture; stronger political rights and participation in government decisions.

MIGRANTS/REFUGEES

In 2002 there were 730 refugees in the country (500 from Nicaragua and 180 from El Salvador).

Some 100,000-250,000 people were displaced in the country. Many people pass through each year, bound for Mexico and the US. The US finances the deportation of immigrants to try and prevent them entering. The Coyote plan, operated by the US Immigration Service, was set up to stop smugglers but it generally results in the imprisonment and deportation of illegal immigrants. Almost all Guatemala's emigrants (95 per cent) are in the US (898,000 men and 335,700 women) living mainly in Los Angeles, New York and Miami.

Money sent by Guatemalans living abroad is 5 per cent of GNP and 30 per cent of all the exports.

DEATH PENALTY

President Portillo postponed the execution of condemned people in 2002.

*Latest data available in *The State of the World's Children* and *Childinfo* database, UNICEF, 2004.

[13] In October 1987, representatives of the URNG and Vinicio Cerezo's government met in Madrid, the first direct negotiations between the Government and guerrilla forces in 27 years of conflict. That year, the National Reconciliation Commission (CNR) played a decisive role in the rapprochement process. The commission was created as a result of the Esquipulas II peace plan for Central America, (signed by Guatemala, Honduras, Nicaragua and Costa Rica). That year in Oslo, guerrillas and government agreed on an operational pattern for CNR and UN mediators. Despite the persistence of political persecution and assassination, a basic agreement was signed in Madrid by the National Commission for Reconciliation, political parties and the URNG.

[14] During the last few months of 1990, negotiations came to a standstill and a high degree of skepticism developed among voters, which led to a 70 per cent abstention rate in the 11 November 1990 presidential elections. During the second round of the elections, in 1991, Jorge Serrano Elías, of the Solidarity Action Movement (MAS), was elected President. The Serrano Government and the URNG decided to take up peace negotiations in Cuernavaca, Mexico, after three decades of violence, committing themselves to reach a lasting agreement. The agenda included topics such as: democratization, human rights, the strengthening of civil groups, rights of the indigenous peoples, constitutional reforms, the resettlement of the landless, the incorporation of the URNG into legal political life.

[15] Human rights organizations reported that in the first nine months of Serrano's rule there had been more than 1,700 human rights violations, including 650 summary executions and the murder of street children.

[16] In July, the US Senate suspended military aid to Guatemala. The URNG demanded that human rights violations cease immediately. Serrano recognized the sovereignty and self-determination of Belize, the former British colony which proclaimed its independence in 1981. The announcement caused the resignation of chancellor Alvaro Arzú, the leader of the National Advancement Party (PAN), and one of the ruling party's main allies.

[17] In 1992, a national debate began on the existence of government armed civilian groups, such as the Civilian Self-Defense

Patrols (PACs). The Catholic Church criticized the Government's economic policy and spoke out in favor of agrarian reform. In the meantime, organizations representing the indigenous peoples demanded the ratification of ILO Agreement 169, dealing with indigenous and tribal peoples. The Government created the *Hunapú* force, made up of the Army, the National Police and the hacienda Guard. In April, members of the Hunapú provoked an incident during a student demonstration demanding improvements in education policies. One student was killed and some injured. The World Bank, the US Government and the European Parliament urged the Guatemala Government to end political violence. That year, at the time of the quincentenary of Columbus' arrival in America, Rigoberta Menchú Tum, a leader from the Quiché people, won the Nobel Peace Prize.

[18] In 1993, President Serrano, backed by a group of military officers, carried out a coup, revoking several articles of the constitution and dissolving Congress and the Supreme Court. After national and international, as well as US, pressure, Serrano was ousted. Former human rights attorney Ramiro De Leon Carpio took over and dismissed Serrano's military supporters. Shortly afterwards, Jorge Carpio Nicolle, the President's cousin, was assassinated. The 1994-95 Government Plan, presented in August, reaffirmed the structural adjustment program prioritizing the end of state intervention in the economy, along with fiscal reform and the privatization of state companies.

[19] Despite the intense campaign against the Civilian Self-Defense Patrols (PACs) and compulsory military service, President De Leon Carpio stated that he would maintain both institutions as long as the situation of armed conflict persisted. The Government said that the records kept on citizens considered a 'danger' to State security had disappeared - thus eliminating evidence against those responsible for human-rights violations. De Leon Carpio's stated goal was to fight corruption in the public sector. In 1994, the President called for the resignation of legislative deputies and members of the Supreme Court, causing a confrontation between the President and Congress. This led to a clash of economic and political interests, culminating in the Executive and Congress agreeing on constitutional reform proposals.

[20] An OAS office was occupied by members of the Committee for Campesino Unity and the National Commission of Widows of

Under-5 mortality
49 per 1,000 live births
2002

Poverty
16.0% of population living on less than $1 per day
2000

Debt service
9.0% exports of goods and services
2001

Maternal mortality
240 per 100,000 live births
2000

Guatemala and some 5,000 members of indigenous groups carried out a march demanding the dissolution of the PACs. In 1994, the Government and guerrillas signed agreements for the resettlement of the population displaced by the armed conflict, without a mediated cease fire. As a result of the accords 800 people were able to settle in the zones of Chalkily, Newton and Huehuetenango, but the majority of the resettlement areas remained still under army control. That year the Minister of Foreign Affairs recognized Belize as an independent State, but upheld Guatemala's territorial claim, meaning no frontier could be established. The Government and URNG agreed to disband the PACs, and to involve the UN in human rights issues. Shortly after, the president of the Constitutional Court - Epaminondas Gonzalez Dubón - was murdered.

[21] The URNG and the Government signed a draft agreement for the resettlement of the People Uprooted by the Armed Confrontation', in Oslo, Norway, in 1994. The Communities of Peoples were recognized as non-fighting civilians and the vital importance of land for these uprooted populations was explicitly stated. The second agreement in Oslo enshrined the principle of not individualizing responsibility for human rights violations as a way of neutralizing the action of those opposed to a negotiated outcome. The UN stated that impunity for the perpetrators was the main obstacle to justice in the case of human rights violations such as illegal detention, torture and execution.

[22] In the 1995 elections, Alvaro Arzú (National Progress Party) won over Alfonso Portillo Cabrera of the FAG. Abstentions reached a record 63 per cent. In 1996, Arzú and the URNG signed a series of peace agreements which put an end - after 36 years - to a civil war which had cost more than 200,000 lives. The cease-fire was respected. Around 80 per cent of the population were living below the poverty threshold at this time.

[23] In 1998, Hurricane Mitch caused more than $5,000,000 worth of damage and left 24,000 dead in the region - 256 from Guatemala. More than 100,000 people were made homeless.

[24] Investigation of human-rights violations during the war produced an avalanche of threats against investigators and members of the judiciary. After presenting a report condemning military officers for several massacres, Bishop Juan Gerardi was murdered in 1998. The public prosecutor working on the case fled to the US where he

requested asylum, claiming he had been under heavy pressure and had received several death threats. That year, the Government ordered hundreds of bodies to be dug up in the grounds of an elite police unit in the capital. A UN report estimated that 96 per cent of the deaths during the war were the responsibility of the army and armed forces. In the second round of the elections held in late December 1999, Alfonso Portillo of the Guatamalan Republican Front (FRG) defeated Oscar Berger of the Great National Alliance (GANA). Abstentions reached 59 per cent.

[25] The drought in 2002 brought famine, killing 41 people. President Portillo declared a state of national disaster, and requested international aid. A UN report estimates that 80 per cent of Guatemalans live in extreme poverty.

[26] Two public prosecutors and a judge investigating the murder of Bishop Gerardi exiled themselves: before leaving, Judge Yassim Barrios sent three soldiers and a bishop to prison for the crime. According to the Supreme Court, in 2001, 23 judges were menaced: Param Cumaraswamy, member of UN Special Envoy for Judicial Independence, said impunity still reigns in Guatemala, and the Government has given no signs of political will to end this situation.

[27] In 2002, the Guatemala Constitutional Court removed parliamentary immunity from Ríos Montt, bringing him closer to trial for changing tax laws to favor an alcoholic drinks company. The Rigoberta Menchú Foundation (FRM) took the case to the Spanish Courts in 2001 to find an alternative route to bring Rios Montt and other officer to trial for the disappearances, torture and deaths of 200,000 people. That year, Guillermo Ovalle de León of the FRM was murdered. Many human rights activists, journalists and other people seeking the truth about the military regimes' crimes were also killed.

[28] In 2002, Guatemala and Belize agreed on a referendum to end the long dispute over borders. President Portillo was accused of diverting public funds to personal accounts abroad. Journalists Rodolfo Flares (*Siglo XXI*, Guatemala) and Roland Rodriguez (*La Prensa*, Panamá) revealed that public officials, friends and relatives of Portillo had opened local and off-shore bank accounts in Panama. Portillo accused the press of making political capital by exaggerating the allegations of corruption.

[29] In 2003 the Spanish courts accepted the FRM's case for the trial of six military officials, including Ríos Montt, and two

citizens on charges of the murder of four priests and three Spanish diplomats. In Guatemala the Center for Human Rights Legal Action (CALDH) laid charges against Ríos Montt for the genocide of indigenous people. Human Rights organizations hope that the Spanish courts will be able to extradite the accused.

[30] That year, the conservative Oscar Berger (GANA), defeated center-left Alvaro Colom, from the National Unity for Hope (UNE). Ríos Montt (FRG) also ran, but was roundly defeated. UN observers reported that activists and opposition leaders had been intimidated, persecuted and murdered during the elections. Former officials from the Civilian Self-Defense Patrols (PACs) contributed to the violence, according to Comité Campesino del Altiplano/CCDA (Altiplano Farmers' Committee).

[31] Berger came to power in a country deep in poverty and insecurity. He promised to strengthen institutions, and to invest in public safety, health, education and technology as well to fight against corruption. He also promised to rebuild the infrastructure - roads, ports and airports; to modernize the National Police, prosecute drug-dealers and organized crime rings.

[32] President Berger repeatedly invited Rigoberta Menchú and Helen Mack Chang (a business administrator who set up many social projects, and whose sister was assassinated) to work together with the Government. Finally, both accepted. Menchu agreed to help oversee the application of the 1996 peace accords. The President said that peace was the necessary precursor for national unity. ■

PROFILE

ENVIRONMENT

The Sierra Madre and the Cuchumatanes Mountains cross the country from east to west, and these are the areas of volcanic activity and earthquakes. Between the mountain ranges there is a high plateau with sandy soil and easily eroded slopes. Although the plateau occupies only 26 per cent of the country's territory, 53 per cent of the population is concentrated there. The long Atlantic coastline is covered with forests and is less populated. In the valleys along the Caribbean coast and in the Pacific lowlands there are banana and sugar plantations.

SOCIETY

Peoples: Approximately 90 per cent are of Mayan descent. Amid the country's great cultural and linguistic diversity, four major peoples can be distinguished: the Ladino (descendants of Amerindians and Spaniards), the Maya, the Garifuna (of the Caribbean region) and the Xinca.
Religions: Mainly Catholic. In recent years a number of Protestant groups have appeared. The Mayan Religion has also survived.
Languages: Spanish is official but most of the population speak one of the 22 Maya dialects.
Main Political Parties: The Guatamalan Republican Front (FRG); Great National Alliance (GANA); National Advancement Party (PAN); National Unity for Hope (UNE); New Nation Alliance (ANN); the Guatemalan National Revolutionary Unity (URNG).
Main Social Organizations: Union of Labor and Popular Associations; National Labor Union Alliance; National Workers' Coordinating Committee; Labor Union of Guatemalan Workers; Altiplano Farmers' Committee; Campesino Unity Committee (CUC). The indigenous people's movement has grown stronger since the 1996 peace accords. It is organized in: National Coordinating Committee of Indigenous Campesinos (CONIC); National Committee for Mayan education (CNEM); Office of Human Rights of the Archbishopric; Centre of Studies of Mayan Culture (CECMA), Communities of People's Resistance.

THE STATE

Official Name: República de Guatemala.
Administrative Divisions: 22 Departments.
Capital: Guatemala City 951,000 people (2003).
Other Cities: Mixco 268,300 people; Villa Nueva 129,600; Quetzaltenango 115,900 (2000).
Government: Oscar Berger Perdomo, President since January 2004. Congress: National Assembly with 113 members (91 departmental constituencies and 22 members elected by proportional representation).
National Holiday: 15 September, Independence Day (1821).
Armed Forces: 44,200 troops (1994). Other: 10,000 National Police, 2,500 Hacienda Guard; 500,000 Territorial Militia.

Arawaks and Caribs: Genocide in Paradise

BEFORE CHRISTOPHER COLUMBUS arrived in the Caribbean islands in 1492, the region had a large indigenous population. Today, virtually none of these people remain.

The story of Columbus' 'discovery' is well known: he thought he had reached the Garden of Eden, paradise, or at least the Spice Islands of southeast Asia by a new route. When his ships arrived, six million Americans (one-fifth of the current population of the zone) survived by hunting, fishing and fighting. Three groups of peoples inhabited the islands: the Ciboneys, in the western parts of modern Cuba and Haiti; the Taino-Arawaks, in the Greater Antilles (now Cuba, Jamaica, Haiti, Dominican Republic, Puerto Rico and Trinidad); and the Caribs, who occupied the present-day Lesser Antilles (to the east of the Greater Antilles).

Next to none of these peoples survive today, except for some 500 Caribs on reservations in the Dominican Republic, most of whom are of mixed African descent. The cultural impact, mass slavery and diseases that the Europeans brought to the area erased these peoples from the islands, mistakenly thought to be the paradise of gold and spices.

The story of the Tainos is typical. They were of the same language group as the Arawaks and occupied an area extending from today's Florida to Paraguay and northern Argentina. And although their history virtually ended with the arrival of the Europeans, it had begun many centuries before. Around the 5th century BC the Arawaks set out from the Orinoco River Basin in the north of South America, settling on the island of Trinidad. From there they spread throughout the Antilles. Later they pushed the Ciboneys westwards and became cultivators and traders. They were organized in communities run by chiefs known as *caciques*, in a social hierarchy with their slaves at the lowest level.

Before the Europeans arrived, the Tainos had been displaced from the Lesser Antilles by the Caribs or *Galibi* who came from the north of South America, like the Arawaks.

The Caribs were mobile, warrior groups with a simple social structure. The Carib women were mostly of Arawak origin, taken through military conquest.

In his first voyage, Columbus reached the Bahamas, and then Hispaniola (now Cuba and the Dominican Republic) where he encountered the Taino. The Admiral, amazed by the islands, the climate, the vegetation and the nakedness of the Americans, thought he had found an earthly paradise. He had read both his bible and the travel writers, particularly Marco Polo's account of his journey to China, and died believing he had reached Asia rather than a continent not shown on European maps. He was ready to be fearful of such beasts as 'man-eaters' and 'man-dogs' recorded in the traveler's notebooks: he thought he had found them in the Carib peoples. According to what he understood from the stories of the Taino-Arawaks, the victims of Carib conquests, there were ferocious warring bands who ate humans (cannibal comes from their language; the Spaniards renamed them 'cannibals'). The tales of Columbus' voyages thus contributed to the creation of the New World myths: of *El Dorado*, the gilded man; of Seven Golden Cities of Cibola; or the riches of the Amazon.

The conquest of paradise meant hell for the Arawaks and Caribs. Within a century, the former declined from a population of 2-3 million people to just a few thousand. The high mortality rate was due to exposure to previously unknown diseases introduced by the Europeans and also to the brutality of the Conquistadors. The Caribs tried to resist the invaders, but this only postponed their extermination until the 17th century.

Though he never found it, Columbus searched obsessively for gold. In its place he brought back some Tainos as slaves, along with spices such as chilies and colorful birds. Queen Isabella, his patron, did not accept the Tainos, considering them subjects of the Spanish Empire. In practice, however, in their own land the Tainos were subjects in name only. They were exploited as slaves and forced to work in conditions that accelerated their demise. As a result of wiping out the indigenous people, the Europeans had no labor force, so they began to import slaves from Africa. Finding paradise on earth meant re-introducing the practice of slavery, which had virtually disappeared in Europe with the introduction of Christianity.

Today, the few surviving Arawaks are found in Guyana, Suriname, French Guiana and Puerto Rico where they are organized in Confederations, Nations and Grand Councils that claim to speak for all the Taino People of the circum-Caribbean and US diaspora. Among them, the US officially recognizes only the Jatibonicu Taino Tribal Nation of Borikén. ∎

Guinea / Guinée

Population:	8,788,030
Area:	245,860 km²
Capital:	Conakry
Currency:	Franc
Language:	French

H unters and gatherers were living in Guinea around 30,000 years ago. Late in the first millennium, the towns of Baga, Koniagi (Coniagui) and Nalu (Nalou) were sacked by Mandinkas (Malinkes) and Sussus. The settlements in upper Guinea had been annexed to Mali since the mid-13th century. From the 16th to the 19th century, Fulbe (Fulani, see Cameroon history), controlled Fouta Djallon, where Bambuk goldmines supported the Mediterranean economy for centuries.

[2]   Samori Touré (1840-1900, Mandinka leader, reformist and warlord), founded a powerful empire of Muslim states which included regions from the present Mali and Côte d'Ivoire. In 1886, Samori confronted French troops which came from Senegal. The *Almani* (the religious and political title he had adopted from1879) fought against colonization until 1898; after that he was expelled from the country to Gabon where he died. His putative grandson, Ahmed Sekou Touré (brought up in a poor and illiterate family) founded de Democratic Party of Guinea (DPG).

[3]   With the loss of Indochina in 1954, Tunisia and Morocco in 1956 and the Algerian revolution in 1954, French colonialism collapsed. In its place, French President

Charles de Gaulle created the French Community in 1958 to protect French interests in sub-Saharan Africa. His approach was neocolonialist, to try and guarantee that the large monopolies remained under the French influence. In the 1958 referendum on the constitution for the French Fifth Republic Guinea voted against membership in the French Community. On 2 October 1958, independence was proclaimed and Sekou Touré became the first President of Guinea. In response, Paris withdrew its qualified technical personnel, thereby paralyzing the infant industries, and blocked trade with Guinea.

[4]   In 1959 the State took control of the economy and created its own currency, freeing the country from the French franc. Industry and agriculture were diversified in an attempt to become self-sufficient; bauxite production exceeded one million tons per year. French aggression continued,

including blocking bank accounts in Paris.

[5]   In 1970, Portuguese mercenaries invaded in an attempt to overthrow the Government. They also wanted to destroy the African Party for the Independence of Guinea and Cape Verde (PAIGC) which was fighting for the independence of Portuguese Guinea. Local Revolutionary Committees were set up to keep control; to strengthen the political campaigns and to stamp out corruption and theft.

[6]   In 1978, the Congress changed the country's official name to the Popular and Revolutionary Republic of Guinea, and re-established relations with France. After a long period of isolation, Sekou Touré visited African and Arab capitals to try and attract investment to extend mineral production, and so help pay the foreign debt. After French-Guinean relations were restored, French companies exploited the ironmines of Nimba Mount, petroleum and bauxite (Guinea became the second largest producer in the world).

[7]   In 1984, Sekou Touré died in the US. The interim president Louis Beavogui was immediately

overthrown Colonel Lansana Conté. who abolished the Party-State, the constitution, labor unions and the Assembly. The PDG was made illegal and the words 'Popular' and 'Revolutionary' were erased from the name of the country. Conté backed the private sector, abolished the state companies and asked France, US and other African states to help re-launch the economy. With a debt of $800,000,000, the *syli* (national currency) was devalued by 100 per cent and public expenditure was cut, a condition for Guinea's entry in the French franc monetary bloc.

[8]   In 1984, Conté reduced the members of the Ministerial Cabinet, and took on the positions of President, Prime Minister and Defense Minister. He prioritized rice cultivation and encouraged commercial, industrial and agriculture enterprises, and an economic recovery program. However, there were food shortages. He also cut public expenditures by sacking many public servants. Discontent in the army increased because of the poor pay. Prices tripled. Demonstrations forced the Government to bring down the prices of essential goods and rents.

[9]   In 1992, 650,000 refugees crossed the border from Sierra Leone and Liberia. The Government increased the number of troops from the Economic Community of West African States (ECOWAS) to prevent the arrival of new refugees.

[10]   That year, a multiparty-system was approved. Opposition leader

LAND USE

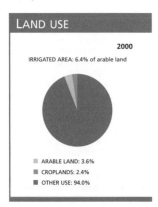

2000

IRRIGATED AREA: 6.4% of arable land

- ARABLE LAND: 3.6%
- CROPLANDS: 2.4%
- OTHER USE: 94.0%

PUBLIC EXPENDITURE

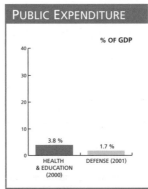

% OF GDP

3.8 % HEALTH & EDUCATION (2000)

1.7 % DEFENSE (2001)

WORKERS

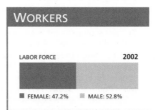

LABOR FORCE   2002

- FEMALE: 47.2%
- MALE: 52.8%

Life expectancy
49.1 years
2000-2005

GNI per capita
$410
2002

Literacy
41% total adult rate
2000

Alpha Conté returned from exile and founded the National Democratic Forum, with 30 opposition groups. Tension and political persecutions continued. Lansana Conté was re-elected in the 1993 elections, with less than 51 per cent of the votes. Alpha Conté accused him of stirring up conflict: there were serious confrontations between police and opposition members. In 1994, many people died in the skirmishes on the Liberian border. In 1995, official parties gained 76 out of 114 seats in the parliamentary elections which were denounced as fraudulent by the opposition. The Paris Club of rich world countries reduced Guinea's debt by $85,000.000 as a result of an improvement in its GDP.

[11] In 1996, an army faction led a rebellion over their low salaries and tried to depose the Government. The rebellion - which took control over the center of Conakry and attacked the presidential palace - was withdrawn. Government representatives, accused of fueling the mutiny, were sent to prison. That year, Sidia Touré (an economist), was appointed Prime Minister and stated that restructuring the economy was first priority. In 1996, the Social Affairs Ministry launched a National Strategy for the Promotion of Women, emphasizing reproductive health through mother and child education as recommended at the Cairo Summit in 1994.

[12] In 1997, thousands of people sought refuge in the country owing to political instability in neighboring countries. In 1998, Human Rights Organizations sent food supplies to the north-east to ease the consequences of a severe drought which killed many people. That year, Sierra Leone and Liberia signed a non-aggression agreement, with the mediation of the envoy from US President Clinton, Jesse Jackson. Each country accused the other of helping and giving shelter to rebel groups. In the 1998 presidential elections in Guinea, Lansana Conté was re-elected. Opposition parties disputed the authenticity of the vote. Opposition leader Alpha Conté was sent to prison until 2001.

[13] Female genital mutilation is still rife, despite the attempts of the Health Ministry and several NGOs in campaigning against it. There has been some modest success in encouraging the village women who perform the 'operation' to sterilize their cutting instruments so as to reduce infection.

IN FOCUS

ENVIRONMENTAL CHALLENGES
Intense mineral exploitation causes soil erosion.

WOMEN'S RIGHTS
Women have been able to vote and stand for election since 1958. In 2000, women held 9 per cent of the parliamentary seats and 8 per cent of the ministerial positions. Their life expectancy was 47 years. They made up 47 per cent of the labor force. Of these, 92 per cent worked in agriculture and 7 per cent in services.

In 2000*, qualified staff attended 35 per cent of births. The maternal mortality rate is 740 for every 100,000 live births*.

CHILDREN
In 2001, 365,000 children were born and 62,000 under-5 died. In 2000*, primary school attendance and enrolment rate was 47 per cent. Some 23 per cent of the children under 5 are moderately or severely underweight*. Although the under-5 death rate is decreasing, illnesses such as diarrhea, malaria and respiratory infections still are

the main cause of child mortality, responsible for 201 child deaths in every 1,000 births*. Guinea is one of the poorest countries in Africa, with weak human resources and low social development.

UNICEF has strongly promoted girls' attendance at school. Girls have also been encouraged to 'bury the knives' in protest at genital mutilation, which affects between 70 and 90 per cent of the female population.

INDIGENOUS PEOPLES/ ETHNIC MINORITIES
The most scattered ethnic group in West Africa, the Fulani (30 per cent of the inhabitants) are divided into two groups: nomads, who rarely intermarry with other groups, and those settled in cities or towns. In Guinea the Fulani people are mainly nomadic. From independence until their leader Sekou Touré's death in 1984, the Malinke people (30 per cent) had a special status in the country. Under Lansana Conté since 1984, the Sussu people have been the dominant ethnic group in Guinea. They control the main positions in the Government and in the armed forces.

MIGRANTS/REFUGEES
Towards the end of 2002, the country hosted more than 180,000 refugees from civil wars in the region (approximately 110,000 from Liberia, who arrived in the 1990s; 70,000 from Sierra Leone, seeking asylum because of human-rights abuses in their country, as well as 2,000 from Côte d'Ivoire after the 2002 war).

Nearly 50,000 were repatriated from Guinea to Sierra Leone during 2002 while 30,000 new refugees arrived from neighboring countries. By the end of 2002, 5,000 people had applied for asylum in industrialized countries. In 2001, around 30,000 who had emigrated to Côte d'Ivoire returned to Guinea. In 2002, more than 20,000 remained displaced in the country; 40,000 were assisted to return by the Red Cross.

DEATH PENALTY
It is still in force for ordinary crimes.

*Latest data available in *The State of the World's Children* and *Childinfo* database, UNICEF, 2004.

[14] Recent economic growth allowed to forward the government goals, stated in the Guinea vision 2010 document from 1999, which aimed to reduce poverty and the development of education and health. A meeting of the Occidental African States Economic Community (OASEC) took place in the Ghanaian capital Accra in 2001: Ghana, Guinea, Nigeria, Sierra Leone, Gambia and

Liberia, agreed to move towards a common currency.

[15] In 2002, Guinea, Sierra Leone and Liberia decided to take security measures on their borders in case of future rebellions. The region has been ravaged by civil war in the last two decades, with a disastrous impact on human development.

[16] New presidential elections were held on 21 December 2003,

under repressive conditions. The Government closed the airport and frontiers in the days running up to the election and only allowed cars with diplomatic or special licenses on the roads. The opposition boycotted the elections, but some of its leaders were still arrested in the lead-up to the election, along with some army officers. President Lansana Conté was duly elected for the third time. ■

PROFILE

ENVIRONMENT
The central massif of Futa-Dyalon, where cattle are raised, separates a humid and densely populated coastal plain, where rice, bananas and coconuts are grown, from a dryer northeastern region, where corn and manioc/cassava are cultivated. Rainfall reaches 3,000-4,000 mm per year along the coast. The country has extensive iron and bauxite deposits.

SOCIETY
Peoples: Guineans comprise 16 ethnic groups, of which Fulani, Mandingo, Malinke and Sussu are the most numerous.
Religions: 65 per cent are Muslim, 33 per cent practice traditional religions, and 2 per cent are Christian and other minor groups.
Languages: French (official). The most widely spoken local languages are Malinke and Sussu.
Main Political Parties: Party for Unity and Progress; Rally of the Guinean People; Party for Renewal and Progress; Union for the New

Republic; National Union for Prosperity of Guinea.
Main Social Organizations: National Confederation of Guinean Workers.

THE STATE
Official Name: République de Guinée.
Administrative Divisions: 33 regions.
Capital: Conakry 1,366,000 people (2003).
Other Cities: Kankan 124,200 people; Labe 90,200; NiZerekore 77,400 (2000).
Government: General Lansana Conté, President since April 1984, (displaced Louis Lansana Beauvogui: elected in the 1993 elections, re-elected in 1999. François Lonseny Fall, Prime Minister since March 2004. Parliament: National Assembly with 114 members, elected for a four year term. **National Holidays:** 2 October, Republic Day (1958); 3 April, The Second Republic Anniversary (1984). **Armed Forces:** 9,700 (1996). Other: People's Militia: 7,000; Gendarmerie: 1,000; Republican Guard: 1,600.

Guinea-Bissau / Guiné-Bissau

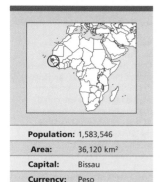

Population:	1,583,546
Area:	36,120 km²
Capital:	Bissau
Currency:	Peso
Language:	Portuguese

Guinea-Bissau was the first Portuguese colony to gain independence in Africa. This was achieved even before the fall of the Portuguese dictatorship in Lisbon, in a successful political and military struggle led by Amilcar Cabral's African Party for the Independence of Guinea and Cape Verde (PAIGC).

[2] After belonging to the Mali and Songhai empires, the peoples in the Geba river valley became independent. This independence was soon threatened by the Portuguese, who had settled on the coast from the end of the 15th century, and by the Fulani, coming from the interior in the 16th century. Inland, the state of Gabu remained autonomous until the 19th century while the coastal population suffered the consequences of the slave trade and forced displacement to the Cape Verde Islands.

[3] Resistance against the European colonists began in 1500 when the Portuguese arrived in Guinea. At that time, the country was inhabited by several different groups, immigrants from the state of Mali along with the Fulani and Mandingo groups, who lived in organized autocratic societies in the savannas. During the 17th century Guineans made their first contact with the inhabitants of the Cape Verde islands, a mandatory stopover for the ships carrying slaves to Brazil.

[4] The Portuguese colonization of Guinea was harsh. As the country was small and poor, the monopoly on trade and agriculture was dealt with by a private company, the Unio Fabril. Guineans were forced to cultivate export crops while massively reducing the acreage available for subsistence farming. In the 1950s, infant mortality reached the remarkable rate of 600 deaths per 1,000 births. There were only 11 doctors in the country and only one per cent of the rural population was literate. In the early 1960s, only 11 Guineans had completed secondary education.

[5] It was against this setting of misery and exploitation that Amilcar Cabral founded the Athletics and Recreational Association in 1954. This organization developed into the African Party for the Independence of Guinea and Cape Verde (PAIGC) two years later. The Party called on all Guineans and inhabitants of Cape Verde to unite in anti-colonial resistance, regardless of color, race or religion. In September 1959, after trying fruitlessly to engage the Portuguese in negotiations for three years, the PAIGC embarked upon guerrilla warfare. The fighting spread quickly and by 1968 the Portuguese were confined to the capital, Bissau, and a few coastal strongholds. A Popular National Assembly was elected and on 24 September 1973, the 'democratic, anti-imperialist and anti-colonialist republic of Guinea' was proclaimed. Two months later the UN General Assembly recognized the independent state.

[6] Amilcar Cabral was assassinated in Conakry, Guinea, in February 1973, by Portuguese agents. He left many books and studies on the struggles for freedom in the African colonies. His successor, Luis Cabral, set up the Government Council in the heart of the liberated area.

[7] The impact of the unilateral independence of Guinea-Bissau and its immediate recognition by the UN shook the infrastructure of Portuguese colonialism. General Spinola, commander of the 55,000 colonial soldiers, demanded that political changes in Portugal were needed. The Captains' Movement was born in Bissau, which later became the Armed Forces'

PROFILE

ENVIRONMENT
The land is flat with slight elevations in the southeast and abundant irrigation from rivers and canals. The coastal area is swampy, suitable for rice. Rice, peanuts, palm oil and cattle are produced in the drier eastern region.

SOCIETY
Peoples: Balante 27.2 per cent; Fulani 22.9 per cent; Malinke 12.2 per cent; Mandyako 10.6 per cent; Pepel 10.0 per cent; other 17.1 per cent. **Religions:** Two-thirds profess traditional African religions; nearly one-third are Muslim and there is a small Catholic minority. **Languages:** Portuguese (official). The crioulo dialect, a mixture of Portuguese and African languages, is used as the lingua franca. The most widely spoken native languages are Mande and Fulah. **Main Political Parties:** The Party for Social Renewal, progressive (PSR); the Resistance of Guinea-Bissau-Bafatá Movement (RGB); the African Independence Party of Guinea and Cape Verde (PAIGC), left; the Democratic Alliance; the Union for Change and the Social Democratic Party. **Main Social Organizations:** National Workers' Union of Guinea-Bissau (UNTG); Confederation of Independent Unions (CSI).

THE STATE
Official Name: República da Guiné-Bissau. **Administrative Divisions:** 8 Regions and 1 Autonomous Sector. **Capital:** Bissau 336,000 people (2003). **Other Cities:** Bafatá 19,400 people; Gabu 12,200 (2000). **Government:** Henrique Rosa, interim President, and Antonio Arthur Sanha, interim Prime Minister, since September 2003, appointed by a military council. Single-chamber legislature: People's National Assembly, with 102 members elected among the members of regional councils. The Assembly was dissolved by former President Ialá in November 2002; legislative elections are set for March 2004. **National Holiday:** 24 September, Independence declared unilaterally (1973). **Armed Forces:** 9,250 (2001). Other: 2,000 Gendarmes.

Movement, the group which was responsible for the coup that overthrew the dictatorial regime in Portugal on 25 April 1974. Four months after the coup, Portugal recognized the independence of Guinea-Bissau.

[8] The PAIGC Government diversified agriculture giving priority to feeding the population. Foreign companies were nationalized, agrarian reform was implemented together with a mass literacy campaign. In foreign relations, the new government opted for non-alignment and unconditional support for the struggle against apartheid and colonialism in Africa. Top priority was given to economic integration with the archipelago of Cape Verde, with a view towards uniting the two countries.

[9] In 1980, João Bernardino (Ninho) Vieira, a former guerrilla commander, staged a coup and installed a Revolutionary Council.

[10] Talks with Cape Verde were cut short while the two countries were discussing a united constitution (See Cape Verde). The new government in Bissau was immediately recognized by the neighboring Republic of Guinea, which had been in dispute with former president Cabral over offshore oil rights in an area presumed to be rich in petroleum deposits.

[11] The first development plan of 1983-86 proposed an initial investment of $118.6 million, of which 75 per cent would be financed by international funds. In 1984, the construction of five ports was started, and the construction of the Bisalanca Airport was completed. The Government started a campaign against corruption and inefficiency in public administration, and as a result in 1984 Vice-President Victor Saude Maria was asked to resign. The Popular Assembly eliminated the position of prime minister, and the Revolutionary Council became the Council of State.

[12] The 1984 stabilization plan failed, causing further deterioration of the economic and financial situation. Sixty per cent of the country's income came from the export of peanuts and dates whose price had fallen sharply.

[13] The Government adopted a 'corrective' policy, including freezing salaries and reducing public investment. This was an attempt to bring it into line with IMF conditions for refinancing the servicing of the foreign debt. The economy was subsequently opened up to foreign capital in the hope of attracting resources from Portugal and France, particularly in the area of telecommunications.

[14] In February 1991, the PAIGC approved a political reform which anticipated elections for 1992.

Life expectancy
45.3 years
2000-2005

GNI per capita
$150
2002

Literacy
38% total adult rate
2000

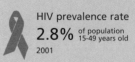
HIV prevalence rate
2.8% of population 15-49 years old
2001

Because of the economic instability and political tensions in 1992, the Government postponed the elections. However, in 1993, they were put back once more after the murder of a high military commander.

[15] Finally, in 1994 João Bernardo Vieira defeated Kumba Ialá of the Party for Social Renewal (PSR). During the campaign, Ialá accused him of supporting tribalism and racism. In the parliamentary elections, Vieira's PAIGC took 64 of the 100 seats at stake. Believing that the ruling party had 'bought' votes, Ialá refused to take part in a national unity government. That same year, the West African Economic Monetary Union (WAEMU) was founded, with eight member countries and a market of 72 million consumers, including Guinea-Bissau.

[16] In 1995, the IMF granted a new $14 million loan in support of economic reforms. In June, the visit of Senegalese President Abdou Diouf led to a rapprochement with Dakar. Both countries agreed to exploit joint energy and mineral resources.

[17] In late 1995, Guinea-Bissau ratified the border agreement signed with Senegal in 1993, resetting its maritime frontiers and stipulating the joint exploitation of an area which was supposedly rich in oil.

[18] Guinea-Bissau continued to house pro-independence rebels from the Senegalese Movement of Democratic Forces of Casamance (MFDC). However, a Guinea-Bissau's military attack on a refugee camp on the frontier with Senegal, in January 1998, fed rumors of rapprochement between Bissau and Dakar.

[19] In November 1998, a peace agreement was signed by both the rebels and the Government, in Abuja, Nigeria. In January 1999, fight was resumed in the capital, between the forces of General Ansumana Mané, who had been accused of supplying weapons to Senegalese rebels, and Vieira's Government troops. After four days of bloody battles, from which many fled, a ceasefire was agreed.

[20] On 4 May, the UN asked 'donor' countries to help Guinea-Bissau recover following eight months of civil war. Three days later, however, General Mané rose up again and Vieira was defeated; he sought political asylum in Portugal. The army accused Vieira of corruption and treason. France condemned the coup and Mané was accused of violating the Abuja and Lomé agreements, signed three months earlier.

[21] In August, the FAO included Guinea-Bissau amongst the 16 African countries with the greatest

IN FOCUS

ENVIRONMENTAL CHALLENGES
The need to increase exports led to over-cultivation of the soil; in addition, rice plantations are replacing part of the coastal forest. Slash-and-burn cultivation, as well as numerous forest fires, have contributed to deforestation.

WOMEN'S RIGHTS
Women have been able to vote and stand for office since 1977. In 2000, 10 per cent of parliamentary seats and 18 per cent of ministerial positions were held by women.

In 2000, women made up 41 per cent of the workforce and were mostly engaged in agriculture.

The adult female illiteracy rate was, in 2000*, 76 per cent, while among men it amounted to 46 per cent. The net primary school enrollment rate for women reached 45 per cent*. In secondary education, only 5 per cent of teachers were women, while in 1980 the figure was 21 per cent.

Seventy-four per cent of pregnant women are anemic, 62 per cent received prenatal care and 35 per cent of births are attended by skilled health staff*. Life expectancy for women was 46.9 years, compared with 40 in 1980.

It is estimated that 50 per cent of women have undergone genital mutilation (between 70 and 80 per cent in areas inhabited by the Fulani and Mandinka and between 20 and 30 per cent in urban areas).

CHILDREN
In 2001, 55,000 children were born and 12,000 under-5s died. In 2000, 23 per cent of children under 5 suffered from moderate and severe low weight. UNICEF is carrying out a campaign to eradicate polio and to create an environment conducive to ensuring immunization services, vitamin A supplementation, malaria control, HIV/AIDS prevention and breastfeeding promotion. At the end of 2001, 1,500 children under 14 were HIV-positive and 4,300 children were orphaned by this disease.

INDIGENOUS PEOPLES/ ETHNIC MINORITIES
The Balante (30 per cent of the population) inhabit the central and northern coastal region. Their political organization is based on the council of family authorities. In 1984, Ntombikte, regarded as a prophet, created the Kiyang-yang movement, whose leaders were arrested by the Government a year later, banning their religious and curative activities.

The Fulani (22 per cent of the population) live in the central region. Meanwhile, the Manjak peoples (14 per cent of the population) are

located in the western and southern area of the Gambia River. The Pepel represent 10 per cent of the population and live on Bissau Island and the southern coastal regions. It is estimated that the Pepel have lived in part of their current territory since the 12th century. Historically, this group had a strong presence in urban areas and in the army.

MIGRANTS/REFUGEES
At the end of 2002, Guinea-Bissau hosted about 7,000 refugees (6,000 were from Senegal and the rest had arrived from Liberia and Sierra Leone). Most refugees resided in local villages along the country's border (320 km) with Senegal. Several hundred lived in Jolmete camp.

According to a report by the UN, although the border area with Senegal remained stable during 2002, the violence there could spill across the border into refugee areas. Authorities of both countries have stated that some refugees and asylum-seekers in the border area are Senegalese rebels.

DEATH PENALTY
This was abolished in 1993.

*Latest data available in *The State of the World's Children* and *Childinfo* database, UNICEF, 2004.

poverty and food shortages, stating that it was facing a serious emergency.

[22] Five months after the coup, a mass grave was found containing 18 bodies in the town of Portogole, including former vice president Correira. Meanwhile, the military junta presented evidence to Portugal of the 'crimes' committed by Vieira in order to get him repatriated. On 17 November, two weeks before the national elections, General Mané stated that 'any president who is elected and does not fulfil his promises will be immediately deposed'.

[23] In the second round of presidential elections on 16 January 2000, Kumba Ialá of the PSR was elected President with 72 per cent of the vote.

[24] In November, Mané proclaimed himself leader of the army and attempted a coup, but he was killed together with eight followers after cross-fire with government forces in Quinhamel, 30 kilometers from Bissau.

[25] The Guinea-Bissau Resistance-Ba Fata Movement (RGB), with the second largest representation in the National Assembly, abandoned the

government coalition in January 2001. In May, both the IMF and the World Bank stopped their monetary help due to the 'loss' of millions of dollars of aid for development. In September, Ialá removed the President of the Supreme Court and three Judges from office. In November, he sacked his Minister of Foreign Affairs for criticizing him. In December, accused of attempting a coup, Prime Minister Faustino Imbali was also dismissed.

[26] In November 2002, Ialá dissolved Parliament and announced he would call the elections as expected. In February 2003, five PAIGC members and other opposition members were arrested while preparing for the elections which were postponed to April, then June, and finally October 2003.

[27] In May 2003, more than 80 per cent of public employees, who were owed more than a year's wages, went on strike. Their actions included closing hospitals and schools and also water and power cuts.

[28] On 14 September, a week after Ialá had postponed elections for the fourth time, the Army Chief,

General Verissimo Correia Seabre, led a bloodless coup. It was condemned by the UN and the African Union, but it was not resisted by the country's population, who were tired of political instability and economic devastation (most people survive on only $0.50 per day).

[29] On 23 September, a military junta appointed the interim authorities to lead the transitional government until the next parliamentary elections, set for March 2004, and presidential elections slated for March 2005. Henrique Rosa, an economist who had headed the Electoral Commission in the country's first free elections in 1994, was appointed interim President. Antonio Arthur Sanha, head of the PRS and an outspoken critic of the deposed president, became the interim Prime Minister.

[30] In January 2004, Judge Maria do Ceu Silva Monteiro was appointed President of the Supreme Court, filling a post that had been vacant for more than two years. The Supreme Court will be charged with validating the results of elections. ∎

Guyana / Guyana

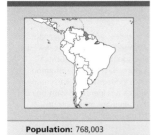

Population:	768,003
Area:	214,970 km²
Capital:	Georgetown
Currency:	Guyana dollar
Language:	English

The original inhabitants of what is now Guyana, the Arawaks, were displaced from the area by the Caribs, warriors who dominated the region before moving on to the nearby islands which were later called after them.

2   Both the Arawaks and the Caribs were nomads. Organized into families of 15 to 20 people, they lived by fishing and hunting. There are thought to have been half a million inhabitants at the time of the arrival of Europeans in Guyana. There are around 45,000 Indians, divided into nine ethnic groups, of which seven maintain their cultural identity and traditions.

3   Led on by the legend of *El Dorado*, in 1616 the Dutch built the first fort. Guyana was made up of three colonies: Demerara, Berbice and Essequibo. But in 1796, the Dutch colony was taken over by the British, who had already begun a wide-scale introduction of slaves. A slave, Cuffy, led a rebellion in 1763 which was brutally put down. To this day, Cuffy is considered a national hero.

4   Those slaves that escaped from the plantations went into the forests to live with the indigenous people, giving rise to the 'bush blacks'. The English brought in Chinese, Javanese and Indian workers as cheap labor. Since 1950, Guyana's population managed to channel independence ideas into a single movement, the People's Progressive Party (PPP), with policies of national independence and social improvements, and long-term aims for a socialist country. Cheddi Jagan, the first Prime Minister of the colony, was in power for three successive terms.

5   After years of violence, Britain recognized Guyana's independence within the Commonwealth on 26 May 1966. By that time, the PPP had split; most of the Afro-Guyanese population joined the People's National Congress (PNC), while indigenous people remained loyal to Jagan. Forbes Burnham, leader of the PNC, took office, supported by other ethnic minorities.

6   This process was influenced by ethnic conflict and by foreign interests, particularly from the US, which felt its hegemony in the Caribbean threatened by Jagan's socialism.

7   Even though Burnham came to power with Washington's blessing, he kept his distance. He declared himself in favor of non-alignment and proclaimed a Cooperative Republic in 1970. The bauxite, timber and sugar industries were nationalized in the first half of the 1970s, and by 1976 the State controlled 75 per cent of the country's economy. At the same time, regional integration was implemented through CARICOM (Caribbean Community), the Latin American Economic System (SELA), and the Caribbean Merchant Fleet.

8   In 1976, Cheddi Jagan stated the need to 'achieve national anti-imperialist unity', when disputes broke out with Brazil over the border. The PPP representatives returned to Parliament, from which they had withdrawn three years earlier to protest over electoral corruption. Afterwards, Burnham announced the creation of a Popular Militia.

9   Elections were postponed in order to hold a constitutional referendum, with Parliament drawing up a new constitution. This led to the PPP's withdrawal from legislative activity for the second time. In 1980 Burnham was elected President. According to international observers, the election had been plagued by fraud. Burnham granted authorization for transnational corporations to carry out oil and uranium operations and he turned to the IMF to obtain credit.

10   In June of the same year, Walter Rodney, the famous Guyanese intellectual and founder of the opposition Working People's Alliance (WPA) was killed by a car bomb. The culprits were never found.

11   In the post-election period, border disputes escalated. Venezuela claimed the Essequibo region, approximately 159,000 sq km (three quarters) of Guyanese territory, arguing that British imperialism illegally deprived Venezuela of that area in the 19th century. In 1983, both countries turned to the UN. In 1985 direct negotiations started again to settle the dispute. Negotiations were focused on an outlet to the Atlantic Ocean for Venezuela.

12   While financial difficulties increased during 1984 and the

Life expectancy
63.2 years
2000-2005

GNI per capita
$840
2002

Literacy
99% total adult rate
2000

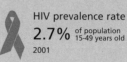
HIV prevalence rate
2.7% of population 15-49 years old
2001

Government faced a new crisis in its relations with labor unions, Burnham resumed contacts with the IMF to obtain a $150 million loan, but considered the conditions on the loan 'unacceptable'. The US invasion of Grenada - and Guyana's criticism of this action - led to a deterioration of the relations between the two countries. Guyana made overtures to the socialist countries.

[13] Burnham died in 1985 and was replaced by Desmond Hoyte. The PNC won the general elections that year, but the opposition complained of alleged fraud. In 1986, five of the six opposition parties formed the Patriotic Coalition for Democracy, whereby all the seats went to the PNC. Hoyte announced in January 1987 that his Government would return to 'Co-operative Socialism'.

[14] Parliament met in December 1991, after the Government declared a state of emergency in order to postpone the elections planned for that month. The state of emergency was extended until June 1992. In October general elections, Cheddi Jagan defeated President Desmond Hoyte (54 per cent to 41 per cent).

[15] Jagan was one of the first Latin American leaders to adopt Marxism in the 1950s, ending 28 years of PNC dominion.

[16] In 1993 President Jagan allowed US troops to train in the forests. He also accepted US military collaboration to combat drug-trafficking and to help bring clean water and sanitation to the interior.

[17] Jagan wanted to modify the economic adjustment plan adopted by Hoyte, in agreement with the IMF. His government defended 'non-conventional' methods of problems solving in land distribution, transport, health, housing and education. He proposed a market economy strategy to resolve the problem of the poverty of 80 per cent of the population. The emigration rate exceeded the demographic growth index, so that the population fell from 1,020,000 in 1989 to 808,000 in 1992.

[18] The nation's wealth still remained nearly intact with large reserves of gold, diamonds, bauxite, forests and great agricultural potential. The fiscal deficit, which caused high inflation, was related to the smuggling of minerals, along with the price policy on exports of sugar, rice and other agricultural products.

[19] The first anniversary of Jagan's Government was tarnished by a strike in the national electricity company as the Government had failed to implement its promise to increase State workers' pay by 300 per cent. The Government claimed the conditions imposed by the IMF

IN FOCUS

ENVIRONMENTAL CHALLENGES
Compared with deforestation elsewhere in the world, Guyana has suffered little and until 1990, only a small fraction of the extensive forests had been felled. However, foreign companies are pressing for the intensification of timber exploitation. In some areas, there has been no reforestation after logging, and this has led to soil erosion. There is water pollution from industrial and agricultural chemicals.

WOMEN'S RIGHTS
Women have been able to stand for election since 1945 and to vote since 1953. In 2000 women held 19 per cent of the Parliamentary seats and 15 per cent of the ministerial positions. They had representation in 30 per cent of the local governments.

In 2000* the female over-15 illiteracy rate was 1.9 per cent, down on the 6.9 per cent reported in 1980.

Women comprised 34 per cent of the workforce in 2000, mainly in services (66 per cent), in agriculture (17 per cent) and in industrial jobs (13 per cent).

Ninety-five per cent of pregnant women received antenatal care and 71 per cent of them are anemic*. In 2000, 4 per cent of women between 15 and 24 years were living with HIV/AIDS.

CHILDREN
17,000 children were born in 2001, while 1,000 under-5s died.

Twelve per cent of the children are underweight at birth*.

By the end of 2001 an estimated of 800 children were HIV-positive while 4,200 were AIDS orphans.

INDIGENOUS PEOPLES/ ETHNIC MINORITIES
Ethnicity has been a key factor in Guyana's political history, even before independence. While the descendents of Africans were assimilated into the dominant European culture, the Indian community maintained its culture. Half of today's population is of Indian descent, 39 per cent are Afro-Guyanan and the rest are of European, Asian or indigenous origin.

African slaves were brought by the Dutch to work on sugar plantations in the 17th century. The British later took over the colony, and after the British Empire abolished slavery in 1838, a labor shortage on the plantations resulted as Afro-Guyanans moved to the cities or established collective farms. To replace slave labor, the British hired workers from China and India. The Indian population eventually became one of the country's dominant groups.

Indian and Afro-Guyanan intermarriage, religious conversion and adoption of each other's cultures have become common. Since independence, each ruling regime has identified with one of the dominant ethnic groups. When the PPP is in power, the Afro-Guyanan minority complains of discrimination; and when the PNC rules, the Indo-Guyanan majority makes the complaints.

Although ethnic tensions seemed to decline between the late 1980s and early 1990s, tension rose during Janet Jagan's months in office, mainly sparked by allegations of electoral fraud; there was also resentment over the fact that she was born outside Guyana, in the US.

MIGRANTS/REFUGEES
There are reports of people migrating to the upper and lower regions of the Mazaruni and Kamarang rivers, for hunting, fishing and farming.

48,608 Guyanans lived in the US in 1980. Ten years later this figure had risen to 120,698.

DEATH PENALTY
The death penalty still applies for ordinary crimes.

*Latest data available in *The State of the World's Children* and *Childinfo* database, UNICEF, 2004.

prevented it from being this generous.

[20] In June 1994, Jagan rejected the ambassador to Georgetown nominated by the US, accusing him of 'subversive activities' during the last few years of British colonial administration.

[21] In 1995, the worst environmental accident in the history of the country occurred, when four million cubic meters of cyanide-contaminated waste fell into the Omai river, a tributary of the Essequibo, the nation's main river.

[22] In 1996 Amnesty International denounced the use of the death penalty by hanging in Guyana, the first such since 1990. That same year the Government had $500 million - nearly a quarter - of its foreign debt pardoned.

[23] Jagan died in 1997 and his wife Janet took over as interim Prime Minister. In the 15 December elections, she was elected President with 55.5 per cent against the 40.6 per cent of Hoyte's PNC. Despite threats of civil disobedience incited by Hoyte, the 77 year-old, US-born Jagan took office on 19 December. Sam Hinds was appointed Prime Minister.

[24] In her first months in office, Janet Jagan had to deal with a drought that affected the country's production (especially of gold), reduced trade, created transportation problems and facilitated forest fires. Rising prices triggered protests, the largest of which gathered outside the state telephone company to denounce rate increases of 400 to 1,000 per cent.

[25] After serving just 20 months of her term, Jagan resigned for health reasons. Economy Minister Bharrat Jagdeo - a youngster at 35 - took her place. The People's National Congress, mostly made up of Afro-Guyanans, criticized the way the power transition was handled.

[26] In March 2000, Venezuelan President Hugo Chávez reiterated his country's claims to the Essequibo region, but affirmed that Venezuela would submit to UN arbitration. Chávez also criticized a US company planning to build a rocket-launching site in the area in question.

[27] The permit granted by Guyana to a Canadian oil company for the exploitation of territorial waters caused conflict with Suriname. After a round of talks mediated by Jamaican Prime Minister Percival

James Patterson, agreement was reached to hold future meetings between both parties to decide the future of the region.

[28] In March 2001, the general election planned for 1997 was held, with international observers who confirmed that virtually everything was in good order, in spite of some irregularities due to the absence of some voters' names in the register. Finally, Jagdeo was re-elected.

[29] According to a World Trade Organization (WTO) report published in October 2003, Guyana's economy is now largely dependent on natural resources such as sugar, gold, bauxite and rice. Production of these resources has been growing very slowly over the last 15 years despite the liberalization of Guyana's trade and investment policies.

[30] In January 2004 the Paris Club of creditor countries agreed to reduce Guyana's debt by $95 million, under the enhanced Heavily Indebted Poor Countries (HIPC) Initiative, created by the IMF and the World Bank. Most creditors also committed to grant additional debt relief to Guyana so that the debt will be reduced by a further $33 million. ∎

Haiti / Haïti

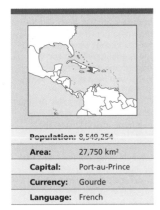

Population:	8,549,254
Area:	27,750 km²
Capital:	Port-au-Prince
Currency:	Gourde
Language:	French

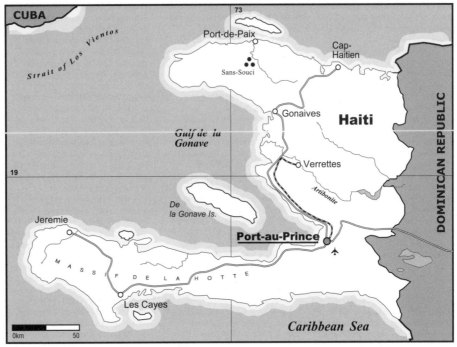

The island of Hispaniola or Quisqueya, its local name, is currently divided into two republics: Haiti and the Dominican Republic (see Dominican Republic). When it was 'discovered' by Christopher Columbus in 1492, the island was inhabited by numerous Arawak peoples, who almost entirely disappeared over the next few decades. Spanish colonists, supported by the Dominican missionaries, called the islands after their patron saint, St Dominic (Santo Domingo). The island was later colonized by the French and other European settlers who were attracted by the sugar plantations. Disputes arose among the Europeans and in 1697 Spain ceded the west of the island to France, under the Treaty of Ryswick.

2   After gaining control of the island, France began to exploit it, introducing about 20,000 African slaves per year, leading to rapid racial mixing. Sugar soon became the principal export product of the region, and during the 18th century Haiti became the most important French possession in the Americas.

3   This prosperity was based on African slave labor. By 1789, the number of African slaves in the colony had reached 480,000. There were 60,000 mulattos and free 'colored' people, while the rich land-owning Europeans

LAND USE

2000

IRRIGATED AREA: 8.2% of arable land

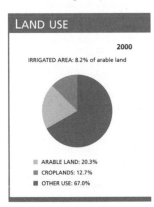

- ARABLE LAND: 20.3%
- CROPLANDS: 12.7%
- OTHER USE: 67.0%

constituted a minority of no more than 20,000. The Haitians were influenced by the revolutionary movement that had started in the colonial capitals and they waged a revolutionary war, led by former slave Toussaint L'Ouverture. The war lasted from 1791 to 1803 and ended with the proclamation of the first black republic in the world.

4   It was L'Ouverture who gave the *marrons or quilombolas* (rebel slaves) their direction, rallying them to the call of 'general freedom for all', transforming the different groups into a disciplined army. On 4 February 1794, taking advantage of the splits in the French colonial system, he succeeded in getting the French National Convention to ratify a decree abolishing slavery in Santo Domingo and appointing himself as a general. After the coup of the 18 Brumaire (1799), Napoleon Bonaparte sent a large military expedition to reconquer the colony and re-establish slavery. L'Ouverture responded with a general uprising, but he was imprisoned and died in exile in France in 1803.

5   Jean-Jacques Dessalines took over leadership of the war of independence, aided by Henri Christophe and Alexandre Pétion, who together radicalized L'Ouvertures's legacy. They succeeded in uniting the Africans and mulattos and after a series of heroic campaigns, they forced the French troops to capitulate. Independence was proclaimed on 28 November 1803, and Haiti

became the first independent state in Latin America.

6   In 1818, JP Boyer was elected president instead of Pétion. Boyer recovered the north of the country in 1820, putting an end to Christophe's monarchic experiment. Two years later he conquered Santo Domingo in the east of the island, thus achieving a fragile reunification, which lasted for a quarter of a century. In 1843, a revolution led by the Santo Domingan Creoles divided the island into two definite, independent States: the Dominican Republic in the east, and the Republic of Haiti in the west.

7   From 1867, a bloody civil war launched a period of political instability and economic crisis which lasted until 1915, when the country was occupied by US marines for non-compliance with 'its commitments'. A year later the US invaded the Dominican Republic, gaining control of the whole island.

8   The invasion of Haiti was heroically resisted by Charlemagne Péralte's 'Revolutionary Army'. Péralte was treacherously murdered in 1919. The US troops finally defeated the resistance and controlled the country until 1934, turning it into a virtual colony. That year, President Vincent succeeded in getting the US troops to withdraw from the island, but he could not eliminate US influence from the country's domestic affairs.

9   The national army, or Garde d'Haiti, took a central role in national politics, staging coups

against presidents Lescot, 1941-1946; Estime, 1946-1950; and Magloire, 1950-1957. In 1957, François Duvalier, a middle-class doctor, seized power supported by the army and the US.

10   The army, the commercial bourgeoisie, the ecclesiastic authorities, the state bureaucracy, and the US State Department used Duvalier to control the country for over 30 years. In 1964, Duvalier or 'Papa Doc' proclaimed himself President-for-life, passing on the title to his son Jean-Claude or 'Baby Doc' on his death in 1971.

11   Assailed on the international level by continual condemnations of human rights violations, and on the domestic level by active opposition, Jean-Claude Duvalier's government called elections in 1984. Sixty-one per cent of the population abstained. The opposition grew, organizing itself into parties and trade unions, while the regime was becoming a burden to the US.

12   Repression grew, and by 1985 it was estimated that Baby Doc's regime had been responsible for 40,000 murders. The country was enveloped by a growing wave of protests and strikes. Duvalier fled the country in a US airforce plane and received temporary asylum in France.

13   A National Governing Council (CNG) led by General Henri Namphu assumed control of the government, promising 'free and direct' elections by the end of 1987.

14   The dictator's flight did not end the mobilization of the

Life expectancy
49.5 years
2000-2005

GNI per capita
$440
2002

Literacy
50% total adult rate
2000

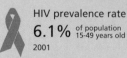

HIV prevalence rate
6.1% of population 15-49 years old
2001

people. Mass lynching by Tontons-Macoutes forced the National Governing Council to dissolve this repressive force.

[15] In October 1986, the CNG called elections to elect a Constituent Assembly to draw up a new constitution. Less than 10 per cent of the 3 million Haitians participated in the election and, in March 1987, a referendum approved the new constitution with 99.8 per cent of the vote. The new constitution established a Parliamentary system, limited the presidential term to 5 years, and divided the power with a prime minister chosen by Parliament.

[16] The elections were to be held in November 1987, but a few hours after the polling stations were opened, they were sabotaged by factions of the armed forces and by former Tontons-Macoutes, and the elections were suspended, finally taking place in January 1988. In a very volatile atmosphere, Leslie Manigat, the 'official' candidate, was elected, only to be deposed in June, in a coup led by General Namphu. In September 1988, a movement of sergeants and soldiers deposed General Namphu, putting Prosper Avril, the éminence grise of the Duvalier period, into power.

[17] In March 1990, General Avril was ousted by General Abraham, who relinquished control to a provisional civilian government headed by Judge Ertha Pascal-Trouillot, the first woman to occupy the presidency in Haiti. The provisional government created suitable conditions to put the Constitution into practice, and called elections for December 1990.

[18] These elections were won by a priest, Jean-Bertrand Aristide, who obtained 67 per cent of the vote as the leader of the National Front for Change and Democracy (FNCD). He was voted in mostly by the poor urban sectors, and took office on 7 February 1991. Aristide, a Liberation Theology activist, had been censured in 1988 by the church authorities and expelled from the Salesian order. His governmental program was based on a war against corruption and drug trafficking, including a thorough literacy campaign, and a project to move from 'extreme poverty to poverty with dignity'.

[19] On 30 September, General Raoul Cédras staged a bloody coup. In protest the Organization of American States (OAS) declared a trade embargo, starting diplomatic negotiations in the region and in the UN. Meanwhile, the rebels tried to avoid

international isolation by officially recognizing the sovereignty and operation of parliament.

[20] In February 1992, OAS representatives, Haitian members of parliament, and the deposed Aristide signed an agreement in Washington to re-establish democracy and reinstate the former president.

[21] In 1993, the UN and OAS special envoy, Dante Caputo, launched a diplomatic campaign for Aristide's return to power. The campaign also included an amnesty for the September 1991 coup leaders and the launching of a development plan outlined by the World Bank.

[22] In January, the de facto government held legislative elections which many people considered illegitimate as they were designed only to partially replace Parliament. Less than 3 per cent of those registered to vote took part. Months later, Marc Bazin resigned as Prime Minister.

[23] In January, the de facto government held legislative elections which were designed only to partially replace Parliament. Less than 3 per cent of

those registered to vote took part. Months later, Marc Bazin resigned as Prime Minister.

[24] On 27 June, indirect talks began in New York between General Cédras and ousted president Aristide. Meanwhile, the UN Security Council imposed a financial, oil and arms embargo on Haiti. In July, Aristide and Cédras signed an agreement that guaranteed the return of the President as well as an amnesty for all military leaders involved in the coup. In accordance with the agreement, Aristide named Robert Malval Prime Minister.

[25] However, a new wave of violence soon broke out in Haiti, to prevent the agreement from going into effect. In October, a US warship patrolled the coast near the capital. An armed mob threatened the American troops, so US President Clinton ordered the ship back to US Guantanamo military base in Cuba. In the meantime, the Security Council reinstated the naval embargo.

[26] Malval's Justice Minister, Guy Malary, was assassinated in 1993. The attack was carried out almost in the same place where Antoine

Izmery, a pro-Aristide businessman, had been killed a month earlier. Those responsible for the killings were members of the pro-military Front for the Advancement and Progress of Haiti, who used the same tactics as the Tontons-Macoutes.

[27] On 15 October 1994, Aristide returned after the coup leaders had gone into exile and the country was occupied by a multinational force led by the US. While in exile, the President had promised to implement a structural adjustment program prescribed by the IMF. In December, troops were demobilized in order to create a new national police force.

[28] In spite of meaning to punish those responsible for human rights abuses, Aristide - under sustained pressure from Washington - was forced to offer merely symbolic gestures in most cases, such as a gravestone in memory of the victims of death squads.

[29] In 1995, a contingent of UN troops replaced the multinational forces. In November, René Préval, an Aristide supporter, won the

IN FOCUS

ENVIRONMENTAL CHALLENGES
Copper extraction ceased in 1976 and bauxite deposits are almost exhausted. The northern coastline has the heaviest rainfall and contains the country's most developed area, though the land there is suffering from serious erosion. The felling of trees in order to use land for agriculture and wood as fuel, has accelerated the process of erosion. Forests make up less than 2 per cent of the land area.

WOMEN'S RIGHTS
Women have been able to vote and stand for office since 1950. In 2000, they held 4 per cent of seats in Parliament and no ministerial positions. That impled a retrogression, taking into account that they held 13 per cent of these positions in 1995. In 2000, they made up 43 per cent of the labor force. Fifty per cent of women worked in agriculture, 38 per cent in the area of services and 9 per cent in industry.

Skilled health staff attends only 24 per cent of births and the maternal mortality rate is 680 dead women per 100,000 live births*. Chronic malnutrition is widely spread among pregnant women and 64 per cent of them suffer from anemia*. The fertility rate is 4.0 children per woman*.

The last national study on violence against women was carried out in 1995. From a sample of 14 municipalities out of a total of 132, a total of 1,935 cases of violence were reported. Violence was classified as physical (33 per cent) and sexual (37 per cent), with rapes representing 13 per cent of the total; others (6 per cent) and not specified (25 per cent). Eighty-one per cent of cases of violence involved women between 10 and 34 years old.

Many women enter the labor market at an early age; about 10 per cent of girls aged between 5 and 9 and 33 per cent aged between 10 and 14 can be considered economically active.

CHILDREN
The under-5 mortality rate is among the 40 highest rates in the world: 123 deaths per 1,000 live births*. Twenty-one per cent of newborn babies suffer from low weight. Over 70 per cent of children under 1 year old are immunized against TB; the percentage of those immunized against polio, measles, diphtheria and tetanus is around 46 per cent.

The main causes of infant mortality are diarrhea, acute respiratory infections and malnutrition. Only half of school-age children attend school, while only 20 per cent of the population has secondary education.

INDIGENOUS PEOPLES/ ETHNIC MINORITIES
When Christopher Columbus arrived, in 1492, numerous Arawak people were living on the island. Over the next few decades they almost entirely disappeared as a result of death and disease.

MIGRANTS/REFUGEES
Some 33,200 Haitians were refugees or asylum-seekers at the end of 2002; most of them (29,200) were awaiting the outcome of pending asylum claims in the US. During the year, 10,600 Haitians sought asylum in the US (8,400), in France (1,900), and also in Canada and the Dominican Republic. The approval rate for Haitian applications before the US Immigration and Naturalization Service was 36 per cent that year.

According to human rights organizations working within the country, in 2002, 6,200 Haitians were internally displaced by repression.

DEATH PENALTY
This was abolished in 1987.

*Latest data available in *The State of the World's Children* and *Childinfo* database, UNICEF, 2004.

Under-5 mortality
123 per 1,000 live births
2002

Malnutrition
17% under-5s
1995-2002

Debt service
5.2% exports of goods and services
2001

Maternal mortality
680 per 100,000 live births
2000

elections with 88 per cent of the vote. The new President took office on 7 February 1996, in a country where 80 per cent of the population was living below the poverty line. Préval requested the UN peace forces to remain for an additional period of time due to the numerous conflicts and acts of violence which involved national police. Kidnappings and murders - including those of eight policemen out of duty - did not stop, while popular uprisings were violently repressed.

30 In July 1996, Claude Raymond, a general and minister in Duvalier's cabinet, was arrested for terrorist activities. Four days later, André Armand, former Army sergeant and leader of the retired soldiers lobby group, was killed by unknown assailants after publicly stating that retired army members were plotting to assassinate Préval and former president Aristide. The resignation of Prime Minister Rosny Smarth in 1997 and the President's decision to dissolve Parliament and govern by decree heightened political tensions and confrontation with the opposition. Jacques-Edouard Alexis, of the Lavalas political organization, was named in March 1999 to take over as Prime Minister.

31 Elections slated for March of that year were postponed until May in order to resolve voter registration problems. One month after the elections and under pressure from violent and strong protests that paralyzed the island, the Electoral Council announced the results which gave Lavalas 16 out of the 17 Senate seats. The US, UN and OAS questioned the recount.

32 In April 2000, the country's most noted journalist, Jean Dominique, owner of Radio Haiti Inter, was assassinated on arrival at work. The case, which had not been resolved two years later, became the best-financed and organized crime investigation in the country's history. A senator loyal to Aristide used his legislative immunity to avoid testimony, evidence for the case disappeared, and one of the witnesses was killed and his body vanished. Months later, another journalist was killed with a machete by presumed government allies.

33 The opposition boycotted the February 2001 presidential elections, forcing their leading candidates not to participate. They appointed an 'alternative president'. Despite the boycott and the lack of international observers, the elections took place and gave an overwhelming victory to Aristide, who thus took office

as President for a third time. Talks between Aristide's governing party and the opposition alliance failed in an attempt to establish a new Electoral Council to review the ballot. The motive of the dispute was the number of parliamentary seats belonging to each party. International economic aid had been suspended since the 2000 elections.

34 In December 2001, a group of heavily-armed former soldiers entered the presidential palace and opened fire on the security personnel in an attempted coup that left 12 people dead. Former policeman Guy Philippe was later arrested in the Dominican Republic after being fingered as the mastermind behind the failed coup.

35 The economic crisis led Prime Minister Cherestal to resign in January 2002. In March, Parliament approved - by broad majority - the appointment of Yvon Neptune to the post. Neptune, a close friend of Aristide, promised to engage in dialogue with the opposition forces in order to pull the country out of political and socio-economic crisis.

36 In 2002, most of Haiti's resources were in the hands of 15 per cent of the population (the one per cent of the population that is of European origin owns half of the country's wealth). Of the remaining 80 per cent that lived in poverty, 73 per cent was living in extreme poverty, lacking access to sanitation, water, and electricity. Two-thirds of Haitians did not eat a proper meal a day, and most of the rest ate only once a day, usually a meal lacking in basic nutrients. According to these figures, Haiti is the poorest country in the Western hemisphere.

37 During 2002, at least 30 journalists were attacked or threatened with death by alleged government supporters, and several journalists and their relatives decided to leave Haiti. In July, journalist Israel Jacky Cantave was kidnapped and beaten; he fled the country in August. In May, the organization Reporters Without Borders put Aristide on its black list of those 'attacking press freedom'. After visiting Haiti in 2002, the Inter-American Commission for Human Rights (ICHR) published a report expressing its concern about the weakness of the state of law in Haiti and about the threats to several journalists. The OAS Special Rapporteur for Freedom of Expression reported an increase in the number of acts of harassment against journalists.

38 On 1 January 2004, Haiti celebrated the 200th anniversary

ENVIRONMENT

Haiti occupies the western third of the island of Hispaniola, the second largest of the Greater Antilles. Two main mountain ranges run from east to west, extending along the country's northern and southern peninsulas, contributing to their shape. The hills and river basins in between form the center of Haiti. The flatlands that open up to the sea in the west, are protected from the humid trade winds by the mountains to the north and east. Coffee is the main export product.

SOCIETY

Peoples: Nearly 95 per cent of Haitians are descendants of African slaves. There are also minorities of European and Asian origin, and integration has produced a small mestizo group. Thousands of Haitians have emigrated in recent years, especially to Colombia, Venezuela and the United States.
Religions: Voodoo, a mixture of Christianity and various African beliefs. Catholics (80 per cent); Protestants (16 per cent).
Languages: French and Creole (both official). French is spoken by less than 20 per cent of the population. Most people speak creole, a combination of Spanish, English, French and African languages.
Main Political Parties: Lavalas Political Organization; Democratic Convergence (group of 15 opposition parties); 'Group of 184' (opposition front of 184 parties and civil society organizations); National Front for Change and Democracy (FNCD); National Alliance for Democracy and Progress (ANDP); National Committee of the Democratic Movements (Konakom).
Main Social Organizations: The 'Grassroots' Church groups, of Catholic origin; Creole Language Movement; Solidarity of the Women of Haiti (SOFA); Confederation of Haitian Workers; Federation of Workers Trade Unions; Movement of Support for Victims of Violence (MAP VIV); Platform of Haitian Human Rights Organizations (POHDH).

THE STATE

Official name: Repiblik Dayti.
Administrative divisions: 9 departments.
Capital: Port-au-Prince 1,961,000 people (2003).
Other Cities: Carrefour 356,400 people; Delmas 301,200; Cap-Haitien 119,400 (2000).
Government: Boniface Alexandre and Gérard Latortue, temporary President and Prime Minister from March 2004. The National Assembly (Legislature) has two chambers: the Chamber of Deputies, with 83 members, and the Senate, with 27 members.
National Holiday: 1 January, Independence Day (1804).
Armed Forces: 1,500.

of independence with large demonstrations throughout the country. The opposition used it as an opportunity to launch a general strike. The opposition - the 'Group 184', which comprises that number of political parties and organizations of Haitian society - took advantage of the anniversary to draw the international community's attention to the possibility of rigged legislative elections in 2004 and of Aristide's attempt to be re-elected in 2005. The President of the Caribbean Community (CARICOM) and Jamaica's Prime Minister, Percival Patterson, sent Aristide a letter, pointing out that the Caribbean 'is worried about reports on the increase of political instability in Haiti'.

39 The uprising against Aristide intensified, while rebels seized

cities and reached the capital in February. Washington and Paris called for Aristide's resignation. Washington sent troops for a multinational army composed mainly of French and Canadian soldiers and contracted a plane to carry Aristide and his small party to the Central African Republic. Once on African soil, Aristide announced he had been kidnapped.

40 Boniface Alexandre and Gérard Latortue were installed as temporary President and Prime Minister in March 2004. In September and October 2004 there was a worrying escalation of violence in Haiti, which resulted in 200 deaths. There was also increasing evidence of repression as known supporters of former President Aristide were reputed to be targeted by police under the control of Latortue. ■

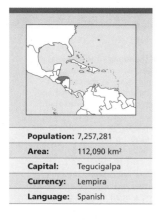

Population:	7,257,281
Area:	112,090 km²
Capital:	Tegucigalpa
Currency:	Lempira
Language:	Spanish

E vidence shows the Copan valley, in the western part of present-day Honduras, has been occupied for about 4,000 years by Maya people, although the city of Copan was inhabited for only about 500 years. Copan reached its peak around 500-800 AD during the Classic Period, when about 15,000 people lived in the area, but like other Maya city-states it was abandoned mysteriously around 900 AD. A variety of other peoples lived in the rest of the territory, including Chibcha (see Colombia) and Lenca.

² Gold stimulated Spanish conquest of the area early in the 16th century. Despite strong resistance from the Native Americans led by Lempira, Pedro de Alvarado - who was in charge of the final Spanish conquest - joined the territory to the Captaincy-General of Guatemala. The initial mining centers were located near the Guatemalan border. The demand for labor led to revolts and accelerated the decimation of the native population. As a result, African slaves were brought in to Honduras, and by 1545 the captaincy may have had as many as 2,000 slaves.

³ For long periods the Spanish utilized a soft defense against the Caribbean pirate attacks; thus, the British came to control the Mosquito region on the Caribbean coast. In the 18th century, however, the Spanish Bourbon kings made a sustained effort to recover these areas, and their success in the Gulf of Honduras was made evident with the completion of a fort at Omoa by 1779.

⁴ In 1821, Honduras gained independence from Spain. Together with the other Central American provinces it joined the short-lived Mexican Empire of Iturbide, which collapsed two years later. Francisco Morazán and other Honduran leaders sought in vain to set up an independent Central American federation. Their efforts were no match for Britain's 'Balkanization' tactics.

⁵ With the liberal reform of 1880, mining became the backbone of the economy. To encourage the development of this sector the country was opened to foreign investment and technology. Toward the end of the 19th century, the United Fruit Company (Unifruco) was established in the country; the US company took over vast tracts of land. It produced almost the entire fruit output of the country, ruled railroads, ships and ports, and dictated many key political decisions.

⁶ US Marines invaded Honduras in 1924, imposing a formal democracy and allowing Unifruco to establish a monopoly in banana production by buying out its main competitor, the Cuyamel Fruit Company. Washington eventually handed power over to Tiburcio Carías Andino, who governed Honduras from 1933 to 1949.

⁷ Border disputes with Guatemala led to US arbitration in 1930. In 1969, friction resulting from Salvadoran peasants emigrating to Honduras led to a further war, which was finally ended with mediation by the Organization of American States (see El Salvador). In 1971, nationalists and liberals signed the Unity Pact. General Osvaldo López Arellano, in power since 1963, permitted elections and Ramón Ernesto Cruz of the National Party was elected President.

⁸ In 1972 López Arellano overthrew the Cruz administration. He demonstrated his sensitivity to peasant demands for land reform and began to impose controls upon United Brands (as Unifruco was now called). The affected parties reacted, and López Arellano was replaced by Colonel Juan A Melgar Castro.

⁹ The army commander-in-chief, General Policarpo Paz García, took power in 1978. This regime became closely allied to that of the dictator Anastasio Somoza in neighboring Nicaragua. Nicaragua's Sandinista Revolution hastened the election of a constituent assembly in Honduras which promptly ratified Paz García as President.

¹⁰ When Roberto Suazo Córdova, assumed the presidency in January 1982, he authorized increases in the price of consumer goods and enacted an 'anti-terrorist' law forbidding strikes as 'intrinsically subversive'. Death squads acted with impunity and opposition political figures 'disappeared' daily.

¹¹ Honduras tolerated the presence of US troops and Nicaraguan counter-revolutionary bases in its territory. It is estimated that, in 1983, the Pentagon had 1,200 soldiers in Honduras. Apart from intervening directly in armed operations, they gave military instruction, logistic support and built infrastructure works. The Nicaraguan 'contras' had some 15,000 fighters, together with some 30,000 Nicaraguan refugees.

¹² Rafael Callejas, candidate for the National Party, had an easy victory in 1989 in elections that were considered fraudulent. Backed by the US and business circles, Callejas began a complete liberalization of the economy.

¹³ In 1990, the Government decreed an amnesty for political prisoners and outlaws. The anti-terrorist law was abolished and a climate of complete political

PROFILE

ENVIRONMENT
Mountains and rainforests cover 80 per cent of the land. Both population and economic activity are concentrated along the Caribbean coast and in the southern highlands, close to the border with El Salvador. The coastal plains have the largest banana plantations in Central America. Coffee, tobacco and corn are grown in the southern part of the country. Electricity is widely available. Approval is underway for a hydroelectric project in Piedras Amarillas, which will be one of the largest in the country, capable of generating 100 mW.

SOCIETY
Peoples: Most Hondurans are of mixed Mayan and European descent. There are 10 per cent of Native Americans and 2 per cent of African descent. The Garifunas, descendants of fugitive slaves and Native Americans, live along the Caribbean coast and on the nearby islands, maintaining their traditional lifestyles.
Religions: Roman Catholic 85 per cent; Protestant 10 per cent.
Languages: Spanish (official), Garifuna, various indigenous languages (such as Lenca and Miskito); a small number of people speak English.
Main Political Parties: National Party (NP), conservative; Liberal Party of Honduras (LPH); Party for

Innovation and Unity-Social-Democracy (PIU); Democratic Unification Party (DUP); Christian Democratic Party of Honduras (CDPH).
Main Social Organizations: The Confederation of Honduran Workers (CTH) founded in 1964 and affiliated to the ORIT (Regional Interamerican Labor Organization). Also: The General Workers' Central Union (CGT), (Social-Christian), the United Federation of Workers (FUT), the Federation of Honduran Workers' Unions (FESITRAH), the Independent Workers' Federation and the United National Peasants' Front of Honduras (FUNACAMPH).

THE STATE
Official Name: República de Honduras.
Administrative Divisions: 18 departments.
Capital: Tegucigalpa 1,007,300 people (2003).
Other Cities: San Pedro Sula 616,500 people; Ceiba 108,900; El Progreso 106,500; Choluteca 93,100 (2000).
Government: Ricardo Maduro, President since January 2002. Unicameral Legislature: National Congress, with 128 members.
National Holiday: 15 September, Independence Day (1821). **Armed Forces:** 18,800, including 13,200 conscripts (1995). Other: 10,000 members of the Public Security Force.

Life expectancy
68.9 years
2000-2005

GNI per capita
$920
2002

Literacy
75% total adult rate
2000

HIV prevalence rate
1.6% of population 15-49 years old
2001

consensus was created. The murder of opposition members and other abuses committed by the military were denounced by the Honduran Committee in Defense of Human Rights.

[14] Opposition candidate Carlos Roberto Reina triumphed in the 1993 elections. One of the Government's first resolutions was the dissolution of the National Board of Investigations, accused of torturing prisoners.

[15] While the armed forces kept policing the cities, the Legislative Assembly began the process of constitutional reform which resulted in granting control of public security forces to the civilian power. The Unit of Criminal Investigation, led by civilians, began operating in January 1995, replacing the secret police dissolved the previous year. The new body, formed initially by 1,500 agents, was trained by Israeli police and the US FBI. At the time, more than 50 people were murdered each day in Honduras.

[16] Senior government officials were jailed in 1995 for their involvement in the sale of official passports. The Supreme Court of Justice revoked former president Callejas' immunity so he could testify regarding the forged documents and misappropriation of public funds. President Reina was also investigated on the use of state funds for private purposes.

[17] On taking office in January 1998, President Carlos Flores was willing to form a national unity government and to reach a truce with the opposition linked to the military. With 80 per cent of the population living in extreme poverty, 228 landowners held more than 75 per cent of the country's lands.

[18] In October that year, the destruction wreaked by Hurricane Mitch amounted to over $5.36 billion. It killed 24,000 people throughout Central America, 14,000 of whom were Hondurans. Likewise, two million Hondurans lost their homes. One year later floods killed 35 people and covered 14,000 hectares of arable land, causing $20 million in losses. The authorities stated that, had they received the aid promised by developed countries after Mitch had struck, they could have dredged the rivers and avoided the new catastrophe.

[19] Conflict between residents in Olancho and the Energisa corporation erupted in 2001. The company was planning to install a hydroelectric project on the Babilonia River, a protected area of the Sierra de Agalta National Park, known as the 'Meso-American biological corridor'. In the face of Government inertia in stopping the

IN FOCUS

ENVIRONMENTAL CHALLENGES
Deforestation and uncontrolled development are contributing to soil deterioration. Mining activities are causing water pollution, especially in Yojoa Lake, the country's largest source of fresh water.

WOMEN'S RIGHTS
Women have been able to vote and stand for office since 1955. Between 1995 and 2000 their representation increased in 1 per cent and reached 9 per cent of the total number of parliamentary seats; in ministerial or equivalent posts representation remained at 11 per cent.

In the year 2000 women comprised 32 per cent of the labor force (9 per cent worked in agriculture, 25 per cent in industry and 66 per cent in services). Thirty-five per cent of pregnant women are anemic; the rate for non-pregnant women is 26 per cent*. The global fertility rate is estimated at 3.7 children per woman, lower than during the period 1970-1975*. Towards the end of 2001*, qualified personnel attended 56 per cent of the births. Some 27,000 women aged 15 to 49 live with HIV/AIDS.

CHILDREN
By 2001, 68 per cent of Honduran families lived in poverty: 75 per cent in rural areas and 57 per cent in cities. Mass unemployment fed the informal economy during the 1990s. In 2001, 384,832 children and adolescents aged 5-18

worked. Of these, 73.6 per cent were boys and 69.2 per cent came from rural areas; almost half were under 15. Only 39 per cent of working children were paid. In 2000*, school attendance was 58.1 per cent, with provision for 35 per cent of pre-schoolers and 84 per cent for elementary students. In 1996, 43 per cent of children under 6 months old were breast-fed only; 29 per cent were underweight and 39 per cent had moderately or severely stunted growth. In 2001, 3,000 children under 14 were living with AIDS, and there were 14,000 orphans due to this illness. During 2001 and 2002 there were many extra-judicial executions of youth gang members, and in total there were over 1,500 deaths of children and young people. In many cases, there was official acquiescence in the security forces' participation.

INDIGENOUS PEOPLES/ ETHNIC MINORITIES
There are eight main groups: the Lenca, Pech, Garifuna, Chortis, Tawahkas, Tolupanes, Xicaques and Miskito - who comprise the majority within the indigenous population - and the English-speaking Afro-American population. In 1998, the estimated indigenous population was of 410,000 people (7 per cent of the total).

Their main claim, and the main reason for their persecution by those with power, is their demand for almost 35,000 acres of land in the west; an issue that is likely to lead to conflict. The Miskito are the poorest sector of society, and they live isolated from the other indigenous peoples in the rural southeast and on the

Caribbean coast. This contributes to their lack of access to educational and health services. The main organization representing them to the Government on environmental issues, their right to land and cultural diversity is the Misquito Asla Takanka (Unity of the Mosquitia) that works particularly with 200 villages around Gracias a Dios.

MIGRANTS/REFUGEES
Internal migration has shown that women mainly migrate toward cities and men toward agricultural areas. Between 1995 and 1989, migration shows a net negative balance: more people left than came into the country.

Honduras is a member of the Proceso de Puebla (Puebla Process), an agreement that since 1995 has tried to regulate migration between some Central American countries and North America. The amounts consigned increased during the 1990s. In 1998, the sums involved approached $1,100 million in El Salvador, $363 million in Guatemala, $128 million in Honduras and $95 million in Nicaragua (or 16 per cent of the GDP of El Salvador, 3 per cent of both Guatemala's and Honduras', and 5 per cent of Nicaragua's).

DEATH PENALTY
The death penalty was abolished in 1956.

*Latest data available in *The State of the World's Children* and *Childinfo* database, UNICEF, 2004.

project, residents organized a campaign that received international support. According to the movement, environmental licenses were granted without thorough environmental impact assessments. Four activists have been murdered to date. Demonstrations are brutally repressed and raids, threats and intimidation of locals by the company still go unpunished.

[20] In January 2002 the National Party candidate, Ricardo Maduro, became the country's new President after receiving 52.2 per cent of the votes. As a result of the economic crisis, the number of thefts had risen, and kidnappings had become a common way to obtain money. Shortly after his coming to office, Maduro - who had promised he would put an end to this type of violence - formed a force of 10,000 soldiers to fight crime.

[21] The Committee of Relatives of Prisoners-Missing Persons in Honduras (COFADEH) said that 16 people's lives were in imminent danger in Gualaco region and 11 communities had been seriously affected there during 2003. In November that year, journalist Germán Antonio Rivas, manager-owner of Corporación Maya Televisión (Maya Television Corporation), from Santa Rosa de Copán city, was murdered. During the 1980s Rivas had been a voluntary worker for the Human Rights Movement. He had previously been targetted in another murder attempt for having denounced the cyanide spill caused by Minerales de Occidente (Western Minerals) in Lara River, which provided fresh water for Santa Rosa de Copán. In the light of this report, the Natural Resources and Environmental Bureau fined the

mining company 1,000,000 lempiras. A further six journalists said there had been murder attempts on their lives between 2000 and 2003.

[22] The year 2004 started with heated public debate on the so-called 'anti-maras' (youth gangs) law, in force in Honduras since 1983 and amended in 1999. The amendment is criticized by some jurists as unconstitutional and by others as discriminatory and repressive. There has been pressure on various fronts to rescind it but President Maduro declared that if the judiciary were to rule the amendment unconstitutional, Congress would pass an equally severe law to replace it. Some 2,000 young people under 23 years old have been killed by death squads that have operated with impunity since 1999 - despite the outcry from human rights organizations and police. ∎

Hungary / Magyarország

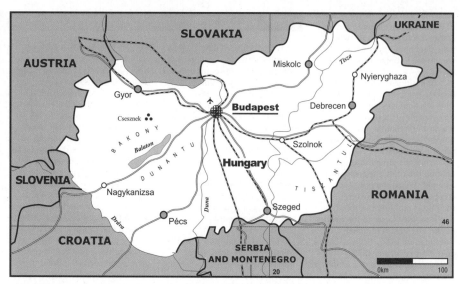

Population:	9,784,352
Area:	93,030 km²
Capital:	Budapest
Currency:	Forint
Language:	Hungarian

I n the days of the Roman Empire, the territory of present-day Hungary belonged to the provinces of Pannonia and Dacia. By the end of the 4th century Rome had lost Pannonia, which had been occupied by German and Slavic peoples. The central plains were inhabited by Huns, Bulgars and Avars, nomadic peoples from the steppes north of the Black Sea. The Avars ruled over the Danube basin during the 7th and 8th centuries, until they were conquered by Charlemagne.

[2] Charlemagne's successors set up a number of duchies in the western and northern parts of the basin, while the southern and eastern parts fell under the sphere of influence of the Byzantine Empire and Bulgaria. The Duchy of Croatia became independent in 869 and Moravia put up stiff resistance to the Carolingians until the appearance of the Magyars. The latter had organized a federation of tribes west of the lower Don. These were made up by several clans led by a hereditary chieftain. The federation was called On-Ogur (Ten Arrows); the term 'Hungarian' is a derivation of this word in the Slavic language. In 892, the Carolingian Emperor Rudolf sought the support of the Magyars to break Moravian resistance.

[3] Led by Arpad, the prince elected by the chiefs of the seven groups of Hungarians, the Magyars crossed the Carpathian mountains and conquered the inhabitants of the central plateau. Moravia was defeated in 906 and Pannonia a year later. The Hungarians then expanded northwards and carried out numerous raids into the rest of Europe. The German Emperor Otto I defeated Arpad in 955 and halted Magyar expansion. Arpad's heirs reunified the groups and adopted Western Christianity. Upon the death of King Andrew III in 1301, the Arpad dynasty came to an end.

[4] Stephen I was crowned by Rome, subsequently putting in place the foundations of the Hungarian State. The fights for succession upon Stephen's death triggered two centuries of instability, but Hungary consolidated its dominions as far as the Carpathian mountains and Transylvania in the north, and the region between the Sava and Drava rivers in the south. In addition, it ruled over Croatia, Bosnia, and Northern Dalmatia (although the latter remained a separate state).

[5] After the Mongol invasion of the 13th century - in which Hungary lost half of its population - the kingdom opened its doors to new settlers. However, it was forced to make various concessions to the Cuman overlords and immigrants, who further weakened it. Finally, the country found stability when Charles Robert of Anjou (1307-1342), the royal candidate who was favored by the Pope, was appointed to the throne. As the struggles between the Holy Roman Empire and the papacy did not involve Hungary, the 14th century was the country's golden age. The kingdom established friendly relations with

Austria, Bohemia and Poland, and strong ties with Bosnia, although it seized Dalmatia from Venice, and other territories from Serbia.

[6] Due to the long absences and arbitrary rule of Sigismund of Luxembourg (1387-1437), who was also a German and Czech king, the Hungarian *Diet* (parliament), which was made up of nobles, was enabled to pass laws. Taxes were continually being exacted from the peasants, who staged revolts in the north and in Transylvania. After another controversial succession, Matthias Corvinus of Prague became king of Hungary in 1458. He ruled his country with an iron fist. With the help of the Black Army, made up of mercenaries, Matthias subdued his enemies within the country and expanded his dominion over Bosnia, Serbia, Walachia, and Moldova, engaging in campaigns against Bohemia and Austria. Upon Matthias' death in 1490, the richest nobles appointed Vladislav II, who was King of Bohemia and known for his weak character. The Black Army was disbanded, but the oppressed peasants rebelled again in 1514, and the rebellion was ruthlessly put down. Austria recovered the southern provinces and established its authority over Hungary.

[7] Hungary was conquered by the Ottoman Empire in 1526. The sultan supported Zapolya of Hapsburg to succeed the king, who had been killed in battle. However, upon Zapolya's death he occupied Budapest himself, and annexed a large portion to the south and center of the country. Croatia and the western and northern strip of the country remained under the rule of Ferdinand of Hapsburg, who had to pay tribute to the Turkish Empire. During the 17th and 18th

centuries, Hungary was under two empires whose only interest in the country lay in the tributes it paid. The conflict intensified when the majority of the population embraced the Reformation, and Vienna attempted to re-establish Catholicism. A new awareness emerged, even among the nobles, against absolutism, the poverty and oppression suffered by the peasants, and the country's stagnation.

[8] Inspired by the 1848 revolution in Paris, the Hungarian Diet passed the so-called April Laws, which introduced changes in agriculture by transferring ownership to those who worked the land, and in fiscal matters by broadening the tax base. In addition, parliament was reorganized on a more representative basis. The reunification of the country and the creation of a separate administration in Budapest were proposed. The reform was met with distrust on the part of large landowners and the Serbian, Romanian, and Croatian minorities. When the revolution was defeated, Austria, aided by Russia, annulled the reforms and regained control over Hungary. When Austria was defeated by Prussia in 1866, Vienna subdivided its empire and accepted the April Laws. A Nationalities Law guaranteed respect for the rights of minorities, giving way to the establishment of the Austro-Hungarian Empire in 1867.

[9] With the collapse of the Hapsburg Empire during World War I, a provisional government took power and proclaimed the Republic of Hungary. But Serbians, Czechs and Romanians seized two-thirds of the country and the central government was paralyzed. In 1919, a Communist rebellion led

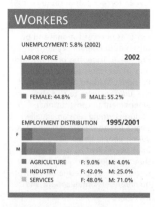

Life expectancy
71.9 years
2000-2005

GNI per capita
$5,280
2002

Literacy
99% total adult rate
2000

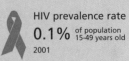
HIV prevalence rate
0.1% of population 15-49 years old
2001

to the formation of a Soviet Republic. Bela Kun's Bolsheviks were forced to flee when the Romanian troops took over the capital. The European powers pushed Romania into withdrawing and installed a provisional government. The 1920 parliament restored the monarchy and appointed Admiral Milkos Horthy as provisional ruler.

[10] In the Trianon Treaty, the victorious allies recognized Hungarian independence, but Yugoslavia, Romania, and Czechoslovakia kept control of most of the country's territory and 60 per cent of its population. Austria, Poland, and Italy also benefited from this partition. Hungary was forced to pay heavy reparations; its industry and productive apparatus were left in a shambles. Unemployment rose to unprecedented levels and nearly 400,000 refugees arrived from the territories it had lost. Middle-class Hungarians and refugees joined together to set up right-wing armed groups, blaming the left for their ruin.

[11] Funds granted by the League of Nations, followed by private investments, alleviated domestic tensions, but the depression of the 1930s had a severe impact on Hungary. Horthy formed an extreme-right government which sided with Germany, while anti-Semitism grew within the country. The alliance with Berlin enabled Budapest to recover part of Slovakia, Ruthenia, and northern Transylvania. Hungary co-operated in the German attacks on Romania, Yugoslavia and the USSR, but nothing could stop the Red Army counter-offensive. In the Treaty of Paris, Hungary was forced to retreat to the borders determined by the Treaty of Trianon, pay reparations and reduce its army, under the supervision of the Russian occupation.

[12] In 1944 a provisional assembly formed a coalition government. Its program included the expropriation of large estates, the nationalization of the banking system and heavy industry, guarantees for small landowners and private initiative, democratic rights and liberties. The Communists, at that time represented by the Workers' Party, assumed control of the government. The constitution of the Peoples' Republic of Hungary was promulgated in 1946. In 1948, agriculture was forcibly collectivized and a series of development plans which put a priority on heavy industry were implemented. In 1953, Matyas Rakosi, head of government, was replaced by Imre Nagy, who

IN FOCUS

ENVIRONMENTAL CHALLENGES
Large investments will be necessary in order to meet EU standards on waste management, energy efficiency and pollution. Oil and natural gas deposits have been found in the Szegia and Zala river basins, and exploitation regulations need to be established. Forty-one per cent of the population is exposed to sulfur dioxide and nitrogen dioxide emissions. The sulfurous emissions are greater than in most western European countries.

WOMEN'S RIGHTS
Women have been able to vote and stand for office since 1918. Between 1995 and 2000, the proportion of seats held by women in parliament fell from 11 to 8 per cent, while their representation in ministerial or equivalent positions rose from 0 to 5 per cent.

In 2000, women made up 45 per cent of the labor force (4 per cent in agriculture, 25 per cent in industry, and 71 per cent in services) and the female unemployment rate was 6.3 per cent, 2.4 per cent down from 1995.

In 2002, international women's rights organizations expressed their concern about alleged cases of exploitation and ill-treatment of women in zones where prostitution is permitted. Since 1990, Hungary has been identified as being involved in the largely forced trafficking of women for the sex trade, as both a country of origin and a destination for victims.

CHILDREN
In 2001, Hungary had 2 million people under 18 and 470,000 under 5. Until 2002, Hungarian law allowed girls between 16 and 18 years old to get married. The UN Convention on the Elimination of All Forms of Discrimination against Women (CEDAW) expressed concern about this in its report on the situation of Hungarian women. In 2001, the basic indicators of child welfare were similar to those of industrialized countries. However, the Roma/gypsy minority children were segregated in several respects, particularly in access to education. Roma children comprised a majority in special needs schools or classes for mentally disabled children.

INDIGENOUS PEOPLES/ ETHNIC MINORITIES
In 2002, the Roma/gypsies in Hungary numbered 572,000 (5.6 per cent of the total population). Geographically dispersed, they are the most disadvantaged minority, suffering the worst discrimination. Culturally, racially and linguistically distinct from the majority population, they have been a frequent target of discrimination and prejudice by the authorities and society as a whole. In 2002, systematic racial discrimination against them was documented. Also noted was the failure of the Hungarian legislature and authorities to protect them against violence and address their needs for access to education, housing and public services. Although their situation is alarming - and in many cases has worsened since the Communist era - the Government has adopted policies, including new systems of self-rule, as well as measures to root out discriminatory behavior in the police force. However, these policies do not go far enough in dealing with the depth of general discrimination suffered by the Roma, who not only face violent attacks by right-wing groups, but also lack of protection and prejudice from the police and courts.

MIGRANTS/REFUGEES
At the end of 2002, the country hosted about 1,200 refugees and asylum-seekers, but only 100 people, almost all of them from Iraq and Afghanistan, had been granted asylum. That year, nearly 6,400 people, mostly from Iraq and Afghanistan, applied for asylum in Hungary, down about 32 per cent from 2001. The authorities granted refugee status in fewer than three per cent of the roughly 4,000 asylum cases in which a decision was reached.

DEATH PENALTY
Capital punishment was abolished in 1990.

promised political changes, generating expectations among the population. In 1955, Nagy was deposed and expelled from the Workers' Party. He was replaced by András Hegedus; Erno Gero remained as first secretary of the party.

[13] The resolutions adopted by the 20th Congress of the Soviet Union Communist Party prompted students to organize a demonstration in Budapest that drew protesters from many other sectors of society. Gero reacted harshly. The police were instructed to open fire on the crowd, the demonstration turned into a popular revolt, backed by the army, and Nagy returned as head of government. He announced Hungary's withdrawal from the Warsaw Pact, and asked the UN to recognize the country's neutrality. In 1956 the Red Army, which had withdrawn during the revolution, reinstated the Communist government, led by Janos Kadar, who closely followed the Soviet line.

[14] Central planning became less strict around 1968. Living standards rose, but bureaucracy and corruption grew. Discrimination against Hungarian women continued, even though they were largely incorporated into the labor market. In 1981, women made up 45 per cent of all workers, although they were paid less than men and their job opportunities were restricted to specific fields. Between 1986 and 1988, Hungarian and Austrian environmentalists protested over the construction of a dam on the Danube, a Hungarian-Czechoslovakian project supported by Austria. In the end, the government in Budapest was forced to shelve the project.

[15] Kadar was elected first secretary of the Hungarian Workers' Socialist Party (WSP) and head of government. In 1988, he faced a demonstration in Budapest in which the protesters demanded reforms. The Government subsequently relaxed press censorship and permitted the formation of trade unions and independent political groups such as the Hungarian Democratic Forum (HDF). As *perestroika* (restructuring) developed in the Soviet Union, in 1989 Hungary's parliament passed a law legalizing strikes, public demonstrations and political associations. The WSP also approved the abolition of the single party system and agreed to celebrate Independence Day on 15 March, the date of the 1848 revolt against Austria. An austerity plan which reduced subsidies and devalued the currency was adopted; as a consequence, unemployment and inflation climbed. About 100,000 people demonstrated in Budapest, demanding elections and the withdrawal of Soviet troops. The opposition candidates won the provincial elections held that year,

and two million workers went on strike, protesting against price increases.

[16] After an agreement between the WSP and the opposition, the Republic of Hungary was proclaimed on 23 October 1989, and the single-party system was abolished. Hungary soon broke its Cold War alliances. Within a short time, Budapest had established relations with Israel, South Korea, and South Africa. In 1989, the WSP had become the Hungarian Socialist Party (MSzP), with one faction deciding to keep its old name. In the 1990 elections, the HDF won 43 per cent of the vote, forming a coalition government with two smaller parties; the MSzP and the WSP took 10.3 and 3.5 per cent of the vote, respectively. Agricultural and industrial output shrank 10 per cent due to IMF policies which stood in the way of domestic capital accumulation and favored foreign investment. In 1990, inflation climbed to 30 per cent, with the average family spending 75 per cent of its income on essential goods. By 1991, the spending had increased to 90 per cent of income. Of the country's 10 million inhabitants, two million were living below the poverty line.

[17] Women's representation in politics declined: in the 1990 elections, women won 7.5 per cent of the seats, down from 21 per cent in 1985. Women made up 46 per cent of the active workforce of 4.85 million, but this began to change with the newly expanding view that the 'natural' order should be restored. However, the idea that women should stay at home clashed with the new economic reality of the country, where two salaries were needed to cover even the most basic needs of a nuclear family.

[18] In 1992, the Government decided to reduce the public deficit, which exceeded $900 million in 1991, by slashing public spending. Growing popular discontent forced center-right Prime Minister Joszef Lantall to back down on planned oil price hikes. The economic crisis fuelled nationalistic and xenophobic demonstrations. The HDF and nearly 70,000 people from different political groupings took part in a pro-democracy march in Budapest: 48 skinheads were convicted of assaults on gypsies and foreigners.

[19] In the 1994 elections, the MSzP led by Gyula Horn won 209 of the 386 seats, and he was sworn in as prime minister. The Alliance of Free Democrats (SzDSz) held on to 70 of its 90 seats while the HDF retained only 37 of its previous 165 seats. In 1995, Horn's honeymoon with the electorate

came to an end when his unpopular package of economic measures was approved. The education budget and unemployment and maternity benefits were cut, in order to reduce the fiscal deficit. Horn continued to forge closer ties with the West. He also requested neighboring countries for more help to Hungarian minorities living within their borders, with a view to preserving their cultural identity. In 1996, Hungary signed an agreement with Slovakia for the protection of ethnic minorities and, soon after, reached a similar accord with Romania.

[20] In 1998, Hungary agreed to the installation of nuclear weapons and NATO troops in Hungarian territory as a pre-condition to joining the military alliance. That year, admission to NATO was approved by 85 per cent of those who voted in a referendum (in which around 4 million people abstained). Bilateral relations with Romania, home to a large Hungarian minority, improved following former communist Ion Iliescu's defeat and the removal of the ultra-nationalist Romanian parties, which were hostile to the Hungarian and Roma/gypsy minorities. In 1998, Hungary continued to focus its diplomatic efforts on admission into the EU. In 1999, Parliament voted overwhelmingly in favor of joining NATO. The extreme right Party for Justice and Life opposed the move. That year, Hungary, Poland and the Czech Republic were admitted into NATO, just before the Alliance bombing of Yugoslavia began.

[21] In 2000, a 100,000 cubic meter cyanide spill - at a mining site in Romania - in the Tisza river valley led to the region's worst environmental catastrophe since the 1986 Chernobyl nuclear disaster. All life along a 40-km stretch of the river was killed, from microbes to fish and plants. The river, which flows into the Danube, contaminated potable water in Yugoslavia, Romania and Hungary. Two smaller acid spills also occurred that year, prompting authorities to take legal action against the Romanian mining company, which went bankrupt almost immediately after the first accident.

[22] In 2000, the National Assembly elected the independent Ferenc Mádl as president, the second democratically elected leader of the country. In 2001, parliament passed a controversial Status Law to authorize Hungarian descendants living in Romania, Ukraine, Croatia and Slovenia to carry a special identity card that would grant them temporary

PROFILE

ENVIRONMENT

The country is a vast plain with a maximum altitude of 1,000 m partially ringed by the Carpathian Mountains. The mountainous region has abundant mineral resources (manganese, bauxite, coal). Between the Danube and its tributary, the Tisza, lies a highly fertile plain, the site of most of the country's farming activity. Cattle are raised on the grasslands east of the Tisza.

SOCIETY

Peoples: Hungarian 92 per cent; and minority groups: Croatian; German; Roma/gypsies; Romanian; Serbian; Slovak and Slovene.
Religions: Roman Catholic 57.8 per cent, Protestant 21.6 per cent; no religion 18.5 per cent; other 1.9 per cent.
Languages: Hungarian (official), 98 per cent; German; Roma; and Slovak.
Main Political Parties: Hungarian Civic Party (Fidesz-MPP); Hungarian Socialist Party (MSzP); Hungarian Workers' Party (MMP); Alliance of Free Democrats (SzDSz); Hungarian Democratic Forum (HDF); Hungarian Truth and Life Party (MIEP).
Main Social Organizations: Autonomous Union Confederation; Democratic Union Confederation; National Confederation of Hungarian Trade Unions; Hungarian Feminist Network.

THE STATE

Official Name: Magyar Koztarsasag (Hungarian Republic).
Administrative Divisions: 19 counties and the capital.
Capital: Budapest 1,708,000 people (2003).
Other Cities: Debrecen 209,600 people; Miskolc 181,900; Szeged 170,600 (2000).
Government: Ferenc Mádl, President since August 2000. Peter Medgyessy, Prime Minister since May 2002. Both are elected by the single-chamber National Assembly (legislature, 386 representatives elected for five-year terms). The Assembly is the supreme authority in the Republic. Eight seats in the Assembly are reserved for each of the country's minorities.
National Holidays: 15 March, Independence Day (1848); 23 October, Declaration of the Hungarian Republic (1989).
Armed Forces: 64,300 (1996). Other: Border Guard, 15,900. Civil Defense Troops, 2,000. Internal Security Troops, 2,500.

work, education, healthcare and travel benefits while they were in Hungary. That year, the Hungarian economy grew 4.2 per cent, with a significant increase in GDP and a steady decline in unemployment, putting it on top of East European countries. In 2001 - the 1,000-year anniversary of Hungary's consolidation as a nation - a monument originally built in 1934 was re-erected to commemorate four major national tragedies: the defeats by the Tatars, Turks and Hapsburgs and the Peace of Trianon, which led to the loss of two-thirds of the territory.

[23] In the 2002 elections - the most hard-fought since the return to democracy - a coalition of Socialists and Liberal Democrats won a majority in parliament, and Peter Medgyessy (a financial expert and former minister of foreign affairs) became prime minister. Former premier Viktor Orbán was criticized by the new government for his decision to sell more than 500,000 hectares of state-owned arable land. Orbán said he had intended to grant land to small farmers before the new government sold the property to large companies. That year,

Medgyessy admitted he had worked as a secret service officer from 1970 to 1982, but denied having collaborated with the KGB. He said his job had been to steer Hungary towards IMF membership without Moscow's knowledge.

[24] In 2003, parliament amended the 2001 Status Law, which neighboring countries had criticized. The coalition government removed several key aspects of the law, including a reference to a 'unified Hungarian nation spanning borders'. Romania and Slovakia, both home to large Hungarian minorities, complained that the law interfered with their sovereignty and discriminated against other ethnic groups. But according to media reports, Hungary amended the law in an attempt to bring it into line with EU guidelines, after the law was criticized by Brussels.

[25] Like the other ten countries which joined the EU on 1 May 2004, Hungary has to solve the issue of the free movement of labor. This issue is highly controversial for the 15 EU current member states, some of which fear a large inflow of 'cheap labor' after EU enlargement. ∎

Iceland / Island

Population:	293,702
Area:	103,000 km²
Capital:	Reykjavik
Currency:	Kronur
Language:	Icelandic

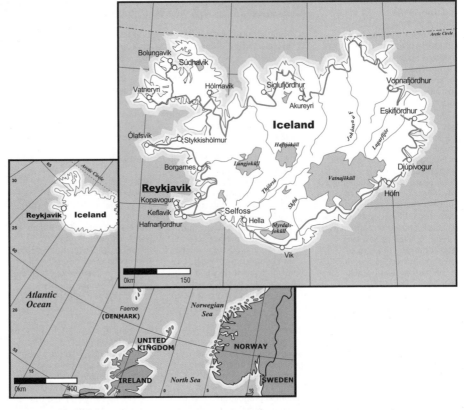

According to accounts written after the territory was discovered in the Viking era, Scandinavian peoples settled in Iceland. The Book of Icelanders (*íslendingabók*) written around 1130 AD places Scandinavian colonization between 870-930 AD. Another source of information from the 12th century, The Book of Settlers (*Landnámabók*), states that the first Scandinavian settler, Ingólfr Arnarson, arrived in Reykjavik in 874 AD. In 930 AD, a constitution was adopted and an assembly *(Althingi)*, the world's first bicameral parliament, was created. Most of Iceland's population is originally of Norwegian, Scottish and Irish descent.

² Iceland was an independent republic until 1262, but under the 'Old Treaty' of 1263 it became part of the kingdom of Norway. In the 14th century Iceland and Norway were conquered by Denmark. Norway separated from the Danish Crown in 1814, but Iceland remained under its dominion. In the late 19th century Iceland had no proper roads or bridges.

³ In 1915 Danish women were allowed to vote and stand for office; for Icelandic women this happened in 1920. In 1918, Iceland became an associate state of Denmark, until it recovered its independence and a republic was proclaimed in June 1944.

⁴ After World War I, agriculture was revitalized through new legislation and the introduction of modern equipment. From 1920 onwards, the fishing industry grew steadily, and communications improved through the building of a network of inland roads.

⁵ In 1949 Iceland joined the Council of Europe and NATO. Since the country had no army or navy, the US provided it with defense forces, within NATO's strategic framework. The island has armed coast guard ships and helicopters to prevent illegal fishing in its territorial waters. In 1952, Iceland, Sweden, Norway, Finland and Denmark founded the Nordic Council in Copenhagen. This was a consultative organization on legislative matters, whose mission was to study and boost Scandinavian regional cooperation.

⁶ Due to the fishing industry's importance for Iceland - it is a major source of employment - and the fear of over-fishing by foreign fleets, Reykjavik extended its territorial waters to 12 nautical miles in 1964, and to 50 miles in 1972. This triggered two serious conflicts known as the 'cod wars' with the United Kingdom. These were settled by a treaty signed in 1973. In 1975, Iceland extended its territorial waters to 200 miles, citing the need to protect the environment and its economic interests. The failure to reach a new agreement led to the third and most serious 'cod war'.

⁷ NATO membership became controversial in the 1970s. The pro-NATO People's Alliance (PA) won the 1978 elections and formed a ruling coalition with the moderate Social Democratic Party (SDP). In 1980, Vigdis Finnbogadottir, an independent candidate opposed to US military bases on the island, won the presidential election with the support of the Left, taking 34 per cent of the vote. She was the country's first female head of state. However the post did not confer on her the power to alter government policy towards NATO membership and the US bases. In 1984 she was re-elected unopposed.

⁸ In 1985, Parliament approved a resolution declaring Iceland a 'nuclear-free zone' thereby barring nuclear weapons from the country. Although Iceland's continuing NATO membership was not actually jeopardized, the air base at Keflavik - a part of the US 'early warning' system - remained controversial. In September 1988, the Icelandic Government announced a moratorium on new military projects.

⁹ That same year, relations between Reykjavik and Washington became tense. The US claimed that Iceland's decision to catch 80 adult and 40 young rorqual whales violated the moratorium imposed by the International Whaling Commission (IWC). Iceland's response was that the whales were captured as part of a scientific program and refused to modify its decision. The US threatened to boycott Icelandic seafood products and two Icelandic whaleboats were sunk by environmental activists in Reykjavik Bay. In 1987, Iceland announced the reduction of its catch to 20 whales. The threats of sanctions continued, and the following year it further reduced the quota.

¹⁰ In 1988, Finnbogadottir was re-elected for a third term, with

WORKERS

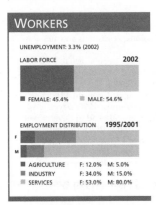

UNEMPLOYMENT: 3.3% (2002)

LABOR FORCE   **2002**

■ FEMALE: 45.4%   ■ MALE: 54.6%

EMPLOYMENT DISTRIBUTION   **1995/2001**

F

M

■ AGRICULTURE	F: 12.0%	M: 5.0%
■ INDUSTRY	F: 34.0%	M: 15.0%
■ SERVICES	F: 53.0%	M: 80.0%

PUBLIC EXPENDITURE

% OF GDP 2000

7.5 % — HEALTH
5.4 % — EDUCATION

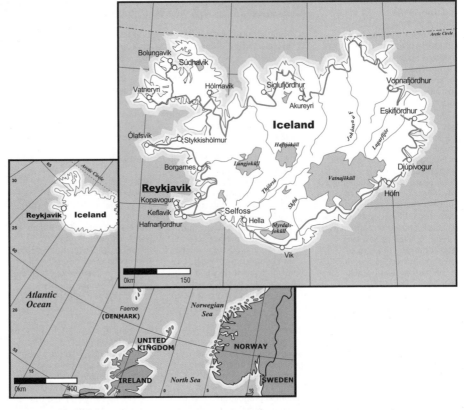

(map labels: Bolungavik, Súdhavik, Hólmavik, Siglufjördhur, Vopnafjördhur, Vatneryri, Akureyri, Eskifjördhur, Ólafsvik, Iceland, Stykkishólmur, Hafsjökull, Langjökull, Djúpivogur, Borgarnes, Vatnajökull, Höfn, Reykjavik, Kopavogur, Keflavik, Selfoss, Hella, Hafnarfjordhun, Myrdals-jökull, Vik, Arctic Circle, 0km 150; Reykjavik, Iceland, Atlantic Ocean, Faeroe (DENMARK), Norwegian Sea, UNITED KINGDOM, NORWAY, IRELAND, North Sea, SWEDEN, 0km 400)

Life expectancy
79.8 years
2000-2005

GNI per capita
$27,970
2002

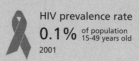
HIV prevalence rate
0.1% of population 15-49 years old
2001

the backing of the main parties and over 90 per cent of the electorate. Steingrimur Hermannsson became Prime Minister, as head of a center-left coalition made up of the SDP and the PA. The new government committed itself to an economic austerity program, designed to curb high inflation and recession. A growth in tourism paved the way for economic recovery.

[11] In 1989, as a result of growing international pressure, including a boycott of Icelandic products organized by Greenpeace, Reykjavik announced a two-year suspension of its whale hunting. The fishing industry went into crisis as certain species, especially cod, suffered from over-fishing. This led to new laws restricting foreign access to territorial waters, causing friction in commercial relations with other countries.

[12] In the 1991 parliamentary elections, Hermannsson's center-left coalition won 32 of the 63 seats in the Althingi. David Oddsson became Prime Minister. Iceland's incorporation into the EU was approved by the Althingi in 1993; that year, laws were passed to protect polar bears which were being exterminated. In 1994 Icelandic fishing boats entered an area of the Barents Sea near Russian and Norwegian territorial waters, giving rise to tension with these two countries, which wanted to allow the fish stocks in the area to recover by reducing catch sizes. In 1993 Iceland left the International Whaling Commission (IWC).

[13] In the April 1995 parliamentary elections, the Independence Party won 25 of the 63 seats and gained a majority in the Althingi in alliance with the Progressive Party, which won 15 seats. The representation of the PA and the Women's Alliance shrank, while the new People's Movement won four seats. The economy enjoyed a slight recovery: GDP grew three per cent and inflation was below two per cent. Unemployment - aggravated by layoffs at the NATO base - rose to five per cent.

[14] After ruling the country for 16 years, Finnbogadottir did not run in the 1996 elections. Olafur Ragnar Grimsson (a former finance minister and member of the PA) won with 41.4 per cent of the vote. That year, fishing quotas were increased after several years of strict limits aimed at preserving the species, fuelling economic growth. GDP grew 5.7 per cent, unemployment fell to four per cent and inflation stood at around three per cent. The

IN FOCUS

ENVIRONMENTAL CHALLENGES
Several aquifers have been polluted by fertilizer runoff. Sewage treatment is not adequate in all cases.

WOMEN'S RIGHTS
Women have been able to vote and stand for election since 1920. From 1995 to 2000, the number of parliamentary seats held by women grew from 25 to 35 per cent, while the proportion of ministerial or equivalent positions fell from 15 to eight per cent. In 2000, women made up 45 per cent of the workforce, with 80 per cent employed in services, 15 per cent in industry and 5 per cent in agriculture. Female unemployment declined from 4.9 per cent of the female labor force in 1995 to 2.6 per cent in 2000; in the same period, male unemployment fell from 4.8 to 1.5 per cent of the male labor force.

CHILDREN
Iceland is a sparsely populated country with low population growth. The fertility rate is low, as is infant mortality. Child welfare is generally good, although more so in urban than rural areas.

INDIGENOUS PEOPLES/ ETHNIC MINORITIES
The population is of Norwegian, Finnish, Scottish and Irish descent. There are no organized indigenous peoples groups or ethnic minorities. However, Iceland forms part of the Arctic Council, which represents the interests of regional indigenous peoples in their respective governments (for example, the Sami in Norway - see that country's *In Focus*)

MIGRANTS/REFUGEES
The country hosted very few refugees and asylum-seekers in late 2000 - no more than 50 people - due to its remote geographic location. Most are from Ukraine, Afghanistan, Romania and Democratic Republic of Congo. Refugees are given special treatment: they are guaranteed lessons in the Icelandic language, receive housing benefits, vocational training, and have the same right to medical and educational services as Icelanders themselves.

DEATH PENALTY
The death penalty was abolished in 1928.

economy continued to grow in 1997 due to expanding domestic consumption, as exports rose only three per cent on the previous year's figures. The bulk of investments were aimed at aluminum production. Several foreign companies - mostly from Switzerland, the US and Norway - intensified exploitation of this mineral resource.

[15] In 1997 Iceland took part in the Kyoto negotiations for reductions in greenhouse gas emissions. Along with Australia and Norway, it was authorized to increase emissions, unlike 'highly polluting' countries such as the US or others from the EU. In 1999 the conservative Independence Party won the Althingi elections with 26 of the 63 seats, followed by the PA (17) made up of feminists, socialists and social democrats, the Liberal Party (12) and the Left-Green Alliance (6).

[16] Four earthquakes shook the southwest of Reykjavik in 2000, causing damage to homes and infrastructure, but no victims. That year, as a member of FATF (Financial Action Task Force on Money-Laundering, the 29-nation group founded in 1989), Iceland launched a review of anti-money laundering measures, which continued through 2001 and 2002.

[17] Despite rejoining the IWC in 2001, Iceland announced it would return to commercial whaling, ignoring the Commission's moratorium. In 2002 the IWC voted by a slight margin to reincorporate Iceland as a full member, since the country planned to restrict the capture of whales for scientific purposes in the near future and to limit commercial whaling after 2006. In the 2003 general elections, Oddsson was re-elected Prime Minister, within the governing coalition. ∎

PROFILE

ENVIRONMENT
Located between the North Atlantic and the Arctic Ocean, Iceland is an enormous plateau with an average altitude of 500 meters. A mountain range crosses the country from east to west passing through an extensive ice-covered region, the source of the main rivers. The coastline falls sharply from the plateau forming fjords. Most of the population lives in the coastal area in the southern and western parts of the country, where ocean currents temper the climate. Reykjavik, the capital and economic center, is located in a fertile plain where the largest cities are found. The northern coast is much colder as a result of Arctic Ocean currents. Geysers and active volcanoes are used as a source of energy. Agricultural output is poor; fishing accounts for 80 per cent of all exports.

SOCIETY
Peoples: 96 per cent of Icelanders are descendants of Norwegian, Scottish and Irish immigrants.
Religions: Protestants (95.8 per cent), mainly evangelical Lutheran (91.5 per cent), who practice the official religion. Catholics (0.9 per cent). No religion (1.5 per cent). Other (1.8 per cent)

Languages: Icelandic.
Main Political Parties: Independence Party (conservative); People's Alliance (socialist); Progressive Party (center-left); Social Democratic Party; Left-Green Alliance.
Main Social Organizations: Icelandic Workers Federation; Confederation of State and Municipal Employees of Iceland.

THE STATE
Official Name: Lydhveldid Island.
Administrative Divisions: 26 districts and 105 municipalities.
Capital: Reykjavik 184,000 people (2003).
Other Cities: Kopavogur 24,400 people; Hafnarfjordhur 19,800 (2000).
Government: Olafur Ragnar Grimsson, President and head of state since August 1996. David Oddsson, prime minister and head of government since April 1991, re-elected in 2003. Unicameral Parliament composed of 63 members, elected by popular vote for a four-year term.
National Holiday: 17 June, Independence Day (1944).
Armed Forces: 120 coastguards (1996). Other: 2,200 NATO troops (1996).

India / Bharat

Population:	1,096,917,184
Area:	3,287,260 km²
Capital:	New Delhi
Currency:	Rupee
Language:	Hindi

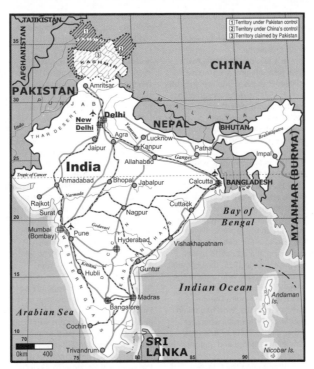

The roots of Indian civilization stretch back to prehistoric times. The earliest human activity in the subcontinent can be traced back to the Early, Middle and Late Stone Ages (400,000-200,000 BC). These peoples were semi-nomadic hunters and gatherers for many millennia. The first evidence of agricultural settlements on the western plains of the Indus is contemporaneous with similar developments in Egypt, Mesopotamia and Persia.

2   The earliest known civilization in India, the starting point in its history, dates back to about 3000 BC. It was a highly developed urban civilization, and two of its towns, Mohenjodaro and Harappa, located in the Indus Valley in present-day Pakistan, represent the high watermark of the settlements. They erected huge temples, engaged in irrigated agriculture and maintained active trade with peoples from the Persian Gulf and Sumeria (Iraq).

3   In the 16th century BC, the Aryans (Indo-Europeans) entered India and subdued the local population. They brought with them horses, iron armor and the Sanskrit language, which is the basis of the majority of Indian languages. Cavalry warfare facilitated the rapid spread of Aryan culture across north India, and allowed the emergence of large empires. The Aryans did not have a written language, but they developed a rich tradition, composing the hymns of the Vedas, the great philosophic poems that are at the heart of Hindu thought. The civilization they created, later called Vedic, was based on a rigid caste system in which the conquerors constituted the dominant nobility.

4   The 6th century BC was a time of social and intellectual ferment in India. It was then that Mahavira Jain and Gautama Buddha started to preach. The two great religions, Jainism and Buddhism, became the cornerstones of the Indian culture. Later, Buddhist monks were to spread their religion to what is now China, Japan, North and South Korea, Sri Lanka and Southeast Asia.

5   By the end of the 3rd century BC, Chandragupta Maurya unified north India and formed the first great Indian empire. Its greatest emperor was Ashoka (286-231 BC).

6   A golden age of Indian culture began with the Gupta empire (c300-500 AD). Art and literature flourished; treatises were written on mathematics, astronomy and medicine. It was during this era that the Kamasutra appeared, the famous work on the art of love.

7   The invasions of the Huns signalled the end of the Gupta empire; north India broke up into a number of separate kingdoms and was not unified again until the arrival of the Muslims.

8   Great rival dynasties that rose in the south were the Cholas, Pandyas and Pallavas; the latter created the baroque-style Dravidian architecture.

9   The Muslim invasions that began in 700 had great impact on Indian culture, including language, dress, architecture and social values. In 1192, Muslim power arrived in India on a permanent basis. The most important Islamic empire was that of the Moghuls, a Central Asian dynasty founded by Babur early in the 16th century. During the reign of Shahjehan, the capital was moved to Delhi and the Taj Mahal was built (around 1650).

10   In 1296 Ala-ud-din Khalji proclaimed himself Sultan of Delhi and by 1311 the whole of India was under the Sultanate. In 1336 the Vijayanagara Empire, the kingdom of Hindu alliance, was founded with its capital at Hampi to counter the Muslim power. Over time uprisings divided the Empire and the Muslim

Sultanates formed a new alliance. In 1565 the Sultanate coalition defeated the Vijayanagar army. As a result, the power in the region passed to Muslim rulers and later their kingdoms were annexed to the Mughal Empire (1529-1857).

11   The arrival of the Europeans marked the next major phase in India's history. In 1687, the British East India Company settled in Bombay and throughout the 18th century, its private army waged war against the French, emerging victorious in 1784. From 1798, Company troops led by Richard Wellesley methodically conquered Indian territory in various campaigns.

12   The British ruled over India through the East India Company. India later became 'the Jewel in the Crown' of the British Empire, giving an enormous boost to the nascent Industrial Revolution by providing cheap raw materials, capital and a large captive market for British industry. The Indian economy was dismantled. Exports of Indian handmade, high-quality cloth were stopped because they impaired the growth of the British textile industry. The ruin of this industry brought widespread impoverishment to the countryside. The land was reorganized under the harsh *Zamindari* (landlord) system to facilitate the collection of taxes to enrich British coffers. Farmers were forced to switch from subsistence farming to commercial crops (indigo, jute, coffee and tea). This resulted in severe famines.

13   By 1820, the English were in control of almost all of India, except for the Punjab, Kashmir and

Peshawar, which were governed by their Sikh ally, Ranjit Singh. After his death in 1849, the British annexed these territories. The 'loyal allies' retained nominal autonomy and were allowed to keep their courts, great palaces and immoderate luxury, much to the satisfaction of European visitors.

14   'Divide and rule' was a motto of British domination. Mercenaries recruited in one region were used to subdue others. Such was the case with Nepalese Gurkhas and Punjabi Sikhs. Religious strife was also fomented; an electoral reform at the beginning of the 20th century stated that Muslims, Hindus and Buddhists could each vote only for candidates of their own faiths. Throughout the colonial period the manipulation led to innumerable social uprisings.

15   The most serious of these were the 1857-1858 rebellions by *sepoys*, Indian soldiers in the British army. These began as a barracks movement, eventually incorporating a range of grievances and growing into a nationwide revolt. Hindus and Muslims joined forces and even proposed the restoration of the ancient Moghul Empire. By the end of the rebellion, the East India Company was dissolved and the country became a British domain ruled by a Viceroy. Queen Victoria was proclaimed Empress of India.

16   The educational system was conceived to train Indians for colonial administration; however, it did not exactly fulfill this purpose. What it did was to create an intellectual élite fully conversant with European culture and thinking. Years later, it was that intelligentsia that formed the Indian National Congress (1885) which included British liberals and, for a long time, limited itself to proposing superficial reforms to improve British administration.

17   When Mohandas K Gandhi, a lawyer educated in England, returned to India in 1915, the independence cause won wide popular support. Gandhi had taken part in the struggle against apartheid in South Africa, where he had developed a technique of non-violent action which he called *satyagraha* (moral domination). He was a devout Hindu and espoused a philosophy of tolerance, brotherhood of all religions and non-violence (*ahimsa*). His ties with the Indian National Congress, where young Jawaharlal Nehru was an activist, strengthened the movement's most radical wing. In 1919, the Amritsar massacre occurred; a demonstration was savagely repressed leaving, according to British sources, 380 dead and 1,200 wounded.

18   Under his leadership, the Congress launched the Non-Cooperation Movement (1920-1922)

Life expectancy
63.9 years
2000-2005

GNI per capita
$480
2002

Literacy
57% total adult rate
2000

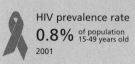
HIV prevalence rate
0.8% of population 15-49 years old
2001

and the Civil Disobedience Movement (1930). One of the most important mass movements was the Salt March, in which Gandhi led a band of followers on a trip to the remote village of Dandi on the west coast to collect salt. This act implied a symbolic violation of British law, which had imposed a monopoly on the collection and selling of the vital mineral.

19   The campaign showed the effectiveness of peaceful civilian opposition. The movement spread nationwide at all levels and included non-participation in elections or administrative bodies, non-attendance at British schools, non-violence, refusal to consume British products, and passive acceptance of the ensuing legal consequences. For the first time, the British saw women flocking to demonstrations. Jails overflowed with prisoners who did not resist arrest, posing an immense problem for the colonial authorities.

20   Gandhi came to be called *Mahatma* (Great Soul) in recognition of his leadership. He became the movement's representative in contacts with the British, who after World War II were left with no option but to negotiate independence. India became independent in August 1947.

21   The Indian Union brought together a great diversity of ethnic, linguistic, and cultural groups, and there was conflict from the start. The massacres that followed were only partially mitigated by Gandhi's hunger strikes, which he continued until his assassination by a fanatical Hindu in 1948. The subcontinent was finally divided into two states: the Indian Union and Pakistan, which was created to concentrate the Muslim population in one area (see Pakistan and Bangladesh). The Sikhs (2 per cent of the population), who had a long list of martyrs in the struggle for independence, also demanded an independent state in the Punjab, which they did not achieve.

22   The division of Pakistan and India led to 562 principalities having to choose which state they would belong to in 1947. The local government in Kashmir - with a largely Muslim population - tried to avoid the question, but an invasion by Pakistani fighters led it to opt for India in return for military aid. After the Indo-Pakistan war in 1948-49, Kashmir was divided into two parts: Azad (Free) Kashmir that remained in Pakistani hands and Jammu and Kashmir state, of Muslim majority, that joined India.

23   After independence, Prime Minister Jawaharlal Nehru, along with Sukarno of Indonesia, Gamal Abdel Nasser of Egypt and Tito of Yugoslavia, advanced the concept of political non-alignment for newly decolonized countries. In India, he

applied development policies based on the notion that the industrialization of society would bring prosperity.

24   In a few decades India made rapid technological progress, which enabled it to place satellites in orbit and, in 1974, to detonate an atom bomb, making India the first nuclear power in the non-aligned movement. However, it did not manage to solve the country's food problems.

25   The Indian economy was severely hit by the oil crisis of the early 1970s, as it was dependent on oil imports. The export-oriented industrial growth was not sufficient to make up for the rising prices of imports and the growing demand for food by a population which was expanding at a rate of 15 million people a year. In 1975, the economic crisis, and popular resistance to the government's mass sterilization campaigns, led Indira Gandhi (Nehru's daughter, who had taken over as prime minister when her father died in 1966) to declare a state of emergency and impose press censorship.

26   Abandoning the Congress Party's traditional populist policies, Indira Gandhi followed World Bank economic guidelines, losing mass support for the government, without winning wholehearted backing from business sectors (particularly those linked to foreign capital), which demanded even greater concessions. The Government was forced to call parliamentary elections in March 1977. The Congress Party was roundly defeated by the Janata Party, a heterogeneous coalition formed by a splinter group of rightwing Congress Party members, the Socialist Party headed by trade union leader George Fernandes, and the Congress for Democracy, led by Jagjivan Ram, a former minister in Indira Gandhi's cabinet.

27   India's foreign policy of non-alignment remained basically unchanged under ageing Prime Minister Morarji Desai, who was unable to fulfill his promises of full employment and economic improvement.

28   Indira Gandhi returned to power in January 1980. Her administration was marked by a growing concentration of power, and accusations of excessive bureaucracy and corruption in the government, which gradually tarnished her image. In the Punjab, the Government faced increasingly strident demands from Sikh separatists. Small groups of militant Sikhs harassed Hindus, to drive them out of the Punjab and create an absolute Sikh majority in the province. After that, the next step would be secession and the formation of independent

'Khalistan'. Indira accused 'forces from abroad' (namely Pakistan and the US) of destabilizing the country.

29   After Indira Gandhi's assassination by militant Sikhs in 1984, thousands of Sikhs fell victim to indiscriminate retaliation by Hindu paramilitary groups. Bypassing party and institutional formalities, Indira's son Rajiv was rapidly promoted to the office of Prime Minister and leader of the Congress Party. In December 1984 a gas explosion at US company Union Carbide factory at Bhopal killed and injured thousands of people.

30   Elections in January 1985 gave Rajiv overwhelming support. Despite the landslide victory, Gandhi lost in Karnataka, Andhra Pradesh and in Sikkim, a Himalayan kingdom annexed to India in the 1970s, where the separatist Sikkim Sangram Parishad party won.

31   The new premier appointed a conciliatory figure as governor of the Punjab, released political prisoners and ordered that militants within his own party who had participated in the anti-Sikh violence should be tried and punished. These measures paved the way for dialogue with Akali Dal, the regional majority party of Sikhs and other dissident groups. The Punjab autonomists proposed that the Indian central government should maintain control over defense and foreign affairs, the emission of currency, mail, highways and telecommunications. Meanwhile, the local government would enjoy greater autonomy than India's other states.

32   In 1987, India intervened in the Sri Lankan conflict. It sent troops to press for a ceasefire agreement between the Tamils and Sinhalese. Three years later, the Indian peacekeeping force was quietly withdrawn after suffering heavy casualties.

33   India's foreign policy remained loyal to non-alignment but a few changes were announced on the domestic front. Rajiv promised the private sector he would lift restrictions on imports and on the purchase of foreign technology.

34   In March 1990, tensions between India and Pakistan mounted as Pakistan increased its support for the Kashmir independence movements. In November, clashes between Hindus and Muslims escalated amidst a general worsening of the economic crisis. Prime Minister Singh was replaced by Chandra Shekhar, also from the Janata Dal.

35   An election campaign during which more than 280 people were killed gave way to parliamentary elections in May 1991. But the elections were adjourned following the assassination of Rajiv Gandhi, who was killed in an attack by a member of the Tamil liberation

movement. A week later, Narasimha Rao was appointed Gandhi's successor as head of the Congress Party. The elections - the most violent in India's history as an independent state - resumed in June. The Congress Party obtained a majority of seats.

36   The new government announced a drastic shift toward liberalism that would change the economic policy in force since independence. Prime Minister Rao opened up India's market to foreign investment, reduced the role of the state, allowed the rupee to float against the dollar, and removed import controls.

37   The process of economic liberalization launched in 1992 has been intensified and has severely damaged the economic, social and cultural rights of the population. The State reduced its role in providing healthcare, education and electricity, and encouraged private companies' participation. The situation is particularly aggravated in the case of water, a resource that was traditionally seen as a public good in a country where two-thirds of the territory is prone to drought.

38   Numerous acts of violence took place in 1992 by Hindu fundamentalists against the Islamic population in the cities of Bombay and Ayodhya. The clashes between communities, prompted by the demolition of Babur's mosque in Ayodhya, left approximately 1,300 dead and extended to neighboring countries such as Pakistan and Bangladesh.

39   Economic reforms triggered protests from several sectors, especially agriculture. Strong resistance was put up to transnational fertilizer and seed companies. As part of the 'green revolution' and capital-intensive agriculture, the World Bank had granted loans for the purchase of genetically engineered seeds while the Government granted subsidies to farmers. Following instructions from the World Bank, the government decided to eliminate those subsidies. The Farmers' Association of the State of Karnataka (KKRS) - with a membership of 10 million farmers - headed rural protests which were responsible for a number of direct attacks against representatives of transnational corporations since 1991.

40   At the International Conference on Rights of Third World Farmers held in Bangalore in October 1993, farmers declared that the 'seeds, plants, biological material and wealth of the Third World form part of the Collective Intellectual Property of the peoples of the Third World'. They pledged to develop these rights in the face of the private patenting system which encourages the spread of monoculture and threatens biodiversity.

Under-5 mortality
93 per 1,000 live births
2002

Poverty
34.7% of population living on less than $1 per day
1999/00

Debt service
11.8% exports of goods and services
2001

Maternal mortality
540 per 100,000 live births
2000

41 In 1994, India signed two agreements with China to reduce the number of troops stationed along the 4,000 km of common borders and to encourage trade relations. When former Pakistani Prime Minister Nawaz Sharif claimed his country had nuclear weapons, relations between New Delhi and Islamabad were strained. Pakistan closed its consulate in Bombay.

42 During 1995, Prime Minister Narasimha Rao changed his cabinet three times. Elections in several states revealed an increasingly weakened Congress Party. Economic stability and assistance schemes announced by Rao, which included a school dinners plan for 110 million children and the construction of 10 million rural homes, were not enough to stop his popularity from plummeting. Rao resigned in May 1996, following his party's defeat in the general elections.

43 The BJP (Bharatiya Janata Party, Hindu nationalist) did not win a large enough majority in parliament to allow it to govern. A new political crisis brought about the appointment and resignation of two other prime ministers (Atal Bihari Vajpayee, HD Deve Gowda). Nearly a month after the fall of Gowda, Inder Kumar Gujral, also of the United Front, was appointed prime minister. In July, KR Narayanan was elected president.

44 In November, Gujral was forced to resign when an official commission revealed alleged links between a governing coalition party, the Dravida Munnetra Kazagham (DMK), and Sri Lanka's Tamil guerrillas, a group involved in the murder of former Prime Minister Rajiv Gandhi.

45 The BJP triumphed in the February 1998 parliamentary elections and Atal Bihari Vajpayee was designated prime minister. In May, a series of nuclear tests in India heightened tensions with Pakistan, and gave the neighboring country the pretext to carry out similar tests that same month.

46 A bill to reserve one third of parliamentary seats for women was boycotted in parliament throughout the month of July. The bill's opponents, led by two socialist parties, protested outside parliament, interrupting proceedings. According to them, the proposal was unacceptable because it did not include quotas for women from the lower castes. The bill's principal defenders were the ruling party and the major opposition force, the Indian National Congress Party, in agreement for the first time.

47 The government coalition collapsed in April 1999. The Tamil AIA-DMK party forced two of its ministers to resign after Prime Minister Vajpayee rejected AIA-DMK demands that Defense Minister

IN FOCUS

ENVIRONMENTAL CHALLENGES
The use of fertilizers and pesticides introduced with the Green Revolution has produced lower soil fertility and yields, while the selection of high-yielding seeds has resulted in the disappearance of traditional crop varieties.

Extensive hunting by the British and Indian rajahs, large-scale clearing of forests for agriculture, poaching, potent pesticides and the ever-increasing population have had a devastating effect on the environment in India. The entire country suffers from a shortage of clean drinking water.

WOMEN'S RIGHTS
Women have been able to vote and stand for office since 1950. Between 1995 and 2000, the share of parliamentary seats held by women increased from seven to nine per cent. In 2000, women made up 32 per cent of the total labor force.

Between 1995 and 2001, 60 per cent of pregnant women received prenatal care and 43 per cent of births were attended by skilled health staff.

In 2000, 88 per cent of pregnant women and 50 per cent of non-pregnant women were anemic.

The percentage of women who could read and write stood at 61 per cent, compared to that of men. Sixty-five per cent of Indian women had completed 5 years of schooling and for every 1,000 women between the ages of 15 and 19, 104 children were born.

In 2000, nearly 3.97 million adults were living with HIV/AIDS. According to UNAIDS with the current disease burden, HIV will emerge as the largest cause of

adult mortality in India this decade, together with an additional 1 million TB cases.

CHILDREN
In 2001, India was the second most populous country in the world, with over 1 billion people. Of the 400 million children under 18, about a quarter were under five years old.

In 2000, 26 per cent of the population was living below the poverty line. Between 1991 and 2001, social gains were achieved as a result of economic development policies. For instance, India's literacy rate rose from 52 to 65 per cent, school attendance rates among children between the ages of six and 14 reached 79 per cent in 1999, and some 83 per cent of households had access to drinking water. India was certified free of Dracunculiasis (guineaworm disease); polio immunization efforts were stepped up; and rapid changes in the world of information technology contributed to the promotion of child rights.

India faces the challenge of reducing infant and maternal mortality rates and increasing immunization coverage for common childhood diseases.

Just below 50 per cent of children under three were malnourished; and only half of all households were using iodized salt. Only 37 per cent of households used adequate toilets, in urban areas, and 19 per cent in rural areas.

INDIGENOUS PEOPLES/ETHNIC MINORITIES
There are around 500 groups of indigenous peoples or *adivasis* including the Kanikar, Muthuvan, Urali and Mala Arayan who have born the brunt of caste oppression. There are also non-*adivasi* minorities such as Kashmiris and

Sikhs, who are involved in disputes particularly over territory on the borders with Pakistan. Muslims are another minority, some emphasizing their religious differences to distinguish themselves from the Hindu majority.

MIGRANTS/REFUGEES
India is not a party to the UN Refugee Convention and does not have national legislation regarding refugees. However, UNHCR is allowed to have an office in the capital. At the end of 2002, nearly 330,000 refugees were living in India, including citizens from Sri Lanka and Burma/Myanmar, as well as Tibetans, Chinese, Bhutanese, Afghans, Bangladeshis and Nepalese. That year, the number of Afghan refugees living in India increased to 40,000. India provided residential permits to many Afghans and citizens from Burma/Myanmar, renewable annually, although the permits do not allow them to work legally or have access to public benefits. In November 2003, Human Rights Watch denounced police abuses during a demonstration by Burmese refugees whose status had been recognized by UNHCR.

Some 600,000 Indians were internally displaced and nearly 17,000 Kashmiris from the Indian-controlled area of Kashmir remained in Pakistan at year's end.

During 2002, 18,000 people from India sought asylum in other countries.

DEATH PENALTY
India is among the countries in which the death penalty is still applied to common crimes.

George Fernandes be removed from office and investigated for having sacked India's Navy Commander, Admiral Vishnu Bhagwat.

48 New confrontations with Pakistan erupted in June after Pakistani forces crossed the border delineated by the UN. Some 1,000 people died in the conflicts. The international organization Human Rights Watch reported serious violations on either side of the border, attributed to officials and agents from both governments. India's security forces were accused of carrying out summary executions, rape and torture.

49 In October 1999, after five electoral rounds, the BJP once again led the administration. Despite the

coalition's victory, this election also marked a BJP decline that benefited leftist and regional parties. More than half of parliamentary seats remained outside the control of the two largest national parties (the BJP and the Congress Party, which suffered the worst defeat in its history).

50 More than a million people were left homeless in an earthquake in Gujarat State in western India in February 2001. At least 30,000 were killed and 55,000 injured in a region that had been devastated by a cyclone in 1998.

51 The battle for control of world food supplies gave a legal victory to the less well-off in a ruling on rights over Basmati rice - which had been

produced on the Indian subcontinent for centuries. The 'rice battle' broke out in 1997, when RiceTech in the US patented 'Kasmati,' a type of Basmati rice, and ended in May 2001 when the US Patent Office rejected RiceTech's application. A ruling the other way would have meant an end to Indian rice exports to the US, and would have forced Asian farmers to pay intellectual property rights on one of their traditional crops.

52 In 2001, a report on AIDS funded by UNICEF but drawn up by the Human Rights Commission of Madhya Pradesh was criticized for suggesting that prostitution is a way of life for the Bedia caste. The view was rejected by non-governmental organizations (NGOs), UNICEF and

Malnutrition
47% under-5s
1995-2002

Water source
84% of population using improved drinking water sources
2000

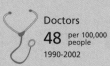
Doctors
48 per 100,000 people
1990-2002

the Bedia community, who demanded that the report be withdrawn on grounds that it promoted caste discrimination. Brinda Karat, of the Joint Action Council and All India Democratic Women's Association (AIDWA), pointed out that 'the very concept of a caste-based survey is repugnant to human rights and democratic thinking as it is premised on a belief that there is something intrinsic to the caste which makes women prostitutes and men pimps'. A year earlier, the founders of the NGO Sahyog, Abhijeet and Yashodhara Das barely escaped lynching in the Himalayan area of Almora for producing a leaflet entitled 'AIDS and Us,' which indicated that incest was widespread in the region. India is, after South Africa, the country with the greatest number of people living with HIV/AIDS.

[53] In July 2001, Vajpayee met Pakistani President Pervez Musharraf in the first summit between the neighboring countries in more than two years. The meeting ended with no resolution to the situation in Kashmir. Chancellor Singh accused Pakistan of standing in the way of an agreement by making the Kashmir issue the main subject of the talks instead of advancing on other bilateral issues. Meanwhile, the Pakistani delegation responded that the main problem was that Indian officials insisted on changing the text of an agreement already approved by the rulers of both countries.

[54] In September, in the wake of the attacks on New York and Washington, the US lifted sanctions it had imposed on India and Pakistan following the nuclear tests staged by the two nations three years previously. This was a 'reward' for the support they offered Washington in its global war on terrorism.

[55] In October 2001, Kashmir was once more the center of conflict when Indian troops fired on Pakistani military posts. Suicide squads attacked parliament in New Delhi, killing several police officers. Both countries made widescale deployments of troops on the frontier, fearing a new war. In early 2002, India ran successful trials of the Agni, a missile with nuclear capacity.

[56] In February 2002, a wave of violence against the Muslim community spread in Gujarat state. More than 2,000 people were killed and women were specially targeted. They were gang-raped before being burned alive. Rebels burned and looted shops, homes, and mosques. Some 15,000 Muslims were driven from their homes. According to the report issued by Amnesty International, the government of Gujarat and the state police took insufficient action to protect civilians, instead colluding with the attackers.

Twenty-one suspects accused of the murder of 14 people burned to death in Baroda were acquitted. After the trial, several witnesses said they lied in court because they had received death threats. The National Human Rights Commission carried out a new investigation and asked the Supreme Court to provide witness protection and to ensure a retrial outside Gujarat to guarantee fair proceedings. In January 2003, the Gujarat government, which had turned a blind eye to the massacre, easily won the elections.

[57] In June 2002, although Defense Minister George Fernandes said Indian troops would remain along the border with Pakistan as long as necessary, there was a marked drop in incursions in Kashmir due to intervention by the US, Russia and other countries.

[58] The new National Water Policy adopted in 2002 laid great emphasis on encouraging private participation in the sector. The Radius Water Limited corporation was granted a concession over the Sheonath river (Durg district), the local population's main source of water for irrigation, fishing, bathing and drinking. The company has forbidden fishing and drawing water for irrigation purposes and has also put in place a system for selling water to villagers.

[59] Most political parties - including the Congress Party and the government coalition - backed the candidacy of Abdul Kalam for president. Kalam is a key researcher in the program that turned India into a nuclear power. On taking office in July, Kalam - who is known as 'the missile man' - became the third Muslim president of the country.

[60] The provisional outcome of the last official census, published in March 2003, showed an increase of 180 million people during the last decade, even if the growth rate had diminished slightly. It is estimated that India will become the world's most populous country within the next 50 years. Two of every three Indians can now read and write, and the number of illiterate people has fallen for the first time since independence.

[61] In 2003, some 29 people were estimated to have been executed (the Government does not release these figures). In March, the promulgation of POTA (Prevention of Terrorism Act) extended capital punishment to acts of 'terrorism' that lead to a person's death. In November, parliament and the central government stated that they favored the extension of the death penalty to the crime of rape.

[62] In January 2004, the Fourth World Social Forum was held in Mumbai (formerly Bombay). Over 15,000 people took part in the event. Many focused on India's realities, such as the caste system in place for

2,000 years. It effectively deprives 240 million people of their rights. Although the term 'untouchable' was abolished in 1950 and replaced by the term *Dalits* (oppressed), their situation remains virtually unchanged. Only seven per cent have access to safe drinking water, electricity and toilets. And a majority of the estimated 40 million bonded laborers (who work virtually as slaves to pay off debts), including 15 million children, are Dalits. They are denied access to land, are forced to work in degrading conditions, and are routinely abused by the police and upper-caste groups, which enjoy the state's protection.

[63] Women also face heavy discrimination, which starts before birth. In 2000, in 27 Indian states,

women from poor families - unable to pay a dowry - underwent abortions of female fetuses. In Bihar and Rajasthan there were only 60 girls for every 100 boys, while the normal ratio would be 100 girls for every 103 boys. Girls and women belonging to the lower castes are often beaten and subjected to degrading treatment in public.

[64] Manmohan Singh, a Sikh, became India's first non-Hindu prime minister in May 2004. Singh, an economist, became premier after Congress leader Sonia Gandhi - Rajiv's widow - refused to accept the post, despite winning the election. Gandhi expressed to the Cabinet that her 'inner voice' revealed that she did not want to become Premier. ■

ENVIRONMENT

The nation is divided into three major geographic regions: the Himalayan mountains, along the northern border; the fertile, densely populated Ganges plain immediately to the south, and the Deccan plateau in the center and south. The Himalayas shelter the country from the cold north winds. The climate is subject to the influence of the monsoons; hot and dry for eight months of the year, and heavy rains from June to September. Rice cultivation is widespread. Coal and iron ore are the main mineral resources. There is a long-standing territorial dispute with Pakistan over Kashmir in the northwest, where important oil deposits are found.

SOCIETY

Peoples: The population of India is a multitude of racial, cultural and ethnic groups. Most are descendants of the Aryan peoples who developed the Vedic civilization. The north still bears the influence of invasions by the Arabs (between the 7th and 13th centuries) and Mongols (12th century). Peoples of Dravidian origin still predominate on the Deccan plateau in the center and south of India.
Religions: 83 per cent Hindu, 11 per cent Muslim, 2.5 per cent Sikh, 2 per cent Christian, 1 per cent Buddhist and 0.5 per cent other.
Languages: 400 registered languages, of which 18 are officially recognized, including Hindi, Bengali, Tamil or Urdu. English is a lingua franca, widely used for administrative purposes. There are 16 official regional languages and an infinity of local variants.
Main Political Parties: The Indian National Congress (INC), founded in 1885, fought for independence from Britain under the leadership of Mahatma Gandhi; the Bharatiya Janata Party (BJP) is a rightwing nationalist party with roots in the militant Rashtriya Swayam Sevak Sangh (RSS); the Communist Party of India-Marxist (CPI-M).
Main Social Organizations: INTUC (Indian National Trade Union Congress); the Bharatiya Mazdoor Sangh; Foundation of Investigation in Science, Technology and Policies of Natural Resources, Chipko Movement, an eco-feminist movement that fights to protect the country's forests. Separatist movements in Kashmir, Punjab and Assam, and the Tamils who support the Tamil Tigers (see Sri Lanka); the All-India Trade Union Congress (AITUC).

THE STATE

Official name: Bharat (Hindi). **Administrative Divisions:** 25 states and 7 union territories. **Capital:** New Delhi 14,146,000 people (2003).
Other Cities: Greater Mumbai (Bombay) 18.1 million; Kolkata (Calcutta) 12.9 million; Hyderabad 6.3 million; Bangalore 6.2 million (2000). **Government:** Federal Republic. Abdul Kalam, president since July 2002. Manmohan Singh, prime minister since May 2004. Bicameral Parliament: Upper House (250 members) and Lower House (545 members). **National Holidays:** 15 August, Independence Day (1947); 26 January, Day of the Republic (1950).
Armed Forces: 1,145,000 troops (1996). Other: 1,421,800: Army, Navy (including naval air force), Air Force, various security or paramilitary forces (Border Security Force, Assam Rifles, Rashtriya Rifles, and National Security Guards).

Indonesia / Indonesia

Population:	225,313,459
Area:	1,904,570 km²
Capital:	Jakarta
Currency:	Rupiah
Language:	Bahasa Indonesia

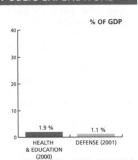

Indonesia has some of the world's earliest *Homo Sapiens* remains. The ancestors of the present-day population were Malay immigrants who arrived on the islands of Java and Sumatra around 400 BC. They brought with them the cultural and religious influences of India. Indonesian civilization reached its height in the 15th century when the kingdom of Majapahit extended far east - beyond Java, Bali, Sumatra, and Borneo - becoming commercially and culturally linked with China.

2   At the end of the 13th century Islam was introduced in the archipelago. It was not imposed through Arab conversion campaigns, but was freely adopted because it represented a simple, egalitarian faith suited to local conditions. When Muslim traders sent Indonesian spices to Europe, the Europeans' interest was aroused, and they set their colonial sights on the region.

3   In 1511, the Portuguese arrived in Melaka; in 1521, the Spanish reached the Moluccas and in 1595, private Dutch merchants organized their first expedition. The Netherlands had just won its independence from Spain and wanted to secure its own supply of spices. In 1602, various Dutch trading groups founded the Dutch East India Company, obtaining a trade monopoly, with a colonial

mandate from the Governor of the region.

4   During the 17th and 18th centuries, Indonesia was fought over by Spain, Portugal, the Netherlands and Britain, the latter creating another private company. Cash crops, coffee and sugar were introduced, yielding excellent profits but seriously upsetting the local socio-economic organization - intact until then - with the subsequent outbreak of anti-colonial revolts. Toward the end of the 19th century, rubber, palm oil and tin became the main export products, though industry only began to develop during World War II, when the Netherlands was unable to meet its production needs at home.

5   In December 1916, nationalist pressure caused the formation of the People's Council or *Volksraad*, a body designed to defend the rights of the local population. Although its proposals were largely ignored, the Council encouraged political participation among the local population.

6   In 1939, eight nationalist organizations formed a coalition called the GAPI - Gabungan Politik Indonesia - demanding democracy, autonomy and national unity within the framework of the anti-Fascist struggle. GAPI adopted the red and white flag and *Bahasa*

Indonesia as the national language.

7   After the outbreak of World War II, the Netherlands were invaded by Germany, and Indonesia by Japan in 1942. The Japanese, who claimed to be the Asiatic brothers of the Indonesians, freed nationalist leaders like Sukarno and Muhammad Hatta who had been imprisoned under Dutch rule. On 11 August 1945 (four days prior to the Japanese surrender) they invested Sukarno and Hatta with full powers to establish a local government.

8   Indonesia proclaimed its independence on 17 August and its intention to be a united, sovereign, just and prosperous republic. The Dutch tried to recover the archipelago, forcing the Indonesians to fight back. The Arab and Indian communities actively supported the pro-independence guerrillas, while Britain backed the Netherlands. The US pressed for a negotiated settlement.

9   Unable to recover military control, the Netherlands accepted a partial transfer of sovereignty in 1949 under a Dutch-Indonesian confederation.

10   In 1954, the Dutch-Indonesian Union, which was never fully implemented, was denounced by the Sukarno Government and the archipelago became fully independent. Sukarno's government soon began its own colonial policies in the region. In 1963, reacting to The Hague's refusal to withdraw from the island of New Guinea, Indonesia occupied West Irian, the former Dutch colony whose territory took up half of the island. The Indonesian independence process, together with the Indian and Pakistani independence, the Cuban Revolution, the nationalization of the Suez Canal, and the French defeats in Vietnam and Algeria, heralded the arrival of the Third World onto the international political scene. Sukarno was one of the main leaders of the movement

for Third World solidarity and in 1955 the Indonesian city of Bandung played host to the first meeting of the main Third World leaders.

11   The Communist Party - which, with three million members, was the second most powerful in Asia after the Chinese - supported Sukarno. He launched nationalist development programs, aimed at raising the living standards of a population with one of the world's lowest per capita incomes. Petroleum provided a strong foundation on which to base economic development; Sukarno created a state petroleum company, PERTAMINA, to break the domination of the Anglo-Dutch transnational, Royal Dutch Shell.

12   In 1965, Indonesian oil deposits were nationalized. In October of that year, a small force of soldiers led by General Suharto seized power under the pretext of stemming the communist penetration. This bloody coup left nearly 700,000 dead, and some 200,000 political activists were imprisoned.

13   Though deprived of any real power, Sukarno remained the nominal president until 1967 - he died in 1970 - when Suharto was officially named Head of State. Suharto opened the doors to foreign oil companies seeking drilling rights. But with the rise in oil prices, the influx of capital, and a liberal economic policy, not only did national income rise; the gap between high and low incomes also widened. Many of the millions of rural dwellers had to leave their lands, enlarging the shantytowns in the large cities.

14   In 1971, defying repression, students took to the streets in protest at the alliance between corrupt generals, Chinese merchants, and Japanese investors. In an attempt to neutralize local dissent under the flag of national unity, in 1975 Suharto invaded East Timor, shortly after its independence from Portugal.

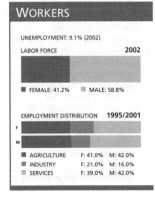

WORKERS

UNEMPLOYMENT: 9.1% (2002)

LABOR FORCE   **2002**

■ FEMALE: 41.2%   ■ MALE: 58.8%

EMPLOYMENT DISTRIBUTION   **1995/2001**

F
M

■ AGRICULTURE   F: 41.0%   M: 42.0%
■ INDUSTRY   F: 21.0%   M: 16.0%
■ SERVICES   F: 39.0%   M: 42.0%

PUBLIC EXPENDITURE

% OF GDP

40

30

20

10

0

1.9 %   1.1 %

HEALTH   DEFENSE (2001)
& EDUCATION
(2000)

| | Life expectancy | | GNI per capita | | Literacy | | HIV prevalence rate |
| | **66.8** years 2000-2005 | | **$710** 2002 | | **87%** total adult rate 2000 | | **0.1%** of population 15-49 years old 2001 |

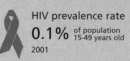

IN FOCUS

ENVIRONMENTAL CHALLENGES
Deforestation caused by the expansion of the paper industry and timber exports affects certain groups such as the indigenous peoples in West Papua (Irian Jaya). There are significant air and water pollution problems, especially in urban areas.

WOMEN'S RIGHTS
Women have been able to vote and run for office since 1945. Between 1995 and 2000 female representation decreased from 13 to 11 per cent and in ministerial posts from 6 to 3 per cent.

In 2000 women comprised 41 per cent of the workforce (42 per cent worked in agriculture, 16 per cent in industry, and 42 per cent in services).

89 per cent of pregnant women received prenatal care (1997*), but only 64 per cent of the births were assisted by trained personnel (1999*).

CHILDREN
Access to social services and housing is jeopardized by the demands of a population growing at an estimated 3 million per annum. The economic crisis and violence in the archipelago caused a mass displacement of people, estimated in 2001 at 1,400,000 women and children.

8.5 per cent (1997*) of the children were born underweight and only 42 per cent of children under 6 months old were solely breastfed. 26 per cent (1999*) of under-5s were underweight.

Child-trafficking, the sexual and labor exploitation of children - the latter even within the family - and the large number of children living on the streets, are the main concerns of child-welfare organizations.

INDIGENOUS PEOPLES/ ETHNIC MINORITIES
The Acehnese, the Chinese and the West Papuans (1.7 per cent, 4 per cent and 0.5 per cent of the population, respectively) are the groups facing the greatest risks. The Acehnese, orthodox Muslims, bear the brunt of the Government's political, economic and religious repression. They have been seeking independence for Aceh province since 1976. Even though Jakarta and the GAM - the group leading the pro-independence movement - signed a peace treaty in 2000, the munber of Acehnese suffering discrimination had not diminished. In 2003 the Government put the province under martial law.

The Chinese and their descendants, mainly Christians, have traditionally enjoyed high economic status. Despite this they have faced political, social and cultural discrimination and repression. Their mother tongue has been outlawed for everyday use and in school since 1966. In 2002 over 20 laws, as well as numerous local and military regulations, were clear examples of discrimination.

Conflict between West Papuans and the Government have been escalating since Indonesia took control in the late 1960s. Between 10,000 and 30,000 Papuans have been killed. Political

abuse and economic repression have been systematic since the occupation. At the beginning of this century, Papuans were still not allowed to form groups or make political statements, and were executed, tortured and abused by the military and the police.

MIGRANTS/REFUGEES
Toward the end of 2002 there were almost 1,000,000 internally displaced people (IDP) in the country. Four provinces - Maluku, Sulawesi, East Java and North Sumatra - accommodated 100,000 IDP each. Another five - North Maluku, North Sulawesi, Aceh, West Kalimantan and Central Sulawesi - accommodated at least 10,000 each. Thousands more were located in other parts of the archipelago. The Government increasingly withdrew its aid to the IDP in certain areas.

In 2002 Indonesia accommodated 29,000 refugees, many from East Timor (Timor-Leste); 500 refugees recognized by UNHCR and another 200 people seeking asylum.

Almost 11,500 Indonesians were refugees or seeking asylum in other countries at the end of 2002.

DEATH PENALTY
Indonesia is one of the countries where the death penalty is still enforced for ordinary crimes.

* Latest data available in The State of the World's Children and Childinfo database, UNICEF, 2004.

time the US granted $2,300,000 for the training of the security forces of Indonesia.

[20] In March 1993 the People's Consultative Assembly chose Suharto - who had also been elected in 1988 - as President for the sixth time.

[21] In 1996 the pre-election debates reached a new low when complaints about the illegal enrichment of the Suharto family and its circle grew. The military saw Islamic groups as well as Sukarno's daughter Megawati Sukarnoputri as the main threats to Suharto's power.

[22] In early 1997, the Indonesian population reached 200 million. The Government announced it would continue its program to transfer the people from over-populated regions to less populated areas.

[23] The ruling Golkar party won the May 1997 parliamentary elections, obtaining 74 per cent of the vote (325 out of 400 seats). The new Parliament included 12 of President Suharto's relatives - six children, two wives, two brothers-in-law, one brother and a cousin - as well as many of the leader's trade partners or cronies. In March 1998, Parliament re-elected Suharto.

[24] A severe stock market crisis increased inflation and caused a risk of hyperinflation. The currency had lost 50 per cent of its value since mid-1997. The price rise affected mostly basic goods and the economic situation deteriorated. Two million workers lost their jobs between October 1997 and March 1998. Following widespread social unrest and severe repression - there were hundreds of dead - Suharto stepped down in May 1998 to be succeeded by Bacharuddin Jusuf Habibie.

[25] In October, violent student protests to demand democracy and the removal of army chief Wiranto overwhelmed the capital. Five students were killed in confrontations with anti-insurrection forces. Also that month, two civilians died during armed conflicts between separatist rebels and police in Aceh province where the army had been accused of committing all kinds of abuses.

[26] Inter-ethnic fighting intensified in Kalimantan, between the Malay, Bugi, Dayak and Chinese on one side and Maduran immigrants on the other, leading to the death of around 70 people in March 1999. In Jakarta the following month, hundreds of Muslims set fire to a community center in retaliation for an explosion at a mosque in Ujung Pandang, the largest in Southeast Asia.

[27] October elections gave the presidency to Abdurraman Wahid,

However, the people of Timor did not see the Indonesians as liberators but as new colonists. The unyielding resistance on the island only deepened Indonesia's internal problems.

[15] In the elections of May 1977, discontent surfaced once again. Despite repression, the banning of leftist parties and press censorship, the official Golongan Karya (Golkar) Party lost in Jakarta to a Muslim coalition which had campaigned against the rampant corruption. The governing party also lost ground in rural areas.

[16] To ensure victory in the election five years later, the regime clamped down on political activity and returned to an electoral system dependent on the Ministry of Home Affairs. In March 1983, in spite of growing opposition, the

People's Consultative Assembly unanimously re-elected Suharto for a fourth 5-year presidential term.

[17] Indonesia adopted a birth control policy that led to a reduction in the population growth rate: while in 1984 it amounted to 2.3 per cent, the average rate between 1980 and 1990 was 1.8 per cent. Even so, demographic pressure, particularly on the island of Java, together with the radical reorientation of the country's economy toward the world market, as well as rapid industrialization, have all led to a deterioration in the quality of the environment and the depletion of agricultural lands. From 1979, the Government reacted to this situation with a population transfer project known as Transmigrasi, which involved

moving 2.5 million Javanese to other less populated islands.

[18] In the 1980s over 300 ethnic groups saw their standards of living drop sharply. The most energetic protests were those of the inhabitants of West Papua (Irian Jaya) who demanded self-determination and freedom of movement to and from the neighboring territory of Papua New Guinea, with which they had a high degree of cultural and historical affinity.

[19] In 1991 the fighting between the army and the Aceh liberation movements in Sumatra became more acute when the Commander of the army called for the annihilation of the insurgents. In March 1992, an armed offensive of several separatist groups was started in West Papua. At the same

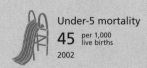 Under-5 mortality
45 per 1,000 live births
2002

 Poverty
7.2% of population living on less than $1 per day
2000

 Debt service
23.6% exports of goods and services
2001

 Maternal mortality
230 per 100,000 live births
2000

who until that time had been leader of the Nahdlatul Ulama Muslim organization. One of Wahid's first acts as President was to offer Aceh broad autonomy and an increase in economic support if the province were to remain a part of Indonesia. He set a seven-month deadline to carry out a referendum, similar to the one held in August 1999 in East Timor (see East Timor). The plan to retain Aceh established that 75 per cent of all income produced there would remain in the province, one of the country's richest regions in natural resources.

[28] In spite of his public promise to eradicate corruption, Wahid immediately was implicated in financial scandals, which in August 2000 led Parliament to launch an unprecedented investigation. The first scandal emerged in May, when it was found that the President's personal masseur had obtained $4.1 million from the national food agency. The second entailed a personal donation to Wahid of $2 million from the Sultan of Brunei that the president failed to make public. In both cases - which the media dubbed Buloggate and Bruneigate - the money was to have been used for humanitarian programs in Aceh, where the separatist rebellion continued. Parliament moved to try Wahid and remove him from office, but abandoned the attempt in February 2001, after thousands of people took to the streets in support of the President and demanding that the opposition Golkar party be dismantled.

[29] In Kalimantan, the following month, combatants of the Dayak peoples took over parts of the province in the worst outbreak of violence in the region since 1997. Within one week, at least 1,000 Madurese refugees were killed and tens of thousands were forced from their homes.

[30] In May, the Parliament - the country's sole legislative body - voted 365 to 4 to begin impeachment proceedings against Wahid, who refused to resign and declared a state of emergency, which was not heeded by the police or the army.

[31] Nearly two years after taking office, and after the Supreme Court ruled the decreed state of emergency unconstitutional, a vote by the MPR (Consultative Assembly) of 591 members present (over a total of 700) removed Wahid in July 2001. Vice-President Megawati Sukarnoputri, Sukarno's daughter, assumed the presidency.

[32] In August, the President issued an apology to the provinces of Aceh and West Papua - which Jakarta had exploited over decades for their natural resources: petroleum and natural gas in Aceh, minerals in West Papua; however, she asserted that these provinces would never be allowed to secede as East Timor had done two years earlier.

[33] In January 2002, Jakarta inaugurated the Human Rights Court to try the army for the atrocities committed in East Timor. Three generals, including the commander at the time of the massacres, Adam Damiri, appeared before the tribunal which, according to its creators, 'is better than an International Court'. East Timor assumed its complete independence in May.

[34] In March, Tommy Suharto, son of the former president, was accused of assassinating a Supreme Court judge who had sentenced him to prison on corruption charges as a tough test of the country's legal and judicial system, still considered vulnerable to corruption.

[35] Over 200 people, most of them tourists, died in October as a result of a bomb attack on a night club in Bali. That same day another bomb exploded near the US Consulate in Sanur, but this time there were no victims. The Jemaah Islamiya (JI) group, allegedly the local branch of the Islamist network al-Qaeda was blamed for the attacks. The Government provided the police with powers to prosecute alleged terrorists. Abu Bakar Ba'asyir, the spiritual leader of the JI, was arrested that same month, accused of having ordered the church bombings and of plotting the assassination of President Sukarnoputri. This led to confrontations between Bakar Ba'asyir's followers and the police.

[36] In December 2002 the Jakarta Government and the separatist Aceh Liberation Movement (GAM) signed a peace treaty in Geneva attempting to put an end to 26 years of violence. In May 2003 the negotiations failed, the Government launched a military attack against rebels and put the province under martial law.

[37] In August 2003 an explosion in front of a hotel in Jakarta killed 14 people. Jemaah Islamiya was blamed for the attack.

[38] In September two members of JI were sentenced to death for the Bali attack. Abu Bakar Ba'asyir was sentenced to 5 years in prison for other crimes; his links to the attacks were not proven, which led many to question Indonesia's commitment to the fight against terrorism. JI came into being in 1970 when Suharto requested Islamic extremists' assistance to fight the 'communist threat'.

[39] In October 2003 the IMF authorized a new loan for Indonesia, after praising its handling of the economy. Months before, the country had announced it would end its association with the organization, since many in Government and the general population objected to its insistence on opening the local market to foreign competition.

[40] In December, Human Rights Watch published a report accusing Indonesia of civil abuse - extrajudicial murders, violent arrests and attacks - in its campaign against the GAM in Aceh. It also denounced a governmental 'veil of silence', since journalists are not allowed access to the area. A week later three soldiers were sentenced to 20 months in prison for beating peasants in an attack on a village.

[41] In September 2004 a car bomb exploded outside the Australian embassy in Jakarta, killing 9 and injuring 180, Jemaah Islamiya was thought to be responsible.

[42] Also in September, the country's first direct presidential election produced a landslide victory for retired general Susilo Bambang Yudhoyono. ∎

PROFILE

ENVIRONMENT

Indonesia is the largest archipelago-state in the world, made up of approximately 13,700 islands. The most important are Borneo (Kalimantan), Sumatra, Java, Celebes, Bali, the Moluccas, West Papua and Timor. Lying either side of the equator, the island group has a tropical, rainy climate and dense rainforest vegetation. The population, the fourth largest in the world, is unevenly distributed: Java has one of the highest population densities in the world (640 people per sq km), while Borneo has fewer than 10 people per sq km. Cash crops - mainly coffee, tea, rubber and palm oil - are cultivated, along with subsistence items, especially rice. Indonesia is the tenth largest oil producer and the third largest tin producer in the world.

SOCIETY

Peoples: Malay, Javanese, Sundanese, Madurese, Balinese, Ambon, Alfur, Toraja, Dayak, Batak, Minahasa and Papuan. There are also Chinese and Indian minorities.

Religions: 86 per cent of the population is Muslim, nearly 10 per cent Christian, 2 per cent Hindu (mostly in Bali), 1 per cent Buddhist, and small minorities that practice traditional beliefs. The State recognizes Islam, Protestant and Catholic Christianity, Hinduism and Buddhism.

Languages: Bahasa Indonesia (official), very similar to Bahasa Malaysia, official language of Malaysia. The governments of both countries have agreed to gradual unification, based on Melayu, the shared mother tongue. Javanese, language of 60 million inhabitants. English, language of business. There are hundreds of regional/local languages - more than 200 are concentrated in the province of West Papua (Irian Jaya).

Main Political Parties: National Awakening Party (PKB). Indonesian Democratic Party in Struggle (PDIP). The governing party during the Suharto era, Golongan Karya (Golkar) was founded in 1971. The United Party for Development (PPP) and the National Mandate Party (PAN), are both moderate Islamic groups. Separatist movements: Free Aceh Movement and Aceh National Liberation Front, there is an indigenous guerrilla group in West Papua (Irian Jaya) - the Free Papua Movement (OPM).

Main Social Organizations: All-Indonesia Workers' Union (SPSI), since 1985, founded in 1973 under the name Labor Federation of Indonesia (FBSI); National Federation of Indonesian Unions; Indonesian Federation of Peasant Unions; Women's Solidarity Movement; Indonesian Environmental Forum.

THE STATE

Official Name: Republik Indonesia.
Administrative Divisions: 26 provinces.
Capital: Jakarta 12,296,000 people (2003).
Other Cities: Surabaya 3,683,200 people; Bandung 3,834,300; Medan 2,977,000 (2000).
Government: Megawati Sukarnoputri, President since July 2001. Elections in July 2004 are by direct vote, in accordance with constitutional changes. Legislature, single-chamber, made up of 500 members, 462 elected by direct popular vote and 38 military representatives, appointed for five-year periods. From July 2004, the 38 military seats will disappear.
National Holiday: 17 August, Independence Day (1945).
Armed Forces: 297,000 (2001). Other: Police, 215,000; Auxiliary Police, (Kamra), 1.5 million.

Iran / Iran

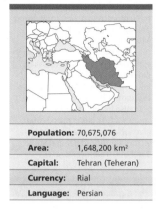

Population:	70,675,076
Area:	1,648,200 km²
Capital:	Tehran (Teheran)
Currency:	Rial
Language:	Persian

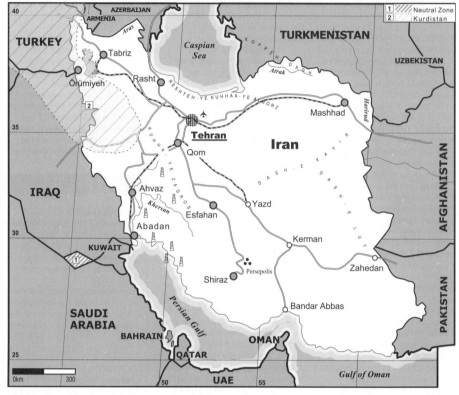

S hortly before the 18th century BC, Indo-European peoples reached the plains of Iran, subduing the shepherds who inhabited the region. Indo-Europeans continued to arrive up until the 10th century, contributing to the Mesopotamian cultural mix. They later became known by different names: Medes, from the name of the ruling group; Iranians, the name they adopted in Persia and India (from Sanskrit *ayriana* meaning nobles); Persians (a Greco-Latin term alluding to Perseus, the mythological ancestor that the Greeks foisted on Iranians), with its corrupted forms: Parsis, Farsis, Fars, or Parthians (according to the time and source). Whatever their names, they first won control of the mountainous region, then conquered the Mesopotamian plains under the reign of Ciaxares. During the rule of Ciro the Great (559-530 BC), this wave of expansion reached as far west as Asia Minor, and as far east as present-day Afghanistan. These borders were later extended as far as Greece, Egypt, Turkestan and part of India.

[2] Towards the end of the 4th century BC, this vast empire fell into the hands of Alexander of Macedonia. Alexander's successors, the Seleucids and Romans (see Syria), lost their hold on the eastern part of the empire to the Persians, who recovered their independence with the Arsacid dynasty (2nd century BC to 3rd AD). They remained independent under the Sassanids until the 7th century, though constantly at war with the Romans and Byzantines.

[3] After the Arab conquest reached the region in 641 (see Saudi Arabia), Islamic thought and practices became dominant. Unlike the people in most other provinces of the Arab Empire, they retained their own language and distinctive styles in arts and literature. With the fall of the Caliphate of Baghdad, Persia attained virtual independence, first under the descendants of Tahir, the last Arab viceroy, and later under the Seleucid Turks and the Persian dynasties. Despite political restlessness, the period was remarkably rich in cultural and scientific progress, personified by the poet, mathematician, philosopher and astronomer, Ummar al-Khayyam.

[4] In 1501 Shi'ism became the state religion in Iran. The Qajar and Pahlavi dynasties would maintain Islam as the state religion. Iran was a Shi'a stronghold in the region, but not being an Arab country and not being on good terms with the Sunni representatives - Arabs at first, Ottomans later - its influence was limited.

[5] The Mongol invasion led by Hulagu Khan that began in 1258 was an altogether different matter. Three centuries of Mongol domination brought dynastic strife between the descendants of Timur Lenk (Tamburlaine) and the Ottomans. The dispute paved the way for Persian Ismail Shah whose grandson Abbas I (1587-1629) succeeded in uniting the country.

He expelled the Turks from the west, the Portuguese from the Ormuz region, and also conquered part of Afghanistan. For a short time Iran ruled a region extending from India to Syria.

[6] A 1909 treaty divided the country into two areas - one of Russian and the other of British economic influence. A British firm was given the opportunity to exploit Iranian oilfields. Military occupation by the two powers during World War I, in addition to government corruption and inefficiency, led to the 1921 revolution headed by journalist Sayyid Tabatabai, and Reza Khan, commander of the national guard. Reza, the revolution's war minister, became prime minister in 1923. Two years later, the National Assembly dismissed Tabatabai, and Reza ousted the Shah, occupying the throne himself.

[7] Reza repealed all treaties granting extra-territorial rights to foreign powers, abolished the obligatory use of the veil by women, reformed the education and health systems, and cancelled oil concessions that favored the British. His attempt to establish a militarily strong, neutral modern state met with fierce resistance. However, he insisted on remaining neutral and did not allow the passage of allied arms to the Soviet Union through

LAND USE

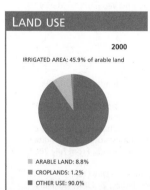

2000

IRRIGATED AREA: 45.9% of arable land

■ ARABLE LAND: 8.8%
■ CROPLANDS: 1.2%
■ OTHER USE: 90.0%

PUBLIC EXPENDITURE

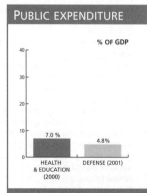

% OF GDP

7.0 %
HEALTH & EDUCATION (2000)

4.8%
DEFENSE (2001)

WORKERS

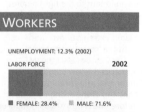

UNEMPLOYMENT: 12.3% (2002)

LABOR FORCE   **2002**

■ FEMALE: 28.4%   ■ MALE: 71.6%

Life expectancy
70.3 years
2000-2005

GNI per capita
$1,710
2002

Literacy
76% total adult rate
2000

HIV prevalence rate
0.1% of population 15-49 years old
2001

Iranian territory. The country was invaded and occupied in 1941 by British and Soviet forces. The Shah was overthrown and sent into exile. He was replaced by his son, Muhammad Reza Pahlevi, more amenable to European interests, who ruled under Anglo-Soviet tutelage until the end of the war.

8 A 1949 constitution curtailed the Shah's authority, and progressive, nationalist forces won seats in parliament. With their support, Prime Minister Muhammad Mossadegh attempted to nationalize oil reserves and expropriate the Anglo-Iranian Oil Company, even though Britain had other suppliers and Iran had no other source of income.

9 In 1953, Mossadegh's audacity was met by an economic embargo and a coup backed by the US Central Intelligence Agency (CIA), which restored the Shah's almost absolute power. Nationalist and left-wing leaders were massacred and thousands were imprisoned. The Shah encouraged multinational corporations in to Iran - citing 'modernization' which consisted of promoting Western consumerism. These measures were resisted by Islamic clergy and several social sectors, notably small farmers and the urban poor. By the end of the 1960s, due to the growing power of foreign corporations and rapidly changing consumption patterns, the Shah had lost the backing of the powerful commercial élites.

10 Opposition groups included the National Front founded by Mossadegh, the Tudeh Communist Party, Fedayin (Marxist) and Mujahedin (Islamic) guerrillas and the exiled cleric Ayatollah Khomeini. The recordings of Khomeini's preaching in Paris became familiar and encouraged the masses to organize. Demonstrations began in secondary schools in 1977 and were widespread by 1978. The Shah was forced to flee in January 1979 and Khomeini made a triumphant return. On 11 February crowds invaded the imperial palace; the Shah's prime minister resigned, and the army accepted the new situation. The Islamic Revolution was introduced as an alternative to Western models and was welcomed enthusiastically throughout the Muslim world.

11 Prime Minister Mehdi Bazargan of the National Front sought to reconcile Muslim traditions with a mixed economy model. However he did not find the required support. Muslim fundamentalists, bolstered by the 'revolutionary guards' and

IN FOCUS

ENVIRONMENTAL CHALLENGES
The main problems are deforestation along the coast of the Caspian Sea; pollution of the sea after the 1991 Gulf War, and air pollution.

WOMEN'S RIGHTS
Women have been able to vote and stand for office since 1963. Between 1995 and 2000, the proportion of seats in parliament held by women rose from 4 to 5 per cent, and in the last term of the Khatami administration several executive positions were held by women. In 2003, Shirin Ebadi was awarded the Nobel Peace Prize. Ebadi was the first woman to preside over a courtroom in Tehran, but after the 1979 Islamic Revolution she was forced to resign. She taught and practised as a lawyer. In 2004 the religious conservatives' electoral victory was a setback for women's rights activists, who favored the reformist Khatami administration. Iranian women who have internet access have been able to debate and analyze subjects that are taboo in their patriarchal and religiously conservative society.

CHILDREN
Children's health has improved in the last two decades. Preventive health services have been extended, reducing maternal and child mortality rates. About 90 per cent are immunized, and polio has been almost totally eradicated. Ninety per cent of births are attended by qualified medical personnel*; 11 per cent of children under 5 years old were moderately to severely underweight and 15 per cent were weak or stunted (1998*). In 2000*, 93 per cent of all households had access to safe drinking water. Some of these indicators were affected after the 2003 Bam earthquake that killed over 40,000. In education, there are inequalities in gender and geographic location. Male school enrolment averaged 98 per cent; while female enrolment stood at 99 per cent in Tehran and 84 per cent in Sistan and Baluchistan. In spite of heavy investment in education, only 15 per cent of children are in preschool.

INDIGENOUS PEOPLES/ ETHNIC MINORITIES
There are three main minority groups: other nationalities (Arab, Azeri, Turkmen, Armenian); religious minorities (Sunni, Bahai, Christian); and ethnic minorities (Kurd, Bakhtiar, Baloch). Discrimination - sometimes oppression - of these groups is based mainly on religious and linguistic differences (*farsi* is the official language; in 2002 about 89 per cent of all Iranians were Sh'ia Muslims).

MIGRANTS/REFUGEES
Iran hosted more than two million refugees and asylum-seekers in 2002, the largest number in the world. Although in early 2000 there was assisted repatriation of 376,000 Afghans, two million Afghans were still in Iran at the end of the year, in addition to 203,000 Iraqis and over 6,000 people of other nationalities. In early 2004 a significant repatriation of Iraqis began. The largest refugee camp (Ashrafi Esfahini), which had housed 12,000 people, closed once it was empty. In 2002, some 38,000 Iranians lived as refugees or asylum-seekers in other countries, including 23,000 in Iraq since the 1980 war, a few thousand in Turkey and less than 1,000 in Austria. Almost 8,000 Iranian refugees in Iraq sought UNHCR assistance for repatriation through a voluntary program launched by the two countries in 2002. In 2003, a similar program was agreed by Iran, Afghanistan and UNHCR to help Afghan refugees return to their country.

DEATH PENALTY
Applicable to a wide range of crimes; according to Amnesty International, 113 people were executed in 2003. The methods used are stoning and hanging.

* Latest data available in The State of the World's Children *and* Childinfo *database, UNICEF, 2004.*

Khomeini's popularity, excluded their former allies from government.

12 In early November 1979, a student group stormed the US embassy in Tehran, taking the staff hostage and showing documentary evidence of CIA meddling in Iranian politics. A US attempt to rescue the hostages was unsuccessful. In 1980, war with Iraq broke out; it continued until 1988.

13 In 1981, the Islamic Revolutionary Party (IRP) won the presidential elections with more than 90 per cent of the vote. A bombing of the party's headquarters killed 72 political leaders, among them the President and the Prime Minister. Ali Khamenei, former secretary-general of the IRP, was elected president. A theocratic regime was imposed, which suppressed opposition. Many people were jailed for political reasons, others went into exile, and still others were executed - between 500 and 1,500 people were sentenced to death in 1989, mostly for drug trafficking.

14 In 1985, Iran posted a huge trade surplus, despite the war with its neighbor. Oil made up almost all the exports.

15 Iran's international image deteriorated in early 1989 when Khomeini issued a *fatwa* - death sentence - against writer Salman Rushdie, citing his *Satanic Verses* book as blasphemous. Rushdie went into hiding, but in 1990 returned to public life and was reconciled with the main Islamic authorities, although the *fatwa* was not formally lifted.

16 Contrary to Western expectations, the death of Ayatollah Khomeini on 3 June 1989 did not lead to widespread instability. As more than eight million mourners gathered to bury him, outgoing President Ali Sayed Khamenei was appointed *faghih* - Iran's spiritual leader - by a vote of the Assembly of Experts.

17 In August, Ali Akbar Hashemi Rafsanjani won a landslide victory in the presidential elections. The new constitution granted the president, until then a largely ceremonial position, real powers. Rafsanjani's election as president meant a strengthening of the 'pro-Western' wing in the regime. Under the Iranian constitution, religious and lay authorities share power.

18 In 1990, Iran condemned the Iraqi invasion of Kuwait, and remained neutral when the Gulf War broke out in 1991. Eventually Iraq was expelled from Kuwait by US military forces in coalition with many other countries. Iran's neutrality was designed to give it an advantage over Baghdad, by gaining acceptance in regional and international diplomacy. Diplomatic relations with Britain were resumed in 1990 and with Saudi Arabia in 1991.This diplomatic initiative was hindered by domestic violence - with multiple political attacks - and by Tehran's links with groups involved in regional conflicts, such as the Lebanon-based Hizbullah.

Under-5 mortality
42 per 1,000 live births
2002

Poverty
<2% of population living on less than $1 per day
1998

Debt service
4.9% exports of goods and services
2001

Maternal mortality
76 per 100,000 live births
2000

[19] To attract foreign investment, Rafsanjani privatized enterprises nationalized by the Islamic Revolution in 1979. With the disintegration of the Soviet Union, Iran set its sights on a new area of influence: the Islamic republics of the Caucasus and Central Asia, signing agreements and opening new channels of communications with its neighbors.

[20] In the April 1992 legislative elections, the 'moderates' who supported President Rafsanjani won a clear victory over the 'radicals'. In July, Iran's spiritual leader Khamenei launched a campaign to 'eradicate Western influence', clashing with Rafsanjani and his more moderate vision of Islam. However, in June 1993, Rafsanjani was confirmed as president by 63 per cent of the vote. In February 1994 he survived an attempt on his life.

[21] Disagreements with Saudi Arabia over the Muslims' annual *haj* (pilgrimage) to Mecca - Islam's main holy site, in Saudi Arabia - affected relations with Riyadh, highlighting the rivalry between the two states in their claim to be the center of the Islamic world.

[22] On the economic front, performance was poor. Oil sales from March 1994 to March 1995 fell compared to the previous year. The Government stopped subsidizing 23 imported products, mostly food and medicine, which led to rising prices. In July 1996, the US toughened its sanctions against Iran, blaming the country for terrorist actions.

[23] The May 1997 elections were won by Muhammad Khatami, regarded as the most pro-Western candidate. The new government took over in August and Khatami announced the country would open up to the West. Masoume Ebtekar, Iran's deputy minister of environmental affairs, denounced in 1998 the oppressive conditions imposed on women by Afghanistan's Taliban regime. In Iran, by contrast with other Muslim countries, women have the right to vote and are increasingly found in decision-making positions.

[24] The Reformists headed by Khatami won the February 2000 general elections by a landslide, taking 226 of the 290 parliamentary seats. In the June elections, which had a low turnout, Khatami was re-elected.

[25] In January 2002, US President George W Bush described Iraq, Iran and North Korea as the 'axis of evil', sponsors of terrorism who wanted to obtain and develop weapons of mass destruction - a charge that was strongly denied by Iran.

[26] The following year, in March, the US invaded and occupied Iraq. The Iranian Government predicted a violent future for the Bush administration if it did not leave the region. 'The US will face more critical times if it decides to extend its presence in Iraq', said Ayatollah Khamenei.

[27] In 2003, Iran faced other problems. In September, the construction of Iran's first nuclear reactor was reported in international fora, causing alarm in several Western nations, especially the US. After complicated diplomatic efforts, Iran accepted UN inspectors, who concluded that the Iranian nuclear program was not for military purposes.

[28] That year, conservative sectors were upset when a woman, Judge Shirin Ebadi, won the Nobel Peace prize. This was taken as a gesture of support for Khatami's reformers in their struggle against Khamenei. Foreign critics also protested since Iran was part of the 'axis of evil'.

[29] In November 2003 Iran broke off cultural and economic ties with Argentina after the Iranian ambassador to Buenos Aires, Hadi Soleimanpour, was detained in London. The arrest was requested by an Argentine judge who suspected Soleimanpour had been involved in the 1994 bombing of AMIA, a Jewish community center in Buenos Aires. A rapprochement took place between the two countries when the ambassador was freed on lack of evidence, but diplomatic relations were not resumed.

[30] In December, an earthquake rocked the city of Bam, declared a UNESCO World Heritage Site. The quake, one of the worst ever, left some 40,000 dead. Global solidarity included an easing of US economic sanctions, although tension remained high between Tehran and Washington.

[31] In early 2004, legislative elections were held amidst controversy: the Council of Guardians - a body similar to the Senate and controlled by the conservative clerics - vetoed more than 2,500 candidates, mostly reformers and Khatami followers. The President's party called for a boycott of the elections, and although about half the registered voters did not show up, this was not enough to delegitimate the conservatives' victory by an absolute majority in Parliament. The outcome triggered social unrest, and around 10 people died in clashes with the police.

PROFILE

ENVIRONMENT

Central Iran is a steppe-like plateau with a harsh climate, surrounded by deserts and mountains (the Zagros on the western border and the Elburz to the north). Underground water irrigates the oases where several varieties of grain and fruit trees are cultivated. The shores of the Caspian Sea are suited for tropical and subtropical crops (cotton, sugar cane and rice). Modern industries (petrochemicals, textiles, building) have grown, but the industry of hand-made rugs and other textiles remains significant.

SOCIETY

Peoples: Persian 51 per cent; Azeris 24 per cent; Kurds 7 per cent; Gilaki and Mazandarani 8 per cent; Lur 2 per cent; Arab 3 per cent; Baloch 2 per cent; Turkmen 2 per cent.
Religions: Shi'a Muslims 89 per cent; Sunni Muslims 10 per cent; Bahai, Christians, Zoroastrians and Jews 1 per cent.
Languages: Persian/Farsi (official) and minority languages (Kurds 7 per cent).
Main Political Parties: Reformist Coalition, whose main party is the Front of Islamic Participation; Islamic conservative parties: Assembly of the Followers of the Imam's Line, Islamic Solidarity of Iran Party, Association of Militant Clergy, and others. Out of Parliament: National Resistence Council; Kurdish Democratic Party; Communist Party; Party of the Masses (Tudeh).
Main Social Organizations: People's Mojahedin is the largest and most active armed militant group, whose philosophy is a mix of Marxism and Islam. With it are the Iranian National Liberation Army and the Union of Islamic Student Societies. Student groups have a significant degree of involvement.

THE STATE

Official Name: Dshumhurije Islâmije Irân.
Administrative Divisions: 28 provinces, 472 towns and 499 municipalities.
Capital: Teheran (Tehran) 7,190,000 people (2003).
Other Cities: Mashhad 2,020,400 people; Isfahan 2,535,000; Tabriz 1,207,600 (2000).
Government: Presidential republic. Muhammad Khatami, president since August 1997, re-elected in 2001. Religious power is exercised by Sayed Ali Khamenei since June 1989. Legislature: Islamic Consultative Assembly single-chamber), with 290 members elected by direct popular vote every four years. The members of parliament are elected by secret, universal ballot.
National Holiday: 1 April, Revolution Day (1979).
Armed Forces: In 2003 there were 12,000,000 personnel available for military service. Other: BASIJ 'Popular Mobilization Army' volunteers, mostly youth; called up in wartime; strength has been as high as 1 million; Gendarmerie: (45,000 border guards).

[32] In June 2004, the International Atomic Energy Agency (IAEA) sharply condemned Teheran for failing to cooperate with the investigation on Iran's nuclear activity. Although the IAEA warned Teheran it was essential to deal with these issues, it neither threatened to report this case to the UN Security Council for possible sanctions nor gave a deadline for Iran to fulfill its obligations.

[33] Teheran had accused the authors of the condemnation report (Britain, France and Germany) of being on Washington's side, which had previously charged the Iranian Government of secretly developing a nuclear weapons program.

[34] Two years had passed since Iran's nuclear program first came to light and, according to the IAEA, some questions still remained outstanding. One of these questions was the lack of a convincing explanation about the uranium contamination found near the uranium enrichment centrifuges, among other places in Iran. Washington maintained that Iran would be carrying out investigations to develop a sophisticated facility that would enrich nuclear fuel to create weapons. However, the Iranian Government reiterated that they were not pursuing nuclear weapons but a program for self-generating electricity: the problem was that the same technology could be used for both purposes. The IAEA board urged Iran to take 'all necessary measures to clarify remaining questions'. ∎

Iraq / Al Iraq

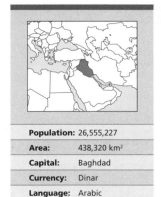

Population:	26,555,227
Area:	438,320 km²
Capital:	Baghdad
Currency:	Dinar
Language:	Arabic

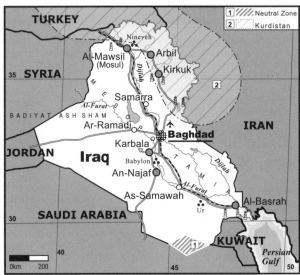

Iraq occupies the territory that was the site of one of the oldest Western civilizations. The Sumerian culture flourished in Mesopotamia around 5000 BC. In 2371 BC, King Sargon of Akkad gained control over the region and established the first Assyrian dynasty. The Assyrian empire expanded its dominion to include modern Turkey, Iran, Syria and Israel. The empire collapsed with the fall of its capital Nineveh (modern-day Mosul) in 612 BC, and was replaced by the Babylonian civilization. King Hammurabi (reigning circa 1792-50 BC), made Babylon the capital and established the first Code of Laws. King Nebuchadnezzar II (c. 605-562 BC), a splendid builder, developed hanging gardens that made Babylon one of the greatest cities of the ancient world.

[2] The Babylonian era came to an end when the Persians, ruled by Cyrus the Great, invaded in 539 BC and dominated the region until Alexander the Great's conquests in 331 BC. His successors, the Seleucids, ruled for 175 years, until the new Persian invasions under the Parthi'ans, who constructed extensive irrigation systems and canals. Later on, the Sassanids established a new capital at Ctesiphon near the Tigris.

[3] After the Arab conquests of the 7th century, Mesopotamia became the center of an enormous empire (see Saudi Arabia). A century later, the new Abbas dynasty moved the capital east from Damascus. Caliph al-Mansur built the new capital, Baghdad, on the banks of the Tigris and for three centuries the city of 'A Thousand and One Nights' was the center of a new culture.

[4] This culture led to the greatest flourishing of the arts and sciences in the Mediterranean region since the days of the Greeks. However, the empire's enormous size led to its collapse after the death of Harun al-Raschid. The African provinces were lost and the region north and east of Persia won independence under the Tahiris (the Kingdom of Khorasan). The caliphs were forced to depend

increasingly on armies of slaves or mercenaries (Sudanese or Turks) to retain their grip on an ever-shrinking empire. When the Mongols assassinated the last caliph in Baghdad in 1258, the title had already lost its political meaning.

[5] The conquests of Genghis Khan devastated the region's agricultural economy, and the region was subsequently ruled in whole or part by Seleucids or Ottomans, Turks, Mongols, Turkomans, Tartars, and Kurds. The movement of steppe peoples (see Afghanistan), brought great instability to the fertile crescent, which finally achieved unification under the Ottoman Turks in the 16th century, having repelled an attack by Timur Lenk (Tamburlaine) in the 14th century.

[6] In the early 16th century, Sunnism held power in Iraq, under Ottoman rule. But the Shi'as from southern Iraq, who identified with the Irani regime, continued to enjoy considerable prestige, which limited Ottoman authority. Efforts were aimed at keeping open the trade routes that ran through the territory, joining East and West to the Mediterranean, as an alternative to the sea routes around Africa. To achieve this, it was necessary to confront the intractable Arab and Kurdish groups as well as the continuous encroachments by Iran. Süleyman imposed strict and direct rule over Iraq with that aim.

[7] In the early 17th century, the authority of local leaders within Iraq had grown significantly. Around that time, Bakr Su Bashi, military chief of a garrison in Baghdad, joined the Safavid Shah Abbas I, who managed to gain control over central Iraq, while Mosul and Shahrizor remained under Ottoman control. The central area was under Safavid rule from 1623-1638.

[8] The Treaty of Qasr-i Shirin (also known as the Treaty of Zuhab) of

1639 brought an end to the conflict, restoring Ottoman control over Baghdad. Aside from unrest between various groups, Iraq maintained a certain level of stability. Control was finally gained over southern Iraq in 1668, and the problems that followed reflected the state of affairs in Istanbul, center of the Ottoman Empire.

[9] The 18th century brought important changes in the region. The reign of Sultan Ahmed III in Istanbul was marked by political stability and reforms influenced by European models.

[10] In Baghdad, Hasan Pasha (1704-1724), of Georgian origin, was succeeded by his son, Ahmed Pasha (1724-1747), who introduced the Mamluks from Georgia. The Mamluks were mostly Christian slaves from the Caucasus, who were trained to perform military and administrative duties. When Ahmed died, the Mamluks assumed power, appointing his son-in-law, Süleyman Abu Layla, as the first Mamluk pasha of Iraq.

[11] From the second half of the 18th century, the Mamluk regime alternated between periods of prosperity and order and periods plagued with internal strife and corruption.

[12] In the early 20th century, Arab Renaissance movements were active in Iraq, paving the way for the rebellion that rocked the Turkish realm during World War I (see Saudi Arabia, Jordan and Syria). The British were keen to expand their influence in the region. With the defeat of the Turks, Iraq entertained hopes of independence. These, however, were dashed when the secret Sykes-Picot treaty of 1916 became known, whereby France and Britain divided the Arab territories between themselves. Faisal, son of sharif Hussein, was expelled from Syria by the French. In 1920, Britain was

awarded a mandate over Mesopotamia by the League of Nations, triggering a pro-independence rebellion.

[13] In 1921, Emir Faisal ibn Hussain was appointed King of Iraq in compensation. In 1930, General Nuri as-Said, who had taken office as Prime Minister, signed a treaty with the British, under which the country became nominally independent on 3 October 1932.

[14] That year, the Baghdad Pact was signed, making Iraq part of a military alliance with Turkey, Pakistan, Iran, Britain and the US. The pact was resisted by Iraqi nationalists. In July 1958, anti-imperialist agitation resulted in a military coup led by Abdul Karim Kassim, which led to the execution of the royal family.

[15] In 1959, the new regime banned all political parties and proclaimed Iraq's annexation of Kuwait. The Arab League, dominated by Egypt, authorized the deployment of British troops to protect the oil-rich enclave.

[16] Close ties with the Soviet Union and China fomented predictions that Iraq could become 'a new Cuba'. Steps towards economic change were taken, the power of landowners was weakened by agrarian reform, and a greater share of the Iraq Petroleum Company's revenues went to the state. In 1963, Kassim was deposed by pan-Arabian sectors within the army. Several unstable governments followed, until July 1968, when a military coup placed the Ba'ath party in power.

[17] Founded in 1947, the Arab Ba'ath Socialist Party (*ba'ath* meaning 'renaissance' in Arabic) was inspired by the ideal of Pan-Arabism, which regarded the Arab World as an indivisible political and economic unit where no country can be self-sufficient. The Ba'athists proclaimed that 'socialism is a need which emerges from the very core of Arab nationalism. It is organized on a national (Arab) level, with several regional leaders in each country.'

[18] Iraq nationalized foreign-owned companies and defended the use of oil as a 'political weapon in the struggle against imperialism and Zionism'. It advocated protected prices and the consolidation of OPEC. A land reform program was launched, and ambitious development plans encouraged the reinvestment of oil money into national industrialization.

[19] In 1970, the Baghdad Government gave the Kurdish language official status, and granted Kurdistan domestic autonomy. However, encouraged by Iran, the traditional regional leaders rose up in arms. In March 1975, the Iran-Iraq border agreement deprived the Kurds of their main foreign support, and the rebels were defeated. The

Life expectancy
60.7 years
2000-2005

Literacy
39% total adult rate
2000

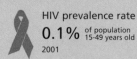
HIV prevalence rate
0.1% of population 15-49 years old
2001

Baghdad Government decreed the teaching of Kurdish in local schools, greater investment in the region, and the appointment of Kurds to key administrative positions.

[20] In July 1979, President Ahmed Hassan al-Bakr resigned and was replaced by Vice-President Saddam Hussein, who attempted to establish Iraq as a leader of the Arab world.

[21] Hussein rejected the Camp David accord between Egypt, Israel and the US, while Iraqi relations with other Arab countries also worsened.

[22] Iraqi forces staged a pre-emptive strike against Iran in September 1980, unleashing a war that lasted for eight years. The West backed Iraq against the fundamentalist regime of Ayatollah Khomeini in Iran.

[23] On 17 June 1981, under the pretext that Iraq was producing nuclear weapons, Israeli planes destroyed the Tamuz nuclear plant.

[24] During the war, the Saudis and Kuwaitis - in an attempt to stop Iranian fundamentalism - granted Baghdad many loans which were used both in the conflict and for strengthening the country's infrastructure. An oil pipeline was built through Turkey as an alternative to the one which ran across Syria to the Mediterranean; Syria had closed the pipeline down in solidarity with Iran. The roads to Jordan were also upgraded.

[25] In November 1984, 17 years after they had broken off diplomatic relations, official ties with the US were re-established. In spite of Washington's declaration of neutrality in the Iran-Iraq conflict, the Iran-Contra scandal (see Nicaragua) revealed the superpower's double-dealing.

[26] Through the 1988 armistice, Iraq retained 2,600 square kilometers of Iranian territory and a powerful and skilful army that soon found another pretext to take action again.

[27] The Iran-Iraq war had been in part the outcome of massive arms-buying by both countries during the 1970s. The oil price rises in the early 1970s had swollen both countries' coffers and the West was keen to recover this money through arms sales. By 1975, Iran had become the single largest purchaser of US arms. Equally, without imported weapons and technology, Saddam Hussein would not have been able to invade Kuwait in 1990, and the Gulf Wars would not have taken place.

[28] Neighboring Kuwait was extracting more oil than allowed from deposits along the border, and refused to establish export quotas. As the US hinted that it would remain neutral in the event of conflict, on 2 August, Iraq invaded Kuwait and took thousands of foreign hostages.

[29] Four days later the UN decided on a total economic and military

IN FOCUS

ENVIRONMENTAL CHALLENGES
A large part of the country's infrastructure was devastated by the successive wars. Tank and troop movements caused major damage to road surfaces and soil, especially in the area along the Saudi Arabian border. Depleted uranium from missiles used by UN forces in the first Gulf War lingers as a health threat in southern Iraq.

There are problems with access to drinking water and soil erosion; salinization and desertification are major concerns.

WOMEN'S RIGHTS
Women have been able to vote and stand for office since 1980. In 2000, only 6 per cent of seats in Parliament were held by women and there was no female representation in ministerial or equivalent positions. Between 1990 and 2000, women accounted for an average of 20 per cent of the total labor force (of these women, 39 per cent worked in agriculture, 9 per cent in industry and 52 per cent in services). While the school enrolment rate for girls is 86 per cent, there is total coverage for boys. Since the 1980s, the maternal mortality rate and the proportion of pregnant women with anemia have increased.

CHILDREN
In 2003, Iraqi people were caught up in an international military conflict for the third time in 20 years. The ten years of economic sanctions imposed by the international community and the impact of war will have repercussions on the general conditions in the country, further increasing the threats to the life and welfare of children and young people. In 2001*, more than half of all Iraqis were under the age of 18. One out of eight children died before reaching the age of five. One-third of children were malnourished and one-fourth of newborns were of low birth weight. Apart from suffering a deterioration in basic life conditions and access to clean water, health care and education, children are exposed to the dangers posed by unexploded ordnance and land mines as well as exploitation and abuse.

The first figures assessing the impact of the attack on Baghdad in March 2003 had not been completed by the end of that year. But it was estimated that 270,000 children born in 2003 had not been vaccinated. In addition, studies carried out in Baghdad in May 2003 found that 7 out of 10 children had had diarrhea in the previous month. Diarrhea is the leading factor in child malnutrition and is linked to the lack of clean water, poor sanitation, and lack of rubbish disposal in the major cities during the conflict.

INDIGENOUS PEOPLES/ ETHNIC MINORITIES
Kurds are a persecuted ethnic minority in Iraq.

In spite of comprising a majority of Iraq's population, Shi'as have historically been dominated by the Sunni minority. Most Shi'as live in the south near the Iranian border. Under Saddam's regime, discrimination against Shi'as occurred in all fields: they were excluded from political participation and they did not have freedom of expression or the right to organize. Shi'as are not allowed to take part in Friday prayers nor to freely distribute Shi'a religious material. Saddam resorted to arbitrary executions, a forced resettlement policy, and a heavy military presence in Shi'a areas. In response, the Shi'as formed militant organizations which at first sought to oust Saddam. Their use of violence gradually decreased, but Shi'as continued small-scale guerrilla activities against religious bans and the assassination of Shi'a clerics in 1999.

MIGRANTS/REFUGEES
In December 2002, the UK Government issued a report portraying Iraq as 'a terrifying place to live' with allegations of torture, rape and persecution of Kurds and Shi'as by the regime. Nevertheless, thousands of Iraqis were denied asylum in the UK and other Western countries that year.

Hundreds of thousands of Iraqis are living as refugees in other countries in the region. More than 200,000 Iraqi Shi'as sought refuge in Iran, Jordan hosted nearly 300,000 fleeing Saddam's regime, and there were over 70,000 in Syria hosted prior to the 2003 attacks on Baghdad. Most of these refugees were undocumented. Many Iraqis live in Europe, either as refugees or asylum-seekers. Many have refused to be repatriated during ceasefire periods, due to the continuing insecurity in Iraq.

DEATH PENALTY
Iraq is one of the countries in which the death penalty still applies for common crimes.

* Latest data available in *The State of the World's Children* and *Childinfo* database, UNICEF, 2004.

embargo until Iraq retreated unconditionally from the occupied territory. Withdrawal was rejected, but a proposal for an international conference to discuss the problems of the Middle East issue was submitted. When Iraq started to release the hostages and to make new attempts at negotiating, the US refused to talk and demanded an unconditional surrender.

[30] On 17 January 1991, an alliance of 32 countries led by the US launched an attack on Iraq. When the land offensive began in March, Saddam Hussein had already announced his unconditional withdrawal. The Iraqi army did not fight back, and merely attempted to stage an organized retreat, yet it suffered great losses. The war ended early in March, with the total defeat of the Iraqis.

[31] Towards the end of the offensive, the US encouraged an internal revolt against Hussein by the southern Shi'a and the northern Kurds. However, the political differences between the two groups stood in the way of an alliance, and the rebels were crushed by the still-powerful Iraqi army. Over one million Kurds sought refuge in Iran and Turkey to escape the troops from Baghdad, and thousands starved or froze to death with the onset of winter.

[32] Between 150,000 and 200,000 people, mostly civilians, died in the war. An estimated 70,000 Iraqis died as a result of the subsequent embargo, including 20,000 children. At the end of 1991, both the Turkish and Iraqi armies were continuing to harass the Kurds in the border area.

[33] The conditions for lifting the embargo became very strict due to the US determination to bring about the downfall of Hussein. In addition, according to *The New York Times* and the *Sunday Telegraph*, the US introduced huge amounts of counterfeit dinars, smuggled across the Jordanian, Saudi Arabian, Turkish and Iranian borders. Baghdad established the death penalty for anyone participating in these operations.

[34] Toward the end of 1991, the Iraqi Government authorized UN inspections of military establishments. In 1992, Iraq was found to be engaged in a uranium enrichment project, which had been developed using German technology. UN inspection teams destroyed 460 x 122 mm warheads armed with sarin, a poisonous gas. They also

Under-5 mortality
125 per 1,000 live births
2002

Malnutrition
16% under-5s
1995-2002

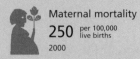
Maternal mortality
250 per 100,000 live births
2000

dismantled the nuclear complex at al-Athir, the uranium enrichment installations at Ash-Sharqat and Tarmiuah, and the chemical weapons plant at Muthana.

35 In 1994 a border crossing was opened with Turkey to allow certain UN authorized foodstuffs and medicines to enter the country - the only exceptions to the trade embargo. But in March 1995, Turkish troops invaded Iraqi Kurdistan - under allied military tutelage - to repress members of the Kurdish Workers Party (PKK).

36 Baghdad's international isolation deepened in 1996, when Jordan's relations with Kuwait and Saudi Arabia improved. However, the UN Security Council voted for the partial lifting of the blockade, to allow restricted sales of crude oil, in order to buy food and medicines for the Iraqi population.

37 A UN report revealed in April 1997 that the number of dead due to hunger or lack of medicines arising from the embargo exceeded one million, of which 570,000 were children. UNICEF reported that 25 per cent of children under 5 were suffering from severe clinical malnutrition.

38 In October, the Security Council threatened to enforce new sanctions if a new inspection was not allowed, with the aim of verifying that the Iraqi administration lacked the capacity to develop chemical and biological weapons. Iraq rejected the presence of US inspectors, which hardened US President Clinton's stance. Clinton, backed by British Prime Minister Tony Blair, launched a missile attack on several Iraqi cities, starting on 16 December. The attack, 'Operation Desert Fox', killed hundreds of Iraqi civilians and troops.

39 In December 1999, the Security Council approved the resumption of weapons inspections in Iraq and the suspension of economic sanctions in case Baghdad decided to cooperate. Russia, France, China and Malaysia abstained from voting. Iraq, alleging it was an attempt by the US to impose its 'evil' will on the Security Council, refused to co-operate and demanded that all sanctions be lifted.

40 When George W Bush took office as US President in January 2001, he announced a hard-line stance and stiffened sanctions against Iraq. After the 11 September 2001 terror attacks on New York and Washington DC, the US attempted to pressure the alliance it was forming into fighting global terrorism, with Baghdad as its main target. However, the allies, including Britain, withheld their support. Meanwhile, Saddam regained popularity in the Arab world by supporting the second Palestinian intifada and proposing that Muslim countries pursue their common interests, especially the

Palestinian cause, through controlling oil prices.

41 In January 2002, in his State of the Union address, Bush dubbed Iraq, Iran and North Korea the 'axis of evil' which, he claimed, sought to obtain weapons of mass destruction (WMD) and sponsored international terrorism.

42 Bush advocated the 'need' to attack Iraq, emphasizing that the danger of Saddam Hussein's regime lay in its 'potential' to develop weapons of mass destruction and in its supposed link to Islamic terrorists. In August, Blair talked Bush into taking the US' case for attacking Iraq to the UN. Meanwhile, Saddam agreed to the resumption of UN weapons inspections.

43 In September, during the 57th UN General Assembly, Bush asked a skeptical audience of world leaders to confront the 'serious and growing threat to peace' posed by the Iraqi regime, or else to allow the US to act. The following month, Baghdad let the UN weapons inspectors visit dozens of 'sensitive' locations. However the UK and US rejected this as they wanted the Security Council to approve a new resolution which would authorize military attacks if Iraq did not comply with the demands.

44 Backed by a new UN resolution, which was more in line with US and UK wishes, the UN weapons inspectors returned to Iraq in November. The January 2003 report found no evidence of the existence of WMD.

45 Even without that evidence or a new resolution by the Security Council explicitly authorizing the use of force, the US, UK and coalition forces launched an attack on Iraq in March 2003, entering the southern part of the country.

46 In April, US troops entered Baghdad and continued to advance towards northern Iraq, meeting strong resistance only in the main cities like Kirkuk and Mosul. Looting became widespread and the allied forces searched for Saddam Hussein and 54 other 'most-wanted' leaders.

47 In May 2003, the UN Security Council lifted economic sanctions against Iraq. The occupation forces destroyed the Ba'ath Party institutions. The US announced the end of major combat operations.

48 In July, the first Interim Governing Council was formed, and in Mosul, Saddam's sons Uday and Qusay were found and killed. They had been intimately bound up with the violence of the Saddam regime.

49 In October, the Security Council approved amendments to the resolution on Iraq, stating that power should be transferred to the Iraqis 'as soon as possible'. Dozens of people were killed in new car bomb attacks, one of which targeted the Red Cross headquarters.

50 On 14 December, it was announced that Saddam Hussein had

been captured in an underground refuge. Images of the former Iraqi leader were broadcast around the world.

51 In February 2004, while Shi'as in al-Basrah continued to demand direct elections, Kofi Annan - in line with Washington's position and in opposition to the Shi'a majority - announced that the best solution for Iraq would be an interim government (to be installed in June 2004). For the first time since World War II, Japanese troops were deployed overseas in a conflict zone, helping with Iraq's reconstruction.

52 By late February 2004, Iraq remained in a state of chaos and uncertainty regarding its future. Public services were ruined, 12 million Iraqis were unemployed, the budget showed a $600 million deficit, the occupying troops were getting tired and morale was dropping, and attacks by the resistance were becoming increasingly successful.

53 Early in March 2004 the Iraqi Council finally agreed a draft of the interim Constitution which would operate until the permanent

Constitution could be drafted by an assembly elected by the Iraqi people.

54 On 1 June 2004, after the unexpected self-dissolution of the Governing Council, the new interim government took office. Ghazi Yacer, a US-educated civil engineer and tribal leader from the northern town of Mosul was appointed as President. Iyad Allawi, known for his close ties to the CIA, took office as Prime Minister.

55 The insurgency intensified despite the installation of the interim administration. Suicide bombings became a regular occurrence, as did kidnappings of foreign workers, many of which ended in their execution when the kidnappers' demands were not met. The heart of the insurgency was in the northern Sunni-dominated city of Falluja. Following US President Bush's re-election in November 2004 a full-scale assault was launched on the city involving 15,000 US and Iraqi troops. The rationale behind the attack was to destroy the insurgency in preparation for elections early in 2005 but it was likely to be just the latest phase in an increasingly bitter war. ∎

PROFILE

ENVIRONMENT

The Mesopotamian region, between the rivers Tigris (Dijlah) and Euphrates (Al-Furat) in the center of the country, is suitable for agriculture, and contains most of the population of Iraq. There are significant oil deposits in the mountainous areas in the north, in Kurdistan. In Lower Mesopotamia, on the Shatt-al-Arab channel, where the Tigris and the Euphrates merge, palm trees produce 80 per cent of the dates sold worldwide.

SOCIETY

Peoples: Three-fourths of the population is Arab. In the north there is a significant Kurdish minority (20 per cent) and the rest are small minorities of Syrians, Armenians and others. **Religions:** Mainly Muslim. About 62 per cent of the population is Shi'a, concentrated in the south. Sunnis are around 35 per cent. Most of the political élite is Sunni. Northern Kurds blend Sunnism with their traditional religion, Yezidi. There is a Christian minority. **Languages:** Arabic (official and predominant); in Kurdistan it is taught as a second language, after Kurdish. **Main Political Parties:** After the end of the 2003 war, the Interim Governing Council established by the occupation forces in July that year was asked to draw up a Constitution and schedule elections. The Council is made up of 24 representatives of ethnic-religious majorities (12 Shi'as, 5 Sunnis, 5 Kurds, 1 Christian and 1 Turk). After the abolition of the Ba'ath Party, the new political reality is complex and in a state of flux. There are various groups, including Islamic fundamentalists, secular, and Kurds with some cross-over between sectors. The real power still resides in the Coalition Provisional Authority (CPA) which has veto power over the Council's resolutions. **Main Social Organizations:** As in the area of politics, the newly emergent order is still formative. The situation regarding trade unions and social organisations had not yet been clearly defined.

THE STATE

Official Name: Al-Jumhuriyah al-'Iraqiyah. **Administrative Divisions:** 15 provinces and 3 autonomous regions. **Capital:** Baghdad 5,620,000 people (2003). **Other Cities:** Mosul 1,099,700 people; al-Basrah 1,004,800; Irbil 692,100; Karkuk (Kirkuk) 688,500 (2000). **Government:** Interim Governing Council (24 members) with powers to draw up a Constitution and call for elections. It operates under the supervision of the Coalition Provisional Authority (CPA). **National Holiday:** 14 July, Proclamation of the Republic (1958). **Armed Forces:** Undergoing reorganization (as is the police).

Ireland / Êire

Population:	4,040,185
Area:	70,270 km²
Capital:	Dublin
Currency:	Euro
Language:	Gaelic, English

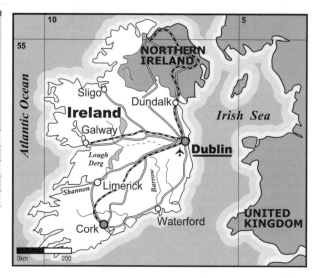

Ireland's original inhabitants were Mesolithic hunter-gatherers who used stone implements. Around 3000 BC, they evolved into Bronze Age people who cultivated crops, raised domestic animals and made weapons, tools and jewelry out of bronze. Starting about 2000 BC, they built the massive stone sanctuaries and tombs (megaliths) that still dot the Irish countryside.

2   The first Celts arrived in Ireland about 1600 BC. Before their arrival, the basic units of Irish society were the *tuatha*, or petty kingdoms; perhaps 150 tuatha for a population of less than 500,000. This societal structure suited the Celts, who were predisposed towards relatively small and autonomous units. At the beginning of the Christian era, the Celts divided Ireland politically into five provinces: Leinster, Munster, Meath, Ulster and Connaught.

3   A bishop and missionary coming from England, St Patrick (c.389-461), arrived in Ireland to convert the inhabitants to Christianity. He was able to make important converts among the royal families and, through the monastery schools, introduced the written word in Latin. By the death of St. Patrick the Irish élite recorded their history in writing. Ireland became almost exclusively Christian, as well as a center of scholarship and culture, but most of this legacy was destroyed in the Viking raids of the 9th and 10th centuries. Pagan customs were incorporated into Christian practice.

4   By the end of the 10th century Brian Boru, the king of a small state called Dal Cais, conquered neighboring Munster and became the strongest king in the southern half of Ireland. But Mael Morda, King of Leinster, began to plot against him and made an alliance with Sitric, the Viking king of Dublin, who got help from the Vikings of the Orkney Islands and the Isle of Man. The battle of Clontarf near Dublin in 1014 ended in victory for Boru's army, but Boru

himself was killed in his tent by Vikings fleeing from the battle.

5   In 1170, a party of Normans coming from England landed near Waterford, which fell in their hands along with Dublin. By 1300, the Normans controlled most of the country but they did not succeed in conquering Ireland because there was no central government that they could take control of. From about 1350, the Irish chieftains - who had acquired many of the weapons used by the Normans and had learnt some of their tactics - began to recover their territories.

6   Queen Mary I was the first English monarch to attempt to subdue Ireland by confiscating land and giving it to English settlers. Her half-sister Elizabeth I continued the policy and sent armed expeditions aimed at subduing rebellion, winning a major battle at Kinsale in 1601.

7   Under King James I from 1608, Ulster was settled by Scottish and English Protestants in a conscious attempt to spread the religion. The leading colonists, who paid rent to the King, were required to clear their estates completely of native Irish inhabitants. Native resentment at the plantation of Ulster led to a major rebellion in 1641. In 1649, following his execution of King Charles I, Oliver Cromwell led a suppressing army and saw atrocities committed in the 1641 rebellion as justification for massacring 4,600 people at Drogheda and Wexford. The power of Protestant landowners was reinforced.

8   When the Catholic King James II was deposed in 1688 he raised an army in Ireland and quickly took control of all but the cities of Derry and Enniskillen. The siege of Protestant Derry became a vital battleground for the whole of Europe: its people held out for eight months before they were relieved, ultimately enabling the

Protestant King William III to confirm his own power and that of Protestants in Ireland at the Battle of the Boyne in 1690.

9   By virtue of the 1 January 1801 Act of Union, Ireland was incorporated into the United Kingdom. During the 19th century most of the population outside the Protestant-dominated northeast supported independence, which led to the formation of a strong nationalist movement.

10   The failure of the potato crop due to blight from 1845 to 1849 resulted in the Great Famine - the diet of the poor was heavily dependent on the tuber. Over 1.1 million Irish - mostly impoverished rural people - died due to undernourishment, typhus and other famine-related diseases, while at least a million others emigrated, mainly to the US. Ireland continued to export food throughout this period - neglect by absentee British landlords and the laissez-faire attitude of the British Government exacerbated the famine.

11   An organized labour movement developed late in Ireland: there was little industry outside the northeast and the political priority was nationalism. The Dublin Lock-out of 1913 marked a sea change: recently unionized workers refused to relinquish union membership and prompted a wave of sympathetic strikes.

12   In 1916, the republican Easter Rising in Dublin was crushed by the occupying forces but it marked the foundation of the Irish Republican Army (IRA) and the final stage of the long struggle for freedom. Although the Rising did not have widespread support, the subsequent execution of many of its leaders and other oppressive measures by the British galvanized support for the republican party

Sinn Fein, which won the majority of seats in the 1918 general election. The IRA's campaign forced the British in 1921 to grant independence to the 26 counties with Catholic majorities. Southern Ireland became a self-governing region within the UK. The remaining six northeastern counties became Northern Ireland, with a devolved government in Belfast and representation in the British parliament in Westminster.

13   Controversy over this settlement caused a bitter civil war in which at least 4,000 died. Though pro-Treaty forces prevailed, relations between the Free State and the British Government remained strained until after World War II, setting back economic development by decades. The 1937 Irish Constitution considered Ireland to be a single country, where all the inhabitants - North and South - have citizenship rights. In 1948 Ireland became a republic, formally breaking from the British Commonwealth.

14   In Northern Ireland, meanwhile, the Protestant majority - which tended to be Unionist, seeing Ulster as part of Britain - had exclusive control, led by the provincial prime minister and a governor acting as a representative of the British Crown. The Catholic minority in Northern Ireland - which tended to be nationalist - was thus excluded from domestic political affairs and faced discrimination. This led to the creation of an active civil rights movement in the 1960s. Although it was non-violent, the civil rights movement was considered a threat to the region's status and their dominant position by Protestant extremists and they reacted to it with violence.

15   In April 1969, amidst growing disturbances, the Northern Ireland Government requested British troops to protect the region's strategic installations. In August, Belfast and London agreed that all the Province's security forces should come under British command.

16   As a counterpart to the Provisional IRA, the 'loyalists' (loyal to the British Crown) formed a number of paramilitary organizations, including the Ulster Volunteer Force and the Ulster Defence Association. Between 1969 and the middle of 1994, more than 3,100 people died at the hands of the Protestant and Catholic paramilitaries, the British army and the Ulster police force, the Royal Ulster Constabulary (RUC).

17   On 30 January 1972 (Bloody Sunday) 13 Catholics were murdered by British troops while demonstrating peacefully in the city of Derry. In the same year, political status was given to

 Life expectancy
77.0 years
2000-2005

 GNI per capita
$23,870
2002

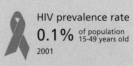 HIV prevalence rate
0.1% of population
15-49 years old
2001

paramilitary prisoners, but this amendment was abolished in 1976.

18   The growing violence provoked London to take over full responsibility for law and order in Northern Ireland. The Government in Belfast was abolished and a system of 'direct rule' from Westminster installed in 1972. In a plebiscite held in 1973, 60 per cent of the population of Northern Ireland voted in favor of union with Britain.

19   At the end of 1973, a Northern Irish Assembly and Executive was created in Belfast in which Protestant and Catholic representatives were supposed to share power. In December, the London and Dublin governments agreed on the establishment of an Irish Council. Both this agreement and the new power-sharing Assembly were bitterly opposed by Unionists. In 1974 a general strike was declared, which resulted in the resignation of the Executive and London took over direct rule once more.

20   In the 1973 election in the Irish Republic, Fianna Fáil (FF) - a party which had been in power for 35 of the previous 41 years - was defeated. A coalition between the conservative Fine Gael (FG) and the Labour Party (LP) took office. It was committed to power-sharing between the two communities in Ulster, but it rejected the

immediate withdrawal of British troops from the region. Ireland joined the European Community in 1973, a decisive shift away from economic dependence on Britain.

21   In 1976, after the IRA murdered the British ambassador in Dublin, and two years after bombings in Dublin and Monaghan killed 33 and injured hundreds more, the Irish Government took stricter anti-terrorist measures. Fianna Fáil was elected in 1977 and it maintained the friendly relations with London established by the previous administration. The new Taoiseach (head of the Irish Government) Jack Lynch supported the creation of a devolved parliament in the North, instead of total unification.

22   In August 1979, Dublin agreed to increase border security after the murders, on the same day, of Lord Mountbatten (a prominent British public figure related to the Royal Family) in the Irish Republic, and 18 British soldiers in Warrenpoint, Northern Ireland. In December, Lynch resigned and was replaced by Charles Haughey, who went back to the old idea of reunification with some form of autonomy in Ulster.

23   A referendum held in 1983 approved a constitutional amendment affirming the ban on abortion. In 1986, a government proposal to remove the constitutional prohibition on

divorce was defeated in a referendum.

24   Talks between the Irish and British heads of Government from 1980 onwards led to the signing of the Anglo-Irish Agreement in 1985. With it, the Dublin Government would have a say in political, judicial, security and border issues in Northern Ireland. Most Unionists in Northern Ireland were strongly opposed, but the Agreement guaranteed that no constitutional change could be made without the consent of the North's population.

25   In the 1980s, the Irish economy suffered high unemployment levels (an average of 16.4 per cent between 1983 and 1988) and emigration levels, added to high inflation rates and industrial recession. Strict austerity measures, applied from 1987, allowed for growth in the second half of the decade.

26   In November 1990, Mary Robinson, the Labour Party candidate and a lawyer who stood up for the rights of gays, women and the legal recognition of illegitimate children, became the first woman president of Ireland.

27   Multi-party negotiations began in Belfast in April 1991, in another attempt to define Northern Ireland's political future, with representatives from Ulster's constitutional parties and the British Government. Sinn Féin, the

political arm of the Provisional IRA, which supported the immediate withdrawal of British troops, the disarmament of the Royal Ulster Constabulary (RUC) police and Ireland's reunification, was excluded from the talks for having refused to condemn the IRA's acts of violence.

28   Meanwhile, the IRA launched one of its largest military offensives, both in Ulster and England. In early 1992, in Ulster, independent Republicans were responsible for several acts of arson in businesses and shops. From late 1991, Protestant paramilitary groups had reinforced their attacks on Catholics. These groups said they were willing to reply with 'an eye for an eye' to every IRA action.

29   During January 1993, Albert Reynolds (FF) was confirmed as head of the FF/Labour Party Government in the Republic. At the same time, a referendum on abortion led two-thirds of voters to support the right to information on birth control and abortion and the right to travel abroad to carry out an abortion.

30   In January 1994, the British Government lifted all restrictions on TV and radio broadcasts of interviews with Sinn Féin members. In August, the IRA declared it was ceasing all military operations.

31   The Reynolds Administration fell in November, after the Labour

IN FOCUS

ENVIRONMENTAL CHALLENGES
Water pollution is the main environmental challenge, particularly in lakes due to agricultural runoff. Even though acid rain decreased by 7 per cent from 1990 to 2001, carbon dioxide emissions increased by 122 per cent as a consequence of a 68-per-cent rise in the number of vehicles.

WOMEN'S RIGHTS
There was a partial franchise for women in 1918, and this was extended to them all in 1928. Between 1995 and 2000 parliamentary seats held by women decreased from 14 to 13 per cent, while their representation in ministerial or equivalent positions increased from 16 to 20 per cent.

In 1985 women comprised 30 per cent of the workforce, increasing to 48.8 per cent in 2002 (1.7 per cent in agriculture, 13.5 per cent in industry and 84.8 per cent in services). Ireland is one of the EU countries with the lowest female participation in the labor market. 30 per cent of women worked part-time in

2002, compared with only 6.5 per cent of the men. Women do most of the childcare and, as their salaries are on average 24 per cent lower than men's, affordable childcare is not an option. In addition, many men get more social benefits related to their employment than women (pensions, better health insurance, mortgage relief and so on). In order to concord with the commitments under the Beijing 1995 convention, in 2002 the Government published its National Plan for Women (2001-2005). Ireland is the only EU country where abortion is illegal.

CHILDREN
Children in the Irish Republic have better access to education, good nutrition, health and housing than their counterparts in the North. There has been an improvement in Northern Ireland's economy since the 1998 peace agreements, as investment levels have increased in the hope of a lasting settlement. In 2001 over 80 per cent of the students finished high school and 50 per cent entered university.

In 2002, surveys confirmed that, as a result of the years of

conflict, even pre-school children from both Catholic or Protestant families showed sectarian or bigoted feelings towards people or symbols of the other faith.

INDIGENOUS PEOPLES/ ETHNIC MINORITIES
Some sectors of the population speak Gaelic and maintain some traditional ways of life, but Ireland's ethnic diversity today comes more from late 20th-century immigration (70 per cent of immigrants are from European countries) than from its original inhabitants.

In spite of the 1998 Good Friday Agreement, many Catholics in Northern Ireland still feel they are socially discriminated against.

MIGRANTS/REFUGEES
By the end of 2002, Ireland hosted more than 6,500 refugees and asylum-seekers in need of protection. These included over 4,500 asylum-seekers with applications pending and about 2,000 persons granted refugee status.

Ireland received 11,634 asylum applications in 2002, almost 12 per cent more than in 2001. According

to the UNHCR, the largest numbers of applications came from Nigeria, Romania, Moldova, Zimbabwe and Ukraine.

Around 7,450 applications were rejected during 2002, while another 8,200 were closed following applicants' failure to attend a second interview.

Almost 300 unaccompanied children sought asylum in Ireland in 2002, less than half the number in 2001.

Since 1998 the hopes for peace and (in the South) its membership of the EU have made Ireland a magnet for migrants as its economy has improved. This is in contrast to its history as a country of emigration. From 1997 to 2000, 66,000 Irish returned home, and more are anticipated. In addition, figures for the 2001 -2006 period project an in-migration of over 300,000 from different nationalities.

DEATH PENALTY
Capital punishment for ordinary crimes was abolished in 1990. The last execution was in 1954.

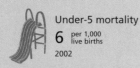

Under-5 mortality
6 per 1,000 live births
2002

$ **Aid**
0.40% Official development assistance as % of donors' GNI
2002

Maternal mortality
5 per 100,000 live births
2000

Party withdrew its support due to the controversy on the delay of extradition to Northern Ireland of a priest accused of pedophilia. The new Prime Minister was John Bruton, who led a coalition of his FG Party with the Labour Party and the Democratic Left.

[32] Widespread sexual and physical abuse of children by priests and religious orders has been exposed over the past decade. Inquiries and compensation tribunals are considering the cases of up to 10,000 victims of abuse over the past 50 years. The state has underwritten the compensation fund - while the religious orders are contributing cash and property transfers, the taxpayer will bear the brunt of the cost.

[33] The Roman Catholic Church, pre-eminent in social and political affairs since before independence, has suffered a major loss in confidence, with mass attendance falling rapidly in the last decade.

[34] In a referendum in 1995, the Irish approved (by 50 to 49 per cent of the vote) a constitutional reform authorizing divorce for couples separated for more than four years.

[35] In the June 1996 round of talks held in Belfast, Irish leader Bruton supported the British proposal to exclude Sinn Féin from the negotiating table, since both governments regarded the IRA's attitude as unconstructive. In February the IRA ended its unilateral ceasefire by setting off a bomb in London that killed two people and hurt several others.

[36] In April 1997, several attacks announced by the IRA on streets, train stations and airports paralyzed the British transport system during the election campaign. Sinn Féin asked the IRA to declare a new ceasefire, which was decided in July. Negotiations were resumed in September, with the inclusion of Sinn Féin.

[37] Fianna Fáil won the June 1997 Irish general election with 77 out of 166 seats, forming a minority coalition with the Progressive Democrats and the support of independents. Bertie Ahern became Prime Minister. Mary McAleese became President.

[38] After tough negotiations, on 10 April 1998 a peace agreement on Northern Ireland was reached in Belfast (the Good Friday Agreement). The text, negotiated by eight political parties, mediated by London, Dublin and Washington, included limited autonomy for Northern Ireland, with the creation of a power-sharing executive (cabinet), legislative assembly and cross-border co-operation bodies. The plan also called for the gradual release of political prisoners and for the disarmament of

paramilitary organizations whose parties took part in the negotiations and the reconstitution of the police force to encourage nationalists to join.

[39] Most political forces, including Sinn Féin and the political wings of loyalist paramilitaries, initially favored the Agreement, which overcame its first hurdle when Ulster Unionist leader David Trimble received the support of his party, the Ulster Unionist Party (UUP). Only two Unionist parties were opposed: the Democratic Unionist Party (DUP), of Dr Ian Paisley, and Robert McCartney's United Kingdom Unionist Party (UKUP).

[40] In late May a referendum ratified the Agreement with 94 per cent of the vote in the Republic and 72 per cent in the North. A month later the first elections were held to form the Assembly as of February 1999. The new agreement paved the way for the people of Ulster to decide the Province's future, through a vote, to reunite with Ireland or to remain within the UK.

[41] In August, a bomb in Omagh, Northern Ireland, killed 30 people and endangered the fragile peace process. But the uproar caused by the attack on both sides of the border led the republican group responsible for the bomb (the Real IRA, a splinter group from the Provisional IRA) to declare a unilateral ceasefire.

[42] The establishment in December 1999 of the first Government of Northern Ireland in 25 years, although 'cross-border', confirmed the 'devolution' of sovereignty to the Province by the British Parliament. This new ruling body (Executive Council) was formed by the Prime Minister, David Trimble, from the UUP, with the deputy Prime Minister, Seamus Mallon, of the Social Democratic and Labour Party (SDLP) and 10 ministers, three belonging to the pro-British UUP and the moderate Catholic SDLP, and two each from Sinn Féin and the DUP. It was the first time representatives from these parties had joint political responsibilities.

[43] Coinciding with the inauguration of the new Government, the Republic of Ireland withdrew its constitutional claim over Northern Ireland, which it had maintained since Ireland's independence from the UK. The commitment was signed while the cross-border bodies were being set up in which Northern and Southern Irish would take part.

[44] Ireland has traditionally been a country of emigration but that situation has reversed to some degree in recent years. The country experienced significant and sustained economic growth in the 1980s and 1990s, and low unemployment turned it into a net

importer of skilled labor. Between 1995 and 2000 more than 250,000 foreigners entered the country.

[45] The Irish economic boom derived in part from significant investment by the European Union and in part from a successful shift into hi-tech industries: Ireland became the largest exporter of computer software outside the US and hosts the European headquarters of the Microsoft, Intel and Dell corporations. The boom of the 'Celtic Tiger' has, however, gone hand in hand with a widening gap between rich and poor: the Irish Republic has the worst economic inequality among OECD countries after the US.

[46] The Nice Treaty, which paved the way for 12 Eastern Europe countries to join the EU, was rejected by the Irish in a referendum held in June 2001 but accepted in a second referendum in October 2002. Unlike Britain, Ireland adopted the euro as its currency in January 2002.

[47] The FF/PD coalition was returned to power with an overall majority in the 2002 general election.

[48] By a margin of less than 2 per cent, a referendum in March 2002

rejected the Government's proposal constitutionally to prohibit any legislation allowing pregnant women allegedly at risk of suicide to have abortions. It was estimated some 40,000 Irish women travel to the UK each year to have an abortion.

[49] In October 2002, Sinn Féin members were arrested in Belfast, charged with espionage and attempting to obtain official information for terrorist purposes. London suspended Ulster's Executive Council and the Legislative Assembly and resumed control of Northern Ireland.

[50] The outcome of November 2003 Northern Ireland Legislative Assembly elections showed gains of 10 seats for the DUP and 6 seats for Sinn Féin, strengthening the two parties at opposite ends of the local political spectrum. London has not yet restored the authority of the Assembly nor of the Executive.

[51] Economic growth in the Republic, which was 8 per cent for the 1995-2002 period, went down to just 2.7 per cent in 2003.

[52] In January 2004 Ireland took over the Presidency of the EU for six months. ■

PROFILE

ENVIRONMENT

The country comprises most of the island of Ireland. The south is made up of rocky hills, none over 1,000 meters in height. The central plain extends from east to west and is irrigated by many rivers and lakes. With a humid ocean climate and poor soil, much of the country is covered with grazing land. Farming is concentrated mainly along the eastern slopes of the hills and the Shannon valleys. The main agricultural products are wheat, barley, oats, potatoes and beet. Meat and milk processing are among the major local industrial activities.

SOCIETY

Peoples: The Irish comprise 94 per cent of the population, with a small English minority. The great famines which struck the island over the last two centuries led to the emigration of about 4 million Irish people, especially to the US.
Religions: 91.6 per cent Catholic, 2.3 per cent Anglican, 0.4 per cent Presbyterian (1991).
Languages: Irish, English and Shelta (language of the Travelers/gypsies/Roma people).
Main Political Parties: Fianna Fáil (FF), conservative; Fine Gael (FG), Christian democratic linked to the rural population; Labour Party; Progressive Democrats; Green Party; the Democratic Left and Sinn Féin, republican movement party based in Northern Ireland.
Main Social Organizations: The Irish Congress of Trade Unions, with 750,000 members and 64 affiliated unions.

THE STATE

Official Name: Poblacht na h'Eireann.
Administrative Divisions: 26 Counties.
Capital: Dublin 1,015,000 people (2003).
Other Cities: Cork 123.100 people; Limerick 54.000; Galway 65.800; Waterford 44.600 (2002).
Government: Mary McAleese, President since November 1997. Bartholomew (Bertie) Ahern, Prime Minister since June 1997, re-elected in May 2002. Bicameral Parliament: the House of Representatives, with 166 members, and the Senate, with 60 members.
National Holiday: 17 March (St Patrick's Day).
Armed Forces: 10.559 (2002).

Israel / Yisra 'el

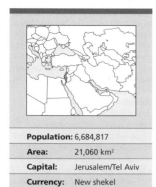

Population:	6,684,817
Area:	21,060 km²
Capital:	Jerusalem/Tel Aviv
Currency:	New shekel
Language:	Hebrew and Arabic

OCCUPIED BY ISRAEL
1. Syria - Golan Heights - occupied in 1967
2. Southern Lebanon - occupied 1983-2000
3. West Bank - occupied in 1967
4. Gaza Strip - occupied 1967-1994
○ Recovered by Palestine from 1994: Gaza Strip, Jericho, Nablus, Ramallah

S ome form of a Jewish national entity, formed out of an amalgamation of Israelite tribal territorial societies, existed intermittently in the region for well over a millennium until the brutal persecution of the Jews by the Roman authorities from 70 AD. It was conquered from the Eastern Roman Empire (Byzantines) by the Caliphate in the 7th century and attracted Arab settlers. Throughout the centuries, the size of the Jewish population in the land fluctuated.

2	By the 1800s, about 25,000 Jews still lived in their ancient homeland, Palestine ('Land of the Philistines', the Latin name given to Judea by the Roman Emperor Hadrian). A rise in European antisemitism and pogroms inspired a new wave of Jewish emigration to Palestine in the 1880s.

3	In 1896 Viennese journalist Theodor Herzl published *The Jewish State*. Influenced by the European nationalism of the 19th century, he envisaged a Jewish nation-state that would put an end to antisemitism. The name Zionism is derived from Zion, one of the biblical names for Jerusalem. Initially, the Zionist movement was not particularly focused on Palestine and explored many possible places to establish a Jewish state through the purchase of land, such as Uganda and Madagascar.

4	During World War I, Britain and France agreed to divide up the remains of the Ottoman Empire in the Middle East. In 1917, British Foreign Secretary Arthur Balfour declared his support for the establishment of a national homeland for the Jewish people in Palestine; as Prime Minister in 1905 he had opposed Jewish immigration into Britain. He stated 'that nothing shall be done which may prejudice the civil and religious rights of existing non-Jewish communities in Palestine' (90 per cent of the population at that time). It was this 1917 Balfour Declaration and the Jewish people's historical ties to the Holy Land which captured the imagination of many ordinary Jews who suffered persecution in Europe,

and Zionism hence became principally focused on Palestine.

5	The Zionist goal of Jewish statehood was violently opposed by local Arab leaders, who saw the Ottoman Turks' defeat as an opportunity either to create their own state or to join a larger Arab entity and revive the old Arab empire of early Islam.

6	At the end of World War II, Britain retained control of Palestine, based on its commitment under the Balfour Declaration. Jewish militias grew, the largest of them being the *Haganah* (Defense), a branch of the Jewish Agency, responsible for bringing Jews to Israel. These militias were associated with political factions from both the Right and Left of Zionist politics. The *Irgun Zvai Leumi* and its more violent splinter group, *Lehi* (also known as the Stern Gang), were affiliated with the ultra-conservative Revisionist Party, founded by Vladimir Zev Jabotinsky. The *Palmach*, though technically an élite arm of the *Haganah*, recruited many of its members from socialist-oriented *kibbutzim*. Yigal Allon, Moshe Dayan, and Yitzhak Rabin were members of these militias.

7	Staunch Zionists regarded Jews the world over as exiles, and they organized migration to Israel from all corners of the globe. At the beginning of the 20th century there were 500,000 Arabs and 50,000 Jews living in Palestine. By the 1930s, the number of Jews had risen to 300,000 - above the British-imposed quotas - largely due to Jewish flight from antisemitic persecutions in Nazi Germany. The British saw their power in Palestine threatened since the Arabs of Palestine had also increased (through high birth rates and immigration) to roughly 1,000,000 in 1940.

8	In 1939 London declared that its aim was to set up an independent Palestinian state with both peoples sharing government. Ships bringing refugees from Hitler's Europe were turned back from Palestinian ports. The Zionists organized acts of sabotage and terrorism, using force to hold Britain to its promise.

9	Using donations from Jews all over the world, the Zionists purchased Palestinian lands from Arab owners living in Beirut or Paris, who cared little about the fate of their tenants, the Palestinian *fellahin*

(peasants). The Jews then arrived, deeds in hand, to expel peasant families that had lived there for generations. They set up co-operative agricultural colonies, *kibbutzim*, defending themselves from a now hostile climate through armed militia.

10	In February 1947, in view of intensified anti-British attacks, London submitted the Palestinian problem to the United Nations. A special committee recommended partition of the territory into two independent states; one Arab, the other Jewish. Jerusalem would remain under international administration.

11	In that Cold War era, the Soviet Union preferred a Jewish state to a British military base, and its support was decisive in the creation of Israel. At the same time, London and Washington considered the partition unfeasible.

12	The UN General Assembly finally approved the partition plan in a 33 to 13 vote (Arab countries and India), with 10 abstentions. Hardline Zionist militias began to expel Palestinians *en masse* from major cities and towns, alleging an imminent Arab attack. This policy culminated in a massacre at the village of Deir Yasin in April 1948, when the *Irgun*, an extremist group led by Menachem Begin, murdered its entire population.

13	On 14 May 1948, the British High Commissioner withdrew from Palestine, and David Ben Gurion proclaimed the State of Israel. The Jordanian, Egyptian, Syrian, Iraqi and Lebanese armies attacked immediately.

14	The war ended in January 1949, and Israel obtained 40 per cent more territory than it had been due under the partition plan. Although weapons and aircraft purchased from the Soviet Union proved decisive in the Israeli victory, the Government of Israel supported the West in the Cold War and formed a strategic alliance with the US. This relationship, lasting to this day, experienced difficult moments when in 1956, Israeli troops backed by France and Britain invaded Egypt in response to the nationalization of the Suez Canal. The US and the USSR firmly opposed the action, forcing the invaders to withdraw with agreement from Egypt that it would stop sending fighters into Israeli territory.

15	Egyptian President Gamal Abdel Nasser, deprived of US credit and arms, turned to the USSR, which led to even closer relations between Israel and the US. Egypt and Syria, who were backed by the Soviet Union, and Jordan, supported by Britain, maintained a constant pressure of guerilla raids on Israeli civilians.

16	Several years later, the border with Syria remained a scene of

Life expectancy
79.2 years
2000-2005

GNI per capita
$16,710
2002

Literacy
95% total adult rate
2000

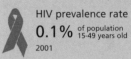
HIV prevalence rate
0.1% of population 15-49 years old
2001

constant conflict, particularly as both sides squabbled over access to fresh water from the Sea of Galilee. It was later revealed that the Soviet Union had intentionally escalated the situation in the Middle East by sending false messages to the various Arab states that the Israelis were massing their forces at the border with Syria.

17 On 17 May 1967, Nasser demanded that the UN Emergency Force (UNEF) - a UN peacekeeping force set up after the 1956 Suez war - leave Egypt, which the then UN Secretary-General U Thant complied with. Nasser immediately began remilitarizing the Sinai Peninsula, increasing tensions with Israel. On 23 May, the Egyptian Navy closed off the Straits of Tiran blockading Israeli shipping and the port of Eilat at the North of the Gulf of Aqaba. Egypt and Jordan had also signed a mutual defense treaty on 30 May (treaties with Syria already existed). Israel launched an attack on Egypt on 5 June and thus the Six-Day War began.

18 The war resulted in the Israeli seizure of the Jordanian-controlled West Bank of the Jordan River and East Jerusalem, Syria's Golan Heights, the Egyptian-controlled Gaza Strip and the Sinai Peninsula. Soon after the end of the Six-Day War, Prime Minister Eshkol's cabinet voted in favor of withdrawing from all the occupied territories (except East Jerusalem) in exchange for a comprehensive peace treaty.

19 In response, in September 1967, 8 Arab leaders agreed the Khartoum Declaration which condemned Israel and guided Arab states' policy towards Israel until the mid-1970s. Specifically, the Declaration called for no peace with Israel, no recognition of Israel, no negotiations with it, and insistence on the rights of the Palestinian people in their own country.

20 Resolution 242 of the UN Security Council (22 November 1967), calls for peace and recognition of the right of every nation to live free from threat within secure and recognized boundaries, in return for Israel's withdrawal from the occupied territories.

21 The armed conflict that broke out in 1973, known as the Yom Kippur war as it took place on one of Judaism's holiest days, began when Egyptian troops crossed the Suez Canal and Syrian forces attempted to regain the Golan Heights. They were supported militarily and financially by many Arab states including Saudi Arabia, Kuwait, Iraq, Algeria, Libya, Tunisia, Sudan and Morocco. The war ended the myth of Israeli military invincibility, but it did not lead to a significant modification of the border lines.

22 In 1977, Menachem Begin was elected Prime Minister, breaking the

historical continuity of Labor Party rule.

23 Begin refused to negotiate with the Palestine Liberation Organization (PLO) and expressed his intention to annex the West Bank. Meanwhile in 1977, the US persuaded Egyptian President Anwar Sadat to sign the Camp David Agreement, leading to peace between Cairo and Tel Aviv and the return of Sinai to Egypt.

24 In June 1982, Israel launched 'Operation Peace for Galilee', invading Lebanon and devastating Beirut, under the pretext of stopping infiltration by Palestinian guerrilla groups. Arafat's forces withdrew from Lebanon in exchange for the deployment of a joint force of Italians, French, and North Americans to guarantee the security of Palestinian civilians.

25 Despite the agreement, in September 1982 hundreds of Palestinian refugees were murdered by right-wing militia in the Sabra and Shatila refugee camps, within Israeli-controlled areas. Dissent in Israel led to a 400,000-strong demonstration sponsored by the group Peace Now. Begin was forced to appoint a commission of inquiry, which found then Defense Minister Ariel Sharon and other military leaders 'indirectly responsible' for the murders.

26 In December 1987, the funerals of several young Palestinians killed in a clash with Israeli military patrols led to further confrontations, general strikes and civil protests. This marked the beginning of the first *intifada* (uprising - literally, 'shaking off') and Middle Eastern politics were shaken from the least expected quarter - the unarmed grassroots.

27 On 17 January 1991, in answer to the start of the first Gulf War, Iraq launched several Scud-missile attacks on Israel, aimed at provoking it to war. However, Israel did not do so, leaving its defense to Patriot anti-missile units operated by US troops.

28 When the war ended in March 1991, the US presented diplomatic circles with a 'land for peace' proposal. Two months later in Damascus, Syria and Lebanon signed a 'brotherhood, co-operation and co-ordination' treaty. To Israel, this treaty constituted a Syrian threat to a region in the north rich in water sources.

29 That year, Israel asked the US to approve loans of $10 billion to ease its economic difficulties, caused by the resettling of between 250,000 and 400,000 Soviet Jews from 1989 to 1991.

30 The Government created new settlements for immigrants on the West Bank where in 1991, despite efforts to create new jobs, unemployment reached 11 per cent.

31 Attempting to promote peace negotiations in the region, Washington imposed the condition that loans granted would not be

invested in settlements in occupied territories.

32 The settlements became a double-edged sword for Yitzhak Shamir's Government. The US loans and new settlements were both vitally important, while Palestinians and other Arabs demanded an end to new settlements, so the peace talks could continue.

33 On 30 October 1991, a Middle East Peace Conference was held in Madrid, sponsored by the US and the USSR. Shortly afterwards, hundreds of thousands of Israelis held demonstrations, calling on their government to maintain a dialogue with the Palestinians and Israel's Arab neighbors. Delegations from Jordan, Lebanon, Syria and Israel attended the conference; the Palestinians formed part of the Jordanian delegation, as Israel refused to negotiate directly with them.

34 In June 1992, Labor won a decisive victory in the general elections and Yitzhak Rabin became prime minister. Construction of housing in the occupied territories came to an abrupt standstill, and the US lifted the embargo on loans for Israel.

35 After months of secret negotiations in Oslo, Norway, Israeli authorities and PLO leaders signed the Declaration of the Principles of the Interim Self-Government Arrangements, in Washington in September 1993. The Oslo Accords foresaw the installation of a limited autonomy system for Palestinians in the Gaza Strip and the city of Jericho for a five-year period, which would then be extended to include all of the West Bank.

36 The agreement was questioned, due to the opposition of *Hamas* and the Iranian-backed *Hizbullah*, two radical Islamist movements. Meanwhile, Jewish settlers in the occupied territories - supplied with arms by the Government - rejected the agreement (as it stipulated their withdrawal, along with that of the Israeli army).

37 In early May 1994, Israeli Prime Minister Rabin and PLO leader Yasser Arafat signed an agreement in Cairo granting autonomy to Gaza and Jericho. Late that month, the Israeli army withdrew from Gaza, ending 27 years of occupation (see Palestine).

38 1995 was marked by a growing division of Israeli society regarding the peace process with the Palestinians, leading to Rabin's assassination by a young far-right Israeli. Shimon Peres, also from the Labor Party, took Rabin's place but was defeated in the general elections of May 1996 by right-wing leader Binyamin Netanyahu.

40 The return to power of the conservatives hindered negotiations with Palestinians and heightened tensions, putting the country on the brink of a new war. In September the

Government authorized the opening of a tunnel under the Temple Mount, the most sacred site to Jews, but also the home of the Al-Aqsa mosque, the third most sacred place of Islam. This provoked a Palestinian reaction with subsequent disturbances and deaths.

41 Netanyahu, harshly critical of Rabin for having held talks with Arafat and the PLO, met with the Palestinian leader on numerous occasions in late 1996 and early 1997 to negotiate the complete withdrawal of Israeli troops from the city of Hebron in the West Bank.

42 In March 1997, the Government announced its plan to build a new settlement in the Har Homa hills, on the Palestinian outskirts of Jerusalem. The Palestine Authority and the US rejected the project (which ran counter to the spirit of the Oslo Accords) and the negotiations stalled.

43 Ehud Barak, a retired general, had replaced Peres as leader of the Labor Party and became leader of the opposition in 1996. The Labor Party wanted an agreement with the conservative Likud Party to form a unity government that would allow the resumption of the peace process, suspended.

44 After strong international pressure, Netanyahu accepted the US proposal to seek an accord to restart the peace process. He met US President Clinton and Arafat at Wye River in the US. It was agreed that Israel would return Palestinian territory in exchange for Arafat's acceptance of supervision by US intelligence organizations in his fight against terrorism by Islamic groups. The accord, which weakened Arafat in the eyes of his internal enemies, also led to the fall of the Likud Government. Labor backed the signing of the accords, but the governing coalition dissolved and several Likud legislators abandoned the party. The elections of 17 May 1999 were won by Barak's Labor Party. Breaking with a 50-year tradition, in November Israel lifted the state of emergency, which had been in effect since 1948.

45 In late May 2000, Prime Minister Barak ordered the total withdrawal of troops from South Lebanon, occupied since 1982.

46 Another summit was held at Camp David in the US from 11-25 July, but failed in part because agreements on Israeli withdrawal did not materialize and the Palestinian territories were blockaded following a terrorist attack committed by extremist groups.

47 On 28 September 2000, Likud leader Ariel Sharon's visit to the Temple Mount (*Al-Haram Ash-Sharif* to Muslims) - sacred to both Muslims and Jews - triggered a new Palestinian uprising, now commonly referred to as the Second Intifada or

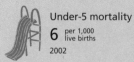
Under-5 mortality

6 per 1,000
live births

2002

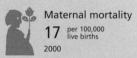
Maternal mortality

17 per 100,000
live births

2000

the Al-Aqsa Intifada. Hundreds of people, mostly Arabs, died in clashes in the following months. This period has also been marked by the increased frequency of suicide bombings against Israeli civilian targets by groups such as Islamic Jihad, Hamas, Hizbullah and the Al-Aqsa Martyrs' Brigade. Ariel Sharon also stepped up his policy of targetted assassinations against Palestinian leaders.

[48] Barak resigned in December to hasten new elections. In a low poll, Sharon won 62 per cent of the vote, and negotiated a unity government with Barak. Sharon took office in March 2001 with Shimon Peres as Foreign Minister. Sharon's mandate turned into one of effective rupture with the Oslo Accords. Arafat tried to meet Israel's security demands by stepping up repression against Islamic extremist organizations, but the critical social situation (including 40 per cent unemployment) breathed new life into the Intifada. In the following

months the armed clashes multiplied and all attempts to reach a truce were frustrated.

[49] The US and Israel withdrew their representatives from the UN-sponsored World Conference Against Racism, held in Durban (South Africa) in early September 2001, when Arab delegations and a majority of the NGO Forum categorized the Jewish State as racist and blamed it for 'crimes of war, acts of genocide and ethnic cleansing.'

[50] After the 11 September 2001 terrorist attacks on Washington and New York, Sharon stepped up the offensive against the Palestinian uprising. The effects of the war began to take a toll on the Israeli economy. Investment fell 65 per cent and some 200,000 people were left without jobs. International tourism dried up, further aggravating the situation. In just one year the tourism revenues shrank by 51 per cent, particularly in Jerusalem and Bethlehem. When it barred Palestinian workers' entry to Israel, Sharon's Government was left not

only without cheap labor, but also without consumers, as the Palestinian territories had been Israel's leading external market.

[51] Israeli Tourism Minister Rehavim Ze'evi was murdered in Jerusalem on 17 October 2001. Israeli forces searched for his murderers in Palestinian territories, and as part of these operations, Yasser Arafat's compound in Ramallah was besieged.

[52] On 29 December Sharon declared that Arafat could not leave his compound until Ze'evi's two alleged murderers - purportedly hiding out with Arafat in Ramallah - were arrested and handed over. Thus, any efforts at negotiation were cut off.

[53] Sharon faced charges of genocide for the 1982 Shabra and Shatila massacre, in a Belgian court. The ruling, due on 6 March 2002, was postponed so that the attorneys could debate, in a new hearing, the International Criminal Court's ruling to grant immunity to sitting heads of state.

[54] Protests against the Israeli reprisals spread around the world.

Thousands of people demonstrated outside Israeli embassies, and in Brazil and Ecuador the supporters of the Palestinian cause burned Israeli flags and protested against the re-occupation of the West Bank cities. In Indonesia, hundreds of youths took to the streets to demand the creation of a Palestinian State.

[55] On 3 January 2002, the Israeli army withdrew from the Palestinian territories, but continued the siege of Arafat's headquarters, shortly before the arrival of US envoy Anthony Zinni.

[56] Hizbullah repeatedly bombed Israeli army positions in the Shebaa Farms in Lebanon, and Israel responded with incursions into southern Lebanon. Sharon declared UN envoy Tarje Larsen *persona non grata* because he had described what occurred in Jenin, a Palestinian refugee camp that had been reduced to rubble after Israeli bombings, as 'a morally repugnant humanitarian disaster'. As a result of incursions into Jenin and other cities under relative control of the Palestinian Authority,

IN FOCUS

ENVIRONMENTAL CHALLENGES

Limited arable land and natural fresh water sources pose serious constraints, making it necessary to import water, mainly from Turkey. Almost ten pesticides forbidden in Western countries were still being used in Israel as of 2001. There is significant air pollution from the burning of fossil fuels in urban and industrial areas. However, solar energy is used for many functions, and research on new energy sources is ongoing. Drip irrigation technology and other water-saving measures are widely used.

WOMEN'S RIGHTS

The status of women within Orthodox Jewish circles is criticized by liberal and modern sectors. Since 1990 the Chief Rabbinate recognized women's right to serve as lawyers in rabbinical courts, which represented a great step forward in a system completely dominated by men. Outside of religion, gender equality is guaranteed by law. Women hold 15 per cent of seats in parliament. The *Histadrut* - the federation of trade unions in Israel - has adopted a resolution declaring that 30 per cent of its leaders must be women. The first Affirmative Action legislation, which applied only to directors of state corporations, was enacted in 1993. In 1995 a broad amendment concerning the entire civil service was passed. Through advocacy and lobbying by women's organizations and legal action,

this progressive legislation is now being more broadly interpreted and more widely enforced. Many political parties now stipulate a minimum number of women on all party lists, but these requirements are not yet implemented at all levels of party activity. Equal rights and duties entail compulsory military service for both men and women - three years for men and two for women. Women who hold strong religious convictions can choose to do their military service in health or education institutions, among other options. Arab women are limited by social norms that impede them from leaving their towns to work (see Palestine). Trafficking of women remains a huge problem. A June 2004 Knesset committee report found that '3,000 women are sold each year in Israel's sex industry', and forced to work in deplorable conditions.

CHILDREN

In education, discrimination is widely reported, especially in terms of resource allocation by the Government. Spending on Jewish children is notoriously higher than spending on Arab children. While 95 per cent of Jewish three-year-olds attend pre-school, only 44 per cent of Arab children do so.

In 2002, 28.1 per cent of the population lived below the poverty line. A great majority of those lived in the Gaza Strip, inhabited by over one million Palestinians whose workplaces are on the Israeli side. Constant closing of the border by the Israeli army due to terrorist

attacks prevents workers from getting to their jobs, leading to an economic slowdown. Another 70,000 people (including 40,000 children) would fall into poverty, according to 2003 projections.

Compulsory military service and familiarity with weapons from an early age lead to, among other things, acts of violence by children and adolescents in school.

INDIGENOUS PEOPLES/ ETHNIC MINORITIES

Almost one million of Israel's inhabitants are Arabs, Druze, Bedouins and Circassians. The situation of Arab citizens, those who remained in Israel after the wars of 1948 and 1967, remains complex (see Palestine).

The Druze (*Mowahhidoon*) broke off from Islam in the 10th century, and have always lived in the Middle East. The Druze community in Israel is officially recognized as a separate religious entity with its own courts (with jurisdiction in matters of personal status - marriage, divorce, maintenance and adoption) and spiritual leadership. In Israel they serve in the army.

The Government is promoting the development of seven southern towns to encourage Bedouins to adopt a sedentary way of life, contrary to their traditions. In the year 2000, half of the 120,000 Israeli Bedouins lived in towns not recognized by the Government, lacking basic services. A minority continues to follow nomadic life in the desert of Judea, living in tents and travelling by camel.

The Circassians arrived from the Balkans in 1880 in service to the Sultan of the Ottoman Empire from the border region of Greece and Bulgaria. About 1,000 Abedzah Circassians live in Reyhaniye, about 2,000 Shapsıg Circassians in Kfar-Kama and scores of families live in various Israeli cities and towns near their jobs. Circassian men serve in the Israeli army and Circassian children go to both Arab and Jewish schools as well as special Circassian language schools.

MIGRANTS/REFUGEES

By the end of 2002, Israel hosted around 2,100 refugees and asylum-seekers with pending applications, half of whom were from Lebanon and the rest mainly from Ethiopia and Sierra Leone.

All Jews are eligible to immigrate and become citizens under Israel's Law of Return. In late 2002, 18,000 Ethiopian Jews immigrated to Israel. The Government is seeking to reduce its reliance on Palestinian workers and is actively recruiting migrant labor, particularly from Southeast Asia, for domestic and agricultural work.

DEATH PENALTY

The death penalty is applicable only in the case of war crimes. Adolf Eichmann was put to death on 31 March 1962 - the only execution carried out since the creation of the Israeli State in 1948.

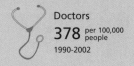
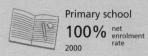
Israel took some 5,000 Palestinians prisoner.

[57] Following the complex game of retaliation and counter-retaliation, on 23 February 2002 missiles fired from Israeli helicopters slammed into Arafat's compound in Ramallah. The Palestinian leader was not hurt. The attack came hours after Palestinian gunmen killed six Israeli soldiers at a West Bank checkpoint.

[58] In May 2002, Likud voted against the creation of a Palestinian State at the request of Netanyahu, Sharon's main rival within the party. Netanyahu argued that a Palestinian State on the West Bank of the River Jordan would pose a 'mortal threat' to Israel, while the top Palestinian negotiator, Saeb Erekat, responded that the vote undermined any attempt to reach a peace agreement. The Likud vote was a heavy blow to Sharon, who had publicly supported the creation of a Palestinian State in the area currently occupied by Israel.

[59] In June and July 2002, terrorist attacks and murders and arrests of Palestinian leaders stepped up. Israel started building a separation wall on the West Bank border, saying this would help prevent suicide bombers from entering Israel. As well as protest about the construction of the wall, there is criticism of its route, seen as an attempt to take more Palestinian land since it does not follow the UN Green Line 1948 borders but cuts into areas of the West Bank.

[60] Tension with Lebanon was re-ignited in September 2002, after Beirut's project to divert 10 per cent of the water in the Wazzani river. The river rises in Lebanon and supplies Israel with potable water. Sharon said the project could lead to war, and filed a complaint with the UN. Lebanon, on the other hand, argued that the volume of water they intended to extract - less than 10 million cubic metres of the 50 million annual flow - was in line with international law.

[61] In October 2002, the Labor Party objected to Sharon's proposal to invest money in Jewish settlements in the Gaza Strip. The Labor Party, under the leadership of Ben-Eliezer, then pulled out of the governing national unity coalition. Sharon's attempt to build a new coalition with right-wing parties failed, forcing him to call elections in January, nine months ahead of schedule.

[62] Likud won the January 2003 elections, taking 37 of 120 seats. The Labor Party's defeat, and reduction in seats from 25 to 19, constituted another problem for Sharon, who was unable to create a coalition with control of parliament. Likud was then again forced to consider an alliance with ultra right-wing and orthodox sectors, which

could damage Israel's relationship with Washington. The US supports the creation of a Palestinian State, but the conservative Israeli political parties do not.

[63] 2003 was marked by the war on Iraq. In Israel, fears that it could be hit by Iraqi missiles compounded concerns over continued Palestinian suicide attacks, while the Israeli army continued its incursions in the Gaza Strip and the West Bank.

[65] In November, with the creation of a new Palestinian Government with Ahmed Qorei as Prime Minister, possibilities for dialogue were renewed. On 27 November, Israeli and Palestinian representatives met in London to launch a new peace plan backed by the US. That day, in statements to the press, Sharon announced positive unilateral steps aimed at easing the tension with Palestinians, and recognized that Israel would have to make painful concessions.

[66] Meanwhile, extra-governmental negotiations were taking place on a Draft Permanent Status Agreement, more commonly known as the Geneva Accord. The unofficial agreement was reached by prominent leaders from peace camps on both sides of the conflict, among them Yossi Beilin, leader of *Yachad* (*lit.* Together) who was also instrumental in bringing about the Oslo Accords, and former Palestinian Authority Minister Yasser Abed Rabbo. As of December 2003, the vast majority (78 per cent) of Palestinians knew little or nothing of the Geneva Accord, published in both the *al-Ayyam* and *al-Quds* newspapers. Of these, less than 10 per cent had read it. Among those who had, a majority disagreed with its central concepts (withdrawal, statehood, Jerusalem, refugees, and ending the conflict).

[67] Among Israelis there is much greater awareness of the Accord's content and it was debated hotly in the Israeli press. Public support of the agreement stands at about 30 per cent, according to radio polls.

[68] Two and a half years after the beginning of the Second Intifada, different reports gave around 5,000 dead and 43,000 injured people on both sides. Of the 3,855 fallen Palestinians, 522 were children and 166 were women. The Israeli army counted 900 dead, 600 of whom were killed in attacks by suicide bombings. There were 60,678 people arrested by Israel in this period.

[69] In February 2004, Prime Minister Sharon unveiled his plan, which included dismantling 17 of the 21 Jewish settlements in Gaza with 5,000 settlers and some others in the West Bank.

[70] In the meantime, giving credence to Palestinian complaints that Sharon was attempting to encroach on West Bank territory,

construction of the wall continued, with some changes to the original route and the dismantling of some sections (such as the one that isolated Baka al-Sharqia for a year, before it returned to the West Bank). The Palestinian Authority denounced a projected second wall along the Jordan river valley.

[71] Reactions for and against the barrier came from virtually every corner of the planet. Attempting to sway public opinion, Palestinians speak of the separation barrier or apartheid wall while Israelis call it a security fence. Meanwhile, new Palestinian suicide bombings took place in Jerusalem, unleashing Israeli military raids on Ramallah.

[72] In October Israeli forces demolished the homes of hundreds of Palestinians and bulldozed infrastructure, killing over 70 in the bloodiest assault on the Gaza Strip in years. The attack was launched after two Israeli children were killed by a Hamas rocket.

[73] In October Sharon's plan to dismantle all 21 Jewish settlements in the Gaza Strip and four small ones in the West Bank, was passed by Parliament thanks to opposition support and despite protests from extremists in his own party. ∎

PROFILE

ENVIRONMENT

Israel, with 20,770 sq km within the pre-1967 borders (see Palestine), is bordered to the west by the Mediterranean Sea. In the south it has a small outlet to the Gulf of Aqaba on the Red Sea. The following territories are currently occupied, both militarily and with settlements of Jewish colonists: Golan Heights (Syria) 1,150 sq km, West Bank 5,879 sq km, Greater Jerusalem 70 sq km. The land comprises four natural regions: the coastal plains; with a Mediterranean climate, the country's agricultural center; a central hilly and mountainous region, stretching from Galilee to Judea; the western lowlands, bound on the north by the Jordan River, which flows into the Dead Sea; and the Negev Desert, to the south, which covers half of the total territory. The main agricultural products are citrus fruits for export, grapes, vegetables, cotton, beets, potatoes and wheat. There is considerable livestock production. Natural resources include timber, potash, copper ore, natural gas, phosphate rock, magnesium bromide, and clays. Industrial production, particularly in the high-tech sector, is growing rapidly and there are serious difficulties with water and pollution. The country has over 2,000 sq km of irrigated land - part of the Negev has been reclaimed through irrigation and afforestation projects.

SOCIETY

Peoples: Jews 80.1 per cent (Europe/America-born 32.1 per cent, Israel-born 20.8 per cent, Africa-born 14.6 per cent, Asia-born 12.6 per cent); Arabs, Druze, Circassians, Armenians, and others 19.9 per cent.
Religions: Judaism (official). Arabs are mostly Muslim with nearly 10 per cent Christian; also Druze (*Mowahhidoon*) and Bahá'í.
Languages: Hebrew and Arabic (official), several languages of the immigrants' countries of origin, especially English, Russian, Yiddish, German, Polish, Romanian, Hungarian, Serbo-Croat and French. Also Ladino (Judeo-Spanish), Circassian, and Amharic.
Main Political Parties: Likud (conservative); HaAvoda (Labor Party and Meimad); Shinui (liberal); Shas (Sephardic Religious Party); National Union (Moledet, Tekuma, Yisrael Beteinu).
Main Social Organizations: The Histadrut Haoudim Haleumit (National Labor Federation) is the main trade union. Gush Emunim, nationalists demanding Jewish settlements in the Gaza Strip and West Bank; Peace Now supports territorial concessions in the West Bank. *Kibbutzim* - co-operative communities - played an significant role in the development of the country, but are now in decline.

THE STATE

Official Name: Medinat Yisra'el (Hebrew); Daulat Isra'il (Arabic).
Administrative Divisions: 6 districts, 31 municipalities, 115 local councils and 49 regional councils. **Capital:** In 1980, Jerusalem (population 686,000 in 2003) was proclaimed the 'sole and indivisible' capital of Israel. The UN condemned the decision. Most diplomatic missions are in Tel Aviv-Yafo (360,400 people). **Other Cities:** Haifa 270,800 people; Rishon LeZiyyon 211,600; Ashdod 187,500.
Government: Ariel Sharon, Prime Minister since March 2001. Moshe Katzav, President since August 2000. Parliamentary system, with 120-member legislature (Knesset). There is no constitution but some of the functions of a constitution are filled by the Declaration of Establishment (1948), the Basic Laws of the Knesset, and the Israeli citizenship law. **National Holiday:** 14 May, Independence Day (1948).
Armed Forces: 175,000 (2004; 430,000 reservists). Other: Border Police (Magav): 6,000.

Italy / Italia

Population:	57,252,557
Area:	301,340 km²
Capital:	Rome (Roma)
Currency:	Euro
Language:	Italian

From 2000 to 1000 BC, the Italian peninsula received Indo-European peoples from Central Europe. In that period two homogenous cultural areas developed: one in the north, characterized by the construction of lake dwellings and the cremation of their dead; and the other, in the south, which was influenced by Mediterranean civilizations. At the end of the second millennium BC strong migratory currents weakened the northern and fragmented the southern cultures. Numerous regional cultures arose (Latin, Ligur, Veneta, Villanovan and Iliric, among others). The foundation of Greek colonies beginning in the 8th century BC was culturally significant. The cities on Sicily and the city of Cagliari, in Sardinia, were founded by the Phoenicians.

2   With the fall of the Hittite empire around 900 BC, the Etruscans established themselves to the north of the Tiber River. Their influence extended throughout the Po valley until the end of the 6th century, when the Celts bore down on them, destroying their territorial unity.

3   According to legend, Romulus founded the city of Rome upon the Palatine hill in the year 753 BC. During the following century, this settlement was united with those on the Quirinal, Capitoline and Esquiline hills. The first form of government was an elective monarchy. Its powers were limited by a senate and a people's assembly of clans which held the power of imperium or mandate to govern.

4   There were two social classes: the patricians, who could belong to the Senate, and the plebeians, who had to band together to protect themselves from the abuses of the large landowners.

5   Under King Tarquinius Priscus (616-578), Rome entered the Latin League. The poverty of the plebeians and the system of debt-induced slavery led to the expulsion of the kings in 509. In the 5th century, the traditional laws were written down. This Law of the Twelve Tables extended to the plebeians, who after a lengthy struggle had managed to win some rights.

6   The Punic Wars against Carthage in the 3rd century allowed Rome to expand its possessions once again; in the early 2nd century, after displacing the Macedonians, Greece became a protectorate. Within a few years, Asia Minor, the northeast of Gaul, Spain, Macedonia and Carthage (including the northern part of Africa) had fallen into Roman hands.

7   Toward the end of the 2nd century, the Gracchi brothers, Tiberius and Gaius - both Roman representatives - were assassinated by the nobles, along with 3,000 followers, for supporting the plebeians.

8   The Roman Empire controlled the land from the Rhine in Germany to the north of Africa, and also included the entire Iberian Peninsula, France, Britain, Central Europe and the Middle East as far as Armenia. The 2nd century brought internal disputes which plunged Rome into chaos.

9   In 330, the Emperor Constantine transferred the capital of the Empire to Byzantium - called New Rome - and converted to Christianity. In 364, the empire split into two parts: the Western and Eastern Roman Empires.

10   The end of the 5th century was marked by the invasions of the Mongols and other northern tribes, and by the attempts of the Byzantine Empire to recover its lost territories. In the mid-6th century, Italy became a province once again, but the Lombards conquered the northern part of the peninsula.

11   When the capital of the empire had been transferred to Byzantium, the bishops of Rome had presented themselves as an alternative to Byzantine power with a separate power base in Rome. When the Lombard kings began taking up arms in defense of Christianity against Rome's enemies, the bishops broke the alliance, in order to maintain their temporal power.

12   In 754, Pope Steven II asked for help from Pepin the Short, and in exchange, crowned him King of the Franks. After the defeat of the Lombards, Pepin turned over the center of the peninsula to the Pope. Charlemagne, Pepin's son, was crowned king and emperor of Rome in 800, but the Muslim invasions which took place mid-century once again left the region without government.

13   Between the 9th and 10th centuries, the Church formed Pontifical States in the central region, including Rome itself. In the 12th century, self-government arose in some cities because of the lack of a centralized power.

14   In the 14th century, when the struggle intensified between the Guelfs (those who favored the Pope) and the Ghibellines (the defenders of the German Empire), the Holy See was transferred to Avignon, where it remained for the next seven papacies. Two centuries later, the prosperity and stability of cities like Venice, Genoa, Florence and Milan produced the intellectual and artistic flowering or the Renaissance.

15   In the early 16th century, the peninsula was attacked by the French, the Spanish and the Austrians, who all craved control of Italy. In 1794, Napoleon Bonaparte entered the country expelling the Austrians. Four years later, he occupied Rome and created the Roman Republic and the Parthenopean Republic, in Naples. Only the two Italian states of Sicily and Sardinia were not under Napoleon's control, as they were governed by Victor Emmanuel I. The French Emperor rescinded the temporal power of the popes and deported Pius VII to Savona.

16   Before the fall of Napoleon in 1815, Victor Emmanuel II named Camillo Benso di Cavour president of the council of ministers. Cavour was to be the architect of Italian unification, forging a single kingdom of Italy from those of Sardinia and Piedmont, with only Rome and Venice remaining outside the realm. In 1870, the Italians invaded Rome and, given Pope Pius IX's refusal to renounce his temporal power, they confined him to the Vatican, where his successors would remain until 1929. In 1878, the King, Humberto I, brought Italy into the Triple Alliance with Austria-Hungary and Germany. Italy's colonial conquest of Eritrea, Ethiopia and Somalia, in eastern Africa, also began.

17   In 1872, influenced by the events of the Paris Commune, Italy's first socialist organization was formed, giving rise in 1892 to the Socialist Party (PSI). The encyclical Rerum Novarum (1891) oriented Catholics towards militant unionization and the union movement expanded rapidly. The Italian invasion of Ethiopia in 1896 ended in defeat for Italy.

18   When World War I broke out, Italy proclaimed its neutrality; however, in the face of growing pressure from nationalist groups on the Left, it ended up declaring war against its former allies of the Triple Alliance.

19   Benito Mussolini, who had been expelled from the PSI for supporting Italy's entry into the war, was able to manipulate resentment over the poor outcome through a blend of nationalism and pragmatism.

20   In 1921, a group headed by Amadeo Bordiga and Antonio Gramsci split off from the PSI to form the Communist Party (PCI), leaving the PSI without its radical wing.

21   Having confronted one government crisis after another, and following Mussolini's impressive march on Rome, Victor Emmanuel III turned over the government to Mussolini. An electoral reform, giving Mussolini's Fascist Party a majority, was denounced by socialist leader Giaccomo Matteotti, who was subsequently assassinated by followers of Il Duce (Mussolini) in 1924. A new constitution established censorship of the press; in 1929 the Pact of Letran was signed with the

Life expectancy
78.7 years
2000-2005

GNI per capita
$18,960
2002

Literacy
98% total adult rate
2000

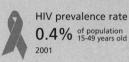
HIV prevalence rate
0.4% of population 15-49 years old
2001

Vatican, re-establishing the temporal power of the popes, and thereby gaining Catholic support for the Government.

[22] Mussolini's foreign policy was directed almost exclusively toward the acquisition of colonies. In 1936, Italy invaded Ethiopia, and a year later the Italian East African Empire was formed. During the Spanish Civil War, closer ties developed with Hitler's Germany, forming the basis for what was to become the Rome-Berlin axis. In April 1939, Italian troops took Albania.

[23] In June 1940 Italy declared war on France and Britain, invading Greece in October. Military defeats in North Africa and Greece brought Germany to its aid. Allied forces invaded Sicily in July 1943. A few days later, the Fascist Grand Council asked the king to reassume his

powers. Humberto I dismissed and jailed Mussolini, naming Pietro Badoglio prime minister. When Badoglio negotiated an armistice with Allied forces, Germany invaded Italy and rescued Mussolini. *Il Duce* then founded the Italian Social Republic (at Salo), where he became a puppet for Hitler until he was captured and executed in April 1945 by the Communist resistance. The resistance, known as partisans, also made up of Christian Democrats, Socialists, Republicans, Radicals and Liberals, played an essential role in the fall of Fascism, especially between 1943 and the end of the war.

[24] At the end of the war, 444,000 Italians were dead - including more than 280,000 civilians - and all of Italy's colonies had been lost. The king handed power over to his son

Humberto II. A June 1946 referendum decided the formation of the republic. Under the leadership of Alcide de Gasperi, the Christian Democrats (DC) managed to form a minority government. These first elections marked the beginning of the Christian Democrats' hold on power. In May 1948, Luigi Einaudi, also of the DC, was elected Italy's first president.

[25] The 1946 International Conference authorized Italy to continue administering Somalia, which it continued to do until 1960. During the 1950s, Italy participated in the reconstruction of Europe. In 1957, it became one of the charter members of the Common Market.

[26] Between 1952 and 1962, the average income of Italians doubled, as a result of the development of industry, which had come to employ 38 per cent of the national workforce. At the same time, agricultural employment dropped by 11 per cent, triggering migration from the countryside to the cities, and from the south to the north. The industrial triangle of Milan, Turin and Genoa attracted a concentration of millions of people, living in overcrowded conditions inferior to those of the rest of Europe.

[27] After successive victories at the polls, in 1961 the DC began opening up to the Left, seeking alliances with the Socialists and Social Democrats. The powerful Communist Party, in spite of its strong electoral presence, was permanently excluded from the cabinet. The economic and institutional crises which took place during that decade led radical groups from the right and left alike to turn to violence as a means of bringing about change: the far right through bombings, while the Red Brigades of the Left used political kidnapping as their main tool. In 1978, the kidnapping and assassination of former Prime Minister Aldo Moro sealed their isolation from mainstream politics.

[28] According to the 1948 constitution, the president must select a prime minister who will have parliamentary support. Until 1978, when socialist Sandro Pertini was elected, all presidents belonged to the DC. Francesco Cossiga, elected in 1985, returned Italy to the tradition of Christian Democrat presidents.

[29] Government cabinets that took lengthy negotiations to form generally only managed to last a few months, with the exception of Bettino Craxi's Socialist administration (1983-1987). Charges against Christian Democrat Arnaldo Forlani's government - linking it to an organization called Propaganda Due - brought the Government down in May 1981.

[30] In February 1991, the PCI became the Democratic Party of the Left (PDS), which sought admission

into the Socialist International. In December 1991, dissenters from the official party line decided to create the Refounded Communist Party (PRC).

[31] In the April 1992 elections, the DC did not achieve a parliamentary majority, the first defeat of a Christian Democratic government since 1946. Days afterwards, Prime Minister Giulio Andreotti announced the dissolution of his government and President Cossiga resigned. The national turmoil caused by the late May assassination of Judge Giovanni Falcone - the Mafia's number one enemy - in Sicily influenced the outcome of the elections, in which DC candidate Oscar Scalfaro, the former president of the chamber of deputies, won a landslide victory.

[32] Two months after Judge Falcone's assassination, the Mafia killed Paolo Borsellino, who on Falcone's death had taken over the investigation against organized crime.

[33] In 1993 an investigation revealed a complex corruption network that involved politicians of all tendencies, members of the business community and the Mafia. More than a thousand political and business leaders were tried under operation Clean Hands, including former Prime Ministers Bettino Craxi and Giulio Andreotti.

[34] Between 1980 and 1992, corruption deprived State coffers of some $20 billion. Because of illegal payments to officials and politicians, Italian public spending was 25 per cent more expensive than in the rest of the European Community.

[35] In 1986, spurred by the opening of Italy's first McDonald's fast-food restaurant in Rome, leftist journalist Carlo Petrini founded the International Slow Food Movement to protest the homogenization of food around the world, and to preserve local foods.

[36] In April 1993, former Central Bank president Carlo Azeglio Ciampi was appointed prime minister.

[37] For the March 1994 legislative elections, within the space of just a few months, media magnate Silvio Berlusconi created the Forza Italia party which, allied with Umberto Bossi's federalist Northern League and Gianfranco Fini's neo-fascist National Alliance (NA), won an absolute majority in parliament.

[38] Berlusconi was appointed prime minister and consolidated his popularity in June when Forza Italia triumphed in the European elections. However, increasingly tense relations with the Northern League, which had persistently criticized Berlusconi, and the NA fascists, began to complicate government action.

[39] In October, the unions opposed retirement pension reforms proposed by the prime minister as, in their view, the reforms limited

PROFILE

ENVIRONMENT
The northern region of the country consists of the Po River plains which extend as far as the Alps. It is the center of the country's economic activity, having the main concentration of industry and farming. Cattle are raised throughout the peninsula; important crops include olives and grapes, with vineyards extending along the southern coastal strip. The country includes not only the peninsula - which is divided by the Apennines - but also the islands of Sicily and Sardinia.

SOCIETY
Peoples: Italians 94 per cent. Others, particularly Sardinians and Germans in Alto Adige and immigrants from Africa.
Religions: Predominantly Catholic (more than 90 per cent); Catholic and Jewish communities are deep-rooted. Growing Muslim community through immigration. **Languages:** Italian (official). Several regional languages, like Neapolitan and Sicilian, are widely spoken. French is spoken in Val d'Aosta and German in Alto Adige. Immigrants speak their own languages, particularly African languages.
Main Political Parties: House of Freedom (which includes: Forza Italia, led by Silvio Berlusconi; National Alliance; Northern League, a regional party; Christian Democratic Center; United Christian-Democrats and the New Italian Socialist Party); L'Ulivo (Olive Tree), center-left electoral coalition linking the Democrats of the Left (former Communist Italian Party); the Italian People's Party; Democrats; Italian Renewal; Democratic Union for Europe; Federation of Greens with the Socialist Italian Party (SIP) and the Party of Italian Communists); the Daisy Alliance, an Olive Tree subdivision, became a party in 2002, joining the Italian People's Party, the Olive Democrats and other centrist parties; the Refounded Communist Party (PRC).
Main Social Organizations: three central unions: CGIL, a Left Democrat affiliate; CISL, centrist; and the UIL, of Social Democratic tendency, represent a combined total of 11 million workers (2004). The three unions signed an agreement with the government and corporations in 1993, to which smaller unions did not adhere, to to hire workers collectively. Organizations representing workers in industry and commerce (Confindustria; Confcommercio), farmers associations (Confcoltivatori, Confagricoltura), Slow Food Movement.

THE STATE
Official Name: Repubblica Italiana. **Administrative Divisions:** 20 Regions divided into 95 Provinces. **Capital:** Rome (Roma) 2,665,000 people (2003). **Other Cities:** Milan (Milano) 4,047,500 people; Naples (Napoli) 3,620,300; Turin (Torino) 1,619,400; Palermo 947,300 (2000). **Government:** Carlo Azeglio Ciampi, President since May 1999. Silvio Berlusconi, Prime Minister since June 2001. Bicameral parliamentary system: The 630-member Chamber of Deputies and the 326-member Senate of the Republic. **National Holiday:** 2 June, Anniversary of the Republic (1946). **Armed Forces:** 216,800 (2001). Other: 111,800. The phasing-out of military service by 2006 was approved in June 2000. The system will be replaced by a professional army in which women will also be able to serve.

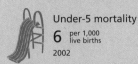

Under-5 mortality
6 per 1,000 live births
2002

Aid
0.20% Official development assistance as % of donors' GNI
2002

Maternal mortality
5 per 100,000 live births
2000

benefits, increased contributions and privatized part of the system. In December, Bossi - who despite a poor showing in the election had nearly a fifth of the deputies behind him - withdrew his support for the Government and Berlusconi resigned.

[40] In April 1996, the center-left Olive Tree Coalition, led by former Christian Democrat Romano Prodi and supported by the PDS, won the elections. Appointed prime minister, Prodi formed a government with prominent PDS leaders and leading conservative personalities like Ciampi and Fini, which also included former communists in the cabinet and support from the Refounded Communists.

[41] The Communist Party threatened to withdraw support for Prodi in October 1997 if the Government would not accept a reduction of the working week to 35 hours. In October 1998 the conflict flared up again, and Prodi resigned. In order to avoid passing power to the right, the center-left alliance proposed Massimo D'Alema, former communist and leader of the PDS, as prime minister. D'Alema was confirmed in his post by President Scalfaro on 21 October.

[42] In July 1998 a Milan court sentenced Silvio Berlusconi and seven other people to 33 months in prison for bribing the financial police. However, none of them served time because the 'Sinconi Act', which had taken effect two weeks earlier, only stipulated imprisonment for those who received sentences of over 3 years in jail.

[43] Former premier Andreotti was acquitted in October 1999 of having used political influence to help the Mafia. Carlo Azeglio Ciampi, a 78-year-old banker and former prime minister, won the presidency with broad support from both right and left in May 1999.

[44] In June 2001, Berlusconi became prime minister once again, leading a center-right coalition, the House of Freedom, in the general elections. The new premier formed a coalition government identical to his previous one (with Bossi and Fini).

[45] Starting in 2000 there was a resurgence of social movements in Italy and protests became more radical. In July 2001 an anti-globalization demonstrator was killed by the security forces in Genoa.

[46] In January 2002, the euro replaced the lira, but Italy was the only country which did not celebrate the change of currency. In response to the unenthusiastic statements by right-wing colleagues in the cabinet, Foreign Minister Renato Ruggiero resigned and was replaced by Berlusconi.

[47] Italian labor law was the most rigid in Europe, and the country was in the vanguard of the European

IN FOCUS

ENVIRONMENTAL CHALLENGES
Air pollution caused by industry emissions (particularly sulfur dioxide), coastal areas and land polluted by industrial effluents and agriculture. Some industrial and domestic waste disposal installations do not provide adequate treatment for waste. Acid rain has damaged lake ecosystems.

WOMEN'S RIGHTS
Women have been able to vote and stand for office since 1945. Female representation in parliament stood at 11 per cent from 1995 to 2000, while in ministerial or equivalent positions it grew from 12 to 13 per cent. In 2000, women made up 39 per cent of the workforce (5 per cent in agriculture, 21 per cent in industry and 74 per cent in services). Women are trafficked from several poor countries (mainly Albania, Ukraine, Moldova and Latin American nations) and exploited as sex workers.

CHILDREN
In Italy, as in other industrialized countries, the indicators show the situation of children to be good.

However, there are differences between the south and the north. Between 1997 and 2000, 12 per cent of Italian families were living below the poverty line. But among families with children under 18, the proportion stood at more than 15 per cent in 2000. At that time 16.9 per cent of children under 18 lived in poverty, although the risk of poverty was higher in the southern provinces; among families with more than three children; with parents who were unemployed or had a low level of education (many of them immigrants).

The number of reports of sexual abuse of children has grown. In 1996, around 200 cases were reported, compared to 700 in 2000.

INDIGENOUS PEOPLES/ ETHNIC MINORITIES
The historical ethnic minorities are the Sards, Tyrolese and Roma (or gypsies). Other minority groups are recent immigrants, a product of economic crisis and military conflicts in less industrialized countries, mostly from the Balkans, Africa and Latin America. Of the latter, many are descendants of Italians who had emigrated to the Americas during World War I and World War II, and have now obtained residency

permits due to their Italian ancestry.

MIGRANTS/REFUGEES
As of late 2002, there were more than 5,200 refugees and asylum-seekers in Italy. More than 3,800 were still awaiting an official decision on their status, while 1,300 had been granted asylum. That year, an additional 7,300 people requested asylum from abroad. Most of the applicants were from Sri Lanka, the former Yugoslavia and Turkey.

In late 2001 and in 2002, the Italian embassies in several Latin American countries struck by severe economic crises (see In Focus for Argentina and Uruguay) were flooded by people of Italian descent who spent whole days and nights queuing on the sidewalks to apply for Italian citizenship, with the goal of emigrating as 'economic exiles'.

DEATH PENALTY
Capital punishment was abolished in 1994, but the country's last execution had taken place in 1947, when the death penalty was abolished for common offenses.

economy. Claiming that economic growth was only sustainable with greater labor flexibility, the Government planned reforms to make it easier for employers to hire and fire employees. In March 2002, the national unemployment rate stood at 9 per cent, while in the south one in five were out of work. On 23 March, more than a million workers demonstrated at Rome's Coliseum protesting that government measures mainly benefited Berlusconi - the richest entrepreneur in the country - and the rest of the business community.

[48] The murder of a government aide, allegedly by the Red Brigades, only widened the breach between government and unions on labor law, and gave rise to fears of a resurgence of the political violence of the 1970s and 1980s.

[49] The country was brought to a halt on 16 April when millions of workers across the country protested the labor laws by joining the first general strike to last more than a day in the past 20 years. In September and October, demonstrations against Berlusconi's government and his pro-US policies were supported by hundreds of thousands of people.

[50] In November 2002 former President Andreotti (84) was sentenced to 24 years in prison for

ordering the Mafia to murder a journalist in 1979. But due to his advanced age, he was not sent to prison.

[51] Despite mass opposition to the war in Iraq, in March 2003 Berlusconi committed troops to the US-led coalition forces.

[52] In May that year Berlusconi testified before a Milan court which was trying him for bribing judges in Rome in connection with the sale of the state-controlled SME food company in 1985. In June, parliament passed an immunity law for high government officials, to save Berlusconi from 'dishonor'. Italy took over the European Union presidency in July. In November, Italians were shocked by the death of 19 soldiers in Nasiriyah, Iraq, killed by a truck bomb that also killed several Iraqis. It was the biggest Italian military loss since World War II. The opposition called for the immediate withdrawal of all troops.

[53] In December Italy was at the center of an international scandal when it emerged that Parmalat, the country's leading foodstuffs corporation, had committed fraud amounting to 14.3 billion euros. The Government intervened to 'protect jobs, not the shareholders or the board of directors' of the empire made up of 197 factories and 36,000 jobs worldwide, including 4,000 in

Italy. As a result of the crisis, some 800,000 Italian investors are estimated to have lost 30 billion euros.

[54] Between December and February 2004, 17 people implicated in the scandal were sent to jail, among them Parmalat's founder, Calisto Tanzi, corporate directors, and officials from consulting company Grant Thornton, which had falsified the company's accounts. Financial institutions such as Citigroup, Bank of America, Deutsche Bank, JP Morgan, Deloitte & Touche and the main Italian banks were also investigated.

[55] On 13 January 2004, the Constitutional Court ruled that the law which granted immunity to Berlusconi and other top government officials during their term of office was unconstitutional.

[56] Controversy arose when a hospital in Florence proposed a less invasive, anesthesized alternative to female genital mutilation, a rite practised by some Muslim immigrant communities, and affecting some 6,000 girls between four and twelve years old. In May 2004, the Government passed a law modifying the Penal Code which penalizes anyone carrying out any kind of infibulation or other form of female genital mutilation. The penalties are harsher if the victim is a minor. ■

Jamaica / Jamaica

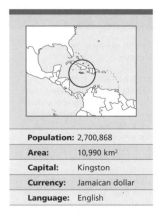

Population:	2,700,868
Area:	10,990 km²
Capital:	Kingston
Currency:	Jamaican dollar
Language:	English

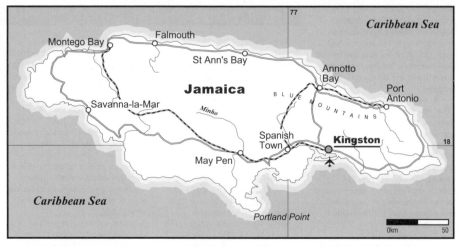

The name Jamaica comes from the Arawak Indian name for the island - Xamayca ('land of springs', 'land of wood and water') a reference to the abundant waters of its luxuriant forests. The Arawaks had pushed out the Guanahatabey, the original inhabitants, who had come from North America. They lived in houses made from palm branches; they were peaceful and carried out self-sufficient farming. They were also skillful sailors, fishers and craftspeople, who carved and polished seashells. Singing and dancing were important activities in their lives. They worshipped idols (*zemis*), but believed in only one God, creator of nature.

² Columbus reached Jamaica on his second voyage to the New World in May 1494, but it was his son, Diego Columbus, who conquered the island in 1509. From then on, the number of Arawaks decreased dramatically. Around 1545, Spanish historian Francisco López de Gomara wrote that 'Jamaica resembles Haiti in all respects - here the Indians have also been wiped out'. Some sources believe there may have been as many as 60,000 Arawaks prior to the Spanish Conquest.

³ The Spanish, now absolute rulers of the island, began to plant sugarcane and cotton, and to raise cattle. There were incursions by

the British in 1596 and 1636 and in 1655 when 6,500 British soldiers under the command of William Penn dislodged the 1,500 Spaniards and Portuguese. Jamaica rapidly became a haven for pirates who ravaged Spanish trade in the Caribbean. The last important enemies that the English had to face on the island were the enclaves of rebel slaves or *quilombos*, hidden in remote areas like the Blue Mountains. In 1760 a general rebellion in the colony was put down, and in 1795 a further revolution shook the island.

⁴ By the late 19th century there were approximately 800 sugar mills and more than 1,000 cattle ranches in Jamaica. The economy was built on the labor of 200,000 African slaves. Anti-slavery and anti-colonial rebellions of the 18th and 19th centuries were followed by labor union struggles in the first few decades of the 20th century. The two main contemporary political parties, the Jamaica Labour Party (JLP) and the People's National Party (PNP), grew out of workers' organizations. Independence was proclaimed in 1962, but successive JLP governments failed to rescue the economy from foreign hands.

⁵ In 1942 rich deposits of bauxite were discovered, and the aluminum transnationals ALCOA, ALCAN, Reynolds and Kaiser quickly established themselves on the island, virtually replacing the sugar industry.

⁶ The transnationals exploited Jamaica's bauxite by shipping the raw metal out of the country,

making all the decisions on production, and paying minimal customs duties.

⁷ After independence a few plants were built to transform bauxite into aluminum, but the bulk of the mineral extracted continued to be shipped unprocessed to the US. In 1973, Jamaica was the second largest

PROFILE

ENVIRONMENT

Jamaica is the third largest of the Greater Antilles (10,991 sq km). A mountain range, occupying two-thirds of the land area, runs across the island from East to West. A limestone plateau covered with tropical vegetation extends to the West. The plains are good for farming and the subsoil is rich in bauxite. The climate is rainy, tropical at sea level and temperate in the eastern highlands.

SOCIETY

Peoples: Most Jamaicans are of African descent. There are small Chinese, Indian, Arab and European minorities.
Religions: Protestants 56 per cent; Catholics 5 per cent, Rastafarians 5 per cent.
Languages: English (official). A dialect based on English called 'patois English' or 'Creole' is also spoken.
Main Political Parties: People's National Party (PNP), founded in 1938 by Norman Manley and led by Prime Minister Percival Patterson, a member of the Socialist International since 1975. The Jamaica Labour Party, founded in 1943 by Alexander Bustamante, is a private sector advocate and is led by Edward Seaga. National Democratic Movement, offshoot of the JLP.
Main Social Organizations: National Workers' Union of Jamaica (NWUJ); Bustamante Industrial Trade Union (BITU). Jamaican Student's Union. Rastafarians groups.

THE STATE

Official Name: Jamaica.
Administrative Divisions: 14 parishes.
Capital: Kingston 575,000 people (2003).
Other Cities: Spanish Town 127,300 people; Montego Bay 90,500 (2000).
Government: Parliamentary monarchy. Head of State: Elizabeth II of Britain. Howard Cooke, Governor General, representing Britain since August 1991. Prime Minister, Percival J Patterson, since March 1992 and re-elected in 1997 and in 2002. Bicameral Legislature: House of Representatives, 60 members elected by direct popular vote every 5 years and the Senate, with 21 members appointed by the Governor General.
National Holiday: 6 August, Independence Day (1962).
Armed Forces: 523,550 available troops for the army, the navy and the air force (2002).

WORKERS

UNEMPLOYMENT: 16.0% (2002)

LABOR FORCE — 2002

■ FEMALE: 46.2%   ■ MALE: 53.8%

EMPLOYMENT DISTRIBUTION   **1995/2001**

F

M

■ AGRICULTURE   F: 30.0%   M: 10.0%
■ INDUSTRY   F: 26.0%   M: 9.0%
■ SERVICES   F: 45.0%   M: 81.0%

LAND USE

2000

IRRIGATED AREA: 9.1% of arable land

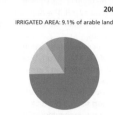

■ ARABLE LAND: 16.1%
■ CROPLANDS: 9.2%
■ OTHER USE: 74.7%

Life expectancy
75.7 years
2000-2005

GNI per capita
$2,820
2002

Literacy
87% total adult rate
2000

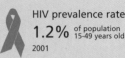

HIV prevalence rate
1.2% of population 15-49 years old
2001

producer of bauxite in the world. The mineral accounted for half of the country's exports but employed only one per cent of the labor force.

[8] The PNP, with a clearly progressive program, won the 1972 elections. The new Prime Minister, Michael Manley, raised the bauxite export tax and began negotiations with the foreign companies to assert greater control over their activities. The PNP Government also supported Caribbean integration. A bi-national bauxite marketing company was created with Venezuela. Jamaica became a member of the Caribbean Multinational Merchant Fleet.

[9] In December 1976 the PNP won again, with an increased majority. Manley advocated socialism within the existing constitutional structure. Jamaica took active part in the Movement of Non-Aligned Countries and supported African anti-colonial movements. This stand strained relations with the US and the transnational mining companies reduced their production, transferring operations to other countries. In consequence, export revenues fell, and with them, funding for government social programs.

[10] In 1979, Manley was forced to seek loans from the IMF, but in February 1980, he suspended negotiations since meeting the Fund's requirements would mean a drastic reduction in living standards for the population. That year elections were held ahead of schedule, in a climate of destabilization generated by the right-wing opposition, which finally won a landslide victory. The new JLP government, headed by Edward Seaga, expelled the Cuban ambassador, and imposed policies that opened the country to unconditional foreign investment. This resulted in an increase in unemployment and the doubling of foreign debt between 1981 and 1983.

[11] In 1983, Jamaica was one of the small group of Caribbean countries that gave diplomatic support and symbolic military assistance to the US invasion of Grenada. A month later, taking advantage of the favorable political atmosphere, Seaga decided to call early parliamentary elections. The PNP boycotted the elections; only the governing party nominated candidates, thereby winning all 60 seats.

[12] In 1989, Michael Manley's PNP came to power again, strengthened by its triumph in the 1986 municipal elections. He presented a very different program from that of 1976, based on free

IN FOCUS

ENVIRONMENTAL CHALLENGES
Soil loss from deforestation and erosion is put at 80 million tons per year. In some metropolitan areas, the lack of sewerage and the dumping of industrial wastes have polluted drinking water supplies, threatening the urban population.

WOMEN'S RIGHTS
In 2000 women held 13 per cent of the parliamentary seats and 12 per cent of the ministerial positions.

In 2000 illiteracy rate among women over 15 years was 9.3 per cent and total female school enrolment rate was 95 per cent*.

Women accounted for 46 per cent of the total workforce of one million, working mainly in services (81 per cent), agriculture (10 per cent) and in industry (9 per cent). Female unemployment rate was 22.5 per cent in that same year.

Fourty per cent of the pregnant women were anemic and 99 per cent received antenatal healthcare (1997*).

CHILDREN
In 2001 54,000 children were born and 1,000 under-5s died*. Primary school enrolment reached 95 per cent for boys and girls in 2000*. However, the quality and efficacy of learning and teaching are a problem. Almost 30 per cent of students,

mostly boys, are functionally illiterate at the end of primary level and only 3.6 per cent in the 0 to 3 year age group are enrolled in pre-schools or playgroups.

Children are 39 per cent of the total population and account for 43 per cent of all poor, most of whom live in rural areas.

By the end of 2001 it was estimated that there were 800 under-14s living with HIV/AIDS and 5,100 children orphaned by AIDS . Four-fifths of the HIV-positive children live in poor households and it is calculated that one out of four will be abandoned. Among adolescents, infection rates have doubled annually since 1995 and girls are three times as likely as boys to become HIV-positive. Sexual initiation can occur as early as 10 years old; only 50 per cent of adolescents use condoms on a regular basis.

About 22,000 children work and almost 2,500 - mostly boys - live on the streets. Sexual exploitation is an emerging problem. Child abuse has increased. Some 2,000 children are in residential institutions where standards of care need more support. High levels of suicide, alcohol abuse and road accidents are major areas of concern.

INDIGENOUS PEOPLES/ ETHNIC MINORITIES
Most Jamaicans (90.9 per cent) are of African descent. There are also

Eastern Indians, Chinese and Europeans. Arawaks or *taínos* were Jamaica's first inhabitants (the name Jamaica comes from the Arawak word *Xamayca*). in 700 BC they reached the Antilles and Jamaica, coming by raft from Guyana.

In the 15th century, by the time Columbus arrived, the Arawak indigenous population had been drastically reduced as a result of a bloody war over land with invading Caribs.

MIGRANTS/REFUGEES
In the year 2000, remittances from the Jamaican diaspora, estimated at 789,299, led to a 10-per-cent increase in GDP. Jamaicans are the third largest Caribbean group living in the US and Canada. Emigration is an old issue: during the 1940s Jamaican farmers were recruited to work in the US. The US has been the destination of choice over the past 30 years, accounting for 589,777 or 59.8 per cent of the official number of Jamaican migrants since 1953. There are also many in the UK.

DEATH PENALTY
Jamaica retains the death penalty for ordinary crimes.

* Latest data available in *The State of the World's Children* and *Childinfo* database, UNICEF, 2004.

enterprise and good relations with the US. Manley re-established relations with Cuba and stated the agreements with the IMF would be respected, although he made it clear he would not accept conditions which would worsen the social inequalities. His aim was to maintain economic growth, but with better wealth distribution.

[13] In April 1992, Percival Patterson replaced Manley as Prime Minister, as the latter resigned following a long period of illness. Promising labor guarantees, in 1992 the Government started the privatization of around 300 state companies and public services. This package included the entire sugar industry.

[14] In March 1993 Patterson was re-elected. The JLP - led once again by Edward Seaga - refused to participate in the partial elections in 1994 because of its disagreement with the electoral system. Defeat hastened the splitting up of the JLP, and the National Democratic Movement was founded. Patterson's policies continued as before, adopting

measures favored by multilateral credit organizations such as the IMF and the World Bank.

[15] Violence has often accompanied Jamaican political campaigns; political leaders seem to have either supported or tolerated it. The violence during the run-up to the 18 December 1997 elections led to the mass resignation of candidates.

[16] Jamaica withdrew from the Inter-American Commission on Human Rights of the Organization of American States in 1998 due to the forum's opposition to the death penalty, still used by Jamaica and other Caribbean countries.

[17] In 1999 the army took to the streets to control riots triggered by the price hike in, for example, fuel which had increased by 30 per cent. Over the last few years, the island's murder rate had become the highest in the world and up to December 2001, there had been a 30 per cent increase in crime.

[18] In 2002, while celebrating the 40th anniversary of Jamaica's independence, Patterson was elected for the third consecutive

time as Prime Minister. This time, the elections were relatively peaceful. Patterson continued his policy of economic liberalism. This gave an initial boost to the financial sector, but it soon faded. On foreign policy, Patterson moved for greater self-determination and in 2003 he proposed a constitutional amendment to make Jamaica a republic, and sever the ties with its colonial past.

[19] The Government faced two significant issues. The first was drug-trafficking, with 100 tons of cocaine traded in 2001. The second was emigration, that in July 2000 was estimated at 20,000 people a year, going mainly to Canada, the US and the UK. Drug-trafficking, mainly of marijuana and cocaine, had increased and some of the police were implicated in those activities. Jamaica has the highest rate in the world of killings by police.

[20] In early 2004, 20 refugees from Haiti arrived, fleeing the violence that shook that country during Jean-Bertrand Aristide's removal from office. ■

Japan / Nihon

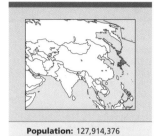

Population:	127,914,376
Area:	377,800 km²
Capital:	Tokyo
Currency:	Yen
Language:	Japanese

The Paleolithic Age in Japan dates back 10,000 to 30,000 years ago. This was followed by the Jomon Neolithic culture which lasted until 200-300 BC and spread throughout the Japanese archipelago. They were hunters and gatherers, creators of fine pottery and stone and bone utensils.

² The arrival of the Yayoi, probably from the continent by land bridges across the straits of Korea, Tsushima, Soya and Tsugaru, introduced rice cultivation, horses and cows, the potter's wheel, weaving and iron tools into Japanese culture.

³ According to Chinese chronicles, at the beginning of the Christian era the Wo region (Wa in Japanese) was divided into more than 100 states. During Himito's reign, some 30 of them were grouped together. The Wa people were divided into social classes and paid taxes. Buildings were technically advanced and there were large markets.

⁴ Isolation from the end of the civil war in 266 until Yamato's consolidation as Emperor in 413 led to the unification of the nation by the middle of the 4th century, a prerequisite for further expansion. In the year 369, Yamato subdued the Korean kingdoms of Paekche, Kaya and Sila, from where he controlled the region. The Yamato Empire suffered a rapid decline, partly as a result of resistance from its Korean subjects but also because of internal fighting within the court.

⁵ The introduction of Buddhism between the years 538 and 552 initially stirred curiosity and admiration because of its majestic temples and supposed magical powers.

⁶ Buddhism (modified through contact with Central Asia, China and Korea) plus the grid system of land division, still visible today, and the characters used in writing are the most important traces of Chinese presence in Japan, which dates back 1,500 years.

⁷ This cultural heritage underwent successive adaptations to the local conditions, language and habits, especially in the 17th and 18th centuries. So-called 'Japanization' was particularly apparent in architecture and language, which shows evidence of very different local linguistic influences.

⁸ In the 9th century, chieftains were replaced by a hereditary court. The aristocracy made Buddhism a controlling force which served to reinforce the power of the State. Japan's first permanent capital was Nara, established in the year 710. After several conflicts, Kammu (781-806) re-established the Empire's independence and transferred the capital to Heian (Kyoto).

⁹ In the new capital, the Fujiwara family consolidated their power and established the Regent as ruling figure, above the Emperor. With imperial approval, the Tendai and Shingon Buddhist sects (closer to Japanese culture) developed in Heian, bringing an end to Nara's religious hegemony.

¹⁰ The imperial land tenure system fell increasingly into private hands. Aristocrats and religious institutions took over large tracts of tax-free land (shoen) and organized private armies for themselves, leading to the creation of a new rural warrior class - the samurai.

¹¹ The predominant Taira and Minamoto clans vied for power in a number of military confrontations. The Taira were in power from 1156 until their defeat in the Gempei War (1180-85). The shogun (general), Minamoto Yoritomo, founded the Kamakura shogunate, the first of a series of military regimes which ruled Japan until 1868.

¹² The Kamakura defeated the Mongol invasions of 1274 and 1281 aided by providential storms, called kamikaze (divine winds). During this period, several new Buddhist sects emerged, such as Pure Land Buddhism, True Pure Land and Lotus.

¹³ In the early 14th century, the Kamakura shogunate was destroyed by Emperor Go-Daigo's Kemmu Restoration. Shortly thereafter military clans expelled Go-Daigo from Tokyo and replaced him with a puppet emperor. Go-Daigo established his court in Yoshino, and for 56 years there were two parallel imperial courts.

¹⁴ The Onin War (1467-77), over succession within the Ashikaga shogunate, became a civil war which lasted almost 100 years. New military chiefs, independent of imperial or shogun authority, established their vassals within fortified cities, leaving the surrounding villages to run themselves and to pay tribute.

¹⁵ In the cities, trade and manufacturing ushered in a new way of life. Portugal began trading with Japan in 1545, and the missionary Francis Xavier introduced Catholicism in 1549. Christianity led to conflict with feudal loyalties, so it was proscribed in 1639. At the same time, all Europeans were banished from Japan, except the Dutch.

¹⁶ In the late 16th century, the warlords became increasingly isolated from the rest of society because of their use of firearms (initially supplied by Europeans), their fortresses, the disarming of peasants, and their tightening of control over the land. This situation helped to pacify and unite the country around a single national authority.

¹⁷ During the 17th century the Tokugawa clan gained supremacy, ruling from the city-fortress of Edo (Tokyo) until 1867. A careful distribution of the land among their relatives and local chieftains guaranteed them the control of the largest cities - Kyoto, Osaka and Nagasaki - as well as of the most important mines.

¹⁸ Local chieftains were compelled to spend half their time on the shogun's affairs while their families remained behind, as hostages. Transformed into military bureaucrats, the samurai were the highest level of a four-class system, followed by the peasants, artisans and traders (who, although despised, were essential in urban life).

¹⁹ A national market arose for textiles, food, handcrafts, books and other products, mainly as a result of the almost total isolation from the outside world effected by the Tokugawas since 1639. Nagasaki was the only exception; here, the Chinese and the Dutch were allowed to open trading posts, although the latter were restricted to a nearby island.

²⁰ In the 19th century, the old economic and social order went into a state of collapse. Peasant revolts were more and more frequent, and the samurai and local chieftains found themselves heavily in debt with the traders. In 1840, the government tried to carry out a series of reforms, but these failed and weakness allowed the United States to prize open its ports.

²¹ Japan was forced out of its isolation by the arrival of US warships under the command of Commodore Matthew Perry. He successfully negotiated the opening up of Japanese markets in 1854. The signing of unfavorable trade agreements with the US and several European countries deepened the crisis. The samurai carried out several attacks against the foreigners and then turned against the shogun, forcing him to resign in 1867.

²² Imperial authority was restored with the young Meiji emperor, in 1868. During the Meiji Restoration, Japan's modernization process began, following the Western model. The US, England, France and Germany exerted influence in education, the sciences, communication and on Japanese culture.

²³ In less than 50 years, the closed, feudal Japan was transformed into an industrialized world power. Western advisers and technology were brought in for

Life expectancy
81.6 years
2000-2005

GNI per capita
$33,550
2002

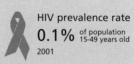

HIV prevalence rate
0.1% of population
15-49 years old
2001

education, trade and industry. An army based on the draft replaced the military authority of the samurai, defeated when they tried to rebel in 1877.

[24] In 1889, succumbing to internal political pressure, the emperor approved a constitution which turned Japan into a constitutional monarchy, with a bicameral legislature (*Diet*). However, only one per cent of the population was eligible for office, and the prime minister and his cabinet were responsible to the emperor (seen as a divine figure).

[25] In the late 19th century and early 20th century, Japan won two major wars: against China (1894-95), which enabled Japan to maintain its control over Korea (annexed in 1910), and in the Russo-Japanese War (1904-05), after which it annexed the Sajalin Peninsula. Japan entered World War I as a British ally, since a treaty had been signed to that effect in 1902.

[26] The war allowed Japan to gain control of several German possessions in East Asia, including the Chinese territory of Kiaochow. In 1915, China was forced to accept Japanese influence over Manchuria and Inner Mongolia. In 1918, Hara Takashi became the head of the first government to have a parliamentary majority.

[27] In 1921-22 Japan signed a naval arms limitation treaty with the US in Washington, replacing an agreement with Britain, and establishing a new balance of power in the Pacific. A new agreement was signed at the Naval Conference in London, in spite of discontent among the Japanese military, who thought it compromised national security.

[28] Economic difficulties caused by the international depression of the 1930s gave militarists the excuse they were seeking to attack the Government. They proposed that the country's problems could only be solved by expanding its military power and conquering new markets for Japanese products and as sources of raw materials.

[29] When Japanese officers occupied Manchuria without official backing in 1931, the Government, unable to deter the military, accepted the creation of the puppet state of Manchukuo in February 1932. Three months later, the Government was turned over to the militarists, who retained it until 1945.

[30] In 1940, Japan invaded Indochina hoping to open up a passage through to Southeast Asia. The US and Britain imposed a total embargo on Japanese merchandise. The Japanese attack on Pearl Harbor, in Hawaii, and on the Philippines, Hong Kong and Malaysia, unleashed the war with

IN FOCUS

ENVIRONMENTAL CHALLENGES
Air pollution - mainly in large urban areas (Tokyo, Osaka and Yokohama) - plus pollution in several coastal areas and acid rain. Acidification in lakes and reservoirs has reduced water quality and threatened habitats. Japan is one of the largest consumers of fish and tropical forest woods, contributing to the depletion of these in Asia.

WOMEN'S RIGHTS
Japanese women have been able to vote since 1947. In 2000, 5 per cent of parliamentary seats were held by women, but there were no women at ministerial level. In 2000 women made up 41 per cent of the 68 million workforce. Unemployment stood at 4.8 per cent of the total population of the labor force (5% for men and 4.5 % for women). In 2000, 72 per cent of the female labor force worked in services, 22 per cent in industry and 6 per cent in agriculture. In 1995*, 100 per cent of births were attended by trained staff.

CHILDREN
In 2001 there were 1,192,000 births, while 6,000 children under 5 died. In 2000*, primary school enrolment and attendance amounted to 100 per cent.

INDIGENOUS PEOPLES/ ETHNIC MINORITIES
The first Koreans arrived in Japan in the early 20th century. During the 1930s and 1940s when Korea was under Japanese rule, several were recruited by Japan. Koreans in Japan receive political support from the governments of South Korea and, to a lesser degree, North Korea. The Korean community is around 710,000 people (85 per cent of the foreign population). They mainly live in Osaka and other urban areas. Koreans face cultural and political restrictions: their education and financial opportunities are limited, and they suffer discrimination, not just from the Government - although they are not allowed to vote - but also from individual and corporate practices. They are mainly concentrated in small communities and do not present a cohesive group. As a result of no employment or low-paid work, their lower income affects nutrition and health. Although some have become integrated into Japanese culture (adopting name, language

and religion), a significant portion resist assimilation and live in Korean neighborhoods, attend Korean schools and take an active part in North and South Korean political relations with Japan.

MIGRANTS/REFUGEES
In 1990 the Japanese Government decreed that all illegal workers were to be deported and their employers sanctioned, with fines ranging from $18,000 to 3 years in jail. Currently there are one million foreigners living in Japan. The total population level is falling, and it is estimated that in 2010 the country will be short of 1.87 million workers. In late 2002 there were more than 6,500 refugees and asylum-seekers in the country (5,900 were Vietnamese and Cambodians admitted before that year, who had remained under temporary status).

DEATH PENALTY
Japan maintains the death penalty for ordinary offenses.

* Latest data available in *The State of the World's Children* and *Childinfo* database, UNICEF, 2004.

the United States and opened up a new phase of World War II.

[31] Japan surrendered on 15 August 1945, after the US had dropped two atomic bombs on Hiroshima and Nagasaki on August 6 and 9. US troops occupied Japan and imposed a government of the Supreme Command of the Allied Powers (SCAP) under the leadership of General Douglas MacArthur, between 1945 and 1952. SCAP forced Japan to abandon the Meiji institutions, to renounce the emperor's claim to divinity, and transfer the Government to a Parliament, which was charged with electing the Prime Minister, and establishing an independent judiciary.

[32] Although imposed upon the Japanese from the outside, the principles laid down in the 1947 constitution were accepted by all sectors of society and in 1952 the country recovered its independence. Japanese sovereignty was restored over the Tokara archipelago in 1951, over the Amami islands in 1953, over the Bonin islands in 1968, and over the rest of the Ryukyu, including Okinawa, in 1972.

[33] SCAP also took other measures to weaken the hierarchical model of the Meiji family-state. These ranged from giving tenants the right to purchase the land they lived on

(until then they had to pay taxes to their lords), and laws aimed at strengthening free trade and preventing the return of monopolies. However, the Japanese financial system remained intact and provided the basis for economic recovery at the end of the occupation.

[34] In 1955, opposing the country's conservative and nationalist sectors, which had supported the war policy, the center-right Liberal Democratic Party (LDP) was formed.

[35] The 1947 Constitution restricted the development of Japanese military power. Japan bowed to US strategy for the region and formed alliances with Taiwan and South Korea. In 1956 it joined the UN and re-established relations with the USSR.

[36] The return to independence found the Japanese economy in a state of growth and change. Although agriculture suffered from small-scale production and urban migration, industrialization and full employment triggered the need for technological innovation.

[37] During the 1960s, Japan specialized in the production of high technology products, establishing trade relations with more industrialized countries instead of its previous Asian partners. The oil crisis of 1973 did

not halt the growth of the Japanese industry, which led the world in steel, ship building, electronics, and automobile manufacturing.

[38] Although Prime Minister Kakuei Tanaka's visit to Beijing in 1972 signalled Japanese recognition of the People's Republic of China, it damaged the country's relations with Taiwan. The scandal following Tanaka's bribing by the Marubeni Corporation (a representative of the US Lockheed Aircraft Corporation), adversely affected the LDP's popularity and in 1976, for the first time in its history, it lost its absolute majority in parliament.

[39] During the 1960s and 1970s, Japan had a large trade surplus in its trade with the US. Japan began to rank first or second with all its trading partners. With direct investment and the establishment of subsidiaries, it expanded worldwide.

[40] The Japanese corporate world is dominated by the Sogo-Shosha system, huge conglomerates which commercialize virtually all kinds of raw material in almost every country in the world, by means of state-of-the-art information systems capable of supplying data for instantaneous decision-making.

[41] The impressive development of the Japanese economy was due not only to this efficiency but also to a

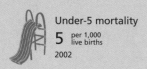
Under-5 mortality
5 per 1,000 live births
2002

$ Aid
0.23% Official development assistance as % of donors' GNI
2002

Maternal mortality
10 per 100,000 live births
2000

policy of foreign investment in projects which quickly deplete non-renewable natural resources. This policy has caused irreversible damage to rainforests and serious alterations to the Third World ecosystem.

42 Emperor Hirohito's death in January 1989 ended the Showa era, begun in 1926. The coronation of Akihito, in the traditional Japanese style, launched the Heisei era (achievement of universal peace). The coronation was attended by more heads of state than had ever gathered together for any such event. The expense incurred generated internal protests.

43 In 1987, Washington protested at Japan's sale of submarine technology to the USSR, between 1982 and 1984. Nevertheless in 1989 Naboru Takeshita was the first head of government to be received by newly-elected US President, George Bush. Takeshita resigned in April after a real estate scandal. His successor, Sosuke Uno, resigned when his affair with a geisha woman was revealed.

44 At the end of the Cold War, Japan emerged as one of the three main world economic powers, together with the US and the EC. At present, it is the country with the largest overseas investment. It is a key participant in the world financial system, and is influential in the exchange of Third World debt funds.

45 On 5 November 1991, Prime Minister Toshiki Kaifu lost the support of the Takeshita clan - the most influential of the official party's five factions - and resigned. Elected in August 1989, he had never been involved in a corruption scandal. He was replaced by 72-year-old Kiichi Miyazawa (also with Takeshita support), who had been elected president of the LDP nine days before.

46 In his inaugural speech, Miyazawa outlined his administration's objectives: expand relations with, and aid to China; negotiate with the US and normalize relations with the former Soviet Union. He announced his willingness to liberalize the rice market, making concessions similar to those already made by the EC and the United States, to ward off a failure of the Uruguay Round of the GATT.

47 In February 1992 the Minister of Postal Services, Hideo Watanabe, admitted to receiving a bribe (previously alleged in 1988) from telecommunications corporation Recruit. Shortly after, four people were arrested with relation to another financial scandal, involving more than 100 members of Miyazawa's government, as well as the mafia group known as Inagawagumi.

48 Toward the middle of the year, after heated debate, a law was passed authorizing troops to be sent abroad for the first time since World War II. In September, some troops joined the UN peacekeeping forces in Cambodia.

49 In early 1993, Miyazawa promised to broaden the scope of Japanese forces, both in terms of funding and personnel, in the UN peacekeeping missions.

50 Also in 1993 the Prime Minister was censured by the Diet for failing to carry out electoral reforms needed to end the endemic corruption in Japanese political life. The official party split, losing 54 seats, and elections were moved up to July.

51 The two dissident groups, led by Tsutomu Hata and Masayoshi Takemura, formed new parties; the Reformation Party and the Pioneer Party.

52 Diplomatic relations with the Russian Government improved slightly when Japan announced that, while not relinquishing its claim to the Kuril Islands (dating from 1950) it would not put conditions on its economic aid to Russia.

53 In March 1993, Shin Kanemaru, the LDP's historic leader, was arrested. He had received bribes in 1992, part of a wider corruption scandal in the Government. Shortly after his arrest he was granted an amnesty.

54 On 18 July, general elections drew the lowest rate of voter participation since the war (67.3 per cent). The LDP, in power since 1955, lost its majority in the *Kokkai* (Diet), This result altered the balance of power in effect since World War II. Miyazawa resigned the LDP's presidency, and assumed responsibility for the defeat. Yohei Kono was named party President.

55 The 'new majority' of the Socialist, Reformation, Komeito (Buddhist), Democratic Socialist, Unified Democratic Socialist and Pioneer parties agreed to form a new Government based upon a limited platform which would not attempt any major changes.

56 Hosokawa, former governor of the province of Kunamoto, was elected Prime Minister in August. On taking office, he announced far-reaching political reforms aimed at fighting corruption and recession, and modernizing the pension and health systems. In his first speech before the Diet, he referred to the aggression with which Japan had treated its Asian neighbors, from the 1930s until the end of World War II. On 15 August, the anniversary of Japan's surrender, he offered condolences and apologies to the victims of Japanese colonialism.

57 When Hosokawa succeeded Miyazawa, the Confederation of Industry announced it would discontinue its contributions to the LDP. According to the local press, these had amounted to $1 billion per year.

58 In August 1993, 165 political leaders and 445 business people were arrested for irregularities committed during the election campaign. 5,500 cases of electoral fraud were brought to court. In October, Shinji Kiyoyama - president of Kajima, the country's second largest construction firm - was arrested for paying a bribe in exchange for a building permit.

59 In December the Japanese Government opened up the rice market, importing 4 per cent of its 10 million tons requirement for domestic consumption.

60 Hosokawa's 'romance' with public opinion lasted until early 1994 when the press became more critical, accusing him of having received money in exchange for favors.

61 In February he was forced to abandon a scheme which he had sponsored, aimed at keeping the Government coalition intact. He had to issue a critique and explanation of what some felt had been reckless actions. A new $140 billion plan to reactivate the economy also drew criticism, and raised doubts about his governance. The press called for solutions to the problems posed by a rapidly ageing population.

62 A summit between Japan and the US ended in failure in March when Hosokawa rejected mandatory quotas to open up the Japanese automobile, telecommunications, pharmaceutical and insurance markets. Japanese businessmen ignored Hosokawa and felt inclined to wage a commercial war with the US before yielding to its pressures. At that time the automobile industry employed 11 per cent of Japan's labor and contributed 30 per cent of the GDP.

63 LDP member of parliament Nakamura was arrested for accepting bribes from Kajima and other construction firms. Hosokawa, unable to shake off accusations from the opposition about his own involvement in illicit business deals, resigned in April and asked 'sincerely for forgiveness from the people of Japan'.

64 Tsutomu Hata was nominated Prime Minister and headed Japan's first minority Government in four decades. The socialists had walked out of the ruling coalition leaving the Government with only 182 of the 512 seats in the lower house.

65 On visits to Europe aimed at establishing closer trade links with the EU, Hata admitted that Japan's trade surplus had caused the trade crisis with the US. After an initial agreement was reached between the two countries, he launched a scheme to promote economic deregulation.

66 Socialist Tomiichi Murayama was elected Prime Minister in June 1994 and took office on 18 July. His party, the Social Democratic Party of Japan (SDPJ) had no parliamentary majority but formed an alliance with its traditional rival, the LDP, and with a new party, the Sakigake.

67 The opening of Kansai airport, located on an artificial island, led to a blossoming of island-city projects in a bid to ease congestion in densely populated cities.

68 On 17 January 1995 an earthquake hit the area of Hanshin. Over 6,000 died, 100,000 buildings were destroyed in the city of Kobe and over 300,000 were left homeless.

69 In March, a series of attacks with poisonous Sarin gas killed 12 people and intoxicated 5,500 others in Tokyo's subways. A similar attack had taken seven lives in Matsumoto in June 1994. Shoko Asahara, the leader of a religious sect called Aum Shinriyko (Supreme Truth), was charged with the attack and arrested along with 16 other leaders from the movement.

70 In January 1996 Ryutaro Hashimoto (LDP president) replaced Murayama as Prime Minister and called for general elections in October, winning a small majority in parliament. In November, Hashimoto formed a cabinet with only LDP members.

71 In a referendum held in late 1997, slightly more than half of the Nago population, on Okinawa island, decided against the construction of a US heliport on the island (held by the US since the Japanese surrender in 1945). Both governments claimed the construction was a step towards the dismantling of a sophisticated air base on the island.

72 The financial and economic crisis which struck Southeast Asia in 1997 also affected Japan, the second world power and first creditor of the world. Hashimoto resigned in July 1998 after the poor electoral results for his LDP. Keizo Obuchi, also of the LDP, obtained sufficient votes in the Lower House and was named the new Prime Minister. The greatest challenges facing the new Government were to cut taxes in order to stimulate consumption and to take action against the bad loans that paralyzed the Japanese banking system.

73 A major radioactive uranium leak at a JCO company reprocessing plant, near the Tokoaimura nuclear plant north of Tokyo, caused radiation levels to rise to 15,000 times higher than normal. The environmental organization

Doctors
197 per 100,000 people
1990-2002

Primary school
100% net enrolment rate
2000

Greenpeace denounced the accident as a symptom of the problems plaguing Japan's nuclear safety system. According to Greenpeace, Japan holds five tons of uranium within its territory, in addition to 30 tons it has purchased but which remain in Europe.

[74] In August, right-wing groups hailed the re-adoption after 50 years of the old imperial flag, while dozens of teachers - who refused to honor imperial symbols from militarist times - were sacked. The growth in nationalism was also reflected in the armed forces, which saw recruitment reach the highest levels for several decades.

[75] Following yet another nuclear accident, this time at the Tokaimura plant in September 1999, Obuchi ordered the inspection of all installations using nuclear fuel. The JCO firm, which recycled nuclear material, admitted that for years it had been using procedures that did not comply with the minimum safety requirements established by the Government. Greenpeace claimed that the plant continued to emit radiation five times higher than recommended safety levels, while Government officials from the nuclear safety area were criticized for their slowness in measuring the contamination. *Yomiuri* newspaper reported that the three operators charged with negligence in the handling of radioactive materials did not even know what a nuclear chain reaction meant.

[76] Obuchi, who had achieved his country's economic revival, went into a coma in April 2000. He was replaced by Yoshiro Mori. In May, days before Obuchi's death, the new Prime Minister spoke at a meeting of Shintoist followers (who during World War II worshipped Emperor Hirohito as a living deity). Mori shocked national and international public opinion with his description of Japan as 'a divine nation that has the Emperor at its center'.

[77] Responding to demands for his resignation from the press, the opposition and factions within his own party, Mori appointed a new cabinet and made administrative reductions. To prop up his eroded power base, Mori gave key positions to former prime ministers Kiichi Miyazawa and Ryutaro Hashimoto.

[78] In February 2001, Mori continued to play golf after hearing that a Japanese fishing vessel had collided with a US nuclear submarine, raising press calls for his resignation due to his 'lack of sensitivity.'

[79] Finally, in April, Mori admitted he had lost public confidence and resigned. He was replaced by Junichiro Koizumi who, as well as promising to revitalize the economy and clean up the government image, included 5 women in his cabinet, including Makiko Tanaka - daughter of former premier - who became the first female foreign minister. This government, with a record female contingent, was classed as a 'Hollywood' cabinet aiming chiefly for popularity. When he came to power, Koizumi had 90 per cent support.

[80] That month, China and South Korea condemned a history book approved by the Japanese authorities. Seoul and Beijing said the text 'glossed over' atrocities by the Japanese army during World War II. The book was written by a group of nationalist historians who stated that Japanese action during the War benefited the South East Asian nations because it prepared them for independence, and that the Nanjing massacre of 1937 - where 300,000 civilians were killed - was 'very far from being a holocaust'. Following the protests, the Japanese Education Minister said 137 changes had been made to the text.

[81] Further friction with China and South Korea was caused by Koizumi's visit to the Shinto altar of Yasukuni. The 2.4 million soldiers honored there include some figures considered war criminals - for example, the executed Prime Minister Hideki Tojo, who led Japan during World War II.

[82] In October, Koizumi visited Seoul and offered apologies for the suffering of that country under the Japanese colonial government.

[83] After this Koizumi tried to avoid the sensitive date of 15 August (the date of Japan's surrender in 1945). However, he visited the temple every year.

[84] South Korea and China also express unease over Koizumi's visit to what they consider 'a monument to militarism'. Sectors of the press accused the Prime Minister of 'intransigent nationalism' and see him as an obstacle to normalizing relations with both countries.

[85] Koizumi's popularity rating was hit by a series of scandals, and fell to 40 per cent in April 2002. In January he had sacked Chancellor Tanaka, whom he accused of lying in an argument with his bureaucrats. This was followed by resignations from allies and ministers, for various reasons, and in April, Yutaka Inoue, speaker of the ruling party in the upper house, also resigned.

[86] In May 2002 Japan, along with the EU, ratified the 1997 Kyoto Protocol on climate change. This gave the Protocol the required number of signatories for it to come into force, despite US refusal to ratify it.

[87] Japan and South Korea co-hosted the soccer World Cup in June 2002 - the first time the competition had been held in the region.

[88] In September 2002 Koizumi became the first Japanese leader to visit North Korea. North Korean leader Kim Jong Il apologized for the abduction of Japanese citizens in the 1970s and 1980s, and confirmed that eight had been killed. A month later, five of the kidnapped were returned to their relatives.

[89] During 2003 Japan had a long trade dispute with the US. The Bush administration set tariffs on steel imports, some as high as 30 per cent, harming Japanese exports. Japan's Trade minister, Soichi Nakagawa, threatened sanctions against US products unless Washington obeyed WTO rules by November.

[90] On 4 December 2003, after joint pressure through the WTO from the EU, China, Brazil and other countries, the US lifted the controversial tariffs, putting an end to the dispute.

[91] That month, the Japanese Government announced it would install a 'purely defensive' US missile-shield. This caused outcry from China, which had already protested when Prime Minister Koizumi appeared in May before the Special Commission on Emergency Legislation of the upper chamber and stated that the Self-Defense Forces were actually 'Japan's army'.

[92] In February 2004, the Government ordered the deployment of 'non-combat' soldiers to Iraq, raising charges of unconstitutionality from the opposition. The order was based on a 1992 law and the precedent of peacekeeping forces in Cambodia. This was the first involvement of Japanese troops in a combat zone since World War II. ∎

PROFILE

ENVIRONMENT

The country is an archipelago made up of 3,400 islands, the most important being Hokkaido, Honshu and Kyushu. The terrain is mountainous, dominated by the so-called Japanese Alps, which are of volcanic origin. Since 85 per cent of the land is taken up by high, uninhabitable mountains, 40 per cent of the population lives on only 1 per cent of the land area, in the narrow Pacific coastal plains, where demographic density exceeds 1,000 inhabitants per sq km. The climate is sub-tropical in the south, temperate in the center and cold in the north. Located where cold and warm ocean currents converge, Japanese waters have excellent fishing, and this activity is important to the countrys economy. Japan's intensive and highly mechanized farming is concentrated along the coastal plains (rice, soybeans and vegetables). There are few mineral resources. Highly industrialized, the countrys economy revolves around foreign trade, exporting manufactured products and importing raw materials.

SOCIETY

Peoples: The Japanese are culturally and ethnically homogeneous, having their origin in the migration of peoples from the Asian continent. There are Korean, Chinese, Ainu and Brazilian minorities.
Religions: Buddhism and Shintoism 84 per cent.
Languages: Japanese.
Main Political Parties: The government coalition is made up of the Liberal Democratic Party (LDP), the Social Democratic Party of Japan (SPDJ) and the New Party Sakigake. The Shinshinto (Japan Renewal Party) has been in opposition since 1994.
Main Social Organizations: The General Council of Japanese Trade Unions has 4,500,000 members.

THE STATE

Official Name: Nihon-Koku
Capital: Tokyo 34,997,000 people (2003).
Other Cities: Yokohama 3,518,000 people; Osaka 2,641,000; Nagoya 2,243,400; Kyoto 1,488,800 (2000).
Government: Parliamentary constitutional monarchy. Emperor Akihito has been Head of State since January 1989, although his official coronation did not take place until 12 November 1990. Junichiro Koizumi, Prime Minister and head of the Government since April 2001. Legislature (The Diet) is bicameral: House of Representatives, made up of 480 members; House of Counsellors, with 252 members, elected by direct popular vote every 4 and 6 years, respectively.
National Holidays: 23 December, Emperor's Birthday (1933). 11 February, Founding of the Country (1889).
Armed Forces: 239,500 (including 8,000 women). Other: 12,000 (non-combat Coast Guard, under the jurisdiction of the Ministry of Transport).

Radioactive homeless people

MORE THAN 70,000 PEOPLE are working in the 17 nuclear power plants and 52 reactors scattered across Japan. Although the nuclear power stations have their own employees in technical positions, more than 80 per cent of the non-technical staff is composed of untrained workers who accept short-term contracts. Homeless people are recruited to perform the most dangerous tasks such as cleaning reactors and decontaminating facilities. The *yakuza* (Japanese mafia) finds, selects and illegally hires the homeless workers for companies which are totally reliant on this workforce to keep their operations going. The most probable fate for these hidden workers is death from bone cancer, caused by the amounts of radioactivity in their bodies, which are higher than those allowed in most countries.

They are called 'nuclear gypsies' on account of the nomadic life they lead, going from one power station to another, until they become ill and then die. To hire these rootless poor people is only possible through the connivance of the Government. The Japanese authorities have stipulated that the annual amount of radioactivity a person can be exposed to is 50 mSv (milli-sieverts). However, the European Union (EU) set 100 mSv as the maximum dosage a worker in a nuclear reactor can be exposed to in five years, while 1 mSv is the annual amount allowed for the general public. According to a report in June 2003 in the Spanish newspaper *El Mundo*, the 'companies operating nuclear stations hire homeless people until they have been exposed to the maximum radiation levels and then they fire them *for the sake of their health*, sending them onto the street again'. Then, within days or months, those same workers are hired again under different names.

MAFIA MOBS

'The *yakuza* (mafia) acts as an intermediary. Companies pay 30,000 yen (216 euros) per working day, but the hired worker only gets 20,000 yen (144 euros). The yakuza get to keep the difference' says Kenji Higuchi, a Japanese journalist who has been investigating this issue for 30 years. Every week, together with Yukoo Fujita, a professor at Keio University, Higuchi visits places where homeless people hang out, to talk to them and warn them about the risks they run by accepting illegal jobs at nuclear power plants, where they are subjected to unhealthy temperature and oxygen conditions, in addition to being exposed to inadmissible levels of radiation. The daily rate of pay for working at power plants - work that is commonly done by robots in other countries - is approximately twice the amount paid in the construction industry. The recruitment of homeless people for such work has been carried out in Japan since the 1970s. According to Fujita, at least half of the 5,000 temporary workers employed by nuclear plants are homeless people.

Up to 17 per 10,000 workers in the power plants have a 100 per cent chance of dying from cancer, and a larger number have a 'high likelihood'. It is estimated that over the last 30 years more than 300,000 temporary staff have been recruited into the Japanese nuclear plants.

GENERATING WORK FOR HOMELESS PEOPLE

Panasonic, Toshiba and Hitachi are among the transnational companies that subcontract homeless people. The soaring demand for electricity in high-tech Japan with its 127.6 million people has fuelled the need for nuclear energy. While the Japanese active working population is around 62 million people, the present unemployment rate is 5 per cent, equivalent to 3.5 million people out of work. The resultant poverty leads to homelessness and people desperate for work - at any cost. ∎

Jordan / Al Urdunn

Population:	5,750,139
Area:	89,210 km²
Capital:	Amman
Currency:	Dinar
Language:	Arabic

B y 2000 BC, groups of Semitic nomads known as Amorites had entered the region that would come to be called Canaan (present-day Jordan). By the middle of the second millennium they settled in the Jordan Valley, which became a Semitic language area. During the 15th to 13th centuries BC, small tribal kingdoms that are mentioned in the Old Testament: Edom, Moab, Bashan, Gilead, dominated Canaan until its complete conquest by the Israelites between 1220 and 1190 BC. In 722 BC Israel fell to the Assyrians, who divided the Jordan region into provinces.

[2] Between the 3rd and 1st century BC, three peoples coexisted in Jordan: Jews, Greeks (veterans from the campaigns of Alexander the Great), and Nabataeans (nomadic Arabs who arrived in Edom in the 7th century BC). The Greeks were mainly veterans of Alexander's military campaigns who fought one another for regional hegemony. By the 1st century BC, Roman legions removed the last Seleucids from Syria, converting the area into a full Roman province.

[3] In order to check Muslim expansion, in the year 636 the Byzantine emperor Heraclius fought the Arabs at the Yarmuk river. Victory gave the Muslims access to the Fertile Crescent (see Saudi Arabia). During the first stage of the Crusades, the western part of the Jordanian territory was used in warfare against the European strongholds.

[4] Between Turkish domination in the 16th century and the start of World War I, the territory formed part of the district of Damascus.

[5] Jordanian peoples joined the widespread Arab rebellion against the Turks, and their participation was decisive in the defeat of the Ottomans. Under the Sykes-Picot Agreement of 1916, Britain controlled Iraq and Palestine, in which present-day Jordan was included. The British had promised

Sherif Hussein of Mecca that they would form a single Arab kingdom with these territories and the Arab Peninsula.

[6] The situation of Faisal - son of the Sherif - in Syria (under French dominion) and his expulsion in 1920, led Prince Abdullah - another of Hussein's sons - to support his brother with Bedouin forces. The British convinced him to accept rule by the Emirate of Transjordan.

[7] This Emirate remained under British mandate until 1928, when the frontiers with Palestine were set and a law was passed giving Abdullah and his heirs power over the State. Foreign affairs and the military remained under British control until 1946, when the Emirate became the 'Hashemite

Kingdom of Transjordan'. After the Arab-Israeli war in 1948, King Abdullah annexed the West Bank of Jordan. The country became known as Jordan, but had new problems regarding the situation of Palestinian refugees, the legal status of Jerusalem, and the doubling in length of its frontier with Israel.

[8] In 1951 Abdullah was assassinated and succeeded by his son Talal. He was anti-British and promised a progressive government, but was deposed a year later. In 1953 his son Hussein took over the throne at the age of 17.

[9] In 1967, the Six Day War - in which Israel on one side fought Egypt, Syria and Jordan on the other - brought serious consequences for Hussein's kingdom. In addition to suffering great military losses, he lost one-third of the most fertile lands and the cities of Bethlehem, Hebron, Jericho, Nablus, Ramallah and Jerusalem.

[10] With the Israeli occupation of Transjordan, the Kingdom received many Palestinians, expelled by the Israelis from their lands initially in 1948 and then (around 200,000) of them, from their refugee camps in 1967. In 1970, a series of guerrilla actions, hijackings and Hussein's desire to replace the Palestine Liberation Organization (PLO) as the Palestinians' representative

PROFILE

ENVIRONMENT

Seventy-five per cent of the country is a desert plateau, between 600 and 900 meters in altitude, which forms part of the Arabian Desert. The western part of this plateau has a series of cleavages at the beginning of the great Rift Valley fault, which crosses the Red Sea and stretches into East Africa. In the past, these fissures widened the Jordan River valley and formed the steep depression that is now the Dead Sea. This region is suitable for agriculture. The country has a a rainy winter and very dry summer. As most of the country is made up of dry plains, farming is limited to cereals (wheat and rye) and citrus fruits. Sheep and goats are also bred.

SOCIETY

Peoples: Most of the population is made up of Palestinians who immigrated following the wars with Israel in 1948 and 1967. Native Jordanians are from 20 large Bedouin ethnic groups of which about one third are still semi-nomadic. There is a Circassian minority (of around 100,000 people) who came from the Caucasus in the 19th century, and now play a major role in trade and administration. Armenians, Kurds, Azeries.

Religions: Muslim (mainly Sunni Muslim but the Shi'a numbers are increasing rapidly) 92 per cent; Christian 8 per cent (mainly orthodox).

Languages: Arabic (official). English.

Main Political Parties: In 1991 political parties were legalized. The most important are: National Constitutional Party (nine party coalition) and the

Jordan Socialist Arab Ba'ath Party. Extra parliamentary: Islamic Action Front, Shi'a; Jordan Democratic Popular Party; Democratic Arab Party of Jordan.

Main Social Organizations: The most important union body is the General Federation of Unions of Jordan. The Union of Jordanian Women has participated in the democratization process and in defense of the political rights of women. Others: National Union of Students of Jordan and the Muslim Brotherhood.

THE STATE

Official Name: al-Mamlakah al-Urdunniya al-Hashimiyah.

Administrative Divisions: 12 provinces.

Capital: Amman 1,237,000 people (2003).

Other Cities: Irbid 537,600 people; Az-Zarqa 471,200; ar-Rusayfah 184,300; as-Salt 64,000 (2000).

Government: Abdullah II, King since February 1999. Faisal al-Fayez, Prime Minister. Legislative branch: National Assembly (bicameral), with a 40 member Senate appointed by the King, and an 80-member Chamber of Deputies elected by direct popular vote; the latter can be dissolved by the King.

National Holiday: 25 May, Independence Day (1946).

Armed Forces: 98,650 personnel (1996). Other: 6,000 soldiers under the authority of the Department of Public Security; 200,000 militia in the 'People's Army'; 3,000 Palestinians in the Palestinian Liberation Army, under the supervision of the Jordanian Army.

Life expectancy
71.0 years
2000-2005

GNI per capita
$1,760
2002

Literacy
90% total adult rate
2000

HIV prevalence rate
0.1% of population 15-49 years old
2001

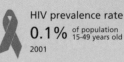

IN FOCUS

ENVIRONMENTAL CHALLENGES
Water scarcity is the most pressing environmental problem. Desertification and urban expansion are leading to the loss of large portions of arable land, especially near the Jordan River.

WOMEN'S RIGHTS
Women have been able to vote and run for office since 1974.

King Abdullah appointed seven women, all liberal professionals, to the 55-seat Senate. As a result, female representation stands at 12 per cent, the highest proportion in the Arab world.

In 2000, women comprised 25 per cent of the total labor force, equivalent to one million people. At the same time, female unemployment amounted to 20 per cent, whereas the male unemployment rate was 11 per cent. The vast majority of women work in services (86 per cent), as opposed to industry (10 per cent) and agriculture (4 per cent).

The illiteracy rate among women over 15 was 15.7 per cent in 2000, three times higher than the rate among men but considerably lower than the 44.6 per cent rate recorded in 1980. In 2000, 50 per cent of expectant mothers were anemic. In 1995, 80 per cent of pregnant women received prenatal care and 97 per cent of all births were assisted by qualified medical personnel.

CHILDREN
Five per cent of children under five were moderately to severely underweight (1997*).

School enrolment among girls is 94 per cent*.

Education is compulsory until the age of 16; however, there are no penalties for parents who fail to comply. Since 2000, Iraqi children are not allowed to attend state schools unless they are either legal residents or refugees recognized as such by the UNHCR.

The State subsidizes food and transport for large or very poor families. There are free vaccination programs and free access to healthcare for minors in state clinics.

Even though it is difficult to determine, sexual abuse within families is more prevalent than reported. Although there are laws prohibiting child labor, it is common to see children hawking their wares on Amman streets. When the police return them to their homes, they are soon back on the streets.

INDIGENOUS PEOPLES/ ETHNIC MINORITIES
Palestinians, who number more than two million (50 per cent of the population) are mainly Sunni Muslim (85 per cent). This population first arrived in 1946 during the incorporation of Palestine into the recently founded Transjordan, during the War of Independence from Israel in 1948, and during and after the Six Day War in 1967, when Israel occupied Palestinian territories. Palestinians in Jordan are dispersed and their status is varied, ranging from prominent individuals completely integrated into Jordanian culture to refugees living in deep poverty.

MIGRANTS/REFUGEES
In late 2002, Jordan received more than 150,000 Palestinian refugees from the Gaza Strip. Of 1,400 refugees registered during that year, some 1,100 were Iraqis. The UNHCR approved 300 applications for refugee status and rejected 2,200. Among the 2,100 pending cases, 1,900 were Iraqis and the rest were Sudanese, Syrians, Egyptians or Algerians.

An estimated 300,000 Iraqis live in Jordan, although it is not clear how many of them are refugees. New contingents arrived in 2002, fleeing the US invasion, economic sanctions and persecution.

There are thought to be 800,000 Palestinians, displaced from the West Bank after the Arab-Israeli War in 1967. They live as Jordanian citizens, unlike the Gaza Palestinians who do not have access to citizenship and remain refugees.

As a result of the global war against terrorism unleashed in 2001, the country began to accept fewer refugees. The Jordanian Government restricted entry of Palestinians with Jordanian documents living on the West Bank. The Government announced the closure of borders against a large inflow of Iraqi refugees during the war. Later on, authorities prepared to receive 70,000 refugees in two camps located near the Iraqi border.

DEATH PENALTY
The death penalty still applies for common crimes.

** Latest data available in
The State of the World's Children
and Childinfo database,
UNICEF, 2004.*

to use an air base within the territory.

[17] King Hussein died on 7 February 1999. He had designated a new heir, his 37-year-old son Abdullah ibn al-Hussein, instead of his brother Hassan.

[18] When Abdullah II took the throne, the Arab-Israeli peace process had reached a stalemate, and Iraq was under attack by the US. Jordan was facing a serious economic crisis while the political parties demanded more openness from the Government.

[19] The second Palestinian *intifada* had a direct impact on Jordan. In October 2001, following clashes between the police and a crowd protesting against the Israeli Government, the Government banned public demonstrations.

[20] The death of an adolescent in police custody in the southern town of Maan in January 2002 unleashed the worst unrest in three years. According to his family, the boy was tortured by the police after they found photographs of al-Qaeda leader Osama bin Laden, and of Palestinians who had died during the *intifada,* in his pockets.

[21] In February, Abdullah II backed Washington's labelling of Iran, Iraq and North Korea 'the axis of terror'. The Government was pressured into taking a less cordial position in relation to Israel. Chancellor Marwan Muasher called the Israeli Ambassador to a meeting in March and threatened to take measures to protest the attack on the Palestine Authority headquarters. Similarly, he asked the UN Security Council for immediate deployment of troops to the Palestinian territories.

[22] In August 2002, an incident with Qatar triggered by a program broadcast by the al-Jazeera TV network ended in the recall of the Jordanian ambassador and the closing of the network's offices in Amman.

[23] In September 2002, in their largest joint initiative to date, Jordan and Israel agreed on an $800 million plan to transport water from the Red Sea to the shrinking Dead Sea.

[24] In October 2002, US diplomat Laurence Foley was shot as he left his home in Amman, in the first assassination of a Western politician in the country.

[25] In the first parliamentary elections of Abdullah II's reign, held in June 2003, the independent candidates who supported the King won two-thirds of the seats.

[26] In August 2003, 11 died and more than 50 were wounded when a bomb went off in the Jordanian Embassy in Baghdad, Iraq. ∎

body were among the reasons leading to the Jordanian army massacre of Palestinians known as 'Black September'.

[11] After the Arab-Israeli war in 1973, the King re-established relations with the PLO, and in 1979 recognized it as the only legitimate representative of Palestine.

[12] In 1985, King Hussein and Palestinian leader Yasser Arafat were reconciled; in July 1988 the King renounced any claim to the West Bank and gave the PLO responsibility for the Israeli-occupied territory.

[13] When Iraq invaded Kuwait in August 1990, Jordan found itself in a difficult position, militarily flanked by Israel and Iraq, with a majority of subjects who supported Iraq, and depending on

Saudi Arabia for finance and on Baghdad for oil. Although it joined the trade embargo against Baghdad, it opposed the use of military force to enforce the UN Security Council resolutions. The country lost $570 million as a result of the embargo. It received 40,000 Kurdish refugees, more than 1,000,000 Iraqis and some 300,000 Jordanians of Palestinian origin who were expelled by Kuwait in response to Jordan's support of Iraq.

[14] On 9 June 1991, Hussein and political representatives signed a new Constitution, which legalized political parties and extended political rights for women.

[15] There was less repression of the growth of Islamic fundamentalism than in other countries of the region. The

Muslim Brotherhood that was allowed to operate initially as a philanthropic organization gained prestige in the area of social welfare: it ran hospitals, schools and several Islamic study centers. The fundamentalists' pressure put obstacles in the way of negotiations with Israel. In 1994, Hussein and Israeli premier Yitzhak Rabin signed a bilateral peace treaty. Israel handed over 300 square kilometers of desert to Jordan and the frontier was established. Even more significant was the granting of custody of sacred Islamic sites in Jerusalem to the care of King Hussein.

[16] Despite its dependence on Iraqi oil, Jordan cut back on trade with Baghdad in 1996. Exports to Iraq were reduced 50 per cent, and the United States was authorized

Kanaky - New Caledonia / Kanaky

Population:	236,979
Area:	18,580 km²
Capital:	Nouméa
Currency:	CFP franc
Language:	French

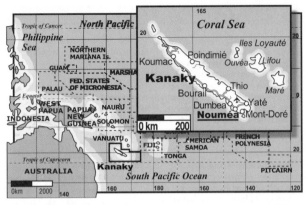

New Caledonia (Kanaky) was populated by Melanesians (Kanaks) 3,000 years ago. The islands were named by Captain Cook in 1774, as the tree-covered hills reminded him of the Scottish - Caledonian - landscape. In 1853, the main island was occupied by the French Navy which organized a local guard to suppress frequent indigenous uprisings. Nickel and chrome mining attracted thousands of French settlers. The colonizers pushed out the original inhabitants, and traditional religions, crafts and social organizations were obliterated. Many landless natives were confined to 'reservations', and the system of terraced fields were trodden over by cattle. The last armed rebellion, stifled in 1917, only accelerated European land appropriation.

² After Algerian independence, in July 1962, colonization increased with the arrival of *pieds-noirs*, the former French colonists in Algeria. By 1946, New Caledonia had become a French Overseas Territory, but the resulting political autonomy did not favor the Kanaks, reduced to a minority group in relation to the *caldoches* (descendants of Europeans who had settled a century ago).

³ In the 1970s, discontent with the economic situation produced by colonial domination generated strikes, land invasions, experiments in co-operative work, and a powerful campaign to restore traditional lands to the local groups. These had been totally occupied by settlers and were used mostly as grazing land for cattle. The rescue of *coutume* (cultural traditions) and the Kanak identity became a priority, and the proposed luxury tourist Club Méditerranée camps were firmly rejected.

⁴ In September 1981, pro-independence leader Pierre Declercq, a Catholic of European origin, was murdered at his home by right-wing extremists, changing the malaise to a full-blown political crisis.

⁵ Another strong reason why France was hesitant to grant Kanaky independence is that it has the

world's second largest nickel deposits, and extensive reserves of other minerals including chrome, iron, cobalt, manganese, and polymetallic nodules, discovered recently on the ocean floor within territorial waters.

⁶ Furthermore, the islands' strategic position is of great military value. Its ports, facilities and bases house 6,000 troops and a small war fleet (including a nuclear submarine), considered by the military command as a 'vital point of support' for the French nuclear-testing site on Mururoa atoll.

⁷ The election of President Francois Mitterrand in 1981 rekindled the hopes of the pro-independence parties. The French socialist leader was supported by most Kanaks, who saw independence as a way to end the unfair income distribution on the island. This stood at $7,000 per capita (the highest in the Pacific except for Nauru) but the vast majority of the money was concentrated in the hands of European - mostly French - business people, the *métros*, who enjoyed fiscal benefits, and the caldoches

who monopolized the top public posts.

⁸ In July 1984, the French National Assembly passed special bills concerning the colony's autonomy, though it rejected amendments submitted by pro-independence parties, confirming Kanak fears that the socialist government of France had no intention of granting independence. In November, the main opposition force, the Socialist Kanak National Liberation Front (FLNKS) called for a boycott of local Territorial Assembly elections, which were sure to endorse the French government plan of postponing Kanak independence indefinitely.

⁹ In December 1984, local government became fully controlled by the caldoches with no indigenous Kanak representation, and the FLNKS unilaterally declared New Caledonia independent, proclaiming it a Kanak state. The resulting election was boycotted by 80 per cent of the Kanak population, forcing the Government to call it off, and prepare for negotiations.

¹⁰ In December 1986, the United Nations General Assembly

proclaimed the right of the Kanak people to self-determination and independence, proposing that the FLNKS be recognized as their legitimate representative.

¹¹ When all attempts at negotiation failed for the Kanaks, the French attacked the island of Ouvéa, and 19 people were killed, most of them apparently executed rather than killed in combat.

¹² In June 1988, FLNKS leader Jean-Marie Tjibaou, and Jacques Lafleur (leader of the Caledonian Popular Assembly for the Republic and strongly opposed to independence) signed Section 1 of the Matignon Accord, supported by French Prime Minister Michel Rocard, in Paris. From July that year direct government over Kanaky was re-established from Paris. Section II of the Accord stipulated the adoption of preparatory measures for voting on self-determination in 1998 and the freezing of the electoral register, to prevent France from increasing the number of voters by sending new colonists.

¹³ The territory was divided into three regions, two with a majority of Kanak voters. One of the aims of this division was to create a Melanesian (Kanak) political and financial 'elite', taking over power from the pro-independence groups in most of the territory.

¹⁴ In a first referendum that same year, the agreements were ratified. In May 1989, Tjibaou and another independence leader who supported the Matignon agreements were assassinated in Ouvéa.

¹⁵ In 1991, the balance of trade was affected by a drop in the international prices of nickel and fish. A new generation of leaders emerged in the provinces controlled by the pro-independence groups, but most Melanesians saw their

---

PROFILE

ENVIRONMENT

The territory consists of the island of New Caledonia (16,700 sq km), the Loyauté/Loyalty Islands (Ouvéa, Lifou, Maré and Walpole), the archipelagos of Chesterfield, Avon, Huon, Belep, and the island of Nouméa. The whole group is located in southern Melanesia, between the New Hebrides (Vanuatu) to the East and Australia to the West. Of volcanic origin, the islands are mountainous with coastal reefs. The climate is rainy, tropical, and suitable for agriculture. The vegetation is dense and the subsoil is rich in nickel deposits.

SOCIETY

Peoples: Indigenous Kanaks/New Caledonians are of Melanesian origin (the Kanaka group), 42.5 per cent; there are French and descendants of French (known as caldoches), 37.1 per cent; as well as Wallisian, 8.6 per cent, Vietnamese, Indonesian, Chinese and Polynesian minorities.
Religions: Roughly 60 per cent Catholic, 16 per cent Protestant and around 5 per cent Muslim.
Languages: French (official) and more than 30 Melanesian and Polynesian dialects.

Main Political Parties: Rally for Caledonia within the Republic (RPCR), anti-separatist; Kanak and Socialist National Liberation Front (FLNKS); Federation of Committees for the Co-ordination of Independentists, separatist; National Front, nationalist. **Main Social Organizations:** The Caledonian Workers' Confederation (CTC); the Federation of New Caledonian Miners' Unions (FSMNC).

THE STATE

Official Name: Territoire d'Outre-Mer de la Nouvelle-Calédonie et Dependances.
Administrative divisions: Three provinces: Loyauté, Nord and Sud. **Capital:** Nouméa 140,000 people (2003). **Other Cities:** Mont-Doré 22,700 people; Dumbéa 15,200; Poindimié 4,700 (2000).
Government: Head of State, French President Jacques Chirac. High Commissioner named by France, Daniel Constantin, since July 2002. Head of Government, Marie- Noëlle Thémereau since June 2004. Legislature: 54-member Territorial Assembly.
National Holiday: 14 July, Bastille Day (1789).
Armed Forces: French troops 3,700 (1993).

Life expectancy
74.9 years
2000-2005

GNI per capita
$14,050
2002

living standards decline even further. The imbalance of income became pronounced amongst the Kanaks and greater access to material goods distanced many Melanesians from their community structures and traditions.

[16]   In the caldoche areas, mainly covering the capital Nouméa, social inequalities also increased, partly due to the arrival of Melanesian farmers who built shanty-towns on the outskirts of the city, but also due to the impoverishment of some caldoches. In a context of increasing social tension, street disturbances became more common.

[17]   The political repercussions of the social gaps were reflected in the 1995 provincial elections. The Palika, one of the members of FLNKS, presented separate lists criticizing the Front representatives' administration of both provinces controlled by the pro-independence groups.

[18]   The exploitation of nickel by the pro-independence groups in the north was successful in the first years of administration, which enabled them to associate with the Canadian company Falconbridge.

IN FOCUS

ENVIRONMENTAL CHALLENGES
Approximately 80 per cent of the territory has been deprived of its original forest and plant cover to serve the mining industry and the production of agricultural exports like rice, pineapples and oranges, which has led to a process of accelerated soil erosion.

WOMEN'S RIGHTS
Ninety-seven per cent of pregnant women receive prenatal healthcare, and 98 per cent of births are attended by qualified medical personnel. Maternal mortality stands at 10 deaths per

100,000 live births. The fertility rate is 2.6 children per woman*.

CHILDREN
The child mortality rate is seven deaths per 1,000 live births, while the average under-five mortality rate is 10 deaths per 1,000 live births*.

DEATH PENALTY
Capital punishment was abolished by France in 1981.

* Latest data available in*The State of the World's Children* and *Childinfo* database, UNICEF, 2004.

[19]   The negotiations for Kanaky independence changed course in April 1998. The FLNKS and Paris established the basis for a general agreement, known as the Nouméa Accord. The coexistence of two different systems - one that follows Kanak traditions and the other imposed by France - proved to be the most difficult issue to resolve. The Kanaks wanted respect for their culture and their traditional

civil society organizations. The Nouméa Accord allowed for the transference of powers that would assure a 'nearly sovereign' territory within 15 to 20 years. The Kanaks and the caldoches agreed to share a common 'citizenship', while France acknowledged the 'blotches' remaining from the colonial period.

[20]   In November, a referendum was held to ratify the Nouméa

agreements. The Yes-voters won with 69.14 per cent of the vote. In December, the text of the law defined the application of the Noumea Accord. On 23 December, the National Assembly voted on the legal foundations of the new country, which covered the creation of new institutions as well as a 'gradual' transfer of state powers.

[21]   In late 2002, a demonstration was held to demand the repeal of a permit for a nickel mine in Prony, granted by French authorities to the Goro Nickel Company, that belonged to the Canadian mining company INCO. The work sites were blocked, and Goro Nickel withdrew its workers from the islands and cancelled the mining operations.

[22]   In 2002 and 2003, environmentalists on the island carried out a campaign to get UNESCO to add the archipelago's coral reef system to its list of world heritage sites. That would affect Goro Nickel's mining interests on the islands. There had already been attempts to hold the company accountable for health and environmental impacts caused by mining operations. ■

Melanesians and Polynesians: surviving cultures

MICRONESIA, Melanesia and Polynesia were originally inhabited by Melanesians and Polynesians. Melanesians live in a group of South Pacific islands which include New Guinea, Kanaky (New Caledonia), Vanuatu, Solomon Islands, and Fiji as well as on the Bismarck and Louisiade archipelagos. They are a homogeneous group, although recent studies link them to the Papuans and even to Aboriginal communities in Australia.

Polynesians come from the same ethnic origins as Melanesians, and while they are physically distinct, there are some common traits in language and appearance although their societies have taken different directions.

The first Melanesians arrived 40,000 years ago, probably from the south of the Asiatic continent. About 9,000 years ago, they began to domesticate indigenous root crops and organize their social life around agriculture. Later on, they also specialized in trade and maritime

technology as well as fishing. They generally moved in small groups, with a stay in any one place limited by the duration of crop cycles.
Polynesians, by comparison, probably descended from Austronesians, ancient seafarers who arrived on the Pacific archipelagos from South Asia around 4,000 BC, populating New Zealand/Aotearoa, the Samoan Islands, French Polynesia, Tonga, Tahiti, Hawaii and other smaller islands where they still live.

The range of languages spoken by Melanesians and Polynesians clearly displays the exceptional linguistic variation of Oceania, where one quarter of all world languages are spoken. Melanesian and Polynesian languages belong to the eastern branch of the Malayo-Polynesian family, which includes over 800 dialects spoken by approximately five million people. Melanesians speak more than 400 of the dialects in this group. In Fiji, the main dialect is spoken by nearly half the

population - some 400,000 people - and it is used in official journals and publications. Other dialects include Motu, Roviana, Bambatana, Tolai and Yabem.

Christianity has been gaining ground and progressively replacing traditional forms of religion, although some communities, Melanesian and Polynesian alike, continue to practice their own religions.

This great cultural, social and linguistic diversity suffered intense political upset with the arrival of the Europeans. Western culture has reached even the most remote villages, where some forms of business and capitalist organization can be seen, along with an increasing dependence on imported products. Traditional culture survives in marginal areas where there is greater resistance to the dominant culture. ■

Kazakhstan / Qazaqstan

Population:	15,364,445
Area:	2,724,900 km²
Capital:	Astana
Currency:	Tengue
Language:	Kazakh

I n the Bronze Age (about 2000 BC), the territory of Kazakhstan was inhabited by people who lived by farming and raising livestock. In the Iron Age, around 500 BC, an alliance was formed among the Saka peoples, who had by then developed the ability to write. In the 3rd century BC, the Usune and Kangli peoples - who lived near the Uighur, Chechen and Alan - subdued the other groups in the area. Later, Attila's Huns occupied the region until they were expelled by the Turks.

[2] In the mid-4th century, the Turkish Kaganate (*Khanate* or kingdom) was formed and later divided into Eastern and Western parts, the latter inhabited by the Turkish-speaking Usune, Kangli, Turguesh and Karluk. The Turkish conquerors built mosques and tried to impose Islam upon the local population. These were times of famous scientists such as Farabi (870-950), Biruni (973-1048) and Makhmud of Kashgar, author of the *Dictionary of Turkish Dialects*.

[3] Between the 9th and 12th centuries, the region was occupied by the Oghuz, Kimak, Kipchak and Karajanid groups. The Kipchaks never achieved political unity and remained outside the realm of Islamic influence, which was concentrated in the cities along the Caspian Sea. Until the 13th century, successive waves of Seleucid, Kidan and Tatar invasions swept across the great steppes. Kipchak chiefs and Muscovite princes joined to resist foreign domination, but did not achieve independence until the fall of the Mongols.

[4] Most of these peoples were nomadic shepherds but gradually settled groups of farmers and artisans formed. The Silk Road, uniting Byzantium, Iran and China, passed through Kazakhstan. Trade relations extended as far as Western Europe, Asia Minor and the Far East.

[5] By the late 15th century, the Khanate of Kazakh had been formed, composed of Elder, Middle and Lesser *zhuzes* (hordes), an alliance of like-minded peoples. By the 16th century, an ethnic identity had been forged among the Kazakhs, whose predecessors were Usune, Kangli, Kipchaks and other groups. The khans of the Kazakh *zhuzes* passed on their power to their heirs, who claimed to be descendants of Juchi, the eldest son of Tenguis-Khan (Genghis Khan).

[6] In the 17th century, the Khanate of Dzhungar occupied and looted in successive raids the Kazakh region. Russian colonial expansion from the north began in the 18th century. The Russians built a line of forts and then began working their way southward, creating a line of defense against the Dzhungars. The Middle and Lesser *zhuzes* fell under Russian protection and lost their autonomy in the 1820s because of frequent rebellions. Defeat of the Elder *zhuze* in 1848 completed Kazakhstan's annexation by the Russian Empire.

[7] Russia installed its government institutions, collected taxes, established areas close to the Kazakhs and built new cities, declaring the entire territory property of the State. The conquest of the 'steppe territory', as Kazakhstan was known, was a long process of wars against local tribes, which were completely defeated in 1880.

[8] In the late 19th and early 20th centuries, Russia built huge railroads across the region, uniting it with distant urban centers and facilitating the exploitation of Kazakhstan's fabulous mineral wealth. The country held a third of Russia's coal reserves, half its copper, lead and zinc reserves, strategic metals like tungsten and molybdenum, iron, and oil in the west and under the Caspian sea.

[9] At the beginning of the 20th century, a small nationalist movement emerged in Kazakhstan, and after the Russian Revolution of 1905 the Kazakhs had their own representatives to the first and second *Duma* (parliament) convened by the Czar. In 1916, when the czarist regime ordered the mobilization of all men between the age of 19 and 43 for auxiliary military service, the Kazakhs rebelled, led by Abdulghaffar and Amangeldy Imanov. The revolt was brutally crushed, but in November 1917, after the triumph of the Soviet revolution in Petrograd, the Kazakh nationalists demanded total autonomy for their country. A nationalist government was installed in Alma-Ata (now Almaty) in 1918, but the country soon became a battleground.

[10] Fighting between the Red Army and the White Russians - the latter defending the overthrown regime - lasted until 1920, when the counter-revolution was defeated. In 1936, Kazakhstan became one of the 15 republics of the USSR and in 1937 the local Communist Party was founded. Kazakhstan received significant migratory inflows of Ukrainians, Belorussians, Germans, Bulgarians, Poles, Jews and Tatars, many of them deported by Joseph Stalin's regime.

[11] In addition to developing its industrial potential, the Soviet regime increased the amount of land under cultivation, which came to constitute 15 per cent of all agricultural land in the USSR. Production included wheat, tobacco, mustard, fruit and cattle (particularly cows). Bringing virgin territory under cultivation was an achievement associated with Leonid Brezhnev, during his period as head of the Communist Party (CP) of Kazakhstan.

[12] Until 1985, the most powerful person in Kazakhstan was Dinmujamed Kunaev, a member of the Politburo of the Soviet Communist Party Central Committee, and first secretary of

PROFILE

ENVIRONMENT

Kazakhstan is bordered to the southeast by China; to the south by Kyrgyzstan; and to the north by the Russian Federation. In the western part of the country lie the Caspian and Turan plains; in the center, the Kazakh plateau; and in the eastern and southeastern regions, the Altai, Tarbagatay, Dzhungarian Alatau and Tien Shan mountains. The country has a continental climate, with average January temperatures of -18°C in the north, and -3°C in the south. In July, the temperature varies from 19°C in the north to 28°C in the south. Major rivers include the Ural, Irtysh, Syr Daríya, Chu and Ili. There is also Lake Balkhash and the Caspian and Aral Seas. The vegetation is characteristic of the steppes, but vast areas have come under cultivation (wheat, tobacco, etc) or are used for cattle-raising. The region's abundant mineral wealth includes coal, copper, semi-precious stones and gold.

SOCIETY

Peoples: Kazakhs, 46.5 per cent; Russians, 35 per cent; Ukrainians 5 per cent; Uzbeks 2 per cent; Tatars 2 per cent.
Religion: Islam and Christian Orthodox.

Languages: Kazakh (official), Russian, German, Ugric, Korean, Tatar. **Main Political Parties:** Republican Party of the Country (OTAN); Civil Party of Kazakhstan; Communist Party of Kazakhstan; Agrarian Party; National Co-operative Party of Kazakstan. **Main Social Organizations:** Birlik Movement, Zheltokso and Semipalatinsk-Nevada, an anti-nuclear movement.

THE STATE

Official Name: Qazaqstan Respublikasy.
Administrative Divisions: 14 regions and 3 cities.
Capital: Astana (formerly called Aqmola, inaugurated as the new capital in December 1997) 332,000 people (2003). **Other Cities:** Almaty (formerly called Alma-Ata) 1,250,000 people (1995); Karaganda 420,500; Pavlodar 300,000; Kokchetav 123,000 (2000). **Government:** Nursultan Nazarbayev, president since April 1990, re-elected in 1999. Daniyal Akhmetov, prime minister since June 2003. Bicameral legislature made up of the 77-member Mazhilis (Assembly) and 47-member Senate.
National Holidays: 16 December, Independence (1991); 25 October, Republic Day (1991).
Armed Forces: 40,000 troops (1996).

Life expectancy
66.3 years
2000-2005

GNI per capita
$1,510
2002

Literacy
99% total adult rate
2000

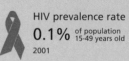
HIV prevalence rate
0.1% of population 15-49 years old
2001

IN FOCUS

ENVIRONMENTAL CHALLENGES

Toxic and radioactive waste - mainly from the armaments industry - have caused serious health problems. A reduction in the water volume of the Aral Sea as a result of the intensive cultivation of cotton on its riverbanks has increased desertification in the area and given rise to a number of environmental problems. Lake Balkhash is suffering similar effects due to the growing industrialization of northern China and the intensive use of water from the Ile river for irrigation. To that is added the continuing thaw of the glaciers in the Tien Shan mountains caused by global warming, leading to a glacial retreat of two cubic kilometers per year, which has affected the volume of water in nearby rivers.

WOMEN'S RIGHTS

Women have been able to vote and stand for election since 1993.

The percentage of women in parliament decreased from 13 per cent in 1995 to 10 per cent in 2000. In the same period, the percentage of women holding ministerial or equivalent positions fell from six to five per cent.

In 2000, women comprised 47 per cent of the total labor force of seven million, with 58 per cent of the women working in the service sector, 21 per cent in agriculture, and 21 per cent in industry. The maternal mortality rate stood at 210 for every 100,000 births*. 27 per cent of pregnant women were anemic and 91 per cent received pre-natal care, while 99 per cent of births were attended by

qualified medical personnel (1999*). An estimated 4,000 to 7,000 women are 'traded' from Kazakhstan to other Asian countries and Western Europe for prostitution. Most of these women come from rural areas and neighboring countries.

CHILDREN

The under 5 mortality rate is 76 per 1,000 live births*, up from 67 per1,000 live births in 1990. Four per cent of children under 5 are underweight, and 96 per cent of all children have been vaccinated against the most common childhood diseases such as poliomyelitis, measles and tetanus*. Kazakhstan is one of the few countries in Asia that forms part of the International Program for the Eradication of Child Labor. Thousands of children in Kazakhstan work in servitude and in hazardous conditions and occupations. Many of them have run away from home, often escaping abuse or parents in the grip of alcoholism or drug abuse, turning to the streets in search of a better life. They frequently end up in the sex trade or involved in other oppressive child labor or exploitation.

The number of 'sex workers' as a result of unemployment has increased since the break-up of the Soviet Union. Authorities are concerned because of the increasing number of children falling into sexual exploitation at an early age - sometimes as young as eight.

According to Amnesty International (AI), under-18 prisoners are exposed to especially cruel conditions. Many are undernourished. The overcrowding is sometimes so severe that prisoners have to sleep in shifts. AI has

denounced torture and beating of prisoners in police stations.

INDIGENOUS PEOPLES/ETHNIC MINORITIES

German and Russian minorities are among the largest of the groups living in Kazakhstan. Most of the Germans are farmers or skilled workers. In the 1990s, more than 350,000 emigrated to Germany, and 70 per cent of those still living in the country would like to emigrate due to unemployment and low salaries, according to opinion polls.

Most of the Russians in Kazakhstan live in the city of Kustana. In the mid-1990s, groups of Russians staged uprisings to demand independence from Kazakhstan. The Government has addressed most of the Russian minority's demands, for example granting them dual citizenship.

MIGRANTS/REFUGEES.

There are around 20,000 refugees in Kazakhstan, mainly Afghans, Chechens and Taikos. Due to the difficult economic conditions in the country, many refugees lack food and housing. International organizations such as the International Red Cross and UNHCR volunteers are working to improve the conditions faced by refugees.

DEATH PENALTY

Capital punishment is applicable to a wide range of crimes, although a moratorium on executions was again adopted in 2004.

*Latest data available in*The State of the World's Children* and *Childinfo* database, UNICEF, 2004.

[21] The country still suffers the environmental and health impact from the more than 500 nuclear tests carried out between 1949 and 1989 by Russia in Semipalatinsk. These caused the discharge of toxic waste and fuel into the sea by rockets launched from Baykonur.

[22] The Kazakh Parliament elected Imangali Tasmagambetov as new Prime Minister in February 2002, after Tokayev's resignation. The former Prime Minister had no choice but to go, because of constant internal divisions in his cabinet.

[23] In Kazakhstan, as in other countries in the region, HIV/AIDS is spreading at an alarming rate, with 3,500 HIV-positive people as of 2001.

[24] Kazakhstan and other countries supported the US-led military actions against Afghanistan and Iraq by sending troops to help deactivate landmines, and by giving the US access to an airport for re-fueling and emergency landings. For its part, the US pledged $5 million in military equipment and training to bolster security for pipelines and oil installations on the shores of the Caspian Sea.

[25] In June 2003, Daniyal Akhmetov was appointed as new premier by parliament after Tasmagambetov was forced to resign due to a dispute over a law governing private land ownership.

[26] Religious tensions persisted in 2003 when the Orthodox Church criticized the opening of two Catholic dioceses in Kazakhstan, accusing the Catholic Church of launching a crusade to gain converts. Some cases of persecution of members of the Baptist Church and Jehovah Witnesses have been documented.

[27] In December 2003, parliament began to discuss a bill to regulate the press. The law established new requirements for obtaining permission to practice journalism, and allowed the Government to intervene in cases in which the media were used for 'propaganda', 'incitement to riot' or 'divulging confidential State information'. Media corporations found to commit such 'crimes' would be subject to temporary or permanent closure. In addition, the law introduced a ban on the 'exhibition of products designed to excite sexual interest'. Although the law was approved, organizations campaigning for press freedom successfully pressed for modifications, although several key articles remained unchanged.

[28] A new moratorium on executions was decreed in January 2004, although the Government said that it was not yet time to abolish the death penalty, as 'the people still supports it'. ■

the CP of Kazakhstan. In 1989, the forced resignation of Kunaev triggered student riots which were crushed by the army.

[13] After the transformations set in motion in the USSR by President Mikhail Gorbachev, Kazakhstan declared its independence. During this period two social movements arose - Birlik and Zheltoksan - as well as the anti-nuclear movement Semipalatinsk-Nevada.

[14] In September 1989, Kazakhstan presented a seven-point plan for the creation of a new union treaty, which was approved by Gorbachev and ten republics. On 1 December 1991, Nazarbayev was elected as the first president of the Republic. The Communist Party became the Socialist Party of Kazakhstan.

[15] Several political groups were formed in 1992, such as the Socialist

Party, the People's Congress Party and the pro-government People's Unity Party. Nazarbayev's party won the first multi-party legislative elections, in March 1994.

[16] In April, the Government launched a vast privatization plan, which included 3,500 state companies, 70 per cent of all state firms. The opening up of the economy and the country's natural resources attracted many foreign investors during 1995.

[17] A customs union between Kazakhstan, Kyrgyzstan, Belarus and the Russian Federation was formed in March 1996, to promote a common market in goods, capital and workers. A year later, Kazakhstan, together with Kyrgyzstan and Tajikistan, signed an agreement to reduce troops and demilitarize borders.

[18] Nazarbayev won the January 1999 Presidential elections with 78 per cent of the vote. Although their fairness was questioned, the elections had an 80 per cent turnout.

[19] Prime Minister Nurlan Balgimbayev resigned in October, after having been censored by Parliament when he sought approval of a very limited budget. Kasymzhomart Tokayev was appointed as the new premier.

[20] The economy had better prospects of growth with the inauguration, in May 2001, of its first large oil pipeline - built by the Kazakh, Russian and American Governments - which would carry 20 million tons of crude oil from the Caspian to the Black Sea, and thence to world markets.

Kenya / Kenya

Population:	32,849,169
Area:	580,370 km²
Capital:	Nairobi
Currency:	Shilling
Language:	English and Swahili

B antu-speaking populations migrated toward the coast from the forests of central Africa 3,000 years ago, settling along the shores of Lake Victoria (east of present-day Kenya). Some 2,000 years later Nilotic and Cushitic peoples (ancestors of the Oromo and Somali) entered from Sudan and Ethiopia and spread throughout the Kenyan territory.

2   In the 16th century, attracted by Kenya's ivory and metals and precious stones from neighboring areas, Arab merchants founded port cities on the shores of the Indian Ocean. They engaged in heavy maritime trade with the Arab world, Persia and India. In coastal cities such as Malindi and Mombasa, the admixture of the merchants and the Bantu people, whose steady expansion had reached the center and the eastern limits of the country, gave birth to the Swahili culture.

3   Malindi and Mombasa were at their height from 1100 to 1500, when Portuguese squadrons attacked both cities. After establishing a network of trade in slaves and ivory, the Portuguese were finally expelled in 1698 by Oman's Sultans, who also took over Zanzibar (a small island off the coast, which later became part of Tanzania) and took advantage of the Portuguese infrastructure and markets.

4   Despite violent attacks by the Masai (a Nilotic shepherd people,

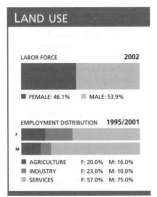
like the Luo), Arabs and Swahilis penetrated the country's hinterland in caravans, reaching Lake Victoria and the extreme southern regions. The country's inner regions, inhabited mostly by Kikuyu and Kamba (Bantu peoples) never developed a culture or organization comparable to those of the coastal area.

5   With the abolition of the slave trade in 1873, and incursions into Kenyan territory by German expeditionaries, Arabs and (the less numerous) Indians began to leave the cities in greater numbers.

6   In 1890 Germany and Britain agreed to divide up the control over East Africa. Kenya went to the British, who already dominated the territory of present-day Uganda. The regime of the protectorate from 1890 - Kenya later became a British Crown colony in 1920 - created the conditions for the development of the British East Africa Company.

7   Railways linking Mombasa with Uganda and Lake Victoria were laid in 1896 and about 5,000 European families settled on land destined for the plantation of coffee and tea, using African labor. These families appropriated four-fifths of Kenya's fertile lands, while the remaining one-fifth was divided up among one million Kikuyu.

8   During World War II, contingents of Kenyans were forced to fight neighboring Italian territories, such as Ethiopia and Somalia, while the British admitted just one local representative to the Legislative Council.

9   In 1944 the Kenya African Union (KAU) was founded. The KAU was an inter-tribal anti-colonialist organization, which

focused on Kikuyu demands. Led by a Kikuyu named Jomo Kenyatta, the KAU organized strikes and peasant marches on the cities.

10   In 1952 massive uprisings were unleashed under the command of a secret society linked to the KAU, called Mau Mau. A state of emergency was declared in 1953 by the colonial administration in response to the increasing attacks on the lives and property of colonists. Political parties were banned, their main leaders arrested - Kenyatta among them - and thousands of Kikuyu were interned in concentration camps.

11   Kenyatta remained in prison until 1959, when he was transferred to house arrest. In 1960 the KAU was legalized under a new name, the Kenyan African National Union (KANU). Kenyatta assumed the presidency of KANU once he was released in 1961.

12   Kenyatta became a member of the Legislative Council in 1962, as part of the British plan for African access to political participation. KANU - supported mainly by the Kikuyu and the Luo, from urban as well as rural areas - won the seat on the Legislative Council in elections in which it faced off with the KADU (Kenyan African Democratic Union), which was supported by several pro-colonialist ethnic groups. The KADU fell apart in 1964.

13   From 1961 on, the British administration set in motion a land sales scheme involving two million hectares. Thus, the colonists - who had been living on Kenyan land - earned $55 million from selling these lands to the people of Kenya. British financial companies opened up credit lines to support the sale of land.

14   General elections were held in May 1963 and Kenyatta became prime minister, while a new constitution, which anticipated the country's autonomy, was approved. After a year of lengthy discussions with London, Kenya achieved formal independence in December. A year later, the republic was proclaimed and Kenyatta was elected president, while Oginga Odinga - of the Luo people - became vice-president.

15   Shortly after Kenyatta took office he was accused of favoring his own ethnic group (Kikuyu) and of neglecting the rest. He encouraged private enterprise and the installation of subsidiaries by transnational corporations. Farmers who had won back their lands lost them again due to their heavy debt burden. A black bourgeoisie with close ties to Kenyatta replaced the white colonists in managing the country's economic affairs.

16   Odinga left KANU in 1966, complaining that it compromised too much, and founded the KPU (Kenyan Popular Union). The KPU was banned after the murder of Tom Mboya, a Luo who had served as a government minister.

17   In the mid-1960s, the Kenyatta Government allowed British military forces to enter the Mombasa port, and permitted the use of the port installations to launch attacks on Uganda. This led to the rupture of diplomatic ties with Uganda, while discrepancies over economic policy generated tension with Tanzania. The East African Community - an ambitious project created in 1967 to integrate the three countries - failed to gel and was dissolved in 1977.

18   Throughout the 1970s, the repression of ethnic movements intensified under the direction of Charles Njonjo. The largest organization of ethnic groups, the GEMA - an association of Kikuyu, Embu and Meru, led by the wealthy Karume Njegay - became a powerful pressure group linking tribal leaders who grew rich doing business with interests from the US and the UK.

19   Kenyatta died at the age of 85 in September 1978. He was succeeded by his vice-president, Daniel Arap Moi, a member of the smaller Kalenjin ethnic group. The climate of distrust continued, aggravated by the tough economic situation: the economic activities engaged in by transnational companies generated structural imbalances, which aggravated the crisis and social tensions. The ruling party, KANU, was the only political force that was allowed to present candidates in the November general elections, in which Moi was confirmed as president.

20   In early 1979, President Moi declared an amnesty for political prisoners and launched a campaign

Life expectancy
44.6 years
2000-2005

GNI per capita
$360
2002

Literacy
82% total adult rate
2000

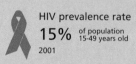
HIV prevalence rate
15% of population 15-49 years old
2001

against corruption. The first measures of the new administration revealed a technocratic approach, which did not tolerate changes in the country's economic policies. In 1980 Njonjo was appointed minister of home affairs.

²¹ At the beginning of Moi's term in office, foreign banks provided credit for planting export crops. Many Kenyan farmers planted sugarcane, coffee, tea and flowers for export under contracts from large US and European firms. As a result, the Government was forced to import enormous quantities of corn and wheat from the US and South Africa.

²² Difficulties caused by a large deficit in public finances prompted President Moi to seek reconciliation with old political rivals who had been driven out of politics. One of the main beneficiaries of the regime's new openness was former vice-president Oginga Odinga, who returned to parliament in 1981 after 11 years of ostracism.

²³ In August 1982, the air force organized a plot that culminated in massive demonstrations and widespread rioting and looting in Nairobi. Moi obtained support from the army, which suppressed the rebellion and disbanded all air force units. The university was closed down indefinitely and Oginga Odinga was placed under house arrest. In June the Legislative Assembly had passed a project declaring Kenya a one-party state.

²⁴ The aborted coup sowed distrust among the different factions in KANU. In May 1983, President Moi denounced an attempted coup d'état by minister Njonjo, who according to Moi had the support of Israel and South Africa. In the midst of the confusion, President Moi called early elections, and won a landslide victory over Njonjo and his supporters.

²⁵ President Moi reopened the border with Tanzania in November 1983, after a summit meeting in Arusha. The summit was meant to be a starting-point for the gradual renewal of economic co-operation between Kenya, Tanzania and Uganda after the failure of the East African Economic Community in 1977.

²⁶ After the 1983 victory, Moi expanded presidential powers, to the detriment of parliament. He made it compulsory for civil servants to join KANU, and in the internal party elections, he replaced the secret ballot with a public vote. The moderate women's opposition group, Mandeleo Ya Wanawake, was taken over by the Government in 1986.

²⁷ In late 1987 Muslim demonstrations in Mombasa triggered a further wave of

repression in which Nairobi University was once again closed. Amnesty International denounced human rights violations in which the Government was implicated, including the torture and the murder of opponents of the Government, especially members of the Mwakenya group.

²⁸ In March 1988, the position of Moi's followers was consolidated in the KANU internal elections. By August, Moi had placed the judiciary under his direct command, and extended the period of preventive detention in which detainees may be held without notifying a judge from 24 hours to 14 days. Male homosexuality - condemned in several of Moi's speeches - was classified as a crime punishable by up to 14 years in prison.

²⁹ Foreign Affairs Minister Robert Ouko, who had denounced corruption within the governing Cabinet, was assassinated in February 1990. An inquest carried out by Scotland Yard disclosed that close advisers of the President took

part in the murder, which triggered a new wave of anti-government protests.

³⁰ Ouko's murder led to an outcry by the international diplomatic community which, added to the numerous reports of human rights violations, prompted Norway to break off diplomatic ties with Kenya in 1991. However, Moi's alignment with the multinational force during the 1991 Gulf War enabled the country to receive economic aid from Britain and military support from Washington. Starting in 1986, Kenya and Uganda engaged in military clashes. Furthermore, the Kenyan Government accused Sudan of protecting groups hostile to Nairobi, and accused Ethiopia of concealing the smuggling of wild animals captured in Kenya.

³¹ In 1990 foreign debt servicing absorbed 30 per cent of export revenues. The trade balance felt the negative impact of the rise in oil import expenditure after the Gulf War and the sharp drop in tourism. The Government helped keep

public spending down by refraining from filling vacancies in state-run companies and by privatizing several public enterprises.

³² In mid-1991, KANU convened the party council to discuss the introduction of democratic reforms. Pressure groups such as the Forum for the Restoration of Democracy (FORD), led by Oginga Odinga, and the Moral Alliance for Peace (MAP), were legally recognized as political parties. However, the setting of a timetable for holding general elections was postponed until late 1992.

³³ Early in 1992, lawyer James Orengo and environmentalist Wangari Maathai were arrested and accused of 'spreading malicious rumors' against the Government. They had stated that President Moi had a plan aimed at cutting short the democratization process that got under way in 1991. That year, a minority opposition group created the Democratic Party (PD), while women's groups demanded access to decision-making positions in the different organizations. Women constituted 52 per cent of voters and 80 per cent of the agricultural work force.

³⁴ The December 1992 general elections were preceded by a march in Nairobi organized by FORD. The Forum, despite its recent break-up into three factions - Kenya, Asili and People - rallied over 100,000 people demanding a definite date for elections and the end of repression and press censorship. Although the six opposition parties took 60 per cent of the vote, they won only 88 seats, compared to KANU's 95 seats. Meanwhile, 2,000 died in western Kenya in conflicts beween ethnic groups.

³⁵ In January 1993 Moi took office for a fourth consecutive term amidst accusations of fraud and corruption. In February the Government engaged in negotiations with the IMF and the World Bank. The agreements led the World Bank to grant the country a $350 million credit. That year, the local currency depreciated 23 per cent and in 1994 Nairobi eliminated exchange controls.

³⁶ In 1994, after the death of Odinga - the leader of FORD-Kenya - opposition groups formed a coalition: the United National Democratic Alliance. The following year Richard Leakey, a paleontologist and member of the opposition, led the SAFINA, which became legal in 1997.

³⁷ In the general elections of December 1997, Moi was re-elected with 40 per cent of the vote, after the dissolution of parliament the previous month. The widespread questioning of the legitimacy of his presidency forced Moi to appoint both Raila Odinga (son of Oginga

PROFILE

ENVIRONMENT

Kenya is located on the east coast of central Africa. There are four main regions, from east to west: the coastal plains with regular rainfall and tropical vegetation; a sparsely populated inland strip with little rainfall which extends towards the north and northwest; a mountainous zone linked to the eastern end of the Rift valley, with a climate tempered by altitude, and volcanic soil fit for agriculture (most of the population and the main economic activities are concentrated here); and the west which is covered by an arid plateau, part of which benefits from the moderating influence of Lake Victoria.

SOCIETY

Peoples: Kenyans are descended from the main African ethnic groups: Bantu, Nilo-Hamitic, Sudanese and Cushitic. Numerically and culturally, the most significant groups are the Kikuyu, the Luyia and the Luo. Others include the Kamba, Meru, Gusii and Embu. There are Indian and Arab minorities.
Religions: 66 per cent of the population are Christian, 6 per cent are Muslim and 20 per cent practice traditional religions.
Languages: English and Swahili are the official languages. There are more than 50 languages spoken, such as Kikuyu and Kamba.
Main Political Parties: Kenya African National Union (KANU) founded in 1943 by Jomo Kenyatta; National Rainbow Coalition (NARC) led by Mwai Kibaki; Forum for the Restoration of Democracy-Asili (FORD-Asili); FORD-People; FORD-Kenya; Democratic Party (DP).
Main Social Organizations: Central Organization of Trade Unions (COTU), founded in 1965, is the only labor federation. Nairobi University Students Organization. Green Belt Movement, environmentalist; several human rights NGOs.

THE STATE

Official Name: Jamhuri ya Kenya.
Administrative Division: 7 provinces and 1 area.
Capital: Nairobi 2,575,000 people (2003).
Other Cities: Mombasa 685,000 people; Kisumu 266,300; Nakuru 319,200; Machakos 173,700 (2000).
Government: Mwai Kibaki, President since 2002 (Head of State and Government); Moody Awori, Vice President since September 2003. Unicameral Legislature: 224-member National Assembly.
National Holiday: 12 December, Independence Day (1963).
Armed Forces: 24,200 troops. Other: 5,000.

Under-5 mortality
122 per 1,000 live births
2002

Poverty
23.0% of population living on less than $1 per day
1997

Debt service
15.4% exports of goods and services
2001

Maternal mortality
1,000 per 100,000 live births
2000

IN FOCUS

ENVIRONMENTAL CHALLENGES
The main environmental problems are soil degradation, erosion and desertification, deforestation and pollution of fresh water sources, mostly near large cities like Nairobi and Mombasa. Meanwhile, thousands of fish in Lake Victoria die each year due to the increased use of pesticides and fertilizers.

WOMEN'S RIGHTS
Women have been able to vote and run for office since 1963, although it was not until 1990 that two women won seats in parliament. In the year 2000, there were seven female members of parliament. That year, 46 per cent of Kenya's total workforce of eight million were women, 75 per cent of whom worked in services, 16 per cent in agriculture and 10 per cent in industry.

Maternal mortality stands at 1,000 for every 100,000 births*. Factors contributing to that high rate include anemia, which affects 35 per cent of pregnant women, and the fact that only 44 per cent of births are attended by qualified medical personnel*.

The literacy rate differs greatly between men and women.

In primary school, the enrolment rates for boys and girls are similar, but in secondary school the proportion of female students drops significantly. Seventy per cent of illiterate people in Kenya are women.

Over 50 per cent of Kenyan women have undergone genital mutilation, a proportion that rises to 80 and 90 per cent in some western districts and in the provinces of Nyanza and Rift Valley.

CHILDREN
The under-five mortality rate increased 26 per cent from 1990 to 2004, to 122 deaths per 1,000 live births*. Eleven per cent of newborns are underweight and 35 per cent are stunted, which tends to lead to anemia, frailty and rickets. Fifty-seven per cent of children under five suffer from acute respiratory infections. Between 80 and 85 per cent of children under the age of one are immunized against the most common childhood diseases, like measles, poliomyelitis, and tetanus.

Of the 2,500,000 people living with HIV/AIDS in Kenya, 220,000 are under 14, and there are over 892,000 children orphaned by AIDS. Only 25 per cent of the population has a clear understanding of how

to prevent HIV/AIDS, and how the disease is transmitted.

Life expectancy has been reduced from 57.7 years in 1985 to 44.6 years in 2005*, as a consequence of the growing HIV/AIDS pandemic.

INDIGENOUS PEOPLES/ ETHNIC MINORITIES
Kenya is home to many minority ethnic groups, the largest of which are the Kalenjin, Kisiis, Luhya, Luo, Masai and Somalians.

Kikuyu are the largest ethnic group, making up 22 per cent of the population. Most of them live in Nairobi. They arrived in Kenya in small groups in the 19th century.

The Masai differ greatly from other ethnic groups in Kenya, with different customs and religious rituals, and they suffer discrimination from the rest of Kenyan society.

The Luo stand out from the rest of the ethnic groups because of their social customs, race and religious beliefs.

MIGRANTS/REFUGEES
In late 2002, Kenya hosted approximately 220,000 refugees and asylum-seekers, including more than 140,000 from Somalia, nearly

70,000 from Sudan, 9,000 from Ethiopia, and about 1,000 from other countries in the region. Over 20,000 new refugees and asylum-seekers arrived in 2002.

Most Somali refugees abandoned their home country during the early 1990s, fleeing civil war and famine. The Kenyan Government has repeatedly blamed Somali refugees for the deterioration of the country's economic situation, which has led to increasing hostility towards them by the local population.

Sudanese, Ethiopians and refugees from other countries depend almost entirely on international aid to survive. Only seven per cent of them have jobs, earning wages of less than a dollar a day.

Political confrontations, land disputes, and ethnic tensions led to the internal displacement of 400,000 Kenyans, mainly farmers, in the last decade.

DEATH PENALTY
The death penalty is applicable to common crimes.

*Latest data available in *The State of the World's Children* and *Childinfo* database, UNICEF, 2004.*

Odinga) and Mwai Kibaki to the office of vice-president.

[38] That year, environmental groups and fishing authorities warned that the environment in the region of Lake Victoria - one of the world's largest fishing reserves - would be seriously damaged if the governments of Kenya, Uganda and Tanzania did not curb the use of toxic chemicals by fisherfolk, which was poisoning fish stocks and polluting water sources.

[39] In August 1998 a bomb killed 248 people at the US Embassy in Nairobi. Three men, allegedly linked to Osama Bin Laden, were held responsible for the attack.

[40] In the year 2000 Kenya suffered the worst drought in a century. The subsequent loss of crops led to food shortages, water rationing and power cuts, in households as well as industry.

[41] That year, President Bush cut US government funding for family planning programs arguing that some of the money intended to promote contraception was actually supporting abortions. In 2002 one out of three deaths of women in Kenya were caused by unsafe illegal abortions, according to the Feminist Majority Foundation. At the same time, the Moi Government ordered the purchase of condoms from a

German firm, using World Bank funds, to help curb the spread of HIV. HIV/AIDS patients occupy half of the hospital beds in the country.

[42] The Kenyan police are responsible for more than 60 per cent of the murders committed in the country in the last five years. In 2001 deaths resulting from police brutality amounted to 90 per cent of all killings. That year, conflicts broke out among ethnic groups over the right to the land located along the Tana river, in the southern part of the country as well as in Nairobi - between Luo and Nubian peoples from Kibera district. Displacement of the population occurred after villages were burnt down.

[43] A law banning female circumcision in girls under 18 and stipulating prison sentences for those found guilty of practising it was passed in February 2002. Genital mutilation, practised in half of the country's rural districts, was traditionally seen as a way to reduce promiscuity among women.

[44] In November 2002 a group of suicide bombers crashed a car-bomb into an Israeli-owned hotel near Mombasa, killing 10 Kenyans and three Israelis. In a simultaneous terrorist attack, an Israeli airliner came under missile fire as it took off from Mombasa airport, but the plane was not hit and landed safely

in Tel Aviv, Israel. The al-Qaeda network claimed responsibility for the attacks and promised there would be further 'lethal' assaults against Israel and the US. Vice-President Musalia Mudavadi said the country had become a battleground for other people's wars.

[45] On 27 December Mwai Kibaki, a 71-year-old former vice-president and finance minister - the candidate of the National Rainbow Coalition - won the presidential elections with 63 per cent of the vote. KANU candidate Uhuru Kenyatta - son of Kenya's first president Jomo Kenyatta, and Moi's hand-picked successor - conceded defeat. This marked the end of Moi's 24-year term in office and of KANU's 40 years in power.

[46] The new president, known for his moderate and conciliatory character, pledged to conduct his duties without fear, favoritism or malice, and to fight corruption. In January 2003, he created an anti-corruption commission that filed legal charges in June against former president Moi for embezzlement, in a case that became a major bank scandal. However, in December the Government granted Moi immunity from prosecution. In November the IMF had granted a loan (the first one in three years) to help finance the commission.

[47] In January 2003 the newly elected government established free and compulsory primary education. Since then an estimated 1.5 million children, who were previously out-of-school, have turned up to attend classes.

[48] The price of coffee, Kenya's main export, plunged to the lowest level in history. In May, during the World Coffee Conference in London, the International Coffee Organization and the World Bank stated that the unparalleled crisis was triggered by a sharp drop in coffee consumption in the US. The humanitarian organization Hermon-Oxfam released a report that stated that the way of life of 25 million coffee producers worldwide was being destroyed.

[49] In October 2004 Wangari Maathai became the first African woman to win the Nobel Peace Prize. The hugely respected environmental campaigner began her work in 1977, starting a women's movement that planted millions of tree seedlings to stop soil erosion, proved fuel and improve the lot of the poor. The Green Belt Movement brought her into conflict with President Moi in the 1990s and she was briefly forced into exile. She is currently assistant environment minister in the Kibaki Government. ▪

Kiribati / Kiribati

Population:	90,159
Area:	730 km²
Capital:	Bairiki
Currency:	Australian dollar
Language:	English and Kiribati

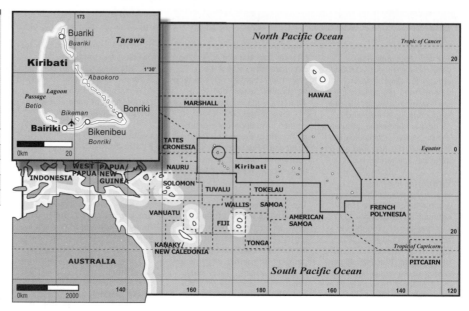

Originally inhabited by Micronesian people, the islands that make up the Republic of Kiribati (Makin, Butaritari, Marakei, Abaiang, Tarawa, Maiana, Abemama, Kuria, Aranuka, Nonouti, Tabiteuea, Beru, Nikunau), witnessed the arrival of the British in the 18th century. In 1765 John Byron landed at Nikunau. In 1788 Thomas Gilbert arrived at Tarawa, and John Marshall at Aranuka. Around 1820 the islands were named the Gilbert Islands.

[2] Missionaries arrived in 1857, and three years later, trade in palm oil and copper began. In 1892 the islands became a British protectorate. In 1915 the islands were joined with the neighboring Ellice archipelago (now Tuvalu), to form the colony of the Gilbert and Ellice Islands.

[3] In 1916 Banaba Island became part of the colony. The island had large deposits of guano (bird droppings rich in phosphate). The fertilizer, exploited by the UK since 1920, was exported to Australia and New Zealand.

[4] In 1943, during World War II, the islands were occupied by the Japanese. The intensity of the fighting led to the evacuation of the Banabans.

[5] Since the open-cast mining of guano had made the island uninhabitable, the evacuees were unable to return. Afterward, they obtained an indemnity of £19 million from the British Government.

[6] In 1957 Britain, as part of its nuclear armament program, detonated three hydrogen bombs near Christmas Island.

[7] The Ellice Islands broke off in 1975 due to their ethnic, historical and cultural differences with the Melanesian majority of the Gilbert Islands.

[8] The inhabitants of the Gilbert Islands proclaimed independence on 12 July 1979 adopting the name: Republic of Kiribati (the equivalent of 'Gilbert' in their 13-letter alphabet). Ieremia Tabai assumed the presidency.

[9] In 1986 Kiribati was recognized by the UN as one of the world's poorest countries, and began negotiations with the IMF. Since the country has the highest-grade manganese deposits in the world, it hoped to exploit its offshore mineral deposits.

[10] A 1989 UN report on global warming and the possible rise in sea level said that unless urgent measures were taken, Kiribati could disappear under the rising sea.

[11] In the 1991 elections, Teatao Teannaki won with 46 per cent of the vote, leading to the first change in president since independence.

[12] Teannaki, accused of misuse of state funds, resigned in May 1994. In July, the opposition coalition Maneaba Te Mauri won a parliamentary majority and in September Teburoro Tito was elected president.

[13] In 1995, due to the continuation of French nuclear tests in Mururoa (French Polynesia), Kiribati broke off ties with France.

[14] In 1996, Kiribati signed a trade agreement with China. The following year Japan contributed $40 million towards the construction of Betio port, one of Kiribati's main ports.

[15] Due to the low elevation of most of the islands - barely a couple of meters above sea level - there is growing concern about the greenhouse effect. If the sea level were to rise, the islands would be partially submerged and would lose their sources of drinking water.

[16] The country joined the UN in 1999 and the International Labour Organization the following year.

[17] Kiribati was the first to see the dawn of the new millennium in 2000. Millennium Island (renamed as such in 1999 to encourage tourism), was the center of celebrations in the hours before the turn of the century.

[18] In March 2002, together with Tuvalu and Maldives, Kiribati announced that it would take measures against the US in the face of its refusal to sign the Kyoto Protocol on greenhouse gas emissions - the cause of global warming and rising seawaters.

[19] In July 2003, after having defeated his brother Harry in the elections, Anote Tong was elected president.

[20] China broke off diplomatic relations with Bairiki after Kiribati established ties with Taiwan in November 2003. ∎

PROFILE

ENVIRONMENT

Kiribati consists of 33 islands and coral atolls, with a total land area of 810 sq km, scattered over 5,000 sq km in Micronesia in the Pacific. The islands include Banaba (Ocean Island), the Phoenix and the Line Islands, except for Jarvis Island, which is a US possession. The sandy soil is made of coral rock, and is only suitable for palm trees. The climate is tropical and rainy, tempered by the effect of sea winds. The country's large phosphate deposits are now virtually exhausted. Fishing (carried out in agreement with Japanese, Taiwanese, US and Korean fleets), and copper are its main export industries. Underwater mineral deposits offer great economic potential.

SOCIETY

Peoples: The population is mostly of Micronesian descent. Kiribati 97.4 per cent; mixed (Kiribati and other) 1.5 per cent; Tuvaluan 0.5 per cent; European 0.2 per cent; other 0.4 per cent.
Religion: Catholics (53.4 per cent); Protestants (39.2 per cent), including Adventists (1.9 per cent) and Mormons (1.6 per cent); Baha'is (2.4 per cent); others (1.5 per cent).
Languages: English and Kiribati (Gilbertese).
Main Political Parties: Maneaban Te Mauri; Boutokaan Te Koaua, and Maurin Kiribati Pati.
Main Social Organizations: there are several labor unions, but the main one since 1979 has been Kiribati General Labor Confederation; Kiribati Student Association.

THE STATE

Official Name: Republic of Kiribati. **Capital:** Bairiki 42,000 people; (2003). **Other Cities:** Bikenibeu 7,000; Abaiang 5,300 (2000).
Government: Anote Tong, president since July 2003. Legislature: House of Assembly, made up of 42 members, one of whom represents the Banabans, elected by direct popular vote.
National Holiday: 12 July, Independence Day (1979).

North Korea

South Korea

(See history and statistics
on the following pages)

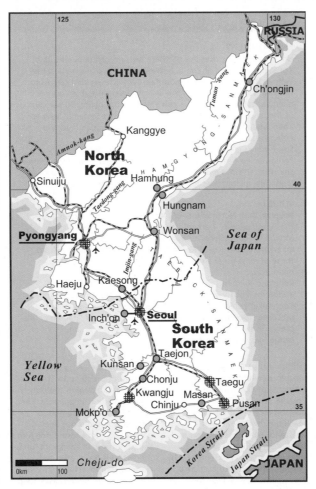

The Korean peninsula lies between China and Japan, and this position has shaped the nation's history and the character of its people. The territory has frequently been the arena of struggles between armies from China, Mongolia and Japan. The peninsula was first inhabited by tribes of the Tungu language who emigrated to Siberia. Between the 10th and 8th centuries BC several tribal states were established, of which the most complex was the one known as Old Choson, in the Taedong river basin. Towards the 4th century BC, Choson developed into a league of tribes grouped between the basins of the Liao and Taedong rivers. At this time, Choson inhabitants used weapons made of iron, harnesses for horses and war carriages. In 108 BC, the Chinese empire defeated the kingdom of Choson and replaced it with four Chinese colonies. During the height of Old Choson, other tribal states flourished in the peninsula: Puyo, in the Manchurian region of the Sungari river basin, and Chin, which arose during the 2nd century BC to the south of the Han river and was later divided into three tribal states (Mahan, Chinhan and Pyonhan).

2   The different leagues expanded through the peninsula which, as of the 1st century BC, was divided into the rival kingdoms of Koguryo, Paekche and Silla. Koguryo (which in the 6th century covered an area similar to present-day North Korea) was founded by Chu-mong in 37 BC. Paekche was founded by Onjo in 18 BC, and Silla by Pak Hyokkose in 57 BC. These three states were consolidated by King Taejo (53-146) in Koguryo, King Koi (204-286) in Paekche and King Naemul (356-402) in Silla. The three kingdoms developed into states through successive wars which led to the organization of centralized military and administrative systems.

3   With the support of the Chinese T'ang dynasty, Silla conquered Paekche in the year 660 and Koguryo in 668. However, the survivors of the defeated Koguryo, led by General Tae Cho-yang, established the Kingdom of Perhae to the north of present-day Manchuria and soon, impeded by China from integrating with the other Korean kingdom, entered into direct confrontation with Silla. The peninsula was divided into two states, one in the north and one in the south, both paying taxes to China. Perhae became a very sophisticated state, called 'the prosperous state of the East' by the Chinese, but after it fell into the hands of the Khitan, a nomad people from the north, its territory no longer participated in the history of Korea.

4   United Silla became an absolute monarchy, which minimized the influence of the aristocracy. The Chinese variant of Avatamsaka Buddhism offered the ideological base for the monarchy and the aristocracy, while the underprivileged were attracted to Pure Land Buddhism, which promised redemption in the next world. In the capital (now Kwangju, in South Korea), the monarchs built giant palaces and royal tombs, while the State's administration was divided, following China's example, into provinces, prefectures and counties.

5   The decline of Silla began towards the end of the 8th century, as a result of peasant uprisings and conflicts with the aristocracy, which had abolished royal despotism. A new system was established which increased the power of some landlords. Two provincial leaders, Konhwon and Kungye, established the kingdoms of Late Koguryo and Late Paechke respectively. During this period, known as the Three Late Kingdoms Period, Zen Buddhism was the most popular religion, with emphasis on individual fulfillment through contemplation. This doctrine was much less hierarchical than that of Avatamsaka Buddhism, and favored individual autonomy.

6   In 918, Wang Kong founded Songak (today's Kaesong, in North Korea) and in 936 he united the peninsula once again, incorporating the survivors of Late Paechke, devastated by the Khitan. Wang Kong proclaimed himself the legitimate successor of Koguryo and repeatedly confronted the Khitan, expanding Koguryo's territory up to the Yalu river. Wang Kong was the founder of the Koryo dynasty, from which the western name Korea derives. The ruling class of Koryo was made up mainly of provincial lords, owners of castles, and by Silla's old aristocracy. Koryo was ruled by a Supreme State Council, formed by aristocrats, who adopted Buddhism as a religion to achieve spiritual goals and personal happiness, while they practiced the political principles and ethical values of Confucianism.

7   A coup broke out in 1170 and, taking advantage of the subsequent chaos, general Ch'oe Ch'ung-hon established a military regime from 1197 to 1258. In the 13th century, Koryo was repeatedly invaded by the Mongols who came to have great influence in the court. In 1392, Confucian master Yi Song-gye overthrew the tottering dynasty and founded the Choson dynasty (also known as the Yi dynasty, after its founder), which lasted until 1910. In 1394, Yi Song-gye founded Seoul and turned it into the capital of the Kingdom.

8   Choson was dominated by an hereditary aristocratic class, called *yangban*, which devoted itself to the study of neo-Confucian doctrines. During the reign of Sejo, the seventh monarch, a government structure emerged, led by the *yangban* ideology. The country was divided into eight provinces and the central government appointed the administrative chiefs of the state. Legal codes were written and the State Council took charge of the administration. During the 15th century many teachers were recruited to serve the government. They criticized the bureaucracy and recommended several radical measures to implement the ideas of Confucius. However, these teachers had to leave the administration due to strong pressure.

9   In 1597, Toyotomi Hideyoshi, a Japanese military leader who had just reunited his country, invaded Shohon under the pretext of invading China. The national crisis made people from all spheres of life - including Buddhist monks - join in the struggle against the invaders. In 1598, with China's help, the Koreans forced the aggressors to retreat, but most of Shohon was devastated. Many palaces, public buildings and homes were burnt, numerous national treasures

destroyed and a large number of craftspeople and experts were kidnapped and taken to Japan. At the beginning of the 17th century, nomad Manchurians invaded Shohon, took over the northern part of the territory, and captured Seoul in 1636, demanding the unconditional surrender of the king. In 1640 the Manchurians overthrew the Ming dynasty in China and replaced it with the Ch'ing dynasty. The taxes Korea paid to the Ming went to the Ch'ing.

[10]   During the second half of the 17th century and throughout the 18th century, Korean society underwent great changes. Rice became widespread and irrigation systems were improved. Agricultural production was increased and the peasants' standard of living improved. Tobacco and ginseng crops encouraged domestic and foreign trade, thus intensifying contacts with European traders and Catholic priests. Meanwhile, radical ideological changes were taking place in Korea, since many teachers no longer concerned themselves only with theoretical speculation but also with matters of practical importance. This gave birth to *silhak* or education based on pragmatism, which urged the Government to undergo changes. Also, a school of silhak devoted itself to the study of the Korean language and history and facilitated, jointly with the development of popular art, the access of the people to written texts. By the end of the 18th century some teachers of silhak had converted to Catholicism, followed by members of the aristocracy. Large sectors of the population, encouraged by the hope of finding equality before God after death, were seduced by the new religion which spread rapidly.

[11]   The decline of the Yi dynasty was characterized by economic and religious factors, plus outside pressures. The yangban or aristocracy had appropriated public lands and did not pay taxes, which led to an increase of taxes on the poor, who could not pay and lost their lands. Also, the State banned Christianity, because of its incompatibility with Confucianism. During the persecutions of 1801, 1839 and 1866, the converted teachers faced death or apostasy, while foreign missionaries were beheaded. At the same time, Japan pressed Korea to open its foreign trade and China increased its interference in the peninsula to counterbalance the Japanese influence. In 1860, the scholar Ch'oe-u founded a popular

PROFILE

ENVIRONMENT

North Korea comprises the northern portion of the peninsula of Korea, located east of China, between the Sea of Japan and the Yellow Sea. The territory is mountainous with wooded ranges to the east, along the coast of the Sea of Japan. Rice, the country's main agricultural product, is cultivated on the plains, 90 per cent of the land being worked under a co-operative system. There are abundant mineral resources (coal, iron, zinc, copper, lead and manganese).

South Korea is located in the southern part of the Korean Peninsula, east of China, between the sea of Japan and the Yellow Sea. The terrain is more level than North Korea's and the arable land area, mainly used for rice farming, is larger.

SOCIETY

Peoples: Both North and South Koreans, probable descendants of the Tungu people, were influenced by their Chinese and Mongolian conquerors over many centuries. Homogeneous ethnic and cultural features in Korea stand out in sharp contrast from those of most other Asian countries. There are no distinct minorities.

Religions: Religious practices are frowned upon in the North. Buddhism, Confucianism (a code of ethics rather than a religion), Chondokio (which combines Buddhist and Christian elements) are practised throughout the country, while traditional Shamanic cults prevail in the interior.

Languages: Korean (official).

religion called Tonhak (oriental teachings) which combined elements of Confucianism, Christianity, Shamanism and Buddhism. Soon, these new teachings, in the name of resistance against foreigners and corruption, gained a large following among peasants and by 1893 had turned into a political movement. In May 1893 the Tonhak followers took the city of Chonju, in the southwest, and the two intervening powers, China and Japan, sent troops to crush them.

[12]   To justify their military presence in the peninsula, Japan proposed that China carry out a joint reform in Korea, but China's negative reply led to a military conflict which ended with a Japanese victory in 1895. Japan occupied Korea in 1905 and in 1910 the country was formally annexed, putting an end to the Yi dynasty.

[13]   Under the Japanese, Korea was used as a supplier of foodstuffs and as a source of cheap labor. Japanese landlords and factory owners settled in Korea, with an infrastructure developed merely to extract the wealth of the country. In the 1930s, the northern part of Korea saw industrial development of war materials, to supply Japan's goal of continental expansion.

[14]   With the defeat of Japan in World War II, Korea was occupied on each side of the 38th parallel: the northern part by Soviet troops and the southern by the United States. Korean hopes for a united, independent country

seemed on the verge of being realized but a complex struggle of interests between the two powers made it impossible. The Soviet Union maintained its influence and did not allow general elections in the north of the peninsula. In the south, under the supervision of a United Nations Temporary Commission, elections were held in May 1948 and Syngman Rhee was elected first president of the Republic of Korea, whose capital was established in Seoul. Meanwhile, the Supreme Assembly of the People of North Korea wrote a new Constitution, which came into effect in August 1948. Kim Il-Sung was appointed Prime Minister and on 9 September the People's Republic of Korea was proclaimed, with its capital in Pyongyang.

[15]   On 12 October the Soviet Union recognized this state as the only legitimate government of Korea. In December, the General Assembly of the United Nations recognized the exclusive sovereignty of the southern Republic of Korea. Most foreign troops left both countries the following year but US troops remained in the south under the UN flag, then dominated by the United States.

[16]   In June 1950, North Korea launched a carefully planned offensive against South Korea. The United Nations convened its members, to put a stop to the invasion. In the meantime US President Truman called his army to assist South Korea, without asking Congress to declare war.

[17]   Likewise, Truman failed to seek UN permission before sending the US Fleet to the Strait of Formosa to protect one of the US Army's flanks and to assist Chiang Kai Shek's anti-Communist Chinese regime. The disastrous military situation of the South Koreans was saved by General Douglas MacArthur, who landed some 160 kilometres south of the 38th parallel and managed to divide and defeat North Korean troops. China, concerned over the advancing allied troops, warned that the presence of the US in North Korea would force it to join the war. MacArthur ignored the warning and in November launched his 'Home by Christmas' offensive.

[18]   However, China sent 180,000 troops to Korea and by mid-December it had driven US troops back, south of the 38th parallel. On 31 December 1951, China launched a second offensive against South Korea, subsequently taking up positions along the former border.

[19]   After differences of opinion on military strategy, MacArthur was relieved of his command by Truman. It was later revealed that MacArthur had outlined plans to use nuclear weapons against Chinese cities, advocating full-scale war with China.

[20]   In 1953, an armistice was signed and Korea was officially divided in two by the 38th parallel. The conflict had lasted 17 months and left approximately four million dead.

[21]   On 8 August 1990, the UN Security Council unanimously approved the admission of both Koreas. On 13 December 1991, Prime Ministers Yon Kyong Muk (North Korea) and Chong Won Shik (South Korea) signed a 'Reconciliation, Non-Aggression, Exchange, and Cooperation Agreement', regarded as an important step towards reunification.

[22]   In late 2002, North Korea reinitiated nuclear activity and, in January 2003, withdrew from the Treaty of Non Proliferation of Nuclear Weapons, straining relations with the US, whose government included Pyongyang among the 'axis of evil' countries. South Korea offered to mediate between both nations, and this was accepted by North Korea.

[23]   In February 2004, the second round of negotiations between China, the United States, Russia, Japan and the two Koreas took place in Beijing. Pyongyang stated it would cease its nuclear program if Washington assured it that no retaliation would be sought. ∎

North Korea / Choson

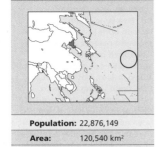

Population:	22,876,149
Area:	120,540 km²
Capital:	Pyongyang
Currency:	Won
Language:	Korean

The Kingdom of Koguryo, the seventh-century state now known as North Korea, had a special way of treating foreign enemies: it avoided direct confrontation and maintained an impressive military capacity within its cities (see history of Korea).

2 The region was invaded several times, including by the Japanese (1592-1598) and the Manchus (1627-1636). Japan annexed the region in 1910, and occupied it until the end of World War II. After this, the USSR occupied Korea north of the 38th parallel, while the US occupied the southern section.

3 On 3 September 1948 the People's Republic of Korea was proclaimed in Pyongyang and Kim Il Sung, leader of the Korean Workers' Party (KWP), was elected Prime Minister. North Korea followed a similar strategy to that of the former kingdom, limiting its contact with the outside world and concentrating on building up its military strength. Despite its geographical proximity to the People's Republic of China, North Korea tried to remain neutral in the Sino-Soviet conflict.

4 The KWP enjoyed uninterrupted power for five decades. The party's philosophy is called *Juche*, a blend of self-reliance, nationalism and centralized control of the economy.

5 Under the socialist regime, agrarian reform collectivized part of the country's agriculture. Industrialization had begun during the Japanese occupation, and large textile, chemical and hydroelectric plants were established.

6 After the devastation of the Korean War (1950-53, see Korea), North Korea started the reconstruction of the country. When Syngman Rhee was ousted in South Korea (1960), North Korea attempted rapprochement with its neighbor, a move interrupted when the military took power in Seoul.

7 Korea adopted a centrally-planned socialist economy, with 90 per cent of industry in the hands of the State and the rest organized in co-operatives.

8 Between 1954 and 1961 North Korea signed military assistance treaties with China and the USSR. In 1972, the new constitution made Kim Il Sung President as well as Prime Minister.

9 Kim Jong Il, Kim Il Sung's son, was named head of the Government in 1980. In 1984 North Korea provided relief to flood victims in South Korea. That same year mixed enterprises were authorized in the construction, technology and tourist sectors.

10 In 1988 North Korea began ideological rectification contrary to the liberalization process introduced by Gorbachev in the USSR.

11 North Korea was internationally isolated, dependent on oil imports and financially tied to Japan, while receiving goods and remittances amounting to $1,000 million a year from 200,000 of the 700,000 North Korean exiles living in Japan.

12 Kim Il Sung's death at 82, in July 1994, complicated talks with the US and delayed the summit planned between the two Koreas. Kim Jong Il succeeded his father without having the same authority, which led to a power struggle among leading cadres.

13 In 1995 widespread floods affecting some five million people, with the loss of almost two million tons of crops, led the North Korean Government to make an unprecedented appeal for foreign aid. Japan donated 300,000 tons of rice and South Korea 150,000 tons.

14 In October 1997 Kim Jong Il, the de facto leader after his father's death, was officially

LAND USE

2000

IRRIGATED AREA: 73.0% of arable land

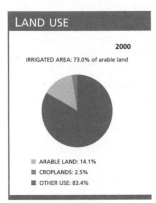

- ARABLE LAND: 14.1%
- CROPLANDS: 2.5%
- OTHER USE: 83.4%

WORKERS

LABOR FORCE   **2002**

- FEMALE: 43.3%   ■ MALE: 56.7%

PROFILE

SOCIETY

Main Political Parties: The Korean Workers' Party (KWP), founded in 1945 with a Marxist-Leninist orientation, is the dominant political organization; the Korean Social Democratic Party and the Chondokio Chong-u party, affiliated to the KWP in a National Front for the Reunification of Korea, created in June 1945; Union of Young Socialist Workers; Democratic Women's Union.

Main Social Organizations: The General Federation of Trade Unions is the only workers' organization, while the Union of Agricultural Workers is a peasants' association.

THE STATE

Official Name: Choson Mintschutschui Inmin Konghwaguk.
Administrative Divisions: 9 Provinces, 1 District.
Capital: Pyongyang 3,228,000 people (2003).
Other Cities: Hamhung 808,300 people; Chongjin 663,400; Sinuiju 371,300; Kaesong 195,300 (2000).
Government: Presidency is vacant since Kim Il Sung died in July 1994. His son, Kim Jong Il, de facto President of the Republic. Kim Yong Nam, Chairman of the Presidium of the Supreme People's Assembly since September 1998. Pak Pong Ju, Premier since September 2003. The State's highest body is the Supreme People's Assembly, with 687 members.
National Holiday: 9 September, Republic Day (1948).
Armed Forces: 1,054,000 (1994). Other: 3,800,000 Peasant Red Guard, 115,000 Security Troops, of the Ministry of Public Security.

Life expectancy
63.1 years
2000-2005

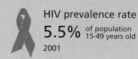

HIV prevalence rate
5.5% of population
15-49 years old
2001

appointed head of the Workers' Party. But due to internal rivalries he was not formally appointed President.

[15] In 1998 it was estimated that some 100,000 people had died of hunger, cold and lack of medical attention since 1995. The daily ration of rice per person was just 100 grams.

[16] In June 2000 an historic summit between the two Koreas was held in Pyongyang. Kim Dae-Jung, South Korea's President, met with Kim Jong Il to discuss security issues. They signed an agreement to work together toward the reunification of the Korean peninsula.

[17] A delegation from the European Union, led by Swedish Prime Minister Göran Persson, visited the two Koreas in May 2001 to support the process of reconciliation between the countries.

[18] US President George W Bush stated in January 2002 that North Korea was part of the 'axis of evil' dedicated to terrorism, along with Iran and Iraq. Pyongyang described Bush's statement as a virtual declaration of war. Military maneuvers carried out jointly by South Korea and the US in March 2002 led the North Korean

Government to threaten to break the nuclear agreement in force since 1994, under which Pyongyang had accepted abandoning its own nuclear program in exchange for US assistance with energy and building nuclear power stations.

[19] In September 2002 Kim Jong Il offered an apology to Japanese Prime Minister Junichiro Koizumi, during his visit to North Korea, for the kidnappings of Japanese citizens in the 1980s and 1990s.

[20] In October 2002 Washington revealed that Pyongyang had admitted having a nuclear weapons program and demanded this be dismantled immediately. The North Korean Government refused to accede to this demand, although it expressed willingness to come to an agreement with Washington. Japan and South Korea agreed that the US should consider the proposal, while China advocated a negotiated agreement.

[21] After the US decided to halt oil shipments to Pyongyang in late 2002, North Korea restarted its Yongbyon nuclear reactor and expelled international inspectors. In January 2003 Pyongyang announced that North Korea was withdrawing from the Nuclear Non-Proliferation Treaty.

[22] In April 2003, in Beijing, North Korea, the US and China embarked on the first talks on the nuclear crisis. In July Pyongyang acknowledged that it had enough plutonium to start manufacturing nuclear weapons.

[23] In October 2003 the Government announced that 8,000 spent fuel rods had been reprocessed, obtaining sufficient material for eight atomic bombs.

[24] Pyongyang offered to freeze its nuclear program in exchange for US concessions. Washington demanded that the program be terminated.

[25] In April 2004, more than 150 people died and 1,300 were injured in a explosion that took place in Ryongchon, near the border with China. According to authorities, the explosion was triggered when a live power cable came into contact with a train carrying chemical explosives. Upon the disaster, several countries including South Korea, Germany, Australia and Japan offered to send aid ranging from food until chemical tools. Even the US, through the Red Cross, promised to send $100,000. This sum, although meaningless, was regarded by analysts as a good will gesture on Washington's part in the middle

of a nuclear crisis in which both countries were involved.

[26] Five young men and women born in North Korea of Japanese parents who had been kidnapped by Pyongyang agents 25 years ago, arrived in Tokyo in May. Until two years ago, these young men and women had been ignorant of their origin and had grown and been educated under the North Korean regime which dominates all aspects of the country's life. It later emerged that their parents had preferred not to tell them about their origin, fearing what might happen to them since Japan is portrayed as a historical enemy by Pyongyang. In September 2002, when the then Japanese Prime Minister, Junichiro Koizumi, traveled to Pyongyang to meet Kim Jong-il, the North Korean leader had admitted that 13 Japanese citizens had been kidnapped in order to train the country's spies in the Japanese language, customs and culture. Of those 13 people, only the five released were still alive. Japan had supplied North Korea with 250,000 tons of rice and $10 million of medical supplies in return for the release of the young 'abductees'. ■

IN FOCUS

ENVIRONMENTAL CHALLENGES
Pollution of rivers, as well as inadequate supplies of safe drinking water result in frequent water-borne diseases, such as diarrhea and cholera. Uncontrolled deforestation leads to soil erosion and degradation and loss of fertile land. Air contamination started becoming a problem in the 1970s, as did pollution of rivers and seas (the country's west coast on the Yellow Sea is severely polluted).

WOMEN'S RIGHTS
Women have had the vote and been eligible for office since 1946.

In the year 2000 women held 20 per cent of seats in Parliament, although they occupied no ministerial posts nor participated in local governments. Despite participating in the Government, women hold only four per cent of seats on the Korean Workers' Party (KWP) Central Committee.

In the year 2000, 43 per cent of the North Korean workforce were women; 42 per cent of them worked in

agriculture, 35 per cent in services and 23 per cent in industry.

Qualified medical personnel assist 97 per cent of births and almost all pregnant women receive antenatal healthcare*. 71 per cent of pregnant women suffer from anemia and maternal mortality stands at 67 per 100,000 live births*.

Reports have condemned the trafficking of women from North Korea to China, on the promise of jobs. Once they reach China their identification documents are taken from them and they are often forced into prostitution.

CHILDREN
The infant mortality rate is 42 deaths for every 1,000 live births*, while under-five mortality stands at 55 for every 1,000 live births*.

Many children are subjected to intense political indoctrination. There have been reports of young children being submitted to military training and compulsory indoctrination at school.

21 per cent of children under five are moderately or severely underweight*. The chronic food shortages affect many children,

causing undernourishment. Throughout 2003 over three million people ate in canteens run by social organizations.

According to the Government, sexual exploitation of children is not a problem in North Korea. However, the US State Department reports that young women and girls are sold as wives in China.

INDIGENOUS PEOPLES/ETHNIC MINORITIES
See South Korea.

MIGRANTS/REFUGEES
At least 100,000 North Korean refugees were living in China in 2002. Although there are no exact figures, there was also a significant number of North Koreans in Russia and elsewhere in Asia, while over 1,100 emigrated to South Korea.

Poverty and the food crisis, which started in the mid-1990s, are the main causes of emigration. Almost 3.5 million North Koreans (nearly 18 per cent of the population) have died since 1994 from hunger or famine-related diseases.

Several international NGOs have suspended operations in

North Korea, citing the Government s failure to provide a transparent food management and distribution system. NGOs accuse the Government of dividing the population into categories based on their loyalty and utility to the regime, and of channelling food aid accordingly. Under the country's Penal Code, desertion is punished with a minimum of seven years in prison and the death penalty applies in the case of deserters who establish contact with South Koreans, Christians or foreigners once they reach China.

The number of internally displaced people is estimated at over 100,000. Despite the Government s policy of controlling internal migration, they move from one place to another to avoid being caught.

DEATH PENALTY
The death penalty applies even for ordinary crimes.

* Latest data available in *The State of the World's Children* and *Childinfo* database, UNICEF, 2004.

South Korea / Han'guk

Population:	48,182,450
Area:	99,260 km²
Capital:	Seoul
Currency:	Won
Language:	Korean

The Republic of South Korea was created on 15 August 1948. Its first President was Syngman Rhee, through elections held with US troops in the country. For 14 years Rhee ruled the country as a dictator, and imposed a Constitution to perpetuate his rule as a constitutional dictator.

[2] The Rhee administration was an unconditional ally of US policy. Americans were very much aware of events in China, where the nationalist Kuomintang had been defeated by the communists who promised rural peoples 'land to the tiller'. They then urged South Korea to carry out a land redistribution scheme, compensating landowners and limited to three hectares per person.

[3] A draconian National Security Law in 1958 enabled Syngman Rhee to imprison political dissidents of all types. Rhee was re-elected in 1952, 1956 and 1960, amid charges of electoral fraud. There were protests in Seoul and the threat of revolution forced Rhee to resign on 27 April 1960.

[4] New elections were held, and Po Sun Yun, a member of the Democratic Party, was elected President. The head of government, John Chang, attempted to lead the country toward effective economic development and put an end to corruption.

[5] In May 1961 a military coup ousted Chang. In July, General Chung Hee Park took command of the junta and proceeded to suspend all democratic freedoms and imprison all members of the previous regime.

[6] The new Government initiated a National Reconstruction policy, including a planned strategy against communism and corruption, and promised free elections upon completion of these 'revolutionary tasks'.

[7] In 1963, Park held elections and won by just 1.4 per cent. He declared martial law to quell the protests that followed, and suppressed all political and labor freedoms.

[8] The military regime established centralized economic planning and, with the help of western technocrats, South Korea became an exporting country. In 1965 the Government signed a treaty with Japan renouncing their claim to war reparations in exchange for economic aid. After the agreement, South Korea started to receive Japanese funds.

[9] The country developed into an industrial economy dominated by large, Korean-owned transnational corporations producing steel, ships, cars and electronics goods. Low grain prices impoverished the peasantry, who were forced into cities. Some of the world's lowest wages, longest hours and most unsafe working conditions were the norm for workers here.

[10] Eighteen years after taking power, having won four fraudulent elections, Park was killed in October 1979, shot by the director of his Intelligence Agency in unclear circumstances.

[11] On 17 May 1980, the military established martial law once again, arresting opposition members. The following day, factory workers and students took control of Kwangju city, in an historic uprising. Repression was brutal: the army killed thousands. Kim Dae Jung, a prominent opposition leader, was sentenced to life imprisonment, charged with instigating the protests.

[12] In the same manner as his predecessor, Chun Doo Hwan held elections in an attempt to legitimize and civilianize his rule; he won the elections in 1981.

[13] In October 1983, several members of the South Korean cabinet were killed by a bomb at the Martyrs' Mausoleum in Burma during a state visit. The Burmese, claiming proof of North Korean involvement, broke off diplomatic relations with Pyongyang.

[14] Opposition to Chun's regime continued to grow as repression escalated, reminiscent of Park's worst excesses. The US withdrew their support of the Marcos regime in the Philippines, after claims of election fraud and human rights abuses, and a worried Korean regime instituted some reforms. Censorship was lifted somewhat and Kim Dae Jung's imprisonment was changed to house arrest.

[15] During 1987, hundreds of thousands of Korean workers joined in strikes and factory occupations in an unprecedented wave of protests. They demanded the right to form democratic unions independent of the government-run Federation of Korean Trade Unions, higher wages, an end to forced overtime and a larger share of the benefits of the nation's spectacular growth.

[16] In July 1987, Chun appointed Roh Tae Woo both as his successor

and as president of the official Democratic Justice Party. Demonstrations followed amid protests that Roh would continue the dictatorship once in power. Demands that Chun face trial for his part in the Kwangju massacre were also voiced.

[17] Faced with the possibility of larger street demonstrations and concern over its international image (South Korea would host the Olympic Games in 1988) political restrictions were eased during the 1987 election campaign.

[18] In the elections, the newly-freed opposition together polled a majority, but failed to unite the two factions, led by Kim Yong Sam of the Reunification Democratic Party and Kim Dae Jung of the Party for Peace and Democracy. The split enabled the incumbent government to win the elections.

[19] In January 1990, opposition groupings formed a merger with the official Democratic Justice Party, and became the Democratic Liberal Party, controlling 220 seats in the 298-member National Assembly. The Party for Peace and Democracy remained the only real parliamentary opposition.

[20] In April 1990, in a new offensive against independent trade unions, police stormed the Hyundai shipyards and arrested over 600 union activists, ending a 72-hour worker occupation protesting the arrest of union leaders. A few days later, 400 striking workers occupying the Korean Broadcasting System's headquarters were also arrested. The resulting nationwide protests precipitated the biggest drop in the history of the country's stock market.

[21] In September 1991, US President George Bush made the decision to withdraw tactical nuclear weapons from South Korea, and in November this was accomplished. This significant step met one of North Korea's requirements before allowing nuclear inspections in its territory.

[22] In December 1991, Seoul and Pyongyang signed a Reconciliation, Non-aggression, Exchange and Cooperation Accord, improving bilateral relations (see Korea).

[23] In May 1992, President Roh Tae Woo named Kim Young Sam, who had obtained 41.4 per cent in the December presidential election, as his successor. Kim's election coincided with a weakening opposition, worsened by the resignation in February 1993 of Chung Ju-Yung, leader of the United People's Party, charged with having accepted illegal contributions from a major corporation during the electoral campaign.

[24] Corruption scandals also reached the Government. Choi Ki Son, a close aide of President Kim, admitted he had embezzled public funds. Furthermore, Suh Eui Hyun, leader of the country's largest Buddhist order, was accused of accepting $10 million from a businessman to hand them over to Kim Young Sam.

[25] In 1995, two former presidents, Chun Doo Hwan (1979-1988) and Roh Tae Woo (1988-1993), were arrested for their role in the coup that put Chun in power in December

PROFILE

SOCIETY

Main Political Parties: Democratic Party (Minju Dang), Grand National Party (Hannara Dang), United Liberal Democrats (Jayu Minju Yonmaeng), Democratic Labour Party (Minjunodong Dang); Our Party (Uri Dang). Other parties: Green Party of South Korea; Socialist Party (Sahe Dang); Democratic People's Party (Minkook Dang).
Main Social Organizations: Legally, all unions must belong to the Government-controlled Federation of Korean Trade Unions (FKTU).

THE STATE

Official Name: Taehaen-min guk (Republic of Korea).
Administrative Divisions: 9 Provinces. **Capital:** Seoul 9,714,000 people (2003). **Other Cities:** Pusan 4,266,100 people, Taegu 2,947,400; Incheon 2,403,700 (2000). **Government:** Goh Kun, acting President since March 2004. Lee Hai Chan, Prime Minister since June 2004. Single-chamber Legislature: National Assembly, with 273 members, elected every 4 years. **National Holiday:** 13 August, Liberation Day (1945).
Armed Forces: 633,000 (1995). Other: 3,500, 000 Civil Defense Corps, 4,500 Coast Guard.

Life expectancy
75.5 years
2000-2005

GNI per capita
$9,930
2002

Literacy
98% total adult rate
2000

HIV prevalence rate
0.1% of population 15-49 years old
2001

1979. They were accused of treason and embezzlement.

²⁶ In December 1996 a Seoul court sentenced former Defense Minister Lee Yanh-ho to four years in prison for accepting illegal commissions from Daewoo, the country's third largest car manufacturer.

²⁷ In 1997 the country was rocked by the Asian financial crisis. The IMF intervened with a $ 67 billion loan, but demanded more flexible labor conditions and the privatization of the *chaebols* (industrial conglomerates such as Samsung, Hyundai, Daewoo, of which most South Korean political and military leaders are shareholders).

²⁸ Kim Dae Jung, of the opposition Democratic Party (DP), won the December presidential elections. Upon taking office he announced an amnesty for political prisoners and a national unity government.

²⁹ A large crowd received Kim Dae Jung upon his return in June from a trip to Pyongyang for an historic summit between the two Koreas. He discussed with the North Korean leader Kim Jong Il issues of security, including the 37,000 US soldiers stationed in South Korea, and missile programs.

³⁰ In October 2000, Kim Dae Jung received the Nobel Peace Prize for his 'work for democracy, for human rights in South Korea and East Asia and for peace and reconciliation with North Korea'.

³¹ In November, the Daewoo car manufacturer declared itself bankrupt. In the previous months, billions of dollars from public coffers had gone toward bailing it out. However, company chairman, Kim Woo Joong, had disappeared with a large portion of those funds in 1999. After the announcement that more employees would be laid off, in February 2001, Daewoo workers went on strike. This was put down violently by the police, leaving hundreds injured and imprisoned.

³² The publication of a Japanese history textbook whitewashing its colonial past and the atrocities committed by its army in Korea, caused protests. A group of women, known as 'comfort girls' - forced to practice prostitution during the occupation - gathered every Wednesday to protest outside the Japanese embassy in Seoul. A South Korean social movement demanded that Japan withdraw the book from circulation.

³³ In spite of these differences, the two countries co-hosted the soccer World Cup in June 2002. Though the event was projected to make 1.3 billion euros in profits, the excessive expenditure in preparing the stadia and the bankruptcy of ISL company, owner of all commercial rights, caused predicted income to plummet.

IN FOCUS

ENVIRONMENTAL CHALLENGES
There is significant air pollution, especially in the big cities. Acid rain affects most of the country. Rivers and part of the seas are polluted by discharge of waste and industrial waters; the west coast on the Yellow Sea is badly affected. Trawling is destroying marine habitats and also threatening species with extinction.

WOMEN'S RIGHTS
Women have been able to vote and stand for election since 1948; in 2000 they held six per cent of seats in parliament. Women comprised 42 per cent of the total labor force that year. Between 1995 and 2000 the proportion of women working in services rose from 61 to 68 per cent, while those in industry fell from 24 to 19 per cent and those in agriculture from 15 to 13 per cent.

Maternal mortality rate is one of the world's lowest at 20 deaths for every 100,000 live births*. Ninety-six per cent of women receive prenatal care and all births are attended by qualified medical personnel*. Widespread violence against women prompted the creation of the Ministry of Gender Equality in 2001, a year in which approximately 7,200 rapes were reported. This move was applauded by women's rights advocates and described as a significant step in the fight against domestic violence. The Ministry has pushed through several laws advocating women's

rights and combating gender discrimination.

CHILDREN
Between 97 and 99 per cent of all children are immunized against diseases such as polio, measles and tetanus*. The under-five mortality rate is the second lowest in Asia, and one of the world's lowest, at five deaths per 1,000 live births*.

In 2000, public education was compulsory until the age of 15 and almost 90 per cent of teenagers had access to secondary education. Children had almost universal access to high quality healthcare.

The 1999 Youth Protection Act provides for up to 10 year prison sentences and $7,750 fines for those who employ youngsters under 19. A sexual protection law was passed in 2000, setting 20 years as the minimum age for practicing prostitution, and also establishing penalties for those who hire prostitutes under 20.

In spite of Government efforts, the sex trade grows daily in South Korea. The Chief of Police, Kim Kang Ja, estimated that in 2003 500,000 of the country's sex workers were underage. Human trafficking from neighboring countries has also increased, mostly of people under 18, who are destined for prostitution in brothels, massage parlors and nightclubs.

INDIGENOUS PEOPLES/ ETHNIC MINORITIES
In constrast with most of the rest of the world, Korea is ethnically, culturally and linguistically homogeneous. However, it has ancestral regional tensions dating

back to the unification of the three Korean Kingdoms in the 7th century. But economic and political differences came to surface after World War II, influenced by the Soviet bloc in the North and the US bloc in the south.

MIGRANTS/REFUGEES
South Korea is highly restrictive towards non-Asian asylum-seekers. In late 2002 it had received more than 1,200 asylum requests, mostly from North Korea (1,141) and from other neighboring countries.

Refugees recognized by the Government receive annual temporary visas, renewable up to three times. After the third time, the refugee can request permanent residence, work and sign up in state health programs, although healthcare does not reach all refugees since according to the Government there are not enough funds to cover both citizens and refugees.

Since 2001 the Government grants a temporary status to those people who, for reasons such as guerrilla insurgency in their own countries, are refused refugee status. Those granted this status do not have the right to work and annual visas are only renewed when the Government deems it necessary.

DEATH PENALTY
The death penalty is applicable to all types of offenses.

* Latest data available in The State of the World's Children and Childinfo database, UNICEF, 2004.

³⁴ Relations between the two Koreas were tested in June 2002 by a naval collision that killed five South Korean sailors and several North Koreans. In July, Pyongyang expressed regret for the incident. Afterwards there were two summits and a detente process began. In May, North and South Korean families were reunited. In an unprecedented gesture, North Korean athletes competed in the Asian Games in September, in Pusan (South Korea). That month, both states agreed on the construction of railway and highway links, and on the de-mining of two points of the border that has separated them since 1953.

³⁵ In February 2003, Roh Mooh Hyun succeeded Kim Dae Jung. The new President stated his desire to continue the rapprochement with Pyongyang and to achieve greater independence from US foreign policy.

³⁶ In April, parliament supported sending non-combat troops to Iraq (300 engineering and medical military personnel) to cooperate with the US in that country's reconstruction. Later on, the opposition and the press accused close presidential aides of corruption. Roh Moo Hyun announced in parliament that he would call a referendum to confirm his popular support.

³⁷ September registered a record high of debtors (3.5 million) of South Korean credit companies, a financial storm which had started in March and rocked the country's economic stability. To fuel consumption, the Government had encouraged the use of credit cards. Debt amounted to $65 billion by that time, equal to 14 per cent of the GDP.

³⁸ The crisis between the US and North Korea (named as one of President Bush's 'axis of evil'

countries) affected South Koreans because of the impact on them of any confrontation. Pyongyang accepted Seoul's offer to mediate in the conflict. In February 2004 the second round of talks between China, the US, Russia, Japan and the two Koreas took place in Beijing, where Pyongyang announced it would suspend its nuclear program if it was assured it would not be attacked.

³⁹ In March 2004, after a heated session, parliament voted in favor of impeaching Mooh Hyun, charged with breaching presidential neutrality by publicly stating his support for the new Uri Dang party (Our Party). Prime Minister Goh Kun was appointed acting president until September.

⁴⁰ On 25 May 2004 Goh Kun resigned as Prime Minister. Lee Jun (Finance Minister and deputy) became acting Prime Minister. ■

Kuwait / Al Kuwayt

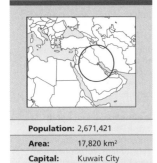

Population:	2,671,421
Area:	17,820 km²
Capital:	Kuwait City
Currency:	Dinar
Language:	Arabic

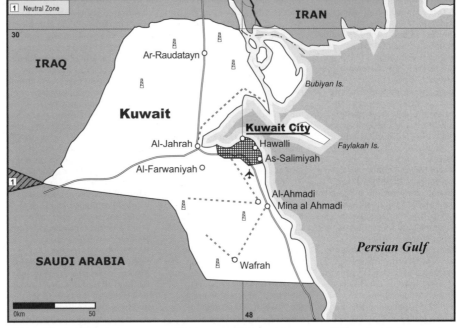

The history of the territory currently known as Kuwait was always intimately linked to that of the Mesopotamian civilizations (see Iraq) but, beginning in the 13th century, after the Mongol invasion caused the collapse of the Caliphate, the region entered a long period of isolation.

[2] In the 18th century, although nominally subject to the Ottoman Empire, the local Arab groups were virtually independent. They decided to elect a *shaij* (sheikh) to conduct sporadic negotiations with the Turks. In 1756, the leader of the Anaiza tribe, Abdul Rahim al-Sabah, founder of the current reigning dynasty, was appointed to this task.

[3] At that time, the place, formerly known as the Qurain (horn), began to be called Kuwait, a diminutive for al-Kout, which is a local Arabic term to describe the fortified houses on the coast.

[4] The Ottoman Empire, in alliance with the Sabah family, ruled the country until the 19th century. But when the Ottomans threatened to annex Kuwait in 1899, the Sabahs requested protectorate status from Britain. In exchange, Britain guaranteed Kuwait's territorial integrity. This treaty and the subsequent British military presence in the region frustrated Turkish attempts to expand the Berlin-Baghdad railway to reach the Gulf through Kuwaiti territory.

[5] At the end of World War I, France and Britain divided up the remains of the Ottoman Empire. Kuwait was now considered a British protectorate, separate from the newly-created kingdom of Iraq, which claimed it as a province, invoking the historical domination of the region by the Government of Baghdad.

[6] In 1938, oil began to flow in Kuwait. After World War II, Emir Ahmad Jabir al-Sabah granted the concession to the Kuwait Oil Company, owned by British BP and US Gulf, and oil was first exported in 1946.

[7] In 1961, independence was negotiated. Emir Sabah proclaimed himself Emir and took up full powers. Iraq refused to recognize the new state, claiming that it was an artificial creation of the British to maintain access to oil. Consequently, the British troops remained to defend the emirate until they were replaced by the troops of the Arab League.

[8] In 1962 a Constitution was adopted creating a National Assembly of 50 members, elected individually by male citizens over the age of 21, whose fathers or grandfathers had resided in Kuwait before 1920.

[9] Oil entirely changed the country. The Bedouins replaced their camels with luxurious air-conditioned cars. Pearl fishing - the main economic activity at the time - disappeared. The entire population settled in brand new cities, where stylized mosque towers stood side-by-side with shopping centers which replaced the old *souks* (markets). The population's educational standards and life expectancy rose. All manual labor and work in the oil industry was done by immigrant workers, who by 1985 outnumbered the Kuwaiti population by almost two-to-one.

[10] Kuwaiti rulers became concerned that so much prosperity in such a poor region could put its legitimacy into question. In 1961 the Arab Fund for Economic Development was created, in order to channel 'soft' loans and donations to Third World countries. When the Organization of Petroleum Exporting Countries (OPEC) succeeded in raising prices in 1973, Kuwait increased its revenue immensely.

[11] Most of the Third World countries supported OPEC. They hoped to receive help to establish a 'New International Economic Order', in which they would obtain better prices for the other raw materials that they supply to the countries of the North. However, instead of investing their oil revenues in their own countries or in other Third World nations, the Gulf monarchs placed their fortunes in transnational banks. This added to the excess liquidity in these banks, which started to grant loans to the Third World quite indiscriminately. This situation was one of the main factors that provoked the 'debt crisis' in 1982.

[12] Within the Gulf area, however, Kuwait was generous with its wealth. By the end of the 1980s, Kuwait had the highest rate of official development assistance in the world, proportional to its gross national product.

[13] In 1981 the new Emir, Jabir al-Sabah, called for national elections in February that year. Out of the 50 seats in the National Assembly, 40 were won by candidates loyal to the ruling family. Only 6.4 per cent of the population was permitted to vote.

[14] When the Iran-Iraq war broke out in 1980, Kuwait

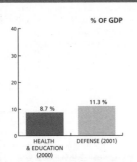

LAND USE

2000

IRRIGATED AREA: 70% of arable land

- ARABLE LAND: 0.4%
- CROPLANDS: 0.1%
- OTHER USE: 99.4%

PUBLIC EXPENDITURE

% OF GDP

- HEALTH & EDUCATION (2000): 8.7 %
- DEFENSE (2001): 11.3 %

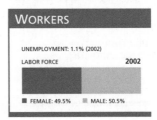

WORKERS

UNEMPLOYMENT: 1.1% (2002)

LABOR FORCE — 2002

- FEMALE: 49.5%
- MALE: 50.5%

Life expectancy
76.6 years
2000-2005

GNI per capita
$18,270
2002

Literacy
82% total adult rate
2000

officially remained neutral, but in fact supported Iraq with large donations and loans. Kuwait considered Iraq to be a 'first line of defense' against the Iranian Islamic revolution.

[15] In 1985, the National Assembly began to oppose government measures such as press control, increases in the prices of public services and educational reforms. In August 1986, the Emir dissolved the Assembly and began to rule by decree.

[16] In the late 1980s, the Kuwait Investments Office (KIO) had capital assets outside the country estimated at $1 billion, which included hotels, art galleries, European and US real estate, and major shares in large transnational corporations: 10 per cent of British Petroleum, 23 per cent of Hoechst, 14 per cent of Daimler-Benz, and 11 per cent of the Midland Bank.

[17] In 1987, alleging that Iraq was using the port of Kuwait to export oil and import weapons, the Iranian navy attacked Kuwaiti merchant ships. In response, Kuwait requested and obtained permission from the major powers - US, France, Britain, and the USSR - to use their flags for the Kuwait merchant navy. The US and

Britain sent their navies to protect Kuwaiti ships in the Gulf.

[18] Once the war between Iran and Iraq came to an end in 1988, tension with Iraq started to mount. Kuwait demanded the payment of $15 billion on account of war loans, which Iraq refused to repay, alleging that those sums had been used to protect Kuwait.

[19] Iraq accused Kuwait of 'stealing' the country's oil from the common deposits which lie under the border, and demanded $2.4 billion in compensation.

[20] On 2 August 1990, Iraq invaded Kuwait. Emir al-Sabah and his family took refuge in Saudi Arabia. Nearly 300,000 Kuwaitis fled the country. A pro-Iraqi provisional government, led by al-Hussein Ali, sought the merging of Iraq and Kuwait. Ten days later, the Emirate was declared an Iraqi province.

[21] The US reacted strongly to the invasion and promoted a series of tough UN Security Council measures. On 6 August, the trading, financial, and military boycott of Iraq was voted through, and on 29 November, the use of force against Iraq was approved if the country refused to withdraw from Kuwait before 15 January 1991. Only Cuba and Yemen abstained from voting.

[22] The ensuing Gulf War devastated the country, not so much in terms of lives lost, for most of the fighting was done in Iraqi territory, but because the bombings and forced withdrawal of the occupation troops left most of Kuwait's oil wells burning and the country was unable to produce any oil until 1992.

[23] Kuwait became an environmental disaster area. The 500 burning oil wells produced 3 million tons of smoke. Huge oil spills along the coast produced major degradation of the air, marine resources and soil. A large oil slick along the coast killed 25,000 birds. The Gulf's ecosystem was seriously affected, especially fish species which form a staple of the local diet.

[24] The Kuwait Institute for Scientific Research stated that 900 km of desert were affected by the traffic of military vehicles, which caused the land to shift, and frequent sandstorms.

[25] It was estimated that the clean-up and reconstruction cost between $150 and 200 billion. Kuwait became a debtor nation, owing $22 billion to the Allied countries.

[26] After the War was over, more than 1,300 people were killed by mines laid during the conflict.

[27] The conflict also affected public health. A government survey among doctors in the six largest hospitals showed that the environmental disaster led to a rise in the incidence of respiratory ailments, miscarriages and underweight infants.

[28] In March 1991 Amnesty International denounced extrajudicial killings, arbitrary detentions and torture of Palestinians, Jordanians and Iraqis living in Kuwait. During US Secretary of State James Baker's visit, the Government pledged to lead the Emirate towards democracy, but no timeframes were mentioned.

[29] In June 1991, Emir Jabir al-Sabah called a National Council to discuss the elections, and female and foreign suffrage. The opposition was still demanding the re-establishment of the 1962 constitution and the formation of a democratic parliament, though no opposition leaders were allowed on the Council.

[30] Women, excluded from politics since independence, make up 67 per cent of all university graduates. In the 1990s, through the Committee of Women's Affairs and the Kuwaiti Women's Cultural and

IN FOCUS

ENVIRONMENTAL CHALLENGES
The worst environmental damage was caused by the burning of oil wells during the Gulf War in 1991. Air and water pollution are problems, as well as a shortage of drinking water, and rapidly advancing soil erosion leading to desertification.

WOMEN'S RIGHTS
Kuwait is the only country in the world where women have no right to vote and cannot run for office. In spite of this, some women hold important positions, such as the Director of Kuwait University, the Ambassador in Austria and the Undersecretary of Higher Education, within the Ministry of Education.

In 2000, women made up 32 per cent of the labor force of 1 million people. Of the women in the workforce, 98 per cent worked in services, while the other 2 per cent were employed in agriculture and industry.

Maternal mortality stands at 5 per 100,000 live births, and

40 per cent of pregnant women are anemic.

CHILDREN
Mortality rates among children are low: 9 per 1,000 live births for infants and 10 per 1,000 in children under 5. Ten per cent of children under 5 are underweight and 24 per cent have stunted growth. Between 94 and 99 per cent of children were immunized in 2002 against common diseases (polio, measles, diphtheria, and tetanus).

Some 66 per cent of all children have access to primary education and 50 per cent to secondary education. The authorities are planning to universalize preschool education, which at present covers only a small fraction of the population.

There are no reliable sources regarding domestic violence, nor available mechanisms to deal with child abuse.

INDIGENOUS PEOPLES/ETHNIC MINORITIES
The Government denies the *Bidun* the rights and guarantees granted to Kuwaiti citizens. Mostly Bedouin, they come from the

northern Arab provinces and arrived in Kuwait in 1920, when the present borders in the region were demarcated.

However, in May 2000, Parliament passed a law to allow some 2,000 *Biduns* the possibility of becoming citizens. The rest will have to obtain passports from their countries of origin to be able to reside in Kuwait.

A significant number of Arab and Iranian nomads living in coastal regions along the Gulf since the 1940s also do not have Kuwaiti citizenship.

MIGRANTS/REFUGEES
Immigrants can request 5-year residence permits, which grant them some advantages over illegal residents. In order to obtain Kuwaiti citizenship they must present a passport and other documentation from their countries of origin, which is difficult for those who have fled their homelands.

In 2002 there were more than 65,000 refugees in Kuwait, mostly from other countries in the region. That total was made up of 50,000 Palestinians, 15,000 Iraqis, and

much smaller groups from Somalia and Afghanistan. But these are only estimates, since Kuwait does not recognize the existence of refugees in its territory, although it tolerates foreign labor. Some 120,000 stateless Arabs, known as *Bidun*, were living in Kuwait in 2002.

Kuwait is not a member of the Office of the United Nations High Commissioner for Refugees (UNHCR), and lacks legislation and proceedings to handle requests or applications from refugees. In spite of this, in 1996 the Kuwaiti Government and UNHCR signed an agreement allowing the UN agency to provide aid to refugees, on its own or in conjunction with other organizations.

Kuwait received thousands of Iraqi refugees during the Gulf War in 1991. Once the conflict was over they were deported to Iraq, accused of collaborating with the Iraqi regime during the occupation of Kuwait.

DEATH PENALTY
Applicable to a wide range of offenses.

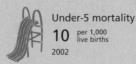
Under-5 mortality
10 per 1,000 live births
2002

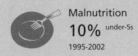
Malnutrition
10% under-5s
1995-2002

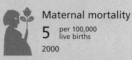
Maternal mortality
5 per 100,000 live births
2000

Social Society, they organized campaigns and mobilized for their citizenship rights.

[31] In November 1999 the Emir passed a law granting women the right to vote and to run for public office, and lowering the legal voting age from 21 to 18. However the law was repealed by the National Assembly.

[32] Kuwaiti women do not only lack political rights. Discrimination is also strong in the civil realm: marriage between Muslim women and non-Muslims is banned, a woman needs her husband's permission to obtain a passport, and, in Islamic courts, the testimony of a man is worth that of two women.

[33] Other discrimination includes the punishment of homosexual relations between men, with jail sentences of 7 to 10 years. The Government also periodically carries out HIV-testing among foreigners living in Kuwait and expels those who are HIV-positive.

[34] When the war ended, the Emir launched the slogan of 're-Kuwaitizing' the country to drastically reduce the number of foreigners. Over 300,000 Palestinians were expelled.

[35] In mid-December 1991, Saudi Arabia, the United Arab Emirates, Oman, Qatar, Bahrain, and Kuwait held a summit aimed at creating a collective security mechanism, and establishing a new defensive framework for the region which holds 40 per cent of the world's oil reserves.

[36] After resuming oil production, Kuwait initially accepted the OPEC quota of two million barrels per day. However in February 1993 it confronted OPEC's other members and unilaterally decided to raise daily production to 2.16 million barrels.

[37] In 1993 the UN finally determined the frontier with Iraq, despite protests by Baghdad. As a response to supposed incursions by Iraqi troops, the US bombed Iraq repeatedly (see Iraq). Washington decided to install missiles in Kuwait and it began building a wall 130 kms long equipped with mines along the new frontier.

[38] In August the ex-chief of the Temporary Free Government imposed by Baghdad, al-Hussein Ali, was condemned to death, as well as five Kuwaitis and 10 Jordanians accused of collaborating with the Iraqi occupation.

[39] The following year, the Government moved towards privatizing State companies and carried out major arms investments.

[40] In February 1996, Amnesty International again denounced summary executions, torture and deportations without trial.

[41] After several legislators threatened to throw out the Minister of Islamic Affairs for errors printed in 120,000 copies of the Qur'an, the Emir dissolved Parliament in May 1999 and called legislative elections in July.

[42] The burning of an oil refinery in early 2002 led to harsh criticisms of the new Petroleum Minister, who was forced to resign. In Parliament, a series of debates on the matter ended in denunciations of corruption, incompetence and nepotism, which for politicians and analysts alike underscored the Government's operational problems. Given the context, the candidates proposed for the ministerial seat refused the offer, paralyzing decision-making at the Petroleum Ministry. The Information Minister, Sheikh Ahmad Fahd al-Sabah, eventually took over the Ministry until the 2003 elections.

[43] After the 11 September 2001 attacks against the US, the Emir expressed his support for the US led anti-terrorism coalition. It was later revealed that the spokesperson for al-Qaeda, Suleiman Abu Ghaith, was a Kuwaiti citizen, and that other Kuwaitis were held at the US military base in Guantanamo, Cuba. In January 2002, US Treasury Secretary Paul O'Neill visited Kuwait to ask the Government to block all sources of financing for al-Qaeda.

[44] The US, UK and coalition forces began the war against Iraq, launching a ground attack from Kuwait in March 2003, amid controversy at home and in the UN. The Arab League unanimously condemned the invasion, with the exception of the Kuwaiti delegation.

[45] According to the Amnesty International 2003 annual report, Kuwait sentenced to death four men, one of them found guilty of murdering a journalist in March 2001. The other three, a Kuwaiti and two Saudis, were convicted of raping and killing a 6-year-old *bidun* (stateless) girl in May. The three testified at the beginning of the trial that they had confessed under torture. In spite of this, the court accepted the confessions. The four were hanged in public and the bodies left on display for some minutes.

[46] In the National Assembly elections of July 2003, Islamic groups won 21 seats,

government supporters 14, independents 13 and Liberals 3.

[47] In February 2004, Japanese soldiers arrived in Kuwait to help with humanitarian activities in Iraq; the first Japanese troops to enter a conflict area since World War II.

[48] After meeting US envoy, former Secretary of State James Baker, Kuwait announced it was prepared to waive a 'significant proportion' of the Iraqi debt. Iraq's debt amounted to $16 billion and, with this gesture, Kuwait aligned with other Gulf states that were also Baghdad creditors such as the United Arab Emirates and Qatar, which had cancelled most part of their debt.

[49] Kuwaiti women, who had been campaigning for their right to vote for decades, were given fresh impetus in May when the Council of Ministers approved a bill allowing women to vote and to stand for parliamentary elections. According to the Council, the proposal was framed within a policy of 'broadening popular participation'. Before being presented to Parliament, the proposal should be approved by the Emir. In 1999, under pressure from tribal groups, Parliament had narrowly defeated a similar move which had been submitted by the Emir.

[50] That same month, religious authorities issued a *fatwa* (religious edict) forbidding concerts with women singers for being considered as 'un-Islamic'. The acts forbidden by the fatwa included women singing to men, the mixing between sexes within the same places when women 'reveal part of their body, use vulgar words and dance'. The ban followed an outcry over a Lebanese TV show, *Star Show*, which is based on a hit French TV show of the same name in which male and female teenagers from different Arab countries live together before competing in a talent contest. ∎

ENVIRONMENT

Nearly all the land is flat, except for a few ranges of dunes. The inland is desert with only one oasis, the al-Jahrah. The coast is low and uniform. The city and port of Kuwait is located in the only deep-water harbor. The hot climate is tempered by ocean currents but the temperature is high in summer. Winters are warm with frequent dust and sand storms. Petroleum is the main economic resource, with three refineries in Shuaiba, Mina al-Ahmadi and Mina Abdulla.

SOCIETY

Peoples: Kuwaitis, of Arab descent, account for less than half of the population, 60 per cent of which is made up of immigrant workers from Palestine, Egypt, Iran, Pakistan, India, Bangladesh, the Philippines and other countries.
Religions: Muslim 85 per cent, of which Sunni account for 70 per cent and Shi'a 30 per cent; other (mostly Christian and Hindu) 15 per cent.
Languages: Arabic (official).
Main Political Parties: There are no legal parties. In the National Assembly are represented: the Islamic Constitutional Movement, a moderate Sunni group; the Kuwaiti Democratic Forum, liberal; the Salafeen, a fundamentalist Sunni group, and the National Islamic Alliance (Shi'a).
Main Social Organizations: Federation of Unions, founded in 1967 with 12,000 members. The Kuwait Students' National Union. Kuwaiti Women's Cultural and Social Society.

THE STATE

Official Name: Dawlat al-Kuwayt. (State of Kuwait).
Administrative Divisions: 5 governances.
Capital: Kuwait City (Al-Kuwayt) 1,222,000 people (2003).
Other Cities: as-Salimiyah 142,700 people; Hawalli 90,100; al-Farwaniyah 58,100 al-Jahra 16,000 (2000).
Government: Constitutional Monarchy. Jabir al-Ahmad al-Sabah, Emir since December 1977; Sabah al-Ahmad al-Jabir al-Sabah, Prime Minister appointed by the Emir in July 2003. The National Assembly has 50 members, elected for a four-year term. Ministers are members of the Legislative Branch.
National Holiday: 25 February, National Day (1950).
Armed Forces: 15,300 (1996). Others: The National Guard has 5,000 troops (Paramilitary).

Kyrgyzstan / Kyrgyzstan

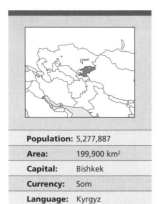

Population:	5,277,887
Area:	199,900 km²
Capital:	Bishkek
Currency:	Som
Language:	Kyrgyz

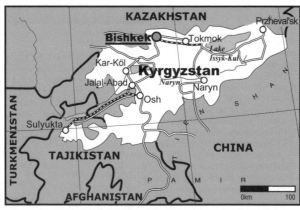

Beginning in the 3rd century BC or earlier, nomadic Kyrgyz shepherds settled on the steppes in eastern Siberia (to the north of present-day Mongolia). They followed shamanistic beliefs - a shaman is a priest using magic to cure people, to control events by communicating with nature spirits and to pass on wisdom.

[2] As they began to move towards the west, starting in the 1st century BC, the Kyrgyz merged with Tashtika - a mix of Asian and European descendants - a process that continued through the 5th century. Between the 6th and 8th centuries, the Kyrgyz populated the land where the Yanisey emerged, in central Siberia.

[3] Between the 6th and 10th centuries, the Kyrgyzstan region remained under the control of different Turkish groups. In 751, the area was the scene of a battle in which Turks, Arabs and Tibetans joined forces to expel the vast army of the Chinese Tang Dynasty (618-907) from Central Asia.

[4] In the 9th century, the Kyrgyz set out on a journey that lasted four centuries. They occupied Tula territory (in the present-day Russia) temporarily and returned to Yanisey in the 12th century. After that, they began to slowly descend into the Yanisey valleys, and reached the territory of modern-day Kyrgyzstan in the 15th century.

[5] In 1207, the Kyrgyz surrendered to Mongol Jochi (Genghis Khan's son) to avoid falling under the dominion of Islamic (Arab and Turkish) peoples spreading from southwestern Asia. Until then, they had managed to escape the Mongol conquest, thanks to their mobility and ability to adapt to the cold, treeless steppes.

[6] In the 16th and 17th centuries, the Kyrgyz occupied both sides of the Tien Shan mountains (the area of the present-day frontier between Kyrgyzstan, China and

Kazakhstan), provoking constant attacks from Zungaros (Mongols from the northeast) starting in 1703. Many Kyrgyz fled to the Kyrgyzstan region. The clashes ended in 1757 when the Manchu Empire under the Ching Dynasty (1644-1911/12) gained formal, but not effective, control over the Tien Shan mountains.

[7] Between 1835 and 1830, the Kyrgyz people were subdued by the Khan of Kokand (from Uzbekistan, to the west of Kyrgyzstan) who founded the city of Bishkek (the future capital). As a consequence, Islam began to be adopted, contributing to the emergence of a kind of national Kyrgyz culture.

[8] Two groups from Tien Shan became entangled in a fratricidal war that lasted from 1835 to 1858. Both groups were supported alternately by the Khanate of

Kokand Khan and the Russians. In 1855, the Russian army intervened.

[9] The mass immigration of Russian serfs after the abolition of serfdom in 1861 was the main cause of the displacement, between 1862 and 1872, of one-third of the Kyrgyz to the Tien Shan mountains. Russian peasants escaping famine set fire to Kyrgyz towns, appropriated their pastureland and applied their own agricultural techniques. In 1875, the Russian Empire annexed the entire territory and granted the colonists legal title to the land.

[10] Tension between the Russians and Kyrgyz over land ownership and the imposition of compulsory military service triggered a revolt that began in 1916 and continued for years after the October Revolution of 1917. Before that, many Kyrgyz sought refuge in China.

[11] In December 1917, the Bolshevik government opened a regional assembly in Bishkek (which was renamed Frunze in honor of a Red Army general). Like their predecessors, the new government continued to draft Kyrgyz soldiers. In 1926, the present borders were drawn up, and Kyrgyzstan was granted the status of Autonomous Soviet Socialist Republic, as part of the USSR.

[12] In 1921, the USSR began to collectivize land and the industrial production of the region's raw materials such as cotton, wool, leather, tobacco, fish, wood, water and metal. Factories were built for processing antimony and other metals. Planned production, tight social control and persecution put an abrupt end to the nomadic Kyrgyz way of life, despite resistance. Many were executed or sent to concentration camps, while others escaped to China.

[13] In 1936, Kyrgyzstan became a Soviet republic.

[14] From 1926 to 1959, the Kyrgyz proportion of the population shrank from 60 to 40 per cent. Russians, Ukrainians and Germans who had been captured by the Red Army in 1941 immigrated to Kyrgyzstan. Industry underwent further expansion, with the production of machinery, electricity and construction materials, although the modernization and improvement of the economy failed to ease the tensions. A Kyrgyz independence movement began to grow rapidly

PROFILE

ENVIRONMENT

Located in the northeastern part of Central Asia, Kyrgyzstan lies in the heart of the Tian Shan mountain range. It is bounded by China and Tajikistan in the south, Kazakhstan in the north, Uzbekistan in the west, the Pamir and Altai mountain ranges in the southwest and the Tian Shan range in the northeast. It has plateaus and valleys: in the north, the Chu and Talas valley; in the south, the Alai Valley; and in the southwest, the Fergana Valley. The climate is continental, with sharp contrasts between day and night temperatures. The eastern part of Tian Shan is dry, while the southwestern slopes of the Fergana range are rainy. The main rivers are the Narym and the Kara-Suu. Lake Issyk-Kul is the most important of the country's lakes. In the mountains there are forests and meadows, while desert and semi-desert vegetation abounds at lower altitudes. Metal deposits include lead and zinc; in addition, there are large coal reserves and some oil and natural gas deposits.

SOCIETY

Peoples: Kyrgyz, 52.4 per cent; Russians, 21.5 per cent; Uzbeks, 12.9 per cent; Ukrainians, 2.5 per cent, Germans 2.4 per cent.
Religions: 75 per cent Muslim (Sunni); 6 per cent Christian (Russian Orthodox Church) and others.

Languages: Kyrgyz (official); Russian (co-official); Uzbek; Dungan; Ukranian and others.
Main Political Parties: Ate-Meken Socialist Party, Party of Communists of Kyrgyzstan; Union of Democratic Forces; Women's Democratic Party of Kyrgyztan; Party of War Veterans in Afghanistan.
Main Social Organizations: Council of Free Trade Unions, Kyrgyz Committee on Human Rights, Movement for the National Democratic Union, Business Union.

THE STATE

Official Name: Kyrgyz Respublikasy (Kyrgyz Republic). **Administrative Division:** 6 provinces and 1 city (Bishkek). **Capital:** Bishkek 806,000 people (2003). **Other Cities:** Osh 217,000 people; Jalal-Abad 73,200; Kara-Köl 66,900; Tokmok 61,800; Narin 41,700 (2000).
Government: Askar Akayev, President since October 1990, re-elected in 1995 and 2000. Nicolay Tanayev, Prime Minister since May 2002, appointed by Parliament after the imprisonment in March 2002 of Kurmanbek Bakiyev. There is a two-chamber Supreme Council: the Legislative Assembly (60 members) and the People's Representatives Assembly (45 members).
National Holiday: 31 August, Independence Day (1991). **Armed Forces:** 12,200 troops (1997).

Life expectancy
68.6 years
2000-2005

GNI per capita
$290
2002

HIV prevalence rate
0.1% of population
15-49 years old
2001

in 1986, at the start of the process of political opening led by Mikhail Gorbachev in Moscow

[15] In the early 1990s, the Kyrgyz Communist Party (PCK) opposed the legalization of non-Communist parties promoted by Moscow. In August 1991, during the attempted coup against Gorbachev staged by the conservative wing of the Communist Party, Askar Akayev, a prominent liberal member of the Kremlin, supported Gorbachev (as did Boris Yeltsin and others). Akayev came from the Russian minority in Kyrgyzstan and was considered one of the brains behind the political reforms undertaken by the USSR in the 1980s.

[16] That same month, Kyrgyzstan became an independent state and Akayev was designated president of the Kyrgyzstan Federal Republic.

[17] The PCK was banned until after the 1991 presidential election in which Akayev's presidency was confirmed unopposed. In December, Kyrgyzstan and ten other former USSR republics signed the founding charter for the Commonwealth of Independent States (CIS), which established, among other conditions, the stationing of joint military forces in each republic.

[18] In 1992, after pledging to preserve democracy - the ban on the PCK was lifted that year - and to modernize the economy, still dependent on Russia through the CIS, Akayev pushed for membership of the UN, IMF and the Organization for Security and Co-operation in Europe. In July, a package of stringent economic measures was adopted in agreement with the IMF, which entailed the privatization of industry and land ownership, as well as the liberalization of the financial and banking system, to develop a fully functioning free market economy.

[19] Exacerbated by the lack of support from the CIS, Akayev's economic policy led to a significant loss of jobs, gave rise to discrepancies and disputes in parliament. In 1993, parliament approved the first Kyrgyz Constitution which established that elections for a single-chamber legislature would be held in 1995.

[20] However, the tension in parliament worsened and forced Akayev to call a referendum in January 1994 to legitimize his authority. The same year he managed to push through a constitutional amendment creating a bicameral legislature. At the same time, a new currency (the som) was released, which

IN FOCUS

ENVIRONMENTAL CHALLENGES
Water pollution caused by mining industry waste is a major concern since one-third of the population is supplied directly from rivers, streams or wells. In the meantime, the salinization of soil is increasing due to the use of salt-water for irrigation.

WOMEN'S RIGHTS
Women have been able to vote and stand for election since 1918. In 2003 they held seven per cent of the seats in parliament. They accounted for 47 per cent of the country's workforce of two million. The majority (53 per cent) work in agriculture, 38 per cent in services and nine per cent in industry.

Ninety per cent of pregnant women receive prenatal care and 98 per cent of births are attended by qualified medical personnel*. Violence against women, including domestic violence, is a serious problem.

According to Interior Ministry statistics, 300 women are murdered each year, although unofficial figures are much higher. Most of the crimes against women go unreported due largely to cultural traditions and psychological pressure.

After Kyrgyzstan gained independence from the Soviet Union in 1991, 'bride abduction' became a frequent practice, especially in the southern part of the country. Each year, between 10 and 30 women are estimated to be kidnapped and forced into marriage.

CHILDREN
The infant mortality rate stands at 52 per 1,000 live births*. Six per cent of newborn babies are underweight and 25 per cent are below average measurements*. Approximately half of the deaths of babies under two are due to tuberculosis.

In 2000*, the literacy rate stood at 97 per cent. Primary education is obligatory and parents are fined or even sentenced to a year of forced labor if they fail to send their children to school.

From 1999 to 2003, 36 people were prosecuted for involvement in child sex exploitation and pornography, and ten were convicted of trafficking in children.

INDIGENOUS PEOPLES/ETHNIC MINORITIES
Russians came to the region as representatives of the Russian Empire in 1861 to supervise the colonization of Central Asia. Russians complain of discrimination. Since the break-up of the Soviet Union, thousands of Russians have left Kyrgyzstan, mainly to Russia and other former Soviet Republics.

Uzbeks are concentrated in the southern regions of Osh, Batken and Jalal-Abad. In 1990, there were armed clashes between Uzbeks and Kyrgyz in the region of Osh. Since 2002, the Kyrgyz Government has been working to grant Uzbeks more participation in politics and to ease tension among the country's three main ethnic groups (Kyrgyz, Russians and Uzbeks).

MIGRANTS/REFUGEES
As of late 2003, 8,300 refugees and asylum-seekers had arrived in Kyrgyzstan. The majority (6,800) were from Tajikistan and the rest from Afghanistan, Chechnya and China. Those from China were Uighurs, a Muslim Turkic people.

Refugees recognized as such by the Government are allowed to live in the country indefinitely, enjoy labor rights, and are eligible for Kyrgyz identity documents.

Of the 6,800 Tajik refugees in Kyrgyzstan, between 90 and 95 per cent arrived after civil war broke out in Tajikistan.

After the 11 September 2001 terror attacks on New York and Washington DC, a number of Afghans were arrested in Kyrgyzstan, including a few who had already been granted official refugee status.

By late 2002, around 500 Chechens had applied for asylum, but the Kyrgyzstan Government rejected their applications to avoid damaging its relations with Russia.

Under bilateral arrangements with the Chinese Government, Kyrgyzstan does not grant asylum to refugees from China.

DEATH PENALTY
Applicable to all kind of crimes.

*Latest data available in *The State of the World's Children* and *Childinfo* database, UNICEF, 2004.

briefly eased inflationary pressures.

[21] In 1995, the President attempted to extend his term through a referendum, but parliament forced him to run in elections in December. Akayev was re-elected, taking more than 60 per cent of the vote. In another referendum in 1996, a broad majority of voters approved constitutional amendments that gave him wider powers. As a result, opposition members and journalists critical of the government were hounded, jailed for slander and even tortured.

[22] In December 1999, the entire cabinet resigned after Akayev and the National Security Council held it responsible for the rising inflation, fiscal deficit and devaluation of the currency. That year, Akayev sent in troops against Muslim Uzbek militants who had occupied towns near Tajikistan.

[23] In February and March 2000, parliamentary elections were held in which the PCK won the majority of votes, followed by the Union of Democratic Forces. International observers and members of the Kyrgyz Human Rights Committee were forced to leave Kyrgyzstan after suffering reprisals for protesting the arrest of parliamentarian Feliks Kulov. He was arrested to keep him from participating in the second round of the elections. Although he was released in August, he was not allowed to run in the October presidential election. He was disqualified for failing a Kyrgyz language test, even though Russian had been made one of the country's official languages in 2000 in order to prevent an exodus.

[24] In September 2001, the Government allowed the installation of a US air base at Manas airport in Bishkek, saying it

was co-operating in the war on Islamic terrorism. In September 2003, Akayev agreed with Moscow to open a rapid reaction military base in Kant, 30 km from Manas, for the same purpose.

[25] In 2002, the imprisonment of opposition leader Azimbek Beknazaror, the 10-year sentence handed down to Kulov, the increase in deaths during crackdowns on street demonstrations and international organizations' constant criticism of human rights' violations, created a situation that led to Akayev's isolation.

[26] According to political observers, Akayev used the war against terrorism as an excuse to strengthen the army, his last bastion of support. In June 2003, parliament approved a law granting presidents and former presidents life-long immunity from prosecution, in order to facilitate his voluntary resignation. ∎

Laos / Lao

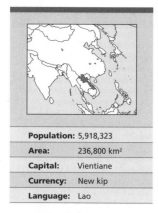

Population:	5,918,323
Area:	236,800 km²
Capital:	Vientiane
Currency:	New kip
Language:	Lao

The earliest inhabitants of Laos were migrants from southern China. From the 11th century onward, parts of Laos fell under the Khmer Empire (in the region now known as Cambodia), and later under Siamese influence from the Sukhothai dynasty. With the fall of Sukhothai in 1345, the first kingdom of Laos emerged under Fa Ngum, a Burmese prince brought up in the court of Angkor Wat. As the Khmer Empire crumbled, Fa Ngum welded together a new empire, founding the flourishing state of Lang Xang, the 'Land of a Million Elephants'. In the late 18th century, the country split into three regions: Champassac, Vientiane and Luang Prabang. In the early 19th century, the Thais had established dominion over those territories. Tiao Anuvong, Prince of Vientiane, led an ill-fated nationalist rebellion in 1827. In 1892, the French invaded and by 1893 had established a protectorate over Luang Praband, with the rest of the country becoming part of French Indochina.

[2] During World War II, Japan occupied Laos and a pro-independence movement arose in Vientiane, led by three princes, Phetsarat, leader of the Free Laos government-in-exile, Suvana Fuma, leader of the National Progressive Party, and Tiao Sufanuvong, head of the Neo Lao Issara (Laos National United Front). In September 1945, they set up a provisional government and declared the independence of Laos.

[3] In 1946, the country was again under French occupation. The Pathet Lao provisional government sought refuge in Bangkok, where the Pathet leaders organized the anti-colonialist struggle through the Lao Issara or 'free Laos' movement.

[4] On 19 July 1949, the Franco-Laotian Convention recognized Laotian independence 'as part of the French Union'. The Pathet Lao leaders saw this as mere formal independence. Suvana Fuma opted for negotiation, but the opposition coalition decided on active resistance; their military victories led to a new treaty in 1953.

[5] Differences between the Lao Issara, Suvana Fuma government, and the Pathet Lao were reconciled in November 1957. An agreement was reached, whereby the latter would participate in the political life of the country under the name 'Neo Lao Haksat' (Laotian Patriotic Front), led by Tiao Sufanuvong.

[6] In 1958, Suvana Fuma's ruling party joined forces with the Independent Party to form the so-called Laotian People's Demonstration, together achieving a small majority in Parliament.

[7] The 1958 elections were won by the left. A center-left coalition government was formed, led by 'neutralist' Suvana Fuma, with Sufanuvong as planning minister.

[8] Opposition from the US and its threat to cut off economic aid destabilized the Government, and in August the leaders of the Committee for the Defense of National Interests took over. The new Government, supported by the US, launched a military offensive against the Pathet Lao, forcing Sufanuvong to return to armed struggle.

[9] In late 1959, the army seized power, while the Pathet Lao controlled the strategic northern provinces and the central Plain of Jars.

[10] General Fumi Nosavang and his troops seized Vientiane on 13 December 1960, driving out Pathet Lao troops, which had taken over the capital for two days.

[11] Thailand and the US supported the Revolutionary Anti-Communist Committee, headed by Fumi Nosavang and Prince Bun Um, which declared itself the legitimate government. On 20 December 1960, however, Princes Suvana Fuma and Sufanuvong signed a declaration in favour of forming a government of national unity.

[12] The 'neutralists' joined forces with the Pathet Lao. By the end of 1960, half of the country's territory was under the control of the Pathet Lao and a similar area had been taken over by 'neutralist' forces.

[13] In Geneva in 1961, Britain and the Soviet Union began negotiations for a peaceful solution, and in January 1962 a final agreement was signed to form a government of national unity.

[14] Growing US intervention resulted in the internationalization of the Vietnam War, which led to bombings in Laos. In nine years Laos was pulverized by more bombs than the whole of Europe during World War II.

[15] The Pathet Lao declared an armistice in 1973, and the Vientiane Government formed a new cabinet, including Pathet Lao members, with a Council of Ministers headed by Suvana Fuma. The US defeat in Vietnam deprived the right-wing groups of the only support they received.

[16] In 1975, the national unity cabinet gave way to a majority of Neo Lao Haksat ministers, and in December a peaceful movement put an end to the monarchy. A People's

PROFILE

ENVIRONMENT

Laos is the only landlocked country in Indochina. The territory is mountainous and covered with rainforests. The Mekong river valley, stretching down the country from north to south, is suited to agriculture, basically rice. It is estimated that 40 per cent of the arable land was left barren as a result of the 25-year war. The climate is tropical and the lowlands are prone to disasters such as the 1978 flood and the 1988 drought.

SOCIETY

Peoples: Three-fifths of Laotians are descendants of the Lao ethnic groups who inhabit the western valleys. The inhabitants of the mountains account for more than one-third of the total population, while five per cent are of Chinese and Vietnamese origin.
Religions: Buddhist 57.8 per cent; traditional religions 33.6 per cent; Christian 1.8 per cent; Muslim 1.0 per cent; atheist/no religion 4.8 per cent; Chinese folk-religions 0.9 per cent. **Languages:** Lao (official); French; English and many minor ethnic group languages. **Main Political Parties:** The Lao People's Revolutionary Party (PPRL), authoritarian communist, in power with 98 of the 99 National Assembly's seats.

Main Social Organizations: Union of Lao People's Revolutionary Youth and the Association of Patriotic Women are mass organizations of the PPRL; Lao Students Movement for Democracy; the Chao Fah, formed by members of the Meo minority - or Hmong - maintains an insurgent group.

THE STATE

Official Name: Sathalanalat Paxathipatai Paxaxon Lao (Lao People's Democratic Republic).
Administrative Divisions: 16 provinces, 1 special zone (Xaisomboun) and 1 municipality (Viangchan).
Capital: Vientiane (Viangchan) 716,000 people (2003). **Other Cities:** Savannakhét 154,900 people; Louangphrabang 116,000 (2000).
Government: Khamtai Siphandon, President since February 1998, elected by the National Assembly for a five-year term. Boungnang Volachit, Prime Minister since March 2001, appointed by the President. Unicameral Legislature: 99-member National Assembly. **National Holiday:** 2 December, Proclamation of the Republic (1975).
Armed Forces: 67,260 troops (conscripts), (1996). Other: 100,000 members of the Self-defense Militia Forces.

Life expectancy
54.5 years
2000-2005

GNI per capita
$310
2002

Literacy
65% total adult rate
2000

HIV prevalence rate
0.1% of population 15-49 years old
2001

Democratic Republic was proclaimed with Prince Sufanuvong as President, led by the renamed Lao People's Revolutionary Party (PPRL). Real power was wielded by Kaysone Phomvihan, the General Secretary of the Party. Entrepreneurs and state bureaucrats left the country en masse, ruining the economy and crippling the public administration.

[17] Within its two first years in power, the PPRL launched different policies, which included the collectivization of agriculture. More than 40,000 people were sent to 're-education' camps and nearly 30,000 were incarcerated for political reasons.

[18] The Government nationalized the banks and reorganized the public sector. Rice production rose from 700,000 tons in 1976 to 1.2 million in 1981, when self-sufficiency in grain was achieved for the first time. To gain access to the sea and to reduce dependence on Thailand, a road was constructed to the Vietnamese port of Danang, and an oil pipeline to Vietnam's refineries. The 1980s were characterized by an 'economic opening'.

[19] In October 1982, General Phoumi Nosavan, a 'conservative' who had been living in exile since 1965, formed an anti-communist government which was named the 'Royal Lao Democratic Government'. Soon after, several exiles and members of the resistance movement who belonged to the United Lao National Liberation Front (ULNLF, created in September 1980), withdrew from the Government and settled in southern Laos.

[20] In 1988 diplomatic relations were renewed with China, and in early 1989 the first co-operation agreements were signed with the US to combat the cultivation and trafficking of opium. By the late 1980s practically all political prisoners had been released and 're-education' camps had been closed.

[21] Upon the disintegration of the Soviet Union, all economic aid was suspended and bilateral trade was reduced by 50 per cent.

[22] In 1991, the economic crisis was exacerbated by floods and pest infestations in a quarter of the country's farmlands.

[23] In that context, Laos established closer ties with Thailand. Also in 1991, the two governments signed a Co-operation and Security Treaty. Thai investments were mainly concentrated in banking and trade.

[24] In December 1992, legislative elections were called; only the PPRL and a few independent government-authorized candidates took part. Scores of government opponents were imprisoned.

[25] Deforestation became a serious environmental problem. The timber felled expanded from 6,000 cubic meters in 1964 to more than 600,000 in 1993. That year, the Government restricted lumber exports. In March 1994 the World Bank granted Laos a loan for reforestation. International environmental groups criticized the project because it gave the funds directly to the Government, with little input from local communities.

[26] In April 1994, the 'Friendship Bridge' over the Mekong River was opened, uniting Laos and Thailand. This reconciliation represented a distancing from Vietnam and an integration with Thailand, a more prosperous nation.

[27] In early 1995, Thailand-based capital dominated investment in Laos. A law passed in March eliminated the last vestiges of the planned economy system. Another law updated labor legislation. However, the Government was determined to maintain its communist identity.

[28] In December 1997, the PPRL retained its dominance, winning 99 seats in the National Assembly. Just four of the 159 candidates were from outside the country's only party.

[29] The stock market crisis affecting several countries in the region hit the Laos economy. Imports and consumer prices increased, particularly for the basic food basket. From 1997, the national currency, the kip, began an accelerated devaluation process that two years later showed a decline of more than 500 per cent with respect to the dollar.

[30] In February 1998, the National Assembly elected Prime Minister Siphandon as the new President. Sisavat Keobounphan became the new Prime Minister.

[31] A wave of bomb attacks shook the country in 2000-2001. According to the Government they were the work of the guerrilla Chao Fa group, or of anticommunist groups based abroad. However, several analysts suspected that the violence could be linked to friction within the regime itself. There were no attacks during the December 2000 celebrations commemorating a quarter-century of communist government. Laos is one of five communist regimes surviving in the world.

[32] In his opening address before the PPRL congress in March 2001, President Siphandon said the party aimed to triple per capita income in Laos by the year 2020, though it recognized the failures in managing the country's fragile economy. A statute passed by the congress reaffirmed the Party's support for socialism and 'opposition to multiparty systems and political pluralism'.

[33] In October 2001, several European activists were arrested in front of the presidential palace in Vientiane for staging a protest against the detention of students in a pro-democracy demonstration the previous year. The European Parliament adopted a resolution which, in spite of not suspending aid, imposed conditions on the future political development of the country.

[34] In September 2001, Japan granted a loan for the construction of the second 'Friendship Bridge' over the Mekong, which was started in early 2002 and should be finished in 2005.

[35] In early 2002, the border conflict between Thailand and Laos - which included the dispute over the Mekong River islets - remained unresolved.

[36] In the February 2002 elections, Khamtay Siphandon was re-elected Head of State. The ruling party confirmed its hold on power, since only 1 out of the 166 candidates was not a member of the LPRP.

[37] In June 2003, three drug traffickers were the first to be sentenced to death since the imposition of the death penalty for drug crimes in 2002.

[38] In July 2003, ministers and delegates from Laos, China, Thailand, Myanmar and India signed a declaration by which they committed to co-operate in the fight against drugs. ∎

IN FOCUS

ENVIRONMENTAL CHALLENGES
The most pressing environmental problem is the intense logging and the resultant dwindling of water supplies and loss of 70 per cent of natural habitats. Less than five per cent of the land is suitable for agriculture, though farming generates 80 per cent of employment.

WOMEN'S RIGHTS
Laotian women have been able to vote and stand for office since 1958. In 2000, 21 per cent of seats in parliament were held by women, while they held no ministerial positions.

Between 1990 and 2000, 81 per cent of women worked in agriculture, 14 per cent in the area of services and 5 per cent in the industrial sector.

In 2000*, the illiteracy rate in women over 15 was 46.6 per cent, while in men it was reduced to 23.8 per cent. Women net primary and secondary school enrollment rates reached 78 per cent and 27 per cent respectively*. Meanwhile, the estimated average time of schooling was seven years.

In 2000, 62 per cent of pregnant women suffered from anemia. The percentage of births attended by skilled health personnel fell from 60 to 19 per cent*. One out of every 1,000 Laotian women between 15 and 24 years old was living with HIV/AIDS.

CHILDREN
In 2000*, 40 per cent of children under five were moderately or severely underweight.

At the end of 2001, there were less than 100 children under 14 living with HIV/AIDS.

The goals to be achieved by 2020 include reducing the infant mortality rate, under-five mortality rate, maternal mortality rate and also malnutrition. To that end, health policies, immunization programs and measures to guarantee vaccine supplies have been implemented. Emphasis has been placed on curbing malaria (leading cause of death among children), diarrhea (second cause) and respiratory infections.

INDIGENOUS PEOPLES/ ETHNIC MINORITIES
The Hmong, also referred to as the Meo, constitute a population of 193,000 people, equivalent to four per cent of the total population. They come from the mountains and live in and around the Plain of Jars. Having been recruited and trained by the CIA for a secret war in the officially neutral Laos, the Hmong aided the US during the Vietnam War. According to UNHCR, 20,000 Hmong soldiers died in combat during the conflict, 50,000 civilians were wounded and 120,000 were displaced from their homes.

In 1975, thousands of Hmong fled to the US, where many of them had to wait more than 25 years to be granted US citizenship in return for their loyalty. Meanwhile, a small group of starving Hmong still live in the jungle, hiding from the persecution of the Laotian army.

MIGRANTS/REFUGEES
Thailand is the destination of many Laotians who emigrate in search of work. In 1990, an estimated 14,000 foreigners were living in Laos, and in 1995 there were 15,000 foreigners living as refugees. Nearly 15 per cent of the population fled the country during the communist repression.

DEATH PENALTY
The death penalty is applicable even for common crimes.

*Latest data available in *The State of the World's Children* and *Childinfo* database, UNICEF, 2004.

Latvia / Latvija

Population:	2,264,965
Area:	64,600 km²
Capital:	Riga
Currency:	Lat
Language:	Latvian

The first inhabitants of present-day Latvia were nomadic hunters, fishers and gatherers who migrated to the forests along the Baltic coast, after the last glaciers had retreated. Around 2,000 BC, these groups were replaced by the Baltic peoples, Indo-Europeans who began farming and established permanent settlements in Latvia, Lithuania and eastern Prussia.

[2] The ancient Baltic peoples had come into contact with the Roman Empire through the amber trade. This activity, which reached its peak during the first two centuries of the Christian era, was brought to a halt by Slav expansion toward central and eastern Europe.

[3] The Swedes and the Russians both claimed these lands during the 10th and 11th centuries and in the 12th century, German warriors and missionaries came to the Latvian coast. As it was inhabited at the time by the Livs, the Germans called it Livonia. In 1202, the bishop of the region, under authorization from Rome, established the Order of the Knights of the Sword (see Estonia).

[4] Before becoming the Knights of the Teutonic Order, in 1237, the Germans had subdued and converted the tribal groups of Latvia and Estonia to Christianity. The Teutonic Knights created the so-called Livonian Confederation, consisting of areas controlled by the Church, free cities and regions governed by knights.

[5] When Russia invaded the region in 1558, to halt Polish-Lithuanian expansion, the Order fell apart and Livonia was partitioned. At the end of the Livonian War in 1583 Lithuania annexed the area north of the Dvina river; the south remained in Polish hands and Sweden kept the north of Estonia. In 1621, Sweden occupied Riga and Jelgava; Estonia and the northern part of Latvia were subsequently ceded to Sweden by the Truce of Altmark (1629).

[6] The region west of Riga, on the Baltic Sea, was organized into the Duchy of Courland, becoming a semi-independent vassal of Poland. In the mid-17th century, Courland became known as a major naval and trade center for northern Europe, and even had colonial aspirations.

[7] Sweden kept these territories until the Great Northern War, when it was forced to cede them to Russia under the Peace of Nystad. In

1795, after the three partitions of Poland, Livonia was finally subdivided into three regions within Russia: Estonia (the northern part of Estonia); Livonia (the southern portion of Estonia and northern portion of Latvia) and Courland. The Russian Revolution of 1905 gave rise to the first expressions of Latvian national sentiment.

[8] The peasants revolted against their German feudal lords, and the Russian rulers. Although the rebellion was put down by czarist troops, it set the stage for the war of independence 13 years later. After the Russian Revolution of 1917, the Latvian People's Council proclaimed the country's independence on 18 November 1918. A government led by the leader of the Farmers' Union, Karlis Ulmanis, was formed.

[9] Far from having its desire for independence and sovereignty respected, Latvia was attacked by German troops and by the Red Army. Only in 1920 was Latvia able

to sign a peace treaty with the USSR, in which the latter renounced its territorial ambitions. In 1922, a constituent assembly established a parliamentary republic. The international economic crisis of the 1930s, and the polarization of socialists and Nazi sympathizers led to the collapse of the Latvian Government. In 1934, Prime Minister Ulmanis suspended parliament and governed under a state of emergency until 1938.

[10] With the outbreak of World War II, according to the secret Russo-German pact, Latvia remained within the USSR's sphere of influence. In 1939, Latvia was forced to sign a treaty permitting the Soviets to install troops and bases on its soil. In 1940, it was invaded by the Red Army, and a new government was formed, which subsequently requested that the republic be admitted to the USSR.

[11] During the German offensive against the USSR, between 1940 and 1944, Latvia was annexed to the German province of Ostland, and its Jewish population was practically exterminated. The liberation of Latvia by the Red Army meant the re-establishment of Soviet government. Before the Soviet forces arrived, 65,000 Latvians fled to Western Europe.

[12] In 1945 and 1946, about 105,000 Latvians were deported to Russia, and the far northeastern corner of Latvia - with its predominantly Russian population - was taken away from Latvia to form part of the USSR. In 1949,

WORKERS

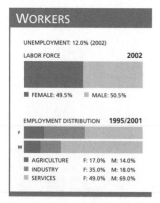

UNEMPLOYMENT: 12.0% (2002)

LABOR FORCE 2002

■ FEMALE: 49.5% ■ MALE: 50.5%

EMPLOYMENT DISTRIBUTION 1995/2001

F

M

■ AGRICULTURE	F: 17.0%	M: 14.0%
■ INDUSTRY	F: 35.0%	M: 18.0%
■ SERVICES	F: 49.0%	M: 69.0%

PROFILE

ENVIRONMENT
Latvia's terrain is characterized by softly rolling hills (highest point: Gaizins, 310 m), and by the number of forests, lakes and rivers, which empty into the Baltic Sea and the Gulf of Riga, in the northeastern part of the country. Latvia has 494 kms of coastline. The country's most fertile lands lie in the Zemgale Plain, which is known as the country's breadbasket. The plain is located in the south, extending as far as the Lithuanian border. The highlands, which make up 40 per cent of the land, lie in the western and northern parts of the country, crossing over into Estonia. The climate is humid and cold, due to cold air masses coming from the Atlantic. Summers are short and rainy, with an average temperature of 17° C; winters last from December to March, with temperatures below zero, sometimes as low as -40° C. Two-thirds of all arable land is used for grain production, and the rest is pastureland. The main industries are metallurgical engineering (ships, automobiles, railway carriages and agricultural machinery), followed by the production of motorcycles, home appliances and scientific research equipment.

SOCIETY
Peoples: Latvians and Lithuanians constitute the two main branches of the Baltic Indo-European peoples, with distinct languages and cultures that

set them apart from the Germans and Slavs. Ethnic Latvians make up 52 per cent of the country's population, followed by Russians, 34 per cent; Poles, Belarussians, Ukrainians, Lithuanians and Estonians account for the remaining 14 per cent.
Religions: The majority is Protestant (Lutheran), followed by Catholics.
Languages: Latvian (official); Russian, Lithuanian and Polish. **Main Political Parties:** New Era (JL), Social Democrats (LSSP), Latvia's Way (LC), Latvia First Party (LPP), Fatherland and Freedom (TB-LNNK), For Civil Rights (PCTVL), People's Party (TP), Union of Greens and Farmers (ZZS). The government is formed by the ZZS, TP and LPP.
Main Social Organizations: Confederation of Free Trade Unions.

THE STATE
Official Name: Latvijas Respublika.
Capital: Riga 733,000 people (2003).
Other Cities: Daugavspils 113,600 people; Liepaja 94,100; Jelgava 70,700; Jurmala 58,900 (2000).
Government: Parliamentary republic. Vaira Vike-Freiberga, President, elected in July 1999. Indulis Emsis, Prime Minister since February 2004. Single-chamber parliament (Saeima), made up of 201 members elected by direct vote.
National Holiday: 18 November, Independence Day (1918). **Armed Forces:** 6,950 troops (1996).

Life expectancy
71.0 years
2000-2005

GNI per capita
$3,480
2002

Literacy
100% total adult rate
2000

HIV prevalence rate
0.4% of population 15-49 years old
2001

forced collectivization of agriculture triggered a mass deportation of Latvians, with about 70,000 being sent to Russia and Siberia. In 1959 the President of Latvia's Supreme Soviet, Karlis Ozolins, was dismissed because of his nationalist tendencies.

[13] Armed Latvian resistance to the Soviet regime was finally put down in 1952. All symbols of Latvian independence - the national anthem, the flag, and national monuments and history - were banned or adapted to the new regime. Russian became the official language, and massive immigration of Russians and other nationalities began. To the nationalists, this was taken to be a deliberate colonization policy, aimed at diminishing the influence of the indigenous population.

[14] Until the 1980s, Latvian resistance was expressed in isolated actions by political and religious dissidents, which were systematically repressed by the regime; in addition, some nationalist campaigns were carried out by exiles. From 1987, the policy of *glasnost* (openness) initiated by Mikhail Gorbachev in the USSR, gave hope to Latvian aspirations, permitting public political demonstrations, and the reinstatement of the national symbols.

[15] In October 1988, close to 150,000 people gathered to celebrate the founding of the Popular Front of Latvia (LTF), which brought together all of Latvia's recently formed social and political groups, as well as militant communists. A month later, for the first time since Soviet occupation, hundreds of thousands of Latvians commemorated the anniversary of the 1918 declaration of independence. The LTF began to have influence with the local government, and with the Moscow authorities.

[16] A year later, the LTF Congress endorsed the country's political and economic independence from the Soviet Union. Despite Moscow's resistance to Latvia's secession, the LTF's policy of carrying out changes peacefully met with widespread popular support from citizens of Russian or other origins. The LTF program for non-violent change included public demonstrations, free elections and change through parliamentary procedure. Latvia's 1938 constitution went into effect once again, for the first time since the 1940 Soviet occupation.

[17] On 4 May 1990 Latvia marked the Declaration of the Re-establishment of Independence, as well as the reinstatement of the 1922 constitution. In September 1991, the new Council of State of

IN FOCUS

ENVIRONMENTAL CHALLENGES
The most pressing challenges are improving the quality of potable water and the sewage disposal system. Toxic waste disposal and curbing air pollution are major concerns. The Government has committed itself to implementing all EU environmental directives by 2010.

WOMEN'S RIGHTS.
Women have been able to vote and stand for election since 1917. From 1995 to 2000, the proportion of seats in parliament held by women rose from nine to 17 per cent, while the percentage of women in ministerial or equivalent positions increased from zero to seven per cent. In 2002, women accounted for 51 per cent of all workers (14 per cent in agriculture, 18 per cent in industry and 69 per cent in services). Unemployment stood at 13.3 per cent among women and 15.5 per cent among men. There is evidence that the country has been a source of women forcibly trafficked into the sex trade since 1990, especially to Lithuania, the final destination of the women or merely a transit point on the way to Western Europe. Sexual harassment in the workplace is reportedly common, even though it is illegal. Cultural factors tend to dissuade women from reporting the problem. A new law prohibits discrimination with regards to labor and wages, but large gender gaps persist.

CHILDREN
In 2002, Amnesty International expressed concern over the number of cases of domestic violence and child abuse, including sexual abuse within the family. An estimated 12 to 15 per cent of all sex workers were between the ages of eight and 18 in 2000. In 1998, the proportion of criminal offences committed by juveniles - under the age of 18 - had climbed to 17 per cent, and Interpol reported that minors were being recruited to take part in organized crime.

INDIGENOUS PEOPLES/ ETHNIC MINORITIES
According to the 2000 census, the population comprised the following ethnic groups: 57.4 per cent Latvian, 30 per cent Russian, four per cent Belorussian, three per cent Ukranian and two per cent Polish. Since 1990, discrimination against Russians has taken the following forms: a 'quota' for the naturalization of minorities, which hinders their access to politics; different rules on property ownership, which puts them at an economic disadvantage; and the restriction on receiving education in their own language. As a result, Russians have come together in their own non-governmental organizations and political parties since 1994, to fight political discrimination and push for the right of their children to be educated in the Russian language.

MIGRANTS/REFUGEES
As of late 2001, Latvia hosted almost no refugees or asylum-seekers. The difficulty of obtaining refugee status has been questioned by the UNHCR since 2002, when the Government decided to modify selection procedures and transferred the responsibility for reaching a decision on applications for asylum to the Interior Ministry. In the view of the UNHCR, the Latvian police lacks the training and experience for the task.

DEATH PENALTY
In May 2003, the country took the first step toward abolishing the death penalty, signing protocol 13 of the European Convention on Human Rights. The last execution was carried out in 1996.

the USSR, in its inaugural session, formally recognized the independence of the Baltic republics.

[18] A new parliament elected in June 1993 appointed Guntis Ulmanis as president. The beginning of an economic liberalization process led to a sharp rise in unemployment. In 1994, foreign investment grew but the economy was still dependent on Russia, its main supplier of fuel and its chief market for exports. Also, in spite of the massive privatization of state companies, the budget and trade balance deficits persisted.

[19] The September 1995 legislative elections did not reveal any clear winner since nine parties obtained between 5 per cent and 16 per cent of the vote. An agreement between the conservative National Block and two left-wing parties led to Andris Skele being appointed Prime Minister in December.

[20] A referendum approved together with the October 1998 elections relaxed the requirement of obligatory fluency in Latvian in order to become a citizen, repealing a restrictive law passed in February. The People's Party, with 21.2 per cent of the vote, beat the Union Latvia's Way, which had garnered 18.1 per cent of the turnout.

[21] A week of commemoration for the victims of Stalin's deportations to Siberia, estimated at 15,000, was carried out in June 2001. The President stressed the need to remember those deportations.

[22] The New Era party, a new center-right party led by Einars Repöe, took the largest share of votes, 23.9 per cent, in the October 2002 parliamentary elections. The party immediately began talks to form a coalition with the other conservative forces. Repöe, famous for having been made president of the Central Bank of Latvia at the young age of 30, pledged to fight the deep corruption in the public administration, rated by Transparency International as among the worst in Europe.

[23] In August 2003, the US suspended military aid to Latvia in response to the Latvian Government's refusal to sign an agreement that would guarantee immunity for US citizens who might be accused of genocide, crimes against humanity and war crimes by the International Criminal Court.

[24] Latvia's admission to the European Union (EU) was approved by 67 per cent of the voters in a referendum on 20 September 2002. The arguments in favor of admission were based on the country's inability to survive in isolation and the assertion that the 'yes' vote represented the final step towards democracy and a break with Latvia's past as a member of the Soviet Union. The 'no' campaign appealed to nationalism and independence, on the grounds that national sovereignty - newly won from Moscow - would be yielded to Brussels.

[25] In February 2004, Prime Minister Repöe was forced to resign after the September 2003 break-up of the ruling coalition. Following the referendum approving Latvia's entry into the EU, three of the four parties in the coalition accused Repöe of using 'extortion, threats and lies' to rule the country. President Vaira Vike-Freiberga appointed Indulis Emsis, of the Peasants Union Alliance-Green Party, as the new Prime Minister.

[26] On 1 May 2004 the country joined the EU. ■

Lebanon / Lubnan

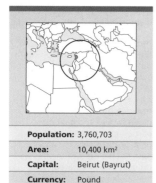

Population:	3,760,703
Area:	10,400 km²
Capital:	Beirut (Bayrut)
Currency:	Pound
Language:	Arabic

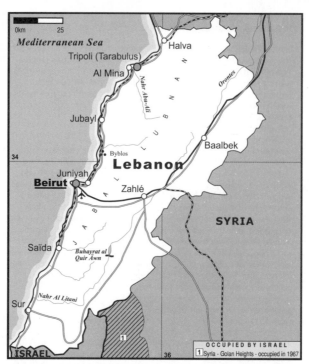

OCCUPIED BY ISRAEL
1 Syria - Golan Heights - occupied in 1967

In 3000 BC, the Hellenes stated that the coastal areas they called Phoenicia were occupied by groups coming from the Persian Gulf. Byblos, the first Phoenician city, was founded between 3050 BC and 2850 BC. Its inhabitants established commercial and religious connections with Egypt as of the 25th century BC.

2   The total destruction of Byblos by fire in 2150 BC, was a consequence of an invasion by the Amorite (a Semitic people), who rebuilt the city and intensified ties with Egypt. In the 18th century BC, new invaders - called Hyksons (a Semitic people) - destroyed the Byblos Amorite government and the Egyptian Middle Kingdom (in 1720 BC).

3   After ousting the Hyksons in 1567 BC, Egypt began its imperial expansion, which created the conditions for the development of Phoenician commerce on a large scale. Under Egyptian guard, Phoenician merchants regularly distributed papyrus, ivory, gems, timber, horses, silk and other goods between the Orient and the Mediterranean Sea.

4   The Egyptian domination of Phoenicia declined during the reign of Ramses III (1187-1156 BC), upon the invasion of Syria by groups from Asia Minor and Europe. Between the withdrawal of Egypt and the advance of the Assyrians (10th century BC), the history of Phoenicia is primarily the history of the city-state of Tyre, that founded colonies on islands and on the African and European coasts of the Mediterranean Sea. The Phoenicians formed connections with the Greeks, to whom they transmitted their arts and their alphabet in the 8th century BC.

5   In 538 BC, the Phoenicians backed the conquest of the Babylonian territories by the Persians, who allowed them to trade there in their own currency. In 332 BC Tyre capitulated to the army of Alexander the Great after resisting for eight months. The surviving local inhabitants were sold into slavery.

6   In 64 BC Phoenicia was incorporated into the Roman province of Syria. During the Roman period, the Phoenician language died out, and Aramaic, spoken by Semitic peoples who arrived from the Orient, was adopted as the local language. During that period, Lebanon produced numerous writers in Greek, among whom the Neo-Platonist Porphyry (3rd century BC) stands out. The Beirut Law School, which flourished in the 6th century, made essential contributions to Roman jurisprudence.

7   Between 608 and 630, Persians and Byzantines disputed supremacy over Lebanon and Syria, whose people accepted the Muslim Arab conquest in 630.

8   The Muslim occupation facilitated the settlement of Arab peoples in southern Lebanon. In the meantime, Monothelitic Christian groups fleeing persecution in Syria settled in the north after being declared heretics in 681. They adopted the Arab language and, together with the indigenous peasants, founded the Maronite Church. Even though they rebelled against the Muslims on various occasions, the Maronites enjoyed their protection against constant attacks from Constantinople until the early 11th century.

9   During the 11th century, the southern Arab settlers, dissidents from the Ismaelian Shi'a Islam (followers of Caliph Ali, 656-661), founded a religion only accessible to the initiated that they called the Druze faith. In the coastal towns the population became mainly Sunni Muslim (orthodox). A great number

of Christians grouped in diverse sects, both in the cities and in the country, where they spoke Arabic as did the Maronites.

10   Throughout a 100-year period (from the late 11th century to 1187) the Muslims lost control of Lebanon to the first Papal crusaders. After it was reconquered, thanks to support from Egypt, the Muslims managed to repel Mongolian attacks. At the end of the 13th century, it became part of the Mamluk state (military oligarchy) of Syria and Egypt, and enjoyed certain autonomy. Trade was promoted, leading to prosperity for the city of Tripoli.

11   After defeating the Mamluks in 1516-17, the Ottoman Turk Empire gained control over Lebanon.

12   Between the 16th and 18th centuries, the Shi'as became secure in the south under the control of Damascus (capital of Syria), as were most of the Druze and some Maronites. Christians and Druze settled along the length of Mount Lebanon, enjoying a semi-autonomous status and finding a common interest in consolidating their power against the coastal Sunni, under the leadership of bureaucrats from Istanbul. The Ottoman Tripoli governed the northern territory of Lebanon.

13   In 1697, the Mount Lebanon notables elected a prince belonging to the Sunni Shihab family, who governed in close cooperation with the Druze until 1842. Throughout this period, European influence over Lebanese politics grew, while the Ottomans suffered the wear of continuous attacks from Egypt. French merchants, settled in

Lebanese ports, influenced the Maronites, who joined the Roman Catholic Church in 1736.

14   As well as sustained economic growth, the 19th century brought social changes and political crises. The Ottoman Turks ended the local rule of the Shihab Dynasty in 1842, irreversibly exacerbating already poor relations between the Maronites (supported by the French) and the Druze (aided by the British). These relations reached a low ebb with the Druze massacre of Maronites in 1860.

15   In 1861, the French, together with the Ottoman authorities, imposed a basic set of laws - which prevailed until World War I (1914-18) - in which the Ottomans established their direct control over Mount Lebanon.

16   In 1923, the League of Nations awarded the administration of Syria and Lebanon to France which, in fact, had never ceased to exercise control over the areas. The first 20 years of French administration were favorable to the Maronites, who made up half of the population of Lebanon. In 1926, the French agreed that the President would be a Maronite, the Prime Minister a Sunni Muslim and the Head of the Senate a Shi'a Muslim.

17   During their first years of management in Lebanon, the French developed production, communications and Jesuit-based education. After the stock market crash and the start of the global depression at the end of the 1920s, both friction and nationalism grew between religious groups in Lebanon. The total withdrawal of the French army took place at the end of 1946. Lebanon immediately became a member of the UN and the Arab League.

18   The Nationalist Maronite President Bishara al-Khuri, elected in 1943 - the year of Lebanon's declaration of independence - was forced to resign in 1952. The escalation of violence, supported by the Syrian Ba'ath Arab Socialist Party (pan-Arabist) since 1949, was the product of the favoritism and corrupt dealings of the Khuri Government (allied with the Sunni) and a controversial constitutional amendment that allowed the President to run for a second term.

19   The presidency of Maronite Camille Chamoun, elected by parliament in place of Khuri, coincided with the presidency of Gamal Abdel Nasser, Egyptian anti-colonialist pan-Arabist leader. When Nasser attempted to seize the Suez Canal from the British in 1956, Chamoun denied Nasser's request to cut off diplomatic ties with Europe. The 1957 parliamentary elections were marked by confrontations between those favoring Lebanon's integration in the United Arab

Life expectancy
73.5 years
2000-2005

GNI per capita
$3,990
2002

Literacy
86% total adult rate
2000

Republic and pro-Western supporters. Parliament was manipulated to ensure the re-election of Chamoun.

[20] By the following year the rioting had escalated into an all-out civil war. In July, Chamoun, who was no longer obeyed by the Muslim members of the army, allowed 10,000 US Marines to disembark. The foreign troops remained in Lebanon until October of that year, when parliament appointed General Chehab as president.

[21] Between 1958 and 1969, the governments of Chehab and subsequently of Helou (both of Maronite extraction) disavowed the traditional system of political-religious representation, and the army was called out to clamp down on the violent protests by civilians.

[22] During that period, due to the influx of peasants - who made up half of the economically active population at the time - Beirut became home to 40 per cent of the country's population. The peasants were forced to abandon their lands which, due to the deterioration resulting from decades of intensive farming, only produced one per cent of GDP. In Beirut, each neighborhood identified with a religious affiliation whose sectarianism was on the rise.

[23] Even though it had received numerous Palestinians evicted from their land by Israel, Lebanon's failure to intervene in the 1967 Arab-Israeli War revived the antagonism among Lebanese people concerning their country's role in the Arab world. The Muslims, most of whom were united under the Muslim Lebanese Nationalist Movement - which backed the Palestine Liberation Organization (PLO) - called for Lebanon's annexation to Syria, as had been demanded prior to the French occupation.

[24] Following the 1973 Arab-Israeli War, Lebanon granted refuge to 300,000 Palestinians who were allowed to settle in the southern part of its territory. Concentrated in camps, between 1973 and 1975 the refugees were the object of segregation and violent attacks by Maronite paramilitary groups. They were also bombed by the Israeli army on several occasions.

[25] The agreement signed by Israel and Egypt in September 1975 raised the possibility that the Palestinians and Lebanon's Muslims would be left on their own by the Arab nations.

[26] In April 1975, a civil war again erupted throughout Lebanese territory. At the beginning of 1976, as a result of the daily armed clashes since the start of the civil war, the central government was dissolved and the Maronites were forced to accept defeat.

[27] According to the Syrian authorities, the prospect of a pro-Palestinian left-wing government in Lebanon in 1976, in addition to the possibility of a division of the Lebanese territory, could trigger an Israeli invasion. As a result, Syrian President Hafez al-Assad backed the restoration of the Maronite Government and refrained from interfering in the attacks on Palestinian refugee camps launched by Maronite militia between July and September.

[28] In September and October 1976, Lebanon was divided by a 'green line' that split Beirut into eastern and western zones, as well as the rest of the country, following the route to Damascus. The northern region remained under the control of the Maronite Government, whose president was Elias Sarkis. The southern region was placed under the administration of left-wing Kamal Jumblat (who was assassinated in March 1977) with the participation of Druzes, Muslims and Palestinians and the intervention of a 30,000-soldier Arab-League peace force.

[29] In 1978 Syria once again gave formal support to the Lebanese pro-Palestinian left. By then the Government was headed by the Phalange Party, which received instructions, weapons and troops from Israel. Notwithstanding the posting of a small contingent by the UN, Israel did not put a halt to its ground forays and bombings in southern Lebanon.

[30] The civil war was a catastrophe for the Lebanese, who witnessed the destruction of Beirut and the country's infrastructure. The tens of thousands of civilian dead included 20,000 Palestinians. In the period between 1975 and 1982, Lebanon's economic losses were almost total, but the oil boom of those years favored some business transactions that partially compensated the deficit.

[31] In July 1981, the Israeli bombing of the PLO general headquarters in West Beirut caused the death of 300 civilians. Despite a conciliatory intervention by the US in June 1982, 60,000 members of the Israeli army invaded Lebanon within the framework of an operation by the Israeli government named 'Peace for Galilee'.

[32] In late August 1982, the PLO withdrew its troops from Beirut under the supervision of US, French and Italian soldiers. On 15 September, in retaliation for the assassination of Phalange President Bashir Gemayel - the sole candidate, elected a few days earlier - the city of Beirut was occupied by Israeli troops. The next day, the Lebanese militia, led by Israeli commanders, burst into the Palestinian refugee camps of Sabra and Shatila and murdered thousands of civilians.

[33] In June 1983, the new Lebanese president, Amin Gemayel (brother of the former president), signed an agreement with Israel which included establishing a 'security zone' (an area of 850 square kms,

IN FOCUS

ENVIRONMENTAL CHALLENGES
Deforestation, desertification and soil erosion are pressing problems in various locations throughout the country. Coastal water is polluted by untreated sewage and occasional oil spills. In Beirut, air pollution from vehicle and industrial emissions is a problem.

WOMEN'S RIGHTS
Women have been able to vote and run for office since 1952. Between 1995 and 2000, women held two per cent of the seats in parliament, and no ministerial or equivalent positions. In 2000, women comprised 30 per cent of the total labor force.

Although in recent years access to education for girls and women has become the same as for boys and men, in 2000 the illiteracy rate stood at seven per cent for women aged 15-24, compared with two per cent for males of the same age group.

Eighty-seven per cent of pregnant women receive prenatal care and 89 per cent of births are attended by qualified personnel*.

CHILDREN
The overall situation with respect to child welfare has improved in the past few years. Ninety-eight per cent of children aged 6-11 attend school, with no gender differentiation, and in 2001, 91 per cent of children between the ages of 3 and 5 were registered in preschool. In the last few years, the mortality rate has decreased considerably both for under-ones and under-fives, as have the malnutrition level and the incidence of infectious-contagious diseases. However, much work is required to rebuild the social sectors and to stimulate economic growth in order for these improvements to be maintained. This includes plans for health and water supply infrastructure, the refurbishing of schools, and improvements in curricula.

After Israeli troops pulled out from southern Lebanon, the area was found to contain many land mines. In 2000 and 2001, some 30 children under the age of 16 died in accidents. Among the survivors, 24 children had lost one or more limbs.

INDIGENOUS PEOPLES/ ETHNIC MINORITIES
In Lebanon the main minorities are religious and/or political groups in addition to ethnic. There are Armenians (4 per cent of the population), Druze (6 per cent), Palestinians (11 per cent), Sunnis (20 per cent), Christian-Maronites (25 per cent), and Shi'a (32 per cent). The future of relations between the groups largely depends on Syria's influence on the country.

Arabic is the common language, and many Maronites also speak French. Maronites have enjoyed a privileged social and political status, especially after World War I, despite being fewer in number than the Shi'a, and a minority religious group as the others are all Muslim.

The Druze practice a branch of Islam that differs from that of the Shi'a and Sunnis in many respects, and have suffered social discrimination because of it in the past.

The '1943 National Pact' - never put down in writing - guarantees the representation of Maronites, Sunnis and Shi'as in the highest-ranking positions in the country (the president is usually Maronite, the prime minister Sunni and the head of Parliament Shi'a). This agreement does not guarantee a position for the Druze, although the commander-in-chief of the armed forces has historically been Druze.

MIGRANTS/REFUGEES
In 2002 the country hosted around 410,000 refugees and people seeking asylum or in need of protection. This amounts to more than 10 per cent of Lebanon's total population. Most of the refugees were Palestinian and 387,000 were registered as such; there were 16,000 unregistered Palestinians and around 3,400 waiting for their status to be acknowledged by UNHCR.

Most Palestinian refugees (more than 220,000) lived in 12 camps throughout the country. The rest of the non-Palestinian refugees were, for the most part, Iraqi or Sudanese.

DEATH PENALTY
In 2003 the death penalty was still applicable in the case of common crimes.

*Latest data available in *The State of the World's Children* and *Childinfo* database, UNICEF, 2004.

Under-5 mortality	Malnutrition	Debt service	Maternal mortality
32 per 1,000 live births 2002	**3%** under-5s 1995-2002	**43.7%** exports of goods and services 2001	**150** per 100,000 live births 2000

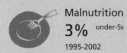

patrolled by Israel) in the south of Lebanon.

³⁴ In July 1984 the Lebanese currency, which had remained relatively stable since the beginning of the war in 1975, crashed, triggering unprecedented inflation. That year, the balance of payments showed a deficit of over $1.5 billion.

³⁵ The Israeli army officially pulled out of Lebanon in 1985 on the condition that the Christian militia would displace the Muslims from southern Lebanon. The Phalangists and the Christians, in general, as well as the Druze-Shi'a alliance and the PLO, divided into factions that supported or opposed Syrian leadership.

³⁶ In September 1988, at the end of Gemayel's presidential term, parliament was unable to reach an agreement on the selection of a new president. Despite continued popular demands that Selim al-Hoss become President, Gemayel appointed Maronite General Michel Aoun as Prime Minister. The country

was governed by two rival administrations: Hoss from West Beirut and Aoun from the eastern portion of the city.

³⁷ In March 1989, Aoun declared what he called the 'liberation war', which aimed to end Syria's presence in Lebanon. In October, the Lebanese parliament met in Saudi Arabia to sign a national reconciliation agreement, granting greater power to the cabinet of ministers. It also determined that there would be an equal number of Christian and Muslim representatives in parliament, and stipulated the partial withdrawal of Syrian troops from Lebanon. General Aoun rejected the agreement because he considered it a 'Syrian ruse'.

³⁸ On 5 November 1989, René Moawad, a Maronite Christian inclined towards an opening to the Arab world, was unanimously elected president. However, Moawad was killed by a car-bomb 17 days before taking office. Two weeks later, Elias Hrawi, another Maronite, was elected president by a

meeting of the Lebanese Parliament held in Syrian-controlled territory.

³⁹ Taking advantage of the new situation created by the Iraqi invasion of Kuwait in 1990, the Syrian-backed forces launched an offensive in October against Aoun, who sought asylum in France upon his defeat. In December, a government of national unity was formed, for the first time since the beginning of the civil war. It incorporated the Lebanese Forces (Christian militia), the Amal (Shi'a), the PSP (Druze), and the pro-Syrian parties.

⁴⁰ The presidents of Lebanon and Syria signed a Brotherhood, Co-operation and Coordination Agreement in Damascus in May 1991. Syria recognized Lebanon as a separate and independent state and agreed to joint co-operation plans in military, cultural and economic matters. In spite of opposition by Israel, the Phalangist party and the Lebanese Forces militia, it was ratified by the majority of the members of the Lebanese Parliament.

⁴¹ In July that year, 6,000 Lebanese army troops took over the territories occupied by the PLO in the south of the country. That month, in spite of the apparent defeat of the PLO, Israel stated that it would not withdraw its forces from the security zone.

⁴² In mid-1992, a general strike against the Government's official economic policy and violent street demonstrations brought about the fall of the pro-Syrian Omar Karame Government. President Elias Hrawi designated Rashid Al Sohl, a moderate Sunni, as the new head of government. He formed his cabinet with an equal number of Christians and Muslims. The August parliamentary elections were boycotted by the Christians. The new parliament included new Hizbullah and Amal representatives. In October, Rafiq al-Hariri, a naturalized Saudi Arabian millionaire, was named Prime Minister.

⁴³ During 1995, government attention was focused on finding a solution to the armed conflict and the reconstruction of Beirut by means of a project that al-Hariri named 'Horizon 2000'. In January of that year, the UN Security Council decided to expand its intervention in the country; simultaneously, Hizbullah and the Southern Lebanon Army resumed their attacks in order to displace Israeli troops and delay negotiations with Syria.

⁴⁴ In the parliamentary elections, held in five rounds between June and September 1996, voter turnout was low and numerous irregularities were reported. The pro-governmental list headed by al-Hariri obtained a majority, and Hizbullah lost one seat.

⁴⁵ The economic situation changed significantly from 1992 to 1996 with the reduction of annual inflation from 170 per cent to 10 per cent and

a 200 per cent increase of foreign currency reserves. Al-Hariri's vision of re-establishing Lebanon as the main financial market in the Middle East began to become reality.

⁴⁶ In October 1998, the National Assembly elected General Emile Lahoud president. Lahoud also had the backing of the Syrian army.

⁴⁷ In 1999, after continuous clashes with Lebanese guerrillas, Israeli Prime Minister Ehud Barak offered a plan to pull out of Lebanese territory, but the plan depended on reaching an agreement with Syria for the return of the Golan Heights. On 25 May 2000, under attack from Hezbollah forces, Israeli troops withdrew from southern Lebanon. The Lebanese Government declared that date a national holiday, the Day of Resistance and Liberation.

⁴⁸ The Israeli Government allowed residents of the former occupied zone to vote for the first time in nearly 30 years in the September parliamentary elections. Christians and Muslims, right and left adhered to former premier al-Hariri's protests against the role of the army in national policy-making and the Government's failure to bring about economic recovery. The multimillionaire and his allies won by a large margin, forcing a reluctant President Lahoud to appoint al-Hariri premier in October.

⁴⁹ In September 2002, to help meet demand for water, the Lebanese Government began work to divert the border Wazzani River - a move that Israel's premier Ariel Sharon warned could start a war.

⁵⁰ In April 2003, Prime Minister al-Hariri tendered his resignation, a decision that some saw as merely tactical, since he was urged by parliament to stay in office and appoint a new cabinet.

⁵¹ During September, Belgium decided to bring charges (for which Lebanon had presented evidence) against Ariel Sharon for his role in the 1982 massacre in Palestinian refugee camps in southern Lebanon. Sharon had been Israel's Minister of Defense at that time. In October, the Arab League condemned the escalation of what it described as state terrorism by Israel, pointing to the constant attacks on Lebanon.

⁵² In November, in the fall-out from the US-led invasion of Iraq, the US Congress adopted economic and diplomatic sanctions against Syria, accusing it of sheltering Iraqi terrorists and of violating Lebanese sovereignty. All Lebanon's political leaders expressed solidarity with Syria, out of fear that Syria could become the next US military target.

⁵³ In October 2004 prime minister Rafik al-Hariri resigned, declining to form a new government that would face international pressure over Syria's interference in Lebanese affairs. ∎

PROFILE

ENVIRONMENT

Lebanon has a fertile coastal plain, situated between the Mediterranean Sea and the Lebanon Mountains, where most of the population lives. The plain has a mild Mediterranean climate marked by winter rains. Between two parallel mountain ranges, the Lebanon Mountains (whose highest peak is Sauda, at 3,083 m) and the Anti-Lebanon Mountains, (with temperate forests on their slopes), lies the fertile Bekaa Valley. Despite the scarce rainfall, the soil is very fertile because of rich alluvial deposits. Along the coast, a dry bush - the *maquis* - grows, and wheat, cotton, olives, oranges and vineyards are cultivated. The cedar tree has become a national symbol. This wood was used to build the Phoenician fleet and temples. Nowadays there are only about 400 cedars left, ranging between 200 and 800 years old.

SOCIETY

Peoples: The Lebanese (80 per cent) are an Arab people. There is a significant Palestinian minority, mostly refugees. There are also Armenians (4 per cent), Syrians, Kurds, Europeans and others (2 per cent). **Religions:** 55.3 per cent Muslim (34 per cent Shi'a and 21.3 per cent Sunni); 37.6 per cent Christian (25.1 per cent Catholic, 19 per cent Maronites and 4.6 per cent Greek-Catholics); 11.7 per cent Orthodox Christian (6 per cent Orthodox-Greeks, 5.2 per cent Apostolic-Armenians); 0.5 per cent Protestant; 7.1 per cent are Druze. **Languages:** Arabic (official); French is widely spoken, Armenian and English are less common. **Main Political Parties:** The Resistance and Development coalition won the last elections; Lebanese Forces and Lebanese Phalange (Maronite Christian); Shi'a organizations Amal and Hizbullah ('party of God'); National Front (Muslim groups; Progressive Socialist Party (mostly Druze). **Main Social Organizations:** Joined Lebanese Employees' and Workers' Syndicates Federation; Lebanon University National Union.

THE STATE

Official Name: al-Jumhouriyah al-Lubnaniyah.
Administrative Divisions: 6 governmental divisions. **Capital:** Beirut (Bayrut) 1,792 ,000 people (2003). **Other Cities:** Tripoli (Tarabulus) 206,500 people; Juniyah 77,400; Zahlah 74,300 (2000).
Government: Emile Lahoud, President since November 1998. Rafiq al-Hariri, Prime Minister since October 2000. Unicameral Legislature: Assembly of Representatives, with 128 members elected for a four-year term by the religious communities. **National Holiday:** 22 November, Independence Day (1943); 25 May, Resistance and Liberation Day (2000). **Armed Forces:** 48,900 personnel (1996). Syrian occupation army: 30,000 soldiers. Other: Hezbollah 3,000.

Lesotho / Lesotho

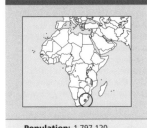

Population:	1,797,120
Area:	30,350 km²
Capital:	Maseru
Currency:	Loti
Language:	Sotho and English

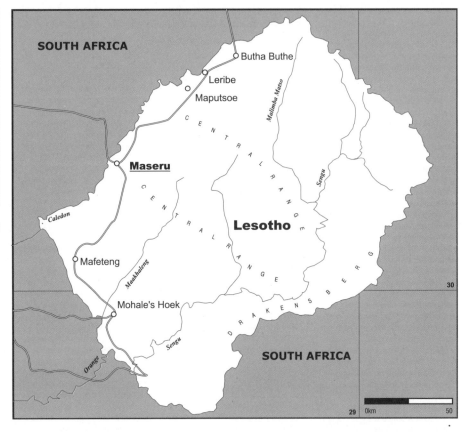

The San, first nomadic peoples of present-day Lesotho, populated southern Africa 2000 years ago. They came into contact with the Bantus, who migrated to these lands around the 4th century AD. By the 16th century, both groups dominated the Caledon river basin.

[2] The Zulu conquests, launched in 1818 by Shaka, affected many Bantu-speaking peoples, among them the North Sotho or Pedi who lived in what became Transvaal in northern South Africa. While some withdrew northwards, the head of the Bakwena tribe, Moshoeshoe, brought other Sothos and groups of dissident Zulus to the Drakensberg mountains. The lengthy war of resistance fought first against the Zulus, and then against the expansionist Boers, consolidated their bonds. These groups gave Moshoeshoe the title of 'Great Leader of the Mountain', and called themselves Basothos.

[3] In the mid-19th century, the Boers (the Dutch colonizers) tried unsuccessfully to force the Basotho to work their land.

[4] Dutch colonization in South Africa seemed destined to fail until the discovery in 1867 of diamonds and, soon afterwards, of gold. The British began to arrive shortly thereafter and in 1868, British missionaries persuaded the Basotho traditional leader Moshoeshoe to turn his kingdom into a protectorate on the pretext of saving the people from the Boers' attempts to convert them into slaves. The territory was administered separately from South Africa, although both were controlled by Britain after the Boer War of 1899-1902.

[5] During World War II (1939-1945), 20,000 Basothos served in the British forces.

[6] Britain had promised the South African government that Basotholand (Lesotho), Bechuanaland (Botswana) and Swaziland would eventually become part of South Africa. However, when the South African Union broke all ties with London in 1961, consolidating apartheid, the British preferred to grant the countries their independence. In 1956, a constitution was promulgated in Basotholand and in 1966 the country proclaimed independence as Lesotho.

[7] As an enclave within South Africa, Lesotho depended on the surrounding country as an outlet for its products. Its currency was the South African rand and South African companies controlled the country's economy and communications.

[8] With imports 10 times higher than exports, the difference was offset by money that migrant workers sent home (45 per cent of the labor force worked in South Africa's gold mines).

[9] This economic situation enabled the opposition Congress Party to win the legislative elections of 1970. Prime Minister Leabua Jonathan dissolved parliament, and sent King Moshoeshoe into exile. He was allowed to return on the promise that he would refrain from political activity.

[10] After the 1976 student uprising in Soweto, South Africa, thousands of young South Africans took refuge in Lesotho. When South

PROFILE

ENVIRONMENT

This small country lies in the Drakensberg mountains, surrounded by South Africa. Landlocked and mountainous, its only fertile land is located in the west where corn, sorghum and wheat are grown. In the rest of the country cattle are raised. Erosion affects 58 per cent of the soil in the lowland areas. Two-thirds of all farmland belongs to migrant laborers; in their absence some is worked by people with little incentive to care for it. The Lesotho Highlands Water Project was developed to make greater use of water from the highlands - the country's main natural resource - through a hydroelectric project that would divert water to South Africa in return for electricity. The first phase was inaugurated in 2004 with the completion of the Mohale Dam. Except for small diamond deposits, there are no mineral resources.

SOCIETY

Peoples: Ethnically homogeneous, the country is inhabited by the Basotho (Sotho) people (85 per cent) and a Zulu minority (15 per cent). There are small communities of Asian and European origin.

Religions: Mainly Christian. Also traditional African beliefs. **Languages:** Sesotho (Southern Sotho) and English (officials), Zulu, Xhosa.
Main Political Parties: Lesotho Congress for Democracy (LCD, former Basotho Congress Party), Basotho National Party, founded in 1958, conservative.
Main Social Organizations: the Lesotho General Workers' Union (LGWU), founded in 1954, is the only central labor organization. Representative Students' Council.

THE STATE

Official Name: Kingdom of Lesotho.
Administrative Divisions: 10 Districts.
Capital: Maseru 170,000 people (2003).
Other Cities: Maputsoe 32,800 people; Mafeteng 29,400 (2000). Government: King Letsie III, Head of State since February 1996. Pakalitha Mosisili, Prime Minister since May 1998. Parliamentary Monarchy. Parliament has two chambers: the 120-member National Assembly and the 33-member Senate.
National Holiday: 4 October, Independence Day (1966). **Armed Forces:** 2,000 troops (1996).

Life expectancy
35.1 years
2000-2005

GNI per capita
$470
2002

Literacy
83% total adult rate
2000

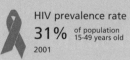
HIV prevalence rate
31% of population 15-49 years old
2001

Africa began its Bantustan policy, Lesotho refused to recognize the puppet state in Transkei. In early 1977, South Africa closed the Lesotho border in retaliation. The economic situation became dramatic and Lesotho appealed for international solidarity.

[11] After Zimbabwean independence in 1980, Lesotho joined the economic integration project promoted by the Front Line states, strengthening relations with Mozambique.

[12] South Africa retaliated by supporting groups opposed to the Jonathan Government, who sought help from the United Nations and the European Economic Community. The official Basotho National Party (BNP) also had to face the opposition of groups linked to the Basotho Congress Party (BCP), led by Ntsu Mokhele.

[13] Incidents triggered by South African military groups trying to prevent African National Congress (ANC) refugees from organizing in Maseru (see South Africa), led to an attack in December 1982 in which 45 people were killed, including 12 children. Three ANC leaders were killed; many of the other victims had no political affiliation.

[14] In 1982, the Government imposed emergency legislation. The army and the police were reinforced and a paramilitary group known as Koeko violently suppressed BCP supporters in the Drakensberg mountains. The BCP abandoned the nationalist stand it had endorsed in the 1970s and fell into deep crisis. Many leaders received aid from South Africa.

[15] In March 1983, an attempt to sabotage the country's main power plant sparked a border incident between troops from Lesotho and South Africa. There was growing South African pressure on Lesotho to sign a non-aggression treaty with Pretoria, similar to those which the apartheid regime had signed with Swaziland and Mozambique. Jonathan was against the treaty, but was forced to compromise due to Lesotho's economic dependence on South Africa.

[16] Towards the end of 1984, the South African Government retained weapons purchased in Europe by Lesotho, and delayed remittances sent home by Lesotho's 400,000 or so migrant workers in South Africa. It also delayed plans to build a dam on the Sengu River, on the border between the two countries. The pressure from South Africa was aimed at intimidating Lesotho's voters and strengthening opposition to the BNP, the conservative Basotho Democratic Party (BDA) and the (ANC-aligned) BCP.

[17] These measures did not satisfy Pretoria and on 20 January 1986 General Justin Lekhanya, head of

IN FOCUS

ENVIRONMENTAL CHALLENGES
Erosion is the country's biggest environmental problem. The scarcity of water is aggravated by a hydropower project in the highlands that would redirect some of the water to South Africa.

WOMEN'S RIGHTS
Women have been able to vote and stand for office since 1965. From 1995 to 2000, the number of seats in parliament held by women amounted to approximately five per cent, and women's share of ministerial or equivalent positions rose to six per cent.

In 2000*, female literacy was equivalent to 127 per cent of the rate among men. That huge gap is not reflected in access to education, which was similar for both sexes.

Prenatal health care in 1995* covered 87.6 per cent of all pregnancies, but still in 2000*, only 59.7 per cent of births were assisted by qualified medical personnel.

CHILDREN
Lesotho is one of the poorest countries in the world. Many child-welfare aspects are in need of improvement. Small advances made in the two last decades are being badly undermined by the HIV/AIDS pandemic.

In 2001, 73,000 children under 14 were orphaned by

AIDS. Life expectancy fell from 53.5 years in 1990 to a projected 35.1 for 2005*.

In 2001, 85,000 children under five were in need of urgent food aid. It was estimated some 30,000 children needed nutritional supplements. More than 4,000 homes and 40 schools were in urgent need of repairs or renovations. More than 2,000 homes and 20 schools needed to improve the quality of their water supplies to prevent the risk of communicable diseases.

INDIGENOUS PEOPLES/ ETHNIC MINORITIES
The majority of the population is Sotho. The San, the original inhabitants of the area, were mainly killed or displaced by the British. Sotho cultural and social traditions remain.

MIGRANTS/REFUGEES
There are no registered refugees in the country. Internal migration is strong, and 13 per cent of males are migrant laborers in South Africa, temporarily in some cases, with better job opportunities.

DEATH PENALTY
In force even for common offenses.

*Latest data available in *The State of the World's Children* and *Childinfo* database, UNICEF, 2004.

Lesotho's paramilitary forces, overthrew the government of Leabua Jonathan and headed the military committee that replaced it.

[18] In 1988, workers living in South Africa sent home remittances totaling more than $350 million, equivalent to 500 per cent of the total value of Lesotho's exports.

[19] In March 1990, the military regime sent King Moshoeshoe into exile, accusing him of hindering the country's democratization program. His son Bereng Mohato Siisa replaced him as Letsie III. On 30 April 1991, another coup toppled Lekhanya's government; a Council was set up chaired by Colonel Elias P Ramaema.

[20] The South African Government blocked remittances from migrant workers in 1991. In May, a demonstration against foreign interference ended with 34 people dead and 425 arrests.

[21] In 1993, a new constitution appointed the King head of state, without granting him either legal or executive powers. In the July legislative elections, the BCP won all the seats. In August, the privatization of six state companies

got under way with a loan from the IMF.

[22] The government plan to integrate the armed wing of the BCP into the army led to the kidnapping and murder of the finance minister by disgruntled soldiers.

[23] The King dissolved Parliament. Demonstrators were injured and killed in the crackdown on protests by soldiers and police. Domestic republican opposition and international pressure forced Letsie III to abdicate in favor of his father. King Moshoeshoe II was restored to the throne in January 1995.

[24] That year, part of the World Bank-financed project to increase the supply of water in the Vaal river valley in South Africa, using the water that descends from the Maloti mountains, was completed.

[25] In January 1996, the King died in a car accident. The Assembly designated his son Letsie III to replace him. Four opposition politicians were charged with treason in March; they were accused of having planned a coup against the Government since September 1995.

[26] Italian non-governmental organizations accused the World Bank in 1998 of violating the human rights of communities and damaging the environment by funding the construction of hydroelectric dams in Lesotho.

[27] The May 1998 elections were won by the ruling party, now called the Lesotho Congress for Democracy (LCD). The opposition, which won one of the 80 disputed seats, complained that the elections were flawed. The Government asked South Africa for help in September when a sector of the army joined the protests. South Africa sent troops who brought the situation under control through the use of force. South Africa charged $1 million for the intervention.

[28] A body with government and opposition representatives was formed in December 1998 to organize new elections and revise the laws governing them. South African troops, along with a small contingent from Botswana, pulled out of the territory by May 1999.

[29] In mid-1999, 12 foreign firms were charged with bribery in tendering for the joint South Africa-Lesotho highlands water project to divert water from the Maloti mountains in the largest infrastructure project in Africa. The process involved expensive contracts for building hydropower dams that would supply electricity to Lesotho and water to South Africa, where industry needed increasing amounts of water. It was estimated the works would damage the environment, crops, pastureland and the local way of life, and would adversely affect the country's mountain water system.

[30] In April 2001, South African President Thabo Mbeki traveled to Lesotho to improve relations between the countries. The visit was not well-received by the opposition due to the 1998 intervention by South African troops.

[31] In March 2002, after months of speculation, the King announced parliamentary elections on 25 May. The LCD obtained 55 per cent of the vote, compared to the PNB's 22 per cent.

[32] In February 2004, Industry and Trade Minister Mpho Malie defied the US and the EU during meetings between African trade ministers and US Trade Representative Bob Zoellick, EU Trade Commissioner Pascal Lamy and WTO Director-General Supachai Panitchpakdi, in Mombasa, Kenya. Malie said Europe and the US could not demand that African countries open up their markets while they continued to protect their own. The ministers aimed to forge a strong common position ahead of the 2005 WTO talks in Hong Kong. ∎

Liberia / Liberia

Population:	3,602,847
Area:	111,370 km²
Capital:	Monrovia
Currency:	Liberian dollar
Language:	English

T he territory of present-day Liberia - formerly known as the Grain Coast - was inhabited by 16 different ethnic groups. The Mande speaking peoples, including the Mandingo, lived in the east and northeast. After the arrival of the Portuguese, Mandingo traders and artisans played an important role as they spread throughout the territory, becoming the principal propagators of Islam.

2   Long before US President Abraham Lincoln freed the slaves in 1865, during the US civil war, emancipated blacks posed a social problem to US southern slaveholders. As a solution to the 'problem' some were 'repatriated'. On the assumption that blacks would feel at home in any part of Africa, plans were made to ship them to the British colony of Sierra Leone.

3   In 1821, the American Colonization Society purchased a portion of Sierra Leone and founded a city which was named Monrovia after James Monroe, president of the United States.

4   Only 20,000 US blacks returned to Africa. The local population distrusted these settlers whose language and religion were those of the colonizers. Supported by US Navy firepower, the newcomers settled on the coast and occupied the best lands. For a long time, they refused to mix with the 'junglemals', whom they considered 'savages'. Today only 20 per cent of the population speak English.

5   In 1841, the US Government approved a constitution for the African territory. It was written by Harvard academics, who called the country Liberia. Washington also appointed Liberia's first African governor: Joseph J Roberts. In July 1847, a Liberian Congress representing the repatriates from the US proclaimed independence. Roberts was appointed president of the country, which had a Harvard-made constitution and a flag which resembled that of the US.

6   The emblem on the Liberian coat of arms reads: 'Love of liberty

brought us here'. However, independence brought little freedom for the original population. For a long time, only landowners were able to vote. The 45,000 descendants of the former US slaves formed the core of the local ruling class, and they had close links to transnational capital. One of the principal exports, rubber, was controlled by Firestone and Goodrich under 99-year concessions granted in 1926. The same was true of oil, iron ore and diamonds. Resistance to this situation was suppressed on several occasions by US Marine interventions to 'defend democracy'.

7   The discovery of extensive mineral deposits, and the use of the

Liberian flag by US ships, heralded a period of economic growth beginning in 1960. This was instantly dubbed an 'economic miracle', but this so-called miracle only reached the American-Liberian sector of the population.

8   The political establishment was shaken in 1979, when a hike in the price of rice triggered demonstrations and unrest. A year later, Sergeant Samuel Doe overthrew the regime of William Tolbert, who was executed by firing squad, along with other 13 members of his government. Doe also suspended the Constitution and banned all political parties.

9   In 1980, the beginning of a democratization process was

announced, followed by the signing of the first agreement with the IMF.

10   Falling exports, increasing unemployment, wage cuts and spiraling foreign debt tipped the country into an enormous crisis that fuelled popular discontent. Between 1980 and 1989, the Doe administration uncovered nine anti-government conspiracies.

11   Elections were held in 1985. With any viable political opposition banned, and accusations of fraud and imprisonment of opposition leaders abounding, Doe obtained 50.9 per cent of the vote. The Liberian People's Party (LPP) and United People's Party (UPP), which represented the major opposition forces, were not allowed to participate.

12   In 1987, most of the funding obtained by the Government came directly from Washington. The US maintained valuable interests in Liberia, such as $450 million in capital goods, military bases, a regional radio station, and a communications base for all US diplomatic services in Africa.

13   In December 1989, the National Patriotic Front of Liberia (NPFL) - unknown until then - launched an armed insurrection led by army officer Charles Taylor. In June 1990, a victory by the NPFL seemed imminent. But in the battle for Monrovia, the rebel front split and an Independent Patriotic Front of Liberia (INPFL) was formed, led by Prince Johnson.

14   In September 1990, President Samuel Doe was murdered by Johnson's troops. In the ensuing confusion, several interim presidents were announced

PROFILE

ENVIRONMENT
The country is divided into three geographic regions: the low, swampy coastal plain, which is home to most of the population; the central plateau, crossed by numerous valleys and covered with dense tropical forests; and the mountainous inland along the border with Guinea. In the fertile coastal areas, rice, coffee, sugarcane, cocoa and palm oil are produced. American companies own large rubber plantations. Liberia is also the leading African iron-ore producer. Deforestation and poaching are unsolved problems. The civil war caused serious damage to the environment.

SOCIETY
Peoples: Most Liberians belong to the Mende, Kwa and Vai ethnic groups, which are split into nearly 30 sub-groups. Of these, the most significant are the Mandingo, Kpelle, Mendo, Kru, Gola and Bassa (the Vai are known for having created one of the few African written languages). The descendants of 'repatriated' US and Caribbean slaves constitute only five per cent of the population. **Religions:** 40 per cent profess traditional African religions; 40 per cent are Christian; 20 per cent are Muslim. **Languages:** English (official), although it is only spoken by 15 per cent of the population. The rest speak African languages (some 30 are spoken throughout the country).

Main Political Parties: National Patriotic Party (NPP); Unity Party; All Liberia Coalition Party; Alliance of Political Parties; United People's Party (UPP); Liberian People's Party (LPP); Liberian Action Party (LAP, Gyude Bryant's party); United Liberation Movement for Democracy in Liberia (ULIMO), founded in 1991 by Samuel Doe's followers; Ulimo-J and Ulimo-K, created after the division of the United Liberian Independence Movement.
Main Social Organizations: Federation of Liberian Trade Unions; National Students Union of Liberia.

THE STATE
Official Name: Republic of Liberia.
Administrative Divisions: 15 Counties.
Capital: Monrovia 573,000 people (2003).
Other Cities: Zwedru 33,800 people; Buchanan 27,000 people (2002). **Government:** Charles Gyude Bryant, interim President since October 2003, was appointed to head a transition government after the resignation in August of Charles Ghankay Taylor, President since July 1997. Bicameral Legislature: the House of Representatives with 64 members elected every six years, and the Senate made up of 26 members elected every nine years.
National Holiday: 26 July, Independence Day (1847).
Armed Forces: Between 11,000 and 15,000 (2001).

Life expectancy
41.4 years
2000-2005

GNI per capita
$150
2002

Literacy
54% total adult rate
2000

IN FOCUS

ENVIRONMENTAL CHALLENGES
The tropical rain forest is subject to deforestation, soil erosion and particularly loss of biodiversity. There is frequent pollution of rivers from the dumping of iron ore tailings and of coastal waters from oil residue and raw sewage.

WOMEN'S RIGHTS
Women have been able to vote and stand for office since 1946. They held eight per cent of seats in Parliament in 1997, the last year for which data was provided.

Domestic violence was widespread throughout the country, but was not perceived as a problem by the Government, the courts or the media.

Prior to the civil war in 1989, approximately 50 per cent of women in rural areas between the ages of eight and 18 had been subjected to genital mutilation. In 2001, a campaign was launched to eradicate this practice, but no significant results were achieved and the Government has provided no support for the campaign.

Women married under traditional laws are considered the property of their husbands and are not entitled to own property or retain custody of their children if their husbands die. In 2001, the Government created the Ministry for Gender and Development, whose mandate included the promotion of the well-being of women and girls. However, there are still clashes between tradition and the state.

CHILDREN
In 2001, 1.05 million of an estimated total of 1.7 million school-age children were enrolled in primary and secondary schools. Half of them were girls. In 2000* the total adult literacy rate stood at 54 per cent: 70 per cent for men, 30 per cent for women (2000)*. During the civil war of the mid-1990s, 50,000 children were killed and many others were wounded, orphaned, or abandoned. A considerable number of orphanages operate in Monrovia.

Unfortunately, various armed militias continue to recruit children. In 2002 and 2003, large-scale campaigns to track down Liberian children were launched in five West African countries. Posters with the pictures of 707 Liberian children were displayed in markets, schools and hospitals with the aim of reuniting the children with their families.

INDIGENOUS PEOPLES/ ETHNIC MINORITIES
Although the constitution bans ethnic discrimination, it also states that only blacks or descendants of blacks may be citizens or own land.

Formerly, the population was made up of more than 16 ethnic groups that spoke different dialects. None of these groups constituted a majority within the population.

Many members of the Muslim Mandingo minority encountered hostility when they sought to return, after the end of the civil war, mainly to villages in Lofa, Bong, and Nimba counties. Many of them were unable to reoccupy their homes, which had been taken over by members of the Lorma, Gio, and Mano minorities who held Mandingos responsible for atrocities committed during the war. Mandingos face arbitrary arrests, ethnic violence and many seek refuge in Guinea.

MIGRANTS/REFUGEES
There were reports that security forces harassed returning refugees and displaced persons, especially in cities in border areas. According to Amnesty International, instead of being able to return to their homes, hundreds of thousands of people are still internally displaced. The number increases day by day as civilians flee their homes in order to avoid killings, rape, beatings, forced labor and looting.

DEATH PENALTY
Liberia maintains and applies the death penalty to punish ordinary crimes.

Latest data available in The State of the World's Children and Childinfo database, UNICEF, 2004.

advances by means of a arms embargo. The two main armed groups and the provisional Sawyer Government agreed a ceasefire in seven months' time and general elections.

[18] In March 1994, the Council of State - a transitional body made up of representatives from the NPFL, ULIMO and the Sawyer administration - took office. Meanwhile, battles raged between rival armed groups and with ECOMOG. Negotiations continued in 1995, Charles Taylor became a member of the Council of State, and a new government was formed.

[19] The civil war broke out again in 1996, particularly in Monrovia. In September, Ruth Perry became the new head of the Council of State, with ECOMOG support. In November, peacekeeping forces began to disarm the rival factions. The war had claimed 200,000 lives. Almost one million Liberians, out of a total population of 2.4 million, had been displaced from their homes or were living as refugees in neighboring countries.

[20] In July 1997, Charles Taylor won the general elections with 75.3 per cent of the vote.

[21] In January 1999, Ghana and Nigeria accused Liberia of backing the brutal Revolutionary United Front (RUF) of Sierra Leone. Taylor accused Guinea of providing financial support to armed groups in the north of Liberia. In April, Guinean troops attacked the city of Voinjama, in Lofa county. The clashes forced more than 25,000 people to flee their homes.

[22] In December 2000, the UN concluded that Taylor was supplying weapons to the RUF in exchange for stolen diamonds. It was estimated that Liberia exported more diamonds smuggled from Sierra Leone than it obtained from its own mines.

[23] In 2001, Amnesty International reported numerous cases of murder and disappearance of human rights activists, journalists and politicians critical of the Government. In March, 40 university students, who had held peaceful anti-government demonstrations on campus, were arbitrarily detained, tortured and raped by special security forces. Many students were forced to take refuge abroad.

[24] That year, the UN imposed an arms embargo on Liberia, boycotted the export of diamonds and prohibited Taylor and members of his inner circle from travelling abroad. In September, Taylor decided to reopen the borders with Guinea and Sierra Leone, which had been closed as a result of mutual accusations by the three neighboring governments that they were supporting the rebel movements within each other's borders.

[25] According to reports by the UN High Commissioner for Refugees (UNHCR), girls and teenagers in the refugee camps of Liberia, Guinea and Sierra Leone were victims of sexual abuse by 67 officials belonging to more than 40 humanitarian organizations, including the UN, several NGOs and officials of the respective governments. The officials traded money or food for sex.

[26] In early 2002, conflict heated up between the Government and the rebel movement Liberians United for Reconciliation and Democracy (LURD), which had led the insurrection in Lofa. In February, as LURD forces were advancing towards the capital, Taylor declared a state of national emergency and human rights abuses worsened.

[27] In March 2003, LURD, which was only 10 km away from Monrovia, called for Taylor's resignation as a condition for a ceasefire agreement. In June, a Sierra Leone court accused Taylor of crimes against humanity and issued an international warrant for his arrest. The rebel groups dominated two-thirds of the territory and hundreds of civilians had been killed but Taylor still refused to resign. In July, Nigerian President Olusegun Obasanjo offered him exile and promised that he would not be handed over to Sierra Leone.

[28] In August, Nigerian peacekeeping troops entered the country, backed by US Marines. On 11 August, Taylor handed over power to Vice-President Moses Blah and left Liberia, siphoning off $100 million, and leaving it, according to the New York Times, the world's poorest nation. The rebel groups signed a peace agreement in Ghana.

[29] In September, the UN approved the creation of the UN Mission in Liberia (UNMIL). It was to be made up of 15,000 peacekeeping troops - mostly from African and Asian countries - and was the largest such force in the world. Its mission was to ensure humanitarian aid and to help 700,000 refugees living in neighboring countries and 450,000 internally displaced - who mainly lived in Monrovia - return to their homes. It was also put in charge of restoring water, electricity, sanitation, education and health services, food supplies, back-paying wages and cutting unemployment, which had soared 85 per cent. More than 40,000 fighters, including 15,000 children, were to be disarmed, educated and reintegrated into society.

[30] On 14 October 2003, Gyude Bryant, a businessman seen as neutral enough to govern until the elections set for October 2005, was appointed President of a caretaker government. ■

simultaneously: Johnson, Taylor, Amos Sawyer and Raleigh Seekie, former head of Doe's presidential guard.

[15] The Economic Community of West African States (ECOWAS) sent a peace force (ECOMOG), composed of 10,000 troops from Nigeria, and supported a provisional government headed by Sawyer (of the LPP) in 1991.

[16] In September 1991, a new rebel movement was formed among Doe's followers: the United Liberation Movement of Liberia for Democracy (ULIMO) that launched attacks from Sierra Leone against the NPFL, based in northeastern Liberia.

[17] In July 1993, a peace agreement was signed in Geneva under the auspices of ECOMOG and the UN, which had hindered military

Libya / Libiyah

Population:	5,768,469
Area:	1,759,540 km²
Capital:	Tripoli (Tarabulus)
Currency:	Dinar
Language:	Arabic

Libya has long been torn between the different political and economic centers of North Africa. The border with Egypt - where two Libyan dynasties ruled between the 10th and 8th centuries BC - permitted cultural contact, but did not lead to a unified state. The establishment of the Carthaginian and then the Roman empires on the western border further stressed this division. After the Arab conquest in the 7th century, Tunisia and Morocco on one side, and Egypt on the other, became the new centers of power, which left Libya's border situation unchanged.

2   The development of maritime trade and the ensuing piracy turned Tripoli (Tarabulus) into one of the major Mediterranean ports, leading to European and Turkish interventions. In 1551, Suleiman the Magnificent annexed the region to the Ottoman Empire. However, a weakened central authority gave increasing autonomy to the governors, precipitating independence movements. Piracy was used as a pretext to bomb Tripoli in 1804 (the first US foreign military intervention).

3   In 1837, Muhammad al-Sanussi founded a clandestine Muslim brotherhood (the Sanussi religious sect) which promoted resistance to Turkish domination, and was also active in Egypt. With the decline of the Ottoman Empire, Italy declared war on Turkey in 1911 and seized the Libyan coast, the last Turkish possession in North Africa. With the outbreak of World War I, Italy occupied the ports of Tripoli and Homs (Al-Khums) while the rest of the territory remained autonomous. At the end of the war, Italy faced the resistance led by Sidi Omar al-Mukhtar, which finally ended in 1931, when al-Mukhtar was captured and executed, and Libya was annexed by the Italian Empire.

4   From Egypt and Tunisia, the Sanussi brotherhood remained active and co-operated with the Allies in World War II. Muhammad Idris al-Sanussi, leader of the brotherhood, was recognized as Emir of Cyrenaica by the British. At the end of the war, the country was divided into a British zone (Tripolitania and Cyrenaica) and a French zone (Fezzan) governed from Chad. In 1949, a UN resolution restored legitimate union to the region and established the independent nation of Libya, with Idris al-Sanussi on the throne.

5   Idris based his power on religious authority and the support of powerful Turkish-Libyan families from the US and Britain (both holding military bases in the country) and transnational oil companies that had settled in the country, as the oil began to flow in great quantities in 1960.

6   In 1966, Muammar al-Qadhafi, the son of Bedouin nomads, founded the Union of Free Officers while studying in London. (He had joined the army as a young nationalist). He returned to Libya and on 1 September 1969 he led an insurrection in Sabha that swiftly overthrew the King.

7   Qadhafi's Revolutionary Council proclaimed itself Muslim, Nasserist and socialist; it eliminated all US and British military bases in Libya, and imposed severe limitations on the almost 60 transnational corporations operating in the country. The production of petroleum and its by-products was placed under state control, although the Government did not totally sever ties with the foreign corporations.

8   Qadhafi launched an ambitious development program, with special emphasis on agriculture. Each rural family was allotted 10 hectares of land, a tractor, a house, tools, and irrigation facilities. Over 1,500 artesian wells were drilled and two million hectares of desert began to be artificially irrigated.

9   Due to its rapid growth, Libya drew workers from other Arab countries and technicians from all over the world. In 1973, following publication of Qadhafi's Green Book - in which he expounds his ethical and political theories, rejecting capitalism and Marxism - he created a complex structure of popular participation through people's committees and a People's General Congress.

10   In the cities, he created a social security system, with free medical assistance and family allowances to encourage large families. He granted industrial workers 25 per cent participation in company profits. According to official records, industrial investment was 11 times

PROFILE

ENVIRONMENT

Most of the country is covered by desert. The only fertile lands are located along the temperate Mediterranean coast, where most of the population live. There are no perennial rivers and rain is scarce. The country has significant oil deposits. Water is scarce and most of it is pumped from underground deposits. One of the largest hydraulic development projects in the world has partially solved this problem. Atmospheric pollution is caused by gases from oil refining. Desertification and erosion are growing.

SOCIETY

Peoples: The indigenous population was Berber. Today, Arabs account for 90 per cent of the population. There is a Berber minority that maintains its traditions. Key immigrant communities: Egyptian, Sudanese, Chadian, Italian, Greek, Pakistani, Turk, Korean and others.
Religions: Islam (official), Sunni. There is a small Christian minority. **Languages:** Arabic (official); regional variations of Berber; languages of the immigrant communities; Italian and English.
Main Political Parties: The Socialist Party of Libya is in power. Other parties are banned. According to Qadhafi's 'Green Book', Libya is headed toward a direct democracy, in which there are no intermediaries. The new political organization is based on the Basic People's Congresses, directly elected, which elect the members of the 46 People's Congresses. These, in turn, select the members of the General People's Congress, the highest government body.
Main Social Organizations: Mass organizations of workers, peasants, students and women.

THE STATE

Official Name: Jamahiriya Al-Arabiya Al-Libiya Al-Shabiya Al-Ishtirakiya Al-Uzma (The Great Socialist People's Libyan Arab Jamahiriya).
Administrative Divisions: 3 provinces, 10 counties and 1,500 communes. **Capital:** Tripoli (Tarabulus) 2,006,000 people (2003). In January 1987, Qadhafi appointed Hun, a village 650 Km to the southeast of Tripoli, as the administrative capital of the country. **Other Cities:** Benghazi 1,041,000 people; Misratah 179,100; az-Zawiyah 175,100 (2000).
Government: Colonel Muammar al-Qadhafi, leader of the Revolution and commander-in-chief of the People's Armed Forces, has been Head of State since September 1969. He named Zintani Muhammad az-Zintani, Secretary of the General People's Congress in 1992, and Mubarak al-Shamikh as the Secretary of the People's Committee in 2000. Single-chamber legislature: the General People's Congress is the highest Government body, with 2,700 representatives of the People's Congresses.
National Holiday: 1 September, Revolution Day (1969). **Armed Forces:** 65,000 actives (1996); 40,000 reservists, popular militia (1993). Other: Revolutionary Guards 3,000.

Life expectancy
72.8 years
2000-2005

Literacy
80% total adult rate
2000

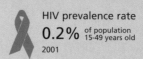
HIV prevalence rate
0.2% of population 15-49 years old
2001

IN FOCUS

ENVIRONMENTAL CHALLENGES
Desertification and the scarcity of natural sources of drinking water are the most pressing problems to be dealt with. The plan to pipe water to the coastal cities from the extensive underground water deposits in the Sahara desert is the most ambitious such project in the world.

WOMEN'S RIGHTS
Women have been able to vote and run for office since 1964.

In 2000, women comprised 23 per cent of the labor force. The maternal mortality rate amounts to 120 for every 100,000 births*.

Mistreatment of women is still a major problem. However, the reports on domestic violence do not reflect that reality. Few complaints are filed, among other reasons because tradition exercises strong pressure to keep family affairs private.

Some groups located far from urban areas continue to practice female genital mutilation on girls.

Although the 1969 constitution ensures equal conditions for women, discrimination persists. For example, women need permission from their husband or another male relative to leave the country.

Female emancipation is a generational phenomenon: women under 35 tend to have modern attitudes toward family and work, something not observed in older women.

There have been reports of Sudanese girls being trafficked and sold as slaves in Libya.

CHILDREN
Military service is compulsory for adults over 18, and all teenagers over 14 receive pre-military training at school. In 1979, a female military academy was created and women take an active part in the army. The illiteracy rate is 32 per cent among women over 15, compared to 9 per cent among men (2000)*. The Government subsidizes education, which is mandatory until the age of 15. There have been cuts in the health budget in recent years.

INDIGENOUS PEOPLES/ ETHNIC MINORITIES
The largest minority are the Berber, divided in three groups: Luata, Nefusa and Adassa. They live in the northeastern part of Libya, near the Mediterranean Sea; some live among the Jebel Nefusa plateaus and hills, as well as in the Fezzan Oasis in the southwest of Libya. The Government manipulates the clans, who are in need of funds and are keen on gaining government posts. It also

tries to keep the groups separated from each other.

There have been frequent allegations of discrimination, especially against the Tuareg and Tamazigh.

MIGRANTS/REFUGEES
There are around 2.5 million foreign workers in Libya. Africans, especially, have been object of resentment and violence.

The Government expelled hundreds of thousands of African immigrants, abandoning them in the desert on the border with Nigeria and Chad.

The law does not grant asylum or refugee status, but there are around 30,000 Palestinians and 3,000 Somalis living in Libya. In 2001, the UNHCR aided the most vulnerable refugees, and the Government co-operated by granting free accommodation to around 850 people.

DEATH PENALTY
Libya retains the death penalty. Death sentences are still handed down, although there have been no recent reports of executions.

*Latest data available in *The State of the World's Children* and *Childinfo* database, UNICEF, 2004.

greater than under the monarchy and agricultural investment was 30 times greater. In just five years, Libya ceased to be the poorest nation in North Africa, and achieved the highest per capita income on the continent, $4,000 per year.

[11] In 1977, the country changed its name to the Socialist People's Libyan Arab Jamahiriya (meaning mass state in Arabic). But while Qadhafi achieved ample positive results internally, similar fruits were not achieved in the field of diplomacy. Attempts at integration with Syria, Egypt and Tunisia met with failure. Qadhafi criticized the rapprochement between Egypt and Israel, which led to friction with the Saudi monarchy, the Emirates and Morocco.

[12] From 1980, Libyan diplomacy and foreign relations focused on sub-Saharan Africa and Latin America. The Government supported the Polisario Front in Western Sahara and participated directly in the civil war in Chad, defending the Transitional Government of National Union, led by Goukouni Oueddei.

[13] US President Ronald Reagan undertook an international campaign to demonstrate the Libyan leader's alleged ties to world

terrorism. In August 1981 in the Gulf of Sidra, the US shot down two Libyan planes. Qadhafi avoided any violent response to the provocation, winning the sympathy of the conservative Arab regimes which had until then been hostile to his government.

[14] In addition to imposing an economic embargo, the US bombed Tripoli and Benghazi in 1986, in an attempt to eliminate Qadhafi.

[15] In November 1991, US and British courts charged the Libyan Government with two terrorist attacks in 1988 against commercial flights: one over Lockerbie, Scotland, involving a Pan Am airliner, which left 270 dead, including 189 Americans. The second was over Nigeria, against a UTA plane, with a death toll of 170. Interpol issued international arrest warrants for two Libyan agents accused of both attacks. In January 1992, Libya announced it was willing to cooperate with the UN in clarifying the bombings.

[16] Qadhafi, however, rejected an extradition request from the UN, and unsuccessfully proposed a trial in Tripoli. The UN gave an ultimatum, demanding that Qadhafi explicitly renounce 'terrorism' by 15 April 1992. When

the deadline expired, the EU and the seven leading industrialized nations adopted economic sanctions. Qadhafi appealed - unsuccessfully - before the International Court of Justice. In 1994, the UN tightened the embargo.

[17] The isolation, however, did not impede the growth of the private sector or foreign investment, mainly in oil projects. One section of the pipeline designed to bring water to remote desert communities began to function in 1996.

[18] In 1998, the Movement of Non-Aligned Countries and the Organization of African Unity supported a Libyan request to try the two suspects of the Lockerbie bombing in a neutral country. After lengthy multilateral negotiations, the UK and the US proposed that the two accused be tried in The Hague by Scottish judges under Scottish law. The proposal was accepted in March 1999, and the UN Security Council lifted the sanctions in April.

[19] In September 1999, more than 20 African and Arab leaders gathered in Tripoli to commemorate the 30th anniversary of the Libyan revolution. Fifteen years after having severed diplomatic relations,

London sent its ambassador to Tripoli in December.

[20] Libya took advantage of this to launch a diplomatic offensive in the region, offering itself as mediator in the Sudan conflict and resuming relations with Chad. In March 2000, Washington sent a high level delegation to study the lifting of obstacles to investments and trips to Libya, banned since 1981.

[21] In September 2000, clashes between Libyans and illegal immigrants left 50 dead. There were 1,000,000 immigrants from other parts of the continent at that time.

[22] After the foiled coup in Central African Republic (CAR) in May 2001, the Qadhafi Government dispatched troops in order to protect President Ange Fèlix Patassé. In November, Patassé once again requested Libya's help. Once peace was restored, CAR demanded the withdrawal of Libyan soldiers.

[23] The US extended sanctions imposed on Libya and Iran for five more years in August 2001, even though it lacked European support. It argued that the sanctions were aimed at preventing the financing of terrorist groups in those countries.

[24] In early 2001, the Scottish court acquitted one of the Lockerbie suspects: Al Amin Khalifa Fhimah. The other, Abdelbaset al-Megrahi was sentenced to life imprisonment. In January 2002, Tripoli sought an appeal, but it was denied. Qadhafi accused the Court of being under the influence of Washington and London and of lacking sufficient evidence.

[25] In April 2002, six Bulgarian and one Palestinian doctors accused of 'deliberately' infecting 400 children with HIV in 1999 as part of an alleged conspiracy led by the CIA against Libyan security were awaiting sentencing. (If declared guilty, they could be sentenced to life in prison).

[26] In January 2003, Libya assumed the chair of the UN Commission on Human Rights, despite US opposition.

[27] After acknowledging its responsibility in the Lockerbie attacks in a letter to the UN Security Council, the Libyan Government established a $2.7 billion indemnification fund in August 2002 for the victims' families. In September, the UN Security Council lifted the sanctions against Libya with 13 votes in favor. France and the US abstained.

[28] In December 2003, the Qadhafi Government announced that it would abandon its programs to develop weapons of mass destruction.

[29] In January 2004, Libya agreed to compensate the victims of a French aircraft shot down in the desert in 1989. ∎

Liechtenstein / Lietchtenstein

Population:	34,077
Area:	160 km²
Capital:	Vaduz
Currency:	Swiss franc
Language:	German

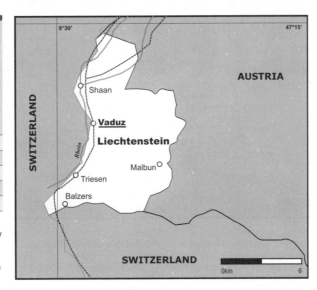

The territory of the present-day principality of Liechtenstein was inhabited by Neolithic times. The Rhaetians settled there in 800 BC, remaining until the Romans arrived in 15 BC. A Roman road traversed the country from north to south and was protected from German incursions by the fortifications of Schaan.

2 In the 4th century AD, Saint Luzius brought Christianity to the province of Churrhaetia. A century later, the Germans invaded the country from the north and eliminated the Romans. Years later, the region passed into the hands of the Germanic Dukedom, forming part of the country of Lower Rhaetia, producing the two feudal domains of Vaduz and Schellenberg, ruled by the Counts of Werdenberg-Vaduz, the Barons of Brandis, the Counts of Sulz and the Counts of Hohenems.

3 Prince Johann Adam of Liechtenstein, founder of the current principality, bought the Schellenberg domain in 1699 and that of Vaduz in 1712. By combining hereditary rights from these Germanic domains he gained a seat and a vote in the Imperial Council of Princes.

4 The principality of Liechtenstein was established on 23 January 1719, when Emperor Charles VI of Germany converted the two counties into a 'principality of the empire' for his servant Anton Florian of Liechtenstein.

5 In 1806 Liechtenstein was made part of the Confederation of the Rhine - a league of 16 states belonging to the German Empire - by Napoleon. He guaranteed them independence and they recognized him as protector.

6 The principality entered the Germanic Confederation under the Congress of Vienna in 1815 and remained there until this was dissolved in 1866, breaking the last juridical links with Germany. Liechtenstein has had no army since 1868. Between 1852 and 1918 (end of World War I) there was a tariff agreement with the Austro-Hungarian empire.

7 Beginning with the reign of Johann (1858-1929), Liechtenstein saw prosperity. Modern development of the country really began with the promulgation of the constitution of 1862 and was reinforced by the Democratic-Liberal Magna Carta of 1921, still in place today. Under Johann's leadership, Liechtenstein signed a tariff agreement with Switzerland in 1923 and in 1924 adopted the Swiss franc as legal currency.

8 Neutrality during World War II saved the collection of works of art that the family held in its Vienna palace, which was removed after the conflict, thus avoiding expropriation by the Czech communist regime.

9 Liechtenstein - the only independent principality of the old Austro-Hungarian Empire - began its process of integration with the rest of Europe and the world after World War II.

10 In 1950 it became a member of the International Court of Justice at the Hague.

11 The country entered the Council of Europe in 1975.

12 Prince Franz Josef II, the first monarch to live permanently in Liechtenstein, died on 13 November 1989, after a reign of 51 years. He was succeeded by his oldest son, Hans-Adam II.

13 Mario Frick (28) became Prime Minister after the 1993 elections.

14 Liechtenstein joined the United Nations in 1990, the European Free Trade Area (EFTA) in 1991 and the European Economic Zone in 1995.

15 In the late 20th century, the combination of low taxes, simple procedures and the protection of bank secrecy laws turned Liechtenstein into a controversial tax haven that was even involved in a money laundering scandal in the 1990s.

16 Mario Frick was re-elected prime minister in the 1997 elections.

17 In 2000 a report by the German secret service (BND) stated that Liechtenstein was the leading money-laundering location in Europe, and among the leaders in the world. The Financial Action Task Force on Money Laundering (FATF) included the principality on a list of money-laundering havens.

18 The Progressive Citizens Party won the elections in February 2001. Otmar Hasler became Prime Minister in April.

19 New fiscal legislation enabled the principality to be removed from the FATF's black list in 2001. However, that year it received 107 requests from abroad for judicial co-operation on matters of economic or financial misconduct. For the first time, the principality's justice system enforced a legal sentence related to the drug trade.

20 Despite the new controls, Liechtenstein's neighbors and international organizations have pressed it to further modify its legislation, as they believe the State still maintains openings for money-laundering and tax evasion. But bankers - including the Prince himself, head of the LGT Bank, the biggest in Liechtenstein - said further banking reform would endanger most of the $70.3 billion held in the principality. Hans-Adam has threatened to move to Austria and take his family assets abroad if the legal reforms demanded threaten his business interests.

21 A March 2003 referendum granted new political powers to Prince Hans-Adam.

22 In August that year the Prince announced he would pass power on to his son, Prince Alois, on 15 August 2004, although he would remain head of state. ■

PROFILE

ENVIRONMENT
This small principality lies between Switzerland and Austria, in the Rhine valley. Wheat, oats, rye, corn, grapes and fruit are produced. 38 per cent of the land is pasture. In recent years, the principality has been transformed into a highly industrialized country, producing textiles, pharmaceutical products, precision instruments and refrigerators among other items.

SOCIETY
Peoples: German 95 per cent; Italian and other 5 per cent.
Religions: Catholic 80 per cent; Protestant 6.9 per cent; other 5.6 per cent.
Languages: German (official).
Main Political Parties: The Progressive Citizens Party (FBP); Patriotic Union (VU); Free List, green.
Main Social Organizations: Trades Union Association (artisans and traders), Agricultural Union.

THE STATE
Official Name: Fürstentum Liechtenstein.
Administrative Divisions: 11 communes.
Capital: Vaduz 5,000 people (2003).
Other Cities: Schaan 5,143; Balzers 3,752; Triesen 3,586 (1995).
Government: Liechtenstein is a constitutional monarchy. Prince Hans-Adam II, Head of State since 13 November 1989; to hand over power to his son, Prince Alois, in August 2004. Otmar Hasler, Head of Government since April 2001. Government functions are carried out by a FBP and VU coalition. Single-chamber legislature: Parliament with 25 members elected every four years. Diplomacy: A member of the European Council, Liechtenstein has a customs and monetary alliance with Switzerland, which is its representative abroad. **National Holiday:** 14 February.

Lithuania / Lietuva

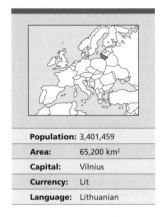

Population:	3,401,459
Area:	65,200 km²
Capital:	Vilnius
Currency:	Lit
Language:	Lithuanian

Lithuanians have lived along the shores of the Baltic Sea since long before the Christian era. Protected by the forests, Lithuanian tribes fiercely resisted German efforts to subdue them in the 13th century, and united under the leadership of Mindaugas, who was crowned king by Pope Innocent IV in 1253.

[2] In the 14th century, Lithuania began its eastward and southern expansion, going into Belarusian lands. Gediminas built the Grand Duchy of Lithuania, which extended from the Baltic Sea to the Black Sea, with its capital at Vilnius. In 1386, Jagiello, Gediminas' grandson, married the Queden of Poland, thus uniting the two kingdoms.

[3] In 1480 with the coronation of Ivan III of Muscovy as the sovereign of all Russia, a new and greater threat emerged for historic Lithuania. Nevertheless, the Lithuanian-Polish union reached its peak in the 16th century, when it was unrivalled in Europe as a political system (see Poland), only to fall in the 17th century, in the course of a series of devastating wars with Sweden, Russia and Turkey as well as peasant rebellions within.

[4] In the 1772 and 1793 partitions of Poland among Russia, Prussia and Austria, Russia kept only Belarus. But the Polish state disappeared in 1795, and all of Lithuania was in Russian hands in 1815. That same year, the Congress of Vienna granted the Russian Emperor the additional titles of King of Poland and Grand Prince of Lithuania.

[5] The czarist regime treated Lithuania as though it were a part of Russia, calling it the Northwest Territory after 1832. Between 1864 and 1905, Russification extended to all aspects of life: books printed in Lithuanian had to use the Cyrillic alphabet, and Catholics were persecuted.

[6] During World War I, Germany occupied a major part of Lithuania. In 1915, a congress - authorized by the occupying Germans - elected the 20-member Council of Lithuania.

The 214 delegates to the congress called for the creation of an independent Lithuanian state within its 'ethnic borders' and with Vilnius as its capital. On 16 February 1918 the Council declared Lithuania's independence and terminated all political ties with other nations.

[7] In 1919, the Red Army entered Vilnius and formed a communist government, which was later forced to withdraw. The new head of the Polish State, Josef Pilsudski, tried to re-establish the former union, but failed. In the end, the League of Nations and the European powers agreed to the separation of Poland and Lithuania in 1923, but Lithuania refused to recognize this line of demarcation.

[8] In 1926, Lithuania and the Soviet Union signed a non-aggression treaty. Lithuania, Latvia and Estonia signed a treaty of good

will and co-operation in Geneva in 1934.

[9] In September 1939, a secret German-Soviet non-aggression treaty brought Lithuania within the USSR's sphere of influence. In October, a mutual assistance treaty was signed in Moscow; according to its terms, Lithuania was forced to accept the installation of Soviet garrisons and air bases on its soil. In 1940, the Soviet Army occupied Lithuania and a number of local political leaders were arrested and deported, while others fled toward Western Europe.

[10] In August 1940, during the term of Prime Minister Justas Paleckis, Lithuania was incorporated as a constituent republic of the USSR. After German occupation in 1941, the Baltic States and Belarus became the German province of Ostland.

[11] During the German occupation, 190,000 Jews were sent to concentration camps. Some 100,000 residents of Vilnius - a third of that city's population, most of them Jews - were killed. Vilnius was known as the 'Jerusalem of Lithuania' and had been considered to be one of the world's most important centers of Jewish culture.

[12] Vilnius was reconquered by the Red Army in 1944 and Lithuania was once again occupied by the Soviets. Almost 20,000 Lithuanians took refuge in Eastern Europe, while a new period of Sovietization began that included deportations to northern Russia and Siberia, amid the forced collectivization of agriculture.

[13] Religious persecution continued even after Stalin's death in 1953. Thus the resistance of the Catholic Church became identified with the nationalist movement. In 1972, the 'Lithuanian Catholic Church Chronicle' (banned by the Government) was published by the Lithuanian Movement for Human Rights.

[14] With the democratization process initiated by Mikhail Gorbachev in the USSR, Lithuania began a period of intense political agitation. In June 1998, the Lithuanian Movement to Support Perestroika (restructuring) was founded; its Executive Committee adopted the name Sejm - the name of the Lithuanian Parliament at the time of independence - also known as Sajudis. The Sajudis installed a kind of 'shadow' government, and demanded a return to the peace

PROFILE

ENVIRONMENT

Situated on the eastern coast of the Baltic Sea, Lithuania is characterized by gently rolling hills and flat plains. The largest of the Baltic 'mini-states', it has more than 700 rivers and streams, abundant forests and around 3,000 lakes. The Nemunas river, which crosses the country from east to west, is an important shipping route. Lithuania has a moderate climate, with an average temperature of around 18° C in the summer, and sub-zero temperatures in winter. Forty-nine per cent of the land is arable; the chief crops are grains, potatoes and vegetables. There are large numbers of livestock. Among the country's leading industries are the food and machine manufacturing industries, as well as the export of energy. Seventy per cent of the country's energy is generated by a nuclear plant of the same type as the one in Chernobyl, Ukraine - the site of the 1986 nuclear accident. Since the 1980s, pollution has increased, especially bacterial pollution of rivers and lakes, which has been linked to the increase in infectious childhood diseases, particularly in the first years of life.

SOCIETY

Peoples: 83 per cent of the population is Lithuanian; the rest include Russians, 8.4 per cent; Poles, 7.0 per cent; Belarusians 1.5 per cent; Ukrainians 1.0 per cent and smaller populations of Germans, Jews,

Latvians, Tatars, Armenians, Moldovans, Roma, Uzbeks and Azeris. **Religion:** Catholic majority (80 per cent); there are Protestant minorities. There are also Orthodox Russians; some evangelical minorities; plus Muslims, Jews and people with no religion. **Languages:** Lithuanian (official); Russian, Polish. **Main Political Parties:** The present Government is made up of a convention of liberal parties (Lithuanian Liberal Union, New Union and Centre Union of Lithuania); Lithuanian Democratic Labor Party (former Communist Party); Social Democrat Party; Russian Union of Lithuania (minority); Conservative Party; Christian Democrat Union. **Main Social Organizations:** Lithuanian Green Movement, Human Rights Association.

THE STATE

Official Name: Lietuvos Respublika.
Administrative Divisions: 44 Districts.
Capital: Vilnius 549,000 people (2003).
Other Cities: Kaunas 411,600 people; Klaipeda 202,400; Siauliai 146,300; Panevezys 133,600 (2000).
Government: Parliamentary republic. Valdas Adamkus, president since July 2004. Algirdas Brazauskas, prime minister since July 2001. Single-chamber parliament (Seimas) made up of 141 members. **National Holiday:** 16 February, Independence Day (1918). **Armed Forces:** 5,100 (1996). Other: Coast Guard, 5,000.

Life expectancy
72.7 years
2000-2005

GNI per capita
$3,660
2002

Literacy
100% total adult rate
2000

HIV prevalence rate
0.1% of population 15-49 years old
2001

treaties that recognized the country's independence.

15   In July, the Lithuanian Freedom League (LFL) emerged from underground activity. The LFL, which dates back to 1978, called for immediate withdrawal of Soviet troops from the country, and the independence of Lithuania, aiming in the long term at integration with the European Union. Police brutality toward participants of a demonstration sponsored by the LFL triggered joint protest actions with the Sajudis, and led to a crisis within the Lithuanian Communist Party leadership.

16   The Lithuanian Government opted not to follow the example set by Estonia's Supreme Soviet, which had made a unilateral decision on the question of sovereignty. Instead, Lithuanian authorities began making concessions to local movements, legalizing the use of the flag and the national anthem, designating Independence Day as a holiday and authorizing public commemoration of that day. In addition, Lithuanian was adopted as the country's official language, and the Vilnius Cathedral and other churches were reopened.

17   In February 1989, the Sajudis demanded a free and neutral Lithuania, within a demilitarized area. That month the first secretary of the CP and the Sajudis attended the official commemoration of the country's independence, side by side. In December, Lithuania's Supreme Soviet did away with the article of the constitution which assigned the CP a leading role; the first decision of its kind within the USSR.

18   In January 1990, Soviet President Mikhail Gorbachev announced in Vilnius that the details of a future relationship with the Union would be established through legislation. In March, the Lithuanian Parliament proclaimed the nation's independence, effective immediately. In September 1991, the new Council of State of the USSR accepted the independence of the three Baltic States, which were immediately recognized by several countries and by the UN.

19   In August 1991, after the failed coup against Gorbachev in the USSR, the Lithuanian Parliament banned the Communist Party, the Democratic Workers' Party and the Lithuanian Communist Youth organization. The following month, President Vytautas Landsbergis issued a call, before the UN, for the withdrawal of Soviet troops from Lithuania.

20   The new constitution was approved by a referendum on 25 October 1992. That year, GNP diminished by over a third and inflation reached almost 1,000 per cent.

IN FOCUS

ENVIRONMENTAL CHALLENGES
Soil and groundwater have been significantly polluted by oil by-products and chemicals. Since 1980 an increase in pollution of the country's aquifers has been reported, especially of bacterial origin, which could threaten a spread of disease through rivers and lakes.

WOMEN'S RIGHTS
Lithuanian women have been able to vote and run for office since 1918. Women have held 18 per cent of seats in Parliament since 1995. Women's share of ministerial or equivalent positions rose from 0 to 6 per cent. In 2000 women comprised 48 per cent of the workforce. That year, female unemployment reached 13 per cent, while male unemployment stood at 17.8 per cent. Since the 1990s, Lithuania has been recognized as a country of origin, destination and transit of women forced into prostitution. The Government stated the need for international assistance at the Council of Europe.

CHILDREN
In 2002, 30,000 children were born. Eight out of every 1,000 die before their first birthday*. Primary school enrolment is 95 per cent of school-age children*. Most of the Lithuanian population is literate. Sexual abuse of youngsters is a problematic issue, particularly within the family. On-line advertisements offering Lithuanian children for adoption, and explaining the legal procedures to be followed, are common.

INDIGENOUS PEOPLES/ ETHNIC MINORITIES
Poles and Russians make up national minorities, and the Roma/gypsies are an ethnic minority. None of these groups has had serious problems with the Government or with Lithuanian society as a result of their ethnic or national origin. Since 1990, Lithuanian policies on minorities have been regarded as the most liberal in the area. A small group of organizations is working to promote Russian culture in Lithuania. Poles live mostly in Vilnius and stand out due to their language, culture and religion. Their most extreme demands include the reinstatement of property rights over land. Their most common demands are related to greater dissemination of Polish language and culture.

The greatest difficulty for the integration of the Roma into Lithuanian society is their nomadic character. Most of the adults lack identity documents and are illiterate. They generally speak Russian. Roma children are not encouraged to finish school and their linguistic differences cause them problems.

MIGRANTS/REFUGEES
In late 2002, Lithuania hosted over 200 refugees and asylum-seekers. During that year, another 300 people requested asylum, mostly Chechens from Russia and a group of Afghans.

A total of 325 cases were considered and 220 were granted temporary residence, 25 were rejected as manifestly unfounded and only one obtained refugee status on first petition. Almost 30 Chechens were sent to Belarus, which the UNHCR considered a violation of the UN Convention on Refugees.

DEATH PENALTY
The death penalty was abolished for all crimes in 1998. The last execution took place in 1995.

*Latest data available in *The State of the World's Children* and *Childinfo* database, UNICEF, 2004.

21   In February 1993, the leader of the former Communist Party, Algirdas Brazauskas, was elected President with 60 per cent of the vote. In 1993 and 1994, Brazauskas continued with the transition policy toward a market economy.

22   In 1995, around 80 per cent of Lithuanians were estimated to be 'poor', 15 per cent 'middle class', and 5 per cent 'rich'. The accentuation of social inequalities was seen as the key factor in the ruling party defeat in local elections that year.

23   The opposition won the 1996 parliamentary elections. In 1998, Valdas Adamkus was elected President, with a slight margin above his rival, the former Communist Arturas Paulauskas.

24   The finance and economy ministers resigned in early October 1999, after the Government approved the sale of the state oil company to the US firm Williams International. Massive demonstrations against the sale forced Prime Minister Rolandas Paksas to resign in October. The President then appointed former vice-president Andrius Kubilius as Prime Minister, and went ahead with the sale.

25   In June 2002, Lithuania promised the EU that it would shut down the Ignalin nuclear plant, whose reactors - similar to those of the Chernobyl plant in the Ukraine - were declared unsafe by Brussels. The closure would take place between 2005 and 2009. The Government demanded greater financial assistance from the EU to offset the devastating economic and social effects of the closure. The plant generated over 70 per cent of Lithuania's electricity.

26   On 5 January 2003, Roland Paksas, leader of the right-wing Social Democratic Party, a former prime minister and mayor of Vilnius, won the presidential elections with 54.9 per cent of the vote. Adamkus, the front-runner in most polls after having guided the former Communist Republic into the UN and NATO, was defeated. Paksas staged an aggressive campaign, promising Lithuanians a better way of life and maintaining a pro-Western foreign policy.

27   On 10 and 11 May 2003 a referendum was held to decide on Lithuania's incorporation to the EU. However, only 64 per cent of voters turned out. After the first day of the referendum, electoral authorities expressed doubts that the 50 per cent of voters needed to ensure the validity of the referendum would be achieved. Paksas and Prime Minister Algirdas Brazauskas were forced to broadcast a nationally televised message urging the population to vote.

28   In November 2003, President Paksas was accused in a military intelligence report of having ties with the Russian Mafia and secret services, of illegal arms sales and of financing international terrorism. The parliamentary commission appointed to investigate the accusations concluded that Paksas had violated the constitution and that he leaked secret information, thus posing a threat to national security. Paksas illegally granted Lithuanian citizenship to Russian entrepreneur Yuri Borisov, who had financed his presidential campaign. Borisov was accused of illegal arms sales and of blackmailing the President in order to obtain a post of confidence. In December 2003 parliament started impeachment proceedings for the President.

29   In February 2004 three Russian diplomats were accused of espionage and expelled from Lithuania. The foreign ministry said they were engaged in illegal activities, under the protection of their diplomatic positions, favoring privatizations and attempting to obtain secret information from members of parliament regarding President Paksas' impeachment. ∎

Luxembourg / Luxembourg

Population:	464,904
Area:	2,600 km²
Capital:	Luxembourg
Currency:	Euro
Language:	French and German

Luxembourg, Belgium, the Netherlands, and part of northern France constitute the Low Countries, and until 1579 they shared a common history (see the Netherlands).

² In the war of the Low Countries against Spain, Luxembourg sided with the southern provinces, acknowledging the authority of Philip II. Luxembourg was conquered by France in 1684, but returned to Spain 13 years later, under the Treaty of Rijswijk. In 1713, it came under control of the Austrian Hapsburgs until the Napoleonic invasion of 1795, when it was annexed by the French Empire.

³ In 1815, after the defeat of Napoleon, the Congress of Vienna handed over the Duchy to William of Orange, who incorporated it as his kingdom's 18th province. After the Belgian revolt in 1831, Luxembourg was divided.

⁴ The largest section was given to Belgium, and the smallest to William as the Grand Duchy of Luxembourg, which he accepted in 1839. Thereafter the Duchy was administered independently until 1867. In 1866, the German Confederation was dissolved and the Treaty of London guaranteed the neutrality of the Grand Duchy.

⁵ Germany occupied the country during and after the two world wars, from 1914 to 1919 and again from 1940 until 1949. After World War II Luxembourg formed an alliance with Belgium and the Netherlands called Benelux.

⁶ In 1949 Luxembourg abandoned its neutrality and became a founding member of NATO.

⁷ In 1957 it became a founding member of the European Economic Community (EEC), which began to operate in 1958.

⁸ In 1964 the Grand Duchess Charlotte abdicated in favor of her son, who became Grand Duke Jean.

⁹ In the 1974 elections, the Christian Social Party (CSP) was replaced in power for the first time since the end of World War I by a coalition of the Socialist Workers' Party (SWP) and the Democratic Party (DP).

¹⁰ In 1979 the CSP regained power, while the country experienced an economic recession.

¹¹ Jacques Santer became prime minister in 1984.

¹² In the June 1989 legislative elections the CSP, SWP and DP took 22 seats. Women - who won the right to vote in 1919 - began to be admitted to the armed forces in October.

¹³ In 1990, the ambassador at NATO, Guy de Muyser, resigned amid accusations that he leaked classified information to the USSR. Border controls were abolished with Belgium, France, Germany and the Netherlands.

¹⁴ A 'financial scandal' broke out in 1991 when the International Bank of Credit and Commerce (BCCI) went bankrupt - an institution which was originally from Luxembourg with its headquarters in the United Arab Emirates.

¹⁵ Luxembourg signed the Maastricht Treaty in 1992, which created the European Union (EU).

¹⁶ In 1994, the CSP and the SWP were returned to power in the general elections, allowing Jacques Santer to continue as Prime Minister.

¹⁷ In 1995, Santer became President of the European Commission and was replaced as Prime Minister by Jean-Claude Juncker.

¹⁸ Unemployment rose to 3.7 per cent in late 1997, which was still the lowest rate among the 15 EU member states. In November, some 30,000 people from various European countries demonstrated in Luxembourg, calling for a Europe 'at the service of employment'.

¹⁹ In March 1998, the Government announced it would increase funding for the plan to extend the rail network for the high-speed train (TGV) to Eastern Europe.

²⁰ In November 1999, along with Belgium and the Low Countries, Luxembourg suggested that the European Union authorize faster integration for a core group of countries, while some countries dragged their feet over monetary integration and border controls. Prime Minister Jean-Claude Juncker, re-elected that year, said the 'two-speed' proposal was a necessity.

²¹ Grand Duke Jean abdicated in September 2000. His son Henri, 45, took office in October.

²² A report by a French parliamentary commission accused Luxembourg in January 2002 of standing in the way of the fight against money-laundering and financial corruption. Among the main obstacles, it mentioned the strict banking secrecy laws, and the administrative delays any time the authorities were asked to co-operate.

²³ The euro became the national currency in January 2002.

²⁴ Prime Minister Juncker traveled to Cyprus in January 2004 to prepare for the island's admission to the EU.

²⁵ In February, Luxembourg prepared for the June elections. Unemployment stood at 4.5 per cent that month.

²⁶ On 1 March 2004 representatives of the workers, the Government and the EU met to define Luxembourg's stand on the Kyoto Treaty and emissions of greenhouse gases. ∎

PROFILE

ENVIRONMENT
Located on the southeastern side of the Ardennes, Luxembourg has two natural regions. The north is a sparsely populated region of valleys and woods, with a maximum altitude of 500 meters, where potatoes and grains are cultivated. The south (Gutland) is a low plain and the country's main demographic corridor, where most of the population, major industries (iron, steel and mining), and cities, including the capital, are located. This part of the country has problems with air and water pollution in urban areas.

SOCIETY
Peoples: Luxemburger 67.4 per cent; Portuguese 12.1 per cent; Italian 4.8 per cent; French 3.5 per cent; Belgian 2.8 per cent; German 2.3 per cent; other 7.1 per cent.
Religions: No official religion. Catholic (94.9 per cent); Protestants (1.1%); Jewish (4%).
Languages: Letzebuergish, French, German, Portuguese and Italian.
Main Political Parties: Christian Social People's Party (center-right); Luxembourg Socialist Workers' Party (center-left); Democratic Party (center-left); Action Committee for Democracy and Justice for Pensioners; Green (Party); The Left and Communist Party.
Main Social Organizations: General Confederation of Luxembourg Workers; National Trade Union Council.

THE STATE
Official Names: Grand-Duché de Luxembourg; Grossherzogtum Luxemburg, Groussherzogtum Lëtzebeurg.
Administrative Divisions: 3 districts and 12 cantons.
Capital: Luxembourg-Ville 77,000 people (2003).
Other Cities: Esch-sur-Alzette 25,500 people; Dudelange 17,000; Differdange 17,700 (2000).
Government: Constitutional monarchy. Multi-party parliamentary system. Grand Duke Henri, Head of State since October 2000; Jean-Claude Juncker, Prime Minister and Head of Government since January 1995. Single-chamber legislature: Chamber of Deputies, with 60 members elected by direct popular vote, every 5 years.
National Holiday: 23 June, National Day (1921).
Armed Forces: 800. Other: 560 (Gendarmes).

PUBLIC EXPENDITURE

% OF GDP

	HEALTH & EDUCATION (2000)	DEFENSE (2001)
	9.3 %	0.8 %

Macedonia, TFYR / Makedonija

Population:	2,075,805
Area:	25,710 km²
Capital:	Skopje
Currency:	Denar
Language:	Macedonian

The area that was historically called Macedonia belongs to the present-day Republic of Macedonia and to the states of Serbia, Bulgaria and Greece. Archaeological finds show evidence of human settlements between 7000 and 3500 BC. Semi-nomadic Indo-European peoples arrived then in the Balkan Peninsula. During the 1st millennium BC, the area was inhabited by Tracians, Illyrians, Dacians and Greeks.

2　Macedonia became the dominant power in Greece during the reign of Philip II (359-336 BC). Under Macedonian hegemony, the League of Corinth was created, linking all Greek city-states with the exception of Sparta.

3　Alexander III ('the Great'), Philip's son and a student of Aristotle, defeated the Persian Empire and led the Macedonian armies to northern Africa and the Arabic peninsula, crossing Mesopotamia and reaching as far east as India. Over 11 years, he built up the largest empire the world had ever seen up to that point. The aim of his empire was the urbanization of the Orient and the fusion of Greek culture with the cultures of the peoples he conquered, giving rise to what is known as Hellenism.

4　After Alexander's death in 323 BC, the succession struggle by his generals led to the division of the empire into three large kingdoms: Egypt, Macedonia and Asia. That period, which began with Alexander's death and lasted until the foundation of the Roman Empire, is known as the Hellenistic age.

5　By the 2nd century BC, the Romans began their expansion into the Balkans, where they arrived in search of metals, slaves and agricultural products.

6　In 168 BC, upon his defeat by the Romans, Perseus was forced to dissolve the kingdom of Macedonia which became a Roman province in 148.

7　The ethnic composition of the Macedonians was not significantly affected by the Goth, Hun and Avar invasions. However, when Slavs arrived in the Balkans, they established permanent settlements throughout Macedonia.

8　Between the 7th and the 14th centuries, Macedonia was successively subdued by the Bulgarian, Byzantine and Latin empires until they were almost completely dominated by the Serbs.

9　In 1389, after the Battle of Kosovo, Serbia recognized Turkish sovereignty, and in 1549 it joined the Ottoman Empire. The Ottomans seized the best lands for themselves and established a feudal system. Christian peasants either became vassals of Muslim lords, to whom they paid a tithe, or were driven onto the less fertile lands.

10　In 1864, the Ottoman Empire divided Macedonia into three provinces: Salonika, Monastir, including parts of Albania, and Kosovo, which extended into 'Old Serbia'. In 1878, Russia forced Turkey into accepting the creation of Bulgaria, which included most of Macedonia, but the other European powers returned this territory to the Ottomans. During the ensuing years, Bulgaria, Serbia and Greece all continued to lay claim to Macedonia.

11　Towards the end of the 19th century, a strong nationalist movement emerged in Macedonia. In 1893, the VMRO (Vatreshna Makedonska Revolutsionna Organizatsia) was created, with the slogan 'Macedonia for the Macedonians'.

12　In 1908, after the fall of the Ottoman Empire, the clamor for possession of Ottoman-Turkish territories in the region culminated in the two Balkan Wars of 1912 and 1913.

13　The Treaty of Bucharest (1913) put an end to the second Balkan War. Bulgaria lost Macedonia which was divided between Greece (Salonika and most of the Macedonian coastal area) and Serbia (central and northern parts of the territory). Albania became an autonomous principality.

14　The Balkans turned into the powder keg of Europe and finally set off World War I. The end of World War I saw the partition of 1913 reconfirmed and Slavic Macedonia was incorporated into the new Serbian, Croat and Slovenian kingdom.

15　In the inter-war period, Serbian domination deepened Yugoslav inter-ethnic conflicts. King Alexander, who assumed dictatorial powers in 1929, was assassinated in Marseilles in 1934 by Croatian nationalists. At the beginning of World War II, when Germany invaded Yugoslavia, these internal divisions meant that the invaders met little resistance.

16　The Yugoslav nationalist struggle intensified during the following years. Guerrillas led by the Yugoslav Communist League (YCL) seized power in May 1945, later proclaiming the Socialist Federal Republic of Yugoslavia, which included six republics (Slovenia, Croatia, Bosnia-Herzegovina, Montenegro, Serbia and Macedonia) and two autonomous regions belonging to Serbia (Kosovo and Voivodina).

17　That year, Tito (Josip Broz) was elected President. Commerce and banking were nationalized and agriculture was collectivized. He distanced himself from Moscow and launched the 'Yugoslav road to socialism'. On the foreign policy front, he was a prominent leader in the movement of non-aligned countries.

18　The Yugoslav system distinguished between 'constituent peoples' of the Federation (Serbs, Croats, Slovenes, Macedonians, etc.) and 'nationalities'. Since the latter had no State or their State of reference did not belong to the Federation, they were considered 'national minorities', regardless of how numerous they were in each region. Albanians were granted this minority status. They formed a clear majority in the province of Kosovo, although they represented a minority in the Republic of Serbia, of which Kosovo formed a part.

19　After Tito's death, conflict broke out among the republics that constituted the Federation. In 1989, the Federal Government withdrew all reference to minorities from the Constitution. In January 1990, a special Congress of the Yugoslavian Communist League did not accept the motion to grant greater autonomy to YCL branches in the republics. The Communist Leagues of

PROFILE

ENVIRONMENT

In the south-central part of the Balkan Peninsula, Macedonia, which is landlocked, is bordered in the north by Serbia and Kosovo, in the east by Bulgaria, in the south by Greece and in the west by Albania. Two mountain ranges cross the region, the Pindo (a continuation of the Alps) and the Rodope, in the center and the east. With a continental climate, the average temperature in the capital is 1°C in winter, and 24°C in summer. The country's main agricultural activity is centered in the Vardar River basin. In the mountain region, sheep and goats are raised. There are some copper, iron and lead deposits.

SOCIETY

Peoples: Macedonians 66.4 per cent; Albanians 23.1 per cent; Turks 3.9 per cent; Roma 2.3 per cent; Serbs 1.9 per cent (1994).
Languages: Macedonian and Albanian (official languages); Roma and Turkish. **Religions:** Christian Orthodox (majority); Muslim and others.
Main Political Parties: There is a coalition between the Internal Macedonian Revolutionary Organization, the Democratic Union for Integration (DUI) and the Democratic Alternative; Social Democratic League of Macedonia; the Socialist Party. Albanian parties: the Democratic Prosperity Party, Democratic Party of Albanians.
Main Social Organizations: Union of Women's Organizations of the Republic of Macedonia. League of Albanian Women.

THE STATE

Official Name: Republika Makedonija. **Administrative Divisions:** 30 districts. **Capital:** Skopje 447,000 people (2003). **Other Cities:** Bitolj (Bitola) 92,300 people; Prilep 81,600; Kumanovo 77,900; Tetovo 54,600 (2000). **Government:** Republican. President Branko Crvenkovski, since May 2004. Prime Minister: Hari Kostov, since May 2004. Unicameral Legislature: the Sobranie (Assembly) integrated by 120 members elected for a four year term. **National Holiday:** 8 September, Independence Day (1991). **Armed Forces:** 10,400 (8,000 conscripts). Other: 7,500 (police).

Life expectancy
73.6 years
2000-2005

GNI per capita
$1,700
2002

Literacy
96% total adult rate
2000

Slovenia, Croatia and Macedonia decided to separate from the YCL and created the Communist League-Democratic Renewal Party.

20   The first republics to become independent were Slovenia and Croatia, at the expense of a conflict with Serbia. On 8 December 1991, a plebiscite was held in which Macedonians pronounced themselves in favor of independence. All Macedonian political parties, except for the Albanian ethnic minority, supported the decision.

21   Greece refused to acknowledge the republic, claiming that the use of the name 'Macedonia' was a 'usurpation' of the name of a Greek province and of part of Greece's history and culture.

22   On 12 January 1992, in a referendum, the Albanian minority of Macedonia voted for the creation of their own independent state. In April, the territory of Macedonia was proclaimed the Independent Republic of Illirida (republic of Albanians resident in Yugoslavia). That year, the UN approved sending troops to control inter-ethnic conflicts.

23   The new Yugoslav Federation withdrew its troops from the country. In July, the entire cabinet resigned, after failing to achieve international recognition. Social Democrat Branko Crvenkovski took over as Prime Minister in August and succeeded in obtaining recognition from Russia, Albania, Bulgaria and Turkey.

24   In April 1993, the country was admitted as a member of the UN with the provisional name of The Former Yugoslav Republic (TFYR) of Macedonia.

25   In 1996, a privatization plan led to the downfall of the ruling coalition. The October-November 1998 parliamentary elections were won by a new coalition, called the Internal Macedonian Revolutionary Organization-Democratic Party for Macedonian National Unity (VMRO-DMPNE), which obtained 28.1 per cent of the vote. The Social-Democratic League took 25.1 per cent, while the Democratic Alternative, with slightly more than 10 per cent, joined the governing coalition.

26   To avoid trouble with the Albanian minority, while tension soared in neighboring Yugoslavia, the Government asked NATO to station troops on the border. When the bombing of Yugoslavia began in March 1999, Macedonia offered NATO the use of its troops and air space and opened the border to Albanian refugees coming from Kosovo.

27   Macedonia's frail economy was severely affected by the war. Yugoslavia was one of its largest markets. Many of its industrial plants depended on the import of raw materials and components for production from Yugoslavia. As a consequence, exports fell and some 40,000 workers lost their jobs.

28   Tito Petkovski, of the (former Communist) Social Democratic Party, won the largest number of votes in the first round of the 1999 presidential elections. But the second round was won by Boris Trajkovski of the ruling coalition, who had taken 25 per cent of the vote in the first round. The opposition and international observers said the elections were seriously flawed.

29   A revolution broke out in March 2001 as people demanded more rights for the Albanian minority, resulting in a wave of refugees and the occupation of territory by the rebel National Liberation Army (NLA). The violence ceased in August, after the international community intervened and demanded the rebels hand over their weapons in exchange for recognition of the Albanian minority.

30   In November, after delays and breaks in the ceasefire, Parliament passed constitutional reforms which granted Albanians broader rights. The constitution would no longer mention the Albanian 'minority', but the 'Albanians that live in the territory of Macedonia'. Albanian was recognized as the second official language, and its use was allowed in Parliament; state institutions - mainly the police - were obliged to open up jobs to Albanians. The operation Essential Harvest was launched under NATO supervision in order to collect weapons from the more than 2,500 Albanian rebels who had promised to lay them down.

31   The international community decided in early 2002 to send more than 500 million euros, twice the initially foreseen amount, for economic reforms and reconstruction, in recognition of the stability achieved by Macedonia six months after the war had ended.

32   On 15 September, international observers took part in a mission to certify the neutrality of the country's first parliamentary elections, after the armed uprising in the northeast. The Social Democratic opposition led by Branko Crvenkovsky won with more than 40 per cent of the vote, while Ljubco Georgievski's nationalist party, the VMRO, took only 24 per cent. President Boris Trajkovski invited Crvenkovski, the new prime minister - who had already held that position between 1992 and 1998 - to create a coalition government. More than half of the Albanian voters supported the Democratic Union for Integration (DUI) - the political heir to the National Liberation Army - led by the former Albanian rebel leader Ali Ahmeti.

33   In 2003, Amnesty International denounced the persistent abuse and ill-treatment of Albanians, especially by members of the 'Lions', a special all-Macedonian police unit set up by the Interior Ministry following the NLA uprising.

34   In February 2004, Trajkvksi died in a plane crash on his way to a conference in Mostar. Bosnian television blamed NATO forces for the accident. He was temporarily replaced by the president of Parliament, Ljubco Jordanovski. ■

IN FOCUS

ENVIRONMENTAL CHALLENGES
Water and air pollution, as well as the generation of industrial waste, particularly in the metallurgical industry, have reached alarming levels.

WOMEN'S RIGHTS
Women have been able to vote and stand for office since 1946, in the former Yugoslavia, and since independence in 1991. In 2000, women held eight per cent of parliamentary seats, and accounted for 42 per cent of the labor force.

Although official documentation is sketchy and confusing, Macedonia is known to be a major transit route from countries of the former USSR and Eastern Europe for women and children trafficked into Western Europe and the Balkans. There is also growing evidence of internal trafficking and of the fact that Macedonia is becoming a final destination for human trafficking.

CHILDREN
In 2002, only 12 per cent of preschool age children had access to adequate educational services, mainly because most parents were unable to afford paying the fees or to travel the long distances that often separated their homes from preschool services.

Parliament passed new legislation concerning primary and secondary education. The most significant changes involve the right of children with disabilities to be integrated into mainstream schools for at least four hours a day.

The movement of children and their families across the border since 2001 has proved that many lack identity documents and had not even been registered at birth. Most of these undocumented children were born outside the country's health system infrastructure and live in rural areas or belong to the Roma ethnic group.

INDIGENOUS PEOPLES/ ETHNIC MINORITIES
The minority groups recognized in Macedonia - either due to ethnic or religious differences distinguishing them from the Macedonian majority - are the Albanians, Roma and Serbs. The Albanians and Macedonians have a long history of peaceful coexistence, although the two groups speak different languages and have different religions and traditions. When Macedonia became independent, the Albanians started to demand greater cultural and political rights, with protests that sometimes ended in violent clashes. Since 1991, slow progress has been made towards addressing their grievances.

The Roma are not concentrated in a particular region of the country. They do not enjoy the right to citizenship, they have no access to education in their own language (unlike other minority groups), they do not take part in politics and, as in many other European countries, they are among the poorest and most neglected groups. However, the Government is making efforts to minimize discrimination and abuses - including police abuse - against the Roma.

The 40,000 Serbs in Macedonia are mainly living in the northern parts of the country, near the border with Serbia. They are demanding greater respect for their cultural rights, but their main demand is protection from the Albanians. During the NATO attack against Serbia, the Government of Macedonia was accused of serving the interests of the Albanian minority, and protests were held by Serbs to express solidarity with people in Serbia.

MIGRANTS/REFUGEES
In late 2002, around 8,500 people remained internally displaced within Macedonia as a result of the conflict in 2001.

Some 5,000 Macedonians sought asylum abroad. Most of them filed applications for refugee status in Switzerland, Austria, Sweden, Germany and Belgium. Around 750 who had fled the 2001 conflict remained in Kosovo at year's end and almost 100 remained in southern Serbia. The majority of Macedonians in Serbia and Kosovo were Albanians, although some were Roma. Macedonia hosted more than 2,700 refugees and asylum-seekers, almost all of them Roma, Ashkali, and Egyptians from Kosovo with temporary humanitarian assisted person status.

DEATH PENALTY
Macedonian law does not provide for the death penalty.

Madagascar / Madagascar

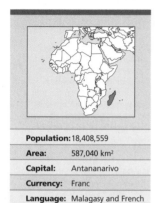

Population:	18,408,559
Area:	587,040 km²
Capital:	Antananarivo
Currency:	Franc
Language:	Malagasy and French

Twentieth century archeological research indicates Madagascar began to be inhabited around 700 AD. Even though this enormous island is geographically close to the area where African Bantu languages are spoken, Malagasy is derived from the Malay-Polynesian languages. The Malagasy people represent a unique mixture of Asian and African cultures. Prior to 1000 AD, important Afro-Arab influences expanded throughout Madagascar. Between the 1st and 5th centuries AD, Malay-Polynesian navigators (see Melanesians and Polynesians), for reasons still unknown, repeatedly took upon themselves the challenge of crossing 8,000 kms of ocean to reach the African coast.

2   During the 14th century, groups of Comoran traders established a series of ports in the northern region of the island, which were subsequently destroyed by the Portuguese. Madagascar is mentioned in the writings of Marco Polo; however, the first European to visit the island in 1500 was Diogo Dias, a Portuguese navigator. Portuguese explorers visited the valley of the River Matitana (in southeastern Madagascar) between 1507 and 1513, witnessing the arrival of an Afro-Arab group (Malindi Arabs). After one or two generations of that group's descendants, who married local Tompontany people, another group, the Antemoro, founded a theocratic state of Madagascar, the only state - in its time - to produce written texts. When the Portuguese found no gold, ivory or spices, they lost interest in the territory.

3   In the 16th century the Sakalawas on the west coast and the Betsilios on the east coast established the first monarchies. In the 17th century the Merina kingdom or Imerina came into being on the eastern edge of the central plateau. A century later it was the Merinas, under their leader Nampoina, who initiated the process of unification which was completed later by Nampoina's son Radama I (1810-1828). Due to more frequent contact with Arabs and Europeans, Radama organized a modern army and adopted the Latin alphabet for the Malagasy language. However, Nampoina's untimely death and the ensuing conflicts over succession paved the way for European occupation of the island by the end of the 19th century. Under the colonial system, huge swathes of forests were cleared to make way for sugarcane, cotton, and coffee plantations. The foreign colonists and companies seized the best lands and forced the peasants to work them in conditions of semi-slavery.

4   Resistance to foreign domination, and the struggle for political rights and economic improvement, led to a major uprising from 1947 to 1948, which was ruthlessly crushed by the French army with the loss of thousands of lives. The defeat of the insurrection enabled the colonial administration to control the transition to autonomy. Independence was finally proclaimed in 1960, with Philibert Tsiranana as president. In the first elections (1960), the Social Democratic Party (PSD) won, and Tsiranana became the first president of the republic, an office to which he was re-elected in 1965 and 1972.

5   In 1972, after a series of serious disturbances, Tsiranana was forced to resign; he turned over full presidential powers to General Gabriel Ramanantsoa, who suspended the National Assembly and the Senate. He also abolished the 1959 constitution. France withdrew its troops in 1973. After three years of instability, in 1975 Commander Didier Ratsiraka became president. He adopted socialist policies, and called a referendum that year, which overwhelmingly approved Ratsiraka's continuation as head of state for seven years, and a Charter from the Malagasy Socialist Revolution was adopted as the basis for a new constitution. On 30 December 1975 the country's name was changed to the Democratic Republic of Madagascar.

6   In 1976, the 12-member Supreme Council of the Revolution was established. The Malagasy Revolutionary Vanguard, called Association for the Rebirth of Madagascar (AREMA, founded in 1975 in support of Ratsiraka) became the leading party within the National Revolutionary Front (union of peoples' parties). Colonel Joel Rakotomalala was appointed prime minister. Upon his death that same year, he was replaced by Justin Rakotoniaina. The legislative function was placed in the hands of a 144-member National Council. In 1977, Désiré Rakotoarijaona replaced Rakotoniaina as prime minister.

7   Eleven years later, Lt-Col Victor Ramahatra succeeded Rakotoarijaona as prime minister. In the 1989 general elections, President Ratsiraka was re-elected president, with 67 per cent of the vote. His

PROFILE

ENVIRONMENT

Madagascar is one of the world's largest islands, separated from the African continent by the Mozambique Channel. The island has an extensive central plateau of volcanic origin which overhangs the hot and humid coastal plains. These are covered with dense rainforest to the east and grasslands to the west. The eastern side of the island is very rainy, but the rest has a dry, tropical climate. The population is concentrated on the high central plateau. Rice and products for export (sugar, coffee, bananas, and vanilla) are cultivated along the coast. Stockbreeding is also an important activity throughout the island. The major mineral resources are graphite, chrome and phosphate.

SOCIETY

Peoples: The Malgaches, 98.9 per cent of the population, are made up of different ethnic groups of Malagasy-Afro-Indonesian origin. Immigrant communities: Indian and Pakistani, 0.2 per cent; French, 0.2 per cent; Chinese, 0.1 per cent, and others. **Religions:** Traditional beliefs 52 per cent; Christian 41 per cent (of which Roman Catholic 21 per cent, Protestant 19 per cent); Muslim 7 per cent. **Languages:** Malagasy and French (official). Hovba and other local dialects are also spoken. **Main Political Parties:** Association for the Rebirth of Madagascar (AREMA); I Love Madagascar (TIM); Militant Party for the Development of Madagascar (MFM); Be Judged by Your Work (AVI); National Union for Development and Democracy (UNDD); Social Democratic Party (PSD). **Main Social Organizations:** Confederation of Malgache Workers (FMM); Confederation of Christian Trade Unions of Madagascar (SEKRIMA); Union of Independent Trade Unions of Madagascar (USAM) and Union of Workers' Trade Unions of Madagascar (FISEMA). National Council of Christian Churches.

THE STATE

Official Names: Repoblikan'i Madagasikara. République Démocratique de Madagascar. **Administrative Divisions:** 6 provinces, 10 districts, 1,252 sub-districts, and 11,333 towns. **Capital:** Antananarivo 1,678,000 people (2003). **Other Cities:** Toamasina 166,000 people; Fianarantsoa 131,600; Mahajanga (Majunga) 128,600 (2000). **Government:** Marc Ravalomanana, President and head of state since April 2002. Jean-Jacques Rasolondraibe, Prime Minister and Head of Government since May 2002. Unicameral Legislature: National Assembly with 160 members elected for a five-year term by direct vote. **National Holiday:** 26 June, Independence Day (1960). Armed Forces: 21,000 (1996). Other: 7,500 (Gendarmerie).

Life expectancy
53.6 years
2000-2005

GNI per capita
$240
2002

Literacy
67% total adult rate
2000

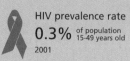

HIV prevalence rate
0.3% of population 15-49 years old
2001

IN FOCUS

ENVIRONMENTAL CHALLENGES
Deforestation is one of the most pressing environmental problems (the forests have been destroyed on 75 per cent of the land). Several aquifers have been polluted as a result of organic waste and limited sanitation. Madagascar is considered a great biological reserve; however, it is endangered due to the type of crops that have been cultivated for centuries. Destruction exceeds the jungle's capacity to regenerate.

WOMEN'S RIGHTS
Women have been able to vote and run for office since 1959. According to data published between 1995 and 2000 the number of seats held by women in parliament increased to 8 per cent and the ministerial or equivalent positions held by women rose from zero to 19 per cent. In 2000, women comprised 45 per cent of the total labor force. The illiteracy rate stood at 23.4 per cent for women aged 15-24, compared to 16.4 per cent among men of the same age group. That year, only 46 per cent of all births were attended by qualified medical personnel.

CHILDREN
In 2000 it was estimated that over 70 per cent of the population lived below the poverty line, and 30 per cent in extreme poverty.

Children suffer chronic problems such as malnutrition. Poverty is aggravated by the lack of funds for health and education. In this context, natural occurrences can create acute emergencies. The Kesiny cyclone had devastating effects. More than 500 children died during an influenza outbreak. The impact of the drought in the south was devastating and forced many men to migrate to other parts of the island, causing the gradual deterioration of homes and villages that had been left to the women's care. This situation led to an increase in malnutrition and impoverishment. In 2000, over 19 per cent of the children and adolescents between the ages of 5 and 14 worked. In 2001, over 6,300 children under the age of 14 were AIDS orphans who had lost both parents.

INDIGENOUS PEOPLES/ ETHNIC MINORITIES
The Madagascan population is made up of several ethnic groups. The Merina, of Asian origin, comprised 25 per cent of the population in 1998; they live in the highlands of the Pacific Area. The coastal peoples, known as *Cotiers,* are of mixed African, Malayo-Indonesian, and Arab ancestry. Among them are the Betsimisaraka, the Tsimihety in the north and the Antandroy in the south. The groups are demanding greater political participation at the center. In the past there was unrest between Merina and the Cotiers; however there have been no reports of violence between them since 1992.

MIGRANTS/REFUGEES
The Government co-operates with UNHCR and other humanitarian organizations by helping a small number of refugees. It also provides assistance to refugees not protected under the 1951 Convention or the 1967 protocols.

DEATH PENALTY
The country has been de facto abolitionist since 1958.

reform-oriented policies restored a multiparty system, and several opposition members were included in his cabinet. In 1991, the opposition united around the Committee of Living Forces (CFV), formed by 16 organizations. A series of street demonstrations and the occupation of the National Radio station led the Government to declare a state of emergency. The Committee called for Ratsiraka's resignation, appointing a transition government. Shortly after, following the detention of two ministers belonging to the transition cabinet, 400,000 people took to the streets and repeated the demand for Ratsiraka's resignation. The demonstration was repressed, with 31 people killed and hundreds injured. Guy Razanamasy took office as prime minister that year, and reopened dialogue with the opposition, appointing a government of national unity.

[8] In 1992, a multiparty forum was created to draw up a new constitution: the new constitution was approved by referendum that year, and presidential elections were set. Albert Zafy was elected president (by a large margin over Ratsiraka) and took office in 1993. The economic and social situation of the country, one of the poorest in the world, was a disaster. Per capita income had grown hardly at all over 16 years, from $200 to $230 per year, while calorie consumption dropped from 108 per cent to 95 per cent. In 1994, the Government introduced a series of austerity measures recommended by the International Monetary Fund (IMF), which further inflamed social tensions. Massive demonstrations were held in opposition to these policies. In 1995, the governor of the Central Bank abandoned his post at the request of the IMF and the World Bank.

[9] In 1995, the Malagasy people approved increased powers for Zafy in a referendum. The debate over the structural adjustment policies coincided with controversy over the use of the nation's natural resources, when the mining transnational RTZ Associates proposed opening a mine on the southern coast of the island to extract titanium dioxide. This sparked strong protests by environmentalists, since unique species of native flora and fauna would be destroyed. In 1996, the National Assembly approved a vote of no confidence in the Government, leading to the formation of a new cabinet. The motion was partly caused by comments made by IMF Managing Director Michel Camdessus, who said the lack of governmental cohesion meant compliance with agreements with the multilateral lender was not guaranteed. Accused of violating the constitution, Zafy resigned in 1996. In the subsequent presidential elections, Ratsiraka was re-elected.

[10] A new constitution, approved by referendum in 1998, gave broader powers to the President and granted economic autonomy to the country's six provinces. The CFV accused the Government of authoritarian tendencies. After that year's legislative elections, Tantely Andranarivo became the new prime minister, replacing Pascal Rakotomavo, both members of AREMA.

[11] The opposition, alleging that voters had not received adequate information, boycotted the 2000 local elections - designed to give local governments control over their development, education and health programs. Seventy per cent of voters stayed home and AREMA won in most provinces. The exception was the capital, under the control of Marc Ravalomanana, a charismatic political leader of humble origins who had become a tycoon through the processing and sale of yoghurt.

[12] In 2001, the police cracked down on demonstrators in the capital, Antananarivo. They were demanding freedom for Jean-Eugene Voninahitsy, deputy chair of parliament, who had been jailed for insulting Ratsiraka and for issuing bad cheques. After Voninahitsy's imprisonment, an opposition bloc was formed in parliament, the Unit for Defense of Democracy in Crisis. After 29 years, the Senate resumed operations, as had been agreed in the new constitution, which included the presidency, the National Assembly and the High Constitutional Court (HCC). In the 2001 presidential elections, Ravalomanana claimed victory without a second round. But Ratsiraka did not accept defeat.

[13] In 2002, Ravalomanana and his followers organized a general strike in the capital and a series of protest demonstrations against the supposed manipulation of votes by Ratsiraka. Ravalomanana proclaimed himself president that year and appointed ministers, who took office in the capital. Due to a series of violent clashes, Ratsiraka declared martial law in Antananarivo. The country was at a standstill and, while Ratsiraka and his ministers left for Toamasina (previously Tamatave, second largest city and port in the country, which they named the new capital) - an economic blockade was imposed on Antananarivo. Ravalomanana took over the Home Ministry, Ratsiraka's last stronghold in Antananarivo, and also proclaimed himself commander-in-chief of the armed forces.

[14] In 2002, the HCC annulled the results of the elections and asked for a recount, which was accepted by both candidates. The HCC finally awarded Ravalomanana 51.46 per cent of the vote, and he took office as president. Ratsiraka - who obtained 35.9 per cent of the vote - ignored the verdict. The province of Toamasina declared its independence and Ratsiraka sought to isolate Antananarivo from the country's ports. The US, Australia, Japan, Germany and France recognized Ravalomanana's government. After seven months of political crisis, Ratsiraka fled to the Seychelles in exile and then to France. Ravalomanana's party, called 'I Love Madagascar', obtained a majority in the parliamentary elections, which were seen as a test of the people's support for his government.

[15] In 2003, the exiled Ratsiraka was sentenced in absentia to ten years imprisonment with forced labor, on charges of misappropriation of public funds. The former Prime Minister Tantely Andrianarivo was sentenced to 12 years under the same conditions, accused of abuse of authority. In 2004 Madagascar requested international aid after a cyclone caused severe damage, especially in the north of the island. As a consequence, around 100,000 people were left homeless, and several died. Madagascar is frequently hit by strong cyclones during the winter season. ∎

Malawi / Malawi

Population:	12,572,372
Area:	118,480 km²
Capital:	Lilongwe
Currency:	Kwacha
Language:	Chewa

I n the 1st century BC, Bantu groups invaded the southeastern region of Africa, inhabited by Twa and Fulani groups. Between the 13th and 15th centuries, there were further migrations of Bantu people, who knew how to work with iron and used this knowledge to dominate the original inhabitants.

2   In 1480, the Bantu groups formed several small states joined together in a federation which encompassed large parts of Zambia, Mozambique and all of present-day Malawi.

3   In the 17th century, the first Portuguese explorers arrived from the area of the present-day Mozambique. From 1790 until 1860, the slave trade grew dramatically in the area.

4   Around 1835, Zulu expansion (see South Africa) pushed the Ngoni-Ndwande to the shores of Lake Malawi, giving rise to 60 years of war.

5   The country was explored by David Livingstone in 1859 and experienced a Portuguese attempt at colonization in 1890 which was checked by the British Government. Britain wanted to keep the territory which would eventually serve as a link in a continuous chain of colonies from South Africa to Egypt. In 1891, it became the protectorate of Nyasaland through Cecil Rhodes' British South African Company.

6   In 1893, its name was changed to the British Central African Protectorate. European settlers were offered land for coffee plantations at very low prices with large tax incentives. Africans worked the plantations in extremely difficult conditions.

7   In 1907, the protectorate reverted to the name of Nyasaland.

8   Nationalist leaders established the Nyasaland African Congress (NAC) in 1944. On 23 October 1953, concerned about their actions and those of white liberal activists, the British unified the territory with the Federation of Rhodesia.

9   In 1958, Hastings Kamuzu Banda, 'the black messiah', returned from the US where he had graduated in medicine, to assume the leadership of the NAC. He landed in prison several times due to clashes with the British authorities.

10   In 1959, the Malawi Congress Party (MCP), headed by Banda, was founded as a successor to the NAC. The party was pro-independence. Two years later, after the MCP scored a victory in the 1961 elections for a constituent assembly, Banda was appointed prime minister.

11   In order to prevent internal divisions, Banda's authority in the Party was expanded. When the colony became independent on 6 July 1964, the MCP and the country remained under Banda's autocratic rule. He established close economic and diplomatic ties with the racist governments of South Africa and Rhodesia, and

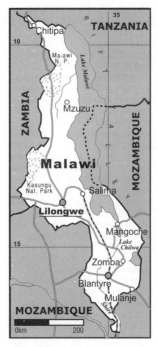

with the colonial administration in Mozambique.

12   South Africa became the main market for Malawi's exports of tea and tobacco, while its investors built roads, railways and a new capital city. South African executives took charge of the airline, news services and development agencies and a large part of the state administration.

13   In 1975, Mozambican independence led to a radical change in Banda's political outlook. He had actively

cooperated with the Portuguese in their struggle against FRELIMO. The closure of the Mozambique-Rhodesia border led to a drastic reduction in Malawi's trade with Rhodesia, and deprived Ian Smith's government of a route to get around the international blockade.

14   In June 1978, in the first election in 17 years, all of the candidates had to belong to the MCP and pass an English test, which immediately excluded 90 per cent of the population.

15   Zimbabwe's independence in 1980 changed things for Malawi. Banda lost his close economic relations with South Africa. Consequently, the Government drew closer to the Front Line states, joining the SADCC association because of Malawi's dependence on the railway lines through Mozambique and Zimbabwe.

16   This situation strengthened the Socialist League of Malawi (LESOMA) which favored breaking economic and political ties with South Africa and an end to Banda's dictatorship. In 1980 the party created a guerrilla force, while the Malawi Freedom Movement (MAFREMO), led by Orton Chirwa, gained strength.

17   In 1983, Chirwa and Attati Mpakati, a LESOMA leader, were accused of conspiracy and sentenced to death. Shortly thereafter, Mpakati was assassinated by South African agents while visiting Harare. Chirwa and his wife were kidnapped in Zambia where they were living in exile, and imprisoned in Blantyre.

LAND USE

2000

IRRIGATED AREA: 1.3% of arable land

- ARABLE LAND: 22.3%
- CROPLANDS: 1.5%
- OTHER USE: 76.2%

PROFILE

Environment
The terrain and the climate are quite varied. The major geological feature is the great Rift fault that runs through the country from north to south. Part of this large depression is filled by Lake Malawi, which takes up one fifth of the land area. The rest is made up of plateaus of varying altitudes. The most temperate region is the southern part, which is also the highest, containing most of the population and economic activities (basically farming). The lowlands are covered by grasslands, forests or rainforests, depending on the amount of rainfall they receive. In March 2002, the Shire River was discovered to be affected by a plague of water hyacinths, threatening to block the flow of the river or divert its course. The Shire, an outlet of Lake Malawi, pours into the Zambezi River and represents an important means of transport and source of food.

Society
Peoples: Maravi (including Nyanja, Chewa, Tonga, and Tumbuka) 58.3 per cent; Lomwe 18.4 per cent; Yao 13.2 per cent; Ngoni 6.7 per cent.
Religions: There is no official religion. Christian, 50 per cent (of which 20 per cent are Protestant and 18 per cent are Roman Catholic); Muslim, 20 per cent. Many people follow traditional religions, but many of them also define themselves as Christians or Muslims.
Languages: Chewa and English (official languages); several Bantu languages - other than Chewa - are spoken by their respective ethnic groups.
Main Political Parties: United Democratic Front (UDF); Alliance for Democracy (Aford); Malawi Congress Party (MCP).
Main Social Organizations: Trade Union Congress of Malawi. Union of Malawian Students.

The State
Official Name: Republic of Malawi.
Administrative Divisions: 24 districts.
Capital: Lilongwe 587,000 people (2003).
Other Cities: Blantyre 518,800 people; Mzuzu 94,400 (2000).
Government: Presidential republic. Bingu wa Mutharika, President since May 2004. Legislature: single-chamber National Assembly, made up of 177 members.
National Holiday: 6 July, Independence Day (1964).
Armed Forces: 9,800 (1996). Other: 1,500.

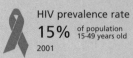
IN FOCUS

ENVIRONMENTAL CHALLENGES

The degradation of the soil and deforestation are the main environmental problems. Drought intensified the lack of water in early 1998. Some water sources are polluted by industrial or agricultural waste as well as untreated sewage. Meanwhile, sedimentation in spawning areas is endangering marine species.

WOMEN'S RIGHTS

Women have been able to vote and stand for office since 1961. In 2000, eight per cent of parliamentary seats were held by women, while their representation in ministerial or equivalent positions amounted to four per cent.

In 2000, 39 per cent of women between the ages of 15 and 24 were illiterate - twice the proportion of men in the same age group who were illiterate.

That year, women made up 49 per cent of the country's labor force; most of them worked in agriculture.

HIV/AIDS poses one of the most serious problems for the population in general; it affects especially women of child-bearing age in rural areas. Only 34 per cent of women between the ages of 15 and 24 have an understanding of how to prevent infection. In 2001, 13.6 per cent of pregnant women between the ages of 15 and 19 were living with HIV, while the rate rose to 25.7 percent among pregnant women between the ages of 20 and 24. In recent years, the shortage of staff and basic equipment and materials has been aggravated by health budget cuts.

CHILDREN

The rural population has been hit hardest by Malawi's humanitarian crisis. In 2001, more than 65 per cent of the population was living below the poverty line.

The food crisis, a consequence of chronic poverty, unfavourable weather conditions and excessive reliance on one-crop farming has led to chronic malnutrition and endemic diseases (cholera, chronic infections, etc) that together with the AIDS epidemic paint an outlook of extreme vulnerability for the entire population, especially children.

By 2001, nearly 400,000 children under the age of 15 had been orphaned by HIV/AIDS. Since 1990, life expectancy has fallen almost 10 years, to the current 37.5 years.

INDIGENOUS PEOPLES/ETHNIC MINORITIES

The main African ethnic groups make up 99.5 per cent of the population and are divided into the Chewa, Nyanja, Tumbuka, Yao, Lomwe, Sena, Tongo and Ngoni. The rest of the population, 0.5 per cent, includes Asian and European minorities.

MIGRANTS/REFUGEES

As of late 2002, Malawi hosted some 13,000 refugees and asylum-seekers, including more than 7,000 from Rwanda, nearly 3,000 from Burundi, and around 3,000 from the Democratic Republic of Congo. Some 6,000 refugees live in Malawi's only refugee camp, Dzaleka, where humanitarian aid workers provide food, water and health services. The majority of refugees, however, face the same food shortages and drought that affect more than three million local residents.

DEATH PENALTY

The death penalty is occasionally imposed, even for common crimes.

[18] Banda created a secret police force, called the Special Branch, with South African and Israeli advisers. The President also personally controlled the economy, owning 33 per cent of all businesses.

[19] Between 1987 and 1988, Malawi received 600,000 refugees from Mozambique, in whose civil war Banda had supported the counter-revolution waged by the National Resistance Movement until he was visited in 1988 by President Chissano of Mozambique.

[20] Also in 1988, Amnesty International denounced the imprisonment of scholars and writers, among them Jack Mapanje, the country's foremost poet. The US cancelled $40 million of foreign debt in November 1989.

[21] The implementation of an IMF structural adjustment program brought down inflation and reduced the balance of payments deficit, while leading to increase in investment. However, the policies made conditions worse for the poor.

[22] In 1990 and 1991, earthquakes and floods exacerbated food shortages among the rural populace, which made up 90 per cent of the total population.

[23] In February 1992, the Catholic Church wrote a pastoral letter criticizing the human rights situation and calling for greater political freedom. A popular uprising in Blantyre was harshly repressed.

[24] In April 1992, opposition leader Chafuka Chihana of the Alliance for Democracy was arrested when trying to return to the country. An international campaign prevented his execution.

[25] In May, a general strike called by textile workers was brutally put down, with 38 deaths and hundreds of injuries. In reprisal, the World Bank discontinued part of its financial aid.

[26] The ruling Congress Party of Malawi, the only party to participate in the June 1992 elections, obtained 114 seats in the National Assembly.

[27] In late 1992, news was received of the death of Orton Chirwa of MAFREMO. He had been in prison since 1983, and died under torture. To keep popular indignation from turning violent, Banda announced that a referendum would be held on opening up the political system.

[28] In June 1993, the Public Affairs Committee (PAC) forced Banda to set the referendum for that month in order to choose between a one-party system and a multiparty system. Nearly two-thirds of voters chose a multiparty system. That month, Banda released Vera Chirwa, widow of the assassinated dissident, and Africa's oldest female political prisoner. Banda did not resign but promised presidential elections would be held in 1994.

[29] On 17 May 1994, four million Malawians elected a new president and 177 members of parliament in the first multipary elections since the country's independence.

[30] Opposition member Bakili Muluzi won the elections, and his party, the United Democratic Front (UDF), won 84 of the 177 seats at stake. In September, having won only 55 seats, Banda decided to retire from political activity.

[31] Malawi suffered the consequences of an intense drought and famine in 1994. In the midst of an increasingly difficult social situation, the Government went ahead with its IMF-sponsored policy to cut public spending. In January 1995, ex-President Banda was arrested, charged with the murder of three former ministers.

[32] In 1996, Malawi entered negotiations to form a free trade area, along with 11 other African nations. The Government announced it would revoke the laws affecting foreign investors in rural areas.

[33] In 1997, the US started to train Malawian troops to create an African peacekeeping force.

[34] The drought, which affected vast regions of Africa, almost totally dried up Malawi's Shire River, one of the country's main rivers. International experts recommended a reduction in the amount of water used in agriculture through the importing of food, and the gradual industrialization of the economy. In 1998, it was estimated the underground water reserves of the region would take 1,400 years to recover.

[35] A cholera epidemic which affected 15,000 people left 500 dead between 1998 and 1999. In April 1999, the country's first television channel began to operate.

[36] After flawed elections, Muluzi was re-elected in June 2002, while his party won 93 of the 192 legislative seats. In late February 2000, the President requested the resignation of his cabinet. Some of his ministers, among them Economic Minister Cassim Chilumpha, were not considered trustworthy by donor countries that provided development aid.

[37] After Muluzi criticized donor states for meddling in the country's domestic policies, Denmark, which had pledged $87 million for the 2000-2004 period, cancelled its aid in January 2002, which blocked the start of new development and environmental programs.

[38] In 2001, a state of national disaster was declared as a consequence of the great death toll caused by the famine. The Government was accused of selling the country's stocks of grain to Kenya and forcing the population to eat unripe grain. The country was facing a risk that the famine would stretch into the following year. Floods and the deterioration of roads and railways made food distribution more difficult. Seventy per cent of the population was going hungry and children and the elderly were those at greatest risk.

[39] In August 2003, the opposition party Genuine Alliance for Democracy was created by parliamentary dissidents. ■

Malaysia / Malaysia

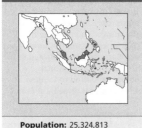

Population:	25,324,813
Area:	329,750 km²
Capital:	Kuala Lumpur
Currency:	Ringgit
Language:	Bahasa Malaysia

The Malay Peninsula and the Borneo states of Sarawak and Sabah were first inhabited by the descendants of pre-Malay immigrants, the *orang asli*, who lived, as some still do, in the forests. The Malays probably came from southern China, via what is now Indonesia.

[2] Immigration from present-day China - made possible by the use of canoes during the second millennium BC - brought metal-working and agricultural techniques, particularly rice-farming, starting in the first millennium AD. The agricultural and fishing surplus contributed to the development of urban cultures, ports and trading with India. Indian influence was all-pervasive, bringing religion, political systems and the Sanskrit language.

[3] The Indianized kingdom of Funan was founded in the Mekong river area in the 1st century AD and Buddhist states eventually developed in the east, trading with China. In the 15th century, the port of Melaka (Malacca) was founded; its rulers, who were the first in the region to convert to Islam, stopped paying taxes to Siam (now Thailand). Trade with Islamic merchants brought prosperity to Melaka. The new faith spread across the rest of present-day Malaysia and Indonesia, replacing Buddhism. At

the beginning of the 16th century, Melaka attracted the Portuguese, who were competing with Arab merchants for the Indian Ocean trade routes.

[4] In 1511 the Portuguese viceroy of India, Alfonso de Albuquerque, seized the port by force. It was of vital strategic importance in the Portuguese struggle to maintain their monopoly on the spice-trade from the Moluccas Islands. These spices were exchanged for Indian textiles and Chinese silk and porcelain. In the 17th century, the Dutch formed an alliance with the Sultan of Johor to drive the Portuguese out of Melaka. This alliance between Johor and the Dutch was established in Batavia (present-day Jakarta) and it succeeded in eliminating European and Asian competition for a hundred years.

[5] Meanwhile, the British began to establish back-up points for their trade with China in northern Borneo (Kalimantan), and in 1786 founded the port of George Town, on the island of Penang (Pulau-Pinang), off the western coast. The British model of free trade proved more successful than the Dutch trade monopoly and Penang attracted a cosmopolitan population of Malays, Sumatrans, Indians and Chinese. In 1819, the British founded Singapore, but at the time they were more interested in safeguarding shipping than in the local spice trade, as their imports from China were being paid for with opium from India. Nevertheless, the Dutch and the British found it difficult to coexist in the region. A treaty drawn up in 1824 granted control of Indonesia to the Dutch, while Malaya was left in British hands.

[6] The colonies of Penang, Melaka and Singapore became the key points of the British colony. The British encouraged Chinese immigration to the ports along the Straits of Malacca in the early 19th century. They intermarried and became known as the Straits Chinese. The Malay peasants and

fishing people continued their traditional activities. From 1870, the British began to sign protectorate agreements with the sultans and in 1895 they encouraged them to form a federation, with Kuala Lumpur as its capital. The sultanates of northern Borneo (Brunei, Sabah and Sarawak, the last ruled by James Brooke, and his heirs) also became British protectorates, administered from Singapore, but without any formal ties with the peninsula.

[7] Towards the end of the 19th century, the British introduced rubber with Hevea seeds smuggled from Brazil, so bringing about an end to the rubber boom in the South American Amazon. They encouraged Tamil immigration from southern India, to get workers for the rubber plantations which faced growing demand from the incipient automobile industries.

[8] In the early 20th century, large numbers of Chinese arrived to work the tin mines and service the urban ports. The multi-ethnic society, with cultural, religious, and language differences, also had different educational systems for Malays, Indians and Chinese. On the economic front, the Malays stayed mainly in rural agriculture, the Chinese in the tin mines and urban service sectors, and the Indians worked on the rubber estates. In the first decades of the 20th century, the Malays joined the Islamic reform movements of the Middle East, the Indians supported the struggles of Mahatma Gandhi, and the Chinese were ideologically influenced first by the nationalism of Sun Yat-Sen and then by the Communist Party. Although the majority favored the Kuomintang, as early as 1927 there were Communist cells among the Chinese in the Strait Settlements.

[9] In 1942, during World War II, the country was occupied by the Japanese. The Japanese tried, like other Southeast Asian movements, to form alliances with the local

nationalist movements to gain support against the European powers. The greatest resistance came from the Chinese, especially the Malayan Communist Party, which organized guerrilla forces to oppose the invading forces.

[10] At the end of the war it was clear that British domination could not continue without changes, but the difficulties of diverse ethnic interests, 'protected' sultanates and ports under direct colonial administration made it difficult to find a suitable political system. The British proposed a Malayan Union with equal citizenship for all. This threatened the position of the Malays, and Malay nationalists gathered around the symbolic figure of the sultans founding the United Malays' National Organization (UMNO), controlled by the dominant class but with popular support.

[11] In 1948, there was a communist-led insurrection that was suppressed by British forces. Its failure was partly due to the view of many poor Malays and Indians that the revolt was a Chinese effort and not the action of a unifying, anti-colonial progressive movement. The Marxist parties were outlawed and their leaders jailed. From 1948 until 1960, the Communist Party waged guerrilla warfare in the northern Malayan Peninsula and in Borneo.

[12] In the early 1950s, journalist and activist Dato Onn made a new attempt at creating a pan-ethnic party. He left UMNO to found the Malayan Independence Party. He was defeated in the 1952 municipal elections by an alliance of UMNO and the Malayan Chinese Association (MCA). The alliance was later broadened to include the Malayan Indian Congress (MIC), winning nationwide elections in 1955.

[13] Faced with the threat of an armed communist insurrection, the British decided to negotiate. This resulted in Malayan independence in 1957. Tunku Abdul Rahman, a prince who led

WORKERS

UNEMPLOYMENT: 3.8% (2002)

LABOR FORCE   **2002**

■ FEMALE: 38.3%   ■ MALE: 61.7%

EMPLOYMENT DISTRIBUTION   **1995/2001**

F

M

■ AGRICULTURE	F: 21.0%	M: 13.0%
■ INDUSTRY	F: 33.0%	M: 29.0%
■ SERVICES	F:46.0%	M: 58.0%

Life expectancy
73.1 years
2000-2005

GNI per capita
$3,540
2002

Literacy
87% total adult rate
2000

HIV prevalence rate
0.3% of population 15-49 years old
2001

the independence movement, became the first prime minister. A federation of 11 states was established with a parliamentary system and a monarch chosen every five years from among the nine state sultans. A constitutional bargain was struck by the three communities: citizenship was granted to the non-Malays, but the Malays were recognized as indigenous people. They were accorded special privileges in education and public-sector employment and Malay would be the official language. The country adopted the free market system and a reliance on foreign capital, which had been established under colonialism, remained dominant.

Malaya was politically pro-Western.

¹⁴ In 1963, the British colonial states of Singapore (south of Malaya), Sabah and Sarawak obtained independence and joined Malaya to form the Federation of Malaysia. There were major disagreements over ethnic policy and Singapore was expelled from the federation in 1965, becoming an independent republic.

¹⁵ The conservative Alliance Party ruled with a large majority from 1957, but in the 1969 elections it lost many seats to the Islamic PAS Party, Gerakan and - mostly - to the Chinese-based Democratic Action Party (DAP). The parliamentary system was suspended and the country was ruled for two years by a National Operations Council.

¹⁶ A new economic policy set targets to increase the share of the economy in the hands of the Malays - *Bumiputeras* ('sons of the soil' - the local people who made up 59 per cent of the population) to 30 per cent by 1990 (from one per cent in 1970), while the share of the economy in the hands of foreign interests was to drop from 70 to 30 per cent and the share of the non-Bumiputeras (mainly Chinese and Indian) would amount to 40 per cent.

¹⁷ During the next two decades, the state companies that represented Bumiputeras acquired shares in British property and mining companies, and became part of joint ventures with transnational corporations. The Bumiputera share of the economy rose to almost 20 per cent by 1989, while foreign ownership fell below 40 per cent. Because of these policies, Malaysians of Chinese descent claimed that they faced discrimination at work, in education and elsewhere.

¹⁸ Dr Mahathir Mohamad took office as prime minister in 1981, and started to develop Malaysian industry. In the late 1980s he faced increasing challenges to his leadership from UMNO (the Front's main party). Some of his opponents left to form a new opposition party, Semangat 46. In 1990 they formed a loose opposition coalition with the Islamic PAS, the DAP and the small left-wing People's Party.

¹⁹ Under Mahathir, the number of political prisoners fell from over 1,000 to a few hundred. In 1987 a major crackdown led to 150 more detentions, including opposition politicians and leaders of social groups, all of whom were released by 1990.

²⁰ Malaysian foreign policy moved from its pro-Western position in the 1960s through non-alignment in the 1970s to a pro-Third World stance in the 1980s. In 1990, Kuala Lumpur hosted the inaugural summit meeting of 15 Third World countries (aiming at fostering concrete South-South co-operation projects). It played a major role in the South Commission and actively supported the Palestine Liberation Organization and South Africa's African National Congress.

²¹ Malaysia is a large tropical wood exporter and dealer, with a growing demand in the industrialized countries, especially Japan. In 1989 its timber exports earned $2.6 billion. More than 80 per cent of this timber came from Sarawak and Sabah, in Borneo. At that time it was estimated that out of the 305,000 square kilometers (sq km) of tropical forests, only 157,000 sq km were left, and the country was losing 5,000 sq km of tropical forest each year. Because of this Malaysia through its multinational companies shifted to logging in other countries (Brazil, DR Congo, Zimbabwe and Papua-New Guinea among others).

²² As hi-tech industries grew, the country experienced a shortage of skilled and semi-skilled labor. Wages increased significantly, accentuating the differences among social sectors.

²³ Tuanku Ja'afar ibni al-Marhum Tuanku Abdul Rahman became king in April 1994. In 1995, Prime Minister Mahathir's National Front coalition took 162 of the 192 seats in the Chamber of Representatives, and 84 per cent of the vote.

²⁴ Malaysia was hit by the 1997 economic crisis caused in part by the collapse of various regional currencies. In early September 1998, after months of debate on the situation, Mahathir removed Economy Minister Anwar Ibrahim from office, and accused him of 'sexual misconduct'. After his dismissal, Anwar led major protests against the Government and was arrested on 20 September. The opposition backed Anwar, seeing him as a liberal and a champion of foreign investment, and showed its support in protests. After he was imprisoned, the opposition leadership passed to his wife, Azizah Ismail. The economy suffered a 7 per cent recession compared to the previous year, and the new Economy Minister called for control over exchange rates and investment in order to stabilize the country.

²⁵ In April 1999, Anwar was sentenced to six years in prison, charged with 'sexual misconduct' and sodomy. Tens of thousands of demonstrators took to the streets of Kuala Lumpur to express solidarity for Anwar.

²⁶ The November 1999 legislative elections gave the absolute majority and more than two thirds of the seats to the ruling party, allowing Mahathir to stay in power until 2005. The Alternative Front, led by Azizah Ismail, received less than 20 per cent of the vote and complained that the Government had permitted just nine days of political campaigning. Meanwhile, the party of the Prime Minister, UMNO, suffered internal divisions, losing ground to its Islamic partner, PAS.

²⁷ In January 2000, once the trial against Anwar resumed, the Government detained four opposition political leaders and the former Economy Minister's

PROFILE

ENVIRONMENT

The Federation of Malaysia is made up of Peninsular Malaysia (131,588 sq km), and the states of Sarawak (124,450 sq km) and Sabah (73,711 sq km) in northern Borneo (Kalimantan), 640 km from the peninsula in the Indonesian archipelago. Thick tropical forests cover more than 70 per cent of the mainland area, and a mountain range stretches from north to south across the peninsula. Coastal plains border the hills on both sides. In Sabah and Sarawak, coastal plains ascend to the mountainous interior. There is heavy annual rainfall. Malaysia's economy is export-orientated. Tin and rubber, the traditional export products, have recently been replaced by petroleum and manufactured goods.

SOCIETY

Peoples: Bumiputera (Malays) and other indigenous peoples including orang asli, Penan, Iban - 56 per cent; Chinese 33 per cent; Indians 11 per cent.
Religions: Islam, the official religion, is practiced by about half the population. Buddhist 17 per cent, Taoist 11 per cent, Hindu 7 per cent, Christian 7 per cent; animist.
Languages: Bahasa Malaysia (Malay) is the official language. Chinese languages, Tamil, English and many orang asli languages.
Main Political Parties: Barisan Nasional (ruling coaltion) includes United Malays National Organization (UMNO), Gerakan Rakyat Malaysia Party (PGRM), Malaysian Chinese Association (MCA), Malaysian Indian Congress (MIC), Sabah Progressive Party (SAPP), Sarawak United People's Party (SUPP). Main opposition parties include Democratic Action Party (DAP); Islamic Party of Malaysia (PAS).
Main Social Organizations: The leading labor organization is the Congress of Malaysia's Unions. Network of Indigenous Peoples of Malaysia.

THE STATE

Official Name: Persekutuan Tanah Malaysia
Administrative Division: 13 states, 3 federal territories and 130 districts.
Capital: Kuala Lumpur 1,352,000 people (2003).
Other Cities: Johor Baharu 691,000 people; Ipoh 552,800; Petaling Jaya 474,600; Melaka 126,100 (2000).
Government: Constitutional, parliamentary and federal monarchy. Tuanku Salehuddin Abdul Aziz Shah ibn al-Marhum Hisamuddin Alam Shah is the current king or *yang di-pertuan agong*, since April 1999. The sovereign is elected every five years from among the nine regents (sultans), and only the sultans can vote. Datuk Abdullah Ahmad Badawi, Prime Minister since 2003. Central bicameral parliament, 69-member Senate, 192-member Chamber of Deputies, with a constitution and a legislative assembly for every state.
National Holiday: 31 August, Independence Day (1957).
Armed Forces: 114,500 (1995). Other: 21,500 Police, Regular, Sea and Air, Auxiliaries.

Under-5 mortality
8 per 1,000 live births
2002

Poverty
<2% of population living on less than $1 per day
1997

Debt service
6.0% exports of goods and services
2001

Maternal mortality
12 per 100,000 live births
2000

IN FOCUS

ENVIRONMENTAL CHALLENGES
Indiscriminate logging and the use of highly toxic herbicides are causes for concern. There are fears that indigenous trees and crops may be irreparably harmed.

WOMEN'S RIGHTS
Women have been able to vote and stand for office since 1955. Between 1995 and 2000, women held 7 per cent of the seats in parliament, while their share of ministerial or equivalent positions increased from 7 per cent to 16 per cent.

In 2002, 40 per cent of the workforce was made up of women, 13 per cent of whom worked in agriculture, 29 per cent in industry and 58 per cent in the service sector.

Malaysia is a country of origin, transit and destination for the trafficking of women and children into the sex trade, including women from Malaysia, Indonesia, the Philippines, Thailand, China, Taiwan, Singapore, Myanmar (Burma), Vietnam, Sri Lanka and Laos. Some Chinese Malaysian women are involved in the sex trade in Hong Kong, Japan, Canada, the US, and Australia.

In 2002 there were an estimated 142,000 women in the sex trade in Malaysia. Despite Islamic influence and the Government's social control, most cities have a red-light district.

CHILDREN
In the last few years the economy developed and priority was put on improvements in the fields of education and healthcare. However, the ILO estimates that in 2000 more than 60,000 children under 14 were economically active, including 28,000 girls, as well as 640,000 adolescents aged 15-19. Most of the children are in the informal sector, selling food and working in night markets; some also work on the rubber and palm oil plantations.

One of the main concerns of non-governmental organizations is how to make HIV/AIDS prevention information available in schools, because this would imply the inclusion of sex education in the curriculum, in a country that although multicultural, is mainly Muslim, and in which there are widely differing views on the subject.

INDIGENOUS PEOPLES/ ETHNIC MINORITIES
There are numerous groups of indigenous peoples (other than the Malays) although they are only approximately 2.1 million or 10.2 per cent of the population. The major issue confronting these ethnic communities is the dispossession of land.

The descendants of pre-Malay immigrants, the *orang asli*, live mainly in the forests of the peninsula and are largely outside the formal economy and social structure. There are many sub-

ethnic groups classified under Negrito, Senoi and Proto-Malay. They numbered 105,000 in 1997 representing just 0.5 per cent of the national population.

In Sarawak, in northern Borneo, there are several groups including the nomadic Penan, numbering about 7,000, who live in the equatorial rainforest. Few still practise hunting and gathering. Another group are the Bidayuh, with just over130,000 people; 8 per cent of Sarawak's population.

The Iban (formerly sometimes called Dayaks) are the most numerous of Sarawak's ethnic groups forming 30 per cent of the state's population. They are Christian. Their main concerns are lack of political representation, the loss of their land, and social, urban and educational problems that hinder the community's development.

The Kadazans in Sabah, also in northern Borneo, are descended from diverse ancestral groups with different languages and a range of social customs. Despite having lived in Sabah since 1800, they have been neglected and lack political representation. They number about 607,000, around 2.9 per cent of Malaysia's total population.

The Indians are geographically dispersed. Since most of them are Hindus, they are a religious as well as an ethnic minority. Chinese and Indians still

face cultural restrictions, mainly due to the Government's aim of assimilating children in the Malay education system. Indian and Chinese political parties, together with the Malays' UMNO and other parties, form the ruling coalition. There is tolerance and celebration of Malaysia's diversity of cultures. However, state policies are still felt broadly to favor Malays.

MIGRANTS/REFUGEES
In late 2002, Malaysia hosted around 59,000 asylum-seekers, the overwhelming majority of whom were Muslims from the Philippines. A total of 1,578 applications for refugee status were pending at UNHCR. Another 400 had already been granted refugee status. In 2002, at least 5,000 Rohingyas and 3,000 Acehnese were living in refugee conditions. The country is not a signatory to the UN convention on refugees, but since 1998 it has not denied protection to those approved by UNHCR.

DEATH PENALTY
The death penalty is mandatory for some offenses, such as murder and drug-trafficking, and discretionary for others. The Islamic PAS party, which in 2003 controlled two out of Malaysia's 13 states, favors implementing full sharia law.

---

defense lawyer, unleashing a wave of protests within and outside the country. Charges against the opposition included sedition and inciting racial violence. In March that year, the Government clamped down on pro-Anwar press. In April, responding to criticism, the Government announced the formation of a National Commission of Human Rights, to take citizens' complaints.
[28] In spite of protests and complaints from environmentalists, in February 2001 the Government went ahead with a mega-dam project in Bakun, Borneo, expected to become the largest in Southeast Asia. Apart from costing $5 billion, the dam would displace 10,000 people and flood large rainforest areas. A private company, jointly linked to the Government, began the preparatory logging.
[29] In March 2001, dozens of people were arrested in a poor Kuala Lumpur suburb during the worst ethnic clashes between Indians and Malays since 1969. Defense minister Najib Tun Razak

tried to minimize the ethnic causes and reduce it to a misunderstanding among neighbors. Kerk Kim Hock, Secretary General of the opposition Democratic Action Party, called for multi-party talks to ease the tension and the 'fragility of ethnic relations'. The Indian community, mostly descending from laborers who had come to work in rubber plantations during colonial times, is the poorest in the country.
[30] Tighter control over capital flows had enabled the Government to ease the effects of the financial crisis and avoid the special loans and rules imposed by international financial institutions (IMF and the World Bank). At UMNO's annual assembly in June, Mahathir lashed out at the West, alluding to the criticism he received for detaining Anwar and opposition members. The Premier accused Anwar Ibrahim's opposition party, Reformasi, of 'using Mafia-style strategies to reach its goals', and the Islamic

PAS of being 'more interested in power than religious values'.
[31] In April 2002 the Government gave illegal immigrants a certain period to 'give themselves up' and avoid punishments such as lashings, jail and fines, while Parliament passed amendments to the Immigration Act. After a conference in Bali, in which Asia-Pacific ministers agreed to take measures against human trafficking, the authorities increased their actions against illegal residents (10 per cent of the labor force), most of them Indonesian and Filipinos.
[32] Before a visit by Mahathir to Washington in May 2002, the police arrested 14 people suspected of being Islamic militants, including the wife of a man accused of aiding hijackers who carried out the 11 September 2001 attacks in the US. This police offensive was applauded by the US, which thanked the Malaysian Government for the support it gave to the US' 'war on terror'.
[33] In June 2002 Mahathir announced that he planned to

resign in 2003. In August 2002, strong regulations against undocumented immigrants took effect and led to the departure of thousands of foreign workers.
[34] In June 2003, Mahathir expressed strong criticism of the US and Britain. In an obvious reference to the war on Iraq, he said that false allegations had been used to justify military action. He also claimed that the West had begun to invade and rule certain countries to exploit their wealth rather than because of security concerns - and that Malaysia could be a target. The speech, which followed categorical opposition to the war in Iraq voiced by the Non-Alignment Countries Conference in Kuala Lumpur in February 2003, angered US President George W Bush, who threatened Malaysia with economic sanctions.
[35] Abdullah Ahmad Badawi became Prime Minister in October 2003, replacing Mahathir Mohamad after 22 years in power. ∎

Maldives / Dhivehi Raajje

Population:	337,722
Area:	300 km²
Capital:	Male
Currency:	Rufiyaa
Language:	Dhivehi

The Maldives archipelago was inhabited as early as the 5th century BC by Buddhist peoples who were probably from Sri Lanka and southern India. In their regions of origin, both groups spoke Indo-Aryan languages - Sinhalese and Dravidian, respectively - from which the Dhivehi language was later derived. Throughout the centuries, traders from Arab countries, Malaysia, Madagascar, Indonesia, and China visited the islands as a stopover destination.

2   Islam was adopted in 1153 AD. Ibn Battutah, a notable North African traveler who resided in the islands in the 1340s, remarked disapprovingly on the freedom enjoyed by women.

3   The Portuguese established themselves by force in Male (today's capital) from 1558 until they were expelled by the local population in 1573.

4   In the 17th century, the islands were a sultanate under the protection of the Dutch rulers of Ceylon (present-day Sri Lanka). The British took possession of Ceylon in 1796, but it was not until 1887 that the incorporation of its territory to the British Crown was formalized.

5   The British had little economic interest in the natural resources of the islands (fishing and tropical fruits). However, the archipelago was of great importance to their maritime transport when they had control over the Suez Canal Company between 1875 and 1956. In order to maintain the transit route under British control at that time (from Gibraltar to Hong Kong), a naval base was set up on Gan Island, at the southern end of the Maldives.

6   Until 1932, absolute power over the local population rested with sultans or sultanas, the only ones to benefit from the relationship with Britain. That year, a Constitution that granted some rights to Maldivians went

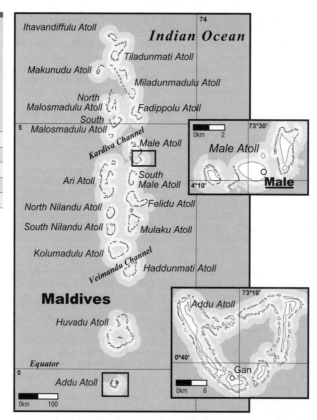

into effect, although the country remained a sultanate. In 1953, a popular revolt overthrew the ruler and a republic was proclaimed. British troops intervened to 'restore order' and three months later the country reverted to a sultanate.

7   In 1957, Britain requested permission to enlarge the Gan naval base and install facilities for fighter planes to land there. The proposal triggered fierce opposition and Prime Minister Ibrahim Ali Didi was forced to

resign. In 1959, rebellion broke out in the southern Maldives, which decided to break away under the name of the Republic of Suvadiva. One year later, the 20,000 Suvadivan republicans were restored to the sultanate with British help.

8   This intervention paved the way for the British to immediately sign a new agreement with the Sultan extending the protectorate, and maintaining and enlarging the military bases.

9   In 1965 the Maldives attained full independence from Britain, receiving immediate recognition from the UN. However, the Gan naval base was not dismantled until 1976, one year after the building of the US' military installations on the neighboring island of Diego García.

10   The sultanate was abolished in a plebiscite held in 1968 and an Islamic republic was established. Amir Ibrahim Nasir, the Sultan's Prime Minister, became President. In March 1975, President Nasir accused Prime Minister Ahmed Zaki of leading a conspiracy; Zaki was immediately exiled to a desert island along with some of his supporters.

11   Once the British withdrew from the Gan naval base, Nasir proposed to rent the unused installations to transnational corporations, but his idea was rejected by the *Majilis* (legislative council). Nasir, who had been elected five years earlier, ended his second presidential term in 1978, without standing for re-election. Maumoon Gayoom, a former Minister of Transport during the Nasir administration who had studied in Sri Lanka and Egypt, was appointed President.

12   Until that time, the Maldives, with a population scattered across 200 islands, had practiced mainly traditional medicine and had only one hospital in Male. Half of the population had access to the Dhivehi-language schools *(makthabs)* which were focused on reading and reciting the Qur'an, while only English-language primary and secondary schools, attended by British descendants, were equipped to teach the standard curriculum.

13   Most of the population subsisted outside the money

PROFILE

ENVIRONMENT
There are nearly 1,200 coral islets in this archipelago, where the land is never more than 3.5 meters above sea level. Vegetation is sparse except for the plentiful coconut palms. A tropical monsoon climate prevails. There are no mineral or energy resources. Fishing is the main natural resource.

SOCIETY
Peoples: The population of the archipelago came from migrations of Dravidian, Indo-Aryan and Sinhalese peoples from India, later followed by Arab peoples.
Religions: Muslim (official and proclaimed universal).
Languages: Dhivehi (official), an Indo-Aryan language related to Sinhalese; English and Arabic are also spoken.
Main Political Parties: There are no political parties. The *Majilis* or parliament is elected by

direct vote and in turn proposes a president whose candidacy is submitted to a referendum.
Main Social Organizations: There are no social organizations.

THE STATE
Official Name: Dhivehi Jumhuriyya (Republic of the Maldives).
Administrative Divisions: 20 districts.
Capital: Male 83,000 people (2003).
Other Cities: Hithadhoo 10,800 people; Fuvahmulah 8,100 (2000).
Government: Presidential republic. Maumoon Abdul Gayoom, President since 1978, re-elected in 1983, 1988, 1993, 1998 and 2003. Legislative Power: the Citizens' Council, with 48 members, 8 of whom are elected by the President.
National Holiday: 26 July, Independence Day (1965).
Armed Forces: About 1,000. The force performs both army and police functions.

Life expectancy
67.4 years
2000-2005

GNI per capita
$2,090
2002

Literacy
97% total adult rate
2000

HIV prevalence rate
0.1% of population 15-49 years old
2001

economy, depending on fishing and the cultivation of tropical fruits. Being excellent boat-builders and sailors, Maldivians held long-standing maritime relations with Sri Lanka, Singapore and India.

[14] In 1979, Gayoom travelled to Europe, the Middle East and Cuba, where he attended the Sixth Summit Conference of the Non-Aligned Movement and became a member of the organization. In 1980, the Maldives signed a scientific and technological co-operation agreement with the Soviet Union. A similar agreement was signed with China in 1981, and also a trade agreement with India. That year, the Maldivian authorities refused to join ASEAN. Meanwhile, in 1982 the Maldives became a member of the British Commonwealth.

[15] During the first five years of his administration, Gayoom founded schools with educational programs following international standard curricula. During that period, the Government set up a fisheries corporation for the processing of canned and frozen tuna which became the main export product together with handmade clothing.

[16] In 1983, upon ending his first presidential term, Gayoom was re-elected in a referendum with 95 per cent of the vote.

[17] In the early 1980s, tourism was promoted and the Maldives became a holiday destination for many Europeans. Within 20 years, the tourism industry grew by 1,600 per cent. In early 2000, 74 islets were set aside exclusively for tourist resort development which, on the negative side, led to increasing pollution of beaches.

[18] In August 1988, three months before he was elected president for the third time, Maumoon Gayoom - with the help of Indian troops - put down another coup attempt, allegedly promoted by Amir Nasir. Seventy-five people were arrested, most of them Sri Lankans.

[19] In 1990, in a cabinet reshuffle, Gayoom removed the minister of defense, trade and industry. The former minister was the president's brother-in-law and was considered the richest person in the Maldives. From 1978 and until the break-up of the Soviet Union (1990-1991), successive Maldivian cabinets had refused to divulge information regarding the amount of loans and subsidies granted by foreign countries.

[20] In 1991, the Maldives fell into an economic crisis caused by a chronic trade deficit. That year,

IN FOCUS

ENVIRONMENTAL CHALLENGES
Global warming and the resulting rise in the sea level are affecting the islands and coral reefs. Only ten per cent of the land is arable. A depletion of freshwater aquifers threatens drinking water supplies.

WOMEN'S RIGHTS
Women have been able to vote and stand for office since 1932. From 1995 to 2000, women held 6 per cent of seats in parliament as well as ministerial positions.

In 2000, women made up 43 per cent of the islands' labor force. Between 1990 and 2000, 20 per cent of pregnant women were anemic. UNICEF's latest data available* shows that 81 per cent of pregnant women receive prenatal care, while 70 per cent of births are attended by qualified health personnel.

Frequently, girls receive no more than seven years of schooling since parents do not allow them to live outside their own island and not all islands have access to secondary and tertiary education.

In 2000, 97 per cent of women were literate.

CHILDREN
In 2001, 75 per cent of the population in the 200 or so inhabited islands was under 25 years old. Malnutrition and inadequate hygiene are

impediments to children's development, in spite of certain improvements in the overall situation in the last decade.

There are substantial disparities in access to basic services between communities on the different atolls. The high costs of transport services and infrastructure, persistent gender inequalities, insufficient data-collection mechanisms, increasing disintegration of the traditional family unit, environmental threats, urban congestion and increasing migration to the main cities are the main factors that threaten the well-being of children.

UNICEF's latest data available* shows that 30 per cent of children under five are moderately or severely underweight. Severe malnutrition affects 7 per cent of children in that age group, while 13 per cent suffers from severe and moderate weakness and 25 per cent suffers from moderate to severely stunted growth.

It is estimated that around 26,000 young people will expect to enter the labor market by 2006; as a result, high youth unemployment rates are expected.

INDIGENOUS PEOPLES/ ETHNIC MINORITIES
In early history - around 500 BC - the Buddhists replaced the ancient sun-worshipping religions, and in

turn Buddhism was displaced in 1153 AD by Islam. The language of the Maldives is Dhivehi. It is related to Sinhala, a Sri Lankan language, but also contains Arabic and Tamil words. The chain of islands has stood out throughout history for being a cultural mosaic of Africans, Arabs and sailors from Southeast Asia.

MIGRANTS/REFUGEES
As a result of the wide socioeconomic disparities between Male and outlying islands, there is a high rate of internal migration to the capital. The limited number of secondary and tertiary-level educational institutions and health facilities mean that a large number of students and medical patients go abroad, mainly to neighboring countries. Other mobile groups include unskilled and skilled labor, looking for better possibilities both within and outside the country.

DEATH PENALTY
The death penalty has not been applied in the case of any type of crime since 1952, the year in which the last execution took place.

*Latest data available in *The State of the World's Children* and *Childinfo* database, UNICEF, 2004.

the Government sold 25 per cent of its shares in the Bank of Maldives and adopted free-market policies, although state control was maintained over exports of frozen and canned fish. To boost revenues, during the first Gulf War (1990-1991) Gayoom allowed the US to use the military installations. In 1994, the country's foreign debt represented 75 per cent of the GDP.

[21] President Gayoom began his fourth term of office in 1993 and remained as head of the ministries of defense, national security and finance. That year, the Government evacuated five small islands that were under threat of being submerged by rising sea levels from the melting of the polar ice caps as a result of global warming.

[22] In 1997, one year prior to his fifth re-election, Gayoom opened the country's first university-level institute. At the same time, telephone connections were established in those islands still without them and the installation

of a water purification plant was announced for the following year.

[23] A new constitution was approved in 1998, establishing that the legislature would elect the president. Choosing from among five candidates, legislators decided in September to re-elect Gayoom; this was confirmed by referendum in November with 90 per cent of the vote. The Government had prohibited political parties from campaigning for their candidates, forcing all of them to run as individuals. The first Maldivian Republic set up the basis for a regulatory framework in which political pluralism was not reflected and government censorship was strengthened.

[24] Since the 1990s, the country has been accused of systematic violations of basic rights. Sexual rights organizations have protested against the punishment - which includes life imprisonment - for male homosexual acts. Likewise, Reporters Without Borders

denounced the imprisonment of journalists who had published articles criticizing the Government. Amnesty International called upon the Maldivian Government to modify its laws to allow the free expression of ideas and respect the right to *habeas corpus*.

[25] In September 2003, a demonstration in Male ended with three people killed, 24 wounded and 100 arrested. The protests were triggered by a prison riot that was sparked by cases of torture and a lack of legal representation for prisoners. Among the inmates were three members of parliament who were going to stand as candidates for the presidential elections and several activists of the outlawed Maldivian Democratic Party.

[26] In the October 2003 presidential referendum, Gayoom, the only candidate, won 90.3 per cent of the vote and started his sixth consecutive term of office. ■

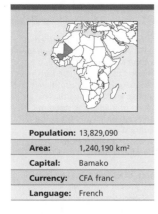

Population:	13,829,090
Area:	1,240,190 km²
Capital:	Bamako
Currency:	CFA franc
Language:	French

The remains of rock paintings and carvings that date from before 5000 BC were found in the region of Malian Sahara (northern half of the territory). A human skeleton found near the city of Timbuktu in 1927 also dates from that era.

2 Since the 3rd century, traders traveled in caravans across the Sahara desert from the Niger River, which was rich in gold deposits, to present-day Morocco and Algeria. They transported feathers, ivory and gold, as well as slaves to work in salt extraction.

3 Between the 4th and 11th centuries, the Saharan trade routes across Mali were controlled by the Soninke kingdom of Ghana, between the Niger and Senegal rivers. Evidence of this black civilization are the terra-cotta statues found in the city of Djenne that were sculpted in the 8th century. In 1076, the Almoravids (a group of religious Muslim warriors and Berber dynasty) overthrew the Soninke empire.

4 In the 12th century, the Almoravids were replaced by the kingdom of Mali (Malinke, black African group). From the middle and northern portions of the Niger River, the Malinke dominated the Saharan trade routes. In 1255, the empire covered what are now Senegal, Gambia, Guinea-Bissau, part of Guinea, half of Mauritania, southern Algeria and all of Mali.

5 The decline of the Malinke empire began in the 15th century with the emergence of the Songhai empire that was settled in the area between Timbuktu and the present-day city of Gao and managed to spread its rule over all of Mali between the 15th and 16th centuries. Under Songhai influence, the cities of Djenne and Timbuktu flourished as centers of both trade and Islamic scholarship.

6 In 1591, the Moroccan army of Ahmad al-Mansur took over the domain of the Songhai empire, imposing its rule for about two centuries. It was during this period that most of Mali's Berber groups such as the Tuaregs - the most numerous group, whose members are still nomadic - and the 'Moors' (Arab Berbers) came to the region.

7 With the destruction of Songhai rule, a time of political chaos ensued. The Moroccans dispersed the manuscripts of Timbuktu's libraries and executed Songhai scholars. They also discontinued the trans-Sahara trade routes. New routes were established to supply gold and slaves to the European posts on the Atlantic coast.

8 The ties between Moroccan authorities and invaders lapsed and in 1737 the Tuaregs managed to seize control of the Niger Bend. In 1833, the Muslim Fulani kingdom, which had spread to Cote d'Ivoire and Senegal since the 17th century, finally defeated the Moroccans. The Fulani were nomadic herders. Those who are still pastoralists are widely dispersed in West Africa; most have retained their original animistic beliefs.

9 The 19th century in Mali was marked by French colonial penetration, from the west (Senegal), and at the same time, by the wars between Islamic groups (*jihads*) prompted by the establishment of a theocratic state by the Fulani dynasty of the Macina region.

10 The French built their first fort in 1855. By combining military incursions and partial alliances with rival local groups, they managed to dominate the territory which would later be called French Sudan (present-day Mali, Burkina Faso, Benin and Senegal).

11 The fact that France was growing weaker, combined with the democratic atmosphere that prevailed after World War II, encouraged the emergence of anti-colonial organizations. In Africa, this was expressed by the formation of the African Democratic Assembly (RDA), at a conference in Bamako in 1945, led by Modibo Keita.

12 In the following decade, under the impact of the defeat of French colonialism at Dien Bien Phu in Vietnam (1954) and the Algerian revolution (1954-1962), Paris embarked on a policy of gradual concessions that led to Mali's independence and to the proclamation of the Republic of Mali in August 1960.

13 That same year, Modibo Keita became President and headed the Federation of Mali, which was joined by the presidents of Senegal (Senghor) and Cote d'Ivoire (Houphouet-Boigny). The three leaders, who had been educated in France, wanted a common program under the banner of 'African socialism'. However, their differences regarding their countries' individual relationship with France and with the USSR and China caused the project to fail.

14 Keita decided to expropriate and nationalize all sectors of the economy. His administration neither managed to change the backward social and economic conditions nor build a strong political structure. In 1967, when the country was on the verge of political and financial collapse, Keita started negotiations with France. In November 1968, the Military Committee for National Liberation (CMLN), headed by Colonel Moussa Traoré, seized power in a coup.

15 Traoré banned all political activity. Until that time, the parliamentary democracy had never been fully exercised. In 1974, a new

PROFILE

ENVIRONMENT

There are three distinct regions: the northern region which is part of the Sahara desert; the central region which consists of the Sahel grasslands, subject to desertification; and the southern region, with humid savannah vegetation, home to most of the population, and irrigated by the two major rivers: the Senegal and the Niger. There are significant gold deposits.

SOCIETY

Peoples: Among the many Malian ethnic groups, the largest are the Mande. Other significant ethnic groups are the Tuareg, Peul, Songhai, Moor, Senufo, Fulani, Dogon and Voltaic. In the north are found the lighter-skinned nomadic population, made up of Berber groups.
Religions: 90 per cent Muslim, 9 per cent practice traditional African religions, and small Christian minority. **Languages:** French (official). Of the African languages, Bambara is the most widely spoken (80 per cent). Arabic and Tuareg are also spoken.
Main Political Parties: Alliance for Democracy in Mali (ADEMA); Party for National Renewal (PARENA); Rally for Mali; Rally for Democracy and Progress; Democratic and Social Convention.
Main Social Organizations: National Workers Union of Mali (UNTM); Alumni and Students Association of Mali (AEEM); National Union of Women of Mali (UNFM); National Union of Mali Youth (UNJM); Movements and Unified Fronts of the Azawads (MFUA), opposition Tuareg groups.

THE STATE

Official Name: République du Mali. **Administrative Divisions:** 8 regions and the district of Bamako. **Capital:** Bamako 1,264,000 people (2003). **Other Cities:** Ségou 132,400 people; Mopti 114,400; Sikasso 125,400; Gao 104,700 (2000). **Government:** Head of state: Amadou Toumani Tourné, President since 8 June 2002. Head of Government: Ousmane Issoufi Maïga, Prime Minister since 2004. The Prime Minister appoints the members of the Cabinet. Legislature: single-chamber: National Assembly, with 129 members, elected every 5 years.
National Holiday: 22 September, Independence Day (1960).
Armed Forces: 7,350 (Gendarmes, Republican Guard, Militia and National Police) (1995)

Life expectancy
48.6 years
2000-2005

GNI per capita
$240
2002

Literacy
26% total adult rate
2000

HIV prevalence rate
1.6% of population 15-49 years old
2001

constitution was approved in a referendum with 99.8 per cent of the vote, which provided for a six-year presidential term. Its Civil Code included a law - still in force in 2004 - that condemned sodomy. The opposition was banned from taking part in the election and Keita's followers were imprisoned. Keita died in prison on 16 May, 1977. In the largest mass demonstration ever seen in Bamako, the people followed Keita's body to the cemetery in open defiance of the military regime.

[16] Also in 1974, Traoré launched a process of liberalization of the economy and relied on loans granted by France, the US, the EEC and OPEC, to finance agricultural production, which employed 80 per cent of the population. But the fluctuations in international prices brought about the collapse of Mali's economy, which required the implementation of emergency plans by the UNDP and the European Development Fund.

[17] In 1979, Traoré's re-election triggered student demonstrations which were harshly repressed. As a result, three students were killed, around 100 arrested and 13 tortured. Immediately after, Traoré embarked upon an austerity program drawn up by the IMF and the international creditor banks, through the Democratic Union of Malian People (the military junta's puppet party).

[18] In June 1985, President Traoré, running as the official party's only candidate, was re-elected with 99.94 per cent of the vote.

[19] In 1988, the foreign debt amounted to 125 per cent of GDP, with debt servicing exceeding a quarter of export revenues. That same year, following IMF guidelines, the Government began the privatization of the banking system with French financial support. The authorities also announced a reduction in the number of public employees, as well as the decision to sell off state enterprises; at the same time, the cabinet was reshuffled. Students, teachers and public employees took to the streets to protest against these measures.

[20] On 10 April 1991, a popular and military revolt against the Traoré regime carried Lt-Col Amadou Toumani Touré to power. He was the leader of the Council of Transition for the Salvation of the People (CTSP), which promised to transfer government to civilians early in 1992.

[21] An uprising in June 1991 by the Tuaregs in the north and the Moors in the east exacerbated the social tensions. In July, an attempted coup by a portion of the armed forces led Toumani Touré to grant a 70 per cent wage raise to the armed forces and civil servants. In April 1992, the premier signed a peace agreement with the Azawad Unified Front and Movements, an umbrella

ENVIRONMENTAL CHALLENGES
The desertification process and soil erosion are aggravated by the lack of water and the deforestation by fire in order to open the way for crops.

WOMEN'S RIGHTS
Women have been able to vote and stand for office since 1959. Between 1995 and 2000, the proportion of seats in parliament held by women increased from 2 to 12 per cent and their representation in ministerial or equivalent positions doubled to 21 per cent. In 2000, women made up 46 per cent of the total labor force.

That year, 74.9 per cent of women between the ages of 15 and 24 were illiterate, compared to 52.7 per cent of men in the same age group.

The last specialized surveys (DHS 1996-2001 and MICS 1999-2002) reported that nearly 90 per cent of women between the ages of 15 and 49 had undergone some form of genital mutilation, except for those living in the regions of Gao and Timbuktu, where the rate was lower. The same surveys revealed that 73 per cent of women had at least one daughter who had also undergone genital mutilation. No differences were found with respect to this practice between

women from rural areas and those from urban areas or among those who belonged to different ethnic groups or religions.

CHILDREN
In 2002, 7.09 million people, more than half of the population, were under 18 years old. Of these, 2.5 million were under five years old. That year, more than 140,000 children under five died. The previous year, 13,000 children under 14 were living with HIV, and 70,000 children under 14 had lost both parents to AIDS. The life expectancy in Mali was 49 years. In 2000, 51 per cent of boys were enrolled in school, with a lower enrollment rate for girls. The school drop-out rate was higher in girls than in boys.

In 1998, the trafficking of thousands of children from Mali to northern Cote d'Ivoire was made public. The children were mostly boys and were trafficked to work in coffee, cotton and cocoa plantations or for domestic labor under abusive conditions. It was estimated that within the last years, 15,000 children between 9 and 12 years old had been sold for such purposes.

INDIGENOUS PEOPLES/ ETHNIC MINORITIES
There are 10 distinct ethnic groups in Mali. Mande is the biggest group, accounting for 50 per cent of the population. The Tuaregs and

Senegalese - a group native to the region and a national minority, respectively - make up six and three per cent of the total population.

More than 600,000 Tuaregs went through a period of rebellion in the mid-1990s. The government repression they suffered reduced the chance of further revolts in recent years, although the authorities remain unwilling or unable to implement development and educational projects to alleviate the social marginalization suffered by the Tuaregs.

MIGRANTS/REFUGEES
Mali hosted some 4,000 refugees and asylum-seekers in late 2002, primarily from Liberia, Sierra Leone, and Cote d'Ivoire. That year, about 5,000 people from Mauritania lived in Mali in refugee-like circumstances. Nearly 3,000 Malians requested asylum in Europe and other industrialized countries in 2002. About 4,000 Malians lived in Mauritania as refugees. The UNHCR closed its office in the country in 2001.

DEATH PENALTY
Mali is considered de facto abolitionist since the last execution dates back to 1980. However, the death penalty is still provided for by law.

organization linking four Tuareg opposition groups.

[22] On 26 April 1992, Alpha Oumar Konaré, leader of the Alliance for Democracy in Mali (ADEMA), was elected President in the first multiparty elections since the country's independence.

[23] Konaré continued cutting public spending and went ahead with the privatization of state companies and the elimination of price controls through successive structural adjustment programs in accordance with IMF guidelines. In 1995, the discovery of new gold deposits attracted foreign investment.

[24] An exodus of 120,000 Tuaregs was provoked by the persecution against them. They fled to Algeria, Mauritania, Niger and Burkina Faso (Mali had confronted this latter country in a border war in 1985). In 2002, Amnesty International reported that thousands of Tuaregs had been executed and imprisoned without trial. In 1995, the Government pursued negotiations with Tuareg groups which led to the demobilization of 2,700 guerrillas in 1996 and to the gradual return of refugees.

[25] In May 1997, Konaré was re-elected president with 95.9 per cent

of the vote. The opposition complained that there was no guarantee of protection if they voted, and so they boycotted the 1998 general and local elections. That year, Moussa Traoré and his wife were charged with misappropriation of funds and abuse of power, and were sentenced to death, although the sentence was later commuted to life imprisonment.

[26] A coup d'etat was foiled in January 2000, but a few days later the President decided to include military officers in his cabinet. One month later, Mande Sidibe, an economist and former IMF official, was appointed Prime Minister.

[27] The April 2002 elections were marred by allegations of fraud and gave the victory to Amadou Toumani Touré with 64.4 per cent of the vote. Touré was very popular for having overthrown Traoré and for having kept his promise to hand over power to civilians in 1992. However, the cabinet of the 'government of national unity' formed by Touré with 22 minority organizations, resigned en masse in October of that year. None of those involved gave a public explanation.

[28] At the WTO ministerial conference held in Cancun in

September 2003, Mali, together with three other African countries, filed a complaint against subsidies granted by the US Government to US cotton producers. The Malian representatives said it was a 'life or death' issue for the frail economy of the West African country, which since the 1970s has achieved a high level of competitiveness in this product.

[29] That month, the president of France paid an official visit and granted a loan to support Mali's textile industry, with the aim of curbing emigration. He also unsuccessfully proposed a co-operation agreement for the repatriation of undocumented Malian immigrants living in France who currently number around 100,000.

[30] At the end of 2003, the Government negotiated the release of 40 hostages (mainly German tourists) who had been kidnapped by an Islamic extremist group, the Salafist Group for Preaching and Combat, as part of an operation against the Algerian Government. The Algerian organization to which the kidnappers belonged was included on Washington's list of terrorist groups. ∎

Malta / Malta

Population:	397,334
Area:	320 km²
Capital:	Valletta
Currency:	Liri
Language:	Maltese and English

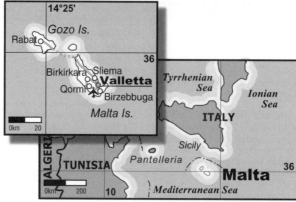

M alta's most valuable 'natural resource' is its geographic location, which has made it the historical focus of every conflict for domination of the Mediterranean. Being situated midway between Tunisia and Sicily, Malta is the key to the sea routes between east and west. In ancient times, Phoenicians, Greeks, Carthaginians, Romans and Saracens successively occupied the island.

[2] In 1090, the Normans conquered the island for the Kingdom of Sicily and 300 years later it fell to the Spanish Kingdom of Aragon. In the 16th century, the defense of the island was entrusted to the order of the Knights of St John of the Hospital (Knights Hospitalers). Kicked out of Palestine, they settled in Malta in 1574. They remained there for more than two centuries, known as the Knights of Malta, until they were driven out by the French in 1798. The Congress of Vienna in 1815 formally recognized the title of 'Sovereign Order of Malta', and consecrated English sovereignty over the island.

[3] From the early 20th century, the Maltese fought for their independence. After a popular uprising in 1921, London agreed to a certain degree of internal autonomy, which was revoked at the beginning of World War II.

[4] Malta was used as a base for the Allied counter-offensive against

Italy. In 1947, London returned the island to a certain level of autonomy.

[5] Independence was formally declared on 8 September 1964 but Britain maintained a strong influence over politics on the island. In 1971, the Labour Party attained power and established broader diplomatic relations. NATO forces were expelled that year, and Malta later joined the Movement of Non-Aligned Countries.

[6] From the beginning of the Labour administration, measures to reduce the Church's power had been introduced. The bishops owned 80 per cent of all property on the island and controlled education. The conflict erupted in 1983 when the Government expropriated all Church property and made secular education obligatory in primary schools. In 1985, the Government and the Church signed an agreement providing for a gradual transition to secular education at the secondary level.

[7] The Nationalist Party gained power in May 1987. Prime Minister Edward Fenech Adami initiated a policy of growing ties with the US. The economy was liberalized and tourism and foreign investment received a boost.

[8] Adami was re-elected in 1992, but he lost his position in the Government in 1996 when the Labour Party won the elections and Alfred Sant became Prime Minister.

Sant pulled the country out of NATO and asserted that Malta would use constitutional neutrality to promote stability and security in the Mediterranean region. He also froze the program for joining the European Union (EU) promoted during the Adami administration, and announced that he would seek a more gradual approach to admission into the bloc.

[9] The Government of Sant lasted for two years. In 1998, a vote of censure by the opposition provoked its collapse and new elections were called. The Nationalist Party's triumph reinstated Adami as Prime Minister. His first measure was to revive the request to join the EU.

[10] On 24 March 1999, Minister of Foreign Affairs Guido de Marco was promoted to President by Parliament. That same year, the EU

formally re-accepted Malta's application at its annual meeting in Brussels, and later authorized the start of final negotiations.

[11] Malta was the first country to abolish the death penalty in the new millennium when it passed the Law of the Armed Forces (Amendment) in March 2000, under which life imprisonment became the maximum penalty.

[12] Pope John Paul II visited Malta in May 2001. Approximately 200,000 people - one half of the population - attended the beatification by him of the three most celebrated Catholics (two priests and a nun). This open-air ceremony brought to a close the Pope's visit to the island, where he was completing his pilgrimage following the footsteps of St Paul.

[13] The debate surrounding accession to the EU was resolved on 8 March 2003 in a referendum in which a narrow majority (53.6 per cent) voted in favor of membership. In March 2004, Lawrence Gonzi took office as prime minister, appointed by President Guido de Marco. In the negotiations for accession, it was agreed that Malta would be granted 272 million euros by the EU for the 2004-2006 period, and would have to contribute around 178 million euros. The positive balance euros was seen by supporters of admission as one of the main reasons to join the EU. Malta formally joined the EU on 1 May 2004. ■

PROFILE

ENVIRONMENT
Malta is made up of five islands, two of which are uninhabited. The inhabited islands are the largest ones: Malta, where the capital is located, 246 sq km, and Gozo, 67 sq km. The archipelago is located in the central Mediterranean Sea, south of Sicily, east of Tunisia and north of Libya. The coast is high and rocky, with excellent natural harbors. The islands' environmental challenges are concentrated precisely in these areas. The problems are caused by the encroachment of urbanization, the development of tourism, the gradual abandonment of farmland, the increase in waste and the water pollution resulting from industrial activity.

SOCIETY
Peoples: The Maltese (95.7 per cent) come from numerous ethnic backgrounds, with strong Phoenician, Arab, Italian and British roots. There is a small British minority (2.1 per cent). **Religions:** Catholic (official); there are minorities of Anglicans and Muslims. **Languages:** Maltese and English, both official. Maltese is a Semitic language written in the Latin alphabet, with Italian elements. **Main Political Parties:** The Nationalist Party; The Labour Party, Alternativa Demokratika/Alliance for Social Justice.

THE STATE
Official Name: Repubblika ta'Malta. **Capital:** Valletta 83,000 people (2003). **Other Cities:** Birkirkara 21,700 people; Qormi 18,100; Sliema 11,800 (2000). **Government:** Parliamentary Republic. Fenech Amadi, president since March 2004. Lawrence Gonzi, Prime Minister since March 2004. Unicameral Legislature: House of Representatives has a minimum of 65 members, elected for a five-year term. The number of seats can increase if no party wins an absolute majority. **National Holiday:** 21 September, Independence Day (1964). **Armed Forces:** 1,950 troops (1996).

LAND USE

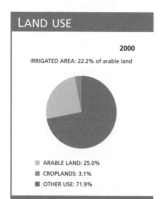

2000

IRRIGATED AREA: 22.2% of arable land

- ARABLE LAND: 25.0%
- CROPLANDS: 3.1%
- OTHER USE: 71.9%

PUBLIC EXPENDITURE

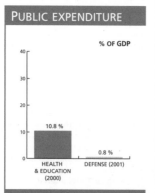

% OF GDP

10.8 %

0.8 %

HEALTH & EDUCATION (2000)

DEFENSE (2001)

Marshall Islands / Marshall Islands

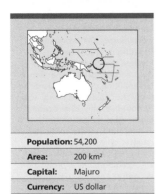

Population:	54,200
Area:	200 km²
Capital:	Majuro
Currency:	US dollar
Language:	Marshallese and English

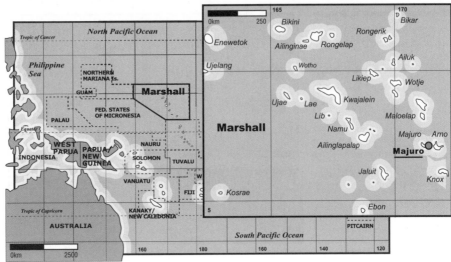

The Kwajalein and Bikini atolls of the Marshall Islands were thrust into modern history in February 1944 when heavy bombing by combined US naval and air force units hit the islands. This was followed by a prolonged and bloody battle which ended with the defeat of the Japanese and the occupation of the islands. Countless lives were lost but the military command considered it was a fair price to pay for the islands given their strategic location.

2 In 1979, the US proposed making the four administrative units an Associated Free State. The Republic of the Marshall Islands (the official name since 1982) was granted jurisdiction over local and foreign affairs but the US declared the islands military territory for specific use. By doing so, they made a de facto situation official: between 1946 and 1958, nuclear tests had been performed on the Bikini and Kwajalein atolls which turned the Marshall Islands into the area with the highest level of radioactive contamination in the world.

3 In 1961, Kwajalein became the Pacific experimental missile target area, especially for intercontinental ballistic missiles launched from California, and early in the 1980s the US chose the atoll as a testing site for its new MX missiles. The local population was evacuated and entry was forbidden to civilians.

4 In the case of the Bikini atoll, 23 nuclear tests were performed there between 1946 and 1958, including the detonation of the first H-bomb. The inhabitants of the atoll insisted on returning to their homeland after having been transferred to the Rongelap atoll. In 1979, testing revealed that 130 of the total 600 inhabitants living on the Bikini atoll were contaminated with extremely dangerous levels of plutonium.

5 The inhabitants of Bikini, together with those living on Rongelap, sued the US Government for $450 million. The charges were filed together with reports compiled by US Government agencies demonstrating that local residents had been intentionally exposed to radioactivity in 1954 in order to study the effects of the bomb on humans. Reports revealed by the US Government in 1995 proved the dangers of exposure were known but this had never been passed on to the people of the Marshall Islands. The US has so far paid nearly $100 million in compensation for damages caused by nuclear testing.

6 In October 1986, the US and the Marshall Islands signed a pact whereby the latter became a Free Associated State, responsible for its own internal political affairs. The US would be responsible for the defense of the new state for a period of 15 years, which would enable the US to set up an important air base on the island, in exchange for financial aid.

7 In the first elections of the new state, held in 1986, Amata Kabua was elected President. In 1988, the Marshall Islands were admitted to the South Pacific Regional Trade and Economic Co-operation Agreement.

8 In April 1990, the US announced that it would use the area to destroy chemical weapons installed in Europe to date. Environmentalists also denounced plans to dispose of 25 million tons of toxic waste on one of the archipelago's atolls between 1989 and 1994. In September of that year, the Marshall Islands were accepted as a member state of the UN.

9 Chancellor Tony de Brun founded the Ralik Ratak Democratic Party in June 1991, after distancing himself from President Kabua who, after being re-elected for a fourth consecutive term, died in December 1996. In January 1997, Parliament appointed Imata Kabua, cousin of the deceased, as the new president.

10 In June, the Opposition won a suspension of the project to store nuclear waste. The Government announced the construction of a large hotel and casino complex, financed by South Korean capital.

11 In February 1998, Asian banks expressed satisfaction with economic reforms which, according to the Government, were linked to the end of US aid. The Marshall Islands Government started talks with Washington on the formation of a Free Association Agreement similar to the one between the US and Micronesia. This would establish the sovereignty of the island, the right of the people to their own constitution and self-determination, and the possibility of withdrawing from the Agreement if either of the parties should so wish.

12 In the legislative elections of November 1999, the United Democratic Party took 18 of the 33 seats.

13 After the 2003 legislative elections, Kessai Note - speaker of the *Nitigela* (Legislature) in 2000 when he was elected president - was re-elected by parliament and took office in January 2004. Note announced that his top priority would be fighting corruption, in response to reports that identified the Marshall Islands as one of the areas with the worst money-laundering problems in the world. ∎

PROFILE

ENVIRONMENT

A total of 1,152 islands grouped in 34 atolls and 870 reefs. The land area covers 180 sq km, but the islands are scattered over a million sq km in the Pacific. The atolls of Mili, Majuro, Maloelap, Wotje and Likiep lie to the north-east. The south-west atolls are: Jaluit, Kwajalein, Rongelap, Bikini and Enewetak among others. The northern islands receive less rainfall than the southern atolls.

SOCIETY

Peoples: Sixty per cent of the population lives on Majuro and Kwajalein. A large number of Kwajalein's residents are US military personnel. Most inhabitants are of native descent (96.9 per cent), with minority communities of Filipino (0.5 per cent) and others (2.6 per cent). **Religions:** There is no official religion. Protestant 90.1 per cent; Roman Catholic 8.5 per cent; other 1.4 per cent. **Languages:** Marshallese (kajin-majol), English. **Main Political Parties:** United Democratic Party; Ralik Ratak Democratic Party; Kabua Party.

THE STATE

Official Name: Republic of the Marshall Islands. **Administrative Divisions:** 33 municipalities. **Capital:** Majuro 25,000 people (2003). **Other Cities:** Ebeye 13,000 people; Jaluit 2,500 (2000). **Government:** Parliamentary Republic. Kessai H Note, President of the local Government since 2000, re-elected in 2003. High Commissioner Janet McCoy is the US Government delegate and handles security, defense and foreign affairs. The Constitution provides for a 33-member parliament which appoints the local president. **National holiday:** 1 May, Proclamation of the Republic (1979); 21 October, Independence Day (1986).

Martinique / Martinique

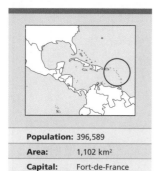

Population:	396,589
Area:	1,102 km²
Capital:	Fort-de-France
Currency:	Euro
Language:	French

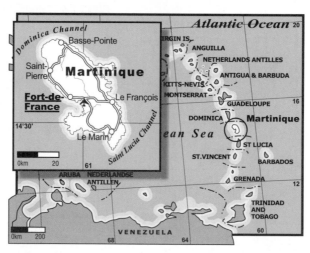

'Madinina' was the name given by the Carib Indians to the largest of the Lesser Antilles; the island came to be known as Martinique in the colonial period.

[2] It was not until a century and a half after the French occupation in 1635 (interrupted by short periods of British rule) that economic activity began, due to the sparse population and an almost complete dearth of precious metals.

[3] Late in the 17th century, sugar cultivation transformed the landscape, effectively ending the era in which fruits and vegetables were gathered rather than cultivated. The slave trade modified the system of production and African slaves replaced indigenous people on the plantations. Monoculture defined Martinique's role within the international labor structure, consolidating colonial ties with France.

[4] A minority of 12,000 European land, sugar mill and business owners controlled 93,000 slave laborers, a situation that led to uprisings. The *Marronuage* - free zones within the colony created by collective rebellions of slaves - appeared. There are records of *quilombos* (see Quilombos in Brazil) on the island in 1811, 1822 and 1833, years when rebellions shook Martinique.

[5] In the early 19th century, the crisis of capitalism put an end to the traditional plantation system, which was incapable of transferring capital to industry, leading to great social disturbances.

[6] In 1937 the formation of Martinique's central labor union provided an organizational framework for social mobilization. Leftist Aimé Césaire was elected mayor of Fort-de-France in 1945 and, in 1946, Martinique's deputy in the National French Assembly. Césaire was co-founder, alongside Senegal's Léopold Sédar Senghor, of the *Négritude* movement that

protested the imposition of French culture.

[7] In 1948 the French Government created the Overseas Department. Martinique's middle-classes wanted the same rights as the French, but differences within the anti-colonialist movement made it impossible to reach a consensus.

[8] While both emigration to France and French foreign aid had always provided support for the Martinique's economy, demands for independence resulted only in the granting of greater autonomy. The visits of Charles de Gaulle (1956, 1960, and 1964) did not smooth over the political

unrest and by the late 1970s France decided to help Martinique become economically self-sufficient in preparation for independence. Despite liberation groups being responsible for several bombings in the 1980s, there were no major protests against colonialism, either in Paris or on the Caribbean islands.

[9] In the March 1986 elections, left-wing parties took 21 out of 41 seats in the regional council. Aimé Césaire was re-elected president of the council. Rodolphe Désiré (Martinique Progressive Party) became the first left-wing Martinique representative in the French Senate.

[10] The creation of a single European market led to a worsening of the economic situation in 1993. Elections resulted in a tie between the right and the pro-independence left coalition. In the plebiscite to ratify the Maastricht treaty, voter turnout was only 25 per cent in Martinique, indicating hostility or at least indifference to deeper integration with the EU.

[11] In 1997, US pressure encouraging banana production in Central America continued, damaging Caribbean exports. In early 1998, unemployment affected 40 per cent of the active population, an all-time record in the country.

[12] French President Jacques Chirac visited the island in March 2000. The people of Martinique demanded greater trade with France and more autonomy in order to trade independently with its Caribbean neighbors.

[13] Michel Cadot became commissioner, replacing Dominique Bellion in July 2000.

[14] The new European currency, the euro, became legal tender in Martinique in January 2001, as it did in France.

[15] In 2002, the French newspaper *Le Parisien* classified the operative conditions of the hotel industry in Martinique and Guadeloupe as a tourist cataclysm. The Accor Hotels Chief Gerard Pelisson informed French President Jacques Chirac about the hostile and aggressive attitude of the staff in Martinican hotels. Workers also carried out work stoppages and went on strike, causing damage to the organization and productivity of those hotels. As a result, nearly 1,500 jobs were lost in 15 important hotels.

[16] Four referendums held by France on 7 December 2003 led to different outcomes in its territories. The reform conferring the status of Overseas Collectivities won in Saint Martin and Saint Bartholomew by 95.5 and 76.1 per cent, respectively. However Guadeloupe and Martinique voted - by 72.9 per cent and 50.4 per cent, respectively - to continue under the previous system by which the islands were overseas departments governed by a general council and a regional council.

[17] The crisis in the banana industry worsened in early 2004, when growers announced that they could not afford to pay social contributions and taxes, and demanded a response from the Government or from France.

[18] Yves Dassonville was appointed Préfet (Commissioner) in February 2004. ∎

PROFILE

ENVIRONMENT

Martinique is a volcanic island, one of the Windward Islands of the Lesser Antilles. Mount Pelée, whose eruption in 1902 destroyed the city of St Pierre, is a dominant feature of the mountainous terrain. The fertile land is suitable for agriculture, especially sugarcane. The tropical, humid climate is tempered by sea winds.

SOCIETY

Peoples: Descendants of former African slaves (90 per cent). There is a minority made up of people of European origin (5 per cent). Indian, Lebanese and Chinese (5 per cent).
Religions: Catholic (95 per cent); Hinduism and traditional African religions (5 per cent). **Languages:** French (official), and Creole.
Main Political Parties: Communist Party of Martinique, (PCM); Progressive Party of Martinique (PPM); Rally for the Republic/Union for French Democracy (RPR-UDF).
Main Social Organizations: General Confederation of Workers (CGT).

THE STATE

Official Name: Département d'Outre-Mer de la Martinique.
Capital: Fort-de-France 93,000 people (2003).
Other Cities: La Trinité 13,100 people; Le Marin 7,400 (2000).
Government: Head of State: President of France (Jacques Chirac). Head of government: Yves Dassonville, French-appointed Préfet (Commissioner) since February 2004. Claude Lise, re-elected in 1998 as president of the general council. The council's 36 members are elected through universal suffrage for a six-year term.

Mauritania / Muritaniyah

Population:	3,068,742
Area:	1,025,520 km²
Capital:	Nouakchott
Currency:	Ouguiya
Language:	Arabic and French

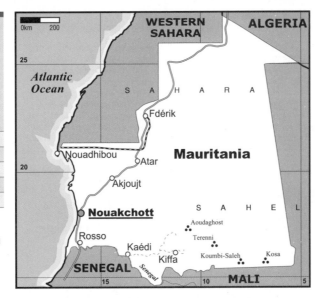

Numerous archaeological remains have been discovered in northern Mauritania dating from the Lower Paleolithic and Neolithic periods. Mauritania was inhabited early on by sub-Saharan peoples and by the Sanhadja Berbers and was the cradle of the Berber Almoravid movement, which in the 11th century AD spread an austere form of Islam throughout the territory and neighboring areas. The caravan route that linked Mauritania with Morocco was followed by Arab peoples that formed several powerful confederations such as Trarza and Brakna, which dominated the Senegal River valley, Kunta in the east, and Rigaibat (Regeibat) in the north. Due to the Almoravid conquest in the first place and later to the Fulani migrations (see Cameroon), the population was integrated and unified.

² In the 14th century, the Beni Hilal, who had invaded North Africa three centuries before, reached Mauritania. For over 200 years, they plundered the region and fought with the Berbers throughout an area including present-day southern Algeria and Sahara, while southern Mauritania belonged to the Mali Empire. In 1644, all the Berber groups in the region joined to fight the Arabs, but the resulting conflict, the Cherr Baba War, ended 30 years later with the defeat of the Berbers. The Arabs became a warrior caste, known as the *Hassani*, monopolizing the use of weapons, while trade, education and other civilian activities were left in the hands of the local population. Beneath these two groups came the Haratan, African shepherds from the south, kept as semi-serfs. Though this rigid social stratification weakened with time, it is still intact among the Arab-Berbers, the Fulani and Soninke from the south.

³ Towards the end of the 17th century various emirates arose, which failed to consolidate the country politically due to internal rivalries and dynastic quarrels. Nevertheless, they provided a minimal degree of order within the region that led to a relative growth of trade caravans. This was due to the cultural unification being carried out by the Zuaias (group of Berber-Marabouts) who devised a simple system of Arabic writing, propagating it along with their religious teachings.

⁴ In the 19th century, growing trade coincided with a French project to concentrate the commercial activities of the former French-Sudan (present-day Mali) in Senegal, which meant the elimination of trans-Saharan trade. Due to the frequent forays into Senegal, the French decided to invade Mauritania. The invasion began in 1858, under General Faidherbe, and the fighting continued until the 20th century. The resistance initially put up by the emirates of Trarza and Brakna was continued by Sheikh Ma al-Aini (see Western Sahara), his sons, and later his cousin Muhammad al-Mamun, the emir of Adrar. Pursued by the French almost 1,000 kilometers into the Sahara, Muhammad al-Mamun died in combat in 1934.

⁵ After World War II, Mauritania became a French Overseas Province, with its own deputies in the French Parliament. In 1955, internal autonomy was granted and independence was declared on 28 November, 1960. Since the country lacked its own infrastructure and administration, its organizational capacity was extremely limited. A French transnational corporation, MIFERMA, was more powerful than the Government, and its iron ore mines supplied 80 per cent of the country's exports and employed one in four wage-earning workers. The progressive wing of the Mauritanian People's Party (PPM), presided over by Moktar Ould Daddah, set in place the foundations for national independence. In 1965, Mauritania withdrew from the Common Afro-Mauritanian Organization (OCAM) through which the French maintained control over their former colonies. In 1966, SOMITEX, the state enterprise with a monopoly on imported consumer products, ended the monopoly held by French traders. Arabic culture began to be revived, and a customs system independent from Senegal was set up. The Arab-Mauritanian Bank was granted the monopoly on foreign trade and, for the first time, the country issued its own currency.

Life expectancy
52.5 years
2000-2005

GNI per capita
$410
2002

Literacy
40% total adult rate
2000

IN FOCUS

ENVIRONMENTAL CHALLENGES
The most pressing environmental problem is the process of desertification and the resultant erosion and growing shortage of water. Desertification is accelerated by overgrazing, deforestation and soil erosion aggravated by lengthy droughts. Mauritania has limited natural fresh water sources. The Senegal River, located along the border with the country of the same name, is the only perennial river.

WOMEN'S RIGHTS
Women have been able to vote and stand for office since 1961, but it was not until 1995 that they won their first seat in parliament. By 2000, they held 4 per cent of parliamentary seats and the same percentage of ministerial positions. In 2000, women made up 42 per cent of the total labor force: 62 per cent in the area of agriculture, 34 per cent in the area of services and 4 per cent in industry.

The maternal mortality rate is among the world's 15 highest: 1,000 women die for every 100,000 live births. Meanwhile, 24 per cent of pregnant women are anemic. In 2000, only 64 per cent of pregnant women received medical care during pregnancy and 57 per cent of births were attended by skilled medical personnel. The global fertility rate was six children per woman.

NGOs say there are a large number of unreported cases of domestic violence. Generally, the cases of violence are resolved within the family unit.

Female genital mutilation is frequently practised, in spite of efforts by the Government and NGOs. It is often performed after the seventh day of birth and almost always before the age of six months. According to studies carried out in 2001 by international organizations, 75 per cent of women between 15 and 49 years old have undergone genital mutilation.

CHILDREN
The infant mortality rate was 120 deaths per 1,000 live births in 2002; while, that same year, under-5 mortality rate was 183 deaths per 1,000 live births, placing Mauritania among the 15 countries with the highest rates in the world.

Fifty per cent of children receive treatment against malaria. Between 58 and 70 per cent of children are immunized against common childhood diseases, such as polio, measles and tetanus.

In 2000, some 64 per cent of children had access to primary education while only 14 per cent had access to secondary education.

There are special programs for the protection and welfare of children, as well as programs to care for abandoned children, however, the lack of financial resources prevents these from having a major impact.

INDIGENOUS PEOPLES/ ETHNIC MINORITIES
Most 'Black Moors' were slaves in the past. At the present time, they are still discriminated against by the so-called 'White Moors' and other African peoples. They are dispersed throughout the country, although

their villages exist mainly in the southern regions.

The Kewri, who are mainly farmers, shepherds, and fisherfolk, are composed of three black ethnic groups - the Peul, the Soninke and the Wolof. They inhabit the southern regions of Mauritania and each group has its own language.

During 1989-1990, the Government expelled thousands of Kewri in a dispute with Senegal. The Kewri were also persecuted by the police and armed forces with hundreds tortured, disappeared, and/or executed.

MIGRANTS/REFUGEES
In 2002, Mauritania hosted about 25,000 refugees from Western Sahara. Meanwhile, some 4,000 refugees from Mali who arrived in Mauritania in the 1990s returned to their country once peace was restored.

The refugees from Western Sahara fled to Mauritania during the 1970s to escape the Moroccan invasion of their country. Sahrawi refugees in Mauritania are mostly self-sufficient, and are not assisted by the UN High Commissioner for Refugees (UNHCR) or other aid agencies.

More than 45,000 Mauritanians were refugees or asylum-seekers at the end of 2002; 40,000 were in Senegal and approximately 7,000 in Europe and other Western countries.

DEATH PENALTY
The death penalty is applicable to a wide range of crimes.

herders in the border area along the Senegal River. In Nouakchott, angry crowds of Mauritanians attacked hundreds of unarmed Senegalese with sticks and stones in 1989. In Dakar, several Senegalese reported murders and mutilations of their compatriots in Mauritania. Radical groups in Senegal reacted by murdering Mauritanian shopkeepers, and looting their shops. Within the country, there have been instances of violence between black African Mauritanians from the south and Arabs and Berbers from the rest of the country: the army supported the Arabs and Berbers, killing hundreds of black African Mauritanians. In 1989, the border incidents prompted Senegal to break off diplomatic relations with Nouakchott.

[9]   In a 1991 referendum, Mauritanians voted in favour of a multiparty system and the establishment of a democratic government. The opposition, concentrated in the United Democratic Front (FDU), exerted pressure on the Government to introduce democracy in the country, but the only response was repression. In spite of the constitutional reform, social tensions caused by the crisis did not decrease and strikes, to which most of the population adhered, were held. In 1992, President Ahmed Taya was re-elected in the first multiparty elections, which were considered flawed by the opposition and international observers. Taya defeated his main rival, Ahmed Ould Daddah (Moktar's brother), winning 63 per cent of the vote. After two rounds of voting in the legislative election, the Democratic and Social Republican Party (PRSD) achieved an absolute majority in the National Assembly, winning 67 of the 79 seats.

[10]   That year, Mauritania re-established diplomatic ties with Senegal and Mali and resumed negotiations on border disputes and the situation of Mauritanian refugees in both neighboring countries. Foreign aid granted by China and France gave new impetus to the discredited Taya Government, accused of being responsible for the country's difficult social conditions. The application of an IMF-sponsored structural adjustment plan further aggravated the mounting tensions. Demonstrations were widespread and were harshly put down by the police. In 1994, the ruling party won the local elections, also considered fraudulent by the opposition. Sixty Islamic leaders were arrested, on charges of creating an atmosphere of fear. The Government ordered all

[6]   In 1974, the iron mines were nationalized. The country started to replace French influence with closer links to Muslim countries, and finally became a member of the Arab League. Saudi Arabia, Kuwait, and Morocco supplied economic assistance. In 1975 Mauritania, fulfilling an old ambition to annex part of 'Spanish' Sahara (now Western Sahara), joined Morocco in an attempt to divide the Spanish possession. With logistical and military support from France, Mauritania and Morocco occupied Western Sahara. The government of Ould Daddah, independent Mauritania's first president (from 1961 to 1978) and the first Mauritanian to graduate from a university, paid a high price because after violent reprisals by the Polisario Front (see Western Sahara), Mauritania was virtually occupied by Moroccan troops. The

economic crisis was intensified and popular discontent led to demonstrations and clashes with the police. The Mauritanian people, who felt a strong affinity with the Saharawis, condemned the intervention in the Western Sahara liberation war. The crisis exploded in 1978 and over the next six years, five coups were mounted. An attempt was made to Arabize the entire population, without recognizing other peoples living in the southern part of the country.

[7]   In 1984, Ould Haidalla (President since 1980) was ousted by a coup led by Maawiya Ould Sid'Ahmed Taya, an army colonel and chief of staff, who officially recognized the Democratic Saharawi Arab Republic. Steps were also taken to dismantle the 'clandestine economy' (only 50 per cent of companies kept legal accounting records). In 1985,

Mauritania was granted a $12 million loan by the IMF, committing itself to the implementation of a stringent structural adjustment program. Due to the continuing desertification process, the country suffers from a persistent grain deficit, which in the 1980s reached 12,000 tons annually. The economic and social outlook deteriorated; the southern farming and grazing lands shrank as the desert expanded, and impoverished nomadic people were driven to the cities. In the fishing sector the Government put the priority on preserving fish stocks and attempted to integrate the fishing industry into the rest of the economy. New licenses were no longer issued to foreign fishing fleets.

[8]   In 1987, clashes broke out between farmers and cattle-

Under-5 mortality
183 per 1,000
live births
2002

Poverty
28.6% of population
living on less
than $1 per
day
1995

Debt service
22.7% exports
of goods
and services
2001

Maternal mortality
32 per 100,000
live births
2000

'fundamentalist' militants to cease political activity.

11 In 1995, thousands of demonstrators rocked Nouakchott, setting cars on fire and looting shops after a new value added tax caused a rise in prices. Mauritania's creditors accepted a re-negotiation of the public debt that was then partially cancelled. In 1996, Taya appointed former Fisheries Minister El Afia Ould Mohamed Khouna as Prime Minister. The opposition boycotted the elections for a new Senate. The PRSD won a majority of seats in the Senate and, in the legislative elections took 71 of the 79 seats in the National Assembly.

12 In 1996, an agreement with the EU gave Mauritania access to set quotas of credit for five years, in return for permission to fish in the country's territorial waters, considered the richest in the world. International bodies said the nation's macroeconomic performance had improved. However, it continued to rank amongst the poorest nations in its social indicators. In 1997, Taya was

re-elected with nearly 90 per cent of the vote, with Mohamed Lemine Ould Guig as Prime Minister. Soon after, Taya called for Guig's resignation, as he had turned out to be extremely unpopular with Mauritanians, and appointed Sheikh Mohamed Khouna as the new Prime Minister. Khouna partially reshuffled the cabinet. Human-rights organizations appealed for an end to slavery in Mauritania in 1998. Human-rights activists were imprisoned for denouncing cases of slavery. Hundreds of black Mauritanian refugees still live at the present time in Dagana (Senegal) and complain that they have been forgotten by both governments and by the UN. They claim that Mauritania is a racist state and that they are treated as second-class citizens.

13 The Paris Club agreed to reduce Mauritania's debt by $620 million. The Club justified its decision by stating the country was making great efforts to reform its economy. The Government announced it would divide the

energy and water company for separate privatization. Communications Minister Rachid Ould Salah reported that he would seek a majority partner for the former, while the water company would remain mostly state-owned. Mauritania also privatized the telecommunications sector following World Bank recommendations.

14 In 2001, the parliamentary and municipal elections gave a majority in the National Assembly to the ruling PRSD. The opposition increased its representation in municipal government and in Parliament (from 1 to 10 seats). During the 1990s, despite a nominally multiparty system, minorities were in fact barred from participation. The new proportional representation system would make for greater electoral transparency. The World Bank granted a loan of $119 million to improve living conditions, especially in Nouakchott and Nouadhibou, and for improvements in education. In 2002, the Government dissolved

the opposition Action for Change party, which defended the rights of slaves' descendants and black Mauritanians, accusing it of posing a threat to national unity and of inciting intolerance.

15 In 2003, Taya was forced to abandon the presidential palace after clashes with rebel soldiers in Nouakchott. The developing of very close ties with Israel since 1984 had apparently earned the Government the hostility of several Islamic countries. Finally, loyal government troops regained control over the capital. That same year, Taya was re-elected President in the general elections, with 67 per cent of the vote, and Sghair Ould M'Bareck became Prime Minister. The number of registered voters was 1.7 million people, who chose between six candidates. Abdi Ould Horma, director of local communities at the ministry of the Interior, said all measures had been taken to assure a transparent election and that the presence of international observers was unnecessary. Once again, the opposition cried fraud. ∎

Still enslaved

A QUARTER OF A CENTURY AGO, in 1981, the Government of Mauritania formally abolished slavery - at its fourth attempt. However, to this day people are still being kidnapped, placed in captivity and then forced into slavery in distant regions of the country. In February 2004 for example a free-born man, Cheikhna Ould Beilil, pleaded for his wife and child to be freed - he said they were enslaved at their owner's place. His was the second case to emerge recently of traditional slavery that international rights groups say still binds hundreds of thousands into servitude in the West African region.

In Mauritania itself, according to different sources, more than 40 per cent of the people are enslaved and exploited by the country's élites. Typically they work on plantations or as domestic servants, in a situation of complete dependency on their masters. Anti-Slavery International (ASI), a UK-based non-governmental organization, notes that there is no sanction against the employment of forced labor.

As the abolition law is fairly recent, one might assume that it would be enforced and that everyone would know about it. Yet a large part of the population

appears not to know of the existence of this legislation. In fact, most former slaves remain in the same conditions as before abolition. Some of them were never freed (90,000, according to the Mauritanian League for Human Rights). In addition, ASI estimated that 300,000 freed slaves returned to their former masters, begging to be taken back as they had become economically and psychologically dependent through servitude.

Slavery was legally abolished following widespread protests against the public sale of a woman. However according to an Amnesty International (AI) report, it still exists in Mauritania, largely because the Government has not taken effective steps to ensure its eradication. So it persists in new and less obvious ways, such as work being paid for in kind rather than in cash - a form of payment that curtails a person's independence and emphasizes the imbalance in their relationship with their employer. Another manifestation of slavery is the way that women and children (in particular) are traded like currency between families and ethnic groups. The outlawing of slavery has not been backed up by the Government with information campaigns for slaves about

their rights; no legal advice was provided for enslaved people to help gain their freedom, nor legal protection for those slaves who escaped. In addition, former slaves have no access to higher education or senior positions.

BORN INTO SLAVERY

In 2002, ASI produced a study that revealed that almost all the cases of slavery involved individuals whose ancestors were enslaved many generations ago. Today, the children of slaves nearly always become slaves - as if born into a slave class. As a result, the children of an enslaved woman become her master's property, even if the father is a free man.

The Government is in denial about slavery in the country, and does not allow investigations by international human rights groups. In the words of Africa Advocacy Director Adotei Akwei: 'The Government of Mauritania refuses to follow through on its responsibility to abolish slavery not only in principle, but in practice. If it wishes to take its place amongst civilized, modern states, the Government must put an end to this miserable assault on human dignity and freedom.' ∎

Mauritius / Mauritius

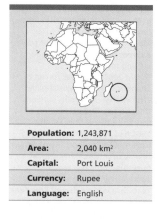

Population:	1,243,871
Area:	2,040 km²
Capital:	Port Louis
Currency:	Rupee
Language:	English

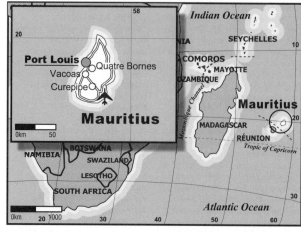

In the 10th century, Phoenician, Malay, Swahili, and Arab navigators visited the island of Mauritius, but did not settle there. In the 15th century, the Arabs named it Dina Robin - 'isle of silver'.

[2] In 1498, the navigator Vasco da Gama landed at the island during his trip around the Cape of Good Hope. In 1510, Portuguese navigator Pedro Mascarenhas used it as a stopover port, naming it Cirne.

[3] Around 1598 the Dutch claimed the island as their own, as an uninhabited island, and named it after their Head of State: Mauricio, Prince of Orange and Count of Nassau. From then until 1710, several attempts by the Dutch to colonize the island failed. In the meantime, pirates used it as a refuge.

[4] In 1721, Mauritius was colonized by the French Bourbons, who renamed it Ile de France. As rivalry surged between France and Britain over India, the island constituted an important strategic base.

[5] During the French Revolution (1789-1799), Mauritius gained a certain degree of autonomy, but in 1810 it fell into British hands. In 1814, after Napoleon's defeat, the Treaty of Paris recognized the island as a British colony. The British introduced sugarcane, which was to become the island's main economic resource right up until the present day.

[6] In the 19th century, sugar cultivation expanded to the extent that treaties were even signed with Madagascar and Mozambique to plant sugarcane in their coastal regions. However, in 1835 the emancipation of slaves, who constituted 70 per cent of the population, led to a serious labor shortage. Emancipation was opposed by the European landowners, who tried to alleviate the situation by bringing in, by the early 20th century, a total of more than 450,000 hired workers from India. In time, a majority of the population of Mauritius was comprised of people of Indian origin.

[7] By the early 20th century, local workers had begun to organize. In 1912, future Indian independence leader Mahatma Gandhi visited the island.

[8] In 1936, the labor movement (mainly made up of people of Indian descent), created the Labor Party, but a series of strikes were brutally repressed, and the party leaders were killed, imprisoned or exiled. Seewoosagur Ramgoolam, a doctor, started his political career as the leader of the Advance group. In the late 1940s, with the support of the colonial administration, he became the head of the Labor Party of Mauritius (PLM).

[9] During World War II, the decline of British colonial power favored the independence movements. At the same time, US political and military influence increased. The inhabitants of Mauritius fought for and achieved representation within the British colonial government. In 1957, a new government structure was created, giving Mauritius its own Prime Minister. In 1959, the first elections with universal suffrage brought the PLM to power, making Seewoosagur Ramgoolam Prime Minister in 1961.

[10] From Mauritius, the British administration ran the islands of Rodrigues, Cargados-Carajos and the Chagos archipelago. In 1965, with the approval of Ramgoolam (knighted by the British Crown), Chagos and other islands became the British Indian Ocean Territories, and the United States established a major naval base on one of its islands, Diego García.

[11] Mauritius became independent in 1968, after a long de-colonization process. Britain wanted merely to grant it limited autonomy, allowing it simply to run its domestic affairs. The 1958 Constitution, still in force, was created by the Colonial Office following the usual model used in the Commonwealth. Mauritius became a monarchy, ruled by Elizabeth II, and the sovereign was represented by a governor-general and a high commissioner.

[12] Until then, the two-party system had been deeply-rooted. The Labor Party, supported by the population of Indian origin, was the majority party up to 1958 when the French-Mauritians and Creoles came together in the Social Democratic Party of Mauritius (PSDM), and Muslim groups founded the Muslim Action Committee. The latter forged closer ties to the Labor Party in the 1960s. Sir Seewoosagur Ramgoolam was re-elected Prime Minister after Indian Labor groups and Muslims formed an alliance for the 1967 elections. Gaetan Duval, the leader of the

WORKERS

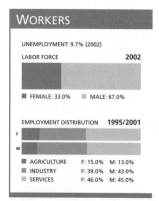

UNEMPLOYMENT: 9.7% (2002)

LABOR FORCE 2002

FEMALE: 33.0% MALE: 67.0%

EMPLOYMENT DISTRIBUTION 1995/2001

AGRICULTURE	F: 15.0%	M: 13.0%
INDUSTRY	F: 39.0%	M: 43.0%
SERVICES	F: 46.0%	M: 45.0%

PROFILE

ENVIRONMENT
The archipelago is located in the Indian Ocean, 800 sq km east of Madagascar, is made up of the island of Mauritius (53 km wide and 72 km long); Rodrigues Island (104 sq km) with 23,000 inhabitants who farm and fish; Agalega (69 sq km) with 400 inhabitants, who produce copra; and Saint Brandon, 22 small islands inhabited by people who fish and collect guano. The islands are of volcanic origin, surrounded by coral reefs. The terrain climbs from a coastal lowland to a central plain surrounded by mountains. Heavy rainfall contributes to the fertility of the red tropical soil. Sugarcane is the main crop.

SOCIETY
Peoples: Indo-Pakistani 68.0 per cent; Creole (mix deriving from British and French with population from the east African coast) 27.0 per cent; Chinese 3.0 per cent.
Religions: 50.6 per cent Hindu; 27.2 per cent Christian (mostly Catholic, with an Anglican minority); 16.3 per cent Muslim; 0.3 per cent Buddhist; 2 per cent others.
Languages: English (official) 29.1 per cent. Creole 21.6 per cent. Hindi 18.6 per cent. Bhojpuri (a Hindi dialect), Urdu, Hakka, French, Chinese, Tamil, Arabic, Marati, Telegu, and other languages are also spoken.
Main Political Parties: Mauritius Socialist Movement (MSM); Militant Mauritius Movement (MMM) - Labor Party.
Main Social Organizations: General Workers' Federation (GWF), affiliated with the Militant Mauritius Movement; Mauritian Women's Committee.

THE STATE
Official Name: State of Mauritius.
Administrative Divisions: 4 islands and 9 districts.
Capital: Port Louis 143,000 people (2003).
Other Cities: Curepipe 81,500 people; Quatre Bornes 78,900 (2000).
Government: Parliamentary republic. Anerood Jugnauth (MSM), President since 2003; Paul Bérenger (MMM), Prime Minister. Legislature: single-chamber: National Assembly with 72 members elected every 5 years.
National Holiday: 12 March, Independence Day (1968).
Armed Forces: non-existent. Other: 1,300 élite forces in charge of internal security.

Life expectancy
72.0 years
2000-2005

GNI per capita
$3,850
2002

Literacy
85% total adult rate
2000

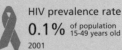

HIV prevalence rate
0.1% of population 15-49 years old
2001

PSDM, led the group which opposed independence. Nevertheless, in 1969, a coalition government was formed with the Labor Party and the PSDM. Duval, the representative of the French elite and the main opponent of independence, became foreign minister.

[13] The Government was characterized by electoral fraud and repression of the trade unions, and by its close ties with Israel and South Africa. Pretoria had a free zone in Port Louis which enabled it to trade with the EEC, thus evading international sanctions.

[14] In 1971, the indigenous people of Diego García were secretly transferred to the outskirts of Port Louis (capital of Mauritius), a move that caused a scandal years later when it was discovered by the US Congress. The island was not returned to Mauritius and its inhabitants were not granted permission to return home.

[15] The political environment became tense in the 1970s when a new opposition group called the Militant Mauritius Movement (MMM) denounced the alliance between the Labor Party and the former French settlers. The legislative elections scheduled for 1972 were not held until 1976. Even though the MMM won the most votes, the Labor Party, through alliances with smaller groups, managed to stay in power. The workers' demonstrations and the social unrest caused by unemployment increased, reaching their peak in 1979.

[16] In the 1982 elections the MMM allied with the Socialist Party of Mauritius (PSM) obtained 62 of the 66 seats and full control of the government. Anerood Jugnauth became Prime Minister. The MMM-PSM alliance promised to increase job opportunities and salaries, nationalize key sectors of the economy, reduce economic ties with South Africa, and demand that the US return Diego García.

[17] The rise in the price of oil, coupled with the drop in the international price of sugar, caused a deficit in the balance of payments equal to 12 percent of the gross domestic product. The Government was forced to turn to the IMF, which approved five stand-by loans between 1979 and 1985.

[18] To receive these loans, the Government had to adopt austerity measures: to postpone part of the planned salary increase and job creation programs, to relinquish part of its control over public expenditure, to cut subsidies on basic foods and to devalue the Mauritian rupee.

[19] All these measures led to clashes between the MMM and the PSM, a situation which eventually resulted in a call for early elections, in August 1983. A new coalition was formed including labor, socialists and Duval's social-democrats. However, this apparent political stability was very weak and was followed by a series of governmental alliances, which failed to consolidate the coalition's position. Majority parties underwent serious divisions, giving rise to new political groups such as the Mauritius Socialist Movement (MSM), a splinter of the PSM, led by Anerood Jugnauth.

[20] In the legislative elections of December 1987, the coalition made up of the MSM, PSDM and Labor won a very narrow victory, giving it a majority in parliament. Anerood Jugnauth was re-elected Prime Minister, and the MMM became the main opposition force.

[21] That year, the newspapers reported scandals concerning the involvement of politic leaders in drug-trafficking and money-laundering. At least one of several attempts to assassinate Jugnauth was blamed on the drug traffickers.

[22] In 1988, in agreement with the Organization of African Unity (OAU), Mauritius insisted on demanding the return of the island of Tromelin, administered by France, and of the Chagos archipelago, along with the demilitarization of the Indian Ocean, which is used for military maneuvers by the big powers. The demands were supported by environmental groups, due to the proliferation of nuclear weapons on the islands.

[23] In the September 1991 legislative elections, the ruling MSM succeeded in maintaining Jugnauth in the post of Prime Minister by reinforcing the traditional alliance with the MMM. In March 1992, Mauritius changed from a constitutional monarchy to a republic, and in June Cassam Uteem became the country's first President.

[24] In August 1993, Foreign Minister Paul Bérenger of the MMM withdrew from the cabinet, leaving Jugnauth without an absolute majority.

[25] In 1994, the economic performance of the island - whose foreign debt accounted for 25 per cent of GDP - was still regarded as satisfactory by the multilateral financial bodies.

[26] In January 1995, Jugnauth appointed representatives of the PMSD to his government. In the December legislative elections, an opposition coalition (MMM-Labor Party) led by Paul Bérenger and Nuvin Rangoolam took two-thirds of the seats. Rangoolam became Prime Minister.

[27] In June 1997, the MMM left the ruling coalition. Rangoolam took over the functions of foreign minister when Bérenger abandoned the post. A few days later, parliament re-elected Cassam Uteem president.

[28] During the visit of Indian Prime Minister Atal Behari Vajpayee in March 2000, which coincided with the celebration of the 30th anniversary of the independence of Mauritius, several agreements were signed by the two countries on the issues of trade and coastal patrols. In the September elections, Jugnauth was re-elected as prime minister.

[29] In November 2000, the High Court of London ruled that the UK had acted illegally in 1966 when it forced the inhabitants of the Chagos archipelago (some of whom had become exiled in Mauritius) to leave their homes.

[30] In January 2001, making the most of preferential tariffs for the import of African textiles to the US - under the African Growth and Opportunities Act (AGOA) -

IN FOCUS

ENVIRONMENTAL CHALLENGES
Monoculture and the use of pesticides are degrading the soil and polluting water sources. That and the deterioration of the coral reefs are the main environmental problems.

WOMEN'S RIGHTS
Women have been able to vote and stand for office since 1956. In the 2000 parliamentary elections, there were 33 women candidates out of a total of 353, which represented an increase of just three per cent over the 1995 elections. There was one female candidate for every 21 men, by electoral district. Female representation in parliament remained steady at eight per cent of the seats, while women held only three per cent of ministerial or equivalent posts. In 2000, women made up 33 per cent of the workforce.

In 2000, the ratio of literate adult women (over 15) to literate adult men was 92 to 100.

Domestic violence is a serious problem. There is a Ministry in charge of guaranteeing women's rights, child development, and family welfare. The law punishes domestic violence and provides the judicial system with wide authority to fight against it. In 2001, a study by an NGO, SOS Femmes, reported that 84 per cent of the women surveyed had suffered physical abuse.

CHILDREN
Significant strides in child welfare have been seen in the past 20 years.

Infant mortality and under-five mortality rates were reduced by more than 50 per cent between 1990 and 2002, to 17 and 19 per cent respectively.

In 2003, UNICEF ended its program in support of the welfare of small children, in place since 1970. However, there are still many challenges. There are pockets of poverty within the population, aggravated by domestic violence, sexual abuse and exploitation of women and children, as well as growing use of drugs and alcohol by young people. Commercial child sex exploitation is also considered a pressing problem.

INDIGENOUS PEOPLES/ ETHNIC MINORITIES
The majority of the population is Indo-Mauritian. The existing tension among the Hindu majority and Christian, Creole and Muslim minorities, persists. However, recent clashes have not been reported. Creoles and Muslims complain of a glass ceiling in the public administration, beyond which they are not allowed to ascend.

MIGRANTS/REFUGEES
The law does not guarantee refugee status to people even if they meet the1951 requirements or the current ones, established in 1967. Although the Government provides protection against the deportation of citizens to their countries of origin, it does not guarantee refuge or political asylum. The reason for this is that it is a small country with limited resources that wants to avoid becoming a shelter for refugees.

DEATH PENALTY
The death penalty was abolished in 1995. The last execution was carried out in 1987.

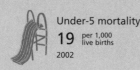

China announced that it would build a textile factory in Mauritius.

[31] In February, President Uteem refused to sign new anti-terrorism legislation; he resigned the same day. His office was transferred to vice-president Angidi Chettiar, who also refused to approve the law and likewise resigned. Arianga Pillay, the third president in one week, signed the new law. Amongst other changes, the law allowed for the detention of suspects for longer periods, and denied terrorism suspects the right to legal representation.

[32] In 2002, Karl Hoffman was elected president of the National Assembly. Information Technology and Telecommunications Minister Geehad Geelchand toured India, the UK, France, and Ireland promoting Mauritius as a new pole for cyber-development.

[33] On 11 September 2003, coinciding with the second anniversary of the terror attacks on the World Trade Center in New York and the Pentagon in Washington, Prime Minister Anerood Jugnauth met US ambassador John Price in Saint Louis, the capital. The fight against terrorism was the main topic of discussion.

[34] In early 2003, Anerood Jugnauth ceded his leadership of the MSM to his son Pravind. In September, Paul Bérenger became Prime Minister, the first non-Indian to hold the post. Jugnauth became President in October of the same year.

[35] In early January 2004, the local police force investigated deposits of $25 million in a Swiss bank, made in 1997. The money had apparently been destined to support the Labor Party, which was in power at that time. Navim Ramgoolam, Prime Minister during that period, and two other leaders of the movement allegedly deposited the funds.

[36] In late January 2004, representatives of small island nations met in the Bahamas to prepare for the summit at the end of the year in Mauritius with more than 300 participants from the Caribbean, the Mediterranean, southern China, and the Pacific, Atlantic, and Indian oceans.

[37] In February 2004, the UNESCO General Director Koichiro Matsuura made a three-day official visit, meeting with delegates of the Forum of African Parliamentarians for Education (FAPED).

[38] In late February, workers demonstrated against the upcoming visit by World Trade Organization (WTO) Director-General Supachai Paritchpakdi, accusing the global body of posing a threat to social rights. ∎

Diego García Is.

Population: 1,300
Area: 52 km²
Language: English

The settlement of Diego García began in 1776 when the French Viscount de Souillac sent a ship there from Mauritius, trying to establish a French presence before the English could get there. French entrepreneurs obtained permission to exploit all of the island's riches: coconuts (for coconut oil), giant tortoises, fish and birds. In exchange. they established a leper colony on the island. With the defeat of Napoleon in 1815, the island passed into the hands of the British Crown together with Mauritius' other dependencies. During the 19th century, many workers came from India and Africa.

[2] Around 1900, there were approximately 500 inhabitants but the population increased radically over the next decades, with the arrival of Africans, Madagascans and Indians. Once they had settled, they developed a culture of their own. They spoke creole, a mixture of their local languages and they took part in the Tamul rituals (of Madagascan origin) even though they were mostly Roman Catholic. The indigenous Chagos community, the Ilois, lived in their traditional manner more or less unchanged until the 1960s.

[3] In 1965, Britain decided to remove Diego García from Mauritius jurisdiction, annexing it to the BIOT (British Indian Ocean Territories). Although this change was condemned by the UN, the British and Mauritius governments made a deal where a large sum changed hands. Two years later, Britain ceded the island to the US for 50 years in exchange for a discount on its purchase of nuclear arms. To make way for the construction of important US air and naval bases, the Ilois were deported to Mauritius in the early 1970s.

[4] The 4,000 or so uprooted Ilois were abandoned as soon as they arrived in Mauritius, finding themselves in a situation of total indigence. They had not been allowed to keep their possessions and even today they are deprived of nationality. Neither the British nor the Mauritius Government recognize them as citizens. The Ilois' attempts to return to their land became increasingly common, as they began to receive the support of international opinion. The situation reached the US Senate in 1975, but both the US and British governments have continued to ignore the problem until recently, each blaming the other for the situation and both spending intermittent sums of money, in order to temporarily alleviate the severity of the situation.

[5] Between 1992 and 1993, the Government issued repeated claims to the Chagos archipelago, including Diego García, before the UN and the International Court of Justice. In reprisal, Britain cut economic aid to the country.

[6] In July 1997, just as the UK returned Hong Kong to Chinese control, Mauritius demanded that the British Prime Minister Tony Blair return Diego García.

[7] In July 2000, the Ilois displaced from the Chagos archipelago brought a lawsuit against the British crown. The 500 or so remaining Ilois want to return to their lands.

[8] In December 2001, the Ilois filed a lawsuit in a federal court in Washington which involved US Defense Secretary Donald Rumsfeld and most of his predecessors at the Pentagon. The suit was filed by three Ilois on behalf of the original inhabitants and their descendants. Charges included illegal deportations, racial discrimination, torture and genocide.

[9] Since 1960, the naval base has been used: during the Cold War against the USSR, in the Gulf War in 1991 and in the Operation Desert Fox in 1998. In 2001 and 2002, the US used the island for refueling and also for B-1 and B-52 bombers during the war against Afghanistan.

[10] In October 2003, a British court ruled that although the Ilois had been treated 'shamefully' in the past, their claims were unfounded. ∎

PROFILE

ENVIRONMENT
The Chagos Archipelago is located some 1,600 km southwest of India, in the middle of the Indian Ocean. The main islands are Diego García (8 km long by 6 km wide), Chagos, Peros, Banhaus and Solomon. The islands are made up of coral formations and are flat; they have a large number of coconut trees, which grow well here because of the tropical climate and year-round rain. The presence of the US naval base has seriously degraded the coral reefs, from the large-scale dredging and construction work.

SOCIETY
Peoples: At the present time, all the inhabitants are US or British military personnel.
Main Social Organizations: Lalit, local movement that demands the de-militarization of all the archipelago's islands and the devolution of Diego García to Mauritius.

THE STATE
Government: Rule is nominally exercised by a Commissioner from the Foreign Office in London.
Armed Forces: 25-strong Royal Navy detachment.

Mexico / México

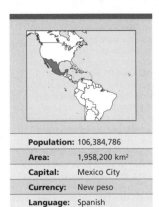

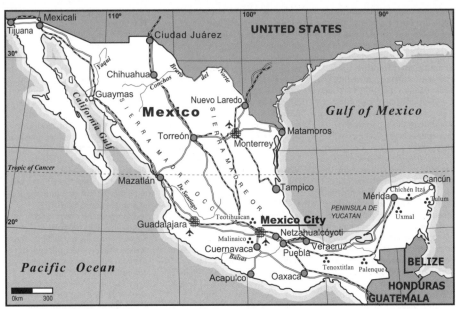

Population:	106,384,786
Area:	1,958,200 km²
Capital:	Mexico City
Currency:	New peso
Language:	Spanish

The 20,000-year history of what we know today as Mexico includes over 2,000 years of urban life. Over this period, Meso-American peoples developed advanced civilizations such as the Olmec, Teotihuacan, Maya and Mexica. These cultures had complex political and social organizations, and advanced artistic, scientific, and technological skills. The Olmecs (1200-200 BC), Mexico's first established culture, developed in the coastal states of Veracruz and Tabasco. Despite the absence of a local supply of stone, they developed massive buildings (La Venta, San Lorenzo, Tres Zapotes) and also created an advanced calendar. Around 1200 BC the Mayan culture emerged, most noted for its complex systems of mathematics and astrology, prolific city-building and complex architecture. By 1400 AD the Mayan state had splintered and almost disappeared, leaving an astonishing collection of ceremonial centers and ancient cities. In the valley of Oaxaca, around 900 BC, the Zapotecs, who were great city builders and artisans, rose; the Mixtec culture conquered the Zapotecs and developed around Mitla and Yagul. By the early 1400s the Mixtecs became vassals of the mighty Aztec empire. These two cultures continue their existence today in the State of Oaxaca, which is inhabited by some 2 million of their descendants.

2   The Toltecs, a civilization of mighty warriors believed by some to have developed from the magnificent Teotihuacan culture, occupied the northern reaches of the Valley of Mexico from around 950-1300 AD. They built one of Mexico's most impressive cities (Tula), were master craftsmen, and strongly influenced later Mayan and Aztec cultures. The Aztec civilization dominated Mexico for nearly 200 years (1345-1521) and was flourishing when Spanish conquerors arrived in 1519. The Aztecs used an elaborate system of

taxing and patronage to subjugate an enormous empire that stretched well into Central America. They borrowed heavily from their Olmec, Toltec, and Mayan predecessors to develop a complex linguistic, religious, artistic, architectural and military heritage.

3   The empire came to a sudden end in 1521, when Spanish explorer Hernán Cortés took advantage of internal strife between the ruling Aztecs and other indigenous peoples who paid them tribute. After killing Moctezuma II, Emperor of the Aztecs, Cortés laid siege to the capital, Tenochtitlan, with the help of a huge army led by the Tlazcaltecs. Once the city fell, Cortés initiated Christianization and Hispanization of the indigenous inhabitants.

4   In the 17th century, the major economic structures of the so-called 'New Spain' were laid down. The hacienda, a landed estate, emerged as the basic production unit, and mining became the basis of a colonial economy conceived to meet the gold and silver needs of the Spanish homeland. The American Indian population was exploited and decimated by hard labor and disease. By 1800, Mexico had become one of the world's richest countries, but with great poverty also.

5   After almost three centuries of colonial domination, the struggle for independence began in 1810, led by criollos (Mexicans of Spanish descent) such as Miguel Hidalgo and José Maria Morelos, two priests. The struggle became a broad-based national movement as Indians and Mestizos (people of mixed European and Indian descent) joined its ranks, but the rebels were soon crushed by the

royal army. The liberal revolution in Spain radically changed the situation. Afraid to lose their privileges, the Spanish residents and the conservative clergy came to an agreement with the surviving revolutionaries. This pact became known as the Iguala Plan, trading independence for a guaranteed continuation of Spanish dominance. In 1821 General Iturbide proclaimed himself Emperor, but was rapidly replaced by General Antonio López de Santa Anna.

6   At the time, Mexico was the most extensive Spanish American country, covering 4.6 million square kilometers, including the Central American provinces, but it was also stricken by economic, political and social problems. In 1824, a Constitution was approved establishing a federal republic, made up of 19 states, four regions and a federal district. In 1836, Santa Anna, elected President three years previously, passed a new Constitution which did away with all vestiges of federalism and the Mexican state of Texas, which had been settled by some 30,000 US citizens, called on the US for support and protection. Santa Anna led his army to victory against the Texans that year at the Alamo, but was defeated by US troops who took him prisoner, later releasing him for a large ransom.

7   In 1845, the US annexed Texas, which led to a break in diplomatic relations with Mexico. It also caused a frontier conflict, since the US claimed that the southern border of Texas was on the Rio Bravo or Rio Grande, not the Rio Nueces (further north) as was commonly accepted. In 1846, the US President James Polk tried to force through a frontier agreement and buy the

state of California - both moves rejected by Mexico. Polk ordered the US army to occupy the disputed lands between the two rivers, leading to a two-year war which was won by the US. The victors annexed all Mexican territory north of the Rio Bravo or Rio Grande. More than half of the Mexican territory was controlled by the US at the end of the war.

8   Between 1821 and 1850, Mexico had 50 different governments. The political instability was not ended by the country's first elections. As in many other Latin American states, the Mexican bourgeoisie supported two political parties: the liberals and the conservatives.

9   The Liberals' victory of 1857 strengthened the republic, instituting a free market economy, putting in place individual rights and guarantees, and expropriating the wealth of the clergy. But the conservatives, supported by the church, took up arms, and civil war - commonly known as the War of the Reform - broke out.

10   Mexico's first Native American president, Benito Juárez, was successful in re-establishing national unity in 1861. However, his decision to suspend payment on all foreign debts triggered armed intervention by France, Britain and Spain. Although Britain and Spain withdrew, France established a monarchy in an attempt to counterbalance US influence over the area. Maximilian of Austria was crowned Emperor of Mexico. The Mexican resistance soon brought the republican troops back together again, and Juarez was reinstated as president in 1867.

11   In 1871, Juan de Wata Rivera started the newspaper The Socialist.

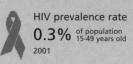
On 10 September, this newspaper published the general statutes of the 1st Marxist International for the first time in Latin America. General Porfirio Díaz, who fought with the Liberals against French intervention, seized power in 1876 and held onto it until 1911. During the 35 years of his dictatorship, the country opened its doors to foreign investment, the economy was modernized and social inequalities increased.

[12] In 1910, Francisco Madero led the Mexican Revolution under the slogan 'effective suffrage, no re-election'. This was the first popular Latin American revolution of the century. In 1913, US ambassador Henry Lane Wilson participated in a conspiracy, resulting in the assassination of Madero. The people responded by taking up arms more vigorously than before. Peasants joined the revolt, led by Emiliano Zapata and Francisco (Pancho) Villa. The principles of this Revolution were set out in the Constitution of 1917, promulgated by Venustiano Carranza. It was the most socially-advanced constitution of its time and many of the principles are still in force today. However, conflict between the various revolutionary factions continued, resulting in the deaths of the major leaders.

[13] In 1929, under President Plutarco Elias Calles, these factions joined to form the National Revolutionary Party. In 1934, General Lázaro Cárdenas took office. He embodied the continuation of the revolutionary process, and was one of the main driving forces behind its accomplishments. The major reforms included land reform, the nationalization of oil (the founding of PEMEX), the expropriation of oil refineries, incentives for new industries, and a national education system. The National Revolutionary Party became the Institutional Revolutionary Party (PRI) and the deeply-rooted revolutionary socialist principles were gradually abandoned.

[14] Conditions created by World War II accelerated the first phase of Mexico's industrialization which reached its peak during Miguel Aleman's term of office (1946-1952). The changes that took place during this period altered the former social balance. Mexico's population remained predominantly rural, with only 40 per cent in the cities, but the rapid development was not able to absorb the quickly growing population. Communal land ownership, which had stimulated solidarity and revolutionary feeling among peasants in the 19th century, was gradually replaced by a new type of individual land

tenure causing the formation of large estates or *latifundios*.

[15] During the following decade, Cardenas' successors, though not always loyal to his principles, stabilized the system by reinforcing those factors responsible for its success in a continent generally afflicted by underdevelopment and stagnation. Strong governmental influence, involving substantial public investment, kept the economy strong. A reasonable balance was maintained between heavy and light industry and tourism was encouraged.

[16] Against the backdrop of the 1968 Mexico Olympics, the students' movement organized protests against the true social situation in the country. A student rally held on the Plaza de las Tres Culturas was dispersed by the army. The order to shoot to kill was given without warning, and hundreds of people died or were injured in the 'Tlatelolco Massacre'.

[17] During the presidency of José Lopez Portillo (1976-1982), important oil deposits were discovered. This bound Mexico, as the US' main oil supplier, more closely to the US.

[18] In 1982, Miguel de la Madrid assumed the presidency implementing an IMF economic adjustment plan. Cuts in subsidies and public spending, changes in the pattern of public investment, and a dual currency exchange rate caused public discontent and the PRI's first electoral defeat since its foundation. In the June 1983 elections, the PRI failed to impose its municipal candidates in the capital and two other major cities.

[19] Under the pressure of foreign debt the trends of 1983 continued: growing inflation; losses in real wages; reductions of public spending; falls in production, and rising unemployment.

[20] The devastating earthquake of September 1985, in which more than 20,000 people were buried alive, further aggravated an already critical situation. The reduction in the oil quota by the US made it necessary to generate alternative sources of income. One of these was tourism, and another was the *maquiladoras* - foreign companies on the border with the US which are exempt from taxes and from paying their workers social insurance, disposing of the products on the vast domestic market.

[21] The internal situation became more difficult for the PRI and it was accused of rigging the 1986 municipal elections. The formation of an independent Labor Union Negotiation Board posed a threat to the PRI's labor wing, which had traditionally formed a bloc within the Labor Congress, the largest

coordinating board of labor federations.

[22] On 6 July 1988, several parties gained a significant vote in the national elections, something which had not happened since 1910. Carlos Salinas de Gortari, the PRI candidate, won the ballot with - according to official figures - 50 per cent of the vote (the lowest percentage in party history). The Left emerged for the first time as a real alternative to the PRI. Cuauhtemoc Cárdenas, the son of the charismatic leader and former Mexican President from 1934-1940, led a coalition of groups operating as a single party, the FDN, representing the masses and opposing the Institutional Revolutionary Party. Cárdenas took second place with 31 per cent of the vote in an election marked by accusations of fraud and irregularities by the opposition. The abstention rate was 49.72 per cent.

[23] In 1989, the FDN split, and Cárdenas founded the Democratic Revolution Party, made up of former members of the PRI, communists and members of smaller organizations. In the meantime, the People's Socialist Party (PPS), the Authentic Party of the Mexican Revolution (PARM) and the Party of the Cardenista Front for National Reconstruction (PFCRN) continued as autonomous organizations which voted with the PRI in Congress.

[24] The PRI administration resolved to open up the country to foreign investment, and also announced a series of measures aimed at controlling inflation. Both these decisions were welcomed by the US Government. Mexico made overtures to the US to sign a free trade agreement, coinciding with Mexico's entry into GATT (now the World Trade Organization - WTO) and the legal authorization for foreign investment in Mexican enterprises to go above the previously stipulated 49 per cent. In May 1990, President Salinas de Gortari privatized the banking system, which had been nationalized eight years earlier.

[25] In the elections of 1991, the PRI proclaimed itself the winner with 61.4 per cent of the vote, amid accusations of fraud. It gained control of the Chamber of Deputies, and power to carry out constitutional reforms.

[26] One of these was the agrarian reform approved in December 1991, which granted property rights to *campesinos* (peasants) who farm state lands known as *ejidos* (co-operative farms ceded by the Zapata Revolution in 1917). According to the PRI, the new system was designed to reduce the annual ten million tons of imported food. According to the opposition, the

reform - which allowed campesinos to sell their lands - would bring about a transfer of small landholdings to larger investors.

[27] On 17 December 1992, the Mexican, US and Canadian governments signed the North American Free Trade Association (NAFTA) Treaty.

[28] During the Salinas administration, inflation was reduced from three figures to a rate of nine per cent in 1993. Between the end of 1988 and mid-1993, the State received some $21 billion from the privatization of state interests. Private foreign debt increased by $11 billion in 1993.

[29] On 1 January 1994, the day the NAFTA agreement came into force, the Zapatista National Liberation Army (EZLN) - whose strength the Government had played down - occupied three towns in the southern state of Chiapas, declaring them a freed zone. Chiapas is one of the states with the largest population of Mayan Indians. It also has the highest level of Spanish-language illiteracy and the lowest incomes. But in addition it has large oil and gas reserves - 21 per cent of the nation's crude oil is extracted in Chiapas. In the poorest state, this band of indigenous people, called *Zapatistas*, rose up to claim the right to defend themselves against a government and a social order which offered them nothing but wanted their land.

[30] The Government initially refused to recognize the scope of the uprising. When the number of dead rose above a thousand - the army had been deployed to the region - and the complaints of summary executions continued, the Government - at the insistence of Catholic Bishop Samuel Ruíz and protests from national and international civil society - agreed to negotiate and unilaterally declared a ceasefire.

[31] In February, negotiations began in San Cristobal de las Casas with the rebels demanding reforms to electoral and agrarian statutes (approved in 1991) and to the Penal Code, besides other reforms to improve the quality of life of indigenous peoples.

[32] The PRI presidential candidate Luis Donaldo Colosio was murdered on 23 March in Tijuana. Three members of his bodyguard were involved. The PRI nominated Ernesto Zedillo as his replacement for the 21 August elections, and Zedillo was voted in by 49 per cent of the electorate. Both the PRD and the EZLN accused the Government of electoral fraud.

[33] In September, PRI secretary-general José Ruiz Massieu was assassinated, and in November his brother Mario resigned from his post as Attorney-General as he

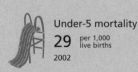

| | Under-5 mortality | | Poverty | | Debt service | | Maternal mortality |
| | **29** per 1,000 live births 2002 | | **8.0%** of population living on less than $1 per day 1998 | | **26.1%** exports of goods and services 2001 | | **83** per 100,000 live births 2000 |

believed Party officials were blocking the criminal investigation. His brother's death increased suspicions that leading PRI figures, and perhaps the drug mafia, were also involved in the murders.

[34] The economy continued to grow until, on 20 December, the new government abandoned the policy of gradually depreciating the currency because of the acceleration of capital flight. By the end of the year, the peso had lost 42 per cent of its value. Its fall caused the stock market to collapse in a crisis that came to be known as 'The Tequila effect'. The crisis led to questioning of the free market and trade liberalization model prescribed by the IMF and threatened other economies in the region.

[35] After negotiations failed in Chiapas, in February, Zedillo launched a military offensive which was halted after protests from various international bodies. The investigations of the Colosio and Ruiz Massieu murders had still gotten nowhere.

[36] Raúl Salinas de Gortari, brother of the former president, was arrested in February accused of masterminding the Ruiz Massieu killing. At the same time, the Government called for the extradition of Mario Ruiz Massieu from the US, on charges of hampering the investigation into his brother's death. Raul Salinas' wife was arrested in Switzerland in November when using false documents to carry out a banking transaction. Mrs Salinas was attempting to transfer funds - presumably from the laundering of drug money - from her husband's account.

[37] The PRI and the two leading opposition parties agreed an electoral reform in December, which included establishing an independent control commission and limiting campaign expenditure.

[38] In September 1996, seven months after the San Andrés accords on rights and indigenous culture had been signed by the federal and state governments and the EZLN, the peace negotiations stalled when the Zapatistas accused the Government of failing to live up to the agreements.

[39] Cuauhtemoc Cárdenas was elected mayor of Mexico City in July 1997, while in the same elections the Democratic Revolution Party (PRD) became the opposition party with most seats in the chamber of deputies, outdoing the National Action Party (PAN). These two parties, along with the Greens and the Workers Party, announced the creation of an opposition alliance against the PRI, from 1 September.

[40] On 22 December, in Acteal, Chiapas, 45 Tzotzil indigenous people of the Las Abejas (the bees)

ENVIRONMENTAL CHALLENGES
The river system is not extensive and is unevenly distributed throughout the country and the pollution of some aquifers has aggravated the problem of access to drinking water. Air and land pollution are significant in industrial areas. Deforestation extends 6,000 sq km a year. The disposal of solid and liquid waste is inadequate. In the capital, land subsidence is a problem, due to the falling level of underground waters.

WOMEN'S RIGHTS
Women have been able to vote and stand for office since 1947. Between 1990 and 2000, the proportion of parliamentary seats held by women rose from 12 to 16 per cent, while they maintained 5 per cent of ministerial or equivalent positions. In 2000, women made up 33 per cent of the labor force. In the 1991-2000 period, women's wages amounted to just 38 per cent of the wages earned by men, in non-agricultural jobs.

The gender gap in educational levels among young people between the ages of 15 and 24 has diminished in the last few decades. In 2000, 3.5 per cent of young women were illiterate, only slightly more than the 2.6 per cent of men in the same age group.

From 1993, more than 370 women have been found murdered in Ciudad Juárez and Chihuahua, while 70 remain missing. They are mostly young women from poor backgrounds, who are kidnapped, held captive and subjected to sexual violence. Amnesty International recommended that any negligence, failure to act, complicity or tolerance on the part of state officials in connection with the disappearances and murders of women in Chihuahua should be investigated and punished.

CHILDREN
Mexico is the most populous Spanish-speaking country in the world. In 2001, more than 43 per cent of the country's population were under the age of 18. In the last 30 years, life expectancy rose from 61 to 76.4 years, while 40 per cent of Mexicans lived below the poverty line.

Many minors are forced to work or migrate, with or without their families, within different rural areas, from rural to urban areas, or to foreign countries, mainly the US.

In 1996, 3.5 million children aged between 12 and 17 formed part of the country's formal or informal labor force. Nearly 130,000 children disappeared from their homes between 1996 and 2000. Most are trafficked to the US and Canada where they are bought for up to $30,000. A large market for body organ sales operates along the northern border. In 2001, in Mexico City alone, there were more than 15,000 children living on the streets.

Cases of commercial child sex exploitation and drug use and dealing among minors have been reported. Street children face abuse at the hands of adults, apart from putting their health at risk by exposing themselves to sexually transmitted diseases, malnutrition, severe skin infections, gastrointestinal and bronchial disorders, and a high rate of problems arising from drug abuse.

INDIGENOUS PEOPLES/ ETHNIC MINORITIES
With more than 50 ethnic groups and over 60 languages, Mexico is among the countries with the strongest indigenous presence in the Americas, with between 10 and 20 million indigenous people. The Aztecas, Choles, Mames, Mayas, Guajiros, Lacandons, Olmecas, Nahuas, Mixtecos, Apaches, Tlpanecos, Tarahumaras, Toltecas, Zapotecas and Zoques stand out on account of their number and cultural legacy.

There are unresolved agrarian conflicts, while indigenous groups face severe discrimination with respect to the administration of justice, as well as persistent threats of eviction and relocation which keep them in a permanent state of vulnerability. Excessive militarization in some indigenous communities and the presence of alleged paramilitary groups have been reported. Extreme poverty, lack of basic services, and difficulties in providing bilingual and intercultural education are key factors hindering the development of these communities.

Indigenous peoples, through groups such as the Zapatistas (see History), are demanding the recognition of their fundamental rights and of the multicultural nature of the nation; the possibility of autonomous economic development, social and political representation; and the right to maintain and develop their cultural practices.

MIGRANTS/REFUGEES
Until the early 21st century no person was considered a refugee in Mexico. In 2001, the 161 recognized refugees in Mexico were from: Albania, Algeria, Bangladesh, Belarus, Colombia, Congo, Cuba, Ethiopia, Guatemala, Honduras, Iran, Iraq, Pakistan, Palestine, Russia, Sierra Leone, Sri Lanka, Somalia, Sudan, Togo, Tunisia and Yemen. Less than half of them (77) were from Latin America (Colombia, Cuba, Guatemala and Honduras). Between 70 and 80 per cent of recognized refugees intend to resettle in another country during the first year after having been granted refugee status. In 2000, it was estimated that 32 million Mexicans were living in the US.

DEATH PENALTY
The death penalty is applicable in the case of exceptional crimes, such as those committed under military law or in wartime. The last execution was carried out in 1937.

pacifist group were massacred by paramilitaries with the compliance of the public security forces. This prompted the resignation of acting governor of the state, Julio Ruiz Ferro, and his secretary, Emilio Chuayffet.

[41] The number of deaths of people trying to cross the border into the US increased fourfold in 1998 over the previous year. The harsh treatment dealt out by US border guards and increased vigilance in places where illegal immigrants tended to cross forced people to attempt much more dangerous routes.

[42] In August 1999, Cuauhtemoc Cárdenas's PDR and the right wing PAN led by Vicente Fox decided to form an alliance to confront PRI dominance, presenting a single candidate for the July 2000 elections.

[43] However, the coalition failed in December after the PAN rejected the proposal of a group of 'notables' on how to elect a common candidate for the coalition. The Right had opposed 25 observations made in a proposal by 14 independent figures who suggested primary elections and four surveys in order to designate a candidate for the eight opposition parties.

[44] The electoral reforms paved the way for the first truly clean elections in the history of the

Malnutrition
8% under-5s
1995-2002

Water source
88% of population using improved drinking water sources
2000

Doctors
130 per 100,000 people
1990-2002

Primary school
100% net enrolment rate
2000

country. The PAN finally joined forces with the Green Party and in a landmark election, Fox was elected President in July, ending more than 70 years of PRI rule. The coalition also gained control of both houses of Congress. Fox declared that his government would be open to honest members of all parties, and warned that corruption would no longer be tolerated in Mexico.

[45] When he took office in December 2000, Fox promised to fight corruption and sought, among other things, to eradicate economic inequity and provide education and health services to the population. His first tour of the Southern Cone region sought to open Mexican economy to foreign trade, especially with the Mercosur countries (Argentina, Brazil, Paraguay and Uruguay) and Chile.

[46] That month, Fox appointed former senator Luis Álvarez as commissioner for peace in Chiapas. By then, peace talks between the guerrillas and the Government were suspended. As he had promised in his campaign, Fox ordered the army to withdraw from indigenous communities. The President also lived up to the promise that the first bill he would send to the legislature would be the one based on the recognition of indigenous rights. EZLN leader Subcomandante Marcos agreed to resume negotiations with the Government.

[47] Fox announced he would lead a national offensive against drug trafficking and organized crime. He also promised to dismantle a corrupt prison system.

[48] Between 24 February and 11 March 2000, a caravan of 24 Zapatista delegates traveled from Chiapas to Mexico City to present its demands to Congress (legal guarantees, bilingual education, mass media that reflect indigenous cultures, autonomy in land use and customs, among others). After several discussions, legislators passed reforms on the Indigenous Act (Cocopa Law), but the EZLN rejected the new law because it did not take into account the indigenous peoples' demands, and announced it would not resume the peace talks.

[49] When the economic crisis worsened in late 2001, the President's popularity fell drastically. It was felt he had not fulfilled his promises - among them to create 1.5 million jobs. It was estimated 9 million people worked in the informal sector, ie one-quarter of the working population who, although they did not pay taxes, contributed with 12.7 per cent of the GDP. Thousands of peasants marched throughout the country in August, to demand

solutions for their sector, one of the worst hit. In Mexico City alone, 30,000 peasants demonstrated at the ministries of Rural Development, Economy, Finance and Agriculture.

[50] In January 2002, the Supreme Court of Justice legalized abortion in cases of rape; when artificial insemination was applied without the woman's consent; and when the fetus had genetic or birth defects. While the Mexican Bishops' Conference stated that the passing of a law does not imply its moral acceptance, women's groups considered the decision important to their health and dignity.

[51] In May 2003, Mexico's Electoral Tribunal (TEPJF) upheld a $90 million fine to the PRI for irregular financing activities during the presidential campaign of 2000. The TEPJF confirmed that the PRI had illegally received more than $45 million from the state-owned oil company PEMEX. The money found its way into the PRI's coffers through the union representing the company's employees.

[52] However, the PRI was the big winner of the parliamentary elections held in July of that year. The PAN's seats in the Chamber of Deputies went down from 207 to 155, while the PRI obtained 15 more seats than in the previous period. Likewise, President Fox's party lost six governors in an election that was marked by a voter turnout of just 40 per cent, the lowest in Mexico's history.

[53] In August 2003, Amnesty International published a report on the 'Juárez femicide': the abduction, rape, torture and murder of more than 370 women in Ciudad Juárez, in Chihuahua state which borders the US. The murdered women were triply vulnerable, being poor, young and female in a violent, patriarchal society. In spite of international pressure, the Mexican Government has not made progress in the investigation into the murders. On the contrary, in many cases it has hampered and delayed investigations by performing inadequate or incomplete forensic tests, falsifying evidence and allegedly torturing people into signing false confessions.

[54] Surrounded by mass demonstrations and protests, the Fifth WTO Ministerial Conference held in September 2003 in Cancun collapsed. The trade talks ended after the rich countries failed to meet the demands of poorer nations who wanted drastic reform of agricultural subsidies with no Western strings attached. The developing world used its new-found bargaining strength to resist the conditions that the US and Europe in particular tried to

impose. The poorer countries' political power was strengthened by the emergence of the G21 group, including China, Brazil and India, which provided a critical counterweight to the huge bargaining power of the US and EU. A brief draft statement was approved instead of the main ministerial text which had been discussed since July of that year.

[55] In February 2004, the federal authorities arrested Miguel Nazar

Haro, former Chief of the Federal Security Directorate (DFS), for his alleged participation in the 1975 forced disappearance of Jesús Piedra Ibarra, presumed member of a leftist guerrilla organization. This was the first arrest obtained by the special prosecutor that President Vicente Fox appointed in November 2001 to investigate and prosecute human rights violations committed under previous governments. ∎

PROFILE

ENVIRONMENT

The country occupies the southern portion of North America. It is mostly mountainous, with the Western Sierra Madre range on the Pacific side, the Eastern Sierra Madre on the Gulf of Mexico, the Southern Sierra Madre and the Sierra Neovolcánica Transversal along the central part of the country. The climate varies from dry desert wasteland conditions in the north to rainy tropical conditions in southeastern Mexico, with a mild climate in the central plateau, where the majority of the population lives. Due to its geological structure, Mexico has abundant hydrocarbon reserves, both on and off shore. The great climatic diversity leads to very varied vegetation. The rainforests in the southeastern zone and the temperate forests on the slopes of the Sierra Neovolcánica are strategic economic centers.

SOCIETY

Peoples: Mexicans are descended from Meso-American peoples and Spanish conquistadors. Indigenous peoples amount to 30 per cent of the national population. Out of the 56 indigenous groups, the main ones are: Tarahumara, Nahua, Huichol, Purepecha, Mixteco, Zapoteca, Lacandon, Otomi, Totonaca, and Maya.
Religions: Mainly Catholic.
Languages: Spanish (official). An estimated six million Mexicans speak indigenous languages.
Main Political Parties: National Action Party (PAN), conservative, founded in 1939, and the Green Ecological Party, joined in an electoral coalition (Alliance for Change); Institutional Revolutionary Party (PRI), was in Government since it was founded in 1929 until 2000; Party of the Democratic Revolution (PRD), traditionally led by Cuauhtemoc Cárdenas, together with the Labor Party, Social Alliance Party, Nationalist Society Party and Convergence for Democracy in another electoral coalition (Alliance for Mexico).
Main Social Organizations: The Labor Congress, a congregation of the large union organizations, was the PRI's support base. The National Peasants' Front was created in 1983 in a merger of the National Confederation of Farmers (CNC), the General Union of Workers and Farmers of Mexico (UGOCM), the National Confederation of Small Landowners (CNPP) and the Independent Farmers' Central Union (CCI). Authentic Labor Front (FAT); Mexican Network of Action against Free Trade (RMALC); National Coordinator of Mexican Students (CNEM); Zapatista National Liberation Front (FZLN) a civic-political group formed in 1995 by the Zapatista National Liberation Army (EZLN). Major indigenous groups: National Indigenous Congress, International Indigenous Press Agency, Plural National Indigenous Assembly for Autonomy.

THE STATE

Official Name: Estados Unidos Mexicanos.
Administrative Divisions: 31 states and a federal district.
Capital: Mexico City 18,660,000 people (2003).
Other Cities: Guadalajara 3,798,800 people; Netzahualcóyotl 1,401,300; Monterrey 3,409,100; Puebla 2,495,100 (2000).
Government: The system is both federal and presidential. Vicente Fox Quesada, President since December 2000. The Congress of the Union (Legislature) has two chambers: the 500-member Chamber of Deputies, and the 128-member Senate.
National Holiday: 16 September, Independence Day (1810).
Armed Forces: 175,000 troops (include 60,000 conscripts), and 300,000 reserves (1996). Other: 14,000 Rural Defense Militia.

Micronesia / Micronesia

Population:	111,465
Area:	700 km²
Capital:	Palikir
Currency:	US dollar
Language:	Kosraean, Yapese, Pohnpeian and Trukese

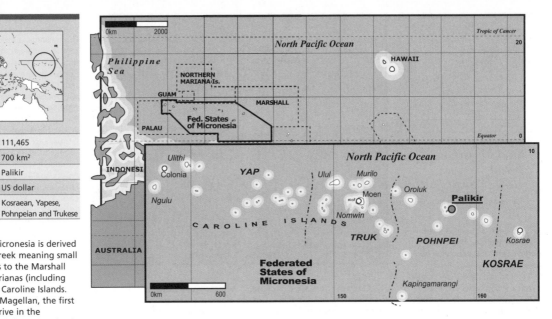

The name Micronesia is derived from the Greek meaning small islands. It refers to the Marshall Islands, the Marianas (including Guam) and the Caroline Islands.

[2] Ferdinand Magellan, the first European to arrive in the Marianas, named them the Islands of Thieves, but they were later renamed after Queen Mariana of Austria, Spanish regent.

[3] In 1885, the Germans tried to impose a protectorate on the islands. The Spanish appealed to the Vatican but lost Guam under the Treaty of Paris of 10 December 1898, which ended the war with the US. Finally, Spain chose to sell the archipelago to Germany for 25 million pesetas.

[4] The Japanese occupied the islands in 1914, and kept the area demilitarized until 1935. Japan launched the attack on Pearl Harbor from Micronesia on 7 December 1941.

[5] In 1947, an agreement with the United Nations allowed the US to keep the islands as a trust territory. A UN mandate forced the US to help develop a national awareness among the island's population to enable them to exercise their right to self-determination.

[6] Under the Commonwealth system, the US was allowed to keep its military bases on the islands and take charge of their defense and foreign affairs. In 1975 a plebiscite was held and in 1978 the Northern Mariana Islands acquired 'Free Associate State' status.

[7] In 1978, another plebiscite led to the creation of the Federated States of Micronesia. Four districts of the trust supported the motion, while Palau and the Marshall Islands remained autonomous states.

[8] Nuclear experiments performed by the US on Bikini and Eniwetok atolls resulted in the displacement of the local inhabitants, who were then unable to return. Tests carried out in 1977 revealed that water, fruit, and vegetables were still too radioactive for consumption.

[9] In October 1982, the US signed a Free Association Agreement with the Marshall Islands and the Federated States of Micronesia, approved by both countries in 1983 and proclaimed in October 1986. The US would be responsible for defense (including the maintenance of military bases) in exchange for financial aid to the islands.

[10] On 17 September 1990 Micronesia joined the United Nations.

[11] After the March 1991 legislative elections, Bailey Olter was elected President in May.

[12] In June 1993 Micronesia joined the IMF.

[13] Leo A Falcam, who was appointed President in May 1999, issued an official statement reiterating Micronesia's opposition to the transportation of plutonium through the region by nations such as Britain, France and Japan, particularly through its own territorial waters.

[14] In 1999, Micronesia and the US resumed negotiations leading to a Free Association Agreement, which would expire in 2001.

[15] Micronesia, together with 13 other nations from the Pacific Island Countries Trade Agreement (PICTA), met in August 2001 to discuss trade issues, the need to lower their customs barriers and to get Australia and New Zealand/Aotearoa, with whom they signed the Pacific Agreement on Closer Economic Relations (PACER), to do the same. The accord is aimed at obtaining financial support for the weaker economies and integrating them into a larger economy.

[16] After he was named president in May 2003, Joseph Urusemal stated in a speech before the UN General Assembly that his country was threatened by the increase in frequency and intensity of Pacific storms due to global climate change.

[17] That year, proposals for a new 20-year-agreement with the US and $1.8 billion in aid were made to Washington. Micronesia asked for fair compensation for the damage to the population from nuclear testing on its atolls, stating that the effects were unknown at the time the original agreement was signed. In May 2003, the Kwajalein community finally accepted a $3 billion deal over the same period for the extended use of this atoll. ■

PROFILE

ENVIRONMENT

Covers an area of 2,500 sq km, more than half of which is taken up by the island of Pohnpei (called Ponape until 1984). The terrain is mountainous, with a tropical climate and heavy rainfall. The Federation is made up of four states, including the Caroline islands, except Palau: Yap,119 sq km; Chuuk (called Truk before 1990), 127 sq km; Pohnpei, 345 sq km; and Kosrae, 100 sq km.

SOCIETY

Peoples: Trukese 41.1 per cent; Pohnpeian 25.9 per cent; Mortlockese 8.3 per cent; Kosraean 7.4 per cent; Yapese 6.0 per cent; Ulithian, or Woleaian, 4.0 per cent; Mokilese, 1.2 per cent and others.
Religions: Christianity is the predominant religion, with the Kosraeans, Pohnpeians, and Trukese being mostly Protestant and the Yapese mainly Roman Catholic.
Languages: local languages; English (official).

THE STATE

Official Name: Federated States of Micronesia.
Administrative Divisions: 4 states (Chuuk/Truk, Kosrae, Pohnpei, Yap).
Capital: Palikir, on the island of Pohnpei 7,000 people (2003).
Other Cities: Weno (Moen) 23,900 people; Tol 10,000; Kolonia 5,800 (2000).
Government: Head of State and Government Joseph Urusemal, President since 4 May 2003; Legislature, single-chamber with 14 members (10 on 2-year terms, 4 on 4-year terms). There are no political parties.
National Holidays: 10 May, Proclamation of the Federated States of Micronesia (1979); 3 November, Independence (1986).
Armed Forces: External defense is guaranteed by the US.

Moldova / Moldova

Population:	4,258,650
Area:	33,850 km²
Capital:	Chisinau
Currency:	Moldovan lei
Language:	Moldovan

Moldovans are descended from the peoples of the southern part of Eastern Europe who had been subdued, and culturally influenced, by the Roman Empire. Byzantine chronicler John Skilitsa (976 AD) mentioned the Vlachs as their forebears. In the mid-14th century, Vlach peoples from the northeast formed their own state, independent of the Hungarian Kingdom, in the territory of South Bukovina. The first *gospodar* (governor) of the Moldovan Principality was Bogdan (1356-1374), although according to legend, it was Dragos who founded the principality.

[2] During the second half of the 14th century, the Moldovans freed themselves from Hungarian domination, and from the Tatar khans. By the early 15th century, Moldova's borders were the Dnestr River (to the west), the Black Sea and the Danube (to the south) and the Carpathian mountains (to the west).

[3] This small principality was subject to the influence and interest of larger states: Hungary, Poland, and the Ottoman Empire.

The Christian Orthodox Church was the official church, and the language - known as Ecclesiastical Slav - was used for church liturgy, for official documents and education.

[4] Moldova achieved its greatest political and economic success under the gospodars Alexander the Good (1400-1432) and Stephen the Great (1457-1504). During this period, Moldova went to war against Hungary, Poland and the Crimean Khanate, but its main threat came from the Turks, who in 1484 stripped it of key territories, gave it the Turkish name Akkerman, and created the *raya* - enclaves ruled over by the Turks.

[5] In the early 16th century, Moldova lost its independence as a state, and recognized the power of the Turkish sultan (although still maintaining considerable autonomy within the Ottoman Empire). Turkish domination over Bukovina lasted until 1775, over Bessarabia

until 1812, and over the rest of the Moldovan Principality until 1878. Turkey seized one Moldovan territory after another; by the mid-18th century, Moldova had lost half of its lands between the Prut and the Dnestr rivers.

[6] Anti-Turkish sentiment grew with Moldova's territorial losses, the increase in tributes paid to the sultans, and invasions by Turkish and Tatar troops, who devastated Moldovan cities and towns. Gospodars Petra Rares (1527-38, 1541-46), Ioann Voda Liuti (1572-74) and Dmitri Kantemir (1710-11) all turned against Turkey. Moldova was forced to ally itself with the large powers that opposed Turkey (Hungary, Austria, Poland, and especially Russia). In 1711, Dmitri Kantemir and his Moldovan army joined forces with Russian czar, Peter the Great.

[7] All the wars between Russia and Turkey in the 18th and 19th centuries were related to Moldova.

Mistrusting the Moldovans, the Ottomans put Greek Phanariotes (from Phanar, a suburb of Istanbul), on the Moldovan throne, who ruled until 1821. There were bloody Russian-Turkish wars on Moldovan soil (1735-39; 1768-74; 1787-91), with many Moldovan volunteers fighting the Turks in Russian ranks.

[8] Under the Treaty of Jassy (1792), the Russians obtained the left bank of the Dnestr, south of the Yagolik River. During the second partition of Poland between Russia, Prussia and Austria in 1793, Russia obtained the other part of the left bank of the Dnestr. After the Russo-Turkish War of 1806-1812 and the Peace of Bucharest, Russia seized the territory between the Prut and the Dnestr rivers (Bessarabia). The Muslim population was deported, thus putting an end to the Turkish invasions of Bessarabia.

[9] During the 19th century, the population of Bessarabia grew from 250,000 to 2,500,000. By the end of the century, Moldovans made up half of the province's population. There were also a significant number of Ukrainians and Russians, as well as Bulgarians, Germans, Jews and Gagauz (Muslims). During the Russian-Turkish wars of 1828-29, 1877-78 and the Crimean War (1853-56), Bessarabia acted as a rearguard for the Russian army. Under the Treaty of Paris (1856), the part of Southern Bessarabia next to the Danube and the Black Sea was incorporated into the Moldovan Principality, which joined Walachia in 1859 to form the State of Romania. In 1878, the Treaty of Berlin returned this territory to Russia.

[10] Moldovan schools began to be closed in the 1840s, and as of 1866 the Moldovan language was no longer taught. After the Russian Revolution of 1905, the teaching of Moldovan was once again authorized. On 2 December, 1917, the People's Republic of Moldova was proclaimed. Romanian troops entered Bessarabia and ousted local Soviet authorities. Between December 1917 and January 1918, first the Soviets and then the Romanians gained control over Moldova. Toward the end of January, the independent Moldovan Republic was proclaimed.

[11] In the 1920s and 1930s, the territory of modern Moldova was divided into two unequal parts. Bessarabia was part of the Romanian Kingdom, while the left bank of the Dnestr belonged to the USSR. On 12 October 1924, the Autonomous Soviet Socialist Republic (ASSR) of Moldavia was formed, in Ukraine. Its first capital was Balta, and after 1929, Tiraspol. Moldavia/Moldova made certain gains in industrial and cultural development, while Bessarabia, as

PROFILE

ENVIRONMENT
Located to the south of Russia, Moldova is bordered on the west by Romania and on the east by Ukraine. Moldova lies at the foot of the Carpathian mountains, and is made up of plateaus of relatively low altitude. The region is drained by the Dnestr and the Prut rivers. The soil is black and very fertile. Average temperature in summer is 19° to 22°C, and in winter, -3° to -5°C. The country's main economic activities are stockbreeding and agriculture - especially vineyards, sugar beet, fruits and vegetables.

SOCIETY
Peoples: Moldovans, 64 per cent; Russians, 14 per cent; Ukrainians, 13.8 per cent; Gagauz, 3.5 per cent; Bulgarians, 1.5 per cent. **Religions:** Christian Orthodox. **Languages:** Moldovan (official), Russian, Ukrainian, Gagauz.
Main Political Parties: Communist Party of Moldova; Braghis Alliance (an alliance of center and socialist parties); Christian Democratic People's Party; Party

for Rebirth and Reconciliation (center); Democratic Party of Moldova; National Liberal Party; Green Alliance. **Main Social Organizations:** Moldovan unions, although independent from government, are not highly representative of workers. The Workers' Confederation, the largest trade union in Moldova, did not support teachers and health workers on strike for a wage rise in 2002. The Solidarity union also lacks the strength of Western unions. There are 2,500 NGOs registered in the country, but only 500 are active.

THE STATE
Official Name: Republica Moldova. **Capital:** Chisinau 662,000 people (2003). **Other Cities:** Tiraspol 205,900 people; Belícy 173,200; Tighina 142,800 (2000). **Government:** Vladimir Voronin, President since April 2001. Vasile Tarlev, Prime Minister since April 2001. Unicameral Parliament, with 101 members elected by popular vote. **National Holiday:** 27 August, Independence Day (1991). **Armed Forces:** 7,210 (2002). Other: 2,500 *Opon* (national guard).

Life expectancy
68.9 years
2000-2005

GNI per capita
$460
2002

Literacy
99% total adult rate
2000

HIV prevalence rate
0.2% of population 15-49 years old
2001

part of Romania, remained at a standstill.

12   On 28 June 1940 - with World War II already under way - the Soviet Government issued an ultimatum whereby Romania was forced to accept Soviet annexation of Bessarabia. On 2 August, the Moldavian Soviet Socialist Republic (Moldavian SSR) was founded as a part of the USSR, uniting the central part of Bessarabia and the ASSR of Moldavia. The northern and southern parts of Bessarabia, and the eastern region of the Moldavian ASSR, remained within Ukraine. In June 1941, Nazi troops invaded the USSR. Romania made an alliance with Hitler and recovered all of Bessarabia, as far as the Dnestr and Odessa. Three years later, the Red Army took on a weakened Germany, recovering Bessarabia and northern Bucovina.

13   Soviet leader Leonid Brezhnev's political career began in Moldavia, where he was leader of the local Communist Party. He was later to become Secretary General of the Communist Party of the Soviet Union (CPSU) and President of the USSR, positions which he held simultaneously until 1983.

14   After the liberalization process initiated by Soviet president, Mikhail Gorbachev, in 1985, political and ethnic problems began to emerge. In 1988, the Democratic Movement in Support of Perestroika (restructuring) began demanding the return to the use of the Latin alphabet instead of the Cyrillic alphabet for writing the Moldovan language. Nationalists called for an end to the political and economic privileges which Russian residents enjoyed, stating that if they could not do without them, they should return to their native land. On 10 November 1989, Parliament approved the Official Language Law, which established Moldavian as the country's official language for political, economic, social and cultural affairs, with Russian to be used only in the press and other mass media.

15   On 27 August 1991, the country declared its independence from the USSR as Moldova. A month later, Dnestr (Transnistria) and Gagauz - opposing both Moldova's independence and the possibility of union with Romania - declared themselves independent republics.

16   In December, Mircea Snegur won the country's first presidential elections. In March 1992, Moldova was admitted to the UN as a new member.

17   The political spectrum split into those supporting unification with Romania and groups preferring independence. In parliamentary elections, pro-independence parties took an ample majority and in

IN FOCUS

ENVIRONMENTAL CHALLENGES
The intensive use of agrochemicals, including banned pesticides such as DDT, contaminate soils and underground water, of which 40 per cent has bacterial pollution. Also, 45 per cent of lakes and water bodies are polluted with chemicals. Extensive agriculture speeds erosion and degradation of fertile soils.

WOMEN'S RIGHTS
Women have been able to vote since 1978 (when Moldova was part of the USSR) and to stand for office since 1993, when a new Constitution was passed. In 2002, 12.9 per cent of seats in parliament were held by women, up from five per cent in 1995 and nine per cent in 2000. However, women did not hold any ministerial or equivalent positions in 2000. That year, women made up 49 per cent of the work force.

Almost 20 per cent of pregnant women were anemic in 2000.

Moldova is a source of women trafficked into forced prostitution in several countries, especially Italy, Turkey, Greece and Kosovo. Although there are no official data, in 2000 advocates of women's rights and members of parliament stated there were more than 10,000 Moldovan women working as prostitutes in other countries.

CHILDREN
Moldova is the poorest country in Europe. A combination of the effects of poverty and the drop in social spending have reduced the ability of families to protect their children. The latest official data revealed that in the first years of this century, more than 12,000 children lived in orphanages and other welfare institutions. About 80 per cent of these children come from vulnerable families unable to take care of them. With no clear government social policy, institutional care is used as a welfare measure to provide housing and education to the children of poor families. The condition of poor children with physical or mental disabilities is especially alarming. In 2002 some 5 per cent of newborn babies were underweight.

INDIGENOUS PEOPLES/ ETHNIC MINORITIES
The Gagauz and Slavs are identified as national minorities. In 1998, the former amounted to three per cent of the population, while the latter made up 27 per cent. The Slavs are a diverse group with Russian, Ukrainian and Bulgarian roots. Whether or not they should be identified as a single ethnic group is a question that is under debate. They are united by the Russian language, and have shown an ability to engage in unified political activity. In surveys from the 1990s, some 76

per cent of Russians had supported a unified USSR, including Moldova; as did 70 per cent of Ukrainians, 95 per cent of Gagauz and 89 per cent of Bulgarians. Slavs are geographically dispersed in Moldova, somewhat more concentrated in Dnestr, on the eastern border with Ukraine. Within the region, Russians and Ukrainians make up 53 per cent of the population, while Romanians make up 40 per cent. The Slav minority clashed with the Government over the leadership of Dnestr until 1998, after eight years of separatist fighting, when a definitive peace agreement was reached. Instead of fighting for independence, the Slavs focus their present demands on gaining more autonomy for the Dnestr region, within Moldova.

MIGRANTS/REFUGEES
Approximately 300 refugees and asylum-seekers were living in Moldova in late 2001. There were also thousands of internally-displaced people, although their precise number is unknown. That year, 5,200 Moldovans sought asylum in Western Europe. Almost 15 per cent of the Moldovan population lived and worked outside the country in early 2002.

DEATH PENALTY
Abolished in 1995.

August the new Constitution declared Moldova an independent democratic state. Two months later an agreement was signed with Moscow for the withdrawal of Russian troops.

18   In 1995, President Snegur accelerated the privatization of public companies and facilitated the inflow of foreign capital, but he failed to rally support and was defeated by Petru Lucinschi in the November 1996 elections. Economic reform continued.

19   In 1999, Lucinschi began a new stage of privatizations with the aim of alleviating enormous recession and the pressure of both domestic and international debt. Sell-offs included the telecommunications monopoly and the electricity sector - the latter plagued by inefficiencies, shortages and appalling levels of non-payment: tens of thousands of consumers were used to not paying. One part of the country had electricity for only two hours a day, while most were supplied through a Soviet-era network from Ukraine where the

energy was purchased. The nation's tobacco and wine industries, a source of national pride, were also up for sale.

20   After the Communist Party won the elections with 49.9 per cent of the vote, Vladimir Voronin became president in April 2001. One of the first measures implemented by the Government was to introduce Russian as the compulsory language from the second grade in schools, sparking controversy in a nation where 70 per cent of the population are Romanian speakers. A month earlier, the Government had ratified a treaty with Russia as a strategic partner, leading to the measure being seen as one more step along the path to 'Russification'.

21   Repeated anti-government marches led to Education Minister Ilie Vancea being ousted in February 2002, despite earlier withdrawal of the obligatory Russian language ruling and changes to the history textbooks. This was swiftly followed by the

resignation of Interior Minister Vasile Dregenel who refused to halt the demonstrations.

22   In November 2003, before and even after President Voronin refused to sign an agreement with Russia granting greater autonomy to Transnistria and putting an end to a 13-year conflict, nationalist opposition forces took to the streets in protest. The opposition accused Voronin of favoring rapprochement with Moscow (which has a 2,500-strong peace force and a large missile and artillery base in the region) and requested US and European peace forces. Meanwhile, Voronin's supporters accused Washington and the EU of using the area's fragility to expand their influence eastwards.

23   In late 2003 Moldova was the poorest country in Europe and had the highest rate of trafficking in both people and organs, especially kidneys (see In focus box). The donors generally undergo surgery in Turkey and their organs are sold to Israelis, Arabs and Western Europeans. ∎

Monaco / Monaco

Population:	35,017
Area:	2 km²
Capital:	Monaco
Currency:	Euro
Language:	French

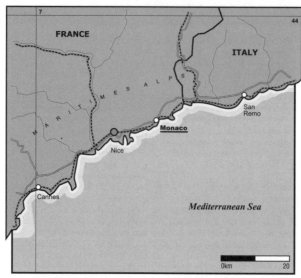

The territory of Monaco (located in a mountainous region on the Mediterranean coast) has been inhabited since the Stone Age. Monaco's Rock was a refuge for numerous peoples; the Ligures were the first settled inhabitants. Monaco's coast and harbor provided them with an outlet to the sea.

2 The region was occupied by Phoenicians, Greeks and Carthaginians and by the end of the 2nd century BC by Romans. Monaco became a part of the Alpes-Maritime area. The Romans built La Turbie, the trophy of Augustus, who was celebrating his triumphant military campaigns. During that same period, Phoenician and Carthaginian sailors brought prosperity to the region. Monaco was annexed to Marseilles and converted to Christianity in the 1st century AD.

3 With the fall of the Roman Empire (5th century), the region was invaded by different peoples. In the 7th century it was a part of the Lombard kingdom and 100 years later it formed part of the kingdom of Arles. It was controlled by Muslims after the Saracen invasion of France. Starting in the 10th century, after the expulsion of the Saracens by the Count of Provence, the coast gradually became inhabited.

4 In 1191, Monaco was ceded to Genoa as a colony. On 8 January 1297 the Grimaldis, a Genoese family of exiles, held on to the fortress and placed the founding stone of their present palace. Emperor Henry VI gave control of the land around the Rock of Monaco to their chief, Fulco del Castello. From then on, the Rock became an object of dispute between the two main parties of Genoa: the Ghibellines (followers of the Emperor) and the Guelfs (followers of the papacy) allied with the Grimaldis.

5 In 1331 Charles I reconquered the Rock and acquired the wealth of the

Spinola (allies of the Ghibellines), and gained control over Menton and Roquebrune. He was considered by many to have been the real founder of the Principality, and first lord of Monaco. Charles died in 1357 and his son Rainier II fought against the Genoese until 1489. Then the King of France and the Duke of Savoy recognized the sovereignty of Monaco.

6 In September 1641 Honorato II, Prince and Lord of Monaco since 1612, and Louis XIII of France signed the Treaty of Peroné, by which the kingdom of

France guaranteed protection to the Prince of Monaco. The same year the Spanish were expelled from the Principality.

7 During the French Revolution the Principality was annexed to France and proclaimed Protectorate of Sardinia from 1815 to 1860 under the Treaty of Vienna. Monaco's sovereignty was recognized by the Franco-Monegasque treaty of 1861.

8 Prince Charles III of Monaco drew the international jet set when the first casino was opened in 1863 and the Monte Carlo center in 1866.

9 Charles III ruled from 1856 to 1889; his son Albert I promulgated the first constitution in 1911.

10 A treaty signed in 1918 contained provisions limiting French protection of Monaco, establishing that its policies as well as its military and economic interests would be in line with those of France.

11 A new constitution, proclaimed in 1962, abolished the death penalty, granted women the right to vote and appointed a Supreme Court in order to ensure basic freedoms.

12 In May 1993 Monaco became an official member of the UN.

13 In 1998, an Israeli citizen was involved in a case of money laundering tied to Latin American drug trafficking, increasing suspicions that the country was a major money laundering center. Given the possibility that Russian mafia money might have entered the country, a short but unsuccessful investigation was carried out.

14 Although not a European Union member, in 1999 Monaco adopted the euro as its official currency, and it participates in the EU market system through its customs union with France.

15 Patrick Leclercq took over as Minister of State in January 2000, replacing Michel Lévêque. In October that year, France threatened to take parliamentary action against Monaco to pressure it to clamp down on money laundering. Paris accused the Principality of hiding essential information by means of bank secrecy laws, but Monaco ignored the criticism.

16 In October 2002 the Financial Action Task Force on Money Laundering (FATF) began to assess worldwide compliance with its recommendations. Monaco was classified as 'somewhat co-operative' - the second category of three, based on degree of commitment to the fight against money laundering - together with Barbados and Bermuda.

17 Prince Albert remarked that he was upset that some people in Monaco were seen as drug traffickers. The business community, meanwhile, accused France of being hypocritical, pointing out that all the money that enters the Principality first passes through the French Central Bank.

18 In 2004, the British law ruled that Stephen Troth (born in Chesterfield and member of the HSBC banking group) would face another two years in prison for siphoning more than $10 million from celebrity clients in Monaco, including among others, racing driver Michael Schumacher. A Monaco court had condemned him to four years in prison in 2002. ■

PROFILE

ENVIRONMENT

The Principality of Monaco is located at the foot of the Alps and bordering the Mediterranean Sea. It shares borders with several French communities of the Alpes-Maritime département: Cap-d'Ail, La Turbie, Beausoleil and Roquebrune-Cap-Martin. Its territory covers an area of 195 hectares.

SOCIETY

Peoples: Around 15 per cent of Monacans are locals; French 47 per cent, Italian 15 per cent, others 12 per cent.
Religion: The State is Catholic. There are also Anglicans, Baha'i, Jews and Protestants.
Language: French is the official language, also Monegasque, English and Italian.
Main Political Parties: National and Democratic Union (UND); National Union for the Future of Monaco.

THE STATE

Official Name: Principality of Monaco.
Administrative Divisions: Four sections or *quartiers*, Monaco-Ville, the old town; La Condamine, the harbor area; Monte Carlo, residential area; Fontvielle, a newer zone reclaimed from the sea. **Capital:** Monaco-Ville 34,000 peoples (2003).
Government: Parliamentary monarchy. Constitution effective since 17 December 1962. Prince Rainier III, sovereign since 9 May 1949, Head of State. Patrick Leclercq, Minister of State and Head of Government since January 2000. Unicameral Legislature: National Council, with 18 members elected for a five-year term.
Armed Forces: Defense is the responsibility of France.

Mongolia / Mongol Uls

Population:	2,666,950
Area:	1,566,500 km²
Capital:	Ulaanbaatar
Currency:	Tughrik
Language:	Khalkha Mongolian

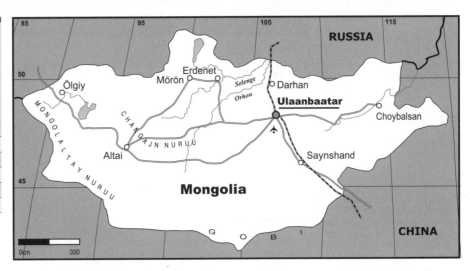

The Mongols are one of the main ethnic groups of northern and eastern Asia, linked by cultural ties and a common language. Dialects vary from one part of the region to another, but most can be understood by a Mongolian.

[2] Direct lineage from a male ancestor gives the family or clan its name, though there was an earlier tradition of female lineages. Intermarriage between members of the same clan was forbidden so there was great need for establishing alliances between clans, who formed tribal groups.

[3] The Mongols were mostly nomadic, with the movement of livestock and campsites determined by pasturage needs throughout the year. Animals were owned individually, while grazing lands were collective property.

[4] The most powerful clans tended to control the tribal groups' activities. The weakest families maintained their own authority and ownership of animals, but they were forced to pay tribute to the dominant clan. They moved, camped, grazed their livestock and went to war under that clan's orders.

[5] Political and military organization was adapted to the needs of each clan or tribe. A person capable of handling a weapon could be a chief or a soldier, according to the needs of the moment. Capturing livestock,

women or prisoners from other tribes was a common means of acquiring wealth.

[6] The Siung-nu, or Huns, were the earliest inhabitants of the Selenga valleys, joining Siberia to the heart of Asia, and they are thought to have settled in this region by 400 BC.

[7] The Huns created a great empire in Mongolia when China was undergoing unification as an imperial state under the Ch'in and Han dynasties (221 BC-220 AD).The Hun Empire warred against China for centuries, until it disintegrated - perhaps due to internal conflicts - around the 4th century.

[8] Some of the southern tribes surrendered to China and settled in Chinese territory, where they were eventually absorbed by the Chinese, while others migrated westward. In the 5th century, Attila's Huns conquered almost all of Europe, reaching Gaul and the Italian peninsula.

[9] The Huns were subsequently displaced by the Turks who established themselves throughout the region. Social organization at the time did not consist only of nomadic tribal groups. The major Hun chieftains set up general headquarters, surrounded by cultivated lands where they bred larger, stronger horses, capable of carrying a warrior in armor.

[10] This led to a differentiation between aristocrats and traditional archers, who rode smaller horses. Agriculture also became more important to the economy.

[11] The term 'Mongol' first appeared in records of different groups written during the T'ang Chinese dynasty. It then disappeared until the 11th century, when the Kidan became the rulers of Manchuria and northern China, controlling almost all of present-day Mongolia.

[12] The Kidan established the Liao dynasty in China (907-1125) and

ruled Mongolia, fostering division between the different groups.

[13] The Kidan were succeeded by the Juchen, who were in turn succeeded by the Tatars, before the era of Genghis Khan (Temujin). Born in 1162, Temujin was the grandson of Qabul (Kublai Khan), who had been the Mongols' greatest leader to date. Temujin inherited several fiefdoms that had been seized from his family.

[14] In 1206, because of his political and military prowess, Temujin was recognized as leader of all the Mongols, and given the title of Genghis Khan. His armies invaded northern China, reaching Beijing. By 1215, the Mongolian Empire extended as far as Tibet and Turkistan.

[15] Upon Genghis Khan's death in 1227 disputes among his successors caused the Mongolian Empire to disintegrate, until the Chinese throne was left in the hands of the Ming dynasty in 1368. China invaded Mongolia and set fire to Karakorum, the former imperial capital, though it was unable to bring the territory under control.

[16] In the 15th and 16th centuries, controlling the areas beyond the Great Wall of China demanded military mobilization.

[17] The Oyrat alliance between groups living in western Mongolia began gaining control of the territory. They conquered several oases in Sinkiang and the Tibet region, and added their own mercantile and administrative expertise to the Mongols' tribal organization.

[18] The separation of the Oyrat from the Jaljas began during this period, with the latter forming the core of what was later to become Outer Mongolia. A tribal league was formed between the Khalkhas in the north and the Chahars in the south, while the leadership passed over to the Ordos, during the reign of Altan Khan (1543-83).

[19] To keep their hold on power, the Mongolian princes thought it useful to be backed up by a religious ideology. They adopted the Tibetan Buddhist religion as Tibet posed no cultural threat, and the Tibetan script was easy to use.

[20] Altan Khan proceeded to invite a Tibetan prelate, whom the Mongols called 'Dalai Lama' to lead the state religion. The merging of religious interests with those of the State was accomplished by claiming that an heir to the Khalkhas clan was the first 'reincarnation' of the Living Buddha of Urga.

[21] In 1644, after consolidating their power in Manchuria, the Manchus seized the Chinese throne, with the help of Mongolian tribes from the far east. Before occupying Beijing, the Manchus took control of southern Mongolia, which was henceforth known as Inner Mongolia.

[22] It took China almost a century to conquer Outer Mongolia. Meanwhile, Inner Mongolia became a part of China, and the Khalkhas' desire to retain power in the south prevented the Oyrats from attaining reunification.

[23] This was the final stage of the great wars among the Mongols; ending in their overall dispersal. Several groups of Khalkhas remained in the south; some Chahars settled in Sinkiang and the Oyrat dispersed in different directions, including czarist Russia.

[24] In the Russo-Japanese War of 1904-05, both armies used Mongolian troops and staff. This served Japanese interests well as a resurgence of Mongolian nationalism could weaken both Russia and China. At the end of the war, Russia secretly recognized Inner Mongolia as belonging to Japan's sphere of influence.

[25] With the outbreak of the Chinese Revolution in 1911, there was a pervading malaise in Mongolia. Until then, the region

LAND USE

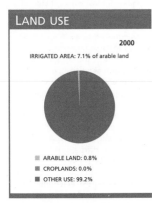

2000

IRRIGATED AREA: 7.1% of arable land

- ARABLE LAND: 0.8%
- CROPLANDS: 0.0%
- OTHER USE: 99.2%

 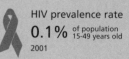
had been the object of disputes between Russia and Japan. However, the Mongolians' social and political discontent was directed against the Manchus and the local government.

26 Led by their Buddhist leader, Mongolia proclaimed independence from China and sought Russian support. However, because of its secret treaties with Japan and Britain, Russia could offer nothing more than mere 'autonomy'. After lengthy negotiations, this status was granted to Outer Mongolia.

27 This situation continued until the Russian Revolution in 1917. China sent in troops and made the Mongolians sign a request for aid from Beijing. But the region was invaded by retreating czarist troops, who expelled the Chinese and mistreated the Mongolians.

28 With the traditional leaders discredited because of their poor handling of the Chinese and White Russian interventions, some groups of Mongolian revolutionaries sought help from the Bolsheviks. Russian and Mongolian troops took the capital, Urga, in July 1921.

29 This was the beginning of the republic, although initially the Living Buddha acted as puppet king, only authorized to endorse the new regime's proposals. Upon his death in 1924, the People's Republic of Mongolia was proclaimed.

30 The Mongolian People's Revolutionary Party (MPRP), made up of conservatives and revolutionary nationalists, wavered between Beijing and Moscow until the defeat of the Chinese Revolution, at the hands of Chiang Kai-shek. At this time, Mongolia began to fall increasingly under the influence of the USSR, and Joseph Stalin.

31 The new republic proclaimed the right of women to vote.

32 Following the Soviet model, the MPRP Government tried to collectivize the economy in order to break the power of the feudal lords and the Buddhist priests. Between 1936 and 1938, the Mongolian regime purged the party and the army, executing many leaders.

33 In 1939, Japan invaded northeastern Mongolia, along the Siberian border. Mongolian troops resisted ferociously until Soviet help arrived.

34 The defeat of Japan was a severe blow to the Axis powers in Berlin and Tokyo. Mongolia and the USSR fought together in the Inner Mongolian and Manchurian campaign, two weeks before the end of World War II.

35 As part of the Yalta agreement, Chiang Kai-shek agreed to hold a plebiscite in Mongolia.

PROFILE

ENVIRONMENT

Comprises the northern area of Mongolia, also known as 'Outer Mongolia' (the southern part, 'Inner Mongolia', comes within Chinese territory under the name of Inner Mongolian Autonomous Region). At the center of the country lies the wide Gobi desert, bordered on the north and south by steppes where there is extensive nomadic sheep, horse and camel raising. The Altai mountain region, in west Mongolia, is rich in mineral resources: copper, tin, phosphates, coal and oil.

SOCIETY

Peoples: Khalkha Mongol 78.8 per cent; Kazakh 5.9 per cent; Dörbed Mongol 2.7 per cent; Bayad 1.9 per cent; Buryat Mongol 1.7 per cent; Dariganga Mongol 1.4 per cent; other 7.6 per cent.
Religions: Buddhism.
Languages: Khalkha Mongolian.
Main Political Parties: Mongolian People's Revolutionary Party (MPRP); Mongolian National Democratic Party (MNDP); Social Democratic Party (SDP); Democratic Union Coalition (DUC) is a coalition created in 1996 by the MNDP and the SDP; Motherland Democracy Coalition (formed in 2003 by the New Social Democratic Party and the Democratic Party).
Main Social Organizations: Central Council of Mongolian Unions; 'Blue Mongolia'; Mongolian Confederation of Free Unions.

THE STATE

Official Name: Bügd Nairamdach Mongol Ard Uls.
Administrative Divisions: 18 provinces and 1 municipality (Ulan Bator).
Capital: Ulaanbaatar (Ulan Bator) 812,000 people (2003).
Other Cities: Darhan 75,000 people; Erdenet 71,200; Choybalsan 37,700; Ölgiy 21,100 (2000).
Government: Parliamentary republic. Natsagiyn Bagabandi, President since June 1997, re-elected in 2001; Tsakhiagiyn Elbegdorj, Prime Minister since August 2004. Legislature: single-chamber Assembly with 76 members elected every 4 years.
National Holiday: 11 July, Independence Day (1921).
Armed Forces: 21,100 (1996). Other: 10,000 (internal security and border guards).

Although the result favored independence, Mongolia failed to receive diplomatic recognition. In 1961, Mongolia was admitted to the UN.

36 In 1960, Government officials in Ulaanbaatar accused the Chinese Government of mistreating Mongolian citizens and of seeking territorial expansion, at Mongolia's expense.

37 Friction continued until 1986, when the Chinese deputy minister of the Council of Ministers visited Mongolia and re-established consular and commercial relations.

38 In March 1988, China and Mongolia signed a treaty aimed at defining the 4,655-kilometre border between the two countries. A year later, during Mongolian premier Tserenpylium Gombasuren's visit, the first in 40 years, relations between the two countries were returned to normal.

39 In 1989, within the framework of Soviet *perestroika* (restructuring), Moscow announced that three-quarters of its troops would be withdrawn in 1990. Shortly afterwards, both governments agreed to the complete withdrawal of all Soviet military personnel and equipment

from Mongolian territory by the end of 1992.

40 Meanwhile, the MPRP leadership admitted that social and economic reforms were inadequate. The ruling party adopted democratic changes in internal elections.

41 In 1989 and 1990, several opposition groups emerged. One of the most active, the Democratic Union of Mongolia, was officially recognized in January 1990. In March, increasingly frequent public demonstrations against the Government triggered a new crisis within the MPRP.

42 The National Assembly approved a constitutional amendment withdrawing the reference to the MPRP as society's 'prime moving force' and approving new electoral legislation; however, no changes were made in relation to political party activity.

43 The legendary figure of Genghis Khan, whose name was forbidden for many years, was rehabilitated as an authentic expression of Mongolian pride and tradition, sentiments which until recently were condemned as being an expression of a narrow-minded 'nationalism'.

44 In spite of 65 years of Soviet aid, Mongolia's economy maintained vestiges of nomadism. In the early 1990s, urbanization was just beginning, and half of Ulaanbaatar's population lived in tents, with rudimentary electric and water supplies.

45 In the first months of 1991, there was a substantial reduction in Mongolia's foreign trade. There were acute shortages of food, medicine and fuel. The currency plummeted, and government income declined sharply, while expenditure steadily increased.

46 In May, Prime Minister Dashiun Byambasuren announced a new economic policy which included incentives to attract foreign investment, the establishment of a national stock exchange, the sale of two-thirds of the state's capital goods, deregulation of prices and changes in the banking system.

47 The chair of the Central Bank of Mongolia, Zhargalsaikhan, was arrested together with a group of new investors in December 1991, for an $82 million fraud as a result of which the country lost most of its reserves. At the same time, Deputy Prime Minister Cabaadorjiyn Ganbold was accused of secretly authorizing the transfer of 4,400 kilograms of gold to a branch of Goldman Sachs - a British merchant bank, as collateral for a $46 million loan, apparently earmarked for covering losses.

48 In 1992, Parliament approved a Government-proposed constitutional reform, adopting the official name 'Republic of Mongolia', and dropping the word 'People's'. The reform also established a pluralistic democratic system, replacing the socialist system.

49 In October 1992, after being defeated in the June elections which were won by a wide margin by the ruling MPRP, the opposition formed the Mongolian National Democratic Party (MNDP). The Social Democratic Party (SDP) preferred to remain independent.

50 In 1992, the withdrawal of Russian troops - begun in 1987 - was completed. Meanwhile, Otchirbat had a rapprochement with the MNDP and the SDP to prepare the presidential elections in June 1993. Thanks to these former members of the opposition, the President was re-elected with almost 58 per cent of the vote and announced the 'Westernization' of the economy.

51 Throughout 1994, disagreements between Otchirbat and the former communist majority in parliament were frequent. According to official estimates 26.5 per cent of the population lacked the minimum subsistence income.

52 The June 1996 elections marked the end of communist

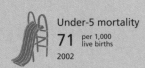

Under-5 mortality
71 per 1,000 live births
2002

$ Poverty
13.9% of population living on less than $1 per day
1995

Debt service
7.7% exports of goods and services
2001

Maternal mortality
110 per 100,000 live births
2000

dominion, with victory for the Democratic Union Coalition (DUC), a coalition formed by the SDP and the MNDP. The DUC took 50 of the 76 seats, while the former communist bloc shrank from 70 to 25 seats. In July, Parliament appointed Mendsayhany Enkhsaikhan as Prime Minister.

[53] After the election, the Government implemented reforms to switch quickly to a market economy. This process had a high social cost, increasing unemployment and poverty, and added to the damage caused by the lack of technical and economic assistance following the disappearance of the Soviet Union.

[54] In May 1997, Natsagiyn Bagabandi, of the MPRP, won the presidential election with 60.8 per cent of the vote. President Punsalmaagiyn Otchirbat, the DUC re-election candidate, took 29.8 per cent. The result was interpreted as a reaction against the 'shock therapy' applied in order to reach a liberalized economy.

[55] A law introduced in June 1998 required the use of surnames in legal documents. The new legislation, which responded to demands for modernization and greater integration with the rest of the world, caused confusion and concern amongst the people. For centuries, most of the population had been made up of nomadic herders, living in small groups, for whom surnames were irrelevant.

[56] The failure to tackle the economic crisis and strong criticism forced the Government to resign, and a new cabinet was formed, headed by Janlaviin Narantsatsralt. Seven months later, in July 1999, following a dispute related to the privatization of a copper mine co-owned by Mongolia and Russia, Narantsatsralt and his ten ministers all resigned. Parliament appointed a new member of the DUC, economist Rinchinnyamiin Amarjargal, as premier.

[57] A report issued in January 2000 by non-governmental organizations estimated there were 4,000 street children, three quarters of whom were spending their days in the sewers of the capital (this number had not changed by 2004). When the country abandoned the Soviet model in 1992 there were only 300 street children. As factories and other workplaces closed, urban poverty increased, compounding rural poverty. According to tradition, when a family of Mongolian herders could not feed the whole group, it would send one or several children to live in the city. This system, which had worked for hundreds of years, became bankrupt as the urban relatives could not feed the

IN FOCUS

ENVIRONMENTAL CHALLENGES

Water is a scarce resource, especially in regions close to the Gobi Desert. Coal burning by power plants has severely polluted the air in the capital city. Deforestation and uncontrolled farming have led to soil erosion. Desertification is another symptom of environmental deterioration. In 2001 frequent forest fires and the *dzuds* - an environmental phenomenon in winter that combines extreme cold spells with blizzards and droughts - led to considerable loss of human life and damage to property.

WOMEN'S RIGHTS

Women have been able to vote and stand for office since 1924. Between 1995 and 2000 women held 8 per cent of seats in Parliament and occupied no top ministerial or equivalent positions. In 2000 women made up 47 per cent of the labor force. In 2000, about 90 per cent of pregnant women received prenatal care, 97 per cent of births were attended by skilled medical personnel and 45 per cent of pregnant women were anemic. International agencies regard the high maternal mortality rate, caused in part by unsafe abortions, and the inexistence of family planning services and counselling to be serious problems.

No effective measures have been taken to combat trafficking in women. Domestic violence is common but the culprits are not punished. Rape within wedlock is not considered an offense in Mongolia. In 1998 women were the victims of 8 per cent of all murders; by 2001 the number had more than doubled, reaching 17 per cent.

CHILDREN

In 2002 there were a million children under 18 in a total population of 2.7 million. UNICEF latest data available* shows that 8 per cent of all children are born underweight. 12.7% of children under a year old are severely or moderately underweight, while two per cent of children in the same age bracket are very severely underweight. Stunted growth is found in 26.4 per cent of children under the age of one, with very severe growth problems among 8.5 per cent of children in the same age bracket.

During the harsh winters of 2002 and 2003 rural children and women were the hardest hit. Their incomes dropped and they had reduced access to food. These families were also psychologically, socially and emotionally affected, suffering in the post-*dzud* period from stress and immunological problems as well as malnutrition and fatigue.

In 1999 the ILO reported that almost 1,700 children up to the age of 14 and 91,800 teenagers between 15 and 19 were working in the country. It was estimated that in 2000 approximately 3,000 boys and 2,000 girls between the ages of 10 and 14 were working.

Some 3,000 children were living on the streets of the capital, who were more vulnerable to being forced to work as prostitutes in other countries, or to being abused by adults in the informal labor market or in unpaid domestic service.

INDIGENOUS PEOPLES/ ETHNIC MINORITIES

Even though Mongolia is inhabited by several ethnic minorities (Lhoton, Kazakh, Uriankhai, Zakhchin, Myangad, Oold and Torguud) the Kazakh, who comprise 4 per cent of the country's population, are the only ethnic, religious or linguistic minority recognized by the Government and whose rights are respected. Most Mongols belong to the Khalakh group, which comprises 85 per cent of the population.

MIGRANTS/REFUGEES

In January 1999 Mongolia had still not signed or ratified international treaties on the status of refugees (the 1951 UN Convention, and the 1967 Protocol relating to the Status of Refugees). Groups of North Koreans enter the country across the Chinese border. The Government co-operates with UNHCR and other humanitarian organizations, however, it has refused entry to several asylum-seekers.

DEATH PENALTY

This is applicable even to ordinary crimes.

*Latest data available in *The State of the World's Children* and *Childinfo* database, UNICEF, 2004.

children either. Ill-health is also a serious threat in the winter in Ulaanbataar, one of the coldest capital cities in the world.

[58] Living conditions became considerably worse after the winter of 2000 - the coldest in 55 years. The Government declared more than half the country a disaster area. More than 2 million head of livestock were lost, the equivalent of $1.65 billion.

[59] In the July 2000 legislative elections the MPRP was elected with 72 of a total 76 seats.

[60] The winter of 2001 was even more severe than the previous one, with heavy blizzards and temperatures plunging below -50°C. More than 6 million head of livestock perished. China, the International Red Cross and the United Nations all appealed for support for the 75,000 families affected, and especially for the thousands of herders whose survival depends almost exclusively on their animals.

[61] In 2001 the IMF approved a $40 million low-interest loan over a three-year term. The loan was to be used in combating poverty, boosting the economy and investing in social plans in Mongolia.

[62] Domestic violence against women is a serious issue: it is estimated that between 10 and 24 per cent of all murders occur within the family. In 1998, women were victims of 8 per cent of all murders, while in 2001 the number had risen to 17 per cent. More than 60 per cent of all cases of family abuse are caused by alcoholism.

[63] In 2001, the Government set up a human rights center to take charge of prison management (in 1999 alone, 200 prisoners had died in custody). That year, 180 prison guards were trained at the center. The Constitution bans all types of torture, degrading treatment or punishment. Although reports of such practices have dropped, the use of unnecessary force in handling prisoners continues, especially in rural areas. In 2002, the prison administration installed cameras in 17 of the 22 state prisons to combat this.

[64] In November 2002, more than 50 demonstrators (members of the Democratic Party) were arrested while protesting against the land privatization act - in effect since May 2003 - which covered one per cent of Mongolian territory.

[65] In January 2004, after two years of negotiations, a new labor plan was implemented, allowing Mongolians to work in Taiwan. That month, of the 7,000 Mongolian workers registered (90 per cent were between 20 and 35 years old, and 55 per cent were men), 3,000 were admitted to the plan. ∎

Montserrat / Montserrat

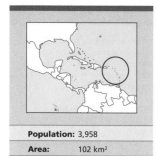

Population:	3,958
Area:	102 km²
Capital:	Plymouth
Currency:	EC dollar
Language:	English

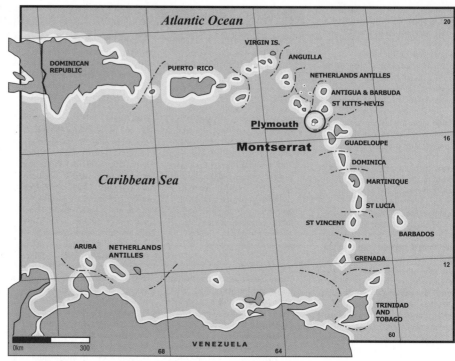

Montserrat, like the rest of the Lesser Antilles, was inhabited by the Caribs (see box 'Arawaks and Caribs'), who were wiped out by colonization. France and Britain fought at length for the island, which was also a haven for pirates, but Britain gained possession of it in 1632.

2   Montserrat was colonized mainly by Irish people following their expulsion from nearby St Kitts. The island was covered by sugar and cotton plantations and large numbers of African slaves were transported to work these from 1651 onwards. In the mid-19th century the island had little more than 10,000 residents, of whom 9,000 were slaves.

3   In the 20th century Montserrat became a British Dependent Territory, though it has been a member of several Caribbean federations, the last being the West Indies Federation, dissolved in 1962. Since 1960 the island has been ruled by an Administrator (retitled Governor in 1971) appointed by the British, who is responsible for defense, external affairs, the public service and international financial services. All other matters are the responsibility of the Executive Council, on which sits the Governor, the chief minister and five other ministers. The Democratic Progressive Party (DPP), founded by William Bramble and later chaired by his son, Austin Bramble, refused to alter this colonial arrangement when Montserrat joined the new grouping of West Indies Associate States in 1967.

4   The DPP lost all its seats in parliament in November 1973 to the then recently created People's Liberation Movement (PLM). In 1979 the new chief minister, John Osborne, announced his plan for total independence for 1982 - though this was never put into practice. Those against independence argued that income from tourism and remittances of Montserrat nationals living abroad

were not enough to cover the trade deficit, paid by the UK.

5   In 1989 there were 347 offshore banks in Montserrat, which yielded huge earnings to promoters and agents but not to the Government, which received only a five per cent share of the sales of licenses that were issued.

6   In 1992, an in-depth probe of banking operations led the UK to close 90 per cent of commercial and offshore banks, on the

grounds that they engaged in illegal transactions and drug money laundering.

7   In 1995 and 1996, the economy was seriously weakened by the constant expulsion of ashes by the Soufriere Hills volcano. The volcano erupted in mid-1997, killing more than 20 people, destroying the capital, Plymouth, and making the greater part of Montserrat uninhabitable. Thousands of people were

evacuated to areas in the north, to Britain, and to other Caribbean countries. Bertrand Osborne resigned as chief minister in August 1997, after residents complained at the way the evacuation of the local population was carried out.

8   The new chief minister, David Brandt, requested a judicial investigation into the UK's decision to evacuate the population of Montserrat instead of aiding those who decided to stay. The results of that investigation held both officials in Montserrat and the UK responsible for contributing to the death of nine farmers, for not granting them land on which they could have taken refuge.

9   Presenting the 2001 budget following another election, the new chief minister John Osborne listed some causes for the economic crisis which affected the island: lack of capacity to generate income, slow implementation of public sector projects, private sector hindrance of the Government, and a -6.3% economic growth rate in fiscal year 2000, among others.

10   In early 2002 the UK passed a bill granting British citizenship to its dependencies. This resulted in increased possibilities for emigration for the people of Monserrat and made the likelihood of winning independence more remote.

11   In July 2003 Deborah Barnes Jones was appointed by the UK to take office as Governor in April 2004. ∎

PROFILE

ENVIRONMENT

Montserrat is one of the Leeward islands in the Lesser Antilles, located 400 km east of Puerto Rico, northwest of Guadeloupe. The terrain is volcanic in origin and quite mountainous, with altitudes of over 1,000 meters. The tropical, rainy climate is tempered by sea winds. The soil of the plains is relatively fertile and suitable for agriculture. Only one-fourth of the land is cultivated and population density in these areas is high. Half of the island is suitable for stockbreeding.

SOCIETY

Most of the population is of African descent, with a small minority of European descendants. Religions: Mostly Christian; Anglicans, Catholics and Methodists predominate.
Languages: English (official). Most people speak a local dialect.
Main Political Parties: New People's Liberation Movement (NPLM); National Progressive Party (NPP).
Main Social Organizations: The Montserrat Allied Workers' Union. There is also a Teachers' Union and Seamen and Waterfront Workers' Union.

THE STATE

Official Name: Montserrat. **Capital:** Plymouth 2,000 people (2003).
Government: Deborah Barnes Jones, appointed in July 2003 to succeed Longrigg in April 2004. John Osborne, chief minister since April 2001. Parliament: Legislative Council with 11 members, 9 of them elected every 5 years.

Morocco / Al Maghrib

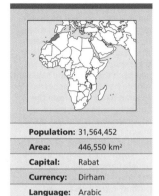

Population:	31,564,452
Area:	446,550 km²
Capital:	Rabat
Currency:	Dirham
Language:	Arabic

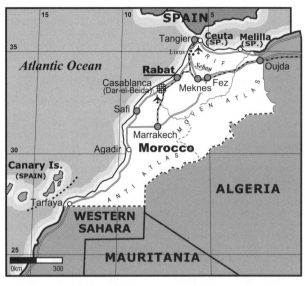

B erbers lived in what is now Morocco long before the Phoenicians invaded the territory in 12th century BC. Although their origin is unknown, the Berber - a name given to them by the Arabs in the 7th century AD which means 'those that are not Arab' - are believed to be Euro-Asians. Throughout the centuries, three main tribes would form dynasties: the Sanhajah, the Masmouda and the Zenata.

2   The nomad and warrying Sanhajah formed the Almoravid dynasty and founded Marrakesh. The peaceful and farming Masmouda lived north and west of the Atlas mountain range and formed the Almohad dynasty. The horseriding and nomad Zenata controlled the area between Tafilalet and present Algeria and founded the Merinides dynasty.

3   Once the Mediterranean Phoenicians sighted North African lands in the 12th century BC, they gradually established trade posts throughout the eastern coast. Fish salting factories - topped by Roman ruins - and other traces of their occupation can be found in Liks, but also in Tangiers, Melilla, Chella, Rahat and Tamuda.

4   The Phoenicians were seafarers and tradesmen, and scarcely conquerors. In the 8th century they founded their main city, Carthage, in present Tunisia, which grew to become a

prosperous kingdom. Some Carthaginians moved to the Moroccan coast, establishing prosperous communities, which took the name of the Garum, an anchovy paste that was to become a major export.

5   The Berber were greatly influenced by the Carthaginians. After the Second Punic war, when Carthage became an African province of Rome, thousands of Carthaginese fled from the Romans seeking refuge in friendly enclaves along the coast. Once Carthage had been taken, the

Romans spread to the Berber kingdoms of Mauritania and Numidia (current Algeria).

6   Cities such as Volubilis, Sala Colonia or Tingis developed a mixed culture, of Mauritanian origin, partially Roman and even Christian. The Vandals and Goths went through the region, on the way to Carthage, without leaving traces.

7   In 683, the Arabs - led by Oqba Ben Nafi, head of the Umayed Dynasty from Damascus - brought Islam to the current Morrocan territory. Ben Nafi

founded the city of Kairwan (current Tunis) and built the first mosque in the African continent. He called the land Maghreb al Aqsa. The Berber accepted the Qur'an and led, along with the Arabs, through the Almohades, Islamic expansion to the south. However, they held on to their language and customs.

8   In 703, the Berber backed the second great Umayed leader in the region, Musa Ibn Nouasser, in his Islamic expansion towards southern Spain and southern Morocco. Some Christian enclaves remained, but most Christians fled to the Iberian peninsula.

9   Idris Ben Abdallah, a descendant of prophet Muhammad, crossed Egypt, Tangiers and Volubilis, by then fully Islamic. The Berber kings proclaimed him King and pledged him their support.

10   When his father died, Idris II was crowned king at the age of 12. He founded Fez, which in 818 received 8,000 Arab families expelled by Spanish Christians from the Emirate of Cordoba. Seven years later, another 2,000 families came from Kairwan. The immigrants' sophistication and skills turned Fez into an intellectual and spiritual center of Islam.

11   After Idris II died, southern Morocco was dominated by the Almoravids, nomads and without farming skills. For a century they

WORKERS

UNEMPLOYMENT: 18.3% (2002)

LABOR FORCE   2002

■ FEMALE: 34.9%   ■ MALE: 65.1%

EMPLOYMENT DISTRIBUTION   1995/2001

F

M

■ AGRICULTURE   F: 38.0% M: 39.0%
■ INDUSTRY   F: 19.0% M: 8.0%
■ SERVICES   F: 43.0% M: 52.0%

PROFILE

ENVIRONMENT
The country has an 800-km coastline. In the eastern part there are two mountain ranges (Atlas and Rif), covered with barren steppes and inhabited by nomadic Berbers. In the foothills lie irrigated lands where citrus fruit, vegetables and grain are cultivated. Stockbreeding is extensive on the western slopes of the Atlas Mountains (Grand Atlas and Anti-Atlas), which are rich in phosphate, zinc and lead deposits. Along the coastal plains, grapes and citrus fruit are grown. Fishing stocks are important, though mainly exploited by foreign fleets. Expansion of farms in marginal areas, overgrazing of pastures by livestock, destruction of vegetation in the quest for firewood, and the conversion of forested areas into cultivated land are all factors that have led to soil erosion. Some efforts have been made to reverse this process, mostly through reforestation.

SOCIETY
Peoples: Arab 70 per cent; Berber 30 per cent.
Religions: Mainly Sunni Muslim (98.7 per cent). Christian (1.1 per cent) and Jewish (0.2 per cent).
Languages: Arab (official) and Berber variations. French and Spanish are also spoken.
Main Political Parties: Socialist Union of Popular Forces (progressive); Independence Party (*Istiqlal*), founded in 1943; Justice and Development Party (Islamic); National Rally of Independents (moderate); Popular Movement (Berber); National Popular Movement (conservative); Constitutional

Union; National Democratic Party (conservative); Front of Democratic Forces; Party of Progress and Socialism (communist).
Main Social Organizations: General Union of Moroccan Workers (UGTM); Moroccan Workers Union; Democratic Labor Confederation; Moroccan Employers Association; Organization of the Muslim Woman in Morocco; Islamic Educational Scientific and Cultural Organization (ISESCO).

THE STATE
Official Name: al-Mamlakah al-Maghribiyah.
Administrative Divisions: 37 provinces and two municipalities, Casablanca and Rabat.
Capital: Rabat 1,759,000 people (2003).
Other Cities: Casablanca (Dar-el-Beida) 3,292,100 people; Fez 900,900; Marrakech 736,500 (2000).
Government: Sayyidi Muhammad VI ibn al-Hasan, King since July 1999. Driss Jettou, Prime Minister since 9 October 2002. In September 1996, constitutional reform inaugurated a bicameral legislative regime. House of Deputies, *Majlis al-Nawwab*, with 325 members elected by direct vote for a 5-year term. The 270 members of the Senate, *Majlis al-Mustasharin*, an advisory body, are elected by indirect vote.
National Holiday: 2 March, Independence from France (1956).
Armed Forces: 194,000 (1996).
Other: Gendarmerie Royale: 40,000; Force Auxiliaire: 10,000.

Life expectancy
68.7 years
2000-2005

GNI per capita
$1,190
2002

Literacy
49% total adult rate
2000

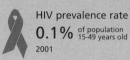

HIV prevalence rate
0.1% of population 15-49 years old
2001

imposed Islam on the black Saharan peoples. Ibn Tachafine founded Marrakesh in 1062 and a large part of Spain joined the Almoravid Empire.

12   The 12th century is considered the golden age of Moroccan history, and coinciding with the emergence of the Almohad dynasty. Marrakesh was spiritually led by Mohamed Ibn Toumart, founder of the Muwahiddin doctrine (utter union with God). Toumar, along with statesman Iacoub Al Mansour, led the country towards a spiritual, intellectual and economic flourishing.

13   Morocco was the cradle of the two North African empires that dominated the Iberian peninsula. It became one of the power centers of the region because of its geographic location: it was close to Spain, and at the northern end of the trans-Saharan trade routes. Although neither Fés nor Marrakech achieved the academic prestige of Cairo, their political influence was felt as far as Timbuktu and Valencia. Their close ties with Spain were culturally enriching during the Cordovan Caliphate, but they brought negative consequences to Morocco in the final stages of the 'Reconquest'. The war moved into Africa and the Spanish and Portugal seized strongholds on the coast (Ceuta in 1415, and Tangier in 1471 and Melilla in 1497). European naval dominance blocked Mediterranean and Atlantic routes to Morocco causing a decline in trade.

14   Unlike Algeria and Tunisia, Morocco was not formally annexed to the Ottoman Empire, but it did benefit from the presence of Turkish corsairs who hampered Luso-Spanish expansion. This precarious balance allowed the sultans to remain autonomous until the 20th century. France's policy of economic penetration meant that France was supervising Moroccan finances, while arguing with Germany over who should have political sway over the area. The French finally won, securing agreements with Spain over the borders of the Spanish Sahara, and Sultan Muley Hafid ended his support of the Saharan rebels (see Western Sahara). In 1912, an agreement between France, Spain and Britain transformed Morocco into a French protectorate, giving Spain the Rif region, to the north (where Ceuta and Melilla are located), and the Ifni region to the south, near the Sahara. In exchange, Britain obtained French consent for its policies in Egypt and Sudan. The city of Tangier was declared an international free port and the sultan became a figurehead.

15   The areas under Spanish control became sanctuaries for the nationalists unhappy with European domination. In 1921, it was on Spanish territory that the Berber revolt led by Emir Abdel Krim (Abd al-Karim al-Khattab) began. Backed by the Third International and the Pan-Islamic Movement, he proclaimed the Republic of the Confederated Tribes of the Rif, induced the inland peoples to rebel, and put Spain on the defensive. The French intervened causing the rebellion to spread throughout the entire country. It took them until 1926 to force the Emir to surrender.

16   In the south, Spanish rule was nominal, and French pressures to close down this 'sanctuary' for Algerian, Moroccan, Saharan and Mauritanian rebels failed (see Western Sahara).

17   During World War II, there was sustained nationalist agitation. Demands for liberation were so pressing that Sultan Sid Muhammad Ben Youssef became the spokesperson for the cause. Growing tension led the French to depose the Sultan in 1953, but this only succeeded in making the nationalist movement more radical. The nationalists raised an army and fought until they achieved Muhammad's return to power as King Muhammad V. In 1956, the French were forced to acknowledge Morocco's independence.

18   On 7 April 1956, Morocco recovered Tangier, as well as the 'special zones' of Ceuta and Melilla, although the ports of these two cities still remain under Spanish control. Ifni was not returned to Morocco until 1969.

19   The goal set by Muhammad V was 'to move forward slowly' gradually modernizing the country's economic and political structures. But his son, Hassan II, who succeeded him in 1961, had more conservative ideas. His family came from the lineage of Muhammad, the prophet, and his theocratic regime, based on a paternalistic system of favors and duties, prevented the development of authentic national commerce. The King also encouraged foreign investment, especially from France, to exploit the nation's natural resources.

20   In 1965, Ben Barka, leader of the powerful National Union of Popular Forces (NUPF) was assassinated on the orders of Hassan II. The NUPF worked for the social and economic welfare of workers and peasants.

21   The death of Ben Barka in Paris was followed by a crackdown on popular organizations.

22   In 1975, the conflicts underlying Moroccan society surfaced when King Hassan ordered the occupation of Spanish Sahara, as it was then called, unleashing a war that has brought about important political changes in North Africa.

23   Funds for the military campaign, the fall in the price of phosphates on the international market, and the loss of financial aid from Saudi Arabia - in retaliation for Hassan's support of the Camp David agreements between Israel and Egypt - deepened the economic crisis.

24   Severe drought in 1980 and 1981 drastically reduced food supplies, forcing the Government to increase food imports. This sent the country's foreign debt soaring to intolerable levels. The IMF assisted the monarchy with emergency loans, which carried a condition eliminating subsidies on food and housing, a measure that increased the hardships faced by the working classes. The Government failed to achieve its ambitious development aims, and the 'export of unemployed workers' was limited by French immigration restrictions.

25   The situation worsened when several moderate opposition parties decided to break the tacit political truce. The Socialist Union of Popular Forces (USFP) staged anti-government demonstrations. In June 1981, Casablanca was the scene of bloody repression known as the 'Casablanca massacre', which led to an open conflict between the King and the leftist parties over the high cost of the Sahara war (over $1 million a day).

26   The stalemate on the battlefield in early 1983 made signs of dissent within the Moroccan armed forces visible. The tension became evident with the assassination of General Ahmed Dlimi, the supreme commander of the Royal Armed Forces.

27   In 1984, the Saharan Arab Democratic Republic (RASD), proclaimed by the Polisario Front's fighters in the former Spanish Saharan colony, was recognized as a full member of the Organization of African Unity (OAU). Morocco reacted by withdrawing from the pan-African organization.

28   In his capacity as religious leader, the Moroccan king became concerned about the rise of Islamic fundamentalism throughout the Arab world.

29   In 1987, the Moroccan monarch suggested to King Juan Carlos of Spain that both governments form a study group designed to consider the future of Ceuta and Melilla. The proposal was not well received in Spain, as there was an insistence on the 'historical nature' of Spain's presence in Ceuta and Melilla.

30   In May 1988, after 12 years of tension, Morocco and Algeria re-established diplomatic relations, through the mediation of Saudi Arabia and Tunisia. The cause of the disruption in their relations had been the war in the Sahara, as Algeria had openly supported the Saharan nationalists from the beginning. Better relations between Algeria and Morocco meant that a gas pipeline was built across the Strait of Gibraltar.

31   Urban migration of a million people per year has exacerbated the urban housing situation, putting a strain on sanitation, water and other services.

32   In March 1992, the Paris Club creditor countries agreed to renegotiate the $21.3 billion foreign debt.

33   The United Nations International Council for the Control of Narcotics condemned the fact that many farmers in countries like Morocco have been pressured into cultivating opium and coca, respectively the raw materials for the production of heroin and cocaine.

34   In Western Sahara, a UN peace plan announced in 1991 led to a ceasefire and plans for a referendum that would give RASD inhabitants the option for independence or integration with Morocco. The Moroccan Government had delayed the referendum, hoping to defeat the Polisario Front (see Western Sahara).

35   Torture and disappearances are common both in Western Sahara and Morocco. Nubier Amau, secretary general of the Democratic Confederation of Labor, was sentenced to two years imprisonment, for slander against the regime. In February 1993, the Moroccan Human Rights Association announced the existence of 750 political prisoners.

36   The opposition won the first parliamentary elections following the 1992 reform of the constitution, taking 99 of the 222 seats, while the ruling party took only 74. Two months later, Hassan held a spectacular inauguration ceremony of one of the biggest mosques in the world, built in Casablanca at a cost of $536 million.

37   Despite the constitutional reform, the King continued to dominate national politics, and in May 1994, he appointed one of his relations by marriage, Abd al-Latif Filali, as prime minister.

38   In early 1996, the Government announced it would submit proposals for constitutional reform to referendum. The changes, which basically aimed at the formation of a bicameral legislature, were approved in

Under-5 mortality
43 per 1,000 live births
2002

Poverty
<2% of population living on less than $1 per day
1999

Debt service
17.8% exports of goods and services
2001

Maternal mortality
220 per 100,000 live births
2000

September. The King still had the right to dissolve the chambers. The privatization policies continued that year with the sale of several companies.

[39] In September 1997 Morocco and the Polisario Front signed an agreement to relaunch a peace plan for Western Sahara, exchange prisoners, release political prisoners, allow refugees to return, and quarter troops. The long-postponed referendum on the status (independence or integration with Morocco) of the territory under dispute was announced.

[40] In February 1998 King Hassan II appointed Abderrahmane El Youssoufi, leader of the Socialist Union of Popular Forces, as prime minister, and in March he appointed a whole new cabinet. A year later, in March 1999, the Government asked the UN to postpone the referendum scheduled for December. The UN General Secretary proposed postponing the referendum - which had originally been scheduled for 1991 but was put off each time the date approached - until an indefinite date before 2002.

[41] The death of Hassan II in July 1999 and the succession of his son Muhammad VI as king brought significant political changes. The first move of the new monarch was to free some 800 political prisoners. In a television address in August, he pledged to fight social inequalities, domestic violence, unemployment and rural emigration. The Polisario Front welcomed the King's first measures and his decision to go ahead with the Western Sahara self-determination referendum. In November Muhammad VI announced his decision to make some form of self-rule possible for the occupied zone.

[42] That same month, the King dismissed Home Minister Driss Basri, who had served throughout King Hassan's reign of almost two decades. Muhammad VI announced the freeing of another 2,000 political prisoners as a goodwill gesture in January 2000, to celebrate the end of Ramadan. The Government's proposals to recognize some rights for women provoked demonstrations both for and against the measures during March 2000.

[43] In August the King announced the discovery of major oil and gasfields along the Eastern border of the kingdom. Independent media had speculated that the underground reserve could contain some 20 billion barrels of oil.

[44] According to a report by the Moroccan Prison Observation Group, published in May 2001, the country's jails were corrupt, violent, disease-ridden and rife with child abuse (some of the victims as young as 12). Moroccan prisons hold some 80,000 inmates in a system that was designed for less than half that number. According to the report, the only food the prisoners get is that taken to them by their relatives.

[45] Tensions with Spain came to light after the 11 September 2001 attacks in New York and Washington. Madrid tightened controls in Ceuta and Melilla, and suggested Rabat make a greater effort to limit the flow of illegal immigrants toward Spain.

[46] Tourism, especially from the US, fell drastically after the 11 September attacks.

[47] In a break with tradition, in January 2002 Muhammad VI announced his wedding, which took place in April, to Salma Bennani, a 24-year-old computer technician, who did not assume the title of Queen. The wedding marked the country's modernization, which would encourage women's participation in public life.

[48] In early 2003 Morocco resumed diplomatic relations with Spain, disrupted in 2001.

[49] In May 2003 terrorist attacks in Casablanca left 45 dead. According to Government sources, the terrorists were members of the Sirat al-Mustaqim (part of he Salafiya-Jhadiya movement), but the alleged responsibility of Al-Qaeda was not ruled out. The Moroccan parliament passed stringent anti-terrorism laws, which extend the definition of terrorism to cover any disturbance of the public order, as a consequence of the Casablanca incidents.

[50] In February 2004 the Polisario Front unilaterally decided to release 100 Moroccan war prisoners as a 'humanitarian gesture' and in favor of peace. This new release raised to 1,743 the number of prisoners set free by the Polisario since the year 2000.

[51] On 24 February 2004 an earthquake measuring 6.5 on the Richter scale hit northeastern Morocco; its epicenter was located about 15 kms from Al Toxemias city. With an outcome of over 564 dead and 300 injured this was the worst earthquake in Morocco since the one that destroyed the city of Agadir (southwest) in 1960, leaving almost 12,000 dead. ∎

IN FOCUS

ENVIRONMENTAL CHALLENGES
Soil erosion resulting from farming of marginal areas, destruction of vegetation and overgrazing have led to land degradation and desertification. Water supplies are contaminated by raw sewage, and pollution of coastal waters by oil spills.

WOMEN'S RIGHTS
Moroccan women have been able to vote and run for office since 1963, although it was not until 1993 that the first woman held a seat in parliament. Thirty seats in the Chamber of Deputies are reserved for women under the new electoral code; thus, female representation grew from 1 per cent in 1995 to 10.8 per cent in 2002. In September 2003 city council elections, women won just 1.7 per cent of the seats.

The illiteracy rate among women over 15 was reduced from 84.5 per cent in 1980 to 69.9 in the year 2000.

Moroccan women comprised 35 per cent of the workforce in 2000, while female unemployment stood at 27.6 per cent.

Forty-two per cent of Moroccan women received prenatal healthcare between 1995 and 2002.

CHILDREN
Between 1998 and 2000, 11 per cent of the children were underweight at birth.

Net primary school enrolment rate stood at 78 per cent between 1996 and 2002. School attendance between the ages of 7 and 13 is compulsory; however a Government study revealed that 800,000 school-aged children did not attend school in 2003.

The practice of 'adoptive servitude', in which urban families adopt rural girls to work as domestic servants (many are orphans; in other cases it is the girl's family who receives her salary), is socially accepted, and it is not regulated by the Government. Since the year 2000, after several accusations of physical and psychological abuse and the complicity of orphanages in the practice, the National Observatory of Children's Rights (ONDE) has conducted an awareness campaign on the matter, which, however, has failed to eradicate the problem.

A problem that has drawn recent attention is the situation of unaccompanied repatriated children. Following their deportation, mostly from Spain, they are subject to abuse on the streets as well as within the country's borders. In December 2003, the Government signed a repatriation agreement with Spain, stating the latter committed itself to helping reunify children with their families and to provide education for them.

INDIGENOUS PEOPLES/ ETHNIC MINORITIES
Almost 60 per cent of the population regard themselves as being of Berber descent, including the royal family. Berber associations claim the Government does not defend their culture, since it refuses to register newborns with their traditional names, does not encourage public usage of their language, limits the activities of members of these associations, and continues the Arabization of the names of cities, towns and geographic locations.

In September 2003, 317 primary and secondary schools started teaching the Berber language.

MIGRANTS/REFUGEES
Sixty-six per cent of the country's revenues come from remittances sent home by Moroccans living abroad. In May 2002, Moroccan Security Forces arrested almost 200 people in a raid on illegal migrant smuggling networks in the city of Tetuan.

For 28 years, over 160,000 Saharawi have been living in refugee camps in the Algerian desert since the Moroccan invasion and occupation of Western Sahara in 1975; the refugees and Saharawis living in the occupied territory demand the right to self-determination but Morocco has consistently blocked a UN-administered referendum.

In late November 2003, Morocco set in motion an operation to expel thousands of undocumented sub-Saharans around Uxda, on the Algerian border. The border, closed since 1994, was crossed daily by smugglers of merchandise and people traffickers.

DEATH PENALTY
The death penalty is applicable in the case of ordinary crimes. The last death sentence was handed down in August 2003, to four alleged terrorists.

Mozambique / Moçambique

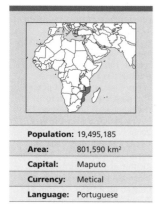

Population:	19,495,185
Area:	801,590 km²
Capital:	Maputo
Currency:	Metical
Language:	Portuguese

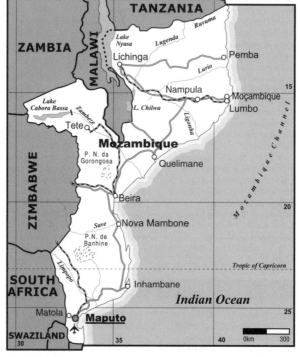

A round the 3rd century AD, agricultural and cattle-herding communities moved into what is present-day Mozambique. Among these people were Bantu speakers from west-central Africa who introduced iron-making technologies and combined cultivation of some grains with knowledge of root and tree crops, providing them with sustenance and favoring their expansion along the Indian Ocean.

2   The city of Sofa (near present-day Beira) was founded by Shirazis towards the end of the 10th century. It became a point of contact between two of the most flourishing developed cultures in Africa: the commercial, Muslim cultures of the east coast and the metallurgical, animist culture of Zimbabwe. As with other civilizations on the continent, the Portuguese presence in Mozambique was fatal: they planned to seize control of the Eastern trade which had nourished the two civilizations for centuries. This led to the destruction of the ports and the stifling of Zimbabwean gold exports. The route to the gold mines was closed by the Changamiras of Zimbabwe. The Monomotapa or Mwene Mutapa - the title given from the 14th to the 17th centuries to a line of kings from an area of south-east Africa between what is now Zimbabwe and Mozambique, who

were the leaders of the Karanga - declared allegiance to the Portuguese in 1629, following which they lost authority in the region.

3   When Zanzibar (a city and port in present-day Tanzania) expelled the Portuguese from the territory under their control, the colonists turned to the slave trade as the only profitable option open to them. Attempts to connect Mozambique and Angola by land failed repeatedly and European control was confined to a coastal strip where their entire 'administration' was limited to granting *prazos* - concessions of huge areas of land - to Portuguese and Indian adventurers who plundered the land and enslaved the natives. These *prazeiros* were given almost a free hand, but, in 1890, when the Portuguese had to prove their authority over the region, which the English were

questioning, threatening to occupy the territory, a long, hard struggle led to the forcible subjugation of the *prazeiros*. The conquest of the interior, however, was not completed until around 1920 when the ruler Mokombe, in the Tete region, was defeated.

4   Mozambique started to supply South African gold mines with migrant workers (up to one million every year) and its ports were open to South African and Rhodesian foreign trade. Portuguese colonialism controlled the country as an 'Overseas Province' and encouraged local group rivalries to prevent anti-European feelings from developing. Split into several movements, the nationalists staged strikes and demonstrations in their struggle for independence. In 1960, a spontaneous and peaceful demonstration in Mueda was fiercely repressed, leaving 500 people dead. This convinced many Mozambicans that peaceful negotiations with the colonial power were pointless.

5   In 1961, Eduardo Mondlane (a UN official) visited his home country and persuaded the pro-independence groups that they

should unify. Finally, the Front for the Liberation of Mozambique (FRELIMO) was created in Tanzania in 1963. FRELIMO was made up of activists and organizations from all regions and ethnic groups in Mozambique. In 1964, FRELIMO, which had a high level of underground organizational and political activity, embarked on a guerrilla war to win 'complete and utter independence'. In 1965, FRELIMO controlled some areas of the country and by 1969, one-fifth of Mozambican territory was under their control. That year, Mondlane was assassinated by colonialist agents. Differences of opinion developed within FRELIMO about the desired form of independence; some wanting a mere 'Africanization' of the established system and others seeking to create a new popular democratic society. FRELIMO's Second Congress, held in the liberated areas, elected Samora Machel as president of the organization. Fighting intensified and spread to other areas.

6   The impossibility of winning the colonial wars in Africa led to the 1974 military uprising in Lisbon, ending the Salazar and Caetano regimes. A transitional government was established in Mozambique and in 1975, the People's Republic of Mozambique was founded. The first President of independent Mozambique and revolutionary leader, Samora Machel, announced that 'the struggle will continue' in solidarity with the freedom fighters in Zimbabwe and South Africa. The FRELIMO Government nationalized education, health care, foreign banks and several transnational corporations. Communal villages were promoted, bringing together the scattered rural population. Collective production methods were organized and health care, education and technical assistance were rationalized. In 1977, FRELIMO's Third Congress in Maputo adopted Marxist-Leninism as the Front's ideology.

7   Mozambique supported Zimbabwe's independence struggle, blockading imports and exports from Ian Smith's regime despite severe repercussions on the Mozambican economy. Zimbabwean freedom fighters were given permission to set up bases within Mozambican territory; the white minority regimes retaliated with air raids and invasions. Zimbabwe's independence in 1980 altered the political outlook of the region, tightening the circle around apartheid and allowing Mozambique to revitalize its economy through greater integration with Zimbabwe, Malawi, Lesotho and Swaziland.

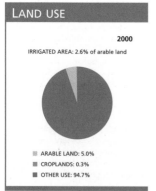

LAND USE

2000

IRRIGATED AREA: 2.6% of arable land

- ARABLE LAND: 5.0%
- CROPLANDS: 0.3%
- OTHER USE: 94.7%

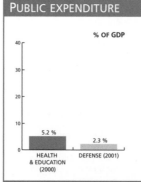

PUBLIC EXPENDITURE

% OF GDP

5.2 % HEALTH & EDUCATION (2000)

2.3 % DEFENSE (2001)

WORKERS

LABOR FORCE   **2002**

- FEMALE: 48.4%
- MALE: 51.6%

Life expectancy	GNI per capita	Literacy	HIV prevalence rate
38.1 years	**$210**	**44%** total adult rate	**13%** of population 15-49 years old
2000-2005	2002	2000	2001

[8] In 1980, Machel launched a political campaign aimed at eliminating corruption, inefficiency and bureaucracy in state agencies and companies. A program for economic development was implemented, calling for investments in agriculture, transport and industry. All of these projects were affected by the increasing deterioration of relations with South Africa, which invaded Mozambique in 1981, attacking the Maputo suburb of Matola. They also backed the Movement of National Resistance (RENAMO), made up of former Salazar followers and mercenaries. South Africa attacked the anti-racist refugees living in Mozambique, while RENAMO aimed to sabotage economic objectives and intimidate the rural population. In 1982, the Government cracked down on the black market and launched a major offensive against RENAMO in the Gorongoza region.

[9] In 1983, FRELIMO's Fourth Congress discussed major changes in the Government's economic program such as the reduction of large agricultural projects and the priority of granting concessions to minor investments. The delegates attending the Congress were mostly rural workers, while the number of women delegates had doubled since the 1977 Congress. The idea of creating small agricultural and industrial units was the result of a major reappraisal of all the large state-run farms. These were charged with excessive centralization, bureaucracy and economic inefficiency.

[10] In 1985, Mozambique suffered terrorist attacks carried out by RENAMO and a severe drought which decimated cattle stock, causing a 70 per cent drop in production and reducing grain production by 25 per cent. Machel denounced South Africa's covert support for RENAMO, saying that it was a violation of the Nkomati agreements of March 1984, when the two countries had signed a non-aggression treaty.

[11] Already tense economic and defense situations were compounded by the death of President Machel on 19 October 1986. His plane crashed while returning from a meeting of Presidents in Zambia. Until the present time it has never been established whether the plane crash was an accident or an act of sabotage. Presidents Kenneth Kaunda (Zambia), Mobutu Sese Seko (Zaire, now DR Congo), José Eduardo Dos Santos (Angola) and Machel had debated joining forces to confront South Africa's aggression toward the

IN FOCUS

ENVIRONMENTAL CHALLENGES
The war devastated the country's entire productive system, especially in the agricultural sector. The use of its mangrove forests for firewood has led to deforestation. Recurrent droughts in the hinterlands have prompted urban migration to coastal areas with adverse environmental consequences for cities there, which are now overcrowded. Another problem in recent years has been the illegal hunting of elephants for the black market trade in ivory.

WOMEN'S RIGHTS
Women have been able to vote and stand for office since 1975.

In 2000, women held 25 per cent of seats in Parliament, while they had no representation in ministerial or equivalent positions.

That year, women made up 48 per cent of the country's labor force. In 1997, 71.4 per cent of women received antenatal healthcare, but during the same year, only 44 per cent of births were attended by skilled medical personnel.

Although there are no official statistics, according to the public health authorities and women's rights advocacy organizations, domestic violence against women - particularly rapes and beatings - is widespread. Many women believe that their husbands have the right to beat them and cultural pressures discourage them from taking legal action against abusive husbands. Besides, there is no law that defines domestic violence as a crime, although it may be punished if reported as occurring outside the home. In

2000, NGOs working on the issue of domestic violence registered 700 requests for assistance of which only 10 could be forwarded to the courts.

CHILDREN
In 2002, more than half of the country's population were children under 18 years old. Seventy per cent of the population were living in absolute poverty, in spite of the growth achieved since 1992, when the armed conflict that had devastated the country ended. Difficulties have been aggravated by heavy rainy seasons in coastal areas and by high HIV/AIDS rates among the population of that region. In May 2003, nearly 660,000 people had serious problems accessing basic food and another 255,000 people were at risk of food insecurity.

UNICEF's latest data showed that 14 per cent of children suffered from low birth weights. Life expectancy has not exceeded 40 years since 1970, and in 2002 a slight drop - to 38 years - was registered.

In 2001, there were 418,000 orphans who had lost both parents to HIV/AIDS. The percentage of children under one year old vaccinated against childhood diseases barely reached 55 per cent in the case of polio and 58 per cent for measles.

INDIGENOUS PEOPLES/ ETHNIC MINORITIES
In 2000, ethnic Shona and Tsonga made up 10 and 23 per cent of the population respectively.

Other minority groups include Portuguese, some Indians and Euro-Asians.

With respect to religion, 39 per cent of the population are Christians and 13 per cent Muslims, while the majority adheres to traditional African religions.

The official language is Portuguese, which is used in the state administration, education and trade. Within the population at large a range of African languages are spoken.

MIGRANTS/REFUGEES
Mozambique was home to about 7,000 refugees and asylum-seekers at the end of 2002 (4,000 from Congo, 2,000 from Rwanda and 1,000 from Burundi). Half of those refugees remained in the capital, where they received little or no humanitarian assistance. Although government officials placed restrictions on property rights, employment, freedom of movement, access to education and other social services, many refugees and asylum-seekers - particularly young males - chose to remain in the Maputo area where they managed to evade some of these restrictions and, in some cases, sought entry into South Africa.

Efforts were directed to encourage 1,000 refugees living in the overcrowded Bobole camp on the outskirts of Maputo to transfer to a relatively new camp in Nampula Province. Some 500 refugees registered for relocation to the new camp, Maratane, and were transferred at the end of 2002. Although the authorities planned to close Bobole camp, it was not possible to do so that year.

Ethnic tensions among Congolese refugees triggered violence at the Maratane camp in September 2002, resulting in several arrests.

DEATH PENALTY
Abolished in 1990. The last execution was carried out in 1986.

independent countries of southern Africa and UNITA and RENAMO attacks in Angola and Mozambique. By the end of that year, FRELIMO's Central Committee had elected Joaquim Chissano (minister of Foreign Relations) as President and Commander-in-Chief of the Armed Forces.

[12] In 1987, the Mozambican Government reconsidered the economic strategy it had followed since independence. A more flexible foreign investment policy was adopted and local producers were encouraged to invest more. This was the first step toward the establishment of a mixed economy, a concept adopted by

the FRELIMO Congress in 1989. The party dropped all references to its Marxist-Leninist orientation. Peace negotiations between RENAMO and the Government in Maputo began in 1990. These negotiations were made easier as the new constitution admitted a multiparty system. The continuation of the single-party system had been one of the arguments used by the rebels to justify their terrorist activity.

[13] In 1991, the authorities of Manica province, one of the most fertile regions of the country, declared a state of emergency because of the drought which destroyed most of the crops. It was

considered the worst drought for 40 years, causing enormous shortages for the 300,000 local inhabitants. That year, a peace protocol was signed by the Government of Mozambique and RENAMO in Rome. It foresaw the recognition of the rebel movement as a legal political party in a protocol that was considered the forerunner to a peace agreement. The refinancing of the $1.6 billion foreign debt was contingent upon the success of these accords. In addition to the promise to hold elections, this agreement introduced new laws regulating political parties and guaranteed the freedom of

 Under-5 mortality
197 per 1,000 live births
2002

 Poverty
37.9% of population living on less than $1 per day
1996

 Debt service
3.4% exports of goods and services
2001

 Maternal mortality
1,000 per 100,000 live births
2000

information, expression and association. Prime Minister Mario da Graça Machungo explained that his country was suffering badly from the cessation of aid from the former USSR and Eastern European countries. RENAMO continued its actions and elections set for 1991 were postponed. Meanwhile the Liberal and Democratic Party of Mozambique, an opposition party, was created. A coup attempt by those opposed to peace negotiations ended in failure. Chissano was re-elected during FRELIMO's 6th Congress, and Feliciano Salamao was named secretary general.

[14] In 1992, the new political party regulations became one of the major hindrances to peace negotiations in Mozambique. Chissano offered RENAMO a special status, guaranteeing their members political rights but the rebels turned down the offer. The armed opposition also refused to accept the terms that established a minimum of a hundred registered members in each province, as well as in the capital, to qualify as a bona fide political party. That year, with Italy as mediator, Chissano and Alfonso Dhlakama (of RENAMO) signed a peace agreement in Rome, putting an end to 16 years of conflict which had caused over a million deaths and five million refugees. The terms of the agreement included the confinement of RENAMO and Government troops to pre-established areas, while weapons were to be turned over to UN soldiers charged with disarming both sides. The agreement also provided for the creation of an army of both Government and guerrilla forces. Also in 1992, differences between the two parties led to direct UN intervention in the elaboration of a new Peace Plan which included civilian observers and 7,500 peace-keeping troops.

[15] In 1993, FRELIMO participated in joint military maneuvers with the US. This change of attitude towards the West favored Mozambique's request for foreign aid. The UN postponed elections until October 1994, hoping to restart the stalled peace process. After negotiations, RENAMO agreed to take part in the elections. Chissano was re-elected with over 53 per cent of the vote. In the parliamentary elections, FRELIMO won with 44.3 per cent, followed by RENAMO with 37.7 per cent. In 1995, the Paris Club promised to give Maputo $780 billion for the country's reconstruction. Social conditions after the civil war were disastrous; the agricultural sector was devastated and fields were ridden with landmines.

[16] During 1996, the Government managed to restore old trade links between Johannesburg and Maputo. Investment was needed to revive the ailing economy. An agreement between Chissano and the South African President Nelson Mandela allowed thousands of South African farmers of European origin to settle in 200,000 hectares in the north of the country, as part of a process resisted by the opposition. The heavy rains of 1997 displaced thousands of people, mostly to Malawi. This water, however, helped maintain cereal production, both for family subsistence and as a main export crop. That same year, the Government's privatization program went ahead: more than 900 of the 1,200 State companies were sold. Inflation reached 5.8 per cent, the lowest figure since the World Bank and IMF began to oversee the national economy.

[17] In 1998, a cholera epidemic killed more than 800 people. The disease spread mostly in the south and the central provinces. The opening of trade relations with South Africa made economic growth possible, which in 1999 was amongst the highest in the world (11 per cent). In the legislative and presidential elections of that year, FRELIMO won and Chissano was re-elected. RENAMO denounced the election as a fraud, and in 2000 more than 40 people were killed during protests staged by the party. Meanwhile, international observers declared that the elections had been fair and free. That year, 82 people died in prisons in the north of the country. Most of them were RENAMO activists, imprisoned after the electoral riots; a preliminary report suggested that they had died of asphyxiation owing to overcrowding.

[18] In 2000, several of the country's largest creditors approved a grace period for repayment of Mozambique's foreign debt. Floods devastated the country during that year. The catastrophe displaced over a million people and killed more than 200. In an act of solidarity, Germany proposed canceling Mozambique's debt of up to $1.5 billion. Journalist Carlos Cardoso, editor of independent daily *Metical*, who was investigating political and corporate corruption, was murdered that year. Months later, six people - among them two leading entrepreneurs - were formally accused of the murder. The federal prosecutor accused the judicial system of incompetence, corruption and abuse of its powers.

[19] In 2002, malaria turned into an epidemic and was the primary cause of death in the country's hospitals, which received an average of 800 patients per day. Some hospitals in Maputo had to place two patients in each bed. That year, floods in the Zambezi valley displaced nearly 70,000 people.

[20] In 2002, FRELIMO elected Armando Guebuza (independent) as candidate for the 2004 presidential elections. Chissano declined to stand for a third term. That year, two people accused of murdering journalist Carlos Cardoso in 2000, alleged during the trial that Nymphine Chissano, son of President Chissano, was linked to the journalist's death. Nymphine Chissano denied knowledge of and participation in Cardoso's murder. In 2003, Brazil pledged to build a plant in Mozambique to produce anti-AIDS drugs to help the Mozambican population ravaged by the disease. More than 13 per cent of adults were infected by the virus and life expectancy fell to just 38 years. Had they not been afflicted by HIV/AIDS, Mozambicans would by now have had a life expectancy of 64 years in line with average global growth.

[21] In February 2004, Lutheran missionary Doraci Edinger was murdered in Nampula, northern Mozambique. She had been threatened after exposing, at the end of 2003, an organ-trafficking network that was operating in the region. A group of Roman Catholic missionary nuns filed a similar complaint with the Mozambique Human Rights League, describing the disappearance of tens of children from the area, whose dead bodies were later found with organs missing (heart, eyes, lungs, kidneys, tongue). The missionaries have received repeated death threats since filing their report. ■

PROFILE

ENVIRONMENT

The wide coastal plain, wider in the south, gradually rises to relatively low inland plateaus. The Tropic of Capricorn runs across the country and the climate is hot and dry. Two major rivers cross the country: the Zambezi in the center and the Limpopo in the south. Due to its geographic location, the country's ports are the natural ocean outlets for Malawi, Zimbabwe and part of South Africa. However, trade has been hampered by wars during the past two decades. Mineral resources are important though scarcely exploited.

SOCIETY

Peoples: The Mozambican population is made up of a variety of ethnic groups, mainly of Bantu origin. The main groups are: Makua 47.3 per cent; Tsonga 23.3 per cent; Malawi 12 per cent; Shona 11.3 per cent; Swahili 9.8 per cent; Yao 3.8 per cent; Makonde 0.6 per cent.
Religions: There is no official religion. The rural population practice traditional religions. Most of the urban population is Christian or Muslim. Islam prevails in the north.
Languages: Portuguese (official). Most of the population speaks Bantu languages, the main ones being Swahili and Macoa-Lomne.
Main Political Parties: Mozambique Liberation Front (FRELIMO), founded in 1962 by Eduardo Mondlane with the integration of three nationalist groups; National Resistance of Mozambique (RENAMO), embarked on armed insurgence against the Government after the declaration of independence; Liberal and Democratic Party of Mozambique (PALMO), created in 1991; National Union of Mozambique (UNAMO), emerged from a split of RENAMO.
Main Social Organizations: Organization of Mozambican Women; Mozambican Youth Organization.

THE STATE

Official Name: República Popular de Moçambique.
Administrative Divisions: 10 provinces.
Capital: Maputo 1,221,000 (2003).
Other Cities: Matola 467,200 people; Beira 437,100; Napula 333,700 (2000).
Government: Joaquim Chissano, President since November 1986, re-elected in 1994 and 1999. Luisa Diogo, Prime Minister since February 2004. The Assembly of the Republic is the main political body. **National Holiday:** 25 June, Independence Day (1975).
Armed Forces: 50,000 (1993).

Myanmar (Burma) / Myanma Naingngandaw

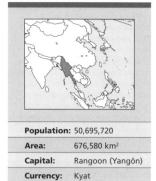

Population:	50,695,720
Area:	676,580 km²
Capital:	Rangoon (Yangôn)
Currency:	Kyat
Language:	Burmese

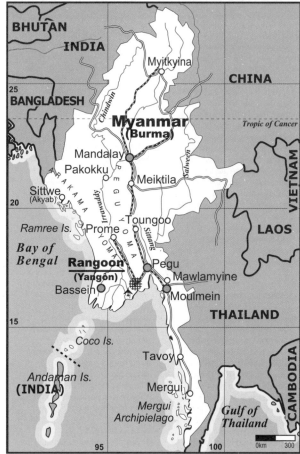

The first evidence of the existence of Burmese civilization dates from the 11th century when the Burmese established the state of Pagan.

2   The following two centuries represented the 'golden age' in Burmese thought and architecture. The Mongols attacked from the north, with aid from the Great Khan in Beijing. In 1283, the Mongol invasion ended the Pagan state and the Mongols remained in power until 1301.

3   Burma remained divided into small ethnic states until the 16th century when Toungoo local leaders reunified the territory. The second of these rulers, Bayinnaung, extended his domain to parts of present-day Laos and Thailand.

4   In 1740, a Toungoo ruler again achieved unification, with the help of the British. But when his successors continued the project of national reconstruction, they clashed with British interests in Assam, India, and a confrontation resulted with their former European allies. The Burmese fought three wars against the British throughout the 19th century. During the last war (1885-1886), Burma was annexed to the British viceroyalty of India and remained a part of it until 1937.

5   The 1930s began with a rising tide of nationalist movements; that of the Buddhist monk, U Ottama, inspired by Gandhi; Saya San's attempt to restore the monarchy; and uprisings organized by the University of Rangoon, bringing together Buddhists and Marxists.

6   Heavy taxes and the collapse of the world rice market in 1930 forced thousands of small farmers into debt and ruin. Discontent led to popular rebellions in 1938 and 1939.

7   When World War II broke out, a group of militant anti-colonialists, known as 'the 30 comrades', led by Aung San, formed the Burma Independence Army (BIA). They joined the Japanese against the British and invaded the capital in 1943. Minority groups of Karen, Kachin and Chin organized guerrilla groups, supported by the British, to combat both the BIA and the Japanese.

8   The Japanese granted Burma independence on 1 August 1943, but soon after friction developed between the Japanese and the socialist wing of 'the 30 comrades'. On 27 March 1945, the BIA declared war on Japan and was recognized by the British as the Patriotic Burmese Forces. On 30 May, they captured Rangoon, this time with the help of the British. Aung San was elected president in 1946. He organized a transition government, and in 1947, a constitution was drafted. On 19 July, a military commando assassinated Aung San

and several aides in the palace, and U Nu stepped in as premier. On 4 January 1948, independence was proclaimed.

9   Over the next period the new government had to face several challenges: the rebellion of ethnic minorities; the presence of Chinese Kuomintang forces, and the armed insurrection of the People's Volunteer Organization, linked to the Communist Party.

10   In 1962, General Ne Win ousted the government in a coup, installing a military revolutionary council. He nationalized the banks, the rice industry (which accounted for 70 per cent of foreign earnings), and trade.

11   In 1972, a new constitution confirmed the ruling Burma Socialist Program Party (BSSP) as the only legal political organization.

12   The socioeconomic crisis unleashed protests and demands for democratization in 1987. A BSSP Congress appointed Sein Lwin as head of state, which triggered new protests that were repressed by the government. Lwin was forced to resign 17 days after he had taken office. His successor, Maung Maung, liberalized the regime.

13   After a coup in 1988 the military formed the State Law and Order Restoration Council (SLORC). They promised to hold free elections but in the meantime announced a state of emergency and suspended the constitution. They also changed the country's name to Union of Myanmar - Burma only refers to the majority ethnic group - and dropped the term 'Socialist'.

14   The National League for Democracy (NLD) won 80 per cent of the vote in the 1990 elections, while the ruling National Unity Party (ex-BSPP) retained only 10 of the 485 seats. The election outcome was disregarded by the Government,

ENVIRONMENT

The country lies between the Tibetan plateau and the Malayan peninsula. Mountain ranges to the east, north and west surround a central valley where the Irrawaddy, Sittang and Salween rivers flow. Most of the population is concentrated in this area, where rice is grown. The climate is tropical with monsoon rains between May and October. Rainforest covers most of the country.

SOCIETY

Peoples: Burmese 69 per cent; Shan 8.5 per cent; Karen 6.2 per cent; Rakhine 4.5 per cent; Mon 2.4 per cent; Chin 2.2 per cent; Kachin 1.4 per cent.
Religions: Buddhist 89.1 per cent, Christian 4-9 per cent, Muslim 3.8 per cent; other 2.2 per cent.
Languages: Burmese (official) and the languages of the minority ethnic groups.
Main Political Parties: Political parties and their activities are generally illegal. The National League for Democracy (NLD) is the main opposition force. The military created the dictatorial National Unity Party (Taingyintha Silonenyinyutye) before the 1990

elections; the Government of the National Coalition of Burmese Unity is made up of parties that won the last elections but were not allowed to exercise power; it currently exists as a government in exile and as a leading opposition force.
Main Social Organizations: All Burma-Students Democratic Front; All Burma-Young Monks' Union; Federation of Trade Unions - Burma (FTUB); The Federation of Trade Unions-Kawthoolei (FTUK).

THE STATE

Official Name: Pyidaungzu Myanma Naingngandaw.
Capital: Rangoon (Yangôn) 3,874,000 people (2003).
Other Cities: Mandalay 1,037,300 people; Mawlamyine 360,400; Bago 223,700; Akyab 161,200 (2000). **Government:** General Than Shwe, President, Head of State (military junta - State Peace and Development Council) since April 1992. Khin Nyunt, Prime Minister since August 2003. Legislature: suspended since 1988. **National Holiday:** 4 January, Independence Day (1948). **Armed Forces:** 286,000 (1995). Other: 85,000 (People's Police, People's Militia).

Life expectancy
57.3 years
2000-2005

Literacy
85% total adult rate
2000

IN FOCUS

ENVIRONMENTAL CHALLENGES
Deforestation has been responsible for the destruction of two-thirds of the country's tropical forest. Air, soil and water pollution is caused by industrial activity and inadequate solid waste disposal. The lack of sewage treatment, at both the industrial and domestic levels, poses a serious problem.

WOMEN'S RIGHTS
Women have been able to vote since 1935 and to stand for office since 1946 but there have been no elections since 1990 when the military refused to hand over power. There are no women holding senior political positions. In 2000, women made up 43 per cent of the country's labor force. That year, 9.5 per cent of women between the ages of 15 and 24 were illiterate, while the illiteracy rate among men in the same age group stood at 8.5 per cent. Between 1990 and 2000, nearly 20 per cent of women over 15 could not read or write.

There are no independent organizations advocating for women's rights. Women have no representation at the governmental level, they are excluded from the army and there are no women in the courts, government ministries or councils.

CHILDREN
Nearly half of the population of the country was under 18 years old in 2002. According to UNICEF, out of the 1.3 million children that are born every year, more than 92,500 will die before their first birthday and another 138,000 before reaching their fifth birthday. The leading causes of infant morbidity and mortality are acute respiratory infections, diarrhea, tuberculosis and malaria. More than 30,000 people die of malaria every year and HIV/AIDS is starting to pose a serious threat to children since more than 2 per cent of pregnant women were HIV-positive in 2002.

Children, mainly those belonging to ethnic or religious minority groups, are used as porters by the army, and are forced to work from the age of 11. Rape of children by soldiers has been condemned.

INDIGENOUS PEOPLES/ ETHNIC MINORITIES
The Kachin, Mon, Rohingya (Muslims) and Zomi are indigenous peoples that inhabit different regions of the country. There are two ethnic-nationalist minorities, the Karen and the Shan, which are the biggest minority groups. With regard to religion, the Muslim minority is under close surveillance by the Government. Buddhism is the main religion.

The Karen and Shan are the minority groups that suffer the most attacks by the army; they are the victims of rape, torture, extortion and murder. Soldiers act with impunity and the Government neither takes steps to prevent abuses nor investigates complaints.

MIGRANTS/REFUGEES
An estimated 600,000 to 1 million people were internally displaced at the end of 2002. The difficulty in gaining access to the country has made it impossible to accurately assess the number of displaced or the conditions in which they were living.

Many Burmese were refugees and asylum-seekers in neighboring countries (335,000 in Thailand, more than 50,000 in India and 120,000 in Bangladesh), and smaller numbers were living in Malaysia, Japan and South Korea. Likewise, nearly 255,000 people lived in refugee-like circumstances in Thailand and Malaysia, most of them because they feared persecution on the basis of ethnic discrimination.

DEATH PENALTY
Myanmar maintains capital punishment for ordinary crimes.

---

which banned opposition activities, imprisoned or banished its leaders, and harshly cracked down on street demonstrations.

[15] In July 1989, the leader of the NLD, Aung San Suu Kyi, Nobel Peace Prize and the daughter of anti-colonial hero Aung San, was sentenced to house arrest.

[16] In September 1991, many students were arrested in demonstrations at Rangoon University campus. Protests erupted after a student who had distributed pamphlets requesting the release of Suu Kyi was brutally beaten by members of the military intelligence service.

[17] In April 1992, General Than Shwe took power, releasing 200 dissidents and permitting 31 universities and schools to reopen. In September, martial law was suspended.

[18] In January 1993, the military invoked a National Convention to draw up a new constitution. At the end of that year, Amnesty International denounced the imprisonment of over 1,550 opposition figures.

[19] An article of the new 1994 constitution stipulated presidential candidates could neither be married to foreigners nor bear children

under foreign citizenship and they should have been residing in Myanmar for the last 20 consecutive years. The regulation was custom-made for Suu Kyi who was married to a British citizen and had lived abroad for several years. The military junta met with her in September 1994 for the first time since she was arrested. No agreement was reached regarding the new constitution.

[21] In July 1995, Suu Kyi was released from house arrest and called on the SLORC to hold a dialogue. The SLORC refused, jailed dozens of dissidents and maintained the ban on political debate.

[22] The fall in early 1996 of Manerplaw, headquarters of the rebel minority, was a major blow to the opposition because it was also a base for activities of other groups. In January, through a secret accord, the Government gained the surrender of Khun Sa, known as the 'opium king'. Later that year the military junta ordered the arrest of 250 NLD members. The regime also approved a law banning NLD political meetings and restricted Suu Kyi's freedom of movement.

[23] Under growing international pressure, mainly from the US and the EU, the SLORC made some

concessions in 1997. In September, the NLD was authorized to hold its first congress after seven years, although only half of its delegates were allowed to participate. By the end of the year, the military junta dissolved itself, appointing a State Peace and Development Council (SPDC). In July, under the influence of neighboring countries India and China, Myanmar had been admitted as a member of the Association of Southeast Asian Nations (ASEAN).

[24] In August 1998, the army launched a virulent press campaign against Suu Kyi, who had been arrested when trying to leave the capital to meet with supporters. The junta labeled her 'public enemy number one'.

[25] Intelligence chief Khin Nyunt visited Thailand in September 2001 in what was declared an improvement in bilateral relations and he announced that the anti-drug fight would pull his country out of the so-called 'Golden Triangle' of drug production (along the shared border with Thailand and Laos) by 2005. Earlier that year, troops from Thailand and Myanmar had clashed along the common border, with Bangkok and Rangoon accusing each other of supporting the narcotics-producing Shan

militias. In May the tensions had reduced due to the growing presence of special US troops on the Thai side of the border. Their declared mission was to train the Thai army to fight drug trafficking.

[26] In May 2002, after 19 months of house arrest, Suu Kyi was released and her right to participate in political activity was renewed, in what was seen as the beginning of a democratic transition process. The UN was an active mediator and proposed the immediate release of all prisoners of conscience, estimated at 1,500 to 2,000.

[27] In May 2003, members of the NLD who were travelling on party business in Upper Myanmar, were attacked by pro-junta supporters. At least four people died and the exact whereabouts of over 100 detained people, including Suu Kyi, were unknown.

[28] A resolution of the Commission on Human Rights of December 2003 expressed concern about the frustrated visit of the Special Rapporteur in March 2003, when listening devices were discovered during interviews with inmates at Insein Prison. The Commission strongly condemned the existence of executions, reports of sexual violence carried out by members of the armed forces, the continued use of torture, detentions for political reasons, the confiscation of land and human rights violations including the use of children for forced labor or military labor. It also criticized the denial of freedom of assembly, association, expression and movement (young people, especially women under 25 years old, are not allowed to leave the country).

[29] After having been appointed Prime Minister in August 2003, Khin Nyunt promoted a reform of the constitution, of a more liberal nature, and the resumption of the National Convention, suspended since 1996. He also proposed to develop a 'road map' to democracy.

[30] From the 1988 uprising until 2003, military authorities have signed ceasefire agreements with more than 20 rebel ethnic armies that include children. One of the groups, the United Wa State Army (UWSA), which was engaged in drug-trafficking, recruited an army of 20,000 soldiers, more than half of whom were children under 12 years old.

[31] In January 2004, the Government and the Karen National Union (a guerrilla group that represents the Karen ethnic group) reached an agreement to put an end to hostilities. In April 2004 Suu Kyi was still in 'protective custody' but hopes increased for her release following the Government's pledge to reconvene a body to draft a constitution. After a 9-year suspension, the National Convention reconvened in May. ■

Namibia / Namibia

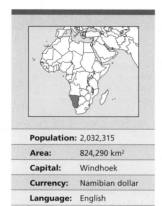

Population:	2,032,315
Area:	824,290 km²
Capital:	Windhoek
Currency:	Namibian dollar
Language:	English

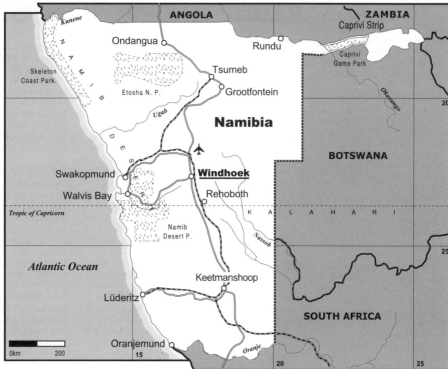

S outhwestern Africa was occupied first by San (Bushmen) and Khoikhoi peoples, Ovambo in the north and the Bantu-speaking Herero. Later the Nama, known as the Red Nation, occupied lands in the south, maintaining close-knit ties between their clans and living from animal-herding. Closely linked to these peoples were the Damara, from Central Africa, who combined herding with hunting and copper-smelting. In the central and north-eastern regions, the Herero built clan alliances, often led by a supreme chief. The Ovambo, farmers who developed several kingdoms along the Kunene river, posed a constant threat to the unity of the Herero.

2 Arid and scarcely populated, the Kalahari desert did not attract European colonization. In 1670, German missionaries, European traders and Norwegian whalers began to arrive on the coast and some ventured into the hinterland. Trade conflicts between the various clans became increasingly violent and facilitated conquest by the Oorlam-Nama, a group from the Cape that arrived in the early 19th century. Their military technology, which was modelled on that of the Afrikaners and included horses, rifles and an army of small commandos,

allowed them to dominate the Nama and the Damara. Halfway through the century, a kingdom was set up by Chief Jonker Afrikaner, of Oorlam and Herero lineage, who had the full backing of the Damara and the Red Nation.

3 In 1870, the British made a treaty with the Herero and flew their flag on the port of Walvis Bay. However, the German Second Reich of Bismarck and William I, occupied the area through dubious treaties, plunder and the strategy of dividing the African peoples. In 1884, Germany annexed the territory under the name of South West Africa. In 1885, Herero resistance forced the Germans back to Walvis Bay, until British support arrived.

4 At the end of the 19th century, German colonists built

railways from Swakopmund and Lüderitz. The country acquired strategic value for the Europeans with the discovery of large reserves of iron, lead, copper and diamonds, which were later augmented by metals of military interest: manganese, tungsten, vanadium, cadmium and great quantities of uranium.

5 The great resistance led by the Herero, from 1904-1907, could barely be stopped by mass hangings and enforced detention in concentration camps, which led to a 90 per cent reduction in Herero numbers by 1910. The Nama, who had been slow to enter the conflict, were defeated in 1907. Only a third of the Nama population survived, confined to concentration camps. The rigid German control did not extend northwards significantly to trouble the Ovambo.

6 During World War I, the British invaded the colony and, by the time the conflict ended, the region became a League of Nations trust territory. Administration of the territory, known as South West Africa, was assigned to the Union of South Africa.

7 Over the years, the South African Boers and German colonists in Namibia overcame the initial resistance.

8 In 1947, South Africa formally announced to the UN its intention to annex the territory. The UN, which had inherited responsibility for League of Nations trust territories, opposed the plan, arguing that 'the African inhabitants of South West Africa have still not achieved political independence'. Until 1961, the UN insisted on this point. Year after year it was systematically ignored by South Africa's racist regime.

9 Between 1961 and 1968, the UN tried to establish the country's independence. Legal pressure was ineffective and the Namibian people, led by the South West Africa People's Organization (SWAPO), embarked on an armed struggle on 26 August 1966.

10 In 1968, the UN finally proclaimed that South African occupation of the country now known as Namibia was illegal. A UN Council was set up as legal representative of the territory until sovereignty could be freely

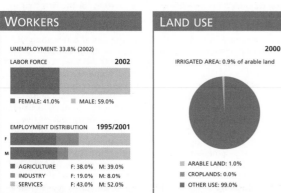

WORKERS

UNEMPLOYMENT: 33.8% (2002)

LABOR FORCE 2002

■ FEMALE: 41.0% ■ MALE: 59.0%

EMPLOYMENT DISTRIBUTION 1995/2001

F
M

■ AGRICULTURE	F: 38.0%	M: 39.0%
■ INDUSTRY	F: 19.0%	M: 8.0%
■ SERVICES	F: 43.0%	M: 52.0%

LAND USE

2000

IRRIGATED AREA: 0.9% of arable land

■ ARABLE LAND: 1.0%	
■ CROPLANDS: 0.0%	
■ OTHER USE: 99.0%	

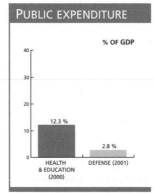

PUBLIC EXPENDITURE

% OF GDP

12.3 % HEALTH & EDUCATION (2000)
2.8 % DEFENSE (2001)

Life expectancy
44.3 years
2000-2005

GNI per capita
$1,780
2002

Literacy
82% total adult rate
2000

HIV prevalence rate
22.5% of population 15-49 years old
2001

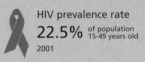

exercised by the people. However, attempts by most members of the UN General Assembly to follow this condemnation with economic sanctions systematically came up against the veto of the Western powers.

[11] Angolan independence, declared in 1975, affected Namibia's struggle for freedom, by providing SWAPO guerrillas with a friendly rearguard. The guerrilla war intensified and the Western powers started to put pressure on Pretoria to seek a 'moderate' solution.

[12] In December 1978, South Africa held elections in Namibia without UN observers and with no SWAPO participation, leading to a total lack of credibility in the results.

[13] The economy had grown in a sustained manner since World War II, reaching a peak of $1,000 per head in the 1970s ($20,000 for Europeans and $150 for black Namibians). Even while incomes in the white enclave soared, the salary of black workers was barely enough to live on. It took until halfway through this decade for workers to be trained to any significant degree in qualified tasks.

[14] The South African administration in Windhoek operated along customary colonial lines of dependence. The country exported corn, meat, fish, minerals and raw materials, while due to the lack of industries, all consumer products that were needed, such as wheat, rice and manufactured goods, had to be imported. Ninety per cent of goods in Namibia came from South Africa.

[15] The *status quo* preserved internal inequalities. Around 90 per cent of the population received 18.8 per cent of the GDP, while the rest, of European origin, received 81.2 per cent. Until independence, three-quarters of agricultural production was in the hands of white farmers. Although average per capita income was one of the highest in Africa - $1,410 - behind this figure were huge inequalities: while whites earned an average of $1,880, the rest of the population did not earn more than $108.

[16] Apart from boycotting the efforts to negotiate Namibia's independence, South Africa upped its military budget by 30 per cent for the conflict against the Namibian People's Liberation Army, SWAPO's armed wing. In the last months of 1982 and early 1983, the war intensified along the border with Angola and southwards, where SWAPO forces

PROFILE

ENVIRONMENT

Mainly made up of plateaus in the desert region along the Tropic of Capricorn. The Namib desert, along the coast, contains rich diamond deposits and is only populated because of mining activities. To the east, the country shares the Kalahari desert with Botswana, an area populated by herders and hunters. The population is densest in the north, and in the central plateau, where rainfall is heaviest. There is a coastal fishing industry which, together with cattle raising, was the mainstay of the economy before mining began in the 1960s. The country has important reserves of copper, lead, zinc, cadmium and uranium.

SOCIETY

Peoples: The Namibian population is divided into 11 ethnic groups; the most numerous are the Ovambo 47.4 per cent; Kavango 8.8 per cent; Herero 7.1 per cent; Damara 7.1 per cent; and others. There is a European minority (4.6 per cent). **Religions:** There is no official religion. Many people practice traditional African religions although there are a large number of Christians (Lutheran 51.2 per cent, Catholics

19.8 per cent, Anglican 5 per cent). **Languages:** English (official); the native population speaks Khoisan and Bantu; German and Afrikaans are also spoken. **Main Political Parties:** Southwest African People's Organization (SWAPO); Congress of Democrats; Democratic Turnhalle Alliance (DTA); United Democratic Front. **Main Social Organizations:** National Union of Workers of Namibia.

THE STATE

Official Name: Republic of Namibia. **Administrative Divisions:** 13 districts. **Capital:** Windhoek 237,000 people (2003). **Other Cities:** Rehoboth 33,800 people; Rundu 28,500; Swakopmund 28,300; Walvis Bay 24,500; Keetmanshoop 20,000 (2000). **Government:** Sam Nujoma, President since March 1990, elected by the Constituent Assembly in November 1989, re-elected in 1999. Theo-Ben Gurirab, Prime Minister since 2002. The Constitution established a presidential regime and a multiparty system. **National Holiday:** 21 March, Independence Day (1990). **Armed Forces:** 8,100 (1996).

launched audacious attacks, even in the so-called 'iron triangle', located near the city of Grootfontein, where the main South African military units were concentrated.

[17] In February 1984, representatives of Angola and South Africa met in Zambia's capital, Lusaka, for peace negotiations. They agreed a planned withdrawal of South African troops from southern Angola, in return for a ceasefire. In May, delegates from SWAPO and other Namibian parties met a South African representative but negotiations failed. The South African withdrawal from Angola did not occur within the deadline and the situation was deadlocked again.

[18] In December 1988, after prolonged US-mediated negotiations, South Africa, Angola and Cuba reached an agreement whereby South African troops would leave Namibia and, at the same time, the Cubans would withdraw their 50,000 soldiers from Angola.

[19] In November 1989, the First Constituent Assembly was elected. Ten political parties stood in the UN-supervised elections. SWAPO won with 60 per cent of the poll, gaining control of the Assembly and appointing the 60-year-old leader Sam Nujoma as first President of Namibia.

[20] Independence was proclaimed on 21 March 1990. The presidential guard of honor

was made up of troops from SWAPO and the SWA Territory Force which had protected the South African regime; both were to be integrated into the new National Army.

[21] The new government had to face up to the inequalities inherited from the South African apartheid system, above all in health and education.

[22] Namibia adopted English as its official language, replacing Afrikaans. The Government organized a Department of Informal Education, which together with UNICEF started to teach women to read and write, first in their own languages and then in English. A rehabilitation plan was developed for some 40,000 disabled people, mostly victims of 23 years of pro-independence guerrilla warfare.

[23] Prepared to play an important role in Southern Africa, Nujoma donated around $3 million in 1991 to the African National Congress (ANC), a sum which was handed over to ANC leader, Nelson Mandela, on a visit he made to Namibia on 31 January.

[24] In 1992 Namibia and South Africa agreed to return the port of Walvis Bay to Windhoek in 1994. One year later the National Council, the upper chamber of Parliament, came into operation. In 1994, the Government approved a land law, which aimed among other things to limit the concentration of wealth. It was estimated that 1 per cent

of the population held 75 per cent of the nation's land.

[25] In December of that year, Nujoma was re-elected President with 70 per cent of popular support. However, in May 1995 his party, SWAPO, split - leading to the creation of the SWAPO for Justice group.

[26] In mid-1997, a SWAPO Congress proclaimed Nujoma President of Namibia for a third term. That year, the Government refused to open an investigation into crimes committed during the period before independence, which created tensions with South Africa.

[27] The number of people living with HIV/AIDS increased alarmingly.

[28] The fishing industry recorded strong growth in 1998. To encourage financial investment, the Government began promoting Namibia as a tourist destination for the first time.

[29] In August 1999, some 200 rebels were detained and tortured after attempting to take over the small town of Katima Mulil. They 'confessed' to being supporters of independence for the Caprivi Strip, Namibia's panhandle territory, hundreds of kilometers long and barely four or five kilometers wide, that divides Botswana from Angola. The Caprivi Strip is inhabited by the Iozi ethnic group, who refused to be led by the country's Ovambo majority, which also dominates SWAPO.

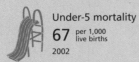

Under-5 mortality
67 per 1,000 live births
2002

Poverty
34.9% of population living on less than $1 per day
1993

Maternal mortality
300 per 100,000 live births
2000

---

30   Also in 1999, the Constitution was modified so that Nujoma could run for a third Presidential term, which he won with 76 per cent of the vote. On taking office in March 2000, apart from announcing he would not run again, Nujoma declared that the country's goals were to achieve a standard of living similar to the industrialized North by the year 2030, and in the immediate term, to fight HIV, which continued to decimate the population.

31   The World Court ruled in favor of Bostwana in December 1999, in a territorial dispute over the Sedudu island situated in the Chobe River.

32   Black community farmers urged the 4,000 commercial farmers, mainly white, to hasten the land reform to avoid what they called 'Zimbabwe-style invasions on their farms'. Only some 35,000 Namibians have been relocated to fertile lands since 1990, because landowners refuse to sell.

33   In January 2002, the Herero community demanded compensation of $2 billion for war crimes committed between 1904-1907 under German rule. Several companies - the best known of which is Deutsche Bank - were accused of forming a 'brutal alliance' with imperial Germany to exterminate more than 65,000 Herero.

34   In March 2002, Nujoma ordered the arrest of all homosexuals and in a speech at the University of Namibia he declared that 'homosexuality or lesbianism are not allowed'.

35   Although the Namibian Constitution provides for press freedom, the state media have been put under pressure from the Government and SWAPO leaders, and self-censorship has also been imposed. In August 2002, President Nujoma declared himself Head of the Information and Broadcasting Ministry.

36   In September, Nujoma attacked Western governments at the Johannesburg summit, stating that Africa no longer needed their investments for development. He also stated that British Prime Minister Tony Blair was responsible for creating the situation in Zimbabwe and demanded the lifting of sanctions imposed against Zimbabwe's President Mugabe.

37   In November 2003, a group of black farmers called off its plans to occupy white-owned lands after reaching an agreement with white farmers' representatives. The Government declared land occupations illegal and announced they would not be allowed.

38   In January 2004, Germany apologized for the massacre of Herero people during its colonial occupation, but refused to pay any reparations.

39   In May 2004, Nujoma fired his Foreign Affairs Minister Hidipo Hamutenya during the SWAPO Congress held at Windhoek in which Nujoma's successor for the November elections was to be chosen. Hamutenya, the favorite candidate of the SWAPO party to become elected as the new President, did not have Nujoma's support for the bid. Of the three nominated candidates, Hamutenya, Nahas Angula and Hifikepunye Pohamba, it was the latter the one who was supported by Nujoma behind the scenes.

After two days of congress, Pohamba won the second round of voting with 341 votes, while his main contender, Hamutenya, received 167 votes. After the congress, Hamutenya was sacked from the Cabinet and no official reason was given for his dismissal. Pohamba, in his victory speech, committed his time and energy to the improvement of the well-being of Namibians.

40   According to SWAPO's track record after having dominated Namibian politics since 1990, Pohamba was highly expected to become the next President. According to some observers, Nujoma, who retained SWAPO's leadership, would continue to run the country's politics even after leaving office.

41   That same month, a new bridge was opened across the Zambezi River (between Namibia and Zambia), which would provide a huge boost to regional trade. The bridge would also link the Democratic Republic of Congo to the Namibian port of Walvis Bay. The new bridge, financed by Germany at a cost of more than $9 million, was included in a broader project that would turn Namibia into an important commercial axis. Previously, the only way of crossing the Zambezi River towards Katima Mulilo (eastern region of the city of Caprivi) was through an old corridor. The celebration was headed by the respective Presidents of Zambia and Namibia. ∎

IN FOCUS

ENVIRONMENTAL CHALLENGES
Long-term droughts have limited natural fresh water resources. Desertification and land degradation have spread to protected areas where wildlife poaching also poses a serious problem.

WOMEN'S RIGHTS
Women have been able to vote since 1989. Their representation in Parliament increased from 8 per cent in 1990 to 18 per cent in 1995 and 22 per cent in 2000. They held 8 per cent of ministerial posts.

In 2000, women made up 41 per cent of the labor force, a percentage that has remained almost unchanged since 1980.

The total illiteracy rate decreased between 1980 and 2000. The 1980 illiteracy rate of 29 per cent among men and 38.2 per cent among women, fell to 17 per cent and 19 per cent respectively in 2000. The illiteracy rate among women between the ages of 15 and 24 stands at 6.7 per cent and among men of the same age group it rises to 10 per cent. Women's literacy programs, which have been implemented since independence (1960) by UNICEF and the Department of Informal Education, account for this reverse gender gap.

Some 91 per cent of pregnant women received prenatal care in 1995-2000, while 78 per cent of births were attended by skilled medical personnel. The prevalence of HIV/AIDS among pregnant women between 14 and 25 years old was 17.9 per cent in 2000.

In recent years there have been reports of state violence against women and children, including rapes and sexual abuse.

CHILDREN
Malnutrition, especially in marginalized areas, and high HIV/AIDS prevalence, are the main health problems affecting children. In 2002, 16 per cent of babies had low birth weight. Vitamin A supplements coverage reached 84 per cent of children between 6 and 59 months. 24 per cent of children under five years old show stunted growth.

According to figures from 2001, out of the 230,000 Namibians living with HIV/AIDS, 13 per cent are children and 47 per cent have been orphaned by AIDS.

Only 30 per cent of San children are enrolled in school, and just 45 per cent of them make it to fifth grade, compared with the national rate of 92 per cent. San and Himba children account for the majority of the 16,500 children not in school. In the Kavango region, girls' dropout rates far exceed boys' throughout primary and secondary school.

INDIGENOUS PEOPLES/ETHNIC MINORITIES
The Namibian population is divided into 11 ethnic groups; the main ones are the Ovambo (47.4 per cent), Kavango (8.8 per cent), Damara (7.1 per cent) and Herero (7.1 per cent). The European minority represents 4.6 per cent of the population. The San were the earliest peoples to occupy Namibia. They are the most marginalized ethnic group in the country, showing high levels of alcoholism. They work on farms established on their own ancestral lands and earn very low wages. The Government of Botswana wants to remove them from central Kalahari in order to exploit mineral riches and tourist safaris. Out of a total of 55,000 San, 25,000 live in Namibia. They speak one of the varieties of click languages, which consists of sounds produced by different positions of the tongue. The situation of the San peoples was discussed at the World Conference Against Racism, held in South Africa in 2001, and a range of NGOs continue to denounce the discrimination suffered by them.

MIGRANTS/REFUGEES
At the end of 2002, there were about 25,000 refugees in Namibia, mainly from Angola. Approximately 1,000 refugees from various other countries also live in Namibia and another 3,000 arrived in 2003, escaping food shortages when Angola's war ended.

About 1,000 Namibians were refugees in Botswana at the end of 2002. Some 1,000 were repatriated during that year.

DEATH PENALTY
Namibia abolished the death penalty for all crimes in 1990, although Nujoma's Government has been accused of constant human-rights violations such as extrajudicial executions and prison deaths.

Nauru / Nauru - Naoero

Population:	13,660
Area:	21 km²
Capital:	No official capital
Currency:	Australian dollar
Language:	English

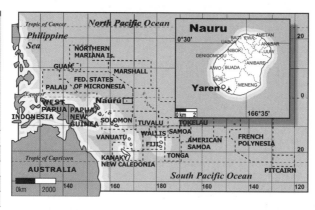

Nauru, which lies in the central Pacific, was originally populated by migrating Polynesian, Micronesian and Melanesian people. The British sailor John Fearn was the first European to visit the island, which he named Pleasant Island. Whaling ships often called at Nauru during the 19th century, until it was annexed by the German Second Reich in 1888.

[2] In 1900, Australian Albert Ellis was sent a stone by a traveler, who thought it might make good marbles for children. Upon analyzing it, Ellis discovered the phosphate that would turn Nauru into a relatively wealthy country. In 1905, an Anglo-German company began mining on the island.

[3] At the beginning of World War I, Australia occupied Nauru. After the war, it became a trust territory administered by Australia on behalf of Australia, Britain and New Zealand. During World War II Nauru was under Japanese control and thousands of Nauruans were sent to forced labor camps on the island of Truk (in present-day Micronesia). At the end of the War, only 700 came back alive. Australia recovered the island, and mining was continued by British, Australian and New Zealand transnational consortia. In 1947, Nauru was made a United Nations Trust Territory under Australian administration.

[4] Traditionally fishing people, the Nauruans did not adjust well to mining and were soon replaced by immigrants, mostly Chinese. Immigrants were so numerous that in 1964, the Australian Government suggested that Nauruans should accept resettlement to a different island or elsewhere in Australia. Nauruans rejected the proposal, deciding to stay on their island and seek autonomy.

[5] The mining sector was nationalized in 1967, which resulted in a large increase in per capita income. Nauru declared independence on 31 January 1968, rejecting Australian attempts at domination. A year later it became a member of the Commonwealth.

[6] Nauru has no taxes. Government expenses and public investment are paid out of a huge legal fund fed by phosphate revenues. Education, medical care and housing are free.

[7] Hammer DeRoburt dominated the political scene and was President from independence in 1968 until the 1976 elections, when he lost to Bernard Dowiyogo, of the Nauru Party. Two years later, DeRoburt was re-elected president and held office from 1978 to 1986. Bernard Dowiyogo won the 1986 ballot in which a woman was elected deputy for the first time since independence.

[8] Nauru established formal diplomatic relations with the Republic of China on 4 May 1980. Since then, both nations maintained close trade and friendship links.

[9] Bernard Dowiyogo's second administration sued the government of Australia for its indiscriminate exploitation of the phosphate mines for 50 years. In 1991, Australia acknowledged the right of Nauru to be indemnified. Britain and New Zealand agreed to collaborate with Australia in the payment of $100 million to Nauru.

[10] In December 1997 then president Godfrey Clodumar re-established diplomatic relations with France, broken off two years previously in protest against nuclear tests in French Polynesia. At the same time, Nauru demanded a drastic cut in the production of greenhouse gases which lead to global warming and a rise in sea levels that would drown the island.

[11] Nauru citizens, who used to enjoy one of the highest per capita incomes in the world, suffered a sharp decrease in their standard of living due to bad investments of the government. Dowiyogo lost Parliament's confidence. In April 1999 René Harris became President. On 14 September, Nauru joined the United Nations.

[12] In August 2001, 460 illegal immigrants, most of them Afghans, and also Sinhalese and Thais, were rescued by a Norwegian cargo ship when the vessel carrying them sank. There was an attempt to land the immigrants on Australian territory at Christmas Island, but Australia refused to accept them. After several days of diplomatic negotiations, New Zealand agreed to accept 150 refugees, while the rest went on to Nauru. Canberra offered to pay the expenses for the refugees heading for the island.

[13] That same year, FATF (Financial Action Task Force) applied countermeasures against Nauru because it had not complied with its commitment to strengthen the laws against money-laundering; it was put on its list of non-cooperative countries and territories. In 2002, the US deplored the fact that $70 billion taken from Russia in 1998 had entered Nauruan transnational accounts.

[14] In April 2004, Australian lawyers due to appear in court in Nauru to challenge the detention of some 300 asylum-seekers were prevented from entering the country by the Nauruan Government, which said that local lawyers could take the cases. However, one of the Australian solicitors said: 'If we win this case, if we ever get a chance to argue this case, then Australia is going to have to find somewhere else to warehouse people and Nauru will lose the huge amount of income it gets from Australia to lock up people there'.

[15] On 23 June 2004, President Harris was unseated by Parliament in a vote of no-confidence, following a dramatic day during which the veteran leader was ousted. Ludwig Scotty was appointed as the new President. Harris stated that he feared that Scotty would surely try to close the controversial refugee camp, which was financed by Australia. ■

LAND USE

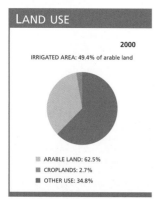

2000

IRRIGATED AREA: 49.4% of arable land

- ARABLE LAND: 62.5%
- CROPLANDS: 2.7%
- OTHER USE: 34.8%

PROFILE

ENVIRONMENT
Nauru is a coral island, 6 km long by 4 km wide, located near Micronesia just south of the Equator. With sandy beaches and a thin belt of fertile land (300 meters wide), the island has a 60-meter high central plateau of guano (bird droppings), rich in phosphoric acid and nitrogen.

SOCIETY
Peoples: Nauruans are descendants of Polynesian, Micronesian and Melanesian immigrants. There are also Australian, Aotearoan/ New Zealand, Chinese and European minorities, and workers from Tuvalu, Kiribati and other neighboring islands. Men outnumber women two to one. **Religions:** Christian. **Languages:** English (official) and Nauruan. **Main Political Parties:** Nauru Party (NP); Democratic Party of Nauru. **Social Organizations:** There are two social organizations: the Nauru Workers' Organization (NWO), founded in 1974 and affiliated to the NP; and the Phosphate Workers' Organization (PWO), founded in 1953.

THE STATE
Official Name: Republic of Nauru. **Administrative Divisions:** 14 districts. **Capital:** There are no population centers and so the island has no formal capital. The Government buildings are located opposite the airport in the Yaren district. **Government:** Ludwig Scotty, President since June 2004, elected for a three-year term by the Legislature. This is unicameral and has 18 members. **National Holiday:** 31 January, Independence Day (1968). **Armed Forces:** Australia is responsible for the island's defense.

Nepal / Nepal

Population:	26,289,096
Area:	147,180 km²
Capital:	Kathmandu
Currency:	Rupee
Language:	Nepali

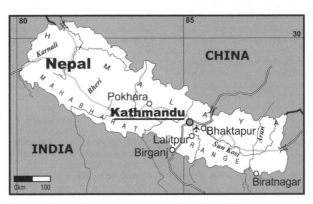

N epal's rich prehistory lies mainly in the legendary traditions of the Newar, an indigenous people native to Nepal Valley (present day Kathmandu Valley). In Nepal Buddhism and Brahman Hinduism originated as related religions (although with different value systems), sharing holidays, events and myths. Nepal is situated between two of the world's most populated countries; India and China. References to Nepal Valley and Nepal's lower hill areas are found in the ancient Indian classics, suggesting that the Central Himalayan hills were closely connected culturally and politically to the Gangetic Plain at least 2,500 years ago. Lumbini, Gautama Buddha's birthplace in southern Nepal, and Nepal Valley also figure prominently in Buddhist accounts. There is substantial archeological evidence of Buddhist influence in Nepal, including a famous column inscribed by Ashoka (Emperor of India, 3rd century BC) at Lumbini and several shrines in the valley.

2   Although there are gaps, the sequence of the Nepal Valley's history can be traced along with the rise of the Licchavi dynasty in the 4th or 5th century AD. While the earlier Kirati dynasty had claimed the status of the Kshatriya caste of rulers and warriors, the Licchavis were probably the first ruling family in that area of Indian plains origin. This set a precedent for what became the normal pattern thereafter (Hindu kings claiming high-caste Indian origin ruling over a population much of which was neither Indo-Aryan nor Hindu).

3   The Licchavi dynastic chronicles, supplemented by numerous stone inscriptions, are detailed from AD 500 to 700. A powerful, united kingdom also emerged in Tibet in this period, and the Himalayan passes to the north of the valley were opened. Extensive cultural, trade and political relations developed, transforming the valley from a relatively remote backwater into the major intellectual and commercial center between South

and Central Asia. Nepal's contacts with China began in the mid-7th century with the exchange of several missions. But intermittent warfare between Tibet and China terminated this relationship; and while there were briefly renewed contacts in subsequent centuries, these were re-established on a continuing basis only in the late 18th century.

4   The middle period in Nepalese history roughly corresponds with the rule of the Malla dynasty (10th-18th century) in Nepal Valley and surrounding areas. Although most of the Licchavi kings were devout Hindus, they did not impose Brahmanic social codes or values on their non-Hindu subjects. The Mallas perceived their responsibilities differently, however. The Malla ruler Jaya Sthiti (reigned c. 1382-95) introduced the first legal and social code influenced by contemporary Hindu principles. His successor Yaksa Malla (reigned 1429-1482) divided

his kingdom among his three sons, creating the independent principalities of Kathmandu, Patan and Bhaktapur (Bhagdaon) in the valley. Each state controlled the territory in the surrounding hill areas, with particular importance attached to the trade routes to Tibet (north) and to India (south) that were vital to their economies. In the western and eastern hill areas there were small independent principalities, which were sustained through a delicate balance of power based upon traditional inter-relationships and in common ancestral origins among the ruling families.

5   In the 16th century virtually all these principalities were ruled by dynasties claiming high-caste Indian origin whose members had left the hills in the wake of Muslim invasions of Northern India. In the 18th century the principality of Gorkha (or Gurkha) had a predominant role in the hills and even posed a challenge to Nepal Valley. The Mallas, weakened by familial dissent and widespread social and economic

IN FOCUS

ENVIRONMENTAL CHALLENGES
Wood-burning accounts for 90 per cent of energy consumption, resulting in deforestation and soil erosion. Urban areas are particularly affected by air and water pollution. The lack of sewerage systems in major cities has also contributed to the deterioration of the environment.

WOMEN'S RIGHTS
Nepalese women have been able to vote and run for office since 1951.

In 2003 women held 9 per cent of seats in Parliament and 6 per cent of ministerial or equivalent posts. There are political restrictions for women of certain castes, but the Constitution states that at least 5 per cent of candidates to the House of the Representatives and 20 per cent to local governments must be women. Women comprised 41 per cent of the workforce, mostly in the agricultural sector.

Only 27 per cent of pregnant women received antenatal healthcare and qualified personnel attended just 11 per cent of births. Even though both indicators show improvement, their evolution has been slow and insufficient between 1991 and 2000.

In 2000, 57.2 per cent of women aged 15 to 24 were illiterate, while among men of the same age the proportion was 23.3 per cent. Among all adult women (older than 15 years old) the

percentage of illiteracy reached 76 per cent.

It is estimated that 40 per cent of girls are married before their 15th birthday. In 2001 at least 200,000 Nepalese women were sexual workers in India alone.

CHILDREN
A lack of legislation, the Maoist insurgency and the resulting pattern of severe human-rights violations and permanent caste-, class-, ethnicity- and gender-based discrimination pose a threat to human security, particularly among children. The impact of the insurgency on education was devastating. Almost 3,000 teachers were displaced, affecting 100,000 students, and 700 schools were closed.

In 2001, 1,500 children under-14 were HIV-positive, and there were 13,000 AIDS orphans among that age group.

In 2000, the number of child laborers was estimated to be more than 2 million. Most of them were working in agriculture, domestic service and small industry. ILO figures showed that 5 out of 100 children aged between 6 and 14 were economically active. Each year about 7,000 Nepalese girls are forced to become sex workers in different parts of the globe.

INDIGENOUS PEOPLES/ ETHNIC MINORITIES
There are over 75 ethnic groups, speaking 50 different languages. The Constitution grants each community the right to preserve and promote its

language, writing and culture. The Government favours Hinduism and proselytizing is not allowed. Members of the lower castes are subject to widespread discrimination all over the country, except in Kathmandu, where differences are less notorious.

MIGRANTS/REFUGEES
During 2002, over 132,000 refugees and asylum-seekers were living in Nepal. These included more than 112,000 Bhutanese, 20,000 Tibetans, and smaller numbers of other nationalities recognized as refugees by the UNHCR.

Between 100,000 and 150,000 Nepalese were internally displaced by the end of 2002. Nearly 1,700 Nepalese were refugees in industrialized countries, while an estimated 10,000 were living in India.

Nepal is not party to the UN Convention on the Status of Refugees. Although the Government allows UNHCR to operate in the country, refugees recognized by the agency have neither legal status nor prospects for local integration. Therefore, UNHCR generally seeks resettlement in other countries for such refugees.

DEATH PENALTY
The death penalty for ordinary crimes was abolished in 1990 and for all types of crimes in 1997. The last execution took place in 1979.

Life expectancy
59.9 years
2000-2005

GNI per capita
$230
2002

Literacy
42% total adult rate
2000

HIV prevalence rate
0.5% of population 15-49 years old
2001

discontent, were no match for the great Gorkha ruler Prithvi Narayan Shah, who conquered the valley in 1769 and moved his capital to Kathmandu, providing the foundation of the modern state of Nepal.

6 The Shah (or Saha) rulers faced persistent problems to centralize an area characterized by extreme diversity and ethnic and regional parochialism. They absorbed dominant regional and local élites into the central administration of Kathmandu, thus neutralizing potentially disintegrative political forces and involving them in national politics. This limited the center's authority in outlying areas because local administration was based upon a compromise division of responsibilities between the local élites and the central administration.

7 The British conquest of India in the 19th century posed a threat to Nepal that was left with no real alternative but to seek an accord with the British to preserve its independence. This was accomplished by the Rana family regime after 1860. Under this *de facto* alliance, Kathmandu recruited Gurkha units for the British Indian Army and accepted British 'guidance' on foreign policy. In exchange, the British guaranteed the Rana regime protection against both foreign and domestic enemies and allowing autonomy in domestic affairs. Nepal maintained a friendly relationship with China and Tibet, for economic reasons.

8 When the British withdrew from India in 1947, the Ranas lost a vital external source of support and the regime was exposed to new dangers. Anti-Rana forces, composed mainly of Nepalese residents in India who had their political apprenticeship in the Indian nationalist movement, formed an alliance with the Nepalese royal family, led by the king. Nepal, India and the UK signed an agreement in Kathmandu in 1947, and Gurkha troops were used by India in the war against China (1961-62), Pakistan in 1965 and 1971, and by the UK against Argentina (1982).

9 In 1951, the Nepalese Congress overthrew the Rana regime with support from King Tribhuvan Bir Bikram Shah Deva, after which the country experimented with different forms of democracy. Political parties were legalized and a general election was held in 1959, based on the Constitution approved by King Mahendra Bir Bikran Shah Deva. Nepal became a member of the United Nations in 1955, and it has been an active member of the Non-Aligned Movement since the Bandung Conference. In 1960, the first elected Prime Minister, B P Koirala, was arrested. Parliament was dissolved, the Constitution was suspended and political parties were

outlawed. In 1962 a non-party or Panchayat system was introduced.

10 In 1979, student protest movements emerged in Kathmandu and other cities. King Birendra Bir Birkram Shah Deva responded by holding a plebiscite to choose between a multiparty system or a reformed Panchayat, the latter obtaining 55 per cent of the vote. The opposition considered the outcome a fraud. By July 1986, 75 countries endorsed a proposal by Birendra that Nepal should be declared a zone of peace. All of its neighbors except India and Bhutan endorsed the proposal. India is Nepal's leading trade partner. The two signed several trade and transit treaties between 1950 and 1989, when the two countries became involved in an undeclared trade war. Nepal clashed with India over its arms imports from China, India suspended all trade with Nepal and closed 19 of the 21 transit routes in 1989, seriously harming the Nepalese economy.

11 The anti-Panchayat protests reached a peak in 1990. Birendra initiated talks with the opposition and agreed to political pluralism. The transition to a parliamentary democracy with a constitutional monarchy was announced by royal decree in April that year. In 1991 the first free elections were held in Nepal after 32 years of semi-monarchic rule. The Communist Party

of Nepal (CPN) and the Nepalese Congress Party (NCP, monarchist and pro-Government) united for the elections, joining forces with other groups. The Communists won 4 of the 5 posts in the capital, but the national majority went to the NCP.

12 Prime Minister Krishna Prasad Bhattarai (appointed in 1990) resigned that same year, and was succeeded by Girija Prasad Koirala (NCP). Koirala promised to launch a mixed economy, earmarking 70 per cent of national income to rural regions and carrying out agrarian reform. He made primary education free. The opposition harshly criticized Koirala for signing certain treaties with India, saying he had 'sold off national interests' given that India would benefit with five hydroelectric projects.

13 To attract foreign investment, in 1993 Koirala promoted the total convertibility of the Nepali rupee (national currency) with foreign currencies, and signed new trade accords with India. Koirala resigned in 1994 due to lack of parliamentary support and infighting in the NCP, and Man Mohan Adhikari was named Prime Minister. In the November elections the CPN won 88 seats in the Chamber of Representatives. In 1995, lacking majority political support, Mohan Adhikari handed over control to NCP leader Sher Bahadur Deuba. In 1996, guerrilla groups describing

themselves as Maoist launched campaigns to 'eradicate feudalism'.

14 In June 2001 Birendra, Queen Aishwarya and other members of the royal family were shot to death by their heir, Prince Dipendra Bir Bikram Shah Deva, 29, who was inebriated and later shot himself in a suicide attempt, but survived in a state of coma. The Royal Council appointed Dipendra King of Nepal and Prince Gyanendra, Birendra's brother, as his Regent. Dipendra died on 4 June and Gyanendra became King. That same year, Koirala resigned due to the growing violence between the insurgent Maoists and the security forces; Sher Bahadur Deuba took over as Prime Minister and declared a ceasefire.

15 In the subsequent negotiations, the Maoists included among their 31 demands the abolition of the 1990 Constitution, the creation of an interim government and the election of a Constituent Assembly to draft a new national charter that would end the monarchy and create a republic. The Government did not accept the demands and violence escalated. The King declared a state of emergency, categorizing the rebels as terrorists. With constitutional guarantees suspended, the death toll among civilians and rebels alike rose. The conflict became civil war and by 2002 had claimed 2,100 lives, and 100,000 refugees fled to neighboring Bhutan.

16 In May 2002 Deuba used the state of emergency as an excuse to dissolve parliament, calling elections for November. In October, after refusing peace talks with the rebels, Deuba suggested that the King postpone the elections for a year, until the insurgents were defeated. King Gyanendra dismissed Deuba and appointed Lokendra Bahadur Chand as Prime Minister while postponing the elections indefinitely.

17 In January 2003, Maoist guerillas offered a truce to launch peace talks. Among their claims - which Kathmandu was likely to concede - they demanded that the Government not label them as 'terrorists' and stop offering rewards for the arrest of rebels. In August, the rebels put an end to the peace talks with the Government and to the seven-month truce, calling a general strike. The political stalemate led to a major outbreak of violence, with clashes between students, activists and the police.

18 In April 2004, opposition groups angry over the King's assumption of executive powers added their voices to the protests of the strikers. Schools and businesses were shut and roads were patrolled by security forces. That same month officials and security personnel captured by the rebels during clashes in north-west Nepal were released.

19 In March 2004 Nepal joined the World Trade Organization (WTO). ∎

PROFILE

ENVIRONMENT
Nepal is a landlocked country in the Himalayas with three distinct geographical regions: the fertile, tropical plains of Terai, the central plateaus, covered with rainforest, and the Himalayan mountains, where the world's highest peaks are located. The climate varies according to altitude, from rainy and tropical, to cold in the high mountains. This diversity allows for the cultivation of rice, sugarcane, tobacco, jute and cereals. Most of the population live from agriculture. Livestock - sheep and buffalo - is also important. Mineral and hydroelectric resources are as yet unexploited.

SOCIETY
Peoples: Nepali 53.2 per cent; Bihari (including Maithili and Bhojpuri) 18.4 per cent; Tharu 4.8 per cent; Tamang 4.7 per cent; Newar 3.4 per cent; Magar 2.2 per cent; Abadhi 1.7 per cent; other 11.6 per cent.
Religions: Hinduism 86.2 per cent (official); Buddhism 7.8 per cent; Muslim 3.8 per cent; Christian 0.2 per cent; other 2 per cent.
Languages: Nepali (official) is spoken by only half the population; many other languages are spoken, corresponding to the different cultural communities, Tibetan being the second most common language. **Main Political Parties:** The Nepalese Congress Party (NCP); the Communist Party of Nepal; National Democratic Party (NDM); Nepalese Goodwill Party; National People's Front.

THE STATE
Official Name: Nepál Adhirajya. **Administrative Divisions:** 5 regions, 14 zones and 75 districts. **Capital:** Kathmandu 741,000 people (2003). **Other Cities:** Biratnagar 203,300 people; Pokhara 157,700; Lalitpur 153,900; Birganj 118,300 (2000). **Government:** Parliamentary Monarchy. Gyanendra Bir Bikram Shah Dev, King (Maharajadhiraja) since June 2001. Surya Bahadur Thapa, Prime Minister since June 2003. Bicameral legislature: The House of Representatives with 205 members elected every five years and The House of the States with 60 members. **National Holidays:** 15 February, (Constitution) and 18 February, (Fatherland); 7 July, Birthday of King (1946). **Armed Forces:** 35,000 (1994). Other: 28,000 (Police Forces).

Netherlands / Nederland

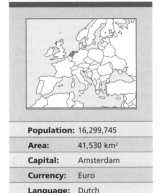

Population:	16,299,745
Area:	41,530 km²
Capital:	Amsterdam
Currency:	Euro
Language:	Dutch

The borders of present-day Netherlands (Holland) were established in 1867. Until then, the region known as the Low Countries (made up of what are now Belgium, Luxembourg, Netherlands and the northern part of France) suffered several political divisions.

[2] In the 4th millennium BC, the first pre-Celtic (Indo-European) tribes emigrated from present-day south-west Germany to the Low Countries. In the 2nd millennium BC, the high level of social and cultural development reached by these tribes found expression in their art which featured curves and arabesques. The Celts were conquered by Frisian and Batavian Germanic peoples in the 3rd century BC.

[3] The Roman Empire never managed to occupy the land of the Frisians, who remained independent north of the Rhine until the 8th century. The Romans instead settled in the Rhine delta, where they founded the province of Gallia Belgica in 54 BC. There they worked the lands around their villas, while the Frisians continued to fish and raise cattle. In the 3rd century BC, a rise in sea levels affected production in the region.

[4] In the 1st century AD, the Batavians rebelled against the Romans, but the latter only withdrew in the 4th century with the invasions of the Saxons (Germanic), who came from eastern Germany, and the Franks (Germanic), who came from the north. The Low Countries, to the south of the Rhine, were split in two, with the southern half under Roman jurisdiction, using a Romance language, and the northern half under Germanic control.

[5] The Franks subdued Roman Gallia (Gaul) in the 5th century and expanded the domain of the Western Empire, in alliance with the Catholic Church. In 695, the Frank Carolingian dynasties set up a bishopric in the city of Utrecht, encroaching on the Frisian region, which it controlled by the end of the following century. In 800, Charlemagne was crowned emperor.

[6] In 911, the northern part of France was ceded to the Vikings from Scandinavia. The Normans, as they became known, founded the duchy of Normandy and conquered other regions such as the Low Countries. As a result territorial sovereignty was divided between several fiefs. Through their expansion the Normans opened up routes for commercial and cultural exchange with the East.

[7] Between the 10th and 13th centuries textile craft industries grew in several communities, accompanied by a growth in population. From the 11th century onwards, the Frisians developed a system to drain the seawater and reclaim land for pasture and agriculture. Cistercian and Premonstraten monks were active in the construction of dykes to reclaim land from the sea.

[8] In 1302, Flanders became independent from France. The centers of production (such as Utrecht, The Hague, Amsterdam and Ghent) gradually expanded and perfected their economies, developing for example a banking system, as well as winning political autonomy.

[9] In the latter half of the 14th century, the dukes of Burgundy allied with the Flemish (from Flanders). Under this prosperous alliance, which lasted until 1477, the arts flourished with painters such as Jan Van Eyck (1395-1441), Rogier van der Weyden (1400-64) and Hugo van der Goes (1440-82) as well as Gothic Flemish sculpture and architecture. In this period, the Duchy of Burgundy's authority was extended throughout the Low Countries.

[10] After the death of Charles the Bold in 1477, his daughter Mary of Burgundy married Maximilian of Austria and the Low Countries came under the control of the Hapsburg dynasty, which expanded its hegemony throughout the Germanic Holy Roman Empire (962-1806).

[11] Charles V (born in Ghent in 1500), son of the archduke of Austria, occupied the throne of Spain in 1517. He was succeeded in 1556 by his son Philip II who inherited the Habsburg lands in Austria, the Holy Roman Empire which included the Netherlands, and also Spain's overseas possessions. In 1566, political and religious struggle led by the Duke of Orange erupted in the Low Countries, where the Protestant Reformation took hold in the north (Netherlands). Two years later the Duke of Alva brutally crushed the revolt. In 1579, the seven northern provinces (Calvinist) proclaimed their independence in the Union of Utrecht and adopted the name

---

WORKERS

UNEMPLOYMENT: 2.7% (2002)

LABOR FORCE   **2002**

- ■ FEMALE: 40.9%   ■ MALE: 59.1%

EMPLOYMENT DISTRIBUTION   **1995/2001**

F

M

■ AGRICULTURE	F: 4.0%	M: 2.0%
■ INDUSTRY	F: 31.0%	M: 9.0%
■ SERVICES	F: 63.0%	M: 84.0%

LAND USE

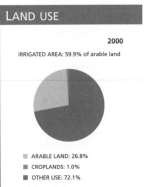

2000

IRRIGATED AREA: 59.9% of arable land

- ■ ARABLE LAND: 26.8%
- ■ CROPLANDS: 1.0%
- ■ OTHER USE: 72.1%

PUBLIC EXPENDITURE

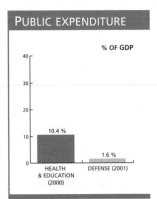

% OF GDP

10.4 % — HEALTH & EDUCATION (2000)

1.6 % — DEFENSE (2001)

Life expectancy
78.3 years
2000-2005

GNI per capita
$23,960
2002

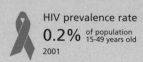

HIV prevalence rate
0.2% of population
15-49 years old
2001

United Provinces of the Netherlands, while the southern provinces (Catholic) remained loyal to Spain.

[12] For most of the period 1568-1648 the United Provinces and Spain were at war. Their battles took place mostly along the sea routes to the Indies, where both colonial powers (like England and France) wanted to prevail.

[13] In 1602, the Netherlands - which had large shipyards along the North Sea coast and major investors - formed the Dutch East India Company, with agencies in Ceylon, India and Indonesia. In 1621, the United Provinces founded the Dutch West India Company. Its profits came largely from the slave trade, and smuggling from Spain's colonies.

[14] In 1648, the Dutch had three large settlements in America: one in the north for the fur trade, another in Brazil and another in Suriname, for the slave trade and smuggling with the Spanish. Of these settlements, in 1700 only the trading posts of Curaçao, St Eustatius and St Maarten remained, and the plantations in Dutch Guyana and Elmina as slave ports.

[15] During the Twelve Years' Truce with Spain (1609-21), controversies within the Union grew. The collaboration between the province of Holland and the House of Orange (German) gave way to a growing rivalry. In 1618, Maurice of Orange executed the leader of the main party in the Netherlands. At the end of the Truce, when the war with Spain was resumed, both rivals were forced to reunite until the signing of the Treaty of Munster in 1648, under which Spain recognized the independence of the United Provinces.

[16] In 1628 French philosopher Descartes - a critic of the dominant method of Scholasticism (based on comparing and contrasting the views of recognized authorities) moved to the Netherlands where he was able to publish *Discourse on Method* (1637).

[17] Dutch maritime power began to decline after the wars against Britain (1652-4 and 1665-7). The country used up part of its capital to buy bonds in foreign governments. Bankers in Amsterdam were among the most powerful in Europe.

[18] In the War of the Spanish Succession (1701-1714) the Dutch allied with the British against the French. In the latter part of the century wars continued between and among the Dutch, French, Spanish and British.

[19] After the French Revolution (1789), Holland became a French protectorate between 1794 and 1806, with a republican system of government. The United Provinces became the Batavian Republic. The new political and economic liberties were welcomed by various sectors of Dutch society, such as the anti-Orange Patriot movement which, under the impact of the first Industrial Revolution, rejected the monarchy.

[20] Between 1806 and 1814, under the Empire of Napoleon Bonaparte, the new Batavian Republic fell victim to political struggles. In 1814, Prince William I of Orange was called on to restore the monarchy and in 1815 he won sovereignty over all of the Low Countries. In 1830, a revolution led Belgium to secede from the Netherlands. In 1831, it annexed the eastern region of Luxembourg, while the Grand Duchy of Luxembourg became independent in 1867.

[21] Throughout the 19th century the Dutch expanded civil rights. The Constitution of 1848 became the foundation of the Netherlands' current democracy. Under its provisions arbitrary personal rule by the monarch was no longer possible and members of the first chamber of parliament, formerly appointed by the King, were thereafter elected by the provincial assemblies. Members of the assemblies and the second chamber of parliament were elected; only people who were tax-payers could vote.

[22] After decades of debate over the school system, Protestants and Catholics allied themselves against the liberals and, in 1888, the first private schools were opened. New political parties were founded, based on the religious ideas and ideologies of the time. To the Liberal, Protestant and Catholic parties were added the Protestant Conservative, the Socialist and the Communist parties. As none could obtain a majority, coalitions became commonplace.

[23] During World War I (1914-1918), the Netherlands declared its neutrality and political parties agreed to a truce in order to dedicate their energies to the domestic economy and foreign trade. The merchant navy had recovered and industry grew, in particular textiles, electronics, and chemicals.

[24] During the postwar period, the Netherlands was a member of the League of Nations, but it re-affirmed its neutrality, a symbol of which was the International Court of Justice at The Hague. During the Versailles negotiations, Belgium tried unsuccessfully to revive an old territorial claim against the Netherlands.

[25] During World War II (1939-45), Germany occupied the Netherlands (and attacked France from Dutch territory). Queen Wilhelmina formed a government-in-exile in London, and all political factions took part in anti-Nazi resistance.

[26] In 1945, an agreement was signed by the Government, companies and trade unions. It lasted 20 years and was aimed at controlling prices and salaries. The Netherlands underwent rapid industrialization especially in steel production, electronics and petrochemicals. In the following years, Dutch transnational companies were consolidated, such as Royal Dutch Shell (petrochemicals), Unilever (world's largest food and soap manufacturer), Philips (electronics), AKZO (chemicals), Heineken (beer), ABN AMRO (banking), and ING (banking and insurance).

[27] In the postwar years, with a Government composed of Labor Party-led (former socialists and Catholics) coalitions, the Netherlands joined NATO, the UN and the European Economic Community. Together with Belgium and Luxembourg it formed the Benelux economic alliance. It granted independence to Indonesia (1949), New Guinea (1963) and Suriname (1975).

[28] The 1960s witnessed struggles for the rights of women and sexual minorities, and public debates were held on the use of drugs. These pressure groups achieved significant changes in legislation and state medical insurance coverage. In the ensuing years abortion and prostitution were legalized, and use of marijuana and heroin decriminalized. To help addicts, information and medical assistance plans were

PROFILE

ENVIRONMENT

The country is a large plain and 38 per cent of its territory is below sea level. Intensive agriculture and cattle-raising produce high quality milk products and crops (particularly flowers). Population density is amongst the highest in the world. Highly industrialized, the country is a major producer of natural gas, and is a dominant influence in petroleum activity. It has large refineries in the Netherlands Antilles and Rotterdam, the world center of the free, or 'spot', crude oil market.

SOCIETY

Peoples: Dutch 91 per cent; Turks 1.3 per cent; Moroccans 1 per cent; Germans 0.3 per cent; and others.
Religions: 31 per cent Catholic; Dutch Reformed Church 14 per cent; Calvinist 8 per cent; Muslim 3.9 per cent; other 4.1 per cent; no religion 39 per cent.
Languages: Dutch (official); Frisian; Turkish, Arab, Kurdish and from other immigrant communities.
Main Political Parties: Labor Party (PvdA), social-democratic, affiliated to the Socialist International; People's Party for Freedom and Democracy (VVD), conservative liberal; Christian-Democratic Appeal (CDA); List Pim Fortuyn (LPF), far right; Democrats 66 (D66), social-liberal; Political Reformed Party (SGP), Christian; Green Left (GL), ecologist and socialist.
Main Social Organizations: Federation of Netherlands Trade Union Movements, which includes Socialist and Catholic trade unions; National Confederation of Christian Trade Unions.

THE STATE

Official Name: Koninkrijk der Nederlanden.
Administrative Divisions: 12 Provinces.
Capital: Amsterdam 1,145,000 people (2003). Although the Government has its seat in The Hague, Amsterdam is still considered the capital. **Other Cities:** Rotterdam 1,125,500 people; The Hague (s'-Gravenhage) 443,700; Utrecht 232,900; Eindhoven 200,600 (2000).
Government: Constitutional and parliamentary monarchy. Queen Beatrix, Head of State since April 1980. Prime Minister Jan Peter Balkenende, since July 2002. Gerrit Zalm and Thom De Graaf, Deputy Prime Ministers since May 2003. The Legislature has two chambers: the First Chamber, with 75 members, and the Second Chamber, with 150 members.
National Holiday: 30 April, Queen's Day (1938).
Armed Forces: 74,400 (1995). Other: 3,600 Royal Military Corps.
Dependencies: See Netherlands Antilles and Aruba.

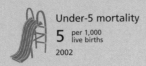 Under-5 mortality
5 per 1,000 live births
2002

 Aid
0.81% Official development assistance as % of donors' GNI
2002

 Maternal mortality
16 per 100,000 live births
2000

IN FOCUS

ENVIRONMENTAL CHALLENGES
Underground water is highly polluted with nitrates, as a result of the widespread use of agrochemicals, and also with heavy metals. Major rivers carry all kinds of organic and industrial waste, especially from European countries. There are significant levels of air pollution, mostly from refineries and automobiles, leading to high levels of acid rain.

WOMEN'S RIGHTS
Women have been able to stand for office since 1917 and to vote since 1919. Between 1995 and 2000 the number of seats in Parliament held by women increased from 31 to 36 per cent, while female representation in ministerial or equivalent posts dropped from 31 to 28 per cent.

In 2000, women made up 41 per cent of the workforce (two per cent in agriculture, nine per cent in industry and 84 per cent in services), while female unemployment fell from 8.8 to 4.9 per cent in the period 1995-2000.

The Netherlands has made more progress than any other country in preventing trafficking of women from countries in the South to the EU as well as in providing support for the women concerned through social security programs and legal, medical and psychological aid, as well as temporary residence permits.

CHILDREN
Educational, health and general welfare needs are covered for Dutch children, making poverty in this group practically non-existent. However children from

ethnic minorities have more problems integrating socially. Those from Turkish, Moroccan or Surinamese families suffer more social segregation in schools, and have greater drop-out rates and learning difficulties.

Traditionally mothers have been responsible for early years child-care, but as in other countries, the Netherlands has seen a greater demand for nurseries. The Government is trying to address this issue.

INDIGENOUS PEOPLES/ETHNIC MINORITIES
The main minority groups are Turks, Moroccans and Surinamese.

MIGRANTS/REFUGEES
In 2002 there were 17,200 refugees and asylum-seekers in the country. Of these, 3,600 had been

granted asylum, 4,200 had been granted temporary leave to remain on humanitarian grounds, and 9,400 were awaiting a decision regarding their asylum requests.

Some 18,700 people requested asylum in 2002, 42 per cent less than in 2001. Most of the requests were from citizens of Angola, Sierra Leone, Afghanistan, Iraq and Iran. The Dutch authorities approved 11 per cent of the 34,300 requests which were decided in 2002.

Immigrants make up 8.7 per cent of the workforce, and they do not always have access to the same benefits as the Dutch population.

DEATH PENALTY
The death penalty was abolished in 1982.

---

implemented, including distribution of condoms, needles and the heroin substitute methadone.

[29] In the 1970s, the electorate voted in center-left governments, which reformed the tax system and increased investment in social policies. However, the size of the defense budget and the installation of NATO atomic missiles in the country caused controversy.

[30] The Netherlands is one of the countries allocating the highest percentage of its GDP to aid for the Third World. It has also pursued policies defending human rights and took a stand against South Africa's apartheid system. Meanwhile, links with Israel have tended to estrange it from some Arab countries.

[31] In 1980, after an embezzlement scandal involving her husband, Queen Juliana abdicated in favor of her daughter Beatrix. In 1985, the Government authorized the installation of nuclear missiles, despite protests by the Dutch people, which continued until the end of the Cold War in 1991.

[32] In 1991, when it held the EU presidency, the Netherlands called on the heads of state and government meeting in Maastricht to condemn racism and to adopt legislation prohibiting xenophobic acts throughout Europe. However, in September 1993 the Netherlands enacted legislation restricting immigrants from outside the EU.

[33] In 1992, the Central Office of Statistics announced the 'green gross national product' (GGNP).

This indicator evaluates losses of natural resources, in relation to the capacity for regeneration, and the effect on local communities.

[34] On 22 August 1994, Wim Kok, from the Labor Party, became Prime Minister, in coalition with two other parties, VVD and Democrats 66. Three months earlier, local election results had shown a growth in support for racist far-right parties.

[35] In 1995, for the second year running, the complex hydraulic system failed, causing flooding of vast areas in southern and central Netherlands. A state of emergency was declared, and 250,000 people were evacuated.

[36] The 1998 elections were won again by Wim Kok.

[37] In April 2001 the first same-sex marriages took place in the Netherlands, and gay couples conquered the right to adopt children. Laws on gay rights were passed by a comfortable majority.

[38] The International Criminal Tribunal for the former Yugoslavia (ICTY), based in The Hague, made headlines around the world in June 2001, when it tried former Yugoslav president Slobodan Milosevic for crimes against humanity committed during the Balkans War (mid 1990s).

[39] In January 2002 the Netherlands adopted the euro as the official currency.

[40] That month, the Netherlands became the first country to legalize euthanasia (a partial regulation had been in place since 1993). The new law permits ending a person's life under strict criteria: he/she must be in

intolerable and constant pain, be of sound mind, and must have made repeated requests to be allowed to die; the doctor in charge has to obtain a second medical opinion. Finally, the death must occur in an appropriate medical way.

[41] The Government resigned on 16 April 2002 after admitting its responsibility for the Srebrenica massacre, during the war in Bosnia in 1995. The 7,600 page-long official report stated that Dutch security forces in the area - under UN command - failed to prevent the killing of 7,000 Bosnian Muslims by Bosnian Serbs. The victims were 'evacuated' from the UN security area by Dutch troops, which ultimately led to them being killed. The report also accused the UN of sending in the troops without a clear mandate or the weapons needed to defend the area. Dutch soldiers' use of force and weapons were limited to self-defense. The Government's resignation took place weeks before the Parliamentary elections set for 15 May.

[42] Far-right leader Pim Fortuyn was murdered in May 2002. However, the Dutch Government decided to go ahead with the elections as planned. Fortuyn, riding high in the polls, had recently declared that Holland should close its borders to immigrants and that Islam was a backward religion. His electoral proposals included laying off 25 per cent of civil servants. The murderer, who received a prison sentence, stated that his victim was a menace to democracy.

[43] On 15 May 2002 the Christian Democrats (CDA) won the parliamentary elections, winning 43 seats. Fortuyn's party - List Pim Fortuyn - came in second place, with 26 seats, and the People for Freedom and Democracy Party (VVD) came in third.

[44] In July 2002, Christian Democrat Jan Peter Balkenende (1959), an economist and devout Calvinist, became Prime Minister. He formed a coalition government with the three largest parties. However, in October the government coalition collapsed after in-fighting. General elections were set for January 2003.

[45] In the 22 January 2003 elections, the Christian Democrats obtained a majority of the vote, while the VVD and the Democrats 66 Party (conservative) came in second and third, respectively. The three parties formed a coalition government headed by Balkenende. The Prime Minister sought to reduce the fiscal deficit and unemployment by cutting state expenditure.

[45] In April 2004, more than 100 pictures that were first looted from Holland by the Nazis, who earmarked them for Hitler's private collection, and then in 1947, were stolen by the Red Army and taken to the former Soviet Union, were officially given back to the Netherlands by Ukrainian President Leonid Kuchma. The pictures had been stored in Kiev for more than 50 years and were presented to Dutch Prime Minister Balkenende at the Mariinsky Palace, in the Ukrainian capital. ∎

Netherlands Antilles / Nederlandse Antillen

Population:	224,407
Area:	800 km²
Capital:	Willemstad
Currency:	Netherlands Antillean guilder
Language:	Dutch

Both Caribs from the 'S' or 'Windward Islands' and Caiquetios (an Arawak nation and original inhabitants of what today are the islands of Aruba, Bonaire and Curaçao) were enslaved and taken to Hispaniola (present-day Haiti and Dominican Republic) by the end of the 19th century, soon after the arrival of Columbus in 1493 and then Alonso de Ojeda in 1499.

[2] Due to the lack of natural resources, only the Windward Islands (particularly Sint Maarten) acquired strategic importance as a port of entry into the Caribbean and also for salt extraction. Ports on the Iberian Peninsula were closed to Holland after the war with Spain and Portugal, so the Dutch were forced to seek alternative sources of salt in the Antilles.

[3] The traffic of Dutch ships was first repressed and then prohibited in 1606 by Spain. Holland created the West Indies Company to establish, manage and defend its colonies. The theft of Spanish ships and their cargoes became an important source of income.

[4] In 1634, the stockholders of the Company decided to invade Curaçao, which thus became a major international center of slave, salt and Brazilwood trading.

[5] In 1648, after three centuries of conflict, the Treaty of Westphalia granted Holland control over these islands. The native populations - particularly those of Curaçao and Bonaire - were replaced by African slaves

to meet the needs of new agricultural operations, and thus became a minority on these islands. Slave rebellions were frequent in the 18th century and unleashed bloody massacres at the hands of colonial troops.

[6] During the Napoleonic wars at the beginning of the 19th century, the islands passed into British hands for two brief periods. Although the slave trade had been prohibited in 1814, it was not abolished in the Dutch colonies until 1863. The lives of 'free' slaves did not change substantially. Many migrated to the Dominican Republic, Panama, Venezuela and Cuba.

[7] In 1876, the Dutch Parliament proposed selling the islands to Venezuela, but negotiations fell through. With the rise of the oil industry at the beginning of the 20th century, refineries were installed because of the proximity to Lake Maracaibo.

[8] This new activity began in the 1920s and radically changed the colony. It attracted thousands of immigrants from Venezuela, Suriname and the British West Indies and brought about the decline of agriculture. In the following decades, automation caused a significant reduction in the number of jobs.

[9] In 1937, political activity was launched when the first local parties were founded. However, it was not until 1948 that the new post-war Dutch Constitution renamed what had been known as Curaçao and dependencies as the Netherlands Antilles, thus bringing about the notion of statehood to the islands.

[10] The issue of independence has long been at the center of local political life. In 1954, a new law established the islands' autonomy over their internal affairs.

[11] On 30 May 1969, with unemployment at 20 per cent, a labor demonstration was broken up by the police, 300 Dutch marines and US marines from the American fleet, which happened to be anchored in the archipelago. As a result of these disturbances, Parliament was dissolved.

[12] The People's Electoral Movement (PEM), founded in 1971 in Aruba, proposed that since the islands had nothing in common (not even a name, because Antilles is the generic designation of the whole region), each island should be free to choose its own constitution and set itself up as an autonomous republic. In a referendum in 1977, the majority of Arubans voted in favor of separation from the other islands.

[13] The Netherlands argued that the federation would ensure

PROFILE

ENVIRONMENT
The Netherlands Antilles are made up of two Caribbean island groups. The main group is composed of Bonaire (288 sq km) and Curaçao (444 sq km). Located near the coast of Venezuela, they are known (together with Aruba) as the Dutch Leeward Islands or the ABC Islands. The smaller group is made up of three small islands of volcanic origin: Sint Eustatius (21 sq km), Saba (13 sq km) and Sint Maarten (34 sq km - the southern part of the island of St Martin which is a dependency of the French island of Guadeloupe). These are known as the S Islands or the Dutch Windward Islands, although in fact they are part of the Leeward group of the Lesser Antilles. In general the climate is tropical, moderated by ocean currents.

SOCIETY
Peoples: Most of the population descend from African slaves. There are also Carib Indians and descendants of Europeans and Asians.
Religions: Mainly Catholic; some Protestants, Jews, Seventh-Day Adventists.
Languages: Dutch (official). The most widely spoken language - in Curaçao and Bonaire - is Papiamento, a local dialect based on Spanish with elements of Dutch, Portuguese, English and some African languages. In St Eustatius, Saba and St Martin, English is the main language. Spanish is also spoken.

Main Political Parties: Workers' Liberation Front/Frente Obrero Liberashon (FOL); Antillean Restructuring Party (PAR); National People's Party (PNP); Labor Party People's Crusade (PLKP); New Antilles Movement (MAN); Democratic Party of Bonaire (PDB); Democratic Party of Curaçao (DP); Democratic Party of Sint Eustatius (DP-St E); Democratic Party of Sint Maarten (DP-St M); Patriotic Union of Bonaire (UPB). *Note:* political parties are indigenous to each island.
Main Social Organizations: National Confederation of Curaçao Trade Unions (AVVC); Central General Di Trahadonan di Corsow (CGTC); General Federation of Bonaire Workers (AFBW); Bonaire Labor Federation (FEDEBON).

THE STATE
Official Name: De Nederlandse Antillen
Capital: Willemstad 143,000 people (2003).
Other Cities: Kralendijk 7,900 people; Philipsburg 6,300 (2000). **Government:** Frits Goedgedrag, Governor since July 2002, appointed by the Dutch Government. Etienne Ys, Prime Minister since June 2004 (second term). Unicameral Legislature: the Staten (States), with 22 members elected every four years. The Netherlands Antilles are part of the Kingdom of the Netherlands, which handles its foreign relations. It has autonomy in internal affairs. **National Holiday:** 30 May, Anti-colonial Movement (1969). **Armed Forces:** The Dutch Crown is responsible for defense.

WORKERS

UNEMPLOYMENT: 14.0% (2002)

LABOR FORCE   **2002**

■ FEMALE: 42.8%   ■ MALE: 57.2%

better economic prospects and political stability. The differences of opinion, also held among islanders themselves, delayed negotiations.

[14]   The delay radicalized the electorate and in 1979 the New Antilles Movement (MAN) achieved a parliamentary majority in Curaçao (7 out of 12 seats). In coalition with the PEM and the UPB (Bonaire Patriotic Union) it formed the first left-of-center government in the islands. The MAN favored a federal formula with considerable autonomy for each of the islands but the PEM insisted on the total separation of Aruba.

[15]   In 1980 it was agreed to set independence for 1990, on condition that each of the six islands submitted the issue to a referendum as soon as possible. Aruba chose to become an individual associated state, breaking away from the federation in January 1986 (see Aruba).

[16]   The Netherlands Antilles became modern trading posts, totally dependent on transnational oil companies, which maintained a monopoly on all oil refining and processing. Exxon and Royal Dutch Shell (an Anglo-Dutch consortium), linked financially and commercially to branches of approximately 2,500 foreign firms registered on the islands, managed to have virtual decision-making authority over 85 per cent of the total imports, 99 per cent of the exports and 50 per cent of the islands' net income.

[17]   At the end of 1984, the announcement that transnational oil companies were withdrawing from the islands spread panic among the people and local political leaders.

[18]   The conflict was partially resolved in October 1985 when the Antilles Government purchased the Curaçao refinery and in turn rented it to Petróleos de Venezuela SA. The deal did not include the Exxon plant on Aruba, which closed down.

[19]   The separation of Aruba favored the 1984 victory of a right-of-center coalition headed by María Liberia Peters of the National People's Party (PNP). This coalition was unable to sustain the minimum consensus necessary to stay in power. Therefore in January 1986, MAN leader, Domenico Martina, became Prime Minister once again. In 1988, María Liberia Peters returned to power.

[20]   In 1990, the Government renewed its contracts with the Venezuelan oil company and introduced a series of austerity

IN FOCUS

ENVIRONMENTAL CHALLENGES
There is little farming; however, a large Venezuelan oil refinery is located on Curaçao. The coastal areas of the islands have suffered the consequences of economic development. The soil has been polluted, and waste disposal is a serious problem due to the lack of proper facilities. Projects for the construction of landfill sites were developed but could not be implemented because of insufficient funding. Curaçao is the most polluted of the islands.

WOMEN'S RIGHTS
Although the islands depend on the Netherlands in several respects, the population elects its own Parliament every four years. Women have been able to vote and stand for office since 1954.

In 1995, 10.9 per cent of women over 15 were illiterate. The difference in educational levels between men and women increases among the oldest sectors of the population.

In 1995, unemployment among women in Curaçao reached 17 per cent while among men it stood at 9.8 per cent.

In 1994, there were 1,144 women registered in the peri-natal information system (37 per cent of all births). Only 25 per cent of prenatal visits were made before the 20th week of

pregnancy and 52 per cent of women began prenatal care in the third trimester. Ninety-nine per cent of births took place in clinics or hospitals.

From 1985 to 1996, 815 HIV/AIDS cases were registered in the islands: 466 (57.2 per cent) were men and 349 (42.8 per cent) were women. More than two-thirds of people living with HIV/AIDS were between 25 and 44 years old and 97.5 per cent of cases were registered in Curaçao and St. Martin. Mother-to-child-transmission affects newborns, while in the 25 to 44 age group transmission was mainly through sex. In Curaçao between 1991 and 1993, AIDS was one of the leading causes of death in the 25 to 44 age group (14 per cent of deaths).

CHILDREN
School attendance is mandatory for children between 6 and 15 years old.

Child labor is prohibited by law for children under 14 with the two following exceptions: when they work in or for the benefit of the family in which they are being raised and in schools, provided these activities are of an educational nature and are not intended to generate a profit. The work should not be physically or mentally demanding or dangerous for the child. Children between 14 and 18 years old should not engage in night work or in work of a dangerous nature (including the risk of

death, injuries and other dangers to health).

INDIGENOUS PEOPLES/ETHNIC MINORITIES
The Arawaks were the first inhabitants in the area. About 85 per cent of Curaçao's population is of African descent. The rest of the population is made up of a mixture of Dutch, Portuguese, North Americans and natives from other Caribbean islands. The major religions include Anglican, Muslim, Protestant, Mormon and Baptist. The Jewish community is one of the oldest in the region, dating back to 1634.

MIGRANTS/REFUGEES
Although refugees should receive the same treatment as in the Netherlands, the problems are not the same. In March 2004, after being held in custody for nearly a year, five Cuban refugees were released and given permission to live on the island while authorities consider their request for political asylum.

It is estimated that 5 per cent of the island's population emigrated in recent years due to economic difficulties. The main country of destination was the Netherlands.

DEATH PENALTY
As in the Netherlands, the death penalty for all crimes was abolished in 1982.

measures designed to cover the deficit generated by the Aruban withdrawal from the federation.

[21]   In the general elections of March 1990, the PNP won seven seats while the MAN of Martina won only two. Peters was re-elected as Prime Minister.

[22]   The election of the Island Councils in 1991 was marked by the defeat of the Democratic Party, which had been in power for 40 years in Sint Maarten (Windward Islands group), as a result of internal divisions, financial irregularities committed by the administration and the fear of a downfall in the tourism boom.

[23]   The Netherlands requested that each island made a separate proposal for constitutional reform in 1993. Accordingly, Curaçao received special status, Sint Maarten was made independent, while Bonaire, Saba and Sint Eustatius continued under Dutch control. The

constitution also dictated that the Treaty of Strasburg, which predicted complete independence for 1999, would not be applied in the islands. A referendum carried out in 1994 supported the continuation of the Federation.

[24]   In 1995 the Netherlands Antilles, with 233 AIDS cases, had the eighth highest infection rate of the 43 Latin American countries. The average rate for the region was 16 cases, while in the Netherlands Antilles it was 117.

[25]   In November 1999, Miguel Pourier was elected Prime Minister for the third time.

[26]   The Netherlands announced a contribution equivalent to $6.24 million to subsidize the tourism industry, which suffered from the reduced air travel in the wake of the 11 September 2001 terrorist attacks in New York. The tax reduction measures proposed by the local government had proved insufficient to boost

tourism, which led to the closing of hotels in the off-season.

[27]   The parliamentary elections of January 2002, were won by the Workers' Liberation Front 30th of May with 23 per cent of the vote, while Prime Minister Pourier's party received 20 per cent of votes.

[28]   In the Curaçao Island Council elections of May 2002, the Party for the Restructured Antilles did not obtain the necessary votes, forcing Etienne Ys to resign as Prime Minister. Mirna Louisa-Godett was appointed in his place, taking over from Ben Komproe who had served as interim Prime Minister.

[29]   In March 2004, the Government began to analyze recommendations made by public health experts to develop a plan to solve problems in this area. The restructuring project aimed at saving 25 million Dutch florins per year and a significant reduction of healthcare costs. ■

New Zealand/Aotearoa
New Zealand/Aotearoa

Population:	3,931,823
Area:	270,530 km²
Capital:	Wellington
Currency:	NZ dollar
Language:	English and Maori

A otearoa, 'the land of the long white cloud', was settled around the 9th century by Maori, who were thought to have arrived there from Polynesia. Maori themselves speak of the arrival of *waka hourua* (voyaging canoes) from the legendary island of Hawaiki (see box 'Melanesians and Polynesians: surviving cultures'). Over the years a distinct culture developed, based on tribal organization and a strong affinity with the land. Maoris saw themselves as guardians of the land for future generations.

² In 1642 Abel Tasman, from Holland, reached the South Island, the larger of Aotearoa's two main islands. However, a misunderstanding with the indigenous population prevented him from going ashore. It was not until 1769 that James Cook from England surveyed the shores of the two larger islands. This opened the door for a growing colonization of the country that Tasman had named 'New Zealand'. The French also took an interest in this new land and set about purchasing land parcels most notably in an area called Akaroa, a

small peninsula on the north-east coast of the South Island. In response, the British signed a 'Declaration of Independence' with 34 northern Maori tribes in 1835, thus declaring New Zealand an independent state under British rule. In response to increasing lawlessness, however, the Treaty of Waitangi was created and New Zealand was formerly annexed by the British Crown as a colony in 1840.

³ In the early 19th century, colonization increased with the arrival of British immigrants and

missionaries. They brought with them new diseases, values and beliefs, which affected the traditional Maori way of life. Trading with settlers initially brought wealth to many Maori communities, but these gains were reversed with interest once the settlers began to alienate significant amounts of Maori land.

⁴ In 1840 the territory of New Zealand was formally annexed by the British crown as a colony. The two larger islands were occupied under different legal arrangements:

the South Island was incorporated by virtue of the right of 'discovery', and the North Island through the Treaty of Waitangi, signed in 1840 by Maori chiefs and representatives of the British Government. According to the text of the treaty - which is different in its English and Maori versions - Maori chiefs accepted the presence of British settlers and the establishment of a government by the Crown to rule the settlers. In exchange, Maori were assured absolute respect for their national sovereignty.

⁵ However, once the Treaty was signed, an extremely violent process of expropriation of Maori lands began. The so-called 'land wars' between Maori and the Europeans were essentially for sovereignty and guaranteed rights to the lands, forests, fisheries and other *taonga* (treasures).

⁶ Massive immigration, land confiscation and legal decisions led to the gradual annexation of Maori land, to the extent that out of the 27 million hectares they owned in 1840, they now have a little over a million left.

⁷ While the north of the country was involved in a series of wars, the South Island settlers went through a period of prosperity because of the discovery of gold. This discovery brought a massive flow of British, Chinese and Australian immigrants, which energized the region's economy.

⁸ After 1840 colonization increased. The Päkehä (non-Maori) usurped the right to fish in the area, thus depriving Maori of one of their main activities. For the Maori, British dominance threatened their cultural extinction, due to the arbitrary imposition of European language, religion and costumes.

⁹ Maori opposition found new expression by the end of the 19th century. They organized petitions, delegations and submitted their claims before local courts and even before the British Crown itself, demanding compliance with the Treaty of Waitangi. These efforts were fruitless. The lands that had once belonged to Maori were now used for farming, which had started to play a central role not only in the life of the settlers but also in the whole economy. New markets for dairy and meat products opened up in the 1880s, with the appearance of cold-storage systems, which made long-distance shipping possible. The rising price of these products constituted the basis of the country's economic development.

¹⁰ By the end of the century, the country's political scene was dominated by the Liberal government. They were the first in the world to grant the vote to women in 1893 and to establish measures to protect the rights of

PROFILE

ENVIRONMENT
New Zealand/Aotearoa is situated in Oceania. Its two principal islands are mountainous. The North Island is volcanic and has plateaus and geysers. The South Island is crossed by the Southern Alps, a mountain chain with peaks of over 3,000 meters. The climate is moderately rainy, with temperatures cooler in the south. The economic base of the country is agricultural, however, tourism is becoming increasingly important.

SOCIETY
Peoples: Most of the population is descended from European settlers (80 per cent). Maori (14 per cent), and Polynesians from other Pacific Islands (6 per cent). **Religions:** Anglican and other Protestant denominations dominate. There are also Catholic, Muslim and various Maori church minorities. **Languages:** English and Maori are the official languages, with English dominant. **Main Political Parties:** A multi-party system, based since 1996 on a mixed-member proportional representation voting system. Parties in government

include Labour, National, New Zealand First, United Future New Zealand, Green Party, ACT and Progressive Coalition. **Main Social Organizations:** The Trade Union Federation and the Council of Trade Unions (CTU), and several Maori organizations.

THE STATE
Official Name: New Zealand (English); Aotearoa (Maori). **Administrative Divisions:** Divided into 15 town and 58 district authorities. **Capital:** Wellington 343,000 people (2003). **Other Cities:** Auckland 1,120,000 people; Christchurch 344,000; Dunedin 111,400; Hamilton 172,400; Palmerston North 75,700 (2002). **Government:** A parliamentary monarchy and member of the British Commonwealth. Governor-General: Silvia Cartwright since 4 April 2001. Helen Clark, Prime Minister and Head of Government since 1999, re-elected in 2002. New Zealand/Aotearoa has a parliamentary system, with a unicameral legislative body of 120 members. **National Holiday:** 6 February, Waitangi Day (1840). **Armed Forces:** 9,870 (2001). Dependencies: Cook Islands, Niue, Tokelau.

Life expectancy
78.3 years
2000-2005

GNI per capita
$13,710
2002

HIV prevalence rate
0.1% of population
15-49 years old
2001

industrial workers, a group which was growing parallel to the development of cities and manufacturing industries.

[11] Until the 20th century there were no political movements to oppose the power of the Liberals who had become a coherent, organized political party after 20 years in power. The Labour Party (LP), with ample working-class and urban middle-class support, came to power for the first time in 1935. The Party also enjoyed the support of Maori even though there was still no legislative recognition of the Treaty of Waitangi.

[12] World War II marked the beginning of a new era for the country, for during that time Britain was unable to guarantee the security of its former colony. This led to closer ties between New Zealand/Aotearoa and the US. Through a series of political and military alliances, US presence was consolidated in the region. In the 1950s and 1960s New Zealand had to pay the price for this relationship, particularly when it found itself involved in the Vietnam War, a conflict that touched the political life of the country very deeply.

[13] Legislation in the 1950s forced many Maori from their land and the 1960s saw their increasing urbanization.

[14] In the 1970s, New Zealand/Aotearoa tried to diversify its production and to enter markets other than the UK and the US. Unemployment rose and inflation reached unprecedented levels due to the failure of the diversification scheme, the rise in the price of oil and financial loans. The year 1975 saw a drastic fall in the purchasing power earned from primary exports. This fall, combined with the foreign loans, increased foreign debt. That year the new National Party (NP) Government closed the doors on immigrants, mainly from the Pacific, whom it blamed for increasing unemployment.

[15] In 1975, growing Maori activism led to the formation of the Waitangi Tribunal to investigate Treaty claims. In 1986 the Labour Government gave it the power to hear claims dating back to the 1840 signing. The Tribunal had no binding powers over the Crown, and by 1992 less than 15 per cent of the recommendations had been implemented.

[16] During the 1980s, the Labour Government introduced a monetarist economic policy, which included the privatization of some public enterprises. These policies alienated many traditional Labour supporters and between1986 to 1999, Aotearoa was an international showcase for neo-liberalism. Public spending was slashed and labor laws restricted trade union activity.

IN FOCUS

ENVIRONMENTAL CHALLENGES
The country faces problems such as deforestation and erosion but also the disappearance of autochthonous flora and fauna species, which were affected by foreign species introduced by the European settlers. The tropical rainforest was devastated by settlers so as to create arable land and pastures. More recently there have been campaigns against nuclear experiments and against genetic engineering in agriculture.

WOMEN'S RIGHTS
New Zealand/Aotearoa was a pioneer in women's suffrage: women have voted since 1893 and been able to stand for election since 1919. However, universal representation is still an object of debate, and in several legislative reforms carried out since then (the last of which took place in the 1990s) a more representative participation of the different ethnic groups has been promoted. In 2002 women occupied 30.8 per cent of parliamentary seats and 18.7 per cent of ministerial offices or equivalents. Women have held the offices of Prime Minister and Governor-General since 1999 and 2001 respectively.

In the 2001 election, women voters outnumbered men by a ratio of 105 to 100. Though in 2001 women represented more than half of the labor force, they earned half what men did.

CHILDREN
In 2002 Maori children amounted to a quarter of the total number of minors in Aotearoa.

One third of infant deaths are caused by Sudden Infant Death Syndrome; in 59 per cent of the cases the mother and/or father is a smoker. In 1998, 2.2 out of 1,000 Maori children and 0.7 non-Maori children died because of this.

INDIGENOUS PEOPLES/ ETHNIC MINORITIES
Maori have inhabited the land they call Aotearoa for more than a thousand years. Tuberculosis, typhoid fever, chickenpox and other diseases unknown to the Maori, together with the introduction of firearms and the constant inter-tribal wars and wars against Europeans led to a significant decrease in their population (there were estimated to be a million Maori in 1800).

In 2002 Maori or their descendants accounted for 16 per cent of the population (597,800 people) and their birth rate is higher than that of people of European origin, but they suffer disproportionately from poverty and unemployment. Some of their current claims are: the creation of an independent Maori state, more participation in the government, protection of Maori land in particular, ownership of the foreshore, fisheries and other *taonga*, and increased promotion of their culture and their language.

MIGRANTS/REFUGEES
The conditions required by those who want to obtain asylum or refugee status in New Zealand/Aotearoa are not very flexible. In 2000, only 311 people were granted the status of refugee out of 2,350 cases considered (13.2 per cent). In 2002 the majority of the aspiring refugees were Thai, Indian and Iranian. The highest number of rejections was met by Thai, Indian and Sri Lankan refugees.

DEATH PENALTY
This was abolished in 1989; the last execution occurred in 1957.

[17] In 1987, New Zealand's nuclear-free status became law, prohibiting the entry of nuclear arms or vessels to the nation's ports, thus questioning the military presence of France and the United States, who used the South Pacific as a nuclear weapons testing ground. This decision suspended indefinitely the 1951 defense treaties between the US, New Zealand/Aotearoa and Australia (ANZUS) although no formal dissolution has ever been announced.

[18] The National Party won the October 1990 elections, but the change in administration did not affect the New Zealand economy. There was an increase in privatizations, protectionism was dismantled even further, and there were large cutbacks in health, education and social benefits. The result was falling inflation, but unemployment also rose. In 1994, New Zealand achieved its first budget surplus in 17 years, the currency became more robust, unemployment fell and inflation settled at 2 per cent.

[19] Between 1994 and 1995 the Goverment compensated Tainui iwi in the North Island both with money and 15,400 hectares of land, for their claims over land colonized in the previous century. Even Britain's Queen Elizabeth apologized for the loss of life during the colonization of

the islands and in 1996 the Crown compensated the major South Island Iwi, Ngai Tahu, with another substantial compensation amount and the return of the lost land.

[20] In 1996 Prime Minister Jim Bolger (leader of the National Party) opposed the atomic tests carried out by France on the Mururoa atoll, responding to the electorate's concerns about peace and the preservation of the environment. He secured another term in Parliament although he was replaced in late1997 by his deputy, Jenny Shipley, who became New Zealand's first female Prime Minister. That same year the first parliament elected by proportional representation increased the number of Maori and female representatives. In 1999 parliament included 16 Maori deputies, 2 gay activists, as well as 35 women with Helen Clark and Shipley occupying the seats of Prime Minister and Leader of the opposition respectively.

[21] In April 2000 the new Labour Government, led by Helen Clark, announced that the titles of Sir and Dame, issued by the British Crown, would no longer be used but would be replaced by titles unique to New Zealand/Aotearoa.

[22] Also that year, to the alarm of consumers, environmentalist and Maori groups, which had organized a campaign to declare the country 'free from genetic engineering', the

Royal Commission on Genetic Modification issued a report supporting the development and use of genetically modified organisms. To placate public concerns, the Government placed a moratorium on unauthorized GM field trials until October 2003.

[23] Queen Elizabeth II visited New Zealand, commemorating her Golden Jubilee. Prime Minister Helen Clark said at the time that it was 'inevitable that New Zealand shall become a republic and that this would reflect the reality that New Zealand is a 21st century state, completely sovereign and 20,000 kilometers away from the United Kingdom'.

[24] In July, during the celebrations of the 40 years of Papua New Guinea's independence, the Prime Minister formally apologized for the treatment Papuans received from New Zealanders during the colonial period.

[25] Clark was elected in July 2002 for a second term of office albeit needing to form a coalition with the center right party, United Future New Zealand, and the support of the Green Party. This election resulted in turmoil for National Party, however, in that this was the worst electoral showing in its 70 years and a debate would ensue over its right to occupy the opposition front bench in Parliament. The Greens called for them to step down and share space with the other opposition parties.

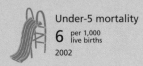
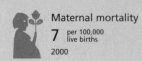
[26] In 1983 New Zealand and Australia signed an agreement to establish Closer Economic Relations (CER), and although still participating in a 'close' relationship, the country has increased its economic participation in Asia, particularly with the flourishing Asian economies. New Zealand/Aotearoa is a 'dialogue partner' of the Association of Southeast Asian Nations (ASEAN) and is an active participant in APEC (Asia-Pacific Economic Co-operation).

[27] The central issues of public debate in the early 2000s were alternative methods of energy generation, genetic engeneering, unemployment, resources for education, what to do with violent and repeat offenders, child abuse, land ownership, access to health services and immigration.

[28] In 2003, the National Commission of Human Rights carried out a study claiming that 70 per cent of New Zealanders have discriminated against Asian immigrants. According to the official estimates, since 1980 more than 200,000 Asian immigrants have arrived in the country, and by the year 2021 more than 13 per cent of the population will have Asian origins. Asians find it extremely difficult to get a job, even those well qualified. In August 2003, the Race Relations Commissioner, Joris de Bres, said that the growth of Asian immigrants was very similar to the growth of Pacific islanders that took place in the 1970s. According to de Bres, discrimination in the early 21st century was now primarily directed at Asians. ■

Niue

Population: 1,896
Area: 260 km²
Capital: Alofi
Currency: NZ dollar
Language: English

N iue was settled by Samoans and Tongans. Captain James Cook named it 'Savage Island' when he visited it in 1774. The indigenous peoples' reputation for fierceness kept missionaries away (the island's first permanent mission dates from 1861), and also the slave traders who caused much suffering in other areas of the Pacific. Emigration to the phosphate mines on other islands in the area initiated an outflow that has continued ever since. In 1900 the island was declared a British protectorate and was annexed by New Zealand/Aotearoa in 1901. It was administered along with the Cook Islands until 1904, when it separated to form a separate possession. In 1974 it became an Autonomous Associated State of New Zealand/Aotearoa. The United Nations recognized this as a legitimate decision and eliminated the 'Niue case' from the Decolonization Committee agenda. As well as economic support from New Zealand, Niue also received help with defense and international affairs.

[2] In 1991, Aotearoa announced a reduction of financial aid. Niue and Australia established diplomatic links during 1992.

[3] In 1999 Niue requested entry to the United Nations Food and Agriculture Organization (FAO).

[4] As had happened before the elections, the Legislative Assembly was dissolved in 2002 and the country was administered by members of the cabinet. Elections were held on 20 April, with Lakatani's Niue People's Action Party winning. In May, Young Vivian became the new premier.

[5] In January 2004 Cyclone Heta - with winds of up to 300km/h - killed at least one person and left 200 people homeless. ■

ENVIRONMENT
Located in the South Pacific in southern Polynesia, 2,300 km north-east of New Zealand/Aotearoa, west of the Cook Islands and east of the Tonga archipelago. Of coral origin, the island is flat and the soil relatively fertile. Its rainy, tropical climate is tempered by sea winds.

SOCIETY
Peoples: The people of Niue are of Polynesian origin.
Religions: Protestant. **Languages:** English (official), local Niue language (national). **Main Political Parties:** Niue People's Party (NPP); Niue People's Action Party (NPAP).

THE STATE
Official Name: Niue. **Capital:** Alofi 1,000 people (2003).
Government: Autonomous associated state. Sandra Lee, Representative of New Zealand since February 2003. Young Vivian, Prime Minister since April 2002. Single-chamber legislature: there is a 20-member Legislative Assembly which is headed by the Prime Minister. New Zealand/Aotearoa controls defense and foreign affairs.
National Holiday: 6 February, Waitangi Day (1840).
Armed Forces: New Zealand/Aotearoa is responsible for the island's defense.

Cook Islands

Population: 18,474
Area: 236 km²
Capital: Avarua
Currency: NZ dollar
Language: English

T he islands, which had already been explored and settled by Polynesians and Spaniards, received their name from the English navigator Captain James Cook , who drew up the first map of the archipelago in 1770.

[2] In 1821, Tahitian missionaries were sent to the islands by the London Missionary Society; a Protestant theocracy was established and all 'pagan' structures were destroyed, as were many of the traditional forms of social organization. The islands were declared a British Protectorate in 1888 and became part of New Zealand/Aotearoa in 1901. The land rights of the indigenous Maori were recognized, and the sale of real estate to foreigners was prohibited. In 1965, the United Nations promoted and supervised a plebiscite, and the population voted against independence, and in favor of maintaining its ties to New Zealand.

[3] Prime Minister Geoffrey Henry governed the country with an iron hand for 15 years before being replaced in 1978 by Thomas Davis, of the Democratic Party (DP), who gave incentives to private fruit exporters. However he was dismissed from office by Parliament in 1987, being replaced by Pupuke Robati, also of the DP. In the 1990 elections, Geoffrey Henry's Cook Islands Party was returned to office, and re-elected in 1994.

[4] The islands' government created a whale sanctuary in 2001, the largest declared by a country in waters of its jurisdiction, to protect these sea mammals from being hunted to extinction.

[7] Tourism provides half of the GDP. The Cook Islands have a ratio of seven tourists per every local islander. ■

ENVIRONMENT
Area: 236.6 sq km. Archipelago located in the South Pacific 2,700 km northeast of New Zealand/Aotearoa, made up of 15 islands which extend over an ocean area of 2 million sq km. They are divided into 2 groups. The northern group is made up of 6 small coral atolls, which are low and arid, with a total area of 25.5 sq km. The southern group comprises 8 larger and more fertile volcanic islands (211 sq km). The capital, Avarua, is located on Rarotonga, the largest of the islands. Every 5 years, for the past 2 decades, the islands have suffered terrible droughts.

SOCIETY
Peoples: The majority of the population is Maori. There are also some Europeans (2.4 per cent). **Religions:** Christian (Cook Islands Church).
Languages: English (official), Cook Island Maori. Language and traditions similar to Maori in New Zealand.
Main Political Parties: Democratic Alliance (DA); The Cook Islands Party (CIP); New Alliance (NA).

THE STATE
Official Name: The Cook Islands. **Capital:** Avarua 13,000 people (2003).
Government: Autonomous associated state. Apenera Short, Representative of Aotearoa. Terepai Moate, Prime Minister since January 1991. Single-chamber legislature; there is a Legislative Assembly, with 25 members elected by direct vote every five years.

Tokelau / Tokelau Islands

Population:	1,521
Area:	12 km²
Capital:	Fakaofo
Currency:	NZ dollar
Language:	Tokelauan

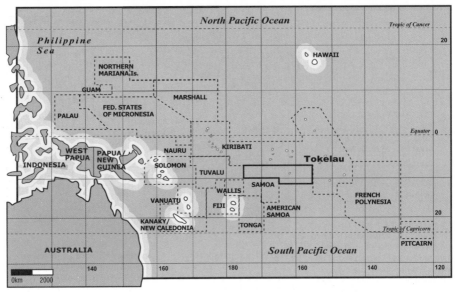

Polynesian peoples arrived in Tokelau around the 9th century, developing a tribal culture in harmony with the land. They called themselves 'land guardians for the future'.

2 English explorer John Byron arrived in 1765. Due to the absence of great riches the islands became a British protectorate only in 1877 and were annexed in 1916, included as part of the colonial territory of the Gilbert and Ellice Islands (now Kiribati and Tuvalu). In 1925, Britain transferred administrative control of the islands to New Zealand/Aotearoa. In 1946, the group was officially designated the Tokelau Islands, and in 1958 full sovereignty passed to New Zealand.

3 New Zealand/Aotearoa adopted policies intended to maintain traditional customs, institutions and communal relations in Tokelau. Until 1990 there was only a single ship calling at the islands from Apia (Samoa) every two or three months. There are no adequate harbors for the development of tourism.

4 In the 1980s, farming underwent a crisis due to a number of adverse climatic conditions. Emigration to New Zealand/Aotearoa and Samoa rose considerably. The New Zealand Government tried to encourage Tokelau immigrants to return to their homeland, but without success.

5 In 1976 and 1981, UN envoys to Tokelau reported that the inhabitants of the islands did not wish to change their relations with New Zealand/Aotearoa. In December 1984, the UN Assembly decided that New Zealand, as administrating power, should report on its management, butcontinue to administer the islands. However, before the UN Special Committee in June 1987, Tokelau expressed a wish to achieve greater political autonomy.

6 A UN report on the consequences of the greenhouse effect included Tokelau among the islands which could disappear under the sea in the 21st century.

7 In February 1990, the country was devastated by Hurricane Ofa, which destroyed all the banana trees and 80 per cent of the coconut plantations, as well as hospitals, schools, houses, and bridges. As a result, emigration increased.

8 In 1991 the first regular maritime transport service was established between the three atolls.

9 In May 1995, the New Zealand Parliament approved extended powers for the local assembly. The satellite telephone system arrived in 1997.

10 New Zealand Official Development Aid (NZODA) set aside a budget of NZ$7.5 million for Tokelau in 2000.

11 The Minister of Pacific Islands from New Zealand/Aotearoa implemented support programs in policy management and development in 2001, to help Tokelau initiate self-rule.

12 Between 2002 and 2003 the budget included additional funds for the construction of the future government buildings.

13 Australia has also maintained co-operation agreements with the islands. During 2002 and 2003, Australian funds were granted for education in Tokelau, as aid for students in the territory, or as scholarships within Australia.

14 With the assistance provided by the Secretariat of the Pacific Community (SPC) and the Government of Samoa, Tokelau started to develop a community-based fisheries management plan which included the three atolls: Fakaofo, Nukunonu and Atafu.

15 The SPC and the Samoa Fisheries Department were in charge of training each community. The atolls still have traditional laws for the preservation of the sea coast and species for the next generations. The scientific methods of this plan would help communities to maximize the traditional institutions, knowledge and fisheries regulatory measures. A key aspect of this plan was the support provided to communities regarding the planning, monitoring and evaluation of the different stages of the project. The management plans were even translated into Tokelauan in order to succeed in approaching communities. ■

PROFILE

ENVIRONMENT
A group of coral islands, comprising three atolls: Atafu 2.02 sq km and 577 people, Nakunono 5.46 sq km and 374 people, Fakaofo 2.63 sq km and 664 people. Geographically, Sivains atoll belongs to the group but is an administrative dependency of American Samoa. The group is located in Polynesia in the South Pacific, to the east of the Tuvalu islands. The islands are flat, with thin, not very fertile soil. Rainfall is erratic and there are frequent droughts. Fishing constitutes the traditional economic activity.

SOCIETY
Peoples: The population is of Polynesian origin.
Religions: Mostly Protestant, 70 per cent.
Languages: Tokelauan (official), English and local dialects.
Main Political Parties: there are no political parties.

THE STATE
Official Name: Tokelau.
Capital: Fakaofo 540 people (1999).
Other Cities: Fenua Fala, and small villages on every island.
Government: All executive and administrative functions are in theory vested in the Administrator of Tokelau, responsible to the New Zealand Minister of Foreign Affairs and Trade. In 1994 these powers were formally delegated to Tokelau's Fono (Parliament with 45 members, representing the three atolls), or to the Council of Faipule (cabinet) when the Fono is not in session. In 1996 the New Zealand Parliament amended the 1948 Act to confer limited legislative power on the Fono, giving Tokelau in practice, and in large measure, administrative and political autonomy. Kolouei O'Brien, Head of Government since 2003. Neil Walter, Administrator since 2002.
National Holiday: 6 February, Waitangi Day (1840).
Armed Forces: Defense is the responsibility of New Zealand.

Nicaragua / Nicaragua

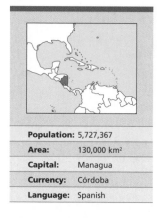

Population:	5,727,367
Area:	130,000 km²
Capital:	Managua
Currency:	Córdoba
Language:	Spanish

Present-day Nicaragua was once a region of influence of the two great Central American cultures: the Chibcha (see Colombia) and the Maya. The Caribbean coast was inhabited by the Miskito, originally called 'Kiribi' - the oldest peoples in Nicaragua - and was visited by Christopher Columbus in 1502. By converting local leaders Nicoya and Nicarao to Christianity and crushing the resistance of Diriangen's armies, the conquistadors Gil Gonzales Dávila and Andrés Nino consolidated Spain's hold over the territory. In 1544 it was incorporated into the Captaincy-General of Guatemala.

² In 1821 Nicaragua became independent, together with the rest of Central America, joining the Mexican Empire. It withdrew in 1824 to form the Federation of the United Provinces of the Center of America.

³ Nicaragua left the Federation in 1839, declaring itself an independent state. The country was divided between two groups: the coffee and sugar oligarchies, and the artisans and small landowners. The former would become the conservatives, and the latter, the liberals who favored free trade.

⁴ In 1856, 120 soldiers landed in Nicaragua under the command of William Walker, an American mercenary. With Washington's tacit support, he proclaimed himself President of Nicaragua. His purpose

was to find new territories for slavery which was on the point of being abolished in the Union. Walker was defeated by the allied armies of Central America in 1857, and later executed. Nicaragua's ports were occupied by Germany in 1875 and Britain in 1895. Britain commandeered Nicaragua's Customs in order to collect on unpaid debts.

⁵ After 30 years of conservative rule the Liberal Party came to power in 1893, and José Santos Zelaya became President. The liberals refused to comply with demands made by the United States, as part of the 'dollar diplomacy' approach adopted by William M Taft's administration. In 1912, Taft sent in US Marines who killed the Liberal Party leader, Benjamín Zeledón, and remained in Nicaragua until 1925. In 1926 they returned to protect President Adolfo Díaz, who was about to be overthrown.

⁶ This second US occupation was resisted by Augusto C Sandino, who raised and commanded a popular army of about 3,000 troops. For more than six years they held out against 12,000 US marines who were supported by the airforce and ground troops of the local oligarchy. Sandino promised that he would lay down arms when the last

marine left Nicaragua. He carried out his promise in 1933, but was assassinated by US-backed Anastasio Somoza García who, after seizing power, ruled despotically until he was killed by the patriot Rigoberto López Pérez in 1956.

⁷ During two decades of dictatorship, Somoza had achieved almost absolute control of the nation's economy. He was succeeded by his son, engineer Luis Somoza Debayle, who in turn handed the Government on to his son, Anastasio, a West Point graduate.

⁸ Anastasio Somoza outlawed all trade unions, massacred members of peasant movements and banned all opposition parties. In the 1960s the Sandinista National Liberation Front (FSLN) was founded. This organized and developed the guerrilla warfare which lasted for 17 years. When opposition leader Pedro Joaquín Chamorro, editor of the daily *La Prensa*, was assassinated on Somoza's orders in January 1978, a nationwide strike was called and there were massive protest demonstrations.

⁹ By March 1979, the Sandinista Front had united its three factions and formed the 'Patriotic Front'. In May 1979 the Front launched the 'final offensive', combining a general strike, a popular uprising, armed combat, and intense diplomatic activity abroad. On 17 July Somoza fled the country, bringing to an end a dynasty that had killed 50,000 people. The Junta for National Reconstruction,

created a few weeks before in Costa Rica, was installed in Managua two days later.

¹⁰ The victorious revolutionaries nationalized Somoza's lands and industrial properties, which constituted 40 per cent of the economic resources of Nicaragua. They also replaced the defeated National Guard with the Sandinista Popular Army. The revolutionary government implemented a literacy campaign and began reconstruction of the devastated economy.

¹¹ In May 1980 two non-Sandinista members of the Junta, Violeta Barrios de Chamorro and Alfonso Robelo, resigned. The Government avoided a crisis by replacing them with Rafael Córdoba and Arturo Cruz, two 'moderate' anti-Somoza activists. The FSLN confirmed it would rule in a context of democratic participation, a non-aligned foreign policy and with respect for civil liberties.

¹² In 1981, US President Ronald Reagan announced his aim of destroying the Sandinistas. Between April and July 1982 deputy interior minister Edén Pastora ('Commander Zero') deserted, and 2,500 former National Guards, supported by the US, invaded Nicaragua from Honduras. From then on Nicaragua was harassed without respite, forcing the authorities to extend the state of emergency, to institute compulsory military service and to ban pro-American political declarations.

¹³ In 1983, President Reagan admitted the existence of secret funds destined for covert CIA operations against Nicaragua. The funds were also used to aid counter-revolutionaries or contras operating from Honduran territory. Reagan referred to the contras as 'freedom fighters'.

¹⁴ Concerned at the serious threat of a war that might escalate throughout Central America, the governments of Colombia, Mexico, Panama and Venezuela sought a negotiated settlement to the conflict. As the 'Contadora Group', these countries' foreign ministers advanced peace plans which won great diplomatic support and prevented an invasion by US forces.

¹⁵ Contra attacks intensified steadily with open US backing. Elections were held in November 1984. Candidates were drawn from the FSLN, the Democratic Conservative Party, the Independent Liberal Party, the Popular Social Christian Party, the Communist Party, the Socialist Party and the Marxist-Leninist People's Action Movement. Over 80 per cent of Nicaragua's 1.5 million registered voters went to the polls and the FSLN obtained 67 per cent

LAND USE

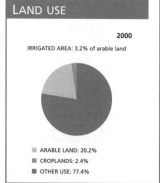

2000

IRRIGATED AREA: 3.2% of arable land

- ARABLE LAND: 20.2%
- CROPLANDS: 2.4%
- OTHER USE: 77.4%

PUBLIC EXPENDITURE

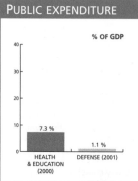

% OF GDP

7.3 %
HEALTH & EDUCATION (2000)

1.1 %
DEFENSE (2001)

WORKERS

UNEMPLOYMENT: 12.2% (2002)

LABOR FORCE   **2002**

- FEMALE: 36.6%
- MALE: 63.4%

Life expectancy
69.5 years
2000-2005

GNI per capita
$370
2002

Literacy
64% total adult rate
2000

HIV prevalence rate
0.2% of population 15-49 years old
2001

of the vote. In November Reagan was re-elected and in April 1985 he declared a trade embargo against Nicaragua and seized its assets.

16   A new Constitution came into effect in January 1987. It provided for a presidential system, with a president elected by direct vote for a six-year term. Legislators would be elected on the basis of proportional representation.

17   In February, with UN and OAS participation, the Central American presidents met for negotiations in Esquipulas, Guatemala. The Esquipulas II Accords stipulated an end to external support for armed opposition groups; the opening of internal dialogue in each of the countries, mediated by the Catholic Church; and an amnesty for those who lay down their arms, with guarantees of political representation.

18   In Nicaragua a National Reconciliation Commission was formed. Contra leader Fernando Chamorro returned from exile; he was granted an amnesty after he renounced violence. Press censorship was lifted and Violeta Chamorro's opposition daily *La Prensa* reappeared. On 7 October, a unilateral cease-fire went into effect in several parts of the country, although contra leaders announced that they would continue hostilities.

19   Throughout 1988, US pressure and the effects of Hurricane Joan worsened the economic situation. Monetary reform and a cut in the Government budget in February did not halt spiraling inflation.

20   In July 1988, the US ambassador to Managua was expelled on the accusation of encouraging anti-Sandinista activities. The US Government responded by expelling Nicaragua's representative in Washington.

21   The Esquipulas II Accords seemed to be doomed, but when the five Central American presidents met at Costa del Sol, El Salvador, in February 1989, President Daniel Ortega embarked on fresh negotiations. The Sandinista proposal was to bring the elections forward to February 1990 and to accept proposed modifications to the 1988 electoral law. The condition was that the contras dismantle their bases in Honduras within three months of an agreement. The US however insisted that the contras continue in Honduras, and President George Bush persuaded Congress to award them $40 million in 'humanitarian aid'.

22   Daniel Ortega was the FSLN presidential candidate. The National Opposition Union (UNO), a 14-party coalition, nominated Pedro Joaquin Chamorro's widow, Violeta Barrios de Chamorro.

IN FOCUS

ENVIRONMENTAL CHALLENGES
Approximately 40 per cent of the territory's water and soil are polluted, and there is significant deforestation. Growing environmental deterioration is aggravating poverty. The country is prone to natural disasters such as earthquakes, volcanic eruptions, floods and droughts.

WOMEN'S RIGHTS
Women have been able to vote and stand for office since 1955. Between 1995 and 2000 the number of seats in Parliament held by women did not reach 10 per cent, while female representation in ministries or equivalent positions dropped from 10 to 5 per cent.

In 2000, women made up 36 per cent of the workforce, and 25 per cent of households were headed by women.

Prenatal healthcare coverage grew from 71.5 per cent in 1993 to 86 per cent in 2001. The work of Médecins Sans Frontières in public health has been extended since 2001 to include a focus on sexual and domestic violence; it has received hundreds of reports of such violence.

CHILDREN
In 2001, 53 per cent of the population was under 18. Extreme poverty and inequity affect mostly children and women. That year, 2.3 million people were living in poverty and 831,000 in extreme poverty, especially in the central and Atlantic regions. One in three children had some degree of

chronic malnutrition, and nine per cent suffered from severe malnutrition.

Only 29 per cent of children finish primary school. Many families cannot afford direct or indirect school costs. Poverty encourages child labor, which in 2001 affected more than 167,000 children and teenagers. Until the same year, 36 per cent of all boys and girls were not officially enrolled in school for administrative, legal and cultural reasons.

Sexual exploitation among children and teenagers, as well as drug abuse and violence have become new causes for concern. The existence of almost 76,000 landmines constitutes a threat for Nicaraguans, especially children.

INDIGENOUS PEOPLES/ ETHNIC MINORITIES
There are two large ethnic minorities in Nicaragua: Afro-Nicaraguans (nine per cent of the population) and Miskitos (five per cent). Some Miskitos speak English and are Protestant, due to the British influence in the area between the 17th and 19th centuries, but most maintain their original language and culture.

There are other smaller communities: the Sumo, Rama and Garifuna (a mix of indigenous peoples and Afro-Nicaraguans). The Creoles are of African descent and live along the Caribbean coast. Most come from Jamaica and the Cayman Islands.

Although relations between Creoles and Miskitos have been tense throughout history, they share a common rivalry against the majority of the population, who

are descendants of native peoples and Spanish colonizers, speak Spanish and are mostly Catholic.

To redress a history of exploitation and discrimination against the country's indigenous peoples, the Nicaraguan Constitution in 1987 provided for a degree of autonomy in the two regions on the eastern coast, granting indigenous communities there local powers and freedoms. However, the social and economic status of these peoples have not improved; in 2001 unemployment among people from the Mosquito Region exceeded 50 per cent.

MIGRANTS/REFUGEES
Internal migration occurs from the countryside to Managua and toward peripheral areas of the country, caused by pressures from the extension of agricultural crops and the low agricultural returns in the dry areas.

In 2002 it was estimated that there were 1.3 migrants per 1,000 Nicaraguans.

After the 1980s, emigration grew considerably due to the national economic situation, the internal armed conflict and the increased openings for unskilled labor in neighboring countries. In 1998, 20 per cent of Nicaraguan homes received remittances sent by relatives or friends working abroad.

DEATH PENALTY
Abolished in 1979; the last execution took place in 1930.

23   All surveys showed the FSLN would win by a wide margin on 25 February 1990. Unexpectedly, the UNO won the elections with 55 per cent of the vote against the FSLN's 41 per cent. Ortega accepted defeat and pledged to hand over power to the new president, Violeta Chamorro.

24   On 25 April, before she took office, the President and the FSLN signed a 'Transition Protocol'. This included respecting the standing Constitution and the social achievements of the revolution, and supporting disarmament of the contras. The new president announced that she would personally assume the Defense Ministry and maintain the Sandinista General Humberto Ortega as commander of the armed forces. This forced the UNO's Vice-President Virgilio Godoy and other members of the coalition to withdraw from the Government.

25   In May 1990, public employees went on strike for wage increases of up to 200 per cent. The Government declared the strike illegal, and revoked the civil service law (under which civil servants could not be fired without just cause) as well as the agrarian reform law passed by the Sandinista Government. Workers responded by extending the strike over the whole country. After a week, the Government partially gave in to the workers' demands, and the strike ended.

26   Since the mid-1990s, the Government has received several offers from international consortia interested in carrying out projects in some 270,000 hectares of tropical rainforests in northern Nicaragua, ranging from the creation of landfill sites for toxic waste, to the exploitation of the region's vast fishing, mineral and forestry resources.

27   When the Government was accused of carrying out secret negotiations with a Taiwanese enterprise, the existence of large mineral deposits was inadvertently revealed. These included gold, silver, copper, tungsten and Central America's largest deposits of calcium carbonate, a raw material used in cement production.

28   In 1991, President Chamorro agreed with the FSLN to recognize agrarian reform and to set aside for workers at least 25 per cent of shares in state enterprises slated for privatization.

29   Inflation fell from 7,000 per cent in 1990 to 3.8 per cent in 1992 due to an IMF and World Bank-sponsored adjustment program. Productive investments and spending in education and health were reduced. Unemployment rose to 60 per cent.

30   Differences between the President and the UNO led them to

Under-5 mortality
41 per 1,000 live births
2002

Poverty
82.3% of population living on less than $1 per day
1998

Debt service
26.2% exports of goods and services
2001

Maternal mortality
230 per 100,000 live births
2000

split in 1993 after which Chamorro received support from the Sandinistas and the UNO's Center Group. The following month, the UNO expelled that group and changed its name to Political Opposition Alliance (APO).

[31] Bypassing the party's leadership, the FSLN parliamentary bloc presented its own bill against nepotism which banned presidential re-election and prohibited relatives of the standing presidents from running for president. This clause put an end to the political aspirations of Chamorro's son-in-law, minister Antonio Lacayo.

[32] The economic crisis was intensified by a drought which led to the loss of 80,000 hectares of crops and left 200,000 farmers without food. Malnutrition affected 300,000 children and some lost their sight through lack of vitamin A.

[33] In January 1994, the UNO, with less than half its founders and unable to obtain the support to set up a constituent assembly, ended a year of boycotting the National Assembly. Violence continued between the army, gangs of criminals and small guerrilla groups.

[34] In August the Assembly passed a new military law aimed at eliminating political involvement by the Sandinista Popular Army and increasing its dependence on civilian authority, although the power was actually left in the hands of a military council. General Humberto Ortega resigned.

[35] Debate on constitutional reform prevailed in 1995. In February, the Assembly proposed to change the army's name, ban compulsory military service and grant guarantees to private property. These measures were supported by President Chamorro but she did not agree with the shift of power from the executive to the legislative branch, regarding the right to raise taxes. The Assembly published the reforms unilaterally in February and began to implement them.

[36] In June, an agreement was reached on a general law for constitutional reforms which stated these had to be supported by a majority of 60 per cent in the Assembly before being signed by the President, who concluded the agreement in July.

[37] Approval of the nepotism law was deferred. President Chamorro's son-in-law announced his plans to leave the Government in order to campaign for the November 1996 presidential elections.

[38] Conservative Arnoldo Alemán, ex-mayor of Managua, won 49 per cent of the vote, defeating Sandinista Daniel Ortega. The

electoral law established that, having obtained more than 45 per cent of the vote, there was no need for a second round.

[39] On assuming the presidency, Alemán promised to create 500,000 new jobs and launched a plan to relieve the debt of the agricultural sector, estimated at $150 million.

[40] In April 1997, the Government and the Sandinista opposition accused each other of arming and training paramilitaries. Despite negotiations, relations remained tense.

[41] In August, the Government announced it would not pass goods confiscated by the Sandinistas in 1979 on to Anastasio Somoza's heirs, in answer to a lawsuit filed by Lilian Somoza, the former dictator's daughter.

[42] According to estimates made in early 1998, the US had once again become Managua's main trading partner. Nicaraguan exports to this country were worth $375 million in 1997, 30 per cent up on two years previously.

[43] Hurricane Mitch struck in November 1998, leaving in its wake 3,000 dead, tens of thousands of people homeless and a devastated economy.

[44] A dispute between Nicaragua and Honduras flared up in late 1999 when Tegucigalpa ratified a border treaty with Colombia on the possession of islands in the Caribbean which, according to Managua, meant a loss of 30,000 square kilometers of its maritime territory. After mediation by the OAS, Managua and Tegucigalpa agreed to suspend the deployment of troops on the land border while the dispute was resolved at the International Court of Justice at The Hague.

[45] The Supreme Court of Justice sentenced six US companies to pay $1 billion to some 4,000 rural workers as compensation for the physical harm (cancer, infertility and physical deformities) they suffered from highly toxic insecticides used between 1968 and 1983.

[46] After winning 53.3 per cent of the vote in the November 2001 elections, Liberal candidate Enrique Bolaños became President; Ortega received 45 per cent. Although he contested the number of seats obtained in the Assembly, which did not tally with those counted by the FSLN, OAS observers said the elections had been fair.

[47] A week after Bolaños took office in January 2002, former president Alemán was elected chairman of the National Assembly. Shortly after, the Assembly did not approve the courts' request to lift Alemán's parliamentary immunity to try him for fraud against the state ($1.3 million), embezzlement

PROFILE

ENVIRONMENT

Nicaragua has both Pacific and Caribbean coastlines. It is crossed by two important mountain ranges: the Central American Andes, running from northwest to southeast, and a volcanic chain with several active volcanoes along the western coast. The Managua and Nicaragua lakes lie between the two ranges. On the eastern slopes, the climate is tropical with abundant rainfall, while it is drier on the western side where the population is concentrated. Cotton is the main cash crop in the mountain area, while bananas are grown along the Atlantic coast.

SOCIETY

Peoples: 69 per cent of Nicaraguans are mixed descendants of American Indians and Spanish colonizers; 17 per cent are of European descent; 9 per cent are African descendants and 5 per cent belong to Indian minorities (Miskitos, Sunos and Ramas).
Religion: Catholics (85 per cent); Protestants (15 per cent)
Languages: Spanish (official and predominant). Miskito, Suno, English and Garifuna are spoken on the Atlantic coast.
Main Political Parties: The Constitutional Liberal Party, conservative (CLP); Sandinista National Liberation Front (FSLN); Conservative Party of Nicaragua (CPN). **Main Social Organizations:** The Nicaraguan Labor Confederation (CTN); the Labor Unity and Action Confederation (CAUS); the Rural Workers' Association (ATC); the Workers' Front (FO); the Unified Labor Confederation (CUS); the National Employees' Union (UNE); the National Confederation of Professionals (CONAPRO); National Union of Nicaraguan Students.

THE STATE

Official Name: República de Nicaragua.
Administrative Division: 9 regions, 15 departments, 143 municipalities. **Capital:** Managua 1,098,000 people (2003).
Other Cities: León 153,200 people; Chinandega 120,400; Masaya 110,000; Granada 88,800; Matagalpa 73,400 (2000).
Government: Enrique Bolaños Geyer, President since January 2002.
Legislature: National Assembly, with 93 members.
National Holidays: 15 September, Independence Day (1821); 19 July, Sandinista Revolution Day (1979). **Armed Forces:** 17,000 troops (1996).

and unlawful association. Alemán had signed in 2000 a controversial agreement with the FSLN leadership to reform the Constitution, enabling him to share government positions with the Sandinistas, receive immunity and a life-long seat in the Assembly.

[48] In 2002, the courts ruled that the charges of sexual abuse and rape brought against former president Ortega in 1998 by his step-daughter Zoilamérica Narváez had lapsed, effectively absolving him. Ortega, an MP in 1998, was protected by National Assembly immunity. The Inter-American Commission on Human Rights accepted Narváez's complaint of lack of justice in Nicaragua.

[49] The number of homeless children and teenagers, who in many cases end up leading a life of crime, has grown in recent years. Some of them have been illegally arrested by the police, while citizens and other groups want to carry out 'social cleansing' - ie murder - as already happens in neighboring Honduras and Guatemala against street children.

[50] On 7 December 2003, former president Alemán was sentenced to 20 years' home arrest and made to pay a $17 million fine for crimes of

corruption, including the use of $100 million of state funds for his electoral campaigns.

[51] On 17 December, Nicaragua, Guatemala, Honduras and El Salvador signed a free-trade agreement with the US to scale back tariffs and other trade barriers in agriculture, foodstuffs, investments, services and intellectual property sectors.

[52] Having qualified for the Highly Indebted Poor Countries (HIPC) initiative, after implementing anti-corruption and structural adjustment plans including privatizations, the World Bank 'pardoned' 80 per cent of the $6,500 million Nicaraguan external debt in January 2004. Critics of privatization stress it has not improved services - at least 50 per cent of people have no access to electricity or communications - and that government policies have not tackled serious social issues. Government spending on health fell from $50 per person in 1983 to $16 in 2000, malnutrition and infant mortality grew, some 840,000 children were not in school in 2003, and unemployment reached 13 per cent. Fifty per cent of the population still lived in poverty. ∎

Niger / Niger

Population:	12,872,813
Area:	1,267,000 km²
Capital:	Niamey
Currency:	CFA franc
Language:	French

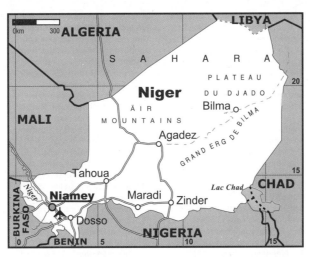

Fossil remains found in what is now Niger indicate that it has been inhabited since prehistoric times. The Nok Empire, reaching its peak in present-day Nigeria between the 15th century BC and the 5th century AD (see Nigeria), left its mark on this territory. From that time onwards, Niger was successively or simultaneously controlled by different kingdoms, empires and city-states in the region. During the 7th century AD, the western stretch of the country became part of the Songhai Empire created by the Berber (see Guinea), who were important propagators of Islam from the 11th century onwards. Between the 14th and 19th centuries the eastern part of the territory belonged to the Kanem-Bornu State, which had been founded by the Kurani in the 8th century (see Chad). Meanwhile, during the 19th century, the Haussa states flourished in the south (see Nigeria), until conquered by the Fulani.

² Throughout the 19th century, the territory was colonized by France which exerted power over the existing kingdoms either by the use of arms or through treaties. In 1922, Niger was formally made a colony. Traditional subsistence crops were replaced by cash crops like peanuts and cotton, which were grown for export, causing food shortages in Niger.

³ In the 1950s, within the context of decolonization in the region, Niger launched its independence movement, led by Hamani Diori. In 1960, the country's first constitution was approved and Niger became an independent state.

⁴ When it broke its colonial ties, Niger was the poorest country in French West Africa, with 80 per cent of the population living in rural areas with persistent drought, soil erosion and population pressure which continue to threaten the country's agriculture and ecology.

⁵ In the new republic's first election in 1960, the Niger Progressive Party (NPP) candidate, Hamani Diori, was elected President. The new Government maintained close economic and political ties with France, to the point of allowing French troops to remain within its territory. In the first years of his presidency, Diori banned the opposition Sawaba (Freedom) party, forcing its leader, Djibo Bakari, into exile and creating a one-party state. Diori's Government was accused of corruption and of harshly repressing the growing political opposition.

⁶ In the early 1970s, in response to the drought which hit the Sahel region, the army distributed food among the people there, thus becoming fully aware of their needs. On 13 April 1974, a Supreme Military Committee took power, suspending the constitution, and naming Lieutenant Colonel Seyni Kountche as head of state; Diori was detained. The first measures it took aimed to fix prices for agricultural products, increase salaries, stop nepotism, redirect investments, and develop education and sanitation services.

⁷ The new Government tried to establish a political base, particularly among young people, through the creation of 'samarias', a traditional form of social group, and signed bilateral agreements with France. The Military Council allowed Djibo Bakary, exiled leader of the Sawaba (Freedom) Party, to return to Niger on condition he did not engage in political activity. He was subsequently arrested and detained until 1984.

PROFILE

ENVIRONMENT
Most of Niger's territory is made up of a plateau with an average altitude of 350 m. The north is covered by the Sahara desert and the south by savannas. There are uranium, iron, coal and tin deposits, and possibly oil. Eighty per cent of the population lives in rural areas. There are nomadic herders in the center of the country, and peanut, rice and cotton farming in the south. Eighty-five per cent of all energy is provided by firewood.

SOCIETY
Peoples: Among the herders of the central steppe, ethnic origins vary from the Berber Tuareg, to the Fulani, including the Tibu (Tubu). In the south there are West African ethnic groups; the Hausa, Djerma (Zarma), Songhai and Kamuri, among others. **Religions:** Muslim; in the south there are traditional African religions and a Christian minority. **Languages:** French (official) and several local languages. **Main Political Parties:** National Movement for the Developing Society (MNSD); Nigerien Party for Democracy and Socialism; Rally for Democracy and Progress (RDP), a coalition made up of nine parties opposed to the MNSD. **Main Social Organizations:** Nigerien National Workers' Union (UNTN).

THE STATE
Official Name: République du Niger. **Administrative Divisions:** 7 Départements. **Capital:** Niamey 890,000 people (2003).
Other Cities: Zinder 185,100 people; Maradi 172,900; Tahoua 87,700 (2000). **Government:** Tandja Mamadou, President since December 1999. Hama Amadou, Prime Minister since January 2000. **Parliament:** National Assembly, with 83 members elected every five years.
National Holiday: 3 August, Independence (1960).
Armed Forces: 5,300 (1996). Other: 5,400 Gendarmes, Republican Guards and National Police.

⁸ During the 1970s the country experienced an economic boom, based on an increase in the international price of uranium, of which Niger is the world's fourth largest producer. This mineral accounted for 90 per cent of the country's exports in 1980, when the so-called 'miracle' came to an abrupt end because of the decline in foreign demand as well as in the price of this product. Economic strength and development programs helped divert attention from the absence of legal political activity.

⁹ The country's foreign debt increased from $207 million to $1 billion between 1977 and 1983. In 1983 Kountche promoted an IMF structural adjustment program, but favorable uranium prices did not result and between 1984 and 1985 the perennial drought in the Sahel region worsened.

¹⁰ In 1983 President Kountche appointed Mamid Algabid, a Tuareg, as the new Prime Minister, and announced limited elections. The Government faced political challenges on different fronts: it put down an attempted coup by former members of the secret police and engaged in combat with the Tuareg people who had resorted to guerrilla warfare in the north.

¹¹ In 1987 Kountche died from a cerebral hemorrhage. The Military Council appointed Ali Saibou as his successor. He appointed ten new ministers and declared an amnesty which provided for the return of political exiles.

¹² On 2 August 1988, the National Movement for a Developing Society (MNSD) was formed as the only government-authorized party, and the National Development Council drew up a new constitution, which was approved in a plebiscite in 1989. In December 1989, Seibou was elected President in the first elections since independence in 1960.

¹³ The new president, Ali Saibou, had a favorable economic outlook on his side, as there were 200,000 tons of surplus grain in 1989. He tried to link his project for a one-party system, capable of uniting Niger's different political tendencies, to his promise to initiate a genuine democratization process. Throughout 1990 there was intense opposition from political actors, labor unions and students. Besides demanding salary increases and educational reform, support for a multiparty system was expressed through massive strikes and demonstrations which were harshly suppressed by the police. In November 1990 a multiparty system of government was approved.

¹⁴ The Government launched a structural adjustment plan, imposed by the World Bank and the IMF, and announced a two-year freeze on

Life expectancy
46.2 years
2000-2005

GNI per capita
$170
2002

Literacy
16% total adult rate
2000

public sector salaries. Workers and students reacted by calling a new series of strikes and holding more demonstrations. In late 1990, Seibou publicly announced his commitment to leading the country towards a multiparty democratic system and he created the National Conference to oversee the political transition.

[15] After four months, the National Conference decided to form a transitional government, headed by a new Prime Minister, Amadou Cheiffou. André Salifou was named president of the High Council of the Republic, the body holding legislative power during the transition period. The drawing up of a new constitution sparked fierce debate between those who wanted Niger identified as an Islamic nation and those who demanded an explicit declaration of a secular state. A compromise identified Niger as a state not subject to any religion. Islamic groups could have no formal role in Niger's political life as the electoral law banned parties with a religious base. The State was bankrupt, no resources were allocated to pay public sector salaries and student scholarships.

[16] In February 1993, the first multiparty elections were held. In April's presidential election, Mahamane Ousmane was elected with 55.4 per cent. The efforts to reach an agreement to end the insurrection by Tuareg guerrillas in the north continued throughout

1993-1994. The fighting continued until an agreement was signed between the main guerrilla group, the Coordination of Armed Resistance, and the Government. The most important result was that the central Government granted autonomy to part of the country inhabited by some 750,000 Tuaregs.

[17] In January 1995, an opposition coalition triumphed in the legislative elections and immediately replaced the Prime Minister, Amadou Cissé, with Hama Amadou. The latter announced that his first move would be to introduce an economic austerity plan, reaching an agreement for settling payment of overdue civil service salaries.

[18] Tension continued to mount between the new Government and the President. In January 1996, a military coup toppled Ousmane, who was replaced by the National Salvation Council, headed by Colonel Ibrahim Baré Mainassara, who appointed Boukary Adji as Prime Minister. In July, Mainassara was elected President with 52 per cent of the vote. He dissolved the Independent National Electoral Commission, leading the main opposition parties to boycott the November legislative elections. In December, following the victory of Mainassara's supporters, Amadou Cissé was made Prime Minister.

[19] Political persecution continued in 1998 with the arrest of several members of the opposition. Social

action was dominated by constant anti-government demonstrations. One year later, the Supreme Court annulled the March election results in some districts and called for a new round of ballots. On 4 April, after a tension-filled week, Mainassara was assassinated by members of his own presidential guard. Coup leader Daouda Malam Wanké was then named President and head of the National Reconciliation Council, who governed the country during the nine-month transition period. Prime Minister Hassane dissolved the National Assembly and political parties were temporarily suspended.

[20] The international community strongly pressured the country to return to democratic rule. In October 1999, Niger held the first round of general elections and, in the second round in November, retired military officer Tandja Mamadou, of the MNSD, won by a large majority over his rival, former prime minister and parliamentary leader Mahamadou Issoufou.

[21] Mamadou's Government faced several problems. One of them was the threat posed by the indiscriminate hunting of endangered species (giraffes, hippopotamuses and lions), a traditional activity in the northern deserts. In February 2001, Environment Minister Issoufou Assoumane, warned that there had been a massacre of animals over the

past ten years and that the Government would be on the alert to control further hunting. The number of hunting licenses sold would also be limited. A year later the National Assembly also penalized clitoridectomy, which was practised by some ethnic groups. According to a 1999 study, about 20 per cent of women in Niger had been subjected to genital mutilation.

[22] In spite of the agreements signed with the Tuaregs, the violence did not end. In July and August 2003 the Niger Delta was the site of armed confrontations among different gangs for control of the illegal trade in oil and derivatives. Between 50 and 100 people died as a result of fighting.

[23] During 2003, Niger's government became involved in an international conflict when intelligence reports furnished by the US and the UK stated that Iraq had bought uranium from Niger to build atomic bombs.

[24] Mamadou demanded that the evidence proving these claims be produced. As this was not forthcoming, CIA Director George Tenet had to admit that the information on the sale of uranium was false. However, the British Government did not retract its accusations, even when a UN delegation of experts concluded that the information provided by the secret services was false. ∎

IN FOCUS

ENVIRONMENTAL CHALLENGES
This region is greatly affected by desertification from intensive grazing and deforestation. Strong winds produce considerable erosion. There is air and water pollution mainly in densely populated urban areas. A range of animals, such as elephants, giraffes, hippopotamuses and lions, are in danger of extinction due to uncontrolled hunting and the destruction of their natural habitat.

WOMEN'S RIGHTS
Women have been able to vote and stand for office since 1948. In 2000, only eight of the 883 members of the National Assembly were women, although they held 10 per cent of ministerial posts. Forty-four per cent of the five-million strong labor force were women; 78 per cent were working in services, 18 per cent in industry and 4 per cent in agriculture.

From 1990-2000, only 30 per cent of pregnant women received prenatal care and 41 per cent suffered from anemia. Maternal

mortality rate is 1,600 deaths per 100,000 live births*. In 2000, only 16 per cent of births are attended by skilled medical personnel.

According to a 1999 World Health Organization study, it was estimated that 20 per cent of women in Niger had undergone some type of genital mutilation, of which clitoridectomy is the most common form. In May 2002, as part of the Penal Code reform, the National Assembly passed a law penalizing the practice. The Government took an active role in combating female genital mutilation and worked closely with local and international NGOs to develop and distribute educational materials at government clinics and maternal health centers, organizing information seminars and campaigns on this issue.

CHILDREN
Niger has the world's second highest under-five mortality rate, with 265 deaths for every 1,000 live births. It also has the world's second highest infant mortality rate (after Sierra Leone) with 156 deaths every 1,000 live births. In 2000, 17 per cent of babies suffered from low birth

weights and 39.8 per cent of children under-five had stunted growth. Between 30 and 51 per cent of children under one are immunized against the most common childhood diseases such as polio, measles, tetanus and diphtheria.

In 2000, only 30 per cent of school-age children attended education centers.

There is evidence that the country is a destination for victims of trafficking, generally, girls, boys and young women who end up in prostitution in the main urban centers. A local NGO has reported incidents of domestic trafficking of rural children, sold by their families to work as servants in other homes.

INDIGENOUS PEOPLES/ETHNIC MINORITIES
The country's population is made up of the Hausa (56 per cent) and Djerma (22 per cent) ethnic groups. Both groups dominate government and business.

Tuaregs, Arabs, Fulani, Toubous, and Kanouris have few representatives in the Government, and many of these ethnic groups

claim that they suffer from discrimination. Minorities have the same access to healthcare as the rest of the population.

MIGRANTS/REFUGEES
There were about 1,000 refugees and asylum-seekers from various African countries in Niger at the end of 2000. In the same year, nearly 1,000 Malians were living in Niger near the Niger-Mali border.

Refugees have access to health clinics, small business loans and scholarships for secondary and tertiary education.

Approximately 10,000 refugees who were living in other countries were repatriated to Niger in the late 1990s after the Government reached a peace accord with armed groups in the north of the country.

DEATH PENALTY
Although this still applies, there have been no executions since 1976.

*Latest data available in *The State of the World's Children* and *Childinfo* database, UNICEF, 2004.

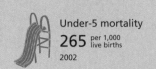
Under-5 mortality
265 per 1,000 live births
2002

Poverty
61.4% of population living on less than $1 per day
1995

Debt service
6.8% exports of goods and services
2001

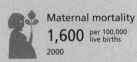
Maternal mortality
1,600 per 100,000 live births
2000

Diamonds of war

AFRICA, although a poor continent, has rich mineral resources. But unregulated, illegal trafficking in diamonds and other precious stones exacerbates conflicts and worsens the poverty that affects the region. The mineral wealth of some African countries is the direct cause of poverty for their people. While the diamond industry has benefited countries such as Botswana - employing 10 per cent of the population and contributing two thirds of government income - it has had tragic consequences for others.

Hundreds of millions of dollars flow from the illegal diamond trade directly into the hands of rebels, corrupt governments and their armies who use the profits to buy arms. The illicit trade feeds war in local conflicts and across borders. The weapons are also used to gain or retain control of mines and the mineral wealth they bring, fueling a vicious cycle.

The result is systematic suffering and poverty of many ordinary African people as the money from diamonds and minerals buys guns and pays mercenaries instead of being spent on social and development projects such as education and health care.

FUNDING THE REBELS
In Angola, Sierra Leone and the Democratic Republic of Congo (DRC), precious stones have been the main source of funds for insurgent movements.

Diamond-generated wealth combines with racial and political motives to feed continuing confrontations between Hutu and Tutsi people in the eastern part of the DRC. Angola, Namibia and Zimbabwe support the DRC Government in return for mining rights in frontier zones. Burundi, Rwanda and Uganda support the rebels, trading diamonds for funds.

Laurent Kabila led his guerrilla force to victory in 1997, ending the long dictatorship of Mobutu Sese Seko. Since then the power struggle has been replaced by conflict over the control of mineral resources including oil, cobalt and diamonds.

Kabila was assassinated in January 2001, shortly after granting the Israel Diamond Industries exclusive rights over DRC's diamond trade. His son and successor Joseph Kabila revoked the move. He then presided over one of the worst diamond-fueled conflicts in Africa. Nearly half a million of the 58 million Congolese make a living directly or indirectly from contraband in precious metals.

In neighboring Angola for the last 30 years, the opposition National Union for the Total Independence of Angola (UNITA) has been fighting government forces for control of natural resources - a conflict which has already cost a million lives.

The 35,000 strong UNITA forces, initially funded by the US to combat the left-wing Luanda Government during the Cold War, survived on the profits of diamond smuggling.

Despite its rich and abundant natural resources of diamonds and oil, Angola ranks 164th out of the 175 nations in the 2003 UN Development Program's Human Development Index. Until the end of the conflict, war was the spending priority: some 86 per cent of Angola's national budget was spent on defense. This had devastating effects on the people: nearly one in four children died before the age of five and only 38 per cent of the population had access to improved water resources. More than 1.2 million people were still internally displaced at the end of 2003, with no access to basic food, housing or health provision.

Over in West Africa, Sierra Leone's diamonds only make up one per cent of world supplies, but they are highly valued because of their quality. The country suffered brutal conflict over control of its diamond fields in the north and east, where rebel Revolutionary United Front (RUF) militias fought for control of tdiamond-rich territory. The RUF was infamous for its use of child soldiers and its terror campaign against civilians. Since the outbreak of conflict in 1991, rebel forces killed, raped, mutilated and abducted tens of thousands of unarmed civilians. Sadly, it is the illegal diamond trafficking from the rebel held zones that kept the RUF in arms. By February 2004 more than 70,000 civil war fighters had been disarmed, and the war crimes trials began in June that year.

CONFLICT OF INTERESTS
There is a lack of transparency in the international trade in precious stones, and too few control mechanisms. Gems do not set off alarms at airports, sniffer dogs cannot detect them and the stones can be rapidly converted into cash. Networks of intermediaries and middle men make the industry a difficult one to monitor.

Antwerp is the Belgian city that handles two thirds of all the world's diamonds. Diamond importers there receive packages of rough stones from African countries, and these are swiftly dispatched on to the rest of Belgium, Britain and India.

The International Committee of the Red Cross, the non-governmental organization (NGO) Intermon/Oxfam and the UN have deplored the current situation and demanded regulation of diamond mining and trade. In July 2000, the UN Security Council imposed a ban on the illegal importation of diamonds from rebel-held zones of Sierra Leone, but the RUF dodged the embargo through weapons trading with Liberia, which exported six million kilograms of gems between 1994 and 1998.

Intermon/Oxfam, Global Witness, Medico International, Netherlands Institute for Southern Africa (NIZA) and the Dutch agency Novib/Oxfam launched a 'Fatal Transactions' campaign which tried to persuade the industry and consumers to choose conflict-free diamonds and demanded the creation of an international certification system to guarantee the origin of stones.

BLOOD DIAMONDS
The Belgian, Israeli and Ukrainian governments are being pressured into tighter controls on transactions taking place in Antwerp, Tel Aviv and Kiev.

In mid-2001, a meeting in Moscow aimed to set up an international system to certify the source of diamonds and help find a solution to the wars in Angola, Sierra Leone and DR Congo. Representatives of 34 governments, the European Commission, the international diamond industry, the World Diamond Council and NGOs met to discuss a system based on the Kimberley process - a certification system proposal initiated by the governments of South Africa, Botswana and Namibia in 2000.

The Diamond High Council (HRD), an organization representing the industry in Belgium, is revising how diamonds are imported, valued and exported. But there are some 4,000 establishments in Antwerp beyond its control, with thousands of traders, jewelers and middle-men, some involved in the illegal trafficking of blood diamonds.

Rigorously applied international legislation could lead to some controls on the illicit trade, but there are many interests in play. Few want to threaten a business with an annual turnover of $50 billion, even though $5 billion goes directly to warring factions in Africa. In a new twist to the tragedy, investigators have alleged that organisations such as al-Qaeda have used the diamond trade to transfer finances outside the scrutiny of the international banking system.

Some sectors of the industry have shown interest in clean diamond dealing, fearing that consumers will stop buying stones tainted by African blood. De Beers, the giant that controls 75 per cent of world diamond trade, is now attempting to guarantee its diamonds come from war-free sources. In 2000, the company closed its offices in DRC and Guinea and demands that its suppliers buy no diamonds from dubious sources. According to the company's director Nicky Oppenheimer, 'a diamond is forever' is a better motto than 'a diamond is for war'. However in March 2004, Global Witness report found that the diamond trade still fuels armed conflicts, mostly in Africa. Its findings were based on research done in the US, where over half the world's diamonds are sold. ∎

Nigeria / Nigeria

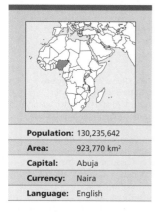

Population:	130,235,642
Area:	923,770 km²
Capital:	Abuja
Currency:	Naira
Language:	English

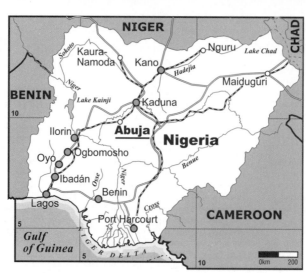

A s heirs to the ancient Nok civilization, the Yoruba lived in walled cities with broad avenues. As early as the 9th century, they had a democratic system of urban administration, with a mayor and a municipal council elected by a citizens' assembly. As art, they produced beautiful ceramics and bronze sculptures. Between the 10th and 11th centuries, Ife, Oyo, Ilorin and Benin (not the present-day nation) were loosely confederated city-states extending their influence from the Niger River to present-day Togo.

2   The city of Ife has enjoyed a reputation as the main religious center of the nation since those times; the Oni of Ife was the High Priest of all Yorubans, whether Nigerian or not.

3   The city of Oyo, strengthened since the 16th century by the slave trade, maintained political power through the *Alafin* (ruler). The dependence on slavery caused its downfall when that institution was abolished.

4   In the northern part of the country, the Hausa states constituted a cultural center of very diverse character. In the south-east, the Igbos were active traders coming from the same group as the Yorubas; however, they did not develop urban civilizations.

5   In 1914, Britain unified all these territories under a single administration, interested in the exploitation of tin and agricultural and timber resources.

6   The British method of indirect colonial administration used the northern Muslim emirs as their agents. Consequently this area, populated by Hausa and Fulani, enjoyed greater political supremacy.

7   Independence in 1960 brought the Northern People's Congress to power, in an alliance with the National Council of Nigerian Citizens, an Igbo organization. However, the federal structure (four states) and the bicameral parliament, based on the British model, afforded the regional governors more effective power than that held by President Nnambi Azikiwe. Progressive parties were pushed aside in a succession of electoral frauds, while political leaders lost their national outlook, encouraging ethnic rivalries.

8   The army came to power when General Yacubu Gowon was appointed president in 1966. In 1967, the oil industry began to develop, just as France was inciting the separatist movement among the Igbo. The civil war in Ibarra that lasted from 1967 until 1970 was a bid for secession, but eventually failed.

9   With Nigeria as the world's 8th largest oil producer, Gowon expropriated 55 per cent of the transnational oil companies, allowing the consolidation of local entrepreneurs.

10   Real power was vested in the nationalist Supreme Military Council, with different presidents. The council closed US military and espionage installations. During Olusegun Obasanjo's presidency, Barclays Bank and British Petroleum assets were nationalized when these companies violated economic sanctions against apartheid South Africa.

11   In 1978, constitutional reform and a call for elections paved the way for a return to civilian government. The Federal Election Commission authorized only five parties, all representing the traditional financial and political elite. Parties with socialist or revolutionary perspectives were barred from the electoral process, under the pretext of avoiding political fragmentation. The National Party of Nigeria (NPN) won the election with 25 per cent of the vote; the Unity Party of Nigeria (UPN) obtained 20 per cent.

12   The new president Shehu Shagari launched a capitalist plan, based exclusively on petrodollars, to transform Nigeria into the development hub of sub-Saharan Africa. His promises included constructing a new capital, doubling elementary and high school enrollment and achieving self-sufficiency in food production via controversial 'green revolution' methods.

13   None of these proposals came to fruition. Economic indicators showed gloomy prospects, and there was an increase in contraband, large urban concentrations of immigrants and poor peasants, high unemployment and the reduction of workers' purchasing power. Another burden were the IMF conditions for refinancing the foreign debt. Shagari was nevertheless re-elected in 1983 as the NPN candidate, amidst accusations of electoral fraud and military conspiracies.

14   On 1 January 1984, Muhamad Buhari staged a fourth coup, accusing the Government of corruption in the petroleum sector, which accounted for 95 per cent of export earnings. There were detentions at all levels, and civilian government officials were replaced by military personnel.

15   The aggravation of the crisis, an external debt of $15 billion, the repression and the expulsion of 600,000 illegal foreigners set the stage for another coup. On 26 August 1985, General Ibrahim Babangida was appointed president.

16   In December 1987, local elections were held with 15,000 independent candidates taking part. The appointed National Election Commission did not achieve an adequate level of organization. As a consequence of the violence, confusion and subsequent allegations of fraud, the elections were annulled.

17   On 7 December 1989, the military government announced that the presidential and legislative elections originally scheduled for the end of the month would be postponed until December 1990. Six months later, the ban on political activism had been lifted, in an attempt to monitor the transition from military to civilian government in 1992.

18   Babangida visited Britain in May 1990, where he obtained $100 million in aid for the Nigerian economy, which is oriented to trade mainly with the US, the UK and France.

19   That same year, the creation of nine states to separate hostile ethnic groups ended in protests, repression, around 300 deaths and a curfew imposed by the Government.

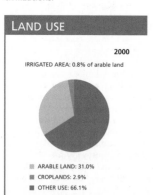

LAND USE

2000

IRRIGATED AREA: 0.8% of arable land

- ARABLE LAND: 31.0%
- CROPLANDS: 2.9%
- OTHER USE: 66.1%

PUBLIC EXPENDITURE

% OF GDP

1.2 % — HEALTH & EDUCATION (2000)

1.1 % — DEFENSE (2001)

WORKERS

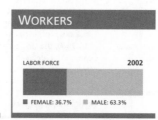

LABOR FORCE   **2002**

- FEMALE: 36.7%   MALE: 63.3%

Life expectancy
51.5 years
2000-2005

GNI per capita
$290
2002

Literacy
64% total adult rate
2000

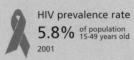

HIV prevalence rate
5.8% of population 15-49 years old
2001

[20] Toward the end of 1991, the internal party elections held to select candidates for governor were annulled due to alleged fraud. In November, a new census eliminated 20 million 'non-existent' voters from the electoral register.

[21] On 14 December, elections for governors were held; the Social Democratic Party (SDP, left-of-center) won in 16 states, and the National Republican Convention (NRC, right-of-center) won in 14. Opposition groups were granted a general amnesty, and 11 well-known dissidents were freed. A law prohibiting former government officials from running for office was revoked.

[22] Early in 1992, the imprisonment of 263 Muslim militants caused protests in the state of Katsina. During this period, there was also an escalation of inter-ethnic conflict between Hausa and Kataj in the state of Kaduna, and territorial conflict between Tiv and Jukin in the Taraba, leaving 5,000 dead.

[23] Legislative elections were held in July 1992. The SDP won 52 seats in the Senate and 314 in the Chamber of Representatives; the NRC won 37 and 275, respectively. The National Assembly was inaugurated in December, allowing the country to enter a transition period after 23 years of military regimes.

[24] In October 1992, the primary presidential elections with candidates from the SDP, the NRC and 23 other parties, were invalidated by President Babangida, claiming fraud. The President proscribed the candidates, deposed the leaders of the SDP and NRC and suspended political activity. These developments jeopardized the planned transfer of power to a civilian government that was to emerge from the elections in early 1993.

[25] In November Babangida postponed until June the elections slated for January 1993. He also ratified the proscription of all the 1992 candidates. Finally, he postponed the transfer of power until August.

[26] On 12 June 1993, the first presidential elections were held since 1983. The military government did not divulge election results until it had concluded an investigation of alleged fraud. The main contest was between the NRC and SDP, who had been authorized to take part in the election with alternative candidates.

[27] Babangida once again invalidated the election results on 23 June, accusing SDP and NRC candidates of 'buying votes'. Moshood Abiola, a Muslim millionaire who was the SDP candidate and who had apparently won the elections, asked for international condemnation of the regime in London.

[28] The US and Britain suspended their economic aid, military training and froze diplomatic relations. This external reaction provided Abiola with the impetus to launch a civil disobedience campaign. Massive protests broke out on the streets of Lagos, the former capital, where at least 25 people were killed by federal troops. Twenty-five opposition groups formed the 'Democracy Campaign'.

[29] Under pressure, the regime set new presidential elections for 14 August 1993 (with the express exclusion of Abiola and Othma Tofa of the NRC), and announced the transfer of power for 27 August.

[30] Clashes continued and on 26 August 1993 Babangida resigned, leaving the country in the hands of Ernest Shonekan, who promised to hold new elections.

[31] The following month, Abiola returned from London and labor unions called a general strike, demanding he be recognized as Nigerian president. Towards the end of 1993 the Minister of Defense, General Sani Abacha, overturned Shonekan, dissolved parliament and banned political activity.

[32] Abacha was a very influential member of the previous military regime and a key figure in the military coup that ousted the Government in 1983. In one of his first statements, he announced he would abandon some of the liberal economic reforms adopted in the 1980s.

[33] Interest rates fell and a new foreign exchange control was established, at a time when any possibility of reaching an agreement with the IMF was increasingly remote. Popular support for Abiola mounted; his arrest in June 1994, triggered a 10-day-strike in the oil sector, the most important in the country.

[34] The execution of nine members of the Movement for the Survival of the Ogoni People in November resulted in the isolation of the military regime. Several countries, including the United States, withdrew their ambassadors from Nigeria.

[35] In 1996 on the basis of a register of political parties drawn up by the National Electoral Commission, Abacha legalized five political groups: the United Nigerian Congress Party, the Committee for National

IN FOCUS

ENVIRONMENTAL CHALLENGES
Nigeria has lost between 70 and 80 per cent of its forests. Only 1.7 per cent of land lies within protected nature reserves. Deterioration of arable land, desertification and air and water pollution are a problem in urban areas. Some water sources have been seriously affected by oil spills.

WOMEN'S RIGHTS
Women have been able to vote and run for office in the south of the country since 1958, and in the north since 1978. In the past decade, considerable efforts have been made to improve health services, although they are still insufficient to guarantee safe childbirth. In 1999, 63.6 per cent of pregnant women received prenatal care and 41.6 per cent of births were attended by qualified personnel.

In 2000, 25 per cent of women between the ages of 15 and 49 had suffered genital mutilation; in addition, 20 per cent of women within this age bracket had at least one daughter who had been subjected to some form of genital mutilation.

There are women who have been formally accused of crimes punishable by death who in some cases remain isolated for prolonged periods awaiting a trial, with no access to legal counsel. According to Amnesty International: 'within the sphere of the ordinary criminal justice system, some women have been imprisoned awaiting execution for periods of up to 10 years'.

CHILDREN
In 2002, there were 62,226,000 children and adolescents under the age of 18, of which over 20 million were under the age of five. In 2000, only 49 per cent of the rural population had access to improved sources of drinking water, while among the urban population the proportion reached 78 per cent.

In 2002, only 25 per cent of infants under one were vaccinated against poliomyelitis and 40 per cent against measles.

Toward the end of 2001, there were 270,000 HIV-positive children between the ages of 0 and 14, and there were 995,000 AIDS orphans.

Nigeria is a country of origin and transit for child-trafficking for the sex-trade in western Africa, Asia and western Europe.

INDIGENOUS PEOPLES/ ETHNIC MINORITIES
The Ibo or Igbo have inhabited the region for thousands of years and are mainly concentrated in the southern states. During the 20th century and the beginning of the 21st century, the implementation of Islamic *Sharia* law has been opposed in the northern regions of the country.

The Ogoni are located on the Delta of the Niger River, in the southern part of the country (their ancestral lands). They have been taking action against the activities of oil companies such as Shell, demanding compensation for damages caused to their lands.

The Yoruba were excluded from political participation until the 1999 elections, when Obasanjo (of Yoruban origin) won the presidency, with the result that many restrictions against this group were lifted. However, until 2001 they still suffered discrimination. Some Yoruban organizations are banned, especially those considered most militant.

The Ijaw live mainly in the Niger Delta and have participated more in regional events during the past years. They pressure the Government to change its economic policy and practices that affect them, and have become involved in campaigns against the oil companies.

MIGRANTS/REFUGEES
Extremely high levels of community violence, linked to political, religious and/or ethnic differences between diverse groups of Nigerians, have caused the displacement of around 100,000 people (2002).

While 30,000 Nigerians sought refuge or asylum in other countries, 10,000 who had fled the country during 2002 returned before the end of the year.

There were over 7,000 refugees in Nigeria in 2002, mainly from Chad, Sierra Leone and Liberia.

DEATH PENALTY
The death penalty is still applicable to all types of crimes and, according to interpretation of the *Sharia*, it also applies in cases of adultery.

Consensus, the National Central Party of Nigeria, the Democratic Party of Nigeria and the 'Grassroots' Democratic Movement.

36 An increase in oil prices stimulated economic growth in 1997. However, official data indicated that 80 per cent of the population was living in poverty.

37 In April 1998, Abacha announced that the August elections were to be replaced by a plebiscite that would determine whether he was to continue in power. His sudden death on 8 June gave rise to widespread rejoicing and expectations of political change. Abiola also died shortly afterwards. General Abdusalam Abu-Bakar, appointed by the military junta as new President, promised to respect the democratic transition.

38 The local elections held in February 1999 were won by the Popular Democratic Party (PDP) of former military ruler General Olusegun Obasanjo. The Alliance for Democracy, which primarily represented the Yoruba ethnic group, in the southeast, won the government of the former capital, Lagos, by a broad margin, while the All People's Party, led by supporters of former dictator Sani Abacha, won in the state of Jigawa. General elections were set for March 1999.

39 Obasanjo also won in March. At first, the opposition attempted to appeal the results before the Electoral Court, but later it backed down. The new president promised to re-evaluate the Government's investment policies and to reform the inefficient and corrupt public sector. Upon taking office in May, Obasanjo called upon Nigerians to join him in a three-day fast to seek divine intervention that would ensure a positive presidential performance. During his first days in office, he deposed 30 military officers and confiscated millions of dollars which he said had been stolen from the public Treasury during previous administrations.

40 In March 2000, Obasanjo visited Lagos, where violent ethnic fighting between the Ijaw and Ilaje peoples ended in hundreds of deaths. The President was able temporarily to end the fighting by establishing a peace committee with their leaders.

41 In June 2001, in the state of Nasarawa, neighboring the capital, ethnic violence was sparked off between the Azara and Tiv minorities by the death of an Azara community leader. Around 40,000 people fled the conflict.

42 Murtullah Mohammed, head of government during the military

PROFILE

ENVIRONMENT

The country's extensive river system includes the Niger and its main tributary, the Benue. In the north, the *harmattan*, a dry wind from the Sahara, creates a drier region made up of plateaus and grasslands where cotton and peanuts are grown for export. The central plains are also covered by grasslands, and are sparsely populated. The southern lowlands, home to most of the country's population, receive more rainfall and have dense tropical forests. Cocoa and oil-palms are grown in this area. The massive delta of the Niger River divides the coast into two separate regions. In the east, oil production is concentrated around Port Harcourt, the homeland of the Igbo, who converted to Christianity and fought to establish an independent Biafra. To the west, the industrial area is concentrated around Lagos and Ibadan. Yoruba are the predominant western ethnic group, and some of them have converted to Islam.

SOCIETY

Peoples: Nigeria is the most populous country in Africa. The 250 or so ethnic groups fall into four main ones: the Hausa and Fulani in the north; the Yoruba in the southwest; and the Igbo in the southeast. **Religions:** The north is predominantly Muslim, while Christians form the majority in the southeast. In the southwest are Muslims, Christians and followers of traditional African religions. **Languages:** English (official). Each region has a main language depending on the predominant ethnic group, Hausa, Igbo or Yoruba. **Main Political Parties:** People's Democratic Party; All People's Party; Alliance for Democracy.
Main Social Organizations: National Labor Congress; National Association of Nigerian Students.

THE STATE

Official Name: Federal Republic of Nigeria.
Administrative Divisions: 30 States.
Capital: Abuja 452,000 people (2003).
Other Cities: Lagos 8,733,100 people; Ibadan 3,587,100; Kano 3,424,100; Ogbomosho 963,300 (2000).
Government: Olusegun Obasanjo, president since May 1999, re-elected in April 2003. Bicameral legislature: the House of Representatives, with 360 members, and the Senate, with 109 members. **National Holiday:** 1 October, Independence Day (1960). **Armed Forces:** 71,100 troops (1995). Other: 7,000 National Guard, 2,000 Port Security Police.

regime, had wasted hundreds of millions of dollars in 1970 which were purportedly to set up a telephone network. Twenty years later, the network had not been established and the money had vanished.

43 In August 2001, Nigeria's telephone system was creaking. Phone lines were so regularly intercepted that even international telephone calls by Cabinet members were interrupted without notice. At that time, the major mobile phone companies of the country, Johannesburg MTN and Wireless Econet promised a 'cable revolution'. However, due to frequent blackouts and excessive voltage, each company needed a generator for its transmission tower. In addition, each company had to pay license fees of $285 million to the government. According to the 2001 Transparency International Index on perceptions of corruption in business, Nigeria was ranked the second most corrupt country after Bangladesh.

44 In October, Obasanjo, together with President Thabo Mbeki of South Africa and Abdelaziz Bouteflika of Algeria formally launched the New Partnership for Africa's Development (NEPAD), which called on the rest of the world to become partners in the development of Africa. NEPAD commitments included instituting transparent and democratic governments in African states, respecting human rights and stopping wars in exchange for more foreign aid and the lifting of trade barriers to African exports.

45 In 2001 and 2002, a radical version of the Islamic *Sharia* code, introduced in a dozen Muslim states, provoked great controversy and violent protests. Stoning, amputation and flogging were some of the punishments included in the law. In January 2002 a man was hanged in Katsina state in the first execution since Islamic law was introduced.

46 In October 2002, the International Court of Justice published its verdict on the border conflict between Nigeria and Cameroon, giving the latter sovereignty over the main territory in dispute - the Bakassi Peninsula. The Nigerian Government announced it would make a detailed study of the ruling and would defend its right to the territory.

47 In November 2002, a confrontation between Christians and Muslims in Kaduna, during the Muslim Ramadan and on the eve of the celebration of the Miss World Contest in Nigeria, was caused by the publication of an article in *This Day* magazine, which suggested that the Prophet Muhammad would have been able to choose a wife among the contestants. The hundreds of dead and injured resulting from the strife forced the organizers to transfer the contest to London.

48 Even before the riots, many countries had called for a boycott of the contest, due to the Katsina state sharia court's decision to stone a woman to death for committing adultery. Amina Lawal had been sentenced in August by this Islamic court in the north of the country, found guilty of having a child out of wedlock.

49 In April 2003 Olusegun Obasanjo, leader of the Popular Democratic Party (PDP), was re-elected president of Nigeria, in an election day marred by violence. The elections were deemed fraudulent by European Union observers, and the results were rejected by the opposition.

50 A countrywide nine-day general strike ended in July 2003 with the reduction of fuel prices that had been increased by the Government. Oluyemi Adeniji took office as Minister of Foreign Affairs.

51 In August 2003 Nigeria declared it would not relinquish the Bakassi Peninsula, awarded to Cameroon in 2002. In January 2004, both Nigeria and Cameroon stationed troops on the border in conflict.

52 In February 2004, Amina Lawal was freed after the sharia court of appeal ruled that her conviction was invalid as she was already pregnant when *Sharia* was implemented in her home province.

53 The beginning of the March 2004 local election campaign was marked by political assassinations and a series of armed attacks.

54 In a new report, Amnesty International denounced discrimination against women in Nigeria and enforcement of the death penalty under national legislation; in July 2003, there were 487 people awaiting execution. ∎

Population:	85,693
Area:	500 km²
Capital:	Saipan
Currency:	US dollar
Language:	English

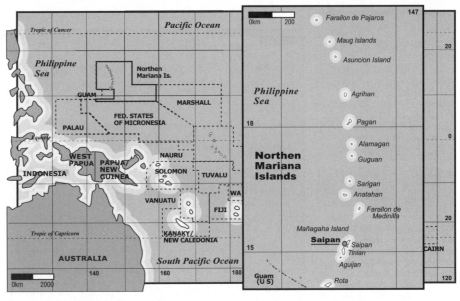

In Saipan, the largest island of the Mariana archipelago, evidence has been found of human habitation from 1500 BC.

2   During his first expedition around the world, Portuguese navigator Ferdinand Magellan sighted the islands in 1521 and claimed them for the Spanish Crown. They were held by the Spanish until ceded to Germany in 1899 as the Spanish empire declined.

3   During World War I the islands came under the control of Japan, which fought with the Allies against Germany. The Japanese occupied the islands until World War II.

4   In June 1944, after fierce fighting, the US took control of Saipan and Tinian because of their strategic location in the North Pacific, on the route between Hawaii and the Philippines. They finally came to form part of the Trust Territory of the Pacific Islands in 1947.

5   The islands had this status until they became a Free Associated State of the US in a referendum held in 1975.

6   In 1978, the islands became self-governing in political union with the US. Washington developed a project to turn two-thirds of Tinian into a military air base and an alternative center for the storage of nuclear weapons. In 1984 the US Government started negotiations with local landowners.

7   When news leaked out that cement deposits containing radioactive waste from Japanese nuclear plants had been dumped in this part of the Pacific, the alarm was sounded on similar US projects that would directly affect the Marianas Islands.

8   In 1984 US President Reagan granted some civil and political rights to the islands' residents, such as equal employment opportunities in the federal government, the civil service and the US armed forces.

9   The Northern Marianas were formally admitted to a Commonwealth arrangement in political union with the US in 1986. The inhabitants were granted US citizenship but not the right to vote in presidential elections. They have a representative in the US Congress with no voting rights.

10   The country's main economic activities are fishing, agriculture (concentrated in smallholdings) and tourism which employs about 10 per cent of the workforce. Some of these activities have often been affected by the typhoons the islands suffer in the rainy season. In January 1988 Rota island was devastated by a typhoon, and the US declared a state of emergency. In January 1990, Typhoon Koryn hit the whole archipelago.

11   In the 1989 local elections, Republicans retained the governorship. Larry Guerrero was elected governor after Pedro P Tenorio had decided to stand down.

12   On 22 December 1990 the UN Security Council voted to dissolve the Trusteeship. Thus, the Northern Marianas became an independent state, associated to the US.

13   In 1992, the US Supreme Court ratified the property ownership system, whereby only nationals could own land. In 1994, Froilan C Tenorio was elected governor.

14   In 1995, there were some 22,600 foreign workers in the country, three times the number of Marianan workers. Unemployment amongst the latter stood at 15 per cent.

15   In January 1998, Pedro P Tenorio was re-elected governor. His victory was questioned by opposition groups, as it was his third period in office following previous terms in 1982 and 1986.

16   Throughout 1999 local officials, backed by key figures from the Republican Party in the US Congress, argued intensely with the Clinton (Democrat) administration, regarding the conditions of slavery and exploitation that immigrant workers were subjected to on the islands. Tensions worsened when local Republican leaders told Clinton officials visiting the islands that the Marianas would not relinquish the exemptions on Federal customs, immigration and labor laws that it enjoyed.

17   Both human rights groups and Washington officials stated that this exemption allowed the growth of slavery in Saipan, as well as terrible working conditions and salaries. In spite of these complaints, in practice Washington condones the conditions of slavery for workers on the island by allowing US capital to invest in Marianas' textile industries; there they avoid tariffs and use cheaper labor, while claiming US origin for their products.

18   Since the 1960s, pollutants from the US Navy have affected the islands' environment. In Saipan, Tanapag locals protested in early 2002 together with activists from the non-governmental organization Greenpeace at the office of the US General Attorney, for what they considered to be 'gross negligence and a crime against the environment'.

19   In April 2004 the US Geological Survey (USGS) warned that ash from a freshly active volcano on Anatahan could pose a serious threat to aviation. ■

PROFILE

ENVIRONMENT
The Marianas archipelago, located in Micronesia, east of the Philippines and south of Japan, consists of 16 islands (excluding the island of Guam), of which only six are inhabited. The most important in size and population are: Saipan (122 sq km), Tinian (101 sq km) and Rota (85 sq km). Of volcanic origin, the islands are generally mountainous. The climate is tropical, with rain forest vegetation. In the northernmost islands, however, these conditions shade gradually into a more temperate climate and brush-like, herbaceous vegetation. Development plans endanger the local fauna. Toxic waste left by the US army have caused health problems in at least one of the country's villages.

SOCIETY
Peoples: The population is mostly indigenous, of Chamorro origin. There are also Japanese, Chinese, Korean, European, Filipino and Micronesian minorities. **Religions:** Catholic (majority); some traditional faiths persist. **Languages:** English (official); 55 per cent speak Chamorro; also Carolinian, Tanapag, Filipino and Japanese. Political Parties: Republican Party; Democratic Party; Reform Party.

THE STATE
Official Name: Commonwealth of the Northern Marianas Islands. **Capital:** Saipan 71,000 people (2003). **Other Islands:** Rota 2,100 people; Tinian 2,100 (2000). **Government:** By virtue of the US Commonwealth status, the President of the US is the Head of State. Juan N Babauta, Governor by direct election, since January 2002. There is a two-chamber legislature with 9 senators and 18 representatives. **National Holiday:** Commonwealth Day, 8 January (1986). **Armed forces:** The US is responsible for defense.

Norway / Norge

Population:	4,569,598
Area:	323,880 km²
Capital:	Oslo
Currency:	Kroner
Language:	Norwegian

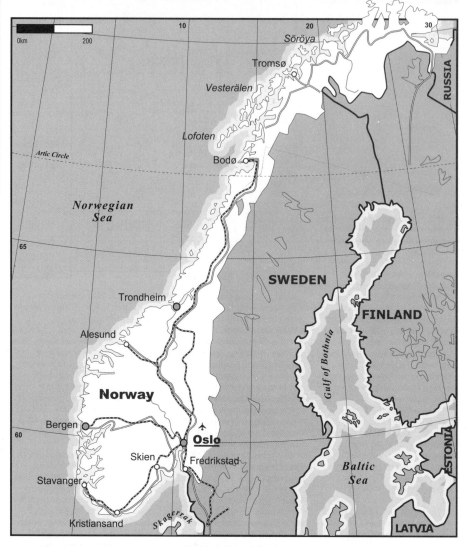

Germanic groups are thought to have emigrated to Norway between the 9th and 7th millennia BC, when the glaciers receded from the northern European coasts. Cave drawings show that they were familiar with navigation and used skis for traveling over the snow. When the Scandinavians arrived around the 1st century AD, the Sami, shepherds that had lived on these lands for thousands of years, were expelled northwards.

[2] Historians believe that Norwegian nationality and conversion to Christianity began between 800 and 1030 AD. The Viking King Harald Harfagre, considered the founder of the nation, took control of a large part of the country after defeating his rivals in a naval battle at Hafrsfjord, near the city of Stavanger.

[3] Viking expeditions extended the Norwegian Empire to Greenland to the west and Ireland to the south. In 1002, Leif Erikson and his followers were the first Europeans to cross the Atlantic and reach North America, which they named Vinland.

[4] At the end of the Viking era, Norway was an independent kingdom in which four regional peasant assemblies (*lagting*) elected the monarch. Legitimate and illegitimate children of the king had equal rights to succession before the *lagtings*. In the 10th and 12th centuries it was common for two kings to rule simultaneously without any conflict arising between them.

[5] King Magnus III Barfot (1093-1103) conquered the Scottish Orkney and Hebrides Islands. His three sons ruled together: they imposed a tithe, founded monasteries and built cathedrals. At the beginning of the 12th century, a 100-year civil war broke out, as a result of the disputes between the monarchy and the church, lasting until the coronation of Haakon IV in 1217.

[6] The new king reorganized the public administration system, imposed a hereditary monarchy, and signed a treaty with Russia over the country's northern border. Greenland and Iceland agreed to a union with the King. With the Scottish islands and the Faeroes included the Norwegian Empire reached its maximum extent.

[7] The Black Death killed close to 50 per cent of Norway's population between 1349 and 1350. The upper classes were decimated; Danes and Swedes were hired to fill the positions left vacant in the higher levels of the Government and the church. However, the King lost control over his dominions and isolated regions organized autonomous administrations.

[8] The ascent of Queen Margrethe of Denmark to the throne in 1387 enabled the union of the Scandinavian countries. In 1389, she was crowned Queen of Sweden and in 1397 her adopted nephew Erik was elected king of all Scandinavia in Kalmar, Sweden. With the Kalmar Union, Norway was gradually subordinated, ultimately becoming a province of Denmark.

[9] After 1523, Norway's administrative council sought greater independence from Denmark. However, the fact that power lay in the hands of the Catholic bishops made it difficult to gain Swedish support. At the end of the civil war, between 1533 and 1536, the council was abolished. In 1537, the Danish King made the Lutheran religion the country's official religion; the Norwegian Church has been a State church ever since.

WORKERS

UNEMPLOYMENT: 3.9% (2002)

LABOR FORCE **2002**

■ FEMALE: 46.5%   ■ MALE: 53.5%

EMPLOYMENT DISTRIBUTION **1995/2001**

F
M

■ AGRICULTURE	F: 6.0%	M: 2.0%
■ INDUSTRY	F: 33.0%	M: 9.0%
■ SERVICES	F: 61.0%	M: 88.0%

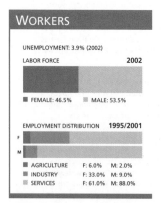

PUBLIC EXPENDITURE

% OF GDP

13.5 %
HEALTH & EDUCATION (2000)

1.8 %
DEFENSE (2001)

Life expectancy
78.9 years
2000-2005

GNI per capita
$37,850
2002

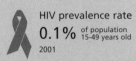
HIV prevalence rate
0.1% of population 15-49 years old
2001

[10] During this period, social conditions in Norway were better than in Denmark. Landlords in the countryside exploited the regional timber resources, and there was a large group of rural wage-earners. Most of Norway's population were peasants and fishing people, and cities no larger than 15,000 people.

[11] At the end of the Napoleonic wars, Denmark unilaterally surrendered control of Norway to Sweden. In 1814, Norway's constituent assembly proclaimed national independence. Sweden re-established its dominance by force, but in 1905 Norway regained its sovereignty without bloodshed.

[12] During the period of Swedish control, most of the laws enacted in 1814 remained in force. The Norwegian constitution is one of the oldest in the world, second only to that of the United States. It is based on the principles of national sovereignty, the separation of powers and the inviolability of human rights.

[13] Under a constitutional amendment in 1884, Norway adopted a parliamentary monarchy. The Danish Prince Carl was elected king of Norway, under the name Haakon VII, in 1905. Up until 1914, the country experienced rapid economic expansion, with the hydroelectric wealth of the region allowing large-scale industrial development.

[14] There was general concern that in 1906, 75 per cent of Norway's hydroelectric dams belonged to foreign investors. In 1909, Parliament passed laws for the protection of the country's natural resources.

[15] Universal suffrage, a term which applied to men only when it was passed in 1898, was extended to women by reforms approved in 1907 and 1913. One consequence of industrialization and universal suffrage was the growth of the Labor Party (LP).

[16] During World War I, Norway tried to remain neutral, but was obliged by the other powers to cut trade with Germany. Anti-German feeling was strong, particularly because of the various accidents caused by German submarines.

[17] Unlike other Western European social democracies, Norway's LP (with a left-wing majority) joined the Third Communist International in 1918. However, it could not agree with the centralization applied by the Soviet Communist Party, and cut its ties with the Comintern in 1923.

[18] Despite economic difficulties and serious labor conflicts (with unemployment reaching 20 per cent in 1938), Norway underwent vigorous industrial expansion in the inter-war years. The Government extended social legislation to include pensions, mandatory leave for workers and unemployment benefits.

[19] In 1940, at the beginning of World War II, Norway was invaded by Germany, after two months of fighting. King Haakon and the Government went into exile in London, co-ordinating the resistance from there. Vidkun Quisling became head of state and decreed martial law for resistance members. German troops left in May 1945 and Quisling was executed for treason, after King Haakon's return. Haakon died in 1957 and was succeeded by his son Olaf V.

[20] The LP governed continuously between 1935 and 1965 (except for the Nazi occupation), when it lost its parliamentary majority and Per Borten, the leader of the Center Party, was named Prime Minister. However, he resigned in 1971 when it was revealed that he had leaked confidential information during EC negotiations.

[21] After the War, Norway abandoned its policy of neutrality, joining NATO in 1949, the Nordic Council in 1952, and the European Free Trade Association (EFTA) in 1960. Large oil deposits were discovered in the North Sea in the late 1960s. Incorporation to the EEC was rejected in a referendum in 1972.

[22] Although its initiative to join the EEC was defeated, the LP remained in power throughout the 1970s and most of the 1980s, sometimes in alliance with the Socialist Left Party (SVP). When Prime Minister Oddvar Nordli resigned in 1981, the LP appointed Gro Harlem Brundtland, the first woman Prime Minister.

[23] From the beginning of the 1970s, Norway and the USSR disagreed over their rights to the Barents Sea. In 1977, Norway extended its territorial waters to 200 miles and designated a protected fishing zone in its territory of Svalbard, which had been dangerously overfished. A temporary agreement signed in 1978 defined a 'grey fishing area' to be jointly administered.

[24] In 1981 an agreement was signed with Iceland on mining and fishing rights. A similar dispute with Denmark, regarding Greenland, was taken to the International Court of Justice.

[25] The LP won the elections in May 1986, after four years of conservative governments, once more under Gro Harlem Brundtland, who appointed 8 women to her 18-member cabinet.

[26] Ties with the US were strained in 1987 after Norwegian state company Kongsberg Vapenfabrikk (KV) exported 'heavy water' used in nuclear reactors, breaking NATO restrictions on the sale of those materials to former Warsaw Pact members and Third World nations.

[27] Romania and the former West Germany, who had re-exported the product to India, pledged, along with Israel, not to resell it without Norwegian authorization, and only to use it for peaceful purposes. The disagreement was overcome in 1988 when Norway banned all its 'heavy water' exports.

[28] That year, the US threat to sanction Norway over whaling was lifted when Norway agreed to limit whale hunting to scientific needs. But in 1990, Oslo announced it would resume traditional whaling.

[29] In 1988 fishing was seriously affected by a rise in the concentration of seaweed in the south and depredation by migrating seals in the north. However, after Sweden suspended fish imports in protest at Norway's hunting of seal pups, Norway banned the practice in 1989.

[30] Acid rain caused by industries in the Kola peninsula, to the east of Norway, and fires that broke out in Soviet nuclear submarines to the north - which the Soviets always denied - triggered protests. In 1989, Norway and the USSR agreed to share information on maritime accidents.

[31] The LP's vote fell from 41 per cent in 1985 to 37 per cent in 1989, due to the economic decline and the austerity measures taken by the Government. Incomes and sales fell, while unemployment reached 6 per cent, unheard of since the end of World War II.

[32] Gro Harlem Brundtland resigned in July 1989, after an agreement was reached between the Conservative, Center and Christian Democratic parties. In elections that year, the Labor and Conservative parties lost votes to the more radical parties. In

PROFILE

ENVIRONMENT

The Scandinavian mountain range runs north-south along the coast of the country. On the western side, glacier erosion has gouged out deep valleys that are way below actual sea level, resulting in the famous 'fjords', narrow, deep inlets walled in by steep cliffs. Maritime currents produce humid, mild winters and cool summers. The population is concentrated in the south, especially round Oslo. Nine-tenths of the territory is uninhabited.

SOCIETY

Peoples: Norwegians 96.3 per cent, Danish 0.4 per cent, British 0.3 per cent, Pakistani 0.2 per cent, Iranian 0.2 per cent, others (including 40,000 Sami, an indigenous people who live chiefly in the northern province of Finnmark) 1.9 per cent.
Religions: 88 per cent of the population belongs to the Church of Norway (Lutheran); there are Muslim, Evangelical and Catholic minorities.
Languages: Two forms of Norwegian are officially recognized; 80 per cent of school children learn the old form 'Riksmaal' (Bokmal, strongly influenced by Danish during the 434 year-long union of the two countries), and 20 per cent learn the neo-Norwegian 'Nynorsk' ('Landsmal', created out of the rural dialects). In the north, the Sami speak their own language.
Main Political Parties: Norwegian Labor Party; Conservative Party; Progress Party; Christian People's Party; Socialist Left Party.
Main Social Organizations: Norwegian Federation of Unions; Organization of Academics (AF); Organization of Trades (YS).

THE STATE

Official Name: Kongeriket Norge.
Administrative Divisions: 19 provinces (Fylker).
Capital: Oslo 795,000 people (2003).
Other Cities: Bergen 200,200 people; Trondheim 140,700; Stavanger 109,900 (2000).
Government: Parliamentary constitutional monarchy. Harald V, King since January 1991. Prime Minister: Kjell Magne Bondevik, appointed by the King in October 2001. Legislative power resides in the Storting, the 165-member unicameral parliament.
National Holiday: 17 May, Constitution Day (1814).
Armed Forces: 29,000 (1995).

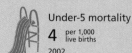

Under-5 mortality
4 per 1,000 live births
2002

Aid
0.89% Official development assistance as % of donors' GNI
2002

Maternal mortality
16 per 100,000 live births
2000

IN FOCUS

ENVIRONMENTAL CHALLENGES

The two main environmental issues are traditional whaling activity - opposed by environmentalists all over the world - and the oil industry, mostly in relation to joint projects with Russia (whose controls are slack) in the Barents Sea, which affect the fragile Arctic environmental balance. Fishing sectors also protest against these projects. In 1986, pollution in rivers and lakes in the south was blamed on sulphur dioxide emissions from the United Kingdom.

WOMEN'S RIGHTS

Women have been able to vote since 1907 (with restrictions) and 1913 (universal suffrage). Since Gro Harlem Brundtland's second term as Prime Minister, in 1986, women have held many government positions, and approximately 40 per cent of ministries. Women make up 46 per cent of the work force.

Approximately 88 per cent of women work in services, 10 per cent in industry, and 2 per cent in agriculture. Prenatal health coverage stands at 100 per cent, as does the proportion of births attended by qualified medical staff.

CHILDREN

Five per cent of children had low birth weight*. A report presented by Norway at the 33rd International Congress of Military Medicine held in Helsinki, Finland, in June 2000, explained the programs implemented to reduce the high number of suicides among Armed Forces recruits below the age of 20. Risk factors were studied and permanent counseling is offered.

INDIGENOUS PEOPLES/ ETHNIC MINORITIES

The Sami, a 40,000-member minority, live mostly in the northern province of Finnmark and belong to the ancient people

of Lapland. Spread throughout Norway, Sweden, Finland and the Kola peninsula in Russia, and with a total population of 80,000, they speak a Uralic language (of the Finno-Ugric family). They arrived in these lands before the Scandinavians, Finnish or Russians, and although they used to practice shamanism, today they are mostly Protestants. The Icelandic sagas of the 18th century include the first references to their existence. Although initially they were hunter-gatherers, for a long time reindeer farming has been their main activity. Only some 7,000 Sami currently herd reindeer, with a total of 500,000 animals. The arrival of hydroelectric, oil and fishing companies on their lands, as well as government efforts to integrate them into Norwegian society, has turned their reindeer-herding more into a business than a way of life. They are represented in Norway by a Council or Parliament elected by the community.

MIGRANTS/REFUGEES

In 2001 Norway received 1,269 refugees sent by UNHCR, and has continued to process asylum requests. In 2003, more than 17,500 asylum requests had been received by the Board of Immigration (UDI), which analyzes and approves them. That number represented a 16 per cent increase on the previous year. Refugees come mostly from Serbia and Montenegro (2,460), the Russian Federation (1,720), Iraq (1,620) and Somalia (1,530). The permits, once granted, can be renewed each year.

DEATH PENALTY

The death penalty for common offenses was abolished in 1905 and for all types of crimes in 1979. The last execution took place in 1948.

*Latest data available in *The State of the World's Children* and *Childinfo* database, UNICEF, 2004.

November 1990 Brundtland was appointed Prime Minister once again.

[33] King Olaf V died in 1991, and was succeeded by his son Harald V.

[34] In January 1992, the Norwegian consulate in South Africa was upgraded to an embassy, after the ending of apartheid brought about in part by trade sanctions imposed by Norway and other countries. Minister of Foreign Affairs, Johan Juergen Holst, served as an intermediary in the Israeli-PLO negotiations.

[35] Despite serious disagreements among Norwegians, Oslo sought entry to the European Union (EU) in late 1992. Labor unions considered that joining the former European Community would threaten national sovereignty, while many entrepreneurs - particularly in the export sector - wanted full access to the EU market.

[36] Entry had to be approved by a referendum, and a date was set for November 1994. The campaign for this vote largely dominated political life for two years and revolved around oil exploitation, and regional and fishing policy.

[37] While only the social democrats and conservatives supported joining the EU, 52.4 per cent of the electorate voted against integration, blocking Norway's membership.

[38] In 1994, the economy continued to expand and

unemployment to fall. In 1995, unemployment reached 4.8 per cent and the trend was expected to continue.

[39] In October 1996, the Labor Party's Thorbjorn Jagland became head of government after Gro Harlem Brundtland resigned.

[40] Following the September 1997 elections, Jagland resigned. The ruling LP took 35 per cent of the vote and 65 seats out of the total 165 in play. The Prime Minister had announced he would stand down if the party could not equal the 36.9 per cent it had achieved in 1993.

[41] Christian Democrat Kjell Magne Bondevik was appointed Prime Minister. A coalition of three centrist parties took control but with only 43 seats in Parliament. Bondevik started by earmarking part of the oil income for investments in health and education.

[42] In 1997, the economy expanded for the fifth year running. However in early 1998, Norway began to suffer the consequences of falling international crude oil prices, following the crisis in Southeast Asia - the biggest oil-importing market in the world.

[43] The installation of natural gas plants became the center of a controversy that led Bondevik to resign in 2000. He maintained that the plants would release too much carbon dioxide into the atmosphere, while the opposition parties insisted on avoiding

increased spending on fuel imports at all costs.

[44] Labor leader Jens Stoltenberg took office as the new Prime Minister on March 2000. Women were appointed to approximately half of Cabinet posts. Norway served as intermediary between the Government of Sri Lanka and Tamil separatists.

[45] In September 2000, the 'other Norwegian nation', the Sami, who for 20 years had tried to clarify their rights to the land, protested against a government plan to tap a gold mine in the northern region of Pasvik. The Sami Parliament - an advisory, non-executive body - demanded to be heard and said the use of the territory by the Government would endanger the community's survival, which was dependent on fishing and reindeer herds. For centuries the Sami had not been allowed to claim any land rights, because the land was restricted to speakers of Norwegian. The Sami language had been taught in schools since 1960.

[46] In early 2001, the Government decided to re-establish exports of whale meat and fat, thus lifting the ban imposed due to international pressure. Environmental organizations argued that endangered species would be affected. The killing of grey wolves, considered a threat to livestock, led to a clash with Sweden, which claimed the wolves

were an endangered species. Meanwhile, the Government promoted seal hunting as a tourist attraction and proposed the killing of dolphins for scientific research.

[47] Benjamin Hermansen, a young Norwegian-Ghanaian anti-racist activist, was stabbed to death in January 2001 by six members of the neo-Nazi group Boot Boys, who were later arrested and tried.

[48] The LP did not gain a majority in the September 2001 general elections. A month later a three-party coalition was formed between Conservatives, the Christian People's Party and Liberals, who jointly supported the right-wing Progress Party and Kjell Magne Bondevik as new Prime Minister.

[49] In 2002, environmentalists continued to try to stop whaling, warning consumers about the harm the hunting caused to several endangered Nordic species. Whale fat was exported mostly to Japan. The Government insisted that it applied controls on whaling.

[50] Norway suspended its participation in the peace process in Sri Lanka in November 2003, after disagreements with that country's leadership.

[51] In December 2003, environmentalists and the fishing industry warned against planned oil exploration in the Barents Sea, fearful of the plan's environmental impact. ∎

Oman / Uman

Population:	3,020,264
Area:	309,500 km²
Capital:	Muscat (Masqat)
Currency:	Omani rial
Language:	Arabic

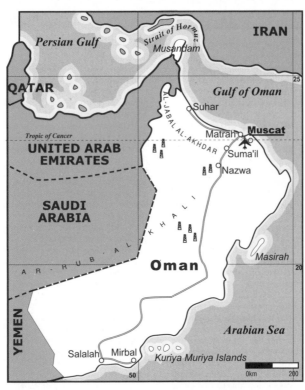

S umerian clay tablets from the third century BC mention Oman as one of the outstanding markets in the economy of the Mesopotamian cities. Omani navigators became the lords of the Indian Ocean, connecting the Gulf to India, Indonesia and Indochina. In the 7th century they also played a major role in the peaceful propagation of Islam. Around 690 AD Abd Al-Malik decided to control the expansion of dissident sects. Consequently, some defeated leaders were forced to abandon the country. One of them, Prince Hamza, migrated to Africa where he founded Zanzibar, beginning a relationship between Oman and the African coast that would last until the 19th century.

² Towards 751, Oman took advantage of the dynastic strife in Damascus to elect an *imam* who gradually evolved from a spiritual leader to a temporal sovereign. Omani wealth gave the *imam* considerable power in the entire Gulf region, but also made Oman the object of successive invasions by the caliphs of Baghdad, the Persians, the Mongols and the local groups of central Arabia, which were all repelled. The Portuguese arrived in 1507, destroying the fleet and coastal fortifications, opening the way for the occupation of the principal cities and the control of the Strait of Hormuz. The Portuguese held control of the region for almost 150 years.

³ In 1630, Imam Nasir ibn Murshid launched an inland struggle against the invaders. His son, Said, concluded this endeavor in 1650 with the expulsion of the Portuguese from Muscat (Musqat) and the recovery of Zanzibar and the African coast of Mombasa in 1698. Thus a powerful state was created which obtained the political unification of the African and Asian territories where a common culture and economy had developed.

⁴ Sultan Said, the third in the Saiyid dynasty, expanded the African territories and moved the capital to Zanzibar in 1832. At the time of his death in 1856, the British presence was already being strongly felt on both continents. Said's sons argued and as a result, the African and Asian parts of the state were separated: the elder son, Thuwaini, kept the sultanate of Oman while his brother Majid took control of Zanzibar. The 1891 Canning Agreement virtually made Oman a British protectorate, weakening the Omani Kingdom.

⁵ In 1913, inland peoples elected their own *imam* in opposition to the sultan's hereditary rule. Despite support from British troops, the sultan could not reconquer the rebel provinces. The struggle came to an end only in 1920, when a treaty was signed acknowledging the country's division in two: the Sultanate of Muscat and the Imamate of Oman. The imam persuaded the sultan to promise not to interfere in Imamate affairs, nor grant asylum to criminals and opposition members who fled

Oman. In exchange Muscat was given control over customs and the right to set taxes on imports coming from the UK.

⁶ Muscat was an extremely poor country, where arable lands accounted for less than one per cent of the total territory, and was artificially divided by colonialism. Between 1932 and 1970, it suffered the despotic rule of Sultan Said ibn Taimur, who fanatically opposed any foreign influence in the country, even in education and healthcare. This did not prevent him from granting control over the country's oil deposits to Royal Dutch Shell.

⁷ Imam Ghaleb ibn Alim, elected in 1954, proclaimed independence and announced his intention to join the Arab League. In 1955, after putting down the nationalist movement, the British invaded the Imamate and reunited the country under the name of Sultanate of Muscat and Oman. Since then a liberation movement has been fighting against the monarchy, particularly in the southern province of Dhofar.

⁸ Taimur was overthrown by his own son Qabus on 23 July 1970. Those who expected the young, Oxford-educated monarch to introduce modernizing changes soon realized that British domination was only being replaced by US domination. The US became a net importer of oil and began to develop an active interest in the area.

⁹ Oil, produced commercially since 1967, provided more than half of the GDP. However more than half of Oman's labor force remained involved in agriculture, in the thin coastal strip that contains the country's only arable land.

¹⁰ With US assistance, Qabus organized a mercenary army but when this force proved incapable of smashing the Popular Front for the Liberation of the Gulf, he signed an agreement with Iran's Shah Reza Pahlevi to secure Iranian intervention in the conflict.

¹¹ The guerrilla fighters were forced to retreat under the superior firepower of Iranian troops. Iranians also placed the Strait of Hormuz under their jurisdiction and stayed in the country establishing a virtual protectorate over Qabus's regime.

¹² At the Shah's downfall, Iranian soldiers were quickly replaced by Egyptian commandos and troops. The Sultan decided to give the US the Masirah island air base, and later the air bases at Ihamrit and Sib and the naval bases at Matrah and Salalah. At that time, two-thirds of the national budget was committed to defense.

¹³ In the 1980s, during the Iran-Iraq war, the US focused on Oman in its efforts to establish influence in the area.

PROFILE

ENVIRONMENT

With its 2,600 km coastline, Oman occupies a strategic position on the southeastern edge of the Arabian Peninsula and flanking the Gulf of Oman, where oil tankers leave the Persian Gulf. It is separated from the rest of the peninsula by the Rub al Khali desert that stretches into the center of the country. Local nomadic groups now live alongside petroleum and natural gas exploitation. Favored by ocean currents, the coastal regions enjoy a better climate. Monsoon summer rains fall in the north.

SOCIETY

Peoples: Omani Arab 73.5 per cent; Pakistani (mostly Baluchi) 18.7 per cent; other 5.5 per cent. **Religions:** Muslim 86 per cent; Hindu 13 per cent; other 1 per cent. **Languages:** Arabic, official and predominant, English, Baluchi and Urdu are also spoken.
Main Political Parties: There are no legal political parties.

THE STATE

Official Name: Saltanat 'Uman (Sultanate of Oman).
Administrative Divisions: 59 Districts. **Capital:** Muscat (Masqat) 638,000 people (2003). **Other Cities:** Nizwa 74,400; Suma'il 42,700; Salalah 163,600 (2000). **Government:** Absolute Monarchy. Qabus bin Said, Sultan since July 1970 and Prime Minister since January 1972. Bicameral Legislature: the Consultative Assembly (*Majlis al-Shura*), with 82 elected members with only consultative tasks, and the Council of State (*Majlis al-Dawla*), with 40 appointed members. **National Holiday:** 19 November, the Sultan's birthday. **Armed Forces:** 43,500 (1996). Other: 3,900.

	Life expectancy		GNI per capita		Literacy		HIV prevalence rate

Life expectancy
72.4 years
2000-2005

GNI per capita
$7,720
2002

Literacy
72% total adult rate
2000

HIV prevalence rate
0.1% of population 15-49 years old
2001

14 In 1989 oil prices became steady and in June, the major oil and gas company Petroleum Development Oman (PDO) discovered the most important natural gas deposits found within the last 20 years.

15 That year Oman adopted a conciliatory policy towards Iran, establishing an economic cooperation agreement, on the condition that political stability be promoted in the country.

16 Following the Iraqi invasion of Kuwait in March 1991, a member of the Gulf Cooperation Council (GCC), Oman suspended aid to Jordan and to the PLO.

17 In 1991, the Government announced that the democratization process was under way; this included the creation of a parliament directly elected by the country's citizens.

18 The Sultan launched a plan to diversify the country's economy, aiming at developing fishing, agriculture and tourism, among other sectors, faced with the prospect of the depletion of oil reserves before the year 2010.

19 The fiscal deficits accumulated by the Government since 1981 led the World Bank to warn that the level of State expenditure was 'unsustainable'.

20 Taking heed of the international financial organization's stand, in 1995 the Sultan announced a program of reforms which included a reduction of state spending, a series of privatizations and measures to attract foreign investment.

21 In 1996, the Government announced a five-year plan to balance the budget by 2000. The project, aiming to free the economy from oil dependence, included privatizations and stimuli to increase foreign investment.

22 That same year, the Sultan established a new succession mechanism. This meant that, if the royal family could not reach agreement on the appointment of a successor within three days of his death, the candidate chosen by the Sultan himself would be accepted.

23 In June 1997 Sultan Qabus expanded women's political rights by royal decree, allowing women to stand for election. In the October 1997 elections, the Government selected two women to serve on the Consultative Council (*Majlis al-Shura*). In December 1997, the Sultan appointed 4 women to the 41-member Council of State (*Majlis Al-Dawla*).

24 Oman became one of the first Arab countries to establish diplomatic and trade relations with Israel in January 1997. A month later, the rapprochement process came to a halt, when the Arab League questioned the Israeli decision to build new settlements in eastern Jerusalem.

IN FOCUS

ENVIRONMENTAL CHALLENGES
Rising soil salinity, coastal pollution from oil spills and very limited water resources are the main environmental challenges the country is facing.

WOMEN'S RIGHTS
2003 saw the first universal elections to the *Majlis al-shura* (Consultative Assembly) for candidates over the age of 21, even though a restricted group of women have been able to run for election since 1994. In short, Oman's history has been marked by an absence of female political representation.

In the year 2000, women constituted 17 per cent of the workforce, working mostly in services.

The Basic Charter prohibits discrimination on the basis of sex, ethnic origin, race, language, sect, place of residence, and social class. Interpretations of Islamic law (*Sharia*) and tradition affect women's rights regarding private property and access to state loans. Only 62 per cent of adult women were able to read and write in the year 2000, while 80 per cent of men were literate. In 2003 female enrolment at tertiary level outnumbered male. In 2002, 54 per cent of students at the country's main university were women. Rape within marriage is not illegal, nor is female genital excision or mutilation, although this practice is declining.

CHILDREN
In 2001 half the country's population comprised children and adolescents aged under 18. Life expectancy has risen over the last 30 years, from 50 to 74.4 years.

In 2003 the Government raised the minimum age for child labor from 13 to 15 years. Adolescents aged 15 to 18 are allowed to work, but not at night, nor weekends or holidays. It is still difficult to control child labor in small family businesses, particularly those in the agriculture and fishing sectors.

Government efforts have led to improvements in access to education, although the quality of preschool education remains poor.

INDIGENOUS PEOPLES/ ETHNIC MINORITIES
Citizens of African origin complained of job discrimination in both the public and private sectors. A Royal Decree ratified the International Convention on the Elimination of All Forms of Racial Discrimination in the year 2000.

Religious freedom is allegedly granted by law, but Hindu or Christian temples are only allowed to be built in locations determined by the Government. The Government prohibited non-Muslims from proselytizing, including publishing religious material, although religious material printed abroad could be brought into the country. Most Omanis are Ibadhi Muslims, followers of Abd Allah ibn Ibad. 25 per cent are Sunni Muslims, and there is a minor group of Shi'a Muslims, most of whom are of Iranian or Iraqi descent. Ibadhism is a form of Islam different in its hierarchical organization from the rest of the Muslim groups. The reason why Oman is in some aspects isolated from its neighbors is the practice of Ibadhism, according to Sunni and Shi'a Muslims.

MIGRANTS/REFUGEES
The extradition of political refugees is prohibited, and there have been no reports of the forced return of people to a country where they feared persecution.

Tight control over the entry of foreigners to the country has limited the entry of refugees and asylum-seekers.

Hundreds or thousands of illegal immigrants, mainly from Iran, Pakistan and Afghanistan are detained each year by the Royal Omani Police and held in special centers until their deportation can be arranged. The Government does not routinely grant protection to refugees or asylum-seekers.

DEATH PENALTY
The death penalty applies even for ordinary crimes.

25 In early 1998, Oman, along with all the other Gulf Cooperation Council (GCC) member nations, debated the possibility of freeing its currency from the dollar to prevent the loss of income on oil sales. The six GCC nations controlled 45 per cent of the world's crude oil reserves, but were losing millions of dollars per year due to falling international exchange rates of the US currency.

26 Oman and the United Arab Emirates signed an accord in May 1999 that defined part of the common border with the Abu Dhabi Emirate. Both parties agreed that, eventually, they would have to delineate more exactly the borders between Oman and the other emirates.

27 In April 2001 the Government announced an amnesty for illegal workers. The amnesty allowed illegal residents not facing any criminal charge to leave Oman after paying a $125 fine at the Labor Ministry, rather than the normal penalty for over-stayers of $25 dollars a day.

28 In July, three Pakistanis were executed at the prison in al-Manouwama, a suburb of Muscat, convicted of smuggling illegal narcotics into the country.

29 In November 2001, in the UN General Assembly, Oman voted in favor of a resolution prohibiting the use of antipersonnel landmines in territories involved in armed conflicts.

30 In August 2002 Oman endorsed the amendment of Article 43 of the Convention on the Rights of the Child, increasing the number of Child Rights Committee members from 10 to 18. In October that year, Muscat ratified the International Convention on the Elimination of Racial Discrimination. The Ministry of Social Development issued a decree for the formation of national social development committees. These committees hold the responsibilities of both promoting voluntary social organizations and through their activities, enhancing awareness of issues relating to childhood and disability, and also finding alternative funding for social programs.

31 In November 2002 Sultan Qabus decreed an extension of voting rights to all citizens over the age of 21. Previously, those allowed to vote were selected from among local leaders, intellectuals and prominent entrepreneurs, with about a quarter of the state's 1.8 million people taking part in elections.

32 In order to reduce unemployment, the Government tried to replace foreign workers with Omanis and encouraged job growth in the private sector. According to official figures, a quarter of the sultanate's population are foreigners.

33 Oman's electric power is generated from domestic oil- and gas-burning plants. Through the use of cutting-edge technology, the country expected to boost its declining oil output and increase production to 50,000 barrels a day. The Government was also seeking ways to take advantage of other energy reserves, such as natural gas to improve the economy.

34 In October 2003 the first elections in which all citizens over the age of 21 were allowed to vote were held. Voters elected the 83 members of the *Majlis al-Shura* (Consultative Council). Two women were among those elected. ∎

Pakistan / Pakistan

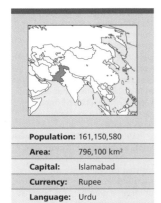

Population:	161,150,580
Area:	796,100 km²
Capital:	Islamabad
Currency:	Rupee
Language:	Urdu

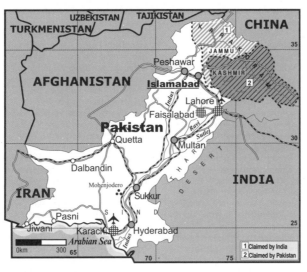

1 Claimed by India
2 Claimed by Pakistan

Pakistan means the land of the pure, as it was religion (Islam) that bound together the people of different ethnic communities and languages. Poet-philosopher Mohammed Iqbal articulated the concept of Pakistan in 1931 when he proposed a separate state for the Muslims in the Indian subcontinent.

2 After the arrival in India of traders from Arabia and Persia, a permanent Muslim foothold was achieved with Muhammad ibn Qasim's conquest of Sind in 711 AD.

3 In 1296 Ala-ud-din Khalji proclaimed himself Sultan of Delhi and by 1311 the whole of India was under the Sultanate. In 1336 the Vijayanagara Empire, the kingdom of Hindu alliance, was founded with its capital at Hampi to counter the Muslim power. Over time uprisings divided the Empire and the Muslim Sultanates formed a new alliance. In 1565 the Sultanate coalition defeated the Vijayanagar army. As a result, the power in the region passed to Muslim rulers and later their kingdoms were annexed to the Mughal Empire (1529-1857).

4 The decline of Muslim power and the rise of the Hindu middle class took place during British colonialism. In October 1906, Muslim leaders searching for an effective political tool, met the British viceroy and demanded a reform of the electoral system with a separate system for Muslims. The All India Muslim League (ML) was founded in Dhaka (in what is now Bangladesh) to defend their political rights and interests. The British conceded the reform in the Government of India Act of 1909, confirming the ML's status as the representative of Indian Muslims.

5 In the 1930s there was a growing awareness of a common identity among Muslims as well as the need to preserve it within a separate territory. Under the leadership of Muhammad Ali Jinnah, ML continued its campaign for Pakistan; a separate homeland in British India. After the general election of April 1946, a convention of newly-elected Muslim parliamentarians reiterated the demand for the establishment of Pakistan at the request of Hussain Shaheed Suhrawardi, then chief minister of Bengal.

6 The Hindu-Muslim relationship was affected by tensions and riots in different parts of India. This convinced the leadership of the Indian National Congress (representing mainly the nationalists) to accept Pakistan as a solution to the problems. On 3 June 1947, after the British withdrawal from India, a Partition Plan was announced and both the ML and the Congress accepted it. On 14 August of the same year, the new state of Pakistan was born comprising West Punjab, Sind, Baluchistan, North-West Frontier Province and East Bengal, surrounding northeastern and northwestern India.

7 Between 1948 and 1949, Pakistan annexed one third of the Indian province of Kashmir. The territory, mostly Muslim, had been annexed to India in 1947, in exchange for military support against Pakistani fighters.

8 Pakistan became a member of the Southeast Asian Treaty Organization (SEATO) in 1954 and the Central Treaty Organization (CENTO) in 1955, two strong military alliances led by the US. Pakistan later withdrew from these alliances, although bilateral relations with the US remained cordial.

9 Since gaining independence, Pakistan has suffered permanent political crises. The first constitution of March 1956 was abrogated by a coup on 7 October 1958, in which martial law was proclaimed. On 27 October 1958, General Ayub Khan introduced 'basic democracy', a system of local self-government and indirect presidential elections. Martial law came to an end in 1962 and a new constitution granted absolute power to the President and declared Pakistan an Islamic Republic. Ayub Khan was forced to resign on 25 March 1969, following a popular uprising. Martial law was again imposed and General Yahya Khan became President.

10 In the first general elections held between October and December 1970, the Awami League (AL) and the Pakistan People's Party (PPP) emerged victorious in East and West Pakistan, respectively. The AL won

---

PROFILE

ENVIRONMENT

Pakistan is mountainous and semi-arid, with the exception of the Indus River basin in the east. This is virtually the only irrigated zone in the country, suitable for agriculture and vital to the local economy. The Indus rises in the Himalayas in the disputed province of Kashmir and flows into the Arabian Sea. The majority of the population live along its banks. The main agricultural products are wheat and cotton, grown under irrigation.

SOCIETY

Peoples: Most Pakistanis are of Indo-European descent, mixed with Persian, Greeks and Arabs (in the Indus Valley), and Turkish and Mongolian (in the mountainous areas). Much Indian immigration has occurred in recent years. There are 5 main ethnic groups: Punjabi, Sindhi, Pashtun, Mujahir and Baluch. **Religions:** Islam is the official religion followed by more than 95 per cent of the population (most belong to the Sunni sect); 2 per cent are Christian;1.6 per cent are Hindu; the remainder belong to other smaller sects. **Languages:** Urdu (official, although it is spoken by only 9 per cent of the population). Other languages are Punjabi, Sindhi, Pashtu, Baluchi, English and more than 50 local languages.
Main Political Parties: Pakistan People's Party (PPP); Awami National Party, Baluchistan National Party; Republican National Party; Jamaa-e-Islami (Islamic Assembly). **Main Social Organizations:** The National Pakistan Federation of Unions.

THE STATE

Official Name: Islam-i Jamhuriya-e Pakistan.
Administrative Divisions: 4 provinces, 1 territory (Tribal Areas) and 1 capital territory (Islamabad).
Capital: Islamabad 698,000 people (2003).
Other Cities: Karachi 11,800,000 people; Lahore 5,470,000; Faisalabad 2,136,000 (2000).
Government: General Pervez Musharraf, self-appointed President since June 2001, confirmed by referendum in 2002. Prime Minister Chaudhry Shujaat Hussain resigns to pave the way for Finance Minister Shaukat Aziz to take over the post. **National Holidays:** 14 August, Independence Day (1947); 23 March, Proclamation of the Republic (1956). **Armed Forces:** 587,000 (1996). Other: 275,000 (National Guard, Border Corps, Maritime Security, Mounted Police).

WORKERS

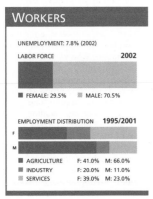

UNEMPLOYMENT: 7.8% (2002)

LABOR FORCE 2002

■ FEMALE: 29.5%   ■ MALE: 70.5%

EMPLOYMENT DISTRIBUTION 1995/2001

F
M

■ AGRICULTURE	F: 41.0%	M: 66.0%
■ INDUSTRY	F: 20.0%	M: 11.0%
■ SERVICES	F: 39.0%	M: 23.0%

Life expectancy
61.0 years
2000-2005

GNI per capita
$410
2002

Literacy
43% total adult rate
2000

HIV prevalence rate
0.1% of population 15-49 years old
2001

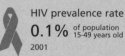

an absolute majority in the parliamentary elections, which gave it control of the federal government. When the opening of parliament was postponed in March 1971, the people of East Pakistan began the movement for an independent Bangladesh. The AL was banned and its leader Sheikh Mujibur Rahman was arrested. A civil war broke out and the AL formed a government in exile in India. The Indian army intervened and on 16 December 1971, Bangladesh was granted independence.

[11] Zulfiqar Ali Bhutto, the leader of the PPP, formed a civilian government in 1972, following the resignation of General Yahya Khan. He encouraged strong public sector participation in the economy, followed a non-aligned foreign policy and approved radical land reforms. The PPP was victorious again in the general election of 1977, but the opposition parties accused the PPP of vote-rigging. At that point, General Zia-ul Haq overthrew the Bhutto Government and proclaimed martial law. Bhutto was arrested and sentenced to death on charges of conspiracy.

[12] Pakistan strenuously opposed Soviet intervention in Afghanistan at the end of 1979.

[13] Zia accelerated the process of Islamicization in all spheres of political and social life. Many political opponents were harassed and detained. A general election without political parties held in February 1985 partially legitimated Zia's Government. Zia was killed in a mysterious air crash in August 1988 and democracy was restored. Benazir Bhutto (PPP), daughter of the former President, took office following general elections in November 1988.

[14] Benazir was the first woman to serve as head of state of a predominantly Islamic country, with two terms in office (1988-1990 and 1993-1996). Under Benazir, Pakistan became a signatory of the International Convention for the Elimination of Discrimination against Women, but some women felt their situation did not improve significantly with a female president. Some felt that she did not make sufficient efforts to push through laws to re-establish a quota of female seats in parliament. However her weak coalition government included conservative religious parties who opposed any such changes. Nonetheless, during her presidency women were appointed for the first time as high-court judges; a campaign

against domestic violence began, and a women's bank was set up.

[15] In mid-1990, there were about three million Afghan refugees living in Pakistan. During the Soviet occupation of Afghanistan, the US used Pakistani territory to supply arms to the *Mujahedin*, rebel groups fighting against the pro-Soviet regime in Kabul. This situation turned Pakistan into a key ally for US regional policy, and resulted in the granting of significant economic assistance.

[16] On 6 August 1990, President Ghulam Ishaq Khan dissolved Benazir's government, charging her administration with nepotism and corruption. The President suspended the National Assembly and named Ghulam Mustafa Jatoi, leader of the Combined Opposition Parties (COP) coalition, head of the interim government.

[17] On 24 October 1990, Nawaz Sharif was elected Prime Minister, with the support of the Muslim League. The Pakistan People's Party (PPP) of Benazir Bhutto (who had also stood) denounced electoral fraud and launched an intense opposition campaign.

[18] When the Gulf War broke out, following the Iraqi invasion of Kuwait, Pakistan sent troops to Saudi Arabia. Surveys showed that the population had strong pro-Iraqi tendencies, but the Government announced that the country's forces would only defend Islamic holy places, and would not take part in combat or go into Iraqi territory.

[19] Shortly after taking office, Sharif approved a plan to encourage private investment that included the privatization of state-run companies. This plan was strongly resisted by the 300,000 public sector workers.

[20] A process of re-Islamization of society, promoted by Sharif, included the introduction of *sharia* or Islamic law with consequent setbacks for women's social and legal status. The Government banned the media from making any reference to a woman's right to divorce.

[21] In November 1991, the opposition accused Nawaz Sharif of embezzling public funds. Sharif was responsible for the bankruptcy of several cooperative credit institutions. Only the unconditional support of President Ishaq Khan prevented the fall of Sharif. The matter was referred to the judiciary and triggered a wave of demonstrations led by the PPP, to which the Government reacted with increased repression.

[22] In February 1992, the ancient dispute over the border territory

of Kashmir brought Pakistan and India to the brink of a new armed conflict. The Jammu and Kashmir Liberation Front, a Muslim group demanding the creation of an independent state, staged a protest march against the division of the territory between the two countries disputing it. The Pakistani Government ordered the army to shoot at the demonstrators, and several people were injured or killed.

[23] When Pakistan developed a nuclear weapon construction project in 1992, the US suspended economic assistance and arms sales to Islamabad. Pakistan announced that China had guaranteed economic and technological support to continue the nuclear research program.

[24] President Ishaq Khan accused Prime Minister Nawaz Sharif of poor administration, corruption and nepotism, forcing him to resign in April 1993. Sharif appealed to the Supreme Court and was reinstated in May. The dissolution of the Assembly was revoked and the call for elections cancelled. Both Khan and Sharif resigned in July.

[25] The interim President, Moin Kureishi, a former World Bank and IMF official, suspended the system whereby members of Parliament had received funds for investment in their own districts, a source of endless corruption, and also taxed large property units. Traditionally, powerful landowners had dominated Pakistan's economy and political system and had exempted themselves from paying taxes. Only one per cent of the 139 million workers paid taxes.

[26] Benazir Bhutto returned to power in October 1993. The PPP won 86 of the Assembly's 217 seats, against 72 obtained by Sharif.

[27] Between 1994 and 1995, Bhutto attempted to democratize the country at a time of more political and ethnic violence than had been seen since the separation of Bangladesh in 1971. Karachi and the northern separatist areas were the center of disputes, in which over 3,500 died.

[28] On 20 September 1996, Murtaza Bhutto, brother of the Prime Minister and leader of a guerrilla group demanding her resignation, died in a confrontation with the police. The Bhuttos had been rivals since their father was overthrown in 1977.

[29] In November, Benazir was forced to resign after being accused of corruption. In the new parliamentary elections, the

followers of former Prime Minister Nawaz Sharif won 136 seats of the 217 at stake. Miraj Khalid led the Government as Deputy Prime Minister until Sharif came to office in early 1997.

[30] Tension with India intensified in May 1998, when that country carried out a series of nuclear tests and Pakistan responded with its own.

[31] While the Indian Government kept claiming its authority over the Kashmir region, Pakistan insisted on calling for a referendum among Kashmiris to determine whether they were in favor of independence.

[32] In October 1999, General Pervez Musharraf, who had been in charge of military operations in Kashmir and had been removed from his post by Sharif, led a coup and imprisoned the Prime Minister, accusing him of kidnapping, terrorism and attempted murder. Pakistan became the first nuclear power under military leadership.

[33] While the military government was trying the former Prime Minister, his defense lawyer Iqbal Raad was murdered. Although Musharraf blamed the murder on terrorists, Sharif's supporters accused the Government of involvement.

[34] On 10 December 1999, Sharif was granted a presidential pardon and exiled in Saudi Arabia in exchange for not returning to Pakistan for ten years and renouncing his personal fortune. He also promised not to participate in the country's politics for 21 years.

[35] The first stage of local elections was held in late December, in 18 of the 106 districts. Analysts observed a change in control of the electoral scene, from political parties to local feudal families.

[36] By March 2000, the second stage of local elections had been held in 20 districts, and the pressure had grown on the President to present a clear schedule to return to a democratic system in October 2002. Meanwhile, the police detained more than 2,000 activists from the Alliance for the Restoration of Democracy and 22 of its leaders, who were planning a demonstration.

[37] Musharraf became head of state and was appointed President of Pakistan in June 2001, announcing he would maintain the powers he had as head of the executive branch, and that he would remain as commander of the army. In October, Musharraf extended his mandate indefinitely as Supreme Commander of the Army.

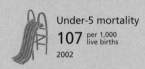

	Under-5 mortality		Poverty		Debt service		Maternal mortality
	107 per 1,000 live births 2002		**13.4%** of population living on less than $1 per day 1998		**25.8%** exports of goods and services 2001		**500** per 100,000 live births 2000

³⁸ After the terrorist attacks on 11 September 2001 against New York and Washington, the US announced it would lift economic and military sanctions it had imposed on India and Pakistan after the nuclear tests of 1998. The measure was motivated by Musharraf's support for the US military operation in Afghanistan, against the Taliban regime of Saudi-born terrorist Osama Bin Laden. The Taliban, which ruled in Kabul, had formerly received direct military, economic and ideological support from Pakistan. The Taliban's assumption of power in 1996 had been considered by members of the Pakistani army as their first 'victory'.

³⁹ The US bombings over Afghanistan caused extensive protests from Islamic Pakistani groups. Musharraf made changes in the army shortly before the US military operations began in the neighboring country, releasing some pro-Islamic generals from strategic posts.

⁴⁰ When US Secretary of State Colin Powell visited Islamabad in October 2001, Musharraf requested Washington's support in the Kashmir conflict, as well as aid for the economic consequences of the huge inflow of Afghan refugees crossing the border.

⁴¹ India blamed Pakistan for the suicide attack on the Indian Parliament in Delhi by Islamic activists on 13 December. Musharraf condemned the attack and denied any link between his Government and those responsible for it. On 26 December 2001, India deployed troops and planes on its border with Pakistan, increasing the tension in Kashmir. While Indian and Pakistani troops exchanged fire along the border, on 30 December Pakistani authorities detained Mohammed Saeed, the leader of one of the activist groups blamed for the attack on Parliament.

⁴² On 18 March 2002, supposed Islamic militants threw grenades inside a Protestant church in Islamabad, killing several people. In April, US journalist Daniel Pearl, who had been kidnapped in January by an Islamic group, was murdered.

⁴³ In April 2002, Musharraf called for a referendum with the support of the Supreme Court. With 97 per cent of the vote he was allowed to extend his presidency for another five years. All observers denounced the elections as fraudulent.

⁴⁴ After tests of medium-range surface-to-surface missiles, capable of transporting nuclear

IN FOCUS

ENVIRONMENTAL CHALLENGES
Pakistan suffers from water shortage and pollution, soil depletion and deforestation.

WOMEN'S RIGHTS
Women have been able to vote since 1947. The situation of gender inequality in the country has varied depending on political circumstances. Benazir Bhutto's governments made some advances that were reversed by military coups and fundamentalist surges in some provincial and national governments. Except for Benazir and four female members of Parliament in 1990, women's political participation has been practically non-existent.

Women's participation in the labor force - about 35 per cent - has remained constant since 1980.

In 2000, the percentage of literate women was 49 per cent.

Forty-three per cent of pregnant women receive prenatal care and only 20 per cent of births are attended by trained health staff.

CHILDREN
In 2002, Pakistan had an under-five mortality rate of 107 deaths per 1,000 live births (the rate was 227 per 1,000 in 1960 and 130 per 1,000 in 1990) and an infant mortality rate of 83 per 1,000. Nineteen per cent of babies had low birth weights. This rate increases in children under five years old, 38 per cent of whom are moderately or severely underweight, while in 37 per cent of cases they suffer from moderately or severely

stunted growth. At the end of 2001, around 2,200 children (under 14 years old) were living with HIV/AIDS and 25,000 were AIDS orphans.

There is a significant gap between boys' and girls' net school enrolment rates. In 2002, the primary school enrolment rate was 83 per cent for boys and 48 per cent for girls. In secondary school, it was 29 per cent and 19 per cent, respectively.

INDIGENOUS PEOPLES/ ETHNIC MINORITIES
The Pashtun are the main ethnic minority. They account for 9.5 million people on the border with Afghanistan, where they make up the majority of the population. They are divided into nomadic and settled groups and speak Pashtu, a language of Indo-European origin. Religion is important to them, as is their genealogy. Women have almost no right or value; they usually represent a form of payment for offenses.

The Hunzakut people, famous for their longevity, are divided into the Wakhi and the Burusho. They live on the banks of the river Hunza, number between 55,000 and 60,000 people and speak Burushaski, an Indo-European language. They consider themselves descendants of Alexander the Great and are Muslims. Their tolerance, festive spirit and equality between the sexes are among their most outstanding social characteristics.

The Hazara, a group of between 110,000 and 220,000 Persian language speakers, live on the border with Afghanistan where they make up 9 per cent of

the total population. They are warlike, self-sufficient people who trade almost exclusively with their Pashtun neighbors. They believe themselves to be descendants of Gengis Khan.

The Kalash are the most enigmatic of ancient peoples. The nearly 6,000 people living in the Pamir mountain range speak Chitrali (a language unknown to their neighbors) and have little in common with the surrounding peoples except for the fact that - like the Hunzakut - they believe themselves to be descendants of Alexander the Great. They practice the only animistic religion in the area, with innumerable gods, angels and spirits.

MIGRANTS/REFUGEES
The migratory flow from Afghanistan has been constant. In the late 1970s it was due to the Soviet occupation, in the mid-1990s it took place when the Taliban regime seized power and since January 2002, it has been caused by US attacks in the search for Osama bin Laden.

In 2003, Pakistan received 1.7 million Afghan refugees and 18,000 refugees from other nationalities including 17,000 from Kashmir. The total number of Afghan refugees is estimated at 2.2 million. During the same year, 10,400 Pakistanis sought asylum in different countries around the world.

DEATH PENALTY
The death penalty is still applied, even for ordinary crimes.

warheads, were carried out by Pakistan, Musharraf declared that the country did not want war but was prepared to defend itself in the event of being attacked.

⁴⁵ Opposition forces accused Musharraf of perpetuating his dictatorship, after he decided to grant himself new powers, among which was the right to dissolve a democratically elected parliament. In the October 2002 elections, the Government imposed restrictions on or proscribed important leaders such as Nawaz Sharif and Benazir Bhutto. The Pakistan People's Party (PPP), which supported the military, won by a slim majority. However, the most critical result was the growth of the Islamist parties, mainly in the areas bordering Afghanistan, which

would render them into a key element in any government coalition.

⁴⁶ In November 2002, the National Assembly appointed Zafarullah Jamali (a close ally of Musharraf) as Prime Minister. In elections to the Senate in February 2003 (the final stage of what the President called transition to democracy) the ruling party won once again.

⁴⁷ In June 2003, *Sharia* law was introduced in the North-West Frontier Province.

⁴⁸ In November 2003, Pakistan declared a Kashmir ceasefire, which was swiftly matched by India. In December, Musharraf miraculously survived an attempt on his life when a bomb exploded under a bridge seconds after his car passed over it.

⁴⁹ In February 2004, the country's leading nuclear scientist Dr Abdul Qadeer Khan admitted to having worked on secret projects for the development of nuclear weapons. He said that the technology had been transferred to Libya, North Korea and Iran.

⁵⁰ US Secretary of State Colin Powell declared in March 2004 that Pakistan was the major non-NATO ally of the US in the fight against terrorism, after intense operations were launched against the al-Qaeda network on the border with Afghanistan.

⁵¹ In March-April 2004, after a 14-year break, test cricket was resumed between India and Pakistan - an important symbol of rapprochement between the two nations. ∎

Palau / Palau - Belau

Population:	21,354
Area:	460 km²
Capital:	Koror
Currency:	US dollar
Language:	English

Five thousand years ago, sailors from Formosa and China peopled the islands of Micronesia, forming highly stratified societies where age, sex and military prowess defined rank and wealth.
2 European colonization in the 19th century destroyed cultural diversity, but it did not totally eliminate the indigenous people of Palau.
3 In 1914, the Japanese took the islands from Germany who had bought them from Spain in 1899 for 25 million pesetas. During World War II, Japan installed its main naval base in Palau and it soon became the scene of fierce combat.
4 By the end of World War II, the indigenous population of Palau had been reduced from 45,000 to 6,000. Micronesia became a US trust territory. The US used the islands as nuclear testing grounds and reneged on promises of self-government, instead fostering economic dependence. Palau's self-determination process was delayed until the late 1970s.
5 In 1978, at the beginning of the transition to self-government, the archipelago opted for separation from Micronesia. In January 1979, the new constitution banned all nuclear weapons installations, nuclear waste storage, and foreign land ownership. A further amendment established a 200-mile area of territorial waters under the UN-approved Law of the Sea, which the US tried to veto.
6 The new constitution was endorsed by 35 of the 38 assembly members, but the US put pressure on the local parliament to use Palau as a military base. In July 1980, a third referendum ratified the original document by a 78 per cent majority.
7 In 1981, Gordon Mochire, owner of International Power Systems (IPESCO) arrived in Palau, aiming to install a 16-megawatt nuclear power plant. The scheme was to be financed by the US, subject to amendments to the anti-nuclear constitution.
8 President Haruo Remliik was persuaded to hold another plebiscite on the Mochire project and a 'Compact of Free Association' with the US. The Compact failed to achieve enough votes. In 1983, the President signed agreements for a loan totaling $37.5 million and in 1984, the power plant was built.
9 In 1985 Remliik refused to call a third referendum when the US proposed to revoke the historic anti-nuclear constitution. A few days later he was assassinated.
10 Succumbing to pressure, the Palau Congress amended the Constitution by a referendum, and on 21 August 1987, a further plebiscite approved the Compact.
11 In 1987 and 1988 several attacks and threats on opposition groups took place.
12 In August 1988 President Salii was found dead from a gunshot wound. The official version was suicide.
13 The status of Free Associated State was approved by referendum in July 1993, with 68 per cent of the vote.
14 In November 1996, Kuniwo Nakamura was elected President in the first presidential poll since independence.
15 Despite Chinese opposition, Palau established diplomatic relations with Taiwan in 1999. This coincided with an aggressive Taiwanese policy of winning recognition from small Pacific States in return for economic aid.
16 In 2001, Tommy Remengesau, who had been Vice-President, was sworn in as leader.
17 Remengesau authorized US naval bases in Palau for personnel deployed in Okinawa, Japan.
18 In 2002 Palau's relations with the US and Taiwan improved. Taiwanese Prime Minister, Chen Shui-bian thanked Palau's legislature spokesperson, Mario S Guilbert, during his visit to Taiwan, for the part he played in getting China to withdraw the missiles it had aimed at Taiwan. Guilbert in turn recognized Taiwanese support in tourism, agriculture, education and culture.
19 Palau joined the 'coalition of the willing' in March 2003 and supported the US-led war on Iraq. Remengesau further offered the US use of Palau's facilities for its military operations. ∎

PROFILE

ENVIRONMENT

Palau comprises almost 350 islands, with a total surface area of 494 sq km. A barrier reef to the west forms a large lagoon dotted with small islands. Coral formations and marine life in this lagoon are among the richest in the world with around 1,500 species of tropical fish and 700 types of coral and anemones. The maritime ecosystem is however being damaged by pollution.

SOCIETY

Peoples: Most are of Polynesian origin. Palauan (83.2 per cent), Filipinos (9.8 per cent), Micronesian (2.9 per cent), Chinese (1.2 per cent), 'white' (0.8 per cent), other (3.0 per cent).
Languages: English, Palauan, Sonsoralese, Tobi, Angaur.
Religion: No official religion. Catholics (40.7 per cent); Protestants (24.7 per cent); local religions, mainly modekngei (27.1 per cent), other (7.5 per cent).
Main Political Parties: The Coalition for Open, Honest and Fair Government is opposed to the proliferation of nuclear arms and toxic wastes in the region and rejected the status of Free Associated State; the Palau Party favored it. National Party of Palau.

THE STATE

Official Name: Republic of Palau (Belu'u era Belau).
Administrative Divisions: 16 States. Capital: Koror 14,000 people (2003).
Other Cities: Meyungs 1,100 (2000).
Government: Tommy Remengesau, President since January 2001. The National Congress (Legislature) has two Chambers: the House of Delegates, with 16 members, and the Senate, with 9 members.
National Holidays: 9 July, Constitution Day (1979); 1 October, Independence Day (1994).
Armed Forces: The US is responsible for defense.

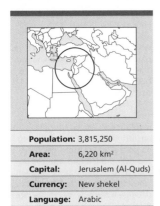

Population:	3,815,250
Area:	6,220 km²
Capital:	Jerusalem (Al-Quds)
Currency:	New shekel
Language:	Arabic

Jewish State, UN Plan, 1947
Arab State, UN Plan, 1947
1 West Bank

Jewish State, UN Plan, 1947
Annexed to Israel in the 1948 war
2 Gaza Strip

Israel's pre-1967 borders
Occupied by Israel in 1967
Recovered by Palestine from 1994: Gaza Strip, Jericho, Nablus, Ramallah

The land now known as Palestine was the site of one of the earliest-known towns, at Jericho, which by around 7000 BC had become a mud-walled settlement with inhabitants who had domesticated animals and begun to rear crops.

2 The area was settled by Semitic peoples who eventually became known as Canaanites and acquired a wide reputation as traders across the Near East. Along with the related Phoenician people – another trading people who settled the coastal area of what is now Lebanon – they were famous for their colored dyes. A Canaanite people, the Jebusites, established a settlement they called Urusalim ('city of peace').

3 Around the 12th century BC an Indo-European sea people called the Philistines settled along the coastal area, building the cities of Gaza, Gath, Ashkelon, Ashdod and Ekron. The word Palestine derives from their name and was later to be applied to the whole land by the Romans.

4 By this time most of the interior of Canaan had been occupied by another Semitic group, the Hebrews, some of whom had returned to the area following a period of captivity in Egypt. The Hebrews were eventually united in their wars against the neighboring Philistines and Ammonites under a chieftain or king called Saul. Under his successor, David, a unified kingdom of Israel was established with the newly conquered Jebusite fortress of Jerusalem as its capital, though after his death it split into two territories, Judaea in the south and Israel in the north. Israel was conquered by the Assyrians in 722 BC and was known thereafter as Samaria. Judaea survived independently until its conquest by the Babylonians in 597 BC. Around 10 years later, following a rebellion, the Babylonian king Nebuchadnezzar sacked Jerusalem, destroyed its temple and deported many skilled workers to Babylon.

5 Over the succeeding centuries, control of the area passed to the Persian Empire and then to the Greeks under Alexander, whose general Ptolemy gained control of Palestine as well as Egypt in the carve-up of territory following Alexander's death. By 200 BC Palestine was under the control of another Greek dynasty, the Seleucids, whose attempt to increase the Hellenization of the local culture eventually met with the Jewish Maccabean Revolt, a guerrilla war which did not properly end until 141 BC. By then a Jewish dynasty of priest-kings had been established, the Hasmoneans, who enlarged their territory to include Samaria, Transjordan and the former coastal lands of the Philistines.

6 Following Jerusalem's capture by Pompey in 63 BC, the territory was effectively a client state of the Roman Empire, from 43 BC under King Herod the Great, who rebuilt the Jewish temple in Jerusalem. Roman misgovernment led in 66 AD to a major revolt, which spread over the whole of Palestine and ended in 70 with the partial destruction of Jerusalem and its temple. Many Jews were massacred or enslaved. A second Jewish revolt from 131 led to the rebuilding of the city under Hadrian as a Greco-Roman city, Aelia Capitolina, from which all Jews were expelled.

7 From 330 AD Palestine came under the control of the Byzantine Empire. In 638 Omar Al-Khattaab entered Jerusalem, ending the era of Byzantine rule and marking the beginning of the Arab-Islamic era. According to Islamic tradition, the prophet Muhammad rose to heaven in Jerusalem, and so the city became a holy place for Muslims alongside Christians and Jews.

8 In 1516, Jerusalem was conquered by the Ottoman Empire, remaining under its control until the end of World War I.

9 From 1878 the Zionist movement began to establish the first Jewish settlements in Palestine. In 1895, the total population of Palestine numbered about 500,000 (453,000 Palestinian Arabs owned 99 per cent of the land and 47,000 Jews owned 5 per cent).

10 The Jewish National Fund, created by the Fifth Zionist Congress, set about buying land and from 1904 to 1914 a second wave of immigrants arrived. In 1909 the first kibbutz (collective farm) was settled to the north of Jaffa.

11 When World War I broke out, the British promised independence to the Arab territories under Ottoman rule, including Palestine, in exchange for their support against Turkey, an ally of Germany.

12 In 1917, the British Foreign Secretary, in the so-called 'Balfour Declaration', agreed to give British support for the creation of a 'Jewish Homeland'. In 1919 the Palestinians held their first Conference at which they rejected the Balfour Declaration and demanded an independent Palestinian State, as the British had promised in exchange for their support during the war.

13 In 1920 the Conference of San Remo approved the British mandate over Palestine. Two years later the League of Nations Council also approved a mandate supporting the creation of a Jewish Homeland on the territory. For six months the Palestinians held strikes and demonstrations in protest at the confiscation of lands and illegal immigration, the objective of which was to increase the Jewish population and thus give force to their claim over the land.

14 The British Government issued a new 'White Paper', limiting Jewish immigration and promising Palestine its independence after 10 years. This was rejected by leading Zionists, who formed militias and launched a bloody campaign against the British and Palestinians. On 9 April 1948, the Irgun organization, led by Menahem Begin, raided the village of Deir Yassin, killing 254 civilians. Terrorized, thousands of Palestinian abandoned their lands.

15 At the end of World War II, the United Nations approved the partition of Palestine (Resolution 181). The Palestinians, who represented 70 per cent of the

Life expectancy
72.4 years
2000-2005

GNI per capita
$930
2002

population and owned 92 per cent of the land, were restricted to 43 per cent of the territory. The rest was given to the Jews, who constituted 30 per cent of the population and owned 8 per cent of the land. Jerusalem fell within the 1 per cent that remained under international control.

[16] On 14 May 1948, the Jews proclaimed the State of Israel. The following day, the first Arab-Israeli war broke out. Palestine was split into three areas: the part occupied by Israel; the West Bank, which came under the control of Jordan; and Gaza, governed by Egypt. About 700,000 Palestinians fled their homes to neighboring countries and settled in refugees camps.

[17] In 1964, the Palestine Liberation Organization (PLO) was created to defend the rights of the Palestinian people and reaffirm their identity both in the region and in the international arena. In 1969, Yasser Arafat was elected president of the PLO.

[18] The clandestine Palestinian organizations, like Al-Fatah, mistrusted this new organization that was being promoted by Arab governments and its emphasis on seeking a diplomatic solution. Convinced that they would only recover their lands by resorting to force, on 1 January 1965, they carried out their first armed attack in Israel.

[19] In 1967, the Six-Day War broke out: Israel took over Jerusalem, the Golan Heights in Syria, the Sinai desert in Egypt and the Palestinian territories in the West Bank and the Gaza Strip. The UN called on Israel to withdraw from the Arab territories that it had occupied by force, and declared the Palestinians' right to return to their lands and to self-determination.

[20] The defeat of the regular Arab armies strengthened the conviction that guerrilla warfare was the only way to reach their goals. In March 1968, during a battle in the village of Al-Karameh, Palestinians forced the Israelis to withdraw. The battle passed into folk history as the first victory of the Palestinian force. The armed groups joined the PLO and obtained the support of Arab governments.

[21] King Hussein of Jordan, who had been a representative and spokesperson of the PLO, regarded the increasing political and military strength of the Palestinians as a threat. In September 1970 this came to blows as Palestinian resistance elements in Jordan known as *fedayeen* (from the Arabic *fida'i*, 'one who is ready to sacrifice one's life for the cause') were attacked by King Hussein's largely Bedouin forces in response to a string of high profile terrorist hijackings of civilian aircraft by the Palestinian Front for the Liberation of Palestine led by George Habash, which drew international anger. A 10-day civil war led to an estimated 3,500 deaths and massive material destruction in Jordan. The PLO was expelled from Jordan and set up headquarters in Beirut.

[22] This new exile reduced the possibility of armed attacks on targets inside Israel, and new radical groups such as 'Black September', named after the fighting between Jordanian government forces and Palestinian *fedayeen*, directed their efforts towards Israeli institutions and businesses in Europe and other parts of the world. Palestinians, until then regarded by world opinion purely as refugees, quickly came to be identified by some as terrorists.

[23] PLO leaders promptly realized the need to change their tactics and, without abandoning armed struggle, launched a large-scale diplomatic offensive, starting to devote much of their energy to consolidating Palestinian unity and identity. The Algiers Conference of Non-Aligned Countries (1973) identified the Palestine problem, and not Arab-Israeli rivalry, as the key to the conflict in the Middle East for the first time.

[24] In 1974, an Arab League summit conference recognized the PLO as 'the only legitimate representative of the Palestinian people'. In October of the same year the PLO was granted observer status in the UN General Assembly, which recognized the right of the Palestinian people to self-determination and independence. On 10 November 1975 the UN General Assembly adopted, by a vote of 72 to 35 (with 32 abstentions), Resolution 3379, which stated that 'Zionism is a form of racism and racial discrimination'. The resolution was revoked on 16 December 1991, with a vote of 111 to 25 (with 13 abstentions).

[25] The PLO Charter agreed in 1968 called for a sustained revolutionary armed struggle against the 'Zionist occupation' to liberate all of Palestine including the internationally recognized pre-1967 borders of the State of Israel which the PLO rejected. 'Armed struggle is the only way to liberate Palestine. This it is the overall strategy, not merely a tactical phase'. This necessarily implied the end of the present State of Israel. Without giving up this ultimate goal, the PLO has gradually come to accept the 'temporary solution' of setting up an independent Palestinian State 'in any part of the territory that might be liberated by force of arms, or from which Israel may withdraw'.

[26] In 1980, Israeli prime minister Menahem Begin, and Egyptian president Anwar Sadat signed a peace agreement, mediated by US president Jimmy Carter, at Camp David. Israel agreed to withdraw its forces from the Sinai peninsula, and return it to Egypt. Soon afterwards, Jewish settlements in the West Bank multiplied on appropriated Palestinian lands, increasing tension in the occupied territories. Successive UN votes against these measures, or for any action against Israel, were stripped of any practical value by the US using its veto in the Security Council.

[27] In July 1982, in an attempted 'final settlement' of the Palestine issue, Israeli forces invaded Lebanon. They sought to destroy the PLO's military structure, and to capture the greatest possible number of its leaders and combatants who had been staging attacks along Israel's northern border. The massacre that took place at the refugee camps of Sabra and Shatila was by the Southern Lebanese Army under orders from Israeli Defense Minister Ariel Sharon. International sympathy with the plight of the Palestinian people surged. The headquarters of the organization were moved to Tunis and Yasser Arafat toured Europe receiving the honors due a head of state in various countries, in particular at the Vatican.

[28] The PLO leadership quietly participated in talks with Israeli leaders receptive to a negotiated settlement with the Palestinians. With the invasion of Lebanon, small but active peace groups emerged in Israel, demanding the initiation of a dialogue with the PLO. Palestinian radicals questioned these overtures,

PROFILE

ENVIRONMENT

Historically Palestine is the 27,000 sq km territory west of the Jordan River which the League of Nations handed over to Britain's mandatory power in 1918. This territory comprises: the area occupied by Israel before 1967, 20,073 sq km; Jerusalem and its surroundings, 70 sq km; the West Bank area, 5,879 sq km and the Gaza Strip, 378 sq km. Many nations now recognize Palestine to be the area under full and partial sovereignty of the Palestinian National Authority, with final status negotiations still in limbo. This is hotly disputed by most Palestinians who see the whole region as indisputably Palestine. It is a land of temperate Mediterranean climate, fertile on the coast and in the Jordan Valley. It is surrounded in the south and the northeast by the Sinai and Syrian deserts respectively.

SOCIETY

Peoples: The Palestinians are a group of mainly Arabic speakers who regard themselves as a distinct group of the Arabic-speaking peoples, with family origin in Palestine being the defining characteristic. As such, the designation is independent of nationality and religion. There are 700,000 Palestinians in Israel; 1,500,000 on the West Bank; 800,000 in the Gaza Strip, and the rest mostly living in Middle Eastern (Jordan 2,170,000; Lebanon 395,000; Syria 360,000; other Arab countries 517,000) and European countries. 33 per cent of the inhabitants of the occupied territories live in refugee camps. There are large Palestinian populations in the US, Chile, Brazil and other countries.

Religions: Muslim (mostly Sunni) 97 per cent; Christians (Eastern Orthodox) 3 per cent.

Languages: Palestinians speak a unique dialect of Levantine Arabic. Hebrew is a common second language, as is English.

Main Political Parties: Palestine Liberation Organization (PLO). Fatah (*lit.* victory or conquest; also a reverse acronym of *Harakat Al-Tahrir Al-Watani Al-Filastini*, Palestinian National Liberation Movement). Hamas (*Harakat Al-Muqawamah Al-Islamiyyah - lit.* Islamic Resistance Movement), very influential in Gaza and the West Bank, is opposed to the Oslo process (1993) and autonomy agreements. Islamic Jihad (*Al-Jihad Al-Islami*).

Main Social Organizations: Palestinian Labor Federation; General Union of Palestine Women; Addamir (prisoners' association).

THE STATE

Official Name: As-Sulta Al-Watania Al-Filistiniya.

Capital: Jerusalem (Al-Quds), 668,000 people (1999). Almost universally seen by Palestinians as their capital; the Palestine National Authority (PNA) is in Jericho, 14,744 people (1997).

Government: Yasser Arafat, President of the Palestinian National Authority since July 1994, re-elected in January 1996. The Autonomous Council acts as parliament.

Armed Forces: No official data available.

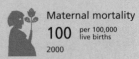

Under-5 mortality
25 per 1,000 live births
2002

Maternal mortality
100 per 100,000 live births
2000

breaking with Yasser Arafat's policies. These factional divisions within the PLO at times led to violent confrontations.

29 Following years of infighting, in 1987, the Palestinian National Congress, held in Algeria, managed to rebuild the PLO's unity.

30 In December 1987, the funerals of several young Palestinians killed in a clash with Israeli military patrols led to further confrontations, general strikes and civil protests. The *Intifada* (uprising, lit. 'shaking off') began in the Gaza Strip, the West Bank and East Jerusalem. The Intifada marked a new stage in the Palestinian struggle: for the first time the population - young people, children, and the elderly - rose up against the occupying army. Many unarmed civilians resorted to throwing stones at Israeli troops, who responded with gunfire, a reaction that shocked the world. The Intifada lasted approximately five years and virtually destroyed the already fragile economies in the occupied territories.

31 On 14 November 1988, the Palestinian National Congress (parliament-in-exile) in Algeria, proclaimed the Independent State of Palestine, in accordance with international law and the 1948 UN Resolution No. 181, which split Palestine into two states, one Jewish, the other Arab-Palestinian. This implied accepting the State of Israel. Ten days later, 54 nations officially recognized the new State of Palestine.

32 Arafat was elected president of Palestine and in that capacity gave an address to the UN General Assembly, in which he rejected terrorism, recognized the State of Israel, and demanded that international troops be sent into the occupied territories. As a result of his speech, US president Ronald Reagan decided to initiate talks with the PLO.

33 When Iraq invaded Kuwait (1991), the Palestinians attempted to draw a parallel between the situations of Kuwait and Palestine: if Iraq was forced to comply with UN resolutions, then Israel also should be.

34 When the Gulf War broke out in 1991, it was clear that the Palestinian people were pro-Iraq. This position deprived the PLO of the financial backing of the rich Gulf emirates, who opposed the Iraqi regime.

35 In September 1991, in the closing session of the Palestine National Council, Yasser Arafat was confirmed as the president of Palestine and of the PLO. The latter accepted the resignation of Abu Abbas, leader of the Palestine Liberation Front. Abbas was given a life sentence in absentia by an Italian tribunal, for the hijacking of

IN FOCUS

ENVIRONMENTAL CHALLENGES
The Palestinian-Israeli conflict is destroying farmlands, particularly olive groves, natural resources and fauna. Gaza suffers water shortages, and refugee camps are highly polluted by refuse and sewage water. Soil is affected by erosion, drains are inadequate and underground water is contaminated.

WOMEN'S RIGHTS
In 1996, Palestinians held democratic elections to choose 86 representatives, five of whom are women.

Polygamy is still allowed. Groups of women's rights advocates demand laws to punish 'honor crimes' since Muslim courts pardoned men who have murdered their wives. Movements like Jerusalem Link bring together Palestinian and Israeli women, who seek to move beyond the conflict to establish bonds and to improve women's situation in general. In 2000, the average age at which Palestinian women married was 18. According to estimates, in 2002 65 per cent of women living in rural communities had not completed primary education and only 7.9 per cent completed secondary school.

Estimates show that 25 per cent of Palestinian women have suffered abuse at least once in their lives. There are no official statistics as women beaten by their male relatives tend not to report the incidents, because this is not perceived by (male) officialdom as abuse or violence, but as men's right. Since the recent escalation of the conflict between Israel and Palestine, the number of pregnant women in Palestine not receiving prenatal care increased 4.5 times to nearly 20 per cent.

CHILDREN
The standard of the education received by Arab Palestinian children is, in almost all aspects, inferior to the education given to Israeli children. One of the consequences of this is lower achievement.

Moderate and severe cases of malnutrition were found in 17.5 per cent of children living in the Gaza Strip, and 3.5 per cent in the West Bank.

Many Palestinian children have been victims of the Israeli-Palestinian conflict, with an estimated 573 Palestinian children killed, 6,000 made homeless and almost 2,000 children arrested, interrogated, detained or imprisoned.

INDIGENOUS PEOPLES/ ETHNIC MINORITIES
Muslims, Jews, Christians, Bedouins, and Druze constitute the indigenous population. Most Druze and Bedouins live in Israel (see Israel). Among the Palestinian population there are mostly Muslims with a sizeable Christian minority. Christian Palestinians live mostly in Bethlehem and the surrounding area, some others have become Israeli citizens and dwell, among other places, in Jerusalem and Haifa. In both cities Arabs and Jews live side-by-side.

MIGRANTS/REFUGEES
Although figures from different sources do not always coincide, according to UNWRA (UN Relief and Works Agency for Palestinian Refugees), in 2002 there were 4,055,758 refugees registered with the agency. One third lives in the Gaza Strip and West Bank, another third, evicted from their homes between 1948 and 1967, fled to Jordan, Syria and Lebanon. Israel and the United States propose that the Palestinian Authority should restrict the return of refugees to the 200,000 Palestinians expelled in 1948, disregarding the individual rights of Palestinians to return to their land. The number of Palestinians and their descendants who have emigrated to other countries in the world, including South America and Europe, is over 7 million.

DEATH PENALTY
The Palestinian Authority applies the death penalty. Mistrials and flawed sentences have been denounced.

---

the *Achille Lauro* cruise liner and the resultant death of wheelchair-bound Jewish American passenger Leon Klinghoffer in 1985.

36 In 1991, the first Middle East Peace Conference was held in Madrid, sponsored by the US and the former USSR. Palestinians and Israelis agreed to mutual recognition.

37 In September that year, Israel and the PLO signed a Declaration of Principles at the White House, which established a five-year deadline for the withdrawal of Israeli forces from the occupied territories, and for negotiating the permanent settlement status of the Gaza Strip, the West Bank and East Jerusalem, and which would be followed by the establishment of an independent Palestinian State.

38 The Israeli Parliament ratified recognition of the PLO and the Declaration of Principles. The PLO Central Committee approved the text concerning autonomy.

39 The agreement was opposed by Hamas and Hizbullah on the

Palestinian side, as well as by settlers in the occupied territories, and by far-right parties on the Israeli side. In a climate of hostility, the Israeli military withdrawal from Gaza and Jericho anticipated for December 13 was postponed.

40 In May 1994 Rabin and Arafat signed the 'Gaza and Jericho first' autonomy agreement, while Israeli withdrawal continued, enabling the return of several contingents of the Palestinian Liberation Army exiled in Egypt, Yemen, Libya, Jordan or Algeria.

41 After 27 years in exile Arafat arrived in Gaza in July as head of the Executive Council of the new Palestinian National Authority (PNA). Those regions under Palestinian control saw an influx of foreign and Palestinian investment - on top of international aid - for housing and infrastructure development in areas inhabited by Palestinians, and to lay the foundation for the future state.

42 The struggle between the historic leader of the PLO and the

Islamic fundamentalist opposition became increasingly violent. Arafat wanted Hamas to participate in the Palestinian general elections in January 1996, which would have further legitimized his leadership. However, the Islamic fundamentalists decided to boycott the elections. Arafat was elected president with 87 per cent of the vote and government candidates won 66 out of a total of 88 seats.

43 Right-wing Likud leader Binyamin Netanyahu's election as Israeli Prime Minister (see Israel) in May 1996 aggravated tension between the countries.

44 The difficult negotiations ended with the withdrawal of Israeli troops from the city of Hebron in 1997. In the same year, in accordance with the agreements between the two sides, Palestinian political prisoners were set free from Israeli jails. At the end of 1997, the peace talks stalled when Netanyahu ignored previous agreements and resumed construction of new illegal

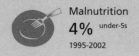
Malnutrition
4% under-5s
1995-2002

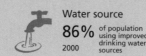
Water source
86% of population using improved drinking water sources
2000

the permanent settlement status of the Palestinian territories, when the five-year term expired he would proclaim an independent Palestinian State, with its capital in East Jerusalem.

⁴⁵ In 2000, US president Bill Clinton invited Arafat and Prime Minister Ehud Barak (Labor Party) to a meeting at Camp David. The US and Israeli proposals for a final agreement did not meet basic Palestinian demands regarding the dismantling of illegal settlements on the West Bank, the return of refugees, and Palestinian border control. Jerusalem, a holy city for both Muslims and Jews, became the biggest stumbling block in the negotiations, since both sides wanted to install their capital city there.

⁴⁶ Tension in the area increased when former Israeli Defense Minister Ariel Sharon visited Haram al-Sharif/Temple Mount in Al Quds/Jerusalem, considered a holy place by both Muslims and Jews. A new Intifada was declared, a string of suicide bombings in Israeli town centers led to numerous Israeli civilian deaths, and Israel resumed its bombing of Palestinian villages, leaving 400 civilians dead.

⁴⁷ Sharon's victory in Israel's February 2001 elections was perceived as another blow to the weakened peace process. That month, the UN Secretary-General issued a document indicating that Israel's economic blockade of the West Bank and Gaza Strip had pushed Arafat's government to the verge of collapse due to lack of revenue.

⁴⁸ The UN special envoy to the Middle East, Terje Road Larsen, warned that if other countries did not provide urgent financial support to the Palestinians (his report estimated that one billion dollars was needed for the rest of that year) violence would increase.

⁴⁹ Fighting increased over the following months. Israel's offensive and the stalled negotiations increased resistance to the occupation. Sharon replied with targetted assassinations of suspected terrorists, and extended his offensive to attacking Palestinian communities and towns with helicopters and gunboats. These attacks were followed by night raids on Palestinian towns, which destroyed homes, airports and hospitals. Several hundred Palestinians died in the conflict, and military operations continued with the occupation of the territories that had been under relative Palestinian control.

⁵⁰ After the 11 September 2001 attacks on the World Trade Center in New York and the Pentagon in Washington, Sharon believed international public opinion and

Western governments could turn in his favor, and - counting on the support of the US - he increased the offensive against the Palestinian uprising. The new US President, George W Bush, needing to attract allies to his anti-terrorist campaign against the Taliban regime in Afghanistan, preferred to keep his distance and avoid confrontations with the Arab world.

⁵¹ Numerous suicide attacks by radical Palestinian militants marked a new stage in the conflict. The suicide bombers of Hamas and Islamic Jihad, among other Islamic groups, chose places attended by Jewish young people to cause the greatest possible harm. To strengthen security, Sharon limited the traffic of goods and people through the borders of the West Bank and Gaza Strip from the beginning of the uprising. The measure affected both Palestinian workers and businesses.

⁵² In December Sharon cut all contact with Arafat. The new Israeli strategy no longer acknowledged the Palestinian leader as a valid negotiator, and the break in relations also put an end to negotiation efforts. In early 2002, with the arrival of a new mediator from the US, Sharon lifted the restrictions imposed on Palestinians from the West Bank and Gaza, regions that were under the control of Jewish forces. On 11 January, Islamic Jihad announced it would step up its actions, while Israel attacked PNA targets by land, sea and air in the largest offensive since the beginning of the second Intifada.

⁵³ Restrictions on the movement of goods and people in Israel and the occupied territories after 18 months of uprising placed the Palestinian economy on the verge of collapse. The continued closure of border checkpoints caused irreparable harm. Unemployment tripled, affecting almost 30 per cent of the Palestinian labor force. In spite of the relatively good financial performance of the PNA, the Government collected taxes that amounted to only one fifth of those collected in previous years. Donations from the Arab League and the European Union had increased in 2001, but not enough. The PNA had a budget deficit of $430 million and the estimated GDP in Gaza and the West Bank fell 12 per cent in the first quarter of 2002.

⁵⁴ A summit of Arab countries was held in Beirut in March, which Arafat could not attend because Sharon kept him cornered in his Ramallah bunker for more than a month. A group of 40 pacifists, 11 of them from the West, defied the Israeli army's siege and formed a 'human shield' to protect the Palestinian leader from a potential Israeli attack.

⁵⁵ In spite of its initial chaos, the summit ended with the approval of a peace plan which included a historic decision. The signatory countries agreed to recognize the State of Israel, as long as it withdrew to its pre-1967 borders and allowed the return of three million Palestinian refugees, as well as the creation of a Palestinian state with a sector of Jerusalem as its capital. Israel called the proposal 'unacceptable'.

⁵⁶ In April, Fatah, Hamas, Islamic Jihad, People's Front and Democratic Front for the Liberation of Palestine, agreed for the first time a common military strategy 'to confront any Israeli attack'. Most of the 82 suicide bombers in Israel and the Jewish settlements since the beginning of the Intifada were militants from these extremist organizations.

⁵⁷ That month, Jenin refugee camp on the West Bank was the scene of bloody bombings by Israel, causing the death of hundreds of Palestinians. Terje Larsen, the UN envoy, called what happened in Jenin a 'morally repugnant humanitarian disaster'. Sharon declared him *persona non grata*. The Jenin camp was reduced to rubble. After the raids on this and other communities under the relative control of the PNA, Israel detained some 5,000 Palestinians.

⁵⁸ After almost 40 days of siege, on 10 May, 126 Palestinians who had taken refuge in the Church of the Nativity in Bethlehem, left it one by one. The first to leave - 13 men considered terrorists by Israel - were flown to Cyprus on a British plane, where they would remain until the EU decided their final destination. Another 26 Palestinians, accused by Israel of minor offenses, were sent to the Gaza strip, while the rest were freed.

⁵⁹ In June 2002 US President George W Bush called on Palestinians to reject Arafat's leadership and to choose a leader who was 'not committed to terrorism'. In December Arafat postponed elections, blaming Israel for the delay.

⁶⁰ In March 2003, Mahmoud Abbas (a moderate politician also known as Abu Mazen) was elected prime minister of the Palestinian Authority. In April, Bush presented Sharon and Abbas with a new peace plan known as the 'Road Map', which was sponsored by the so-called Middle East Quartet (US, EU, UN and the Russian Federation). This plan proposed the creation of a Palestinian State and the resolution of all outstanding issues by 2005. Abbas resigned in July, accused by the radicals of making too many concessions to Israel.

⁶¹ The violence increased. For the first time, a young woman, mother

of two children, carried out a suicide attack. Prime Minister Sharon resumed the attacks on and destruction of Palestinian villages, and construction started on a separation wall in the West Bank. The reaction of the international community to this issue was at best permissive. While the UN General Assembly demanded that Israel stop work on the wall, the EU and US asked that the International Court of Justice refrain from giving an advisory opinion regarding the legality of the wall. The barrier deprives thousands of Palestinians of access to basic services like water, medical care and education, as well as to their means of livelihood, such as farming and other jobs. The Israeli decision prompted an international movement against 'the wall of shame', including Israeli pacifist organizations, such as Ta'ayush and the Israeli Peace Bloc.

⁶² In March 2004, Hamas carried out a double suicide attack in the port of Ashdod. Israel retaliated with a series of attacks, consisting of 'targeted assassinations' of Palestinian political leaders. In an operation supervised by Sharon, Israel killed the spiritual leader of Hamas, disabled 67-year-old Sheikh Ahmed Yassin, as he left a mosque in Sabra (Gaza). Although this murder was unanimously rejected by the international community, the US vetoed a UN Security Council motion condemning the assassination.

⁶³ In April 2004, Sharon announced a 'Plan of unilateral disengagement from Palestinian areas' which included the evacuation of settlements in the Gaza Strip and the dismantling of six settlements in the West Bank. In exchange, Israel sought US support to keep 'settlement blocs' in the West Bank, home to most of the 230,000 Israeli settlers, and a declaration by President Bush denying Palestinian refugees the right to return.

⁶⁴ In October Israeli forces demolished the homes of hundreds of Palestinians and bulldozed infrastructure, killing over 70 in the bloodiest assault on the Gaza Strip in years. The attack was launched after two Israeli children were killed by a Hamas rocket.

⁶⁵ In October 2004 Yasser Arafat was taken seriously ill and was flown to Paris to receive hospital treatment. He died on 11 November. His official funeral was held in Cairo, Egypt. He was then buried in the compound in which he had long been imprisoned in Ramallah, on the West Bank. Mahmoud Abbas took over as head of the PLO, while parliamentary speaker Rawhi Fattuh and prime minister Ahmed Qureia divided the presidential powers within the Palestine Authority until elections could be held. ∎

Panama / Panamá

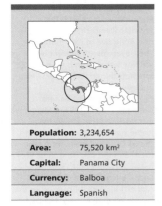

Population:	3,234,654
Area:	75,520 km²
Capital:	Panama City
Currency:	Balboa
Language:	Spanish

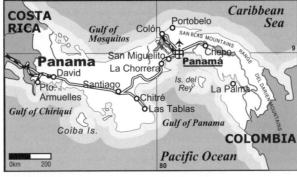

The Chibcha civilization, which developed in the isthmus of Panama, was one of America's great cultures. The Chibchans had a highly stratified society, developed elaborate architecture, crafted gold and had a wide scientific knowledge.

2   In 1508, Diego de Nicuesa was given the task of colonizing what was known as the Gold Coast (present day Panama and Costa Rica). The enterprise ended in complete failure. In 1513, Vasco Nuñez de Balboa was sent to look for what was assumed to be a 'South Sea', and on 25 September he found the Pacific.

3   The isthmus soon acquired great geopolitical significance due to the proximity of the Atlantic and Pacific oceans. Panama became an important commercial center for the Spanish monopoly. After sailing from Spain, ships arrived in Portobelo, in the Caribbean Sea, from where the cargo crossed the isthmus by mule to Panama City. Once in Panama, the merchandise was distributed throughout America from San Francisco to Santiago. The concentration of riches attracted English pirates and buccaneers; Francis Drake razed Portobelo in 1596 and Henry Morgan set fire to Panama in 1671.

4   Panama was dependent upon the viceroyalty of Peru until 1717, when the Bourbons transferred it to the new viceroyalty of Granada;

this was later to be a part of Greater Colombia when the country became independent from Spain in 1821.

5   In 1826, Panama was selected by Simón Bolívar as the site of the Congressional Assembly which was to seal the continent's unity. But the economic decadence of the end of the 18th century, coupled with the change in commercial routes meant that Panama did not maintain its strategic importance after breaking with Spain, and did not become an independent nation with the disintegration of Greater Colombia in 1830.

6   In 1831 Panama seceded from New Granada for a year, with the intention of forming a Colombian Confederation while maintaining autonomy. The state of Panama was created in 1855 within the Federation of New Granada (present-day Colombia).

7   The first direct reference to the US 'right' to intervene militarily in Panama, was the Mallarino-Bidlak Treaty of 1864, signed by the Governments of Washington and Bogotá. The document authorized the US to obtain a faster means of uniting the east coast with the west by building a railroad across the isthmus. It also allowed the US to offset the British presence in the area, especially in Nicaragua.

8   On 1 January 1880, a French company, the Universal Company of the Panama Canal led by Ferdinand de Lesseps, started to build the canal. In 1891, the company was

accused of fraud in its dealings, causing its bankruptcy, though 33 km of the project had already been completed. In order to complete the project, three years later, the New Panama Canal Company was founded.

9   In 1902, the US bought out the French company, and in January 1903, the Hay-Herran Treaty was signed with a representative of the Colombian Government. The treaty spelled out the terms of the construction and administration of the canal, granting the US the right to rent a 9.5 km-wide strip across the isthmus in perpetuity.

10   The Colombian Senate rejected the treaty unanimously, considering it improper and an affront to Colombia's sovereignty. Only a revolution allowed the US to remain. The 'revolutionaries', supported by US marines, declared Panama's independence in November 1903, and the US recognized the new state within three days. While Theodore Roosevelt was President, the 'Big Stick' policy of sending troops into Central American states was common practice.

11   A new treaty, the Hay-Buneau Varilla Treaty, granted the US full authority over a 16 km-wide strip and the waters at either end of the canal in perpetuity. Buneau Varilla, a former shareholder of the canal company and a French citizen, signed as the official representative of Panama. He received payment for his services in Washington, and did not return to Panama. The canal, covering a distance of 82 km, was officially opened on 15 August 1914, and from then on was administrated and governed by the US.

12   The Canal Zone brought incalculable wealth to the US, not so much in toll fees but in time and distance saved by vessels traveling between California and the East Coast. US military bases in Panama functioned as an effective means of control over Latin America. Against the backdrop of the Cold War, American military instructors lectured Latin American military officers on the National Security

Doctrine, a politico-military system which ousted legally constituted governments and imposed military dictators. Also, the financial center created in the isthmus became an initial foothold for the expansion of US transnational corporations and money laundering.

13   In January 1964, 21 students who died in an attempt to raise Panama's flag in the Canal Zone were transformed into national martyrs. The demand for full sovereignty over the Zone was taken up by the Government of General Omar Torrijos. He rose to power in 1969, upon the dissolution of a three-member Military Junta which had overthrown President Arnulfo Arias in 1968. The diplomatic battle against the colonial enclave was waged in all the international forums and gained the support of the Latin American countries, the Movement of Non-Aligned Countries and the UN.

14   The struggle for sovereignty united Panamanians, stimulating nationalistic feelings repressed by decades of foreign cultural penetration, control of the economy and US military intervention. At the same time, the Torrijos Government initiated a process of transformation aimed at establishing a more equitable social order. The most important changes introduced included reforms in agriculture and education, and the nationalization of copper exploitation. A 'banana war' to obtain fairer prices was waged against transnational fruit companies such as the United Fruit Company, which was later named 'United Brands'.

15   The US finally agreed to open negotiations in favor of a new canal treaty, as the Panama issue was damaging its image in Latin America. The 1977 Torrijos-Carter Treaty abrogated the previous one and provided for the canal to become fully Panamanian from the year 2000. Amendments introduced by the US Senate, however, added provisions to the treaty that were contrary to Panamanian sovereignty. The US retained the right to intervene 'in defense of the Canal' even after expiration of the treaty, scheduled for 31 December 1999.

16   On 31 July 1981, Torrijos died in a suspicious airplane accident. Unconfirmed reports suggested that the plane's instruments were interfered with from the ground. President Aristides Royo, who succeeded Torrijos in 1978, lost the support of the National Guard and was forced to resign by his new commander-in-chief, Ruben Paredes. He started realigning the country's policies, adopting a pro-US stance. The role of the US in the

WORKERS

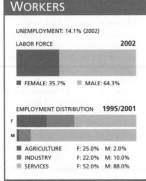

UNEMPLOYMENT: 14.1% (2002)

LABOR FORCE   2002

■ FEMALE: 35.7%   ■ MALE: 64.3%

EMPLOYMENT DISTRIBUTION   1995/2001

F

M

■ AGRICULTURE	F: 25.0%	M: 2.0%
■ INDUSTRY	F: 22.0%	M: 10.0%
■ SERVICES	F: 52.0%	M: 88.0%

PUBLIC EXPENDITURE

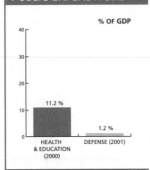

% OF GDP

11.2 %   HEALTH & EDUCATION (2000)

1.2 %   DEFENSE (2001)

Life expectancy
74.7 years
2000-2005

GNI per capita
$4,020
2002

Literacy
92% total adult rate
2000

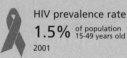
HIV prevalence rate
1.5% of population 15-49 years old
2001

Malvinas (Falklands) War and the launching of the Contadora Group - set up to try and mediate in the region's conflicts, with Panama as the first host - led to new frictions in relations between the two nations. The island of Contadora had already gained a certain notoriety as the hideout chosen by the US for the exiled Shah of Iran, Reza Pahlevi, after he was overthrown.

[17] In 1983, Paredes was replaced as commander-in-chief of the National Guard by General Manuel Noriega. The 1984 presidential and legislative elections were narrowly won by Nicolas Barletta, the candidate of the Democratic Revolutionary Party, which was founded by Torrijos and supported by the armed forces. The opposition, led by veteran politician Arnulfo Arias, made accusations of fraud.

[18] Barletta encountered growing opposition to his economic policies, and resigned toward the end of 1985. He was succeeded by Eric del Valle, but the driving force continued to be General Noriega, a former protégé of the US Government whom the US now aimed to overthrow for refusing to collaborate in plans to invade Nicaragua. A 'settling of accounts'

began, in which Noriega was accused of links with drug-traffickers and other crimes. The opposition united behind the National Civil Crusade, made up of parties of the right and center with the broad support of the business community.

[19] In 1987, Washington withdrew its economic and military aid. In 1988, it froze Panama's assets in the US and imposed economic sanctions, including the cessation of payments for Canal operations. In March all the Panamanian banks closed for several weeks, provoking a financial crisis. The American military presence increased. Del Valle overthrew Noriega, but the National Assembly backed the commander-in-chief and removed the President, replacing him with the Minister of Education, Manuel Solís Palma.

[20] Elections were called for 5 May 1989. The official candidate was Carlos Duque and the opposition, the so-called Democratic Alliance of Civilian Opposition, put forward Guillermo Endara. Amid interference from the White House, which discredited the electoral process and its results even before it had taken place, the results of the ballot were kept secret for several days and, because they

favored the opposition, the election was declared null and void.

[21] Solís declared that the US' objective was to set up a puppet government regardless of the election results and retain control of the Canal Zone, going back on the commitments it had assumed under the Torrijos-Carter Treaty.

[22] An anti-Noriega uprising by a group of young officers failed in October 1989. Economic sanctions were followed by a US military invasion of the country without warning or prior declaration of war. Endara was installed as President at Fort Clayton, the American base, at the start of the invasion.

[23] This was the largest US military operation since the Vietnam War (1964-1973), with the mobilization of 26,000 troops. Panamanian resistance proved to be stronger than the invaders had anticipated, which prolonged the military operation. Indiscriminate bombing damaged heavily-populated neighborhoods and killed many civilians - 560 according to official figures; between 4,000 and 10,000 according to the opposition. Losses were estimated at more than $2 billion and about 5,000 Panamanians were temporarily imprisoned. Noriega took refuge within the Vatican Embassy and was later extradited and transferred to the US.

[24] The Government of Guillermo Endara replaced the National Defense Force with a minor police agency, called the Public Force. In order to disarm the population, $150 was paid for each weapon that was turned in. US economic aid, which the new government had counted on, did not materialize and Endara himself began a hunger strike in order to obtain it. The Government had to accept the presence of US 'supervisors' in the ministries and the actions of the Southern Command troops outside the canal zone in order to fight drug trafficking and Colombian guerrilla warfare.

[25] Washington's interest in the region waned after the defeat of the Sandinistas in Nicaragua, and so the economic crisis in Panama at the time of the invasion was never overcome.

[26] The Organization of American States called the invasion 'deplorable' and called for a vote on the withdrawal of troops; there were 20 votes in favor, one against (the US) and six abstentions. Britain supported the invasion and France vetoed the UN Security Council denunciation. In Latin America, only El Salvador supported the US invasion.

[27] In March 1991, a Panamanian took over the administration of the canal for the first time.

[28] In April, Endara announced the end of his alliance with the Christian Democrat Party (PDC), dismissing five of its ministers. The Government's precarious stability was shaken by five coup attempts during its first two years in power.

[29] In the course of General Noriega's trial, in 1991 in Miami, it was disclosed that the former leader had close connections with the US Drug Enforcement Agency (DEA) and the CIA. That same year it was discovered that President Endara's legal office had connections with 14 companies that laundered drug money. The DEA also disclosed that drug dealings had increased since the invasion. In June 1992, Noriega was sentenced to 40 years in prison.

[30] The Government suffered a serious setback when a referendum on constitutional reform on 15 November 1992 was defeated by 63.5 per cent of votes against 31.5 per cent. The people rejected, among other things, the formal abolition of the Defense Force (Public Force).

[31] Foreign Minister Julio Linares was forced to resign in August 1993 as he had been involved in the sale of weapons to Serbian forces in Bosnia through the Panamanian consulate in Barcelona.

[32] Economist Ernesto Pérez Balladares, former minister and admirer of Omar Torrijos, was elected President in 1994 with 34 per cent of the vote. These were the first general elections held after the US invasion.

[33] In June 1994, the Cuna and Embera indigenous groups rejected the construction of a road through their autonomous territory. They were supported by environmentalist groups and the Catholic Church. The highway was to have crossed the 550,000 hectares of rainforest called 'Darien's Barrier' - declared a world heritage site by UNESCO. The 108-km highway would link Panama with Colombia. For years, this forest endured illegal logging of oak, cedar and mahogany. Likewise, the area was devoted to coca cultivation and arms smuggling.

[34] A plan to assassinate Pérez Balladares and several cabinet members was uncovered in January 1995. Ten National Police members were arrested on charges of conspiracy but the investigation was shelved for lack of evidence.

[35] The country continued to have an active role in arms and drug trafficking as well as money laundering. The explosion of a package during a routine drug inspection killed three officials and injured 25. The explosives, grenades and ammunition, were being sent to Ecuador, supposedly to guerrilla

PROFILE

ENVIRONMENT

The country is bordered by the Caribbean in the north and the Pacific in the south. A high mountain range splits the country into two plains, a narrow one covered by rainforests along the Atlantic slopes and a wider one with forests on the Pacific slopes. Canal navigation and the trading and financial activities connected to it constitute the main economic resource of the country. Tropical products are cultivated and copper is mined at the large Cerro Colorado mines.

SOCIETY

Peoples: 64 per cent of the inhabitants are descendants from native Americans and European colonist immigrants. 14 per cent are of African descent. The three main indigenous groups are the Cunas on the island of San Blas in the Caribbean, the Chocoes in the province of Darien and the Guaymies, in the provinces of Chiriqui, Veraguas and Bocas del Toro. **Religions:** 80 per cent Catholic, 10 per cent Protestant (mainly Evangelist), 5 per cent Muslim, 1 per cent Baha'i, 0.3 per cent Jewish, 3.7 per cent others. **Languages:** Spanish, official; several indigenous languages; most of the population speaks English. **Main Political Parties:** Revolutionary Democratic Party (RDP); Arnulfist Party; Solidarity Party; Nationalist Republican Liberal Movement. **Main Social Organizations:** Workers' Confederation of the Republic of Panama (CTRP); United Unions of Panama (SCS); Federation of Panamanian Students (FEP); Panamanian Workers' National Central (CNTP); Dobbo Yala Foundation (indigenous NGO).

THE STATE

Official Name: República de Panamá. **Administrative Divisions:** 9 provinces and 4 indigenous territories. **Capital:** Panama City 930,000 people (2003). **Other Cities:** San Miguelito 331,692 people; Colón 59,746; David 79,100 (2000). **Government:** Martín Torrijos, President since September 2004. Single-chamber parliament: Legislative Assembly, made up of 71 members, elected every 5 years by direct vote. **National Holiday:** 3 November, Independence (1903). **Armed Forces:** The National Guard was declared illegal in June 1991. US soldiers in the Canal Zone were withdrawn and military bases were returned to Panama. Other: 11,000 National Police.

Under-5 mortality
25 per 1,000
live births
2002

Poverty
7.6% of population
living on less
than $1 per
1998 day

Debt service
12.9% exports
of goods
and services
2001

Maternal mortality
160 per 100,000
live births
2000

groups. Two arms deposits were found in the capital, belonging to a Colombian citizen.

[36] The reform of the labor code, aimed at attracting foreign investment, led to an atmosphere of social violence and strikes, since it would reduce labor security and the freedom to unionize and negotiate collectively. Confrontations of workers and students with the police left 4 dead and 86 injured in August. However, the law was passed.

[37] The announcement that US troops would remain in Panama was made after it became known that Balladares had received money from the Colombian Cali cartel to fund his 1994 election campaign. The President admitted the fact but denied having known of the origin of the funds. This scandal was followed by the forced closure of the Agro-Industrial and Commercial Bank due to its excessive debts and drug money-laundering activities.

[38] In September 1997, after 80 years' presence in Panama's territory, the Southern Command headquarters returned to the US. The Government released statements guaranteeing that the operation of the Panama Canal would not be affected by its return to national ownership. It also announced plans for building a third set of lock gates in early 2000, due to the increase in traffic and the tonnage of the ships.

[39] After Balladares was defeated in a referendum in which he proposed to change the Constitution to allow for his re-election, the main candidates for the May 1999 elections were Mireya Moscoso, the widow of Arnulfo Arias, and Martín Torrijos, son of General Omar Torrijos. Moscoso won on a manifesto of eradicating corruption and politicking in the administration of the Canal and allowing the participation of both workers and shipowners.

[40] On 14 December, a ceremony was held to celebrate the return of the Canal to Panamanian jurisdiction. Moscoso and former US President Jimmy Carter - who had signed the treaty agreeing to return the Canal with Omar Torrijos in 1977 - put their seal on diplomatic addenda which ratified this. Carter stated it was 'one of the most important historic occasions in the hemisphere' and that with the vigorous development of trade, Panama now had the chance to 'become the Singapore of the region', making the most of the Canal, and the international financial center, which contained the offices of 120 of the world's banks.

[41] After being criticized for having granted asylum to two Haitian officers accused of human rights violations, the Government decided in November 2000 not to grant asylum to Vladimiro Montesinos. He was a former advisor to Peru's President Fujimori, accused in his country of serious human rights abuses.

[42] Protests called in May 2001 by labor and student unions against the 66 per cent hike in public transport charges led to clashes with the police which left more than 100 injured and dozens arrested. The Government also raised taxes on essential services such as electricity, gasoline and telephones. Finally, after negotiations mediated by the Church, the measure was suspended.

[43] After the peace process with Colombian guerrillas ended, Panama increased its security forces along the border with Colombia, in case the conflict expanded to its territory. Panama also hosts hundreds of Colombian refugees who have fled the guerrillas.

[44] In April 2002, the Truth Commission of Panama delivered its report. It had been formed by Moscoso to investigate what happened to the disappeared during the 1968-1989 military government, and clarified 110 of the 189 cases which had not been solved. The Commission carried out 35 excavations in old barracks and airports, finding 48 bodies. Some of the documents were supplied by the US Defense Department, which blamed the Defense Forces of the time for the crimes committed.

[45] Juan Jované, Director of the Social Security Fund, was removed from his post for his opposition to the Government's privatization plans (following the adjustment policies dictated by the IMF and the World Bank to counteract the serious crisis affecting the social security system). On 23 September 2003, workers replied with a general strike that paralyzed the country. More than 40 people were injured in clashes with the police.

[46] While it had military bases in Panama, the US took part in two world wars and fought several wars of its own (Korea, Vietnam, Persian Gulf, and the 1983 invasion of Grenada). The bases were used to train troops and for bombing practice - activities unrelated to the 'protection and defense of the Canal', the pretext under which they had been created. The accumulation of unexploded missiles and ordnance during 96 years has resulted in dangerous environmental pollution. So, in spite of having recovered its territorial integrity after the withdrawal of foreign bases, Panama's economic activity is impeded.

[47] The Revolutionary Democratic Party (RDP) through its candidate Martín Torrijos, son of former dictator Omar Torrijos, won the May 2004 presidential elections. Voter turnout reached 80 per cent. Torrijos defeated Endara, who stressed he was 'happy because (Panamanian) democracy emerged … untouched.' from the elections. ∎

IN FOCUS

ENVIRONMENTAL CHALLENGES

Water pollution from contaminants used in agriculture is threatening fishing. There is growing deforestation in areas of tropical rainforest. Land degradation and soil erosion are threatening to silt the Panama Canal. There is air pollution in urban areas and mining is damaging natural resources.

WOMEN'S RIGHTS

Women have been able to vote and stand for office since 1945. In 2000, women held 10 per cent of total seats in Parliament and 6 per cent of ministerial or equivalent posts.

The proportion of women employed as salaried workers in the labor market fell from 45 per cent in 1990 to 41 per cent in 2001, while female workers' wages during that period were equivalent to 42 per cent of average male wages.

In 1998, 72.2 per cent of pregnant women receive prenatal care, and 97 per cent of births are attended by skilled health staff*.

There were few convictions for domestic violence compared with the number of reported cases. In November 2003, 1,500 cases of domestic violence and more than 500 rapes had been registered. The real number of cases of sexual harassment and/or abuse is estimated to be higher since only 20 per cent of victims report them to the authorities, especially if they occur at home.

Although the labor code prohibits gender-based discrimination, there are reports of women being sexually harassed in the workplace.

CHILDREN

At the end of 2001, there were nearly 1,000 children between 0 and 14 years old living with HIV/AIDS and 8,000 within the same age group had been orphaned by AIDS.

Life expectancy rose to 74.7 years in 2002 (it was 65 years in 1970). However, there are still wide disparities between geographic regions, with the eastern province on the border with Colombia being the poorest. In 2000, the Government estimated that 27,000 children between the ages of 12 and 14 were economically active. This figure rose to 83,244 among the 15-19 year-olds. According to the ILO, 66 per cent of child workers are in rural areas and 34 per cent in urban areas. 2002 marked the third year of a recession which had negative impacts on all social programs and public policy. A power struggle paralyzed the country and resulted in a drop in standards of services for children, health and education.

INDIGENOUS PEOPLES/ ETHNIC MINORITIES

Indigenous peoples face discrimination as well as having reduced access to health services and low literacy levels.

The Guaymis (70,000) live mostly in the provinces of Bocas del Toro, Chiriqui and Veraguas, and today mainly work on the coffee plantations. The Cuna (45,000) are one of the most politically active indigenous groups in Latin America. Their main problems are poor healthcare and sanitation facilities. They preserve their culture but have freely mixed with Europeans and mestizos. The Chocoes, the smallest group with only a few thousand people, are the most seriously affected by the conflict in Colombia. Regular waves of refugees cross the border and frequently settle on their land.

The Panamanian Chinese community is fully integrated, contributing to Panamanian society by, for example, making donations to the most disadvantaged sectors.

MIGRANTS/REFUGEES

At the end of 2002, Panama was home to 1,700 refugees, 100 asylum-seekers whose claims were pending, and 900 Colombians who had 'Temporary Humanitarian Status'. However, the number of Colombians who fled to Panama is over 60,000. Many Salvadorans and Nicaraguans have settled in the country since entering as refugees in the second half of the 1990s.

DEATH PENALTY

There is no death penalty. According to Amnesty International, the last time it was applied was in 1903.

*Latest data available in The State of the World's Children and Childinfo database, UNICEF, 2004.

Papua New Guinea / Papua New Guinea

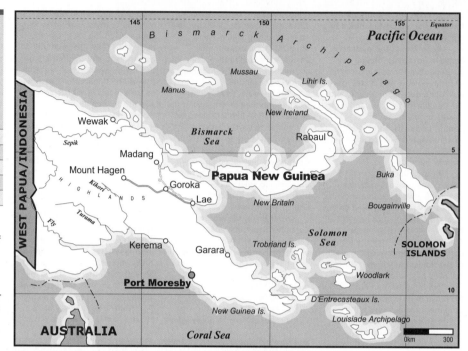

Population:	5,959,257
Area:	462,840 km²
Capital:	Port Moresby
Currency:	Kina
Language:	English

The island of New Guinea, located on the eastern side of the Malay archipelago, was probably occupied 50,000 years ago by Melanesian peoples. With almost 800,000 sq km, it is the world's second largest island after Greenland. It has high mountains (the highest peak is over 5,000 meters above sea level) and deep valleys. The climate is tropical, with heavy rainfall, and climatic disasters, such as typhoons and tidal waves (*tsunamis*), are not uncommon. Traditionally, its population lived in groups scattered throughout the dense tropical jungle, cut off from the outside world. As a result, over 700 dialects are spoken on the islands of New Guinea.

2   The western part of the island (now West Papua) was explored by Indonesian and Asian navigators centuries before the arrival of Europeans. The first Europeans were the Portuguese and Spanish. In 1526, Portuguese sailor Jorge de Meneses named the island *Ilhas dos Papuas*. Twenty years later, Spaniard Iñigo Ortiz Retes renamed the island 'New Guinea', since he thought the islanders resembled the people of Guinea in Africa. Even though European sailors continued to visit and explore the area, little was known about the inhabitants before the 19th century.

3   In the second half of the 19th century the island was disputed by Holland, Germany and Britain, as a result of which the territory was divided into areas called quadrants. Britain ceded its part to Australia in 1904 and it was renamed Territory of Papua. After World War I, the League of Nations officially handed the German part over to Australia as a mandated territory. Australia regained control of the German and British areas after World War II and unified them under the name 'Territory of Papua New Guinea'. Holland continued to rule the western part of the island, known as Irian Barat, which was annexed to Indonesia after a referendum in 1969 and became known as the province of Irian Jaya.

4   In 1971, the eastern territory was officially named Papua New Guinea (PNG), but continued under Australian rule until its independence in 1975. Michael Somare, leader of the Pangu party, who had won the first elections three years before, headed the separatist movement. Secessionist movements, operating both internally and from outside, had rocked the country since independence. Even though Bougainville island had declared its independence some days before Papua New Guinea, Australia and PNG prevented it from gaining international recognition, leading to an armed conflict some years later.

5   In May 1988, Papua New Guinea, together with Vanuatu and the Solomon Islands, signed an agreement to defend and preserve traditional Melanesian cultures. Relations with Indonesia, which occupies the western portion of the island, are

PUBLIC EXPENDITURE

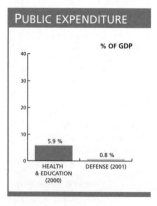

% OF GDP

HEALTH & EDUCATION (2000): 5.9 %

DEFENSE (2001): 0.8 %

PROFILE

ENVIRONMENT

Located east of Indonesia, just south of the Equator, the country is made up of the eastern portion of the island of New Guinea (the western part is the Indonesian territory of West Papua) plus a series of smaller islands: New Britain, New Ireland and Manus, in the Bismarck archipelago; Bougainville, Buka and Mussau, which form the northern part of the Solomon Islands group; the Louisiade and D'Entrecasteaux archipelagos; and the islands of Trobriand/Kiriwina and Woodlark, southeast of New Guinea. The terrain is volcanic and mountainous, except for the narrow coastal plains. The climate is tropical and the vegetation is equatorial rainforest. The country suffers from deforestation, due to large-scale indiscriminate felling.

SOCIETIES

Peoples: Papuans 85 per cent; Melanesians 15 per cent. **Religions:** Many people follow local traditional religions but they also belong to Catholic (32.8 per cent) and Protestant (58.4 per cent) communities.

Languages: English (official). A local Pidgin, with many English words and Melanesian grammar, is widely spoken, as well as 700 other local languages.
Main Political Parties: National Democrat Alliance (NDA), Popular Democratic Movement (PDM); Pangu Pati (PP); Popular Action Party; Popular Progressive Party (PPP).

THE STATE

Official Name: Independent State of Papua New Guinea.
Administrative Divisions: 20 Provinces.
Capital: Port Moresby 275,000 people (2003).
Other Cities: Lae 112,400 people; Madang 33,900; Wewak 27,400; Goroka 17,900 (2000).
Government: Queen Elizabeth II, Head of State, represented since June 2004 by Governor General Sir Paulias Matane, sworn in as governor-general. Michel Somare, Prime Minister since August 2002. Single-chamber legislature: Parliament, with 109 members.
National Holiday: 16 September, Independence Day (1975). **Armed Forces:** 3,700 troops (1996).

troubled. The Free Papua independence movement operates in this province, and Indonesian military operations here in 1984 led 12,000 inhabitants to seek refuge in Papua New Guinea. Many of them still live on the border with Indonesia.

[6] In early 1989 the dispute with Bougainville island's secessionist movement became militarized. The Porgera mines in Bougainville, which exploit important gold and copper deposits, are under Australian control. Over half of export earnings are generated by mining in the islands of Papua New Guinea, which constitutes an essential element of the national economy. Oilfields are also important.

[7] In the following years PNG sent troops to Bougainville and the conflict worsened, but the secessionists retained control over Porgera's copper mine. It was in this context of violence that Parliament reinstated the death penalty in 1991, 34 years after it had been abolished. This decision was strongly rejected by different social movements. In October 1996, when peace envoy Theodore Miriung was murdered, the conflict with Bougainville deepened. In early 1997, Prime Minister Julius Chan resigned when it was revealed that he had contracted international mercenaries to quell the secessionist uprising.

[8] John Giheno replaced Chan on an interim basis, and a few weeks later Parliament appointed Bill Skate as Head of Government. In July 1997, in New Zealand/Aotearoa, the Government and secessionist rebels brought the Bougainville crisis to an end by signing a definitive peace agreement, including the demilitarization of the island and the deployment of UN peace-keeping troops. Australia promised funds for the rebuilding of Bougainville. Casualties of the nine-year conflict are estimated at 20,000.

[9] The political system of this young nation has been a concern from the very beginning. Formally a democratic and parliamentary monarchy, the country's party system was weak and fragmented. Switches in party loyalty were frequent, as was the creation of new coalitions and alliances, occasionally leading to governments being overturned through parliamentary votes of no confidence. In 11 years (from 1977 to 1988) Papua New Guinea had five different prime ministers.

[10] Skate's decision to ask Taiwan to grant a credit worth $2.5 billion prompted Parliament to request his resignation in 1999.

IN FOCUS

ENVIRONMENTAL CHALLENGES
Deforestation is affecting the rainforests, as a result of increasing commercial demand for wood from tropical climates. There are high levels of pollution caused by quarrying, but the most serious environmental problem is drought.

WOMEN'S RIGHTS
Women have been eligible for office since 1963 and have been able to vote since 1964. Female political participation is minimal, with only one of the 109 seats in Parliament held by a woman. There are no women in the Supreme Court nor in the provincial governments. Although the Constitution guarantees equal protection regardless of gender or race, women commonly face discrimination in a range of areas. There are frequent incidents of gang rape and domestic violence (although the latter is a crime, in the majority of communities this type of aggression is regarded as a private issue). Few victims report these crimes. It is estimated that 65 per cent of women prisoners have been convicted of assaulting or killing another woman, crimes that are common in those areas where polygamy is prevalent. Even in urban areas, Papuan women are often regarded as second-class citizens. Adultery is a crime and women tend to receive harsher sentences than men. In many rural communities women are treated as property, being sold as wives, and are often denied their

rights. Sexual harassment, which is widespread, is not considered a crime, 57 per cent of women are literate, compared to 71 per cent of men. Maternal mortality is 300 per 100,000 live births*.

CHILDREN
70 children in every thousand die before the age of one*. There is widespread sexual abuse of minors.

Primary education is not free, nor universal, and fees are high. In 1999 it was estimated that 91 per cent of boys and 78 per cent of girls were enrolled at primary school, but the majority later drop out.

The Government does not assign sufficient resources to the rights and welfare of children. Following budget cuts, the Government stopped providing medical supplies to the population and free healthcare was suspended, hitting rural areas especially hard.

INDIGENOUS PEOPLES/ETHNIC MINORITIES
The indigenous population is one of the most diverse in the world, comprising several hundred distinct communities, the majority of which number a few hundred people. The ethnic make-up of the population is very complex, with more than 700 groups, divided by language, traditions and customs. Many of these communities have been in conflict with their neighbors for centuries. The mountainous terrain adds to the isolation of these groups.

The principal division is between the Papuans (80 per cent of the population) and the Melanesians (19 per cent). Small ethnic communities, comprising mainly Micronesians or

Polynesians, live in the outlying islands.

There are over 715 languages in use, most of them spoken on the island of New Guinea, which is divided between Papua New Guinea and West Papua. Almost 650 languages have been identified and it was discovered that only between 350 and 450 are related. Most of these languages, spoken by hundreds or thousands of people, have extremely complex grammar. The Enga language, from the province of Enga, is spoken by 130 thousand people.

The Catholic faith has taken root in the indigenous communities, but there are still many missionaries in the country. The non-Christian indigenous population practice different religions, but on the whole maintain their traditional culture, animism and ancestor worship.

MIGRANTS/REFUGEES
By the end of 2002, Papua New Guinea was home to approximately 5,200 refugees and asylum-seekers. Almost 5,100 came from West Papua (formerly Irian Jaya). The other 100 refugees were mainly Iraqis who had been unable to reach Australia.

DEATH PENALTY
The death penalty was reinstated in 1991, since when there have not been any executions, although several people have been sentenced to death.

*Latest data available in *The State of the World's Children* and *Childinfo* database, UNICEF, 2004.

He was succeeded by Mekere Morauta, who sought new loans from the World Bank and the IMF, causing tension between Papua New Guinea and China.

[11] According to analysts, the November 2002 general elections were the most important ones since independence, for it was the first time a president had completed a full term in office since 1975, in a country marked by political instability and violence. Due to PNG's difficult terrain and inaccessible tropical forest, mountain and volcanic areas, national elections require a long electoral process.

[12] The results of the chaotic elections were issued one month

later, with the veteran Michael Somare obtaining the majority and becoming Prime Minister for the third time. One of his first resolutions as Prime Minister was to stop Morauta's privatization program, arguing that he needed more time to evaluate the conditions of the program and its advantages for the State. Both the World Bank and the IMF were ardent promoters of privatization. The policy objectives of Somare's new Government included the adoption of urgent measures against poverty, endemic unemployment and widespread crime.

[13] Given the Australian Government's rising concern over

terrorism - 88 Australians died in October 2003 in an attack in Bali, Indonesia - Australia decided to intervene in neighboring states, such as the Solomon Islands and Papua New Guinea. An agreement signed by PNG and Australia in December 2003 stated that 230 police and 70 military officers from Australia would be deployed on the island in 2004. Even though during the talks the PNG Government considered the plan to be neo-colonialist, Somare had to give in when John Howard's Government threatened to block all forms of aid unless the proposal was fully accepted. The first Australian contingent arrived in December 2003. ■

Paraguay / Paraguay

Population:	6,159,680
Area:	406,750 km²
Capital:	Asunción
Currency:	Guaraní
Language:	Spanish and Guaraní

B efore the 15th century, Guaraní Indians lived in the region between the Paraguay river (which divides modern Paraguay into its western and eastern regions) and the Paraná river, the natural border with today's Brazil. The Guaranís spoke Tupí, the most widely used language in South America when the Spanish arrived. Women cultivated corn, cassava and sweet potatoes while men engaged in fishing, hunting and the defense of their villages.

[2] In the late 15th century, persistent attacks mostly by Tupí-Payaguá groups who moved out of the barren region of Gran Chaco (a strip of forest along the borders between Paraguay, Argentina and Bolivia) were forcefully repelled by Guaranís, carrying the conflict into the margins of the Inca empire.

[3] The Guaranís' peaceful reception of the Spanish explorers, who came through Brazil and the Río de la Plata (silver river) in the next century, was mainly due to their need to prevent new incursions by the Payaguás.

[4] Although the region of Paraguay did not have precious metals, the Spanish colonizers made it their administrative center for South America because of its strategic location and lack of local opposition. In 1537, Martínez de Irala founded the fort of Nuestra Señora de Asunción, which was later to become the country's capital.

[5] From Asunción, Irala limited Portuguese expansion through a line of forts and established the first settlements in the present-day Argentinean cities of Santa Fe, Corrientes and Buenos Aires.

[6] Spanish conquistadors and Guaranís lived together peacefully on the basis of a subsistence economy which was strengthened by the technical advances and work ethic introduced by the Jesuits in the early 17th century. The 32 missions where up to 100,000 Guaranís came to live became centers of religious conversion, agricultural production, manufacturing and trade, and within a few decades they comprised an autonomous administrative entity.

[7] The Guaranís' military prowess allowed them to defend the missions from attacks launched by both Portuguese slave raiders and armies from Asunción. Between 1721 and 1735, the two colonial powers enforced a territorial partition of the mission settlements. In 1767, the Jesuits were finally expelled from South America and

many Guaranís were sold into slavery.

[8] The port of Buenos Aires became the epicenter of trade between Europe - whose industrial expansion fuelled a demand for leather, and later on wool, from the Río de la Plata region - and the southern cone of America. As a result, Buenos Aires was proclaimed capital of the Viceroyalty of Río de la Plata in 1776. When Buenos Aires proclaimed its independence from Spain in 1810, Paraguayans resisted the capital's authority, while at the same time taking advantage of the weakening of local Spanish authorities. On 14 May 1811, Paraguay proclaimed its independence under the leadership of Captains Caballero and Yegros.

[9] Yegros established a junta with lawyer Gaspar Rodríguez de Francia, who imposed an isolationist policy toward both Buenos Aires and Brazil, in order to preserve territorial sovereignty and protect the Paraguayan economy from French and British products that were then flooding the continent. The Republic was proclaimed in 1813, and in 1816, the Congress appointed Francia dictator for life.

[10] Francia ('El Supremo') secularized institutions, confiscated church property and made the State the nation's largest landowner. He also promoted production within the context of a strict autarchy. Upon Francia's death in 1840, Paraguayans enjoyed a healthy economy and an equitable distribution of wealth.

[11] Carlos Antonio López became leader with popular backing, and after his participation in a civilian-military consulate between 1841 and 1844, Congress appointed him

President of the Republic, and at the same time approved a presidential Constitution.

[12] After the death of Francia and the fall of the Governor of Buenos Aires, Juan Manuel de Rosas - hostile to Britain and France - in 1852, the economic and military powers that were disputing control over the region (Britain, US, France and Brazil) developed new strategies for intervention in Paraguayan affairs.

[13] Carlos Antonio López, threatened by the escalating attacks from Brazil, concentrated on developing the arms industry and communications in the country, with the support of the US. In 1858, the US navy sent a fleet and US representatives took part in several negotiations. Upon López's death, in 1862, Paraguay had the most developed arsenal and infrastructure (railroads, telegraph system and hospitals) in the southern cone of America.

[14] Paraguay had long-standing border and trade disputes with both the Brazilian Empire and the Government of Buenos Aires. These two powers saw Paraguay not only as territory to annex but also as a strong ally of the countries that opposed their attempts to dominate the region. The Uruguayans for example had also struggled to maintain independence, particularly from Argentina.

[15] In 1864 Brazil helped the leader of Uruguay's Colorado Party to oust the Blanco Party opponent. In response, Paraguay's president Francisco Solano López (who succeeded his father Carlos Antonio López) went to war with Brazil which he saw as threatening the regional balance of power. Bartolomé Mitre, president of Argentina, then organized an alliance with Brazil and Colorado-controlled Uruguay (the Triple Alliance), and together they declared war on Paraguay on 1 May 1865.

[16] The War of the Triple Alliance, which ended in 1870, was the bloodiest in South America's history. Paraguay's population fell from over half a million to around 220,000 and the country's state apparatus was destroyed. The end of the conflict was followed by six years of Brazilian occupation, during which time Paraguay became deeply indebted to British banks and allowed uncontrolled extraction of *quebracho* (used for tanning) and rubber by foreign companies.

[17] Argentina and Brazil had annexed part of Paraguay and demanded reparations. In 1887, in the aftermath of defeat, the main Paraguayan parties were founded: the Colorado Party and the

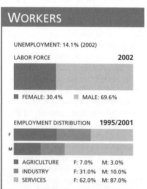

WORKERS

UNEMPLOYMENT: 14.1% (2002)

LABOR FORCE   **2002**

■ FEMALE: 30.4%   ■ MALE: 69.6%

EMPLOYMENT DISTRIBUTION   **1995/2001**

F

M

■ AGRICULTURE	F: 7.0%	M: 3.0%
■ INDUSTRY	F: 31.0%	M: 10.0%
■ SERVICES	F: 62.0%	M: 87.0%

LAND USE

2000

IRRIGATED AREA: 2.8% of arable land

■ ARABLE LAND: 5.8%	
■ CROPLANDS: 0.2%	
■ OTHER USE: 94.0%	

Life expectancy
70.9 years
2000-2005

GNI per capita
$1,170
2002

Literacy
93% total adult rate
2000

Authentic Liberal Radical Party (ALRP). The latter was founded by Faustino Sarmiento, President of Argentina during the War of the Triple Alliance, who settled in Paraguay in 1874 (until his death in 1888). Sarmiento promoted a new Paraguayan political class and, putting into practice the ideas laid out in his book *Civilization and Barbarism*, pushed for the prohibition of the Guaraní language and customs.

18   The Colorado Party ruled from 1887 until 1904 when the ALRP seized power, holding on to it during the next three decades. From the War of the Triple Alliance onwards, foreign dependency and corruption were endemic to the Paraguayan State, as demonstrated by the border war with Bolivia (Chaco War, 1932-1935).

19   The Chaco War cost Paraguay 50,000 lives and was orchestrated by rival oil multinationals - Standard Oil and Shell - disputing the territories of Gran Chaco that were supposedly rich in oil deposits. This war, as a result of which Paraguay won control over two-thirds of the Bolivian Chaco, came to an end through the diplomatic intervention of the US and Britain.

20   Between 1936 and 1954, there were two coups (in 1936 and 1940, led by Generals Estigarribia and Morínigo, respectively), a civil war (in 1947, as a result of the ALRP rebellion) and seven popularly elected presidencies which had no political continuity. In 1948, an alliance between a majority of the army and the Colorado Party was formed which brought General Alfredo Stroessner (then Commander-in-Chief of the armed forces) to the presidency in 1954 through a new coup.

21   Stroessner was backed by the US Government, within the framework of the National Security Doctrine, until the late 1970s. During his regime, which lasted until 1989, all freedoms were suppressed and state terrorism was applied (murder, disappearances, imprisonment without trial and torture). This was revealed in the 'Archives of Terror' found by the Paraguayan justice system in 1992.

22   These archives provided clear evidence of thousands of human rights abuses both in isolated cases and as part of international plans of repression, such as Operation Condor (in the 1970s) in which Stroessner co-operated with the US and military regimes in Chile, Argentina, Brazil and Uruguay.

23   Stroessner managed to orchestrate a puppet opposition and had himself re-elected seven times. Under his rule, Paraguay became home to World War II criminals, as well as the Nicaraguan dictator Anastasio Somoza, after

IN FOCUS

ENVIRONMENTAL CHALLENGES
Widespread deforestation, water pollution and the loss of wetlands are the country's most serious environmental problems. The inadequate waste treatment poses health risks for urban residents.

WOMEN'S RIGHTS
Women have been able to vote and stand for office since 1961. In 2000, they held 3 per cent of the seats in Parliament, while their representation in ministerial or equivalent positions amounted to 7 per cent. That year, women made up 30 per cent of the country's labor force.

From 1990, the ratio of women's earnings to men's was about 40 per cent in non-agricultural sectors. It is precisely in those sectors where women represent a majority that their salaries are considerably lower than men's. In 1990, 83.9 per cent of pregnant women received prenatal care; since then, considerable efforts have been made to improve healthcare for pregnant women, and the rate of coverage increased to 89 per cent in 1998.

CHILDREN
The Children's Code approved in mid-2001 is being implemented and the new National Secretariat for Children and Adolescents was given ministerial rank. However, no progress was made on issues

such as state reform, decentralization, and other reforms essential for providing better services for children and young people. The Pan American Health Organization (PAHO) has supported the introduction of the combination vaccine against five major childhood killer diseases (diphtheria, tetanus, whooping cough, hepatitis B and influenza hemophilus), although in 2002 only part of the infant population was covered. The country's economic crisis has reduced the already weak capacity of social services to effectively protect children's rights. According to UNICEF, 1 in 3 children aged between 7 and 17 worked in 2001 - a total of some 462,000. Forty-two per cent of these children had started working by the age of 8 and nearly 37 per cent of the total do not attend school. Many children take part in family agricultural production. In urban areas, thousands of children under 12 work selling newspapers, washing windscreens and as prostitutes. Many of them regularly suffer from malnutrition and diseases.

INDIGENOUS PEOPLES/ ETHNIC MINORITIES
Ninety per cent of the population are mestizo, descending from the Spanish and indigenous peoples belonging to the Guaraní family. According to the last census carried out in 2001, the indigenous population comprises 80,000 people. There are 17 ethnic groups descended from five linguistic

families: Tupí-Guaraní, Enxet-Maskoy, Mataguayo, Zamuco, and Guaicurú; the Tupí-Guaraní are the most numerous. Thirteen of these peoples live in the Chaco, where deforestation is destroying the indigenous habitat, while the other four live in the eastern region. While only 1.2 per cent identify themselves as indigenous, indigenous culture is deeply rooted in Paraguay where Guaraní is one of the two official languages and is spoken by most of the population, in both rural and urban areas.

Although the Constitution provides for their protection and recognition, they are affected by many problems such as poor healthcare, housing and malnutrition.

MIGRANTS/REFUGEES
One million Paraguayans live abroad.

The Government cooperates with the UN High Commissioner for Refugees in receiving refugees and asylum-seekers on a case-by-case basis. According to the NGO Committee of Churches, 21 people were granted refugee status while another 11 requests were pending; 27 of the 32 requests were from Russia, Vietnam and Cuba.

DEATH PENALTY
The death penalty was abolished in 1992 and the last execution was in 1928.

the Sandinista revolution in 1979. Paraguay became a cocaine-trafficking center with the drug from Peru and Bolivia going on to Brazil, Argentina and the US.

24   In the early 1980s, Stroessner ordered the creation of a tax-free area on the border with Brazil, the main center of which was Ciudad del Este. According to Brazilian media investigations, foreign exchange houses in Ciudad del Este have laundered about $100 million per year. Security forces assigned to this city and surrounding areas were then and still are inadequate to cover the hundreds of reports filed each year denouncing the organized groups trafficking in women, children, drugs, arms and stolen vehicles.

25   The construction of the world's largest hydroelectric plant (Itaipú) near Ciudad del Este, opened by Stroessner in 1984, drew accusations of illegal expropriation of lands, as a result of investigative reports written mostly by Brazilian

journalists, whose work was systematically obstructed by death threats and murders.

26   Most of the companies and foreign settlers (nearly 400,000 in 2003) congregated around Ciudad del Este on a strip of land 1,200 km long and 65 km wide, where Portuguese and Brazilian currency are commonly used. At the end of 2001, the US Government labelled this region as an 'area of terrorist activity', where Hamas and Hizbullah groups purportedly operate.

27   The democratization process in Latin America promoted by the US during the presidency of Jimmy Carter (1977-1981), contributed to the emergence of opposition groups. In Paraguay it was supported by the Paraguayan Catholic Church as well as the Inter-Union Labor Movement, a Permanent Assembly of Landless Rural Workers (APCT), the Rural Women's Co-ordination Group and several indigenous peoples' organizations.

28   On 3 February 1989, Stroessner was overthrown by a coup headed by his son's father-in-law, army commander General Andrés Rodríguez, who called elections in May. The elections were open to all political parties except the still-banned Communist Party.

29   In the elections, General Rodríguez - who had been frequently linked to drug-trafficking, even by the US Drug Enforcement Administration (DEA) - was elected with 68 per cent of the vote, while the ALRP won 21 per cent. Despite the presence of foreign observers, voting was plagued by countless irregularities, attributed to the Colorado Party.

30   In the elections for the National Constituent Assembly held in December 1991, the Colorado Party took 60 per cent of the vote and the ALRP, 29 per cent. The Constitution of June 1992, which replaced the one introduced by Stroessner in 1967, included clauses protecting human rights and

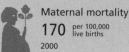

Under-5 mortality	Poverty	Debt service	Maternal mortality
30 per 1,000 live births 2002	**19.5%** of population living on less than $1 per day 1998	**12.5%** exports of goods and services 2001	**170** per 100,000 live births 2000

banned the death penalty for ordinary crimes. The Presidents of the Republic, the Supreme Court and Congress did not attend the public meeting held to promulgate the new constitution.

[31] In December 1992, Paraguay signed an agreement with Argentina, Brazil and Uruguay to create a common market (Mercosur) which came into operation in 1995. Nevertheless, the country's economic indicators (among the poorest in America) showed a steady decline.

[32] In the May 1993 elections, the ruling party's civilian candidate Juan Carlos Wasmosy was elected with 40 per cent of the vote. A year later, Parliament approved a law which banned the military from party politics. The Government and military high command took immediate action to have the law declared unconstitutional.

[33] In 1994, General Ramón Rozas Rodríguez, who had been appointed head of the anti-drugs campaign the previous year, was assassinated when he was supposed to present a report on illegal activities involving the military leadership, including General Lino Oviedo. In April 1996, the President retired eight high-ranking officers. General Oviedo resisted the order and holed up with a group of officers, while Wasmosy took refuge in the US embassy.

[34] In the Colorado Party internal elections in September 1997, Oviedo was elected presidential candidate with 36.8 per cent of the vote against 35 per cent for Luis María Argaña and 22.5 per cent for Wasmosy's candidate Carlos Facetti. In October, Oviedo was arrested on charges of sedition and in April 1998 he was sentenced to 10 years in prison.

[35] The May 1998 elections, with Oviedo in prison, gave 46.8 per cent of the vote to the Colorado Party's Raúl Cubas and Luis María Argaña, against 38.2 per cent for the Democratic Alliance (ALRP and others). One of the first measures taken by the new president was to release Oviedo. However, in December, the Supreme Court ruled that this action was unconstitutional.

[36] In early March 1999, President Cubas found himself facing a possible vote of no confidence in Parliament. However, on 23 March, Vice President Argaña was assassinated by unknown troops. Following several days of street rioting, Cubas resigned and took refuge in Brazil, while Oviedo was granted safe passage to Argentina.

[37] The head of Congress, (Colorado Party), took over the presidency on 28 March 1999. A ruling by the Supreme Court allowed Luis González Macchi to replace Cubas for the remainder of his term, due to end in 2003.

[38] In the late 1990s, the World Rain Forest Movement denounced the virtual extinction of the Ayoreo Indians, who originally occupied 2,800 hectares of the Gran Chaco. Since the 1970s, entrepreneurs belonging to the Paraguayan Mennonite community (about 25,000 people), as well as the companies Falabella and Veragilma - interested in the exploitation of *palosanto* wood (or holy wood) - have devastated and appropriated Ayoreo lands.

[39] In May 2000, the Government foiled a coup attempt by Oviedo, who was later arrested on the Brazliian border and placed under house arrest in Brasilia. Oviedo, who was accused of Argaña's assassination and of plotting the 1996 coup attempt, was placed near Stroessner's residence in Brasilia, where the former dictator had lived since 1989. In spite of the numerous charges filed against him, Stroessner has received regular pension payments since 1993 as a former minister of the Paraguayan state.

[40] In 2001, Amnesty International reported cases of torture of prisoners, including juveniles. In 2002, Human Rights Watch revealed that 112 soldiers had died in unexplained circumstances during the previous 13 years and demanded that the Paraguayan authorities establish a minimum age for conscription of 18 years.

[41] In July 2002, the Paraguayan Government decreed a state of emergency that lasted for a week, in order to control street protests. People demanded the resignation of President González Macchi for his alleged participation in the illegal investment of $16 million of state funds, which were wired from the Central Bank of Paraguay to his Citibank account in New York. Two people were killed and 300 were arrested as a result of the confrontations.

[42] In December that year, the Supreme Court of Justice passed a law preventing impeachment proceedings against President González Macchi over charges of alleged corruption. González Macchi, for his part, accused the Vice-President, Julio César Franco (of the ALRP), of having conspired with Oviedo to destabilize the country.

[43] In the April 2003 elections, the Colorado Party's candidates Nicanor Duarte Frutos and Luis Castiglioni won a majority with 37 per cent of the vote, followed by the ALRP with 24 per cent and Oviedo's National Union of Ethical Colorados with 13.5 per cent of votes. Duarte, who had been Minister of Culture between 1993 and 1997 and between 1999 and 2001, promised to fight corruption and promote a state investment policy in agriculture, the country's main productive sector.

[44] On leaving office in August 2003 González Macchi was subpoenaed and ordered to remain in the country to face public trial on a range of charges of violating the Constitution. In November that year, 20 accusations of constitutional offenses, conspiring to commit crimes and money-laundering were filed against six members of Paraguay's Supreme Court of Justice. By April 2004, three of the magistrates allegedly involved had handed in their resignations.

[45] In August 2004 more than 420 people died and hundreds were injured in a fire at Ikua Bolaños shopping mall, in Asuncion. President Frutos announced three days of national mourning. The police stated that the tragedy - which stretched the emergency services to their limit - was caused by the explosion of a gas cylinder in one of the mall's kitchens. Troops and some 1,000 police joined the firefighters in the rescue operations. Police spokespeople confirmed that the complex lacked enough emergency exits.

[46] According to the Paraguayan chief of police, several people saw the building's doors being closed and confirmed that the emergency door was welded shut. One of the mall's security guards confirmed that the order to close the doors had come from the owners, Juan Pio Paiva and his son, to prevent people from leaving without paying.

[47] The owners were accused of voluntary manslaughter by the public prosecutor. Several countries, among them Uruguay, Chile, France, the US and Spain sent aid to Asunción. Pope John II and several presidents sent their condolences. ∎

PROFILE

ENVIRONMENT

A landlocked country in the heart of the Río de la Plata basin, Paraguay is divided into two distinct regions by the Paraguay River. To the east lie fertile plains irrigated by tributaries of the Paraguay and Paraná rivers, and covered with rainforest. This is the main farming area, producing soybeans (the major export crop), wheat, corn and tobacco. The western region or Northern Chaco is dry savanna, with cotton and cattle.

SOCIETY

Peoples: Paraguayans are mostly mestizo (90 per cent), from the Spanish and indigenous peoples. The indigenous population (which comprises 80,000 people) belongs to the large Guaraní family, with linguistic and cultural variants. At present there are movements that defend the Guaraní ethnic identity. Immigration has produced German, Italian, Argentine and Brazilian minorities. Brazilians occupy a growing area on the border with their home country. A million Paraguayans live abroad, of whom approximately 200,000 emigrated for political reasons.

Religions: Mainly Catholic, official. Protestant groups.

Languages: Spanish and Guaraní (both official); most Paraguayans are bilingual.

Main Political Parties: Colorado Party; Authentic Radical Liberal Party; National Union of Ethical Colorados; Party for a Country of Solidarity; National Agreement; White Party.

Main Social Organizations: The Paraguayan Labor Confederation; the United Workers' Central (CUT), uniting labor unions and the Rural Workers' Movement; the Paraguayan Women's Union; Guaraní Ñanduti Rogue; Paraguayan Students Union; Swindled Savers in Action.

THE STATE

Official Name: República del Paraguay.

Administrative Divisions: 17 departments and the capital city.

Capital: Asunción 1,639,000 people (2003).

Other Cities: Ciudad del Este 254,300 people; San Lorenzo 224,900; Lambaré 167,900; Fernando de la Mora 160,300 (2000).

Government: Head of state and government, Nicanor Duarte Frutos, President elected in April 2003 for a five-year term. Luis Castiglioni, Vice-President, elected In April 2003. The National Congress (Legislature) has two chambers: the Chamber of Deputies, with 80 members, and the Chamber of Senators, with 45 members.

National Holiday: 14 May, Independence Day (1811).

Armed Forces: 20,200 (1996). Others: 8,000 (Police).

Peru / Perú

Population:	27,968,365
Area:	1,285,220 km²
Capital:	Lima
Currency:	New sol
Language:	Spanish, Quechua and Aymara

Evidence of human life dating back over 15,000 years was found in caves near Ayacucho, in what is now Peru. The Chavin civilization, that reached its peak between 1400 and 200 BC, excelled at urban planning. The Paraca (700 to 100 BC) were skilled anatomists and embalmers. The Mochica built adobe temples in the Mocha valley, and it is thought their direct descendants were the Chimu (1000 to 1400 AD) who were great metalworkers. The Nazca culture (200 BC to 800 AD) developed agriculture with large-scale irrigation systems and built enormous calendars that are still discernible from the heights. The Tiahuanaco-Huari culture (600 BC to 1000 AD), based in what is currently Bolivia, expanded into the Peruvian highlands.

2   The 12th century marked the zenith of the Inca empire, which politically united the various cultures and languages of the region, resettling many subjects in other parts of the empire and imposing Quechua as a common language. As with the rest of the Andean civilizations, the Incas' cultural legacy was destroyed by Spanish colonization, but its history was preserved down the generations by oral tradition and texts written after the conquest. The founders of the Inca dynasty, Manco Capac and Mama Oclo, settled in Cuzco, which later became the capital of the empire. In the 14th century, during the reign of the fourth Emperor (or Inca), Mayta Capac, they attacked neighboring populations.

3   Capac Yupanqui was the first to extend Inca influence beyond the Cuzco valley. With the eighth emperor, Viracocha Inca, the empire began a program of permanent conquest, establishing garrisons amongst the conquered peoples. In 1438, Pachacuti Inca Yupanqui, one of the sons of Viracocha Inca, usurped the throne from his brother Inca Urcon and the empire expanded beyond Lake Titicaca, subjugating the Chanca, Quechua and Chimu

peoples and taking over the kingdom of the Shiri - the Cara sovereigns - in Quito.

4   During the reign of Topa Inca Yupanqui (1471-1493) the Inca extended their power southwards, towards what is now central Chile. On the death of Topa Inca a war of succession broke out, which was won by Huayna Capac (1493-1525). He extended the northern frontier up to the river Ancasmayo (the current frontier between Ecuador and Colombia) before dying of a disease that was probably introduced by the Spanish. Tahuantisuyu, as the Incan Empire was known, governed around 13 million people.

5   The death of Huayna Capac caused another war of succession between Huascar, governor in Cuzco, and his younger brother Atahualpa, a son of Huayna Capac and a Shiri princess, who ruled the northern part of the empire from Quito. In 1532 the scales were tipped in favor of Atahualpa, but a group of 180 Spanish led by Francisco Pizarro and Diego de Almagro, disembarked in Tumbes. The Spanish killed those loyal to Atahualpa and, recognizing him as the legitimate governor of the empire, met with him in Cajamarca, kidnapped him and demanded a large ransom in silver and gold. While imprisoned Atahualpa had Huascar killed, before he himself was strangled in 1533; the forces of the empire were thus paralyzed. The Spanish reached Cuzco, where they crowned Topa Hualpa, with the intention of reigning through an Inca emperor.

However, Topa Hualpa was an ally of Huascar, and so the Europeans were committed to the faction they initially had not wanted to support.

6   Topa Hualpa died shortly afterwards and the Spanish reinforced their alliance with the pro-Huascar faction by putting his brother Manco Capac on the throne and dispersing the last of Atahualpa's army. In 1535, Pizarro prohibited Manco Capac from re-establishing control over the dominions along the coast and in the north, which were either still loyal to Atahualpa or lacked central control. Manco Capac then understood that the Spanish were a far greater threat than any of Atahualpa's followers and in 1536 he besieged Cuzco for a year. But his forces were finally disbanded by Diego de Almagro, returning from an expedition to Chile.

7   Manco Capac founded an independent Inca state in the Amazon regions which lasted until 1572, with the death by poisoning of Titu Cusi Yupanqui, the last Inca. The days of the Tahuantisuyu (the Inca Empire) were numbered from the moment Pizarro founded Lima on the coast in 1535, which operated as the center of Spanish power. The Spanish administration radically changed the property and land-use rules; the payment of tributes and forced labor broke up the bases of the old society and the old gods were officially replaced with Catholicism, although cults of minor deities did not disappear. Similarly, regions and cities of the old empire

survived beyond the reach of the Spanish Crown for centuries. The most notable example of this was the fortress of Machu Picchu, 80 kilometers north-east of Cuzco, which was only re-discovered in 1911 by Hiram Bingham, a Yale University professor.

8   Due to the conflicts between the *conquistadores* (the Spanish conquerors), the Spanish Crown could not fully establish its authority for decades. Almagro, disillusioned by losing his chances to conquer lands in Chile, besieged Cuzco until he was beaten and executed in 1538. His allies conspired with his son and attacked Pizarro's palace. Pizarro was assassinated in 1541. The Spanish Crown refused to recognize the young Almagro, who was captured and executed in 1542. The conquistadores, led by Gonzalo Pizarro, Francisco's brother, unhappy with the Spanish King's new laws (aiming to impede feudalism, and thereby threatening their wealth and power) rebelled in 1542, remaining independent from the Crown to all intents and purposes until 1544, when Gonzalo Pizarro was defeated and executed.

9   It was only with the appointment of Viceroy Francisco de Toledo in 1569 that Spain consolidated its dominion in the region. The American institutions were adapted to Spanish authority and for a long time the chiefs of the various Andean nations administered the interests of their communities while collecting tributes and providing indigenous workforce for the mines. Since they was no chance of peaceful cohabitation, when the son of Manco Capac, Tupac Amaru, led the indigenous rural population in an uprising, the Crown had him captured and executed in 1571.

10   Once Toledo's administration was over, the Viceroyalty in Peru assumed the form it maintained until the 18th century, including all of South America except Venezuela and Brazil. The discovery of the silver mines in Potosí in 1545 was followed by those of Huancavelica in 1563. With the exception of the gold from New Granada (Colombia), mineral production was concentrated in Peru itself, or in Upper Peru (Bolivia). The Spanish Crown prioritized these areas, which became the most developed and richest parts of the continent.

11   During the 16th and 17th centuries, Lima was the center of power and wealth for all of Spanish-controlled South America. Based on the labor of the indigenous workforce, the Court of Lima - where the King's justice was meted out - attracted the rich, religious orders, intellectuals and artists. It was in Lima that the tribunals of the Inquisition worked most avidly and cruelly. With the advent of the

Life expectancy
69.8 years
2000-2005

GNI per capita
$2,050
2002

Literacy
90% total adult rate
2000

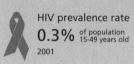

HIV prevalence rate
0.3% of population 15-49 years old
2001

Bourbon dynasty in 1700, replacing the Hapsburgs as rulers of Spain, measures were taken to promote the development of the colonies and to achieve better government of the continent. The creation of the Viceroyalty of New Granada meant the Viceroyalty of Peru lost control over the port of Quito as well as the territory constituting modern day Colombia. The creation of the Viceroyalty of the River Plate in 1777 also removed control over Upper Peru and what are today Argentina, Paraguay and Uruguay. Chile, meanwhile, became an independent Captaincy of the Viceroy of Peru.

[12] Reforms to the mercantile system, allowing the Pacific and Atlantic ports to trade directly with Spain, weakened the condition of the Viceroyalty even further. In 1780, the *cacique* (indigenous leader) José Gabriel Condorcanqui had a *corregidor* (chief magistrate) arrested on charges of cruelty. He led a general uprising of indigenous people against the authority of the Viceroyalty in 1780 under the name of Tupac Amaru II, even gaining the support of some *criollos* (descendants of the Spanish). The rebellion, which spread to Bolivia and Argentina, lost support when it turned into a violent battle between the indigenous people and the whites. Tupac II was captured in 1781 and taken to Cuzco where, after being forced to witness the execution of his wife and children, he was quartered and beheaded. The revolution continued, however, until the Spanish Government approved a general pardon for the insurgents.

[13] The concentration of the Crown's military power in Lima; the conservative attitude of the local oligarchy, and the effective suppression of the indigenous uprisings, meant that Peru remained loyal to Spain when the rest of its colonies in South America began the fight for independence between 1810 and 1821. The forces which finally expelled the Spanish came from beyond Peruvian borders. General José de San Martín freed Chile in 1818 and used it as a base to attack Peru by sea with the aim of securing Buenos Aires' control over the mines of Upper Peru and of assuring independence for the Argentine provinces. Toward the end of 1820, he occupied the port of Pisco and the Viceroy withdrew his troops into the interior of the country. San Martín entered Lima and declared independence on 28 July 1821.

[14] San Martín asked for the help of Venezuela's Simón Bolívar to attack the large Spanish contingents in the interior of Peru, but the latter would not agree to share the leadership. Bolívar (who had liberated the northern part of South America) took over in Peru to

PROFILE

ENVIRONMENT

The Andes divide the country into three regions. The desert coastal area, with large artificially irrigated plantations and some natural valleys, has historically been the most modern and westernized. Half the population live in the *sierra* (highlands), between two ranges of the Andes. Numerous peasants here are still organized into *ayllus* (communities) with Incan roots. There is subsistence farming of corn and potatoes, with traditional llama and alpaca rearing forced to move to higher slopes, due to expanding mining and sheep rearing. The eastern region, comprising the Amazon lowlands, with a tropical climate and rainforests, is sparsely populated. Peru is one of the largest producers of coca, a medicinal and energizing plant. Coca - traditionally consumed among Indians who chew its leaves - once chemically refined and developed into a different substance, becomes the basis of cocaine.

SOCIETY

Peoples: Nearly half of all Peruvians are of indigenous origin, mostly Quechua and Aymara, living on the sierra. Along the coast, most of the population are mixed descendants of indigenous indians and Spaniards, and there are also small groups of descendants of African slaves. There are several indigenous groups in the East Amazon jungle. There are also Chinese and Japanese immigrant minorities.
Religions: Catholic (official), with syncretic expressions related to Indian beliefs. **Languages:** Spanish, Quechua and Aymara (all official).
Main Political Parties: Possible Peru (led by Alejandro Toledo); American Revolutionary People's Alliance (APRA); National Unity; Moralizing Independent Front.
Main Social Organizations: The Peruvian Workers General Central Union (CGTP), founded in 1928 and predominantly communist; the Peruvian Workers' Central Union (CTP), founded in 1944, linked to APRA; the independent National Workers' Confederation (CNT).

THE STATE

Official Name: República del Perú. **Administrative Divisions:** 25 Departments, 155 Provinces and 1,586 Districts. **Capital:** Lima 7,899,000 people (2003). **Other Cities:** Arequipa 720,400 people; Trujillo 590,700; Chiclayo 481,100; Cuzco 279,600 (2000).
Government: Alejandro Toledo Manrique, president since July 2001. Carlos Ferrero Costa, prime minister since December 2003. Unicameral legislature: The Congress, with 120 members. **National Holiday:** 28 July, Independence (1821). **Armed Forces:** 125,000 troops (65,000 conscripts), 188,000 reserves (1996). Other: National Police: 60,000 members. Coast Guard: 600 members. Campesino Rounds: the campesino self-defense forces, made up of 2,000 groups mobilized within emergency zones.

continue the fight. In the battles of Junín and Ayacucho, in 1824, the Spanish were defeated and Peru became politically independent. The first years of independence were spent in constant battles between the conservative oligarchy, yearning for the times of the viceroyalty, and the liberals. The wars with Colombia in 1827, and with Bolivia, took place against that backdrop. The unification of Peru with Bolivia, attempted by Bolivian President Andrés Santa Cruz in 1835, failed both socially and economically.

[15] Marshal Ramón Castilla, who ruled the country from 1845 to 1862, shaped the modern Peru, after abolishing slavery and proclaiming the Constitution. In 1864, Spain attempted to establish enclaves on the Peruvian coast. Peru, Chile, Bolivia and Ecuador declared war on the country. The Spanish fleet bombarded Valparaíso in Chile and El Callao in Peru, before being defeated in 1866.

[16] From 1845, with the silver mines exhausted, guano - bird feces used as fertilizer - became Peru's main export product. When the guano 'boom' was over, it was replaced by saltpeter from the southern deserts. This wealth was to bring about the Pacific War (1879-1883). Peru and Bolivia joined forces against Chile, which exploited the saltpeter, with the support of British companies. Peru and Bolivia lost the war and with it the provinces of Arica, Tarapac and Antofagasta.

[17] The 20th century marked the beginning of large-scale copper mining, particularly by the North American Cerro de Pasco Copper Corporation. Foreign capital was also involved in oil exploitation in the north, and sugarcane and cotton in the north and center. The anachronistic agrarian structures, however, continued unchanged. Within this context, the APRA (American Popular Revolutionary Alliance), a Marxist-inspired party

committed to Latin Americanism, achieved widespread popular support. Víctor Haya de la Torre, its main leader, was in favor of merging class boundaries and debated with José Carlos Maritegui, founder of the Peruvian Communist Party (PC). Triumphant in several elections, APRA never actually came into power due to successive military coups.

[18] In 1968, a military faction headed by General Juan Velasco Alvarado ousted President Fernando Belaúnde Terry and started a process of change by nationalizing oil production. This also included recovery of natural resources and fishing, co-operative based agrarian reform, worker participation in company ownership, the creation of socially owned enterprises, the expropriation of the press - planning to hand the latter over to organized social sectors - and an independent non-aligned foreign policy. An ailing Velasco gradually lost control of the process and the trust of his allies. He was overthrown by his Prime Minister General Francisco Morales Bermúdez in 1975. Under pressure from the IMF and an oligarchy keen on regaining power, Morales called elections. Belaunde's Acción Popular (AP), which had boycotted the constituent elections, triumphed in the 1980 presidential elections and established IMF guidelines. That year armed violence reappeared with the Sendero Luminoso ('Shining Path') guerrillas and in 1984 with the Tupac Amaru Revolutionary Movement (MRTA).

[19] In the 1985 elections, the APRA candidate Alan García came in first with 46 per cent. With a foreign debt of $14 billion, García announced he would limit payments to 10 per cent of the annual export income and would negotiate directly with the creditors, without IMF mediation.

[20] The 1989 general elections were won by the unknown outsider, Alberto Fujimori, who was elected with 56.4 per cent of the vote. On assuming power, Fujimori implemented a severe anti-inflationary plan and, without parliamentary support, began to govern by decree. In 1992, Fujimori led a coup claiming that Parliament was corrupt and inoperative and that the judicial system was obstructing national reconstruction. The imprisonment of Abimael Guzmán, founder and leader of Sendero Luminoso, dealt a major blow to the guerrilla group, which was willing to start peace talks.

[21] In 1995, Peru and Ecuador waged an undeclared war along their common border at the Condor mountain range. Peace talks were held under the Río Protocol, with Argentina, Brazil, Chile and the US as guarantors. Re-elected that year,

Under-5 mortality
39 per 1,000 live births
2002

Poverty
15.5% of population living on less than $1 per day
1996

Debt service
22.0% exports of goods and services
2001

Maternal mortality
410 per 100,000 live births
2000

Fujimori amnestied members of the army and police who had been convicted for human rights violations in the fight against the guerrillas since 1980. The so-called 'faceless judges', who remained anonymous during trials, convicted more than 2,000 people in 1992-1995. In 1998, three years after the armed conflict, Peru and Ecuador agreed on a peace treaty based on new border lines proposed by Argentina, Brazil, Chile and the US.

[22] In spite of the constitutional ban on further re-election, Fujimori's candidacy was made official. Peruvians took part in the 2000 elections knowing that Fujimori's political machine had presented one million forged signatures supporting his re-election. The opposition candidate, economist and former shoeshine boy of indigenous origin Alejandro Toledo (with 41 per cent of the vote) claimed Fujimori (48.7 per cent) had misused state funds to finance his campaign and prevented the opposition's access to the media. Toledo headed a large protest in Lima, to force a second electoral round. Finally, he announced he would not take part in the elections until their fairness could be guaranteed. With no international observers, in the second round the only candidate, Fujimori was declared President by the Electoral Court. The number of spoiled ballots - with the words 'no to fraud', at Toledo's request - and the votes for the self-excluded candidate, showed that 54 per cent had voted against Fujimori, who was strongly criticized by the Organization of American States (OAS) and the US.

[23] The OAS supported a schedule of institutional changes in Peru: freedom of the press, independence of the courts, modifications in the electoral system and civilian control of the army and intelligence services. Fujimori promised US Secretary of State Madeleine Albright he would implement the changes. In response to the scandal involving National Intelligence director Vladimiro Montesinos - according to many, the real 'power behind the throne' - (a video had shown Montesinos bribing a legislator), Fujimori announced he would call new elections in 2001, in which he would not take part. Fujimori resigned, from Japan where he was now residing, at the same time as he was deposed by Parliament in Lima. Valentín Paniagua, of Popular Action, was appointed interim president. In 2001, Congress accused Fujimori of abandoning his post.

[24] Having won the cleanest elections in many years, Toledo became the first freely elected President of indigenous origin. On taking office in 2001, he had a country heavily indebted, with fiscal

IN FOCUS

ENVIRONMENTAL CHALLENGES
The country suffers from soil degradation. Some species of fish are endangered due to uncontrolled fishing. The coastline has been polluted by industrial and urban waste. A lack of coherent, high-quality environmental services is especially evident in Lima, where there are also high levels of air pollution.

WOMEN'S RIGHTS
Women have been able to vote and run for office since 1955.

Between 1995 and 2000 women held 10 per cent of seats in parliament, while their share of ministerial or equivalent posts increased from 6 to 10 per cent.

In 2000 women comprised more than 30 per cent of the labor force, but their wages (on average equivalent to a quarter of what men earn) had not increased since 1990.

Although there were no gender differences in access to education, there was still a gender gap in literacy rates among young people aged between 15 and 24: 4.8 per cent of women in that age group were illiterate, compared to 1.8 per cent of men.

Violence against women is a chronic problem. Rape, harassment by partners or others, and the sexual, physical and psychological abuse of Peruvian women is aggravated by the perpetrators' impunity before judicial authorities. It is estimated that half of migrants are women. A rise in the number of single mothers and divorced or separated women has led to an increase in the number of female heads of households.

CHILDREN
Children are the most vulnerable and unprotected sector of the population. Of the 3.8 million people living in extreme poverty, 2.1 million are minors. The work of ministries responsible for social policies was disrupted by restructuring and budget cuts.

The country is still characterized by huge socio-economic differences and exclusion, and child labor remains a serious problem. In 2000 it was estimated that there were 250,000 formal or informal workers under 18 in Lima, 80 per cent of whom were under 12. There were over one million economically active minors in the country as a whole.

INDIGENOUS PEOPLES/ ETHNIC MINORITIES
The majority of the indigenous population lives in the central and southern area of the Andes and comprises 38 per cent of the total population. There are nearly 80 languages including Aymara (22 per cent), Quechua (30 per cent), Arawak, Cahuapana, Harakmbet, Huitoto, Jibaro and Pano.

Traditionally their control over the land and the defense of their culture and traditions has been limited. Following the 1993 Constitution, a law abolishing the inalienability of native lands was put into effect, as a result of which sale of their lands is no longer prohibited. Discrimination is rife and many indigenous people do not have birth certificates or documents that would enable them to take an active part in society. The indigenous population living near the Amazon (between 200,000 and 300,000 people) is geographically isolated, a situation exacerbated by the centralized nature of Government administration. Deficiencies in healthcare and education mean bleak prospects for future generations. African-Peruvians earn less than the white population.

MIGRANTS/REFUGEES
By the end of 2002, there were 900 refugees in the country, mostly Cubans, former-Yugoslavians and Iranians. Between 1980 and 1990 attacks by the Sendero Luminoso (Shining Path) guerrillas devastated large parts of the rural areas. The conflict left 25,000 dead and 800,000 internally displaced people; thousands returned to their homes during the 1990s, but around 600,000 remained in the new settlements (especially in Metropolitan Lima, which became home to up to 40 per cent of the displaced population, coming originally from the poorest regions - Ayacucho, Huancavelica and Apurimac).

The Peruvian Government estimates that over 2 million Peruvians live abroad and that 75 per cent are illegal immigrants. This number has quadrupled over the last 20 years. The main destinations are the US, western European countries, Argentina, Chile and Japan.

DEATH PENALTY
The death penalty was abolished in 1979.

problems, a severe recession and 54 per cent of the population living in extreme poverty. According to the forecast of Toledo's own economic team, poverty in Lima had increased from 35 to 45 per cent between 1997-2000. A Truth and Reconciliation Commission analyzed thousands of cases of human rights violations that had occurred over the last two decades. The authorities issued a second international arrest warrant (the first had been issued three months earlier) against Fujimori, on charges of corruption and human rights violations.

[25] Days before the visit of US President George W Bush in 2002, nine people were killed when a bomb exploded near the US embassy in Lima. According to the Peruvian Government, the goal of Bush's visit was to support the Toledo administration and its plans for a free market economy.

[26] That same year, Health Minister Fernando Carbone reported the conclusions of the Commission on Voluntary Surgical Contraception Activities, which indicated that a forced sterilization plan had been put into effect in rural parts of the country during Fujimori's mandate. It is estimated that between 1996 and 2000, the National Program of Family Planning and Reproductive Health sterilized over 280,000 people, mainly indigenous, against their will or in exchange for food.

[27] In 2002 there were violent protests against the privatization of two powerful Peruvian electricity companies, during which one person died and hundreds were repressed. After two weeks of conflict, the Minister of the Interior, Fernando Respigliosi, resigned and Toledo suspended the privatizations.

[28] In 2003 a court in Lima sentenced Vladimiro Montesinos to eight years in jail on the charge of embezzlement (in 2002 he had been incarcerated for abuse of power and for having illegally taken over the function of Intelligence Chief). Montesinos is awaiting trial on other charges.

[29] Prime Minister Beatriz Merino resigned in 2003 accused of involvement in corruption scandals, which she denied. Toledo requested Merino's resignation, and she was replaced by Carlos Ferrero (an experienced legislator from the Possible Peru party). Merino had been held in high regard by the population due to her efforts to reform state institutions and the tax system.

[30] In April 2004, at least six people died and 1,500 tourists were trapped in landslides near Machu Picchu. The avalanche of mud blocked routes between the historic site and Cuzco. President Toledo personally helped co-ordinate the rescue operation. ∎

Philippines / Pilipinas

Population:	82,808,513
Area:	300,000 km²
Capital:	Manila
Currency:	Peso
Language:	Pilipino and English

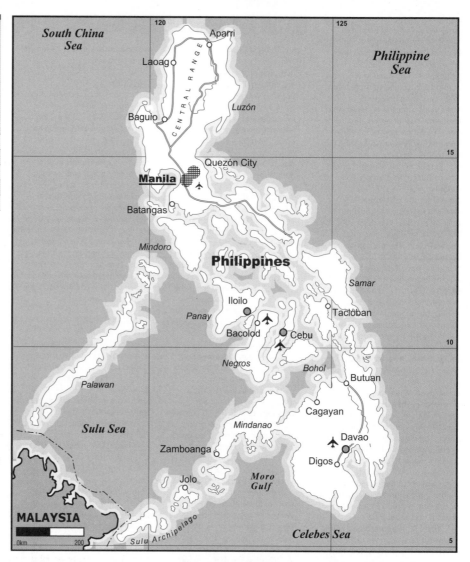

The Philippine archipelago was first inhabited in Paleolithic times, and the Neolithic culture on the islands began around 900 BC. Native peoples, such as the Aeta and the Igorot, probably subsisted without being assimilated by the later groups of migrants.

2 Between the 2nd and 15th centuries AD, migrants from Indonesia and Malaysia settled on the islands, gathering in clans. They were virtually uninfluenced by the classical Indian culture which had touched others in the region. Between the 11th and 13th centuries the coastal areas were raided by Muslim, Japanese and Chinese merchant ships, bringing traders and craftspeople to the islands. The southern islands adopted Islam and sultanates soon appeared.

3 The archipelago was 'discovered' by Ferdinand Magellan in 1521 but the explorer was killed on one of its beaches and Spanish possession of the islands, which were also coveted by the British and the Dutch, was not secured until 1564. The Igorot of the Cordillera region and the Islamic population of Mindanao were never fully incorporated by European colonization, and most of the rural population preserved their subsistence economy, never even paying tribute to the Europeans. Several uprisings by these communities and the Chinese were repressed by the Spaniards.

4 Spanish colonization in the Philippines followed similar patterns to that in the Americas. However, the Philippines had two distinguishing features; they were located on the oceanic trading routes, in a position that received merchandise from all over Southeast Asia on its way to Europe, and they were ruled by the Viceroyalty of Mexico.

5 Late in the 19th century, a local independence movement developed, led by the native bourgeoisie, who wanted the political power which was denied them. Other oppressed sectors

soon followed their lead. Anti-colonial revolution erupted in 1896 and independence was proclaimed on 12 July 1898. However, the US immediately started diplomatic negotiations to seize control of the archipelago, which resulted in the signing of the Treaty of Paris, on 10 December 1898, ending the Spanish-US war. In meetings, which barred Filipino delegates, Spain decided to cede the archipelago to the US in exchange for compensation.

6 Between 1899 and 1911, one million Filipinos died in the struggle against US occupying troops. During World War II, the archipelago was occupied by Japan but US troops returned after the end of the war. The archipelago was eventually granted formal independence in 1946 but the Philippines have remained under US economic domination ever since.

7 Nor did independence bring about any social changes. The

hacienda system - large estates farmed by sharecroppers - persisted in the country. More than half the population were peasants, and 20 per cent of the population owned 60 per cent of the land. Although the sharecropper was supposed to receive half of the harvest, most of the peasant's actual income went to pay off the debts incurred with the cacique (the landowner).

8 The Nationalist Party, a conservative party of landowners, remained in power until 1972, when Ferdinand Marcos, president since 1965, declared Martial Law. In 1986 a coalition of opposition forces rebelled against the continuous abuses of Ferdinand Marcos, paving the way for democratization. During his presidency repression grew both against armed movements (the Muslim independent groups of Mindanao and the New People's Army led by the Maoist Communist Party), and against

political and trade union opposition. This repression often had the military support of the US.

9 Due to its long presence in the country, the Catholic Church is deeply rooted in Filipino society. This is reflected in the fact that 75 per cent of Filipinos over the age of 10 have learnt to read in institutions dependent on the Church. The Church played an active role in the denunciation of fraud when the 1976 referendum supported the imposition of martial law. Five years later, 45 political and trade union organizations united to boycott the fraudulent and unconstitutional elections that Marcos used to stay in power. In September 1981 thousands of people demonstrated in Manila, demanding an end to the dictatorship and the withdrawal of US military bases.

10 On 21 August 1983, opposition leader Benigno Aquino (People's Power party, social-democratic) was murdered at

Life expectancy	GNI per capita	Literacy	HIV prevalence rate
70.0 years 2000-2005	**$1,020** 2002	**95%** total adult rate 2000	**0.1%** of population 15-49 years old 2001

Manila airport as he stepped off the plane that had brought him back after a prolonged exile in the US. His murder was attributed to Marcos. More than 500,000 mourners followed his coffin to the cemetery. This event triggered a popular uprising which did not desist until the dictator was ousted.

[11] Amidst a scenario of increased violence and repression, a large section of the population put pressure on Marcos, demanding early elections in 1986, and supporting the candidacy of Corazón Aquino, widow of the assassinated leader.

[12] Elections were held in February 1986, but widespread fraud prevented 'Cory' Aquino from winning, and she subsequently called for civil disobedience. Marcos' Minister of Defense, Juan Ponce Enrile, attempted a coup against the dictator, but failed. A million supporters surrounded the rebels, led by Enrile, in the field where they had taken refuge. Marcos opted for exile and Corazón Aquino assumed the presidency with Enrile as her Minister of Defense.

[13] The new constitution was approved by a large majority in the February 1987 plebiscite. The charter granted autonomy to the Mindanao and Cordillera regions, thus paving the way for a truce with guerrilla groups operating in those areas. In early 1990 the New People's Army (NPA) representatives left the negotiating table, after several acts of provocation against mass organizations and attempts on the lives of civilian leaders. Agrarian reform, which should have been the cornerstone of the Government's plan for social transformation, was diluted after going through a legislature where many of the members were landowners. The debate over the future of the Clark and Subic Bay American military bases began in April 1988, as the contracts were due to expire in September 1991.

[14] Large-scale natural disasters and social conflicts exposed the population, particularly children, to extreme insecurity. In 1990, 39 per cent of the Filipino population were under the age of 14, and in spite of NGO efforts, only a third of their basic needs were met. A number of Government 'internal refugee' camps were created to provide basic assistance to some 1,250,000 homeless people.

[15] During 1991 increasing pressure from regional and ethnic groups, the urgent need for a more equitable distribution of land and wealth and, possibly, the approaching presidential elections of May 1992, led Corazón Aquino to create a Bureau of Northern Communities. The Bureau was concerned with the mountain and ethnic groups, particularly in Luzón. There was also a Bureau of Southern Cultural Communities, excluding the Muslims. The staff of the Bureaus were recruited from within the communities in question.

[16] In June 1991, the eruption of Mount Pinatubo shook the country, claiming the lives of over 700 Filipinos, flattening entire villages, forcing the evacuation of over 300,000 people, and burying the evacuated Clark US air force base under the ashes.

[17] With its airbase unusable, and faced with the prospect of difficult negotiations as the contract approached its expiry date, the US opted to abandon the base of its own accord. On 26 November 1991, Clark airbase was formally abandoned. It had employed over 40,000 Filipinos, most of whom had carried out menial work.

[18] Of the 32 million Filipinos entitled to vote, 25 million took part in the May 1992 elections which were considered the calmest and cleanest in the country's history. The winner was Fidel Ramos, former Defense Minister in the Aquino administration.

[19] In 1994, the Ramos Government had to seek the opposition's support to control evasion of the 10 per cent VAT tax. This measure won him the IMF's support - including a loan - and prompted a five per cent growth in GNP. The campaign against crime, now headed by Vice President Estrada, led to two per cent of the police force, who were implicated in criminal activities, being discharged, while another five per cent were kept under investigation. The NPA communist guerrillas lost strength due to an amnesty for its members and to internecine conflicts regarding the amnesty.

[20] In 1995 Imelda Marcos was elected to the Chamber of Deputies, in spite of the many corruption charges against her. Swiss banks returned $475 million to the country which had been deposited by her husband Ferdinand Marcos during dictatorship, but the Government was convinced that billions remained in other accounts.

[21] The elimination of restrictions on investments, the reduction in customs barriers and the presence of skilled and cheap labor, attracted investors which led to

IN FOCUS

ENVIRONMENTAL CHALLENGES
Indiscriminate deforestation, mostly due to lumber production, and soil erosion are the most important problems in non-urban areas. Manila has significant water and air pollution.

WOMEN'S RIGHTS
Filipino women have been able to vote and stand for office since 1937. Between 1995 and 2000, women held around 11 per cent of total seats in Parliament, while their representation in ministerial or equivalent positions rose slightly from 8 to 10 per cent. In 2000, women made up 38 per cent of the labor force. Between 1990 and 2001, waged women workers constituted about 40 per cent of the total non-agricultural labor force, while their average salaries represented 49 per cent of men's earnings in the same jobs. Violence against women, both inside and outside the home, remained a serious social problem. Between January and June 2001, an average of seven women per day were raped. Since by law rape is punishable by the death penalty, it is thought that many women refrain from pressing charges when the rapist is a relative. Among the 1,815 people sentenced to death in 2001, 52 per cent had been convicted of rape. In 2001, Amnesty International reported that Filipino women in custody were particularly vulnerable to sexual harassment and physical violence by members of the police force.

CHILDREN
In 2002, 34 million Filipinos were under 18 years old and 9,790,000 were under 5 years old. Between 1990 and 2001, there was a 42 per cent reduction in the under-5 mortality rate. In 2003, 68 per cent of children were well-nourished and 64 per cent were immunized against all common childhood diseases. UNICEF's latest data available showed that 28 per cent of children under five were moderately or severely underweight and approximately 2 million children were exposed to hazardous working environments (mines, docksides or quarries). Sexual exploitation and trafficking in children for the sex industry are serious problems.

Some NGOs estimate that approximately 60,000 Filipino children are involved in the commercial sex industry. In addition, official figures report at least 22,000 street children. Of the more than 10,000 victims of child abuse attended in 2000, more than 70 per cent were girls, among whom 44 per cent were victims of sexual abuse; most of the remaining boys and girls had been abandoned, neglected or exploited as laborers.

INDIGENOUS PEOPLES/ ETHNIC MINORITIES
Throughout the archipelago there are small concentrations of Negrito peoples. Aetas are the most discriminated among the indigenous groups. The terms Igorots and Cordilleras are used to refer collectively to a number of indigenous groups including the Bontoc, Kalinga, Ibaloy, Ifugao, Apayao/Isneg and Tinggians. Group members speak multiple languages and their customs differ from the Filipino majority. The Moro inhabit the Philippines' southern region, mainly the islands of the Sulu archipelago. Since the 11 September 2001 terrorist attacks, the Moro have remained under close surveillance and US soldiers have been deployed in the Philippines to assist in quashing them. Confrontations between Christian and Moro groups have decreased and several groups have chosen to disarm. The Moro have the country's lowest life expectancy and are the most disadvantaged group in terms of political and economic participation. They still demand the right to self-determination.

MIGRANTS/REFUGEES
At least 45,000 Filipinos remain internally displaced. During 2003, nearly 90,000 people were displaced. Some of them had returned home by the end of the year. Most displaced people and refugees were Muslims who had fled fighting between the Philippines' Armed Forces and Muslim insurgent groups. Some 57,000 Filipino refugees were living in Malaysia, while 160 refugees and asylum-seekers had fled to the Philippines.

DEATH PENALTY
The death penalty is still applied, even for ordinary crimes.

six-per-cent growth in GNP. Remittances totaling $2 billion from 4.2 million workers living abroad - mainly domestics - came into the country in 1995.

²² In late 1995, there was an unprecedented food crisis, with a 70 per cent increase in rice prices. More than two-thirds of the population were estimated to be living below the poverty line. Farmers' organizations blamed the Government for their incoherent and corrupt agricultural policy, calling for agrarian reform, including the industrialization of rural activity, food self-sufficiency and protection of the environment.

²³ Despite protests from representatives of the Christian Filipinos, who make up the majority of the nation, the Government and the Muslim guerrillas signed a peace agreement on 30 September 1996. Nur Misuari, leader of the Moro Islamic Liberation Front (MILF), became governor of Mindanao, an autonomous region which covers around a quarter of national territory.

²⁴ In January 1998, thousands of children from various countries marched through the streets of Manila in protest against exploitative child labor. This sparked a worldwide campaign for better conditions for the world's 250 million child laborers.

²⁵ In May, Vice President Joseph Estrada was elected President with 37 per cent of the vote. In March 2000, Salamat Hashim, leader of the largest Islamic rebel group in the Philippines, called for a referendum on the self-determination of Muslims in the South. Muslims make up five per cent of the country's population and live mostly in Mindanao.

²⁶ Tens of thousands of Filipinos took to the streets of Manila to demand Estrada's resignation in October, while the opposition requested the President's impeachment, after a former crony denounced Estrada for receiving millions of dollars in kickbacks from an illegal gambling racket.

²⁷ Parliament started impeachment proceedings against the President. The process revealed that Estrada had hundreds of millions of dollars in bank accounts under false names. In the midst of massive mobilizations, which led to Estrada's fall, Vice President Gloria Macapagal-Arroyo assumed the Presidency on 20 January 2001.

²⁸ Corruption charges tainted the President when, in October 2001, her husband was accused of taking bribes. A former presidential palace employee accused lawyer José Miguel Arroyo

of having accepted a bribe of more than $900,000 from a telecommunications firm, in exchange for lifting the presidential veto on a franchise agreement. Both the President and the accused authorized a formal investigation into the case.

²⁹ A state of emergency was declared in April 2002 in the city of General Santos, south of Mindanao, after several bombs killed 14 people. The police detained two suspects and concluded that the attacks had been carried out by the MILF.

³⁰ In June the US Government pressed charges against five leaders of the Philippine Abu Sayyaf rebel group, linked to the al-Qaeda network and Osama bin Laden, for the kidnap and murder of two US citizens. A Filipino nurse had also been kidnapped by Abu Sayyaf at the same time and had been murdered during a rescue operation carried out by Filipino troops.

³¹ In October 2002, Abu Sayyaf - whose main objective was the creation of a Muslim state in the south of the Philippines - perpetrated a series of attacks against stores and a Christian temple which left 8 people dead and 170 injured. At least five people were arrested and taken to Manila.

³² On 23 January 2003, Rómulo Kintanar was murdered at a restaurant in Manila. Kintanar had been a Communist Party leader in the 1980s but no longer belonged to the institution. The Party claimed responsibility for the killing, attributing it to its armed wing, the New People's Army.

³³ In a report published in January of that year, Amnesty International condemned the use of torture on political prisoners in Filipino prisons. Those most at risk of being tortured included alleged members of armed groups, their suspected sympathizers as well as ordinary criminals and members of poor or marginalized communities.

³⁴ In March 2004, according to President Gloria Macapagal-Arroyo, four Abu Sayyaf members were arrested, while 36 kilos of high explosive trinitrotoluene (TNT) were confiscated, averting a terrorist bombing on the scale of the Madrid attacks perpetrated on 11 March. As Arroyo stated, one of the arrested men had claimed responsibility for the 27 February explosion aboard the SuperFerry 14 that killed over 100 people. The suspects, who had probably received military training from the terrorist network Jemaah Islamiah, linked to al-Qaeda, planned to launch attacks on trains and shops in Manila, which is home to 10 million people. ■

PROFILE

ENVIRONMENT

Of the 7,107 islands that make up the archipelago, spread over 1,600 kilometres from north to south, 11 account for 94 per cent of the total area and are home to most of the population. The archipelago is located approximately 100 kilometres southeast of the Asian continent; it is bordered on the east by the Philippine Sea, on the west by the South China Sea, and on the south by the Celebes Sea. Luzón and Mindanao are the most important regions. The archipelago is of volcanic origin, forming part of the 'Ring of Fire of the Pacific'. The terrain is mountainous with large coastal plains where sugarcane, hemp, copra and tobacco are grown. The local climate is humid and tropical. The mean annual temperature is around 26.5° C. Filipinos recognize three seasons: *Tag-init* or *Tag-araw* (summer; March to May), *Tag-ulan* (rainy season; June to November), and *Tag-lamig* (cold season; December to February). Abundant rains favor the growth of dense forests. It is the main producer of iron ore in Southeast Asia, and also has oil, chromium, copper, nickel, cobalt, silver and gold.

SOCIETY

Peoples: The vast majority of the population originates from the first migration waves from Malaysia and Indonesia. Some 200,000 Chinese traders settled there from the 11th century onwards. Islamic communities from Borneo entered the territory in the 15th century and resisted the evangelization of the Spanish conquistadors (who arrived in 1521), who had a significant cultural influence over the rest of the population. Some communities of Malay origin, in different stages of evolution, also resisted Christianization. After 1898, US colonization had a strong influence on Filipino society and culture.
Religions: Catholics 83 per cent; Muslims 5 per cent; Protestants 5 per cent; Independent Filipino Church 3 per cent; Animists, Buddhists and other 4 per cent.
Languages: Some 55 per cent of the population speaks Pilipino (official), based on the Tagalog language, of Malay origin. English, spoken by 45 per cent, is also official, and is compulsory in the education system. But 90 per cent of the population speaks one of the following languages: Cebuano (6 million); Hiligaynon (3 million); Bicolano (2 million); Waray-Waray (1 million). Spanish and Chinese are minority languages.
Main Political Parties: Laban ñg Demokratikong Pilipino (Struggle of Filipino Democrats, LDP); Lakas ñg Edsa (National Union of Christian Democrats), known as Lakas; the Liberal Party; Nationalist People's Coalition (NPC); the BISIG, socialist movement of Tagalog speakers that founded the socialist organization; the People's Reform Party (PRP); the Nationalist Party; the National Democratic Front (NDF), led by the Philippine Communist Party and its military wing, the New People's Army (NPA); an NPA splinter group, the Cordillera People's Liberation Army (CPLA), organized the Cordillera Bodong Association (CBA) which demands full autonomy for the north; in the southern Muslim areas, the Moro Islamic Liberation Front (MILF) pursues its goal of autonomy through guerrilla warfare.
Main Social Organizations: Labor is divided between the left-wing Kihusan Mayo Uno (May Day Confederation) and the Trade Union Congress of the Philippines (TUCP), affiliated to AFL-CIO. The Philippines has over 700 voluntary organizations and church groups, which constitute the Green Forum.

THE STATE

Official Name: Republika ñg Pilipinas.
Administrative Division: 12 regions, 73 provinces.
Capital: Metro Manila 10,352,000 people (2003).
Other Cities: Cebu 1,172,800 people; Davao 1,145,600; Bacolod 739,600; Cagayan 407,800; Zamboanga 147,200 (2000).
Government: Presidential republic. Gloria Macapagal-Arroyo, President since January 2001. Teofisto Guingona, Vice President since January 2001. The Congress (Parliament) has two chambers: House of Representatives, 260 members; Senate, 24 members.
National Holiday: 4 July, Independence Day (from the US, 1946); 12 July, Independence Day (from Spain, 1898).
Armed Forces: 107,500 troops (1996). Others: National Police (Home Ministry): 40,500. Coast Guard: 2,000.

Pitcairn / Pitcairn

Population:	47
Area:	5 km²
Capital:	Adamstown
Currency:	NZ dollar
Language:	English

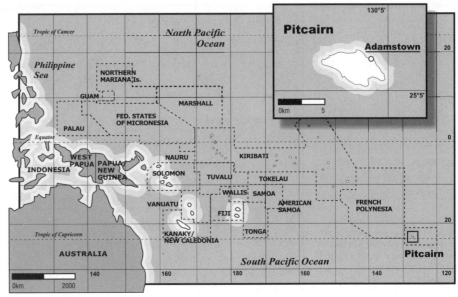

A s on most of the islands in the region, Pitcairn's first settlers were Polynesians (see 'Melanesian and Polynesian' box). The first European to visit the island was the English voyager Robert Pitcairn who sailed along its coasts in 1767.

[2] In 1789, part of the crew of HMS Bounty mutinied on their return to Britain from six months in Tahiti. The captain and the rest of the crew were given a small boat and the other men returned to Tahiti. They stayed there a short time and then transferred to Pitcairn Island.

[3] The group, led by Fletcher Christian, was made up of eight crew members, six Tahitian men and 12 women. Ten years later, only one of the mutineers, John Adams, was still alive, with 11 women and 23 children. Adams christened the children and peopled Pitcairn, which later became a British colonial dependency.

[4] The population reached 200 in 1937, but decreased in recent times as young islanders emigrated to New Zealand/Aotearoa in search of work.

[5] Pitcairn was under the jurisdiction of the Governor of Fiji between 1952 and 1970, when it became a dependency of the British High Commissioner in New Zealand/Aotearoa.

[6] Despite the lack of communications, education in the islands was important and primary school was compulsory for all children between the ages of 5 and 15. A single teacher from New Zealand/Aotearoa is appointed for a two-year period and is also responsible for publishing the Pitcairn Miscellany, a four-page bulletin.

[7] There is no racial discrimination on the island and equal rights are ensured by the law. The island's Administrative Council is made up of 10 representatives of mixed descent, half of whom are chosen from inhabitants over the age of 18 who have lived on the island for at least 3 years.

[8] The islanders work almost exclusively at subsistence fishing and farming. The fertile valleys produce a wide variety of fruit and vegetables, including citrus, sugar cane, watermelons, bananas, potatoes, and beans. However, the island's main source of income is the export of postage stamps for sale to stamp collectors.

[9] In 1987, the British High Commissioner in Fiji, acting on behalf of Pitcairn, joined representatives from the US, France, New Zealand/Aotearoa and six Pacific island states in signing the South Pacific Regional Environment Protection Convention, designed to prevent the disposal of nuclear waste in the region.

[10] In early 1992, deposits of manganese, iron, copper, zinc, silver and gold were identified in underwater volcanoes within the island's territorial waters. Exploitation of this mineral wealth could dramatically change the island's economy.

[11] The population of Pitcairn has been shrinking in recent years. In January 1998, there were just 30 people, only eight of whom were working. Ten had emigrated the year before.

[12] The survival of the island is dependent on the boats which ship in the necessary goods, as there is no airstrip. The lack of crews for the boats could accelerate depopulation. The UK aimed to avoid this happening by building an emergency air strip.

[13] The 44 inhabitants of Pitcairn discovered that the UK no longer had any interest in them in January 2000, when the Crown issued an edict to remove the last subsidies on electricity and the tariffs for unloading provisions, which had

allowed the islanders to survive. The population then began to consider the possibility of becoming a French overseas colony.

[14] Richard Fell became the Governor in 2001.

[15] In October 2004 six Pitcairn citizens, including the mayor, Steve Christian, were found guilty of 32 offences of sexual assault following a month-long trial conducted under British and Pitcairn flags. The offences had been uncovered by a policewoman from Kent, England, who was on Pitcairn to train members of the local police force. She had found evidence that sexual

abuse of girls between 12 and 15 years old was standard practice on the island. In August 2004 some island residents broke silence to explain to the press that the practice was a tradition and that in Pitcairn children are sexually active from an early age. The Kent police officer who led the investigation stated: 'These judgments today have sent a clear message that the abuse of children is not acceptable in any culture anywhere, and Pitcairn Island is no exception.' All six of the convicted men claim to be descendants of the original mutineers on the Bounty. ∎

PROFILE

ENVIRONMENT

Four islands of volcanic origin, of which only Pitcairn is inhabited. The others are: Henderson, Ducie and Oeno. The group is located in the eastern extreme of Polynesia, slightly south of the Tropic of Capricorn, east of French Polynesia. The economy is based on subsistence agriculture, fishing, handicrafts, and there are very few export products. The rainy, tropical climate is tempered by sea winds. The islands are subject to typhoons between November and March.

SOCIETY

Peoples: The population consists of descendants of mutineers from HMS Bounty and Polynesian women from Tahiti.
Religion: Seventh Day Adventist (100 per cent).
Languages: English (official). A Tahitian-English dialect is spoken.
Main Political Parties: None.

THE STATE

Official Name: Pitcairn, Henderson, Ducie and Oeno Islands.
Capital: Adamstown.
Government: Queen Elizabeth II (Chief of State) represented by UK High Commissioner to New Zealand/Aotearoa and Governor Richard Fell (since 2001). Jay Warren, magistrate and president of the Council since 1990, re-elected in 1999. The Council is made up of ten members. Randy Christian, president of the Council since 2004.
National Holiday: Second Saturday in June, Queen Elizabeth II's birthday (1926).
Armed Forces: The UK is responsible for defense.

Poland / Polska

Population:	38,515,955
Area:	323,250 km²
Capital:	Warsaw (Warzawa)
Currency:	Zloty
Language:	Polish

The name Poland comes from the Polanian people ('people of the plains') who lived in the heartland of what became Poland, ruled by the Piast dynasty.

2   In the 10th century, the Polanians subdued the Kujavians, the Mazovians, the Ledzians, the Pomeranians, the Vistulans, and the Silesians. Mieszko I (960-992) Duke of the Piast, united neighboring peoples and thus founded the first Polish State.

3   Poland was a hereditary monarchy until the 12th century, with an army of élite warriors and a large peasantry, who were mobilized as they were needed and paid taxes to support the system.

4   Mieszko submitted in the face of the expanding German Empire, in exchange for recognition of his sovereignty. As compensation, he appealed for Papal protection and in 1,000 AD he founded the first Polish ecclesiastical city state.

5   The Roman Catholic Church was a crucial element in the political structure of the Polish State until the 12th century, when the State began to fragment.

6   During the feudal period, Poland was subdivided into several duchies, ruled by the Piasts, and some 20 overlords, who became increasingly autonomous as the power of the Church grew. This was also a period of great demographic growth.

7   The arrival of German settlers changed the country's ethnic composition, for up to then the population had been of Slavic stock. From the 13th century, the population of the towns became increasingly German and Jewish, who brought in their own legal systems, their capital, their crafts and their agricultural skills.

8   Under the reign of Casimir the Great (1333-70), Poland became a monarchy divided into estates, with the King acting as an arbiter between the nobility, the clergy, the bourgeoisie, and the peasants.

In 1399 the monarchy became elective.

9   Through a royal marriage in 1386, Poland joined with Lithuania, although the differences between the two countries were upheld. In 1410, the Teutonic Order forces were defeated at Grunwald. This secured Poland's power, and at the same time left the Teutons weakened after the Peace of Torun in 1411.

10   In 1466, after a new victory over the Teutons, Poland recovered Pomerania of Gdansk and Malbork, Elblag, and the Land of Chelm; it also gained the territory of Warmia. In recognition of their assistance during the war, Poland granted autonomy to Pomerania and some privileges to the towns. A period of economic prosperity and cultural renaissance began.

11   During the 15th century the General Diet (parliament) of Poland and Lithuania was created. It had two houses: a lower house, comprising members of the nobility, and an upper house, or royal council, presided over by the King. The two states shared the King, the diet, and the management of foreign affairs, while administration, justice, finance and the army remained separate.

12   The 16th or 'Golden' century is also known as the period of the Royal Republic, for the King had to consult the nobles before fixing taxes or declaring war. The rights of the bourgeoisie and the peasantry were curtailed in favor of the nobility and the clergy.

13   In 1573, with the end of the Jagiellon dynasty, the Diet approved the free election of the King and guaranteed religious tolerance, at a time when Europe was being shaken by religious wars. King Stephen Bathory (1576-86) gave up his role as arbitrator and the nobility started to elect their own courts.

14   During the 17th century, while Sweden fought Poland for control of the Baltic, and Russia entered into conflict with Lithuania, Turkish and Austrian ambitions in central Europe also put pressure on Poland.

15   On the lower Dnepr, on the border with the Ukraine, free peasants and impoverished nobles became the first Cossacks, warriors who lived by pillaging. In 1648,

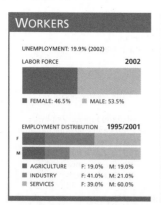

WORKERS

UNEMPLOYMENT: 19.9% (2002)

LABOR FORCE   2002

■ FEMALE: 46.5%   ■ MALE: 53.5%

EMPLOYMENT DISTRIBUTION   1995/2001

F
M

■ AGRICULTURE   F: 19.0%   M: 19.0%
■ INDUSTRY   F: 41.0%   M: 21.0%
■ SERVICES   F: 39.0%   M: 60.0%

LAND USE

2000

IRRIGATED AREA: 0.7% of arable land

■ ARABLE LAND: 46.0%
■ CROPLANDS: 1.1%
■ OTHER USE: 52.9%

Life expectancy
73.9 years
2000-2005

GNI per capita
$4,570
2002

Literacy
100% total adult rate
2000

HIV prevalence rate
0.1% of population 15-49 years old
2001

they started a national revolt. The King made unsuccessful attempts to reach an agreement with the rebels, whose victories weakened the republic.

[16] The Cossacks formed occasional alliances with the Turks and the Russians. In 1654, Russian troops entered Polish territory. Sweden invaded the rest of the country a year later. King John Casimir fled to Silesia, and Austria aided Poland, while the peasants organized an armed resistance.

[17] The Swedes and the Turks were expelled from the country and the Cossacks were defeated. Russia kept Smolensk and the Ukraine, the left bank of the Dnepr and the city of Kiev. The wars devastated the land, decimated the population and split the republic.

[18] In 1772, Russia, Prussia, and Austria partitioned Poland. There was a second partition in 1793, after a new Russian invasion annulled the 1791 Constitution and put an end to attempts to reorganize the State.

[19] A patriotic insurrection was crushed in 1794, and was followed by the third partition. The Polish State disappeared from the map, although the people retained a sense of national identity.

[20] In the 19th century there were several attempts to free Poland. National conscience and Catholicism, both under persecution, became stronger. New political parties emerged (peasants', workers' and national) and resistance was expressed through art and culture.

[21] The Russian Revolution in 1917 brought Poland the support of the Western powers. In 1918 a provisional government, led by Jozef Pilsudski, established an eight-hour working day and equal rights for men and women.

[22] A sense of national identity had emerged in the Ukraine, Lithuania and Belarus. The creation of a federation failed as a result of the Soviet counter-offensive. The Peace of Riga, signed in 1921, granted the independence of the Baltic states and fixed Poland's eastern border at Zbrucz.

[23] The 1921 Constitution adopted a parliamentary system.

[24] Social and economic instability benefited the Communist Party, banned in 1923. Its main military leader, Jozef Pilsudski, staged a coup in 1926. The ensuing prosperity ended with the impact of the 1929 Wall Street crash.

[25] The German-USSR non-aggression pact, signed in August 1939, threatened Poland. Britain and France had a treaty with Poland which promised retaliation if any of them was attacked.

ENVIRONMENTAL CHALLENGES
The country has high levels of air pollution partly because of its location in the center of Europe. It absorbs polluted water and air 'in transit' from other countries. Sulfur dioxide emissions from coal-fired power plants, and the resulting acid rain has damaged forests. The attempt to reduce pollution levels to EU-acceptable levels implies substantial costs for business and the Government.

WOMEN'S RIGHTS
Polish women have been able to vote since 1918. Since 1990 they have held 13 per cent of seats in parliament. Women's representation in ministerial and similar positions grew from seven per cent in 1995 to 17 per cent in the year 2000.

Women's participation in the workforce has been stable since 1980 (46 per cent). In 2000, the female enrolment rate was high in both primary and secondary education (98 and 92 per cent respectively).

Ninety-nine per cent of girls finished 5th grade. The same year, 99 per cent of births were attended by qualified medical personnel.

CHILDREN
UNICEF's latest data available* showed that six per cent of newborn babies are underweight. The mortality rate for infants (under-ones) fell from 62 to 8 per 1,000 live births between 1960 and 2002. Among children under five the mortality rate was reduced from 70 to 9 per thousand over the same period.

INDIGENOUS PEOPLES/ ETHNIC MINORITIES
Poles descend from a mixture of different ethnic groups (Slavonic, Polanie or 'people of the plain', Lithuanian, Finnish, Gothic and Celtic peoples). Some 96 per cent of the population are Poles and the rest are Belarusian, Ukrainian, Ruten and Jewish. There are small Greek (114,000), Russian (60,000), Slovak (38,000) and Lithuanian (11,500) communities. The upheavals in Poland's political

history created several linguistic communities. Polish Roma/gypsies have several languages: Baltic Romany (30,000), Carpathian Romany, Sinte Romany and Vlach Romany (5,000).

MIGRANTS/REFUGEES
In late 2002, Poland sheltered some 300 refugees. In 2003, 5,200 persons filed asylum applications: from the Russian Federation (mostly Chechens) (3,000), Afghanistan (600), Armenia (220), and India (200). 4,700 applications were rejected, of which 710 had no legal basis, according to the Government. Throughout the 20th century, there were high rates of Polish migration (mostly Jewish) to every part of the world.

DEATH PENALTY
The death penalty was abolished for all crimes in 1997. The last execution was in 1988.

*Latest data available in *The State of the World's Children* and *Childinfo* database UNICEF, 2004.

When Germany invaded Poland on 1 September 1939 Britain and France declared war.

[26] In the occupied territories millions of Poles died, especially Jews, some of whom were taken to German concentration camps. Many others starved or were executed.

[27] The Polish government-in-exile led the resistance. A military contingent fought on the western front, while the Home Army carried out subversive actions. After the German invasion, the USSR accepted the creation of a Polish army under its jurisdiction.

[28] The Soviet counter-offensive modified bilateral relations. The government-in-exile demanded an inquiry into the murders of Polish officers, and the USSR broke diplomatic relations and shifted to military occupation.

[29] After Germany's defeat, the allies gathered at Yalta and agreed on a Provisional Polish Government of National Unity (made up by representatives from pro-Soviet and exiled groups) which was to call elections. The Polish Workers' Party dominated the Government.

[30] In 1945 the provisional Government and the USSR signed an agreement establishing the Polish eastern border, along the Curso line. The allies fixed the western border along the Oder-

Neisse line of Lusetia.

[31] The Polish Workers' Party and the Socialist Party of Poland combined to form the Polish United Workers' Party (PUWP). The Polish Peasants' Party disintegrated, and elections were postponed.

[32] The PUWP governed the country, modeling itself on the Soviet Communist Party (CPSU) in the USSR. Industry and commerce were nationalized, the State built great steel and metal works, and forcibly collectivized agriculture. Women were incorporated into the workforce.

[33] The CPSU crisis, after the denunciation of Stalin's crimes in the 20th Congress of 1956, had repercussions on the PUWP. In November of that year Wladyslaw Gomulka was elected party first secretary and promised to take a 'Polish path towards socialism'. Gomulka freed Cardinal Stefan Wyszynski - head of the Catholic Church - stirring up popular expectations.

[34] In 1970, West Germany recognized the Polish borders established after the War. East Germany had done so in 1950.

[35] In 1970, strikes broke out due to an increase in prices. The Government gave orders to open fire on the workers and started another crisis within the PUWP. Gomulka was replaced by Edward Gierek, but the regime underwent

new crises over corruption and internal fights within the party.

[36] In 1976, new strikes broke out, which were repressed not through the use of firearms but by imposing long prison sentences. In 1979, the Polish Pope John Paul II visited his native land, and was welcomed by massive gatherings.

[37] The strike at Gdansk's Lenin Dockyard in August 1980 was led by Lech Walesa and turned into a general strike. The Government was forced to negotiate and two months later recognized Solidarity, a workers' union with 10 million members. Rural Solidarity was created, to represent three million peasants.

[38] The PUWP appointed Wojciech Jaruzelski, then Prime Minister, to the post of party first secretary. In December 1981, martial law was declared, Solidarity was banned and its leaders went underground.

[39] Martial law was lifted in 1983, but the Constitution was modified to include a state of emergency. With the Catholic Church acting as mediator, government and Solidarity representatives went back to negotiations in 1989, while the USSR was embarking on *perestroika* (restructuring).

[40] In the elections in June that year, the PUWP only obtained the number of representatives that had been agreed on with the opposition. Mazowiecki, a

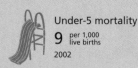

Under-5 mortality
9 per 1,000 live births
2002

Poverty
<2% of population living on less than $1 per day
1998

Debt service
28.0% exports of goods and services
2001

Maternal mortality
13 per 100,000 live births
2000

moderate member of Solidarity, was appointed the first president of a non-communist government in the East European bloc.

⁴¹ Poland re-established diplomatic relations with the Vatican and with Israel. The US and East Germany promised financial assistance. German reunification caused some alarm, but the negotiations ratified the postwar Polish borders.

⁴² In December 1989, the National Assembly approved reinstating the name the Republic of Poland. In January 1990, the PUWP was dissolved and the Social Democracy of the Republic of Poland and the Polish Social Democratic Union were created.

⁴³ In January 1990, Poland started an economic adjustment program agreed with the IMF, requested entry to the Council of Europe and established relations with the EU. Poland's entry to NATO was made dependent on the results of its economic reforms and the upgrading of its military capability.

⁴⁴ In May 1990, the first strike against the Government was held in Gdansk. Walesa accused Mazowiecki of having forgotten his days as a worker. Solidarity split into several political parties.

⁴⁵ In the first direct presidential elections, held in December 1990, Lech Walesa won with 75 per cent of the vote. In August 1991, new Prime Minister Jan Krysztof Bielecki resigned, upsetting the precarious balance of political transition. The former Communist Party and a small peasant party were ready to accept his resignation, but Walesa backed the Prime Minister and insisted on giving him special powers, by threatening to dissolve the Diet.

⁴⁶ In December 1991, Jan Olszewski was appointed Prime Minister. The cabinet was not ratified by the Diet until 23 December, and then only by a narrow margin of 17 votes.

⁴⁷ As of November 1991, Poland became the twenty-sixth member of the European Council, a Western European organization which also includes Turkey, the Czech Republic, and Hungary.

⁴⁸ In mid-June, at Walesa's request, Parliament deposed Olszewski and appointed as Prime Minister Hanna Suchocka, from the Democratic Union (DU), supported by a seven-party coalition.

⁴⁹ Suchocka applied strict monetary controls and promoted the August 1992 privatization act. Walesa, under pressure from the Church, revoked the right to abortion in February 1993.

⁵⁰ The September elections saw the return to power of those who had supported the communist

regime: the Democratic Left Alliance (SLD), the Union of Labor (UP) and the Polish Peasants' Party (PSL) together won 73 of the 100 seats in the Senate. Walesa appointed PSL leader Waldemar Pawlak Prime Minister.

⁵¹ In 1994, beset by conflicts with Parliament, Walesa slowed the pace of the reforms and economic liberalization policies to reduce their social impact.

⁵² The former communists' return to power was concluded in November 1995 when Aleksander Kwasniewski won the second round of presidential elections, with 52 per cent of the vote.

⁵³ Prime Minister Josef Olesky, who replaced Pawlak, was forced to resign in January 1996, after the Interior Minister accused him of having been a collaborator with the Soviet KGB. The following month, Wlodzimierz Cimoszewicz replaced him.

⁵⁴ Right-wing factions of several parties formed a coalition headed by Marian Krzaklewski, called Solidarity Electoral Action (AWS).

⁵⁵ In the 1997 parliamentary

elections, the AWS defeated the ruling Democratic Left Alliance (SLD), with 33.8 per cent of the vote. Jerzy Buzek, a chemical engineer from Silesia, who designed the AWS's economic program, was named Prime Minister.

⁵⁶ Poland's aspiration to join the EU gave rise to a debate on agricultural production in 1998. In February 1999 Parliament approved entry to NATO by an overwhelming 409 to 7 votes.

⁵⁷ Government reforms in preparation for EU entry left thousands of people out of work. In September 1999 more than 30,000 farmers and workers held a protest march in Warsaw, demanding that Prime Minister Buzek bring elections forward.

⁵⁸ Despite Buzek's declaration that Poland had met all the requirements for EU membership in April 2000, the ratification process implied delays in getting full membership before 2003.

⁵⁹ In October, Kwasniewski, now leader of the SLD, comprising former communists, became the first president to be re-elected

since the transition to democracy, with almost 54 per cent of the vote. Adrei Olechowski, his main opponent, won only 17.3 per cent. Walesa failed to get 1 per cent of the vote and retired from politics.

⁶⁰ The lowest vote in Poland's brief democratic history occurred a year later in the parliamentary elections with barely 41 per cent turnout. Corruption scandals under Solidarity and the poor state of the economy, especially in rural areas, led to increased support for radical anti-Europeans, and Andrzej Lepper's Self Defense Movement of the Polish Republic (SDM) took an unexpected 10.2 per cent of the vote. The ultra-Catholic League of Polish Families also did well with 7.87 per cent. However, the SLD took the bulk of the vote with 41 per cent.

⁶¹ A coalition government formed by the SLD and the Polish Peasants' Party (PSL) - which took 9 per cent of the vote - made Leszek Miller prime minister in October 2001. In December, the EU Summit included Poland on the list of 10 countries hoping to become full members in May 2004.

⁶² Skepticism about EU membership increased after Germany and Austria voiced their fear of a flow of cheap foreign labor from the East. It was made clear that citizens of new member states would have to wait seven years before being allowed to work in other EU countries. In rural areas, there were likewise fears of a flood of people from other EU states, particularly Germany, as Polish land was 30 times cheaper than in many EU countries. In April 2002, Poland agreed with Brussels that foreigners would be barred from buying land in Poland for 12 years after it joined the EU.

⁶³ In March 2003 Miller expelled the PSL from the Government coalition, for not supporting his proposed tax reform.

⁶⁴ In a referendum held in June 2003 Polish citizens voted to join the EU.

⁶⁵ A helicopter with Prime Minister Miller on board crashed in December 2003. Miller was injured but survived.

⁶⁶ In early 2004, as reward for providing troops for the US-led coalition in Iraq, Poland was given command over one of Iraq's four reconstruction zones.

⁶⁷ President Kwasniewski declared in March 2004 that Poland had been deceived by the US and UK regarding the existence of weapons of mass destruction in Iraq. However Polish troops continued to participate in the reconstruction of Iraq.

⁶⁸ On 1 May 2004 Poland joined the EU. ∎

PROFILE

ENVIRONMENT
On the extensive northern plains, crossed by the Vistula (Wisla), Warta and Oder (Odra) rivers, there are coniferous woodlands, rye, potato and flax plantations. The fertile soil of central Poland's plains and highlands yield a considerable agricultural production of beet and cereals. The southern region, on the northern slopes of the Carpathian Mountains, is less fertile. Poland has large mineral resources: coal in Silesia; sulfur in Tarnobrzeskie; copper; zinc and lead. Major industries are steel, chemicals and shipbuilding.

SOCIETY
Peoples: Polish, 96 per cent; Ukrainian, 0.8 per cent; Belarusian, 0.8 per cent; German, 0.5 per cent; Swedish, 0.5 per cent.
Religions: Catholic, 90.7 per cent; Orthodox, 1.4 per cent. Protestant and other (7.9 per cent).
Languages: Polish.
Main Political Parties: Democratic Left Alliance (SLD); Union of Labor (UP), Citizens Platform (PO); Self Defense Movement of the Polish Republic (SDM, Samoobrona); Law and Justice (PiS); Polish Peasants' Party (PSL).
Main Social Organizations: Union affiliation has declined greatly. Two main groups with political affiliation: Poland Trade Union Alliance and Solidarity. Independent unions like the Central Union of Agricultural Groups.

THE STATE
Official Name: Polska Rzeczpospolita.
Administrative Divisions: 49 provinces.
Capital: Warsaw (Warzawa) 2,200,000 people (2003).
Other Cities: Lódz 1,017,300 people; Kraków 784,800; Wroclaw 634,600; Poznan 580,200 (2000).
Government: Aleksander Kwasniewski, President and Head of State since December 1995, re-elected in 2000. Marek Belka, Chairman of the Council of Ministers (Premier) and Head of Government since May 2004. Bicameral Legislature: the *Diet*, with 460 members, and the Senate, with 100 members.
National Holiday: 11 November, Independence Day (1918); 3 May, Constitution Day (1791).
Armed Forces: 241,750 (1997). Other: 23,400 Border Guard, Police, Coast Guard.

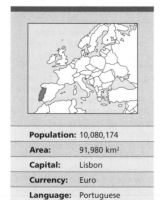

Population:	10,080,174
Area:	91,980 km²
Capital:	Lisbon
Currency:	Euro
Language:	Portuguese

I n ancient times Portugal was inhabited by Lusitanians, an Iberian people whose cultural influence extended over a vast area including the whole western shore of the Iberian Peninsula. The coastal areas were occupied by successive invaders from the Middle East.

2 During the 2nd century BC the Romans settled in the territory, ruling over it until the fall of the Empire around the 5th century AD. Like the rest of Europe, Portugal was invaded by Northern European peoples (generically called Barbarians), who raided the Roman dominions. Among these peoples were the Visigoths. They had a developed culture and settled on the Iberian Peninsula dividing the territory into various kingdoms, and spreading the Christian faith. Their domination over the whole region lasted for nearly six centuries.

3 In the 8th century AD Arab peoples invaded the region, meeting resistance from the inhabitants. In spite of the Arab political and cultural dominance this was a period of religious tolerance and a flowering of art.

4 During the 11th century the reconquest of the Lusitanian territory started, ending with the expulsion of the Arabs a hundred years later. With Muslim domination over, the territory was politically unified and Portugal entered a period of great economic prosperity. This reached its height during the 15th and 16th centuries, with great maritime expeditions and conquests of vast territories in America, Africa, and the Far East.

5 Its maritime superiority enabled Portugal to develop active worldwide trade and achieve a privileged economic position within Europe. A long time elapsed before other nations like Britain and the Netherlands were in a position to threaten Portugal's naval supremacy.

6 Following a series of dynastic struggles, in 1581 the country was made subject to Philip II, King of Spain. The two kingdoms remained united until 1688 when Portugal succeeded in having its independence recognized in the Treaty of Lisbon. Unity with Spain brought the decline of Portugal's power. Most of the maritime empire collapsed, besieged by the British and the Dutch, who started to control most of the trading routes and outposts.

7 By the time Portugal recovered its independence in 1640, it had been devastated by 30 years of war against Spain. The country was forced to look on while the new maritime powers seized most of its colonies in Africa and Asia. Brazil remained under Portuguese rule. The position of Britain as the leading maritime power became painfully obvious when Portugal was forced to sign the Treaty of Methuen, which established Portugal's political and economic dependence on the British. Pombal, an adviser of Jose I, carried out economic reforms. Like the Spanish Bourbons, Pombal had been influenced by the ideas of the French Enlightenment and he changed colonial management. The discovery and exploitation of gold mines in Brazil enabled the country to enjoy a period of great economic prosperity. But in spite of Pombal, Portugal finally went into decline.

8 Dependence on Britain was further consolidated when Portugal was forced to seek support to end Napoleonic occupation, which lasted from 1807 to 1811. French domination led to the independence of Brazil; the Portuguese court had fled there in exile. Brazil had enjoyed a significant expansion in trade, in particular with Britain. At the end of the Napoleonic period in Europe, the rising Brazilian bourgeoisie was not ready to be displaced, so in 1821 Brazil declared independence. Meanwhile a civil war broke out in Portugal between those who wanted the restoration of absolutism and liberal groups preferring greater political participation.

9 While other countries embarked on rapid industrialization which would quickly put them in an economically powerful position, Portugal maintained its traditional agrarian structure. Thus, it reached the end of the 19th century economically stagnant, deprived of the richest and largest part of its colonial empire, and suffering from an acute internal political crisis.

10 The monarchy was unable to ensure the stability needed to start economic recovery, and was definitively overthrown by liberal opposition forces in 1910. This started the Republican period. Once they had attained their objective, the alliance of Liberal and Republican groups started to fragment and internal differences prevented them from achieving a common governmental agenda. One of the few things they shared was active opposition to the Church, which had been a traditional ally of the *ancien régime* and had had important privileges and powers, including the control of education. The inefficiency of the Liberals, together with the ruthless persecution of representatives of the ancien régime, encouraged the formation of a vast opposition movement.

11 Portugal sided with Britain in World War I. This only deepened the economic crisis and increased popular discontent. Political instability and economic stagnation were the most salient features of the period. In 1926 this led to a coup bringing a right-wing military group to power. They set up an authoritarian corporatist regime which they called the 'New State'. With a few changes, it was to rule the country for over 40 years. Political opposition was proscribed, with major figures imprisoned or exiled. Trade unions were dissolved and replaced by corporatist organizations similar to those in fascist Italy.

12 The most significant figure of this period and the true ruler behind the military was economist Antonio de Oliveira Salazar, who occupied various positions and dominated Portuguese political and economic life. The country remained neutral during the Spanish Civil War and World War II, which could both have jeopardized its barely stable economy.

WORKERS

UNEMPLOYMENT: 5.1% (2002)

LABOR FORCE   **2002**

■ FEMALE: 44.1%   ■ MALE: 55.9%

EMPLOYMENT DISTRIBUTION   **1995/2001**

F
M

	F	M
■ AGRICULTURE	11.0%	14.0%
■ INDUSTRY	44.0%	24.0%
■ SERVICES	45.0%	62.0%

LAND USE

2000

IRRIGATED AREA: 24.0% of arable land

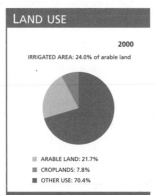

■ ARABLE LAND: 21.7%
■ CROPLANDS: 7.8%
■ OTHER USE: 70.4%

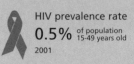
The agricultural system remained unchanged throughout the whole period, causing much migration towards the major cities of Portugal and Europe. The 1950s saw the start of decolonization and the country was faced with the possibility of losing its last dominions in Africa. Salazar's regime sought to repress the rebellions in the colonies, which led to Portugal being isolated internationally.

The human and economic cost of these colonial wars accelerated the internal attrition of Salazar's government. Repressive measures had to be increased to halt the growing opposition. His death in 1970 and the deepening of the economic crisis showed that the end of the regime was close at hand.

In 1974, amidst the opposition of many social groups and political parties, a significant number of dissatisfied army officers gathered under the Armed Forces Movement (*Movimento das Forças Armadas* - MFA). In April, they staged a coup intending to end the wars in Africa and start the democratization process.

The military government that emerged from this 'Carnation Revolution' had vast popular support. The new Government quickly recognized the independence of Angola, Mozambique, and Guinea-Bissau. Meanwhile it actively sought international recognition and attempted to improve the country's image abroad. It legalized left-wing political parties, decreed an amnesty for political prisoners and passed a series of land laws aimed at breaking up large rural estates and modernizing agricultural production.

After a year in office, dissent between the Socialist and Communist parties, which were the main supporters of the new regime, interrupted the process of democratization. In the 1976 general elections, the Socialist Party led by Mario Soares won the majority of votes, becoming Portugal's first democratic constitutional government in the 20th century. However, the continuing economic crisis, Soares' harsh economic adjustment program and strong political and trade union opposition, wore the Socialist Government down very quickly.

The 1980s witnessed the continuation of the process of transition and political integration with Europe. The electorate approved a new constitution and eliminated all the special bodies created under military rule. Portugal joined NATO and the EEC in 1986. That year, the Socialist Party lost power again, this time to its one-time ally, the center-left Social Democratic Party (PSD).

By the end of the 1980s Portugal was experiencing significant economic growth, but still far below the average for the rest of Europe. Changes accelerated after the electoral victory of the PSD, which used its ample parliamentary majority to liberalize the economy. The new economic policy met with strong opposition, particularly from workers in the public sector, who saw the PSD's reforms as a threat to their jobs.

The trade union movement brought the country to a standstill on several occasions. It opposed the privatization of public companies, and the attempt to repeal labor and land reform legislation enacted in 1974. In 1984, demanding respect for the achievements of the 'Carnation Revolution' an extreme left-wing group, called the Popular Forces of April 25 (FP-25), also started to take action against these measures.

In April 1987, the governments of Portugal and the People's Republic of China signed an agreement charging Portugal with the administration of Macau until 1999. Sovereignty was then transferred to China, under the 'one country, two systems' principle (see Macau).

In 1988, the PSD and the Socialist Party agreed to modify the constitution to allow the re-privatization of various companies nationalized during the 'Carnation Revolution' and to further reduce presidential powers. President Mario Soares opposed these reforms, which led to his distancing from the PS leadership and to a permanent clash with Prime Minister Anibal Cavaco Silva.

Portuguese politics became polarized between the ruling PSD and the PS. The latter was a more viable left-wing alternative after the collapse of real socialism. However, in the October 1991 parliamentary elections, the PSD won over 50 per cent of the vote. Cavaco Silvas' political victory was due to the social democratic slant with which he disguised his orthodox liberal economic orientation.

In January 1992, Portugal took over the presidency of the European Community. The new President, Luis Mira de Amaral, Portuguese minister of industry and energy, announced he would promote industrial co-operation with Latin America, Africa and central Europe and the signing of the Maastricht Treaty between the members of the Community.

In August 1993, the Assembly restricted the right to seek asylum and enabled the expulsion of foreigners from the country. The legislation was based on the defense of the job market and was opposed by President Soares.

A plan financed by the EU was approved for the 1993-1997 period for the poorest members, including Portugal, providing investment in education, transport, industrial retrofitting and job creation.

Portuguese politics were rocked by intense student protests and strikes for higher wages in the public sector. The 50-per-cent increase in the toll charged at Lisbon's access bridge prompted several protests blocking the route.

The October 1995 general elections were won by the Socialist Party which gained an absolute majority at the Assembly. Antonio Guterres replaced Prime Minister Anibal Cavaco. After 10 years of PSD dominance, oriented toward European integration and economic liberalism, the PS capitalized on domestic discontent with education and health and assured the financial market it would not interfere with the goals regarding monetary union and privatization.

The Socialist Jorge Sampaio took over the presidency of the

PROFILE

ENVIRONMENT

The country includes the Iberian continental territory and the islands of the Azores and Madeira archipelagos. The Tagus, the country's largest river, divides the continental region into two separate areas. The northern region is mountainous, with abundant rainfall and intensive agriculture: wheat, corn, vines and olives are grown. In the valley of the Douro, the major wine-growing region in the country, large vineyards extend in terraces along the valley slopes. The city of Oporto is the northern economic center. The South, Alentejo, with extensive low plateaus and a very dry climate, has large wheat and olive plantations and sheep farming. The cork tree woods, which made Portugal a great cork producer, are found here. Fishing and shipbuilding are major contributors to the country's economy. Mineral resources include pyrite, tungsten, coal and iron.

SOCIETY

Peoples: The Portuguese (99.5 per cent) came from the integration of various ethnic groups: Celts, Arabs, Berbers, Phoenicians, Carthaginians and others. Immigrants come from Africa (0.2 per cent) and the Americas (Brazilians 0.1 per cent, US Americans 0.1 per cent). There is substantial migration by Portuguese towards richer countries in the continent.

Religions: Catholic (94.5 per cent); Protestants (0.6 per cent); other Christians mostly Catholic Apostolic and Jehovah Witnesses (0.9 per cent); Jewish (0.1 per cent); Muslims (0.1 per cent).

Language: Portuguese; there are two small areas where two dialects are spoken: 'Mirandes' (derived from Asturian-Leonese) and 'Barranquenho'.

Main Political Parties: Social Democrat Party, center-right; Socialist Party, center-left; People's Party; Unitarian Democratic Coalition (with the Portuguese Communist Party and the Greens). The Left Bloc, formed by the Democratic People's Union, the Revolutionary Socialist Party and Politics XXI, extreme left.

Main Social Organizations: The General Confederation of Portuguese Workers (CGTP), a nationwide multi-union organization with 287 union members (represents 80 per cent of the organized workers); the General Union of Portuguese Workers (UGT-P), which combines 50 unions; National Agriculture Confederation (CNA).

THE STATE

Official Name: República Portuguesa.

Administrative Divisions: 18 districts, 2 autonomous regions (Azores and Madeira).

Capital: Lisbon 1,962,000 people (2003).

Other Cities: Oporto 1,206,800 people; Amadora 123,400; Vila Nova de Gaia 74,800 (2000). **Government:** Jorge Sampaio, President since March 1996, re-elected in 2001. Pedro Santana Lopes, Prime Minister since July 2004. Unicameral Legislature: Assembly of the Republic, with 230 members.

National Holidays: 10 June, Portugal Day (1580); 5 October, Independence Day (1910); 25 April, Liberty Day (1975).

Armed Forces: 43,600 (2002). Other: 20,900 Republican National Guard; 20,000 Public Security Police; 8,900 Border Security Guard.

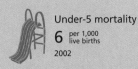

	Under-5 mortality			Poverty			Aid			Maternal mortality

Under-5 mortality
6 per 1,000 live births
2002

Poverty
<2% of population living on less than $1 per day
1994

Aid
0.27% Official development assistance as % of donors' GNI
2002

Maternal mortality
5 per 100,000 live births
2000

country in March 1996. The Government brought in an economic plan in line with EU demands, particularly regarding the budget deficit.

30   A successful campaign against tax evasion meant increased spending on health, education and social policies. The privatization program was intensified, selling shares in telecommunications, electricity and roads. Unemployment fell to 6.7 per cent of the active population.

31   In February 1998, Parliament approved a law legalizing abortion up to 10 weeks of pregnancy. The Government called a referendum and voters rejected the law by 50.91 per cent to 49 per cent, with a turnout of 32 per cent.

32   After 442 years' governing the island, Portugal handed Macao over to China on 20 December 1999. President Sampaio was present at the ceremony, along with his Chinese counterpart Jiang Zemin. This act signified the end of the Portuguese empire, as well as the end of all European control in Asia. Portugal, which had been the first European power to control Asian territories, was also the last to withdraw.

33   Sampaio visited Xanana Gusmao, East Timor's pro-independence leader, in February 2000 and promised to help the Timorese to restore their education system. This was the first visit of a Portuguese head of state since Portugal pulled out of Timor in 1974.

34   Prime Minister Antonio Guterres took over as president of the EU until July 2000. His leadership led the EU to impose diplomatic isolation on Austria when the fascist-sympathizing Liberty Party, led by Jörg Haider, joined the Austrian governing coalition.

35   In April 2001, Sampaio's presidential electoral victory confirmed his continuing popularity, consolidating the control of the Socialists led by Guterres.

36   December saw the inauguration of the Alqueva hydroelectric project on the Guadiana river. It created the greatest artificial lake in Europe, and was condemned by several environmental groups as too big, destructive and unnecessary. Although the project would irrigate the southern wasteland of the country, it would also flood the habitat of its unusual wild life (including eagles, wild boar, falcons and Iberian lynxes) as well as submerging 160 Stone Age period rocks. The Alqueva project dated from 1957, the time of Oliveira Salazar's dictatorship. The politicians endorsed the project

IN FOCUS

ENVIRONMENTAL CHALLENGES
The poor quality of the soil is exacerbated by the effects of erosion. There are very high levels of air pollution in urban areas due to vehicle emissions, and in areas near cellulose and cement factories. There are also reports of water contamination, particularly in coastal areas.

WOMEN'S RIGHTS
Women have been able to vote and run for office since 1976, although a select group was allowed to vote from 1931.

From 1995 to 2000, the percentage of seats in parliament held by women increased from 13 to 19 per cent, while female representation in ministerial or equivalent positions remained constant at 10 per cent. In the year 2000 women comprised 44 per cent of the workforce, mostly working in services and agriculture.

In 2002, 57 per cent of the almost 400,000 students enrolled in tertiary education were women.

In non-agricultural sectors the average salary was 30 per cent lower for women than for men. Domestic violence, sexual harassment at work, abuse and trafficking of women into forced prostitution are issues of concern for the Government and society.

Portugal is a transit and destination country, mostly for people from Eastern Europe. In 2003 there were several reports of women trafficked from Brazil

and forced to work in prostitution. Prostitution is not illegal in Portugal, but human trafficking, procurement and the distribution of pornography involving minors are.

CHILDREN
In 2002 over 2 million inhabitants were under the age of 18 and more than 500,000 were under five. Life expectancy at birth rose from 67 years in 1970 to 78 years in 2002.

The Government implemented programs for children's welfare and in defense of the rights of the child in 2003, mostly in public education and health services. Education is compulsory, free and universal for 9 years, up to the age of 15, and 98% of school-age children were enrolled in 2000. In addition, there is also free, public pre-school education, for children from the age of 4 until primary school. The number of children in pre-school grows annually. There are public nurseries for 3 months to 3 years of age, which have been improving both in number and quality.

Throughout 2003 Portugal was a transit country for African children, particularly from Angola, who were trafficked to other European countries.

INDIGENOUS PEOPLES/ ETHNIC MINORITIES
Portugal's main minority are the Roma or gypsies. Their community numbers 50,000, and they are the sector of the population that most suffers discrimination, particularly at the hands of the police.

There have been reports of segregation of the Afro-Portuguese population. The Government has passed laws against racism and discrimination.

Some 5 per cent of the total population are immigrants, who are also considered minorities. In late 2000, there were 47,217 Cape Verdeans, 22,411 Brazilians, 20,468 Angolans and 16,006 Guineans living in Portugal.

MIGRANTS/REFUGEES
Some 200 people from Sierra Leone, Angola and Afghanistan applied for asylum in 2002. An estimated 2,500 people - former refugees from Guinea-Bissau's 1998 civil war - finally received their residence permits under an amendment of Portugal's laws on alien immigrants. These people were left in a legal void in 2000, when they lost their temporary protected status, but continued residing illegally in the country.

The Government tightened immigration controls in 2002 and 2003, which were aimed at combating the network for forced labor operating in Western Europe. Most of the trafficking victims were men from Eastern Europe (plus the abovementioned cases of African children and Brazilian women).

DEATH PENALTY
The death penalty was abolished for all kinds of crime in 1976.

arguing that it was essential for irrigating the wasteland areas of the country, but some environmentalists highlighted that only 48 per cent of the irrigated land would be useful for crops or pasture. The environmental group Quercus advocated the dam should be filled only to 139 meters and not to its maximum 152 meters in order to save the trees.

37   The poor economic performance of Guterres' government led him to make repeated changes in the cabinet, which, together with charges of corruption within the Socialist Party, lost him popularity. In December 2001, after the drastic defeat in the local election, Guterres resigned and Parliament was dissolved.

38   Elections were brought forward and, in March 2002, the social-democratic candidate Manuel Durão Barroso won. The

new Prime Minister formed a center-right coalition government. At the time of his taking office he promised to cut corporate taxes and reduce public expenditure, as well as to privatize public services including health.

39   In late 2002 an investigative journalism report revealed a child-sex network, involving diplomats, politicians, sportsmen and journalists. The network had been covered up for two decades with the State's complicity, since the victims were children from Casa Pia (Pious House), Portugal's main state orphanage. Investigators stated that 128 boys and girls had been subjected to sexual abuse. Ten people had been arrested by the end of 2003, including Carlos Cruz, a famous Portuguese TV presenter; Jorge Ritto, former Portuguese ambassador to South Africa and Carlos 'Bibi' Silvino, a former employee of Casa Pia,

charged with 35 crimes of sexual abuse.

40   In August 2003 fire devastated almost 215,000 hectares of the country - an area the size of Luxembourg. It is estimated that the ecological repercussions of this disaster, with 12.5 million tons of earth washing into the rivers, will continue to pollute soil and waters for at least a year.

41   Four bills to legalize abortion were rejected on 5 March 2004 in parliament with PSD and PP votes. However, the Government ordered a study of the number, causes and complications arising from illegal abortions to try and modify opinion on the existing law. Eleven thousand women required medical treatment after having illegal abortions in 2002, according to the Ministry of Public Health. The number of abortions is estimated at 30,000 a year. ∎

Puerto Rico / Puerto Rico

Population:	3,915,379
Area:	8,950 km²
Capital:	San Juan
Currency:	US dollar
Language:	Spanish and English

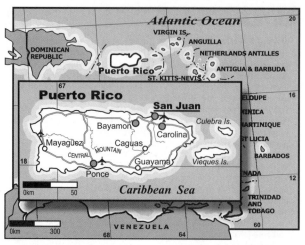

In 1508, 15 years after Christopher Columbus landed, the island of Borinquen (as Puerto Rico was called by the Arawaks/Tainos who lived there) became a colony and has continued so up to the present day. Puerto Rico is the easternmost of the Greater Antilles and because of its strategic location at the entrance to the Caribbean, the island endured 400 years of Spanish rule. It also suffered repeated attacks by pirates and regular naval forces, whether British, Dutch or French, and finally remained under US administration after the Spanish-American War of 1898.

[2] As in neighboring islands, the local Taino people were exterminated by war, disease and overwork. African slaves were brought in to take their place in the fields where most food supplies for Spanish expeditions to the mainland were produced. Thus, Puerto Rican culture became a blend of its African and Spanish heritage.

[3] Spanish rule was continually challenged by external attacks and internal rebellions by both the Tainos and enslaved African workers. The latter rebelled successively in 1822, 1826, 1843, and 1848. The struggle for independence in the rest of Latin America had its counterpart in Puerto Rico's struggle for administrative reform (1812-1840), but Spanish troops ruthlessly stifled the uprising.

[4] In 1868, five years before slavery was finally abolished, a group of patriots led by Ramón Emeterio Betances moved things nearer to liberation. In the town of Lares they proclaimed Puerto Rico's independence and took up arms to free the island. Despite their defeat, the Lares revolt signalled the birth of the Puerto Rican nation.

[5] The independence movement continued to gain strength in the following years. The Cubans were already up in arms in 1897, led by José Martí in a movement that reached Puerto Rico. US military intervention in the war against Spain, in 1898, hastened Spain's defeat but for Puerto Rico it only meant the imposition of a new ruler.

[6] US colonial administrations, first military and then civilian, imposed English as the official language and attempted to turn the island into a sugar plantation and military base. Puerto Ricans were made US citizens in 1917, though they were given no participation in the island's government. As a result, resistance to colonial rule grew. In 1922 the pro-independence Nationalist Party (PN) was founded. PN-led uprisings in 1930 and 1950 were harshly repressed.

[7] In 1947, intense internal and international pressure forced the US to allow Puerto Rico to elect its own governor. The 1948 elections gave the post to Luis Muñoz Marín, leader of the Popular Democratic Party (PPD), who favored turning the country into a self-governing commonwealth or free associated state. The US Government authorized the drafting of a constitution in 1959, which was approved by a plebiscite and later ratified by the US. Muñoz Marín's program was thus sanctioned.

[8] With the institution of Commonwealth status, US administrations were freed from the obligation of reporting on Puerto Rico's status to the UN Decolonization Committee. Moreover, in this way the UN tacitly endorsed the arrangement declaring the 'end' of colonial rule. In September 1978, the Decolonization Committee reconsidered the situation. In December that year a UN General Assembly resolution once again defined Puerto Rico as a colony and demanded self-determination for its people.

[9] Muñoz Marín promoted industrialization on the island through massive US private investment enticed by government tax incentives. During the 1950s, Puerto Rican agriculture was destroyed by an influx of US products, resulting in over 50 per cent of the island's food being imported. The newly-formed labor reserve was more than enough to supply cheap hands for the

LAND USE

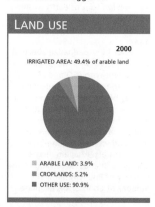

2000

IRRIGATED AREA: 49.4% of arable land

- ARABLE LAND: 3.9%
- CROPLANDS: 5.2%
- OTHER USE: 90.9%

PROFILE

ENVIRONMENT

The smallest and easternmost island of the Greater Antilles. A central mountain range, covered with rainforests, runs across the island. In the highlands, subsistence crops are grown (corn, cassava/manioc); on the western slopes there are large coffee plantations and in the central region small tobacco farms. On the northern slopes citrus and pineapples are grown for export to the US. The main crop is sugarcane, which is cultivated on the best farmlands along the coastline. The islands of Vieques (43 sq km), Mona (40 sq km) and Culebra also belong to Puerto Rico.

SOCIETY

Peoples: Most Puerto Ricans are mestizos, descendants of Spanish colonizers, African slaves, Taino people and other small immigrant groups. In the 1940s, about 3 million Puerto Ricans emigrated to the US in search of better economic opportunities. This tendency began to decrease over the years until it has been almost reversed at the present time as a result of the favorable economic situation. **Religions:** No official religion. Catholics (85.3 per cent), Protestants (4.7 per cent), others (10 per cent). **Languages:** Spanish and English (both official). English is used in all matters related to political relations with the US. The forced introduction of English in education, public administration and communications was given support in 1993, when it was made an official language alongside Spanish.

Main Political Parties: The New Progressive Party (PNP), led by Pedro Rosselló, advocating total integration - or annexation - to the US as the 51st state of the Union; the Democratic People's Party (PPD), founded in 1938 by Luis Muñoz Marín, supports the current 'Commonwealth' status; the Puerto Rican Independence Party (PI), founded in 1946 from a breakup of the PPD, social-democrat. **Main Social Organizations:** The Labor Federation of Puerto Rico, which is affiliated to the US AFL-CIO. Federation of Pro-Independence University Students (FUPI); Committee for the Rescue and Development of Vieques.

THE STATE

Official Name: Estado Libre Asociado de Puerto Rico. **Capital:** San Juan 2,332,000 people (2003). **Other Cities:** Bayamon 205,400 people; Carolina 169,800; Ponce 156,500; Caguas 89,500 (2000). **Government:** Sila María Calderón, since January 2001, the first woman Governor. Bicameral National Assembly: Chamber of Representatives with 51 members and the Senate with 28 members. **National Holiday:** 25 July, Constitution (1952); 23 September, the Battle of Grito de Lares (start of the anti-colonial armed revolt in 1868); 4 July, US Independence (1776). **Armed Forces:** 5,000 US Army troops (2003).

Life expectancy
75.6 years
2000-2005

GNI per capita
$10,950
2002

growing US corporate community, and Puerto Ricans soon began migrating en masse to the US, and especially to New York in search of work.

[10] With the great social upheavals of the 1960s, the struggle for independence flowered anew on the island. Despite the revival of the independence movement, a 1967 plebiscite confirmed the Commonwealth status. Moreover, elections the following year gave the governorship to the New Progressive Party (PNP) which favored making the island the 51st state of the US. After the 1972 elections, the PPD returned to power led by Rafael Hernández Colón. In 1976, supporters of the US statehood option returned to the governorship. Carlos Romero Barceló announced that if he were re-elected for a second term, he would call a pro-statehood referendum. Barceló was re-elected in 1980, but by such a slim margin that plans for a statehood plebiscite were abandoned.

[11] Puerto Rico has one representative in the US Congress, but with no voting rights other than in committees. US citizenship only gave Puerto Ricans the right to participate in the 1980 presidential elections, although residents in the US are able to vote in all elections.

[12] Rafael Hernández Colón was elected governor on 6 November 1984. He promised a 'four-year term of struggle against corruption and unemployment'. He renewed Puerto Rico's Commonwealth status thus rejecting his predecessor's intention to integrate into the Union. Hernández Colón was re-elected in 1988, with 48.7 per cent of the vote, against 45.8 per cent for those in favor of annexation by the US, and 5.3 per cent for those who favored independence.

[13] In April 1991, Governor Hernández Colón passed a law granting official status to the Spanish language. Soon after, the Puerto Rican people were granted the Prince of Asturias award by the Spanish crown, 'in recognition of the country's efforts to defend the Spanish language'.

[14] In the plebiscite carried out late in 1991, various strategies were proposed to promote development on the island. Hernández Colón succeeded in rallying moderate nationalists and supporters of independence, who campaigned together. They were in favor of self-determination, the end of subjection to US jurisdiction, the affirmation of Puerto Rican identity, regardless of any future referendum decisions, and the maintenance of US

IN FOCUS

ENVIRONMENTAL CHALLENGES
The main environmental problems are soil erosion and occasional droughts which result in lack of water for human consumption.

WOMEN'S RIGHTS
Puerto Rico has its own constitution and local governmental autonomy. Women have been able to vote since 1928. In 2000, they made up 37 per cent of the country's labor force and were mostly engaged in services.

That year, there were fewer women unemployed (7.8 per cent) than men (11.9 per cent).

Among women over 15, 5.6 per cent were illiterate in 2000, a proportion that matched the illiteracy rate among men. Boys and girls had equal access to education.

Domestic violence against women remained an issue of concern in 2003 and civil society organizations were particularly concerned with raising awareness about, preventing and punishing this type of abuse.

CHILDREN
In the 1990s, the number of Puerto Ricans under 18 decreased by 5 per cent, from 1,154,527 to 1,092,000, while in the US the figure increased by 14 per cent. This change is due to a drop in overall fertility rates in

Puerto Rico and the migration of Puerto Rican families to the US.

Also between 1990 and 2000, the proportion of female-headed households increased from 22 to 27 per cent.

In 1999, more than half of Puerto Rican families with children - 58 per cent - were living below the poverty line. American Samoa was the only US dependent territory with a higher child poverty rate than Puerto Rico.

That year, the percentage of poor families with children in the US was 18 per cent. The percentage of teenagers between the ages of 16 and 19 who dropped out of high school was 14 per cent, down 12 per cent on 1990 figures.

In 1999, the child poverty rate was highest in Vieques (81 per cent) and lowest in Trujillo Alto (40 per cent). Child poverty rates tended to be higher in rural than in urban areas.

INDIGENOUS PEOPLES/ ETHNIC MINORITIES
Traces of Taino physical characteristics can be found in Taino descendants who live in areas of Borinquen. Their written language took the form of petroglyphs which can still be found in some Puerto Rican caves. After 200 years' absence from official records, Tainos reappeared in a military census carried out in 1790: 2,000 natives were still living on the island of Mona, where they had been

relocated by the Spanish after the conquest.

MIGRANTS/REFUGEES
According to the 1990 US census, 2.7 million Puerto Ricans were living in that country. Half of them had been born in Puerto Rico. In 2004, many Puerto Rican soldiers were serving at US military bases in Iraq.

In January 2004, 325 immigrants were intercepted at sea when trying to enter the US illegally through Puerto Rico's northern and western coasts.

DEATH PENALTY
Puerto Rico banned capital punishment two years after the execution of a man in 1927 and ratified this prohibition in the 1952 constitution, which confirmed Puerto Rico's self-governing commonwealth status. The question of capital punishment on the island is a matter of constant debate, due to its political relationship with the US. Virtually no local politician or public figure speaks out in favor of the death penalty. The nearly four million people that live in this US territory do not have representatives with voting rights in the US Congress, which passed a law reinstating the death penalty for drug barons in 1984 and broadened its reach to other types of crimes in 1992.

citizenship. However, all this effort came to nothing in the polls, when 55 per cent of the voters supported the PNP's position that a break with Washington had to be avoided. Given this result, Hernández' position within his party was weakened, strengthening the hand of more pro-independence sectors and Hernández finally resigned the PPD leadership.

[15] Pedro Roselló, a supporter of Puerto Rico's integration into the US, was elected governor in 1992. His plan to make English the only official language on the island - replacing Spanish - caused massive protest demonstrations. Finally in 1993 English was made an official language alongside Spanish.

[16] In November 1993, a referendum was held to decide on the political future of the island. Those wanting to maintain the 'free associated state' status won a narrow victory, with 48.4 per cent of the vote, while the group supporting the transformation of Puerto Rico into the 51st US state took 46.2 per cent. Independence

supporters had a mere 4 per cent. Five years later, a new plebiscite was carried out which registered virtually the same result.

[17] Tens of thousands of people protested in February 2000 against renewed military exercises by the US army on the Puerto Rican island of Vieques. This island had been used by the US for military exercises including bomb target practice for 50 years, but these had been suspended after the accidental death of a civilian in April 1999. President Clinton and Governor Sila María Calderón, of the PPD, who took office in January 2000, had made an agreement to resume maneuvers, but the church authorities organized a protest group to camp in the target area, thus interrupting the 'war games'.

[18] The controversy over US military training in Vieques continued until January 2003, the date set by Clinton's successor, George W Bush, for the last military exercises by the US Navy on the island. Most of the 8,000 Vieques residents celebrated the

Navy's departure, as did Calderón. However, the area remained under the control of the US Department of the Interior.

[19] Another source of tension between the US and Puerto Rican authorities was partially resolved in July 2003. A murder in Puerto Rico prompted US prosecutors, led by John Ashcroft, to attempt to apply the death penalty, which had been abolished in 1929 in the territory, to the Puerto Ricans accused of the crime. The US initiative was strongly rejected by the islanders. Although the alleged murderers were absolved, US judicial authorities continued their attempt to reinstate capital punishment on the island.

[20] In 2004, an electoral year, a new political party emerged: the Catañeses United Party (PCU), a group from the region of Cataño, formed by several former PNP members. The PCU supported Pedro Roselló as candidate for governor and presented a 'pro-statehood' position, that is to say, in favor of US annexation of the island. ∎

Qatar / Qatar

Population:	627,567
Area:	11,000 km²
Capital:	Doha (Ad-Dawhah)
Currency:	Riyal
Language:	Arabic

L ike the neighboring island of Bahrain, ever since ancient times the Qatar peninsula has participated in the Persian Gulf trade between Mesopotamia and India. Islamicized in the 7th century (see Saudi Arabia), at the time of the Caliphate of Baghdad, Qatar had already obtained autonomy which was maintained until 1076 when it was conquered by the Emir of Bahrain. From the 16th century, after a brief period of Portuguese occupation, the country lived in great prosperity due to the development of pearl fishing which attracted immigrants. Settled on the coasts, under the leadership of the al-Thani family, these settlers succeeded in politically uniting the country in the 18th century, though it remained subject to Bahrain's sovereignty. The process of independence, begun in 1815 by Sheikh Muhammad and his son Jassim, culminated in 1868 with the mediation of the English; the al-Thanis agreed to end the war in exchange for guaranteed territorial integrity.

[2] The Turkish sultans, nominal sovereigns of the entire Arabian peninsula since the 16th century, feared the increasing British penetration in the Gulf. Consequently, they named the reigning Sheikh (Jassim al-Thani) governor of the province of Qatar as a pretext for establishing a small military garrison in Dawhah (Doha). Neither Qatar nor Britain were concerned about this formal affirmation of sovereignty and the garrison remained until World War I without the slightest effect on British influence in the region.

[3] In 1930, the price of pearls dropped when the Japanese flooded the market with a cheaper version of cultivated pearls. Consequently Sheikh Abdullah sold all the country's oil prospecting and exploitation rights, and granted a 75-year lease on its territorial waters, for £400,000. The Anglo-Iranian Oil Company discovered oil in 1939 but actual production only began after World War II, attracting other companies that purchased parts of the original concession. The immense wealth obtained by Royal Dutch Shell did not seem to concern Sheikh Ahmad ibn Ali al-Thani as oil and tariff revenues increased his personal fortune by £15 million.

[4] Shortly thereafter, Ahmad was ousted by his own family. They replaced him with his cousin Khalifa, giving him the task of removing any elements that were opposed to progress and modernization.

[5] Sheikh Khalifa created a Council of Ministers and an Advisory Council to share the responsibilities of his absolute power and promised social justice and stability. Redistributing the oil revenues, he exempted all inhabitants from taxation and provided free education and medical attention. His greatest achievement has perhaps been the subsidizing and promotion of productive activities at the beginning of his mandate.

[6] To reduce Qatar's dependency on a single product, the fishing industry was revitalized, industrialization was accelerated with new cement and fertilizer plants, plus iron and steel mills. The country took advantage of its strategic position to provide commercial and financial services to the economies of the entire region. In addition, a large part of the country's financial surplus was invested abroad (in Europe and the US). In 1980, it was estimated that income from this exportation of capital would eventually equal all oil revenues. In this way Qatar sought to ensure its future when the oil wells ran dry.

[7] As a tool of control, a state oil company - the Qatar Petroleum Producing Authority (QPPA) - was set up in 1972. By February 1977, all foreign oil installations had been expropriated.

[8] Qatar's economic expansion required the large-scale immigration of foreign technical experts and workers - the former were mainly European and American; the latter Iranian, Pakistani, Indian and Palestinian. About 60 per cent of the economically active population in Qatar are foreigners. To avoid any profound transformation of the local culture, the Government has preferred and promoted immigration from Arab countries.

[9] Since 1981, together with Bahrain, Kuwait, Oman, the United Arab Emirates and Saudi Arabia, Qatar has participated in the Gulf Cooperation Council (GCC), an organization designed to coordinate the area's policies on political, economic, social, cultural and defense issues.

[10] Following OPEC policy, in 1982 the country cut crude oil production by 25 per cent. Consequently exports decreased, reflected in a considerable reduction in volume of petrodollars invested in the West, in public spending and in industrial expansion. Nevertheless, Qatar's iron and steel plant in the industrial center of Umm Said - producing 450,000 tons a year at the beginning of the decade - and a liquid gas plant made the Government decide to go ahead with a $6 billion natural gas project for use in its energy and desalinization programs.

[11] In April 1986, tensions flared between Bahrain and Qatar over the artificial island of Fasht ad-Dibal.

PROFILE

ENVIRONMENT

The country consists of the Qatar Peninsula, on the eastern coast of the Arabian Peninsula in the Persian Gulf. The land is flat and the climate is hot and dry. Farming is possible only along the coastal strip. The country's main resource is its huge oil wealth on the western coast.

SOCIETY

Peoples: Qatari Arabs make up 20 per cent of the population. A further 25 per cent are Arab immigrants from Palestine, Egypt and Yemen. The remaining 55 per cent are immigrants from non-Arab states, mostly from Pakistan, India and Iran.
Religions: Muslim (official and predominant). The majority are Sunni, with mainly Shi'a Iranian immigrants. There are also Christian and Hindu minorities. **Languages:** Arabic (official and predominant). Urdu is spoken by Pakistani immigrants, and Farsi by Iranians. English is the business language. **Main Political Parties:** There are no organized political parties.

THE STATE

Official Name: Dawlat Qatar. **Capital:** Doha (Ad-Dawhah) 286,0700 people (2003). **Other Cities:** Al-Rayyan 183,000 people; Al-Wakrah 22,900; Umm Said (Musay'id)18,100 (2000). **Government:** Hamad ibn Khalifah al-Thani, Emir and Head of State since June 1995. Sheikh Abdullah ibn Khalifah al-Thani, Prime Minister since October 1996. Legislative Power: a Consultative Council with 45 members, 30 of them elected by universal suffrage to four-year terms and the rest appointed by the Emir. **National Holiday:** 3 September, Independence Day (1971). **Armed Forces:** 12,400 (2002).

Life expectancy
72.2 years
2000-2005

Literacy
94% total adult rate
2000

This conflict was resolved through negotiations sponsored by the GCC. French troops were then recruited and under Qatar's uniform they participate in the defense of the Emirate. In November 1987, the Government renewed diplomatic relations with Egypt, which had been cut off when Egypt signed the Camp David accords with Israel.

[12] In March 1991, after the Iraqi invasion of Kuwait, the GCC suspended all economic aid to Jordan and the Palestine Liberation Organization (PLO). That month, the Foreign Ministers of Egypt, Syria, and the six Arab countries of the GCC signed in Saudi Arabia an agreement with the US that projected a common military strategy between the US and the Arab countries in the anti-Iraqi coalition, mechanisms to avoid arms proliferation, acceptance of a peace treaty by Israel and a new economic program for the development of the region.

[13] In September 1991 Qatar inaugurated North Field, an off-shore deposit of natural gas, and so became a major producer of this fuel, with an estimated reserve of ten billion cubic meters (five per cent of the world's total).

[14] In December, a group of 53 eminent people signed a petition to the Emir of Qatar asking for free parliamentary elections, a written constitution and increased personal and political freedoms.

[15] By the end of 1991 Qatar and Bahrain became involved in another territorial dispute, this time over Hawar Island, and more especially underground rights to Dibval and Qitat, both potentially rich in oil.

[16] In 1993, the fall in the price of oil on the international market triggered an almost 20 per cent decrease in fiscal income. Thus, in 1994 al-Thani negotiated new agreements with several Asian companies for the exploitation of natural gas.

[17] In June 1995, heir to the throne Hamad ibn Khalifa al-Thani overthrew his father to become Emir of Qatar. He promised to step up efforts to resolve the territorial disputes with Saudi Arabia and Bahrain.

[18] The Al-Jazeera 'independent' television channel, founded at the personal initiative of the Emir in 1996, was an immediate success in Middle Eastern countries, with its pro-Arab and pro-Muslim stance and the broadcasting of information ignored by the major Western TV channels and the gagged state TV stations.

[19] In 1997, Qatar froze relations with Israel. However, it offered its capital Doha as the venue for the Economic Conference of the Middle East and North Africa to be held in November, as part of the peace

IN FOCUS

ENVIRONMENTAL CHALLENGES
Qatar suffered the polluting effects of the oil fires which occurred during the first Gulf War. Drinking water resources are scarce so that dependence on large scale desalinization units is increasing.

WOMEN'S RIGHTS
Women have no political representation. In 2003, they comprised just 26 per cent of the total workforce. Women are not paid at the same rate as men, but they generally obtained the same extra benefits, such as travel or household expenses. Even though the law did not impose restrictions, until 2003 it was hard for a woman to travel abroad without a male companion. During that year there were no arrests or charges against men for domestic violence, which does not mean it does not exist. Muslim law punishes rapists with the death penalty, unless the rape is within marriage when it is not seen as rape. Some employers have ill-treated their female domestic employees, most of whom come from South Asia or the Philippines. Foreign countries' embassies have been refuges for female employees, victims of their bosses' abuse. In several

cases, charges were not laid for fear of losing a job. The legal system allows men to commit 'honor murders' if they feel offended by the immodest behavior of their partners.

CHILDREN
Gulf states have made major progress with regard to the situation of children. Economic prosperity during the 1970s and the early 1980s was used to establish socio-economic infrastructures, which have been the basis for the development, distribution and availability of basic services such as education, health services, drinking water, sanitation and electricity-generating power plants. Education is compulsory and free for every child from 6 to 18 years.

Youngsters between 15 and 18 are allowed to work under family supervision, but in 2003 there were no estimates available for the number of children at work.

Forced labor is forbidden, but the plight of some children forced to work as camel-jockeys - and of some girls in domestic service - is well known. Generally these children come from African countries, Pakistan or Bangladesh and are accompanied by adults who train them and claim to be their parents, so the Government does not intervene in this kind of child

abuse. However, for the camel racing, in 2002 the Government set minimal safety standards and set up a school and health service for the jockeys.

INDIGENOUS PEOPLES/ ETHNIC MINORITIES
Non-citizens are discriminated against in terms of their jobs, education, housing and health services. While Qataris get free basic services, non-citizens have to pay for electricity, water, health services and education. They are also not allowed to own land. The major groups are Indian, Pakistani and Iranian, as well as Arabs from other countries.

MIGRANTS/REFUGEES
The constitution grants the right of return to the country. Foreigners are subject to restrictions, designed to limit the size of the workforce, when entering or leaving the country. Illegal entry is not allowed, even to asylum-seekers from neighboring countries.

DEATH PENALTY
Death penalty applies according to the interpretation of the Sharia (Muslim law) even for ordinary crimes.

process. In October, Sheikh Abdullah ibn Khalifa al-Thani was appointed Prime Minister, a post previously occupied by Emir Hamad.

[20] In November 1998 a plan for constitutional reform was unveiled, with the goal of creating a parliament elected by direct vote. At this time only men aged over 18 years old were eligible to vote. In the March 1999 local elections, women were allowed the vote, but none of the six female candidates was elected.

[21] The rebels responsible for a 1996 coup attempt against the Emir were sentenced to life imprisonment in February 2000. Amongst them was the Emir's cousin, Sheikh Hamad ibn Jassem al-Thani, an ally of the deposed father of the current monarch.

[22] In March 2001, Qatar solved its border conflicts with Bahrain and Saudi Arabia. The International Court of Justice at The Hague found in favor of Bahrain's ownership of Hawar islands, while it acknowledged the rights of Qatar over the city of Zubarah. Both countries signed an agreement in Doha, which demarcated the 60 km common border of sea and land crossed by Bedouin.

[23] The Emir was not satisfied with the judicial sentences for those involved in the coup and in May 2002 the Appeal Court passed death sentences on the Emir's cousin and another 18 men, 20 life sentences and 29 acquittals. At that time, Qatar had not applied the death penalty for a decade.

[24] During the 2002 US bombing on Afghanistan, while the US established its largest operation center in the Gulf in Qatar, Al-Jazeera was paradoxically the only TV channel authorized by the (Afghan) Taliban regime to broadcast in the areas under its control and to spread propaganda messages and threats by terrorist network al-Qaeda leader, Osama bin Laden.

[25] Even though the summit of the Islamic Organization conference held in Doha on 5 March 2003 condemned the imminent strike on Iraq, the Emir allowed the use of the US military base in Qatar as a planning center for the attack. Meanwhile, Al-Jazeera reported the invasion and broadcast tapes by Iraq's leader Saddam Hussein - whose whereabouts were unknown - calling for resistance.

[26] The new constitution was approved on 29 April 2003, by 96 per cent of the 85,000 votes that comprised the electoral roll. The reforms, which were less than expected, did not create a parliament, but a *Majlis ash-Shura* (consultative assembly). Women were given the right to vote and to hold public posts, and information and religious freedoms were granted, but political parties remained banned.

[27] Even though Hamad had, in 1996, appointed the third of his ten sons, Jassim (born 1978) as his heir, in August 2003 he replaced him with the next son, Tamim (born 1979).

[28] In February 2004 former Chechen president and separatist leader Zelimkhan Yanderbiyev was assassinated in a car bomb explosion in Doha, where he had lived for the previous three years. Qatar accused the Russian secret services of the murder, but they denied the accusation and attributed it to internal fighting among different separatist factions. Russia had asked for Yanderbiyev's extradition and had accused him of participating in the armed raids on Dagestan in 1999 and the siege of a theater in Moscow in 2002. ∎

Réunion / Réunion

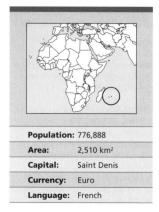

Population:	776,888
Area:	2,510 km²
Capital:	Saint Denis
Currency:	Euro
Language:	French

The island of Réunion was uninhabited until the beginning of the 17th century when Arab explorers arrived, calling it Diva Margabin. Its subsequent name-changes reflect the colonial power struggle: the Portuguese renamed it Ilha Santa Apolonia in 1513; French settlers called it Bourbon in 1600. After the French Revolution it was given its current name of Réunion.

[2] The French colonial regime replaced subsistence farming with the export commodities of sugarcane and coffee, cultivated by slave labor. The island's fish stocks were depleted by the over-exploitation of several species. From the 19th century the island was an important French military base in the Indian Ocean, together with other dependencies such as Djibouti and Comoros Islands.

[3] In March 1946 Réunion was designated a French Overseas Department. This was backed by the Left, both in Réunion and in France. The local middle class and the French colonists supported the integration of Réunion into French territory.

[4] Later, conservative political changes in France led to a realignment of political forces on the island. While sectors linked to colonial interests defended the island's Department status, the Réunion Communist Party (PCR) changed its stance, and in 1959 campaigned for partial autonomy. For ten years, the PCR was the sole supporter of gradual independence.

[5] In 1978, the UN supported full independence for Réunion. The dispute between the island and France became an international issue. That year, in a meeting with other anti-imperialist and anti-colonialist organizations in the Indian Ocean area, a Permanent Liaison Committee was formed as part of their common struggle against foreign domination. In June 1979, during elections for the European Parliament, Paul Vergés - PCR leader - raised the issue of

dual colonialism, claiming that Réunion was not only dominated by the French, but forced to serve the interests of the entire European Community.

[6] A demographic explosion on the island, whose population grew by 20 per cent in a decade, caused a production crisis and a rise in unemployment. Increasing social unrest led to frequent rioting. In 1991, eight people died in clashes with the police in protest over the closure of the underground television station Tele Free-DOM, run by Camille Sudre. Sudre, a French national settled in Réunion, won the regional elections in 1992. Backed by the PCR, he occupied one of the two main executive posts on the island.

[7] However, France's supreme court annulled the elections for alleged irregularities and banned Sudre from standing again. The 1993 regional elections were won by the Free-DOM party, led by Marguerite Sudre, Camille's wife. The new president formed links with the French Right and was appointed to the cabinet by conservative Edouard Balladur (1993-1995) in Paris.

[8] Unemployment soared in 1996 to an all-time high of 40 per cent, and it was estimated to be even higher among young people (39 per cent of the population is under 20). In 1997, social discontent found expression in frequent demonstrations. In 1998, PCR leader Paul Vergés was elected head of the Regional Council, beating right-

wing candidate Jean-Paul Virapoullé by a narrow margin.

[9] In June 2001 Gonthier Friederici took office as prefect. In 2002 the island was devastated by cyclone Dina, with major damage to agriculture and housing.

[10] Although sugar exports continue to be the island's main economic resource, the service sector has grown considerably in recent years. The Government has tried to develop tourism to stem

unemployment, which in 2004 affected one-third of the workforce. The economy is still largely dependent on French financial aid.

[11] There is a huge gap between rich and poor - a source of constant social tension. The white and Indian communities enjoy European-type standards of living, while African descendants are affected by poverty and unemployment levels similar to those in the poorest countries in Africa. ∎

PROFILE

ENVIRONMENT

Located in the Indian Ocean, 700 km east of Madagascar, Réunion is a volcanic, mountainous island. It has a tropical climate, heavy rainfall and numerous rivers. These conditions favor the cultivation of sugarcane, the main economic activity. Tourism also contributes to the economy.

SOCIETY

Peoples: Mostly of African descent (63.5 per cent); Indian 28.3 per cent; Europeans 2.2 per cent; Chinese 2.2 per cent.
Religion: Mainly Catholic (94 per cent). Muslim, Hindu and Buddhist minorities. **Languages:** French (official) and Creole.
Main Political Parties: Free-DOM Movement; Communist Party of Réunion; Union for French Democracy; Socialist Party.

THE STATE

Official Name: Département d'Outre-Mer de la Réunion.
Administrative Divisions: 5 Arrondissements.
Capital: Saint Denis 178,000 people (2003).
Other Cities: St Paul 91,600 people; St Pierre 72,000; Le Tampon 63,000; St André 44,800 (2000). **Government:** Gonthier Friederici, Prefect appointed by the French Government in July 2001 (representing French President Jacques Chirac). There are two local councils: the 47-member General Council, and the 45-member Regional Council. The island has 5 representatives and 3 senators in the French parliament. **National Holiday:** 20 December, Abolition of slavery (1848). **Armed Forces:** 4,000 French troops (1995).

Romania / România

Population:	22,227,813
Area:	238,390 km²
Capital:	Bucharest
Currency:	Lei
Language:	Romanian

The origins of Romanians date back to the Dacians or Getae (sold as slaves in Athens in the 4th century BC), after whom the Roman province of Dacia was named. The province was located in the Carpathian mountains and in Transylvania, in the northeastern territory of present-day Romania.

2 In the first century BC, the Dacians established a powerful kingdom, and in alliance with other peoples they fiercely resisted the Romans, who were interested in the region's mineral wealth. Rome finally triumphed over the Dacians in 106 AD, annihilating them or expelling them to the north.

3 The province was first a consulate and then subdivided into Upper Dacia and Lower Dacia. Emperor Marcus Aurelius withdrew from the region by the year 270, but the influence of Roman culture and language still remains.

4 Between the 3rd and the 12th centuries, the region underwent successive invasions by Germanic tribes, Slavs, Avars and others. Bulgarian rule, which lasted over 200 years, established a certain social organization and introduced Greek Orthodox Christianity. In the late 9th century, the Magyars expelled the Bulgarians.

5 Hungary conquered Transylvania during the 11th century, but the Tatar-Mongol invasion of 1241 wiped out all trace of the first inhabitants of this region. The Vlachs from Transylvania reappeared in the 13th century to the south of the Carpathian Mountains, in Walachia and Moldova.

6 The state of Walachia was created in 1290, when a prince from Fagaras and his followers crossed the mountains and established themselves in Cimpulung, moving on later to Curtea de Arges. The emigration southwards can be attributed to the arrival of Germanic peoples and to the consolidation of Hungarian feudal power in Transylvania.

7 The new principality fought for its independence from Hungary until the rule of Mircea the Elder (1386-1418), when the Ottoman Empire became a greater threat. In the wars against Hungary, Walachia allied itself with Bulgaria and Serbia, but both kingdoms were about to be absorbed by the Turks.

8 After defeating the Serbs in Kosovo in 1389, the Ottoman Empire began closing in on Walachia, with intensifying pressure after the fall of Bulgaria in 1393. Walachia became a vassal state of Sultan Mehmed I in 1417, though Prince Mircea maintained his claim to the throne and the Christian religion remained intact.

9 Prince Mircea's death in 1418 was followed by a rapid succession of princes, until the Turks appointed a Romanian prince of their choice to the throne. After the Battle of Mohacs in 1526, the Turks ruled Walachia through an imperial governor.

10 In 1594, the Turkish inhabitants of Walachia were massacred by Prince Michael in alliance with Moldova, and with Transylvania's support he went on to invade Turkish territory. Faced with the collapse of his counter-offensive, the Sultan had no choice but to recognize the sovereignty of Walachia, which subsequently became linked to Hungary.

11 In 1600, Michael conquered Moldova, proclaiming himself regent. Rudolf II recognized the claim, although he later tried to take over Transylvania and Moldova.

12 In the 17th and 18th centuries, Walachia and Moldova fell under Turkish rule again and were administered by the Greeks for certain periods, until Russia occupied the region in 1769. Austria forced Russia to return the principalities to the Sultan in 1774.

13 In 1806, Russia invaded the region, but under the Treaty of Bucharest in 1812, it only retained the southeastern part of Moldova - Bessarabia.

14 Another war broke out between Russia and Turkey in 1828. The following year, the Treaty of Adrianopolis maintained the principalities as tributaries of the Sultan, but under Russian occupation. Russian troops remained in the region, and the princes began to be appointed for life.

15 The local nobility drew up a constitution known as the 'Reglement organique', which was passed in Walachia in 1831 and in Moldova in 1832. After the Sultan's approval in 1834 Russia withdrew.

16 During the European revolutions of 1848, nationalist sentiment in Moldova and Walachia was stimulated by peasant rebellions. These reached a climax in May with the protests at Blaj, which were put down by Turkish and Russian troops, restoring the 'Reglement organique'.

17 Russian troops extended their occupation for three more years. During the Crimean War the three Romanian principalities were occupied alternately by Russian and Austrian troops. The Treaty of Paris in 1856 maintained the ancient statutes of the principalities until it was revised in 1857.

18 The local delegates proposed that the provinces be autonomous, joining together under the name 'Romania'; that a foreign king be elected, with the right to hereditary succession; and that the country be neutral. In August 1858, despite the Sultan's opposition, the Treaty of Paris created a commission to carry out the unification process.

19 In 1859, the principalities elected a single prince, Alexandru Ion Cuza, who was recognized by the major powers and by the Sultan in 1861. The Constitution of 1863 established a bicameral legislative body, granting property holders greater electoral power.

20 When the war between Russia and Turkey resumed in 1877, Russia rejected the alliance with Romania and threatened to invade its territory. Romania authorized the transit of Russian troops through its territory in April and declared war on Turkey in May. Romania contributed to the Russian victory, but it was not admitted to the subsequent peace talks.

21 The 1878 Treaty of Berlin respected Romania's independence, but failed to return Bessarabia to Romania, instead giving it Dobrudja, a small region on the Danube delta. The Government reinforced its loyalty to the Romanian crown.

22 When the Balkan War broke out in 1912, tension from territorial disputes in past wars persisted between Romania and its neighbors. After the first few battles, Bucharest demanded a ratification of its borders in Dobrudja. The St Petersburg Conference of 1913 gave Romania Silistra, much to Bulgaria's displeasure.

23 Romania took advantage of the second Balkan War to shore up its position. The Treaty of Bucharest gave Romania the southern part of Dobrudja. At the beginning of World War I, Romania wavered between taking Bessarabia or Transylvania, finally opting for the latter.

24 In 1916, Romania allied itself with Britain, France, Russia and Italy, declaring war on Austria and Hungary. After the occupation of Bucharest, King Ferdinand and the Romanian Government and army took refuge in Moldova, under the Czar's protection. The defeat of the Central Powers in 1918 made it possible for Romania to incorporate Transylvania, Bessarabia, Bucovina and Banat. That year, the King made voting obligatory for men over the age of 21, and introduced the secret ballot.

25 Social upheaval, and the landowners' fear of having their lands expropriated, led General Averescu (the hero of two wars) to take harsh measures. The general strike of 1920 was put down and the Communist Party was declared illegal in 1924.

26 In the 1928 election, the National Peasant Party (NPP) obtained 349 out of 387 seats. The Government abolished martial law and press censorship, also decentralizing public administration, a measure supported by the ethnic minorities. It also authorized the sale of land, and foreign investment in the country.

27 The council of regency which had been formed upon Ferdinand's death, was dissolved when King Carol assumed the throne in 1930, a succession agreed to by the major political parties. The King took advantage of the emergence of the

Life expectancy
70.5 years
2000-2005

GNI per capita
$1,850
2002

Literacy
98% total adult rate
2000

HIV prevalence rate
0.1% of population 15-49 years old
2001
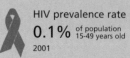

Iron Guard, a fascist Moldovan group, to weaken the traditional parties.

28 In 1938, after a fraudulent plebiscite, Carol passed a new corporative constitution. Seeking closer ties with Germany, he met Hitler in November and upon his return he had 13 officials of the Iron Guard assassinated, along with its leader. Carol founded his own party, the National Renaissance Front (NRF).

29 Carol affirmed that he was being forced by Hitler and obtained French and British assurances of the country's territorial integrity. By the time of Poland's invasion in 1939, Romania had not only renounced the mutual defense treaty which it had signed with Warsaw, but had also detained Polish authorities as they fled across Romanian territory.

30 Between June and September 1940, Romania was forced to turn Bessarabia and Bucovina over to the USSR, Transylvania to Hungary, and Dobrudja to Bulgaria. Because of his disastrous foreign policy, Carol had to abdicate in September, leaving his son Michael on the throne and turning over the Government of the country to General Antonescu. Romania was occupied by German troops, and was proclaimed a 'national legionary state'.

31 Romanian troops cooperated with the abortive German offensive against the USSR, but when the Red Army mounted the counter-offensive, Bucharest abruptly changed sides. In March 1944, the Peasant, Liberal, Social Democratic and Communist Parties created the National Bloc and in August, King Michael ousted Antonescu and declared war on Germany.

32 In September, with most of its territory occupied since late August by Soviet troops, Romania signed an armistice with the Allies. At the Potsdam Conference, the Allies decided to resume relations with Romania, provided its government was 'recognized and democratic'. The USSR granted it immediate recognition while the US and Britain adopted a 'wait-and-see' attitude. The Government arrested, prosecuted and sentenced leaders and members of the Social Democratic and National Peasant parties. In 1947, King Michael was forced to abdicate.

33 In 1948, the Communists and some Social Democrats formed the Romanian Workers' Party (RWP) which joined the Ploughers' Front and the Hungarian People's Union to form the People's Democratic Front (PDF). In the March election that year, the PDF won 405 of the 414 seats of the National Assembly. In April the People's Republic of Romania was proclaimed, and a socialist constitution was adopted. In June, the Government adopted centralized economic planning.

34 Between 1948 and 1949, Bucharest signed friendship and cooperation treaties with the European socialist bloc, and joined the Council for Mutual Economic Assistance. In 1955, Romania joined the Warsaw Pact, but in 1963 it began to drift away from the Soviet fold.

35 In 1951 the First Five Year Plan was started, aimed at socialist industrialization of steel, coal, and oil. In 1952, the new regime started to consolidate under President Groza and Prime Minister Gheorghiu-Dej, head of state from 1961.

36 Gheorghe Maurer was appointed Prime Minister in 1961. He tried to achieve greater economic and political independence, so Romania did not take sides in the Chinese-Soviet dispute. In 1962 the land collectivization policy was ended, and trade with the US, France, and Germany began.

37 In 1965, when Gheorghiu-Dej died, Nicolae Ceausescu was elected First Secretary of the RWP, which changed its name to the Romanian Communist Party (RCP) in June. The Constitution was reformed, and the National Assembly changed the name of the country to the Socialist Republic of Romania. In 1967, Ceausescu was elected President of the State Council.

38 Ceausescu placed some distance between Romania and the USSR. In 1966, he affirmed that his country was continuing its struggle for independence. Romania established diplomatic relations with West Germany and, unlike other members of the Warsaw Pact, it did not break off relations with Israel in 1967, nor did it participate in the Soviet invasion of Czechoslovakia in 1968.

39 In the 1970s and early 1980s, Ceausescu was re-elected several times as president of the country. Economic hardships, accentuated by administrative corruption, led to growing discontent.

40 From 1987, difficult living and labor conditions triggered marches and strikes. These were put down by the security forces. In 1988 and 1989, several government scandals broke out; various cabinet ministers and government authorities were subsequently tried and dismissed.

41 With the beginning of *perestroika* in the USSR and the crisis of the European socialist bloc, Ceausescu became progressively more discredited in world opinion. Towards the end of 1989, confrontations between civilians and the army in Timisoara left many dead or injured; the international press spoke of hundreds of deaths, and the news had strong repercussions within Romania. The Government declared a state of emergency, but a faction within the regime carried out a coup with massive popular support. Accused of 'genocide, corruption and destruction of the economy', Ceausescu and his wife were secretly executed by army soldiers. The National Salvation Front (NSF) assumed control of the government.

42 NSF leaders were called into question and resistance towards the new government increased, leading to violent confrontations in the streets. In the May 1990 elections, the NSF obtained 85 per cent of the vote, but international observers confirmed fraud allegations.

43 In September 1991 Prime Minister Peter Roman and his entire cabinet were forced to resign, under pressure from thousands of miners who marched towards Bucharest to protest against the Government's privatization policy. Demonstrators were heavily repressed during the three-day demonstration and it is estimated that there were at least three deaths and over a hundred people injured.

44 After announcing he would fulfill some of the miners' claims, President Iliescu appointed Theodor Stolojan - former Minister of Finance - as Prime Minister. This appointment was interpreted as an attempt to pacify foreign investors and international financial organizations.

45 In 1991, 77 per cent of the electorate approved the new constitution which turned Romania into a multiparty presidential democracy. In Transylvania, however, the new constitution received scant support.

46 In January 1992, the cooperative farming system created by the Ceausescu regime ceased to exist legally, but it continued to operate de facto.

47 Western countries and international financial organizations continued to voice their discontent with the Government for its alleged sluggishness in implementing economic reforms. Thirty per cent of the land still belonged to the State in 1994. After two years of deliberation, Bucharest passed a law to privatize state enterprises in June 1995.

48 After years of fruitless negotiations, Bucharest and Budapest signed a treaty in

PROFILE

ENVIRONMENT

The country is crossed from north to center by the Carpathian Mountains, the westernmost peaks of which are known as the Transylvanian Alps. The Transylvanian plateau is contained within the arc formed by the Carpathian Mountains. The Moldavian plains extend to the east, while the Walachian plains stretch to the south, crossed by the Danube, which flows into a large delta on the Black Sea. The mountain forests supply raw material for a well-developed timber industry. With its abundant mineral resources (oil, natural gas, coal, iron ore and bauxite), Romania has begun extensive industrial development. Its economy still depends to a great extent on the export of raw materials and agricultural products. It is one of Europe's largest oil producers.

SOCIETY

Peoples: Romanian 89.5 per cent, Hungarian 6.6 per cent, German 0.3 per cent, Ukrainian 0.3 per cent, Turkish, Greek and Croatian. These data do not include the Roma people, who represent between 5 and 10 per cent of the population, but who are usually considered as Romanian in the census.
Religions: Mainly Romanian-Orthodox (86.8 per cent). There are Catholic (5 per cent) and Protestant (3.5 per cent) minorities. **Languages:** Romanian (official language, spoken by the majority); ethnic minorities often speak their own languages, particularly Hungarian and Romany.
Main Political Parties: Social Democratic Party (PSD coalition); Romania Mare Party (xenophobic), Democratic Party; National Liberal Party; Democratic Alliance of Hungarians in Romania.
Main Social Organizations: General Union of Trade Unions

THE STATE

Official Name: România.
Administrative Divisions: 41 Districts and the Municipality of Bucharest.
Capital: Bucharest 1,853,000 people (2003).
Other Cities: Timisoara 338,900 people; Constanza 339,300; Iasi 353,600 (2000). **Government:** Ion Iliescu, President and Head of State since January 2001. Adrian Nastase, Prime Minister and Head of Government since January 2001. Legislature, bicameral: Senate, 143 members; Deputies, 341 members, 13 representing ethnic minorities.
National Holiday: 1 December, Unification Day. (1918). **Armed Forces:** 228,400 (1996). Other: 43,000 Border Guard, Gendarmes, Construction Troops.

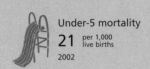

Under-5 mortality
21 per 1,000 live births
2002

Poverty
2.1% of population living on less than $1 per day
2000

Debt service
18.8% exports of goods and services
2001

Maternal mortality
49 per 100,000 live births
2000

September 1996 regarding the 1.6 million Hungarians living in Romania. Hungary had to agree to accept Romania's commitment to 'guarantee the rights of the minority', and give up its demand of 'autonomy' for Transylvanian Hungarians. Although ultranationalist tendencies diminished with the defeat of Iliescu in the November elections (Hungary installed a consulate in Cluj, the capital of Transylvania) problems arose again when the Romanian senate voted against a university education project for the minorities.

[49] The new government of Emil Constantinescu, the President elected in November 1996, announced it would attack corruption and organized crime. Prime Minister Victor Ciorbea implemented an economic and structural adjustment program based on IMF prescriptions: balanced state finance, increased privatizations and decentralization of the administration.

[50] After disagreements between members of the government coalition and faced with growing popular discontent, Ciorbea resigned in March 1998. He was replaced by Radu Vasile, who proposed accelerating the privatization of state enterprises, wiping out corruption and reducing bureaucracy. In the international sphere, sights were set on gaining admission to NATO and the European Union (EU).

[51] The new government coalition failed to achieve economic or political stability. Minister of Finance Daniel Daianu resigned. The party representing the Hungarian minority threatened to withdraw from the government if the university project was not approved. In the end it was agreed to open a multicultural university that would operate in Hungarian and German.

[52] In December 1999, a mining strike and internal disagreements in the coalition caused the Cabinet to collapse. Vasile was forced to resign on 14 December. His place was temporarily filled by Alexandru Athanasiu, and later by Mugur Isarescu.

[53] In January 2000, tens of thousands of liters of cyanide spilled into the Somes River, a tributary of the Tisza and the Danube, killing flora and fauna along hundreds of kilometers of the rivers in the worst water contamination catastrophe in Europe in a decade. The accident occurred at the Aurul gold mine, located near Baia Maresobre. Drinking water supplies in Hungary, Ukraine, Yugoslavia and Bulgaria were affected by the contamination.

[54] Promising to speed up reforms that would help the country enter

IN FOCUS

ENVIRONMENTAL CHALLENGES
Soil erosion and degradation, water and air pollution by solid or gaseous industrial wastes and the contamination of the Danube delta wetlands are the most significant environmental challenges.

Copsa Mica, in the center of Romania, is considered to be one of the areas with the highest levels of industrial pollution in Europe.

WOMEN'S RIGHTS
Women have been able to vote and run for office since 1946. Female suffrage, albeit with some restrictions, had already been introduced in 1929.

From 1995 to the year 2000, only 10 per cent of parliamentary seats have been held by women, while in ministerial and similar posts their representation has grown from nil in 1995 to eight per cent in 2000. Romania is a country of origin and transit for girls and women who are sexually exploited in Turkey, Italy, Greece and other Balkan countries. This phenomenon, already in existence during the 1990s, has been steadily increasing since the year 2000.

CHILDREN
Children and women are among those who are most vulnerable to the problems experienced since the transition. Despite deterioration in the quality of the health services, children's health has improved, as shown by the slight reduction in the mortality rate, which went down to 19 per 1000 live births. However, in the rural areas infant mortality rates continue to be significantly higher than in the cities. In 2003 only 60 per cent of Romanians aged from 16 to 59 had a job and 30 per cent of the population lived in poverty. In the same year, 42,777 boys and girls lived in public or private institutions; 76 per cent of them were aged between 10 and 18. In addition, 43,783 boys and girls lived in protected family environments, such as foster families or extended families. Some of these children had been abandoned by their families, but most of them enter these institutions due to poverty, undernourishment, school desertion, social exclusion, disabilities, HIV/AIDS and unhealthy lifestyles. In 2001 over 4,000 children were living with HIV/AIDS.

The minimum working age is 16, but parental or tutorial consent is needed and physical and psychological fitness must be taken into account, as well as the pre-requisite of job safety and a timetable that allows continuation of the child's education. Up to the year 2003 there are no accurate statistics on infant or juvenile work. Working is frequent among Roma (Gypsy) children of all ages, including begging and informal street jobs.

INDIGENOUS PEOPLES/ ETHNIC MINORITIES
Ethnic minorities are recognized by law. There are 18 political organizations that represent different ethnic groups. Hungarians (1,434,377 according to the 2002 census) have parliamentary representation, while the Roma do not have as much due to internal troubles as to the low level of voting. The Roma are territorially dispersed and have relatively little organization. Originally they were brought to the country as slaves, and they have to face discrimination even today. The National Committee against Discrimination fined two companies that did not allow Roma to enter, and some schools were regarded as discriminatory.

MIGRANTS/REFUGEES
Some 9,200 Romanians, mostly Roma, sought asylum during 2002, including some 1,900 in the United States, 1,600 in the United Kingdom, and 1,700 in Ireland, among other destinations. Romania hosted 75 refugees and asylum seekers in need of protection; 39 cases remain pending.

A new law which came into effect in November 2000 exempts asylum seekers from penalties for illegal entry or residence. Refugee status is granted to applicants who meet the UN Refugee Convention standard.

DEATH PENALTY
The last execution was carried out in 1989, when the death penalty was abolished for all crimes.

the EU, Iliescu easily won the December presidential elections, beating the ultra-nationalistic and xenophobic Corneliu Vadim Tudor, of the Greater Romania Party. Adrian Nastase, also a Social Democrat, was appointed Prime Minister.

[55] In January 2001, nearly 250,000 state buildings and properties, which had been nationalized during the Communist regime, were included in a property restoration list approved by Parliament. Numerous buildings, such as hospitals and schools, were excluded from the list. The property was to be returned to the original owners. The Hungarian minority (mostly Catholic and Calvinist) welcomed the measure because the law entitled them to reclaim several church-related buildings. The Romanian Orthodox Church has been a loyal servant of nationalist state policy.

[56] A debate on the limits on respect for cultural traditions and human rights was set up in October 2003 by the forcible marriage of the under-14-year-old daughter of a Roma Gypsy King, which was annulled by the Government four days afterwards, as a result of the pressures exerted by the EU.

[57] On 18 and 19 October 2003, Romanians voted in a referendum on a new constitution meant to bring their country into line with members of the EU, which Romania hopes to join by 2007. The referendum was declared valid since 54.4 per cent of the almost 18-million electorate had cast their votes. It was estimated that 20 per cent of the voters of the impoverished eastern and northern regions had left the country to look for better living conditions within the EU.

[58] In October, while Transparency International ranked Romania among the three most corrupt countries in Europe, where citizens complained of having to bribe doctors and nurses at hospitals so that their relatives could be operated on, three ministers resigned. The Health Minister was expelled from the university where he taught for plagiarizing medical textbooks; the Minister for European Integration was accused of improper usage of EU funds by her family and a third minister resigned because several of his aides had accepted bribes.

[59] Several railway and mine workers strikes, protesting against the laying off of 20,000 workers made it less certain that the Social Democratic Party (PSD) would win the 2004 elections.

[60] Romania, along with Bulgaria, Slovakia, Slovenia, Lithuania, Latvia and Estonia joined the North Atlantic Treaty Organization (NATO) in March 2004. Romania's strategic location and its navy and air bases on the Black Sea, as well as its support for the US in the war in Iraq, made the country an attractive candidate for NATO membership. ∎

Russia / Rossiya

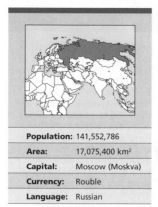

Population:	141,552,786
Area:	17,075,400 km²
Capital:	Moscow (Moskva)
Currency:	Rouble
Language:	Russian

The southern part of present-day Russia was inhabited from ancient times by Sarmatians and Scythians. The Slavs (Indo-Europeans) invaded the northern regions during the first centuries of the Roman Empire. In the 3rd century, the Goths conquered the region situated between the Baltic and Black seas but were later expelled by the Huns in the 4th century. Russia was then invaded by different nomadic peoples from the north who later brought down the Roman Empire.

² In the early 9th century, the Varangians (Vikings from Sweden) established small kingdoms in the region of Lake Ladoga, constituting a commercial and warrior aristocracy that subjugated the local population. The territories under Varangian control were unified into the kingdom of Novgorod under the leadership of Norman chief Rurik.

³ In 882, Oleg 'the Wise' united Novgorod (in the north) and Kiev (in the south) and created the first Russian State, known as the 'Ancient Rus' with Kiev as its capital. In the 9th century, the route between the Baltic and Black seas, known as 'the route of the Varangians and the Greeks', became important for European trade.

⁴ In 944 after a failed incursion into Constantinople, Igor (913-945) signed a commercial treaty with Byzanz and opened the principality to Christian influence.

⁵ Vladimir (980-1015) consolidated the judicial and territorial organization of the Russian State. In 988, he was converted to orthodox Christianity and made it the official religion.

⁶ Svyatopolk, Vladimir's successor, killed three of his brothers in order to consolidate his own power, but Yaroslav, the fourth brother, ousted Svyatopolk and assumed power in Kiev. After his death in 1054, Russia was divided into a series of principalities that were dominated by conflicts and rivalries. Muscovy (the principality of Rostov-Suzdal) was first mentioned in historical chronicles in 1147.

⁷ The 12th and 13th centuries were characterized by a political, economic and cultural decline. Except for Novgorod and Pakov, all the principalities were devastated by Teutons and Mongols. In 1242, Prince Alexander of Novgorod defeated the Teutons in the famous 'battle on ice' on Lake Chudskoye, near the Neva River, winning the title Prince of Nevsky as a result.

⁸ In 1245, Mongol (Tatar) rule over Russia was consolidated. In 1380, Muscovite Prince Dmitry defeated the Mongols in the battle of Kulikov, near the Don river, marking the beginning of the liberation process.

⁹ In 1439, the Russians abandoned the Greek Orthodox Church and established their own church (Russian Orthodox).

¹⁰ In 1480, Ajmat, the last of the Golden Horde's khans, retreated from a confrontation with the troops of Prince Ivan III. This finished the process of unification of Russian lands under Muscovite authority.

¹¹ In 1547, Ivan IV came to the throne. He was known as Ivan 'the Terrible' for his tyrannical behavior. He established serfdom (whereby peasants were bound to the land by debt) murdered or deported members of boyar clans (nobility) and attempted to create a universal empire. On his death, the kingdom fell into anarchy as a result of the struggles over succession.

¹² In 1598, after the death of Ivan's son, Fyodor, the ruling dynasty came to an end. The boyar Boris Godunov was elected as Czar and a period marked by famine and turmoil began, which became known as the 'Time of Troubles' (1605-1613). 'False Dmitri', an impostor supported by Poles, claimed to be Ivan's son and led an uprising against Boris. After he was killed by boyars, a second 'False Dmitri' appeared.

¹³ In 1612, a patriotic uprising expelled the Polish troops who had occupied Moscow. The Zemsky Sobor (parliament) elected boyar Michael Romanov as the new Czar, thus beginning the Romanov dynasty.

¹⁴ Under the Romanovs, Russia became an absolute monarchy, administered by an efficient bureaucracy and an oligarchy (made

PROFILE

ENVIRONMENT
The largest country in the world, Russia is divided into five vast regions: the European region, the Ural area, Siberia, Caucasia and the Central Asian region. The European region is the richest, lying between Russia's western border and the Ural Mountains (the conventional boundary between Europe and Asia); it is a vast plain crossed by the Volga, Don and Dnepr rivers. The Urals, which extend from north to south, have important mineral and oil deposits in their outlying areas. The third region, Siberia, lies between the Urals and the Pacific coast. It is rich in natural resources, but sparsely populated because of its harsh climate. Caucasia is an enormous steppe which extends northward from the mountains of the same name, between the Black and Caspian Seas. Finally, the Central Asian region is a large depression of land made up of deserts, steppes and mountains. Grain, potatoes and sugar beet are grown on the plains; cotton and fruit in Central Asia; tea, grapes and citrus fruit in the subtropical Caucasian and Black Sea regions. The country's vast mineral resources include oil, coal, iron, copper, zinc, lead, bauxite, manganese and tin, found in the Urals, Caucasia and Central Siberia.

SOCIETY
Peoples: Russians, 81.5 per cent; Tatars, 3.8 per cent; Ukrainians, 2.9 per cent; over 100 other nationalities, including Chuvash, Bashkirs, Belarusians, Moldovans, and Chechens (1996).

Religions: Orthodox Christianity is predominant. There are also Muslim, Protestant and Jewish minorities.
Languages: Russian (official); there are almost as many languages as nationalities.
Main Political Parties: Communist Party of the Russian Federation; Unity Interregional Movement; Fatherland-All Russia, a coalition of two parties; Union of Rightist Forces; Liberal Democratic Party, Nationalist conservative; Yabloko ('the Apple'); Russia Our Home, neo-liberal; Congress of Russian Communities and the Movement of Y. Boldurev.
Main Social Organizations: Federation of Independent Labor Unions of Russia (FNPR), with more than 40 million workers; All-Russian Confederation of Labor; Russian Confederation of Labor.

THE STATE
Official Name: Rossiyskaya Federatsiya.
Administrative Divisions: The federation is made up of 26 autonomous republics.
Capital: Moscow (Moskva) 10,469,000 people (2003).
Other Cities: St Petersburg 4,656,900 people; Nizhnij Novgorod 1,351,800; Novosibirsk 1,397,800 (2000).
Government: Parliamentary republic. Vladimir Putin, President since 1999, re-elected in 2004; Mikhail Fradkov, Prime Minister since March 2004. Bicameral Legislature: the Federal Assembly is formed by the State Duma, with 450 members, and the Federation Council, with 178 members.
National Holiday: 12 June, Russia Day (1990).
Armed Forces: 1,270,000. Other: 220,000.

Life expectancy	GNI per capita	Literacy	HIV prevalence rate
66.8 years	**$2,140**	**100%** total adult rate	**0.9%** of population 15-49 years old
2000-2005	2002	2000	2001

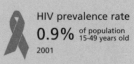

up of nobles, merchants and bishops) which was integrated into the Government structure. Under Czar Alexis, a schism took place in the Russian Orthodox Church when Patriarch Nikon tried to adapt it to the Greek Orthodoxy in 1653. Members of the traditional clergy known as the 'Old Believers' refused to accept the changes and their spokesperson, Archpriest Habacuc, was burnt at the stake.

[15] During the 17th century the economy grew rapidly, as a result of territorial expansion, and the exploitation of Siberia's natural resources. A market also developed for Russia's forest products and semi-manufactured goods, primarily in Britain and Holland.

[16] Under Peter I, who reigned from 1689 to 1725, Russia entered the Modern Age. The Czar attempted to 'Westernize' Russia in his despotic manner. He established an espionage network in his administration, essential for maintaining his strict autocracy. He put down the boyars in Moscow, and had his own son, Alexei, tortured and executed for joining them. In 1703, Peter founded St Petersburg, where he established the imperial capital.

[17] In foreign policy, Russia gained access to the sea after the Great Northern War against Sweden (1700-1721). After winning the war against Persia, Peter extended Russia's southern borders as far as the Caspian Sea. The territorial, economic and commercial expansion which characterized this period made Russia one of the major European powers but also created a mosaic of ethnic and cultural groups which could not easily be assimilated into a single unit.

[18] In 1762, Catherine II 'the Great' came to the throne. She disseminated the principles of the Enlightenment but also signed the Charter of the Nobility which legalized the privileges of the nobles. The Empire's conquests continued, with the annexation of parts of Ukraine, Poland, Lithuania and Crimea.

[19] While the Russian State and nobility grew richer - court expenses amounted to 50 per cent of the state budget - impoverishment of the peasants and serfs increased.

[20] The French Revolution and the fight against absolutism influenced the Russian intelligentsia, which began demanding freedoms and social equality. Emperor Pavel I (1796-1801) reacted with extreme severity and imposed cultural censorship, internal exile and even banned trips to foreign countries.

[21] Alexander I began his reign with the implementation of liberal reforms. In 1812, Napoleon's troops invaded Russia. The 'War for the Motherland' in which peasant fighters were also involved, ended with the triumph of the Russian army commanded by Marshal Kutuzov. This

IN FOCUS

ENVIRONMENTAL CHALLENGES

The country's main rivers are being polluted by the indiscriminate use of toxic agrochemicals and the lack of treatment of waste and sewage waters. Chelyabinsk, a city lying in the Ural Mountains, has high levels of radioactivity, due to leaks in its plutonium plant. Lake Baikal is contaminated by the dumping of industrial waste.

WOMEN'S RIGHTS

Women have been able to vote and stand for office since 1918. From 1995 to 2000, women held between 8 and 10 per cent of total seats in parliament. They occupied no ministerial or equivalent positions in 1995, and 8 per cent in 2000. In the same year, women made up 49 per cent of the labor force. However, between 1990 and 2001 their salaries remained 36 per cent lower than men's. In 2002, more than one million women suffered from some type of domestic violence. Official statistics reported more than 250,000 crimes against women but this type of offense is generally underreported.

For the sex industry, Russian women were trafficked to almost 50 different destinations, such as Western Europe, the US, Canada and other former Soviet republics. Some highly educated and skilled women agreed to be taken abroad to work in the sex industry, but most insisted that they had no idea of the appalling conditions, the slavery, or abuse they would be subjected to.

HIV spread has become an increasing problem. By the end of

2002, a total of 229,000 people had been diagnosed with HIV. Almost a quarter (50,400) of that total was added in 2002 alone, indicating that the epidemic is growing at a frightening rate. Women account for an increasing share of newly diagnosed HIV infections - 33% in 2002, compared to 24% a year earlier. One consequence is a sharp rise in mother-to-child transmission of HIV.

CHILDREN

There is evidence of a considerable rise in substance and drug abuse among young people as well as of rapid growth of HIV/AIDS. Falling funding levels threaten the quality of education. Poverty, neglect and abuse within the home mean that many children end up in state care or on the street. According to official reports, 253,000 parents had abandoned their children in 2001.

In 2000, between 10,000 and 16,000 children were engaged in informal jobs in St. Petersburg. Nearly 6,000 children were taken to temporary detention centers in Moscow during 2003.

There are reports of children being kidnapped or purchased from their parents for sexual abuse, child pornography or organ trafficking. The Government has verified foreign adoptions of Russian children who are later forced to work in the sex industry.

INDIGENOUS PEOPLES/ ETHNIC MINORITIES

Russia is home to more than 100 ethnic groups. Less than eight per cent of the country's population is made up of the peoples living in the Volga River basin and the Urals area - Bashkirs, Kalmyks, Komis, Maris,

Mordovans, Tatars, Udmurts and Chuvash. Of these almost half are Tatars, the second largest nationality in Russia. The traditional religion of the Tatars and Bashkirs is Islam, the Kalmyks practice Buddhism, and the most common religion among the rest of the population is Orthodox Christianity.

The peoples living in the North Caucasus - Abazians, Adygeis, Balkars, Ingushetians, Kabardins, Karachayevs, Ossetians, Cherkessians, Chechens, and the ethnic groups from Dagestan (Avars, Aguls, Dargins, Kumyks, Laks, Lezgins, Nogays, Rutuls, Tabasarans and Tsakhurs) - make up less than three per cent of the Russian population.

The peoples living in Siberia and the far North - Altais, Buryats, Tuvas, Khakass, Shors, Yakuts - and the 30 or so groups in the far North constitute 0.6 per cent of the entire population.

MIGRANTS/REFUGEES

Of the 17,400 refugees and asylum-seekers in the Russian Federation at the end of 2002, 13,800 were registered with the Ministry of the Interior. Eighty per cent of them were refugees from Georgia. That year, 371,000 people remained internally displaced. Meanwhile, 25,300 Russian asylum-seekers filed applications in other countries during 2002, a 30 per cent increase over the previous year.

DEATH PENALTY

Russia is considered abolitionist in practice by Amnesty International. The last known execution was carried out in 1999.

victory transformed Russia into the continent's major power.

[22] As a reaction to absolutism, secret societies were formed that fought for the liberation of the peasantry, the distribution of land and the enacting of a constitution. Nikolai I, 'the policeman of Europe', started his government by brutally repressing the 'Decembrist revolt' that became a symbol for young revolutionaries. Since the Czar strongly believed in the divine right of the monarchy, he was intent on perpetuating the class privileges of the aristocracy and preventing the advance of liberalism.

[23] His foreign policy was mainly focused on the suppression of revolutionary movements that emerged in Poland, Germany and Hungary in 1848 as well as on the division of Turkey which prompted the Crimean War against Britain and France (1853-1856). The war was

badly managed on both sides and revealed the weakness of the Russian administration, army and economy.

[24] Czar Alexander II began a series of reforms (1856-1874): he abolished serfdom which affected 40 million peasants, reformed the judicial system, reduced censorship and accepted autonomy for the University. However, the peasantry continued to suffer from lack of land and poverty, which fomented revolutionary ideas. Several secret societies emerged such as the 'Land and Freedom' or 'People's Will' groups. The latter assassinated Czar Alexander II in 1881 and its main leaders were hanged.

[25] Alexander III maintained autocratic rule in Russia, supported by the church and the political police (*ochrana*), which kept social institutions, from schools to the judicial system, under strict control. His policy was also oriented towards a

radical russification of border areas.

[26] Socialist ideas reached Russia by way of Plekhanov who was in touch with Marx and Engels and founded the first social democratic group. In 1898, the Social Democratic Workers' Party of Russia (SDWPR) was banned but was later reorganized abroad around exiles Plekhanov, Vera Zasulich, Pavel Axelrod and Vladimir Ilich Ulyanov (known as 'Lenin').

[27] In the second Congress held at Brussels and London in 1903, the Party was split into two factions: the 'Mensheviks' who shared the idea of an evolutionary socialism and the 'Bolsheviks', led by Lenin, who proclaimed insurrection and rule by the proletariat.

[28] The war against Japan (1904-1905) led to the First Russian Revolution. On 9 January 1905, the army opened fire on thousands of demonstrators in St Petersburg. The uprising became generalized. There

<table>

Under-5 mortality **21** per 1,000 live births 2002 | Poverty **6.1%** of population living on less than $1 per day 2000 | Debt service **14.5%** exports of goods and services 2001 | Maternal mortality **67** per 100,000 live births 2000

The Chechens: always resisting

LOCATED IN southwestern Russia, the Chechen Republic of Ichkeria (Chechnya) is an area of 15,000 sq km on the eastern flank of the North Caucasus. It borders North Ossetia and Ingushetia to the west, Dagestan to the east, and Georgia to the south. The northern and western regions are lowlands. Agriculture is mainly concentrated in the Terek and Sunzha river valleys. Chechnya and the region are rich in oil and gas.

The million or so inhabitants are predominantly Chechens. Ingush and Russians are the other two main groups in the country. More than 370,000 people live in Grozny, the capital.

CHECHEN PEOPLE
The Chechens were one among the several ethnic groups that made up the Alan state from the 8th century until its destruction by the Mongols in the 13th century. About two hundred years later they descended to the plains, where they fought and traded with Russia and Georgia. Sunni Islam has been the religion since the 18th century.

Chechens call themselves Nokhchi and their language, Chechen, belongs to the Nakh branch of the northeast Caucasian language family. Chechen was written in Arabic script until the 1920s when it was replaced with Russian Cyrillic script with the rise of the Soviet Union; the Latin alphabet was also used for written Chechen. With Soviet dominance, the Cyrillic alphabet replaced the Latin alphabet in 1938, and after the declaration of the Chechen Republic in 1991 the Latin alphabet became standard again.

HISTORY OF RESISTANCE
From the 16th to the 18th century, Caucasia was fought over by Russian Czars, the Ottoman Empire and Persia. It was then that the resistance movement against invaders came into existence under the leadership of Sheikh Mansur (the legendary national hero). Mansur was captured by the Russians in 1791 and died some years later.

In spite of having trading relationships with Russia, Chechnya resisted Czarist attempts at domination. From 1840, Imam Shamil led a rebellion of Caucasians that held off the imperial troops of Nicholas I and Alexander II for over a decade. But eventually, in 1859, the Russian Empire annexed Chechnya. Shamil was captured and later died in exile.

SOVIET PERIOD
After the 1917 Russian Revolution, the Chechens fought in the civil war locally against both the Cossacks - the anti-Communist or White Russians - and the Communists. Once Soviet authority was established, the Chechens joined with other Caucasian peoples to form the Republic of the Mountain Peoples in 1920. The Soviets abolished the Republic in 1924, having separated the Chechen Autonomous Oblast from it in 1922.

Many Chechens were forced onto collective farms in the 1930s and suffered religious persecution. They responded by fighting to protect their way of life. In 1934 the Soviets united the Chechens and Ingush in the Chechen-Ingush Autonomous Oblast which became an autonomous republic in 1936.

During World War II, Josef Stalin accused the Chechen and Ingush of collaboration with the Nazis. They were deported to Central Asia in 1944 and the Republic abolished. It was not restored until 1957 when its former inhabitants were allowed to return from exile.

FIRST CHECHEN-RUSSIAN WAR
The Caucasian region's rich oil deposits lie at the heart of the modern conflict. Russia wants to keep control over the production and transport of oil and gas from the region in the face of Chechen secessionists and Western corporations.

In October 1991, General Dzhokhar Dudayev, who had expelled the Communist Government in Grozny, won a resounding victory in the elections, and Chechnya declared itself independent. However, Moscow refused to recognize it; the Ingush set up their own republic, and Dudayev did not manage to obtain international support.

In December 1994, Boris Yeltsin launched an invasion of Chechnya. Grozny was almost completely destroyed as a result of bombings and the Russian Federation army finally occupied it in February 1995, with thousands dead. Dudayev was forced into hiding, but his rebel forces continued to fight.

In May 1996, Yeltsin and Chechen President Zelimkhan Yandarbiyev agreed to a ceasefire. By this time, some 40,000 people including civilians had been killed and 300,000 Chechens had fled. Later, Chechnya's autonomy was recognized by the Russian Federation, but it was not allowed to secede. While some Chechens wanted to support the settlement, the rebels continued the fight for full independence. In August the Chechens launched a major offensive, defeating the Russian forces to retake Grozny. By December, the humiliated Russian troops had been withdrawn.

Aslan Maskhadov won Chechnya's elections of January 1997. In May, a peace treaty was signed along the lines of the 1996 agreement. Maskhadov lost control to more radical rebels and anarchy followed.

The ending of the first war allowed the Russians to repair and reopen the Chechen section of the oil pipeline from Baku to Novorossiysk. This pipeline is vital to Russia, for not only does the Russian 'Transneft' monopoly earn transit fees of up to $300 million annually from it, its successful operation will determine routes of future oil and gas pipelines. The pipeline was reopened in October 1997.

SECOND WAR
In August 1999, Vladimir Putin became Russia's Prime Minister. In that period, Islamic secessionist guerrillas entered Chechnya from Dagestan, occupying some villages and declaring the region an Islamic area. Russian forces took back the villages, but Chechen fighters joined the struggle for an Islamic state. A series of bomb attacks in Moscow was blamed on Chechen Islamic terrorists by Putin and used as the pretext for Moscow's new assault on Grozny. Rebel leader Shamil Basayev denied responsibility for the attacks.

Putin's elevation to the presidency at the end of 1999 strengthened Russia's intention to keep Chechnya in the Federation. The bitter fighting between the Russian army and the 2,000 Chechen rebels continued until early February 2000, by which time Grozny was in ruins, but in Russian control. Around half the surviving rebels fled to the mountains of southern Chechnya where they continued to fight.

The capital was transferred to Gudermes. Captured Chechens were sent to the detention centers in Chernokosovo, in northern Chechnya, and Mozdok, in Ingushetia. According to various human rights organizations, they were

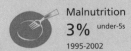
Malnutrition
3% under-5s
1995-2002

Water source
99% of population using improved drinking water sources
2000

Doctors
423 per 100,000 people
1990-2002

tortured. In May 2000, Moscow appointed Akhmad Kadyrov to replace Maskhadov.

The conflict continued through 2001 amid allegations of human-rights abuses by Russian troops. After the 11 September attacks on the US, Putin re-framed his war in Chechnya as an 'anti-terrorist operation' against Islamic extremists linked to al-Qaeda. In this way, he gained the backing of some Western countries that had previously ignored or been against the war.

In October 2002, a band of 50 Chechen guerrillas took 800 civilians hostage at the Duvrovka Theater in Moscow, threatening to kill them if the Russian army did not withdraw from Chechnya. Russian special forces stormed the theater, after filling it with a disabling gas which killed more than 100 Russian theater-goers. All the Chechens were killed, and some 700 hostages were released.

After this crisis, Putin announced a referendum for May 2003 on a new constitution that would give Chechnya the status of a republic within the Russian Federation. The majority of Chechens voted in favor. The rebels rejected the decision and vowed to continue the struggle for full independence.

Control over oil continued to fuel conflict in the region. While oil production was badly disrupted in the wars, US oil giants such as Exxon have been busily prospecting and claiming new oil fields. The EU is just as keen to get its hands on Caucasian oil and there is substantial European investment. With these predators around, Russia is unlikely to loosen its grip on Chechnya or its neighbors. ∎

were strikes and rebellions such as that by sailors from the battleship Potemkin in Odessa and the revolt in the Kronstadt garrison.

29   Nicholas II promised to enact a new Constitution and convene a national Parliament (*Duma*). The Duma's political and social demands were rejected by the Czar who dissolved it and put down the revolution.

30   In 1907, the second Duma was elected, with the participation of the SDWPR. The main political issue continued to be land. Prime Minister Stolipin promoted agrarian reform, in order to create a class of land-owning peasants (*kulaks*). However, he was unsuccessful and was assassinated. The second Duma was also dissolved. An electoral reform guaranteed that the Duma committees which followed also had a conservative majority.

31   Russia's entry into World War I precipitated a crisis within the regime. The losses brought about by war, and the lack of food, simply deepened popular discontent and ended in the February 1917 revolution. Soldiers joined the revolution and the first Workers' and Soldiers' Council (Soviet) was created in St Petersburg.

32   Nicholas II abdicated and the Duma committee established a new Provisional Government, while local soviets multiplied. Lenin returned to Russia in a sealed railway car with the help of the German Government. Once in Russia he launched his April Thesis ('All power to the soviets'), proclaiming the constitution of a socialist republic of soviets, the nationalization of the banking system and the abolition of private ownership. Soon after, the Bolsheviks' influence within the soviets began to grow, and a power split emerged between the councils and Alexander Kerensky's Provisional Government.

33   The government decision to continue the war together with the difficulties suffered by the population made the Provisional Government lose credibility. The Bolsheviks exhorted the people to 'turn the world war into a civil war'. On 25 October, Lenin led the uprising which brought down the Government, and the first socialist republic was established. In early 1918, the Bolsheviks dissolved the Constituent Assembly, in which the revolutionary socialists held a majority.

34   The Soviet Government (Council of People's Commissars) approved a peace 'without annexation or indemnities', the abolition of private ownership of land (150 million hectares were expropriated without indemnities), which was turned over to the peasantry, and the nationalization of the banking system. Other measures were approved, including the control of factories by their workers, the

creation of a militia and of revolutionary tribunals, the abolition of class-based privileges and inheritance rights, the separation of the Church and the State and equal rights for men and women.

35   In July 1919, the Russian Soviet Federal Socialist Republic (RSFSR) was created with the adoption of a Constitution based on the system of soviets and the dictatorship of the proletariat. That same month, Czar Nicholas II and his family were executed.

36   Immediately afterward, anti-Bolshevik groups ('White Russians') led by former Czarist generals attempted to restore the previous regime with the support of Germany, France and Britain, which prompted the outbreak of civil war (1918-1920). The Red Army under the command of Leon Trotsky, the People's Commissar for Defense, defeated the foreign intervention force and brought the war to an end.

37   During this period, the Soviet Government imposed the policy of 'war communism' which resulted in the nationalization of the means of production and the centralization of economic planning. The failure of this policy, which brought about a fall in industrial and agricultural production and threatened the country with economic collapse, prompted the 10th Party Congress of the Russian Communist Party to approve the New Economic Policy (NEP). This consisted of a return to the laws of a market system ('state capitalism'); freedom was granted to determine salaries, constitute small private companies and develop domestic trade and foreign investment. The State retained control over foreign trade, heavy industry and infrastructure (state property). The Communist Party dictatorship was strengthened with the prohibition of all opposition within the Party in 1921 and the creation of the *Tcheka* (Soviet secret police).

38   In April 1922, Joseph Stalin became secretary general of the Party. After Lenin's death in 1924, Trotsky and Stalin vied for power; Stalin effectively became the ruler. He abandoned the NEP and re-established the system of centralized planning (five-year plans) and forcibly imposed the collectivization of agriculture by means of the system of *kolkhoses* and *sovkhoses* (collective farms).

39   In December 1922, the Union of Soviet Socialist Republics (USSR) was founded, comprising Russia, Ukraine, Belarus and the Transcaucasia Federation (Azerbaijan, Armenia and Georgia). Stalin ruled as absolute dictator and eliminated all opposition. Trotsky was expelled from the USSR and took refuge in Mexico where he was murdered in 1940. It is estimated that during the purges of 1935-1938 alone, nearly ten million

people died. The victims of the different waves of purges totaled at least 20 million.

40   In 1939, a secret agreement with Germany (the Molotov-Ribbentrop Pact), allowed the USSR to occupy part of Poland, as well as Romania, Estonia, Latvia and Lithuania. In 1941, Hitler launched a large-scale attack against Moscow, sending in thousands of troops, as well as German air power. At a cost of between 25 and 30 million lives, the Red Army was able to repel the German troops and finally took Berlin in May 1945.

41   In 1945, at the Yalta conference, the Western powers and the USSR 'carved up' their respective areas of influence in Europe. In those countries occupied by the Red Army (Bulgaria, Hungary, Romania, Czechoslovakia, Poland and East Germany), the Communists took power and proclaimed first 'people's republics', then socialist republics, following the model of the Communist Party of the Soviet Union (CPSU).

42   In 1956, at the 20th Party Congress of the CPSU, Nikita Krushchev began a de-Stalinization process (denouncing the Stalinist personality cult and dogmatism), which came to an abrupt end when Leonid Brezhnev ousted Krushchev in October 1964.

43   The strategy of the Cold War devised by the US in the post-war period fuelled the arms race. The Warsaw Pact between the USSR and its Eastern European allies was created in 1955. The East-West confrontation eventually included nuclear weapons and the control of outer space, where the US and the USSR actively pursued their own space programs in the 1960s and 1970s, with neither one actually taking a lead.

44   In December 1979, the USSR embarked on the war in Afghanistan. It was the first time since World War II that the Soviet army had taken part in a conflict outside Eastern Europe. The military action turned into a disaster for the invaders: the invasion was condemned by 104 votes in the UN General Assembly; 55 countries boycotted the Moscow Olympic Games; 13,300 Soviet soldiers died in Afghanistan and the USSR did not manage to win the war.

45   In 1985, Mikhail Gorbachev became Secretary-General of the CPSU. He initiated a period of drastic changes based on the restructuring of the economy (*perestroika*) and increased transparency in cultural and political affairs (*glasnost*). His reform program included opening up the country to a free-market economy and to foreign capital, internal democratization of the Party and constitutional reform to allow for a multi-party system. In

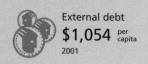

External debt
$1,054 per capita
2001

Imports (millions)
$78,025 goods and services
2002

Exports (millions)
$108,763 goods and services
2002

the area of foreign policy, he withdrew Soviet troops from Afghanistan, improved relations with China, signed arms control accords with the US and in 1990 co-operated with Washington in driving Iraq - its former ally - out of Kuwait during the first Gulf War.

[46] In April 1986, there was a serious accident at the Chernobyl nuclear power plant in Ukraine. Some 135,000 people were evacuated and by 1993 7,000 people had died (see Ukraine).

[47] In June 1991, Boris Yeltsin was elected President. After a failed coup, in August, the CPSU was dissolved after 70 years in power. The changes within the USSR unleashed similar processes in Eastern Europe.

[48] In 1991, Deputy Prime Minister Yegor Gaidar continued the rapid liberalization of the economy ('shock therapy') with the support of the US and international financial institutions. The effects were devastating for ordinary people: between 1990 and 1999 the number of people living on less than $2 a day more than tripled.

[49] On 8 December, Yeltsin and the rulers of Belarus and Ukraine laid the USSR to rest, proclaiming the Commonwealth of Independent States (CIS) to take its place. Russia assumed the formal representation of the former USSR in foreign affairs. Latvia, Estonia and Lithuania withdrew and were recognized as separate countries by the UN.

[50] President Yeltsin declared that the US was no longer a 'strategic rival', and continued the reform of the economy that Gorbachev had begun, including the liberalization of prices, and the privatization of industry, agriculture and trade.

[51] In March 1993, the Parliament tried unsuccessfully to limit Yeltsin's powers. Following further disagreements, Yeltsin dissolved Parliament on 21 September. Communists and nationalists staged violent demonstrations in Moscow. With US blessing, Yeltsin put down the revolt: tanks surrounded the Russian parliament building which was bombed and taken by force, causing the deaths of 138 people.

[52] A few days later, Yeltsin called for new elections and organized a referendum to increase his own powers. The December elections marked the defeat of those sectors faithful to Yeltsin, but 60 per cent of the voters approved the constitutional reform which granted him greater powers.

[53] Fearful of defeat in the July 1996 presidential elections, Yeltsin tried to modify his policies, stopping the privatizations and nominating Yevgeny Primakov - a diplomat from the Soviet era who was an ally of Gorbachev - as foreign minister. In the electoral campaign all the opposition candidates from Gorbachev to the Communists, criticized the unlimited financial speculation, corruption and 'clannishness' of Yeltsin and his allies. In the second round of the July elections, Yeltsin took 53.8 per cent of the vote through an unexpected alliance with Alexandr Lebed, an opposition candidate who had received 11 million votes.

[54] Lebed was appointed as Security Council Secretary and immediately started negotiations to end the war in Chechnya which had caused the death of 80,000 people.

[55] Yeltsin returned in March 1997, following a long absence. He reformed his cabinet and launched a far-reaching plan to cut back State spending and privatizations. The living conditions of the population continued to worsen. The chaotic change to a market economy damaged the production mechanisms, dismantled the social protection systems, and fed the rise of the mafias. In that year 73 per cent of the banking sector was under mafia control, and one of their most lucrative lines was the trafficking of nuclear material.

[56] In September 1998, Yevgeny Primakov was appointed Minister of Foreign Affairs. Primakov, an economist, refinanced debts with international organizations, without promising concrete changes. Fiscal controls were reinstated and the Government began to intervene in the economy. In the international field, Primakov introduced a policy less dependent on Washington and stood up to the US and Britain after their attacks against Iraq in December 1998.

[57] Primakov's popularity, which outshone Yeltsin's, convinced the President that a change in the administration was needed. In May 1999, during the bombing of Yugoslavia, he decided to replace Primakov with Sergei Stepashin. In August, Stepashin was replaced by Vladimir Putin, a former member of the State Security Committee (KGB) during the Soviet period.

[58] Between 1992-2000, the Russian population had fallen by 2.8 million. In 2001 it fell by a further 700,000. Vladimir Zhirinovsky, a far right leader who had in the past proposed stimulating population growth through polygamy - 'allowing men to have up to four women each' - called for a halt to the 'reduction in population' and for abortion to be made illegal.

[59] According to official statistics, almost one in every three Russians was living in poverty, the average pension had fallen below basic survival levels and more than 60 per cent of pensioners were at risk. Minister of Labor and Social Development, Alexander Pochinok, admitted in July 2001 that civil servants were among those with the lowest salaries, with many of them unable to cover their families' basic needs. An Amnesty International Report published in 2002 revealed that 800 million Russians were living in poverty and that the income gap also had a geographical dimension: the income of a Muscovite was 17 times higher than that of a resident of Ingushetia. The same report stated that economic and business activity was still being developed with little regard for the law, transparency and honesty.

[60] In December 2001, the Duma passed the first non-deficit budget since the demise of the Soviet Union. However, the fall in gas and oil prices after the September 2001 terrorist attacks in the US forced the Ministry of Finance to review its estimates, since the price of oil had fallen since then. Russia had become the second-largest oil exporter in the world, after Saudi Arabia.

[61] In January 2002, the TV station TV-6, the last national independent station, was forced to shut down at the request of a minor stockholder. The Supreme Court of Moscow refused an appeal. The station's largest stockholder was Boris Berezovsky, one of Russia's new oligarchs and a critic of Putin. Journalists and opposition politicians claimed it was another attempt by the President to gain control of the country's independent media.

[62] With parliamentary approval in July, and for the first time since the 1917 Revolution, the sale of farmlands was allowed in the country, as long as the purchasers were Russian.

[63] In March 2003, Russia opposed the intervention in Iraq led by the US and supported by the UK and other allies. According to Russian Foreign Minister Igor Ivanov, intervention in Iraq without UN approval would weaken the anti-terrorist coalition formed after the 11 September 2001 attacks in the US.

[64] During the first six months of the year, 12,700 Russian citizens requested asylum at foreign embassies.

[65] In March 2004, Putin was re-elected President with over 70 per cent of the vote. He defined economic growth and a reduction of at least 12 per cent in poverty levels as his Government's goals. He also proposed to fight the 'drug mafia' which poses a serious problem to the country. According to unofficial figures, there were about five million drug addicts in Russia. In the area of foreign policy, he insisted on the need to withdraw coalition troops from Iraq. The Deputy Minister of Foreign Affairs identified Russia and the US as the two countries with special responsibility for international security, implying the need for co-operation between the two countries in the fight against terrorism.

[66] That month, terrorist attacks intensified within Russia. One of the attacks was in Uzbekistan and another on a Moscow subway train, killing 40 people.

[67] Between January and March 2004, there were 43 disappearances in Chechnya, including that of human rights activist Aslan Davletukaev. He was beaten and kidnapped by 50 Russian soldiers and his body was found on the side of a road on 16 January. Gangs of Russian soldiers and men loyal to Chechen President Kadyrov loot and rape after curfew every night in Grozny.

[68] The Foreign Ministry called on all Russian workers in Iraq to leave the country for security reasons. Nearly 500 people were evacuated in April. However, the Russian Embassy in Baghdad did not reduce its personnel, believing they were secure.

[69] Today, while ordinary Russians grow poorer, Moscow has more billionaires than any other city in the world, mainly as a result of the smash and grab of public wealth that took place in the Yeltsin years of rapid privatization.

[70] In September, an armed group held hostage for more than 48 hours some 1,000 students, parents and teachers who were taking part of the first day of school celebrations at a school in Beslan, southern Russia. The kidnappers demanded the freedom of militants jailed in the neighboring community of Ingushetia - located between Chechnya to the south, North Ossetia to the west and bordering with Georgia - and the withdrawal of Russian troops from Chechnya.

[71] More than 394 people, including 156 children, died when Russian special forces stormed into the school. Putin, who decreed two days of national mourning over the tragedy, declared: 'We have not reacted appropriately, we have shown weakness, and the weak lose'. The EU requested explanations on the behavior of the special forces dealing with civilians and 'rebels', causing a furious reply from Moscow which, among other things, stated that they were 'terrorists'.

[70] President Putin claimed that Russia was 'in a state of war' and announced reforms that entrenched his own power, including the appointment (rather than election) of regional governors.

[71] In October Putin announced his intention to ratify the Kyoto protocol on reducing greenhouse gas emissions, leaving the US internationally isolated on the issue. ∎

Rwanda / Rwanda

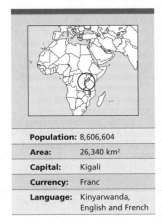

Population:	8,606,604
Area:	26,340 km²
Capital:	Kigali
Currency:	Franc
Language:	Kinyarwanda, English and French

U ntil the 14th century, the only human beings to occupy the territory of what is now Rwanda were the Twa (or Batwa) Pygmies. The Twa lived as hunter-gatherers and potters and were subjugated by Bantu ethnic groups from Central Africa and the Watutsi (or 'Tutsi') from Ethiopia, who migrated to Rwanda, Burundi, Tanzania, Zaire and Uganda in several waves over the course of two centuries.

2   Before the German occupation of Rwanda, Burundi and Tanzania in 1897, mixed marriages between the Bantu and Watutsi led to integration between these groups.

3   Academic studies of the Kinyarwanda language - the only language spoken by 80 per cent of people in present-day Rwanda - in which the word *Tutsi* originally meant 'cattle-raiser' and the word *Hutu* 'a subordinate', as well as studies of the coexistence of present-day myths and cults among all Rwandans (with the exception of the Twas) conclude that the pre-colonial society of their ancestors had effective mechanisms of social cohesion and mobility.

4   This oral culture - rich in poetry, rhetoric, songs and dances - lasted in its original form until the mid-1920s. In 1916, Belgium occupied the region

encompassing Rwanda and Burundi and seven years later it took official control of these territories by mandate of the League of Nations.

5   Until the 1920s, Europeans used Rwandan territory - which had small gold deposits - as a transit zone for precious stones, metals and ivory that were extracted in neighboring regions. For this purpose, they used slave labor and classified people based on their height and skin color, according to an ethnocentric scale, ignoring the idiosyncratic native system.

6   Under this system, Rwanda was ruled and administered through participation in the main productive sectors: agriculture and livestock farming. The shortage of pasture lands (by then Rwanda already had a high population density) meant they were assigned temporarily to individuals who were in permanent competition on the

basis of their productive output. So, the 'Tutsi' status, which meant that the person had a reputation for being a productive worker, was granted or withdrawn by village courts (*gacacas*) that operated on a weekly basis.

7   The Tutsis won the right to create armies in order to expand their territories. Kigeri Rwabugiri

was the king to achieve the greatest power between 1860 and 1895.

8   In the mid-1920s, persistent threats to the Tutsis who had been invested with a degree of authority in trading posts by the Belgians (they were Bantus, chosen because of their greater height) led the settlers to

LAND USE

2000

IRRIGATED AREA: 0.4% of arable land

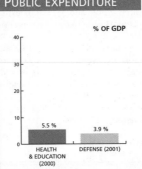

- ARABLE LAND: 36.5%
- CROPLANDS: 10.1%
- OTHER USE: 53.4%

PUBLIC EXPENDITURE

% OF GDP

5.5 %	3.9 %
HEALTH & EDUCATION (2000)	DEFENSE (2001)

Life expectancy
39.3 years
2000-2005

GNI per capita
$230
2002

Literacy
67% total adult rate
2000

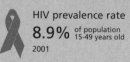

HIV prevalence rate
8.9% of population 15-49 years old
2001

establish a tutelary monarchy and put an end to the local system of administration. Belgium also sent missionaries to educate the Rwandan people (who were first redistributed geographically and banned from entering the jungle) through religious instruction and servile labor in coffee plantations.

9   Together with the clergy, this new Tutsi elite (15 per cent of the population) was eager to inculcate a distorted version of the history of Rwanda among the inhabitants of the Belgian protectorate of Rwanda-Urundi. In this way, the first written history of Rwanda laid the foundations for the segregation of the Hutus and Twas.

10   From 1930, the Hutus and Twas were identified at birth and deprived of all rights except for access to primary schools and Catholic churches. Likewise, until 1961, Hutus were only authorized to study and pursue an ecclesiastical career in which they came to represent 30 per cent of members.

11   Also from that year, the ratio of Hutus to Tutsis among priests and nuns was inverted (80 per cent Hutus to 20 per cent Tutsis). This change within the Rwandan Catholic Church - which had the largest congregation on the African continent until the late 20th century - paralleled political events that led to the replacement of the Tutsi

monarchy by a racist Hutu dictatorship.

12   During the 1950s, in line with a plan for democratization and the subsequent withdrawal of the European authorities, the UN urged Belgium to increase the participation of Hutus in public life.

13   By 1959, the Belgians had replaced with Hutus half of Tutsi high-level officials, who had enjoyed uninterrupted participation in the trafficking of diamonds to the metropolis. After gaining access to the diamond market, the Hutus were able to obtain arms.

14   In the same year, the Hutus founded the Party of the Hutu Emancipation Movement (Parmehutu) and the monarchic Tutsis created the National Rwandese Union (UNAR), amidst violent confrontations.

15   In early 1960, two years before the proclamation of the Republic of Rwanda and its separation from Burundi, the UN supervised elections in which the Hutu-dominated party won a large majority.

16   Between 1961 and 1973, the Parmehutu killed 20,000 Tutsis and forced 300,000 to flee to Burundi, Uganda, Tanzania and what was then Zaire. The remaining Tutsis had their lands confiscated and were excluded from all state institutions, as well as being demonized for allegedly collaborating in ten invasions

carried out by exiled Tutsi groups belonging to the UNAR during that period.

17   In 1973, a coup was plotted by factions of the Parmehutu that disagreed with President Gregoire Kayibanda's foreign policy and unequal distribution of privileges. On 5 July that year, Kayibanda was ousted by his Minister of Defense, Colonel Juvenal Habyarimana.

18   Some days later, Habyarimana dissolved the Parmehutu and ordered the execution of 50 members of Kayibanda's Government. In 1975, the new President of Rwanda officially created a one-party state with himself at the head of the National Revolutionary Movement for Development (MRND).

19   From that date, all Rwandans were compulsorily enrolled in the MRND. In this way, and through massive propaganda campaigns, Habyarimana strictly controlled and manipulated the circulation of people and property, while the Tutsis were subjected to a covert segregation campaign that induced 300,000 of them to go into exile.

20   In 1978, the one-party Constitution was ratified in a referendum and Habyarimana was elected President. Five years after taking power, Habyarimana had an army of 7,000 troops, 1,300 elite squads, and a personal guard of 1,000 men.

21   By the late 1980s, the sudden fall in coffee prices, which represented 75 per cent of Rwanda's exports, brought about a socio-economic collapse as well as a wave of denunciations by journalists, claiming the existence of nepotism and abuse of power, which Habyarimana did not manage to silence.

22   In 1988, Habyarimana was re-elected and women won 15 per cent of seats in the Chamber of Deputies.

23   In 1989, under US pressure when spokespeople for the 600,000 Tutsi refugees made public denunciations and threats, Habyarimana initiated negotiations for the return of exiles.

24   In October 1990, 7,000 Rwandan Patriotic Front (FPR) soldiers trained in Uganda (their country of asylum) invaded Rwanda. This invasion, which failed to reach the capital (Kigali) was led by Paul Kagame, a Rwandan born in 1957, who had been head of Ugandan army intelligence since 1986.

25   President Habyarimana repelled the Tutsi offensive thanks to the intervention of troops from Belgium (traditionally linked to the Tutsis), France (a beneficiary of the Hutu hegemony) and Zaire, which had a Hutu President at that time, and also through the diplomatic intervention of Belgian Prime Minister, Wilfried Martens.

Rwanda - 1994: The West's genocidal negligence

ON 7 APRIL, 1994, Rwandan official radio called for the annihilation of all Tutsis - 'the nation's enemies', as they had been called since Rwandan independence - and of all those who were unwilling to kill them. The Army and the militias, together with Hutu and Twa civilians, murdered more than 10,000 people a day, until 15 July 1994, when Paul Kagame's Tutsi troops took the capital city (Kigali). Abandoned to their fate by the Catholic and Anglican churches, as well as by the UN, between 800,000 and one million Rwandans died in that period, 90 per cent of them Tutsi, under horrendous circumstances. Only those who took refuge in the 250 Rwandan mosques managed to survive.

Three months before the genocide was launched, Canadian general Romeo

Dallaire, leading the Belgian, French and US blue helmet forces present in Rwanda on a UN peace mission, personally informed Kofi Annan, the UN Secretary General, that lists of names were circulating in Rwanda in order to implement the murder of 1,000 Tutsis every 20 minutes. Dallaire's report and his request for reinforcements obtained no response from the UN. On the contrary, the organization ordered the withdrawal of all its troops in Rwanda, just hours after the assassination of President Juvenal Habyarimana when his plane was shot down on 6 April, 1994, in an incident that was never fully explained and that triggered the massacres.

The International Criminal Tribunal for Rwanda - created in 1995 by the UN,

after the organization apologized for not having intervened during the genocide in 1994 - and the Rwandan courts, which in 1996 had only 81 judges, had only ruled on 21 cases by 2004. This leads to the belief that the identification and trial of those who orchestrated the genocide will take several decades.

The Red Cross estimated that half of all Rwandan homes in 2004 were headed by children under 15, and that one fourth of those homes were headed by widows. ■

Under-5 mortality
183 per 1,000 live births
2002

Poverty
35.7% of population living on less than $1 per day
1983/85

Debt service
11.4% exports of goods and services
2001

Maternal mortality
1,400 per 100,000 live births
2000

Although Belgium and Zaire withdrew their troops the following month, the French troops remained in Rwandan territory.

26 In June 1991, the President signed a new Constitution which provided for a multi-party system, established the separation of state powers and limited presidents to two terms in office.

27 In August 1992, in view of the systematic violation of the Constitution, and repeated armed confrontations and insistent attempts by Tutsi refugees to return to their country, the UN (represented by Belgium, France and the US) negotiated a ceasefire and called for peace talks to be held in early 1993 in Arusha (Tanzania).

28 In February 1993, in spite of the presence of UN officials in Rwanda, the FPR managed to gain control of most of the country.

29 On 6 April 1994, Habyarimana and the President of Burundi (also a Hutu) died when the plane carrying them was attacked. A few hours later, the UN troops - who had suffered ten casualties - abandoned Rwanda together with 600 French citizens resident in the capital.

30 The death of President Habyarimana triggered a genocide against the Tutsis, as well as moderate Hutus and Twas, which cost the lives of between 800,000 and 1.5 million people, 90 per cent of whom were Tutsis, within a period of 100 days (see box).

31 In early July, the FPR army seized control of Kigali and the UN sent in troops again to guarantee the establishment of a government of national unity. That same month, Major General Kagame became both Vice-President and Minister of Defense while Pasteur Bizimungu (Hutu) was appointed President.

32 Between 1994 and 1996, French soldiers and Hutu militias oversaw the transfer of two million Rwandan Hutus to the eastern territories of what was then Zaire, from where the Hutu leadership planned to launch an offensive on Rwanda and unleashed a genocide of Zairean Tutsis.

33 In November 1995, the UN described the 1994 killings in Rwanda as 'genocide' and in 1996 an International Criminal Tribunal for Rwanda (ICTR) was established which started proceedings against military officers, clergy, political leaders and directors of the state-run radio station. Until 2004, the ICTR had only delivered 21 verdicts. In

IN FOCUS

ENVIRONMENTAL CHALLENGES
Excessive grazing in lowlands has caused erosion and a considerable loss of natural vegetation. Ninety per cent of the energy consumed by Rwandans comes from natural firewood resources, leading to deforestation.

WOMEN'S RIGHTS
Women have been able to vote and stand for office since 1961. At the end of 2003, they held 48 per cent of the parliamentary seats. In addition, 9 of the 32 members of the cabinet of ministers were women.

Almost 20 per cent of women between 15 and 24 years old could not write or read, compared to an illiteracy rate of 14 per cent for men of the same age group.

More than 90 per cent of pregnant women receive some kind of prenatal care but only 31 per cent of births are attended by skilled health staff*. The fertility rate is 5.8 born children per woman*.

Women continue to face social discrimination. Traditionally, they have played a fundamental role in subsistence activities in rural areas and since the 1994 genocide have had to assume greater responsibilities as heads of household.

CHILDREN
Rwanda is the most densely populated country in Africa and has few natural resources and minimal industry. The 1994 genocide caused the collapse of Rwanda's fragile economy, severely impoverishing the population, particularly women, and eroding the country's human resource base. The HIV/AIDS has had a devastating impact on life expectancy which plunged from 50 years in 1990 to just 39 years in 2002.

In 2001, more than 65,000 children under 14 were living with HIV/AIDS and some 264,000 had been orphaned by AIDS.

In 2000, 37 per cent of children between the ages of 5 and 14 worked. Many children had to become heads of household and some engaged in prostitution or domestic service as a solution. NGOs reported that more than 2,100 children were engaged in prostitution in different cities and that, although close estimates are lacking, there are thousands of street children.

INDIGENOUS PEOPLES/ ETHNIC MINORITIES
The Hutu are the largest ethnic group, while the number of Tutsis can not be accurately estimated since they have intermarried for generations. The 1994 mass killings and migrations affected the ethnic composition of the population. The Twa (or Batwa), descendants of the Pygmies, number approximately 23,000. The Twa demand access to land, housing and education, as well as the eradication of discrimination against them. There have been bloody conflicts between Hutus and Tutsis since 1962, resulting in hundreds of thousands of deaths. In 1994, a genocide of Tutsis was carried out under the direction of the dominant Hutus.

MIGRANTS/REFUGEES
The Government has intimidated refugees who refused to abandon the country voluntarily. More than 80,000 Rwandans remain outside Rwanda. According to the UN High Commissioner for Refugees (UNHCR), 8,000 Rwandans voluntarily returned to their country from DR Congo and another 2,000 were repatriated from Tanzania. An agreement was signed to organize a network for the return of Rwandan refugees from countries such as Zambia, Uganda, DR Congo, Republic of the Congo, Malawi, Namibia, Zimbabwe and Mozambique. More than 400 former Hutu fighters were repatriated. Rwanda collaborates with the UNHCR and provides temporary protection to approximately 33,000 people, mostly Congolese refugees who fled their country in 1996.

DEATH PENALTY
The death penalty is still applied, in some cases even for ordinary crimes.

*Latest data available in *The State of the World's Children* and *Childinfo* database, UNICEF, 2004.

1996, Rwanda's judicial system comprised only 81 judges and some 150 courts.

34 From July 1994, skirmishes between the Rwandan army and Hutu militias caused hundreds of deaths per year. Amnesty International denounced the participation of children in the fighting.

35 In 1998, having sent troops to DR Congo the previous year - as did Uganda - to overthrow President Mobutu, an ally of the Rwandan Hutu, Kagame ordered the occupation of half of its territory. Laurent Kabila, who had succeeded Mobutu, had not managed to neutralize the Democratic Liberation Forces (FDLR) of Rwandan Hutu refugees as Kagame had expected.

36 In April 2000, President Bizimungu resigned while Prime Minister Pierre Rwigema (a moderate Hutu) was replaced by Bernard Makuza (another moderate Hutu).

37 That same month, Paul Kagame was elected President of the National Transitory Assembly.

38 In 2000, the UN, which had apologized to Rwanda and Belgium in 1999 for its lack of action during the genocide, blamed Kagame for the attack that killed Habyarimana in 1994.

39 In 2001, Kabila was assassinated while Rwandan troops controlled most of the territory of DR Congo. Under a peace treaty signed in December 2002, Kagame agreed to withdraw Rwandan forces and DR Congo promised to disarm the FDLR.

40 In August 2003, Kagame was elected President in a plebiscite with 95.5 per cent of the vote. In October of that year, the FPR won an absolute majority in the first multi-party parliamentary elections. EU observers said the poll was marred by irregularities.

41 Rwandan media remained under state control and Kagame banned several political parties including the Democratic Renovation Party and the MRND.

42 In 2003, 60 per cent of Rwanda's population, which registered Africa's highest demographic growth in 2003, were living below the poverty line. That year, 500,000 victims of a volcanic eruption immigrated from DR Congo.

43 On 7 April 2004 in Kigali Kagame inaugurated a ceremony in remembrance of the 100-day genocide in 1994.

44 On 24 April, Kagame violated the peace treaty signed in 2002 when he sent Rwandan troops to attack DR Congo. ∎

St Helena / Saint Helena

Population:	5,049
Area:	122 km²
Capital:	Jamestown
Currency:	Pound sterling
Language:	English

S t Helena was uninhabited when Portuguese navigators arrived in 1502. In 1659 it became a British colony when an outpost of the British East India Company was established on the island. Of scant economic interest, the island acquired notoriety as the location of Napoleon's second exile, from 1815 until his death in 1821.

2   The Malvinas/Falklands War put it back on the map, a century and a half later. A British representative stated: 'It was only with the help of Ascension Island and the labor force provided by St Helena, that we could recover the Falklands'. This may justify the expensive maintenance of this British enclave through the Overseas Development Administration.

3   In December 1984, the UN General Assembly urged Britain to bolster the fishing industry, handicrafts and reforestation on the island and to foster awareness of the right to independence. Washington and London both voted against the resolution. The UN also questioned the existence of the military base on Ascension Island since there should be no bases in non-autonomous territories.

4   In January 1989 a new constitution was instituted conferring greater powers on the members of the Legislative Council and enabling civil servants to stand for election with the approval of the Governor. The new constitution also lowered the voting age to 18.

5   The island's only export is fish, but there has been a decline in the total catch in recent years.

6   St Helena is of scientific interest because of its rare flora and fauna. The island has some 40 plant species unknown in the rest of the world.

7   In 1997 unemployment rose to 18 per cent. In 1999 the UK announced it would grant citizenship to the residents of dependent territories.

8   The British Government had decades earlier acquired a ship, the RMS St Helena, to link the islands to the rest of the world. It has been the only means of reaching St Helena. An airport was planned, but the islanders opposed the idea, as it would harm the natural habitat.

9   St Helena is the only British Overseas Territory that receives periodic economic aid from the Crown to overcome the deficit generated by its limited economy.

10   In May 2002 the island celebrated the 500th anniversary of its discovery with a series of maritime and cultural events, including the opening of a museum in Jamestown, the capital city. On display in the museum are graphic panels telling the island's history.

11   In late 2003 the British Crown appointed a new Governor. Michael Clancy was to become Governor and Commander-in-Chief in October 2004, replacing David Hollamby.

12   In April 2004 the UK Government rejected as unviable four public-private tenders for development of air access. Most islanders would prefer air access after the *St Helena* ship is withdrawn in 2010. ∎

Ascension Island

A scension Island is of volcanic origin, with a surface area of 88 sq km. Its importance derives from its strategic location in the South Atlantic, 1,200 km northwest of St Helena. It is a communication relay center between South Africa and Europe, and the United States maintains a missile tracking station - Wideawake Airfield - there under an agreement with the UK. The island's naval installation and airbase were vital to Britain during the Malvinas/Falklands Islands war (April-June 1982) and afterwards as a base for the ships and planes that supplied the British troops occupying the islands claimed by Argentina.

2   There is no indigenous population and the majority of residents are employees of the St Helena Government. In 1988, out of the 1,099 inhabitants, 765 were from St Helena, 222 were British, 102 were American and 10 were of other nationalities. These figures do not include British military personnel. The main religion is Protestant and the official language is English. The island's administrator, Andrew Kettlewell, has represented the Government of St Helena since November 2002. ∎

Tristan da Cunha

T he most important of a group of South Atlantic islands 2,400 km west of Cape Town, South Africa, and under the administration of St Helena. The islands total 201 sq km (Tristan da Cunha 98 sq km; Inaccessible Island, 10 sq km, 32 km west of the main island; Nightingale Islands, 25 sq km, 32 km south of Tristan da Cunha, and Diego Alvarez or Gough Island, 91 sq km, 350 km south of the main island).

2   The approximately 300 inhabitants (in 2000) are concentrated on Tristan da Cunha, the majority employed by the Government and in a lobster-processing factory. There were volcanic eruptions in 1961 and the island was evacuated, though the population returned in 1963. On Diego Alvarez there is a small weather station run by the South African Government. The main religion is Protestant and the official language is English. The administrator, Brian P Baldwin, represents the Government of St Helena. An advisory council with executive and legislative duties, comprises eight elected and three appointed members. Of the eleven government departments in Tristan Da Cunha, four are headed by women.

3   A ten-year contract to operate Tristan da Cunha's lucrative lobster-fishing concession, which was awarded in 1996 to a South African firm, went into effect on 1 January 1997. The residents of Tristan da Cunha - like those of St Helena - demanded British citizenship during the annual visit by St Helena's Governor.

4   In May 2001 the island was hit hard by a storm that destroyed the entire infrastructure. The UK earmarked $106,000 to begin reconstruction. According to the World Conservation Union (IUCN) catalogue, issued in November 2003, some native species of fauna in Tristan da Cunha and Ascension islands are disappearing because of the loss of their natural habitat through encroachment by domestic animals. ∎

St Kitts-Nevis / Saint Kitts-Nevis

Population:	41,578
Area:	360 km²
Capital:	Basseterre
Currency:	EC dollar
Language:	English

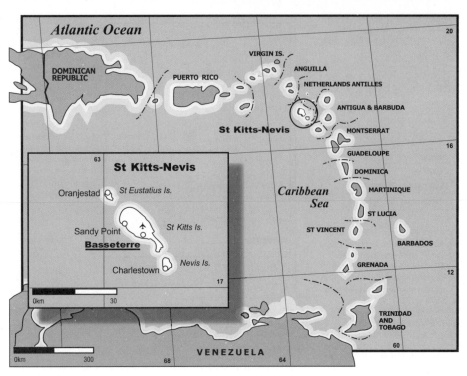

The island of Liamuiga, or 'fertile land' in the language of the Carib Indians who originally lived there, was renamed St Christopher by Columbus on his second voyage to America, in 1493. It was colonized by the Europeans in 1623, when the adventurer Thomas Walker established the first English settlement in the Caribbean. The neighboring island of Nevis was colonized five years later. After the rapid extermination of the Caribs, the English started to grow plantation crops, especially sugarcane, for which they used slaves from Africa.

[2] In the 20th century, the decolonization process following World War II gave the islands total internal autonomy, while foreign relations and defense were left to the colonial capitals. These islands joined the Associated States of the West Indies. In 1980, Anguilla formally separated from St Kitts and Nevis (see Anguilla); after this the islands were governed by a Prime Minister and a parliament, both elected by universal suffrage.

[3] The Labor Party had been in office since 1967, but suffered a major defeat in the 1980 election at the hands of an opposition coalition of the People's Action Movement (PAM) and the Nevis Reformation Party (NRP). Kennedy Alphonse Simmonds became Prime Minister. The opposition victory meant that independence, planned for June 1980 had to be postponed, as the NRP opposed a post-independence federation with St Kitts. The 1976 plebiscite showed that 99.4 per cent of the population of Nevis favored separation. In the 1984 elections, Kennedy Simmonds and his government increased their parliamentary representation. Simmonds was re-elected in March 1989, in line with the US interests in the region.

[4] In 1990, strikes broke out among agricultural workers who had been refused a ten per cent wage increase. Sugar companies responded by hiring close to 1,000 workers from St Vincent and the Grenadines.

[5] In 1992, the Concerned Citizens' Movement won the election in Nevis, ousting the Nevis Reformation Party (NRP) led by Daniel Simeon. Together with the People's Action Movement, the NRP made up the main coalition. Weston Paris, Governor-General Sir Clement Athelston's representative on Nevis, died in circumstances which were unclear.

[6] The November 1993 election was inconclusive. Further elections were held in July 1995, and were won by the St Kitts-Nevis Labor Party led by Denzil Douglas. In 1998 the Concerned Citizens' Movement, led by Vance Amory, Prime Minister of Nevis, failed to win the necessary two-thirds of the vote to achieve independence.

[7] Hurricane George, in late 1998, caused serious damage to 80 per cent of homes. Reconstruction on the islands took many months.

[8] In late 2000, UNESCO declared the Fort in Brimston Hill National Park a Historic Heritage of Humanity site. It was built in 1690 and is a vivid reminder of the clashes between the Spanish and the French for control in the Caribbean.

[9] Prime Minister Douglas was awarded the 2001 Gandhi-King-Ikeda Peace Prize, by the Martin Luther King International Chapel at Morehouse College, for his work for unity and peace.

[10] In March 2004, Douglas visited the Dominican Republic to take part in a regional meeting on AIDS organized by the Caribbean Community (CARICOM). As part of an emergency plan to address the pandemic in the Caribbean, the US will contribute $15 million over five years. Douglas said 'stigma is a challenge that blocks the progress of AIDS programs in the Caribbean', and that 'discrimination and exclusion leave many without access to treatment'. ■

St Lucia / Saint Lucia

Population:	151,509
Area:	620 km²
Capital:	Castries
Currency:	EC dollar
Language:	English

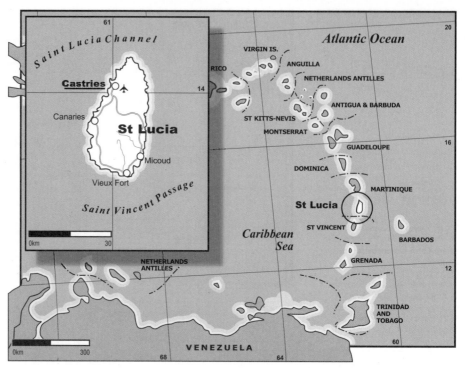

B efore Christopher Columbus named it Santa Lucia in 1502, the East Caribbean island had already been conquered by the Caribs, who had expelled the first inhabitants, Arawak indians from South America.

2 Neither the Spaniards nor the British defeated local resistance. In 1660 the French settled on the island, starting a dispute with Britain which lasted 150 years. Over this period, the flag of St Lucia changed 14 times.

3 In 1814, the Treaty of Paris transferred the island from France to Britain, which ruled until independence in 1978. France left the legacy of *patois*, a pidgin language of mixed African and French.

4 Under British rule, St Lucia became one big sugarcane plantation populated by African slave laborers. Agriculture is still the main economic resource but sugar gave way to banana cultivation. There are also cocoa and coconut crops.

5 The island was part of the Colony of the Windward Islands, and between 1959 and 1962 St Lucia formed part of the West Indies Federation. In 1967 the island became more autonomous and adopted a new constitution as one of the Federated States of the Antilles, negotiating its independence separately.

6 In 1979, in the first elections held as an independent nation, the St Lucia Labor Party (SLP) beat Prime Minister John G M Compton and his United Workers Party (UWP).

7 The new Prime Minister, Allen Louisy, promised to help workers and peasants and to encourage small business as a means of curbing unemployment. George Odlum, Deputy Prime Minister and also leader of the SLP's 'new left' wing, promoted the country's entry to the Non-Aligned Movement and established diplomatic relations with Cuba and North Korea.

8 After repeated political crises, the UWP won the 1982 and 1987 elections. Compton returned to power with a conservative platform: a market economy and adjustment measures recommended by the IMF. The increase in exports and tourism revenues was not enough to leave economic crisis behind, which continued through the 1990s.

9 The years 1994 and 1995 were marked by protests from workers on plantations growing bananas - the island's main export - and also by dock employees, demanding higher wages. In 1996, Vaughn Allen Lewis (UWP) was elected Prime Minister.

10 In 1997, the SLP won the elections. Upon taking office as Prime Minister, Kenny Anthony formed a commission to investigate corruption during the UWP administration.

11 The summit of Caribbean nations in 1998 decided to remove custom tariffs between member countries to compensate for the reduction of US support. During the summit Anthony stated his 'deep discomfort' over the US policy of not including Caribbean textile industries in the North American Free Trade Agreement (NAFTA).

12 St Lucia, supported by other countries, withdrew from the talks at the WTO in Geneva (1999), after the WTO refused to discuss US sanctions against the European Union (EU) regarding the special treatment given by the EU to Caribbean banana exports, as against those from Latin America.

13 In 2000, churchgoers in Castries were attacked with machetes by a group who murdered a nun, injured 13 others and then set fire to the building. The attackers said that 'God had told them to carry out the attack, because of the corruption within the Catholic Church'.

14 In 2002, a tropical storm destroyed almost half of the banana crop. In some areas, whole plantations were wiped out.

15 In 2004, two British subjects visiting the island were sentenced to a six-year prison term for trying to smuggle 2.5 kilos of cocaine from St Lucia on a flight to London. ■

PROFILE

ENVIRONMENT
One of the volcanic Windward Islands of the Lesser Antilles, south of Martinique and north of St Vincent. The climate is tropical with heavy rainfall, tempered by ocean currents. The soil is fertile; bananas, cocoa, sugarcane and coconuts are grown.

SOCIETY
Peoples: Most inhabitants descend from African slaves and their integration with European colonists. There is also a minority of Europeans.
Religions: Roman Catholic 79 per cent; Protestant 15 per cent, of which Seventh-Day Adventist 6.5 per cent, Pentecostal 3 per cent; other 5.5 per cent.
Languages: English (official) and a local patois derived from French and African elements.
Main Political Parties: The St Lucia Labor Party (SLP); The United Workers' Party (UWP).

THE STATE
Official Name: St Lucia.
Capital: Castries 14,000 people (2003).
Other Cities: Vieux Fort 4,600 people; Micoud 3,700 (2000).
Government: Calliopa Pearlette Louisy, Governor-General appointed by the British Crown in 1999. Kenny Anthony, Prime Minister since March 1997.
National Holiday: 13 December, Independence Day (1978), and discovery by Christopher Columbus.

St Vincent and the Grenadines / Saint Vincent

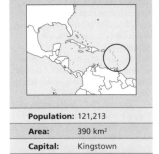

Population:	121,213
Area:	390 km²
Capital:	Kingstown
Currency:	EC dollar
Language:	English

The island's first inhabitants were Arawaks; they were displaced by the Caribs, who lived on the island when Columbus arrived in 1498. In 1783, St Vincent became a British colony. However, the local people resisted European conquest. Former slaves who had rebelled on the neighboring islands and had taken refuge on St Vincent joined the Caribs to oppose the invaders. In 1796, they were defeated and exterminated or deported.

[2] The island developed a plantation economy using slave labor, the chief crops being sugarcane, cotton, coffee and cocoa, and in 1833 became part of the Windward Islands colony. In 1960, together with the Grenadine Islands, it was granted a new constitution with substantial internal autonomy.

[3] St Vincent became a self-governing state in association with the UK in 1969. The post of head minister - similar to that of Prime Minister, but with more limited powers - was held then by Milton Cato, together with the pro-US St Vincent Labor Party (SVLP). Defense and foreign relations continued to be controlled by Britain. Independence was declared in October 1979.

[4] The elections in December 1979 reinforced the predominance of the SVLP, while Ebenezer Joshua's neo-colonial People's Political Party (PPP) received only 2.4 per cent of the vote.

[5] The new government faced an armed rebellion of Rastafarians led by Lennox 'Bumba' Charles on Union Island. This rebellion was quickly put down by troops from Barbados.

[6] In 1980, the Government faced a serious socio-economic crisis, enabling the popular movements to gain ground. In May 1981, the National Committee in Defense of Democracy was formed, supported by several opposition parties, the labor unions and other organizations. Several days later, the Government attempted to impose repressive legislation designed to maintain 'public order', triggering mass protests.

[7] Cato's government supported the US invasion in Grenada and sent a police detachment to join the occupation forces (see Grenada). Cato called early elections, but the economic crisis resulted in the New Democratic Party (NDP) winning the election. James Mitchell became Prime Minister.

[8] In the May 1989 election, James Mitchell (NDP) was re-elected, going on to sign an agreement with the Prime Ministers of Dominica, St Lucia and Grenada to create a new state of the four islands in 1990 (see Dominica).

[9] Given the Grenadinians' secessionist feelings, which had already erupted in violence in 1980, Mitchell created a Ministry of Grenadine Affairs and appointed Herbert Young, a Grenadinian, as Minister of Foreign Affairs.

[10] Pressure from Washington led to a flash operation in December 1998 lasting ten days in which an army battalion wiped out marijuana crops. Cannabis growers complained the destruction left them without a source of income. More than 25,000 banana growers (bananas are the country's main crop) protested in 1999 against US attempts to pressure the World Trade Organization to revoke what the US considered European privileges for banana producers in the Caribbean.

[11] In 2000 the unemployment rate reached 30 per cent. Arnhim Eustace was appointed the new Prime Minister in October. The March 2001 elections led to the defeat of the New Democratic Party (NDP) after 17 years in power, and its replacement by the Unity Labor Party (ULP), led by Ralph Gonsalves.

[12] In March 2002 the island declared as its main national hero Caribbean leader Joseph Chatoyer, 200 years after his death. Chatoyer led the nationalist movement against English colonization and fought until his death.

[13] In March 2004 Deputy Prime Minister Louis Straker met with Cuban officials to sign technical cooperation agreements - training of qualified personnel in Cuba to promote educational development in St Vincent - and to intensify cooperation in the agricultural and construction sectors. St Vincent and the Grenadines has enjoyed diplomatic relations with Cuba since 1992. ∎

PROFILE

ENVIRONMENT

Comprises the island of St Vincent (345 sq km) and the northern part of the 32 Grenadines islands (43 sq km) including Bequia, Canouan, Mustique, Matreau, Quatre, Savan and Union. They are part of the Windward Islands of the Lesser Antilles. Of volcanic origin, the islands have fertile rolling hills. The climate, tropical with heavy rainfall and tempered by ocean currents, is fit for plantation crops. St Vincent is a leading arrowroot producer, a plant with starch-rich rhizomes, used in the manufacture of a type of paper used in electronics. Bananas are the main export. The population is mainly concentrated on the island of St Vincent. There are severe pollution problems in the coastal waters.

SOCIETY

Peoples: Descendants of African slaves 82 per cent, mixed 14 per cent; there are also European, Asian, and indigenous minorities.
Religions: Anglican and other Protestant; Catholic.
Languages: English (official); also a local dialect.
Main Political Parties: The New Democratic Party (NDP); the Unity Labor Party, social-democratic (ULP); the People's Independent Movement.

THE STATE

Official Name: St Vincent and The Grenadines.
Capital: Kingstown 29,000 people (2003).
Other Cities: Georgetown 1,600 people; Byera 1,300 (2000).
Government: Head of State, Queen Elizabeth II. Charles Antrobus, Governor General appointed by Britain, since 1996. Ralph Gonsalves, Prime Minister, elected in March 2001; Louis Straker, Deputy Prime Minister. There are 21 members in the House of Assembly. **National Holiday:** 27 October, Independence Day (1979).

LAND USE

2000

IRRITATED AREA: 9.1% of arable land

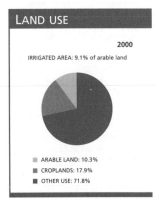

- ARABLE LAND: 10.3%
- CROPLANDS: 17.9%
- OTHER USE: 71.8%

PUBLIC EXPENDITURE

% OF GDP 2000

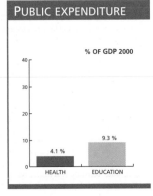

HEALTH	EDUCATION
4.1 %	9.3 %

Samoa / Samoa

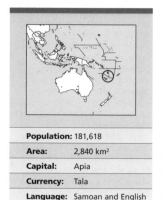

Population:	181,618
Area:	2,840 km²
Capital:	Apia
Currency:	Tala
Language:	Samoan and English

The archipelago of Samoa has been inhabited since at least 1000 BC. The first Samoans of the Polynesian ethnic group (See table on Melanesians and Polynesians) developed a complex social structure organized around the family and its heads, the Matai. Four of these local groups still hold a privileged position: the Malietoa, the Tamasese, the Mataafa and the Tuimalealiifano. Their heads self-designate themselves as being 'descended from kings' (*tama aiga*).

[2] The Dutch were the first Europeans to visit the islands in 1722, but colonization did not begin until the end of the 19th century.

[3] For decades the US, Britain and Germany were in dispute over Samoa. In 1855, Germany finally occupied the islands. German merchants bought copra with Bolivian and Chilean currency valued at ten times less than its real worth. In 1889 a new treaty recognized US rights over the part of Samoa located east of meridian 171; 'rights' which the US still retains. The western half remained under German rule.

[4] In 1914, upon the outbreak of World War I, New Zealand occupied the German part of the island, which was later granted to New Zealand/Aotearoa by the League of Nations as a trust territory.

[5] In 1920, an influenza epidemic killed 25 per cent of the population. The 'Mau' movement

that began to spread throughout the archipelago, in resistance to the foreign governments, carried out a nine-year-long civil disobedience campaign, which eventually became a vigorous pro-independence movement.

[6] In 1961 after intense protests and pressure from the UN, a plebiscite was held for Samoans to vote on independence. This was achieved the following year, with a Constitution based largely on the traditional social structure and the executive power in the hands of two rulers, Tupua Tamasase Meoble and Malietoa Tanumafili. Only the leading group (Matai), around 8,500 people, were eligible to vote.

[7] After being elected Prime Minister in 1970, Tupua Tamasese Lealofi launched a battle against the Matai. He also backed the establishment of foreign corporations on the archipelago, despite strong opposition.

[8] The 1976 elections were won by the opposition. Tupuola Tais became Prime Minister. In 1979 he retained office by only one vote in parliament.

[9] In February 1982, Va'al Kolone, leader of the Party for the Protection of Human Rights, became Prime Minister. In September he was removed from government, amid accusations of corruption and abuse of power.

[10] In April 1988, Tofilau Eti Alesana came to power. His political

party won an absolute majority in the legislature in the 1985 elections when it obtained 31 of the 47 seats.

[11] A plebiscite held in 1990 granted most women the right to vote. Cyclone Ofa left 10,000 people homeless.

[12] The 1991 constitutional reform extended the parliamentary term from three to five years, and increased the number of seats from 47 to 49. Fiame Naomi became Minister of Education that year, the first woman to be appointed to the cabinet.

[13] In the 1996 election, Prime Minister Tofilau Eti Alesana, in spite of having lost support, kept his post and continued to liberalize the economy, eliminating customs controls and reducing taxes. In 1998 the partial burning of forests by farmers went out of control and destroyed 25 per cent of the

natural forests. Prime Minister Tofilau Eti had to resign in November of that year due to complications from cancer. He was replaced by Tuilaepa Sailele Malielegaoi.

[14] In July 1997, a constitutional amendment changed the name of the country to Samoa, eliminating the adjective 'Western'.

[15] In April 2000, Leafa Vitale and Toi Aukuso, respectively the Minister for Women's Affairs and a former Minister of Communications, were sentenced to death by hanging for murdering a Cabinet colleague. According to the charges, they had killed the Minister of Public Works, Levaula Kamu, during a political rally held the previous year.

[16] After a close-run electoral race, Tuilaepa Sailele Malielegaoi was re-elected in March 2001 for a second term.

[17] In 2001, the Organization for Economic Cooperation and Development (OECD) intensified its pressure on Samoa to identify its banks' customers and to introduce financial controls. Samoa is one of the countries that the OECD categorizes as the 'black boxes' of the global finance system, so called because they hide illegal transactions that are evading taxes in their home countries.

[18] In August 2002 the Government submitted a bill to reduce ministries and government agencies by almost 50 per cent so as to cut expenditure and improve the efficiency of the services. ∎

PROFILE

ENVIRONMENT
Includes the islands of Savai'i, 1,690 sq km, 40,000 people; Upolu, 1,100 sq km, 110,000 people; Manono and Apolina, in Polynesia, northeast of Fiji. The eastern portion of the Samoa archipelago is under US administration. The islands are of volcanic origin, mountainous, with fertile soil in the lowland areas. The climate is tropical, tempered by sea winds.

SOCIETY
Peoples: Samoans are mostly Polynesian (92.6 per cent). 'Euronesians' (a result of European and Polynesian integration) make up 10 per cent of the population. There are also Europeans and Pacific islanders. **Religions:** Congregational 47.2 per cent; Roman Catholic 22.3 per cent; Methodist 15.1 per cent; Mormon 8.6 per cent; other 6.8 per cent. **Languages:** Samoan and English are the official languages. **Main Political Parties:** The Human Rights Protection Party (HRPP); the Samoa National Development Party; the Samoa All People's Party, founded in 1996.

THE STATE
Official Name: Samoa i Sisifo. Capital: Apia 40,000 people (2003).
Other Cities: Falelatai 1,800 people; Safotulafai 1,800 (2000).
Government: Malietoa Tanumafili II, Head of State for life since April 1963. Tuilaepa Sailele Malielegaoi, Prime Minister since November 1998, re-elected in 2001. Unicameral Legislature: Legislative Assembly, with 49 members elected for a five-year term; 47 members are Matais (traditional heads of families) and two members are non-Samoan nationals. According to the Constitution, after the death of Tanumafili II, the President will be elected for a five-year term by the parliament.
National Holiday: 10 June, Independence Day (1962)

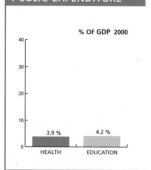

LAND USE

2000

- ARABLE LAND: 19.4%
- CROPLANDS: 23.7%
- OTHER USE: 56.9%

PUBLIC EXPENDITURE

% OF GDP 2000

3.9 %	4.2 %
HEALTH	EDUCATION

Population:	64,819
Area:	200 km²
Capital:	Pago Pago
Currency:	US dollar
Language:	Samoan and English

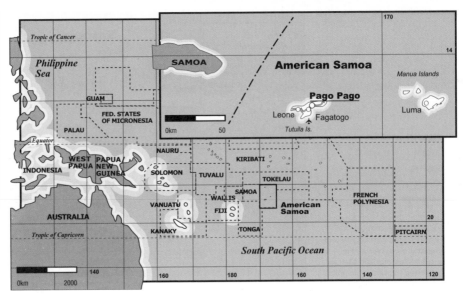

Inhabited since the 7th century BC by Melanesians (see box: 'Melanesians and Polynesians'), the island was reached by Europeans in the 18th century. The colonial powers Germany, Britain and the US were in dispute over its possession 150 years later. A treaty in 1899 settled the conflict, granting the United States the seven islands east of meridian 171. Traditional social structures were maintained but agriculture was not stimulated so the population became totally dependent on the external colonial economy. This situation resulted in an increasing number of emigrants; over half of the Samoan population currently lives in Hawaii and other parts of the United States.

2   On 5 December 1984, the UN General Assembly considered Eastern Samoa's right to self-determination and independence. A unanimous vote reiterated that factors such as territory, geographic location, population and meager resources should not hinder independence. The US, in its role as administrative power, was urged to hasten the decolonization process and to implement an educational program to assure Samoans' full awareness of their rights. The islanders, however, seemed to be content with their existing status, which allowed them to emigrate to the US without restrictions. There were no organized pro-independence groups.

3   In 1984, Governor Coleman (elected in the first elections for governor held in 1977) submitted proposals for a new Constitution in American Samoa for ratification by the US Congress. The proposals were withdrawn in May of the same year, because it was feared that they would be harmful to the interests of US citizens. In November, AP Lutali was elected Governor and Faleomavaega Eni Hunkin became Vice-Governor.

4   In October 1988, the delegate to the US House of Representatives, Fofo Sunia, was sentenced to a 5 to 15 week term in prison for fraud. Hence, Eni Hunkin replaced Sunia. In November, Coleman was re-elected

for his third term and Galeani Poumele replaced Hunkin as Vice-Governor.

5   Despite reforms to the 1967 Constitution during the 1980s, proposed changes were not ratified by the US Congress. According to the Constitution currently in effect, in addition to a governor, who is elected for a four-year term, there is also a legislature, or *Fono* with an 18-member Senate elected every four years by the *matai*, or clan heads. There is also a 20-member House of Representatives elected by direct popular vote for two-year terms. Women do not have the right to vote. Samoans are considered US 'nationals', but not 'citizens' of that country, that is without the right to vote. They do send a delegate to Congress - also without the right to vote.

6   After his re-election as Governor in 1992, Lutali took measures to cut public spending, especially by reducing the number of government employees. The projected social security reform in the US and its dependencies led to a debate in the second half of 1996 about the consequences for the inhabitants of American Samoa.

7   In November 1996, Tauese Pita Sunia was elected Governor with 51 per cent of the vote, to replace AP Lutali. Togiola Tulafano became Vice-Governor. Both took office in January 1997.

8   Later that year, in November, the Government in Pago Pago imposed a curfew between 9:00pm and 6:00am, after expressing concern over the apparent rise in crime rates. In February 1998, a senior official in the Education Ministry accused the Governor of diverting funds meant for school building improvements in order to install a sauna in his official residence. In September, the Opposition tried to challenge the

Governor on the charges of 'abuse of power'. Republican Eni Faleomavaega was re-elected senator to the US with 86 per cent of the vote during the month of November.

9   The Government had to impose austerity measures in order to reduce the deficit, including a shortened workweek, a rise in taxes and cost reductions.

10   In November 2000, Governor Tauese P Sunia, from the Democrat Party, was elected with 50.7 per cent of the vote.

11   In February 2003, the owner of a factory producing clothing for the

US chains Sears and JC Penney was declared guilty of abuse and trafficking of persons, money laundering and extortion. The factory employed illegal Vietnamese and Chinese immigrants who were beaten, poorly fed and threatened with deportation if they protested. The director of the Labor Committee, located in Washington, pointed out that the ambiguous situation of Samoa made it into an ideal place for worker exploitation.

12   In March 2003, Sunia died before ending his mandate and in April his deputy, Togiola Tulafona, took up the post. ■

PROFILE

ENVIRONMENT
The island occupies 197 sq km of the eastern part of the Samoan archipelago, located in Polynesia, slightly to the east of the International Date Line, northwest of the Fiji islands. The most important islands are Tutuila (where the capital is located), Tau, Olosega, Ofu, Annuu, Rose and Swains. Of volcanic origin, the islands are mountainous with fertile soil on the plains. The climate is rainy and tropical, tempered by sea winds. There is dense, woody vegetation and major streams of shallow waters. The main export product is fish, especially tuna. Bananas and crafts are also exported.

SOCIETY
Peoples: Samoans are mostly Polynesians (89 per cent); Tongans 4 per cent; other 5 per cent. **Religions:** Christian (Protestant 50 per cent, Catholic 20 per cent); others 30 per cent. **Languages:** Samoan, predominant, and English are the official languages. **Main Political Parties:** Democratic Party; Republican Party

THE STATE
Official Name: Territory of American Samoa. **Capital:** Pago Pago (on Tutuila) 52,000 people (2003). **Other Cities:** Tafuna 7,100 people; Nu'uuli 5,300; Fagatogo 3,800 (2000). **Government:** Head of State, President George W Bush. Togiola Tulafono became acting Governor in April 2003, following the death of Tauese P Sunia - who had been re-elected by popular vote in 2000 - until the 2004 elections. There is a bicameral legislature: the House of Representatives with 21 members and the Senate composed of 18 members. Samoans are considered US 'nationals', but do not have the right to vote in US presidential elections while living on the islands. **National Holiday:** 17 April, Territorial Flag Day (1900). **Armed Forces:** Defense is the responsibility of the US.

San Marino / San Marino

Population:	28,108
Area:	61 km²
Capital:	San Marino
Currency:	Euro
Language:	Italian

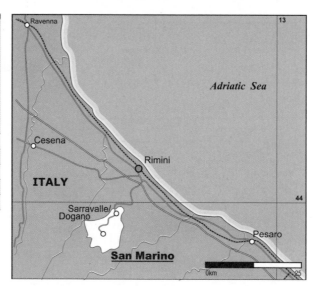

Adriatic Sea

ITALY

Ravenna

Cesena

Rimini

Sarravalle/Dogano

Pesaro

San Marino

0km   25

According to archaeological evidence, the territory of San Marino, located between the provinces of Romana and Marca, was inhabited in prehistoric times. The city was founded in 301 AD by a Dalmatian stonemason from the island of Arbe, called Marinus, who after converting to Christianity and escaping religious persecution by emperor Diocletian, took refuge with other Christians on Mount Titano, in the Apennines. Marinus built a community there that, in time, acquired the features of a small state. In memory of the stone cutter, the land was christened 'Land of San Marino', later to be called 'Community of San Marino', until it finally received its current name.

2   The original system of government was made up of an assembly, the *Arengo*, consisting of the heads of each family. In 1243, two posts of Captain-Regent (*Capitani Reggenti*) were created as joint heads of state. After the fall of the Roman Empire (5th century

AD) the lack of a central power favored self-rule for several Italian cities from the 12th century, as well as the development of trade, manufacturing and crafts. San Marino followed this path, with the difference being that it is the only city to remain independent today.

3   In the 15th century, San Marino's territory grew with support from the Duke of Urbino and through an alliance against Sigismondo Pandolfo Malatesta, lord of Rimini. When the alliance won, Pope Pius II awarded San Marino the castles of Fiorentino, Montegiardino and Serravalle.

4   The Constitution of San Marino dates from the year 1600, and the Sammarinese regard themselves as the oldest republic in the world.

5   In 1739 Cardinal Giulio Alberoni invaded the territory, as part of his

campaign to recover Italian possessions, but civil disobedience acts and secret messages sent to the Pope appealing for justice achieved their goal of papal recognition of San Marino's autonomy and the restoration of its independent status.

6   San Marino remained on the sidelines of Italian unification (1830-1870) and stayed independent, signing a Friendship Treaty with Italy in 1862.

7   The state did not take part in World War I (1914-1918) but the conflict affected the country's economy. At the end of the war, unemployment - already high - and inflation rose considerably.

8   In 1923, two years after Benito Mussolini came to power, the General Council was dissolved, giving way to the fascist Sovereign

and Supreme Council. However, San Marino survived the expansion of Italian fascism and remained neutral during World War II (1939-1945). German troops bombed the republic in July 1944, but Nazi occupation ended after a large demonstration, putting an end to the Supreme Council and paving the way for new elections. During the War, San Marino received more than 100,000 refugees.

9   After the War, the Communists came to power. In 1945 the Communist Party and the San Marino Socialist Party (PSS) formed a coalition which held power for 12 years.

10   In 1957 a centrist alliance dominated by the San Marino Christian Democratic Party (PDCS) won control of the government until 1973.

11   A PDCS-PSS coalition governed for the next five years until in November 1977 the Socialists accused the Christian Democrats of not solving the country's economic problems. They then formed a coalition with the Communists. Early elections were called in May 1978, and the leftist coalition ruled San Marino setting up a highly advanced social welfare system.

12   San Marino reinforced its links with the West and joined the European Union (EU) and the European Council in 1988. In 1992 it became a member state of the United Nations, and joined the IMF.

13   In 1990 the Communist Party renamed itself the Progressive Democratic Party, and remained in the coalition with the Christian Democrats, who in 1992 formed a new coalition with the Socialists. This coalition won the 1993 and 1998 elections.

14   One of the oldest sources of income in the tourist sector is the sale of historic coins and stamps. San Marino issued its first commemorative stamps in 1894.

15   Today, agricultural activities are focused on cereals, grapes and fruit, as well as livestock (cattle and pigs). Apart from the tourist industry, most of San Marino's income comes from the manufacture and export of ceramics, furniture, textile products, paintings and wines.

16   In 2000, San Marino had an enviable standard of living and healthcare system, considered one of the world's best. The Government sought to maintain these through an economic development program to support traditional craftspeople and agriculture.

17   On 1 April 2003, Piermarino Menicucci and Giovanni Giannoni were elected Captains-Regent, while Augusto Casali was appointed Secretary of State and Minister of Foreign Affairs. ∎

PROFILE

ENVIRONMENT

Located in Italy, San Marino is an independent enclave, south of Rimini near the Adriatic coast. The hilly terrain is dominated by the Apennine peak of Mount Titano (738 m). The climate is Mediterranean. The little industrial activity (mostly in construction) is concentrated in the capital, San Marino, a population center which spreads across Titano's western slope. The main source of income is tourism, including crafts and stamps. Also significant are the remittances sent by the emigrant population, settled mostly in Italy and other neighboring countries.

SOCIETY

People: Sammarinese; Italians. **Language:** Italian (local) and a local dialect. **Religion:** Catholic 95 per cent. **Main Political Parties:** San Marino Christian Democrat Party (PDCS); San Marino Socialist Party (PSS); Progressive Democratic Party (PDP); Popular Alliance of Democrats (APD); Socialists for Reform (SR); Communist Refoundation (RC).
Social organizations: Unity Trade Union Central, Democratic General Confederation of Workers, General Confederation of Labor.

THE STATE

Official Name: Serenisima Repubblica di San Marino.
Capital: San Marino, 5,000 inhabitants (2003).
Administrative Divisions: 9 municipalities (castelli); Acquaviva, Borgo Maggiore, Chiesanuova, Domagnano, Faetano, Fiorentino, Monte Giardino, San Marino, Serravalle. Other cities: Serravalle/Dogano 4,726 inhabitants; Boego Maggiore 2,366 inhabitants (1996).
Government: Presidential republic. The executive branch consists of the Council of State, with 10 members, chaired by two Captains-Regent Piermarino Menicucci and Giovanni Giannoni (since April 2003); Augusto Casali is Secretary of State and Minister of Foreign Affairs (2003). Unicameral legislature: the Great General Council, with 60 members elected for a five-year term by proportional representation.
National Holiday: 3 September, Foundation of the Republic (301 AD)
Armed Forces: Volunteers. Military service is voluntary, but all citizens aged between 16 and 65 may be drafted if the State requires them for national defense. Police force.

São Tomé and Príncipe / São Tomé e Príncipe

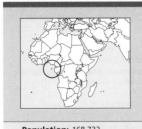

Population:	168,732
Area:	960 km²
Capital:	São Tomé
Currency:	Dobra
Language:	Portuguese

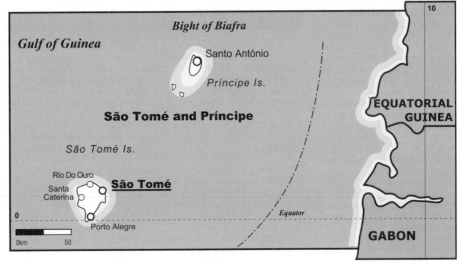

T hese islands were probably uninhabited when first visited by European navigators in the 1470s. Thereafter, the Portuguese began to settle convicts and exiled Jews there and established sugar plantations, using slave labor from the African mainland. Strategically located 300 kilometers off the African coast, the islands' natural ports were used by the Portuguese as supply stops for ships in the 15th century. Dutch, French, Spanish, British and Portuguese slave traders bought enslaved African laborers to be sold in the American colonies. Some of the slaves remained on the islands, and later became the leading African producers of sugarcane.

2   Rebellions broke out and a slave named Amador led a revolt that succeeded in taking over two-thirds of the island of São Tomé, where he proclaimed himself ruler.

3   Soon defeated, the rebels hid in *quilombos* (guerrilla shelters in the forest) after burning their crops.

4   Agriculture virtually disappeared for three centuries. In the 17th century the islands were briefly held by the Dutch before reverting to Portuguese control. The islands were used to hold slaves in transit, until they recovered their prosperity in the late 19th century with the

cultivation of cocoa and coffee. Even after abolition was declared in 1869, slavery continued in a disguised manner ('free' workers signed contracts for nine years at fixed salaries), leading to revolts and an international boycott against the 'cocoa slavery' of the Portuguese colony in the early 20th century.

5   This neo-slavery system continued until the mid-1900s. A Society for Immigration of São Tomé organized the modern slave trade, 'hiring' plantation workers in other Portuguese colonies: Angola, Cape Verde, Guinea and Mozambique. This flow 're-Africanized' the country as the *filhos da terra* (sons of the earth),

the result of several centuries of intermixing between the native people and the Portuguese, mixed with the African immigrants. During the colonial regimes of Salazar and Caetano, repression was particularly harsh. In February 1953, over 1,000 people were killed in Batepá in less than a week.

6   This massacre demonstrated the need for the rebels to join forces, and in 1969 the Movement for the Liberation of São Tomé and Príncipe (MLSTP) was founded, with two main objectives: independence and land reform.

7   Foreign companies owned 90 per cent of São Tomé land and, despite the fertile soil, most food was imported due to the island's monoculture policy. Rural workers were one of the major pillars of the MLSTP, and held a 24-hour strike in August 1963, which paralyzed all the plantations.

8   As the island's terrain did not favor guerrilla warfare, the MLSTP launched an intensive underground political campaign that resulted in its recognition by the OAU (Organization of African Unity) and the Non-Aligned Nations. Together with the MPLA of Angola, the PAIGC of Guinea and Cape Verde, and FRELIMO of Mozambique, the MLSTP joined the Conference of National Organizations of the Portuguese Colonies. It was the only legitimate group in existence when, after the 1974 revolution, Portugal began to free its colonies.

9   The MLSTP joined a transition government in 1974 and in the following year declared independence. Its accomplishments were impressive: banks and farms were nationalized, medicine was socialized, a national currency was created, a major

PROFILE

ENVIRONMENT
The country comprises the islands of São Tomé (857 sq km) and Príncipe (114 sq km), and the smaller islands of Rólas, Cabras, Bombom and Bone de Joquei in the Bay of Biafra of the Gulf of Guinea, facing the coast of Gabon. The islands are mountainous, of volcanic origin, with dense rainforests, a tropical climate and heavy rainfall. Cocoa, copra and coffee are the main export crops.

SOCIETY
Peoples: Most are Africans of Bantu origin traditionally classified in five groups formed as a result of different migratory waves: the *Filhos da terra* (sons of the earth), descendants of the first enslaved workers brought to the islands and intermingled with the Portuguese; the Angolares, thought to descend from Angolans who came to the islands in the 16th Century; the Fôrros, descendants of freed slaves when slavery was abolished; the Serviçais, migrant workers from Mozambique, Angola and Cape Verde; and the native Tongans. Since independence, these categories have begun to disappear.

Religions: Roman Catholic, about 80.8 per cent; remainder mostly Protestant, predominantly Seventh-Day Adventist and an indigenous Evangelical Church.

Languages: Portuguese (official); Fôrro; Crioulo, a dialect with Portuguese and African elements, is widely spoken.

Main Political Parties: Movement for the Liberation of São Tomé and Príncipe-Social Democratic Party (MLSTP-PSD); Democratic Coalition, Christian Democratic Front.

Main Social Organizations: Women's, Youth and Pioneers Organizations linked to the MLSTP.

THE STATE
Official Name: República Democrática de São Tomé e Príncipe.

Administrative Divisions: 7 Districts.

Capital: São Tomé 54,000 people (2003).

Other Cities: Trinidade 14,200 people; Santana 7,700; Neves 7,400 (2000).

Government: Fradique de Menezes, President since September 2001, re-elected in 2003. Maria das Neves, Prime Minister since July 2003. Unicameral Legislature: National Assembly, with 55 members.

National Holiday: 12 July, Independence Day (1975).

LAND USE

2000

IRRIGATED AREA: 23.1% of arable land

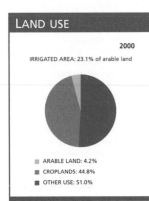

- ARABLE LAND: 4.2%
- CROPLANDS: 44.8%
- OTHER USE: 51.0%

Life expectancy
69.9 years
2000-2005

GNI per capita
$290
2002

administrative reform was launched to reorganize public administration, and numerous centers of popular culture, based on the culture-building educational methods of Brazilian Paulo Freire, were created as part of a literacy campaign.

[10] Opposing these reforms was a rightwing faction led by Health Minister Carlos da Graça, who fled to Gabon to plot a mercenary invasion of the islands in early 1978. The MLSTP's first congress in August, aimed at strengthening the rank and file, eventually led to the formation of a People's Militia and the creation of mass organizations to 'defend the revolution'.

[11] In March 1986, two opposition groups based outside the country - the São Tomé e Príncipe Independent Democratic Union (UDISTP) and the more radical São Tomé e Príncipe National Resistance Front (FRNSTP), founded by Carlos da Graça - announced the formation of an alliance called the Democratic Opposition Coalition. Its aim was to put pressure on the Government to hold free elections. A month later, a fishing vessel with 76 members of the FRNSTP on board arrived in Walvis Bay, the South African enclave in Namibia. They asked the Pretoria Government to supply military aid needed to destabilize the São Tomé Government. These events led to Carlos da Graça's resignation as president of the FRNSTP. In May, he announced his willingness to cooperate with the Government, on condition that Cuban and Angolan troops stationed in the country be withdrawn.

[12] In 1985, in the midst of the worst drought in the country's history, the Government sought to open up the economy: new legislation was designed to promote foreign investment. Gradually the State relinquished economic control, previously heavily dependent upon such key products as cocoa, coffee and bananas. The Government sought ways to attract foreign capital to the agricultural, fishing and tourism sectors.

[13] In March 1990, the People's National Assembly approved amendments to the Constitution, later to be submitted to a referendum. These changes made possible a move to a multiparty system. Independent candidates were admitted in the legislative elections, and the tenure of the President was limited to no longer than two five-year terms.

[14] The first parliamentary elections after independence were held in January 1991. The

IN FOCUS

ENVIRONMENTAL CHALLENGES
Deforestation and soil erosion are significant. Dwindling natural resources, that determine the population's living conditions, affect the country and other island nations. São Tomé and Príncipe has environmental protection legislation.

WOMEN'S RIGHTS
Women have been able to vote and stand for election since 1975. According to the latest World Bank and UNDP data, the percentage of women in government posts fell from 13 to 9 per cent in the last term. Approximately 79 per cent of births are assisted by qualified personnel, but a shortage in doctors prevents extensive pre-natal care. The birth rate in 2002 was 4 children per woman.

Domestic violence is a problem, including rape in marriage. The scope of the problem is unknown, since most cases go unreported as women do not come forward to claim their rights, which include the possibility of suing their husbands. Marital disputes tend to remain within the home.

The Constitution grants the same political, economic and social rights to men and women. On 6 September 2000, the country signed the United Nations Human Rights Charter and followed up with information programs, including distribution of copies of the Convention on the Elimination of All Forms of Discrimination against Women.

CHILDREN
Child labor is common throughout the country, especially on the plantations, where conditions are very harsh. The infant mortality rate is to 75 per 1,000 live births.

The under-5 mortality rate is 11 per 1,000 live births. Thirteen per cent of children under five are malnourished.

The Constitution states that health is a right of all citizens and the Government's duty is to provide it, but after 1980 the health services collapsed. Currently it is estimated there is one doctor for every 1,600 people.

Half of all primary school teachers and more than 80 per cent of secondary teachers lack an adequate training. Education receives only 0.4 per cent of the GDP.

The poor literacy is exacerbated by the lack of books, libraries, newspapers and magazines. There is limited publishing activity.

INDIGENOUS PEOPLES/ ETHNIC MINORITIES
Since the 15th century, the population is based on intermarriage between Portuguese convicts, Jews that arrived after 1496, when King Emmanuel I of Portugal ordered their expulsion, and slaves from the African coast that were used as labor.

MIGRANTS/REFUGEES
According to data published in December 2000 by the Embassy of São Tomé and Príncipe in Lisbon, there were 14,251 São Tomé citizens registered in the Consulate, mainly working in the construction, health or education sectors. Five per cent are professionals, and many are doctors and nurses who practice in Portugal. The Embassy estimates there are some 20,000 citizens living in Portugal illegally.

DEATH PENALTY
It was abolished in 1990.

opposition Democratic Convergence of Leonel d'Alva was voted into power. In March, the former prime minister Miguel Trovoada returned from exile and was unopposed in the presidential elections.

[15] The social and economic situation of the country worsened as the result of an IMF and World Bank imposed austerity plan. Public sector salaries were frozen, a third of all civil servants were dismissed and the local currency was devalued by 80 per cent. While inflation fell, the price of basic foodstuffs quadrupled and unemployment reached 30 per cent.

[16] The São Tomé economy was sustained in 1997 by international assistance, largely from Europe, financing 60 per cent of the budget. The European Development Fund backed a program to create jobs and to set up and provide equipment for medical centers. The country's external debt in 1998 reached $270 million, more than five times its annual GDP, around $50 million.

[17] The November 1998 elections marked the MLSTP's return to the Government. Upon taking office in January 1999, Prime Minister

Guilherme Posser da Costa stated that his center-left administration would have to implement an 'austerity package' while seeking to reactivate the economy through oil exploration and agricultural development. Overwhelmed by the national economic crisis, state employees launched a strike in December 2000 to demand payment of back-wages and a salary hike to compensate for the effects of inflation.

[18] In April 2002 Gabriel Costa was sworn in as Prime Minister after winning the March elections. The Government was shared by the MLSTP and a coalition called MDFM/MPCD.

[19] In April 2003 Menezes was re-elected as President. In July, Maria das Neves was elected Prime Minister.

[20] On July 2003, while President Menezes was on visit to Nigeria, military troops took control of the archipelago, arrested the main government authorities and set up a 'national salvation junta'.

[21] Nine days later, the coup's leaders accepted international mediation and returned power to the President. An amnesty was agreed for the coup leaders, as well as the establishment of a

new government and new elections.

[22] On September 2003, Menezes launched a complete revamping of the Armed Forces and publicly criticized the Army for not having protected democracy during the brief but intense *coup d'etat*.

[23] In May 2004, São Tomé was granted a $6.5 million World Bank loan to fund basic health and education programs, prior to the launching of new challenges regarding the imminent development of crude oil production in the country. These funds would be devoted to the development of social programs aimed at the poorest social sectors and to the promotion of cooperation among the public sector, civil society and communities.

[24] In July, Menezes agreed with his Nigerian counterpart, Olusegun Obasanjo, to develop the exploration and exploitation of São Tomé's crude oil reserves. During a meeting held in Rivers State (the heart of Nigeria's hydrocarbon industry), both Presidents signed an agreement that would promote oil activity in the area, hoping it would also serve as a cooperation model for African countries. ■

Saudi Arabia / Al Arabiyah as Suudiyah

Population:	25,625,687
Area:	2,149,690 km²
Capital:	Riyadh
Currency:	Riyal
Language:	Arabic

A rabia was drawn into the orbit of western Asiatic civilization toward the end of the 3rd millennium BC. Caravan trade between south Arabia and the Fertile Crescent began about the middle of the 2nd millennium BC. The domestication of the camel around the 12th century BC made desert travel easier and gave rise to a flourishing society in south Arabia, centered around the state of Saab (Sheba). In eastern Arabia the island of Dolman (Bahrain) had become a thriving entrepot between Mesopotamia, south Arabia, and India as early as the 24th century BC. With the discovery by the Mediterranean peoples of the monsoon winds in the Indian Ocean, Roman and Byzantine seaborne trade between the northern Red Sea ports and south Arabia flourished, extending to India and beyond. In the 5th and 6th centuries AD, successive invasions by Christian Ethiopians and counter-invasions by the Sasanian kings disrupted the states of south Arabia.

2   In the 6th century Quraysh - the noble and holy house of the confederation of the Hejaz controlling the sacred enclave of Mecca - contrived a series of agreements with the northern and southern peoples. Under this aegis, caravans moved freely from the southern Yemen coast to Mecca and thence northward to Byzantium or eastward to Iraq. As a result of the Quraysh's dominant position, members of the house of 'Abd Manaf concluded pacts with Byzantium, Persia, and rulers of Yemen and Ethiopia, promoting commerce outside Arabia. Quraysh had some sanctity as lords of the Meccan temple (the Ka'bah) and were themselves known as the Protected Neighbors of Allah. The people on pilgrimage to Mecca were called the Guests of Allah.

3   The Ka'bah, through the additions of other cults, developed into a pantheon, the cult of other gods perhaps being linked with political agreements between Quraysh - worshippers of Allah - and the other clans.

4   Muhammad, the prophet of Islam, was born in 570 of the Hashimite branch of the noble house of 'Abd Manaf. Though orphaned at an early age, he never lacked protection by his clan. Marriage to a wealthy widow improved his position as a merchant, but he began to make his mark in Mecca by preaching the oneness of Allah. Rejected by the Quraysh lords, Muhammad sought affiliation with other groups; he was unsuccessful until he managed to negotiate a pact with the chiefs of Medina. He obtained their protection and became theocratic head and arbiter of the Medina confederation (*ummah*). Those Quraysh who joined him there were known as *muhajirun* (refugees or emigrants), while his Medina allies were called *ansar* (supporters). The Muslim era dates from the *hijrah* (hegira) - Muhammad's move to Medina in AD 622.

5   Muhammad's supporters attacked a Quraysh caravan in AD 624, thus breaking the vital security system established by the 'Abd Manaf house, and hostilities broke out against his Mecca kin. In Medina he faced both the necessity to enforce his role as arbiter and to raise supplies for his moves against Quraysh. He overcame internal opposition and, externally, his rising power was demonstrated after Quraysh's failure to overrun Medina, when he declared it his own sacred enclave. Muhammad foiled Quraysh offensives and marched back to Mecca. After taking Mecca in AD 630 he became lord of the two sacred sites. However, even though he broke the power of some Quraysh lords, he then sought reconciliation with his Quraysh kin.

6   After Muhammad's entry into Mecca the groups linked with Quraysh came to accept Islam; this meant little more than giving up their local deities and worshipping only Allah. They had to pay the tax, but this was not new since the chiefs had already been taxed to protect the Meccan enclave. From then on Islam was destined for a world role.

7   Under Muhammad's successors, the expansionist urge of different groups, temporarily united around the nucleus of the two sacred sites, coincided with the weakness of Byzantium and Sasanian Persia. Those who converted to Islam launched a career of conquest that promised to satisfy the mandate of their new faith as well as the desire for booty and lands. With families and flocks, they left the peninsula. Such large population movements affected all Arabia; in Hadhramaut they possibly caused neglect of irrigation works, resulting in erosion of fertile lands. In Oman, too, when Arabs evicted the Persian ruling class, its complex irrigation system suffered.

8   As the conquests far beyond Arabia poured loot into the Holy Cities (Mecca and Medina), they became wealthy centers of a sophisticated Arabian culture. Medina became a center for Qur'anic (Koranic) study, the evolution of Islamic law, and historical record. Under the caliphs - Muhammad's successors - Islam began to assume its characteristic shape. Paradoxically, outside the cities it made little difference to Arabian life for centuries. After the Prophet's death, the second caliph Omar led the Arab conquest. Within ten years the Arabs occupied Syria, Palestine, Egypt and Persia. With Muawiya, the caliphate became hereditary in the family of the Ummaias and the Arabs became a privileged caste which ruled over the conquered nations.

9   In the 8th century, the borders of the Arabian Empire reached from North Africa and Spain to the west, to Pakistan and Afghanistan in the east. Upon moving the capital to Damascus, Syria became the cultural, political and economic center of the Empire. Greco-Roman, Persian and Indian components blended into a mix in which science played an important role. Contrary to Muhammad's expectations, the Arabian peninsula was to remain on the sidelines within the enormous empire, except in religious matters. Mecca, although failing to match Baghdad or Damascus in socio-economic and cultural importance, continued to be the center of Islam and the destination for large pilgrimages from all over the world.

10   This situation remained unchanged for centuries. The Empire split up; the capital moved to Baghdad and the power of the caliphs passed to the viziers, while culturally Arabic civilization attained the highest standards in all fields of knowledge and artistic creation. Arabic became the language of scholars from Portugal to India. In the peninsula, nomadic groups continued to herd their flocks, the settled population kept up their commerce, and rivalries

LAND USE

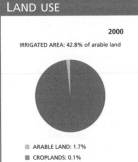

2000

IRRIGATED AREA: 42.8% of arable land

- ARABLE LAND: 1.7%
- CROPLANDS: 0.1%
- OTHER USE: 98.2%

PUBLIC EXPENDITURE

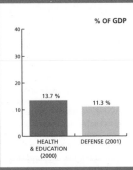

% OF GDP

13.7 % HEALTH & EDUCATION (2000)

11.3 % DEFENSE (2001)

Life expectancy
72.3 years
2000-2005

GNI per capita
$8,460
2002

Literacy
76% total adult rate
2000

between the two were frequently settled through war. As in Muhammad's time, demographic growth was channeled towards conquest, with the emigration of whole communities, such as the Bani Hilals in the 11th century. Trading caravans carrying supplies to Mecca became much more frequent, while the ports became more active as a result of trade with Africa. The peninsula was governed from Egypt, first by Saladin and later by the Mamelukes. The Turks ruled from the 16th century to the 20th century, without introducing any major changes in the socio-economic pattern of the Arab nation.

[11] Under Turkish rule the provinces of Hidjaz and Asir on the Red Sea had some autonomy due to the religious prestige of the shereefs of Mecca, descendants of Muhammad. The interior, with Riyadh as the main urban center, became the Emirate of Najd at the end of the 18th century, through the efforts of the Saud family supported by the Wahabite sect (known as the Islamic Puritans). In the 19th century, with Turkish assistance, the Rated clan forced Abd al-Rahman ibn Saud out of power; the ousted leader sought exile in Kuwait. In 1902, his son Abd al-Aziz, again backed by the Wahabites, organized a religious-military sect, the Ikhwan, in which he enlisted nearly 50,000 Bedouins to reconquer Najd. Twelve years later the Saudis defeated the Rachidis and added the Al-Hasa region on the Persian Gulf which had been controlled by the Turks, against whom the Saudi forces fought during World War I. At the end of the conflict, Britain - the major power in the area - faced a difficult situation. In exchange for Abd al-Aziz's continued anti-Turk campaign, Britain had promised to guarantee the integrity of his state. But for the same reason it had also promised to make Hussein ibn Ali (the shereef of Mecca) king of a nation that would encompass Palestine, Jordan, Iraq and the Arabian peninsula.

[12] The Emir of Najd thought that Britain would not keep its word to Hussein. Such a powerful kingdom, ruled by the Prophet's family with the capital in the holy city, would alter the regional balance of power. But in 1924 Hussein proclaimed himself caliph (see Jordan). Abd al-Aziz invaded his territory immediately, despite British opposition, and in January 1926 was declared King of Hidjaz and Sultan of Nadj in the great mosque of Mecca. Six years later the 'Kingdom of Hidjaz, of Nedj and its dependencies' was formally unified under the name of Saudi Arabia.

PROFILE

ENVIRONMENT

The country occupies up to 80 per cent of the Arabian peninsula. There are two major desert regions: the An Nefud in the north, and the Rub al-Khali in the south. Between the two lies the Nejd massif, of volcanic origin, and the plain of El Hasa, the country's only fertile region, where wheat and dates are cultivated. The country's cultivated land amounts to less than 0.3 per cent; 90 per cent of agricultural products consumed are imported. Oil extraction, concentrated along the shores of the Persian Gulf shores, is the source of its enormous wealth.

SOCIETY

Peoples: Saudis are mainly of Arab origin. In recent years there has been large immigration of Iranians, Pakistanis and Palestinians who have settled in the new eastern industrial areas, bringing the number of foreigners to an estimated five million (1992).
Religions: Islam, Sunni orthodox Wahabism (official) 91 per cent; Shi'a 8 per cent; Christians 1 per cent. **Languages:** Arabic, with dialect variations; languages of other communities, particularly of foreign workers, include Farsi and Urdu.
Political Parties: Not permitted, but there exist opposition groups, most of them in the diaspora. **Social Organizations:** Not permitted.

THE STATE

Official Name: al-Mamlakah al-'Arabiyah as-Saudiyah.
Administrative Divisions: 13 regions (Al-Baha, Al-Jouf, Asir, Eastern, Hail, Jizan, Madinah, Makkah, Najran, Western Border, Qasim, Riyadh and Tabouk). **Capital:** Riyadh (Ar-Riyad) (royal capital) 5,126,000 people (2003). **Other Cities:** Jeddah (administrative center) 2,604,500 people; Mecca (Makkah - religious center) 1,229,200 (2000). **Government:** Absolute monarchy. King Fahd ibn Abd al-Aziz al-Saud, Head of State and of the Government since 13 June 1982. Crown Prince and Regent Abdullah ibn Abd al-Aziz al Saud since 1996. Advisory Council, with advisory role to the King. The National Assembly (Majlis al-Shura) has two chambers: the Assembly of Deputies (Majlis al-Nuwaab) with 80 members elected by popular suffrage and the Assembly of Senators (Majlis al-Aayan) with 40 members appointed by the king. **National Holiday:** 23 September, National Unification (1932). **Armed Forces:** 105,000 (plus 57,000 active National Guard). Other: 10,500; Coast Guard, 4,500; Special Security Force, 500.

[13] In 1930, the monarch gave US companies permission to drill for oil. When he died in 1953, his son Saud squandered the Kingdom's Aramco oil company revenues on his playboy lifestyle. In 1964 the country was on the verge of bankruptcy when Saud was ousted by his brother Faisal, an able diplomat who had also proved a valiant soldier in the wars. Monogamous, deeply religious and very austere, Faisal gave new life to the country's economy and began to invest petrodollars in ambitious development programs, though maintaining the traditional feudal structure headed by the autocratic ruler. Under him, the Emirs ruled the provinces, with the support of chiefs and their desert armies. Other sectors of the population had no say in government.

[14] Faisal rejected the Soviet Union and any other system linked with atheism, including Nasser's nationalism in Egypt, as well as Iraqi or Syrian Ba'athism. His strategic alliance with the US was seen as 'natural', but was undermined by US support for Israel after the 1967 war and

rivalries with neighboring Iran, which under the Shah Pahlevi also played watchdog for Washington's interests in the Gulf.

[15] During the 1973 Arab-Israeli war, Faisal supported an oil embargo on the countries backing Israel, including the US. The sudden oil shortage allowed the Organization of Petroleum Exporting Countries (OPEC) to hike oil prices rapidly, heralding a new era in international relations. In 1975, Faisal was murdered by an apparently insane nephew. His brother Khaled was named as his successor. However, due to the latter's ill health, his brother Crown Prince Fahd ibn Abd al-Aziz became the ruler.

[16] Oil revenue, which amounted to $500 million a year when Faisal was crowned in 1964, had grown to almost $30 billion when he died. New cities, universities, hospitals, freeways and mosques sprouted up everywhere. Yet there was surplus money available. Instead of planning oil production to meet the country's needs, which would have avoided the fall in prices and the weakening of OPEC during the

1980s, fortunes accumulated in Western banks. Thus, Saudi Arabia tied its fortune to the industrialized capitalist world. In addition it created a surplus of money in circulation, which the banks lent to various Third World countries for some questionable projects and ventures. When the countries defaulted on their huge debts, this created the 1984-85 foreign debt crisis, with a rise in interest rates.

[17] Muslim fundamentalist groups denounced the Saudi dynasty for allegedly betraying Islam, leading to violent confrontations in 1979. Analysts interpreted these incidents as a symptom of widespread discontent. The theological basis which legitimized the ruling autocracy was undermined by the progressive rise to power of new members of the ruling family, trained in European and US universities and military academies, rather than in the traditional desert-tent Qur'anic schools.

[18] After the overthrow of the Shah of Iran in 1979, the Saudi Government drew closer to the US. With King Khaled's death, in 1982, his brother Fahd - the architect of Saudi Arabia's modernization - became king.

[19] The year before, Fahd had created a peace plan for the Middle East which had been approved by several Arab countries, the PLO and the US, though it collapsed after Israeli opposition. This plan proposed the creation of a Palestinian State with Jerusalem as its capital, the withdrawal of Israel from the occupied Arab territories, and the dismantling of the Jewish colonies set up in 1967, as well as the recognition of the right of every state in the region to live peaceably. On 26 September 1982, during the Haj or pilgrimage to Mecca, Fahd condemned Israeli intervention in Lebanon. He also criticized the 1979 Soviet intervention in Afghanistan and accused Iran's Ayatollah Khomeini of attempting to destabilize the regime through sabotage.

[20] Naval bases in Jubail and Jeddah were built under the supervision of the US Army. Also, investments and bank deposits by the Saudi State and nobility were closely linked with the performance of the US economy: two-thirds of the huge amount of Saudi petrodollars invested abroad went into corporation stocks, treasury bonds and bank deposits in the US.

[21] The 1985-89 five-year plan promised a 'wide income redistribution'. Yet that intention coincided with the first signs of economic trouble in the Kingdom. In 1984, due to another drop in the price of crude, the official budget closed with a deficit for the first time. The Minister of Industry,

 Under-5 mortality
28 per 1,000 live births
2002

 Malnutrition
14% under-5s
1995-2002

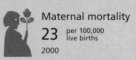 Maternal mortality
23 per 100,000 live births
2000

Ghazi Al Gosaibi, was forced to resign after writing a poem which made reference to corruption.

[22] During the Iran-Iraq war (1980-1990), Saudi Arabia backed Iraq financially, afraid that the Iranian Islamic revolution might spread through the Gulf. Fahd changed his title to Guardian of the Holy Sites, but every year some pilgrims to Mecca protested about the alliance between Riyadh and Washington and by what they considered a commercialization of holy places, surrounded today by shopping centers, highways and other symbols of transnational culture. In 1987, Saudi police fired on a march by Iranian women and disabled war veterans in Mecca, killing hundreds of pilgrims. In retaliation, the embassies of Saudi Arabia and Kuwait in Tehran were attacked and burned, and relations between both countries grew very tense, remaining so until 2000, when an economic co-operation treaty was signed.

[23] After the Iraqi invasion of Kuwait in August 1990 Saudi Arabia was the scene of a huge military deployment by a multinational coalition led by the US. Apart from the loss of human lives, the war caused a huge ecological disaster as oilfields burned.

[24] In March 1992, Fahd issued several decrees called 'The Basic System of Government', aimed at decentralizing political power. It established an Advisory Council, with the right to review all matters of national policy, and the *mutawein*, religious police whose mandate was to ensure the observance of Islamic customs.

[25] Growing social inequalities aggravated tensions among the Saudis, even though they are privileged compared with the millions of foreign workers living in the country. An attack against the offices of US advisors in Riyadh in November 1992 killed at least six people and was seen as proof of those tensions. The hostility of one segment of the population toward the US grew stronger, reaching a critical point with the attack on the US El Khobar base in June 1996 that left 19 soldiers dead.

[26] Due to his failing health, in 1996 Fahd transferred power to his brother Abdullah bin Abd al-Aziz al Saud - who had been confirmed as heir four years earlier.

[27] In September 2001, the terrorist attacks on New York and Washington, perpetrated by several Saudi citizens (among others) who were supporters of bin Laden's al-Qaeda network, cast a shadow on the Saudi-US alliance.

[28] In December Saudi women won the right to their own identity documents (ID). Previously, they had been included in a family ID as dependants of the husband or father. Women have to have family permission to undergo surgical procedures. However, they are allowed to control their own money and to inherit wealth, as stated in Islamic law.

[29] In September 2002, with the prospect of a second Gulf War, Prince Saud Al-Faisal, the Saudi Foreign Minister, said that Saudi Arabia would only allow the use of its territory for military action against Iraq if that action was supported by a UN Security Council resolution. On October the borders between Saudi Arabia and Iraq were officially opened for the first time since the invasion of Kuwait in 1990.

[30] The US invasion of Iraq in March 2003 had a catastrophic impact on the balance in the Persian Gulf region, and contributed to an increase in suicide attacks in Iraq and Saudi Arabia. In May 2003 car bombs killed more than 30 people in Riyadh. In November, another attack killed 17. Terrorist violence continued throughout 2004 and the first attack on a government building took place in April, when a car bomb blew up next to the agency in charge of General Security in the Kingdom. A month later there was a confrontation between attackers and Saudi security forces in the city port of Yanboa.

[31] Calls for political reform mounted, backed by the West which saw this as the way to shore up their allies in Saudi Arabia, faced with growing unrest and terrorist attacks. In late 2003, the authorities announced that elections (municipal) would be held for the first time in the Kingdom's history. According to the official statement, the measure aimed to 'increase citizen participation in local political mangement through the empowering of municipal councils'. Rising demands for reform resulted in the announcement in March 2004 that women would be able to vote and run for office, although the announcement was made through the Saudi embassy in London, and the statement said it was hoped that both men and women 'would have the chance to vote'.

[32] A series of terrorist attacks in Riyadh, carried out according to estimates by the al-Qaeda network in May and June 2004, apart from generating confusion in the country, resulted in a rise in the price of oil, which reached record levels. The country's capital witnessed violent attacks against the Al-Khobar Petroleum Center, the Organization of Arab Petroleum Countries, and also against the luxurious Oasis Resort, which was considered as a heavily fortified site. In June, the decapitation of the American contractor Paul Johnson showed that Islamic militants were rapidly changing tactics by attacking both the royal family and the George W Bush administration in Washington, deeply involved in a 'global war on terror'. ∎

IN FOCUS

ENVIRONMENTAL CHALLENGES
Oil production has increased water pollution levels, which grew during the first Gulf War, when 640 kilometers of coast and wetlands were affected by a 4.5 million-barrel oil spill, killing thousands of fish and birds. Water resources are being depleted by a vast agricultural irrigation system.

WOMEN'S RIGHTS
In late 2003, the authorities announced that municipal elections would be held for the first time. In March 2004 it was announced that women would be able to vote and run for office, but this has not yet been implemented.

Saudi Arabia signed and ratified in 2000 the Convention on the Elimination of All Forms of Discrimination Against Women, but there are no reports on its implementation. No measures were taken against discrimination in legislation, education or daily life (women are not represented in the *Majlis*

al Shura [National Assembly], cannot travel abroad without written permission from a male relative, cannot drive since 1990, and are arrested if they break the dress code). Women make up 16 per cent of the labor force. Between 1995 and 2000, 9.7 per cent of women between 15 and 24 years of age could not read or write. Some 10 per cent of births were not attended by qualified personnel.

CHILDREN
Programs are needed to stop the transmission of disease during the Haj (pilgrimage), the spread of HIV/AIDS, drug use, accidents and obesity. UNICEF has proposed the implementation of programs to address hepatitis epidemics and the growing incidence of cancer.

Although there is one teacher to every 13 students, the figure is not uniform throughout the country, since urban schools have many more pupils than rural schools.

In 2002 the UN Committee on the Rights of the Child recommended that hotlines and

shelters for women and children fleeing domestic violence be set up. That year, the religious police whipped teenagers who had allegedly flirted, whistled or talked in public to women they did not know. Hundreds of teenagers were punished publicly where they had committed their 'offenses'.

INDIGENOUS PEOPLES/ ETHNIC MINORITIES
The Shi'a are a minority religious group, constituting 15 per cent of the population in 2000. They were still subject to discrimination in the political, social and economic realms. Until 2000 there were restrictions on their political organization, they had no right to freedom of expression and had no access to the same public positions as the Sunni majority.

There are several Shi'a advocacy groups, that make various types of demands on the Saudi Government. The Reform Movement acts from abroad and seeks: Shi'a recognition as an Islamic sect, freedom of religion, the provision for Shi'a education in their region, freedom

of speech, an end to government harassment and the same powers for Shi'a and Sunni courts in issues such as marriage, divorce, and inheritance.

MIGRANTS/REFUGEES
After the first Gulf War, some 33,000 Iraqis took refuge in the country. Although some 25,000 were sent to other countries, 5,200 ended up in the Rafha camp, in a small desert strip, with extreme temperatures and sandstorms. Some 40 per cent of camp residents were under 18. In 2002 they had spent 10 years in the camp. In 2002 the UNHCR requested that the US take 3,000 refugees from Rafha, but Washington refused.

In 2002 there were some 246,000 refugees from other countries, among them Palestinians with legal residence but without assistance or refugee status from the UNHCR.

DEATH PENALTY
The death penalty is applied, even for ordinary offenses.

Senegal / Sénégal - Sounougal

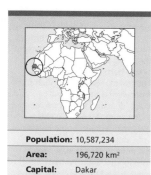

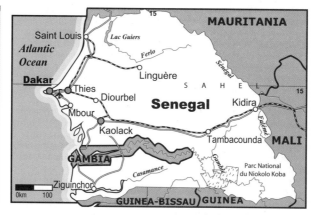

Population:	10,587,234
Area:	196,720 km²
Capital:	Dakar
Currency:	CFA franc
Language:	French

The banks of the Senegal River were inhabited early on by peoples who had converted to Islam through contact with neighboring Arab countries, parts of which make up the region known as the Sahel. The Wolof (who constitute more than a third of the population), Fulani (see Cameroon), Pulaar and other peoples, all lived within the area of modern Senegal. When the French occupied it during the 17th century, Senegal was incorporated into a triangular world trade pattern whereby European manufactured goods were exchanged in Africa for slaves. The slaves were sold in the Caribbean for rum and sugar to go back to Europe.

[2] After slavery was abolished by the French Revolution of 1848, the Senegalese became 'second class citizens' of the French Empire, with one political representative in Paris. Senegal exported thousands of tons of peanuts per year and supplied the French army with soldiers. During the second half of the 19th century, there were frequent rebellions among the Muslim leaders, and it was only in 1892

that the French managed to fully 'pacify' the country.

[3] The Pan-African movement inspired Senegal's Léopold Sédar Senghor and Martinique's Aimé Césaire, to create in 1933 the concept of *négritude* against the imposition of French culture, which proclaimed itself as 'universal'. As 'an effective liberation tool', *négritude*, in Senghor's view, had to escape 'peculiarism' and achieve a specific political identity.

[4] Senghor had been a member of the French resistance during World War II, and in 1945 was elected representative to the French National Assembly. In 1948 he led the foundation of the Senegalese Democratic Bloc (later on Senegalese Progressive Union), which demanded greater autonomy for the colonies, although not independence.

[5] Finally, on 4 April 1960, Senegal declared its independence, and on 5 September adopted a republican system. Senghor was elected president and through successive re-elections he stayed in power for two decades. He applied an ideology of African socialism based on the collectivist essence of

traditional African agrarian society. Senghor believed that 'socialism' already existed on the continent and therefore did not need to be imposed. In the global economy, this 'collectivism' actually served to provide cheap labor for the export-oriented production of peanuts and cotton, while 82 per cent of the nation's industry was French-controlled.

[6] In an effort to keep up with political change in France, Senghor sought membership of the Socialist International, and reformed the constitution establishing a three-party system: a 'liberal democratic' party (the Senegalese Democratic Party), a 'Marxist-Leninist' party (the African Party for Independence) and his own, renamed the Senegalese Socialist Party (PSS).

[7] In the early 1980s the Government gave in to pressure from the US, France, the World Bank and the IMF to accept a structural adjustment plan. The elimination of agricultural subsidies triggered a rise in production costs and prices of basic consumer goods. The country has faced a series of serious droughts, seen as part of

the desertification process caused by climatic conditions and the French-imposed substitution of export crops for traditional food crops.

[8] In 1981 Senghor was replaced by then prime minister Abdou Diouf. The new President brought flexibility to the political system. Fourteen new parties were created, preventing the regime's main rival, Abdoulaye Wade's Senegalese Democratic Party (PDS), from uniting all the Government opposition forces. Meanwhile, in the southern province of Casamance a new separatist movement emerged in 1982: the Casamance Movement of Democratic Forces (MFDC), led by abbot Austin Diamacoune Senghor. The people in Casamance, mainly Dioles, were proud of their independence and resistance to the Islamic hierarchical societies of the north. In 1983, after successive confrontations with the Senegalese police forces, Diamacoune and other separatist leaders were detained.

[9] In 1988 the PSS won another electoral victory, obtaining 73 per cent of the vote, while the PDS - which obtained a mere 26 per cent - questioned the legitimacy of the election. Several PDS leaders were detained, and Wade was forced to go into exile in Paris, returning to Senegal in 1989. That year, a border conflict broke out with Mauritania triggered by violence between peasants and farmers, causing hundreds of casualties and forcing some 70,000 refugees to enter Senegal. The conflict stopped integration with Gambia. Both countries had planned on creating the Senegambia Federation. Diouf criticized the neighboring country for harboring the Casamance guerrillas and for signing a defense treaty with Nigeria (see Gambia).

[10] In 1991, Diouf was elected President of ECOWAS (Economic Community of the Western African States), which includes 17 countries in the region. That year, the US Government wrote off $42 million of Senegal's foreign debt after Diouf supported the allies in the Gulf War and contributed to the 'peace troops' stationed in Liberia. The IMF approved a new $5.7 million loan. The office of Prime Minister was restored and members of opposition parties were appointed to two cabinet posts. After negotiations with opposition parties, a consensus was reached to reform the electoral laws.

[11] In 1993, amid allegations of widespread fraud, Diouf won the presidential elections in the first round ballot, with 58.4 per cent of the vote. In the legislative elections, his PSS party maintained control of the National Assembly, with 84 of

PROFILE

ENVIRONMENT
Located on the west coast of Africa, embracing Gambia, its northern border formed by the Senegal River, the country's population is concentrated in the less arid western part, close to Dakar. The Senegal Valley is still under-populated as a result of slave trade which was very intense in this region.

SOCIETY
Peoples: Wolof 42 per cent; Serer 14.9 per cent; Diola 10 per cent; Peul (Fulani) 9.3 per cent; Malinke (Mandingo) 3.6 per cent. Approximately 3 per cent are immigrants from non-African countries, mainly France, Lebanon and Syria.
Religions: 94 per cent Muslim, 5 per cent Christian, traditional African religions and others 1 per cent. **Languages:** French (official). The most widely spoken indigenous languages are Wolof, Peul and Ful. **Main Political Parties:** 'Sopi' or 'Change' Coalition, headed by the Senegalese Democratic Party (PDS, liberal), of President

Abdoulaye Wade; Alliance of Progress Forces (AFP); Socialist Party of Senegal (PSS), founded by Léopold Senghor; several other minority parties.
Main Social Organizations: National Federation of Senegalese Workers (CNTS); Union of Free Senegalese Workers (UTLS).

THE STATE
Official Name: République du Sénégal.
Administrative Divisions: 10 Districts.
Capital: Dakar 2,167,000 people (2003).
Other Cities: Thies 255,200 people; Kaolack 221,400; Ziguinchor 200,700; Saint Louis 144,100 (2000).
Government: Parliamentary Republic. Abdoulaye Wade, President and Chief of State since April 2000. Macky Sall, Prime Minister and Head of Government since April 2004. Parliament: 120 member National Assembly and 60 member Senate.
National Holiday: 4 April, Independence Day (1960).
Armed Forces: 13,400, and 1,200 French troops (1996).

| Life expectancy
52.9 years
2000-2005 | GNI per capita
$470
2002 | Literacy
37% total adult rate
2000 | HIV prevalence rate
0.5% of population 15-49 years old
2001 |

the 120 seats. The main opposition party - the PDS - won 27 seats.

12 Senegal's economic and financial situation worsened during 1993, partly because international prices for Senegalese export products fell considerably. The trade deficit grew, which was offset by new loans taking the foreign debt to $3.5 billion, more than 60 per cent of GDP.

13 The 100 per cent devaluation of the CFA franc agreed by France and the IMF accentuated social tensions in early 1994. The opposition Co-ordination of Democratic Forces organized an anti-government demonstration which ended in confrontations with the police. Six police died and dozens of people were injured. Some 180 people were arrested for their alleged responsibility for the riots, including opposition leaders Wade and Landing Savané, who were declared innocent and freed after five months in prison. The Government's repressive action was criticized by human rights organizations, the European Parliament and US Congress.

14 Wade joined Diouf's cabinet in 1995, after negotiating with the Government. International finance institutions supported the President when he announced legislation to encourage foreign investment and accelerate privatization.

15 In spite of support from France and the US, Government troops made no progress against the Casamance guerrillas. Observers said the MFDC was popular among Casamance youth and that the region's geography made it impossible for Dakar to win. Neither would the 'regionalization' of the country planned in 1996 mean a political resolution to the conflict. In 1997 guerrilla action led to the mobilization of 2,500 soldiers against MFDC bases, along the frontier with Guinea-Bissau.

16 That year, Senegal extended its protocol with the EU for four more years, under which it would receive nearly $11 million per year in compensation. In 1998, Amnesty International denounced the reigning 'terror' in Casamance which was decimating a farming population and ruining an area considered prosperous before the war.

17 After 40 years of one-party rule, Wade won the 2000 presidential elections with a campaign denouncing the corruption and inefficiency of the PSS government. Senegalese youth were the most affected by unemployment. New independent radio stations monitored the voting, turning it into one of the most transparent and peaceful elections the region had ever known. Upon taking office Wade appointed a former

opposition veteran, Mustafa Niasse, as his Prime Minister. The Government's main priority was to stop the separatist conflict by peaceful means, but violence increased in Casamance with successive attacks by MFDC factions opposed to the conciliatory stance of some of their leaders.

18 A referendum passed a new Constitution in 2001. This limited the president's term of office from seven to five years, reducing the presidency to a maximum of two consecutive periods and stating that any member of parliament who left their party would lose their seat. It also enabled the President to dissolve the National Assembly (lower chamber) without the support of a majority of its members. Shortly after, Wade dissolved the Assembly, preparing for parliamentary elections that year: the 'Sopi' - or 'Change' - coalition, formed by parties loyal to Wade and led by the PDS, won by a landslide. The new Senegalese Prime Minister - the first woman to hold that office in the country - Mame Madior Boye, announced the composition of her new government. Ten of the posts went to PDS members.

19 In 2001, Wade announced he would hand over Hissene Habré, former president of Chad facing war crime charges, if a third country would be willing to give him a fair trial. Human rights groups held Habré responsible for some 40,000 executions and the torture of 200,000 people during his rule between 1982 and 1990. Jean-Marie Francois Biagui resigned as Secretary-General of the MFDC, claiming lack of loyalty from its members. Biagui had been appointed during an MFDC congress which tried to overcome internal differences in order to resume the peace talks. However, those differences impeded the creation of a joint front and Biagui was never accepted by some factions loyal to Diamacoune.

20 In 2002 the *Joola* (ferry named after the Joola or Diola people) capsized and sank off Gambia's coast, causing one of the largest disasters in maritime history. Over 1,800 people were killed.

21 After the fatal shipwreck, Wade dismissed Prime Minister Idrissa Seck and the rest of his cabinet - a 1996 decree had authorized the *Joola* to use 'its own resources' for maintenance and repairs. In 2002 the euro began to officially operate in Senegal.

22 In 2003, Sidy Badji, MFDC founder, died at his home in Ziquinchor, a few days before peace talks began between the rebels and the Government. That year, MFDC leader Jean-Marie Francois Biagui announced the end of the

separatist war before hundreds of rebel delegates in Ziguinchor. Both parties were firmly committed to ending over 20 years of violence.

23 The armed section of the MFDC did not take part in the talks and, according to some sources, peace would only be possible when

the strongest factions were willing to talk. In April 2004, MFDC rebels ambushed a group of Senegalese soldiers who were removing landmines in the south. Three soldiers were killed and another five injured. That month Macky Sall replaced Seck. ∎

IN FOCUS

ENVIRONMENTAL CHALLENGES
Deforestation and desertification. A hydroelectric dam project in a valley north of the Senegal river poses a serious threat for environmental balance. There are few regulations governing the use of most natural resources: there is poaching, excessive fishing and shepherding.

WOMEN'S RIGHTS
Women have been able to vote and run for office since 1945.

Female representation in Parliament remained at 12 per cent between 1995 and 2000, but women held only 7 per cent of ministerial posts. In 2003 they made up 43 per cent of the workforce, but more than half were unpaid or received wages far below those of men.

Although the Constitution includes gender equity, discrimination is rampant. Women have the right to choose their husbands, but in practice almost half are in polygamous marriages.

According to UNICEF's latest data available*, only 28 per cent of women over 15 years of age could read and write, compared with 47 per cent of men in that age group. Female genital mutilation is common in rural areas, although the largest ethnic group, the Wolofs, does not practice it.

Women in the cities have more access to education and possibilities of participation. In urban areas it is easier to have access to the legal rights of divorce, alimony and equal pay.

CHILDREN
The Ministry of Family, Social Development and Solidarity is responsible for the promotion of child welfare. The Government has built more schools and pursued programs to encourage the enrollment and attendance of girls in school. In 2000, only 63 per cent of children were enrolled in primary school, although education is compulsory and free between the ages of 6 and 16.

Child labor is banned, but practised. The minimum age for employment was not particularly

respected in the informal sector or within family businesses, where the Government did not impose a minimum age.

INDIGENOUS PEOPLES/ ETHNIC MINORITIES
The Wolof are the largest ethnic minority (42 per cent) and 75 per cent of the population speak their language. The Lebu, who basically live off fishing, live in the Cape Verde and Saint Louis peninsula. The Serer constitute almost 15 per cent of the total population and are Muslims, except for a group living along the Petite-Côte.

The Malinke live in Eastern Senegal; the Sininke in the border zones with Mali and Mauritania.

The Diola comprise 10 per cent of the population and live mostly in Casamance. They continue to suffer repression and exclusion from political processes. The Government makes few efforts to improve their conditions or meet their demands for better infrastructure, education and economic opportunities.

MIGRANTS/REFUGEES
The conflict in Casamance province, which lasted until late 2002, forced more than 10,000 Senegalese to take refuge in other countries: 6,000 in Guinea-Bissau and almost 5,000 in Gambia. There were an estimated 5,000 internally displaced people in Senegal.

Senegal harbored some 45,000 refugees and asylum-seekers, most of them from Mauritania in 1990. Refugee leaders stated that the population had no intention of repatriating from Senegal, until the Mauritanian Government ensured their citizenship and compensated them for the loss of their properties.

DEATH PENALTY
Although the death penalty is still in force, the last execution took place in 1967.

*Latest data available in *The State of the World's Children* and *Childinfo* database, UNICEF, 2004.

Serbia and Montenegro / Srbija i Crna Gora

Population:	10,513,058
Area:	102,000 km²
Capital:	Belgrade
Currency:	Dinar (Serbia); Euro (Montenegro and Kosovo)
Languages:	Serb, Montenegrin

In the 4th century BC, the Balkan Peninsula and the Adriatic coast were inhabited by Illyrian, Thracian and Panonian groups, and they were also the site of Greek colonies. In the mid-2nd century, Rome defeated the alliance of the Illyrian peoples and began colonizing the new province of Illyria. Important Roman cities developed, such as Emona (now Ljubljana), Mursa (Osijek) and Singidunum (Belgrade). When the Roman Empire split into Eastern and Western regions, the border between the two ran through what is now Serbia-Montenegrin territory. Towards the end of Roman domination, Christianity was established in the region.

[2] In the 5th and 6th centuries AD, these territories were invaded by a number of nomadic tribes: Visigoths, Huns, Ostrogoths, Avars, Bulgars and Slavs. They imposed their own religious beliefs upon the people, but Christianity gradually took hold again between the 9th and 11th centuries. From the 7th to the 13th centuries there were several feudal states. The Serbs were separate from these states, although they were unable to resist external pressure. Bosnia was subdued by Hungary, and the rest of the territory, as far as the state of Ducla, by Byzantium. Macedonia was divided up between Byzantium and Bulgaria (see Bosnia-Herzegovina, and Croatia).

[3] In the mid-11th century, under the reign of Stephen Nemanja (1168-1196), Serbia freed itself from Byzantine domination. The Serbian rulers of the Nemanja dynasty fought against the non-Christian

religions which had been spread by the Bulgars. They received a royal title from the Pope in 1217, but the hoped-for propagation of the Catholic faith did not follow. In 1219, the Serbian Orthodox Church was founded, and mass began to be celebrated in Serbian. Under the reign of Stefan Dusan (1331-1355) the medieval Serbian State reached its apogee when it occupied Albania and Macedonia.

[4] The Ottoman Empire began its conquest of the Balkans in the mid-14th century, after the Battle of Kosovo in 1389. In the 14th and 15th centuries, the first of a series of migrations began from Serbia and Bosnia to neighboring Slav regions and ultimately to Russia. In 1395, all of Macedonia came under the Ottoman Empire. Bosnia, which had been a part of the Hungarian kingdom since the 12th century, was conquered in 1463. The Slav population of Bosnia became Muslim within a relatively short period of time. In 1465, the Turks occupied Herzegovina. By this time, Venetia had annexed the territories of Neretva and Zetina, along the coast. The city-state of Dubrovnik came under Hungarian control, and then, after 1526, became a part of the Ottoman Empire for 489 years.

[5] Between the 16th and 18th centuries, all of what was to become Yugoslavia's territories were divided up. Serbia, Bosnia, Herzegovina, Montenegro and Macedonia were part of the Ottoman Empire; Croatia, Slovenia, Slavonia, part of Dalmatia and Vaivodina belonged to the Hapsburgs; and Istria and Dalmatia to the Venetian Republic. After the 1690 revolution was put down in Old Serbia, some 70,000 people

took refuge in the Hapsburg Empire. The Ottoman Empire transferred Albanian Muslims to the abandoned territories of Kosovo and Motojia.

[6] After the Russo-Turkish war of 1768-74, Russia obtained the right to sponsor the Orthodox population of the Ottoman Empire, through the Treaty of Kuchuk-Kainardzhi. Austria seized the Balkans in 1797, as a result of the Napoleonic Wars, The Balkan *pashalik* (the north of Serbia), which belonged to the Ottoman Empire after the first Serbian uprising (1804-13), the Russo-Turkish war (1806-12) and the second Serbian uprising (1815), was granted internal autonomy. The political and military leaders Gueorgui Cherny (Karadjordje) and Milos Obrenovic founded Serbia's ruling dynasties. In 1829, Serbia became an independent principality within the Ottoman Empire, with Milos Obrenovic as its prince.

[7] In the 1878 Congress of Berlin, the Great Powers recognized the full independence of Serbia and Montenegro, which became kingdoms in 1882 and 1905 respectively. In the first Balkan war in 1912, Serbia, Montenegro, Greece, Romania and Bulgaria formed an alliance. In the second, in 1913, they fought against each other over the Ottoman Empire's domains. The end result was Macedonia's partition between Serbia, Greece and Bulgaria, while Serbia and Montenegro expanded their territories.

[8] Serbian resistance to the Austro-Hungarian Empire led to the assassination of the Austrian archduke Franz Ferdinand in 1914, in Sarajevo, the event that marked

the beginning of World War I. After the War, which saw the end of Austria-Hungary's empire, a kingdom of Serbs, Croats and Slovenes was founded, including Serbia, Montenegro and the territories of Slovenia, Croatia, Slavonia, Bosnia and Herzegovina.

[9] In 1929, the nation began to be called Yugoslavia: the land of the southern Slavs. The Government remained in the hands of Serbians, and under the reign of Alexandr Karagueorgevich, it became an absolute monarchy. The regime's exclusivist policies gave rise to a strong anti-Serbian movement among Croats and other ethnic minorities, which led to the King's assassination in Marseilles in 1934.

[10] At the beginning of World War II, Yugoslavia was neutral. In 1941, when Hitler attacked Yugoslavia, the country was so divided internally that it was easily subdued within a few days. The King and the members of the government fled the country, and the German Command carried out a policy of extermination against the Serbian and Muslim population.

[11] Two groups which were hostile towards each other launched the resistance movement: the nationalists loyal to the King - called *chetniks* - led by Draza Mihajlovic, and the partisans under the leadership of Josip Broz, a Croat better known by his *nom de guerre*, Tito. This group was made up of communists in favor of a united Yugoslavia, and anti-Nazi forces from all the republics with the exception of Serbia; it later became the Yugoslav League of Communists (YLC).

[12] After bloody fighting against occupation troops and the Croatian *ustasha* (fascist) movement allied to the Germans, Tito emerged victorious. After the liberation of the country in May 1945, a Provisional Government was formed led by Tito and supported by the Soviet Union and Britain.

[13] During the war 2,000,000 Yugoslavians were killed and 3,500,000 were left homeless. When the war finally ended, the country was in ruins.

[14] On 29 November 1945, a Constituent Assembly abolished the monarchy, proclaiming a federation of six republics: Slovenia and Croatia in the North, Serbia in the East, Bosnia-Herzegovina and Montenegro at the center, and Macedonia in the South. It also founded two autonomous provinces: Voyvodina and Kosovo, to the northeast and southeast of Serbia, respectively.

[15] The YLC joined the Cominform (Communist and Workers' Parties' Information Bureau) in 1947, but withdrew in the Spring of 1948 over disagreements with the Soviet

WORKERS

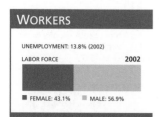

UNEMPLOYMENT: 13.8% (2002)

LABOR FORCE   **2002**

■ FEMALE: 43.1%   ■ MALE: 56.9%

CP leadership. The USSR initiated an embargo against Yugoslavia, which led to the strengthening of its ties with the West and the Third World.

[16] After a phase of economic centralization including the forced collectivization of agriculture in 1950, Tito introduced the concept of 'self-management'. Its goals were to ensure workers direct, democratic participation in all decision-making processes concerning their living and working conditions, and to protect social democracy against the distortions and abuses of 'statism' - bureaucracy and technocracy.

[17] Tito was one of the founders of the Non-Aligned Movement, set up in 1961. The Yugoslav leader defined non-alignment as the process whereby countries which were not linked to political or military blocs could take part in international issues, without being satellites of the major powers.

[18] The Yugoslavian leadership was charged with revisionism and isolated from the international Communist movement because of its neutral foreign policy and heterodox model of social and economic organization. Relations with the USSR slowly returned to normal after Stalin's death in 1953.

[19] That same year, an Agrarian Reform Law was approved authorizing private farming, and 80 per cent of the land returned to private hands. The combination of private economic activity and the self-management system led to average annual GNP growth rates of 8.1 per cent, between 1953 and 1965. In 1968, industrial production was 12 times greater than in 1950. In terms of the economy, industrial production was three times as important as agricultural production. As a result, Yugoslavia's social and economic model was of great interest to the European Left.

[20] The country's growth rate declined slightly toward the end of the 1960s. Even so, until the end of the 1970s, the annual growth rate exceeded five per cent.

[21] President Tito was aware of the inter-ethnic tensions in the Yugoslavia of his day, as well as the sharp contrasts between the socio-economic situation of the industrialized north and that of the underdeveloped south. In 1970, he announced that after he stepped down, the country's leadership should be exercised by a body made up of the federated republics and the autonomous provinces.

[22] In 1971 and 1972, ethnic conflicts worsened, especially between Serbs and Croats, and Croatia presented a formal complaint against the confederated system. After 1974, there was an increase in separatist activity by Kosovo's Albanian majority.

[23] After Tito's death in April 1980, the executive power was vested in a collective presidential body, made up of a representative of each republic and autonomous province, and the president of the YLC with a rotating annual presidency. The new regime ratified Tito's policies of self-management socialism and non-alignment.

[24] Despite a strong economic position during the 1960s, both Serbia and Croatia became exporters of labor. Yugoslavia continued to export labor, and cash remittances from Yugoslavian workers in Western Europe together with revenues from tourism constituted an essential source of foreign currency to improve the balance of payments. This became more important in 1980 when the economic situation worsened.

[25] In March and April 1981, there were riots in the autonomous province of Kosovo (bordering on Albania) and these recurred in 1988 and 1990. In Kosovo, 90 per cent of the population (1.9 million) at this time was of Albanian origin. It was the poorest region of Yugoslavia, with unemployment reaching 50 per cent in 1990, with a per capita GNP of $730 while Serbia's was $2,200.

[26] According to the federal government, Kosovo housed nationalist forces and separatist extremists inspired and instigated from abroad, whose final objective was secession from Serbia and Yugoslavia. Many Serbs and Montenegrins left the area. Repression of the uprisings in Kosovo, which left a number of people dead and injured, led to mutual diplomatic recrimination between Belgrade and Tirana (the Albanian capital) and the resignation of Kosovo's governor, Jusuf Zejnullahu, in March 1990. There was also tension in other republics due to the growth of militant Muslim and Catholic groups.

[27] Ethnic conflicts - coupled with inflation, which reached 90 per cent in 1986 and four figures in 1989 - were considered by the central committee of the Communist League to be rooted in deeper contradictions. During these years, several lawsuits dealing with government corruption exposed the fact that the system was crumbling. The Communist parties of Slovenia and Croatia announced their withdrawal from the YLC. In its January 1990 congress, the Yugoslavian League of Communists renounced its constitutional single-party role, and called on parliament to draft a new constitution, eliminating the

IN FOCUS

ENVIRONMENTAL CHALLENGES
The war and in particular the NATO bombings in 1999 caused a series of environmental problems, the worst being contamination from depleted uranium used in NATO missiles. There is an alarming degree of air pollution in Belgrade and pollution of coastal waters, especially in tourist areas such as Kotor Bay. Industries dump their waste into the Sava River, a tributary of the Danube.

WOMEN'S RIGHTS
At the beginning of 2004, 10 of the 126 seats in the Serbian and Montenegrin parliament were held by women, while they had 27 out of the 250 seats in the Serbian parliament. Women are active in political organizations and occupy 10 per cent of ministerial level posts.

Violence against women is reflected in the high rates of domestic violence. In 2002, the criminal code was amended to criminalize rape between partners.

According to the International Helsinki Federation, women's salaries are on average 11 per cent lower than men's.

Patriarchal ideas regarding gender roles, particularly in rural areas, lead to discrimination. In minority communities, women cannot own property. Almost all births are attended by qualified personnel. Data on prenatal care have not been published.

CHILDREN
Nine years of free, compulsory education are provided. However, economic difficulties affect both children's education and health. The worst affected are Roma children who do not have access to preschool education. The main problem for them is that very often they do not speak Serbian due to lack of schooling, and they may even be sent to schools for children with emotional problems if they do not pass the standard examination (which all Serb children must take).

It is estimated that approximately 30 per cent of children are abused in some way. Although teachers are instructed to expose abuse, frequently they do not. The Government provides psychological and legal assistance, and has even established a center for treating trauma caused by incest.

The trafficking of children for sexual exploitation continues to be a serious problem.

INDIGENOUS PEOPLES/ ETHNIC MINORITIES
Although a Law for the Protection and Rights of National Minorities was passed in February 2003, discrimination against the Roma continues. In addition to a disproportionately high rate of unemployment, they are frequently attacked by racist groups and the authorities take no measures to tackle this problem. Most of the Roma who fled from Kosovo after July 1999 continue to face serious problems, worsened by difficulties in registering. Information published by Amnesty International also mentions that Roma who lack documentation or proof of citizenship, have been denied medical and social benefits, and children have been discriminated against in their access to education.

MIGRANTS/REFUGEES
In 2004, Serbia and Montenegro continued to be the epicenter of displacement in the Balkans, hosting more than a half million uprooted people, (543,100) from its several wars in the Balkans. It recorded 291,100 refugees, 189,400 from Croatia, 99,700 from Bosnia and 1,500 ethnic Albanians from Macedonia in Kosovo. More than 248,000 of these were ethnic Serbs. Serbia had an estimated 252,000 internally displaced persons. In addition, 70,100 of the country's nationals were refugees or asylum seekers abroad, the majority from Kosovo. Serbia and Montenegro had 224,800 internally displaced persons from Kosovo, 70% ethnic Serbs, 13% Roma, and 6% Montenegrins. Another 22,200 Kosovars were displaced, but had remained within Kosovo. In addition, Kosovo hosted about 5,000 mostly Albanians displaced from the Presevo Valley in southern Serbia, most during the conflict in the valley that ended in 2001.

DEATH PENALTY
In January 2003, the Serbian parliament abolished the death penalty for all crimes. The Montenegrin parliament abolished it in June.

Under-5 mortality
19 per 1,000 live births
2002

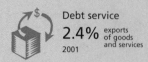
Debt service
2.4% exports of goods and services
2001

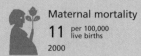
Maternal mortality
11 per 100,000 live births
2000

leading role assigned to the League in all spheres of Yugoslav life.

[28] In April of the same year, in the first multiparty elections to be held in Yugoslavia since World War II, nationalist groups demanding either secession or a confederated structure won in all of the republics except Serbia and Montenegro. In 1989, Yugoslavia's last socialist prime minister, Ante Markovic - a Croat and a neo-liberal - launched a series of structural reforms in order to put an end to the crisis.

[29] As of 1990, the situation began to deteriorate even further. Industrial production fell by 18-20 per cent in Serbia and 13 per cent in Montenegro - while the gross foreign debt of the Federation as a whole reached $16.295 million. Of this, more than $5.5 million arose from Serbia and Montenegro.

[30] With mounting social pressures because of the economic situation and the disintegrating state, Yugoslavian politics were polarized by two fundamentally opposed concepts. Kucan in Slovenia argued for decentralization to relieve the wealthier regions of the obligation to subsidize the more backward areas, while Slobodan Milosevic, charismatic president of the Serbian Communist League, proposed greater centralization and solidarity in the Federation.

[31] In December 1990, the Croatian Parliament adopted a new constitution which established the right to withdraw from the Federation. At the same time, a referendum in Slovenia endorsed independence. In the following months, there was disagreement over the reform of the federal system and the appointment of the President.

[32] On 8 September 1991, Croatia and Slovenia declared their independence from the Federation, and the Serbian population within Croatia declared its intention of separating from Croatia. The federal army, whose officials answered primarily to Serbia, intervened in Slovenia and Croatia, stating that separation was a threat to Yugoslavia's integrity. War broke out, with many victims on both sides (see Croatia).

[33] War led to the destruction by federal troops of entire cities - like Osijek, Vukovar and Karlovac - as well as the occupation of nearly a quarter of Croatia's total land area. Areas affected included the territories of West and East Slavonia, as well as the area known as Krajina, which toward the end of 1991 proclaimed itself the 'Republic of Serbian Krajina'.

[34] In December, the president of the governing council, Stjepan Mesic, and Prime Minister Markovic, both Croats and the last

representatives of a united government, resigned. By the end of 1991, there was a total of 550,000 refugees, 300,000 of them from occupied areas of Croatia.

[35] In 1992, within the territory which still defined itself as Yugoslavia, Serbian president Milosevic shored up his position by retiring 70 generals and admirals of the federal armed forces whose loyalty to him was in question. He also won Montenegrin support for his plan to establish a unified Yugoslavia with its capital in Belgrade, through a plebiscite in that republic. The 1 March referendum was boycotted by the opposition.

[36] On 15 January 1992, the European Community recognized Croatia and Slovenia as sovereign states. On 27 April, the parliament of Serbian and Montenegrin deputies announced the foundation of the new Federal Republic of Yugoslavia, a federation between Serbia and Montenegro with a parliamentary system of government.

[37] In the meantime, fighting continued in the regions characterized by inter-ethnic strife. Since April 1992, the heart of the fighting had been the republic of Bosnia-Herzegovina, which was recognized by the EC on 7 April. In order to divest itself of responsibility for the aggression in Croatia and Bosnia-Herzegovina, in early May Belgrade announced that it was no longer in control of troops from what had formerly been the federal army, now fighting in the independent republics. Far from having the desired effect, Serbia's position led the EC to declare a trade embargo against Yugoslavia on 28 May.

[38] However, the general elections held in the new federation on 31 May served to further strengthen Milosevic's position. His Socialist Party of Serbia (SPS) won 70.6 per cent of the vote in Serbia, while the Socialist Democratic Party of Montenegro won 76.6 per cent. The democratic opposition, as well as the Albanian minorities and the Muslims of Sandchak, boycotted the elections; only 56 per cent of the electorate participated.

[39] From 1993, a series of purges began within Serbian government institutions. The intransigence of the Serbian Government was evident in Kosovo, where any attempt at independence was met with repression within a framework policy of cultural annihilation.

[40] As Milosevic and the ruling SPS party grew more authoritarian, international pressure increased and the social and economic crisis deepened. In 1993, 80 per cent of the federal budget was earmarked for the armed forces, and 20 per

cent of the country's GNP went to supporting the Serbs in Bosnia and Croatia.

[41] The power of Milosevic's SPS party increased from 1994 onwards. In the parliamentary elections in December 1993 they gained the majority in the Assembly. The Serb President imprisoned his most important political rivals and tried to take a less central role in the war. This line of action included selective collaboration with the war crimes trials in The Hague.

[42] Milosevic's main aim was that the UN should suspend its sanctions on Yugoslavia from May 1992. On 24 September 1994, the international organization decided to partially lift the measures for 100 days, allowing international flights, and cultural and sporting exchanges. This diplomatic coup by Milosevic - who was previously accused of being the main instigator of the war in the Balkans - contributed to his increasing popularity in the Federation.

[43] The Yugoslav President Zoran Lilic continued to play an important role in the peace process in Bosnia-Herzegovina during 1995. The political distancing between Yugoslavia and the Bosnian Serb leaders Radovan Karadzic and Ratko Mladic was at odds with the attitude adopted on the military front.

[44] Milosevic's popularity soared again following the signing of the peace agreement in Dayton, Ohio, though his major triumph came on 14 December 1995 when the US suspended the sanctions on Yugoslavia as a result of the signing of the Paris agreement. During the embargo, per capita income had fallen to half the previous amount and more than one and a half million people were unemployed.

[45] The year 1997 was marked by confrontations between the federal army and the population of Kosovo (90 per cent of Albanian origin). Milosevic called a referendum, in all of Serbia, on the need for foreign mediation on this conflict. This move was rejected by 75 per cent of the voters (with a boycott by the Albanian-speaking population of Kosovo).

[46] In April 1998, Yugoslav army soldiers killed two Albanian citizens trying to enter the Federation, claiming they were 'terrorists'. This aggravated tension between Yugoslavia and Albania - accused by Belgrade of arming the Kosovan Liberation Army (KLA). A week later, members of the 'contact group', the US, France, Italy, Germany, Russia and Britain, meeting in Rome to agree a common stance, confirmed they would seek dialogue between the parties. The US stated its support for a fresh embargo on Belgrade if Milosevic refused dialogue,

including a ban on weapons deliveries and a ban on investments. This proposal was not accepted by Russia.

[47] Later confrontations in Kosovo in June 1998 led Britain and other NATO member countries to issue a call for intervention in the region. After a brief truce in the second half of the year, which the KLA forces used to establish an independent policy of persecuting the Serb minority, the Yugoslav army re-entered the territory. The failure of negotiations held in Rambouillet, France, through which the European countries and the US wanted to make Yugoslavia a protectorate, paved the way for war. Yugoslavia, as the party guilty of failing to agree the Rambouillet accords, remained under NATO observation and isolated from its old ally, Russia.

[48] In March 1999 the Alliance launched air strikes on Yugoslav targets in Serbia, Montenegro and the province of Kosovo. The UK and US, the main military forces, also had air, naval and logistical support from Germany, Italy, France and Turkey amongst others. Bombs dropped from beyond the reach of anti-aircraft fire caused hundreds of deaths amongst Kosovars and Serbs. The air attack unleashed a campaign of revenge attacks against Kosovars, who fled in their tens of thousands to neighboring countries and Montenegro. NATO air attacks with 'smart' bombs destroyed hundreds of civilian buildings, including a state TV station, schools, a hospital and the Chinese embassy in Belgrade. The violence between Serb and Kosovar civilians grew from the start of the bombing.

[49] At the beginning of June, the Group of Eight richest countries sent former Russian prime minister Viktor Chernomyrdin and former Finnish president Martti Ahtisaari to negotiate conditions for a ceasefire. The bombing ended on 10 June and the Yugoslav forces accepted the presence of a UN force, KFOR, made up of some 35,000 troops. According to the agreement, Yugoslav sovereignty was recognized over the province, but in practice it was a protectorate under NATO military control and the political coverage of the UN.

[50] Ethnic cleansing of Serbs and Roma led to dozens of deaths after KFOR arrived, and the force was unable to totally disarm the KLA, integrating this into the police force. Several thousand members of these communities had to move from their homes, while a large number of Kosovar refugees returned to the province.

[51] The Serb opposition was unable to unite against Milosevic, and despite demonstrations after

the arrival of KFOR troops in which up to 10,000 people demanded his resignation, the movement split and then disappeared.

[52] The railway line from Montenegro to Serbia was reopened in October 1999, while the ban on commercial flights between third party countries and Yugoslavia was lifted in February 2000. In November, Montenegro adopted the German mark as its currency, while it remained in confrontation with Belgrade.

[53] Arkan - real name Zeljko Raznjatovic - one of the Serb paramilitary leaders and president of the Serbian Unity Party, was assassinated in January 2000 in a hotel in Belgrade. This prompted a cycle of political killings that also took the Defense Minister, the Montenegrin Pavle Bulatovic, in February that year.

[54] In June the Yugoslav legislature approved constitutional changes under which the President would be elected by popular vote instead of by the Assembly. After the elections, the opposition claimed that their candidate, Vojislav Kostunica, had won by a majority and that a second-round election was not needed. But after three days of silence, the electoral commission gave Kostunica 48.22 per cent of the vote, to Milosevic's 40.23 per cent, making a run-off vote necessary. The US and EU denounced the election as fraudulent and demanded that Milosevic acknowledge defeat.

[55] A popular uprising, organized by the opposition, joined by the police and army, forced Milosevic to flee. After intense negotiations with the former president's supporters, Kostunica was finally sworn in as President. A new Parliament, elected in early November, appointed a Milosevic supporter, Zoran Zizic, as Prime Minister.

[56] After the Socialist Party lost the parliamentary elections by a broad margin to the Democratic Opposition of Serbia (DOS) coalition, in January 2001 Milosevic was placed under house arrest. In April he was transferred to a prison in Belgrade. Prosecutors announced there would be charges brought against him. The following month, US President George W Bush said economic aid to Yugoslavia was conditional upon Milosevic being handing over to the International Criminal Tribunal for the Former Yugoslavia (ICTFY) in The Hague. On 28 June the former president was extradited, prompting Premier Zizic to resign in protest. In his first appearance before the ICTFY, Milosevic refused to recognize the legitimacy of the court and said that the objective of the trial was 'to produce false justifications for

the war crimes that NATO committed in Yugoslavia'.

[57] As part of the reforms intended to revitalize the economy, the first large layoff in 50 years took place in Serbia in August. Since the end of World War II lifetime employment had been guaranteed, but that ended when, after several weeks of talks between the Government and labor unions at the Zastava car factory in the city of Kragujevac, an agreement was reached to lay off 8,000 of its 12,000 workers. The Milosevic regime had never made workers redundant, but had ensured that they had received a minimum salary of $10 a month, even during the war.

[58] Although the GDP of the Yugoslav Federation had grown an estimated five per cent in 2001, this was just half the growth recorded in 1989. The Paris Club - rich world creditor nations - had canceled $3 billion, two-thirds, of Yugoslavia's official debt. This opened possibilities of recovery for the economy - which continued to be one of the most devastated on the continent. The Government's highest expectations were placed on an increase in foreign capital investment, in hopes that it would accelerate recovery.

[59] Fear in Europe about new fragmentation in the Balkans prompted the EU to draft an interim plan for the dissolution of the Federal Republic of Yugoslavia, but declarations of independence were postponed. In March 2002 Yugoslavia, Montenegro and Serbia signed an accord under which the name 'Yugoslavia' would disappear, provisionally creating a new state called 'Serbia and Montenegro'. At the end of the year, each would vote on new Constitutions and each would have its own President, Defense Minister and Foreign Minister. These semi-independent states would also take charge of their own economies. After three years, each would hold a referendum to decide whether or not to seek independence.

[60] In February 2003 the parliament approved the constitutional charter for the new union of Serbia and Montenegro. The two republics still used separate currencies. The issue of Kosovo, an international protectorate but legally part of Serbia, remained unresolved.

[61] In March Prime Minister Zoran Djindjic was assassinated by snipers. More than 200,000 people attended his funeral.

[62] The unified parliament of Serbia and Montenegro elected Svetozvar Marovic, the Montenegrin deputy chair person of the Democratic Party of Socialists (DPS), as the country's first

PROFILE

ENVIRONMENT

Most of the country is mountainous, with one important plain north of the Sava River, a tributary of the Danube, where agriculture is concentrated. The climate is continental in this area, and Mediterranean along the coast. Rich deposits of bauxite, coal, lead, copper and zinc in the mountains, together with tourism in the Adriatic coast of Montenegro are major sources of income.

SOCIETY

Peoples: Serb 62.6 per cent; Albanian 16.5 per cent; Montenegrin 5.0 per cent; multiethnic 3.4 per cent; Hungarian 3.3 per cent; Muslim 3.3 per cent; Roma (Gypsy) 1.3 per cent; Croat 1.1 per cent; other 3.5 per cent. In Kosovo - under UNMIK (Interim Administration Mission in Kosovo) - up to 90 per cent of the population is of Albanian origin. These rates are subject to error because of the exceptional political situation.
Religions: 65 per cent Serb-Orthodox, 19 per cent Muslim, 4 per cent Catholic.
Languages: Serb, Montenegrin (official), Albanian, Hungarian, Slovakian and Roma.
Main Political Parties: Socialist Party of Serbia (SPS); Serbian Radical Party; Reformist Party, neo-liberal; Democratic Movement of Serbia; Socialist Party of Voivodina; Hungarian Democratic League of Voivodina; Green Party, among others.
Social Organizations: League of Unions.

THE STATE

Official Name: Srbija i Crna Gord (Serbia and Montenegro).
Capital: Belgrade 1,118,000 people (2003).
Other Cities: Pristina 190,500 people; Nis 184,400; Novi Sad 176,100 (2000).
Government: The country is a confederal parliamentary democratic republic, with two constituent states, the Republic of Serbia (Republika Srbije) and the Republic of Montenegro (Republika Crna Gora). Both republics have a common foreign, defense, trade and human rights policy. Each republic has a separate parliament in addition to the central parliament. After three years, their respective populations are to be asked in a referendum whether they want to continue to be part of this new federation, or opt for independence. President: Svetozar Marovic, since March 2003. Serbian Prime Minister: Zoran Zivkovic. Montenegrin Prime Minister: Milo Djukanovic. The 126 member parliament (Assembly of Serbia and Montenegro) that elected Marovic was itself elected for a four year term in February by the parliaments of Serbia (91 seats) and Montenegro (35 seats). Representation is distributed among parties and coalitions in proportion to the number of seats they hold in Serbia's and Montenegro's national parliaments. Kosovo is under the UN interim administration mission presided over by former Finnish premier Harri Holkeri, in office since August 2003.
National Holiday: 29 November, Proclamation of the Republic (1945).
Armed Forces: 126,500 (60,000 recruits) (1995).

president. The Assembly of Serbia and Montenegro which elected Marovic has been itself elected in February by the parliaments of Serbia and Montenegro.

[63] In spite of difficulties in harmonizing some economic policies, such as foreign tariffs, trade between Serbia and Montenegro increased by 47.1 per cent between January and November 2003, with respect to the same period the previous year.

[64] In February 2004, the legal provision establishing a minimum participation of 50 per cent of the electorate to make elections valid was eliminated in Serbia after the failure of three successive presidential elections due to the high rate of abstentions. The post had been vacant since President

Milan Milutinovic was deposed in December 2002 and after that it was filled temporarily by the presidents of the parliament.

[65] In March 2004, Kosovo - still under UN guardianship - was again the scene of violent confrontations between the Albanian majority and the Serbian minority. The Albanian-Kosovar leaders, among them their president, Ibrahim Rugova, announced that their aim was independence, although the UN and the EU had stated that they were in favor of autonomy within the Federation. Meanwhile, in Serbia various leaders demanded partition of the province between Serbs and Albanians, another solution resisted by Western foreign ministers. ■

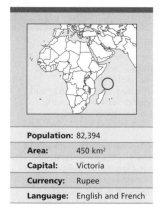

Population:	82,394
Area:	450 km²
Capital:	Victoria
Currency:	Rupee
Language:	English and French

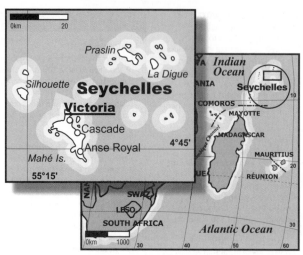

P rior to exploration by
Portuguese sailors in the 16th
century, the archipelago had
already been visited by Persian
Gulf merchants. French and British
colonists fought violently over this
Indian Ocean colony during the
18th century. After expelling the
French in 1794, the British paid
little attention to it, and it was
governed from the island of
Mauritius until 1903. The
Seychelles archipelago gained
strategic significance within the
context of European colonial
expansion during the second half
of the 19th century.
2   The Seychelles People's
United Party (SPUP) founded in
1964 gave the local population
- most of them descendants of
enslaved Africans and Indian
workers - a new sense of
nationalism. Meanwhile, the
colonial interests organized
themselves into the Seychelles'
Taxpayers Association. It was later
renamed the Seychelles
Democratic Party and, led by
James Mancham, it opposed
independence.
3   In the legislative elections of
April 1974, the SPUP won 47.6
per cent of the vote. However,
the peculiar colonial 'democratic'
system awarded the Party only 2
of the 15 seats and Mancham
remained Prime Minister. In spite
of this, it was too late to stem
the tide of nationalism and in

1976 Mancham agreed to the
British Foreign Office's suggestion
that he become the first
President of the Republic of
Seychelles. Shortly before
independence, he had agreed to
'return' the strategic British
Indian Ocean Territory (BIOT)
islands to the UK. The British in
turn had promised to pass them
on to the US, which planned to
set up the important Diego
Garcia naval base there.
4   Aware that the people would
not accept this deal, Mancham
postponed the elections until
1979, arguing that they were not
necessary as all of the parties
were in favor of independence.
5   Mancham's foreign policy was
directed at cementing a strong
alliance with South Africa, the
source of most of its tourists,
while domestic policy destroyed
tea and coconut plantations to
make room for new five-star
hotels, owned by foreign
companies. Entire islands were
sold off to foreigners like Harry
Oppenheimer, the South African

gold magnate, and the actor
Peter Sellers.
6   In 1977, while Mancham was
maneuvering to postpone the
elections yet again, the SPUP took
over the country 'with the
collaboration of the local police
force' while Mancham was out of
the country. Accused of 'leading a
wasteful life while his people
worked hard', Mancham was
replaced by SPUP leader Albert
René.
7   René renewed his support for
the Non-Aligned Movement,
which had recognized the SPUP as
a legitimate liberation movement
prior to independence. The new
Government turned to socialism,
promising to reorganize tourism,
give priority to self-sufficiency in
agriculture and fishing, increase
education, and reduce the high
unemployment rates which were
affecting nearly half the working
population.
8   In mid-1978, in response to
the changing political context, the
SPUP became the People's
Progressive Front of Seychelles

(FPPS). In June 1979, the FPPS won
the national elections with 98 per
cent of the vote. After the victory,
President René demanded that
the US base on Diego Garcia be
closed and the island returned to
Mauritius.
9   In August 1978, a land reform
law was passed calling for the
expropriation of all uncultivated
land. René also nationalized the
water and electricity services, the
construction industry and
transportation, which led to a
rapid economic recovery in the
Seychelles. In spite of not having
any mineral or oil wealth, by
1979-1980 they had the largest
per capita income of any of the
islands in the region.
10   This economic growth was
encouraged and supported by
tourism and effective
administration. At this time the
Seychelles received an average of
80,000 tourists a year. During the
Mancham's time in office most of
them were South Africans, but
after René became president
more Europeans came.
11   The opponents of Albert
René, mainly the South African
apartheid regime, did not give up
their efforts to overthrow the
socialist government of the
Seychelles. In November 1981, a
group of 45 mercenaries led by
former colonel Mike Hoare tried
to invade the island and oust the
Government. The coup plotted by
former President Mancham failed
and the mercenaries had to hijack
an Indian airliner to escape to
South Africa.
12   After the unsuccessful
invasion, the Seychelles
Government declared a state of
emergency and imposed a curfew.
13   The failed invasion and the
economic recession in Europe
caused tourism to decline by
approximately ten per cent.
In August 1982, the situation

PUBLIC EXPENDITURE

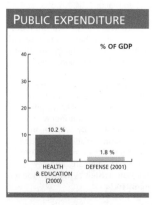

% OF GDP

HEALTH & EDUCATION (2000): 10.2 %
DEFENSE (2001): 1.8 %

PROFILE

ENVIRONMENT
An archipelago of 92 islands: Mahé, Praslin, and
La Digue are the largest islands, made of granite;
the rest are of coral. The climate is tropical with
plentiful vegetation and heavy rainfall. Only the
largest islands are inhabited, but some economic
use is made of the other islands.

SOCIETY
Peoples: Most Seychellois are descended from
Africans and Europeans. There are minorities of
European, Chinese and Indian origin.
Religions: Roman Catholic 88.6 per cent; other
Christian (mostly Anglican) 7.7 per cent; Hindu 0.7
per cent; other, 3 per cent (1996).
Languages: English and French (official); most of
the population speak Creole, a local dialect with
European and African influences.
Main Political Parties: People's Progressive Front
of Seychelles (FPPS); Seychelles National Party

(SNP), continuation of the United Opposition (OU,
centrist), in turn formed by the National Alliance
Party; Rally of the People of Seychelles for
Democracy; Democratic Party (PD).
Main Social Organizations: The National Workers'
Union.

THE STATE
Official Name: Repiblik Sesel.
Capital: Victoria 25,000 people (2003).
Other Cities: Anse Royal 3,700 people; Cascade
2,500 (2000).
Government: France-Albert René, President since
June 1977, re-elected in 1993, 1998 and 2001.
Single-chamber legislature: National Assembly,
with 34 members.
National Holiday: 28 June, Independence Day
(1976).
Armed Forces: 300 (1996). Other: 1,300 National
Guard.

deteriorated further when military personnel plotted an unsuccessful rebellion, strengthening rumors of another possible mercenary conspiracy. European conservative groups organized a smear campaign to support these rumors. In June 1984, Albert René was re-elected with 93 per cent of the vote.

[14] In September 1986, there was another coup attempt. Albert René, who was in Zimbabwe at a Non-Aligned Countries summit, returned immediately and put down the rebellion. Most of those responsible were arrested, including the main leader, Minister of Defense Colonel Ogilvy Berlouis.

[15] The Seychelles Government promoted the creation of a peace zone in the Indian Ocean and demanded that all warships wishing to call at its ports be 'nuclear-free'. As a result, the US and British naval fleets stopped calling.

[16] In the presidential elections of June 1989, René was the only candidate and was re-elected for a third term, with 96 per cent of the vote.

[17] The opposition forced President René to accept a multi-party system. The first experiment was carried out in July 1992, when a commission was elected to draw up the new constitution. The People's Progressive Front of Seychelles (FPPS), the ruling party, took 13 of the 23 seats. Former president Mancham's Democratic Party (PD) won eight seats.

[18] The Government continued with its authoritarian ways. The PD soon withdrew from the commission and the first draft constitution was rejected. The project was suspended until the PD returned to the commission in June 1993, and the text was written with support from both parties; 73.6 per cent of the voters approved the new constitution.

[19] The constitution officially established a multi-party system, a 33-member National Assembly and a five year presidential term. René won the July 1993 elections and his party had an overall majority in the National Assembly.

[20] Tourism continued to be the main source of income. The annual number of visitors was higher than the national population in 1993 and 1994. Oil derivatives and tinned tuna made up more than 80 per cent of the islands' exports during this period.

[21] Although according to the United Nations Development Program (UNDP) Seychelles ranked in 1998 as the African country with the highest human development index, it was only 56th in the world.

IN FOCUS

ENVIRONMENTAL CHALLENGES
The water supply - which is limited and precious - depends on catchments to collect rainwater.

WOMEN'S RIGHTS
Women have been able to vote and stand for office since 1948. In 2000, female representation in Parliament was around 24 per cent of seats and they held 33 per cent of ministerial or equivalent positions.

Domestic violence against women continues to be a problem. Police refuse to intervene in domestic disputes, unless it involves a weapon or major assault. In the few cases that reached court, the perpetrator was released or given only a light sentence. In general, acts of domestic violence are not considered criminal offenses. Societal concern about such violence prompted different NGOs to sponsor awareness campaigns for women and girls. Although prostitution is illegal, its incidence is growing. Seychelles' society is largely matriarchal, and does not discriminate against single mothers. In 2003, 76 per cent of births were to single mothers and many fathers were required by law to support their children.

CHILDREN
In 2002, there were 42,000 children under 18 years old and 14,000 under five. The Government has made efforts to invest money in education and to encourage children and young people to attend school. Education is free until the age of 18, and includes some teaching materials.

The minimum age of consent for marriage was 14 for women (girls), and 14 per cent of all births during the year were to mothers under 20. Girls are not allowed to attend school when they are pregnant, and many do not return to school after the birth of a child.

Sexual abuse of children, usually in low-income families, was a serious problem. However, only a few cases were reported during the year and they were generally perpetrated by stepfathers or older brothers. The Ministry of Health and the press published reports indicating that there had been a significant number of rapes of girls under 15, but only a few cases were actually prosecuted in court.

INDIGENOUS PEOPLES/ ETHNIC MINORITIES
There is no indigenous culture in the Seychelles, but some customs of African origin have survived. A large number of Seychellois are Catholic; however, there is widespread belief in the supernatural and in the power of the *gris* (spirits). Witchcraft was outlawed in 1958, but there are many traditional practicners (*bonhommes and bonfemmes du bois*) with their cures and curses. The majority of the population are mulattos, descendants of mixed African and European origin. There are minority groups of European, Chinese and Indian origin. Most of the population speak Creole, a local dialect with European and African influences.

MIGRANTS/REFUGEES
A growing number of immigrants has been admitted since 2003 - particularly Chinese, Indians, Filipinos, Thai and Madagascans - to work in the construction and fishing sectors. Reports allege that these workers are paid lower wages and forced to work longer hours than citizens.

The law grants refugee or asylum status to those people who fulfill the definitions of the 1951 Convention and 1967 Protocols; it also grants protection against the forced return of refugees.

DEATH PENALTY
Capital punishment was abolished for all crimes in 1993. No executions have been carried out since independence.

[22] With a view to proving the country's political stability to investors, René called elections two years early. In September 2001, he was re-elected to his third consecutive term since the establishment of the multi-party system. Wavel Ramkalawan, the opposition candidate of the Seychelles National Party, challenged the results saying voters had been intimidated or had been bribed to support the FPPS.

[23] Global warming is one of the pressing problems Seychelles faces today. Several plant and animal species, such as birds, giant turtles, coconut palms and others have already been affected by the rising temperatures and sea levels. Most of the coral around the islands has died. The country's biodiversity makes it an important tourist destination, and tourism is a major source of income. The Government has made environmental protection a top priority and the population is educated from a young age about the importance of nature conservation.

[24] In January 2002, the Seychelles National Party's bid to annul the previous year's presidential election on the grounds of alleged irregularities was denied by the Constitutional Court.

[25] In April 2002, the Consultative Council on Tourism, which had operated as a government advisory body since 1999, was reorganized. Simone de Comarmond, Minister of Tourism and Transportation, stated that the Government was committed to taking the necessary steps to develop tourism. She stated that in the wake of the 11 September 2001 terrorist attacks in the US it was more necessary than ever to ensure that the Seychelles tourism industry remained competitive.

[26] The international organization Reporters Without Borders protested against the Government in 2002 for the libel suit filed against the independent *Regar* newspaper. The newspaper had published an article accusing Vice-President James Michel of corruption.

[27] In July 2003, the Government implemented an economic reform program aimed at reducing the country's budget deficit. Three overseas embassies were closed and a new tax was placed on imports as well as on local goods and services. The police arrested four members of the Seychelles National Party, including Jean-François Ferrari, of the *Regar* newspaper, for collecting signatures for a petition against the new tax.

[28] In September that year, the body of Thérese Blanc-Payet, Ferrari's sister-in-law, was found on a beach. In response, the European Parliament's Committee for Development and Co-operation requested that President René provide a report on the political and human-rights situation in Seychelles.

[29] In July 2004, Seychelles withdraw from the SADC (Southern African Development Community) and from the IOR (Indian Ocean Rim association for regional cooperation). The Government also declared the cessation of the diplomatic missions in the United Kingdom, South Africa and Malaysia. Seychelles was spending 1.5 million euros annually to sustain the missions. ∎

Sierra Leone / Sierra Leone

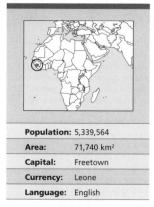

Population:	5,339,564
Area:	71,740 km²
Capital:	Freetown
Currency:	Leone
Language:	English

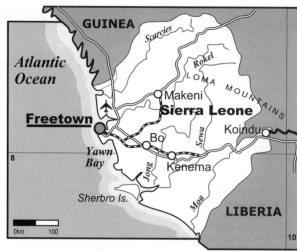

The Portuguese reached Sierra Leone ('lion mountains') in 1462. In the early 16th century it was a regular stop for European traders of cloth and metal goods, ivory, timber, and some slaves. Around that time, Mande-speaking people migrated from present-day Liberia, and they eventually established the states of Bullom, Loko, Boure, and Sherbro. In the 17th century British traders arrived. A century later, Fulani and Mande-speaking traders from the Fouta Djallon region of what is now Guinea converted numerous Temne to Islam, which became firmly established in the north and spread through the rest of the country.

[2] In the late 18th century, Britain decided to 'return' runaway and freed slaves from the Caribbean to Africa, and selected the recently acquired territory of Sierra Leone for the purpose. Abolitionist leader Granville Sharp purchased an area of 250 sq km for £60 from the local rulers, where he established an agricultural society based on democratic principles, but which quickly became a British colonial company in 1791. Over the next 50 years, the population of Freetown swelled with the arrival of 70,000 slaves, in addition to migration from the interior of the country.

[3] The country became a crown colony in 1808, and in 1821, it was merged with Gambia and Gold Coast (present-day Ghana) to create the British West African Territories.

[4] The creoles sought to emulate European culture and considered themselves superior to the 'savages' of the interior, acting as brokers for British colonialism. In 1896 Sierra Leone became a British protectorate.

[5] In 1898 resistance leader Bai Buré rallied most of the inland population, already angered by a British tax on their dwellings. However, British military superiority overwhelmed the insurgents after nearly a year of fighting.

[6] With the drawing up of the constitution, the first election for a parliamentary council took place in 1924.

[7] In 1953 the ministerial system was introduced, and Sir Milton Margai, leader of the Sierra Leone People's Party (SLPP), was appointed chief minister the following year.

[8] In 1960, the British wanted to withdraw from Sierra Leone, and an agreement was negotiated with the traditional leaders to protect their interests. In 1961, Sir Milton Margai became the first prime minister of an independent Sierra Leone.

[9] Although they lost their political power, the creoles, together with British and Syrian-Lebanese merchants, retained control over the economy.

[10] When Margai died in 1964, his brother Albert headed a government tainted by widespread corruption. The diamond trade and crime became major sources of income.

[11] In 1967 the All Peoples' Congress (APC) party led by Siaka Stevens won the elections. The conservative creoles, traditional leaders, and British neo-colonialists united to prevent change. Stevens was overthrown by a military coup and forced into exile in Guinea (Conakry).

[12] In April 1968, a group of low-ranking officers took power through the so-called Sergeants' Revolt. They brought back Stevens who in 1971 broke all ties with Britain and declared Sierra Leone a republic, becoming its first President.

[13] Stevens nationalized the lumber industry and the State seized majority control of the diamond trade. To protect the price of iron ore and bauxite, Sierra Leone joined the associations of iron and bauxite producing countries.

[14] In 1978 a plebiscite approved the establishment of a one-party political system. The APC incorporated prominent members of the SLPP within its ranks, granting them posts within the Government.

[15] The economic and political crisis peaked in 1979, as a result of a fall in exports, growing inflation and declining standards of living, together with authoritarian measures and government corruption, which undermined Stevens' popularity.

[16] In September 1981 the Sierra Leone Labour Congress (SLLC) declared a general strike, demanding immediate changes in economic policy. The strike spread throughout the country and nearly toppled the Government, which had to make several concessions.

[17] In urban areas, the scarcity of food and services became chronic. Smuggling grew as the purchasing power of salaried workers fell by 60 per cent. A dynamic black market emerged.

[18] Powerful Lebanese traders controlled the black market and more than 70 per cent of the country's exports. Gold and diamond smuggling was estimated at nearly $150 million per year while official exports amounted to $14 million in 1984.

[19] In November 1985, Siaka Stevens handed over the presidency to Joseph Momoh, a member of his cabinet; the change did not affect the country's critical economic situation.

[20] The Government declared a state of economic emergency in 1987. This gave the State the sole right to market gold and diamonds; a 15 per cent surcharge on imports, and a cut in the salaries of public employees.

[21] In March 1991, rebel forces operating from Liberia occupied two border towns. Guerrilla groups from Burkina Faso, Liberia, and Sierra Leone joined them, occupying one third of the country.

[22] A referendum held in August approved a new constitution establishing a multiparty system, while the economic crisis and corruption continued.

[23] In 1992, the Government launched an IMF-imposed

PROFILE

ENVIRONMENT
The country is divided into three regions. The coastal strip, nearly 100 kilometers long, is a swampy plain that includes the island of Sherbro.

SOCIETY
Peoples: The Temne and Mende account for nearly one-third of the population. Lokko, Sherbro, Limba, Sussu, Fulani, Kono and Krio are other important groups. The Krio - whose name comes from the English word 'creole' - are descendants of African slaves freed in the 19th century who settled in Freetown. There are also Arab, European, Chinese and Indian minorities.
Religions: Most of the people practise traditional African religions; nearly one-third are Muslims, concentrated in the north; the Catholic minority is located in the capital.
Languages: English (official). The most widely spoken native languages are Temne, Mende and Krio. The latter serves as the language of commerce in the capital.
Main Political Parties: All Peoples' Congress (APC); Sierra Leone People's Party (SLPP).
Main Social Organizations: Sierra Leone Labour Congress.

THE STATE
Official Name: Republic of Sierra Leone.
Capital: Freetown 921,000 people (2003).
Other Cities: Koidu 109,900 people; Bo 79,700; Kenema 69,900 (2000).
Government: Ahmad Tejan Kabbah, President since March 1996, re-elected in 2002. Unicameral Legislature: House of Representatives, with 112 members.
National Holiday: 19 April, Republic Day (1971).
Armed Forces: 13,000 troops (1995).

Life expectancy	GNI per capita	Literacy	HIV prevalence rate
34.2 years	**$140**	**36%** total adult rate	**7%** of population 15-49 years old
2000-2005	2002	2000	2001

structural adjustment program. James Funa, a former World Bank executive, was named Finance Minister. He implemented monetary control, incentives for natural resource exploration by foreign companies, widespread privatization, and an overhaul of the state apparatus affected by widespread corruption.

[24] That year, Captain Valentine Strasser seized power through a coup. He suspended the constitution, created the National Provisional Governing Council and confirmed Funa in his post.

[25] The United Liberation Movement for Democracy in Liberia used the eastern part of Sierra Leone as a base from which to carry out attacks against Charles Taylor's forces (see Liberia). In the meantime, the Revolutionary United Front of Sierra Leone (RUF) was operating in the southeast, waging civil war to gain control of the diamond-producing areas and funding itself from the illicit sale of the stones.

[26] Guerrilla actions led to an abrupt decline in legal mining activity; diamonds' share of the country's exports dropped from 54.7 per cent in 1987 to a mere seven per cent in 1990. Per capita GDP dropped from $320 in 1980 to $210 in 1991.

[27] The Government promise to call elections did not convince the RUF, which extended its armed struggle to the rest of the country in 1995. Government forces won back the Sierra Rutile titanium mine, whose production amounted to 50 per cent of Freetown's foreign trade. But the Government seemed unable to defeat the guerrillas. Between 1991 and 1996, the war caused 10,000 deaths and two million refugees.

[28] In January 1996, following a bloodless coup, Strasser was replaced by Brigadier-General Julius Maada Bio. The presidential elections held in February as planned were won by Ahmad Tejan Kabbah of the SLPP in the second round with nearly 60 per cent of the vote.

[29] Rebel troops led by Major-General Johnny Paul Koroma ousted President Kabbah on May 1997. The Organization of African Unity, meeting in Namibia, criticized the coup and began negotiations to force the leaders to step down.

[30] In September 1997, former president Kabbah asked the UN for help to re-establish his government. In March 1998, the UN ECOMOG troops - paradoxically mostly Nigerians who at that time were ruled by dictator Sani Abacha - took the main cities and regions of Sierra Leone, forcing out Koroma and his military junta.

IN FOCUS

ENVIRONMENTAL CHALLENGES
The central rainforest, crossed by many rivers, has been cut down to create land for agriculture, resulting in soil degradation. In the eastern plateau there are diamond reserves. Widespread deforestation has led to the loss of 85 per cent of natural habitats.

WOMEN'S RIGHTS
In 2000 women held nine per cent of seats in parliament and 10 per cent of ministerial posts.

Female participation in the labor force has been stable since 1980, accounting for 37 per cent of the total in 2000.

Literacy among women improved in the 1990-2000 period* (from 14 to 23 per cent), although it is still far below the male literacy rate (which rose from 40 to 51 per cent over the same period).

Some 68 per cent of pregnant women received pre-natal care, and 42 per cent of births were attended by qualified personnel.

CHILDREN
According to latest UNICEF's available data*, 27 per cent of children under five are underweight, while 10 per cent are undernourished and 34 per cent show stunted growth. At the end of 2001, 16,000 children under 15 were HIV-positive, and 42,000 had been orphaned by AIDS.

There was a 41 per cent enrolment rate in primary education between 1996 and 2002. Some 57 per cent of children between the ages of 5 and 14 work. This percentage rises to 60 per cent in rural areas and falls to 48 per cent in urban areas.

INDIGENOUS PEOPLES/ETHNIC MINORITIES
The Mende and Temne are the dominant ethnic groups, but there are many more minority groups. In Freetown some 5,000 residents speak Bassa (no relation to the Basa in Nigeria, Ghana, Cameroon and Benin) and practice a traditional religion. The Fulani, herders and nomadic traders of Caucasian origin, comprise five per cent of the population and are spread throughout the land, but mostly concentrated in the north. The Gola live on the border with Liberia in the provinces of Kenema and Pujehun. They number about 9,000, speak Gola and practice Islam (75 per cent) and traditional religions. The Kissi make up three per cent of the population, living mainly in the north-west. Eight per cent are Muslim. The Krio Fula, descendants of freed slaves live in the western peninsula, and on the Banana, York and Bonthe islands. They were the most politically powerful group during colonial times, despite being only three per cent of the total population. The Limba, 9 per cent, shared power with the Krio in the late 1960s. Malinke people, around 2.5 per cent of the population, live in the Kabala region. Their Maninka language is spoken quite widely. They became part of a national state only when they joined the Mali Empire in the 13th century. The Sussu live in the northern province, and the Vai live on the Atlantic coast, numbering 18,000.

MIGRANTS/REFUGEES.
There were over 130,000 refugees from Sierra Leone in other countries in late 2002. Guinea had 70,000, Liberia 40,000, Ghana and Gambia 5,000 each, Nigeria 2,000, and the US and other developed countries approximately 10,000. More than 200,000 returned to Sierra Leone once the war ended; 90,000 during 2002. Of these, 40,000 returned from Liberia.

DEATH PENALTY
The death penalty is still applicable.

*Latest data available in The State of the World's Children and Childinfo database,UNICEF, 2004.

[31] The Kabbah administration achieved stability and in March 1998 it ordered a halt to all gold and diamond mining - which had been largely controlled by foreign companies for the last 60 years - except by Sierra Leonean concerns. In the final months of the year another rebel offensive took control of part of Freetown, the capital. The arrival of Nigerian troops brought the conflict to an impasse. The two sides signed a ceasefire in January 1999.

[32] The new RUF rebel leader, Foday Sankoh, signed a peace treaty with the Government in July to put an end to nine years of civil war. Under the treaty, Sankoh was appointed director of the Strategic Minerals Commission and Vice-President, though a 1998 UN resolution banned him from traveling without its authorization.

[33] The rebels resumed fighting in May 2000. Foday Sankoh was captured and imprisoned. The UN estimated that only half of the 45,000 rebel soldiers had turned in their weapons. In August, the regional leaders replaced Sankoh with Issa Sesay. Kabbah and presidents Olusegun Obasanjo of Nigeria and Alfa Oumar Konare of Mali held meetings with Sankoh.

[34] An armed splinter group, 'West Side Boyz', previously loyal to Koroma, took seven British soldiers hostage in August. The following month, British forces liberated the hostages and captured the group's leader, Foday Kallay.

[35] Claiming that the continued state of insecurity made free and fair elections impossible, in January 2001 the Government postponed elections scheduled for February and March. For the first time, UN troops began a peaceful deployment in rebel territory in March, and in May initiated the disarmament of the 45,000 rebel soldiers, which was completed by January 2002.

[36] General elections were held in May 2002, after the President lifted the state of emergency, in force for the previous four years. The National Electoral Commission confirmed Kabbah's victory with 70 per cent of the vote. His SLPP also won the parliamentary elections, taking 83 of the 112 seats. Koroma's party won 27 seats. Sankoh's RUF won no seats and only 1.7 per cent of the vote for him as presidential candidate.

[37] In July, UN British troops started to leave Sierra Leone, but two months later the UN Security Council decided to extend the military mission's stay in the country on request from President Kabbah, who was concerned about instability caused by the civil war in neighboring Liberia.

[38] Foday Sankoh died in July 2003, while awaiting trial for war crimes.

[39] The disarmament and rehabilitation of over 70,000 civilian fighters was officially completed in February 2004.

[40] In March a UN-backed war crimes tribunal began hearing cases against the RUF and government-backed militias, together responsible for some 50,000 deaths in the ten-year civil war. So far, the tribunal has not been able to arrest former Liberian president Charles Taylor, now exiled in Nigeria, who is thought to have funded the RUF. His lawyers stated that the tribunal's jurisdiction should not extend beyond Sierra Leone's borders. ∎

Population:	4,371,513
Area:	620 km²
Capital:	Singapore
Currency:	Singapore dollar
Language:	Malay and English

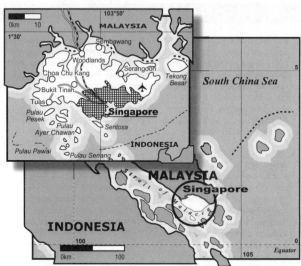

One of the earliest references to Singapore as Temasek, or Sea Town, was found in the Javanese 'Nagarakretagama' of 1365. The name was also mentioned in a Vietnamese source at around the same time. By the end of the 14th century, the Sanskrit name, Singapura (Lion City), became commonly used. By that time Singapore was caught in the struggles between Siam (now Thailand) and the Java-based Majapahit Empire for control of the Malay Peninsula. According to the Malay Annals, Singapore was defeated in one Majapahit attack, but Iskandar Shah, or Parameswara, a prince of Palembang, later killed the local chieftain and installed himself as the island's new ruler. Shortly after, he was driven out and fled north to Muar in the Malay Peninsula, where he founded the Malacca Sultanate.

2   From 1819 Singapore became an extremely important base for the British, when Sir Thomas Stamford Raffles established the local headquarters of the British East India Company there.

3   In 1824, the island of Singapore and the adjacent islets were purchased as a single lot by Raffles from the Sultan of Johore (see Malaysia). The Company appointed Prince Hussein as the new ruler of Singapore. In gratitude, he granted the Company royal authorization to improve the port. Chinese immigrants soon constituted the majority of the local population.

4   Singapore was part of the British colony called 'the Straits Settlements', together with the ports of Penang and Melaka (Malacca). In 1946, Penang and Melaka joined the Malayan Union and Singapore became a crown colony.

5   Japan occupied Singapore in February 1942 but was defeated in 1945 by British forces and a strong internal resistance group, organized by a revolutionary movement and led by the Communist Party of Malaya (CPM). The name Malaya included both Singapore and the Malay peninsula; the separation of the two was always questioned by the Left.

6   Once the war was over, the Malay sultanates and the former Straits Settlements attempted to form a union or federation, with a view to attaining independence for the territory. However, the conflicting interests of the Chinese and Malay communities, and the conservative and progressive forces, made progress difficult. In January 1946, the Singapore Labor Union declared a general strike and in 1948 the Communist Party led an anti-colonial uprising which failed to gain the support of the Malays and the poorer sectors of the Indian population. Marxist parties were outlawed and had to take refuge in the forests, where they resorted to guerrilla warfare.

7   As the first step towards the self-government of the city-state, municipal elections were held in 1949. Only English-speaking people were allowed to vote until 1954, when the People's Action Party (PAP) was founded. Anti-imperialism advocated by the PAP brought citizens of British and Chinese backgrounds together for the first time. In 1959, the Chinese were allowed to vote; full internal autonomy was granted, and the PAP obtained an overwhelming victory. Lee Kuan Yew, founder of the party, became Prime Minister, campaigning on a platform of social reforms and independence. He planned a federation with Malaya, which had been independent since 1957.

8   The PAP split into a socialist faction, led by Lim Chin Siong, and the 'moderates' of Lee Kuan Yew, who encouraged the promotion of private enterprise and foreign investment.

9   In 1961, the left wing of the PAP founded Barisan Sosialis (the Socialist Front), which opposed the project of uniting Singapore and Malaya under British control. In September 1963, the Federation of Malaysia, consisting of Singapore,

PROFILE

ENVIRONMENT

Singapore consists of one large island and 54 smaller adjacent islets. The country is connected to Malaysia by a causeway across the Johore Strait. The terrain, covered by swampy lowlands, is not conducive to farming and the population traditionally works in business and trade. The climate is tropical with heavy rainfall. In its strategic geographical location, central to the trade routes between Africa, Asia and Europe, the island has become a flourishing commercial center. Economically, the main resources of the country have been its port, the British naval base and, more recently, industrial activity: textiles, electronic goods and oil refining.

SOCIETY

Peoples: 76 per cent of Singaporeans are of Chinese origin. Malaysians account for 15 per cent and 6 per cent are from India and Sri Lanka.
Religions: Buddhist 28 per cent; Christian 19 per cent; Islam 13 per cent; Taoist 13 per cent; Hindu 5 per cent. There are Sikh and Jewish minorities.
Languages: Malay, English, Chinese (Mandarin) and Tamil are the official languages. Malay is considered the national language but English is spoken in the public administration and serves as a unifying element for the communities. Various Chinese dialects are spoken, as are Punjabi, Hindi, Bengali, Telegu and Malayalam in the Indian communities.
Main Political Parties: The People's Action Party (PAP); Singapore Democratic Alliance; Singapore Democratic Party.
Main Social Organizations: The major national trade union is the Congress of Singapore Labor Unions.

THE STATE

Official Name: Hsin-chia-p'o Kung-ho-kuo (Mandarin); Republik Singapura (Bahasa Malaysia); Singapore Kudiyarasu (Tamil); Republic of Singapore.
Capital: Singapore 4,253,000 people (2003).
Government: Parliamentary republic. Sellapan Ramanathan, President since September 1999; Lee Hsien Loong, Prime Minister since August 1994. Unicameral Legislature, with 90 members.
National Holiday: 9 August, Independence Day (1965).
Armed Forces: 55,500, inc. 34,800 conscripts. Other: 11,600 Police and Maritime Police (estimate). 100,000 Civil Defense Force.

LAND USE

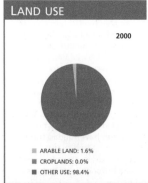

2000

- ARABLE LAND: 1.6%
- CROPLANDS: 0.0%
- OTHER USE: 98.4%

PUBLIC EXPENDITURE

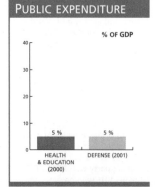

% OF GDP

HEALTH & EDUCATION (2000)	DEFENSE (2001)
5 %	5 %

Life expectancy
78.1 years
2000-2005

GNI per capita
$20,690
2002

Literacy
92% total adult rate
2000

HIV prevalence rate
0.2% of population 15-49 years old
2001

the Malay peninsula, Sarawak and Sabah (both in the north and northeast of Borneo) was set up, after those opposed to the Federation had been conveniently purged.

10 As a Federation member, Singapore depended heavily on the peninsula; even its water supply came from there. Integration at that time was not feasible because of profound disagreements between Singapore's Chinese community and the Malay community of the rest of the Federation. On 9 August 1965, after several ethnic conflicts, Prime Minister Lee decided to withdraw from the Federation.

11 In 1965, there were serious internal conflicts caused by the mistreatment of the Malay population and other ethnic minorities. There were also intense struggles with the left-wing opposition, whom the Government classified as 'communist subversives'. The island became an independent republic, and a Commonwealth member. A mutual assistance and defense treaty was signed with Malaysia, and on 15 October of the same year Singapore became a member of the United Nations.

12 The first years of independence witnessed substantial economic growth. The island was turned into an 'enclave' for the export of products manufactured by transnationals, and into an international financial center which controlled the regional economy.

13 In 1974 the oil crisis upset Singapore's export scheme. Singapore was the fourth largest port in the world, with the second highest per capita income in Asia, after Japan. The ensuing economic deterioration brought about public demonstrations by students and workers. These protests were fiercely repressed, to the extent that the Socialist International expelled the PAP from its ranks in 1975.

14 In order to placate criticism from the opposition, the regime approved a reform which allowed the incorporation of two representatives from the Workers' Party and the Democratic Party of Singapore, respectively.

15 Despite the sustained economic growth from 1987, the Government expelled thousands of Thai and Filipino workers, blaming them for taking over the jobs of natural citizens.

16 The decision to ban foreign publications judged detrimental by the Government, the imprisonment of opposition members and a Security Law allowing imprisonment without trial for two years, renewable indefinitely, raised

IN FOCUS

ENVIRONMENTAL CHALLENGES
Industrialization has caused serious air and water pollution. There is little land available, making the final disposal of solid waste difficult. There are periods of smog, resulting from frequent forest fires in Indonesia.

WOMEN'S RIGHTS
Women have been able to vote and stand for election since 1947.

Female representation in politics is scanty. In 2000 only four per cent of Parliament seats were held by women, and no women held ministerial or equivalent positions.

In 2001, although the proportion of waged women in non-agricultural sectors rose to 46 per cent, female wages were half of those for men. Women may not transmit their citizenship to their offspring born abroad, although they may request it for their child, while men transmit it automatically. Since 1999, women have been able to sponsor the citizenship of their foreign husbands.

In 2003, most of the country's sex workers were foreign, especially from Malaysia, Thailand, Philippines, China,

Indonesia, Vietnam, India and Sri Lanka. Most had come to the country for that purpose, but the authorities investigated several cases of women forced into the sex trade that year.

CHILDREN
The under-18 population amounted in 2002 to 1,046,000, and the under-5 to 253,000.

Life expectancy at birth rose from 69 in 1990 to 80 in 2002. The under-five mortality rate was halved in the 1990s, with only four deaths for every 1,000 children in 2002.

The Government has shown it is strongly committed to children's rights and welfare, especially by investing in health and education. Six years of primary public education are compulsory by law.

In 2002, there were more than 70 cases of prostitution among minors, most of whom were foreigners aged under 18. Sexual intercourse between adults and females under 16 is banned, but concessions are made for those girls 'aware' of being involved in the sex trade at 16 or 17. However, the authorities have the power to pursue those who organize or benefit from prostitution, who traffic women into the country for

that purpose or who deceive women or girls into participating in the trade.

INDIGENOUS PEOPLES/ ETHNIC MINORITIES
More than 75 per cent of the population is Chinese, while the rest are Malaysians, Indonesians, Pakistanis and Indians. A small number of Europeans are concentrated in the capital and nearby urban centers.

MIGRANTS/REFUGEES
Since its creation Singapore's population was determined by immigration, which diminished throughout the 20th century. The 1947 census showed that 56 per cent of the population was born in the country, while in the 1980 census the proportion had grown to 78 per cent.

Most of the immigrant population is from Malaysia, Thailand, Philippines, Sri Lanka and India, employed in the labor sectors, while immigrants with a university education come mostly from Japan, Eastern Europe, North America and Australia.

DEATH PENALTY
It is applicable even for ordinary offenses.

countless reports of human rights violations.

17 In the 1988 elections the opposition vote grew, but due to the electoral system its parliamentary representation diminished. In 1991, the PAP again won an overwhelming majority of seats. In November, Goh Chok Tong replaced Lee Kuan Yew as Prime Minister, but the latter nevertheless retained considerable political weight. At his initiative, Singapore offered Washington the possibility of installing bases in the country when the Filipino Congress decided to close US military bases in the Philippines.

18 In 1994 and 1995 relations were strained between Singapore and the US, Philippines and the Netherlands when a Dutch engineer was hanged on heroin trafficking charges, a US man was sentenced to a beating with a rattan cane for vandalism, and a Filipina maid was executed for murdering a colleague. In the case of the domestic worker, the crime was proved and diplomatic relations were re-established. The US citizen's sentence was reduced in terms of the number of strokes and months in prison.

19 In June 1996 the 'Speak Mandarin' campaign was

challenged by ethnic minorities, concerned that the language was becoming a condition of employment. The Government's concern shifted to the declining standard of English spoken by the population, and in 1999 launched a campaign against *singlish*, the local linguistic version of English.

20 That year, Singapore played a key role in shoring up the region's faltering economy, dedicating part of its huge reserves and the trade surplus to support the baht and the rupiah, the Thai and Indonesian currencies, respectively.

21 In the August 1999 presidential elections, only Sellapan Ramanthan Nathan, the PAP candidate, was declared eligible to run. Nathan took office in September.

22 Some 2,000 people engaged in an unprecedented political rally in April 2001 protesting against the Government and to collect funds for popular parliamentarian JB Jeyaretnam, who was on the verge of bankruptcy. It was the first legally sanctioned demonstration in Singapore outside of electoral periods.

23 The free trade accord signed by Singapore and Japan in January 2002 was seen as a 'milestone' by Singaporean authorities because it marked Japan's commitment to the

region. Singaporean investors won access to the Japanese service market. Under the terms of the agreement, companies based in Singapore could freely transfer investment in and out of Japan.

24 In September 2002 Amnesty International reported that 22 people charged with drug dealing had been executed during the previous year, taking the total number of executions to 369 since 1991. Singapore has one of the world's highest execution rates in relation to its population.

25 The Government launched two television programs to promote sex, one of them offering sexual therapy, in a desperate attempt to increase the birth rate, one of the lowest in the world at 1.24 children born per woman, in 2003.

26 The deadly SARS virus pandemic, which caused turmoil in Asian markets, weakened the economy in 2003, which had already sustained a ten per cent drop in 2002. However, in May 2004 the Trade and Industry minister announced a recovery due to external factors, such as low interest rates and growth in foreign trade and investment. According to the Government, the US, China and Japan had been the motors of Singapore's economic growth. ■

Slovakia / Slovensko

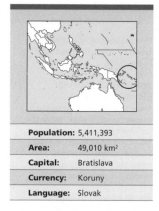

Population:	5,411,393
Area:	49,010 km²
Capital:	Bratislava
Currency:	Koruny
Language:	Slovak

The Slovak territory was populated between 500 and 100 BC by the Cotini, Celts from western Europe. Later, between 100 BC and 400 AD, the Quadi, a Germanic people, formed satellite states of the Roman Empire north of the Danube, remaining part of Bohemia with the Marcomani, until they were pushed out by the Huns led by Attila around 400 AD.

[2] Slovaks from the eastern region of the Vistula who were closely related to the Czechs, began to settle the territory between the 6th and 7th centuries. They soon had to defend themselves from the Avars, nomads from lower Panonia, until the Frankish trader Samo united the Slavs and was chosen as their King. In 805, the Christian King, Charlemagne formed an alliance with the Czech leaders of Bohemia and Moravia to defeat the Avars. In return for their help, Charlemagne distributed dukedoms amongst the Czechs, who took control over the regions of Moravia, Bohemia and Slovakia. The first monarch of the kingdom of Moravia, Mojmir I, ruled from 830 to 846, and Christianity was adopted under his rule.

[3] His nephew Rotislav I succeeded him, ruling from 846 to 870. He expanded the kingdom to include all of Bohemia and founded Great Moravia, unifying the Slav territories in the region for the first time. Rotislav consolidated relations with the Frankish Empire, which answered to Rome, and maintained contact with the Byzantine Empire. In 863, the Byzantine Emperor sent the monks Constantine (Cyril) and Methodius to the region. The monks translated the gospels and designed the first Slav alphabet (see Czech Republic).

[4] During the reign of Svatopluc (870-894) the frontiers of Moravia were extended to include the western part of present-day Hungary and southern Poland. Svatopluc terminated relations with the Byzantine Empire, and Methodius' disciples were forced to abandon the kingdom, taking

refuge in the Balkans (see Czech Republic).

[5] Great Moravia came to an end in 906, when it was destroyed by the German king Arnulf in alliance with the Magyars, a nomadic tribe from the Upper Volga who controlled most of the territories of modern-day Hungary. The western part of the old kingdom remained in the possession of the Czech dukes of Bohemia, while the area between the Carpathians and the Danube - the Slovakia of today - was occupied by the Magyars. Despite repeated attempts to conquer it by the dukes of

Bohemia, for ten centuries it continued to be Hungarian.

[6] The Slovaks continued to have cultural links with the Czechs. During the 15th century, the University of Prague exercised considerable influence. The Hussites of Bohemia (see Czech Republic) repeatedly invaded Hungary, and introduced the custom of conducting the liturgy in the national language instead of Latin in Slovakia.

[7] The Hussite incursions prepared the ground for the advent of Protestantism, based on the teaching of the Kralice Bible

translated by the Bohemian Brethren. In the early 16th century most of the Slovaks had adopted Calvinism. However, when Hungary was invaded by the Ottoman Empire in 1525, Slovakia was governed by the House of Austria, which Germanized Slovak culture to a large extent and strengthened the Counter-Reformation throughout the region.

[8] In 1620, the Magyars recovered Slovakia for the Kingdom of Hungary. The conquest of central Hungary by the Ottoman Empire increased Magyar influence in Slovakia as Hungarian nobles fleeing Turkish power settled in Slovak villages and initiated Hungarian customs.

[9] In the 17th century Turkish dominion in Hungary was replaced by the House of Hapsburg. At the end of the 18th century the Emperor Joseph II changed the Kingdom of Hungary by Germanizing the bureaucracy and limiting the power of the Hungarian authorities. This helped the Slovaks recover their Slav origins and their cultural links with the Czechs.

[10] The nationalist fever across Europe following the Napoleonic Wars also reached the Austrian territories and caused conflict between Slovaks and Hungarians. In 1834, Magyar replaced Latin as the official language. In 1848, the Slovaks, allied with Czechs and German Republicans, rose up against the Magyars, who had in turn rebelled against the Austrians. Within this period, the Slovaks took over control of their secondary education and founded their first scientific society, the Matica Slovaka.

[11] In the late 19th century, the Hungarian authorities banned the Slovak language from public life, replacing it with Magyar. Slovak leaders, especially editors of journals, were persecuted and many were imprisoned. In 1907, the Appony law made Slovak-speaking primary schools adopt Magyar.

[12] The Slovaks supported the Allies in World War I. Tens of thousands of Slovak soldiers forced to serve in the Hungarian army joined the Allies against the Austro-Hungarian Empire. In 1915, the Czech Alliance and the Slovak League (in the US) reached an agreement in Cleveland proclaiming the liberation of the Czech and Slovak nations and their federate union, with complete independence for Slovakia, which would have its own parliament and administration with Slovak as its official language.

[13] Once the War had ended with the Allied victory in 1918, the nationalist efforts of the Slovak doctor Thomas G Masaryk, the

PROFILE

ENVIRONMENT

The terrain is mountainous, dominated by the Carpathian mountain range. Mountainous areas are covered by forests which supply an important timber industry. Agriculture is concentrated in the fertile plains of the Danube and Uh rivers. There are abundant mineral resources, including copper, zinc, lead and mercury, as well as oil and natural gas deposits. Industrial pollution and sulfur emissions are the main environmental problems.

SOCIETY

Peoples: Slovak 85.7 per cent; Hungarian 10.6 per cent; Roma 1.6 per cent; Czech 1.1 per cent; Ruthenian, 0.3 per cent; Ukrainian 0.3 per cent; German 0.1 per cent; other 0.3 per cent (1994).
Religions: Roman Catholic 60.3 per cent; non-religious and atheist 9.7 per cent; Protestant 7.9 per cent, of which Slovak Evangelical 6.2 per cent and Reformed Christian 1.6 per cent; Greek Catholic 3.4 per cent; Eastern Orthodox 0.7 per cent; other 18 per cent.
Languages: Slovak is the official language; Hungarian is also spoken.
Main Political Parties: Movement for a Democratic Slovakia; Slovak Christian Democrat Union, Direction Party-Third Way, Hungarian Coalition Party. **Main Social Organizations:** Confederation of Trade Unions of the Slovak Republic (KOZ-SR), Slovak Union of Nature and Landscape Protectors (environmentalist).

THE STATE

Official Name: Slovenska Republika.
Administrative Divisions: 3 regions divided into 38 municipalities and the capital zone. **Capital:** Bratislava 425,000 people (2003).
Other Cities: Kosice 244,400 people; Presov 95,300; Zilina 87,600; Nitra 87,400; Banská Bystrica 84,400 (2000).
Government: Parliamentary republic, according to the constitution effective since January 1993. Ivan Gasparovic, President since April 2004. Mikulás Dzurinda, prime minister since October 1998, re-elected in September 2002. Unicameral legislature: National Council of the Slovak Republic, with 150 members elected for a four-year term by proportional representation. **National Holiday:** 1 September, Constitution Day (1992). **Armed Forces:** 47,000 (1995). Other: Border Guards: 600; Internal Security Forces: 250; Civil Defense Troops: 3,100.

| Life expectancy **73.7** years 2000-2005 | GNI per capita **$3,950** 2002 | Literacy **100%** total adult rate 2000 | HIV prevalence rate **0.1 %** of population 15-49 years old 2001 |

scientist Milan Stefanik (a Slovak living abroad), and the Czech Eduard Benes, working with the opposition forces in Czech and Slovak lands, led to the creation of the Republic of Czecho-Slovakia on 28 October of that year.

14 In November 1918, Masaryk was elected President of the new Republic, a position he held until 1935. During his term in office - and also that of his successor, Eduard Benes - the Slovaks felt they were relegated within a State controlled by the Czechs.

15 The occupation of Czechoslovakia by Nazi troops in 1939 put the history of the Republic on hold. With the occupation of the Sudetenland in 1938, Benes was forced to resign and go into exile in London. Czechoslovakia was dismembered: Bohemia became a German province and Carpathian Russia was taken by the Hungarians. In March 1939, Slovak independence was proclaimed, with Hitler's puppet President Joseph Tiso in power.

16 After the Allied victory in 1945 and with Soviet forces in the territory, Benes returned to the presidency. Unity was guaranteed by its membership of the Soviet bloc (see under Czech Republic) until, in 1991, with the fall of the Soviet regime and its system of alliances, the Czech and Slovak peoples divided to develop separate political lives.

17 In February 1993 Michal Kovac was elected President of the new Republic of Slovakia. Vladimir Meciar, leader of the Movement for a Democratic Slovakia (MED) and the architect of Czechoslovakian separation, was named Prime Minister.

18 Meciar's administration was marked by controversy and accusations of authoritarianism from the opposition. He re-nationalized the newspaper *Smena*, and created a compulsory television slot for the broadcasting of government news and propaganda. He enforced compliance with an old law obliging Hungarian women to add the suffix 'ova' to their surnames, as with Slovak names, and opposed the teaching of Hungarian in schools.

19 Jozef Moravcik was appointed Prime Minister in March 1993. The new Government attempted to keep Meciar out of power and accept the general principles of European democracy. However, the coalition's inner differences weakened this project and, in the October 1994 elections, Meciar once again became Prime Minister (with 35 per cent of the vote) and cancelled the privatization policy begun by his predecessor.

20 In late 1997 five opposition parties founded the Slovak

IN FOCUS

ENVIRONMENTAL CHALLENGES
Pollution from industry (chemicals, machinery and the paper industry) and sulfur emissions are the main environmental problem, affecting the health of half the population. Acid rain is damaging the forests.

WOMEN'S RIGHTS
Women have been able to vote since 1920. Their parliamentary participation was relatively stable between 1995 (15 per cent) and 2000 (13 per cent), while there was an increase in the proportion of ministerial-level posts held by women over the same period, from 5 per cent to 19 per cent.

Women represented 45 per cent of the labor force in 1980 and 48 per cent between 1990 and 2000. As it is for men, the female literacy rate was 100 per cent between 1990 and 2000, according to World Bank data.

According to UNICEF's latest data available*, 98 per cent of pregnant women received prenatal care.

CHILDREN
From 1960 to 2002, under-five mortality per 1,000 live births decreased from 40 to 9. Over the same period, infant mortality dropped from 33 to 8.

Low birthweight is relatively rare, as is HIV/AIDS. It is estimated that fewer than 100 people aged between 0 and 49 were HIV-positive at the end of 2001.

INDIGENOUS PEOPLES/ ETHNIC MINORITIES
Almost 11 per cent of the population are Hungarian, the largest minority in the country. Although minority rights are mentioned in the Constitution, the law allows for unequal treatment of foreigners. A law regarding the official language, for instance, was transformed in practice into a legal tool for discrimination, as it banned the use of Hungarian in official documents, such as school certificates, as well as in any oral communication between civil servants and the public. This implied, for example, that a police officer had to address a civilian in Slovak (although both of them might be Hungarian). The same applied to doctors, teachers or any other official. In 1996, after lengthy negotiations between Hungary and Slovakia an agreement was reached to modify the situation, authorizing the use of minorities' languages in any situation, public or private, oral or written and also by the media.

There are also Roma/gypsy (1.6 per cent), Czech (1.1 per cent), Ruthenian (0.3 per cent), Ukrainian (0.3 per cent) and German (0.1 per cent) minorities.

The relationship between the Government and the Roma is especially problematic. In February 2004, in response to unrest in the east of the country the police raided Roma settlements, leading to complaints of maltreatment, racial violence, and solitary confinement of those arrested. Organizations such as Amnesty International have demanded that the Slovak Government carry out independent investigations and adhere to international human rights resolutions.

MIGRANTS/REFUGEES
At the end of 2002, there were over 4,500 refugees in Slovakia, almost all of them awaiting the decision of the Immigration Office. Some 4,100 Roma Slovaks left the country to escape discrimination. During 2003, 9,700 requests for asylum were received: 1,800 from China, 1,700 Afghanistan, 1,600 from India and 1,200 from Iraq. The Immigration Office issued 330 initial decisions in 2002, granting asylum in 20 and rejecting the rest.

DEATH PENALTY
The death penalty was abolished for all crimes in 1990.

*Latest data available in *The State of the World's Children* and *Childinfo* database, UNICEF, 2004.

Democratic Coalition (SDK) and signed an agreement with Coexistence, a coalition made up of the Hungarian Christian Democratic Movement, the Hungarian People's Party and the group known as Coexistence. President Kovak, whose relations with Meciar were already strained, joined in criticizing the Prime Minister, urging him in January 1998 to improve relations with the US and the European Union. After his defeat in Parliamentary elections, Meciar resigned and the two main opposition parties, the Slovak Democratic Opposition and the Democratic Left, formed a new Government in October, with Mikulás Dzurinda as Prime Minister.

21 The planned installation of a nuclear reactor in Mochovce, near the Austrian frontier in June 1998, led to protests from Vienna.

22 In May 1999, Rudolf Schuster won the first direct presidential elections, which had been established through constitutional reform in January.

23 Protesting against discrimination, some 1,000 Slovakian Roma people sought asylum in Finland in July 1999. President Schuster recognized the demand as legitimate. The Government adopted immediate measures to improve this minority's situation and avoid a large outflow.

24 The Czech and Slovak Governments reached an agreement in November putting an end to financial differences arising from the separation. Prague promised to deliver 4.5 tons of gold to Bratislava and acknowledged having a $1.5 billion debt with Slovakia.

25 In February 2001 Parliament approved important reforms to the constitution, preparatory to joining the EU and NATO. The new constitution decentralized power, granted more authority to the office that monitors and audits the Government, and strengthened the independence of the judiciary. Russia immediately said it was opposed to Slovakia's possible integration into NATO, seeking to keep that organization away from its borders.

26 In January 2002, eight new regional parliaments were established, continuing the reforms in readiness for entry to the EU.

27 In April 2002, the EU suspended financial aid to Slovakia, expressing doubts over how it was being used. The announcement was made after Roland Toth, Slovak official in charge of the funds, resigned amid accusations of corruption. The suspension compromised Slovakia's intentions of joining the EU.

28 Mikulás Dzurinda's center-right Slovak Democratic Coalition (SDK) won the September 2002 elections in the second round. During the November Prague summit, Slovakia was formally invited to join NATO.

29 In December 2002 in Copenhagen, the country was invited to join the EU in 2004.

30 In May 2003, following a referendum with a vote just above the required 50 per cent, entry to the Union was approved.

31 In February 2004, in the east of the country, government forces faced a revolt by the Roma/gypsy population, demanding their citizens' rights.

32 Finally, in 1 May, 2004 Slovakia joined the EU. ∎

Slovenia / Slovenija

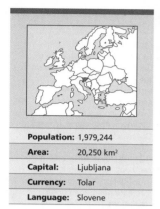

Population:	1,979,244
Area:	20,250 km²
Capital:	Ljubljana
Currency:	Tolar
Language:	Slovene

One of the southern Slav groups, the Slovenes occupied what is now Slovenia and the land to the north of this region in the 6th century AD. Subdued by the Bavarians around the year 743, they were later incorporated into the Frankish Empire of the Carolingians. With the division of the Empire in the 9th century, the Slovenes were reduced to serfdom and the region north of the Drava River was completely dominated by the Germans.

2   The Slovene people preserved their cultural identity because of the educational efforts of their intellectuals who were mostly Catholic monks and priests. The House of Austria gradually established itself in the region, from the latter part of the 13th century onwards.

3   Between the 15th and 16th centuries, the Slovenes participated in several peasant revolts - some, like the 1573 revolt, in conjunction with the Croats - leading the Hapsburgs to improve the system of land tenure.

4   After 1809, a large part of the territory fell within the Napoleonic Empire's Illyrian provinces. After Napoleon's defeat in 1814, Hapsburg (House of Austria) rule was restored within the region. With the 1848 Revolution, the Slovenes called for the creation of a united Slovene province within the Austrian Empire. The first glimmer of hope for a union of southern Slavs (Slavs, Serbs and Croats) emerged in the 1870s.

5   In the 1890s, the Slovene People's Party (Catholic), and the Progressive (Liberal) and Socialist parties were formed. Members of the Catholic clergy also promoted a large-scale organization of peasants and artisans into co-operatives.

6   In 1917 the Austrian Parliament, representing Slovenes and other southern Slav peoples, defended the unification of these territories into a single autonomous political entity, within the Hapsburg realm.

7   At the end of World War I, amid widespread enthusiasm over the fall of the Austro-Hungarian Empire, the Slovenes supported the creation of a kingdom of Serbs, Croats and Slovenes, known from 1929 as Yugoslavia (land of the southern Slavs). Nevertheless at the Paris Peace Conference the victorious powers handed Gorica to Italy despite the presence of a large Slovene population.

8   The St Germain Treaty, signed between the victorious powers and Austria, gave Yugoslavia only a small part of southern Carintia. Two plebiscites were to define the future of the remainder. However, when the southern region opted to join Austria in 1920, the second plebiscite was not held, and both regions remained part of Austria.

9   Serbian hegemony within the Yugoslav kingdom gave rise to some resentment among Slovenes, although less than among the Croats, and that led to an anti-Serbian movement there. In World War II, Slovenia was partitioned between Italy (the southwest), Germany (the northeast) and Hungary (a small area north of the Mura River). The most prominent group within the Slovene resistance movement was the Liberation Front, led by the Communists.

10   The communist guerrillas fought on two fronts at the same time: against the foreign invaders and against anti-communist military units, organized by the occupation with the participation of the local population. After the defeat of the Axis powers (Germany, Italy and Japan), the major part of old Slovenia was returned to Yugoslavia.

11   Upon the foundation of the Federated People's Republic of Yugoslavia, in 1945, Slovenia became one of the Federation's six republics, with its own governing and legislative bodies. Legislative power was made up of a republican council, elected by all citizens, and the council of producers, elected from among Slovenian industrial workers and officials.

12   Although such entities did not add up to an autonomous government, Slovenia managed to maintain a high degree of cultural and economic independence through this self-management brand of socialism (led by the Yugoslav League of Communists). In 1974, changes in the Yugoslavian federal constitution made Slovenia a Socialist Republic.

13   Slovenia became one of the most industrialized of the Federation's republics, especially in the area of steel production and the production of heavy equipment. Yugoslavia's first nuclear power plant was completed in 1981 in Krsko, with the assistance of a private US firm.

14   In the late 1980s, influenced by the changes in Eastern Europe, Slovenia evolved toward a multiparty political system. In January 1989, the Slovene League of Social Democrats was founded, the country's first legal opposition party, and in October Slovenia's National Assembly approved a constitutional amendment permitting Slovenia to secede from Yugoslavia.

15   The Slovene League of Communists left the Yugoslav League in January 1990, becoming the Democratic Renewal Party. In April, in the first multiparty elections to be held in Yugoslavia since World War II, the victory went to Demos, a coalition of sectors united in their aim of achieving separation from the federation.

16   Slovenia and Croatia declared their independence on 25 June 1991. In the hours that followed, federal troops attacked Slovenian territory and occupied frontier posts. After fierce fighting and the bombing of

PROFILE

ENVIRONMENT

Bordered in the west by Italy, in the north by Austria, in the northeast by Hungary and in the south and southeast by Croatia, Slovenia is characterized by mountains, forests and deep, fertile valleys. The Sava River flows from the Julian Alps (highest peak: Mt Triglav, 2,864 meters), in the northwest of the country, to the southeast, crossing the coal-mining region. The Karavanke mountain range is located along the northern border. The region lying between the Mura, Drava, Savinja and Sava rivers is known for its vineyards and wine production. To the west and southwest of Ljubljana, all along the Soca river (known as 'Isonzo' on the Italian side), the climate is less continental, and more Mediterranean. The capital has an average annual temperature of 9°C, with an average of -1°C in the winter and 19°C in summer. The country's main mineral resources are coal and mercury, which contribute to the country's high level of industrialization.

SOCIETY

Peoples: Slovenian 87.8 per cent; Croats 2.8 per cent; Serbs 2.4 per cent; Bosnians 1.4 per cent; Roma 1. 7 per cent; Hungarians 0.4 per cent; and Italian 0.1 per cent. Minorities are officially recognized, 10,000 Roma people live in the country.
Religions: Christian-Catholics are a majority (83.6 per cent), including followers of the traditional Catholic church of Slovenia; Christians from the Eastern Orthodox Church (16.4 per cent). **Languages:** Slovene (official), Serbo-Croat, Hungarian, Italian, German, Czech, Romany.
Main Political Parties: Liberal Democrat Party (LDS) center-left, originally Communist Youth; List of Social Democrats of Slovenia (SDS); People's Party (SLS+SKD) rightist conservative; New Christian People's Party (NSi) previously Demos, the first opposition party to the Communist Party; Social Democratic Party (ZLSD), right-wing.
Main Social Organizations: Two large trade unions, and an independent one, successor of the communist trade union (Association of Free Trade Unions).

THE STATE

Official Name: Republika Slovenija. **Administrative Divisions:** 62 Districts. **Capital:** Ljubljana 256,000 people (2003).
Other Cities: Maribor 97,800 people; Celje 38,300; Kranj 35,500; Velenje 26,400 (2000). **Government:** Janez Drnovsek, President since December 2002. Anton Rop, Prime Minister since December 2002. Unicameral Legislature: the Assembly of Slovenia is formed by 90 members, 40 elected by direct vote and 50 by proportional representation. The State Council is a consultative body with limited legislative powers (40 members). **National Holiday:** 25 June, Independence Day (1991). **Armed Forces:** 9,000 (2002). Other: 4,500 Police (2002).

Ljubljana airport, Belgrade announced that it controlled the federation's borders. However the 21,000-strong Slovenian territorial army caused considerable Yugoslav losses over the next ten days.

[17] On 7 July 1991 a cease-fire went into effect, brokered by the European Community (EC) on the Yugoslav island of Brioni. The agreement reaffirmed the sovereignty of Yugoslav peoples, the federal army agreed to withdraw from Slovenia and Ljubljana promised a three-month freeze of the independence process. In October 1991, the Slovenian Parliament finally approved the end of its official commitment to Yugoslavia. Slovenia implanted its own currency, the Tolar, its national institutions and applied various measures to establish its independence.

[18] While it was part of Yugoslavia, the Slovenian population amounted to a mere 8 per cent of the total population, but accounted for 25 per cent of the country's industrial production.

[19] In January 1992, the EC recognized Slovenia and Croatia as independent states, although civil war continued in Croatia. The homogeneity of the Slovenian population made its secession the least painful in the Yugoslavian dissolution process. International recognition was among the clearest as the country controlled its borders, maintained its own armed forces and issued its own national currency. Following withdrawal of the Yugoslav troops, the Government headed by Milan Kucan reinitiated the task of economic reconstruction without interference from the former Yugoslav Government.

[20] In April 1992, the centrist leader Janez Drnovsek was appointed Prime Minister. In the December elections, Drnovsek's Liberal Democrat Party won and he formed a coalition Government with the Christian Democrats.

[21] With a view to coming closer to the EU, Slovenia began to define itself as a 'European, not Balkan' State. Its shortfall in tax revenue dropped to two per cent of the GNP, inflation was below five per cent and the balance of payments had a deficit of only $70 million. At the beginning of 1994, when unemployment reached 14 per cent, the Government decided to privatize 2,500 state companies.

[22] Slovenia requested association with the EU. This was opposed by Italy which demanded compensation for the nationalization of property belonging to 150,000 Italians between 1945 and 1972. The Catholic Church also demanded the return of property that had been nationalized by the communist regime. In June 1996 Slovenia signed

IN FOCUS

ENVIRONMENTAL CHALLENGES
Mineral and chemical plants have caused severe pollution of the Sava River and the coast, as well as deforestation due to acid rain. Untreated domestic sewage contributes to this water pollution.

WOMEN'S RIGHTS
Women have been able to vote and stand for office since 1945. Until 2000, women's representation in parliament did not exceed 8 per cent of the seats. Of the 5 per cent ministerial or equivalent posts they had managed to occupy in 1995, none was occupied in 2000. That year women comprised 47 per cent of the country's workforce. However, in 2001 in non-agricultural sectors (where their representation was highest, with 61 per cent of the female workforce employed in services and 28 per cent in industry), their salary was still 30 per cent lower than for men.

Although domestic violence against women is not always reported, awareness of it has increased as a result of work by civil society organizations. The Government partially subsidizes three shelters for battered women, operating with limited capacity. Even in 2003, a serious problem is the trafficking of women - to and from the country - for sexual exploitation.

CHILDREN
Over the past few years, the Government has committed itself to the protection of children's rights and welfare. There is free, universal and compulsory education from the age of 6 to 15. According to the Ministry of Education, in 2003, all school-aged children were enrolled in and attended school.

During the year, the police investigated close on 200 sexual attacks on minors; however this does not necessarily prove that such abuse is widespread. The law provides for special protection for children who have been exploited or maltreated. The trafficking of girls for sexual exploitation however continues to be a problem (see Women's Rights).

Children are able to work from the age of 16, although during the harvest or for other kinds of farm work, some younger children may work during the year. Urban employers are more regulated and in the cities the age limit is more respected.

There is some segregation of Roma children and in general they attend separate schools; frequently these are for children with learning difficulties.

INDIGENOUS PEOPLES/ ETHNIC MINORITIES
The Constitution provides for special rights and protection of Italian and Hungarian ethnic minorities, and they have representation in Parliament. Unlike these minorities, the Roma/Gypsies have no special rights. Although Roma representatives have participated for several years in talks to improve their situation, no substantial progress has been made. It is estimated that 40 per cent of the Roma population came from Serbia, Croatia, Bosnia and Albania. Discriminatory attitudes towards the Roma have been denounced by human rights organizations.

MIGRANTS /REFUGEES
The 2002 census indicates that almost 17 per cent of the population is foreign: 35,642 Croats, 38,964 Serbs, 21,542 Muslim Bosnians and 10,467 Muslims are the largest communities. There are over 3,000 Hungarians, Albanians and Italians.

At the end of 2002, Slovenia harbored 380 refugees and asylum-seekers, of whom 200 had their cases pending.

Asylum or refuge was requested by 640 people, less than half the number in 2001. Of these, 132 requests came from Iraqis.

DEATH PENALTY
This was abolished in 1989.

an agreement of association with the EU, with the condition that Slovenia would allow foreigners to purchase property in the country.

[23] In January 1997, Parliament ratified Janez Drnovsek as Prime Minister. President Milan Kucan was re-elected for a further five-year period in November.

[24] During the bombings of Kosovo and Serbia in 1999, Slovenia allowed NATO the use of its airspace. According to a Slovenian research group, RIS, approximately ten per cent of the working population - some 80,000 people - worked via the internet that year.

[25] In April 2000, Drnovsek lost the confidence of Parliament. He was replaced by Andrej Bajuk, leading a conservative coalition. However, the October parliamentary elections returned Drnovsek to power.

[26] In June 2001, Presidents Putin, of Russia, and Bush, of the US, met for the first time in Slovenia, in what used to be the residence of President Tito, the former Yugoslavian leader.

[27] At a summit meeting held in Copenhagen in November 2002, Slovenia was formally invited to join the EU.

[28] On 1 December 2002 Drnovsek won the second round of the presidential elections with 56.4 per cent of the votes. The Minister of Finance, Anton Rop replaced him as Prime Minister.

[29] On 23 March 2003 the Slovenians voted in two plebiscites in favor of joining the EU and NATO. Over 92 per cent of the voters supported joining the EU - the most favorable result among countries joining in 2004 - and over 60 per cent voted to join NATO. Slovenia was the only country to submit the NATO decision to a referendum. It also refused to help the US during the Iraq war; 80 per cent of Slovenians were against the war. The murder of the Serbian Prime Minister, Zoran Djindjic, a reminder of the instability of security in the Balkans, was seen as a factor influencing the vote.

[30] In February 2004, a constitutional court ordered restitution of the right of residence and other civil rights to 18,000 Croats, Bosnians and Serbians, who had effectively been erased from the records following independence in 1992, leaving them without work, without health and social security benefits and without a state of their own.

[31] On 29 March 2004, Slovenia and six other countries from the former Communist bloc joined NATO, the largest increase in membership in the history of the now 26 member-strong organization.

[32] In April 2004, a referendum promoted by the Right voted strongly in favor of revoking Parliament's decision to restore civil rights to ethnic minorities, drawing disapproval from human rights organizations and embarrassing the Government as it prepared for entry to the EU.

[33] On 1 May 2004 the EU welcomed ten new members, among them Slovenia, the only member of the former Yugoslavia to be invited. It joined as a '2nd level of development' country. Its average wealth is 70 per cent that of EU countries; a higher per capita GDP than Greece and lower unemployment than Germany and France are seen as factors that make Slovenia likely to contribute more than it takes out. ∎

Solomon Islands / Solomon Islands

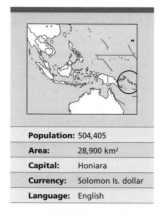

Population:	504,405
Area:	28,900 km²
Capital:	Honiara
Currency:	Solomon Is. dollar
Language:	English

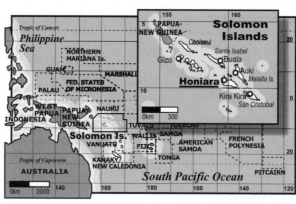

The earliest known occupation of the Solomon Islands is circa 28,000 BC by Australoid hunter-gatherers. The islanders developed a complex social organization based on the *wantok* or extended family system.

[2] The Spaniard Alvaro de Mendaña arrived in 1567, searching for *El Dorado* - the land of gold. In the 18th and 19th centuries, the islands were used as a source of slave labor for the sugar plantations of Fiji and Australia.

[3] Solomon Islands was declared a British Protectorate after World War I. It was occupied by the Japanese in 1942. After World War II, the archipelago was recovered and divided in two. The eastern part, some 14,000 sq km, was placed under Australian administration, and later annexed to Papua New Guinea.

[4] The struggle for independence led by the People's Progressive Party (PPP), headed by Solomon Mamaloni, and the Solomon Islands United Party (SIUPA) led by Peter Kenilorea, ended in 1976 when the islands were granted internal autonomy. Independence was finally declared on 7 July 1978, with Kenilorea as Prime Minister.

[5] Mamaloni was elected Prime Minister in 1981 and established five ministries dedicated to regional affairs.

[6] After the 1984 election, Kenilorea led a coalition government. He patched up relations with the US, but resigned in 1986 amid allegations of accepting French aid for repair work on his home village, damaged by a cyclone. He named Ezequiel Alebua (SIUPA) as his successor. After taking office, Alebua followed Kenilorea's policies.

[7] In 1989, Mamaloni, whose party was now called the People's Alliance Party (PAP), was re-elected Prime Minister.

[8] Francis Billy Hilly replaced him in 1994 but was forced to step down in October after a vote of no confidence. He claimed the logging industry was tainted by government corruption. The new Prime Minister, Mamaloni, ordered the felling of all trees on Pavuvu island, resettling its inhabitants on other islands.

[9] In 1997, Prime Minister Bartholomew Ulufa'alu nationalized the logging industry and ordered an investigation into the use of development funds by the previous administration.

[10] In the first half of 1999, long-simmering disputes over land ownership and access to education, employment and economic development erupted into armed conflict around Honiara on Guadalcanal island.

[11] The Isatabu Freedom Movement (IFM) - representing Guadalcanal interests - demanded compensation for the use of their land as national capital. When the compensation payment was not forthcoming, the IFM evicted people squatting on their land and forced businesses to close. The group most affected were islanders from Malaita, who held most of the jobs and controlled the power structures. The Malaitans retaliated by forming a private army, the Malaita Eagle Force (MEF), which seized arms and gunboats from the SI Police Force. Prime Minister Ulufa'alu, a Malaitan, offered to pay over $500,000 to the Guadalcanal Provincial Government as compensation.

[12] Months later, a peace agreement was reached between both militias, to be enforced by Australia and New Zealand/Aotearoa.

[13] In December 2001, Allan Kemakeza became Prime Minister. Australia warned it would not grant any economic aid until the islands achieved significant political stability (compliance with the law, restoring order), and budgetary and economic reforms.

[14] In late 2002, Cyclone Zoe, the strongest ever recorded in the region, struck the islands, causing major damage to the Tikopia and Anuta atolls. The impoverished SI Government was unable to send aid, relying largely on Australia and New Zealand for help.

[15] In July 2003 an armed intervention by the Australian-led Regional Assistance Mission to Solomon Islands (RAMSI) put an end to four years of confrontation. Days before the operation, Harold Keke, the guerrillas' leader, declared a ceasefire and freed three of the seven hostages taken in June. A month later the rebel commander surrendered to the RAMSI. ∎

PROFILE

ENVIRONMENT

Solomon Islands comprises most of the island group of the same name, except for those in the northwest which belong to Papua New Guinea, the archipelago of Ontong Java (Lord Howe Atoll), the Rennell Islands and the Santa Cruz Islands. The Solomon Islands are part of Melanesia, east of New Guinea. The major islands, of volcanic origin, are: Guadalcanal (with the capital Honiara), Malaita, Florida, New Georgia, Choiseul, Santa Isabel and San Cristobal. The land is mountainous and there are several active volcanoes. Fishing and subsistence agriculture are the traditional economic activities. Deforestation is severe. Heavy rains cause soil erosion, particularly in exposed areas. Coral reefs are being heavily damaged.

SOCIETY

Peoples: Most of the population is of Melanesian origin (93 per cent). There are also Polynesians (4 per cent), Micronesians (1.5 per cent) and Chinese and European minorities.
Religions: Anglicans (45 per cent), Catholic (18 per cent), Methodist and Presbyterian (12 per cent) Baptist (9 per cent), Seventh Day Adventists (7 per cent). Other Protestant 5 per cent, local traditional beliefs 4 per cent.
Languages: English (official, only spoken by 1-2 per cent of the population), pidgin (local language derived from English) and over 120 local languages and dialects.
Main Political Parties: People's Action Party (PAP); Liberal Party; Alliance Party; Nationalist Front for Progress (NFP); Labor Party; National Unity, Reconciliation, and Progressive Party (SINURP).
Main Social Organizations: The Solomon Islands Council of Trade Unions (SICTU), formed in 1986, made up of 6 trade unions.

THE STATE

Official Name: Solomon Islands.
Administrative Divisions: 8 provinces and the capital.
Capital: Honiara 56,000 people (2003).
Other Cities: Gizo 7,000 people; Auki 5,000; Kira Kira 3,800; Buala 3,000 (2000). **Government:** Queen Elizabeth II, Head of State; Nathaniel Waena Governor-General since July 2004, appointed by the British Government. Allan Kemakeza, Prime Minister since December 2001. The National Parliament, has 50 members for a four-year term. **National Holiday:** 7 July, Independence Day (1978).

LAND USE

2000

- ■ ARABLE LAND: 1.5%
- ■ CROPLANDS: 0.6%
- ■ OTHER USE: 97.9%

PUBLIC EXPENDITURE

% OF GDP 2000

5.6 %	3.6 %
HEALTH	EDUCATION

Somalia / Soomaaliya

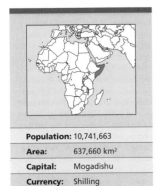

Population:	10,741,663
Area:	637,660 km²
Capital:	Mogadishu
Currency:	Shilling
Language:	Somali and Arabic

Around 2000 BC, Egypt began trading with the Somali territory called Puntland. Centuries later, the Romans called it 'the land of aroma' because of the incense produced there.

2 This commercial tradition took on new dimensions from the 8th century when Arab refugees founded settlements on the coast.

3 In the 13th century, after converting to Islam, and led by Yemeni immigrants, Somalis founded a state which they called Ifat. It paid tribute to Ethiopia, and its principal center was in Zeila. Ifat quickly consolidated its independence and annexed new territories, becoming the Sultanate of Adal.

4 Links with Arab markets and the southern coast of Zandj (East Africa) contributed to the vigorous commercial activity. At the same time, the sultans tried to enlarge their dominion, at the expense of the Ethiopian Empire. As from 1439, the religious implications of conflict prompted the Abyssinians to seek help from European Christians.

5 However, it was not until 1541 that the Portuguese Government, in an attempt to monopolize Indian Ocean trade, sent its fleet. Backed up by the Ethiopian army, the Portuguese razed the city of Zeila, going on to destroy Mogadishu (Muqdisho), Berbera and Brava.

6 The Portuguese destroyed but did not occupy the area, though the presence of their armada hindered

economic reconstruction. Adal was divided into a series of minor sultanates, the northern ones controlled by the Ottoman Empire, while the ones in the south accepted the sovereignty of the Sultan of Zanzibar after the expulsion of the Portuguese in 1698.

7 The Suez Canal gave new strategic value to the 'Horn of Africa' (now Somalia, Somaliland, Puntland, Djibouti, Eritrea and Ethiopia). In 1862, the French bought the port of Obock, leading to the creation of present-day Djibouti. In 1869 the Italians settled in Aseb and later extended their

control over Eritrea. The British took Zeila and Berbera in 1885. In 1906, in compensation for their defeat in Ethiopia, the Italians obtained Somalia's southern coast.

8 In 1889, Italy created a protectorate over central Somalia and southern territories given up by the Sultan of Zanzibar.

9 The British colony was the main center of resistance to occupation. Sheikh Muhammad bin Abdullah Hassan organized an Islamic revolutionary movement, which defeated the British troops on four occasions between 1900 and 1904. The British finally gained control of

the territory in 1920 using airplanes for the first time in Africa.

10 In 1925, the lands to the east of the River Juba passed from Kenya to become an Italian protectorate.

11 With the union of a Somali-speaking part of Ethiopia, Italian East Africa was created in 1936.

12 In 1940, the Italians occupied the British part of the country, and in 1941, the British conquered the Italian part.

13 In 1950, Italian Somalia became a UN territory under Italian control. In 1956 it obtained internal autonomy, under the name of Somalia.

14 The British and Italian regions became independent and were merged as the United Republic of Somalia. Aden Abdullah Osman Daar was the first president.

15 Between 1963 and 1964 the country broke off relations with Britain and disputed its frontiers with Kenya and Ethiopia.

16 Abdi Rashid Ali Shermarke was elected president in 1967. Two years later he was assassinated and Muhammad Siad Barre took on the presidency. In 1970 Somalia adopted socialism, nationalizing part of the economy. In 1974, the country entered the Arab League.

17 In July 1976, Somalia invaded Ogaden (Ethiopia), supposedly in support of the Front for the Liberation of Western Somalia. The Ethiopian army, with the support of Cuban troops, repelled the invasion. Somalia broke off relations with Cuba.

18 The war and the 1978-79 drought brought the country to the brink of collapse.

19 In October 1980 Barre declared a state of emergency and reinstated the Supreme Revolutionary Council, which had ceased functioning in 1976.

LAND USE

2000

IRRIGATED AREA: 18.7% of arable land

- ARABLE LAND: 1.7%
- CROPLANDS: 0.0%
- OTHER USE: 98.3%

Life expectancy
47.9 years
2000-2005

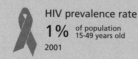

HIV prevalence rate
1% of population
15-49 years old
2001

[20] In 1985, problems with Ethiopia increased because of the dispute over the Ogaden plains and the flow of refugees into Somali camps.

[21] Said Barre was re-elected in December 1986 by 99 per cent of the vote. In 1998 peace was signed with Ethiopia.

[22] In January 1991, the opposition formed the United Somali Congress (USC) and ousted the President, replacing him with Ali Mahdi Mohammed, of the Hawiye clan, who represented business interests.

He fled the capital in November following confrontations between USC factions. The capital remained in the hands of General Mohamed Farah Aideed, leader of the military wing of the USC and of another subdivision of the same clan. It was the start of faction warfare, which was to leave thousands of people dead or in exile.

[23] In March 1992, nine *ugas* or kings of the Hiraan region met for the first time over a hundred years to discuss how to bring peace to

their country. The territory of the former British colony declared independence in May as the Republic of Somaliland. Without international recognition, it suffered from the same inter-clan violence.

[24] In 1992, power remained in the hands of the warlords and armed bands of looters throughout the country.

[25] That same year, under the UN's Operation Restore Hope, 28,000 US troops went to assist under the pretext of re-establishing the supply

of food and to encourage the factions to disarm. In 1993 UN soldiers from Pakistan, India and other Majority World countries took over and US troops withdrew in 1994; the UN forces in 1995. The intervention was seen as disastrous by many, especially in the US, and continues to affect its foreign policy.

[26] In 1995, Somaliland continued to function; elsewhere the factions regrouped around the Somali Salvation Alliance (SSA), led by Ali Mahdi Mohammed, and the SNA, led by Farah Aideed, both claiming power. Farah Aideed died in August 1996 and was succeeded by his son, Hussein. Farah's former right-hand, Osman Hassan Ali ('Ato'), emerged as a new force, though associated with Ali Mahdi.

[27] In January 1997 in Ethiopia, political leaders affiliated with the SSA, with the support of the Organization of African Unity, established a National Salvation Council. Both Hussein Aideed and Mohammed Ibrahim Egal, re-elected President of Somaliland in March, refused to recognize the decision.

[28] In June 1998 a conference of 300 northeastern leaders in the Garowe district elected Colonel Abdullah Yussuf Ahmed as President and Mohammed Abdi Hashi as Vice-President. The so-called Puntland administration would include the Garowe, Bari and Galkayo areas, with Garowe as a possible capital.

[29] In August 2000, a peace conference in Djibouti, involving several factions, elected 245 members of Parliament, and chose Abdiqasim Salat Hassan as the new President. In October, in Mogadishu the new Prime Minister, Ali Khalif Galaydh, announced his Cabinet of 25 ministers, all men and representing the various Somali clans, which he called a 'reconciliation government'.

[30] In May 2001 a referendum in Somaliland voted by a large majority for independence. The country still lacked recognition from the international community.

[31] In late 2001, the US froze some assets of Somalia's largest corporation, Barakaat, due to its apparent links with terrorist network al-Qaeda leader Osama bin Laden. The UN warned that this was aggravating Somalia's already desperate situation. The country was on the verge of total economic collapse due to the conflict, prolonged drought and the ban on exporting livestock.

[32] In May 2002 Mohammed Egal died in a hospital in South Africa, leading to fears that his death could prompt the re-emergence of old rivalries. Dahir Riyale Kahin was designated President of Somaliland.

[33] In October 2002, the 21 factions at war and the Somalia Government agreed to a ceasefire, while further negotiations took place.

Somaliland

Population: 3,500,000
Area: 137,600 km²
Capital: Hargeisa
Currency: Somali shilling
Language: Somali

Somaliland declared its independence from Somalia in 1993, claiming authority within the old British colonial borders and differentiating itself from the Italian colonial territories of Somalia (see history).

[2] Since then, the autonomous government has pursued its demand for international recognition. However, the various UN bodies refer to this territory as 'Somalia's Northwest Zone', in an attempt to preserve the illusion of a future reunification of the former country, devastated by more than 12 years of civil war, with neither strong government institutions, nor representative or stable social organizations.

[3] Within this reality, the Government of Somaliland has made enormous efforts to achieve a multiparty democratic organization and lasting peace, on the domestic front, as well as building diplomatic and commercial relations with the rest of the world.

[4] The death of President Mohamed Ibrahim Egal, in May 2002, threatened to halt the independence process. Egal's successor, Dahir Riyale Kahin, took office and continued the democratization policy and peace process.

[5] The party of President Dahir won the second round of the April 2003 elections by only 80 votes in a ballot of 488,543. The peaceful acceptance of the result by the main opposition party was evidence of a significant advance towards cementing the country's democracy.

[6] In spite of the relative freedom of expression, in June 2003, General Jama Mohamed Ghalib, former chief of police who advocated the return of Somaliland to a federal Somalia, was detained and deported. Several of his supporters were arrested after a shoot-out with Somaliland security forces and remained detained without charge or trial at the end of the year.

[7] The murder of several international aid workers in October 2003 dented the image of a safe and peaceful country that the Government wanted to portray to the rest of the world. The authorities accused foreign agents of infiltrating the country and trying to upset the attempts to gain international recognition that had been worked on for many years.

[8] The disputes with Puntland (another northern semi-autonomous territory) have prevented Somaliland from defining its borders. Military incursions led by Colonel Abdullahi Yussuf in the Sool and Sanaag areas, are aimed at taking over an area where the population belongs to the Darod clan, while in Somaliland most of the population are Isak members.

[9] In January 2004, Puntland forces advanced to within eight kilometres of the Sool regional capital, Las Anod, and kidnapped the brother of the Minister for Rural Affairs, Fou'ad Adan Ade. The Government's weak response to the attacks drew criticism from the opposition and the press.

[10] In May 2004, President Kahin set parliamentary elections for March 2005. According to the authorities, this will be the last step in the democratization process and will help Somaliland obtain recognition as an independent state.

[11] Somaliland not only faces difficulties arising from its pursuit of recognition and state-building, but also the problems of being located in one of the world's poorest areas.

[12] It is hard to engage people's interest in the complex political issues beyond those of group and clan loyalties, among a population of 3.5 million people, of whom 90 per cent led nomadic lives until a short time ago, and who are still suffering the consequences of a long civil war.

[13] The gross national income per capita is $120 (estimated for Somalia by the World Bank). The infant mortality rate is 133 per 1,000 live births. Barely 34 per cent of births are attended by skilled personnel and 95 per cent of girls suffer genital mutilation.

[14] Most people are Muslim. Women have traditionally suffered genital multilation and been semi-secluded. However, their key role in the rebuilding of post-war civil society has recently begun to be recognized.

[15] The literacy rate is 24 per cent. These rates fall abruptly in rural areas where people's contact with schools and modern lifestyles is sporadic. However, at least there is now relative peace, which allows the country to concentrate on achieving the economic development necessary for dealing with the serious crisis faced by its population. ■

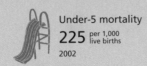
Under-5 mortality
225 per 1,000
live births
2002

Malnutrition
26% under-5s
1995-2002

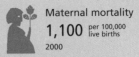
Maternal mortality
1,100 per 100,000
live births
2000

34 By a close margin, Dahir Riyale was elected President of Somaliland in April 2003. In July the Government of Somalia continued with the peace negotiations in Kenya.

35 In January 2004, the talks reached an agreement between the military chiefs and the politicians to set up a new parliament, seen as a major step towards lasting peace.

36 More than 100 people died in June 2004 as a result of clashes between ethnic militias in the town of Bula Hawo, in southern Somalia. Two factions of the SNF (Somali National Front) started fighting over control of the town. Bula Hawo is of key importance to the commercial routes that join Mogadishu with both Kenya and Ethiopia. The fighting, which took place very near the Kenyan border, also affected the Kenyan town of Mandera, where seven people were killed. The Kenyan Government reacted by arresting suspects in the area and police forces were deployed along the border to prevent militias from crossing over. However, hundreds of Somalis crossed the border and sought refuge in the neighboring country.

37 In July 2004, a group of about 150 Somalis met in Mogadishu in order to discuss the rebuilding of the country, after more than a decade of civil war and of total lack of legislation. Those taking part in these talks included academics, entrepreneurs from several parts of the region as well as Somalis living overseas. But with no real government, no police forces and a bad transport network, Somalia was not able to improve its economy. These matters were discussed in the talks, which were held at the Mogadishu Center for Research and Dialogue (CRD).

38 In June of that year, the Government of the United Kingdom decided to return six Somalis who had fled the war back to Somalia. Amnesty International (AI) condemned this decision and asked for clarification, considering this move as an unannounced change in British policy. The organization regarded the argument used by the United Kingdom that those returned to their country would not be risking their lives as unrealistic. Somalia was the country with the highest number of asylum applications to the United Kingdom: more than 4,500 Somalis had submitted applications in 2003.

39 Not only AI, but also the UNHCR regarded the situation in Somalia as highly risky as a result of the new wave of fighting between factions. More than 1.5 million Somalis had gone into exile or had been displaced since the beginning of the war.

40 Peace talks aimed at resolving the conflict continued in Nairobi through 2004. Eventually, on 10 October, Ethiopian-backed warlord Abdullahi Yusuf was elected the President by the peace talks representatives. He immediately called on the international community to help disarm the militias. ∎

Puntland

Population: 2,500,000
Area: 300,000 km²
Capital: Garowe
Currency: Somali shilling
Language: Somali

Puntland, in northeastern Somalia, was self-declared a federal regional state in 1998. Its internal organization is precarious, even more so than Somalia's. Its poor economic situation, reflecting that in Somalia, as well as the violence - both internal and arising from border disputes with Somaliland - pose major obstacles to resuming normal daily life and to arousing the population's interest in participation in their new autonomy.

2 Puntland took part in peace talks for Somalia and supported a federal constitution. In May 2003, a peace agreement was signed between Puntland President Abdullahi Yusuf Ahmed and an armed opposition group, the Puntland Salvation Council, headed by General Mahamoud Musse Hersi ('Ade'). Opposition political leaders were integrated into the Government and all captured soldiers were released.

3 The situation showed a slight improvement in late 2003. Independent expert Ghanim Alnajjar submitted a report to the UN on his visit to Kenya and Somalia in August-September that year. He met the Minister of Commerce, UN members in the country and local NGOs; he also visited the police HQ, the port, the main prison and camps for internally displaced people. He reported that the country was relatively peaceful at this time, which allowed authorities to concentrate on urgent internal issues.

4 In early 2004, President Abdullahi Yusuf Ahmed travelled to Italy, Malaysia and Lybia. In Italy, he discussed Somalia's peace situation with government authorities. In Malaysia, he signed bilateral trade agreements and in Libya, he met President Muammar al-Qadhafi, who supported the fight against the Siad Barre regime (see history of Somalia). ∎

IN FOCUS

ENVIRONMENTAL CHALLENGES
The effects of the most recent droughts have been exacerbated by overgrazing. The sharp increase in livestock numbers. has triggered desertification. Fishing using explosives has damaged coral reefs and aquatic vegetation. The destruction of the habitat of several fish species could threaten future catches. There are 74 endangered species in Somalia, including mammals, plants and birds. There is serious water pollution.

WOMEN'S RIGHTS
Women have been able to vote since 1956. Their active political participation is practically non-existent. Between 1980 and 2000, women have comprised 43 per cent of the labor force. During the last decade, the primary school education rate was only 10 per cent. Pre-natal medical care reaches 32 per cent and specialized personnel attend 34 per cent of births*. Sixty per cent of pregnant women are vaccinated against tetanus*. The maternal mortality rate is 1,100 per 100,000 live births*.

CHILDREN
Twenty-six per cent of the under-fives are moderately or seriously under-weight and 23 per cent are moderately or seriously under-size*. Infant inoculation in 2002 was: tuberculosis, 60 per cent; triple viral, 40 per cent; polio, 34 per cent; measles, 45 per cent. Primary schooling stands at 7 per cent for girls and 13 per cent for boys*.

Over the period 1999-2001, 29 per cent of the boys and 36 per cent of the girls aged between 5 and 14 worked.

Since the start of the war in 1991, over 300,000 children have been killed in the fighting.

INDIGENOUS PEOPLES/ ETHNIC MINORITIES
Somalis make up 64 per cent of the population. This ethnic group is divided into various subclans: Dir, Darood, Issaq, Hawiye, Rahanweyn, Digil. The latter comprise 16 per cent of the population and speak three different languages, which until 1921 were grouped under the name of Somali: Maay, Tunni and Jiddu.

The Afars number 60,000. They have occupied the territory for the past 2,800 years. They are mainly nomadic, and speak Afaraf, an Afro-Asiatic language.

In the Gedo region there are some 3,000 Borana. They are united by the concept of *nagya borana* (Borana peace), and try to maintain internal harmony despite external conflicts. Their social organization, known as *gada*, is divided into age groups. They are camel herders and farmers.

A small number of Tikuu-speaking people, the Bajun, a fishing community, are mostly located in Kenya.

Gosha people, one per cent of the population, live in the south, in the Jamaame district, Juba region and in the urban centers of Kismaayo and Mogadishu. In Somali the name means 'forest people'. They are descendants of the Bantu-speaking slaves imported to Somalia from Tanzania and Mozambique.

MIGRANTS/REFUGEES
Over 1.5 million people have gone into exile or abandoned their homes since the start of the war in 1991.

At the end of 2002, close on 300,000 Somalis lived as refugees in various countries: over 140,000 in Kenya; almost 80,000 in Yemen, 21,000 in Djibouti, some 20,000 in Ethiopia; 7,000 in South Africa; 7,000 in Egypt; over 3,000 in Tanzania; 3,000 in Libya; over 2,000 in Eritrea; 1,000 in Uganda and over 15,000 in Europe and the US. At the end of 2003 there were about 350,000 displaced persons within the country. Some 20,000 were repatriated during the year, mainly in the north.

DEATH PENALTY
This is still applied.

*Latest data available in *The State of the World's Children* and *Childinfo* database, UNICEF, 2004.

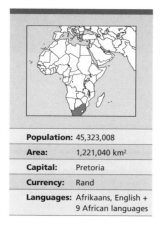

Population:	45,323,008
Area:	1,221,040 km²
Capital:	Pretoria
Currency:	Rand
Languages:	Afrikaans, English + 9 African languages

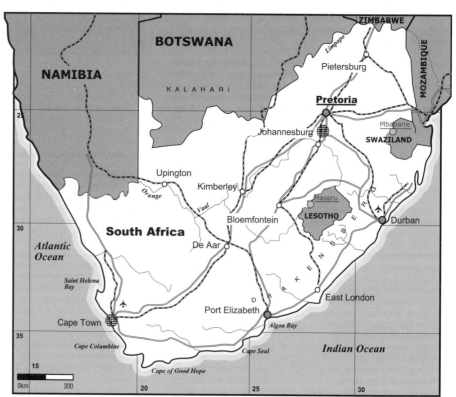

For most of the past 100,000 years, the territory of present-day South Africa has been occupied by the *San*, small mobile groups of hunting and gathering people who expressed their beliefs, rituals and activities in richly abundant rock art. They were gradually displaced by the *Khoikhoi*, agro-pastoralists whose presence goes back 2,000 years. About the year 500 AD, immigrant *Bantu*-speakers began to work the soil, mainly in the river valleys of south-eastern Africa where summer rainfall predominates. Techniques first learnt further north came to be applied to the growing of edible crops such as millet and squash.

² Domestication of cattle created new possibilities as societal and political systems arose. The Bantu-speaking chiefs expanded their power through control of their women as producers, and the youth as workers and soldiers. Wealth in cattle made patronage possible, and was also used as *lobola*, bride-price, by the bridegroom's people to the father or guardian of the bride. Metallurgical skills gave the chiefs an additional valuable trading commodity and greater military potential.

³ The first Dutch settlers arrived at Cape Town in 1652, more than 150 years after the Portuguese sailor Vasco da Gama rounded the Cape of Good Hope. Jan van Riebeeck was the first of the Dutch to challenge the *Khoikhoi*. He landed in Cape Town and established a colony supplying ships on their way to Indonesia. In 1688, nearly 600 farmers had settled there, dividing their energies between farming and the war against the *Khoikhoi*. Being such a small minority, the first Dutch colonists were fiercely united and aggressive, two characteristics which pervaded *boer* (farmer) society in southern Africa.

⁴ The Dutch who worked for the Dutch East India Company (VOC) were not allowed to trade with the local people and had to deliver all their production to the Company's ships. They gradually came into conflict with their overseas bosses, who would not loosen the grip of their monopoly. The Boers won the dispute, and towards the end of the 17th century the so-called free colonists or burghers were in the majority. The population of European origin split between those linked to foreign trade and those who moved inland in search of new lands.

⁵ In 1806, with the Dutch colonial empire on the wane, the British settled in Cape Town. They moved ahead on agreements to trade goods, incorporated the African leaders as intermediaries and ended slavery. This rapidly led to conflict with the slavery maintained by the intransigent Boers, who had begun calling themselves Afrikaners, to distinguish themselves from the colonists. In 1834, nearly 14,000 Afrikaners emigrated to the interior, starting the Great Trek which would take them to what became Transvaal, the Orange Free State and Natal, endeavoring to exploit slave labor without foreign interference. They established the state of Transvaal in 1852 and Orange Free State in 1854.

⁶ The British recognized the independence of the two regions, as the settling of new lands by Europeans increased Cape Town's security. Furthermore, the Boers necessarily had to trade through ports operated by the British. In their expansion northward, the Afrikaners confronted Xhosas and Zulus. The latter, led by military genius Shaka, blocked the colonists' advance over a period of 50 years. Shaka became the head of a great empire which collapsed shortly before the Great Trek, due to internal strife over the royal succession.

⁷ Peace between the Boers and the British Crown ended in 1867 when rich gold and diamond fields were discovered in Transvaal. Certain that the region held great economic and strategic value, Britain proposed a federation between the Cape Colony and the two Free States. The Boers refused, leading to war in 1899. Britain was supported by most of its colonies, while the Boers had German backing. After three years of war, with nearly 50,000 Afrikaners dead and double that number confined to concentration camps, they surrendered, accepting British domination, while maintaining a certain independence for their regions. The British victory signaled the end of the hegemony

LAND USE

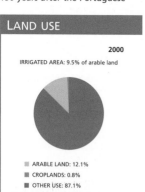

2000

IRRIGATED AREA: 9.5% of arable land

- ■ ARABLE LAND: 12.1%
- ■ CROPLANDS: 0.8%
- ■ OTHER USE: 87.1%

PUBLIC EXPENDITURE

% OF GDP

40

30

20

10

0

9.2 %
HEALTH & EDUCATION (2000)

1.6 %
DEFENSE (2001)

WORKERS

UNEMPLOYMENT: 30.0% (2002)

LABOR FORCE   **2002**

- ■ FEMALE: 37.9%   ■ MALE: 62.1%

of landed Boer farmers in the Orange Free State and Transvaal and the beginning of mining's importance in the economy.

8   For some Boers, the African peoples were 'savages' who had to be tamed and made into slaves. White supremacy and racial segregation were established to justify the subjugation of the black population and to guarantee a supply of cheap farm labor from tenants. Boer farms could not compete with British farming as practised in the Cape and Natal and therefore they needed very cheap labor.

9   The British focus on trade and liberalism made them see slavery as a restraint on the creation of consumer markets. This did not prevent them from erecting rigid barriers to exclude black South Africans from economic and social advancement. The labor legislation from 1809 imposed severe controls on worker mobility. The 1843 Master and Servant Act made it a criminal act to break a work contract.

10   Around 1850, the British also contracted black workers in the territories of present-day Mozambique, Lesotho, Botswana, as well as Indians and Chinese. These 'imported' workers were not allowed to bring their families; pay was poor and they had to return to their own countries if they lost their jobs.

11   In 1894, work taxes were introduced, payable in cash, unless a person could certify having worked outside their home districts for a given time. This was decreed to force Africans to work for a salary far lower than that paid to those of European origin. Another law levied an annual tax on peasants, also payable in cash, which they could only get by selling their produce to the Europeans. Salaries were kept low, destroying the traditional African ways of life.

12   When the gold and diamond mines began to be exploited, the European capitalists had to employ qualified white workers. Most of them were former Boer farmers who had lost everything in the war. Others came from Europe attracted by 'gold fever'. Both of these groups were used to the workings of the industrial capitalist system, and made demands for better pay and conditions. The mining companies promised benefits to these white workers as long as they fell in with the exploitation of the black workforce.

13   In 1896, the so-called color bar was in place in the mining sector and in the urban centers where the British were in the majority. In 1910, the Constitution

IN FOCUS

ENVIRONMENTAL CHALLENGES
Water resources are over-exploited, desertification is in process in some zones. Salinization is the greatest threat in dry regions. Erosion is a major problem, while the air in the cities is very polluted and high levels of acid rain have been recorded.

WOMEN'S RIGHTS
White women have been able to vote since 1930, Asian and mixed-race women since 1984 and black women since 1994. Between 1995 and 2000, women's representation in Parliament increased from 25 per cent to 30 per cent of the seats. They hold 6 per cent of ministerial-level positions. In 2000, women accounted for 38 per cent of the labor force. The country has served as a place of transit and destination for the trafficking of individuals, particularly women and children from other countries of Africa, Asia and Eastern Europe for their exploitation as forced labor, including prostitution. During 2003, women and children were illegally brought into the country by local and international criminal associations for the sex trade. The scope of these operations is unknown. Some countries in conflict were providers of women and children: refugees or asylum-seekers who ended up by becoming involved in the trafficking network; these have

mainly come from Mozambique, Thailand, China and some Eastern European countries.

CHILDREN'S RIGHTS
In 1996, almost 57 per cent of the population, mainly black people, lived in poverty. The per capita income among white people is almost nine times higher than black people's income, showing that racial inequality still exists.

In 2003, the infant mortality rate was 45 deaths per 1,000 live births. For under-fives, the mortality rate for the black population was 63 per 1,000 while for the white population it stood at 15 per 1,000.

The secondary school enrolment rate was over 80 per cent, but there were also high rates of school drop-outs, repetition at all levels and adult illiteracy (33 per cent).

It was estimated that during 2003, there were 28,000 children practising prostitution. The minors are sought after by clients in the belief that there is less risk of HIV/AIDS infection. There are gangs that specifically force children to work in prostitution; on some occasions the family itself exploits them to obtain income for the household. Although the Government has made efforts to fight against child prostitution, up until 2004 the situation had not yet been contained.

INDIGENOUS PEOPLES/ ETHNIC MINORITIES
The word 'ethnic' is representative of a conflictive time in the history of the country; the concept of

'tribe' possesses derogatory connotations related to *apartheid*. In addition to the Zulu, who represent 20 per cent of the total population, other large ethnic groups are the Hottentot, Ndebele, Sotho, Swazi, Tsonga, Tswana, Venda and Xhosa.

During the last elections in April 2004, Zulus and Xhosas were murdered in political confrontations. President Mbeki is Xhosa and the Minister of the Interior, Buthelezi, is Zulu.

MIGRANTS/REFUGEES
Towards the end of 2002, South Africa was sheltering 65,000 refugees and asylum-seekers. Of these, 25,000 had been recognized and the other 40,000 were waiting for a reply to their application. Of those recognized, 8,000 were from the Congo, 7,000 from Somalia, 5,000 from Angola, almost 2,000 from Burundi and 1,000 from Rwanda. In 2004 it was estimated that between 1 and 8 million foreigners lived in the country. Many refugees were afraid of the locals, living in fear for their lives. At the 2001 South African Episcopal Conference, violent action by South Africans against refugees was reported (people thrown off moving trains, injured by acid thrown at their faces, etc.).

DEATH PENALTY
It was abolished for common crimes in 1995 and all types of crimes in 1997.

of the Union of South Africa - a federation of Cape Province, Natal, the Orange Free State and Transvaal - deprived most black people of the right to vote or to own land. In 1930, nine-tenths of the arable land was in the hands of Europeans or their descendants.

14   From 1910, segregationist legislation increased. The Native Labor Act pushed urban workers into a system of submission similar to that operating on rural estates. The 1913 Native's Land Act, earmarked seven per cent of national territory for the blacks - the so-called Bantustans - as reserves which became home to 75 per cent of the population. The remaining 93 per cent of the land was reserved for whites who only made up ten per cent of the population. In the overcrowded black reservations subsistence agriculture was the main activity.

The rest, under white control, was exploited under intensive farming with the reserves providing a permanent source of cheap labor. The 1923 Native Urban Act tightly regulated blacks' lives in cities which were considered white strongholds. The movements of black people became subject to absolute control.

15   From the time South Africa started on the road to independence in 1934 until 1984, political participation was limited to less than 17 per cent of the population. Constitutional Reform in 1984 extended the vote to the Asians - mainly Indians - and the 'Colored' or mixed race groups. Black South Africans - almost two-thirds of the population - remained without the right to vote.

16   At the outset of World War I, the white economy was based on

mining and intensive agriculture. The post-war recession obliged the large mining companies to hire blacks, leading to racial confrontations within the workforce. The Rand strike in 1922 was harshly put down by the Government. Most of the strikers were poor whites, descendants of both English and Boers. Frustrated by their defeat in the war and the loss of their lands, with no easy way of entering the nascent industrial structure, Afrikaners were attracted by the ultra-nationalist propaganda of the far right.

17   The Nationalists, triumphant in the 1924 elections along with their English-speaking allies, broke with the traditional liberal economic policy and imposed protectionism. State capitalism promoted by the Nationalists - with steel works, railways and electricity - made rapid national

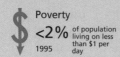
growth possible, something many saw as an 'economic miracle'.

18 Toward the end of the 1920s the falling gold price on the international market led to a crisis between the Nationalists and the Labor party. The Nationalists joined forces with previously despised foreign capital and maintained the racial segregation system which guaranteed cheap workers. The ensuing industrial take-off brought with it an increased number of black employees, leading to racial conflict. A secret society, the Afrikaner Broederbond - Brotherhood - became the bastion of white right-wing politics.

19 The recession following World War II led to a repeat of events: poor whites, threatened by unemployment, rebelled. Racism flourished under the slogan 'Gevaar KKK' (Beware blacks, Indians and communism - Kafir, Koelie, Komunism). In 1948, the Nationalists formed a government by themselves, imposing even harsher restrictions on the black population.

20 The first national political organization of South African blacks had appeared in 1912. The African National Congress (ANC) was created by a group of former students from schools run by missionaries and by people who had studied or gained degrees in North American and European universities. They believed the Afrikaners could be persuaded of the unfairness of the racial segregation laws and that the Anglophile liberals would allow blacks to participate in politics.

21 In the 1940s, the failure of this first strategy led the ANC to adopt a strategy of non-violent resistance to the race laws. In 1955, the anti-racist front was broadened with the Freedom Charter, proclaimed at a multiracial gathering in Kliptown. The Charter included a radical denunciation of *apartheid* (separateness) and called for its abolition, along with wealth redistribution.

22 In 1958, sectors of the ANC that disagreed with its multiracial policy created the Pan African Congress (PAC), which in 1960 held a demonstration in the city of Sharpeville to protest against the pass laws that restricted the movement of black workers in areas reserved for whites. The march was brutally repressed, leaving 70 dead.

23 Following this incident, the PAC, ANC and the Communist Party were all outlawed. The African National Congress (ANC) formed an armed group, the Umkhonto we Sizwe (Spear of the Nation), while the PAC set up another, Poqo (Only Us). In 1963, the main leaders of the ANC were arrested; Nelson Mandela was sentenced to life imprisonment and Oliver Tambo, in exile, took over leadership of the movement. The Government's repressive violence and the lack of supply bases in neighboring countries - dominated by regimes allied to the Afrikaners - prevented the guerrillas from making enough progress to attract greater numbers of recruits.

24 The racist system was largely upheld by the interests of international capitalism in the region, attracted by cheap labor. Foreign investments, especially from the US, increased five times in value between 1958 and 1967. The Afrikaners' protectionist policies created the infrastructure necessary for large industries to be set up, with the aim of developing an industrial center capable of supplying all southern Africa.

25 During the 1960s the number of black rural workers migrating to the cities increased, driven by the poverty of the 'Homelands' or Bantustans, some of which had only poor quality soils, and the lack of social services. This affected the expectations of other urban sectors, such as the Colored people, who saw their hopes of integration into the white economy threatened.

26 In 1976, the black community in the suburbs of Johannesburg erupted. The youth rebellion in Soweto - the South West Township - made the whites realize the crisis had reached the cities where they had previously felt safe. In 1970, 75 per cent of workers in agriculture, mining or the services were black, and the participation of non-whites in specialized jobs had tripled over the last 20 years though blacks earned 5-10 times less than whites for the same work. The governing minority proposed making some reforms to apartheid, in an attempt to prevent further conflicts among migrant workers in the cities.

27 The Pretoria regime declared four Bantustans - Transkei, Ciskei, Venda and Bophuthatswana - to be 'independent states', hoping to halt the internal migration of the unemployed. Eight million people were thus deprived of their South African nationality and converted into foreigners by decree. However very few countries recognized these newly 'independent states'.

28 The independence of Angola and Mozambique in 1975 and that of Zimbabwe in 1980 radically affected the situation in southern Africa. The ANC found the support bases it desperately needed in these countries, and in the other Frontline states of Botswana, Tanzania and Zambia. South Africa, with an economy three times bigger than that of those independent countries combined, initiated a destabilization campaign which included economic pressure, sabotage, support for rebel movements and invasion. All this was in order to force them to deny support to the anti-apartheid movement and block attempts by the newly independent countries to escape South African domination.

29 One of the main arenas of the conflict in southern Africa was Namibia, a former German colony which South Africa occupied during World War I and later annexed. In 1966, the UN ruled that South Africa had to grant Namibia its independence - a demand which the Organization of African Unity (OAU) and the Frontline countries continued to make, despite the delaying tactics of South Africa and the Western powers. It took until March 1990 for Namibia to become independent.

30 To enable South Africa to impose its economic and military strength on southern Africa, the support it received from the US was crucial. Close on 400 US companies had interests in the country, and US capital and technology were vital for developing its industrial and military might.

31 On the domestic front, PW Botha, Prime Minister from 1978 to 1989, began reforming the apartheid system. Between 1982 and 1984, he brought in constitutional reform granting the vote to Indians and colored people and creating two more chambers in parliament for these groups. Blacks were still excluded, with their participation limited to a local level. Many non-whites boycotted the reform, abstaining from voting.

32 The gradual liberalization of apartheid was widely opposed. Repression against blacks did not diminish and was further complicated by inter-ethnic confrontations. In July 1985, the Government declared a state of emergency in 36 districts. By the end of 1986, more than 750 had died and several thousands of the Government's opponents were in prison.

33 Public opinion in the US and Europe forced Western governments and an increasing number of companies and banks to limit their activities in South Africa. The US Congress lifted the veto imposed by President Reagan on economic sanctions, forcing a change in his policy of 'constructive engagement'. Within South Africa, political opposition led to the creation of the United Democratic Front (UDF), which brought together more than 600 organizations working together within the law.

34 From early 1988 the Botha Government came down more heavily on the opposition, outlawing all the constituent groups and imprisoning religious leaders opposed to apartheid, including the black Archbishop, Desmond Tutu, a Nobel Peace Prize winner.

35 In August 1989, cornered by an internal crisis in his party - that had governed for 41 years - Botha resigned. He was replaced by Frederik de Klerk, who declared himself in favor of changing South Africa's racist image. In September, parliamentary elections were held under the State of Emergency which had been operating since 1986.

36 The Mass Democratic Movement (MDM), an anti-apartheid coalition of legal organizations, called a general strike. Despite police raids and threats, three million black South Africans stopped work in the largest protest ever held there. A few days later, the first mass legal demonstration against apartheid since 1959 took place. The growing momentum was accompanied by repression and killings. But by now increasing numbers of the white minority were joining the protests.

37 The opposition agreed to establish the principle of 'one person, one vote' for any negotiations with the Government.

38 In February 1990, De Klerk legalized the ANC and other opposition groups. Nelson Mandela was released on 11 February after 27 years in prison. A period of negotiations began. Mandela resumed his role as leader of the black majority, a post not without its difficulties. Some were related to confrontations - which had caused 5,000 deaths since 1986 - between the ANC and members of the Zulu Inkatha movement. Inkatha had government backing in terms of arms, funds and training.

39 In May, Mandela announced an agreement between the ANC and the Government to end the violence and bring political life back to normal. He called on the international community to maintain economic sanctions and other forms of pressure on the South African Government. He renounced the policy of creating Bantustans - ten had been set up.

In December ANC president Oliver Tambo returned to the country after 30 years of exile.

[40] In April 1991, the European Community (EC) considered lifting the economic blockade and set 30 June as the deadline for starting democratization. On that day, the Government abolished the Population Registration Act and the Land Acts, which had prevented blacks from owning land. De Klerk also promised to begin negotiations for a new Constitution. The US went ahead and lifted the blockade. The EC planned to follow suit, but Denmark and Spain, which had received a visit from Mandela, vetoed the move.

[41] In 1993 the Inkatha Freedom Party (IFP), the Afrikaaner National Front (NFA) and the Conservative Party abandoned negotiations on the Constitution and attempted to boycott the electoral process. Bophuthatswana President Lucas Mangope - in the midst of a strike by public employees - declared he would join the boycott and received military support from the ultra-right Afrikaner Resistance Movement (AWB). The resistance of black civilians and local forces obliged them to withdraw. Mangope was deposed and the South African army took control.

[42] Meanwhile Inkatha boycotted ANC activities and clashed bitterly with Mandela's supporters. Its leader, Mangosuthu Buthelezi, tried unsuccessfully to control another Bantustan, also in Natal; however, he did get the constitution to recognize his nephew Goodwill Zwelethini as King of the Zulus, and he finally agreed to participate in the election.

[43] In October, the UN lifted sanctions against the South African regime. The United States immediately withdrew its financial restrictions.

[44] The provisional Constitution created a 400-seat National Assembly and a Senate with 90 members. The President would be elected by the Assembly for a five-year term. The country was newly divided into nine provinces, each with a governor and legislature, absorbing the ten abolished Bantustans.

[45] The first multiracial elections in South Africa were held in April 1994. The ANC won 63 per cent of the vote.

[46] The Government of National Unity (GNU) included members of the NP and IFP. The minister of finance and the governor of the South African Reserve Bank from the previous government were retained in their posts.

[47] Despite the removal of the barriers of apartheid, economic and cultural obstacles remained. Black workers earned nine times less than whites and unemployment was 33 per cent and 3 per cent respectively. The overall infant mortality was 50 per 1,000 live births (1998) but the rate for blacks was far higher.

[48] Among the measures to be applied at the beginning of his term, Mandela proposed free health care for children aged under six and for pregnant women, a basic diet for schoolchildren and the provision of electricity to 350,000 homes. New legal guidelines for education were established. In October it was announced that 3.5 million people would be given access to water services over the next 18 months. The first GNU budget gave 47 per cent to social services, education took 26 per cent, investment in housing doubled and military spending was reduced.

[49] Ambitious land reform was implemented by Land Affairs Minister Derek Hanekom, a farmer. A labor relations act was approved, guaranteeing the right to strike and set up discussion fora in the workplace. There were far fewer strikes than in previous years.

[50] In January 1995, the ANC withdrew immunity guaranteed before the elections to two former cabinet ministers and 3,500 police officers who were to be investigated by the Truth and Reconciliation Committee (TRC). The trial of a former police colonel for 121 murders, kidnappings and frauds, provided new evidence of police incitement of political violence during the former regime. Prominent Inkatha leaders were implicated in payments made to the security police. A report by the Goldstone Commission was presented to De Klerk in 1994, reiterating these charges. In June, the under-secretary of the IFP was arrested for murders committed in 1987.

[51] The local elections of November 1995 favored the ANC throughout the country. In May 1996, the NP left the Government to join the opposition, for the first time since 1948.

[52] The National Assembly approved a new Constitution which attempted to consolidate the transition to democracy. During the production of the new text, demonstrations attended by thousands of workers and businesspeople led to the elimination of a clause in the final text which gave bosses the right to close their factories.

[53] In 1995 the Truth and Reconciliation Commission was set up, under the presidency of former Archbishop Desmond Tutu, collecting evidence of human rights violations committed between 1960 and 1993. During the investigations, several police officers admitted the use of torture in the 1980s and the hiring of mercenaries. Those responsible were offered an amnesty provided they clarified their part in the events.

[54] The Government announced a strategy aimed at creating 800,000 jobs by the year 2000. Throughout 1996, GDP grew 3 per cent. By November, some two million hectares of land had been redistributed under the Government agrarian reform program.

[55] In October 1997, Mandela visited Libya to mediate in the conflict between Tripoli, Washington and London over the 1992 embargo against Libya resulting from the Lockerbie airplane bombing (see Libya). Mandela supported Libya's stance in calling for a trial in a neutral country, although he made it clear he did not back the unconditional lifting of the embargo.

[56] During his June 1998 farewell message at the Organization of African Unity, Mandela demanded 'the right and the duty to intervene whenever behind sovereign borders people are being massacred to protect tyranny'. These statements contradicted the founding

PROFILE

ENVIRONMENT

Located on the southern tip of the African continent, with coastlines on the Indian and Atlantic Oceans, South Africa has several geographic zones. A narrow strip of lowland lies along the east coast, with a hot and humid climate and large sugarcane plantations. In the Cape region there are vineyards and fynbos vegetation. The vast semi-arid and arid Karoo, with cattle and sheep ranching, makes up over 40 per cent of the total territory, extending inland. The Highveld extends to the north and is the richest arable area. It surrounds the Witwatersrand, a mining area in Gauteng (formerly Transvaal) where large cities and industries are found. The country's economic base lies in the exploitation of mineral resources: South Africa is the world's largest producer of gold and diamonds; the second largest producer of manganese; and the eighth largest producer of coal.

SOCIETY

Peoples: Over 76 per cent of the population is of African origin, of which Zulu 22 per cent, Xhosa 18 per cent, Pedi 9 per cent, Sotho 7 per cent, Tswana 7 per cent, Tsonga 3.5 per cent, Swazi 3 per cent, Ndebele 2 per cent, and Venda 2 per cent. There are also descendants of whites, slaves and Khoisan, called 'Colored'. European descendants account for 13 per cent of the total. Asian groups, predominantly Hindu, make up less than 3 per cent.

Religions: Christianity is predominant (68 per cent) including African independent churches. African beliefs (28 per cent); Islam (2 per cent).

Languages: 11 official languages: Afrikaans, English, isi Ndebele, Sepedi, Sesotho, siSwati, Xitsonga, Setswana, Tshiven da, isi Xhosa, isi Zulu.

Main Political Parties: African National Congress (ANC), New National Party; African Christian Democratic Party; Freedom Front (FF) representing the Afrikaner minority; Pan-African Azanian Congress (PAC).

Main Social Organizations: South African Students' Congress (SASCO), the Congress of South African Trade Unions (COSATU), the National Congress of Trade Unions. Azanian Peoples Organization, advocating black identity.

THE STATE

Official Name: Republic of South Africa.

Administrative Divisions: 9 provinces.

Capital: Pretoria (administrative) 1,209,000 people; Cape Town (legislative) 2,967,000 (2003); Bloemfontein (judicial).

Other Cities: Johannesburg 4,927,200 people; Durban 2,314,100; Port Elizabeth 1,029,400 (2000).

Government: Thabo Mbeki, re-elected in April 2004. Bicameral Legislature: the National Assembly, with 400 members, and the National Council of Provinces, with 90 members.

National Holiday: 27 April, Freedom Day (1994).

Armed Forces: 136,900 (1995).

External debt	Imports (millions)	Exports (millions)
$541 per capita 2001	**$27,761** good and services 2002	**$29,384** good and services 2002

principle of the OAU of non-intervention in the internal affairs of member countries.

[57] That year, during hearings of the Truth and Reconciliation Commission, a plan was revealed, created by apartheid scientists to undermine Mandela's health when he was imprisoned. The plan also included the development of fertility-inhibiting chemical agents and also diseases which would attack the black population.

[58] Attacks on white farmers broke out again as the black population began to express its anger over the slow changes. During the ANC congress, Mandela and his deputy, Thabo Mbeki, warned that the era of formal reconciliation would end at the same time as Mandela's term of office, and that a second ANC government would take tougher measures.

[59] Although the June 1999 elections gave the ANC solid control of Parliament, it did not achieve the two-thirds majority needed to unilaterally amend the constitution. The opposition leadership in the National Assembly fell into the hands of the mainly white Democratic Party (DP). Thabo Mbeki became the new President and appointed Jacob Zuma, also ANC, as deputy President.

[60] Although the Constitution had banned the main forms of discrimination since 1994, a new law approved by Parliament in January 2000 implemented, for the first time, non-discrimination in relations between individuals. The law also prohibited all discrimination based on age, sexual orientation, culture, pregnancy, marital status, matters of conscience and language.

[61] In spite of the fact that since 1994 South Africa had announced restriction policies with regard to the export and import of weapons, and was one of the world leaders in the implementation of the Convention on the Ban, Use, Storage, Production and Transfer of anti-Personnel Mines and their Destruction in 1997, at the end of 2000 Human Rights Watch accused Pretoria of selling weapons to countries with human rights abuses and where the flow of arms could imply an increase of such abuse. In May 2001 an official panel began to investigate accusations of corruption in a weapons deal which had involved Pretoria with British, German, French, Swedish and South African firms. On concluding the process, the Government was acquitted of any responsibility.

[62] Reacting to an official who said the Indian community was unable to carry out certain responsibilities, in early 2001 Mandela accused members of the black majority of using their political power to frighten ethnic minorities and urged the ANC to change the situation.

[63] In September 2001, the World Conference Against Racism took place in Durban, where, faced with the demand by African countries for economic reparation by the former colonizing countries, most of the European states - which at first had been in favor - considered the demand 'unreasonable'.

[64] Over 2,000 minors were reported as having been raped during 2001. To face this problem the Government set up special police units, installed legal protection for the victims of rape and established special courts to deal with sexual offenses.

[65] In April 2002, South African justice absolved Wouter Basson, known by the South African media as 'Doctor Death'. He was notorious for having developed the Costa Project, seeking to create 'intelligent' bacteria that would only kill black people. He had accumulated sufficient cholera and anthrax reserves to cause an epidemic. The weapons he invented included sugar containing salmonella, cigarettes containing anthrax, chocolates containing botulism and whisky containing weed-killer. During the hearings, Basson claimed he was innocent and maintained that he had only obeyed orders, although he did not show any remorse.

[66] Between five and seven million South Africans will die of AIDS by 2010, according to a report issued by the South African Council of Medical Research, and life expectancy by then may be only 36 years. Mbeki disputed the research and tried to prevent its publication. South Africa has one of the highest rates of HIV infection in the world, with 5.3 million people affected. In sub-Saharan Africa as a whole, there are more than 12 million AIDS orphans.

[67] In March 2001 the leaders of the Democratic Alliance asked Mbeki to declare a state of emergency so HIV carriers could receive generic medicines. The South African law that allows the import of such drugs in case of emergency had never been implemented, due to a lawsuit filed by major multinational pharmaceutical firms, which make the drugs. However, international pressure led the 39 companies to withdraw their lawsuit - a

decision marking an important precedent for poor countries needing to import cheap drugs to fight the pandemic.

[68] South Africa's economy continued to struggle, except for some exports - wine, arms, vehicles - which benefited from a weak rand. Political turmoil in neighboring Zimbabwe reduced foreign investment in the region. Drought in 2002 exacerbated food shortages in southern Africa, and poverty was compounded by HIV/AIDS.

[69] In July 2002, the Constitutional Court ruled - in a case brought by the Treatment Action Campaign (TAC) started in 1998 - that the Government is now legally obliged to implement a comprehensive nationwide program for the prevention of mother-to-child transmission of HIV, to include provision of the anti-retroviral drug nevirapine.

[70] July 2002 saw the inauguration, in Durban, of the African Union (AU). The AU replaced the Organization of African Unity, seen as 'the dictators' club', whereas the focus of the AU was placed on people's progress and good governance. The 53-member AU was loosely modeled on the EU. It has the right to intervene in the affairs of its member states, in cases of genocide and war crimes and will have a peace-keeping force and a court of justice. Mbeki was appointed as the AU's first president, while South Africa became a key player in the organization's Peace and Security Council.

[71] In April 2004, after a decade of democracy, the ANC won the elections for the third consecutive time. Mbeki took up office for the second time.

[72] That same year, the Provincial Council (NPC) found itself - for the first time in its history - under the dominion of an ANC majority, leaving all the provinces under the effective control of the governing party.

[73] During the first decade of democracy, the Government built 1.6 million houses for underprivileged people, 70 per cent of which had electricity.

[74] As a measure to reduce unemployment (which had reached 30 per cent in 2002), the Government submitted a project in 2004 to extend the civil service, generating some one million new jobs over a 5-year period.

[75] In May 2004, three years after the start of the *MSF* (Doctors without Frontiers) program to give free medication to people living with HIV/AIDS, 1,000 patients had access to anti-retroviral drug treatment (ART).

In 2002 only 30 patients had access to this medication and in 2003 the number had increased to 776 (of whom 84 were children).

[76] That same month, the former Haitian President, Jean Bertrand Aristide was given asylum by the South African Government. In March that year, South Africa had asked for a UN investigation to be opened into the circumstances surrounding the President's departure. After he left, he had accused the United States and France of obliging him to go into exile.

[77] In April 2004, in the third multi-racial general elections since the end of apartheid, the ANC secured nearly 70 per cent of the vote. Mbeki became re-elected and promised not to disappoint those citizens who granted the ANC a majority.

[78] Also in May, Mbeki promised that his government would grant electricity and running water to all South African households that had been expecting these services for five to eight years. Likewise, he stressed that 113 HIV/AIDS health centers had already become operational and would be treating 53,000 people by March 2005. Mbeki was being then strongly criticized by different national and international sectors, for not doing enough to combat AIDS. The Government, acknowledging criticism, promised to lay emphasis on the improvement of home-based care and to provide increasingly cheaper medicines.

[79] In July 2004, the Cape Floral region, located in Cape Province, was recognized by UNESCO as one of the richest areas for aquatic plants and flora in the world. That tiny South African area, which is a biodiversity treasure and was declared a UNESCO protected area, hosts 20 per cent of Africa's flora and is a living example of how the evolution of species develops in all terms. At least 70 per cent of the 9,000 plant species are unique to Cape Floral and are not found anywhere else in the world. The South African Government expressed willingness to increase responsible tourism to the area, which would result in more employment opportunities and in an increase of foreign currency income.

[80] Also in July, a food security report carried out by Famine Early Warning Systems Networks (FEWS), pointed out that the country would continue to face critical conditions in the supply of food to the population throughout 2004 and 2005. ∎

Spain / España

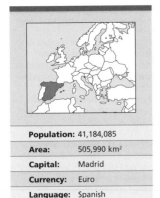

Population:	41,184,085
Area:	505,990 km²
Capital:	Madrid
Currency:	Euro
Language:	Spanish

The territory of what is present-day Spain has been inhabited by numerous cultures. Originally, the peninsula was settled by peoples from northern Africa and western Europe. From 1100 BC, the peninsula attracted seafaring civilizations, such as Phoenicians, Greeks and Carthaginians, who founded settlements and trading posts, especially along the eastern and southern coasts. The seafarers found a diversity of peoples, collectively called Iberians (name probably derived from the Greek name for the river Ebro), who lacked a common culture or language.

2   Between the 9th and 7th centuries BC, the Celts settled in the center and west of the peninsula (see box 'The Celts'). Later on, during the 6th and 5th centuries BC, the Iberian culture developed in the southern part of the territory and the fusion of these two cultures produced what is known as the Celtiberian civilization. They were then colonized by the Carthaginians, who in the 3rd century BC took over most of the peninsula. The Carthaginians were expelled by the Romans, who by the 1st century BC had, for the first time, established a unified authority governing the whole of Iberia. The Iberian élites adopted the Roman culture and became citizens of Rome, especially in the south, where the imperial presence was stronger.

3   The fall of the Roman Empire around 350 AD coincided with the spread of Christianity and, more importantly, with the invasion of Europe by groups from the north. The Iberian peninsula was occupied by the Visigoths who ruled the area for 300 years.

4   In 700 AD the peninsula was invaded by Arabs who defeated Rodrigo, the last Visigoth king, marking the start of the era of Muslim domination. The descendants of the Visigoths lived in the north of the territory and set up kingdoms like Castile, Catalonia, Navarre, Aragon, Leon and Portugal. Over the centuries these kingdoms gradually unified, a process that culminated with their joint military stand against the Arabs.

5   The Arabs called the lands in the south of the Iberian peninsula al-Andalus, a region that reached its peak during the 10th century. In contrast with the rest of impoverished rural Europe, its cities - and Córdoba in particular - prospered through active trade with the East. Religious tolerance enabled Muslims, Jews, and Christians to live side by side, and science, medicine, and philosophy developed. Copies and translations of the Greek classics were made, paving the way for the 15th century European Renaissance.

6   In 1492, a triple process of national unification took place in Spain, through the marriage between Isabel of Castile and Fernando of Aragon, the expulsion of the Moors, and the conquest and subsequent colonization of the new American territories. The uniting of the country's political power and the creation of the Kingdom of Spain were carried out at the expense of the Jews (and members of other cultures) who were expelled from Spain after having lived there for many centuries. Both the Inquisition and centralized power were institutionalized under the new system, while the new American colonies supplied precious metals, sustaining three centuries of economic bonanza. The Crown imposed Christianity on the indigenous population in America. Many native peoples died as a result of the exploitation they were subjected to through forced labor, and also from European diseases to which they had no immunity.

7   The economic prosperity provided by the colonies was reflected in a period of great cultural development in Spain. Literature in particular developed extensively during the 16th and 17th centuries, which were dubbed the Spanish Golden Age. Portugal was annexed to the Spanish Kingdom for the period 1580-1688.

8   In the 18th century, the Bourbons came to the Spanish throne. They reorganized the domestic and colonial administrations, ruling in accordance with the principles of the Enlightenment, as the liberal ideas of the French Revolution spread throughout Europe and America. Combined with Napoleonic expansion, this view contributed to the disintegration of the Spanish colonies after the wars of independence.

9   At the end of the Napoleonic era, there was great conflict between the liberal sectors seeking political and economic modernization, and the absolutists who wished to preserve the traditional order. The disputes between these groups weakened the power of the Empire, making way for independence movements in Spanish America.

10   By the end of the 19th century Spain had renounced its last American territories and had come to terms with the loss of its privileges.

11   At the beginning of the 20th century, Spain was plunged into a deep political, social, and economic crisis; this was exacerbated by World War I (1914-1918). In an atmosphere of extreme polarization, Primo de Rivera's dictatorship, following a coup in 1923, attempted to halt any further demands from workers or regional groups seeking autonomy. The dictatorship, closely resembling the Italian fascist model, retained power until 1931. Its end came about as a result of existing contradictions within the Church, the armed forces and industry, who were all fascist supporters, rather than because of the continuous opposition from political and labor organizations. The end of the dictatorship marked the end of the monarchy, and the dawn of a new republican era.

12   The 'Second Republic' was born into a series of complex political and economic difficulties. In 1936, after two moderate governments, the People's Front, of socialists, republicans, communists and anarchists, won a narrow electoral victory, causing friction with their political opponents.

13   Immediately after the elections, the army, Church and powerful sectors of Spanish economy started working to overthrow the Government, which was weakened by internal differences. In 1936 a sector of the army, led by General Francisco Franco, rose up against the Republic and a three-year long civil war ensued. The republican Government waited in vain for help from the European democracies, but these opted for a policy of non-intervention. Only the Soviet Union provided material support, and many volunteers from America and Europe joined the ranks of the republican army.

14   Franco's forces won the civil war in March 1939, aided by the republicans' internal divisions, the military superiority of his troops, and German and Italian support.

15   When the Civil War ended, Franco became head of the new state. He set up an authoritarian regime along fascist lines, with a corporatist state, a personality cult, and extreme nationalism. Franco ruled over a deeply divided society and an economy that had been devastated by the Civil War.

16   From the beginning of the Cold War in the early 1950s, the US tried to secure Spanish support and Spain became a member of the United Nations in 1955, confirming a change in Franco's foreign policy towards improving the country's international image.

17   In the 1960s, Franco opened Parliament to other groups and movements. During those years key figures from Opus Dei, an ultra-conservative Catholic movement, occupied important posts in the Government and influenced economic policies.

18   Spain ended its economic isolation and liberalized its

WORKERS

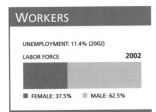

UNEMPLOYMENT: 11.4% (2002)

LABOR FORCE   2002

■ FEMALE: 37.5%   ■ MALE: 62.5%

	Life expectancy		Life expectancy

Life expectancy
79.3 years
2000-2005

GNI per capita
$14,430
2002

Literacy
98% total adult rate
2000

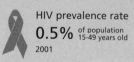
HIV prevalence rate
0.5% of population 15-49 years old
2001

economy by abolishing some state control. The urban middle classes enjoyed improvements in their standard of living, which led to a political relaxation. However, the peasants were still extremely poor and many migrated to the major Spanish and European cities.

19 Franco died in 1975, and power was handed to his successor, the heir to the Spanish throne, Juan Carlos I of Bourbon. The new monarch immediately started negotiations with the political opposition to re-establish the democratic system overthrown in 1939.

20 Between 1976 and 1981 Adolfo Suarez, the leader of the Center Democratic Union (UCD), was Prime Minister. In December 1978 during his term in office, a plebiscite was held which turned Spain into a parliamentary monarchy, re-establishing political freedom, and guaranteeing the right of autonomy to some Spanish regions. Several politicians, intellectuals and artists were able to return to the country after up to 40 years in exile.

21 In February 1981, a group of Civil Guard officers took the *Cortes* (parliament) by force. The firm reaction of all the democratic political groups and in particular of King Juan Carlos, who had the support of the army, guaranteed the failure of the coup and the consolidation of the democratization process.

22 The Spanish Socialist Workers' Party (PSOE) won the October 1982 elections, with a solid majority in the Cortes. Felipe González became President of the Government, the equivalent of Prime Minister in other countries. He was subsequently re-elected in 1988 and 1993.

23 Despite some setbacks, the PSOE's parliamentary majority enabled it to push through an ambitious adjustment and growth plan which deeply transformed the Spanish economy and gave large social sectors access to unprecedented levels of consumption. However, this modernization resulted in high unemployment and social tensions, which led to a split between the

Government and the UGT, the trade union that had supported the PSOE.

24 The Spanish Government was active in international affairs, joining the European Economic Community and NATO in 1986. While it was in the opposition, PSOE had opposed Spain's becoming a member of NATO, but once in power the party defended the decision, which was confirmed through a plebiscite.

25 Spain spent $10 billion in 1992 to celebrate the 500th anniversary of the conquest of America, while it intensified its political shift toward Europe.

26 ETA, the Basque separatist group which has often resorted to violence to achieve its political goals, suffered serious setbacks in 1993. Co-operation between French and Spanish security forces led to the arrest of some of its leaders,

and the discovery in Bayonne, France, of the organization's main arsenal.

27 After a series of corruption scandals, in 1995 the socialist Government lost a key sector of its parliamentary backing. Although he defended his own and his Government's record in office, González called elections a year early.

28 The conservative People's Party (PP) won the Parliamentary elections in March 1996 with 38.9 per cent of the vote. On 5 April, the PP leader, José María Aznar, took office as Prime Minister.

29 In August 1997, an ETA cell kidnapped Miguel Ángel Blanco, a PP activist and councilor in the Basque Country. ETA warned that he would be executed within 48 hours if the Spanish Government did not order the transfer of ETA

Ceuta

Population: 74,093
Area: 19 km²
Currency: Euro
Language: Arabic and Spanish

This is an enclave on the Mediterranean coast of Morocco facing Gibraltar (Spain). The climate is Mediterranean with hot summers and moderate winters. There is sparse rainfall in winter.

2 Occupied by troops of Portuguese King John in 1415, Ceuta was transferred to Spain in 1688 and retained by the Spanish after Moroccan independence in 1956. Despite many UN-backed claims and negotiations before the UN Decolonization Committee, the port is still in Spanish hands, who use most of the territory for military purposes.

3 Estimates indicate that in the period 1995-1999 more than 3,000 people - seeking better work conditions - died while trying to cross the strait of Gibraltar to go to Europe. Between 2001 and 2003, Amnesty International accused the Ceuta authorities of the repeated abuse of underaged immigrants.

4 The continued flow of undocumented immigrants from Morocco entering Spain through Ceuta caused a diplomatic crisis between Madrid and Rabat in 2001. In December 2003, the Moroccan authorities accepted the reforms of the Spanish Law on Foreign Persons, which called for the immediate return of unaccompanied minors found in Spanish territory. ■

SOCIETY
Peoples: 80 per cent of the population is Spanish, born in Ceuta.
Religions: Catholic (majority), Muslim and others. There are also Muslims and Jews. **Languages:** Arabic and Spanish.

THE STATE
Government: Civil authority is exercised by the Spanish Home Affairs Ministry, as part of Cádiz Province. Military authority lies in the hands of a General Commander. The territory has one representative in the Spanish parliament.

Melilla

Population: 69,184
Area: 12 km²
Currency: Euro
Language: Arabic and Spanish

Melilla is a small peninsula on the Mediterranean coast of Morocco with two adjacent island groups. The climate is similar to that of Ceuta. Melilla is an ancient walled town built upon a hill with a modern European-style city on the plain. It is an important port which, like Ceuta, hopes to be a tourist attraction.

2 Founded by Phoenicians and successively held by Romans, Goths and Arabs, Melilla was occupied by Spain in 1495. It was repeatedly besieged by the Riffs, a Berber group that opposed French and Spanish domination, most recently in 1921. It has been claimed by Morocco and, like Ceuta, is used for military purposes.

3 On the northern Moroccan coast the Spanish also hold Peñón (rock) de Vélez de la Gomera, which had 60 inhabitants in 1982; Peñón de Alhucemas with 61 inhabitants in 1982, (with the islets of Mar and Tierra); and the Chafarinas Archipelago (Islands of Congreso, Isabel II and Rey), 1 sq km in area and with a population of 191 inhabitants in 1982.

4 The Spanish Government approved a statute of autonomy for Melilla in 1995, replacing the city council with an assembly, similar to those of other autonomous regions of Spain.

5 In 2000, Melilla received 16.95 per cent of the regional fund that Catalunya, the Balearic Islands, as well as Basque and Navarre provided to support other regions. Ceuta and Extremadura also benefited from this fund.

6 On June 2004 the University of Education at a Distance (UNED) had a debate on drug dealing and immigration, since a significant part of drugs and migration flows arriving to the peninsula and the rest of Europe would come from Melilla. The debate focused on the legal reforms needed to address the issue. ■

SOCIETY
Peoples, languages, religions and other features of the population are similar to those of Ceuta.

THE STATE
Government: A representative of the Spanish Government is responsible for administrating the territory's civilian affairs. There is a military command in charge of military affairs. Like Ceuta, Melilla has a representative in the Cortes, the Spanish parliament.

Under-5 mortality
6 per 1,000 live births
2002

 Aid
0.26% Official development assistance as % of donors' GNI
2002

Maternal mortality
4 per 100,000 live births
2000

prisoners to Basque jails. The deadline passed and Blanco was murdered, sparking huge countrywide protest demonstrations. The Government and opposition, with the exception of Herri Batasuna (HB), a political group close to ETA, reached an agreement not to condone violence.

[30] ETA declared a ceasefire in September 1998. All the Basque nationalist groups, including the Basque Nationalist Party and former members of Herri Batasuna, signed the Estella Pact, an alliance of Basque nationalist parties that, under the slogan 'Self-rule for Basques', won local elections in 1999. ETA resumed armed actions in September - exploding several bombs and killing three people - which ended the non-violence pact.

[31] The fall in unemployment achieved by the Aznar Government's economic policy and Spain's entry into the European currency system, helped the PP to win an overall majority in March 2000.

[32] The Foreigners' Act, passed in August 2000, was strongly criticized by political parties and non-governmental organizations, and caused wide protest. The law sought to regulate the rights and obligations of foreign residents, including the right to freedom of movement, education, employment and social security, trade union membership and soon. As a result, by January 2001, between 30,000-100,000 foreigners were left in disadvantaged legal and labor conditions.

[33] Inflation started rising in late 2000. Although unemployment fell during the Aznar administration, it remained around 14 per cent, the highest in the EU. In 2001, the Spanish economy was one of the fastest growing in the EU. Despite inflation of around 4 per cent, the strong economy helped Aznar face a difficult year in political terms. Problems stemmed from various financial scandals involving public officials, difficulties in the implementation of the Foreigners' Act, and the controversial university reforms that, late that year, caused strikes, demonstrations and sit-ins by students and faculty members.

[34] Tensions with Morocco came to the fore as a result of Madrid's reaction to the 11 September 2001 attacks in New York and Washington. Spain tightened controls on its enclaves of Ceuta and Melilla (on Morocco's coast), and suggested that Rabat 'do more' to limit the flow of illegal immigrants to Spain. Likewise, signs in 2002 of an agreement between Madrid and London regarding the future status of

IN FOCUS

ENVIRONMENTAL CHALLENGES
The Mediterranean is polluted by sewage and emissions from overseas oil and gas production plants, and there has been a proliferation of illegal toxic and dangerous waste dumps near population centers, mainly in rural areas of the peninsula. Environmental pollution, deforestation and desertification affect various areas of the country. Approximately 22 per cent of Spain's forests have suffered some degree of defoliation. Oil spills have affected coastal marine life.

WOMEN'S RIGHTS
Spanish women participate in political life; they have been able to vote and stand for office since 1931. In 2004 the Vice-President is Maria Teresa Fernández de la Vega, and women currently occupy half the 16 ministerial posts. With 126 women in the Lower Chamber, female representation in parliament in 2004 stands at 36 per cent. However violence against women continues to be a problem. The Government has implemented protective measures, including shelters and civil guards, and a telephone hot line.The Government of Cataluña has decreed that immigrant women who are likely to have undergone genital mutilation must be examined by

a doctor. Also, if a girl has been circumcised her parents may lose custody of her. Women represent 38.33 per cent of the workforce and 16.13 per cent hold managerial posts. A law was passed exempting employers from paying social security contributions, in an attempt to boost the number of women in sectors where they are under-represented.

CHILDREN
Children's rights and welfare are promoted through the public education and health systems. Education is compulsory up to the age of 16 and free up to 18. However, many Roma children do not go to school.

INDIGENOUS PEOPLES/ ETHNIC MINORITIES
Following the banishment of the two largest minorities - the Jews, exiled by the Catholic Monarchs in 1492, and the Moors, exiled by Phillip II in 1609 - the Spanish population has been homogeneous in terms of religion. Ceuta and Melilla are home to communities from Morocco and other African countries.

Roma/gypsy citizens continue to face discrimination and exclusion, especially in access to jobs, education and housing. It is estimated that almost 46 per cent of the gypsy population are unemployed. In the Basque country, Galicia and Valencia laws require

the promotion of their respective languages in schools and other institutions. In Cataluña, a percentage of radio and TV broadcasts must be in Catalan.

MIGRANTS/REFUGEES
The Government receives requests for refuge and asylum from within the country and from abroad. It also grants temporary humanitarian status to people who do not qualify as refugees or who apply for political asylum. In 2003, of the 5,767 requests for asylum submitted, only 250 were accepted, placing Spain second to bottom of EU countries in the number of refugees it took. In January 2003, the foreign population comprised 2,672,596 people (6.2 per cent of the population). The most numerous were Ecuadorians (14.6 per cent), followed by Moroccans (14.17 per cent), Colombians, British and Romanians. Between 2002 and 2003 the number of Argentinians in Spain increased by 55.16 per cent. Only 43,000 Argentinians were documented, compared to the almost 110,000 recorded in the town council censuses, suggesting that over 80,000 are illegal residents.

DEATH PENALTY
The death penalty was abolished for all crimes in 1995. The last execution took place in 1975.

Gibraltar intensified the discontent of Morocco, which claims sovereignty over Ceuta and Melilla. On 27 October, days before Moroccan king Muhammad VI began an official visit to Western Sahara (annexed by Morocco in 1975), Rabat called its ambassador in Madrid 'for consultations' and cancelled a bilateral summit with Spain, scheduled for December.

[35] In spite of economic growth, inequality persists between the coastal and interior regions in infrastructure, employment and other sectors. An example of this growing gap has been the project to channel the waters of the Ebro, Spain's largest river, toward the golf courses and specialized agriculture of the coastal areas. Despite parliamentary opposition, protests by the Aragonese (for whom the Ebro is their only water source) and huge demonstrations in Zaragoza and Madrid, the Government has gone ahead with the project.

[36] In 2001 poverty in Spain affected 22.1 per cent of the population (7.5 points higher than

the average for the EU); 44 per cent of the poor are under 25. It is estimated that child labor in the country affects some 300,000 children. In November 2001, UNICEF estimated that approximately 100,000 children in Spain 'work in inhuman conditions'.

[37] In January 2002 Spain took over the presidency of the EU. Anti-terrorism became a priority of Aznar's European agenda, although the operation of the euro and the expansion of the EU were also difficult issues for his administration. In March, the Spanish Government suggested that it would be inconvenient to hold the annual state of the nation debate during its European presidency. The PSOE demanded the immediate staging of the debate and its parliamentary spokesperson, Jesús Caldera, added that the Government should account for the economic, employment, educational and social state of the country, and the 'dangerous counter-reforms it is implementing, rather than just its anti-terrorist measures'.

[38] The sinking of the oil tanker *Prestige* off the Galician coast in November 2002 caused a major ecological disaster, which also affected the coast of south-east France. Two months later another ship - the *Spabunker IV* - sank near Gibraltar, also causing an oil spill. These accidents gave rise to an internal controversy over the Government's lack of contingency plans for such disasters and also the risks of transporting large amounts of oil in territorial waters.

[39] On 16 March 2003, in line with his policy of increasing closeness to Washington, Aznar attended a summit with US president George W Bush and British Prime Minister Tony Blair in the Azores. There, the three leaders gave the UN Security Council 24 hours to adopt a resolution demanding the immediate disarming of Iraq - which they accused of having weapons of mass destruction - as an alternative to an invasion led by the US. The Security Council rejected the ultimatum and the invasion that followed was endorsed by Aznar's Government, which

Doctors
436 per 100,000 people
1990-2002

Primary school
100% net enrolment rate
2000

provided logistical support and later 1,300 soldiers to the occupation forces, although surveys had shown that 90 per cent of Spaniards were against the war.

[40] On 11 March 2004, three days before the general elections, bombs on passenger trains exploded in and near the Madrid station of Atocha. According to official figures, 190 people died, of whom a quarter were foreigners. The next day, over 11 million Spaniards took to the streets to demonstrate their rejection of terrorism. Although the al-Qaeda network claimed responsibility for the attacks in retaliation for Spain's support for the US, the Government and some media insisted that ETA was responsible. On the eve of the elections, thousands of demonstrators gathered at PP premises around the country to demand information on the investigations.

[41] The turnout for the elections on 14 March was far higher than anticipated before the bombings and resulted in unexpected victory for José Luis Rodríguez Zapatero, the PSOE candidate. However, he did not win an absolute majority. He promised to realign Spanish foreign policy towards Europe, emphasise social issues in his economic policies, and withdraw Spanish troops from Iraq unless the UN took over command of the occupation. The withdrawal from Iraq was one of the first measures implemented by the new President of the Government on taking office in April 2004. ■

Gibraltar

Population: 27,271
Area: 6 km²
Capital: Gibraltar
Currency: Gibraltar pound
Language: English and Spanish

A peninsula on the southern coast of Spain, only 32 km from Morocco, Gibraltar's strategic position allows it to control maritime trade between the Mediterranean and the Atlantic ocean.

[2] Gibraltar was occupied by England in 1704 and ceded by Spain in 1714, following the Treaty of Utrecht. Since 1964 Spain has tried to regain political control of the area. In 1967, a plebiscite opted for continued colonial dependency. In 1968 the UN voted in favor of the Spanish re-incorporation of Gibraltar. Since 1972, the two countries have started negotiations several times, but no significant progress has yet been made.

[3] The most recent attempt took place in May 2002 when President José María Aznar met Prime Minister Tony Blair in London. In July, British Foreign Secretary Jack Straw declared that the UK was willing to share sovereignty with Spain. But in a referendum held in November, only 187 of the 17,900 voters accepted the proposal. The outcome was welcomed by Gibraltar residents.

[4] In early 2004 the proposal to share sovereignty was given new impetus after talks between Tony Blair and Mariano Rajoy, Spanish PP candidate and possible successor to President Aznar. ■

SOCIETY

Peoples: Most of the permanent population is of British origin. The non-permanent population are mainly Spanish workers.
Religions: Anglican and Catholic.
Languages: English (official) and Spanish.

STATE

Official Name: Gibraltar.
Government: Non-autonomous territory under UN's control. Governor-General appointed by the British crown: Francis Richards since May 2003. Chief minister: Peter Caruana, since May 1996 - re-appointed in February 2000 by the 15-member advisory council. In the council's last election, held in February 2000, the Social Democrat Party obtained 58.3 per cent of the vote, while the second political force, the Socialist Labor Party, was supported by 41 per cent of the electorate. Britain has made Gibraltarian independence dependent upon an agreement with Spain. In September 1996, NATO Headquarters acknowledged that in the future military control over the peninsula would be exercised by Spain.
National holiday: 10 September (national referendum).

PROFILE

ENVIRONMENT

Spain comprises 82 per cent of the Iberian Peninsula and includes the Balearic and Canary Islands. The center of the country is a plateau which rises to the Pyrenees in the north, forming a natural border with France. The Betica mountain ranges extend to the south. Inland the Central Sierras separate the plateaus of New and Old Castile. In the Ebro River basin, to the north, lie the plains of Cataluña and Valencia, with Murcia in the south-east. The Guadalquivir River basin, to the south, forms the plains of Andalusia. The climate is moderate and humid in the north and north-west, where there are many woodlands. In the interior, the climate is dry in the south and east. Forty per cent of the land is arable. Approximately five per cent of the total land area is under environmental protection. Natural resources include coal, some oil and natural gas, uranium and mercury. Industry is concentrated in Cataluña and the Basque Provinces. Per capita emissions of air and water pollutants exceed Western European averages. Since 1970, the use of nitrogen fertilizers has doubled. Nitrate concentrations in the Guadalquivir River are 25 per cent above 1975 levels. The percentage of the population serviced by sewage systems rose from 14 per cent in 1975, to 48 per cent in the late 1980s. This fact, together with industrial wastes from oil refining plants and natural gas production, has increased the level of pollution in the Mediterranean. The Government has launched a reforestation plan to increase production and stop erosion. With more trees, there has been an exponential increase in forest fires. There is considerable mono-cropping, particularly of eucalyptus, that does not take biodiversity into account.

SOCIETY

Peoples: Castilians, Asturians, Andalusians, Valencians, Catalans, Aragonese, Extremadurans, Basques and Galicians, of mixed descent from the Iberian people of the Mediterranean, the Celts of Central Europe and the Arabs of North Africa. There is a Roma minority and immigrant communities, especially Latin Americans, North Africans and Asians.
Religion: The vast majority of Spaniards are Catholic (95.2 per cent). Muslims 1.2 per cent.
Languages: Spanish or Castilian (official national); there are also official regional languages, such as Basque, Catalan, Valencian, Aranese (or Gascón) and Galician. Non-official languages: Aragonese, Asturian, Bable, Castuo, Canarian, Caló, Portuguese, Romany.
Main Political Parties: Spanish Socialist Workers' Party (PSOE); Peoples' Party (PP); United Left. Political platforms of nationalist movements represented in Parliament: Convergence and Union, Basque Nationalist Party, Galician Nationalist Bloc, Canarian Coalition, Andalusian Party, Republican Left of Cataluña, Basque Solidarity, Aragonese Junta.
Main Social Organizations: The largest labor federations are the General Union of Workers (UGT) and Workers' Confederation (CCOO), along with the anarchist National Labor Confederation (CNT) and General Labor Confederation (CGT). COAG farmers' union, environmental and women's groups.

THE STATE

Official Name: Reino de España (Kingdom of Spain).
Administrative Divisions: Spain is divided into 17 autonomous regions: the Basque Country, Cataluña, Galicia, Andalusia, the Principality of Asturias, Cantabria, La Rioja, Murcia, Valencia, Aragon, Castile, La Mancha, the Canaries, Navarre, Extremadura, the Balearic Islands, Madrid and Castilla-León. Each region has its own local authorities, including an executive branch and a unicameral legislature.
Capital: Madrid 5,103,000 people (2003).
Other Cities: Barcelona 3,855,300 people; Valencia 1,406,600; Seville 1,130,600; Zaragoza 605,900 (2000).
Government: Hereditary monarchy, with King Juan Carlos I of Bourbon as Head of State. Prime Minister José Luis Rodríguez Zapatero since April 2004. Bicameral parliament (Cortes): the Senate, with 255 members, and the Chamber of Deputies with 350 members elected by proportional representation.
National Holiday: 12 October, Hispanic Day.
Armed Forces: 206,000 (1995). Other: Civil Guard 66,000 (3,000 conscripts).

Sri Lanka / Sri Lanka

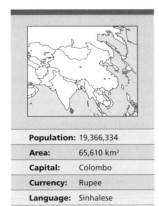

Population:	19,366,334
Area:	65,610 km²
Capital:	Colombo
Currency:	Rupee
Language:	Sinhalese

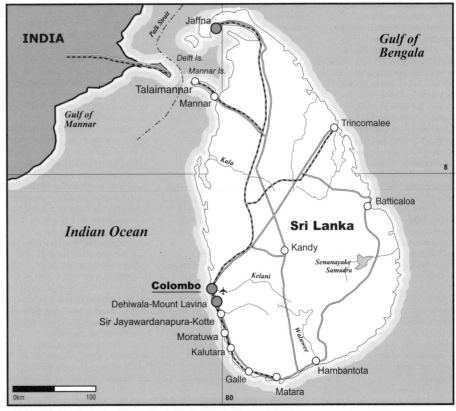

The island of Ceylon was populated by the indigenous Vedda in ancient times. It was then successively invaded by the Sinhalese, Indo-Europeans and Tamils, who laid the foundations of an advanced civilization. When the Portuguese arrived in 1505, the island was divided into seven autonomous local societies.

2 The Dutch expelled the Portuguese from their coastal trading posts 150 years later, but it was the British - already in possession of neighboring India - who finally made the island a colony in 1796. Even then, it took them until 1815 to subdue all the local governments, who fought hard to remain autonomous. The British then introduced new export crops such as coffee and tea-products that gave Ceylon a worldwide reputation because of their excellent quality.

3 In the 20th century, a strong nationalist movement developed. In 1948, Ceylon became independent and joined the British Commonwealth.

4 Under the leadership of Sir John Kotelawala and Prime Minister Solomon RD Bandaranaike, the country pursued a vigorous anti-colonial foreign policy. In August 1954, Bandaranaike met in Colombo with India's Nehru, Muhammad Ali of Pakistan, U Nu of Burma and Indonesia's Sastroamidjojo. The meeting was of

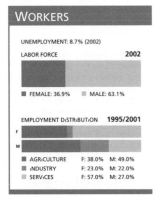

WORKERS

UNEMPLOYMENT: 8.7% (2002)

LABOR FORCE   2002

■ FEMALE: 36.9%   ■ MALE: 63.1%

EMPLOYMENT DISTRIBUTION   1995/2001

F

M

■ AGRICULTURE   F: 38.0%   M: 49.0%
■ INDUSTRY   F: 23.0%   M: 22.0%
■ SERVICES   F: 57.0%   M: 27.0%

great political importance as it led to the 1955 summit conference of Afro-Asian countries in Bandung, heralding the Movement of Non-Aligned Countries.

5 In the late 1950s, the Tamil minority staged a series of secessionist uprisings and in September 1959 the Prime Minister was assassinated. His widow Sirimavo Bandaranaike led the Sri Lanka Freedom Party to electoral victory at the beginning of 1960, although she had no previous political experience.

6 Sirimavo Bandaranaike became the first woman in the world to head a government. In coalition with the Communist and Trotskyist parties, in 1962 she nationalized various US oil and other companies. In 1965, she was defeated by a right-wing coalition but regained power in 1970, in a landslide election victory.

7 She was faced with a 'Guevarist' (after Che Guevara) guerrilla uprising which she crushed ruthlessly. Consistent with her anti-imperialist stand in 1972 she declared Sri Lanka a republic, cutting all ties with the British Commonwealth and launching a land reform program which nationalized British-owned tea plantations but did not substantially change the standard of living of the rural population.

8 Conflict between the Sinhalese majority and the Tamil minority,

descended from the Dravidians of south India, has persisted throughout all of the island's history. The Sinhalese account for 74 per cent of the country's population, while the Tamils comprise 22 per cent and are divided into two groups: the Sri Lankan Tamils and the Indian Tamils. The Tamils reached the island some 2,000 years ago. They settled principally in the northern and eastern provinces. The Indian Tamils are more recent immigrants. Both groups, possessing common characteristics, sought regional autonomy or even the formation of a separate Tamil nation. The Tamil United Liberation Front (TULF) founded on 4 May 1972, joined together three Tamil parties: the Federal Party, the Tamil Congress and the pro-Indian Ceylon Workers' Congress.

9 Bandaranaike organized the Non-Aligned Conference in Colombo in 1976 and was appointed president of the Movement. However, the difficult economic situation, accusations of nepotism, and censorship of the press and emergency measures in force since 1971, weakened her government and enabled the opposition to win the July 1977 election. In spite of his socialist leanings, the new prime minister, Junius Jayewardene (United National Party) opened the door to transnational capital.

10 After a presidential commission had found her guilty of 'abuse of authority' during her coalition government, between 1970 and July 1977, in October 1978 Bandaranaike was expelled from Parliament and deprived of her political rights for seven years.

11 One month later a constitutional reform made Jayewardene Sri Lanka's first president. In November 1980, a series of International Monetary Fund (IMF)-approved economic measures began to be applied, with disastrous consequences for the country.

12 Sri Lanka's first presidential election, in October 1982, gave Jayewardene a clear victory, with 52.5 per cent of the vote. His campaign was backed by the state apparatus and benefited from the division and internal strife of the Freedom Party. In some parts of the country, the political upheaval meant that elections had to be held under state of emergency conditions.

13 The project to turn Sri Lanka into an export center like Hong Kong or Formosa led to the creation of a free zone in Latunyabe where considerable foreign investment was recorded.

14 In early 1982, in spite of earlier denials and the Government's outspoken commitment to non-alignment, the US Navy was granted permission to use Sri

Life expectancy
72.6 years
2000-2005

GNI per capita
$840
2002

Literacy
92% total adult rate
2000

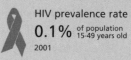
HIV prevalence rate
0.1% of population 15-49 years old
2001

Lanka's refuelling facilities in Trincomalee, a vital spot linking eastern and western sea routes through the Suez Canal.

[15] Early in 1983, the ethnic conflict worsened. In July, the death of 13 soldiers in a Liberation Tigers of Tamil Eelam (LTTE) ambush led to a wave of Sinhalese violence against the Tamils - according to the latter with the complicity of the Government - in Colombo and Jaffna. It is estimated that between 400 and 3,000 people died and over 100,000 were left homeless. More than 40,000 Tamils fleeing the conflict sought refuge in the Indian state of Tamil Nadu.

[16] The ethnic war worsened during 1985, discouraging foreign investors and affecting tourism, one of the main sources of income for this 'fiscal paradise'.

[17] In late July 1987, presidents Rajiv Gandhi (of India) and Junius Jayewardene signed an accord in Colombo granting a certain autonomy to the Tamil minority of the northern and eastern provinces of Sri Lanka, providing for the merger of the two provinces under a single government, and giving Tamil the status of a national language.

[18] In November 1988, the official party's hold on power was ratified by 50.4 per cent of the votes. Jayewardene, at the age of 82, ceded his post to Ranasinghe Premadasa, who was Prime Minister at the time. Political violence was so pervasive that only 53 per cent of the electorate actually voted. Elections were boycotted by both the Tamil guerrillas and the Popular Liberation Front (made up of Sinhalese who were violently opposed to any kind of concessions to ethnic minorities). Political opposition to the Government increased, partly fuelled by a strong student movement which was eventually harshly repressed in early 1989.

[19] In 1990, the Indian Government withdrew the last of its 60,000-strong peacekeeping force, stationed there since 1987. More than 1,000 troops had died on the island. Amnesty International reported that in 1990, the Sri Lankan Government had killed thousands of civilians in the region.

[20] In May 1991, the Tamil Tigers were accused of murdering the Indian President Rajiv Gandhi in a suicide mission. He had become their enemy after the Indian peace forces attacked the rebels. The Tigers denied any involvement.

[21] In the November 1994 presidential elections, the Popular Alliance candidate Chandrika Bandaranaike Kumaratunga, daughter of two former prime ministers, became the first woman president of Sri Lanka.

[22] In August 1995 Kumaratunga presented a plan for state reform, supported by the Tamil parliamentarians. It included transforming Sri Lanka into a federation of eight regions. The central government was to keep control over defense, foreign relations and international economic relations. Increasing military action prevented the project from being adopted.

[23] The city of Jaffna, on the peninsula of the same name, was at the center of the fighting from October 1995. On occupation by Government forces on 5 December the city had been practically abandoned by its 140,000 inhabitants. By mid-1996, half the peninsula's Tamil population had returned to their homes.

[24] The Government and the Tigers agreed to start negotiations in January 1995, but the pact was broken by the Tamils. The guerrillas initiated a new series of attacks against government forces in April.

[25] The Government offered to suspend the military offensive and discuss proposals to increase the autonomy of regional councils administered by Tamils and Muslims. However, it demanded the surrender of the LTTE, something the guerrillas considered unacceptable.

[26] Despite efforts at mediation, the civil war worsened in March 1998, with dozens killed on both sides. In December, government troops carried out a major offensive and forced the the LTTE to retreat to inhospitable areas and abandon several northern cities.

[27] Clashes between government troops and Tamil rebels intensified at the end of 1999. The LTTE took control of the important northern city of Oddusudan in November. In December, just four days after escaping an assassination attempt, President Chandrika Kumaratunga was re-elected for a new term, beating her main rival, Ranil Wickremesinghe, from the UNP. The high turnout (70 per cent of 11.5 million registered) surprised political analysts, who expected a higher level of abstention due to the LTTE attacks days before the election which had caused 33 dead and more than 130 injured - one of them Kamaratunga herself.

[28] Both the President and Wickremesinghe promised during their campaign to put an end to the 16-year-old civil war. Although Tamil voters had supported Kumaratunga in her 1994 victory, this time they followed LTTE's recommendation to vote for Wickremasinghe.

[29] While Kumaratunga and Wickremesinghe met in March 2000 to discuss a possible political agreement to put an end to the ethnic conflict, Tamil rebels captured a key government position on the Jaffna peninsula after a 12-hour battle. The LTTE openly rejected the government peace plan, but agreed to take part in conversations if Norway acted as mediator.

[30] By May the rebels had practically all Jaffna under control. Lack of commitment by government forces was one of the reasons cited for their repeated defeats in the peninsula. Kumaratunga asked India for help. The request for military support was rejected but humanitarian aid was offered. The Government imposed stringent security measures, gave the army greater powers and renewed press censorship of foreign media.

[31] In July 2001, the LTTE carried out suicide attacks, first on the air-force base at Katunayake and then on Bandaranaike international airport, killing 17 people and causing serious damage to the national airline and the tourist industry.

[32] In October, to avoid a vote of censure, President Kumaratunga dissolved Parliament and called for elections to be held on 5 December in which the Popular Alliance lost their majority.

[33] For the first time since the beginning of the civil war, in November 2001 the LTTE publicly renounced its demand for independence of the Tamil provinces. Velupillai Prabhakaran, leader of the rebels, said that autonomy allowing the Tamils to make political and economic decisions would be enough. The UN High Commissioner for Refugees (UNHCR) stated that in spite of the peace process the situation in Sri Lanka was still too delicate to promote the return of the 100,000 Tamil refugees living in southern India.

[34] The alliance led by Wickremesinghe won the December 2001 parliamentary elections with promises to try to negotiate an end to the conflict with the separatists and to reactivate the economy.

[35] The Central Bank of Sri Lanka announced that the country began the year 2002 with the worst recession since independence from Britain. Over the last 20 years the Government's war expenditure reached $2.6 million and an additional $457,000 was spent on refugee assistance. The Government

PROFILE

ENVIRONMENT

An island in the Indian Ocean, southeast of India, separated from the sub-continent by the Palk Channel. The land is flat, except for a central mountainous region. These mountains divide the island into two distinct regions and also block the monsoon winds which are responsible for the tropical climate. The southwest area receives abundant rainfall, and the remainder of the island is drier. Large tea plantations cover the southern mountain slopes, and other major crops are rice, for domestic consumption, and rubber, coconuts and cocoa, for export. Deforestation and soil erosion are important environmental problems. Air pollution is also on the increase, due to industrial gas emissions.

SOCIETY

Peoples: 74 per cent of Sri Lankans are Sinhalese; Tamils are the largest minority group, 18 per cent, and there are Arab (7.7 per cent) and Vedda (1 per cent) minorities. **Religions:** 70 per cent Buddhist; 15.5 per cent Hindu; 7.6 per cent Muslim; 7.5 per cent Christian; and 1 per cent other religions. **Languages:** Sinhalese (official). Also Tamil and English. **Main Political Parties:** United Peoples' Freedom Alliance (UPFA), Popular Party, United National Party (center), Tamil Government Party/National Tamil Alliance (regionalist), National Heritage Party (Buddhist).
Main Social Organizations: Workers' Congress, Trade Union Federation, Trade Union Council, Labor Federation of Workers. Pressure groups exist, such as the Buddhist clergy, the insurgent Liberation Tigers of Tamil Eelam/LTTE ('Tamil Tigers') and Sinhalese groups such as the Nationalist Anti-Terrorism Movement.

THE STATE

Official Name: Sri Lanka Prajathanthrika Samajavadi Janarajaya. **Administrative Divisions:** 9 Provinces, 24 Districts. **Capital:** Colombo 648,000 people (2003). **Other Cities:** Dehiwala-Mount Lavinia 218,500 people; Moratuwa 204,500; Maha Nuwara 150,700; Kotte 127,000 (2000). **Government:** Chandrika Kumaratunga, President since November 1994, re-elected in 1999. Mahinda Rajapakse, Prime Minister since April 2004. Unicameral Legislature: National Assembly, with 225 members. **National Holiday:** 4 February, Independence Day (1948). **Armed Forces:** 118.000-123.000 (including Reservists) (2001). Para-military forces: 88.600.

Under-5 mortality
19 per 1,000 live births
2002

Poverty
6.6% of population living on less than $1 per day
1995/96

Debt service
9.7% exports of goods and services
2001

Maternal mortality
29 per 100,000 live births
2000

IN FOCUS

ENVIRONMENTAL CHALLENGES
Deforestation and soil erosion are considerable. Air pollution is on the increase due to industrial gas emissions. The living conditions of the indigenous population are affected by poaching and increasing urbanization. Mining activities have degraded the coasts and water resources are contaminated by untreated industrial solid and liquid wastes. The levels of air pollution are high in the capital.

WOMEN'S RIGHTS
Women have been able to vote and stand for election since 1932. In 1960 Sirimavo Bandaranaike became the first woman in the world to head an elected government. In 2003 there were 10 women in the 225-seat Parliament. Women held two seats in the Supreme Court. The President is Chandrika Kumaratunga, who once appointed her mother as Prime Minister, the first time a mother and daughter have held the highest positions in a nation.

Women suffer from constant discrimination. They are victims of abuse and trafficking. During 2002, complaints of maltreatment and even rape by the police and security forces were lodged. The Government maintains unjust and discriminatory laws regarding individual rights, age of consent, divorce and land tenure.

CHILDREN
Approximately 800,000 individuals, of whom one third were children, have been displaced. Of the 2.5 million people living in zones directly affected by the conflict, approximately one million are under 18.

Children who have returned after being refugees are particularly vulnerable. UNICEF estimates that in the zones controlled by LTTE, one third of the school-age children have either dropped out or have never been to school.

In the regions controlled by the LTTE, there is a lack of healthcare staff and medical supplies. Chronic malnutrition is high among women and children in parts of Sri Lanka, but particularly among the internally displaced persons returning to their homes.

Exploitation and sexual exploitation of children is a serious problem. The Government estimates that there are 2,000 child prostitutes in the country, particularly in coastal zones. NGOs claim that the figure is considerably higher.

The LTTE recruits and uses children as soldiers.

INDIGENOUS PEOPLES/ ETHNIC MINORITIES
The Tamils originating from Sri Lanka are a majority in the northeast of the country and account for 12 per cent of the population. The group has remained in its region of origin, with scant migratory movements, but has been very much affected by the migratory flow of Sinhalese towards their traditional lands of residence over the past few years. This group is distinct from the Tamils of Indian descent, accounting for 6 per cent of the total population, who reside in central regions. They are considered to be two distinct groups although they share a common language and religion (both are Hindus and communicate in Tamil, while the Sinhalese are generally Buddhists and have their own language).

The problems of the Tamils of Indian origin are different from those originating in Sri Lanka (formerly Ceylon). Since independence, the former have been denied rights of citizenship. In general, they are perceived by the majority of the Sinhalese as foreigners. Efforts have been made between India and Sri Lanka to give these people the rights of citizenship in one or the other country since the Bandaranaike-Gandhi agreement in 1974. In 1980, 500,000 Tamils of Indian origin were repatriated to India. Most of those remaining in the country were recognized as having Sinhalese citizenship, but in 2000 there were still 200,000 stateless Tamils. Furthermore, this community has suffered economic problems based on discrimination against the group, expressed as restrictions on access to certain jobs, in addition to the historical political discrimination.

As most of the Tamils are estate workers, privatization of the tea plantations in the mid-1990s had repercussions on the group. Since then social and cultural concerns include the possibility of Tamil dealings with the Government, freedom of worship, security and the possibility of protection from attacks from the dominating community.

In an effort to protect their culture and ensure equal rights, the Tamils started exerting pressure to achieve autonomy. Political parties, (such as TULF) used conventional methods such as participation in Government coalitions to achieve their objectives; however, more militant Tamils sought the creation of a totally independent state in the northeast (See History).

MIGRANTS/REFUGEES
There were close on 563,000 internally displaced Sri Lankan citizens at the end of 2002. Some 143,000 people had also taken refuge in India. Most of the displaced people and refugees were Hindu Tamils, although thousands of Muslims and some Buddhist Sinhalese were also obliged to move during the armed conflict.

The 2002 ceasefire and the prospects of lasting peace following decades of civil war in the country enabled close on 237,000 internally displaced persons to return to their homes and some 1,000 refugees to return from India.

During 2002, nearly 11,000 Sinhalese sought asylum in industrialized countries, particularly the United Kingdom, France and Canada.

DEATH PENALTY
In practice the country is considered as abolitionist, as no executions have been reported since 1976. In June 2003, the Government promised to continue automatically commuting all death sentences.

---

increased taxes, with a subsequent rise in inflation. The only ones who benefited from the conflict, according to Caritas of Sri Lanka, were the arms traffickers and manufacturers and many young people - Sinhalese and Tamils alike - who found work by joining the army.

[36] In January 2002 the Government eased the embargo on food and medicine for the northern areas, after a seven-year blockade. The measure was a condition the LTTE had imposed for the peace talks. The LTTE began its transition from guerrilla force to political organization. In February, under Norwegian mediation, the Government and the rebels signed a permanent ceasefire treaty.

[37] Thousands of the opposition marched in Colombo in April in protest against the peace process. The rally, organized by the leftist People's Liberation Front and Kumaratunga's Popular Alliance, was the first major expression of discontent with the Government's efforts to reach a peace treaty. During the march, the President accused the Prime Minister of having made concessions that threatened Sri Lanka's sovereignty.

[38] After 12 years, early in 2002 the highway uniting the Jaffna peninsula with the rest of Sri Lanka was reopened and flights to the peninsula started up again.

[39] In September Prime Minister Wickremesinghe lifted the prohibition on the LTTE which had prevented them taking part in negotiations on an equal footing since 1998. On 16 September 2002, in Thailand, negotiations were started to end the 20-year long civil war that had claimed 65,000 lives. In December in Oslo (Norway) the Government and the LTTE agreed on the establishment of a federal system within a united Sri Lanka.

[40] The Tamils suspended peace talks in May 2003, complaining of the Government's lack of interest. However they later stated their willingness to reinitiate talks and submitted a proposal for a transitional autonomous administration. This idea was not welcomed by the parliamentary opposition party, Kumaratunga's Popular Alliance.

[41] Some 4,000 people were left homeless and over 200 were killed during the May 2003 floods.

[42] On 4 November, Kumaratunga dismissed the Ministers of Defense, Interior and Information, ordered the deployment of troops, suspended Parliament and declared a state of emergency, considering that Wickremesinghe had endangered the 'country's territorial security, stability and integrity' through his concessions to the rebels. She also criticized the international monitors and asked for the withdrawal of the Norwegian general who was presiding over the process. Parliament was restored two weeks later, but negotiations with the Tamils were suspended.

[43] The third legislative elections in four years in Sri Lanka took place in April 2004. Kumaratunga's UPFA won 105 of the 225 seats, but did not achieve an absolute majority. Mahinda Rajapakse, a Buddhist lawyer, became Prime Minister.

[44] In an unexpected turn of events, the Popular Alliance recognized the Tamil Tigers, tacitly endorsing them as the sole representatives of the Tamil minority. Peace talks were due to start up again in June. ∎

Sudan / As-Sudan

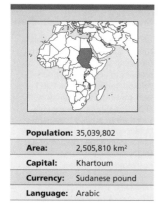

Population:	35,039,802
Area:	2,505,810 km²
Capital:	Khartoum
Currency:	Sudanese pound
Language:	Arabic

The first people settled in what is now Sudan during the Paleolithic period (30,000-7,000 BC). Their descendants began domesticating animals between 10,000-3,000 BC. There was trade in gold, slaves, ivory and granite from this region along the Nile to the Mediterranean.

2   At the end of the 4th millennium BC, north Sudan was colonized by the First Dynasty of the Old Egyptian Empire, causing the black people of the Nile to assimilate elements of their imperial culture.

3   Between 2181 and 1938 BC, immigrants from what is now Libya began farming in this region.

4   A new Nubian (Kushite) culture, which emerged in 2150 BC, arose from the amalgamation of these three ethnic groups, after the decline of the Old Egyptian Empire.

5   In 1580 BC the Egyptians again took over the region, remaining for 500 years. Despite the presence of imperial Egypt, Nubian traditions were maintained; their art - with its distinctive African slant - flourished.

6   Nubians occupied prominent positions in the Pharaonic bureaucracy that divided Nubia/Kush into two districts: Wawat in the north, and Kush in the south, where gold and emeralds could be found, and where a new syncretic Nubio-Egyptian culture forged its own alphabet.

LAND USE

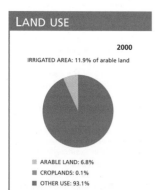

2000

IRRIGATED AREA: 11.9% of arable land

- ARABLE LAND: 6.8%
- CROPLANDS: 0.1%
- OTHER USE: 93.1%

WORKERS

LABOR FORCE   **2002**

- FEMALE: 30.0%
- MALE: 70.0%

7   In the 11th century BC, the viceroys of Kush took advantage of the decline of the New Egyptian Empire to obtain their virtual independence. In 748 BC, their descendants conquered Egypt, remaining until they were expelled in 591 BC.

8   The Persians controlled Egypt and the Kush region from 500 BC.

9   From 300 AD, the inhabitants began to convert to Christianity. The missionaries Nobatia, Dongola and Alodia brought the religion to the black kingdoms of the mid-Nile river region before withdrawing in 675 AD in the face of the Islamic invasion that established the Fatimid dynasty in the 7th century. Despite the Muslim influence, the Nubians mainly remained Christian. The Fatimids were conquered by the Ottoman Turks around 1300.

10   Towards the 15th century, recurrent looting by nomadic Arab groups (Bedouins), together with confrontations between the latter and the Ottoman Empire and the Mamelukes (Egyptian oligarchy, 1250-1517), led to the devastation of Nubia.

11   Between the 13th and 15th centuries, when the Christian kingdoms collapsed, there was a massive immigration of Muslim Arab groups, who in turn became the majority of the population in the northern Sudan territory.

12   From that period until 1820, Sudanese territory fell into two main regions: that of the Muslims, where the Sufi brotherhood were in charge of Islamization, and that of the Fujis (non-Muslims from Ethiopia), whose Islamized aristocracy had governed the central region since the beginning of the 17th century.

13   In 1820, the Egyptian Viceroy under the Ottoman Empire, Muhammad Ali, sent in troops searching for gold and slaves. By 1876, his successors controlled the entire Sudanese territory and had established a centralized bureaucracy in Khartoum. They also implemented a taxation system that constituted a virtual confiscation of gold and agricultural produce, and established commercial routes.

14   The appointment of British General Charles Gordon as Governor of Sudan in 1877 by the Egyptian Viceroy, was as much due to the latter's financial commitments with Britain as to the corruption amongst occupying Egyptian authorities.

15   Gordon set out to enforce compliance with an 1877 Convention, to end the lucrative slave trade, with a view to establishing a capitalist economy in Sudan.

16   The loss of this source of income, the arbitrary repression by British troops and the general discontent among the Sudanese brought about by the imposition of taxes and of foreign religious practices (Egyptian Orthodox Islam

Life expectancy
55.6 years
2000-2005

GNI per capita
$350
2002

Literacy
58% total adult rate
2000

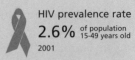
HIV prevalence rate
2.6% of population 15-49 years old
2001

and British-style Christianity), paved the way for Sufi spiritual leader Muhammad Ahmad, who proclaimed himself *Mahdi* (savior) of his people in 1881.

[17] Ahmad's popular forces rose up, took the city of Khartoum, expelled Gordon from Sudanese territory, and established the first nationalist theocracy.

[18] In 1898, the Egyptian authorities under British military intervention, together with the British Crown, made the territory an Anglo-Egyptian Condominium. Egyptian troops occupied it again, under a policy of *closed districts,* which prevented any contact between north and south.

[19] Early in this period, the British introduced extensive cotton cultivation (still Sudan's main crop), and expanded its communications. At the same time, they allowed freedom of worship, in order to eliminate religion as a source of unrest. They also opened elementary and polytechnic schools and, in 1902, inaugurated the Gordon Memorial College (later the University of Khartoum), where an élite began acquiring a British curricular education. Many were appointed to key posts and belonged to the Graduates' General Congress, which evolved into a fledgling political organization.

[20] In 1936, England demanded that Egypt sign an agreement prohibiting entry to Sudan by any Egyptian military suspected of fomenting unrest with Egyptian nationalists or Sudanese groups. The Congress wanted to participate in these negotiations.

[21] When it was not recognized by the British, Congress divided into two groups: one, with the majority, was moderate, well-disposed toward Britain; the other, led by Ismael al-Azhari, was radical, tending toward Egypt.

[22] Towards 1943, Azhari and his followers won the majority vote in the congress and constituted the first Sudanese political party, Ashiqa (Brothers - National Unionist Party - as of 1951). Shortly after, the moderate group organized under the Ummah (Nation) Party led by Arman al-Mahdi, son of the *mahdi* deposed by the British in 1898.

[23] In 1951, Egypt revoked the Anglo-Egyptian Condominium Treaty and proclaimed its sovereignty over Sudanese territory. It was hostile to Britain's threat to grant some independence to the Christian and animist south, while not to the Arab and Muslim north. Despite Egypt's objections, in 1953 Sudan received a degree of autonomy.

[24] In 1955 parliamentary elections were held and the National

IN FOCUS

ENVIRONMENTAL CHALLENGES
Around 60 per cent of the land is affected by desertification. There are periodic droughts and the soil is extremely eroded. Industrial waste has contaminated coasts and rivers, thus endangering fresh water reserves. Indigenous people are affected by indiscriminate hunting.

WOMEN'S RIGHTS
Women have been able to vote and run for office since 1964.

In the year 2000, only five per cent of the parliamentary seats were occupied by women; there were none in ministerial positions and they comprised 30 per cent of the country's labor force. The illiteracy rate was over 28 per cent in women between 15 and 24, whereas for men in the same age range it was 17 per cent.

In 2003, women displaced from the southern regions were more vulnerable to harassment, rape and sexual abuse. Some pregnant women were sentenced to jail for adultery. In the north, female genital mutilation (FGM) is practised on a wide scale: more than 90 per cent of girls and women had undergone some kind of cutting. Infibulation - one of the most dangerous and painful practices - was the most widely used. The Government does not support FGM, but it has not intervened in the areas where it is performed. The trafficking and kidnapping of women and children for forced labor, as domestics or for sexual slavery, still continues.

CHILDREN
In 2003, children and women continued to be deeply affected by the civil war and the resultant humanitarian crisis. Many children were forced into slavery or drafted into the armies. The Government itself forced children to take part in the civil war as soldiers. There were few and slow official efforts to improve basic child-welfare conditions, which are uneven depending on the region. In 2003, only 26 per cent of children were enrolled in elementary schools in the south, while in Khartoum the rate was 78 per cent among school-age children. In the north, access to school was equal for girls and boys. However, some low-income families, unable to pay for schooling for all their children, only educate their sons.

INDIGENOUS PEOPLES/ ETHNIC MINORITIES
There are more than 600 ethnic groups in the country, with over 400 languages. There is widespread ethnic cleansing by the government-backed militias - Janjawid, Murahelin and the People's Defense Forces - against inhabitants in Darfur. These are the Masaalit, Zaghawa, Tama, Tanjur and Dajo people, who constitute the Fur ethnic group. The Arab forces, sympathetic to the north and backed by the Government, attack the African people in the south. The Human Rights Watch organization has accused the Government of 'crimes against humanity'. On the 10th anniversary of the Rwanda genocide in 2004, human rights defenders see the same thing in Sudan. Killings, bombings, mass rape of women and girls and blocking of humanitarian aid were some of the accusations made in 2004.

MIGRANTS/REFUGEES
There are over 100,000 Sudanese refugees along the Sudan and Chad border. In May 2004, an estimated 700,000 people had fled from the conflict in Darfur. According to the UN, 90 per cent were women and children who had moved to refugee camps in Chad. Not everyone wanted to move and over 60,000 live in desperate conditions. Domestically displaced persons face hunger; the Government prevents the access of humanitarian aid. Women who seek shelter in towns risk sexual abuse.

DEATH PENALTY
The death penalty is still enforced, even as a punishment for common crimes.

Unionist Party, backed by nationalist Egyptian president Nasser, won by a wide margin over the Ummah. This was followed in 1956 with a declaration of independence by Azhari and his parliamentary majority. The provisional constitution consolidated the northerners' position and reneged on promises of a federation.

[25] The southern Christians and animists, whose hopes of representation in the Assembly were negated by the Constitution, initiated a civil war which continued until 1972.

[26] In 1958, General Ibrahim Abbud seized power in a coup. After freeing the price of cotton and dissolving the political parties, he installed a Supreme Council that ensured compliance with orthodox Islamic laws throughout Sudanese territory, where he also imposed the Arabic language. In 1962, he evicted the Christian missionaries from southern Sudan schools.

[27] In the south, these measures provoked rebellion. Numerous opposition groups in Khartoum joined the mobilizations to demand democracy and to protest against the liberalization of cotton prices.

[28] In October 1964, Abbud was forced to resign and a transitional government took over.

[29] The 1965 elections brought Muhammed Mahjud, Ummah Party leader, to the presidency. In his four years in office, he did not improve Sudan's economic situation. At the same time, the different factions of the parliament were irreconcilable and the southerners launched new offensives, following the failure to fulfill promises of political participation.

[30] In 1969, General Gaafar al-Nimeiry seized power through a coup.

[31] In 1971, by which time Anya Nya controlled most rural areas, its military leaders formed a political organization, the Southern Sudan Liberation Movement (SSLM).

[32] The Nimeiri regime recognized that the escalating civil strife in the south was a debilitating drain on the country's resources and a serious impediment to Sudan's economic development. In 1971 Nimeiri agreed to negotiate a compromise with the SSLM. Several sessions of mediated discussions culminated in peace negotiations in Addis Ababa, Ethiopia, in February and March 1972. Under the provisions of the Addis Ababa accords, the central government and the SSLM agreed to a ceasefire, and Khartoum recognized the regional autonomy of the three southern provinces.

[33] The 1972 peace and the subsequent rise in oil prices attracted investment from various Arab countries, and this was directed to cultivation in well-irrigated areas and infrastructure development. In 1977, Nimeiry was re-elected, but his government's incompetence and corruption had sunk Sudan in debt. This reached eight billion that year and sealed its bankruptcy in 1978, after the suspension of all IMF credit.

[34] In 1983, when experts from the US company Chevron discovered oil deposits in the south, Nimeiry revoked the Addis Ababa Agreement and, under the

Under-5 mortality
94 per 1,000 live births
2002

Malnutrition
17% under-5s
1995-2002

Debt service
2.3% exports of goods and services
2001

Maternal mortality
580 per 100,000 live births
2000

influence of the (Sunni) Muslim Brotherhood of the National Islamic Front (NIF), imposed *Sharia* (Islamic law). That same year, Nimeiry was re-elected amid widespread accusations of fraud.

[35] These measures sparked renewed fighting in the south. An offensive by John Garang's Sudanese People's Liberation Army (SPLA), the most powerful of the 12 organizations in the region, forced the withdrawal of all foreign companies prospecting for oil.

[36] The NIF and the northern opposition parties - on the one hand - and the international financial organizations - on the other - intensified their criticism of Nimeiry's application of the Sharia, with its restraints on political freedom and effects on the financial systems.

[37] In April 1985, while Nimeiry was in the US, his minister of defense and army chief of staff, Abdul al-Dahab seized power and called for elections the following year.

[38] The Party of the People (Ummah) won the April 1986 elections, and its leader Sadiq al-Mahdi was elected Prime Minister.

[39] The SPLA then demanded Mahdi's resignation and the formation of a provisional government. Its 12,000 guerrillas were besieging government garrisons in the southern provinces. They took control of the region, frequently blocking aid to the most desperate people affected by the violence, who lacked food and medicines.

[40] In June 1989, in the midst of the war between the Sudanese People's Liberation Movement (SPLM) (the armed wing of the SPLA) and the government army, General Omar al-Bashir ousted the regime then in power, dissolved political parties and created a military junta with the participation of the National Islamic Front (NIF), renamed the National Congress Party (NCP).

[41] In 1995, when the civil war had taken over one million lives and forced three million people to flee to neighboring countries, the African Rights humanitarian organization accused Khartoum of the genocide of the Nubians.

[42] In the March 1996 elections, al-Bashir was re-elected with 76 per cent of the vote.

[43] In January 1998, after proving that Sudan had sheltered the al-Qaeda terrorist network leader, Osama bin Laden, at the beginning of the 1990s, the US announced an economic embargo on Sudan. After the bombings of US embassies in Tanzania and Kenya, it accused Khartoum of supporting international terrorism, and a few months later bombed a supposed

PROFILE

ENVIRONMENT

The largest African country, Sudan has three distinct geographic regions: the Sahara and Nubian deserts in the north, the flatlands of the central region and the rainforests of the south. Most of the population lives along the Nile (Nahr an-Nil), where cotton is grown. Port Sudan (Bur Sudan), on the Red Sea, handles all the country's foreign trade. Desertification has affected nearly 60 per cent of the territory. Industrial waste has contaminated coastal areas and some rivers.

SOCIETY

Peoples: There are over 570 ethnic groups. Arabs, who live in the center and north of the country, together with Nubians, account for nearly half of the population. Among the other groups, the most important are the Nilote, Nilo-Hamitic and some Bantu-speaking peoples. **Religions:** Islam is the predominant religion among Arabs and Nubians with a majority of Sunni Muslims. In the south, traditional African religions are practised and there are Christian communities in both north and south. **Languages:** Arabic (official and spoken by most of the population); the different ethnic groups speak over 100 different languages.
Main Political Parties: Opposition parties have been proscribed since 1989. National Congress Party (former National Islamic Front); National People's Congress; 20 smaller parties.
Main Social Organizations: Political associations were allowed in 1998. Democratic Unionist Party; National Democratic Alliance; Sudan People's Liberation Movement; Ummah Party.

THE STATE

Official Name: Jumhuriyat as-Sudan.
Administrative Divisions: 9 states, 66 Provinces and 281 Local Government Areas. **Capital:** Khartoum (Al-Khartum) executive and ministerial, 4,286,000 people (2003); Omdurman (Umm-Durman), legislative, 1,599,300 people (2000). **Other Cities:** Port Sudan (Bur Sudan) 384,100; Kassala 295,100 (2000). **Government:** General Omar Hassan Ahmad al-Bashir, President since 30 June 1989, after overthrowing the civilian government; re-elected in 1996 and 2000. Unicameral Legislature: National Assembly, with 360 members.
National Holiday: 1 January, Independence Day (1956).
Armed Forces: 118,500 personnel (1995). Other: 30,000 to 50,000 (People's Defense Force). **Opposition Forces:** 30,000 to 50,000 personnel (Sudanese People's Liberation Army).

terrorist target (in fact a chemical plant) near the capital.

[44] In 1999, al-Bashir declared a state of siege and renewed his Cabinet.

[45] That same year China - importer of 55 per cent of all Sudanese exports in 2004 - in addition to a Malaysian and a Canadian company, agreed to finance an oil pipeline to the Red Sea. This was expected to yield a net annual revenue to Sudan of $500 million, from 2003.

[46] Between 1998 and 2002, hunger and war caused the daily displacement of hundreds of people seeking humanitarian aid centers.

[47] In February 2001, al-Bashir took office once again, having obtained 86.5 per cent of the vote in the December 2000 elections, which were boycotted by most of the opposition parties.

[48] In December 2001, after a six-month campaign by human rights organizations, the Khartoum authorities reported they had released over 14,500 slaves.

[49] One month later, the SPLA signed an alliance with its southern rival, the Sudanese People's Defense Force, forming a common front against the Government.

[50] In October, the start of peace negotiations in Kenya between the Sudanese Government and the SPLA marked the end of 19 years of civil war that had taken the lives of around two million people. On that occasion, US Secretary of State Colin Powell, whose officials had declared access to African oil to be a matter of national interest, threatened to triple the US contribution to the SPLA to $300 million and to maintain the embargo on Sudan, if peace were not reached by March 2003. Largely as a result of war, in 2003 92 per cent of Sudanese were living below the poverty line.

[51] For his part, SPLA head Colonel John Garang wanted the vice-presidency of Sudan in place of Osman Ali Taha. He also wanted to reclaim the southern provinces of Nuba, Abyei and Blue Nile, which had fallen under northern jurisdiction in 1972, but this remains unresolved.

[52] Between April and December 2003, the Sudanese Government and the SPLA made a pact to combine their troops in a 39,000-strong army; to share oil profits as of January 2004; to draw up a new constitution during 2004; to award administrative autonomy to the south as of that same year and to call for a referendum in 2010 on southern independence. Hassan al-Turabi, leader of the NIF who had been imprisoned several years earlier, was released in October 2003, at the same time as the proscription on his party was lifted.

[53] While peace between north and south was being brokered, government troops launched an offensive in January 2004 on Darfur in western Sudan, an area under both northern and southern jurisdictions. They attacked the Sudanese Liberation Movement/Army (SLM/A, formerly Darfur Liberation Movement).

[54] The SLM/A had been founded the year before, in response to systematic attacks on the Fur region by groups of Arab pastoralists belonging to the Janjawid people who had been driven out of the Sahel (their region of origin) by desertification, and who wanted to evict the Muslim black ethnic groups (Masaalit, Fur and Zaghawa) from their well-irrigated lands.

[55] The Janjawid were armed and trained by the Sudanese Government to pursue a scorched earth policy. By May 2004, this operation had cost 10,000 lives, destroyed huge tracts of land, and forced a million people to flee. Many of these destitute refugees crossed into Chad; many were beaten, raped and tortured on the way. The World Organization Against Torture denounced the torturing of refugee children from Darfur.

[56] In March 2004, al-Turabi and his political and military followers were again arrested by al-Bashir.

[57] In May 2004, the Chad army was attacked on the border by Sudanese government forces.

[58] That same month, political observers warned of a possible anti-government alliance between the armed groups of Darfur and those of Nuba, Abyei and Blue Nile, and of the subsequent eruption of fighting throughout Sudan.

[59] In April 2004, the UN Human Rights Commission refrained from applying sanctions on the Sudanese Government. However, the following month, the UN's food assistance program announced that three million people were affected by famine and disease as result of war, in a major humanitarian disaster.

[60] By September, according to the World Health Organization, 10,000 people a month were dying of disease in the camps. ■

Suriname / Suriname

Population:	442,351
Area:	163,270 km²
Capital:	Paramaribo
Currency:	Surinamese dollar
Language:	Dutch, English and Sranang (creole)

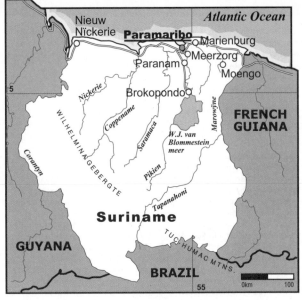

B efore the arrival of the Europeans, the region was inhabited by the Caribs. They were warriors, living in small communities where they existed by hunting, fishing and small-scale farming.

2 Dutch traders arrived in the region in the 17th century, but the first colonies were established by the British, who brought slaves to work in their plantations. In the 19th century Suriname came under definitive Dutch control.

3 In 1863, when slavery was abolished in Dutch territories it was replaced by another source of cheap labor, Asian Indian and Javanese immigrants. This gave rise to a complex ethnic structure in Guyana, with a majority of Indians strongly attached to their cultural heritage. Then there were smaller groups: the Creoles or Afro-Americans, the Javanese, the 'bush people' whose ancestors had rebelled against slavery and fled the plantations, indigenous people and a small European minority.

4 These ethnic, cultural and linguistic differences hindered the development of a national identity. The Creoles formed the NPK (National Party Combination), a coalition of four center-left parties, and they led the fight for independence after World War II. Jaggernauth Lachmon's Vatan Hitakarie represented the Indian population of shop owners and business people, and they sought to postpone independence.

5 In October 1973, the independence faction won the elections. Hanck Arron, leader of the NPS (National Surinamese Party) became the first Prime Minister of the local Government, which had enjoyed a certain degree of autonomy since 1954.

6 Independence was finally proclaimed in 1975. Many middle-income Surinamese took advantage of their status as Dutch citizens to emigrate to the ex-colonial power. Nearly a third of the population left, causing a serious shortage of technical, professional and administrative personnel. The country lost nearly all its much-needed qualified labor, with the sole exception of the workers employed by SURALCO and Billiton, two transnationals which monopolized local bauxite mining and indeed, the country's economic life. Economic activity decreased and agriculture declined to dangerously low levels.

7 In February 1980, the Prime Minister was overthrown by a coup (the 'sergeants' revolution'). The National Military Council (NMC) summoned opposition leaders to form a government and several leftwing leaders took up cabinet posts.

8 Another coup in February 1981 led to Lt-Colonel Desiré Delano (Desi) Bouterse taking power. The Government established relations with Cuba, in the face of domestic opposition and external opposition from the US and from the Netherlands.

9 Labor unions, merchants and professional groups began to express their discontent in 1982. In December of that year, 15 journalists, intellectuals and trade union leaders were executed without trial in Fort Zeeland for allegedly conspiring against the State. The 'December murders' are considered to be the most traumatic event in the country's history.

10 In January 1983, Bouterse formed a new government, which appointed Errol Halibux, a nationalist and member of the Farmers and Labor Union, as Prime Minister. After the American invasion of Grenada, the Suriname Government did an about-face in its relations with Cuba, asking Havana to recall its ambassador and suspending all agreements for co-operation between the countries.

11 In an effort to reduce Suriname's isolation, the Government joined CARICOM as an observer and re-established relations with Cuba, Grenada, Nicaragua, Brazil and Venezuela. It also became a member of SELA, the OAS and the Amazon Pact.

12 In 1986 violence broke out again. On 29 November, a special military unit attacked the village of Moiwana, burning down the home of the leader of the armed opposition, Ronnie Brunswijk, and killing 35 people, mostly women and children. Years later, in 1990, the investigation was reopened and Inspector Herman Gooding, responsible for ordering the new investigation, was murdered and his body was left outside Colonel Bouterse's offices. In April 1987 the National Assembly approved a Constitution, providing for a return to institutional government. The draft constitution was supported by the three main political parties and the army.

13 The United Front for Democracy and Development won the 1988 elections. In July 1989, President Ramsewak Shankar granted an amnesty to the guerrilla movement, allowing them to keep their weapons as long as they remained in the forests. Bouterse and the NDP (National Democratic Party) opposed this agreement, arguing that it legalized an autonomous military force.

14 In December 1990, a coup deposed Ramsewak Shankar. Bouterse, who had resigned a week prior to the coup, resumed his leadership of the army. The National Assembly, which had been set up in September 1987 for a period of five years, appointed the NPS's Johan Draag as provisional president.

PROFILE

ENVIRONMENT
The coastal plain, low and subject to floods, is suitable for agriculture. Rice, sugar and other crops are grown. Land has been reclaimed from the sea by means of drainage and dykes. Inland, the terrain is hilly with dense tropical vegetation, rich in bauxite deposits. Year-round heavy rainfall feeds an important system of rivers, some of which are used to generate hydro-electric power for the aluminum industry.

SOCIETY
Peoples: Suriname Creole 30 per cent; Indo-Pakistani 33 per cent; Javanese 16 per cent; 'Bush People' 10 per cent; Amerindian 3 per cent; other 3 per cent. **Religions:** Christian 44 per cent (21.6 per cent Catholic, 18 per cent Protestant); Muslim 18.6 per cent; Hindu 26 per cent; other 15.8 per cent. **Languages:** Dutch (official), English (for business), Hindi, Javanese, and a form of Creole are spoken. This, called either Taki-Taki or Sranang-Tongo, is based on African languages mixed with Dutch, Spanish and English. **Main Political Parties:** New Front for Democracy (NF); Millennium Combination (MC); Democratic National Platform 2000 (DNP2000); Democratic Alternative '91 (DA'91). **Main Social Organizations:** Suriname Trade Union Federation; Central Organization of Civil Servants.

THE STATE
Official Name: Republiek Suriname.
Administrative Divisions: 9 Districts.
Capital: Paramaribo 253,000 people (2003).
Other Cities: Nieuw Nickerie 13,100 people; Meerzorg 6,400; Marienburg 4,300 (2000).
Government: Parliamentary Republic. President, Ronald Venetiaan since August 2000. Prime Minister, Jules Rattankoemar Ajodhia since August 2000. Unicameral Parliament: 51-member National Assembly. **National Holiday:** 25 November, Independence Day (1975).
Armed Forces: 1,800 (1996).

Life expectancy
71.1 years
2000-2005

GNI per capita
$1,960
2002

Literacy
94% total adult rate
2000

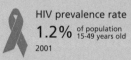

HIV prevalence rate
1.2% of population 15-49 years old
2001

IN FOCUS

ENVIRONMENTAL CHALLENGES
Progressive deforestation is occurring because of extensive logging for timber exportation. Some rivers are polluted due to small-scale mining activities.

WOMEN'S RIGHTS
Women have been able to vote and stand for election since 1948. Out of 51 seats in Parliament, 10 are held by women. The cabinet includes women in foreign affairs and domestic affairs, and a woman is minister for social affairs. In 2001 the first woman member of the court of justice was sworn in.

No mechanisms exist to control domestic violence. The average battered woman is aged between 25 and 50, has two or three children and is a low-wage employee. The police are not inclined to intervene in domestic cases and the victims do not always lodge a complaint. Discrimination against women is particularly manifest in the economy, where men earn considerably more. Over 60 per cent of women workers have jobs that are traditionally considered feminine, such as secretaries or administrative posts. The Government has taken no measures to prevent economic discrimination. Some nightclubs have recruited women from Brazil, Colombia and the Dominican Republic.

CHILDREN
Education is obligatory up to the age of 12, although many children do not attend school because there are none nearby or because they lack resources to go to the nearest one. Although education is free in theory, many schools in practice charge between $4 and $24. In urban zones, close on 80 per cent of children go to primary school, while in rural areas school attendance is considerably lower. Economic pressures oblige children to leave school in order to work.

Although there are many cases of malnutrition among poorer children, the problem has not been quantified. While sexual exploitation is not frequent, when a campaign was launched, it gave rise to a series of complaints. The age of sexual consent is 14. However in order to marry without parental consent, it is 30 years of age.

INDIGENOUS PEOPLES/ ETHNIC MINORITIES
Close on 13 per cent of the Surinamese are traditional peoples or their direct descendants. Between 3 and 5 per cent are indigenous peoples. There are 9 distinguishable indigenous groups, the largest of which are the Arawak, the Caribs, the Trio and the Wayanas. They are divided into 35 communities all over the country. The Caribs and the Arawak are located in coastal zones and in the savannah belt between the coast and the inland tropical forest. The Trio and the Wayanas live in the southern tropical forest zone.

Furthermore, 6 groups of Maroones people live in the country, including the Saramaka, the N'djuca, the Matawi, the Kwinti, the Aluku and the Paramaka. These make up almost 15 per cent of the country's total population. Since the 18th century they have maintained a culture based on a mixture of African and Amerindian traditions.

All these ethnic groups claim their ancestral territories, but particularly those living inland in the dense forest zones. Although they are a majority in these regions, they have very few recognized rights and are not even mentioned in economic development plans that directly threaten their habitat and form of life. The greatest problem faced by the indigenous and traditional population in Suriname is the rampant exploitation of mineral and raw material reserves - in particular gold and timber - on their lands. They are seeking official recognition of their long-term land tenure over their original lands and other basic human rights. Suriname is the only country in the western hemisphere that does not recognize the basic rights of its indigenous population.

DEATH PENALTY
The last execution was carried out in 1982.

---

15 The New Front (NF) won the May 1991 elections held to choose the National Assembly. One of its major proposals was the re-establishment of relations with the Dutch Government.

16 On 16 September, Ronald Venetiaan of the NF was elected President and in October launched a cut in spending on defense and the armed forces. A peace process, including UN-sponsored guerrilla disarmament, was started under the supervision of Brazil and Guyana.

17 In 1993 the country suffered the consequences of a drop in the price of bauxite and between 1980 and 1990 the economy shrank at an average annual rate of 2.6 per cent. The new civil government adopted a harsh structural adjustment program, leading to considerable discontent among the population.

18 Poverty and unemployment in the rural agricultural communities formed the background for the occupation of the Afobakka dam, 100 kilometers south of Paramaribo, in March 1994. The rebels, who called for the resignation of the Government, were expelled by government troops after a four-day occupation. Another important movement took place in rural areas in 1995, when representatives of Indians and *Cimarrones* (runaway slaves living in the forest in their own communities) gathered to protest against the environmental damage caused by a Canadian mining company and an Indonesian timber company.

19 The Netherlands issued an international warrant in April 1997 for former dictator Desi Bouterse, under suspicion of links with drug-trafficking. In response, President Wijdenbosch appointed the former dictator State Councillor, granting him diplomatic immunity.

20 Toward the end of that year, a failed coup ended in the arrest of 17 low-ranking officers. The coup attempt was related to the working conditions of the troops, which had deteriorated, with low salaries and outdated equipment.

21 Social unrest and an unprecedented economic crisis intensified during the first months of 1999, leaving the country practically paralyzed. In February, several political groups boycotted Parliament, preventing the necessary quorum for passage of any bill. There was a 200-per-cent devaluation, inflation reached 20 per cent and the public health system broke down. There were major protest demonstrations, particularly by state employees, who represented ten per cent of the population. Due to the State's debts with the health system, doctors in private hospitals refused to treat patients who had state health insurance. The Government was obliged to hire Cuban doctors.

22 Parliament was shaken from its lethargy by the biggest general strike in Suriname's history and massive protests endured for months in Paramaribo. In June it deposed the Wijdenbosch Cabinet, blaming the officials for the country's economic collapse.

23 In May 2000, Venetiaan's NF won the elections and in August he was elected President with 37 of the National Assembly's 51 votes. Jules Ajodhia was elected Vice-President and Prime Minister.

24 Tensions between Suriname and Guyana, dating back decades due to disputes over territorial waters, reached a peak in June 2000 when a Surinamese vessel forced the withdrawal of the Canadian company CGX Energy, to which Guyana had granted oil exploration rights. In July, after the leaders of the two countries failed to reach an accord in several days of negotiations in Jamaica, the Canadian company called off the project.

25 In November 2000, the High Court of Amsterdam ruled that coup leader Desi Bouterse would be prosecuted - again in absentia - for leading a cocaine-smuggling ring during his time in office and for the 1982 assassinations. Suriname had begun investigating the executions and asked the Netherlands for cooperation and assistance. Because there was no extradition treaty between the two countries, Suriname was not obliged to send Bouterse to Amsterdam for the trial.

26 During a handing over of command ceremony held in mid-2001, the former National Army commander, Glenn Sedney, offered his apologies to the Surinamese community for the 'wounds and divisions' caused in the past by the military.

27 A series of mutinies called attention to the serious situation in the prison system. In January a mutiny took place at the police station in Geyersvlijt where, according to reports, overcrowding was very serious. This mutiny was followed by a similar one in March at the police station in Limesgracht.

28 Financial misfortune added to low market prices led to State banana companies closing down in April 2002, triggering protests and demands by the workers.

29 In May 2002, President Venetiaan stated the need to monitor respect for freedom of expression and to recognize the fact that during the 1980s and 1990s, journalists, newspaper directors and radio broadcasting companies had been intimidated. Venetiaan signed the 'Chapultepec Declaration' regarding freedom of expression. Members of the Journalist Association welcomed the measure, stressing the need to reform some laws in accordance with the guidelines set out in the Declaration.

30 In January 2004, in a maneuver seeking to strengthen the economy, the Surinamese dollar was established as the valid currency, replacing the Dutch guilder. ∎

Swaziland / Swaziland

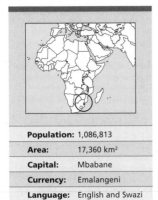

Population:	1,086,813
Area:	17,360 km²
Capital:	Mbabane
Currency:	Emalangeni
Language:	English and Swazi

S waziland, to a greater degree
than nearby Lesotho (see
Lesotho) was born as a nation in
the 19th century, when peoples of
very different origins joined
together. Zulu expansion led
Sobhuza, head of the Dlamini, to
bring together several groups
(including Zulu deserters and San
who remained in the region). They
became a powerful force in the
northeastern part of today's
KwaZulu-Natal province in South
Africa. At his death, shortly after
the Zulus' defeat by the Boers
(1839), his son Mswati continued
the task of keeping the nation
together in the face of threats
from the Afrikaners. He allied
himself with the British shortly
before his death so as to avoid
defeat. After almost 30 years of
resistance the people took the
name of their king as the name of
their country.

2   In 1867, Swaziland became a
British protectorate, like
Basutoland (Lesotho) and
Bechuanaland (Botswana). When
Britain defeated the Boers it
imposed separate colonial
administrations over the whole of
South Africa. The Swazi authorities
were formally recognized in 1941
in accordance with the British
policy of making use of 'local'
intermediaries in its
administration.

3   When the Union of South
Africa broke off relations with

Britain and toughened racial
segregation policies in 1961,
London accelerated the
decolonization process in the
region. Swaziland was granted
internal autonomy in 1967 and
formal independence the
following year. Sobhuza II was
recognized as head of state and
governed with two legislative
chambers. In April 1973, he
dissolved Parliament, suspended
the constitution inherited from the
British, banned the action of all
political parties and proclaimed
himself absolute monarch.
Sobhuza also announced a state of
emergency that is still in place.

4   In 1978 the Swazi Liberation
Movement (SWALIMO) was
founded, led by Ambrose Swane,
who had escaped from prison in
the capital, Mbabane. The
strengthening of the opposition
led to a rapid growth of the
armed forces, from 1,000 in 1975
to over 5,000 in 1979.

5   The growing opposition was
bolstered by, amongst other
things, the consolidation of a

socialist regime in Mozambique,
but this also led Swaziland to
develop closer military relations
with South Africa and Israel.
Sobhuza II was one of only three
African rulers who never severed
diplomatic relations with Tel Aviv.

6   The Constitution was
reformed and re-introduced in

1978 without approval from or
consultation with the electorate.
Following tradition, the actual
approval process consisted of
consultation with the heads of the
40 clans a fortnight before its
application. It banned opposition
parties and established a weak
parliament.

7   After 1980, the economic
situation in Swaziland was
affected by the world recession.
The prices of imported goods
increased and corn, sugar and
wood export prices dropped.
Minerals fell from 40 per cent of
total exports to only 10 per cent
due to the depletion of iron ore
reserves. Various new coal deposits
were discovered in 1980 but their
exploitation has been slow as
there are few resources available
for this.

8   In August 1982, Sobhuza II
died. His successor, Prince
Makhosetive was only 15 years
old, which led to a power struggle
within the royal family and the
deposing of the Prime Minister,
Prince Mabandla Dlamini. He was
succeeded by Bhekimpi Dlamini, a
pro-South African conservative,
who began persecuting anti-
apartheid South African refugees.

9   In August 1983, Ntombi, one
of Sobhuza's widows, overthrew
Queen Dzellue and took power,
strengthening the conservative

PROFILE

ENVIRONMENT

The country is divided into three distinct geographical regions
known as the high, middle and low veld (plain), all approximately
the same size. The western region is mountainous with a central
plateau and flatlands to the east. The main crops are sugarcane,
citrus fruits and rice (irrigated), cotton, maize corn (the basic
foodstuff), sorghum and tobacco.

SOCIETY

Peoples: 84.3 per cent of the population are Swazis. Zulus account
for 9.9 per cent; Tonga and Shangaan another 3 per cent; there
are Indian (0.8 per cent), Pakistani (0.8 per cent) and Portuguese
(0.2 per cent) minorities.
Religions: 77 per cent of the population are Christian, the rest
follow traditional African religions.
Languages: Swazi and English (official); ethnic minorities speak
their own languages.
Main Political Parties: Popular United Democratic Movement
(PUDEMO); Swaziland Progressive Party; Swaziland Democratic
Alliance; National Congress of Ngwane Liberation. All political
parties and activities were banned by King Sobhuza II in 1973.
Main Social Organizations: Swaziland Federation of Trade Unions
(SFTU); Swaziland Youth Congress.

THE STATE

Official Name: Umbuso wakaNgwane.
Administrative Divisions: 210 Tribal Areas, including 40 traditional
communities. **Capital:** Mbabane 70,000 people (2003).
Other Cities: Manzini 22,500 people; Big Bend 14,300; Lobamba
14,000 (2000).
Government: King Mswati III, crowned on 25 April 1986. Absalom
Themba Dlamini, Prime Minister since November 2003. Parliament
has two chambers: The House of Assembly has 65 members and
the Senate has 30 non-partisan members.
National Holiday: 6 September, Independence Day (1968).
Armed Forces: 2,657 (1983).

LAND USE

2000

IRRIGATED AREA: 36.8% of arable land

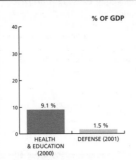

- ARABLE LAND: 10.3%
- CROPLANDS: 0.7%
- OTHER USE: 89.0%

PUBLIC EXPENDITURE

% OF GDP

9.1 %
HEALTH & EDUCATION (2000)

1.5 %
DEFENSE (2001)

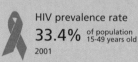
faction. Two months later, the people voted for a new parliament through a complicated indirect electoral system called *tinkhundla*. Prince Dlamini was successful in an election where no political parties participated and in which the voters did not fully know what they were voting for. The election resulted in closer ties with South Africa. Parliament had less influence than the *Liqoqo*, the powerful tribal assembly which operated as the Supreme State Council. That year the illegal People's United Democratic Movement (PUDEMO) was founded; one of its key demands was for a multiparty system.

[10] The repression of anti-apartheid militants increased in 1984, with their detention and return to the Pretoria Government.

[11] During the second half of 1984, the Government closed down the university. Prime Minister Bhekimpi Dlamini's authoritarianism stimulated the revival of SWALIMO, led by Clement Dumisa Dlamini, a much respected nationalist leader and former secretary-general of the Progressive Party. He was exiled to England.

[12] In April 1986, Prince Makhosetive was crowned, taking the name King Mswati III and maintaining the conservative

position of his predecessor. He dissolved the *Liqoqo*, and replaced Prime Minister Bhekimpi with Sotsha Dlamini.

[13] In September 1987, the King dissolved Parliament, announcing elections for November, a year ahead of schedule. The 40 members of Parliament and 10 senators were elected by an electoral college. The King disputed the election of the senators, and insisted the process be repeated.

[14] From the late 1980s the country's economic situation improved noticeably. The economy grew and foreign investment continued. A significant part of the food produced was sold to the European Community. This improvement (a direct consequence of trade sanctions against South Africa) allowed the manufacturing sector to increase production, and raised the economic growth rate to 3.5 per cent per year.

[15] There was growing civil unrest throughout 1990. In 1992, PUDEMO with the support of Matsapa Shongue's Swaziland United Front and Elmond Shongue's Swaziland National Front, officially took up the opposition, forcing the establishment of a Commission to

propose political reforms. In October that year, the King dissolved parliament, announcing plans for a multiparty system.

[16] In 1992-3, drought destroyed the corn crop and generated further unemployment.

[17] In September 1993 the country's first multiparty elections resulted in Prime Minister Obed Dlamini failing to win a seat in Parliament. In November Jameson Mbilini Dlamini became Prime Minister.

[18] During 1994, protests against Mswati III continued. After the fire-bombing of the parliament building in February 1995, 40,000 people took part in a demonstration in March, in support of a two-day general strike.

[19] In February 1996, amid rumors of possible South African military intervention, the King agreed to authorize political parties. The Swaziland Federation of Trade Unions called for an end to the absolute monarchy and the establishment of a multiparty democracy.

[20] Mid-year, the King called for an end to the unrest, repeating that he would reconsider the banning of the political parties. He also said that citizens would be given the opportunity to

participate in drawing up a new Constitution. He replaced Prime Minister Mbilini Dlamini with Barnabas Sibusiso Dlamini in July.

[21] The situation did not change substantially in 1997. In March the King let down the opposition by not sending delegates to the agreed negotiations. In July, he created a 30-member committee, charged with drafting a constitution, asking for all related initiatives to be referred to this body. These delaying tactics intensified the protests. The King reacted, ordering the security forces to fire live ammunition on demonstrators. The clashes produced large numbers of wounded and several union leaders were arrested.

[22] In October 1997, fresh strikes broke out in strategic areas, such as the sugar sector. The unions also called for the committee on constitutional revision to be dissolved.

[23] In April 1998, the King put an environmental conservation plan into action, with public and private sector participation. At the same time, bidding was opened on large-scale public works projects including bridges, the re-routing of major watercourses, and irrigation for areas hit by drought.

[24] In October 2000, the Government evicted 40 families from their land, which was then given to the King's brother. This caused demonstrations that paralyzed the country for two days, as protestors demanded their civil and labor rights.

[25] In mid 2001, a royal decree empowered Mswati to ban any publication not in line with 'Swazi morality and ideals'. Two opposition publications were immediately banned.

[26] In March 2002, an urgent appeal was made for food aid for over 200,000 people at risk of dying from hunger. The crisis arose as the countries of southern Africa were suffering variously from drought, flooding, mis-government and devastated economies.

[27] In October 2003, elections were held once again and the King appointed Absalom Themba Dlamini as Prime Minister. No parties are allowed and most opposition politicians boycotted the elections. Africa's last absolute monarchy remains the only southern African country without an elected government.

[28] At the beginning of 2004, Mswati asked for $15 million to build a palace for each one of his 11 wives. At the same time, the Prime Minister announced that the country was facing a humanitarian crisis because of scant rainfall over the previous three years. ∎

IN FOCUS

ENVIRONMENTAL CHALLENGES
In the low veld, water-borne infections are one cause of the high mortality rate. Wildlife was largely wiped out by European hunters in the first half of the last century, and the remaining animals are being killed by poachers. Swaziland suffers from serious soil erosion due to overgrazing and deforestation and has very limited sources of drinking water.

WOMEN'S RIGHTS
Women have been able to vote and stand for election since 1968. In 2000, only 3 per cent of the seats in Parliament and 6 per cent of ministerial or equivalent posts were held by women. They comprise 38 per cent of the labor force (40 per cent in agriculture, 30 per cent in services, 29 per cent in industry and 1 per cent in various other areas).
    The fertility rate is 4.6 children per woman*. Seventy per cent of pregnant women receive prenatal care, and the same percentage of the births are assisted by qualified personnel*. Maternal mortality is 370 deaths per 100,000 live

births. In spite of legislation, domestic violence against women is widespread. To counter ingrained sexist attitudes, some schools organize discussions and other ways of addressing the subject while the university encourages seminars and workshops on gender issues.

CHILDREN
Infant mortality stands at 106 deaths per 1,000 live births* and the under-5 mortality rate is 149 deaths per 1,000 live births*. Life expectancy has dropped steeply from 47 years in 1995 to 34 years predicted for 2005, due to HIV/AIDS and poverty-related problems. Only between 72 and 77 per cent of infants have been vaccinated against the most common childhood diseases, such as polio, measles and diphtheria. Medical care for children is inadequate. The hospitals are generally over-crowded. Staff and medication are also scarce, particularly in rural areas.
    Child abuse is a serious problem: one third of rape victims are under 10 years of age. There are also many children living in the streets who are increasingly vulnerable to sexual exploitation and

prostitution as a means of survival.

INDIGENOUS PEOPLES/ ETHNIC MINORITIES
There is both social and government discrimination against non-ethnic Swazis (both white and of mixed origin). Although there are no official statistics on this, it is estimated that approximately 2 per cent of the population are non-ethnic Swazis. They have difficulty in obtaining official documents, such as a passport.

MIGRANTS/REFUGEES
The law grants the status of refugee or asylum-seeker to individuals who are protected under the 1951 UN Convention and the 1967 Protocol. In 2003, there were approximately one thousand refugees in the country, mainly from Central Africa and Angola.

DEATH PENALTY
It continues to be applied to all types of crimes.

*Latest data available in *The State of the World's Children* and *Childinfo* database,UNICEF, 2004.

Sweden / Sverije

Population:	8,894,851
Area:	449,960 km²
Capital:	Stockholm
Currency:	Kronor
Language:	Swedish

According to archeological research, the first inhabited area in Sweden is thought to have been the southern part of the country, with occupation dating back to 10,000 years BC. Between 8,000 and 6,000 BC, the region was inhabited by peoples who made a living by hunting and fishing, using simple stone tools. The Bronze Age (1,800-500 BC) brought with it cultural development, reflected in particular in the richness of the tombs of that period.

2   In 500 AD, in Lake Malaren valley, the Sveas created the first important center of political power. From the 6th century BC until 800 AD the population went through a migration period, later becoming settled, with agriculture becoming the basis of economic and social activities.

3   Between the 9th and 11th centuries, the Swedish Vikings reached the Baltic shores on trade expeditions as well as pirate raids and also went as far as what is now Russia, reaching the Black and Caspian Seas. There they established relations with the Byzantine and Arab empires.

4   During the same period, Christian missions from the Carolingian empire (led by the missionary, Ansgar) converted most of Sweden. However, the gods of the ancient local mythologies survived into the 12th century. Sweden had its first archbishop in 1164.

5   Between 1160 and 1250, the fiefdoms of Sverker and Erik alternated in power as each fought to gain control of the Swedish kingdom. The feudal chieftains remained relatively autonomous until the second half of the 13th century, when the King enforced nationwide laws and annexed Finland.

6   The Black Death brought the country's growth to a standstill in 1350, a situation that lasted until the second half of the 15th century. In that period the foundries in the central region became important. During the 15th and 16th centuries

the German Hanseatic League dominated Swedish commerce and encouraged the founding of several cities.

7   In 1397, the royal power of Norway, Sweden and Denmark was handed over to Danish Queen Margaret, who proclaimed the Union of Kalmar. The ensuing conflicts between the central Danish power and the rebellious Swedish nobility, townspeople and peasants ended in 1523, with the accession of Gustav Vasa to the throne of Sweden.

8   Under the reign of Vasa, the monarchy ceased to be elected by the nobility and became hereditary. A German administrative model was adopted and the foundations were laid for a nation state. The possessions of the Church went to the state, in the wake of the Protestant Reformation. From then on, Sweden aspired to becoming

the main power in the Baltic region.

9   In 1630, after intervening successfully in the Thirty Years' War, Sweden waged two more wars to conquer the Danish regions of Skane, Halland, Blekinge, and the Baltic island of Gotland, as well as the Norwegian islands of Bohuslan, Jamtland, and Harjedalen.

10   Sweden thus became a great power in northern Europe, as it now ruled over Finland, several northern German provinces, and the Baltic provinces of Estonia, Latvia and Lithuania. However, the country was still basically rural and lacked resources to maintain its position or power indefinitely.

11   After its defeat in the Great Northern War (1700-21), the Swedish Empire lost most of the provinces to the south and east of the Gulf of Finland. It was reduced to the territories roughly

corresponding to modern Sweden and Finland, with Finland being ceded to Russia during the Napoleonic Wars.

12   In 1718, after the death of Charles XII, a parliament (*Riksdag*) made up of nobles did away with the absolute monarchy, assuming power itself. However, the new king Gustav II staged a coup in 1772, and finally re-established full monarchic powers in 1789.

13   Inspired by the success of the Dutch and British East India Companies, the Swedish East India company was founded in 1731 to trade in east Asia. It was Sweden's largest company in the 18th century, before its demise in 1813.

14   In compensation for the losses incurred during the Napoleonic Wars, Norway was ceded to Sweden. After a short war, it was forcibly annexed by Sweden in 1814. After a series of conflicts, the union dissolved peacefully in 1905 with Norway winning back its independence.

15   In the second half of the 19th century, Sweden continued to be a poor country, with 90 per cent of the population engaged in agriculture. At this point, a great emigration movement began: one million out of a total of five million Swedes left, mainly for North America.

16   During this period the liberal majority in parliament, supported by King Oscar I, established universal education (1842), the free enterprise system and the liberalization of foreign trade (1846). Legislation was also passed establishing sexual equality in inheritance law (1845), the rights of unmarried women (1858), and religious freedom (1860).

17   Several social movements emerged, such as the temperance league, women's rights advocates, and especially the workers' movement, which grew with industrialization and influenced the Government through the creation of the Social Democratic Party (SAP) in 1889.

18   From 1890 onwards, with the support of foreign capital, industrialization accelerated in Sweden. The country had one of the most thriving economies in that part of Europe. Finished products using Swedish technical innovations quickly became the country's main exports.

19   Alfred Nobel had a major influence in this process. A renowned scientist and inventor, up to 300 patents were registered under his name, including the patent for dynamite in 1867. Most of the fortune from his inventions and companies was set aside, after his death in 1896, for the Foundation that carries his name and which every year awards the

Life expectancy
80.1 years
2000-2005

GNI per capita
$24,820
2002

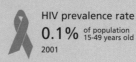

HIV prevalence rate
0.1% of population
15-49 years old
2001

IN FOCUS

ENVIRONMENTAL CHALLENGES
Coastal areas on the North and Baltic seas are highly polluted. Extremely high levels of acid rain damage the soil and pollute sources of drinking water.

WOMEN'S RIGHTS
All women have been able to vote and stand for election since 1921; female suffrage was first granted in 1919, albeit with restrictions.

The percentage of female representation in politics is one of the highest in the world. In 2000, 43 per cent of seats in parliament and ministerial or equivalent positions were held by women.

Violence against women continued to be a problem, with almost 17,000 cases of assault or harassment reported in 2003, not including rapes. Every year an average of 30 women or girls are murdered, often by someone close to the victim. Almost 2,000 rapes against females over 14 years of age were reported in 2002.

Every year between 200 and 500 women arrive in Sweden from the Baltic countries, Central Europe and Russia, to work as domestic employees or in the sex industry.

CHILDREN
The Government is committed to welfare policies and to protecting children's rights. Programs implemented are continuously monitored to ensure that they meet satisfactory child welfare standards. Education is free, universal and compulsory for children from six to 16. Medical and dental healthcare is also free until the age of 16. Parents receive around $1,300 per year for each child under 16 in the family. The amount increases if the family has three or more children.

In 2003 there was concern about the growing number of child abuse cases. That year more than 7,000 cases involving children under 15 were reported. Of these, 300 were rapes and 1,000 were cases of other types of sexual abuse (half the figure for 2002).

INDIGENOUS PEOPLES/ ETHNIC MINORITIES
The Sami descend from nomadic peoples that for thousands of years migrated throughout the north of Scandinavia. The largest community is in Norway, but they are also a minority in Sweden. Until a few years ago, reindeer were the basis of their economy. However, the abandonment of their nomadic lifestyle has substantially altered their customs.

MIGRANTS/REFUGEES
In late 2002, the country sheltered some 24,900 refugees and asylum-seekers. Some 23,600 were awaiting an official decision on their cases. Eighteen had been granted asylum because they had been persecuted for their gender identity or sexual orientation.

Most of the refugees come from former Yugoslavia and Iraq.

DEATH PENALTY
Capital punishment was abolished for ordinary offenses in 1921 and for all offenses in 1972.

Nobel prizes in areas such as physics, medicine, literature and peace.

[20] In the early 20th century, the SAP became a major political force. In 1917 its leaders won posts in public bodies and in 1920 Hjalmar Branting headed the first government by the party of the working class. The party consolidated its power in the 1930s, although this process was not without conflicts. In 1931, in the northern mining city of Ådalen, firepower was used to repress the Workers' Day demonstration and five workers died, in what came to be known as the Ådalen Tragedy.

[21] The SAP's rise to power was accompanied by a policy of seeking consensus for a major social reform program (including state pension funds, free education and public healthcare) and the establishment of a Welfare State, characterized by strong state intervention in the economy and a social security system that aimed to give 'cradle -to -grave' protection. A crucial step towards that goal took place in 1938 in Saltsjöbaden, when employers and workers agreed to resolve their differences peacefully and through institutional channels. This deal symbolized the birth of the 'Swedish Model'.

[22] The model was progressively implemented from the 1930s until 1976, when the SAP lost its first elections since 1936. Prime ministers Per Albin Hansson and Tage Erlander played a major role in that historical process. Erlander led three consecutive governments, from 1946 until 1969.

[23] Since World War I, Sweden has refused to take part in peacetime alliances in order to stay neutral in times of war. This policy relies on Sweden's strong defense system and compulsory national service for men.

[24] Trade routes were disrupted during World War II, resulting in serious food shortages. This provoked a protectionist agricultural policy, for strategic security reasons, that is maintained even today. Swedish neutrality was upheld, but at the price of allowing some one million Nazi soldiers to cross the territory to invade and occupy Norway.

[25] Sweden favored a thaw in East-West relations during the Cold War, and worked actively for international disarmament. One of the cornerstones of its foreign policy is its support for the UN. After Dag Hammarskjöld became UN Secretary-General in 1953, the UN played an important role as mediator in several international crises, such as the Suez Canal crisis in 1956. Hammarskjöld died in a plane crash in 1961, in Africa.

[27] In the 1970s there was a slow-down of economic growth, due partly to the increasing cost of oil imports to satisfy half the country's energy needs. Employers and political parties representing the interests of the bourgeoisie used the economic crisis to express their discontent with the Swedish Model.

[28] In 1976 the SAP lost power to a coalition of three moderate, liberal and conservative parties. Six years later, the Social Democrats returned to power and were re-elected in 1988. In 1986, charismatic leader Olof Palme was shot dead in a murder case that has still not been solved. Ingvar Carlsson succeeded him as prime minister.

[29] In the years that followed, Parliament investigated an alleged case of bribery - involving the Palme administration and Bofors, an arms manufacturer - in connection with the sale of weapons to the Middle East and India. The country's laws banned such sales, as well as trade with areas where there are military tensions or with countries at war. The investigation found that SAP members had carried out illegal espionage operations, embezzled funds and spread false information regarding Palme's assassination.

[30] In the September 1991 elections, the Social Democrats lost their parliamentary majority. Led by Prime Minister Carl Bildt, a conservative administration sought to dismantle the Welfare State and abandoned the full employment policy that had been implemented for decades by the SAP. The crisis, reflected in high unemployment rates, was the background to a wave of xenophobia and assaults on foreigners, unprecedented in Sweden.

[31] On 26 August 1993, the King opened a new parliament for the Sami population of Lapland who numbered 17,000, out of a total Sami population of 60,000, resident in Norway (40,000), Finland, Russia and Sweden. A major dispute with

PROFILE

ENVIRONMENT
Sweden lies on the eastern side of the Scandinavian Peninsula. In the wooded northern part of the country are iron mines and paper mills. The central region has fertile plateaus and plains. The main industrial area is located in the south of the country where there is also agricultural production of wheat, potatoes and sugar-beet as well as cattle. The southern region is also the most densely populated.

SOCIETY
Peoples: Swedes 89.4 per cent; Finn and Sami minorities. There are refugees from Iran and former Yugoslavia. **Religion:** Lutheran (official) 89 per cent; Catholics 1.8 per cent; Pentecostal Church 1.1 per cent. Other 10.6 per cent. **Languages:** Swedish (official); Finnish and Lapp.
Main Political Parties: The left-of-center Social Democratic Party; the Center Party; the Moderate Party (conservative); the Green Party; the right-wing Liberal People's Party; Christian Democratic Party (center-right), New Democracy Party, Communist Workers' Party, Left Party (formerly Communist Party). **Main Social Organizations:** Confederation of Swedish Trade Unions, Confederation of Professional Associations, Central Wage Earners' Organization.

THE STATE
Official Name: Konungariket Sverige.
Administrative Divisions: 24 provinces.
Capital: Stockholm 1,697,000 people (2003).
Other Cities: Göteborg 744,300 people; Malmö 242,700; Uppsala 125,400 (2000).
Government: Hereditary constitutional monarchy. Sovereign: Carl XVI Gustaf, since 15 September 1973. Göran Persson, Prime Minister since March 1996, re-elected in 1998 and September 2002. Unicameral Legislature: the *Riksdag*, with 349 members. **National Holiday:** 6 June, Swedish Flag Day. **Armed Forces:** 16,000 annual conscripts and a regular force of 20,000 officers (2003). Other: Coast Guard: 600 (1993).

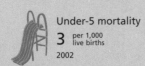 Under-5 mortality
3 per 1,000 live births
2002

 $ Aid
0.83% Official development assistance as % of donors' GNI
2002

 Maternal mortality
2 per 100,000 live births
2000

the Government arose over the abolition of the Sami's exclusive hunting rights over their lands.

[32] The SAP were re-elected in 1994 after a contentious electoral campaign. In a referendum that year, 52 per cent of voters approved Sweden's entry into the EU. A significant part of the political establishment and a number of entrepreneurs supported entry, while left-wing groups and environmentalists were against it. Sweden joined the EU on 1 January 1995. A year later, former Finance Minister Göran Persson replaced Carlsson as Prime Minister.

[33] In August 1997 it was revealed that some 60,000 people, mostly women, had been sterilized between 1935 and 1976, as part of a government plan to prevent 'inferior' humans from reproducing. The concept of the 'purity' of the Swedish race had been defined in 1922 by the Uppsala Institute of Racial Biology. The Government authorized a parliamentary investigation into the sterilization issue.

[34] Persson was re-elected in 1998 with 36 per cent of the vote, the lowest obtained by the SAP in almost 60 years. A bridge between Malmö and the Danish capital Copenhagen was built in 2000, linking the two countries by a short car-journey. In 2001, Sweden occupied the EU presidency and in June a summit of EU leaders was held in Göteborg. More than 50,000 people protested against economic globalization, with some outbreaks of violence and damage to property.

[35] Persson was elected yet again in the 2002 elections. A new referendum was called to decide if Sweden should join the European Monetary Union (EMU) and adopt the euro as its currency, replacing the kronor. Foreign Affairs Minister Anna Lindh was stabbed to death in September while shopping. Her death was initially linked to the controversial referendum, to be held a few days later. However, the murderer, Mijailo Mijailovic, the son of Serbian immigrants, was found to be mentally unstable.

[36] The Swedes voted against joining the EMU, which was a major setback for the Persson administration and had repercussions throughout Europe and especially in the UK, which also opposed the proposed single European currency. Persson said another referendum on issues relating to European integration was unlikely, since most Swedes were strongly opposed to the idea.

[37] In January 2004 the Israeli ambassador in Stockholm, Zvi Mazel, destroyed a work of art, which he considered to be antisemitic, in one of the city's museums. The incident sparked a diplomatic row between the two countries. In April, four people were arrested for alleged links to terrorist groups, drawing strong protests from representatives of the more than 40,000 Muslims living in Sweden. ∎

Ombudsman: arbiter between government and citizens

THE WORD OMBUDSMAN is of Swedish origin, coming from umbodhsmadhr, and has several related meanings: 'representative', 'trustworthy commissioner', 'agent who looks after the interests of a group or business' and 'one who speaks on behalf of another'. In a classical sense, it was originated in Sweden in the 18th century, though a similar kind of post already existed in Turkey at about the same time. King Charles XII is credited with its creation and it has been speculated that he was influenced by the Turkish model after spending several years in Turkey. The Ombudsman institution was soon spread throughout Scandinavia.

The Swedish constitution of 1809 established the Ombudsman's office for the purpose of respecting people's dignity. Through the Ombudsman's office it sought to exert additional control over the fulfillment of laws, to supervise how these laws were being really applied by the administration and to create a new, agile and informal way in which individuals could claim against the abuses and violations committed by state authorities and officials. In the early 19th century, Swedish citizens faced an administration that neither acknowledged its faults nor agreed to correct them, with a very slow and difficult-to-access judicial system and a Parliament overloaded with functions and responsibilities, which found it hard to deal with individual cases and requirements. All these factors contributed to the progressive introduction of the Ombudsman institution, which prompted the resolution of citizens' claims in a flexible and expeditious way.

SWEDEN AND BEYOND

In recent decades, three developments have strongly suggested that this institution is becoming more common and important in international terms. First, the Ombudsman institution was adopted by two countries that were removing long dictatorial regimes: Portugal in 1975 and Spain in 1981. Second, following the fall of the Berlin Wall in 1989, a significant number of Eastern European countries set up similar offices.

Finally, in Latin America, a region disrupted by the systematic violation of human rights and with a slow process of democratic transition in countries such as Guatemala, Colombia, Argentina, Peru, Honduras, Mexico and El Salvador, the creation of Ombudsman Offices has further consolidated the institution.

FUNCTIONS

The Ombudsman in countries like Sweden, Spain, Germany, Guatemala, Peru, Honduras, and the US is appointed by Parliament, although he/she acts with total independence, and his/her mission is to defend the rights of citizens and to supervise acts of the authorities. The Ombudsman intervenes upon another person's request and should do so without having any personal interest in the matter he/she was called upon to deal with.

The Ombudsman should be independent and should arbitrate between government and citizens. In spite of having a wide jurisdiction, he/she can only perform an advisory role. The Ombudsman can suggest the government should make changes but cannot order them. In all countries that have adopted this institution, it lacks executive authority.

Traditionally, the Ombudsman has flourished in parliamentary systems where on account of its functions and fields of competence it finds a natural constitutional harmony. In those presidential systems that have established this institution, a parliamentary association is also maintained since, in most of cases, the person to hold such office is appointed by Parliament.

An Ombudsman receives a large number of complaints per year, apart from those he/she investigates on his/her own initiative. Most of these complaints are rejected without any investigation being carried out. In a significant number of cases, citizens are unable to make a sufficiently specific claim. In other cases, the complaint falls outside the jurisdiction of the Ombudsman, who can only advise the citizen about where to make the complaint. At the same time, he/she serves as an advocate for poorer people in the area of administrative law.

In view of the neutrality of his/her function, the Ombudsman should maintain strict confidentiality about matters that are brought to his/her attention, unless given permission to do otherwise. The only exceptions that are left at the sole discretion of the Ombudsman are situations that present an imminent threat of serious harm. The Ombudsman should take all reasonable measures to prevent anybody, including the administration, from having access to confidential records and files.

Sources: *Encyclopedia Britannica, U.N., University of Guanajuato* (http://www.ugto.com)

Switzerland / Schweiz - Suisse - Svizzera

Population:	7,156,665
Area:	41,290 km²
Capital:	Bern
Currency:	Swiss franc
Language:	German, French and Italian

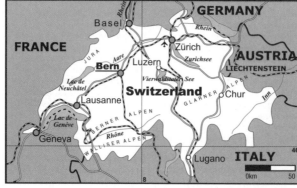

Celtic peoples, the most significant being the Helvetians, occupied the territory of what is now Switzerland before Roman colonization. The Alpine valleys north of the Italian peninsula were conquered by Julius Caesar in 58 BC because of their strategic importance for Rome as access to parts of the Empire.

[2] The Germanic peoples north of the Rhine invaded from the year 260 onwards. Between the 5th and 6th centuries the Germans permanently occupied the region east of the Aar river, together with Burgundian and Frankish groups. By 639 they had founded the kingdoms that would later become France.

[3] The Christian survivors from Roman times had completely disappeared when St Columba and St Gall arrived in the 6th century. These missionaries created the dioceses of Chur, Sion, Basel, Constance and Lausanne. Monasteries were built, in Saint-Gall, Zurich, Disentis and Romainmotier.

[4] Until the partition of Verdun in 843 these territories belonged to Charlemagne's empire. Thereafter, the region west of the Aar was allotted to Lothair, while the east remained in the hands of Louis the German. The French and German influence formed a peculiar blend with the Latin tradition of the Roman Catholic Church.

[5] Around 1033, for dynastic and political reasons, Helvetia became a part of the Holy Roman Empire, remaining so during the Middle Ages. In the 11th century the region was divided after the re-establishment of imperial authority and its disputes with the Papacy. Dukes, counts, and bishops exerted virtually autonomous local power.

[6] Walled cities served as administrative and commercial centers, and protected powerful families seeking to expand their possessions through wars against other lords and kingdoms. In the 13th century, Rudolf IV of Hapsburg conquered most of the territories of Kyburg and became the most powerful lord in the region.

[7] In the cities independence developed in opposition to the nobility. However, it was stronger among the peasant communities in the most inaccessible valleys who practiced economic cooperation to survive the harsh conditions, rejecting forced labor and payment of tithes in cash or kind.

[8] In 1231 the canton (area) of Uri fell under the authority of the Holy Roman Empire, and in 1240 Schwyz and Nidwald were subjected to Emperor Frederick II, although retaining the right to choose their own magistrates. The Hapsburg overlords questioned this freedom and uncertainty remained until Rudolf of Hapsburg was crowned king of Germany in 1273. He exercised his imperial rights in Uri and inherited rights over Schwytz and Unterwald until his death in 1291. These regions thereafter constituted the Perpetual League.

[9] This was an agreement for dispute arbitration, putting law above armed strength. The honorary magistrates had to be residents of those cantons.

[10] The league of the Uri, Schwyz, and Unterwald cantons was joined by the city of Zurich, constituting the first historic antecedent of the Swiss Confederation. This confederation was consolidated with the victory of Margarten in 1315, defeating an army of knights sent to impose imperial law in the region by the Hapsburgs.

[11] The Confederation was supported by new alliances. In 1302 the League signed a pact with the city of Luzern, previously dependent on Vienna. In 1315 Zurich reaffirmed its union and in 1353 it was joined by Bern, followed by the Glarus and Zug cantons, thus forming the core of an independent state within the Germanic Empire.

[12] During the second half of the 14th century, the rural oligarchy was defeated and their lands and laws given over to city councils. This democratic rural movement gave birth to the 'Landesgemeinde', a sovereign assembly of canton inhabitants and a similar movement was led by the city guilds. From then on, the Confederation launched into territorial conquest. During the 15th century the union grew to 13 cantons, it made alliances with other states, and the institution of government known as the *Diet* was formed where each canton was represented by two seats and one vote.

[13] In 1516, after the defeat of the Helvetians, the King of France forced a peace treaty with the cantons. In 1521 an alliance gave France the right to recruit Swiss soldiers. Only Zurich refused to sign this alliance, maintaining military and economic links with the Old Confederation until its end in 1798.

[14] The Reformation came to Switzerland with Huldrych Zwingli, a priest who preached against the mercenary service and the corruption and power of the clergy. Popular support for Zwingli strengthened the urban bourgeoisie. The Reformation became more radical in rural areas where harsh repression re-established the domination of cities over peasants.

[15] Zwingli's attempt to alter the federal alliance to benefit the reformed cities was frustrated by the military victory of the Catholic rural areas. The second national peace of Kappel, signed in 1531 granted the Catholic minority advantages over the Protestant majority.

[16] The areas where both religions coexisted were subject to constant tension, but cooperation was required to preserve the union of the federation. In Catholic regions agriculture prevailed, while in Protestant areas trade and industry flourished, aided by French, Italian and Dutch refugees.

[17] The ownership of real estate, trade and industry, together with the recruiting of mercenary troops, gave great wealth and power to a small group of families, while the small peasants had no rights, and were obliged to work mediocre lands or as farm laborers.

[18] Popular consultation disappeared in the 17th century. The power of the cities caused uprisings, such as the great peasant revolt of 1653, which were harshly repressed. Three years later when a further war ensued the prerogatives of the Catholic cantons were re-established.

[19] During the European conflicts of the 17th and 18th centuries Switzerland remained neutral because of its religious division and its mercenary armies. Neutrality became a condition for the Confederation's existence. The policy of armed neutrality, which still holds, was first formulated by the Diet in 1674.

[20] In 1712 the Protestant victory in the second battle of Villmergen ended religious struggles, ensuring the hegemony of cities which were undergoing industrial expansion. Switzerland became the most industrialized country in Europe. Industry was based on labor at home, completely transforming work in the countryside.

WORKERS

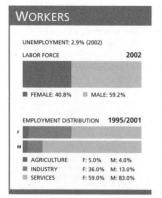

UNEMPLOYMENT: 2.9% (2002)

LABOR FORCE 2002

FEMALE: 40.8% ■ MALE: 59.2%

EMPLOYMENT DISTRIBUTION 1995/2001

	F	M
AGRICULTURE	5.0%	4.0%
INDUSTRY	36.0%	13.0%
SERVICES	59.0%	83.0%

LAND USE

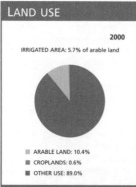

2000

IRRIGATED AREA: 5.7% of arable land

ARABLE LAND: 10.4%
CROPLANDS: 0.6%
OTHER USE: 89.0%

Life expectancy
79.1 years
2000-2005

GNI per capita
$37,930
2002

HIV prevalence rate
0.5% of population
15-49 years old
2001

IN FOCUS

ENVIRONMENTAL CHALLENGES
There is considerable water pollution due to fertilizer and pesticide use.

WOMEN'S RIGHTS
Women have been able to vote and stand for office since 1971. In 2004 they held 25 per cent of the seats in Parliament.

Abortion has been legalized; women are able to end pregnancy during the first 12 weeks. The authorities consider that between 1,500 and 3,000 women are victims of human trafficking. They generally originate from Latin America and Eastern Europe.

In the 1970s, forced sterilization of low-income women or women with mental disabilities was practised. Many are still claiming compensation and the problem remains unresolved.

Domestic violence continues to be a major problem. In October 2003, sentences for this type of crime were increased.

Registered prostitution is legal. In 2002, 467 new registrations were recorded in Zurich, and the total is 3,000. However, there are many unregistered prostitutes; 300 were arrested in that year.

CHILDREN
The public education system and basic health care are provided by the Government. Education is free. Almost all children attend primary school.

Some cases of child abuse have been reported, but it is not a generalized problem. In 2002, laws increasing sentences for this type of crime came into force. An anti-pedophile operation was also carried out: 600 cases have already gone to court, 63 men to prison and another 163 men have had to pay fines. Some 400 cases are still pending. Cycos is a program that receives complaints by individuals who come across child pornography on the internet; approximately 500 complaints a month are recorded. The police can remove certain material from a site.

INDIGENOUS PEOPLES/ ETHNIC MINORITIES
The canton of Jura is located in the northeast of the country. It was created on separation from a larger canton - Bern - in 1979 in an attempt to attenuate the language and religious differences between the German Protestants who remained in what is now Bern and the Roman Catholic Jurassians, of mainly French origin. There is still some tension between the two groups, as some Germans remained in the south of Jura. Furthermore, not all the Francophone and Catholic inhabitants were included in the new canton, causing conflict between the cantons of Jura and Bern.

MIGRANTS/REFUGEES
At the end of 2002, the country sheltered some 44,200 refugees and asylum-seekers. This figure included very few people who had officially been granted the status of refugee or asylum-seeker. In that year, the submission of requests for refuge or asylum increased by 27 per cent over the previous year. Most of the requests were from former Yugoslavian, Turkish, Bosnian and Iraqi citizens.

The federal office for refugees assessed over 21,000 cases during 2002, granting asylum to 8 per cent, 4 per cent less than in 2001. Many of the applications were not investigated and some 3,200 people were deported because the Swiss Government considered that the situation in their countries of origin had returned to normal and that their personal security was not compromised.

Foreign workers are mostly of Spanish, Portuguese, Turkish and Italian origin, in addition to some refugees from the Balkans or Iraq that have arrived in the country over the past 50 years. Towards the end of the 1960s, citizens organized some groups to defend their rights.

DEATH PENALTY
The death penalty was abolished for ordinary crimes in 1942, and the last execution was in 1944. Abolition for any type of crime finally came into force in 1992.

---

[21] Throughout the 18th century, a series of popular revolts against the urban oligarchy called for the reform of the Swiss Constitution. In March 1798, the Old Confederation fell under pressure from Napoleon's army. The Helvetic Republic was proclaimed 'whole and indivisible' with sovereignty for the people. Between the unitary Republic and the 1848 Federal Constitution, Switzerland was shaken by coups, popular revolts, and civil wars. The new federal pact marked a final victory for liberalism in the country. Two legislative bodies were established guaranteeing the rights of the small Catholic cantons.

[22] A state monopoly was created for custom duties and coin minting, while weights and measures were standardized, so satisfying the industrial and commercial bourgeoisie's economic requirements. The 1848 Constitution thus removed the obstacles to capitalist expansion.

[23] Nepotism and the concentration of capital benefited only the few and fuelled growing opposition to the institutional system. The 1874 Constitution partially addressed these issues, and introduced the mechanism of referendum as an element of direct democracy.

[24] Expansion of the home labor system delayed workers' organization as the country industrialized. The Swiss Workers' Federation, created in 1873, had only 3,000 members, and the Swiss Workers' Union, which replaced it in 1880, only exceeded this figure ten years later. The first achievement of the workers' movement was factory legislation, passed by parliament in 1877. The working day was limited to 11 hours with improved working conditions, until then men, women and children worked 14 hours without even basic hygiene and safety conditions.

[25] In 1888 the creation of the Socialist Party prompted liberals in 1894 and conservatives in 1894 and 1912 to organize all over the country. For several decades, the Socialist Party's main demand was the incorporation of proportional representation.

[26] In 1910, 15 per cent of the workers in Switzerland were foreign. Many were anarchists and socialists who had suffered persecution in their own countries and they encouraged radical positions in the workers' movement.

[27] World War I brought great internal tensions to Switzerland, especially between the French and German-speaking regions. Under the leadership of Ulrich Wile, the Swiss army cooperated with Germany. Tension only decreased after the French victory, when Switzerland formally approached the allies and became a member of the League of Nations. The 1918 general strike, although lifted three days later under pressure from the armed forces, led the bourgeoisie to form an anti-Socialist bloc. That year proportional representation was introduced.

[28] The elections in 1919 marked the end of the liberal hegemony, in place since 1848. The Socialists obtained 20 per cent of the vote, leading liberals to ally with the peasants who had 14 per cent, while the conservatives became the second power in the Federal Council.

[29] The 48-hour week was included in factory legislation, while in 1925 an article on old-age pensions was added to the constitution. Assistance to the unemployed improved and collective work contracts became more common.

[30] During World War II, the European powers recognized Swiss armed neutrality and it kept out of the conflict.

[31] After the War, the West reproached Switzerland for its links with Nazi Germany, and the USSR refused to re-establish diplomatic relations, broken off in 1918. However, the country's financial power paved the way for its return to the international community. During the Cold War, Switzerland sided with the West but did not join the UN, in order to maintain its neutrality.

[32] The Swiss economy expanded greatly during the postwar period. The chemical, food, and machinery exporting industries became large transnational corporations. In 1973 Switzerland was placed fourth in direct foreign capital investments, after the US, France, and Britain.

[33] The Swiss economic expansion attracted workers from Italy, Spain and other southern European countries. Between 1945 and 1974 the number of immigrants rose from 5 to 17 per cent. Anti-immigrant feeling was demonstrated in several referenda and the 1974-1976 crises forced several thousands of people back to their countries.

[34] Due to its political neutrality, Switzerland did not join the European Economic Community in 1957. However, it has been a member of EFTA (European Free Trade Association) since 1960.

[35] In 1959, the socialists joined the Federal Council with two representatives. Since then the Executive has remained practically unchanged with 80 per cent of the electorate represented in government.

[36] The population became less interested in elections because Switzerland was mainly governed by political agreements. In 1979 participation was below 50 per cent.

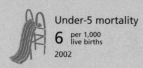
Under-5 mortality
6 per 1,000 live births
2002

Aid
0.32% Official development assistance as % of donors' GNI
2002

Maternal mortality
7 per 100,000 live births
2000

PROFILE

ENVIRONMENT

A small landlocked state in continental Europe, Switzerland is a mountainous country made up of three natural regions. To the northwest, on the French border, are the Jura mountains, an agricultural and industrial area. Industry is concentrated in the Mitteland, a sub-Alpine depression between the Jura and the Alps, with numerous lakes of glacial origin. It is also an agricultural and cattle-raising region. The Alps cover more than half of the territory and extend in a west-east direction with peaks of over 4,000 meters. The main activities of this region are dairy farming and tourism.

SOCIETY

Peoples: Two-thirds of the population are of German origin, while 18 per cent and 13 per cent are French and Italian, respectively. 17.1 per cent of the country's citizens or permanent residents are Italian, from former Yugoslavia, Portuguese, German, Turkish or other nationalities. **Religions:** 47.1 per cent Catholic, 40 per cent Protestant, 2.2 per cent Muslim, 1 per cent Orthodox Christian. **Languages:** German, French and Italian. A very small minority (0.4 per cent) in certain parts of the Grisons canton to the east speak Rhaeto-Romanic (or Romansch), of Latin origin.
Main Political Parties: Freethinking Democratic Party, Democratic Union of the Center (Swiss People's Party); Social Democratic Party; Christian Democratic People's Party; Green Party of Switzerland (ecologist). **Main Social Organizations:** The Swiss Federation of Trade Unions; the Confederation of Christian Trade Unions; the Federation of Swiss Employees' Societies; environmentalist and anti-economic globalization organizations.

THE STATE

Official Name: Confoederatio Helvetica (Romansch); Schweizerische Eidgenossenschaft (German); Confederation Suisse (French); Confederazione Svizzera (Italian).
Administrative Divisions: 20 Cantons, 6 Sub-Cantons.
Capital: Bern (administrative) 320,000 people; Lausanne (judicial) 114,600 (2003). **Other Cities:** Zurich 958,100 people; Geneva 172,900; Basel 163,600 (2000). **Government:** Parliamentary republic with strong direct democracy. Joseph Deiss, Federal President since January 2004; Samuel Schmid, First Vice President since January 2004. The Federal Assembly (Legislature) has two chambers: the National Council, with 200 members, and the Council of States, with 46 members. The Federal Council (executive collegiate), made of 7 members appointed by the United Federal Assembly for a 4-year term. The presidency rotates each year among the coalition in power's councillors. **National Holiday:** 1 August, Foundation of the Swiss Confederation (1291). **Armed Forces:** 3,400 regular troops (1995) 28,000 annual conscripts (15-week courses). Other: 480,000 Civil Defense.

[37] The 1980s saw new groups arise, including the feminist movement and campaigners against nuclear power, which in 1981 incorporated equal rights for men and women in the Constitution - as well as violent demonstrations by juvenile groups against the consumer society.
[38] Women gained the right to vote in 1971, but some cantons retained male-only suffrage until 1985. In 1984, Elisabeth Kopp became the first minister.
[39] Increased poverty amid the wellbeing of the majority, and rising numbers of immigrants, encouraged the growth of the extreme right. The small Swiss Democratic Party and the Party of Drivers, xenophobic and opposed to social policies, gained support in the early 1990s.

[40] In May 1992, a plebiscite approved Switzerland's integration into the IMF and World Bank. In June 1993, Parliament approved the idea of incorporating Swiss troops into the UN peacekeeping forces. This represented a change in the traditional policy of Swiss neutrality. However, most voted against this proposal in a 1994 referendum.
[41] In July 1997, Swiss banks - the targets of international lawsuits filed by individuals - released a list of names of account-holders with funds untouched since World War II. Most of these belonged to Jews who had been exterminated by the Nazis. The World Jewish Congress, the main plaintiff, said the presentation was only a symbolic gesture compared with the profit the banks had made by holding the money for 50 years.

[42] A scandal that involved the embezzlement of millions of dollars by a former intelligence officer for organizing a clandestine army led the Government to suspend the military intelligence chief on charges of masterminding the operation. Defense Minister Adolf Ogi was in charge of the investigation.
[43] Under Ogi's leadership, the Democratic Union of the Center (also known as the Swiss People's Party) won 44 of the 200 parliamentary seats in the October 1999 elections. The Social Democratic Party also won 51 seats, the Freethinking-Democratic Party won 43 seats, while the Christian Democrat People's Party won 35 seats. The four parties formed the Confederation, which has an annual rotating presidency, held by Ogi beginning in January 2000.
[44] A 1998 government report established that antisemitism had re-emerged in Switzerland due to the controversy over its relations with Nazi Germany and also over the question of what Swiss banks had done with the accounts of the Holocaust victims. In January 2000, a study revealed that 16 per cent of the Swiss population had antisemitic views, an increase during the previous decade.
[45] On taking office as President in January 2001, Social Democrat Moritz Leuenberger faced serious criticisms from the press and politicians, mainly because of the Government's crack-down on anti-capitalist protesters who surrounded the World Economic Forum meeting of world economic and business leaders in Davos, a winter resort where the conference had been held annually since 1971.
[46] In March 2001, a referendum overwhelmingly rejected the 'Yes to Europe' proposal that had been presented by the Socialist Party and youth groups, with 77 per cent voting against. The governing coalition opposed the plan, saying that negotiations to become an EU member should not begin before the 2003-2007 legislative period.
[47] A new referendum in June approved a measure allowing Swiss soldiers to carry weapons during peace missions abroad. The electorate also decided that the armed forces could cooperate in military training exercises under NATO. That month, Swiss troops were serving in Kosovo and were themselves protected by Austrian troops because they were not allowed to carry weapons. The Government wanted its army to be able to work on equal footing with the other NATO forces.

[48] In 2001 the Swiss economy was shaken by restructuring measures, causing thousands of layoffs, with unemployment reaching 2 per cent. In October, Swissair, the country's flagship airline, filed for bankruptcy protection after an expansion plan failed. The Government, banks and several private companies launched a multi-million-dollar rescue package to create a new national airline, arising from Swissair regional subsidiary Crossair. Kaspar Villiger, of the Freethinking-Democratic Party, took office as President.
[49] In 2002, 72 per cent of the population voted in favor of legalizing abortion.
[50] That same year, 55 per cent voted to join the UN and the country became the 190th member of the organization.
[51] The Bergier Commission (made up of nine members from Switzerland, UK, US and Israel) which had been established in 1996 by the Swiss Parliament to investigate the country's relationship with the Axis powers, reported that the Swiss authorities had held secret talks with Nazi Germany that helped prolong World War II, that it had refused to give refuge to thousands of Jews - although aware of the existence of concentration camps - and contributed to the expansion of the Nazi economy through the establishment of commercial and financial agreements with Germany.
[52] In 2003 an initiative to reform national legislation on asylum was rejected by a small majority. This initiative would have made the Swiss asylum system one of the most restrictive in the industrialized world.
[53] During 2003, both the Commission for the Prevention of Torture (CPT) and Amnesty International voiced their concern over police abuse of foreigners. That same year a report denounced violence and racist insults against asylum-seekers. Complaints of maltreatment of minors and of people in police custody were also reported. The CPT stated that the way in which certain police operations were conducted could often result in inhuman and degrading treatment.
[54] Amnesty International criticized police behavior with demonstrators near Geneva and Lausanne in June 2003. This led AI to request guarantees for the welfare of demonstrators at the World Economic Forum in Switzerland in January 2004.
[55] Ironically, that same year the 60th UN Human Rights session was held in Geneva. ∎

Syria / Suriyah

Population:	18,650,334
Area:	185,180 km²
Capital:	Damascus
Currency:	Syrian pound
Language:	Arabic

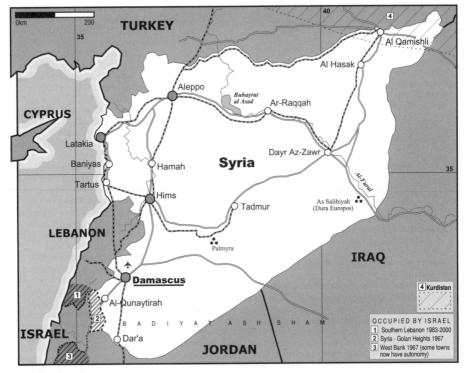

S yria was once the name for the entire region between the peninsulas of Anatolia (Turkey) and Sinai, including the fertile crescent. Ancient civilizations coveted the territory: the Egyptians wanted it as a port, while the Persians considered the region a bridge to their plans for a universal empire.

2   Between the 12th and 7th centuries BC, the Phoenician civilization developed on the central coastal stretch of the territory; a society of sailors and traders without expansionist aims. Phoenician cities were always independent, although some exercised temporary hegemony over others, and they developed the world's first commercial economy.

3   The Phoenicians invented an alphabet, constructed ocean-going ships, practised large-scale ceramic and textile manufacturing, expanded and systematized geography, sailing around the coast of Africa. Their propagation throughout the Mediterranean helped form what would later be called 'Western civilization', of which the Greeks were the main exponents.

4   After the death of Alexander the Great in 323 BC, his vast empire was divided and Syria became the center of a Seleucidan state (named for Seleucus Nicator, one of Alexander's generals) that

initially stretched as far as India. The eastern part was later lost to the Parthians. In the Roman era the province of Syria was a border zone constantly shaken by fierce local wars.

5   The Arabization of the territory was carried out by the Ummaia Caliphs, who, between the years 660 and 750, turned Damascus (Dimashq) into the capital of the empire (see Saudi Arabia), and fostered a strong national spirit. When the Abbas defeated the Ummaias, the capital was transferred to Baghdad, where the new caliphs enjoyed greater support. Although still economically and culturally important, the loss of political power proved significant in the 11th century: when Europeans invaded during the Crusades, the caliphs of Baghdad reacted with indifference. Local emirs were left to their own resources, and disagreements among them allowed a small Christian force to conquer the area, leading to 200 years of occupation.

6   In the 13th century, the Egyptians initiated the process of driving out the Europeans. One result was that Syria became a virtual Egyptian province and center stage for a confrontation with Mongol invaders. In the 16th century, the country became a part of the Ottoman Empire.

7   The Crusaders left behind a significant Christian community, especially with the Maronites, serving as sufficient cause for European interference from the

17th century onwards. The Egyptian Khedive Muhammad (Mehemet) Ali conquered Syria in 1831, and heavy taxes and compulsory military service provoked revolt among both Christian and Muslim communities. The European powers used the repression of Christians as an excuse for intervention. Ali's offensive was suppressed and the 'protection of Syrian Christians' was entrusted to the French. A withdrawal of Egyptian troops took place in 1840, along with the restoration of Ottoman domination and the establishment of Christian missions and schools subsidized by Europeans.

8   In 1858, Maronite Christians gathered in the mountainous region between Damascus and Jerusalem rebelled against the ruling class and eliminated the traditional system of land ownership. Their Muslim neighbors, particularly the Druze, moved to repress the movement before it spread further, triggering a conflict that culminated in the deaths of a large number of Christians in June 1860.

9   A month later, French troops disembarked in Beirut and forced the Turkish Government to create a separate province called 'Little Lebanon'. This was to be governed by a Christian appointed by the Sultan but with the approval of the European powers, with its own police force, and traditional privileges were abolished in the territory. The social conflict thus became a confrontation between

confessional groups with the Christians in 'Little Lebanon' placed in a position of superiority over the local Muslim population.

10   When an Arab rebellion broke out during World War I (see Saudi Arabia, Jordan and Iraq), Emir Faisal was proclaimed king of Syria. At the time French and British intentions were unknown, but the Sykes-Picot agreement divided the fertile crescent giving Syria (with Lebanon) to France, and Palestine (including Jordan) and Iraq to Britain.

11   In 1920, France occupied Syria, forcing Faisal to retreat. Two months later, Syria was divided into five states: Greater Lebanon (adding other regions to the province of 'Little Lebanon'), Damascus, Aleppo, Djabal Druza and Alawis (Latakia). The latter four were reunified in 1924.

12   A Syrian President and Parliament were elected in 1932, but France made it clear that autonomy was unacceptable. This attitude engendered political agitation and confrontation, which only ended with a 1936 agreement with the French. France recognized certain Syrian demands, chiefly reunification with Lebanon. However, the French Government never ratified the agreement, and this led to new waves of violence, which culminated in the 1939 resignation of the Syrian President and a French order to suspend the 1930 Constitution that governed both Syria and Lebanon.

LAND USE

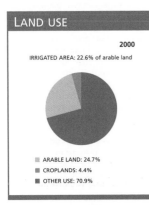

2000

IRRIGATED AREA: 22.6% of arable land

- ■ ARABLE LAND: 24.7%
- ■ CROPLANDS: 4.4%
- ■ OTHER USE: 70.9%

Life expectancy
71.9 years
2000-2005

GNI per capita
$1,130
2002

Literacy
74% total adult rate
2000

PROFILE

ENVIRONMENT

To the west, near the sea, lies the Lebanon mountain range. To the south there are semi-desert plateaus and to the north low plateaus along the basin of the Euphrates River. Farming - grains, grapes and fruit - is concentrated in the western lowlands that receive adequate rainfall. In the south, the volcanic plateaus of the Djebel Druze are extremely fertile farmlands, as are some of the oases surrounding the desert, the main one being that of Damascus. Cotton and wool are exported. Exploitation of oil fields is the country's chief industry.

SOCIETY

Peoples: Syrians are mostly Arabs, with minority ethnic groups in the north: Kurds, Turks and Armenians. At the end of 2002, more than 400,000 Palestinian refugees living in the country were registered with UN agencies. The Jewish population was authorized to emigrate in 1992.

Religions: Mainly Muslims, mostly Sunni, followed by Alamites, Shi'a and Ismailites. Also minor communities of eastern Christian religions.

Languages: Arabic (official). Minority groups speak their own languages.

Main Political Parties: The Ba'ath Arab Socialist Party, founded in Damascus in 1947 by Michel Aflaq, including the National Progressive Front and other minor parties. The armed political-religious opposition is represented by the Muslim Brotherhood, a fundamentalist Sunni sect. Communist Party of Syria, (government controlled); Arab Socialist Unity, (government controlled); Socialist Unity Movement, (government controlled); Arab Socialist Party, (government controlled); Socialist Unionist Democratic Party (government controlled).

Main Social Organizations: The General Federation of Labor Unions unites ten workers' federations; Committee for the Defense of Democratic Freedoms and Human Rights in Syria.

THE STATE

Official Name: Al-Jumhouriya al Arabiya as-Suriya.
Administrative Divisions: 14 Districts.
Capital: Damascus (Dimashq) 2,228,000 people (2003).
Other Cities: Aleppo (Halab) 2,319,800 people; Homs (Hims) 698,800; Latakia 391,300; Hamah 350,900 (2000).
Government: Bashar al-Assad, President since July 2000. Muhammad Naji al-Otari, Prime Minister since September 2003. Unicameral Legislature: People's Assembly, with 250 members.
National Holidays: 17 April, Independence Day (1946); 16 November, Revolution Day (1978); 25 May, Resistance and Liberation Day (2000).
Armed Forces: 421,000 troops (1996). Other: 8,000 Gendarmes.

---

[13] In 1941, French and British troops occupied the region to flush out Nazi collaborators. In 1943 Chikri al-Quwatli was elected President of Syria and Bechara al-Kuri President of Lebanon. Bechara al-Kuri proposed elimination of the mandate provisions from the constitution; however, he and his cabinet members were imprisoned by the ever-present French troops. Violent demonstrations followed in both Lebanon and Syria, and the British pressed for withdrawal of the French. In March 1946, the UN finally ordered the European forces to withdraw and the end of the French mandate was declared.

[14] In 1948 Syrian troops fought to prevent the partition of Palestine, and in 1956 joined Egypt in the battle against Israeli, French

and British aggression. This aggression was the answer to Egyptian President Gamal Abdel Nasser's decision to nationalize the Suez Canal.

[15] In 1958, Syria joined Egypt in founding the United Arab Republic, but Nasser's ambitious integration project collapsed in 1961. Ten years later the scheme was reactivated with greater flexibility, and the Federation of Arab Republics was created including Libya.

[16] In 1963, after a revolution, the Ba'ath Arab Socialist Party, founded in 1947 by Christian leader Michel Aflaq, came to power. Its main tenet was that the Arab countries were merely 'regions' of a larger Arab Nation. In November 1970, General Hafez al-Assad became President. He launched a modernization campaign, including a series of

social and economic changes. The subsequent party congress named Assad party leader and proposed 'accelerating the stages towards socialist transformation of different sectors'. This guideline was adopted and became part of the new constitution which was approved in 1973.

[17] Syria took an active part in the Arab-Israeli wars of 1967 and 1973, during which Israeli troops occupied the Golan Heights. Syria also resisted US efforts to impose a 'settlement' in the Middle East, together with Algeria, Iraq, Libya, Yemen and the Palestine Liberation Organization (PLO). They also opposed the Camp David agreement (see Egypt). Syrian troops formed a major part of the Arab Deterrent Force that intervened in Lebanon in 1976 to prevent partition of the country.

[18] In 1978, the Syrian and Iraqi branches of the Ba'ath Party drew closer, but negotiations for creation of a single state disintegrated. In late 1979, at the congress of the Syrian branch of the Ba'ath Party, the Muslim Brotherhood (a right-wing Islamic movement) was harshly censured and labeled 'Zionist agents'.

[19] In 1982 the army launched an offensive; thousands of Brotherhood members were killed and the Syrian Government blamed Iraq for arming the rebels. In April, the border between the two countries was closed.

[20] The virtual alliance formed in 1980 between Saudi Arabia, Iraq and Jordan and tensions between those three countries and Syria were exacerbated by the outbreak of the Iran-Iraq War. Assad charged Iraq with being the aggressor and diverting attention from what he called the major regional issue - the Palestinian question. Toward the end of the year, Syrian accusations of Jordanian support for the Brotherhood brought the two countries to the verge of war. The mediation of Saudi prince Abdalla ibn Abdul-Aziz averted armed conflict.

[21] In 1981 the 'missile crisis' broke out in Syria, when the Christian Phalangist Movement sought to extend their area of authority to include the region around the Lebanese city of Zahde. An Arab Deterrent Force, led by Syria, attempted to prevent the advance. Syria installed Soviet missiles, triggering an Israeli reaction. The crisis was finally averted, but in 1983 Israel invaded Lebanon, and destroyed the Syrian missile bases. Syrian forces (approximately 30,000 troops) remained in Lebanon and only agreed to retreat on condition that all Israeli troops were

previously withdrawn.

[22] In mid-1983 there was a crisis between the Syrian authorities and the PLO leadership. This encouraged Syria to support the Palestinian groups opposed to Yasser Arafat's leadership. The fall in oil prices further aggravated the economic problems caused by the war which forced the Government to set up strict austerity measures in 1984.

[23] In 1985, President al-Assad won a new seven-year term with 99.8 per cent of the vote (a similar percentage to those of the 1971 and 1978 elections). In spite of this, in 1987 a political crisis broke out which forced Prime Minister Abdul Rauf al-Kassem to resign amid charges of corruption.

[24] In May 1990, Syria finally re-established diplomatic relations with Egypt. Some observers considered this a result of a reduction in Soviet military support to Damascus.

[25] When Iraq invaded Kuwait, Syria immediately sided with the anti-Iraqi alliance and sent troops to Saudi Arabia. Diplomatic relations with the US improved noticeably. During the crisis Syria increased its influence over Lebanon and strengthened the allied government in that country; they were also successful in disarming most of the autonomous militias.

[26] In May 1991 Syria and Lebanon signed a cooperation agreement whereby Syria recognized Lebanon as an independent and separate state, for the first time since both countries gained independence from France.

[27] On 2 December 1991, al-Assad was re-elected for the fourth time, by 99.98 per cent of the vote, in elections in which he was the sole candidate. A fortnight later, the Government announced the pardon of 2,800 political prisoners, members of the Muslim Brotherhood.

[28] In 1992, the Government allowed the emigration of 4,000 Jews.

[29] New legislation favored investments in the private sector, which saw significant growth between 1991 and 1993.

[30] Syria stayed away from the first stages of the regional peace process, which facilitated the establishment of a limited autonomy for Palestine and the signing of agreements between Israel and Jordan in July 1994. In January, a 'historic' meeting took place between US President Clinton and al-Assad in Geneva and in September, the Syrian Minister of Foreign Affairs was interviewed for the first time on Israeli television.

Under-5 mortality
28 per 1,000 live births
2002

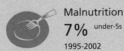
Malnutrition
7% under-5s
1995-2002

Debt service
3.4% exports of goods and services
2001

Maternal mortality
160 per 100,000 live births
2000

[31] In June 1995, official negotiations with Israel failed to return the Golan Heights to Syria, as Tel Aviv wanted to maintain limited military presence in the region indefinitely. In October, a Hizbullah ambush of Israeli troops in southern Lebanon complicated negotiations again.

[32] As part of a policy to stimulate the Syrian private sector economy, key state sectors, including electricity generation, cement production and pharmaceuticals were opened up to private capital.

[33] In November 1997, Damascus unexpectedly strengthened relations with Baghdad at the threat of fresh US military intervention in Iraq - a strategy designed to work against the rapidly consolidating Turkish-Israeli alliance. Iran joined the Syrian-Iraqi negotiations on security issues in April 1998.

[34] Al-Assad was re-elected for his seventh consecutive five-year presidential period in 1999. In March 2000, all 37 cabinet members resigned and Muhammad Mustafa Mero, a veteran leader of the Ba'ath party, was appointed the new Premier.

[35] The sudden death of al-Assad on 10 June plunged the country into mourning for the only leader most Syrians had ever known. He was succeeded by his son, Bashar al-Assad, who took office in July.

[36] Among the first measures of the new President was the April 2001 authorization to establish a private banking system and shortly after, a private radio station was granted broadcast rights for music only. No political content was allowed.

[37] In May, Pope John Paul II visited Syria, and at the reception ceremony al-Assad strongly criticized Israel, comparing the suffering of the Arabs to the persecution of Christ. In response, John Paul II called upon all parties in the conflict to seek a new understanding, including respect among Christians, Muslims and Jews.

[38] With the unanimous support of Asian and African countries, Syria obtained a seat at the UN Security Council in October 2001, in spite of Israel's opposition. Washington's strategy after the 11 September 2001 attacks prevailed in order to convince the most influential Arab countries to join its global campaign against terrorism.

[39] Damascus engaged intensely in international relations in 2001. After heavy pressure from the Lebanese government, Syrian troops withdrew from Beirut and were deployed in other parts of Lebanon. In August, Syria's Premier Miro visited Iraq in the first high-level visit to that country since relations had cooled as a result of Syrian support for Iran during the 1980-1988 Iran-Iraq war. British Prime Minister Tony Blair visited Damascus in November to try to rally Syrian support for the US-led anti-terrorism campaign. However, Blair and al-Assad could not reach agreement on the definition of 'terrorism' and the British leader returned to his country empty-handed.

[40] The November release of dozens of political prisoners belonging to the Muslim Brotherhood, after more than two decades behind bars, was applauded by Amnesty International as a 'satisfactory step towards respect for human rights in Syria'. Nearly all the prisoners had been kept incommunicado in degrading conditions and subjected to torture and mistreatment.

[41] In April 2002, the Syrian radar station in Lebanon was bombed by Israeli aircraft in response to an attack by Hizbullah guerrillas. The offensive raised fear of a military escalation which finally did not take place.

[42] In May, US senior official John Bolton included Syria in a list of states that made up the so-called 'axis of evil', accusing Damascus of trying to obtain weapons of mass destruction. In April 2003, when the Iraq invasion was already in progress, Washington threatened Syria with economic and diplomatic sanctions, alleging that it was helping fugitive Iraqis. The Syrian Government denied US allegations.

[43] In January 2004, al-Assad became the first Syrian leader to visit Turkey in a trip that marked the end of frosty relations with Ankara.

[44] On 8 March, the Committee for the Defense of Democratic Freedoms and Human Rights in Syria organized a rare protest in Damascus to demand democracy and freedom for political prisoners. Two members of the organization, Ahmad Jazen and Hassan Wattfa, were arrested and spent two months in prison. Akhtam Naisse, President of the Committee, was arrested on 14 April after issuing a declaration in which he accused the authorities of arresting more than 1,000 Kurds in an operation launched against that minority group and demanded the Government to put an end to 'illegal and terrorist practices'.

[45] Also in April, following an explosion in a disused UN building in Damascus, in unclear circumstances, one civilian, one policeman and two of the four activists involved were killed in the subsequent shooting. The Government blamed the attack on Islamic fundamentalists.

[46] In May, the US imposed economic sanctions on the country over what it called Syria's support for terrorism and failure to stop militants entering Iraq. In spite of Washington's decision, the EU announced it was sending a trade delegation to Damascus to improve co-operation in the export of oil and gas to Europe. ∎

IN FOCUS

ENVIRONMENTAL CHALLENGES
The dumping of toxic substances pollutes Syria's water and threatens the scarce drinking water resources. Overgrazing, desertification and soil erosion pose further environmental problems which affect large regions of the country.

WOMEN'S RIGHTS
Women have been able to vote and stand for election, subject to conditions and restrictions, since 1953. They hold 9.6 per cent of seats in Parliament and constitute 7 per cent of judges and 10 per cent of lawyers. Domestic violence occurs but there are no figures; very few cases are reported and victims are reluctant to seek assistance outside the family. There are a few private shelters for battered women. Rape is a felony; however, there are no laws against spousal rape. Prostitution and sexual harassment are prohibited by law. The Constitution provides protection against labor and salary discrimination. The punishment for adultery by a woman is double that for a man committing the same crime. Polygamy is legal.

CHILDREN
Primary education is compulsory and school net enrolment rates are high; 94 per cent for girls and 99 per cent for boys in 2000. However, geographic disparities persist. The quality of health services is poor. The drop-out rates for girls are remarkably high.

Military service is compulsory, even for boys still under 18 years old, including those who were born in other countries.

Security forces have broken into Kurdish schools, arresting adults and even torturing them.

Medical care is provided for children until the age of 18. The law provides for severe penalties for those found guilty of abuses against children. Child trafficking and prostitution are rare.

INDIGENOUS PEOPLES/ ETHNIC MINORITIES
Alawis gave themselves this name which means 'those who adhere to the teachings of Ali', the son-in-law of the Prophet Muhammad. They were formerly called the *Nusayris*, a name that accentuates their differences from traditional Islamic practices. This name is still used by those who are unsympathetic to them.

Kurds are the largest minority group. The Government constantly victimizes them and violates their rights, preventing them from fully enjoying their own culture and language. Their freedom of expression is restricted and they allegedly suffer violations of their basic human rights.

MIGRANTS/REFUGEES
At the end of 2002, Syria hosted more than 482,000 refugees and asylum-seekers. These included 400,000 Palestinians who were registered with UN agencies. The Syrian Government estimated the number of Iraqis who were not registered with the UNHCR by the end of 2002 to range between 40,000 and 45,000, many of whom could be refugees. On the other hand, there were around 200,000 Kurds who lived in the country in a refugee-like situation. At the end of the year, a government commission prepared to receive a million Iraqi refugees on the Syrian border as a result of the war against Iraq, and asked the UN for help in supporting the civil victims of the war. UNHCR continues to work in two refugee camps in northeastern Syria, the Al-Hawl and Al-Hasakah camps, which had accommodated more than 15,000 refugees after the Gulf War in 1991. Nearly 4,000 Syrians sought asylum in industrialized countries, mainly in Western Europe and the US. About half of them filed their requests in Germany.

DEATH PENALTY
Syria maintains the death penalty as legal punishment, even for ordinary crimes.

Tajikistan / Tojikiston

Population:	6,356,089
Area:	143,100 km²
Capital:	Dushanbe (Dusanbe)
Currency:	Rouble
Language:	Tajik

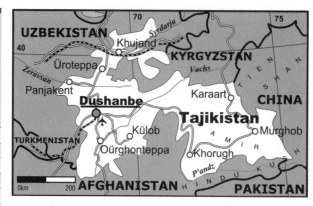

Around 500 BC, Central Asia and southern Siberia's first centers of settled civilization arose in what is now Tajikistan. The Bactrian State was located in the upper tributaries of the Amu Darya. In the Zeravshan river basin and the Kashkadarya river valley lay the nucleus of another State, Sogdiana. The inhabitants of these early civilizations built villages, with adobe and stone houses all along the rivers that they used for irrigating their crops. These included wheat, barley and millet, and a variety of fruits. Navigation was well developed and the cities that lay along the route of the caravans uniting Persia, China and India became important trading centers.

[2] In the 6th century BC these lands were annexed by the Persian Achaemenid Empire. In the 4th century BC, Alexander the Great conquered Bactria and Sogdiana. With the fall of his empire in the 3rd century, the Greco-Bactrian State and the Kingdom of Kushan emerged, and subsequently fell to the onslaught of the advancing Yuechzhi and Tojar steppe tribes. In the 4th and 5th centuries AD, Sogdiana was invaded by the Eftalites, and in the 6th and 7th centuries, by Central Asian Turkish peoples. In the 7th century, Tajikistan came under the control of the Arab Caliphate. After its demise, the region was incorporated into the Tahirid and Samanid kingdoms. In the 9th and 10th centuries, the Tajik people emerged as an identifiable ethnic group.

[3] From the 10th to the 13th centuries AD, Tajikistan formed part of the Gaznevid and Qarakhanid empires, as well as the realm of the Shah of Khwarezm. In the early 13th century, Tajikistan was conquered by Genghis Khan's Mongol Tatars. In 1238, Tarabi, a Tajik artisan, led a popular revolt. From the 14th to the 17th centuries, the Tajiks were under the control of the Timurids and the Uzbek Shaybanid dynasty. From the 17th to the 19th centuries, the land was divided into small fiefdoms whose chieftains alternately revolted against the khans of Bukhara.

[4] In the 1860s and 1870s, the Russian Empire conquered Central Asia, and annexed the northern part of Tajikistan. The Tajik population of Kuliab, Guissar, Karateguin and Darvaz became a province (Eastern Bukhara) of the Bukhara Khanate. Oppression by the Russian bureaucracy and the local feudal lords triggered a wave of peasant revolts toward the end of the 19th century and beginning of the 20th century, the most important of which was the 1885 uprising led by Vose.

[5] In 1916, during World War I, the population of Central Asia and Kazakhstan revolted over the mobilization of their people for rearguard duty with the Russian army. After the triumph of the Bolshevik Revolution in October 1917, Soviet power was established in northern Tajikistan. In April 1918, this territory became a part of the Soviet Republic of Turkistan. Nevertheless, a large number of Tajiks remained under the power of the Emirate of Bukhara, which existed until 1921. In early 1921, the Red Army took Dushanbe, but in February it was forced to withdraw from eastern Bukhara.

[6] Having broken Alim Khan's resistance in 1922, Soviet power was proclaimed throughout Tajikistan. On 16 November 1929, Tajikistan became a federated republic of the Soviet Union. In the 1920s and 1930s, land and water reforms were carried out. The collectivization of agriculture was followed by industrialization, and the so-called 'cultural revolution' campaign.

[7] After World War II, the Soviet regime carried out a series of large construction projects, including a water system linked to the neighboring republic of Uzbekistan, meant to develop the region's cotton crops. In the 1970s and 1980s, the effects of mismanagement and economic stagnation were felt in Tajikistan, one of the poorest regions in the USSR. It suffered a high rate of unemployment, especially among the young, who made up most of the population.

[8] From 1985, the changes promoted by President Mikhail Gorbachev gave way to the expression of long-suppressed ethnic and religious friction in Tajikistan. In February 1990, there were violent incidents in the capital, with more than 30 people killed.The Government decreed a state of emergency, which remained in effect during that year's Supreme Soviet (Parliament) elections, in which the Communist Party won 90 per cent of the available seats. Muslims and Democrats called for the dissolution of the Soviet, because the elections had been held while a state of emergency was in effect.

[9] After the February violence, there was a flight of Russian and Ukrainian professionals, forcing half the hospitals, schools and factories to close down, and compounding the country's socio-economic ills.

[10] In August 1990, Parliament passed a vote of no confidence against President Majkamov, accusing him of supporting those responsible for the Moscow coup, and forcing him to resign. He was succeeded by Kadridin Aslonov as interim president of the republic.

[11] In September 1991, Parliament passed the declaration of independence and the new Constitution, decreed a state of emergency and banned the Islamic Revival Party, which pledged a State respectful of political and religious freedoms, but based on Islam, and advocated the enforcement of the

Life expectancy
68.8 years
2000-2005

GNI per capita
$180
2002

Literacy
99% total adult rate
2000

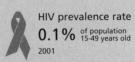

HIV prevalence rate
0.1% of population 15-49 years old
2001

Sharia, the religious, moral and legal Islamic code.

12   Tajikistan's religious revival was stronger than in the rest of the former Soviet Union republics. In the early 1980s, there were 17 mosques; 10 years later there were 128 mosques, 2,800 places of prayer, an Islamic institute and five centers offering religious instruction. Since 1991, the Government has instituted the celebration of several important Muslim holy days.

13   In November 1991, in the first presidential elections Rajmon Nabiev was confirmed in his post by 58 per cent of the vote.

14   On 21 December Tajikistan entered the Commonwealth of Independent States (CIS). At the same time, the Autonomous region of Gorno-Badakhshan requested the status of an autonomous province. Like neighboring Afghanistan, the majority of this region's inhabitants are Shi'a Muslims.

15   In March 1992 large anti-government protests erupted in Dushanbe. These spread outside the capital in April and took on civil war proportions. In this context, a protest demonstration against Nabiev led to his resignation on 8 September. But pro-communist forces in the north launched a major offensive, leading to the fall of the capital and the formation, in December, of a new government controlled by the Popular Front (a paramilitary group). Some 300,000 people fled to other CIS republics and Afghanistan. The persecution and massacre of members of the opposition only diminished in February 1993.

16   Moscow recognized the new regime, led by Imomali Rakhmonov. In March bombing started from Afghanistan and there were incursions of opposition detachments across the frontier controlled by Russian troops. Rakhmonov proposed a draft for a new Constitution, approved by referendum in November. The President was re-elected at the same time, but the Islamic opposition accused the Government of fraud.

17   The civil war officially ended on 27 June 1997, with the signing of a peace agreement between the Government and the opposition - grouped together in the United Tajik Opposition (UTO). The agreement guaranteed the opposition 30 per cent of posts in the cabinet, presence in the legal authorities and an amnesty for all those accused of war crimes.

18   The war caused 20,000 deaths and 600,000 internally displaced people, while another 300,000 fled to Afghanistan, Russia and other CIS countries. The conflict destroyed most of the economy, turning the country into the poorest in the CIS.

IN FOCUS

ENVIRONMENTAL CHALLENGES
Since 1960, irrigated land has increased by 50 per cent, but as in other countries where cotton is the only crop, soil salinity has also risen. Pesticides are overused for farming and industrial pollution affects the air and water. Sewage and drinking water supply systems are inadequate.

WOMEN'S RIGHTS
Women have been able to vote and stand for election since 1924. Women hold 12 of the 97 parliamentary seats. Violence against women is common. The kidnapping of young women who are forced to have sex, and even marry the kidnappers, is frequent. Trafficking of women for sexual exploitation is growing.

CHILDREN
Funds earmarked by the Government are inadequate to maintain the necessary social support system for children. Education is compulsory until 16, but the law is not always enforced. State schools are run down and parents prefer sending their children to private schools or hiring private teachers. One in every eight children works, according to the World Bank.

Healthcare is no longer free, due to legislation changes. The quality and quantity of medical services is extremely limited.

In 1997, cotton production - the main crop - reached only 60 per cent of the projected amount. In February 1998, the Government announced it would speed up privatization programs.

19   Akbar Turayonzoda - second in command in the UTO - returned from exile in Iran to become the first deputy minister. He proposed allowing the Islamic Revival Party to join political life with full rights, including participation in elections. Parliament passed a law banning the creation of parties based on religious movements, and while the President vetoed the law, he made it clear he would not allow an Islamic government in the country.

20   The elections slated for November 1999 went ahead despite strong protests from Usmon, the only opposition candidate. Other candidates could not raise the number of signatures required for them to run for office, and the opposition blamed this on government pressure. Rakhmonov took 96 per cent of the vote.

21   In January 2001, the minimum monthly salary in Tajikistan trebled, reaching slightly more than $1.

According to UNICEF's latest data available*, the under-five mortality rate is 72 per 1,000 live births. Fifteen per cent of newborns are underweight. Sexual exploitation of children, compounded by poverty, is also growing.

INDIGENOUS PEOPLES/ ETHNIC MINORITIES
The largest ethnic minorities are Uzbeks and Russians. Uzbeks and Tajiks have been considered separate nationalities only since 1929, and this differentiation was consolidated in 1991, with the fall of the Soviet Union. Uzbeks are concentrated to the north of the capital, in the Ferghana valley. There are other Uzbek communities in the province of Khatlon, a rural region to the southwest which is one of the poorest in the country. They suffer severe social discrimination and some official restrictions. Their language and culture are considered marginal and are not adequately represented in the political system. Uzbeks do not usually have access to high political posts.

After the peace treaty that ended the civil war was signed in 1997, killings of Uzbeks continued in the Pani district. While the Government has tried to improve relations between Tajiks and Uzbeks, these murders have not been taken to court.

Russians are not oppressed by the Government and are not politically organized. Although they

Approximately 80 per cent of Tajiks lived in poverty, with an average monthly income of about $10. Tajikistan was trying to overcome the effects of civil war and a devastating drought started in 2000.

22   In September 2001, Tajikistan's culture minister, Abdurakhim Rakhimov, was assassinated in Dushanbe. Habib Sanginov, deputy Minister of the Interior, had also been killed in April.

23   That same month, following the terrorist attacks in New York and Washington, Tajikistan offered its support for the anti-terrorism coalition led by the US. In addition, Rakhmonov closed the border with Afghanistan to prevent terrorist infiltration. In February 2002, Tajikistan became the last former soviet republic to join NATO.

24   In November 2002, Boris Gryzlov, Russian Interior Minister, deported 117 Tajik citizens and declared severe measures would be adopted against illegal immigrants. According to estimates, some one million Tajiks emigrate each summer to Russia looking for jobs.

25   With 90 per cent of the vote, a referendum in June approved 50

maintain a group identity, this has not translated into political action.

MIGRANTS/REFUGEES
In 2002 the country harbored 3,500 refugees and asylum seekers, almost all of them Afghans registered at the national migrations bureau - in the Labor and Social Welfare Ministry - as refugees.

That year, more Afghans requested refugee status, but this was refused by the authorities. Also, some 12,000 Afghans were repatriated from Tajikistan, most of them with UNHCR assistance. Some 2,000 Afghans went back to Afghanistan on their own, while 15 family heads were deported.

In 2002 there were 53,000 Tajik refugees, most of them in neighboring countries: 30,000 in Uzbekistan, 12,000 in Turkmenistan, 7,000 in Kyrgyzstan and 4,000 in Kazakhstan.

DEATH PENALTY
It is applicable even for ordinary offenses. In July 2003 Parliament passed a law banning capital punishment for women and reducing the number of cases in which it could apply to men. In April 2004, the President declared a moratorium on the death penalty.

*Latest data available in *The State of the World's Children* and *Childinfo* database,UNICEF, 2004.

amendments to the Constitution, including the potential re-election of Rakhmonov for another double-term (a further 17 years in power), and the suppression of constitutional guarantees of free health care and university education.

26   In July 2003, the deputy president of the Islamic Revival Party (IRP), Shamsiddin Shamsiddinov, was sentenced to 16 years in prison for organizing crime rings and other 'serious' crimes. His party claimed it was a political arrest, rather than religious. Concerned about fundamentalism, Rakhmonov jailed more than 200 members of the radical Hizb ut-Tahrir in 2003, and confiscated 'tons of subversive texts' which promoted the creation of an Islamic caliphate in Central Asia.

27   In March 2004, the UN warned in its annual report on the illegal drug trade that the 6,000 tons of heroin confiscated on the Tajik border with Afghanistan in 2003 - 1,000 times more than in 1996 - are a tiny percentage of the drug shipments that pass from Afghanistan towards Central Asia and Europe. ■

Tanzania / Tanzania

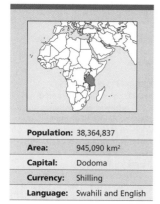

Population:	38,364,837
Area:	945,090 km²
Capital:	Dodoma
Currency:	Shilling
Language:	Swahili and English

The oldest human fossils were found in the Olduvai gorge, in the north of Tanzania. These remains date from millions of years ago, yet little is known about life on most of modern Tanzania's mainland before the 7th century.

² A mercantile civilization, heavily influenced by Arab culture, flourished in this region between 695 and 1550 but was eventually destroyed by Portuguese invaders. A century and a half later, under the leadership of the Sultan of Oman, the Arabs drove out the Portuguese, but the rich cultural and commercial life of past times did not return. As the slave trade grew, Kilwa and Zanzibar became the leading trade centers.

³ Between 1698 and 1830, Zanzibar and the coast were under the rule of the Oman Sultanate, with the Sultan living in Zanzibar. His sons, under British pressure, later split the inherited domain, dividing the old Sultanate in two.

⁴ In the late 19th century a German adventurer set up a company which immediately received imperial endorsement, leasing out the mainland coastal strip to the sultan of Zanzibar. The British had also made a similar deal, so the Berlin Conference, where the European powers distributed Africa among themselves, agreed upon the 'cession of German rights' in favor of Britain.

⁵ The areas of influence were delimited in 1886. Tanganyika, Rwanda and Burundi were recognized as German possessions while Zanzibar formally became a British protectorate in 1890. German troops and British warships joined efforts to stifle a Muslim rebellion on the coast of Tanganyika in 1905.

⁶ After Germany's defeat in World War I, the League of Nations placed Tanganyika under British mandate. Resistance came from traditional chiefs and also from those opposed both to the British and indigenous authorities. The Tanganyika African Association (TAA) was established in 1929 as a forum for trade unionists and co-operative

farmers who opposed British rule. In 1951 the British rulers began to implement a program to remove African homesteaders to make way for post-war British settlers, a policy that swelled an incipient nationalist movement.

⁷ Nationalist feelings were later channeled into TANU (Tanganyika African National Union), a party founded in 1954 by Julius Nyerere, a primary school teacher known by the people as *Mwalimu*, the teacher.

⁸ After seven years of organizing and fighting against racial discrimination and the appropriation of lands by European settlers, independence was achieved in 1961, and Nyerere became President, elected by an overwhelming majority.

⁹ Meanwhile, in Zanzibar, two nationalist organizations, which had been active since the 1930s, merged to form the Afro-Shirazi Party in February 1957. In December 1963, the British transferred power to the Arab minority, and a month later this government was overthrown by

the Afro-Shirazi. In April, Tanganyika and Zanzibar formed the United Republic of Tanzania.

¹⁰ Under Nyerere's leadership, Tanzania based its foreign policy on non-alignment, standing for African unity, and providing unconditional support to liberation movements, particularly FRELIMO in neighboring Mozambique.

¹¹ In February 1967, TANU proclaimed socialism as its objective in the Arusha Declaration, which laid down the principle of self-sufficiency and gave top priority to the development of agriculture, on the basis of communal land ownership, a traditional system known in Swahili as *ujamaa*, which means community.

¹² Ten years later TANU and the Afro-Shirazi Party merged into the Chama Cha Mapinduzi (CCM), which officially incorporated the aim of building socialism on the basis of self-sufficiency.

¹³ In October 1978, Tanzania was invaded by Ugandan troops in an attempt by dictator Idi Amin to distract attention from his internal problems and divert Tanzanian energies from supporting the liberation struggles in Southern Africa. The aggression was repelled in a few weeks, and Tanzanian troops co-operated closely with the Ugandan National Liberation Front to overthrow Idi Amin.

LAND USE

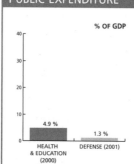

2000

IRRIGATED AREA: 3.2% of arable land

- ARABLE LAND: 4.5%
- CROPLANDS: 1.1%
- OTHER USE: 94.4%

PUBLIC EXPENDITURE

% OF GDP

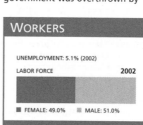

4.9 %
HEALTH & EDUCATION (2000)

1.3 %
DEFENSE (2001)

WORKERS

UNEMPLOYMENT: 5.1% (2002)

LABOR FORCE   **2002**

- FEMALE: 49.0%
- MALE: 51.0%

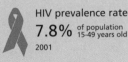
14   The cost of mobilizing the army and maintaining troops in Uganda weighed heavily on the State budget, which was facing serious difficulties by the end of the 1970s. The falling price of Tanzania's main exports; coffee, spices, cotton, pyrethrum and cashew nuts, plus the growing cost of imported products, caused serious financial imbalances.

15   Ujamaa villages were conceived as the nucleus of the Tanzanian economy and were designed to be self-sufficient. Despite Nyerere's enormous efforts, various factors hindered the progress of ujamaa which grew slowly. They continued to depend upon imported foodstuffs and as Government aid was cut, many of them collapsed.

16   In 1983 Edward Sokoine was appointed Prime Minister and immediately launched a campaign against corruption while adopting a more flexible policy towards foreign investment. Sokoine also arranged for Tanzania and Kenya to resume relations that had broken down in 1977 when the East African Economic Community of Tanzania, Kenya and Uganda was dissolved.

17   A national debate was organized to discuss constitutional reform to reorganize the executive power, grant greater political participation to women, strengthen democracy along CCM lines and prohibit more than two successive presidential terms.

18   On 5 November 1985, after 24 years as head of state, President Julius Nyerere passed power on to Ali Hassan Mwinyi, elected with 92.2 per cent of the vote.

19   In 1986, an economic recovery plan went into effect, following IMF and World Bank guidelines. The measures emphasized the reduction of tariff barriers on imports and included incentives for private capital. Agricultural production improved and some industrial enterprises increased their profits.

20   Meanwhile, the ujamaa village model was in crisis due to diminishing yields and to people's increasing resistance to the resettlement, sometimes compulsory, of entire villages. Economic recovery now depended on the loans promised by international institutions in exchange for the introduction of structural reforms.

21   The development of private capital and incentives to create such capital caused new problems. According to UNICEF studies, half the children in the country at that time were

IN FOCUS

ENVIRONMENTAL CHALLENGES
The need to increase exports has led to intensification of farming even in semi-arid areas, causing increasing soil erosion. Forestry continues apace despite the resultant severe desertification. The destruction of coral reefs threatens sea habitats. Animals are threatened by hunting and illegal trade, especially by the ivory trade.

WOMEN'S RIGHTS
Women have been able to vote and stand for election since 1959. In 2000 they held 16 per cent of the seats in parliament and 13 per cent of ministerial posts. By law, 49 of the 296 parliament seats are earmarked for women appointed by the parties. Women comprise 49 per cent of the total labor force, with 90 per cent in agriculture, eight per cent in services and two per cent in industry.

According to UNICEF's latest data available*, some 59 per cent of pregnant women are anemic, and only 36 per cent of births are attended by qualified personnel. This causes a high maternal death rate: 1,500 for every 100,000 births.

Domestic violence is a serious problem, the more so because the law does not ban husbands from mistreating their wives. According to unofficial surveys carried out by women's rights NGOs, more than 60 per cent of women are abused by their spouses.

Between 10 and 18 per cent of women were subjected to female genital mutilation. The proportion rises to 85 per cent in some rural regions. The law bans the practice in women below 18. However, in most regions it is carried out at an early age.

CHILDREN
According to UNICEF's latest data available*, Tanzania is among the 30 countries with the highest under-five mortality rate: 165 per 1,000 live births. Infant mortality stands at 104 per 1,000 live births. Life expectancy at birth is 44.1, due mainly to HIV/AIDS and lack of food.

Approximately 53 per cent of children under-five suffer from malaria. There are two million orphans or abandoned children, most of them as a result of the HIV/AIDS pandemic.

INDIGENOUS PEOPLES/ETHNIC MINORITIES
The people of Zanzibar and Pemba islands, which became part of Tanzania in 1964, are of Arab, African or mixed (Shirazi) descent. Before independence, Arabs dominated trade and political life, in spite of comprising less than 20 per cent of the total population in Zanzibar, and only two per cent of the country's population. Many Tanzanians are Muslim, but not necessarily Arab. Most residents of mainland Tanzania are Christian and speak Swahili. Africans and Arabs on the islands do not always get along, but not necessarily for ethnic reasons.

Both Africans and Arabs are actively separatist, but conficts arise between those who wish to separate from Tanzania and those who do not. Most Arabs would prefer an independent state, in contrast with the African community.

MIGRANTS/REFUGEES
In late 2002 there were some 520,000 refugees in Tanzania: more than 370,000 from Burundi, 140,000 from the Democratic Republic of the Congo, 3,000 from Somalia and Rwanda. There were also 400,000 Burundi nationals living in western Tanzania, not recognized as refugees by the authorities.

Since 1998, the Government has tried to 'encourage' refugee repatriation in several ways. Armed conflicts in Burundi have compromised the safety of refugees and Tanzanian nationals. In 2002, less than 700 refugees were resettled in developed countries such as Canada, Sweden, Norway and the United States, with the help of UNHCR, other international refugee agencies and the governments involved.

DEATH PENALTY
It is still applicable, even for ordinary offenses.

*Latest data available in *The State of the World's Children* and *Childinfo* database,UNICEF, 2004.

malnourished. Tanzania remained among the 30 poorest countries in the world, although it managed to escape the famine that hit other Central African nations.

22   Agricultural tasks have traditionally been carried out chiefly by women. While nearly half the workforce is made up of women, they do 85 per cent of all agricultural work. In the outlying areas around the major cities, the female population is increasingly opting for work in the underground economy.

23   At the beginning of 1990, former president Julius Nyerere abandoned his opposition to a multiparty democracy, arguing that the absence of an opposition party contributed to the fact that the CCM had abandoned its program and its commitments. In February 1991 a commission was formed to oversee the country's transition period.

24   In its 1991 report, Amnesty International disclosed the existence of at least 40 political prisoners on the island of Zanzibar. Mwinyi's government denied that any political arrests had been made, and invited the human rights organization to prove its claims.

25   In December, after a 23-year exile in England, opposition leader Oscar Kambona announced his plan to return to Tanzania and lead the fight for a multiparty system. He announced the founding of the Democratic Alliance of Tanzania party. However, the national elections held in April 1993 confirmed yet again the predominance of the ruling CCM, which obtained 89 per cent of the vote.

26   The Government promised the IMF it would implement a strict program of economic adjustment that included the elimination of 20,000 public

sector jobs and a reduction of the budget deficit. It thus reduced education spending - which in 1960 had been 30 per cent - to 5 per cent of total public expenditure and in February 1994, authorized a 68 per cent raise in electricity and 233 per cent increase of several local taxes.

27   In March, the World Bank praised Tanzania as its second-best African student after Ghana. The country's harsh social conditions were aggravated by an influx of Rwandan refugees, fleeing from the genocide that killed over 500,000.

28   1995 was dominated by the multiparty legislative and presidential elections held in October, where the CCM triumphed again due to Nyerere's support. Benjamin Mkapa became the new President and appointed Frederick Sumaye Prime Minister.

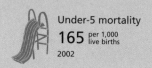

29   In December 1996, the Government decided to expel the majority of the 540,000 Rwandan refugees from the country. Most of them faced death, from the same conflicts they had fled three years before. Tanzania still had 230,000 Hutu refugees from Burundi, and some 50,000 from the Democratic Republic of the Congo (formerly Zaire).

30   A bomb at the US embassy in Dar es Salaam killed 11 and injured 80 people in August. It was linked with the global terror network al-Qaeda.

31   The death of Julius Nyerere in October 1999 brought tributes from political leaders all over the world. A draft plan for semi-autonomous local government on the mainland presented in December - to run alongside national government and Zanzibar's own semi-autonomous regime - led to conflict between the President and defenders of the project. The idea of a federation of autonomous regions had been criticized by Nyerere but his death paved the way for renewed discussion. Such a system would allow the mainland population equal rights to the islanders, who already had semi-autonomous government.

32   Mkapa was re-elected with 72 per cent of the vote in the

October 2000 elections. In Zanzibar the CCM candidate Amani Karume was victorious, but flagrant irregularities in the monitoring on the island meant the opposition did not recognize the result. After violent protests where at least 30 people died, and a re-run of elections in two districts, Karume was sworn in as President of Zanzibar in November.

33   In March 2001, the CCM signed an agreement with the main opposition party in Zanzibar, the United Civic Front (UCF), aiming to end the political violence in the semi-autonomous islands. The parties agreed to form a joint committee to re-establish peace and encourage the 2,000 or so refugees in Kenya to return home. In April Dar es Salaam witnessed the first joint demonstration by opposition parties in decades. The opposition pressed for constitutional reform. The Labor Party demanded a new constitution and independent electoral commissions.

34   An enormous new gold mine - the Bulyanhulu mine - opened in Tanzania in July 2001, which made the country the third biggest African producer. Bulyanhulu was taken over by the Canadian Barrick Gold Corporation and, after investing $280 million, production

forecasts were made of 400,000 ounces of gold per year.

35   In November 2001 Mkapa founded an East African regional parliament and court with the presidents of Uganda and Kenya in Arusha. The agreement between Tanzania, Uganda and Kenya was seen as a step toward the creation of a common market across three countries (see para 38).

36   In early 2002, the governor of the Central Bank Doaud Ballali said there had been great progress in macroeconomic stability over the last seven years. According to Ballali, inflation had fallen from 30 per cent in 1995 to 4.7 per cent in 2002 and by this date the economy was growing by more than 5 per cent per year (above the African average). In the financial sector there was an increasing number of banks - there had been only one before 1993, and 20 by early 2002 - complemented by a further 12 non-banking financial institutions.

37   In January 2004 Zanzibar celebrated the 40th anniversary of its independence, while the UCF accused the Government of economic mismanagement. The average income of Zanzibaris was $0.60 per day.

38   In March, Tanzania signed a customs union treaty with Kenya

and Uganda, forming a bloc of 90 million people with a GDP of $25 billion.

39   In April 2004, Tanzania celebrated the 40th anniversary of the union between Zanzibar and the mainland. President Mkapa issued a call to keep the union at all costs. Shortly before this, Zanzibar's autonomous government had announced the island would have its own flag by the end of the year, alleging that the Constitution allowed it to 'have its own identity'.

40   In May, in Dar es Salaam (Tanzania's main port and city with the largest number of Internet cafes), an official website of the Government called Parliamentary Online Information System (POLIS) was launched. This website is dedicated to explaining the activities planned by Parliament and to making politics more understandable and accessible to the public. The Government expressed hopes that Polis would turn into one of the most visited sites in the country. POLIS was funded by the UN Development Program (UNDP); Marc Malloch Brown, the UNDP administrator, declared that it would extend the tentacles of democracy.

41   Pius Msekwa, speaker of the Tanzanian Parliament, agreed that the launching of POLIS was important for the country's democracy. According to Msekwa, providing people with access to parliamentary information would be crucial to strengthen the democratic process and would bring transparency to the government administration.

42   According to 2002 reports from different organizations, only 300,000 out of the 35 million Tanzanians would have access to the Internet. As of 2004, there were 23 Internet service providers and most people would access the web via Internet cafes, where access was cheaper than in other African countries.

43   On the other hand, the main leader of the opposition in Parliament, Wilfred Lwakatare, declared that the undertaking was part of a show, since several government members have no computers in their offices.

44   In July, wildlife authorities investigated the death of more than 10,000 flamingos at the Lake Manyara National Park (located to the east of the Rift Valley). Reports showed that the deaths were caused by toxins in algae. Among the more than 300 bird species that inhabit the lake, there are more than 3 million flamingos. ∎

PROFILE

ENVIRONMENT

The country is made up of the former territory of Tanganyika plus the islands of Zanzibar and Pemba. The offshore islands are made of coral. The coastal belt, where a large part of the population live, is a flat lowland along the Indian Ocean with a tropical climate and heavy rainfall. To the west lies the central plateau, dry and riddled with tsetse flies. The north is a mountainous region with slopes suited for agriculture. Around Lake Victoria, a heavily populated area, there are irrigated farmlands. Large plantations of sisal and sugarcane stretch along the coastal lowlands. Mount Kilimanjaro, the highest peak in Africa at 6,000 m, is located in the northern highlands.

SOCIETY

Peoples: Tanzanians are mostly of Bantu origin, subdivided into around 120 ethnic groups. On the mainland there are also Nilo-hamitic groups in the west; there is a Shirazi minority of Persian origin in Zanzibar. Both regions have groups of Arab, Indian, Pakistani and European immigrants.
Religions: Muslim 35 per cent; traditional religions 35 per cent; Christian 30 per cent. Zanzibar is 99 per cent Muslim, Shi'a and Sunni.
Languages: Swahili (official - the *lingua franca* of Central and Eastern Africa of Bantu origin). English (official), Arabic and more than 100 local languages.
Main Political Parties: Revolutionary Party of Tanzania (CCM-Chama Cha Mapinduzi), socialist

orientation, emerged 5 February 1977, from the fusion of the Tanganyika - later Tanzania - African National Union (TANU), founded by Julius K Nyerere in 1954, and the Afro-Shirazi Party of Zanzibar. Since 1992, there is a multiparty system that includes, amongst others, the Civic United Front (CUF, regionalist of Zanzibar); Party for Democracy and Progress (CHADEMA).
Main Social Organizations: Organization of Tanzanian Trade Unions (OTTU); Union of Women of Tanzania (UWT); Tanzanian Association of NGO's (TANGO), National Union of Students of Tanzania (MUWATA).

THE STATE

Official Name: Jamhuri ya Muungano wa Tanzania.
Administrative Divisions: 25 Divisions.
Capital: Dodoma 155,000 people (2003). Official capital since 1974, functions as seat of legislature.
Other Cities: Dar es Salaam (former capital) 2,372,200 people; Mwanza 291,100; Zanzibar 247,500; Tanga 202,900 (2000).
Government: Benjamin Mkapa, President since November 1995, re-elected in 2000. Frederick Sumaye, Prime Minister since November 1995. Amani Karume, the second Vice-President since November 2000, is also President of Zanzibar and Pemba. Unicameral Legislature: 296-member National Assembly.
National Holiday: 26 April, Union Day (1964).
Armed Forces: 34,600 (1996). Other: 1,400 Rural Police, 85,000 Militia.

Thailand / Prathet Thai

Population:	64,081,371
Area:	513,120 km²
Capital:	Bangkok
Currency:	Baht
Language:	Thai

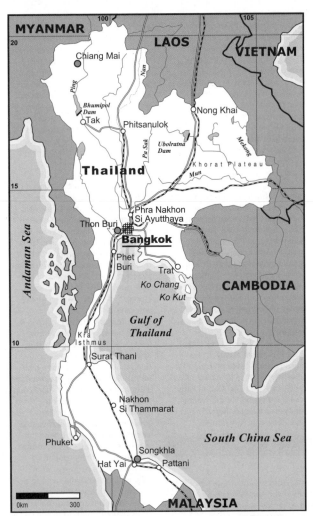

Archeological evidence indicates almost continuous human occupation of Thailand for the last 20,000 years. Thai-speaking peoples migrated southward from China around the 10th century AD. By the 13th century, the Thais emerged as a dominant force in the region, slowly absorbing the weakened empires of the Mons and Khmers. By 1238, the first Thai kingdom, Sukhothai, was established. King Ramkamhaeng the Great, noted as an administrator, legislator and statesman, is credited with the invention of the Thai script. The Sukhothai period saw the Thais for the first time developing a distinctive civilization with their own administrative institutions, art and architecture. Sukhothai Buddha images, characterized by refined facial features, lineal fluidity, and harmony of form, are considered to be the most beautiful and original examples of Thai artistic expression.

2   In 1350 the more powerful state of Ayutthaya exerted its influence over Sukhothai; formerly a vassal state, it usurped administrative power, leaving Sukhothai a deserted kingdom. The Ayutthaya kings became very powerful, moving east to take Lopburi - a former Khmer stronghold - and then in 1431 to Angkor, the capital of the Khmer Empire. The Ayutthaya kings adopted Khmer court customs, language and culture. Unlike the paternal rulers of Sukhothai, Ayutthaya's kings were absolute monarchs and assumed the title *devaraja* or God King. Ayutthaya became one of the greatest and wealthiest cities in Asia. From the early 16th century the Portugese established trade, supplied mercenaries and taught the Thais cannon foundry and musketry.

3   The Burmese were the most powerful rival of the Ayutthaya kingdom and in 1569 they defeated Ayutthayan forces, occupied their capital, and ruled the kingdom for 15 years. Ayutthayan rule ended in 1767 when, after a siege of 14 months, a new Burmese invasion sacked the city, burning and looting and melting down the gold from

Buddha images and taking 90,000 captives. After expelling the Burmese occupying forces, Thai general Phya Taksin moved his capital to the west bank of the Chao Phraya river, known as Thonburi, and was proclaimed king. During his reign Phya Taksin liberated Chiang Mai and the rest of northern Thailand from the Burmese.

4   Rama I (1782-1809), founder of the Chakkri dynasty which still reigns in Thailand, moved his capital across the Chao Phraya River to Bangkok (Krung Thep), which at the time was still a small village. By the mid-19th century, Bangkok had become a city of some 400,000 people, swollen by the huge numbers of Chinese who had poured into Siam (as Thailand was then called) during those years. Rama II re-established relations with the West, allowing the Portuguese to construct the first Western embassy in Bangkok. His successor, Rama III, extended the Thai Empire south along the Malay Peninsula, north into Laos and southeast into Cambodia, while he continued to reopen the country to foreigners, successfully promoting trade with China.

5   The name Thailand means 'land of the free', and throughout the country's 800-year history, the Thai people have never been colonized. While Rama IV (1851-68) opened the country to Western influence and initiated reforms and modern development, control of Siam was disputed by the French and the British. In 1896, the two powers agreed to leave the state formally independent. In World War I, Siam fought alongside the Allies and later joined the League of Nations.

6   On 24 June 1932, a coup curtailed the power of the monarchy, creating a parliament elected by universal suffrage. The country's name was changed to Thailand with the advent of a democratic government in 1939, but the democratic experience was short-lived and in 1941, during World War II, the Bangkok Government allowed Japan to use its territory, becoming a virtual satellite of that country. During the conflict, Siamese troops occupied part of Malaysia, but were forced to abandon it in 1946, after the allied victory.

7   In June that year, King Ananda Mahidol was assassinated in

mysterious circumstances. US maneuvering succeeded in putting his brother, Rama IX, into power. Born in the US, the new king had never hidden his pro-US leanings. Since then, Thailand has remained under Washington's patronage.

8   US interests in Thailand were essentially strategic as its geographical location and plans for a projected channel through the Kra Isthmus made the country critical to US military policy in the area. In 1954, the Southeast Asian Treaty Organization (SEATO), a military pact designed to counterbalance the growing power of revolutionary forces in the region, established its headquarters in Bangkok.

9   In 1961, large numbers of US troops entered the country in reaction to an insurrection in Laos. The US military maintained its presence in Thailand for 14 years, resulting in strong ties being forged between the Thai and US armed forces. In exchange for their participation in the anti-communist struggle, the Thai military enjoyed greater political influence and impunity from their corrupt activities, which included control of the drug trade from the famous 'golden triangle' in the north.

10   Between 1950 and 1975, US support of military regimes in Thailand cost it over $2 billion. On 14 October 1973, a popular uprising by students brought down the Government. As a result, in 1975 the first civilian government in 20 years was formed. Elections brought Prince Seni Pramoj to power. He demanded the immediate withdrawal of US troops, the dismantling of military bases and an improvement of relations with neighboring revolutionary governments.

11   The Thai military disagreed with the new government, and in October 1976 Pramoj was overthrown in a bloody coup planned by right-wing navy officers. Thousands of students and intellectuals joined a guerrilla struggle led by the Communist Party in the rural areas, and Thai relations with neighbors became extremely tense. Finally, in October 1977, a second coup brought the 'civilized right wing' of the military to power. They took a liberal line in policy-making as they were eager to attract new transnational investments. In 1979, Thailand granted asylum to Cambodian refugees. Refugee camps along the border became the rearguard of Cambodian strongman Pol Pot's Khmer Rouge guerrillas; a large part of international humanitarian aid was unwittingly channeled to them. Thailand thus served US interests in the region, as a base for new attacks against communist Vietnam which supported the anti-Khmer forces.

12   On 1 April 1981, another military coup shook Bangkok. This

Life expectancy	GNI per capita	Literacy	HIV prevalence rate
69.3 years 2000-2005	**$1,980** 2002	**96%** total adult rate 2000	**1.8%** of population 15-49 years old 2001

time it was led by General Sant Chitpatima with the support of young middle-ranking officers demanding institutional democracy and social change. The King and Prime Minister General Prem had been asked to lead the coup and had apparently accepted. However, they finally opposed the uprising, and it was put down after three days of great tension.

13 The young officer's revolt, rooted in the military establishment, was basically a reaction to government measures bringing in forced retirement for certain senior generals. Nevertheless, the short-lived coup gained unusually strong support from trade unions and student groups - and this support in itself was extraordinary since the coup was instigated by the military.

14 At the same time, the left-wing opposition was severely weakened by an internal split in the Communist Party into the pro-Vietnamese and pro-Chinese factions.

15 Towards the end of 1984, the currency was sharply devalued, sparking discontent from General Arthit Kamlang-Ek and other hardline generals, who threatened to withdraw military support for Prem. Some timely political maneuvering by the Prime Minister, offering incentives to the officers for their support, allowed Prem to isolate Arthit.

16 After a further coup attempt in September 1985, Prem relieved Arthit of his command and designated General Chaovalit Yongchaiyut as the head of the armed forces.

17 Political instability continued in Bangkok, with several cabinet changes and requests for early legislative elections on two separate occasions. In May 1986, the Democrat Party obtained enough of a majority to form a coalition, presided over once again by General Prem as Prime Minister.

18 While General Chaovalit's stature continued to grow, enhanced by his forceful attacks on corruption, the Government called for early elections in April 1988, to avoid Prem being censured. The main criticisms of his administration were his questionable management of public funds and overall incompetence, particularly in the handling of the border war with Laos several months earlier, which had escalated from a dispute over the control of three villages.

19 In the first general election since 1976, amid massive vote-buying campaigns (a practice considered normal by almost all candidates), the Thai Nation Party won the election. King Bhumibol Adulyahed asked General Chatichai Choonhavan to form a new

government, which he did by arranging a six-party coalition.

20 Thailand's new leading force and its most successful entrepreneur, Chatichai, introduced important policy changes, breaking with the traditional focus on internal affairs and security. His main idea was to convert what had once been the Indochinese battlefield into a huge regional market. Tempted by the possibility of Cambodia and Laos opening up their markets, he invested considerably in those countries.

21 This formula further fuelled the Thai economy, and in 1989 the growth rate exceeded 10 per cent. Thailand then challenged Western Europe and its subsidy policies for agricultural export products. There were also disagreements with the United States over Bangkok's refusal to accept North American trade criteria on intellectual property, especially with regard to computer programs.

22 In March 1991, the military carried out another coup led by General Sunthorn Kongsompong, who presented King Bhumibol Adulyahed with a draft for a new constitution. The latter approved the draft, and justified the military coup on the grounds of 'growing corruption' within the civilian government. The King also agreed with the military on the need for calling new elections. As an indirect result of the military coup in Thailand, peace negotiations in neighboring Cambodia came to a standstill, with the Cambodian government denouncing Thailand for its renewed support of the Cambodian armed opposition.

23 Throughout 1991, Thailand remained under the command of the National Peace Keeping Council (NPKC), a body of the military commanded by Sunthorn. In December, the King approved the new constitution which stipulated that elections to replace the NPKC Government would be held within 120 days. However, the military junta reserved the right to directly appoint 270 senators out of a total of 360, giving it total control over the new government.

24 In elections held on 22 March 1992, the majority of votes went to the opposition. There were 15 parties, with a total of 2,740 candidates, and 32 million out of 57 million Thais turned out to vote.

25 In early April, General Suchinda Kraprayoon, commander-in-chief of the army at the time, became Prime Minister, backed by a small majority made up of five pro-military parties. In his 49-member cabinet, Suchinda included 11 former ministers who had been accused of embezzlement during Chatichai's government.

26 At the end of May, what began as an anti-government

demonstration ended in a massacre, with hundreds of people killed and injured. Army troops fired into a crowd gathered at the Democracy Monument and political leaders such as Chamlong Srimuang were imprisoned. The protests continued until an unexpected television appeal for national reconciliation was made by the Thai King. Suchinda, in the meantime, announced his support for a constitutional amendment whereby the Prime Minister would have to be an elected member of Parliament, a clause which would disqualify even Suchinda from holding the post. Srimuang was subsequently freed, and an amnesty announced for those who had been arrested. With a curfew still in effect in Bangkok, Parliament initiated discussion of the constitutional amendment and the King appointed General Prem Tinsulanonda to supervise the process.

27 On 24 May, Suchinda resigned and his Vice President, Mitchai Ruchuphan, became interim president. Constitutional amendments approved in June reduced military participation in the Government and King Bhumibol named Anand Panyarachun Prime Minister. Panyarachun, who enjoyed a great deal of prestige in Thailand, had been Prime Minister after the 1991 military coup.

28 Parliament accepted the King's nomination of Panyarachun, who appointed a number of technocrats to cabinet positions and requested the resignations of the 12 military officers responsible for the May massacre.

29 In June 1992, the King dissolved Parliament and called early elections to be held in September, which were won by the Democratic Party (DP) with 79 seats in the House of Representatives. On 23 September, a parliamentary majority was formed (177 seats), comprising the DP, the Palang Dharma (PD) and the New Aspiration Party (NAP), which appointed anti-military leader Chuan Leekpai as Prime Minister. Shortly after, the pro-military Social Action Party joined this coalition.

30 The Muslim separatist movement in southern Thailand is supported by fundamentalist leader Nik Abdulaziz Nikmat, Governor of the state of Kelatan in Malaysia and opposer of the central government of Prime Minister Mahathir Mohamad. Several violent incidents, of a religious nature, were registered during 1993. Concerned about the role played by his country within the region, Chuan strengthened ties with China and Indonesia and, in October, he officially withdrew all support provided to the Khmer Rouge since 1979.

31 Although in 1994 the economy of Thailand was among the fastest

PROFILE

ENVIRONMENT

Thailand is located in central Indochina. From the mountain ranges in the northern and western zones, the Ping and Nan Rivers flow down to the central valley and then through extensive deltas, into the Gulf of Thailand. The plains are fertile with large commercial rice plantations. The southern region occupies part of the Malay Peninsula. Severe deforestation of the area has resulted in decreased production of rubber and timber, and has been responsible for migration of part of the native population.

SOCIETY

Peoples: The Thai group constitutes the majority of the population. The most important minority groups are the Chinese, 12 per cent and, in the south, the Malay, 13 per cent. Other groups are Khmer, Karen, Indians and Vietnamese. **Religions:** Most people (94 per cent) practise Buddhism. Muslims, concentrated in the south, make up about 4 per cent of the population. There is a Christian minority. **Languages:** Thai or Siamese (official). Minority groups speak their own languages. **Main Political Parties:** Phak Thai Rak Thai (TRT-Thais Love Thais Party); Democratic Party; Thai Nation Party; National Development Party. **Main Social Organizations:** Forum of the Poor; Thai Network for Community Rights and Biodiversity (BIOTHAI).

THE STATE

Official Name: Muang Thai, or Prathet Thai (Kingdom of Thailand). **Administrative Division:** 5 regions and 73 provinces. **Capital:** Bangkok (Krung Thep) 6,486,000 people (2003). **Other Cities:** Ratchasima 207,500 people; Chiang Mai 170,300; Khon Kaen 143,200; Nakhon Pathorn 122,500 Thanyaburi 115,500 (2000). **Government:** King Bhumibol Adulyadej, Head of State, since June 1946. Thaksin Shinawatra, Prime Minister and Head of Government since February 2001. The National Assembly (Parliament) has two chambers: the House of Representatives, with 438 members, and the Senate, with 200 members. **National Holiday:** 5 December, the King's birthday (1927). **Armed Forces:** 254,000 troops (1996). Other: 141,700 (National Security Volunteer Force, Air Police, Frontier Police Patrols, Province Police and 'Hunter Soldiers').

Under-5 mortality
28 per 1,000 live births
2002

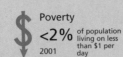

Poverty
<2% of population living on less than $1 per day
2001

Debt service
25.1% exports of goods and services
2001

Maternal mortality
44 per 100,000 live births
2000

growing in the world, it was in political turmoil. The first parliamentary session of 1995 brought an exchange of accusations and the tense political atmosphere led to the dissolution of Parliament. On 2 July early elections took place. The Thai Nation Party obtained 25 per cent of the seats and the Democrats 22 per cent. Banham Silapa-archa, leader of the winning party, formed a government supported by several small parties.

[32] In November 1996, Chavalit Yonchaiyudh (NAP) was elected Prime Minister, with 125 of the 393 seats in the Chamber of Representatives. Chuan Leekpai's DP, took 123 seats. A coalition with the Chart Pattana (52), Social Action (20), Prachakorn Thai (18) plus two minor parties, allowed Chavalit to secure a majority weeks later.

[33] Thailand was hit by a financial crisis in 1997, exacerbated by scandals and attempts to salvage the banks - leading to the resignation of the economy minister and the closure of businesses - and by Chavalit's proposal for constitutional reform in order to avoid a vote of no confidence lodged by the opposition.

[34] In August 1997, the constitutional reform project was completed. It aimed to limit corruption, put citizens' rights into law, and eliminate army influence from the Senate. Alarmed by the perceived loss of power, the governing parties initially rejected this project, but they were forced to accept it given the agreement between the army and King Bhumibol. The new Constitution was passed in a General Assembly on 11 October.

[35] When the new prime minister Chuan Leekpai took office in November 1997, the Thai currency, the baht, had devaluated 37 per cent. The crisis lasted throughout the following year, which closed with an 8 per cent drop in Gross National Product. Unemployment affected 1.8 million people (6 per cent of the population), while the Government proposed making 200,000 of its 1.5 million employees redundant. The $17.2-billion loan granted by the IMF involved a series of counterpart demands. As well as redundancies in the state sector, the Government put 59 state companies up for sale, including telecommunications, electricity, petrochemicals and finances.

[36] In March the Prime Minister survived a vote of no confidence and even extended the base of his alliance, by incorporating Chart Pattana, which had 51 votes in parliament, into the Government. The Government decided not to renew the work permits of half a million immigrant workers, but finally gave in to pressure from rice-growers and other entrepreneurs

IN FOCUS

ENVIRONMENTAL CHALLENGES
Air pollution has increased for several reasons: exhaust emissions from vehicles in cities, industrial pollution, lack of disposal mechanisms for waste matter, unrestricted industrial development, etc. Waterways are polluted due to the dumping of organic and industrial waste; tree felling continues to aggravate soil erosion. Several animal species are endangered by massive illegal hunting.

WOMEN'S RIGHTS
Women have had the vote and been eligible for office since 1932. In 2003, 9.6 per cent of parliamentary seats were occupied by women, as were 5.7 per cent of ministerial or equivalent positions. Women make up 46 per cent of the workforce (50 per cent in agriculture, 31 per cent in the services sector and 17 per cent in industry).

The maternal mortality rate is 44 per 100,000 live births. Fifty-seven per cent of pregnant women suffer from anemia, while 77 per cent receive prenatal care and 85 per cent of deliveries are attended by qualified personnel.

Although it is illegal, prostitution is increasing very fast. According to government departments, 200,000 people are involved. NGOs claim that the figure may be as high as 800,000 (including 200,000 children). In the 1980s there were 70,000 female prostitutes in Bangkok alone.

CHILDREN
Twenty-eight children under five die per 1,000 infants born alive. The moderate and severe malnutrition rate is under 1 per cent while the rate of infants underweight at birth is 8.5 per cent. Access to safe drinking water and sewerage is practically universal. In 1998 gross school matriculation was 91 per cent.

According to government estimates, 5 per cent of minors forced into prostitution are male. Although the number of children made to work has diminished, it is estimated that in the first quarter of 1999 there were about one million boys and girls in the workforce. The figure for 1992 was 2.6 million.

Mother-to-child transmission is already responsible for some 30,000 children living with HIV/AIDS. Additionally, in some regions HIV/AIDS has caused an increase in mortality rates for children under five.

INDIGENOUS PEOPLES/ ETHNIC MINORITIES
The largest minorities are the Chinese (12 per cent) and South Malaysians. The former arrived in Thailand in the late 19th and early 20th centuries and currently control 85 to 90 per cent of the country's businesses. Additionally, since the early 1990s, they have acquired political power and currently occupy 86 of a total of 347 parliamentary seats.

The South Malaysians (Muslims) are a religious minority in a country where Buddhism is the official religion. Successive military régimes have attempted to foster generalized nationalism in the country, among other things teaching only in Thai and encouraging Buddhist practices. Malaysians were thus left out, as 80 per cent do not speak Thai. Furthermore, the Malaysians have practically no political representation, they are perceptibly poorer, and their access to health services is less secure than for the rest of the population.

MIGRANTS/REFUGEES
In late 2002 Thailand took in some 336,000 refugees and asylum seekers, more than 335,000 of them from Burma. There are some 2 million illegal immigrants from Burma living in the country.

In 2001 the Government initiated a registration program for immigrants lacking legal documentation, which allowed them to remain in the country on a transitory basis. Simultaneously a harassment and deportation campaign was started against those who did not register.

DEATH PENALTY
Applicable for all kinds of crimes.

who employ cheap labor, granting 95,000 new permits.

[37] The March 2000 elections for the direct appointment of senators were plagued with irregularities. The electoral authority disqualified 78 of the 200 legislators elected, accusing them of corruption and fraud. Two of the disqualified senators were the wives of the Interior and Justice ministers. It was the first time senators had been elected by popular vote.

[38] The Thais Love Thais Party (TRT), headed by media magnate Thaksin Shinawatra, won the January 2001 parliamentary elections but did not obtain an absolute majority. The TRT took 248 of the 500 seats in contention. Although the elections took place under a new Constitution, designed to reduce electoral fraud, accusations of irregularities forced the electoral commission to hold new balloting in 62 districts. In February, Parliament elected Shinawatra Prime Minister.

[39] In early 2001, Thai and Burmese troops clashed along the shared border - the Mae Sai-Tachilek crossing - and Bangkok and Rangoon accused each other of supporting drug-producing militias. Shinawatra had made combating drug-trafficking a government priority. In May 2001 the tensions escalated as the presence of special US troops increased on the Thai side of the border. Their stated mission was to train the Thai army in anti-drug trade techniques. That same month, near the border with Burma/Myanmar, more than 20,000 US and Thai soldiers carried out their annual joint maneuvers. In June, Shinawatra traveled to Rangoon to discuss the border problems, resulting in the reopening of Mae Sai-Tachilek.

[40] The jewelry and precious stones industry suffered a major contraction in early 2002. US consumption, which represented 50 per cent of the global market for cut gems, had collapsed in the wake of the September 2001 terrorist attacks in New York and Washington. For Thailand, one of the leading world exporters, the consequences were severe. By March 2002, the recession in that market had left some 200,000 Thais out of work.

[41] In July 2003 Thailand repaid IMF loans two years ahead of schedule.

[42] In early 2003 Shinawatra resumed the anti-drug war. Over a three-month period 2,500 suspected drug-traffickers died; according to critics extra-judicial deaths multiplied.

[43] In 2004 the country has suffered escalating violence, starting in January with an attack on a military arsenal. In the following months, attacks have become an almost daily event, leaving over 100 dead. Authorities attribute the attacks to a new outbreak of Islamic separatism.

[44] In April 2004 a series of simultaneous disturbances took place in Yala, Pattani and Songkhla (the three provinces with Muslim majorities). As a result, 108 supposedly mostly Islamic militants died at the hands of security forces.

[45] In May the army sent 500 members of the deployment force on a 'search and destroy' mission against 5,000 Muslim militants in the south. Two 1,000-man battalions were sent as backup. ∎

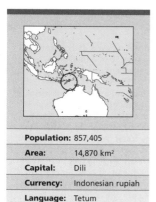

Population:	857,405
Area:	14,870 km²
Capital:	Dili
Currency:	Indonesian rupiah
Language:	Tetum

B efore the arrival of Vasco da Gama, the Chinese and Arabs knew Timor as an 'inexhaustible' source of precious woods which were exchanged for axes, pottery, lead and other goods of use to the local inhabitants.

[2] Timor's traditional society consisted of five categories: the *Liurari* (kings and chiefs), the *Dato* (nobles and warriors), the *Ema-reino* (freemen) the *Ata* (slaves) and the *Lutum* (nomadic shepherds).

[3] The local population opposed colonialism with armed insurrections in 1719, 1895 and 1959, all of which were put down. In 1859, Portugal and the Netherlands agreed to divide the territory between them. The Portuguese kept the eastern part, under an accord ratified in 1904. Passive resistance by the Maubere enabled their culture to survive five centuries of colonialism. After the devastation of the forests of precious woods, the cultivation of coffee became Timor's economic mainstay.

[4] In the mid-1970s, an independence movement was organized and the struggle for national liberation began, bringing together nationalist political forces and several social organizations.

[5] In April 1974, when the clandestine struggle against colonial rule had already grown and gained broad support, the 'Carnation Revolution' took place in Lisbon. With the fall of the fascist colonial regime in the metropolis the political scene in Timor changed and the patriotic movement was legalized. In September, the Revolutionary Front for the Independence of East Timor (FRETILIN) was created.

[6] The new Portuguese Government promised independence but the colonial administration favored the creation of the Democratic Union of Timor (UDT), which supported the colonial *status quo* and 'federation' with Portugal. At the same time, the Indonesian consulate in Dili encouraged a group of Timorese to organize the Timor Popular

Democratic Association (APODETI) which supported integration with Indonesia.

[7] A period of conflict ensued between Portuguese neocolonial interests, Indonesian annexationists and the independence movement. In August, the UDT attempted a coup causing FRETILIN to issue a call for general armed insurrection, and the Portuguese administration withdrew from the country. FRETILIN achieved territorial control and declared independence on 28 November 1975, proclaiming the Democratic Republic of East Timor. Portugal's withholding of official recognition

had important diplomatic and political implications, which continue until the present time.

[8] On 7 December 1975, Indonesia invaded Timor. A few hours earlier, US President Gerald Ford had visited Jakarta, capital of Indonesia, where he had probably learned of, and endorsed, Indonesian president General Suharto's expansionist plans. FRETILIN was forced to withdraw from the capital, Dili, and from the major ports. On 2 June 1976, a so-called 'People's Assembly', made up of UDT and APODETI members, approved Timor's annexation as a province of Indonesia. The

annexation was not recognized by the United Nations Decolonization Committee, which still regarded Portugal as the island's ruler.

[9] In December 1978, Nicolás dos Reis Lobato, President of the Republic and FRETILIN leader, died in combat. Despite this blow, the liberation movement continued the struggle.

[10] In an attempt to set the Maubere against each other, the Indonesian army recruited young Timorese. But the young Timorese answered calls from the Front and mutinied to join FRETILIN. In 1983 a ceasefire was signed between FRETILIN commander in chief Xanana Gusmão and head of the expeditionary corps Colonel Purwanto. Suharto did not recognize the agreement and guerrilla warfare continued.

[11] In 1988, rapprochement between FRETILIN and the TDU culminated in the creation of a joint Nationalist Convergence and Gusmão was confirmed as commander in chief of the liberation army. This body was instrumental in Portugal, actively raising the Timorese question with the European Parliament and the European Commission (EC). Europe rejected Indonesian occupation and backed Maubere self-rule along with a negotiated solution to the conflict.

[12] In October 1989 the UN Human Rights Sub-commission approved a motion condemning Indonesian occupation and repression in East Timor. When Pope John Paul II visited Dili that month a group of youths unrolled a FRETILIN banner, a few meters away from the platform where he was leading Mass. Indonesian security forces repressed the students shouting anti-occupation slogans.

[13] Timorese families were forced to hang a list of household members' names on their doors so that occupation forces could check who was present at any time of day or night. Thousands of Maubere women were were sterilized against their will. The Indonesian authorities applied policies aimed at reducing the Maubere people to a minority. Mass graves of Maubere proved the occupation forces had carried out wide-scale executions.

[14] On 12 November 1991, a large funeral procession accompanying the remains of a young student who had been killed turned into a bloodbath when the army machine-gunned the crowd, killing at least 50 and leaving countless people injured. When the Portuguese Government heard the news they called on the EC to cut trade with Indonesia - which had a preferential trade agreement - and call a UN Security Council meeting. Portugal produced veiled criticism of the body for not confronting Indonesia

PROFILE

ENVIRONMENT

Located between Australia and Indonesia, Timor-Leste comprises the eastern portion of Timor Island, the dependency of Oecusse, located on the northwestern part of the island, the island of Atauro to the North, and the islet of Yaco to the East. Of volcanic origin, the island is mountainous and covered with dense rainforest. The climate is tropical with heavy rainfall, which accounts for the extensive river system. The southern region is flat and suitable for farming. Agriculture is the basis of its export-oriented economy, and copra, coffee, rice, cotton, tobacco and sandalwood are its main crops.

SOCIETY

Peoples: The Maubere people are descended from Melanesian and Malayan populations. In 1975 there was a Chinese minority of 20,000, who had arrived during the 20th century, as well as 4,000 Portuguese. Amnesty International estimates that 210,000 people have died as a result of the Indonesian occupation. There are 6,000 Maubere refugees in Australia and 1,500 in Portugal. **Religions:** Most of the population follows traditional practices. 30 per cent are Catholic.
Languages: Tetum is the national language. There are some 40 dialects. Indonesian occupation had banned the use of these languages in education, and virtually all the teaching was done in Bahasa Indonesia, the Indonesian language. This situation was reversed after official Independence in 2002. A minority also speaks Portuguese.
Main Political Parties: Revolutionary Front for the Independence of East Timor (FRETILIN); Democratic Party (PD); Social-Democratic Party (PSD); Timorese Social-Democratic Association (ASDT).

THE STATE

Official Name: República de Timor Leste. **Capital:** Dili 49,000 people (2003). **Other Cities:** Dare 17,500 people; Baucau 14,500 (2000). **Government:** Xanana Gusmão, President elected in April 2002, took office on 20 May that year, when the country became formally independent. That same day the Transitional Authority imposed by UN in 1999 ceased functioning. Mari Alkatiri, Chief Minister since September 2001. Legislature: 88-member Parliament.
National Holiday: 28 November, Independence Day (1975).

Life expectancy
49.5 years
2000-2005

GNI per capita
$270
2002

and acting as it had when Iraq invaded Kuwait in August 1990.

[15] In late 1991, claims came to light in Portugal that Jakarta and Canberra had signed a contract with 12 companies for the extraction of a billion barrels of crude oil in the Timor Sea. This list of companies was headed by Royal Dutch Shell (British and Dutch capital) and the US Chevron company. These were followed by six Australian companies, Japan's Nippon Oil and the transnationals Phillips Petroleum, Marathon and the Enterprise Oil Company. Opposition leaders accused the companies' home countries of collaborating with Jakarta in playing down the genocide and silencing the international press for the benefit of their own economic interests.

[16] In December 1996, exiled activist José Ramos Horta and Catholic bishop Carlos Filipe Ximenes Belo received the Nobel Peace Prize in Oslo. Indonesian authorities planned to boycott the ceremony, but the problem of East Timor hit the headlines all around the world.

[17] Suharto's resignation in Jakarta in June 1998 and his replacement by Bacharuddin Jusuf Habibie acted as a catalyst for instability on the island. Habibie announced a plan to give East Timor greater autonomy and to this end, a date was set for a referendum.

[18] The referendum was finally held on 30 August 1999, amidst a campaign of violence by Indonesian paramilitaries, backed by some of the army. 78.5 per cent of the voters were in favor of independence, and this outcome spurred a fresh wave of paramilitary violence.

[19] Following discussion with Jakarta, the UN decided to send a peace mission headed by Australian troops. This force (known as Interfet) arrived in Dili two weeks after the referendum, ousting paramilitaries from the capital and surrounding areas, and setting up posts along the frontier. Sovereignty was finally handed over on 25 October.

[20] The UN made Sergio Vieira de Melo head of the Timor Transition Authority. Vieira created a 15-member Consultative Council, which included Gusmão. In February 2000, Interfet ceded control of large areas of the territory to the Transition Authority, which remained under Vieira's responsibility.

[21] In March 2000, Indonesia and the UN stated that those responsible for the violence in August and September 1999 must stand trial. In late February 2000 the Aitarak leaders - one of the pro-Indonesian paramilitary groups - had a meeting with military leaders and FALINTIL (Forças Armadas de Libertaçao Nacional de Timor Leste, pro independence guerrilla led by Xanana Gusmão) politicians in

Singapore. The refugee issue was mentioned at the meeting, as were paths to reconciliation.

[22] The United Nations evacuated all human rights workers in August, after three of them were killed by pro-Jakarta militias. Meanwhile the Indonesian Red Cross office in Kupang said terrorist attacks were preventing it from providing aid to the 120,000 refugees in the western part of the island.

[23] In August 2001, FRETILIN won the parliamentary elections with 57 per cent of the vote, taking 55 of the 88 seats in the Assembly. This new body would draw up the Constitution and become the first parliament when East Timor proclaimed independence on 20 May 2002.

[24] In January 2002, East Timor inaugurated the Truth and Reconciliation Commission (TRC) to investigate crimes committed by the Indonesian forces during the 25 years of occupation. In Vieira's words, the TRC would give an 'official hearing' to the population's complaints, recognizing past suffering and providing an opportunity for genuine and lasting reconciliation between victim and persecutors. However, no amnesty was offered to those admitting crimes like murder or rape. These cases would be transferred to the regular courts so that criminals could be tried. Between 100,000 and 200,000 Timorese died in the first years of the occupation, many through starvation or disease.

[25] Also in January 2002, Jakarta officially inaugurated a human rights court to try military officers and others involved in atrocities

committed in East Timor following the 1999 pro-independence vote there. Indonesia had been under international pressure to try at least 18 military and paramilitary leaders accused of encouraging pro-Indonesian forces in East Timor to commit murder.

[26] In February 2002, the assembly approved a draft Constitution for the country to adopt on formal independence. The project divided the authorities into executive, legislative and judicial bodies and stipulated that the military must be politically neutral. The document also stated that the predominantly Catholic nation would have no state religion, and press freedom would be guaranteed. After long debate, Portuguese and Tetum were designated official languages, while English and Bahasa Indonesia would be used as working languages.

[27] The same month, Indonesia and the UN administration in East Timor signed two agreements in order to 'smooth' relations between the two countries after East Timorese independence. The two parties reached agreement in a meeting in Bali, Indonesia.

[28] In April, Xanana Gusmão won the presidential elections with 82.7 per cent of the vote, while his only rival, Francisco Xavier do Amaral, took 17.3 per cent of the vote. Gusmão took office as the country's first President on 20 May. Shortly after this, Gusmão met with Indonesian President Megawati Sukarnoputri in Jakarta, and offered her a personal invitation to the independence celebrations.

[29] In early May, a UN Development Program report revealed that after

independence East Timor would be the poorest country in Asia and that it would rank among the 20 poorest nations of the world. At that time, most Timorese depended on subsistence fishing and agriculture. The country has no industry and practically no exportable products. Per capita GDP stood at $478 in early May and half the population earned less than 55 cents per day.

[30] That same month, East Timor presented international lenders - with whom meetings had already been held in 1999 in Tokyo, in 2000 in Lisbon and Brussels and in 2001 in Canberra and Oslo - with a multimillion-dollar development aid plan for its first years of independence. The call for aid came at a conference hosted by the World Bank and the UN in Dili, with representatives from 27 countries and multilateral organizations.

[31] In August 2002, Abilio Soares was sentenced to three years in prison. He had been Governor of the former Indonesian province during the violence after the 1999 independence referendum. He was found guilty on two counts of gross rights violations.

[32] On 5 August 2003, General Adam Damiri, former East Timor military commander, was sentenced to three years in prison by the Human Rights Court in Jakarta. Damiri was one of the 18 high-ranking Indonesian officers accused by this court for their alleged role in atrocities committed in East Timor during the 1999 referendum.

[33] The Government announced that it wished the new country to be known internationally as Timor-Leste. ■

IN FOCUS

ENVIRONMENTAL CHALLENGES
The felling and clearing of trees have led to deforestation and land erosion. As a result of the independence struggles, sandalwood forests were destroyed, lagoons polluted and domestic animals hunted. More sandalwood forests, the only ones still existing in the South Pacific, were devastated during the 20 years of Indonesian occupation than during the 450 years of Portuguese colonization.

WOMEN'S RIGHTS
In the Constituent Assembly elected in 2001, women won 26 per cent of seats. Rural women are marginalized, living in extreme poverty, and lacking access to adequate health and pre-natal care. They do not participate in decision-making at government level nor in educational programs. According

to Natércia Godinho-Adams, a representative of organizations for women's rights, the election process needs to be monitored to end the pressure on rural women to vote for their village leaders.

CHILDREN
In October 1999, the immunization campaign coordinated by UNICEF, Médecins Sans Frontières International and the World Health Organization (WHO), reached about 4,000 children under the age of five in Dili. Measles spreads rapidly in mobile populations; children who are moving around and poorly fed have weakened immune systems.

UNHCR estimates that some 800 East Timorese children who had been separated from their parents since 1999 were still in orphanages and other institutions in Indonesia or East Timor in 2002. UNHCR is now trying to locate them and negotiate

with the Indonesian Government for their return.

MIGRANTS/REFUGEES
Although East Timor became party to the UN Refugee Convention in 2002, UNHCR is processing claims for refugee status. During 2002, UNHCR received 35 applications for refugee status.

The number of East Timorese refugees in West Timor was significantly reduced in 2002: nearly 32,000 people voluntarily returned to East Timor, encouraged by assistance and repatriation bonuses from the Indonesian Government and international donors.

Of the more than 250,000 East Timorese who fled to West Timor in 1999, nearly 90 percent had been repatriated by the end of 2002.

DEATH PENALTY
It was abolished in 1999.

Togo / Togo

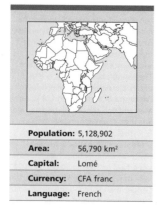

Population:	5,128,902
Area:	56,790 km²
Capital:	Lomé
Currency:	CFA franc
Language:	French

B etween the 4th and 10th centuries, Togo was peopled by the Ewe (of the same origin as the Igbo and Yoruba of Nigeria and the Ashanti of Ghana). The Ewe were a relatively poor and peaceful people with simple social structures like the Dagomba kingdoms in the north.

² The slave trade gave the region the name of Slave Coast, and millions of people were shipped to slavery between the 16th and 19th centuries.

³ Togo became a German colony in 1884 under 'treaties' signed with local chieftains. Occupied by Anglo-French troops during World War I, the territory was divided between the two powers with the endorsement of the League of Nations. The western part was annexed to Ghana in 1956, while the eastern part remained under French rule and became an Overseas Territory.

⁴ In 1958, Sylvanus Olympio, (a member of the Togolese Unity party) won the elections. The 1960 proclamation of independence seemed to overlook a contract signed in 1957 with the Benin Mines Company, in which the French consortium had seized control of Togo's phosphate reserves, its main natural resource. When Olympio confronted this situation in 1963, proposing a series of basic reforms - doubtless influenced by

Nkrumah's radical pro-independence program in Ghana - he was assassinated in a military revolt with the participation of army officer Etienne Gnassingbé Eyadéma.

⁵ Olympio's successor, the neo-colonialist Nicholas Grunitzky, from the opposition Togolese Progress Party, was overthrown by a further coup in 1967, led by (now) General Gnassingbé Eyadéma, who became the new head of state.

⁶ In 1969, the Togo People's Group (RPT) brought in a one-party system with Eyadéma as President. His government adopted nationalist measures which were later modified. In 1972 a law gave the State 35 per cent of shares of the mining company, which was raised to 51 per cent in 1975 and in 1976 the production and export of phosphate was nationalized.

⁷ In December 1979, a new presidential Constitution was approved and Eyadéma was re-elected for a seven-year term. His government was confident of improving the economy, basing its optimism on tourism, oil and a rise in world phosphate prices. However in 1981 phosphate prices dropped by 50 per cent and a worldwide economic recession reduced the number of European tourists. A serious balance of payments deficit increased the foreign debt to $1 billion.

⁸ In June 1984 a refinancing agreement with stringent conditions was reached with the Paris Club and the IMF. This brought about salary freezes, a large reduction of government investments and more taxes, including a so-called 'solidarity

tax' which took five per cent of the population's incomes.

⁹ In January 1985 the Lomé III agreements were signed in Togo's capital, regulating cooperation between ACP (Africa, Caribbean and Pacific) countries and the EEC.

¹⁰ In January 1986 Eyadéma was re-elected with 99.95 per cent of the vote. In 1988, Togo signed new agreements with the IMF. In 1990, the Government began a program of privatization of state-

run companies, to tackle the trade deficit and a foreign debt of $1.27 billion.

¹¹ In 1991, more than 10,000 peasants in the northern district of Keran Oti lost their lands to create an 80 sq km game reserve for hunting.

¹² In April 1991, more than a thousand people took over one of Lomé's neighborhoods, demanding Eyadéma's resignation. The police reacted violently, killing dozens of demonstrators. A few days later, opposition parties were legalized and Eyadéma announced an amnesty for political prisoners.

¹³ In August 1991, a National Conference named Kokou Koffigoh - a human-rights leader - as provisional Prime Minister. A legislative assembly was established which ousted Eyadéma as head of the armed forces and blocked his candidacy in the upcoming 1992 elections.

¹⁴ The dissolution of the RPT by the legislative assembly prompted a military coup in November 1991. The armed forces took over the Government, dissolved the legislative assembly and kidnapped Koffigoh for several hours. Political parties and opposition organizations organized the resistance against a return to dictatorship.

¹⁵ Amidst political, economic, social and ethnic problems, negotiations began to make the transition to a civilian government by 1992. A timetable was established for a return to democracy and all citizens were re-registered to vote.

¹⁶ The opposition split from Koffigoh in January 1993 and nominated a government-in-exile

PROFILE

ENVIRONMENT

The country is a long, narrow strip of land with distinct geographical regions. In the south, a low coastline with lakes, typical of the Gulf of Guinea; a densely populated plain where manioc, corn, banana and palm oil are produced. In the north, subsistence crops are gradually giving way to coffee and cocoa plantations. The Togo Mountains run through the country from north-east to south- west.

SOCIETY

Peoples: The main ethnic groups are the Ewe (43.1 per cent), Kabye (26.7 per cent), Gurma (16.1 per cent), Kebu (3.8 per cent) and Ana (Yoruba, 3.2 per cent). The descendants of formerly enslaved Africans who returned to Togo from Brazil are called Brazilians. They form a caste with great economic and political influence. The small European minority (0.3 per cent) is concentrated in the capital.

Religions: The majority follow traditional African religions (50 per cent). There are Christian (35 per cent) and Muslim (15 per cent) minorities.

Languages: French (official). The main local languages are Ewe, Kabye, Twi and Hausa.

Main Political Parties: Rally of the Togolese People (RTP), was the only legal party from 1969 until 1991; Rally for Democracy and Development (RSDD); Union for Democracy and Social Progress (UDPS); Juvento; Movement of the Believers of Peace and Equality (MOCEP).

Main Social Organizations: National Confederation of Togolese Workers (CNT).

THE STATE

Official Name: République Togolaise.

Administrative Divisions: 5 Regions and 21 Prefectures. **Capital:** Lomé 799,000 people (2003). Other Cities: Sokodé 115,100 people; Kpalimé 47,100; Atakpamé 40,300 (2000).

Government: Gnassingbé Eyadéma, President since April 1967, re-elected in 1998 and 2003. Koffi Sama, Prime Minister since 2002. Unicameral Legislature: 81-member National Assembly. **National Holiday:** 27 April, Independence Day (1960). **Armed Forces:** 6,950 (1997). Other: 750 gendarmes.

LAND USE

2000

IRRIGATED AREA: 0.3% of arable land

- ARABLE LAND: 46.1%
- CROPLANDS: 2.2%
- OTHER USE: 51.6%

	Life expectancy		GNI per capita		Literacy		HIV prevalence rate
	49.7 years		**$270**		**57%** total adult rate		**6%** of population 15-49 years old
	2000-2005		2002		2000		2001

IN FOCUS

ENVIRONMENTAL CHALLENGES
There are signs of serious deforestation attributable to agriculture and the use of wood for fuel. Water pollution poses health risks and a threat to the fishing industry. Air pollution is a growing problem in cities.

WOMEN'S RIGHTS
Women have been able to vote since 1945. There is almost no female representation in Parliament. In 2000, women held 9 per cent of ministerial positions.

They make up 40 per cent of the country's labor force.

Although the gender gap in education was reduced over the period 1990-2000, there are still serious disparities. According to UNICEF's latest data available*, the primary school enrollment rate for men increased from 87 to 100 per cent, while in the case of women it increased from 62 to 82 per cent. In secondary education, the gap is still wider: male enrollment rose from 26 to 32 per cent, while female enrollment increased from 10 to 14. The illiteracy rate fell between 1980 and 2000. Among men it fell from 33 to 28 per cent and among women from 65 to 57.5 per cent.

According to the same databases, seventy-three per cent of pregnant women received prenatal healthcare but only 49 per cent of births were attended by trained health staff. In 2001, 5.4 per cent of pregnant women were HIV-positive.

CHILDREN
According to UNICEF's latest data available*, 15 per cent of newborns suffer from low birth weight. Among children under-5, 25 per cent are moderately or severely underweight and 22 per cent show stunted growth. The infant mortality rate is 87 per 1,000 live births, although it decreased between 1960 and 2002. The under-5 mortality rate decreased from 267 to 140 per 1,000 live births and the under-1 mortality rate fell from 158 to 79 per 1,000 live births.

At the end of 2001, out of the 150,000 people living with HIV/AIDS, 10 per cent were under 14 years of age.

Sixty per cent of children between the ages of 5 and 14 work. In downtown Lomé there is an area known as the 'Child Market' where child prostitution is widely practised. Girls as young as nine are offered for sex for $2 or $3 and some police demand sex in

exchange for not arresting them. Child trafficking is one of Togo's main problems, particularly across the border with Benin. In mid-2001, the Togolese Government was funding a child protection agency and had also increased the number of police officers and army patrol vehicles devoted to controlling this traffic.

INDIGENOUS PEOPLES/ETHNIC MINORITIES
The Akposso people inhabit southern Togo and number about 102,000 people who practise a traditional religion based on a very rich mythology.

Gurma people make up three per cent of the population, living mainly in northern Togo. They are Muslims; mostly pastoralists leading a semi-nomadic life.

The Mamprusi have a population of about 8,000 people. They combine Islam with traditional religion and belong to an ethnic group that is mostly found in Ghana.

Dagombas have a population of about 30,000 and inhabit the western central area. They settled in the 16th century and after a long dispute with Gonja people, managed to occupy what is now their territory. They practise Islam and traditional religions.

There are 11,400 Hausas (the largest group in Central Africa with more than 40 million Hausa-speakers). The largest number of Hausa live in Nigeria and Niger.

The Mossi, in the north-east, have a population of some 23,000. Most Mossi people live in Burkina Faso, making up 53 per cent of its population.

MIGRANTS/REFUGEES
At the end of 2002, nearly 11,000 refugees were living in Togo, the vast majority from Ghana. These Ghanaian refugees remained after the ethnic conflict in their country forced some 15,000 of them to cross the border. Although the Government of Ghana invited the refugees to repatriate in 1999, some 10,000 remained in Togo.

Approximately 5,000 Togolese exiles are found in Benin (1,000), Ghana (1,000) and Western countries.

DEATH PENALTY
Capital punishment has been abolished in practice.

*Latest data available in *The State of the World's Children* and *Childinfo* database, UNICEF, 2004.

---

in Benin. In this same month the presidential guard killed some hundred demonstrators in Lomé, which led to thousands of people fleeing to Ghana and Benin.

[17] In an atmosphere of civil war, Eyadéma won the elections with 96.5 per cent of the vote, in a poll denounced as fraudulent by the opposition. The protests in the streets intensified, and in January 1994, Eyadéma survived unharmed an assassination attempt which left 67 people dead.

[18] The opposition triumphed in the February legislative elections, but Eyadéma barred Prime Minister Edem Kodjo from forming a government without ruling party members. The Action Committee for Renewal, an alliance of opposition groups, decided to boycott the Government for almost a year.

[19] In July 1997 the opposition joined forces to defeat Eyadéma, who had been in power since 1967. Even the military applied pressure on him to liberalize the political system. The following year, the Legislative Assembly approved new press legislation, banning the arbitrary arrest of journalists, as well as other police abuses. The June presidential

elections were considered fraudulent by the opposition; Eyadéma won with 52 per cent of the vote. Over the next months the capital was shaken by constant opposition demonstrations against the election results.

[20] In January 2000, the West African Economic and Monetary Union (WAEMU) member countries - eight West African states that use the CFA franc as national currency (Benin, Burkina Faso, Côte d'Ivoire, Guinea-Bissau, Mali, Niger, Senegal and Togo) - created a customs union and eliminated tariff barriers within the bloc.

[21] The meeting of Francophone nations of West Africa in March 2000 was a diplomatic success for the Eyadéma Government, as Benin, Niger, Burkina Faso and Côte d'Ivoire all attended. In September, Agbeyome Messan Kodjo was made Prime Minister.

[22] In February 2001, an international commission denounced systematic human rights violations in the country - including summary executions, the torture of prisoners, rapes and abductions - following the 1998 elections.

[23] In August 2001, Eyadéma announced he would respect the Constitution and end his term in 2003, the year in which he could no longer legally stand as President. Premier Kodjo supported the possibility of constitutional change allowing Eyadéma to stand again.

[24] After planned legislative elections failed to be held in October, in March 2002 the Joint Commission of Inquiry - created from ruling party and opposition members - met in Lomé to 'revive political dialogue' through the organization of elections. The opposition had refused to participate in the National Electoral Commission until attorney Yawovi Agboyibo - leader of the Togolese opposition imprisoned since 3 August 2001 - was freed. On 16 March 2002, Agboyibo was finally liberated.

[25] In April 2002, WAEMU member countries signed a trade agreement with the US. The countries of the union had previously had closer trade relations with the European Union (EU).

[26] The ruling party won the parliamentary elections held in

October 2002. The main opposition parties staged a boycott in protest at the way the poll was conducted. In December, Parliament reformed the Constitution, removing a clause which barred Eyadéma from seeking a third term as president.

[27] In February 2003, the EU offered support to help organize the June elections provided the Government showed a clear commitment to the democratic process and assured free and fair elections with the participation of all political groups.

[28] Again amid accusations of fraud, Eyadéma was re-elected in the June 2003 elections with 57 per cent of the vote. The EU had decided against sending observers because the preconditions for a free and fair election had not been met. EU aid was suspended until October when the ACP states, arguing that the election had been 'democractic enough', asked that humanitarian aid be resumed.

[29] Eyadéma - now Africa's longest-serving dictator (35 years) - is thought to be ill, and apparently has not been seen in public since Liberation Day celebrations in January. ∎

Tonga / Tonga

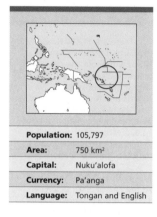

Population:	105,797
Area:	750 km²
Capital:	Nuku'alofa
Currency:	Pa'anga
Language:	Tongan and English

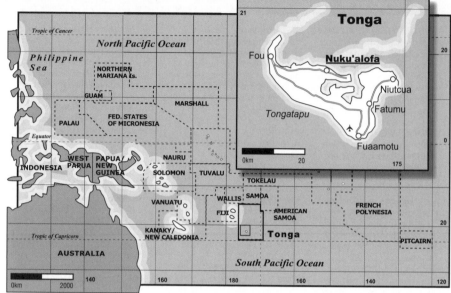

Tonga was inhabited over 1,000 years ago by immigrants from Samoa who created a complex society, with a monarch in charge. The first ruler was Ahoeitu, in the latter half of the 10th century. Towards the 15th century, religious and social roles were separated. That is why the Dutch found two rulers when they came to the islands in 1616. In 1773 British explorer James Cook named the archipelago the 'Friendly Isles'.

[2] In the mid-19th century, after a civil war, King Taufa'ahau Tupou (who after converting to Christianity became George I) secured political union, which had not existed since the 18th century. Backed by European missionaries, he seized Vavau and Tongatopu, introduced a parliamentary system and a land reform which granted each adult male in the country 3.3 hectares of arable land. In the current system, with no more lands to distribute, families share the lots.

[3] In 1889, Britain and Germany signed a treaty which gave Tonga over to Britain. In 1890 the archipelago was made a 'protectorate' of the British Crown, though the monarchy was kept with limited powers.

[4] Queen Salote, great-grand-daughter of George I, was crowned in 1918 and in 1960 she gave women the right to vote in legislative elections.

[5] The British transformed the country's agriculture and fishing, orienting it towards copra and banana crops for export.

[6] Present King Taufa'ahau Tupou IV was crowned in 1967, and in 1970 Tonga obtained independence. A social security system which included free education and medical services for all was implemented.

[7] In the mid-1970s thousands of Tongans emigrated to New Zealand/Aotearoa. Natural disasters, such as the Isaac cyclone in 1992, destroyed part of the crops.

[8] Opposition groups founded the Pro-Democracy Movement (PDM) in 1992, which won six of the nine seats in the National Assembly in the 1993 elections.

[9] In 1994, the PDM became the Tonga Democratic Party, led by 'Akilisi Pohiva.

[10] The King, in spite of promises to the contrary, kept his grip on power almost unchanged.

[11] Demonstrations in favor of political liberalization in 1997 led to the arrest of several political leaders and journalists.

[12] In March 1998, Minister of Lands Fakafanua was arrested and charged with mismanagement of public funds and corruption. He was released a few days later, though barred from leaving the country.

[13] Prince Ulukalala Lavaka Ata was appointed Prime Minister in January 2000, by his father.

[14] The King of Tonga granted research rights to an Australian company in December 2000 to study the islanders' genes. This was in exchange for the benefits of the research being applied free to the Tongans. Scientists are interested in the island's population as there is a high percentage of obese people.

[15] In October 2001, two ministers, including the deputy Prime Minister, were forced to step down after the Government discovered that some $26 million could not be accounted for. A US businessman, Jesse Bogdonoff, who had been appointed official Court Jester by the King, was involved in the financial scandal.

[16] A Constitutional amendment in October 2003 granted more powers to the King and increased state control over the media.

[17] In February 2004 Bogdonoff agreed to pay one million dollars to settle his dispute with Tonga. ■

PROFILE

ENVIRONMENT
The archipelago was known as the 'Friendly Isles' and is located in western Polynesia, east of the Fiji Islands, slightly north of the Tropic of Capricorn. It comprises approximately 169 islands, only 36 of which are permanently inhabited. It includes three main groups of islands: Tongatapu, the southernmost group where more than half of the population live; Vavau, to the north, and Haapai in between. The volcanic islands are mountainous while the coral ones are flat. The climate is mild and rainy with very hot summers. The fertile soil is suitable for growing banana, copra and coconut trees.

SOCIETY
Peoples: Polynesian, European (around 300). It is estimated that 20 per cent of Tongans now live abroad. **Religions:** Free Wesleyan, 43.6 per cent; Roman Catholic, 16.0 per cent; Mormon, 12.1 per cent; Free Church of Tonga, 11.0 per cent; Church of Tonga, 7.3 per cent. **Languages:** Tongan and English are official.
Main Political Parties: Human Rights and Democracy Movement (HRDM, formerly People's Party).

THE STATE
Official Name: Pule'anga Fakatu'i o' Tonga. Kingdom of Tonga.
Administrative Divisions: 23 Districts. Capital: Nuku'alofa 35,000 people (2003). **Other Cities:** Neiafu 4,000 people; Haveloloto 3,200; Vaini 2,800; Tofoa-Koloua 2,400 (2000).
Government: Monarchy, limited by the power of the nobles (the five ministries are lifetime terms). Taufa'ahau Tupou IV, King since 1965; Prince Lavaka Ata 'Ulukalala, Prime Minister since January 2000. Unicameral Legislative Assembly that includes 5 ministers, governors of Háapai and Vavau, 7 nobles (elected by their 33 peers) and 7 deputies elected by male taxpayers aged over 21.
National Holiday: 4 June, Independence Day (1970).
Armed Forces: Tonga Defense Services, comprising the Royal Marines, the Royal Guards and the Maritime Force.

PUBLIC EXPENDITURE

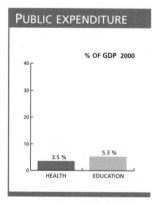

% OF GDP 2000

- HEALTH: 3.5 %
- EDUCATION: 5.3 %

Trinidad and Tobago / Trinidad and Tobago

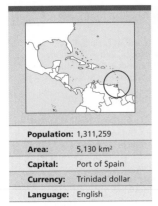

Population:	1,311,259
Area:	5,130 km²
Capital:	Port of Spain
Currency:	Trinidad dollar
Language:	English

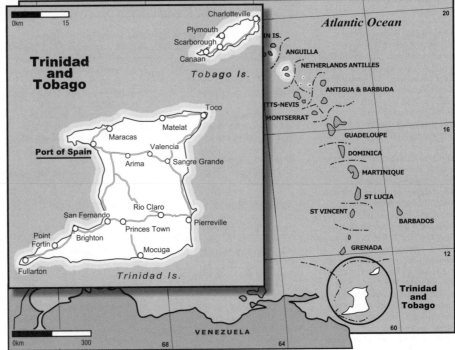

Although the islands of Trinidad and Tobago form a single nation, their histories are different. Trinidad, 12 kilometers from the mouth of the Orinoco River, was claimed by Columbus for Spain in 1498. Tobago had been inhabited by Carib indians, but when the Dutch arrived in 1632, they found it uninhabited. Shortly thereafter the Spanish took the island to prevent the Dutch from using it as a base for exploring the Orinoco, where there was thought to be gold.

2 Like the region's other colonies, the islands underwent numerous Dutch, French and British invasions. Instability and minimal demographic growth were the rule: in 1783 the population consisted of 126 Europeans, 605 Africans (of whom 310 were slaves) and 2,032 Amerindians. Trinidad became a British colony in 1802, as did Tobago in 1814.

3 Once slavery was abolished in 1834, Africans were replaced by workers from India and China on the sugar-cane plantations, which were central to the economy. As a result most of the African population became urban workers, while the majority of rural workers were Indian. Some black workers still living in the countryside developed a mutual aid system called *gayap*, similar to those of other Latin American communities with Amerindian, African or mixed-blood roots.

4 1924 saw the first moves toward autonomy, and the colonial administration allowed limited suffrage for certain minor positions. Trade unions were organized at this time, and they raised the issue of independence.

5 The sugar-cane based economy began to decline in the early 20th century and sugar was gradually replaced by oil, which had become the main economic activity by 1940.

6 In 1950, internal autonomy having been won, the People's National Movement (PNM) won the elections and Dr Eric Williams was appointed Prime Minister.

7 After a brief period as a part of the West Indian Federation (1958-1962), Trinidad and Tobago became independent in 1962.

8 Dramatic increases in oil prices during the 1970s changed the economy and society radically. Worker mobilization also grew.

9 In 1975 worker protests gave way to major strikes which brought together workers from the oil and sugar-cane sectors,

WORKERS

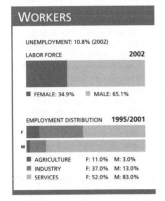

UNEMPLOYMENT: 10.8% (2002)

LABOR FORCE   **2002**

■ FEMALE: 34.9%   ■ MALE: 65.1%

EMPLOYMENT DISTRIBUTION   **1995/2001**

F

M

■ AGRICULTURE	F: 11.0%	M: 3.0%
■ INDUSTRY	F: 37.0%	M: 13.0%
■ SERVICES	F: 52.0%	M: 83.0%

PROFILE

ENVIRONMENT
The country is an archipelago located near the Orinoco River delta off the Venezuelan coast, at the southern end of the Lesser Antilles in the Caribbean. Trinidad, the largest island (4,828 sq km), is crossed from east to west by a mountain range that is an extension of the Andes. One-third of the island is covered with sugar and cocoa plantations. Petroleum and asphalt are also produced. Tobago, 300 sq km with a small central volcanic mountain range, is flanked by Little Tobago (1 sq km), the islet of Goat and the Bucco Reef. In the archipelago the prevailing climate is tropical with rains from June to December, but tempered by the sea and east trade winds. Rivers are scarce, but dense forest vegetation covers the mountains.

SOCIETY
Peoples: There is a large minority of African origin (43 per cent), and a slight majority descended from Asian Indians (40 per cent) brought during the 19th century as contract workers. Mestizo (14 per cent), European (1 per cent) and Chinese (1 per cent) groups make up a small minority. **Religions:** There is no official religion. Catholic 29.4 per cent; Protestant 29.7 per cent; Hindu 23.7 per cent; Muslim 5.9 per cent; other 11.3 per cent.

Languages: English (official). Hindi, Urdu, French and Spanish.
Main Political Parties: The People's National Movement (PNM); United National Congress (UNC); Citizen Alliance (CA); National Alliance for Reconstruction (NAR).
Main Social Organizations: Trinidad and Tobago Labor Congress (TTLC) is the only trade union center, with 80,000 members; Jamaat-al-Muslimeen.

THE STATE
Official Name: Republic of Trinidad and Tobago. **Administrative Divisions:** 7 Counties, 4 Cities with own government, 1 semi-autonomous island, Tobago. **Capital:** Port of Spain 55,000 people (2003). Scarborough is the main town on Tobago. **Other Cities:** San Fernando 29,600 people; Arima 26,400; Point Fortin 17,500 (2000). **Government:** Maxwell Richards, President since March 2003. Patrick Manning, Prime Minister since December 2001, re-elected in October 2002. The Parliament of the Republic of Trinidad and Tobago (Legislature) has two chambers: the House of Representatives, with 36 members, and the Senate, with 31 members. **National Holiday:** 31 August, Independence Day (1962). **Armed Forces:** 2,100 (1996). Other: 4,800 Police.

Life expectancy
71.3 years
2000-2005

GNI per capita
$6,490
2002

Literacy
98% total adult rate
2000

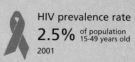

HIV prevalence rate
2.5% of population 15-49 years old
2001

overcoming ethnic rivalry. The movement was defeated when the Government brought out the army to distribute gasoline.

[10] In August 1976 a new constitution proclaimed Trinidad and Tobago a republic. At that time oil-industry nationalization was initiated, and prices were brought into line with OPEC's, while investment from transnationals was encouraged.

[11] In May 1981 Dr Eric Williams died, after 31 years as Prime Minister. George Chambers took over from him.

[12] From 1982 onwards dependence on oil brought about instability and other serious problems. Factors causing the crisis were the international recession and fall in oil prices, as well as falling demand, competition from refineries on the south and east coasts of the US and declining production.

[13] In 1983 the Government confronted the situation with austerity policies, which meant public investment cuts, public salary controls, and doing away with subsidies.

[14] In October the Chambers Government opposed the US invasion of Grenada, and did not contribute to the expeditionary force from six Caribbean nations. The rival National Alliance for Reconstruction (NAR) won the December 1986 elections, taking 33 of 36 parliamentary seats.

[15] Arthur Napoleon Robinson's government proposed a 5-year 'readjustment' plan as of December 1990, designed to hasten integration with CARICOM (Caribbean Community and Common Market) countries.

[16] An austerity plan agreed upon with the IMF, from whom the Government received 110 million dollars in 1988 and a standby loan of 128 million dollars in 1989, led to major strikes in the oil sector, as well as a general strike in March 1989.

[17] The Robinson Administration (committed to reducing inflation to 5 per cent a year, restructuring public enterprises, reducing the size of the state and further liberalizing the economy) abolished export licenses, freed prices (except for basic foodstuffs and pharmaceuticals) and reduced public sector salaries by 10 per cent.

[18] In July 1990 the country's first attempted coup d'état took place when some 100 Muslims occupied parliament and demanded the Prime Minister's resignation. On 1 August the rebel group surrendered and the Government granted them amnesty.

IN FOCUS

ENVIRONMENTAL CHALLENGES
Waters are polluted by agricultural chemicals, industrial waste and raw sewage. Deforestation and soil erosion are also major problems.

Geographic proximity to a major route for maritime traffic leading from the Caribbean and the Gulf of Mexico out into the Atlantic has caused petroleum pollution on the coast.

WOMEN'S RIGHTS
Women have had the vote and been eligible for office since 1946. In 2001, 32 per cent of parliamentary seats and 9 per cent of ministerial level positions were occupied by women.

Participation in the workforce is 34 per cent.

Female primary school enrollment is 92 per cent, and 75 per cent in secondary.

Prenatal medical attention is available to 92 per cent of pregnant women, and 96 per cent of deliveries are attended by qualified personnel.

CHILDREN
The child mortality rate dropped between 1960 and 2002. In the case of children under 5 it fell from 73 to 20 per thousand, and for infants under one from 61 to 17 per thousand.

Twenty-three per cent of newborn babies are underweight.

In late 2001, children accounted for 300 of 17,000 people living with HIV/AIDS.

Net schooling rates are 93 per cent for boys and 92 per cent for girls.

Two per cent of minors aged between 5 and 14 work.

INDIGENOUS PEOPLES/ ETHNIC MINORITIES
The Yaio, Nepuyo, Chaima, Warao, Kalipuna, Carinepogoto, Garani and Arawak tribes, generically known as Caribs, inhabited the islands some 6,000 years before the arrival of the first Europeans. There were some 40,000 when the Spanish settled in 1592. In 1699, the Indian Revolt of Arena (led by Chief Hyarima) was the first major insurrection in favor of the islands' independence. In 1783 they were forced off their land, to make way for sugar plantations worked by African slaves.

Many Carib names are still current, as names of rivers (Caroni and Oropouche), of mountains (Tamana and Aripo), and of locations (Arima, Paria, Arouca, Caura, Tunapuna, Tacarigua, Couva, Mucurapo, Chaguanas, Carapichaima, Guaico, Mayaro, Guayaguayare).

Currently some 12,000 descendants of the original inhabitants live in northeast Trinidad. St Rose Carib Community brings together people who try to preserve ancestral customs and lifestyles.

MIGRANTS/REFUGEES
In April 2004, 7 Liberian citizens sought asylum in Port of Spain, claiming that they ran risk of death in Liberia. These applicants were arrested and held incommunicado at Golden Grove. Amnesty International received reports that the prisoners were mistreated and held in inhuman conditions. Although Trinidad and Tobago is a signatory state of the 1951 Convention on the Statute of Refugees and its 1967 Protocol, the country was apparently not complying with the international agreement.

DEATH PENALTY
Still applicable.

[19] 1990 saw a slight economic recovery, stemming from increases in oil exports due to the Gulf crisis. These allowed the Government to cancel the public sector salary reduction in early 1991.

[20] In December 1991 the PNM won the elections with 46 per cent of the vote. Patrick Manning became Prime Minister. The United National Congress (UNC) took 26 per cent of the vote while Robinson's NAR took 25 per cent. A high number of abstentions were observed. Foreign debt stood at 2.51 billion dollars and unemployment at 24 per cent.

[21] The Government's economic adjustment and privatization plans sparked massive protest demonstrations in January 1993. Manning called out the army to keep matters under control.

[22] The amnesty Robinson had granted the participants in the 1990 attempted coup (114 members of the Muslim group Jamaat-al-Muslimeen) was annulled. This was a largely symbolic measure given that the court ruled that the accused would not be tried or arrested.

[23] Believing that the economic and political situation was favorable to him, Manning called early elections in November 1995. He was, however, mistaken, for the PNM took 17 parliamentary seats, as did Basdeo Panday's opposition UNC.

[24] After making an alliance with the NAR, Panday became Trinidad and Tobago's first prime minister of Indian immigrant stock.

[25] In early 1997 two PNM members of parliament joined the government coalition as independents. This desertion left the PNM only 15 seats to the coalition's 21.

[26] In February 1997 former prime minister Robinson was elected President.

[27] In May that same year British legal authorities prevented the hanging of nine people charged with murders committed in 1996. The UK Privy Council was still the highest legal authority.

[28] The December 2001 general elections ended in a tie between the UNC and the PNM (with 18 parliamentary seats each). Panday and Manning agreed that Robinson should decide who would be Prime Minister. The President chose Manning, but Panday (claiming that the ruling party should continue in power in the case of a draw) requested new elections in six months' time.

[29] Manning called on parliament to appoint a spokesperson to break the deadlock that had been paralyzing the political system for almost four months. However, UNC and PNM members of parliament had still not managed to do so by April 2002, and Panday requested new elections due to the lack of parliamentary support. Manning meanwhile claimed that simply opening parliament would be sufficient to meet constitutional requirements.

[30] Manning won the October 2002 elections, the third in under two years. After a hotly contested race, the PNM won 20 parliamentary seats, while Panday took the remaining 16.

[31] Maxwell Richards was sworn in as President in March 2003, after having been appointed by the electoral college.

[32] In August 2003 over 8,000 jobs were lost with the closure of the state-owned sugar enterprise Caroni, one of the country's largest. ■

Tunisia / *Tunisie*

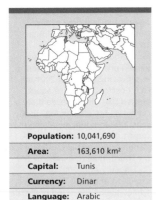

Population:	10,041,690
Area:	163,610 km²
Capital:	Tunis
Currency:	Dinar
Language:	Arabic

From the 12th century BC the Phoenicians had ports in North Africa. Carthage was founded in the 8th century BC and by the 6th century the Carthaginian kingdom encompassed most of present-day Tunisia. Carthage became part of Rome's African province in 146 BC after the Punic Wars. Roman rule lasted until the Muslim Arab invasions in the mid-7th century AD.

[2] In Tunisia the Arabs met the strongest resistance to their advance, but this region eventually became one of the best-cultivated and developed of their cultural centers; the city of Kairuan is associated with some of the most outstanding names in Islamic architecture, medicine and historiography. During the dissolution of the Almohad Empire, Tunisia attained independence under the Berber dynasty of the Hafsids who, between the 13th and 16th centuries, extended their power over the Algerian coast.

[3] European maritime trade attracted Turkish corsairs. The most famous, Khayr ad-Din (known as Red Beard), set up his headquarters in Tunisia, placing the Tunisian-Algerian coast under the authority of the Ottoman sultans. The inland regions, however, remained in the hands of the Berbers, allied to Constantinople (now Istanbul). The need to work with them allowed the Bey (designated governor) to act with a large degree of autonomy and to become in practice a hereditary ruler. The Murad family ruled between 1612 and 1702, and

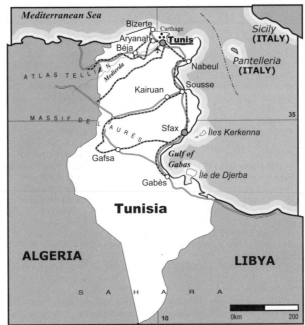

from 1705 until after independence in 1957, this role was filled by the Husseinite family.

[4] After the French occupation of Algeria (1830), European economic penetration became increasingly evident as did indebtedness. In 1869 the burden of the foreign debt forced the Bey to allow an Anglo-French-Italian commission to supervise the country's finances.

[5] In 1882, 30,000 French soldiers invaded the country, under an agreement whereby Britain, which had just occupied Egypt, 'transferred its rights' to Tunisia, to compensate France for its loss of control over the Suez Canal. In 1883 the country formally became a French protectorate.

[6] The Tunisians launched a campaign in 1925 for a Constitution (Destur 1), which would bring autonomy to the country.

[7] Habib Bourguiba, a lawyer, founded the pro-independence party Neo-Destur in 1934. He was imprisoned by the French for 11 years, and again at the end of World War II.

[8] In 1942, during World War II, German troops arrived to fight against the Allies in Algeria; in 1943 the last troops withdrew from the country.

[9] After the War, the Neo-Destur party grew and a series of demonstrations and anti-colonial uprisings led to armed struggle between 1952 and 1955. In 1955, Bourguiba was released and

France granted home rule under the Bey's regime. The Bey was deposed in 1957 by a constituent assembly. A republic was proclaimed with Bourguiba as President. He started an energetic campaign against the French presence at the Bizerte naval base, finally dislodging them in 1964. The Neo-Destur Party became the Destur Socialist Party (PSD) and until 1981 was the only legal political organization.

[10] Between 1963 and 1969, there was a program of collectivization of small farms and trading companies, and nationalized foreign enterprises. Tunisia opposed recognition of Israel by the Arab League in 1968.

[11] In 1969, the collectivization process was aborted and the Tunisian economy was opened up to foreign investment. A 1972 law effectively turned the whole country into a duty-free zone for export industries. Habib Bourguiba, the 'Supreme Warrior', was appointed president for life.

[12] Towards the end of the 1970s, the economy suffered the effects of declining phosphate exports, and protectionist measures applied in the European Economic Community against textile imports. In January 1978, the General Union of Tunisian Workers (UGTT) - the oldest labor union in Africa - called a general strike and street fighting left dozens dead. Union leaders, including the President, Habib Achour, were arrested.

[13] Tunisia, like other Arab states, broke off diplomatic relations with Egypt following the Camp David accords in 1979 which were seen as a betrayal of the Palestinians.

[14] Appointed Prime Minister in 1980, Mohammed Mzali initiated a program of liberalization. Political parties were allowed to reorganize and labor unions and

WORKERS

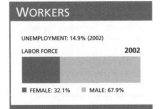

UNEMPLOYMENT: 14.9% (2002)

LABOR FORCE   2002

■ FEMALE: 32.1%   ■ MALE: 67.9%

PROFILE

ENVIRONMENT
Tunisia is the northernmost African state. The eastern coastal plains are heavily populated and intensively cultivated with olives, citrus fruit and vineyards. The interior is dominated by the mountainous Tell and Aures regions populated by nomadic shepherds. The Sahara desert, in the south, has phosphate and iron deposits, while dates are cultivated in the oases.

SOCIETY
Peoples: 93 per cent of Tunisians are Arab, 5 per cent are Berber and 2 per cent are European.
Religions: 99.4 per cent Sunni Muslim. There are also Jewish and Catholic groups.
Languages: Arabic (official). French, Tamazight (Berber). **Main Political Parties:** Democratic Constitutional Rally (RCD); Movement of Socialist Democrats; Unionist Democratic Union; Party of People's Unity; Movement for Renewal; Social-Liberal Party.

Main Social Organizations: General Union of Tunisian Workers (UGTT).

THE STATE
Official Name: Al-Jumhuriyah at-Tunisiyah.
Administrative Divisions: 25 Government Regions.
Capital: Tunis 1,996,000 people (2003).
Other Cities: Safaqis (Sfax) 262,000 people; Aryanah 203,500; Sousse 149,200 (2000).
Government: Zine al-Abidine Ben Ali, who became President after a bloodless coup in November 1987; he was elected as President in April 1989, re-elected in 1994 and 1999. Mohamed Ghannouchi, Prime Minister since November 1999. Unicameral Legislature: Chamber of Deputies, with 182 members.
National Holiday: 20 March, Independence Day (1956).
Armed Forces: 35,500 (1997). Other: 13,000, National Police; 10,000, National Guard.

Life expectancy
72.8 years
2000-2005

GNI per capita
$2,000
2002

Literacy
71% total adult rate
2000

the UGTT were revived. General elections were held in November 1981 in which the ruling National Front won 94 per cent of the vote and all of the seats. Irregularities were reported.

[15] The country received Palestinian militants expelled from Beirut in 1982, and subsequently hosted the official headquarters of the PLO (Palestine Liberation Organization).

[16] In January 1984, the Government decided to end some food subsidies. The price of bread rose 115 per cent and violent demonstrations left more than 100 dead. Bourguiba cancelled the price increases. In 1985, there was further labor unrest and the UGTT was placed under government control. There were also violent confrontations with an emerging Islamic fundamentalist movement that ended with some death sentences.

[17] From 1986 onwards, the process of Westernization (the most far-reaching in the Arab world) was questioned. The Islamic response confronted the public with the issues of religion in the life of the individual and the community, and Tunisia's identity as an Arab-Muslim country. Female emancipation and the influence of tourism were questioned.

[18] Colonel (later General) Zine al-Abidine Ben Ali began his rise to power in 1985. He was appointed Prime Minister in 1987 and in November that year he removed President Bourguiba, who was declared mentally and physically unfit to govern. Ben Ali took over as President. The period of national reconciliation meant greater press freedom and the liberation of hundreds of political prisoners. The PSD, still playing a dominant role, was renamed the Democratic Constitutional Rally (RCD).

[19] The presidential and legislative elections of 2 April 1989 were considered by observers to be the most free and fair since independence, even though 1,300,000 citizens were not registered to vote. The electorate was split between the Government RCD (with 80 per cent of the vote and all the seats) and the Hezb Ennahda Islamic movement, whose independent candidates won 15 per cent. President Ben Ali was elected with 99 per cent of the vote.

[20] In 1991, religious parties were banned. A restrictive law of association was adopted in March 1992 and in July members of Hezb Ennahda were sentenced to life imprisonment.

[21] In November 1993, Ben Ali passed another law limiting 'basic freedoms'. In this political climate,

IN FOCUS

ENVIRONMENTAL CHALLENGES
Inadequate toxic waste dumps are causing serious environmental damage. There is water pollution, deforestation and overgrazing, which causes soil erosion and desertification.

WOMEN'S RIGHTS
Women have been able to vote since 1959. Female representation in parliament slowly increased between 1990 (4 per cent), 1995 (7 per cent) and the year 2003 (12 per cent); 10 per cent of ministerial-level posts were held by women.

In 2000, they comprised 32 per cent of the total labor force. Although 95 per cent of girls attend primary school, the rate drops to 70 per cent in secondary school. The illiteracy rate among women aged 15-24 is 37 per cent, while among the total population it is 26.8 per cent. Prenatal healthcare coverage is 92 per cent, and 90 per cent of births are attended by specialized personnel.

CHILDREN
At birth, seven per cent of babies are underweight. Twelve per cent of under-fives are moderately underweight. The mortality rate for under-fives decreased from 254 per 1,000 in 1960, to 26 per 1,000 in 2002, and for infants under-one from 170 to 21 per 1,000 over the same period. Primary school enrollment and attendance in 2002 was 99 per cent.

INDIGENOUS PEOPLES/ ETHNIC MINORITIES
The Bedouins, located in the city of Gafsa (Qafsa) in the center of the country and the southern region, number around 2,100,000. They have mostly adopted a semi-nomadic form of life and in the winter raise cattle and carry out traditional trading with caravans across the desert. In the summer they crop-farm on the edges of the desert. They are Muslim, mostly Sunni, although some have adopted Sufism.

The Berbers, who speak Tamazight, amount to some 4,500 inhabitants, mostly living on the Island of Jerba, in the Gabes Gulf, to the southwest of Tunis, where they have lived for thousands of years. Europeans and Jews make up 2 per cent of the population.

MIGRANTS/REFUGEES
The country grants refugee status and considers requests for asylum, in line with international recommendations. Extradition of political refugees is prohibited. In the few cases that it was requested, extradition was refused and asylum-seekers were not obliged to return to countries where they had suffered persecution. The UNHCR estimates that there are 120,000 Algerians and 75,000 Iraqis living in the country as refugees.

DEATH PENALTY
In practice, the country has abolished the death penalty. The last execution took place in 1991.

he was re-elected with 99 per cent of the vote in the March 1994 general elections, while the ruling party took control of 88 per cent of seats in parliament.

[22] The plan for economic liberalization and hard-line political policy was continued. One of the main opposition political leaders, Mohamed Moada, was sentenced to 11 years in prison in October 1995 for having published an account of the curtailment of freedoms in Tunisia and for maintaining secret relations with Libya.

[23] At the first multi-party elections, held in October 1999, President al-Abidine Ben Ali took 99.4 per cent of the vote. His party, the DCR, won 148 of the 182 seats, while the other six parties shared the remaining 34 seats. One of the first measures

passed by the new administration was the freeing of 600 political prisoners, mainly those from the al-Nahda Movement and the Workers' Communist Party.

[24] The death of Habib Bourguiba in April 2000 brought together political leaders from Europe and the Arab countries, including Presidents Jacques Chirac of France, Abdelaziz Bouteflika of Algeria and Yasser Arafat of Palestine.

[25] In March 2001, Amnesty International (AI) called on Tunisia to stop the escalation of harassment and pressure on human-rights activists. In its report, AI stated that the pressure began when the Tunisian League of Human Rights was suspended in November 2000. From then on, all League meetings were prevented by the security forces

and legal action was started against the president of the Human Rights League, Moktar Trifi, and others.

[26] Although the constitution limited presidents to three terms in office, in September 2001 the DCR Central Committee again elected Ben Ali as presidential candidate for 2004. In May that year, a referendum modifying the constitution enabled Ben Ali to stand as presidential candidate for the fourth time running.

[27] In early April 2002 an explosion in the old Ghriba synagogue on the island of Djerba left 19 dead. The authorities blamed the attack on two Tunisians, one living in the French city of Lyon, and the other in Tunisia.

[28] At the beginning of 2003, President Ben Ali made several appeals for a peaceful solution to the Iraq problem and supported the UN Security Council resolutions on this issue.

[29] In October, the Government condemned the attacks by Israel on Syria and demanded strict compliance with international legislation to avoid the escalation of violence in the Middle East.

[30] During US Secretary of State Colin Powell's visit to Tunisia in December 2003, issues related to the crisis in the region were discussed and Ben Ali was invited to visit the US in February 2004.

[31] Following the arrest of Iraqi leader Saddam Hussein in December 2003, Tunisia called for efforts to find a way to enable Iraq to recover its sovereignty and find peace. The same month parliament adopted an anti-terrorist and anti-money-laundering law.

[32] In February 2004, Ben Ali visited Washington, where he had discussions on bilateral issues and the situation in the Middle East.

[33] In 2004, General Habib Ammar was designated president of the organizing committee for the World Summit on the Information Society to be held in Tunisia in 2005. Ammar - a commander in the National Guard and later Minister of the Interior after Ben Ali's coup - has criminal charges hanging over him. These were lodged by the World Organization Against Torture (OMCT) and the Swiss Association Against Impunity (TRIAL) before the Geneva General Prosecutor, and accuse him of turning police stations into detention centers, and torturing opposition members, including the press.

[34] The March Arab Summit in Tunis was postponed at short notice after officials failed to agree on ways to reform the Middle East. ■

Turkey / Türkiye

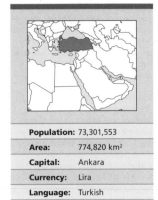

Population:	73,301,553
Area:	774,820 km²
Capital:	Ankara
Currency:	Lira
Language:	Turkish

The territory that in 1923 became the Turkish Republic has been inhabited by many different peoples since before the 10th millennium BC.

2   Animal figures carved in caves near Anatolia (the name given to the Asian territory of modern Turkey, as well as Asia Minor) are the oldest traces of human habitation here. Representations of humans from the 7th millenium BC have been found in Hacilar.

3   Wall paintings in the prehistoric city of Catalhoyuk show the customs, dress and deities of an agricultural indigenous people from the mid-7th and 6th centuries BC, who raided the Mediterranean Sea area.

4   Between 5500 and 4500 BC the fortification, sculpture and painting on pottery from Mersin reached a peak of inventiveness. In the latter half of that period, people's lives were revolutionized by the development of metallurgy in copper, bronze, iron, silver and gold.

5   From the 4th millennium BC until 2300 BC Indo-European invaders - mostly Achaeans from Thessalia, in the north of modern Greece - settled on the southeast coast and in the center of the territory of modern Turkey. The kingdoms of Troy (now Hihsarlik), Alisar Huyuk (in central Anatolia), Beycesultan and Cilicia (in the southeast) were prominent.

6   Achaean architecture and artforms - which included a repertoire of cuneiform symbols arising from their diplomatic and trade relations with Assyria and Mesopotamia - inspired the later foundation of the Mycenaean culture (15th century BC) by the Achaeans in modern Greece.

7   In the 17th century BC, the Hatti culture of Alisar Huyuk was extinguished by the settling of the Indo-European Hittite Empire, which shared hegemony with the Arameans (nomadic semitic groups) as it expanded into Syria. The region of Cilicia remained under the control of the Armenian kingdom of Urartu, until 250 BC, when it was conquered by Parthians (Iranian). The latter were displaced by the Romans in 224.

8   The Hittite empire collapsed in the 12th century BC, as a result of several invasions from Balkan Phrygians and Thracians, among others, who had occupied Greece. In the 8th and 7th centuries BC their expeditions from Greece set forth throughout the Mediterranean, and they founded Byzantium - now Istanbul - among many other cities.

9   In the 7th century BC, the Thracians founded the kingdom of Lydia (now southwest Turkey). Its prosperous gold trade led to the introduction of currency in Greece.

10   Between 546 BC and 334 BC, Anatolia (Cilicia had been annexed in 250 BC) remained under control of the Persian Achaemenian empire, which forced its mostly Greek inhabitants to fight against Athens during the Peloponnesian War.

11   Alexander the Great invaded Asia Minor in 334 BC, but his empire there was short-lived, since some regions were fiercely defended by local princes and others by the Syrians. In the two following centuries, Celtic peoples arrived in the area, while the Romans also started to take territories. The Romans annexed Anatolia as a province of the Roman Empire in the 1st century BC.

12   Asia Minor remained under Christianity's political, religious and cultural dominion from the reconstruction of Byzantium when it became Constantinople, the capital of the Eastern Roman Empire (334/340-1453), until the partial occupation of Asia Minor by Turkish-Mongolian Oguz peoples in the 11th century.

13   The (orthodox) Persian Sunni Muslim house of the Seleucids had Islamized the Oguz during the 10th century. However, the Oguz - like the old inhabitants of Asia Minor - refused to accept the bureaucratic regulations the Persians tried to impose along with their religious practices.

14   In 1299, the Mongolian Turkish leader Osman founded an independent state in Anatolia which, under the name of the Ottoman Empire, would later extend to Asia, Europe - through the Balkan peninsula - and Africa.

15   In 1375, after repelling an invasion by the Mameluke army (in power in Egypt and Syria between 1250 and 1517), the Ottomans defeated the Byzantine Empire (weakened by the Crusades) by taking Constantinople in 1453. It was renamed Istanbul by Mehmed II, the Conqueror, as the capital of his empire.

16   Sultan Selim I, when appointed Caliph (king and religious chief of Islam), extended the Ottoman Empire to Syria, Egypt and part of Mesopotamia, between 1512 and 1520.

17   The reign of Selim's successor, Sultan Suleyman the Magnificent (1520-1566) marked the pinnacle of the Ottoman Empire. During this period, his court developed a culture that blended the Byzantine and Seleucid traditions, as shown in the architecture of the city of Sinan, (Mimar). The Empire became a French ally and thus dominated the

WORKERS

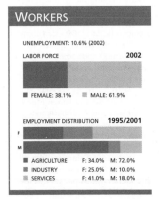

UNEMPLOYMENT: 10.6% (2002)

LABOR FORCE   2002

■ FEMALE: 38.1%   ■ MALE: 61.9%

EMPLOYMENT DISTRIBUTION   1995/2001

F

M

■ AGRICULTURE	F: 34.0%	M: 72.0%
■ INDUSTRY	F: 25.0%	M: 10.0%
■ SERVICES	F: 41.0%	M: 18.0%

LAND USE

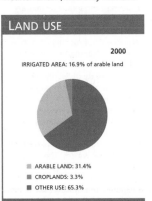

2000

IRRIGATED AREA: 16.9% of arable land

■ ARABLE LAND: 31.4%	
■ CROPLANDS: 3.3%	
■ OTHER USE: 65.3%	

PUBLIC EXPENDITURE

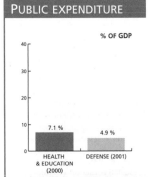

% OF GDP

7.1 % HEALTH & EDUCATION (2000)

4.9 % DEFENSE (2001)

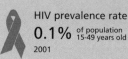
Mediterranean region, occupying Morocco, Algeria, Tunisia, Libya, Hungary, and even laying siege to Vienna.

[18] After Suleyman's death, the Ottoman Empire declined, in part because of the prosperity brought to Western Europe by American gold and silver and the expansion of British and Dutch trade.

[19] In 1571, the victory at the sea battle of Lepanto signalled the triumph of the Christians through the Holy League - led by John of Austria, with Spanish and Venetian and papal support - and effectively ended the Ottoman navy's control of the Mediterranean. The Ottomans tried to take Vienna once again in 1683. Under the treaty of Karlowitz (1699) Lepanto was returned to them but they had to give Hungary over to Austria, as well as part of Ukraine and Podolia to Poland. Also, they lost their territories north of the Black Sea in several defeats against Russia.

[20] In the 19th century, the remains of the Ottoman Empire went through permanent crisis: its Christian regions sought independence, while many regional *Pashas* (administrative authorities) rebelled. The only thing that prevented the Empire from falling apart was the rivalry between Russia and Britain over the control of Christian insurgents.

[21] Greek independence (1831-32) was followed by Egypt's (1839-41).

The treaty of San Stefano ended the Russian-Turkish wars (1877-78), with great territorial losses for the Ottomans. Also at the Congress of Berlin (1878), European power forced the Turks to withdraw from Serbia, Montenegro, Romania, Bulgaria, Bosnia, Herzegovina and Cyprus, which remained under British control.

[22] In the Tanzimat ('reorganization') period from 1839-1876, the Ottomans borrowed large sums from the British for revitalizing the economy. The debts undermined the reforms and suppression followed. A parliamentary monarchic Constitution was accepted by the Sultan in 1876 but never promulgated.

[23] In 1908, a reform movement of university and military academy students - the Young Turks - rebelled, demanding the implementation of the 1876 Constitution. In 1909, Sultan Abdul Hamid was deposed by Muhammad V, but the sultans' power was now limited. The Young Turks' reforms included the secularization of Muslim schools and courts and the introduction of women's rights during World War I (1914-1918). The modern state apparatus of the Tanzimat was democratized, while management of the economy, industry and agriculture were developed.

[24] In 1911-12, Italy occupied Libya, Turkey's last African possession, and Rhodes, among other islands in the Aegean sea. After the Balkan Wars in 1912-13, Turkey was left with only Eastern Thrace in Europe.

[25] In World War I (1914-18), the Ottoman Empire sided with Germany and the Austro-Hungarian Empire. Minority ethnic groups that remained in Turkey were brutally repressed by the Young Turk Government, which killed some one million Armenians in 1915 in the first genocide of the 20th century. Armenians and Greeks had controlled much industry and business before the War.

[26] In 1919, a Turkish nationalist movement organized by military leader Mustafa Kemal (later known as Ataturk: father of all Turks) formed a revolutionary government in Ankara, leading the Turkish War of Independence (1918-1923).

[27] The Treaty of Sèvres (1920) took away all the Ottoman Asian dependencies, Eastern Thrace (except Istanbul and its suburbs), Gallipoli, its Aegean islands and Smyrna, while the Bosphorus strait and the Dardanelles were declared international waters. The Treaty also granted autonomy to the Turkish region of Armenia and the area inhabited by Kurds (20 million people in 2004), which was then called Kurdistan (spread between Turkey, Iraq, Iran and Syria), where oil had been found. The area holds 100 per cent of Turkish oil and 74 per cent of Iraqi oil. The Treaty was not recognized by Ataturk's movement.

[28] After repulsing a Greek incursion into Asia Minor in 1922, Ataturk deposed Sultan Muhammad VI and negotiated a new treaty, signed in Lausanne in 1923, which exempted his country from paying war reparations, cancelled the privileges enjoyed by foreign traders, and set Turkey's current borders, ignoring Kurdistan's autonomy.

[29] In 1923, Ataturk proclaimed the Republic of Turkey and was elected President by the National Assembly, where Ataturk's Republican People's Party (CHP) held a majority until 1950.

[30] Ataturk banned the two opposition parties that were formed before his death. The Kurdish separatist movement, that rebelled in 1925, 1930 and 1937, was the only organization that challenged his regime.

[31] Implementing his party's program (identical to the 1937 Constitution) between 1924 and 1937, Ataturk imposed a new national identity that sought to undermine imperial traditions and build on the Young Turks' reforms. Measures included the use of Turkish as the official language and prohibition of other languages, use of the Latin alphabet and Gregorian calendar.

[32] Turkey, which had regained the Bosphorus and Dardanelles in the 1936 Montreux Conference, declared its neutrality when World War II (1939-45) began.

[33] The centralized economy of Ataturk's autocratic regime exacerbated the low productivity that had contributed to the fall of the Ottoman Empire. After his death in 1938, his successor Ismet Inonu (1884-1973) saw the risk of losing territory near the Black Sea to the USSR after World War II, and accepted US military bases and loans from 1947. The Turkish President adopted liberalization measures in exchange.

[34] In 1947, Inonu reinstated the Democratic Party (DP - split from the CHP), the National Party (NP - pro-Ataturk) and some newspapers that operated under censorship. Like Kemal, he also repressed separatist, religious, socialist and communist activity. Among those jailed was poet Nazim Hikmet (1902-63) whose work - known in Turkey after his death - synthesized Turkish oral poetry.

[35] In the 1950 elections, the DP candidate Celal Bayar was chosen president with 54 per cent of the vote. The president of the outgoing

PROFILE

ENVIRONMENT

The country is made up of a European part, Eastern Thrace, and an Asiatic part, the peninsula of Anatolia and Turkish Armenia, separated by the Dardanelles, the Sea of Marmara and the Bosphorus. Eastern Thrace, located in the southeast of the Balkan Peninsula, makes up less than one-thirtieth of the country's total land area, including an arid steppe plateau, the Istranca mountains to the east, and a group of hills suitable for farming. Anatolia is a mountainous area with many lakes and wetlands. The Ponticas range in the north and the Taurus range in the south form the natural boundaries of the Anatolian plateau, which extends eastward to form the Armenian plateaus. The east is occupied by the Armenian massif, around the lake region of Van, where there is much volcanic activity and occasional earthquakes. Parallel to the Taurus there are a number of ranges known as Antitaurus, which run along the borders of Georgia, together with the Armenian mountains. The country is mainly agricultural. The lack of natural resources, and absence of capital and appropriate infrastructure, have been major obstacles to industrialization.

SOCIETY

Peoples: Most are descendents of ethnic groups from Central Asia that began to settle in Anatolia in the 11th century. The largest minority is Kurdish (20 per cent), followed by Arabs (1.5 per cent), Jews, Greeks, Georgians and Armenians (0.3 per cent). Their cultural autonomy is limited.
Religions: Mainly Islamic (80 per cent Sunni, 20 per cent Shi'a, of which 14 per cent are Alevi, non-orthodox Shi'a); Christians (0.2 per cent).
Languages: Turkish (official) and some 30 languages of ethnic minorities, such as Kurmanji spoken by the Kurdish minority.
Main Political Parties: Justice and Development Party (AKP); Republican People's Party (CHP); True Path Party; Nationalist Action Party; Motherland Party.
Main Social Organizations: Confederation of Public Sector Unions; Confederation of Revolutionary Workers Unions; Moral Rights Workers Union; Turkish Confederation of Employers' Unions; Women for Women's Rights.

THE STATE

Official Name: Túrkiye Cumhuriyeti.
Administrative Divisions: 74 Provinces.
Capital: Ankara 3,428,000 people (2003).
Other Cities: Istanbul 9,500,000 people; Izmir (Smyrna) 2,272,500; Bursa 1,164,400; Adana 1,137,100; Gaziantep 778,200 (2000).
Government: Head of State: Ahmet Necdet Sezer, President since 5 May 2000. Head of Government: Recep Tayyip Erdogan, Prime Minister since March 2003. The Great National Assembly of Turkey has 550 seats.
National Holiday: 29 October, Republic Day (1923).
Armed Forces: 639,000 troops (1996); 390,000 conscripts (1996). Other: 70,000 Gendarmes-National Guard; 50,000 Reserves.

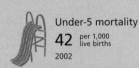

Under-5 mortality
42 per 1,000 live births
2002

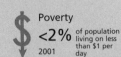

Poverty
<2% of population living on less than $1 per day
2001

Debt service
40.0% exports of goods and services
2001

Maternal mortality
70 per 100,000 live births
2000

Senate, Menderes (executed in 1961) allowed some Sunni Islamic practices that were strictly monitored.

[36] The Bayar administration (1950-60) increased Turkey's economic and political dependence on the US. Turkey joined NATO in 1952. Annual average inflation rose to 15 per cent in that period, when Turkish emigration to Europe (mainly Germany, where 2.5 million Turks lived in 2004) began.

[37] The 1959 British-Turkish-Greek agreement on Cyprus included British withdrawal but did not determine the issue of sovereignty over the island in a way that satisfied both Turks and Greeks. That, added to a series of corruption accusations against the DP cabinet and growing unemployment, caused widespread protests that led to a military coup on 28 April 1960.

[38] After the coup, the military imposed martial law and formed the National Unity Committee, where Muslims and non-religious wrote a secular Constitution which was approved the following year by referendum.

[39] The October 1961 elections were marked by confusion and fear. They were won by the successors to the banned DP (Justice Party - JP, Party of the New Turkey and Peasants' Party), which had been heavily rejected 18 months earlier. General Gursel was elected president, with a coalition government led by Inonu.

[40] Civil liberties continued to improve slightly until the Government resigned in 1965. In 1964, legislation was brought in to prevent the consolidation of the JP in Parliament. Between 1962 and 1964, the Turkish Government amnestied the DP's political prisoners and legalized trade unions.

[41] The UN prevented an armed conflict between Turkey and Greece in 1963 when a civil war broke out in Cyprus.

[42] The JP won the 1965 elections with 51 per cent of the vote. It was formed by Muslims and secular groups, both for and against state intervention in the economy.

[43] The outgoing president, Suleiman Demirel (JP - re-elected in 1969) was able to reconcile opposing interests and attracted foreign investment, but the army forced him to resign in March 1971 after an escalation of violence between the leftist Federation of Turkish Revolutionary Youth and the Turkish People's Liberation Army (founded in 1969), and radical groups from the JP that in 1970 had formed the DP.

[44] In April 1971, a new government coalition formed by the army decreed martial law until

IN FOCUS

ENVIRONMENTAL CHALLENGES
Istanbul is polluted with high levels of sulfur dioxide and the Marmara Sea is contaminated with mercury. Uncontrolled logging also contributes to environmental degradation.

WOMEN'S RIGHTS
Women have been able to vote and run for office since 1930. In the year 2000 they held 4 per cent of Parliament seats and 5 per cent of ministerial positions.

Turkish women comprise 38 per cent of the workforce. 59 per cent of them work in agriculture; 27 per cent in the service sector and 14 per cent in industries.

Violence against women, particularly within marriage, is a major problem. According to the Government's Family Research Institute, beating in the home is the most frequent form of violence against women. Nearly one-third (31.5 per cent) of married and/or divorced women have been beaten by their husbands; 21.5 per cent of them were often beaten by their parents before marrying and 41 per cent of their marriages were arranged or forced. Spousal abuse is considered an extremely private matter, involving societal notions of family honor. Few women go to the police or other institutions seeking help.

'Honor killings' - the murder of women by male family members when they are suspected or proven to be unfaithful or of having sex before marriage - continue in rural areas. According to medical reports there are dozens of this kind of murder each year, and they are more frequent among Kurd families in the southeast.

Spousal rape is not considered a crime. Rapists can evade punishment if they agree to marry their victims. Punishment for sexual assault is more severe if the victim is married rather than than single or not a virgin.

CHILDREN
According to UNICEF's latest data available*, the infant mortality rate is 36 deaths per 1,000 live births and under-5 mortality is 42 deaths per 1,000 live births. Sixteen per cent of newborns are underweight and the same percentage is also undersized. Between 77 and 82 per cent of children under one year old are immunized against the commonest childhood diseases such as poliomyelitis, measles and tetanus.

According to the Government, 92 per cent of girls and 100 per cent of boys attend primary school. However, in rural areas the enrolment rate for girls is significantly lower than that for boys.

The number of workers between 12 and 17 years old dropped from 1.5 million in 2001 to 948,000 in 2003, thanks to the enforcement of new laws which prohibit the employment of children younger than 15.

INDIGENOUS PEOPLES/ ETHNIC MINORITIES
Kurds comprise 20 per cent of the country's population. Most of them live in the southeast, although thousands have given up public expressions of their culture, have been assimilated into Turkish society, and live in Istanbul. Kurds living in Turkey are mostly Sunni Muslims, although a Shi'a minority also exists. Southeastern Kurds depend on agriculture for their livelihoods and continue to be semi-nomadic.

Kurds in Turkey face a great deal of social, cultural, economic and political discrimination. For a long time the Government has marginalized the southeastern region of the country by allocating it meager budgets. Until 1991, speaking Kurdish in public was outlawed. In 2003 the Turkish Government, pressured by EU demands, allowed a few Kurdish language courses and broadcasts.

MIGRANTS/REFUGEES
In late 2002 there were about 10,000 refugees and asylum seekers in Turkey, mostly from Iran (4,800) and Macedonia (between 3,000 and 4,000), and, to a lesser extent, from Iraq and former Yugoslavia.

Almost 44,300 Turks, mostly Kurds, are seeking asylum around the world.

DEATH PENALTY
Abolitionist for ordinary crimes. There have been no executions since 1984.

*Latest data available in *The State of the World's Children* and *Childinfo* database, UNICEF, 2004.

the 1973 elections, when the army replaced military courts by 'special security courts' that were still active in 2004.

[45] No party obtained a majority in the 1973 elections. Bulent Ecevit, of the Social Democratic People's Party, founded in 1972 by Ismet Inonu, was the candidate with the most votes. The pro-Ataturk Inonu and his CHP followers had proclaimed themselves social-democrats, calling upon their traditional following among Turkish peasants. Inonu sought to modify his public image after his close association with army, The JP and the Islamic National Salvation Party (NSP) came in second and third.

[46] Ecevit ruled in coalition with the NSP between January and September 1974.

[47] Turkish military intervention in Cyprus caused that island to divide in July 1974, provoking cabinet splits. The cabinet was replaced with a crisis committee which alternated in government with Ecevit and Demirel, while clashes with guerrillas and right-wing extremists intensified in the interior.

[48] On 12 September 1980 General Kenan Evren dissolved Parliament and applied martial law with a brutality that resulted in thousands of accusations of human rights violations by several Western European organizations.

[49] In 1982, the official return to democracy was heralded with a new constitution that included a one-chamber Parliamentary system. However, 200 candidates were banned from the 1983 elections and martial law was still in place in 1987.

[50] The 1983 elections were won by Turgut Ozal (a former World Bank official), leading the new center-right coalition of the Motherland Party. Ozal embraced economic liberalism with the aim of gaining access to the European Economic Community (EEC).

[51] In 1984, Kurdish separatists founded the Kurdistan Workers Party (PKK), launching an armed struggle in southeast Turkey. That year, the Government recognized the Northern Republic of Cyprus.

[52] In 1987 inflation reached 87 per cent. However, Ozal was helped by the fact that Turkey's application to join the EEC was accepted. He obtained 36 per cent of the vote in the elections, followed by Demirel with 29 per cent and the True Path Party (TPP).

[53] The EEC made Turkey's admission conditional on its ratification of human rights treaties, the normalization of its relations with Greece (which implied negotiations on the status of Cyprus and the Aegean Sea oil), and the reduction of unemployment.

[54] In 1988, Istanbul was freed from 8 years of martial law, after the Government pledged itself to enforce human rights at the European Council and the UN.

Malnutrition
8% under-5s
1995-2002

Water source
82% of population using improved drinking water sources
2000

Doctors
127 per 100,000 people
1990-2002

55 In October 1989, Ozal was re-elected President, in spite of having been defeated in the March municipal elections due to accusations of corruption.

56 In August 1990, when Iraq was blockaded after the invasion of Kuwait, Turkey interrupted the flow of Iraqi oil to the Mediterranean by blocking the oil pipeline through its territory. It also allowed the use of its military airports and US bases for the bombing of Iraq.

57 In October 1991, 20,000 Turkish soldiers entered northern Iraq in order to attack PKK bases. Kurdish representatives accused the Turkish Government of bombing the civilian population.

58 The October 1991 parliamentary elections were won by Suleyman Demirel's True Path Party (TPP) with 27 per cent of the vote. Demirel sought an alliance with Erdal Inonu's Social Democratic Populist Party (SDPP), which came in third, to become Prime Minister. The Motherland Party (ANAP), which obtained 24 per cent of the vote, formed the opposition, although it would support any measure leading to Turkey's admission into the EEC.

59 In mid-March 1992, the banned PKK announced the formation of a war government and a national assembly in the territory they claimed as the core of Kurdistan. In April, Turkey and Syria announced an agreement to fight against the PKK. Syria closed its PKK training camps and carried out stricter controls along its borders.

60 In 1992, the Council of Europe urged the Government to reduce repression against the Kurdish community. The Turkish authorities subsequently granted an amnesty to 5,000 political prisoners and authorized the use of the Kurdish language in public places. In November, the EEC set 1996 as the date for Turkish admission to the Customs Union, a first step toward eventual membership.

61 Upon the death of President Turgut Ozal in April 1993, Demirel was chosen as his successor. Tansu Ciller, minister of economic affairs, assumed the leadership of the DYP and was named Prime Minister. Ciller, the first woman to head a government in Turkey, announced she would cut back state spending. In July, some 700,000 civil servants carried out strikes and demonstrations for several days in Ankara, Istanbul and Izmir.

62 In 1995 the Government used 35,000 soldiers to launch its largest offensive against the PKK, with support from Iranian Kurds from the Kurdistan Democratic Party in order to dismantle PKK bases and attack Kurdish towns. By 2004, some 4,000 Kurdish towns had been destroyed.

63 Prime Minister Ciller's TPP and the ANAP formed a government coalition, led by Mesul Yilmaz from the ANAP, who took office in March 1996. In April Turkey signed a military agreement with Israel. On 24 April, a few days before a Muslim festival, Ankara shut off the water supply to Damascus (Syria), alleging technical difficulties at one of its dams.

64 In June 1996, the alliance was dissolved and the TPP chose to rule with the fundamentalists (PP). Necmettin Erbakan became became the first Muslim head of government in Turkey since 1923. The PP had obtained 158 of the 550 seats, pledging to create Islamic organizations to balance the influence of NATO and the EU in Turkish domestic affairs.

65 The President replaced Erbakan with Mesut Yilmaz (ANAP) in June 1997, but Yilmaz was forced to resign over accusations of corruption in January 1998. He was replaced by Bulent Ecevit (SDP).

66 In January 1998, the Constitutional Court, which had accused Erbakan the previous year of leading the country to the brink of civil war and conspiring against the secular regime (while the army claimed the PP leader was connected to underground Islamic organizations), banned him from politics for five years and dissolved his party. The PP then became the Islamic Virtue Party (VP).

67 In September 1998, the Islamic mayor of Istanbul, Recep Tayyip Erdogan, was sentenced to 10 months in prison, having been accused of reading religious verses at a public event, while the Government was getting ready to celebrate the Republic's 75th year and commemorate the 60th anniversary of Ataturk's death.

68 In July 1999, PKK leader Abdullah Ocalan was sentenced to death after his extradition five months earlier from the Greek embassy in Kenya, where he had requested asylum. That year, Greece lifted its veto on Turkey's admission into the EU and announced it was willing to negotiate the unification of Cyprus.

69 Two earthquakes in the northwestern city of Ismit killed some 20,000 people that year.

70 The Party of the Democratic Left (DSP) led by Ecevit won 22 per cent of the vote, and Ahmet Necder Sezer became President.

71 Sezer, an independent, began a seven year term in May 2000. Although he defended the military's secularism, Sezer had been in favor of eliminating clauses that curbed civil liberties from the 1982 Constitution in order to facilitate Turkey's integration into the EU. The following month, Ecevit was appointed Prime Minister.

72 In July 2001 a new pro-Islamic party, called Saadet - 'happiness' - was founded by members of the VP, which had been banned in June by the Constitutional Court.

73 That year, the European Human Rights Constitutional Court declared Turkey was guilty of human rights violations against the Greek population of Cyprus during its occupation of that island's northern sector. In March 2002, Turkey allowed a gas pipeline through its territory to supply Greece.

74 In January 2002, Turkish women recovered the rights of property and inheritance that had been eliminated at the time of Ataturk's death.

75 In the November 2002 elections, the Islamic vote, through the Party for Justice and Development (AKP), won 365 of the 550 Parliament seats with 34.3 per cent of the vote, followed by the CHP with 19.4 per cent.

76 Although the AKP leader, Erdogan, was not allowed to take part in the 2002 elections, his party campaigned for the elimination of secular principles from the Constitution.

77 Abdullah Gul (AKP), who became Prime Minister in November 2002, handed over the post to Erdogan in March 2003, after legislative reforms enabled this move.

78 Erdogan's popularity was based on his self-made image: he started life in a poor family, went to university and became mayor of Istanbul. Erdogan said that as Prime Minister he would direct his administration in such a way as to allow Turkey to become a full member of the EU by 2012.

79 The year before, inflation had reached 45 per cent, while 50 per cent of the Government's spending was used to pay the interest on foreign debts. A new IMF loan was contracted, on condition that public spending would be reduced and taxes would be increased.

80 When Erdogan took office in March 2003, Parliament prevented the US from using its military bases in Turkey to attack Iraq, although it allowed US planes to fly over Turkish territory.

81 In July 2003, Parliament passed laws in respect of Kurdish rights and abolished the death penalty. This changed Ocalan's situation, and his sentence was commuted to life imprisonment. In September, the Kurdish Congress for Liberty and Democracy in Kurdistan (former PKK) ended a ceasefire that had been in force since 2001, arguing that the authorities were not implementing Kurdish rights.

82 In November 2003 a car bomb next to a synagogue in Istanbul killed 25 people and injured more than 200. Two days later, two coordinated attacks against the Brisith consulate and a British bank killed another 25 people in the capital, where in January 2002 two people had been killed by what was apparently a suicide bomb attack at a Masonic lodge.

83 In February 2004 the European Council presented Ankara with a project for the effective enforcement of Kurdish rights based on an Amnesty International report that accused the Turkish authorities of more than 30,000 deaths, thousands of 'disappearances', torture, sexual violence against women and so on.

84 The European Council also urged the Government to ratify the Rome Statute of the International Criminal Court, to limit the number of military officers in the National Security Council - which monitors government institutions - and to dissolve the 'special security courts' accused of human rights abuses. The Council also asked Turkey to negotiate a rapid redress of abuses against the Greek population in Cyprus.

85 In April 2004, the Turkish and Greek inhabitants of Cyprus voted in a referendum to decide on unification between south (Greek) and north (Turkish), and on integration into the EU. The Greek population voted against the first issue - in effect preventing unification - and in favor of the second one, while the Turkish residents voted for both. The EU promised to study the implementation of an economic development plan for the Turkish population of Cyprus, which can only trade with Turkey and is almost totally isolated.

86 In the last two decades the Turkish drug cartels have been in control of most of the heroin used by some 30 million Europeans. They have turned Turkey into the main drug dealing hub between Asia and Europe.

87 In April 2004 with Bulgaria's admission to NATO Turkey was no longer the only member country with land access to the Black Sea.

88 In June 2004 Istanbul hosted a NATO summit under heavy security. Four people died and several were injured in attacks during the summit, which provoked protest from pacifists and environmentalists. The US did not persuade Turkey to intervene in Iraq. Ankara only offered bilateral help to its neighbor country. The refusal of Germany, and especially of French President Jacques Chirac, was decisive in this matter (see history of Iraq).

89 In October 2004 Turkey was finally accepted as a formal candidate for European Union membership, despite continued doubts expressed about its human-rights record. ∎

Turkmenistan / Türkmenistan

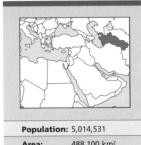

Population:	5,014,531
Area:	488,100 km²
Capital:	Ashkhabad
Currency:	Manat
Language:	Turkmen

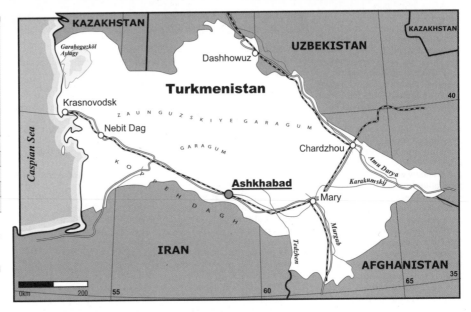

From 1000 BC onwards, the area now known as Turkmenistan formed part of different states: first the Persian Empire (controlled by the Achaemenid dynasty) and later the empire of Alexander the Great. In the third century AD it was conquered by the Sassanids, an Iranian dynasty.

² Between the 5th and 8th centuries, there were successive invasions by the Eftalites, the Turks and the Arabs. From the 6th to the 8th century, the whole Caspian Sea area was controlled by the Arab Caliphate. When that declined in the 9th and 10th centuries, the territory became a part of the Tahirid and Sassanid states. In the mid-11th century, the Seljuk Empire was formed in Turkmenistan. During this period, the Turkmens emerged as an ethnic group through the fusion of Oguz Turks and local groups, and towards the end of the 12th century they were conquered by the Khwarazm Shah dynasty.

³ In the early 13th century, Genghis Khan invaded Turkmenistan and his heirs divided it. The northern regions were taken by the Mongol Tatars. In the 14th and 15th centuries, the country fell under the Timurids (of Tamerlane), who were succeeded by the Uzbek khans of the Shaybani dynasty. From the 16th to the 18th centuries, Turkmenistan was divided among the khanates of Khiva and Bukhara, and the Persian Safavid state.

⁴ In the 1880s, the territory was conquered by the Russians and became part of the Trans-Caspian region and the province of Turkistan, but the lands inhabited by the Turkmens passed to Khiva and Bukhara, which were Russian protectorates.

⁵ Resistance to Russian domination in Turkmenia lasted until the Battle of Geok-Tepe in 1881, in which the rebels were defeated. The Turkmens were active participants in the 1916 uprising against the Czar. In the city of Tedzhen, several Russian residents and government officials were executed by the local population.

⁶ The fall of the Czar in 1917 left the Trans-Caspian region under the control of the Russian Provisional Government. In December 1917, after the Bolshevik take-over in St Petersburg, Worker Council (Soviet) power was proclaimed.

⁷ In July 1918, Britain re-established the Provisional Government in Trans-Caspia. After two years of civil war, Soviet power was reinstated in 1920 and on 14 February 1924, the Soviet Socialist Republic of Turkmenistan was founded, as a member of the Soviet Union (USSR).

⁸ Up until that time, Turkmenistan had never had national political unity. Clan membership was the only form of social organization, and most of

LAND USE

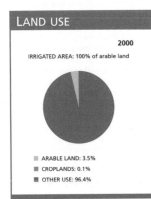

2000

IRRIGATED AREA: 100% of arable land

- ARABLE LAND: 3.5%
- CROPLANDS: 0.1%
- OTHER USE: 96.4%

PROFILE

ENVIRONMENT

Turkmenistan is in an arid zone, with a dry continental climate, located in the south-eastern part of Central Asia between the Caspian Sea to the west, the Amu Darya River to the east, the Ustiurt mountains to the north and the Kopet-Dag and Paropamiz mountain ranges to the south. The land is flat and most of the territory (80 per cent) lies within the Kara-Kum desert. Topographically, 90 per cent of Turkmenistan is sandy plain. On the eastern shore of the Caspian Sea lie the Major and Minor Balkan ranges, of relatively low altitude. The Amu Darya river crosses Turkmenistan from east to west. The Kara-Kum Canal diverts the waters of the Amu Darya to the irrigation systems of the Murgab and Tedzhen oases, as well as those of the Mary and Ashkhabad areas. Turkmenistan is bounded by Kazakhstan to the north - west, Uzbekistan to the east and Afghanistan and Iran to the south. There are rich mineral deposits, including natural gas and oil.

SOCIETY

Peoples: Turkmenis 77 per cent; Russians 6.7 per cent; Uzbeks 9.2 per cent; Kazakhs 2 per cent; Tatars 0.8 per cent; other 6.6 per cent (1996).
Religions: Sunni Muslim (87 per cent); Russian Orthodox 6.4 per cent. Under the 1996 religion law, only these two were allowed to register. Unregistered religious activity is a criminal offense.

Languages: Turkmen (official), Russian.
Main Political Parties: Democratic Party (DP, split off from the former Communist Party); Party for Democratic Development; Agzibirlik (Unity). The only party allowed to present candidates in the December 1999 elections was the DP.
Main Social Organizations: Independent labor unions in process of formation.

THE STATE

Official Name: Türkmenistan Jumhuriyäti.
Administrative Divisions: 3 provinces and 1 Dependent Region (Ashkhabad).
Capital: Ashkhabad (Aschabad) 574,000 people (2003).
Other Cities: Chardzhou (Cardzou) 166,000 people, Tedzhen.
Government: Saparmurad Niyazov Turkmenbashi, President since October 1990. The Constitution adopted in 1992 gave the President the powers of Head of State and Head of Government. The epithet 'Turkmenbashi' - 'Leader of the Turkmen people' - was conferred on the President in 1993. In 1999 Parliament decided that 'Turkmenbashi will be president for life'. Unicameral Legislature: Parliament or Islamic Assembly, with 50 members elected by direct election every five years.
National Holiday: 27 October, Independence Day (1991).
Armed Forces: 18,000.

Life expectancy
67.1 years
2000-2005

GNI per capita
$1,200
2002

HIV prevalence rate
0.1% of population
15-49 years old
2001

the population was nomadic. The Soviet regime imposed secularization, industrialization and collective agriculture. During the 1920s and 1930s there were several armed uprisings against Moscow's measures.

[9] After World War II, the economy grew, accompanied by increases in oil and gas production and cotton farming. But during Leonid Brezhnev's administration from 1963-83, political problems worsened and the economy entered a period of stagnation (particularly in those republics where the Soviets had adopted a mono-cropping policy, as in the case of Turkmenistan with the cultivation of cotton).

[10] From 1985, the changes promoted in the USSR by President Mikhail Gorbachev led to an Islamic renaissance, which found expression in the construction of a number of mosques.

[11] After the coup attempt in the USSR in August 1991, the Communist Party of Turkmenistan lost its legitimacy to govern. President Saparmurad Niyazov called a plebiscite that led to the declaration of independence in October and the adoption of a presidential system. In November, Turkmenistan joined the Commonwealth of Independent States (CIS), and the Communist Party changed its name to the Democratic Party.

[12] Niyazov prioritized the country's relations with Turkey, with whom it had cultural links. Niyazov was re-elected in June 1992 and 1994. Without distancing itself from Russia, Turkmenistan drew closer to Iran, through the construction of the Ashkhabad-Teheran railway, amongst other things. It also achieved the status of most favored nation with the US. Several opposition leaders took refuge in Moscow. The Russian Government was concerned by Niyazov's rapprochement with Iran.

[13] In December 1997, the first oil pipeline was opened between Turkmenistan and Iran, to export Turkmeni oil and gas to the countries of the Mediterranean and the Persian Gulf.

[14] In February 1998 Niyazov announced his plans to give Parliament more authority and less to the presidency. However only the ruling DP party was allowed to field candidates in the parliamentary elections, causing the Organization for Security and Cooperation in Europe (OSCE) to withdraw its offer to supervise the elections. Ninety-five per cent of registered electors turned out to vote.

IN FOCUS

ENVIRONMENTAL CHALLENGES
There is contamination of soils and groundwater from pesticides and agricultural chemicals, tree loss due to poor irrigation, and pollution in the Caspian Sea. The re-routing of the Am Darya river for irrigation means the Aral Sea does not receive water. There is desertification.

WOMEN'S RIGHTS
Women have been able to vote since 1927. In 2000, they held 26 per cent of seats in parliament and barely 4 per cent of ministerial level posts. Between 1980 and 2000, women represented 46 per cent of the country's labor force.

The net rate of female primary school attendance for the period was 84 per cent. According to UNICEF's latest data available* 98 per cent of women receive prenatal care and 97 per cent of births are attended by skilled health personnel.

CHILDREN
According to UNICEF's latest data available*, at birth, some 5 per cent of babies are underweight. Twelve per cent of children under-five are moderately or severely underweight and 22 per cent suffer from moderately or severely stunted growth. Under-five mortality stands at 88 per 1,000 live births, and under-one mortality at 71 per 1,0000 live births.

The primary school enrollment rate was 87 per cent.

INDIGENOUS PEOPLES/ ETHNIC MINORITIES
The Russian minority amounts to almost seven per cent of the population. Although the Constitution guarantees equal rights for all inhabitants, in practice Russians are discriminated against and do not feel represented, for example in the civil service or the army. The lack of social and political organizations prevents an organized struggle for their rights. Use of the Russian language is severely restricted and it is almost not taught at school. Its use is almost exclusively limited to the business community. Furthermore, the Russian language media has

gradually been closed down. This situation led to many Russian citizens leaving the country at the beginning of the 1990s.

MIGRANTS/REFUGEES
At the end of 2002, there were almost 13,700 refugees in the country. Of these, 12,300 come from Tajikistan and the rest from Afghanistan. During 2003, the UNHCR helped to repatriate 110 refugees from Tajikistan and 150 from Afghanistan. To start with, refugees are lodged in rural areas and enjoy the same rights as citizens. In November 2002, Niyazov issued a decree authorizing the internal deportation of people who had committed crimes, or were suspected of causing unrest, engaging in 'immoral' conduct or not working to help the country's economy.

DEATH PENALTY
Capital punishment was abolished for all crimes in 1999.

*Latest data available in *The State of the World's Children* and *Childinfo* database, UNICEF, 2004.

[15] In 1999 Parliament voted in favor of making Niyazov president for life but he announced that he would step down in 2010, when he turned 70.

[16] In October that year, Niyazov said that the country would not privatize the oil and gas industries for at least the next 10 to 15 years, adding that he expected the industry to continue as the economic mainstay of the country. In February 2001, shortly after gas supplies to Russia had been stopped after disagreements on pricing, Turkmenistan agreed to supply the Russian company Itera with 10 billion cubic meters at the price originally agreed.

[17] In May 2001 the exploitation of natural resources in the Caspian Sea led to conflict with Azerbaijan, which was working in oilfields claimed by Turkmenistan. Negotiations between experts from both nations could not resolve the dispute and in June Turkmenistan withdrew its ambassador from Baku.

[18] After the September 2001 terrorist attacks on New York and Washington, and the US military response against Afghanistan, Turkmenistan stood by its neutrality and refused to allow its airspace to be used to carry out

attacks. However, Niyazov did allow international humanitarian aid through to Afghanistan. The Imam-Nazar frontier crossing became a central point on transport routes. By the end of October, the United Nations World Food Program had already sent dozens of trucks of food through to be distributed in northern Afghanistan. The UNICEF operation for northern Afghanistan also moved through Imam-Nazar.

[19] The turnover in government ministers that had begun in 2000 gathered pace in 2001. By the end of that year few office-holders had been in their jobs for more than a year. One of the most significant changes was the concentration of power in the hands of the president of the National Security Committee, who was made deputy Prime Minister, responsible for defense, law and order, and foreign affairs, as well as special legal advisor to the President.

[20] In late 2001 and early 2002 the Government had hopes that the relative stability in Afghanistan could provide Turkmenistan with a pipeline route to the coast of Pakistan. Despite cordial relations with Moscow, Turkmenistan's continuing lack of economic

development was partly due to Russia's refusal to allow gas exports to more competitive markets.

[21] In November 2002, the President survived a machine-gun attack on his vehicle. Exiled opposition leaders were accused of planning the operation. Former minister of foreign affairs, Boris Shikhmuradov, was detained together with 40 other activists, accused of conspiracy and condemned to life imprisonment.

[22] Niyazov's visit to Moscow in April 2003, led to the signing of an agreement whereby Russia agreed to purchase 60,000 million cubic meters of natural gas annually from Turkmenistan. Diplomatic relations between the two countries were soured by Niyazov's decision to cancel dual nationality, allowed since a common agreement in 1993.

[23] Early in 2004, a series of bizarre laws were enacted, including a ban on unkempt beards and hair, and a tax for foreigners wishing to marry Turkmeni women.

[24] In April in Geneva the UN denounced the human-rights situation in Turkmenistan. Allegations were made about political assassinations designed to keep President Niyazov in power. ■

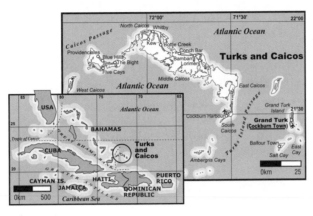

Population:	22,028
Area:	430 km²
Capital:	Cockburn Town
Currency:	US dollar
Language:	English

Turks and Caicos are two island chains separated by a deep water channel, lying approximately 150 km north of Haiti at the southernmost tip of the Bahamas chain. Like many of the smaller Caribbean islands, these were first inhabited by Arawak peoples. Some researchers claim it was East Caicos or Grand Turk that Columbus first set foot on when he reached the New World in 1492. The first Europeans to settle on the islands were salt-rakers from Bermuda in 1678.

[2] During the following century, Turks and Caicos faced several invasions by both French and Spanish forces. The islands were a refuge during this period for both pirates and their merchant-vessel victims, Spanish galleons carrying American wealth to Europe. By 1787, colonial settlers had established cotton plantations and imported African slaves, and British domination was consolidated. Both archipelagos remained British colonies.

[3] Turks and Caicos were administered from the Bahamas until the Separation Act of 1848. After 1874, the islands were annexed to Jamaica, remaining a dependency until independence in 1962, when they again became a separate colony. During World War II, the United States built an airstrip on South Caicos and in 1951 the islands' authorities signed an agreement permitting the US to establish a missile base and a Navy base on Grand Turk island.

[4] After the Bahamas' independence in 1972, Turks and Caicos received their own governor. Further autonomy achieved through the 1976 constitution provided for a Governor, a Legislative Council, a Supreme Court and a Court of Appeals.

[5] In the 1976 elections, the pro-independence People's Democratic Movement (PDM), led by Jafs McCartney, won against the pro-US Progressive National Party (PNP). The PDM favored a new constitution that granted internal autonomy as a step towards eventual independence.

[6] In 1980, the next election year, Britain showed an interest in granting independence to the islands, which receive $2 million a year in aid. The overwhelming electoral triumph of the PNP was attributed to the failure of the PDM to solve the country's economic crisis, including a 30 per cent unemployment rate and the local population's fears that the economy could worsen with independence.

[7] The new head minister, entrepreneur Norman Saunders, convinced Britain to shelve the idea of independence. He concentrated on bringing new business to the islands: tourism talks with the French Club Méditerranée; the development of light industry and offshore banking; and finally an agreement with BCM Ltd, for construction of an oil refinery with a capacity of 125,000 barrels per day.

[8] Internal differences arose within the Government with regard to economic policy. However, these differences were quickly forgotten when Saunders and Stafford Missik, his development minister and a key opposition figure within the Government, were arrested in Miami. They were in the process of creating an international drug network, using the islands as a bridge between the US and South America.

[9] The British Government suspended the ministerial system until 1988, when a general election was held. PDM's Oswald Skippings won the election, with 11 of the 13 parliamentary seats going to his party. The election marked the end of direct British administration of the islands.

[10] Unemployment reached 12 per cent of the active population in 1992. In 1993 imports cost $42.8 million and exports were worth $6.8 million.

[11] Martin Bourke was appointed Governor in 1993, and Derek H Taylor became Prime Minister in 1995.

[12] Tourism registered a 10 per cent increase in the first three months of 1995 compared with the same period of 1994. Some 70 per cent of the total 60,000 tourists were US citizens. The economy of the islands was also supported by fishing and international financial services.

[13] Haitian refugee ships reaching the islands in 1998 and 1999 were systematically rejected by the archipelago's maritime authorities. One of these ships was sunk in June 1998 and six people died as a result of a confrontation with the coastguards. The survivors accused the coastguards of firing without warning.

[14] The December 1999 Legislative Council elections resulted in a majority for the People's Democratic Movement. Mervyn Jones was appointed Governor in January 2000.

[15] A new financial scandal arose in April that year when a lawyer disappeared leaving no trace of the money from a Christian foundation that he had managed. There are 7,000 offshore financial companies registered on the islands, which deal with business considered shady by other countries. The UK, the US and several European countries have complained that this financial system enables the laundering of millions of dollars produced daily by drug dealing and other criminal activities.

[16] After the 11 September 2001 attacks in the United States, tourism was significantly reduced on the islands, leading Governor Jones to implement a support plan for the islands' hotels and airlines. ■

PROFILE

ENVIRONMENT

An archipelago of more than 30 islands comprising the southeastern part of the Bahamas. Only eight are inhabited: Grand Turk, Salt Cay, South Caicos, Central Caicos, North Caicos, Providenciales, Pine Cay and Parrot Cay. The climate is tropical with heavy rainfall, moderated by ocean currents. The islands are on the hurricane path and were particularly devastated in 1928, 1945 and 1960. Fishing is the main economic activity.

SOCIETY

Peoples: The majority is of African descent. There is a white minority and a significant number of Haitian immigrants.
Religions: Baptists 41.2 per cent; Methodists 18.9 per cent; Anglicans 18.3 per cent; Seventh Day Adventists 1.7 per cent; other, 19.9 per cent.
Languages: English.
Main Political Parties: Progressive National Party (PNP), majority; the People's Democratic Movement (PDM); the National Democratic Alliance (NDA) and the United Democratic Party (UDP).

THE STATE

Official Name: Turks and Caicos Islands.
Capital: Cockburn Town on Grand Turk Island 6,000 people (2003).
Other Cities: The islands with the largest populations are: Providenciales 7,900 people; Grand Turk 5,000; North Caicos 1,900; South Caicos 1,700 (2000).
Government: Mervyn Jones, Governor appointed by Britain, since January 2000. Derek H Taylor, Chief Minister since January 1995, re-elected in 1999. The Legislative Council has 20 members.
National Holiday: 30 August, Constitution Day (1976).
Armed Forces: Defense is the responsibility of the United Kingdom.

Tuvalu / Tuvalu

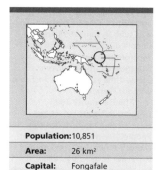

Population:	10,851
Area:	26 km²
Capital:	Fongafale
Currency:	Australian dollar
Language:	Tuvaluan and English

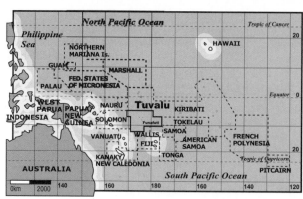

Around 30,000 BC, peoples from Southeast Asia started their expansion toward the Pacific islands. By the 9th century AD, they had spread throughout practically all of Polynesia. The inhabitants of the archipelago then known as 'Funafuti' came there from the islands of Samoa and Tonga.

[2] In the 16th century the Europeans reported seeing the islands but did not settle on them due to the lack of exploitable resources. Years later, a European named the atolls the Ellice Islands.

[3] Between 1850 and 1875, thousands of islanders were captured by slave traders and sent to the phosphate (guano) works in Peru and the saltpeter mines in Chile. Within a few years, the population had shrunk from 20,000 to 3,000 inhabitants. As a source of slave labor, the Polynesian islands offered direct access to markets on the Pacific coast.

[4] A new wave of invasions began in 1865, with the arrival of British and North American missionaries. By 1892 the islands had become a British protectorate. In 1915, with their neighbors, the Gilbert Islands (see Kiribati), the British formed the Colony of the Gilbert and Ellice Islands. This arbitrary merger was decided on administrative grounds. In a 1974 referendum, 90 per cent of the Ellice islanders voted in favor of separate administrations. The split became official in October 1975, and the first elections in independent Tuvalu were held in August 1977. Toaripi Lauti was named Prime Minister.

[5] The archipelago became independent on 1 October 1978, adopting the name Tuvalu, which in the local language means 'united eight', symbolizing the eight inhabited islands which make up the country. The islands became autonomous from London, but they fell under the

economic influence of Australia, which had already started to hold considerable sway over the economy.

[6] Under a friendship treaty of 1979 Washington relinquished its claim over the islands of Nurakita, Nukulaelae, Funafuti and Nukufetau.

[7] Tuvalu is the smallest of the Less Developed Countries, in both population and land area. One of its main sources of foreign exchange is the sale of stamps, which are valuable collectors' items, and the granting of fishing licenses to

foreign fleets which earns some $100,000 per year.

[8] Faced with a lack of natural resources, a sparse population and an almost total lack of internal sources of savings or investment, the country depends heavily on foreign aid, mostly from Australia, to finance its regular and its development budget. In 1989, the State was able to meet only about 10 per cent of its expenses. Most of this money was sent home by the quarter of the islands' population who lived on neighboring islands working in the phosphate mines.

[9] A 1989 report by the UN included Tuvalu in a list of countries most likely to disappear under the sea in the 21st century as a result of global warming.

[10] In August 1991 the Government announced it would seek compensation from the UK for damages caused when that country authorized the US to build landing strips on the islands during World War II. The army dug trenches that left 40 per cent of the land area in Funafuti unfit to live on.

[11] During the Independence Day celebrations, in October 1995, a new flag was hoisted, replacing the British Union Jack. In 1996, the new Prime Minister, Bikenibeu Paeniu, once again made the British flag official.

[12] A fire swept through a residential village for students in Vaitupu island, causing the death of 18 girls and their supervisor in March 2000.

[13] In September, Tuvalu was formally admitted to the UN as its 189th member, one week after having left the British Commonwealth.

[14] Lagitupu Tuilimu replaced Ionatana Ionatana as Prime Minister after the latter died in December 2000.

[15] The Government hired out its Internet domain - identified by the letters 'tv' - to a company from California for a yearly rent of several million dollars. Part of the money has already been used to pave streets (which were made of smashed corals) and build schools.

[16] Some Tuvaluans are buying land in Fiji, Australia and New Zealand/Aotearoa, anticipating the moment when - as a result of the rise in sea levels due to global warming - the water will no longer be fit to drink. In March 2001 Tuvalu, jointly with Kiribati and Maldives, filed a lawsuit against the US Government because it did not sign the Kyoto Protocol that seeks to reduce the emissions of gases causing the greenhouse effect. Since then, the Tuvalu Government has campaigned against the emission of these gases by developed countries.

[17] Former finance minister Saufato Sopoanga was elected Premier in August 2002, after defeating Koloa Telake in the general elections.

[18] In May 2004 Sopoanga announced he would hold a referendum to turn Tuvalu into a republic, thus replacing the Queen of the UK as head of state. ∎

PROFILE

ENVIRONMENT

Five coral atolls and four islands, with a maximum height of five meters over sea level, stretch out over 560 km, from northeast to southeast, within an ocean area of 1,060,000 sq km. The archipelago is situated slightly south of the equator, 4,000 km northeast of Australia, south of the Gilbert Islands, between Micronesia and Melanesia. It comprises the islands of Funafuti, Nanumanga, Nanumea, Niutao, Nui, Nukufetau, Nukulaelae, Nurakita and Vaitupu. The climate is tropical with heavy rainfall. The islands are completely flat with a thin layer of topsoil suffering from severe erosion. Fishing and coconut farming are traditional activities. The rising sea level, caused by global warming, is ruining crops and contaminating drinking water with salt.

SOCIETY

Peoples: Tuvaluans are mainly Polynesians (96 per cent), from Samoa and Tonga; 4 per cent are Micronesian.
Religion: Church of Tuvalu (Congregational) 85.4 per cent; Seventh-Day Adventist 3.6 per cent; Baha'i 1 per cent; Roman Catholic 1.4 per cent.
Languages: Tuvaluan and English (spoken mostly on Funafuti).
Main Political Parties: Prominent families control Tuvalu's politics. They are not formally organized into parties.

THE STATE

Official Name: Tuvalu.
Capital: Fongafale on Funafuti's atoll 6,000 people (2003).
Other Atolls: Vaitupu 1,231 people; Niutao 904; Nanumea 879; Nukufetau 694 (1985).
Government: General Faimalaga Luka, Governor-General and Chief of State, since September 2003; Saufatu Sopoanga, Prime Minister since August 2002. Tuvalu has a parliamentary government modeled on the British system. Parliament has 15 members, elected for 4-year terms.
National Holiday: 1 October, Independence Day (1978).

Uganda / Uganda

Population:	27,623,190
Area:	241,040 km²
Capital:	Kampala
Currency:	Shilling
Language:	Swahili

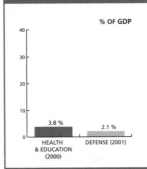

I n present-day Uganda the ruined mud walls of the Kingdom of Bigo show evidence of urban civilizations dating from the 10th century.

2 The ruins of sizeable hilltop fortresses still remain. These fortifications mark the lines of penetration from the North of the Bacwezi, a nation of Nilotic herders, who subdued the Bantu peoples of the area around the 13th century. Their fortresses - in some cases up to 300 meters in diameter - were built to protect their cattle - their main source of wealth and status. Gradually, the conquerors mixed with the local people, adopted a Bantu language, and came to be called Bahima but continued their nomadic lifestyle.

3 Between the 17th and 18th centuries, the kingdoms of Bunyoro, Buganda, Busoga and Ankole were founded. A dispute for supremacy arose between Bunyoro, supported by the Swahili traders, and Buganda, linked to the 'Shirazis' of Zanzibar. At the beginning of the 19th century Bunyoro lost some of its allies, who formed the independent state of Toro, leading to the undisputed hegemony of Buganda.

4 In the mid-19th century Buganda was governed by Kabakas or traditional leaders, who were in theory absolute rulers but in practice were limited by the Lukiko, a council representing the higher castes. Buganda had a standing army which guaranteed its regional autonomy. It had a relatively equitable society, in which caste privileges were more honorary and political than economic, and a sound agricultural economy that allowed it to survive the decline of the slave trade.

5 HM Stanley, the British adventurer and journalist, arrived in 1875. He denounced the spread of Islam in the region and reported an alleged request by Kabaka Mutesa I asking Europe to send missionaries to halt Egyptian-Sudanese religious infiltration.

6 These missionaries soon arrived: English Protestants in 1877 and French Catholics in 1879. They quickly converted part of the Bugandese hierarchy, splitting the power élite into three factions. Two of these reflected the rivalry between missionaries - in local dialect the 'Franza' and 'Ingleza' parties - while the third (moderate and Islamic) assumed the defense of national interests. The main impact was the consolidation of the European presence.

7 The missionaries succeeded in deposing the Muslim Kabaka Mwanga in 1888, and shortly afterwards the Imperial British East Africa Company (IBEA) arrived, a typical colonial trading company, forerunner for the British Government.

8 The 1886 Anglo-German agreements had ceded the states in the lakes area to the British, who established them as a Protectorate in 1893.

9 The other organized local groups were forced to adopt political systems similar to Buganda's, as the British thought that the Lukiko resembled their own parliamentary system. With the intention of developing a ruling élite to serve as intermediaries for the colonial power, the British undertook 'land reform', privatizing communally owned land, which left the rural population landless and benefited the Lukiko-based bureaucracy.

10 In 1894, Buganda became a British protectorate. An agreement signed in 1900 transformed it into a constitutional monarchy, controlled by the Protestants.

11 In 1902 the western province of the country became part of Kenya.

12 The cultivation of cotton as a cash crop started in 1904.

13 During the first half of the 20th century, until the end of World War II, the country was governed indirectly, through the local power structures. London allowed the creation of labor union-type organizations, which brought together the more active militants. Their modern nationalist tendencies subsequently led to the development of anti-colonialist feelings.

14 The severe disruption in food production caused by the confiscation of lands was aggravated by the introduction of export cash crops in the post-War period. Many export crops were new to the region, and their prominence in agricultural production resulted in a steady decline in people's living standards until the 1960s, when the decolonization movement brought about Ugandan independence. Kabaka Mutesa II of Buganda was the first President and Dr Milton Obote the Prime Minister.

15 In 1965, Obote reformed the Constitution, assuming greater powers, and eliminated the federal system imposed by the British. He also adopted policies that favored the poorest sectors, arousing fierce opposition from the Asian population - a minority of some 40,000, holding British passports - who controlled almost all commercial activity in the country.

16 Obote supported regional economic integration with Tanzania and Kenya and the East African Community was established (1967-1977).

17 In January 1971, Obote was overthrown in a coup led by deputy commander of the army, Idi Amin Dada. Obote took refuge in Tanzania. In the economic crisis the Government faced opposition from the Asian minority (which he expelled en masse in 1972) and transnational corporations.

18 Amin's attitudes and measures were controversial: he maintained trade relations with the US and Britain, but also cultivated good relations with the socialist world. Similarly, while he supported several African liberation movements, he opposed Angola's bid for membership of the Organization of African Unity (OAU) and adopted a permanently hostile attitude toward Nyerere's government in Tanzania. He also expropriated land and property from members of the Jewish community and made overtures toward the Arab countries.

19 In the mid-1970s Amin declared himself President-for-Life. In 1978, he provoked a war with Tanzania by annexing land in

LAND USE

2000

IRRIGATED AREA: 0.1% of arable land

- ARABLE LAND: 25.7%
- CROPLANDS: 9.6%
- OTHER USE: 64.7%

PUBLIC EXPENDITURE

% OF GDP

- HEALTH & EDUCATION (2000): 3.8 %
- DEFENSE (2001): 2.1 %

WORKERS

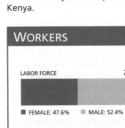

LABOR FORCE   **2002**

- FEMALE: 47.6%   ■ MALE: 52.4%

Life expectancy
46.2 years
2000-2005

GNI per capita
$250
2002

Literacy
67% total adult rate
2000

HIV prevalence rate
5% of population 15-49 years old
2001

the north. In April 1979, he was forced to flee Kampala, after a joint offensive launched by Tanzanian troops and opposition activists united in the Ugandan National Liberation Front (FNLU), an umbrella movement uniting efforts aimed at ending Idi Amin's reign of terror.

[20] The new Government's main body, a National Advisory Council led by Yusuf Lule, a politically inexperienced university professor with conservative tendencies, lasted 68 days. Lule was replaced by Godfrey Binaisa, a FNLU leader. However, Binaisa was unable to reconcile the conflicting tendencies within the movement. He was even less capable of confronting the growing prestige of Milton Obote, whose Uganda People's Congress party (UPC) continued to enjoy wide popular support.

[21] The President brought forward the elections scheduled for 1981, and tried to ban Obote's candidacy. This fuelled a crisis that exploded in May 1980 when the army replaced Binaisa with a Military Commission entrusted with maintaining the electoral schedule and enforcing the democratic principles of the movement that had overthrown Amin. The Commission, under the orders of General David Oyite Ojok, supervised the elections in December 1980, and as predicted the UPC won an overwhelming majority, with Obote as President.

[22] Obote inherited a bankrupt country. The copper mines had not been worked for several years and corruption was rife. Despite the reaffirmation of his support in the elections, in 1981 the defeated parties initiated a destabilization campaign that turned into a guerrilla movement.

[23] The Government authorized the return of Asian businesses, regulated the participation of foreign capital and embarked upon a reorganization of the economy, fighting corruption and speculation. Despite the intensification of political violence in 1985, it achieved the withdrawal of Tanzanian troops which had been in Uganda since the fall of Amin.

[24] Between 1981 and July 1985, major military offensives were launched against the strongholds of the National Resistance Army (NRA) - the military wing of the National Resistance Movement (NRM) founded by former president Yusuf Lule and led by Yoweri Museveni - and other opposition groups.

[25] In 1981 the Government took steps to prevent cattle smuggling by the nomadic peoples across the Kenyan border, which was causing

PROFILE

ENVIRONMENT

The land is made up of a number of plateaus, gently rolling towards the Nile River in the north-west. There are volcanic ranges and numerous rivers, the largest of which is the Nile. Nearly 18 per cent of the territory is covered by rivers, lakes and swamps. The climate is tropical, tempered by altitude. Timber is taken from the rainforest that covers 6.2 per cent of the land. In addition to subsistence farming of rice and corn/maize, coffee, cotton, tea and tobacco are cultivated as cash crops. Lake Victoria is one of the largest fish reservoirs in the world. There is widespread draining of swamp land for agricultural use.

SOCIETY

Peoples: Most Ugandans descend from a mix of various African ethnic groups, mainly the Baganda, Bunyoro and Batoro, and some San, and Sudanese. There are also minorities of Indian and European origin.
Religions: More than half the people are Christian (62 per cent), 19 per cent practise traditional religions and 15 per cent are Muslims. Others: 1 per cent.
Languages: English, the official language, is spoken by a minority. Swahili and Luganda are the most widely spoken.
Main Political Parties: National Resistance Movement (NRM), led by Yoweri Museveni. All other parties have been disenfranchised by the Government (endorsed by a referendum in 2000); the main ones are the Ugandan People's Congress (UPC) (former President Obote's party); the Democratic Party (DP) and the Ugandan Patriotic Movement.
Main Social Organizations: National Organization of Trade Unions (NOTU); women's groups and other civil society organizations.

THE STATE

Official Name: Republic of Uganda.
Capital: Kampala 1,246,000 people (2003).
Other Cities: Jinja 85,200 people; Mbale 70,600; Masaka 64,900 (2000).
Government: Yoweri Museveni, President since January 1986 (after the overthrow of Tito Okello), elected as President in 1996 and re-elected in 2001. Apolo Nsibambi (NRM), Prime Minister since April 1999. Unicameral Legislature: National Parliament, with 292 members.
National Holiday: 9 October, Independence Day (1962).
Armed Forces: 55,000 (1997).

starvation among thousands in Karamoja province.

[26] In spite of guerrilla activity, Uganda's economy grew by an annual average of five per cent from 1982 and exports increased 45 per cent after 1983.

[27] The anticipated victory of the UPC in the general elections (scheduled for December 1985) was thwarted by General Bazilio Olara Okello's coup in July 1985. The new president (from the Acholi ethnic group) accused Obote (of Lango origin) of unilateral tribal domination and called elections to form a broad-based government within six months.

[28] After the coup, the National Resistance Army intensified its actions, occupying Kampala in January 1986. On 30 January, NRA leader Yoweri Museveni assumed the presidency and in March announced the fall of the northern town of Gulu, the last bastion of forces loyal to Okello.

[29] Museveni was faced with the reconstruction of a country virtually destroyed, with almost a million dead, two million refugees, 600,000 injured and incalculable damage to property.

[30] In addition to the lack of resources there was an extremely high incidence of HIV/AIDS, at epidemic proportions in some parts of the country.

[31] Uganda's foreign debt rose to $1.2 billion in 1987. In an attempt to establish economic independence and avoid the International Monetary Fund (IMF) Museveni resorted to exchange arrangements with other African states. Some Western countries disapproved of Uganda's relations with Cuba and Libya. The US pressed Tanzania and Rwanda into ending the exchange operations that they had with Uganda.

[32] In February 1992, local human rights organizations pushed for multiparty democracy in the

country. The Government's response was that it wanted to build a democracy based on traditional ethnic structures, and that political parties were therefore unnecessary.

[33] Faced with pressure from the opposition and some international agencies, in February 1993 the Government announced the election of a Constituent Assembly for 1995, charged with studying the draft of a new constitution. The text drafted by the Government was criticized by the opposition (Democratic Party and former President Obote's party, the UPC) for maintaining the partial ban on political parties for a seven-year period.

[34] In an endeavor to win the support of the Baganda people, Museveni authorized the restoration of the monarchy. During Prince Ronald Muenda Mutebi's coronation ceremony as Kabaka, on 31 July, authorities returned all royal property, which had been confiscated during former president Obote's administration. At the end of the year Museveni was accused by the opposition of having ordered the assassination of opposition leader Amon Bazira in Kenya in August.

[35] In the March 1994 elections Museveni's supporters won around half the seats, and the direct appointment of some of the posts gave Museveni a broad majority in the new assembly. Continuing with his policy of restoring local authorities, he authorized the creation in June of an independent kingdom for the Bunyoros, a people in the north of the country.

[36] In 1995 Museveni continued to claim that a multiparty system would only exacerbate 'tribal divisions'. International funding organizations said they were satisfied with the economic performance of Uganda. Foreign investment grew, but budget cuts worsened the situation of most of the population who were already living below the poverty line.

[37] On 9 May 1996, Museveni was re-elected president by more than 75 per cent of the electorate, with a 72.6 per cent turnout, defeating Paul Semogerere and Muhammad Mayanja. Museveni was victorious again in the May legislative elections, with his party winning 156 of the 196 seats at stake. The new government was appointed in July, with Kintu Musoke as Prime Minister.

[38] Museveni's economic reforms meant Uganda topped the World Bank's list of aid to 20 debtor countries in 1997. It was estimated that $24 million would be needed to tackle hunger in the country. The Franco-Australian LaSource

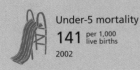
Under-5 mortality
141 per 1,000 live births
2002

Poverty
82.2% of population living on less than $1 per day
1996

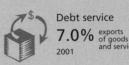
Debt service
7.0% exports of goods and services
2001

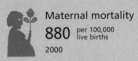
Maternal mortality
880 per 100,000 live births
2000

company paid Uganda for the right to exploit its cobalt mines, and the nation received loans from the European Union and North Korea for the construction of a hydroelectric plant.

[39] In mid-1998, the Ugandan army entered neighboring Democratic Republic of Congo (DRC) and joined the rebels fighting President Laurent Kabila. In October 1999, Ugandan Defense Minister Stephen Kavuma stated that the troops would remain in DRC until peace was restored.

[40] In November 1999, in the Tanzanian city of Arusha, the presidents of Kenya, Tanzania, and Uganda signed a treaty that established the East African Community (EAC) in 2001.

[41] Museveni hosted the African Development Forum 2000, held in Addis Ababa. At the Forum Museveni made reference to the alarming rates of HIV/AIDS in sub-Saharan Africa, where 25 million people were living with HIV/AIDS. The prevalence of HIV in Uganda was one of the highest in the world, but through information services and a media campaign titled 'Loving with care' the Government began to control the epidemic.

[42] A referendum was held in June 2000 to decide on the establishment of a multiparty system. In spite of a boycott by the Democratic Party (DP) and other political groups, 80 per cent of voters (50 per cent of the registered electorate) supported the 'democracy without parties' formula defended by Museveni in the campaign, which meant that Uganda maintained its system of government, unique in the continent. This did not prevent, in practice, the NRM (now simply called the 'Movement') from acting as a state party. The system gave Museveni absolute power.

[43] Amnesty International denounced violations of the human rights of Ugandan gays, bisexuals and transsexuals. In June 2000, the police murdered a member of Lesgabix, a group of lesbians and gays from Kampala.

[44] In the March 2001 presidential elections, Museveni was re-elected with 69.3 per cent of the vote, followed by 27.8 per cent for Kizza Besigye, a former colonel of the NRM. International observers estimated that there had been up to 15 per cent electoral fraud, and confirmed that the elections had taken place in a climate of intimidation. On 12

May Museveni took office for a new term until 2006, which, according to the Constitution, would be his last.

[45] In July 2001, Museveni held a meeting with the political leader of the Democratic Republic of Congo, Laurent Kabila's son Joseph, in Dar es Salaam, accelerating the withdrawal of the Ugandan army from that country and the stationing of UN soldiers along the front lines.

[46] A report by the World Trade Organization (WTO) indicated that the economic reforms carried out by the Museveni administration, including liberalization of the trade regime, had attracted foreign investment and contributed to the country's growth. GDP had grown, until 2001, by about 6 per cent per year; the fiscal deficit and inflation were reduced, improving the economic outlook. The agricultural sector accounted for 42 per cent of GDP and provided 80 per cent of jobs. The European Union was Uganda's main trading partner. Regional integration favored an increase in trade between Uganda and other sub-Sahara African countries.

[47] In March 2002, Uganda signed an agreement with Sudan to fight the Lord's Resistance

Army (LRA), a group led by the 'prophet' Joseph Kony, whose aim was to govern the country according to the Ten Commandments. The rebel movement, located along the border between the two countries, used systematic kidnapping of thousands of Ugandan children as part of its tactics.

[48] In October 2002, the escalation of the conflict with the LRA led the army to evacuate over 400,000 citizens from the combat area. In December, after five years of negotiations, a peace treaty was signed with rebel movement Uganda National Rescue Front (UNRF II), made up of Amin's former soldiers.

[49] In May 2003, the last Ugandan troops withdrew from DR Congo and tens of thousands of citizens sought asylum in Uganda. In August the former dictator, Idi Amin Dada died in hospital in Jeddah, Saudi Arabia.

[50] In February 2004 at least 200 people were killed by LRA rebels in a refugee camp in the north of the country. The President apologized for mistakes in coordination by the army to prevent the massacre. ∎

IN FOCUS

ENVIRONMENTAL CHALLENGES
Environmental problems include deforestation, soil erosion and overgrazing. Lake Victoria is being throttled by water-hyacinths. Poaching is widespread. Swamp lands are being indiscriminately drained for agricultural use.

WOMEN'S RIGHTS
Women have been able to vote since 1962. Their political representation increased slightly between 1990 (12 per cent of seats) and 2000 (18 per cent). In 1995, 10 per cent of ministerial posts were held by women, increasing to 13 per cent in 2000. Between 1980 and 2000, women represented a stable 48 per cent of the labor force.
   Although female illiteracy has steadily decreased, according to UNICEF latest data available*, it is still very high and much higher than for men (43 per cent for women and 22 per cent for men)
   According to the mentioned databases, 92 per cent of women receive prenatal care. However,

specialist health personnel attend only 39 per cent of births.

CHILDREN
In 2002, the under-five mortality rate was 141 per 1,000 live births and 82 per 1,000 live births for infants. Twelve per cent of all newborn babies were underweight, 23 per cent of under-fives were moderately or seriously underweight and 39 per cent were moderately or seriously stunted. Of the 600,000 people living with HIV/AIDS at the end of 2001, 110,000 were children aged between 0 and 14, and there were 480,000 AIDS orphans.
   According to data for 1995-1999, only 45 per cent of children reached the 5th year of primary school.
   Child labor for the 5 to 14 age-range reached 34 per cent between 1999 and 2001
   The Lord's Resistance Army (LRA) has kidnapped thousands of children as part of its guerrilla warfare strategy.

INDIGENOUS PEOPLES/ ETHNIC MINORITIES
There are at least 43 different ethnic groups in Uganda. Among the smaller groups are the Batwa, native to the region. The

estimated 2,100 survivors of this Banda-speaking group in Uganda have been evicted from the lands in the Bwindi and Mgahinga Parks, to free new areas for cultivation. At present they are almost all living as beggars in the cities. Some 18,000 Nubians live in the Bombo area, 60 km from Kampala. They claim descent from the Kingdom of Kush and the Egyptian Kushites, and speak Kenuzi-Dongola as well as Arabic. They arrived in the region at the end of the 19th century, when they received land in Uganda and Kenya in return for helping the British suppress revolts in Sudan and Egypt. Among the larger groups are the Baganda people whose original lands were to the north-east and north of Lake Victoria. Their highly structured society made them an ideal instrument for British domination. The Baganda and Bunyoro have elected kings, in line with government policy to reintroduce traditional systems of local rule.

MIGRANTS/REFUGEES
Between 600,000 and 700,000 Ugandans were displaced by the fighting between the Government and the LRA.

Approximately 27,000 took refuge abroad: 20,000 in DR Congo, 5,000 in Sudan and 2,000 in industrialized countries. In turn, the country has received some 220,000 refugees from other countries: 170,000 from Sudan, 20,000 from Rwanda, almost 10,000 from DRC, some 1,000 from Somalia and 20,000 from various other countries. These refugees live in the capital city. Conditions worsened for internally displaced people during 2002, due to increased fighting. Thousands of homeless people are caught in crossfire as they search for food and water. The high level of insecurity makes it practically impossible for humanitarian organizations to provide support.
   The LRA has murdered people in refugee camps in the north.

DEATH PENALTY
The death penalty is still applied.

*Latest data available in *The State of the World's Children* and *Childinfo* database, UNICEF, 2004.

Ukraine / Ukrayina

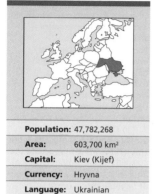

Population:	47,782,268
Area:	603,700 km²
Capital:	Kiev (Kijef)
Currency:	Hryvna
Language:	Ukrainian

B etween the 9th and 12th centuries AD, most of present-day Ukraine belonged to the Kievan (Kijef) Rus, which grouped together several alliances of Eastern Slavic peoples. Its nucleus was the Russian alliance, with its capital at Kiev. The ancient Russian people gave rise to the three main eastern Slav nations: Russia, Ukraine and Belarus. In the 12th century, the Kievan Rus separated into the principalities of Kiev, Chernigov, Galich and Vladimir-Volynski, all in what is now Ukrainian territory. In the 14th century, the Grand Principality of Lithuania annexed the territories of Chernigov and Novgorod-Severski, Podolia, Kiev and a large part of Volin. The Khanate of Crimea emerged in the southern part of Ukraine and Crimea, and expanded into Galicia and Podolia. After the 11th century, Hungary began seizing the Transcarpathian territories.

[2] The Ukrainians emerged as an identifiable people in the 15th century. Their name was derived from *krai*, meaning border, which in 1213 was the name given to the territories along the Polish border.

In the 16th century, the use of the name was extended to the entire Ukrainian region. Historically, there were close ties between Ukrainians and Russians, who had fought together against the Polish and Lithuanian feudal kingdoms and against the Tatars in Crimea. The Ukrainian territories (Volin, eastern Podolia, Kiev and part of the left bank of the Dnepr) were incorporated into the Rzecz Pospolita (the union of Poland and Lithuania), which imposed Roman Catholicism.

[3] During the first half of the 17th century, the struggle for independence from Poland and Lithuania intensified. The war of the Ukrainian people (1648-1654) under Bohdan Khmelnytsky ended with the unification of Ukraine and Russia. In March 1654, Ukrainian autonomy within the Russian Empire was ratified.

[4] In 1783, the Khanate of Crimea - home of the Tatars - was annexed by Russia. After the partition of Poland between Russia, Prussia and Austria (1793-95), the right bank of the Dnepr became a part of Russia and Ukraine's autonomy was

abolished at the end of the 18th century. In 1796, the left bank of Ukraine became the Province of Malo-Rossiya (Little Russia).

[5] After the end of czarist rule in 1917, a dual system emerged in Ukraine, with power being divided between the Provisional Government of St Petersburg and the Ukrainian Central Rada (council) in Kiev. In December, after the Bolshevik Revolution, the First Congress of Ukrainian Soviets formed a government. The Ukrainian Central Rada supported the Austro-German troops which invaded the country in the spring of 1918. Until 1920, Ukraine was the scene of major fighting between the Soviets and their internal and external enemies. In December 1922, Ukraine attended the first All-Union Congress of the Soviets, held in Moscow, where the founding of the Union of Soviet Socialist Republics (USSR) was ratified.

[6] In the period between the world wars, the Soviet Government carried out rapid industrialization and collectivization of agriculture.

[7] The secret clauses of the 1939 Soviet-German non-aggression pact

incorporated western Ukraine into the USSR. In 1940, Ukraine was enlarged through the addition of Bessarabia and Northern Bukovina. Germany invaded Ukraine in 1941, when a strong guerrilla resistance began. By the end of World War II, all areas inhabited by ethnic Ukrainians became part of the USSR. Ukraine participated in the founding of the UN as a charter member.

[8] In 1954, Crimea - which had formerly belonged to the Russian Federation - was turned over to Ukraine by the Soviet centralized authority. The leader of the Soviet Communist Party at the time was Nikita Krushchev, formerly first secretary of the Ukrainian Communist Party.

[9] On 26 April 1986, the nuclear plant at Chernobyl - 130 kilometers north of Kiev - was the scene of the worst nuclear accident in history when one of its reactors exploded, affecting an area inhabited by 600,000 people. By 1993, 135,000 were evacuated and 7,000 had died of radiation-related diseases. The reactor was sealed in cement. Chernobyl's radioactive fallout contaminated Ukraine, Russia, Belarus, Poland and regions of Sweden and Finland. In the following years, researchers recorded an increase in cancers and other radioactivity-related diseases.

[10] In 1985 within the framework of the reforms in the USSR, Communist leaders and Ukrainian nationalists founded the Ukrainian People's Movement for *Perestroika* (restructuring) (RUKH), which demanded greater political and economic autonomy. In the March 1990 legislative elections, RUKH candidates received massive support from the population. On 16 July 1990, the Ukrainian Supreme *Soviet* (Parliament) proclaimed the sovereignty of the republic. On 24 August 1991, the Ukrainian Parliament approved the republic's independence, and convened a plebiscite to ratify or reject the decision.

[11] In December 1991, 90 per cent of Ukrainians ratified their independence and elected Leonid Kravchuk, formerly first secretary of the Ukrainian Communist Party, as President.

[12] On 8 December 1991, the presidents of Ukraine, the Russian Federation and Belarus pronounced the end of the USSR, founding the Commonwealth of Independent States (CIS).

[13] In 1992, Ukraine deregulated prices, created a new currency, made bids for arms factories and encouraged foreign investment.

[14] On 5 May, the Crimea peninsula declared independence, but it was vetoed by the Ukrainian Parliament. Crimea yielded and withdrew the declaration. Russia reacted to the

PROFILE

ENVIRONMENT

Ukraine is bordered by Poland, Slovakia, Hungary, Romania and Moldova in the west and southwest; by Belarus in the north and Russia in the east and northeast. The Black Sea and the Sea of Azov (Acovsko More) are located in the south. It is mostly made up of flat plains and plateaus, with the Carpathian Mountains (max. altitude 2,061 m) along the country's southwestern borders, and the Crimean Mountains (max. altitude 1,545 m) in the south. The climate is moderate and mostly continental. There is black soil; both wooded and grassy steppes in the south. Much of the north is made up of mixed forest areas (such areas occupy 14 per cent of the republic's total land surface).

SOCIETY

Peoples: Ukrainians, 72.7 per cent; Russians, 22.1 per cent; Belarusians, 0.9 per cent; Moldovans, 0.6 per cent, Poles, 0.4 per cent.
Religions: Mainly Christian Orthodox. Catholics, Protestants, Jews. **Languages:** Ukrainian (official), Russian. **Main Political Parties:** Viktor Yushchenko Our Ukraine Bloc; Communist Party of Ukraine (KPU);

Ukrainian Social-Democratic Party; Socialist Party of Ukraine; For a United Ukraine.
Main Social Organizations: Confederation of Free Trade Unions of Ukraine (KVPU, with 18 trade unions); League of Ukrainian Women; Ukrainian National Committee of Youth Organizations (UNKMO).

THE STATE

Official Name: Ukrayina.
Administrative Divisions: 25 Regions, the Republic of Crimea has special status as well as great internal autonomy. **Capital:** Kiev (Kijef) 2,618,000 people (2003). **Other Cities:** Kharkov (Char'cov) 1,692,700 people; Donetsk 1,764,000; Dnipropetrovsk 1,483,300; Odessa 1,121,500 (2000).
Government: Leonid Kuchma, President and Head of State since July 1994, re-elected in 1999. Viktor Yanukovich, Prime Minister since November 2002. Legislature, single-chamber: Supreme Council, with 450 members. **National Holiday:** 24 August, Independence (1991). **Armed Forces:** 387,400 (1997). Other: 72,000 National Guard and Border Guard.

Life expectancy **69.7** years 2000-2005	GNI per capita **$770** 2002	Literacy **100%** total adult rate 2000	HIV prevalence rate **1%** of population 15-49 years old 2001

situation in June, annulling the 1954 decree by which it had ceded Crimea to Ukraine, demanding that it be returned. Kiev refused, but granted Crimea economic autonomy.

15   Prime Minister Vitold Fokin resigned in September 1993 over the failure of his economic policies. He was replaced by Leonid Kuchma, the former president of the Union of Industrialists and Entrepreneurs.

16   The liberal policies of the new government and its privatization scheme soon came up against the dual obstacles of the Supreme Council - dominated by former communists - and worker resistance.

17   In June, in a direct challenge to Kravchuk's moderate foreign policy, the Supreme Council announced the appropriation of the entire ex-USSR nuclear arsenal in Ukraine. With the disintegration of the Soviet Union, Ukraine became the world's third most important nuclear power.

18   Finding himself politically vulnerable, in September 1993 Kravchuk agreed to cede Ukraine's Black Sea fleet to Russia, in compensation for debts incurred through oil and gas purchases from Moscow. In addition, he accepted help from Russia in dismantling the 46 intercontinental SS24 missiles which Ukraine had wanted to keep as a last bastion against any possible future expansionist schemes on the part of Russia. However, opposition in Kiev led to the invalidation of the settlement.

19   In the meantime, the economy went out of control with inflation reaching 100 per cent per month and Kuchma resigned.

20   The first presidential elections of the post-Soviet era took place in June and July 1994. Former Prime Minister Leonid Kuchma defeated Kravchuk with 52 per cent of the vote, after which he declared his intention to strengthen links with Russia and enter fully into the Commonwealth of Independent States (CIS).

21   The Communist Party of Ukraine (KPU) obtained 113 seats (24.7 per cent) in the March 1998 Parliamentary elections, effectively becoming a left and center-left parliamentary majority. President Kuchma, an independent, was re-elected in the second round of the presidential elections on 14 December 1999, with 56 per cent of the vote. He promised to continue with market reforms and pro-Western policies, better ties with Eastern Europe, the US and NATO. International observers reported that the elections were far from free and fair.

22   On November 26 Kuchma urged the European Union (EU) to take Ukraine into account when the bloc discussed expansion plans in December. In late December, after striking a deal with the opposition, Kuchma appointed Viktor

IN FOCUS

ENVIRONMENTAL CHALLENGES
Air and water pollution are significant; deforestation is becoming a serious problem. Approximately 2.8 million people live in areas contaminated with radiation from the 1986 accident in the Chernobyl atomic plant, in the northeast.

WOMEN'S RIGHTS
Although women have been able to vote and stand for election since 1919, it was only in 2000 that Ukrainian women held Parliament seats. That same year, they had five per cent of ministerial or equivalent posts. Women comprise 49 per cent of the total labor force. According to UNICEF latest data available*, prenatal and care at childbirth are universal. The maternal mortality rate is 35 per 100,000 live births.

The problem of violence against women has not been solved. The Institute of Sociological Research stated in September 2000 that 12 per cent of women under 28 had suffered violence.

Figures from the United Nations Development Program (UNDP) show that the number of rapes reported in 2003 fell significantly over previous years, but some NGOs believe that most rapes and other abuses are underreported. The mass media rarely cover violence against women, in spite of the efforts made by human rights advocates to address it.

CHILDREN
According to UNICEF latest data available*, the infant mortality rate is 16 per 1,000 live births, and 20 per 1,000 live births among children under five. Six per cent of the newborn are underweight and 15 per cent are stunted. Between 98 and 99 per cent of children under one year old are immunized against diseases such as polio, tetanus and measles.

Some 100,000 children lived on the streets in 2001, of which those under 7 comprised 14 per cent of the total. Most had fled from domestic violence or sought a better financial situation. According to a survey made by the State Family and Youth Institute, 43 per cent of minors say they have suffered some type of violence. Most of the abuses are related to child prostitution. Human trafficking has been growing during last years, and girls are the main victims.

INDIGENOUS PEOPLES/ ETHNIC MINORITIES
Russians comprise slightly more than 22 per cent of the population. They live mostly in the eastern regions of Ukraine. They have a strong group identity and are politically mobilized, constantly demonstrating for union with Russia. They have formed political parties, but have not achieved their aims. Since separation from the USSR, the government established Ukrainian as the official language and closed all Russian-speaking education centers. The use of the Russian language by the mass media and in government areas is not encouraged.

MIGRANTS/REFUGEES
In 2002, Ukraine received some 3,600 refugees and asylum seekers. Of these, some 3,000 were recognized as refugees, 400 are waiting for a decision on their case and 200 were transferred to the UNHCR, after being rejected by the Ukrainian authorities. Most of the refugees came from Afghanistan (1,572), Armenia (244), Azerbaijan (232), Russia (228), Georgia (116), Sudan (67) and Iraq (66).

Ever since a ministerial resolution in 1996, Ukraine has a temporary protection regulation for all war refugees. Currently there are 3,021 people, including hundreds of children, in this situation.

DEATH PENALTY
Abolished in 2000.

*Latest data available in *The State of the World's Children* and *Childinfo* database,UNICEF, 2004.

Yushchenko, then head of the National Bank of Ukraine, as Prime Minister. In February 2000, Yushchenko announced Ukraine would restructure its foreign debt with tougher fiscal policies and a massive privatization plan. The President abolished the death penalty on 22 March, following European Council demands. On 16 April in a referendum, 90 per cent of the population backed the alliance and reform initiatives proposed by Kuchma, who was now able to dissolve Parliament without a majority.

23   After the disappearance of a journalist critical of the regime, opposition politicians alleged that there was a tape in which the President, prior to the disappearance, discussed the 'solution' to the problematic reporter with security officials. In February 2001 massive demonstrations requested Kuchma's resignation. Ukraine's rapprochement with the West was frozen when the journalist's decapitated body was found. Demonstrations against Kuchma continued and grew.

24   In April 2001 Parliament removed Yushchenko, the best ally of the market reforms demanded by the West, causing a serious political crisis. This revealed the tensions among three sectors: pro-Russian forces trying to return Kiev to the Kremlin's sphere, pro-Western forces who wanted to continue with the reforms and movement towards the EU and NATO, and organized crime, whose goal was to maintain the instability that benefited it. That month, Ukraine signed a technology and military cooperation agreement with Russia.

25   Fourteen per cent of Ukrainian people were disabled, being either war veterans from Afghanistan or victims of the Chernobyl nuclear disaster or of the frequent accidents in the Donbass coal mining region. According to an ILO report, the death rate for that year amounted to 5 workers for every million tons of coal extracted, the highest in all Europe.

26   In the March 2002 Parliamentary elections, Viktor Yushchenko's Our Ukraine Bloc won with 23.6 per cent of the vote, followed by the Communists, with 20 per cent. The pro-government For United Ukraine took third place. The Liberal opposition accused Ukrainian authorities of fraud. Yushchenko announced he would contest the results, saying he had been robbed of 12 per cent of the vote.

27   In August 2003, Ukraine announced it would send 1,600 soldiers to Iraq, to help the coalition led by the US that had invaded that country in March.

28   Ukraine - although still wanting to join the EU and NATO - agreed in September to form a Common Economic Space with Russia, Belarus and Kazakhstan, despite domestic opposition and fears that the agreement would hinder its pro-European integration policy.

29   In March 2004, the Ukraine Confederation of Free Trade Unions reported serious violations of labor freedom in the country, after the son of the organization's president was assaulted by unidentified persons.

30   In November 2004 the presidential election – of dubious transparency, according to international observers – produced such a close result that the two leading candidates (prime minister Viktor Yanukovich and opposition Viktor Yuschenko) agreed to hold a second run-off vote. ∎

United Arab Emirates / Al Imarat al Arabiyah al Muttahidah

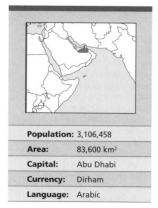

Population:	3,106,458
Area:	83,600 km²
Capital:	Abu Dhabi
Currency:	Dirham
Language:	Arabic

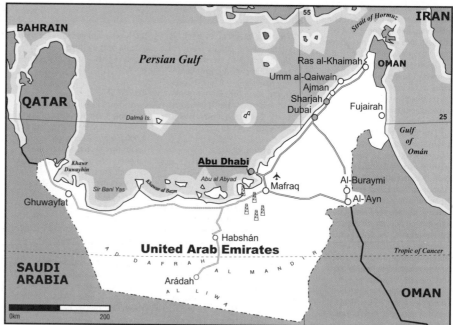

In the southeastern corner of the Arab peninsula, the Rub al-Khali desert occupies part of the territory of present-day Saudi Arabia and almost all that of the United Arab Emirates.

2   By the 6th century the oases supplied water to a small stable population that spoke different Arabic dialects. Some were farmers, others were merchants or craftspeople from small villages and others (generically known as 'Bedouins') were nomads who raised camels, sheep and goats. Along with these activities, the coastal peoples also fished in Gulf waters.

3   The Bedouins - a mobile, tribally organized and armed group - together with the merchants, dominated the farmers and craftspeople.

4   Among herders and farmers, religion had become another type of social control. Local gods were identified with the heavenly bodies and could incarnate into

rocks, trees or animals. Some families, by interpreting the language of the gods, managed to exercise control over others.

5   Up until the 7th century, the Byzantine and Sassanid empires waged a long war in the peninsula, although this did not directly involve the territory of the present-day Emirates. Such activity, as well as the opening of trade routes, attracted merchants, dealers and craftspeople who brought knowledge of the foreign world and its cultures.

6   Islam was adopted during the Prophet Muhammad's lifetime.

Tribal chiefs secured their power without significantly changing the lifestyle of the few inhabitants.

7   Upon the Prophet's death, various groups disputed his spiritual inheritance. The Ibadis (who claimed to be his direct descendants), created the Uman (Oman) imanate in the mid-8th century. At the end of the 9th century it was suppressed by the Abassids, caliphs who claimed a universal authority and whose capital was in Baghdad.

8   After the 11th century, the Sunni form of Islam gradually

spread from being the religion of the ruling groups, to reach the population at large. The Ibadis continued to exert strong religious authority until the 15th century.

9   The Gulf ports were used for trading in textiles, glass, porcelain and spices from China, which were transported to the Red Sea through a chain of oases.

10   During the 17th and 18th centuries, the Ibadis reinstated their imanate under a Yaribi dynasty, remaining on the borders of the Ottoman Empire. To the north, Bahrain was under Iranian domination.

11   While the Ottomans were occupied with constant wars in Europe, Africa and Asia, the southeastern region was devoted to trade. Ruling families linked directly with merchants appeared and piracy developed, benefiting from the natural advantages of the coasts (known since that period as the 'Pirate Coast').

12   When European fleets increased their use of the maritime route round the Cape, British influence grew. British ships used the Gulf ports as harbors on the way to India, and helped to combat piracy.

13   At the beginning of the 19th century, Britain gained complete control over the region through agreements reached with the local chiefs and small governors of the ports. The Trucial States, (the Pirate Coast's new name) included Abu Dhabi, Dubai and Sharjah. Relations with Britain continued in the same way until the first decades of the 20th century.

PROFILE

ENVIRONMENT
Located in the southeastern part of the Arabian peninsula, stretching from the Qatar peninsula toward the strait of Hormuz, the land is mostly desert with few oases and *wadis* (dry and rocky river beds). The coastal areas are very hilly lowlands with coral islands offshore and sand dunes. This is where most of the operating oilfields are, and therefore, where the highest levels of coastal pollution occur. The country is one of the world's main oil producers.

SOCIETY
Peoples: Only 19 per cent of the population are Arabs from the UAE; the remaining 23 per cent of Arabs come from other countries. Fully 50 per cent of the population are migrant workers from South Asia. Europeans and US 5 per cent. 80 per cent live in Dubai, attracted by the oil wealth.
Religions: Muslim 94.9 per cent (Sunni 80 per cent, Shi'a 14.9 per cent); Christian 3.8 per cent; others 1.3 per cent.
Languages: Arabic (official); Persian, Hindi and Urdu are also spoken. English is spoken among immigrants and for business reasons.
Main Political Parties: No political parties or

trade unions are allowed.

THE STATE
Official Name: Daulat al-Imarat al-'Arabiya al-Muttahida.
Administrative Divisions: 7 emirates: Abu Dhabi; Dubai; Sharjah; Ajman; Umm al-Qaiwain; Ras al-Khaimah and Fujairah.
Capital: Abu Dhabi (Abu Zaby) 1,305,000 people (2004).
Other Cities: Dubai 947,600 people; Sharjah 562,700; Ras al-Khaimah 203,000; Ajman 167,000 (2004).
Government: Parliamentary Republic with a president of the federation as a Head of State: Sheikh Khalifa bin Zayed Al Nahayan, Emir of Abu Dhabi, since November 2004. Vice President and Prime Minister: Sheikh Maktoum ibn Rashid al-Maktoum, Emir of Dubai, since November 1990. Unicameral Legislature: Federal National Council with 40 members appointed by the emirs.
National Holiday: 2 December, Independence Day and Proclamation of the Union (1971).
Armed Forces: 64,500 (1997).

Life expectancy
74.7 years
2000-2005

Literacy
76% total adult rate
2000

14 Around 1914, the Saudi state re-emerged in Central Arabia. Russia, France and Germany also sought to intensify their presence in the area. This led the British to formalize relations with the Trucial States of Bahrain, Oman and Kuwait, which let the Government in London handle their external affairs.

15 World War I did not alter these relationships. Britain was the real power behind Abd al-Aziz's government in the new kingdom of Saudi Arabia, controlling the southern and southeastern coasts of the peninsula. With the development of air routes, the Gulf's airfields and those of Egypt, Palestine and Iraq took on an important role.

16 After World War II, relations among Arab countries changed. The League of Arab States was formed in 1945 by those countries that had some form of independence.

17 At the beginning of the 1960s, the Middle East's oil deposits were known to be among the largest in the world. The United States joined Britain in keeping control over the Gulf States, whose revenues depended almost entirely on oil.

18 The growing influence of the Pan-Arabist Egyptian President Gamal Abdel Nasser led Britain to allow greater local participation in the governments of several states of the Protectorate. In 1968, it withdrew its military forces from the region. That same year, the OPEAC - a branch of OPEC (Organization of Oil Exporting Countries) - was created, formed exclusively by oil-exporting Arab states.

19 In 1971, Abu Dhabi began a large-scale exploitation of its oil wells. The clear establishment of borders between the territories became indispensable. Under British influence, the United Arab Emirates were created that year without the participation of Qatar or Bahrain.

20 The new state had to face a conflict with Iran which, claiming historical rights, occupied the islands of Abu Mussa, Tunb al-Cubra and Tunb al-Sughra on the Strait of Hormuz. During the first decade, oil production rose (mainly in Abu Dhabi, Dubai and Sharjah). National participation in the control of oil exploitation also grew.

21 When OPEC decided in 1973 to raise the price of oil by 70 per cent and reduce supply by 5 per cent, a new era in the oil-rich states' relations with the world began. The results of this policy were explosive. The UAE's annual growth rate in the 1970s was over 10 per cent due to oil revenues.

22 There was a rapid growth of cities with state-of-the-art highways, oil pipelines and banks, and many immigrants were attracted by the region's possibilities. Little was left of the ancient pursuits of fishing or diving for pearls on the coast.

23 The 1980s began with the Iran-Iraq war. Although the United Arab Emirates maintained an apparently neutral stand, they gave economic support to Iraq to avoid a possible 'Iranization' of the region. Once the conflict had ended, the UAE had become the Middle East's third largest oil producer, after Saudi Arabia and Libya.

24 As from 1981 the Government tried to develop other industrial fields to reduce dependence on oil production.

25 The country was a member of the Non-Aligned Movement and supported Palestinian claims. In late 1986, diplomatic relations were established with the Soviet Union and the People's Republic of Benin. In 1987, relations with Egypt were reinstated. These had been broken off after the Camp David agreements with Israel.

26 During the Gulf War (1991), the Emirates supported the fight against Iraq, which had occupied Kuwait.

27 In March 1991, the Gulf Co-operation Council signed an agreement with the US which included a common military strategy and mechanisms to prevent arms proliferation in the zone.

28 In 1992, with Syrian mediation, Iran modified its claims over the islands of the Strait of Hormuz. The conflict was placed under international arbitration, following pressure by the Emirates.

29 The influence of Islamic fundamentalism increased in the UAE between 1993 and 1996. Sheikh Zayed, President of the Union, was keen to extend 'integral' Islam. In February 1994, he decided to extend *Sharia* (Islamic law) to criminal cases which had previously been dealt with by civil courts.

30 In 1997, in view of the US threat of an armed intervention in Iraq, Sheik Zayed stated that the Iraqi people deserved a 'new chance' and that measures of this type would be 'unacceptable'.

31 In the field of domestic policy, economic liberalization continued, leading among other things to the establishment of a free trade zone in 1998 in the city of Ras al-Khaimah; the first in the Middle East. In April 2000, the UAE embassy in Iraq was reopened.

32 The fall in oil prices was the main reason that GDP growth in the Emirates dropped in 2001. The country achieved some diversification of its economic activity in sectors not related to oil - such as aluminum, tourism, telecommunications and aviation - which still contribute two thirds of the GDP and 30 per cent of exports.

33 After an Iraqi boat with smuggled oil was shipwrecked in April 2002, the UAE decided to ban oil tankers belonging to 10 countries blacklisted by the International Maritime Organization from its territorial waters.

34 In May 2003, it was announced that the Emirates' trade with Turkey had increased by 20 per cent during 2002. The annual business volume of Turkish companies in the country was in excess of $1,000 million.

35 In June 2003, the UAE Red Crescent announced a donation of $110,000 for the construction of housing for the victims of floods in Bangladesh, and $52,700 for social support programs in Asia and regions of the Pacific.

36 In February 2004, experts announced that the 2003 fiscal balance had been extremely positive, continuing the trend observed over the past 4 years. Surplus in current accounts amounted to around $10,700 million in 2002 and $12,200 million in 2003.

37 In November 2004 the President, Sheikh Zayed – considered the father of the nation – died at the age of 86. His son Sheikh Khalifa bin Zayed Al Nahayan, the Crown Prince of Abu Dhabi, succeeded him as President.

38 There are still no democratically elected institutions or political parties but a cabinet reshuffle in November brought a woman into government for the first time with the appointment of Shaikha Lubna al-Qasimi as economy and planning minister. ∎

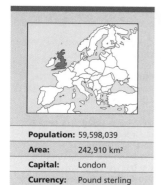

Population:	59,598,039
Area:	242,910 km²
Capital:	London
Currency:	Pound sterling
Language:	English

T he first known inhabitants of what is now Britain were Paleolithic hunters, following herds of wild animals. After the final ice age, agriculturalists began to settle on the island. Over thousands of years, these people and the many others who migrated from the continent evolved toward increasingly complex social systems.

2   In 44 AD the Romans invaded southern Britain. In 90 AD they created the province of Britannia, and founded London between 70 and 100 AD. In the early 5th century they abandoned the island, leaving it largely defenseless against the raids of Angles, Saxons and Jutes. These Germanic peoples pushed the Celts westwards, taking over the southern part of the island and establishing Anglo-Saxon kingdoms.

3   During the 5th century, the inhabitants of Ireland and Wales adopted Christianity. In the 7th century, the British church came under the power of Rome.

4   During the 7th and 9th centuries Danish invaders overran the eastern part of England. In the 11th century, the Normans, led by William the Conqueror, invaded England and secured the throne. Successive Anglo-Norman kings maintained their power by establishing various forms of vassalage over the feudal lords, though under John (1199-1216), these barons, in alliance with the clergy, were able to restrict the power of the monarchy through the Magna Carta, signed in 1215.

5   The Magna Carta laid the foundations of the British parliamentary system. It also marked the beginning of a continuous power struggle between the monarchy and the nobility. The growing power of the land-owning class and later the bourgeoisie eventually led to the consolidation of a parliamentary monarchy. The Welsh came under English control in 1382.

6   Frequent dynastic conflicts, disputes over territories in France belonging to the English Crown, commercial rivalry between England and France in Flanders, and French aid to Scotland in its wars with England paved the way for the Hundred Years' War (1337-1453), which culminated in the loss of the English possessions on the continent.

7   The negative effects of the War increased the unpopularity of the monarchy which faced at the same time an anti-Papal movement led by the followers of Wycliffe (a precursor of Luther) and a peasant rebellion. The peasants, led by Wat Tyler, rose up against the payment of tribute and the power of the feudal lords. In 1381, Tyler and his followers managed to enter London and negotiate directly with the King, Richard II. The Peasants' Revolt was unsuccessful however and Tyler was later executed.

8   The period following the Hundred Years' War was dominated by a long struggle for control of the throne between the royal Houses of Lancaster and of York. This led to the War of the Roses which ended with the coming to power of the Welsh House of Tudor in 1485. The Tudor period is considered the beginning of the modern British state. One of the Tudor kings, Henry VIII (1509-47), broke away from the Church of Rome, founding the Anglican Church. The desire to extend English authority and the religious Reformation to Ireland led to the subjugation of Ulster by Henry's daughter Elizabeth I (1558-1603).

Tudor involvement in Ireland laid the foundations for centuries of religious and political conflict in the country.

9   Under the reign of Elizabeth I, poetry and the theatre flourished with playwrights such as Ben Jonson, Marlowe and Shakespeare. Industry and trade developed, and the country embarked upon its 'colonial adventure', the beginning of its future empire. After defeating the Spanish fleet - the 'Invincible Armada' - in 1588, the British Navy 'ruled the waves', with no other fleet capable of opposing it.

10   British merchant ships involved in the slave trade, or laden with colonists or belonging to pirates and privateers sailed the oceans freely. Markets multiplied, demand grew rapidly, and producers were forced to seek new techniques in order to accelerate production. It was a prelude to the industrial revolution which was to take place in the country at the beginning of the 18th century.

11   In 1603, the crowning of James I (James VI of Scotland) put an end to the independent Scottish monarchy. The religious intolerance of James' son Charles I, led to a Scottish uprising and increasing discontent in England. This culminated in the English Civil War, which broke out in 1642. The deteriorating political situation led to the Puritans forming an army supported by Parliament; led by Oliver Cromwell, they

defeated the royal forces in 1646 and again in 1648.

12   In 1649, Parliament executed the King and proclaimed Cromwell 'Lord Protector', establishing a republic known as the Commonwealth. Radical egalitarian ideas came to the fore within the parliamentary movement, notably among the Levellers, who advocated political democracy and the abolition of the English class system. But their ideas were suppressed and their leaders imprisoned by Cromwell. After Cromwell's death, in 1658, the monarchy was restored with Charles II.

13   The priorities of the new regime were the colonization of North America and trade with America, the Far East and the Mediterranean. The slave trade - the kidnapping, trafficking and selling of slaves from Africa to buyers in America and other places - which had started in the 16th century, became one of the main sources of income for the empire.

14   The absolutism of Charles II's successor, James II, and his espousal of Catholicism were opposed by the Protestant Parliament which deposed James through the 'Glorious Revolution'. Parliament invited the Dutch prince William of Orange to assume the English throne. William III was forced to sign the Declaration of Rights (1689), limiting royal powers and guaranteeing the supremacy of Parliament.

15   In this period John Locke summarized revolutionary ideals, proposing that people have basic natural rights: to property, life, liberty and personal security. Government, created by society to protect these rights, must fulfill its mission; if it fails to do so, the people have the right to resist its authority.

16   In 1707, the parliaments of Scotland and England were joined together, creating the United Kingdom of Great Britain. Britain intervened in the war of succession in Spain, obtaining Minorca, Gibraltar and Nova Scotia through the Treaty of Utrecht (1713). In 1765, increased taxes imposed by the Stamp Act triggered the rebellion and secession of the American colonies, which declared their independence in 1776.

17   During this period, the two large political parties were formed: the Conservatives (Tories), representing the interests of the large landowners, and the Liberals (Whigs), representing the merchant class. The ideas forming the basis of economic liberalism were developed at this time by Adam Smith. The liberal doctrine provided the political ideology for British imperialism, which used the concept of 'free trade' as a justification for forcing open the ports and markets of the Third World, often with the use of

Life expectancy
78.2 years
2000-2005

GNI per capita
$25,250
2002

HIV prevalence rate
0.1% of population
15-49 years old
2001

naval force. Perhaps the most notorious example of this was the Opium Wars fought against China in the mid-19th century.

18 After the crushing of a nationalist rebellion in Ireland in 1798, the United Kingdom of Great Britain and Ireland was created in 1801 with the dissolution of the Irish Parliament (see Ireland).

19 The 18th century gave rise to the agricultural 'revolution', which introduced important innovations in farming techniques, as well as major changes in land tenure. The large landowners enclosed their properties, eliminating communal lands which had hitherto been used by small farmers, and introducing a more capitalist agricultural economy.

20 At the same time, the industrial revolution began, with the textile manufacturers being the first to confront the problem of meeting a growing demand for cloth overseas. The introduction of machinery changed the way in which work was done, and the medieval shop was replaced by the factory. On the heels of the textile industry came mining and metallurgy. The mechanization process was consolidated with the invention of the steam engine, the use of coal as a fuel and the substitution of first iron, then steel, for wood in construction.

21 This period was characterized by population growth (up from 10,900,000 in 1801 to 21,000,000 in 1850), increasing demand and expanding trade, improvements in the transport system, capital accumulation, the creation of a vast colonial empire, scientific advances and the golden age of the bourgeoisie. Britain became the world's premier manufacturing nation. Its colonial policy helped to prevent competition against its factories; for example it established regulations which destroyed the Indian textile industry.

22 The United Kingdom obtained new territories from its wars with France, particularly its triumph over Napoleon at Waterloo (1815).

23 One result of the industrial revolution was increasing discontent among the rapidly growing working class, due to low salaries, unhealthy working conditions, unsatisfactory housing, malnutrition, job insecurity and the long and tiring working days to which men, women and children were subjected. In many cases, popular uprisings were characterized by violence, and were met with equally violent repression.

24 In the early stages of the industrial revolution, spontaneous movements arose, like the 'Luddites' - textile workers who destroyed machinery to prevent it from destroying their cottage industry. Trade unions began to appear later.

25 In 1819 a demonstration in Manchester was ruthlessly put down

(the Peterloo massacre), and repressive legislation followed, limiting the right of association and freedom of the press. Nevertheless, resistance movements continued their activity. One of the main movements of this period was the nationalist Irish Association led by Daniel O'Connell.

26 The most important of the mass movements was the Chartist Movement, made up primarily of workers. It took its name from the People's Charter, published in 1838 at a mass assembly in Glasgow, Scotland. This movement brought a number of issues to the fore, both political - universal suffrage, use of the secret ballot, reform of voting registers - and social - better salaries and better working conditions. After its demonstrations and strikes, 'Chartism' faded away. However, it had a far-reaching influence and its grievances were subsequently taken up by some members of parliament.

27 Robert Owen (1771-1858), considered to be the founder of socialism and the English co-

operative movement, argued that the predominance of individual interests led to the impoverishment of the masses. From 1830 on, he devoted himself to the establishment of co-operatives and the organization of labor into trade unions.

28 During the long reign of Queen Victoria (1837-1901), the traditional nobility strengthened its alliance with the industrial and mercantile bourgeoisie, and the first socialist movements emerged. Trade unions were legalized in 1871 and shortly afterwards some labor legislation was approved.

29 Beginning in 1873, the rising population numbers led to a food shortage, making imports necessary. At the same time industry began to feel the competition from the US and Germany. Britain increased its imperial activities in Africa, Asia and Oceania, not only for economic reasons, but also because of the political ambition to build a great empire. The Boer or South African War (1899-1902), fought to secure

control over southern Africa, was the most expensive regional conflict of the 19th century.

30 The first quarter of the 20th century saw the birth of the women's liberation movement. The militancy of the suffragettes led to some women obtaining the right to vote in 1917. The most famous example of their militancy was the suicide of Emily Davison, who threw herself in front of the King's horse during a race in 1913.

31 In Ireland, the majority Catholic population were stripped of their lands, restricted in their civil rights because of their religion, and deprived of their political autonomy. Millions emigrated, and political unrest periodically resulted in violent uprisings. Not until 1867 were the privileges of the Anglican Church eliminated; at the same time, measures were taken to improve the situation of the peasants. The 1916 Easter Rising in Dublin was ruthlessly put down by the British, but the Crown forces were unable to win the ensuing guerrilla war which began in

IN FOCUS

ENVIRONMENTAL CHALLENGES
This highly industrialized country has serious environmental contamination problems, principally air pollution. A nuclear re-processing plant on the Irish Sea appears to be linked to the high incidence of leukemia in the areas located on both coasts of this sea. The great amount of domestic garbage is another important environmental problem.

WOMEN'S RIGHTS
Women have been able to vote and run for office since 1918. In the year 2000, 24 per cent of ministerial positions and/or equivalent were occupied by women (in 1995, they only amounted to 9 per cent). Women comprise 44 per cent of the country's total labor force: 87 per cent worked in services, 12 per cent in industry, and 1 per cent in agriculture.

According to UNICEF's latest data available*, the maternal mortality rate is 13 out of every 100,000 live births and 99 per cent of births are attended by qualified personnel.

Since May 2002, the police has registered 11,411 rapes and 24,811 complaints of domestic violence. Isolated cases of female genital mutilation have been registered.

The law allows for equal opportunities; however, on average women earn 80 per cent of men's hourly salary for doing the same job.

CHILDREN
According to UNICEF's databases *, the infant mortality rate is 5 deaths per thousand live births; among under-fives, it is 7 per thousand. Eight per cent of newborns are underweight. In 2003, between 85 and 94 per cent of babies under 12 months old had been vaccinated against illnesses such as measles, poliomyelitis and tetanus.

Pedophilia is very much on the increase. Reports from different NGOs abound, concerning child trafficking from other countries to the UK; they are used as household servants or messengers for gangs linked to drug trafficking, and are also forced to work in factories, restaurants and/or as beggars. Young people under 16 are not allowed to work for more than a few hours a week except as part of educational programs.

The country is also used as a destination by gangs trafficking in women, mainly girls and adolescents, to work in prostitution. A report from the Home Office estimated that 1,500 girls and adolescents were trafficked into the country in the year 2000 for this purpose.

INDIGENOUS PEOPLES/ ETHNIC MINORITIES
Afro-Caribbean migration to the UK increased after World War II. The largest communities are located in the south of England, mainly in London. In spite of their proficiency in the English language, the Afro-Caribbeans have had to endure much discrimination and violence.

Asian immigrants started arriving in great numbers in the

1950s. They are mostly from South Asia (India, Pakistan and Bangladesh) and are concentrated in the large English cities. They suffer great social discrimination at the hands of the majority groups and encounter obstacles which prevent their access to high government positions.

MIGRANTS/REFUGEES
Towards the end of 2002, the UK had around 79,200 refugees and asylum-seekers, including over 52,600 applicants with their cases pending. An estimated 26,500 people were granted asylum in 2002. Several NGOs have published reports documenting the poverty, precarious health coverage, isolation, racial violence and abuses that asylum-seekers have been subjected to. A survey taken among the organizations helping them showed that over three-quarters of these people have suffered regularly from hunger.

The applicants must fill in forms at the borders, at the time of entry into the UK. These must be completed in English; otherwise, they are refused.

DEATH PENALTY
It was abolished in 1965 but the death penalty was technically retained for treason, piracy and crimes committed under military jurisdiction. The UK became completely abolitionist in 1998.

* Latest data available in *The State of the World's Children* and *Childinfo* database, UNICEF, 2004.

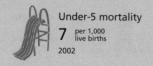

Under-5 mortality

7 per 1,000 live births

2002

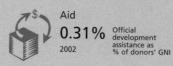

Aid

0.31% Official development assistance as % of donors' GNI

2002

1918, and Britain finally granted Ireland independence in 1921. Six counties in the north-east, with Protestant majorities, remained under British control with a devolved administration in Belfast.

32 Economic and political rivalry between the European powers led to the outbreak of World War I (1914-18). The Central Powers of Austro-Hungary and Germany, joined subsequently by Turkey and Bulgaria, fought against the Allied powers of France, Britain, Russia, Serbia and Belgium, with Italy, Japan, Portugal, Romania, the United States and Greece joining during the course of the War.

33 Despite its victory, Britain emerged from the War in a weakened condition. It had invested $40 billion in military expenditure, mobilized 7,500,000 troops, suffered a loss of 1,200,000 soldiers and acquired an enormous foreign debt.

The deep economic depression in the post-War years led to renewed unrest among workers, which reached its height in the General Strike of 1926. The Conservative Government declared the strike illegal, but did not take any measures to revive British industry. In the elections of 1929, the Labour Party came to power for the first time.

34 In the aftermath of World War I, Britain supported the creation of the League of Nations. In 1931, the British Community of Nations (Commonwealth) was established under the Statute of Westminster. This formally recognized the independence of Canada, Australia, New Zealand and South Africa.

35 On 1 September 1939, Germany invaded Poland and two days later Britain declared war on Germany, marking the beginning of its participation in World War II (1939-45). In May 1940 a coalition cabinet

was formed, with Winston Churchill as Prime Minister. From 1939 to 1941, Britain and France were ranged against Germany which was joined by Italy in 1940. Hungary, Romania, Bulgaria and Yugoslavia participated in the war as 'lesser' allies of the Nazis.

36 In 1941, the Soviet Union, Japan and the US entered the conflict. On 8 May 1945, Germany surrendered. The UK, US and the USSR emerged as the major victors from the war. However, the British Empire was eclipsed by the rising power of the US, which became the undisputed economic, technological and military leader.

37 In May 1945, the Labour Government of Clement Attlee, who won the elections with the slogan 'We won the war, now we will win the peace', nationalized the coal mines, the Bank of England and the iron and steel industries. It also established the National Health Service, which offered free health care to all.

38 Pakistan was formed and India became independent in 1947, although both remained members of the British Commonwealth. During the following decade, most of Britain's overseas colonies obtained their independence. Britain was a founder member of NATO in 1949.

39 The Franco-British military intervention in the Suez Canal Zone in 1956, which failed due to a lack of US support, was met by strong criticism from both inside and outside Britain (see Egypt). The following year, the UK detonated its first hydrogen bomb in the Pacific Ocean.

40 The general election of 1964 was won by the Labour Party under the leadership of Harold Wilson. His government faced serious problems, such as the declaration of independence by Southern Rhodesia (today Zimbabwe), and the severing of diplomatic relations with nine other African countries.

41 In 1967, having been denied entry to the Common Market, and faced with economic problems and rapidly increasing unemployment, Wilson withdrew British troops from South Yemen, evacuated all bases east of Suez except for Hong Kong, discontinued arms purchases from the US and implemented a savage austerity budget.

42 In Northern Ireland in 1969, the latent conflict erupted. A number of people were killed and wounded in riots between Catholics and Protestants. The Catholics demanded equal political rights, and better access to housing, schools and social security. The Protestant-controlled Northern Irish Government responded by sending in their armed police reserves against the Catholic demonstrators. The British Government sent in their troops to

separate the two sides and took control of police and reserve forces away from the Belfast Government.

43 In August 1971, Prime Minister of Northern Ireland Brian Faulkner opened internment camps and authorized the detention of suspects without trial. Protests against these measures resulted in more than 25 deaths. On 30 January 1972, 'Bloody Sunday', British soldiers opened fire on a peaceful protest march in Derry (Londonderry), killing 13 Catholics and injuring hundreds more. The Irish Republican Army (IRA) responded with numerous assassinations.

44 In March 1973, the people of Northern Ireland voted in a referendum to remain within the UK rather than join a united Ireland. There was a high abstention rate of 41.4 per cent.

45 In the 1970s, social conflict in Britain intensified, and Edward Heath's Conservative Government (1970-74) was faced with strikes in key public enterprises. The dockers, coal miners and railway workers all went on strike. Inability to deal with this labor unrest led to his resignation in 1974, and the Labour Party won the following elections. In January 1973 a majority of the electorate voted in favor of entering the European Economic Community (EEC). A policy of progressive integration with Europe began, as well as a search for new markets for ailing British industry.

46 A new divorce law was passed in 1975. The same year, feminists campaigned successfully against restrictions being added to the 1967 abortion law.

47 In 1979, voters in Scotland and Wales turned down autonomy for their regions in referenda organized by James Callaghan's Labour Government.

48 In May of that year, after the 'winter of discontent' characterized by strikes, the Conservative Party won the election, with Margaret Thatcher as its leader. The new Prime Minister brought in a severe monetarist policy to bring down inflation. She began to reverse the nationalization process carried out under Labour, and returned to a free market policy.

49 In 1981, a group of IRA prisoners began a hunger strike as part of their campaign to win recognition as political prisoners. The Government refused to accept the prisoners' demands. The strike resulted in 12 deaths.

50 In April 1982, Thatcher sent a Royal Navy force, including aircraft carriers and nuclear submarines, to the Malvinas islands (Falklands) which had been occupied by troops from the military junta in Argentina. After 45 days of fighting the British recovered the islands for the Crown (see Argentina).

PROFILE

ENVIRONMENT

The country consists of Britain (England, Scotland, and Wales) and Northern Ireland, and several smaller islands. The Pennines, a low mountain range, run down the northern center of England. The Grampian mountains are located in Scotland and the Cambrian mountains in Wales. The largest plains are in the southeast, around London. The climate is temperate. Farming is highly mechanized and is now a subsidiary activity. The service industry, especially insurance, finance and tourism, are big income earners. The huge coal and iron ore deposits which made the Industrial Revolution possible have nearly run out, but gas and oil finds in the North Sea turned the UK into an exporter of these products.

SOCIETY

Peoples: English, Scots, Welsh and Irish. Minorities including Indians (1.5 per cent), Pakistanis (0.9 per cent) and Afro-Caribbean (0.8 per cent), among others. **Religions:** Protestant 53.4 per cent (Anglican 43.5 per cent; Presbyterian 4.5 per cent; Methodist 2.2 per cent); Roman Catholic 9.8 per cent; Orthodox 1 per cent; other Christians 1.7 per cent; Muslim 2.6 per cent; Hindu 0.6 per cent, Sikh 0.5 per cent; Jewish 0.5 per cent; other/no religion 29.9 per cent. **Languages:** English (official), Welsh, Gaelic and the languages of various immigrant groups. **Main Political Parties:** Labour Party, social democrat, led by Tony Blair, in government. Conservative Party, opposition. Liberal Democrat Party, center-left; British National Party, extreme right. In Northern Ireland, Ulster Unionist Party, conservative; Social Democratic and Labor Party (SDLP), liberal-left; Democratic Unionist Party (DUP), ultra conservative; Sinn Féin, Irish nationalist. **Main Social Organizations:** The Trade Union Congress (TUC) has 12 million members. National Alliance of Women's Organizations, which unites organizations defending women's rights.

THE STATE

Official Name: United Kingdom of Great Britain and Northern Ireland.
Administrative Divisions: 39 Counties and 7 Metropolitan Districts.
Capital: London 7,619,000 people (2003). **Other Cities:** Birmingham 2,642,300 people; Leeds 1,502,100; Sheffield 1,106,400; Glasgow 1,083,600; Bristol 615,100; Liverpool 468,300 (2000).
Government: Constitutional parliamentary monarchy. Elizabeth II, Queen and Head of State since February 1952. Tony Blair, Prime Minister since May 1997, re-elected in 2001. Bicameral Legislature: the House of Commons, with 659 members elected for a five-year term, and the unelected House of Lords, with 703 members, 586 life peers and 91 hereditary members and 26 bishops (2004).
Armed Forces: 206,380 (2004). Dependencies: Anguilla, Bermuda, Gibraltar (contested by Spain), the Falkland Islands/Malvinas (contested by Argentina), British Virgin Islands, Northern Ireland, Montserrat, Cayman Islands, Guernsey, Jersey, Isle of Man, Turks and Caicos, St Helena, British Territories in the Indian Ocean (Mauritius) and Pitcairn (Oceania).

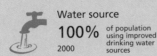
Water source
100% of population using improved drinking water sources
2000

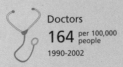
Doctors
164 per 100,000 people
1990-2002

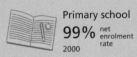
Primary school
99% net enrolment rate
2000

51 In October 1983, the British Government decided to withdraw its troops from Belize. The following year, in agreement with a treaty dating back to the First Opium War, Britain ceded sovereignty over Hong Kong to the People's Republic of China, with effect from June 1997.

52 During the Thatcher Administration, the trade union movement suffered serious setbacks, hampered by increasingly restrictive laws and the loss of affiliates in the industrial sector, itself in decline. The 1984/85 miners' strike culminated in defeat for the union after a year of violent internal strife and confrontation with the police.

53 In 1987, Thatcher was elected to her third consecutive term in office. She continued her policies as before: radical economic liberalization, privatization of state corporations, tax reform and opposition to union demands. In foreign affairs, Britain opposed greater European Community integration and continued to align itself closely with the US.

54 In mid-1989, after several years of growth, inflation reached high levels, unemployment continued to rise steeply, productive investments fell and the balance of payments deficit grew. At the same time, the introduction of a new Poll Tax and other projected reforms produced strong popular resistance.

55 In February 1990, the UK and Argentina renewed diplomatic relations and their representatives met in Madrid to negotiate the issue of the return of the Malvinas/Falklands.

56 In November 1990 Thatcher was replaced as head of the Government and Tory leader by her former minister, John Major. On taking office, Major declared himself to be in favor of capitalism with a human face, thus setting himself apart from the 'Iron Lady's' (Thatcher) harsher version of capitalism.

57 In 1991, Major announced that the Poll Tax would be replaced and promoted legal protection for the sick, working women, consumers and families. However, Major continued most of Thatcher's reforms, including the selling-off of nationalized industries such as the railways.

58 In European affairs, the Prime Minister distanced himself from his predecessor. In 1991, London gave its backing to European agreements on monetary union. However, the fidelity which British diplomacy showed towards the US remained unaltered, as proven by British participation alongside the US in the Gulf War against Iraq.

59 The Government managed to bring down inflation (which dropped from 10 per cent to 3.8 per cent between 1990 and 1991) and interest rates (which decreased from 15 per cent to 9.5 per cent), but economic

activity remained stagnant. In 1991, industrial production declined and numerous small businesses failed. Unemployment continued to rise (over 9 per cent by late 1991), and now affected white-collar workers and professionals, groups which had supported Thatcher's neo-liberal policies.

60 Despite this growing unpopularity, Major's Conservative Party unexpectedly won the general election in 1992 - the Party's fourth consecutive victory - plunging progressive forces into despair.

61 From 1993 the Conservatives began to suffer a series of electoral defeats in local by-elections against a backdrop of economic recession and three million unemployed. On 15 December, London signed a joint declaration with Dublin on Northern Ireland, paving the way for peace talks (see Ireland). A series of scandals in 1994, such as the illegal funding of a dam in Malaysia, further sullied the Tories' image. Meanwhile, Parliament lowered the age of consent for homosexuals from 21 to 18, ignoring calls to match the legal age of 16 for heterosexual sex.

62 Successive Labour local election victories in 1996 heralded the general election victory in May 1997, which saw Tony Blair become Prime Minister. The crushing defeat of the Tories, who only obtained 30 per cent of the vote, against Labour's 43.1 per cent (the biggest landslide victory of the century), forced leadership changes within the party.

63 Referenda in Wales and Scotland in 1997 supported greater devolution to the regions. In early 1998, talks on Northern Ireland brought a new peace plan. A referendum in Northern Ireland in May showed 70 per cent support for the plan. In London, that same month, people gave their approval for direct election to a new post, the Mayor of London.

64 Under the 'Good Friday' agreements, Northern Ireland would have its own legislative assembly, directly elected by the population, as in Wales and Scotland. A referendum in Ireland put an end to territorial claims over the North. The nomination of Northern Ireland MPs David Trimble (Ulster Unionist) and John Hume (Social Democratic and Labour Party, sympathetic to the nationalists) for the Nobel Peace Prize in October 1998 helped create the feeling of a common goal between Protestant and Catholic communities.

65 The Spanish courts called for Scotland Yard to arrest General Augusto Pinochet - the former Chilean dictator - as he recovered from a back operation in hospital in London. After a year and a half of legal wrangling, Pinochet was freed. Home Secretary Jack Straw said Pinochet's poor health meant he

would be unable to stand the strain of extradition to Spain and the ensuing trial.

66 During 1999 the Northern Irish unionist and nationalist parties made commitments on joint government, which culminated with the installation of a power-sharing executive in December that year. The two-community cabinet operated under the leadership of David Trimble as Prime Minister, with the participation of Sinn Féin. Gerry Adams and Martin McGuinness sat on the executive until February 2000 when Reverend Ian Paisley's Democratic Unionist Party (DUP) withdrew, and the administration was suspended. Sovereignty, which had been devolved to the province in December, returned to London.

67 Internal elections for Labour's candidate as Mayor of London ended in a split between Ken Livingstone - representative of the Labour left - and Tony Blair's preferred candidate, Frank Dobson. The Labour Party finally expelled Livingstone, but despite that he was elected Mayor in May 2000.

68 A UNICEF report published in September revealed that one in three British children live in poverty. These figures implied that five million children and their families could not satisfy their basic needs. One year before, the British Government had promised that, over a two-year term, 700,000 of the poorest children would have more money for better homes, clothes and food.

69 In June 2001 Blair's Labour Government won a second massive victory at the general election, prompting further soul-searching and another change of leader in the Conservative Party.

70 In October 2001, in order to stop the spread of an outbreak of foot and mouth disease, 3,915,000 animals were slaughtered. This epidemic followed the outbreak of 'mad cow disease' (Bovine Spongiform Encephalopathy - BSE) which had peaked in 1996 and forced the health authorities to kill four and a half million cows. Exports of British beef dropped dramatically and have not regained the levels attained before 1996, when exports to the EU were banned.

71 Following the September 2001 attacks on Washington and New York, Britain offered support for the US-launched 'war on terror'. Blair spearheaded the US offensive on Afghanistan, under the application of Article 5 of the NATO members' mutual defense clause, which states that member states must support another member who comes under attack. Similarly, in March 2002, Blair declared jointly with US vice-president Dick Cheney that Iraq was a threat to world stability, making it possible for Britain to support Washington in attacks on Iraq.

72 In the May 2002 local elections, the far-right British National Party gained its first three seats in nine years, in Burnley. The Conservatives took 34 per cent and Labour 33 per cent, with the Liberal Democrats taking 27 per cent. Even though 5,889 seats had been up for election, BNP leader Nick Griffin saw the result as a 'triumph' and denied the party was using urban racial tension to its benefit, although he confirmed his Party's objective was to keep Britain 'white'.

73 In July 2002, Foreign Secretary Jack Straw announced that the UK was to supply parts to the US for its F-16 jet fighters destined for Israel. This outraged activists who saw the move as another nail in the coffin of Labour's supposed 'ethical' foreign policy.

74 In January 2003 Blair stated that an attack on British soil was inevitable and assured he had evidence that would link Saddam Hussein and the al Qaeda network. Notwithstanding France and Germany's reluctance to accompany Washington in the war against Iraq, and the fact that the surveys indicated most British people were opposed, Blair decided to go out on a limb with Bush, prompting severe criticism even within his own party. The anti-war demonstration in London on 16 February 2003 was the biggest such protest in British history, involving at least one million people.

75 The US, UK and coalition forces invaded Iraq in March 2003 in spite of the strong international opposition to the war. Both nations were the only permanent members of the UN Security Council in favor of the invasion.

76 The controversy surrounding the arguments wielded by Blair to lend support to the invasion of Iraq was reawakened in July 2003 with the suicide of David Kelly, a scientist and adviser to the Ministry of Defense. Kelly had been pinpointed as the main source of a press investigation accusing the British Government of distorting intelligence reports to exaggerate the threat posed by Baghdad. The death of the scientist, added to the impossibility of finding the weapons of mass destruction in Iraq that London and Washington accused Saddam Hussein of possessing, caused Blair's popularity to plunge, even though an official investigation concluded that there had been no information manipulation on the part of the government.

77 Confronted with opinion polls indicating that a great number of British people were opposed to the adoption of a common constitution for the European Union, Blair announced that a referendum would be held regarding this matter in 2005. ∎

Population:	300,037,902
Area:	9,629,090 km²
Capital:	Washington D.C.
Currency:	Dollar
Language:	English

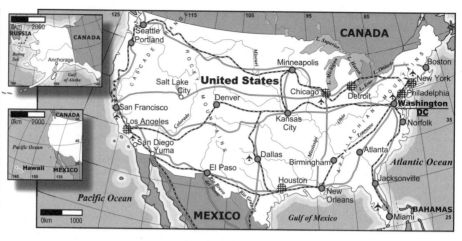

The continental territory occupied by the United States was inhabited 30,000 years before the arrival of the Europeans by peoples who probably came from Asia across the Bering Strait. The various Native American groups spread across the landmass, adapting their lifestyle to local conditions from the desert areas in the southwest through the plains to the eastern woodlands.

2   In the deserts and on the plains, they were primarily hunters and gatherers, living in small tribes with a simple social structure. Where the lands were more fertile, agriculture developed and relatively large towns were established (Cahokia, close to present-day St Louis, had 40,000 people in the year 1000 AD).

3   The religious beliefs of these peoples were rooted in a cosmic conception in which the Earth belongs to the Universe, and is considered a living being, with both material and spiritual powers. The shamans, calling upon these forces, could foretell the future, lead their people or heal the sick.

4   The first Europeans to come to America - Scandinavian - did not settle permanently in the region. After the voyage of Christopher Columbus in 1492, Spaniards established the colonies of St Augustine in Florida and Santa Fe in New Mexico; they also explored Texas and California. Then came the British, French and Dutch, all bent on territorial conquest.

5   In 1540, Hernando De Soto wrote in his journals of having found among the Cherokee an advanced agricultural society, linked to the peoples of the Ohio, the Mississippi and even the Aztecs.

6   There were an estimated 1,500,000 Native Americans in the 15th century. Two centuries later, the large plantations of the South began buying slaves, and by 1760 there was a total of 90,000 Africans - twice the number of whites in that part of the country. The total number of British settlers on the Atlantic coast at the time was 300,000, far outnumbering the French in the Mississippi Valley.

7   Most British immigrants left their country fleeing from poverty, religious persecution and political instability. Yet the birth of the colonies was marked by war against the native peoples and other European colonists. By 1733, there were 13 English colonies, whose chief economic activities were agriculture, fishing and trade.

8   In 1763, with the European wars behind them, France ceded its colonies east of the Mississippi to Britain, while its possessions west of that river went to Spain.

9   War with Britain broke out in 1775. The Declaration of Independence, which marked the birth of the United States, was signed on 4 July 1776. The war continued, but in the end the United States won (aided by its ally, France). England recognized US sovereignty in 1783.

10   In 1787, the Philadelphia Constitutional Convention drew up the first federal constitution, which came into effect in 1788. George Washington, commander of the Continental Army, was elected President in April 1789. In 1791, ten amendments dealing with individual freedoms and 'states' rights' were added to the original constitution.

11   The West was conquered simply by staking claims on the land, without previous ownership. The presidents in power at the time justified this as being the US 'Manifest Destiny' to become a great nation.

12   In 1803, the Louisiana purchase (from the French) doubled the size of the Union. Between 1810 and 1819, the US went to war against Spain in order to annex Florida. In 1836, the Texans rebelled against Mexico and set up a republic, subsequently joining the Union in 1845. After a new war, the US took over half of the Mexican territory. California became a state in 1850, and Oregon in 1853.

13   Westward expansion meant another tragedy for the original inhabitants of the region, who were decimated by successive waves of gold fever and multiple treaties that were ignored by new settlements in native lands. In 1838, 14,000 Cherokee people were forced off their lands by the army, 4,000 perishing in a march to their new territory.

14   In 1850, of the six million inhabitants of European origin in the South, only 345,525 were slave owners. However, most whites were pro-slavery, remembering the slave rebellions which had taken place in South Carolina (1822) and Virginia (1800 and 1831).

15   The Civil War (or War of Secession), from 1861-65 revolved around the question of slavery, but it was in fact a struggle between the two economic systems prevailing in the country. While the industrial North sought to free an important source of labor and protect the domestic market, the slave-owning and agricultural South's interest was to maintain its cheap labor force and continue to enjoy free access to foreign markets.

16   With the election of Abraham Lincoln in 1860, the Southern states seceded. Committed to preserving the Union, and with a superior industrial base and superior weapons, the North finally triumphed over the South in the Civil War, although a million people were killed on both sides. Slavery was abolished, but racial discrimination and ill-feeling between the two regions persisted, leading to the assassination of Lincoln in 1865.

17   After the War, the Native Americans of the Great Plains, especially the Lakota (Sioux), fought for their lands. The sovereignty treaties of 1851 and 1868 were ignored after the discovery of gold in the area. In spite of a major Lakota victory at Little Big Horn in 1876, the occupation of their territory was completed by 1890, when the native peoples were finally defeated.

18   In the 1880s, the remaining Native Americans were confined to reservations on arid, barren lands. Years later, when uranium, coal, oil, natural gas and other minerals were discovered on some of the reservations, the issue of 'rights' to the land was once again brought up by mining companies.

19   Between 1870 and 1920, the population of the United States grew from 38 to 106 million, and the number of states increased from 37 to 48. It was a period of rapid capitalist expansion, triggered by the growth of the railroads as huge companies. An agrarian country was transformed into an industrial society.

20   A two-party system of government had been established, with the Republican and Democratic parties alternately in power. Despite their different traditions, both parties have historically maintained a large degree of consensus on major national and international issues, leading to a highly coherent foreign policy. The long struggle for women's suffrage began in 1889, being achieved in 1920.

21   Having reached domestic stability, the US ventured onto the international scene. The US justified its interventions under the Monroe Doctrine and the slogan 'America for the Americans'. France was forced to withdraw its troops that protected Emperor Maximilian in Mexico, and Britain had to drop a territorial dispute with Venezuela. In 1890, the first Pan-American conference was held, paving the way for the inter-American system later set up.

22   The Spanish-American War in 1898, fought in Cuba and the Philippines, marked the beginning of a US imperial era. The occupation of Panama, and subsequent construction of the

Life expectancy
77.1 years
2000-2005

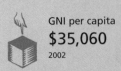

GNI per capita
$35,060
2002

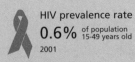

HIV prevalence rate
0.6% of population
15-49 years old
2001

Panama Canal and a series of military bases turned Central America - an area of 'vital security interest' to the US - into a kind of protectorate.

23   During World War I, the US broke its neutrality in 1917 when it declared war on Germany, Austria and Turkey. In 1918, President Woodrow Wilson was one of the architects of the Treaty of Versailles, which established the framework for a new European peace. He also sought to guarantee peace by establishing the League of Nations. However, in 1920 US entry into the League of Nations was blocked by Congress.

24   The 1921-1933 period comprised the so-called 'lawless' years because gangsterism practically governed many major cities and the Ku Klux Klan (KKK) terrorized the black population in the southern states. A controversial law that banned the production and consumption of alcoholic beverages - Prohibition - gave way to smuggling, clandestine production and gangsterism.

25   In 1924, J Edgar Hoover was appointed Director of the Bureau of Investigations, a special police force created by Attorney General Charles Bonaparte in 1908 during the Theodore Roosevelt administration. Hoover tried to obtain more power for his agents - who were not allowed to carry firearms - in their fight against crime.

26   The Great Crash on Wall Street (the US Stock Exchange) in 1929 led many banks to fail, affected industry and trade severely and produced a global economic crisis. Unemployment figures rose to 11 million. Under Franklin Roosevelt's presidency (1933-45), the Government managed to bring the financial crisis under control through the New Deal policy, which involved massive investment in public works.

27   In 1935 Hoover's aspiration gave way to a Congress resolution creating the Federal Bureau of Investigations (FBI), with national jurisdiction and allowing its agents to carry firearms.

28   In 1935, while Europe prepared for another war, Congress passed a law proclaiming US neutrality. Roosevelt amended the law in order to allow arms shipments to France and Britain. In 1941, the Japanese attack on the US military base at Pearl Harbor in Hawaii precipitated US entry into World War II.

29   The War acted as a dynamo for the US economy. With 15 million soldiers at the Front, employment grew from 46.5 million to 53 million with the military industry. To meet the demand for workers, six million people migrated from the

IN FOCUS

ENVIRONMENTAL CHALLENGES
Air pollution causes acid rain. The US is the world's largest emitter of carbon dioxide into the atmosphere. Pesticides and fertilizers have polluted the water. Water resources are limited, especially in the west. There is desertification.

WOMEN'S RIGHTS
Women have been able to stand for election since 1788, and to vote since 1920. Some 14 per cent of seats in Congress are held by women.

In 2000, women comprised 46 per cent of the labor force, with 86 per cent working in services, 12 per cent in industry and only 1 per cent in agriculture.

The percentage of men and women was similar at all education levels, except in higher education, where the enrolment rate among women amounted to 83 per cent, compared to 63 per cent among men. According to UNICEF's latest data available*, prenatal health care covers 99 per cent of women, and 99 per cent of births are attended by qualified personnel.

CHILDREN
There are no significant malnutrition problems among children but levels of obesity cause increasing concern. According to UNICEF's latest data available*, approximately eight per cent are born underweight. Under-five mortality fell from 30 per 1,000 live births in 1960 to 8 per 1,000 live births in 2000. Primary school enrolment

standed at 94 per cent among boys and 96 per cent among girls. Some 99 per cent of all children reached 5th grade (2000*).

In late 2001 there were 10,000 children under 15 living with HIV/AIDS.

INDIGENOUS PEOPLES/ ETHNIC MINORITIES
The country comprises multiple territories that were originally under indigenous control. After the bloody repression of indigenous resistance in the 19th century, most of the ancestral ethnic groups have descendants among the present population. Many reside in reservations negotiated with the Government or directly established by it, but others are relatively integrated into US society. Cherokees are a special case, being a wealthy nation with a high quality of life.

The main ethnic groups are: Cherokee (16 per cent of total Native American population), Navajo (12), Chippewa (5), Lakota (5), Choctaw (4), Pueblo, Apache, Iroquois, Lumbee, Creek (3), Blackfoot (2).

The states with indigenous reservations are: Washington, Idaho, Montana, North Dakota, South Dakota, Minnesota, Wisconsin, Michigan, New York, Oregon, Wyoming, Nebraska, California, Nevada, Utah, Colorado, Kansas, Arizona, New Mexico, Oklahoma, North Carolina, Mississippi and Florida.

MIGRANTS/REFUGEES
Some 638,000 refugees and asylum seekers were in the country in late 2002. Among them, 407,000 were cases pending with the Immigration

and Naturalization Service (INS) and 120,000 awaited a ruling by immigration judges. The INS approved 49 per cent of all requests in 2001 (19,200) and denied the rest (20,000). Of the new requests, 22,700 are from China, more than 20,000 from Mexico, 17,400 from Colombia, 8,400 from Haiti, 4,000 from Guatemala and 3,800 from India. The largest approval rates in asylum requests have been obtained by Ethiopians (75 per cent), Afghans and Iraqis (72 per cent), Cubans (69 per cent) and Iranians (67 per cent).

The US Patriot Act 2001 authorizes the detention and deportation of non-citizens suspected of terrorist activity, extending the refusal of asylum to the spouse and children of the detained. Persons without documentation who are detained in Caribbean waters are taken to the Guantanamo (Cuba) naval base, according to new government regulations which particularly affect Haitians.

DEATH PENALTY
As of 2004, 38 US states have the death penalty, though 6 of these have not used it since 1976. In addition, 3 federal executions took place under the Bush Administration - the first since 1963. The country continues to violate international standards by executing people who were under 18 at the time they committed their crime.

*Latest data available in *The State of the World's Children* and *Childinfo* database, UNICEF, 2004.

countryside to the cities and many women worked outside the home. In spite of a labor 'truce', there were 15,000 strikes during the War, which led Congress to pass a law limiting the right to strike.

30   At that time, the FBI persuaded President Roosevelt to investigate a Soviet conspiracy against the US which included massive espionage.

31   With Germany defeated in 1945, President Harry Truman (who had assumed the presidency upon Roosevelt's death in 1944) wanted to put an end to the war with Japan. Thus, on 6 and 9 August, he gave the order to wipe out the cities of Hiroshima and Nagasaki with history's first atomic bombs. That same year, at Yalta and Potsdam, Britain, the United States and the Soviet Union divided up the areas which would come under

their respective spheres of influence.

32   Truman presided over the opening of the United Nations in 1946, and was re-elected President in 1948. As the number one Western power, and in the context of the 'Cold War', the US assumed a global confrontation with the USSR. The Inter-American Treaty of Reciprocal Assistance was signed, and the North Atlantic Treaty Organization (NATO) was created. The US took it upon itself to safeguard the global capitalist system, with the support of international institutions such as the World Bank and the IMF, as well as armed intervention around the world.

33   Addressing the country's new needs, in 1947 Truman created the Central Intelligence Agency (CIA), whose mandate was to provide the

President with reliable information on all domestic or foreign activities related to national security. The Marshall Plan was implemented in 1948 to reactivate the post-war European economies, at a cost of $13 billion over four years.

34   Hoover took advantage of the domestic and global situation to increase his influence, and in 1950 Senator Joseph McCarthy began to persecute Communist sympathizers in Washington. The FBI opened files on politicians, intellectuals, journalists and ordinary citizens suspected of 'un-American' activities (mostly Communist). So-called McCarthyism, through the House Committee on Un-American Activities (HUAC), carried out a major 'witch-hunt' which saw a 'red' and potential Soviet spy in any dissident. The FBI files were filled with thousands of pages of

Under-5 mortality
8 per 1,000 live births
2002

Aid
0.13% Official development assistance as % of donors' GNI
2002

Maternal mortality
17 per 100,000 live births
2000

information on citizens from all walks of life.

35 In 1952, General Dwight Eisenhower, commander-in-chief of American forces in Europe during the War and head of NATO, was elected President. The Korean War (1950-53), the partition of Germany, popular uprisings in Poland and Hungary, and the delicate balance of nuclear weapons served to maintain tension with the USSR. In 1954, the Senate put an end to McCarthyism, censoring McCarthy, but the FBI continued to maintain its files on citizens.

36 In 1956, the US offered South Vietnam's government military support. In 1960, a summit meeting between Eisenhower and Soviet leader Khruschev was cancelled when an American U-2 spy plane flying over Soviet territory was brought down.

37 The election of Democratic presidential candidate John F Kennedy in 1960 brought hope for relief from domestic and foreign tensions. However, influenced by CIA reports, Kennedy supported the Bay of Pigs invasion of Cuba in 1961, and initiated the economic blockade of that country. He also supported the National Aeronautics and Space Administration's (NASA) drive to overtake the USSR (which had launched the first satellite and put the first man into orbit) in the space race and to put a man on the Moon before the decade was over.

38 Kennedy was assassinated in Dallas, Texas, in 1963. Although Lee Harvey Oswald was jailed for the crime and later murdered, other suspects for the assassination were the Mafia, Cuban agents (pro and anti-Castro), the CIA and the Army.

39 With regard to Latin America, President Kennedy had launched the Alliance for Progress in Uruguay in 1961, in an attempt to prevent 'a new Cuba'. However, the funds earmarked for this project were insufficient to effect real change. Faced with growing guerrilla activity in the region, the US, through the CIA (and its global presence) supported the regional armies.

40 Lyndon Johnson was elected President in 1964. The war in Vietnam escalated, causing a wave of protests throughout the US. Racial segregation led to increasing confrontation, underlined by the assassinations of black civil rights leaders Martin Luther King and Malcolm X.

41 In 1968, the American Indian Movement (AIM) was founded by two Chippewa leaders. In 1969, AIM occupied the abandoned prison on Alcatraz Island in San Francisco to call attention to their demands and denounce the mistreatment of their

people. The hippie movement and student protests reflected a deep cultural renewal.

42 In 1968 Richard Nixon (Eisenhower's Vice-president and fomer HUAC chairman) was elected President. In 1969, two astronauts from NASA's Apollo program set foot on the Moon, leading the US to win the space race.

43 In 1972, Nixon visited Moscow and Beijing. Also that year, after 48 years as head of the FBI, Hoover died, leaving behind him millions of files of citizens under investigation, including his own and those of the eight presidents he had worked for.

44 In 1973, Nixon was re-elected and in 1974 he signed the final withdrawal of US troops from Vietnam - the effective defeat by the North Vietnamese forces was seen as a major blow to the American psyche. Nixon was forced to resign the same year, following the discovery that Republicans had spied on Democrat election campaign headquarters located in the Watergate Hotel.

45 Latin American dictatorships - initially supported by Washington - had their heyday in the latter half of the 1970s. However, the Democratic administration of Jimmy Carter signified the beginning of the end for them. His pressure on the issue of human rights undermined the dictatorships.

46 On the international front, Carter organized the meeting between Egyptian President Mohammed Anwar al Sadat and Israeli Prime Minister Menachim Begin, in Camp David, signed the Salt II agreement to restrict the number of nuclear weapons held by the US and the USSR, and established full diplomatic relations with China. However, economic inflation and the lengthy US hostage crisis in Iran caused his electoral defeat in 1980.

47 During the Republican administration of Ronald Reagan (1980-88) the military-industrial complex energized the whole economy and partly made up for lagging behind Japan and Western Europe on other fronts. In 1983 the US invaded Grenada in response to its rapprochement with Cuba.

48 The Irangate scandal erupted in 1986, with the illegal use of weapons to support counter-revolutionary forces in Nicaragua. In spite of his 'peace through strength' doctrine, Reagan agreed with USSR leader Mikhail Gorbachev to limit the number of mid-range missiles.

49 George Bush won the 1988 elections. In 1989 he invaded Panama, toppled the government and arrested its leader, the former CIA informer Manuel Noriega. In February 1991, the US led the multinational force which expelled

Iraq after its invasion of Kuwait. The Gulf War consolidated US military supremacy.

50 Bill Clinton, Democrat Governor of Arkansas, was elected President in November 1992, with a majority in both chambers of Congress. The North American Free Trade Agreement (NAFTA) with Mexico and Canada went into

operation in January 1994. The economy recovered and unemployment fell.

51 For the first time in 40 years, the Democratic Party lost the election to both chambers of Congress in 1994. Clinton led a military intervention in Bosnia-Herzegovina and imposed the Dayton (Ohio) agreements in

PROFILE

ENVIRONMENT

There are four geo-economic regions. The East includes New England, the Appalachian Mountains and part of the Great Lakes and the Atlantic coast, a sedimentary plain which stretches from the mouth of the Hudson River to the peninsula of Florida. To the west are the Appalachian mountains, where mineral deposits (iron ore and coal) abound. This is the most densely populated and industrialized area, where the country's largest steel plants are located. High-technology agriculture provides food for the large cities. The Midwest stretches from the western shores of Lake Erie to the Rocky Mountains, also including the middle Mississippi. Formed by the grasslands of the central plain, the Midwest is the country's largest agricultural area; horticulture and milk production predominate in the north, while wheat, corn and other cereals are cultivated in the south, side by side with cattle ranches where cows and pigs are raised. Major industrial centers are located near the Great Lakes, near the area's agricultural production and large iron ore and coal deposits. The South is a subtropical flatland area, comprising the south of the Mississippi plain, the peninsula of Florida, Texas and Oklahoma. Large plantations (cotton, sugarcane, rice) predominate here, while there is extensive cattle-raising in Texas. The region is also rich in mineral deposits (oil, coal, aluminum, etc.). The West is a mountainous, mineral-rich area (oil, copper, lead, zinc). There is considerable horticultural production along the fertile valleys of the Sacramento and San Joaquin rivers in California. Large industrial centers are located along the Pacific coast. In addition, the US has two states outside its original contiguous area: Alaska, on the continent's northwest where Mt McKinley is located (Mt 'Denali', in the indigenous Atabasco language), the highest peak in North America, and Hawaii, an archipelago in the Pacific Ocean.

SOCIETY

Peoples: There are 1.9 million Native Americans, half of whom live in 300 reservations. The white population were originally immigrant Europeans including British, Germans, Irish, Russian and Italian, now mixed with immigrants from all parts of the world. The largest minorities are of African origin, 11 per cent of the total population; Hispanic 10 per cent; and Asian 8 per cent. **Religions:** Protestant (58 per cent); Catholic (26 per cent); Jewish (2 per cent); Muslims (2 per cent); other (2 per cent); non-religious (10 per cent).
Languages: English; Spanish; Native American languages and those of each immigrant group. **Main Political Parties:** Republican Party, Democratic Party, Green Party, Reform Party, Libertarian Party (right-wing). **Main Social Organizations:** The American Federation of Labor - Congress of Industrial Organizations (AFL-CIO) is the country's largest workers' organization, with 13,500,000 members. Many of the country's rural laborers, especially those of Mexican origin, are organized in the United Farm Workers (UFW) labor union, founded by César Chávez.

THE STATE

Official Name: United States of America.
Administrative Divisions: Federal State, 50 States and 1 Federal District, Columbia.
Capital: Washington, DC 4,098,000 people (2003).
Other Cities: New York 8,008,278; Los Angeles 3,694,820; Chicago 2,896,016; Houston 1,953,631; Philadelphia 1,517,550 (2000).
Government: Presidential government, federal system. George W Bush, President since January 2001. Dick Cheney, Vice-president since 2001. There is a bicameral Congress: the House of Representatives, with 435 members, and the Senate, with 100 members.
National Holiday: 4 July, Independence (1776).
Armed Forces: 1,547,300 (1995). Other: 68,000 Civil Air Control.

Malnutrition
1% under-5s
1995-2002

Water source
100% of population using improved drinking water sources
2000

Doctors
276 per 100,000 people
1990-2002

Primary school
95% net enrolment rate
2000

November 1995. That year, a bomb in Oklahoma killed 160 people, in the worst terrorist attack in the country up to that point. In October 1996, Clinton supported talks between Israelis and Palestinians in Washington. In November, he was re-elected with 49.2 per cent of the vote.

52   In 1998 Clinton had to contest the charge of perjury brought against him by independent counsel Kenneth Starr. In February 1999 the Senate voted against impeaching Clinton. Between March and June, the US led the NATO forces that bombed Yugoslavia in response to Serb persecution of Albanian citizens in Kosovo.

53   The November Presidential elections marked a critical point for the electoral system. One of the tightest elections ever, scarred with irregularities, pitched Republican candidate George W Bush, governor of Texas and son of the former president, against Democrat Vice-President Al Gore. The uncertainty went on for weeks after the state of Florida, which had had 6 million votes, ordered a limited recount.

54   On December 2000 the US Supreme Court ruled in favor of Bush. The difference between electoral votes and the popular vote underlined the need to revise the country's electoral system.

55   On 11 September 2001 the US suffered the most serious terrorist attack ever made on its territory. Four commercial airplanes were hijacked by suicide bombers, of which two crashed into the World Trade Center twin towers in New York, which collapsed, and another into the Pentagon building in Washington. More than 3,000 died and direct economic destruction amounted to an estimated $1 billion. The US population was traumatized.

56   The Bush Government reacted by declaring a 'global war on terror'. Washington increased the military budget by 20 per cent, and then a further 15 per cent. The US military budget was thus larger than the total of the military budgets of all of its 18 allies in NATO.

57   On 7 October 2001, the US initiated what would amount to 24,000 air raids against the Taliban Government in Afghanistan (see Afghanistan), accused by Washington of harboring al-Qaeda terrorists. The US deposed the Taliban regime on November 13, but without achieving its two main goals: capturing dead or alive al-Qaeda leader Osama Bin Laden and the leader of the Taliban, Mullah Muhammad Omar.

58   The bankruptcy of energy giant Enron in 2001 took down with it the auditing firm Andersen

and called into question the complex financing system of the country's economy. In 2002, major companies such as WorldCom, Xerox, Adelphia, Tyco, Global Crossing and Merrill Lynch were under investigation, suspected of artificially inflating their profits.

59   In January 2002, Bush identified North Korea, Iran and Iraq as enemy nations and members of an 'axis of evil', although only an attack on Iraq was anticipated. The September 11 attacks revealed major flaws in US intelligence services, which were restructured along Cold War lines though updated through electronic espionage.

60   Bush, supported only by Britain, proclaimed the 'need' to attack Iraq, mainly on the basis that Iraqi President Saddam Hussein had a program to develop weapons of mass destruction. In August, British Prime Minister Tony Blair persuaded Bush to take to the UN the US case for attacking Iraq. In early September 2002, during the 57th UN General Assembly, Bush asked the UN Security Council to act or step aside and let the US take the necessary actions.

61   In October 2002, Baghdad agreed to let the UN weapons inspectors visit dozens of 'sensitive' locations. The UK and US rejected this and demanded that the Security Council approved a new resolution which would authorize military action if Iraq did not comply with their demands.

62   That month, the 'axis of evil' gained a new front when Washington revealed that North Korea had admitted it was developing a nuclear weapons program. Washington demanded these weapons be immediately dismantled, but North Korea initially refused to do so. China, which had been silent on Iraq, stressed that in the North Korean/US case the parties needed to arrive to a peaceful agreement through dialogue and negotiation.

63   Bush popularity levels after 9/11 reached 90 per cent, leading the Republicans to obtain a majority in the November 2002 elections for Congress.

64   The US deficit reached its worst level in 2003 since the end of World War II, forcing state governors to drastically reduce budgets and to lay off thousands of state employees.

65   Although UN inspectors found no weapons of mass destruction in Iraq, Bush announced in January 2003 he was willing to attack Iraq even without the support of his European allies.

66   The US, the UK and the coalition forces gathered by Washington and London invaded Iraq in March 2003 despite

controversy as well as at the UN. Other permanent members of the Security Council did not support the war, and France and Germany were openly opposed.

67   The Allied forces rapidly advanced on Baghdad. On 1 May, on board the USS Abraham Lincoln, Bush announced the end of the first stage of the conflict and the start of Iraq's 'democratic reconstruction' (see Iraq).

68   In February 2004, the President admitted that the alleged weapons of mass destruction which had been used to justify the invasion had not yet been found. After the proclaimed 'end of the war', the number of US troops killed by resistance forces kept growing. For the first time, Bush spoke of the need for UN intervention.

69   By April 2004 occupation forces were being attacked from

some unexpected quarters: Iraqi Sh'ia forces (oppressed by Hussein's regime and supposedly 'liberated' by the US). Bush had to struggle against two resistance fronts and also the protests within the US of students, who felt deceived by Washington. The Polish Government also declared it had been deceived.

70   The terrorist attacks in Spain in early 2004 showed that terrorism was as strong and violent as it had been before the invasion of Iraq.

71   In April 2004, the new Spanish government ordered the immediate withdrawal of its 1,400 soldiers supporting the occupation in Iraq. The US death toll in Iraq passed 1,000 in September.

72   In November Bush narrowly won a second term of office as President, defeating Democratic challenger John Kerry. ∎

US DEPENDENCIES

JOHNSTON:
Coral atoll of 2.6 sq km, made up of the Johnston island and the Sand, East and North islets, located approximately 1,150 km west-southwest of Honolulu (Hawaii). With an Air Force base the population (all military) is approximately 1,000. The atoll was uninhabited when it was discovered by British Captain Johnston in 1807. In 1858, Hawaii claimed sovereignty, but that same year US companies started exploitation of phosphate. Since 1934, the atoll has been administered by the US Navy. Civilians are not admitted.

MIDWAY:
A round atoll which comprises two islands: Sand and Eastern, with 5 sq km of total area and 2,300 inhabitants (1985) almost exclusively military. In 1867, they were annexed by the US and are currently administered by its Navy. The islands are used for military purposes and operate as a refueling base for trans-Pacific flights. In 1942 during World War II, an important sea battle took place here.

WAKE:
Together with neighboring Wilkes and Peale, they make up an atoll with an area of 6.5 sq km and an estimated population of 1,600 inhabitants, mainly military personnel. Located between Midway and Guam, the island was seized by the United States during the 1898 war with Spain. It has a large airport which used to be a stopover for trans-Pacific flights, but nowadays it is not used for business purposes. Since 1972 it has been administered by the Air Force which now uses it as a missile testing station.

HOWLAND, JARVIS & BAKER:
Located in central Polynesia, in the Equatorial Pacific, they were occupied by the US in the middle of the 19th century. The islands have been uninhabited since the end of World War II as major phosphate deposits had been depleted. There is a lighthouse in Howland. The islands are administered by the US Fishing and Wild Life Service.

PALMIRA & KINGMAN:
The northernmost islands of the Line archipelago. Palmira is an atoll surrounded by more than 50 coral islets covered with exuberant tropical vegetation. It was annexed in 1898 during the war with Spain and is now a private property, dependent on the US Department of the Interior. Kingman is a reef, located north of Palmira, annexed by the US in 1922. The total area of both islands is 7 sq km. Although uninhabited, the US-Japanese project to turn them into deposits of radioactive waste raised protests throughout the Pacific region in the 1980s.

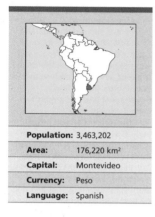

Population:	3,463,202
Area:	176,220 km²
Capital:	Montevideo
Currency:	Peso
Language:	Spanish

The territory of what is now part of Uruguay was discovered by Spanish explorer Juan Díaz de Solís in 1516. At that time, the country was inhabited by the Charrúa, the Chaná and the Guaraní. The Charrúa were nomadic hunters, while the Chaná developed a rudimentary form of agriculture and the Guaraní practised agriculture and mastered ceramics and navigation of rivers.

² Solís sailed into the Río de la Plata which he called the *Mar Dulce* (Freshwater Sea). Ambushed by Indians, Solís and all the other members of the expedition were killed.

³ Spanish colonization was slow since settlers considered the region as a 'land of no profit' because it did not have the mineral wealth of Mexico and Peru. In 1611, the Governor of Asunción, Hernando Arias de Saavedra (Hernandarias) introduced cattle and horses, which - thanks to the good pasture and climate - thrived and transformed the region into what was known as the *Vaquería del Mar* (Cattle Ranch of the Sea). The Jesuits, a Christian religious order which had begun to establish missions in Paraguay in the 17th century, started to expand towards the eastern side of the Uruguay River in 1632. From 1667, seven missions were founded to the east of the river.

⁴ In 1680, the Portuguese founded Colonia do Sacramento on the shore opposite Buenos Aires. This settlement caused constant friction between Portugal and Spain. The border disputes gave rise to the city of Montevideo, the only natural port in the Río de la Plata, which was founded in 1724 by the Governor of Buenos Aires, Bruno Mauricio de Zabala.

⁵ The cattle attracted the *faeneros* - leather workers - from Brazil and Buenos Aires. The spread of cattle gave rise to the skilled horsemen/cowboys known as *gauchos*, who were usually of mixed European and indigenous ancestry.

⁶ The widespread cattle-ranching led to the extinction of some indigenous mammals, a reduction of plant diversity and soil degradation. The indigenous people were displaced and moved into the Jesuit missions further north. In 1831, the Charrúas were exterminated in Salsipuedes by the first independent Government of Uruguay. The survivors of this ethnic group were taken as slaves and a few of them, who became known as 'the last Charrúas' were sent to France and exhibited there as fairgound-ground type curiosities.

⁷ The May Revolution which broke out in Buenos Aires in 1810 was rejected by the Montevideans, who supported the trade monopoly with Spain. In contrast, small and medium-scale producers from the countryside and the landless people rose up in arms. The rebels were led by a former *criollo* captain of the Spanish army, José Artigas. His republican and federal ideas as well as his close relationship with Indians and slaves and his land distribution program turned him into the leader of the Federal League, which comprised what is now Uruguay and the Argentine provinces of Cordoba, Corrientes, Entre Ríos, Misiones and Santa Fe.

⁸ Uruguay was invaded by the Portuguese in 1816, with the tacit approval of Buenos Aires and Montevideo, whose governments were alarmed by the events known as the 'Artigan chaos'. Once defeated, Artigas sought refuge in Paraguay in 1820, where he died 30 years later.

⁹ When Brazil became independent from Portugal in 1823, Uruguay became the Brazilian 'Cisplatine Province'.

¹⁰ In 1825 the *orientales* renewed their independence campaign against the Brazilian Empire. On 25 August independence was declared and the *orientales* decided to return to the United Provinces of the Río de la Plata.

¹¹ Since the British diplomatic service was interested in preventing both Río de la Plata territories from belonging to Argentina in order to protect Britain's commercial interests, it promoted the creation of a small state within the region. In 1828, through the mediation of Lord Ponsonby, the war was brought to an end and the independence of the country was approved.

¹² The first Constitution of Uruguay was adopted in 1830. The new Constitution established a republican government but most of the population (who were illiterate, rural workers) were denied the right to vote.

¹³ The rest of the 19th century was riven by civil wars between two political parties: the *Blanco* (White) or National Party, linked to the country and to land owners, and the *Colorado* (Red but not communist), linked to European capital and liberal ideas. The successive uprisings that followed were favored by a weak state and rural workers used to warfare.

¹⁴ In 1865, Colorado dictator Venancio Flores signed an agreement with Brazil and Argentina and created the Triple Alliance, breaking Paraguayan isolation - with European support - and forcing Paraguay to open its borders to foreign trade (see Paraguay).

¹⁵ In 1876, Colonel Lorenzo Latorre ushered in a period of militarism. In that period (1876-1879), state power was strengthened thus preventing armed uprisings by monopolizing the use of force. Also, the countryside was enclosed with fences, resulting in the land being completely appropriated by the private sector, and leaving no room for the gaucho, who was transformed into a hired hand.

¹⁶ In 1903 the Colorado José Batlle y Ordoñez assumed the presidency and was determined to modernize the state. The last rural uprising, led by the *caudillo* (leader) of the Blancos Aparicio Saravia, took place one year later. Saravia died during the confrontation and Batlle laid the foundations for the modern Uruguayan state.

¹⁷ The State became the main employer. A large liberal middle-class developed, educated in State schools.

¹⁸ The Church and the State were separated and divorce legalized. A collegiate system of government was introduced in 1917 and women's suffrage was enacted in 1932. This open legislation earned the country the title 'the Switzerland of South America'.

¹⁹ Uruguayan exports grew during both World Wars. Meat and its products were supplied first to the Allies, who were fighting against Nazism and Fascism in Europe, and later to US troops fighting in Korea.

²⁰ Trade balance surpluses secured the country large foreign currency reserves. The welfare policy of subsidies encouraged the emergence of relatively strong import-substitution industries. Meanwhile, a prosperous building industry helped maintain high employment. However, the cattle and sheep sector, which generated most exports, did not expand but remained at the production levels of 1908.

²¹ Land owners invested their profits abroad, engaging in financial speculation and superfluous consumption. In the 1950s, the industrial sector stagnated - a situation that proved impossible to reverse.

²² The first Blanco Government, in 1959, accepted IMF economic guidelines which accelerated the recession. The social conflict was intensified in 1968 when the Colorado Government of Jorge Pacheco Areco, curbed the spending power of wage-earners and tried to eliminate the trade unions' bargaining power. A broad movement led by the National Workers' Convention and the student organizations opposed such policies. At the same time the Tupamaro (MLN) guerrilla movement was active throughout the country. In 1971 the Frente Amplio (Broad Front), a left-wing coalition, was founded. It promoted a progressive government program, and nominated a retired general, Liber Seregni, in the presidential elections of that year.

Life expectancy
75.3 years
2000-2005

GNI per capita
$4,370
2002

Literacy
98% total adult rate
2000

HIV prevalence rate
0.3% of population 15-49 years old
2001

23   Juan María Bordaberry became President in 1972. Parliament declared a state of emergency which allowed homes to be searched without warrants, the suspension of habeas corpus and the referral of civilians to military courts. In 1972 the Tupamaros were defeated. A campaign including the systematic use of torture rapidly dismantled the clandestine organization. In June 1973, President Bordaberry and the armed forces staged a coup. Parliament was dissolved, and a civilian-military government was formed. Left-wing parties and unions were banned; torture and arbitrary detentions of people opposed to the regime were commonplace.

24   During the ensuing dictatorship the concentration of wealth in transnational corporations increased. Salaries lost 50 per cent of their purchasing power, whilst foreign debt reached $5 billion.

25   In 1980, the Government submitted an authoritarian constitution to a referendum. The defeat suffered by the military marked the beginning of the end of the dictatorship.

26   Social organizations sprang up again in 1983: the struggle against the military regime became open and took to the streets. One of the most important protest mobilizations was called by the newly-formed Inter-union Plenary of Workers (PIT) which celebrated May Day for the first time since 1973, under the banner of Freedom, Work, Salary and Amnesty.

27   That same month, the military started negotiations with the three political parties recognized as legal, excluding the Broad Front, whose president Liber Seregni had been in prison since the coup, and the Blanco Party leader Wilson Ferreira Aldunate, who was to be arrested on his return to the country after an 11-year exile.

28   In the November 1984 elections some leaders and political parties remained proscribed. The elections were won by the conservative leader of the Colorado Party, Julio María Sanguinetti, who became President. The new government restored freedoms and political rights and, in response to popular demand, Parliament approved an amnesty law whereby all political prisoners were freed. Uruguay resumed diplomatic relations with Cuba and Venezuela, which had been broken off since the kidnapping of schoolteacher Elena Quinteros from the Venezuelan Embassy in Montevideo.

29   A parliamentary commission was created to investigate the fate of those Uruguayans who had disappeared both in the country and abroad. The civilian courts summoned the officers allegedly responsible for human rights abuses. Then, Parliament approved the Expiry Law of the Punitive Powers of the State, which exempted all military and police personnel responsible for human rights crimes from punishment. A national referendum ratified the law with 56 per cent of the vote.

30   In 1989, a structural adjustment policy was implemented, marked by the deregulation of the market. The Government signed a secret agreement with the World Bank, in exchange for rescheduling Uruguay's debt. The Government committed itself to reduce expenditure on social security; to privatize bankrupt banks absorbed by the State, and to reform public companies making them profitable and attractive for privatization.

31   In 1989, the Blanco/National Party won the elections and Luis Alberto Lacalle took office as President. The Broad Front won in Montevideo with its candidate Tabaré Vázquez. The Left assumed responsibility for municipal administration for the first time in the history of the country.

32   Lacalle carried out his neo-liberal policy: taxes were increased and the privatization of state-run companies was encouraged. In March 1991, Argentina, Brazil, Paraguay and Uruguay approved the Mercosur common market agreement.

33   A committee convened by the labor union movement, constituted by members of several parties, managed to submit the state enterprise privatization law, previously approved by Parliament, to a plebiscite. In December 1992, 72 per cent of the population voted to repeal the law. However, the Government managed to privatize certain state enterprises, including the national airline, the gasworks and the sugarcane plantations in the north of the country.

34   In the 1994 elections Sanguinetti was elected as President once again by a small majority.

35   The Broad Front won the Mayoralty of Montevideo (government of the capital) for the second time. At national level, results showed a country divided into three parts: Colorado Party, 31.2 per cent; Blanco/National Party, 30 per cent; and Progressive Encounter-Broad Front, 29.8 per cent.

36   In October 1999, Argentine poet Juan Gelman requested Sanguinetti to investigate the fate of his daughter-in-law María Claudia García, who had been kidnapped in Buenos Aires in 1976 and later illegally transferred to Montevideo. Gelman also asked him to investigate the whereabouts of the child María Claudia had given birth to at the Military Hospital. In response to the indifference showed by the Uruguayan Government, an international campaign was launched, with the support of hundreds of intellectuals, artists and citizens from all over the world, demanding that Sanguinetti follow up the investigations.

37   In the presidential elections of 1999, the left Progressive Encounter-Broad Front became the majority political party in the first round. To prevent a victory by the left, the National Party allied itself with the Colorado Party and voted for the Colorado candidate, Jorge Batlle, who became President with 52 per

IN FOCUS

ENVIRONMENTAL CHALLENGES
There is increasing pollution in the northern regions as a result of emissions from a thermoelectric plant in Candiota (Brazil), while rivers and streams are contaminated by agro-chemicals and waste from the meat industry. An increasing loss of ecosystems on the plains and in the eastern wetlands has been observed, due to monocultures of forestry and rice, respectively.

WOMEN'S RIGHTS
Women have been able to vote and stand for office since 1932. They hold 11.6 per cent of seats in Parliament, but none in ministries or local governments. They make up 42 per cent of the country's labor force; 85 per cent work in services, 13 per cent in industry and 2 per cent in agriculture.

The maternal mortality rate is 27 deaths per 1,000 live births. Twenty per cent of pregnant women suffer from anemia and 94 per cent of them receive prenatal care. More than 99 per cent of births are attended by skilled health staff.

Women have equality under the law but they often face discrimination arising from traditional attitudes and practices. At work, the same applies: they are usually in the lowest-paid jobs. Their salaries are on average two-thirds of those of men. On the other hand, approximately 60 per cent of the students at university are women, although they are under-represented in professional positions.

CHILDREN
According to UNICEF's latest data available*, the infant mortality rate is 14 deaths per 1,000 live births, while the under-5 mortality rate is 15 deaths per 1,000 live births. Between 94 and 99 per cent of infants under one year old are immunized against diseases such as tetanus, measles and polio.

Education is free and primary education is compulsory; 95 per cent of children completed their primary education at the age of 12.

UNICEF has revealed that 40 per cent of children under five live in the poorest 20 per cent of homes. While not yet a major problem, child sexual exploitation has increased in recent years, particularly in the areas bordering Brazil and Argentina as well as in tourist centers such as Punta del Este, Maldonado and Montevideo.

The Child Labor Code protects children, and the Ministry of Labor and Social Security is responsible for enforcing this law. However, most child labor occurs in the informal sector (40 per cent of total employment in the country). Some children work as street vendors in the informal sector or in the agrarian sector, which are generally less strictly regulated and offer lower pay.

Uruguay has the highest suicide rate in Latin America and fluctuates between the top four to seven highest suicide rates in the world. Some 500 Uruguayans kill themselves every year.

INDIGENOUS PEOPLES/ ETHNIC MINORITIES
The Afro-Uruguayan minority, estimated at 8 per cent of the population, faces societal discrimination. A study carried out by the NGO Mundo Afro found that the illiteracy rate among Afro-Uruguayan women was twice the national average. Afro-Uruguayans are virtually unrepresented in the bureaucratic and academic sectors.

MIGRANTS/REFUGEES
According to different statistics, more than 450,000 Uruguayans live abroad - between 12 and 13 per cent of the population, although some estimates put the number of emigrants even larger. Emigration is affecting the population growth rate and as a result some experts predict that the country may start experiencing negative population growth in a few years' time. Most emigrants are between 20 and 29 years old.

DEATH PENALTY
This was abolished for all crimes in 1907.

*Latest data available in *The State of the World's Children* and *Childinfo* database, UNICEF, 2004.

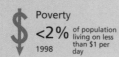

| Under-5 mortality **15** per 1,000 live births 2002 | Poverty **<2%** of population living on less than $1 per day 1998 | Debt service **36.3%** exports of goods and services 2001 | Maternal mortality **27** per 100,000 live births 2000 |

cent of the vote in the November elections.

[38] In March 2000, President Batlle declared that building peace and trust among Uruguayans was essential. Forty days later, he informed Gelman that his granddaughter was indeed in Montevideo. The 23-year old woman had been given to a police officer after the murder of her mother in December 1976. The news confirmed the cooperation of the armed forces of Uruguay and Argentina in the repression of political opponents beyond national borders.

[39] In August, the Peace Commission was created by presidential decree, and charged with taking all possible steps to investigate the fate of Uruguayans who 'disappeared' during the military dictatorship. The work of the Commission, which was questioned by human rights organizations, ended with a final report approved in April 2003, that confirmed the 'action of state agents' in the illegal repression.

[40] In early 2001, an outbreak of foot-and-mouth disease affected Uruguay's cattle and forced the country to lose its standing as a country free from the disease. The rapid spread of the virus forced the authorities to vaccinate at least 500,000 animals, while 10,200 affected beasts were killed.

[41] The year 2002 was poor economically with a considerable downturn in most people's quality of life. The Argentine economic crisis and the shrinking of the Brazilian market posed serious problems to Uruguay, raising the possibility of a default within the short term.

[42] In March 2002, the IMF approved a $443 million loan to help Uruguay out of the recession and to protect it from the Argentine economic crisis. Uruguay agreed to achieve fiscal balance in 2004. The IMF urged Uruguay to privatize its state monopolies, such as electricity, oil, telecommunications and railroads.

[44] That month, Sara Méndez, a Uruguayan woman who had been kidnapped in Buenos Aires in 1976 and illegally transported to Uruguay, managed to find her son, Simón Riquelo, who had been kidnapped with her shortly after his birth and had disappeared. The boy had been given to an Argentinian chief of police who had brought him up as his own child. This ended Méndez's 25-year search for her son - something she had done with the help of human rights organizations but without the cooperation of Uruguayan justice. A huge crowd gathered in Montevideo to celebrate the reunion of mother and son.

[45] In April, Uruguay sponsored a UN resolution against Cuba regarding the human rights situation on the island. The motion caused protests from Havana against President Batlle whom

Fidel Castro called a 'wretched Judas'. As a result, both countries broke off diplomatic relations.

[46] That same month, for the first time in 20 years, employers and workers joined in a major demonstration against the Government's economic policy. The demonstrators protested against the bankruptcy filed by 35 per cent of businesses since 1998 and the closing of 15 ranches every day, overcome by debt. They also pointed out that over 75,000 workers had been laid off.

[47] Emigration intensified as a result of the economic crisis. It is estimated that some 450,000 Uruguayans, 13 per cent of the population, are living abroad. Most emigrants are young with good educational level and professional qualifications, which accentuates the country's aging demographic profile.

[48] In May, Batlle announced economic emergency measures, intended to ease the effects of the crisis. The initiative increased business incomes, imposed VAT on the public supply of drinking water and public transport and increased the tax on personal earnings of working and retired employees. These measures prompted a *caceroleo* ('pot-banging' demonstation) in Montevideo, since

the President had promised that the fiscal adjustment carried out in February was to be the last one in his administration.

[49] The value of the dollar rocketed on 20 June, increasing by 40 per cent, after the Ministry of Economy Alberto Bensión unexpectedly announced the decision to change the exchange rate policy. The free flotation of the US dollar was praised by the US and the IMF, but local outrage was shown in several demonstrations.

[50] Alejandro Atchugarry was appointed as the new Minister of Economy to deal with the economic crisis. On 30 July, the Central Bank of Uruguay declared a bank holiday, the first one in several decades, to prevent the outflow of deposits that was precipitating the collapse of the banking system. A month earlier, a large private bank had been ordered to suspend activity, for illiquidity and an alleged diversion of funds.

[51] Amid increasing rumors of a possible *corralito* (restrictions on withdrawals) the bank holiday was extended until 5 August, when the US confirmed it would provide Uruguay with a loan of $1,500 million as direct economic assistance.

[52] In October 2002, former Minister of Foreign Affairs, Juan Carlos Blanco,

was prosecuted for his part in the disappearance of schoolteacher Elena Quinteros, kidnapped from the Venezuelan Embassy 26 years previously. Blanco was the only civilian or military officer during the dictatorship to be prosecuted for the human rights violations committed during that period. The former Minister was released eight months later when Carlos Ramela, Batlle's representative on the Peace Commission, appeared in court to state that, according to investigations, the schoolteacher had been murdered without the knowledge of the Armed Forces or the government of the time.

[53] Diplomatic relations between Uruguay and Argentina deteriorated during this period. In 2002, during an interview for Argentinian television, Batlle stated 'off the record' that all Argentinian politicians were thieves. This statement was broadcast and forced Batlle to travel to Buenos Aires to publicly apologize for his mistake. Another issue was the difference in economic policy between Argentinian President Néstor Kirchner and Batlle and also on the way of resolving human rights violations. Kirchner's Government declared that the resolution of the 'Gelman case' implied that the Uruguayan authorities had known the truth about the disappearance of María Claudia García. Batlle promised to cooperate with investigations; however, some months later he ordered the case to be dismissed.

[54] In August 2003, in an historic decision the Supreme Court ruled to proceed with the prosecution of former dictator Bordaberry for his alleged responsibility in the June 1973 coup and in the murder of eight communist workers in April 1972.

[55] In December 2003, citizens voted in a referendum to confirm or repeal a law that abolished the fuel import monopoly of the state-run company ANCAP and opened it up to investment by private companies. The 'yes' option to repeal the law was supported by 63 per cent of voters. For the first time, an electoral option supported by both the Blanco and Colorado Parties was defeated at the polls.

[56] In April 2004, the Senate began to debate the Law for the Defense of Reproductive Health (legalization of abortion) which had been passed by the Chamber of Deputies two years earlier. In view of the impossibility of obtaining a majority, and with a previously announced presidential veto, the Senate agreed to submit the issue to a referendum.

[57] Opinion polls indicated the likely victory of the leftist Broad Front in the 30 October elections, sufficient to enable it to govern without having to seek support from groups on the right. ■

PROFILE

ENVIRONMENT

Uruguay has a gently rolling terrain, crossed by characteristic low hills - an extension of Brazil's southern plateau - belonging to the ancient Guayanic-Brazilian massif. Its average altitude is 300 meters above sea level. This, together with its location and latitude, determines its temperate, subtropical, semi-humid weather, with rainfall throughout the year. The vegetation is made up almost entirely of natural grasslands, suitable for cattle and sheep raising. The territory is well irrigated by many rivers, and has over 1,100 km of navigable waterways, in particular on the rivers Negro and Uruguay, and on the Plata estuary. The coast is made up of many sandy beaches that attract a large number of tourists.

SOCIETY

Peoples: Most Uruguayans are descendants of Spanish, Italian and other European immigrants. Recent historical and genetic research show that a significant part of the population also has American Indian ancestry. Afro-American descendants make up about 8 per cent of today's population. **Religions:** Catholics 66 per cent; Protestants 2 per cent; Jews 2 per cent. Afro-Brazilian cults are also practiced. **Languages:** Spanish. **Main Political Parties:** Colorado Party (Red); National/Blanco Party (White); Broad Front/Progressive Encounter (Frente Amplio/Encuentro Progresista); New Space (Nuevo Espacio); Civic Union (Unión Cívica). **Main Social Organizations:** PIT-CNT (Inter-Union Workers' Bureau - National Workers' Convention). FUCVAM (Uruguayan Federation of Housing Construction by Mutual Help). Federation of University Students (FEUU).

THE STATE

Official Name: República Oriental del Uruguay.
Administrative Divisions: 19 Departments. **Capital:** Montevideo 1,341,000 people (2003). **Other Cities:** Salto 86,600 people; Paysandú 76,400; Las Piedras 70,700; Rivera 69,400; Maldonado 40,600 (2000).
Government: Presidential system. Jorge Batlle, President since March 2000. Bicameral Legislature: the Chamber of Senators, with 31 members, and the Chamber of Deputies, with 99 members. The Vice-President chairs the Senate. **National Holidays:** 25 August, Independence Day (1825); 18 July, Constitution Day (1830).
Armed Forces: 25,600 (1997). Other: 700 Metropolitan Guard, 500 Republican Guard.

Uzbekistan / Özbekiston

Population:	26,868,064
Area:	447,400 km²
Capital:	Tashkent
Currency:	Som-Kupon
Language:	Uzbek

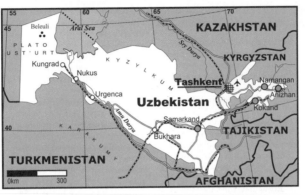

I n the 10th century BC agricultural centers such as Khwarezm (on the lower Amur-darya), Ma Wara an-Nahr (between mid Amur-darya and Sir-Darya) and the Fergana Valley became the first Indo-European-speaking states. Between the 6th century BC and the 7th century AD they successively formed part of the Persian Achaemenid empire, Alexander the Great's empire, the Greco-Bactrian kingdom and the white Eftalite Hunnish Kushan kingdom.

² Nomadic Turks annexed most of Central Asia to their Turkish Khanate from the 6th to the 8th century. Turkish speakers arrived in Uzbek territory, and intermarried with local inhabitants. In the mid 8th century they were conquered by the Arabs, who spread Islam, especially in the cities.

³ From the 9th century to the early 13th century, when the caliph's power declined and that of the local Samanids, Karajanids and the shas of Khwarezm increased, the Muslims reached a significant level of development in agriculture and crafts. The cities of Bukhara, Samarkand and Urgenca were prosperous trading centers for caravans following the Great Silk Route, from China to Byzantium.

⁴ Between 1219 and 1221 Khwarezm was devastated by the Mongols and handed over to Genghis Khan's oldest son. His

second son, Chagatai, took control of Ma Wara an-Nahr and Fergana. Inhabitants were now called Chagatais. Turkish and Mongol tribes took refuge in the steppes. In the second half of the 14th century, Timur, the head of one of these tribes, occupied Ma Wara an-Nahr and made Samarkand his imperial capital.

⁵ The union of the Uzbek nomadic peoples took place in the 15th century in Central Kazakhstan. The new arrivals gave their name to all the country's inhabitants. Once the State of Shaybani was dissolved, the khanates emerged (feudal theocracies made up of Uzbeks, Turkmen, Tajiks, Kyrgyz and Karakalpaks). In 1512 the Khanate of Khiva emerged, whose military élite were from the Kungrats, an Uzbek people. In 1806 their leader, Mohammed Amin, founded the dynasty that was to govern Khiva until 1920.

⁶ In the mid-16th century the Khanate of Bukhara emerged,

headed by the Uzbek Manguite military élite. In 1753 the Manguite leader Muhammad Rajim founded a dynasty that ruled until 1920. The Bujara Khanate reached its apogee during the reign of the Khan Nasrula (1826-1860). At the beginning of the 19th century the Emirs of Fergana, of the Ming Dynasty, founded the Khanate of Kokand.

⁷ These states, which had no fixed borders, were unable to command the complete loyalty of their regional leaders. The Emirs of Khiva and Bukhara exercised nominal sovereignty over the Turkish groups of the Kara Kum Desert (slave-traders in Iran). Although they were at their highest level of organization, they were unable to resist the advancing European expansion in the heart of Central Asia, where there was a clash of British and Russian interests over cotton.

⁸ The 1860 Russian offensive was hampered by the states' geographical isolation, such as

Khiva, located in the middle of the desert. In 1867 the Czar created the Province of Turkistan, with its center in Tashkent, belonging to Kokand, which he annexed in 1875. In the late 19th century the province included Samarkand, Syr-Darya and Fergana. In August 1873 the Khan of Khiva, and then in September the Emir of Bukhara, accepted Russian protectorate status. The harsh living conditions imposed by Moscow triggered several uprisings, such as those in Andizhan in 1898 and Central Asia in 1916.

⁹ After the fall of the Czar in 1917, power passed first to the Committee of the Provisional Government and the *soviets* and then, after the success of the October revolution in Petrograd, to the Soviet of Tashkent. In 1918, the Red Army thwarted the attempt to establish an autonomous Muslim government in Kokand and crushed the rebellion by the 'Turkistan Union for the Struggle Against Bolsheviks'. The army occupied Khiva in April 1920 and Bukhara in September. Land reform started in 1921. Military operations continued until mid-1922, when the impact of the reforms led to a loss of support for the rebels.

¹⁰ In 1924 Moscow reorganized Central Asian frontiers along ethnic lines, creating the Soviet Socialist Republic of Uzbekistan (SSRU). In May 1925 Uzbekistan became part of the Union of Soviet Socialist Republics (USSR). Tajikistan formed part of Uzbekistan (as an autonomous republic) until 1929, when it became part of the USSR.

LAND USE

2000

IRRIGATED AREA: 88.3% of arable land

- ■ ARABLE LAND: 10.8%
- ■ CROPLANDS: 0.9%
- ■ OTHER USE: 88.3%

PROFILE

ENVIRONMENT

Uzbekistan is bordered to the north and north-west by Kazakhstan, to the south-east by Tajikistan, to the north-east by Kyrgyzstan and to the south by Afghanistan. There are two main rivers and more than 600 streams, some of which are diverted for irrigation, while others are used for hydroelectric projects. In the north-west and center of the country there are plains (the Ustyurt Plateau, the Amu Darya Valley and the Kyzylkum desert) and there are mountains in the south-east (the Tien-Shan and Gissar and Alay ranges). The climate is hot and dry on the plains and more humid in the mountains. There are large deposits of natural gas, oil and coal. Among the most pressing environmental problems are the salinization of the soil as a result of monoculture, desertification, and contamination of drinking water and air pollution.

SOCIETY

Peoples: Uzbeks 75.8 per cent; Russians 6 per cent; Tajiks 4.8 per cent; Kazakhs 4.1 per cent, Kyrgyz 0.9 per cent; Ukrainians 0.6 per cent; Turks 0.6 per cent; other 7.2 per cent (1995).
Religions: Muslim (Sunni), 88 per cent; Orthodox, 1 per cent; other (mostly non-religious), 11 per cent.
Languages: Uzbek (official), Russian, Tajik.

Main Political Parties: Popular Democratic Party (Chalk Demokratik); Self-Sacrifice (Fidokorlar); Motherland Progress Party; Justice (Adilat); National Revival (Millyi Tiklanish).
Main Social Organizations: There are no independent trade unions. State enterprise workers are members of the Trade Union Federation of Uzbekistan. Human Rights Society of Uzbekistan (HRSU).

THE STATE

Official Name: Uzbekistan Jumhuriyati.
Administrative Division: 12 regions, 1 capital city and 1 autonomous republic (Qoraqalpoghiston).
Capital: Tashkent 2,155,000 people (2003).
Other Cities: Samarkand 362,000 people; Namangan 333,000; Andizhan 313,000; Bukhara 235,000 (1995).
Government: Islam Karimov, President since March 1990, elected in 1991 (shortly after Uzbek independence) and reelected in 2000. Shavkat Mirziyayev, Prime Minister since December 2003. Unicameral Legislature: National Assembly, with 250 members.
National Holiday: 1 September, Independence Day (1991).
Armed Forces: 65,000 (1995). Other: (National Guard) 700.

Life expectancy
69.7 years
2000-2005

GNI per capita
$450
2002

Literacy
99% total adult rate
2000

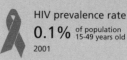

HIV prevalence rate
0.1% of population 15-49 years old
2001

IN FOCUS

ENVIRONMENTAL CHALLENGES
The Aral Sea is shrinking after years of intensive irrigation for agriculture, with resultant concentration of chemical pesticides (including DDT) and salt. Desertification and soil salinization are increasing. Industrial waste pollutes water sources, endangering human health. Monoculture, mainly cotton, has degraded the soil.

WOMEN'S RIGHTS
Women have been able to vote since 1938. In 2000 women occupied 7 per cent of seats in parliament, and 3 per cent of ministerial-level posts.

Between 1980 and 2000 female participation in the workforce remained steady at around 47 per cent.

According to UNICEF latest available data*, prenatal healthcare coverage is 97 per cent and 96 per cent of births are attended by skilled health personnel. Net female primary school enrollment was 78 per cent in 2000.

CHILDREN
According to UNICEF latest available data* (2002), the mortality rate was 68 per 1,000 for children under-five, and 52 per 1,000 for those under-one. Nineteen per cent of under-fives were moderately or seriously underweight, 12 per cent were moderately or seriously emaciated and 31 per cent were moderately or seriously below normal height. In 2000, the primary school enrollment was 78 per cent and 89 per cent of students reach 5th grade.

In 2001, 15 per cent of children between 5 and 14 worked. Child labor rates in rural areas were double those of urban areas.

INDIGENOUS PEOPLES/ ETHNIC MINORITIES
The dominant ethnic group are the Uzbeks who, since the fall of the communist regime, have been attempting to recover their cultural identity. This ethnic group extends to Afghanistan and Turkey, and was a part of Genghis Khan's Mongol forces, playing a key role in his conquests. Uzbeks make up 80 per cent of the population and are one of the groups who originally settled in the territory. During the era of Soviet domination, Moscow used their traditional enemies, the Tajiks, to keep them under control. Russians, who settled in the country during the Soviet period and still enjoy great political influence, account for 5 per cent of the population. The remaining 15 per cent is made up by Tajiks, Kasajos and Tatars.

MIGRANTS/REFUGEES
At the end of 2002, the country harbored a total of 38,000 refugees (30,000 from the Tajikistan civil war and 8,000 Afghans).

Between 2000 and 2001 approximately 3,000 Muslim citizens from villages on the borders with Afghanistan and Tajikistan were relocated within the country by government order. In an attempt to prevent potential consolidation of Islamic movements in the country, evacuees have been banned from visiting their former homes (some of which were demolished or burnt down).

Some 2,700 Uzbeks requested asylum abroad, mostly in the US (1,000) and Switzerland (640).

DEATH PENALTY
The death penalty is still in force.

*Latest data available in *The State of the World's Children* and *Childinfo* database,UNICEF, 2004.

During Josef Stalin's regime several Uzbeks were sentenced to death, including the prime minister, Fayzullah Khodzhayev, and the first secretary of the Communist Party (CP), Akmal Ikramov (both were later rehabilitated in 1953). During the 1930s the capital was transferred from Samarkand to Tashkent.

[11] Reforms designed to develop the region's agricultural potential (since 1956 based on cotton monoculture) through the construction of huge irrigation canals and dams turned the country into the USSR's main cotton supplier and the third-largest producer in the world. However, in less than 30 years this intensive irrigation dried up the Aral Sea, the world's fourth-largest inland body of water.

[12] Sharaf Rashidov governed from 1956 to 1983, a period of great stability for the republic.

[13] When Leonid Brezhnev took over the CP leadership in the USSR in 1983, he appointed new people to the Uzbekistan Government. The new local first secretary revealed that official figures for earlier cotton crops had been false.

[14] The resulting scandal led to arrests, proceedings against 4,000 public employees and expulsions from the ruling party, but no structural changes.

[15] From 1985, the reforms introduced by Mikhail Gorbachev, together with the deteriorating economic situation and the diminishing centralized authority of the USSR CP, led to ethnic and religious clashes in Uzbekistan, stemming from the majority Sunni Muslims' resistance to the USSR CP's anticlericalism.

[16] The Soviet invasion of Afghanistan (1979-1989), in which Sunni Muslims fought, had increased hostility towards Moscow and the Russian minority resident in Uzbekistan. The most serious consequences were the conflict in Fergana in June 1989 and clashes in Namangan in December 1990.

[17] Islam Karimov, who became First Secretary of the Uzbekistan CP in 1989, was appointed president of the SSRU in 1990. In August 1991 the Uzbek Soviet approved the Independence Law and in December, in Almaty (Kazakhstan), the Uzbek delegation signed the creation of the Commonwealth of Independent States (CIS). That same month, with most opposition parties proscribed, Karimov was elected president.

[18] Karimov's style proved authoritarian, stamping out dissidence, and he adopted the Southeast Asian model as the basis for Uzbekistan's new path to development, moving towards a market-based economy. A privatization plan was approved in January 1994 and the price of basic foodstuffs and electricity increased by up to 300 per cent.

[19] Attempts were made to limit Russian and Iranian influence in the region, in particular after 1995. Karimov supported the US embargo against Iran and called for the creation of a 'common Turkistan' to counter Russia imperialist pretensions. In late 1997, Uzbekistan voted with the US and Israel against ending the economic embargo against Cuba in the UN General Assembly.

[20] In November 1998 Karimov supported Russia in the war against Chechnya. The Islamic Movement of Uzbekistan (IMU), led by a member of the Taliban, began an offensive with the objective of creating an Islamic state in the north-east of the country. The Government accused the IMU of setting off several car-bombs in Uzbekistan during 1999.

[21] On 9 January 2000, Karimov was re-elected, with 92 per cent of the vote. The Organization for Cooperation and Security in Europe (OCSE) had refused to send observers, criticizing the electoral system, while the US described the elections as 'neither free nor fair'. Human Rights Watch denounced the Government for carrying out a 'brutal campaign' against religious activists. Nonetheless, Karimov requested India's cooperation in fighting international terrorism in Afghanistan and other Central Asian countries.

[22] Uzbekistan's entry to the Shanghai Five Group - China, Russia, Kazakhstan, Kyrgyzstan and Tajikistan - in June 2001 signaled the creation of the Shanghai Cooperation Organization (SCO), which agreed to fight ethnic and religious fundamentalism.

[23] Karimov was a key ally when the US attacked Afghanistan in October 2001. Karimov hoped to build a railroad to the Indian Ocean (the only access to the sea being to the north, by way of Russia). Karimov allowed US forces to use Uzbek airspace and military bases for deployment. After substantial international pressure was brought to bear, Karimov opened the border with Afghanistan to international aid from the UN and other humanitarian organizations. In exchange for support, the US promised $160 million in economic aid.

[24] In January 2002 a referendum passed Karimov's proposal to extend the presidential term from five to seven years. The West suspected that Karimov had ambitions to become president-for-life.

[25] President Karimov visited the US, where he signed several cooperation agreements. Five years after it was founded, the Human Rights Society of Uzbekistan (HRSU) was officially recognized as the country's first fully independent human-rights organization. According to its activists, the Government's decision was the result of international pressure and the presidential trip to the US.

[26] IMU leader Juma Namangoniy was murdered in August 2002.

[27] In September of the same year, an old frontier dispute with Kazakhstan was settled.

[28] Despite having been banned in 1992, the opposition Freedom party (Erk) had its first formal gathering in June 2003. In December Shavkat Mirziyayev replaced Otkir Sultanov as prime minister.

[29] In March 2004, the Uzbek Government blamed Islamic extremists for the deaths of some 20 people in a bomb and gun attack. ∎

Vanuatu / Vanatu

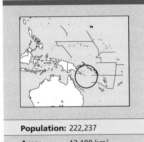

Population:	222,237
Area:	12,190 km²
Capital:	Vila
Currency:	Vatu
Language:	Bislama, English and French

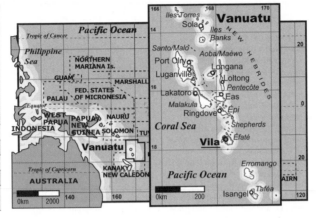

The first colonization of Polynesia and Melanesia is still unclear to anthropologists and historians (see box 'Melanesians and Polynesians'). Sailing westwards, Polynesians reached Vanuatu around 1400 BC. These navigators crossed and populated the entire Pacific Ocean from Antarctica to Hawaii and as far as Easter Island on the eastern edge of the Pacific Ocean. Their culture was highly developed; they domesticated animals and developed some subsistence crops; they manufactured ceramics and textiles, organized their societies into a caste system and, in some cases, possessed a historical knowledge which had been orally transmitted down the generations for centuries.

2   On 29 April 1605 the Portuguese-Spanish navigator, Pedro Fernández de Quiros, was the first European to sight mountains which he believed to be part of the Great Southern Continent for which he was searching; he named the place 'Tierra del Espíritu Santo' (Land of the Holy Spirit).

3   A century and a half later, Frenchman Louis Antoine de Bougainville sailed around the region and demonstrated that it was not part of Australia but rather a series of islands. In 1774, British captain James Cook drew the first map of the archipelago, calling it the New Hebrides.

4   Shortly thereafter traders arrived and felled the forests and the islands became the source of a semi-enslaved labor force. The workers were either taken by force or purchased from local leaders in exchange for tobacco, mirrors and firearms.

5   During almost all of the 19th century, the archipelago was on the dividing line between the French (in New Caledonia) and British (in the Solomon Islands) zones of influence, and the two nations finally decided to share the islands. In 1887, a Joint Naval Commission was established, and in 1906, the Condominium was formalized, which envisaged joint provision of some basic services: post, radio, customs, public works, but left each power free to develop other services. Consequently, there were two police forces, two monetary systems, two health services and two school systems ruled by two representatives on the islands.

6   The local inhabitants, Melanesians, were relegated to being 'stateless' in their own country. They were not considered citizens until a legislative assembly was established in the territory in 1974. Until then only British or French people were entitled to citizenship and land ownership.

7   Most of the neighboring archipelagos achieved independence in the 1970s. This encouraged the foundation of the National Party of the New Hebrides (now the Vanuaaku Pati [VP] - Our Land Party) in 1971. It organized grassroots groups on all the islands. The Party became the country's leading political force and demanded full independence, in opposition to various 'moderate' pro-French parties that preferred to maintain colonial status. When the Party won two-thirds of the vote in 1979, the UK accepted the outcome.

8   Independence was declared on 30 July 1980. Measures were immediately taken to return the land held by foreigners to the Melanesians; the school system was unified and a national army was created.

9   At this time government revenues depended heavily on foreign aid and the country's exports covered only half of the cost of its imports. Since it was a tax haven with more than 60 banks established in Vila there was no firm strategy to raise taxes.

10   Ombudsman Marie-Noelle Ferrieux-Patterson reported in 1996 that the Government had diverted aid for cyclone victims, issued false passports and misappropriated monies from pensions funds. These accusations provoked street demonstrations and the Government declared a state of emergency.

11   In early 2002, an earthquake measuring 7.2 on the Richter scale cut the power and water supply in most neighborhoods, destroyed buildings and bridges, and injured several people.

12   Former Prime Minister Barak Sope was sentenced, in July 2002, to three years in prison for issuing false government guarantee certificates - valued at Aus $46 million - but was pardoned three months later for health reasons.

13   In May 2003, the OECD took Vanuatu off its tax haven list, as a reward for its efforts to improve tax accountability.

14   Alfred Masing Nalo was elected President in April 2004, but was removed in May by the Supreme Court, as he was on trial for criminal complicity and embezzlement.

15   In May 2004 Prime Minister Edward Natapei lost his majority in Parliament. The acting president, Roger Abiut, dissolved Parliament and called for elections in July. ∎

PUBLIC EXPENDITURE

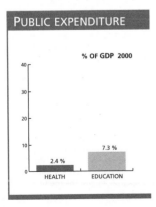

% OF GDP 2000

HEALTH 2.4 %
EDUCATION 7.3 %

PROFILE

ENVIRONMENT

Vanuatu is a Melanesian archipelago of volcanic origin, comprising more than 70 islands and islets, many of them uninhabited. It stretches for 800 km in a north-south direction in the South Pacific about 1,200 km east of Australia. Major islands are: Espiritu Santo, Malekula, Epi, Pentecost, Aoba, Maewa, Paama, Ambrym, Efate, Erromango, Tanna and Aneityum. Active volcanoes are found in Tanna, Ambrym and Lopevi and the area is subject to earthquakes. The land is mountainous and covered with dense tropical forests. The climate is tropical with heavy rainfall. The subsoil of Efate is rich in manganese and the soil is suitable for farming. Fishing is a traditional economic activity. The land tenure system has contributed to general soil depletion due to deforestation and erosion. Rising sea levels will affect both inhabited and uninhabited coastal areas. There is also a risk that rising tides will seep into ground water, threatening water supplies.

SOCIETY

Peoples: Most people are Melanesian (98 per cent), with 1 per cent European (British and French) and smaller groups from Vietnam, China and other Pacific islands. **Religions:** Presbyterian (36.7 per cent), Anglican (15 per cent), Catholic (15 per cent), indigenous religions (7.6 per cent), other (15.7 per cent). **Languages:** Bislama, English and French are official. More than 100 Melanesian languages are also spoken. **Main Political Parties:** Vanuaaku Pati (VP)/Party of Our Land; Union of Moderate Parties; Vanuatu National United Party; Melanesian Progressive Party.
Main Social Organizations: Vanuatu Trade Union Congress (VTUC); Vanuatu Association of Non Governmental Organizations (VANGO).

THE STATE

Official Name: Ripablik blong Vanuatu. République de Vanuatu, Republic of Vanuatu. **Administrative Divisions:** 6 provinces: Malampa, Penama, Sanma, Shefa, Tafea, and Torba. **Capital:** Vila, on Efate Island, 34,000 people (2003). **Other Cities:** Luganville (Santo) 8,400 people; Port Olry 1,200; Isangel 1,200 (2000). **Government:** Roger Abiut, acting president since May 2004. Unicameral Legislature, with 52 members elected for a four-year term. **National Holiday:** 30 July, Independence Day (1980).

Vatican City / Città del Vaticano

Population:	440
Area:	1 km²
Capital:	Vatican City
Currency:	Euro
Language:	Italian and Latin

In ancient times, the territory now known as the Vatican City, to the west of the Tiber river, was known as the Ager Vaticanus (Vatican fields). Some sources say the name Vatican comes from a former Etruscan town on the site called Vaticum, others say it derives from the Latin *vates* (seer), and that in the past there was a hill called Vatican inhabited by soothsayers who predicted the fate of passers-by.

2 Due to the persecution of Christians and the destruction of Church documents in Rome by Emperor Diocletian in 303, today there are few traces of the first Christians' presence in the area.

3 Emperor Constantine the Great (307-337) made peace with the Church, allowing Christianity to abandon its clandestine status and hold a privileged juridical standing.

4 In the 4th century construction began, at the foot of Vatican Hill, of what would later be known as St Peter's Basilica. According to archaeological evidence, the first pope was buried there. Medieval pontiffs purchased the territory and built a bridge, the Pons Aelius, to link the lands with Rome.

5 The landscape and building architecture were developed by each pope. The pontiffs became rulers of the city of Rome and the surrounding areas.

6 In the year 756 this domain was officially granted to Pope Stephen II by Pippin the Short, King of the Franks, in appreciation for having appointed him king. Papal possessions increased through donations, acquisitions and conquest and in this way the future Papal States, legally established by Charlemagne in the IX century, covered almost all of the central zone of Italy.

7 In 847, Pope Leon IV erected a large wall, named Leonine, to defend the Vatican against the Saracens. This wall turned the St Peter's area into walled grounds protecting the Basilica and its treasures, smaller churches, monasteries, homes of the clergy, and the orchards of its inhabitants. It

turned the city into a *sui generis* district, different from the rest of Rome.

8 Between 1309 and 1377, the popes lived mostly in Avignon, due to constant conflicts in Rome. Pressed by Philip IV of France, Pope Clement V moved the pontiff's capital to Avignon, then belonging to the pope's vassals and which in 1348 became property of the pontiffs. The seven popes of that period were French, as well as 111 of the 134 cardinals.

9 After Gregory XI re-established the pontifical capital in Rome, Clement VII led the cardinals who in 1378 declared invalid the election of Urban VI, and was elected anti-pope, occupying the empty throne in Avignon. Europe was divided in its support for both pontiffs: while France backed Clement, England supported Urban, a dispute that would continue throughout the 100 Years War (1337-1453) and would lead to the period known as the Great Schism, in which several anti-popes were named, and which would finally end in 1417.

10 Most of the annexations to the Vatican territory were kept under pontifical rule until 1797, when Napoleon Bonaparte took the territory, creating the Roman Republic.

11 In 1801 Pope Pius VII recovered some of his power and in 1815 after the fall of Napoleon, the Congress of Vienna returned almost all of the papacy's possessions.

12 The first Vatican Council was held in 1869 and decreed the dogma of papal infallibility. A year later, the

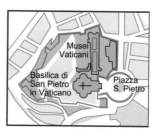

Papal States were finally dissolved when Victor Emmanuel II annexed them to the unified kingdom of Italy, including Rome. The papacy's jurisdiction was limited to the Vatican, in which each of the successive pontiffs remained, in protest, as self-imposed prisoner. This voluntary reclusion continued until 1929 when the Lateran Treaty, signed between the Holy See and the Kingdom of Italy - ruled then by Benito Mussolini - acknowledged the sovereignty and international status of the Vatican City State. This state is different from the Holy See, since the latter is the executive organ of the Catholic Church, and the former is the physical territory over which that government rules. Thus, the pontiff's political authority was consolidated.

13 Throughout the centuries, and especially during the Renaissance (14th-mid 17th centuries), Papal patronage turned the Vatican into one of the world's most important cultural hubs, with architectural works such as St Peter's, the Sistine Chapel, decorated by Michelangelo, Botticelli and other artists, and the *Stanza della Segnatura* frescoes by Raphael.

14 During World War II, Pope Pius XII took the Vatican's definition of 'neutrality' to the limit, provoking criticism to this day of the relationship with Hitler's Germany and in particular the Vatican's knowledge of and response to the Holocaust.

15 In 1982, banker Roberto Calvi was found dead in London. This led to the collapse of his huge, privately-owned bank, Banco Ambrosiano, revealing a 'black hole' in its balance sheet of some $1.3 billion. A large part of the missing money was later found in accounts owned by the Vatican Bank. The death of Calvi - 'God's banker' - exposed links with masons, mafia and Vatican fraud.

16 The Vatican's resources came from the 1,750 million lira that the Lateran Treaty determined as compensation for the territories lost in 1870, and donations from all over the world, especially from the US and Germany. These funds are administered by the Institute for Religious Works - better known as the Vatican Bank - restructured after the scandals caused by collapse of the Banco Ambrosiano. It is believed to have a capital of $11 billion, and countless real estate properties throughout the world.

17 In 1993, the budget had a $91.7 million deficit, exceeding the $86.1 million planned. For the first time, Vatican workers demonstrated for a wage and pension rise. During a visit by Pope John Paul II to the US, in June, his image was sold on posters and T-shirts, and in 1995, the Vatican sold Papal prayers on CD. In 1995 the Vatican's economy had overcome its deficit.

18 During the last decade of the 20th century, scandals arising from allegations of pedophilia against Catholic priests rocked the Vatican. The victims received a total of $119.6 million in damages, the largest compensation awarded in the history of sexual abuse cases.

19 In October 2002 the Pope beatified Mother Teresa of Calcutta. In what was seen as a fairly political move, he also canonized the outspoken José Escrivá de Balaguer, founder of Opus Dei - the conservative order that wields great power within the Church.

20 In October 2003 Pope John Paul II, aged 83, celebrated the 25th year of his Papacy. He has been much criticized for his conservatism, particularly in the area of contraception. He has presided over a period in which the number of Roman Catholics grew from 750 million to one billion worldwide. The most significant growth took place in Africa, the region with the highest rates of HIV/AIDS and child deaths and where the Catholic Church campaigns against the use of condoms. ■

PROFILE

ENVIRONMENT

Located within the city of Rome, next to the Tiber river, it includes St Peter's basilica and square, Vatican palaces and gardens, the church and palace of St John in Lateran, the papal 'villa' of Castelgandolfo, and 13 buildings outside this area which are considered extraterritorial.

SOCIETY

People: Vatican citizens are members of the Papal and Catholic Church administration who live there because of their work. Most of the permanent officials are Italians, a large number are Swiss and the rest come from different countries.
Religion: Catholic. **Languages:** Italian (the state) and Latin (official).

THE STATE

Official Name: Stato della Città del Vaticano.
Administrative Divisions: Two parallel administrations: Holy See (supreme organ of the Catholic Church); Vatican City (physical headquarters of the church) **Capital:** Vatican City, 900 residents (est 2003). **Government:** monarchy elected for life. Pope John Paul II (Karol Wojtyla, Polish), sovereign elected on 16 October 1978 by the College of Cardinals (in secret meeting). He is the first non-Italian Pope in 456 years. The equivalent of the head of government is the Secretary of State, Cardinal Angelo Sodano since 1991, who chairs a commission of five cardinals. The Pope is also the Bishop of Rome and supreme head of the Catholic Church. The Church administration is advised by the College of Cardinals and the Bishops' Synods, who meet when the pontiff wishes. The Church's administrative bodies are 9 Holy Congregations, 3 Secretariats and several commissions, prefectures or courts, which are jointly known as the Roman Curia.

Venezuela / Venezuela

Population:	26,639,527
Area:	912,050 km²
Capital:	Caracas
Currency:	Bolívar
Language:	Spanish

Cumanagotos, Tamaques, Maquiritares, Arecunas, and other Carib groups inhabited the northern tip of South America when the Spanish arrived in 1498. Local buildings, constructed on stilts, reminded the Spaniards of Venice, so they named the country Venezuela (Little Venice).

2 During the colonial period, Venezuela was organized as a Captaincy General of the Viceroyalty of New Granada. Its agricultural economy, based on cocoa and slave labor, forged a society dominated by a local aristocracy of *mantuanos*, with a majority of *pardos* (African slaves and their descendants).

3 The first phase of the revolution for freedom started in April 1810 with Francisco de Miranda. He sought independence from Spain and the creation of a vast American Confederacy to be known as Colombia, which would crown an Inca emperor. Miranda failed, was captured by the Spaniards in 1811 and later died in prison.

4 The second revolutionary stage was initiated by Simón Bolívar who, backed by the *mantuano* oligarchy, installed a government in Caracas. His plans for independence did not include changes in social structure, and he was not supported by the *pardos*, most of whom hated their white creole owners. Their liberation movement was led by the Spanish loyalist General José Tomás Boves, who defeated Bolívar in 1814. Boves abolished slavery and redistributed the land among the people. It was the end of the First Republic.

5 Bolívar went into exile and on returning to Venezuela, championed popular demands and won mass support. Accompanied by other military leaders like Antonio José de Sucre, Santiago Mariño, José A Páez and Juan B Arismendi, he carried out successful military campaigns in the northern half of the continent.

6 In 1819, the Angostura Congress created the new republic of 'Gran Colombia', uniting Colombia, Ecuador, Panama and Venezuela. In 1830, shortly before Bolívar's death, General José Antonio Páez declared Venezuela's secession from Gran Colombia.

7 For decades, Venezuelan politics revolved around the *caudillo* or leader, Páez. His political successor, Antonio Guzmán Blanco, was determined to modernize the country. He succeeded to a certain extent, introducing new technology, new means of communication, and reforming the legal code.

8 Juan Vicente Gómez took power in 1908, ruling for 17 years as a dictator. He gave free access to the foreign oil companies, which operated primarily in the Lake Maracaibo oil fields. In 1935 General Eleazar López Contreras took office. He was succeeded in 1941 by General Isaías Medina Angarita, who laid the foundations for greater political activity by legalizing the Democratic Action (AD) party. He supported the Allies during World War II.

9 In 1945 a civilian-military movement took power, led by Rómulo Betancourt, the leader of AD, and General Marcos Pérez Jiménez. The country's first free elections were held in 1947. Writer Rómulo Gallegos (AD) was elected President but overthrown in 1948 by yet another military coup, installing the harsh dictatorship of Marcos Pérez Jiménez.

10 In 1958, Pérez Jiménez was overthrown and the country then entered a stable 'democratic' period under a coalition government formed by the Punto Fijo Pact (1958) which enabled the AD and COPEI (the Christian Democrats) to alternate in power for decades. This stability was largely achieved because of massive oil revenues, improved relations with the US, and expanded political rights.

11 Unfortunately, the ensuing economic growth brought little change to the lives of the poor majority. Popular discontent resulted in guerrilla warfare led by the Communist Party, the Movement of the Revolutionary Left (which split from AD), and other groups.

12 In 1960, Venezuela sponsored the formation of the Organization of Petroleum Exporting Countries (OPEC). Sixteen years later, during the presidency of social democrat Carlos Andrés Pérez, Venezuelan oil was nationalized. Pérez also supported the creation of the Latin American Economic System (SELA) and argued in favor of a New International Economic Order.

13 Although Venezuela was the world's third largest oil exporter and received its highest prices during the governments of Pérez and Christian Democrat Luis Herrera Campins, the Government was unable to manage the enormous amounts of money coming into the country. Huge state-run companies were created for the manufacture of iron, aluminum, cement, and for hydroelectric power, while most private companies were being subsidized.

14 In 1982, a sharp decrease in oil revenues, foreign debt, and a flight of private capital forced the Government to take control of exchange rates and foreign trade. Inflation, unemployment, and housing shortages started to rise, while extreme poverty rose too.

15 The 1983 presidential elections were won by the AD's Jaime Lusinchi, who gained 56 per cent of the vote, defeating COPEI's Rafael Caldera.

16 In response to the economic problems, Lusinchi's policy comprised an austerity plan which gave meagre results, and a flawed 'social pact' between employers and unions and, towards the end of his term, increasing state control over the economy.

17 The AD's candidate in the 1988 elections, Carlos Andrés Pérez, won the presidency backed by the Confederation of Venezuelan Workers (CTV).

18 Social tension increased and 25 days later the poorest people took to the streets in a wave of riots and looting. Police repression left more than 1,000 dead (246 according to the Government), and 2,000 wounded or jailed.

19 IMF-backed economic restructuring was initiated, which lost the Government popular support. In December 1989, these policies were blamed for abstention rates of nearly 70 per cent and broad gains by the Christian Democrats and left-wing parties, when Venezuelans elected their 20 state governors and 369 mayors for the first time.

20 Although the Government recognizes indigenous peoples' land rights, there has not been adequate protection of the indigenous population. They suffer persecution from landowners, farmers and

LAND USE

2000

IRRIGATED AREA: 16.9% of arable land

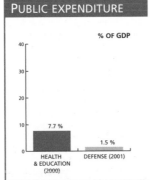

- ARABLE LAND: 2.8%
- CROPLANDS: 1.1%
- OTHER USE: 96.1%

PUBLIC EXPENDITURE

% OF GDP

7.7 %
HEALTH & EDUCATION (2000)

1.5 %
DEFENSE (2001)

WORKERS

UNEMPLOYMENT: 15.8% (2002)

LABOR FORCE   2002

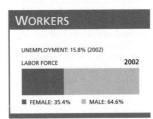

- FEMALE: 35.4%   ■ MALE: 64.6%

Life expectancy
73.7 years
2000-2005

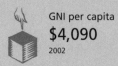
GNI per capita
$4,090
2002

Literacy
93% total adult rate
2000

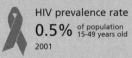
HIV prevalence rate
0.5% of population 15-49 years old
2001

[20] government officials, while Brazilian miners continue to invade their land prospecting for gold within Venezuelan territory.

[21] Early in 1992, the popularity of the Pérez Government was at its lowest, with the AD party distancing itself from imposing further economic measures. Congress exercised its controlling function by investigating crimes, but due to the corruption and inefficiency of the judiciary these investigations very rarely led to prosecutions.

[22] On 4 February 1992, a military coup against the President was led by Francisco Arias. While the attempt failed, it showed that administrative corruption and the economic crisis were the causes of instability. Arias and parachute commander Hugo Chávez, both belonging to the Bolívar-200 Military Movement, were arrested.

[23] The Government suspended all constitutional rights. An agreement was reached with the teachers' unions, putting an end to a fortnight of strikes and police repression of students and teachers.

[24] Another coup attempt by Chávez took place in November 1992. The air force played a key role in controlling the rebels.

[25] President Pérez was suspended from office on 21 May 1993, charged with misappropriation of funds. Shortly after he was tried for corruption and sentenced to house arrest. After serving time, he returned to politics in 1996.

[26] Ramón Velázquez became deputy President until former President Rafael Caldera won the 1994 general elections. The abstention rate reached 40 per cent.

[27] In the 1990s, Caracas had become one of Latin America's most violent cities. A feeling of insecurity prevailed as the number of murders rose. In 1995 it was estimated that 10 per cent of Caracas residents carried a weapon.

[28] The economic crisis worsened in February 1993, with the fall of the Banco Latino, the country's second commercial bank. In August 1995, 18 out of the 41 private banks had been investigated and 70 per cent of the deposits were being managed by the Government.

[29] President Caldera suspended constitutional guarantees regarding real estate, private property and business. He also restricted trips abroad, meetings and the immunity against arbitrary arrests. Despite Congress' vote to reinstate these rights, the President restricted them once more to prevent speculation and capital flight.

[30] On 6 December 1998, Hugo Chávez was elected constitutional president with 56.5 per cent of the vote. In his inaugural speech, he

PROFILE

ENVIRONMENT

The country comprises three main regions. In the north and west are the Andes and other mountain chains, and there are more high mountains to the south. The central Orinoco Plains are a livestock farming area. In the southeast, highlands of ancient rock and sandstone extend to the borders with Brazil and Guyana, forming Venezuelan Guyana. This is a sparsely inhabited area with thick forests, savannas, rivers, and some peculiar features: the tepuyes or plateau mountains, and the rare Sarisarinama depths. Most of the population lives in the hilly north. The main oil basins are: Lake Maracaibo (Zulia), Orinoco River Basin (Delta Amacuro, Monagas, Guárico), Falcón Basin (Falcón), Apuré-Barinas Basin (Apure and Barinas states) and Cariacó Basin (Sucre). In the Gulf of Paria and the center of the State of Anzoátegui there are natural gas reserves. The country produces iron ore, manganese, bauxite, tungsten and chrome, gold and diamonds.

SOCIETY

Peoples: Venezuelans are descended from the integration of indigenous peoples, Afro-Caribbean and European settlers. Today, indigenous peoples and Afro-Caribbeans each account for less than 7 per cent of the population. In recent times, Venezuela has received more immigrants than any other South American country.
Religions: Mainly Catholic, 92.7 per cent.
Languages: Spanish, official and predominant; 31 local languages are spoken.
Main Political Parties: Movement for the Fifth Republic; Democratic Action (AD), member of the Socialist International; the Movement Towards Socialism (MAS), the Social Christian Party of Venezuela (COPEI), a member of the Christian Democrat International; Communist Party of Venezuela; Radical Cause.
Main Social Organizations: The Venezuelan Confederation of Workers (CTV) is the main trade union, and is controlled by AD. There are other trade unions which are clearly linked to political parties. Unitary Workers Confederation of Venezuela (CUTV); Confederation of Autonomous Trade Unions (CODESA).

THE STATE

Official Name: República Bolivariana de Venezuela.
Administrative Divisions: 21 states with partial autonomy (including the Federal District), 2 Federal territories.
Capital: Caracas 3,226,000 people (2003).
Other Cities: Maracaibo 1,847,000 people; Valencia 1,719,500; Barquisimeto 1,027,700; Guyana City 748,200 (2000). Government: Presidential System. Hugo Chávez, President since February 1999, re-elected in 2000. Unicameral Legislature: National Assembly, with 165 members.
National Holiday: 5 July, Independence Day (1811).
Armed Forces: 79,000, including 18,000 conscripts (1997). Other: Co-operation Army 23,000.

announced he would replace what he described as a 'dead' constitution through a 'peaceful revolution' to fight poverty and restructure foreign debt, standing at more than $23 billion. In order to do this there would be a National Constituent Assembly (NCA) which would draw up a new constitution in six months.

[31] In early 1999, Chávez publicized his 'peaceful revolution' through his diplomatic corps and through a television program which received and directly 'resolved' the concerns of the public. On 25 July, in elections for the NCA, 75 per cent of the population voted for the Chávez' Movement for the Fifth Republic, giving it the absolute majority in the body.

[32] In September, the country hosted the second meeting

between Colombia's National Liberation Army (ELN) and the Colombian governmental authorities. Chávez, who played an important role in the Colombian conflict, turned down a US request to use his air bases to 'combat drug trafficking' there. It was widely believed the US aimed to invade Colombia and destroy insurgent groups.

[33] Although there was a 54 per cent abstention rate and opposition from the Catholic Church, the business sector and followers of the old political system, 70 per cent of those who turned out to vote approved the new constitution. Thus was born the 'Bolivarian Republic of Venezuela'. The high abstention rate was due, amongst other factors, to floods which killed 50,000 people.

[34] In June 2000 Chávez was re-elected by an overwhelming majority for a term ending in 2006. In August, he met the leaders of the main oil exporting countries. The re-elected President faced harsh criticism from the US for meeting Iraqi president Saddam Hussein in Baghdad. Chávez was the first democratically elected head of state to visit Iraq since the 1991 Gulf War.

[35] Chávez announced measures in early 2002 aimed at stimulating the economy and achieving social justice. These included reforms of the Lands Law and fossil fuels legislation. The latter doubled the royalties paid by foreign investors from 16 per cent to 30 per cent, and reserved for the state at least 51 per cent of the shares of joint ventures. The Lands Law allowed the Government to expropriate tracts of land over 5,000 hectares and give them to peasants. Chávez's personalist approach to politics and socioeconomic reforms made him clash with many sectors: trade unionists, entrepreneurs, mass media and the Catholic Church.

[36] The Gross Domestic Product grew by 2.8 per cent and economic activity - excluding crude oil - jumped by about 4 per cent in 2001. However Chávez was unable to capitalize on the high oil prices to shift revenues to development programs for the most vulnerable people. His bold statements led to an increase in capital flight - nearly $3 billion in the first three months of his term.

[37] In February 2002, to confront the crisis, Chávez enacted a strict adjustment package that was applauded by the IMF. He announced that the currency exchange rate would be floated, after parity with the dollar had been tied at a 10-per cent annual depreciation of the bolívar, which represented a devaluation of more than 25 per cent. The budget was reduced by 22 per cent and public spending by 7 points. He also agreed additional taxes. Many Venezuelans reacted against the price hikes, especially on items of mass consumption.

[38] As a result of his ties with Cuba, Iraq and Libya, and his hesitation to condemn the September 2001 attacks on the US, Chávez ended up in direct confrontation with the superpower. He had almost single-handedly rebuilt OPEC by committing Venezuela to adhere to its OPEC sales quotas, causing world oil prices to double to over $20 per barrel. Venezuela is one of the most important oil suppliers to the US.

[39] The President moved to take control of the state oil company Petróleos de Venezuela (PDVSA) - nominally owned by the Government, but actually in thrall

Under-5 mortality
22 per 1,000 live births
2002

Poverty
15.0% of population living on less than $1 per day
1998

Debt service
24.6% exports of goods and services
2001

Maternal mortality
96 per 100,000 live births
2000

to the foreign operators. He removed several of its managers and appointed a new board of directors. This move provoked a new crisis. In April 2002 a general strike was called by employers and trade unions, with massive demonstrations.

40 The armed forces joined civilian protests. Army commander Efraín Vázquez announced he was no longer loyal to the President and Chávez was overthrown. He was kidnapped and sent to Orchila island, where - it was later revealed - they planned to assassinate him.

41 The coup put Pedro Carmona, head of the country's main business association, into the presidency. He dissolved Parliament and the Supreme Court, annulled the Constitution, called presidential elections to take place in a year and convened legislative elections for December, under a decree of 'reorganizing the public powers'. These announcements came with the figures on the previous day's violence: 15 dead and 350 injured, according to the fire department. On 14 April, at midnight, troops loyal to Chávez's legitimate government entered the Miraflores presidential palace and waited for the operation that would rescue Chávez and return him to power. Carmona was forced to step down and was arrested.

42 The US did not condemn the coup against Chávez until he returned to power. The British *Guardian* newspaper reported that US intelligence had been studying the possibility of removing Chávez from office for over a year; also that on the day of the coup, the US navy on the Venezuelan coast had tuned in to communications in Caracas. Washington's stance on Venezuela fed fears of 'coup contagion' throughout the region.

43 Amnesty International reported that, after Chávez was reinstated, the Government did not try any of the National Guard members accused of the deaths during the conflict. It also denounced torture and police abuse against opposition followers and human rights advocates.

44 In July 2002 former US President Jimmy Carter travelled to Venezuela and met with Chávez to start negotiations between those involved in the conflict, but the opposition did not show up.

45 New threats to political stability were posed in October when a group of 14 high-ranking military men called for 'civil and military disobedience'. The group demanded that the President's authority should not be respected and that either he should leave office or that his term in power should be decided by referendum.

46 In late October the Secretary-General of the Organization of American States (OAS), former Colombian president César Gaviria, arrived in Caracas to try and mediate in the military-political crisis. Negotiations got nowhere. The business association, the CTV, and the opposition coalition Democratic Coordinator (CD), called for a general strike to press for a referendum to decide whether or not Chávez should remain in office. The measure caused the loss of $50 million per day in oil exports. The opposition called for civil disobedience and non-payment of state services.

47 The Government rejected the referendum arguing that it was unconstitutional to call it before the presidential mid-term, in August 2003.

48 Although the 62-day strike put the country on the verge of bankruptcy, Chávez managed to stay in power. The strike was lifted, even though the Government rejected all proposals that included a referendum before

August 2003. Former US President Carter had proposed that the presidential term should be shortened via a constitutional amendment.

49 UNICEF reported that the political crisis had a strong impact on children, who missed 30 per cent of school lessons due to the endless strikes. There were outbreaks of diseases that were believed to have been eradicated, such as measles.

50 In May 2003 the Government and the CD signed a 19-point agreement, including a referendum to revoke the Presidency, the creation of the National Electoral Council (CNE), the disarmament of civil society and the setting up of a Truth Commission.

51 The opposition gathered 3.4 million signatures, of which the CNE only validated 1.83 million, less than the number required for the vote. The opposition protested in the streets against what it believed was a fraud by the CNE, and suffered violent Government repression. In June 2004, the CNE

accepted 2.44 million signatures, which enabled the referendum to take place in August 2004.

52 Since the political crisis started the Government withstood strong pressure from the Venezuelan mass media (dominated by the Cisneros group), which played a decisive role in the 2003 coup. Chávez also denounced in his program *Aló Presidente* a hostile policy by CNN, which had 'poisoned' the airwaves. That is why in April 2004 he declared a 'communications war' on Ted Turner's network.

53 In May 2004 security forces detained 88 Colombian paramilitaries charged with training to overthrow Chávez. Former President Carlos Andrés Pérez's home was raided, who after returning from Miami denied being involved in the conspiracy, but stated that Chávez had to be overthrown by force.

54 In August Chávez triumphed over his opponents, winning 59 per cent of the vote in the long-awaited 'recall' referendum. ■

IN FOCUS

ENVIRONMENTAL CHALLENGES
Deforestation and soil degradation are some environmental problems. A lack of water treatment in the main urban and industrial centers has increased the pollution of lakes Maracaibo and Valencia, and the Caribbean Sea. Rainforests are seriously threatened by mining activity.

WOMEN'S RIGHTS
Women have been able to vote and stand for election since 1947. In 2000 they held 7 per cent of local government posts and 3 per cent of ministerial posts. Women comprised 35 per cent of the total labor force, with 85 per cent working in the service sector, 13 per cent in industry and 2 per cent in agriculture.

According to UNICEF's latest data available*, the maternal mortality rate stood at 96 for every 100,000 births. Some 29 per cent of pregnant women were anemic, and 90 per cent received pre-natal care, while 94 per cent of births were assisted by qualified personnel.

Domestic violence against women is widespread and has grown in recent years.

CHILDREN
As of UNICEF's latest data available*, the mortality rate among children was 19 per 1,000 live births; the under-5 mortality

rate was 22 per 1,000 live births. Seven per cent of newborns were underweight; between 63 and 78 per cent of children under one year of age are immunized against polio, tetanus and measles, among other diseases. In 2001 there were 170,000 AIDS orphans.

Seven per cent of children between the ages of 5 and 14 work, especially in the informal sector, generally as street vendors or beggars. UNICEF reports there are 240,000 children on the streets. However, social organizations believe that number amounts to 500,000.

There are reports that children from other South American countries, mostly Ecuador, have been trafficked to work in Caracas as street-sellers, domestics and prostitutes.

INDIGENOUS PEOPLES/ ETHNIC MINORITIES
There are at least 2 million Afro-Venezuelans, who suffer mostly social discrimination. Discrimination tends to be on economic division rather than race. Most Afro-Venezuelans live in the Barlovento region, on the Caribbean coast, where they were brought between the 16th and 19th centuries to work as slaves. There are approximately 27 different indigenous groups, of which only four communities have more than 10,000 residents. Indigenous peoples, since the conquest of America, have lived in poverty:

most lack access to health care and education, and are undernourished. During the 1990s there were considerable achievements in protection for indigenous rights, both cultural and political. In spite of this, in the political realm there are several communities without access to the system. For many years indigenous groups have called for a system of proportional representation that allows ethnic minority participation. As they are excluded from the Venezuelan Congress, they have created the Congress of Indigenous Peoples of Venezuela to protect and claim their rights.

MIGRANTS/REFUGEES
During 2002, Venezuela received 1,100 refugees and asylum-seekers, mostly Colombian. It is estimated that 1.5 million Colombians have settled in Venezuela since the 1970s.

The social and political crisis which began in late 2002 forced many Venezuelans to emigrate to the US and other countries, but in small numbers according to experts.

DEATH PENALTY
Capital punishment was abolished in 1863.

* Latest data available in *The State of the World's Children* and *Childinfo* database, UNICEF, 2004.

Vietnam / Viêt Nam

Population:	83,584,512
Area:	331,690 km²
Capital:	Hanoi
Currency:	Dong
Language:	Vietnamese

The Vietnamese nation was born out of centuries of war: in the 9th century against the Chinese Han dynasty, ending nearly a thousand years of subjugation; against the Chams in the 11th and 12th centuries; driving back Genghis Khan and his grandson Kublai Khan in the 13th century; the Chinese Ming and Ching dynasties in the 15th and 17th centuries; and the Khmers in the 18th century.

2 When France began its conquest of Indochina in 1860, it encountered sporadic but disorganized and poorly armed resistance, delaying victory by 30 years. By around 1900 the French had consolidated their position in the peninsula and Vietnam was divided into Tonkin in the north, Annam in the center and Cochinchina in the south. To counter Chinese influence, the use of *Quoc Ngu* - Vietnamese written in Latin script - was encouraged. This provided nationalists with a powerful tool to popularize knowledge and modernize the culture, which reduced printing costs and made reading easier, compared with publishing in Chinese script.

3 In 1929 several Marxist-Leninist parties emerged, which were unified the following year by Nguyen Ai Quoc (Ho Chi Minh) in the Indochina Communist Party. Later this party split into three

national sections, corresponding to Laos, Cambodia and Vietnam. The last was called the Workers' Party until 1976, when it took the name of Communist Party of Vietnam (CPV).

4 During World War II the communists organized the resistance to the Japanese occupation, collaborating with the Allies. Meanwhile, in 1941, Ho Chi Minh founded the Viet Minh or League for Independence.

5 After the defeat of Japan, the Viet Minh had a powerful

army and enjoyed widespread popular support. August 1945 saw the start of a general insurrection. Two weeks later the revolutionaries, who controlled Hanoi, proclaimed independence for the country and the founding of the Republic. Emperor Bao Dai abdicated and offered his services as adviser to the new regime.

6 The March 1946 agreement with the French (who controlled Cochinchina) recognized the Vietnamese Government and granted the country free state status in the French Union. However France proclaimed Cochinchina an independent republic in June 1946 and united it with the North, proclaiming the Associated State of Vietnam and appointing former emperor Bao Dai head of state. The Viet

Minh waged a nine-year-long guerrilla war and were finally victorious in 1954 with the defeat of French forces at Dien Bien Phu garrison.

7 The 1954 Geneva Agreement stipulated French withdrawal and general elections in Vietnam for 1956. The Viet Minh was to redeploy north of Parallel 17. In the South, the US set up the Ngo Dinh Diem regime in Saigon, and the promised elections did not take place. In 1960, democrats, socialists, nationalists and Marxists united in the National Liberation Front (NLF) (Vietcong), headed by Nguyen Huu Tho, a lawyer. The 'second resistance' was launched, against successive military governments in Saigon and the US, who first sent Saigon arms and advisors, and later troops (580,000 in 1969). A larger tonnage of bombs was dropped than during the whole of World War II, and chemical and bacteriological weapons were experimented with. Ho Chi Minh died in 1969.

8 Over the course of the 15-year-long war, the US spent $150 billion, destroyed 70 per cent of northern villages and left 10 million hectares of land barren. Nevertheless, Saigon was taken by the Vietcong in April 1975 and renamed Ho Chi Minh City. On 2 July 1976 the territory was reunited under the name Socialist Republic of Vietnam.

9 Vietnam did not enjoy long-lasting peace. In January 1979 it was forced to go to war with Pol Pot's Cambodian Government which claimed part of its territory (see History of Cambodia). In the same year, after Vietnamese protege Heng Samrin replaced Pol Pot, China (a staunch ally of the defeated Pol Pot) invaded the North, supposedly to protect the Chinese population from a 'Vietnamization' campaign. New frontier skirmishes in 1980 demonstrated Vietnamese military power, and frontiers remained unaltered.

10 From 1981, President Ronald Reagan blocked a UN assistance program and prevented a US charity from making shipments to Vietnam.

11 After 1985 Hanoi freed several political prisoners and grew closer to ASEAN and the US, becoming more receptive to US requests to search for unidentified war dead and for the children of US soldiers.

12 Le Duan, secretary-general of the CPV since 1969 and a close associate of Ho Chi Minh, died in 1986. Congress appointed former Vietcong strategist Nguyen Van Linh his successor.

LAND USE

2000

IRRIGATED AREA: 40.8% of arable land

- ARABLE LAND: 17.7%
- CROPLANDS: 4.9%
- OTHER USE: 77.4%

PUBLIC EXPENDITURE

% OF GDP

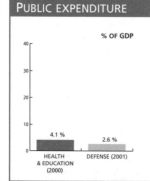

4.1 %	2.6 %
HEALTH & EDUCATION (2000)	DEFENSE (2001)

WORKERS

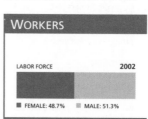

LABOR FORCE — **2002**

- FEMALE: 48.7%
- MALE: 51.3%

Life expectancy
69.2 years
2000-2005

GNI per capita
$430
2002

Literacy
93% total adult rate
2000

HIV prevalence rate
0.3% of population 15-49 years old
2001

[13] Political change in East Europe in the late 1980s led to internal pressure to open up the country politically. As of 1989 dissenting voices within Congress were calling for change towards a multi-party parliamentary system.

[14] In August 1989 Nguyen Van Linh called for a rejection of bourgeois liberalization, political pluralism and non-socialist opposition parties. Even so, non-communist candidates were allowed to run in the 1989 National Assembly elections. In 1990 the Vietnamese Veterans' Association was formed with government authorization. The dominant role of the CPV was reaffirmed, with the arrest of many defenders of political pluralism and the dismissal of 18,000 public employees charged with corruption.

[15] In 1989 the British started deporting the thousands of Vietnamese refugees living in shelters in Hong Kong, until international pressure brought the measure to a halt.

[16] The 1991 CPV Congress reiterated its commitment to socialism, considering it 'the only option'. Secretary-general Van Linh was replaced by Du Muoi who continued the renewal *(Doi Moi)* initiated in 1986.

[17] After the disintegration of the USSR the CPV declared that the one-party system would be maintained, but decided to go ahead with some political and economic changes, including conditional acceptance of private enterprise and foreign investment.

[18] In October 1991 a UN initiative ended the deadlock with Cambodia, with an agreement signed in Paris. This also represented the first step toward the normalization of relations with China, which had been cool following the 1963 break between Beijing and Moscow, and were broken off completely with the overthrow of the Khmer Rouge in Cambodia (who were supported by China).

[19] In November 1991 the British resumed the deportation of 64,000 Vietnamese in Hong Kong camps.

[20] The new April 1992 constitution allowed independent candidates to run for election. Even so, in July, 90 per cent were CPV members. The new president named by the Assembly in September was General Le Duc Anh, an ally of prime minister Vo Van Kiet. In November a delegation of US senators arrived to discuss the issue of more than 2,000 missing POWs.

IN FOCUS

ENVIRONMENTAL CHALLENGES

Slash-and-burn methods in use in agriculture have caused deforestation and soil degradation. Pollution and overfishing threaten marine life. Underground waters are contaminated, limiting availability of drinking water. Growing industrialization and migration to cities damage the environment, principally in Hanoi and Ho Chi Minh City. The most important damage, especially in the North, was originally caused by the war, including the use of chemical defoliants (Agent Orange).

WOMEN'S RIGHTS

Women have been able to vote since 1946. In 1990, women occupied 18 per cent of National Assembly seats and in 2000, 26 per cent.

From 1980 to 2000 female workers represented 49 per cent of the labor force.

According to UNICEF's latest data available*, female primary school enrollment was 92 per cent, compared to a 98 per cent male enrollment rate. Female illiteracy rates dropped steadily from 13 per cent in 1990 to 9 per cent in 2000. In the same period, the male illiteracy rate was around 5 per cent.

Sixty eight per cent of pregnant women received prenatal healthcare, and 70 per cent of births were attended by specialist personnel*.

CHILDREN

According to current UNICEF databases*, mortality rates for children under-five decreased between 1960 and 2002, from 105 to 39 per 1,000 live births. In the case of infants under-one, the rate fell from 70 to 30 per 1,000.

Nine per cent of babies had low birth weights. Thirty three per cent of children under-five were moderately or seriously underweight, and 36 per cent were stunted*. The primary school enrollment rate was 95 per cent*.

In late 2001, 2,500 of the 130,000 people living with AIDS were children, and there were 22,000 AIDS orphans.

From 1999 to 2001, 23 per cent of children aged between 5 and 14 worked.

Children are most seriously at risk from undetonated wartime explosives in the territory (which caused 40,000 deaths over 25 years).

INDIGENOUS PEOPLES/ ETHNIC MINORITIES

The Chinese minority numbers around 500,000 and is relatively well integrated into society although many have been through difficult periods (including significant migration within the country or abroad). After the 1975 unification of the country they had to adapt to the communist regime which hindered their commercial activity, although the situation improved for those in the north, especially peasant farmers near the Chinese border.

The minority which has challenged the Government most has been the original *Montagnard* inhabitants from the highlands in the center of the country. Historically the relationship between the indigenous population and the Government has been violent, in particular since the mid-1960s when the United Front for the Oppressed Minorities' Struggle was founded.

MIGRANTS/REFUGEES

In late 2002 there were an estimated 16,000 refugees from Cambodia, comprising 13,000 members of Vietnamese ethnic groups who arrived in 1993-94, and 3,000 descendants of Chinese.

Nearly 295,000 Vietnamese refugees (the majority of Chinese ethnic origin) were split between 1,000 living in Hong Kong and the remaining 294,000 on the continent. In June 2002 Hong Kong closed down the last remaining refugee camp and granted the 1,000 Vietnamese refugees there permanent resident permits.

Over 100 *Montagnards* fled to Cambodia from Vietnam in 2001 and hope to be resettled; an unknown number of people from Vietnam's more than 1,000 ethnic minorities from the highlands in the center of the country, mainly Christians, are still in hiding on the Cambodian border.

The Cambodian Government repatriated 250 refugees in an attempt to avoid further border-crossing. UNHCR arrived at an agreement with the two Governments to set up a refugee camp in January 2002 in order to repatriate 1,000 people. Neither country complied with the agreement, in spite of which 400 refugees arrived in the settlement, where UNHCR has reported ongoing pressure and mistreatment on the part of the Vietnamese Government, including trials for illegal emigration. This situation led to a further exodus to Cambodia in 2003.

The US took in 2,500 Vietnamese refugees during 2002.

DEATH PENALTY

Capital punishment is still in force.

* Latest data available in *The State of the World's Children* and *Childinfo* database, UNICEF, 2004.

[21] Privatizations and the liberalization of foreign investment led to 8.3 per cent growth in GDP in 1992.

[22] The boom in rice production mostly benefited the South, and emphasized the inequality between the two regions. With over five million inhabitants (almost twice as many as Hanoi), Ho Chi Minh city was the economic capital and seemed to adapt to the new model better than the North. The Government granted long-term loans and lease contracts, tax breaks and the right to inherit up to three hectares of land.

[23] In the mid 1990s a large part of the country was still devastated by napalm or the defoliant 'Agent Orange'. Telecommunications systems, highways and electric power facilities were in the process of recovery, with loans from the World Bank and the Asian Development Bank. Undetonated landmines were a serious problem, particularly in the central region.

[24] In 1995 diplomatic relations were established with the US. President Bill Clinton expressed concern about the 2,000 US citizens still unaccounted for in Southeast Asia.

[25] The 1996 rapprochement between Hanoi and Washington led many transnationals to express their interest in the Vietnamese market once the liberalization of the economy was consolidated.

[26] In September 1997 Tran Duc Luong was elected president, and Phan Van Khai prime minister. In December three CPV leaders were replaced, former president Le Duc

Under-5 mortality
39 per 1,000 live births
2002

Poverty
17.7% of population living on less than $1 per day
1998

Debt service
6.7% exports of goods and services
2001

Maternal mortality
130 per 100,000 live births
2000

Anh, former prime minister Vo Van Kiet and veteran leader Du Muoi, whose position as secretary-general was taken over by Le Kha Phieu.

[27] In April 1998 drought destroyed 7,000 of 260,000 hectares of coffee plantations, from which produce had been exported to Europe and the US since 1980.

[28] The 1998 regional crisis caused a relatively modest drop in growth, from 8.8 per cent in 1997 to 6.1 per cent, but in order to maintain export competitiveness two currency devaluations were deemed necessary. Foreign direct investment fell 70 per cent. In September the country became a full member of Asia-Pacific Economic Cooperation (APEC).

[29] A typhoon and exceptionally heavy rains in 1998, followed by floods in 1999, affected the country's economy. Environmental organizations also pointed out that matters had been aggravated by the indiscriminate felling of forests. Prime Minister Khai pointed out that the crisis had been influenced by low consumer demand, growing production stocks and the inefficiency of State enterprises.

[30] A land-frontier agreement with China was signed in December 1998, after an eight-year negotiation process. The settling of sea-borders was left for later talks.

[31] Corruption was recognized as a national problem in 1998 and identified as a by-product of economic liberalization. In January three Tamexco employees with close CPV ties were executed for corruption, including former director Pham Huy Phuoc. In 1999 the CPV demanded the resignation of deputy prime minister Ngo Xuan Loc (who returned to the cabinet five months later) and punishment of former Central Bank governor Cao Sy Kiem for misappropriation of funds.

[32] The CPV politburo acknowledged in 2000 that relatives of its own members were involved in corruption and that this was commonplace throughout party ranks. It became compulsory for leaders to declare their wealth and an autonomous monitoring body was set up to gather complaints. This body reported judicial lack of independence, lack of information about legislation in force and the need for an independent parliament, with a true voice in politics.

[33] In April 2001 reformer Nong Duc Manh (former National

PROFILE

ENVIRONMENT

A long narrow country covering the eastern portion of Indochina along the Gulf of Tonkin and the South China Sea. The monsoon-influenced climate is hot and rainy. Rainforests predominate and there is a well-supplied river system. The northern region is comparatively higher. There are two river deltas: the Song Koi in the north, and the Mekong in the south. Most of the people are farmers, and rice is the main crop. The north is rich in anthracite, lignite, coal, iron ore, manganese, bauxite and titanium. Textile manufacture, food products and mining are the major economic activities. The felling of trees for domestic use (firewood) and construction have contributed to deforestation. However, the most significant losses - particularly in the northern part of the country - are a result of the Vietnam War, specifically from the use of such chemical defoliants as 'Agent Orange'. Vietnamese Government policy - started after 1975 and reaching its peak in the mid-1980s - that moved millions of former North Vietnamese to what was thought to be the relatively underpopulated central highlands took a heavy toll on the environment, including widespread deforestation.

SOCIETY

People: Vietnamese make up most of the population. The remainder is made up of mountain people, consisting of several ethnic groups - Tho, Hoa, Tai, Khemer, Muong, Nung - and descendants of Chinese.

Religions: Mainly Buddhist; traditional religions. There are some 2 million Catholics and 3 million followers of the Hoa-Hao and Cao-Dai sects.

Languages: Vietnamese (official) and languages of the ethnic minorities.

Main Political Parties: The Communist Party of Vietnam (DCSV - Dang Cong San Vietnam), Democratic and Socialist Parties of Vietnam, Coalition of Vietnamese National Parties, Nationalist Party.

Main Social Organizations: The Federation of Unions of Vietnam (Tong Cong Doan Vietnam), founded in 1946, is the only union confederation and a WFTU member; the Vietnamese Women's Union, founded in 1930.

THE STATE

Official Name: Công hòa xã hôi chu' nghî'a Viêt Nam.

Administrative Divisions: 39 Provinces, including the urban areas of Hanoi, Haiphong and Ho Chi Minh City.

Capital: Hanoi 3,977,000 people (2003).

Other Cities: Ho Chi Minh City (formerly Saigon) 5,566,900 people; Haiphong 1,763,300; Da-Nang 762,800 (2000).

Government: Tran Duc Luong, President and head of state since September 1997, re-elected in 2002. Phan Van Khai, Prime Minister and head of government since September 1997. Nong Duc Manh, secretary-general of the Communist Party since April 2001. Unicameral Legislature: National Assembly with 498 members. Executive power is exercised by a council of ministers.

National Holiday: 2 September, Independence Day (1945).

Armed Forces: 572,000 troops (1995). Other: 5,000,000 (Urban Defense Units, Rural Defense Units).

Assembly president) was appointed CPV secretary-general.

[34] During his official visit in November 2000, President Clinton promised more US assistance in clearing the territory of undetonated explosives. In June 2001 Tran Duc Luong signed an agreement with the US in Hanoi during a donors' meeting.

[35] In April 2002, 59 people faced charges of bank fraud for $100 million in Ho Chi Minh City, involving hundreds of individuals and organizations. The trial was regarded by Transparency International as part of the

Government's effort to change the situation in a country ranked among the most corrupt on the planet.

[36] In May 2002 the Russians gave up their naval base in Cam Ranh Bay, which had been the biggest Soviet facility outside the Warsaw Pact.

[37] President Tran Duc Luong was re-elected by the Assembly for a second term in July 2002. This meant a second term for Prime Minister Phan Van Khai, too.

[38] Six organized crime bosses from Ho Chi Minh city were

sentenced to death in June 2003, including *capo* Nam Can, and government officials were sentenced to long prison terms.

[39] In November, for the first time since the war, a US vessel entered Vietnamese waters near Ho Chi Minh City.

[40] In January 2004, the reemergence and expansion in Vietnam (and Thailand) of a pandemic disease called 'chicken flu', a subtype of the flu virus that first infected humans in Hong Kong, in 1997, put the government's health system on the alert.

[41] In March, weeks after Hanoi had declared the eradication of the disease, the Vietnamese Ministry of Agriculture, reported the detection of the virus in various chickens of a farm located in southern Vietnam. That same month, the virus death toll hit 16. Both WHO and FAO would have warned Hanoi about not reopening poultry farms and not declaring itself free of disease too soon.

[42] In July, the UN refugee agency, UNHCR, found more than 40 Montagnards (Christian minority group) hiding in the jungle in Cambodia. Human rights groups claimed there was a large number of Montagnards still living secretly in the province of Ratanakiri, located in northeast Cambodia. The Cambodian Government declared the Montagnards to be illegal migrants and refused to provide humanitarian assistance. Under pressure from Cambodian King Norodom Sihanouk, diplomats, human rights groups and the UNHCR, the latter was allowed to reopen its office in the city of Banlung (capital of Ratanakiri), in order to aid Montagnard people.

[43] According to the UNHCR, several Montagnards were ill and exhausted after having lived hiding in the trees, suffering shortage of food, water and clothes. According to Pen Bunna, official of the Cambodian Human Rights and Development Association (ADHOC), Montagnard people survived by eating tree leaves and wild mushrooms. Those who were found in the worst conditions were sent to Phnom Penh in order to receive medical treatment.

[44] The Montagnards have been persecuted by the Vietnamese Government due to their collaboration with the US during the war for nearly 30 years. Their situation got worse since April 2004, after peaceful demonstrations in which they demanded land and religious rights. ∎

Virgin Islands (US) / Virgin Islands

Population:	113,466
Area:	340 km²
Capital:	Charlotte Amalie
Currency:	US dollar
Language:	English

As is the case in other Caribbean islands, the Virgin Islands were originally inhabited by Carib and Arawak indians. The only gold on the islands was seen in the ornaments worn by the inhabitants and was of little economic interest. From the time of Columbus' arrival in 1493 onwards, the local population was persecuted and massacred, and was destroyed by the second half of the 16th century.

2 The western part of the archipelago was claimed by other countries after the departure of the Spaniards. The Netherlands gained control in the 18th century and organized crop cultivation; first of sugar cane and then of cotton. They imported African slave workers as in many other parts of Latin America and the Caribbean. At the height of Dutch colonization, there were 40,000 African slaves on the islands.

3 During Abraham Lincoln's second presidential term, the United States failed to acquire the islands. But in 1917, after World War I when the US wanted to consolidate its presence in the area, $25 million was paid to the Dutch for the islands and the 26,000 former African slaves who inhabited them.

4 From that time on, the US initiated a series of changes in the territorial administration, ranging from the continuation of the legislation established by the Dutch, to the new law approved in 1969. This instituted the election of a Governor and Vice-Governor, the election of a non-voting Congressional delegate and the right of its inhabitants to vote in American elections. In a 1981 referendum, a proposed Constitution was voted against by 50 per cent of the registered voters. In December 1984, the UN General Assembly reiterated the right of the islands to self-determination, and urged the local population to exercise their right to independence.

5 The local economy depended on the US. It largely revolved around an oil refinery owned by US-Amaranda Hess Corporation on the island of St Croix. The refinery is the largest of its kind in the world and produces over 700,000 barrels a day. The company's influence on local politics was very important, as it had 1,300 permanent and 1,700 temporary employees and supplied all the islands' energy needs. In spite of this, tourism was still the island's main source of income.

6 A referendum scheduled for November 1989 was to decide the future status of the islands. However, it was not held because in September 1989 the islands were severely damaged by Hurricane Hugo. According to official estimates, 80 per cent of the buildings were destroyed. The disaster caused an outbreak of looting and unrest. Armed bands wandered the streets; some members of the police and National Guard also took part in the pillaging. The US sent more than 1,000 troops to the area, but the disturbances had virtually ceased by the time they arrived. In the words of local people, there was nothing left to steal.

7 The US Government declared the islands a disaster area and granted $500 million in humanitarian aid. However, damages were estimated at $1 billion. The island's reconstruction temporarily revitalized the labor market, particularly in construction jobs.

8 An aluminum oxide plant, which had been closed in 1985, was purchased in 1989 by an international group trading in raw materials. The plant has a capacity for an annual production of 700,000 metric tons. Shipments to the US and Europe began in 1990.

9 Alexander A Farrelly, who had governed the islands since 1987, quit his post in 1995 and was replaced by Roy L Schneider. In the following elections, in November 1998 Charles Turnbull won with 58.9 per cent of the vote, while Schneider took the remaining 41.1 per cent. In elections for the senate, Turnbull's Democrat Party took 6 seats while the Republicans kept 2 and the pro-region Independent Citizens' Movement took one seat. The independents drew even with the Democrats, holding six seats.

10 Hurricane Lenny lashed the islands in November 1999 causing four deaths in St Croix and serious damage to buildings and roads.

11 Fourteen counts of embezzlement, fraud and falsifying documents against former Governor Schneider and three top officials of his administration were dismissed by Judge Ive Swan in March 2000.

12 The US Virgin Islands are among the 16 territories of the world that still remain colonies. In May 2004, the UN launched a campaign of reaffirmation of the principle of equality of rights and self-determination of peoples. However, neither the US Virgin Islands nor the British ones, have expressed the desire to become independent, particularly fearing a breakdown of the lucrative tourist industry and a rise of taxes, since any products or raw materials from the islands are admitted tax-free into the US. ■

LAND USE

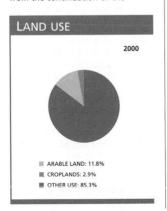

2000

- ARABLE LAND: 11.8%
- CROPLANDS: 2.9%
- OTHER USE: 85.3%

PROFILE

ENVIRONMENT
The western part of the Virgin Islands group, east of Puerto Rico, the territory includes three main islands - St Thomas, St John and St Croix - and approximately 50 uninhabited small islands. The mountainous terrain is of volcanic origin. The climate is tropical, but irregular rainfall makes farming difficult. A small amount of fruit and vegetables are grown in St Croix and St Thomas. Tourism is an important economic activity. There is a large oil refinery in St Croix, supplying the US market.

SOCIETY
Peoples: Most of the population is English-speaking and of African origin with a small Spanish-speaking Puerto Rican minority. 35 to 40 per cent of the inhabitants are from other Caribbean islands; 10 per cent from the US.
Religions: Protestant and Catholic.
Languages: English, official; also Spanish and Creole.

Main Political Parties: There are local representatives of the US Republican and Democrat parties and an Independent Citizens Movement (ICM).

THE STATE
Official Name: Virgin Islands of the United States.
Capital: Charlotte Amalie 51,000 people (2003).
Other Cities: Anna's Retreat 13,500 people; Charlotte Amalie West 8,000 (2000).
Government: Charles Turnbull, Governor since January 1999. The unicameral legislature is made up of 15 representatives (7 from St Thomas, 7 from St Croix and 1 from St John).
National Holiday: 27 March , Transfer Day (from The Netherlands to the US, 1917).
Armed Forces: The US is responsible for the defense of the islands. The naval bases have been under local jurisdiction since 1967, but the US retains the right to occupy them at any time, as well as to recruit local residents for US armed forces.

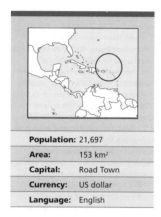

Population:	21,697
Area:	153 km²
Capital:	Road Town
Currency:	US dollar
Language:	English

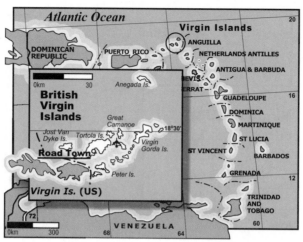

The Virgin Islands, were named by Christopher Columbus in 1493 in honour of St Ursula. At that time the islands were inhabited by Caribs and Arawaks, but by the mid-16th century they had all been exterminated by the Europeans.

[2] In the 18th century, the British gained control of the easternmost islands of the archipelago and, using African slave labor, they began cultivating sugarcane, indigo and cotton. By the mid-18th century, the islands' slave population had reached 7,000, outnumbering the European colonists 6 to 1. Slavery was eventually abolished there in the 1830s.

[3] In 1872 the islands joined the British colony of the Leeward Islands, which was administered under a federal system. This federation was dissolved in July 1956, but the Governor of the Leeward Islands continued to be responsible for the administration of the Virgin Islands until 1960. In that year direct control over the islands passed into the hands of an administrator designated by the British Crown. The British Virgin Islands did not belong to the East Indies Federation, which existed between 1958 and 1962, preferring to develop links with the American Virgin Islands, under US control.

[4] The colony was governed under several constitutions during the 20th century. The ministerial form of government began in 1967 with the first open elections. In 1977 the Constitution was modified, granting greater autonomy and carrying out changes in the electoral system. Responsibility for defense, internal security and foreign affairs remained in the hands of the British-appointed governor.

[5] In the 1980s tourism accounted for 45 per cent of the national income, while fishing was the traditional economic activity. Gravel and sand were important exports, and a 'tax-haven' banking facility was established.

[6] In August 1986, the British Government dissolved the Legislative Council, calling a new election several days after the opposition presented a vote of no confidence in the Chief Minister Cyril Romney. In September the Virgin Islands Party (VIP) won 5 of the 9 seats and the United Party (UP) won 2. Lavity Stott, the VIP leader, was named Chief Minister.

[7] In March 1988, Chief Minister Omar Hodge resigned over accusations of corruption, and was replaced by Ralph O'Neal. Hodge denied the charges against him. In March 1989 Hodge created a new party, the Independent People's Movement (IPM). In early 1990 he was cleared of the charges against him.

[8] In the November elections, the VIP increased its majority to 6 seats, while the IPM obtained 1 seat, and the independents 2. Stoutt maintained his post as chief minister, and O'Neal was re-elected Chief Minister.

[9] Due to the increase in drug trafficking, and following recommendations by the British Government, legislation was introduced to control the operations of international financial companies. These would need a license to operate on the islands and their activities would be subject to periodic inspections, as the authorities believed most of the investments were coming from the drug trade.

[10] In October 1991, Peter Alfred Penfold was named Governor.

[11] In the legislative elections of February 1995, the VIP took 6 seats, the IPM 3, the Concerned Citizens' Movement (CCM) took 2, as did the UP. On May 15 1995, following the death of H Lavity Stoutt, Ralph O'Neal took over as Chief Minister. In June 1995, David Mackilligin was appointed Governor.

[12] In July 1997, the Government approved a three-year development plan, which included a $2 million plan to extend the port and the construction of two tourist centers.

[13] The British Crown appointed Frank Savage Governor in 1998, and in the May 1999 elections the VIP took 8 seats with 38 per cent of the vote. The National Democratic Party took 5 with 36.9 per cent of the vote, while the remainder of the vote went to the CCM (4 per cent). Independent candidates took 13.4 per cent of the vote, but none had enough support to win a seat on the Legislative Council.

[14] The Government started road works and other infrastructural projects on the outer islands. In December 2001 Chief Minister Ralph T O'Neal presented the 2002 budget and underscored the importance of these infrastructural works for developing tourism in Virgin Gorda, Anegada and Jost Van Dyke.

[15] In May 2004, a new agency was launched in order to fight money laundering in the islands. Chief Minister Orlando Smith stated that the Financial Investigation Agency strengthened its administration with the strong purpose of upholding honesty and transparency in business. ∎

PROFILE

ENVIRONMENT

The eastern portion of the Virgin Islands comprises 36 islands and reefs, 16 of which are inhabited. The larger ones are Tortola, Anegada, Virgin Gorda and Jost Van Dyke, which are home to most of the population. The islands' rolling terrain is of volcanic origin. Agricultural production is limited to fruit and vegetables as a result of erratic rainfall. The major economic activities are fishing and tourism. The coral reefs are threatened by tourist activities.

SOCIETY

Peoples: Most are descendants of African slaves. There is also a small British minority. 86 per cent of the population are concentrated on Tortola Island, 9 per cent live on Virgin Gorda, 3 per cent on Anegada and 2 per cent on Jost Van Dyke.
Religions: Mainly Protestant (45 per cent Methodist, 21 per cent Anglican, 7 per cent Church of God, 5 per cent Seventh-Day Adventists, 4 per cent Baptist, 2 per cent Jehovah's Witnesses, 2 per cent other Protestant); 6 per cent Roman Catholic; 6 per cent other religions (1981).
Languages: English (official).
Main Political Parties: The Virgin Islands Party (VIP), led by Ralph T O'Neal; National Democratic Party; the United Party (UP); the Concerned Citizens' Movement (CCM).

THE STATE

Official Name: British Virgin Islands.
Capital: Road Town 12,000 people (2003).
Other Cities: East End-Long Look 4,900 people (2000).
Government: Frank Savage, British-appointed Governor since 1998. Ralph O'Neal is the Chief Minister, re-elected in 1999. There is a Legislative Council of 9 elected and 4 appointed members.
National Holiday: 1 July, Territory Day.
Armed Forces: Defense is the responsibility of the United Kingdom.

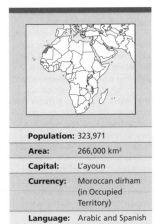

Population:	323,971
Area:	266,000 km²
Capital:	L'ayoun
Currency:	Moroccan dirham (in Occupied Territory)
Language:	Arabic and Spanish

From the 5th century, the far west of the Sahara has been populated by Moors, Tuaregs and Tubus, resulting from migratory flows prompted by desertification, which has affected the region since the Neolithic Era. Their presence is documented by the Tassili stone carvings and other relics. In the 9th century, waves of migrants arrived from Yemen and intermarried with the local population. Four hundred years on, the first confederation of Saharawi peoples appeared.

2   The arrival of the Spanish on this coast had a strategic motive: the defense of the eastern coast of the Canary Islands. Colonization was mostly limited to Villa Cisneros (present-day Dakhla) until 1886, when, as a result of the Berlin Conference (see box in Congo Republic), Madrid resolved not to let an 'empty space' fall to another power. However, after an agreement with France was reached in 1904, establishing the borders of Spanish Sahara, the situation returned to what it had been. Colonialism divided the territory into four countries, where the nomadic ethnic groups continued to live completely independently, ignoring the frontiers imposed.

3   In 1895, Sheikh Ma al-Aini founded the Smara citadel and fought the Franco-Spanish presence with the support of the Sultan of Morocco until 1910, when the latter gave in to European pressure and suspended assistance to the rebels, who expanded their actions into Morocco and even threatened Marrakech. The French counter-attack consisted of an invasion of 'Spanish' territory and the conquest of Smara in 1913, though resistance continued until 1920.

4   The French pressed Spain to increase its control over the territory, and in 1932 L'ayoun was founded. In 1933, the victory of the forces under Mohammed al Mamun, cousin to Ma al-Aini and Emir of Adrad, forced a change in colonialist tactics. France occupied the rebel base at Tindouf oasis and advanced into Algeria, Mauritania and Morocco, while Spanish troops took Smara, overcoming the insurgents in 1934.

5   When the French deposed Sultan Mohammed V, the National Liberation Army (ALN) was created in Morocco, and its Southern Division operated in close cooperation with the Saharawi people. Following Morocco's independence in 1956, and the dissolution of the ALN, the Saharawis were left to face Spain and the French air force on their own, leading to a withdrawal of resistance in 1958.

6   At that time, phosphate exploitation began at Boucraa, where ten billion tons of what is considered to be the best quality phosphate in the world had been discovered. Transnational capital,

with the consent of Spain's fascist Franco regime, invested more than $160 million, transforming the country, particularly its population distribution. In 1959, L'ayoun had 6,000 residents, but had reached 28,000 by 1974, while the nomadic population dropped from 90 per cent to 16 per cent of the country's total in that same period.

7   With the decline of the traditional nomadic way of life, ties and relationships began to weaken, though the colonial administration maintained latent divisions through political recognition of the *shiuj* (clan chiefs) and notables of the different groups and also specified in the national identity document which people or faction the holder belonged to. However, a new national identity slowly developed, transcending traditional divisions.

8   The Saharawis founded the Al Muslim movement in 1967, and the Sahara Liberation Front a year later. In 1973, the revolutionary leadership decided to pursue armed struggle, creating the Polisario Front (the Popular Front for the Liberation of Saguia al Hamra and Rio de Oro), which was led by Elwali Mustafa Sayed until he died in combat. The war and the resolutions of the UN,

IN FOCUS

ENVIRONMENTAL CHALLENGES

Heat and drought are problems inherent to the zone, causing a scarcity of arable land. The sirocco blows during the fall and winter; this dry Sahara wind blows towards the coast of Western Africa between November and March, causing frequent fogs, severely restricting visibility. The opportunity presented by the recent discovery of oil has been grasped by Morocco, which has started to exploit this resource, as it does fishing and phosphates.

WOMEN'S RIGHTS

Saharawi women in the occupied territories are subjected to torture and rape. The health of women in the refugee settlements in Algeria is threatened by the scarcity of food. Women's role in society has been transformed by life in refugee exile. Most men are required to serve in the Polisario resistance army, leaving women to take primary responsibility for running the refugee 'towns' outside Tindouf. Women traditionally received no education in Saharawi society or Spanish colonial schools but the younger generation are among the most literate, educated girls and women in the Muslim world. Many visit or study in foreign

countries. There are, as yet, very few women in positions of political power but this is changing as the more educated generation gains more influence. Women do not wear a veil but are expected to wear some hair-covering.

INDIGENOUS PEOPLES/ ETHNIC MINORITIES

The Saharawis are one of the nomadic tribes descending from African slaves, Arab Bedouins and Berbers from Sanhanja. They are mainly Sunni Muslims, and speak Hassania, one of the purest forms of the Arabic language. Ethnic status is an explosive political issue in Western Sahara. In occupied Western Sahara the Saharawi face both discrimination and severe repression from the Moroccan authorities. Moroccans have for three decades been offered financial inducements by their Government to settle in Western Sahara so as to entrench colonial control - and to confound the workings of a referendum on self-determination which was originally only supposed to include Saharawis resident at the time of the 1975 invasion. Recently Saharawi leaders have reluctantly accepted a new UN plan which would allow Moroccan settlers to vote - but Morocco continues to block the referendum regardless.

MIGRANTS/REFUGEES

The Saharawi refugee settlements in the bleak desert region of Tindouf - named after the main cities of their occupied land - are unique in that they are controlled by their own government rather than by an international agency or the host country. Algeria effectively cedes autonomy over the area to the Saharawi Arab Democratic Republic, a fellow founding member of the African Union. Organization of the camps is efficient and both education and health services have been prioritized. But the near 200,000 refugees that live here are entirely dependent on international food aid and the quantity and quality of this have recently been reduced. As a result, 35 per cent of children suffer from chronic malnutrition, and 13 per cent from acute malnutrition. There is a high rate of stunted growth and life expectancy is 45 years for women and 47 years for men.

DEATH PENALTY

Saharawis may face the death penalty under Moroccan rule in the occupied territories but not in the areas governed by the Saharawi Arab Democratic Republic.

which favored the independence movement, prompted the Franco Government to prepare to withdraw from the colony, recognizing the right of self-determination and organizing a census prior to a referendum. The census showed that there were 73,497 Saharawis living in the territory.

[9] In 1974, the World Bank classified Western Sahara as potentially the richest territory in the Maghreb region for its extensive fisheries and phosphate reserves.

[10] With one eye on the fishing and phosphate reserves and the other on the advantage of unifying his troubled nation around an external cause, King Hassan II of Morocco claimed sovereignty over Western Sahara. The International Court of Justice at The Hague overruled its claims and ordered decolonization. King Hassan responded by organizing what was dubbed the 'Green March', a propaganda move that mobilized 350,000 Moroccans to head south, crossing the border, to press for a reversal of The Hague ruling. Within days these were replaced by Moroccan soldiers. As General Franco lay on his deathbed, Spain signed a secret agreement which handed over the territory to Morocco and Mauritania.

[11] Tens of thousands of ordinary Saharawis fled into the desert from the invading Moroccan forces, setting up their own makeshift refugee camps. Many, like the 25,000 who gathered at Guelta Zemmour, were determined to stay on Western Saharan territory but were repeatedly bombed by Moroccan planes using napalm. In the face of this onslaught the refugees had to walk hundreds of kilometers across the desert to the Algerian town of Tindouf. There the Algerian Government ceded effective control over a swathe of its own territory to Polisario, which built and administered its own refugee settlements.

[12] On 27 February 1976 the Saharawi proclaimed the Saharawi Arab Democratic Republic (SADR). The new African republic was born in Bir Lahlu, a desert post in Saguia El Hamra, a few kilometers from the Mauritanian border. Just hours earlier, in L'ayoun, the last representative of the colonial administration had officially announced the end of the Spanish presence.

[13] Several countries recognized the new nation, but it triggered a war against Morocco and Mauritania. In 1979, Mauritania, on the verge of collapse, decided to halt fighting and sign a peace treaty with the Polisario Front. Hassan's troops, however, stepped up attacks with French and US support.

[14] The Polisario Front's military victories led to a diplomatic success in July 1980 at the conference of the Organization of African Unity (OAU) in Freetown, where 26 African countries announced official recognition of the SADR as the legitimate state of the Saharawi people. Four months later the UN issued a resolution requesting Morocco's withdrawal. In 1981 Morocco began the construction of a defensive sand wall - known as a *berm* - dividing occupied Western Sahara from the liberated zones. Eventually the *berm* ran the length of the country and was over 1,500 kilometers long (longer than the Great Wall of China); it was guarded by 120,000 soldiers and two million mines.

[15] The SADR was accepted in November 1984 as a full member of the OAU. Morocco withdrew from the organization, as it had announced it would. On 14 November 1985 the UN Decolonization Committee recognized the Saharawi people's right to self-determination.

[16] In August 1988, Moroccans and Saharawis agreed on a peace plan presented by the UN and the OAU, which included a ceasefire and a referendum on self-determination.

[17] In July 1990, representatives from Morocco and the Polisario Front debated in Geneva a procedural code for holding a referendum to allow the Saharawis to decide their own future. The greatest challenge was how to define who could vote. The most recent census of the Saharan population dated to 1974, and Morocco wanted its people in the occupied zone to be authorized to vote.

[18] On 29 April 1991, the UN approved the establishment of MINURSO (United Nations Mission for the Referendum in Western Sahara) and established 6 September of the same year as the date for the ceasefire to come into force and 26 January 1992 for the referendum.

[19] The parties also agreed on an end to hostilities for the referendum, the gradual reduction of Moroccan troops in the territory - estimated at 160,000 - to 25,000, and the withdrawal of the remaining forces 24 hours after the announcement of

Western Sahara: Norway nets big fisheries deal

Norwegian companies are trying to get a slice of the growing fisheries industry in Moroccan-occupied Western Sahara. Backed by Norwegian capital and know-how, they are investing in the industry and thereby reinforcing Morocco's position in occupation, despite protests by the Sahrawis.

The continental platform of Western Sahara is one of the richest fishing grounds in the world. It comprises an area of more than 150,000 sq km with a great diversity of species. There are 200 varieties of fish, 60 types of mollusk and several species of cephalopods and crustaceans. This marine wealth allowed Morocco to develop an export trade without putting in large amounts of capital or investment in the occupied territory - which could have had beneficial spin-offs for Western Sahara's economy.

RICH TRAWL
In July 2004, the Norwegian Ambassador in Morocco, Arne Aasheim, visited L'ayoun, the capital of Western Sahara. During his visit, he had meetings with the Moroccan authorities and representatives of the fishing industry. According to reports, the main aim of these meetings was to work out how Norwegian companies could boost their involvement in the booming Moroccan fisheries.

Norway is a major player in all aspects of the industry, including ship-building, fishing technology, processing and distribution. Morocco, on the other hand, has only recently identified it as one of its most promising sectors for economic development. Since 2001, it has invested approximately 150 million euros in its fisheries. And of course the focus of this burgeoning business is the rich marine resources off the coast of Western Sahara. However, the revenues are being used to strengthen Morocco's grip on the territory rather than being channeled into development for the Sahrawi people and their land. In the same way, virtually the entire fisheries workforce in Western Sahara is of Moroccan origin, and the growth in the industry means that more and more Moroccans settle there.

According to research by Norway-based fishing news service IntraFish, in 2002 the Norwegian Government has been giving financial support to its exporters to help them penetrate the Moroccan market. At least 4 million euros were made available to finance Norwegian technology and infrastructure for the fisheries sector.

SHOCKED SAHRAWIS
The news about Norwegian investments in Western Sahara came as a shock to the Saharawi government-in-exile, the Polisario Front. Polisario considers any transaction between the occupying power (Morocco) and any other entity or government as illegal under international law. They condemn any action that reinforces the Moroccan occupation of their land.

For them and the Saharawi people, Norway's action was particularly offensive as the country is known for its defense of human rights and the right of self-determination.

The Norwegian authorities refused both to issue a statement, and to provide any information about the negotiations. For Polisario, the UN's legal opinion on oil exploration in Western Sahara, announced in 2001, was critical to this case. The UN had ruled that Morocco had no right to act on behalf of Western Sahara and market its resources. But, as has been so often the case, the occupying power has carried on regardless - now with Norway's help. ∎

the referendum results. The Polisario Front, meanwhile, would withdraw its forces to an area near Tindouf, in Algeria.

[20] In the following months, the Moroccan Government settled thousands of Moroccan citizens in Saharawi territory to make them eligible voters, repeatedly violated the ceasefire, stepped up repression against the Saharawis and obstructed the work of international journalists.

[21] MINURSO was entrusted with drawing up the electoral roster based on the 1974 census. This implied that an undetermined number of Saharawis could not vote in the referendum, but nor could the Moroccans who immigrated after 1976. The Saharawis of voting age who were living in refugee camps in Algeria would be transported back to their towns of origin.

[22] By January 1992, when the referendum was slated to take place, MINURSO was far from completing its program for identifying voters and the Saharawi repatriation plan could not be finalized. Meanwhile, 60,000 Moroccan soldiers remained in Western Sahara. In the ensuing years Morocco continued to obstruct moves towards the referendum. Brahim Hakim, member of the Polisario Front's directorate, ended his exile in Algeria and returned to Morocco. Hakim stated that armed struggle had become futile and ordered his followers to lay down their weapons. In recent years, a growing number of rebels had distanced themselves from the Front as military defeats continued.

[23] The refugee settlements near Tindouf were, by the early 1990s, well established and efficiently run by Polisario, though entirely dependent on international food aid due to the barrenness of this part of the desert. Most families by now had built houses of mud brick alongside their traditional nomadic tents. Saharawis have made education a priority, with many of its young people studying in the universities of friendly nations such as Algeria, Libya and Cuba. Schoolchildren from the camps are hosted every year by solidarity groups in western Europe to give them a sense of the world beyond the desert.

[24] In March 1997 UN Secretary-General Kofi Annan appointed former US Secretary of State James Baker as his personal envoy to Western Sahara, entrusting him with relaunching the peace process. Morocco and the Polisario Front agreed on 16 September 1997 to reactivate the peace plan for Western Sahara, exchange prisoners and release political prisoners. The referendum date was set for 7 December 1998.

[25] Under the UN plan, Morocco and the Polisario Front agreed to accept that if Morocco won, the UN would disarm the Saharawi combatants, while if the Polisario Front won, it would supervise the withdrawal of Moroccan troops and administration from Western Sahara. The resettlement of the 200,000 Saharawis exiled since the 1970s, mostly in Tindouf, was a matter left pending. Not keen on a referendum that seemed likely to deliver a Saharawi victory, Morocco successfully sought to bog down the procedures for voter registration and stall the referendum indefinitely.

[26] The death of King Hassan II of Morocco in July 1999 and accession of his son, Muhammad VI, fostered hopes of political changes in the country. The monarch's first messages showed signs of greater openness on Western Sahara, and some political prisoners were released.

[27] The UN Security Council again suspended the referendum scheduled for July 2000. Morocco expressed its intention of negotiating with the Polisario Front to grant it a certain degree of autonomy, but closed the door to the referendum.

[28] Having previously seemed to be firmly in favour of a referendum on self-determination, James Baker and the UN started to put pressure on the Saharawis to accept some form of autonomy within Morocco. In 2001, following the failure of several attempts at negotiation in London and Berlin, the Polisario Front rejected the Framework Agreement for the Sahara Statute, known as the Baker Plan, which granted a certain degree of autonomy to the zone, but under Moroccan sovereignty. The referendum had already been postponed 12 times.

[29] In October 2001, King Muhammad VI made his first trip to the Western Sahara region since coming to the throne. This trip coincided with an agreement between Morocco and French and US oil companies to explore along the Sahara coast. President Muhammad Abdelaziz of the SADR described this trip - which coincided with a new anniversary of the Green March - as a provocation and announced the peace process would deteriorate.

[30] French President Chirac, visiting Morocco, declared that the disputed territory was part of that country. Chirac's words were the first of a major power in support of Morocco's claims and against UN resolutions.

[31] In February 2002 Algeria rejected the Baker Plan and proposed that the UN should administrate Western Sahara. Kofi Annan proposed four options to solve the conflict: continue with the Arrangement Plan which included the self-determination referendum; continue with the Framework Agreement, with slight changes; start negotiations for the participation of the territory; and the withdrawal of MINURSO, meaning that the peace plan - which had already cost 560 million Euros and 11 years of sterile efforts - had failed.

[32] Over the past few years, substantial natural gas and oil reserves have been found, covering a territory of some 210,000 square kilometers off the Saharawi coast. Morocco has made a deal with the French trans national company, Total Fina Elf and the US company Kerr-McGee for extraction, despite the fact that the UN may take reprisals as, theoretically, Rabat does not have administrative power over the Western Sahara. The Saharawis accuse Morocco of signing these deals to get powers with authority in the UN Security Council involved and thus legitimate their invasion. For its part, in 2002 the SADR signed a treaty with the Anglo-Australian company Fusion Oil to assess the potential oil reserves.

[33] In January 2003, Baker submitted a new plan which foresees the Saharawi territory becoming, by means of autonomous elections, an autonomous region of Morocco for at least four years. Morocco would retain sovereignty over the region, while the Saharawi would manage their own domestic affairs and local institutions. Following this period, a referendum for self-determination would be held, in 2007 or 2008, in which the Saharawis included in the Spanish census of 1974 and the settlers arriving with the 'Green March'

(some 150,000), would participate to decide on independence or integration. The Polisario Front accepted the proposal - a major concession - and freed 243 Moroccan prisoners. Morocco refused to consider it.

[34] On 30 January 2004, coinciding with the 30th anniversary of the Polisario Front, the UN extended MINURSO's mission in the Sahara until 30 April.

[35] Early in 2004 the UNHCR established a phone connection between the refugee settlements in Algeria and the occupied capital of L'ayoun. This was followed, on 5 March, by the first in a long-awaited programme of family exchanges between Saharawis in the refugee camps and the occupied territories: 21 Saharawis, from 9 families, flew from Tindouf to L'ayoun while a similar number travelled in the opposite direction. The exchanges continued to happen on a weekly basis during 2004, with priority given to acute cases where a close relative is seriously ill. The UN soon hopes to institute a regular mail service.

[36] In June, James Baker announced his resignation, frustrated at Morocco's refusal to take the latest referendum plan seriously, despite Polisario's concessions.

[37] In September South Africa announced that it was formally recognizing the Saharawi Arab Democratic Republic. The announcement was a major coup for Polisario and a severe blow to Morocco, which withdrew its ambassador from Pretoria in protest. ∎

PROFILE

ENVIRONMENT
The country is almost completely desert and is divided into two regions: Saguia el Hamra in the north and Río de Oro in the south. It has one of the world's largest fishing reserves, but the principal source of wealth is mining, especially phosphate deposits.

SOCIETY
Peoples: The Polisario Front estimates the dispersed Saharawi population at one million. These are traditionally nomadic groups that differ from the Tuaregs and Berbers in their social and cultural organization. **Religion:** Islam. **Languages:** Arabic and Spanish (official). Many Saharawis also speak Hassania.
Main Political Parties: The People's Liberation Front of Saguia al-Hamra and Rio de Oro (Polisario Front) founded on 10 May 1973 by Elwali Mustafa Sayed. **Main Social Organizations:** The Saguia al-Hamra and Rio de Oro General Workers' Union (UGTSARIO).

THE STATE
Official Name: Saharawi Arab Democratic Republic.
Capital: L'ayoun (Layoune) 187,000 people (2003).
Other Cities: Dakhla 40,200 people; Smara 36,100; Boucraa 27,800 (2000). **Government:** Muhammad Abdelaziz, President of the Republic since 1982, is also Secretary-General of the Polisario Front. Bouchraya Hammoudi Bayoune, Prime Minister since 1999. The National Assembly (parliament) has 101 members, elected by local and regional conferences and acts as a check on the executive branch. Polisario is committed to multi-party democracy when it gains independence.
National Holiday: 27 February, Proclamation of the Republic (1976).

West Papua / Papua

Population:	1,800,000
Area:	418,000 km²
Capital:	Jayapura
Currency:	Indonesian rupiah
Language:	250 living languages, Bahasa Indonesia

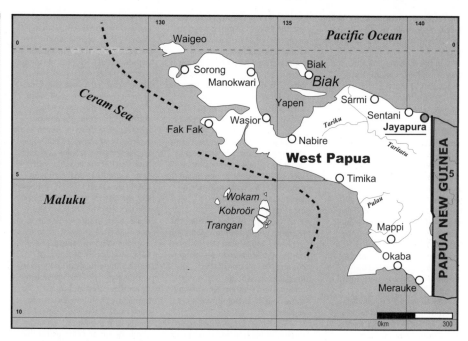

Humans first settled New Guinea at least 50,000 years ago. It was connected to Australia by a land bridge until about 10,000 years ago. There is evidence of agriculture from possibly as early as 9,000 years ago, which makes the island one of the earliest independent centers for the domestication of several varieties of sweet potato and fruit-bearing trees.

[2] The British were the first Europeans who attempted to settle the western part of the island (which the indigenous people now call West Papua). In 1793 a short-lived British colony was set up near present-day Manokwari but it was evacuated within two years. A unilateral proclamation was made by the Dutch on the 24th of August 1828 at the newly founded Fort du Bus on West Papua's south coast: the natives of the western half of New Guinea were to be subjects of the King of the Netherlands from this point forward.

[3] The Dutch were not initially concerned with colonizing West Papua, but opened Fort du Bus to protect their lucrative trade in the surrounding spice islands (the Dutch East Indies) from other European powers. Fort du Bus was abandoned after only ten years. Until the turn of the twentieth century, the Dutch governed West Papua indirectly through the Sultan of Tidore, and did not establish a continuous settlement in West Papua until 1897, nor did they engage in any substantial development within the country until the 1950s.

[4] On 27 November 1949 the Dutch ceded sovereignty of the Dutch East Indies to the Indonesian Republic, but excluded Dutch New Guinea (West Papua). Throughout the 1950s, the Dutch argued that West Papua was geographically and ethnically different from Indonesia and the Papuans should - over time - be given self-determination. By contrast, the Indonesians argued that Dutch New Guinea had already been transferred to them in 1949, and had achieved independence then. In 1962, 1,500 Indonesians 'invaded'.

[5] Under the auspices of the UN, the US urged Indonesia and the Netherlands to the negotiating table. Retired US diplomat Ellsworth Bunker drew up a plan to transfer the administrative authority for West Papua from the Netherlands to a neutral administrator, and thence to Indonesia. No West Papuans were involved in these negotiations. This 'New York Agreement' was signed by the Indonesians and the Dutch at UN headquarters on 15 August 1962.

[6] In 1968, a UN team arrived to 'assist, advise and participate' in the 'Act of Free Choice', which took place the following year. Only 1,025 West Papuans were chosen to vote in open meetings. UN Secretary-General U Thant later reported that without dissent the West Papuans had pronounced themselves in favor of remaining with Indonesia.

[7] It is estimated that at least 100,000 people have been killed by the Indonesian armed forces since then. Indonesia's harsh regime is responsible for murders, torture, forced migrations and the 'export' of Muslim Indonesians to the island. Most of the profit obtained from the world's biggest gold mine and the third biggest copper deposit ends up in Indonesia. Only a fifth of this revenue has been returned to West Papua.

[8] In February 2000, 400 delegates including representatives of the armed wing of West Papua's most long-standing separatist movement (the OPM) met in Sentani and openly discussed a strategy to take West Papua towards independence. This meeting rejected the 1969 Act of Free Choice as fraudulent and illegal.

[9] Throughout these developments, Jakarta has consistently opposed independence. In 2001, Indonesian troops murdered Theys Eluay, then President of the Papuan Council, which brought together all groups calling for self-determination in the territory. In 2003, the assassins were found guilty by an Indonesian military court but received light sentences of no more than three-and-a-half years. Indonesia has proposed dividing West Papua into three provinces, saying that this will promote autonomy in the region when it will actually undermine it. The military presence in the territory has recently increased, as have detentions and killings of West Papuans. ■

PROFILE

ENVIRONMENT
Located in the Pacific Ocean directly north of Australia, West Papua, together with the eastern half of its island landmass, Papua New Guinea, comprises the second largest island in the world and contains rainforests second only in size to those of the Amazon. West Papua has an abundance of natural resource wealth such as oil, gold, copper and wood. While it comprises 21 per cent of the total landmass of Indonesia, it is home to only 1 per cent of its population.

SOCIETY
Peoples: The indigenous population is of Melanesian - (South Pacific Islands) - descent. Total population: 2.1 million (2.5 million)*. Indigenous: 62 per cent (60 per cent). Migrants and transmigrants born in other parts of Indonesia (called 'Javanese'): 17 per cent (40 per cent). **Religion:** Reflecting an exposure to Dutch missionaries, Christianity is threaded through the belief system of many indigenous West Papuans. Indonesian migrants and transmigrants are predominantly Muslim. **Languages:** Bahasa Indonesia (official). There are 253 tribal languages. West Papua and its neighbour, Papua New Guinea, contain 15 per cent of all the world's known languages.

THE STATE
Official Name: Papua, formerly Irian Jaya (West Papua).
Capital: Jayapura. **Government:** Effectively controlled by Indonesia. The Papua Council and its Presidium (Executive), which once acted as a figurehead for the independence movement, no longer has the backing of all the organizations advocating independence in West Papua. The local legislature, with a native Papuan upper house, has limited real power: it cannot propose legislation and has limited veto rights. Effective law-making power is retained in Jakarta.
National Holiday: 1 December, Independence Day.
Armed Forces: The military presence has more than doubled in the last five years to 12,000.

(*) NOTE: The information from Indonesia often differs from that from West Papuans. Where there are discrepancies, the Indonesian version is given first, then the West Papuan version in brackets.

Yemen / Al Yaman

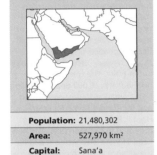

Population:	21,480,302
Area:	527,970 km²
Capital:	Sana'a
Currency:	Rial
Language:	Arabic

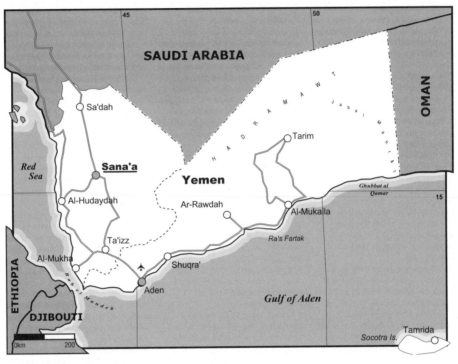

G eographically located on the Indian, African and Mediterranean trade routes, Yemen was famous in antiquity because of its trade in incense, perfume and myrrh. Its main cities (Ma'in, Marib, Timna, and Najzan), stretched along the caravan routes that brought aromatic fragrances from Dhufar (presently part of Oman) and Punt (Somalia). These extensive trade routes continued along the coast of the Red Sea as far as the Mediterranean markets, and from Taima towards Mesopotamia.

2   These cities were united in kingdoms, first Mina and later the better-known Saba (Sheba), cited in the Bible. In the year 20 BC the Romans, who had already conquered Egypt, unsuccessfully attempted to extend their dominion to Saba.

3   At the beginning of the 2nd century, the Greek geographer and mathematician Ptolemy started to refer to this zone as 'Happy Arabia' because of its vegetation (distinguishing it from the rest of the peninsula) and its wealth, resulting from trade.

4   In the 3rd century, the Kingdom of Saba fell under the control of the Himyarite dynasty (Kingdom of Himyar). A century later, Christian missionaries started arriving in Yemen.

5   The last Himyarite King was Jewish. He launched a violent persecution of the Christian community, leading to the intervention and occupation in 522 by the Ethiopian King of Aksum, who was a Christian. The Kings of Aksum spoke Greek and had been converted to Christianity in 333, establishing the traditional Christian foundations of the future Abyssinia (Ethiopia).

6   In 572, the Persians invaded Arabia, driving out the Ethiopians and turning Yemen into a Persian *satrapy* (province).

7   When Islamic domination reached the country in the 7th century, the country had suffered almost three centuries of conflict and invasions, resulting in the loss of its splendor. It was governed from Damascus by the Omeyas and later from Baghdad by the Abasids.

8   By the end of the 8th century the borders of the Arabian Empire reached from North Africa and Spain in the west, to Pakistan and Afghanistan in the east. Damascus in Syria became the capital of the empire, where the foundations of a new culture were laid. Greco-Roman, Persian and Indian components blended to form the new dominant culture, with the Arabs reaching high levels of scholarship and philosophy. The Arabs formed the social élite, the ruling class, though little changed in the lives of the Yemenis and other subject peoples.

9   In the 15th century the Portuguese arrived in Arabia, blocking trade routes in the Red Sea and controlling the spice route where Yemen held a strategic position. In 1516 they conquered Aden and established themselves there until 1538. With Aden in its power, Portugal controlled the entry to the Red Sea.

10   Then, in the 16th century, the Ottoman expansion started. The Turks occupied a few coastal spots on the Red Sea, leaving inland areas and the southern coast independent, governed by an *imam* (priest). In 1618, the British arrived and established the East India Company in the port of al-Mukha (*Mocha*: origin of the name for a type of coffee).

11   In the 19th century the British expanded their presence. As a consequence of Muhammad Ali's conquest of the country, the British occupied the entire extreme south-western region (see Egypt) and took Aden (in 1839), the best harbor in the region, to monitor Turkish activities. Meanwhile the Turks consolidated their inland dominion, which was finally achieved in 1872. Concessions were made to allow the imam to retain his position and also make the post hereditary rather than elective. This division set in train the process by which Yemen and the Yemeni people were split into two countries.

12   Towards 1870, with the opening of the Suez Canal and the consolidation of Turkish domination over the northern part of Yemen, the Aden settlement acquired new importance in British global strategy; it was a key port on the Red Sea and ultimately gave them access to the new canal.

13   In the early 20th century, Turkey and Britain established a border between their territories, which came to be called North and South Yemen, respectively. Friendship and protectorate treaties were gradually signed with local leaders, but it was a slow process, only completed in 1934 when the British gained control of the southern territory, as far as the border with Oman.

14   In 1911, Imam Yahya Hamid ad-Din led a nationalist rebellion; and two years later the Turks recognized his authority over the territory in exchange for the formal acceptance of Turkish sovereignty.

15   During World War I the Imam allied himself with the Ottoman

LAND USE

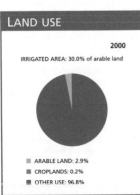

2000

IRRIGATED AREA: 30.0% of arable land

- ARABLE LAND: 2.9%
- CROPLANDS: 0.2%
- OTHER USE: 96.8%

PUBLIC EXPENDITURE

% OF GDP

- HEALTH & EDUCATION (2000): 12.1 %
- DEFENSE (2001): 6.1 %

WORKERS

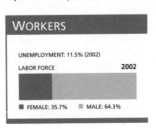

UNEMPLOYMENT: 11.5% (2002)

LABOR FORCE   2002

- FEMALE: 35.7%   ■ MALE: 64.3%

Life expectancy
60.0 years
2000-2005

GNI per capita
$490
2002

Literacy
46% total adult rate
2000

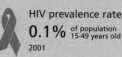
HIV prevalence rate
0.1% of population 15-49 years old
2001

Empire and remained loyal to it until the end of the war. When the Empire broke up, Yemen recovered its independence (November 1918) and Hamid ad-Din was proclaimed King.

[16] In 1925, Britain recognized Yemen's independence and in the 1934 peace treaty, its sovereignty was guaranteed. Taking advantage of treaties with peoples in the surrounding areas, the British first turned Aden into a protectorate and in 1937, into a British colony.

[17] The birth of the nationalist Free Yemeni Movement in the mid-1940s was provoked by the autocratic rule of the imams. In 1945, North Yemen became a founding member of the Arab League and two years later it became a member of the United Nations (UN).

[18] There was an aborted uprising in 1948 in which Imam Yahya was killed, followed in 1955 by a coup against Imam Ahmad. In 1958, six governors of South Yemen established the Federation of South Arabia, which by 1965 with British support, comprised the region's 17 states.

[19] That same year Imam Ahmad ash-Shams who ruled North Yemen, joined the United Arab Republic formed by Egypt and Syria, remaining in it until 1961. He was succeeded by his son Muhammad al-Badr, who was deposed by the Nasserist military in 1962, when the Yemen Arab Republic (YAR) was proclaimed under the leadership of Abdullah al-Sallal.

[20] The former ruler, al-Badr, received both Saudi and British support, initiating a long civil war against the republican government that was backed by Egypt. A coup within the Republicans placed the moderate al-Iryani in power. Meanwhile, in South Yemen, the National Liberation Front, established in 1963, took the port of Aden in 1967 and proclaimed independence, launching a socialist revolution.

[21] South Yemen became the People's Republic of Yemen (PR Yemen), closed all the British bases in 1969, nationalized the banking system, took control of foreign trade and the shipbuilding industry and initiated agrarian reform. Its foreign policy closely linked it to the USSR. In its efforts to isolate the 'Cuba of the East', Saudi Arabia considered that al-Iryani was the lesser of all the possible evils and resigned itself to accepting him.

[22] In October 1972, despite ideological and political differences between North and South Yemen, al-Iryani signed a treaty with the revolutionary government of what was now called the People's Democratic Republic of Yemen (PDRY) for a future merger of the two states.

[23] This ran counter to Saudi strategy and in June 1974 Colonel Ibrahim al-Hamadi forced al-Iryani to resign and installed himself as ruler in Sana'a. Although initially accepted by Saudi's King Faisal, the young officer made a powerful

enemy when he challenged the landlords of the north in an effort to centralize power. After surviving three assassination attempts, he was killed on 11 October 1977 together with his brother.

[24] A junta led by Lt-Colonel Ahmed al-Gashmi, with Prime Minister Aziz Abdel Ghani and Major Abdul al-Abdel Aalim, took power vowing to continue their predecessor's policies. Al-Gashmi was killed in a bomb attack in June 1978 and consequent unrest led to war between the two Yemens.

[25] In October 1978 the National Liberation Front (NLF) established the Yemen Socialist Party at a congress with considerable support from the population. In December the first general elections were held since independence, to appoint the 111 members of the People's Revolutionary Council from among 175 candidates.

[26] Saudi Arabia's constant hostility increased when it claimed parts of PDRY, precisely those areas where the Algerian state oil company had discovered oil-fields. Tension heightened with the increasing US military presence in Saudi Arabia.

[27] Major Ali Abdullah Saleh was appointed President of YAR in 1978 but was unable to prevent internal dissent leading to armed conflict in January 1979. The National Democratic Front, which included the nation's progressive sectors, was on the brink of taking power, so with Saudi provocation the conflict was diverted into a war with the

South (PDRY). Syria, Iraq and Jordan intervened and their mediation led to a cease-fire and negotiations for the unification of the two Yemeni states, which had been suspended since 1972.

[28] In January 1986 civil war broke out in PDRY. The confrontation was brief but left 10,000 dead. President Muhammad al-Hasani was ousted and the former Prime Minister Haydar Bakr al-Attas was elected president in October 1986. The new head of state pledged to maintain the alliance with Ethiopia and Syria.

[29] Finally, on 22 May 1990, the republics united as the Republic of Yemen. The political capital was established in Sana'a (former capital of the Arab Republic of Yemen) and the economic capital in Aden (former capital of the Democratic Republic of Yemen).

[30] In a joint session of the Legislative Assemblies of the two states, held in Aden, a Presidential Council was elected, made up of General Ali Abdullah Saleh (former president of YAR/North Yemen), Abdel Karim Abdullah al-Arashi, Salem Saleh Mohammed and Abdul Aziz Abdel Ghani. The members of the Council elected Ali Abdullah Saleh president of the united republic. Ali al-Beidh was vice-president and General Haydar Bakr al-Attas, former president of PDRY/South Yemen, was also given a post in the new government.

[31] In May 1991, the Constitution was ratified in a national referendum: an overwhelming majority voted for freedom of expression and political pluralism. Islamic fundamentalist groups opposed to unification called for a boycott, finding the absence of *shari'a* (Islamic law) unacceptable, and also the introduction of voting rights for women.

[32] A few months after its installation, the provisional Government of the Republic of Yemen protested over the presence of foreign armies, massing in Saudi Arabia to prevent the invasion of Kuwait. The Saudi Arabian Government expelled 850,000 Yemeni migrant workers. The returning workers worsened the state of the national economy. Over 2 million people out of a total population of 10.5 million, were unemployed.

[33] In March 1993, Ali Abdullah Saleh's General People's Congress (GPC) won the parliamentary elections.

[34] In order to weaken Yemen, seen as a 'bad example' by the region's monarchies, Saudi Arabia supported the fight for secession led by vice-president al-Beidh. In May 1994, secessionists proclaimed a southern Yemen democratic republic and requested the support of Saudi Arabia. However they were

PROFILE

ENVIRONMENT

The Republic of Yemen is formed by the union of the People's Democratic Republic of Yemen (South) and the Yemen Arab Republic (North). The north has the most fertile lands of the Arabian Peninsula. For that reason the country, together with the Hadhramaut Valley, used to be called 'Happy Arabia'. Beyond a semi-desert coastal strip along the Red Sea, lies a more humid mountainous region where the agricultural lands are found (sorghum is grown for internal consumption and cotton for export). The traditional coffee crop has been replaced by *qat*, a narcotic herb. The climate is tropical with high temperatures especially in Tihmah - where rainfall is heavy - and in the eastern region. The country has no mineral resources. The southern territory is dry, mountainous and lacks permanent rivers. Two-thirds of the land area is either desert or semi-desert. Agriculture is concentrated in the valleys and oases (1.2 per cent of the country). Fishing is an important commercial activity. Yemen's territory includes the island of Socotra, which is important strategically because of its location at the entrance to the Gulf of Aden. This island, which became part of South Yemen in 1967, has 17,000 inhabitants spread over 3,626 sq km.

SOCIETY

Peoples: Nearly all Arab. A small Persian minority lives along the coast.

Religions: Islam, official (Shi'a, 53 per cent and Sunni, 46.9 per cent).
Languages: Arabic, official.
Main Political Parties: General People's Congress (GPC); Yemeni Congregation for Reform (Islah); Nasserite Unionist People's Organization; Arab Socialist Rebirth Party; the Yemeni Socialist Party.
Main Social Organizations: General Federation of Yemen Workers' Trade Unions, Association of Yemeni Students.

THE STATE

Official Name: al-Jumhuriya al-Yamaniya.
Administrative Divisions: 16 Provinces.
Political Capital: Sana'a 1,469,000 people (2003).
Economic Center: Aden.
Other Cities: Aden 562,000 people; Al-Hudaydah (Hodeida) 246,000; Taiz 290,107 (1995).
Government: Ali Abdullah Saleh, President since May 1990, re-elected in 1994 and 1999. Abdul Kader Bajammal, Prime Minister since March 2001. Since unification of the Yemen Arab Republic (North) and the People's Democratic Republic of Yemen (South) in May 1990, Presidential Council made up of 5 members (3 from the North, 2 from the South). Unicameral Legislature: Assembly of Representatives, with 301 members.
National Holiday: 22 May, unification (1990).
Armed Forces: 66,300 (1997). Other: 20,000 (Central Organization for Security); 20,000 (tribal forces).

defeated by forces loyal to the Government. In July, the council of ministers adopted a plan of general amnesty in order to protect political pluralism. The Government named Aden as the country's economic capital, which was regarded as a gesture towards southern Yemenis. In September, Socialist Party members were forced to leave the Government, while the Islamist Yemeni Congregation for Reform (Islah) obtained six new places in the cabinet. The Constitution was modified to make shari'a law the basis of all Yemeni legislation.

[35]   In February 1995, 11 parties formed a new alliance, the Democratic Opposition Coalition, seeking to obtain power. The Government signed a draft agreement with Saudi Arabia in which both states expressed their will to set permanent common borders and promote bilateral relations.

[36]   The landing of Eritrean forces on the Hanish Islands in the Red Sea in December led to a war. Egypt's President Hosni Mubarak offered to mediate and in March 1996 Yemen and Eritrea accepted international arbitration to resolve the disagreement. At the end of that year, however, the key points had still not been resolved.

[37]   In 1997, the GPC won the parliamentary elections and on 15 May the new Prime Minister, Faraj Said ibn Ghanem took office.

[38]   That year the Government implemented a structural adjustment plan to revive an economy suffering the effects of civil war and the reduction of aid from many Western and Arab nations. The privatizations earned the Government funding from the World Bank and the International Monetary Fund.

[39]   Abdul Karim al-Iryani took over as Prime Minister in May 1998. A Saudi attack on a Yemeni detachment on the island of Duwaima, in the Red Sea, in July, further worsened relations between the two neighbors. In October the international court in The Hague ruled in favor of Yemeni ownership of the Hanish islands, also claimed by Eritrea.

[40]   The September 1999 elections gave a clear victory to Ali Abdullah Saleh, who was re-elected with 96.3 per cent of the vote.

[41]   The abduction of 28 mostly British tourists in December 1998 raised controversy over the method used by some clans to make their claims known to the central authorities. Kidnapping was becoming a common practice in order to get government attention and to force it to give in to local demands. In the 1990s some 200 tourists or executives from European or US companies were

IN FOCUS

ENVIRONMENTAL CHALLENGES
Fresh water sources are very limited, the use of groundwater beyond its replacement capacity has led to a drop in its level. Extensive grazing has caused soil erosion and very acute desertification.

WOMEN'S RIGHTS
Women have been able to vote and stand for election since 1967. They represent 28 per cent of the total workforce in the country, with 88 per cent working in agriculture, 9 per cent in the service area and 3 per cent in industry.

According to UNICEF's latest data available*, only 22 per cent of births are assisted by qualified personnel and 34 per cent of pregnant women receive prenatal care. Maternal mortality stands at 570 deaths per 100,000 live births.

The law prohibits violence against women, but in fact this is little respected. Domestic violence is considered a family matter and is rarely reported to the police. Female genital mutilation is prohibited by law, but is still practised in parts of the country. The majority of cases are in communities with strong African influence.

CHILDREN
According to current UNICEF databases*, the infant mortality

rate is 79 deaths per 1,000 live births, while under-5 mortality is 107 deaths per 1,000 live births. Between 73 and 79 per cent of infants are vaccinated against diseases such as polio, diphtheria, measles and tetanus. Although the Government tries to protect children's rights, it lacks the necessary resources to ensure adequate child medical care, education and welfare services. Furthermore, malnutrition is common among children. The law stipulates universal education; however, the school attendance rate for primary education was 67 per cent, while for secondary education it barely reached 37 per cent (2000*).

INDIGENOUS PEOPLES/ ETHNIC MINORITIES
Yemen is a Muslim country with both *Sunni* and *Shi'a*. Most people are Sunni from the *Shafi'i* school (an orthodox branch of Muslim jurisprudence; its name comes from *ash-Shafi'i*, an Islamic jurist who lived between 767 and 820), while the Zaydi minority, living in the northern provinces around *Sa'da*, is *Shi'a*.

There is also a small group of Ismailites (a *Shi'a* sect), representing around 1 per cent of the population. Differences between the various religious factions are based on different interpretations of the *shari'a* or Islamic law. There are small non-Muslim minorities:

Christians (around 4 per cent), Hindus and Jews, who remained when their communities left the country after independence.

MIGRANTS/REFUGEES
In 2002, Yemen received around 81,700 refugees. Most of them were Somali (79,000), Ethiopian (1,500), Palestinians(149) plus some Eritreans, Sudanese and Syrians.

Yemen is the only country in the Arab peninsula to be a member of the UN High Commissioner for Refugees (UNHCR). Although the condition of refugees is satisfactory in Yemen, the high poverty rate has led to displacement of the population towards the Gulf countries. For its part, UNHCR has supplied limited help and basic medical care to 10,000 refugees living in camps.

Many Yemeni (between 20 and 25 per cent of the population) migrate to various countries in search of work. The remittances sent by emigrants to their families are one of the population's main sources of income.

DEATH PENALTY
It is applicable to all types of crimes.

* Latest data available in *The State of the World's Children* and *Childinfo* database, UNICEF, 2004.

taken in this manner. In February 2000, a new law was introduced making the abduction of foreigners a capital offence.

[42]   In October 2000, 17 US soldiers were killed in Aden in a suicide attack on the US warship USS Cole. The radical Islamist Osama bin Laden, a Saudi of Yemeni descent, was blamed for masterminding the attack. That same month, a bomb exploded at the British embassy. Four Yemenis were imprisoned after declaring they had carried out the attack in solidarity with the Palestinian cause.

[43]   Violence marked the municipal elections of February 2001, which were accompanied by a referendum on extending the presidential term to seven years. Clashes among factions and with the police, as a result of the vote recount, left 30 people dead. The recount resulted in approval for the constitutional reform and Saleh's term in office was extended.

[44]   In May, without explanation, the President restructured the Cabinet and deposed Premier Abdul-Karim al-Iryani, naming

former foreign minister Abdul Kader Bajammal in his place. Wahiba Fare took over the Human Rights portfolio and became the first woman in Yemen history to head a ministry.

[45]   In November, Saleh traveled to Washington to reassure his US counterpart that Yemen would participate in the coalition of nations that Washington was organizing to fight terrorism. Following this, the Government arrested many Yemenis and foreigners.

[46]   Amnesty International reported that Yemen's war on terrorism had made the State forget to protect human rights. The organization deplored intimidation of journalists and widespread use of torture, in addition to the continuation of the death penalty, flogging and mutilation.

[47]   In March 2002, the Government expelled more than 100 Islamic students, including French and British citizens, as part of its campaign against terrorism and against members of the al-Qaeda network, headed by bin Laden. The US agreed to send

military advisers to train Yemeni forces in anti-terrorism tactics. According to Washington, Yemen, like Afghanistan, could foster al-Qaeda's growth.

[48]   At least 5,000 people staged a protest in April, burning Israeli and US flags and effigies of US President Bush and Israel's Prime Minister Ariel Sharon, and demanding the closure of the US embassy. An explosion and a grenade attack had recently occurred at the embassy compound.

[49]   In October 2002 a French oil tanker exploded off the coast of Yemen and revived fears about al-Qaeda activity. To avoid any US intervention and ensure continuation of financial support, the Government promoted a campaign to capture al-Qaeda followers.

[50]   One month later, a missile launched on Yemen from an un-piloted plane killed six people, among them someone that the US (who authorized the operation) had accused of being the al-Qaeda leader in Yemen. In May 2004, Yemeni security forces arrested two suspected al-Qaeda leaders. ■

Zambia / Zambia

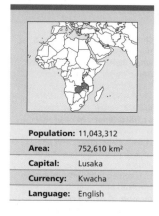

Population:	11,043,312
Area:	752,610 km²
Capital:	Lusaka
Currency:	Kwacha
Language:	English

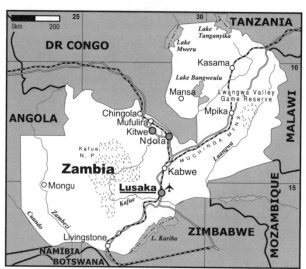

E vidence of *Homo sapiens rhodesiensis* going back 100,000 years has been found in near Broken Hill, Kabwe. Like many African countries whose boundaries were demarcated in the colonial period, modern-day Zambia includes the descendants of many different peoples, including the San. Migrants from the north - possibly Bantu-speaking groups - settled in the region with their agriculture, use of metal, pottery and domesticated animals in the1st millennium AD. Over time, the settled Bantu-speakers displaced some of the hunting and gathering peoples. Around the year 1,000, a copper currency was in use. Burial objects, including gold ornaments, signal the existence of social hierarchies towards the 14th century.

2   Waves of Bantu-speaking immigrants - the Luba and Lunda peoples - arrived from today's DR Congo and Angola in the 18th century. By the 19th century, before colonization, they - like the Bemba who settled in the northeast and the Lozi (Barotse) along the Zambezi river - formed powerful centralized state structures. In the 19th century Portuguese attempts to establish authority over the area were resisted, but many communities were disrupted by Arab and Mozambican slave traders.

3   In 1851, David Livingstone, a British missionary and explorer, reached the Victoria Falls. He opened the way for merchants and adventurers. Cecil Rhodes and his British-South Africa Company (BSA) were looking to expand northwards from South Africa, and established a mining and trade monopoly in the area in 1889. A year later, Rhodes signed a treaty with the Lozi ruler Lewanika and the resulting protectorate was soon transformed through colonial domination into Northern Rhodesia.

4   The BSA protectorate won support from British because it prevented the Portuguese from linking their colonies of Angola and Mozambique. The BSA's prime concern in Northern Rhodesia was to exploit the rich copper deposits around Ndola and Kitwe in the north. By 1909 a railway line was built linking the copper belt with the capital, Lusaka, and the southern African network. In 1924, Britain assumed direct control of the region. South African and US mining companies increased their investment in copper. The miserable working conditions of black miners led to the formation of labor unions, which gave rise to

the first independence movements, such as the Northern Rhodesia African National Congress (NRANC).

5   In 1952, primary school teacher Kenneth Kaunda, became NRANC Secretary-General with Harry Nkumbula as President. In 1953, the British created a federation of Northern Rhodesia (now Zambia), Southern Rhodesia (now Zimbabwe) and Nyasaland (now Malawi). Zambia's African nationalists felt that their country's

copper wealth was being used to underpin the settler-controlled federation, and they campaigned for it to be dismantled. They fought for independence and against racial discrimination. Kaunda broke away from Nkumbula to form the Zambia African Congress (ZAC).

6   The ZAC refused to cooperate with the British on a gradual transfer of power. It was outlawed and Kaunda was arrested in 1959. The ZAC became the United National Independence Party (UNIP), which Kaunda chaired when he was released in 1960. As the Party gained widespread support, violence broke out in 1961.

7   One year later, the British announced a constitutional review. The nationalist platform was thus strengthened and succeeded in dissolving the Federation in 1964. The UNIP won the elections and proclaimed independence in October 1964.

8   Independent Zambia had one of the largest mining sectors in Africa at this time and was becoming one of the most urbanized countries. It nationalized its copper reserves, was a founding member of the Organization of Copper Exporting Countries (OCEC), and hosted the 3rd Summit

PROFILE

ENVIRONMENT

A high plateau extends from Malawi in the east to the swamp region along the border with Angola in the west. The Zambezi River flows from north to south and provides hydroelectric power at the Kariba Dam. The climate is tropical, tempered by altitude. Mining is the main economic activity, as there are large copper deposits. Shanty towns account for 45 per cent of housing in Lusaka, with attendant problems like the lack of drinking water and adequate health care, factors which contributed to the 1990 and 1991 cholera epidemics.

SOCIETY

Peoples: 98 per cent of Zambians are descendants of Bantu-speaking migrants, in some 70 ethnic groups. There are about 15,000 Europeans and a small Asian population.
Religions: Traditional African religions are practised. There are Christian and Muslim and Hindu minorities.
Languages: English (official). The 70 or so local languages include Bemba, Kaonda, Lozi, Lunda, Luvale, Nyanja and Tonga.
Main Political Parties: Movement for Multiparty Democracy (MMD); United Party for National Development (UPND); United National Independence Party (UNIP); Forum for Democracy and Development (FDD).
Main Social Organizations: The Trade Union Congress of Zambia comprises 16 unions. The newly-created Workers' Trade Union has 2 million members.

THE STATE

Official Name: Republic of Zambia.
Capital: Lusaka 1,394,000 people (2003).
Other Cities: Ndola 346,500 people; Kitwe 762,700; Mufulira 130,400 (2000).
Government: Levy Mwanawasa, President since January 2002. Unicameral Legislature: National Assembly, with 159 members.
National Holiday: 24 October, Independence Day (1964).
Armed Forces: 21,600 (1997). Other: Police Mobile Unit (PMU): 700; Police Paramilitary Unit (PPMU): 700.

LAND USE

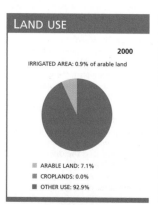

2000

IRRIGATED AREA: 0.9% of arable land

- ARABLE LAND: 7.1%
- CROPLANDS: 0.0%
- OTHER USE: 92.9%

PUBLIC EXPENDITURE

% OF GDP

5.8 %

0.6 %

HEALTH & EDUCATION (2000)   DEFENSE (2001)

Life expectancy	GNI per capita	Literacy	HIV prevalence rate
32.4 years 2000-2005	**$330** 2002	**78%** total adult rate 2000	**21.5%** of population 15-49 years old 2001

Meeting of the Non-Aligned Countries Movement in 1970. It actively supported liberation movements in neighboring countries.

9   As a land-locked country, trapped in a railway network controlled by the white minority governments of South Africa and Rhodesia, Zambia (together with Tanzania) accepted Chinese aid to construct a major new line. In 1974, with the inauguration of the Tan-Zam Railway, Zambia gained access to Indian Ocean ports. In the same year, the Portuguese colonial-fascist regime was overthrown and Zambia's neighbors Angola and Mozambique embarked on their paths to independence.

10   By the late 1970s Zambia's economic fortunes had taken a downturn. The OPEC oil crisis hit the country hard and copper prices fell. Zimbabwean independence in 1980 was welcomed by Zambia. However, white-ruled South Africa (SA) punished Kaunda's support for his neighbor by boycotting Zambia. SA also sent in troops because Zambia sheltered members from the liberation movements of Namibia (SWAPO) and South Africa (ANC).

11   In October 1980, after a failed coup attempt, which was supported by South Africa, the Government declared a state of emergency and imposed a curfew. Government officials, businesspeople and foreigners were arrested. After a long trial, seven were hanged.

12   Kaunda surrounded himself with former comrades-at-arms. His critics questioned the need for a state of emergency and the one-party system. Allegations grew of government corruption. The tension diminished after the 1983 elections, in which President Kaunda won 93 per cent of the vote.

13   Kaunda was re-elected in 1988. But in the 1991 elections, which were brought forward two years because of economic crisis and followed a constitutional reform establishing a multiparty system, Kaunda was defeated by Frederick Chiluba, of the Movement for Multiparty Democracy (MMD). Chiluba, a former union leader, won 81 per cent of the vote and 125 of the 150 seats in Parliament. Kaunda resigned as UNIP party leader in 1992.

14   Chiluba declared Christianity the official religion and banned the creation of a Islamic fundamentalist party in spite of there being more than 2 million Muslim Zambians (both Shi'as and Sunnis) in the country.

15   Accusations of corruption and the agricultural crisis led the President to request his Lands Minister to step down and the

IN FOCUS

ENVIRONMENTAL CHALLENGES
Wildlife is threatened by poaching, as well as by the lack of resources with which to maintain protected areas. Mining has damaged the environment. Soil erosion and loss of fertility are associated with the overuse of fertilizers. Air pollution results in acid rain in mining areas.

WOMEN'S RIGHTS
Women have been able to vote since 1962. Women's participation in formal politics is low. Only 3 per cent of government positions at ministerial level are held by women.

According to UNICEF's latest data available*, 65 per cent of girls are enrolled in primary school. Some 75 per cent of them reach fifth grade. Illiteracy among women between 15 and 24 years of age stands at 14.5 per cent.

In spite of the fact that 93 per cent of pregnant women receive prenatal care, only 43 per cent of births are attended by skilled health staff. Nineteen per cent of pregnant women between 15 and 24 are living with HIV/AIDS. Between 1980 and 2000, women made up 45 per cent of the country's labor force.

CHILDREN
UNICEF's latest data available* showed that ten per cent of newborn babies are underweight. The child mortality rate is 192 deaths per 1,000 live births for children under-five and 108 deaths per 1,000 live births among infants under-one. Some 28 per cent of under-5s are underweight and 47 per cent are stunted. There are 150,000 children between 0 and 14 years old living with HIV/AIDS, out of a total number of 1,200,000 people who are HIV-positive. As many as 572,000 children have been orphaned by AIDS.

INDIGENOUS PEOPLES/ ETHNIC MINORITIES
Zambia is an ethnically varied country with over 70 groups. The Bemba (2 million), Nyanja and Tonga (around 1 million each) are the main peoples.

The Kavango population, mainly around the borders with Namibia and Angola, number around 10,000 in Zambia. They are cultivators and herders who practise traditional religions.

The Lozi/Barotse (500,000) are located in the western and southern provinces, near Livingstone.

The Luba people (250,000) live in north-western Zambia. They are the descendants of a powerful empire which dates from the 15th

century.
Lunda people live in the Luapula area and the north west.

Ngoni people came to Zambia from the south.The Tabwa peoples are in the north and practise Islam, Christianity and traditional religions.

The Chokwe peoples are also located in the north-western province and have a population of 56,000. They are descendants of the Mbundi and Mbuti pygmies, who emigrated from the upper reaches of the Kasai river, towards 1600. They practise traditional religion.

MIGRANTS/REFUGEES
At the end of 2002, Zambia sheltered nearly 250,000 refugees, including 190,000 from Angola, more than 50,000 from DR Congo, 5,000 from Rwanda, 1,000 from Burundi, and 1,000 from other countries. Angolan refugees, expelled after 25 years of civil war, have been arriving in Zambia since the 1970s. Nearly half of them live in cities and the rest live in camps in western Zambia.

DEATH PENALTY
Capital punishment still in force.

* Latest data available in The State of the World's Children and Childinfo

other ministers to declare their incomes. Shortly afterwards, he removed the director of the Bank of Zambia for suddenly devaluing the currency, the kwacha, by more than 20 per cent. Chiluba blamed the crisis on foreign debt payments, which consumed 40 per cent of the country's GDP.

16   In March 1996 the Paris Club cancelled 67 per cent of Zambia's debt. The IMF/World Bank structural adjustment program in 1997 increased rural poverty levels and at least 150,000 workers lost their jobs as a result of the privatization of state enterprises.

17   In November 1997, dozens of people - including Kaunda, disqualified from possible re-election by a constitutional amendment - were arrested for allegedly taking part in a failed coup. A state of emergency was imposed and later extended to March 1998. Kaunda was released from house arrest in June and the charges against him were withdrawn.

18   In 1999, a high court sentenced 59 soldiers to death after they were found guilty of treason for the failed coup attempt in 1997.

19   In May 2001, political divisions - resulting from the debate on whether Chiluba should run for a third term as President - prompted some 80 MMD members to create the Forum for Democracy and Development (FDD).

20   In July 2001, Paul Tembo, previously Chiluba's campaign manager and a member of the FDD, was murdered shortly before he was to testify in a high-level corruption case.

21   Also in July, Zambia issued an urgent appeal for food aid to feed some two million people in the wake of poor harvests caused by flooding and drought in different parts of the country. Vice-President Enock Kavindele stated that some 100,000 tons of maize/corn were needed.

22   In January 2002, MMD candidate Levy Mwanawasa was declared President amid controversy arising from the close presidential and parliamentary elections of December 2001. Ten opposition parties protested over alleged fraud. Mwanawasa won 28.7 per cent of the vote, while Anderson Mazoka, of the United Party of National Development (UPND), won 26.7 per cent.

23   Parliament, encouraged by President Mwanawasa, voted to lift former president Chiluba's immunity from prosecution in July 2002.

24   In October, the Government said it would not accept genetically modified maize to help alleviate the food shortages faced by the poorest 3 million people in the country.

25   In February 2003, former President Chiluba was arrested and charged on 59 counts, including abuse of office and the theft of $30 million. In December, he went on trial on corruption charges. That same month, the Supreme Court confirmed the death sentences of 40 out of the 59 soldiers involved in the 1997 failed coup.

26   In June 2004, British debt campaign group, the World Development Movement, reported that: 'The evidence suggests that the past 20 years of IMF and World Bank intervention have exacerbated rather than ameliorated Zambia's debt crisis. Ironically, in return for debt relief, Zambia is required to do more of the same. The country has been condemned to debt'. ∎

Zimbabwe / Zimbabwe

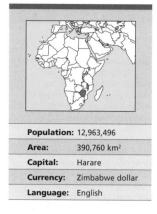

Population:	12,963,496
Area:	390,760 km²
Capital:	Harare
Currency:	Zimbabwe dollar
Language:	English

In the region known today as Zimbabwe there are many signs of ancient African civilizations, including mines, irrigation and terracing.

2   Among the ruins, the major archaeological sites are Mapungubwe and Great Zimbabwe, with its monumental walled enclosure. The ancestors of today's Shona people, Bantu-speaking ironworkers who had settled in the region before the 5th century, built these walls in later centuries.

3   They discovered gold, copper and tin deposits, and developed sophisticated techniques for working these metals. They traded with Arab-influenced centers on the coast, such as Sofala in present-day Mozambique, and this trade facilitated an expansion of their culture. The Mutapas, or kings, extended their influence over most of the region.

4   The height of Great Zimbabwe was 14th-16th century. This civilization established trading connections as far as Asia. By the time the Portuguese conquered the coastal settlements in the 16th century, Great Zimbabwe was in decline and the center of gravity of a more devolved Zimbabwean culture moved northwards under the Rozvi kings. Khami, in the south, was another major center

after the fall of Great Zimbabwe.

5   Shona society was deeply disrupted in the 1830s by the invasion of the Ndebele from Zululand (in what is now South Africa), escaping the military might of Zulu king Shaka.

6   The Zulu-speaking Ndebele established a kingdom in the southeast by conquering and incorporating the local, mainly Shona people. In the first half of the 19th century, the territory was divided between the Shona people in the north-east, and the Ndebele. When white settlers arrived in the late 19th century they negotiated with Lobenguela, the Ndebele king. He granted exclusive rights for the exploitation of the country's mineral resources and land to imperial entrepreneur Cecil Rhodes' British-South Africa

Company (BSA) in exchange for money.

7   Britain authorized the BSA to take control over the territory and open it for settlers, and a 'pioneer column' moved into a fortified camp called Salisbury.

8   In 1893, the Ndebele rebelled. Rhodes 'police' attacked Lobengula's capital Bulawayo and destroyed it. He was captured.

9   In 1896-7 a major uprising by Shona people was brutally repressed and the country (Southern Rhodesia) came under the secure control of the BSA.

10   In 1923 it became a settler-run state which emulated South Africa in many aspects of racial segregation. Its intensive agriculture and gold mines made it the second richest country in colonial Africa.

11   In 1953 Southern Rhodesia formed a Central African Federation with its neighbors Northern Rhodesia (now Zambia) and Nyasaland (now Malawi). Through the Federation the British hoped to create a counterweight to Afrikaaner-

dominated apartheid in South Africa.

12   When the decolonization process began in Africa in the late 1950s, Europeans (5 per cent of the population) owned around half the land. Zambia and Malawi gained independence in 1964. In Southern Rhodesia, the African National Congress (ANC) also intensified the struggle for self-determination under majority rule. The settler Government of Ian Smith refused to countenance black rule or British attempts to compromise and announced a unilateral declaration of independence in 1965. This provoked the turn to armed struggle by the African liberation movements ZAPU (Zimbabwe African Peoples Union, led by Joshua Nkomo) and ZANU (Zimbabwe African National Union, led by Robert Mugabe from 1975).

13   Smith's rebel Rhodesian Front regime faced a UN embargo, though the blockade was systematically violated with the co-operation of the white government in South Africa. Following Mozambique's independence in 1975, the armed struggle was stepped up and Zimbabwean guerrillas penetrated from camps outside the country. Smith retaliated against Zambia and Mozambique. These countries together with Angola, Botswana and Tanzania, had suffered significant political

LAND USE

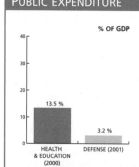

2000

IRRIGATED AREA: 3.5% of arable land

- ARABLE LAND: 8.3%
- CROPLANDS: 0.3%
- OTHER USE: 91.3%

PUBLIC EXPENDITURE

% OF GDP

- HEALTH & EDUCATION (2000): 13.5 %
- DEFENSE (2001): 3.2 %

WORKERS

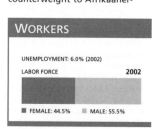

UNEMPLOYMENT: 6.0% (2002)

LABOR FORCE   **2002**

- FEMALE: 44.5%
- MALE: 55.5%

Life expectancy
33.1 years
2000-2005

GNI per capita
$470
2002

Literacy
89% total adult rate
2000

HIV prevalence rate
33.7% of population 15-49 years old
2001

and economic destabilization as 'Front Line' states against the region's white regimes.

14   Under increasing international pressure, in 1978 Smith and some African leaders signed an internal settlement. However, this was unacceptable to the liberation movements whose success forced the Government to negotiate. London supervised the February 1980 free elections, won by Robert Mugabe. In line with the April 1980 Lancaster House agreements, Britain transferred power to ZANU. The white Zimbabweans retained some privileges, including their land and protected seats in Parliament.

15   Mugabe began by abolishing racist legislation and reconstructing the economy, affected by seven years of war, which had reduced cattle to one third, devastated roads, and exacerbated diseases such as malaria. Mugabe advocated reconciliation and his cabinet included ZAPU and white leaders. He set an ambitious Development Plan and in the first few years there was rapid growth, especially in farm production. However, Mugabe was hampered by South Africa's blockade on Zimbabwe's agricultural exports and political dissent between ZANU and Nkomo's ZAPU whose mainly Ndebele former guerrillas were unhappy with ZANU and Shona dominance. A serious drought in 1983 was an additional setback.

16   African farmers' hopes for a true agrarian reform clashed with the limitations imposed by the Lancaster House agreement which ensured that white land had to be purchased (not expropriated) by the Government.

17   Towards the end of June 1985, Mugabe's Zimbabwe African National Union (ZANU) obtained a comfortable victory in parliamentary elections throughout the country, except in the Ndebele area of Matabeleland; the majority of the whites voted for the Rhodesian Front. At this time, Zimbabwe played a key role in the development of the regional trading and cooperation organization, the Southern African Development and Cooperation Council (SADCC), which tried to counteract apartheid South Africa's regional economic might.

18   In 1986, 4,500 farmers (most of them white) still owned 50 per cent of the country's most productive land, employing black farm-workers who lived on the farms. Over four million Africans

IN FOCUS

ENVIRONMENTAL CHALLENGES
There is deforestation, soil erosion and degradation, and air and water pollution. Poaching is decimating the herds of black rhinoceros (among the largest in the world). Small-scale mining produces heavy metal pollution and toxic waste.

WOMEN'S RIGHTS
Women have been able to vote since 1957 and run for office since 1978. In the year 2000, 14 per cent of seats in Parliament and 12 per cent of ministerial positions were held by women. Between 1980 and 2000, women comprised 45 per cent of the total labor force.

According to UNICEF's latest data available*, female enrollment in primary school is 80 per cent, but only 39 per cent in secondary school. Illiteracy among women stands at 15 per cent. 93 per cent of pregnant women receive prenatal healthcare and 73 per cent of births are attended by qualified personnel.

There were 1,100 maternal deaths per 100,000 live births (1995*). In the year 2001, 25.2 per cent of pregnant women were HIV-positive.

CHILDREN
The high child mortality rate has not decreased significantly over recent decades. In 1960, for every 1,000 live births 159

children under-five and 97 infants under-one died. According to UNICEF's latest data available*, the rate stands at 123 and 76 respectively. Eleven per cent of babies have low birth weight.

By the end of 2001, among the 2,300,000 people living with HIV/AIDS in the country, 240,000 were children and there were 782,000 AIDS orphans.

The primary school enrollment rate was 80 per cent*.

INDIGENOUS PEOPLES/ ETHNIC MINORITIES
Only about 10 per cent of the population are not Shona or Ndebele people. These other ethnic groups include Shangaan, Venda and Tsonga people. There are also some Tswa (San). Shona remain the largest population of approximately 70 per cent to which most politicians in power, including President Robert Mugabe, belong. Ndebeles from Matabeleland constitute approximately 20 per cent, but are a powerful group.

MIGRANTS/REFUGEES
By the end of 2002, around 10,000 foreign refugees were living in Zimbabwe: 5,000 from DR Congo, 3,000 from Rwanda, 1,000 from Burundi and 1,000 from other African countries. Refugees mainly live in urban areas and are subject to all many restrictions. The Government has requested help with providing for the refugees. It has taken steps to prevent sexual exploitation of female refugees. UNHCR has provided food and

water in the in the neediest areas.

In Zimbabwe, since 2000, between 100,000 and 200,000 people were relocated by the Government, as part of its agrarian reform program. They were mainly settled on land illegally expropriated from white farmers. The US Committee for Refugees estimated that the events of 2002 caused approximately 150,000 to 200,000 people to flee their homes, and that 100,000 or more Zimbabweans were internally displaced at year's end, many of them black farm-workers from white farms who fled after threats from landless pro-government protesters.

Around 10,000 Zimbabwean nationals applied for asylum in the UK in the last 10 years; most arrived after 1999. In 2002, Zimbabweans were the second largest group of asylum seekers to the UK, with some 7,695 asylum applications. According to official figures in Harare, more than 3 million Zimbabweans live overseas. Many are refugees or illegals in neighboring Botswana, South Africa, Zambia and Mozambique.

DEATH PENALTY
Capital punishment is still applied.

* Latest data available in *The State of the World's Children* and *Childinfo* database, UNICEF, 2004.

were squeezed onto communally owned tribal trust lands, which were poor, situated in dry regions and lacking infrastructure and communications.

19   The (white) Commercial Farmers Union generated 90 per cent of all agricultural production, paid a third of Zimbabwe's wages and exported 40 per cent of the country's goods. Its insistence on the 'willing-buyer, willing-seller' principle for land transfers slowed the process of land reform and redistribution.

20   Two constitutional reforms were enacted in September 1987, through which the 30 parliamentary seats protected for whites were abolished and executive authority was transferred to the president, elected by Parliament for a six-year period.

21   Mugabe played an important role in the summit of the

Movement of Non-Aligned Countries held in September in Harare (the capital, formerly Salisbury). He requested the widespread adoption of sanctions against South Africa. In addition, he supported Mozambique's government against the rebel National Resistance of Mozambique (RENAMO) with some 12,000 troops.

22   In December 1987, Mugabe and Nkomo reached a unification agreement (ratified in April 1988) creating the Patriotic Front of the Zimbabwe African National Union (ZANU-PF).

23   In the March 1990 elections, ZANU-PF won 116 of the 119 parliamentary seats. Mugabe interpreted this result as the people's support for a one-party system. However, only 54 per cent of the electorate went to the polls and the newly formed opposition Zimbabwe Unity Movement (ZUM) obtained 15

per cent of the votes. The opposition gained the majority of its votes in Harare (almost 30 per cent) and other urban centers, while ZANU held the rural areas.

24   In 1990, Parliament approved a land reform law authorizing the Government to expropriate land held by whites at a price fixed by the State, and to redistribute it among black Zimbabweans. The majority of the African population supported the law, deeming it an act of racial and economic justice. Nevertheless ZANU-PF moved away from Marxist-Leninist doctrine, maintaining a social democratic and mixed economy in which whites had an important role.

25   In 1992, the Mozambican conflict came to an end which removed the threat of destabilization for Zimabawe.

26   The April 1996 elections (with an abstention rate of 68

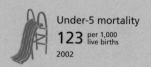
Under-5 mortality
123 per 1,000 live births
2002

Poverty
36.0% of population living on less than $1 per day
1990/91

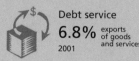
Debt service
6.8% exports of goods and services
2001

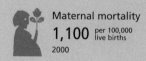
Maternal mortality
1,100 per 100,000 live births
2000

PROFILE

ENVIRONMENT

The country consists mainly of a high rolling plateau. Most of the urban population live in the High Veld, an area of fertile land, with moderate rainfall and mineral wealth. The climate is tropical, tempered by altitude.

SOCIETY

Peoples: The majority of Zimbabweans (70 per cent) are of Bantu origin from the Shona (founders of the first nation in the region) and Ndebele (20 per cent) a Zulu-speaking people that arrived in the 19th century. Others include Venda, Shangaan, Tsonga and San.
Religions: African traditional beliefs (55 per cent); Christian (45 per cent).
Languages: English (official); Shona, Zulu and other languages.
Main Political Parties: Zimbabwe African National Union-Patriotic Front (ZANU-PF); Movement for Democratic Change (MDC); Regional ZANU-Ndonga party (ZANU-N).
Main Social Organizations: Organization of Rural Associations for Progress; Council of Trade Unions of Zimbabwe, National Students Union of Zimbabwe.

THE STATE

Official Name: Republic of Zimbabwe.
Administrative Divisions: 8 Provinces.
Capital: Harare 1,469,000 people (2003).
Other Cities: Bulawayo 794,600 people; Chitungwiza (outside Harare) 390,600; Mutare 168,100 (2000).
Government: Robert Mugabe, President since December 1987, re-elected in 1990, 1996 and 2002. Unicameral Legislature: the House of Assembly, with 150 members.
National Holiday: 18 April, Independence Day (1980).
Armed Forces: 39,000 (1997). Other: 15,000 (Republican Police Force), 2,000 (Police Support Unit), 4,000 (National Militia).

per cent) gave Mugabe the victory with 93 per cent of the votes.

27 After Laurent Kabila came to power in DR Congo (DRC) in 1997, civil conflict there persisted, Mugabe became increasingly involved in supporting Kabila against rebels - which drained Zimbabwe's public finances.

28 IMF-imposed structural adjustment programs cutting public spending, and economic stagnation, made it increasingly difficult for the Government to provide its supporters with basic services. Although about 30 per cent of white-owned land had been redistributed, pressure mounted from the war veterans who felt they had been neglected since Independence. In June 1996 they forcibly took over six farms east of Harare.

29 In July the Government announced a new plan to settle 100,000 families on five million hectares to be purchased from white farmers. The IMF and EU, although recognizing the need for land reform, rejected the plan, saying it was too ambitious, and agreed only to support a two-year pilot project. Mugabe changed his mind yet again in November, ordering the expropriation of 841 farms.

30 In October 1999 a special 3-per cent tax was imposed on salaries. The Government stated it would be used to treat people with HIV/AIDS (25 per cent of the country's adult population). The measure was seen by many as a scheme to finance the 11,000 troops that Mugabe sent to back the Kabila regime in the DRC. Corruption by the ruling élite was widely reported in the media.

31 Mugabe suffered a shock defeat by a new opposition party - the Movement for Democratic Change (MDC) in February 2000's constitutional referendum. This had been designed to enhance presidential powers and allow for the confiscation of white farms without compensation.

32 ZANU-PF was galvanized into retaliatory action. In March 2000, 420 white-owned farms were occupied by black war veterans. The Commercial Farmers Union accused Mugabe of orchestrating the occupations to hide the failure of the land distribution projects. The Government owned nearly two million acres of uncultivated farmland. Mugabe responded that the country could not pay for the division of land into smaller plots or to provide minimal infrastructure, such as waterworks and roads.

33 In May, as a platform for the June parliamentary elections, Mugabe launched a manifesto stating that he would not give in to international pressure and that he would not reverse or prevent the land invasions. Anxious to prevent foreign scrutiny, his government decided to slash the number of election observers. Despite allegedly rigging the elections, ZANU won only five more seats than the trade-union backed and largely urban opposition Movement for Democratic Change (MDC). In the elections, Mugabe encountered real opposition for the first time since 1980, and determined to suppress it.

34 In 2001, the Mugabe regime was the target of charges of human rights violations, including the right to information. The British media and several NGOs reported that many judges and journalists had been forced to leave Zimbabwe and that several opposition leaders had been assassinated.

35 Renewed international pressure led Mugabe to slow the illegal land occupations in September 2001 in exchange for major financial aid from Britain to compensate the white farmers whose land had been expropriated. The reluctance of companies to invest in the country had fuelled unemployment, and inflation reached 70 per cent by the end of the year.

36 The Government, which had censored the state-owned broadcast media, introduced a bill in January 2002 for an Information Access and Privacy Protection Act. This sought to silence the independent press and foreign journalists before the upcoming presidential elections. National and international pressure led the Government to withdraw the bill - but it promptly returned an amended version to Parliament.

37 Mugabe won the March 2002 presidential elections with 56.2 per cent of the vote, beating Morgan Tsvangirai of the opposition MDC, which won 41.9 per cent of votes. The opposition, independent election observers and the international community again disputed the result. Weeks after the elections, the Commonwealth expelled Zimbabwe for one year, following recommendations by electoral observers that the voting had been obstructed by government-inspired violence. The EU and the US announced that they would impose severe sanctions against Zimbabwe in 2002. Denmark closed its embassy

in Harare. Like the EU, Switzerland froze the assets of some senior government figures and refused them entry.

38 In August 2002, 3,000 white farmers were told to quit their lands and in September Parliament passed a series of laws to speed up the expropriation process, which was to end in a month's time. Some 2,500 farmers decided not to obey the order, defying the Government, and violence ensued. Inflation soared in response to the economic crisis. Morgan Tsvangirai was charged with treason, allegedly for plotting to overthrow the President.

39 In March 2003, observers reported unprecedented levels of repression in the widespread confrontations over land expropriation. The trade unions and the MDC attempted to stage mass strikes and actions to pressure Mugabe to retire early. The protests met with severe government repression.

40 Mugabe, still securely in power, stepped up his anti-West rhetoric and propaganda war. The Daily News, the only independent daily, was closed down in October. Many journalists have been imprisoned and beaten. In December 2003, the Commonwealth extended Zimbabwe's expulsion indefinitely.

41 In February 2004, Morgan Tsvangirai's treason trial came to an end but the judgement was not expected for several months. A month later, the EU renewed sanctions and extended its list of officials banned from entry to its states. In June, the World Association of Newspapers (WAN) condemned Zimbabwe's draconian press laws and called on Mugabe to end the ban on independent media within the country.

42 That same month, several Zimbabwean civil rights groups expressed discontent over a decision by the African Union (AU), which during the summit held in Ethiopia suspended publication of a report that denounced human rights abuses in the country. The report, prepared in 2002 by the AU Commission on Human Rights, contained allegations of government complicity in cases of torture, arbitrary arrest of opposition members of parliament and human rights lawyers.

43 In October Morgan Tsvangirai was acquitted of plotting to assassinate President Mugabe, ending a two-and-a-half year case that could have led to his execution. ∎

The world in figures

2005/2006

	AREA (SQUARE KM) [1]	TOTAL POPULATION (THOUSANDS) [2]	DEMOGRAPHIC GROWTH 1985-2000 (%) [2]	DEMOGRAPHIC GROWTH TO YEAR 2015 (%) [2]	TOTAL POPULATION ESTIMATE FOR YEAR 2015 (THOUSANDS) [2]	POPULATION DENSITY [2]	URBAN POPULATION AS % OF TOTAL [2]	URBAN POPULATION, ANNUAL GROWTH (%) [2]	2015 URBAN POPULATION AS % OF TOTAL POPULATION [2]
	2002	2005	1985-2000	2000-2015	2002	2005	2005	2000-2005	2002
Afghanistan	652,090	25,971	3.1	3.4	35,473	39.8	24.3	6.9	30.5
Albania	28,750	3,220	0.3	0.7	3,440	112.0	45.0	2.0	51.2
Algeria	2,381,740	32,877	2.2	1.5	38,142	13.8	60.0	3.2	65.3
Andorra	453	75	2.8	2.4	95	166.4	91.3	3.5	91.1
Angola	1,246,700	14,533	2.7	2.9	19,268	11.7	37.2	4.9	44.9
Anguilla	96	12	2.8	1.5	14	127.6	100.0	3.6	100.0
Antigua	440	74	0.8	0.4	76	167.3	38.4	1.3	43.4
Argentina	2,780,400	39,311	1.3	1.1	43,450	14.1	90.6	1.5	92.2
Armenia	29,800	3,043	-0.5	-0.3	2,963	102.1	64.1	0.8	64.2
Aruba	190	103	2.6	1.9	123	543.2	44.7		43.7
Australia	7,741,220	20,092	1.4	0.8	21,747	2.6	92.7	0.9	94.9
Austria	83,860	8,120	0.4	0.0	8,058	96.8	65.8	0.5	67.2
Azerbaijan	86,600	8,527	1.3	1.0	9,450	98.5	49.9	1.5	51.3
Bahamas	13,880	321	1.7	1.0	351	23.1	90.0	1.9	91.6
Bahrain	710	754	3.3	1.9	900	1,062.4	90.2	1.8	91.4
Bangladesh	144,000	152,593	2.4	1.8	181,428	1,059.7	25.0	4.0	29.6
Barbados	430	272	0.4	0.3	280	633.1	52.9	1.5	59.1
Belarus	207,600	9,809	0.0	-0.4	9,427	47.2	71.6	0.3	75.2
Belgium	33,100	10,359	0.3	0.1	10,470	313.0	97.3	0.1	97.5
Belize	22,960	266	2.6	1.8	315	11.6	48.6	3.4	51.8
Benin	112,620	7,103	2.9	2.5	9,093	63.1	46.1	4.4	53.5
Bermuda	50	83	0.8	0.6	87	1,654.6	100.0	0.8	100.0
Bhutan	47,000	2,392	2.2	2.6	3,043	50.9	9.1	6.0	12.6
Bolivia	1,098,580	9,138	2.2	1.8	10,831	8.3	64.4	3.0	69.0
Bosnia-Herzegovina	51,130	4,209	-0.2	0.5	4,284	82.3	45.3	2.3	51.1
Botswana	581,730	1,801	2.6	-0.1	1,712	3.1	52.5	2.2	57.5
Brazil	8,547,400	182,798	1.6	1.1	201,970	21.4	84.2	1.8	88.4
Brunei	5,770	374	2.7	2.0	453	64.9	77.6	2.4	82.8
Bulgaria	110,910	7,763	-0.7	-0.8	7,167	70.0	70.5	-0.1	74.0
Burkina Faso	274,000	13,798	2.9	3.0	18,562	50.4	18.6	5.6	23.2
Burundi	27,830	7,319	1.7	3.0	9,834	263.0	10.6	5.9	14.6
Cambodia	181,040	14,825	3.2	2.2	18,421	81.9	19.7	4.2	26.1
Cameroon	475,440	16,564	2.7	1.5	18,860	34.8	52.9	4.0	59.9
Canada	9,970,610	31,972	1.2	0.7	34,133	3.2	81.1	1.1	84.0
Cape Verde	4,030	482	2.1	1.9	577	119.6	57.6	4.0	64.8
Cayman Is.	260	43	3.7	2.7	55	164.6	100.0	3.4	100.0
Central African Rep.	622,980	3,962	2.3	1.4	4,586	6.4	43.8	3.0	50.3
Ceuta	19	75				3,947.4			
Chad	1,284,000	9,117	3.0	2.9	12,138	7.1	25.8	4.2	31.1
Chile	756,630	16,185	1.6	1.1	18,019	21.4	87.7	1.5	90.2
China	9,598,050	1,322,273	1.2	0.6	1,402,321	137.8	40.5	2.3	49.5
Christmas Is.	135	0.4				3.2			
Cocos	14	0.6				45.0			
Colombia	1,138,910	45,600	1.9	1.4	52,190	40.0	77.4	2.2	81.3
Comoros	2,230	812	2.9	2.6	1,042	364.3	36.3	4.4	43.0
Congo D.R.	2,344,860	56,079	2.8	2.8	74,160	23.9			
Congo R.	342,000	3,921	3.3	2.8	5,215	11.5	32.7	4.5	39.7
Cook Is.	236	18	0.2	0.1	19	78.3	73.3	1.0	83.1
Coral Sea Is.									
Costa Rica	51,100	4,327	2.5	1.6	5,030	84.7	61.7	2.6	66.8
Côte d'Ivoire	322,460	17,165	2.8	1.5	19,837	53.2	45.8	3.4	51.0
Croatia	56,540	4,405	0.0	-0.3	4,275	77.9	59.9	0.6	64.6
Cuba	110,860	11,353	0.7	0.2	11,525	102.4	76.0	0.5	78.1
Cyprus	9,250	813	1.3	0.6	861	87.9	69.5	1.7	71.6
Czech Republic	78,870	10,216	0.0	-0.1	10,076	129.5	74.5	0.0	75.7
Denmark	43,090	5,386	0.3	0.2	5,447	125.0	85.5	0.2	86.8
Diego Garcia	52	1.3				25.0			
Djibouti	23,200	721	3.7	1.5	839	31.1	84.6	2.4	87.6
Dominica	750	79	0.4	0.2	80	105.3	72.7	0.5	76.2
Dominican Republic	48,730	8,998	1.7	1.3	10,121	184.7	60.1	2.3	64.6
Ecuador	283,560	13,379	2.1	1.3	15,155	47.2	62.8	3.0	67.6
Egypt	1,001,450	74,878	2.1	1.9	89,996	74.8	42.3	2.3	44.9
El Salvador	21,040	6,709	1.8	1.3	7,560	318.9	60.1	2.7	64.2
Equatorial Guinea	28,050	521	2.5	2.5	662	18.6	50.0	4.5	58.2
Eritrea	117,600	4,456	2.1	3.1	5,914	37.9	20.8	4.6	26.5
Estonia	45,100	1,294	-0.7	-1.1	1,159	28.7	69.6	-1.0	71.4
Ethiopia	1,104,300	74,189	3.1	2.4	93,845	67.2	16.2	5.0	19.8
Faeroe Is.	1,400	47	0.0	0.6	50	33.9	39.3	0.6	43.5
Fiji	18,270	854	0.9	0.8	919	46.8	53.2	2.9	60.1
Finland	338,150	5,224	0.4	0.1	5,284	15.4	60.9	0.9	62.1
France	551,500	60,711	0.5	0.4	62,841	110.1	76.7	0.6	79.0
French Guiana	90,000	187	4.2	2.2	230	2.1	75.6	4.3	77.5
French Polynesia	4,000	252	2.0	1.2	287	162.9	51.9	2.3	53.2
Gabon	267,670	1,375	2.9	1.8	1,645	5.1	85.2	3.1	89.1
Gambia	11,300	1,499	3.5	2.3	1,851	132.7	26.1	4.5	27.8
Georgia	69,700	5,026	0.0	-0.7	4,724	72.1	51.5	0.8	51.6
Germany	357,030	82,560	0.4	0.0	82,497	231.2	88.5	0.2	90.0
Ghana	238,540	21,833	2.6	2.0	26,359	91.5	46.3	4.2	51.1
Gibraltar	6	27	0.2	0.0	27	4,545.2	100.0	-0.7	100.0
Greece	131,960	10,978	0.6	0.0	10,944	83.2	61.4	0.4	65.2
Greenland	341,700	57	0.4	0.2	58	0.2	82.9	0.4	85.5
Grenada	340	80	-0.5	-0.3	77	235.2	42.2	1.8	49.5
Guadeloupe	1,705	446	1.3	0.6	471	261.9	99.8	1.2	99.9
Guam	550	168	1.8	1.4	192	305.2	94.0	2.5	95.2
Guatemala	108,890	12,978	2.6	2.3	16,197	119.2	47.2	3.4	51.9
Guinea	245,860	8,788	2.8	2.2	11,233	35.7	36.5	4.5	44.2
Guinea-Bissau	36,120	1,584	2.8	2.9	2,104	43.8	35.6	4.0	43.5
Guyana	214,970	768	0.0	0.0	761	3.6	38.5	2.3	44.2
Haiti	27,750	8,549	1.8	1.3	9,694	308.1	38.8	3.4	45.5
Honduras	112,090	7,257	2.9	2.0	8,762	64.7	46.4	4.2	51.3
Hungary	93,030	9,784	-0.4	-0.5	9,324	105.2	65.9	0.0	70.0
Iceland	103,000	294	1.0	0.6	311	2.9	93.0	1.0	94.1
India	3,287,260	1,096,917	1.9	1.4	1,246,351	333.7	28.7	2.8	32.2
Indonesia	1,904,570	225,313	1.6	1.1	250,428	118.3	47.9	3.6	57.8
Iran	1,648,200	70,675	2.1	1.4	81,422	42.9	68.1	1.8	73.9
Iraq	438,320	26,555	2.8	2.6	34,226	60.6	66.8	3.3	66.8
Ireland	70,270	4,040	0.5	0.9	4,398	57.5	60.4	1.2	63.6
Israel	21,060	6,685	2.6	1.7	7,772	317.4	91.7	1.8	92.4
Italy	301,340	57,253	0.1	-0.2	55,507	190.0	67.5	0.1	69.2
Jamaica	10,990	2,701	0.8	1.0	2,977	245.8	52.2	1.7	54.2
Japan	377,800	127,914	0.3	0.0	127,224	338.6	65.7	0.3	67.7
Jordan	89,210	5,750	4.1	2.2	6,982	64.5	79.3	3.5	81.1
Kanaky-New Caledonia	18,580	237	2.2	1.7	278	12.8	61.6	2.8	64.7
Kazakhstan	2,724,900	15,364	-0.1	-0.1	15,328	5.6	55.9	0.2	58.2
Kenya	580,370	32,849	2.9	1.3	36,864	56.6	41.6	4.1	51.8
Kiribati	730	90	1.8	1.3	102	123.5	50.2	2.7	61.9
Korea, North	120,540	22,876	1.2	0.4	23,706	189.8	61.7	1.6	65.7
Korea, South	99,260	48,182	0.9	0.4	49,672	485.4	80.8	1.4	83.0
Kuwait	17,820	2,671	1.8	2.7	3,352	149.9	96.4	2.3	96.9
Kyrgyzstan	199,900	5,278	1.4	1.3	5,949	26.4	33.7	0.9	35.4
Laos	236,800	5,918	2.5	2.1	7,282	25.0	21.6	4.9	27.4
Latvia	64,600	2,265	-0.6	-0.9	2,064	35.1	65.9	-1.0	66.3
Lebanon	10,400	3,761	1.8	1.3	4,207	361.6	88.0	1.7	90.1
Lesotho	30,350	1,797	1.4	-0.3	1,713	59.2	18.2	4.6	21.0
Liberia	111,370	3,603	2.0	3.1	4,713	32.4	47.9	4.9	54.1
Libya	1,759,540	5,768	2.2	1.8 .	6,886	3.3	86.9	2.6	89.0
Liechtenstein	160	34	1.3	0.7	36	213.0	21.8	3.1	24.0
Lithuania	65,200	3,401	-0.1	-0.6	3,222	52.2	66.6	-0.1	67.5

DEMOGRAPHY

	AREA (SQUARE KM) [1]	TOTAL POPULATION (THOUSANDS) [2]	DEMOGRAPHIC GROWTH 1985-2000 (%) [2]	DEMOGRAPHIC GROWTH TO YEAR 2015 (%) [2]	TOTAL POPULATION ESTIMATE FOR YEAR 2015 (THOUSANDS) [2]	POPULATION DENSITY [2]	URBAN POPULATION AS % OF TOTAL [2]	URBAN POPULATION, ANNUAL GROWTH (%) [2]	2015 URBAN POPULATION AS % OF TOTAL POPULATION [2]
	2002	2005	1985-2000	2000-2015	2002	2005	2005	2000-2005	2002
Luxembourg	2,600	465	1.1	1.2	522	178.8	92.4	1.1	94.1
Macedonia, TFYR	25,710	2,076	0.7	0.4	2,160	80.7	59.7	1.3	62.0
Madagascar	587,040	18,409	2.9	2.7	24,000	31.4	27.0	4.8	30.7
Malawi	118,480	12,572	3.0	1.9	15,165	106.1	17.2	7.3	22.2
Malaysia	329,750	25,325	2.6	1.7	29,563	76.8	65.1	2.8	71.0
Maldives	300	338	3.1	2.9	447	1,125.7	29.7	3.5	35.2
Mali	1,240,190	13,829	2.7	3.1	18,986	11.2	33.7	4.6	40.9
Malta	320	397	0.8	0.4	411	1,241.7	92.1	0.9	93.7
Malvinas-Falklands	11,410	3	3.1	0.4	3	0.3	84.9	1.2	91.3
Marshall Is.	200	54	2.0	1.1	60	271.0	66.7	3.7	69.5
Martinique	1,102	397	0.8	0.4	412	359.9	96.2	0.9	97.4
Mauritania	1,025,520	3,069	2.5	2.7	3,988	3.0	64.3	4.3	73.9
Mauritius	2,040	1,244	1.0	0.8	1,340	609.7	43.8	1.6	47.3
Mayotte Is.	400	163,366				408,415.0			
Melilla	12	69				5,765.3			
Mexico	1,958,200	106,385	1.8	1.3	119,618	54.3	76.0	1.7	78.8
Micronesia	700	111	1.5	0.7	119	159.2	30.0	3.2	35.2
Moldova	33,850	4,259	0.1	-0.1	4,206	125.8	46.3	0.3	50.0
Monaco	2	35	1.1	0.8	38	17,508.5	100.0	1.0	100.0
Mongolia	1,566,500	2,667	1.8	1.3	3,051	1.7	57.0	2.3	59.5
Montserrat	102	4	-7.1	0.2	4	38.8	13.8	2.5	16.9
Morocco	446,550	31,564	1.9	1.5	36,496	70.7	58.8	2.8	64.8
Mozambique	801,590	19,495	2.0	1.6	22,537	24.3	38.0	4.1	48.5
Myanmar-Burma	676,580	50,696	1.6	1.1	55,762	74.9	30.6	2.9	37.6
Namibia	824,290	2,032	3.4	1.0	2,196	2.5	33.5	2.8	39.8
Nauru	21	14	2.7	2.1	17	650.5	100.0	1.8	100.0
Nepal	147,180	26,289	2.3	2.1	32,011	178.6	15.8	5.1	20.5
Netherlands	41,530	16,300	0.6	0.4	16,791	392.5	66.8	0.3	71.4
Netherlands Antilles	800	224	1.1	0.7	240	280.5	70.1	1.4	73.1
New Zealand-Aotearoa	270,530	3,932	1.0	0.7	4,173	14.5	86.0	1.0	87.0
Nicaragua	130,000	5,727	2.7	2.2	7,027	44.1	58.1	3.4	62.8
Niger	1,267,000	12,873	3.3	3.6	18,317	10.2	23.3	5.5	29.7
Nigeria	923,770	130,236	2.9	2.3	161,726	141.0	48.3	4.1	55.5
Niue	260	2	-2.0	-1.3	2	7.3	36.7	-0.6	43.2
Norfolk Is.	36	2				51.5			
Northern Marianas	500	86	6.2	3.4	117	171.4	94.7	5.6	96.2
Norway	323,880	4,570	0.5	0.4	4,719	14.1	80.5	0.9	86.4
Oman	309,500	3,020	3.6	2.7	3,908	9.8	78.6	4.4	82.6
Pakistan	796,100	161,151	2.7	2.4	204,465	202.4	34.8	4.1	39.5
Palau	460	21	2.3	1.9	26	46.4	68.2	2.7	68.1
Palestine	6,220	3,815	3.9	3.3	5,260	613.4	71.9		75.6
Panama	75,520	3,235	2.0	1.7	3,790	42.8	57.8	2.0	61.7
Papua New Guinea	462,840	5,959	2.5	2.0	7,169	12.9	13.2	4.0	14.5
Paraguay	406,750	6,160	2.8	2.2	7,653	15.1	58.5	3.6	64.3
Peru	1,285,220	27,968	1.9	1.4	31,965	21.8	74.6	2.1	78.0
Philippines	300,000	82,809	2.2	1.6	96,338	276.0	62.6	3.1	69.2
Pitcairn	5	0	1.6	0.0	0	13.2		0.0	
Poland	323,250	38,516	0.3	-0.1	38,173	119.2	62.0	0.7	64.0
Portugal	91,980	10,080	0.0	0.0	10,030	109.6	55.6	1.7	60.9
Puerto Rico	8,950	3,915	0.8	0.4	4,044	437.5	97.5	1.2	99.1
Qatar	11,000	628	3.2	1.3	711	57.1	92.3	1.7	93.6
Réunion	2,510	777	1.8	1.2	862	309.5	92.3	1.9	94.9
Romania	238,390	22,228	-0.1	-0.3	21,649	93.2	54.7	0.2	56.4
Russia	17,075,400	141,553	0.1	-0.6	133,429	8.3	73.3	0.2	74.3
Rwanda	26,340	8,607	1.7	2.1	10,565	326.8	21.8	4.2	40.5
Sahara, Western	266,000	324							
Samoa	2,840	182	0.6	1.1	203	64.0	22.5	2.8	24.7
Samoa, American	200	65	2.6	2.2	80	324.1	91.1	4.4	93.8
San Marino	61	28	1.2	0.9	30	460.8	88.7	1.1	89.1
São Tomé and Príncipe	960	169	2.4	2.3	212	175.8	37.9	3.3	40.3
Saudi Arabia	2,149,690	25,626	3.6	2.6	32,728	11.9	88.5	3.4	91.1
Senegal	196,720	10,587	2.6	2.2	13,159	53.8	51.0	4.0	57.9
Serbia and Montenegro	102,000	10,513	0.5	-0.1	10,445	103.1	52.3	0.6	55.5
Seychelles	450	82	1.1	0.8	88	183.1	50.2	2.2	53.3
Sierra Leone	71,740	5,340	1.4	2.5	6,399	74.4	40.2	4.0	47.6
Singapore	620	4,372	2.6	1.1	4,707	7,050.8	100.0	1.0	100.0
Slovakia	49,010	5,411	0.3	0.1	5,441	110.4	58.0	0.5	60.8
Slovenia	20,250	1,979	0.4	-0.2	1,931	97.7	50.8	0.3	52.6
Solomon Is.	28,900	504	3.2	2.6	643	17.5	17.1	5.6	20.9
Somalia	637,660	10,742	1.8	3.7	15,263	16.8	35.9	5.2	42.7
South Africa	1,221,040	45,323	1.9	0.0	44,266	37.1	57.9	1.3	62.7
Spain	505,990	41,184	0.4	0.1	41,167	81.4	76.7	0.2	78.1
Sri Lanka	65,610	19,366	1.2	0.7	20,640	295.2	21.0	2.8	22.5
St Helena	122	5	-0.6	0.0	5	41.4	36.1	2.3	40.4
St Kitts-Nevis	360	42	0.0	-0.4	40	115.5	31.9	-0.1	32.5
St Lucia	620	152	1.2	0.7	162	244.4	31.3	2.0	36.8
St Pierre and Miquelon	242	6	0.2	0.0	6	26.3	89.0	0.4	89.7
St Vincent	390	121	0.8	0.5	127	310.8	60.5	2.6	68.6
Sudan	2,505,810	35,040	2.2	1.8	41,430	14.0	40.8	4.5	49.3
Suriname	163,270	442	0.7	0.7	471	2.7	77.2	1.3	81.6
Swaziland	17,360	1,087	2.6	0.2	1,075	62.6	23.9	4.0	27.0
Sweden	449,960	8,895	0.4	0.1	8,983	19.8	83.4	0.3	84.3
Switzerland	41,290	7,157	0.6	-0.2	7,010	173.3	67.5	0.6	68.7
Syria	185,180	18,650	2.9	2.2	23,018	100.7	50.3	3.3	52.4
Taiwan	36,960	22,370				605.2			
Tajikistan	143,100	6,356	1.9	1.2	7,252	44.4	24.2	1.3	24.4
Tanzania	945,090	38,365	3.0	1.8	45,909	40.6	37.5	5.4	46.8
Thailand	513,120	64,081	1.2	0.9	69,585	124.9	32.5	2.7	36.7
Timor-Leste	14,870	857	0.4	2.7	1,060	57.7	7.8	2.2	9.5
Togo	56,790	5,129	2.9	2.2	6,351	90.3	36.3	4.2	43.3
Tokelau	12	2	-0.5	-0.1	2	126.8		0.0	
Tonga	750	106	0.2	0.9	115	141.1	34.0	1.8	38.2
Trinidad and Tobago	5,130	1,311	0.6	0.3	1,342	255.6	76.2	1.1	79.7
Tunisia	163,610	10,042	1.7	1.0	11,116	61.4	64.4	2.3	68.1
Turkey	774,820	73,302	1.8	1.2	82,150	94.6	67.3	2.6	71.9
Turkmenistan	488,100	5,015	2.4	1.5	5,820	10.3	45.8	2.1	50.0
Turks and Caicos	430	22	4.3	3.0	29	51.2	47.4	4.2	53.4
Tuvalu	26	11	1.5	1.1	12	417.3	57.0	4.3	64.7
Uganda	241,040	27,623	3.2	3.4	39,335	114.6	12.4	5.7	14.2
Ukraine	603,700	47,782	-0.2	-0.8	44,368	79.1	67.3	-0.1	68.9
United Arab Emirates	83,600	3,106	4.0	1.6	3,588	37.2	85.5	2.0	87.2
United Kingdom	242,910	59,598	0.3	0.3	61,275	245.4	89.2	0.2	90.2
United States	9,629,090	300,038	1.0	1.0	329,669	31.2	80.8	1.0	83.6
Uruguay	176,220	3,463	0.7	0.6	3,683	19.7	93.0	0.9	94.4
Uzbekistan	447,400	26,868	2.1	1.4	30,718	60.1	36.4	1.6	37.0
Vanuatu	12,190	222	2.7	2.2	275	18.2	23.7	4.0	28.6
Vatican	0.44	1	0.4	0.0	1	1,784.1	100.0	0.0	100.0
Venezuela	912,050	26,640	2.3	1.7	31,189	29.2	88.1	2.1	90.0
Vietnam	331,690	83,585	1.9	1.3	94,742	252.0	26.7	2.2	32.4
Virgin Is. (Am.)	340	113	0.5	0.8	122	333.7	94.1	0.1	95.8
Virgin Is. (Br.)	153	22	2.2	1.6	25	141.8	65.4	3.9	71.8
Wallis and Futuna	274	15	0.8	0.5	16	54.3		0.0	
Yemen	527,970	21,480	4.0	3.5	30,677	40.7	26.3	4.7	31.3
Zambia	752,610	11,043	2.6	1.3	12,670	14.7	36.5	2.6	40.8
Zimbabwe	390,760	12,963	2.4	0.2	13,031	33.2	35.9	2.9	41.4

1. World Development Indicators 2003, World Bank / 2. World Population Prospects-The 2002 Revision. United Nations

	LIFE EXPECTANCY AT BIRTH (YEARS) [1]	LIFE EXPECTANCY AT BIRTH - MALE (YEARS) [1]	LIFE EXPECTANCY AT BIRTH - FEMALE (YEARS) [1]	TOTAL FERTILITY RATE (CHILDREN PER WOMAN) [2]	CRUDE BIRTH RATE (PER 1,000 PEOPLE) [1]	CRUDE DEATH RATE (PER 1,000 PEOPLE) [1]	% OF MARRIED WOMEN OF CHILDBEARING AGE USING CONTRACEPTIVES [2]	MATERNAL MORTALITY (PER 100,000 LIVE BIRTHS) [2]	BIRTHS ATTENDED BY TRAINED HEALTH PERSONNEL (%) [2]	INFANT MORTALITY RATE (PER 1,000 LIVE BIRTHS) [2]
	2000-2005	2000-2005	2000-2005	2002	2000-2005	2000-2005	1995-2002	2000	1995-2002	2002
Afghanistan	43.1	43.0	43.3	6.8	47	21	5	1,900	12	165
Albania	73.7	70.9	76.7	2.3	18	5	58	55	99	26
Algeria	69.7	68.1	71.3	2.8	23	5	64	140	92	39
Andorra										6
Angola	40.1	38.8	41.5	7.2	52	24	6	1,700	45	154
Anguilla										
Antigua										
Argentina	74.2	70.6	77.7	2.5	19	8	53		100	12
Armenia	72.4	69.0	75.6	1.2	10	8	74	82	98	16
Aruba							61	55	97	30
Australia	79.2	76.4	82.0	1.7	12	7	76	8	100	6
Austria	78.5	75.4	81.5	1.3	9	10	51	4	100	5
Azerbaijan	72.2	68.7	75.5	2.1	18	6	55	94	84	74
Bahamas	67.1	63.9	70.3	2.3	19	8	62	60	99	13
Bahrain	74.0	72.5	75.9	2.7	20	3	62	28	98	13
Bangladesh	61.4	61.0	61.8	3.5	29	8	54	380	12	51
Barbados	77.2	74.5	79.5	1.5	12	8	55	95	91	12
Belarus	70.1	64.9	75.3	1.2	9	13	50	35	100	17
Belgium	78.8	75.7	81.9	1.7	11	10	78	10	100	5
Belize	71.4	69.9	73.0	3.2	27	5	56	140	83	34
Benin	50.6	48.4	53.0	5.7	42	14	19	850	66	93
Bermuda										
Bhutan	63.2	62.0	64.5	5.1	35	9	31	420	24	74
Bolivia	63.9	61.8	66.0	3.9	29	8	53	420	69	56
Bosnia-Herzegovina	74.0	71.3	76.7	1.3	10	8	48	31	100	15
Botswana	39.7	38.9	40.5	3.7	31	21	48	100	94	80
Brazil	68.1	64.0	72.6	2.2	20	7	77	260	88	30
Brunei	76.3	74.2	78.9	2.5	23	3		37	99	6
Bulgaria	70.9	67.4	74.6	1.1	8	15	42	32		14
Burkina Faso	45.7	45.2	46.2	6.7	48	17	12	1,000	31	107
Burundi	40.9	40.4	41.4	6.8	44	21	16	1,000	25	114
Cambodia	57.4	55.2	59.5	4.8	34	10	24	450	32	96
Cameroon	46.2	45.1	47.4	4.7	35	17	26	730	60	95
Canada	79.3	76.7	81.9	1.5	10	8	75	6	98	5
Cape Verde	70.2	67.0	72.8	3.4	28	5	53	150	89	29
Cayman Is.										
Central African Rep.	39.5	38.5	40.6	5.0	38	22	28	1,100	44	115
Ceuta										
Chad	44.7	43.7	45.7	6.7	48	20	8	1,100	16	117
Chile	76.1	73.0	79.0	2.4	18	6	56	31	100	10
China	71.0	68.9	73.3	1.8	15	7	87	56	76	31
Christmas Is.										
Cocos										
Colombia	72.2	69.2	75.3	2.6	22	5	77	130	86	19
Comoros	60.8	59.4	62.2	4.9	37	8	26	480	62	59
Congo D.R.	41.8	40.8	42.8	6.7	50	21	31	990	61	129
Congo R.	48.2	46.6	49.7	6.3	44	15		510		81
Cook Is.							63		100	19
Coral Sea Is.										
Costa Rica	78.1	75.8	80.6	2.3	19	4	75	43	98	9
Côte d'Ivoire	41.0	40.8	41.2	4.8	35	20	15	690	63	102
Croatia	74.2	70.3	78.1	1.6	11	12		8	100	7
Cuba	76.7	74.8	78.7	1.6	12	7	73	33	100	7
Cyprus	78.3	76.0	80.5	1.9	13	8		47	100	5
Czech Republic	75.4	72.1	78.7	1.2	9	11	72	9	99	4
Denmark	76.6	74.2	79.1	1.8	12	11	78	5	100	4
Diego Garcia										
Djibouti	45.7	44.7	46.8	5.7	40	18		730		100
Dominica							50		100	13
Dominican Republic	66.7	64.4	69.2	2.7	23	7	65	150	98	32
Ecuador	70.8	68.3	73.5	2.8	23	6	66	130	69	25
Egypt	68.8	66.7	71.0	3.3	27	6	56	84	61	35
El Salvador	70.7	67.7	73.7	2.9	25	6	60	150	90	33
Equatorial Guinea	49.1	47.8	50.5	5.9	43	17		880	65	101
Eritrea	52.7	51.2	54.2	5.5	40	12	8	630	21	47
Estonia	71.7	66.5	76.8	1.2	9	14	70	63		10
Ethiopia	45.5	44.6	46.3	6.2	43	18	8	850	6	114
Faeroe Is.										
Fiji	69.8	68.1	71.5	2.9	24	5	44	75	100	17
Finland	78.0	74.4	81.5	1.7	11	10	77	6	100	4
France	79.0	75.2	82.8	1.9	13	9	75	17	99	4
French Guiana	75.1	72.5	78.3		24	4				
French Polynesia	71.0	68.9	73.4		20	5				
Gabon	56.6	55.8	57.5	4.0	32	11	33	420	86	60
Gambia	54.1	52.7	55.5	4.8	36	13	10	540	55	91
Georgia	73.6	69.5	77.6	1.4	10	10	41	32	96	24
Germany	78.3	75.2	81.2	1.3	9	11	75	8	100	4
Ghana	57.9	56.5	59.3	4.2	32	10	22	540	44	57
Gibraltar										
Greece	78.3	75.7	80.9	1.3	9	10		9		5
Greenland										
Grenada							54		99	20
Guadeloupe	78.3	74.8	81.7		16	6				
Guam	74.5	72.4	77.0		20	5				
Guatemala	65.8	63.0	68.9	4.5	34	7	38	240	41	36
Guinea	49.1	48.8	49.5	5.9	43	16	6	740	35	109
Guinea-Bissau	45.3	43.8	46.9	7.1	50	20	8	1,100	35	130
Guyana	63.2	60.1	66.3	2.3	22	9	37	170	86	54
Haiti	49.5	49.0	50.0	4.0	30	15	27	680	24	79
Honduras	68.9	66.5	71.4	3.8	30	6	62	110	56	32
Hungary	71.9	67.7	76.0	1.2	9	14	77	16		8
Iceland	79.8	77.6	81.9	2.0	14	7		0		3
India	63.9	63.2	64.6	3.1	24	8	47	540	43	67
Indonesia	66.8	64.8	68.8	2.4	21	7	53	230	64	33
Iran	70.3	68.9	71.9	2.4	20	5	74	76	90	35
Iraq	60.7	59.2	62.3	4.8	35	9	44	250	72	102
Ireland	77.0	74.4	79.6	1.9	14	8		5	100	6
Israel	79.2	77.1	81.0	2.7	20	6	68	17	99	6
Italy	78.7	75.5	81.9	1.2	9	11	60	5		4
Jamaica	75.7	73.7	77.8	2.4	20	6	66	87	95	17
Japan	81.6	77.9	85.1	1.3	9	8	59	10	100	3
Jordan	71.0	69.7	72.5	3.6	28	4	56	41	97	27
Kanaky-New Caledonia	74.9	72.5	77.7		19	5				
Kazakhstan	66.3	60.9	71.9	2.0	16	9	66	210	99	61
Kenya	44.6	43.5	45.6	4.1	33	17	39	1,000	44	78
Kiribati							21		85	51
Korea, North	63.1	60.5	66.0	2.0	16	11	62	67	97	42
Korea, South	75.5	71.8	79.3	1.4	12	6	81	20	100	5
Kuwait	76.6	74.9	79.0	2.7	20	2	50	5	98	9
Kyrgyzstan	68.6	64.8	72.3	2.7	22	7	60	110	98	52
Laos	54.5	53.3	55.8	4.8	36	13	32	650	19	87
Latvia	71.0	65.6	76.2	1.1	8	14	48	42	100	17
Lebanon	73.5	71.9	75.1	2.2	19	5	63	150	89	28
Lesotho	35.1	32.3	37.7	3.9	31	26	30	550	60	64
Liberia	41.4	40.7	42.2	6.8	50	22	10	760	51	157
Libya	72.8	70.8	75.4	3.1	23	4	45	97	94	16
Liechtenstein										10
Lithuania	72.7	67.5	77.6	1.3	9	12	47	13		8

HEALTH

	UNDER-5 MORTALITY RATE (PER 1,000 LIVE BIRTHS) [2]	% OF INFANTS WITH LOW BIRTH WEIGHT (2500 GM) [2]	% OF MALNUTRITION (UNDER 5 YEARS OLD) [2]	UNDERNOURISHED PEOPLE AS % OF TOTAL POPULATION [5]	% OF WOMEN WHO BREASTFEED FOR SIX MONTHS [2]	DAILY CALORIE CONSUMPTION PER CAPITA	DOCTORS PER 100,000 PEOPLE [3]	NURSES PER 100,000 PEOPLE [4]	% OF POPULATION WITH ACCESS TO IMPROVED WATER SOURCES [2]	% OF POPULATION WITH ACCESS TO SANITATION SERVICES [2]
	2002	1998-2002	1995-2002	1998-2000	1995-2002	2001	1990-2002	1990-1998	2000	2000
Afghanistan	257		48	70				18	13	12
Albania	30	3	14	8	6	2,900	133	380	97	91
Algeria	49	7	6	6	13	2,987	85	298	89	92
Andorra	7							283	100	100
Angola	260	12	31	50	11	1,953	5	115	38	44
Anguilla										
Antigua	14	8	10			2,381	17	330	91	95
Argentina	19	7	5			3,171	294	77		
Armenia	35	7	3	46	30	1,991	305	481		
Aruba										
Australia	6	7				3,126	260	830	100	100
Austria	5	7				3,799	302	532	100	100
Azerbaijan	105	11	7	23	7	2,474	357	767	78	81
Bahamas	16	7				2,777	106	230	97	100
Bahrain	16	8	9		34		169	283		
Bangladesh	77	30	48	35	46	2,187	20	11	97	48
Barbados	14	10	6			2,992	121	330	100	100
Belarus	20	5		2		2,925	457	1,182	100	
Belgium	6	8				3,682	395	1,075		
Belize	40	6	6		24	2,886	55	82	92	50
Benin	156	16	23	13	38	2,455	10	20	63	23
Bermuda						2,904				
Bhutan	94	15	19				16	39	62	70
Bolivia	71	9	10	23	39	2,267	130	69	83	70
Bosnia-Herzegovina	18	4	4	6		2,845	140	452		
Botswana	110	10	13	25	34	2,292	26	219	95	66
Brazil	36	10	6	10	42	3,003	158	41	87	76
Brunei	6	10				2,814	85	402		
Bulgaria	16	10		15		2,626	344	713	100	100
Burkina Faso	207	19	34	23	6	2,485	3	20	42	29
Burundi	190	16	45	69	62	1,612	1		78	88
Cambodia	138	11	45	36	12	1,967	30	74	30	17
Cameroon	166	11	21	25	12	2,242	7	37	58	79
Canada	7	6				3,176	186	897	100	100
Cape Verde	38	13	14		57	3,308	17	56	74	71
Cayman Is.										
Central African Rep.	180	14	24	44	17	1,949	4	9	70	25
Ceuta										
Chad	200	17	28	32	10	2,245	3	15	27	29
Chile	12	5	1	4	73	2,868	115	47	93	96
China	39	6	11	9	67	2,963	167	99	75	40
Christmas Is.										
Cocos										
Colombia	23	9	7	13	32	2,580	109	48	91	86
Comoros	79	25	25		21	1,735	7	34	96	98
Congo D.R.	205	12	31	73	24	1,535	7	44	45	21
Congo R.	108		14	32	4	2,221	25	185	51	
Cook Is.	23	3			19			200	100	100
Coral Sea Is.										
Costa Rica	11	7	5	5	35	2,761	178	109	95	93
Côte d'Ivoire	176	17	21	15	10	2,594	9	31	81	52
Croatia	8	6	1	18	23	2,678	229	474		
Cuba	9	6	4	13	41	2,643	590	678	91	98
Cyprus	6					3,302	269	447	100	100
Czech Republic	5	7	1			3,097	308	886		
Denmark	4	5				3,454	339	722	100	
Diego Garcia										
Djibouti	143		18			2,218	13	74	100	91
Dominica	15	10	5			2,995	49	416	97	83
Dominican Republic	38	14	5	26	11	2,333	216	30	86	67
Ecuador	29	16	15	5	29	2,792	138	70	85	86
Egypt	41	12	11	4	57	3,385	218	233	97	98
El Salvador	39	13	12	14	16	2,512	121	35	77	82
Equatorial Guinea	152	13	19		24		25	40	44	53
Eritrea	89	21	44	58	52	1,690	5	16	46	13
Estonia	12	4				3,048	307	625		
Ethiopia	171	15	47	44	55	2,037	3		24	12
Faeroe Is.										
Fiji	21	10	8		47	2,789	36	195	47	43
Finland	5	4				3,202	306	2,162	100	100
France	6	7				3,629	303	497		
French Guiana						2,889				
French Polynesia										
Gabon	91	14	12	8	6	2,602			86	53
Gambia	126	17	17	21	26	2,300	4	13	62	37
Georgia	29	6	3	16	18	2,247	487	474	79	100
Germany	5	7				3,567	354	957		
Ghana	100	11	25	12	31	2,670	6	72	73	72
Gibraltar										
Greece	5	8				3,754	392	257		
Greenland										
Grenada	25	9			39	2,749	50	368	95	97
Guadeloupe										
Guam										
Guatemala	49	13	24	25	39	2,203	90	27	92	81
Guinea	169	12	23	32	11	2,362	13	56	48	58
Guinea-Bissau	211	22	25		37	2,481	17	109	56	56
Guyana	72	12	14	14	11	2,515	48	84	94	87
Haiti	123	21	17	50	24	2,045	25	11	46	28
Honduras	42	14	17	21	35	2,406	83	26	88	75
Hungary	9	9	2			3,520	361	385	99	99
Iceland	4	4				3,231	326	865		
India	93	30	47	24	37	2,487	48	45	84	28
Indonesia	45	10	26	6	42	2,904	16	50	78	55
Iran	42	7	11	5	44	2,931	110	259	92	83
Iraq	125	15	16	27	12			236	85	79
Ireland	6	6				3,666	226	1,593		
Israel	6	8				3,512	378	613		
Italy	6	6				3,680	567	296		
Jamaica	20	9	6	9		2,705	140	65	92	99
Japan	5	8				2,746	197	745		
Jordan	33	10	5	6	34	2,769	205	296	96	99
Kanaky-New Caledonia						2,770				
Kazakhstan	76	8	4	8	36	2,477	339	649	91	99
Kenya	122	11	21	44	5	2,059	14	90	57	87
Kiribati	69	5	13		80	2,922		236	48	48
Korea, North	55	7	21	34	97	2,201			100	99
Korea, South	5	4				3,055	173	291	92	63
Kuwait	10	7	10	4	12	3,170	160	475		
Kyrgyzstan	61	7	11	8	24	2,882	288	750	77	100
Laos	100	14	40	24	23	2,309	61	108	37	30
Latvia	21	5		5		2,809	313	549		
Lebanon	32	6	3	3	27	3,184	274	100	100	99
Lesotho	87	14	18	26	15	2,320	7	60	78	49
Liberia	235		26	39	35	1,946		6		
Libya	19	7	5			3,333	120	360	72	97
Liechtenstein	11									
Lithuania	9	4		3		3,384	394	884		

HEALTH

	LIFE EXPECTANCY AT BIRTH (YEARS) [1]	LIFE EXPECTANCY AT BIRTH - MALE (YEARS) [1]	LIFE EXPECTANCY AT BIRTH - FEMALE (YEARS) [1]	TOTAL FERTILITY RATE (CHILDREN PER WOMAN) [2]	CRUDE BIRTH RATE (PER 1,000 PEOPLE) [1]	CRUDE DEATH RATE (PER 1,000 PEOPLE) [1]	% OF MARRIED WOMEN OF CHILDBEARING AGE USING CONTRACEPTIVES [2]	MATERNAL MORTALITY (PER 100,000 LIVE BIRTHS) [2]	BIRTHS ATTENDED BY TRAINED HEALTH PERSONNEL (%) [2]	INFANT MORTALITY RATE (PER 1,000 LIVE BIRTHS) [2]
	2000-2005	2000-2005	2000-2005	2002	2000-2005	2000-2005	1995-2002	2000	1995-2002	2002
Luxembourg	78.4	75.1	81.4	1.7	13	8		28	100	5
Macedonia, TFYR	73.6	71.4	75.8	1.9	14	8		23	97	22
Madagascar	53.6	52.5	54.8	5.7	42	13	19	550	46	84
Malawi	37.5	37.3	37.7	6.1	45	24	31	1,800	56	114
Malaysia	73.1	70.8	75.7	2.9	23	5	55	41	97	8
Maldives	67.4	67.8	67.0	5.4	36	6	32	110	70	58
Mali	48.6	48.0	49.1	7.0	50	16	8	1,200	41	122
Malta	78.4	75.9	80.7	1.8	12	8		0	98	5
Malvinas-Falklands										
Marshall Is.							37		95	54
Martinique	79.1	75.8	82.3		14	7				
Mauritania	52.5	50.9	54.1	5.8	42	14	8	1,000	57	120
Mauritius	72.0	68.4	75.8	2.0	16	7	26	24	99	17
Mayotte Is.										
Melilla										
Mexico	73.4	70.4	76.4	2.5	22	5	70	83	86	24
Micronesia	68.6	68.0	69.1	3.8	28	6	45		93	20
Moldova	68.9	65.5	72.2	1.4	11	11	62	36	99	27
Monaco										4
Mongolia	63.9	61.9	65.9	2.4	22	7	67	110	97	58
Montserrat										
Morocco	68.7	66.8	70.5	2.8	23	6	59	220	40	39
Mozambique	38.1	36.6	39.6	5.7	41	23	6	1,000	44	125
Myanmar-Burma	57.3	54.6	60.2	2.9	24	11	33	360	56	77
Namibia	44.3	42.9	45.6	4.6	33	18	44	300	78	55
Nauru										25
Nepal	59.9	60.1	59.6	4.3	33	10	39	740	11	66
Netherlands	78.3	75.6	81.0	1.7	12	9	79	16	100	5
Netherlands Antilles	76.3	73.3	79.2		15	6				
New Zealand-Aotearoa	78.3	75.8	80.7	2.0	14	8	75	7	100	6
Nicaragua	69.5	67.2	71.9	3.8	32	5	69	230	67	32
Niger	46.2	45.9	46.5	8.0	55	19	14	1,600	16	156
Nigeria	51.5	51.1	51.8	5.5	39	14	15	800	42	110
Niue									100	
Norfolk Is.										
Northern Marianas										
Norway	78.9	76.0	81.9	1.8	12	10	74	16	100	4
Oman	72.4	71.0	74.4	5.0	32	3	32	87	95	11
Pakistan	61.0	61.2	60.9	5.1	36	10	28	500	20	83
Palau							47		100	24
Palestine	72.4	70.8	74.0	5.6	39	4	51	100	97	23
Panama	74.7	72.3	77.4	2.7	23	5	58	160	90	19
Papua New Guinea	57.6	56.8	58.7	4.1	32	9	26	300	53	70
Paraguay	70.9	68.6	73.1	3.9	30	5	57	170	71	26
Peru	69.8	67.3	72.4	2.9	23	6	69	410	59	30
Philippines	70.0	68.0	72.0	3.2	25	5	50	200	58	29
Pitcairn										
Poland	73.9	69.8	78.0	1.3	10	10	49	13	99	8
Portugal	76.2	72.6	79.6	1.5	11	11	66	5	100	5
Puerto Rico	75.6	71.2	80.1		14	8				
Qatar	72.2	70.5	75.4	3.3	17	4	43	7	98	11
Réunion	75.2	71.2	79.3		19	5				
Romania	70.5	67.0	74.2	1.3	10	12	64	49	98	19
Russia	66.8	60.8	73.1	1.2	9	15		67	99	18
Rwanda	39.3	38.8	39.7	5.8	44	22	13	1,400	31	96
Sahara, Western										
Samoa	70.0	66.9	73.4	4.2	29	5	30	130	100	20
Samoa, American										
San Marino										4
São Tomé and Príncipe	69.9	67.0	72.8	4.0	33	6	29		79	75
Saudi Arabia	72.3	71.1	73.7	4.6	32	4	32	23	91	23
Senegal	52.9	50.8	55.1	5.0	37	12	11	690	58	79
Serbia and Montenegro	73.2	70.9	75.6	1.7	12	11	58	11	99	16
Seychelles										12
Sierra Leone	34.2	33.1	35.5	6.5	50	29	4	2,000	42	165
Singapore	78.1	75.9	80.3	1.4	10	5	74	30	100	3
Slovakia	73.7	69.8	77.6	1.3	10	10	74	3		8
Slovenia	76.3	72.6	79.8	1.2	8	10	74	17	100	4
Solomon Is.	69.2	67.9	70.7	4.5	33	5	11	130	85	20
Somalia	47.9	46.4	49.5	7.3	52	18	1	1,100	34	133
South Africa	47.7	45.1	50.7	2.6	23	17	56	230	84	52
Spain	79.3	75.9	82.8	1.2	9	9	81	4		4
Sri Lanka	72.6	69.9	75.9	2.0	16	7	71	92	97	17
St Helena										
St Kitts-Nevis							41		99	20
St Lucia	72.5	70.8	74.1	2.3	20	6	47		100	17
St Pierre and Miquelon										
St Vincent	74.1	72.6	75.6	2.2	20	6	58		100	22
Sudan	55.6	54.1	57.1	4.4	33	12	7	590	86	64
Suriname	71.1	68.5	73.7	2.5	22	6	42	110	85	31
Swaziland	34.4	33.3	35.4	4.6	34	25	28	370	70	106
Sweden	80.1	77.6	82.6	1.6	10	11	78	2	100	3
Switzerland	79.1	75.9	82.3	1.4	9	10	82	7		5
Syria	71.9	70.6	73.1	3.4	28	4	48	160	76	23
Taiwan										
Tajikistan	68.8	66.2	71.4	3.1	24	6	34	100	71	53
Tanzania	43.3	42.5	44.1	5.2	39	18	25	1,500	36	104
Thailand	69.3	65.3	73.5	1.9	17	7	79	44	99	24
Timor-Leste	49.5	48.7	50.4	3.9	24	13	8	660	24	89
Togo	49.7	48.2	51.1	5.4	38	15	26	570	49	79
Tokelau										
Tonga	68.6	68.0	69.1	3.8	27	7	41		92	16
Trinidad and Tobago	71.3	68.4	74.4	1.6	14	7	38	160	96	17
Tunisia	72.8	70.8	74.9	2.0	17	5	66	120	90	21
Turkey	70.5	68.0	73.2	2.5	21	6	64	70	81	36
Turkmenistan	67.1	63.9	70.4	2.7	22	6	62	31	97	76
Turks and Caicos										
Tuvalu									99	38
Uganda	46.2	45.4	46.9	7.1	51	17	23	880	39	82
Ukraine	69.7	64.7	74.7	1.2	8	14	89	35	100	16
United Arab Emirates	74.7	73.3	77.4	2.9	17	2	28	54	96	8
United Kingdom	78.2	75.7	80.7	1.6	11	10	82	13	99	5
United States	77.1	74.3	79.9	2.1	14	8	76	17	99	7
Uruguay	75.3	71.6	78.9	2.3	17	9	84	27	100	14
Uzbekistan	69.7	66.8	72.5	2.5	22	6	67	24	96	52
Vanuatu	68.8	67.5	70.5	4.2	30	5	15	130	89	34
Vatican										
Venezuela	73.7	70.9	76.7	2.7	23	5	77	96	94	19
Vietnam	69.2	66.9	71.6	2.3	20	6	74	130	70	30
Virgin Is. (Am.)	78.0	74.2	82.0		14	6				
Virgin Is. (Br.)										
Wallis and Futuna										
Yemen	60.0	58.9	61.1	7.0	45	9	21	570	22	79
Zambia	32.4	32.7	32.1	5.7	42	28	34	750	43	108
Zimbabwe	33.1	33.7	32.6	4.0	32	27	54	1,100	73	76

1. World Population Prospects-The 2002 Revision. United Nations / 2. The State of the World's Children 2004, UNICEF

HEALTH

	UNDER-5 MORTALITY RATE (PER 1,000 LIVE BIRTHS) [2] — 2002	% OF INFANTS WITH LOW BIRTH WEIGHT (2500 GM) [2] — 1998-2002	% OF MALNUTRITION (UNDER 5 YEARS OLD) [2] — 1995-2002	UNDERNOURISHED PEOPLE AS % OF TOTAL POPULATION [5] — 1998-2000	% OF WOMEN WHO BREASTFEED FOR SIX MONTHS [2] — 1995-2002	DAILY CALORIE CONSUMPTION PER CAPITA — 2001	DOCTORS PER 100,000 PEOPLE [3] — 1990-2002	NURSES PER 100,000 PEOPLE [4] — 1990-1998	% OF POPULATION WITH ACCESS TO IMPROVED WATER SOURCES [2] — 2000	% OF POPULATION WITH ACCESS TO SANITATION SERVICES [2] — 2000
Luxembourg	5	8					253	782		
Macedonia, TFYR	26	5	6	4	37	2,552	300	488		
Madagascar	136	14	33	40	41	2,072	11	22	47	42
Malawi	183	16	25	33	44	2,168		113	57	76
Malaysia	8	10	12		29	2,927	68	113		
Maldives	77	22	30		10	2,587	40	113	100	56
Mali	222	23	33	20	38	2,376	5	13	65	69
Malta	5	6				3,496	263	1,100	100	100
Malvinas-Falklands										
Marshall Is.	66	12			63			149		
Martinique										
Mauritania	183	42	32	12	20	2,764	14	62	37	33
Mauritius	19	13	15	5	16	2,995	85	233	100	99
Mayotte Is.										
Melilla										
Mexico	29	9	8	5	38	3,160	130	87	88	74
Micronesia	24	18			60			279		
Moldova	32	5	3	10		2,713	325	874	92	99
Monaco	5							1,621	100	100
Mongolia	71	8	13	42	51	1,974	254	307	60	30
Montserrat										
Morocco	43	11	9	7	66	3,046	49	105	80	68
Mozambique	197	14	26	55	30	1,980	6		57	43
Myanmar-Burma	109	15	35	6	11	2,822	30	26	72	64
Namibia	67	16	24	9	26	2,745	29	168	77	41
Nauru	30							588		
Nepal	91	21	48	19	69	2,459	4	5	88	28
Netherlands	5					3,282	251	902	100	100
Netherlands Antilles						2,565				
New Zealand-Aotearoa	6	6				3,235	226	771		
Nicaragua	41	13	10	29	31	2,256	61	92	77	85
Niger	265	17	40	36	1	2,118	4	23	59	20
Nigeria	183	12	36	7	17	2,747	19	66	62	54
Niue		0						478	100	100
Norfolk Is.										
Northern Marianas						3,382	413	1,840	100	
Norway	4	5					137	325	39	92
Oman	13	8	24		16	2,457	68	34	90	62
Pakistan	107	19	38	19				144	79	100
Palau	29	9			59				86	100
Palestine	25	9	4		29				90	92
Panama	25	10	7	18	25	2,386	117	144	90	92
Papua New Guinea	94	11	35	27	59	2,193	7	67	42	82
Paraguay	30	9	5	14	7	2,576	117	24	78	94
Peru	39	11	7	11	71	2,610	117	115	80	71
Philippines	38	20	28	23	37	2,372	124	418	86	83
Pitcairn										
Poland	9	6				3,397	233	527		
Portugal	6	8				3,752	312	379		
Puerto Rico							220	289		
Qatar	16	10	6		12					
Réunion						3,407	191	409	58	53
Romania	21	9	6			3,014	423	821	99	
Russia	21	6	3	5		2,086			41	8
Rwanda	183	9	27	40	84					
Sahara, Western										
Samoa	25	4					70	155	99	99
Samoa, American								508		
San Marino	6									
São Tomé and Príncipe	118		13		56	2,567	47	127		
Saudi Arabia	28	11	14	3	31	2,841	153	330	95	100
Senegal	138	18	23	25	24	2,277	10	22	78	70
Serbia and Montenegro	19	4	2	8	11	2,778			98	100
Seychelles	16		6			2,461	132	468		
Sierra Leone	284		27	47	4	1,913	9	33	57	66
Singapore	4	8	14				135	492	100	100
Slovakia	9	7				2,894	322	708	100	100
Slovenia	5	6				2,935	215	681	100	
Solomon Is.	24	13	21		65	2,272	13	119	71	34
Somalia	225		26	71	9			20		
South Africa	65	15	12		7	2,921	443	472	86	87
Spain	6	6				3,422	436	458		
Sri Lanka	19	22	29	23	54	2,274	41	103	77	94
St Helena										
St Kitts-Nevis	24	9			56	2,997	117	498	98	96
St Lucia	19	8	14			2,849	518	263	98	89
St Pierre and Miquelon										
St Vincent	25	10				2,609	88	239	93	96
Sudan	94	31	17	21	16	2,288	16	58	75	62
Suriname	40	13	13	11	9	2,643	45	156	82	93
Swaziland	149	9	10	12	24	2,593	15			
Sweden	3	4				3,164	311	821	100	100
Switzerland	6	6				3,440	336	779	100	100
Syria	28	6	7	3	81	3,038	142	189	80	90
Taiwan										
Tajikistan	72	15		64	14	1,662	207	484	60	90
Tanzania	165	13	29	47	32	1,998	4	85	68	90
Thailand	28	9	19	18	4	2,486	24	87	84	96
Timor-Leste	126	10	43		44					
Togo	141	15	25	23	18	2,287	8	30	54	34
Tokelau								315	100	
Tonga	20	0			62	2,756	79	287	90	99
Trinidad and Tobago	20	23	7	12	2	3,293	70	286	80	84
Tunisia	26	7	4		46	3,343	127	109	82	90
Turkey	42	16	8		7	2,738	300	587		
Turkmenistan	98	6	12	8	13					
Turks and Caicos								300	100	100
Tuvalu	52	5				2,398	5	19	52	79
Uganda	141	12	23	21	65	3,008	299	736	98	99
Ukraine	20	5	3	5	22	3,341	177	341		
United Arab Emirates	9	15	14		34				100	100
United Kingdom	7	8				3,368	164	497	100	100
United States	8	8	1			3,766	276	972	98	94
Uruguay	15	8	5	3		2,848	375	70	85	89
Uzbekistan	68	7	19	19	16	2,197	300	1,011	88	100
Vanuatu	42	6	20		50	2,565	12	260		
Vatican										
Venezuela	22	7	5	21	7	2,376	203	64	83	68
Vietnam	39	9	33	18	31	2,533	52	56	77	47
Virgin Is. (Am.)										
Virgin Is. (Br.)										
Wallis and Futuna										
Yemen	107	32	46	33	18	2,050	22	51	69	38
Zambia	192	10	28	50	40	1,885	7	113	64	78
Zimbabwe	123	11	13	38	33	2,133	14	129	83	62

3. Human Development Report 2003, UNDP / 4. WHOSIS - WHO Statistical Information System, Web Site WHO 2002 / 5. FAOSTAT - Statistical Database - Web Site FAO 2004

EDUCATION

	LITERACY (TOTAL ADULT LITERACY RATIO %) [2]	LITERACY (TOTAL ADULT MALE LITERACY RATIO %) [2]	LITERACY (TOTAL ADULT FEMALE LITERACY RATIO %) [2]	PRIMARY SCHOOL NET ENROLMENT RATIO [1]	PRIMARY SCHOOL NET ENROLMENT RATIO (MALE) [1]	PRIMARY SCHOOL NET ENROLMENT RATIO (FEMALE) [1]	SECONDARY SCHOOL NET ENROLMENT RATIO [1]	SECONDARY SCHOOL NET ENROLMENT RATIO (MALE) [1]	SECONDARY SCHOOL NET ENROLMENT RATIO (FEMALE) [1]	TERTIARY GROSS ENROLMENT RATIO [1]	PRIMARY PUPIL TO TEACHER RATIO [1]
	2000	2000	2000	1997-2000	1997-2000	1997-2000	1997-2000	1997-2000	1997-2000	1997-2000	2000
Afghanistan	36	51	21							2	43
Albania				98	98	97	74	73	75	15	22
Algeria	63	75	51	98	100	97	62	60	63	15	28
Andorra											
Angola				37	39	35				1	35
Anguilla											35
Antigua	82	80	83								19
Argentina	97	97	97	107	108	107	79	77	82	48	22
Armenia	98	99	98	69	68	70	64	62	65	20	19
Aruba				97	98	96	72	70	74	30	19
Australia				96	95	96	90	88	91	63	18
Austria				91	90	92	89	89	88	58	14
Azerbaijan	97	99	96	91	90	93	78	78	78	22	19
Bahamas	95	95	96	83	86	79	72	72	71	25	14
Bahrain	88	91	83	96	95	97	92	89	95	25	17
Bangladesh	40	49	30	89	88	90	43	42	44	7	57
Barbados	100	100	100	105	105	105	85	86	84	38	17
Belarus	100	100	100	108	109	107	76	76	76	56	17
Belgium				101	101	100				57	12
Belize	93	93	93	100	98	102	63	61	66		23
Benin	37	52	24	70	83	57	17	24	11	1	54
Bermuda										4	9
Bhutan	47	61	34								41
Bolivia	85	92	79	97	97	97	68	69	67	36	24
Bosnia-Herzegovina	93	98	89								16
Botswana	77	75	80	84	82	86	70	65	74	5	27
Brazil	87	87	87	97	100	94	71	69	74	17	26
Brunei	92	95	88							14	15
Bulgaria	98	99	98	94	95	93	88	88	87	41	18
Burkina Faso	24	34	14	36	42	29	8	10	6	1	47
Burundi	48	56	40	54	59	49				1	50
Cambodia	68	80	57	95	100	90	17	21	12	3	53
Cameroon	71	79	64							5	63
Canada				99	98	99	98	98	98	60	15
Cape Verde	74	85	66	99	98	99	48	47	48		28
Cayman Is.											15
Central African Rep.	47	60	35	55	64	45					74
Ceuta										2	15
Chad	43	52	34	58	70	47	8	12	4	1	71
Chile	96	96	96	89	89	88	75	84	64	38	25
China	85	92	78	93	92	95				7	20
Christmas Is.											
Cocos											
Colombia	92	92	92	89	89	88	57	54	59	23	27
Comoros	56	63	49	56	60	52				1	36
Congo D.R.	61	73	50	33	33	32	12	15	9	1	26
Congo R.	81	88	74							5	51
Cook Is.											25
Coral Sea Is.											
Costa Rica	96	96	96	91	91	91	49	47	52	16	25
Côte d'Ivoire	49	60	37	64	73	55				7	48
Croatia	98	99	97	84	85	84	79	78	80	29	18
Cuba	97	97	97	97	98	97	82	80	84	24	11
Cyprus	97	99	95	95	95	95	88	87	89	20	17
Czech Republic				90	90	90				30	18
Denmark				99	99	99	89	88	91	59	10
Diego Garcia											
Djibouti	65	76	54	33	37	28				1	36
Dominica											21
Dominican Republic	84	84	84	93	92	93	40	35	45	23	41
Ecuador	92	93	90	99	99	100	48	47	49	18	23
Egypt	55	67	44	93	95	90	79	80	77	39	22
El Salvador	79	82	76	81	75	87	39	40	39	18	26
Equatorial Guinea	83	93	74	72	76	68	26	38	14	3	42
Eritrea	56	67	45	41	44	38	22	25	19	2	45
Estonia	100	100	100	98	98	97	83	82	84	58	14
Ethiopia	39	47	31	47	53	41	13	15	10	2	55
Faeroe Is.											
Fiji	93	95	91	99	99	100				14	23
Finland				100	100	100				74	16
France				100	100	100	95	94	95	54	19
French Guiana											
French Polynesia										3	14
Gabon	71	80	62	88	89	87				8	49
Gambia	37	44	30	69	71	66	35	41	29	2	38
Georgia	100	100	99	95	95	95	73	72	73	35	16
Germany				87	86	87	88	87	88	46	15
Ghana	72	80	63	58	60	57	31	33	28	3	33
Gibraltar											
Greece	97	99	96	97	97	97	87	86	89	50	13
Greenland											
Grenada				84			46				21
Guadeloupe											
Guam											
Guatemala	69	76	61	84	86	82	26	27	25	8	33
Guinea	41	55	27	47	52	41	12	17	6	1	44
Guinea-Bissau	38	54	24	54	63	45					44
Guyana	99	99	98	98	99	97				0	26
Haiti	50	52	48							12	35
Honduras	75	75	75	88	87	88				1	34
Hungary	99	100	99	90	91	90	87	87	88	40	11
Iceland				102	102	102	83	81	86	49	11
India	57	68	45							10	40
Indonesia	87	92	82	92	93	92	48	49	46	15	22
Iran	76	83	69	74	74	73				10	25
Iraq	39	55	23	93	100	86	33	40	26	14	21
Ireland				90	90	90				48	22
Israel	95	97	93	101	101	101	88	88	89	53	12
Italy	98	99	98	100	100	100	91	90	91	50	11
Jamaica	87	83	91	95	95	95	74	73	76	16	36
Japan				101	101	101	101	100	101	48	20
Jordan	90	95	84	94	93	94	76	73	78	29	21
Kanaky-New Caledonia											
Kazakhstan	99	100	99	89	89	88	83	84	82	5	20
Kenya	82	89	76	69	68	69	23	23	23	31	19
Kiribati											30
Korea, North	98	99	96								24
Korea, South	98	99	96	99	99	100	91	91	91	78	32
Kuwait	82	84	80	66	68	65	50	49	50	21	14
Kyrgyzstan				82	84	81				41	25
Laos	65	76	53	81	85	78	30	33	27	3	30
Latvia	100	100	100	92	92	92	74	72	77	63	15
Lebanon	86	92	80	74	74	74	70	67	73	42	17
Lesotho	83	73	94	78	75	82	21	16	25	3	48
Liberia	54	70	37	83	96	71	25	30	20	3	36
Libya	80	91	68							49	8
Liechtenstein											
Lithuania	100	100	100	95	95	94	89	88	89	52	16

EDUCATION

	LITERACY (TOTAL ADULT LITERACY RATIO %) [2]	LITERACY (TOTAL ADULT MALE LITERACY RATIO %) [2]	LITERACY (TOTAL ADULT FEMALE LITERACY RATIO %) [2]	PRIMARY SCHOOL NET ENROLMENT RATIO [1]	PRIMARY SCHOOL NET ENROLMENT RATIO (MALE) [1]	PRIMARY SCHOOL NET ENROLMENT RATIO (FEMALE) [1]	SECONDARY SCHOOL NET ENROLMENT RATIO [1]	SECONDARY SCHOOL NET ENROLMENT RATIO (MALE) [1]	SECONDARY SCHOOL NET ENROLMENT RATIO (FEMALE) [1]	TERTIARY GROSS ENROLMENT RATIO [1]	PRIMARY PUPIL TO TEACHER RATIO [1]
	2000	2000	2000	1997-2000	1997-2000	1997-2000	1997-2000	1997-2000	1997-2000	1997-2000	2000
Luxembourg				97	96	97	78	75	81	9	12
Macedonia, TFYR	96	97	94	92	92	92	81	82	80	24	22
Madagascar	67	74	60	68	67	68	11	11	12	2	50
Malawi	60	75	47	101	97	104	25	27	23	0	56
Malaysia	87	91	83	98	98	99	70	67	74	28	18
Maldives	97	97	97	99	99	99	31	29	33		23
Mali	26	36	16	43	51	36				2	63
Malta	92	91	93	99	98	100	79	81	77	21	19
Malvinas-Falklands											
Marshall Is.											15
Martinique											
Mauritania	40	51	30	64	66	62	14	16	13	4	42
Mauritius	85	88	81	95	95	95	64	63	65	11	26
Mayotte Is.											
Melilla											
Mexico	91	93	89	103	103	104	60	57	62	21	27
Micronesia	67	66	67							15	23
Moldova	99	100	98	78	79	78	68	67	69	28	20
Monaco											16
Mongolia	98	99	98	89	87	91	58	53	64	33	32
Montserrat											
Morocco	49	62	36	78	82	74	30	33	27	10	28
Mozambique	44	60	29	54	59	50	9	11	8	1	64
Myanmar-Burma	85	89	81	83	83	83	37	38	35	12	32
Namibia	82	83	81	82	79	84	38	32	44	6	32
Nauru											
Nepal	42	59	24	72	77	67				5	37
Netherlands				100	101	99	90	90	90	55	10
Netherlands Antilles				95	101	88	74	64	83	22	18
New Zealand-Aotearoa				99	99	99	92	91	93	69	16
Nicaragua	64	64	64	81	80	81	36	33	38	12	36
Niger	16	24	9	30	36	24	5	6	4	1	42
Nigeria	64	72	56							4	34
Niue	81	80	83								
Norfolk Is.											
Northern Marianas											
Norway				101	101	102	95	95	95	70	
Oman	72	80	62	65	65	64	59	59	60	8	24
Pakistan	43	57	28	66	83	48				4	40
Palau				111	113	109	101	98	105	31	15
Palestine											
Panama	92	93	91	100	100	100	62	59	65	35	25
Papua New Guinea	64	71	57	84	88	80	21	24	18	2	36
Paraguay	93	94	92	92	92	92	47	45	48	10	20
Peru	90	95	85	104	105	104	61	62	61	29	25
Philippines	95	95	95	93	92	93	53	48	57	31	35
Pitcairn											
Poland	100	100	100	98	98	98	91	89	92	56	11
Portugal	92	95	90				85	82	89	50	13
Puerto Rico										41	
Qatar	94	94	94	95	95	96	78	75	82	25	13
Réunion											
Romania	98	99	97	93	93	93	80	79	81	27	20
Russia	100	100	99							64	17
Rwanda	67	74	60	97	97	97				2	51
Sahara, Western											
Samoa	99	99	98	97	98	95	68	65	71	11	24
Samoa, American											15
San Marino											5
São Tomé and Príncipe											34
Saudi Arabia	76	83	67	58	60	56	51	52	50	22	12
Senegal	37	47	28	63	66	60				4	51
Serbia and Montenegro	98	99	97							24	20
Seychelles											15
Sierra Leone	36	51	23				26	29	24	2	44
Singapore	92	96	88							44	25
Slovakia	100	100	100	89	89	90	75	75	75	30	20
Slovenia	100	100	100	93	94	93	89	87	90	61	14
Solomon Is.										3	24
Somalia											
South Africa	85	86	85	89	90	88	57	54	60	15	34
Spain	98	99	97	102	102	103	94	92	95	59	14
Sri Lanka	92	94	89	97	97	97				5	28
St Helena											
St Kitts-Nevis											19
St Lucia				100	100	100	80	70	90	25	22
St Pierre and Miquelon											
St Vincent											25
Sudan	58	69	46	46	50	42				7	27
Suriname	94	96	93	92	94	90	43	40	46	7	17
Swaziland	80	81	79	93	92	94	44	40	47	5	33
Sweden				102	103	102	96	94	98	70	11
Switzerland				99	99	99	88	90	85	42	14
Syria	74	88	60	96	99	94	39	41	37	6	24
Taiwan											
Tajikistan	99	100	99	103	107	98	76	82	69	14	22
Tanzania	75	84	67	47	46	48	5	5	5	1	40
Thailand	96	97	94	85	87	84				35	21
Timor-Leste											
Togo	57	72	43	92	101	83	23	32	14	4	34
Tokelau											
Tonga				91	92	90	70	68	73	4	21
Trinidad and Tobago	98	99	98	92	92	92	71	68	73	6	20
Tunisia	71	81	61	99	100	99	70	69	72	22	23
Turkey	85	93	77							15	28
Turkmenistan										19	
Turks and Caicos											
Tuvalu											
Uganda	67	78	57	109	113	106	12	14	10	3	59
Ukraine	100	100	100	72	72	71				43	21
United Arab Emirates	76	75	79	87	86	87	67	64	72	12	16
United Kingdom				99	99	99	94	93	95	60	18
United States				95	94	96	88	87	89	73	15
Uruguay	98	97	98	90	90	91	70	66	74	36	21
Uzbekistan	99	100	99							37	21
Vanuatu				96	92	100	23	21	25	0	24
Vatican											
Venezuela	93	93	92	88	87	89	50	46	55	28	21
Vietnam	93	95	91	95	98	92	62			10	28
Virgin Is. (Am.)											18
Virgin Is. (Br.)											
Wallis and Futuna											
Yemen	46	68	25	67	84	49	37	52	21	11	30
Zambia	78	85	72	66	66	65	19	20	18	2	45
Zimbabwe	89	93	85	80	80	80	40	42	39	4	37

1. World Development Indicators 2003, World Bank / 2. World Population Prospects-The 2002 Revision. United Nations

COMMUNICATIONS

	NEWSPAPERS PER 1,000 PEOPLE [1]	RADIOS PER 1,000 PEOPLE [1]	TV SETS PER 1,000 PEOPLE [1]	TELEPHONES (MAINLINES) PER 1,000 PEOPLE [1]	COMPUTERS PER 1,000 PEOPLE [1]
	1996	1997	2001	2001	2001
Afghanistan	5	114	14	1.5	
Albania	35	260	123	49.7	7.6
Algeria	27	244	110	61.0	7.1
Andorra			462	438.3	
Angola	11	74	19	5.9	1.3
Anguilla					
Antigua	91	543	443	481.3	
Argentina	37	681	326	223.8	91.1
Armenia	5	264	230	140.3	7.9
Aruba			224	350.3	
Australia	293	1,999	731	518.9	515.8
Austria	296	753	542	468.1	335.4
Azerbaijan	27	22	321	111.3	
Bahamas	99	744	247	400.3	
Bahrain	112	81	402	246.6	141.8
Bangladesh	53	49	17	4.3	1.9
Barbados	200	749	325	476.3	92.3
Belarus	152	199	342	278.8	
Belgium	160	793	543	497.9	232.8
Belize		613	183	144.4	135.2
Benin	5	441	44	9.2	1.7
Bermuda			1,086	869.2	495.4
Bhutan		50	26	25.4	5.8
Bolivia	55	676	121	62.2	20.5
Bosnia-Herzegovina	152	243	111	110.7	
Botswana	27	150	30	91.5	38.7
Brazil	43	434	349	217.8	62.9
Brunei	69	297	642	264.0	74.6
Bulgaria	116	543	453	359.4	44.3
Burkina Faso	1	433	103	4.9	1.5
Burundi	2	220	30	2.9	
Cambodia	2	119	8	2.5	1.5
Cameroon	7	163	35	6.7	3.9
Canada	159	1,047	700	675.8	459.9
Cape Verde		182	101	142.7	68.6
Cayman Is.			200	821.2	
Central African Rep.	2	80	6	2.4	1.9
Ceuta					
Chad		236	2	1.4	1.6
Chile	98	759	286	232.5	106.5
China		339	312	137.4	19.0
Christmas Is.					
Cocos					
Colombia	46	549	286	170.5	42.1
Comoros		174	4	12.2	5.5
Congo D.R.	3	386	2	0.4	
Congo R.	8	123	13	7.1	3.9
Cook Is.					
Coral Sea Is.					
Costa Rica	91	816	231	229.7	170.2
Côte d'Ivoire	16	183	60	18.0	7.2
Croatia	114	340	293	365.2	85.9
Cuba	118	185	251	51.0	19.6
Cyprus	111	526	181	630.9	246.6
Czech Republic	254	803	534	375.1	145.7
Denmark	283	1,400	857	719.2	540.3
Diego Garcia					
Djibouti		87	71	15.4	10.9
Dominica		634	220	290.6	75.0
Dominican Republic	27	181	97	110.2	
Ecuador	96	413	225	103.7	23.3
Egypt	31	339	217	103.6	15.5
El Salvador	28	478	201	93.4	21.9
Equatorial Guinea	5	427	116	14.7	5.3
Eritrea		464	39	8.2	1.8
Estonia	176	1,136	629	352.1	174.8
Ethiopia		189	6	4.3	1.1
Faeroe Is.		2,222	996	554.5	67.1
Fiji	52	681	116	112.3	60.9
Finland	445	1,624	678	547.6	423.5
France	201	950	632	573.5	337.0
French Guiana					
French Polynesia	109	571	195	222.6	280.0
Gabon	30	501	326	29.5	11.9
Gambia	2	396	3	26.2	12.7
Georgia	5	568	474	158.6	
Germany	305	570	586	634.2	382.2
Ghana	14	710	118	11.6	3.3
Gibraltar					
Greece	23	478	519	529.2	81.2
Greenland	18	482	411	467.4	107.4
Grenada		597	375	327.5	130.0
Guadeloupe					
Guam	193	1,511	725	508.9	
Guatemala	33	79	62	64.7	12.8
Guinea		52	45	3.2	4.0
Guinea-Bissau	5	204	36	9.8	
Guyana	75	559	81	91.9	26.4
Haiti	3	18	6	9.7	
Honduras	55	413	96	47.1	12.2
Hungary	465	690	445	374.0	100.3
Iceland	336	1,081	509	663.9	418.1
India	60	120	83	37.5	5.8
Indonesia	23	159	153	34.5	11.0
Iran	28	281	163	168.7	69.7
Iraq	19	222	83	28.6	
Ireland	150	695	399	484.5	390.7
Israel	290	526	335	476.3	245.9
Italy	104	878	494	471.5	194.8
Jamaica	62	796	194	197.3	50.0
Japan	578	956	731	597.1	348.8
Jordan	75	372	111	127.4	32.8
Kanaky-New Caledonia	122	560	506	231.2	
Kazakhstan		411	241	113.1	
Kenya	10	221	26	10.4	5.6
Kiribati		388	35	42.1	23.2
Korea, North	208	154	59	22.5	
Korea, South	393	1,034	363	485.7	256.5
Kuwait	374	624	482	239.7	131.9
Kyrgyzstan	27	110	49	77.9	
Laos	4	148	52	9.8	3.0
Latvia	135	700	840	308.3	153.1
Lebanon	107	183	336	194.9	56.2
Lesotho	8	54	16	10.3	
Liberia	12	274	25	2.2	
Libya	15	273	137	109.3	
Liechtenstein			469	608.2	
Lithuania	29	524	422	312.9	70.6
Luxembourg	325	392	664	779.9	517.3

	NEWSPAPERS PER 1,000 PEOPLE [1]	RADIOS PER 1,000 PEOPLE [1]	TV SETS PER 1,000 PEOPLE [1]	TELEPHONES (MAINLINES) PER 1,000 PEOPLE [1]	COMPUTERS PER 1,000 PEOPLE [1]
	1996	1997	2001	2001	2001
Macedonia, TFYR	21	205	282	263.5	
Madagascar	5	216	24	3.6	2.4
Malawi	3	499	4	5.2	1.3
Malaysia	158	420	201	195.8	126.1
Maldives	20	109	120	99.4	21.9
Mali	1	180	17	4.3	1.2
Malta	126	666	566	530.0	229.6
Malvinas-Falklands				59.8	50.0
Marshall Is.					
Martinique		149	96	7.2	10.3
Mauritania				7.2	
Mauritius	119	379	301	257.4	109.1
Mayotte Is.				69.8	
Melilla					
Mexico	94	330	283	137.2	68.7
Micronesia		71	20	84.0	
Moldova	13	758	296	154.0	15.9
Monaco		671			
Mongolia	30	50	72	51.8	14.6
Montserrat					
Morocco	28	243	159	40.8	13.7
Mozambique	2	44	5	4.4	3.5
Myanmar-Burma	9	65	8	6.1	1.1
Namibia	19	141	38	65.7	36.4
Nauru					
Nepal	12	39	9	13.1	3.5
Netherlands	306	980	553	621.1	428.4
Netherlands Antilles	338		335	372.3	
New Zealand-Aotearoa	362	997	558	477.1	392.6
Nicaragua	30	270	69	31.2	9.6
Niger		121	37	1.9	0.5
Nigeria	24	200	68	4.6	6.8
Niue					
Norfolk Is.				395.9	
Northern Marianas				720.4	508.0
Norway	569	3,324	883	720.4	508.0
Oman	29	621	563	89.7	32.4
Pakistan	40	105	148	23.3	4.1
Palau					
Palestine			134	77.6	
Panama	62	300	194	148.3	37.9
Papua New Guinea	14	86	20	11.7	56.7
Paraguay	43	188	218	51.2	14.2
Peru		269	148	77.5	47.9
Philippines	82	161	173	42.4	21.7
Pitcairn					
Poland	102	523	401	295.1	85.4
Portugal	32	304	415	426.8	117.4
Puerto Rico	126	761	330	336.4	
Qatar	175	488	869	274.5	163.9
Réunion					
Romania	300	358	379	183.8	35.7
Russia	105	418	538	243.3	49.7
Rwanda		85	0	2.7	
Sahara, Western					
Samoa	1,063	141 64.1	6.7		
Samoa, American	85		228	211.3	
San Marino	70				
São Tomé and Príncipe		318	228	36.3	
Saudi Arabia	326	326	264	144.8	62.7
Senegal	5	126	79	24.5	18.6
Serbia and Montenegro	107	297	282	228.8	23.4
Seychelles	39	543	202	261.1	146.5
Sierra Leone	4	259	13	4.7	
Singapore	298	672	300	471.4	508.3
Slovakia	131	965	407	288.0	148.1
Slovenia	169	405	367	400.9	275.7
Solomon Is.		147	24	17.1	50.9
Somalia	1	60	14	3.5	
South Africa	32	338	152	112.5	68.5
Spain	100	330	598	431.1	168.2
Sri Lanka	29	215	117	44.3	9.3
St Helena					
St Kitts-Nevis		676	260	568.8	174.5
St Lucia		742	365	313.5	146.8
St Pierre and Miquelon					
St Vincent		685	234	219.6	116.1
Sudan	26	466	386	14.2	3.6
Suriname	68	729	261	175.8	45.5
Swaziland	26	162	128	31.4	
Sweden	410	2,811	965	739.1	561.2
Switzerland	373	1,002	554	745.6	540.2
Syria	20	276	67	103.0	16.3
Taiwan					
Tajikistan	20	141	326	35.9	
Tanzania	4	406	42	4.1	3.3
Thailand	64	235	300	98.7	27.8
Timor-Leste					
Togo	2	265	37	10.3	21.5
Tokelau					
Tonga		653	66	109.2	
Trinidad and Tobago	123	532	340	239.9	69.2
Tunisia	23	158	198	108.9	23.7
Turkey	111	470	319	285.2	40.7
Turkmenistan	7	256	196	80.2	
Turks and Caicos					
Tuvalu					
Uganda	2	127	28	2.8	3.1
Ukraine	175	889	456	212.1	18.3
United Arab Emirates	156	318	252	339.7	135.5
United Kingdom	329	1,446	951	588.0	366.2
United States	213	2,117	835	667.1	625.0
Uruguay	293	603	530	282.9	110.1
Uzbekistan	3	456	276	65.8	
Vanuatu		346	12	33.6	
Vatican					
Venezuela	206	294	185	109.3	52.8
Vietnam	4	109	186	37.6	11.7
Virgin Is. (Am.)		996	594	563.7	
Virgin Is. (Br.)					
Wallis and Futuna					
Yemen	15	65	283	22.1	1.9
Zambia	12	175	113	8.0	7.0
Zimbabwe	18	362	30	18.6	12.1

1. World Development Indicators 2003, World Bank

LABOR FORCE

	LABOR FORCE AS % OF TOTAL POPULATION [1]	UNEMPLOYMENT AS % OF LABOR FORCE [3]	% OF WOMEN IN LABOR FORCE [1]	% OF MALE EMPLOYMENT IN AGRICULTURE [2]	% OF MALE EMPLOYMENT IN INDUSTRY [2]	% OF MALE EMPLOYMENT IN SERVICES [2]	% OF FEMALE EMPLOYMENT IN AGRICULTURE [2]	% OF FEMALE EMPLOYMENT IN INDUSTRY [2]	% OF FEMALE EMPLOYMENT IN SERVICES [2]
	2002	2002	2002	1995-2001	1995-2001	1995-2001	1995-2001	1995-2001	1995-2001
Afghanistan	41.8		35.8						
Albania	50.4	15.8	41.5						
Algeria	35.0	27.3	29.0						
Andorra									
Angola	46.1		46.2						
Anguilla		7.8							
Antigua									
Argentina	41.4	19.6	34.4		10	89	1	34	65
Armenia	63.7	9.4	48.6						
Aruba									
Australia	51.0	6.3	44.0	3	10	86	6	31	63
Austria	46.8	4.0	40.4	7	14	79	6	43	52
Azerbaijan	45.7	1.3	44.7						
Bahamas	55.0	7.7	47.4	1	5	93	6	24	69
Bahrain			21.6						
Bangladesh	53.4	3.3	42.5	78	8	11	54	11	34
Barbados	53.5	10.3	45.9	3	11	85	5	31	64
Belarus	53.2	3.0	48.9						
Belgium	41.4	7.5	41.1	2	13	86	3	37	60
Belize	35.2	12.8	24.3	6	12	81	37	19	44
Benin	45.4		48.3						
Bermuda									
Bhutan	48.0		40.0						
Bolivia	41.2	7.4	38.0	2	16	82	2	40	58
Bosnia-Herzegovina	46.9		38.2						
Botswana	44.7	15.8	45.1						
Brazil	46.8	9.4	35.5	19	10	71	26	27	47
Brunei	45.8		36.3						
Bulgaria	51.5	17.6	48.0						
Burkina Faso	49.0		46.5						
Burundi	55.0	14.0	48.6						
Cambodia	53.2	1.8	51.5						
Cameroon	40.9		38.2						
Canada	53.6	7.7	46.0	2	11	87	5	32	63
Cape Verde	42.0		38.8						
Cayman Is.									
Central African Rep.	48.3								
Ceuta									
Chad	48.5		44.8						
Chile	41.6	7.8	34.5	5	14	82	19	31	49
China	60.1	4.0	45.2						
Christmas Is.									
Cocos									
Colombia	44.4	15.7	39.1		20	80	2	30	68
Comoros	46.0		42.2						
Congo D.R.	41.5		43.3						
Congo R.	41.5		43.5						
Cook Is.									
Coral Sea Is.									
Costa Rica	40.5	6.1	31.6	4	17	79	22	27	51
Côte d'Ivoire	40.4		33.6						
Croatia	47.3	14.8	44.4	17	22	61	16	38	46
Cuba	49.9		39.9						
Cyprus	48.7	3.3	38.9	10	18	71	11	30	58
Czech Republic	55.9	7.3	47.2	4	28	69	6	49	48
Denmark	54.4	4.7	46.5	2	15	83	5	37	58
Diego Garcia									
Djibouti									
Dominica				14	10	72	31	24	40
Dominican Republic	44.8	15.9	31.4	3	20	77	24	27	49
Ecuador	40.0	9.3	28.7	2	14	84	11	26	63
Egypt	39.0	9.2	31.0	35	9	56	29	25	46
El Salvador	44.3	6.2	37.3	6	25	69	37	24	38
Equatorial Guinea	41.9		35.7						
Eritrea	50.4		47.4						
Estonia	56.1	10.3	48.9	7	23	70	11	40	49
Ethiopia	43.0		41.0	88	2	11	89	2	9
Faeroe Is.									
Fiji	41.6	5.4	31.8						
Finland	49.7	9.1	48.2	4	14	82	8	40	52
France	45.4	8.9	45.3		13	86	2	35	63
French Guiana									
French Polynesia									
Gabon	45.3	18.0	44.8						
Gambia	50.7		45.2						
Georgia		12.3	46.8						
Germany	49.8	8.7	42.4	2	19	79	3	46	50
Ghana	47.9		50.4						
Gibraltar									
Greece	43.4	9.6	38.2	20	12	67	16	29	54
Greenland									
Grenada				10	12	77	17	32	46
Guadeloupe									
Guam		5.5							
Guatemala	37.7	1.8	30.1	14	19	68	37	26	38
Guinea	47.4		47.2						
Guinea-Bissau	46.9		40.5						
Guyana	44.5		34.4						
Haiti	43.9		42.8						
Honduras	38.6	4.2	32.6	9	25	67	50	21	30
Hungary	47.8	5.8	44.8	4	25	71	9	42	48
Iceland	56.5	3.3	45.4	5	15	80	12	34	53
India	44.8		32.5						
Indonesia	49.2	9.1	41.2	42	16	42	41	21	39
Iran	32.2	12.3	28.4						
Iraq	28.2		20.4						
Ireland	42.9	4.6	35.0	2	15	83	12	38	50
Israel	44.0	10.3	41.7	1	13	86	3	35	61
Italy	44.5	9.0	38.7	5	21	74	6	39	55
Jamaica	53.1	16.0	46.2	10	9	81	30	26	45
Japan	53.5	5.4	41.7	6	22	73	5	38	57
Jordan	30.4		25.6						
Kanaky-New Caledonia		18.6							
Kazakhstan	49.4	9.3	47.1						
Kenya	52.0		46.1	16	10	75	20	23	57
Kiribati									
Korea, North	52.4		43.3						
Korea, South	51.6	3.1	41.8	13	19	68	10	34	56
Kuwait	41.9	1.1	32.1						
Kyrgyzstan	44.1		47.2	53	8	38	52	14	34
Laos	47.9								
Latvia	55.1	12.0	50.5	14	18	69	17	35	49
Lebanon	36.1		30.1						
Lesotho	41.4		37.0						
Liberia	40.0		39.6						
Libya	28.8		24.0						
Liechtenstein									
Lithuania	52.3	13.8	48.0	16	40	63	24	33	43

	LABOR FORCE AS % OF TOTAL POPULATION [1]	UNEMPLOYMENT AS % OF LABOR FORCE [3]	% OF WOMEN IN LABOR FORCE [1]	% OF MALE EMPLOYMENT IN AGRICULTURE [2]	% OF MALE EMPLOYMENT IN INDUSTRY [2]	% OF MALE EMPLOYMENT IN SERVICES [2]	% OF FEMALE EMPLOYMENT IN AGRICULTURE [2]	% OF FEMALE EMPLOYMENT IN INDUSTRY [2]	% OF FEMALE EMPLOYMENT IN SERVICES [2]
	2002	2002	2002	1995-2001	1995-2001	1995-2001	1995-2001	1995-2001	1995-2001
Luxembourg	42.4	3.0	36.8						
Macedonia, TFYR	47.3	31.9	42.0						
Madagascar	47.4		44.7						
Malawi	48.1		48.4						
Malaysia	42.3	3.8	38.3	13	29	58	21	33	46
Maldives	40.8		43.5						
Mali	48.9		46.1						
Malta	37.9	6.8	28.3						
Malvinas-Falklands									
Marshall Is.									
Martinique									
Mauritania	46.3		43.5						
Mauritius	43.3	9.7	33.0	13	43	45	15	39	46
Mayotte Is.									
Melilla									
Mexico	41.9	1.9	33.8	7	22	71	23	29	47
Micronesia									
Moldova	50.7	6.8	48.4						
Monaco									
Mongolia	50.9	3.4	47.1						
Montserrat									
Morocco	40.8	18.3	34.9	6	40	54	6	32	63
Mozambique	52.0		48.4						
Myanmar-Burma	53.5		43.4						
Namibia	41.3	33.8	41.0	39	8	52	38	19	43
Nauru									
Nepal	46.7		40.5						
Netherlands	46.2	2.7	40.9	2	9	84	4	31	63
Netherlands Antilles		14.0	42.8						
New Zealand-Aotearoa	50.1	5.2	45.2	6	12	81	11	32	56
Nicaragua	41.5	12.2	36.6						
Niger	47.1		44.3						
Nigeria	39.9		36.7	2	11	87	4	30	67
Niue									
Norfolk Is.									
Northern Marianas									
Norway	51.8	3.9	46.5	2	9	88	6	33	61
Oman	26.7		18.9						
Pakistan	38.1	7.8	29.5	66	11	23	41	20	39
Palau									
Palestine		31.3							
Panama	42.8	14.1	35.7	2	10	88	25	22	52
Papua New Guinea	49.3		42.4						
Paraguay	40.1	14.7	30.4	3	10	87	7	31	62
Peru	38.8	7.9	31.9	3	11	86	8	25	67
Philippines	42.8	9.8	38.0	27	13	61	47	18	36
Pitcairn									
Poland	51.6	19.9	46.5	19	21	60	19	41	39
Portugal	50.7	5.1	44.1	14	24	62	11	44	45
Puerto Rico	38.2	12.3	37.8						
Qatar	53.1		16.4						
Réunion		34.4							
Romania	48.1	8.4	44.5	45	22	33	39	33	29
Russia	53.8	8.9	49.2	8	23	69	15	36	49
Rwanda	59.1	0.6	48.7						
Sahara, Western									
Samoa									
Samoa, American									
San Marino		3.6							
São Tomé and Príncipe									
Saudi Arabia	33.1	4.6	17.7						
Senegal	44.9		42.6						
Serbia and Montenegro	48.1	13.8	43.1						
Seychelles									
Sierra Leone	37.5		37.1						
Singapore	49.2	5.2	39.2		23	77		33	67
Slovakia	54.9	18.5	47.7	5	26	69	10	49	42
Slovenia	50.5	5.9	46.6	11	28	61	11	46	42
Solomon Is.	51.3		46.4						
Somalia	42.8		43.4						
South Africa	39.9	30.0	37.9						
Spain	44.3	11.4	37.5	5	14	81	8	41	51
Sri Lanka	44.3	8.7	36.9	49	22	27	38	23	37
St Helena									
St Kitts-Nevis									
St Lucia				16	14	71	27	24	49
St Pierre and Miquelon									
St Vincent									
Sudan	40.3		30.0						
Suriname	39.1	14.0	34.2	3	10	86	7	32	56
Swaziland	37.1		37.8						
Sweden	53.8	4.0	48.1	1	12	87	4	38	59
Switzerland	53.9	2.9	40.8	4	13	83	5	36	59
Syria	32.9	11.7	27.6						
Taiwan		4.6							
Tajikistan	40.6	2.7	45.2						
Tanzania	51.5	5.1	49.0						
Thailand	60.8	2.6	46.2	47	17	36	50	20	31
Timor-Leste			44.7						
Togo	41.6		40.0						
Tokelau									
Tonga									
Trinidad and Tobago	45.6	10.8	34.9	3	13	83	11	37	52
Tunisia	40.5	14.9	32.1						
Turkey	46.7	10.6	38.1	72	10	18	34	25	41
Turkmenistan	44.3		45.9						
Turks and Caicos									
Tuvalu									
Uganda	49.1		47.6						
Ukraine	51.1	10.1	48.8						
United Arab Emirates	49.2	2.3	15.9						
United Kingdom	50.0	5.1	44.3	1	12	87	2	36	61
United States	51.4	5.8	46.2	1	12	86	4	32	64
Uruguay	46.2	17.0	42.2	1	14	85	6	34	61
Uzbekistan	43.4	0.4	46.9						
Vanuatu									
Vatican									
Venezuela	41.7	15.8	35.4	2	13	85	16	29	55
Vietnam	52.0		48.7						
Virgin Is. (Am.)		5.9							
Virgin Is. (Br.)									
Wallis and Futuna									
Yemen	31.8	11.5	28.3						
Zambia	42.9		44.6						
Zimbabwe	46.6	6.0	44.5						

1. World Development Indicators 2003, World Bank / 2. Human Development Report 2003, UNDP / 3. LABORSTA database, ILO Web Site

ECONOMY

	% OF POPULATION LIVING UNDER ONE DOLLAR PER DAY	SURVEY YEAR	GNI PER CAPITA ($, ATLAS METHOD) [1]	GDP PER CAPITA (PPP, CURRENT $) [1]	GDP, ANNUAL GROWTH (%) [1]	AVERAGE ANNUAL INFLATION (%) [1]	CONSUMER PRICE INDEX (ALL ITEMS 1995=100) [1]	IMPORTS OF GOODS AND SERVICES (CURRENT MILLION $) [1]	EXPORTS OF GOODS AND SERVICES (CURRENT MILLION $) [1]	TOTAL EXTERNAL DEBT (THOUSANDS $) [1]	PER CAPITA EXTERNAL DEBT ($)	DEBT SERVICE (% OF EXPORTS OF GOODS AND SERVICES) [1]
			2002	2002	2002	2002	2002	2002	2002	2001	2001	2001
Afghanistan												
Albania			1,380	3,973	4.7	6.5	7.8	2,058	923	1,094	350	2.2
Algeria	<2	1995	1,720	5,536	4.1	0.5	1.4	13,044	18,630	22,503	732	21.2
Andorra												
Angola			660	2,053	17.1	102.6	108.9	5,888	7,057	9,600	752	27.6
Anguilla												
Antigua			9,390	10,596	2.7	1.3		541	470			
Argentina			4,060	10,594	-10.9	30.8	25.9	27,315	30,694	136,709	3,643	66.3
Armenia	12.8	1998	790	2,957	12.9	2.3	1.1	1,085	692	1,001	324	8.3
Aruba					6.0	3.7	3.3					
Australia			19,740	27,756	3.5	2.3	3.0	88,371	88,780			
Austria			23,390	28,611	1.0	1.3	1.8	99,141	98,444			
Azerbaijan	3.7	2001	710	3,115	10.6	0.5	1.5	3,198	2,306	1,219	148	5.3
Bahamas			14,860	16,554	4.5	1.8	2.2					
Bahrain			11,130	16,593		-0.4	-0.7	4,695	6,404			
Bangladesh	36.0	2000	360	1,737	4.4	2.7	4.9	9,061	6,850	15,216	108	7.3
Barbados			9,750	16,024	1.5	3.4	2.6	1,447	1,311	701	2,610	4.5
Belarus	<2	2000	1,360	5,344	4.7	41.9	42.5	8,723	8,290	869	87	2.8
Belgium			23,250	26,695	0.7	1.8	1.6	186,182	193,831			
Belize			2,960	5,907	3.7	0.3	1.2	597	444	708	2,886	25.1
Benin			380	1,032	5.3	2.4	2.5	719	385	1,665	261	7.9
Bermuda					3.1	2.1						
Bhutan			590		7.7	6.8	6.8	229	122	265	125	4.2
Bolivia	14.4	1999	900	2,360	2.5	2.0	0.9	1,952	1,462	4,682	552	31.1
Bosnia-Herzegovina			1,270	5,538	3.9			2,658	1,410	2,226	547	19.1
Botswana	23.5	1993	2,980	8,244	3.5	4.5	8.1	3,223	3,296	370	211	1.7
Brazil	9.9	1998	2,850	7,516	1.5	8.5	8.4	72,339	67,141	226,362	1,301	75.4
Brunei			24,100	17,019	1.0	-0.2						
Bulgaria	4.7	2001	1,790	6,909	4.3	5.0	5.8	9,297	7,996	9,615	1,197	17.3
Burkina Faso	61.2	1994	220	1,012	5.6	2.9	2.2	720	288	1,490	122	11.8
Burundi	58.4	1998	100	613	3.6	12.9	-1.4	136	47	1,065	166	39.8
Cambodia			280	1,649	4.5	3.1	3.2	2,091	1,814	2,704	201	1.3
Cameroon	33.4	1996	560	1,712	4.4	0.7	2.8	2,534	2,465	8,338	540	12.6
Canada			22,300	28,699	3.3	1.1	2.2	268,355	304,276			
Cape Verde			1,290	4,787	4.0	2.4	3.7	322	146	360	808	5.5
Cayman Is.					5.3	3.1						
Central African Rep.	66.6	1993	260	1,198	4.2	1.4	3.4	177	129	822	218	11.9
Ceuta												
Chad			220	1,008	10.9	3.7	5.2	1,218	235	1,104	136	7.9
Chile	<2	1998	4,260	9,561	2.1	2.6	2.5	21,700	23,043	38,360	2,488	28.1
China	16.1	2000	940	4,475	8.0	-1.2	0.5	313,802	332,367	170,110	132	7.8
Christmas Is.												
Cocos												
Colombia	14.4	1998	1,830	6,068	1.5	7.0	6.3	15,694	15,984	36,699	857	35.3
Comoros			390	1,640	3.0	7.1		79	38	246	339	3.6
Congo D.R.			90	606	3.0	23.3	31.5	1,224	1,047	11,392		1.7
Congo R.			700	967	3.5	-0.7	4.4	1,512	2,309	4,496	1,269	4.2
Cook Is.												
Coral Sea Is.												
Costa Rica	6.9	1998	4,100	8,470	2.8	9.8	9.2	7,259	6,900	4,586	1,143	9.0
Côte d'Ivoire	12.3	1995	610	1,500	-0.9	4.7	3.1	3,701	4,448	11,582	719	13.5
Croatia	<2	2000	4,640	9,967	5.2	2.9	2.0	10,691	9,466	10,742	2,417	27.9
Cuba					5.6	2.6						
Cyprus			12,320	17,725	2.0	2.8	2.8	4,465	4,112			
Czech Republic	<2	1996	5,560	15,148	2.0	2.6	1.8	41,903	40,345	21,691	2,115	11.2
Denmark			30,290	29,975	1.6	1.1	2.4	63,294	73,654			
Diego Garcia												
Djibouti			900	2,028	1.6	2.0		347	247	262	385	5.5
Dominica			3,180	5,265	-2.8	0.9	1.9	168	135	207	2,642	11.5
Dominican Republic	<2	1998	2,320	6,197	4.1	5.8	8.9	6,801	5,072	5,093	600	6.0
Ecuador	20.2	1995	1,450	3,446	3.0	12.4	12.5	6,608	5,613	13,910	1,103	21.4
Egypt	3.1	2000	1,470	3,701	3.0	4.0	2.7	21,014	16,397	29,234	423	8.9
El Salvador	21.4	1997	2,080	4,675	2.3	1.7	1.9	5,892	3,977	4,683	742	6.3
Equatorial Guinea			700	23,086	0.2	11.8		791	464	239	510	0.1
Eritrea			160	958	9.2	1.1		531	118	410	106	1.7
Estonia	<2	1998	4,130	11,712	5.8	4.3	3.6	5,944	5,685	2,852	2,108	7.4
Ethiopia	81.9	99/00	100	724	5.0	-6.3	1.6	2,005	909	5,697	85	18.5
Faeroe Is.												
Fiji			2,160	5,347	4.4	2.5	4.3	1,035	1,132	188	229	2.0
Finland			23,510	25,859	1.6	1.3	1.6	38,163	48,804			
France			22,010	26,151	1.0	1.3	1.9	345,072	365,625			
French Guiana												
French Polynesia			16,150	24,362	4.0	1.0		835	169			
Gabon			3,120	6,350	3.0	5.9	0.5	1,962	2,957	3,409	2,658	13.9
Gambia	59.3	1998	280	1,723	-0.6	16.9	0.8	268	209	489	362	3.8
Georgia	<2	1998	650	2,190	5.4	4.4	5.6	1,302	901	1,714	328	7.8
Germany			22,670	26,324	0.2	1.6	1.3	610,572	645,542			
Ghana	44.8	1999	270	2,050	4.5	20.2	14.8	4,042	3,069	6,759	338	13.0
Gibraltar												
Greece			11,660	18,184	4.0	3.7	3.6	36,863	27,967			
Greenland												
Grenada			3,500	6,989	-0.5	4.5	0.2	279	234	215	2,664	8.2
Guadeloupe												
Guam												
Guatemala	16.0	2000	1,750	3,927	2.0	9.1	8.0	5,746	3,817	4,526	386	9.0
Guinea			410	2,026	4.3	2.4		1,004	868	3,254	395	12.3
Guinea-Bissau			150	779	-4.2	7.9	3.8	147	81	668	475	41.1
Guyana	<2	1998	840	4,086	0.3	3.1	2.6	777	663	1,406	1,846	6.6
Haiti			440	1,578	-0.9	10.2	9.9	1,247	469	1,250	154	5.2
Honduras	23.8	1998	920	2,520	2.0	7.3	7.7	3,511	2,447	5,051	763	11.2
Hungary	<2	1998	5,280	13,129	3.3	10.7	5.5	32,512	31,400	30,289	3,039	37.2
Iceland			27,970	29,614		5.2	5.2	3,154	3,118			
India	34.7	99/00	480	2,571	4.4	4.0	4.4	82,909	78,156	97,320	94	11.8
Indonesia	7.2	2000	710	3,138	3.7	7.2	11.5	49,363	61,210	135,704	633	23.6
Iran	<2	1998	1,710	6,339	5.9	21.7	14.3	19,066	28,848	7,483	111	4.9
Iraq					-50.6							
Ireland			23,870	32,960	3.6	6.5	4.7	83,145	98,541			
Israel			16,710	20,055	6.0	1.7	5.6	51,813	44,147			
Italy			18,960	25,570	0.4	2.7	2.5	290,358	307,805			
Jamaica	<2	2000	2,820	3,774	1.0	7.1	7.1	4,344	3,228	4,956	1,904	14.3
Japan			33,550	25,650	-0.7	-0.2	-0.9	406,428	432,547			
Jordan	<2	1997	1,760	4,106	4.9	0.4	1.8	6,665	4,192	7,479	1,443	10.7
Kanaky-New Caledonia			14,050	21,955	2.1	-0.6		1,009	400			
Kazakhstan	1.5	1996	1,510	5,769	9.5	5.3	5.8	11,938	11,129	14,372	925	31.6
Kenya	23.0	1997	360	992	1.8	4.9	2.0	3,835	3,098	5,833	188	15.4
Kiribati			810		2.8	2.7		39	4			
Korea, North												
Korea, South	<2	1998	9,930	16,465	6.3	1.7	2.8	183,885	190,741	110,109	2,336	13.9
Kuwait			18,270	16,328	-1.0	-7.5	1.4	12,266	17,952			
Kyrgyzstan	2.0	2000	290	1,572	-0.5	2.3	2.1	691	630	1,717	344	29.8
Laos	26.3	97/98	310	1,678	5.0	9.2	10.6	612	467	2,495	462	9.0
Latvia	<2	1998	3,480	8,965	6.1	1.8	1.3	4,526	3,843	5,710	2,429	13.6
Lebanon			3,990	4,243	1.0	2.5		7,065	2,399	12,450	3,520	43.7
Lesotho	43.1	1993	470	2,272	3.8	8.0	33.8	704	398	592	330	12.4
Liberia			150		4.2	31.5				1,987	641	0.5
Libya							2.6	5,279	12,140			
Liechtenstein												
Lithuania	<2	2000	3,660	10,015	6.7		0.3	7,038	6,212	5,248	1,506	31.0

ECONOMY	TOTAL NET OFFICIAL DEVELOPMENT ASSISTANCE RECEIVED ($ MILLION) [2]	TOTAL NET OFFICIAL DEVELOPMENT ASSISTANCE RECEIVED ($ PER CAPITA) [2]	TOTAL NET OFFICIAL DEVELOPMENT ASSISTANCE RECEIVED (% OF GDP) [2]	TOTAL NET OFFICIAL DEVELOPMENT ASSISTANCE DISBURSED (% OF GDP) [2]	TOTAL NET OFFICIAL DEVELOPMENT ASSISTANCE DISBURSED ($ MILLION) [2]	ENERGY USE CONSUMPTION (OIL EQUIVALENT) PER CAPITA (KG) [1]	ENERGY IMPORTS AS % OF CONSUMPTION [1]	HEALTH SERVICES (AS % OF GDP) [2]	EDUCATION SERVICES (AS % OF GDP) [2]	DEFENSE (AS % OF GDP) [1]
	2001	2001	2001	2001	2001	2000	2000	1990	2000	2001
Afghanistan								0.6		
Albania	269	86	6.5			521	50	2.1	3.1	1.2
Algeria	182	6	0.3			956	-415	3.0	4.8	3.5
Andorra								6.8		
Angola	268	21	2.8			584	-470	2.0	2.7	3.1
Anguilla										
Antigua	9	119	1.3					3.3	3.2	
Argentina	151	4	0.1			2	-32	4.7	4.0	1.4
Armenia	212	69	10.0			662	69	3.2	2.9	3.1
Aruba								4.7		
Australia				0.3	873	6	-111	6.0	4.7	1.7
Austria				0.3	533	4	66	5.6	5.8	0.8
Azerbaijan	226	28	4.1			1	-62	0.7	4.2	2.6
Bahamas	9	28						4.4	3.2	
Bahrain	18	26	0.2			10	-14	2.8	3.0	4.1
Bangladesh	1,024	7	2.2			142	19	1.4	2.5	1.3
Barbados	-1	-4						4.2	7.1	
Belarus	39	4	0.3			2	86	4.7	6.0	1.4
Belgium				0.4	867	6	78	6.2	5.9	1.3
Belize	21	87	2.7					2.1	6.2	1.5
Benin	273	43	11.5			377	23	1.6	3.2	
Bermuda										
Bhutan	59	28	11.1					3.7	5.2	
Bolivia	729	86	9.1			592	-20	4.9	5.5	1.6
Bosnia-Herzegovina	639	157	13.4			1	25	3.1		9.5
Botswana	29	17	0.6					3.8	8.6	3.5
Brazil	349	2	0.1			1	22	3.4	4.7	1.5
Brunei	0	1				6	-866	2.5	4.8	6.1
Bulgaria	346	43	2.6			2	47	3.0	3.4	2.7
Burkina Faso								3.0	1.5	1.6
Burundi								1.7	3.4	8.1
Cambodia	409	30	12.0					2.0	1.9	3.0
Cameroon	398	26	4.7			427	-100	1.1	3.2	1.4
Canada				0.2	1,533	8	-49	6.6	5.5	1.2
Cape Verde	77	172	13.0					1.8	4.4	0.8
Cayman Is.										
Central African Rep.								1.4	1.9	1.2
Ceuta										
Chad	179	22	11.2					2.5	2.0	1.5
Chile	58	4	0.1			2	66	3.1	4.2	2.9
China	1,460	1	0.1			905	3	1.9	2.9	2.3
Christmas Is.										
Cocos										
Colombia	380	9	0.5			681	-159	5.4	3.5	3.8
Comoros	28	38	12.5					3.2	3.8	
Congo D.R.						292	-4	1.1		
Congo R.	75	21	2.7			296	-2	1.5	4.2	
Cook Is.										
Coral Sea Is.										
Costa Rica	2	1				861	52	4.4	4.4	
Côte d'Ivoire	187	12	1.8			433	12	1.0	4.6	0.9
Croatia	113	25	0.6			2	54	8.0	4.2	2.6
Cuba	51	5				1	54	6.1	8.5	
Cyprus	50	63	0.5			3	98	4.3	5.4	3.1
Czech Republic	314	31	0.6			4	26	6.6	4.4	2.1
Denmark				1.0	1,634	4	-43	6.8	8.2	1.6
Diego Garcia										
Djibouti	55	81	9.6						3.5	4.4
Dominica	20	255	7.6					4.3	5.1	
Dominican Republic	105	12	0.5			932	82	1.8	2.5	
Ecuador	171	14	1.0			647	-175	1.2	1.6	2.1
Egypt	1,255	18	1.3			726	-24	1.8	4.7	2.6
El Salvador	235	37	1.7			651	47	3.8	2.3	0.8
Equatorial Guinea	13	28	0.7					2.3	0.6	2.1
Eritrea	280	73	40.7					2.8	4.8	27.5
Estonia	69	51	1.2			3	36	4.7	7.5	
Ethiopia						291	6	1.8	4.8	6.2
Faeroe Is.										
Fiji	26	32	1.5					2.5	5.2	2.2
Finland				0.3	389	6	54	5.0	6.1	1.2
France				0.3	4,198	4	49	7.2	5.8	2.5
French Guiana										
French Polynesia									0.5	
Gabon	9	7	0.2			1	-975	2.1	3.9	0.3
Gambia	51	38	13.0					3.4	2.7	1.0
Georgia	290	56	9.2			543	74	0.8		0.7
Germany				0.3	4,990	4	60	8.0	4.6	1.5
Ghana	652	33	12.3			400	24	2.3	4.1	0.6
Gibraltar										
Greece				0.2	202	3	64	4.6	3.8	4.6
Greenland										
Grenada	12	143	2.9					3.4	4.2	
Guadeloupe										
Guam										
Guatemala	225	19	1.1			628	27	2.3	1.7	1.0
Guinea	272	33	9.1					1.9	1.9	1.7
Guinea-Bissau	59	42	29.4					2.6	2.1	3.1
Guyana	102	134	14.6					4.2	4.1	0.8
Haiti	166	20	4.4			256	24	2.4	1.1	
Honduras	678	102	10.6			469	49	4.3	4.0	
Hungary	418	42	0.8			2	55	5.2	5.0	1.8
Iceland						12	27	7.5	5.4	
India	1,705	2	0.4			494	16	0.9	4.1	2.5
Indonesia	1,501	7	1.0			706	-58	0.6	1.3	1.1
Iran	115	2	0.1			2	-115	2.6	4.4	4.8
Iraq						1	-384	2.2		
Ireland				0.3	287	4	85	5.1	4.4	0.7
Israel	172	28	0.2			3	97	8.3	7.3	7.7
Italy				0.2	1,627	3	84	6.0	4.5	2.0
Jamaica	54	21	0.7			2	88	2.6	6.3	
Japan				0.2	9,847	4	80	6.0	3.5	1.0
Jordan	432	83	4.9			1	94	4.2	6.1	8.6
Kanaky-New Caledonia									0.6	
Kazakhstan	148	10	0.7			3	-100	2.7	4.4	1.0
Kenya	453	15	4.0			515	21	1.8	6.4	1.8
Kiribati								8.0		
Korea, North						2	8	1.6		
Korea, South	-111	-2				4	83	2.7	3.8	2.8
Kuwait	4	2				11	-434	2.6	6.1	11.3
Kyrgyzstan	188	38	12.3			497	41	2.2	5.4	1.7
Laos	243	45	13.8					1.3	2.3	2.1
Latvia	106	45	1.4			2	66	3.5	5.9	1.2
Lebanon	241	68	1.4			1	97	2.5	3.0	5.5
Lesotho	54	30	6.8					5.2	13.0	3.1
Liberia								3.1		31.2
Libya	10	2				3	-350	1.6		
Liechtenstein										
Lithuania	130	37	1.1			2	55	4.3	6.4	1.8

ECONOMY

	% OF POPULATION LIVING UNDER ONE DOLLAR PER DAY	SURVEY YEAR	GNI PER CAPITA ($, ATLAS METHOD) [1]	GDP PER CAPITA (PPP, CURRENT $) [1]	GDP, ANNUAL GROWTH (%) [1]	AVERAGE ANNUAL INFLATION (%) [1]	CONSUMER PRICE INDEX (ALL ITEMS 1995=100) [1]	IMPORTS OF GOODS AND SERVICES (CURRENT MILLION $) [1]	EXPORTS OF GOODS AND SERVICES (CURRENT MILLION $) [1]	TOTAL EXTERNAL DEBT (THOUSANDS $) [1]	PER CAPITA EXTERNAL DEBT ($)	DEBT SERVICE (% OF EXPORTS OF GOODS AND SERVICES) [1]
			2002	2002	2002	2002	2002	2002	2002	2001	2001	2001
Luxembourg			38,830	56,546	0.8	2.1	2.1	25,424	29,384			
Macedonia, TFYR	<2	1998	1,700	6,262	0.3	1.9	0.1	2,160	1,431	1,423	699	12.9
Madagascar	49.1	1999	240	735	-11.9	15.4	15.9	1,028	764	4,160	253	43.3
Malawi	41.7	97/98	160	586	1.8	12.2	27.2	912	442	2,602	224	7.8
Malaysia	<2	1997	3,540	8,922	4.2	3.7	1.8	91,696	108,261	43,351	1,845	6.0
Maldives			2,090		2.3	1.0	0.9	442	545	235	783	4.6
Mali	72.8	1994	240	878	9.6	4.4	5.0	1,119	834	2,890	236	8.8
Malta			9,200	16,817	-0.7	4.9	2.9	3,335	3,172	1,531	3,916	3.5
Malvinas-Falklands												
Marshall Is.			2,350			4.0	1.9		69	8			
Martinique												
Mauritania	28.6	1995	410	1,511	5.1	-1.3	3.8	517	362	2,164	795	22.7
Mauritius			3,850	10,530	4.4	5.1	6.7	2,868	2,877	1,724	1,440	6.9
Mayotte Is.												
Melilla												
Mexico	8.0	1998	5,910	8,707	0.7	4.8	5.0	185,154	170,588	158,290	1,576	26.1
Micronesia			1,980		2.0	-1.1		114	62			
Moldova	22.0	2001	460	1,431	7.2	8.1	5.1	1,206	799	1,214	284	19.3
Monaco												
Mongolia	13.9	1995	440	1,651	3.7	21.1	8.0	839	672	885	350	7.7
Montserrat												
Morocco	<2	1999	1,190	3,768	4.5	2.6	2.8	13,362	11,152	16,962	573	17.8
Mozambique	37.9	1996	210		9.9	14.3	16.8	2,012	1,070	4,466	245	3.4
Myanmar-Burma					9.7	22.6	57.1			5,670	118	3.1
Namibia	34.9	1993	1,780	6,410	3.0	7.1	11.3	1,692	1,332			
Nauru												
Nepal	37.7	1995	230	1,323	-0.6	3.1	2.6	1,610	1,017	2,700	112	4.9
Netherlands			23,960	27,275	0.1	3.4	3.5	227,048	247,328			
Netherlands Antilles							0.4					
New Zealand-Aotearoa			13,710	20,455	3.8	0.7	2.7	17,813	18,657			
Nicaragua	82.3	1998	370	2,139	4.1	13.0	4.0	1,665	761	6,391	1,228	26.2
Niger	61.4	1995	170	774	3.0	3.0	2.6	548	350	1,555	140	6.8
Nigeria	70.2	1997	290	851	-0.9	11.6	12.9	18,977	16,406	31,119	264	12.4
Niue												
Norfolk Is.												
Northern Marianas												
Norway			37,850	36,048	2.0	-0.7	1.3	49,253	75,394			
Oman			7,720	13,247	2.2	-1.5	-0.7	4,494	5,594	6,025	2,242	14.2
Pakistan	13.4	1998	410	2,014	4.4	4.5	3.3	10,900	10,735	32,019	219	25.8
Palau			7,140		3.0	3.0		99	18			
Palestine			930		-19.1	23.6		3,085	604			
Panama	7.6	1998	4,020	5,972	0.8	1.2	1.1	3,659	3,570	8,245	2,742	12.9
Papua New Guinea			530	2,141	-2.5	13.6	11.8	1,503	1,611	2,521	462	12.7
Paraguay	19.5	1998	1,170	4,419	-2.2	12.0	10.5	2,755	1,676	2,817	503	12.5
Peru	15.5	1996	2,050	4,924	5.2		0.2	9,342	8,548	27,512	1,044	22.0
Philippines	14.6	2000	1,020	4,022	4.6	4.5	3.1	36,874	37,714	52,356	679	18.7
Pitcairn												
Poland	<2	1998	4,570	10,187	1.2	1.5	1.9	48,029	36,386	62,393	1,614	28.0
Portugal	<2	1994	10,840	17,808	0.4	4.6	3.5	45,286	34,733			
Puerto Rico			10,950	24,268	5.6	5.3		68,199	54,836			
Qatar							1.4	4,052	4,080			
Réunion												
Romania	2.1	2000	1,850	6,326	4.3	22.0	22.5	18,803	15,519	11,653	519	18.8
Russia	6.1	2000	2,140	7,926	4.3	15.2	15.8	78,025	108,763	152,649	1,054	14.5
Rwanda	35.7	83/85	230	1,221	9.4		2.5	435	140	1,283	159	11.4
Sahara, Western												
Samoa			1,420	5,374	1.3	2.5	8.1	193	77	204	1,170	10.8
Samoa, American												
San Marino												
São Tomé and Príncipe			290		3.0	6.8		42	19	313	2,045	22.9
Saudi Arabia			8,460	11,516	1.2	-2.4	-0.5	45,589	78,214			
Senegal	26.3	1995	470	1,535	2.4	2.6	2.2	1,833	1,449	3,461	360	13.3
Serbia and Montenegro			1,400		4.0	25.5		5,724	2,854	11,740		2.4
Seychelles			6,530		-2.4	6.0	0.2	608	535	215	2,700	2.6
Sierra Leone	57.0	1989	140	509	6.3	3.9	-3.3	334	127	1,188	260	102.0
Singapore			20,690	23,394	2.2	0.2	-0.4					
Slovakia	<2	1996	3,950	12,426	4.4	3.9	3.3	19,112	17,242	11,121	2,062	17.0
Slovenia	<2	1998	9,810	17,748	2.9	7.9	7.5	11,374	11,300			
Solomon Is.			570	1,516	-4.0	9.4	8.3			163	361	6.9
Somalia										2,532	279	
South Africa	<2	1995	2,600	10,133	3.0	8.5	10.6	27,761	29,384	24,050	541	11.6
Spain			14,430	20,697	1.8	4.3	3.1	182,681	174,076			
Sri Lanka	6.6	95/96	840	3,447	3.0	8.6	9.7	6,964	5,825	8,529	455	9.7
St Helena												
St Kitts-Nevis			6,370	10,844	-4.3	3.7	3.9	250	151	189	4,505	12.6
St Lucia			3,840	5,487	-0.5	0.2	0.1	405	318	238	1,620	6.5
St Pierre and Miquelon												
St Vincent			2,820	5,364	0.7	2.8	0.8	220	163	194	1,641	7.8
Sudan			350	1,967	10.6	0.9	16.0	2,023	1,649	15,348	477	2.3
Suriname			1,960		2.7	24.1	98.9	644	518			
Swaziland			1,180	4,503	1.8	14.3	5.9	840	713	308	291	2.7
Sweden			24,820	25,315	1.9	1.3	2.2	85,108	97,463			
Switzerland			37,930	28,359	-0.2	0.4	0.6	101,620	112,355			
Syria			1,130	3,385	3.1	2.5	0.4	6,467	7,785	21,305	1,256	3.4
Taiwan												
Tajikistan	10.3	1998	180	916	9.1	21.6		855	745	1,086	177	11.2
Tanzania	19.9	1993	280	557	5.8	4.2	4.6	2,290	1,533	6,676	188	10.3
Thailand	<2	2000	1,980	6,788	5.2	0.7	0.6	72,709	81,865	67,384	1,095	25.1
Timor-Leste			520		-0.5	0.2						
Togo			270	1,459	3.0	1.5	3.1	693	458	1,406	300	6.6
Tokelau												
Tonga			1,410	6,365	1.6	8.0	10.4	71	29	63	624	2.8
Trinidad and Tobago	12.4	1992	6,490	9,114	2.7	-0.1	4.2	3,799	4,841	2,422	1,872	4.7
Tunisia	<2	1995	2,000	6,579	1.9	2.7	2.8	10,666	9,634	10,884	1,131	12.9
Turkey	<2	2000	2,500	6,176	7.8	43.5	45.0	46,425	52,663	115,118	1,661	40.0
Turkmenistan	12.1	1998	1,200	4,622	14.9	12.0		2,807	2,777	2,259		31.8
Turks and Caicos												
Tuvalu												
Uganda	82.2	1996	250	1,354	6.3	-3.2	-0.3	1,636	699	3,733	154	7.0
Ukraine	2.9	1999	770	4,714	4.5	3.4	22.7	22,442	23,178	12,811	260	10.6
United Arab Emirates					-5.7			31,314	31,314			
United Kingdom			25,250	25,672	1.5	3.0	1.6	416,944	386,216			
United States			35,060	35,158	2.3	1.2	1.6	1,466,900	1,103,100			
Uruguay	<2	1998	4,370	12,118	-10.8	18.8	14.0	3,712	3,478	9,706	2,883	36.3
Uzbekistan	19.1	1998	450	1,611	4.2	45.5		3,786	3,829	4,627	183	25.9
Vanuatu			1,080	2,807	-0.3	2.1	3.7	122	101	66	326	1.0
Vatican												
Venezuela	15.0	1998	4,090	5,226	-8.9	31.6	22.4	21,942	28,316	34,660	1,400	24.6
Vietnam	17.7	1998	430	2,240	7.1	3.3	3.8	18,677	18,008	12,578	159	6.7
Virgin Is. (Am.)												
Virgin Is. (Br.)												
Wallis and Futuna												
Yemen	15.7	1998	490	783	4.2	15.9	7.9	2,937	2,682	4,954	266	4.9
Zambia	63.7	1998	330	806	3.0	19.7	24.8	1,662	1,087	5,671	536	11.7
Zimbabwe	36.0	90/91	470	2,322	-5.6	107.5	76.7	1,807	1,999	3,780	296	6.8

ECONOMY

	TOTAL NET OFFICIAL DEVELOPMENT ASSISTANCE RECEIVED ($ MILLION) [2]	TOTAL NET OFFICIAL DEVELOPMENT ASSISTANCE RECEIVED ($ PER CAPITA) [2]	TOTAL NET OFFICIAL DEVELOPMENT ASSISTANCE RECEIVED (% OF GDP) [2]	TOTAL NET OFFICIAL DEVELOPMENT ASSISTANCE DISBURSED (% OF GDP) [2]	TOTAL NET OFFICIAL DEVELOPMENT ASSISTANCE DISBURSED ($ MILLION) [2]	ENERGY USE CONSUMPTION (OIL EQUIVALENT) PER CAPITA (KG) [1]	ENERGY IMPORTS AS % OF CONSUMPTION [1]	HEALTH SERVICES (AS % OF GDP) [2]	EDUCATION SERVICES (AS % OF GDP) [2]	DEFENSE (AS % OF GDP) [1]
	2001	2001	2001	2001	2001	2000	2000	1990	2000	2001
Luxembourg				0.8	141	8	98	5.3	4.0	0.8
Macedonia, TFYR	248	122	7.2					5.1	4.1	7.0
Madagascar	354	22	7.7					2.5	3.2	1.2
Malawi	402	35	23.0					3.6	4.6	0.8
Malaysia	27	1				2	-55	1.5	6.2	2.2
Maldives	25	83	4.3					6.3	3.9	
Mali								2.2	2.8	2.0
Malta	2	4				2		6.0	4.8	0.8
Malvinas-Falklands										
Marshall Is.								5.8	16.6	
Martinique										
Mauritania	262	96	26.0					3.4	3.0	2.1
Mauritius	22	18	0.5					1.9	4.2	0.2
Mayotte Is.										
Melilla										
Mexico	75	1				2	-50	2.5	4.2	0.5
Micronesia								5.6	5.5	
Moldova	119	28	8.1			671	98	2.9	4.0	0.4
Monaco								3.6		
Mongolia	212	84	20.2					4.6	2.3	2.3
Montserrat										
Morocco	517	18	1.5			359	94	1.3	5.5	4.1
Mozambique						403	-1	2.7	2.5	2.3
Myanmar-Burma	127	3				262	-21	0.4	0.5	2.3
Namibia	109	57	3.5			587	72	4.2	8.1	2.8
Nauru										
Nepal	388	16	7.0			343	13	0.9	3.7	1.1
Netherlands				0.8	3,172	5	24	5.5	4.9	1.6
Netherlands Antilles										
New Zealand-Aotearoa				0.3	112	5	17	6.2	6.1	1.2
Nicaragua	928	178				542	43	2.3	5.0	1.1
Niger								1.8	2.7	1.1
Nigeria	185	2	0.4			710	-119	0.5	0.7	1.1
Niue										
Norfolk Is.										
Northern Marianas										
Norway				0.8	1,346	6	-778	6.7	6.8	1.8
Oman	2	1				4	-516	2.3	3.9	12.2
Pakistan	1,938	13	3.3			463	26	0.9	1.8	4.5
Palau								5.7		
Palestine	865	261	21.8							
Panama	28	9	0.3			892	71	5.3	5.9	1.2
Papua New Guinea	203	37	6.9					3.6	2.3	0.8
Paraguay	61	11	0.9			746	-75	3.0	5.0	0.9
Peru	451	17	0.8			489	25	2.8	3.2	1.7
Philippines	577	8	0.8			554	51	1.6	4.2	1.0
Pitcairn										
Poland	966	25	0.5			2	12	4.2	5.0	1.9
Portugal				0.3	268	2	87	5.8	5.8	2.1
Puerto Rico										
Qatar	1	2				27	-270	2.5	3.6	
Réunion										
Romania	648	29	1.7			2	22	1.9	3.5	2.5
Russia	1,110	8	0.4			4	-57	3.8	3.5	3.8
Rwanda	291	36	17.1					2.7	2.8	3.9
Sahara, Western										
Samoa	43	247	16.9					3.9	4.2	
Samoa, American								10.0		
San Marino								1.6		
São Tomé and Príncipe	38	248	80.8							
Saudi Arabia	27	1				5	-363	4.2	9.5	11.3
Senegal	419	44	9.0			324	44	2.6	3.2	1.5
Serbia and Montenegro						1	26	2.9	5.1	4.9
Seychelles	14	170	2.4					4.2	6.0	1.8
Sierra Leone								2.6	1.0	3.6
Singapore	1	0				6	100	1.3	3.7	5.0
Slovakia	164	31	0.8			3	66	5.3	4.2	1.9
Slovenia	126	63	0.7			3	53	6.8	5.8	1.4
Solomon Is.	59	131	22.2					5.6	3.6	
Somalia								0.9		
South Africa	429	10	0.4			3	-34	3.7	5.5	1.6
Spain				0.3	1,737	3	74	5.4	4.5	1.2
Sri Lanka	330	18	2.1			437	44	1.8	3.1	3.9
St Helena										
St Kitts-Nevis	11	253	3.1					3.1	3.3	
St Lucia	16	111	2.5					2.7	5.8	
St Pierre and Miquelon										
St Vincent	9	73	2.4					4.1	9.3	
Sudan	172	5	1.4			521	-46	1.0	7.6	3.0
Suriname	23	54	3.1					5.5	3.6	
Swaziland	29	28	2.3					3.0	6.1	1.5
Sweden				0.8	1,666	5	35	6.5	8.0	2.0
Switzerland				0.3	908	4	56	6.0	5.5	1.1
Syria	153	9	0.8			1	-79	1.6	4.1	6.2
Taiwan										
Tajikistan	159	26	15.1			470	57	1.0	2.1	1.2
Tanzania	1,233	35	13.2			457	5	2.8	2.1	1.3
Thailand	281	5	0.2			1	44	2.1	5.4	1.4
Timor-Leste										
Togo	47	10	3.7			338	32	1.5	4.8	2.9
Tokelau										
Tonga								3.5	5.3	
Trinidad and Tobago	-2	-1				7	-106	2.6	4.0	
Tunisia	378	39	1.9			825	11	2.9	6.8	1.6
Turkey	167	2	0.1			1	66	3.6	3.5	4.9
Turkmenistan	72	15	1.2			3	-231	4.6		3.8
Turks and Caicos										
Tuvalu										
Uganda	783	32	13.8					1.5	2.3	2.1
Ukraine	519	11	1.4			3	41	2.9	4.4	2.7
United Arab Emirates	3	1				10	-386	2.5	1.9	2.5
United Kingdom				0.3	4,579	4	-17	5.9	4.7	2.5
United States				0.1	11,429	8	27	5.8	4.8	3.1
Uruguay	16	5	0.1			923	67	5.1	2.5	1.3
Uzbekistan	153	6	1.4			2	-10	2.6	7.7	1.1
Vanuatu	32	157	14.8					2.4	7.3	
Vatican										
Venezuela	45	2				2	-280	2.7	5.0	1.5
Vietnam	1,435	18	4.4			471	-25	1.3	2.8	2.6
Virgin Is. (Am.)										
Virgin Is. (Br.)										
Wallis and Futuna										
Yemen	426	23	4.6			201	-525	2.1	10.0	6.1
Zambia	374	35	10.3			619	5	3.5	2.3	0.6
Zimbabwe	159	13	1.8			809	15	3.1	10.4	3.2

1. World Development Indicators 2003, World Bank / 2. Human Development Report 2003, UNDP

	FOREST AND WOODLAND AS % OF LAND AREA [1]	ARABLE LAND AS % OF LAND AREA [1]	CROPLANDS AS % OF LAND AREA [1]	OTHER USES OF THE LAND AS % OF LAND AREA [1]	IRRIGATED AREA AS % OF ARABLE LAND [1]	FERTILIZER USE (KGS PER HA) [1]
	2000	2000	2000	2000	2000	2000
Afghanistan	2	12	0	88	30	0.6
Albania	36	21	4	74	49	16.1
Algeria	1	3	0	97	7	12.0
Andorra		2				
Angola	56	2	0	97	2	0.5
Anguilla						
Antigua	20	18				
Argentina	13	9	1	90	6	33.0
Armenia	12	18	2	80	51	14.1
Aruba		11				
Australia	21	7	0	93	5	45.7
Austria	47	17	1	82	0	0.2
Azerbaijan	13	19	3	78	76	1.3
Bahamas	84	1	0	99		42.9
Bahrain		3	6	92	67	0.2
Bangladesh	10	63	3	35	49	0.2
Barbados	5	37	2	60	6	0.2
Belarus	45	30	1	70	2	0.1
Belgium		25	1	74	4	0.4
Belize	59	3	1	96	3	95.9
Benin	24	18	2	80	1	18.1
Bermuda						
Bhutan	64	3	0	97	25	
Bolivia	49	2	0	98	6	3.8
Bosnia-Herzegovina	45	10	3	87	0	83.6
Botswana	22	1	0	99	0	12.4
Brazil	63	6	1	92	4	0.1
Brunei	84	1	1	99	14	
Bulgaria	33	40	2	58	17	32.9
Burkina Faso	26	14	0	86	1	8.9
Burundi	4	35	14	51	6	3.9
Cambodia	53	21	1	78	7	
Cameroon	51	13	3	85	0	8.0
Canada	27	5	0	95	2	54.4
Cape Verde	21	10	0	90	7	3.0
Cayman Is.	50					
Central African Rep.	37	3	0	97		0.3
Ceuta						
Chad	10	3	0	97	1	5.0
Chile	21	3	0	97	78	0.2
China	17	13	1	85	40	0.3
Christmas Is.						
Cocos						
Colombia	48	3	2	96	19	0.2
Comoros	4	35	22	43		3.8
Congo D.R.	60	3	1	97	0	0.1
Congo R.	65	1	0	99	0	28.6
Cook Is.						
Coral Sea Is.						
Costa Rica	39	4	5	90	21	0.9
Côte d'Ivoire	22	9	14	77	1	24.7
Croatia	32	26	2	72	0	0.2
Cuba	21	33	8	59	19	37.3
Cyprus	13	11	5	85	28	0.1
Czech Republic	34	40	3	57	1	97.3
Denmark	11	54	0	46	20	0.2
Diego Garcia						
Djibouti	0					
Dominica	61	4	16	80		1.0
Dominican Republic	28	23	10	67	17	79.0
Ecuador	38	6	5	89	29	0.1
Egypt	0	3	0	97	100	0.4
El Salvador	6	27	12	61	5	0.1
Equatorial Guinea	62	5	4	92		
Eritrea	16	5	0	95	4	21.9
Estonia	49	26	0	73	0	25.9
Ethiopia	5	10	1	89	2	15.7
Faeroe Is.		2				
Fiji	45	11	5	84	1	37.5
Finland	72	7	0	93	3	0.1
France	28	34	2	64	11	0.2
French Guiana						
French Polynesia	29	1	5	94	4	0.4
Gabon	85	1	1	98	3	0.9
Gambia	48	23	1	77	1	3.5
Georgia	43	11	4	85	44	50.4
Germany	30	33	1	66	4	0.2
Ghana	28	16	10	74	0	3.3
Gibraltar						
Greece	28	21	9	70	38	0.2
Greenland						
Grenada	15	3	29	68		
Guadeloupe						
Guam	38	11	11	78		
Guatemala	26	13	5	82	7	0.2
Guinea	28	4	2	94	6	3.6
Guinea-Bissau	78	11	2	88	5	8.0
Guyana	86	2	0	97	30	26.2
Haiti	3	20	13	67	8	25.8
Honduras	48	10	3	87	6	0.2
Hungary	20	50	2	48	4	0.1
Iceland	0	0				3.0
India	22	54	3	43	32	0.1
Indonesia	58	11	7	81	14	0.1
Iran	4	9	1	90	46	92.1
Iraq	2	12	1	87	64	71.4
Ireland	10	15	0	85		0.6
Israel	6	16	4	80	46	0.3
Italy	34	27	10	63	25	0.2
Jamaica	30	16	9	75	9	0.1
Japan	66	12	1	87	55	0.3
Jordan	1	3	2	95	19	81.2
Kanaky-New Caledonia	20	0	0	99		0.1
Kazakhstan	4	8	0	92	11	1.7
Kenya	30	7	1	92	1	35.3
Kiribati	38		51			
Korea, North	68	14	2	83	73	0.2
Korea, South	63	17	2	81	60	0.5
Kuwait	0	0	0	99	70	78.6
Kyrgyzstan	5	7	0	93	75	21.2
Laos	54	4	0	96	18	9.9
Latvia	47	30	0	70	1	27.4
Lebanon	4	19	14	68	31	0.3
Lesotho	0	11				16.9
Liberia	36	4	2	94	1	
Libya	0	1	0	99	22	31.4
Liechtenstein	44	25				
Lithuania	31	45	1	54	0	54.6

	FOREST AND WOODLAND AS % OF LAND AREA [1]	ARABLE LAND AS % OF LAND AREA [1]	CROPLANDS AS % OF LAND AREA [1]	OTHER USES OF THE LAND AS % OF LAND AREA [1]	IRRIGATED AREA AS % OF ARABLE LAND [1]	FERTILIZER USE (KGS PER HA) [1]
	2000	2000	2000	2000	2000	2000
Luxembourg						
Macedonia, TFYR	36	22	2	76	9	82.3
Madagascar	20	5	1	94	31	3.1
Malawi	28	22	1	76	1	15.6
Malaysia	59	6	18	77	5	0.8
Maldives	3	3	7	90		
Mali	11	4	0	96	3	11.2
Malta	0	25	3	72	22	93.8
Malvinas-Falklands						
Marshall Is.						
Martinique						
Mauritania	0	0	0	100	10	
Mauritius	8	49	3	48	19	0.4
Mayotte Is.						
Melilla						
Mexico	29	13	1	86	24	73.9
Micronesia						
Moldova	10	55	11	33	14	2.8
Monaco						
Mongolia	7	1	0	99	7	2.9
Montserrat						
Morocco	7	20	2	78	13	41.3
Mozambique	39	5	0	95	3	3.7
Myanmar-Burma	52	15	1	84	19	21.2
Namibia	10	1	0	99	1	0.4
Nauru						
Nepal	27	20	0	79	38	26.2
Netherlands	11	27	1	72	60	0.5
Netherlands Antilles		10				
New Zealand-Aotearoa	30	6	6	88	9	0.5
Nicaragua	27	20	2	77	3	11.9
Niger	1	4	0	96	1	1.0
Nigeria	15	31	3	66	1	6.6
Niue						
Norfolk Is.						
Northern Marianas						0.2
Norway	29	3				0.3
Oman	0	0	0	100	78	0.1
Pakistan	3	28	1	72	82	
Palau	76	22				
Palestine						
Panama	39	7	2	91	5	67.1
Papua New Guinea	68	0	1	98		57.1
Paraguay	59	6	0	94	3	28.5
Peru	51	3	0	97	28	65.8
Philippines	19	19	15	66	15	0.1
Pitcairn						
Poland	31	46	1	53	1	0.1
Portugal	40	22	8	70	24	0.1
Puerto Rico	26	4	5	91	49	
Qatar	0	2	0	98	62	27.8
Réunion						
Romania	28	41	2	57	27	39.0
Russia	50	7	0	92	4	11.4
Rwanda	12	36	10	53	0	0.3
Sahara, Western						
Samoa	37	19	24	57		89.2
Samoa, American	60	10	15	75		
San Marino		17				
São Tomé and Príncipe	28	4	45	51	21	0.1
Saudi Arabia	1	2	0	98	43	19.2
Senegal	32	12	0	88	3	82.9
Serbia and Montenegro						39.0
Seychelles	67	2	13	84		0.3
Sierra Leone	15	7	1	92	5	3.0
Singapore	3	2	0	98		
Slovakia	42	30	3	67	11	61.0
Slovenia	55	9	2	90	1	0.4
Solomon Is.	91	2	1	98		
Somalia	12	2	0	98	19	0.5
South Africa	7	12	1	87	10	51.4
Spain	29	27	10	64	20	0.2
Sri Lanka	30	14	16	70	35	0.3
St Helena						
St Kitts-Nevis	11	19	3	78		0.2
St Lucia	15	5	23	72	18	1.8
St Pierre and Miquelon						
St Vincent	15	10	18	72	9	1.0
Sudan	26	7	0	93	12	2.3
Suriname	90	0	0	100	76	0.1
Swaziland	30	10	1	89	37	32.6
Sweden	66	7				0.1
Switzerland	30	10	1	89	6	0.2
Syria	3	25	4	71	23	80.5
Taiwan						
Tajikistan	3	5	1	94	84	12.3
Tanzania	44	5	1	94	3	5.6
Thailand	29	29	6	65	28	0.1
Timor-Leste	34	5	1	95		
Togo	9	46	2	52	0	7.9
Tokelau						
Tonga	6	24	43	33		
Trinidad and Tobago	50	15	9	76	2	78.7
Tunisia	3	19	14	68	8	38.3
Turkey	13	31	3	65	17	86.6
Turkmenistan	8	3	0	96	106	64.7
Turks and Caicos						
Tuvalu						
Uganda	21	26	10	65	0	0.9
Ukraine	17	56	2	42	7	13.5
United Arab Emirates	4	1	2	97	31	0.6
United Kingdom	11	24	0	75	2	0.3
United States	25	19	0	80	13	0.1
Uruguay	7	7	0	92	13	97.8
Uzbekistan	5	11	1	88	88	0.2
Vanuatu	37	2	7	90		
Vatican						
Venezuela	56	3	1	96	17	0.1
Vietnam	30	18	5	77	41	0.4
Virgin Is. (Am.)	41	12	3	85		0.2
Virgin Is. (Br.)						
Wallis and Futuna						
Yemen	1	3	0	97	30	12.2
Zambia	42	7	0	93	1	5.8
Zimbabwe	49	8	0	91	3	51.3

1. World Development Indicators 2003, World Bank

	CEREAL IMPORTS (METRIC TONS) [3]	FOOD PRODUCTION PER CAPITA INDEX (1981-91=100) [1]	FOOD IMPORTS AS % OF MERCHANDISE IMPORTS [1]	IMPORTS OF CONVENTIONAL WEAPONS ($ MILLION, 1990 PRICES) [2]	EXPORTS OF CONVENTIONAL WEAPONS ($ MILLION, 1990 PRICES) [2]
	2002	2001	2001	2002	2002
Afghanistan					
Albania	470,073		19.4		
Algeria	8,610,899	139	28.2	464	
Andorra			20.1		
Angola	581,013	149		5	1
Anguilla					
Antigua	6,758	99	21.8		
Argentina	14,626	146	5.7	210	
Armenia	420,090	71	25.3		
Aruba	6,623		19.1		
Australia	64,745	145	5.0	614	30
Austria	767,312	104	6.1	79	124
Azerbaijan	728,234	86	16.2		
Bahamas	15,743	140	15.6		
Bahrain	138,683	139	11.8	51	
Bangladesh	2,574,625	141	15.3	21	
Barbados	56,765	100	17.2		
Belarus	859,079	61	11.8		
Belgium	6,146,162	112	8.9	29	14
Belize	27,251	176	14.0		
Benin	184,377	159	20.4		
Bermuda	2,004	78	19.8		
Bhutan	34,434	118	17.9		
Bolivia	489,503	147	15.0		
Bosnia-Herzegovina	518,932				
Botswana	2,956	96			
Brazil	7,809,248	151	5.8	154	18
Brunei	29,120	205	16.5		
Bulgaria	177,225	65	5.2		20
Burkina Faso	110,816	137	22.3		
Burundi	22,269	96	23.0		
Cambodia	100,824	157			
Cameroon	364,556	132	15.5		
Canada	4,564,376	119	5.7	359	318
Cape Verde	62,682	136	33.7		
Cayman Is.	687	85			
Central African Rep.	52,951	143	12.3		
Ceuta					
Chad	70,997	135	24.0		
Chile	1,694,649	145	7.4	56	1
China	9,430,873	179	3.8	2,307	818
Christmas Is.					
Cocos					
Colombia	3,644,651	122	11.7	119	
Comoros	69,906	122	21.9		
Congo D.R.	331,099	83		14	
Congo R.	249,408	130	20.8		
Cook Is.	814				
Coral Sea Is.					
Costa Rica	812,406	149	7.5		
Côte d'Ivoire	1,081,550	134	17.2	7	
Croatia	88,959	68	8.9	2	
Cuba	1,684,818	61			
Cyprus	583,641	129	16.6		
Czech Republic	155,380	79	4.7	53	85
Denmark	1,140,837	105	11.6	7	9
Diego Garcia					
Djibouti	274,768	90	27.0		
Dominica	7,381	85	22.5		
Dominican Republic	1,398,788	118			
Ecuador	885,072	162	8.1	1	
Egypt	10,322,252	158	25.9	638	
El Salvador	716,033	114	16.7		
Equatorial Guinea	10,255	115			
Eritrea	228,211	127		180	
Estonia	213,339	43	10.6	1	
Ethiopia	697,017	142	7.0	20	
Faeroe Is.	8,679	97	20.3		
Fiji	138,130	99	15.7		
Finland	334,481	90	5.5	24	12
France	1,563,953	102	8.2	22	1,617
French Guiana	0				
French Polynesia	38,896	93	20.1		
Gabon	169,296	117	18.5		
Gambia	121,891	153	34.5		
Georgia	242,744	79			
Germany	3,631,290	99	6.8		
Ghana	740,786	174	18.2		
Gibraltar					
Greece	2,246,199	102	11.9	567	
Greenland	2,662	106	18.2		
Grenada	11,615	94	20.1		
Guadeloupe	0				
Guam	11,989	129			
Guatemala	1,135,767	138	14.1		
Guinea	429,590	159	23.5		
Guinea-Bissau	33,251	145	43.6		
Guyana	37,940	194	6.9		
Haiti	735,809	100			
Honduras	452,109	113	17.7		
Hungary	57,293	84	3.1		
Iceland	63,724	110	9.8		
India	2,805	129	4.8	1,668	
Indonesia	7,927,166	117	9.9	51	70
Iran	6,550,800	130	16.1	298	
Iraq		68			
Ireland	762,477	114	6.8	20	
Israel	3,072,451	115	5.4	226	178
Italy	9,803,141	103	8.8	308	490
Jamaica	478,640	119	15.5		
Japan	26,605,400	92	13.0	154	
Jordan	1,227,522	139	17.7	149	
Kanaky-New Caledonia	39,642	129	15.1		
Kazakhstan	60,917	74	9.2	69	
Kenya	707,824	106	13.9		
Kiribati	60,429	134	36.8		
Korea, North	1,825,472				
Korea, South	13,388,837	130	5.7	229	22
Kuwait	593,159	229	17.0	27	
Kyrgyzstan	254,611	121	13.6		
Laos	43,102	170			
Latvia	31,199	42	12.4	3	
Lebanon	765,267	148	17.5		
Lesotho	57,675	129			
Liberia	221,716				
Libya	2,257,322	163	27.5		11
Liechtenstein		91			
Lithuania	182,278	56	9.2	7	3

	CEREAL IMPORTS (METRIC TONS) [3]	FOOD PRODUCTION PER CAPITA INDEX (1981-91=100) [1]	FOOD IMPORTS AS % OF MERCHANDISE IMPORTS [1]	IMPORTS OF CONVENTIONAL WEAPONS ($ MILLION, 1990 PRICES) [2]	EXPORTS OF CONVENTIONAL WEAPONS ($ MILLION, 1990 PRICES) [2]
	2002	2001	2001	2002	2002
Luxembourg	44,763				
Macedonia, TFYR	94,914	87	13.8		
Madagascar	126,487	107	13.7		
Malawi	305,133	163	20.1		
Malaysia	5,123,885	148	5.4	213	
Maldives	37,513	130	23.0		
Mali	127,735	125	19.0		
Malta	169,249	118	11.0		
Malvinas-Falklands					
Marshall Is.					
Martinique	0				
Mauritania	428,795	112	26.2		
Mauritius	307,239	112	15.8		
Mayotte Is.					
Melilla					
Mexico	14,092,111	138	5.4	19	
Micronesia	9,415	18,866			
Moldova	80,331	46	14.3		
Monaco					
Mongolia	315,987	103	16.6		
Montserrat	349				
Morocco	5,032,115	106	13.7	169	
Mozambique	694,970	124	14.0		
Myanmar-Burma	113,709	171	14.7	208	
Namibia	138,566	115		11	
Nauru	465				
Nepal	27,371	133	12.6	8	
Netherlands	7,759,754	101	10.5	236	260
Netherlands Antilles	202,684	164	9.1		
New Zealand-Aotearoa	446,208	133	8.7	17	
Nicaragua	277,323	155	16.4		
Niger	129,577	146	44.2		
Nigeria	3,711,664	157	20.2	2	
Niue	65				
Norfolk Is.	167				
Northern Marianas					
Norway	450,847	89	7.1	82	203
Oman	521,981	159	22.4	48	
Pakistan	285,380	144	12.5	1,278	8
Palau					
Palestine	832,765				
Panama	400,414	104	12.2		
Papua New Guinea	578,525	124	18.3		
Paraguay	16,221	144	14.4		
Peru	2,491,230	176	13.3	4	5
Philippines	4,620,238	136	8.5	17	
Pitcairn					
Poland	648,162	86	6.2	258	43
Portugal	3,325,124	100	11.3	103	
Puerto Rico		84			
Qatar	143,833	178	11.1	8	
Réunion	0				
Romania	371,867	100	7.6	186	
Russia	1,424,420	66	20.5	170	5,941
Rwanda	30,460	110			
Sahara, Western					
Samoa	10,592	99			
Samoa, American	105	96			
San Marino					
São Tomé and Príncipe	13,352	166			
Saudi Arabia	5,673,790	83	15.6	478	
Senegal	1,176,309	137	26.8		
Serbia and Montenegro	20,631	104	9.3		
Seychelles	13,781	138	19.7		
Sierra Leone	96,427	80			
Singapore	836,135	40	3.7	227	2
Slovakia	80,889	73	5.7	27	40
Slovenia	373,729	114	6.2		
Solomon Is.	9,443	147	16.3		
Somalia					
South Africa	2,771,719	105	4.6		34
Spain	12,299,681	115	10.0	132	65
Sri Lanka	1,292,523	123	14.4	9	
St Helena	76				
St Kitts-Nevis	4,494	94	17.4		
St Lucia	35,178	74	27.0		
St Pierre and Miquelon	14				
St Vincent	28,694	77	26.7		
Sudan	1,326,454	168	15.1		
Suriname	39,886	77	18.1		
Swaziland	162,389	87			
Sweden	304,753	97	7.3	45	120
Switzerland	552,076	93	5.5	36	11
Syria	1,189,177	153	19.0	162	
Taiwan					
Tajikistan	454,448	55			
Tanzania	537,954	104	16.2		
Thailand	991,623	120	5.0	150	
Timor-Leste	12				
Togo	223,283	132	22.8		
Tokelau	0				
Tonga	8,587	98	32.5		
Trinidad and Tobago	216,462	115	8.8		
Tunisia	3,544,323	127	8.3	7	
Turkey	2,645,500	110	3.7	721	29
Turkmenistan	10,468	137	11.7		
Turks and Caicos					
Tuvalu	1,707				
Uganda	205,588	137	12.2		
Ukraine	387,787	53			270
United Arab Emirates	2,096,378	291	9.9	452	
United Kingdom	3,489,282	89	8.0	575	719
United States	5,014,779	122	4.4	346	3,941
Uruguay	399,514	134	11.4	2	
Uzbekistan	238,200	124		5	170
Vanuatu	21,031	111	21.9		
Vatican					
Venezuela	1,527,792	123	11.5	50	
Vietnam	1,423,167	155		69	
Virgin Is. (Am.)	0	103			
Virgin Is. (Br.)	278				
Wallis and Futuna	1,181				
Yemen	2,298,947	136	34.8	496	
Zambia	367,321	108	7.7		
Zimbabwe	685,847	110	8.8		

1. World Development Indicators 2003, World Bank / 2. Human Development Report 2003, UNDP / 3. LABORSTA database, ILO Web Site

	FEMALE PROFESSIONAL AND TECHNICAL WORKERS (AS % OF TOTAL) [1]	% OF WOMEN LEGISLATORS, SENIOR OFFICIALS AND MANAGERS [1]	EARNED INCOME SHARED (% TO WOMEN) [1]	% OF MINISTERIAL POSTS OCCUPIED BY WOMEN [1]	% OF PARLIAMENTARY SEATS OCCUPIED BY WOMEN [1]
	2003	2003	2003	2000	2003
Afghanistan					
Albania				15	6
Algeria				0	6
Andorra					
Angola				15	16
Anguilla					
Antigua				0	8
Argentina				7	31
Armenia					3
Aruba					
Australia	45	25	1	20	27
Austria	48	29	1	31	31
Azerbaijan				3	11
Bahamas	56	31	1	17	23
Bahrain					6
Bangladesh	25	8	1	10	2
Barbados	55	40	1	14	20
Belarus				26	18
Belgium	50	19	0	19	25
Belize	53	33	0	11	14
Benin				11	6
Bermuda					
Bhutan					9
Bolivia	40	36	0		18
Bosnia-Herzegovina					12
Botswana	52	35	1	27	17
Brazil	62			0	9
Brunei				0	
Bulgaria				19	26
Burkina Faso				9	12
Burundi				5	19
Cambodia	33	14	1	7	9
Cameroon				6	9
Canada	53	35	1	24	24
Cape Verde				35	11
Cayman Is.					
Central African Rep.					7
Ceuta					
Chad					6
Chile	50	24	0	26	10
China				5	22
Christmas Is.					
Cocos					
Colombia	49	38	0	47	11
Comoros					
Congo D.R.					
Congo R.					11
Cook Is.					
Coral Sea Is.					
Costa Rica	28	53	0	29	35
Côte d'Ivoire				9	9
Croatia	50	25	1	16	16
Cuba				11	36
Cyprus	43	18	0		11
Czech Republic	53	26	1		16
Denmark	51	21	1	45	38
Diego Garcia					
Djibouti				5	11
Dominica				0	19
Dominican Republic	49	31	0		15
Ecuador	44	25	0	20	16
Egypt	29	10	0	6	2
El Salvador	47	33	0	15	10
Equatorial Guinea					5
Eritrea				12	22
Estonia	70	35	1	14	18
Ethiopia				22	8
Faeroe Is.					
Fiji				21	6
Finland	57	28	1	44	37
France				38	12
French Guiana					
French Polynesia					
Gabon				12	11
Gambia				31	13
Georgia	60	23	0	10	7
Germany	50	27	1	36	31
Ghana				9	9
Gibraltar					
Greece	47	25	0	7	9
Greenland					
Grenada				25	18
Guadeloupe					
Guam					
Guatemala				7	9
Guinea				11	19
Guinea-Bissau				8	8
Guyana					20
Haiti				18	9
Honduras	51	36	0	33	6
Hungary	61	34	1	36	10
Iceland	55	31	1	33	35
India				10	9
Indonesia				6	8
Iran				9	4
Iraq					
Ireland	49	28	0	19	14
Israel	54	27	1	6	15
Italy	44	19	0	18	10
Jamaica				13	14
Japan	45	9	0	6	10
Jordan				0	3
Kanaky-New Caledonia					
Kazakhstan				18	9
Kenya				1	7
Kiribati					
Korea, North					
Korea, South	34	5	0	7	6
Kuwait				0	0
Kyrgyzstan					7
Laos				10	23
Latvia	68	38	1	7	21
Lebanon				0	2
Lesotho					17
Liberia					
Libya				13	
Liechtenstein					
Lithuania	69	47	1	19	11

WOMEN'S SITUATION

	FEMALE PROFESSIONAL AND TECHNICAL WORKERS (AS % OF TOTAL) [1]	% OF WOMEN LEGISLATORS, SENIOR OFFICIALS AND MANAGERS [1]	EARNED INCOMES HARED (% TO WOMEN) [1]	% OF MINISTERIAL POSTS OCCUPIED BY WOMEN [1]	% OF PARLIAMENTARY SEATS OCCUPIED BY WOMEN [1]
	2003	2003	2003	2000	2003
Luxembourg				29	17
Macedonia, TFYR				11	18
Madagascar				13	6
Malawi				12	9
Malaysia	45	20	0		15
Maldives	40	15			6
Mali				33	10
Malta				5	9
Malvinas-Falklands					
Marshall Is.					
Martinique				14	3
Mauritania				9	6
Mauritius					
Mayotte Is.					
Melilla					
Mexico	40	25	0	11	16
Micronesia					
Moldova	66	37	1		13
Monaco					
Mongolia				10	11
Montserrat				5	6
Morocco					30
Mozambique					
Myanmar-Burma					
Namibia	55	30	1	16	21
Nauru					
Nepal				15	8
Netherlands	48	26	1	31	33
Netherlands Antilles					
New Zealand-Aotearoa	53	38	1	44	29
Nicaragua				23	21
Niger				10	1
Nigeria				23	3
Niue					
Norfolk Is.					
Northern Marianas					
Norway	48	26	1	42	36
Oman					
Pakistan	26	9	0		21
Palau					
Palestine	32	11			..
Panama	46	33	0	20	10
Papua New Guinea				0	1
Paraguay	54	23	0		8
Peru	44	27	0	16	18
Philippines	62	58	1		17
Pitcairn					
Poland	60	32	1	19	21
Portugal	50	32	1	10	19
Puerto Rico					
Qatar				0	
Réunion					
Romania	57	29	1	20	10
Russia	64	37	1		6
Rwanda				13	26
Sahara, Western					
Samoa					
Samoa, American					
San Marino					9
São Tomé and Príncipe					
Saudi Arabia					
Senegal				16	19
Serbia and Montenegro					
Seychelles				23	29
Sierra Leone				8	15
Singapore	43	24	1	6	12
Slovakia	61	31	1	19	19
Slovenia	54	31	1	15	12
Solomon Is.					0
Somalia					
South Africa				38	30
Spain	45	32	0	18	27
Sri Lanka	49	4	1		4
St Helena					
St Kitts-Nevis				0	13
St Lucia				18	21
St Pierre and Miquelon					
St Vincent				0	23
Sudan				5	10
Suriname	51	28			18
Swaziland				13	6
Sweden	49	30	1	55	45
Switzerland	43	24	1	29	22
Syria				11	10
Taiwan					12
Tajikistan					22
Tanzania					10
Thailand	55	27	1	6	10
Timor-Leste				7	7
Togo					
Tokelau					
Tonga					
Trinidad and Tobago	51	40	0	9	25
Tunisia				10	12
Turkey	31	8	0	0	4
Turkmenistan					26
Turks and Caicos					
Tuvalu					
Uganda				27	25
Ukraine	63	37	1		5
United Arab Emirates	25	8	0		0
United Kingdom	43	30	1	33	17
United States	54	46	1	32	14
Uruguay	52	37	1		12
Uzbekistan				4	7
Vanuatu					2
Vatican					
Venezuela	58	24	0	0	10
Vietnam					27
Virgin Is. (Am.)					
Virgin Is. (Br.)					
Wallis and Futuna					
Yemen	15	4	0		1
Zambia				6	12
Zimbabwe				36	10

1. World Development Indicators 2003, World Bank

The World Guide 2005/2006 National Distributors

AUSTRALIA
New Internationalist Australia
28 Austin Street
Adelaide
SA 5000
Tel: +61 (0) 8 8232 1563
Fax: +61 (0) 8 8232 1887
Email: helenp@newint.com.au

For Australian bookshop distribution:

Bush Books
PO Box 1958
Gosford South
NSW 2250
Tel: +61 (0) 2 4323 3223
Fax: +61 (0) 2 4323 3274
Email: bushbook@ozemail.com.au

BELGIUM
11.11.11
Vlasfabriekstraat 11
1060 Brussel
Tel: +32 (0) 2 539 2620
Fax: +32 (0) 2 539 1343

CANADA and UNITED STATES
New Internationalist Canada
401 Richmond Street West
Studio 393
Toronto, Ontario
M5V 3A8
Tel: +1 416 588 6478
Fax: +1 416 588 4285
Email: nican@web.ca

For Canadian bookshop distribution:

Garamond Press
63 Mahogany Court
Aurora, Ontario
L4G 6M8
Tel: +1 905 841 1460
Fax: +1 905 841 3031
Email: garamond@web.net

NEW ZEALAND / AOTEAROA
PO Box 35038
Christchurch
Tel/Fax: + 64 (0) 3 386 3153
Email: newint@chch.planet.org.nz

NORWAY
Arning Publikasjoner
P.O.Box 35
7315 Lensvik
Norway
www.arning.no

UNITED KINGDOM
New Internationalist Publications
55 Rectory Road
Oxford
OX4 1BW
Tel: +44 (0) 1865 811400
Fax: +44 (0) 1865 793152
Email: ni@newint.org

For UK bookshop distribution:

Turnaround
Unit 3, Olympia Trading Estate
Coburg Road, Wood Green
London
N22 6TZ
Tel: +44 (0) 20 8829 3000
Fax: +44 (0) 20 8829 5088
Email: orders@turnaround-uk.com

For UK educational distribution:

Carel Press
4 Hewson Street
Carlisle
CA2 5AU
Tel: +44 (0) 1228 538928
Fax: +44 (0) 1228 591816
Email: info@carelpress.co.uk

URUGUAY
Instituto del Tercer Mundo
Juan D Jackson 1136
CP 11200
Montevideo
Tel: +59 8 2419 6192
Fax: +59 8 2411 9222
Email: item@chasque.net